Introduction to Psychology

GATEWAYS TO MIND AND BEHAVIOR

Dennis Coon
John O. Mitterer
Brock University

Australia • Brazil • Japan • Korea • Mexico • Singapore • Spain • United Kingdom • United States

***Introduction to Psychology: Gateways to Mind and Behavior*, Thirteenth Edition**
Dennis Coon / John O. Mitterer

Senior Publisher: Linda Schreiber-Ganster
Publisher: Jon-David Hague
Sr. Development Group Manager: Jeremy Judson
Developmental Editor: Shannon LeMay-Finn
Assistant Editor: Kelly Miller
Editorial Assistant: Sheli DeNola
Senior Media Editor: Mary Noel
Senior Marketing Manager: Jessica Egbert
Marketing and Communications Director: Talia Wise
Senior Content Project Manager: Pat Waldo
Design Director: Rob Hugel
Art Director: Vernon Boes
Manufacturing Planner: Karen Hunt
Rights Acquisitions Specialist: Dean Dauphinais
Production Service: Kate Mannix, Graphic World Inc.
Text Designer: Diane Beasley
Photo Researcher: Roman Barnes
Text Researcher: Pablo D'Stair
Copy Editor: Graphic World Inc.
Cover Designer: Lawrence R. Didona
Cover Image: Main image, Masterfile/Royalty-free, and inset images, PhotoDisc
Compositor: Graphic World Inc.

Library of Congress Control Number: 2011932716

Student Edition:

ISBN-13: 978-1-111-83363-3

ISBN-10: 1-111-83363-X

Loose-leaf Edition:

ISBN-13: 978-1-111-83483-8

ISBN-10: 1-111-83483-0

Wadsworth
20 Davis Drive
Belmont, CA 94002-3098
USA

Cengage Learning is a leading provider of customized learning solutions with office locations around the globe, including Singapore, the United Kingdom, Australia, Mexico, Brazil, and Japan. Locate your local office at **www.cengage.com/global.**

Cengage Learning products are represented in Canada by Nelson Education, Ltd.

To learn more about Wadsworth, visit **www.cengage.com/Wadsworth.**
Purchase any of our products at your local college store or at our preferred online store **www.CengageBrain.com.**

Printed in Canada
1 2 3 4 5 6 7 15 14 13 12 11

To the many instructors and students who have used various editions of this book, all the way up to lucky thirteen. We offer our heartfelt thanks for the trust you have put in us.

About the Authors

Dr. Dennis Coon is the author of *Psychology: Modules for Active Learning* and *Psychology: A Journey,* as well as *Introduction to Psychology*. Together, these texts have been used by more than 2 million students. Dr. Coon frequently serves as a reviewer and consultant to publishers, and he edited the best-selling trade book *Choices.* He also helped design modules for PsychNow!, Cengage's interactive CD-ROM.

In his leisure hours, Dr. Coon enjoys hiking, photography, painting, woodworking, and music. He also designs, builds, and plays classical and steel string acoustic guitars. He has published articles on guitar design and occasionally offers lectures on this topic, in addition to his more frequent presentations on psychology.

John O. Mitterer was awarded his Ph.D. in cognitive psychology from McMaster University. Currently, Dr. Mitterer is faculty member at Brock University, where he has taught more than 25,000 introductory psychology students. He is the recipient of the 2003 Brock University Distinguished Teaching Award, a 2003 Ontario Confederation of University Faculty Associations (OCUFA) Teaching Award, a 2004 National 3M Teaching Fellowship, the 2005 Canadian Psychological Association Award for Distinguished Contributions to Education and Training in Psychology, and the 2010 Brock University Don Ursino Award for Excellence in the Teaching of Large Classes. He also held a three-year Brock Chancellor's Chair for Teaching Excellence from 2006 to 2009.

His first love is in applying cognitive principles to the improvement of undergraduate education. In support of his introductory psychology course, he has been involved in the production of textbooks and ancillary materials such as CD-ROMs and websites for both students and instructors. Dr. Mitterer has published and lectured on undergraduate instruction throughout Canada and the United States.

In his spare time, Dr. Mitterer strives to become a better golfer and to attain his life goal of seeing all the bird species in the world. To this end, he recently traveled to Papua New Guinea, Uganda, the Galapagos, and China.

Brief Contents

Introduction: The Psychology of Studying — Reflective Learning 1

1 Introduction to Psychology and Research Methods 13
Psychology in Action: Psychology in the Media — Are You Fluent in Klingon? 44

2 Brain and Behavior 51
Psychology in Action: Handedness — Are You Sinister or Dexterous? 77

3 Human Development 83
Psychology in Action: Effective Parenting — Always Kiss Your Children Goodnight 117

4 Sensation and Perception 125
Psychology in Action: Pay Attention! — Becoming a Better Eyewitness to Life 160

5 States of Consciousness 167
Psychology in Action: Exploring and Using Dreams 198

6 Conditioning and Learning 205
Psychology in Action: Behavioral Self-Management — A Rewarding Project 234

7 Memory 241
Psychology in Action: Mnemonics — Memory Magic 268

8 Cognition, Language, and Creativity 275
Psychology in Action: Enhancing Creativity — Brainstorms 297

9 Intelligence 303
Psychology in Action: Intelligent Intelligence Testing — User Beware! 323

10 Motivation and Emotion 331
Psychology in Action: Emotional Intelligence — The Fine Art of Self-Control 363

11 Sex, Gender, and Sexuality 369
Psychology in Action: Sexual Problems — When Pleasure Fades 393

12 Personality 403
Psychology in Action: Barriers and Bridges — Understanding Shyness 435

13 Health, Stress, and Coping 441
Psychology in Action: Stress Management 468

14 Psychological Disorders 475
Psychology in Action: Suicide — Lives on the Brink 505

15 Therapies 511
Psychology in Action: Self-Management and Seeking Professional Help 538

16 Social Thinking and Social Influence 547
Psychology in Action: Assertiveness Training — Standing Up for Your Rights 570

17 Prosocial and Antisocial Behavior 575
Psychology in Action: Multiculturalism — Living with Diversity 597

18 Applied Psychology 603
Psychology in Action: Human Factors Psychology — Who's the Boss Here? 626

Appendix: Behavioral Statistics 633

References R-1

Name Index I-1

Subject Index/Glossary S-1

Contents

Preface xvi

Starting Off on the Right Foot 1

Reflective Reading — How to Tame a Textbook 2

How to Use *Introduction to Psychology: Gateways to Mind and Behavior* 3

Reflective Note Taking — LISAN Up! 4

Using and Reviewing Your Notes 5

Reflective Study Strategies — Making a Habit of Success 5

Self-Regulated Learning — Academic All-Stars 6

Procrastination — Avoiding the Last-Minute Blues 6

Time Management 6

Goal Setting 7

Make Learning an Adventure 7

Reflective Test-Taking — Are You "Test Wise"? 7

General Test-Taking Skills 7

Using Digital Media — Netting New Knowledge 8

Psychology CourseMate 8

CengageNOW 9

Psychology Resource Center 9

Psychology Websites 9

A Final Word 10

Chapter in Review: Gateways to Psychology 11

Gateway Questions Revisited 11

Media Resources 11

1 Introduction to Psychology and Research Methods 13

Fly Like an Eagle 13

Psychology — Behave Yourself! 14

Seeking Knowledge in Psychology 14

Psychological Research 15

Psychology's Goals 15

Critical Thinking — Take It with a Grain of Salt 17

Critical Thinking Principles 17

Pseudopsychologies — Palms, Planets, and Personality 18

Problems in the Stars 19

Scientific Research — How to Think Like a Psychologist 20

The Scientific Method 20

Research Ethics 22

A Brief History of Psychology — Psychology's Family Album 23

Structuralism 24

Functionalism 24

Behaviorism 24

Gestalt Psychology 25

Psychoanalytic Psychology 26

Humanistic Psychology 26

The Role of Diversity in Psychology 27

Psychology Today — Three Complementary Perspectives on Behavior 28

The Biological Perspective 29

The Psychological Perspective 29

The Sociocultural Perspective 30

Psychologists — Guaranteed Not to Shrink 31

Helping People 34

Other Mental Health Professionals 34

The Psychology Experiment — Where Cause Meets Effect 35

Variables and Groups 35

Evaluating Results 37

Double Blind — On Placebos and Self-Fulfilling Prophecies 37

Research Participant Bias 37

Researcher Bias 38

Nonexperimental Research Methods — Different Strokes 39

Naturalistic Observation 39

Correlational Studies 40

The Clinical Method 41

Survey Method 42

Psychology in Action: Psychology in the Media — Are You Fluent in Klingon? 44

Chapter in Review: Gateways to Psychology 46

Gateway Questions Revisited 46

Media Resources 48

Feature Boxes (Highlights)

- Critical Thinking: Testing Commonsense Beliefs 15
- Human Diversity: Who's WEIRD? 28
- Discovering Psychology: Is a Career in Psychology Right for You? 33

2 Brain and Behavior 51

A Stroke of Bad Luck 51

Neurons — Building a "Biocomputer" 52
- Parts of a Neuron 52
- The Nerve Impulse 52
- Synapses and Neurotransmitters 54
- Neural Networks 56

The Nervous System — Wired for Action 56

Research Methods — Charting the Brain's Inner Realms 60
- Mapping Brain Structure 60
- Exploring Brain Function 61

The Cerebral Cortex — My, What a Wrinkled Brain You Have! 64
- Cerebral Hemispheres 64
- Hemispheric Specialization 65
- Lobes of the Cerebral Cortex 67

The Subcortex — At the Core of the (Brain) Matter 71
- The Hindbrain 71
- The Forebrain 73
- The Whole Person 74

The Endocrine System — My Hormones Made Me Do It 74

Psychology in Action: Handedness — Are You Sinister or Dexterous? 77

Chapter in Review: Gateways to Brain and Behavior 80

Gateway Questions Revisited 80

Media Resources 81

Feature Boxes (Highlights)
- Critical Thinking: You Can Change Your Mind, But Can You Change Your Brain? 57
- Brainwaves: Repairing Your Brain 59
- The Clinical File: Mirror, Mirror in the Brain 68
- Human Diversity: His and Her Brains? 70
- The Clinical File: Trapped! 72

3 Human Development 83

It's a Girl! 83

Nature and Nurture — It Takes Two to Tango 84
- Heredity 84
- Environment 86
- Reaction Range 88

The Newborn — More Than Meets the Eye 89
- Motor Development 90
- Perceptual and Cognitive Development 91
- Emotional Development 92

Social Development — Baby, I'm Stuck on You 93
- Attachment 94
- Day Care 95
- Attachment and Affectional Needs 96

Parental Influences — Life with Mom and Dad 96
- Parenting Styles 96
- Maternal and Paternal Influences 96
- Ethnic Differences: Four Flavors of Parenting 97

Language Development — Who Talks Baby Talk? 98
- Language and the Terrible Twos 99
- The Roots of Language 99

Cognitive Development — Think Like a Child 101
- Piaget's Theory of Cognitive Development 101
- Piaget Today 104
- Vygotsky's Sociocultural Theory 106

Adolescence and Young Adulthood — The Best of Times, the Worst of Times 107
- Puberty 107
- The Search for Identity 108
- Emerging Adulthood 109

Moral Development — Growing a Conscience 110
- Levels of Moral Development 110

The Story of a Lifetime — Rocky Road or Garden Path? 111
- Erikson's Psychosocial Theory 111

Middle and Later Adulthood — You're an Adult Now! 113
- Other Challenges of Adulthood 113
- A Midlife Crisis? 114
- Facing the Challenges of Adulthood 114
- Old Age 114

Death and Dying — The Final Frontier 115
- Reactions to Impending Death 115
- Implications 116

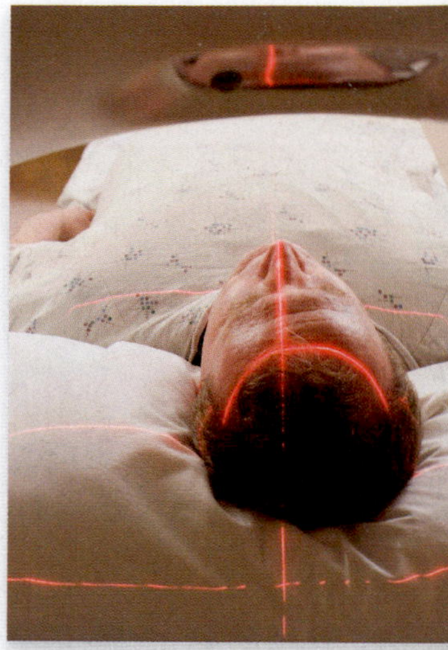

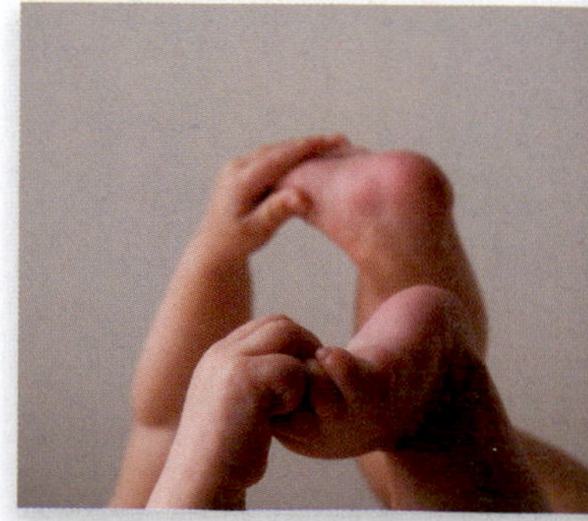

Psychology in Action: Effective Parenting—Always Kiss Your Children Goodnight 117

Chapter in Review: Gateways to Human Development 120

Gateway Questions Revisited 120

Media Resources 122

Feature Boxes (Highlights)

- **Discovering Psychology:** What's Your Attachment Style? 95
- **Critical Thinking:** Theory of Mind: I'm a *Me*!....and You're a *You*! 105
- **Human Diversity:** Ethnic Diversity and Identity 108
- **Critical Thinking:** The Twixters 109

4 Sensation and Perception 125

The Trees Have Eyes 125

Sensory Processes—The First Step 126

Selection 126
Sensory Adaptation 126
Sensory Analysis 127
Sensory Coding 127

Vision—Catching Some Rays 128

Structure of the Eye 129
Rods and Cones 129
Color Vision 131
Seeing in the Dark 132

Hearing—Good Vibrations 134

How We Hear Sounds 134

Smell and Taste—The Nose Knows When the Tongue Can't Tell 137

The Sense of Smell 137
Taste and Flavors 138

The Somesthetic Senses—Flying by the Seat of Your Pants 138

The Skin Senses 139
Pain 139
The Vestibular System 141

Perception—The Second Step 142

Bottom-Up and Top-Down Processing 144
Gestalt Organizing Principles 144
Perceptual Constancies 147

Selective Attention—Tuning In and Tuning Out 148

Depth Perception—What If the World Were Flat? 149

Binocular Depth Cues 150
Monocular Depth Cues 151

Perceptual Learning—Believing Is Seeing 154

Perceptual Expectancies 154
Motives, Emotions, and Perception 155
Perceptual Habits 155

Extrasensory Perception—Do You Believe in Ghosts? 158

An Appraisal of ESP 158

Psychology in Action: Pay Attention!—Becoming a Better Eyewitness to Life 160

Chapter in Review: Gateways to Sensation and Perception 163

Gateway Questions Revisited 163

Media Resources 164

Feature Boxes (Highlights)

- **Brainwaves:** The Matrix: Do Phantoms Live Here? 140
- **The Clinical File:** Staying in Touch with Reality 144
- **Human Diversity:** Do They See What We See? 155

5 States of Consciousness 167

A Visit to Several States (of Consciousness) 167

States of Consciousness—The Many Faces of Awareness 168

Altered States of Consciousness 168

Sleep—Catching a Few ZZZs 168

The Need for Sleep 168
Sleep Patterns 170

Stages of Sleep—The Nightly Roller Coaster 171

Sleep Stages 171
The Dual Process Hypothesis of Sleep 172

Sleep Disturbances—The Sleepy Time Blues 174

Insomnia 174
Sleepwalking, Sleeptalking, and Sleepsex 176
Nightmares and Night Terrors 176
Sleep Apnea 176
Narcolepsy 177

Dreams—A Separate Reality? 177

REM Rebound 177
Dream Theories 178
Dream Worlds 179

Hypnosis—Look into My Eyes 179

Theories of Hypnosis 180
The Reality of Hypnosis 180
Stage Hypnosis 182

Meditation and Sensory Deprivation—Chilling, the Healthy Way 183

Meditation 183
Sensory Deprivation 183
Positive Psychology: Mindfulness and Well-Being 184

Drug-Altered Consciousness—The High and Low of It 185

Drug Dependence 186
Patterns of Abuse 187

Uppers—Amphetamines, Cocaine, MDMA, Caffeine, Nicotine 187

Amphetamines 187
Cocaine 189
MDMA ("Ecstasy") 190
Caffeine 190
Nicotine 191

Downers — Sedatives, Tranquilizers, and Alcohol 192
Barbiturates 192
GHB 192
Tranquilizers 193
Alcohol 193
Hallucinogens — Tripping the Light Fantastic 196
LSD and PCP 196
Marijuana 196
Psychology in Action: Exploring and Using Dreams 198
Chapter in Review: Gateways to Consciousness 201
Gateway Questions Revisited 201
Media Resources 202
Feature Boxes (Highlights)
- Human Diversity: Consciousness and Culture 169
- Critical Thinking: They Came from Outer Space? 173
- Discovering Psychology: Swinging Suggestions 180
- Brainwaves: How Psychoactive Drugs Affect the Brain 186

6 Conditioning and Learning 205

Rats! 205
What Is Learning — Does Practice Make Perfect? 206
Types of Learning 206
Classical Conditioning — Does the Name Pavlov Ring a Bell? 207
Pavlov's Experiment 207
Principles of Classical Conditioning — Leonard Studies Lemon Juice 209
Acquisition 209
Expectancies 209
Extinction and Spontaneous Recovery 210
Generalization 210
Discrimination 210
Classical Conditioning in Humans — An Emotional Topic 211
Conditioned Emotional Responses 211
Vicarious, or Secondhand, Conditioning 212
Operant Conditioning — Can Pigeons Play Ping-Pong? 212
Positive Reinforcement 213
Acquiring an Operant Response 213
The Timing of Reinforcement 214
Shaping 215
Operant Extinction 216
Negative Reinforcement 216
Punishment 216
Operant Reinforcers — What's Your Pleasure? 217
Primary Reinforcers 218
Secondary Reinforcers 218
Feedback 219
Learning Aids 219
Partial Reinforcement — Las Vegas, a Human Skinner Box? 221
Schedules of Partial Reinforcement 222
Stimulus Control — Red Light, Green Light 224
Punishment — Putting the Brakes on Behavior 225
Variables Affecting Punishment 226
The Downside of Punishment 226
Using Punishment Wisely 227
Cognitive Learning — Beyond Conditioning 229
Cognitive Maps 229
Latent Learning 230
Modeling — Do as I Do, Not as I Say 231
Observational Learning 231
Modeling and the Media 232
Psychology in Action: Behavioral Self-Management — A Rewarding Project 234
Chapter in Review: Gateways to Conditioning and Learning 236
Gateway Questions Revisited 236
Media Resources 238
Feature Boxes (Highlights)
- The Clinical File: In the Blink of an Eye 208
- Critical Thinking: Are We Less Superstitious Than Pigeons? 214
- Brainwaves: Tickling Your Own Fancy 217
- Discovering Psychology: Learning and Conservation 220
- Critical Thinking: Are Animals Stuck in Time? 223
- Critical Thinking: You Mean Video Games Might Be Bad for Me? 233

7 Memory 241

Fuhgeddaboudit 241
Stages of Memory — Do You Have a Mind Like a Steel Trap? Or a Sieve? 242
Sensory Memory 242
Short-Term Memory 242
Long-Term Memory 243
Short-Term Memory — Do You Know the Magic Number? 244
Chunking 245
Rehearsing Information 245
Long-Term Memory — A Blast from the Past 246
Elaborating False Memories 246
Organizing Memories 248
Types of Long-Term Memory 250

Measuring Memory—The Answer Is on the Tip of My Tongue 251
Recalling Information 252
Recognizing Information 252
Relearning Information 253
Implicit and Explicit Memories 253
Forgetting—Why We, Uh, Let's See; Why We, Uh... Forget! 254
When Encoding Fails 255
When Memory Storage Fails 256
When Retrieval Fails 256
Memory and the Brain—Some "Shocking" Findings 260
Consolidation 260
Long-Term Memory and the Brain 262
Exceptional Memory—Wizards of Recall 263
Eidetic Imagery 263
Strategies for Remembering 264
Memory Champions 265
Improving Memory—Keys to the Memory Bank 265
Encoding Strategies 265
Retrieval Strategies 267
A Look Ahead 268
Psychology in Action: Mnemonics—Memory Magic 268
Chapter in Review: Gateways to Memory 271
Gateway Questions Revisited 271
Media Resources 272
Feature Boxes (Highlights)
- **Human Diversity:** Horses, Memories, and Culture 244
- **Critical Thinking:** Do You Like Jam with Your Memory? 247
- **Critical Thinking:** Telling Wrong from Right in Forensic Memory 248
- **Discovering Psychology:** Card Magic! 255
- **The Clinical File:** The Recovered Memory/False Memory Debate 260
- **Critical Thinking:** The Long-Term Potential of a Memory Pill 262

8 Cognition, Language, and Creativity 275
Color Is the Keyboard 275
What Is Thinking?—Brains over Brawn 276
Some Basic Units of Thought 276
Mental Imagery—Does a Frog Have Lips? 276
The Nature of Mental Images 276
Concepts—I'm Positive, It's a Whatchamacallit 278
Forming Concepts 278
Types of Concepts 279
Language—Say What? 281
The Structure of Language 283
Animal Language 284
Problem Solving—Getting an Answer in Sight 285
Mechanical Solutions 286
Solutions by Understanding 286
Heuristics 286
Insightful Solutions 286
Common Barriers to Problem Solving 289
Experts and Novices 289
Creative Thinking—Down Roads Less Traveled 290
Tests of Creativity 291
Stages of Creative Thought 292
Positive Psychology: The Creative Personality 293
Intuition—Mental Shortcut? Or Dangerous Detour? 293
Intuition 294
Psychology in Action: Enhancing Creativity—Brainstorms 297
Chapter in Review: Gateways to Cognition, Language, and Creativity 300
Gateway Questions Revisited 300
Media Resources 301
Feature Boxes (Highlights)
- **Critical Thinking:** What's North of My Fork? 281
- **Human Diversity:** Bilingualism—*Si o No, Oui ou Non,* Yes or No? 282
- **Human Diversity:** How to Weigh an Elephant 288
- **Critical Thinking:** Have You Ever Thin Sliced Your Teacher? 294
- **Critical Thinking:** Extra Hot, Decaf, Double-Shot... 296

9 Intelligence 303
Homo Sapiens 303
Defining Intelligence—Intelligence Is... You Know, It's... 304
Defining Intelligence 304
Reliability and Validity 305
Testing Intelligence—The IQ and You 306
Five Aspects of Intelligence 306
The Wechsler Tests 306
Group Tests 307
Intelligence Quotients 309
Variations in Intelligence—The Numbers Game 310
IQ and Sex 311
IQ and Age 311
IQ and Achievement 311
The Intellectually Gifted—Smart, Smarter, Smartest 312
Gifted Children 312
Intellectual Disability—A Difference That Makes a Difference 313
Levels of Intellectual Disability 313
Causes of Intellectual Disability 314

Heredity and Environment — Super Rats, Family Trees, and Video Games 316
Hereditary Influences 317
Environmental Influences 317
Beyond Psychometric Intelligence — Intelligent Alternatives to "g" 319
The Intelligent Nervous System 319
Intelligent Information Processing 320
Artificial Intelligence 320
Multiple Intelligences 321
Psychology in Action: Intelligent Intelligence Testing — User Beware! 323
Chapter in Review: Gateways to Intelligence 326
Gateway Questions Revisited 326
Media Resources 328
Feature Boxes (Highlights)
- **Human Diversity:** Intelligence — How Would a Fool Do It? 308
- **The Clinical File:** Meet the Rain Man 314
- **Critical Thinking:** You Mean Video Games Might Be Good for Me? 318

10 Motivation and Emotion 331

No Need to Tell Lady Gaga 331
Motivation — Forces That Push and Pull 332
A Model of Motivation 332
Biological Motives and Homeostasis 333
Circadian Rhythms 333
Hunger — Pardon Me, My Hypothalamus Is Growling 334
Internal Factors in Hunger 335
External Factors in Hunger and Obesity 337
Dieting 338
Eating Disorders 339
Culture, Ethnicity, and Dieting 342
Biological Motives Revisited — Thirst, Sex, and Pain 342
Thirst 342
Pain 342
The Sex Drive 343
Stimulus Motives — Skydiving, Horror Movies, and the Fun Zone 344
Arousal Theory 344
Levels of Arousal 345
Learned Motives — The Pursuit of Excellence 346
Opponent-Process Theory 346
Social Motives 346
The Key to Success? 347
Motives in Perspective — A View from the Pyramid 348
Intrinsic and Extrinsic Motivation 349
Turning Play into Work 349
Inside an Emotion — How Do You Feel? 350
Primary Emotions 351
Emotion and the Brain 352
Physiology and Emotion — Arousal, Sudden Death, and Lying 352
Fight or Flight 353
Sudden Death 353
Lie Detectors 354
Expressing Emotions — Making Faces and Talking Bodies 355
Facial Expressions 355
Theories of Emotion — Several Ways to Fear a Bear 358
The James-Lange Theory 358
The Cannon-Bard Theory 358
Schachter's Cognitive Theory of Emotion 359
Emotional Appraisal 360
The Facial Feedback Hypothesis 360
A Contemporary Model of Emotion 361
Psychology in Action: Emotional Intelligence — The Fine Art of Self-Control 363
Chapter in Review: Gateways to Motivation and Emotion 364
Gateway Questions Revisited 364
Media Resources 366
Feature Boxes (Highlights)
- **Brainwaves:** Your Brain's "Fat Point" 336
- **Discovering Psychology:** What's Your BMI? (We've Got Your Number.) 337
- **Discovering Psychology:** Behavioral Dieting 340
- **Discovering Psychology:** True Grit 347
- **Critical Thinking:** Crow's-Feet and Smiles Sweet 356
- **The Clinical File:** Suppressing Emotion — Don't Turn Off the Music 361

11 Sex, Gender, and Sexuality 369

Pink and Blue? 369
Sexual Development — Circle One: *XX* or *XY*? 370
Dimensions of Sex 370
Sexual Orientation — Who Do You Love? 371
The Stability of Sexual Orientation 372
Homosexuality 372
Gender Development — Circle One: Masculine or Feminine 374
Acquiring Gender Identity 375
Gender Roles 375
Gender Role Socialization 377
Androgyny — Are You Masculine, Feminine, or Androgynous? 378
Psychological Androgyny 378

When Sex and Gender Do Not Match — The Binary Busters 379

Sexual Behavior — Mapping the Erogenous Zones 380

Sexual Arousal 380

Human Sexual Response — Sexual Interactions 383

Female Response 384

Male Response 384

Comparing Male and Female Responses 384

Atypical Sexual Behavior — Trench Coats, Whips, Leathers, and Lace 385

Paraphilias 385

Contemporary Attitudes and Sexual Behavior — For Better or Worse 387

A Sexual Revolution? 387

The Crime of Rape 389

STDs and Safer Sex — Choice, Risk, and Responsibility 390

HIV/AIDS 390

Behavioral Risk Factors for STDs 392

Safer Sex 392

Psychology in Action: Sexual Problems — When Pleasure Fades 393

Chapter in Review: Gateways to Sex, Gender, and Sexuality 398

Gateway Questions Revisited 398

Media Resources 400

Feature Boxes (Highlights)

- Brainwaves: Genes, Hormones, and Sexual Orientation 373
- Human Diversity: High Test 375
- Human Diversity: What's Love Got to Do with It? 381
- Critical Thinking: Are We Oversexualizing Young Girls? 388
- Critical Thinking: Gender Role Stereotyping and Rape 389

12 Personality 403

At the Core 403

The Psychology of Personality — Do You Have Personality? 404

Traits 404

Types 404

Self-Concept 405

Self-Esteem 406

The Whole Human: Personality Theories 406

The Trait Approach — Describe Yourself in 18,000 Words or Less 407

Predicting Behavior 407

Classifying Traits 407

The Big Five 408

Psychoanalytic Theory — Id Came to Me in a Dream 411

The Structure of Personality 411

The Dynamics of Personality 412

Personality Development 413

The Neo-Freudians 414

Humanistic Theory — Peak Experiences and Personal Growth 417

Maslow and Self-Actualization 417

The Whole Person: Positive Personality Traits 418

Carl Rogers' Self Theory 419

Humanistic View of Development 420

Learning Theories of Personality — Habit I Seen You Before? 421

How Situations Affect Behavior 422

Personality = Behavior 422

Social Learning Theory 423

Behaviorist View of Development 424

Nature and Nurture — The Great Personality Debate 425

Do We Inherit Personality? 425

Is Personality Affected by Environment? 427

Traits, Consistency, and Situations 427

Personality Theories — Overview and Comparison 428

Personality Assessment — Psychological Yardsticks 429

Interviews 429

Direct Observation and Rating Scales 430

Personality Questionnaires 431

Projective Tests of Personality 433

Psychology in Action: Barriers and Bridges — Understanding Shyness 435

Chapter in Review: Gateways to Personality 437

Gateway Questions Revisited 437

Media Resources 438

Feature Boxes (Highlights)

- Human Diversity: Self-Esteem and Culture — Hotshot or Team Player? 406
- Discovering Psychology: What's Your Musical Personality? 408
- Discovering Psychology: Which Personality Are You (and Which Is Best)? 410
- The Clinical File: Telling Stories about Ourselves 420
- Critical Thinking: The Amazing Twins 426

13 Health, Stress, and Coping 441

Mee Jung's Amazing Race 441

Health Psychology — Here's to Your Good Health 442

Behavioral Risk Factors 442

Health-Promoting Behaviors 443

Early Prevention 445

Community Health 445

Positive Psychology: Wellness 445

Stress—Thrill or Threat? 446
General Adaptation Syndrome 446
Stress, Illness, and Your Immune System 447
When Is Stress a Strain? 448
Appraising Stressors 449
Coping with Threat 450
Frustration—Blind Alleys and Lead Balloons 451
Reactions to Frustration 452
Coping with Frustration 453
Conflict—Yes, No, Yes, No, Yes, No, Well, Maybe 453
Managing Conflicts 455
Psychological Defense—Mental Karate? 456
Learned Helplessness and Depression—Is There Hope? 458
Learned Helplessness 458
Depression 459
Depression: Why Students Get the Blues 460
Recognizing Depression 460
Coping with the College Blues 460
Stress and Health—Unmasking a Hidden Killer 461
Life Events and Stress 461
Psychosomatic Disorders 463
Biofeedback 464
The Cardiac Personality 465
Hardy Personality 467
Positive Psychology: Hardiness, Optimism, and Happiness 467
Psychology in Action: Stress Management 468
Chapter in Review: Gateways to Health, Stress, and Coping 472
Gateway Questions Revisited 472
Media Resources 473
Feature Boxes (Highlights)
- **Discovering Psychology:** Unhealthy Birds of a Feather 444
- **Human Diversity:** So You Think You're Poor 450
- **The Clinical File:** Coping with Traumatic Stress 451
- **Human Diversity:** Acculturative Stress—Stranger in a Strange Land 463
- **Critical Thinking:** It's All in Your Mind 464

14 Psychological Disorders 475

Beware the Helicopters 475
Normality—What's Normal? 476
Core Feature of Disordered Behavior 477
Insanity and the Insanity Defense 478
Classifying Mental Disorders—Problems by the Book 478
An Overview of Psychological Disorders 479
General Risk Factors 482
Disorders in Perspective—Psychiatric Labeling 482
Social Stigma 482
Psychotic Disorders—The Dark Side of the Moon 484
The Nature of Psychosis 484
Delusional Disorders—An Enemy Behind Every Tree 486
Paranoid Psychosis 486
Schizophrenia—Shattered Reality 486
Disorganized Schizophrenia 487
Catatonic Schizophrenia 487
Paranoid Schizophrenia 488
Undifferentiated Schizophrenia 488
The Causes of Schizophrenia 488
Implications 491
Mood Disorders—Peaks and Valleys 492
Major Mood Disorders 492
What Causes Mood Disorders? 493
Anxiety-Based Disorders—When Anxiety Rules 495
Adjustment Disorders 495
Anxiety Disorders 496
Obsessive-Compulsive Disorder 498
Stress Disorders 498
Dissociative Disorders 499
Somatoform Disorders 499
Anxiety and Disorder—Four Pathways to Trouble 501
Psychodynamic Approach 501
Humanistic-Existential Approaches 501
Behaviorist Approach 502
Cognitive Approach 502
Personality Disorders—Blueprints for Maladjustment 502
Maladaptive Personality Patterns 503
Antisocial Personality 503
Psychology in Action: Suicide—Lives on the Brink 505
Chapter in Review: Gateways to Psychological Disorders 507
Gateway Questions Revisited 507
Media Resources 509
Feature Boxes (Highlights)
- **Discovering Psychology:** Crazy for a Day 477
- **Human Diversity:** Running Amok with Cultural Maladies 480
- **Critical Thinking:** A Disease Called Freedom 483
- **Brainwaves:** The Schizophrenic Brain 490
- **The Clinical File:** Sick of Being Sick 500

15 Therapies 511

Paddle Like a Duck 511
Origins of Therapy—Bored Out of Your Skull 512
Psychoanalysis—Expedition into the Unconscious 513
Psychoanalysis Today 514
Dimensions of Therapy—Let Me Count the Ways 514
Dimensions of Psychotherapy 514

Humanistic Therapies—Restoring Human Potential 516
- Client-Centered Therapy 516
- Existential Therapy 516
- Gestalt Therapy 517

Cognitive Therapy—Think Positive! 517
- Cognitive Therapy for Depression 518
- Rational-Emotive Behavior Therapy 518

Therapies Based on Classical Conditioning—Healing by Learning 520
- Aversion Therapy 521
- Desensitization 522

Operant Therapies—All the World Is a Skinner Box? 524
- Nonreinforcement and Extinction 525
- Reinforcement and Token Economies 525

Medical Therapies—Psychiatric Care 527
- Drug Therapies 527
- Electrical Stimulation Therapy 528
- Psychosurgery 528
- Hospitalization 529
- Community Mental Health Programs 530

Therapies—Human to the Core 530
- Core Features of Psychotherapy 531
- Basic Counseling Skills 532

The Future of Therapy—Magnets, Groups, and Smartphones 534
- New Medical Therapies 534
- Group Therapy 534
- Therapy at a Distance 536

Psychology in Action: Self-Management and Seeking Professional Help 538

Chapter in Review: Gateways to Therapies 542

Gateway Questions Revisited 542

Media Resources 544

Feature Boxes (Highlights)
- **Discovering Psychology:** Ten Irrational Beliefs—Which Do You Hold? 519
- **The Clinical File:** Overcoming the Gambler's Fallacy 520
- **Discovering Psychology:** Feeling a Little Tense? Relax! 522
- **Critical Thinking:** How Do We Know Therapy Actually Works? 531
- **Human Diversity:** Therapy and Culture—A Bad Case of "Ifufunyane" 534

16 Social Thinking and Social Influence 547

Six Degrees of Separation 547

Humans in a Social Context—People, People, Everywhere 548
- Roles 548
- Group Structure, Cohesion, and Norms 548

Social Cognition—Behind Our Masks 550
- Social Comparison Theory 551
- Attribution Theory 552
- Actor and Observer 552

Attitudes—Belief + Emotion + Action 554
- Forming Attitudes 554
- Attitudes and Behavior 555
- Attitude Measurement 556

Attitude Change—Why the Seekers Went Public 556
- Persuasion 556
- Cognitive Dissonance Theory 557

Social Influence—Follow the Leader 559
- Social Power 559

Mere Presence—Just Because You Are There 560
- Social Facilitation and Loafing 560
- Personal Space 560
- Spatial Norms 560

Conformity—Don't Stand Out 561
- The Asch Experiment 562
- Group Factors in Conformity 563

Compliance—A Foot in the Door 563

Obedience—Would You Electrocute a Stranger? 564
- Milgram's Obedience Studies 565

Coercion—Brainwashing and Cults 567
- Brainwashing 567
- Cults 567

Psychology in Action: Assertiveness Training—Standing Up for Your Rights 570

Chapter in Review: Gateways to Social Thinking and Social Influence 572

Gateway Questions Revisited 572

Media Resources 573

Feature Boxes (Highlights)
- **Critical Thinking:** Solitude 549
- **The Clinical File:** Self-Handicapping—Smoke Screen for Failure 553
- **Critical Thinking:** Groupthink—Agreement at Any Cost 562
- **Discovering Psychology:** The Car Game 565
- **Discovering Psychology:** Moo Like a Cow 566

17 Prosocial and Antisocial Behavior 575

Love and Hate 575

Prosocial Behavior—Come Together 576

Interpersonal Attraction—Social Magnetism? 576
- Finding Potential Friends 576
- Getting to Know One Another 577
- Social Exchange Theory 578

Loving—Dating and Mating 578
Love and Attachment 579
Evolution and Mate Selection 580
Helping Others—The Good Samaritan 581
Bystander Intervention 582
Who Will Help Whom? 583
The Whole Human: Everyday Heroes 583
Antisocial Behavior—The World's Most Dangerous Animal 584
Instincts 584
Biology 585
Frustration 585
Social Learning 586
Media Violence 586
Preventing Aggression 587
Prejudice—Attitudes That Injure 589
Becoming Prejudiced 589
The Prejudiced Personality 590
Intergroup Conflict—The Roots of Prejudice 591
Experiments in Prejudice 593
Psychology in Action: Multiculturalism—Living with Diversity 597
Chapter in Review: Gateways to Prosocial and Antisocial Behavior 599
Gateway Questions Revisited 599
Media Resources 600
Feature Boxes (Highlights)
- **Critical Thinking:** Pornography and Aggression Against Women—Is There a Link? 587
- **Discovering Psychology:** I'm Not Prejudiced, Right? 590
- **Human Diversity:** Choking on Stereotypes 592
- **Critical Thinking:** Terrorists, Enemies, and Infidels 593
- **Human Diversity:** Is America Purple? 594

18 Applied Psychology 603
In Touch with Knowledge 603
Industrial/Organizational Psychology—Psychology at Work 604
Theories of Leadership 604
Job Satisfaction 606
Job Enrichment 607
Organizational Culture 608
Personnel Psychology 608
Environmental Psychology—Life on Spaceship Earth 611
Environmental Influences on Behavior 612
Stressful Environments 613
Human Influences on the Environment 615
Sustainable Lifestyles 616
Social Dilemmas 617
Environmental Problem Solving 618
Conclusion 618
Educational Psychology—An Instructive Topic 619
Elements of a Teaching Strategy 620
Psychology and Law—Judging Juries 620
Jury Behavior 620
Jury Selection 622
Sports Psychology—The Athletic Mind 623
Motor Skills 624
The Whole Human: Peak Performance 624
Psychology in Action: Human Factors Psychology—Who's the Boss Here? 626
Chapter in Review: Gateways to Applied Psychology 629
Gateway Questions Revisited 629
Media Resources 631
The Whole Human: Psychology and You 631
Feature Boxes (Highlights)
- **Critical Thinking:** From Glass Ceiling to Labyrinth 605
- **The Clinical File:** Desk Rage and Healthy Organizations 608
- **Discovering Psychology:** Surviving Your Job Interview 610
- **Critical Thinking:** Territoriality 612
- **Discovering Psychology:** Reuse and Recycle 617
- **Human Diversity:** Peanut Butter for the Mind—Designing Education for Everyone 621
- **Critical Thinking:** Death-Qualified Juries 622

Appendix: Behavioral Statistics 633
References R-1
Name Index N-1
Subject Index/Glossary S-1

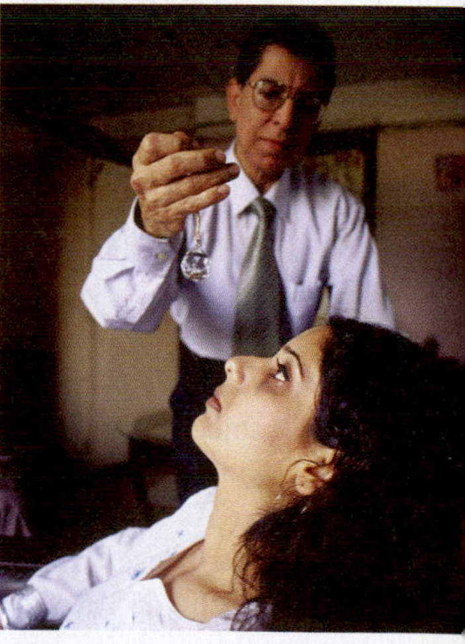

Preface

To the Student — An Invitation to Learn Psychology

Greetings from your authors! We look forward to being your guides as you explore the exciting field of psychology and our ever-evolving understanding of human behavior. In a very real sense, we wrote this book about you, for you, and to you. We sincerely hope you will find, as we do, that what you learn is at once familiar, exotic, surprising, and challenging.

Reading Introduction to Psychology: Gateways to Mind and Behavior

In *Gateways to Mind and Behavior,* we have done all we could imagine to make it enjoyable for you to read this book. We trust you will find your first journey through psychology to be quite interesting and useful to you in your everyday life. Each chapter of this book will take you into a different realm of psychology, such as personality, abnormal behavior, memory, consciousness, or human development. Each realm is complex and fascinating in its own right, with many pathways, landmarks, and interesting detours to discover. Like any journey of discovery, your exploration of psychology will help you to better understand yourself, others, and the world around you. It's definitely a trip worth taking.

Studying Introduction to Psychology: Gateways to Mind and Behavior

None of us likes to start a new adventure by reading a manual. We just want to step off the airplane and begin our vacation, get right into that new computer game, or just start using our new camera or cell phone. You might be similarly tempted to just start reading this textbook. Please be patient. Successfully learning psychology depends on how you study this book, as well as how you read it.

Psychology is about each of us. It asks us to adopt a reflective attitude as we inquire, "How can we step outside of ourselves to look objectively at how we live, think, feel, and act?" Psychologists believe the answer is through careful thought, observation, and inquiry. As simple as that may seem, thoughtful reflection takes practice to develop. It is the guiding light for all that follows.

Gateways to Mind and Behavior, then, is your passport to an adventure in active learning, not just passive reading. To help you get off to a good start, we strongly encourage you to read our short "manual," *Introduction: The Psychology of Studying,* which precedes Chapter 1. This introduction describes a variety of study skills, including the *reflective SQ4R* method, which you can use to get the most out of this text, your psychology course, and your other courses as well. It also explains how you can explore psychology through digital media such as the Internet, electronic databases, and interactive CD-ROMs.

To the Instructor — An Invitation to Teach Psychology

Thank you for choosing *Introduction to Psychology: Gateways to Mind and Behavior* for your students and for your course. Marcel Proust wrote, "The real voyage of discovery consists not in seeing new landscapes but in having new eyes." It is in this spirit that we have written this book to promote not just an interest in human behavior but also an appreciation for the perspective of the psychologist.

As we point out to your students in *Introduction: The Psychology of Studying,* which precedes Chapter 1, there is a big difference between experiencing and reflecting on experience (Norman 1993). For John Dewey (1910), reflective thinking is the "active, persistent and careful consideration of any belief or supposed form of knowledge in the light of the grounds that support it, and the further conclusion to which it tends." The psychologist's perspective, of course, involves reflecting on human behavior in a variety of ways. When it comes to studying psychology, reflective cognition requires actively thinking about what you have just read, which results in deeper understanding and memory. (Please consider taking a look at our *Introduction* as it explains to your students in some detail how to become a more reflective student, as well as outlining how they can get the most out of this book. By the way, we encourage you, if at all possible, to assign your students to read it as well.)

Throughout this text, we have tried to select only the very "best" material from the many topics that could be presented. Nevertheless, *Gateways to Mind and Behavior* covers not only the heart of psychology, but also many topics at the cutting edge of current knowledge, including a focus on the practical applications of psychology, the growing importance of neuroscience, and the richness of human diversity. New information, anecdotes, perspectives, and narratives appear throughout the 13th edition. The result is a concise text that is readable, manageable, informative, and motivating. At the same time, we have structured this book to help students consolidate the skills to learn efficiently and to become better critical thinkers. Without such skills, students cannot easily go, as Jerome Bruner (1973) put it, "beyond the information given."

The Teaching Challenge

Wouldn't it be nice if all of our students came to our courses highly motivated to explore psychology and well prepared to cope with the learning challenges we create for them? As the authors of this textbook, we have together accumulated some 60 years of classroom experience, teaching tens of thousands of college and university students. Although we have found most students to be generally well-intentioned, our modern world certainly does immerse them in their work, careers, families, intimate relationships, popular culture, and life in general. As we compete for ever more limited student attention, we must do more than just lecture in psychology. We must also motivate our students to read and learn, as well as to educate them about how to learn effectively (Matthew & Sternberg, 2009; Paternoster & Pogarsky, 2009).

We have explicitly designed and written the 13th edition of *Gateways to Mind and Behavior* to foster deeper student engagement with the field of psychology, better memory for what has been read and studied, and a deeper understanding of how to become more reflective learners and thinkers. To help you and your students reach these goals, we have organized our design philosophy around three core principles:

1: Readability and Narrative Emphasis

Many introductory psychology students are reluctant readers. Selecting a textbook is half the battle in teaching a successful course. A good text does much of the work of imparting information to your students. This frees class time for your discussion, extra topics, or media presentations. It also leaves students asking for more. When a book overwhelms students or cools their interest, teaching and learning suffer. If students won't read the textbook, they can't very well be reflective about what they have read.

That's why we've worked hard to make this a clear, readable, and engaging text. *Gateways to Mind and Behavior* is designed to give students a clear grasp of major concepts without burying them in details. At the same time, it offers a broad overview that reflects psychology's rich heritage of ideas. We think students will find this book informative and intellectually stimulating.

Because we want students to read this book with genuine interest and enthusiasm, not merely as an obligation, we have made a special effort to weave narrative threads through every chapter. Everyone loves a good story, and the story of psychology is among the most compelling to be told. Throughout *Gateways to Mind and Behavior,* we have used intriguing anecdotes and examples to propel reading and sustain interest.

Practical Applications

To make psychology even more inviting to students, we have emphasized the many ways that psychology relates to practical problems in daily life. For example, a major feature of this book is the *Psychology in Action* sections found at the end of each chapter. These high-interest discussions bridge the gap between theory and practical applications. We believe it is fair for students to ask, "Does this mean anything to me? Can I use it? Why should I learn it if I can't?" The Psychology in Action sections show students how to solve practical problems and manage their own behavior. This allows them to see the benefits of adopting new ideas, and it breathes life into psychology's concepts.

2: Integrated Support for Active Learning

Studying, rather than reading, a textbook requires the active engagement that psychologist Donald Norman (1993) calls *reflective cognition*. Being reflective when you read a textbook involves asking yourself if you understand what you are reading, how it might relate to things you already know, what new questions your reading might trigger, and so on. The resulting elaboration of the just-read new information is, perhaps, the best way to foster understanding and form lasting memories (Anderson, 2010a; Gadzella, 1995; Goldstein, 2011).

Gateways to Mind and Behavior was the first college text with an SQ4R active-learning format. Over the years, Dennis Coon's pioneering books have made learning psychology a rewarding experience for more than 2 million students. With their feedback, and generous help from many professors, we have continued to refine the unique features of *Gateways to Mind and Behavior*.

In keeping with this tradition of pedagogical innovation, we have redesigned this edition of *Gateways to Mind and Behavior* to encourage students to become more reflective, active learners. To achieve this important pedagogical goal, the traditional SQ4R method has been updated to *reflective SQ4R,* an active-learning format, to make studying psychology an even more rewarding experience. As students explore concepts, they are encouraged to think critically about ideas and relate them to their own experiences. Notice how the steps of the reflective SQ4R method—*survey, question, read, recite, reflect,* and *review*—are incorporated into the chapter design:

Survey

Features at the beginning of each chapter help students build cognitive maps of upcoming topics, thus serving as advance organizers (Ausubel, 1978). A photograph and short preview arouses interest, gives an overview of the chapter, and focuses attention on the task at hand. A *Gateway Theme* and a list of more detailed *Gateway Questions* are then given to guide reading. These questions are now also numbered, making it easier for students and instructors to relate the Gateway Questions to a matched set of learning objectives that appear throughout the materials that accompany this textbook.

The answers to Gateway Questions are what we think of as *Gateway Concepts*. In other words, they open intellectual pathways and summarize psychology's "big ideas." Ultimately, the Gateway

Concepts provide a good summary of what students have learned. If they remember most of them 10 years after finishing reading this book, we will be happy authors, indeed. With these chapter-opening features, we invite students to read with a purpose and actively process information.

Question

How can questioning be built into a textbook? Each major chapter section begins with one or more Gateway Questions. As students read a chapter, they can try to discover the answers to these questions. They can then compare their answers with the ones listed in the chapter summary.

Further, throughout each chapter, italicized *Dialogue Questions,* like the one just above, also serve as advance organizers. That is, Dialogue Questions prompt students to look for important ideas as they read, thus promoting active learning. They also establish a dialogue in which the questions and reactions of students are anticipated. This clarifies difficult points in a lively give-and-take between questions and responses.

Read

We've made every effort to make this a clear, readable text. To further aid comprehension, we've used a full array of traditional learning aids. These include boldface terms (with phonetic pronunciations), bulleted summaries, a robust illustration program, summary tables, a name index, and an integrated subject index and glossary. As an additional aid, figure and table references in the text are marked with small geometric shapes. These "place-holders" make it easier for students to return to the section they were reading after they have paused to view a table or figure.

We have made the glossary function in this edition even more powerful. All glossary items are bolded and defined in-text as a term is first encountered. This aids reading comprehension because students get clear definitions when and where they need them — in the general text itself. In addition, a parallel *Running Glossary* defines key terms in the margins of the relevant pages. The Running Glossary makes it easier for students to find, study, and review important terms. Finally, the *Main Glossary,* at the end of the book, has been integrated with the *Subject Index,* making it easier to link important definitions to where they are discussed in the text.

Recite

Throughout each chapter, strategically placed built-in study guides called *Knowledge Builders* give students a chance to test their recall and further develop their understanding of preceding topics. Each Knowledge Builder includes a *Recite* section, a short, noncomprehensive quiz, to help students actively process information and assess their progress. Recite questions, which are not as difficult as in-class tests, are meant to offer a sample of what students could be asked about various topics. Students who miss any items are encouraged to backtrack and clarify their understanding before reading more. In other words, completing Recite questions serves as a form of recitation to enhance learning.

Reflect

Of course, simple recitation is usually not sufficient to foster deeper understanding. Accordingly, in each chapter, we invite students to engage in two distinct types of reflection, self-reflection and critical thinking:

- **Self-Reflection** Self-reflection (or self-reference) makes new information more meaningful by relating it to what is already known (Klein and Kihlstrom, 1986). We provide many opportunities for self-reflection throughout *Gateways to Mind and Behavior*. The text is written with many contemporary references, examples, and stories to make it easier for students to relate what they are reading to their own life experience. As we mentioned previously, each chapter ends with a Psychology in Action section that invites students to relate psychology to practical problems in their own daily lives.

  Discovering Psychology boxes in many chapters are "try-it" demonstrations that enable students to observe interesting facets of their own behavior or do self-assessment exercises. In this way, students are given yet another way to link new information to concrete experiences. Finally, to help students further elaborate their new understanding, each Knowledge Builder includes a series of *Self-Reflect* questions that encourage students to connect new concepts with personal experiences and prior knowledge.

- **Critical Thinking** Being reflective about psychology involves more than self-reflectively asking "What does this have to with me and what I already know?" It also involves reflecting more deeply about the field. Our book also invites students to think critically about psychology.

  The active, questioning nature of the reflective SQ4R method is, in itself, an inducement to critical thinking. In addition, every Knowledge Builder also includes *Think Critically* questions. These stimulating questions challenge students to think critically and analytically about psychology. Each is followed by a brief answer with which students can compare their own thoughts. Many of these answers are based on research and are informative in their own right. Many of the Dialogue Questions that introduce topics in the text also act as models of critical thinking.

  Further, Chapter 1 contains a discussion of critical thinking skills and a rational appraisal of pseudopsychologies. In addition, the discussion of research methods in Chapter 1 is actually a short course on how to think clearly about behavior. It is augmented by suggestions about how to critically evaluate claims in the popular media. Chapters 8 and 9, which cover cognition, language, creativity, and intelligence, include many topics related to critical thinking.

  Throughout the text, many boxed highlights promote critical thinking about specific topics that students should approach with healthy skepticism. The *Critical Thinking* boxes model a reflective approach to the theoretical and empirical foundations of critical thinking in psychology. In addition, *Human Diversity* boxes encourage reflection on the variability of the human experience, *The Clinical File* boxes encourage reflection on the clinical applications of psychology, and *Brainwaves* boxes foster deeper insight into the brain structures and processes that underlie psychological phenomena. Taken together, these features will help students think more reflectively about your course and the field of psychology, while also gaining thinking skills of lasting value.

Review

As we noted previously, all important terms appear in a Running Glossary throughout the book, which aids review. We have also integrated the Main Glossary with the Subject Index. When reviewing, students can easily link definitions of concepts with the appropriate section of text in which those concepts are introduced and discussed.

As also noted, a Psychology in Action section shows students how psychological concepts relate to practical problems, including problems in their own lives. The information found in Psychology in Action helps reinforce learning by illustrating psychology's practicality.

To help students further consolidate their learning, each chapter *Summary* restates all of the major ideas presented earlier in the chapter, organized around the same Gateway Questions found at the beginning of the chapter. In this way, we bring the reflective SQ4R process full-circle and reinforce the learning objectives for the chapter.

3: *Integrative Themes:* The Whole Person

No one linear chapter organization can fully capture the interconnectedness of our field. This edition of *Gateways to Mind and Behavior* continues to offer *Bridges,* clearly marked in-text links to other material relevant to the reading at hand. For example, a student reading about the Freudian theory of dreams will encounter a Bridge to a relevant discussion of psychoanalysis in a later chapter.

In addition, to convey some of this richness we have woven a number of broad themes throughout the chapters of this book. Starting in Chapter 1, we explore the idea that human behavior is better understood when examined from three complementary perspectives: the biological perspective, the psychological perspective, and the sociocultural perspective. We express the idea that insights from one perspective can often be combined with insights from another throughout the book, in periodic, short, integrative sections entitled *The Whole Person*. Furthermore, we explore this natural complexity throughout chapters in a variety of more detailed themes. You may choose to explicitly present these themes to your students. Alternatively, you might leave these for your students to explore and unconsciously absorb.

The Biological Perspective: The Growing Importance of Neuroscience

Our students, partly because of popular media, are increasingly aware that the brain and the nervous system play a role in shaping human behavior. While our chapter on *Brain and Behavior* deals with the usual topics, such as methods of studying the brain, neural functioning, synaptic transmission, the structure of the nervous system and brain, and the endocrine system, we deliberately include a discussion of the biological perspective in many of the other chapters comprising this book. One way we do this is to incorporate a *Brainwaves* box into some of those chapters. ■ Table A.1 gives a chapter-by-chapter list of topics that are discussed from the biological perspective.

The Psychological Perspective: The Centrality of Self-Knowledge

There are many ways we have threaded the psychological perspective throughout this book. It is, of course, central to psychology. In this edition of *Gateways to Mind and Behavior,* we have chosen to place a special thematic emphasis on the self. In doing so, we respond to Timothy Wilson's (2009) criticism that introductory psychology courses do not spend enough time exploring the issue of self-knowledge despite the fact that students are terribly interested in learning more about themselves. Besides, as you may have already noted, our focus on active, reflective learning is also designed to improve our students' self-awareness. Throughout the book, we follow the development of the self from the beginnings of self recognition in infancy to the development of wisdom in old age. ■ Table A.1 gives a chapter-by-chapter list of the relevant discussions.

The Sociocultural Perspective: Human Diversity, Culture, and Gender

Of course, no introductory psychology textbook would be complete without a discussion of human diversity and the multicultural, multifaceted nature of contemporary society. In *Gateways to Mind and Behavior,* students will find numerous discussions of human diversity, including differences in race, ethnicity, culture, gender, abilities, sexual orientation, and age. Too often, such differences needlessly divide people into opposing groups. Our aim throughout this text is to discourage stereotyping, prejudice, discrimination, and intolerance. We've tried to make this book gender neutral and sensitive to diversity issues. All pronouns and examples involving females and males are equally divided by gender. In artwork, photographs, and examples, we have tried to portray the rich diversity of humanity. In addition, a boxed feature, *Human Diversity,* appears throughout the book, providing students with examples of how to be more reflective about human diversity.

In short, many topics and examples in this book encourage students to appreciate social, physical, and cultural differences and to accept them as a natural part of being human. ■ Table A.1 gives a chapter-by-chapter list of discussions of issues of human diversity and culture, while ■ Table A.1 does the same for issues of gender.

TABLE A.1 Modules for Active Learning

Chapter	Neuroscience in *Introduction to Psychology*	Self-Knowledge in *Introduction to Psychology*	Human Diversity and Culture in *Introduction to Psychology*	Gender in *Introduction to Psychology*
Chapter 1 Introduction to Psychology and Research Methods	Neuroscience and biopsychology, evolutionary psychology, the biological perspective, EEG and dreaming, links between brain and behavior, phrenology, Phineas Gage and case studies	Importance of self-knowledge, ethical research, psychological perspective, self-actualization, testing common sense, critical thinking, personal freedom, scientific thinking, introspection, behaviorism, humanism, eclecticism	Cultural psychology, human diversity, appreciating social and cultural differences, the impact of culture, cultural relativity, a broader view of diversity, human diversity and representative samples	The psychology of gender, gender differences in communication, gender bias in research, women in psychology, unbiased sampling in research, gender and social norms
Chapter 2 Brain and Behavior	Neural function, synaptic transmission, neurotransmitters, parts of nervous system and brain, localization of function, methods of studying the brain, endocrine system, handedness	Brain and self, localization of function including self, self-directed neuroplasticity, locked-in syndrome, truth and lies, split-brain and consciousness, intelligence, frontal lobes, strokes and self, hemispheres and self, mirror neurons, thinking styles, emotions	Biological treatments for people with spinal injuries, hypopituitary dwarfism, acromegaly, handedness and laterality, brain interfaces for people with total paralysis, diagnosis of neurological conditions, cultural experiences shape the brain, handedness and culture	Specialization of men's and women's brains, sex differences in lateralization, hormonal differences, sex and steroids
Chapter 3 Human Development	Biological factors in heredity and development, readiness, maturation, prenatal biological influences, sensitive periods, enriched environments and the brain, reaction range, temperament, biological predisposition to language, cognitive stages and brain maturation, puberty, physical changes in old age	Temperament, newborn sensitivity, imitation, attachment, terrible twos, egocentrism, theory of minds, self-awareness, turn-taking in language development, self-recognition, search for identity, moral development, role confusion, self-acceptance, personal growth, self-esteem reactions to impending death	Culture and evolution, ethnic differences in child-rearing, relationship between culture and babbling, parentese in different cultures, sociocultural influences on cognitive development, scaffolding, zone of proximal development, adolescent status and culture, diversity and the adolescent search for identity, ethnicity and personal identity, culture and moral reasoning, ageism and myths about the elderly	Prenatal development, maternal and paternal parenting styles, emotional attachment patterns, gender-role development, gender and puberty, male and female moral reasoning, male and female midlife transitions
Chapter 4 Sensation and Perception	Sensory filtering, transduction, sensory localization in the brain, electrical stimulation of sensory experiences in the brain and sensory nerves, physiology of various sense receptors and sensory pathways, sensory gating, neuromatrix theory, perceptual construction and learning	Perceptual experiences, psychophysics, reality testing, perceptual awareness, perceptual learning, perceptual habits and top-down processing	The "other race" effect in facial recognition, culture and the recognition of pictorial depth cues, culture and the Müller-Lyer illusion, cross-racial perceptions (eyewitness accuracy), cultural differences in perception	Sex differences in color deficiency
Chapter 5 States of Consciousness	EEG, stages of sleep, REM and dreaming, biological theories of sleep and dreaming, effects of "sleeping pills," narcolepsy, EEG and hypnosis, brain scans and meditation, how psychoactive drugs affect the brain and neurotransmitters, drug addiction	Consciousness, self-awareness and heightened self-awareness, self-control under hypnosis, autosuggestion, self-control mindfulness, analyzing dreams, lucid dreaming	States of consciousness and culture, culture and interpretations of dreams and hypnopompic imagery, the cultural context of drug use	REM sleep and dreaming in men and women, caffeine and pregnancy, effects of alcohol on sexual performance
Chapter 6 Conditioning and Learning	Eyeblink conditioning, the brain and diagnosis of autism and minimal consciousness, conditioned emotional reactions and the amygdala, primary reinforcement and intracranial self-stimulation	Awareness of cognitive learning vs. unconscious nature of associative learning, self-managed behavior	Spanking and culture, comparing U.S. television content with cultures that limit televised violence	Effects of television on children's perceptions of sex roles, effects of television on children's level of aggression

Chapter 7 Memory	Penfield, brain stimulation and memory, amnesia and types of memory, cerebellum and procedural memory, brain trauma and amnesia, consolidation, long-term potentiation, role of hippocampus in declarative memories, limbic system and flashbulb memories, cortex and long-term memory	Episodic memory, elaborative encoding, experience of partial retrieval, self-reference and memory, mnemonics	Aging and memory, cultural influences on memory, eyewitnesses and cross-racial recognition, labeling and the ability to remember people from other social groups	Recovered memories vs. false memories
Chapter 8 Cognition, Language, and Creativity	Synesthesia, imagery and the brain, kinesthetic imagery, sign language and the brain, creativity vs. mental illness	Synesthesia, imagery, kinesthetic images, cognitive effects of bilingualism, linguistic relativity, insight, intuition, creativity	Linguistic misunderstandings between cultures, the pros and cons of bilingualism, linguistic relativity, cultural differences in the use of phonemes, the deaf community and gestural languages, cultural barriers to problem solving	Stereotypes and cognition
Chapter 9 Intelligence	Lou Gehrig's disease and intelligence, IQ and cortical area, organic causes of mental disability, RT and intelligence, heredity and intelligence	Giftedness, self-respect and intellectual disability, multiple intelligences, wisdom	Age and IQ; the developmentally disabled; race, culture, ethnicity, and intelligence; cultural differences in intelligence (as taught to children); culture-fair intelligence testing	Fragile X, sex differences in IQ, men, women, and the definition of intelligence
Chapter 10 Motivation and Emotion	Needs as internal deficiencies, biological motives, homeostasis, circadian rhythms, role of melatonin, biological factors in hunger, hypothalamus and thirst, types of thirst, estrus, sex hormones, physiological changes and emotion, physiological arousal, moods, emotion and the limbic system, including the amygdala, role of autonomic nervous system and arousal, parasympathetic rebound, polygraphy, brain scans and lying	Intrinsic motivation and creativity, meta-needs, self-actualization, emotional expression and health, higher emotional intelligence	Cultural values and food preferences; culture, ethnicity, and dieting; pain avoidance and cultural conditioning; the influence of culture on emotional expressions; cultural differences in the occurrence of emotion; cultural differences in facial expressions; cultural learning and body language	Eating disorders and gender, how hormones affect sex drive, gender differences in emotion, alexithymia
Chapter 11 Sex, Gender, and Sexuality	Biology of sexual development, prenatal sex development, genes, the brain and sexual orientation, prenatal biological basing effect, differing skills of men and women, testosterone and sexual behavior	Androgyny and self-expression, sexual self-awareness, sexually responsible behavior, communication skills, sexuality and self-esteem	Sexual orientation, gender-role stereotypes, culture and gender roles, androgyny, gender variance, casual sex in America, sexual attitudes and behavior across cultures, oversexualization of children, rape "culture", AIDS worldwide	Psychosocial differences between men and women, intersexuality, controversy about gender differences in ability (left brain/right brain), gender roles, gender-role stereotypes, culture and gender roles, gender-role socialization, androgyny, sexual arousal (after watching erotic films), sexual activity, sexual orientation, role of hormones in sex drive, gender differences in sexual response, sexual double standard, gender-role stereotyping and rape, rates of HIV/AIDS infection and death
Chapter 12 Personality	Behavioral genetics and personality, Big 5 traits, brain systems and neurotransmitters, limbic system and the unconscious	Long-term consistency of self, self-concept, self-esteem, self-confidence, Freudian ego, free choice, self-actualization, positive personality traits, self-image	Acculturative stress, character and culture, self-esteem and culture, common traits and culture	Social learning of male and female traits, Oedipus vs. Electra complexes

Continued

TABLE A.1 Modules for Active Learning *(continued)*

Chapter	Neuroscience in *Introduction to Psychology*	Self-Knowledge in *Introduction to Psychology*	Human Diversity and Culture in *Introduction to Psychology*	Gender in *Introduction to Psychology*
Chapter 13 Health, Stress, and Coping	Stress reaction, general adaptation syndrome, psychoneuroimmunology, psychosomatic disorders, biofeedback	Self-screening for illnesses, self-control, wellness, cognitive appraisal, coping, hardiness, optimism, happiness, stress management, humor	Culture shock and acculturative stress, scapegoating of ethnic group members	Sex differences in seeking social support
Chapter 14 Psychological Disorders	Biological risk factors, organic psychosis, Alzheimer's disease, hereditary and biological causes of schizophrenia, the schizophrenic brain, biology and depression, the psychopathic brain, diathesis-stress model	Congruence (between self-image and ideal self), possible selves, self-efficacy, self-reinforcement	How culture affects judgments of psychopathology, culture-bound syndromes from around the world, ethnic group differences in psychopathology	How gender affects judgments of psychopathology, gender differences in rates of anxiety disorders, sex differences in rates of clinical depression, gender differences in suicide (attempt and completion)
Chapter 15 Therapies	Drug therapies, ECT, brain stimulation therapy, psychosurgery, future of medical therapies, transcranial magnetic stimulation	Insight, personal growth and psychotherapy, human potential, choosing to become, courage, overcoming irrational beliefs, the fully functioning person, behavioral self-management	Cultural issues in counseling and psychotherapy, culturally aware therapists	
Chapter 16 Social Thinking and Social Influence	"Brainwashing"	Social comparison, self-disclosure, self-assertion, solitude	Culture, social roles, in-groups vs. out-groups, social status, attitudes	Upward comparison among women, self-handicapping and gender
Chapter 17 Prosocial and Antisocial Behavior	Homogamy, evolution and mate selection, aggression, biology, and the brain	Prosocial behavior, superordinate goals, overcoming stereotypes and prejudice, self-identity multiculturalism	Male-female differences in mate preferences, racial prejudice and discrimination, ethnocentrism, social stereotypes, cultural differences in hostility and aggression, symbolic prejudice, rejection and demonization of out-groups, experiments in creating and reducing prejudice, multiculturalism, breaking the prejudice habit, cultural awareness	Influence of physical attractiveness, male-female differences in mate preferences, evolutionary perspectives on male and female mate selection, levels of testosterone and aggression, effects of pornography on sexual violence against women
Chapter 18 Applied Psychology		Self-management, communication skills, beyond self-interest, sports and physical self-esteem, peak performance, flow, satisficing	Corporate "culture", cultural differences in norms governing personal space, attentional overload in urban settings, resource consumption in different cultures, universal instructional design	Gender role stereotypes and leadership, women as leaders, sex and jury composition

A Full Set of Learning and Teaching Supplements

The 13th edition of *Introduction to Psychology: Gateways to Mind and Behavior* is supported by a full set of learning and teaching supplements, ranging from a traditional study guide and instructor's manual to electronic resources such as a test bank and access to a variety of web-based materials. While these supplements are further described later in this preface, a few bear mentioning now.

To encourage further reflection, students will find a section called *Web Resources* at the end of each chapter. The websites described there invite students to go beyond the text to explore a wealth of interesting information on topics related to psychology. In addition, the *Interactive Learning* section at the end of each chapter directs students to *CengageNOW,* a powerful online study tool that provides students with a rich assortment of interactive learning experiences, animations, and simulations. *CengageNOW* is a web-based personalized study system that provides a pretest and a posttest for each chapter and separate chapter quizzes.

To ensure students really read and comprehend course material, *Aplia* for *Introduction to Psychology* helps students understand psychology as a science through fresh and compelling content, brief engagement activities that illustrate key concepts, and thought-provoking questions. *Aplia* includes auto-graded homework that is tailored to test quantitative and conceptual understanding of key topics.

Students can also visit *Psychology CourseMate*, where they can access an integrated eBook and chapter-specific learning tools, including flashcards, quizzes, videos, and more.

At *CengageBrain.com,* students can select from more than 10,000 print and digital study tools, including the option to buy individual e-chapters and e-books. The first e-chapter is free!

Introduction to Psychology: Gateways to Mind and Behavior—What's New?

Thanks to psychology's vitality, this edition is, once again, improved in many ways. To begin, we celebrate the longevity of this book, as reflected by the fact that this is the 13th edition, the "superstition edition." Throughout the book, students will find occasional references to superstition in general and superstitions about the number 13 in particular. We trust that students will find it amusing to track down these references.

This edition also features an updated reflective SQ4R system, outlined earlier in this Preface. The result will foster a better link between remembering the material in the book on the one hand and thinking reflectively and critically about psychology on the other hand.

Finally, the 13th edition of *Introduction to Psychology: Gateways to Mind and Behavior* also features some of the most recent and interesting information in psychology, drawing on an extensively updated and expanded reference list. More than two-thirds of the expanded reference list is dated 2000 or newer. The following annotations highlight just a few of the new topics and features that appear in this edition.

Introduction: The Psychology of Studying

- This section is now structured just like any other chapter, with Gateway Questions and a Summary section. Students are invited to practice what they are learning about reading a textbook while still reading in this section.
- We have once again updated our SQ4R framework; it is now known as *reflective SQ4R.*
- The Knowledge Builders have been restructured so that students can more easily see the connection with the reflective SQ4R method. Specifically, *Relate* questions have been renamed *Self-Reflect* questions and *Critical Thinking* questions have been renamed *Think Critically* questions to make it clearer that relating new information to personal experience and thinking critically about new information are both forms of reflective cognition.
- In addition, the updated Introduction shows students how to be more reflective as they read effectively, study more efficiently, take good notes, prepare for tests, take tests, create study schedules, and avoid procrastination.

Chapter 1: Introduction to Psychology and Research Methods

- This chapter has been revised and reorganized to make integration between critical thinking, the scientific method, and psychology easier for students to follow.
- The chapter opener has been reworked to include a new example and to introduce the idea of superstition.
- Previously scattered material on commonsense beliefs has been collected together and reworked into a section on commonsense beliefs.
- For greater clarity, critical thinking has now been redefined in terms of the relationship between logical analysis (theory) and systematic observation (data). The main section on critical thinking has been reorganized as well.
- The section on research specialties (including the small section on animal research) has been moved to the section on psychology as a career.
- The section on pseudopsychology now includes a definition of superstition. The objections to astrology have been reorganized into two parts: theoretical objections and empirical objections.
- The more common term *confirmation bias* has replaced *fallacy of positive instances*. The chapter has been thoroughly rewritten to more clearly reflect the role of confirmation bias in pseudopsychology and the role of disconfirmation in critical thinking and scientific psychology.
- The topic of research ethics has been integrated into the section on the scientific method.

- The previous section on the role of women in psychology is now a section on diversity. The first male and female African-American PhDs are introduced. Material on research bias can now be found here as well.
- The section on specialties in psychology now includes material on research specialties and animal research, which has been updated to feature Orca conservation.

Chapter 2: Brain and Behavior

- This chapter has been lengthened to reflect the growing importance of neuroscience in contemporary psychology. Additional neuroscience content can also be found in most subsequent chapters (most noticeably in *Brainwaves* boxes).
- A new chapter-opening photo and vignette highlight the centrality of the brain and how a stroke makes that clear to us.
- Glial cells are now mentioned as support structures in the brain.
- Neurotransmitters are given more extensive coverage, including a new table; they are referred to more often later in the book as well.
- The *Brainwaves* box about neurogenesis has been updated.
- Neurological soft signs are now discussed in a section on clinical case studies.
- The distinction between MRI and fMRI has been clarified.
- The idea that brain size relative to body size is related to intelligence has been clarified.
- A new *Clinical File* box, *Trapped!,* now collects together the information on locked-in syndrome.
- The hormone oxytocin is now covered in the section on the endocrine system.

Chapter 3: Human Development

- Height, which is determined by almost 200 genes acting in concert, is given as an example of a polygenic trait.
- It is now made clearer that the biological process of maturation can be either forced too early or delayed too late, using toilet training as an example.
- The section on teratogens has been updated and now includes a slightly revised definition.
- The material on the newborn has been reorganized to better track the idea that much early development is due to maturation. It also allows for a clearer association between early reflexes and later motor development.
- The importance of developing self-recognition now receives greater stress.
- The section on Hispanic parenting is now organized around the concept of "familismo."
- New examples are provided to help students better understand assimilation and accommodation.
- A new *Critical Thinking* box is now devoted to Theory of Mind, an important developmental topic.
- The section on midlife has been compressed and simplified.

Chapter 4: Sensation and Perception

- Following extensive reviewer feedback, Chapter 4 now combines material on sensation and perception, which were previously presented in two chapters.
- Core topics previously covered in two chapters continue to be covered in the same sequence, albeit in somewhat shortened form.
- The new chapter opens with a new photo and vignette.
- Combining sensation and perception has made possible a clearer treatment of the interaction between bottom-up and top-down processing in perception.
- The fundamentals of sensation, including thresholds, have been further refined.
- A new example of an artificial retina is now included.

Chapter 5: States of Consciousness

- A modified opening vignette and subsequent section better reflects the notion of levels of consciousness as well as altered states of consciousness.
- The definition of consciousness has been updated to more clearly reflect the current consensus that normal consciousness is of the external world and the internal world.
- A new theory of the function of sleep spindles is now given.
- The health risks of sleep apnea are clarified.
- The risk of co-sleeping is articulated.
- A new section on polydrug abuse highlights drug interactions. The case of Heath Ledger is featured.
- A small caveat about some possible benefits of psychoactive drug use counters an appropriately negative coverage of psychoactive drugs and their abuse.
- The first study of the long-term effects of Ecstasy is discussed.
- The use of amphetamines as "study drugs" is now discussed.
- The Psychology in Action section has been revised. Several theorists have been omitted, and Ernest Hartmann's Contemporary Theory of Dreaming has been added.

Chapter 6: Conditioning and Learning

- A new *Clinical File* box, *In the Blink of an Eye,* offers compelling examples of real-world applications of classical conditioning and links to other chapters as well.
- A new *Critical Thinking* box, *Are We Less Superstitious Than Pigeons?,* elaborates on animal and human superstitious conditioning.
- The section on learning aids has been updated and better linked to the pedagogy in textbook.
- The section on modeling in the media has been updated.

Chapter 7: Memory

- The chapter-opening photo and vignette have been updated.
- The section on stages of memory was extensively reorganized to make it easier to understand the Atkinson-Schiffrin model.

- The example in the *Human Diversity* box now refers to the memory consequences of being a *gaucho,* a South American cowboy.
- The term *constructive processing* has been changed to *elaborative processing*. The word *elaboration* is now consistently used throughout the chapter and the text to refer to the flexibility of long-term memory. In addition, *elaborative encoding* has been subsumed under the term *elaborative processing*.
- New glossary additions for *false memory* and *source confusion* allow for a better description of a major downside of elaborative memory processing.
- A new section, *From Encoding to Retrieval in Long-Term Memory,* better links encoding strategies to retrieval consequences.
- A new section, *Memory and Emotion,* now better describes the formation of flashbulb memories. The new section is part of a longer section on memory and the brain.

Chapter 8: Cognition, Language, and Creativity

- The treatment of the topics of cognition, imagery, language, problem solving, and creativity has been separated from the treatment of intelligence, which is presented in Chapter 9.
- A new chapter opener features synesthesia and the artist Kandinsky.
- The section on language has been expanded and now includes a new *Critical Thinking* box, *What's North of My Fork?,* which introduces a charming illustration of the linguistic relativity hypothesis.
- A new section on expertise now ends the revised section on problem solving.
- The section on intuition has been reorganized and now includes a new *Critical Thinking* box, *Extra Hot, Decaf, Double-Shot...,* on the difficulty of making choices in the modern world.
- A section on brainstorming has been added to the material on problem solving.

Chapter 9: Intelligence

- The treatment of intelligence has been separated from the treatment of the topics of cognition, imagery, language, problem solving, and creativity, which are presented in Chapter 8.
- Aptitude tests are now covered and distinguished from tests of general intelligence.
- Qualities of good tests (reliability, validity, standardization) are now covered.
- Stability of IQ across the lifespan is discussed.
- A new section discusses the relationship of IQ with sex, age, and occupation.
- The section on giftedness is now expanded.
- The section on intellectual disability has been dramatically expanded and includes coverage of a number of organic factors.
- Early childhood education is now championed.
- A new section on alternatives to psychometric intelligence has been created. Coverage of artificial intelligence and multiple intelligences can be found here along with new sections on cognitive psychology and IQ and the brain and IQ.

Chapter 10: Motivation and Emotion

- The opening vignette is new; previous material on alexithymia has been incorporated in the body of the chapter.
- The discussion of the trait of sensation-seeking has been revised.
- A new *Discovering Psychology* box, *True Grit,* highlights our need for achievement.
- The section on sudden death has been rewritten and expanded.
- The section on polygraphy introduces the guilty knowledge test.
- The relationship between attribution and appraisal has been clarified.
- The emotional effects of Botox are now considered in the section on the facial feedback hypothesis.
- The material on eating disorders has been updated in anticipation of the publication of the DSM-5.

Chapter 11: Gender and Sexuality

- The opening vignette has been updated.
- The treatment of sex reassignment has now been reorganized into a new section on transexuality.
- *Androgen insensitivity* is now more appropriately labeled *androgen insensitivity syndrome*. Similarly, *androgenital syndrome* is more accurately referred to as *congenital adrenal hyperplasia*.
- Figures on sexual anatomy have been combined and simplified.
- The chapter now reflects changes likely to appear in the DSM-5 with respect to the definitions of gender identity disorder, paraphilias, and sexual dysfunctions.
- Data on sexuality, including graphs, has been updated.
- Asexuality is introduced as a fourth sexual orientation.
- The material on behavioral risk factors for STDs is now couched more broadly.
- Hypersexual disorder is now discussed in the Psychology in Action section.

Chapter 12: Personality

- The opening section has been reorganized and shortened to more quickly transition to the main discussion of the four personality theories.
- Material on heredity has been moved to a later, new section, *Nature and Nurture—The Great Personality Debate.*
- Humanist theory is now treated before behavioral theory.
- The notion of biological predispositions is introduced. Trait theory and psychoanalytic theory are contrasted with learning theory and humanist approaches in their stress on personality consistencies as being due to innate dispositions.

- A new *Discovering Psychology* box, *Which Personality Are You (and Which is Best)?*, explores the common misconception that some personality traits are more desirable than others.
- Freudian slips are identified as such; an illustration cartoon has been added.

Chapter 13: Health, Stress, and Coping

- An updated vignette is reflected throughout the chapter.
- Health statistics have been updated throughout.
- The material on burnout has been reworked.
- A new *Human Diversity* box, *So You Think You're Poor,* features the interesting topic of the health effects of relative poverty.
- The section on recognizing depression now follows NIMH guidelines.
- The material on social support has been reworked and appears in the Psychology in Action section.
- The *Undergraduate Stress Questionnaire* is now included in the Psychology in Action section so students can measure their own stress levels.

Chapter 14: Psychological Disorders

- Mental health statistics have been updated throughout the chapter.
- This chapter has been updated to reflect the upcoming DSM-5 including a new section on the DSM-5, a discussion of some issues about adding new disorders, and updated tables including new naming conventions.
- The first section has been reorganized to better reflect the DSM-5 definition of mental disorders, the placement of the treatment of "insanity," and to discuss the dangers inherent in psychiatric labeling.
- New material on the insanity defense has been added.
- A new Japanese disorder, *hikikomori,* has been added to the section on culture-bound syndromes.
- Senator John McCain is offered as an example of a triskadekaphobe (someone who fears the number 13).
- The list of warning signs for suicide has been updated.

Chapter 15: Therapies

- The opening section is now labeled *Treating Psychological Distress*. It begins with a history of therapy and psychoanalysis and ends with a look at how therapies differ.
- The opening discussion of the basic aspects of therapy now better aligns with the dimensions of therapy listed in Table 15.3. These dimensions are now referred to more consistently throughout the chapter.
- Humanistic and cognitive therapies are now covered in successive sections and treated as two contrasting types of "talk" therapies.
- The two successive sections on behavior therapies are now more clearly identified as based on classical and operant conditioning respectively.
- The section on medical therapies has been updated. Table 15.2 includes a new column on Mode of Action linking back to Chapter 2 and major neurotransmitter systems.
- The section on medical therapies has been updated to include a discussion of electrical stimulation of the brain (other than ECT) in the somatic therapy section.
- A major new section now overviews psychotherapy and examines the future of psychotherapy, including a new section on TMS (transcranial magnetic stimulation). This section positions both group therapies and Internet therapy as the future of psychotherapy.

Chapter 16: Social Thinking and Social Influence

- The chapter-opening vignette has been updated.
- The term "status" has been clarified with a change to "social status."
- A new *Critical Thinking* box on solitude helps students distinguish between loneliness and being alone.
- Discussions of social comparison, attribution, and attitude formation have been collected together as forms of social cognition. To do so, material on social comparison is now covered in Chapter 16 (not Chapter 17).
- The term *buyer's regret* has been introduced in the analysis of cognitive dissonance.
- The factors that lead to compliance have been more clearly separated from particular compliance techniques. The result is greater clarity and a better explanation of how compliance techniques work.
- The chapter now includes an update on the Milgram studies.

Chapter 17: Prosocial and Antisocial Behavior

- The chapter-opening vignette has been revised and better integrated throughout the chapter itself.
- Material on social comparison was moved to Chapter 16, allowing for a clearer exposition of the more affective factors influencing interpersonal attraction.
- The section on interpersonal attraction has now been organized into two subsections: one on finding friends and one on getting to know each other.
- Reciprocity has been added to the list of factors shaping attraction.
- The section on helping others now opens with a more recent story than that of Kitty Genovese, whose case is still included.
- Bullying is treated as a form of aggression in a new section.
- Following contemporary theory, authoritarianism has been split into two dimensions: right wing authoritarianism and social dominance orientation.
- The concept of self-stereotyping has been introduced into the discussion on the damage inflicted by stereotyping.

Chapter 18: Applied Psychology

- The opening vignette on new digital developments has been updated and reflected throughout the chapter.
- Downsizing is now mentioned (in the context of caring companies).
- The notion of employee empowerment is now mentioned.

- Smart meters are introduced in the section on conservation, which now stresses control as well as feedback.
- The idea of learning styles now complements existing material on teaching styles.

Appendix: Behavioral Statistics

- A new opening vignette follows a student grappling with statistics. The vignette is woven throughout the Appendix. The result is a more engaging approach to traditionally dry material.

A Complete Course—Teaching and Learning Supplements

A rich array of supplements accompanies *Introduction to Psychology: Gateways to Mind and Behavior,* including several that make use of the latest technologies. These supplements are designed to make teaching and learning more effective. Many are available free to professors or students. Others can be packaged with this text at a discount.

Student Support Materials

Introductory students must learn a multitude of abstract concepts, which can make a first course in psychology difficult. The materials listed here will greatly improve students' chances for success.

Gateways to Psychology: Concept Maps and Concept Reviews

Concept Maps created by Claudia Cochran of El Paso Community College and quiz items updated by Shawn Talbot of Kellogg Community College appear for each chapter of the text on CourseMate. This includes a Gateways concept map.

Careers in Psychology: Opportunities in a Changing World, 2e

This informative booklet, written by Tara L. Kuther, is a Wadsworth exclusive. The pamphlet describes the field of psychology, as well as how to prepare for a career in psychology. Career options and resources are also discussed. *Careers in Psychology* can be packaged with this text at no additional cost to students (ISBN 0-495-60074-1).

Online Resources

The Internet is providing new ways to exchange information and enhance education. In psychology, Wadsworth is at the forefront in making use of this exciting technology.

Psychology CourseMate

Cengage Learning's *Psychology CourseMate* brings course concepts to life with interactive learning, study, and exam preparation tools that support the printed textbook. Watch student comprehension soar as your class works with the printed textbook and the textbook-specific website. *Psychology CourseMate* goes beyond the book to deliver what students need!

Aplia for *Introduction to Psychology* helps students understand psychology as a science through fresh and compelling content, brief engagement activities that illustrate key concepts, and thought-provoking questions.

Key features include:

- Auto-assigned, auto-graded homework holds students accountable for the material before they come to class, increasing their effort and preparation.
- Exercises include experiments with questions that test students' ability to interpret data and draw conclusions, graph-based questions that test quantitative understanding, and applications that gauge conceptual understanding.
- Customized images correspond to textbook visuals, providing a consistent look.
- Immediate, detailed explanations for every answer enhance comprehension.
- Grades are automatically recorded in your Aplia gradebook; analytics allow you to monitor and address performance on a student-by-student and topic-by-topic basis.

CENGAGENOW™

CengageNOW is an online teaching and learning resource that gives you more control in less time and delivers better outcomes—NOW. Students have access to an integrated eBook, interactive quizzing and practice, videos, and other multimedia tools to help them get the most out of your course.

InfoTrac® College Edition

InfoTrac College Edition is a powerful online learning resource, consisting of thousands of full-text articles from hundreds of journals and periodicals.

WebTUTOR™

WebTutor™

Jumpstart your course with customizable, rich, text-specific content within your Course Management System. Whether you want to Web-enable your class or put an entire course online, *WebTutor™* delivers. *WebTutor* offers a wide array of resources, including integrated eBook, media assets, quizzing, weblinks, and more! Visit webtutor.cengage.com to learn more.

Essential Teaching Resources

As every professor knows, teaching an introductory psychology course is a tremendous amount of work. The supplements listed here should not only make life easier for you, they should also make it possible for you to concentrate on the more creative and rewarding facets of teaching.

Instructor's Resource Manual

The *Instructor's Resource Manual* contains resources designed to streamline and maximize the effectiveness of your course preparation. In a three-ring binder format for the first time, this IRM is a treasure trove — from the introduction section, which includes a Resource Integration Guide, to a full array of chapter resources. Each chapter includes learning objectives, discussion questions, lecture enhancements, role-playing scenarios, "one-minute motivators," broadening-our-cultural-horizons exercises, journal questions, suggestions for further reading, media suggestions, and web links (ISBN: 1-111-83484-9).

Test Bank

The *Test Bank* was prepared by Jeannette Murphey. It includes more than 4,500 multiple-choice questions organized by chapter and by learning objectives. All items, which are classified as factual, conceptual, or applied, include correct answers and references from the text. All questions new to this edition are identified by an asterisk (ISBN: 1-111-83485-7).

PowerLecture with ExamView

The fastest, easiest way to build powerful, customized media-rich lectures, PowerLecture provides a collection of book-specific PowerPoint lectures and class tools to enhance the educational experience. JoinIn™ content for Response Systems allows you to transform your assessment tools with instant in-class quizzes and polls. Wadsworth's exclusive agreement to offer TurningPoint® software lets you pose book-specific questions and display students' answers seamlessly within the Microsoft PowerPoint slides of your own lecture, in conjunction with the "clicker" hardware of your choice (ISBN: 1-111-83485-7).

Videos

Wadsworth offers a variety of videos to enhance classroom presentations. Many video segments in the Wadsworth collection pertain directly to major topics in this text, making them excellent lecture supplements.

Wadsworth Film and Video Library for Introductory Psychology

Adopters can select from a variety of continually updated film and video options. The Wadsworth Film and Video Library includes selections from the *Discovering Psychology* series, the *Annenberg* series, and *Films for Humanities*. Contact your local sales representative or Wadsworth Marketing at 1-877-999-2350 for details.

ABC News on DVD: Introductory Psychology, Volumes 1–3 CD-ROM

ABC Videos feature short, high-interest clips from current news events as well as historic raw footage going back 40 years. Perfect for discussion starters or to enrich your lectures and spark interest in the material in the text, these brief videos provide students with a new lens through which to view the past and present, one that will greatly enhance their knowledge and understanding of significant events and open up to them new dimensions in learning. Clips are drawn from such programs as *World News Tonight*, *Good Morning America*, *This Week*, *PrimeTime Live*, *20/20*, and *Nightline*, as well as numerous ABC News specials and material from the Associated Press Television News and British Movietone News collections.

Wadsworth Media Guide for Introductory Psychology

This essential instructor resource, edited by Russell J. Watson, contains hundreds of video and feature film recommendations for all major topics in Introductory Psychology (ISBN: 0-534-17585-6).

Supplementary Books

No text can cover all of the topics that might be included in an introductory psychology course. If you would like to enrich your course, or make it more challenging, the Wadsworth titles listed here may be of interest.

Challenging Your Preconceptions: Thinking Critically about Psychology, Second Edition

This paperbound book (ISBN: 0-534-26739-4), written by Randolph Smith, helps students strengthen their critical-thinking skills. Psychological issues such as hypnosis and repressed memory, statistical seduction, the validity of pop psychology, and other topics are used to illustrate the principles of critical thinking.

Writing Papers in Psychology: A Student Guide

The sixth edition of *Writing Papers in Psychology* (ISBN: 0-534-52395-1) by Ralph L. Rosnow and Mimi Rosnow is a valuable "how to" manual for writing term papers and research reports. This new edition has been updated to reflect the latest APA guidelines. The book covers each task with examples, hints, and two complete writing samples. Citation ethics, how to locate information, and new research technologies are also covered.

Cross-Cultural Perspectives in Psychology

How well do the concepts of psychology apply to various cultures? What can we learn about human behavior from cultures different from our own? These questions lie behind a collection of original articles written by William F. Price and Rich Crapo. The Fourth Edition of *Cross-Cultural Perspectives in Psychology* (ISBN: 0-534-54653-6) contains articles on North American ethnic groups as well as cultures from around the world.

Summary

We sincerely hope that both teachers and students will consider this book and its supporting materials a refreshing change from the ordinary. Creating it has been quite an adventure. In the pages that follow, we believe students will find an attractive blend of the theoretical and the practical, plus many of the most exciting ideas in psychology. Most of all, we hope that students using this book will discover that reading a college textbook can be entertaining and enjoyable.

Acknowledgments

Psychology is a cooperative effort requiring the talents and energies of a large community of scholars, teachers, researchers, and students. Like most endeavors in psychology, this book reflects the efforts of many people. We deeply appreciate the contributions of the following professors who have, over the years, supported this text's evolution:

Faren R. Akins
University of Arizona

Avis Donna Alexander
John Tyler Community College

Clark E. Alexander
Arapahoe Community College

Tricia Alexander
Long Beach City College

Dennis Anderson
Butler Community College

Lynn Anderson
Wayne State University

Nancy L. Ashton
R. Stockton College of New Jersey

Scott A. Bailey
Texas Lutheran University

Frank Barbehenn
Bucks County Community College

Michael Bardo
University of Kentucky

Larry W. Barron
Grand Canyon University

Linda M. Bastone
Purchase College, SUNY

Brian R. Bate
Cuyahoga Community College

Hugh E. Bateman
Jones Junior College

Evelyn Blanch-Payne
Oakwood College

Cheryl Bluestone
Queensborough Community College–CUNY

Galen V. Bodenhausen
Michigan State University

Aaron U. Bolin
Arkansas State University

Tom Bond
Thomas Nelson Community College

John Boswell
University of Missouri, St. Louis

Anne Bright
Jackson State Community College

Soheila T. Brouk
Gateway Technical College

Derek Cadman
El Camino Community College

James F. Calhoun
University of Georgia

Dennis Cogan
Texas Tech University

Lorry Cology
Owens College

William N. Colson
Norfolk State College

Chris Cozby
California State University, Fullerton

Corinne Crandell
Broome County Community College

Thomas L. Crandell
Broome County Community College

Charles Croll
Broome County Community College

Daniel B. Cruse
University of Miami

Keith E. Davis
University of South Carolina–Columbia

Diane DeArmond
University of Missouri, Kansas City

Patrick T. DeBoll
St. John's University

Dawn Delaney
University of Wisconsin–Whitewater

Jack Demick
Suffolk University

Lorraine P. Dieudonne
Foothill College

H. Mitzi Doane
University of Minnesota–Duluth

Wendy Domjan
University of Texas at Austin

Roger A. Drake
Western State College of Colorado

John Dworetzky
Glendale Community College

Bill Dwyer
Memphis State University

Thomas Eckle
Modesto Community College

David Edwards
Iowa State University

Raymond Elish
Cuyahoga Community College

Diane Feibel
University of Cincinnati–Raymond Walters College

Paul W. Fenton
University of Wisconsin, Stout

Dave Filak
Joliet Junior College

Oney D. Fitzpatrick, Jr.
Lamar University

Linda E. Flickinger
Saint Clair County Community College

William F. Ford
Bucks County Community College

Marie Fox
Metropolitan State College of Denver

Chris Fraser
Gippsland Institute of Advanced Education

Christopher Frost
Southwest Texas State University

Eugenio J. Galindro
El Paso Community College

Irby J. Gaudet
University of Southwestern Louisiana

David Gersh
Houston Community College

David A. Gershaw
Arizona Western College

Andrew R. Getzfeld
New Jersey City University

Carolyn A. Gingrich
South Dakota State University

Perilou Goddard
Northern Kentucky University

Michael E. Gorman
Michigan Technological University

Peter Gram
Pensacola Junior College

David A. Gries
State University of New York, Farmingdale

R.J. Grisham
Indian River Community College

John Grivas
Monash University

Anne Groves
Montgomery College

Michael B. Guyer
John Carroll University

Janice Hartgrove-Freile
Lone Star College, North Harris

Raquel Henry
Kingwood College

Callina Henson
Oakland Community College–Auburn Hills

Anne Hester
Pennsylvania State University–Hazleton Campus

Gregory P. Hickman
The Pennsylvania State University–Fayette

Don Hockenbury
Tulsa Junior College

Sidney Hockman
Nassau Community College

Karen Y. Holmes
Norfolk State University

Barbara Honhart
Lansing Community College

John C. Johanson
Winona State University

James A. Johnson
Sam Houston State University

Myles E. Johnson
Normandale Community College

Pat Jones
Brevard Community College

Richard Kandus
Menifee Valley Campus

Bruno M. Kappes
University of Alaska–Anchorage

Charles Karis
Northeastern University

John P. Keating
University of Washington

Patricia Kemerer
Ivy Tech Community College

Cindy Kennedy
Sinclair Community College

Shaila Khan
Tougaloo College

Yuthika Kim
Oklahoma City Community College

Richard R. Klene
University of Cincinnati

Ronald J. Kopcho
Mercer Community College

Mary Kulish
Thomas Nelson Community College

Billie Laney
Central Texas College

Phil Lau
DeAnza College

Robert Lawyer
Delgado Community College

Walter Leach
College of San Mateo

Christopher Legrow
Marshall University

Lindette I. Lent
Arizona Western College

Elizabeth Levin
Laurentian University

Julie Lewis
Georgian College

Mei-Ching Lien
Oregon State University

Elise B. Lindenmuth
York College of Pennsylvania

Linda Lockwood
Metropolitan State College of Denver

Philip Lom
West Connecticut State University

Cheryl S. Lynch
University of Louisiana–Lafayette

Salvador Macias, III
University of South Carolina, Sumter

Abe Marrero
Rogers State University

Al Mayer
Portland Community College

Michael Jason McCoy
Cape Fear Community College

Edward R. McCrary, III
El Camino College

Yancy B. McDougal
University of South Carolina, Spartanburg

Mark McGee
Texas A&M University

Angela McGlynn
Mercer County Community College

Mark McKinley
Lorain County Community College

Chelley Merrill
Tidewater Community College

Beth Moore
Madisonville Community College

Feleccia R. Moore-Davis
Houston Community College System

Edward J. Morris
Owensboro Community College

Edward Mosley
Pasiac County Community College

James Murray
San Jacinto University

Gary Nallan
University of North Carolina–Ashville

Andrew Neher
Cabrillo College

Don Nelson
Indiana State University

Steve Nida
Franklin University

Peggy Norwood
Tidewater Community College

James P. B. O'Brien
Tidewater Community College

Frances O'Keefe
Tidewater Community College

Steve G. Ornelas
Central Arizona College

Laura Overstreet
Tarrant County College

Darlene Pacheco
Moorpark College

Lisa K. Paler
College of New Rochelle

Debra Parish
Tomball College

Cora F. Patterson
University of Southwestern Louisiana

Leon Peek
North Texas State University

John Pennachio
Adirondack Community College

Peter Phipps
Sullivan County Community College

Steven J. Pollock
Moorpark College

Jack Powell
University of Hartford

Ravi Prasad
Texas Tech University

Derrick L. Proctor
Andrews University

Douglas Pruitt
West Kentucky Community College

Robin Raygor
Anoka-Ramsey Community College

Richard Rees
Glendale Community College

Paul A. Rhoads
Williams College

Harvey Richman
Columbus State University

Robyn R. Rogers
Texas State University, San Marcos

Marcia Rossi
Tuskegee University

Jeffrey Rudski
Mulhenberg College

James J. Ryan
University of Wisconsin, La Crosse

John D. Sanders
Butler County Community College

Nancy Sauerman
Kirkwood Community College

Michael Schuller
Fresno City College

Pamela E. Scott-Johnson
Spelman College

Jillene G. Seiver
Bellevue College

Carol F. Shoptaugh
Southwest Missouri State University

Maria Shpurik
Florida International University

Harold I. Siegel
Rutgers University

Richard Siegel
University of Massachusetts, Lowell

Nancy Simpson
Trident Technical College

Madhu Singh
Tougaloo College

Glenda Smith
North Harris Community College

Steven M. Smith
Texas A&M University

Francine Smolucha
Moraine Valley Community College

Michael C. Sosulski
College of DuPage

Lynn M. Sprott
Jefferson Community College

Donald M. Stanley
North Harris County College

Julie E. Stokes
California State University–Fullerton

Catherine Grady Strathern
University of Cincinnati

Harvey Taub
Staten Island Community College

Christopher Taylor
University of Arizona

Carol Terry
University of Oklahoma

Laura Thompson
New Mexico State University

Richard Townsend
Miami-Dade Community College–Kendall Campus

Bruce Trotter
Santa Barbara City College

Susan Troy
Northeast Iowa Community College

Pat Tuntland
Pima College

Paul E. Turner
David Lipscomb University

A.D. VanDeventer
Thomas Nelson Community College

Mark Vernoy
Palomar College

Charles Verschoor
Miami-Dade Community College–Kendall Campus

Frank Vitro
Texas Women's University

John Vojtisek
Castleton State College

Francis Volking
Saint Leo University

David W. Ward
Arkansas Tech University

Paul J. Wellman
Texas A&M University

Sharon Whelan
University of Kentucky

Robert Wiley
Montgomery College

Thomas Wilke
University of Wisconsin, Parkside

Carl D. Williams
University of Miami

Glenda S. Williams
Lone Star College North Harris

Don Windham
Roane State Community College

Kaye D. Young
North Iowa Area Community College

Michael Zeller
Mankato State University

Margaret C. Zimmerman
Virginia Wesleyan College

Otto Zinser
East Tennessee State College

Producing *Introduction to Psychology: Gateways to Mind and Behavior* and its supplements was a formidable task. We are especially indebted to each of the following individuals for supporting this book: At Cengage, we are especially grateful to our editor, Jon-David Hague, for his wit, wisdom, and support. Jon-David has unmistakably contributed to this book.

We also wish to thank the many individuals at Cengage who have so generously shared their knowledge and talents over the past year. These are the people who made it happen: Jeremy Judson, Vernon Boes, Pat Waldo, Mary Noel, Kelly Miller, and Sheli DeNola.

It has been a pleasure to work with such a gifted group of professionals and many others at Cengage. We want to single out Jeremy Judson. As our developmental editor, Jeremy has gracefully kept us on track and offered many deeply appreciated suggestions. Our other developmental editor, Shannon LeMay-Finn, has kept the train on the rails day in and day out. Her detailed editorial comments have immeasurably improved the final result. Thank you, Shannon. Thank you also Kate Mannix from Graphic World Inc.

Last but not least, at home, Heather Mitterer, Kayleigh Hagerman, Barbara Kushmier, and Tammy Stewart helped in oh, so many ways.

Gateway THEME

It is possible to study more efficiently and effectively by being a reflective learner who engages in active processing.

Introduction

The Psychology of Studying—Reflective Learning

Starting Off on the Right Foot

You're actually reading this! As your authors, we're glad (honest!). Too often, students just jump in and plough through a textbook from the first assigned chapter to the last. That's a shame because it's far better to study a textbook, not just read it. Think about it: How much do you typically remember after you've read straight through a whole chapter? If the answer is "nada," "zilch," or simply "not enough," it may be because *reading* is not the same as *studying*. Even if you're an excellent student, you may be able to improve your study skills. Students who get good grades tend to work smarter, not just longer or harder (Santrock & Halonen, 2010). They also tend to understand and remember more of what they've learned long after their exams are over. Psychology is for their lives, not just for their exams. To help you get a good start, let's look at several ways to improve studying.

Gateway QUESTIONS

I.1 What is the best way to read a textbook?
I.2 How can learning in class be improved?
I.3 What is the best way to study?
I.4 What is self-regulated learning?
I.5 How can procrastination be overcome?
I.6 What are some ways to be a more effective test-taker?
I.7 Can digital media help with reflective processing?

Reflective Reading—How to Tame a Textbook

Gateway Question I.1: *What is the best way to read a textbook?*

What's the difference between reading a textbook and studying it? Have you ever spent an evening "vegging out" in front of the TV? Although it was likely great fun, you may have noticed that you didn't think very much about what you were watching and that your subsequent memories were not very detailed. Psychologist Donald Norman (1993) uses the term **experiential cognition** to refer to the style of thinking that occurs during passive experience. Even though this is the appropriate way to experience entertainment, it doesn't work so well if your goal is to learn while, say, reading a textbook.

In contrast, suppose a TV special about global warming really gets you thinking. You might wonder how global warming will affect your own future. Perhaps you are skeptical about some of the program's predictions. Didn't you read something different recently? You spend some time googling global warming. Now you are reacting "mindfully" and "going beyond the information given" (Bruner, 1973; Siegel, 2007). This is **reflective cognition** (Norman, 1993). Rather than just having an experience, you *actively think* about it. Similarly, you will learn more from a textbook if you mindfully reflect on what you read. Reflective thinking can help you better understand and remember details about an experience in the future. (In memory terms, the consequence of reflective thinking is called *elaborative processing,* which you will learn more about in Chapter 7.)

How can I be more reflective while reading? One powerful way to be more reflective is through a form of self-reflection called **self-reference.** As you read, you should relate new facts, terms, and concepts to your own experiences and information you already know well. Doing this will make new ideas more personally meaningful and easier to remember. Critical thinking is another powerful way to be more reflective. **Critical thinkers** pause to evaluate, compare, analyze, critique, and synthesize what they are reading (Chaffee, 2010). You should, too. In Chapter 1, we will learn how to think critically about psychology.

"I'm too busy going to college to study."

These ways to improve learning can be combined into the **reflective SQ4R method.** SQ4R stands for *survey, question, read, recite, reflect,* and *review.* These six steps can help you study more effectively:

S = *Survey.* Skim through a chapter before you begin reading it. Start by looking at topic headings, figure captions, and summaries. Try to get an overall picture of what lies ahead. Because this book is organized into short sections, you can survey just one section at a time if you prefer.

Q = *Question.* As you read, turn each topic heading into one or more questions. For example, when you read the heading "Stages of Sleep" you might ask, "Is there more than one stage of sleep?" "What are the stages of sleep?" "How do they differ?" Asking questions prepares you to read with a purpose.

R1 = *Read.* The first R in SQ4R stands for read. As you read, look for answers to the questions you asked. Read in short "bites," from one topic heading to the next, then stop. For difficult material you may want to read only a paragraph or two at a time.

R2 = *Recite.* After reading a small amount, you should pause and recite or rehearse. Try to mentally answer your questions. Also, summarize what you just read in brief notes. Making notes will reveal what you do and don't know, so you can fill gaps in your knowledge (Peverly et al., 2003).

If you can't summarize the main ideas, skim over each section again. Until you can understand and remember what you just read, there's little point to reading more. After you've studied a short "bite" of text, turn the next topic heading into questions. Then read to the following heading. Remember to look for answers as you read and to recite or take notes before moving on. Ask yourself repeatedly, "What is the main idea here?"

Repeat the question–read–recite cycle until you've finished an entire chapter (or just from one *Knowledge Builder* to the next, if you want to read shorter units).

R3 = *Reflect.* As you read, reflect on what you are reading. As stated earlier, two powerful ways to do this are self-reference and critical thinking. This is the most important step in the reflective SQ4R method. The more mindfulness and genuine interest you can bring to your reading, the more you will learn (Hartlep & Forsyth, 2000; Van Blerkom, 2011).

R4 = *Review.* When you're done reading, skim back over a section or the entire chapter, or read your notes. Then check your memory by reciting and quizzing yourself again. Try to make frequent, active review a standard part of your study habits (see ● Figure I.1).

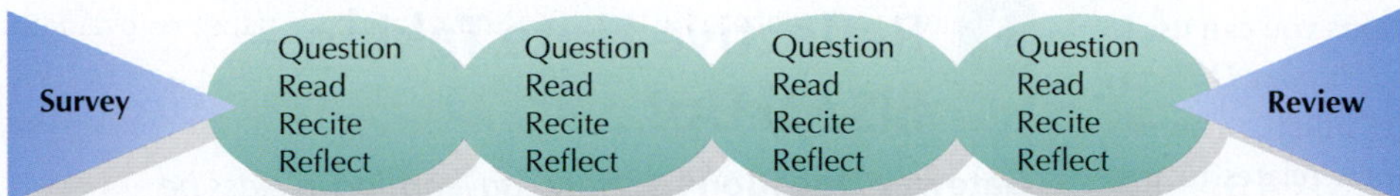

• Figure I.1 The reflective SQ4R method promotes active learning and information processing. You should begin with a survey of the chapter or section, depending on how much you plan to read. Then you should proceed through cycles of questioning, reading, reciting, and reflecting, and conclude with a review of the section or the entire chapter. Copyright © Cengage Learning 2013

Does this really work? You bet! Using a reflective reading strategy improves learning and course grades (Taraban, Rynearson, & Kerr, 2000). It also results in enhanced long-term understanding. Simply reading straight through a chapter can give you "intellectual indigestion." That's why it's better to stop often to survey, question, recite, reflect, review, and "digest" information as you read.

How to Use Introduction to Psychology: Gateways to Mind and Behavior

You can apply the reflective SQ4R method to any text. However, we have specifically designed this textbook to help you *actively* learn psychology. In fact, this *Introduction* has been designed just like the rest of the book. Please consider trying out the following suggestions as you work through this section:

Survey

Each chapter opens with a chapter survey that includes a *Gateway Theme,* a short opening story introducing what will be covered, and a list of *Gateway Questions.* You can use these features to identify important ideas as you begin reading. The short opening story should help you get interested in the topics you will be reading about. The *Gateway Theme* and *Gateway Questions* are good guides to the kinds of information to look for as you read. In fact, answers to the *Gateway Questions* are a good summary of the core concepts in each chapter. If, years from now, you still remember those *Gateway* concepts, your authors will be very happy indeed. Anyway, after you've studied the *Gateway Questions,* take a few minutes to do your own survey of the chapter, including the figure captions and chapter-ending material. You should also notice that each major chapter heading is usually accompanied by one or more of the *Gateway Questions.* Taken together, this will help you build a "mental map" of upcoming topics.

Question

How can I use the reflective SQ4R method to make reading more interesting and effective? Try to actively interact with your textbooks as you read. Perhaps the most important way to do this is to ask yourself a lot of questions as you read. For example, as noted earlier, major chapter sections begin with headings; try turning them into questions. One Chapter 1 heading is "Critical Thinking—Take It with a Grain of Salt." Turn this into a question that occurs to you, such as "Why should I be skeptical of what I read?" If you read to answer your questions, you will be much more likely to "get" the key points in what you are reading. *Dialogue Questions* like the one that began this paragraph will also help you focus on seeking information as you read. These questions are very much like those running through the minds of students like you as they read this book. Similarly, the *Gateway Questions* are repeated throughout each chapter to help you recognize key topics. Try to anticipate these questions. Even better, be sure to ask your own questions.

Read

As an aid to reading, important terms are printed in **boldface type** and defined when they first appear. (Some are followed by pronunciations—capital letters show which syllables are accented.) You'll also find a *running glossary* in the lower right-hand corner of pages you are reading, so you never have to guess about the meaning of technical terms. If you want to look up a term from a lecture or another chapter, check the main *Subject Index/Glossary.* This "mini-dictionary" is located near the end of the book. Perhaps you should take a moment to find it now. In addition, many figures and tables will help you quickly grasp important concepts.

Recite and Reflect

To help you study in smaller "bites," this book is divided into short sections that end with a study guide called a *Knowledge Builder.* By answering "Recite" questions in the *Knowledge Builder* you can check how well you remember what you just read. Additionally, *Think Critically* questions invite you to reflect more deeply about the how and why of what you have just read, and *Self-Reflect* questions help you connect new ideas to your own life. (Don't forget to also take notes and recite and reflect on your own.)

This book also provides other opportunities for you to reflect on what you are reading. Each chapter ends with a *Psychology in Action* section. These discussions are filled with practical ideas you can relate to your own life. In many chapters, *Discovering Psychology* boxes also invite you to relate psychology to your own behavior.

Experiential cognition Style of thought arising during passive experience.

Reflective cognition Style of thought arising while actively thinking about an experience.

Self-reference The practice of relating of new information to prior life experience.

Critical thinking An ability to evaluate, compare, analyze, critique, and synthesize information.

Reflective SQ4R method An active study-reading technique based on these steps: survey, question, read, recite, reflect, and review.

Critical Thinking boxes present intriguing questions you can use to sharpen your critical thinking skills. In addition, *Human Diversity* boxes encourage you to reflect on the rich variability of human experience; *Brainwaves* boxes show how the brain relates to psychology; and *The Clinical File* boxes show how psychology can be applied to treat clinical problems.

Review

Each chapter concludes with *Gateways to Psychology,* a detailed chapter review. There you will find the *Gateway Questions* restated, along with point-by-point answers, which are summaries of psychology's "big ideas" and enduring principles. The first time you finish a chapter, don't feel obligated to memorize the *Gateway* concepts. However, be sure to take a moment to think about them. Ultimately, they will provide a good, high-level summary of what you learned in this course. By making these ideas your own, you will gain something of lasting value: You will learn to see human behavior as psychologists do.

For further review, you can use the running glossary in the margin, as well as boldface terms, figures, and tables. ■ Table I.1 summarizes how this text helps you apply the reflective SQ4R method. Even with all this help, there is still much more you can do on your own.

TABLE I.1 Using the Reflective SQ4R Method

SURVEY
- Gateway Theme
- Chapter-Opening Story
- Gateway Questions
- Topic Headings
- Figure Captions

QUESTION
- Topic Headings
- Gateway Questions

READ
- Boldface Terms
- Running Glossary (in margin)
- Figures and Tables

RECITE
- Recite Questions (in *Knowledge Builders*)
- Practice Quizzes (online)
- Notes (make them while reading)

REFLECT
- Think Critically Questions (in *Knowledge Builders*)
- Self-Reflect Questions (in *Knowledge Builders*)
- Psychology in Action sections (throughout the text)
- Boxed Highlights (throughout the text)

REVIEW
- Italicized Gateways Concepts
- Boldface Terms
- Running Glossary (in margin)
- Figures and Tables
- Practice Quizzes (online)
- Study Guide

Reflective Note Taking—LISAN Up!

Gateway Question I.2: *How can learning in class be improved?*

Reading strategies may be good for studying, but what about taking notes in class? Sometimes it's hard to know what's important. Just as studying a textbook is best done reflectively, so too is learning in class (Norman, 1993). Like effective reading, good notes come from actively seeking information. People who are **active listeners** avoid distractions and skillfully gather ideas. Here's a listening/note-taking plan that works for many students. The letters LISAN, pronounced like the word *listen,* will help you remember the steps:

L = *Lead. Don't follow.* Read assigned materials before coming to class. Try to anticipate what your teacher will say by asking yourself questions. If your teacher provides course notes or PowerPoint overheads before lectures, survey them before coming to class. Reflective questions can come from those materials or from study guides, reading assignments, or your own curiosity.

I = *Ideas.* Every lecture is based on a core of ideas. Usually, an idea is followed by examples or explanations. Ask yourself often, "What is the main idea now? What ideas support it?"

S = *Signal words.* Listen for words that tell you what direction the instructor is taking. For instance, here are some signal words:

There are three reasons why . . .	Here come ideas
Most important is . . .	Main idea
On the contrary . . .	Opposite idea
As an example . . .	Support for main idea
Therefore . . .	Conclusion

A = *Actively listen.* Sit where you can get involved and ask questions. Bring questions you want answered from the last lecture or from your text. Raise your hand at the beginning of class or approach your professor before the lecture. Do anything that helps you stay active, alert, and engaged.

N = *Note taking.* Students who take accurate lecture notes tend to do well on tests (Williams & Eggert, 2002). However, don't try to be a tape recorder. Listen to everything, but be selective and write down only key points. If you are too busy writing, you may not grasp what your professor is saying. When you're taking notes, it might help to think of yourself as a reporter who is trying to get a good story (Ryan, 2001; Wong, 2011).

Actually, most students take reasonably good notes—and then don't use them! Many students wait until just before exams to review. By then, their notes have lost much of their meaning. If you don't want your notes to seem like "chicken scratches," it pays to review them daily (Ellis, 2011).

Using and Reviewing Your Notes

When you review, you will learn more if you take the extra steps listed here (Burka & Yuen, 2008; Ellis, 2011; Santrock & Halonen, 2010):

- As soon as you can, reflectively improve your notes by filling in gaps, completing thoughts, and looking for connections among ideas.
- Remember to link new ideas to what you already know.
- Summarize your notes. Boil them down and *organize* them.
- After each class session, write down several major ideas, definitions, or details that are likely to become test questions. Then, make up questions from your notes and be sure you can answer them.

Summary

The letters LISAN are a guide to active listening, but listening and good note taking are not enough. You must also review, organize, reflect, extend, and think about new ideas. Use active listening to get involved in your classes and you will undoubtedly learn more (Van Blerkom, 2011).

Reflective Study Strategies—Making a Habit of Success

Gateway Question I.3: *What is the best way to study?*

Grades depend as much on effort as they do on "intelligence." However, don't forget that good students work more *efficiently*, not just harder. Many study practices are notoriously unreflective, such as recopying lecture notes, studying class notes but not the textbook (or the textbook but not class notes), outlining chapters, answering study questions with the book open, and "group study" (which often becomes a party). The best students emphasize *quality:* They study their books and notes in depth and attend classes regularly. It's a mistake to blame poor grades on events "beyond your control." Students who are motivated to succeed usually get better grades (Perry et al., 2001). Let's consider a few more things you can do to improve your study habits.

Study in a Specific Place

Ideally, you should study in a quiet, well-lit area free of distractions. If possible, you should also have at least one place where you *only study.* Do nothing else there: Keep magazines, MP3 players, friends, cell phones, pets, MSN Messenger, video games, puzzles, food, lovers, sports cars, elephants, pianos, televisions, Facebook, and other distractions out of the area. In this way, the habit of studying will become strongly linked with one specific place. Then, rather than trying to force yourself to study, all you have to do is go to your study area. Once there, you'll find it is relatively easy to get started.

Use Spaced Study Sessions

It is reasonable to review intensely before an exam. However, you're taking a big risk if you are only "cramming" (learning new information at the last minute). Spaced practice is much more efficient (Anderson, 2010). **Spaced practice** consists of a large number of relatively short study sessions. Long, uninterrupted study sessions are called **massed practice.** (If you "massed up" your studying, you probably messed it up too.)

Cramming places a big burden on memory. Usually, you shouldn't try to learn anything new about a subject during the last day before a test. It is far better to learn small amounts every day and review frequently.

Try Mnemonics

Learning has to start somewhere, and memorizing is often the first step. Many of the best ways to improve memory are covered in Chapter 7, especially the last few sections. Let's consider just one type of technique here.

A **mnemonic** (nuh-MON-ik) is a memory aid. There are many ways to create mnemonics. Most mnemonics link new information to ideas or images that are easy to remember. For example, what if you want to remember that the Spanish word for duck is *pato* (pronounced POT-oh)? To use a mnemonic, you could picture a duck in a pot or a duck wearing a pot for a hat. Likewise, to remember that the cerebellum controls coordination, you might picture someone named "Sarah Bellum" who is very coordinated. For best results, make your mnemonic images exaggerated or bizarre, vivid, and interactive (Macklin & McDaniel, 2005; Radvansky, 2011).

Test Yourself

A great way to improve grades is to take practice tests before the real one in class (Karpicke & Blunt, 2011). In other words, reflective studying should include **self-testing,** in which you pose questions to yourself. You can use flash cards, *Knowledge Builder* Recite,

Mnemonics make new information more familiar and memorable. Forming an image of a duck wearing a pot for a hat might help you remember that *pato* is the Spanish word for duck.

Active listener A person who knows how to maintain attention, avoid distractions, and actively gather information from lectures.
Spaced practice Practice spread over many relatively short study sessions.
Massed practice Practice done in a long, uninterrupted study session.
Mnemonic A memory aid or strategy.
Self-testing Evaluating learning by posing questions to yourself.

Think Critically, and Self-Reflect questions, online quizzes, a study guide, or other means. As you study, ask many questions and be sure you can answer them. Studying without self-testing is like practicing for a basketball game without shooting any baskets.

For more convenient self-testing, your professor may make a *Study Guide* or a separate booklet of *Practice Quizzes* available. You can use either to review for tests. Practice quizzes are also available on *Psychology CourseMate*, as described later. However, don't use practice quizzes as a substitute for studying your textbook and lecture notes. Trying to learn from quizzes alone will probably *lower* your grades. It is best to use quizzes to find out what topics you need to study more (Brothen & Wambach, 2001).

Overlearn

Many students *underprepare* for exams, and most *overestimate* how well they will do. A solution to both problems is **overlearning,** in which you continue studying beyond your initial mastery of a topic. In other words, plan to do extra study and review *after* you think you are prepared for a test. One way to overlearn is to approach all tests as if they will be essays. That way, you will learn more completely, so you really "know your stuff."

Self-Regulated Learning—Academic All-Stars

Gateway Question I.4: *What is self-regulated learning?*

Think of a topic you are highly interested in, such as music, sports, fashion, cars, cooking, politics, or movies. Whatever the topic, you have probably learned a lot about it—painlessly. How could you make your college work more like voluntary learning? An approach called self-regulated learning might be a good start. **Self-regulated learning** is deliberately self-reflective and active self-guided study (Hofer & Yu, 2003; Kaplan, 2008). Here's how you can change passive studying into reflective, goal-oriented learning:

1. *Set specific, objective learning goals.* Try to begin each learning session with specific goals in mind. What knowledge or skills are you trying to master? What do you hope to accomplish (Burka & Yuen, 2008)?
2. *Plan a learning strategy.* How will you accomplish your goals? Make daily, weekly, and monthly plans for learning. Then put them into action.
3. *Be your own teacher.* Effective learners silently give themselves guidance and ask themselves questions. For example, as you are learning, you might ask yourself, "What are the important ideas here? What do I remember? What don't I understand? What do I need to review? What should I do next?"
4. *Monitor your progress.* Self-regulated learning depends on self-monitoring. Exceptional learners keep records of their progress toward learning goals (pages read, hours of studying, assignments completed, and so forth). They quiz themselves, use study guides, make sure they follow the reflective SQ4R system, and find other ways to check their understanding while learning.
5. *Reward yourself.* When you meet your daily, weekly, or monthly goals, reward your efforts in some way, such as going to a movie or downloading some new music. Be aware that self-praise also rewards learning. Being able to say, "Hey, I did it!" or "Good work!" and knowing that you deserve it can be very rewarding. In the long run, success, self-improvement, and personal satisfaction are the real payoffs for learning.
6. *Evaluate your progress and goals.* It is a good idea to frequently evaluate your performance records and goals. Are there specific areas of your work that need improvement? If you are not making good progress toward long-range goals, do you need to revise your short-term targets?
7. *Take corrective action.* If you fall short of your goals, you may need to adjust how you budget your time. You may also need to change your learning environment to deal with distractions such as watching TV, daydreaming, talking to friends, or testing the limits of your hearing with your iPod.

If you discover that you lack necessary knowledge or skills, ask for help, take advantage of tutoring programs, or look for information beyond your courses and textbooks. Knowing how to regulate and control learning can be a key to life-long enrichment and personal empowerment (Van Blerkom, 2011).

Procrastination—Avoiding the Last-Minute Blues

Gateway Question I.5: *How can procrastination be overcome?*

All these study techniques are fine. But what can I do about procrastination? A tendency to procrastinate is almost universal. (When campus workshops on procrastination are offered, many students never get around to signing up!) Even when procrastination doesn't lead to failure, it can cause much suffering (Wohl, Pychyl, & Bennett, 2010). Procrastinators work only under pressure, skip classes, give false reasons for late work, and feel ashamed of their last-minute efforts. They also tend to feel frustrated, bored, and guilty more often (Blunt & Pychyl, 2005).

Why do so many students procrastinate? Many students equate grades with their *personal worth.* That is, they act as if grades tell whether they are good, smart people who will succeed in life. By procrastinating they can blame poor work on a late start, rather than a lack of ability (Beck, Koons, & Milgrim, 2000). After all, it wasn't their best effort, was it?

Perfectionism is a related problem. If you expect the impossible, it's hard to start an assignment. Students with high standards often end up with all-or-nothing work habits (Onwuegbuzie, 2000).

Time Management

Most procrastinators must eventually face the self-worth issue. Nevertheless, most can improve by learning study skills and better time management. We have already discussed general study skills, so let's consider time management in a little more detail.

A **weekly time schedule** is a written plan that allocates time for study, work, and leisure activities. To prepare your schedule, make a chart showing all the hours in each day of the week. Then fill in times that are already committed: sleep, meals, classes, work, team practices, lessons, appointments, and so forth. Next, fill in times when you will study for various classes. Finally, label the remaining hours as open or free times.

Each day, you can use your schedule as a checklist. That way you'll know at a glance which tasks are done and which still need attention (Burka & Yuen, 2008).

You may also find it valuable to make a **term schedule** that lists the dates of all quizzes, tests, reports, papers, and other major assignments for each class.

The beauty of sticking to a schedule is that you know you are making an honest effort. It will also help you avoid feeling bored while you are working or guilty when you play.

Be sure to treat your study times as serious commitments, but respect your free times, too. And remember, students who study hard and practice time management *do* get better grades (Rau & Durand, 2000).

Goal Setting

As mentioned earlier, students who are reflective, active learners set **specific goals** for studying. Such goals should be clear-cut and measurable (Burka & Yuen, 2008). If you find it hard to stay motivated, try setting goals for the semester, the week, the day, and even for single study sessions. Also, be aware that more effort early in a course can greatly reduce the "pain" and stress you will experience later. If your professors don't give frequent assignments, set your own day-by-day goals. That way, you can turn big assignments into a series of smaller tasks that you can actually complete (Ariely & Wertenbroch, 2002). An example would be reading, studying, and reviewing 8 pages a day to complete a 40-page chapter in 5 days. For this textbook, reading from one *Knowledge Builder* to the next each day might be a good pace. Remember, many small steps can add up to an impressive journey.

Make Learning an Adventure

A final point to remember is that you are most likely to procrastinate if you think a task will be unpleasant (Pychyl et al., 2000). Learning can be hard work. Nevertheless, many students find ways to make schoolwork interesting and enjoyable. Try to approach your schoolwork as if it were a game, a sport, an adventure, or simply a way to become a better person. The best educational experiences are challenging, yet fun (Ferrari & Scher, 2000; Santrock & Halonen, 2010).

Virtually every topic is interesting to someone, somewhere. You may not be particularly interested in the sex life of South American tree frogs. However, a biologist might be fascinated. (Another tree frog might be, too.) If you wait for teachers to "make" their courses interesting, you are missing the point. Interest is a matter of *your attitude* (see ● Figure I.2 for a summary of study skills).

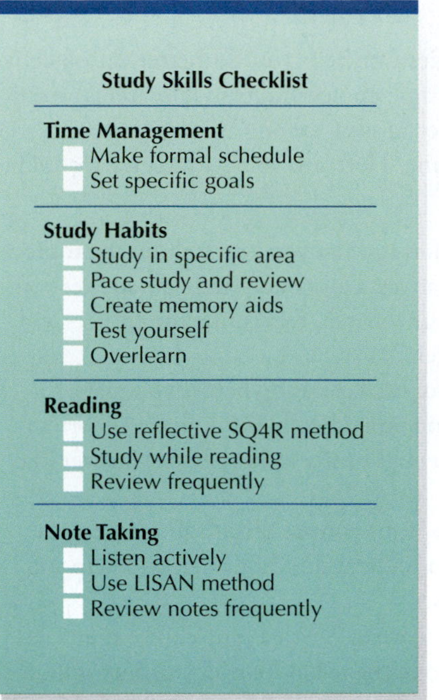

● **Figure I.2** Study skills checklist. Copyright © Cengage Learning 2013

Reflective Test-Taking—Are You "Test Wise"?

Gateway Question I.6: *What are some ways to be a more effective test-taker?*

If I read and study effectively, is there anything else I can do to improve my grades? You must also be able to show what you know on tests. Here are some ways to improve your test-taking skills.

General Test-Taking Skills

You'll do better on all types of tests if you observe the following guidelines (Wood & Willoughby, 1995; Van Blerkom, 2011):

1. Read all directions and questions carefully. They may give you good advice or clues.
2. Quickly survey the test before you begin.
3. Answer easy questions before spending time on more difficult ones.
4. Be sure to answer all questions.
5. Use your time wisely.
6. Ask for clarification when necessary.

Overlearning Continuing to study and learn after you think you've mastered a topic.

Self-regulated learning Deliberately self-reflective and active self-guided study.

Weekly time schedule A written plan that allocates time for study, work, and leisure activities during a one-week period.

Term schedule A written plan that lists the dates of all major assignments for each of your classes for an entire semester or quarter.

Specific goal A goal with a clearly defined and measurable outcome.

Objective Tests

Several additional strategies can help you do better on objective tests. Objective tests (multiple-choice and true-false items) require you to recognize a correct answer among wrong ones or a true statement versus a false one. Here are some strategies for taking objective tests.

1. First, relate the question to what you know about the topic. Then, read the alternatives. Does one match the answer you expected to find? If none match, reexamine the choices and look for a *partial* match.
2. Read *all* the choices for each question before you make a decision. Here's why: If you immediately think that *a* is correct and stop reading, you might miss seeing a better answer like "both *a* and *d*."
3. Read rapidly and skip items you are unsure about. You may find "free information" in later questions that will help you answer difficult items.
4. Eliminate certain alternatives. With a four-choice multiple-choice test, you have one chance in four of guessing right. If you can eliminate two alternatives, your guessing odds improve to 50-50.
5. Unless there is a penalty for guessing, be sure to answer any skipped items. Even if you are not sure of the answer, you may be right. If you leave a question blank, it is automatically wrong. When you are forced to guess, don't choose the longest answer or the letter you've used the least. Both strategies lower scores more than random guessing does.
6. There is a bit of folk wisdom that says "Don't change your answers on a multiple-choice test. Your first choice is usually right." This is *false*. If you change answers, you are more likely to gain points than to lose them. This is especially true if you are uncertain of your first choice or it was a hunch, and if your second choice is more reflective (Higham & Gerrard, 2005).
7. Remember, you are searching for the one *best* answer to each question. Some answers may be partly true, yet flawed in some way. If you are uncertain, try rating each multiple-choice alternative on a 1–10 scale. The answer with the highest rating is the one you are looking for.
8. Few circumstances are *always* or *never* present. Answers that include superlatives such as *most, least, best, worst, largest,* or *smallest* are often false.

Essay Tests

Essay questions are a weak spot for students who lack organization, don't support their ideas, or don't directly answer the question (Van Blerkom, 2011). When you take an essay exam try the following:

1. Read the question carefully. Be sure to note key words, such as *compare, contrast, discuss, evaluate, analyze,* and *describe*. These words all demand a certain emphasis in your answer.
2. Answer the question. If the question asks for a definition and an example, make sure you provide both. Providing just a definition or just an example will get you half marks. Giving three examples instead of the one asked for will not earn you any extra marks.
3. Reflect on your answer for a few minutes and list the main points you want to make. Just write them as they come to mind. Then rearrange the ideas in a logical order and begin writing. Elaborate plans or outlines are not necessary.
4. Don't beat around the bush or pad your answer. Be direct. Make a point and support it. Get your list of ideas into words.
5. Look over your essay for errors in spelling and grammar. Save this for last. Your *ideas* are of central importance. You can work on spelling and grammar separately if they affect your grades.

Short-Answer Tests

Tests that ask you to fill in a blank, define a term, or list specific items can be difficult. Usually, the questions themselves contain little information. If you don't know the answer, you won't get much help from the questions.

The best way to prepare for short-answer tests is to overlearn the details of the course. As you study, pay special attention to lists of related terms.

Again, it is best to start with the questions whose answers you're sure you know. Follow that by completing the questions whose answers you think you probably know. Questions whose answers you have no idea about can be left blank.

Again, for your convenience, Figure I.2 provides a checklist summary of the main study skills we have covered.

Using Digital Media—Netting New Knowledge

Gateway Question I.7: *Can digital media help with reflective processing?*

Digital media offer another way to be more reflective. Search the Internet for any psychological term, from *amnesia* to *zoophobia,* and you will find a vast array of information. Websites range from the authoritative, like the one provided by the American Psychological Association, to Wikipedia entries and personal blogs. However, be aware that information on the Internet is not always accurate. It is wise to approach all websites with a healthy dose of skepticism.

Psychology CourseMate

How would I find information about psychology on the Internet? Your first stop on the Internet should be *Psychology CourseMate.*

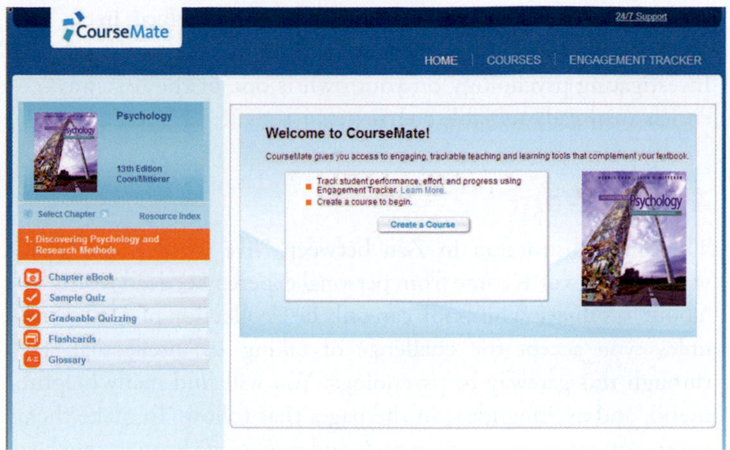

Psychology CourseMate **gives you online access to a variety of valuable learning aids and interesting materials.** Copyright © Cengage Learning 2013

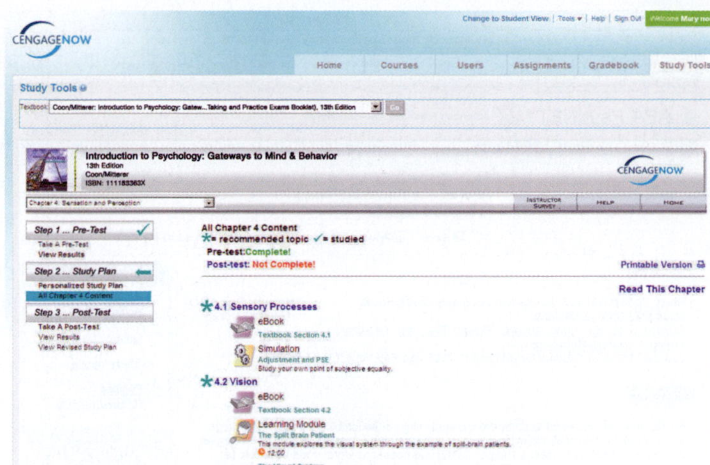

● Figure I.3 A sample screen from *CengageNOW*. Copyright © Cengage Learning 2013

There you will find an interactive eBook that allows you to take notes, highlight, bookmark, search the text, and use in-context glossary definitions. You can also access interactive teaching and learning tools, including:

- Quizzes
- Flashcards
- Videos
- Learning Modules
- and more

Psychology CourseMate is located at **www.cengagebrain.com**. Be sure to visit this site for valuable information about how to improve your grades and enhance your appreciation of psychology.

CengageNOW

Students can also make use of *CengageNOW for Coon/Mitterer's Psychology: Gateways to Mind and Behavior 13e. CengageNOW* is a web-based, personalized study system that provides a pretest and a posttest for each chapter. *CengageNOW* also creates personalized study plans, which include media such as videos, animations, learning modules, and links to the eBook. These materials can help you master the topics you need to study most (see ● Figure I.3). Go to **www.cengagebrain.com**.

Psychology Resource Center

Do you like videos, simulations, and animations? Do you learn best when you get actively involved in psychology? The Cengage Psychology Resource Center brings psychology to life with a full library of original and classic video clips plus interactive learning modules tied to all of the topics covered in your introductory psychology course. Go to **www.cengagebrain.com**.

Psychology Websites

You'll find the titles of interesting websites you may want to explore at the end of each chapter in this book, including this one. The best way to reach these sites is through *Psychology CourseMate*. We have not included website addresses in the book because they often change or may become inactive. At *Psychology CourseMate*, you'll find up-to-date links for websites listed in this book. The sites we've listed are generally of high quality.

PsycINFO

Psychological knowledge can also be found through specialized online databases. One of the best is PsycINFO, offered by the American Psychological Association (APA). **PsycINFO** provides summaries of the scientific and scholarly literature in psychology. Each record in PsycINFO consists of an abstract (short summary), plus notes about the author, title, source, and other details (see ● Figure I.4). All entries are indexed using key terms. Thus, you can search for various topics by entering words such as *drug abuse, postpartum depression,* or *creativity.*

Almost every college and university subscribes to PsycINFO. If this is the case, you can usually search PsycINFO from a terminal in your college library or computer center—for free. PsycINFO can also be directly accessed (for a fee) through the Internet via APA's PsycINFO Direct service.

PsycINFO A searchable online database that provides brief summaries of the scientific and scholarly literature in psychology.

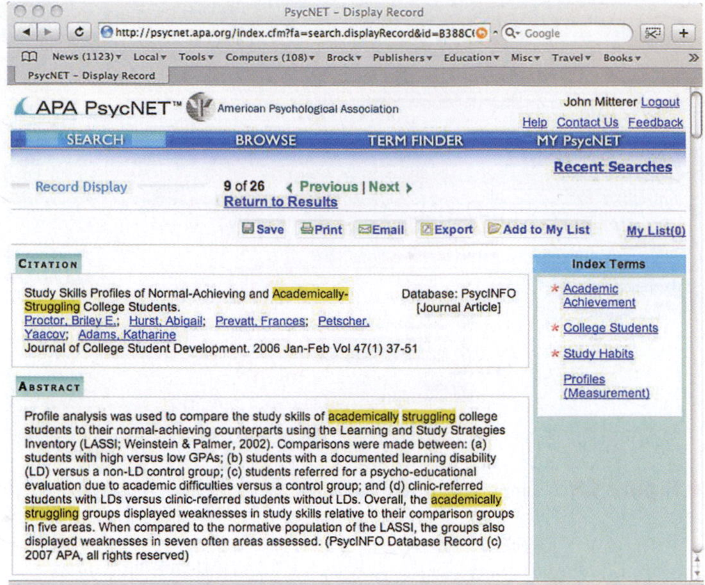

Figure I.4 This is a sample abstract from the PsycINFO database. If you search for the term *study skills,* you will find this article and many more in PsycINFO. (This record is reprinted with permission of the American Psychological Association, publisher of the PsycINFO Database, all rights reserved. May not be reproduced without prior permission.)

The APA Website

The APA also maintains an online library of general interest articles on aging, anger, children and families, depression, divorce, emotional health, kids and the media, sexuality, stress, testing issues, women and men, and other topics. It is well worth consulting when you have questions about psychological issues. For links to recent articles in newspapers and magazines, be sure to check the APA's PsycPORT page.

Please do explore the "digital gateways" described here. You might be surprised by the fascinating information that awaits you. Investigating psychology on your own is one of the best ways to enrich an already valuable course.

A Final Word

There is a distinction in Zen between "live words" and "dead words." Live words come from personal experience; dead words are "about" a subject. This book can only be a collection of dead words unless you accept the challenge of taking an intellectual step through this gateway to psychology. You will find many helpful, useful, and exciting ideas in the pages that follow. To make them yours, you must set out to *actively* and *reflectively* learn as much as you can. The ideas presented here should get you off to a good start. Good luck!

For more information, consult any of the following books:

Burka, J. B., & Yuen, L. M. (2008). *Procrastination: Why you do it, what to do about it*. Cambridge, MA: Perseus.

Chaffee, J. (2010). *Thinking critically* (10th ed.). Belmont, CA: Cengage Learning/Wadsworth.

Ellis, D. (2011). *Becoming a master student: Concise* (13th ed.). Belmont, CA: Cengage Learning/Wadsworth.

Rosnow, R. L. (2011). *Writing papers in psychology: A student guide to research papers, essays, proposals, posters, and handouts* (9th ed.). Belmont, CA: Cengage Learning/Wadsworth.

Santrock, J. W., & Halonen, J. S. (2010). *Your guide to college success: Strategies for achieving your goals* (6th ed.). Belmont, CA: Cengage Learning/Wadsworth.

Van Blerkom, D. L. (2011). *College study skills: Becoming a strategic learner* (7th ed.). Belmont, CA: Cengage Learning/Wadsworth.

Wong, W. (2011). *Essential study skills* (7th ed.). Belmont, CA: Cengage Learning/Wadsworth.

Knowledge Builder — Study Skills

RECITE

1. The four Rs in reflective SQ4R stand for "read, recite, reflect, and review." T or F?
2. When using the LISAN method, students try to write down as much of a lecture as possible so that their notes are complete. T or F?
3. Spaced study sessions are usually superior to massed practice. T or F?
4. According to research, you should almost always stick with your first answer on multiple-choice tests. T or F?
5. To use the technique known as overlearning, you should continue to study after you feel you have begun to master a topic. T or F?
6. Setting learning goals and monitoring your progress are important parts of ________________ learning.
7. Procrastination is related to seeking perfection and equating self-worth with grades. T or F?

REFLECT

Think Critically

8. How are the reflective SQ4R method and the LISAN method related?

Self-Reflect

Which study skills do you think would help you the most? Which techniques do you already use? Which do you think you should try? To what extent do you already engage in self-regulated learning? What additional steps could you take to become a more active, goal-oriented learner?

Answers: 1. T **2.** F **3.** T **4.** F **5.** T **6.** self-regulated **7.** T **8.** Both encourage people to be reflective and to actively seek information as a way of learning more effectively.

Chapter in Review Gateways to Psychology

Gateway QUESTIONS REVISITED

I.1 What is the best way to read a textbook?

I.1.1 Reflective reading, which involves actively thinking about what is being read, is better than passive reading.

I.1.2 One way to be a more active reader is to follow the six steps of the reflective SQ4R method: Survey, question, read, recite, reflect, and review.

I.2 How can learning in class be improved?

I.2.1 Reflective learning in class involves active listening.

I.2.2 One way to be a more active listener in class is to follow the five steps of the LISAN method: lead, don't follow; ideas; signal words; actively listen; note taking.

I.3 What is the best way to study?

I.3.1 More reflective studying involves studying in a specific place, using spaced study sessions, trying mnemonics, testing yourself, and overlearning.

I.4 What is self-regulated learning?

I.4.1 Self-regulated learning is deliberately self-reflective and active self-guided study.

I.5 How can procrastination be overcome?

I.5.1 Procrastination can be overcome through time management, setting goals, and making learning an adventure.

I.6 What are some ways to be a more effective test-taker?

I.6.1 A variety of guidelines are available for improving general test-taking skills.

I.6.2 More specialized strategies are available for objective tests, essay tests, and short-answer tests.

I.7 Can digital media help with reflective processing?

I.7.1 Digital media offer another way to be more reflective, as long as care is taken to approach all websites with a healthy dose of skepticism.

MEDIA RESOURCES

Web Resources

Internet addresses frequently change. To find an up-to-date list of URLs for the sites listed here, visit your Psychology CourseMate.

How to Succeed as a Student Advice on how to be a college student. Topics from studying to housing to preparation for work are included.

Library Research in Psychology Hints on how to do library research in psychology.

Psychology Glossary This glossary provides definitions for common psychological terms.

Tools for Reflection More advice on how to become a more reflective learner.

Interactive Learning

Log in to **CengageBrain** to access the resources your instructor requires. For this book, you can access:

CourseMate brings course concepts to life with interactive learning, study, and exam preparation tools that support the printed textbook. A textbook-specific website, ***Psychology CourseMate*** includes an ***integrated interactive eBook*** and other ***interactive learning tools*** including quizzes, flashcards, videos, and more.

CENGAGE**NOW**™

CengageNOW is an easy-to-use online resource that helps you study in less time to get the grade you want—NOW. Take a pre-test for this chapter and receive a personalized study plan based on your results that will identify the topics you need to review and direct you to online resources to help you master those topics. Then take a post-test to help you determine the concepts you have mastered and what you will need to work on. If your textbook does not include an access code card, go to CengageBrain.com to gain access.

WebTUTOR™

More than just an interactive study guide, **WebTutor** is an anytime, anywhere customized learning solution with an eBook, keeping you connected to your textbook, instructor, and classmates.

If your professor has assigned **Aplia** homework:

1. Sign in to your account.
2. Complete the corresponding homework exercises as required by your professor.
3. When finished, click "Grade It Now" to see which areas you have mastered and which need more work, and for detailed explanations of every answer.

Visit **www.cengagebrain.com** to access your account and purchase materials.

Gateway THEME

Psychology is a science and a profession. Scientific observation is the most powerful way to critically answer questions about behavior.

Introduction to Psychology and Research Methods

1

Fly Like an Eagle

Just about every weekend, Henry can be found jumping from airplanes. Not content to be a mere parachutist ("It's so *boring!*" he insists), he wears a skin-tight "wing suit" so he can soar headfirst as fast and as far as he can before deploying his tiny parachute at the last possible moment. Being a bit superstitious, Henry never jumps without his lucky 1986 American silver eagle dollar, minted the year of his birth, safely tucked in his pocket. Yup, that's him hurtling toward the ground at a frighteningly high rate of speed. Henry is an extreme skydiver.

Why, you might wonder, would Henry do anything that crazy even once, much less again and again? But then, you might equally wonder why people get married, join the army, travel to different countries, grow roses, become suicide bombers, go to school, or live out their lives in monasteries. And what's with the silver dollar?

You might even wonder, at least sometimes, why *you* do the things you do. In other words, just like your authors, the odds are you are curious about human behavior. That may even be a part of the reason you are taking a course in psychology and reading this book.

Psychology is an ever-changing panorama of people and ideas. You really can't call yourself educated without knowing something about it. And, although we might envy those who have walked on the moon or explored the ocean's depths, the ultimate frontier lies much closer to home. Psychology can help you better understand yourself and others. This book is a guided tour of human behavior. We hope you enjoy the adventure.

Gateway QUESTIONS

1.1 *What is psychology and what are its goals?*
1.2 *What is critical thinking?*
1.3 *How does psychology differ from false explanations of behavior?*
1.4 *How is the scientific method applied in psychological research?*
1.5 *How did the field of psychology emerge?*
1.6 *What are the contemporary perspectives in psychology?*
1.7 *What are the major specialties in psychology?*
1.8 *How is an experiment performed?*
1.9 *What is a double-blind experiment?*
1.10 *What nonexperimental research methods do psychologists use?*
1.11 *How good is psychological information found in the popular media?*

Psychology—Behave Yourself!

Gateway Question 1.1: *What is psychology and what are its goals?*

Those of us wondering about Henry's extreme skydiving are not the first humans ever to be curious about human behavior. The word *psychology* itself is thousands of years old, coming from the ancient Greek roots *psyche,* meaning "mind," and *logos,* meaning "knowledge or study." However, have you ever actually seen or touched a "mind"? Because the mind can't be studied directly, **psychology** is now defined as the scientific study of behavior and mental processes.

What does "behavior" *refer to in the definition of psychology?* Anything you do—eating, hanging out, sleeping, talking, or sneezing—is a behavior. So are studying, gambling, watching television, tying your shoes, giving someone a gift, learning Spanish, reading this book, and, yes, extreme skydiving. Naturally, we are interested in *overt behaviors* (directly observable actions and responses) like these. But psychologists also study *covert behaviors.* These are private mental events, such as thinking, dreaming, and remembering (Jackson, 2011).

Today, psychology is both a *science* and a *profession.* As scientists, some psychologists do research to discover new knowledge. Others apply psychology to solve problems in fields such as mental health, business, education, sports, law, medicine, and the design of machines (Coolican et al., 2007). Still others are teachers who share their knowledge with students. Later we will return to the profession of psychology. For now, let's focus on how psychologists create knowledge. Whether they work in a lab, a clinic, or a classroom, all psychologists rely on critical thinking and especially information gained from scientific research.

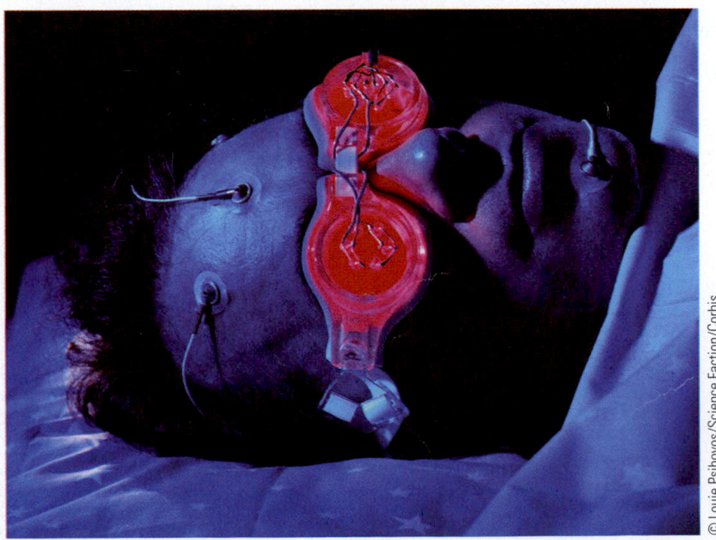

© Louie Psihoyos/Science Faction/Corbis

Psychologists are highly trained professionals who have specialized skills in counseling and therapy, measurement and testing, research and experimentation, statistics, diagnosis, treatment, and many other areas. Here, psychologist Steven LaBerge wears goggles designed to alert him that he is dreaming, in order to increase his chances of having a lucid dream (Holzinger, LaBerge, & Levitan, 2006). (See Chapter 5 for more details.)

Seeking Knowledge in Psychology

Isn't psychology really just a matter of using your common sense? Actually, much "commonsense" wisdom is pure B.S. (B.S., of course, stands for *Before Science*). Many people regard themselves as expert "people watchers" and form their own commonsense theories of behavior. However, you may be surprised to learn how often self-appointed authorities and long-held commonsense beliefs about human behavior are wrong (Lilienfeld et al., 2010). Take a moment and read "Testing Commonsense Beliefs" for more information.

But how could common sense be wrong so often? We'll spend quite a bit of time in this chapter exploring why this might be so. One problem is that much of what passes for common sense is vague and inconsistent. Suppose that your friend marries someone very different from her. What do people say? "Ah. . . opposites attract." And what do they say if she gets divorced soon after? "Well, she should have known that birds of a feather flock together." Let's examine another commonsense statement. It is frequently said that "every cloud has a silver lining." With this in mind, you use your lover's worrisome absences as a chance to spend more time with your family. You take comfort in this "silver lining" until a family member cautions, "Where there's smoke, there's fire!" Also notice that, like these examples, most of these commonsense statements work best after the fact.

Another problem with common sense is that it often depends on limited personal observations. For example, have you ever had someone tell you he heard that the food in New York City (or Mexico, or Canada, or Paris, or wherever) is terrible? But this might mean no more than that someone didn't like the food in one restaurant on one visit. Like such casual observation, psychologists rely on **scientific observation,** which is also based on gathering *empirical evidence* (information gained from direct observation). However, unlike our everyday personal experiences, scientific observation is *systematic,* or carefully planned. Scientific observations are also *intersubjective,* which means they can be confirmed by more than one observer.

Basically, the empirical approach says, "Let's take a more objective look" (Stanovich, 2010). Psychologists study behavior directly and collect data (observed facts) so they can draw valid conclusions. Would you say it's true, for instance, that "Absence makes the heart grow fonder"? Why argue about it? As psychologists, we would simply get some people who are separated ("absent hearts") and some who see each other every day ("present hearts") and find out who is fonder of their loved ones!

Here's an example of gathering empirical evidence: Have you ever wondered whether people become more hostile when it's boiling hot outside? John Simister and Cary Cooper (2005) decided to find out. They obtained data on temperatures and criminal activity in Los Angeles over a 4-year period. When they graphed air temperature and the frequency of aggravated assaults, a clear relationship emerged (see ● Figure 1.1). Assaults and temperatures rise and fall more or less in parallel (so there may be something to the phrase "hot under the collar").

Critical Thinking — Testing Commonsense Beliefs

It may appear that psychological research "discovers" what we already know from everyday experience. Why waste time and money confirming the obvious? Actually, commonsense beliefs are often wrong. See if you can tell which of the following commonsense beliefs are true and which are false (Landau & Bavaria, 2003):

- Babies love their mothers because mothers fulfill their babies' physiological need for food. True or False?
- Most humans use only 10 percent of their potential brainpower. True or False?
- Blind people have unusually sensitive organs of touch. True or False?
- The more motivated you are, the better you will do at solving a complex problem. True or False?
- The major cause of forgetting is that memory traces decay or fade as time passes. True or False?
- Psychotherapy has its greatest success in the treatment of psychotic patients who have lost touch with reality. True or False?
- Personality tests reveal your basic motives, including those you may not be aware of. True or False?
- To change people's behavior toward members of ethnic minority groups, we must first change their attitudes. True or False?

Actually, research has shown that *all* these beliefs are false. Yet in a survey, *all* the beliefs were accepted as common sense by many college students (Landau & Bavaria, 2003). How did you do?

We can all benefit from being more reflective as we evaluate our beliefs. It's valuable to ask whether they make logical sense or whether there is any evidence supporting them (Jackson & Newberry, 2012). Do any of the concepts in this book apply to the belief? Can you imagine how you could collect evidence that might get you closer to the truth? *Critical Thinking* boxes like this one will help you be more reflective about human behavior.

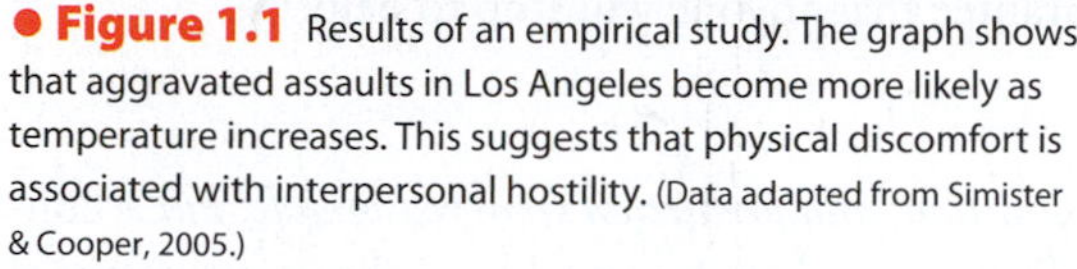

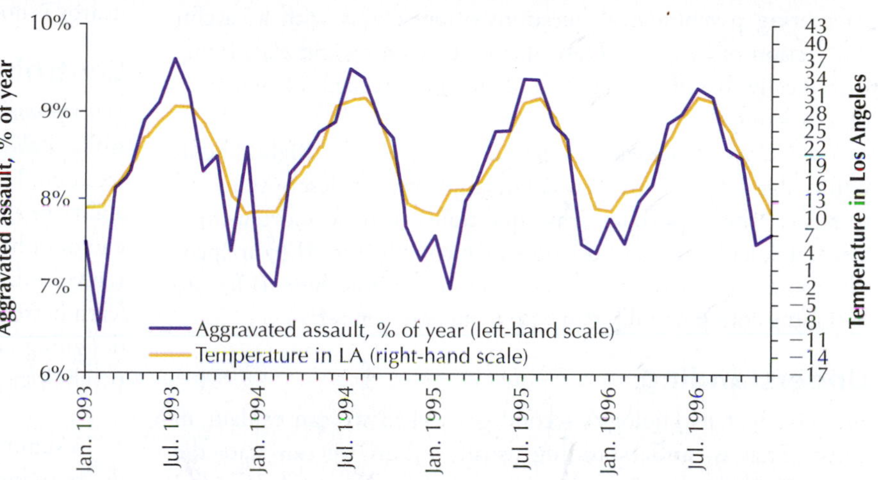

● **Figure 1.1** Results of an empirical study. The graph shows that aggravated assaults in Los Angeles become more likely as temperature increases. This suggests that physical discomfort is associated with interpersonal hostility. (Data adapted from Simister & Cooper, 2005.)

Isn't the outcome of this study fairly predictable? Not if you started out believing otherwise. Sometimes, the results of studies match our personal observations or commonsense beliefs and sometimes they come as a surprise. In this instance, you may have guessed the outcome. Your suspicions were confirmed by scientific observation. However, hostile actions that require more extreme physical exertion, such as fistfights, might become *less* likely at very high temperatures. Without systematically gathering data, we wouldn't know for sure whether overheated Angelenos become sluggish or more aggressive.

Psychological Research

Many fields, such as history, law, art, and business, are also interested in human behavior. How is psychology different? Psychology's great strength is that it uses scientific observation to systematically answer questions about all sorts of behaviors (Stanovich, 2010). Of course, studying some topics may be impractical or unethical. More often, questions go unanswered for lack of a suitable **research method**—a systematic approach to answering scientific questions. In the past, for example, we had to take the word of people who say they never dream. Then the EEG (electroencephalograph, or brainwave machine) was invented. Certain EEG patterns, and the presence of eye movements, can reveal whether a person is dreaming. People who "never dream," it turns out, dream frequently. If they are awakened during a dream, they vividly remember it. Thus, the EEG helped make the study of dreaming more scientific.

Psychology's Goals

What do psychologists hope to achieve? As scientists, our ultimate goal is to benefit humanity (O'Neill, 2005). More specifically, the goals of psychology are to *describe, understand, predict,* and *control* behavior. What do psychology's goals mean in practice? Let's see.

Psychology The scientific study of behavior and mental processes.

Scientific observation An empirical investigation structured to answers questions about the world in a systematic and intersubjective fashion (observations can be reliably confirmed by multiple observers).

Research method A systematic approach to answering scientific questions.

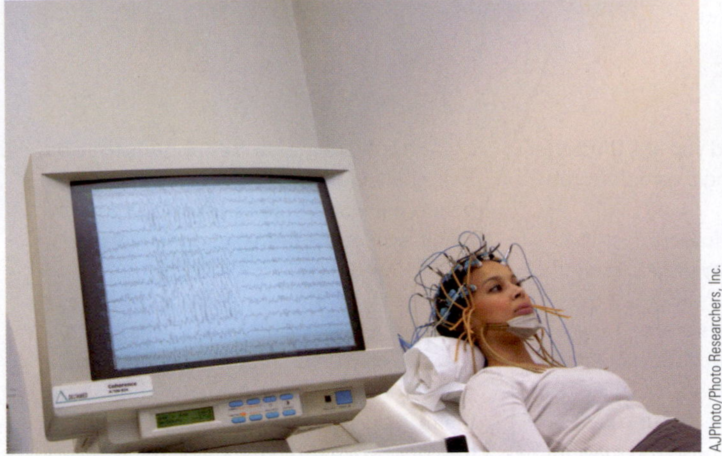

AJPhoto/Photo Researchers, Inc.

The scientific study of dreaming was made possible by use of the EEG, a device that records the tiny electrical signals generated by the brain as a person sleeps. The EEG converts these electrical signals to a written record of brain activity. Certain shifts in brain activity, coupled with the presence of rapid eye movements, are strongly related to dreaming. (See Chapter 5 for more information.)

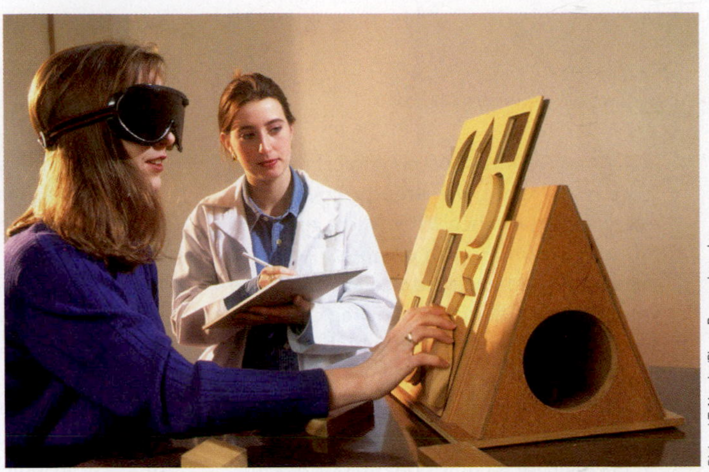

Richard T. Nowitz/Photo Researchers, Inc.

Some psychologists specialize in administering, scoring, and interpreting psychological tests, such as tests of intelligence, creativity, personality, or aptitude. This specialty, which is called psychometrics, is an example of using psychology to predict future behavior.

Description

Answering psychological questions often begins with a careful description of behavior. **Description**, or naming and classifying, is typically based on making a detailed record of scientific observations.

But a description doesn't explain anything, does it? Right. Useful knowledge begins with accurate description, but descriptions fail to answer the important "why" questions. *Why* do more women attempt suicide, and *why* do more men complete it? *Why* are people more aggressive when they are uncomfortable? *Why* are bystanders often unwilling to help in an emergency?

Understanding

We have met psychology's second goal when we can explain an event. That is, **understanding** usually means we can state the causes of a behavior. For example, research on "bystander apathy" reveals that people often fail to help when *other* possible helpers are nearby. Why? Because a "diffusion of responsibility" occurs. Basically, no one feels personally obligated to pitch in. As a result, the more potential helpers there are, the less likely it is that anyone will help (Aronson, Wilson, & Akert, 2010; Darley, 2000). Now we can explain a perplexing problem.

BRIDGES

Bystander apathy and conditions that influence whether people will help in an emergency are of great interest to social psychologists. **See Chapter 17, pages 581–583, for details.**

Prediction

Psychology's third goal, **prediction**, is the ability to forecast behavior accurately. Notice that our explanation of bystander apathy makes a prediction about the chances of getting help. If you've ever been stranded on a busy freeway with car trouble, you'll recognize the accuracy of this prediction: Having many potential helpers nearby is no guarantee that anyone will stop to help.

Control

Description, explanation, and prediction seem reasonable, but is control *a valid goal?* "Control" may seem like a threat to personal freedom. However, to a psychologist, **control** simply refers to the ability to alter the conditions that affect behavior. If a clinical psychologist helps a person overcome a terrible fear of spiders, control is involved. If you suggest changes in a classroom that help students learn better, you have exerted control. Control is also involved in designing cars to keep drivers from making fatal errors. Clearly, psychological control must be used wisely and humanely.

In summary, psychology's goals are a natural outgrowth of our desire to understand behavior. Basically, they boil down to asking the following questions:

- What is the nature of this behavior? (description)
- Why does it occur? (understanding and explanation)
- Can we forecast when it will occur? (prediction)
- What conditions affect it? (control)

Knowledge Builder The Science of Psychology

RECITE

To check your memory, see if you can answer these questions. If you miss any, skim over the preceding material before continuing to make sure you understand what you just read.

1. Psychology is the ________________ study of ____________________ and ____________ processes.

2. Commonsense beliefs are often
   a. vague *b.* inconsistent *c.* based on limited observations *d.* all of the above
3. The best psychological information is typically based on
   a. forecasting behavior *b.* opinions of experts and authorities *c.* anthropomorphic measurements *d.* empirical evidence.
4. Which of the following questions relates most directly to the goal of *understanding* behavior?
   a. Do the scores of men and women differ on tests of thinking abilities? *b.* Why does a blow to the head cause memory loss? *c.* Will productivity in a business office increase if room temperature is raised or lowered? *d.* What percentage of college students suffer from test anxiety?

REFLECT

Think Critically

5. All sciences are interested in controlling the phenomena they study. T or F?

Self-Reflect

At first, many students think that psychology is primarily about abnormal behavior and psychotherapy. Did you? How would you describe the field now?

Answers: 1. scientific, (overt) behavior, (covert) mental **2.** *d* **3.** *d* **4.** *b* **5.** False. Astronomy and archaeology are examples of sciences that do not share psychology's fourth goal. Think about it for a moment: No one can *control* the stars or the past.

Critical Thinking—Take It with a Grain of Salt

Gateway Question 1.2: *What is critical thinking?*

How does critical thinking play a role in psychology? Most of us would be skeptical when offered a "genuine" Rolex watch or expensive designer sunglasses for just a few dollars on eBay. And most of us easily accept our ignorance of subatomic physics. But because we deal with human behavior every day, we tend to think that we already know what is true in psychology. All too often, we are tempted to "buy" commonsense beliefs, urban legends, and even outrageous claims about the powers of "healing" crystals, "miraculous" herbal remedies, astrology, psychics describing people's personalities and predicting their future, and so forth.

For this, and many more reasons, learning to think critically is one of the lasting benefits of a college education. **Critical thinking** in psychology is a type of reflection (you DID read the *Psychology of Studying*, on pages 1–11, right?) that involves asking whether a particular belief can be supported by scientific theory and observation (Yanchar, Slife, & Warne, 2008). Critical thinkers are willing to challenge conventional wisdom by asking hard questions (Jackson & Newberry, 2012). For example, everyone knows that women are more talkative than men, right? Critical thinkers might immediately ask: "Is there any theory to explain why women might talk more than men? Is there any empirical evidence that supports this 'wisdom'?" What could we do to find out for ourselves? (Be on the lookout later in this chapter for some evidence concerning this belief.)

Critical Thinking Principles

The heart of critical thinking is a willingness to actively *reflect* on ideas. Critical thinkers evaluate ideas by probing for weaknesses in their reasoning and analyzing the evidence supporting their beliefs. They question assumptions and look for alternate conclusions. True knowledge, they recognize, comes from constantly revising our understanding of the world.

Critical thinking relies on the following basic principles (Elder, 2006; Jackson & Newberry, 2012; Kida, 2006):

1. *Few "truths" transcend the need for logical analysis and empirical testing.* Whereas religious beliefs and personal values may be held as matters of faith, most other ideas can and should be evaluated by applying the rules of logic, evidence, and the scientific method.
2. *Critical thinkers often wonder what it would take to show that a "truth" is false.* Critical thinkers actively seek to *falsify* beliefs, including their own. They are willing to admit when they are wrong. As Susan Blackmore (2001) said when her studies caused her to abandon some long-held beliefs, "Admitting you are wrong is always hard—even though it's a skill that every psychologist has to learn." At the same time, critical thinkers can be more confident in beliefs that have survived their attempts at falsification.
3. *Authority or claimed expertise does not automatically make an idea true or false.* Just because a teacher, guru, celebrity, or authority is convinced or sincere doesn't mean you should automatically believe or disbelieve that person. Naïvely accepting (or denying) the word of an "expert" is unscientific and self-demeaning without asking, "Is this a well-supported explanation or is there a better one? What evidence convinced her or him?"
4. *Judging the quality of evidence is crucial.* Imagine you are a juror in a courtroom, judging claims made by two battling lawyers. To decide correctly, you can't just weigh the *amount* of evidence. You must also critically evaluate the *quality* of the evidence. Then you can give greater weight to the most credible facts.
5. *Critical thinking requires an open mind.* Be prepared to consider daring departures and go wherever the evidence leads. However, don't become so "open-minded" that you are simply gullible. As astronomer Carl Sagan once noted, "It seems to me that what is called for is an exquisite balance between two conflicting needs: the most skeptical scrutiny of all hypotheses that are served up to us and at the same time a great openness to new ideas" (Kida, 2006, p. 51).

Description In scientific research, the process of naming and classifying.
Understanding In psychology, understanding is achieved when the causes of a behavior can be stated.
Prediction An ability to accurately forecast behavior.
Control Altering conditions that influence behavior.
Critical thinking (in psychology) A type of reflection involving the support of beliefs through scientific explanation and observation.

To put these principles into action, here are some questions to ask as you evaluate new information (Browne & Keeley, 2010; Jackson & Newberry, 2012):

1. What claims are being made? What are their implications?
2. Are the claims understandable? Do they make logical sense? Is there another possible explanation? Is it a simpler explanation?
3. What tests (if any) of these claims have been made? What was the nature and quality of the tests? Can they be repeated? Who did the tests? How reliable and trustworthy were the investigators? Do they have conflicts of interest? Do their findings appear to be objective? Has any other independent researcher duplicated the findings?
4. How good is the evidence? (In general, scientific observations provide the highest quality evidence.)
5. Finally, how much credibility can the claim be given? High, medium, low, provisional?

A course in psychology naturally enriches thinking skills. In this book, all upcoming chapters include *Think Critically* questions based on the ones you have seen here. Take the time to tackle these questions. The effort will sharpen your thinking abilities and make learning more lively. For an immediate thinking challenge, let's take a critical look at several nonscientific systems that claim to explain behavior.

Pseudopsychologies—Palms, Planets, and Personality

Gateway Question 1.3: *How does psychology differ from false explanations of behavior?*

A **pseudopsychology** (SUE-doe-psychology) is any unfounded system that resembles psychology. Many pseudopsychologies give the appearance of being scientific but are actually false. (*Pseudo* means "false.") Pseudopsychologies are types of **superstitions**, unfounded beliefs held without evidence or in the face of falsifying evidence.

Unlike "real" psychology, pseudopsychologies change little over time because followers seek evidence that appears to confirm their beliefs and avoid evidence that falsifies them. Critical thinkers, scientists, and psychologists, in contrast, are skeptical of their own theories (Schick & Vaughn, 2011). They actively look for contradictions as a way to advance knowledge.

Can you give some examples of false psychologies? One pseudopsychology, known as *phrenology*, was popularized in the nineteenth century by Franz Gall, a German anatomy teacher. Phrenology claimed that personality traits are revealed by the shape of the skull. Psychological research has long since shown that bumps on the head have nothing to do with talents or abilities. In fact, the phrenologists were so far off that they listed the part of the brain that controls hearing as a center for "combativeness"! *Palmistry* is a similarly falsified system that claims lines on the hand reveal personality traits and predict the future. Despite the overwhelming evidence against phrenology and palmistry, these pseudopsychologies are still practiced today. Palmists, in particular, can still be found separating the gullible from their money in many cities.

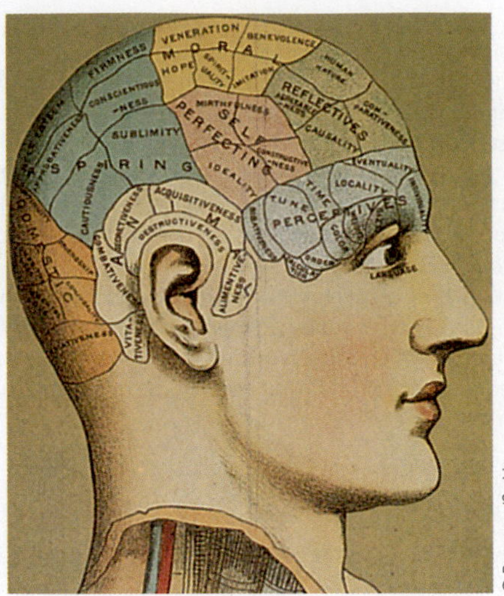

Phrenology was an attempt to assess personality characteristics by examining various areas of the skull. Phrenologists used charts such as the one shown here as guides. Like other pseudopsychologists, phrenologists resisted attempts to empirically verify their concepts.

At first glance, a pseudopsychology called *graphology* might seem more reasonable. Some graphologists claim that personality traits are revealed by handwriting. Based on such claims, some companies even use graphologists to select job candidates. This is troubling because graphologists score close to zero on tests of accuracy in rating personality (Dazzi & Pedrabissi, 2009; Furnham, Chamorro-Premuzic, & Callahan, 2003). In fact, graphologists do no better than untrained college students in rating personality and job performance (Neter & Ben-Shakhar, 1989). Even a graphological society recommends that handwriting analysis should not be used to select people for jobs (Simner & Goffin, 2003). (By the way, graphology's failure at revealing personality should be separated from its value for detecting forgeries.)

Graphology might seem harmless enough until you imagine being denied a job because a graphologist didn't like your handwriting. This false system has been used to determine who is hired, given bank credit, or selected for juries. In these and similar situations, pseudopsychologies do, in fact, harm people.

Would you hire this man? Here's a sample of your author's handwriting. What do you think it reveals? Your interpretations are likely to be as accurate (or inaccurate) as those of a graphologist.

If pseudopsychologies have no scientific basis, how do they survive and why are they popular? There are several reasons, all of which can be illustrated by a critique of astrology.

Problems in the Stars

Arguably the most popular pseudopsychology, astrology holds that the positions of the stars and planets at the time of one's birth determine personality traits and affect behavior. Like other pseudopsychologies, astrology has repeatedly been shown to have no scientific validity, either theoretically or empirically (Kelly, 1999; Rogers & Soule, 2009):

1. **The theory of astrology is unconvincing.** Astrology is based on a zodiac map invented several thousand years ago in an ancient civilization called Babylon. Unlike scientific theories, which are regularly falsified and rejected or revised accordingly, the basic underpinnings of astrology have remained relatively unchanged. To date, no astrologer has offered a convincing explanation of *how* the positions of the planets at a person's birth could affect his or her future. Astrologers have also failed to explain *why* the moment of birth should be more important than, say, the moment of conception. (Perhaps it is because it is relatively easy to figure out the moment of birth and much trickier to determine the moment of conception.) Besides, the zodiac has shifted in the sky by one full constellation since astrology was first set up. (In other words, if astrology calls you a Scorpio you are really a Libra, and so forth.) However, most astrologers simply ignore this shift (Martens & Trachet, 1998).
2. **The evidence against astrology *is* convincing.** One study of more than 3,000 predictions by famous astrologers found that only a small percentage were fulfilled. These "successful" predictions tended to be vague ("There will be a tragedy somewhere in the east in the spring") or easily guessed from current events (Culver & Ianna, 1988). Similarly, if astrologers are asked to match people with their horoscopes, they do no better than would be expected by chance. In one famous test, astrologers could not even use horoscopes to distinguish murderers from law-abiding people (Gauquelin, 1970). In fact, there is no connection between people's astrological signs and their intelligence or personality traits (Hartmann, Reuter, & Nyborg, 2006). There is also no connection between the "compatibility" of couples' astrological signs and their marriage and divorce rates or between astrological signs and leadership, physical characteristics, or career choices (Martens & Trachet, 1998).

In short, astrology doesn't work.

Then why does astrology often seem to work? Even the daily horoscopes printed in newspapers can seem uncannily accurate. For many people this apparent accuracy can only mean that astrology is valid. Unfortunately, such *uncritical acceptance* overlooks a much simpler psychological explanation (see, for example, Rogers & Soule, 2009). The following discussion explains why.

Uncritical Acceptance

Perceptions of the accuracy of horoscopes are typically based on **uncritical acceptance**—the tendency to believe claims because they seem true or because it would be nice if they were true. Horoscopes are generally made up of mostly flattering traits. Naturally, when your personality is described in *desirable* terms, it is hard to deny that the description has the "ring of truth." How much acceptance would astrology receive if a birth sign read like this:

> **Virgo:** You are the logical type and hate disorder. Your nitpicking is unbearable to your friends. You are cold, unemotional, and usually fall asleep while making love. Virgos make good doorstops.

Confirmation Bias

Even when an astrological description contains a mixture of good and bad traits, it may seem accurate. To find out why, read the following personality description.

> **Your Personality Profile**
>
> You have many personality strengths, with some weaknesses to which you can usually adjust. You tend to be accepting of yourself. You are comfortable with some structure in your life but do enjoy diverse experiences from time to time. Although on the inside you might be a bit unsure of yourself, you appear under control to others. You are sexually well-adjusted, although you do have some questions. Your life goals are more or less realistic. Occasionally you question your decisions and actions because you're unsure that they are correct. You want to be liked and admired by other people. You are not using your potential to its full extent. You like to think for yourself and don't always take other people's word without thinking it through. You are not generally willing to disclose to others because it might lead to problems. You are a natural introvert, cautious, and careful around others, although there are times when you can be an extrovert who is the "life of the party."

Does this describe your personality? A psychologist read a similar summary individually to college students who had taken a personality test. Only 5 students out of 79 felt that the description was inaccurate. Another classic study found that people rated the "personality profile" as more accurate than their actual horoscopes (French et al., 1991).

Reread the description and you will see that it contains both sides of several personality dimensions ("You are a natural introvert . . . although there are times when you can be an extrovert . . ."). Its apparent accuracy is an illusion based on **confirmation bias,** in which we remember or notice things that confirm our expectations

Pseudopsychology Any false and unscientific system of beliefs and practices that is offered as an explanation of behavior.

Superstition Unfounded belief held without evidence or in spite of falsifying evidence.

Uncritical acceptance The tendency to believe claims because they seem true or because it would be nice if they were true.

Confirmation bias The tendency to remember or notice information that fits one's expectations but to forget discrepancies.

and forget the rest (Lilienfeld, Ammirati, & Landfield, 2009). The pseudopsychologies thrive on this effect. For example, you can always find "Aquarius characteristics" in an Aquarius. If you looked, however, you could also find "Gemini characteristics," "Scorpio characteristics," or whatever. Perhaps this explains why, in an ironic twist, 94 percent of those sent the full 10-page horoscope of a famous mass murderer accepted it as their own (Gauquelin, 1970).

Confirmation bias is also relied on by various "psychic mediums" who claim that they can communicate with the deceased friends and relatives of audience members. An analysis shows that the number of "hits" (correct statements) made by these people tends to be very low. Nevertheless, many viewers are impressed because of our natural tendency to remember apparent hits and ignore misses. Of course, particularly embarrassing misses are often edited out before such shows appear on television (Nickell, 2001).

Non Sequitur

The Barnum Effect

Pseudopsychologies also take advantage of the **Barnum effect,** which is a tendency to consider personal descriptions accurate if they are stated in general terms (Kida, 2006). P. T. Barnum, the famed circus showman, had a formula for success: "Always have a little something for everybody." Like the all-purpose personality profile, palm readings, fortunes, horoscopes, and other products of pseudopsychology are stated in such general terms that they can hardly miss. There is always "a little something for everybody." To observe the Barnum effect, read *all 12* of the daily horoscopes found in newspapers for several days. You will find that predictions for other signs fit events as well as those for your own sign do. Try giving a friend the wrong horoscope sometime. Your friend may still be quite impressed with the "accuracy" of the horoscope.

Astrology's popularity shows that many people have difficulty separating valid psychology from systems that seem valid but are not. The goal of this discussion, then, has been to make you a more critical observer of human behavior and to clarify what is, and what is not, psychology. Here is what the "stars" say about your future:

> Emphasis now on education and personal improvement. A learning experience of lasting value awaits you. Take care of scholastic responsibilities before engaging in recreation. The word *psychology* figures prominently in your future.

Pseudopsychologies may seem like no more than a nuisance, but they can do harm. For instance, people seeking treatment for psychological disorders may become the victims of self-appointed "experts" who offer ineffective, pseudoscientific "therapies" (Kida, 2006; Lilienfeld, Ruscio, & Lynn, 2008). Valid psychological principles are based on scientific theory and evidence, not fads, opinions, or wishful thinking.

Scientific Research—How to Think Like a Psychologist

Gateway Question 1.4: *How is the scientific method applied in psychological research?*

Thinking critically about psychology begins with the careful recording of facts and events, the heart of all sciences. To be *scientific,* our observations must be *systematic,* so that they reveal something reliable about behavior (Stanovich, 2010). To use an earlier example, if you are interested in the relationship between heat and aggression, you will learn little by driving around and making haphazard observations of aggressive behavior. To be of value, your observations must be planned and systematic.

The Scientific Method

The **scientific method** is a form of critical thinking based on careful collection of evidence, accurate description and measurement, precise definition, controlled observation, and repeatable results

Dan McCoy/Rainbow

Applying the scientific method to the study of behavior requires careful observation. Here, a psychologist videotapes a session in which a child's thinking abilities are being tested.

(Jackson, 2011; Yanchar, Slife, & Warne, 2008). In its ideal form, the scientific method has six elements:

1. Making observations
2. Defining a problem
3. Proposing a hypothesis
4. Gathering evidence/testing the hypothesis
5. Theory building
6. Publishing results

Let's take a closer look at some elements of the scientific method. Earlier we ran across the commonsense belief that women are chattier than men. How might a psychologist seek to confirm or disconfirm this belief? All the basic elements of the scientific method are found in this example, from University of Arizona psychologist Mathias Mehl and his colleagues (2007).

Making Observations

The commonsense belief under examination is that women are more talkative than men. Is there any truth to this belief? The researchers reviewed previously published studies and noted that a few reports do seem to support this stereotype.

Defining a Problem

However, the researchers also noticed that none of the studies had actually recorded men's and women's normal conversations over long time periods. Thus, they defined their problem as, "Will women talk more than men if we record natural conversations over longer time spans without bothering people and perhaps biasing our observations?"

Proposing a Hypothesis

What exactly is a "hypothesis"? A **hypothesis** (hi-POTH-eh-sis) is a tentative statement about, or explanation of, an event or relationship. In common terms, a hypothesis is a *testable* hunch or educated guess about behavior. For example, you might hypothesize "Frustration encourages aggression." How could you test this hypothesis? First you would have to decide how you are going to frustrate people. (This part might be fun.) Then you will need to find a way to measure whether they become more aggressive. (Not so much fun if you plan to be nearby.) Your observations would then provide evidence to confirm or disconfirm your hypothesis.

Because we cannot see or touch frustration, we must define it operationally. An **operational definition** states the exact procedures used to represent a concept. Operational definitions allow unobservable ideas, such as covert behaviors, to be tested in real-world terms (see • Figure 1.2). For example, since you can't measure frustration directly, you might define frustration as "interrupting an adult before he or she can finish a puzzle and win a free movie pass." And aggression might be defined as "the number of times a frustrated individual insults the person who prevented work on the puzzle." In other words, covert behaviors are operationally defined in terms of overt behavior so they can be observed and studied scientifically.

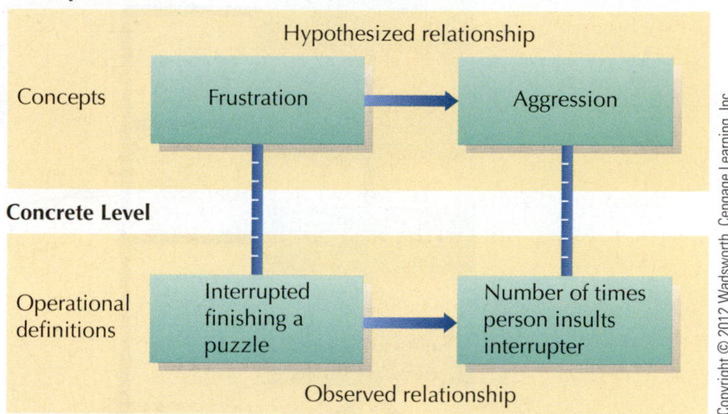

• Figure 1.2 Operational definitions are used to link concepts with concrete observations. Do you think the examples given are reasonable operational definitions of frustration and aggression? Operational definitions vary in how well they represent concepts. For this reason, many different experiments may be necessary to draw clear conclusions about hypothesized relationships in psychology.

Gathering Evidence/Testing the Hypothesis

Now let's return to the question of whether women talk more than men do. To gather data, the researchers used an electronically activated recorder to track people's conversations. This device automatically recorded sounds for 30 seconds every 12.5 minutes. Since participants could not tell when they were being recorded, they soon got used to wearing the recorders and acted and spoke normally. The number of words recorded was counted and used to estimate the total number of words spoken each day. On average, women spoke 16,215 words a day, with men close behind at 15,699. Since this difference is too small to be meaningful, we can conclude, as the researchers did, that this study provides no evidence in support of the hypothesis that women talk more than men do (Mehl et al., 2007).

Theory Building

What about theory building? In research, a **theory** is a system of ideas designed to interrelate concepts and facts in a way that summarizes existing data and predicts future observations. Good theories summarize observations, explain them, and guide further research (• Figure 1.3). Without theories of forgetting, personal-

Barnum effect The tendency to consider a personal description accurate if it is stated in very general terms.

Scientific method A form of critical thinking based on careful measurement and controlled observation.

Hypothesis A statement of the predicted outcome of an experiment or an educated guess about the relationship between variables.

Operational definition Defining a scientific concept by stating the specific actions or procedures used to measure it. For example, "hunger" might be defined as "the number of hours of food deprivation."

Theory A system of ideas designed to interrelate concepts and facts in a way that summarizes existing data and predicts future observations.

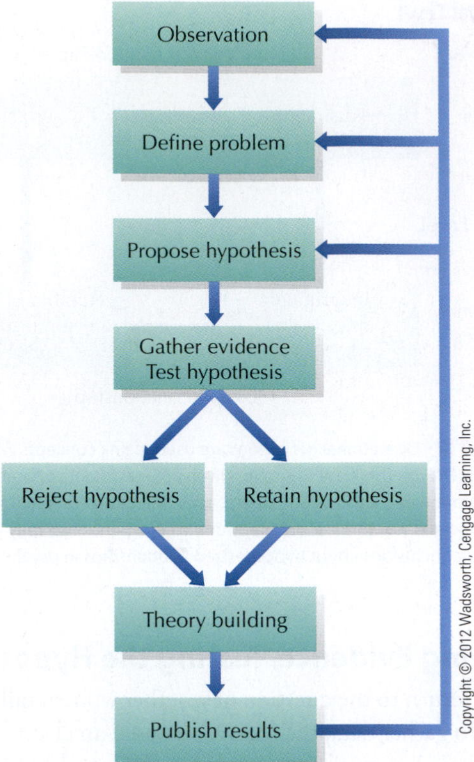

● **Figure 1.3** Psychologists use the logic of science to answer questions about behavior. Specific hypotheses can be tested in a variety of ways, including naturalistic observation, correlational studies, controlled experiments, clinical studies, and the survey method. Psychologists revise their theories to reflect the evidence they gather. New or revised theories then lead to new observations, problems, and hypotheses.

ity, stress, mental illness, and the like, psychologists would drown in a sea of disconnected facts (Stanovich, 2010).

BRIDGES

One of the major limitations of Freudian personality theory is that many of its concepts are not testable or falsifiable. **See Chapter 12, pages 414–415.**

Although Mehl and his colleagues did not present a theory of why some people talk more or less, they did discuss how their findings might affect such a theory. For instance, they pointed out that they studied only university students, and that older men and women might differ in how much they talk each day. Such findings invite others to study talkativeness in other age groups and to propose theories to explain any differences that might be observed.

Publishing Results

Because scientific information must always be *publicly available,* the results of psychological studies are usually published in professional journals (see ■ Table 1.1). That way, other researchers can read about the results and make their own observations if they doubt the study's findings (Jackson, 2011). If others are able to *replicate* (repeat) the results of a study, those results become more credible.

■ TABLE 1.1 Outline of a Research Report

- **Abstract** Research reports begin with a very brief summary of the study and its findings. The abstract allows you to get an overview without reading the entire article.
- **Introduction** The introduction describes the question to be investigated. It also provides background information by reviewing prior studies on the same or related topics.
- **Method** This section tells how and why observations were made. It also describes the specific procedures used to gather data. That way, other researchers can repeat the study to see if they get the same results.
- **Results** The outcome of the investigation is presented. Data may be graphed, summarized in tables, or statistically analyzed.
- **Discussion** The results of the study are discussed in relation to the original question. Implications of the study are explored and further studies may be proposed.

In a scholarly article published in the journal *Science,* Mehl and his colleagues (2007) describe the question they investigated, the methods they used, and the results of their study on male and female talkativeness.

Research Ethics

Aren't there also rules about how scientists have to treat the people they study? You are absolutely right. Psychology experiments sometimes raise *ethical* questions. Three areas of ethical concern in behavioral research are the use of *deception, invasion of privacy,* and the risk of *lasting harm.* Deception and potential harm are illustrated by a classic study of obedience. Participants were ordered to give what they thought were painful electric shocks to another person (no shocks were actually given) (Milgram, 1963). Believing that they had hurt someone, many people left the experiment shaken and upset. A few suffered guilt and distress for some time afterward.

BRIDGES

Stanley Milgram undertook his infamous studies to better understand just how willing people are to obey an authority. **See Chapter 16, pages 564–567.**

Such experiments raise serious ethical questions. Did the information gained justify the emotional costs? Was deception really necessary? As a reply to such questions, American Psychological Association guidelines state that "Psychologists must carry out investigations with respect for the people who participate and with concern for their dignity and welfare" (see ■ Table 1.2). Similar guidelines apply to animals—investigators are expected to "ensure the welfare of animals and treat them humanely" (American Psychological Association, 2002, 2010a). To assure this, most university psychology departments have ethics committees that oversee research. Nevertheless, no easy answers exist for the ethical questions raised by psychology, and debate about specific experiments is likely to continue.

Knowledge Builder: Critical Thinking and the Scientific Method in Psychology

RECITE

1. Most of psychology can rightfully be called common sense because psychologists prefer informal observation to systematic observation. T or F
2. *Confirmation bias* refers to graphology's accepted value for the detection of forgeries. T or F
3. Personality descriptions provided by pseudopsychologies are stated in general terms, which provide "a little something for everybody." This fact is the basis of the
   a. palmist's fallacy
   b. uncritical acceptance pattern
   c. confirmation bias
   d. Barnum effect
4. A psychologist does a study to see whether exercising increases sense of well-being. In the study, he will be testing an
   a. experimental hypothesis
   b. operational definition
   c. empirical definition
   d. anthropomorphic theory
5. ____________ behaviors are operationally defined in terms of ____________ behavior
   a. Overt, covert
   b. Observable, overt
   c. Covert, overt
   d. Covert, abstract

REFLECT

Think Critically

6. Can you think of some "commonsense" statements that contradict each other?
7. Try constructing a few "Barnum statements," personality statements that are so general that virtually everyone will think they apply to themselves. Can you string them together to make a "Barnum profile"? Can you adapt the same statements to construct a "Barnum horoscope"?
8. Each New Year's Day, phony "psychics" make predictions about events that will occur during the coming year. The vast majority of these predictions are wrong, but the practice continues each year. Can you explain why?

Self-Reflect

It is nearly impossible to get through a day without encountering people who believe in pseudopsychologies or who make unscientific or unfounded statements. How stringently do you evaluate your own beliefs and the claims made by others?

How might you scientifically test the old saw that you can't teach an old dog new tricks? Follow the steps of the scientific method to propose a testable hypothesis and decide how you would gather evidence. (Well, OK, you don't have to publish your results.)

Answers: 1. F **2.** F **3.** *d* **4.** *a* **5.** c **6.** There are many examples. Here are a few more to add to the ones you thought of: "He (or she) who hesitates is lost" versus "Haste makes waste;" "Never too old to learn" versus "You can't teach an old dog new tricks." **7.** The term "Barnum statement" comes from Levy (2003; but see also Rogers & Soule, 2009), who offers the following examples: You are afraid of being hurt. You are trying to find a balance between autonomy and closeness. You don't like being overly dependent. You just want to be understood. **8.** Because of confirmation bias, people only remember predictions that seemed to come true and forget all the errors. Incidentally, "predictions" that appear to be accurate are usually easily deduced from current events or are stated in general terms to take advantage of the Barnum effect.

TABLE 1.2 Basic Ethical Guidelines for Psychological Researchers

Do no harm.
Accurately describe risks to potential participants.
Ensure that participation is voluntary.
Minimize any discomfort to participants.
Maintain confidentiality.
Do not unnecessarily invade privacy.
Use deception only when absolutely necessary.
Remove any misconceptions caused by deception (debrief).
Provide results and interpretations to participants.
Treat participants with dignity and respect.

A Brief History of Psychology—Psychology's Family Album

Gateway Question 1.5: *How did the field of psychology emerge?*

As we noted previously, people have been informally observing human behavior and philosophizing about it for thousands of years. In contrast, psychology's history as a science dates back only about 130 years to Leipzig, Germany. There, Wilhelm Wundt (VILL-helm Voont), the "father of psychology," set up a laboratory in 1879 to study conscious experience.

What happens, Wundt wondered, when we experience sensations, images, and feelings? To find out, he systematically observed and measured stimuli of various kinds (lights, sounds, weights). A **stimulus** is any physical energy that affects a person and evokes a response (stimulus: singular; stimuli [STIM-you-lie]: plural). Wundt then used **introspection,** or "looking inward," to probe his reactions to various stimuli. (Stop reading, close your eyes, carefully examine your thoughts, feelings, and sensations, and you will be introspecting.)

Over the years, Wundt studied vision, hearing, taste, touch, memory, time perception, and many other topics. By insisting on systematic observation and measurement, he asked some interesting questions and got psychology off to a good start (Schultz & Schultz, 2012).

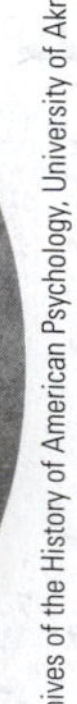

Wilhelm Wundt, 1832–1920. Wundt is credited with making psychology an independent science, separate from philosophy. Wundt's original training was in medicine, but he became deeply interested in psychology. In his laboratory, Wundt investigated how sensations, images, and feelings combine to make up personal experience.

Stimulus Any physical energy sensed by an organism.
Introspection To look within; to examine one's own thoughts, feelings, or sensations.

Structuralism

Wundt's ideas were carried to the United States by Edward Titchener (TICH-in-er). Titchener called Wundt's ideas **structuralism** and tried to analyze the structure of mental life into basic "elements" or "building blocks."

How could he do that? You can't analyze experience like a chemical compound, can you? Perhaps not, but the structuralists tried "mental chemistry," mostly by using introspection. For instance, an observer might hold an apple and decide that she had experienced the elements "hue" (color), "roundness," and "weight." Another example of a question that might have interested a structuralist is "What basic tastes mix together to create complex flavors as different as broccoli, lime, bacon, and strawberry cheesecake?"

Introspection proved to be a poor way to answer most questions (Benjafield, 2010). Why? Because no matter how systematic the observations, the structuralists frequently *disagreed.* And when they did, there was no way to settle differences. Think about it. If you and a friend both introspect on your perceptions of an apple and end up listing different basic elements, who would be right? Despite such limitations, "looking inward" is still used as one source of insight in studies of hypnosis, meditation, problem solving, moods, and many other topics.

Functionalism

American scholar William James broadened psychology to include animal behavior, religious experience, abnormal behavior, and other interesting topics. James's brilliant first book, *Principles of Psychology* (1890), helped establish the field as a separate discipline (Hergenhahn, 2009).

The term **functionalism** comes from James's interest in how the mind functions to help us adapt to the environment. James regarded consciousness as an ever-changing *stream* or *flow* of images and sensations—not a set of lifeless building blocks, as the structuralists claimed.

The functionalists admired Charles Darwin, who deduced that creatures evolve in ways that favor survival. According to Darwin's principle of **natural selection,** physical features that help plants and animals adapt to their environments are retained in evolution. Similarly, the functionalists wanted to find out how the mind, perception, habits, and emotions help us adapt and survive.

What effect did functionalism have on modern psychology? Functionalism brought the study of animals into psychology. It also promoted educational psychology (the study of learning, teaching, classroom dynamics, and related topics). Learning makes us more adaptable, so the functionalists tried to find ways to improve education. For similar reasons, functionalism spurred the rise of industrial/organizational psychology, the study of people at work.

William James, 1842–1910. William James was the son of philosopher Henry James, Sr., and the brother of novelist Henry James. During his long academic career, James taught anatomy, physiology, psychology, and philosophy at Harvard University. James believed strongly that ideas should be judged in terms of their practical consequences for human conduct.

Archives of the History of American Psychology, University of Akron

BRIDGES

Today, educational psychology and industrial/organizational psychology remain two major applied specialties (Coolican et al., 2007). **See Chapter 18 for more information about applied psychology.**

Behaviorism

Functionalism and structuralism were soon challenged by **behaviorism,** the study of observable behavior. Behaviorist John B. Watson objected strongly to the study of the "mind" or "conscious experience." He believed that introspection is unscientific precisely because there is no way to settle disagreements between observers. Watson realized that he could study the overt behavior of animals even though he couldn't ask them questions or know what they were thinking (Benjafield, 2010). He simply observed the relationship between *stimuli* (events in the environment) and an animal's **responses** (any muscular action, glandular activity, or other identifiable aspect of behavior). These observations were objective because they did not involve introspecting on subjective experience. Why not, he asked, apply the same objectivity to study human behavior?

Watson soon adopted Russian physiologist Ivan Pavlov's (ee-VAHN PAV-lahv's) concept of *conditioning* to explain most behavior. (A *conditioned response* is a learned reaction to a particular stimulus.) Watson claimed, "Give me a dozen healthy infants, well-formed, and my own special world to bring them up in and I'll guarantee to take any one at random and train him to become any type of specialist I might select—doctor, lawyer, artist, merchant-chief, and yes, beggarman and thief" (Watson, 1913/1994).

Would most psychologists agree with Watson's claim? No. The behaviorists believed that all responses are *determined* by stimuli. Today, this is regarded as an overstatement. Just the same, behaviorism helped make psychology a natural science, rather than a branch of philosophy (Benjamin, 2009).

John B. Watson, 1878–1958. Watson's intense interest in observable behavior began with his doctoral studies in biology and neurology. Watson became a psychology professor at Johns Hopkins University in 1908 and advanced his theory of behaviorism. He remained at Johns Hopkins until 1920, when he left for a career in the advertising industry!

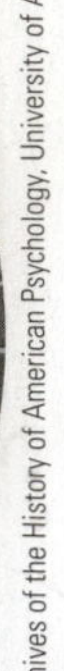

Archives of the History of American Psychology, University of Akron

Radical Behaviorism

The best-known behaviorist, B. F. Skinner (1904–1990), believed that our actions are controlled by rewards and punishments. To study learning, Skinner created his famous conditioning chamber, or "Skinner box." With it, he could present stimuli to animals and record their responses. Many of Skinner's ideas about learning grew out of work with rats and pigeons. Nevertheless, he believed that the same laws of behavior apply to humans. As a "radical behaviorist," Skinner also believed that mental events, such as thinking, are not needed to explain behavior (Schultz & Schultz, 2012).

BRIDGES

See Chapter 6, pages 211–229, for more information about operant conditioning.

Behaviorists deserve credit for much of what we know about learning, conditioning, and the proper use of reward and punishment. Skinner was convinced that a "designed culture" based on positive reinforcement could encourage desirable behavior. (Skinner opposed the use of punishment because it doesn't teach correct responses.) Too often, he believed, punishment and misguided rewards lead to destructive actions that create problems such as overpopulation, pollution, and war.

B. F. Skinner, 1904–1990. Skinner studied simple behaviors under carefully controlled conditions. The "Skinner box" you see here has been widely used to study learning in simplified animal experiments. In addition to advancing psychology, Skinner hoped that his radical brand of behaviorism would improve human life.

Cognitive Behaviorism

Radical behaviorists have been criticized for ignoring the role that thinking plays in our lives. One critic even charged that Skinnerian psychology had "lost consciousness"! However, many criticisms have been answered by **cognitive behaviorism,** a view that combines cognition (thinking) and conditioning to explain behavior (Zentall, 2002). As an example, let's say you frequently visit a particular website because it offers free streaming videos. A behaviorist would say you visit the site because you are rewarded by the pleasure of watching interesting videos each time you go there. A cognitive behaviorist would add that, in addition, you *expect* to find free videos at the site. This is the cognitive part of your behavior.

Gestalt Psychology

Imagine that you just played "Happy Birthday" on a low-pitched tuba. Next, you play it on a high-pitched flute. The flute duplicates none of the tuba's sounds. Yet we notice something interesting: The melody is still recognizable—as long as the *relationship* between notes remains the same. Now, what would happen if you played the notes of "Happy Birthday" in the correct order, but at a rate of one per hour? What would we have? Nothing! The separate notes would no longer be a melody. Perceptually, the melody is more than the individual notes that define it.

It was observations like these that launched the Gestalt school of thought. German psychologist Max Wertheimer (VERT-hi-mer) was the first to advance the Gestalt viewpoint. It is inaccurate, he

Max Wertheimer, 1880–1941. Wertheimer first proposed the Gestalt viewpoint to help explain perceptual illusions. He later promoted Gestalt psychology as a way to understand not only perception, problem solving, thinking, and social behavior, but also art, logic, philosophy, and politics.

Structuralism The school of thought concerned with analyzing sensations and personal experience into basic elements.

Functionalism The school of psychology concerned with how behavior and mental abilities help people adapt to their environments.

Natural selection Darwin's theory that evolution favors those plants and animals best suited to their living conditions.

Behaviorism The school of psychology that emphasizes the study of overt, observable behavior.

Response Any muscular action, glandular activity, or other identifiable aspect of behavior.

Cognitive behaviorism An approach that combines behavioral principles with cognition (perception, thinking, anticipation) to explain behavior.

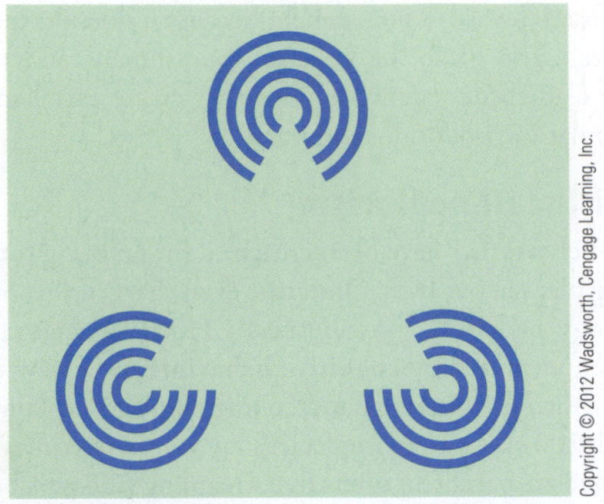

● **Figure 1.4** The design you see here is entirely made up of broken circles. However, as the Gestalt psychologists discovered, our perceptions have a powerful tendency to form meaningful patterns. Because of this tendency, you will probably see a triangle in this design, even though it is only an illusion. Your whole perceptual experience exceeds the sum of its parts.

said, to analyze psychological events into pieces, or "elements," as the structuralists did. Accordingly, **Gestalt psychologists** studied thinking, learning, and perception as whole units, not by analyzing experiences into parts. Their slogan was, "The whole is greater than the sum of its parts" (see ● Figure 1.4). In fact, the German word *Gestalt* means "form, pattern, or whole."

Like a melody, many experiences cannot be broken into smaller units, as the structuralists proposed. For this reason, studies of perception and personality have been especially influenced by the Gestalt viewpoint.

Psychoanalytic Psychology

As American psychology grew more scientific, an Austrian doctor named Sigmund Freud was developing radically different ideas that opened new horizons in art, literature, and history, as well as psychology (Chessick, 2010; Jacobs, 2003). Freud believed that mental life is like an iceberg: Only a small part is exposed to view. He called the area of the mind that lies outside of personal awareness the **unconscious.** According to Freud, our behavior is deeply influenced by unconscious thoughts, impulses, and desires—especially those concerning sex and aggression.

Freud theorized that many unconscious thoughts are **repressed,** or held out of awareness, because they are threatening. But sometimes, he said, they are revealed by dreams, emotions, or slips of the tongue. ("Freudian slips" are often humorous, as when a student who is tardy for class says, "I'm sorry I couldn't get here any later.")

Sigmund Freud, 1856–1939. For more than 50 years, Freud probed the unconscious mind. In doing so, he altered modern views of human nature. His early experimentation with a "talking cure" for hysteria is regarded as the beginning of psychoanalysis. Through psychoanalysis, Freud added psychological treatment methods to psychiatry.

Like the behaviorists, Freud believed that all thoughts, emotions, and actions are *determined.* In other words, nothing is an accident: If we probe deeply enough, we will find the causes of every thought or action. Unlike the behaviorists, he believed that unconscious processes (not external stimuli) were responsible.

Freud was also among the first to appreciate that childhood affects adult personality ("The child is father to the man"). Most of all, perhaps, Freud is known for creating **psychoanalysis,** the first fully developed psychotherapy, or "talking cure." Freudian psychotherapy explores unconscious conflicts and emotional problems.

It wasn't very long before some of Freud's students began to promote their own theories. Several who modified Freud's ideas became known as neo-Freudians (*neo* means "new" or "recent"). **Neo-Freudians** accept much of Freud's theory but revise parts of it. Many, for instance, place less emphasis on sex and aggression and more on social motives and relationships. Some well-known neo-Freudians are Alfred Adler, Anna Freud (Freud's daughter), Karen Horney (HORN-eye), Carl Jung (yoong), Otto Rank (rahnk), and Erik Erikson. Today, Freud's ideas have been altered so much that few strictly psychoanalytic psychologists are left. However, his legacy is still evident in various **psychodynamic theories,** which continue to emphasize internal motives, conflicts, and unconscious forces (Gedo, 2002; Moran, 2010).

Humanistic Psychology

Humanism is a view that focuses on subjective human experience. Humanistic psychologists are interested in human potentials, ideals, and problems.

How is the humanistic approach different from others? Carl Rogers, Abraham Maslow, and other humanists rejected the Freudian idea that we are ruled by unconscious forces. They were also uncomfortable with the behaviorist emphasis on conditioning. Both views have a strong undercurrent of **determinism**—the idea that behavior is determined by forces beyond our control. In contrast, the humanists stressed **free will**, our ability to make voluntary choices. Of course, past experiences do affect us. Nevertheless, humanists believe that people can freely *choose* to live more creative, meaningful, and satisfying lives.

Abraham Maslow, 1908–1970. As a founder of humanistic psychology, Maslow was interested in studying people of exceptional mental health. Such self-actualized people, he believed, make full use of their talents and abilities. Maslow offered his positive view of human potential as an alternative to the schools of behaviorism and psychoanalysis.

Humanists are interested in psychological needs for love, self-esteem, belonging, self-expression, creativity, and spirituality. Such needs, they believe, are as important as our biological urges for food and water. For example, newborn infants deprived of human love may die just as surely as they would if deprived of food.

How scientific is the humanistic approach? Initially, humanists were less interested in treating psychology as a science. They stressed subjective factors, such as one's self-image, self-evaluation, and frame of reference. (*Self-image* is your perception of your own body, personality, and capabilities. *Self-evaluation* refers to appraising yourself as good or bad. A *frame of reference* is a mental perspective used to interpret events.) Today, humanists still seek to understand how we perceive ourselves and experience the world. However, most now do research to test their ideas, just as other psychologists do (Schneider, Bugental, & Pierson, 2001).

Maslow's concept of self-actualization is a key feature of humanism. **Self-actualization** refers to developing one's potential fully and becoming the best person possible. According to humanists, everyone has this potential. Humanists seek ways to help it emerge. ■ Table 1.3 presents a summary of psychology's early development.

■ TABLE 1.3 The Early Development of Psychology

Perspective	Date	Notable Events
Experimental psychology	1875	• First psychology course offered by William James
	1878	• First American Ph.D. in psychology awarded
	1879	• Wilhelm Wundt opens first psychology laboratory in Germany
	1883	• First American psychology lab founded at Johns Hopkins University
	1886	• First American psychology textbook written by John Dewey
Structuralism	1898	• Edward Titchener advances psychology based on introspection
Functionalism	1890	• William James publishes *Principles of Psychology*
	1892	• American Psychological Association founded
Psychodynamic psychology	1895	• Sigmund Freud publishes first studies
	1900	• Freud publishes *The Interpretation of Dreams*
Behaviorism	1906	• Ivan Pavlov reports his research on conditioned reflexes
	1913	• John Watson presents behaviorist view
Gestalt psychology	1912	• Max Wertheimer and others advance Gestalt viewpoint
Humanistic psychology	1942	• Carl Rogers publishes *Counseling and Psychotherapy*
	1943	• Abraham Maslow publishes "A Theory of Human Motivation"

The Role of Diversity in Psychology

Were all early psychologists Caucasian men? Although women and ethnic minorities were long underrepresented among psychologists (Minton, 2000), there *were* pioneers. In 1894, Margaret Washburn became the first woman to be awarded a Ph.D. in psychology. By 1906 in America, about 1 psychologist in 10 was a woman. In 1920, Francis Cecil Sumner became the first African American man to earn a doctoral degree in psychology. Inez Beverly Prosser, the first African American female psychologist, was awarded her Ph.D. in 1933.

Margaret Washburn, 1871–1939. In 1908 Margaret Washburn published an influential textbook on animal behavior, titled *The Animal Mind.*

Archives of the History of American Psychology, University of Akron

Archives of the History of American Psychology, University of Akron

Francis Cecil Sumner, 1895–1954. Francis Sumner served as chair of the Psychology Department at Howard University and wrote articles critical of the underrepresentation of African Americans in American colleges and universities.

Archives of the History of American Psychology, University of Akron

Inez Beverly Prosser, ca. 1895–1934. Inez Beverly Prosser was one of the early leaders in the debate about how to best educate African American children.

Gestalt psychology A school of psychology emphasizing the study of thinking, learning, and perception in whole units, not by analysis into parts.

Unconscious Contents of the mind that are beyond awareness, especially impulses and desires not directly known to a person.

Repression The unconscious process by which memories, thoughts, or impulses are held out of awareness.

Psychoanalysis A Freudian approach to psychotherapy emphasizing the exploration of unconscious conflicts.

Neo-Freudian A psychologist who accepts the broad features of Freud's theory but has revised the theory to fit his or her own concepts.

Psychodynamic theory Any theory of behavior that emphasizes internal conflicts, motives, and unconscious forces.

Humanism An approach to psychology that focuses on human experience, problems, potentials, and ideals.

Determinism The idea that all behavior has prior causes that would completely explain one's choices and actions if all such causes were known.

Free will The idea that human beings are capable of freely making choices or decisions.

Self-actualization The ongoing process of fully developing one's personal potential.

Human Diversity — Who's WEIRD?

As you read through this book, you may find yourself wondering whether a particular concept, theory, or research finding applies equally well to women and men, to members of various races or ethnic groups, or to people of different ages or sexual orientations. "Human Diversity" boxes like this one will help you be more reflective about our multicultural, multifaceted world.

Biases concerning the race, ethnicity, age, and sexual orientation of researchers and participants in psychological research have definitely limited our understanding (Denmark, Rabinowitz, & Sechzer, 2005; Guthrie, 2004). Far too many conclusions have been created by and/or based on small groups of people who do not represent the rich tapestry of humanity. For example, to this day, the vast majority of human participants in psychology experiments are recruited from introductory psychology courses. This fact led the distinguished psychologist Edward Tolman to note that much of psychology is based on two sets of subjects—rats and college sophomores—and to joke that rats are certainly not people and that some college sophomores may not be either! Further, most of these participants have, over the years, been Caucasian members of the middle class, and most of the researchers themselves have been Caucasian males (Guthrie, 2004). Although none of this automatically invalidates the results of psychology experiments, it may place limitations on their meanings.

Perhaps the most general research bias of all becomes clear when you ask about people who live in the oddest societies in the world. The answer is just plain WEIRD (Western, Educated, Industrialized, Rich, and Democratic). According to Henrich, Heine, and Norenzayan (2010), we have a strongly ingrained tendency to assume that what Western researchers discover studying Western research participants is the norm in human behavior and that the behavior of those in other societies is unusual. However, after a careful review of studies comparing Westerners with people from other societies, Henrich, Heine, and Norenzayan concluded that exactly the opposite is the case. We are WEIRD and should be careful to assume that what we learn from studying behavior in our society illuminates the behavior of people in non-Western societies.

Fortunately, the solution to problems of bias is straightforward: We need to encourage a much wider array of people to become researchers and, when possible, researchers need to include a much wider array of people in their studies. In recognition of human diversity, many researchers are doing just that (Lum, 2011; Reid, 2002).

The predominance of early Caucasian male psychologists is worrisome because it inadvertently introduced a narrowness into psychological theory and research. As one example, Laurence Kohlberg (1969) proposed a theory about how we develop moral values. His studies suggested that women were morally "immature" because they were not as concerned with justice as men were. However, few women were involved in doing the studies, and Kohlberg merely *assumed* that theories based on men also apply to women. In response, Carol Gilligan (1982) provided evidence that women were more likely to make moral choices based on caring, rather than justice. From this point of view, it was men who were morally immature.

BRIDGES

Today, we recognize that both justice and caring perspectives may be essential to adult wisdom. **See Chapter 3, pages 110–111, for more details.**

Kohlberg's oversight is just one form of **gender bias in research**. This term refers to the tendency for females to be underrepresented as research subjects and female topics to be ignored by many investigators. Consequently, investigators assume that conclusions based on men also apply to women. But without directly studying women, it is impossible to know how often this assumption is wrong. A related problem occurs when researchers combine results from men and women. Doing so can hide important male–female differences. An additional problem is that unequal numbers of men and women may volunteer for some kinds of research. For example, in studies of sexuality, more male college students volunteer to participate than females (Wiederman, 1999). What a surprise! What shouldn't surprise you is that the same charge of bias also arises when it comes to people of different ages, sexual orientations, races, and ethnic groups. To find out more, see the nearby "Who's WEIRD?" box.

Fortunately, since 2000, over 70 percent of all undergraduate and graduate degrees in psychology have been awarded to women. Similarly, 25 percent of all undergraduate degrees and 16 percent of doctorates in psychology were awarded to persons of color (American Psychological Association, 2003a). Increasingly, psychology is coming to reflect the rich diversity of humanity (Hyde, 2007).

Psychology Today—Three Complementary Perspectives on Behavior

Gateway Question 1.6: *What are the contemporary perspectives in psychology?*

At one time, loyalty to each school of thought in psychology was fierce, and clashes were common. Now, some early systems, such as structuralism, have disappeared entirely, whereas new ones have gained prominence. Also, viewpoints such as functionalism and Gestalt psychology have blended into newer, broader perspectives. The three broad views that shape modern psychology are the *biological, psychological,* and *sociocultural* perspectives (■ Table 1.4).

■ TABLE 1.4 Contemporary Ways to Look at Behavior

Biological Perspective

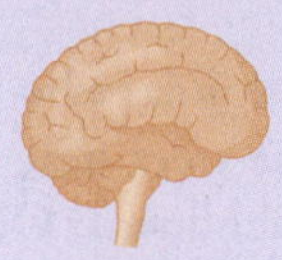

Biopsychological View

Key Idea: *Human and animal behavior is the result of internal physical, chemical, and biological processes.*

Seeks to explain behavior through activity of the brain and nervous system, physiology, genetics, the endocrine system, and biochemistry; neutral, reductionistic, mechanistic view of human nature.

Evolutionary View

Key Idea: *Human and animal behavior is the result of the process of evolution.*

Seeks to explain behavior through evolutionary principles based on natural selection; neutral, reductionistic, mechanistic view of human nature.

Psychological Perspective

Behavioral View

Key Idea: *Behavior is shaped and controlled by one's environment.*

Emphasizes the study of observable behavior and the effects of learning; stresses the influence of external rewards and punishments; neutral, scientific, somewhat mechanistic view of human nature.

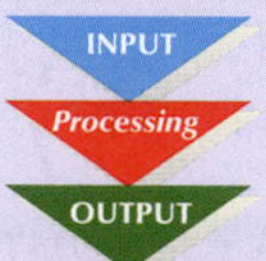

Cognitive View

Key Idea: *Much human behavior can be understood in terms of the mental processing of information.*

Concerned with thinking, knowing, perception, understanding, memory, decision making, and judgment; explains behavior in terms of information processing; neutral, somewhat computer-like view of human nature.

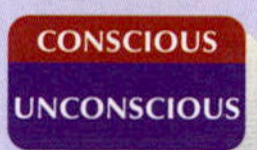

Psychodynamic View

Key Idea: *Behavior is directed by forces within one's personality that are often hidden or unconscious.*

Emphasizes internal impulses, desires, and conflicts—especially those that are unconscious; views behavior as the result of clashing forces within personality; somewhat negative, pessimistic view of human nature.

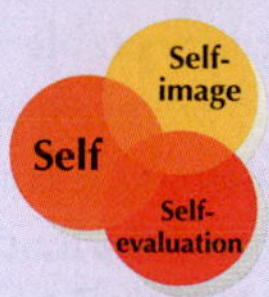

Humanistic View

Key Idea: *Behavior is guided by one's self-image, by subjective perceptions of the world, and by needs for personal growth.*

Focuses on subjective, conscious experience, human problems, potentials, and ideals; emphasizes self-image and self-actualization to explain behavior; positive, philosophical view of human nature.

Sociocultural Perspective

Sociocultural View

Key Idea: *Behavior is influenced by one's social and cultural context.*

Emphasizes that behavior is related to the social and cultural environment within which a person is born, grows up, and lives from day to day; neutral, interactionist view of human nature.

The Biological Perspective

The **biological perspective** seeks to explain our behavior in terms of biological principles such as brain processes, evolution, and genetics. By using new techniques, *biopsychologists* are producing exciting insights about how the brain relates to thinking, feelings, perception, abnormal behavior, and other topics. Biopsychologists and others who study the brain and nervous system, such as biologists and biochemists, together form the broader field of **neuroscience. Evolutionary psychologists** look at how human evolution and genetics might explain our current behavior.

The Psychological Perspective

The **psychological perspective** views behavior as the result of psychological processes within each person. This view continues to emphasize objective observation, just as the early behaviorists did. However, the psychological perspective now includes cognitive psychology, which seeks to explain how mental processes affect our thoughts, actions, and feelings (Goldstein, 2011). Cognitive psychology has gained prominence in recent years as researchers have devised ways to objectively study covert behaviors, such as thinking,

Gender bias in research A tendency for females and female issues to be underrepresented in research, psychological or otherwise.

Biological perspective The attempt to explain behavior in terms of underlying biological principles.

Neuroscience The broader field of biopsychologists and others who study the brain and nervous system, such as biologists and biochemists.

Evolutionary psychology The study of how human evolution and genetics might explain our current behavior.

Psychological perspective The traditional view that behavior is shaped by psychological processes occurring at the level of the individual.

memory, language, perception, problem solving, consciousness, and creativity. With a renewed interest in thinking, it can be said that psychology has finally "regained consciousness" (Robins, Gosling, & Craik, 1998).

Freudian psychoanalysis continues to evolve into the broader *psychodynamic view.* Although many of Freud's ideas have been challenged or refuted, psychodynamic psychologists continue to trace our behavior to unconscious mental activity. They also seek to develop therapies to help people lead happier, fuller lives. The same is true of humanistic psychologists, although they stress subjective, conscious experience and the positive side of human nature, rather than unconscious processes.

Positive Psychology

Psychologists have always paid attention to the negative side of human behavior. This is easy to understand because of the pressing need to solve human problems. However, more and more psychologists, some of them inspired by the humanists, have begun to ask, "What do we know about love, happiness, creativity, well-being, self-confidence, and achievement?" Together, such topics make up **positive psychology,** the study of human strengths, virtues, and optimal behavior (Compton, 2005; Seligman & Csikszentmihalyi, 2000). Many topics from positive psychology can be found in this book. Ideally, they will help make your own life more positive and fulfilling (Simonton & Baumeister, 2005).

The Sociocultural Perspective

As you can see, it is helpful to view human behavior from more than one perspective. This is also true in another sense. The **sociocultural perspective** stresses the impact that social and cultural contexts have on our behavior. We are rapidly becoming a multicultural society, made up of people from many nations. How has this affected psychology? Meet Jerry, who is Japanese American and is married to an Irish-Catholic American. Here is what Jerry, his wife, and their children did one New Year's Day:

> We woke up in the morning and went to Mass at St. Brigid's, which has a black gospel choir. . . . Then we went to the Japanese-American Community Center for the Oshogatsu New Year's program and saw Buddhist archers shoot arrows to ward off evil spirits for the year. Next, we ate traditional rice cakes as part of the New Year's service and listened to a young Japanese-American storyteller. On the way home, we stopped in Chinatown and after that we ate Mexican food at a taco stand (Njeri, 1991).

Jerry and his family reflect a new social reality: Cultural diversity is becoming the norm. Over 100 million Americans are now African American, Hispanic, Asian American, Native American, or Pacific Islander (U.S. Census Bureau, 2007). In some large cities, such as Detroit and Baltimore, "minority" groups are already the majority.

Cultural Relativity

Imagine that you are a psychologist. Your client, Linda, who is a Native American, tells you that spirits live in the trees near her home. Is Linda suffering from a delusion? Is she abnormal? Obviously, you will misjudge Linda's mental health if you fail to take her cultural beliefs into account. **Cultural relativity**—the idea that behavior must be judged relative to the values of the culture in which it occurs—can greatly affect the diagnosis and treatment of mental disorders (Lum, 2011). Cases like Linda's teach us to be wary of using narrow standards when judging others or comparing groups.

BRIDGES

Psychotherapy can be less effective if a therapist and client come from different cultures. **See Chapter 15, pages 533–534, for a discussion of the impact of culture on therapy.**

A Broader View of Diversity

In addition to cultural differences, age, ethnicity, gender, religion, disability, and sexual orientation all affect the **social norms** that guide behavior. Social norms are rules that define acceptable and expected behavior for members of various groups. As we mentioned earlier, often, the unstated standard for judging what is "average," "normal," or "correct" has been the behavior of white, middle-class Western males (Henrich, Heine, & Norenzayan, 2010). To fully understand human behavior, psychologists need to know how people differ, as well as the ways in which we are all alike. To be effective, psychologists must be sensitive to people who are ethnically and culturally different from themselves (American Psychological Association, 2003b). For the same reason, an appreciation of human diversity can enrich your life, as well as your understanding of psychology (Denmark, Rabinowitz, & Sechzer, 2005).

As illustrated by this photo from the inauguration of President Barack Obama in 2009, America is becoming more diverse. To fully understand human behavior, personal differences based on age, race, culture, ethnicity, gender, and sexual orientation must be taken into account.

The Whole Human

Today, many psychologists realize that a single perspective is unlikely to fully explain complex human behavior. As a result, they are *eclectic* (ek-LEK-tik) and draw insights from a variety of perspectives. As we will see throughout this book, insights from one perspective often complement insights from the others, as we seek to better understand the whole human. In a moment, we will further explore what psychologists do. First, here are some questions to enhance your learning.

Knowledge Builder — History and Contemporary Perspectives

RECITE

Match:

1. ______ Philosophy
2. ______ Wundt
3. ______ Structuralism
4. ______ Functionalism
5. ______ Behaviorism
6. ______ Gestalt
7. ______ Psychodynamic
8. ______ Humanistic
9. ______ Cognitive
10. ______ Biopsychology

A. Against analysis; studied whole experiences
B. "Mental chemistry" and introspection
C. Emphasizes self-actualization and personal growth
D. Interested in unconscious causes of behavior
E. Interested in how the mind aids survival
F. Studied stimuli and responses, conditioning
G. Part of psychology's "long past"
H. Concerned with thinking, language, problem solving
I. Used introspection and careful measurement
J. Relates behavior to the brain, physiology, and genetics

11. A psychotherapist is working with a person from an ethnic group other than her own. She should be aware of how cultural relativity and ______________________ affect behavior.
 a. the anthropomorphic error *b.* operational definitions *c.* biased sampling *d.* social norms
12. Studying the behavior of American undergraduates and then drawing conclusions about how people around the world might behave
 a. is scientifically appropriate *b.* is an example of cognitive behaviorism *c.* could easily result in misleading generalizations *d.* is an example of multiculturalism

REFLECT

Think Critically

13. Modern sciences like psychology are built on observations that can be verified by two or more independent observers. Did structuralism meet this standard? Why or why not?

Self-Reflect

Which school of thought most closely matches your own view of behavior? Do you think any of the early schools offers a complete explanation of why we behave as we do? What about the three broad contemporary perspectives? Can you explain why so many psychologists are eclectic?

A group of psychologists were asked to answer this question: "Why did the chicken cross the road?" Their answers are listed next. Can you identify their theoretical orientations?

The chicken had been rewarded for crossing road in the past.

The chicken had an unconscious wish to become a pancake.

The chicken was trying to solve the problem of how to reach the other side of the road.

The chicken felt a need to explore new possibilities as a way to actualize its potentials.

The chicken's motor cortex was activated by messages from its hypothalamus.

Answers: 1. G **2.** I **3.** B **4.** E **5.** F **6.** A **7.** D **8.** C **9.** H **10.** J **11.** *d* **12.** *c* **13.** No, it did not. The downfall of structuralism was that each observer examined the contents of his or her own mind—which is something that no other person can observe.

Psychologists—Guaranteed Not to Shrink

Gateway Question 1.7: *What are the major specialties in psychology?*

Do all psychologists do therapy and treat abnormal behavior? Only about 59 percent are clinical and counseling psychologists. Regardless, all **psychologists** are highly trained in the methods, knowledge, and theories of psychology. They usually have earned a master's degree or a doctorate, typically requiring several years of postgraduate training. Twenty-nine percent are employed full-time at colleges or universities, where they teach and do research, consulting, or therapy. The remainder give psychological tests, do research in other settings, or serve as consultants to business, industry, government, or the military (see ● Figure 1.5).

At present, the American Psychological Association (APA) consists of more than 50 divisions, each reflecting special skills or areas of interest. No matter where they are employed or what their area of specialization, many psychologists do research. Some do *basic research,* in which they seek knowledge for its own sake. For example, a psychologist might study memory simply to understand how it works. Others do *applied research* to solve immediate practical problems, such as finding ways to improve athletic performance (Coolican et al., 2007). Some do both types of research. Some of the major specialties are listed in ■ Table 1.5.

Have you ever wondered what it takes to become a psychologist? See "Is a Career in Psychology Right for You?"

Positive psychology The study of human strengths, virtues, and effective functioning.

Sociocultural perspective The focus on the importance of social and cultural contexts in influencing the behavior of individuals.

Cultural relativity The idea that behavior must be judged relative to the values of the culture in which it occurs.

Social norms Rules that define acceptable and expected behavior for members of a group.

Psychologist A person highly trained in the methods, factual knowledge, and theories of psychology.

TABLE 1.5 Kinds of Psychologists and What They Do

Specialty		Typical Activities	Sample Research Topic
Biopsychology	B*	Does research on the brain, nervous system, and other physical origins of behavior.	"I've been doing some exciting research on how the brain controls hunger."
Clinical	A	Does psychotherapy; investigates clinical problems; develops methods of treatment.	"I'm curious about the relationship between early childhood trauma and their adult relationships so that I can help adults be more successful in their marriages."
Cognitive	B	Studies human thinking and information processing abilities.	"I want to know how reasoning, problem solving, memory, and other mental processes relate to computer game playing."
Community	A	Promotes community-wide mental health through research, prevention, education, and consultation.	"How can we prevent the spread of sexually transmitted diseases more effectively? That's what I want to better understand."
Comparative	B	Studies and compares the behavior of different species, especially animals.	"Personally, I'm fascinated by the communication abilities of porpoises."
Consumer	A	Researches packaging, advertising, marketing methods, and characteristics of consumers.	"My job is to improve the marketing of products that are environment friendly."
Counseling	A	Does psychotherapy and personal counseling; researches emotional disturbances and counseling methods.	"I am focused on better understanding why people become hoarders and how to help them stop."
Cultural	B	Studies the ways in which culture, subculture, and ethnic group membership affect behavior.	"I am interested in how culture affects human eating behavior, especially the foods we eat and whether we eat with a spoon, chopsticks, or our fingers."
Developmental	A, B	Conducts research on infant, child, adolescent, and adult development; does clinical work with disturbed children; acts as consultant to parents and schools.	"I'm focusing on transitions from the teenage years to early adulthood."
Educational	A	Investigates classroom dynamics, teaching styles, and learning; develops educational tests, evaluates educational programs.	"My passion is to figure out how to help people with different learning styles be effective learners."
Engineering	A	Does applied research on the design of machinery, computers, airlines, automobiles, and so on, for business, industry, and the military.	"I'm studying how people use movement-based computer interfaces, like the Kinect."
Environmental	A, B	Studies the effects of urban noise, crowding, attitudes toward the environment, and human use of space; acts as a consultant on environmental issues.	"I am concerned about global warming and want to understand what impact rising temperatures have on human culture."
Evolutionary	B	Studies how behavior is guided by patterns that evolved during the long history of humankind.	"I am studying some interesting trends in male and female mating choices."
Forensic	A	Studies problems of crime and crime prevention, rehabilitation programs, prisons, courtroom dynamics; selects candidates for police work.	"I am interested in improving the reliability of eyewitness testimony during trials."
Gender	B	Does research on differences between males and females, the acquisition of gender identity, and the role of gender throughout life.	"I want to understand how young boys and girls are influenced by gender stereotypes."
Health	A, B	Studies the relationship between behavior and health; uses psychological principles to promote health and prevent illness.	"How to better help people overcome drug addictions is my field of study."
Industrial-organizational	A	Selects job applicants; does skills analysis; evaluates on-the-job training; improves work environments and human relations in organizations and work settings.	"Which plays a greater role in successful management styles, intelligence or emotion? That is my question."
Learning	B	Studies how and why learning occurs; develops theories of learning.	"Right now I'm investigating how patterns of reinforcement affect learning. I am especially interested in superstitious conditioning."
Medical	A	Applies psychology to manage medical problems, such as the emotional impact of illness, self-screening for cancer, and compliance in taking medicine.	"I want to know how to help people take better charge of their own health."
Personality	B	Studies personality traits and dynamics; develops theories of personality and tests for assessing personality traits.	"I am especially interested in the personality profiles of people willing to take extreme risks."
School	A	Does psychological testing, referrals, emotional and vocational counseling of students; detects and treats learning disabilities; improves classroom learning.	"My focus is finding out how to keep students in school instead of having them drop out."
Sensation and perception	B	Studies the sense organs and the process of perception; investigates the mechanisms of sensation; develops theories about how perception occurs.	"I am using a perceptual theory to study how we are able to recognize faces in a crowd."
Social	B	Investigates human social behavior, including attitudes, conformity, persuasion, prejudice, friendship, aggression, helping, and so forth.	"My own interest is interpersonal attraction. I place two strangers in a room and analyze how strongly they are attracted to each other."

*Research in this area is typically applied (A), basic (B), or both (A, B).

Discovering Psychology — Is a Career in Psychology Right for You?

As you read this book, we encourage you to frequently reflect on new ideas by relating them to your own life in order to better understand and remember them. "Discovering Psychology" boxes like this one are designed to help you be more reflective about how psychology relates to your own life. Answer the following questions to explore whether you would enjoy becoming a psychologist:

1. I have a strong interest in human behavior. True or False?
2. I am good at recognizing patterns, evaluating evidence, and drawing conclusions. True or False?
3. I am emotionally stable. True or False?
4. I have good communication skills. True or False?
5. I find theories and ideas challenging and stimulating. True or False?
6. My friends regard me as especially sensitive to the feelings of others. True or False?
7. I enjoy planning and carrying out complex projects and activities. True or False?
8. Programs and popular books about psychology interest me. True or False?
9. I enjoy working with other people. True or False?
10. Clear thinking, objectivity, and keen observation appeal to me. True or False?

If you answered "True" to most of these questions, a career in psychology might be a good choice. And remember that many psychology majors also succeed in occupations such as management, public affairs, social services, business, sales, and education (Kuther & Morgan, 2010).

(a) Specialties in Psychology

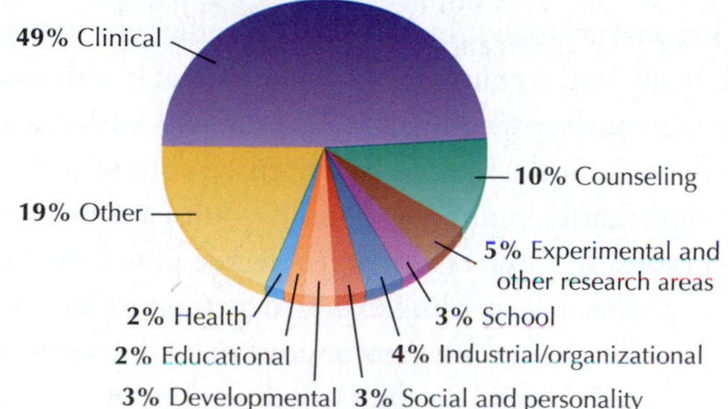

(b) Where Psychologists Work

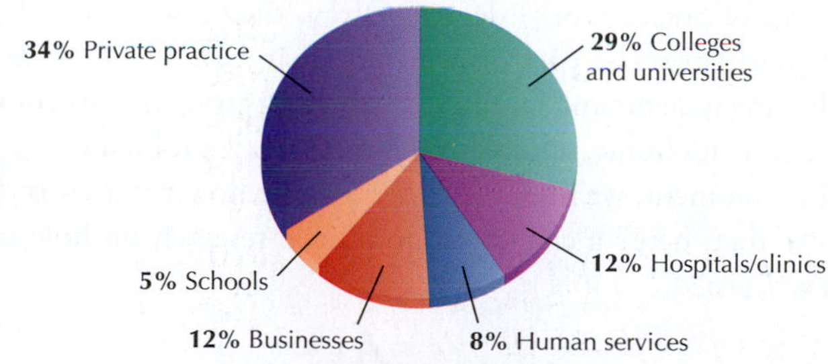

(c) What Psychologists Do (Primary Activity)

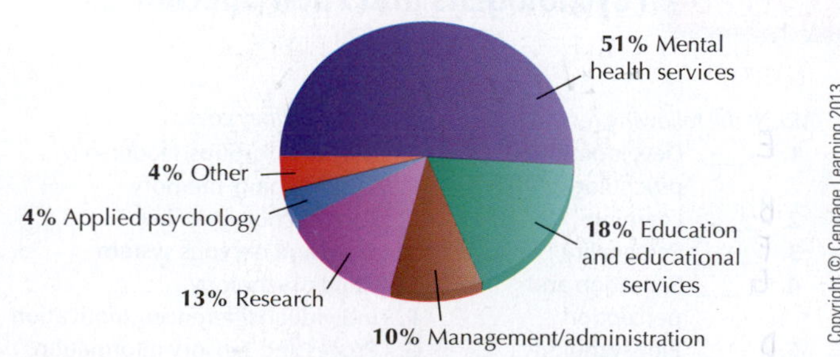

• **Figure 1.5** (a) Specialties in psychology (American Psychological Association, 2007a). Percentages are approximate. (b) Where psychologists work (Cheal et al., 2009). (c) This chart shows the main activities psychologists do at work. Any particular psychologist might do several of these activities during a work week. As you can see, most psychologists specialize in applied areas and work in applied settings (Cheal et al., 2009).

Animals and Psychology

Research involving animals was mentioned in some of the preceding examples in Table 1.5. Why is that? You may be surprised to learn that psychologists are interested in the behavior of *any* living creature—from flatworms to humans. Indeed, some comparative psychologists spend their entire careers studying rats, cats, dogs, parrots, or chimpanzees.

Although only a small percentage of psychological studies involve animals, they include many different types of research (Ord et al., 2005). Some psychologists use **animal models** to discover principles that apply to humans. For instance, animal studies have

Killer whales living along the Pacific coast near the border between the United States and Canada are listed as endangered. Studies of their social behavior are enhancing our efforts to conserve these magnificent creatures (Parsons et al., 2009).

Animal model In research, an animal whose behavior is used to derive principles that may apply to human behavior.

helped us understand stress, learning, obesity, aging, sleep, and many other topics. Psychology can also benefit animals. Behavioral studies can help us better care for domestic animals and those in zoos, as well as conserve endangered species in the wild.

Helping People

Although most psychologists help people in one way or another, those interested in emotional problems usually specialize in clinical or counseling psychology (see ■ Table 1.5). **Clinical psychologists** treat psychological problems or do research on therapies and mental disorders. In contrast, **counseling psychologists** tend to treat milder problems, such as troubles at work or school. However, such differences are fading, and many counseling psychologists now work full time as therapists.

To become a clinical psychologist, it is best to have a doctorate (Ph.D., Psy.D., or Ed.D.). Most clinical psychologists have a Ph.D. degree and follow a scientist-as-practitioner model. That is, they are trained to do either research or therapy. Many do both. Other clinicians earn the Psy.D. (Doctor of Psychology) degree, which emphasizes therapy skills rather than research (Peterson, 2001).

Does a psychologist have to have a license to offer therapy? At one time it was possible in many states for anyone to "hang out a shingle" as a "psychologist." Now psychologists must not only meet rigorous educational requirements, they must meet stringent legal requirements as well. To work as a clinical or counseling psychologist, you must have a license issued by a state examining board. However, the law does not prevent you from calling yourself anything else you choose—therapist, rebirther, primal feeling facilitator, cosmic aura balancer, or life skills coach—or from selling your "services" to anyone willing to pay. Beware of people with self-proclaimed titles. Even if their intentions are honorable, they may have little training. A licensed psychologist who chooses to use a particular type of therapy is not the same as someone "trained" solely in that technique.

Psychologists are often inaccurately portrayed in the media as incompetent therapists. Some films have featured psychologists who are more disturbed than their patients (such as Jack Nicholson's character in *Anger Management*) or psychologists who are bumbling buffoons (such as Billy Crystal's character in *Analyze This*). In the movie comedy *Prime*, a therapist listens to a patient describe intimate details of her relationship with a man but fails to tell the patient that the man is her son. Such characters may be dramatic and entertaining, but they seriously distort public perceptions of responsible and hardworking psychologists (Schultz, 2004).

Real clinical and counseling psychologists follow an ethical code that stresses (1) high levels of competence, integrity, and responsibility; (2) respect for people's rights to privacy, dignity, confidentiality, and personal freedom; and, above all, (3) protection of the client's welfare (American Psychological Association, 2002, 2010a; Barnett et al., 2007). Psychologists are also expected to use their knowledge to contribute to society. Many do volunteer work in the communities in which they live.

Other Mental Health Professionals

Clinical psychologists are not the only people who work in the field of mental health. Often they coordinate their efforts with other specially trained professionals. What are the differences among psychologists, psychiatrists, psychoanalysts, counselors, and other mental health professionals? Each has a specific blend of training and skills.

Psychologists are all shrinks, right? Nope. "Shrinks" (a slang term derived from "head shrinkers") are **psychiatrists**, medical doctors who treats mental disorders, often by doing psychotherapy. Psychiatrists can also prescribe drugs, which is something psychologists usually cannot do. However, this is changing. Psychologists in New Mexico and Louisiana can now legally prescribe drugs. It will be interesting to see whether other states grant similar privileges (Munsey, 2008).

To be a psychoanalyst, you must have a moustache and goatee, spectacles, a German accent, and a well-padded couch—or so the media stereotype goes. Actually, to become a **psychoanalyst** you must have an M.D. or Ph.D. degree plus further training in Freudian psychoanalysis. In other words, either a physician or a psychologist may become an analyst by learning a specific type of psychotherapy.

In many states, counselors also do mental health work. A **counselor** is an adviser who helps solve problems with marriage, career, school, work, or the like. To be a licensed counselor (such as a marriage and family counselor, a child counselor, or a school counselor) typically requires a master's degree plus 1 or 2 years of full-time supervised counseling experience. Counselors learn practical helping skills and do not treat serious mental disorders.

Psychiatric social workers play an important role in many mental health programs where they apply social science principles to help patients in clinics and hospitals. Most hold an M.S.W. (Master of Social Work) degree. Often, they assist psychologists and psychiatrists as part of a team. Their typical duties include evaluating patients and families, conducting group therapy, or visiting a patient's home, school, or job to alleviate problems.

In a moment, we'll take a closer look at how research is done. Before that, here's a chance to do a little research on how much you've learned.

Knowledge Builder: Psychologists and Their Specialties

RECITE

Match the following research areas with the topics they cover.

1. E_____ Developmental psychology
2. B_____ Learning
3. F_____ Personality
4. G_____ Sensation and perception
5. D_____ Biopsychology
6. A_____ Social psychology
7. H_____ Comparative psychology

A. Attitudes, groups, leadership
B. Conditioning, memory
C. The psychology of law
D. Brain and nervous system
E. Child psychology
F. Individual differences, motivation
G. Processing sensory information
H. Animal behavior

8. In psychological research, animal ______________ may be used to discover principles that apply to human behavior.
9. A psychologist who specializes in treating human emotional difficulties is called a ______________ psychologist.
10. Which of the following can always prescribe drugs to treat mental disorders?
    a. a psychologist *b.* a psychiatrist *c.* a psychotherapist *d.* a counselor

REFLECT

Think Critically

11. If many psychologists work in applied settings, why is basic research still of great importance?

Self-Reflect

Which specialty in psychology is most interesting to you? What is it about that specialty that most attracts you?

Answers: 1. E **2.** B **3.** F **4.** G **5.** D **6.** A **7.** H **8.** models **9.** clinical or counseling **10.** *b* **11.** Practitioners benefit from basic psychological research in the same way that physicians benefit from basic research in biology. Discoveries in basic science form the knowledge base that leads to useful applications.

The Psychology Experiment—Where Cause Meets Effect

Gateway Question 1.8: *How is an experiment performed?*

To get beyond description and fully understand behavior, psychologists must to be able explain *why* we act the way we do. To discover the *causes* of behavior, we must usually conduct an **experiment.** An experiment is a formal trial undertaken to confirm or disconfirm a hypothesis about the causes of behavior (although causes are sometimes revealed by naturalistic observation or correlations). Experiments allow psychologists to carefully control conditions and bring cause-and-effect relationships into sharp focus. Hence, they are generally accepted as the most powerful scientific research tool. To perform an experiment you would do the following:

1. Directly vary a condition you think might affect behavior.
2. Create two or more groups of subjects. These groups should be alike in all ways *except* the condition you are varying.
3. Record whether varying the condition has any effect on behavior.

Suppose you want to find out if using cell phones while driving a car affects the likelihood of having an accident. First, you would form two groups of people. Then you could give the members of one group a test of driving ability while they are using a cell phone. The second group would take the same test without using a cell phone. By comparing average driving ability scores for the two groups, you could tell if cell phone use affects driving ability.

As you can see, the simplest psychological experiment is based on two groups of **experimental subjects**—animals or people whose behavior is investigated. Human subjects are also called **participants.** One group is called the *experimental group;* the other becomes the *control group.* The experimental group and the control group are treated exactly alike except for the condition (or *variable*) you intentionally vary.

Variables and Groups

What are the different kinds of variables? A **variable** is any condition that can change and that might affect the outcome of the experiment. Identifying causes and effects in an experiment involves three types of variables:

1. **Independent variables** are conditions that are altered or varied by the experimenter, who sets their size, amount, or value. Independent variables are suspected *causes* for differences in behavior.
2. **Dependent variables** measure the results of the experiment. That is, they reveal the *effects* that independent variables have on *behavior.* Such effects are often revealed by measures of performance, such as test scores.
3. **Extraneous variables** are conditions that a researcher wishes to prevent from affecting the outcome of the experiment.

We can apply these terms to our cell phone/driving experiment in this way:

1. Cell phone use is the independent variable—we want to know if cell phone use affects driving ability.
2. Driving ability (defined by scores achieved on a test of driving ability) is the dependent variable—we want to know if the ability to drive well depends on whether a person is using a cell phone.

Clinical psychologist A psychologist who specializes in the treatment of psychological and behavioral disturbances or who does research on such disturbances.

Counseling psychologist A psychologist who specializes in the treatment of milder emotional and behavioral disturbances.

Psychiatrist A medical doctor with additional training in the diagnosis and treatment of mental and emotional disorders.

Psychoanalyst A mental health professional (usually a medical doctor) trained to practice psychoanalysis.

Counselor A mental health professional who specializes in helping people with problems not involving serious mental disorder; for example, marriage counselors, career counselors, or school counselors.

Psychiatric social worker A mental health professional trained to apply social science principles to help patients in clinics and hospitals.

Experiment A formal trial undertaken to confirm or disconfirm a hypothesis about cause and effect.

Experimental subjects Humans (also referred to as **participants**) or animals whose behavior is investigated in an experiment.

Variable Any condition that changes or can be made to change; a measure, event, or state that may vary.

Independent variable In an experiment, the condition being investigated as a possible cause of some change in behavior. The values that this variable takes are chosen by the experimenter.

Dependent variable In an experiment, the condition (usually a behavior) that is affected by the independent variable.

Extraneous variables Conditions or factors excluded from influencing the outcome of an experiment.

3. All other variables that could affect driving ability are extraneous. Examples of extraneous variables are the number of hours slept the night before the test, driving experience, and familiarity with the car used in the experiment.

By the way, psychologist Davis Strayer and his colleagues have confirmed that almost all drivers talking on cell phones drive no better than people who are legally drunk, and that texters are even worse (Drews et al., 2009; Strayer, Drews, & Crouch, 2006; Watson & Strayer, 2010).

As you can see, an **experimental group** consists of participants exposed to the independent variable (cell phone use in the preceding example). Members of the **control group** are exposed to all conditions except the independent variable.

Let's examine another simple experiment. Suppose you notice that you seem to study better while listening to your iPod. This suggests the hypothesis that listening to music improves learning. We could test this idea by forming an experimental group that studies with music. A control group would study without music. Then we could compare their scores on a test.

Is a control group really needed? Can't people just study while listening to their iPods to see if they do better? Better than what? The control group provides a *point of reference* for comparison with the scores in the experimental group. Without a control group, it would be impossible to tell whether music had any effect on learning. If the average test score of the experimental group is higher than the average of the control group, we can conclude that music improves learning. If there is no difference, it's obvious that the independent variable had no effect on learning.

In this experiment, the amount learned (indicated by scores on the test) is the *dependent variable.* We are asking, Does the independent variable *affect* the dependent variable? (Does listening to music affect or influence learning?)

Experimental Control

How do we know that the people in one group aren't more intelligent than those in the other group? It's true that personal differences might affect the experiment. However, they can be controlled by randomly assigning people to groups. **Random assignment** means that a participant has an equal chance of being in either the experimental group or the control group. Randomization evenly balances personal differences in the two groups. In our musical experiment, this could be done by simply flipping a coin for each participant: Heads, and the participant is in the experimental group; tails, it's the control group. This would result in few average differences in the number of people in each group who are women or men, geniuses or dunces, hungry, hung over, tall, music lovers, or whatever.

Other *extraneous,* or outside, variables—such as the amount of study time, the temperature in the room, the time of day, the amount of light, and so forth—must also be prevented from affecting the outcome of an experiment. But how? Usually this is done by making all conditions (except the independent variable) *exactly* alike for both groups. When all conditions are the same for both groups—*except* the presence or absence of music—then any difference in the amount learned *must* be caused by the music (● Figure 1.6).

Cause and Effect

Now let's summarize. In an experiment, two or more groups of subjects are treated differently with respect to the independent variable. In all other ways they are treated the same. That is, extraneous variables are equated for all groups. The effect of the independent variable (or variables) on some behavior (the dependent variable) is then measured. In a carefully controlled experiment, the independent variable is the only possible *cause* for any *effect* noted in the dependent variable. This allows clear cause-and-effect connections to be identified (● Figure 1.7).

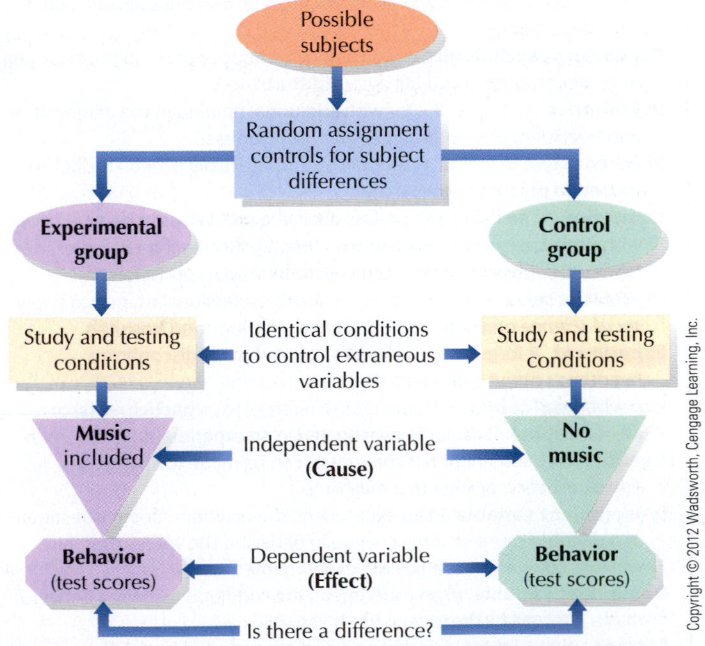

● **Figure 1.6** Elements of a simple psychological experiment to assess the effects of music during study on test scores.

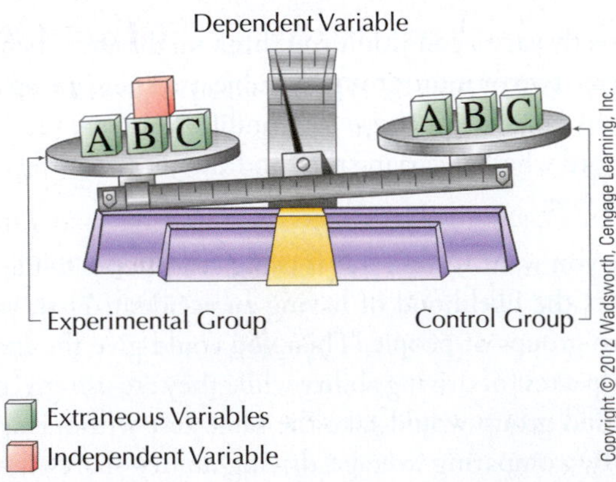

● **Figure 1.7** Experimental control is achieved by balancing extraneous variables for the experimental group and the control group. For example, the average age (A), education (B), and intelligence (C) of group members could be made the same for both groups. Then we could apply the independent variable to the experimental group. If their behavior (the dependent variable) changes (in comparison with the control group), the change must be caused by the independent variable.

Evaluating Results

How can we tell if the independent variable really made a difference? This problem is handled statistically. Reports in psychology journals almost always include the statement, "Results were **statistically significant.**" What this means is that the obtained results would occur very rarely by chance alone. To be statistically significant, a difference must be large enough so that it would occur by chance in less than 5 experiments out of 100. Of course, findings also become more convincing when they can be *replicated* (repeated) by other researchers.

BRIDGES

See the Statistics Appendix for more information on inferential statistics.

Meta-Analysis

As you might guess, numerous studies are done on important topics in psychology. Although each study adds to our understanding, the results of various studies don't always agree. Let's say we are interested in whether males or females tend to be greater risk takers, like our skydiver friend, Henry. A computer search would reveal that more than 100 studies have investigated various types of risk-taking (for example, smoking, fast driving, or unprotected sex).

Is there a way to combine the results of the studies? Yes, a statistical technique called **meta-analysis** can be used to combine the results of many studies as if they were all part of one big study (Cooper, 2010). In other words, a meta-analysis is a study of the results of other studies. In recent years, meta-analysis has been used to summarize and synthesize mountains of psychological research. This allows us to see the big picture and draw conclusions that might be missed in a single, small-scale study. Oh, and about that risk-taking question: A meta-analysis showed that males do tend to take more risks than females (Byrnes, Miller, & Schafer, 1999). (The most frequent last words uttered by deceased young males is rumored to be, "Hey, watch this!")

Double Blind—On Placebos and Self-Fulfilling Prophecies

Gateway Question 1.9: *What is a double-blind experiment?*

Suppose a researcher hypothesizes that the drug amphetamine (a stimulant) improves learning. She explains her hypothesis to her participants and gives experimental group participants an amphetamine pill before they begin studying. Control group members get nothing. Later, she assesses how much each participant learned. Does this experiment seem valid? Actually, it is seriously flawed for several reasons.

Why? The experimental group took the drug and the control group didn't. Differences in the amount they learned must have been caused by the drug, right? No, because the drug wasn't the only difference between the groups. For a start, because of what they were told, participants in the experimental group likely *expected* to learn more. Any observed differences between groups then may reflect differences in expectation, not the actual effect of the drug.

Research Participant Bias

In a well-designed experiment, you must be careful about what you tell participants. Small bits of information might create **research participant bias,** or changes in participants' behavior caused by the influence of their expectations. Notice also that experimental group participants swallowed a pill, and control participants did not. This is another form of research participant bias. It could be that those who swallowed a pill unconsciously *expected* to do better. After all, pills are medicine, aren't they? This alone might have created a **placebo** (plah-SEE-bo) **effect**—changes in behavior caused by belief that one has taken a drug or received some other treatment. Suppose the researcher had not given the experimental group an amphetamine pill and instead had given them a **placebo,** or fake drug. Inactive substances such as sugar pills and saline (saltwater) injections are commonly used as placebos. If a placebo has any effect, it must be based on suggestion, rather than chemistry (McBurney & White, 2010). Placebo effects can be quite powerful. For instance, a saline injection is 70 percent as effective as morphine in reducing pain. That's why doctors sometimes

The placebo effect is a major factor in medical treatments. Would you also expect the placebo effect to occur in psychotherapy? (It does, which complicates studies on the effectiveness of new psychotherapies.)

Experimental group In a controlled experiment, the group of subjects exposed to the independent variable or experimental condition.

Control group In a controlled experiment, the group of subjects exposed to all experimental conditions or variables *except* the independent variable.

Random assignment The use of chance (for example, flipping a coin) to assign subjects to experimental and control groups.

Statistical significance Experimental results that would rarely occur by chance alone.

Meta-analysis A statistical technique for combining the results of many studies on the same subject.

Research participant bias Changes in the behavior of research participants caused by the unintended influence of their own expectations.

Placebo effect Changes in behavior due to participants' expectations that a drug (or other treatment) will have some effect.

Placebo An inactive substance given in the place of a drug in psychological research or by physicians who wish to treat a complaint by suggestion.

prescribe placebos—especially for complaints that seem to have no physical basis. Placebos have been shown to affect pain, anxiety, depression, alertness, tension, sexual arousal, cravings for alcohol, and many other processes (Wampold et al., 2005).

How could an inert substance have any effect? Placebos alter our expectations, both conscious and unconscious, about our own emotional and physical reactions. Because we associate taking medicine with feeling better, we expect placebos to make us feel better, too (Benedetti, 2009). After a person takes a placebo, there is a reduction in brain activity linked with pain, so the effect is not imaginary (Wager et al., 2004).

Controlling Research Participant Bias

How can you avoid research participant bias? To control for research participant bias, we could use a **single-blind experiment.** In this case, participants do not know whether they are in the experimental or the control group or whether they are receiving a real drug or a placebo. All participants are given the same instructions and everyone gets a pill or injection. People in the experimental group get a real drug, and those in the control group get a placebo. Because participants are *blind* as to the hypothesis under investigation and whether they received the drug, their expectations (conscious *and* unconscious) are the same. Any difference in their behavior must be caused by the drug. However, even this arrangement is not enough, because researchers themselves sometimes affect experiments by influencing participants. Let's see how this occurs.

Researcher Bias

How could a researcher influence participants? As we saw above, when the experimenter explained her hypothesis to the participants, she likely biased the results of the study. But even if a researcher uses a single-blind procedure to avoid deliberately biasing participants, **researcher bias**—changes in behavior caused by the unintended influence of a researcher—remains a problem. In essence, experimenters run the risk of finding what they expect to find. This occurs because humans are very sensitive to hints about what is expected of them (Rosenthal, 1994).

Researcher bias even applies outside the laboratory. Psychologist Robert Rosenthal (1973) reports an example of how expectations influence people: At the U.S. Air Force Academy Preparatory School, 100 airmen were randomly assigned to five different math classes. Their teachers did not know about this random placement. Instead, each teacher was told that his or her students had unusually high or low ability. Students in the classes labeled "high ability" improved much more in math scores than those in "low ability" classes. Yet, initially, all of the classes had students of equal ability.

Although the teachers were not conscious of any bias, apparently they subtly communicated their expectations to students. Most likely, they did this through tone of voice, body language, and by giving encouragement or criticism. Their "hints," in turn, created a self-fulfilling prophecy that affected the students. A **self-fulfilling prophecy** is a prediction that prompts people to act in ways that make the prediction come true. For instance, many teachers underestimate the abilities of ethnic minority children, which hurts the students' chances for success (Weinstein, Gregory, & Strambler, 2004). In short, people sometimes become what we prophesy for them. It is wise to remember that others tend to live *up* or *down* to our expectations for them (Jussim & Harber, 2005).

The Double-Blind Experiment

Because of research participant bias and researcher bias, it is common to keep both participants and researchers "blind." In a **double-blind experiment,** neither subjects nor researchers know who is in the experimental group or the control group, including who received a drug and who took a placebo. This not only controls for research participant bias, it also keeps researchers from unconsciously influencing participants.

How can the researchers be "blind"; it's their experiment, isn't it? The researchers who designed the experiment, including preparing the pills or injections, typically hire research assistants to collect data from the participants. Even the research assistants are blinded in that they do not know which pill or injection is drug or placebo or whether any particular participant is in the experimental or control group.

Double-blind testing has shown that about 50 percent of the effectiveness of antidepressant drugs, such as the "wonder drug" Prozac, is due to the placebo effect (Kirsch & Sapirstein, 1998). Much of the popularity of herbal health remedies is also based on the placebo effect (Seidman, 2001).

BRIDGES

For more information about how psychologists study placebos see Chapter 13, pages 464–465.

Knowledge Builder — The Psychology Experiment

RECITE

1. To understand cause and effect, a simple psychological experiment is based on creating two groups: the ______________ group and the ______________ group.
2. There are three types of variables to consider in an experiment: ______________ variables (which are manipulated by the experimenter); ______________ variables (which measure the outcome of the experiment); and ______________ variables (factors to be excluded in a particular experiment).
3. A researcher performs an experiment to learn whether room temperature affects the amount of aggression displayed by college students under crowded conditions in a simulated prison environment. In this experiment, the independent variable is which of the following?
   a. room temperature *b.* the amount of aggression *c.* crowding *d.* the simulated prison environment
4. A procedure used to control both research participant bias and researcher bias in psychological experiments is the
   a. correlation method *b.* controlled experiment *c.* double-blind experiment *d.* random assignment of subjects

REFLECT

Think Critically

5. There is a loophole in the statement, "I've been taking vitamin C tablets, and I haven't had a cold all year. Vitamin C is great!" What is the loophole?
6. People who believe strongly in astrology have personality characteristics that actually match, to a degree, those predicted by their astrological signs. Can you explain why this occurs?

Self-Reflect

In a sense, we all conduct little experiments to detect cause-and-effect connections. If you are interested in cooking, for example, you might try adding a particular spice to a meal on one occasion but not another. The question then becomes, "Does the use of the spice (the independent variable) affect the appeal of the meal (the dependent variable)?" By comparing a spiced meal (the control group) with an unspiced meal (the experimental group) you could find out if that spice is worth using. Can you think of at least one informal experiment you've run in the last month? What were the variables? What was the outcome?

Answers: 1. experimental, control **2.** independent, dependent, extraneous **3.** *a* **4.** *c* **5.** The statement implies that vitamin C prevented colds. However, not getting a cold could just be a coincidence. A controlled experiment with a group given vitamin C and a control group not taking vitamin C would be needed to learn whether vitamin C actually has any effect on susceptibility to colds. **6.** Belief in astrology can create a self-fulfilling prophecy in which people alter their behaviors and self-concepts to match their astrological signs (van Rooij, 1994).

Nonexperimental Research Methods—Different Strokes

Gateway Question 1.10: *What nonexperimental research methods do psychologists use?*

Determining cause-and-effect relationships between variables lies at the heart of discovering not just *what* we do, but explaining *why* we do it. For this reason, psychologists place a special emphasis on controlled experimentation **(experimental method).** However, because it is not always possible to conduct experiments, psychologists gather evidence and test hypotheses in many other ways (Jackson, 2011). They observe behavior as it unfolds in natural settings **(naturalistic observation)**; they make measurements to discover relationships between events **(correlational method)**; they study psychological problems and therapies in clinical settings **(clinical method)**; and they use questionnaires to poll large groups of people **(survey method).** Let's see how each of these is used to advance psychological knowledge.

Naturalistic Observation

Psychologists sometimes rely on *naturalistic observation,* the active observation of behavior in a *natural setting* (the typical environment in which a person or animal lives). For example, in 1960, Jane Goodall first observed a chimpanzee use a grass stem as a tool to remove termites from a termite mound (Van Lawick-Goodall, 1971). Notice that naturalistic observation provides only *descriptions* of behavior. In order to *explain* observations, we may need information from other research methods. Just the same, Goodall's discovery showed that humans are not the only tool-making animals (Rutz et al., 2010).

Chimpanzees in zoos use objects as tools. Doesn't that demonstrate the same thing? Not necessarily. Naturalistic observation allows us to study behavior that hasn't been tampered with or altered by outside influences. Only by observing chimps in their natural environment can we tell whether they use tools without human interference.

Limitations

Doesn't the presence of human observers affect the animals' behavior? Yes. The observer effect is a major problem. The **observer effect** refers to changes in a subject's behavior caused by an awareness of being observed. Naturalists must be very careful to keep their distance and avoid "making friends" with the animals they are watching. Likewise, if you are interested in why automobile drivers have traffic accidents, you can't simply get in people's cars and start taking notes. As a stranger, your presence would probably change the drivers' behaviors. When possible, the observer effect can be minimized by concealing the observer.

Another solution is to use hidden recorders. One naturalistic study of traffic accidents was done with video cameras installed in 100 cars (Dingus et al., 2006). It turns out that most accidents are caused by failing to look at the traffic in front of the car (eyes forward!). Hidden stationary video cameras have also provided valuable observations of many animal species. As recording devices have become miniaturized, it has even become possible to attach "critter cams" directly to many species, allowing observations to be in a wide range of natural environments (● Figure 1.8). For example, zoologist Christian Rutz and his colleagues outfitted shy New Caledonian crows with "crow cams" to better understand their use

Single-blind experiment An arrangement in which participants remain unaware of whether they are in the experimental group or the control group.

Researcher bias Changes in participants' behavior caused by the unintended influence of a researcher's actions.

Self-fulfilling prophecy A prediction that prompts people to act in ways that make the prediction come true.

Double-blind experiment An arrangement in which both participants and experimenters are unaware of whether participants are in the experimental group or the control group, including who might have been administered a drug or a placebo.

Experimental method Investigating causes of behavior through controlled experimentation.

Naturalistic observation Observing behavior as it unfolds in natural settings.

Correlational method Making measurements to discover relationships between events.

Clinical method Studying psychological problems and therapies in clinical settings.

Survey method Using questionnaires and surveys to poll large groups of people.

Observer effect Changes in a subject's behavior brought about by an awareness of being observed.

● **Figure 1.8** New Caledonian crows wearing tiny "crow cams" barely half the weight of a silver dollar have been recorded using twigs to forage for food (Rutz et al., 2007).

of tools to forage for food (Rutz et al., 2007, 2010). Not only can these clever crows use twigs to reach food, they can use a shorter twig to get a longer twig to get food (Wimpenny et al., 2009). Apparently, humans and other primates are not the only tool-using species.

Observer bias is a related problem in which observers see what they expect to see or record only selected details (Jackson, 2011). For instance, teachers in one classic study were told to watch normal elementary school children who had been labeled (for the study) as "learning disabled," "mentally retarded," "emotionally disturbed," or "normal." Sadly, teachers gave the children very different ratings, depending on the labels used (Foster & Ysseldyke, 1976). In some situations, observer bias can have serious consequences (Spano, 2005). For example, a police officer expecting criminal behavior might shoot a person who is reaching for his wallet because he appears to be reaching for a gun.

A special mistake to avoid when observing animals is the **anthropomorphic** (AN-thro-po-MORE-fik) **error.** This is the error of attributing human thoughts, feelings, or motives to animals—especially as a way of explaining their behavior (Waytz, Epley, & Cacioppo, 2010). The temptation to assume that an animal is "angry," "jealous," "bored," or "guilty" can be strong. If you have pets at home, you probably already know how difficult it is to avoid anthropomorphizing, but it can lead to false conclusions. For example, if your dog growls at your date, you might assume the dog doesn't like your companion. But it's possible that your date is merely wearing a cologne or perfume that irritates the dog's nose.

Psychologists doing naturalistic studies make a special effort to minimize bias by keeping an **observational record,** or detailed summary of data and observations. As suggested by the study of traffic accidents and the use of "critter cams," video recording often provides the most objective record of all. Despite its problems, naturalistic observation can supply a wealth of information and raise many interesting questions. In most scientific research it is an excellent starting point.

Correlational Studies

Let's say a psychologist notes an association between the IQs of parents and their children, or between beauty and social popularity, or between anxiety and test performance, or even between crime and the weather. In each case, two observations or events are **correlated,** or linked together in an orderly way. The Los Angeles study of crime and temperature mentioned earlier in this chapter is an example of a **correlational study.** First, two factors are measured. Then, a statistical technique is used to find their degree of correlation. For example, we could find the correlation between the number of hours spent practicing and sports performance during competitions. If the correlation is large, knowing how much a person practices would allow us to predict his or her success in competition. Likewise, success in competition could be used to predict how much an athlete practiced.

Correlation Coefficients

How is the degree of correlation expressed? The strength and direction of a relationship can be expressed as a **coefficient of correlation.** This can be calculated as a number falling somewhere between +1.00 and −1.00. Drawing graphs of relationships can also help clarify their nature (see ● Figure 1.9). If the number is zero or close to zero, the association between two measures is weak or nonexistent (see ● Figure 1.9*c*). For example, the correlation between shoe size and intelligence is zero. (Sorry, size 12 readers.) If the correlation is +1.00, a perfect positive relationship exists (see ● Figure 1.9*e*); if it is −1.00, a perfect negative relationship has been discovered (see ● Figure 1.9*a*).

BRIDGES

For more detail about calculating and graphing correlations see the Statistics Appendix.

Correlations in psychology are rarely perfect. But the closer the coefficient is to +1.00 or −1.00, the stronger the relationship. For example, identical twins tend to have almost identical IQs. In contrast, the IQs of parents and their children are only generally similar. The correlation between the IQs of parents and children is .35; between identical twins, it's .86.

BRIDGES

Correlations between the IQs of family members are used to estimate the degree to which intelligence is affected by heredity and environment. **See Chapter 9, pages 317–318.**

What do the terms "positive" and "negative" correlation mean? In a **positive correlation**, higher scores on one measure are matched by higher scores on the other. For example, there is a moderate positive correlation between high school grades and college grades; students who do well in high school tend to do well in college (and the reverse) (see • Figure 1.9*d*). In a **negative correlation,** higher scores on one measure are associated with lower scores on the other. We might observe, for instance, a moderate negative correlation between the number of hours that students play computer games and their grades. That is, more play is associated with lower grades. (This is the well-known computer-game-zombie effect.) (• Figure 1.9*b*).

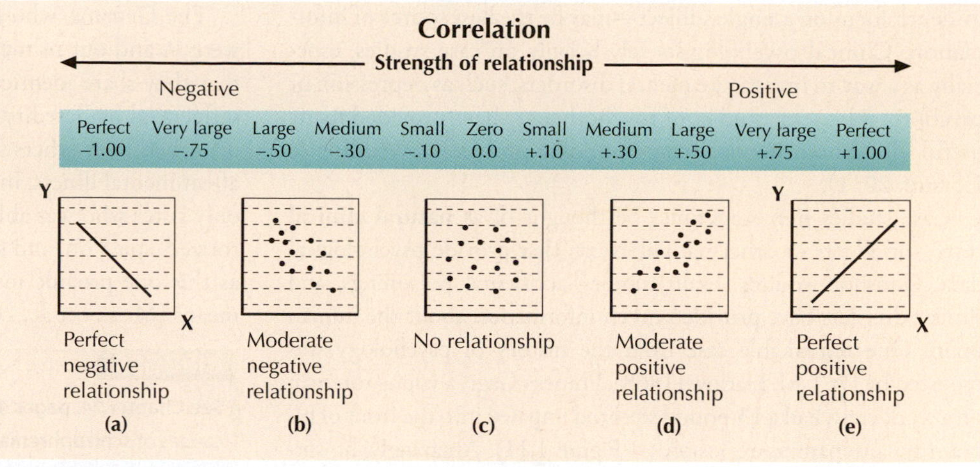

• **Figure 1.9** The correlation coefficient tells how strongly two measures are related. These graphs show a range of relationships between two measures, X and Y. If a correlation is negative (a), increases in one measure are associated with decreases in the other. (As Y gets larger, X gets smaller.) In a positive correlation (e), increases in one measure are associated with increases in the other. (As Y gets larger, X gets larger.) The center-left graph (b "moderate negative relationship") might result from comparing time spent playing computer games (Y) with grades (X): More time spent playing computer games is associated with lower grades. The center graph (c "no relationship") would result from plotting a person's shoe size (Y) and his or her IQ (X). The center-right graph (d "moderate positive relationship") could be a plot of grades in high school (Y) and grades in college (X) for a group of students: Higher grades in high school are associated with higher grades in college.

Wouldn't that show that playing computer games too much causes *lower grades?* It might seem so, but as we saw previously, the best way to be confident that a cause-and-effect relationship exists is to perform a controlled experiment.

Correlation and Causation

Correlational studies help us discover relationships and make predictions. However, correlation *does not* demonstrate **causation** (a cause-effect relationship) (Jackson & Newberry, 2012). It could be, for instance, that students who aren't interested in their classes have more time for computer games. If so, then their lack of study and lower grades would be the result of disinterest, and not excessive game playing (which would be another result of disinterest in classes). Just because one thing *appears* to be directly related to another does not mean that a cause-and-effect connection exists.

Here is another example of mistaking correlation for causation: What if a psychologist discovers that the blood of patients with schizophrenia contains a certain chemical not found in the general population? Does this show that the chemical *causes* schizophrenia? It may seem so, but schizophrenia could cause the chemical to form. Or both schizophrenia and the chemical might be caused by some unknown third factor, such as the typical diet in mental hospitals (see • Figure 1.10). To reiterate, just because one thing *appears* to cause another does not *confirm* that it does. The best way to be confident that a cause-and-effect relationship exists is to perform a controlled experiment.

• **Figure 1.10** A correlation between two variables might mean that X causes Y, that Y causes X, or that some other, third, variable, Z causes *both* X and Y.

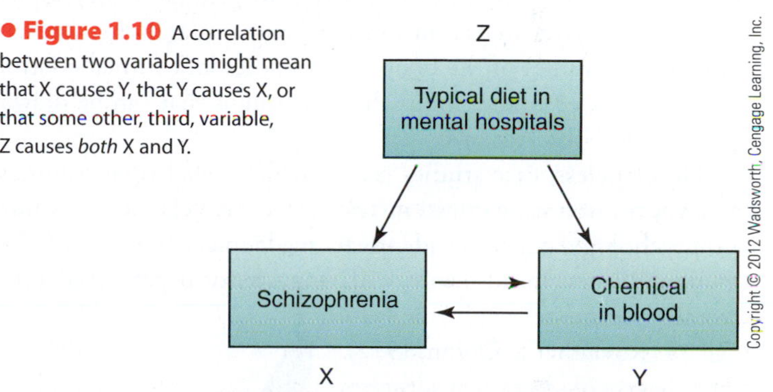

Observer bias The tendency of an observer to distort observations or perceptions to match his or her expectations.

Anthropomorphic error The error of attributing human thoughts, feelings, or motives to animals, especially as a way of explaining their behavior.

Observational record A detailed summary of observed events or a videotape of observed behavior.

Correlation The existence of a consistent, systematic relationship between two events, measures, or variables.

Correlational study A nonexperimental study designed to measure the degree of relationship (if any) between two or more events, measures, or variables.

Coefficient of correlation A statistical index ranging from −1.00 to +1.00 that indicates the direction and degree of correlation.

Positive correlation A statistical relationship in which increases in one measure are matched by increases in the other (or decreases correspond with decreases).

Negative correlation A statistical relationship in which increases in one measure are matched by decreases in the other.

Causation The act of causing some effect.

Case study An in-depth focus on all aspects of a single person.

The Clinical Method

It may be impractical, unethical, or impossible to use the experimental method to study rare events, such as unusual mental disorders, childhood "geniuses," or "rampage" school shootings (Harding, Fox, & Mehta, 2002). In such instances, a **case study**—an in-depth focus on a single subject—may be the best source of information. Clinical psychologists rely heavily on case studies, especially as a way to investigate mental disorders, such as depression or psychosis. Also, case studies of psychotherapy have provided many useful ideas about how to treat emotional problems (Wedding & Corsini, 2011).

Case studies may sometimes be thought of as **natural clinical tests**—accidents or other natural events that provide psychological data. Gunshot wounds, brain tumors, accidental poisonings, and similar disasters have provided much information about the human brain. One remarkable case from the history of psychology was reported by Dr. J. M. Harlow (1868). Phineas Gage, a young foreman on a work crew, had a 13-pound steel rod impaled into the front of his brain by a dynamite explosion (● Figure 1.11). Amazingly, he survived the accident. Within 2 months Gage could walk, talk, and move normally, but the injury forever changed his personality. Instead of the honest and dependable worker he had been before, Gage became a surly, foul-mouthed liar. Dr. Harlow carefully recorded all details of what was perhaps the first in-depth case study of an accidental frontal lobotomy (the destruction of front brain matter).

When a Los Angeles carpenter named Michael Melnick suffered a similar injury, he recovered completely, with no lasting ill effects. Melnick's very different reaction to a similar injury shows why psychologists prefer controlled experiments and often use lab animals for studies of the brain. Case studies lack formal control groups. This, of course, limits the conclusions that can be drawn from clinical observations.

Nevertheless, case studies can provide special opportunities to answer interesting questions. For instance, a classic case study in psychology concerns identical quadruplets, known as the Genain sisters. In addition to having identical genes, all four women became schizophrenic before age 25 (Rosenthal & Quinn, 1977). The chances of identical quadruplets all becoming schizophrenic are about 1 in 1.5 billion.

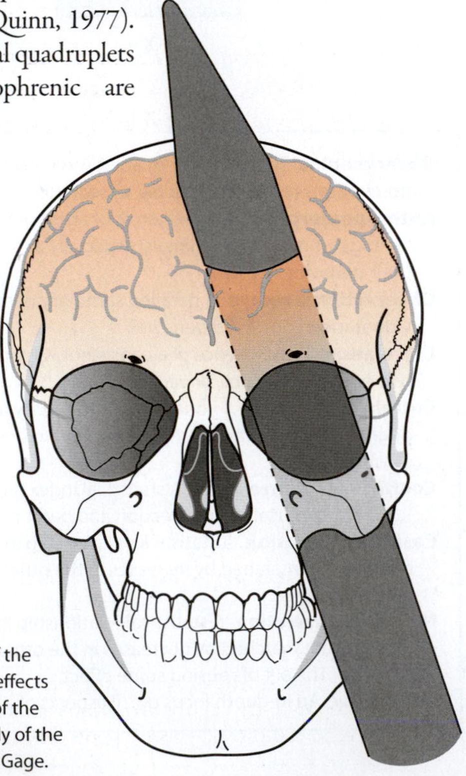

● Figure 1.11 Some of the earliest information on the effects of damage to frontal areas of the brain came from a case study of the accidental injury of Phineas Gage.

The Genains, who have been studied for more than 40 years, were in and out of mental hospitals most of their lives. The fact that they share identical genes suggests that mental disorders are influenced by heredity. The fact that some of the sisters are more disturbed than others suggests that environmental conditions also affect mental illness. Indeed, Myra, the least ill of the four, was the only sister who was able to avoid her father, an alcoholic who terrorized, spied on, and sexually molested the girls. Thus, cases such as this one provide insights that can't be obtained by any other means (Mirsky et al., 2000).

BRIDGES

See Chapter 14, pages 488–491, for more information about the causes of schizophrenia.

Survey Method

Sometimes psychologists would like to ask everyone in the world a few well-chosen questions: "Do you sky dive? Why would you say you do this?" "What form of discipline did your parents use when you were a child?" "What is the most dishonest thing you've done?" Honest answers to such questions can reveal much about people's behavior. But, because it is impossible to question everyone, doing a survey is often more practical.

Surveys, or public polling techniques, are often used to answer psychological questions (Tourangeau, 2004). Typically, people in a representative sample are asked a series of carefully worded questions. A **representative sample** is a small group that accurately reflects a larger population. A good sample must include the same proportion of men, women, young, old, professionals, blue-collar workers, Republicans, Democrats, whites, African Americans, Native Americans, Latinos, Asians, and so on as found in the population as a whole.

A **population** is an entire group of animals or people belonging to a particular category (for example, all college students or all single women). Ultimately, we are interested in entire populations. But, by selecting a smaller sample we can draw conclusions about the larger group without polling each and every person. Representative samples are often obtained by *randomly* selecting who will be included (● Figure 1.12). (Notice that this is similar to randomly assigning participants to groups in an experiment.)

How accurate is the survey method? Modern surveys like the Gallup and Harris polls are quite accurate. The Gallup poll has erred in its election predictions by only 1.5 percent since 1954. However, if a survey is based on a biased sample, it may paint a false picture. A **biased sample** does not accurately reflect the population from which it was drawn. Surveys done by magazines, websites, and online information services can be quite biased. Surveys on the use of guns done by *O: The Oprah Magazine* and *Guns and Ammo* magazine would probably produce very different results—neither of which would represent the general population. That's why psychologists using the survey method go to great lengths to ensure that their samples are representative. Fortunately, people can often be polled by telephone or the Internet, which makes it easier to obtain large samples. Even if one person out of three refuses to answer survey questions, the results are still likely to be valid (Hutchinson, 2004).

■ **TABLE 1.6 Comparison of Psychological Research Methods**

	Advantages	Disadvantages
Experimental Method	Clear cause-and-effect relationships can be identified; powerful controlled observations can be staged; no need to wait for natural event.	May be somewhat artificial; some natural behavior not easily studied in laboratory (field experiments may avoid these objections).
Naturalistic Observation	Behavior is observed in a natural setting; much information is obtained, and hypotheses and questions for additional research can be formed.	Little or no control is possible; observed behavior may be altered by the presence of the observer; observations may be biased; causes cannot be conclusively identified.
Correlational Method	Demonstrates the existence of relationships; allows prediction; can be used in lab, clinic, or natural setting.	Little or no control is possible; relationships may be coincidental; cause-and-effect relationships cannot be confirmed.
Clinical Method	Takes advantage of "natural clinical trials" and allows investigation of rare or unusual problems or events.	Little or no control is possible; does not provide a control group for comparison; subjective interpretation is often necessary; a single case may be misleading or unrepresentative.
Survey Method	Allows information about large numbers of people to be gathered; can address questions not answered by other approaches.	Obtaining a representative sample is critical and can be difficult to do; answers may be inaccurate; people may not do what they say or say what they do.

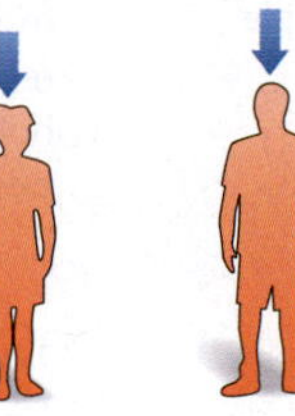
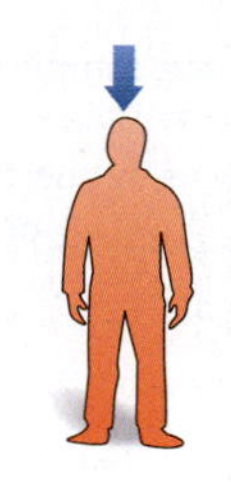
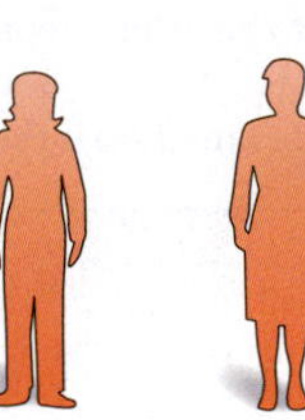
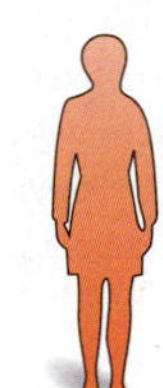
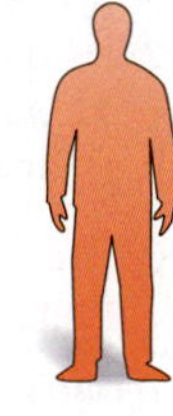

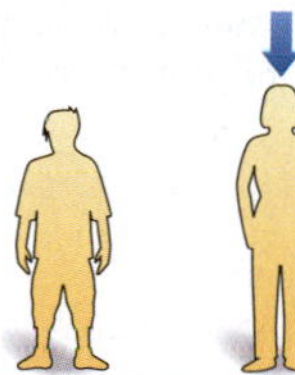

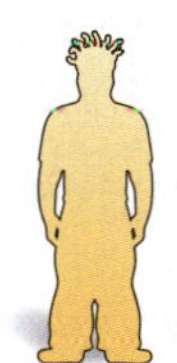
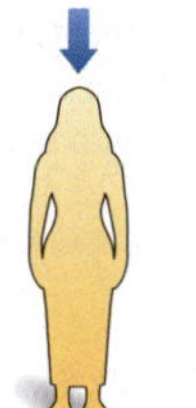

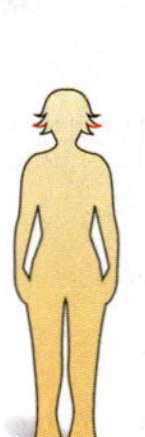

● **Figure 1.12** If you were conducting a survey in which a person's height might be an important variable, the upper, nonrandom sample would be very unrepresentative. The lower sample, selected using a table of random numbers, better represents the group as a whole.

Internet Surveys

Recently, psychologists have started doing surveys and experiments on the Internet. Web-based research can be a cost-effective way to reach very large groups of people, especially people who are not easy to survey any other way (Smyth et al., 2010). Internet studies have provided interesting information about topics such as anger, decision making, racial prejudice, what disgusts people, religion, sexual attitudes, and much more. Biased samples can limit web-based research (because it isn't easy to control who actually answers your online questionnaire), but psychologists are getting better at gathering valid information with it (Birnbaum, 2004; Lewis, Watson, & White, 2009).

Social Desirability

Even well-designed surveys may be limited by another problem. If a psychologist were to ask you detailed questions about your sexual history and current sexual behavior, how accurate would your replies be? Would you exaggerate? Would you be embarrassed? Replies to survey questions are not always accurate or truthful. Many people show a distinct *courtesy bias* (a tendency to give "polite" or socially desirable answers). For example, answers to questions concerning sex, drinking or drug use, income, and church attendance tend to be less than truthful. Likewise, the week after an election, more people will say they voted than actually did (Hutchinson, 2004).

Summary

Despite their limitations, surveys frequently produce valuable information. For instance, one survey explored the vulnerability of U.S. retail malls to terrorist attacks with the goal of improving our capacity to prevent and respond to an attack (Rigakos et al., 2009). To sum up, the survey method can be a powerful research tool. Like other methods, it has limitations, but new techniques and strategies are providing valuable information about our behavior (Kahneman et al., 2004).

Is so much emphasis on science really necessary in psychology? In a word, yes. As we have seen, science is a powerful way of asking questions about the world and getting trustworthy answers. (■ Table 1.6 summarizes many of the important ideas we have covered.)

Natural clinical test An accident or other natural event that allows the gathering of data on a psychological phenomenon of interest.

Survey In psychology, a public polling technique used to answer psychological questions.

Representative sample A small, randomly selected part of a larger population that accurately reflects characteristics of the whole population.

Population An entire group of animals or people belonging to a particular category (for example, all college students or all married women).

Biased sample A subpart of a larger population that does not accurately reflect characteristics of the whole population.

A Look Ahead

To help you get the most out of psychology, each chapter of this text includes a "Psychology in Action" section like the one that follows. There you will find ideas you can actually use, now or in the future. To complete the topics we have been discussing, let's take a critical look at information reported in the popular press. You should find this an interesting way to conclude our opening tour of psychology and its methods.

Knowledge Builder — Nonexperimental Research Methods

RECITE

1. Two major problems in naturalistic observation are the effects of the observer and observer bias. T or F?
2. The ____________________ error involves attributing human feelings and motives to animals.
3. Correlation typically does not demonstrate causation. T or F?
4. Which correlation coefficient represents the strongest relationship? *a.* −0.86 *b.* +0.66 *c.* +0.10 *d.* +0.09
5. Case studies can often be thought of as natural tests and are frequently used by clinical psychologists. T or F?
6. For the survey method to be valid, a representative sample of people must be polled. T or F?
7. A problem with the survey method is that answers to questions may not always be ____________________ or ____________________.

REFLECT

Think Critically

8. A psychologist conducting a survey at a shopping mall (The Gallery of Wretched Excess) flips a coin before stopping passersby. If the coin shows heads, he interviews the person; if it shows tails, he skips that person. Has the psychologist obtained a random sample?
9. Attributing mischievous motives to a car that is not working properly is a thinking error similar to anthropomorphizing. T or F?

Self-Reflect

Google "critter cam" and find one you can watch. What species are you watching? What behaviors might you observe and record?

See if you can identify at least one positive correlation and one negative correlation that involves human behavior.

Have you ever known someone who suffered a brain injury or disease? How did his or her behavior change? Was the change clear-cut enough to serve as a natural clinical test?

Have you ever been asked to complete a survey? Did you do it or did you refuse? If you refused, do you think your refusal influenced the final results of the survey? What would it say about accuracy if lots of people refused to complete the survey? If you completed the survey, were you honest about your answers? What would it say about accuracy if lots of people refused to answer accurately?

Answers: 1. T **2.** anthropomorphic **3.** T **4.** *a* **5.** T **6.** T **7.** accurate, truthful **8.** The psychologist's coin flips *might* produce a reasonably good sample of people *at the mall*. The real problem is that people who go to the mall may be mostly from one part of town, from upper income groups, or from some other nonrepresentative group. The psychologist's sample is likely to be seriously flawed. **9.** Yes. It appears to be difficult for humans to resist thinking of other species and even machines in human terms.

Psychology in Action

Psychology in the Media—Are You Fluent in Klingon?

Gateway Question 1.11: *How good is psychological information found in the popular media?*

Psychology is a popular topic in contemporary media. Unfortunately, much of what you encounter is based on entertainment value rather than critical thinking or science. Here are some suggestions for separating high-quality information from misleading fiction.

Suggestion 1: Be skeptical. Have you ever played the game called "telephone" or "pass it down"? One person whispers a sentence to someone else who, in turn, whispers it on down the line. Usually, when the person at the end of the line repeats the message it has been humorously distorted. Similarly, modern media—especially the Internet—function as a giant "echo chamber" awash with rumors, hoaxes, half-truths, and urban legends like the one about giant alligators living in New York sewers (Hughes, 2008).

One of our all-time favorites was a story about the health department in Oregon seeking a Klingon interpreter for mental health patients who only spoke in the fictional language used on the *Star Trek* television series. This tale started when a newspaper reported that Klingon was on a list of languages that some psychiatric patients claimed they could speak. The article specifically noted that "in reality, no patient has yet tried to communicate in Klingon." Nevertheless, as the story echoed around the web, the idea that Oregon was looking for someone fluent in Klingon had become a "fact" (O'Neill, 2003).

Reports in the popular media tend to be made uncritically and with a definite bias toward reporting "astonishing" findings and telling interesting stories. Remember, saying, "That's incredible" means, "That's not believable"—which is often true.

Suggestion 2: Consider the source of information. It should come as no surprise that information used to sell a product often reflects a desire for profit rather than the objective truth. Here is a typical advertising claim: "Government tests prove that no sleep medicine is stronger or more effective than Coma." A statement like this usually means that there was *no difference* between Coma and the other products tested. No other sleep aid was stronger or more effective. But none was weaker either.

Remember that psychological services may be merchandised as well. Keep the source in mind when reading the claims of makers of home biofeedback machines, sleep-learning devices, subliminal CDs, and the like. Be wary of expensive courses that promise instant mental health and happiness, increased efficiency, memory, extrasensory perception (ESP) or psychic ability, control of the unconscious mind, an end to smoking, and so on. Usually they are promoted with a few testimonials and many unsupported claims (Lilienfeld, Ruscio, & Lynn, 2008).

Psychic claims should be viewed with special caution. Google magician James Randi's Million Dollar Challenge. Randi has long offered $1,000,000 to anyone demonstrating such abilities under controlled conditions. Did you know that no one has even passed the preliminary tests yet?

Stage mentalists make a living by deceiving the public. Understandably, they are highly interested in promoting belief in their nonexistent powers. The same is true of the so-called psychic advisers promoted in TV commercials. These charlatans make use of the Barnum effect (the tendency to consider personal descriptions accurate if they are stated in general terms) to create an illusion that they know private information about the people who call them (Nickell, 2001).

Suggestion 3: Beware of oversimplifications, especially those motivated by monetary gain. Courses or programs that offer a "new personality in three sessions," "six steps to love and fulfillment in marriage," or some newly discovered "secret for unlocking the powers of the mind and the universe" should be immediately suspect.

An excellent example of oversimplification is provided by websites devoted to a video that promises to reveal "the secret to unlimited joy, health, money, relationships, love, youth: everything you have ever wanted." According to these sites, all you need to do is put your desires out to the universe and the universe must respond by granting your wishes. And all it will cost you is the price of ordering the video. (It's no secret that the promoters are the real winners in this game.)

Suggestion 4: Remember, "for example" is no proof. After reading this chapter you should be sensitive to the danger of selecting single examples. If you read, "Law student passes state bar exam using sleep-learning device," don't rush out to buy one. Systematic research showed long ago that these devices are of little or no value (Druckman & Bjork, 1994). A corollary to this suggestion is to ask: Are the reported observations important or widely applicable? Similarly, in 2002, baseball pitcher Randy Johnson began wearing a particular metal-impregnated twisted rope necklace designed to "stabilize the electricity flow through the body." By the 2010 World Series, hundreds of players were superstitiously wearing one, all without any scientific explanation of, or evidence for, their efficacy (Carroll, 2010).

Examples, anecdotes, single cases, and testimonials are all potentially deceptive. According to numerous testimonials, believers in the power of the "secret" described above have been showered with money, success, and happiness immediately after viewing the video. Unfortunately, such *individual cases* (or even several) tell us nothing about what is true *in general* (Stanovich, 2010). How many people *didn't* win the lottery after buying the video? How many people bought the "magic necklace" to no avail? Similarly, studies of large groups of people show that smoking increases the likelihood of lung cancer. It is less relevant if you know a lifelong heavy smoker who is 95 years old. The general finding is the one to remember.

Suggestion 5: Ask yourself if there was a control group. The key importance of a control group in any experiment is frequently overlooked by the unsophisticated—an error to which you are no longer susceptible. The popular media are full of reports of "experiments" performed without control groups: "Talking to Plants Speeds Growth," "Special Diet Controls Hyperactivity in Children," "Graduates of Firewalking Seminar Risk Their Soles."

Consider the last example for a moment. Expensive commercial courses have long been promoted to teach people to walk barefoot on hot coals. (Why anyone would want to do this is itself an interesting question.) Firewalkers supposedly protect their feet with a technique called "neurolinguistic programming." Many people have paid good money to learn the technique, and most do manage a quick walk on the coals. But is the technique necessary? And is anything remarkable happening? We need a comparison group.

Fortunately, physicist Bernard Leikind has provided one. Leikind showed with volunteers that anyone (with reasonably callused feet) can walk over a bed of coals without being burned. The reason is that the coals, which are light, fluffy carbon, transmit little heat when touched. The principle involved is similar to briefly putting your hand in a hot oven. If you touch a pan, you will be burned because metal transfers heat efficiently. But if your hand stays in the heated air you'll be fine because air transmits little heat (Kida, 2006; Mitchell, 1987). Mystery solved.

Felix Ordonez/Reuters/Landov

Firewalking is based on simple physics, not on any form of supernatural psychological control. The temperature of the coals may be as high as 1,200°F. However, coals are like the air in a hot oven: They are very inefficient at transferring heat during brief contact.

Suggestion 6: Look for errors in distinguishing between correlation and causation. As you now know, it is dangerous to presume that one thing *caused* another just because they are correlated. In spite of this, you will see many claims based on questionable correlations. Here's an example of mistaking correlation for causation: Jeanne Dixon, a well-known astrologer, once answered a group of prominent scientists—who had declared that there is no scientific foundation for astrology—by saying, "They would do well to check the records at their local police stations, where they will learn that the rate of violent crime rises and falls with lunar cycles." Dixon, of course, believes that the moon affects human behavior.

If it is true that violent crime is more frequent at certain times of the month, doesn't that prove her point? Far from it. Increased crime could be due to darker nights, the fact that many people expect others to act crazier, or any number of similar factors. Besides, direct studies of the alleged "lunar effect" have shown that it doesn't occur (Dowling, 2005). Moonstruck criminals, influenced by "a bad moon rising," are a fiction (Iosif & Ballon, 2005).

Suggestion 7: Be sure to distinguish between observation and inference. If you see a person *crying,* is it correct to assume that she or he is *sad?* Although it seems reasonable to make this assumption, it could easily be wrong. We can observe objectively that the person is crying, but to *infer* sadness may be in error. It could be that the individual has just peeled 5 pounds of onions. Or maybe he or she just won a million-dollar lottery or is trying contact lenses for the first time.

Psychologists, politicians, physicians, scientists, and other experts often go far beyond the available facts in their claims. This does not mean that their inferences, opinions, and interpretations have no value; the opinion of an expert on the causes of mental illness, criminal behavior, learning problems, or whatever can be revealing. But be careful to distinguish between fact and opinion.

Summary

We are all bombarded daily with such a mass of new information that it is difficult to absorb it. The available knowledge in an area like psychology, biology, or medicine is so vast that no single person can completely know and comprehend it. With this situation in mind, it becomes increasingly important that you become a critical, selective, and informed consumer of information (Lilienfeld et al., 2010).

Knowledge Builder: Psychology in the Media

RECITE

1. Popular media reports usually stress objective accuracy. T or F?
2. Stage mentalists and psychics often use deception in their "acts." T or F?
3. Blaming the lunar cycle for variations in the rate of violent crime is an example of mistaking correlation for causation. T or F?
4. If a psychology student uses a sleep-learning device to pass a midterm exam, it proves that the device works. T or F?

REFLECT

Think Critically

5. Mystics have shown that fresh eggs can be balanced on their large ends during the vernal equinox when the sun is directly over the equator, day and night are equal in length, and the world is in perfect balance. What is wrong with their observation?
6. Many parents believe that children become "hyperactive" when they eat too much sugar, and some early studies seemed to confirm this connection. However, we now know that eating sugar rarely has any effect on children. Why do you think that sugar appears to cause hyperactivity?

Self-Reflect

How actively do you evaluate and question claims found in the media? Could you be a more critical consumer of information? *Should* you be a more critical consumer of information?

Answers: 1. F **2.** T **3.** T **4.** F **5.** The mystics have neglected to ask if eggs can be balanced at other times. They can be balanced any time you like. The lack of a control group gives the illusion that something amazing is happening, but the equinox has nothing to do with egg balancing (Halpern, 2003). **6.** This is another case of mistaking correlation for causation. Children who are hyperactive may eat more sugar (and other foods) to fuel their frenetic activity levels.

Chapter in Review Gateways to Psychology

Gateway QUESTIONS REVISITED

1.1 *What is psychology and what are its goals?*

1.1.1 Psychology is the science of behavior and mental processes.

1.1.2 Psychologists are professionals who create and apply psychological knowledge.

1.1.3 Psychologists engage in critical thinking as they systematically gather and analyze empirical evidence to answer questions about behavior.

1.1.4 Psychologists gather scientific data in order to describe, understand, predict, and control behavior.

1.2 *What is critical thinking?*

1.2.1 Critical thinking is central to the scientific method, to psychology, and to the everyday understanding of behavior.

1.2.2 Critical thinking in psychology is a type of open-minded reflection involving the support of beliefs with scientific explanation and observation.

1.2.3 The validity of beliefs can be judged through logical analysis, evaluating evidence *for* and *against* the claim, and evaluating the *quality* of the evidence.

1.2.4 Critical thinkers seek to falsify claims by making up their own minds rather than automatically taking the word of "experts."

1.3 *How does psychology differ from false explanations of behavior?*

1.3.1 Pseudopsychologies are unfounded systems that are frequently confused with valid psychology.

1.3.2 Unlike psychology, pseudopsychologies change little over time because followers seek evidence that appears to confirm their beliefs and avoid evidence that contradicts their beliefs.

1.3.3 Belief in pseudopsychologies is based in part on uncritical acceptance, confirmation bias, and the Barnum effect.

1.4 *How is the scientific method applied in psychological research?*

1.4.1 In the scientific method, systematic observation is used to test hypotheses about behavior and mental events. A powerful way to observe the natural world and draw valid conclusions, scientific research provides the highest quality information about behavior and mental events.

1.4.2 Psychological research begins by defining problems and proposing hypotheses. Concepts must be defined operationally before they can be studied empirically.

1.4.3 Next, researchers gather evidence to test hypotheses. The results of scientific studies are made public so that others can evaluate them, learn from them, and use them to suggest new hypotheses, which lead to further research.

1.4.4 Psychological research must be done ethically, in order to protect the rights, dignity, and welfare of participants.

1.5 *How did the field of psychology emerge?*

1.5.1 The field of psychology emerged 130 years ago when researchers began to directly study and observe psychological events.

1.5.2 The first psychological laboratory was established in Germany in 1879 by Wilhelm Wundt, who studied conscious experience.

1.5.3 The first school of thought in psychology was structuralism, a kind of "mental chemistry" based on introspection.

1.5.4 Structuralism was followed by functionalism, behaviorism, and Gestalt psychology.

1.5.5 Psychodynamic approaches, such as Freud's psychoanalytic theory, emphasize the unconscious origins of behavior.

1.5.6 Humanistic psychology accentuates subjective experience, human potentials, and personal growth.

1.5.7 Because most of the early psychologists were Caucasian men, bias was inadvertently introduced into psychological research. Today, more women and minorities are becoming psychologists and being studied as research participants.

1.6 *What are the contemporary perspectives in psychology?*

1.6.1 Three complementary streams of thought in modern psychology are the biological perspective, including biopsychology and evolutionary psychology; the psychological perspective, including behaviorism, cognitive psychology, the psychodynamic approach, and humanism; and the sociocultural perspective.

1.6.2 Psychologists have recently begun to formally study positive aspects of human behavior, or positive psychology.

1.6.3 Most of what we think, feel, and do is influenced by the social and cultural worlds in which we live.

1.6.4 Today, there is an eclectic blending of many viewpoints within psychology.

1.7 *What are the major specialties in psychology?*

1.7.1 There are dozens of specialties in psychology including biopsychology, clinical, cognitive, community, comparative, consumer, counseling, cultural, developmental, educational, engineering, environmental, evolutionary, forensic, gender, health, industrial-organizational, learning, medical, personality, school, sensation and perception, and social psychology.

1.7.2 Psychological research may be basic or applied.

1.7.3 Psychologists may be directly interested in animal behavior, or they may study animals as models of human behavior.

1.7.4 Although psychologists, psychiatrists, psychoanalysts, counselors, and psychiatric social workers all work in the field of mental health, their training and methods differ considerably.

1.8 *How is an experiment performed?*

1.8.1 Experiments involve two or more groups of subjects that differ only with regard to the independent variable. Effects on the dependent variable are then measured. All other conditions (extraneous variables) are held constant.

1.8.2 Since the independent variable is the only difference between the experimental group and the control group, it is the only possible cause of a change in the dependent variable

1.8.3 The design of experiments allows cause-and-effect connections to be clearly identified.

1.8.4 To be taken seriously, the results of an experiment must be statistically significant (they would occur very rarely by chance alone). It also strengthens a result if the research can be replicated or if it contributes to the conclusions of a meta-analysis.

1.9 *What is a double-blind experiment?*

1.9.1 Research participant bias is a problem in some studies; the placebo effect is a source of research participant bias in experiments involving drugs.

1.9.2 A related problem is researcher bias. Researcher expectations can create a self-fulfilling prophecy, in which a participant changes in the direction of the expectation.

1.9.3 In a double-blind experiment, neither the research participants nor the researchers collecting data know who was in the experimental group or the control group, allowing valid conclusions to be drawn.

1.10 *What nonexperimental research methods do psychologists use?*

1.10.1 Psychologists also rely on naturalistic observation, the correlational method, case studies, and the survey method.

1.10.2 Unlike controlled experiments, nonexperimental methods usually cannot demonstrate cause-and-effect relationships.

1.10.3 Naturalistic observation is a starting place in many investigations. Two problems with naturalistic observation are the effects of the observer on the observed and observer bias.

1.10.4 In the correlational method, relationships between two traits, responses, or events are measured and a correlation coefficient is computed to gauge the strength of the relationship. Relationships in psychology may be positive or negative. Correlations allow prediction but do not demonstrate cause and effect.

1.10.5 Case studies provide insights into human behavior that can't be gained by other methods.

1.10.6 In the survey method, people in a representative sample are asked a series of carefully worded questions. Obtaining a representative sample of people is crucial when the survey method is used to study large populations.

1.11 *How good is psychological information found in the popular media?*

1.11.1 Information in the mass media varies greatly in quality and accuracy and should be approached with skepticism and caution.

1.11.2 It is essential to critically evaluate information from popular sources (or from any source, for that matter) in order to separate facts from fallacies.

1.11.3 Problems in media reports are often related to biased or unreliable sources of information, uncontrolled observation, misleading correlations, false inferences, oversimplification, use of single examples, and unrepeatable results.

MEDIA RESOURCES

Web Resources

Internet addresses frequently change. To find an up-to-date list of URLs for the sites listed here, visit your Psychology CourseMate.

Definition of "Psychology" Provides definitions of *psychology* and *psychologist.*

Self-Quiz on Psychology and Science. A 10-item online test (with answers) about psychology and science.

What is Psychology? Discusses psychology as a science, with links to other articles about various branches of psychology.

Critical Thinking in Everyday Life: 9 Strategies. Some useful critical thinking strategies, along with many other articles on aspects of critical thinking.

Skeptic's Dictionary Check out Robert Carroll's skeptical view of all things pseudoscientific.

The Power of Belief Streaming video of Dr. Michael Shermer, of the Skeptics Society, discussing skepticism and explaining why we are vulnerable to believing weird things.

Today in the History of Psychology Events in the history of psychology by the date, including podcasts.

Classics in the History of Psychology Original articles by a wide range of psychologists from Allport to Yerkes, including Sigmund Freud, B. F. Skinner, and Carl Rogers.

Women's Intellectual Contributions to the Field of Psychology Information about women's contributions to the field of psychology from a historical perspective.

Divisions of the American Psychological Association The difference specialties in psychology.

Careers in Psychology Page Marky Lloyd's Careers in Psychology Page.

For Students of Psychology Information for students interested in psychology from the American Psychological Association.

The Simple Experiment Description of a basic two-group experimental design.

Ethical Principles of Psychologists and Code of Conduct The full text of the ethical principles that guide professional psychologists.

Placebo Effects Read more about the power of placebo effects.

Psychological Research on the Net Find and complete a survey study.

The Jane Goodall Institute Information about Goodall's work at Gombe, in Tanzania, where she has studied and protected wild chimpanzees for over 40 years.

Research Methods and the Correlation Explore different research methods in psychology.

That's Infotainment! Article about sensationalism in the news media.

The Oregon UFO Wave That Wasn't A discussion of the role of media in a wave of UFO sightings in 1896-1897.

Psychology and the News Media: Reflections on a Ten Year Initiative Article on the presentation of psychology in the news media.

Interactive Learning

Log in to **CengageBrain** to access the resources your instructor requires. For this book, you can access:

CourseMate brings course concepts to life with interactive learning, study, and exam preparation tools that support the printed textbook. A textbook-specific website, ***Psychology CourseMate*** includes an ***integrated interactive eBook*** and other ***interactive learning tools*** including quizzes, flashcards, videos, and more.

CENGAGE**NOW**™

CengageNOW is an easy-to-use online resource that helps you study in less time to get the grade you want—NOW. Take a pre-test for this chapter and receive a personalized study plan based on your results that will identify the topics you need to review and direct you to online resources to help you master those topics. Then take a post-test to help you determine the concepts you have mastered and what you will need to work on. If your textbook does not include an access code card, go to CengageBrain.com to gain access.

WebTUTOR™

More than just an interactive study guide, **WebTutor** is an anytime, anywhere customized learning solution with an eBook, keeping you connected to your textbook, instructor, and classmates.

If your professor has assigned **Aplia** homework:

1. Sign in to your account.
2. Complete the corresponding homework exercises as required by your professor.
3. When finished, click "Grade It Now" to see which areas you have mastered and which need more work, and for detailed explanations of every answer.

Visit www.cengagebrain.com to access your account and purchase materials.

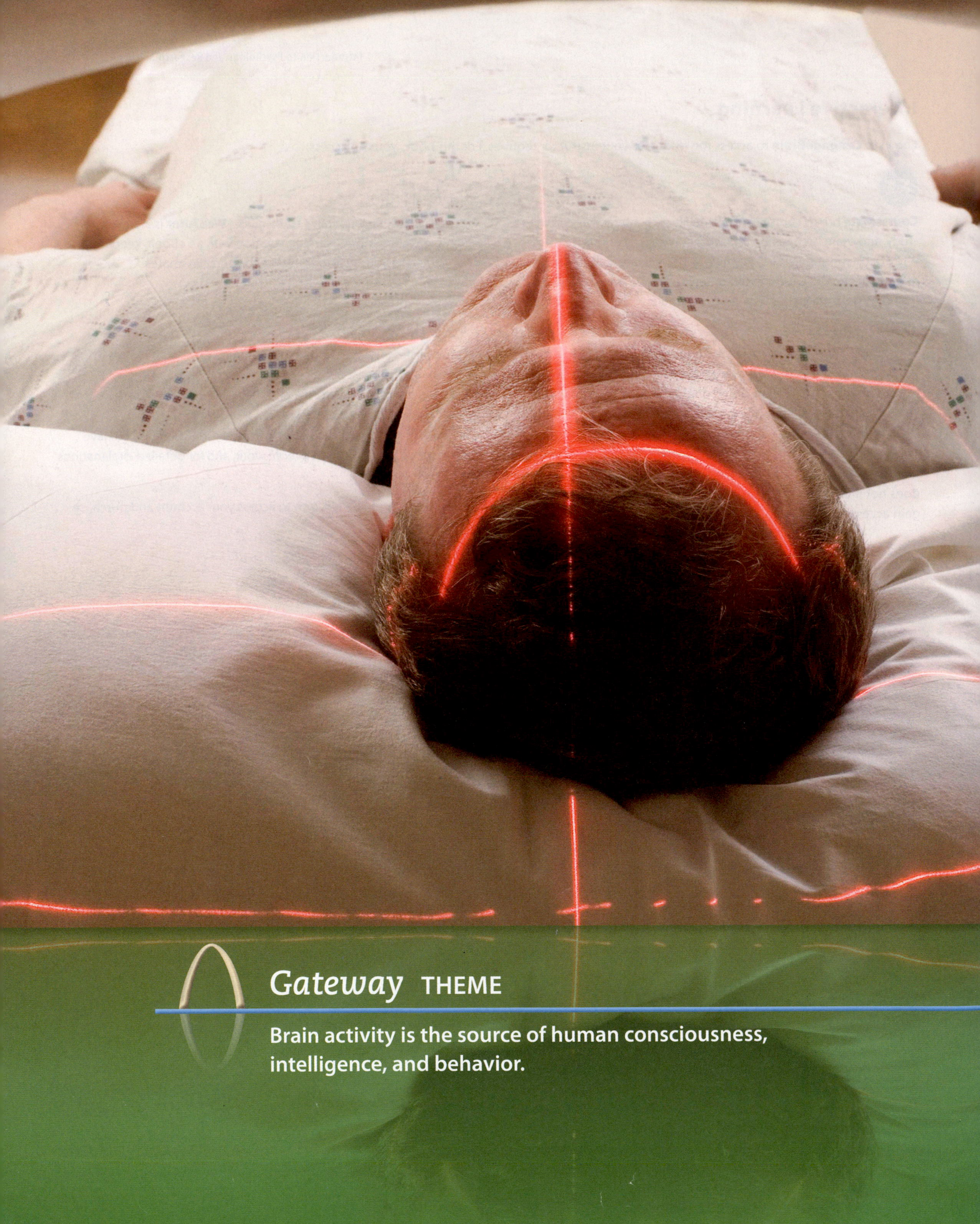

Gateway THEME

Brain activity is the source of human consciousness, intelligence, and behavior.

2 Brain and Behavior

A Stroke of Bad Luck

One morning Bryan Kolb lost his left hand. Up early to feed his cat, he could not see his hand, or anything else to his upper left side. Kolb, a Canadian neuroscientist, instantly realized that he had suffered a stroke at a specific location on the right side of his brain. (A stroke occurs when an artery carrying blood in the brain bleeds or becomes blocked, causing some brain tissue to die.) He drove to the hospital where he argued with the doctors about his own diagnosis. He was right, of course! He eventually resumed his career and even wrote a fascinating account of his own case (Kolb, 1990).

We don't normally notice the central role the brain plays in all that is human. But a stroke or other brain injury can change that in a flash. Almost instantly, victims realize that something is wrong. You would, too, if you suddenly found that you couldn't move, feel parts of your body, see, or speak. However, some brain injuries are not so obvious. Many involve less dramatic, but equally disabling, changes in personality, thinking, judgment, or emotions.

Your 3-pound brain is wrinkled like a walnut, the size of a grapefruit, and the texture of tofu. The next time you are in a market that sells beef brains, stop and have a look. What you will see is similar to your own brain, only smaller. How could such a squishy little blob of tissue allow us to become neuroscientists? To make music of exquisite beauty? To seek a cure for cancer? To fall in love? Or to read a book like this one?

Each of the billions of neurons—or nerve cells—in your brain is linked to thousands of others. The resulting network allows you to process immense amounts of information. In fact, there may be more *possible* pathways between the neurons in your brain than there are stars in the visible universe! Undeniably, the human brain is the most amazing of all computers. Let's visit this fascinating realm.

Gateway QUESTIONS

- *2.1 How do neurons operate and communicate?*
- *2.2 What are the major parts of the nervous system?*
- *2.3 How are different parts of the brain identified and what do they do?*
- *2.4 How do the left and right hemispheres differ and what are the different functions of the lobes of the cerebral cortex?*
- *2.5 What are the major parts of the subcortex?*
- *2.6 Does the glandular system affect behavior?*
- *2.7 In what ways do left- and right-handed individuals differ?*

Neurons—Building a "Biocomputer"

Gateway Question 2.1: *How do neurons operate and communicate?*

The brain consists of some 100 billion **neurons** (NOOR-ons), or individual nerve cells. In fact, who you are can be traced back to electrical impulses flashing through the spidery branches of neurons within your brain. Although these neurons may seem far removed from daily life, everything you think, feel, and do begins with these tiny cells (Banich & Compton, 2011). Your 100 billions of neurons are accompanied by about the same number of *glial cells*, cells that support neurons in a variety of ways (Carlson, 2010). Neurons carry input from the senses to the brain, where the input is processed. Neurons also carry output from the brain in order to activate muscles and glands. Yet, a single neuron is not very smart—it takes many just to make you blink. Literally billions of neurons may be involved when a singer like Lady Gaga sings a tune.

Your brainpower arises because individual neurons link to one another in spidery webs. Each neuron receives messages from many others and sends its own message on to many others. When neurons form vast networks, they produce intelligence and consciousness. Let's see how neurons operate and how the nervous system is "wired."

Parts of a Neuron

What does a neuron look like? What are its main parts? No two neurons are exactly alike, but most have four basic parts (● Figure 2.1). The **dendrites** (DEN-drytes), which look like tree roots, are neuron fibers that receive messages from other neurons. The **soma** (SOH-mah), or cell body, does the same. In addition, the soma sends messages of its own (via nerve impulses) down a thin fiber called the **axon** (AK-sahn).

Some axons are only 0.1 millimeter long. (That's about the width of a pencil line.) Others stretch up to a meter through the nervous system. (From the base of your spine to your big toe, for instance.) Like miniature cables, axons carry messages through the brain and nervous system. Altogether, your brain contains about 3 million miles of axons (Breedlove, Watson, & Rosenzweig, 2010).

Axons "branch out" into smaller fibers ending in bulb-shaped **axon terminals**. By forming connections with the dendrites and somas of other neurons, axon terminals allow information to pass from neuron to neuron.

Now let's summarize with a metaphor. Imagine that you are standing in a long line of people who are holding hands. A person on the far left end of the line wants to silently send a message to the person on the right end. She does this by pressing the hand of the person to her right, who presses the hand of the person to his right, and so on. The message arrives at your left hand (your dendrites). You decide whether to pass it on. (You are the soma.) The message goes out through your right arm (the axon). With your right hand (the axon terminals), you squeeze the hand of the person to your right, and the message moves on.

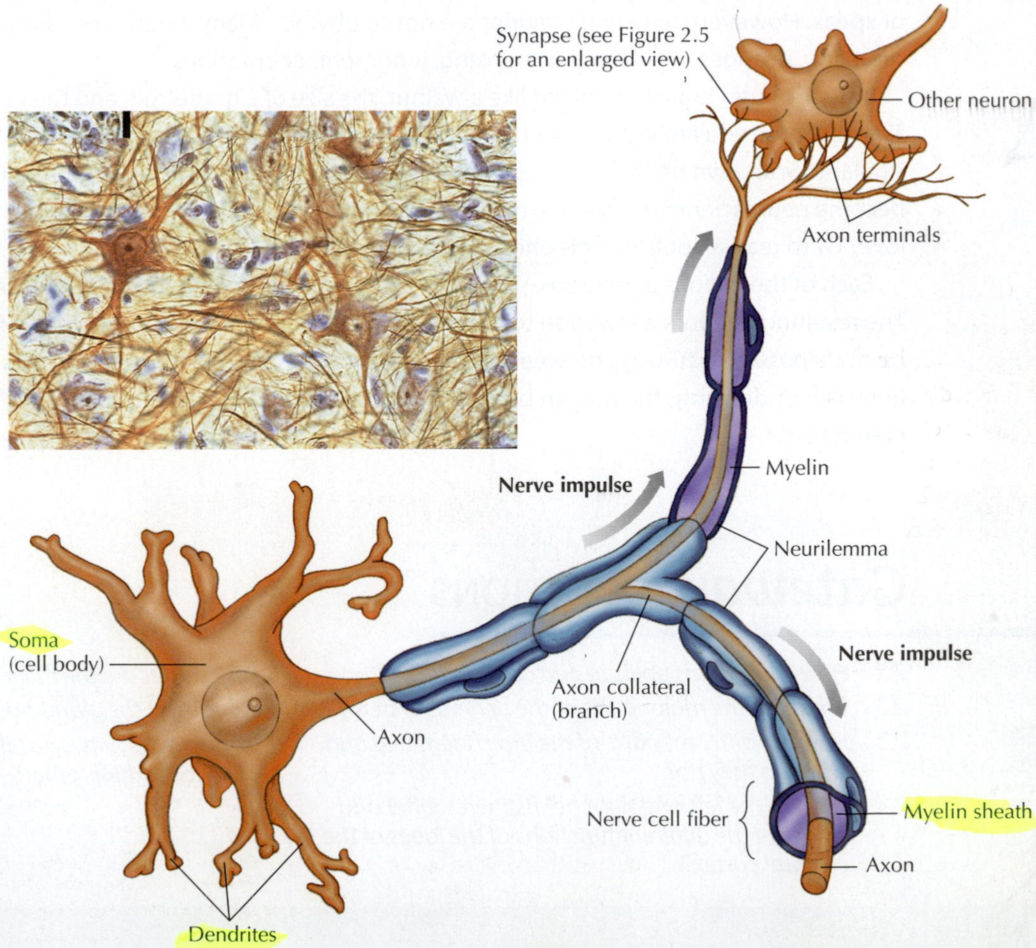

The Nerve Impulse

Electrically charged molecules called *ions* (EYE-ons) are found inside each neuron. Other ions lie outside the neuron. Some ions have a positive electrical charge, whereas others have a negative

● Figure 2.1 A neuron, or nerve cell. In the right foreground you can see a nerve cell fiber in cross section. The upper left photo gives a more realistic picture of the shape of neurons. Nerve impulses usually travel from the dendrites and soma to the branching ends of the axon. The nerve cell shown here is a motor neuron. The axons of motor neurons stretch from the brain and spinal cord to muscles or glands of the body.

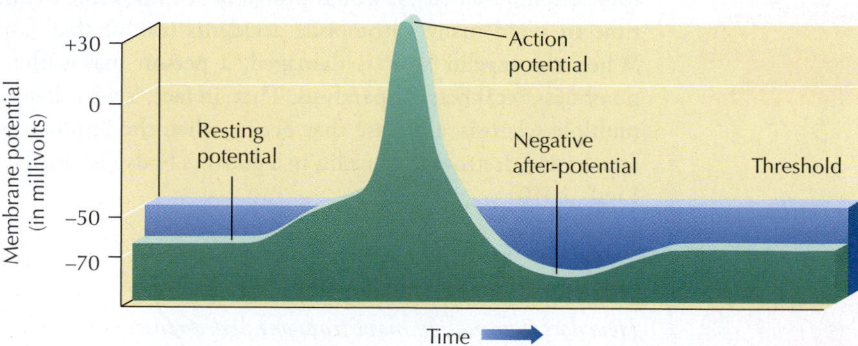

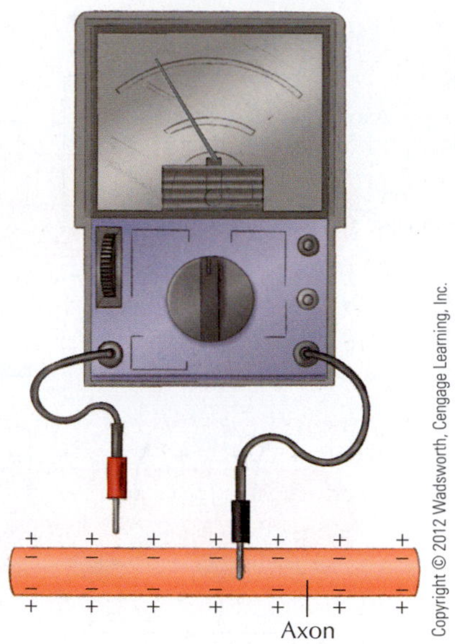

● **Figure 2.2** Electrical probes placed inside and outside an axon measure its activity. (The scale is exaggerated here. Such measurements require ultra-small electrodes, as described in this chapter.) The inside of an axon at rest is about −60 to −70 millivolts, compared with the outside. Electrochemical changes in a neuron generate an action potential. When sodium ions (Na^+) that have a positive charge rush into the cell, its interior briefly becomes positive. This is the action potential. After the action potential, positive potassium ions (K^+) flow out of the axon and restore its negative charge. (See Figure 2.3 for further explanation.)

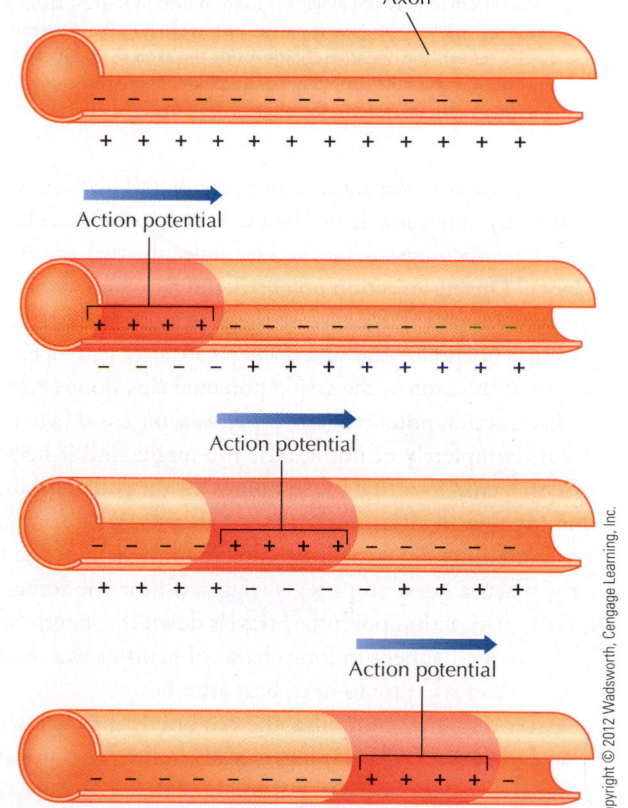

● **Figure 2.3** The inside of an axon normally has a negative electrical charge. The fluid surrounding an axon is normally positive. As an action potential passes along the axon, these charges reverse so that the interior of the axon briefly becomes positive. This process is described in more detail in Figure 2.4.

1. In its resting state, the axon has a negatively charged interior.
2. During an action potential, positively charged atoms (ions) rush into the axon. This briefly changes the electrical charge inside the axon from negative to positive. Simultaneously, the charge outside the axon becomes negative.
3. The action potential advances as positive and negative charges reverse in a moving zone of electrical activity that sweeps down the axon.
4. After an action potential passes, positive ions rapidly flow out of the axon to quickly restore its negative charge. An outward flow of additional positive ions returns the axon to its resting state.

charge. When a neuron is inactive (or resting), more of these "plus" charges exist outside the neuron and more "minus" charges exist inside. As a result, the inside of each resting neuron in your brain has an electrical charge of about −60 to −70 millivolts at the axon. (A millivolt is one thousandth of a volt.) This charge allows each neuron in your brain to act like a tiny biological battery (● Figure 2.2).

The electrical charge of an inactive neuron is called its **resting potential**. But neurons seldom get much rest: Messages arriving from other neurons raise and lower the resting potential. If the electrical charge rises to about −50 millivolts, the neuron will reach its **threshold**, or trigger point for firing (see ● Figure 2.2). It's as if the neuron says, "Ah ha! It's time to send a message to my neighbors." When a neuron reaches its threshold, an **action potential**, or nerve impulse, sweeps down the axon at up to 200 miles per hour (● Figure 2.3). That may seem fast, but it still takes at least a split second to react. That's one reason why hitting a 100-mile-per-hour professional baseball pitch is so difficult.

Neuron An individual nerve cell.
Dendrites Neuron fibers that receive incoming messages.
Soma The main body of a neuron or other cell.
Axon Fiber that carries information away from the cell body of a neuron.
Axon terminals Bulb-shaped structures at the ends of axons that form synapses with the dendrites and somas of other neurons.
Resting potential The electrical charge of a neuron at rest.
Threshold The point at which a nerve impulse is triggered.
Action potential The nerve impulse.

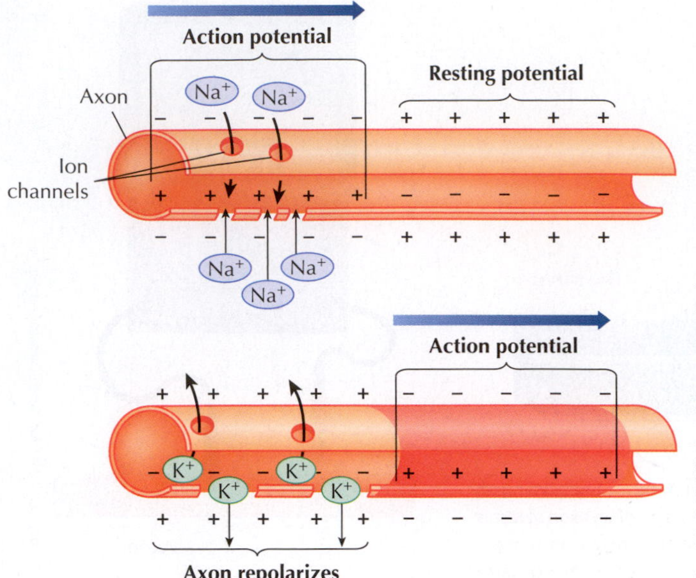

• Figure 2.4 The interior of an axon. The right end of the top axon is at rest. Thus, it has a negative charge inside. An action potential begins when ion channels open and sodium ions (Na^+) rush into the axon. In this drawing, the action potential would travel from left to right along the axon. In the lower axon, the action potential has moved to the right. After it passes, potassium ions (K^+) flow out of the axon. This quickly renews the negative charge inside the axon so that it can fire again. Sodium ions that enter the axon during an action potential are pumped out more slowly. Removing them restores the original resting potential.

What happens during an action potential? The axon membrane is pierced by tiny tunnels or "holes," called **ion channels**. Normally, these tiny openings are blocked by molecules that act like "gates" or "doors." During an action potential, the gates pop open. This allows sodium ions (Na^+) to rush into the axon (Carlson, 2010). The channels first open near the soma. Then gate after gate opens down the length of the axon as the action potential zips along (• Figure 2.4).

Each action potential is an *all-or-nothing event* (a nerve impulse occurs completely or not at all). You might find it helpful to picture the axon as a row of dominoes set on end. Tipping over the dominoes is an all-or-nothing act. Once the first domino drops, a wave of falling blocks will zip rapidly to the end of the line. Similarly, when a nerve impulse is triggered near the soma, a wave of activity (the action potential) travels down the length of the axon. This is what happens in long chains of neurons as a dancer's brain tells her feet what to do next, beat after beat.

After each nerve impulse, the cell briefly dips below its resting level and becomes less willing or ready to fire. This **negative after-potential** occurs because potassium ions (K^+) flow out of the neuron while the membrane gates are open (• Figure 2.4). After a nerve impulse, ions flow both into and out of the axon, recharging it for more action. In our model, it takes an instant for the row of dominoes to be set up again. Soon, however, the axon is ready for another wave of activity.

Saltatory Conduction

The axons of some neurons (such as the one pictured in Figure 2.1) are coated with a fatty layer called **myelin** (MY-eh-lin). Small gaps in the myelin help nerve impulses move faster. Instead of passing down the entire length of the axon, the action potential leaps from gap to gap, a process called **saltatory conduction.** (The Latin word *saltare* means to jump or leap.) Without the added speed of salutatory action potentials, it would probably be impossible to brake in time to avoid many automobile accidents (or hit that fastball). When the myelin layer is damaged, a person may suffer from numbness, weakness, or paralysis. That, in fact, is what happens in multiple sclerosis, a disease that occurs when the immune system attacks and destroys the myelin in a person's body (Khan, Tselis, & Lisak, 2010).

Synapses and Neurotransmitters

How does information move from one neuron to another? The nerve impulse is primarily electrical. That's why electrically stimulating the brain affects behavior. To prove the point, researcher José Delgado once entered a bullring with a cape and a radio transmitter. The bull charged. Delgado retreated. At the last instant the speeding bull stopped short. Why? Because Delgado had placed radio activated electrodes (metal wires) deep within the bull's brain. These, in turn, stimulated "control centers" that brought the bull to a halt (Horgan, 2005).

In contrast to nerve impulses, communication *between* neurons is *chemical.* The microscopic space between two neurons, over which messages pass, is called a **synapse** (SIN-aps) (• Figure 2.5). When an action potential reaches the tips of the axon terminals, **neurotransmitters** (NOOR-oh-TRANS-mit-ers) are released into the synaptic gap. Neurotransmitters are chemicals that alter activity in neurons.

Let's return to our metaphor of people standing in a line. To be more accurate, you and the others shouldn't be holding hands. Instead, each person should have a squirt gun in his or her right hand. To pass along a message, you would squirt the left hand of the

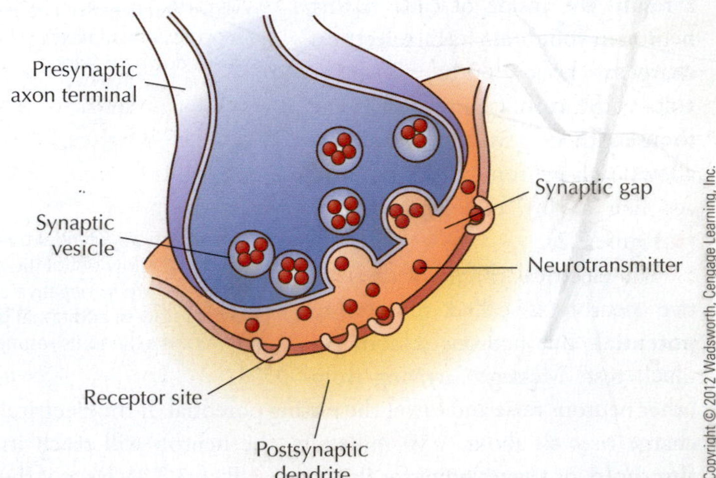

• Figure 2.5 A highly magnified view of a synapse. Neurotransmitters are stored in tiny sacs called synaptic vesicles (VES-ih-kels). When a nerve impulse reaches the end of an axon, the vesicles move to the surface and release neurotransmitters. These molecules cross the synaptic gap to affect the next neuron. The size of the gap is exaggerated here; it is actually only about one millionth of an inch. Some transmitter molecules excite the next neuron and some inhibit its activity.

TABLE 2.1 Major Neurotransmitters

Neurotransmitter	Main Mode of Action	Function in the Brain	Effects of Imbalance
Acetylcholine	Excitatory neurotransmitter	Participates in movement, autonomic function, learning, and memory.	Deficiency may play a role in Alzheimer's disease.
Dopamine	Excitatory neurotransmitter	Participates in motivation, reward, and planning of behavior.	Deficiency may lead to Parkinson's disease, reduced feelings of pleasure; excess may lead to schizophrenia.
GABA	Inhibitory neurotransmitter	Major inhibitory effect in the central nervous system; participates in moods.	Deficiency may lead to anxiety.
Glutamate	Excitatory neurotransmitter	Major excitatory effect in the central nervous system; participates in learning and memory.	Excess may lead to neuron death and autism; deficiency may lead to tiredness.
Norepinephrine	Excitatory neurotransmitter	Participates in arousal and vigilance, and mood.	Excess may lead to anxiety.
Serotonin	Inhibitory neurotransmitter	Participates in mood, appetite, and sleep.	Deficiency may lead to depression and/or anxiety.

(Adapted from Freberg, 2010; Kalat, 2009.)

person to your right. When that person notices this "message," he or she would squirt the left hand of the person to the right, and so on.

When chemical molecules cross over a synapse, they attach to special receiving areas on the next neuron (● Figure 2.5). These tiny **receptor sites** on the cell membrane are sensitive to neurotransmitters. The sites are found in large numbers on neuron cell bodies and dendrites. Muscles and glands have receptor sites, too.

Do neurotransmitters always trigger an action potential in the next neuron? No, but they do change the likelihood of an action potential in the next neuron. Some neurotransmitters *excite* the next neuron (move it closer to firing). Others *inhibit* it (make firing less likely). More than 100 neurotransmitter chemicals are found in the brain. Some examples are acetylcholine, dopamine, GABA, glutamate, norepinephrine, and serotonin (see ■ Table 2.1).

Why are there so many neurotransmitters? Some neurotransmitters are used by specific "pathways" that interlink regions of the brain. It is as if different pathways speak different languages. Perhaps this helps prevent confusing "crosstalk" or intermixing of messages. For example, the brain has a reward or "pleasure" system that mainly "speaks" dopamine (although other neurotransmitters are also found in the system) (Opland, Leinninger, & Myers, 2010; Salamone, 2007).

Slight variations in neurotransmitter function may be related to temperament differences in infancy and personality differences in adulthood (Ashton, 2007). Outright disturbances of any neurotransmitter can have serious consequences. For example, too much dopamine may cause schizophrenia (Di Forti, Lappin, & Murray, 2007), whereas too little serotonin may underlie depression (Merens et al., 2008).

Many drugs mimic, duplicate, or block neurotransmitters. For example, the chemical structure of cocaine is similar to that of dopamine. In the short run, cocaine can trigger an increase in dopamine in the reward system, resulting in a drug "high" (Briand et al., 2008). In the long run, the overuse of recreational drugs like cocaine overstimulates the reward system and disturbs dopamine function, resulting in drug addiction (Volkow et al., 2007).

As another example, the drug curare (cue-RAH-ree) causes paralysis. Acetylcholine (ah-SEET-ul-KOH-leen) normally activates muscles. By attaching to receptor sites on muscles, curare blocks acetylcholine, preventing the activation of muscle cells. As a result, a person or animal given curare cannot move—a fact known to South American Indians of the Amazon River Basin, who use curare as an arrow poison for hunting. Without acetylcholine, a baseball pitcher couldn't even move, much less throw a baseball.

Neural Regulators

More subtle brain activities are affected by chemicals called **neuropeptides** (NOOR-oh-PEP-tides). Neuropeptides do not carry messages directly. Instead, they *regulate* the activity of other neurons. By doing so, they affect memory, pain, emotion, pleasure, moods, hunger, sexual behavior, and other basic processes. For example, when you touch something hot, you jerk your hand away. The messages for this action are carried by neurotransmitters. At the same time, pain may cause the brain to release neuropeptides called *enkephalins* (en-KEF-ah-lins). These opiate-like neural regulators relieve pain and stress. Related neuropeptide chemicals called *endorphins* (en-DORF-ins) are released by the pituitary gland. Together, these chemicals reduce the pain so that it is not too disabling (Drolet et al., 2001).

Ion channels Tiny openings through the axon membrane.
Negative after-potential A drop in electrical charge below the resting potential.
Myelin A fatty layer coating some axons.
Saltatory conduction The process by which nerve impulses conducted down the axons of neurons coated with myelin jump from gap to gap in the myelin layer.
Synapse The microscopic space between two neurons, over which messages pass.
Neurotransmitter Any chemical released by a neuron that alters activity in other neurons.
Receptor sites Areas on the surface of neurons and other cells that are sensitive to neurotransmitters or hormones.
Neuropeptides Brain chemicals, such as enkephalins and endorphins, that regulate the activity of neurons.

We can now explain the painkilling effect of placebos (fake pills or injections); they raise endorphin levels (Stewart-Williams, 2004). A release of endorphins also seems to underlie "runner's high," masochism, acupuncture, and the euphoria sometimes associated with childbirth, painful initiation rites, and even sport parachuting (Janssen & Arntz, 2001). In each case, pain and stress cause the release of endorphins. In turn, these induce feelings of pleasure or euphoria similar to being "high" on morphine. People who say they are "addicted" to running may be closer to the truth than they realize. And more important, we may at last know why some hardy souls take hot saunas followed by cold showers! Ultimately, neural regulators may help explain depression, schizophrenia, drug addiction, and other puzzling topics.

BRIDGES

Read more in Chapter 4, pages 139–141, about how pain can sometimes produce feelings of relaxation or euphoria.

Neural Networks

Let's put together what we now know about the nerve impulse and synaptic transmission to see how **neural networks**, interlinked collections of neurons, process information in our brains. • Figure 2.6 shows a small part of a neural network. Five neurons synapse with a single neuron that, in turn, connects with three more neurons. At the point in time depicted in the diagram, the single neuron is receiving one stronger and two weaker excitatory messages (+) as well as two inhibitory ones (−). Does it fire an impulse? It depends: If enough "exciting" messages arrive close in time, the neuron will reach its threshold and fire—but only if it doesn't get too many "inhibiting" messages that push it *away* from its trigger point. In this way, messages are *combined* before a neuron "decides" to fire its all-or-nothing action potential.

Let's try another metaphor. You are out shopping with five friends and find a pair of jeans you want to buy. Three of them think you should buy the jeans; your best friend is especially positive (+); and two think you shouldn't (−). Because, on balance, their input is positive, you go ahead and buy the jeans. Maybe you even tell some other friends they should buy those jeans as well. Similarly, any single neuron in a neural network "listens" to the neurons that synapse with it and combines that input into an output. At any instant, a single neuron may weigh hundreds or thousands of inputs to produce an outgoing message. After the neuron recovers from the resulting action potential, it again combines the inputs, which may have changed in the meantime, into another output, and another, and another.

In this way, each neuron in your brain functions as a tiny computer. Compared with the average laptop computer, a neuron is terribly simple and slow. But multiply these events by 100 billion neurons and 100 trillion synapses, all operating at the same time, and you have an amazing computer—one that could easily fit inside a shoebox.

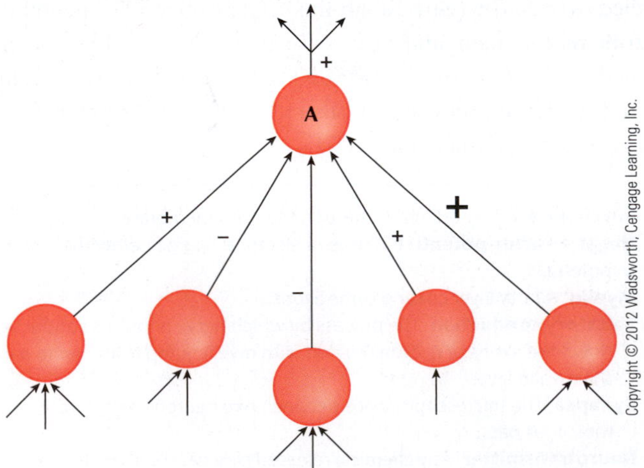

• Figure 2.6 A small neural network. Neuron A receives inputs from two weaker and one stronger excitatory connections (+) and two inhibitory connections (−) and combines the inputs into a "decision" to launch an action potential, which may help trigger further synaptic transmissions in other neurons.

Neuroplasticity

The neural networks in your brain constantly change. The term **neuroplasticity** refers to the capacity of our brains to change in response to experience. New synapses may form between neurons, or synaptic connections may grow stronger. (• Figure 2.6 shows one particularly strong synapse—the large +.) Other synaptic connections may weaken and even die. Every new experience you have is reflected in changes in your brain. For example, rats raised in a complex environment have more synapses and longer dendrites in their brains than rats raised in a simpler environment (Kolb, Gibb, & Gorny, 2003). Or consider Nico and Brooke, teenagers who had a large portion of their brains removed as infants. Today they are functioning well; over the years their brains have compensated for their losses (Immordino-Yang, 2008).

Are adult brains also "neuroplastic"? Although adult brains are less neuroplastic, they can still be changed with patience and persistence. See "You Can Change Your Mind, But Can You Change Your Brain?"

The Nervous System—Wired for Action

Gateway Question 2.2: *What are the major parts of the nervous system?*

Harry and Maya are playing catch with a football. This may look fairly simple. However, in order to merely toss the football or catch it, a huge amount of information must be sensed, interpreted, and directed to countless muscle fibers. As they play, Harry's and Maya's neural networks are ablaze with activity. Let's explore the "wiring diagram" that makes their game of catch possible.

As you can see in • Figure 2.7, the **central nervous system (CNS)** consists of the brain and spinal cord. The brain carries out most of the "computing" in the nervous system. Harry must use his brain to anticipate when and where the football will arrive. Harry's brain communicates with the rest of his body through a large

Critical Thinking — You Can Change Your Mind, But Can You Change Your Brain?

You can always change your mind. But does that have anything to do with your brain? According to scientists who study the brain, the answer must be "yes" since they believe that every mental event involves a brain event.

In one study, people suffering from an intense fear of spiders (arachnophobia) could actually touch spiders after undergoing cognitive behavior therapy. Images of their brains revealed reduced activity in brain areas related to the phobia (Paquette et al., 2003). Not only did they change their minds about spiders, they literally changed their brains.

Another study focused on patients with language difficulties caused by damage to the left sides of their brains. To aid their recovery, the patients were trained in language comprehension, which did, in fact, improve their ability to understand language. In addition, brain images revealed that the right sides of their brains had become more active to compensate for their left-brain damage (Musso et al., 1999). Again, a learning experience changed their brains.

Every time you learn something, you are reshaping your living brain (Begley, 2006). There is even a fancy phrase to describe what you are doing: *self-directed neuroplasticity*. Just think: As you study this psychology textbook, you are changing your mind—and your brain—about psychology.

"cable" called the spinal cord. From there, messages flow through the **peripheral nervous system (PNS)**. This intricate network of *nerves* carries information to and from the CNS.

Are neurons the same as nerves? No. Neurons are tiny nerve cells with one axon. You would need a microscope to see one. **Nerves** are large bundles of many neuron axons. You can easily see nerves without magnification.

Nerves in the peripheral nervous system can regrow if they are damaged. The axons of most neurons in nerves outside the brain and spinal cord are covered by a thin layer of cells called the **neurilemma** (NOOR-rih-LEM-ah). (Return to • Figure 2.1.) The neurilemma forms a "tunnel" that damaged fibers can follow as they repair themselves. Because of this, patients can expect to regain some control over severed limbs once they have been reattached.

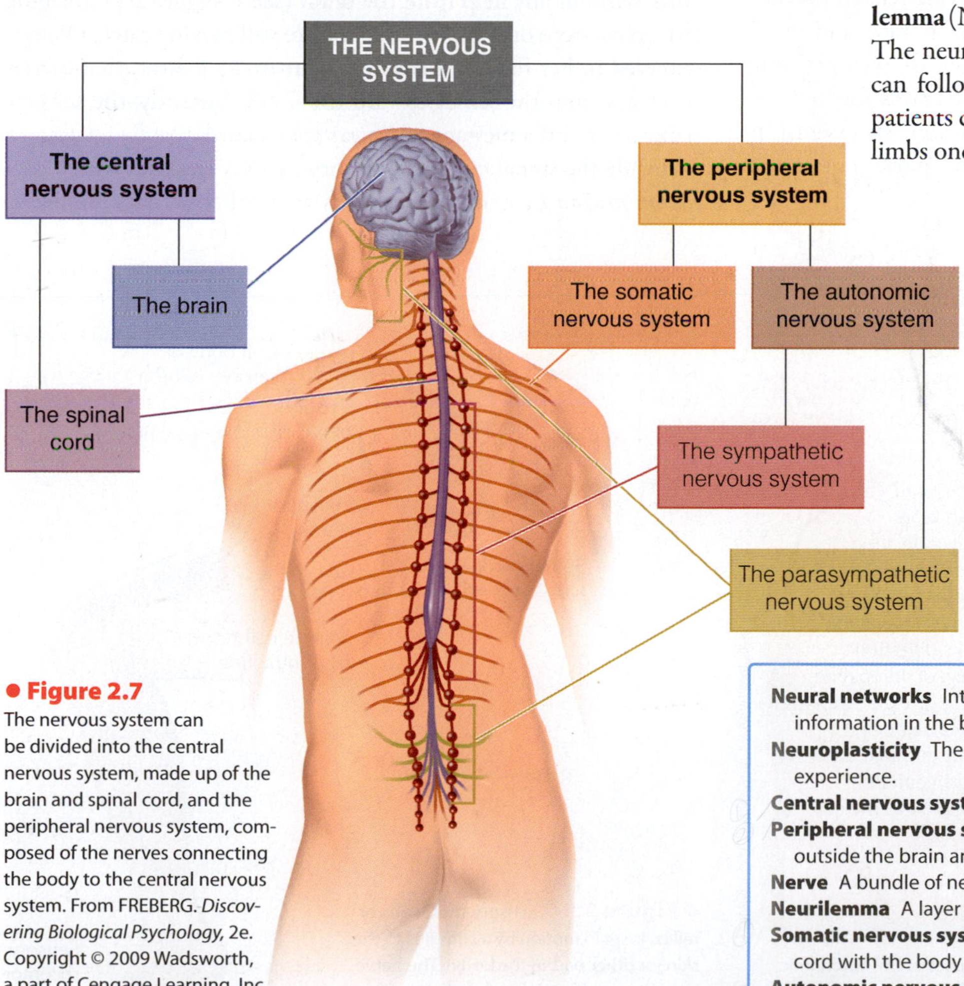

• Figure 2.7 The nervous system can be divided into the central nervous system, made up of the brain and spinal cord, and the peripheral nervous system, composed of the nerves connecting the body to the central nervous system. From FREBERG. *Discovering Biological Psychology*, 2e. Copyright © 2009 Wadsworth, a part of Cengage Learning, Inc. Reproduced by permission. www.cengage.com/permission

The Peripheral Nervous System

The peripheral nervous system can be divided into two major parts (see • Figure 2.7). The **somatic nervous system (SNS)** carries messages to and from the sense organs and skeletal muscles. In general, it controls voluntary behavior, such as when Maya tosses the football or Rafael Nadal hits a tennis ball. In contrast, the **autonomic nervous system (ANS)** serves the internal organs and glands. The word *autonomic* means "self-governing." Activities governed by the autonomic ner-

Neural networks Interlinked collections of neurons that process information in the brain.

Neuroplasticity The capacity of the brain to change in response to experience.

Central nervous system (CNS) The brain and spinal cord.

Peripheral nervous system (PNS) All parts of the nervous system outside the brain and spinal cord.

Nerve A bundle of neuron axons.

Neurilemma A layer of cells that encases many axons.

Somatic nervous system (SNS) The system of nerves linking the spinal cord with the body and sense organs.

Autonomic nervous system (ANS) The system of nerves carrying information to and from the internal organs and glands.

vous system are mostly "vegetative" or automatic, such as heart rate, digestion, and perspiration. Thus, messages carried by the somatic system can make your hand move, but they cannot cause your eyes to dilate. Likewise, messages carried by the ANS can stimulate digestion, but they cannot help you carry out a voluntary action, such as writing a letter. If Harry feels a flash of anger when he misses a catch, a brief burst of activity will spread through his autonomic nervous system.

BRIDGES

The ANS plays a central role in our emotional lives. In fact, without the ANS, a person would feel little emotion. **See Chapter 10, pages 350–351, for more information about the ANS and emotion.**

The SNS and ANS work together to coordinate the body's internal reactions to events in the world outside. For example, if a snarling dog lunges at you, your SNS will control your leg muscles so that you can run. At the same time, your ANS will raise your blood pressure, quicken your heartbeat, and so forth. The ANS can be divided into the *sympathetic* and *parasympathetic* branches.

How do the branches of the autonomic system differ? Both the sympathetic and the parasympathetic branches are related to emotional responses, such as crying, sweating, heart rate, and other involuntary behavior (• Figure 2.8). However, the **sympathetic branch** is an "emergency" system. It prepares the body for "fight or flight" during times of danger or high emotion. In essence, it arouses the body for action. In contrast, the **parasympathetic branch** quiets the body and returns it to a lower level of arousal. It is most active soon after an emotional event. The parasympathetic branch also helps keep vital processes such as heart rate, breathing, and digestion at moderate levels.

Of course, both branches of the ANS are always active. At any given moment, their combined activity determines if your body is more or less relaxed or aroused.

The Spinal Cord

As mentioned earlier, the spinal cord connects the brain to other parts of the body. If you were to cut through this "cable," you would see columns of *white matter* (bundles of axons covered with myelin). This tissue is made up of axons that eventually leave the spinal cord to form the peripheral nervous system nerves. Thirty-one pairs of **spinal nerves** carry sensory and motor messages to and from the spinal cord. In addition, 12 pairs of **cranial nerves** leave the brain directly without passing through the spinal cord. Together, these nerves keep your entire body in communication with your brain.

Is the spinal cord's only function to connect the brain to the peripheral nervous system? Actually, the spinal cord can do some simple "computing" of its own. A **reflex arc** occurs when a stimulus provokes an automatic response. Such reflexes arise within the spinal cord, without any help from the brain (see • Figure 2.9). Imagine that Maya steps on a thorn. (Yes, they're still playing catch.) Pain is detected in her foot by a **sensory neuron**—a neuron that carries messages from the senses toward the CNS. Instantly, the sensory neuron fires off a message to Maya's spinal cord.

Inside the spinal cord, the sensory neuron synapses with a *connector neuron* (a neuron that links two others). The connector

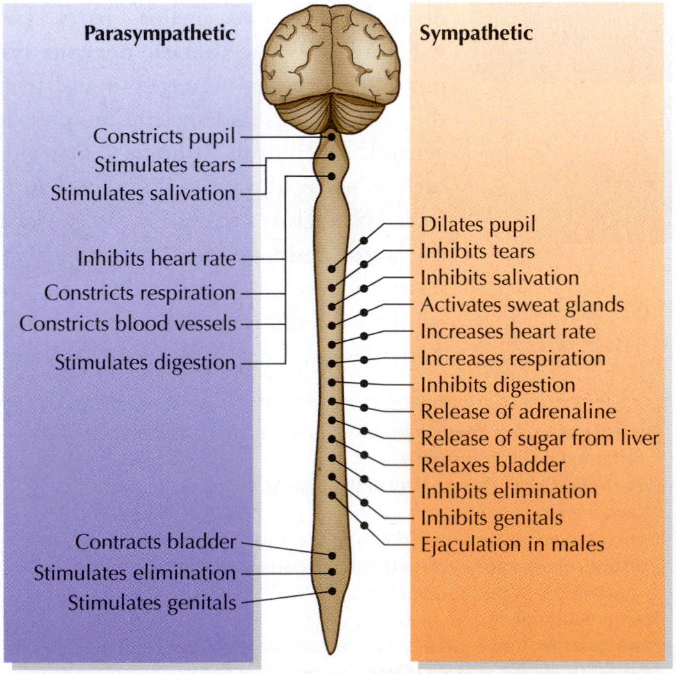

Parasympathetic
Constricts pupil
Stimulates tears
Stimulates salivation
Inhibits heart rate
Constricts respiration
Constricts blood vessels
Stimulates digestion
Contracts bladder
Stimulates elimination
Stimulates genitals

Sympathetic
Dilates pupil
Inhibits tears
Inhibits salivation
Activates sweat glands
Increases heart rate
Increases respiration
Inhibits digestion
Release of adrenaline
Release of sugar from liver
Relaxes bladder
Inhibits elimination
Inhibits genitals
Ejaculation in males

• **Figure 2.8** Sympathetic and parasympathetic branches of the autonomic nervous system. Both branches control involuntary actions. The sympathetic system generally activates the body. The parasympathetic system generally quiets it. The sympathetic branch relays its messages through clusters of nerve cells outside the spinal cord.

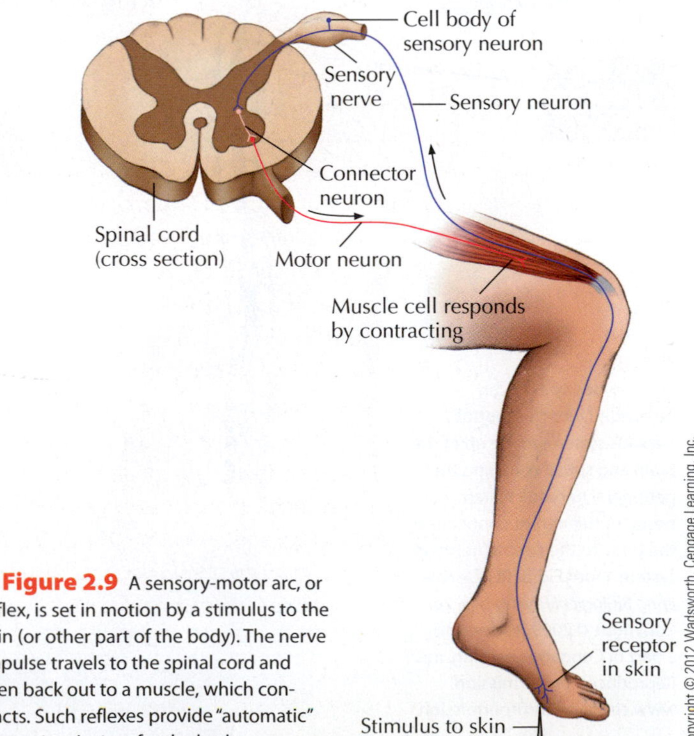

• **Figure 2.9** A sensory-motor arc, or reflex, is set in motion by a stimulus to the skin (or other part of the body). The nerve impulse travels to the spinal cord and then back out to a muscle, which contracts. Such reflexes provide "automatic" protective devices for the body.

Brainwaves: Repairing Your Brain

Until only a few years ago, it was widely believed that we are born with all the brain cells we will ever have (Ben Abdallah, 2010). This led to the depressing idea that we all slowly go downhill, as the brain loses thousands of neurons every day. Rather than facing a steady decline, we now know that a healthy 75-year-old brain has just as many neurons as it did when it was careening through life in the body of a 25-year-old. Although it is true that the brain loses cells daily, it simultaneously grows new neurons to replace them. This process is called **neurogenesis** (noor-oh-JEN-uh-sis), the production of new brain cells (Kempermann, 2005). Each day, thousands of new cells originate deep within the brain, move to the surface, and link up with other neurons to become part of the brain's circuitry. This was stunning news to brain scientists, who must now figure out what the new cells do. Most likely they are involved in learning, memory, and our ability to adapt to changing circumstances (Canales, 2010).

Before neurogenesis was discovered, it was assumed that neuron transplants might be the only way to treat brain damage (Wong, Hodges, & Horsburgh, 2005). Imagine that a patient named Bobby M. has suffered a stroke (like Bryan Kolb), causing partial paralysis in his left arm. What could be done to help Bobby recover? One remedy involves injecting stem cells into his damaged brain areas. This would allow the new cells to link up with existing neurons in order to repair Bobby's stroke damage (Davies et al., 2008; Zhang, Zhang, & Chopp, 2005).

The discovery of neurogenesis in adult brains is leading to new treatments for some types of brain damage. For example, an approach called *constraint-induced movement therapy* could be used to speed Bobby M.'s recovery. In this case, Bobby's good right arm would be restrained, forcing his impaired left arm to be more active. By using his left arm, Bobby could increase neurogenesis in the damaged part of his brain (Taub, 2004). In another approach, drugs that speed up neurogenesis could be injected into the damaged area of Bobby's brain (Zhang, Zhang, & Chopp, 2005). Such techniques are beginning to offer new hope for people suffering from a variety of other disabilities, such as blindness and Parkinson's disease (Brinton & Wang, 2006; Burke et al., 2007).

But don't these treatments assume that Bobby's brain is still capable of neurogenesis? What if it isn't? Brilliant! Although a stroke most likely doesn't damage the brain's ability to repair itself, it is quite possible that other brain disorders do arise from impaired neurogenesis (Thompson et al., 2008). In fact, that is exactly the theory proposed by neuroscientists Carla Toro and Bill Deakin to explain the serious mental disorder schizophrenia (Toro & Deakin, 2007). The brains of schizophrenic persons are usually smaller than normal, indicating that they have fewer neurons. Toro and Deakin's idea is that the schizophrenic brain may be unable to continually create new neurons to replace old ones that have died. If they are right, new therapies to promote neurogenesis may hold the key to treating schizophrenia, one of the most devastating mental illnesses. (For more on schizophrenia, see Chapter 14.)

neuron activates a *motor neuron* (a neuron that carries commands from the CNS to muscles and glands). The muscle fibers are made up of *effector cells* (cells capable of producing a response). The muscle cells contract and cause Maya's foot to withdraw. Note that no brain activity is required for a reflex arc to occur. Maya's body will react automatically to protect itself.

In reality, even a simple reflex usually triggers more complex activity. For example, muscles of Maya's other leg must contract to support her as she shifts her weight. Even this can be done by the spinal cord, but it involves many more cells and several spinal nerves. Also, the spinal cord normally informs the brain of its actions. As her foot pulls away from the thorn, Maya will feel the pain and think, "Ouch, what was that?"

Perhaps you have realized how adaptive it is to have a spinal cord capable of responding on its own. Such automatic responses leave the brains of our football stars free to deal with more important information—such as the location of trees, lampposts, and attractive onlookers—as they take turns making grandstand catches.

Although peripheral nerves can regrow, a serious injury to the brain or spinal cord is usually permanent. However, scientists are starting to make progress repairing damaged neurons in the CNS. For instance, they have partially repaired cut spinal cords in rats by establishing "cellular bridges" to close the gap. Strategies include coaxing severed nerve fibers to grow across the gap (Cheng, Cao, & Olson, 1996), grafting nerve fibers to fill the gap (Féron et al., 2005), and injecting stem cells (immature cells that can mature into a variety of specialized cells, such as neurons) into the gap (Davies et al., 2008).

Research with mice and rats has already been followed up with some human trials. Imagine what that could mean to a person confined to a wheelchair. Although it is unwise to raise false hopes, solutions to such problems are beginning to emerge. Nevertheless, it is wise to take good care of your own CNS. That means using seat belts when you drive, wearing a helmet if you ride a motorcycle or bicycle, wearing protective gear for sports, and avoiding activities that pose a risk to your head or spinal cord.

Can brain damage also be repaired? Although we will be exploring the brain itself in more detail later on in the chapter, we can, for now, answer with an optimistic but cautious *yes* (see "Repairing Your Brain").

Sympathetic branch The branch of the ANS that arouses the body.
Parasympathetic branch The branch of the ANS that quiets the body.
Spinal nerves Major nerves that carry sensory and motor messages in and out of the spinal cord.
Cranial nerves Major nerves that leave the brain without passing through the spinal cord.
Reflex arc The simplest behavior, in which a stimulus provokes an automatic response.
Sensory neuron A neuron that carries information from the senses toward the CNS.
Neurogenesis The production of new brain cells.

Before we go on to explore some of the research tools biopsychologists use, take some time to check out how much you've learned.

Knowledge Builder: Neurons and the Nervous System

RECITE

1. The ____________ and ____________ are the receiving areas of a neuron where information from other neurons is accepted.
2. Nerve impulses are carried down the ______________ to the ____________ ____________.
3. The ____________ potential becomes a(n) ____________ potential when a neuron passes the threshold for firing.
4. Neuropeptides are transmitter substances that help regulate the activity of neurons. T or F?
5. The somatic and autonomic nervous systems are part of the ____________ nervous system.
6. Sodium and potassium ions flow through ion channels in the synapse to trigger a nerve impulse in the receiving neuron. T or F?
7. The simplest behavior sequence is a ____________ ____________.
8. The parasympathetic nervous system is most active during times of high emotion. T or F?

REFLECT

Think Critically

9. What effect would you expect a drug to have if it blocked passage of neurotransmitters across the synapse?
10. Where in all the brain's "hardware" do you think the mind is found? What is the relationship between mind and brain?

Self-Reflect

To cope with all of the technical terms in this chapter, it might help to think of neurons as strange little creatures. How do they act? What excites them? How do they communicate?

To remember the functions of major branches of the nervous system, think about what you *couldn't* do if each part were missing. How does a neural network differ from the central processing unit of a computer?

Answers: 1. dendrites, soma **2.** axon, axon terminals **3.** resting, action **4.** T **5.** peripheral **6.** F **7.** reflex arc **8.** F **9.** Such a drug could have wide-ranging effects, depending on which neurotransmitter(s) it blocked. If the drug blocked excitatory synapses, it would depress brain activity. If it blocked inhibitory messages, it would act as a powerful stimulant. **10.** These questions, known as the mind-body problem, have challenged thinkers for centuries. One recent view is that mental states are "emergent properties" of brain activity. That is, brain activity forms complex patterns that are, in a sense, more than the sum of their parts. Or, to use a rough analogy, if the brain were a musical instrument, then mental life would be like music played on that instrument.

Research Methods—Charting the Brain's Inner Realms

Gateway Question 2.3: *How are different parts of the brain identified and what do they do?*

Biopsychology is the study of how biological processes, especially those occurring in the nervous system, relate to behavior. In their research, many biopsychologists try to learn which parts of the brain control particular mental or behavioral functions, such as being able to recognize faces or move your hands. That is, they try to learn where functions are localized (located) in the brain. Many techniques have been developed to help identify brain structures and the functions they control.

Mapping Brain Structure

Anatomists have learned much about brain structure by dissecting (cutting apart) autopsied human and animal brains and examining them under a microscope. Dissection reveals that the brain is made up of many anatomically distinct areas or "parts." Less intrusive newer methods, such as the CT scan and the MRI scan, can be used to map brain structures in living brains.

CT Scan

Computerized scanning equipment has revolutionized the study of brain structures and made it easier to identify brain diseases and injuries. At best, conventional X-rays produce only shadowy images of the brain. **Computed tomographic (CT) scanning** is a specialized type of X-ray that does a much better job of making the brain visible. In a CT scan, X-rays taken from a number of different angles are collected by a computer and formed into an image of the brain. A CT scan can reveal the location of strokes, injuries, tumors, and other brain disorders.

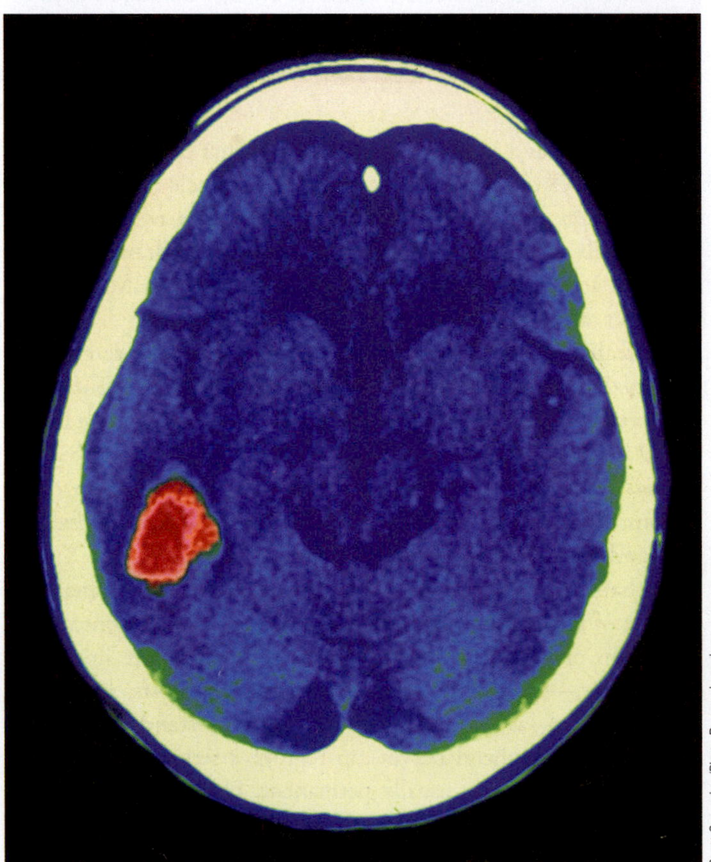

Scott Camazine/Photo Researchers, Inc.

This brain in this photo was damaged by a stroke (shown in red). The location of the stroke will determine what mental or behavioral functions.

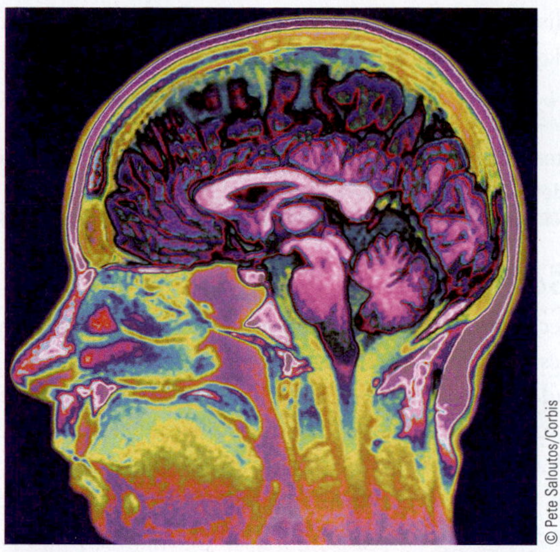

● **Figure 2.10** A colored MRI scan of the brain reveals many details. Can you identify any brain regions?

MRI Scan

Magnetic resonance imaging (MRI) uses a very strong magnetic field, rather than X-rays, to produce an image of the body's interior. During an MRI scan, the body is placed inside a magnetic field. Processing by a computer then creates a three-dimensional model of the brain or body. Any two-dimensional plane, or slice, of the body can be selected and displayed as an image on a computer screen. MRI scans produce more detailed images than are possible with CT scans, allowing us to peer into the living brain almost as if it were transparent (see ● Figure 2.10).

Exploring Brain Function

Although it is valuable to be able to examine images of different brain structures, such as those made possible by CT scans and MRIs, it is another matter entirely to visualize what role those structures play in normal brain function.

What parts of the brain allow us to think, feel, perceive, or act? To answer questions like this, we must **localize function** by linking psychological or behavioral capacities with particular brain structures. In many instances, this has been done through **clinical case studies.** Such studies examine changes in personality, behavior, or sensory capacity caused by brain diseases or injuries. If damage to a particular part of the brain consistently leads to a particular loss of function, then we say the function is localized in that structure. Presumably, that part of the brain controls the same function in all of us.

Although major brain injuries are easy enough to spot, psychologists also look for more subtle signs that the brain is not working properly. **Neurological soft signs**, as they are called, include clumsiness, an awkward gait, poor hand-eye coordination, and other problems with perception or fine muscle control (Morgan & Ricke, 2008). These telltale signs are "soft" in the sense that they aren't direct tests of the brain, like a CT scan or MRI scan. Bryan Kolb initially diagnosed himself as having had a stroke

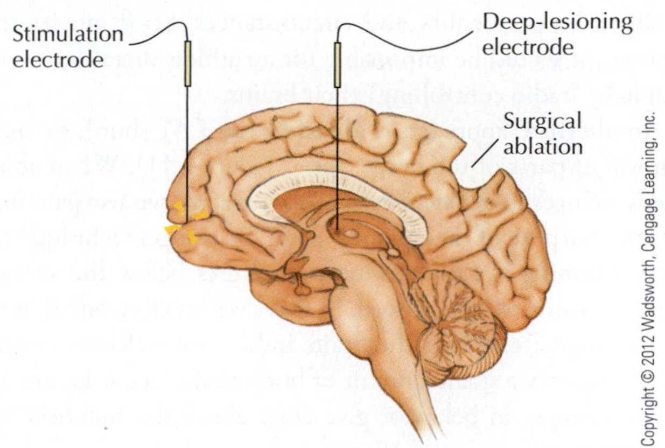

● **Figure 2.11** The functions of brain structures are explored by selectively activating or removing them. Brain research is often based on electrical stimulation, but chemical stimulation is also used at times.

entirely with soft signs. Likewise, soft signs help psychologists diagnose problems ranging from childhood learning disorders to full-blown psychosis (Stuss & Levine, 2002).

Instead of relying on clinical studies, researchers have learned much from **electrical stimulation of the brain (ESB)** (● Figure 2.11). For example, the surface of the brain can be "turned on" by stimulating it with a mild electrical current delivered through a thin insulated wire called an **electrode**. When this is done during brain surgery, the patient can describe what effect the stimulation had. (The brain has no pain receptors, so surgery can be done while a patient is awake. Only local painkillers are used for the scalp and skull. Any volunteers?) Even structures below the surface of the brain can be activated by lowering a stimulating electrode, insulated except at the tip, into a target area inside the brain. ESB can call forth behavior with astonishing power. Instantly, it can bring about aggression, alertness, escape, eating, drinking, sleeping, movement, euphoria, memories, speech, tears, and more.

Could ESB be used to control a person against his or her will? It might seem that ESB could be used to control a person like a robot. But the details of emotions and behaviors elicited by ESB are

Computed tomographic scan (CT scan) A computer-enhanced X-ray image of the brain or body.

Magnetic resonance imaging (MRI) An imaging technique that results in a three-dimensional image of the brain or body, based on its response to a magnetic field.

Localization of function The research strategy of linking specific structures in the brain with specific psychological or behavioral functions.

Clinical case study A detailed investigation of a single person, especially one suffering from some injury or disease.

Neurological soft signs Subtle behavioral signs of brain dysfunction, including clumsiness, an awkward gait, poor hand-eye coordination, and other perceptual and motor problems.

Electrical stimulation of the brain (ESB) Direct electrical stimulation and activation of brain tissue.

Electrode Any device (such as a wire, needle, or metal plate) used to electrically stimulate or destroy nerve tissue or to record its activity.

modified by personality and circumstances. Sci-fi movies to the contrary, it would be impossible for a ruthless dictator to enslave people by "radio controlling" their brains.

An alternate approach is **ablation** (ab-LAY-shun), or surgical removal of parts of the brain (see ● Figure 2.11). When ablation causes changes in behavior or sensory capacity, we also gain insight into the purpose of the missing "part." By using a technique called **deep lesioning** (LEE-zhun-ing), structures below the surface of the brain can also be removed. In this case, an electrode is lowered into a target area inside the brain and a strong electric current is used to destroy a small amount of brain tissue (see ● Figure 2.11). Again, changes in behavior give clues about the function of the affected area.

To find out what individual neurons are doing, we need to do a microelectrode recording. A *microelectrode* is an extremely thin glass tube filled with a salty fluid. The tip of a microelectrode is small enough to detect the electrical activity of a *single* neuron. Watching the action potentials of just one neuron provides a fascinating glimpse into the true origins of behavior. (The action potential shown in ● Figure 2.2 was recorded with a microelectrode.)

Are any less invasive techniques available for studying brain function? Whereas CT scans and MRIs cannot tell us what different parts of the brain *do*, several other techniques allow us to observe the activity of parts of the brain without doing any damage at all. These include the EEG, PET scan, and fMRI. Such techniques allow biopsychologists to pinpoint areas in the brain responsible for thoughts, feelings, and actions.

EEG

Electroencephalography (ee-LEK-tro-in-SEF-ah-LOG-ruh-fee) measures the waves of electrical activity produced near the surface of the brain. Small disk-shaped metal plates are placed on a person's scalp. Electrical impulses from the brain are detected by these electrodes and sent to an **electroencephalograph (EEG)**. The EEG amplifies these very weak signals (brain waves) and records them on a moving sheet of paper or a computer screen (● Figure 2.12). Various brain-wave patterns can identify the presence of tumors, epilepsy, and other diseases. The EEG also reveals changes in brain activity during sleep, daydreaming, hypnosis, and other mental states.

BRIDGES

Chapter 5, pages 171–172, explains how changes in brain waves help define various stages of sleep.

PET Scan

A newer technology, called positron emission tomography (PET), provides much more detailed images of activity both *near* the surface and *below* the surface of the brain. A **PET scan** detects positrons (subatomic particles) emitted by weakly radioactive glucose (sugar) as it is consumed by the brain. Because the brain runs on glucose, a PET scan shows which areas are using more energy. Higher energy use corresponds with higher activity. Thus, by placing positron detectors around the head and sending data to a computer, it is possible to create a moving, color picture of changes in brain activity. As you can see in ● Figure 2.13, PET scans reveal that very specific brain areas are active when you see, hear, speak, or think.

BRIDGES

PET scans suggest that different patterns of brain activity accompany major psychological disorders, such as depression or schizophrenia. **See Chapter 14, pages 489–491 and 504.**

More active brains are good, right? Although we might assume that hardworking brains are smart brains, the reverse appears to be true (Neubauer & Fink, 2009). Using PET scans, psychologist Richard Haier and his colleagues first found that the brains of people who perform well on a difficult reasoning test consume less energy than those of poor performers (Haier et al., 1988) (● Figure 2.14). Haier believes this shows that intelligence is related to brain efficiency: Less efficient brains work harder and still accomplish less (Haier, White, & Alkire, 2003). We've all had days like that!

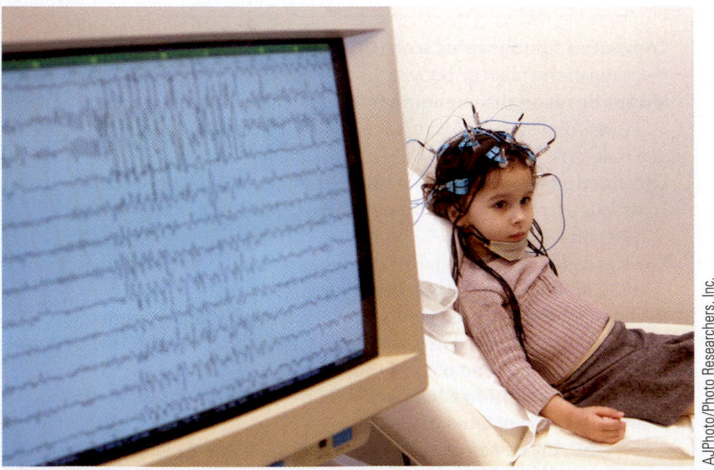

AJPhoto/Photo Researchers, Inc.

● **Figure 2.12** An EEG recording.

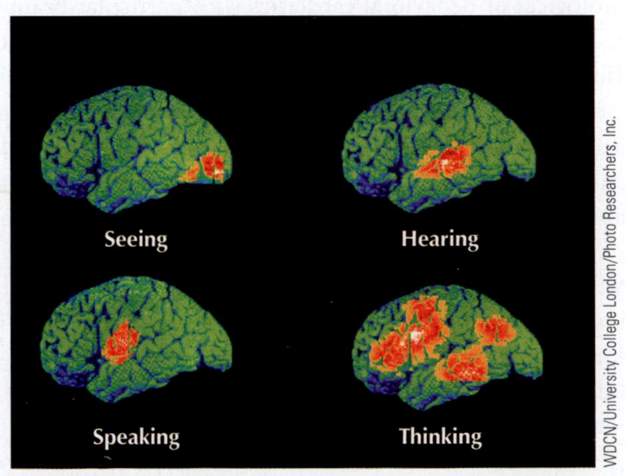

WDCN/University College London/Photo Researchers, Inc.

● **Figure 2.13** Colored PET scans reveal different patterns of brain activation when we engage in different tasks.

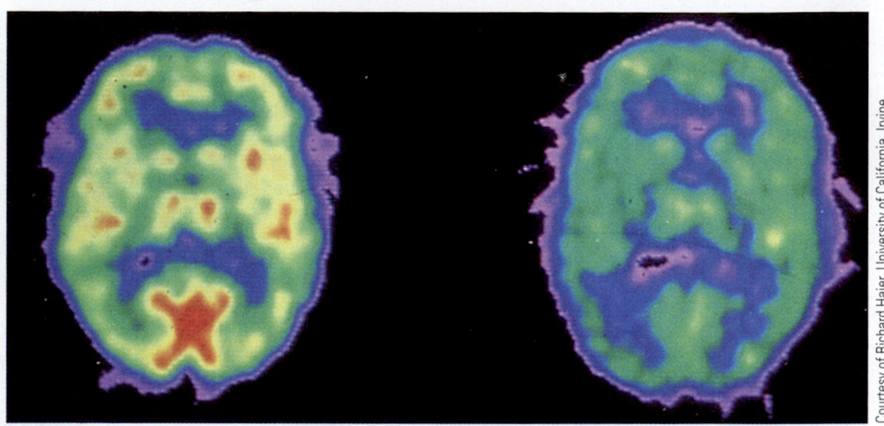

● Figure 2.14 In the images you see here, red, orange, and yellow indicate high consumption of glucose; green, blue, and pink show areas of low glucose use. The PET scan of the brain on the left shows that a man who solved 11 out of 36 reasoning problems burned more glucose than the man on the right, who solved 33.

Courtesy of Richard Haier, University of California, Irvine

Is it true that most people use only 10 percent of their brain capacity? This is one of the lasting myths about the brain. Brain scans show that all parts of the brain are active during waking hours. Obviously, some people make better use of their innate brainpower than others do. Nevertheless, there are no great hidden or untapped reserves of mental capacity in a normally functioning brain.

fMRI

A **functional MRI (fMRI)** uses MRI technology to make brain activity visible. Like PET scans, fMRIs also provide images of activity throughout the brain. For example, if we scanned Bryan Kolb while he was reading a journal article, areas of his brain that control his hands would be highlighted in an fMRI image. (In contrast, if we used MRI, rather than fMRI, we would get a beautiful image of his brain structure without any clues as to which parts of his brain were more or less active.)

Psychiatrist Daniel Langleben and his colleagues (2005; Hakun et al., 2009) have even used fMRI images to tell whether a person is lying. As ● Figure 2.15 shows, the front of the brain is more active when a person is lying, rather than telling the truth. This may occur because it takes extra effort to lie, and the resulting extra brain activity is detected with fMRI. Eventually, fMRI may help us distinguish between lies, false statements made with the intention to deceive, and *confabulations*, which are false claims believed to be true (Hirstein, 2005; Langleben, Dattilio, & Gutheil, 2006).

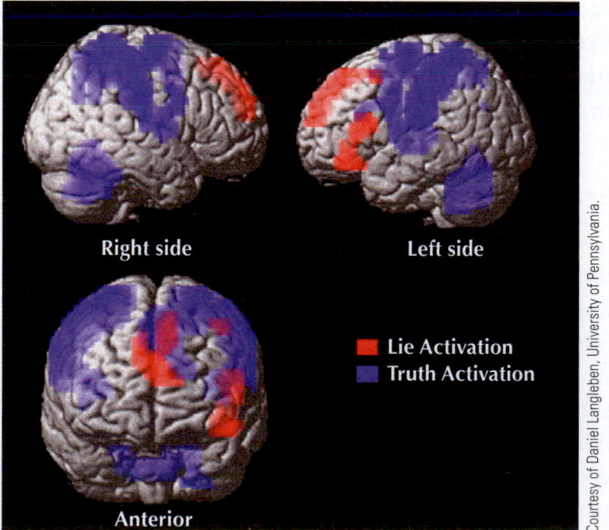

Courtesy of Daniel Langleben, University of Pennsylvania.

● Figure 2.15 Participants were asked to tell the truth or to lie while fMRI images of their brains were taken. When compared with telling the truth (*shown in blue*), areas toward the front of the brain were active during lying (*shown in red*). (Adapted from Langleben et al., 2005.)

As they learn more about the human brain, researchers are creating digital three-dimensional brain maps. These "atlases" show brain structures and even their accompanying psychological functions. They promise to be valuable guides for medical treatment, as well as for exploring the brain (Jagaroo, 2009; Jellinger, 2009). Clearly, it is just a matter of time until even brighter beacons are flashed into the shadowy inner world of thought.

Knowledge Builder: Brain Research

RECITE

1. Which of the following research techniques has the most in common with clinical studies of the effects of brain injuries?
   a. EEG recording *b.* deep lesioning *c.* microelectrode recording *d.* PET scan
2. CT scans cannot determine which part of your brain plays a role in speech because CT scans
   a. use X-rays *b.* reveal brain structure, not brain activity *c.* reveal brain activity, not brain structure *d.* use magnetic fields
3. The strategy that seeks to link brain structures to brain functions is called ______ ______ ______.
4. People only use 10 percent of their brain capacity. T or F?

REFLECT

Think Critically

5. Deep lesioning is used to ablate (or remove) an area in the hypothalamus of a rat. After the operation, the rat seems to lose interest in food and eating. Why would it be a mistake to automatically conclude that the ablated area is a "hunger center"?

Continued

Ablation Surgical removal of tissue.
Deep lesioning Removal of tissue within the brain by use of an electrode.
Electroencephalograph (EEG) A device that detects, amplifies, and records electrical activity in the brain.
Positron emission tomography (PET) An imaging technique that results in a computer-generated image of brain activity, based on glucose consumption in the brain.
Functional MRI (fMRI) MRI technique that records brain activity.

Self-Reflect

You suspect that a certain part of the brain is related to risk-taking. How could you use clinical studies, ablation, deep lesioning, and ESB to study the structure?

You are interested in finding out how single neurons in the optic nerve respond when the eye is exposed to light. What technique will you use?

You want to know which areas of the brain's surface are most active when a person sees a face. What methods will you use?

Answers: 1. *b* **2.** *b* **3.** Localization of function **4.** F **5.** Because other factors might explain the apparent loss of appetite. For example, the taste or smell of food might be affected, or the rat might simply have difficulty swallowing. It is also possible that hunger originates elsewhere in the brain and the ablated area merely relays messages that cause the rat to eat.

The Cerebral Cortex—My, What a Wrinkled Brain You Have!

Gateway Question 2.4: *How do the left and right hemispheres differ and what are the different functions of the lobes of the cerebral cortex?*

In many ways we are pretty unimpressive creatures. Animals surpass humans in almost every category of strength, speed, and sensory sensitivity. However, we do excel in intelligence.

Does that mean humans have the largest brains? Surprisingly, no. Mammals do have the largest brains of all animals. But we humans are not the mammalian record holders. That honor goes to whales, whose brains tip the scales at around 19 pounds. At 3 pounds, the human brain seems puny—until we compare brain weight to body weight. We then find that a sperm whale's brain is 1/10,000 of its weight. The ratio for humans is 1/60. And yet, the ratio for tree shrews (very small squirrel-like insect-eating mammals) is about 1/30. So our human brains are not noteworthy in terms of either absolute or relative weight (Coolidge & Wynn, 2009).

So having a larger brain doesn't necessarily make a person smarter? That's right. Although a small positive correlation exists between intelligence and brain size, overall size alone does not determine human intelligence (Johnson et al., 2008; Witelson, Beresh, & Kigar, 2006). In fact, many parts of your brain are surprisingly similar to corresponding brain areas in lower animals, such as lizards. It is your larger **cerebral** (seh-REE-brel or ser-EH-brel) **cortex** that sets you apart.

The cerebral cortex, which looks a little like a giant, wrinkled walnut, consists of the two large hemispheres that cover the upper part of the brain. The two hemispheres are divided into smaller areas known as lobes. Parts of various lobes are responsible for the ability to see, hear, move, think, and speak. Thus, a map of the cerebral cortex is in some ways like a map of human behavior, as we shall see.

The cerebral cortex covers most of the brain with a mantle of *gray matter* (spongy tissue made up mostly of cell bodies). Although the cortex is only 3 millimeters thick (one tenth of an inch), it contains 70 percent of the neurons in the central nervous system.

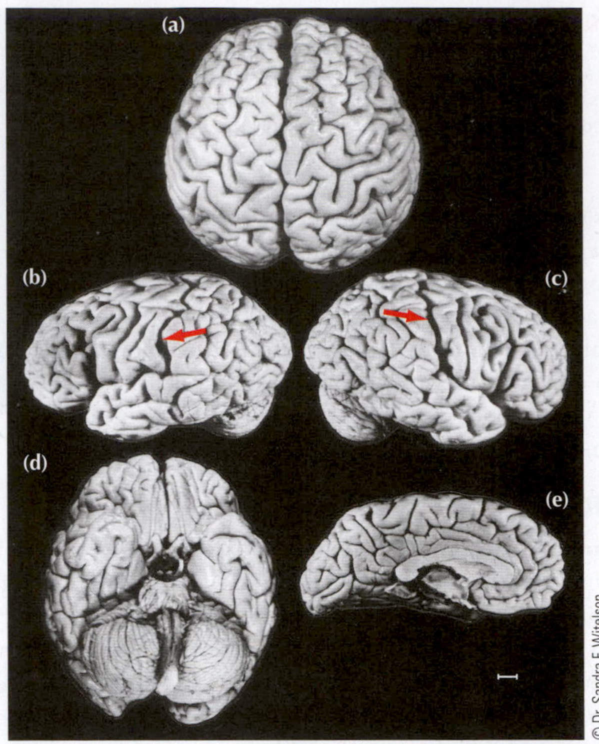

Photographs of views of Einstein's brain: from the top *(a)*, left *(b)*, right *(c)*, bottom *(d)*, and middle section *(e)*. Overall brain size was within normal limits. However, the parts of the brain necessary for spatial reasoning in the parietal lobe (see arrows in b & c) had a unique anatomy and were larger than in control brains. (Adapted from Witelson, Kigar & Harvey, Lancet, 1999, and reprinted with permission of S.F. Witelson.)

It is largely responsible for our ability to use language, make tools, acquire complex skills, and live in complex social groups (Coolidge & Wynn, 2009). In humans, the cortex is twisted and folded, and it is the largest brain structure. In lower animals, it is smooth and small (see ● Figure 2.16). The fact that humans are more intelligent than other animals is related to this **corticalization** (KORE-tih-kal-ih-ZAY-shun), or increase in the size and wrinkling of the cortex. Without the cortex, we humans wouldn't be much smarter than toads.

Cerebral Hemispheres

The cortex is composed of two sides, or *cerebral hemispheres* (half-globes), connected by a thick band of axon fibers called the *corpus callosum* (KORE-pus kah-LOH-sum) (● Figure 2.17). The left side of the brain mainly controls the right side of the body. Likewise, the right brain mainly controls left body areas. When our friend Marge had a stroke, her right hemisphere suffered damage. In Marge's case, the stroke caused some paralysis and loss of sensation on the left side of her body. (Her stroke was more severe than the one Bryan Kolb suffered and her paralysis was similar to Bobby M's, only more widespread.)

Damage to one hemisphere may also cause a curious problem called *spatial neglect.* A patient with right hemisphere damage may pay no attention to the left side of visual space (see ● Figure 2.18). Often, the patient will not eat food on the left side of a plate. Some

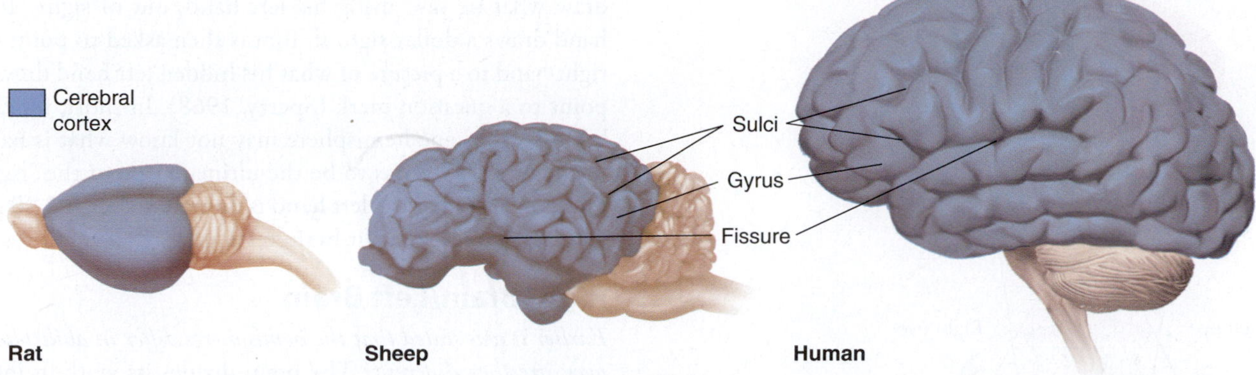

● **Figure 2.16** A more wrinkled cortex has greater cognitive capacity. Extensive corticalization is the key to human intelligence. From FREBERG. Discovering Biological Psychology 2/e. Copyright © 2009 Wadsworth, a part of Cengage Learning, Inc. Reproduced by permission. www.cengage.com/permission.

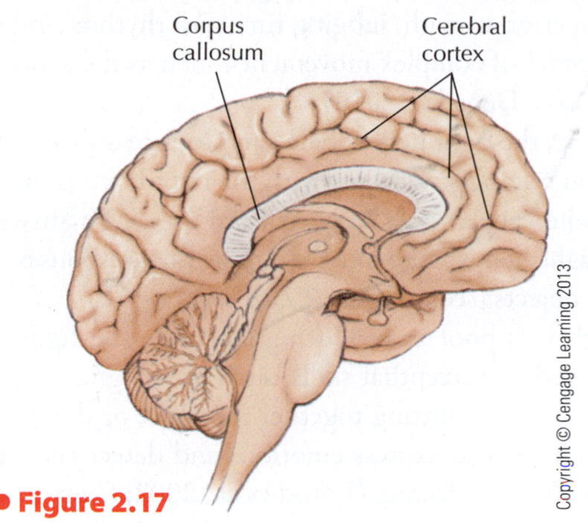

● **Figure 2.17**

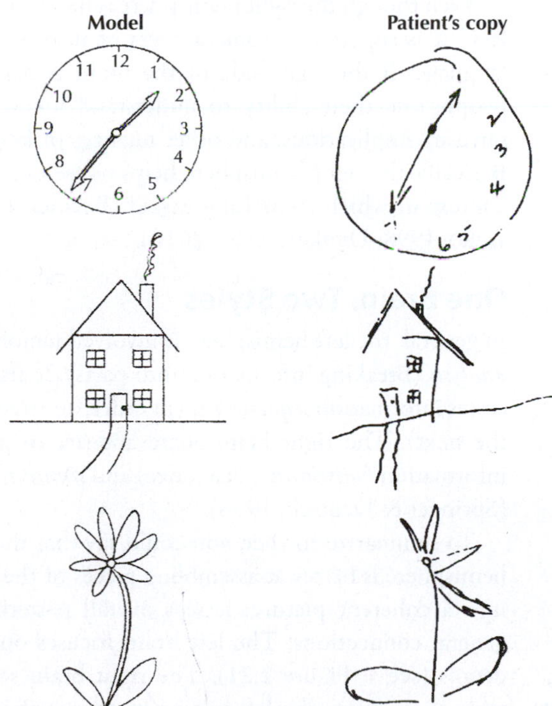

● **Figure 2.18** Spatial neglect. A patient with right-hemisphere damage was asked to copy three model drawings. Notice the obvious neglect of the left side in his drawings. Similar instances of neglect occur in many patients with right-hemisphere damage. From *Left Brain, Right Brain* (5th ed.) by Sally P. Springer & Georg Deutsch. © 1981, 1985, 1989, 1993, 1998 by Sally P. Springer and Georg Deutsch. Used with permission of W. H. Freeman and Company.

even refuse to acknowledge a paralyzed left arm as their own (Hirstein, 2005). If you point to the "alien" arm, the patient is likely to say, "Oh, that's not my arm. It must belong to someone else."

Hemispheric Specialization

In 1981, Roger Sperry (1914–1994) won a Nobel Prize for his remarkable discovery that the right and left brain hemispheres perform differently on tests of language, perception, music, and other capabilities (Colvin & Gazzaniga, 2007).

"Split Brains"

How is it possible to test only one side of the brain? One way is to work with people who've had a **"split-brain" operation**. In this rare type of surgery, the corpus callosum is cut to control severe epilepsy. The result is essentially a person with two brains in one body (Gazzaniga, 2005). After the surgery, it is possible to send information to one hemisphere or the other (see ● Figure 2.19). After the right and left brain are separated, each hemisphere will have its own separate perceptions, concepts, and impulses to act.

How does a split-brain person act after the operation? Having two "brains" in one body can create some interesting dilemmas. When one split-brain patient dressed himself, he sometimes pulled his pants up with one hand (*that* side of his brain wanted to get dressed…) and down with the other (… while *this* side didn't). Once, he grabbed his wife with his left hand and shook her violently. Gallantly, his right hand came to her aid and grabbed the aggressive left hand (Gazzaniga, 1970). However, such conflicts are actually rare. That's because both halves of the brain normally have about the same experience at the same time. Also, if a conflict arises, one hemisphere usually overrides the other.

Split-brain effects are easiest to see in specialized testing. For example, we could flash a dollar sign to the right brain and a question mark to the left brain of a patient named Tom (● Figure 2.19 shows how this is possible). Next, Tom is asked to

Cerebral cortex The outer layer of the brain.
Corticalization An increase in the relative size of the cerebral cortex.
"Split-brain" operation Cutting the corpus callosum.

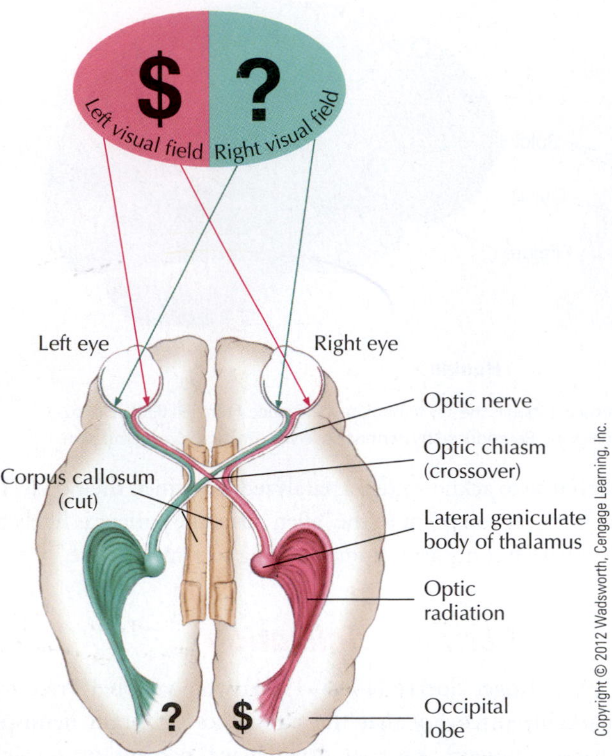

● **Figure 2.19** Basic nerve pathways of vision. Notice that the left portion of each eye connects only to the left half of the brain; likewise, the right portion of each eye connects to the right brain. When the corpus callosum is cut, a "split brain" results. Then visual information can be sent to just one hemisphere by flashing it in the right or left visual field as the person stares straight ahead.

Left Brain

- Language
- Speech
- Writing
- Calculation
- Time sense
- Rhythm
- Ordering of complex movements

Right Brain

- Nonverbal
- Perceptual skills
- Visualization
- Recognition of patterns, faces, melodies
- Recognition and expression of emotion
- Spatial skills
- Simple language comprehension

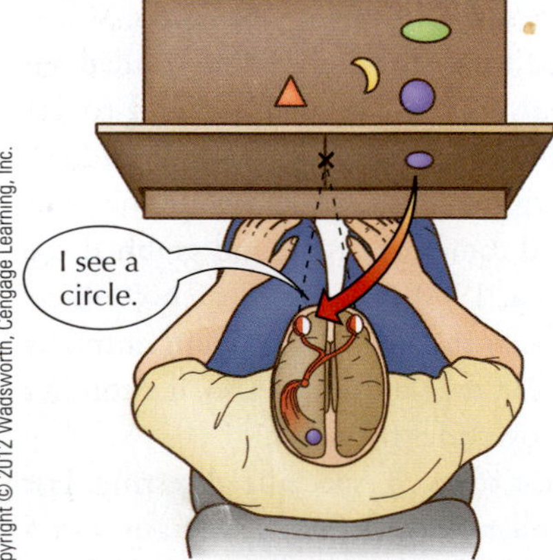

● **Figure 2.20** A circle is flashed to the left brain of a split-brain patient and he is asked what he saw. He easily replies, "A circle." He can also pick out the circle by merely touching shapes with his right hand, out of sight behind a screen. However, his left hand can't identify the circle. If a triangle is flashed to the patient's right brain, he can't say what he saw (speech is controlled by the left hemisphere). He also can't identify the triangle by touch with the right hand. Now, however, the left hand has no difficulty picking out the triangle. In other tests, the hemispheres reveal distinct skills, as listed above the drawing.

draw what he saw, using his left hand, out of sight. Tom's left hand draws a dollar sign. If Tom is then asked to point with his right hand to a picture of what his hidden left hand drew, he will point to a question mark (Sperry, 1968). In short, for the split-brain person, one hemisphere may not know what is happening in the other. This has to be the ultimate case of the "right hand not knowing what the left hand is doing"! ● Figure 2.20 provides another example of split-brain testing.

Right Brain/Left Brain

Earlier it was stated that the hemispheres differ in abilities. In what ways are they different? The brain divides its work in interesting ways. Roughly 95 percent of us use our left brain for language (speaking, writing, and understanding). In addition, the left hemisphere is superior at math, judging time and rhythm, and coordinating the order of complex movements, such as those needed for speech (Pinel & Dehaene, 2010).

In contrast, the right hemisphere can produce only the simplest language and numbers. Working with the right brain is like talking to a child who can say only a dozen words or so. To answer questions, the right hemisphere must use nonverbal responses, such as pointing at objects (see ● Figure 2.20).

Although it is poor at producing language, the right brain is especially good at perceptual skills, such as recognizing patterns, faces, and melodies; putting together a puzzle; or drawing a picture. It also helps you express emotions and detect the emotions that other people are feeling (Borod et al., 2002; Castro-Schilo & Kee, 2010).

Even though the right hemisphere is nearly "speechless," it is superior at some aspects of understanding language. If the right side of the brain is damaged, people lose their ability to understand jokes, irony, sarcasm, implications, and other nuances of language. Basically, the right hemisphere helps us see the overall context in which something is said (Beeman & Chiarello, 1998; Dyukova et al., 2010).

One Brain, Two Styles

In general, the left hemisphere is involved mainly with *analysis* (breaking information into parts). It also processes information *sequentially* (in order, one item after the next). The right hemisphere appears to process information *holistically* (all at once) and *simultaneously* (Springer & Deutsch, 1998).

To summarize further, you could say that the right hemisphere is better at assembling pieces of the world into a coherent picture; it sees overall patterns and general connections. The left brain focuses on small details (see ● Figure 2.21). The right brain sees the wide-angle view; the left zooms in on specifics. The focus of the left brain is local, the right is global (Hübner & Volberg, 2005).

Do people normally do puzzles or draw pictures with just the right hemisphere? Do they do other things with

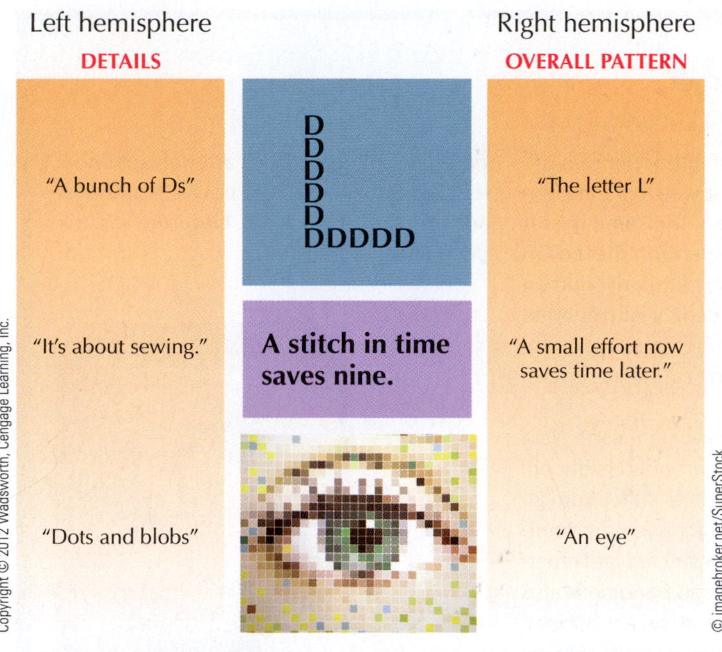

● **Figure 2.21** The left and right brain have different information processing styles. The right brain gets the big pattern; the left focuses on small details.

only the left? Numerous books have been written about how to use the right brain to manage, teach, draw, ride horses, learn, and even make love (Clark, Boutros, & Mendez, 2005). But such books drastically oversimplify right brain and left brain differences. People normally use both sides of the brain at all times. It's true that some tasks may make *more* use of one hemisphere or the other. But in most "real world" activities, the hemispheres share the work. Each does the parts it does best and shares information with the other side.

A smart brain is one that grasps both the details and the overall picture at the same time. For instance, during a concert, a violinist will use her left brain to judge time and rhythm and coordinate the order of her hand movements. At the same time, she will use her right brain to recognize and organize melodies.

Lobes of the Cerebral Cortex

Each of the two hemispheres of the cerebral cortex can be divided into several smaller *lobes*. Some of the **lobes of the cerebral cortex** are defined by larger fissures on the surface of the cortex. Others are regarded as separate areas because their functions are quite different (see ● Figure 2.22).

The Frontal Lobes

The **frontal lobes** are associated with higher mental abilities and play a role in your sense of self. This area is also responsible for the control of movement. Specifically, an arch of tissue at the rear of the frontal lobes, called the **primary motor area** (or **primary motor cortex**), directs the body's muscles. If this area is stimulated with an electrical current, various parts of the body will twitch or move. The drawing wrapped around the motor cortex in ● Figure 2.23 is out of proportion because it reflects the *dexterity*

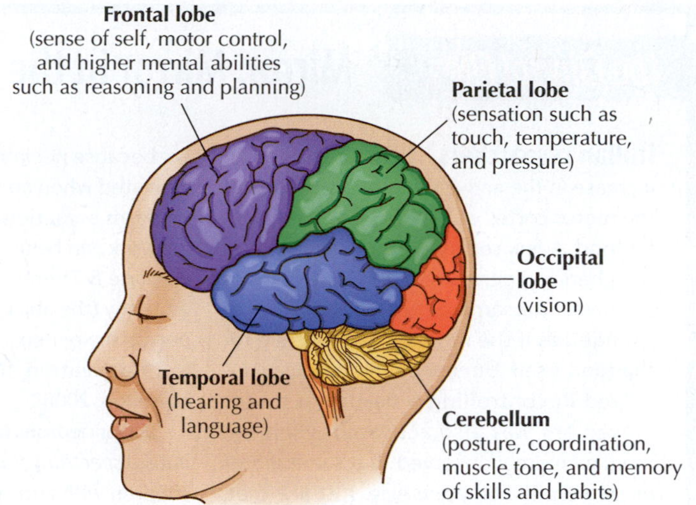

● **Figure 2.22**

of body areas, not their size. The hands, for example, get more area than the feet (see ● Figure 2.23). If you've ever wondered why your hands are more skilled or agile than your feet, it's partly because more motor cortex is devoted to the hands. Incidentally, due to neuroplasticity, learning and experience can alter these "motor maps." For instance, violin, viola, and cello players have larger "hand maps" in the cortex (Hashimoto et al., 2004).

Motor cortex is one brain area that contains **mirror neurons**. These are neurons that become active when we perform an action *and* when we merely observe someone else carrying out the same action (for more information about mirror neurons, see "Mirror, Mirror in the Brain").

The rest of the frontal lobes are often referred to as *frontal association areas*. Only a small portion of the cerebral cortex (the primary areas) directly controls the body or receives information from the senses. All the surrounding areas, which are called **association areas** (or **association cortex**), combine and process information. For example, if you see a rose, association areas will help you connect your primary sensory impressions with memories, so that you can recognize the rose and name it. Some association areas also contribute to higher mental abilities, such as language. For example, a person with damage to association areas in the left hemisphere may suffer **aphasia** (ah-FAZE-yah), or an impaired ability to use language.

Lobes of the cerebral cortex Areas on the left and right cortex bordered by major fissures or defined by their functions.

Frontal lobes Areas of the cortex associated with movement, the sense of self, and higher mental functions.

Primary motor area (primary motor cortex) A brain area associated with control of movement.

Mirror neuron A neuron that becomes active when a motor action is carried out *and* when another organism is observed carrying out the same action.

Association areas (association cortex) All areas of the cerebral cortex that are not primarily sensory or motor in function.

Aphasia A speech disturbance resulting from brain damage.

The Clinical File Mirror, Mirror in the Brain

Italian researchers had just recorded an increase in the activity of a single neuron in the motor cortex of a monkey as it reached for food. A few seconds later, one of the researchers happened to reach for a snack of his own. The same neuron obligingly responded as if the monkey had reached for the food itself. Unexpectedly, a neuron involved in controlling a particular motor movement was also activated when the monkey merely observed that same motor movement in someone else. Just like that, the Italians discovered *mirror neurons* (Rizzolatti, Fogassi, & Gallese, 2006). Because they *mirror* actions performed by others, such neurons may explain how we can intuitively understand other people's behavior. They may also underlie our ability to learn new skills by imitation (Pineda, 2009; Rizzolatti & Craighero, 2004).

The discovery of mirror neurons has triggered a flood of interest. Recently, researchers have confirmed that mirror neurons are found in various areas of the brain and appear to exist in the human brain as well (Bertenthal & Longo, 2007). In addition, neuroscientists speculate that newborn humans (and monkeys) are able to imitate others because networks of mirror neurons are activated when an infant watches someone perform an action. Then, the same mirror network can be used to perform that action (Lepage & Théret, 2007). Similarly, human empathy (the ability to identify with another person's experiences and feelings) may arise from activation of mirror neurons (de C. Hamilton, 2008).

Mirror neurons may even partially explain *autism spectrum disorders*. In early childhood, children with autism begin to suffer from an impaired ability to interact and communicate with other people. Restricted and repetitive behavior, such as head banging is also common. According to the "*broken mirrors*" hypothesis, autism may arise in infants whose mirror neuron system has been damaged by genetic defects or environmental risk factors (Ramachandran & Oberman, 2006). This explanation is attractive because autism's primary features of impaired communication and social interaction appear to be related to the role that mirror neurons play in reflecting the actions and words of others.

To date, these are just hypotheses that await empirical confirmation. More importantly, such possibilities are only just now leading to proposals for new therapies for autism (Wan et al., 2010). Nevertheless, the possibilities are exciting.

Attila Kisbenedek/AFP/Getty Images

A chimpanzee imitates researcher Jane Goodall.

One type of aphasia is related to **Broca's** (BRO-cahs) **area**, a "speech center" that is part of the left frontal association area (for 5 percent of all people, the area is part of the right frontal association area). Damage to Broca's area causes *motor (or expressive) aphasia*, a great difficulty in speaking or writing (Grodzinsky & Santi, 2008). Generally, the person knows what she or he wants to say but can't seem to fluently utter the words (Geschwind, 1979). Typically, a patient's grammar and pronunciation are poor and speech is slow and labored. For example, the person may say "bife" for bike, "seep" for sleep, or "zokaid" for zodiac.

The very front of the frontal association region is known as the **prefrontal area** (or **prefrontal cortex**). This part of the brain is related to more complex behaviors (Banich & Compton, 2011). If the frontal lobes are damaged, a patient's personality and emotional life may change dramatically. Remember Phineas Gage, the railroad foreman described in Chapter 1? It's likely that Gage's personality changed after he suffered brain damage because the prefrontal cortex generates our sense of self, including an awareness of our current emotional state (Kawasaki et al., 2005; Moran et al., 2006).

Reasoning or planning may also be affected (Roca et al., 2010). Patients with damage to the frontal lobes often get "stuck" on mental tasks and repeat the same wrong answers over and over (Stuss & Knight, 2002). PET scans suggest that much of what we call intelligence is related to increased activity in the frontal areas of the cortex (Duncan, 2005). Reduced frontal lobe function also leads to greater impulsivity, including increased risk for drug addiction (Crews & Boettiger, 2009). In turn, drug abuse can further damage this important area of the brain (Liu et al., 1998).

The Parietal Lobes

Bodily sensations register in the **parietal** (puh-RYE-ih-tal) **lobes**, located at the top of the brain. Touch, temperature, pressure, and other somatic sensations flow into the **primary somatosensory** (SO-mat-oh-SEN-so-ree) **area** (or **primary somatosensory cortex**) of the parietal lobes. Again, we find that the map of bodily sensations is distorted. In the case of somatosensory cortex, the drawing in ● Figure 2.23 reflects the *sensitivity* of body areas, not their size. For example, the lips are large in the drawing because of their great sensitivity, whereas the back and trunk, which are less sensitive, are much smaller. Notice that the hands are also large in the map of body sensitivity—which is obviously an aid to musicians, typists, watchmakers, massage therapists, lovers, and brain surgeons.

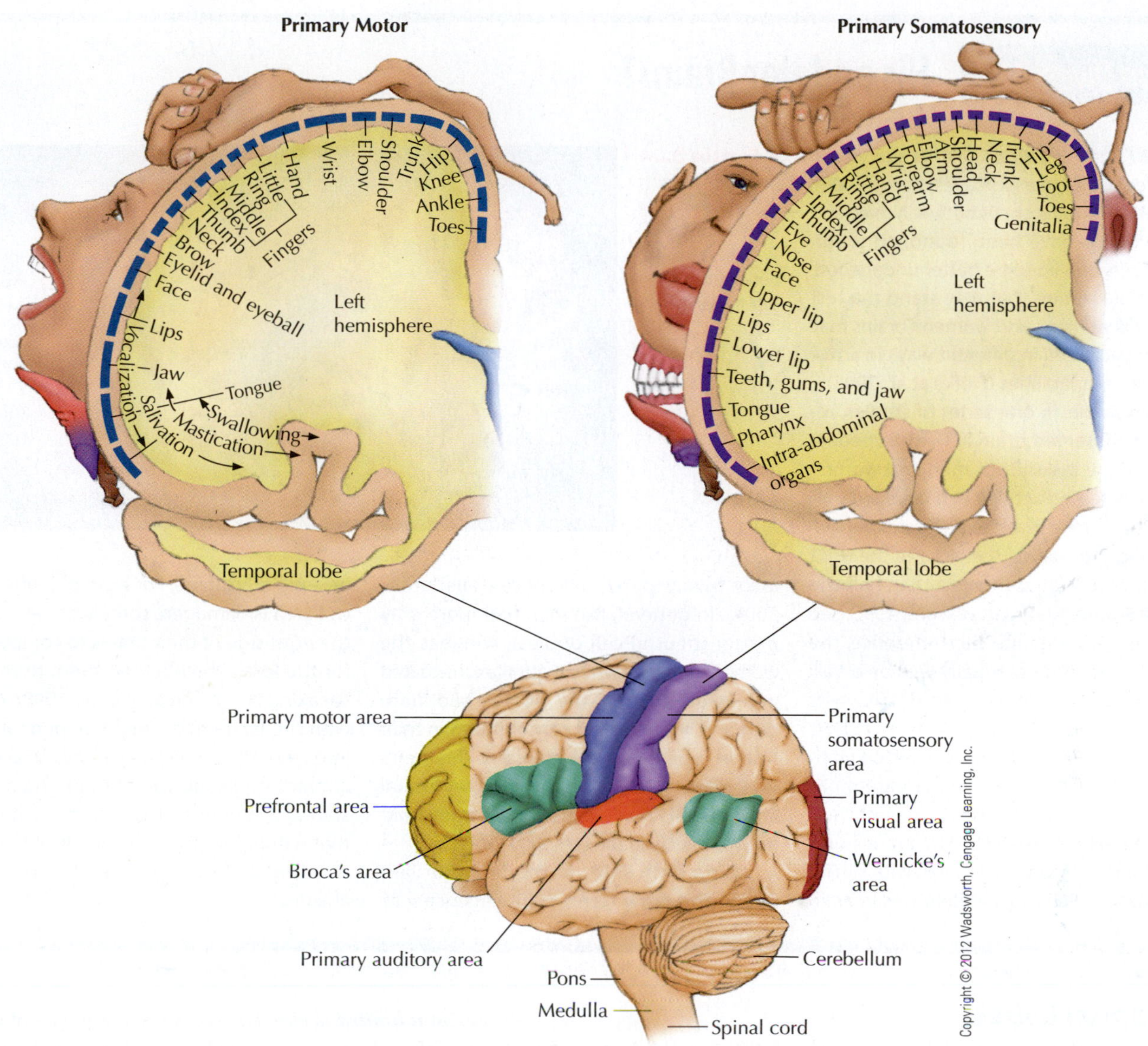

• **Figure 2.23** The lobes of the cerebral cortex and the primary sensory, motor, visual, and auditory areas on each. The top diagrams show (in cross section) the relative amounts of cortex "assigned" to the sensory and motor control of various parts of the body. (Each cross section, or "slice," of the cortex has been turned 90 degrees so that you see it as it would appear from the back of the brain.)

The Temporal Lobes

The **temporal lobes** are located on each side of the brain. Auditory information projects directly to the **primary auditory area**, making it the main site where hearing first registers. If we did a PET scan of your brain while you listened to your favorite song, your primary auditory area would be the first to light up, followed by association areas in your temporal lobes. Likewise, if we could electrically stimulate the primary auditory area of your temporal lobe, you would "hear" a series of sound sensations.

An association area, called **Wernicke's** (VER-nick-ees) **area**, lies on the left temporal lobe (see • Figure 2.23; again, for 5 percent of all people, the area is on the right temporal lobe). Wernicke's area also functions as a language site. If it is damaged, the result is a *receptive (or fluent) aphasia*. Although the person can hear speech, he or she has difficulty understanding the meaning of words. Thus, when shown a picture of a chair, someone with Broca's aphasia might say "tssair." In contrast, a Wernicke's patient might *fluently*, but incorrectly, identify the photo as "truck" (Tanner, 2007).

Broca's area A language area related to grammar and pronunciation.

Prefrontal area (prefrontal cortex) The very front of the frontal lobes; involved in sense of self, reasoning, and planning.

Parietal lobes Areas of the cortex in which bodily sensations register.

Primary somatosensory area (primary somatosensory cortex) A receiving area for body sensations.

Temporal lobes Areas of the cortex that include the sites in which hearing registers in the brain.

Primary auditory area Part of the temporal lobe in which auditory information is first registered.

Wernicke's area A temporal lobe brain area related to language comprehension.

Human Diversity His and Her Brains?

***Are men's and women's brains** specialized in different ways?* In a word, yes (Cahill, 2006). Many physical differences between male and female brains have been found, although their effects remain to be better understood. One generalization that may stand the test of time is that men's and women's brains may well be specialized in different ways to arrive at the same capabilities (Piefke et al., 2005).

For example, in one series of studies, researchers observed brain activity as people did language tasks. Both men and women showed increased activity in Broca's area, on the left side of the brain, exactly as expected. Surprisingly, however, the left *and* the right brain were activated in more than half the women tested (Shaywitz & Gore, 1995; see ● Figure 2.24). Despite this difference, the two sexes performed equally well on a task that involved sounding out words (Shaywitz et al., 1995).

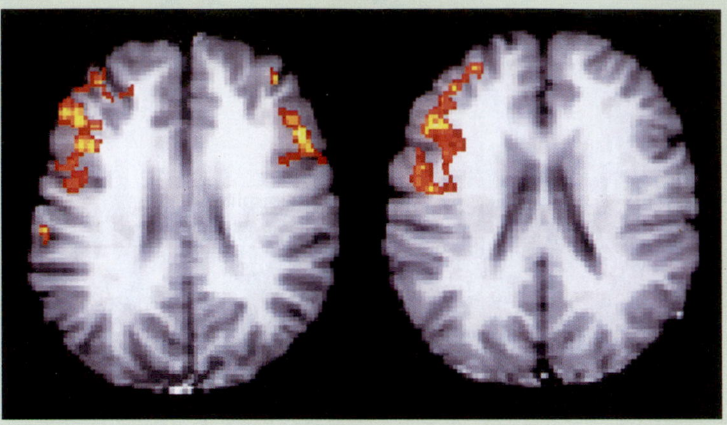

● Figure 2.24 Language tasks activate both sides of the brain in many women but only the left side in men.

Shaywitz et al., 1995 NMR Research/Yale Medical School

Another study, this time focused on intelligence, also found that women are more likely than men to use both sides of their brains (Tang et al., 2010). In a different study, brain images of men and women with similar IQ scores revealed major differences in brain areas involved in intelligence (Haier et al., 2004). In general, the men had more gray matter (neuron cell bodies), whereas the women had more white matter (axons coated in myelin). Further, the women had more gray and white matter concentrated in their frontal lobes than the men did. The men's gray matter was split between their frontal and parietal lobes, whereas their white matter was mostly in the temporal lobes.

Using both sides of the brain for language and other forms of intelligence may be a big advantage. For example, when Broca's area is damaged, some women can use the right side of their brains to compensate for the loss, which allows them to resume speaking (Hochstenbach et al., 1998). A man with similar damage might be permanently impaired. Thus, when a man says, "I have half a mind to tell you what I think," he may be stating a curious truth. Regardless, it seems that nature has given the brains of men and women different routes to the same abilities.

The Occipital Lobes

At the back of the brain, we find the **occipital** (awk-SIP-ih-tal) **lobes**, the area of cortex concerned with vision. Patients with tumors (cell growths that interfere with brain activity) in the **primary visual area**, the part of the cortex to first receive input from the eyes, experience blind spots in their vision.

Do the primary visual areas of the cortex correspond directly to what is seen? Images are mapped onto the cortex, but the map is greatly stretched and distorted (Carlson, 2010). That's why it's important to avoid thinking of the visual area as a little television screen in the brain. Visual information creates complex patterns of activity in neurons; it does *not* make a television-like image.

One of the most fascinating results of brain injury is **visual agnosia** (ag-KNOW-zyah), an inability to identify seen objects. Visual agnosia is often caused by damage to the association areas on the occipital lobes (Farah, 2004). This condition is sometimes referred to as "mindblindness." For example, if we show Alice, an agnosia patient, a candle, she can see it and can describe it as "a long narrow object that tapers at the top." Alice can even draw the candle accurately, but she cannot name it. However, if she is allowed to feel the candle, she will name it immediately. In short, Alice can still see color, size, and shape. She just can't form the associations necessary to perceive the meanings of objects.

Are agnosias limited to objects? No. A fascinating form of "mindblindness" is **facial agnosia**, an inability to perceive familiar faces (Farah, 2006; Sacks, 2010). One patient with facial agnosia couldn't recognize her husband or mother when they visited her in the hospital, and she was unable to identify pictures of her children. However, as soon as visitors spoke she knew them immediately by their voices.

Areas devoted to recognizing faces lie in association areas on the underside of the occipital lobes. These areas appear to have no other function. Why would part of the brain be set aside solely for identifying faces? From an evolutionary standpoint it is not really so surprising. After all, we are social animals, for whom facial recognition is very important. This specialization is just one example of what a marvelous organ of consciousness we possess.

How much do individual brains differ? Could we find different specializations from brain to brain? Perhaps. "His and Her Brains?" explains why.

In summary, the bulk of our daily experience and all of our understanding of the world can be traced to the different areas of the cortex. The human brain is among the most advanced and sophisticated of the brain-bearing species on earth. This, of course, is no guarantee that our marvelous "biocomputer" will be put to full use. Still, we must stand in awe of the potential it represents.

Hemispheres and Lobes of the Cerebral Cortex

RECITE

See if you can match the following:

1. _____ Corpus callosum
2. _____ Occipital lobes
3. _____ Parietal lobes
4. _____ Temporal lobes
5. _____ Frontal lobes
6. _____ Association cortex
7. _____ Aphasias
8. _____ Corticalization
9. _____ Left hemisphere
10. _____ Right hemisphere
11. _____ "Split brain"
12. _____ Agnosia

A. Visual area
B. Language, speech, writing
C. Motor cortex and abstract thinking
D. Spatial skills, visualization, pattern recognition
E. Speech disturbances
F. Causes sleep
G. Increased ratio of cortex in brain
H. Bodily sensations
I. Treatment for severe epilepsy
J. Inability to identify seen objects
K. Fibers connecting the cerebral hemispheres
L. Cortex that is not sensory or motor in function
M. Hearing

REFLECT

Think Critically

13. If you wanted to increase the surface area of the cerebral cortex so that more would fit within the skull, how would you do it?
14. If your brain were removed, replaced by another, and moved to a new body, which would you consider to be yourself, your old body with the new brain, or your new body with the old brain?

Self-Reflect

Learning the functions of the brain lobes is like learning areas on a map. Try drawing a map of the cortex. Can you label all the different "countries" (lobes)? Can you name their functions? Where is the primary motor area? The primary somatosensory area? Broca's area? Keep redrawing the map until it becomes more detailed and you can do it easily.

Answers: 1. K **2.** A **3.** H **4.** M **5.** C **6.** L **7.** E **8.** G **9.** B **10.** D **11.** I **12.** J **13.** One solution would be to gather the surface of the cortex into folds, just as you might if you were trying to fit a large piece of cloth into a small box. This, in fact, is probably why the cortex is more convoluted (folded or wrinkled) in higher animals. **14.** Although there is no "correct" answer to this question, your personality, knowledge, personal memories, and self-concept all derive from brain activity—which makes a strong case for your old brain in a new body being more nearly the "real you."

The Subcortex—At the Core of the (Brain) Matter

Gateway Question 2.5: *What are the major parts of the subcortex?*

You could lose large portions of your cerebral cortex and still survive. Not so with the **subcortex**, the brain structures immediately below the cerebral cortex. Serious damage to the subcortex, or lower brain, can be fatal. Hunger, thirst, sleep, attention, sex, breathing, and many other vital functions are controlled by parts of the subcortex. Let's take a quick tour of these brain areas, which can be divided into the brainstem (or hindbrain), the midbrain, and the forebrain. (The forebrain also includes the cerebral cortex, which we discussed separately because of its size and importance.) For our purposes, the midbrain can be viewed as a link between the forebrain and the brainstem. Therefore, let's focus on the rest of the subcortex (see ● Figure 2.25).

The Hindbrain

Why are the lower brain areas so important? As the spinal cord joins the brain, it widens into the brainstem. The **brainstem** consists mainly of the medulla (meh-DUL-ah) and the cerebellum (ser-ah-BEL-uhm). The **medulla** contains centers important for the reflex control of vital life functions, including heart rate, breathing, swallowing, and the like. Various drugs, diseases, and injuries can disrupt the medulla and end or endanger your life. You can also be left locked-in (see "Trapped!").

The **pons**, which looks like a small bump on the brainstem, acts as a bridge between the medulla and other brain areas. In addition to connecting with many other locations, including the cerebellum, the pons influences sleep and arousal.

The cerebellum, which looks like a miniature cerebral cortex, lies at the base of the brain. Although there is growing evidence of a role in cognition and emotion (Schmahmann, 2010), the **cerebellum** primarily regulates posture, muscle tone, and muscular coordination. The cerebellum also stores memories related to skills and habits (Christian & Thompson, 2005). Again, we see that experience shapes the brain: Musicians, who practice special motor skills throughout their lives, have larger than average cerebellums (Hutchinson et al., 2003).

BRIDGES

In general, the cerebellum stores "know how" or "skill memories." "Know what" memories, such as remembering a person's name or knowing what the cerebellum does, are stored elsewhere in the brain. **See Chapter 7, pages 262–263.**

What happens if the cerebellum is injured? Without the cerebellum, tasks like walking, running, or playing catch become impossible. The first symptoms of a crippling disease called *spinocerebellar degeneration* are tremor, dizziness, and muscular weakness. Eventually, victims have difficulty merely standing, walking, or feeding themselves.

Occipital lobes Portion of the cerebral cortex in which vision registers in the brain.

Primary visual area The part of the occipital lobe that first receives input from the eyes.

Visual agnosia An inability to identify seen objects.

Facial agnosia An inability to perceive familiar faces.

Subcortex All brain structures below the cerebral cortex.

Brainstem The lowest portions of the brain, including the cerebellum, medulla, pons, and reticular formation.

Medulla The structure that connects the brain with the spinal cord and controls vital life functions.

Pons An area on the brainstem that acts as a bridge between the medulla and other structures.

Cerebellum A brain structure that controls posture, muscle tone, and coordination.

The Clinical File Trapped!

At the age of 33, Kate Adamson had a stroke that caused catastrophic damage to her brainstem. This event left her with *locked-in syndrome:* Just before the stroke she was fine, and the next moment she was totally paralyzed, trapped in her own body and barely able to breathe (Laureys & Boly, 2007; Smith & Delargy, 2005). Unable to move a muscle, but still fully awake and aware, she was unable to communicate her simplest thoughts and feelings to others.

Kate thought she was going to die. Her doctors, who thought she was *brain dead*, did not administer painkillers as they inserted breathing and feeding tubes down her throat. However, in time Kate discovered that she could communicate by blinking her eyes. After a recovery that has been miraculous by any measure, she went on to appear before the U.S. Congress and even wrote about her experiences (Adamson, 2004).

Not everyone is so lucky. Just think what might have befallen Kate had she not even been able to blink her eyes. In one chilling study, coma researcher Steven Laureys and his colleagues used fMRI to reexamine 54 patients previously diagnosed as being in a *persistent vegetative state* (known as brain dead). Patients were repeatedly asked to imagine swinging a tennis racquet or walking down a familiar street. Five of the patients showed clearly different brain activity to the two tasks despite being unable to communicate with doctors in any other way (Monti et al., 2010).

What if they could "will" a computer to speak for them? Right on! These results suggest that not all totally locked-in patients are brain dead and hold out the hope that we may eventually be able to develop brain interfaces to help free them from their bodily prisons (Hinterberger et al., 2003; Karim et al., 2006).

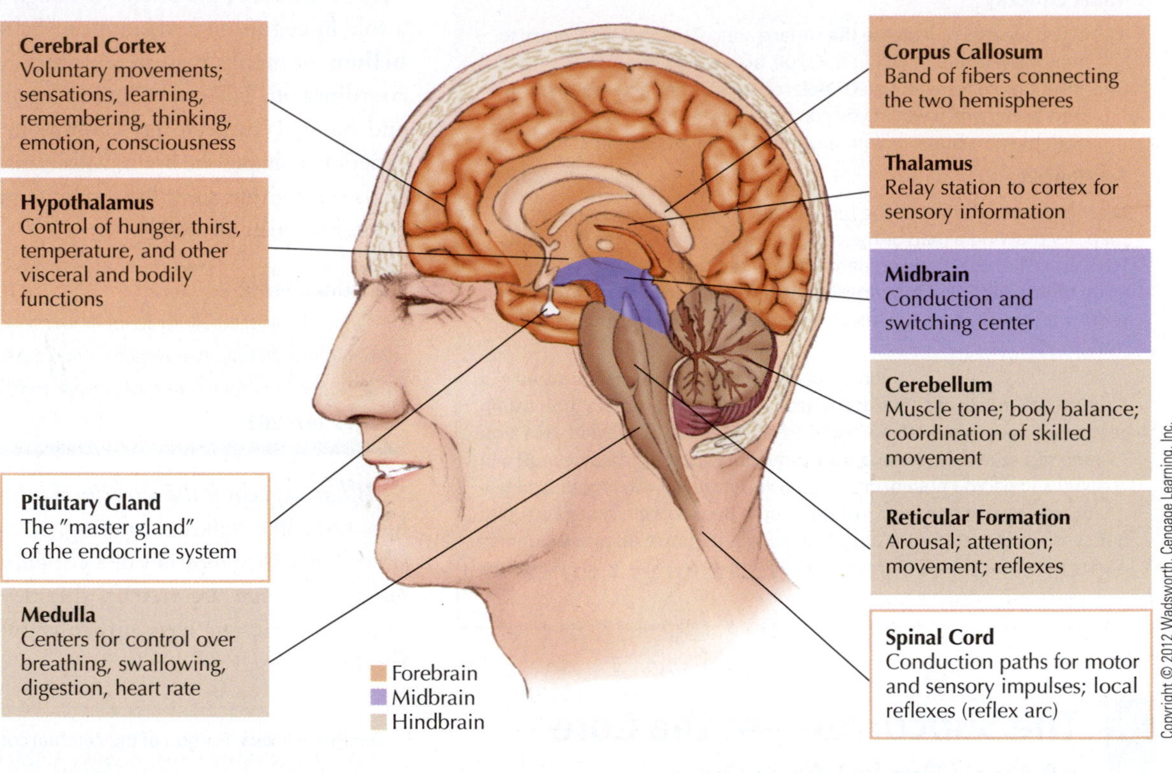

• Figure 2.25 This simplified drawing shows the main structures of the human brain and describes some of their most important features. (You can use the color code in the foreground to identify which areas are part of the forebrain, midbrain, and hindbrain.)

Reticular Formation

A network of fibers and cell bodies called the **reticular** (reh-TICK-you-ler) **formation (RF)** lies inside the medulla and brainstem. As messages flow into the brain, the RF gives priority to some while turning others aside (Kalat, 2009). By doing so, the RF influences *attention.* The RF doesn't fully mature until adolescence, which may be why children have such short attention spans. The RF also modifies outgoing commands to the body. In this way, the RF affects muscle tone, posture, and movements of the eyes, face, head, body, and limbs. At the same time, the RF controls reflexes involved in breathing, sneezing, coughing, and vomiting.

The RF also keeps us vigilant, alert, and awake. Incoming messages from the sense organs branch into a part of the RF called the **reticular activating system (RAS)**. The RAS bombards the cortex with stimulation, keeping it active and alert. For instance, let's say a sleepy driver rounds a bend and sees a deer standing in the road. The driver snaps to attention and applies the brakes. She can thank her RAS for arousing the rest of her brain and averting an accident. If you're getting sleepy while reading this chapter, try pinching your ear—a little pain will cause the RAS to momentarily arouse your cortex.

The Forebrain

Like buried treasure, two of the most important parts of your body lie deep within your brain. The thalamus (THAL-uh-mus) and an area just below it called the hypothalamus (HI-po-THAL-uh-mus) are key parts of the forebrain (see ● Figure 2.25).

How could these be any more important than other areas already described? The **thalamus** acts as a final "switching station" for sensory messages on their way to the cortex. Vision, hearing, taste, and touch all pass through this small, football-shaped structure. Thus, injury to even small areas of the thalamus can cause deafness, blindness, or loss of any other sense, except smell.

The human hypothalamus is about the size of a small grape. Small as it may be, the **hypothalamus** is a kind of master control center for emotion and many basic motives (Carlson, 2010).

BRIDGES

The hypothalamus affects behaviors as diverse as sex, rage, temperature control, hormone release, eating and drinking, sleep, waking, and emotion. **See Chapter 10, pages 334–335.**

The hypothalamus is basically a "crossroads" that connects many areas of the brain. It is also the final pathway for many kinds of behavior. That is, the hypothalamus is the last place where many behaviors are organized or "decided on" before messages leave the brain, causing the body to react.

The Limbic System

As a group, the hypothalamus, parts of the thalamus, the amygdala, the hippocampus, and other structures make up the limbic system (● Figure 2.26). The **limbic system** has a major role in producing emotion and motivated behavior. Rage, fear, sexual response, and intense arousal can be localized to various points in the limbic system. Laughter, a delightful part of human social life, also has its origins in the limbic system (Cardoso, 2000).

During evolution, the limbic system was the earliest layer of the forebrain to develop. In lower animals, the limbic system helps organize basic survival responses: feeding, fleeing, fighting, or reproduction. In humans, a clear link to emotion remains. The **amygdala** (ah-MIG-dah-luh), in particular, is strongly related to fear. For example, during medical testing, one woman reacted with a sudden outburst of fear and anger when the amygdala was stimulated, saying, "I feel like I want to get up from this chair! Please don't let me do it! I don't want to be mean! I want to get something and just tear it up!" (King, 1961).

The amygdala provides a primitive, "quick pathway" to the cortex. Like lower animals, we can be startled and, as such, are able to react to dangerous stimuli before we fully know what is going on (Fellous & LeDoux, 2005). In situations in which true danger exists, such as in military combat, the amygdala's rapid

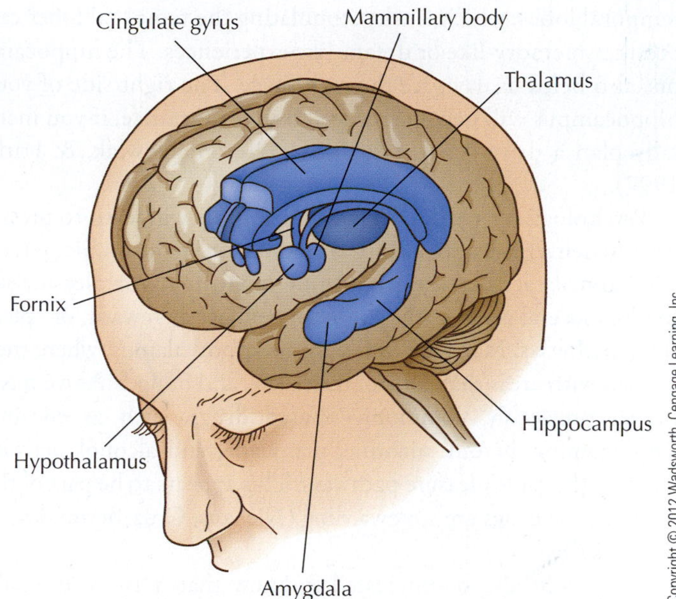

● **Figure 2.26** Parts of the limbic system. Although only one side is shown here, the hippocampus and the amygdala extend out into the temporal lobes at each side of the brain. The limbic system is a sort of "primitive core" of the brain strongly associated with emotion.

response may aid survival. However, disorders of the brain's fear system can be very disruptive. An example is the war veteran who involuntarily dives into the bushes when he hears a car backfire. The role of the amygdala in emotion may also explain why people who suffer from phobias and disabling anxiety often feel afraid without knowing why (Lamprecht et al., 2009; Schlund & Cataldo, 2010).

BRIDGES

Unconscious fear produced by the amygdala seems to explain why people who survive horrible experiences, such as a plane crash, can have debilitating fears years later. **See the discussion of stress disorders in Chapter 14, pages 498–499.**

Some parts of the limbic system have taken on additional, higher-level functions. A part called the **hippocampus** (HIP-oh-CAMP-us) is important for forming lasting memories (Kumaran & Maguire, 2005). The hippocampus lies inside the

Reticular formation (RF) A network within the medulla and brainstem; associated with attention, alertness, and some reflexes.
Reticular activating system (RAS) A part of the reticular formation that activates the cerebral cortex.
Thalamus A brain structure that relays sensory information to the cerebral cortex.
Hypothalamus A small area of the brain that regulates emotional behaviors and motives.
Limbic system A system in the forebrain that is closely linked with emotional response.
Amygdala A part of the limbic system associated with fear responses.
Hippocampus A part of the limbic system associated with storing memories.

temporal lobes, which is why stimulating the temporal lobes can produce memory-like or dream-like experiences. The hippocampus also helps us navigate through space. The right side of your hippocampus will become more active, for instance, if you mentally plan a drive across town (Maguire, Frackowiak, & Frith, 1997).

Psychologists have discovered that animals will learn to press a lever to deliver a dose of electrical stimulation to the limbic system. The animals act like the stimulation is satisfying or pleasurable. Indeed, several areas of the limbic system act as reward, or "pleasure," pathways. Many are found in the hypothalamus, where they overlap with areas that control thirst, sex, and hunger. As we mentioned previously, commonly abused drugs, such as cocaine, amphetamine, heroin, nicotine, marijuana, and alcohol, activate many of the same pleasure pathways. This appears to be part of the reason these drugs are so rewarding (Niehaus, Cruz-Bermúdez, & Kauer, 2009).

You might also be interested to know that music you would describe as "thrilling" activates pleasure systems in your brain. This may explain some of the appeal of music that can send shivers down your spine (Blood & Zatorre, 2001). (It may also explain why people will pay so much for concert tickets!)

Punishment, or "aversive," areas have also been found in the limbic system. When these locations are activated, animals show discomfort and will work hard to turn off the stimulation. Because much of our behavior is based on seeking pleasure and avoiding pain, these discoveries continue to fascinate psychologists.

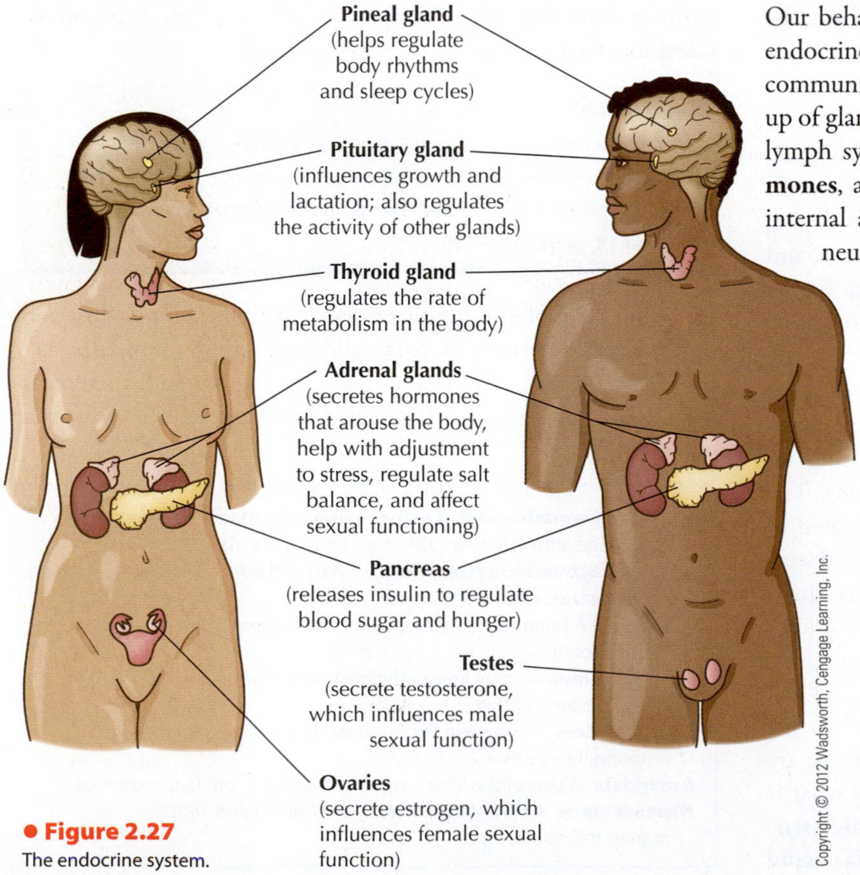

• Figure 2.27
The endocrine system.

The Whole Person

We have seen that the human brain is an impressive assembly of billions of sensitive cells and nerve fibers. The brain controls vital bodily functions, keeps track of the external world, issues commands to the muscles and glands, responds to current needs, regulates its own behavior, and even creates the "mind" and the magic of consciousness—*all* at the same time.

Two final notes of caution are now in order. First, for the sake of simplicity, we have assigned functions to each "part" of the brain as if it were a computer. This is only a half-truth. In reality, the brain is a vast information-processing system. Incoming information scatters all over the brain and converges again as it goes out through the spinal cord, to muscles and glands. The overall system is much, much more complicated than our discussion of separate "parts" implies. Second, we have stressed how the brain underlies all human experience. Again, this is only a half-truth. Human experience also shapes the brain's circuits (Kolb & Whishaw, 2011). For example, as we have seen, practicing cultural knowledge, such as mathematics or music, will not only improve performance, it will also result in a changed brain (Merlin, 2008).

The Endocrine System—My Hormones Made Me Do It

Gateway Question 2.6: *Does the glandular system affect behavior?*

Our behavior is not solely a product of the nervous system. The endocrine (EN-duh-krin) glands form an equally important parallel communication system in the body. The **endocrine system** is made up of glands that secrete chemicals directly into the bloodstream or lymph system (see • Figure 2.27). These chemicals, called **hormones**, are carried throughout the body, where they affect both internal activities and visible behavior. Hormones are related to neurotransmitters. Like other transmitter chemicals, hormones activate cells in the body. To respond, the cells must have receptor sites for the hormone. Hormones affect puberty, personality, dwarfism, jet lag, and much more.

How do hormones affect behavior? Although we are seldom directly aware of them, hormones affect us in many ways (Carlson, 2010). Here is a brief sample: Hormone output from the adrenal glands rises during stressful situations; androgens ("male" hormones) are related to the sex drive in both males and females; hormones secreted during times of high emotion intensify memory formation; at least some of the emotional turmoil of adolescence is due to elevated hormone levels; different hormones prevail when you are angry, rather than fearful. Even disturbing personality patterns may be linked to hormonal irregularities (Evardone, Alexander, & Morey, 2007).

In fact, something as routine as watching a movie can alter hormone levels. After watching violent scenes from *The Godfather*, men had higher levels of the male hormone testosterone. For both men and women, watching a romantic film boosted a hormone that's linked to relaxation and reproduction (Schultheiss, Wirth, & Stanton, 2004). Because these are just samples, let's consider some additional effects hormones have on the body and behavior.

The **pituitary** is a pea-sized globe hanging from the base of the brain (see ● Figure 2.27). One of the pituitary's more important roles is to regulate growth. During childhood, the pituitary secretes a hormone that speeds body development. If too little **growth hormone** is released, a person may remain far smaller than average. If this condition is not treated, a child may be 6 to 12 inches shorter than age-mates. As adults, some will have *hypopituitary* (HI-po-pih-TU-ih-ter-ee) *dwarfism*. Such individuals are perfectly proportioned, but tiny. Regular injections of growth hormone can raise a hypopituitary child's height by several inches, usually to the short side of average.

Too much growth hormone produces *gigantism* (excessive bodily growth). Secretion of too much growth hormone late in the growth period causes *acromegaly* (AK-row-MEG-uh-lee) a condition in which the arms, hands, feet, and facial bones become enlarged. Acromegaly produces prominent facial features, which some people have used as a basis for careers as character actors, wrestlers, and the like.

Oxytocin, another important hormone released by the pituitary, plays a broad role in regulating many behaviors generally involved in happiness (Viero et al., 2010). These include pregnancy, parenthood, sexual activity, social bonding, trust, and even reducing stress reactions (Gordon et al., 2010; Kingsley & Lambert, 2006; Mikolajczak et al., 2010).

The pituitary is often called the "master gland" because it influences other endocrine glands (especially the thyroid, adrenal glands, and ovaries or testes). These glands in turn regulate such bodily processes as metabolism, responses to stress, and reproduction. But the master has a master: The pituitary is directed by the hypothalamus, which lies directly above it. In this way, the hypothalamus can affect glands throughout the body. This, then, is the major link between the brain and hormones (Kalat, 2009).

© Corbis Sygma

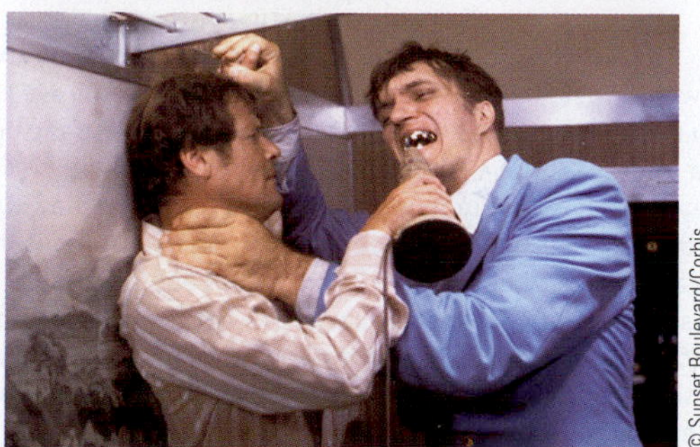

© Sunset Boulevard/Corbis

Underactivity of the pituitary gland may produce a dwarf. Two foot, eight inch Verne Troyer (top), best known for playing Mini-Me in the *Austin Powers* movies, has enjoyed an impressive career as an actor. Overactivity of the pituitary gland may produce a giant. Seven foot, two inch Richard Kiel (bottom) has had a similarly impressive career. He is best known for playing Jaws in several James Bond movies.

The **pineal** (pin-EE-ul) **gland** was once considered a useless remnant of evolution. In certain fishes, frogs, and lizards, the gland is associated with a well-developed light-sensitive organ, or so-called third eye. In humans, the function of the pineal gland is just now coming to light (so to speak). The pineal gland releases a hormone called **melatonin** (mel-ah-TONE-in) in response to daily variations in light. Melatonin levels in the bloodstream rise at dusk, peak around midnight, and fall again as morning approaches. As far as the brain is concerned, it's bedtime when melatonin levels rise (Norman, 2009).

BRIDGES

Melatonin can be used to reset the body's "clock" and minimize jet lag for long-distance pilots, aircrews, and travelers. **See Chapter 10, pages 333–334.**

The **thyroid gland**, located in the neck, regulates metabolism. As you may remember from a biology course, metabolism is the rate at which energy is produced and expended in the body. By altering metabolism, the thyroid can have a sizable effect on personality. A person suffering from *hyperthyroidism* (an overactive thyroid) tends to be thin, tense, excitable, and nervous. An underactive thyroid (*hypothyroidism*) in an adult can cause inactivity, sleepiness, slowness, obesity, and depression (Joffe, 2006).

BRIDGES

In infancy, hypothyroidism limits development of the nervous system, leading to severe intellectual disability. **See Chapter 9, pages 315–316.**

When you are frightened or angry, some important reactions prepare your body for action: Your heart rate and blood pressure rise, stored sugar is released into the bloodstream for quick energy, your muscles tense and receive more blood, and your blood is pre-

Endocrine system Glands whose secretions pass directly into the bloodstream or lymph system.

Hormone A glandular secretion that affects bodily functions or behavior.

Pituitary gland The "master gland" whose hormones influence other endocrine glands.

Growth hormone A hormone, secreted by the pituitary gland, that promotes body growth.

Oxytocin A hormone, released by the pituitary gland, that plays a broad role in regulating pregnancy, parenthood, sexual activity, social bonding, trust, and even reducing stress reaction.

Pineal gland Gland in the brain that helps regulate body rhythms and sleep cycles.

Melatonin Hormone released by the pineal gland in response to daily cycles of light and dark.

Thyroid gland Endocrine gland that helps regulate the rate of metabolism.

pared to clot more quickly in case of injury. As we discussed earlier, these changes are controlled by the autonomic nervous system. Specifically, the sympathetic branch of the ANS causes the hormones *epinephrine* and *norepinephrine* to be released by the adrenal glands. **Epinephrine** (ep-eh-NEF-rin), which is associated with fear, tends to arouse the body. (Epinephrine is also known as adrenaline, which may be more familiar to you.) **Norepinephrine** (which also functions as a neurotransmitter in the brain) also tends to arouse the body, but it is linked with anger.

The **adrenal glands** are located just under the back of the rib cage, atop the kidneys. The *adrenal medulla*, or inner core of the adrenal glands, is the source of epinephrine and norepinephrine. The *adrenal cortex*, or outer "bark" of the adrenal glands, produces a set of hormones called corticoids (KOR-tih-coids). One of their jobs is to regulate salt balance in the body. A deficiency of certain corticoids can evoke a powerful craving for the taste of salt in humans. The corticoids also help the body adjust to stress, and they are a secondary source of sex hormones.

An oversecretion of the adrenal sex hormones can cause *virilism* (exaggerated male characteristics). For instance, a woman may grow a beard or a man's voice may become so low it is difficult to understand. Oversecretion early in life can cause *premature puberty* (full sexual development during childhood). One of the most remarkable cases on record is that of a 5-year-old Peruvian girl who gave birth to a son (Strange, 1965).

Since we are on the topic of sex hormones, there is a related issue worth mentioning. One of the principal androgens, or "male" hormones, is testosterone, which is supplied in small amounts by the adrenal glands. (The testes are the main source of testosterone in males.) Perhaps you have heard about the use of anabolic steroids by athletes who want to "bulk up" or promote muscle growth. Most of these drugs are synthetic versions of testosterone.

Although there is some disagreement about whether steroids actually improve athletic performance, it is widely accepted that they may cause serious side effects (Sjöqvist, Garle, & Rane, 2008). Problems include voice deepening or baldness in women and shrinkage of the testicles, sexual impotence, or breast enlargement in men (Millman & Ross, 2003). Dangerous increases in hostility and aggression ("roid rage") have also been linked with steroid use (Hartgens & Kuipers, 2004). Also common when steroids are used by younger adolescents are an increased risk of heart attack and stroke, liver damage, and stunted growth. Understandably, almost all major sports organizations ban the use of anabolic steroids.

In this brief discussion of the endocrine system, we have considered only a few of the more important glands. Nevertheless, this should give you an appreciation of how completely behavior and personality are tied to the ebb and flow of hormones in the body.

A Look Ahead

In the upcoming *Psychology in Action* section, we will return to the brain to see how hand preference relates to brain organization. You'll also find out if being right- or left-handed affects your chances of living to a ripe old age.

Knowledge Builder: Subcortex and Endocrine System

RECITE

1. Three major divisions of the brain are the brainstem or ______________, the ______________, and the ______________.
2. Reflex centers for heartbeat and respiration are found in the *a.* cerebellum *b.* thalamus *c.* medulla *d.* RF
3. A portion of the reticular formation, known as the RAS, serves as an ______________ system in the brain. *a.* activating *b.* adrenal *c.* adjustment *d.* aversive
4. The ______________ is a final relay, or "switching station," for sensory information on its way to the cortex.
5. "Reward" and "punishment" areas are found throughout the ______________ system, which is also related to emotion.
6. Undersecretion from the thyroid can cause both *a.* dwarfism *b.* gigantism *c.* obesity *d.* intellectual disability
7. The body's ability to resist stress is related to the action of the adrenal ______________.

REFLECT

Think Critically

8. Subcortical structures in humans are quite similar to corresponding lower brain areas in animals. Why would knowing this allow you to predict, in general terms, what functions are controlled by the subcortex?
9. Where in all the brain's "hardware" do you think the mind is found? What is the relationship between mind and brain?

Self-Reflect

If Mr. Medulla met Ms. Cerebellum at a party, what would they say their roles are in the brain? Would a marching band in a "reticular formation" look like a network? Would it get your attention? If you were standing in the final path for behavior leaving the brain, would you be in the thalamus? Or in the hy-*path*-alamus (please forgive the misspelling)? When you are emotional, do you wave your limbs around (and does your limbic system become more active)?

Name as many of the endocrine glands as you can. Which did you leave out? Can you summarize the functions of each of the glands?

Answers: 1. hindbrain, midbrain, forebrain **2.** c **3.** *a* **4.** thalamus **5.** limbic **6.** c, *d* (in infancy) **7.** cortex **8.** Because the subcortex must be related to basic functions common to all higher animals: motives, emotions, sleep, attention, and vegetative functions, such as heartbeat, breathing, and temperature regulation. The subcortex also routes and processes incoming information from the senses and outgoing commands to the muscles. **9.** This question, known as the mind–body problem, has challenged thinkers for centuries. One recent view is that mental states are "emergent properties" of brain activity. That is, brain activity forms complex patterns that are, in a sense, more than the sum of their parts. Or, to use a rough analogy, if the brain were a musical instrument, then mental life would be like music played on that instrument.

Psychology in Action

Handedness—Are You Sinister or Dexterous?

Gateway Question 2.7: *In what ways do left- and right-handed individuals differ?*

Throughout history, left-handedness has been frowned upon. "Lefties" have often been characterized as clumsy, awkward, unlucky, or insincere. The Latin word for left is actually *sinister*! In contrast, right-handedness is the paragon of virtue. The Latin word for right is *dexter* and "righties" are more likely to be referred to as dexterous, coordinated, skillful, and just. But is there any basis in fact for these attitudes?

What causes **handedness**, a preference for the right or left hand? Why are there more right-handed than left-handed people? How do left-handed and right-handed people differ? Does being left-handed create any problems—or benefits? The answers to these questions lead us back to the brain, where handedness begins. Let's see what research has revealed about handedness, the brain, and you.

Assessing Handedness

Write your name on a sheet of paper, first using your right hand and then your left. You were probably much more comfortable writing with your dominant hand. This is interesting because there's no real difference in the strength or dexterity of the hands themselves. The agility of your dominant hand is an outward expression of superior motor control on one side of the brain. If you are right-handed, there is literally more area on the left side of your brain devoted to controlling your right hand. If you are left-handed, the reverse applies.

The preceding exercise implies that you are either entirely right- or left-handed. But handedness is a matter of degree. To better assess your handedness, complete a few questions adapted from the *Waterloo Handedness Questionnaire* (Brown et al., 2006) by putting a check mark in the Right, Left, or Either column for each question. The more "Rights" you circle, the more right-handed you are.

Are You Right- or Left-Handed?

	Right	Left	Either
1. Which hand would you use to spin a top?	____	____	____
2. With which hand would you hold a paintbrush to paint a wall?	____	____	____
3. Which hand would you use to pick up a book?	____	____	____
4. With which hand would you use a spoon to eat soup?	____	____	____
5. Which hand would you use to flip pancakes?	____	____	____
6. Which hand would you use to pick up a piece of paper?	____	____	____
7. Which hand would you use to draw a picture?	____	____	____
8. Which hand would you use to insert and turn a key in a lock?	____	____	____
9. Which hand would you use to insert a plug into an electrical outlet?	____	____	____
10. Which hand would you use to throw a ball?	____	____	____

About 90 percent of all humans are right-handed; 10 percent are left-handed. Most people (about 75 percent) are strongly right- or left-handed. The rest show some inconsistency in hand preference. Which are you?

Is there such a thing as being left-footed? Excellent question. Do you have "two left feet"? **Sidedness** is often measured by assessing hand, foot, eye, *and* ear preference (Greenwood et al., 2006). We also generally prefer breathing through one nostril over the other and even have a preference for which direction we lean our head when kissing (Barrett, Greenwood, & McCullagh, 2006). (Do you "kiss right"?) Nevertheless, handedness remains the single most important behavioral indicator of sidedness.

If a person is strongly left-handed, does that mean the right hemisphere is dominant? Not necessarily. It's true that the right hemisphere controls the left hand, but a left-handed person's language-producing, **dominant hemisphere** may be on the opposite side of the brain.

Brain Dominance

About 95 percent of right-handers process speech in the left hemisphere and are left-brain dominant. A good 70 percent of left-handers produce speech from the left hemisphere, just as right-handed people do. About 19 percent of all lefties and 3 percent of righties use their right brain for language. Some left-handers (approximately 12 percent) use both sides of the brain for language processing. All told, 90 percent of the population uses the left brain for language (Coren, 1992; Willems, Peelen, & Hagoort, 2010).

Is there any way for a person to tell which of his or her hemispheres is dominant? One classic clue is the way you write (see ● Figure 2.28). Right-handed individuals who write with a straight hand, and lefties who write with a hooked hand, are usually left-brain dominant for language. Left-handed people who write

Epinephrine An adrenal hormone that tends to arouse the body; epinephrine is associated with fear. (Also known as adrenaline.)

Norepinephrine Both a brain neurotransmitter and an adrenal hormone that tends to arouse the body; norepinephrine is associated with anger. (Also known as noradrenaline.)

Adrenal glands Endocrine glands that arouse the body, regulate salt balance, adjust the body to stress, and affect sexual functioning.

Handedness A preference for the right or left hand in most activities.

Sidedness A combination of preference for hand, foot, eye, and ear.

Dominant hemisphere A term usually applied to the side of a person's brain that produces language.

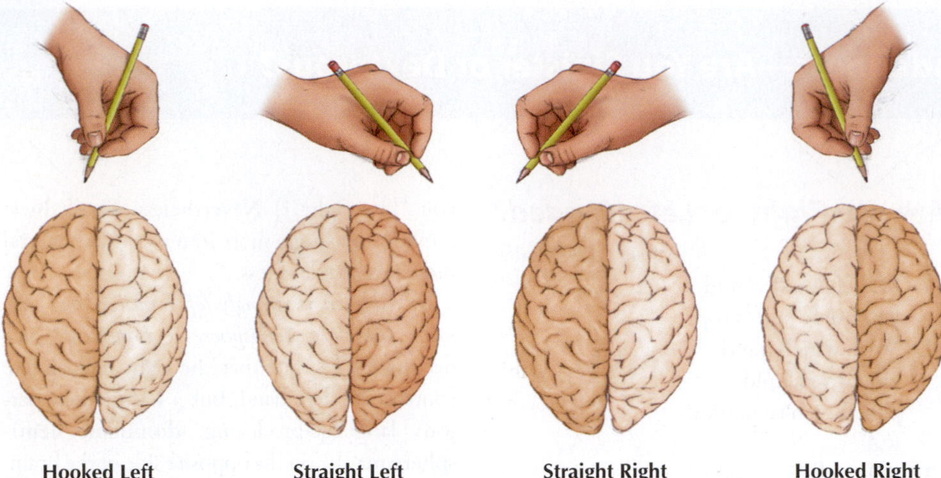

● **Figure 2.28** Research suggests that the hand position used in writing may indicate which brain hemisphere is used for language. (Redrawn from an illustration by M. E. Challinor.)

with their hand below the line, and righties who use a hooked position, are usually right-brain dominant (Levy & Reid, 1976). Another hint is provided by hand gestures. If you gesture mostly with your right hand as you talk, you probably process language in your left hemisphere. Gesturing with your left hand is associated with right-brain language processing (Hellige, 1993).

Are your friends right brained or left brained? Before you leap to any conclusions, be aware that writing position and gesture are not foolproof. The only sure way to check brain dominance is to do medical tests that involve assessing one cerebral hemisphere at a time (Kirveskari, Salmelin, & Hari, 2006).

Causes of Handedness

Is handedness inherited from parents? Yes, at least partly. Clear hand preferences are apparent even before birth, as can be seen in a fetal ultrasound image (● Figure 2.29). According to British psychologist Peter Hepper, prenatal handedness preferences persist for at least 10 years after birth (Hepper, Wells, & Lynch, 2005). This suggests that handedness cannot be dictated. Parents should not try to force a left-handed child to use his or her right hand. To do so may create speech or reading problems (Klöppel et al., 2010).

Studies of identical twins show that hand preferences are not directly inherited like eye color or skin color, however (Ooki, 2005; Reiss et al., 1999). Yet, two left-handed parents are more likely to have a left-handed child than two right-handed parents are (McKeever, 2000). The best evidence to date shows that left-handedness is more common in males and is influenced by a single gene on the X (female) chromosome (Papadatou-Pastou et al., 2008).

On the other hand, environmental factors such as learning, birth traumas, and social pressure to use the right hand can also affect which hand you end up favoring (Bailey & McKeever, 2004). In the past, many left-handed children were forced to use their right hand for writing, eating, and other skills. This is especially true in collectivist cultures like India and Japan, where left-handedness is viewed as especially negative. Not surprisingly, the proportion of left-handers in these societies is only about half that found in individualist cultures such as the United States and Canada (Ida & Mandal, 2003).

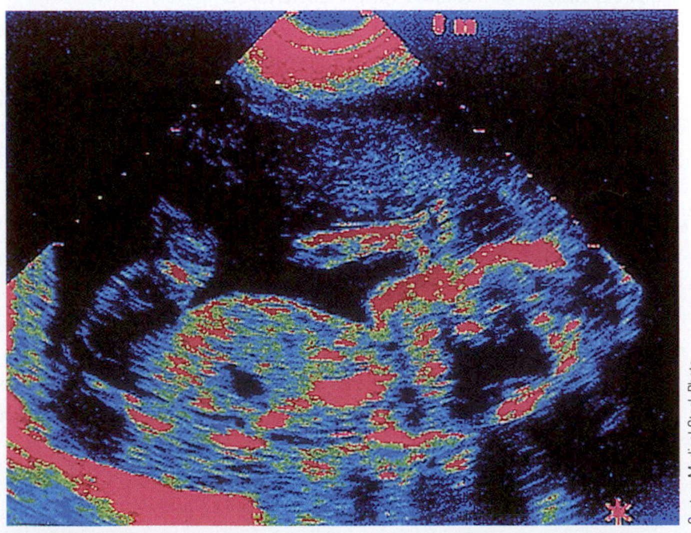

● **Figure 2.29** In this ultrasound image, a 4-month-old fetus sucks her right thumb. Research by British psychologist Peter Hepper suggests that she will continue to prefer her right hand long after she is born and that she will be right-handed as an adult.

Custom Medical Stock Photo

Advantage Right

Are there any drawbacks to being left-handed? A small minority of lefties owe their hand preference to birth traumas (such as prematurity, low birth weight, and breech birth). These individuals have higher rates of allergies, learning disorders, and other problems (Betancur et al., 1990). Similarly, people with inconsistent handedness (as opposed to consistent left-handers) may be at risk for more immune-related diseases (Bryden, Bruyn, & Fletcher, 2005). (Inconsistent handedness means doing some things better with one hand and other things better with the other.)

Is it true that right-handed people live longer than left-handed people? It is true that there is a shortage of very old lefties. One possible explanation lies in the widespread finding that left-handers are more accident-prone (Dutta & Mandal, 2005). However, the supposed clumsiness of lefties may well be a result of living in a right-handed world. One study showed that left-handed locomotive engineers have higher accident rates and suggested that the cause was due to the design of locomotive controls (Bhushan & Khan, 2006). If it can be gripped, turned, or pulled, it's probably designed for the right hand. Even toilet handles are on the right side. On the other hand, the shortage of very old lefties may just reflect the fact that, in the past, more left-handed children were forced to become right-handed. That makes it look like many lefties don't survive to old age. In reality, they do, but many of them are masquerading as righties (Martin & Freitas, 2002)!

Advantage Left

Are there any advantages to being left-handed? Actually, there are some clear advantages to being left-handed (Faurie et al., 2008). Throughout history, a notable number of artists have been lefties, from Leonardo da Vinci and Michelangelo to Pablo Picasso and M. C. Escher. Conceivably, because the right hemisphere is superior at imagery and visual abilities, there is some advantage to using the left hand for drawing or painting (Springer & Deutsch, 1998). At the least, lefties are definitely better at visualizing three-dimensional objects. This may be why there are more left-handed architects, artists, and chess players than would be expected (Coren, 1992). Similarly, being right-handed does not guarantee sports superiority. Left-handers have done well in a variety of professional sports including boxing, fencing, handball, and tennis (Coren, 1992; Dane & Erzurumluoglu, 2003; Holtzen, 2000).

Lateralization refers to specialization in the abilities of the brain hemispheres. One striking feature of lefties is that they are generally less lateralized than the right-handed. In fact, even the physical size and shape of their cerebral hemispheres are more alike. If you are a lefty, you can take pride in the fact that your brain is less lopsided than most! In general, left-handers are more symmetrical on almost everything, including eye dominance, fingerprints—even foot size (Bourne, 2008; Polemikos & Papaeliou, 2000).

In some situations, less lateralization may be a real advantage. For instance, individuals who are moderately left-handed or are ambidextrous (can do things equally well with both hands) seem to have better than average pitch memory, which is a basic musical skill. Correspondingly, more musicians are ambidextrous than would normally be expected (Springer & Deutsch, 1998).

Math abilities may also benefit from fuller use of the right hemisphere. Students who are extremely gifted in math are much more likely to be left-handed or ambidextrous (Benbow, 1986). Even when ordinary arithmetic skills are concerned, lefties seem to excel (Annett, 2002; Annett & Manning, 1990).

The clearest advantage of being left-handed shows up when there is a brain injury. Because of their milder lateralization, left-handed individuals typically experience less language loss after damage to either brain hemisphere, and they recover more easily (Geschwind, 1979). Maybe having "two left feet" isn't so bad after all.

Friedemann Vogel/Bongarts/Getty Images

Left-handers, such as 2010 U.S. Open tennis champion Rafael Nadal, have an advantage in sports such as fencing and tennis. Most likely, their movements are less familiar to opponents, who usually face right-handers.

Lateralization Differences between the two sides of the body, especially differences in the abilities of the brain hemispheres.

Knowledge Builder — Handedness and Brain Lateralization

RECITE

1. About 95 percent of left-handed people process language on the left side of the brain, the same as right-handed people do. T or F?
2. Left-handed individuals who write with their hand below the writing line are likely to be right-brain dominant. T or F?
3. People basically learn to be right- or left-handed. T or F?
4. In general, left-handed individuals show less lateralization in the brain and throughout the body. T or F?

REFLECT

Think Critically

5. News reports that left-handed people tend to die younger have been flawed in an important way: The average age of people in the left-handed group was younger than that of subjects in the right-handed group. Why would this make a difference in the conclusions drawn?

Self-Reflect

Think for a moment about what you "knew" about handedness and left-handed people before you read this section. Which of your beliefs were correct? How has your knowledge about handedness changed?

Answers: 1. F **2.** T **3.** F **4.** T **5.** Because we can't tell if handedness or average age accounts for the difference in death rates. For example, if we start with a group of 20- to 30-year-old people, in which some die, the average age of death has to be between 20 and 30. If we start with a group of 30- to 40-year-old people, in which some die, the average age of death has to be between 30 and 40. Thus, the left-handed group might have an earlier average age at death simply because members of the group were younger to start with.

Chapter in Review Gateways to Brain and Behavior

Gateway QUESTIONS REVISITED

2.1 *How do neurons operate and communicate?*

2.1.1 The dendrite and soma of a neuron combine neural input and send it down the axon to the axon terminals for output across the synapse to other neurons.

2.1.2 The firing of an action potential (nerve impulse) is basically an electrical event.

2.1.3 Communication between neurons is chemical: Neurotransmitters cross the synapse, attach to receptor sites, and excite or inhibit the receiving cell.

2.1.4 Chemicals called neuropeptides regulate activity in the brain.

2.1.5 All behavior can be traced to networks of neurons.

2.1.6 The brain's circuitry is not static. The brain can "rewire "itself and even grow new nerve cells in response to changing environmental conditions.

2.2 *What are the major parts of the nervous system?*

2.2.1 The nervous system can be divided into the central nervous system (CNS) and the peripheral nervous system (PNS). The CNS is made up of the brain, which carries out most of the "computing" in the nervous system, and the spinal cord, which connects the brain to the PNS.

2.2.2 The PNS, includes the somatic nervous system (SNS), which carries sensory information to the brain and motor commands to the body, and the autonomic nervous system (ANS), which controls "vegetative" and automatic bodily processes. The ANS has a sympathetic branch and a parasympathetic branch.

2.2.3 The spinal cord can process simple reflex arcs.

2.2.4 Neurons and nerves in the peripheral nervous system can often regenerate. At present, damage in the central nervous system is usually permanent, although scientists are working on ways to repair damaged neural tissue.

2.3 *How are different parts of the brain identified and what do they do?*

2.3.1 Biopsychologists study how processes in the body, brain, and nervous system relate to behavior.

2.3.2 A major brain research strategy involves the localization of function to link specific structures in the brain with specific psychological or behavioral functions.

2.3.3 Brain structure is investigated though dissection and less intrusive CT scans and MRI scans.

2.3.4 Brain function is investigated through clinical case studies, electrical stimulation, ablation, deep lesioning, electrical recording, and microelectrode recording, as well as less intrusive EEG recording, PET scans, and fMRI scans.

2.4 *How do the left and right hemispheres differ and what are the different functions of the lobes of the cerebral cortex?*

2.4.1 The human brain is marked not by overall size but by advanced corticalization, or enlargement of the cerebral cortex.

2.4.2 "Split brains" can be created by cutting the corpus callosum. The split-brain individual shows a remarkable degree of independence between the right and left hemispheres.

2.4.3 The left hemisphere is good at analysis and it processes small details sequentially. It contains speech or language "centers" in most people. It also specializes in writing, calculating, judging time and rhythm, and ordering complex movements.

2.4.4 The right hemisphere detects overall patterns; it processes information simultaneously and holistically. It is largely nonverbal and excels at spatial and perceptual skills, visualization, and recognition of patterns, faces, and melodies.

2.4.5 The frontal lobes contain the primary motor area (which includes many mirror neurons) and many association areas, which combine and process information. Damage to one association area—Broca's area—results in motor aphasia, a difficulty speaking or writing. Prefrontal cortex is related to abstract thought and one's sense of self.

2.4.6 The parietal lobes contain the primary sensory area, which processes bodily sensations.

2.4.7 The temporal lobes contain the primary auditory area and is responsible for hearing and language. Damage to Wernicke's area results in fluent aphasia, a difficulty understanding meanings of words.

2.4.8 The occipital lobes contain the primary visual area is responsible for vision.

2.4.9 Men's and women's brains are specialized in different ways.

2.5 *What are the major parts of the subcortex?*

2.5.1 The brain can be subdivided into the forebrain, midbrain, and hindbrain. The subcortex includes hindbrain and midbrain brain structures as well as the lower parts of the forebrain, below the cortex.

2.5.2 The medulla contains centers essential for reflex control of heart rate, breathing, and other "vegetative" functions. The pons links the medulla with other brain areas.

2.5.3 The cerebellum maintains coordination, posture, and muscle tone.

2.5.4 The reticular formation directs sensory and motor messages, and part of it, known as the RAS, acts as an activating system for the cerebral cortex.

2.5.5 The thalamus carries sensory information to the cortex.

2.5.6 The hypothalamus exerts powerful control over eating, drinking, sleep cycles, body temperature, and other basic motives and behaviors.

2.5.7 The limbic system is strongly related to emotion. It also contains distinct reward and punishment areas and an area known as the hippocampus that is important for forming memories.

2.6 *Does the glandular system affect behavior?*

2.6.1 Endocrine glands serve as a chemical communication system within the body. The ebb and flow of hormones from the endocrine glands entering the bloodstream affect behavior, moods, and personality.

2.6.2 Many of the endocrine glands are influenced by the pituitary (the "master gland"), which is in turn influenced by the hypothalamus. Thus, the brain controls the body through both the faster nervous system and the slower endocrine system.

2.7 *In what ways do left- and right-handed individuals differ?*

2.7.1 The vast majority of people are right-handed and therefore left-brain dominant for motor skills. Over 90 percent of right-handed persons and about 70 percent of the left-handed also produce speech from the left hemisphere.

2.7.2 Brain dominance and brain activity determine if you are right-handed, left-handed, or ambidextrous.

2.7.3 Most people are strongly right-handed. A minority are strongly left-handed. A few have moderate or mixed hand preferences or they are ambidextrous. Thus, handedness is not a simple either/or trait.

2.7.4 Left-handed people tend to be less strongly lateralized than right-handed people (their brain hemispheres are not as specialized).

MEDIA RESOURCES

Web Resources

Internet addresses frequently change. To find an up-to-date list of URLs for the sites listed here, visit your Psychology CourseMate.

The Nervous System Explore an overview of the major divisions of the nervous system.

Neural Transmission View a series of animations about neural transmission illustrating the action potential and the resting potential.

Synaptic Transmission Read more detail about synaptic transmission or view an animation.

The Whole Brain Atlas View images of various parts of the brain.

The PET Scan Read more about PET scans.

Introduction to fMRI Learn about fMRI; includes fMRI images.

Split Brain Consciousness Explore the cerebral hemispheres and what happens when they are split.

Probe the Brain Explore the motor homunculus of the brain interactively.

Brain Maps Learn about the functions of a healthy cortex and some effects of brain injury.

The Patient's Journey: Living with Locked-In Syndrome Meet Nick, who describes living with locked-in syndrome after suffering brainstem damage.

Endo 101: The Endocrine System Read a description of the endocrine system and hormones.

Anabolic Steroid Abuse Learn about steroids and steroid abuse from the National Institute on Drug Abuse.

What Is "Handedness"? Read about handedness and brain laterality, including a list of famous left handers.

The Sinister Hand Watch an interview on handedness with Dr. Michael Corballis.

Left Brain, Right Brain Read about popular conceptions of the differences between brain hemispheres.

Interactive Learning

Log in to **CengageBrain** to access the resources your instructor requires. For this book, you can access:

CourseMate brings course concepts to life with interactive learning, study, and exam preparation tools that support the printed textbook. A textbook-specific website, ***Psychology CourseMate*** includes an ***integrated interactive eBook*** and other ***interactive learning tools*** including quizzes, flashcards, videos, and more.

CENGAGE**NOW**™

CengageNOW is an easy-to-use online resource that helps you study in less time to get the grade you want—NOW. Take a pre-test for this chapter and receive a personalized study plan based on your results that will identify the topics you need to review and direct you to online resources to help you master those topics. Then take a post-test to help you determine the concepts you have mastered and what you will need to work on. If your textbook does not include an access code card, go to CengageBrain.com to gain access.

WebTUTOR™

More than just an interactive study guide, **WebTutor** is an anytime, anywhere customized learning solution with an eBook, keeping you connected to your textbook, instructor, and classmates.

If your professor has assigned **Aplia** homework:

1. Sign in to your account.
2. Complete the corresponding homework exercises as required by your professor.
3. When finished, click "Grade It Now" to see which areas you have mastered and which need more work, and for detailed explanations of every answer.

Visit www.cengagebrain.com to access your account and purchase materials.

Gateway THEME

The principles of development help us better understand not only children, but our own behavior as well.

Human Development 3

It's a Girl!

With those words, Carol catches her first glimpse of Samantha, her tiny newborn baby. Frankly, at the moment Samantha looks something like a prune, with pudgy arms, stubby legs, and lots of wrinkles. Yet she looks so perfect—at least in her parents' eyes. As Carol and her husband, David, look at Samantha, they wonder: How will her life unfold? What kind of a person will she be? Will Samantha be a happy teenager? Will she marry, become a mother, find an interesting career? David and Carol can only hope that by the time Samantha is 83, she will have lived a full and satisfying life.

What if we could skip ahead through Samantha's life and observe her at various ages? What could we learn? Seeing the world through her eyes would be fascinating and instructive. For example, a child's viewpoint can make us more aware of things we take for granted. Younger children, in particular, are very literal in their use of language. When Samantha was 3 years old, she thought her bath was too hot and said to David, "Make it warmer, Daddy." At first, David was confused. The bath was already fairly hot. But then he realized that what she really meant was, "Bring the water closer to the temperature we call *warm.*" It makes perfect sense if you look at it that way.

Research tells a fascinating story about human growth and development. Let's let Carol, David, and Samantha represent parents and children everywhere, as we see what psychology can tell us about the challenges of growing up, maturing, aging, and facing death. Tracing Samantha's development might even help you answer two very important questions: How did I become the person I am today? and Who will I become tomorrow?

Gateway QUESTIONS

- *3.1 How do heredity and environment affect development?*
- *3.2 What can newborn babies do?*
- *3.3 Of what significance is a child's emotional bond with adults?*
- *3.4 How important are parenting styles?*
- *3.5 How do children acquire language?*
- *3.6 How do children learn to think?*
- *3.7 Why is the transition from adolescence to adulthood especially challenging?*
- *3.8 How do we develop morals and values?*
- *3.9 What are the typical tasks and dilemmas through the life span?*
- *3.10 What is involved in well-being during middle and later adulthood?*
- *3.11 How do people typically react to death?*
- *3.12 How do effective parents discipline and communicate with their children?*

Nature and Nurture—It Takes Two to Tango

Gateway Question 3.1: *How do heredity and environment affect development?*

When we think of development, we naturally think of children "growing up" into adults. But even as adults, we never really stop changing. **Developmental psychology**, the study of progressive changes in behavior and abilities, involves every stage of life from conception to death (or "the womb to the tomb"). Heredity and environment also affect us throughout life. Some events, such as Samantha's achieving sexual maturity, are governed mostly by heredity. Others, such as Samantha's learning to swim, read, or drive a car, are matters primarily of environment.

But which is more important, heredity or environment? Actually, neither. Biopsychologist Donald Hebb once offered a useful analogy: To define the area of a rectangle, what is more important, height or width? Of course, both dimensions are absolutely essential. Without height *and* width, there is no rectangle. Similarly, if Samantha grows up to become a prominent civil rights lawyer, her success will be due to both heredity and environment.

Although heredity gives each of us a variety of potentials and limitations, these are, in turn, affected by environmental influences, such as learning, nutrition, disease, and culture. Ultimately, the person you are today reflects a continuous *interaction,* or interplay, between the forces of nature and nurture (Freberg, 2010). Let's look in more detail at this dance.

Identical twins. Twins who share identical genes (identical twins) demonstrate the powerful influence of heredity. Even when they are reared apart, identical twins are strikingly alike in motor skills, physical development, and appearance. At the same time, twins are less alike as adults than they were as children, which shows environmental influences are at work (Freberg, 2010; Larsson, Larsson, & Lichtenstein, 2004).

Heredity

Heredity ("nature") refers to the transmission of physical and psychological characteristics from parents to their children through genes. An incredible number of personal features are set at conception, when a sperm and an ovum (egg; plural, ova) unite.

How does heredity operate? The nucleus of every human cell contains **DNA,** or **deoxyribonucleic acid** (dee-OX-see-RYE-bo-new-KLEE-ik). DNA is a long, ladder-like chain of pairs of chemical molecules (● Figure 3.1). The order of these molecules, or organic bases, acts as a code for genetic information. The DNA in each cell contains a record of all the instructions needed to make a human—with room left over to spare. In 2003, a major scientific milestone was reached when the Human Genome Project completed sequencing all 3 billion chemical base pairs in human DNA (U.S. Department of Energy Office of Science, 2008).

Human DNA is organized into 46 **chromosomes.** (The word *chromosome* means "colored body.") These thread-like structures hold the coded instructions of heredity (● Figure 3.2). Notable exceptions are sperm cells and ova, which contain only 23 chromosomes. Thus, Samantha received 23 chromosomes from Carol and 23 from David. This is her genetic heritage.

Genes are small segments of DNA that affect a particular process or personal characteristic. Sometimes, a single gene is responsible for an inherited feature, such as Samantha's eye color. Genes may be dominant or recessive. When a gene is **dominant,** the feature it controls will appear every time the gene is present. When a gene is **recessive,** it must be paired with a second recessive gene before its effect will be expressed. For example, if Samantha got a blue-eye gene from David and a brown-eye gene from Carol,

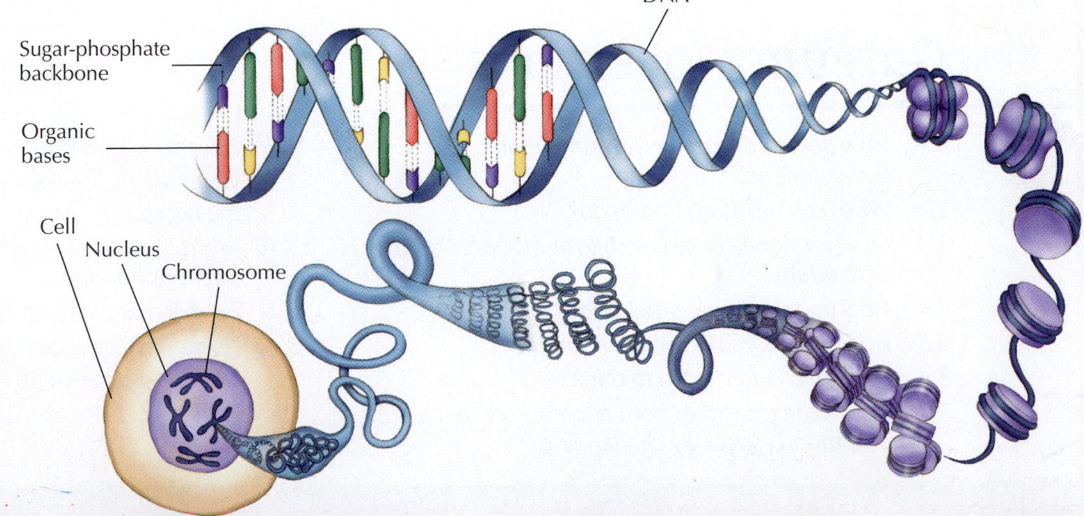

● Figure 3.1 *(Top left)* Linked molecules (organic bases) make up the "rungs" on DNA's twisted "molecular ladder." The order of these molecules serves as a code for genetic information. The code provides a genetic blueprint that is unique for each individual (except identical twins). The drawing shows only a small section of a DNA strand. An entire strand of DNA is composed of billions of smaller molecules. *(Bottom left)* The nucleus of each cell in the body contains chromosomes made up of tightly wound coils of DNA. (Don't be misled by the drawing: Chromosomes are microscopic, and the chemical molecules that make up DNA are even smaller.)

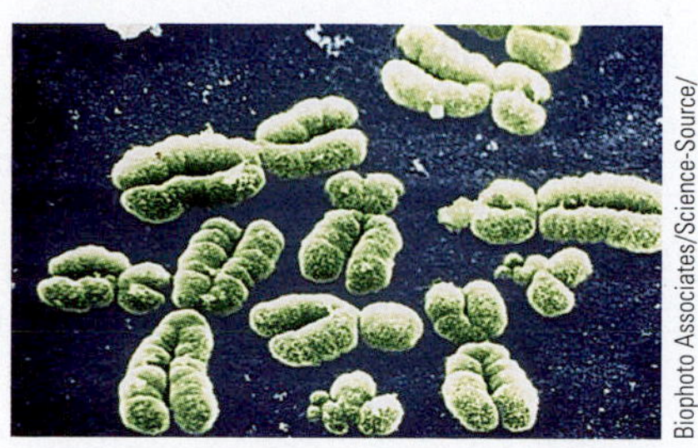

● **Figure 3.2** This image, made with a scanning electron microscope, shows several pairs of human chromosomes. (Colors are artificial.)

Samantha will be brown-eyed, because brown-eye genes are dominant.

If brown-eye genes are dominant, why do two brown-eyed parents sometimes have a blue-eyed child? If one or both parents have two brown-eye genes, the couple's children can only be brown-eyed. But what if each parent has one brown-eye gene and one blue-eye gene? In that case, both parents would have brown eyes. Yet, there is one chance in four that their children will get two blue-eye genes and have blue eyes (● Figure 3.3).

In actuality, few of our characteristics are controlled by single genes. Instead, most are **polygenic** (pol-ih-JEN-ik), or controlled by many genes working in combination. So, for example, there is no one "tall" or "short" gene; in fact, almost *two hundred* genes have already been shown to play a role in determining height (Allen et al., 2010). Through the expression of genes, heredity determines eye color, skin color, and susceptibility to some diseases. Also, genes can switch on (or off) at certain ages or developmental stages. In this way, heredity continues to exert a powerful influence throughout **maturation**, the physical growth and development of the body, brain, and nervous system (Cummings, 2011). As the *human growth sequence* unfolds, genetic instructions influence body size and shape, height, intelligence, athletic potential, personality traits, sexual orientation, and a host of other details (see ■ Table 3.1).

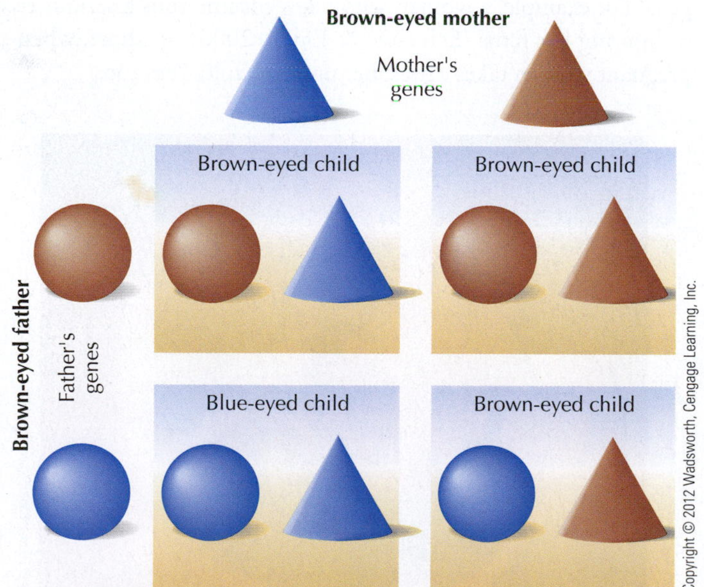

● **Figure 3.3** Gene patterns for children of brown-eyed parents, where each parent has one brown-eye gene and one blue-eye gene. Since the brown-eye gene is dominant, on average 1 child in 4 will be blue-eyed. Thus, there is a chance that two brown-eyed parents will have a blue-eyed child.

■ **TABLE 3.1 Human Growth Sequence**

Period	Duration	Descriptive Name
Prenatal Period	From conception to birth.	Zygote
Germinal period	First 2 weeks after conception.	Embryo
Embryonic period	2–8 weeks after conception.	Fetus
Fetal period	From 8 weeks after conception to birth.	Neonate
Neonatal Period	From birth to a few weeks after birth.	Infant
Infancy	From a few weeks after birth until child is walking securely; some children walk securely at less than a year, while others may not be able to until age 17–18 months.	
Early Childhood	From about 15–18 months until about 2–21/2 years.	Toddler
	From age 2–3 to about age 6.	Preschooler
Middle Childhood	From about age 6 to age 12.	School-age child
Pubescence	Period of about 2 years before puberty.	Adolescent
Puberty	Point of development at which biological changes of pubescence reach a climax marked by sexual maturity.	
Adolescence	From the beginning of pubescence until full social maturity is reached (difficult to fix duration of this period).	
Adulthood	From young adulthood to death; sometimes subdivided into other periods as shown at left.	Adult
Young adulthood (20–34)		
Middle adulthood (35–64)		
Late adulthood (65 plus)		

*Note: There is no exact beginning or ending point for various growth periods. The ages are approximate, and each period may be thought of as blending into the next.

Table courtesy of Tom Bond.

Developmental psychology The study of progressive changes in behavior and abilities from conception to death.

Heredity ("nature") The transmission of physical and psychological characteristics from parents to offspring through genes.

DNA (deoxyribonucleic acid) A molecular structure that contains coded genetic information.

Chromosomes Thread-like "colored bodies" in the nucleus of each cell that are made up of DNA.

Genes Specific areas on a strand of DNA that carry hereditary information.

Dominant gene A gene whose influence will be expressed each time the gene is present.

Recessive gene A gene whose influence will be expressed only when it is paired with a second recessive gene.

Polygenic characteristics Personal traits or physical properties that are influenced by many genes working in combination.

Maturation The physical growth and development of the body, brain, and nervous system.

Readiness

At what ages will Samantha be ready to feed herself, to walk alone, or to say goodbye to diapers? Such milestones tend to be governed by a child's **readiness** for rapid learning. That is, minimum levels of maturation must occur before some skills can be learned. Parents are asking for failure when they try to force a child to learn skills too early or too late (Joinson et al., 2009; Schum et al., 2002).

It is more difficult, for instance, to teach children to use a toilet before they have matured enough to control their bodies. Current guidelines suggest that toilet training goes most smoothly when it begins between 18 and 24 months of age. Consider the overeager parents who toilet trained a 14-month-old child in 12 trying weeks of false alarms and "accidents." If they had waited until the child was 20 months old, they might have succeeded in just 3 weeks. Parents may control when toilet training starts, but maturation tends to dictate when it will be completed (Schum et al., 2002). On the other hand, parents who delay the onset of toilet training may fare no better. The older a child is before toilet training begins, the more likely he or she is to fail to develop full bladder control and become a daytime "wetter" (Joinson et al., 2009). So why fight nature?

Environment

Our environment also exerts a profound influence on our development. **Environment ("nurture")** refers to the sum of all external conditions that affect a person. For example, the brain of a newborn baby has fewer *dendrites* (nerve cell branches) and *synapses* (connections between nerve cells) than an adult brain (● Figure 3.4). However, the newborn brain is highly *plastic* (capable of being altered by experience). During the first 3 years of life, millions of new connections form in the brain every day. At the same time, unused connections disappear. As a result, early learning environments literally shape the developing brain, through "blooming and pruning" of synapses (Nelson, 1999).

Although human culture is accelerating the rate at which human DNA is evolving, modern humans are still genetically quite similar to cave dwellers who lived 30,000 years ago (Cochran & Harpending, 2009; Hawks et al., 2007). Nevertheless, a bright baby born today could learn to become almost anything—a ballet dancer, an engineer, a gangsta rapper, a skydiver, or a biochemist who likes to paint in watercolors. But, with few exceptions, an Upper Paleolithic baby could have become only a hunter or food gatherer.

Prenatal Influences

Environmental factors actually start influencing development before birth. Although the *intrauterine* environment (interior of the womb) is highly protected, environmental conditions can nevertheless affect the developing child. For example, when Carol was pregnant, Samantha's fetal heart rate and movements increased when loud sounds or vibrations penetrated the womb (Kisilevsky et al., 2004).

Had Carol experienced excess stress during her pregnancy, Samantha might have been a smaller, weaker baby at birth (Schetter, 2011). If Carol's health or nutrition had been poor or if she had had German measles, syphilis, or HIV, had used drugs, or had been exposed to X-rays or radiation, Samantha's growth sequence might have also have been harmed. In such cases, babies can suffer from **congenital problems,** or "birth defects." These environmental problems affect the developing fetus and become apparent at birth. In contrast, **genetic disorders** are inherited from parents. Examples are sickle-cell anemia, hemophilia, cystic fibrosis, muscular dystrophy, albinism, and some types of mental retardation.

How is it possible for the embryo or the fetus to be harmed? No direct intermixing of blood takes place between a mother and her unborn child. Yet some substances—especially drugs—do reach the fetus. Anything capable of disturbing normal development in the womb is called a **teratogen** (teh-RAT-uh-jen). Sometimes women are exposed to powerful teratogens, such as radiation, lead, pesticides, or polychlorinated biphenyls (PCBs), without knowing it. But pregnant women do have direct control over many teratogens. For example, a woman who takes cocaine runs a serious risk of injuring her fetus (Schuetze & Eiden, 2006). In short, when a pregnant woman takes drugs, her unborn child does too.

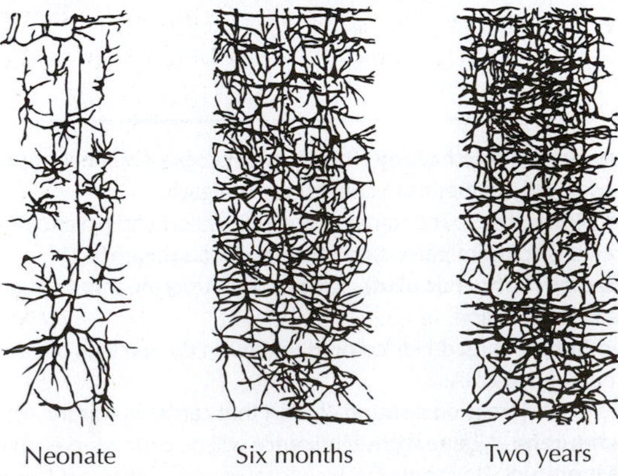

● **Figure 3.4** A rapid increase in brain synapses continues until about age 4. At that point, children actually have more brain synapses than adults do. Then, after age 10, the number slowly declines, reaching adult levels at about age 16. (Reprinted by permission of the publisher from *The Postnatal Development of the Human Cerebral Cortex, Vols. I–VIII* by Jesse LeRoy Conel, Cambridge, MA: Harvard University Press, Copyright © 1939, 1941, 1947, 1951, 1955, 1959, 1963, 1967 by the President and Fellows of Harvard College. Copyright renewed 1967, 1969, 1975, 1979, 1983, 1987, 1991.)

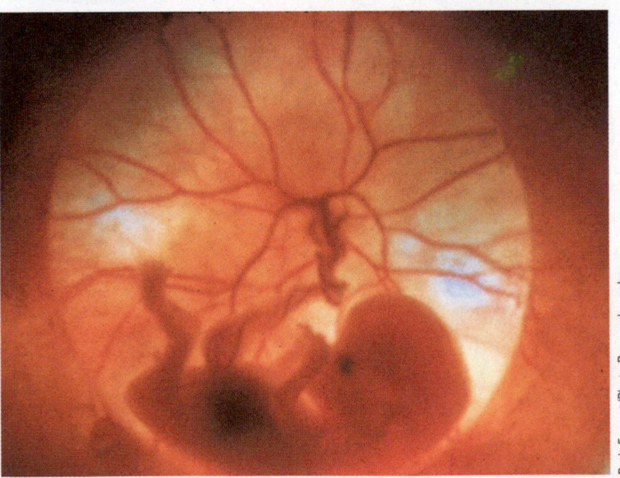

An 11-week-old fetus. Because of the rapid growth of basic structures, the developing fetus is sensitive to a variety of diseases, drugs, and sources of radiation. This is especially true during the first trimester (3 months) of gestation (pregnancy).

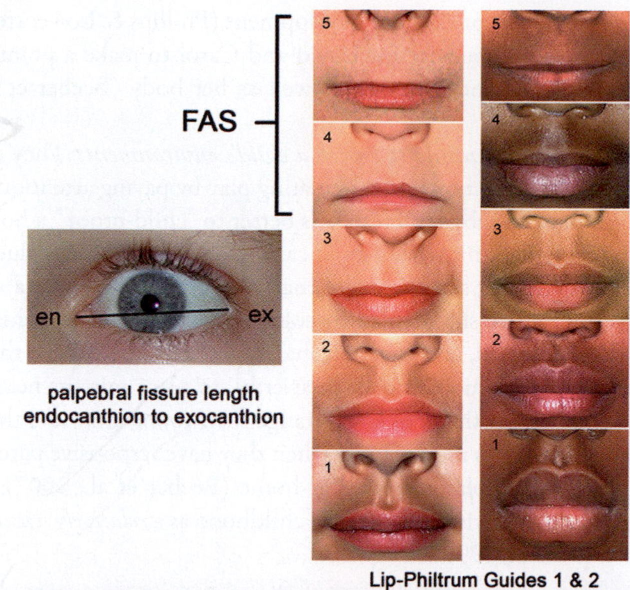

Children of different ethnicities all show typical features of children suffering from fetal alcohol syndrome, including a small non-symmetrical head, a short nose, a flattened area between the eyes, oddly shaped eyes, and a thin upper lip. Many of these features become less noticeable by adolescence. However, mental retardation and other problems commonly follow the FAS child into adulthood.

Unfortunately, in the United States, drugs are one of the greatest risk factors facing unborn children (Coles & Black, 2006; Keegan et al., 2010). In fact, repeated heavy drinking during pregnancy is the most common cause of birth defects in the United States (Liles & Packman, 2009). Affected infants have *fetal alcohol syndrome (FAS)*, including low birth weight, a small head, bodily defects, and facial malformations. Many also suffer from emotional, behavioral, and mental handicaps (Golden, 2005).

If a mother is addicted to morphine, heroin, or methadone, her baby may be born with an addiction. Tobacco is also harmful. Smoking during pregnancy greatly reduces oxygen to the fetus. Heavy smokers risk miscarrying or having premature, underweight babies who are more likely to die soon after birth. Children of smoking mothers score lower on tests of language and mental ability (Huijbregts et al., 2006). In other words, an unborn child's future can go "up in smoke." That goes for smoking marijuana as well (Viveros et al., 2005).

Sensitive Periods

Early experiences can have particularly lasting effects. For example, children who are abused may suffer lifelong emotional problems (Goodwin, Fergusson, & Horwood, 2005). At the same time, extra care can sometimes reverse the effects of a poor start in life (Bornstein & Tamis-LeMonda, 2001). In short, environmental forces guide human development, for better or worse, throughout life.

Why do some experiences have more lasting effects than others? Part of the answer lies in **sensitive periods.** These are times when children are more susceptible to particular types of environmental influences. Events that occur during a sensitive period can permanently alter the course of development (Michel & Tyler, 2005). For example, forming a loving bond with a caregiver early in life seems to be crucial for optimal development. Likewise, babies who don't hear normal speech during their first year may have impaired language abilities (Thompson & Nelson, 2001).

Deprivation and Enrichment

Some environments can be described as *deprived* or *enriched*. **Deprivation** refers to a lack of normal nutrition, stimulation, comfort, or love. **Enrichment** exists when an environment is deliberately made more stimulating, loving, and so forth.

What happens when children suffer severe deprivation? Tragically, a few mistreated children have spent their first years in closets, attics, and other restricted environments. When first discovered, these children are usually mute, retarded, and emotionally damaged (Wilson, 2003). Fortunately, such extreme deprivation is unusual.

BRIDGES

Adults experience a number of disruptive effects when they are deprived of sensory stimulation. **See Chapter 6, pages 183–184, for details.**

Nevertheless, milder perceptual, intellectual, or emotional deprivation occurs in many families, especially those that must cope with poverty (Matthews & Gallo, 2011). Poverty can affect the development of children in at least two ways (Huston & Bentley, 2010; Sobolewski & Amato, 2005). First, poor parents may not be able to give their children needed resources such as nutritious meals, health care, or learning materials. As a result, impoverished children tend to be sick more often, their mental development lags, and they do poorly at school. Second, the stresses of poverty can also be hard on parents, leading to marriage problems, less positive parenting, and poorer parent-child relationships. The resulting emotional turmoil can damage a child's socioemotional develop-

Readiness A condition that exists when maturation has advanced enough to allow the rapid acquisition of a particular skill.

Environment ("nurture") The sum of all external conditions affecting development, including especially the effects of learning.

Congenital problems Problems or defects that originate during prenatal development in the womb.

Genetic disorders Problems caused by defects in the genes or by inherited characteristics.

Teratogen Anything capable of altering fetal development in noninheritable ways that cause birth defects.

Sensitive period During development, a period of increased sensitivity to environmental influences; also, a time during which certain events must take place for normal development to occur.

Deprivation In development, the loss or withholding of normal stimulation, nutrition, comfort, love, and so forth; a condition of lacking.

Enrichment In development, deliberately making an environment more stimulating, nutritional, comforting, loving, and so forth.

ment. In the extreme, it may increase the risk of mental illness and delinquent behavior.

Adults who grew up in poverty often remain trapped in a vicious cycle of continued poverty. Because over 40,000,000 Americans fell below the poverty line in 2009, this grim reality plays itself out in millions of American homes every day (U.S. Census Bureau, 2010).

Can an improved environment enhance development? To answer this question, psychologists have created *enriched environments* that are especially novel, complex, and stimulating. Enriched environments may be the "soil" from which brighter children grow. To illustrate, let's consider the effects of raising rats in a sort of "rat wonderland." The walls of their cages were decorated with colorful patterns, and each cage was filled with platforms, ladders, and cubbyholes. As adults, these rats were superior at learning mazes. In addition, they had larger, heavier brains, with a thicker cortex (Benloucif, Bennett, & Rosenzweig, 1995). Of course, it's a long leap from rats to people, but an actual increase in brain size is impressive. If extra stimulation can enhance the "intelligence" of a lowly rat, it's likely that human infants also benefit from enrichment. Many studies have shown that enriched environments improve abilities or enhance development (Phillips & Lowenstein, 2011). It would be wise for David and Carol to make a point of nourishing Samantha's mind, as well as her body (Beeber et al., 2007).

What can parents do to enrich a child's environment? They can encourage exploration and stimulating play by paying attention to what holds the baby's interest. It is better to "child-proof" a house than to strictly limit what a child can touch. There is also value in actively enriching sensory experiences. Infants are not vegetables. Babies should be surrounded by colors, music, people, and things to see, taste, smell, and touch. It makes perfect sense to take them outside, to hang mobiles over their cribs, to place mirrors nearby, to play music for them, or to rearrange their rooms now and then. Children progress most rapidly when they have responsive parents and stimulating play materials at home (Beeber et al., 2007). In light of this, it is wise to view all of childhood as a *relatively sensitive period* (Nelson, 1999).

Children who grow up in poverty run a high risk of experiencing many forms of deprivation. There is evidence that lasting damage to social, emotional, and cognitive development occurs when children must cope with severe early deprivation.

Reaction Range

One way to visualize the interplay of heredity and environment is through the concept of **reaction range,** the limits that one's environment places on the effects of heredity (● Figure 3.5). Let's suppose that Samantha was born with genes for a normal level of intelligence. If Samantha grows up in a deprived environment, she might well end up with lower than average adult intelligence. If Carol and David provide her with an enriched environment, she

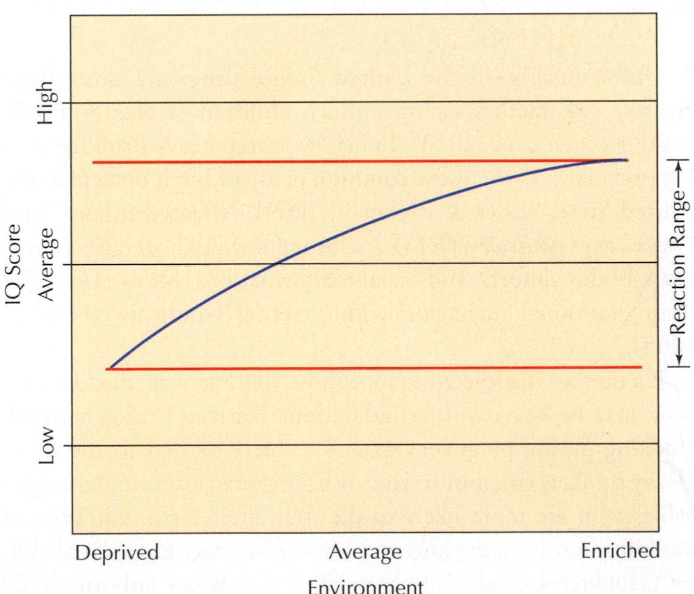

● **Figure 3.5** The effect of heredity on the development of human traits, such as intelligence, can often influenced by environmental circumstances. A child with average genes for intelligence growing up in an average environment might have an average IQ score as an adult. However, growing up in a deprived environment might result in a somewhat lower IQ score and growing up in an enriched environment might result in a somewhat higher IQ score. In this way, the environment sets a range within which our hereditary potential is actually expressed. This range is called the *reaction range*.

will probably have normal, or even above normal, intelligence. Even though Samantha might not be genetically capable of becoming a child prodigy, the environment her parents provide for her will also determine her developmental path.

The Whole Person

Nurture often affects the expression of hereditary tendencies through ongoing reciprocal influences. A good example of such influences is the fact that growing infants influence their parents' behavior at the same time they are changed by it.

Newborn babies differ noticeably in **temperament.** This is the inherited, physical core of personality. It includes sensitivity, irritability, distractibility, and typical mood (Kagan, 2004). About 40 percent of all newborns are *easy children* who are relaxed and agreeable. Ten percent are *difficult children* who are moody, intense, and easily angered. *Slow-to-warm-up children* (about 15 percent) are restrained, unexpressive, or shy. The remaining children do not fit neatly into a single category (Chess & Thomas, 1986).

Because of differences in temperament, some babies are more likely than others to smile, cry, vocalize, reach out, or pay attention. As a result, babies rapidly become active participants in their own development. For example, Samantha is an easy baby who smiles frequently and is easily fed. This encourages Carol to touch, feed, and sing to Samantha. Carol's affection rewards Samantha, causing her to smile more. Soon, a dynamic relationship blossoms between mother and child. Similarly, good parenting can reciprocally influence a very shy child who, in turn, becomes progressively less shy.

The reverse also occurs: Difficult children may make parents unhappy and elicit more negative parenting (Parke, 2004). Alternately, negative parenting can turn a moderately shy child into a very shy one. This suggests that inherited temperaments are dynamically modified by learning (Bridgett et al., 2009; Kagan, 2005).

A person's **developmental level** is his or her current state of physical, emotional, and intellectual development. To summarize, three factors combine to determine your developmental level at any stage of life. These are *heredity, environment,* and your *own behavior,* each tightly interwoven with the others.

Knowledge Builder: The Interplay of Heredity and Environment

RECITE

1. Areas of the DNA molecule called genes are made up of dominant and recessive chromosomes. T or F?
2. Most inherited characteristics can be described as polygenic. T or F?
3. If one parent has one dominant brown-eye gene and one recessive blue-eye gene and the other parent has two dominant brown-eye genes, what is the chance that their child will have blue eyes?
a. 25 percent *b.* 50 percent *c.* 0 percent *d.* 75 percent
4. The orderly sequence observed in the unfolding of many basic responses can be attributed to ____________.
5. A ____________ ____________ is a time of increased sensitivity to environmental influences.
6. "Slow-to-warm-up" children can be described as restrained, unexpressive, or shy. T or F?
7. As a child develops, there is a continuous ____________ between the forces of heredity and environment.

REFLECT

Think Critically

8. Environmental influences can interact with genetic programming in an exceedingly direct way. Can you guess what it is?

Self-Reflect

Can you think of clear examples of some ways in which heredity and environmental forces have combined to affect your development?

How would maturation affect the chances of teaching an infant to eat with a spoon?

What kind of temperament did you have as an infant? How did it affect your relationship with your parents or caregivers?

Answers: 1. F **2.** T **3.** c **4.** maturation **5.** sensitive period **6.** T **7.** Interaction or interplay **8.** Environmental conditions sometimes turn specific genes on or off, thus directly affecting the expression of genetic tendencies (Keller, 2010; Lickliter & Honeycutt, 2010).

The Newborn—More Than Meets the Eye

Gateway Question 3.2: *What can newborn babies do?*

At birth, the human *neonate* (NEE-oh-NATE; newborn infant) will die if not cared for by adults. Newborn babies cannot lift their heads, turn over, or feed themselves. Does this mean they are inert and unfeeling? Definitely not! Contrary to common belief, newborn babies are not oblivious to their surroundings. Infants have physical and mental capacities that continue to surprise researchers and delight parents. The emergence of many of these capacities is closely related to maturation of the brain, nervous system, and body. Likewise, a baby's early emotional life unfolds on a timetable that is largely controlled by maturation.

Neonates like Samantha can see, hear, smell, taste, and respond to pain and touch. Although their senses are less acute, babies are very responsive. Samantha will follow a moving object with her eyes and will turn in the direction of sounds.

Samantha also has a number of adaptive infant reflexes (Siegler, DeLoache, & Eisenberg, 2011). To elicit the *grasping reflex,* press an object in a neonate's palm and she will grasp it with surprising strength. Many infants, in fact, can hang from a raised bar, like little trapeze artists. The grasping reflex aids survival by helping infants to avoid falling. You can observe the *rooting reflex* (reflexive head turn-

Reaction range The limits environment places on the effects of heredity.
Temperament The physical core of personality, including emotional and perceptual sensitivity, energy levels, typical mood, and so forth.
Developmental level An individual's current state of physical, emotional, and intellectual development.

Newborn babies display a special interest in the human face. A preference for seeing their mother's face develops rapidly and encourages social interactions between mother and baby.

ing and nursing) by touching Samantha's cheek. Immediately, she will turn toward your finger, as if searching for something.

How is such turning adaptive? The rooting reflex helps infants find a bottle or a breast. Then, when a nipple touches the infant's mouth, the *sucking reflex* (rhythmic nursing) helps her obtain needed food. Like other reflexes, this is a genetically programmed action. At the same time, food rewards nursing. Because of this, babies quickly learn to nurse more actively. Again, we see how the interplay of nature and nurture alters a baby's behavior.

The *Moro reflex* is also interesting. If Samantha's position is changed abruptly or if she is startled by a loud noise, she will make a hugging motion. This reaction has been compared to the movements baby monkeys use to cling to their mothers. (We leave it to the reader's imagination to decide if there is any connection.)

Motor Development

As we just noted, the emergence of many basic abilities is closely tied to *maturation*, which will be evident, for example, as Samantha learns motor skills, such as crawling and walking. Of course, the *rate* of maturation varies from child to child. Nevertheless, the *order* of maturation is almost universal. For instance, Samantha will be able to sit without support from David before she has matured enough to crawl. Indeed, infants around the world typically sit before they crawl, crawl before they stand, and stand before they walk (● Figure 3.6).

What about my weird cousin Na'vi who never crawled? Like cousin Na'vi, a few children substitute rolling, creeping, or shuffling for crawling. A very few move directly from sitting to standing and walking. Even so, their motor development is orderly. In general, muscular control spreads in a pattern that is *cephalocaudal* (SEF-eh-lo-KOD-ul; from head to toe) and *proximodistal* (PROK-seh-moe-DIS-tul; from the center of the body to the extremities).

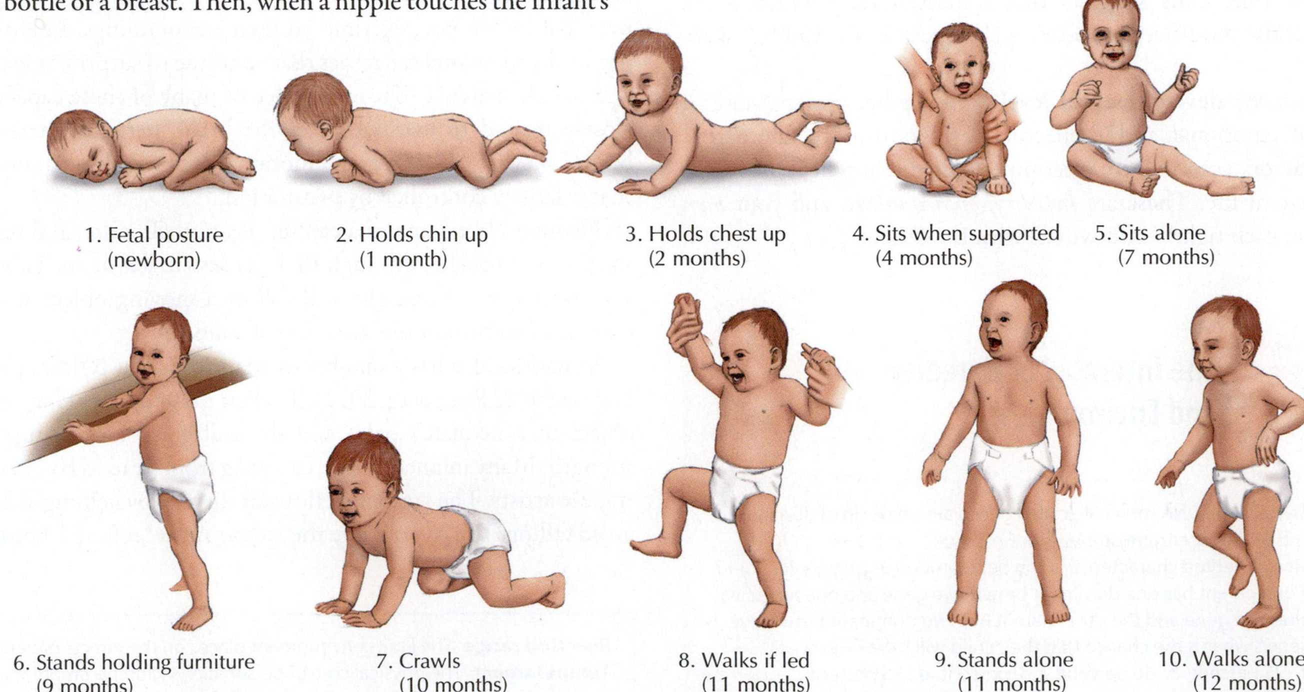

● **Figure 3.6** Motor development. Most infants follow an orderly pattern of motor development. Although the order in which children progress is similar, there are large individual differences in the ages at which each ability appears. The ages listed are averages for American children. It is not unusual for many of the skills to appear 1 or 2 months earlier than average or several months later (Piek, 2006). Parents should not be alarmed if a child's behavior differs some from the average.

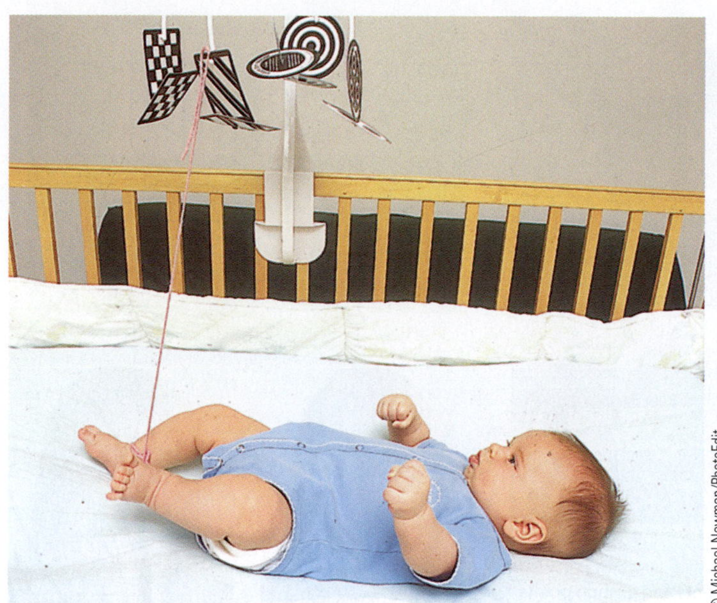

© Michael Newman/PhotoEdit

● **Figure 3.7** Psychologist Carolyn Rovee-Collier has shown that babies as young as 3 months old can learn to control their movements. In her experiments, babies lie on their backs under a colorful crib mobile. A ribbon is tied around the baby's ankle and connected to the mobile. Whenever babies spontaneously kick their legs, the mobile jiggles and rattles. Within a few minutes, infants learn to kick faster. Their reward for kicking is a chance to see the mobile move (Hayne & Rovee-Collier, 1995).

Even if cousin Na'vi flunked Elementary Crawling, his motor development followed the standard top-down, center-outward pattern (Piek, 2006).

Although maturation has a big impact, motor skills don't simply "emerge." Samantha must learn to control her actions. When babies are beginning to crawl or walk, they actively try new movements and select those that work. Samantha's first efforts may be flawed—a wobbly crawl or some shaky first steps. However, with practice, babies "tune" their movements to be smoother and more effective. Such learning is evident from the very first months of life (Piek, 2006; see ● Figure 3.7).

Perceptual and Cognitive Development

Thirty years ago, many people thought of newborn babies as mere bundles of reflexes, like the ones previously described. But infants are capable of much more. For example, psychologist Andrew Meltzoff has found that babies are born mimics. ● Figure 3.8 shows Meltzoff as he sticks out his tongue, opens his mouth, and purses his lips at a 20-day-old girl. Will she imitate him? Videotapes of babies confirm that they imitate adult facial gestures while they can see them. As early as 9 months of age, infants can now remember and imitate actions a day after seeing them (Heimann & Meltzoff, 1996; Meltzoff, 2005). Such mimicry obviously aids rapid learning in infancy.

How intelligent are neonates? Babies are smarter than many people think. From the earliest days of life, babies are learning how the world works. They immediately begin to look, touch, taste, and otherwise explore their surroundings. From an evolutionary perspective, a baby's mind is designed to soak up information, which it does at an amazing pace (Meltzoff & Prinz, 2002).

In the first months of life, babies are increasingly able to think, to learn from what they see, to make predictions, and to search for explanations. For example, Jerome Bruner (1983) observed that 3- to 8-week-old babies seem to understand that a person's voice and body should be connected. If a baby hears his mother's voice coming from where she is standing, the baby will remain calm. If her voice comes from a loudspeaker several feet away, the baby will become agitated and begin to cry.

Another look into the private world of infants can be drawn from testing their vision. However, such testing is a challenge because infants cannot talk. Robert Fantz invented a device called a *looking chamber* to find out what infants can see and what holds their attention (● Figure 3.9*a*). Imagine that Samantha is placed on her back inside the chamber, facing a lighted area above. Next, two objects are placed in the chamber. By observing the movements of Samantha's eyes and the images they reflect, we can tell what she is looking at. Such tests show that adult vision is about 30 times sharper, but babies can see large patterns, shapes, and edges.

Fantz found that 3-day-old babies prefer complex patterns, such as checkerboards and bull's-eyes, to simpler colored rectangles. Other researchers have learned that infants are excited by circles, curves, and bright lights (● Figure 3.9*b*) (Brown, 1990). When Samantha is 6 months old, she will be able to recognize categories of objects that differ in shape or color. By 9 months of age, she will

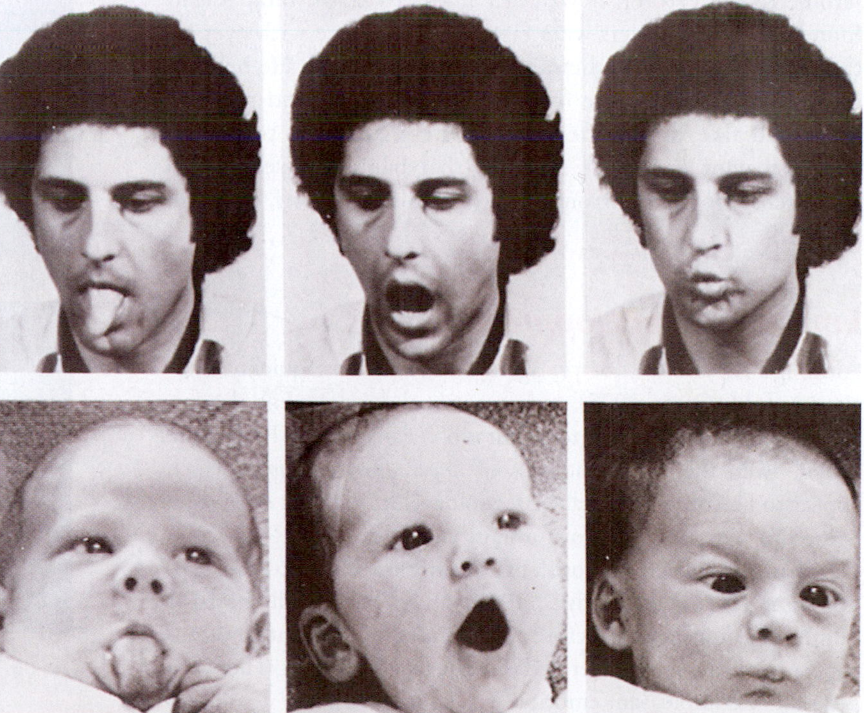

● **Figure 3.8** Infant imitation. In the top row of photos, Andrew Meltzoff makes facial gestures at an infant. The bottom row records the infant's responses. Videotapes of Meltzoff and of tested infants helped ensure objectivity. (Photos courtesy of Andrew N. Meltzoff.)

be able to tell the difference between dogs and birds or other groups of animals (Mandler & McDonough, 1998). By 1 year of age, she will see as well as her parents (Sigelman & Rider, 2009). So, there really is a person inside that little body!

Neonates can most clearly see objects about a foot away from them. It is as if they are best prepared to see the people who love and care for them (Gopnik, Meltzoff, & Kuhl, 2000). Perhaps that's why babies have a special fascination with human faces. Just *hours* after they are born, babies begin to prefer seeing their mother's face rather than a stranger's (Walton, Bower, & Bower, 1992). When babies are only 2 to 5 days old, they will pay more attention to a person who is gazing directly at them rather than one who is looking away (Farroni et al., 2004) (● Figure 3.9*c*).

In a looking chamber, most infants will spend more time looking at a human face pattern than a scrambled face or a colored oval (● Figure 3.9*d*). When real human faces are used, infants prefer familiar faces to unfamiliar faces. However, this reverses at about age 2. At that time, unusual objects begin to interest the child. For instance, in one classic study, Jerome Kagan (1971) showed face masks to 2-year-olds. Kagan found that the toddlers were fascinated by a face with eyes on the chin and a nose in the middle of the forehead. He believes the babies' interest came from a need to understand why the scrambled face differed from what they had come to expect. Such behavior is further evidence that babies actively try to make sense of their surroundings (Gopnik, Meltzoff, & Kuhl, 2000).

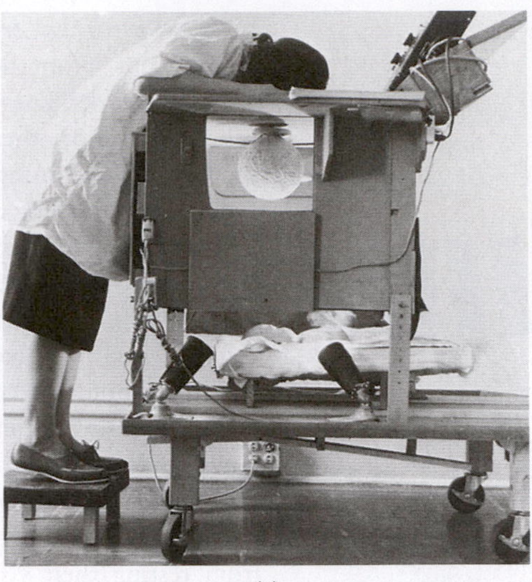

(a)

(b)

(c)

(d)

● Figure 3.9 *(a)* Eye movements and fixation points of infants are observed in Fantz's "looking chamber." *(b)* Thirteen-week-old infants prefer concentric and curved patterns like those on the left to nonconcentric and straight-line patterns like those on the right. *(c)* When they are just days old, infants pay more attention to the faces of people who are gazing directly at them. *(d)* Infants look at the normal face longer than at the scrambled face and at both faces longer than at the design on the right. (Photo *a* courtesy of David Linton. Drawing by Alex Semenoick from "The Origin of Form Perception" by Robert L. Fantz, Copyright © 1961 by Scientific American, Inc. All rights reserved.)

Emotional Development

Although experts do not yet agree on exactly how quickly emotions unfold (Oster, 2005), early emotional development also follows a pattern closely tied to maturation (Panksepp & Pasqualini, 2005). Even the basic emotions of *anger, fear,* and *joy*—which appear to be unlearned—take time to develop. General *excitement* is the only emotion newborn infants clearly express. However, as David and Carol can tell you, a baby's emotional life blossoms rapidly. One researcher (Bridges, 1932) observed that all the basic human emotions appear before age 2. Bridges found that emotions appear in a consistent order and that the first basic split is between pleasant and unpleasant emotions (● Figure 3.10).

Psychologist Carroll Izard thinks that infants can express several basic emotions as early as 10 weeks of age. When Izard looks carefully at the faces of babies, he sees abundant signs of emotion

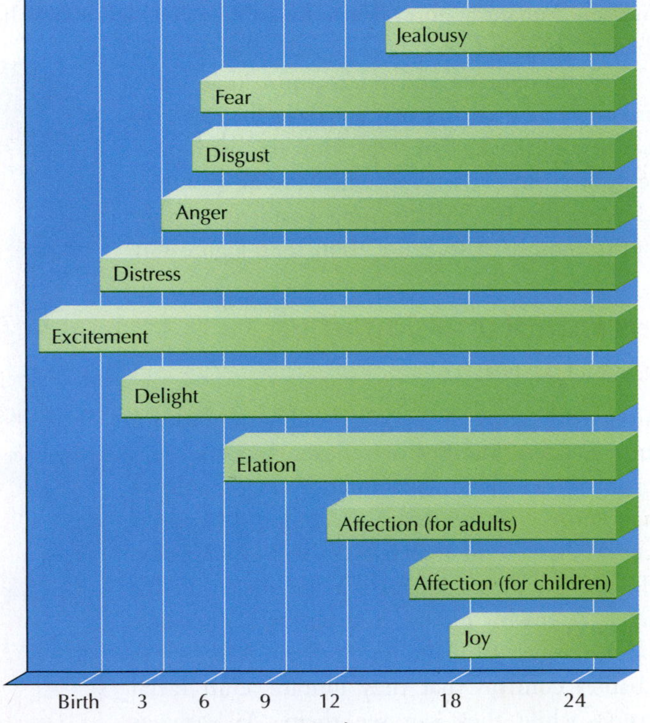

● Figure 3.10 The traditional view of infancy holds that newborns are initially able to show only general excitement but rapidly become able to express a variety of emotions. (K. M. B. Bridges, 1932. Reprinted by permission of the Society for Research in Child Development, Inc.)

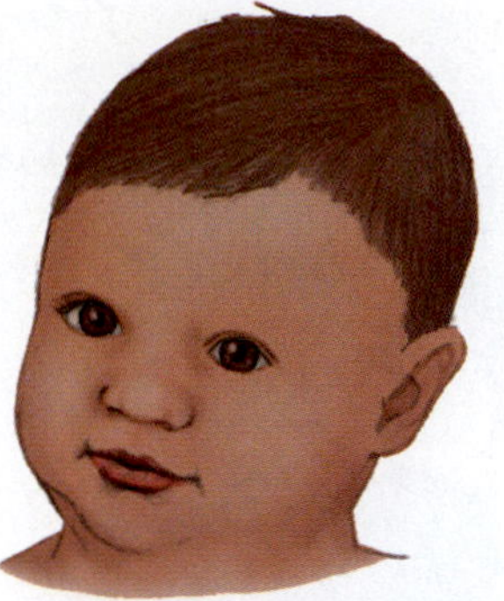
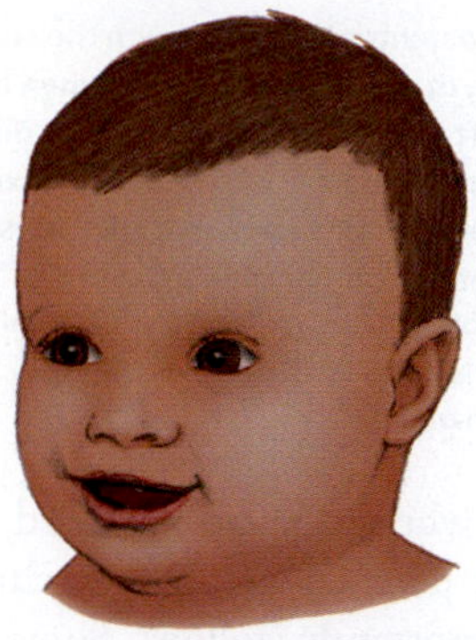
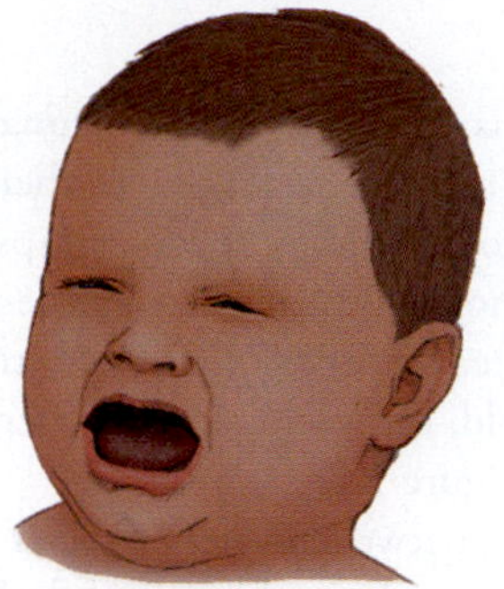
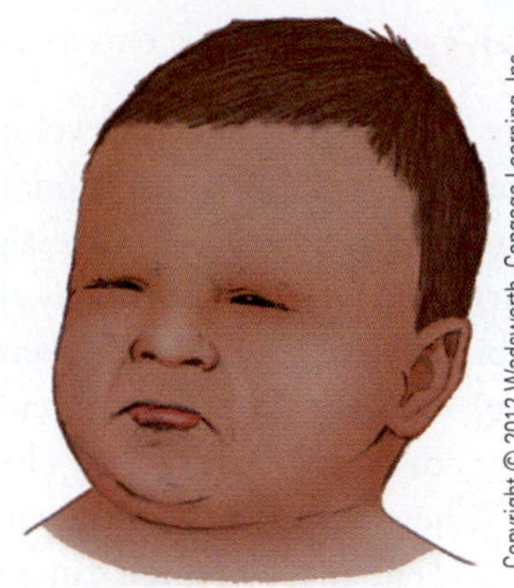

● **Figure 3.11** Infants display many of the same emotional expressions as adults do. Carroll Izard believes such expressions show that distinct emotions appear within the first months of life. Other theorists argue that specific emotions come into focus more gradually, as an infant's nervous system matures. Either way, parents can expect to see a full range of basic emotions by the end of a baby's first year.

(see ● Figure 3.11). The most common infant expression, he found, is not excitement, but *interest*—followed by *joy, anger,* and *sadness* (Izard et al., 1995).

If Izard is right, then emotions are "hardwired" by heredity and related to evolution. Perhaps that's why smiling is one of a baby's most common reactions. Smiling probably helps babies survive by inviting parents to care for them (Izard et al., 1995).

At first, a baby's smiling is haphazard. By the age of 8 to 12 months, however, infants smile more frequently when another person is nearby (Jones & Hong, 2001). This **social smile** is especially rewarding to parents. Infants can even use their social smile to communicate interest in an object, like the time Samantha smiled when her mother held up her favorite teddy bear (Venezia et al., 2004). On the other hand, when new parents see and hear a crying baby, they feel annoyed, irritated, disturbed, or unhappy. Babies the world over, it seems, rapidly become capable of letting others know what they like and dislike. (Prove this to yourself sometime by driving a baby buggy.)

With dazzling speed, human infants are transformed from helpless babies to independent persons. By her third year, Samantha will have a unique personality, and she will be able to stand, walk, talk, and explore. At no other time after birth does development proceed more rapidly. During the same period, Samantha's relationships with other people will expand as well. Before we explore that topic, here's a chance to review what you've learned.

Knowledge Builder: The Neonate and Early Maturation

RECITE

1. If an infant is startled, he or she will make movements similar to an embrace. This is known as the
   a. grasping reflex *b.* rooting reflex *c.* Moro reflex *d.* adaptive reflex
2. During infancy, a capacity for imitating others as they watch them first becomes evident at about 9 months of age. T or F?
3. After age 2, infants tested in a looking chamber show a marked preference for familiar faces and simpler designs. T or F?
4. General excitement or interest is the clearest emotional response present in newborn infants, but meaningful expressions of delight and distress appear soon after. T or F?
5. Neonates display a social smile as early as 10 days after birth. T or F?

THINK CRITICALLY

Reflect

6. If you were going to test newborn infants to see if they prefer their own mother's face to that of a stranger, what precautions might you take?

Relate

What infant reflexes have you observed? Can you give an example of how heredity and environment interact during motor development?

To know what a baby is feeling, would it be more helpful to be able to detect delight and distress (Bridges) or joy, anger, and sadness (Izard)?

Answers: 1. c **2.** F **3.** F **4.** T **5.** F **6.** In one study of the preferences of newborns, the hair color and complexion of strangers were matched to those of the mothers. Also, only the mother's or stranger's face was visible during testing. And finally, a scent was used to mask olfactory (smell) cues so that an infant's preference could not be based on the mother's familiar odor (Bushnell, Sai, & Mullin, 1989).

Social Development—Baby, I'm Stuck on You

Gateway Question 3.3: *Of what significance is a child's emotional bond with adults?*

Like all humans, babies are social creatures. Their early **social development** is rooted in emotional attachment and the need for physical contact. As infants form their first emotional bond with an adult, usually a parent, they also begin to develop self-awareness and to become aware of others. This early social development lays a foundation for subsequent relationships with parents, siblings, friends, and relatives (Shaffer & Kipp, 2010).

Social smile Smiling elicited by social stimuli, such as seeing a parent's face.

Social development The development of self-awareness, attachment to parents or caregivers, and relationships with other children and adults.

Attachment

The real core of social development is found in the **emotional attachment**, or close emotional bond, that babies form with their primary caregivers. To investigate mother–infant relationships, Harry Harlow separated baby rhesus monkeys from their mothers at birth. The real mothers were replaced with **surrogate** (substitute) **mothers**. Some were made of cold, unyielding wire. Others were covered with soft terry cloth (● Figure 3.12).

When the infants were given a choice between the two mothers, they spent most of their time clinging to the cuddly terry-cloth mother. This was true even when the wire mother held a bottle, making her the source of food. The "love" and attachment displayed toward the cloth replicas was identical to that shown toward natural mothers. For example, when frightened by rubber snakes, wind-up toys, and other "fear stimuli," the infant monkeys ran to their cloth mothers and clung to them for security. These classic studies suggest that attachment begins with **contact comfort**, the pleasant, reassuring feeling infants get from touching something soft and warm, especially their mother.

There is a sensitive period (roughly the first year of life) during which attachment must occur for optimal development. Returning to Samantha's story, we find that attachment keeps her close to Carol, who provides safety, stimulation, and a secure "home base" from which Samantha can go exploring.

Mothers usually begin to feel attached to their baby before birth. For their part, as babies mature, they become more and more capable of bonding with their mothers. For the first few months, babies respond more or less equally to everyone. By 2 or 3 months, most babies prefer their mothers to strangers. By around 7 months, babies generally become truly attached to their mothers, crawling after them if they can. Shortly thereafter, they begin to form attachments to other people as well, such as their father, grandparents, or siblings (Sigelman & Rider, 2009).

A direct sign that an emotional bond has formed appears around 8 to 12 months of age. At that time, Samantha will display **separation anxiety**—crying and signs of fear—when she is left alone or with a stranger. Mild separation anxiety is normal. When it is more intense, it may reveal a problem. At some point in their lives, about 1 in 20 children suffer from *separation anxiety disorder* (Dick-Niederhauser & Silverman, 2006). These children are miserable when they are separated from their parents, whom they cling to or constantly follow. Some fear that they will get lost and never see their parents again. Many refuse to go to school, which can be a serious handicap. Children tend to grow out of the disorder (Kearney et al., 2003), but if separation anxiety is intense or lasts for more than a month, parents should seek professional help for their child (Allen et al., 2010).

Most parents are familiar with the storm of crying that sometimes occurs when babies are left alone at bedtime. Bedtime distress can be a mild form of separation anxiety. As many parents know, it is often eased by the carefully monitored presence of "security objects," such as a stuffed animal or favorite blanket (Donate-Bartfield & Passman, 2004).

© Michael Newman/PhotoEdit

Attachment Quality

According to psychologist Mary Ainsworth (1913–1999), the quality of attachment is revealed by how babies act when their mothers return after a brief separation. Infants who are **securely attached** have a stable and positive emotional bond. They are upset by the mother's absence and seek to be near her when she returns. **Insecure-avoidant** infants have an anxious emotional bond. They tend to turn away from the mother when she returns. **Insecure-ambivalent** attachment is also an anxious emotional bond. In this case, babies have mixed feelings: They both seek to be near the returning mother and angrily resist contact with her. (See ● Figure 3.13.)

Attachment can have lasting effects (Bohlin & Hagekull, 2009). Infants who are securely attached at the age of 1 year show resiliency, curiosity, problem-solving ability, and social skills in preschool (Collins & Gunnar, 1990). In contrast, attachment failures can be quite damaging. Consider, for example, the plight of children raised in severely overcrowded orphanages (Wilson, 2003). These children get almost no attention from adults for the first year or two of their lives. Once adopted, many are poorly attached to their new parents. Some, for instance, will wander off with strangers, are anxious and remote, and don't like to be touched or to make eye contact with others (O'Conner et al., 2003). In short,

● **Figure 3.12** An infant monkey clings to a cloth-covered surrogate mother. Baby monkeys become attached to the cloth "contact-comfort" mother but not to a similar wire mother. This is true even when the wire mother provides food. Contact comfort may also underlie the tendency of children to become attached to inanimate objects, such as blankets or stuffed toys.

Courtesy of Harry Harlow, University of Wisconsin Primate Laboratory.

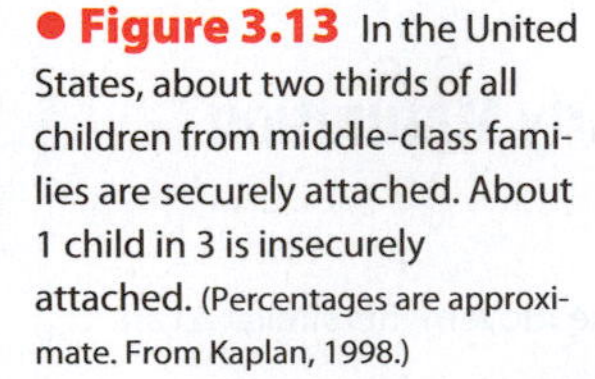

● **Figure 3.13** In the United States, about two thirds of all children from middle-class families are securely attached. About 1 child in 3 is insecurely attached. (Percentages are approximate. From Kaplan, 1998.)

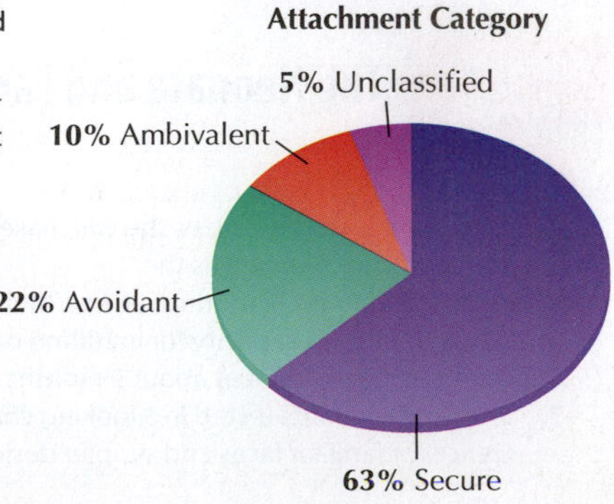

Discovering Psychology: What's Your Attachment Style?

Do our first attachments continue to affect us as adults? Some psychologists believe they do, by influencing how we relate to friends and lovers (Bohlin & Hagekull, 2009; Sroufe et al., 2005). Read the following statements and see which best describes your adult relationships.

Secure Attachment Style

I think most other people are well intentioned and trustworthy.
I find it relatively easy to get close to others.
I am comfortable relying on others and having others depend on me.
I don't worry much about being abandoned by others.
I am comfortable when other people want to get close to me emotionally.

Avoidant Attachment Style

I tend to pull back when things don't go well in a relationship.
I am somewhat skeptical about the idea of true love.
I have difficulty trusting my partner in a romantic relationship.
Other people tend to be too eager to seek commitment from me.
I get a little nervous if anyone gets too close emotionally.

Ambivalent Attachment Style

I have often felt misunderstood and unappreciated in my romantic relationships.
My friends and lovers have been somewhat unreliable.
I love my romantic partner but I worry that she or he doesn't really love me.
I would like to be closer to my romantic partner, but I'm not sure I trust her or him.

Do any of the preceding statements sound familiar? If so, they may describe your adult attachment style (Welch & Houser, 2010). Most adults have a secure attachment style that is marked by caring, supportiveness, and understanding. However, it's not unusual to have an avoidant attachment style that reflects a tendency to resist intimacy and commitment to others (Collins et al., 2002). An ambivalent attachment style is marked by mixed feelings about love and friendship (Tidwell, Reis, & Shaver, 1996). Do you see any similarities between your present relationships and your attachment experiences as a child?

for some children, a lack of affectionate care early in life leaves a lasting emotional impact well into adulthood (see "What's Your Attachment Style?").

Promoting Secure Attachment

One key to secure attachment is a mother who is accepting and sensitive to her baby's signals and rhythms. Poor attachment occurs when a mother's actions are inappropriate, inadequate, intrusive, overstimulating, or rejecting. An example is a mother who tries to play with a drowsy infant or who ignores a baby who is looking at her and vocalizing. The link between sensitive caregiving and secure attachment appears to apply to all cultures (Posada et al., 2002).

What about attachment to fathers? Fathers of securely attached infants tend to be outgoing, agreeable, and happy in their marriage. In general, a warm family atmosphere—one that includes sensitive mothering *and* fathering—produces secure children (Belsky, 1996; Gomez & McLaren, 2007).

Day Care

Does commercial day care interfere with the quality of attachment? It depends on the quality of day care. Overall, *high-quality* day care does not adversely affect attachment to parents. In fact, high-quality day care can actually improve children's social and mental skills (Mercer, 2006; National Institute of Child Health and Human Development, 2010). Children in high-quality day care tend to have better relationships with their mothers and fewer behavior problems. They also have better cognitive skills and language abilities (Burchinal et al., 2000; Vandell, 2004).

However, all the positive effects just noted are *reversed* for low-quality day care. Low-quality day care *is* risky and *may* weaken attachment (Phillips & Lowenstein, 2011). Poor-quality day care can even create behavior problems that didn't exist beforehand (Pierrehumbert et al., 2002). Parents are wise to carefully evaluate and monitor the quality of day care their children receive.

What should parents look for when they evaluate the quality of day care? Parents seeking quality day care should look for responsive and sensitive caregivers who offer plenty of attention and verbal and cognitive stimulation (Phillips & Lowenstein, 2011). This is more likely to occur in daycares with *at least* the following: (1) a small number of children per caregiver, (2) small overall group size (12 to 15), (3) trained caregivers, (4) minimal staff turnover, and (5) stable, consistent care. (Also, avoid any child-care center with the words *zoo, menagerie,* or *stockade* in its name.)

Emotional attachment An especially close emotional bond that infants form with their parents, caregivers, or others.

Surrogate mother A substitute mother (often an inanimate dummy in animal research).

Contact comfort A pleasant and reassuring feeling human and animal infants get from touching or clinging to something soft and warm, usually their mother.

Separation anxiety Distress displayed by infants when they are separated from their parents or principal caregivers.

Secure attachment A stable and positive emotional bond.

Insecure-avoidant attachment An anxious emotional bond marked by a tendency to avoid reunion with a parent or caregiver.

Insecure-ambivalent attachment An anxious emotional bond marked by both a desire to be with a parent or caregiver and some resistance to being reunited.

Attachment and Affectional Needs

A baby's **affectional needs**—needs for love and affection—are every bit as important as more obvious needs for food, water, and physical care. All things considered, creating a bond of trust and affection between the infant and at least one other person is a key event during the first year of life. Parents are sometimes afraid of "spoiling" babies with too much attention, but for the first year or two, this is nearly impossible. In fact, a later capacity to experience warm and loving relationships may depend on it.

Parental Influences—Life with Mom and Dad

Gateway Question 3.4: *How important are parenting styles?*

From the first few years of life, when caregivers are the center of a child's world, through to adulthood, the style and quality of mothering and fathering are very important.

Parenting Styles

Psychologist Diana Baumrind (1991, 2005) has studied the effects of three major **parental styles**, which are identifiable patterns of parental caretaking and interaction with children. See if you recognize the styles she describes.

Authoritarian parents enforce rigid rules and demand strict obedience to authority. Typically they view children as having few rights but adult-like responsibilities. The child is expected to stay out of trouble and to accept, without question, what parents regard as right or wrong. ("Do it because I say so.") The children of authoritarian parents are usually obedient and self-controlled. But they also tend to be emotionally stiff, withdrawn, apprehensive, and lacking in curiosity.

Overly permissive parents give little guidance, allow too much freedom, or don't hold children accountable for their actions. Typically, the child has rights similar to an adult's but few responsibilities. Rules are not enforced, and the child usually gets his or her way. ("Do whatever you want.") Permissive parents tend to produce dependent, immature children who misbehave frequently. Such children are aimless and likely to "run amok."

Baumrind describes **authoritative parents** as those who supply firm and consistent guidance, combined with love and affection. Such parents balance their own rights with those of their children. They control their children's behavior in a caring, responsive, nonauthoritarian way. ("Do it for this reason.") Effective parents are firm and consistent, not harsh or rigid. In general, they encourage the child to act responsibly, to think, and to make good decisions. This style produces children who are *resilient* (good at bouncing back after bad experiences) and develop the strengths they need to thrive even in difficult circumstances (Bahr & Hoffmann, 2010; Kim-Cohen et al., 2004). The children of authoritative parents are competent, self-controlled, independent, assertive, and inquiring. They know how to manage their emotions and use positive coping skills (Eisenberg et al., 2003; Lynch et al., 2004). To read more about effective parenting, see this chapter's "Psychology in Action" section.

"Your father and I have come to believe that incarceration is sometimes the only appropriate punishment."

Peter Steiner/Cartoonbank

Maternal and Paternal Influences

Don't mothers and fathers parent differently? Yes. Although **maternal influences**—all the effects a mother has on her child—generally have a greater impact, fathers do make a unique contribution to parenting (Santrock, 2009). Although fathers are spending more time with their children, mothers still do most of the nurturing and caretaking, especially of young children (Craig, 2006).

Studies of **paternal influences**—the sum of all effects a father has on his child—reveal that fathers are more likely to play with their children and tell them stories. In contrast, mothers are typically responsible for the physical and emotional care of their children (● Figure 3.14).

It might seem that the father's role as a playmate makes him less important. Not so. Samantha's playtime with David is actually very valuable. From birth onward, fathers pay more visual attention to

Fathering typically makes a contribution to early development that differs in emphasis from mothering.

BananaStock/SuperStock

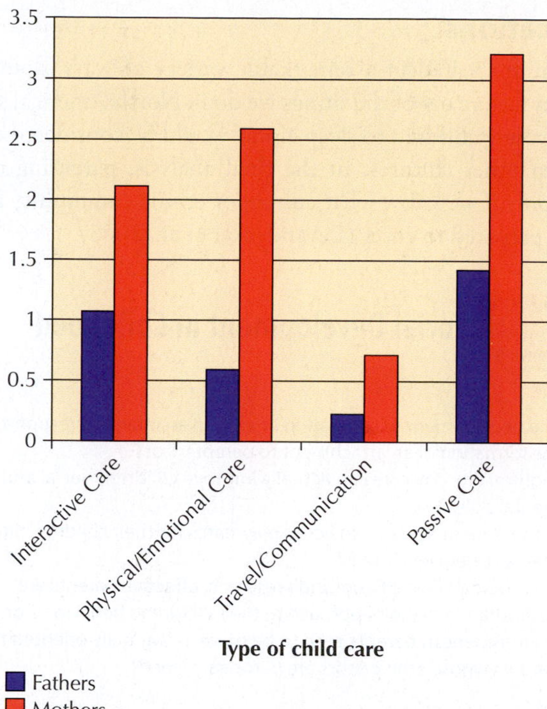

● Figure 3.14 Mother-child and father-child interactions. This graph shows what occurred on routine days in a sample of over 1,400 Australian homes. Mothers spend about twice as long each day on childcare compared with fathers. Further, mothers spend more time on physical and emotional care (e.g., feeding, bathing, soothing) than on interactive care (e.g., playing, reading, activities) while fathers show the reverse pattern. Finally, mothers spend more time on travel (e.g., driving children to sports or music lessons), communication (e.g., talking to teachers about their children), and passive care (e.g., supervising children while they play). (Adapted from Craig, 2006.)

children than mothers do. Fathers are much more tactile (lifting, tickling, and handling the baby), more physically arousing (engaging in rough-and-tumble play), and more likely to engage in unusual play (imitating the baby, for example). In comparison, mothers speak to infants more, play more conventional games (such as peekaboo), and, as noted, spend much more time in caregiving. Young children who spend a lot of time playing with their fathers tend to be more competent in many ways (Paquette, 2004; Tamis-LeMonda et al., 2004).

Overall, fathers can be as affectionate, sensitive, and responsive as mothers are. Nevertheless, infants and children tend to get very different views of males and females. Females, who offer comfort, nurturance, and verbal stimulation, tend to be close at hand. Males come and go, and when they are present, action, exploration, and risk-taking prevail. It's no wonder, then, that the parental styles of mothers and fathers have a major impact on children's gender role development (Holmes & Huston, 2010; Videon, 2005).

Ethnic Differences: Four Flavors of Parenting

Do ethnic differences in parenting affect children in distinctive ways? Diana Baumrind's work provides a good overall summary of the effects of parenting. However, her conclusions are probably most valid for families whose roots lie in Europe. Child rearing in other ethnic groups often reflects different customs and beliefs. Cultural differences are especially apparent with respect to the meaning attached to a child's behavior. Is a particular behavior "good" or "bad"? Should it be encouraged or discouraged? The answer depends greatly on parents' cultural values (Leyendecker et al., 2005).

Making generalizations about groups of people is always risky. Nevertheless, some typical differences in child-rearing patterns have been observed in North American ethnic communities, as we discuss here (Kaplan, 1998; Parke, 2004).

African-American Families

Traditional African-American values emphasize loyalty and interdependence among family members, security, developing a positive identity, and not giving up in the face of adversity. African-American parents typically stress obedience and respect for elders (Dixon, Graber, & Brooks-Gunn, 2008). Child discipline tends to be fairly strict (Parke, 2004), but many African-American parents see this as a necessity, especially if they live in urban areas where safety is a concern. Self-reliance, resourcefulness, and an ability to take care of oneself in difficult situations are also qualities that African-American parents seek to promote in their children.

Hispanic Families

Like African-American parents, Hispanic parents tend to have relatively strict standards of discipline (Dixon, Graber, & Brooks-Gunn, 2008). They also place a high value on *familismo*: the centrality of the family, with a corresponding stress on family values, family pride, and loyalty (Glass & Owen, 2010). Hispanic families are typically affectionate and indulgent toward younger children. However, as children grow older, they are expected to learn social skills and to be calm, obedient, courteous, and respectful (Calzada, Fernandez, & Cortes, 2010). In fact, such social skills may be valued more than cognitive skills (Delgado & Ford, 1998). In addition, Hispanic parents tend to stress cooperation more than competition. Such values can put Hispanic children at a disadvantage in highly competitive, European-American culture.

Affectional needs Emotional needs for love and affection.

Parental styles Identifiable patterns of parental caretaking and interaction with children.

Authoritarian parents Parents who enforce rigid rules and demand strict obedience to authority.

Overly permissive parents Parents who give little guidance, allow too much freedom, or do not require the child to take responsibility.

Authoritative parents Parents who supply firm and consistent guidance combined with love and affection.

Maternal influences The aggregate of all psychological effects mothers have on their children.

Paternal influences The aggregate of all psychological effects fathers have on their children.

Asian-American Families

Asian cultures tend to be group oriented, and they emphasize interdependence among individuals. In contrast, Western cultures value individual effort and independence. This difference is often reflected in Asian-American child-rearing practices (Chao & Tseng, 2002). Asian-American children are often taught that their behavior can bring either pride or shame to the family. Therefore, they are obliged to set aside their own desires when the greater good of the family is at stake (Parke, 2004). Parents tend to act as teachers who encourage hard work, moral behavior, and achievement. For the first few years, parenting is lenient and permissive. However, after about age 5, Asian-American parents begin to expect respect, obedience, self-control, and self-discipline from their children.

Arab-American Families

In Middle Eastern cultures, children are expected to be polite, obedient, disciplined, and conforming (Erickson & Al-Timimi, 2001). Punishment may consist of spankings, teasing, or shaming in front of others. Arab-American fathers tend to be strong authority figures who demand obedience so that the family will not be shamed by a child's bad behavior. Success, generosity, and hospitality are highly valued in Arab-American culture. The pursuit of family honor encourages hard work, thrift, conservatism, and educational achievement. The welfare of the family is emphasized over individual identity. Thus, Arab-American children are raised to respect their parents, members of their extended family, and other adults as well (Medhus, 2001).

© Jeff Greenberg/PhotoEdit

In other ethnic communities, norms for effective parenting often differ in subtle ways from parenting styles in Euro-American culture.

Implications

Children are reared in a remarkable variety of ways around the world. In fact, many of the things we do in North America, such as forcing young children to sleep alone, would be considered odd or wrong in other cultures. In the final analysis, parenting can be judged only if we know what culture or ethnic community a child is being prepared to enter (Leyendecker et al., 2005).

Knowledge Builder — Social Development in Childhood

RECITE

1. The development of separation anxiety in an infant corresponds to the formation of an attachment to parents. T or F?
2. High-quality day care can actually improve children's social and mental skills. T or F?
3. Fathers are more likely to act as playmates for their children, rather than as caregivers. T or F?
4. According to Diana Baumrind's research, effective parents are authoritarian in their approach to their children's behavior. T or F?
5. Asian-American parents tend to be more individually oriented than parents whose ethnic roots are European. T or F?

REFLECT

Think Critically

6. Can emotional bonding begin before birth?
7. Which parenting style do you think would be most likely to lead to eating disorders in children?

Self-Reflect

Do you think that your experiences as a child, such as your early attachment pattern, affect your life as an adult? Can you think of any examples from your own life?

Do you know any parents who have young children and who are authoritarian, permissive, or authoritative? What are their children like?

Do you think parenting depends on ethnicity? If so, why? If not, why not?

Answers: 1. T **2.** T **3.** T **4.** F **5.** F **6.** It certainly can for parents. When a pregnant woman begins to feel fetal movements, she becomes aware that a baby is coming to life inside of her. Likewise, prospective parents who hear a fetal heartbeat at the doctor's office or see an ultrasound image of the fetus begin to become emotionally attached to the unborn child (Santrock, 2009). **7.** Both authoritarian and permissive styles are more likely to lead to eating disorders in children. Parents who are too controlling about what their children eat or too willing to withdraw from conflicts over eating can create problems for their children (Haycraft & Blissett, 2010).

Language Development—Who Talks Baby Talk?

Gateway Question 3.5: *How do children acquire language?*

There's something almost miraculous about a baby's first words. As infants, how did we manage to leap into the world of language? Even a quick survey like this one reveals that both maturation (nature) and social development (nurture) provide a foundation for language learning.

Language development is closely tied to maturation (Carroll, 2008; Gleason & Ratner, 2009). As every parent knows, babies can cry from birth on. By 1 month of age, they use crying to gain attention. Typically, parents can tell if an infant is hungry, angry, or in pain from the tone of the crying (Kaplan, 1998). Around 6 to 8 weeks of age, babies begin *cooing* (the repetition of vowel sounds such as "oo" and "ah").

By 7 months of age, Samantha's nervous system will mature enough to allow her to grasp objects, to smile, laugh, sit up, and *babble.* In the babbling stage, the consonants *b, d, m,* and *g* are combined with the vowel sounds to produce meaningless language sounds: *dadadadada* or *bababa.* At first, babbling is the same around the world. But soon, the language spoken by parents begins to have an influence. That is, Japanese babies start to babble in a way that sounds like Japanese, Mexican babies babble in Spanish-like sounds, and so forth (Gopnik, Meltzoff, & Kuhl, 2000; Kuhl, 2004).

At about 1 year of age, children respond to real words such as *no* or *hi.* Soon afterward, the first connection between words and objects forms, and children may address their parents as "Mama" or "Dada." By age 18 months to 2 years, Samantha's vocabulary may include a hundred words or more. At first there is a *single-word stage,* during which children use one word at a time, such as "go," "juice," or "up." Soon after, words are arranged in simple two-word sentences called *telegraphic speech:* "Want-Teddy," "Mama-gone."

Language and the Terrible Twos

At about the same time that children begin to put two or three words together, they become much more independent. Two-year-olds understand some of the commands parents make, but they are not always willing to carry them out. A child like Samantha may assert her independence by saying "No drink," "Me do it," "My cup, my cup," and the like. It can be worse, of course. A 2-year-old may look at you intently, make eye contact, listen as you shout "No, no," and still pour her juice on the cat.

During their second year, children become increasingly capable of mischief and temper tantrums. Thus, calling this time "the terrible twos" is not entirely inappropriate. One-year-olds can do plenty of things parents don't want them to do. However, it's usually 2-year-olds who do things *because* you don't want them to (Gopnik, Meltzoff, & Kuhl, 2000). Perhaps parents can take some comfort in knowing that a stubborn, negative 2-year-old is simply becoming more independent. When Samantha is 2 years old, Carol and David would be wise to remember that "this, too, shall pass."

After age 2, the child's comprehension and use of words takes a dramatic leap forward. From this point on, vocabulary and language skills grow at a phenomenal rate (Fernald, Perfors, & Marchman, 2006). By first grade, Samantha will be able to understand around 8,000 words and use about 4,000. She will have truly entered the world of language.

The Roots of Language

What accounts for this explosion of language development? Linguist Noam Chomsky (1975, 1986) has long claimed that humans have a **biological predisposition,** or hereditary readiness, to develop language. According to Chomsky, language patterns are inborn, much like a child's ability to coordinate walking. If such inborn language recognition does exist, it may explain why children around the world use a limited number of patterns in their first sentences. Typical patterns include (Mussen et al., 1979):

Identification:	"See kitty."
Nonexistence:	"All gone milk."
Possession:	"My doll."
Agent-Action:	"Mama give."
Negation:	"Not ball."
Question:	"Where doggie?"

Does Chomsky's theory explain why language develops so rapidly? It is certainly part of the story. But many psychologists feel that Chomsky underestimates the importance of learning (Tomasello, 2003) and the social contexts that shape language development (Hoff, 2006, 2009). *Psycholinguists* (specialists in the psychology of language) have shown that imitation of adults and rewards for correctly using words (as when a child asks for a cookie) are an important part of language learning. Also, babies actively participate in language learning by asking questions, such as "What dis?" (Domingo & Goldstein-Alpern, 1999).

When a child makes a language error, parents typically repeat the child's sentence, with needed corrections (Bohannon & Stanowicz, 1988; Hoff, 2006), or ask a clarifying question to draw the child's attention to the error (Saxton, Houston-Price, & Dawson, 2005). More important is the fact that parents and children begin to communicate long before the child can speak. A readiness to interact *socially* with parents may be as important as innate language recognition. The next section explains why.

Biological predisposition The presumed hereditary readiness of humans to learn certain skills, such as how to use language, or a readiness to behave in particular ways.

Early Communication

How do parents communicate with infants before they can talk? Parents go to a great deal of trouble to get babies to smile and vocalize. In doing so, they quickly learn to change their actions to keep the infant's attention, arousal, and activity at optimal levels. A familiar example is the "I'm-Going-to-Get-You" game. In it, the adult says, "I'm gonna getcha . . . . I'm gonna getcha . . . . I'm gonna getcha . . . . Gotcha!" Through such games, adults and babies come to share similar rhythms and expectations (Carroll, 2008). Soon a system of shared **signals** is created, including touching, vocalizing, gazing, and smiling. These help lay a foundation for later language use (Tamis-LeMonda, Bornstein, & Baumwell, 2001). Specifically, signals establish a pattern of "conversational" *turn-taking* (alternate sending and receiving of messages).

Carol	*Samantha*
"Oh what a nice little smile!"	(smiles)
"Yes, isn't that nice?"	
"There."	
"There's a nice little smile."	(burps)
"Well, pardon you!"	
"Yes, that's better, isn't it?"	
"Yes."	(vocalizes)
"Yes."	(smiles)
"What's so funny?"	

From the outside, such exchanges may look meaningless. In reality, they represent real communication. Samantha's vocalizations and attention provide a way of interacting emotionally with Carol and David. One study found that 6-week-old babies gaze at an adult's face in rhythm with the adult's speech (Crown et al., 2002). Infants as young as 4 months engage in vocal turn-taking with adults (Jaffe et al., 2001). The more children interact with parents, the faster they learn to talk and the faster they learn thinking abilities (Dickinson & Tabors, 2001; Hoff & Tian, 2005). Unmistakably, social relationships contribute to early language learning (Hoff, 2006, 2009).

Gary Conner/PhotoLibrary

As with motherese, parents use a distinctive style when singing to an infant. Even people who speak another language can tell if a tape-recorded song was sung to an infant or an adult (Trehub, Unyk, & Trainor, 1993).

Parentese

When they talk to infants, parents use an exaggerated pattern of speaking called **motherese** or **parentese.** Typically, they raise their tone of voice, use short, simple sentences, repeat themselves, and use frequent gestures (Gogate, Bahrick, & Watson, 2000). They also slow their rate of speaking and use exaggerated voice inflections: "Did Samantha eat it A-L-L UP?"

What is the purpose of such changes? Parents are apparently trying to help their children learn language (Soderstrom, 2007). When a baby is still babbling, parents tend to use long, adult-style sentences. But as soon as the baby says its first word, they switch to parentese. By the time babies are 4 months old, they prefer parentese over normal speech (Cooper et al., 1997).

In addition to being simpler, parentese has a distinct "musical" quality (Trainor & Desjardins, 2002). No matter what language mothers speak, the melodies, pauses, and inflections they use to comfort, praise, or give warning are universal. Psychologist Anne Fernald has found that mothers of all nations talk to their babies with similar changes in pitch. For instance, we praise babies with a rising, then falling pitch ("BRA-vo!" "GOOD girl!"). Warnings are delivered in a short, sharp rhythm ("Nein! Nein!" "Basta! Basta!" "Not! Dude!"). To give comfort, parents use low, smooth, drawn-out tones ("Oooh poor baaa-by." "Oooh pobrecito.") A high-pitched, rising melody is used to call attention to objects ("See the pretty BIRDIE?") (Fernald, 1989).

Parentese helps parents get babies' attention, communicate with them, and teach them language (Thiessen, Hill, & Saffran, 2005). Later, as a child's speaking improves, parents tend to adjust their speech to the child's language ability. Especially from 18 months to 4 years of age, parents seek to clarify what a child says and prompt the child to say more.

In summary, some elements of language are innate. Nevertheless, our inherited tendency to learn language does not determine if we will speak English or Vietnamese, Spanish or Russian. Environmental forces also influence whether a person develops simple or sophisticated language skills. The first 7 years of life are a sensitive period in language learning (Hoff, 2009). Clearly, a full flowering of speech requires careful cultivation.

Knowledge Builder: Language Development in Childhood

RECITE

1. The development of speech and language usually occurs in which order?
   a. crying, cooing, babbling, telegraphic speech
   b. cooing, crying, babbling, telegraphic speech
   c. babbling, crying, cooing, telegraphic speech
   d. crying, babbling, cooing, identification

2. Simple two-word sentences are characteristic of ______________________________ speech.
3. Noam ______________________ has advanced the idea that language acquisition is built on innate patterns.
4. Pre-language turn-taking and social interactions would be of special interest to a psycholinguist. T or F?
5. The style of speaking known as ______________________________ is higher in pitch and has a musical quality.

REFLECT

Think Critically

6. The children of professional parents hear more words per hour than the children of welfare parents, and they also tend to score higher on tests of mental abilities. How else could their higher scores be explained?

Self-Reflect

In order, see if you can name and imitate the language abilities you had as you progressed from birth to age 2 years. Now see if you can label and imitate some basic elements of parentese.

In your own words, state at least one argument for and against Chomsky's view of language acquisition.

You are going to spend a day with a person who speaks a different language than you do. Do you think you would be able to communicate with the other person? How does this relate to language acquisition?

Answers: 1. a **2.** telegraphic **3.** Chomsky **4.** T **5.** Parentese or motherese **6.** Children in professional homes receive many educational benefits that are less common in welfare homes. Yet, even when such differences are taken into account, brighter children tend to come from richer language environments (Hart & Risley, 1999).

Cognitive Development—Think Like a Child

Gateway Question 3.6: *How do children learn to think?*

Now that we have Samantha talking, let's move on to a broader view of intellectual development. Swiss psychologist and philosopher Jean Piaget (Jahn pea-ah-ZHAY) (1896–1980) provided some of the first great insights into how children develop thinking abilities when he proposed that children's cognitive skills progress through a series of maturational stages. Also, many psychologists have become interested in how children learn the intellectual skills valued by their culture. Typically, children do this with guidance from skilled "tutors" (parents and others).

Piaget's Theory of Cognitive Development

Piaget's ideas have deeply affected our view of children (Feldman, 2004). According to Piaget (1951, 1952), children's thinking is, generally speaking, less abstract that that of adults. They tend to base their understanding on particular examples and objects they can see or touch. Also, children use fewer generalizations, categories, and principles. Piaget also believed that all children mature through a series of distinct stages in intellectual development. Many of his ideas came from observing his own children as they solved various thought problems. (It is tempting to imagine that Piaget's illustrious career was launched one day when his wife said to him, "Watch the children for a while, will you, Jean?")

Jean Piaget (1896–1980)—philosopher, psychologist, and keen observer of children.

Yves De Braine/stockphoto.com

Mental Processes

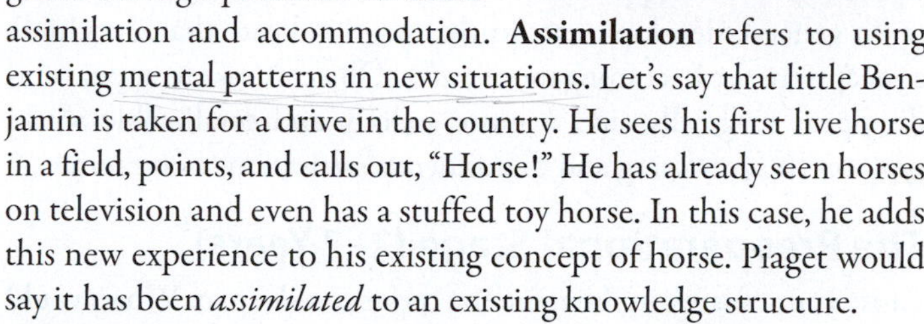

Piaget was convinced that intellect grows through processes he called assimilation and accommodation. **Assimilation** refers to using existing mental patterns in new situations. Let's say that little Benjamin is taken for a drive in the country. He sees his first live horse in a field, points, and calls out, "Horse!" He has already seen horses on television and even has a stuffed toy horse. In this case, he adds this new experience to his existing concept of horse. Piaget would say it has been *assimilated* to an existing knowledge structure.

In **accommodation,** existing ideas are modified to fit new requirements. For instance, suppose a month later Benjamin goes to the zoo, where he sees his first zebra. Proudly, he again exclaims, "Horse!" This time, his mother replies, "No dear, that's a zebra." Little Benjamin has *failed to assimilate* the zebra to his horse concept. He must now *accommodate* by creating a new concept, *zebra*, and modifying his concept of horse (*not* black and white stripes).

The Sensorimotor Stage (0–2 Years)

Look up from this book until your attention is attracted to something else in the room. Now close your eyes. Is it still there? How do you know? As an adult, you can keep an image of the object in your "mind's eye." According to Piaget, newborn babies cannot create *internal representations* such as mental images. As a result, they lack **object permanence**, an understanding that objects continue to exist when they are out of sight.

Signal In early language development, any behavior, such as touching, vocalizing, gazing, or smiling, that allows nonverbal interaction and turn-taking between parent and child.

Motherese (or parentese) A pattern of speech used when talking to infants, marked by a higher-pitched voice; short, simple sentences; repetition; slower speech; and exaggerated voice inflections.

Assimilation In Piaget's theory, the application of existing mental patterns to new situations (that is, the new situation is assimilated to existing mental schemes).

Accommodation In Piaget's theory, the modification of existing mental patterns to fit new demands (that is, mental schemes are changed to accommodate new information or experiences).

Sensorimotor stage Stage of intellectual development during which sensory input and motor responses become coordinated.

Object permanence Concept, gained in infancy, in which objects continue to exist even when they are hidden from view.

BRIDGES

Concepts and language are other types of internal representation. **See Chapter 8, pages 276–277, for more information.**

For this reason, in the first 2 years of life, Samantha's intellectual development will be largely nonintellectual and nonverbal. She will be concerned mainly with learning to coordinate information from her senses with her motor movements. But sometime during their first year, babies begin to actively pursue disappearing objects. By age 2, they can anticipate the movement of an object behind a screen. For example, when watching an electric train, Samantha will look ahead to the end of a tunnel rather than staring at the spot where the train disappeared.

In general, developments in this stage indicate that the child's conceptions are becoming more *stable*. Objects cease to appear and disappear magically, and a more orderly and predictable world replaces the confusing and disconnected sensations of infancy.

The Preoperational Stage (2–7 Years)

Close your eyes again. Imagine the room you sleep in. What would it look like if you were perched on the ceiling and your bed was missing? You have now mentally operated on your image by *transforming* it. According to Piaget, even though preoperational children can form mental images or ideas, they are preoperational because they cannot easily **transform** those images or ideas in their minds.

This is why, although children begin to think *symbolically* and use language before the age of 6 or 7, their thinking is still very concrete and **intuitive** (it makes little use of reasoning and logic). (Do you remember thinking as a child that the sun and the moon followed you when you took a walk?) Such thinking is also often labeled *superstitious*, especially when it persists into later childhood and adulthood (Wargo, 2008).

Let's visit Samantha at age 5: If you show her a short, wide glass full of milk and a taller, narrow glass full of milk, she will most likely tell you that the taller glass contains more milk (even if it doesn't). Samantha will tell you this even if she watches you pour milk from the short glass into an empty taller glass. Older children can easily mentally transform the pouring of the milk by mentally *reversing* it, to see that the shape of the container is irrelevant to the volume of milk it contains. But Samantha is preoperational; she cannot engage in the mental operation of transforming the tall, narrow glass of milk back into a short, wide glass. Thus, she is not bothered by the fact that the milk appears to be transformed from a smaller to a larger amount. Instead, she responds only to the fact that *taller* seems to mean *more* (see ● Figure 3.15).

After about age 7, children are no longer fooled by this situation. Perhaps that's why age 7 has been called the "age of reason." From age 7 on, we see a definite trend toward more logical, adult-like thought (Flavell, 1992).

During the preoperational stage, the child is also quite **egocentric**, or unable to take the viewpoint of other people. The child's ego seems to stand at the center of his or her world. To illustrate, show Samantha a two-sided mirror. Then hold it between you and her, so she can see herself in it. If you ask her what she thinks *you* can see, she imagines that you see *her* face reflected in the mirror, instead of your own. She cannot mentally transform the view she sees into the view you must be seeing.

Such egocentrism explains why children can seem exasperatingly selfish or uncooperative at times. If Benjamin blocks your view by standing in front of the TV, he assumes that you can see it if he can. If you ask him to move so you can see better, he may move

● **Figure 3.15** Children under age 7 intuitively assume that a volume of liquid increases when it is poured from a short, wide container into a taller, thinner one. This boy thinks the tall container holds more than the short one. Actually each holds the same amount of liquid. Children make such judgments based on the height of the liquid, not its volume.

Crossing a busy street can be dangerous for the preoperational child. Because their thinking is still egocentric, younger children cannot understand why the driver of a car can't see them if they can see the car. Children under the age of 7 also cannot consistently judge speeds and distances of oncoming cars. Adults can easily overestimate the "street smarts" of younger children. It is advisable to teach children to cross with a light, in crosswalks, or with assistance.

so that he can see better! Benjamin is not being selfish in the ordinary sense. He just doesn't realize that your view differs from his.

In addition, the child's use of language is not as sophisticated as it might seem. Children have a tendency to confuse words with the objects they represent. If Benjamin calls a toy block a "car" and you use the block to make a "house," he may be upset. To children, the name of an object is as much a part of the object as its size, shape, and color. This seems to underlie a preoccupation with name-calling. To the preoperational child, insulting words may really hurt. Samantha was once angered by her older brother. Searching for a way to retaliate against her larger and stronger foe, she settled on, "You panty-girdle!" It was the worst thing she could think of saying.

The Concrete Operational Stage (7–11 Years)

The hallmark of this stage is the ability to carry out mental operations such as *reversing* thoughts. A 4-year-old boy in the preoperational stage might have a conversation like this (showing what happens when a child's thinking *lacks* reversibility):

"Do you have a brother?"
"Yes."
"What's his name?"
"Billy."
"Does Billy have a brother?"
"No."

Reversibility of thought allows children in the concrete operational stage to recognize that if $4 \times 2 = 8$, then 2×4 does, too. Younger children must memorize each relationship separately.

The development of mental operations allows mastery of **conservation**—the concept that mass, weight, and volume remain unchanged when the shape of objects changes. Children have learned conservation when they understand that rolling a ball of clay into a "snake" does not increase the amount of clay. Likewise, pouring liquid from a tall, narrow glass into a shallow dish does not reduce the amount of liquid. In each case, the volume remains the same despite changes in shape or appearance. The original amount is *conserved.* (See ● Figure 3.15.)

During the concrete operational stage, children begin to use concepts of time, space, and number. The child can think logically about very concrete objects or situations, categories, and principles. Such abilities help explain why children stop believing in Santa Claus when they reach this stage. Because they can conserve volume, they realize that Santa's sack couldn't possibly hold enough toys for millions of girls and boys.

The Formal Operational Stage (11 Years and Up)

After about the age of 11, children begin to break away from concrete objects and specific examples. Thinking is based more on abstract principles, such as "democracy," "honor," or "correlation." Children who reach this stage become self-reflective about their own thoughts, and they become less egocentric. Older children and young adolescents also gradually become able to consider hypothetical possibilities (suppositions, guesses, or projections). For example, if you ask a younger child, "What do you think would happen if it suddenly became possible for people to fly?" the child might respond, "People can't fly." Older children are better able to consider such possibilities.

Full adult intellectual ability is attained during the stage of formal operations. Older adolescents are capable of inductive and deductive reasoning, and they can comprehend math, physics, philosophy, psychology, and other abstract systems. They can learn to test hypotheses in a scientific manner. Of course, not everyone reaches this level of thinking. Also, many adults can think formally about some topics, but their thinking becomes concrete when the topic is unfamiliar. This implies that formal thinking may be more a result of culture and learning than maturation. In any case, after late adolescence, improvements in intellect are based on gaining specific knowledge, experience, and wisdom rather than on any leaps in basic thinking capacity.

How can parents apply Piaget's ideas? Piaget's theory suggests that the ideal way to guide intellectual development is to provide experiences that are only slightly novel, unusual, or challenging. Remember, a child's intellect develops mainly through accommodation. It is usually best to follow a *one-step-ahead strategy,* in which your teaching efforts are aimed just beyond a child's current level of comprehension (Brainerd, 2003).

Parents should avoid *forced teaching,* or "hothousing," which is like trying to force plants to bloom prematurely. Forcing children to learn reading, math, gymnastics, swimming, or music at an accelerated pace can bore or oppress them. True intellectual enrichment respects the child's interests. It does not make the child feel pressured to perform.

■ Table 3.2 briefly summarizes each Piagetian stage. To help you remember Piaget's theory, the table describes what would happen at each stage if we played a game of *Monopoly* with the child. You'll also find brief suggestions about how to relate to children in each stage.

Preoperational stage Period of intellectual development during which children begin to use language and think symbolically, yet remain intuitive and egocentric in their thought.

Transformation The mental ability to change the shape or form of a substance (such as clay or water) and to perceive that its volume remains the same.

Intuitive thought Thinking that makes little or no use of reasoning and logic.

Egocentric thought Thought that is self-centered and fails to consider the viewpoints of others.

Concrete operational stage Period of intellectual development during which children become able to use the concepts of time, space, volume, and number, but in ways that remain simplified and concrete, rather than abstract.

Conservation In Piaget's theory, mastery of the concept that the weight, mass, and volume of matter remains unchanged (is conserved) even when the shape or appearance of objects changes.

Formal operational stage Period of intellectual development characterized by thinking that includes abstract, theoretical, and hypothetical ideas.

TABLE 3.2 Piaget—A Guide for Parents

Piaget	*Monopoly* Game	Guidelines for Parents
Sensorimotor Stage (0–2 Years) The stage during which sensory input and motor responses become coordinated.	The child tries to put houses, hotels, and dice in her mouth and plays with "Chance" cards.	Active play with a child is most effective at this stage. Encourage explorations in touching, smelling, and manipulating objects. Peekaboo is a good way to establish the permanence of objects.
Preoperational Stage (2–7 Years) The period of cognitive development when children begin to use language and think symbolically, yet remain intuitive and egocentric.	The child plays *Monopoly,* but makes up her own rules and cannot understand instructions.	Specific examples and touching or seeing things continue to be more useful than verbal explanations. Learning the concept of conservation may be aided by demonstrations with liquids, beads, clay, and other substances.
Concrete Operational Stage (7–11 Years) The period of cognitive development during which children begin to use concepts of time, space, volume, and number, but in ways that remain simplified and concrete.	The child understands basic instructions and will play by the rules but is not capable of hypothetical transactions dealing with mortgages, loans, and special pacts with other players.	Children are beginning to use generalizations, but they still require specific examples to grasp many ideas. Expect a degree of inconsistency in the child's ability to apply concepts of time, space, quantity, and volume to new situations.
Formal Operations Stage (11 Years and Up) The period of intellectual development marked by a capacity for abstract, theoretical, and hypothetical thinking.	The child no longer plays the game mechanically; complex and hypothetical transactions unique to each game are now possible.	It is now more effective to explain things verbally or symbolically and to help children master general rules and principles. Encourage the child to create hypotheses and to imagine how things could be.

Piaget Today

Today, Piaget's theory remains a valuable "road map" for understanding how children think. On a broad scale, many of Piaget's ideas have held up well. However, there has been disagreement about specific details. For example, according to learning theorists, children continuously gain specific knowledge; they do not undergo stage-like leaps in general mental ability (Feldman, 2004; Siegler, 2005). On the other hand, the growth in connections between brain cells occurs in waves that parallel some of Piaget's stages (see ● Figure 3.16). Thus, the truth may lie somewhere between Piaget's stage theory and modern learning theory.

In addition, it is now widely accepted that children develop cognitive skills somewhat earlier than Piaget originally thought (Bjorklund, 2005). For example, Piaget believed that infants under the age of 1 year cannot think (use internal representations). Such abilities, he believed, emerge only after a long period of sensorimotor development. Babies, he said, can have no memory of people and objects that are out of sight. Yet we now know that infants begin forming representations of the world very early in life. For example, babies as young as 3 months of age appear to

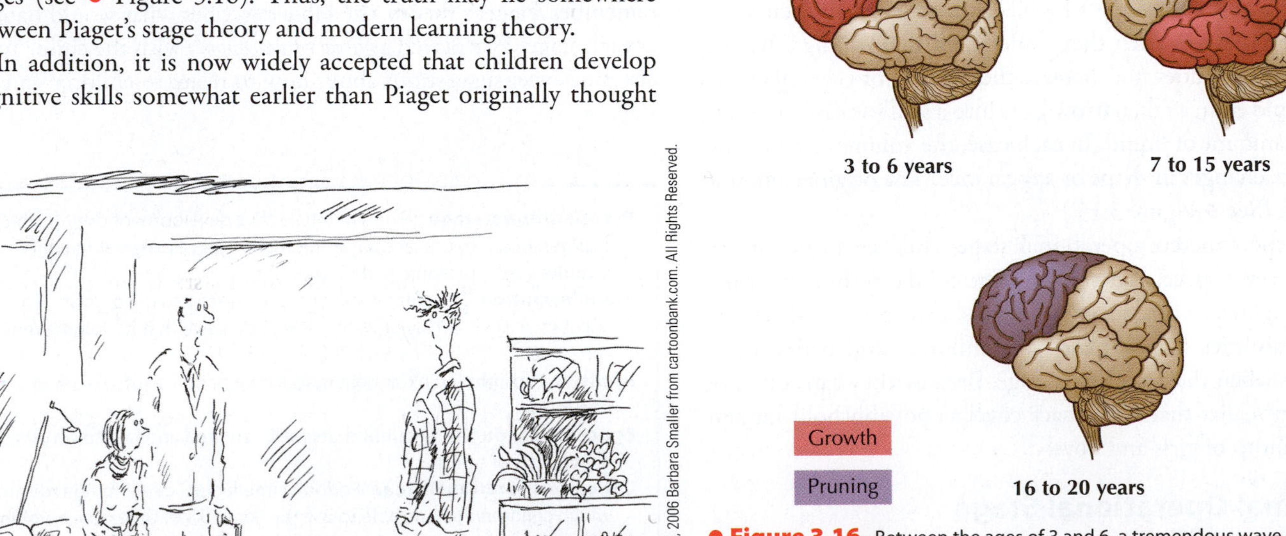

"Young man, go to your room and stay there until your cerebral cortex matures."

● **Figure 3.16** Between the ages of 3 and 6, a tremendous wave of growth occurs in connections among neurons in the frontal areas of the brain. This corresponds to the time when children make rapid progress in their ability to think symbolically. Between the ages of 7 and 15, peak synaptic growth shifts to the temporal and parietal lobes. During this period, children become increasingly adept at using language, a specialty of the temporal lobes. In the late teens, the brain actively destroys unneeded connections, especially in the frontal lobes. This pruning of synapses sharpens the brain's capacity for abstract thinking (Restak, 2001). (Courtesy of Dr. Paul Thompson, Laboratory of Neuro Imaging, UCLA School of Medicine.)

Critical Thinking — Theory of Mind: I'm a *Me*!.... and You're a *You*!

A major step in human development is becoming aware of oneself as a person. When you look in a mirror, you recognize the image staring back as your own—except, perhaps, early on Monday mornings. Like many such events, initial self-awareness depends on maturation of the nervous system. In a typical test of self-recognition, infants are shown images of themselves on a television. Most infants have to be 18 months old before they recognize themselves (Nielsen & Dissanayake, 2004).

But just because a 2-year-old knows he is a *me* doesn't mean he knows you are a *you*. At age 3, Eric once put his hands over his eyes and exclaimed to his friend, Laurence, "You can't see me now!" He knew he had a point of view but did not know his friend's point of view could be different from his own.

Earlier, we saw that Piaget used the term *egocentrism* to refer to this endearing feature of young children and proposed that young children remain egocentric until they enter the concrete operational stage at about age 7. More recent evidence suggests that children become less egocentric beginning at about age 4 (Baron-Cohen, 1985; Doherty, 2009). As noted above, this developing capacity is called *theory of mind* (Gopnik, 2009).

One way to assess if a child understands that other people have their own mental states is the false-belief (or "Sally-Anne") task. A child is shown two dolls, Sally and Anne. Sally has a basket and Anne has a box. Sally puts a coin in her basket and goes out to play. In the meantime, Anne takes the coin from Sally's basket and puts it into her box. Sally comes back and looks for the coin. To assess theory of mind, the child is asked where Sally will look for her coin. Although the child knows the coin is in Anne's box, the correct answer is that Sally will look in her basket. To answer correctly, the child must understand that Sally's point of view did not include what the child saw (Baron-Cohen, 1985).

Theory of mind develops over time. It takes further development to appreciate that other people may lie, be sarcastic, make jokes, or use figures of speech. Some adults are not good at this. In fact, the available evidence suggests that children with autism spectrum disorders are particularly poor at this task (O'Hare et al., 2009).

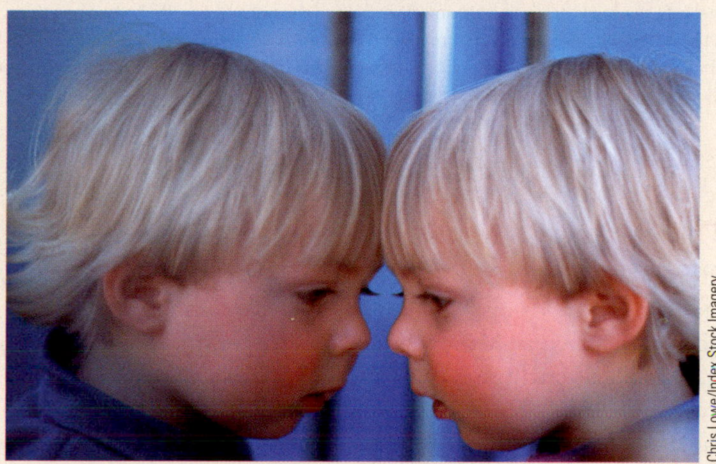

Chris Lowe/Index Stock Imagery

A sense of self, or self-awareness, develops at about age 18 months. Before children develop self-awareness, they do not recognize their own image in a mirror. Typically, they think they are looking at another child. Some children hug the child in the mirror or go behind it looking for the child they see there (Lewis, 1995).

know that objects are solid and do not disappear when out of view (Baillargeon, 2004).

Why did Piaget fail to detect the thinking skills of infants? Most likely, he mistook babies' limited *physical* skills for *mental* incompetence. Piaget's tests required babies to search for objects or reach out and touch them. Newer, more sensitive methods are uncovering abilities Piaget missed. One such method takes advantage of the fact that babies, like adults, act surprised when they see something "impossible" or unexpected occur. To use this effect, psychologist Renee Baillargeon (1991, 2004) puts on little "magic shows" for infants. In her "theater," babies watch as possible and impossible events occur with toys or other objects. Some 3-month-old infants act surprised and gaze longer at impossible events. An example is seeing two solid objects appear to pass through each other. By the time they are 8 months old, babies can remember where objects are (or should be) for at least 1 minute (● Figure 3.17).

Similarly, Piaget thought that children remain egocentric during the preoperational stage, becoming aware of perspectives other than their own only at age 7. Researchers have since begun to refer to this development as **theory of mind**, the understanding that people have mental states, such as thoughts, beliefs, and intentions, and that other people's mental states can be different from one's own. Psychologists currently believe that children as young as age 4 can understand that other people's mental states differ from their own (Doherty, 2009). (To read more about this fascinating development, see "Theory of Mind: I'm a Me!.... and You're a You!")

Another criticism of Piaget is that he underestimated the impact of culture on mental development. The next section tells how Samantha will master the intellectual tools valued by her culture.

Theory of mind The understanding that people have mental states, such as thoughts, beliefs, and intentions, and that other people's mental states can be different from one's own.

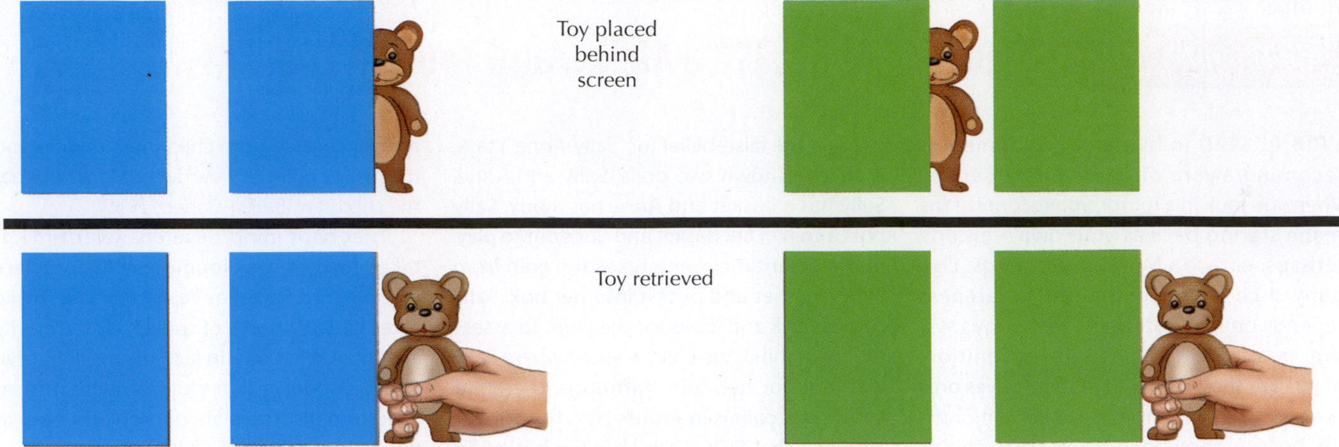

● **Figure 3.17** The panels on the left show a possible event, in which an infant watches as a toy is placed behind the right of two screens. After a delay of 70 seconds, the toy is brought into view from behind the right screen. In the two panels on the right, an impossible event occurs. The toy is placed behind the left screen and retrieved from behind the right. (A duplicate toy was hidden there before testing.) Eight-month-old infants react with surprise when they see the impossible event staged for them. Their reaction implies that they remember where the toy was hidden. Infants appear to have a capacity for memory and thinking that greatly exceeds what Piaget claimed is possible during the sensorimotor period. (Adapted from Baillargeon et al., 1989.)

Vygotsky's Sociocultural Theory

While Piaget stressed the role of maturation in cognitive development, Russian scholar Lev Vygotsky (1896–1934) focused on the impact of sociocultural factors. Many psychologists are convinced that Piaget gave too little credit to the effects of the learning environment. For example, children who grow up in villages where pottery is made can correctly answer questions about the conservation of clay at an earlier age than Piaget would have predicted. Vygotsky's (1962, 1978) key insight is that children's thinking develops through dialogues with more capable persons.

How does that relate to intellectual growth? So far, no one has published *A Child's Guide to Life on Earth.* Instead, children must learn about life from various "tutors," such as parents, teachers, and older siblings. Even if *A Child's Guide to Life on Earth* did exist, we would need a separate version for every culture. It is not enough for children to learn how to think. They must also learn specific intellectual skills valued by their culture.

Like Piaget, Vygotsky believed that children actively seek to discover new principles. However, Vygotsky emphasized that many of a child's most important "discoveries" are guided by skillful tutors. Psychologists David Shaffer and Katherine Kipp (2010) offer the following example:

> Tonya, a 4-year-old, has just received her first jigsaw puzzle as a birthday present. She attempts to work the puzzle but gets nowhere until her father comes along, sits down beside her, and gives her some tips. He suggests that it would be a good idea to put together the corners first, points to the pink area at the edge of one corner piece, and says, "Let's look for another pink piece." When Tonya seems frustrated, he places two interlocking pieces near each other so that she will notice them, and when Tonya succeeds, he offers words of encouragement. As Tonya gradually gets the hang of it, he steps back and lets her work more and more independently (p. 283).

Interactions like this are most helpful when they take place within a child's **zone of proximal development.**

What did Vygotsky mean by that? The word *proximal* means close or nearby. Vygotsky realized that, at any given time, some tasks are just beyond a child's reach. The child is close to having the mental skills needed to do the task, but it is a little too complex to be mastered alone. However, children working within this zone can make rapid progress if they receive sensitive guidance from a skilled partner (LeBlanc & Bearison, 2004). (Notice that this is similar to the one-step-ahead strategy described earlier.)

Vygotsky also emphasized a process he called **scaffolding.** A scaffold is a framework or temporary support. Vygotsky believed that adults help children learn how to think by "scaffolding," or supporting, their attempts to solve problems or discover principles (Daniels, 2005). To be most effective, scaffolding must be responsive to a child's needs. For example, as Tonya's father helped her with the puzzle, he tailored his hints and guidance to match her evolving abilities. The two of them worked together, step by step, so that Tonya could better understand how to assemble a puzzle. In a sense, Tonya's father set up a series of temporary bridges that helped her move into new mental territory. As predicted by Vygotsky's theory, the reading skills of 8- to 10-year-old children are closely related to the amount of verbal scaffolding their mothers provided at ages 3 and 4 (Dieterich et al., 2006).

During their collaborations with others, children learn important cultural beliefs and values. For example, imagine that a boy wants to know how many baseball cards he has. His mother helps him stack and count the cards, moving each card to a new stack as they count it. She then shows him how to write the number on a slip of paper so he can remember it. This teaches the child not only about counting, but also that writing is valued in our culture. In other parts of the world, a child learning to count might be shown how to make notches on a stick or tie knots in a cord.

Implications

Vygotsky saw that grown-ups play a crucial role in what children know. As they try to decipher the world, children rely on adults to help them understand how things work. Vygotsky further noticed that adults unconsciously adjust their behavior to give children the information they need to solve problems that interest the child. In this way, children use adults to learn about their culture and society (Gredler & Shields, 2008; LeBlanc & Bearison, 2004).

Knowledge Builder

Cognitive Development in Childhood

RECITE

Match each item with one of the following stages.

A. Sensorimotor B. Preoperational C. Concrete operational D. Formal operations

1. _____ egocentric thought
2. _____ abstract or hypothetical
3. _____ purposeful movement
4. _____ intuitive thought
5. _____ conservation
6. _____ reversibility thought
7. _____ object permanence
8. _____ nonverbal development
9. *Assimilation* refers to applying existing thought patterns or knowledge to new situations. T or F?
10. Newer methods for testing infants' thinking abilities frequently make note of whether an infant is _____________ by seemingly _____________ events.
11. Vygotsky called the process of providing a temporary framework of supports for learning new mental abilities _____________.

REFLECT

Think Critically

12. In Western cultures, children as young as age 4 can understand that other people have mental states that differ from their own. In other words, they have developed a *theory of mind*. Is this ability uniquely Western, or might children from other cultures also develop a theory of mind?

Self-Reflect

You are going to make cookies with children of various ages. See if you can name each of Piaget's stages and give an example of what a child in that stage might be expected to do.

You have been asked to help a child learn to use a calculator to do simple addition. How would you go about identifying the child's zone of proximal development for this task? How would you scaffold the child's learning?

Answers: 1. B **2.** D **3.** A **4.** B **5.** C **6.** C **7.** A **8.** A **9.** T **10.** surprised, impossible **11.** scaffolding **12.** All humans need to be able to base their actions on their understanding of the intentions, desires, and beliefs of others. In fact, children from Micronesia, a group of small islands in the Pacific Ocean, also develop a theory of mind at around 4 years of age (Oberle, 2009).

Adolescence and Young Adulthood—The Best of Times, the Worst of Times

Gateway Question 3.7: *Why is the transition from adolescence to adulthood especially challenging?*

Adolescence and young adulthood is a time of change, exploration, exuberance, and youthful searching. It can also be a time of worry and problems, especially in today's world. It might even be fair to describe this period as "the best of times, the worst of times." During adolescence, a person's identity and moral values come into sharper focus, even as the transition to adulthood is occurring at ever-later ages.

Adolescence is the culturally defined period between childhood and adulthood. Socially, the adolescent is no longer a child, yet not quite an adult. Almost all cultures recognize this transitional status. However, the length of adolescence varies greatly from culture to culture. For example, most 14-year-old girls in North America live at home and go to school. In contrast, many 14-year-old females in rural villages of many poorer countries are married and have children. In our culture, 14-year-olds are adolescents. In others, they may be adults.

Is marriage the primary criterion for adult status in North America? No, it's not even one of the top three criteria. Today, the most widely accepted standards are: (1) taking responsibility for oneself, (2) making independent decisions, and (3) becoming financially independent. In practice, this typically means breaking away from parents by taking a job and setting up a separate residence (Arnett, 2010).

Puberty

Many people confuse adolescence with puberty. However, puberty is a *biological* event, not a social status. During **puberty**, hormonal changes promote rapid physical growth and sexual maturity. Biologically, most people reach reproductive maturity in the early teens. Social and intellectual maturity, however, may lie years ahead. Young adolescents often make decisions that affect their entire lives, even though they are immature mentally and socially. The tragically high rates of teenage pregnancy and drug abuse are prime examples. Despite such risks, most people do manage to weather adolescence without developing any serious psychological problems (Rathus, 2011).

Zone of proximal development Refers to the range of tasks a child cannot yet master alone, but that she or he can accomplish with the guidance of a more capable partner.

Scaffolding The process of adjusting instruction so that it is responsive to a beginner's behavior and supports the beginner's efforts to understand a problem or gain a mental skill.

Adolescence The culturally defined period between childhood and adulthood.

Puberty The biologically defined period during which a person matures sexually and becomes capable of reproduction.

Human Diversity — Ethnic Diversity and Identity

Ethnic heritage is an important aspect of personal identity (Weisskirch, 2005). For adolescents of ethnic descent, the question is often not just "Who am I?" Rather, it is "Who am I at home? Who am I at school? Who am I with friends from my neighborhood?"

As ethnic minorities in America continue to grow in status and prominence, adolescents are less and less likely to feel rejected or excluded because of their ethnic heritage as they try to find their place in society. This is fortunate because ethnic adolescents have often faced degrading stereotypes concerning their intelligence, sexuality, social status, manners, and so forth. The result can be lowered self-esteem and confusion about roles, values, and personal identity (Charmaraman & Grossman, 2010). At the same time, the increasingly multicultural nature of contemporary American society raises new questions for adolescents about what it means to be American (Schwartz, 2008).

In forming an identity, adolescents of ethnic descent face the question of how they should think of themselves. Is Lori an American or a Chinese American or both? Is Jaime a Latino, a Chicano, or a Mexican American? The answer typically depends on how strongly adolescents identify with their family and ethnic community. Teens who take pride in their ethnic heritage have higher self-esteem, a better self-image, and a stronger sense of personal identity (Roberts et al., 1999; Tse, 1999). They are also less likely to engage in drug use (Marsiglia et al., 2004) or violent behavior (French, Kim, & Pillado, 2006).

Group pride, positive models, and a more tolerant society could do much to keep a broad range of options open to *all* adolescents.

How much difference does the timing of puberty make? For boys, maturing early is generally beneficial. Typically, it enhances their self-image and gives them an advantage socially and athletically. Early-maturing boys tend to be more relaxed, dominant, self-assured, and popular. However, early puberty does carry some risks because early-maturing boys are also more likely to get into trouble with drugs, alcohol, and antisocial behavior (Steinberg, 2001).

For girls, the advantages of early maturation are less clear-cut. In elementary school, fast-maturing girls are *less* popular and have poorer self-images, perhaps because they are larger and heavier than their classmates (Deardorff et al., 2007). This is a growing problem as more American girls are reaching puberty at earlier ages (Biro et al., 2010). By junior high, however, early development includes sexual features. This leads to a more positive body image, *greater* peer prestige, and adult approval (Brooks-Gunn & Warren, 1988). Early-maturing girls tend to date sooner and are more independent and more active in school. However, like their male counterparts, they are also more often in trouble at school and more likely to engage in early sex (Negriff & Trickett, 2010).

As you can see, there are costs and benefits associated with early puberty. One added cost of early maturation is that it may force premature identity formation. When Samantha is a teenager and she begins to look like an adult, she may be treated like an adult. Ideally, this change can encourage greater maturity and independence. However, if the search for identity ends too soon, it may leave Samantha with a distorted, poorly formed sense of self (● Figure 3.18).

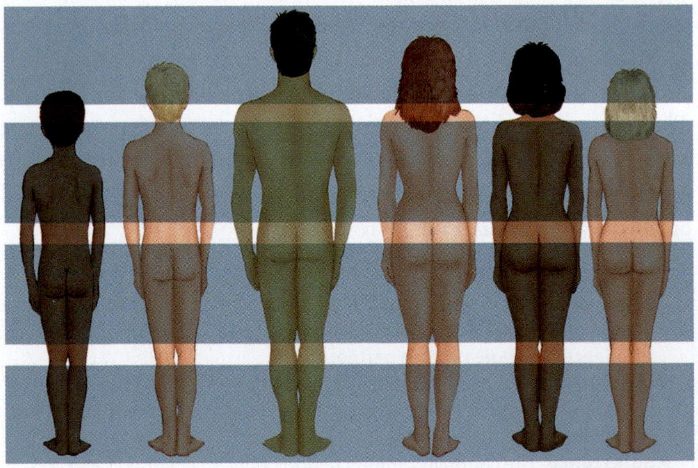

● **Figure 3.18** Dramatic differences in physical size and maturity are found in adolescents of the same age. The three boys pictured are all 16, the three girls are all 13. Maturation that occurs earlier or later than average can affect the "search for identity." (Adapted from "Growing Up" by J. M. Tanner. Copyright © September 1973 by Scientific American, Inc. All rights reserved. Reprinted with permission of Nelson Prentiss)

The Search for Identity

Identity formation is a key challenge faced by adolescents (Schwartz, 2008). Of course, problems of identity occur at other times too. But in a very real sense, puberty signals that it's time to begin forming a new, more mature self-image (Rathus, 2011). Many problems stem from unclear standards about the role adolescents should play within society. Are they adults or children? Should they be autonomous or dependent? Should they work or play? Such ambiguities make it difficult for young people to form clear images of themselves and of how they should act.

Answering the question "Who am I?" is also spurred by cognitive development. After adolescents have attained the stage of formal operations, they are better able to ask questions about their place in the world and about morals, values, politics, and social relationships. Then too, being able to think about hypothetical possibilities allows the adolescent to contemplate the future and ask more realistically, "Who will I be?" (Côté, 2006b). (See "Ethnic Diversity and Identity.")

Critical Thinking: The Twixters

As you read this text, we encourage you to reflect on new ideas and concepts by thinking critically about them. Consider, for example, the term *adulthood.* Is becoming an adult strictly a biological event? Meet 22-year-old Kirsten:

> "When our mothers were our age, they were engaged.... They at least had some idea what they were going to do with their lives.... I, on the other hand, will have a dual degree in majors that are ambiguous at best and impractical at worst (English and political science), no ring on my finger and no idea who I am, much less what I want to do.... I realize that having nothing ahead to count on means I now have to count on myself; that having no direction means forging one of my own" (Page, 1999).

Kirsten is a "twixter," or an emerging adult: twentysomething, still living at home, not yet married, with no children, and no settled career. Indeed, it is no longer uncommon to meet 27-year-olds who still live at home, have not settled into careers, or formed committed relationships. In England, twixters are called "kippers" (Kids In Parents' Pockets Eroding Retirement Savings). In Australia, they are "boomerang kids" (they always come back home). And in Germany they are "nesthocker" (nest squatters). Are such people still adolescents who are taking longer to find their identity? Or are they young adults avoiding their need to enter the adult world? Are they self-indulgent individuals trapped in a "maturity gap" (Galambos, Barker, & Tilton-Weaver, 2003)?

According to psychologist Jeffrey Arnett, emerging adulthood is increasingly common in affluent Westernized cultures that allow young people to take longer to settle into their adult roles (Arnett, 2004). However, in less affluent countries, as in poorer parts of America, most adolescents continue to "become adults" at much younger ages (Arnett & Galambos, 2003). Thus, words like *adolescent* or *adulthood* cannot be defined solely in terms of physical maturation. Sociocultural factors also play a role in defining when we stop being children or become adults (Arnett, 2010).

Emerging Adulthood

Today the challenge of identity formation is further complicated by the fact that more and more young people are deferring young adulthood, preferring to prolong identity explorations into their twenties before they commit to long-term choices in love and work (Arnett, 2010). Western industrialized societies, like the United States and Canada, are becoming increasingly tolerant of **emerging adulthood**, a socially tolerated period of extended adolescence (Arnett, 2010; Côté, 2006a). (See "The Twixters.")

Samantha may live with Carol and David until her mid-twenties, delaying her transition to adulthood. Alternatively, she may make the transition to young adulthood during the traditional 18-to-21 period. Regardless, she will eventually face the primary adult issues of marriage, children, and career. How she manages, especially in her core relationships, will determine whether she feels a sense of intimacy or feels isolated from others.

In many ways adolescence and young adulthood are more emotionally turbulent than midlife or old age. One important aspect of the emotional turbulence of adolescence and young adulthood is the struggle with right and wrong—in other words, the need to develop moral values.

Emerging adulthood A socially tolerated period of extended adolescence now quite common in Western societies.

Moral Development—Growing a Conscience

Gateway Question 3.8: *How do we develop morals and values?*

A person with a terminal illness is in great pain. She is pleading for death. Should extraordinary medical efforts be made to keep her alive? A friend of yours desperately needs to pass a test and asks you to help him cheat. Will you do it? These are *moral* questions, or questions of conscience.

Moral development starts in childhood and continues into adulthood (Turiel, 2006). Through this process, we acquire values, beliefs, and thinking patterns that guide responsible behavior (King, 2009). Moral values are especially likely to come into sharper focus during adolescence and the transition to adulthood, as capacities for self-control and abstract thinking increase (Hart & Carlo, 2005). Let's take a brief look at this interesting aspect of personal development.

Levels of Moral Development

How are moral values acquired? In an influential account, psychologist Lawrence Kohlberg (1981) held that we learn moral values through thinking and reasoning. To study moral development, Kohlberg posed dilemmas to children of different ages. The following is one of the moral dilemmas he used (Kohlberg, 1969, adapted):

> A woman was near death from cancer, and there was only one drug that might save her. It was discovered by a druggist who was charging 10 times what it cost to make the drug. The sick woman's husband could pay only $1,000, but the druggist wanted $2,000. He asked the druggist to sell it cheaper or to let him pay later. The druggist said no. So the husband became desperate and broke into the store to steal the drug for his wife. Should he have done that? Was it wrong or right? Why?

Each child was asked what action the husband should take. Kohlberg classified the reasons given for each choice and identified three levels of moral development. Each is based not so much on the choices made, but on the reasoning used to arrive at a choice.

At the lowest, **preconventional level**, moral thinking is guided by the consequences of actions (punishment, reward, or an exchange of favors). For example, a person at this level might reason, "The man shouldn't steal the drug because he could get caught and sent to jail" (avoiding punishment) or "It won't do him any good to steal the drug because his wife will probably die before he gets out of jail" (self-interest).

At the second, **conventional level**, reasoning is based on a desire to please others or to follow accepted authority, rules, and values. For example, a person at this intermediate level might say, "He shouldn't steal the drug because others will think he is a thief. His wife would not want to be saved by thievery" (avoiding disapproval) or "Although his wife needs the drug, he should not break the law to get it. Everyone has to obey the law. His wife's condition does not justify stealing" (traditional morality of authority).

At the highest, **postconventional level**, moral behavior is directed by self-chosen ethical principles that tend to be general, comprehensive, or universal. People at this level place high value on justice, dignity, and equality. For example, a highly principled person might say, "He should steal the drug and then inform the authorities that he has done so. He will have to face a penalty, but he will have saved a human life" (self-chosen ethical principles).

Does everyone eventually reach the highest level? People advance at different rates, and many fail to reach the postconventional level of moral reasoning. In fact, some may not even reach the conventional level. For instance, a significant number of men in their first-year of college think unwanted sexual aggression is acceptable (Tatum & Foubert, 2009).

The preconventional level is most characteristic of young children and delinquents (Forney, Forney, & Crutsinger, 2005). Conventional, group-oriented morals are typical of older children and most adults. Kohlberg estimated that only about 20 percent of the adult population achieves postconventional morality, representing self-direction and higher principles. (It would appear that few of these people enter politics!)

Developing a "moral compass" is an important part of growing up. Many of the choices we make every day involve fundamental questions of right and wrong. The ability to think clearly about such questions is essential to becoming a responsible adult.

Justice or Caring?

Carol Gilligan (1982) pointed out that Kohlberg's system is concerned mainly with *justice*. Based on studies of women who faced real-life dilemmas, Gilligan argued that there is also an ethic of *caring* about others. As one illustration, Gilligan presented the following story to 11- to 15-year-old American children:

> Seeking refuge from the cold, a porcupine asked to share a cave for the winter with a family of moles. The moles agreed. But, because the cave was small, they soon found they were being scratched each time the porcupine moved about. Finally, they asked the porcupine to leave. But the porcupine refused, saying, "If you moles are not satisfied, I suggest that you leave."

Boys who read this story tended to opt for justice in resolving the dilemma: "It's the moles' house. It's a deal. The porcupine leaves." In contrast, girls tended to look for solutions that would keep all parties happy and comfortable, such as "Cover the porcupine with a blanket."

Gilligan's point is that male psychologists have, for the most part, defined moral maturity in terms of justice and autonomy. From this perspective, a woman's concern with relationships can look like a weakness rather than a strength. (A woman who is concerned about what pleases or helps others would be placed at the conventional level in Kohlberg's system.) But Gilligan believes that caring is also a major element of moral development, and she suggests that males may lag in achieving it (Botes, 2000; Gilligan & Attanucci, 1988).

Does the evidence support Gilligan's position? Several studies have found little or no difference in men's and women's overall moral reasoning abilities (Glover, 2001; Levenson, 2009). Indeed, both men and women may use caring *and* justice to make moral decisions. The moral yardstick they use appears to depend on the situation they face (Wark & Krebs, 1996). Just the same, Gilligan deserves credit for identifying a second major way in which moral choices are made. It can be argued that our best moral choices combine justice and caring, reason and emotion—which may be what we mean by wisdom (Pasupathi & Staudinger, 2001).

Knowledge Builder

Adolescence, Young Adulthood, and Moral Development

RECITE

1. In North America, the primary criterion for the transition from adolescence to adulthood is marriage. T or F?
2. Identify formation is spurred by ________________ and ________________.
3. According to Jeffrey Arnett, the trend in affluent Westernized cultures towards allowing young people to take longer to settle into their adult roles is best referred to as
   a. emerging adulthood *b.* hurried childhood *c.* a maturity gap *d.* extended adolescence
4. According to Kohlberg, the conventional level of moral development is marked by a reliance on outside authority. T or F?
5. Self-interest and avoiding punishment are elements of postconventional morality. T or F?
6. About 80 percent of all adults function at the postconventional level of moral reasoning. T or F?
7. Gilligan regards gaining a sense of justice as the principal basis of moral development. T or F?

REFLECT

Think Critically

8. Are labels like "adolescent" or "young adult" reflective of heredity or environment?

Self-Reflect

To what extent does the concept of identity formation apply to your own experience during adolescence?

Do you know any emerging adults? (Are you one?) Do you think emerging adults are adolescents taking longer to find their identity or young adults avoiding their need to establish themselves in the world of adults?

At what stage of moral development do you think most terrorists function?

Answers: 1. F **2.** puberty, cognitive development **3.** a **4.** T **5.** F **6.** F **7.** F **8.** Environment, rather than heredity, is the better answer. Even better, the meanings of terms like "adolescence" or "adult" vary considerably from culture to culture, indicating that it is really a matter of definition (Côté, 2006 a,b).

The Story of a Lifetime—Rocky Road or Garden Path?

Gateway Question 3.9: *What are the typical tasks and dilemmas through the life span?*

Every life is marked by a number of developmental milestones (Kail & Cavanaugh, 2010). These are notable events, markers, or turning points in personal development. Some examples include graduating from school, voting for the first time, getting married, watching a child leave home (or move back!), the death of a parent, becoming a grandparent, retirement, and one's own death. Thus far, we have traced Samantha's progress through childhood, adolescence, and young adulthood. What challenges lie ahead for her?

Erikson's Psychosocial Theory

Perhaps the best way to get a preview of Samantha's life is to consider some of the major psychological milestones and challenges she is likely to encounter. Broad similarities can be found in the life stages of infancy, childhood, adolescence, young adulthood, middle adulthood, and old age. Each developmental stage confronts a person with new **developmental tasks**, specific challenges that must be mastered for optimal development. Examples are learning to read in childhood, adjusting to sexual maturity in adolescence, and establishing a vocation as an adult.

In an influential book entitled *Childhood and Society*, personality theorist Erik Erikson (1903–1994) suggests that we face a specific *psychosocial dilemma,* or "crisis," at each stage of life. A

© Ted Streshinsky/Corbis

Personality theorist Erik Erikson (1903–1994) is best known for his life-stage theory of human development.

Moral development The development of values, beliefs, and thinking abilities that act as a guide regarding what is acceptable behavior.

Preconventional moral reasoning Moral thinking based on the consequences of one's choices or actions (punishment, reward, or an exchange of favors).

Conventional moral reasoning Moral thinking based on a desire to please others or to follow accepted rules and values.

Postconventional moral reasoning Moral thinking based on carefully examined and self-chosen moral principles.

Developmental task Any skill that must be mastered, or personal change that must take place, for optimal development.

■ **TABLE 3.3** **Erikson's Psychosocial Dilemmas**

Age	Characteristic Dilemma
Birth to 1 year	Trust versus mistrust
1–3 years	Autonomy versus shame and doubt
3–5 years	Initiative versus guilt
6–12 years	Industry versus inferiority
Adolescence (12–19 years)	Identity versus role confusion
Young adulthood (20–34 years)	Intimacy versus isolation
Middle adulthood (35–64 years)	Generativity versus stagnation
Late adulthood (65 years and older)	Integrity versus despair

psychosocial dilemma is a conflict between personal impulses and the social world. Resolving each dilemma creates a new balance between a person and society. A string of "successes" produces healthy development and a satisfying life. Unfavorable outcomes throw us off balance, making it harder to deal with later crises. Life becomes a "rocky road," and personal growth is stunted. ■ Table 3.3 lists Erikson's (1963) dilemmas.

What are the major developmental tasks and life crises? A brief description of each psychosocial dilemma follows.

Stage One, First Year of Life: Trust Versus Mistrust

During the first year of life, children are completely dependent on others. Erikson believes that a basic attitude of trust or mistrust is formed at this time. **Trust** is established when babies are given warmth, touching, love, and physical care. **Mistrust** is caused by inadequate or unpredictable care and by parents who are cold, indifferent, or rejecting. Basic mistrust may later cause insecurity, suspiciousness, or an inability to relate to others. Notice that trust comes from the same conditions that help babies become securely attached to their parents.

Stage Two, 1–3 Years: Autonomy Versus Shame and Doubt

In stage two, children express their growing self-control by climbing, touching, exploring, and trying to do things for themselves. David and Carol fostered Samantha's sense of **autonomy** by encouraging her to try new skills. However, her first efforts were sometimes crude, involving spilling, falling, wetting, and other "accidents." If David and Carol had ridiculed or overprotected Samantha, they might have caused her to feel **shameful** about her actions and **doubt** her abilities.

Stage Three, 3–5 Years: Initiative Versus Guilt

In stage three, children move beyond simple self-control and begin to take initiative. Through play, children learn to make plans and carry out tasks. Parents reinforce **initiative** by giving children freedom to play, ask questions, use imagination, and choose activities. Feelings of **guilt** about initiating activities are formed if parents criticize severely, prevent play, or discourage a child's questions.

Stage Four, 6–12 Years: Industry Versus Inferiority

Many events of middle childhood are symbolized by that fateful day when you first entered school. With dizzying speed, your world expanded beyond your family, and you faced a whole series of new challenges.

The elementary school years are a child's "entrance into life." In school, children begin to learn skills valued by society, and success or failure can affect a child's feelings of adequacy. Children learn a sense of **industry** if they win praise for productive activities, such as building, painting, cooking, reading, and studying. If a child's efforts are regarded as messy, childish, or inadequate, feelings of **inferiority** result. For the first time, teachers, classmates, and adults outside the home become as important as parents in shaping attitudes toward oneself.

Stage Five, Adolescence: Identity Versus Role Confusion

As we have noted, adolescence is often a turbulent time. Erikson considers a need to answer the question "Who am I?" the primary task during this stage of life. As Samantha matures mentally and physically, she will have new feelings, a new body, and new attitudes. Like other adolescents, she will need to build a consistent **identity** out of her talents, values, life history, relationships, and the demands of her culture (Côté & Levine, 2002). Her conflicting experiences as a student, friend, athlete, worker, daughter, lover, and so forth must be integrated into a unified sense of self. Persons who fail to develop a sense of identity suffer from **role confusion,** an uncertainty about who they are and where they are going.

Stage Six, Young Adulthood: Intimacy Versus Isolation

In stage six, the individual feels a need for *intimacy* in his or her life. After establishing a stable identity, a person is prepared to share meaningful love or deep friendship with others (Beyers & Seiffge-Krenke, 2010). By **intimacy,** Erikson means an ability to care about others and to share experiences with them. In line with Erikson's view, 75 percent of college-age men and women rank a good marriage and family life as important adult goals (Bachman & Johnson, 1979). And yet, marriage or sexual involvement is no guarantee of intimacy: Many adult relationships remain shallow and unfulfilling. Failure to establish intimacy with others leads to a deep sense of **isolation**—feeling alone and uncared for in life. This often sets the stage for later difficulties.

Stage Seven, Middle Adulthood: Generativity Versus Stagnation

According to Erikson, an interest in guiding the next generation provides emotional balance in middle adulthood. Erikson called this quality **generativity.** It is expressed by caring about oneself,

© Ale Ventura/PhotoAlto/Corbis

According to Erikson, an interest in future generations characterizes optimal adult development.

one's children, and future generations. Generativity may be achieved by guiding one's own children or by helping other children (as a teacher or coach, for example). Productive or creative work can also express generativity. In any case, a person must broaden his or her concerns and energies to include the welfare of others and society as a whole. Failure to do this is marked by a **stagnant** concern with one's own needs and comforts. Life loses meaning, and the person feels bitter, dreary, and trapped (Friedman, 2004).

Stage Eight, Late Adulthood: Integrity Versus Despair

Late adulthood is a time of reflection. According to Erikson, when Samantha grows old, she must be able to look back over her life with acceptance and satisfaction. People who have lived richly and responsibly develop a sense of **integrity**, or self-respect. This allows them to face aging and death with dignity. If previous life events are viewed with regret, the elderly person experiences **despair,** or heartache and remorse. In this case, life seems like a series of missed opportunities. The person feels like a failure and knows it's too late to reverse what has been done. Aging and the threat of death then become sources of fear and depression.

The Whole Human

To squeeze a lifetime into a few pages, we had to ignore countless details. Although much is lost, the result is a clearer picture of an entire life cycle. Is Erikson's description, then, an exact map of Samantha's past and her future—or your own? Probably not. Still, psychosocial dilemmas are major events in many lives. Knowing about them may allow you to anticipate typical trouble spots in your own life. You may also be better prepared to understand the problems and feelings of friends and relatives at various points in the life cycle.

Middle and Later Adulthood—You're an Adult Now!

Gateway Question 3.10: *What is involved in well-being during middle and later adulthood?*

Although Erikson's dilemmas extend into adulthood, they are not the only challenges adults face, as we'll discuss in this section.

Other Challenges of Adulthood

Middle-aged adults (those aged from about 35 to 64) and *later adults* (those aged 65 and above) face life challenges such as financial pressures, legal conflicts, and personal tragedies, to name but a few. However, most challenges of adulthood revolve around health, work, marriage, children, and parents (Santrock, 2010).

Health

David just came back from his physiotherapy appointment. He put his knee out in a game of touch football (he could swear the other guy didn't just "touch" him!). A high school football star, 40-year-old David has encountered the obvious: he is getting older. Although some adults face far more serious health issues, from heart attacks to cancer, every adult faces the routine wear and tear of aging. How one deals with the inevitable slow declines of adulthood strongly influences that adult's degree of life satisfaction (Lachman, 2004). Fortunately, most of the time, declines happen slowly enough that they can be offset by increased life experience. Most adults learn to work "smarter," both physically and mentally (Miller & Lachman 2000).

Work

The work adults do—as homemakers, volunteers, hourly workers, or in careers—is also critical to feeling successful (Sterns & Huyck, 2001). While peak earnings commonly occur during these years, growing expenses may continue to create financial pressures, from

Psychosocial dilemma A conflict between personal impulses and the social world.

Trust versus mistrust A conflict early in life about learning to trust others and the world.

Autonomy versus shame and doubt A conflict created when growing self-control (autonomy) is pitted against feelings of shame or doubt.

Initiative versus guilt A conflict between learning to take initiative and overcoming feelings of guilt about doing so.

Industry versus inferiority A conflict in middle childhood centered on lack of support for industrious behavior, which can result in feelings of inferiority.

Identity versus role confusion A conflict of adolescence involving the need to establish a personal identity.

Intimacy versus isolation The challenge of overcoming a sense of isolation by establishing intimacy with others.

Generativity versus stagnation A conflict of middle adulthood in which self-interest is countered by an interest in guiding the next generation.

Integrity versus despair A conflict in old age between feelings of integrity and the despair of viewing previous life events with regret.

child care to tuition fees for children and from rent to mortgages. This is one reason why career difficulties and unemployment can pose such serious challenges to adult well-being. Another reason, of course, is that many adults derive much of their identity from their work (Santrock, 2010).

Marriage, Children, and Parents

Most adult Americans identify their social relationships—especially with children, spouses, and parents—as another important aspect of adult life (Markus et al., 2004). Creating and sustaining social relationships can involve working through the stresses of child-rearing, becoming "empty nesters" when children move away, becoming grandparents, experiencing marital strife or divorce, living as singles or in blended families, seeing parents grow old, need support, and die, to mention some of the more common social challenges faced by adults.

A Midlife Crisis?

Don't people face a "midlife crisis" at this point in their lives? Although adulthood brings its fair share of life's challenges, only about a quarter of men and women believe they have experienced a midlife crisis (Wethington, Kessler, & Pixley, 2004). It is more common to make a "midcourse correction" at midlife than it is to survive a "crisis" (Freund & Ritter, 2009; Lachman, 2004). Ideally, the midlife transition involves reworking old identities, achieving valued goals, finding one's own truths, and preparing for old age. Taking stock may be especially valuable at midlife, but reviewing past choices to prepare for the future is helpful at any age. For some people, difficult turning points in life can serve as "wake-up calls" that create opportunities for personal growth (Weaver, 2009; Wethington, 2003).

Facing the Challenges of Adulthood

How do people maintain a state of well-being as they run the gauntlet of modern life? Psychologist Carol Ryff believes that well-being during adulthood has six elements (Ryff & Singer, 2009; van Dierendonck et al., 2008):

1. Self-acceptance
2. Positive relations with others
3. Autonomy (personal freedom)
4. Environmental mastery
5. A purpose in life
6. Continued personal growth

Ryff found that, for many adults, age-related declines are offset by positive relationships and greater mastery of life's demands (Ryff & Singer, 2009). Thus, sharing life's joys and sorrows with others, coupled with a better understanding of how the world works, can help carry people through midlife and into their later years (Lachman et al., 2008; Ryff, Singer, & Palmersheim, 2004). It is important to note that despite the emphasis on youth in our culture, middle age and beyond can be a rich period of life in which people feel secure, happy, and self-confident (Rubenstein, 2002).

Old Age

After the late 50s, physical aging complicates personal development. However, it is wrong to believe that most elderly people are sickly, infirm, or senile. (Nowadays, 60 is the new 40, an idea with which both of your authors wholeheartedly agree!) Only about 5 percent of those older than 65 are in nursing homes. Mentally, many elderly persons are at least as capable as the average young adult. On intellectual tests, top scorers over the age of 65 match the average for men younger than 35. What sets these silver-haired stars apart? Typically they are people who have continued to work and remain intellectually active (Hooyman & Kiyak, 2011; Salthouse, 2004). *Gerontologist*—a psychologist who studies aging and the aged—Warner Schaie (1994, 2005) found that you are most likely to stay mentally sharp in old age if:

1. You remain healthy.
2. You live in a favorable environment. (You are educated and have a stimulating occupation, an above-average income, and an intact family.)
3. You are involved in intellectually stimulating activities (reading, travel, cultural events, continuing education, clubs, and professional associations).
4. You have a flexible personality.
5. You are married to an intelligent spouse.
6. You maintain your perceptual processing speed by staying active.
7. You were satisfied with your accomplishments in midlife.

A shorter summary of this list is "Those who live by their wit die with their wits."

Successful Aging

What are the keys to successful aging? The keys to successful aging are not unlike the elements of well-being at midlife. The psychological characteristics shared by the healthiest, happiest older people are (de Leon, 2005; Vaillant, 2002):

1. Optimism, hope, and an interest in the future
2. Gratitude and forgiveness; an ability to focus on what is good in life
3. Empathy; an ability to share the feelings of others and see the world through their eyes
4. Connection with others; an ability to reach out, to give and receive social support

Actually, these are excellent guidelines for well-being at any stage of adulthood.

In summary, enlightened views of aging call for an end to the forced obsolescence of the elderly. As a group, older people represent a valuable source of skill, knowledge, and energy that we can't afford to cast aside. As we face the challenges of this planet's uncertain future, we need all the help we can get!

Alberto E. Rodriguez/Getty Images

At age 88, Betty White was named Associated Press Entertainer of the Year, in 2010. Shown here attending the premiere of her movie "You Again," White's 70 years as an entertainer show that aging does not inevitably bring an end to engaging in challenging activities.

Aging and Ageism

Ageism, which refers to discrimination or prejudice based on age, can oppress the young as well as the old (Bodner, 2009). For instance, a person applying for a job may just as well be told "You're too young" as "You're too old." In some societies, ageism is expressed as respect for the elderly. In Japan, for instance, aging is seen as positive, and greater age brings more status and respect. In most Western nations, however, ageism tends to have a negative impact on older individuals.

Ageism is often expressed through patronizing language. Older people are frequently spoken to in an overly polite, slow, loud, and simple way implying that they are infirm, even when they are not (Nelson, 2005). Popular stereotypes of the "dirty old man," "meddling old woman," "senile old fool," and the like also help perpetuate myths about aging. But such stereotypes are clearly wrong: A tremendous diversity exists among the elderly—ranging from the infirm to aerobic-dancing grandmothers.

In many occupations, older workers perform well in jobs that require *both* speed and skill. Of course, people do experience a gradual loss of *fluid abilities* (those requiring speed or rapid learning) as they age, but often this can be offset by many *crystallized abilities* (learned knowledge and skills), such as vocabulary and stored-up facts, which may actually improve—at least into the 60s (Schaie, 2005). Overall, very little loss of job performance occurs as workers grow older. In the professions, wisdom and expertise can usually more than compensate for any loss of mental quickness (Ericsson, 2000). Basing retirement solely on a person's age makes little sense.

Death may be inevitable, but it can be faced with dignity and, sometimes, even humor. Mel Blanc's famous sign-off, "That's all folks," is engraved on a marble headstone over his grave. Blanc was the voice of Bugs Bunny, Porky Pig, and many other cartoon characters.

© Michael Newman/PhotoEdit

Death and Dying—The Final Frontier

Gateway Question 3.11: *How do people typically react to death?*

> "I'm not afraid of dying. I just don't want to be there when it happens."
> Woody Allen

The statistics on death are very convincing: Everyone dies. In spite of this, most of us are poorly informed about a process that is as basic as birth. We have seen throughout this chapter that it is valuable to understand major trends in the course of development. With this in mind, let's explore emotional responses to death, the inevitable conclusion of every life.

Reactions to Impending Death

Many people have little direct experience with death until they, themselves, are fairly old. It might seem that as people grow older they would fear death more. However, older persons actually have fewer death fears than younger people. Older people more often fear the *circumstances* of dying, such as pain or helplessness, rather than death itself (Thorson & Powell, 1990). These findings seem to show a general lack of death fears, but they may actually reflect a widespread denial of death. Notice how denial is apparent in the language used to talk about death: Often we speak of a dead person as having "passed away," "expired," "gone to God," or "breathed one's last."

A highly influential account of emotional responses to death comes from the work of Elisabeth Kübler-Ross (1926–2004). Kübler-Ross was a *thanatologist* (THAN-ah-TOL-oh-jist), or a person who studies death. Over the years she spent hundreds of hours at the bedsides of the terminally ill, where she observed

Ageism Discrimination or prejudice based on a person's age.

five basic emotional reactions to impending death (Kübler-Ross, 1975).

1. **Denial and isolation.** A typical first reaction is to deny death's reality and isolate oneself from information confirming that death is really going to occur. Initially, the person may be sure that "It's all a mistake." "Surely," she or he thinks, "the lab reports have been mixed up or the doctor made an error." This sort of denial may proceed to attempts to avoid any reminder of the situation.
2. **Anger.** Many dying individuals feel anger and ask, "Why me?" As they face the ultimate threat of having life torn away, their anger may spill over into rage toward the living. Even good friends may temporarily evoke anger because their health is envied.
3. **Bargaining.** In another common reaction, the terminally ill bargain with themselves or with God. The dying person thinks, "Just let me live a little longer and I'll do anything to earn it." Individuals may bargain for time by trying to be "good" ("I'll never smoke again"), by righting past wrongs, or by praying that if they are granted more time they will dedicate themselves to their religion.
4. **Depression.** As death draws near and the person begins to recognize that it cannot be prevented, feelings of futility, exhaustion, and deep depression may set in. The person realizes she or he will be separated from friends, loved ones, and the familiar routines of life, and this causes a profound sadness.
5. **Acceptance.** If death is not sudden, many people manage to come to terms with dying and accept it calmly. The person who accepts death is neither happy nor sad but at peace with the inevitable. Acceptance usually signals that the struggle 0with death has been resolved. The need to talk about death ends, and silent companionship from others is frequently all the person desires.

Not all terminally ill persons display all these reactions, nor do they always occur in this order. Individual styles of dying vary greatly. Generally, there does tend to be a movement from initial shock, denial, and anger toward eventual acceptance. However, some people who seem to have accepted death may die angry and raging against the inevitable. Conversely, the angry fighter may let go of the struggle and die peacefully. In general, one's approach to dying will mirror his or her style of living (Yedidia & MacGregor, 2001).

It is a mistake, then, to think that Kübler-Ross's list is a series of stages to go through in order or that there is something wrong if a person does not show all these emotions. Rather, the list describes typical reactions to impending death. Note, as well, that many of the same reactions accompany any major loss, be it divorce, loss of a home due to fire, death of a pet, or loss of a job.

Implications

How can I make use of this information? First, it can help both the dying and survivors to recognize and cope with periods of depression, anger, denial, and bargaining. Second, it helps to realize that close friends or relatives may feel many of the same emotions before or after a person's death because they, too, are facing a loss.

Perhaps the most important thing to recognize is that the dying person needs to share feelings with others and to discuss death openly. Too often, dying persons feel isolated and separated from others. Adults tend to "freeze up" with someone who is dying. For such people, thanatologist Kirsti Dyer (2001) has this advice:

- Be yourself and relate person to person.
- Be ready to listen again and again.
- Be respectful.
- Be aware of feelings and nonverbal cues.
- Be comfortable with silence.
- Be genuine.
- Most of all, be there.

Today, many terminally ill individuals also benefit from *hospice* care, which can improve the quality of life in a person's final days. Hospices typically offer support, guidance, pain relief, and companionship (Broom & Cavenagh, 2010). In short, the dying person is made comfortable, and feels loved and respected (Lynn, 2001). The same is often true for the dying person's caregivers (Manslow & Vandenberghe, 2010). As each of us faces the end of life, to die well may be no less an accomplishment than to live well.

Knowledge Builder: Challenges Across the Life Span

RECITE

As a way to improve your memory, you might find it helpful to summarize Erikson's eight life stages and crises. Complete this summary and compare your answers to those given below.

Stage	Crisis	Favorable Outcome
First year of life	1. ________ vs. 2. ________	Faith in the environment and in others
Ages 1–3	Autonomy vs. 3. ________	Feelings of self-control and adequacy
Ages 3–5	4. ________ vs. guilt	Ability to begin one's own activities

Stage	Crisis	Favorable Outcome
Ages 6–12	Industry vs. 5. ______________	Confidence in productive skills, learning how to work
Adolescence	6. ______________ vs. role confusion	An integrated image of oneself as a unique person
Young adulthood	Intimacy vs. 7. ______________	Ability to form bonds of love and friendship with others
Middle adulthood	Generativity vs. 8. ______________	Concern for family, society, and future generations
Late adulthood	9. ______________ vs. 10. ______________	Sense of dignity and fulfillment, willingness to face death

11. Nearly everyone experiences a midlife crisis sometime around age 40. T or F?
12. After age 65, a large proportion of older people show significant signs of mental disability and most require special care. T or F?
13. Job performance tends to decline rapidly in older workers. T or F?
14. In the reaction that Kübler-Ross describes as bargaining, the dying individual asks, "Why me?" T or F?

REFLECT

Think Critically

15. Trying to make generalizations about development throughout life is complicated by at least one major factor. What do you think it is?

Self-Reflect

See if you can think of a person you know who is facing one of Erikson's psychosocial dilemmas. Now see if you can think of specific people who seem to be coping with each of the other dilemmas.

Describe three instances of ageism you have witnessed.

Answers: 1. Trust **2.** mistrust **3.** shame or doubt **4.** Initiative **5.** inferiority **6.** Identity **7.** isolation **8.** stagnation **9.** Integrity **10.** despair **11.** F **12.** F **13.** F **14.** F **15.** Different *cohorts* (groups of people born in the same year) live in different historical times. People born in various decades may have very different life experiences. This makes it difficult to identify universal patterns (Stewart & Ostrove, 1998).

Psychology in Action

Effective Parenting—Always Kiss Your Children Goodnight

Gateway Question 3.12: *How do effective parents discipline and communicate with their children?*

Authoritative parents help their children grow up with a capacity for love, joy, fulfillment, responsibility, and self-control through *positive parent-child interactions*. Positive interactions occur when parents spend enjoyable time encouraging their children in a loving and mutually respectful fashion (Dinkmeyer, McKay, & Dinkmeyer, 1997; Takeuchi & Takeuchi, 2008).

However, as any parent can tell you, it is all well and good to talk about positive interactions until little Johnny misbehaves (and he will, count on it!). As children mature and become more independent, parents must find ways to control their children's behavior ("No, you may not smear banana pudding on Daddy's face"). When parents fail to provide *discipline* (guidance regarding acceptable behavior), children become antisocial, aggressive, and insecure. And yet, it is not easy to have a positive interaction while disciplining your child. This is one reason why overly permissive parents avoid disciplining children.

Effective discipline socializes a child without destroying the bond of love and trust between parent and child. Children should feel free to express their deepest feelings. However, this does not mean they can do whatever they please. Rather, the child is allowed to move freely within consistent, well-defined boundaries for acceptable behavior.

© Image Source/Corbis

Effective Discipline

Parents typically discipline children in one of three ways. **Power assertion** refers to physical punishment or a show of force, such as taking away toys or privileges. As an alternative, some parents use **withdrawal of love,** or withholding affection, by refusing to speak to a child, threatening to leave, rejecting the child, or otherwise acting as if the child is temporarily unlovable. **Management techniques** combine praise, rec-

Power assertion The use of physical punishment or coercion to enforce child discipline.

Withdrawal of love Withholding affection to enforce child discipline.

Management techniques Combining praise, recognition, approval, rules, and reasoning to enforce child discipline ognition, approval, rules, reasoning, and the like to encourage desirable behavior. Each of these approaches can control a child's behavior, but their side effects differ considerably.

What are the side effects? Power-oriented techniques—particularly harsh or severe physical punishment—are associated with fear, hatred of parents, and a lack of spontaneity and warmth (Hergenhahn & Olson, 2009). Most children show no signs of long-term damage from spanking—*if* spanking is backed up by supportive parenting (Baumrind, Larzelere, & Cowan, 2002). However, emotional damage does occur if spankings are severe, frequent, or coupled with harsh parenting. In addition, frequent spanking tends to increase aggression, and it leads to *more* problem behaviors, not fewer (Aucoin, Frick, & Bodin, 2006; Thomas, 2004). After reviewing many studies, psychologist Elizabeth Gershoff (2002) concludes that parents should minimize spanking or avoid it entirely.

BRIDGES

Punishment also has important effects on learning. **For more tips on how to use punishment wisely, see Chapter 6, pages 227–228.**

Withdrawal of love produces children who tend to be self-disciplined. You could say that such children have developed a good conscience. Often, they are described as "model" children or as unusually "good." But as a side effect, they are also frequently anxious, insecure, and dependent on adults for approval.

Management techniques also have limitations. Most important is the need to carefully adjust to a child's level of understanding. Younger children don't always see the connection between rules, explanations, and their own behavior. Nevertheless, management techniques receive a big plus in another area: There is a direct connection between discipline and a child's self-esteem.

How does discipline affect self-esteem? If you regard yourself as a worthwhile person, you have **self-esteem.** In school, children with high self-esteem tend to be more popular, cooperative, and successful in class. Children with low self-esteem are more withdrawn and tend to perform below average (Amato & Fowler, 2002).

Low self-esteem is related to physical punishment and the withholding of love. And why not? What message do children receive if a parent beats them or tells them they are not worthy of love? Thus, it is best to minimize physical punishment and avoid withdrawal of love. In contrast, high self-esteem is promoted by management techniques. Children who feel that their parents support them emotionally tend to have high self-esteem (Amato & Fowler, 2002).

Can self-esteem ever get too high? Many modern parents try to "empower" their children by imposing few limits on behavior, making them feel special, and giving them everything they want (Mamen, 2004). But such good intentions can backfire, leaving parents with children who have developed an artificially high level of self-esteem and a sense of entitlement. That is, overly permissive parenting produces spoiled, self-indulgent children who have little self-control (Baumrind, 1991). Their sense of entitlement can lead them to bully other children to get their way or even to engage in criminal activity. As adults, such children may become addicted to seeking ways to enhance their self-esteem. For example, they may place excessive importance on being physically attractive, leading to stress, drug and alcohol use, and eating disorders (Crocker & Park, 2004).

Consistent Discipline Individual parents choose limits on behavior that are more "strict" or less "strict." But this choice is less important than **consistency**—maintaining stable rules of conduct. Consistent discipline gives a child a sense of security and stability. Inconsistency makes the child's world seem insecure and unpredictable.

What does consistent discipline mean in practice? To illustrate the errors parents often make, let's consider a few examples of inconsistency (Fontenelle, 1989):

> Saying one thing and doing something else. You tell the child, "Bart, if you don't eat your Brussels sprouts you can't have any dessert." Then you feel guilty and offer him some dessert.
>
> Making statements you don't mean. "If you don't quiet down, I'm going to stop the car and make you walk home."
>
> Responding differently to the same misbehavior. One day a child is sent to his room for fighting with his sister. The next day the fighting is overlooked.

Inconsistency gives children the message: "Don't believe what I say because I usually don't mean it."

Using Discipline Constructively At one time or another, most parents use power assertion, withdrawal of love, or management techniques to control their children. Each mode of discipline has its place. However, physical punishment and withdrawal of love should always be used with caution. (Remember, too, that it is usually more effective to reward children when they are being good than it is to punish them for misbehavior.) Here are some guidelines:

1. State specifically what misbehavior you are punishing. Explain why you have set limits on this kind of conduct.
2. Parents should separate disapproval of the act from disapproval of the child. Instead of saying, "I'm going to punish you because *you are bad,*" say, "I'm upset about *what you did.*" Also remember that the message "I don't love you right now" can be more painful and damaging than any spanking.
3. Punishment should never be harsh or injurious. Don't physically punish a child while you are angry. If you do use physical punishment, reserve it for situations that pose an immediate danger to younger children; for example, when a child runs onto the street.
4. Spanking and other forms of physical punishment are not particularly effective for children younger than age 2. The child will only be confused and frightened. Spankings also become less effective after age 5 because they tend to humiliate the child and breed resentment.
5. Punishment, such as a scolding or taking away privileges, is most effective when done immediately. This is especially true for younger children.

After age 5, management techniques are the most effective form of discipline, especially techniques that emphasize communication and the relationship between parent and child (Bath, 1996).

Communicating Effectively with Children

Effective communication with children depends on *I-messages* and a reliance on *logical consequences.*

I-Messages Child psychologist Thomas Gordon (2000) believes that parents should send *I-messages* to their children rather than *you-messages*.

What's the difference? **You-messages** take the form of threats, name-calling, accusing, bossing, lecturing, or criticizing. Generally, you-messages tell children what's "wrong" with them. An **I-message** tells children what effect their behavior had on you. For example, after a hard day's work, Maria wants to sit down and rest awhile. She begins to relax with a newspaper when her 5-year-old daughter starts banging loudly on a toy drum. Many parents would respond with a you-message such as "You go play outside this instant" (bossing) or "Don't you ever make such a racket when someone is reading" (lecturing). Gordon suggests sending an I-message such as, "I am very tired, and I would like to read. I feel upset and can't read with so much noise." This forces the child to accept responsibility for the effects of her actions (Dinkmeyer, McKay, & Dinkmeyer, 1997).

Logical Consequences It is worth avoiding direct *power struggles*. Suppose a child refuses to eat. A parent would be better off not leading off with something like "I'm your parent. Now eat your supper." It is better to recognize that some events automatically discourage misbehavior. For example, a child who refuses to eat dinner will get uncomfortably hungry (Fontenelle, 1989). In such instances, a child's actions have **natural consequences,** or intrinsic effects. Another possibility is to set up **logical consequences**, or rational and reasonable effects. For example, a parent might say, "You can play on your Wii once you've eaten your supper."

The concept of logical, parent-defined consequences can be combined with I-messages to handle many day-to-day instances of misbehavior. The key idea is to use an I-message to set up consequences and then give the child a choice to make: "Michelle, I'm trying to watch TV. You can settle down and watch with me or go play elsewhere. You decide which you'd rather do" (Dinkmeyer, McKay, & Dinkmeyer, 1997).

How could Maria have dealt with her 5-year-old—the one who was banging on a drum? A response that combines an I-message with logical consequences would be, "I would like for you to stop banging on that drum; otherwise, please take it outside or else I will put it away." If the child continues to bang on the drum inside the house, then she has caused the toy to be put away. If she takes it outside, she has made a decision to play with the drum in a way that respects her mother's wishes. In this way, both parent and child have been allowed to maintain a sense of self-respect and a needless clash has been averted.

After you have stated consequences and let the child decide, be sure to respect the child's choice. If the child repeats the misbehavior, you can let the consequences remain in effect longer. But later, give the child another chance to cooperate.

With all child management techniques, remember to be firm, kind, consistent, respectful, and encouraging. And most of all, try every day to live the message you wish to communicate.

Self-esteem Regarding oneself as a worthwhile person; a positive evaluation of oneself.
Consistency With respect to child discipline, the maintenance of stable rules of conduct.
You-message Threatening, accusing, bossing, lecturing, or criticizing another person.
I-message A message that states the effect someone else's behavior has on you.
Natural consequences The effects that naturally tend to follow a particular behavior.
Logical consequences Reasonable consequences that are defined by parents.

Knowledge Builder: Effective Parenting

RECITE

1. Effective discipline gives children freedom within a structure of consistent and well-defined limits. T or F?
2. One good way to maintain consistency in child management is to overstate the consequences for misbehavior. T or F?
3. Spankings and other physical punishments are most effective for children under the age of 2. T or F?
4. Giving recognition for progress and attempts to improve is an example of parental ______________________.
5. I-messages are a gentle way of accusing a child of misbehavior. T or F?
6. In situations where natural consequences are unavailable or do not discourage misbehavior, parents should define logical consequences for a child. T or F?

REFLECT

Think Critically

7. Several Scandinavian countries have made it illegal for parents to spank their own children. Does this infringe on the rights of parents?
8. If power assertion is a poor way to discipline children, why do so many parents use it?

Self-Reflect

What do you think are the best ways to discipline children? How would your approach be classified? What are its advantages and disadvantages?

Parents can probably never be completely consistent. Think of a time when your parents were inconsistent in disciplining you. How did it affect you?

Think of a you-message you have recently given a child, family member, roommate, or spouse. Can you change it into an I-message?

Answers: 1. T **2.** F **3.** T **4.** encouragement **5.** F **6.** T **7.** Such laws are based on the view that it should be illegal to physically assault any person, regardless of their age. Although parents may believe they have a "right" to spank their children, it can be argued that children need special protection because they are small, powerless, and dependent (Durrant & Janson, 2005). **8.** Most parents discipline their children in the same ways that they themselves were disciplined. Parenting is a responsibility of tremendous importance, for which most people receive almost no training.

Chapter in Review Gateways to Human Development

Gateway QUESTIONS REVISITED

3.1 How do heredity and environment affect development?

3.1.1 Heredity (nature) and environment (nurture) are interacting forces that are both necessary for human development. However, caregivers can only influence environment.

3.1.2 The chromosomes and genes in each cell of the body carry hereditary instructions. Most characteristics are polygenic and reflect the combined effects of dominant and recessive genes.

3.1.3 Maturation of the body and nervous system underlies the orderly development of motor skills, cognitive abilities, emotions, and language. Many early skills are subject to the principle of readiness.

3.1.4 Prenatal development is influenced by environmental factors, such as various teratogens, including diseases, drugs, and radiation, as well as the mother's diet, health, and emotions.

3.1.5 During sensitive periods in development, infants are more sensitive to specific environmental influences.

3.1.6 Early perceptual, intellectual, or emotional deprivation seriously retards development, whereas deliberate enrichment of the environment has a beneficial effect on infants.

3.1.7 In general, environment sets a reaction range within which maturation unfolds.

3.1.8 Temperament is hereditary. Most infants fall into one of three temperament categories: easy children, difficult children, and slow-to-warm-up children.

3.1.9 A child's developmental level reflects heredity, environment, and the effects of the child's own behavior.

3.2 What can newborn babies do?

3.2.1 Infant development is strongly influenced by heredity. However, environmental factors such as nutrition, parenting, and learning are also important.

3.2.2 The human neonate has a number of adaptive reflexes, including the grasping, rooting, sucking, and Moro reflexes. Neonates begin to learn immediately, and they appear to be aware of the effects of their actions.

3.2.3 The rate of maturation varies from person to person. Also, learning contributes greatly to the development of basic motor skills.

3.2.4 Tests in a looking chamber reveal a number of visual preferences in the newborn. The neonate is drawn to bright lights and circular or curved designs.

3.2.5 Infants prefer human face patterns, especially familiar faces. In later infancy or early childhood, interest in the unfamiliar emerges.

3.2.6 Emotions develop in a consistent order, starting with generalized excitement in newborn babies. Three of the basic emotions—fear, anger, and joy—may be unlearned.

3.3 Of what significance is a child's emotional bond with adults?

3.3.1 Emotional attachment of human infants is a critical early event.

3.3.2 Infant attachment is reflected by separation anxiety. The quality of attachment can be classified as secure, insecure-avoidant, or insecure-ambivalent.

3.3.3 Secure attachment is fostered by consistent care from parents who are sensitive to a baby's signals and rhythms.

3.3.4 High-quality day care is not harmful and can even be helpful to preschool children. Low-quality care can be risky.

3.3.5 Meeting a baby's affectional needs is as important as meeting needs for physical care.

3.4 *How important are parenting styles?*

3.4.1 Three major parental styles are authoritarian, permissive, and authoritative (effective). Studies suggest that parental styles have a substantial impact on emotional and intellectual development. Authoritative parenting appears to benefit children the most.

3.4.2 Whereas mothers typically emphasize care giving, fathers tend to function as playmates for infants. Both caregiving styles contribute to the competence of young children.

3.4.3 Parenting styles vary across cultures. The ultimate success of various parenting styles depends on what culture or ethnic community a child will enter.

3.5 *How do children acquire language?*

3.5.1 Learning to use language is a cornerstone of early intellectual development. Language development proceeds from crying to cooing, then babbling, the use of single words, and then to telegraphic speech.

3.5.2 The underlying patterns of telegraphic speech suggest a biological predisposition to acquire language. This innate tendency is augmented by learning.

3.5.3 Pre-language communication between parent and child involves shared rhythms, nonverbal signals, and turn-taking.

3.5.4 Motherese or parentese is a simplified, musical style of speaking that parents use to help their children learn language.

3.6 *How do children learn to think?*

3.6.1 The intellect of a child is less abstract than that of an adult. Jean Piaget theorized that intellectual growth occurs through a combination of assimilation and accommodation.

3.6.2 Piaget also held that children mature through a fixed series of cognitive stages. The stages and their approximate age ranges are sensorimotor (0–2), preoperational (2–7), concrete operational (7–11), and formal operational (11–adult).

3.6.3 Caregivers should offer learning opportunities that are appropriate for a child's level of cognitive development.

3.6.4 Learning principles provide an alternate explanation that assumes cognitive development is continuous; it does not occur in stages.

3.6.5 Studies of infants under the age of 1 year suggest that they are capable of thought well beyond that observed by Piaget. Similarly, children begin to outgrow egocentrism as early as age 4.

3.6.6 Lev Vygotsky's sociocultural theory emphasizes that a child's mental abilities are advanced by interactions with more competent partners. Mental growth takes place in a child's zone of proximal development, in which a more skillful person may scaffold the child's progress.

3.7 *Why is the transition from adolescence to adulthood especially challenging?*

3.7.1 The timing of puberty can complicate the task of identity formation, a major task of adolescence.

3.7.2 Identity formation is even more challenging for adolescents of ethnic descent.

3.7.3 In Western industrialized societies, the transition into adulthood is further complicated as it is increasingly delayed well into the 20s.

3.8 *How do we develop morals and values?*

3.8.1 Developing mature moral standards is also an important task of adolescence.

3.8.2 Lawrence Kohlberg identified preconventional, conventional, and postconventional levels of moral reasoning.

3.8.3 Most people function at the conventional level of morality, but some never get beyond the selfish, preconventional level. Only a minority of people attain the highest, or postconventional level, of moral reasoning.

3.8.4 Carol Gilligan distinguished between Kohlberg's justice perspective and a caring perspective. Mature adult morality likely involves both.

3.9 *What are the typical tasks and dilemmas through the life span?*

3.9.1 Erik Erikson identified a series of challenges that occur across the life span. These range from a need to gain trust in infancy to the need to live with integrity in old age.

3.9.2 Successful resolution of the dilemmas produces healthy development whereas unsuccessful outcomes make it harder to deal with later crises.

3.10 *What is involved in well-being during middle and later adulthood?*

3.10.1 Physical aging starts early in adulthood. Every adult must find ways to successfully cope with aging.

3.10.2 Only a minority of people have a midlife crisis, but midlife course corrections are more common.

3.10.3 Well-being during adulthood consists of six elements: self-acceptance, positive relations with others, autonomy, environmental mastery, having a purpose in life, and continued personal growth.

3.10.4 Intellectual declines associated with aging are limited, at least through one's 70s. This is especially true of individuals who remain mentally active.

3.10.5 Successful lives are based on happiness, purpose, meaning, and integrity.

3.10.6 Ageism refers to prejudice, discrimination, and stereotyping on the basis of age. It affects people of all ages but is especially damaging to older people. Most ageism is based on stereotypes, myths, and misinformation.

3.11 *How do people typically react to death?*

3.11.1. Typical emotional reactions to impending death include denial, anger, bargaining, depression, and acceptance, but not necessarily in that order or in every case.

3.11.2 Death is a natural part of life. There is value in understanding it and accepting it.

3.12 How do effective parents discipline and communicate with their children?

3.12.1 Positive parent-child interactions occur when parents spend enjoyable time encouraging their children in a loving and mutually respectful fashion.

3.12.2 Effective parental discipline tends to emphasize child management techniques (especially communication), rather than power assertion or withdrawal of love. Effective parents allow their children to express their feeling but place limits on their behavior.

3.12.3 Consistency is also an important aspect of effective parenting.

3.12.4 Much misbehavior can be managed by use of I-messages and the application of natural and logical consequences.

MEDIA RESOURCES

Web Resources

Internet addresses frequently change. To find an up-to-date list of URLs for the sites listed here, visit your Psychology CourseMate.

Heredity Versus Environment Read more about the interplay of nature and nurture.

Diving into the Gene Pool Learn more about modern genetics from the Exploratorium.

Human Genome Project Learn more about your human genetic heritage.

The Parent's Page Visit links for expectant couples and new parents.

Parenthood.com A comprehensive site for parents.

Crack Babies A photostory by Ken Kobre.

Harry Harlow Read more about Harry Harlow and his famous experiments on maternal deprivation in monkeys.

Attachment Theory Read more on attachment styles.

How to Choose a Daycare That's Right for Your Child An information resource about day care options.

Language Development In Children Much more information about language development in children.

How Does Your Child Hear and Talk? Discover a milestone chart for hearing and talking.

Speech & Language: Talk to Me Explore the role parents play in early language development.

Jean Piaget and Cognitive Development Read a more complete account of Piaget's theory.

Theory of Mind Watch a video illustrating the false-belief test used to assess young children's theory of mind.

Scaffolding as a Teaching Strategy Download a paper on the application of Vygotsky's idea of scaffolding to teaching.

A Positive Approach to Identity Formation of Biracial Children Join the debate about multi-ethnicity and identity formation.

Delayed Adulthood Read two articles about delayed adulthood.

Kohlberg Dilemmas Try your hand at answering several moral dilemmas.

Welcome to Middle Age Home page of middleage.org.

The AARP Home page of the American Association of Retired Persons.

Hospice A website of information about death, bereavement, and hospices.

Nine Steps to More Effective Parenting Read some more good advice on effective parenting.

Discipline: Logical & Natural Consequences Read about ways to effectively structure discipline.

Ten Reasons Not to Hit Your Kids Some reasons to avoid a heavy reliance on power-oriented discipline techniques.

Interactive Learning

Log in to **CengageBrain** to access the resources your instructor requires. For this book, you can access:

CourseMate brings course concepts to life with interactive learning, study, and exam preparation tools that support the printed textbook. A textbook-specific website, ***Psychology CourseMate*** includes an ***integrated interactive eBook*** and other ***interactive learning tools*** including quizzes, flashcards, videos, and more.

CENGAGENOW™

CengageNOW is an easy-to-use online resource that helps you study in less time to get the grade you want—NOW. Take a pre-test for this chapter and receive a personalized study plan based on your results that will identify the topics you need to review and direct you to online resources to help you master those topics. Then take a post-test to help you determine the concepts you have mastered and what you will need to work on. If your textbook does not include an access code card, go to CengageBrain.com to gain access.

WebTUTOR™

More than just an interactive study guide, **WebTutor** is an anytime, anywhere customized learning solution with an eBook, keeping you connected to your textbook, instructor, and classmates.

If your professor has assigned **Aplia** homework:

1. Sign in to your account.
2. Complete the corresponding homework exercises as required by your professor.
3. When finished, click "Grade It Now" to see which areas you have mastered and which need more work, and for detailed explanations of every answer.

Visit **www.cengagebrain.com** to access your account and purchase materials.

Gateway THEME

We actively construct our perceptions out of the information provided by our senses and our past experience; the resulting perceptions are not always accurate representations of events.

4

Sensation and Perception

The Trees Have Eyes

Right now, you are bathed in a swirling kaleidoscope of electromagnetic radiation, heat, pressure, vibrations, molecules, and mechanical forces. Unless your senses translate these forces into a form your brain can understand, you will experience only a void of silence and darkness. The next time you drink in the beauty of a sunset, a flower, or a friend, remember that sensation makes it all possible.

But are our senses enough to give us a completely accurate "picture" of reality? One of your authors was once admiring a flower in a beautiful tropical rainforest when he had the uncanny impression he was being watched. For several minutes he fruitlessly searched around, taking in the lush scene. Nothing. No, wait, there it was. Hanging not more than a foot from his own head was the head of a snake, staring straight at him. Yikes! How on earth could he have missed it? Slowly backing away, he marveled at how the snake was perfectly *camouflaged*, hanging motionless from an overhanging branch, looking for all the world like just another green vine (this species isn't called a green vine snake for nothing).

As this story shows, sensing the world is really just a first step in perceiving the world. Even though his eyes were picking up the basic visual information he needed to perceive the snake, his brain couldn't put the perceptual puzzle together. Sensory information can be interpreted (and misinterpreted) in various ways. That's step two in experiencing the world. We begin this chapter with the first step, sensation. Then we'll explore the second step, perception. Our perceptions create faces, melodies, works of art, illusions, and occasionally, snakes, out of the raw material of sensation.

Gateway QUESTIONS

- 4.1 *In general, how do sensory systems function?*
- 4.2 *How does the visual system function?*
- 4.3 *What are the mechanisms of hearing?*
- 4.4 *How do the chemical senses operate?*
- 4.5 *What are the somesthetic senses?*
- 4.6 *In general, how do we construct our perceptions?*
- 4.7 *Why are we more aware of some sensations than others?*
- 4.8 *How is it possible to see depth and judge distance?*
- 4.9 *How is perception altered by expectations, motives, emotions, and learning?*
- 4.10 *Is extrasensory perception possible?*
- 4.11 *How can I learn to perceive events more accurately?*

Sensory Processes—The First Step

Gateway Question 4.1: *In general, how do sensory systems function?*

Physical energy in the form of light or heat or sound strikes your senses. An instant later you notice a snowball whiz past your nose or the warmth of the sun on your face or a catchy new tune on the radio. In that instant, a remarkable series of events will have transpired as you detect, analyze, and interpret sensory information. Before we examine specific senses in more detail, let's explore how the senses reduce the amount of information the brain must process.

The primary function of the senses is to act as biological **transducers**, devices that convert one kind of energy into another (Fain, 2003). Each sense translates a specific type of external energy into patterns of activity (action potentials) in neurons. Information arriving from the sense organs creates **sensations**. Then the brain processes these messages. When the brain organizes sensations into meaningful patterns, we speak of **perception**. It is fascinating to realize that "seeing" and "hearing" take place in your brain, not in your eyes or ears.

Let's further explore sensation before we move on to perception. Consider, for example, vision, which gives us amazingly wide access to the world. In one instant, you can view a star light years away, and in the next, you can peer into the microscopic universe of a dewdrop. Yet, vision also narrows what we can possibly observe. Like the other senses, vision acts as a *data reduction system*. It selects and analyzes information in order to code and send to the brain only the most important data (Goldstein, 2010).

Selection

How does sensory data reduction take place? Considerable selection occurs because sensory receptors do not transduce all of the energies they encounter. For example, a guitar transduces string vibrations into sound waves. Pluck a string and the guitar will produce a sound. However, stimuli that don't cause the string to move will have no effect. If you shine a light on the string, or pour cold water on it, the guitar will remain silent. (The owner of the guitar, however, might get quite loud at this point!) In a similar way, the eye transduces electromagnetic radiation, the ear transduces sound waves, and so on. Many other types of stimuli cannot be sensed directly because we lack sensory receptors to transduce their energy. For example, humans cannot sense the bioelectric fields of other living creatures, but sharks have special organs that can (Fields, 2007). (Do they *hear* the fields or *feel* them or what?)

In the field of **psychophysics**, physical energy (such as sound waves or electromagnetic radiation) is measured and related to dimensions of the resulting sensations we experience (such as loudness or brightness). Psychophysical research has shown that sense receptors transduce only part of their target energy range (Fain, 2003). For example, your eyes transduce only a tiny fraction of the entire range of electromagnetic energies—the part we call the *visible spectrum.* The eyes of honeybees can transduce, and therefore see, parts of the electromagnetic spectrum invisible to us humans. Likewise, bats "shout" at a pitch too high for humans to transduce. But they can hear their own reflected echoes. This ability, called *echolocation,* allows bats to fly in total darkness while avoiding collisions and catching insects.

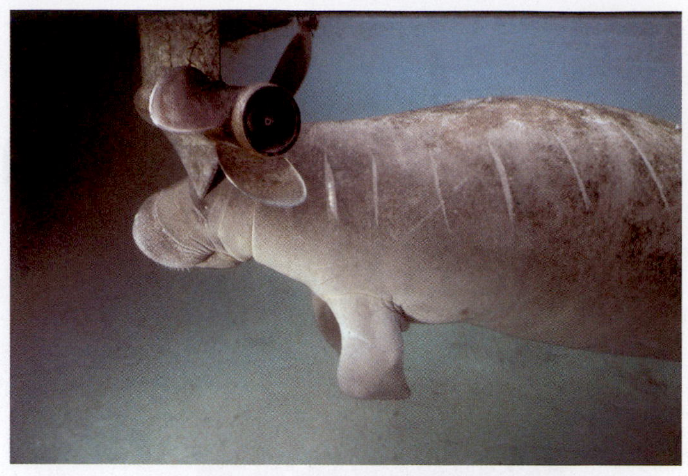

Absolute thresholds define the sensory worlds of humans and animals, sometimes with serious consequences. The endangered Florida manatee ("sea cow") is a peaceful, plant-eating creature that can live for more than 60 years. For the last decade, the number of manatees killed by boats has climbed alarmingly. The problem? Manatees have poor sensitivity to the low-frequency sounds made by slow-moving boats. Current laws require boats to slow down in manatee habitats, which may actually increase the risk to these gentle giants (Gerstein, 2002).

Similarly, energy below a certain minimum intensity is necessary for a sensation to occur. The necessary minimum defines the **absolute threshold** for a sensory system. For example, very soft sounds (which could be heard if they were just a little louder) fall below the absolute threshold for human hearing. Of course owls, who hunt at night, have much lower absolute thresholds for hearing. As you can see, our rich sensory experiences are only a small part of what *could* be sensed and what some animals *can* sense.

Sensory Adaptation

The flow of sensations to the brain is reduced in another way. Think about walking into a house in which fried fish, sauerkraut, and head cheese were just prepared for dinner. (Some dinner!) You would probably pass out at the door, yet people who had been in the house for some time wouldn't be aware of the food odors. Why? Because sensory receptors respond less to unchanging stimuli, a process called **sensory adaptation**.

Fortunately, the olfactory (smell) receptors adapt quickly. When exposed to a constant odor, they send fewer and fewer nerve impulses to the brain until the odor is no longer noticed. Adaptation to pressure from a wristwatch, waistband, ring, or glasses is based on the same principle. Since there is usually little reason to keep reminding the brain that a sensory input is unchanged, sensory receptors generally respond best to *changes* in stimulation. No one wants or needs to be reminded 16 hours a day that his or her shoes are on.

Sensory Analysis

What we experience is also influenced by **sensory analysis**. As they process information, the senses divide the world into important **perceptual features**, or basic stimulus patterns. The visual system, for example, has a set of *feature detectors* that are attuned to very specific stimuli, such as lines, shapes, edges, spots, colors, and other patterns (Hubel & Wiesel, 2005). Look at ● Figure 4.1 and notice how eye-catching the single vertical line is among a group of slanted lines. This effect, which is called *pop-out,* occurs because your visual system is highly sensitive to these perceptual features (Adler & Orprecio, 2006).

Similarly, frog eyes are highly sensitive to small, dark, moving spots. In other words, they are basically "tuned" to detect bugs flying nearby (Lettvin, 1961). But the insect (spot) must be moving, or the frog's "bug detectors" won't work. A frog could starve to death surrounded by dead flies.

Our sensitivity to perceptual features is an innate characteristic of the nervous system. Like other inborn capacities, this sensitivity is also influenced by experiences early in life. For instance, Colin Blakemore and Graham Cooper of Cambridge University raised kittens in a room with only vertical stripes on the walls. Another set of kittens saw only horizontal stripes. When returned to normal environments, the "horizontal" cats could easily jump onto a chair, but when walking on the floor, they bumped into chair legs. "Vertical" cats, on the other hand, easily avoided chair legs, but they missed when trying to jump to horizontal surfaces. The cats raised with vertical stripes were "blind" to horizontal lines, and the "horizontal" cats acted as if vertical lines were invisible (Blakemore & Cooper, 1970). Other experiments show that there is an actual decrease in brain cells tuned to the missing features (Grobstein & Chow, 1975).

● **Figure 4.1** Visual pop-out. Pop-out is so basic that babies as young as 3 months respond to it. (Adapted from Adler & Orprecio, 2006.)

Sensory Coding

As they select and analyze information, sensory systems *code* it. **Sensory coding** refers to converting important features of the world into neural messages understood by the brain (Hubel & Wiesel, 2005). For example, not every difference between two stimuli can be coded; instead, the difference must be sufficiently large. Psychophysics also involves the study of **difference thresholds**. Here we are asking, "How different must two stimuli be before the difference becomes noticeable and, hence, codable?" For example, if you were to put one extra grain of sugar in your coffee, would you notice difference? How much would it take? A few grains? A half spoonful? A spoonful?

To see coding at work, try closing your eyes for a moment. Then take your fingertips and press firmly on your eyelids. Apply enough pressure to "squash" your eyes slightly. Do this for about 30 seconds and observe what happens. (Readers with eye problems or contact lenses should not try this.)

Did you "see" stars, checkerboards, and flashes of color? These are called *phosphenes* (FOSS-feens), visual sensations caused by mechanical excitation of the retina. They occur because the eye's receptor cells, which normally respond to light, are also somewhat sensitive to pressure. Notice, though, that the eye is prepared to code stimulation—including pressure—only into visual features. As a result, you experience light sensations, not pressure. Also important in producing this effect is *sensory localization* in the brain.

Sensory localization means that the type of sensation you experience depends on which brain area is activated. Some brain areas receive visual information; others receive auditory information, and still others receive taste or touch. Knowing which brain areas are active tells us, in general, what kinds of sensations you are feeling.

Transducers Devices that convert one kind of energy into another.

Sensation A sensory impression; also, the process of detecting physical energies with the sensory organs.

Perception The mental process of organizing sensations into meaningful patterns.

Psychophysics Study of the relationship between physical stimuli and the sensations they evoke in a human observer.

Absolute threshold The minimum amount of physical energy necessary to produce a sensation.

Sensory adaptation A decrease in sensory response to an unchanging stimulus.

Sensory analysis Separation of sensory information into important elements.

Perceptual features Basic elements of a stimulus, such as lines, shapes, edges, or colors.

Sensory coding Codes used by the sense organs to transmit information to the brain.

Difference threshold The minimum difference between two stimuli that is detectable to an observer.

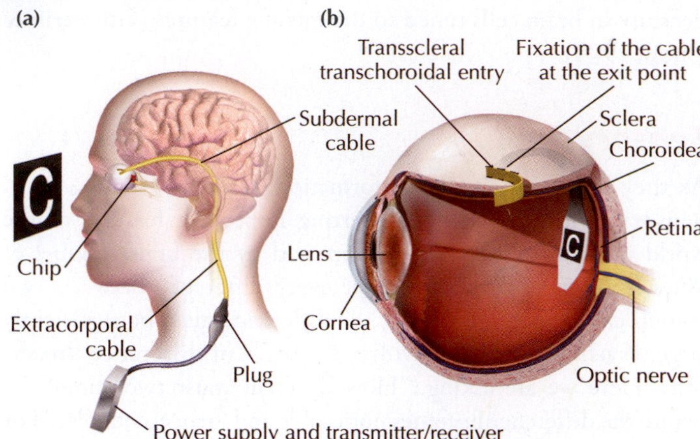

• Figure 4.2 An artificial retina. A light-sensitive grid translates light into electrical impulses that stimulate the optic nerve, resulting in rudimentary visual experiences. From Eberhart Zrenner et al. "Subretinal Electronic Chips Allow Blind Patients to Read Letters and Combine Them to Words (Figure 2)." *Proceedings of the Royal Society B.* Copyright © 2010 by The Royal Society. Reprinted by permission.

BRIDGES

For more information about which brain areas receive various sensory inputs, **see Chapter 2, pages 67–71.**

Sensory localization is beginning to make it possible to artificially restore sight, hearing, or other senses. In one approach, researchers have used a miniature television camera to send electrical signals to directly stimulate to the brain (Dobelle, 2000; Warren & Normann, 2005). In another approach, a grid of light-sensitive elements is implanted into the retina so that it can electrically stimulate the optic nerve instead (• Figure 4.2). Using such technologies, people who have lost their vision are now able to "see" letters, words, and some common objects like knives and forks (Zrenner et al., 2010).

Although the senses supply raw data to the brain, these data remain mostly meaningless until they are interpreted. It's as if the senses provide only the jumbled pieces of a complex puzzle. In the remaining sections of this chapter, we will further explore the various senses and how we put the puzzle together.

Knowledge Builder Sensory Processes

RECITE

1. Sensory receptors are biological ________________, or devices for converting one type of energy to another.
2. As time passes, nerve endings in the skin under your wristwatch send fewer signals to the brain and you become unable to feel the watch. This process is called
   a. transduction *b.* difference threshold *c.* reverse attention *d.* sensory adaptation
3. Lettvin found that a frog's eyes are especially sensitive to phosphenes. T or F?
4. Important features of the environment are transmitted to the brain through a process known as
   a. phosphenation *b.* coding *c.* detection *d.* programming

REFLECT

Think Critically

5. William James once said, "If a master surgeon were to cross the auditory and optic nerves, we would hear lightning and see thunder." Can you explain what James meant?

Self-Reflect

How does sensation affect what you are experiencing right now? Try to imagine how overwhelmed you would be if data reduction didn't occur?

What if, like some other animals, you could transduce other energies? What if your senses were tuned to detect different perceptual features? How would the sensory world you live in change? What would it be like to be a bat?

As you sit reading this book, which sensory inputs have undergone adaptation? What new inputs can you become aware of by shifting your focus of attention?

Answers: 1. transducers **2.** *d* **3.** F **4.** *b* **5.** The explanation is based on sensory localization: Even if a lightning flash caused rerouted messages from the eyes to activate auditory areas of the brain, we would experience a sound sensation. Likewise, if the ears transduced a thunderclap and sent impulses to the visual area, a sensation of light would occur. Amazingly, some people, called *synesthetes*, naturally experience sensory inputs in terms of other senses. For example, one synesthete experiences pain as the color orange, whereas for another the taste of spiced chicken is pointy (Dixon, Smilek, & Merikle, 2004).

Vision—Catching Some Rays

Gateway Question 4.2: *How does the visual system function?*

In the morning when you first open your eyes, you effortlessly become aware of the visual richness of the world around you. But the ease with which normally sighted people can *see* conceals incredible complexity. Vision is an impressive sensory system, worthy of a detailed discussion.

What are the basic dimensions of light and vision? The *visible spectrum*—the spread of electromagnetic energies to which the eyes respond—is made up of a narrow range of wavelengths of electromagnetic radiation. Visible light starts at "short" wavelengths of 400 *nanometers* (nan-OM-et-er: one billionth of a meter), which we sense as purple or violet. Longer light waves produce blue, green, yellow, orange, and red, which has a wavelength of 700 nanometers (• Figure 4.3).

The term *hue* refers to the basic color categories of red, orange, yellow, green, blue, indigo, and violet. As just noted, various hues (or color sensations) correspond to the wavelength of the light that reaches our eyes (Mather, 2008). White light, in contrast, is a mixture of many wavelengths. Hues (colors) from a narrow band of wavelengths are very *saturated*, or "pure." (An intense "fire-engine" red is more saturated than a muddy "brick" red.) A third dimension of vision, *brightness*, corresponds roughly to the amplitude, or height of light waves. Waves of greater amplitude are "taller," carry more energy, and cause the colors we see to appear brighter or more intense. For example, the same "brick" red would look bright under intense, high-energy illumination and drab under dim light.

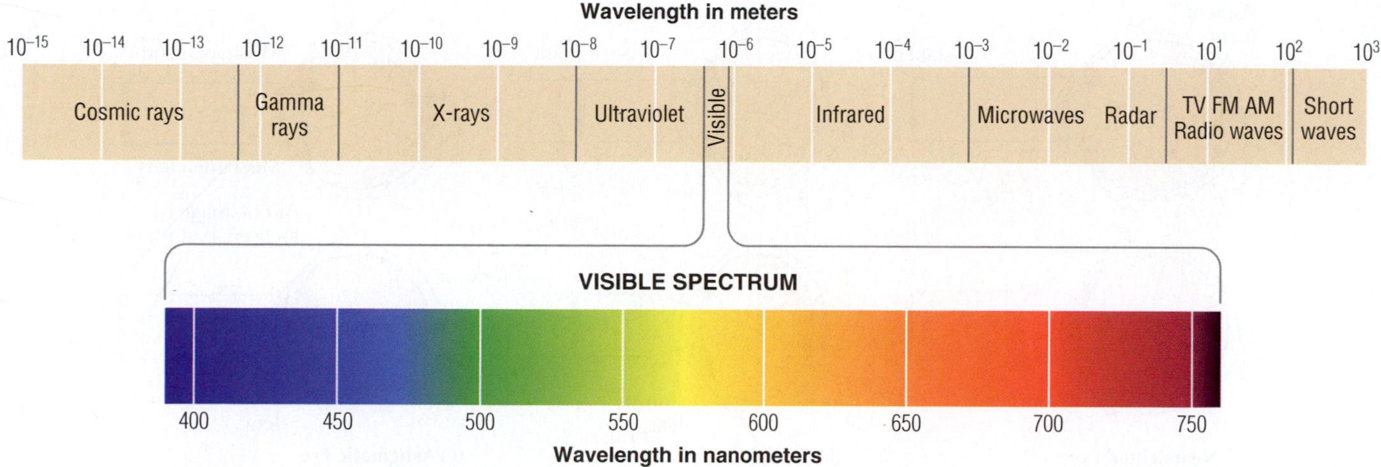

● **Figure 4.3** The visible spectrum. From FREBERG. *Discovering Biological Psychology, 2e*. Copyright © 2010 Wadsworth, a part of Cengage Learning, Inc. Reproduced by permission. www.cengage.com/permissions

Structure of the Eye

Although the visual system is much more complex than any digital camera, both cameras and eyes have a *lens* to focus images on a light-sensitive layer at the back of an enclosed space. In a camera, it is a layer of light-sensitive pixels in the digital image sensor. In the eye, it is a layer of *photoreceptors* (light-sensitive cells) in the **retina**, an area about the size and thickness of a postage stamp (● Figure 4.4).

How does the eye focus? Most focusing is done at the front of the eye by the *cornea,* a clear membrane that bends light inward. The lens makes additional, smaller adjustments. Your eye's focal point changes when muscles attached to the lens alter its shape. This process is called **accommodation.** In cameras, focusing is done more simply—by changing the distance between the lens and the image sensor.

Visual Problems

Focusing is also affected by the shape of the eye. If your eye is too short, nearby objects will be blurred, but distant objects will be sharp. This is called **hyperopia** (HI-per-OPE-ee-ah), or farsightedness. If your eyeball is too long, images fall short of the retina and you won't be able to focus distant objects. This results in **myopia** (my-OPE-ee-ah), or nearsightedness. When the cornea or the lens is misshapen, part of vision will be focused and part will be fuzzy. In this case, the eye has more than one focal point, a problem called **astigmatism** (ah-STIG-mah-tiz-em). All three visual defects can be corrected by placing glasses (or contact lenses) in front of the eye to change the path of light (● Figure 4.5).

As people age, the lens becomes less flexible and less able to accommodate. The result is **presbyopia** (prez-bee-OPE-ee-ah), from the Latin for "old vision," or farsightedness due to aging. Perhaps you have seen a grandparent or older friend reading a newspaper at arm's length because of presbyopia. If you now wear glasses for nearsightedness, you may need bifocals as you age. (Just like your authors. Sigh.) Bifocal lenses correct near vision *and* distance vision.

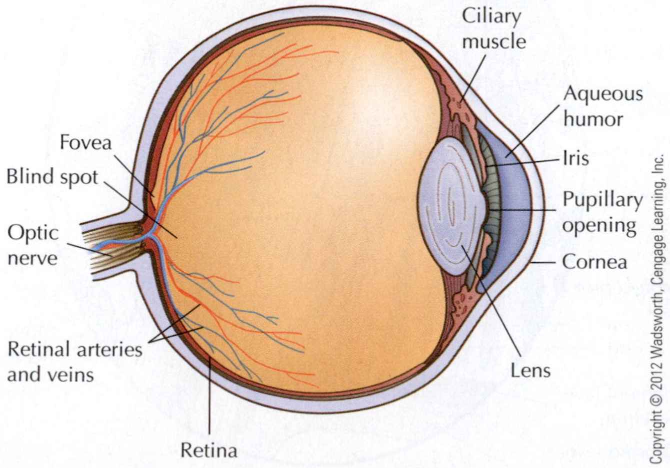

● **Figure 4.4** The human eye, a simplified view.

Rods and Cones

The eye has two types of "image sensors," consisting of receptor cells called *rods* and *cones* (Mather, 2008). The 5 million **cones** in each eye work best in bright light. They also produce color sensations and fine details. In contrast, the **rods**, numbering about 120 million, can't detect colors (● Figure 4.6). Pure rod vision is black and white. However, the rods are much more sensitive to light than the cones are. The rods, therefore, allow us to see in very dim light.

Retina The light-sensitive layer of cells at the back of the eye.
Accommodation Changes in the shape of the lens of the eye.
Hyperopia Difficulty focusing nearby objects (farsightedness).
Myopia Difficulty focusing distant objects (nearsightedness).
Astigmatism Defects in the cornea, lens, or eye that cause some areas of vision to be out of focus.
Presbyopia Farsightedness caused by aging.
Cones Visual receptors for colors and daylight visual acuity.
Rods Visual receptors for dim light that produce only black and white sensations.

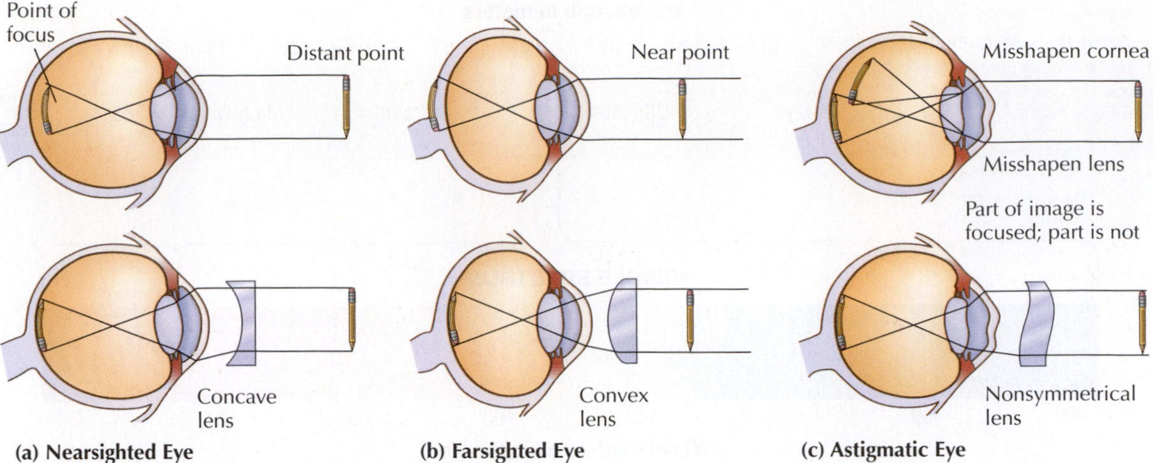

● **Figure 4.5** Visual defects and corrective lenses: *(a)* A myopic (longer than usual) eye. The concave lens spreads light rays just enough to increase the eye's focal length. *(b)* A hyperopic (shorter than usual) eye. The convex lens increases refraction (bending) to focus light on the retina. *(c)* An astigmatic (lens or cornea not symmetrical) eye. In astigmatism, parts of vision are sharp and parts are unfocused. Lenses that correct astigmatism are nonsymmetrical.

Surprisingly, the retina has a "hole" in it: Each eye has a *blind spot* because there are no receptors where the optic nerve passes out of the eye and blood vessels enter (● Figure 4.6, right side). The blind spot shows that vision depends greatly on the brain. If you close one eye, some of the incoming light will fall on the blind spot of your open eye. Why isn't there a gap in your vision? The answer is that the visual cortex of the brain actively fills in the gap with patterns from surrounding areas (● Figure 4.7). By closing one eye, you can visually "behead" other people by placing their images on your blind spot. (Just a hint for some classroom fun.) The brain can also "erase" distracting information. Roll your eyes all the way to the right and then close your right eye. You should clearly see your nose in your left eye's field of vision. Now, open your right eye again and your nose will nearly disappear as your brain disregards its presence.

● **Figure 4.6** Anatomy of the retina. Note that light does not fall directly on the rods and cones. It must first pass through the cornea, the lens, the vitreous humor (a jelly-like substance that fills the eyeball), and the outer layers of the retina. Only about one half of the light at the front of the eye reaches the rods and cones—testimony to the retina's amazing sensitivity. The lower left photograph shows rods and cones as seen through an electron microscope. In the photograph the cones are colored green and the rods blue.

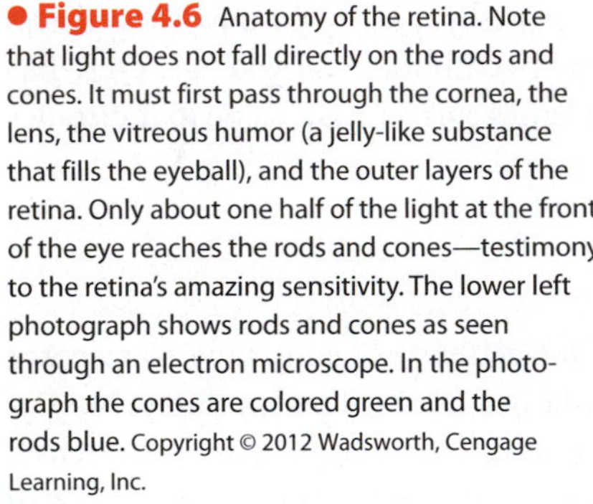

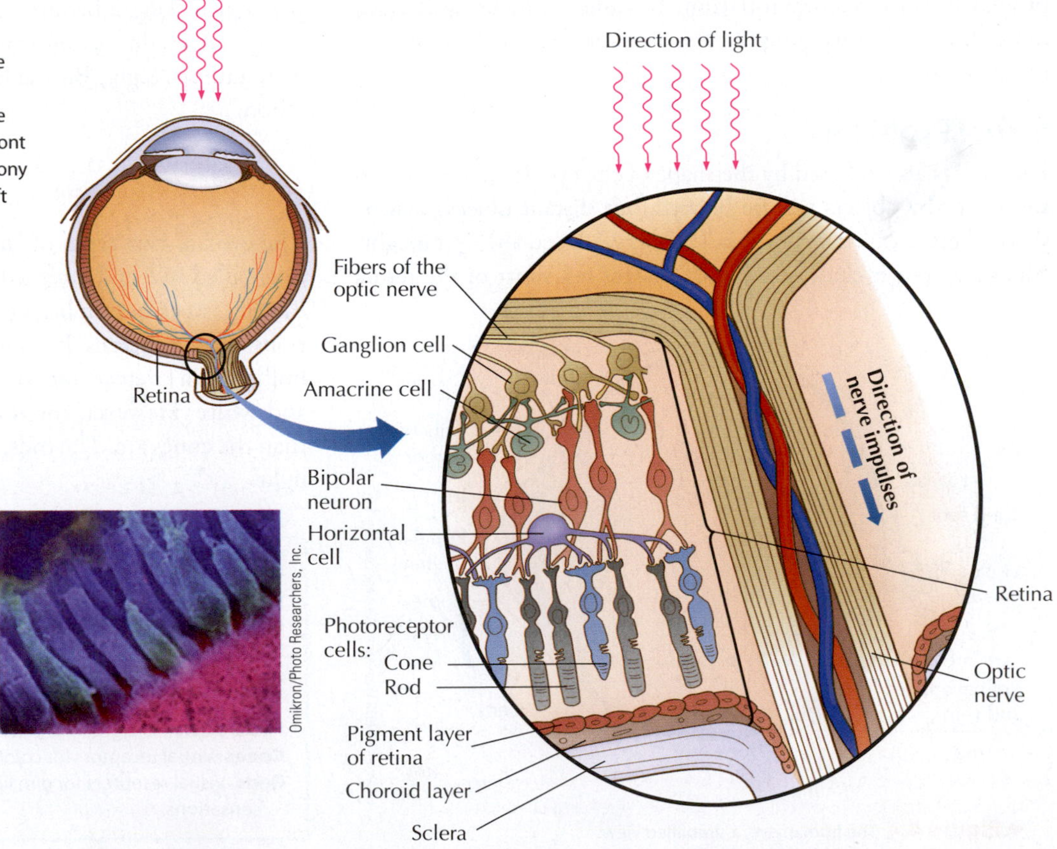

● **Figure 4.7** Experiencing the blind spot. *(a)* With your right eye closed, stare at the upper-right cross. Hold the book about 1 foot from your eye and slowly move it back and forth. You should be able to locate a position that causes the black spot to disappear. When it does, it has fallen on the blind spot. With a little practice, you can learn to make people or objects you dislike disappear too! *(b)* Repeat the procedure described, but stare at the lower cross. When the white space falls on the blind spot, the black lines will appear to be continuous. This may help you understand why you do not usually experience a blind spot in your visual field.

Visual Acuity

The rods and cones also affect **visual acuity**, or sharpness (Foley & Matlin, 2010). The cones lie mainly at the center of the eye. In fact, the *fovea* (FOE-vee-ah), a small cup-shaped area in the middle of the retina, contains only cones—about 50,000 of them. Like high-resolution digital sensors made of many small pixels, the tightly packed cones in the fovea produce the sharpest images. Normal acuity is designated as 20/20 vision: At 20 feet in distance, you can distinguish what the average person can see at 20 feet (● Figure 4.8). If your vision is 20/40, you can see at 20 feet only what the average person can see at 40 feet. If your vision is 20/200, everything is a blur and you need glasses! Vision that is 20/12 would mean that you can see at 20 feet what the average person must be 8 feet nearer to see, indicating better than average acuity. American astronaut Gordon Cooper, who claimed to see railroad lines in northern India from 100 miles above the earth, had 20/12 vision.

Peripheral Vision

What is the purpose of the rest of the retina? Areas outside the fovea also get light, creating a large region of **peripheral** (side) **vision**. The rods are most numerous about 20 degrees from the center of the retina, so much of our peripheral vision is rod vision. Although rod vision is not very high resolution, the rods are quite sensitive to *movement* in peripheral vision. To experience this characteristic of the rods, look straight ahead and hold your hand beside your head, at about 90 degrees. Wiggle your finger and slowly move your hand forward until you can detect motion. You will become aware of the movement before you can actually "see" your finger. Seeing "out of the corner of the eye" is important for sports, driving, and walking down dark alleys. People who suffer from *tunnel vision* (a loss of peripheral vision) feel as if they are wearing blinders (Godnig, 2003).

The rods are also highly responsive to dim light. Because most rods are 20 degrees to each side of the fovea, the best night vision comes from looking *next to* an object you wish to see. Test this yourself some night by looking at, and next to, a very dim star.

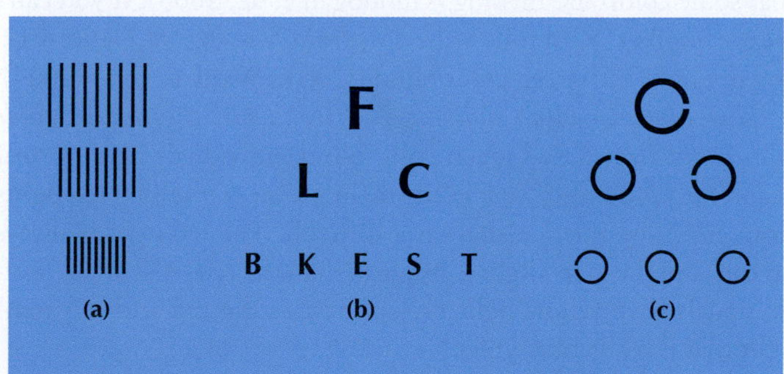

● **Figure 4.8** Tests of visual acuity. Here are some common tests of visual acuity. In *(a)*, sharpness is indicated by the smallest grating still seen as individual lines. The Snellen chart *(b)* requires that you read rows of letters of diminishing size until you can no longer distinguish them. The Landolt rings *(c)* require no familiarity with letters. All that is required is a report of which side has a break in it.

Color Vision

How do the cones produce color sensations? The **trichromatic** (TRY-kro-MAT-ik) **theory** of color vision holds that there are three types of cones, each most sensitive to either red, green, or blue. Other colors result from combinations of these three.

A basic problem with the trichromatic theory is that four colors of light—red, green, blue, and yellow—seem to be primary (you can't get them by mixing other colors). Also, why is it impossible to have a reddish green or a yellowish blue? These problems led to the development of a second view, known as the **opponent-process theory**, which states that vision analyzes colors into "either-or" messages (Goldstein, 2010). That is, the visual system can produce

Visual acuity The sharpness of visual perception.
Peripheral (side) vision Vision at the edges of the visual field.
Trichromatic theory Theory of color vision based on three cone types: red, green, and blue.
Opponent-process theory Theory of color vision based on three coding systems (red or green, yellow or blue, black or white).

● **Figure 4.9** Negative afterimages. Stare at the dot near the middle of the flag for at least 30 seconds. Then look immediately at a plain sheet of white paper or a white wall. You will see the American flag in its normal colors. Reduced sensitivity to yellow, green, and black in the visual system, caused by prolonged staring, results in the appearance of complementary colors. Project the afterimage of the flag on other colored surfaces to get additional effects. Copyright © 2012 Wadsworth, Cengage Learning, Inc.

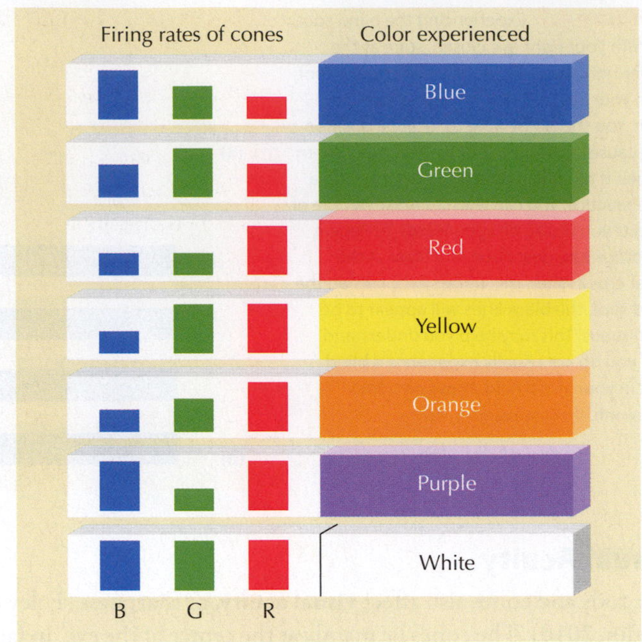

● **Figure 4.10** Firing rates of blue, green, and red cones in response to different colors. The taller the colored bar, the higher the firing rates for that type of cone. As you can see, colors are coded by differences in the activity of all three types of cones in the normal eye. (Adapted from Goldstein, 2010.)

messages for either red or green, yellow or blue, black or white. Coding one color in a pair (red, for instance) seems to block the opposite message (green) from coming through. As a result, a reddish green is impossible, but a yellowish red (orange) can occur.

According to opponent-process theory, fatigue caused by making one response produces an afterimage of the opposite color as the system recovers. *Afterimages* are visual sensations that persist after a stimulus is removed—like seeing a spot after a flashbulb goes off. To see an afterimage of the type predicted by opponent-process theory, look at ● Figure 4.9 and follow the instructions there.

Which color theory is correct? Both! The three-color theory applies to the retina, in which three different types of cone have been found. Each contains a different type of iodopsin (i-oh-DOP-sin), a light-sensitive pigment that breaks down when struck by light. This triggers action potentials and sends neural messages to the brain. The three types of cones are most sensitive to red, green, or blue. Other colors result from combinations of these three. As predicted, each form of iodopsin is most sensitive to light in roughly the red, green, or blue region. Thus, the three types of cones fire nerve impulses at different rates to produce various color sensations (● Figure 4.10).

In contrast, the opponent-process theory better explains what happens in optic pathways and the brain *after* information leaves the eye. For example, some nerve cells in the brain are excited by the color red and inhibited by the color green. So both theories are "correct." One explains what happens in the eye itself. The other explains how colors are analyzed after messages leave the eye (Gegenfurtner & Kiper, 2003).

Color Blindness and Color Weakness

Do you know anyone who regularly draws hoots of laughter by wearing clothes of wildly clashing colors? Or someone who sheepishly tries to avoid saying what color an object is? If so, you probably know someone who is color blind.

What is it like to be color blind? What causes color blindness? A person who is **color blind** cannot perceive colors. It is as if the world were a black-and-white movie. The color-blind person either lacks cones or has cones that do not function normally (Deeb, 2004). Such total color blindness is rare. In **color weakness**, or partial color blindness, a person can't see certain colors. Approximately 8 percent of Caucasian males (but fewer Asian, African, and Native American males and less than 1 percent of women) are red-green color blind (Delpero et al., 2005). These people see reds and greens as the same color, usually a yellowish brown (see ● Figure 4.11). Another type of color weakness, involving yellow and blue, is extremely rare (Hsia & Graham, 1997).

Surprisingly, some people reach adulthood without knowing that some colors are missing (Gündogan et al., 2005). If you can't see the number "5" or follow the dots from X-to-X in ● Figure 4.12, you might be red-green color blind (Coren, Ward, & Enns, 2004).

How can color-blind individuals drive? Don't they have trouble with traffic lights? Red-green color-blind individuals have normal vision for yellow and blue, so the main problem is telling red lights from green. In practice, that's not difficult. The red light is always on top, and the green light is brighter than the red. Also, "red" traffic signals have yellow light mixed in with the red and a "green" light that is really blue-green.

Seeing in the Dark

What happens when the eyes adjust to a dark room? **Dark adaptation** is the dramatic increase in retinal sensitivity to light that occurs after a person enters the dark (Goldstein, 2010). Consider walking into a theater. If you enter from a brightly lit lobby, you practically need to be led to your seat. After a short time, however, you can see the entire room in detail (including the couple kissing over in the corner). It takes about 30 to 35 minutes of complete darkness to reach maximum visual sensitivity (● Figure 4.13). At that point, your eye will be 100,000 times more sensitive to light.

What causes dark adaptation? Like cones, which contain *iodopsin*, rods also contain a light-sensitive visual pigment, rhodopsin (row-DOP-sin), which allows them to see in black and white. When struck by light, visual pigments bleach, or break down chemically. The afterimages you have seen after looking at a flashbulb are a result of this bleaching. In fact, a few seconds of exposure to bright white light can completely wipe out dark adaptation. That's why you should be sure to avoid looking at oncoming headlights when you are driving at night—especially the new bluish-white xenon lights. To restore light sensitivity, the rhodopsin in the rods must recombine, which takes time.

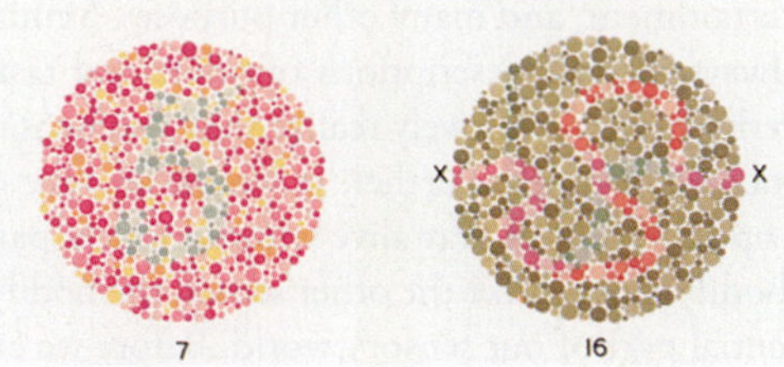

● **Figure 4.12** A replica of two images from the widely used Ishihara test for red-green color blindness. Copyright © 2012 Wadsworth, Cengage Learning, Inc.

● **Figure 4.11** Color blindness and color weakness. *(a)* Photograph illustrates normal color vision. *(b)* Photograph is printed in blue and yellow and gives an impression of what a red-green color-blind person sees. *(c)* Photograph simulates total color blindness. If you are totally color blind, all three photos will look nearly identical.

Is there any way to speed up dark adaptation? The rods are *insensitive* to extremely red light. That's why submarines, airplane cockpits, and ready rooms for fighter pilots are illuminated with red light. In each case, people can move quickly into the dark without having to adapt. Because the red light doesn't stimulate the rods, it is as if they had already spent time in the dark.

The Other Senses

We depend so much on vision that we sometimes neglect the other senses. But you only need to wear earplugs for a short time to appreciate how much we rely on hearing for communication, navi-

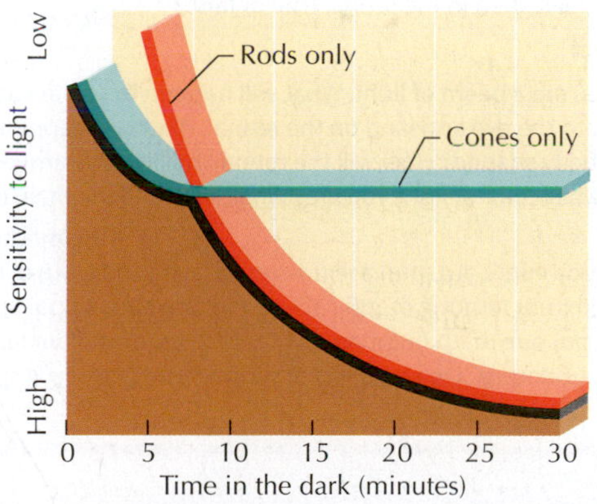

● **Figure 4.13** Typical course of dark adaptation. The dark line shows how the threshold for vision lowers as a person spends time in the dark. (A lower threshold means that less light is needed for vision.) The green line shows that the cones adapt first, but they soon cease adding to light sensitivity. Rods, shown by the red line, adapt more slowly. However, they continue to add to improved night vision long after the cones are fully adapted. Copyright © 2012 Wadsworth, Cengage Learning, Inc.

Color blindness A total inability to perceive colors.
Color weakness An inability to distinguish some colors.
Dark adaptation Increased retinal sensitivity to light.

gation, entertainment, and many other purposes. Similarly, skilled novelists always include descriptions of odors and tastes in their writings. Perhaps they intuitively realize that a scene is incomplete without smells and tastes. Further, it would be very difficult to move, stay upright, or even stay alive without touch, pain, balance, and other bodily senses. Like the other senses, the bodily senses are also an essential part of our sensory world. Before we examine the other senses in more detail, let's see if you have gained any insights into vision.

Knowledge Builder: Vision

RECITE

1. Match:
   - ____ Myopia
   - ____ Hyperopia
   - ____ Presbyopia
   - ____ Astigmatism

   A. Farsightedness
   B. Elongated eye
   C. Farsightedness due to aging
   D. Lack of cones in the fovea
   E. Misshapen cornea or lens
2. In dim light, vision depends mainly on the ________________. In brighter light, color and fine detail are produced by the ________________.
3. The greatest visual acuity is associated with the ________ and the ________.
   a. trichromat, rods *b.* vitreous humor, cones *c.* fovea, cones *d.* nanometer, cones
4. Colored afterimages are best explained by
   a. trichromatic theory *b.* the effects of astigmatism *c.* sensory localization *d.* opponent-process theory
5. Dark adaptation is directly related to an increase in
   a. rhodopsin *b.* astigmatism *c.* accommodation *d.* saturation

REFLECT

Think Critically

6. Sensory transduction in the eye takes place first in the cornea, then in the lens, then in the retina. True or false?

Self-Reflect

Pretend you are a beam of light. What will happen to you at each step as you pass into the eye and land on the retina? What will happen if the eye is not perfectly shaped? How will the retina know you've arrived? How will it tell what color of light you are? What will it tell the brain about you?

Answers: **1.** B, A, C, E **2.** rods, cones **3.** *c* **4.** *d* **5.** *a* **6.** F. Although the cornea and lens prepare incoming light rays by bending them and focusing them on the retina, they do not change light to another form of energy. No change in the *type* of energy takes place until the retina converts light to nerve impulses.

Hearing—Good Vibrations

Gateway Question 4.3: *What are the mechanisms of hearing?*

Rock, classical, jazz, rap, country, hip-hop—whatever your musical taste, you have probably been moved by the riches of sound. Hearing also collects information from all around the body, such as detecting the approach of an unseen car (Yost, 2007). Vision, in all its glory, is limited to stimuli in front of the eyes (unless, of course, your "shades" have rearview mirrors attached).

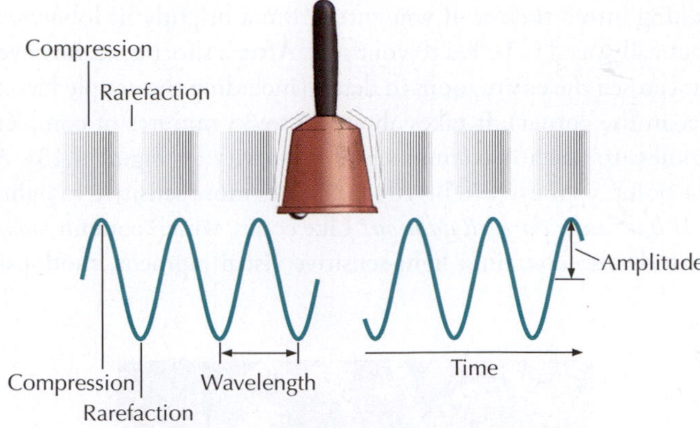

● **Figure 4.14** Waves of compression in the air, or vibrations, are the stimulus for hearing. The frequency of sound waves determines their pitch. The amplitude determines loudness.

What is the stimulus for hearing? If you throw a stone into a quiet pond, a circle of waves will spread in all directions. In much the same way, sound travels as a series of invisible waves of *compression* (peaks) and *rarefaction* (RARE-eh-fak-shun: valleys) in the air. Any vibrating object—a tuning fork, the string of a musical instrument, or the vocal cords—will produce sound waves (rhythmic movement of air molecules). Other materials, such as fluids or solids, can also carry sound. But sound does not travel in a vacuum or the airless realm of outer space. Movies that show characters reacting to the "roar" of alien starships or titanic battles in deep space do so solely for dramatic effect.

The *frequency* of sound waves (the number of waves per second) corresponds to the perceived *pitch* (higher or lower tone) of a sound. The *amplitude,* or physical "height," of a sound wave tells how much energy it contains. Psychologically, amplitude corresponds to sensed *loudness* (sound intensity) (● Figure 4.14).

How We Hear Sounds

How are sounds converted to nerve impulses? Hearing involves an elaborate chain of events that begins with the *pinna* (PIN-ah), the visible, external part of the ear. In addition to being a good place to hang earrings or balance pencils, the pinna acts like a funnel to concentrate sounds. After they are guided into the ear canal, sound waves collide with the *tympanic membrane* (eardrum), setting it in motion. This, in turn, causes three small bones, the *auditory ossicles* (OSS-ih-kuls), to vibrate (● Figure 4.15). The ossicles are the malleus (MAL-ee-us), incus, and stapes (STAY-peas). Their common names are the hammer, anvil, and stirrup. The ossicles link the eardrum with the *cochlea* (KOCK-lee-ah), a snail-shaped organ that makes up the inner ear. The stapes is attached to a membrane on the cochlea called the *oval window*. As the oval window moves back and forth, it makes waves in a fluid inside the cochlea.

Inside the cochlea, tiny **hair cells** detect waves in the fluid. The hair cells are part of the **organ of Corti** (KOR-tee), which makes

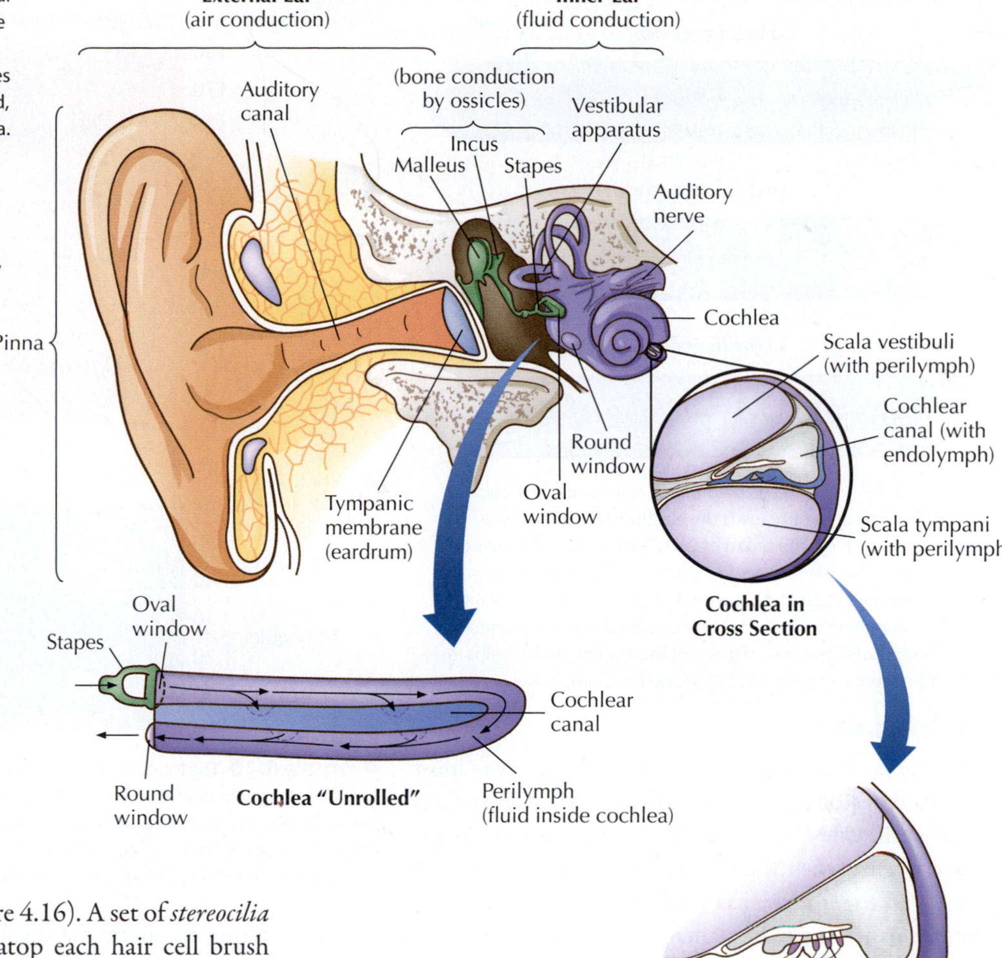

• Figure 4.15 Anatomy of the ear. The entire ear is a mechanism for transducing waves of air pressure into nerve impulses. The inset in the foreground ("Cochlea 'Unrolled'") shows that as the stapes moves the oval window, the round window bulges outward, allowing waves to ripple through fluid in the cochlea. The waves move membranes near the hair cells, causing cilia, or "bristles," on the tips of the cells to bend. The hair cells then generate nerve impulses carried to the brain. (See an enlarged cross section of cochlea in Figure 4.16.) Copyright © 2012 Wadsworth, Cengage Learning, Inc.

up the center part of the cochlea (• Figure 4.16). A set of *stereocilia* (STER-ee-oh-SIL-ih-ah), or "bristles," atop each hair cell brush against the tectorial membrane when waves ripple through the fluid surrounding the organ of Corti. As the stereocilia are bent, nerve impulses are triggered, which then flow to the brain.

How are higher and lower sounds detected? The **frequency theory** of hearing states that as pitch rises, nerve impulses of a corresponding frequency are fed into the auditory nerve. That is, an 800-hertz tone produces 800 nerve impulses per second. (*Hertz* refers to the number of vibrations per second.) This explains how sounds up to about 4,000 hertz reach the brain. But what about higher tones? **Place theory** states that higher and lower tones excite specific areas of the cochlea. High tones register most strongly at the base of the cochlea (near the oval window). Lower tones, on the other hand, mostly move hair cells near the narrow outer tip of the cochlea (• Figure 4.17). Pitch is signaled by the area of the cochlea most strongly activated. Place theory also explains why hunters sometimes lose hearing in a narrow pitch range. "Hunter's notch," as it is called, occurs when hair cells are damaged in the area affected by the pitch of gunfire.

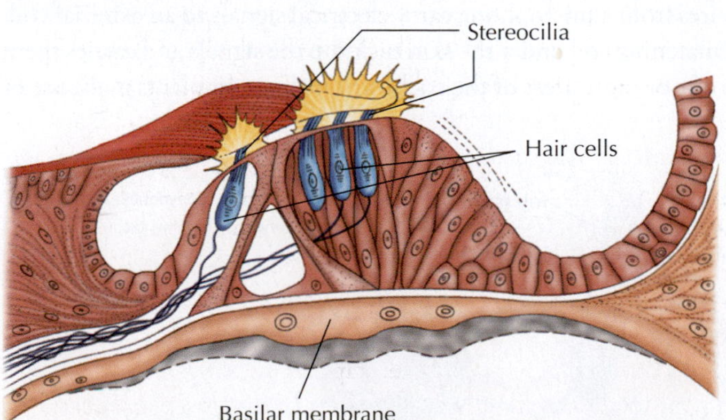

• Figure 4.16 A closer view of the hair cells shows how movement of fluid in the cochlea causes the bristling "hairs," or cilia, to bend, generating a nerve impulse. Copyright © 2012 Wadsworth, Cengage Learning, Inc.

Hair cells Receptor cells within the cochlea that transduce vibrations into nerve impulses.

Organ of Corti Center part of the cochlea, containing hair cells, canals, and membranes.

Frequency theory Holds that tones up to 4,000 hertz are converted to nerve impulses that match the frequency of each tone.

Place theory Theory that higher and lower tones excite specific areas of the cochlea.

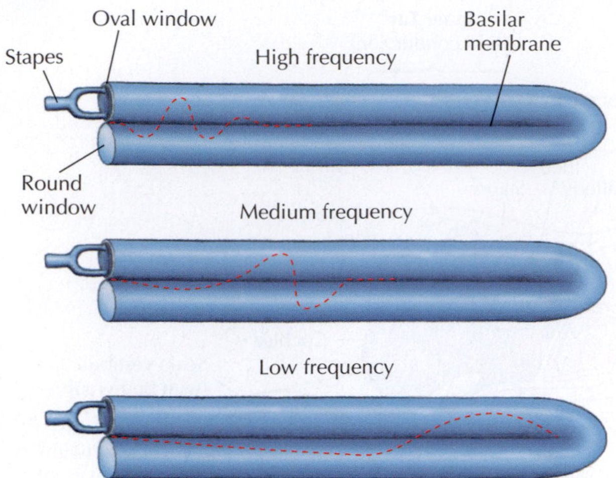

● **Figure 4.17** Here we see a simplified side view of the cochlea "unrolled." The basilar membrane is the elastic "roof" of the lower chamber of the cochlea. The organ of Corti, with its sensitive hair cells, rests atop the basilar membrane. The colored line shows where waves in the cochlear fluid cause the greatest deflection of the basilar membrane. (The amount of movement is exaggerated in the drawing.) Hair cells respond most in the area of greatest movement, which helps identify sound frequency.

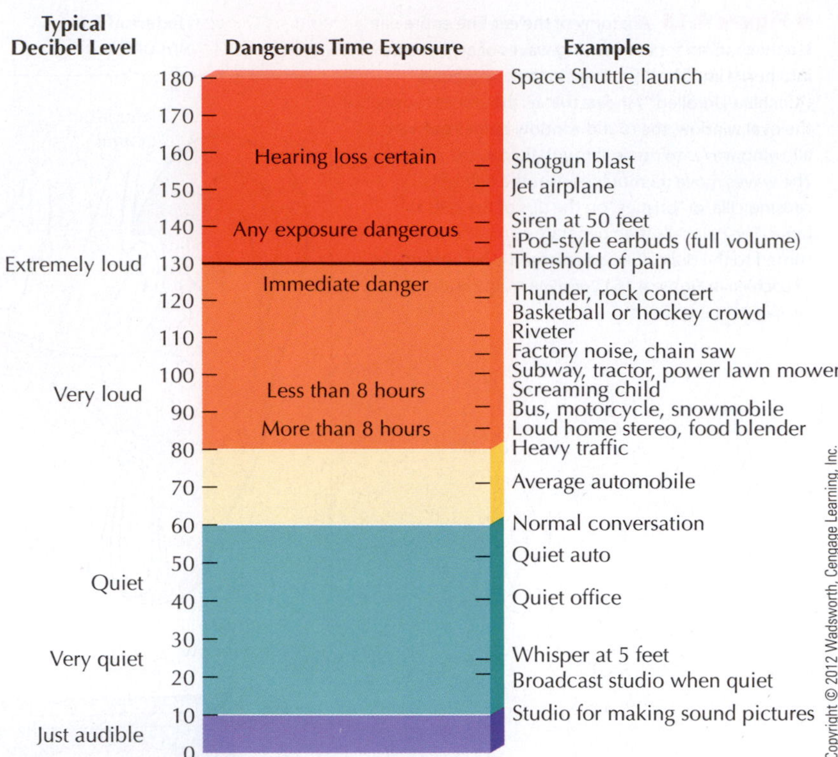

● **Figure 4.18** The loudness of sound is measured in decibels. Zero decibels is the faintest sound most people can hear. Sounds of 110 decibels are uncomfortably loud. Prolonged exposure to sounds above 85 decibels may damage the inner ear. Some rock concerts, which can reach 120 decibels, have caused hearing loss in musicians and may affect audiences as well. Sounds of 130 decibels pose an immediate danger to hearing.

Hearing Loss

What causes other types of hearing loss? The two most common types of hearing loss afflict some 278 million people worldwide (Tennesen, 2007). **Conductive hearing loss** occurs when the transfer of vibrations from the outer ear to the inner ear is weak. For example, the eardrums or ossicles may be damaged or immobilized by disease or injury. In many cases, conductive hearing loss can be overcome with a hearing aid, which makes sounds louder and clearer.

Sensorineural hearing loss results from damage to the inner ear hair cells or auditory nerve. Many jobs, hobbies, and pastimes can cause **noise-induced hearing loss**, a common form of sensorineural hearing loss that occurs when very loud sounds damage hair cells (as in hunter's notch). The hair cells, which are about as thin as a cobweb, are very fragile.

If you work in a noisy environment or enjoy loud music, motorcycling, snowmobiling, hunting, or similar pursuits, you may be risking noise-induced hearing loss. Dead hair cells are never replaced: When you abuse them, you lose them. By the time you are 65, more than 40 percent of them will be gone, mainly those that transduce high pitches (Chisolm, Willott, & Lister, 2003). This explains why younger students are beginning to download very high-pitched ring tones for their cell phones: If their teacher has an aging ear, the students can hear the ring tone but their teacher cannot. (Your authors may have experienced this effect without knowing it!)

How loud must a sound be to be hazardous? Daily exposure to 85 decibels or more may cause permanent hearing loss (Mather, 2008). *Decibels* are a measure of sound intensity. Every 20 decibels increases the sound pressure by a factor of 10. In other words, a rock concert at 120 decibels is 1,000 times stronger than a voice at 60 decibels. Even short periods at 120 decibels can cause temporary hearing loss. Brief exposure to 150 decibels (a jet airplane nearby) may cause permanent hearing loss. You might find it interesting to check the decibel ratings of some of your activities in ● Figure 4.18. Be aware that amplified music concerts, iPod-style earbuds, and car stereos can also damage your hearing.

Artificial Hearing

Hearing aids are of no help in cases of sensorineural hearing loss because auditory messages are blocked from reaching the brain. In many cases, however, the auditory nerve is actually intact. This finding has spurred the development of cochlear implants that bypass hair cells and stimulate the auditory nerves directly (● Figure 4.19). Wires from a microphone carry electrical signals to an external coil. A matching coil under the skin picks up the signals and carries them to one or more areas of the cochlea. The latest implants make use of

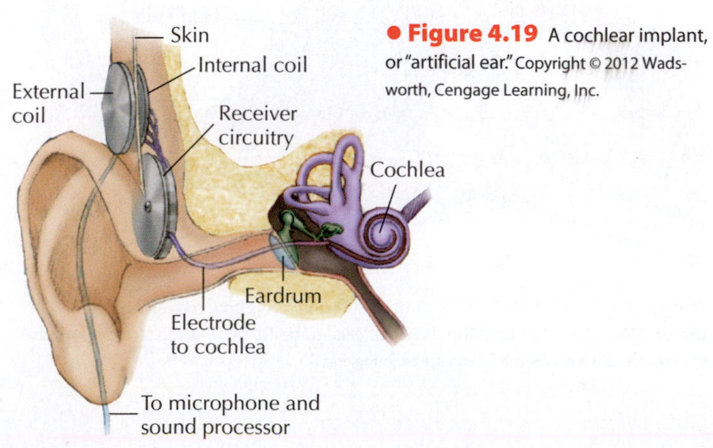

● **Figure 4.19** A cochlear implant, or "artificial ear."

● **Figure 4.20** Receptors for the sense of smell (olfaction). *(a)* Olfactory nerve fibers respond to gaseous molecules. Receptor cells are shown in cross section to the left. *(b)* Olfactory receptors are located in the upper nasal cavity. *(c)* On the right, an extreme close-up of an olfactory receptor shows fibers that sense gaseous molecules of various shapes.

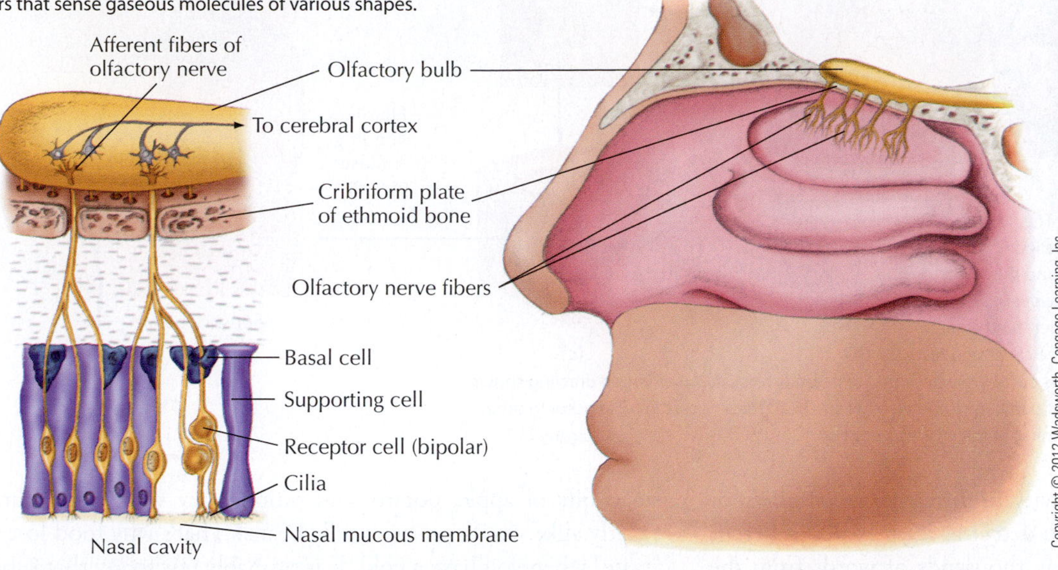

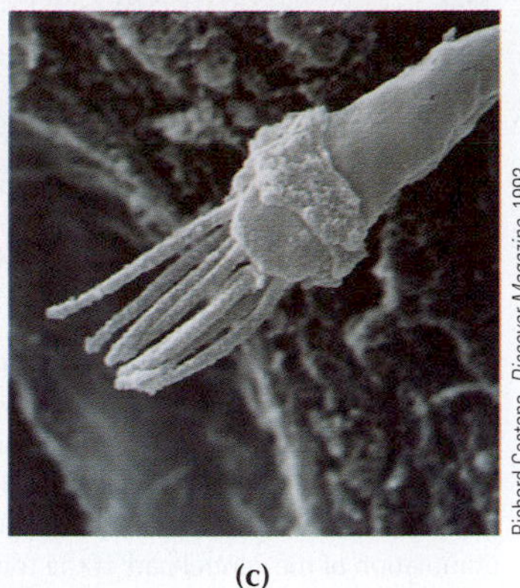

place theory to separate higher and lower tones into separate channels. This has allowed some formerly deaf persons to hear human voices, music, and other higher frequency sounds. About 60 percent of all multichannel implant patients can understand some spoken words and appreciate music (Leal et al., 2003; Foley & Matlin, 2010). Some deaf children with implants learn to speak. Those who receive a cochlear implant before age 2 learn spoken language at a near normal rate (Dorman & Wilson, 2004).

At present, artificial hearing remains crude. All but the most successful cochlear implant patients describe the sound as "like a radio that isn't quite tuned in." In fact, 30 percent of all adults who have tried implants have given up on them. But cochlear implants are improving. And even now, it is hard to argue with enthusiasts like Kristen Cloud. Shortly after Kristen received an implant, she was able to hear a siren and avoid being struck by a speeding car. She says simply, "The implant saved my life."

Smell and Taste—The Nose Knows When the Tongue Can't Tell

Gateway Question 4.4: *How do the chemical senses operate?*

Unless you are a wine taster, a perfume blender, a chef (Ramsay?), or a gourmet, you may think of **olfaction**, or smell, and **gustation**, or taste, as minor senses. Certainly you could probably survive without these *chemical senses* (receptors that respond to chemical molecules). But don't be deceived, life without these senses can be difficult (Drummond, Douglas, & Olver, 2007). One person, for instance, almost died because he couldn't smell the smoke when his apartment building caught fire. Besides, olfaction and gustation add pleasure to our lives. Let's see how they operate.

The Sense of Smell

Smell receptors respond to airborne molecules. As air enters the nose, it flows over roughly 5 million nerve fibers embedded in the lining of the upper nasal passages (● Figure 4.20). Receptor proteins on the surface of the fibers are sensitive to various airborne molecules. When a fiber is stimulated, it sends signals to the brain.

How are different odors produced? This is still an unfolding mystery. One hint comes from a type of *dysosmia* (dis-OZE-me-ah: defective smell), a sort of "smell blindness" for a single odor. Loss of sensitivity to specific types of odors suggests there are receptors for specific odors. Indeed, the molecules that produce a particular odor are quite similar in shape. Specific shapes produce the following types of odors: floral (flower-like), camphoric (camphor-like), musky (have you ever smelled a sweaty musk ox?), minty (mint-like), and etherish (like ether or cleaning fluid).

Does this mean that there are five different types of olfactory receptors? Actually, in humans, about 1,000 types of smell receptors are believed to exist (Bensafi et al., 2004). It appears that different-shaped "holes," or "pockets," exist on the surface of olfactory receptors. Like a piece fits in a puzzle, chemicals produce odors when part of a molecule matches a hole of the same shape. This is the **lock and key theory of olfaction.**

Conductive hearing loss Poor transfer of sounds from the eardrum to the inner ear.
Sensorineural hearing loss Loss of hearing caused by damage to the inner ear hair cells or auditory nerve.
Noise-induced hearing loss Damage caused by exposing the hair cells to excessively loud sounds.
Olfaction The sense of smell.
Gustation The sense of taste.
Lock and key theory of olfaction Holds that odors are related to the shapes of chemical molecules.

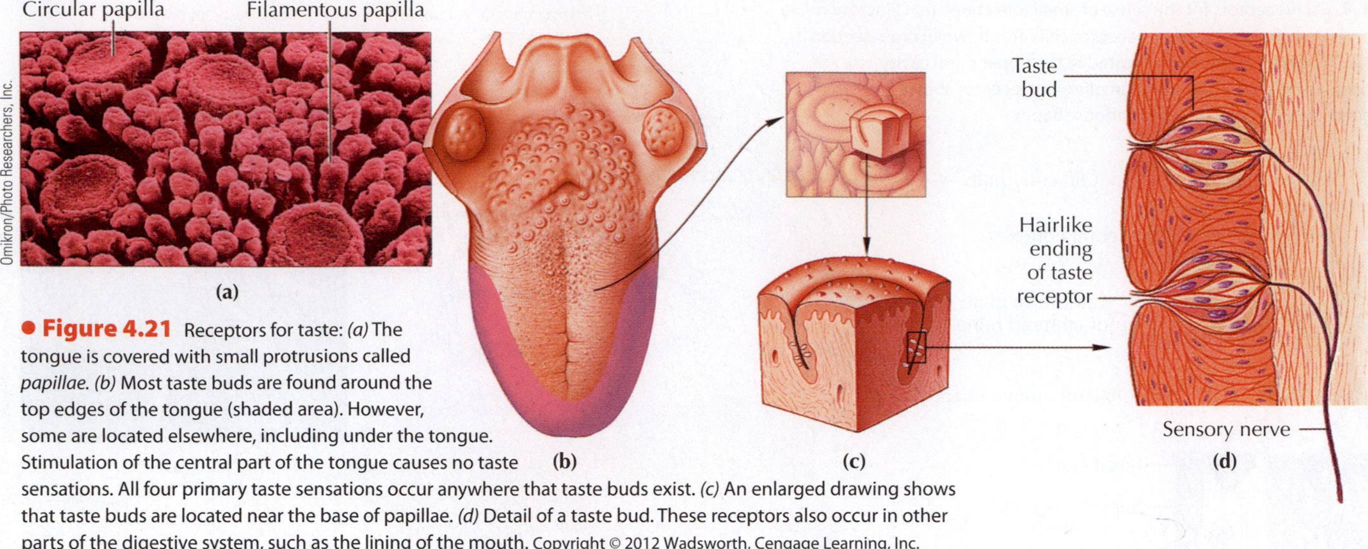

• Figure 4.21 Receptors for taste: *(a)* The tongue is covered with small protrusions called *papillae. (b)* Most taste buds are found around the top edges of the tongue (shaded area). However, some are located elsewhere, including under the tongue. Stimulation of the central part of the tongue causes no taste sensations. All four primary taste sensations occur anywhere that taste buds exist. *(c)* An enlarged drawing shows that taste buds are located near the base of papillae. *(d)* Detail of a taste bud. These receptors also occur in other parts of the digestive system, such as the lining of the mouth.

Further, molecules trigger activity in different *combinations* of odor receptors. Thus, humans can detect at least 10,000 different odors. Just as you can make many thousands of words from the 26 letters of the alphabet, many combinations of receptors are possible, resulting in many different odors. Scents are also identified, in part, by the *location* of the receptors in the nose that are activated by a particular odor. And finally, the *number of activated receptors* tells the brain how strong an odor is (Bensafi et al., 2004). The brain uses these distinctive patterns of messages it gets from the olfactory receptors to recognize particular scents (Laurent et al., 2001).

What causes dysosmia? Five people out of 100 experience some degree of dysosmia, including *anosmia*, the total loss of smell (Bramerson et al., 2004). Risks include infections, allergies, and blows to the head (which may tear the olfactory nerves). Exposure to chemicals such as ammonia, paints, solvents, and hairdressing potions can also cause dysosmia. If you value your sense of smell, be careful what you breathe (Drummond, Douglas, & Olver, 2007; Herz, 2001).

Taste and Flavors

There are at least four basic taste sensations: *sweet, salty, sour,* and *bitter.* We are most sensitive to bitter, less sensitive to sour, even less sensitive to salt, and least sensitive to sweet. This order may have helped prevent poisonings when most humans foraged for food, because bitter and sour foods are more likely to be inedible.

Most experts now believe that a fifth taste quality exists (Chandrashekar et al., 2006). The Japanese word *umami* (oo-MAH-me) describes a pleasant savory or "brothy" taste associated with certain amino acids in chicken soup, some meat extracts, kelp, tuna, human milk, cheese, and soybeans. The receptors for *umami* are sensitive to glutamate, a substance found in monosodium glutamate (MSG) (Sugimoto & Ninomiya, 2005).

If there are only four or five tastes, how can there be so many different flavors? Flavors seem more varied because we tend to include sensations of texture, temperature, smell, and even pain ("hot" chili peppers) along with taste. Smell is particularly important in determining flavor (Shepherd, 2006). If you plug your nose and eat small bits of apple, potato, and onion, they will "taste" almost exactly alike. So do gourmet jelly beans! That's why food loses its "taste" when you have a cold. It is probably fair to say that subjective flavor is half smell.

Interestingly, MSG's reputation as a "flavor enhancer" likely arises when the savory odors of, say, chicken soup, combine with the taste of glutamate (which does not taste very pleasant by itself) (McCabe & Rolls, 2007). At the very least, we may finally know why chicken soup is such a "comfort food." But remember to smell it first!

Taste buds, or taste-receptor cells, are located mainly on the top side of the tongue, especially around the edges. However, a few are found elsewhere inside the mouth (• Figure 4.21). As food is chewed, it dissolves and enters the taste buds, where it sets off nerve impulses to the brain (Northcutt, 2004). Much like smell, sweet and bitter tastes appear to be based on a lock-and-key match between molecules and intricately shaped receptors. Saltiness and sourness, however, are triggered by a direct flow of charged atoms into the tips of taste cells (Lindemann, 2001).

If smell and taste are seen as minor senses, then the somesthetic senses are the unnoticed senses. Let's turn our attention to the somesthetic senses and see why they merit our careful attention.

The Somesthetic Senses—Flying by the Seat of Your Pants

Gateway Question 4.5: *What are the somesthetic senses?*

A gymnast "flying" through a routine on the uneven bars may rely as much on the **somesthetic senses** as on vision (*soma* means "body," *esthetic* means "feel"). Even the most routine activities, such as walking, running, or passing a sobriety test, would be impossible without the **skin senses** (touch), the **kinesthetic senses** (receptors in muscles and joints that detect body position and movement), and the **vestibular senses** (receptors in the inner ear for balance, gravity, and acceleration). Because of their importance, let's begin with the skin senses (• Figure 4.22).

The Skin Senses

It's difficult to imagine what life would be like without the sense of touch, but the plight of Ian Waterman gives a hint. After an illness, Waterman permanently lost all feeling below his neck. Now, in order to know what position his body is in, he has to be able to see it. If he moves with his eyes closed, he has no idea where he is moving. If the lights go out in a room, he's in big trouble (Gallagher, 2004).

Skin receptors produce at least five different sensations: *light touch, pressure, pain, cold,* and *warmth.* Receptors with particular shapes appear to specialize somewhat in various sensations (see ● Figure 4.22). However, free nerve endings alone can produce all five sensations (Carlson, 2010). Altogether, the skin has about 200,000 nerve endings for temperature, 500,000 for touch and pressure, and 3 million for pain.

Does the number of receptors in an area of skin relate to its sensitivity? Yes. Your skin could be "mapped" by applying heat, cold, touch, pressure, or pain to points all over your body (Hollins, 2010). Such testing would show that the number of skin receptors varies, and that sensitivity generally matches the number of receptors in a given area. Broadly speaking, important areas such as the lips, tongue, face, hands, and genitals have a higher density of receptors. Of course, the sensation you ultimately feel will depend on brain activity.

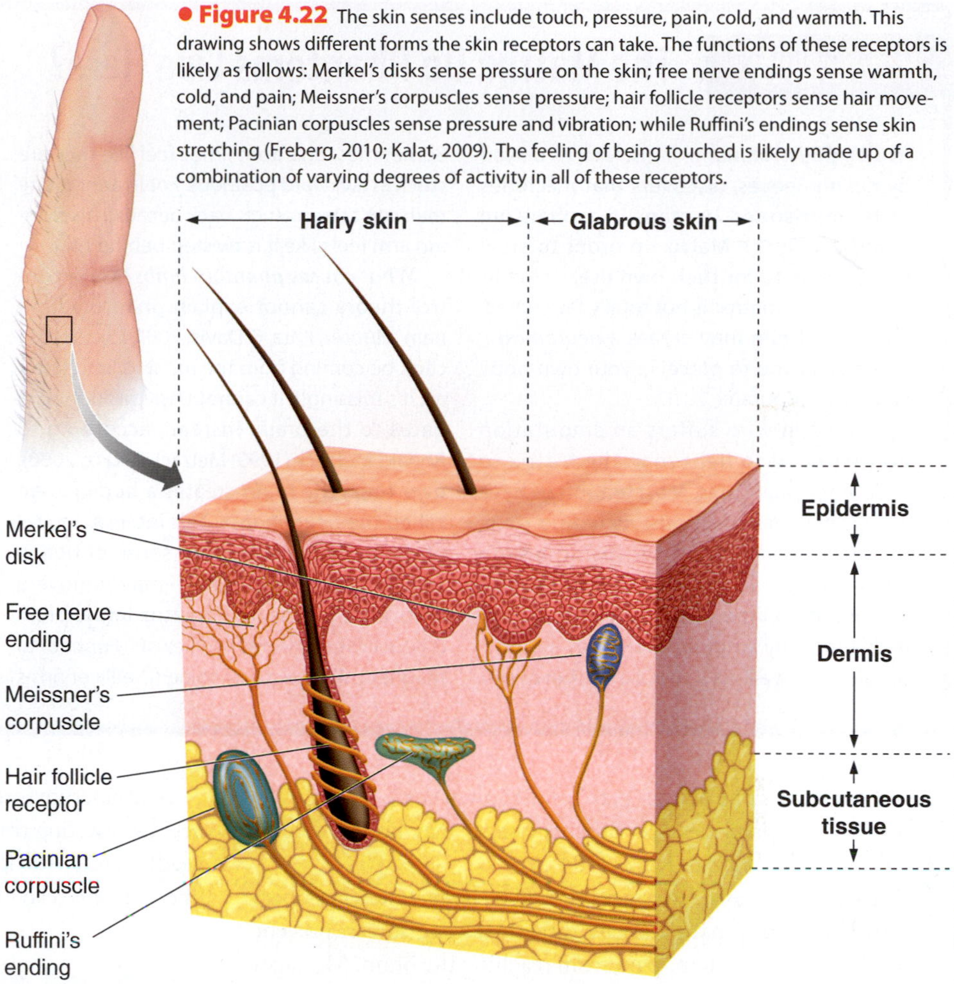

● Figure 4.22 The skin senses include touch, pressure, pain, cold, and warmth. This drawing shows different forms the skin receptors can take. The functions of these receptors is likely as follows: Merkel's disks sense pressure on the skin; free nerve endings sense warmth, cold, and pain; Meissner's corpuscles sense pressure; hair follicle receptors sense hair movement; Pacinian corpuscles sense pressure and vibration; while Ruffini's endings sense skin stretching (Freberg, 2010; Kalat, 2009). The feeling of being touched is likely made up of a combination of varying degrees of activity in all of these receptors.

Pain

The number of pain receptors also varies, right? Yes, like the other skin senses, pain receptors vary in their distribution. About 230 pain points per square centimeter (about a half inch) are found behind the knee, 180 per centimeter on the buttocks, 60 on the pad of the thumb, and 40 on the tip of the nose. (Is it better, then, to be pinched on the nose or behind the knee? It depends on what you like!)

Pain carried by *large nerve fibers* is sharp, bright, and fast, and seems to come from specific body areas (McMahon & Koltzenburg, 2005). This is the body's **warning system**. Give yourself a small jab with a pin and you will feel this type of pain. As you do this, notice that warning pain quickly disappears. Much as we may dislike warning pain, it is usually a signal that the body has been, or is about to be, damaged. Without warning pain, we would be unable to detect or prevent injury. Children who are born with a rare inherited insensitivity to pain repeatedly burn themselves, break bones, bite off parts of their tongues, and become ill without knowing it (Cox et al., 2006). As you might imagine, it's also hard for people with *congenital pain insensitivity* to have empathy for the pain of others (Danziger, Prkachin, & Willer, 2006).

A second type of somatic pain is carried by *small nerve fibers.* This type of pain is slower, nagging, aching, widespread, and very unpleasant (McMahon & Koltzenburg, 2005). It gets worse if the pain stimulus is repeated. This is the body's **reminding system**. It reminds the brain that the body has been injured. For instance, lower back pain often has this quality. Sadly, the reminding system can cause agony long after an injury has healed, or in terminal illnesses, when the reminder is useless.

The Pain Gate

You may have noticed that one type of pain will sometimes cancel another. Ronald Melzack and Patrick Wall's (1996) **gate control theory** suggests that pain messages from the different nerve fibers

Taste bud The receptor organ for taste.

Somesthetic senses Sensations produced by the skin, muscles, joints, viscera, and organs of balance.

Skin senses The senses of touch, pressure, pain, heat, and cold.

Kinesthetic senses The senses of body movement and positioning.

Vestibular senses The senses of balance, gravity, and acceleration.

Warning system Pain based on large nerve fibers; warns that bodily damage may be occurring.

Reminding system Pain based on small nerve fibers; reminds the brain that the body has been injured.

Gate control theory Proposes that pain messages pass through neural "gates" in the spinal cord.

Brainwaves — The Matrix: Do Phantoms Live Here?

In the popular *Matrix* films, Neo, as played by Keanu Reeves, discovers that machines have imprisoned humans in a phantom world called the Matrix, in order to steal human energy for their own use. Actually, the idea of a "matrix" is not totally farfetched. Your own brain may create a *neuromatrix* that allows you to perceive your own body (Iannetti & Mouraux, 2010).

A person who suffers an amputation doesn't need to believe in the Matrix to encounter phantoms. Most amputees have *phantom limb* sensations, including pain, for months or years after losing a limb (Fraser, 2002; Murray et al., 2007). Because the phantom limb feels so "real," a patient with a recently amputated leg may inadvertently try to walk on it, risking further injury. Sometimes, phantom limbs feel like they are stuck in awkward positions. For instance, one man can't sleep on his back because his missing arm feels like it is twisted behind him.

What causes phantom limbs? Gate control theory cannot explain phantom limb pain (Hunter, Katz, & Davis, 2003). Since pain can't be coming from the missing limb (after all, it's missing!), it cannot pass through pain gates to the brain. Instead, according to Ronald Melzack (1999; Melzack & Katz, 2006), over time, the brain creates a body image called the *neuromatrix*. This internal model of the body generates our sense of bodily self. Although amputation may remove a limb, as far as the neuromatrix in the brain is concerned, the limb still exists. Functional magnetic resonance imaging (fMRI) confirms that sensory and motor areas of the brain are more active when a person feels a phantom limb (Rosen et al., 2001). Even though pain signals no longer come from the amputated limb, the neuromatrix evidently interprets other sensory experiences as pain from the missing limb (Giummarra et al., 2007).

Sometimes the brain gradually reorganizes to adjust for the sensory loss (Wu & Kaas, 2002). For example, a person who loses an arm may at first have a phantom arm and hand. After many years, the phantom may shrink, until only a hand is felt at the shoulder. Perhaps more vividly than others, people with phantom limbs are reminded that the sensory world we experience is constructed, moment-by-moment, not by some futuristic machines, but by our own brain activity.

pass through the same neural "gate" in the spinal cord. If the gate is "closed" by one pain message, other messages may not be able to pass through (Melzack & Katz, 2004).

How is the gate closed? Messages carried by large, fast nerve fibers seem to close the spinal pain gate directly. Doing so can prevent slower, "reminding system" pain from reaching the brain. Messages from small, slow fibers seem to take a different route. After going through the pain gate, they pass on to a "central biasing system" in the brain. Under some circumstances, the brain then sends a message back down the spinal cord, closing the pain gates (● Figure 4.23). Melzack and Wall believe that gate control theory may also explain the painkilling effects of *acupuncture* (but see "The Matrix: Do Phantoms Live Here?").

● Figure 4.23 Diagram of a sensory gate for pain. A series of pain impulses going through the gate may prevent other pain messages from passing through. Or pain messages may relay through a "central biasing mechanism" that exerts control over the gate, closing it to other impulses.

Pain sensation
Central biasing mechanism
Spinal cord
Sensory gate
Small nerve fibers
Brainstem
Large nerve fibers

Acupuncture is the Chinese medical art of relieving pain and illness by inserting thin needles into the body. As the acupuncturist's needles are twirled, heated, or electrified, they activate small pain fibers. These relay through the biasing system to close the gates to

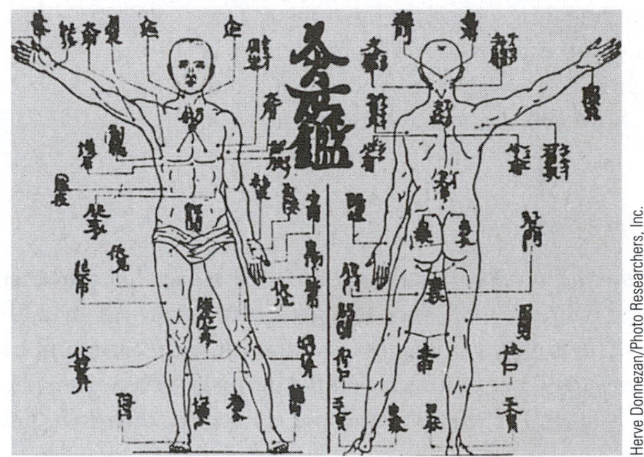

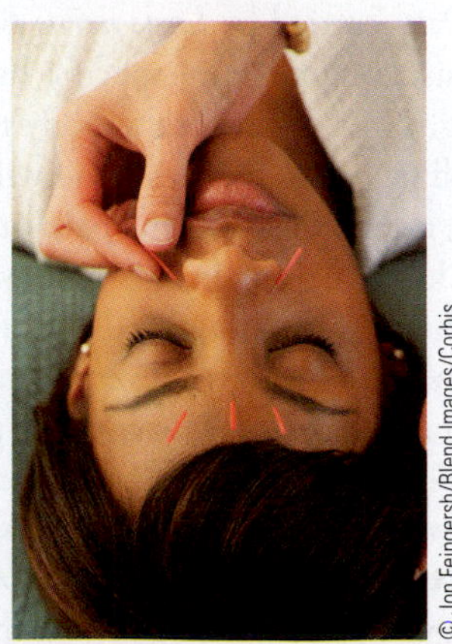

(Above) An acupuncturist's chart. *(Right)* Thin stainless steel needles are inserted into areas defined by the chart. Modern research has begun to explain the painkilling effects of acupuncture (see text). Acupuncture's claimed ability to cure diseases is more debatable.

intense or chronic pain (Melzack & Wall, 1996). Studies have shown that acupuncture produces short-term pain relief for 40 to 80 percent of patients tested (Ernst, 1994; Weidenhammer et al., 2007). (However, its ability to cure illness is much more debatable.)

Pain Control

Gate control theory helps explain *counterirritation*, one widely used pain control technique. Pain clinics use it by applying a mild electrical current to the skin. This causes only a mild tingling, but it can greatly reduce more agonizing pain (Köke et al., 2004). For more extreme pain, the electrical current can be applied directly to the spinal cord (Linderoth & Foreman, 2006).

You can use counterirritation to control your own pain (Schmelz, 2010). For instance, if you are having a tooth filled, try itching or pinching yourself, or digging a fingernail into a knuckle, while the dentist is working. Focus your attention on the pain you are creating, and increase it anytime the dentist's work becomes more painful. This strategy may seem strange, but it works. Generations of children have used it to take the edge off a spanking.

In some cultures, people endure tattooing, stretching, cutting, and burning with little apparent pain. How do they do it? Very likely the answer lies in a reliance on psychological factors that anyone can use to reduce pain, such as anxiety reduction, control, and attention (Mailis-Gagnon & Israelson, 2005).

In general, unpleasant emotions such as fear and anxiety increase pain; pleasant emotions decrease it (Rainville, 2004). Anytime you can anticipate pain (such as a trip to the doctor, dentist, or tattoo parlor), you can lower anxiety by making sure you are *fully informed*. Be sure everything that will happen is explained. In general, the more control you *feel* over a painful stimulus, the less pain is experienced (Vallerand, Saunders, & Anthony, 2007). To apply this principle, you might arrange a signal so your doctor, dentist, or body piercer will know when to start and stop a painful procedure. Finally, distraction also reduces pain. Instead of listening to the whirr of a dentist's drill, for example, you might imagine that you are lying in the sun at a beach, listening to the roar of the surf. Or take an iPod along and crank up your favorite MP3s (Bushnell, Villemure, & Duncan, 2004). At home, music can also be a good distractor from chronic pain (Mitchell et al., 2007).

The Vestibular System

Although space flight might look like fun, you are about 70 percent likely to throw up during your first experience in orbit.

But why? Weightlessness and space flight affect the vestibular system, often causing severe motion sickness. Within the vestibular system, fluid-filled sacs called *otolith* (OH-toe-lith) *organs* are sensitive to movement, acceleration, and gravity (● Figure 4.24). The otolith organs contain tiny crystals in a soft, gelatin-like mass. The tug of gravity or rapid head movements can cause the mass to shift. This, in turn, stimulates hair-like receptor cells, allowing us to sense gravity, acceleration, and movement through space (Lackner & DiZio, 2005).

Three fluid-filled tubes called the *semicircular canals* are the sensory organs for balance. If you could climb inside these tubes, you would find that head movements cause the fluid to swirl about. As the fluid moves, it bends a small "flap," or "float," called the *crista*, that detects movement in the semicircular canals. The bending of each crista again stimulates hair cells and signals head rotation.

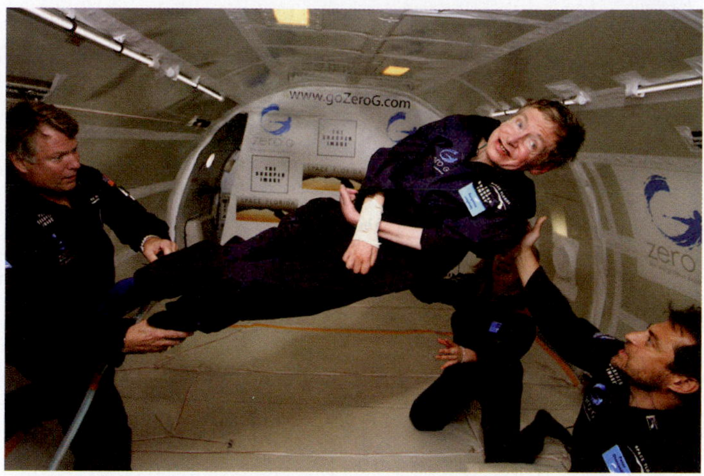

AP Photo/Zero Gravity Corp.

Weightlessness presents astronauts with a real challenge in sensory adaptation. In 2007, world-famous physicist Stephen Hawking, who suffers from amyotrophic lateral sclerosis (ALS, or Lou Gehrig's disease), fulfilled a lifelong dream of experiencing weightlessness. He took a flight on the "Weightless Wonder," NASA's official nickname for the high-flying airplane that provides short periods of weightlessness to train astronauts. (Unofficially it is called the "Vomit Comet.")

What causes motion sickness? According to **sensory conflict theory**, dizziness and nausea occur when sensations from the vestibular system don't match sensations from the eyes and body (Flanagan, May, & Dobie, 2004). On solid ground, information

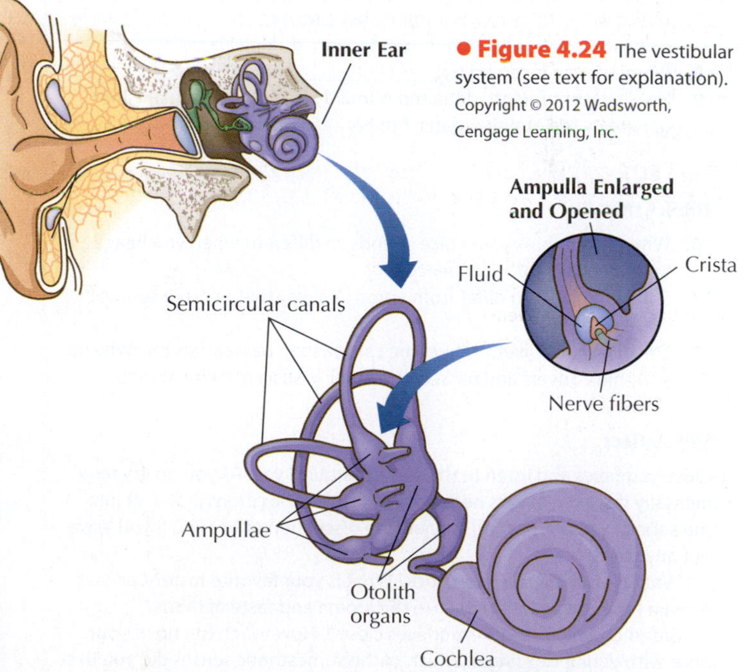

● Figure 4.24 The vestibular system (see text for explanation). Copyright © 2012 Wadsworth, Cengage Learning, Inc.

Sensory conflict theory Explains motion sickness as the result of a mismatch among information from vision, the vestibular system, and kinesthesis.

from the vestibular system, vision, and kinesthesis usually matches. However, in a heaving, pitching boat, car, or airplane, or even playing a videogame, a serious mismatch can occur—causing disorientation and heaving of another kind (Merhi et al., 2007; Stoffregen et al., 2008).

Why would sensory conflict cause nausea? You can probably blame (or thank) evolution. Many poisons disturb the vestibular system, vision, and the body. Therefore, we may have evolved so that we react to sensory conflict by vomiting to expel poison. The value of this reaction, however, may be of little comfort to anyone who has ever been "green" and miserable with motion sickness. To minimize such conflicts, try to keep your head still, fix your vision on a distant immobile object, and lie down if you can (Harm, 2002).

Knowledge Builder

Hearing, the Chemical Senses, and the Somesthetic Senses

RECITE

1. The frequency of a sound wave corresponds to how loud it is. T or F?
2. Which of the following is not a part of the cochlea?
   a. ossicles *b.* pinna *c.* tympanic membrane *d.* all of the above
3. Sensorineural hearing loss occurs when the auditory ossicles are damaged. T or F?
4. Daily exposure to sounds with a loudness of _______ decibels may cause permanent hearing loss.
5. Olfaction appears to be at least partially explained by the _______________ _______________ theory of molecule shapes and receptor sites.
6. The term *umami* refers to
   a. smell blindness *b.* temporary damage to the hair cells *c.* secondary olfaction *d.* a taste quality
7. Which of the following is a somesthetic sense?
   a. gustation *b.* olfaction *c.* rarefaction *d.* kinesthesis
8. Warning pain is carried by _______________ nerve fibers.
9. Head movements are detected primarily in the semicircular canals, gravity by the otolith organs. T or F?

REFLECT

Think Critically

10. Why do you think your voice sounds so different when you hear a tape recording of your speech?
11. Smell and hearing differ from vision in a way that may aid survival. What is it?
12. Drivers are less likely to become carsick than passengers are. Why do you think drivers and passengers differ in susceptibility to motion sickness?

Self-Reflect

Close your eyes and listen to the sounds around you. As you do, try to mentally trace the events necessary to convert vibrations in the air into the sounds you are hearing. Review the discussion of hearing if you leave out any steps.

What is your favorite food odor? What is your favorite taste? Can you explain how you are able to sense the aroma and taste of foods?

Stand on one foot with your eyes closed. Now touch the tip of your nose with your index finger. Which of the somesthetic senses did you use to perform this feat?

Can you think of any ways in which you have used counterirritation to lessen pain?

Imagine you are on a boat ride with a friend who starts to feel queasy. Can you explain to your friend what causes motion sickness and what she or he can do to prevent it?

Answers: 1. F **2.** *d* **3.** F **4.** 85 **5.** lock and key **6.** *d* **7.** *d* **8.** large **9.** T **10.** The answer lies in another question: How else might vibrations from the voice reach the cochlea? Other people hear your voice only as it is carried through the air. You hear not only that sound, but also vibrations conducted by the bones of your skull. **11.** Both smell and hearing can detect stimuli (including signals of approaching danger) around corners, behind objects, and behind the head. **12.** Drivers experience less sensory conflict because they control the car's motion. This allows them to anticipate the car's movements and to coordinate their head and eye movements with those of the car.

Perception—The Second Step

Gateway Question 4.6: *In general, how do we construct our perceptions?*

While driving at night, a woman slams on her brakes to avoid hitting a deer. As she skids to a stop, she realizes that the "deer" is actually a bush on the roadside. Such misperceptions are common. The brain must continuously find patterns in a welter of sensations. How do we organize sensations into meaningful perceptions? Our brain creates our perceptions by using preexisting knowledge such as the principles of perceptual grouping and perceptual constancies to help us make sense out of sensations.

Are you born able to create perceptions out of sensations? Imagine what it would be like to have your vision restored after a lifetime of blindness. Actually, a first look at the world can be disappointing because the newfound ability to *sense* the world does not guarantee that it can be *perceived*. Newly sighted persons must *learn* to identify objects, to read clocks, numbers, and letters, and to judge sizes and distances (Gregory, 2003). For instance, Mr. S. B. was a cata-

Visual perception involves finding meaningful patterns in complex stimuli. If you look closely at this photomosaic by Robert Silver, you may see that it is entirely made up of small individual photos. An infant or newly sighted person might well see only a jumble of meaningless colors. But because the photos form a familiar pattern, you should easily see the American flag.

● **Figure 4.25** It is difficult to look at this simple drawing without perceiving depth. Yet the drawing is nothing more than a collection of flat shapes. Turn this page counterclockwise 90 degrees and you will see 3 Cs, one within another. When the drawing is turned sideways, it seems nearly flat. However, if you turn the page upright again, a sense of depth will reappear. Clearly, you have used your knowledge and expectations to *construct* an illusion of depth. The drawing itself would only be a flat design if you didn't invest it with meaning.

ract patient who had been blind since birth. After an operation restored his sight at age 52, Mr. S. B. struggled to use his vision.

Mr. S. B. soon learned to tell time from a large clock and to read block letters he had known only from touch. At a zoo, he recognized an elephant from descriptions he had heard. However, handwriting meant nothing to him for more than a year after he regained sight, and many objects were meaningless until he touched them. Thus, Mr. S. B. slowly learned to organize his *sensations* into meaningful *perceptions.* Cases like those of Mr. S. B. show that your experiences are **perceptual constructions**, or mental models of external events, that *are actively created by your brain.*

Of course, perceptions can be misconstructed as they are filtered through our needs, expectations, attitudes, values, and beliefs (● Figure 4.25). One of your authors was once approached in a supermarket by a young girl screaming, "Help! Someone is killing my father!" He followed her to see two men struggling. The guy on top had his victim by the throat. There was blood everywhere. It was a murder in progress! Soon, however, it turned out that the "guy on the bottom" had passed out, hit his head, and was bleeding. The "guy on top" saw the first man fall and was loosening his collar.

Obviously, the girl had misperceived what was happening to her father. Because of the dramatic influence of her words, so did your author. As this story shows, sensory information can be interpreted in various ways. The girl's description completely shaped his own initial perceptions. This perhaps is understandable. But he'll never forget the added shock he felt when he met the "murderer." The man he had seen a few moments before as vicious and horrible-looking was not even a stranger. He was a neighbor whom your author had seen dozens of times before. Clearly, we don't just believe what we see. We also see what we believe.

Illusions

Perceptual *mis*construction is responsible for many illusions. In an **illusion**, length, position, motion, curvature, or direction is consistently misjudged. For example, because we have seen thousands of rooms shaped roughly like a box, we habitually construct perceptions based on this assumption. This need not be true, however. An *Ames room* (named for the man who designed it) is a lopsided space that appears square when viewed from a certain angle (● Figure 4.26). This illusion is achieved by carefully distorting the proportions of the walls, floor, ceiling, and windows. Because the left corner of the Ames room is farther from a viewer than the right, a person standing in that corner looks very small; one standing in the nearer, shorter right corner looks very large. A person who walks from the left to the right corner will seem to "magically" grow larger.

Notice that illusions are distorted perceptions of stimuli that actually exist. In a **hallucination**, people perceive objects or events that have no external reality (Boksa, 2009). For example, they hear voices that are not there (see "Staying in Touch with Reality"). If you think you are experiencing an illusion or a hallucination, try engaging in some reality testing.

What do you mean by reality testing? In any situation having an element of doubt or uncertainty, **reality testing** involves obtaining

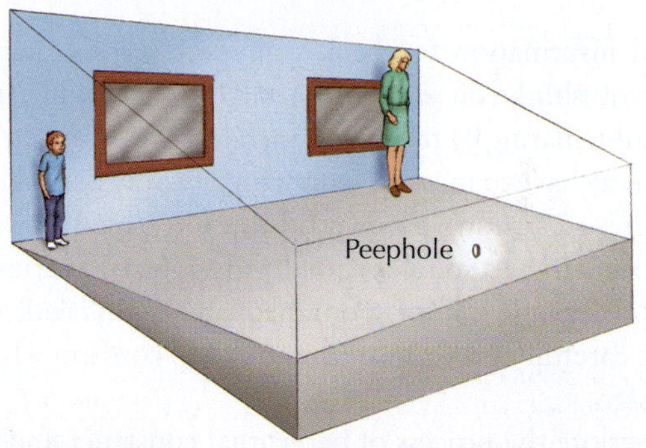

● **Figure 4.26** The Ames room. From the front, the room looks normal; actually, the right-hand corner is very short, and the left-hand corner is very tall. In addition, the left side of the room slants away from viewers. The diagram shows the shape of the room and reveals why people appear to get bigger as they cross the room toward the nearer, shorter right corner.

Perceptual construction A mental model of external events.
Illusion A misleading or misconstructed perception.
Hallucination An imaginary sensation—such as seeing, hearing, or smelling something that does not exist in the external world.
Reality testing Obtaining additional information to check on the accuracy of perceptions.

The Clinical File Staying in Touch with Reality

Just imagine that often, and without warning, you hear a voice shouting, "Buckets of blood!" or see blood spattering across the walls of your bedroom. Chances are people would think you are mentally disturbed. Hallucinations are a major symptom of psychosis, dementia, epilepsy, migraine headaches, alcohol withdrawal, and drug intoxication (Spence & David, 2004). They are also one of the clearest signs that a person has "lost touch with reality."

Yet consider the case of mathematician John Nash (the subject of *A Beautiful Mind,* the winner of the 2002 Oscar for best film). Even though Nash suffered from schizophrenia, he eventually learned to use his *reality testing* to sort out which of his experiences were perceptions and which were hallucinations. Unlike John Nash, most people who experience full-blown hallucinations have a limited ability to engage in reality testing (Hohwy & Rosenberg, 2005).

Curiously, "sane hallucinations" also occur. *Charles Bonnet syndrome* is a rare condition that afflicts mainly older people who are partially blind, but not mentally disturbed (Cammaroto et al., 2008). Animals, buildings, plants, people, and other objects may seem to appear and disappear in front of their eyes. One older man suffering from partial blindness and leukemia complained of seeing animals in his house, including cattle and bears (Jacob et al., 2004). However, people experiencing "sane hallucinations" can more easily tell that their hallucinations aren't real because their capacity for reality testing is not impaired.

Such unusual experiences show how powerfully the brain seeks meaningful patterns in sensory input and the role that reality testing plays in our normal perceptual experience.

additional information to check your perceptions (Landa et al., 2006). If you think you see a 3-foot-tall butterfly, you can confirm you are hallucinating by trying to touch its wings. To detect an illusion, you may have to measure a drawing or apply a straight-edge to it. ● Figure 4.27 shows a powerful illusion called Fraser's spiral. What appears to be a spiral is actually made up of a series of closed circles. Most people cannot spontaneously see this reality. Instead, they must carefully trace one of the circles to confirm what is "real" in the design.

Let's explore the process of perceptual construct and some factors that shape or even distort it.

Courtesy of Dr. Akiyoshi Kitaoka, Department of Psychology, Ritsumeikan University

● **Figure 4.27** The limits of pure perception. Even simple designs are easily misperceived. Fraser's spiral is actually a series of concentric circles. The illusion is so powerful that people who try to trace one of the circles sometimes follow the illusory spiral and jump from one circle to the next. (After Seckel, 2000.)

Bottom-Up and Top-Down Processing

Moment by moment, our perceptions are typically constructed in both *bottom-up* and *top-down* fashion. Think about the process of building a house: Raw materials, such as lumber, doors, tiles, carpets, screws, and nails, must be painstakingly fit together. At the same time, a building plan guides how the raw materials are assembled.

Our brain builds perceptions in similar ways. In **bottom-up processing**, we start constructing at the "bottom," with raw materials. That is, we begin with small sensory units (features), and build upward to a complete perception. The reverse also occurs. In **top-down processing**, preexisting knowledge is used to rapidly organize features into a meaningful whole (Goldstein, 2010). If you put together a picture puzzle you've never seen before, you are relying mainly on bottom-up processing: You must assemble small pieces until a recognizable pattern begins to emerge. Top-down processing is like putting together a puzzle you have solved many times: After only a few pieces are in place, your past experience gives you the plan to rapidly fill in the final picture.

Both types of processing are illustrated by ● Figure 4.28. Also, look ahead to ● Figure 4.31. The first time you see this photo, you will probably process it bottom-up, picking out features until it becomes recognizable. The next time you see it, because of top-down processing, you should recognize it instantly.

An excellent example of perceptual construction is found in the Gestalt organizing principles.

Gestalt Organizing Principles

How are sensations organized into perceptions? The Gestalt psychologists proposed that the simplest organization involves grouping some sensations into an object, or figure, that stands out on a plainer background. **Figure-ground organization** is probably inborn, because it is the first perceptual ability to appear after cataract patients like Mr. S. B. regain sight. In normal figure-ground perception, only one figure is seen. In *reversible figures*, however,

• **Figure 4.28** Check out this abstract design. If you process it "bottom-up," all you will likely see is three small dark geometric shapes near the edges. Would you like to try some top-down processing? Knowing the title of the design will allow you to apply your knowledge and see it in an entirely different way. The title? It's *Special K*. Can you see it now? Copyright © 2012 Wadsworth, Cengage Learning, Inc.

figure and ground can be switched. In • Figure 4.29, it is equally possible to see either a wineglass on a dark background or two facial profiles on a light background. As you shift from one pattern to the other, you should get a clear sense of what figure-ground organization means.

• **Figure 4.29** A reversible figure-ground design. Do you see two faces in profile, or a wineglass? Copyright © 2012 Wadsworth, Cengage Learning, Inc.

BRIDGES

See Chapter 1, pages 25–26, for a brief history of Gestalt psychology.

Are there other Gestalt organizing principles? The Gestalt psychologists identified several other principles that bring some order to your perceptions (• Figure 4.30).

1. **Nearness.** All other things equal, stimuli that are near each other tend to be grouped together (Quinn, Bhatt, & Hayden, 2008). Thus, if three people stand near each other and a fourth person stands 10 feet away, the adjacent three will be seen as a group and the distant person as an outsider (see • Figure 4.30*a*).
2. **Similarity.** "Birds of a feather flock together," and stimuli that are similar in size, shape, color, or form tend to be grouped together (see • Figure 4.30*b*). Picture two bands marching side by side. If their uniforms are different colors, the bands will be seen as two separate groups, not as one large group.
3. **Continuation, or continuity.** Perceptions tend toward simplicity and continuity. In • Figure 4.30*c*, it is easier to visualize a wavy line on a squared-off line than it is to see a complex row of shapes.
4. **Closure.** Closure refers to the tendency to *complete* a figure, so that it has a consistent overall form. Each of the drawings in • Figure 4.30*d* has one or more gaps, yet each is perceived as a recognizable figure. The "shapes" that appear in the two right drawings in • Figure 4.30*d* are *illusory figures* (implied shapes that are not actually bounded by an edge or an outline). Even young children see these shapes, despite knowing that they are "not really there." Illusory figures reveal that our tendency to form shapes—even with minimal cues—is powerful.
5. **Contiguity.** A principle that can't be shown in • Figure 4.30 is contiguity, or nearness in time *and* space. Contiguity is often responsible for the perception that one thing has *caused* another (Buehner & May, 2003). A psychologist friend of ours demonstrates this principle in class by knocking on his head with one hand while knocking on a wooden table (out of sight) with the other. The knocking sound is perfectly timed with the movements of his visible hand. This leads to the irresistible perception that his head is made of wood.
6. **Common region.** As you can see in • Figure 4.30*e*, stimuli that are found within a common area tend to be seen as a group (Palmer & Beck, 2007). On the basis of similarity and nearness, the stars in • Figure 4.30*e* should be one group and the dots another. However, the colored backgrounds define

Bottom-up processing Organizing perceptions by beginning with low-level features.

Top-down processing Applying higher-level knowledge to rapidly organize sensory information into a meaningful perception.

Figure-ground organization Organizing a perception so that part of a stimulus appears to stand out as an object (figure) against a less prominent background (ground).

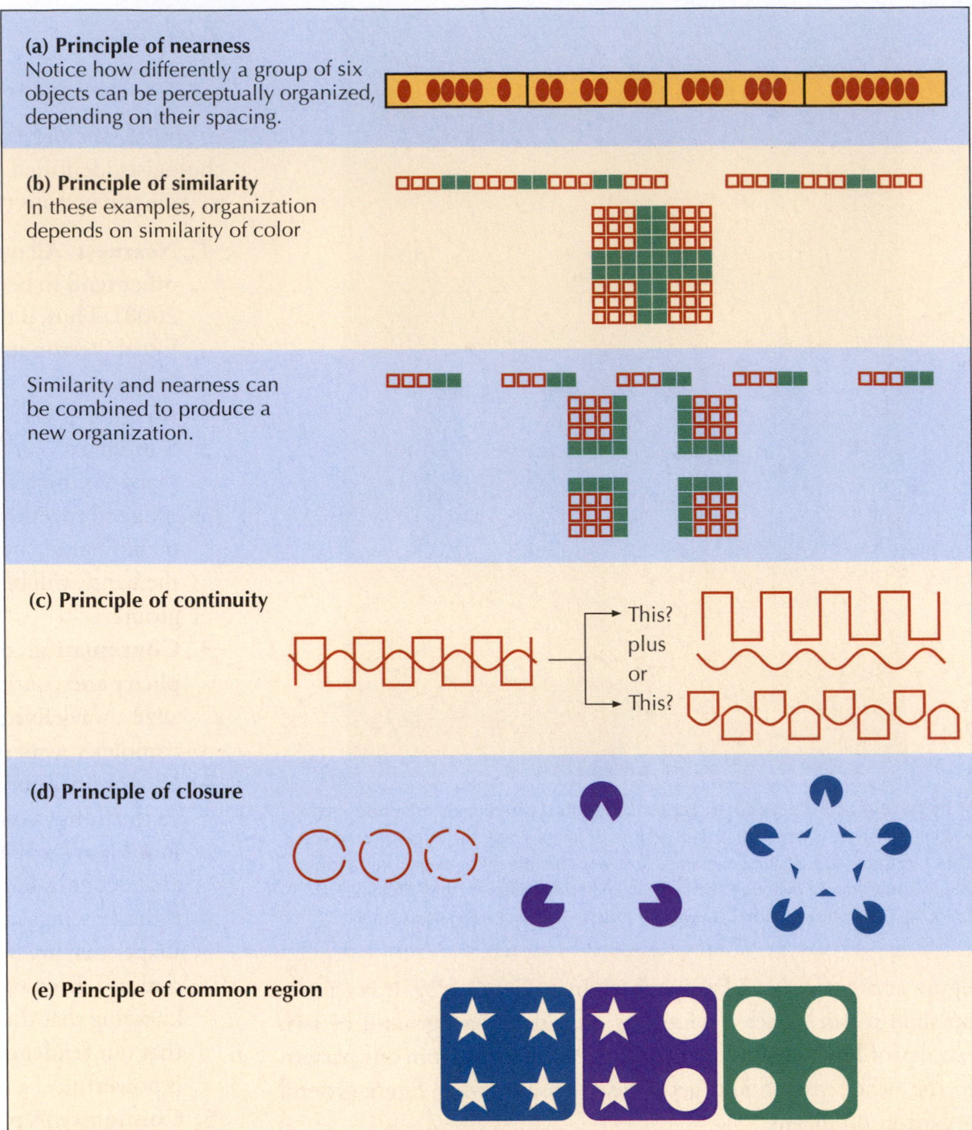

• **Figure 4.30** Some Gestalt organizing principles.

regions that create three groups of objects (four stars, two stars plus two dots, and four dots). Perhaps the principle of common region explains why we tend to mentally group together people from a particular country, state, province, or geographic region.

Clearly, the Gestalt principles offer us some basic "plans" for organizing parts of our day-to-day perceptions in top-down fashion. Take a moment and look for the camouflaged animal pictured in • Figure 4.31 (camouflage patterns break up figure-ground organization). Have you already seen this photo? If you had never seen similar animals before, could you have located this one? Mr. S. B. would have been at a total loss to find meaning in such a picture.

In a way, we are all detectives, seeking patterns in what we see. In this sense, a meaningful pattern represents a **perceptual hypothesis**, or initial plan or guess about how to organize sensations. Have you ever seen a "friend" in the distance, only to have the person turn into a stranger as you drew closer? Preexisting ideas and expectations *actively* guide our interpretation of sensations (Most et al., 2005).

The active, constructive nature of perception is perhaps most apparent for *ambiguous stimuli* (patterns allowing more than one interpretation). If you look at a cloud, you may discover dozens of ways to organize its contours into fanciful shapes and scenes. Even clearly defined stimuli may permit more than one interpretation. Look at the Necker cube in • Figure 4.32 if you doubt that perception is an active process. Visualize the top cube as a wire box. If you stare at the cube, its organization will change. Sometimes it will seem to project upward, like the lower left cube; other times it will project downward. The difference lies in how your brain interprets the same information. In short, we actively *construct* meaningful perceptions; we do not passively record the events and stimuli around us (Rolls, 2008).

• **Figure 4.31** A challenging example of perceptual organization. Once the camouflaged insect (known as a giant walkingstick) becomes visible, it is almost impossible to view the picture again without seeing the insect.

E. R. Degginger/Animals Animals

In some instances, a stimulus may offer such conflicting information that perceptual organization becomes impossible. For example, the tendency to make a three-dimensional object out of a drawing is frustrated by the "three-pronged widget" (• Figure 4.33), an *impossible figure*. Such patterns cannot be organized into stable, consistent, or meaningful perceptions. If you cover either end of the drawing in • Figure 4.33, it makes sense perceptually. However, a problem arises when you try to organize the entire drawing. Then, the conflicting information it contains prevents you from constructing a stable perception.

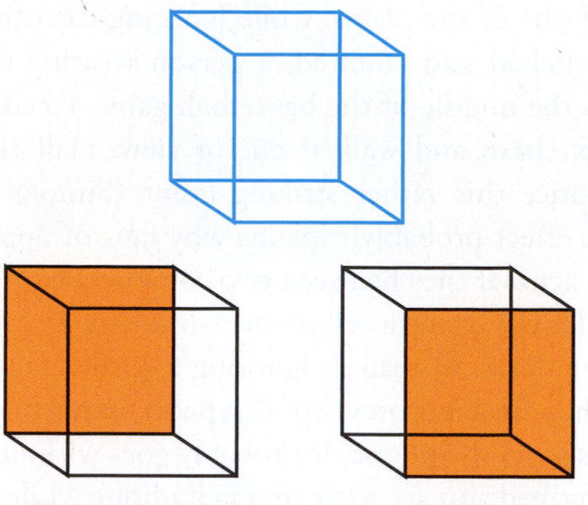

● **Figure 4.32** Necker cube. Copyright © 2012 Wadsworth, Cengage Learning, Inc.

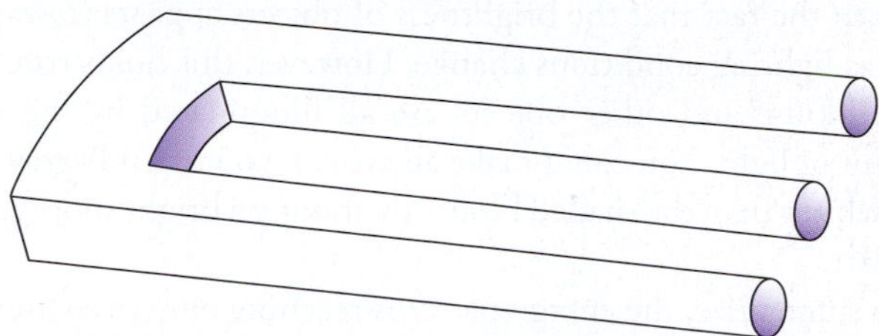

● **Figure 4.33** An impossible figure—the "three-pronged widget." Copyright © Cengage Learning 2013

Learning to organize his visual sensations was only one of the hurdles Mr. S. B. faced in learning to see. In the next section, we will consider some others.

Perceptual Constancies

When Mr. S. B. first regained his vision, he could judge distance in only familiar situations (Gregory, 1990). One day he was found crawling out of a hospital window to get a closer look at traffic on the street. It's easy to understand his curiosity, but he had to be restrained. His room was on the fourth floor!

Why would Mr. S. B. try to crawl out of a fourth-story window? Couldn't he at least tell distance from the size of the cars? No, you must be visually familiar with objects to use their size to judge distance. Try holding your left hand a few inches in front of your nose and your right hand at arm's length. Your right hand should appear to be about half the size of your left hand. Still, you know your right hand did not suddenly shrink, because you have seen it many times at various distances. We call this **size constancy**: The perceived size of an object remains the same, even though the size of its image on the retina changes.

To perceive your hand accurately, you had to draw on past experience to provide a top-down plan for constructing your perception. Some of these plans are so basic they seem to be *native* (inborn). An example is the ability to see a line on a piece of paper. Likewise, even newborn babies show some evidence of size constancy (Granrud, 2006; Slater, Mattock, & Brown, 1990). However, many of our perceptions are *empirical*, or based on prior experience. For instance, cars, houses, and people look like toys when seen from a great distance or from an unfamiliar perspective, such as from the top of a skyscraper. This suggests that although some size constancy is innate, it is also affected by learning (Granrud, 2004).

In **shape constancy** the shape of an object remains stable, even though the shape of its retinal image changes. You can demonstrate shape constancy by looking at this page from directly overhead and then from an angle. Obviously, the page is rectangular, but most of the images that reach your eyes are distorted. Yet, though the book's image changes, your perception of its shape remains constant (for additional examples, see ● Figure 4.34). On the highway, alcohol intoxication impairs size and shape constancy, adding to the accident rate among drunk drivers (Goldstein, 2010).

Let's say that you are outside in bright sunlight. Beside you, a friend is wearing a gray skirt

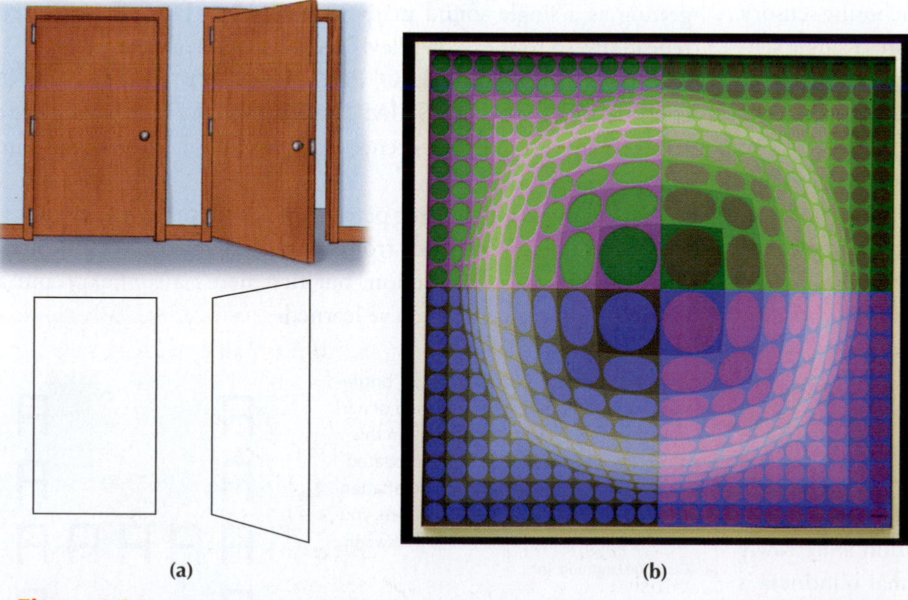

● **Figure 4.34** Shape constancy. *(a)* When a door is open, its image actually forms a trapezoid. Shape constancy is indicated by the fact that it is still perceived as a rectangle. *(b)* With great effort you may be able to see this design as a collection of flat shapes. However, if you maintain shape constancy, the distorted pentagrams strongly suggest the surface of a sphere. (Paz-Ket [oil on canvas], Vasarely, Victor [1908–1997]/Museo de Bellas Artes, Bilbao, Spain/ © DACS/The Bridgeman Art Library International.)

Perceptual hypothesis An initial guess regarding how to organize (perceive) a stimulus pattern.

Size constancy The perceived size of an object remains constant, despite changes in its retinal image.

Shape constancy The perceived shape of an object is unaffected by changes in its retinal image.

and a white blouse. Suddenly a cloud shades the sun. It might seem that the blouse would grow dimmer, but it still appears to be bright white. This happens because the blouse continues to reflect a larger *proportion* of light than nearby objects. **Brightness constancy** refers to the fact that the brightness of objects appears to stay the same as lighting conditions change. However, this holds true only if the blouse and other objects are all illuminated by the same amount of light. You could make an area on your friend's gray skirt look whiter than the shaded blouse by shining a bright spotlight on the skirt.

To summarize, the energy patterns reaching our senses are constantly changing, even when they come from the same object. Size, shape, and brightness constancy rescue us from a confusing world in which objects would seem to shrink and grow, change shape as if made of rubber, and light up or fade like neon lamps.

Selective Attention—Tuning In and Tuning Out

Gateway Question 4.7: *Why are we more aware of some sensations than others?*

Although the senses reduce a mixture of sights, sounds, odors, tastes, and touch sensations to more manageable amounts, they are still too much for the brain to handle. That's why sensory information must also be filtered by *selective attention*. For example, as you sit reading this page, receptors for touch and pressure in the seat of your pants are sending nerve impulses to your brain. Although these sensations have been present all along, you were probably not aware of them until just now. This "seat-of-the-pants phenomenon" is an example of **selective attention**—voluntarily focusing on a specific sensory input. Selective attention appears to be based on the ability of brain structures to select and divert incoming sensory messages (Mather, 2008). We are able to "tune in on" a single sensory message while excluding others.

Another familiar example of this is the "cocktail party effect." When you are in a group of people, surrounded by voices, you can still select and attend to the voice of the person you are facing. Or if that person gets dull, you can eavesdrop on conversations all over the room. (Be sure to smile and nod your head occasionally!) Actually, no matter how interesting your companion may be, your attention will probably shift away if you hear your own name spoken somewhere in the room (Conway, Cowan, & Bunting, 2001). We do find what others say about us to be very interesting, don't we?

At times, we can even suffer from **inattentional blindness**, a failure to notice a stimulus because attention is focused elsewhere (Most et al., 2005). Not seeing something that is plainly before your eyes is most likely to occur when your attention is narrowly focused (Bressan & Pizzighello, 2008). Inattentional blindness is vividly illustrated by a study in which participants were shown a film of two basketball teams, one wearing black shirts and the other wearing white. Observers were asked to watch the film closely and count how many times a basketball passed between members of one of the teams, while ignoring the other team. As observers watched and counted, a person wearing a gorilla suit walked into the middle of the basketball game, faced the camera, thumped its chest, and walked out of view. Half the observers failed to notice this rather striking event (Simons & Chabris, 1999). This effect probably explains why fans of opposing sports teams often act as if they had seen two completely different games.

In a similar way, using a cell phone while driving can cause inattentional blindness. Instead of ignoring a gorilla, you might miss seeing another car, a motorcyclist, or a pedestrian while your attention is focused on the phone. It probably goes without saying, but the more engaged you are with your cell phone while driving (say, texting instead of just having a conversation), the greater the problem (Fougnie & Marois, 2007).

You might find it helpful to think of selective attention as a *bottleneck*, or narrowing in the information channel linking the senses to perception. When one message enters the bottleneck, it seems to prevent others from passing through (see ● Figure 4.35). Imagine, for instance, that you are driving a car and approaching an intersection. You need to be sure the traffic light is still green. Just as you are about to check it, your passenger points to a friend at the side of the road. If you then fail to notice the light just changed to red, an accident may be seconds away.

Are some stimuli more attention getting than others? Yes. Very *intense* stimuli usually command attention. Stimuli that are brighter, louder, or larger tend to capture attention: A gunshot in a library would be hard to ignore. If a brightly colored hot-air balloon ever lands at your college campus, it will almost certainly draw a crowd.

Repetitious stimuli, repetitious stimuli, repetitious stimuli, repetitious stimuli, repetitious stimuli, repetitious stimuli are also attention getting. A dripping faucet at night makes little noise by normal standards, but because of repetition, it may become as attention getting as a single sound many times louder. This effect is used repeatedly, so to speak, in television and radio commercials.

ATTENTION IS ALSO **FREQUENTLY** RELATED TO contrast OR *change* IN STIMULATION. The contrasting type styles in the preceding sentence draw attention because they are *unexpected*.

One of the most amazing perceptual feats is our capacity to create three-dimensional space from flat retinal images. We'll explore that topic in the next section, but first here's a summary and a chance to rehearse what you've learned.

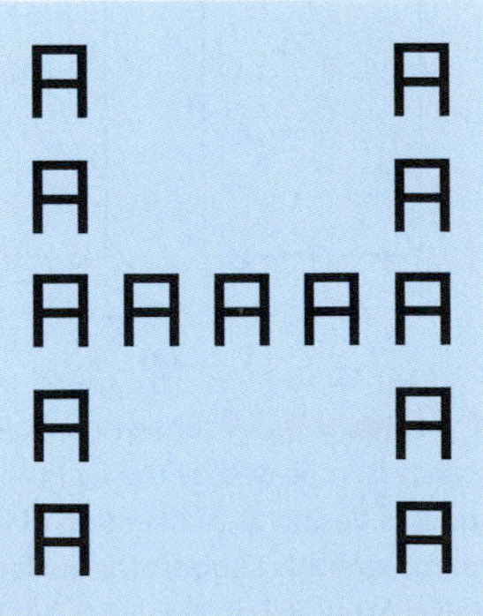

● **Figure 4.35** The attentional "bottleneck," or "spotlight," can be widened or narrowed. If you focus on local details in this drawing you will see the letter *A* repeated 13 times. If you broaden your field of attention to encompass the overall pattern, you see the letter *H*. Copyright © 2012 Wadsworth, Cengage Learning, Inc.

Knowledge Builder

Perceptual Processes and Attention

RECITE

1. In top-down processing of information, individual features are analyzed and assembled into a meaningful whole. T or F?
2. The first and most basic perceptual organization to emerge when sight is restored to a blind person is
   a. continuity *b.* nearness constancy *c.* recognition of numbers and letters *d.* figure-ground
3. At times, meaningful perceptual organization represents a ______________________, or "guess," held until the evidence contradicts it.
4. The design known as the Necker cube is a good example of an impossible figure. T or F?
5. Which among the following are subject to basic perceptual constancy?
   a. figure-ground organization *b.* size *c.* ambiguity *d.* brightness *e.* continuity *f.* closure *g.* shape *h.* nearness
6. The brain-centered ability to influence what sensations we will receive is called
   a. sensory adaptation *b.* psychophysics *c.* selective attention *d.* sensory biasing
7. Which of the following stimuli are more effective at getting attention?
   a. unexpected stimuli *b.* repetitious stimuli *c.* intense stimuli *d.* all of the above

REFLECT

Think Critically

8. People who have taken psychedelic drugs, such as LSD or mescaline, often report that the objects and people they see appear to be changing in size, shape, and brightness. This suggests that such drugs disrupt which perceptual process?

Self-Reflect

As you look around the area in which you are now, how are the Gestalt principles helping to organize your perceptions? Try to find a specific example for each principle.

If you needed to explain the perceptual constancies to a friend, what would you say? Why are the constancies important for maintaining a stable perceptual world?

Can you pay attention to more than one sensory input at once?

Answers: **1.** F **2.** *d* **3.** hypothesis **4.** F **5.** *b, d, g* **6.** *c* **7.** *d* **8.** Perceptual constancies (size, shape, and brightness).

Depth Perception—What If the World Were Flat?

Gateway Question 4.8: *How is it possible to see depth and judge distance?*

Cross your eyes, hold your head very still, and stare at a single point across the room; your surroundings will appear to be almost flat, like a 2-D painting or photograph. This is the world that neuroscientist Susan Barry, cross-eyed from birth, lived with until, at the age of 48, she learned to see in 3-D (Barry & Sacks, 2009). Now, uncross your eyes. Suddenly, the 3-D perceptual world returns. Let's explore the mechanisms that underlie our ability to perceive depth and space.

© Mark Richards/PhotoEdit

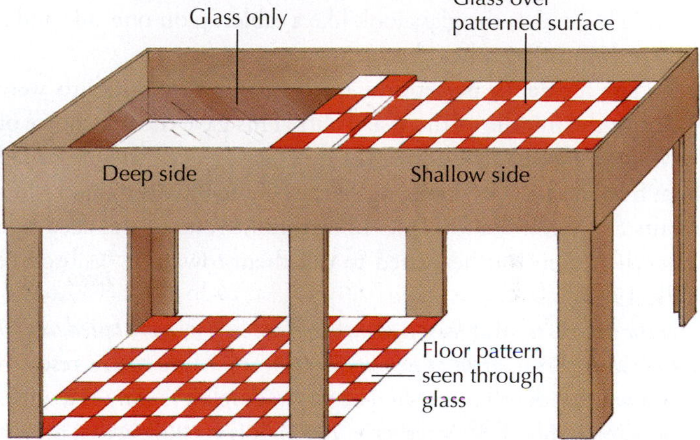

● Figure 4.36 Human infants and newborn animals refuse to go over the edge of the visual cliff. Copyright © 2012 Wadsworth, Cengage Learning, Inc.

Depth perception is the ability to see three-dimensional space and to accurately judge distances. Without depth perception, another form of perceptual construction, the world would look like a flat surface. You would have great difficulty driving a car or riding a bicycle, playing catch, shooting baskets, threading a needle, or simply navigating around a room (Howard & Rogers, 2001a).

Mr. S. B. had trouble with depth perception after his sight was restored. Is depth perception learned? Studies done with a *visual cliff* suggest that depth perception is partly learned and partly innate (Witherington et al., 2005). Basically, a visual cliff is a glass-topped table (● Figure 4.36). On one side, a checkered surface lies directly beneath the glass. On the other side, the checkered surface is 4 feet

Brightness constancy The apparent (or relative) brightness of objects remains the same as long as they are illuminated by the same amount of light.

Selective attention Giving priority to a particular incoming sensory message.

Inattentional blindness A failure to notice a stimulus because attention is focused elsewhere.

Depth perception The ability to see three-dimensional space and to accurately judge distances.

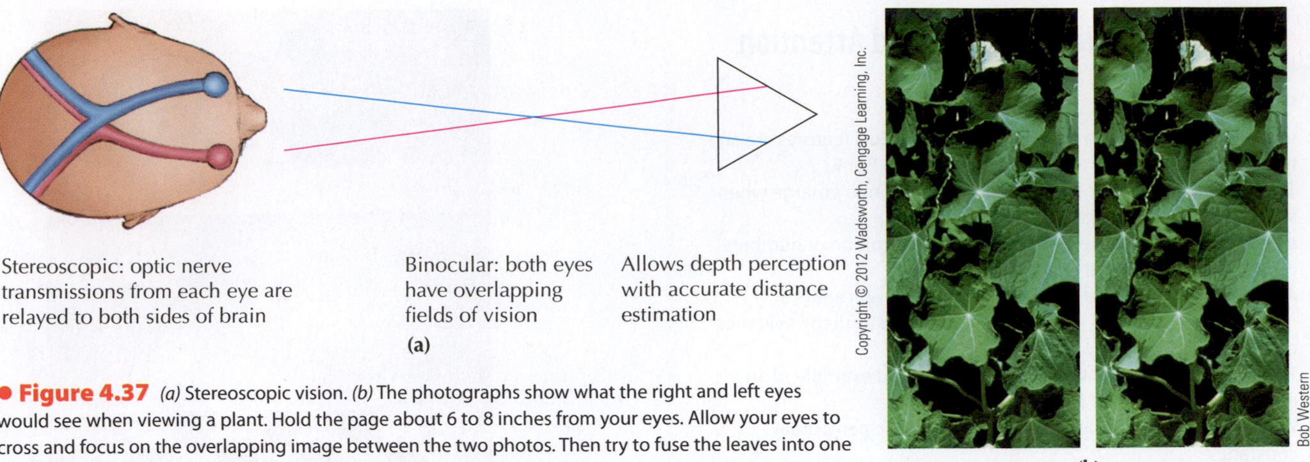

● **Figure 4.37** *(a)* Stereoscopic vision. *(b)* The photographs show what the right and left eyes would see when viewing a plant. Hold the page about 6 to 8 inches from your eyes. Allow your eyes to cross and focus on the overlapping image between the two photos. Then try to fuse the leaves into one image. If you are successful the third dimension will appear like magic.

below. This makes the glass look like a tabletop on one side and a cliff, or drop-off, on the other.

To test for depth perception, 6- to 14-month-old infants were placed in the middle of the visual cliff. This gave them a choice of crawling to the shallow side or the deep side. (The glass prevented them from doing any "skydiving" if they chose the deep side.) Most infants chose the shallow side. In fact, most refused the deep side even when their mothers tried to call them toward it (Gibson & Walk, 1960).

If the infants were at least 6 months old when they were tested, isn't it possible that they learned to perceive depth? Yes. More recent research has shown that depth perception begins to develop as early as 2 weeks of age (Yonas, Elieff, & Arterberry, 2002). It is very likely that at least a basic level of depth perception is innate. Yet, the development of depth perception is not complete until about 6 months, suggesting that it depends on both brain maturation and individual experience.

But don't some older babies crawl off tables or beds? As soon as infants become active crawlers, they refuse to cross the deep side of the visual cliff. However, older infants who have just learned to walk must again learn to avoid the "deep" side of the visual cliff (Witherington et al., 2005). Besides, even babies who perceive depth may not be able to catch themselves if they slip. A lack of coordination—not an inability to see depth—probably explains most "crash landings" after about 4 months of age.

We learn to construct our perception of three-dimensional space by using a variety of *depth cues.* **Depth cues** are features of the environment and messages from the body that supply information about distance and space. Some cues require two eyes (**binocular depth cues**), whereas others will work with just one eye (**monocular depth cues**).

● **Figure 4.38** *Avatar,* released in 2009, is the most successful 3-D film to date. One of the tools director James Cameron developed specially for this film was a stereoscopic camera that simulates retinal disparity and creates a sensation of depth. When viewed through polarized goggles, the resulting film appears fully three-dimensional.

Binocular Depth Cues

The most basic source of depth perception is *retinal disparity* (a discrepancy in the images that reach the right and left eyes). Retinal disparity, which is a binocular cue, is based on the fact that the eyes are about 2.5 inches apart. Because of this, each eye receives a slightly different view of the world. Try this: put a finger in front of your eyes and as close to your nose as you can. First close one eye and then the other, over and over again. You should notice that your finger seems to jump back and forth as you view the different images reaching each eye. However, when the two different images are fused into one overall image, **stereoscopic vision** (3-D sight) occurs (Howard & Rogers, 2001b). The result is a powerful sensation of depth (● Figure 4.37 and ● Figure 4.38).

Convergence is a second binocular depth cue. When you look at a distant object, the lines of vision from your eyes are parallel. You are normally not aware of it, but whenever you estimate a distance under 50 feet (as when you play catch or shoot trash can hoops with the first draft of your essay), you are using convergence. How? Muscles attached to the eyeball feed information on eye position to the brain to help it judge distance (● Figure 4.39).

You can feel convergence by exaggerating it: Focus on your fingertip and bring it toward your eyes until they almost cross. You can actually feel the muscles that control eye movement working harder and harder as your fingertip gets closer.

Can a person with one eye perceive depth? Yes, but not as well as a person with two eyes. Overall, stereoscopic vision is 10 times bet-

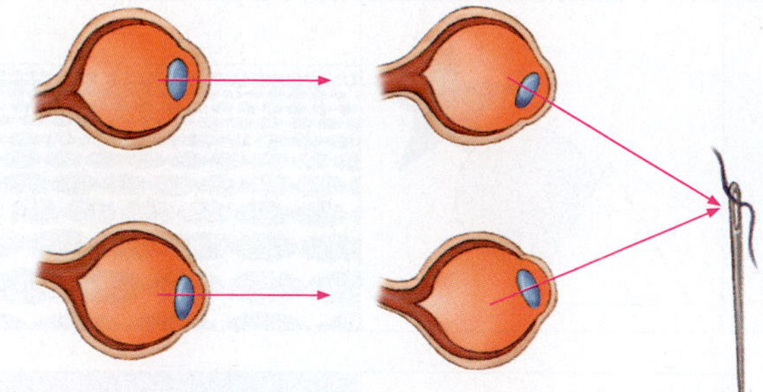

● **Figure 4.39** The eyes must converge, or turn in toward the nose, to focus close objects. The eyes shown are viewed from above the head.

ter for judging depth than perception based on just one eye (Rosenberg, 1994). Try driving a car or riding a bicycle with one eye closed. You will find yourself braking too soon or too late, and you will have difficulty estimating your speed. ("But officer, my psychology text said to . . .") Despite this, you will be able to drive, although it will be more difficult than usual. This is possible because your single eye can still make use of monocular depth cues.

Monocular Depth Cues

As their name implies, monocular depth cues can be perceived with just one eye. One such cue is *accommodation*, the bending of the lens to focus on nearby objects. Sensations from muscles attached to each lens flow back to the brain. Changes in these sensations help us judge distances within about 4 feet of the eyes. This information is available even if you are just using one eye, so accommodation is a monocular cue. Beyond 4 feet, accommodation has limited value. Obviously, it is more important to a watchmaker or a person trying to thread a needle than it is to a basketball player or someone driving an automobile. Other monocular depth cues are referred to as pictorial depth cues, because a good movie, painting, or photograph can create a convincing sense of depth where none exists.

How is the illusion of depth created on a two-dimensional surface? **Pictorial depth cues** are features found in paintings, drawings, and photographs that impart information about space, depth, and distance. To understand how these cues work, imagine that you are looking outdoors through a window. If you trace everything you see onto the glass, you will have an excellent drawing, with convincing depth. If you then analyze what is on the glass, you will find the following features:

1. **Linear perspective.** This cue is based on the apparent convergence of parallel lines in the environment. If you stand between two railroad tracks, they appear to meet near the horizon, even though they actually remain parallel. Because you know they are parallel, their convergence implies great distance (see ● Figure 4.40*a*).
2. **Relative size.** If an artist wishes to depict two objects of the same size at different distances, the artist makes the more distant object smaller (see ● Figure 4.40*b*). Special effects in films create sensational illusions of depth by rapidly changing the image size of planets, airplanes, monsters, or what have you.
3. **Height in the picture plane.** Objects that are placed higher (closer to the horizon line) in a drawing tend to be perceived as more distant. In the upper frame of ● Figure 4.40*b,* the black columns look like they are receding into the distance partly because they become smaller, but also because they move higher in the drawing.
4. **Light and shadow.** Most objects are lighted in ways that create clear patterns of light and shadow. Copying such patterns of light and shadow can give a two-dimensional design a three-dimensional appearance (see ● Figure 4.40*c*). (Also, look ahead to ● Figure 4.41 for more information on light and shadow.)
5. **Overlap.** Overlap (or *interposition*) occurs when one object partially blocks another object. Hold your hands up and ask a friend across the room which is nearer. Relative size will give the answer if one hand is much nearer to your friend than the other. But if one hand is only slightly closer than the other, your friend may not be able to tell—until you slide one hand in front of the other. Overlap then removes any doubt (see ● Figure 4.40*d*).
6. **Texture gradients.** Changes in texture also contribute to depth perception. If you stand in the middle of a cobblestone street, the street will look coarse near your feet. However, its texture will get smaller and finer if you look into the distance (see ● Figure 4.40*e*).
7. **Aerial perspective.** Smog, fog, dust, and haze add to the apparent distance of an object. Because of aerial perspective, distant objects tend to be hazy, washed out in color, and lacking in detail. Aerial haze is often most noticeable when it is missing. If you have ever seen a distant mountain range on a crystal-clear day, it might have looked like it was only a few miles away. In reality, you could have been viewing them through 50 miles of crystal-clear air.
8. **Relative motion.** Relative motion, also known as *motion parallax* (PAIR-ah-lax), can be seen by looking out a window and moving your head from side to side. Notice that nearby objects appear to move a sizable distance as your head moves. Trees, houses, and telephone poles that are farther away appear to move slightly in relation to the background. Distant objects like hills, mountains, or clouds don't seem to move at all.

When combined, pictorial cues can create a powerful illusion of depth (see ■ Table 4.1 for a summary of all the depth cues we have discussed).

Depth cues Features of the environment and messages from the body that supply information about distance and space.
Binocular depth cues Perceptual features that impart information about distance and three-dimensional space which require two eyes.
Monocular depth cues Perceptual features that impart information about distance and three-dimensional space which require just one eye.
Stereoscopic vision Perception of space and depth due to the fact that the eyes receive different images.
Pictorial depth cues Monocular depth cues found in paintings, drawings, and photographs that impart information about space, depth, and distance.

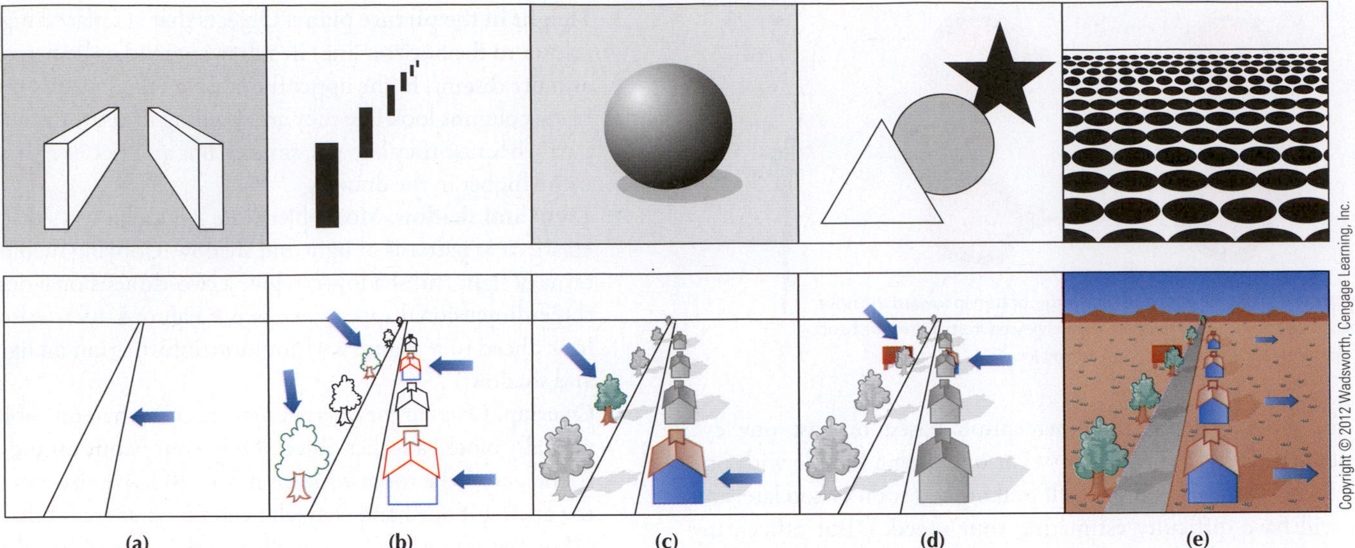

● Figure 4.40 *(a)* Linear perspective. *(b)* Relative size. *(c)* Light and shadow. *(d)* Overlap. *(e)* Texture gradients. Drawings in the top row show fairly "pure" examples of each of the pictorial depth cues. In the bottom row, the pictorial depth cues are used to assemble a more realistic scene.

● Figure 4.41 *(Left)* When judging depth we usually assume that light comes mainly from one direction, usually from above. Squint a little to blur the image you see here. You should perceive a collection of globes projecting outward. If you turn this page upside down, the globes should become cavities. (After Ramachandran, 1995.) *(Right)* The famed Dutch artist M. C. Escher violated our assumptions about light to create the dramatic illusions of depth found in his 1953 lithograph *Relativity*. In this print, light appears to come from all sides of the scene. (Courtesy of the Collection Haags Gemeente Museum, The Hague. © 1994 M. C. Escher/Cordon Art, Baarn, The Netherlands. All rights reserved.)

Is motion parallax really a pictorial cue? Strictly speaking, it is not—except in the world of two-dimensional movies, television, or animated cartoons. However, when parallax is present, we almost always perceive depth. Much of the apparent depth of a good movie comes from relative motion captured by the camera. ● Figure 4.42 illustrates the defining feature of motion parallax. Imagine that you are in a bus and watching the passing scenery (with your gaze at a right angle to the road). Under these conditions, nearby objects will appear to rush *backward*. Those farther away, such as distant mountains, will seem to move very little or not at all. Objects that are more remote, such as the sun or moon, will appear to move in the *same* direction you are traveling. (That's why the sun appears to "follow" you when you take a stroll.)

The Moon Illusion

How do the depth perception cues relate to daily experience? We constantly use both pictorial cues and bodily cues to sense depth and judge distances. Consider an intriguing effect called the *moon illusion* (perceiving the moon as larger when it is low in the sky). When the moon is on the horizon, it tends to look like a silver dollar. When it is directly overhead, it looks more like a dime. Con-

■ TABLE 4.1 **Summary of Visual Depth Cues**

Binocular Cues
- Retinal disparity
- Convergence

Monocular Cues
- Accommodation
- Pictorial depth cues (listed below)
  - Linear perspective
  - Relative size
  - Height in the picture plane
  - Light and shadow
  - Overlap
  - Texture gradients
  - Aerial perspective
  - Relative motion (motion parallax)

● **Figure 4.43** The Ponzo illusion may help you understand the moon illusion. Picture the two white bars as resting on the railroad tracks. In the drawing, the upper bar is the same length as the lower bar. However, because the upper bar appears to be farther away than the lower bar, we perceive it as longer. The same logic applies to the moon illusion. Copyright © 2012 Wadsworth, Cengage Learning, Inc.

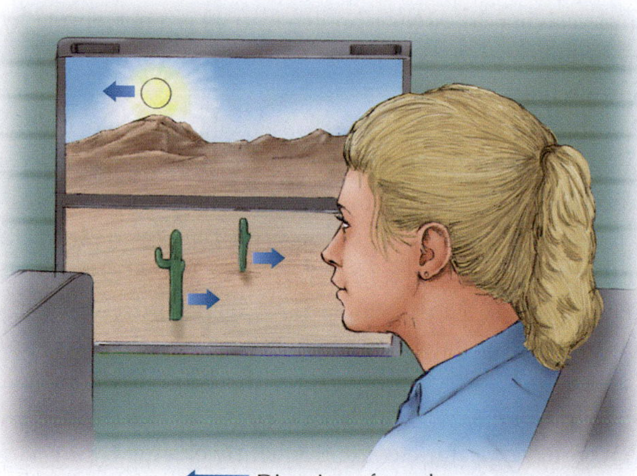

● **Figure 4.42** The apparent motion of objects viewed during travel depends on their distance from the observer. Apparent motion can also be influenced by an observer's point of fixation. At middle distances, objects closer than the point of fixation appear to move backward; those beyond the point of fixation appear to move forward. Objects at great distances, such as the sun or moon, always appear to move forward. Copyright © 2012 Wadsworth, Cengage Learning, Inc.

trary to what some people believe, the moon is not magnified by the atmosphere. But the moon *looks* nearly twice as large when it's low in the sky (Ross & Plug, 2002). This occurs, in part, because the moon's *apparent distance* is greater when it is near the horizon than when it is overhead (Jones & Wilson, 2009).

But if it seems farther away, shouldn't it look smaller? No. When the moon is overhead, few depth cues surround it. In contrast, when you see the moon on the horizon, it is behind houses, trees, telephone poles, and mountains. These objects add numerous depth cues, which cause the horizon to seem more distant than the sky overhead. Picture two balloons, one 10 feet away and the second 20 feet away. Suppose the more distant balloon is inflated until its image matches the image of the nearer balloon. How do we know the more distant balloon is larger? Because its image is the same size as a balloon that is closer. Similarly, the moon makes the same-size image on the horizon as it does overhead. However, the horizon seems more distant because more depth cues are present. As a result, the horizon moon must be perceived as larger (Kaufman & Kaufman, 2000; see ● Figure 4.43).

This explanation is known as the **apparent-distance hypothesis** (the horizon seems more distant than the night sky). You can test it by removing depth cues while looking at a horizon moon. Try looking at the moon through a rolled-up paper tube, or make your hands into a "telescope" and look at the next large moon you see. It will immediately appear to shrink when viewed without depth cues (Ross & Plug, 2002).

Knowledge Builder: Depth Perception

RECITE

1. The visual cliff is used to test for infant sensitivity to linear perspective. T or F?
2. Write an *M* or a *B* after each of the following to indicate whether it is a monocular or binocular depth cue.
accommodation _____ convergence _____ retinal disparity _____
linear perspective _____ motion parallax _____ overlap _____
relative size _____
3. Which of the depth cues listed in Question 2 are based on muscular feedback? _______________
4. Interpretation of pictorial depth cues requires no prior experience. T or F?

Continued

Apparent-distance hypothesis An explanation of the moon illusion stating that the horizon seems more distant than the night sky.

5. The apparent-distance hypothesis provides a good explanation of the
   a. moon illusion *b.* horizontal-vertical illusion *c.* Zulu illusion *d.* effects of inattentional blindness
6. Size-distance relationships appear to underlie which illusion? ____________________

REFLECT

Think Critically

7. What hearing ability would you say is most closely related to stereoscopic vision?
8. What size object do you think you would have to hold at arm's length to cover up a full moon?

Self-Reflect

Part of the rush of excitement produced by action movies and video games is based on the sense of depth they create. Return to the list of pictorial depth cues. What cues have you seen used to portray depth? Try to think of specific examples in a movie or game you have seen recently.

Answers: 1. F **2.** accommodation (M), convergence (B), retinal disparity (B), linear perspective (M), motion parallax (M), overlap (M), relative size (M) **3.** accommodation and convergence **4.** F **5.** *a* **6.** moon illusion **7.** If you close your eyes, you can usually tell the direction and perhaps the location of a sound source, such as a hand-clap. Locating sounds in space is heavily dependent on having two ears, just as stereoscopic vision depends on having two eyes. **8.** The most popular answers range from a quarter to a softball. Actually, a pea held in the outstretched hand will cover a full moon (Kunkel, 1993). If you listed an object larger than a pea, be aware that perceptions, no matter how accurate they seem, may distort reality.

Perceptual Learning—Believing is Seeing

Gateway Question 4.9: *How is perception altered by expectations, motives, emotions, and learning?*

Various processes distort our perceptions, which are far from a perfect model of the world. Let's investigate some factors that affect the accuracy of our perceptual experiences. As we just saw, we use Gestalt organizing principles, perceptual constancies, and depth cues to construct our visual perceptions. All of these processes, and others, make up the common, partly inborn, core of our perceptual abilities. In addition, we each have specific life experiences that can, in top-down fashion, affect our perceptions. For instance, what you perceive can be altered by *perceptual expectancies,* motives, emotions, and *perceptual habits.*

Perceptual Expectancies

What is a perceptual expectancy? If you are a runner in the starting blocks at a track meet, you are *set* to respond in a certain way. If a car backfires, runners at a track meet may jump the gun. Likewise, past experience, motives, context, or suggestions may create a **perceptual expectancy** (or **set**) that prepares you to perceive in a certain way. As a matter of fact, we all frequently jump the gun when perceiving. In essence, an expectancy is a perceptual hypothesis we are *very likely* to apply to a stimulus—even if applying it is inappropriate.

Perceptual sets often lead us to see what we *expect* to see. For example, let's say while driving you just made an illegal lane change (or texted on your cell phone!?). You then see a flashing light. "Rats," you think, "busted," and wait for the police car to pull you over. But as the car draws nearer, you see it was just a car with a vivid turn signal. Most people have had similar experiences in which expectations altered their perceptions. To observe perceptual expectancies firsthand, perform the demonstration described in ● Figure 4.44.

Perceptual expectancies are frequently created by *suggestion.* In one study (wine snobs take note), participants given a taste of a $90 wine reported that it tasted better than a $10 wine. Functional MRI images confirmed that brain areas related to pleasure were indeed more active when participants tasted the more expensive wine (Plassmann et al., 2008). The twist is that exactly the same wine was served in both cases: Suggesting that the wine was expensive created a perceptual expectancy that it would taste better. And so it did (advertisers also take note). In the same way,

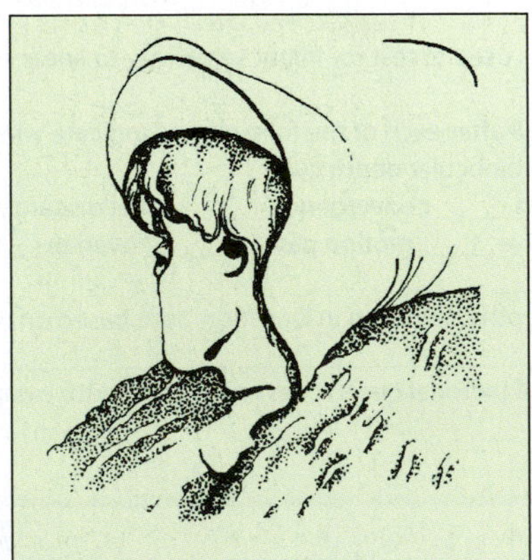

View I

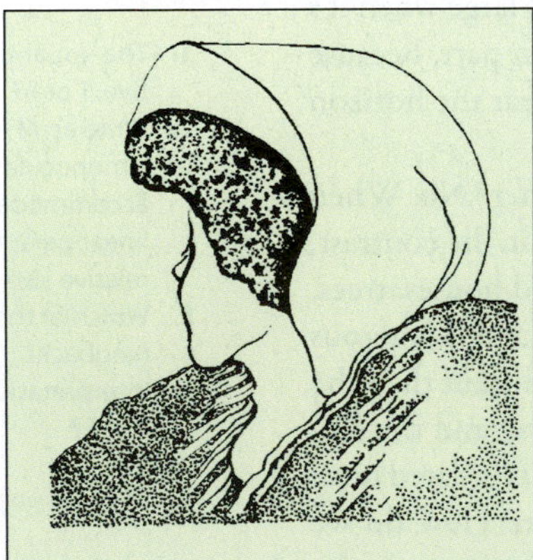

View II

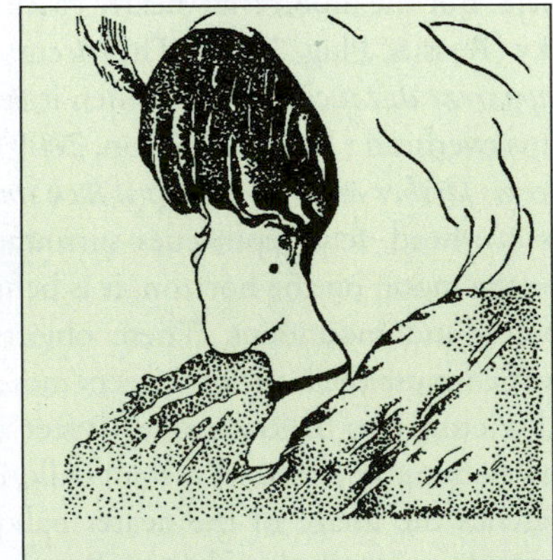
View III

● **Figure 4.44** "Young woman/old woman" illustrations. As an interesting demonstration of perceptual expectancy, show some of your friends view I and some view II (cover all other views). Next show your friends view III and ask them what they see. Those who saw view I should see the old woman in view III; those who saw view II should see the young woman in view III. Can you see both? (After Leeper, 1935.)

Human Diversity: Do They See What We See?

According to psychologist Richard Nisbett and his colleagues, people from different cultures do, in fact, perceive the world differently. European Americans are individualistic people who tend to focus on themselves and their sense of personal control. In contrast, East Asians are collectivist people who tend to focus on their personal relationships and social responsibilities. As a consequence, European Americans tend to perceive actions in terms of internal factors ("she did it because she chose to do it"). In comparison, East Asians tend to explain actions in terms of their social context ("he did it because it was his responsibility to his family") (Norenzayan & Nisbett, 2000).

Do such cultural differences affect our everyday perception of objects and events? Apparently they do. In one study, American and Japanese participants were shown drawings of everyday scenes, such as a farm. Later, they saw a slightly changed version of the scene. Some of the changes were made to the focal point, or figure, of the scene. Other changes altered the surrounding context, or ground, of the scene. Americans, it turns out, were better at detecting changes in the figure of a scene. Japanese participants were better at finding alterations in the background (Nisbett & Miyamoto, 2005).

To explain this difference, Chua, Boland, and Nisbett (2005) presented American and Chinese participants with pictures of a figure (such as a tiger) placed on a ground (such as a jungle) and monitored their eye-movement patterns. The Americans focused their eye movements on the figure; Chinese participants made more eye movements around the ground. In other words, Westerners have a relatively narrow focus of attention, whereas Easterners have a broader focus of attention (Boduroglu, Shah, & Nisbett, 2009). Apparently, the society we live in can, indeed, influence even our most basic perceptual habits. This difference in perceptual style even influences the artistic and aesthetic preferences expressed in Eastern and Western art (Masuda et al., 2008).

labeling people as "gang members," "mental patients," "queers," "illegal immigrants," "bitches," and so on, is very likely to distort perceptions.

Motives, Emotions, and Perception

Our motives and emotions also play a role in shaping our perceptions. For example, if you are hungry, food-related words are more likely to gain your attention than nonfood-related words (Mogg et al., 1998). Advertisers take advantage of two motives that are widespread in our society: *anxiety* and *sex*. Everything from mouthwash to automobile tires is merchandised by using sex to gain attention (LaTour & Henthorne, 2003). Other ads combine sex with anxiety. Deodorant, soaps, toothpaste, and countless other articles are pushed in ads that play on desires to be attractive, to have "sex appeal," or to avoid embarrassment.

Our emotions can also shape our perceptions. According to psychologist Barbara Frederickson, negative emotions generally narrow our perceptual focus, or "spotlight," increasing the likelihood of inattentional blindness. In contrast, positive emotions can actually broaden the scope of attention (Fredrickson & Branigan, 2005). For example, positive emotions can affect how well people recognize people from other races. In recognizing faces, a consistent *other-race effect* occurs. This is a sort of "They all look alike to me" bias in perceiving persons from other racial and ethnic groups. In tests of facial recognition, people are much better at recognizing faces of their own race than others. But when people are in positive moods, their ability to recognize people from other races improves (Johnson & Fredrickson, 2005).

The main reason for the other-race effect is that we typically have more experience with people from our own race. As a result, we become very familiar with the features that help us recognize different persons. For other groups, we lack the perceptual expertise needed to accurately separate one face from another (Sporer, 2001). Such differences indicate the importance of perceptual learning, a topic we turn to next.

Okay, so maybe members of different races or ethnic groups have developed perceptual sets that lead them to see in-group faces differently, but we all see everything else the same, right? For an answer, see "Do They See What We See?"

Perceptual Habits

England is one of the few countries in the world where people drive on the left side of the road. Because of this reversal, it is not unusual for visitors to step off curbs in front of cars—after carefully looking for traffic in the *wrong* direction. As this example suggests, learning has a powerful impact on top-down processing in perception.

How does learning affect perception? The term **perceptual learning** refers to changes in the brain that alter how we construct sensory information into perceptions (Moreno et al., 2009). For example, to use a computer, you must learn to pay attention to specific stimuli, such as icons and cursors. We also learn to tell the difference between stimuli that seemed identical at first. An example is the novice chef who discovers how to tell the difference between dried basil, oregano, and tarragon. In other situations, we learn to focus on just one part of a group of stimuli. This saves us

Perceptual expectancy (or set) A readiness to perceive in a particular manner, induced by strong expectations.

Perceptual learning Changes in perception that can be attributed to prior experience; a result of changes in how the brain processes sensory information.

Lars Baron/Getty Images

In many sports, expert players are much better than beginners at paying attention to key information. Compared with novices, experts scan actions and events more quickly, and they focus on only the most meaningful information. This makes experts to make decisions and react more quickly (Bard, Fleury, & Goulet, 1994).

from having to process all the stimuli in the group. For instance, a linebacker in football may be able to tell if the next play will be a run or a pass by watching one or two key players, rather than the entire opposing team (Seitz & Watanabe, 2005).

In general, learning creates **perceptual habits**—ingrained patterns of organization and attention—that affect our daily experience. Stop for a moment and look at • Figure 4.45. The left face looks somewhat unusual, to be sure. But the distortion seems mild—until you turn the page upside down. Viewed normally, the face looks quite grotesque. Why is there a difference? Apparently, most people have little experience with upside-down faces. Perceptual learning, therefore, has less impact on our perceptions of an upside-down face. With a face in the normal position, you know what to expect and where to look. Also, you tend to see the entire face as a recognizable pattern. When a face is inverted, we are forced to perceive its individual features separately (Caharel et al., 2006).

The Müller-Lyer Illusion

Can perceptual habits explain other illusions? Perceptual habits play a role in explaining some illusions. In general, size and shape constancy, habitual eye movements, continuity, and perceptual habits combine in various ways to produce the illusions in • Figure 4.46. Rather than attempt to explain all of them, let's focus on one deceptively simple example.

Consider the drawing in • Figure 4.46*a*. This is the familiar **Müller-Lyer** (MEOO-ler-LIE-er) **illusion** in which the horizontal line with arrowheads appears shorter than the line with V's. A quick measurement will show that they are the same length. How can we explain this illusion? Evidence suggests it is based on a lifetime of experience with the edges and corners of rooms and buildings. Richard Gregory (2000) believes you see the horizontal line with the V's as if it were the corner of a room viewed from inside (• Figure 4.47). The line with arrowheads, on the other hand, suggests the corner of a room or building seen from outside. In other words, cues that suggest a three-dimensional space alter our perception of a two-dimensional design.

Earlier, to explain the moon illusion, we said that if two objects make images of the same size, the more distant object must be larger. This is known formally as *size-distance invariance* (the size of an object's image is precisely related to its distance from the eyes). Gregory believes the same concept explains the Müller-Lyer illusion. If the V-tipped line looks farther away than the arrowhead-tipped line, you must compensate by seeing the V-tipped line as longer. This explanation presumes that you have had years of experience with straight lines, sharp edges, and corners—a pretty safe assumption in our culture.

Is there any way to show that past experience causes the illusion? If we could test someone who saw only curves and wavy lines as a child, we

• Figure 4.45 The effects of prior experience on perception. The doctored face looks far worse when viewed right side up because it can be related to past experience.

© Bettmann/Corbis

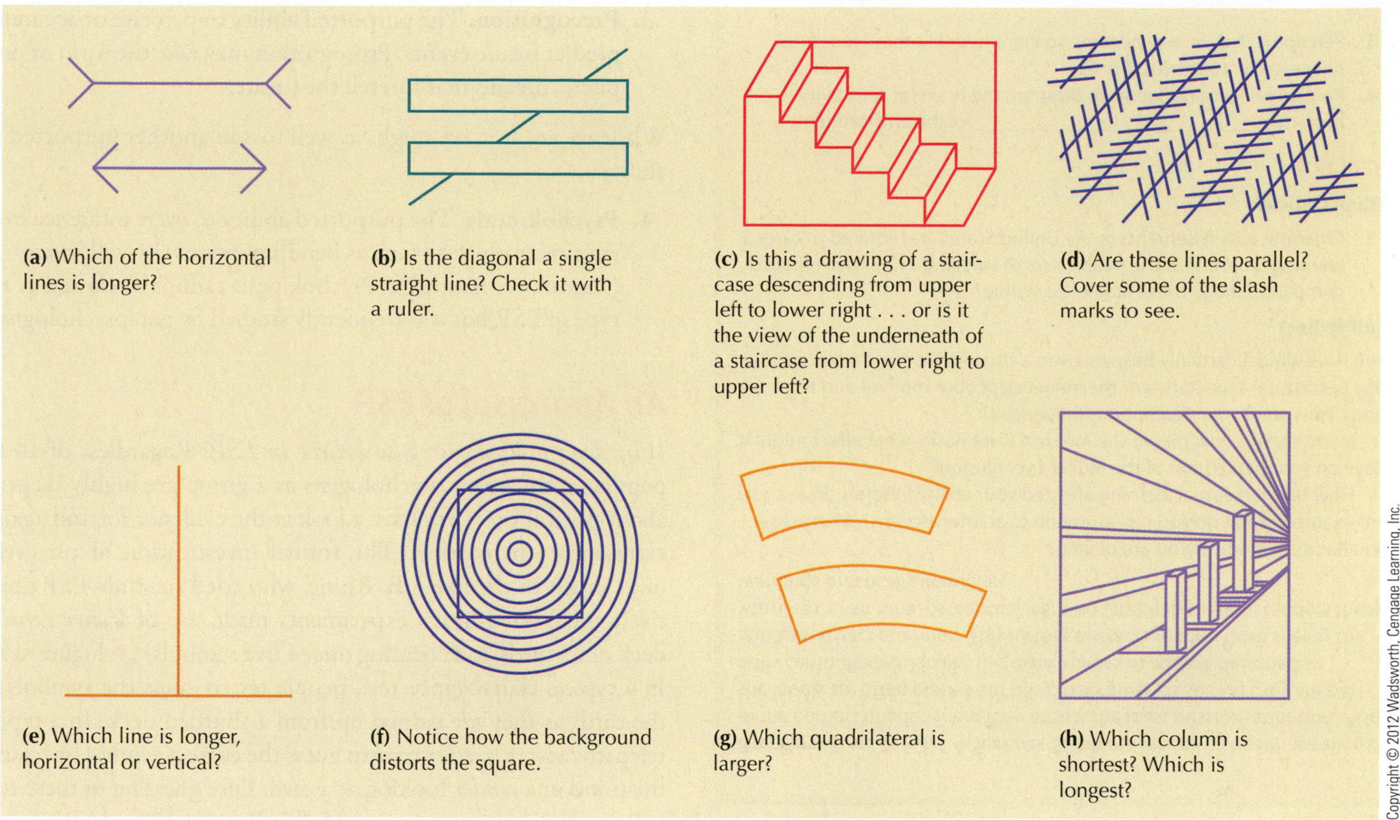

● **Figure 4.46** Some interesting perceptual illusions. Such illusions reveal that perceptual misconstructions are a normal part of visual perception.

would know if experience with a "square" culture is important. Fortunately, the Zulus, a group of people in South Africa, live in a "round" culture. In their daily lives, traditional Zulus rarely encounter a straight line: Their houses are shaped like rounded mounds and arranged in a circle, tools and toys are curved, and there are few straight roads or square buildings.

What happens if a Zulu looks at the Müller-Lyer design? The typical Zulu villager does not experience the illusion. At most, she or he sees the V-shaped line as *slightly* longer than the other (Gregory, 1990). This seems to confirm the importance of perceptual habits in determining our view of the world.

In the next section, we will go beyond normal perception to ask, "Is extrasensory perception possible?" Before we do that, here's a chance to answer the question, "Is remembering the preceding discussion possible?"

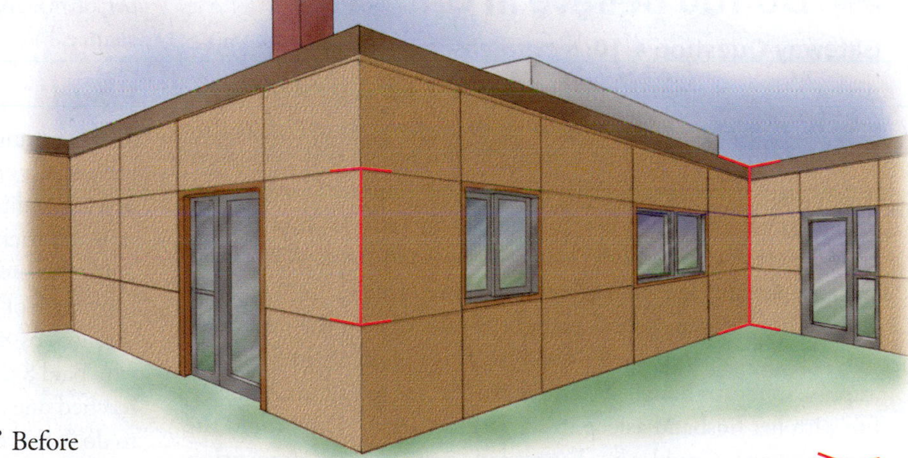

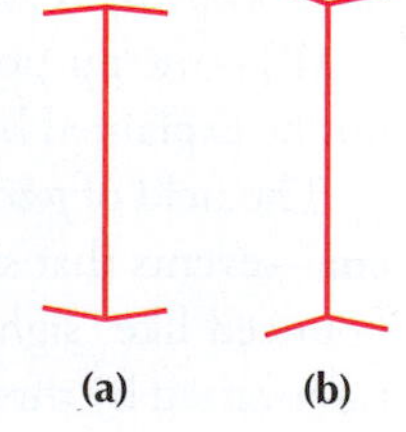

● **Figure 4.47** Why does line *(b)* in the Müller-Lyer illusion look longer than line *(a)*? Probably because it looks more like a distant corner than a nearer one. Because the vertical lines form images of the same length, the more "distant" line must be perceived as larger. As you can see in the drawing on the right, additional depth cues accentuate the Müller-Lyer illusion. (After Enns & Coren, 1995.)

Perception and Objectivity

RECITE

1. When a person is prepared to perceive events in a particular way, it is said that a perceptual expectancy or _______________ exists.
2. People around the world perceive in the same way regardless of culture. T or F?

Continued

Perceptual habits Ingrained patterns of organization and attention that affect our daily experience.

Müller-Lyer illusion Two equal-length lines tipped with inward or outward pointing V's appear to be of different lengths.

3. Perceptual habits may become so ingrained that they lead us to misperceive a stimulus. T or F?
4. Perceptual learning seems to program the brain for sensitivity to important ______________ of the environment.

REFLECT

Think Critically

5. Cigarette advertisements in the United States are required to carry a warning label about the health risks of smoking. How have tobacco companies made these labels less visible?

Self-Reflect

You have almost certainly misperceived a situation at some time because of a perceptual expectancy or the influence of your motives and emotions. How were your perceptions influenced?

If you spent a year hiking the Amazon River Basin, what effect might it have on your perception of the Müller-Lyer illusion?

How has perceptual learning affected your ability to safely drive a car? For example, what do you pay attention to at intersections? Where do you habitually look as you are driving?

Answers: 1. set **2.** F **3.** T **4.** features **5.** Advertisers place health warnings in the corners of ads, where they attract the least possible attention. Also, the labels are often placed on "busy" backgrounds so that they are partially camouflaged. Finally, the main images in ads are designed to strongly attract attention. This further distracts readers from seeing the warnings. Over time, perceptual learning (and habituation) renders these warnings practically invisible.

Extrasensory Perception—Do You Believe in Ghosts?

Gateway Question 4.10: *Is extrasensory perception possible?*

About half of the general public believes in the existence of extrasensory perception (Wiseman & Watt, 2006). Yet very few psychologists share this belief. Actually, it's surprising that even more people aren't believers. ESP and other paranormal events are treated as accepted facts in many movies and television programs. Stage entertainers routinely "astound" their audiences. What is the evidence for and against extrasensory perception?

Let's consider an actual example. Once, during the middle of the night, a woman away for a weekend visit suddenly had a strong impulse to return home. When she arrived, she found the house on fire with her husband asleep inside (Rhine, 1953). How could she have known? Could she have used **extrasensory perception (ESP)**—the purported ability to perceive events in ways that cannot be explained by known sensory capacities?

The field of *parapsychology* studies ESP and other **psi phenomena**—events that seem to defy accepted scientific laws. (Psi is pronounced like "sigh.") Parapsychologists seek answers to the questions raised by three basic forms that ESP could take. These are:

1. **Telepathy.** The purported ability to communicate directly with another person's mind. When the other person is dead, the communications are called *mediumship*.
2. **Clairvoyance.** The purported ability to perceive events or gain information in ways that appear unaffected by distance or normal physical barriers.
3. **Precognition.** The purported ability to perceive or accurately predict future events. Precognition may take the form of prophetic dreams that foretell the future.

While we are at it, we might as well toss in another purported psi ability:

4. **Psychokinesis.** The purported ability to exert influence over inanimate objects (such as bending spoons) by willpower ("mind over matter"). (Psychokinesis cannot be classed as a type of ESP, but it is frequently studied by parapsychologists.)

An Appraisal of ESP

Why don't psychologists also believe in ESP? Regardless of all the popular enthusiasm, psychologists as a group are highly skeptical about psi abilities. Let's have a look at the evidence for and against extrasensory perception. The formal investigation of psi events owes much to the late J. B. Rhine, who tried to study ESP objectively. Many of Rhine's experiments made use of *Zener cards* (a deck of 25 cards, each bearing one of five symbols) (● Figure 4.48). In a typical clairvoyance test, people try to guess the symbols on the cards as they are turned up from a shuffled deck. In a typical telepathy test, a *receiver* tries to guess the correct symbol by reading the mind of a *sender* looking at a card. Pure guessing in these tests will produce an average score of 5 "hits" out of 25 cards. Rhine and others since have reported results much greater than might be expected by chance alone.

Doesn't evidence like that settle the issue? No it doesn't, for a number of reasons, including fraud, poorly designed experiments, and chance.

Fraud

Fraud continues to plague parapsychology. The need for skepticism is especially great anytime there's money to be made from purported psychic abilities. Stage demonstrations of ESP are based on deception and tricks, as are other "for profit" enterprises. For example, in 2002 the owners of the "Miss Cleo" TV-psychic operation were convicted of felony fraud. "Miss Cleo," supposedly a Jamaican-accented psychic, was really just an actress from Los Angeles. People who paid $4.99 a minute for a "reading" from "Miss Cleo" actually reached one of several hundred operators. These people were hired to do "cold readings" through ads that read, "No experience necessary." Despite being entirely faked, the "Miss Cleo" scam brought in more than $1 billion before it was shut down.

Anyone can learn to do "cold readings" well enough to produce satisfied customers (Wood et al., 2003). *Cold reading* is a set of techniques that are used to lead people to believe in the truth of

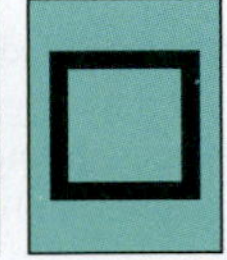

● **Figure 4.48** ESP cards used by J. B. Rhine, an early experimenter in parapsychology. Copyright © 2013 Cengage Learning, Inc.

what a psychic or medium is saying about them. These include a reliance on many of the same techniques used by astrologers, such as uncritical acceptance, confirmation bias, and the Barnum effect. (Remember Chapter 1?)

The "psychic" begins a "reading" by making general statements about a person. The psychic then plays "hot and cold" by attending to the person's facial expressions, body language, or tone of voice. When the psychic is "hot" (on the right track), he or she continues to make similar statements about the person. If the person's reactions signal that the psychic is "cold," the psychic drops that topic or line of thought and tries another (Hyman, 2007).

Poorly Designed Experiments

Unfortunately, some of Rhine's most dramatic early experiments used badly printed Zener cards that allowed the symbols to show faintly on the back. It is also very easy to cheat, by marking cards with a fingernail or by noting marks on the cards caused by normal use. There is also evidence that early experimenters sometimes unconsciously gave people cues about cards with their eyes or facial gestures. In short, none of the early studies in parapsychology were done in a way that eliminated the possibility of deliberate fraud or the accidental "leakage" of helpful information (Alcock, Burns, & Freeman, 2003).

Modern parapsychologists are now well aware of the need for double-blind experiments, security and accuracy in record keeping, meticulous control, and repeatability of experiments (Milton & Wiseman, 1997; O'Keeffe & Wiseman, 2005). In the last 10 years, hundreds of experiments have been reported in parapsychological journals. Many of them seem to support the existence of psi abilities (Aldhous, 2010).

Chance

Then why do most psychologists still remain skeptical about psi abilities? The most important reason has to do with chance. Remember the woman who had a premonition that something bad was about to happen to her husband? She returned home early to find her house on fire with him sleeping inside. An apparent clairvoyant or telepathic experience like this is certainly striking, but it does not confirm the existence of ESP. Such *coincidences* occur quite often. On any given night, many people might act on a "premonition." If, by coincidence, one person's hunch turns out to be correct, it may be *reinterpreted* as clairvoyance (Marks, 2000; Wiseman & Watt, 2006). Then you read about it in the news the next day. No one reports the vast majority of false premonitions, which are simply forgotten.

Inconsistency in psi research is a related problem. For every published study with positive results, there are others that fail and are never reported (Alcock, 2003). Even experimental "successes" are weak. Many of the most spectacular findings in parapsychology simply cannot be *replicated* (reproduced or repeated) (Hyman, 1996a). Furthermore, improved research methods usually result in fewer positive results (Hyman, 1996b; O'Keeffe & Wiseman, 2005).

Even when a person does seems to show evidence of psi ability, it is rare—in fact, almost unheard of—for him or her to maintain that ability over any sustained period of time (Alcock, Burns, & Freeman, 2003). This is likely because a person who only temporarily scores above chance has just received credit for a **run of luck**—a statistically unusual outcome that could occur by chance alone.

To understand the run-of-luck criticism, imagine that you flip a coin 100 times and record the results. You then flip another coin 100 times, again recording the results. The two lists are compared. For any 10 pairs of flips, we would expect heads or tails to match 5 times. Let's say you go through the list and find a set of 10 pairs in which 9 out of 10 matched. This is far above chance expectation. But does it mean that the first coin "knew" what was going to come up on the second coin? The idea is obviously silly. Now, what if a person guesses 100 times what will come up on a coin. Again, we might find a set of 10 guesses that matches the results of flipping the coin. Does this mean that the person, for a time, had precognition—then lost it?

You may be surprised to learn that some ESP researchers believe this "decline effect" shows that parapsychological skills are very fragile, like a weak cell phone connection, fading in and out over time. If a person has a good short run of guessing, it is assumed that the person, for a time, had precognition. A subsequent run of poor guesses is interpreted to mean the person's precognition has temporarily faded out.

In fact, creative interpretation is a common problem when it comes to psi. For example, former astronaut Edgar Mitchell claimed he did a successful telepathy experiment from space. Yet, news accounts never mentioned that on some trials Mitchell's "receivers" scored above chance, whereas on others they scored *below* chance. Although you might assume that below-chance trials were failures to find telepathy, Mitchell reinterpreted them as "successes," claiming that they represented intentional "psi missing." But, as skeptics have noted, if both high scores and low scores count as successes, how can you lose?

Implications

After close to 130 years of investigation, it is still impossible to say conclusively whether psi events occur. As we have seen, a close look at psi experiments often reveals serious problems of evidence, procedure, and scientific rigor (Alcock, Burns, & Freeman, 2003; Hyman, 2007; Stokes, 2001). The more closely psi experiments are examined, the more likely it is that claimed successes will evaporate (Alcock, 2003; Stokes, 2001). As one critic put it, positive ESP results usually mean "Error Some Place" (Marks, 2000).

What would it take to scientifically demonstrate the existence of ESP? Quite simply, a set of instructions that would allow any

Extrasensory perception (ESP) The purported ability to perceive events in ways that cannot be explained by known capacities of the sensory organs.

Psi phenomena Events that seem to lie outside the realm of accepted scientific laws.

Run of luck A statistically unusual outcome (as in getting five heads in a row when flipping a coin) that could still occur by chance alone.

competent, unbiased observer to produce a psi event under standardized conditions that rule out any possibility of fraud or chance (Schick & Vaughn, 2001). Undoubtedly, researchers will continue their attempts to supply irrefutable evidence. Others remain skeptics and consider 130 years of inconclusive efforts reason enough to abandon the concept of ESP (Marks, 2000). Yet, being a skeptic does not mean a person is against something. It means that you are unconvinced. The purpose of this discussion, then, has been to counter the *uncritical* acceptance of psi events that is reported in the popular press or by researchers who are uncritical "true believers." (But then, you already knew we were going to say that, didn't you!)

Of course, in many ESP tests, the outcome is beyond debate. A good example is provided by ESP experiments done through newspapers, radio, and television. The results of more than 1.5 million ESP trials done through the mass media are easy to summarize: There was no significant ESP effect (Milton & Wiseman, 1999). Clearly, state lottery organizers have nothing to fear!

A Look Ahead

In these last few sections we have moved from basic sensations to the complexities of perceiving people and events. We have also probed some of the controversies concerning ESP. In the *Psychology in Action* section, we will return to "everyday" perception, for a look at perceptual awareness.

Knowledge Builder: Extrasensory Perception

RECITE

1. Four purported psi events investigated by parapsychologists are clairvoyance, telepathy, precognition, and ____________________.
2. The Zener cards were used in early studies of *a.* psi phenomena *b.* inattentional blindness *c.* the Müller-Lyer illusion *d.* top-down processing
3. Natural, or "real life," occurrences are regarded as the best evidence for the existence of ESP. T or F?
4. Skeptics attribute positive results in psi experiments to statistical runs of luck. T or F?
5. Replication rates are very high for ESP experiments. T or F?

REFLECT

Think Critically

6. What would you estimate is the chance that two people will have the same birthday (day and month, but not year) in a group of 30 people?
7. A "psychic" on television offers to fix broken watches for viewers. Moments later, dozens of viewers call the station to say that their watches miraculously started running again. What have they overlooked?

Self-Reflect

Let's say that a friend of yours is an avid fan of TV shows that feature paranormal themes. See if you can summarize for her or him what is known about ESP. Be sure to include evidence for and against the existence of ESP and some of the thinking errors associated with nonskeptical belief in the paranormal.

Answers: 1. psychokinesis **2.** *a* **3.** F **4.** T **5.** F **6.** Most people assume that this would be a relatively rare event. Actually, there is a 71 percent chance that two people will share a birthday in a group of 30. Most people probably underestimate the natural rate of occurrence of many seemingly mysterious coincidences (Alcock, Burns, & Freeman, 2003). **7.** When psychologists handled watches awaiting repair at a store, 57 percent began running again, with no help from a "psychic." Believing the psychic's claim also overlooks the impact of big numbers: If the show reached a large audience, at least a few "broken" watches would start working merely by chance.

Psychology in Action

Pay Attention!—Becoming a Better Eyewitness to Life

Gateway Question 4.11: *How can I learn to perceive events more accurately?*

In the courtroom, eyewitness testimony can be a key to proving guilt or innocence. The claim "I saw it with my own eyes" still carries a lot of weight with a jury. Too many jurors (unless they have taken a psychology course) tend to assume that eyewitness testimony is nearly infallible (Brewer & Wells, 2006; Durham & Dane, 1999). Even U.S. judges are vulnerable to overoptimism about eyewitness testimony (Wise & Safer, 2004; 2010). But, to put it bluntly, eyewitness testimony is frequently wrong (Wells & Olson, 2003). Recall, for instance, that one of your authors would have sworn in court that he had seen a murder taking place at the supermarket—*if* he hadn't received more information to correct his misperceptions.

What about witnesses who are certain that their perceptions were accurate? Should juries believe them? Actually, having confidence in your testimony has almost no bearing on its accuracy (Brewer & Wells, 2006)! Psychologists are gradually convincing lawyers, judges, and police that eyewitness errors are common (Yarmey, 2003). Even so, thousands of people have been wrongfully convicted (Scheck, Neufeld, & Dwyer, 2000).

Unfortunately, perception rarely provides an "instant replay" of events. Impressions formed when a person is surprised, threatened, or under stress are especially prone to distortion (Yuille & Daylen, 1998). One study of eyewitness cases found that the *wrong person* was chosen from police lineups 25 percent of the time (Levi, 1998).

Wouldn't the victim of a crime remember more than a mere witness? Not necessarily. A revealing study found that eyewitness accuracy is virtually the same for witnessing a crime (seeing a pocket calculator stolen) as it is for being a victim (seeing one's own watch stolen) (Hosch & Cooper, 1982). Placing more weight on the testimony of victims may be a serious mistake. In many crimes, victims fall prey to *weapon focus*. Understandably, they fix their entire attention on the knife, gun, or other weapon used by an attacker. In doing so, they fail to notice details of appearance, dress, or other clues to identity (Pickel, French, & Betts, 2003). Additional factors that consistently lower eyewitness accuracy are summarized in ■ Table 4.2 (Kassin et al., 2001; Wells & Olson, 2003).

Implications Now that DNA testing is available, more than 200 people who were convicted of murder, rape, and other crimes in the United States have been exonerated. Most of these innocent people were convicted mainly on the basis of eyewitness testimony. Each also spent *years* in prison before being cleared (Foxhall, 2000). How often are everyday perceptions as inaccurate or distorted as those of an emotional eyewitness? The answer we have been moving toward is very frequently. Bearing this in mind may help you be more tolerant of the views of others and more cautious about your own objectivity. It may also encourage more frequent reality testing on your part.

■ TABLE 4.2 Factors Affecting the Accuracy of Eyewitness Perceptions

Sources of Error	Summary of Findings
1. Wording of questions	An eyewitness's testimony about an event can be affected by how questions put to the witness are worded.
2. Postevent information	Eyewitness testimony about an event often reflects not only what was actually seen but also information obtained later.
3. Attitudes, expectations	An eyewitness's perception and memory for an event may be affected by his or her attitudes and expectations.
4. Alcohol intoxication	Alcohol intoxication impairs later ability to recall events.
5. Cross-racial perceptions	Eyewitnesses are better at identifying members of their own race than they are at identifying people of other races.
6. Weapon focus	The presence of a weapon impairs an eyewitness's ability to identify the culprit's face.
7. Accuracy-confidence	An eyewitness's confidence is not a good predictor of his or her accuracy.
8. Exposure time	The less time an eyewitness has to observe an event, the less well she or he will perceive and remember it.
9. Unconscious transference	Eyewitnesses sometimes identify as a culprit someone they have seen in another situation or context.
10. Color perception	Judgments of color made under monochromatic light (such as an orange street light) are highly unreliable.
11. Stress	Very high levels of stress impair the accuracy of eyewitness perceptions.

Adapted from Kassin et al., 2001.

If you have ever concluded that someone was angry, upset, or unfriendly without checking the accuracy of your perceptions, you have fallen into a subtle trap. Personal objectivity is an elusive quality, requiring frequent reality testing to maintain. At the very least, it pays to ask a person what she or he is feeling when you are in doubt. Clearly, most of us could learn to be better "eyewitnesses" to daily events.

AP/Wide World Photos

Even in broad daylight, eyewitness testimony is untrustworthy. In 2001 an airliner crashed near Kennedy International Airport in New York. Hundreds of people saw the plane go down. Half of them said the plane was on fire. Flight recorders showed there was no fire. One witness in five saw the plane make a right turn. An equal number saw it make a left turn! As one investigator noted, the best witness may be a "kid under 12 years old who doesn't have his parents around." Adults, it seems, are easily swayed by their expectations.

Positive Psychology: Perceptual Awareness

Do some people perceive things more accurately than others? Humanistic psychologist Abraham Maslow (1969) believed that some people perceive themselves and others with unusual accuracy. Maslow characterized these people as especially alive, open, aware, and mentally healthy. He found that their perceptual styles were marked by immersion in the present; a lack of self-consciousness; freedom from selecting, criticizing, or evaluating; and a general "surrender" to experience. The kind of perception Maslow described is like that of a mother with her newborn infant, a child at Christmas, or two people in love.

In daily life, we quickly **habituate**, or respond less, to predictable and unchanging stimuli. Habituation is a type of learning—basically, we learn to cease paying attention to familiar stimuli. For instance, when you download a new song from iTunes, the music initially holds your attention all the way through. But when the song becomes "old," it may play without your really attending to it. When a stimulus is repeated *without change*, our response to it habituates, or decreases. Interestingly, creative people habituate *more slowly* than average. We might expect that they would rapidly become bored with a repeated stimulus. Instead, it seems that creative people actively attend to stimuli, even those that are repeated (Colin, Moore, & West, 1996).

The Value of Paying Attention Whereas the average person has not reached perceptual restriction of the "if you've seen one tree, you've seen them all" variety, the fact remains that most of us tend to look at a tree and classify it into the perceptual category of "trees in general" without really appreciating the miracle standing before us. How, then, can we bring about **dishabituation**—a reversal of habituation—on a day-to-day basis? The deceptively simple key to dishabituation is this: Pay attention. The

Habituation A decrease in perceptual response to a repeated stimulus.
Dishabituation A reversal of habituation.

following story summarizes the importance of attention:

> One day a man of the people said to Zen Master Ikkyu: "Master, will you please write for me some maxims of the highest wisdom?"
>
> Ikkyu immediately took his brush and wrote the word "Attention."
>
> "Is that all?" asked the man. "Will you not add something more?"
>
> Ikkyu then wrote twice running: "Attention. Attention."
>
> "Well," remarked the man rather irritably, "I really don't see much depth or subtlety in what you have just written."
>
> Then Ikkyu wrote the same word three times running: "Attention. Attention. Attention." Half angered, the man demanded, "What does that word 'Attention' mean anyway?"
>
> And Ikkyu answered gently: "Attention means attention." (Kapleau, 1966)

How to Become a Better "Eyewitness" to Life

Here's a summary of ideas from this chapter to help you maintain and enhance perceptual awareness and accuracy:

1. *Remember that perceptions are constructions of reality.* Learn to regularly question your own perceptions. Are they accurate? Could another interpretation fit the facts? What assumptions are you making? How might your assumptions be distorting your perceptions?
2. *Break perceptual habits and interrupt habituation.* Each day, try to get away from habitual, top-down processing and do some activities in new ways. For example, take different routes when you travel to work or school. Do routines, such as brushing your teeth or combing your hair, with your nonpreferred hand. Try to look at friends and family members as if they are persons you just met for the first time.
3. *Seek out-of-the-ordinary experiences.* The possibilities here range from trying foods you don't normally eat to reading opinions very different from your own. Experiences ranging from a quiet walk in the woods to a trip to an amusement park may be perceptually refreshing.
4. *Beware of perceptual sets.* Anytime you pigeonhole people, objects, or events, there is a danger that your perceptions will be distorted by expectations or pre-existing categories. Be especially wary of labels and stereotypes. Try to see people as individuals and events as unique, one-time occurrences.
5. *Be aware of the ways in which motives and emotions influence perceptions.* It is difficult to avoid being swayed by your own interests, needs, desires, and emotions. But be aware of this trap and actively try to see the world through the eyes of others. Taking the other person's perspective is especially valuable in disputes or arguments.
6. *Make a habit of engaging in reality testing.* Actively look for additional evidence to check the accuracy of your perceptions. Ask questions, seek clarifications, and find alternate channels of information. Remember that perception is not automatically accurate. You could be wrong—we all are frequently.
7. *Pay attention.* Make a conscious effort to pay attention to other people and your surroundings. Try to get in the habit of approaching perception as if you are going to have to testify later about what you saw and heard.

Knowledge Builder

Perceptual Awareness and Accuracy

RECITE

1. Most perceptions can be described as active constructions of external reality. T or F?
2. Inaccuracies in eyewitness perceptions obviously occur in "real life," but they cannot be reproduced in psychology experiments. T or F?
3. Accuracy scores for facts provided by witnesses to staged crimes may be as low as 75 percent correct. T or F?
4. Victims of crimes are more accurate eyewitnesses than are impartial observers. T or F?
5. *Reality testing* is another term for dishabituation. T or F?
6. A good antidote to perceptual habituation can be found in conscious efforts to
   a. reverse sensory gating *b.* pay attention *c.* achieve visual accommodation *d.* counteract shape constancy

REFLECT

Think Critically

7. Return for a moment to the snake incident described at the beginning of this chapter. What perceptual factors were involved? Why was it so hard for your author to see the snake?

Self-Reflect

Because perceptions are reconstructions or models of external events, we should all engage in more frequent reality testing. Can you think of a recent event when a little reality testing would have saved you from misjudging a situation?

In order to improve your own perceptual awareness and accuracy, which strategies would you emphasize first?

Answers: 1. T **2.** F **3.** T **4.** F **5.** F **6.** *b* **7.** Your author's inexperience with green vine snakes made it harder for him to quickly construct a more accurate perception. Besides, the snake's camouflage evolved precisely to make it harder for potential predators and prey (for a moment your author wasn't sure which he was) to see it.

Chapter in Review Gateways to Sensation and Perception

Gateway QUESTIONS REVISITED

4.1 In general, how do sensory systems function?

4.1.1 The senses act as selective data reduction systems in order to prevent the brain from being overwhelmed by sensory input.

4.1.2 Sensation begins with transduction in a receptor organ; other data reduction processes are sensory adaptation, analysis, and coding.

4.1.3 Sensation can be partially understood in terms of sensory localization in the brain.

4.2 How does the visual system function?

4.2.1 The eye is a visual system, not a photographic one. The entire visual system is structured to analyze visual information.

4.2.2 Four common visual defects are myopia, hyperopia, presbyopia, and astigmatism.

4.2.3 The rods and cones are photoreceptors in the retina of the eye.

4.2.4 The rods specialize in peripheral vision, night vision, seeing black and white, and detecting movement. The cones specialize in color vision, acuity, and daylight vision.

4.2.5 Color vision is explained by the trichromatic theory in the retina and by the opponent-process theory in the visual system beyond the eyes.

4.2.6 Total color blindness is rare, but 8 percent of males and 1 percent of females are red-green color blind or color weak.

4.2.7 Dark adaptation is caused mainly by an increase in the amount of rhodopsin in the rods.

4.3 What are the mechanisms of hearing?

4.3.1 Sound waves are the stimulus for hearing. They are transduced by the eardrum, auditory ossicles, oval window, cochlea, and ultimately the hair cells.

4.3.2 Frequency theory explains how we hear tones up to 4,000 hertz; place theory explains tones above 4,000 hertz.

4.3.3 Two basic types of hearing loss are conductive hearing loss and sensorineural hearing loss. Noise-induced hearing loss is a common form of sensorineural hearing loss caused by exposure to loud noise.

4.4 How do the chemical senses operate?

4.4.1 Olfaction (smell) and gustation (taste) are chemical senses that respond to airborne or liquefied molecules.

4.4.2 The lock and key theory of olfaction partially explains smell. In addition, the location of the olfactory receptors in the nose helps identify various scents.

4.4.3 Sweet and bitter tastes are based on a lock-and-key coding of molecule shapes. Salty and sour tastes are triggered by a direct flow of ions into taste receptors.

4.5 What are the somesthetic senses?

4.5.1 The somesthetic senses include the skin senses, vestibular senses, and kinesthetic senses (receptors that detect muscle and joint positioning).

4.5.2 The skin senses are touch, pressure, pain, cold, and warmth. Sensitivity to each is related to the number of receptors found in an area of skin.

4.5.3 Distinctions can be made between warning pain and reminding pain.

4.5.4 Selective gating of pain messages takes place in the spinal cord, as explained by gate control theory.

4.5.5 Pain can be reduced through counterirritation and by controlling anxiety and attention.

4.5.6 According to sensory conflict theory, motion sickness is caused by a mismatch of visual, kinesthetic, and vestibular sensations. Motion sickness can be avoided by minimizing sensory conflict.

4.6 In general, how do we construct our perceptions?

4.6.1 Perception is an active process of constructing sensations into a meaningful mental representation of the world.

4.6.2 Perceptions are based on simultaneous bottom-up and top-down processing. Complete percepts are assembled out of small sensory features in "bottom-up" fashion guided by preexisting knowledge applied "top-down" to help organize features into a meaningful whole.

4.6.3 Separating figure and ground is the most basic perceptual organization.

4.6.4 The following Gestalt principles also help organize sensations: nearness, similarity, continuity, closure, contiguity, and common region.

4.6.5 A perceptual organization may be thought of as a hypothesis held until evidence contradicts it.

4.6.6 In vision, the image projected on the retina is constantly changing, but the external world appears stable and undistorted because of size, shape, and brightness constancy.

4.7 Why are we more aware of some sensations than others?

4.7.1 Incoming sensations are affected by selective attention, a brain-based process that allows some sensory inputs to be selected for further processing while others are ignored.

4.7.2 Don't use your cell phone while driving!

4.8 *How is it possible to see depth and judge distance?*

4.8.1 A basic, innate capacity for depth perception is present soon after birth.

4.8.2 Depth perception depends on binocular cues of retinal disparity and convergence.

4.8.3 Depth perception also depends on the monocular cue of accommodation.

4.8.4 Monocular "pictorial" depth cues also underlie depth perception. They are linear perspective, relative size, height in the picture plane, light and shadow, overlap, texture gradients, aerial haze, and motion parallax.

4.8.5 The moon illusion can be explained by the apparent-distance hypothesis, which emphasizes that many depth cues are present when the moon is near the horizon, and few are present when it is overhead.

4.9 *How is perception altered by expectations, motives, emotions, and learning?*

4.9.1 Suggestion, motives, emotions, attention, and prior experience combine in various ways to create perceptual sets, or expectancies.

4.9.2 Personal motives and values often alter perceptions by changing the evaluation of what is seen or by altering attention to specific details.

4.9.3 Perceptual learning influences the top-down organization and interpretation of sensations.

4.9.4 One of the most familiar of all illusions, the Müller-Lyer illusion, seems to be related to perceptual learning, linear perspective, and size–distance invariance relationships.

4.10 *Is extrasensory perception possible?*

4.10.1 Parapsychology is the study of purported psi phenomena, including telepathy (including mediumship), clairvoyance, precognition, and psychokinesis.

4.10.2 Research in parapsychology remains controversial because of a variety of problems and shortcomings. The bulk of the evidence to date is against the existence of ESP.

4.10.3 The more carefully controlled an ESP experiment is, the less likely it is to produce evidence that ESP occurs.

4.11 *How can I learn to perceive events more accurately?*

4.11.1 Eyewitness testimony is surprisingly unreliable. Eyewitness accuracy is further damaged by weapon focus, and a number of similar factors.

4.11.2 When a stimulus is repeated without change, our response to it undergoes habituation.

4.11.3 Perceptual accuracy is enhanced by reality testing, dishabituation, and conscious efforts to pay attention. It is also valuable to break perceptual habits, to broaden frames of reference, to beware of perceptual sets, and to be aware of the ways in which motives and emotions influence perceptions.

MEDIA RESOURCES

Web Resources

Internet addresses frequently change. To find an up-to-date list of URLs for the sites listed here, visit your Psychology CourseMate.

Amazing Animal Senses Discover the sensory capacities of other animals.

Psychophysics Explore absolute and discrimination thresholds as well as other psychophysics phenomena.

Video of Units in Visual Cortex Download and view a video of some of the original research by David Hubel and Torsten Wiesel on sensory coding in vision.

Eye Anatomy and Information about Eye Conditions A guide to the parts of the eye and eye conditions.

Organization of the Retina and Visual System A detailed description of the entire vertebrate visual system.

The Joy of Visual Perception An online book about visual perception, including information on the eye.

Virtual Tour of the Ear This site provides educational information about the ear and hearing and provides quick access to ear and hearing Web resources.

Taste and Smell Disorders Read about various disorders of taste and smell and what can be done about them.

American Pain Foundation Find out more about pain and its treatment.

Form and Contour Explore interactive demonstrations of the Gestalt principles and other curious phenomena.

Figure/Ground in Graphic Design Explore the use of the figure-ground principle in graphic design.

Selective Attention Read about and experience dichotic listening.

The Third Dimension Explore a variety of depth cues.

Gallery of Illusions An interesting and fun website that presents illusory stimuli that are fun to view and that provides a basis to learn about sensation and perception.

3-D Stereograms Find the 3-D images hidden in these pictures.

Context and Expectations Read about the effect of context on perception.

Perceptual Learning Explore an example of perceptual learning through wine tasting.

Ames Room Explore the Ames room illusion.

James Randi Education Foundation Win $1,000,000 for proving, under scientifically controlled conditions, that you have ESP.

The Skeptic's Dictionary: ESP Read more about the responses of skeptics to claims of paranormal abilities.

The Skeptic's Dictionary: Cold Reading Learn to recognize when purported psychics are using cold reading techniques.

What Jennifer Saw Explore the evidence in a case of mistaken identity.

The Innocence Project Read about real cases of people convicted through eyewitness testimony but later exonerated by DNA evidence.

Avoiding Habituation Read about how advertisers apply the idea of habituation to the design of advertisements.

Interactive Learning

Log in to **CengageBrain** to access the resources your instructor requires. For this book, you can access:

CourseMate brings course concepts to life with interactive learning, study, and exam preparation tools that support the printed textbook. A textbook-specific website, ***Psychology CourseMate*** includes an ***integrated interactive eBook*** and other ***interactive learning tools*** including quizzes, flashcards, videos, and more.

CENGAGE**NOW**™

CengageNOW is an easy-to-use online resource that helps you study in less time to get the grade you want—NOW. Take a pre-test for this chapter and receive a personalized study plan based on your results that will identify the topics you need to review and direct you to online resources to help you master those topics. Then take a post-test to help you determine the concepts you have mastered and what you will need to work on. If your textbook does not include an access code card, go to CengageBrain.com to gain access.

More than just an interactive study guide, **WebTutor** is an anytime, anywhere customized learning solution with an eBook, keeping you connected to your textbook, instructor, and classmates.

aplia™

If your professor has assigned **Aplia** homework:

1. Sign in to your account
2. Complete the corresponding homework exercises as required by your professor.
3. When finished, click "Grade It Now" to see which areas you have mastered and which need more work, and for detailed explanations of every answer.

Visit **www.cengagebrain.com** to access your account and purchase materials.

Gateway THEME

Understanding states of consciousness can promote self-awareness and enhance personal effectiveness.

5

States of Consciousness

A Visit to Several States (of Consciousness)

- **In New York City,** an aspiring actor consults a hypnotist for help in reducing her stage fright.
- In a Rio de Janeiro hospital, a man lies deep in a coma after surviving a horrendous traffic accident.
- In Yellowstone National Park in northern Wyoming, a college student spends a day walking through the wilderness, in a quiet state of mindfulness meditation.
- In Minnesota, a college student drifts into a pleasant daydream while sitting at the back of class.
- In New Zealand, a Maori tohunga (priest) performs a nightlong ritual to talk to the spirits who created the world in the mythical period the Aborigines call "Dreamtime".
- In Montreal, Canada, three businesswomen head for a wine bar after a particularly stressful day.
- In the American Southwest, a Navajo elder gives his congregation peyote tea, a sacrament in the Native American Church, as a drumbeat resounds in the darkness.
- In Los Angeles, an artist spends 2 hours in a flotation chamber to clear her head before resuming work on a large painting.
- At a park in Amsterdam, a group of street musicians smoke a joint and sing for spare change.
- In Northern Ireland, a nun living in a convent spends an entire week in silent prayer and contemplation.
- In Tucson, Arizona, one of your authors brews himself another cup of cappuccino.

Each of these people is experiencing a different state of consciousness. Some have no choice and some are deliberately seeking to bend their minds—to alter consciousness—in different ways, to different degrees, and for different reasons. As these examples suggest, consciousness can take many forms. In the discussion that follows, we will begin with the familiar realms of sleep and dreaming and then move on to more exotic states of consciousness.

Gateway QUESTIONS

5.1 *What is consciousness?*
5.2 *What are the effects of sleep loss or changes in sleep patterns?*
5.3 *What are some functions of sleep?*
5.4 *What are some sleep disorders and unusual sleep events?*
5.5 *Do dreams have meaning?*
5.6 *What is hypnosis?*
5.7 *Do meditation and sensory deprivation have any benefits?*
5.8 *What are the effects of the more commonly used psychoactive drugs?*
5.9 *How can dreams be used to promote personal understanding?*

States of Consciousness—The Many Faces of Awareness

Gateway Question 5.1: *What is consciousness?*

To be *conscious* means to be aware. **Consciousness** consists of your sensations and perceptions of external events and your self-awareness of mental events including thoughts, memories, and feelings about your experiences and yourself (Morin, 2006; Robinson, 2008). Take, for example, Eric's big moment at the Grand Canyon. As he first looked over the rim he was "blown away" as he surveyed the bottom a mile down and experienced deep feelings of insignificance and awe. At that moment, he was also fully aware that he *was* being "blown away," as he realized he was experiencing a deeply moving moment.

Although this definition of consciousness may seem obvious, it is based on your own subjective, *first-person* experience. You are the expert on what it feels like to be you. But what about other people? What does it feel like to be President Obama? Or your mother? Or someone in a coma? What runs through a dog's mind when it sniffs other dogs? Does it feel joy?

You simply can't answer these questions about *other minds* through your own first-person perspective. The difficulty of knowing other minds is one reason why the early behaviorists distrusted introspection. (Remember Chapter 1?) Instead, psychologists adopt an objective, *third-person* point of view. A key challenge for psychology is to use objective studies of the brain and behavior to help us understand the mind and consciousness, which are basically private phenomena (Koch, 2004; Robinson, 2008). This chapter summarizes some of what we have learned about different states of consciousness.

Altered States of Consciousness

We spend most of our lives in **waking consciousness**, a state of clear, organized alertness. In waking consciousness, we perceive times, places, and events as real, meaningful, and familiar. But states of consciousness related to fatigue, delirium, hypnosis, drugs, and euphoria may differ markedly from "normal" awareness (Chalmers, 2010). Everyone experiences at least some altered states, such as sleep, dreaming, and daydreaming (Blackmore, 2004). Some people experience dramatically altered states, such as the lower levels of awareness associated with strokes and other forms of brain damage (Morin, 2006). In everyday life, changes in consciousness may even accompany long-distance running, listening to music, making love, or other circumstances.

How are altered states distinguished from normal awareness? During an **altered state of consciousness (ASC)**, changes occur in the *quality* and *pattern* of mental activity. Typically there are distinct shifts in our perceptions, emotions, memories, time sense, thoughts, feelings of self-control, and suggestibility (Siegel, 2005). Definitions aside, most people know when they have experienced an ASC. In fact, heightened self-awareness is an important feature of many ASCs (Revonsuo, Kallio, & Sikka, 2009).

Are there other causes of ASCs? In addition to the ones mentioned, we could add: sensory overload (a rave, Mardi Gras crowd, or mosh pit), monotonous stimulation (such as "highway hypnotism" on long drives), unusual physical conditions (high fever, hyperventilation, dehydration, sleep loss, near-death experiences), restricted sensory input (extended periods of isolation), and many other possibilities. In some instances, altered states have important cultural meanings (see "Consciousness and Culture" for more information).

An unconscious person will die without constant care. Yet as crucial as consciousness is, we can't really explain how it occurs (Robinson, 2008; Schwitzgebel, 2011). Nevertheless, it is possible to identify various states of consciousness and to explore the role they play in our lives. Let's begin with a look at the most common altered state, sleep and dreaming.

Sleep—Catching a Few ZZZs

Gateway Question 5.2: *What are the effects of sleep loss or changes in sleep patterns?*

Each of us will spend some 25 years of life asleep. Because sleep is familiar, many people think they know all about it. But many common-sense beliefs about sleep are false. For example, you are not totally unresponsive during sleep. A sleeping mother may ignore a jet thundering overhead but wake at the slightest whimper of her child. Likewise, you are more likely to awaken if you hear your own name spoken instead of another. It's even possible to do simple tasks while asleep. In one experiment, people learned to avoid an electric shock by touching a switch each time a tone sounded. Eventually, they could do it without waking. (This is much like the basic survival skill of turning off your alarm clock without waking.) Of course, sleep does impose limitations. Don't expect to learn math, a foreign language, or other complex skills while asleep—especially if the snooze takes place in class (Froufe & Schwartz, 2001; González-Vallejo et al., 2008). But do expect that a good sleep will help you remember what you learned the day before (Fenn, Nusbaum, & Margoliash, 2003; Saxvig et al., 2008).

The Need for Sleep

How strong is the need for sleep? Sleep is an innate **biological rhythm** that can never be entirely ignored (Mistlberger, 2005; see • Figure 5.1). Of course, sleep will give way temporarily, especially at times of great danger. As comedian and filmmaker Woody Allen once put it, "The lion and the lamb shall lie down together, but the lamb will not be very sleepy." However, there are limits to how long humans can go without sleep. A rare disease that prevents sleep always ends with stupor, coma, and death (Zhang et al., 2010).

How long could a person go without sleep? With few exceptions, 4 days or more without sleep becomes hell for everyone. The world record is held by Randy Gardner, who at age 17 went 264 hours (11 days) without sleep. (Although others have gone even longer

Human Diversity

Consciousness and Culture

Throughout history, people everywhere have found ways to alter consciousness (Siegel, 2005). A dramatic example is the sweat lodge ceremony of the Sioux Indians. During the ritual, several men sit in total darkness inside a small chamber heated by coals. Cedar smoke, bursts of steam, and sage fill the air. The men chant rhythmically. The heat builds. At last, they can stand it no more. The door is thrown open. Cooling night breezes rush in. And then? The cycle begins again—often to be repeated four or five times more.

Like the yoga practices of Hindu mystics or the dances of the Whirling Dervishes of Turkey, the ritual "sweats" of the Sioux are meant to cleanse the mind and body. When they are especially intense, they bring altered awareness and personal revelation.

People seek some altered states purely for pleasure, as is often true of drug intoxification. Yet, as the Sioux illustrate, many cultures regard altered consciousness as a pathway to personal enlightenment. Indeed, all cultures and most religions recognize and accept some alterations of consciousness. However, the meaning given to these states varies greatly—from signs of "madness" and "possession" by spirits to life-enhancing breakthroughs. Thus, cultural conditioning greatly affects what altered states we recognize, seek, consider normal, and attain (de Rios & Grob, 2005).

Expuesto-Nicolas Randall/Alamy.

In many cultures, rituals of healing, prayer, purification, or personal transformation are accompanied by altered states of consciousness. This Whirling Dervish is entering a trance state to free himself from distracting thoughts.

without sleep, Randy still holds the "official" record because *The Guinness Book of Records* no longer recognizes sleep deprivation competitions due to possible health risks.) Surprisingly, Randy needed only 14 hours of sleep to recover. As Randy found, most symptoms of **sleep deprivation** (sleep loss) are reversed by a single night's rest (Sallinen et al., 2008).

What are the costs of sleep loss? At various times, Randy's speech was slurred, and he couldn't concentrate, remember clearly, or name common objects (Coren, 1996). Sleep loss also typically causes trembling hands, drooping eyelids, inattention, irritability, staring, increased pain sensitivity, and general discomfort (Doran, Van Dongen, & Dinges, 2001).

Most people experience **hypersomnia** (hi-per-SOM-nee-ah), or excessive daytime sleepiness, after even a few hours of sleep loss. Hypersomnia is a common problem during adolescence (Carskadon, Acebo, & Jenni, 2004). Rapid physical changes during puberty increase the need for sleep. However, the quality and quantity of sleep time tends to decrease during the teen years (Fukuda & Ishihara, 2001).

Most people who have not slept for a day or two can still do interesting or complex mental tasks. But they have trouble paying attention, staying alert, and doing simple or boring routines (Trujillo, Kornguth, & Schnyer, 2009). They are also susceptible to **microsleeps**, which are brief shifts in brain activity to the pattern normally recorded during sleep. Imagine placing an animal on a moving treadmill over a pool of water. Even under these conditions, animals soon drift into repeated microsleeps. For a pilot or machine operator, this can spell disaster (Hardaway & Gregory, 2005). If a task is monotonous (such as factory work or air traffic control), no amount of sleep loss is safe. In fact, if you lose just 1 hour of sleep a night, it can affect your mood, memory, ability to pay attention, and even your health (Maas, 1999). Sleep helps keep the body, including the brain, healthy by regulating its temperature and immune system, conserving energy, and aiding

Timothy Ross/The Image Works.

• Figure 5.1 Not all animals sleep, but like humans, those that do have powerful sleep needs. For example, dolphins must voluntarily breathe air, which means they face the choice of staying awake or drowning. The dolphin solves this problem by sleeping on just one side of its brain at a time! The other half of the brain, which remains awake, controls breathing (Jouvet, 1999).

Consciousness Mental awareness of sensations and perceptions of external events as well as self-awareness of internal events including thoughts, memories, and feelings about experiences and the self.

Waking consciousness A state of clear, organized alertness.

Altered state of consciousness (ASC) A condition of awareness distinctly different in quality or pattern from waking consciousness.

Biological rhythm Any repeating cycle of biological activity, such as sleep and waking cycles or changes in body temperature.

Sleep deprivation Being prevented from getting desired or needed amounts of sleep.

Hypersomnia Excessive daytime sleepiness.

Microsleep A brief shift in brain-wave patterns to those of sleep.

development and repair (Faraut et al., 2011; Freberg, 2010). According to **repair/restorative theories of sleep**, lowering body and brain activity and metabolism during sleep may help conserve energy and lengthen life. Biologically, sleep is a necessity, not a luxury.

When you drive, remember that microsleeps can lead to macroaccidents. Even if your eyes are open, you can fall asleep for a few seconds. A hundred thousand crashes every year are caused by sleepiness (Rau, 2005). Although coffee helps (Kamimori et al., 2005), if you are struggling to stay awake while driving, you should stop, quit fighting it, and take a short nap.

Severe sleep loss can even cause a temporary **sleep-deprivation psychosis**—a loss of contact with reality. Confusion, disorientation, delusions, and hallucinations are typical of this reaction. Fortunately, such "crazy" behavior is uncommon. Hallucinations and delusions rarely appear before 60 hours of wakefulness (Naitoh, Kelly, & Englund, 1989).

How can I tell how much sleep I really need? Pick a day when you feel well rested. Then sleep that night until you wake without an alarm clock. If you feel rested when you wake up, that's your natural sleep need. If you're sleeping fewer hours than you need, you're building up a sleep debt (Basner & Dinges, 2009).

Sleep Patterns

Sleep was described as an innate biological rhythm. What does that mean? Daily sleep and waking periods create a variety of *sleep patterns*. Rhythms of sleep and waking are so steady that they continue for many days, even when clocks and light-dark cycles are removed. However, under such conditions, humans eventually shift to a sleep-waking cycle that averages slightly more than 24 hours (Czeisler et al., 1999; see ● Figure 5.2). This suggests that external time markers, especially light and dark, help tie our sleep rhythms to days that are exactly 24 hours long. Otherwise, many of us would drift into our own unusual sleep cycles (Duffy & Wright, 2005).

BRIDGES

Daily sleep cycles can be disrupted by rapid travel across time zones (jet lag) and by shift work. **See Chapter 10, pages 333–334, for more information.**

What is the normal range of sleep? A few rare individuals can get by on an hour or two of sleep a night—and feel perfectly fine. Only a small percentage of the population are *short sleepers*, averaging 5 hours of sleep or less per night. On the other end of the scale, we find *long sleepers*, who doze 9 hours or more (Grandner & Kripke, 2004). The majority of us sleep on a familiar 7- to 8-hour-per-night schedule. Urging everyone to sleep 8 hours would be like advising everyone to wear medium-size shoes.

We need less sleep as we get older, right? Yes, total sleep time declines throughout life. Those older than 50 average only 6 hours of sleep a night. In contrast, infants spend up to 20 hours a day sleeping, usually in 2- to 4-hour cycles. As they mature, most children go through a "nap" stage and eventually settle into a steady cycle of sleeping once a day (● Figure 5.3). Perhaps we should all continue to take an afternoon "siesta." Midafternoon sleepiness is a natural part of the sleep cycle. Brief, well-timed naps can help maintain alertness in people like truck drivers and hospital interns, who often must fight to stay alert (Ficca et al., 2010).

Busy people may be tempted to sleep less. However, people on *shortened* cycles—for example, 3 hours of sleep to 6 hours awake—often can't get to sleep when the cycle calls for it. That's why astronauts continue to sleep on their normal Earth schedule while in

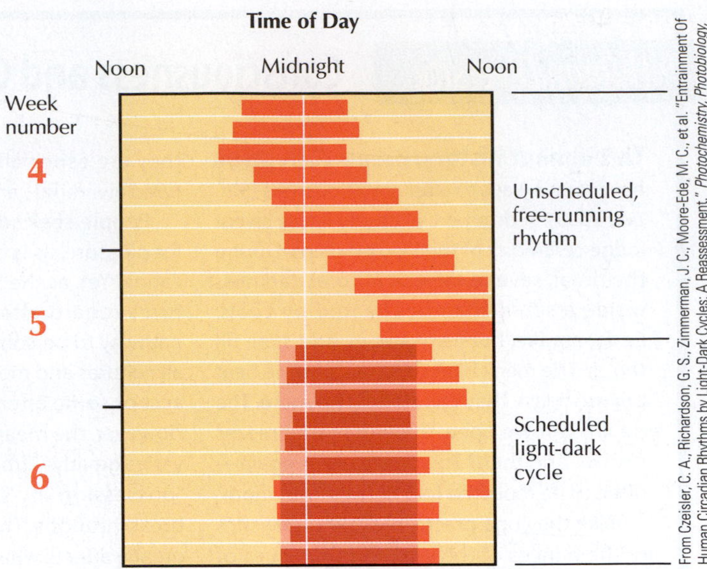

● **Figure 5.2** Sleep rhythms. Bars show periods of sleep during the fourth, fifth, and sixth weeks of an experiment with a human subject. During unscheduled periods, the subject was allowed to select times of sleep and lighting. The result was a sleep rhythm of about 25 hours. Notice how this free-running rhythm began to advance around the clock as they fell asleep later each day. When periods of darkness (shaded area) were imposed during the fifth week, the rhythm quickly resynchronized with 24-hour days.

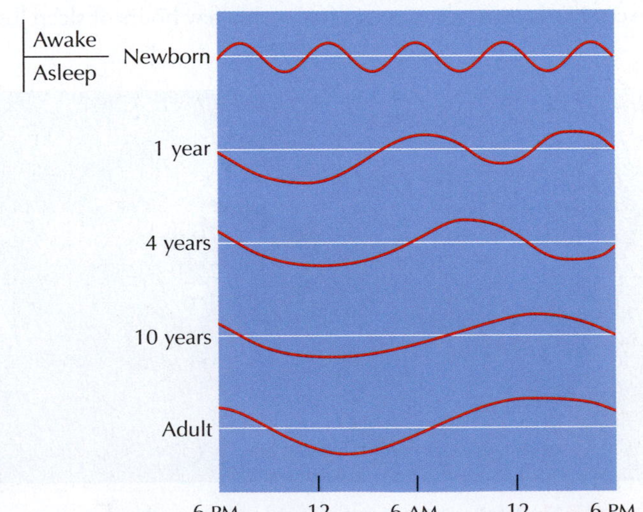

● **Figure 5.3** Development of sleep patterns. Short cycles of sleep and waking gradually become the night-day cycle of an adult. Although most adults don't take naps, midafternoon sleepiness is a natural part of the sleep cycle. From Williams, Agnew, & Webb et al. "Sleep Patterns in Young Adults: An EEG Study." *Electroencephalography & Clinical Neurophysiology*, vol. 17, pp. 376-381. Copyright © 1964. Reprinted with permission from Elsevier.

space. Adapting to *longer*-than-normal days is more promising. Such days can be tailored to match natural sleep patterns, which have a ratio of 2 to 1 between time awake and time asleep (16 hours awake and 8 hours asleep). For instance, one study showed that 28-hour "days" work for some people. Overall, sleep patterns may be bent and stretched, but they rarely yield entirely to human whims (Åkerstedt, 2007).

Stages of Sleep—The Nightly Roller Coaster

Gateway Question 5.3: *What are some functions of sleep?*

What causes sleep? Whether you are awake or asleep right now depends on the *balance* between separate sleep and waking systems. Brain circuits and chemicals in one of the systems promote sleep (Lagos et al., 2009; Steiger, 2007). A network of brain cells in the other system responds to chemicals that inhibit sleep. The two systems seesaw back and forth, switching the brain between sleep and wakefulness. Note that the brain does not "shut down" during sleep. Rather, the *pattern* of activity changes.

Sleep Stages

How does brain activity change when you fall asleep? Changes in tiny electrical signals (brainwaves) generated by the brain can be amplified and recorded with an **electroencephalograph** (eh-LEK-tro-en-SEF-uh-lo-graf), or **EEG**. When you are awake and alert, the EEG reveals a pattern of small fast waves called **beta waves** (● Figure 5.4). Immediately before sleep, the pattern shifts to larger and slower waves called **alpha waves**. (Alpha waves also occur when you are relaxed and allow your thoughts to drift.) As the eyes close, breathing becomes slow and regular, the pulse rate slows, and body temperature drops. Soon after, we descend into *slow-wave sleep* through four distinct **sleep stages**.

Stage 1

As you enter **light sleep** (Stage 1 sleep), your heart rate slows even more. Breathing becomes more irregular. The muscles of your body relax. This may trigger a reflex muscle twitch called a *hypnic* (HIP-nik: sleep) *jerk*. (This is quite normal, so have no fear about admitting to your friends that you fell asleep with a hypnic jerk.) In Stage 1 sleep, the EEG is made up mainly of small, irregular waves with some alpha waves. Persons awakened at this time may or may not say they were asleep.

Stage 2

As sleep deepens, body temperature drops further. Also, the EEG begins to include **sleep spindles**, which are short bursts of distinctive brainwave activity generated by the thalamus (Fogel et al., 2007). Sleep spindles may help prevent the sleeping brain from being aroused by external stimuli, thus marking the true boundary of sleep (Dang-Vu et al., 2010). Within 4 minutes after spindles appear, most people will say they were asleep.

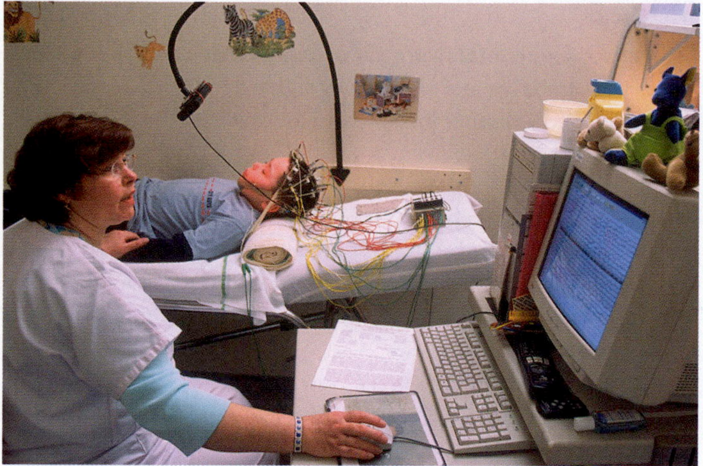

BSIP/Photo Researchers, Inc.

(a)

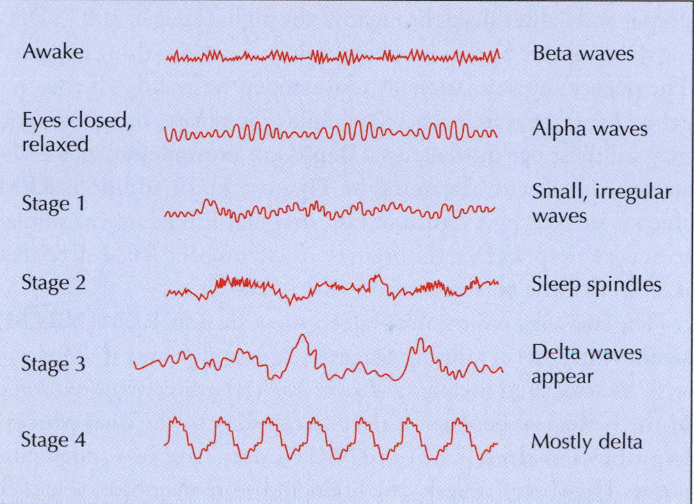

(b)

● **Figure 5.4** *(a)* Photograph of an EEG recording session. The boy in the background is asleep. *(b)* Changes in brainwave patterns associated with various stages of sleep. Actually, most wave types are present at all times, but they occur more or less frequently in various sleep stages. Copyright © 2012 Wadsworth, Cengage Learning, Inc.

Repair/restorative theories of sleep Propose that lowering body and brain activity and metabolism during sleep may help conserve energy and lengthen life.

Sleep-deprivation psychosis A major disruption of mental and emotional functioning brought about by sleep loss.

Electroencephalograph (EEG) A device designed to detect, amplify, and record electrical activity in the brain.

Beta waves Small, fast brainwaves associated with being awake and alert.

Alpha waves Large, slow brainwaves associated with relaxation and falling asleep.

Sleep stages Levels of sleep identified by brain-wave patterns and behavioral changes.

Light sleep Stage 1 sleep, marked by small irregular brainwaves and some alpha waves.

Sleep spindles Distinctive bursts of brainwave activity that indicate a person is asleep.

Stage 3

In Stage 3, a new brainwave called delta begins to appear. **Delta waves** are very large and slow. They signal a move to deeper slow-wave sleep and a further loss of consciousness.

Stage 4

Most people reach **deep sleep** (the deepest level of normal sleep) in about 1 hour. Stage 4 brainwaves are almost pure slow-wave delta, and the sleeper is in a state of oblivion. If you make a loud noise during Stage 4, the sleeper will wake up in a state of confusion and may not remember the noise.

The Dual Process Hypothesis of Sleep

There is much more to a night's sleep than a simple descent into Stage 4. Fluctuations in sleep hormones cause recurring cycles of deeper and lighter sleep throughout the night (Steiger, 2007). During these repeated periods of lighter sleep, a curious thing happens: The sleeper's eyes occasionally move under the eyelids. (If you ever get a chance to watch a sleeping child, roommate, or spouse, you may see these eye movements.) **Rapid eye movements**, or **REMs**, are associated with dreaming (● Figure 5.5). In addition, **REM sleep** is marked by a return of fast, irregular EEG patterns similar to Stage 1 sleep. In fact, the brain is so active during REM sleep that it looks as if the person is awake (Rock, 2004).

The two most basic states of sleep, then, are **non-REM (NREM) sleep**, which occurs during Stages 1, 2, 3, and 4, and REM sleep, with its associated dreaming (Rock, 2004). Earlier, we noted some of the biological benefits of sleep. According to the **dual process hypothesis of sleep**, REM and NREM sleep have two added purposes: They help "refresh" the brain and store memories (Ficca & Salzarulob, 2004).

The Function of NREM Sleep

What is the function of NREM sleep? NREM sleep is dream-free about 90 percent of the time and is deepest early in the night during the first few Stage 4 periods. Your first period of Stage 1 sleep usually lacks REMs and dreams. Later Stage 1 periods typically include a shift into REM sleep. Dreamless, slow-wave NREM sleep increases after physical exertion and may help us recover from bodily fatigue. It also appears to "calm" the brain during the earlier part of a night's sleep (Tononi & Cirelli, 2003).

According to the dual process hypothesis, we are bombarded by information throughout the day, which causes our neural networks to become more and more active. As a result, your brain requires more and more energy to continue functioning. Slow wave sleep early in the night brings overall brain activation levels back down, allowing a "fresh" approach to the next day.

Consider for a moment the amazing jumble of events that make up a day. Some experiences are worth remembering (like what you are reading right now, of course), and others are not so important (like which sock you put on first this morning). As slow-wave sleep reduces overall activation in the brain, less important experiences may fade away and be forgotten. If you wake up feeling clearer about what you studied the previous night, it might be because your brain doesn't "sweat the small stuff"!

The Function of REM Sleep

What, then, is the purpose of REM sleep? According to the dual process hypothesis, whereas NREM sleep "calms" the brain, REM sleep appears to "sharpen" our memories of the previous day's more important experiences (Saxvig et al., 2008). Daytime stress tends to increase REM sleep, which may rise dramatically when there is a death in the family, trouble at work, a marital conflict, or other emotionally charged events. The value of more REM sleep is that it helps us sort and retain memories, especially memories about strategies for solving problems (Walker & Stickgold, 2006). This is why, after studying for a long period, you may remember more if you go to sleep, rather than pulling an all-nighter. (REMember to get some REM!)

Early in life, REM sleep may stimulate the developing brain. Newborn babies have lots of new experiences to process so they spend a hearty 8 or 9 hours a day in REM sleep. That's about 50 percent of their total sleep time.

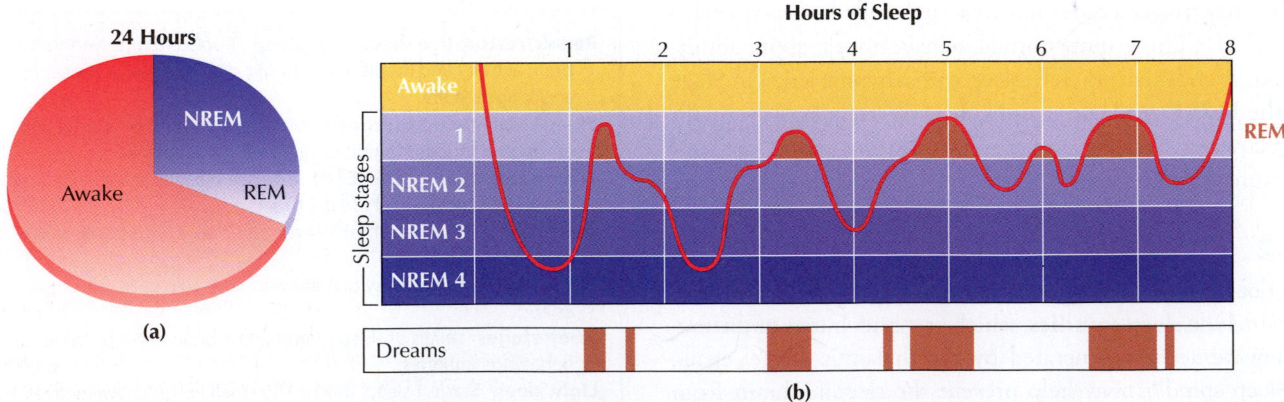

● **Figure 5.5** *(a)* Average proportion of time adults spend daily in REM sleep and NREM sleep. REM periods add up to about 20 percent of total sleep time. *(b)* Typical changes in stages of sleep during the night. Notice that dreams mostly coincide with REM periods.

Critical Thinking They Came from Outer Space?

"Imagine opening your eyes shortly before dawn, attempting to roll over in your bed, and suddenly realizing that you are entirely paralyzed. While lying helplessly on your back and unable to cry out for help, you become aware of sinister figures lurking in your bedroom. As they move closer to your bed, your heart begins to pound violently and you feel as if you are suffocating. You hear buzzing sounds and feel electrical sensations shooting throughout your body. Within moments, the visions vanish and you can move once again. Terrified, you wonder what has just happened" (McNally & Clancy, 2005).

Sleep paralysis, which normally prevents us from moving during REM sleep, can also occur just as you begin to wake up. During such episodes, people sometimes have *hypnopompic* (hip-neh-POM-pik: "upon awakening") *hallucinations*. According to psychologist Al Cheyne (2005), these hallucinations may include bizarre experiences, such as sensing that an alien being is in your bedroom; feeling something pressing on your chest, suffocating you; or feeling like you are floating out of your body.

Although most of us shrug off these weird experiences, some people try to make sense of them. Earlier in history, people interpreted these hallucinated intruders as angels, demons, or witches and believed that their out-of-body experiences were real (Cheyne & Girard, 2009; Cheyne, Rueffer, & Newby-Clark, 1999). However, as our culture changes, so do our interpretations of sleep experiences. Today, for example, some people who have sleep-related hallucinations believe they have been abducted by space aliens or sexually abused (McNally & Clancy, 2005).

Superstitions and folklore often develop as attempts to explain human experiences, including some of the stranger aspects of sleep. By studying hypnopompic hallucinations, psychologists hope to offer natural explanations for many experiences that might otherwise seem supernatural or paranormal (Cheyne & Girard, 2009).

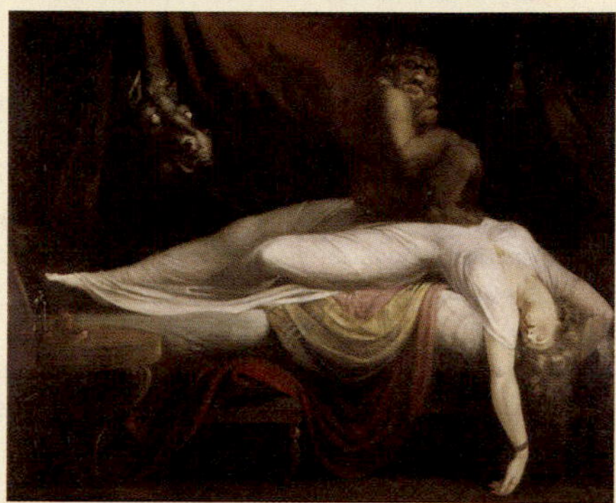

Swiss artist Henry Fuseli drew on hypnopompic imagery as an inspiration for his famous painting, *The Nightmare*.

REM Sleep and Dreaming

Roughly 85 percent of the time, people awakened during REMs report vivid dreams. Some eye movements correspond to dream activities. Dream that you are watching a tennis match, and you will probably move your eyes from side to side. However, people who were born blind still have REMs, so eye movements are not just a result of "watching" dream images (Shafton, 1995). REM sleep is easy to observe in pets, such as dogs and cats. Watch for eye and face movements and irregular breathing. (You can forget about your pet iguana, though. Reptiles show no signs of REM sleep.)

Dreams during REM sleep tend to be longer, clearer, more detailed, more bizarre, and more "dream-like" than thoughts and images that occur in NREM sleep (Hobson, Pace-Schott, & Stickgold, 2000). Also, brain areas associated with imagery and emotion become more active during REM sleep. This may explain why REM dreams tend to be more vivid than NREM dreams (Rock, 2004).

Speaking very loosely, it's as if the dreaming brain were reviewing messages left on a telephone answering machine to decide which are worth keeping. During the day, when information is streaming in, the brain may be too busy to efficiently select useful memories. When the conscious brain is "off-line," we are better able to build new memories.

What happens to the body when a person dreams? REM sleep is a time of high emotion. The heart beats irregularly. Blood pressure and breathing waver. Both males and females appear to be sexually aroused: Men usually have an erection, and genital blood flow increases in women. This occurs for all REM sleep, so it is not strictly related to erotic dreams (Jouvet, 1999).

During REM sleep, your body becomes quite still, as if you were paralyzed. Imagine for a moment the results of acting out some of your recent dreams. Very likely, REM-sleep paralysis prevents some hilarious—and dangerous—nighttime escapades. When it fails, some people thrash violently, leap out of bed, and may attack their bed partners. A lack of muscle paralysis during REM sleep is called *REM behavior disorder* (Ochoa & Pulido, 2005). One patient suffering from the disorder tied himself to his bed every night. That way, he couldn't jump up and crash into furniture or walls (Shafton, 1995). And yet sometimes sleep paralysis can go a little too far. See "They Came from Outer Space?" to find out why.

Delta waves Large, slow brainwaves that occur in deeper sleep (Stages 3 and 4).

Deep sleep Stage 4 slow-wave sleep; the deepest form of normal sleep.

Rapid eye movements (REMs) Swift eye movements during sleep.

REM sleep Sleep marked by rapid eye movements and a return to Stage 1 EEG patterns.

Non-REM (NREM) sleep Non–rapid eye movement sleep characteristic of Stages 2, 3, and 4.

Dual process hypothesis of sleep Proposes that NREM sleep reduces the overall level of brain activation, allowing unimportant memories to be forgotten while REM sleep sharpens memory for important events from the previous day.

In a moment we will survey some additional sleep problems—if you are still awake. First, here are a few questions to check your memory of our discussion so far.

Knowledge Builder: States of Consciousness and Sleep

RECITE

1. Changes in the quality and pattern of mental activity define a(n)
   a. EEG *b.* REM *c.* SIDS *d.* ASC
2. Delusions and hallucinations typically continue for several days after a sleep-deprived individual returns to normal sleep. T or F?
3. Alyssa experiences a microsleep while driving. Most likely, this indicates that she
   a. was producing mostly beta waves *b.* had high levels of sleep hormones in her bloodstream *c.* switched from delta waves to alpha waves *d.* was sleep deprived
4. Older adults, and particularly the elderly, sleep more than children do because the elderly are more easily fatigued. T or F?
5. Alpha waves are to presleep drowsiness as ______________ ______________ are to Stage 4 sleep.
6. Rapid eye movements indicate that a person is in deep sleep. T or F?
7. Which of the following would normally be most incompatible with moving your arms and legs while asleep?
   a. REM sleep *b.* sleep spindles *c.* delta waves *d.* NREM sleep
8. Sharpening memories and facilitating their storage is one function of
   a. activation-synthesis cycles *b.* REM sleep *c.* deep sleep *d.* NREM sleep

REFLECT

Think Critically

9. Why might it be better for the unscheduled human sleep–waking cycle to average more than 24 hours, instead of less?
10. In addition to helping restore the body and store memories, what direct evolutionary advantage might sleeping provide?

Self-Reflect

Make a quick list of some altered states of consciousness you have experienced. What do they have in common? How are they different? What conditions caused them?

Imagine that you are a counselor at a sleep clinic. You must explain the basics of sleep and dreaming to a new client who knows little about these topics. Can you do it?

Answers: 1. *d* **2.** F **3.** *d* **4.** F **5.** delta waves **6.** F **7.** *a* **8.** *b* **9.** Sleep experts theorize that the 25-hour average leaves a little "slack" in the cycle. External time markers can then retard the body cycle slightly to synchronize it with light-dark cycles. If the body cycle were shorter than 24 hours, we all might have to "stretch" every day to adjust. **10.** Natural selection may have favored sleep because animals that remained active at night probably had a higher chance of being killed (Freberg, 2010). (We'll bet they had more fun, though.)

Sleep Disturbances—The Sleepy Time Blues

Gateway Question 5.4: *What are some sleep disorders and unusual sleep events?*

Sleep quality has taken a beating in North America. Artificial lighting, frenetic schedules, exciting pastimes, smoking, drinking, overstimulation, and many other factors have contributed to a near epidemic of sleep problems. Sleep disturbances are a serious risk to health and happiness (Shneerson, 2005). Sleep clinics treat thousands of people each year who suffer from sleep disorders or complaints. Let's explore some of the more interesting problems these people face. These disturbances range from daytime sleep attacks to sleepwalking and terrifying nightmares (see ■ Table 5.1).

TABLE 5.1 Sleep Disturbances—Things That Go Wrong in the Night

Hypersomnia	Excessive daytime sleepiness. This can result from depression, insomnia, narcolepsy, sleep apnea, sleep drunkenness, periodic limb movements, drug abuse, and other problems.
Insomnia	Difficulty in getting to sleep or staying asleep; also, not feeling rested after sleeping.
Narcolepsy	Sudden, irresistible, daytime sleep attacks that may last anywhere from a few minutes to a half hour. Victims may fall asleep while standing, talking, or even driving.
Nightmare disorder	Vivid, recurrent nightmares that significantly disturb sleep.
Periodic limb movement syndrome	Muscle twitches (primarily affecting the legs) that occur every 20 to 40 seconds and severely disturb sleep.
REM behavior disorder	A failure of normal muscle paralysis, leading to violent actions during REM sleep.
Restless legs syndrome	An irresistible urge to move the legs to relieve sensations of creeping, tingling, prickling, aching, or tension.
Sleep apnea	During sleep, breathing stops for 20 seconds or more until the person wakes a little, gulps in air, and settles back to sleep; this cycle may be repeated hundreds of times per night.
Sleep drunkenness	A slow transition to clear consciousness after awakening; sometimes associated with irritable or aggressive behavior.
Sleep terror disorder	The repeated occurrence of night terrors that significantly disturb sleep.
Sleep-wake schedule disorder	A mismatch between the sleep-wake schedule demanded by a person's bodily rhythm and that demanded by the environment.
Sleepwalking disorder	Repeated incidents of leaving bed and walking about while asleep.

Adapted from Carney, Geyer, & Berry, 2005; Shneerson, 2005.

Insomnia

Staring at the ceiling at 2 AM is pretty low on most people's list of favorite pastimes. Yet about 60 million Americans have frequent or chronic insomnia (National Institute of Neurological Disorders and Stroke, 2007). **Insomnia** includes difficulty in falling sleep, frequent nighttime awakenings, waking too early, or a combination of these problems. Insomnia can harm people's work, health, and relationships (Ebben & Spielman, 2009).

Types and Causes of Insomnia

Worry, stress, and excitement can cause *temporary insomnia* and a self-defeating cycle. First, excess mental activity ("I can't stop turning things over in my mind") and heightened arousal block sleep. Then, frustration and anger over not being able to sleep cause more worry and arousal. This further delays sleep, which causes more frustration, and so on (Sateia & Nowell, 2004). A good way to beat this cycle is to avoid fighting it. Get up and do something useful or satisfying when you can't sleep. (Reading a textbook might be a good choice of useful activities.) Return to bed only when you begin to feel that you are struggling to stay awake. If sleeping problems last for more than 3 weeks, then a diagnosis of *chronic insomnia* can be made.

Drug-dependency insomnia (sleep loss caused by withdrawal from sleeping pills) can also occur. There is real irony in the billion dollars a year North Americans spend on sleeping pills. Nonprescription sleeping pills such as Sominex, Nytol, and Sleep-Eze have little sleep-inducing effect. Barbiturates are even worse. These prescription sedatives decrease both Stage 4 sleep and REM sleep, drastically lowering sleep quality. In addition, many users become "sleeping-pill junkies" who need an ever-greater number of pills to get to sleep. Victims must be painstakingly weaned from their sleep medicines. Otherwise, terrible nightmares and "rebound insomnia" may drive them back to drug use. It's worth remembering that although alcohol and other depressant drugs may help a person get to sleep, they greatly reduce sleep quality (Nau & Lichstein, 2005). Even newer drugs, such as Ambien and Lunesta, which induce sleep, have drawbacks. Possible side effects include amnesia, impaired judgment, increased appetite, decreased sex drive, depression, and even sleepwalking, sleep eating, and sleep driving. Rebound insomnia is also a risk, making these drugs at best a temporary remedy for insomnia.

"It's only insomnia if there's nothing good on."

Behavioral Remedies for Insomnia

If sleeping pills are a poor way to treat insomnia, what can be done? Sleep specialists prefer to treat insomnia with lifestyle changes and behavioral techniques (Montgomery & Dennis, 2004). Treatment for chronic insomnia usually begins with a careful analysis of a patient's sleep habits, lifestyle, stress levels, and medical problems. All the approaches discussed in the following list are helpful for treating insomnia (Ebben & Spielman, 2009; Nau & Lichstein, 2005):

1. **Stimulus control.** Insisting on a regular schedule helps establish a firm body rhythm, greatly improving sleep. This is best achieved by exercising **stimulus control**, which refers to linking a response with specific stimuli. It is important to get up and go to sleep at the same time each day, including weekends (Bootzin & Epstein, 2000). In addition, insomniacs are told to avoid doing anything but sleeping when they are in bed. They are not to study, eat, watch TV, read, pay the bills, worry, or even think in bed. (Lovemaking is okay, however.) In this way, only sleeping and relaxation become associated with going to bed at specific times.
2. **Sleep restriction.** Even if an entire night's sleep is missed, it is important not to sleep late in the morning, nap more than an hour, sleep during the evening, or go to bed early the following night. Instead, restricting sleep to normal bedtime hours avoids fragmenting sleep rhythms (Shneerson, 2005).
3. **Paradoxical intention.** Another helpful approach is to remove the pressures of *trying* to go to sleep. Instead, the goal becomes trying to keep the eyes open (in the dark) and stay awake as long as possible (Nau & Lichstein, 2005). This allows sleep to come unexpectedly and lowers performance anxiety (Taylor & Roane, 2010).
4. **Relaxation.** Some insomniacs lower their arousal before sleep by using a physical or mental strategy for relaxing, such as progressive muscle relaxation, meditation, or blotting out worries with calming images. It is also helpful to schedule time in the early evening to write down worries or concerns and plan what to do about them the next day, in order to set them aside before going to bed.

BRIDGES

Learning how to achieve deep relaxation is a highly useful skill. **See Chapter 15, pages 522–523, for more information.**

5. **Exercise.** Strenuous exercise during the day promotes sleep (Brand et al., 2010). However, exercise within 3 to 6 hours of sleep is helpful only if it is very light.

Insomnia Difficulty in getting to sleep or staying asleep.
Stimulus control Linking a particular response with specific stimuli.

6. **Food intake.** What you eat can affect how easily you get to sleep. Eating starchy foods increases the amount of tryptophan (TRIP-tuh-fan: an amino acid) reaching the brain. More tryptophan, in turn, increases the amount of serotonin in the brain, which is associated with relaxation, a positive mood, and sleepiness (Silber & Schmitt, 2010). Thus, to promote sleep, try eating a starchy snack, such as cookies, bread, pasta, oatmeal, pretzels, or dry cereal. If you really want to drop the bomb on insomnia, try eating a baked potato (which may be the world's largest sleeping pill!).
7. **Stimulant avoidance.** Stimulants, such as coffee and cigarettes, should be avoided. It is also worth remembering that alcohol, although not a stimulant, impairs sleep quality.

Sleepwalking, Sleeptalking, and Sleepsex

Sleepsex? As strange as it may seem, many waking behaviors can be engaged in while asleep, such as driving a car, cooking, playing a musical instrument, and eating (Plazzi et al., 2005). The most famous, sleepwalking, is eerie and fascinating in its own right. **Somnambulists** (som-NAM-bue-lists: those who sleepwalk) avoid obstacles, descend stairways, and on rare occasions may step out of windows or in front of automobiles. Sleepwalkers have been observed jumping into lakes, urinating in garbage pails or closets (phew!), shuffling furniture around, and even brandishing weapons (Schenck & Mahowald, 2005).

The sleepwalker's eyes are usually open, but a blank face and shuffling feet reveal that the person is still asleep. If you find someone sleepwalking, you should gently guide the person back to bed. Awakening a sleepwalker does no harm, but it is not necessary.

Does sleepwalking occur during dreaming? No. Remember that people are normally immobilized during REM sleep. EEG studies have shown that somnambulism occurs during NREM Stages 3 and 4 (Stein & Ferber, 2001). Sleeptalking also occurs mostly during NREM sleep. The link with deep sleep explains why sleeptalking makes little sense and why sleepwalkers are confused and remember little when awakened.

Oh, yes, you're curious about sleepsex. There is, of course, an official name for it: *sexsomnia* (Klein & Houlihan, 2010). Sexsomnia is not as exciting as it might sound: Just imagine being startled wide awake by your bed partner, who is asleep but attempting to have sex with you (Andersen et al., 2007; Mangan, 2004).

Nightmares and Night Terrors

Stage 4 sleep is also the realm of night terrors. These frightening episodes are quite different from ordinary nightmares. A **nightmare** is simply a bad dream that takes place during REM sleep. Frequently occurring nightmares (one a week or more) are associated with higher levels of psychological distress (Levin & Fireman, 2002). During Stage 4 **night terrors**, a person suffers total panic and may hallucinate frightening dream images into the bedroom. An attack may last 15 or 20 minutes. When it is over, the person awakens drenched in sweat but only vaguely remembers the terror. Because night terrors occur during NREM sleep (when the body is not immobilized), victims may sit up, scream, get out of bed, or run around the room. Victims remember little afterward. (Other family members, however, may have a story to tell.) Although night terrors are more common in childhood, they are not uncommon in adulthood (Belicki, Chambers, & Ogilvie, 1997; Kataria, 2004).

How to Eliminate a Nightmare

Is there any way to stop a recurring nightmare? A bad nightmare can be worse than any horror movie. It's easy to leave a theater, but we often remain trapped in terrifying dreams. Nevertheless, most nightmares can be banished by following three simple steps. First, write down your nightmare, describing it in detail. Next, change the dream any way you wish, making sure to spell out the details of the new dream. The third step is *imagery rehearsal*, in which you mentally rehearse the changed dream before you fall asleep again (Krakow & Zadra, 2006). Imagery rehearsal may work because it makes upsetting dreams familiar while a person is awake and feeling safe. Or perhaps it mentally "reprograms" future dream content. In any case, the technique has helped many people.

Sleep Apnea

Some sage once said, "Laugh and the whole world laughs with you; snore and you sleep alone." Nightly "wood sawing" is often harmless, but it can signal a serious problem. A person who snores loudly, with short silences and loud gasps or snorts, may suffer from apnea (AP-nee-ah: interrupted breathing). In **sleep apnea**, breathing stops for periods of 20 seconds to 2 minutes. As the need for oxygen becomes intense, the person wakes a little and gulps in air. She or he then settles back to sleep. But soon, breathing stops again. This cycle is repeated hundreds of times a night. Although snoring might be funny, sleep apnea is no joke. As you might guess, apnea victims are extremely sleepy during the day (Collop, 2005). They can also have a harder time functioning during the day (Grenèche et al., 2011) and, in the long run, may suffer damage to their oxygen-hungry brains (Jo et al., 2010).

What causes sleep apnea? Some cases occur because the brain stops sending signals to the diaphragm to maintain breathing. Another cause is blockage of the upper air passages. One of the most effective treatments is the use of a continuous positive airway pressure (CPAP) mask to aid breathing during sleep. The resulting improvement in sleep will often result in improved daytime function (Tregear et al., 2010). Other treatments include weight loss and surgery for breathing obstructions (Collop, 2005).

SIDS

Sleep apnea is suspected as one cause of **sudden infant death syndrome (SIDS)**, or "crib death." In the "typical" crib death, a slightly premature or small baby with some signs of a cold or cough is bundled up and put to bed. A short time later, parents find the child has died. A baby deprived of air will normally struggle to begin breathing again. However, SIDS babies seem to have a weak arousal reflex. This prevents them from changing positions and

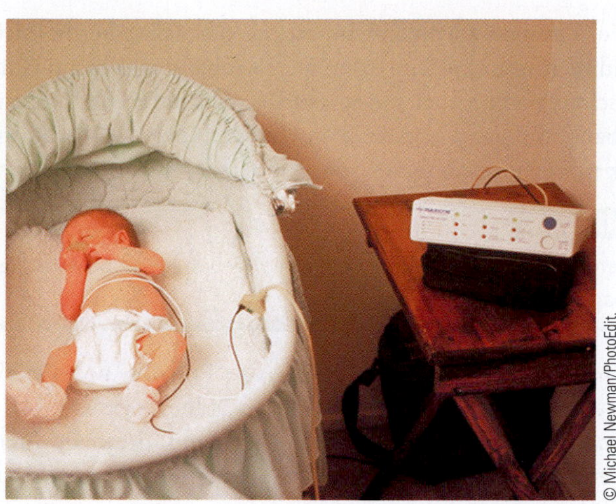

● **Figure 5.6** Infants at risk for SIDS are often attached to devices that monitor breathing and heart rate during sleep. An alarm sounds to alert parents if either pulse or respiration falters. SIDS rarely occurs after an infant is 1 year old. Babies at risk for SIDS should be placed on their backs. (Photo courtesy of Healthdyne, Inc.)

resuming breathing after an episode of apnea (Horne et al., 2001). SIDS is the leading cause of death in children between 1 month and 1 year of age (National Institute of Child Health and Human Development, 2010).

Babies at risk for SIDS must be carefully watched for the first 6 months of life. To aid parents in this task, a special monitor may be used that sounds an alarm when breathing or pulse becomes weak (● Figure 5.6). Babies at risk for SIDS are often premature, have a shrill, high-pitched cry, engage in "snoring," breath-holding, or frequent awakening at night, breathe mainly through an open mouth, or remain passive when their face rolls into a pillow or blanket.

"Back to Sleep"

Sleeping position is another major risk factor for SIDS. Healthy infants are best off sleeping on their backs (sides are not as good but much better than face down) (Shapiro-Mendoza et al., 2009). (Premature babies, those with respiratory problems, and those who often vomit may need to sleep facedown. Ask a pediatrician for guidance.) Remember, "*back* to sleep" is the safest position for most infants (Hauck et al., 2002). It is also worth noting that up to 15 percent of all SIDS cases can be attributed to accidental suffocation and strangulation in bed, which includes suffocation by overly soft bedding or pillows; strangulation, such as an infant's head being caught in crib railings; and *overlaying* (which occurs when a sleeping adult rolls over on top of an infant). (Shapiro-Mendoza et al., 2009).

Narcolepsy

One of the most dramatic sleep problems is **narcolepsy** (NAR-koe-lep-see), or sudden, irresistible sleep attacks. These last anywhere from a few minutes to a half hour. Victims may fall asleep while standing, talking, or even driving. Emotional excitement, especially laughter, commonly triggers narcolepsy. (Tell an especially good joke and a narcoleptic may fall asleep.) Many victims also suffer from **cataplexy** (CAT-uh-plex-see), a sudden temporary paralysis of the muscles, leading to complete body collapse (Peterson & Husain, 2008). It's easy to understand why narcolepsy can devastate careers and relationships (Thorpy, 2006).

Because sudden paralysis happens during dreaming, is there a connection between narcolepsy and REM sleep? Yes, narcoleptics tend to fall directly into REM sleep. Thus, the narcoleptic's sleep attacks and paralysis appear to occur when REM sleep intrudes into the waking state (Mignot, 2001).

Fortunately, narcolepsy is rare. It runs in families, which suggests that it is hereditary (Chabas et al., 2003). In fact, this has been confirmed by breeding several generations of narcoleptic dogs. (These dogs, by the way, are simply outstanding at learning the trick "Roll over and play dead.") There is no known cure for narcolepsy, but a drug named sodium oxybate reduces the frequency and intensity of attacks (Lammers et al., 2010).

Dreams—A Separate Reality?

Gateway Question 5.5: *Do dreams have meaning?*

When REM sleep was discovered in 1952, it ushered in a "golden era" of dream inquiry. To conclude our discussion of sleep, let's consider some age-old questions about dreaming.

Does everyone dream? Do dreams occur in an instant? Most people dream four or five times a night, but not all people remember their dreams. "Nondreamers" are often surprised by their dreams when first awakened during REM sleep. Dreams are usually spaced about 90 minutes apart. The first dream lasts only about 10 minutes; the last averages 30 minutes and may run as long as 50. Dreams, therefore, occur in real time, not as "flashes" (Shafton, 1995).

REM Rebound

How important is REM sleep for dreaming? To answer this question, sleep expert William Dement awakened volunteers each time they entered REM sleep. Soon, their need for "dream time" grew more urgent. By the fifth night, many had to be awakened 20 or 30 times to prevent REM sleep. When the volunteers were finally allowed to sleep undisturbed, they dreamed extra amounts. This effect, called a **REM rebound**, explains why alcoholics have horrible nightmares after they quit drinking. Alcohol reduces sleep quality

Somnambulists People who sleepwalk; occurs during NREM sleep.
Nightmare A bad dream that occurs during REM sleep.
Night terror A state of panic during NREM sleep.
Sleep apnea Repeated interruption of breathing during sleep.
Sudden infant death syndrome (SIDS) The sudden, unexplained death of an apparently healthy infant.
Narcolepsy A sudden, irresistible sleep attack.
Cataplexy A sudden temporary paralysis of the muscles.
REM rebound The occurrence of extra rapid eye movement sleep following REM sleep deprivation.

by suppressing REM sleep, thus setting up a powerful rebound when it is withdrawn (Stein & Friedmann, 2005).

Dement's volunteers complained of memory lapses, poor concentration, and anxiety. For a while, it was thought that people deprived of REM sleep might go crazy. But later experiments showed that missing *any* sleep stage can cause a rebound for that stage. In general, daytime disturbances are related to the *total amount* of sleep lost, not to the *type* of sleep lost (Devoto et al., 1999).

Dream Theories

How meaningful are dreams? Some theorists believe that dreams have deeply hidden meanings. Others regard dreams as nearly meaningless. Yet others hold that dreams reflect our waking thoughts, fantasies, and emotions. Let's examine all three views.

Psychodynamic Dream Theory

Psychodynamic theories of dreaming emphasize internal conflicts and unconscious forces (Jones, 2007). Sigmund Freud's (1900) landmark book, *The Interpretation of Dreams*, first advanced the idea that many dreams are based on **wish fulfillment**—an expression of unconscious desires. One of Freud's key proposals was that dreams express unconscious desires and conflicts as disguised **dream symbols** (images that have deeper symbolic meaning). Understanding a dream, then, requires analyzing the dream's **manifest content** (obvious, visible meaning) to uncover its **latent content** (hidden, symbolic meaning).

© Christie's Images/Corbis

According to psychodynamic theory, dream imagery often has symbolic meaning. How would you interpret Italian artist Mimmo Paladino's dream-like image, titled *Vespero*? The fact that dreams don't have a single unambiguous meaning is one of the shortcomings of Freudian dream theory.

For instance, a woman who dreams of stealing her best friend's wedding ring and placing it on her own hand may be unwilling to consciously admit that she is sexually attracted to her best friend's husband. Similarly, a journey might symbolize death, and horseback riding or dancing, sexual intercourse.

BRIDGES

Interpreting dreams is an important part of Freudian psychoanalysis. **See Chapter 15, page 513.**

Do all dreams have hidden meanings? Probably not. Freud realized that some dreams are trivial "day residues" or carryovers from ordinary waking events. On the other hand, dreams do tend to reflect a person's current concerns, so Freud wasn't entirely wrong.

The Activation-Synthesis Hypothesis

Psychiatrists Allan Hobson and Robert McCarley have a radically different view of dreaming, called the **activation-synthesis hypothesis**. They believe that during REM sleep, several lower brain centers are "turned on" (*activated*) in more or less random fashion. However, messages from the cells are blocked from reaching the body, so no movement occurs. Nevertheless, the cells continue to tell higher brain areas of their activities. Struggling to interpret this random information, the brain searches through stored memories and manufactures (*synthesizes*) a dream (Hobson, 2000, 2005). However, frontal areas of the cortex, which control higher mental abilities, are mostly shut down during REM sleep. This explains why dreams are more primitive and more bizarre than daytime thoughts (Hobson, 2000).

How does that help explain dream content? According to the activation-synthesis hypothesis, dreams are usually meaningless. Let's use the classic chase dream as an example. In such dreams we feel we are running but not going anywhere. This occurs because the brain is told the body is running, but it gets no feedback from the motionless legs. To try to make sense of this information, the brain creates a chase drama. A similar process probably explains dreams of floating or flying.

So dreams have no meaning? The activation-synthesis hypothesis rejects the idea that dreams are deliberate, meaningful messages from our unconscious. It does not rule out the possibility that we can find meaning in some dreams. Because dreams are created from memories and past experiences, parts of dreams can sometimes reflect each person's mental life, emotions, and concerns (Hobson, 2000).

Neurocognitive Dream Theory

Can't dreams just be about normal day-to-day stuff? Yes they can. William Domhoff offers a third view of dreaming. According to his **neurocognitive dream theory**, dreams actually have much in common with waking thoughts and emotions. Indeed, most dreams do reflect ordinary waking concerns. Domhoff believes this is true because many brain areas that are active when we are awake remain active during dreaming (Domhoff, 2001, 2003). From this perspective, our dreams are a conscious expression of REM sleep processes that are sorting and storing daily experiences. Thus, we shouldn't be surprised if a student who is angry at a teacher dreams of embarrassing the teacher in class, a lonely person dreams of romance, or a hungry child dreams of food. It is not necessary to seek deep symbolic meanings to understand these dreams.

Dream Worlds

Which dream theory is the most widely accepted? Each theory has strengths and weaknesses (MacDuffie & Mashour, 2010). However, studies of dream content tend to support neurocognitive theory's focus on the continuity between dreams and waking thought. As noted above, rather than seeming exotic or bizarre, most dreams reflect everyday events (Domhoff & Schneider, 2008; Pesant & Zadra, 2006). For example, athletes tend to dream about the previous day's athletic activities (Erlacher & Schredl, 2004). In general, the favorite dream setting is a familiar room in a house. Action usually takes place between the dreamer and two or three other emotionally important people—friends, enemies, loved ones, or employers. Dream actions are also mostly familiar: running, jumping, riding, sitting, talking, and watching. About half of all dreams have sexual elements. Dreams of flying, floating, and falling occur less frequently. However, note that such dreams lend some support to the activation-synthesis hypothesis, because they are not everyday events (unless you are a trapeze artist).

Even if many dreams can be viewed as just a different form of thought, many psychologists continue to believe that some dreams have deeper meaning (Halliday, 2010; Wilkinson, 2006). There seems to be little doubt that dreams can make a difference in our lives: Veteran sleep researcher William Dement once dreamed that he had lung cancer. In the dream, a doctor told Dement he would die soon. At the time, Dement was smoking two packs of cigarettes a day. He says, "I will never forget the surprise, joy, and exquisite relief of waking up. I felt reborn." Dement quit smoking the following day. (For more information about dreaming, see the *Psychology in Action* section later in this chapter.)

Knowledge Builder: Sleep Disturbances and Dreaming

RECITE

1. Which of the following is ***not*** a behavioral remedy for insomnia?
   a. daily hypersomnia *b.* stimulus control *c.* progressive relaxation *d.* paradoxical intention
2. Eating a snack that is nearly all starch can promote sleep because it increases __________ in the brain.
   a. beta waves *b.* tryptophan *c.* EEG activity *d.* hypnic cycling
3. Night terrors, sleepwalking, and sleeptalking all occur during Stage 1, NREM sleep. T or F?
4. Sleep ________________ is suspected as one cause of SIDS.
5. People who suffer from sudden daytime sleep attacks have which sleep disorder?
   a. narcolepsy *b.* REM behavior disorder *c.* somnambulism *d.* sleep spindling
6. According to the activation-synthesis hypothesis of dreaming, dreams are constructed from ________________________ to explain messages received from nerve cells controlling eye movement, balance, and bodily activity.
7. The favored setting for dreams is
   a. work *b.* school *c.* outdoors or unfamiliar places *d.* familiar rooms
8. The most widely accepted theory of dreaming is
   a. REM rebound theory *b.* neurocognitive theory *c.* psychodynamic theory *d.* activation-synthesis

REFLECT

Think Critically

9. Even without being told that somnambulism is an NREM event, you could have predicted that sleepwalking doesn't occur during dreaming. Why?

Self-Reflect

Almost everyone suffers from insomnia at least occasionally. Are any of the techniques for combating insomnia similar to strategies you have discovered on your own?

How many sleep disturbances can you name (including those listed in Table 5.1)? Are there any that you have experienced? Which do you think would be most disruptive?

Do you think the activation-synthesis theory provides an adequate explanation of your own dreams? Have you had dreams that seem to reflect Freudian wish fulfillment? Do you think your dreams have symbolic meaning or reflect everyday concerns?

Answers: 1. *a* **2.** *b* **3.** F **4.** apnea **5.** *a* **6.** memories **7.** *d* **8.** *b* **9.** Because people are immobilized during REM sleep and REM sleep is strongly associated with dreaming. This makes it unlikely that sleepwalkers are acting out dreams.

Hypnosis—Look into My Eyes

Gateway Question 5.6: *What is hypnosis?*

"Your body is becoming heavy. You can barely keep your eyes open. You are so tired you can't move. Relax. Let go. Relax. Close your eyes and relax." These are the last words a textbook should ever say to you, and the first a hypnotist might say.

Psychodynamic theory Any theory of behavior that emphasizes internal conflicts, motives, and unconscious forces.

Wish fulfillment Freudian belief that many dreams express unconscious desires.

Dream symbols Images in dreams that serve as visible signs of hidden ideas, desires, impulses, emotions, relationships, and so forth.

Manifest content (of dreams) The surface, "visible" content of a dream; dream images as they are remembered by the dreamer.

Latent content (of dreams) The hidden or symbolic meaning of a dream, as revealed by dream interpretation and analysis.

Activation-synthesis hypothesis An attempt to explain how dream content is affected by motor commands in the brain that occur during sleep but are not carried out.

Neurocognitive dream theory Proposal that dreams reflect everyday waking thoughts and emotions.

Discovering Psychology Swinging Suggestions

Here's a demonstration you can use to gain insight into hypnosis. Tie a short length of string (about 6 inches) to a small, heavy object, such as a ring or a small metal nut. Hold the ring at eye level, about a foot from your face. Concentrate on the ring and notice that it will begin to move, ever so slightly. As it does, focus all your attention on the ring. Narrow your attention to a beam of energy and mentally push the ring away from you. Each time the ring swings away, push on it, using only mental force. Then release it and let it swing back toward you. Continue to mentally push and release the ring until it is swinging freely. For the best results, try this now, before reading more.

Did the ring move? If it did, you used *autosuggestion* to influence your own behavior in a subtle way. Suggestions that the ring would swing caused your hand to make tiny micromuscular movements. These, in turn, caused the ring to move—no special mental powers or supernatural forces are involved.

As is true of hypnotic suggestion, the ring's movement probably seemed to be automatic. Obviously, you could just intentionally swing the ring. However, if you responded to suggestion, the movement seemed to happen without any effort on your part. In the same way, when people are hypnotized, their actions seem to occur without any voluntary intent. Incidentally, autosuggestion likely underlies other phenomena, such as how Ouija boards answer questions without any conscious movements by the person using the pointer. Autosuggestion also plays a role in many forms of self-therapy.

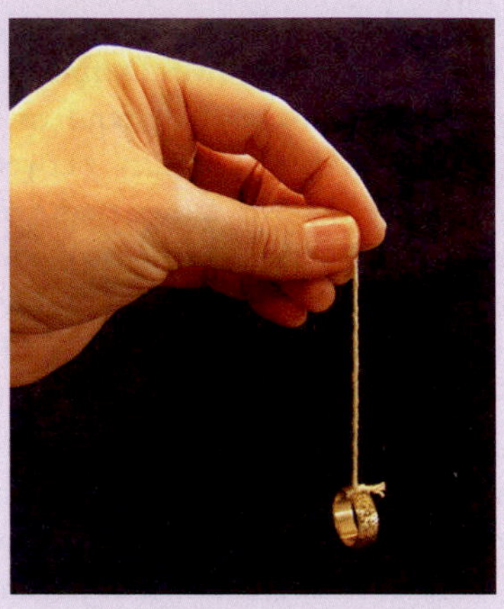
Dennis Coon.

Interest in hypnosis began in the 1700s with Austrian doctor Franz Mesmer, whose name gave us the term *mesmerize* (to hypnotize). Mesmer believed he could cure disease with magnets. Mesmer's strange "treatments" are related to hypnosis because they actually relied on the power of suggestion, not magnetism (Benjafield, 2010; Waterfield, 2002). For a time, Mesmer enjoyed quite a following. In the end, however, his theories of "animal magnetism" were rejected and he was branded a fraud.

The term *hypnosis* was later coined by English surgeon James Braid. The Greek word *hypnos* means "sleep," and Braid used it to describe the hypnotic state. Today, we know that hypnosis is *not* sleep. Confusion about this point remains because some hypnotists give the suggestion, "Sleep, sleep." However, brain activity recorded during hypnosis is different from that observed when a person is asleep or pretending to be hypnotized (Oakley & Halligan, 2010).

Theories of Hypnosis

If hypnosis isn't sleep, then what is it? That's a good question. **Hypnosis** is often defined as an altered state of consciousness, characterized by narrowed attention and an increased openness to suggestion (Kallio & Revonsuo, 2003). Notice that this definition assumes hypnosis is a distinct state of consciousness.

The best-known *state theory* of hypnosis was proposed by Ernest Hilgard (1904–2001), who argued that hypnosis causes a *dissociative state*, or "split" in awareness. To illustrate, he asked hypnotized subjects to plunge one hand into a painful bath of ice water. Subjects told to feel no pain said they felt none. The same subjects were then asked if there was any part of their mind that did feel pain. With their free hand, many wrote, "It hurts," or "Stop it, you're hurting me," while they continued to act pain-free (Hilgard, 1977, 1994). Thus, one part of the hypnotized person says there is no pain and acts as if there is none. Another part, which Hilgard calls the *hidden observer*, is aware of the pain but remains in the background. The **hidden observer** is a detached part of the hypnotized person's awareness that silently observes events.

In contrast, *nonstate theorists* argue that hypnosis is not a distinct state at all. Instead, it is merely a blend of conformity, relaxation, imagination, obedience, and role playing (Kirsch, 2005; Lynn & O'Hagen, 2009). For example, many theorists believe that all hypnosis is really self-hypnosis (*autosuggestion*). From this perspective, a hypnotist merely helps another person to follow a series of suggestions. These suggestions, in turn, alter sensations, perceptions, thoughts, feelings, and behaviors (Lynn & Kirsch, 2006; see "Swinging Suggestions").

Regardless of which theoretical approach finally prevails, both views suggest that hypnosis can be explained by normal principles. It is not mysterious or "magical," despite what stage hypnotists might have you think.

The Reality of Hypnosis

How is hypnosis done? Could I be hypnotized against my will? Hypnotists use many different methods. Still, all techniques encourage a person (1) to focus attention on what is being said; (2) to relax and feel tired; (3) to "let go" and accept suggestions easily; and (4) to use vivid imagination (Barabasz & Watkins, 2005). Basically, you must cooperate to become hypnotized.

What does it feel like to be hypnotized? You might be surprised at some of your actions during hypnosis. You also might have mild feelings of floating, sinking, anesthesia, or separation from your body. Personal experiences vary widely. A key element in hypnosis is the **basic suggestion effect**—a tendency of hypnotized persons to carry out suggested actions as if they were involuntary. Hypnotized persons feel like their actions and experiences are *automatic*—they seem to happen without effort. Here is how one person described his hypnotic session:

> I felt lethargic, my eyes going out of focus and wanting to close. My hands felt real light ... I felt I was sinking deeper into the chair ... I felt like I wanted to relax more and more ... My responses were more automatic. I didn't have to *wish* to do things so much or *want* to do them ... I just did them ... I felt floating ... very close to sleep (Hilgard, 1968).

Contrary to the way hypnosis is portrayed in movies, hypnotized people generally remain in control of their behavior and aware of what is going on. For instance, most people will not act out hypnotic suggestions that they consider immoral or repulsive (such as disrobing in public or harming someone) (Kirsch & Lynn, 1995).

Hypnotic Susceptibility

Can everyone be hypnotized? About 8 people out of 10 can be hypnotized, but only 4 out of 10 will be good hypnotic subjects. People who are imaginative and prone to fantasy are often highly responsive to hypnosis (Kallio & Revonsuo, 2003). But people who lack these traits may also be hypnotized. If you are willing to be hypnotized, chances are good that you could be. Hypnosis depends more on the efforts and abilities of the hypnotized person than the skills of the hypnotist. But make no mistake: People who are hypnotized are not merely faking their responses.

Dennis Coon.

● **Figure 5.7** In one test of hypnotizability, subjects attempt to pull their hands apart after hearing suggestions that their fingers are "locked" together.

Hypnotic susceptibility refers to how easily a person can become hypnotized. It is measured by giving a series of suggestions and counting the number of times a person responds. A typical hypnotic test is the *Stanford Hypnotic Susceptibility Scale*, shown in ■ Table 5.2. In the test, various suggestions are made, and the person's response is noted. For instance, you might be told that your left arm is becoming more and more rigid and that it will not bend. If you can't bend your arm during the next 10 seconds, you have shown susceptibility to hypnotic suggestions (also see ● Figure 5.7).

■ **TABLE 5.2 Stanford Hypnotic Susceptibility Scale**

Suggested Behavior	Criterion Of Passing
1. Postural sway	Falls without forcing
2. Eye closure	Closes eyes without forcing
3. Hand lowering (left)	Lowers at least 6 inches by end of 10 seconds
4. Immobilization (right arm)	Arm rises less than 1 inch in 10 seconds
5. Finger lock	Incomplete separation of fingers at end of 10 seconds
6. Arm rigidity (left arm)	Less than 2 inches of arm bending in 10 seconds
7. Hands moving together	Hands at least as close as 6 inches after 10 seconds
8. Verbal inhibition (name)	Name unspoken in 10 seconds
9. Hallucination (fly)	Any movement, grimacing, acknowledgment of effect
10. Eye catalepsy	Eyes remain closed at end of 10 seconds
11. Posthypnotic (changes chairs)	Any partial movement response
12. Amnesia test	Three or fewer items recalled

Adapted from Weitzenhoffer & Hilgard, 1959

Effects of Hypnosis

What can (and cannot) be achieved with hypnosis? Many abilities have been tested during hypnosis, leading to the following conclusions:

1. **Strength.** Hypnosis has no more effect on physical strength than instructions that encourage a person to make his or her best effort (Chaves, 2000).

Hypnosis An altered state of consciousness characterized by narrowed attention and increased suggestibility.

Hidden observer A detached part of the hypnotized person's awareness that silently observes events.

Basic suggestion effect The tendency of hypnotized persons to carry out suggested actions as if they were involuntary.

Hypnotic susceptibility One's capacity for becoming hypnotized.

2. **Memory.** There is some evidence that hypnosis can enhance memory (Wagstaff et al., 2004). However, it frequently increases the number of false memories as well. For this reason, many states now bar persons from testifying in court if they were hypnotized to improve their memory of a crime they witnessed.

BRIDGES

Should the police use hypnosis to enhance the memories of witnesses? The evidence generally says no. **See Chapter 7, page 248.**

3. **Amnesia.** A person told not to remember something heard during hypnosis may claim not to remember. In some instances, this may be nothing more than a deliberate attempt to avoid thinking about specific ideas. However, brief memory loss of this type actually does seem to occur (Barnier, McConkey, & Wright, 2004).
4. **Pain relief.** Hypnosis can relieve pain (Hammond, 2008; Keefe, Abernethy, & Campbell, 2005). It can be especially useful when chemical painkillers are ineffective. For instance, hypnosis can reduce phantom limb pain (Oakley, Whitman, & Halligan, 2002). (As discussed in Chapter 4, amputees sometimes feel phantom pain that seems to come from a missing limb.)
5. **Age regression.** Given the proper suggestions, some hypnotized people appear to "regress" to childhood. However, most theorists now believe that "age-regressed" subjects are only acting out a suggested role.
6. **Sensory changes.** Hypnotic suggestions concerning sensations are among the most effective. Given the proper instructions, a person can be made to smell a small bottle of ammonia and respond as if it were a wonderful perfume. It is also possible to alter color vision, hearing sensitivity, time sense, perception of illusions, and many other sensory responses.

Hypnosis is a valuable tool. It can help people relax, feel less pain, and make better progress in therapy (Chapman, 2006). Generally, hypnosis is more successful at changing subjective experience than it is at modifying behaviors such as smoking or overeating.

Stage Hypnosis

On stage, the hypnotist intones, "When I count to three, you will imagine that you are on a train to Disneyland and growing younger and younger as the train approaches." Responding to these suggestions, grown men and women begin to giggle and squirm like children on their way to a circus.

How do stage entertainers use hypnosis to get people to do strange things? They don't. Little or no hypnosis is needed to do a good hypnosis act. **Stage hypnosis** is often merely a simulation of hypnotic effects. Stage hypnotists make use of several features of the stage setting to perform their act (Barber, 2000).

1. **Waking suggestibility.** We are all more or less open to suggestion, but on stage people are unusually cooperative because they don't want to "spoil the act." As a result, they will readily follow almost any instruction given by the entertainer.
2. **Selection of responsive subjects.** Participants in stage hypnotism (all *volunteers*) are first "hypnotized" as a group. Then, anyone who doesn't yield to instructions is eliminated.
3. **The hypnosis label disinhibits.** Once a person has been labeled "hypnotized," she or he can sing, dance, act silly, or whatever, without fear or embarrassment. On stage, being "hypnotized" takes away personal responsibility for one's actions.
4. **The hypnotist as a "director."** After volunteers loosen up and respond to a few suggestions, they find that they are suddenly the stars of the show. Audience response to the antics on stage brings out the "ham" in many people. All the "hypnotist" needs to do is direct the action.
5. **The stage hypnotist uses tricks.** Stage hypnosis is about 50 percent taking advantage of the situation and 50 percent deception. One of the more impressive stage tricks is to rigidly suspend a person between two chairs. This is astounding only because the audience does not question it. Anyone can do it, as is shown in the photographs and instructions in ● Figure 5.8. Try it!

To summarize, hypnosis is real, and it can significantly alter private experience. Hypnosis is a useful tool in a variety of settings. Nightclubs, however, are not one of these settings. Stage "hypnotists" entertain; they rarely hypnotize.

Dennis Coon.

● **Figure 5.8** Arrange three chairs as shown. Have someone recline as shown. Ask him to lift slightly while you remove the middle chair. Accept the applause gracefully! (Concerning hypnosis and similar phenomena, the moral, of course, is "Suspend judgment until you have something solid to stand on.")

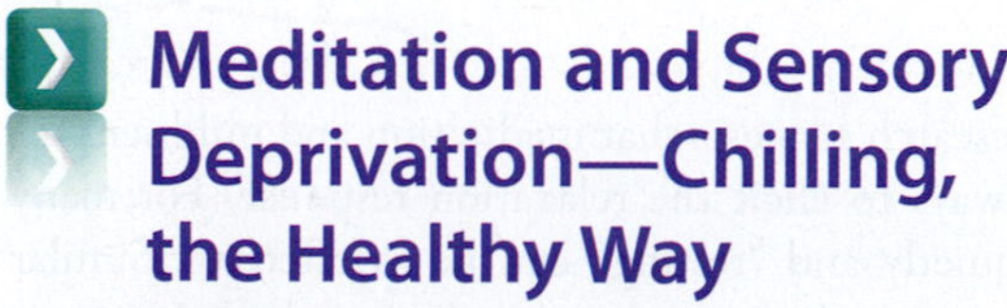

Meditation and Sensory Deprivation—Chilling, the Healthy Way

Gateway Question 5.7: *Do meditation and sensory deprivation have any benefits?*

Throughout history, meditation and sensory deprivation have been widely used as a means of altering consciousness through deep relaxation. Let's see what they have in common and how they differ.

Meditation

Meditation is a mental exercise used to alter consciousness. In general, meditation focuses attention and interrupts the typical flow of thoughts, worries, and analysis. People who use meditation to reduce stress often report less daily physical tension and anxiety (Andresen, 2000; Sears & Kraus, 2009). Brain scans (PET and fMRI) reveal changes in the activity of the frontal lobes during meditation, which suggests that it may be a distinct state of consciousness (Cahn & Polich, 2006; Farb et al., 2007).

Meditation takes two major forms. In **concentrative meditation**, you attend to a single focal point, such as an object, a thought, or your own breathing. In contrast, **mindfulness meditation** is "open," or expansive. In this case, you widen your attention to embrace a total, nonjudgmental awareness of the world (Lazar, 2005). An example is losing all self-consciousness while walking in the wilderness with a quiet and receptive mind. Although it may not seem so, mindfulness meditation is more difficult to attain than concentrative meditation. For this reason, we will discuss concentrative meditation as a practical self-control method.

Performing Concentrative Meditation

How is concentrative meditation done? The basic idea is to sit still and quietly focus on some external object or on a repetitive internal stimulus, such as your own breathing or humming (Blackmore, 2004). As an alternative, you can silently repeat a *mantra* (a word used as the focus of attention in concentrative meditation). Typical mantras are smooth, flowing sounds that are easily repeated. A widely used mantra is the word "om." A mantra could also be any pleasant word or a phrase from a familiar song, poem, or prayer. If other thoughts arise as you repeat a mantra, just return attention to it as often as necessary to maintain meditation.

The Relaxation Response

The benefits of meditation include lowered heart rate, blood pressure, muscle tension, and other signs of stress (Lazar et al., 2000). Medical researcher Herbert Benson believes that the core of meditation is the **relaxation response**—an innate physiological pattern that opposes your body's fight-or-flight mechanisms. Benson feels, quite simply, that most of us have forgotten how to relax deeply. People in his experiments learned to produce the relaxation response by following these instructions:

> Sit quietly and comfortably. Close your eyes. Relax your muscles, beginning at your feet and progressing up to your head. Relax them deeply. Become aware of breathing through your nose. As you breathe out, say a word like "peace" silently to yourself. Don't worry about how successful you are in relaxing deeply. Just let relaxation happen at its own pace. Don't be surprised by distracting thoughts. When they occur, ignore them and continue repeating "peace." (Adapted from Benson, 1977; Lazar et al., 2000.)

As a stress-control technique, meditation may be a good choice for people who find it difficult to "turn off" upsetting thoughts when they need to relax. In one study, a group of college students who received just 90 minutes of training in the relaxation response experienced greatly reduced stress levels (Deckro et al., 2002). The physical benefits of meditation include lowered heart rate, blood pressure, muscle tension, and other signs of stress (Zeidan et al., 2010), as well as improved immune system activity (Davidson et al., 2003).

According to Shauna Shapiro and Roger Walsh (2006), meditation has benefits beyond relaxation. Practiced regularly, meditation may foster mental well-being and positive mental skills such as clarity, concentration, and calm. In this sense, meditation may share much in common with psychotherapy. Indeed, research has shown that mindfulness meditation relieves a variety of psychological disorders, from insomnia to excessive anxiety. It can also reduce aggression and the illegal use of psychoactive drugs (Shapiro & Walsh, 2006). Regular meditation may even help people develop better control over their attention, heightened self-awareness, and maturity (Hodgins & Adair, 2010; Travis, Arenander, & DuBois, 2004).

Sensory Deprivation

The relaxation response can also be produced by brief sensory deprivation. **Sensory deprivation (SD)** refers to any major reduction in the amount or variety of sensory stimulation.

What happens when stimulation is greatly reduced? A hint comes from reports by prisoners in solitary confinement, arctic explorers, high-altitude pilots, long-distance truck drivers, and radar operators. When faced with limited or monotonous stimulation, people sometimes have bizarre sensations, dangerous lapses in attention,

Stage hypnosis Use of hypnosis to entertain; often, merely a simulation of hypnosis for that purpose.

Meditation A mental exercise for producing relaxation or heightened awareness.

Concentrative meditation Mental exercise based on attending to a single object or thought.

Mindfulness meditation Mental exercise based on widening attention to become aware of everything experienced at any given moment.

Relaxation response The pattern of internal bodily changes that occurs at times of relaxation.

Sensory deprivation (SD) Any major reduction in the amount or variety of sensory stimulation.

and wildly distorted perceptions. Intense or prolonged SD is stressful and disorienting. Yet, oddly enough, brief periods of sensory restriction can be very relaxing.

Psychologists have explored the possible benefits of sensory restriction using small isolation tanks like the one pictured in • Figure 5.9. An hour or two spent in a flotation tank, for instance, causes a large drop in blood pressure, muscle tension, and other signs of stress (van Dierendonck & Te Nijenhuis, 2005). Of course, it could be argued that a warm bath has the same effect. Nevertheless, brief SD appears to be one of the surest ways to induce deep relaxation (Suedfeld & Borrie, 1999).

Like meditation, sensory deprivation may also help with more than relaxation. Mild SD can help people quit smoking, lose weight, and reduce their use of alcohol and drugs (van Dierendonck & Te Nijenhuis, 2005). Psychologist Peter Suedfeld calls such benefits **Restricted Environmental Stimulation Therapy (REST)**. Deep relaxation makes people more open to suggestion, and sensory deprivation interrupts habitual behavior patterns. As a result, REST can "loosen" belief systems and make it easier to change bad habits (Suedfeld & Borrie, 1999).

REST also shows promise as a way to stimulate creative thinking (Norlander, Bergman, & Archer, 1998). Other researchers have reported that REST sessions can enhance performance in skilled sports, such as gymnastics, tennis, basketball, darts, and marksmanship (Norlander, Bergman, & Archer, 1999). There is also evidence that REST can relieve chronic pain and reduce stress (Bood et al., 2006). Clearly, there is much yet to be learned from studying "nothingness."

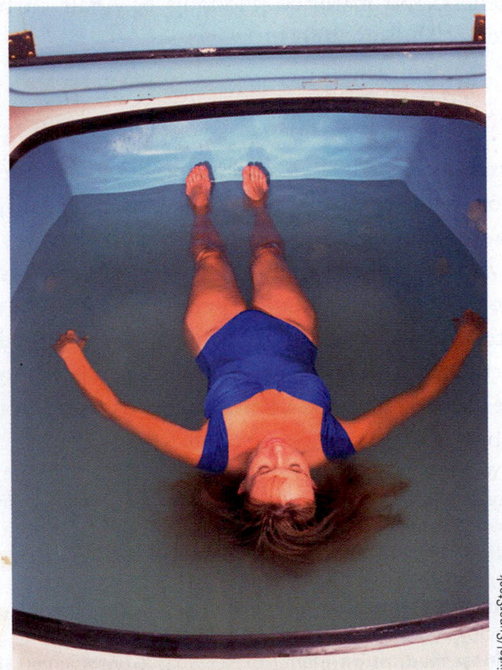

Pixtal/SuperStock

• **Figure 5.9** A sensory isolation chamber. Small flotation tanks like the one pictured have been used by psychologists to study the effects of mild sensory deprivation. Subjects float in darkness and silence. The shallow body-temperature water contains hundreds of pounds of Epsom salts, so that subjects float near the surface. Mild sensory deprivation produces deep relaxation.

Summary

To summarize, research suggests that meditation and mild sensory deprivation are ways to elicit the relaxation response. For many people, sitting quietly and "resting" can be as effective. Similar stress reduction occurs when people set aside time daily to engage in other restful activities, such as muscle relaxation, positive daydreaming, and even leisure reading. However, if you are the type of person who finds it difficult to ignore upsetting thoughts, concentrative meditation might be a good way to promote relaxation. Practiced regularly, meditation and REST may even help improve overall mental health—something almost everyone could use in our fast-paced society.

Positive Psychology: Mindfulness and Well-Being

Did you "space out" anytime today? Most of us have occasional moments of reduced awareness. **Mindfulness** is the opposite of such mindless moments: It involves an open, nonjudgmental awareness of current experience. In other words, everyday mindfulness is very similar to the state sought by people who engage in mindfulness receptive meditation. A person who is mindful is fully present, moment by moment (Siegel, 2007). She or he is acutely aware of every thought, emotion, or sensation, but does not judge it or react to it. The person is fully "awake" and attuned to immediate reality.

Psychologists interested in positive mental states have begun to study the effects of mindfulness. For example, cancer patients who are taught mindfulness meditation have lower levels of distress and a greater sense of well-being. Such benefits apply to healthy people, too. In general, mindfulness is associated with self-knowledge and well-being (Brown & Ryan, 2003; Siegel, 2010). Anyone who has a tendency to sleepwalk through life—and that's most of us at times—would be wise to be mindful of the value of mindfulness.

Knowledge Builder: Hypnosis, Meditation, and Sensory Deprivation

RECITE

1. In Ernest Hilgard's dissociative state theory of hypnosis, awareness is split between normal consciousness and
   a. disinhibition *b.* autosuggestion *c.* memory *d.* the hidden observer
2. Tests of hypnotic susceptibility measure a person's tendency to respond to
   a. suggestion *b.* imagery rehearsal *c.* stimulus control techniques *d.* the activation-synthesis effect
3. Which of the following can most definitely be achieved with hypnosis?
   a. unusual strength *b.* pain relief *c.* improved memory *d.* sleep-like brainwaves
4. The focus of attention in concentrative meditation is "open," or expansive. T or F?

5. Mantras are words said silently to oneself to end a session of meditation. T or F?
6. Which terms do not belong together?
   a. concentrative meditation—relaxation response *b.* mindfulness meditation—mantra *c.* sensory deprivation—REST
   d. meditation—alter consciousness
7. The most immediate benefit of meditation appears to be its capacity for producing the relaxation response. T or F?
8. Prolonged periods of extreme sensory deprivation lower anxiety and induce deep relaxation. T or F?

REFLECT

Think Critically

9. What kind of control group would you need in order to identify the true effects of hypnosis?
10. Regular meditators report lower levels of stress and a greater sense of well-being. What other explanations must we eliminate before this effect can be regarded as genuine?

Self-Reflect

How have your beliefs about hypnosis changed after reading the preceding section? Can you think of specific examples in which hypnosis was misrepresented? For example, in high school assemblies, stage acts, movies, or TV dramas?

Various activities can produce the relaxation response. When do you experience states of deep relaxation coupled with a sense of serene awareness? What similarities do these occurrences have to meditation?

Have you experienced any form of sensory restriction or sensory deprivation? How did you react? Would you be willing to try REST in order to break a bad habit?

Answers: 1. *d* **2.** *a* **3.** *b* **4.** F **5.** F **6.** *b* **7.** T **8.** F **9.** Most experiments on hypnosis include a control group in which people are asked to simulate being hypnotized. Without such controls, the tendency of subjects to cooperate with experimenters makes it difficult to identify true hypnotic effects. **10.** Studies on the effects of meditation must control for the placebo effect and the fact that those who choose to learn meditation may not be a representative sample of the general population.

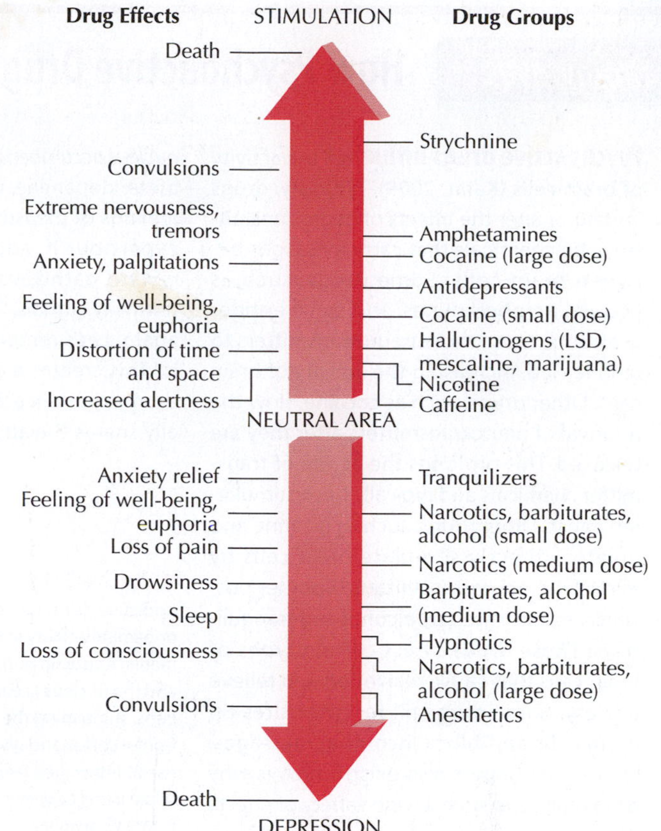

● **Figure 5.10** Spectrum and continuum of drug action. Many drugs can be rated on a stimulation-depression scale according to their effects on the central nervous system. Although LSD, mescaline, and marijuana are listed here, the stimulation-depression scale is less relevant to these drugs. The principle characteristic of such hallucinogens is their mind-altering quality.

Drug-Altered Consciousness—The High and Low of It

Gateway Question 5.8: *What are the effects of the more commonly used psychoactive drugs?*

The most common way to alter human consciousness is to administer a **psychoactive drug**—a substance capable of altering attention, judgment, memory, time sense, self-control, emotion, or perception. In fact, most Americans regularly use consciousness altering drugs (don't forget that caffeine, alcohol, and nicotine are mildly psychoactive). Psychoactive drugs alter consciousness by directly influencing brain activity (Maisto, Galizio, & Connors, 2011; see "How Psychoactive Drugs Affect the Brain"). Many psychoactive drugs can be placed on a scale ranging from stimulation to depression (● Figure 5.10). A **stimulant** (upper) is a substance that increases activity in the body and nervous system. A **depressant** (downer) does the reverse.

Because drugs that can ease pain, induce sleep, or end depression have a high potential for abuse, the more powerful psychoactive drugs are controlled substances (Goldberg, 2010). Nevertheless, nearly 22 million Americans are currently illicit drug users (Substance Abuse and Mental Health Services Administration, 2010). Drug abuse has been one of the most persistent of all social problems in Western nations.

Why is drug abuse so common? People seek drug experiences for many reasons, ranging from curiosity and a desire to belong to a group to a search for meaning or an escape from feelings of inadequacy. Many abusers turn to drugs in a self-defeating attempt to cope with life. All the frequently abused drugs produce immediate feelings of pleasure. The negative consequences follow much later. This combination of immediate pleasure and delayed punishment allows abusers to feel good on demand.

Restricted Environmental Stimulation Therapy (REST) A form of sensory deprivation that results in a variety of psychological benefits.

Mindfulness A state of open, nonjudgmental awareness of current experience.

Psychoactive drug A substance capable of altering attention, memory, judgment, time sense, self-control, mood, or perception.

Stimulant (upper) A substance that increases activity in the body and nervous system.

Depressant (downer) A substance that decreases activity in the body and nervous system.

Brainwaves: How Psychoactive Drugs Affect the Brain

Psychoactive drugs influence the activity of brain cells (Kalat, 2009). Typically, drugs imitate or alter the effects of neurotransmitters, the chemicals that carry messages between brain cells. Some drugs, such as Ecstasy, amphetamines, and some antidepressants, cause more neurotransmitters to be released, increasing the activity of brain cells. Other drugs, such as cocaine, slow the removal of neurotransmitters after they are released. This prolongs the action of transmitter chemicals and typically has a stimulating effect. Other drugs, such as nicotine and opiates, directly stimulate brain cells by mimicking neurotransmitters. Another possibility is illustrated by alcohol and tranquilizers. These drugs affect certain types of brain cells that cause relaxation and relieve anxiety. Some drugs fill receptor sites on brain cells and block incoming messages. Other possibilities also exist, which is why drugs can have such a wide variety of effects on the brain (Julien, 2011).

Nearly all addictive drugs stimulate the brain's reward circuitry, producing feelings of pleasure (Freberg, 2010). In particular, addictive drugs stimulate a brain region called the *nucleus accumbens* to release the neurotransmitter dopamine, which results in intensified feelings of pleasure (● Figure 5.11). As one expert put it, addictive drugs fool brain-reward pathways. As a result, the reward pathway signals, "That felt good. Let's do it again. Let's remember exactly how we did it." This creates a compulsion to repeat the drug experience. It's the hook that eventually snares the addict (National Institute on Drug Abuse, 2010b). In the end, the addictive drug physically changes the brain's reward circuitry, making it even harder for the addict to overcome his or her addiction (Henry et al., 2010; Niehaus, Cruz-Bermudez & Kauer, 2009). Adolescents are especially susceptible to addiction because brain systems that restrain their risk taking are not as mature as those that reward pleasure seeking (Chambers, Taylor, & Potenza, 2003).

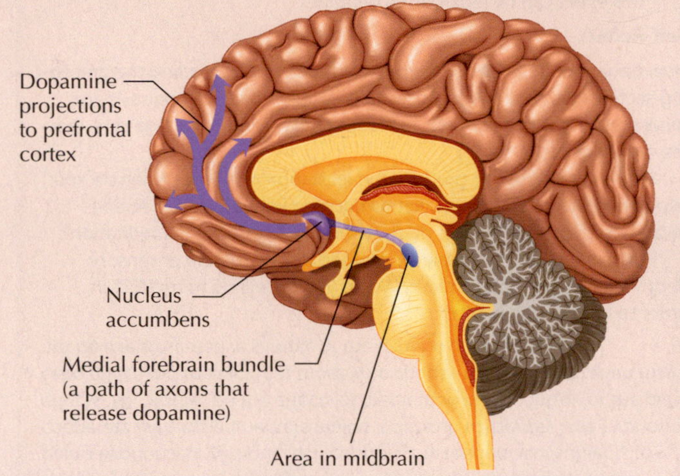

● Figure 5.11 Addictive drugs increase dopamine activity in the medial forebrain bundle and the nucleus accumbens, stimulating the frontal cortex and giving rise to intensified feelings of pleasure. Copyright © 2012 Wadsworth, Cengage Learning, Inc.

In time, of course, most of the pleasure goes out of drug abuse and the abuser's problems get worse. But if an abuser merely feels better (however briefly) after taking a drug, drug taking can become compulsive (Higgins et al., 2004). In contrast, people who stop using drugs often say that they quit because the drawbacks had come to exceed the benefits (Toneatto et al., 1999).

The best predictors of adolescent drug use and abuse are drug use by peers, parental drug use, delinquency, parental maladjustment, poor self-esteem, social nonconformity, and stressful life changes. One study found that adolescents who abuse drugs tend to be maladjusted, alienated, impulsive, and emotionally distressed (Masse & Tremblay, 1997). Antisocial behavior, school failure, and risky sexual behavior are also commonly associated with drug abuse (Ary et al., 1999). Such patterns make it clear that taking drugs is a symptom, rather than a cause, of personal and social maladjustment (Hart, Ksir , & Ray, 2009).

Drug Dependence

Another reason why drug abuse is so common is that taking most psychoactive drugs tends to create dependencies. Once you get started, it can be very hard to stop (Calabria, 2010). Drug dependence falls into two broad categories (Maisto, Galizio, & Connors, 2011). When a person compulsively uses a drug to maintain bodily comfort, a **physical dependence** (addiction) exists. Addiction occurs most often with drugs that cause **withdrawal symptoms** (physical illness that follows removal of a drug). Withdrawal from drugs such as alcohol, barbiturates, and opiates can cause violent flu-like symptoms of nausea, vomiting, diarrhea, chills, sweating, and cramps. Addiction is often accompanied by a **drug tolerance**, a reduced response to a drug. This leads users to take larger and larger doses to get the desired effect.

Persons who develop a **psychological dependence** feel that a drug is necessary to maintain their comfort or well-being. Usually, they intensely crave the drug and its rewarding qualities (Winger et al., 2005). Psychological dependence can be just as powerful as physical addiction. That's why some psychologists define addiction as any compulsive habit pattern. By this definition, a person who has lost control over drug use, for whatever reason, is addicted. In fact, most people who answer yes to both of the following questions have an alcohol or drug problem and should seek professional help:

- In the last year, did you ever drink or use drugs more than you meant to?
- Have you felt you wanted or needed to cut down on your drinking or drug use in the last year?

Patterns of Abuse

Some drugs, of course, have a higher potential for abuse than others. Heroin is certainly more dangerous than caffeine. However, this is only one side of the picture. It can be as useful to classify drug-taking *behavior* as it is to rate drugs. For example, some people remain social drinkers for life, whereas others become alcoholics within weeks of taking their first drink (Robinson & Berridge, 2003). In this sense, drug use can be classified as *experimental* (short-term use based on curiosity), *social-recreational* (occasional social use for pleasure or relaxation), *situational* (use to cope with a specific problem, such as needing to stay awake), *intensive* (daily use with elements of dependence), or *compulsive* (intense use and extreme dependence). The last three categories of drug taking tend to be damaging no matter what drug is used.

Polydrug Abuse

There is one more pattern of drug abuse that bears mentioning: the abuse of more than one drug at the same time. According to the Florida Medical Examiners Commission (2008), polydrug abuse accounts for the "vast majority" of deaths due to drug overdose. When mixed, the effects of different drugs are multiplied by **drug interactions**—one drug enhances the effect of another—that are responsible for thousands of fatal drug overdoses every year (Goldberg, 2010). This is true whether the mixed drugs were legally or illegally obtained.

Drugs of Abuse

Many, if not all, of the drugs discussed in this section have legitimate uses (Hart, Ksir, & Ray, 2009; Goldberg, 2010). Some have been used for centuries in various cultures, in search of insight. Others were developed specifically to treat various mental illnesses. Still others have a variety of health benefits. The key to healthy drug use is moderation and it is truly unfortunate that it is so very hard to keep "the monkey off your back." That is why so many people make a special effort to never get started.

Be that as it may, ■ Table 5.3 reveals that the drugs most likely to lead to physical dependence are alcohol, amphetamines, barbiturates, cocaine, codeine, heroin, methadone, morphine, and tobacco (nicotine). Using *any* of the drugs listed in ■ Table 5.3 can result in psychological dependence. Note also that people who take drugs intravenously are at high risk for developing hepatitis and AIDS. The discussion that follows focuses on the drugs most often abused by students.

Warner Bros/DC Comics/The Kobal Collection.

Heath Ledger's Oscar-winning performance as the *Joker* in one of the Batman films was one of his last. His career was one of many to be cut short by polydrug abuse.

BRIDGES

See Chapter 11, pages 390–392, for more information about AIDS.

Uppers—Amphetamines, Cocaine, MDMA, Caffeine, Nicotine

Now let's turn our attention to the drugs referred to as *uppers*, including amphetamines, cocaine, MDMA, caffeine, and nicotine.

Amphetamines

Amphetamines are synthetic stimulants. Some common street names for amphetamine are "speed," "bennies," "dexies," "amp," and "uppers." These drugs were once widely prescribed for weight loss or depression. Today, the main legitimate medical use of amphetamines is to treat childhood hyperactivity and overdoses of depressant drugs. Illicit use of amphetamines is widespread, however, especially by people seeking to stay awake and by those who rationalize that such drugs can improve mental or physical performance (DeSantis & Hane, 2010; Iversen, 2006).

Adderall and Ritalin, two popular "study drugs," are both mixes of amphetamines used to treat **attention deficit/hyperactivity disorder (ADHD)**. People with ADHD have difficulty controlling their attention and are prone to displaying hyperactive and impulsive behavior (American Psychiatric Association, 2000). Increasing numbers of normal college students are illegally taking these drugs in the hopes they will also be able to focus better while doing school work (McCabe et al., 2005).

I did read about those drugs, but is it true that they actually can help students study? Taking amphetamines as "study drugs" may produce slight improvements in problem-solving performance (Elliott et al., 1997); however, this may be offset by a slight loss of creativity (Farah et al., 2009). Most importantly, the side effects of all amphetamines are worrisome, as we will see shortly.

Methamphetamine is a more potent variation of amphetamine. It can be snorted, injected, or eaten. Of the various types of amphet-

Physical dependence (addiction) Physical addiction, as indicated by the presence of drug tolerance and withdrawal symptoms.

Withdrawal symptoms Physical illness and discomfort following the withdrawal of a drug.

Drug tolerance A reduction in the body's response to a drug.

Psychological dependence Drug dependence that is based primarily on emotional or psychological needs.

Drug interaction A combined effect of two drugs that exceeds the addition of one drug's effects to the other.

Attention deficit/hyperactivity disorder (ADHD) A behavioral problem characterized by short attention span, restless movement, and impaired learning capacity.

TABLE 5.3 Comparison of Psychoactive Drugs

Name	Classification	Medical Use	Usual Dose	Duration Of Effect
Alcohol	Sedative-hypnotic	Solvent, antiseptic	Varies	1–4 hours
Amphetamines	Stimulant	Relief of mild depression, control of narcolepsy and hyperactivity	2.5–5 milligrams	4 hours
Barbiturates	Sedative-hypnotic	Sedation, relief of high blood pressure, anticonvulsant	50–100 milligrams	4 hours
Benzodiazepines	Anxiolytic (antianxiety drug)	Tranquilizer	2–100 milligrams	10 minutes–8 hours
Caffeine	Stimulant	Counteract depressant drugs, treatment of migraine headaches	Varies	Varies
Cocaine	Stimulant, local anesthetic	Local anesthesia	Varies	Varied, brief periods
Codeine	Narcotic	Ease pain and coughing	30 milligrams	4 hours
GHB	Sedative-hypnotic	Experimental treatment of narcolepsy, alcoholism	1–3 grams (powder)	1–3 hours
Heroin	Narcotic	Pain relief	Varies	4 hours
LSD	Hallucinogen	Experimental study of mental function, alcoholism	100–500 milligrams	10 hours
Marijuana (THC)	Relaxant, euphoriant; in high doses, hallucinogen	Treatment of glaucoma and side effects of chemotherapy	1–2 cigarettes	4 hours
MDMA	Stimulant/hallucinogen	None	125 milligrams	4–6 hours
Mescaline	Hallucinogen	None	350 micrograms	12 hours
Methadone	Narcotic	Pain relief	10 milligrams	4–6 hours
Morphine	Narcotic	Pain relief	15 milligrams	6 hours
PCP	Anesthetic	None	2–10 milligrams	4–6 hours, plus 12-hour recovery
Psilocybin	Hallucinogen	None	25 milligrams	6–8 hours
Tobacco (nicotine)	Stimulant	Emetic (nicotine)	Varies	Varies

Question marks indicate conflict of opinion. It should be noted that illicit drugs are frequently adulterated and thus pose unknown hazards to the user.

amine, methamphetamine has created the largest drug problem. "Bergs," "glass," "meth," "crank," or "crystal," as it is known on the street, can be made cheaply in backyard labs and sold for massive profits. In addition to ruining lives through addiction, it has fueled a violent criminal subculture.

Amphetamines rapidly produce a drug tolerance. Most abusers end up taking ever-larger doses to get the desired effect. Eventually, some users switch to injecting methamphetamine directly into the bloodstream. True speed freaks typically go on binges lasting several days, after which they "crash" from lack of sleep and food.

Abuse

How dangerous are amphetamines? Amphetamines pose many dangers. Large doses can cause nausea, vomiting, extremely high blood pressure, fatal heart attacks, and disabling strokes. It is important to realize that amphetamines speed up the use of the body's resources; they do not magically supply energy. After an amphetamine binge, people suffer from crippling fatigue, depression, confusion, uncontrolled irritability, and aggression. Repeated amphetamine use damages the brain. Amphetamines can also cause *amphetamine psychosis*, a loss of contact with reality. Affected users have paranoid delusions that someone is out to get them. Acting on these delusions, they may become violent, resulting in suicide, self-injury, or injury to others (Iversen, 2006).

A potent smokable form of crystal methamphetamine has added to the risks of stimulant abuse. This drug, known as "ice" on the street, is highly addictive. Like "crack," the smokable form of cocaine, it produces an intense high. But also like crack (discussed in a moment), crystal methamphetamine leads very rapidly to compulsive abuse and severe drug dependence.

Effects Sought	Long-Term Symptoms	Physical Dependence Potential	Psychological Dependence Potential	Organic Damage Potential
Sense alteration, anxiety reduction, sociability	Cirrhosis, toxic psychosis, neurologic damage, addiction	Yes	Yes	Yes
Alertness, activeness	Loss of appetite, delusions, hallucinations, toxic psychosis	Yes	Yes	Yes
Anxiety reduction, euphoria	Addiction with severe withdrawal symptoms, possible convulsions, toxic psychosis	Yes	Yes	Yes
Anxiety relief	Irritability, confusion, depression, sleep disorders	Yes	Yes	No, But can affect fetus
Wakefulness, alertness	Insomnia, heart arrhythmias, high blood pressure	No?	Yes	Yes
Excitation, talkativeness	Depression, convulsions	Yes	Yes	Yes
Euphoria, prevent withdrawal discomfort	Addiction, constipation, loss of appetite	Yes	Yes	No
Intoxication, euphoria, relaxation	Anxiety, confusion, insomnia, hallucinations, seizures	Yes	Yes	No?
Euphoria, prevent withdrawal discomfort	Addiction, constipation, loss of appetite	Yes	Yes	No*
Insightful experiences, exhilaration, distortion of senses	May intensify existing psychosis, panic reactions	No	No?	No?
Relaxation; increased euphoria, perceptions, sociability	Possible lung cancer, other health risks	Yes	Yes	Yes?
Excitation, euphoria	Personality change, hyperthermia, liver damage	No	Yes	Yes
Insightful experiences, exhilaration, distortion of senses	May intensify existing psychosis, panic reactions	No	No?	No?
Prevent withdrawal discomfort	Addiction, constipation, loss of appetite	Yes	Yes	No
Euphoria, prevent withdrawal discomfort	Addiction, constipation, loss of appetite	Yes	Yes	No*
Euphoria	Unpredictable behavior, suspicion, hostility, psychosis	Debated	Yes	Yes
Insightful experiences, exhilaration, distortion of senses	May intensify existing psychosis, panic reactions	No	No?	No?
Alertness, calmness, sociability	Emphysema, lung cancer, mouth and throat cancer, cardiovascular damage, loss of appetite	Yes	Yes	Yes

*Persons who inject drugs under nonsterile conditions run a high risk of contracting AIDS, hepatitis, abscesses, or circulatory disorders.

Cocaine

Cocaine ("coke," "snow," "blow," "snuff," "flake") is a powerful central nervous system stimulant extracted from the leaves of the coca plant. Cocaine produces feelings of alertness, euphoria, well-being, power, boundless energy, and pleasure (Julien, 2011). At the turn of the 20th century, dozens of nonprescription potions and cure-alls contained cocaine. It was during this time that Coca-Cola was indeed the "real thing." From 1886 until 1906, when the U.S. Pure Food and Drug Act was passed, Coca-Cola contained cocaine (which has since been replaced with caffeine).

How does cocaine differ from amphetamines? The two are very much alike in their effects on the central nervous system. The main difference is that amphetamine lasts several hours; cocaine is snorted and quickly metabolized, so its effects last only about 15 to 30 minutes.

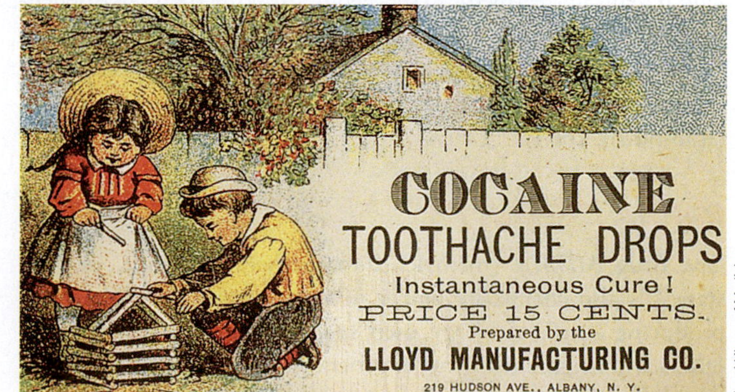

National Library of Medicine.

Cocaine was the main ingredient in many nonprescription elixirs before the turn of the 20th century. Today cocaine is recognized as a powerful and dangerous drug. Its high potential for abuse has damaged the lives of countless users.

Abuse

How dangerous is cocaine? Cocaine's capacity for abuse and social damage rivals that of heroin. When rats and monkeys are given free access to cocaine, they find it irresistible. Many, in fact, end up dying of convulsions from self-administered overdoses of the drug. Even casual or first-time users risk having convulsions, a heart attack, or a stroke (Lacayo, 1995). Cocaine increases the chemical messengers dopamine (DOPE-ah-meen) and noradrenaline (nor-ah-DREN-ah-lin). Noradrenaline arouses the brain, and dopamine produces a "rush" of pleasure. This combination is so powerfully rewarding that cocaine users run a high risk of becoming compulsive abusers (Ridenour et al., 2005).

A person who stops using cocaine does not experience heroin-like withdrawal symptoms. Instead, the brain adapts to cocaine abuse in ways that upset its chemical balance, causing depression when cocaine is withdrawn. First, there is a jarring "crash" of mood and energy. Within a few days, the person enters a long period of fatigue, anxiety, paranoia, boredom, and **anhedonia** (an-he-DAWN-ee-ah: an inability to feel pleasure). Before long, the urge to use cocaine becomes intense. So, although cocaine does not fit the classic pattern of addiction, it is ripe for compulsive abuse. Even a person who gets through withdrawal may crave cocaine months or years later (Washton & Zweben, 2009). If cocaine were cheaper, 9 out of 10 users would progress to compulsive abuse. In fact, rock cocaine ("crack," "rock," or "roca"), which is cheaper, produces very high abuse rates. Here are some signs of cocaine abuse:

- *Compulsive use.* If cocaine is available—say, at a party—you can't say no to it.
- *Loss of control.* Once you have had some cocaine, you will keep using it until you are exhausted or the cocaine is gone.
- *Disregarding consequences.* You don't care if the rent gets paid, your job is endangered, your lover disapproves, or your health is affected; you'll use cocaine anyway.

Anyone who thinks she or he has a cocaine problem should seek advice at a drug clinic or a Cocaine Anonymous meeting. Although quitting cocaine is extremely difficult, three out of four abusers who remain in treatment do succeed in breaking their coke dependence (Simpson et al., 1999; Sinha et al., 2006). There is also hope on the horizon in the form of a vaccine currently undergoing clinical trials that prevents cocaine from stimulating the nervous system (Kampman, 2005).

MDMA ("Ecstasy")

The drug *MDMA* (methylenedioxymethamphetamine, or "Ecstasy") is also chemically similar to amphetamine. In addition to producing a rush of energy, users say it makes them feel closer to others and heightens sensory experiences. Ecstasy causes brain cells to release extra amounts of serotonin as well as prolonging its effects. The physical effects of MDMA include dilated pupils, elevated blood pressure, jaw clenching, loss of appetite, and elevated body temperature (National Institute on Drug Abuse, 2010a). Although some users believe that Ecstasy increases sexual pleasure, it *diminishes* sexual performance, impairing erection in 40 percent of men and retarding orgasm in both men and women. (Zemishlany, Aizenberg, & Weizman, 2001).

Abuse

Ecstasy use in North America has declined slightly from a peak around 2002, perhaps because of widespread negative publicity. Regardless, in 2009, more than 700,000 Americans tried Ecstasy for the first time (Substance Abuse and Mental Health Services Administration, 2010). Every year, emergency room doctors see many MDMA cases, including MDMA-related deaths. Some of these incidents are caused by elevated body temperature (hyperthermia) or heart arrhythmias, which can lead to collapse. Ecstasy users at "rave" parties try to prevent overheating by drinking water to cool themselves. This may help to a small degree, but the risk of fatal heat exhaustion is real. MDMA can also cause severe liver damage, which can be fatal (National Institute on Drug Abuse, 2010a). In addition, Ecstasy users are more likely to abuse alcohol and other drugs, to neglect studying, to party excessively, and to engage in risky sex (Strote, Lee, & Wechsler, 2002). Ironically, Ecstasy use at "rave" parties actually does intensify the impact of the music. We say ironically because the end result is often overstimulation of the brain, which can result in a "rebound" depression (Iannone et al., 2006).

Enough time has passed to assess the long-term effects of Ecstacy use. Feelings of anxiety or depression can persist for months after a person stops taking Ecstasy. In addition, heavy users typically do not perform well in tests of learning and memory and show some signs of underlying brain damage (National Institute on Drug Abuse, 2010a; Quednow et al., 2006). Fortunately, however, the long-term consequences are not as severe as once feared (Advisory Council on the Misuse of Drugs, 2009).

Caffeine

Caffeine is the most frequently used psychoactive drug in North America. (And that's not counting Seattle!) Many people have a hard time starting a day (or writing another paragraph) without a cup since caffeine suppresses drowsiness and increases alertness (Wesensten et al., 2002), especially when combined with sugar (Adan & Serra-Grabulosa, 2010). Physically, caffeine causes sweating, talkativeness, tinnitus (ringing in the ears), and hand tremors (Nehlig, 2004). Caffeine stimulates the brain by blocking chemicals that normally inhibit or slow nerve activity (Maisto, Galizio, & Connors, 2011). Its effects become apparent with doses as small as 50 milligrams, the amount found in about one-half cup of brewed coffee.

How much caffeine did you consume today? It is common to think of coffee as the major source of caffeine, but there are many others. Caffeine is found in tea, many soft drinks (especially colas), chocolate, and cocoa. More than 2,000 nonprescription drugs also contain caffeine, including stay-awake pills, cold remedies, and many name-brand aspirin products.

Abuse

Are there any serious drawbacks to using caffeine? Overuse of caffeine may result in an unhealthy dependence known as **caffeinism**. Insomnia, irritability, loss of appetite, chills, racing heart, and elevated body temperature are all signs of caffeinism. Many people with these symptoms drink 15 or 20 cups of coffee a day. However, even at lower dosages, caffeine can intensify anxiety and other psychological problems (Hogan, Hornick, & Bouchoux, 2002).

Caffeine poses a variety of health risks. Caffeine encourages the growth of breast cysts in women, and it may contribute to bladder cancer, heart problems, and high blood pressure. Pregnant women should consider giving up caffeine entirely because of a suspected link between caffeine and birth defects. Pregnant women who consume as little as two cups coffee a day increase the risk of having a miscarriage (Cnattingius et al., 2000).

It is customary to think that caffeine is not a drug. But as few as 2.5 cups of coffee a day (or the equivalent) can be a problem. People who consume even such modest amounts may experience anxiety, depression, fatigue, headaches, and flu-like symptoms during withdrawal (Juliano & Griffiths, 2004). About half of all caffeine users show some signs of dependence (Hughes et al., 1998). It is wise to remember that caffeine *is* a drug and to use it in moderation.

Nicotine

Nicotine is a natural stimulant found mainly in tobacco. Next to caffeine and alcohol, it is the most widely used psychoactive drug (Julien, 2011).

How does nicotine compare with other stimulants? Nicotine is a potent drug. It is so toxic that it is sometimes used to kill insects! In large doses it causes stomach pain, vomiting and diarrhea, cold sweats, dizziness, confusion, and muscle tremors. In very large doses, nicotine may cause convulsions, respiratory failure, and death. For a nonsmoker, 50 to 75 milligrams of nicotine taken in a single dose could be lethal. (Chain smoking about 17 to 25 cigarettes will produce this dosage.) Most first-time smokers get sick on one or two cigarettes. In contrast, regular smokers build a tolerance for nicotine. A heavy smoker may inhale 40 cigarettes a day without feeling ill.

Abuse

How addictive is nicotine? A vast array of evidence confirms that nicotine is very addictive (Spinella, 2005). The average age of first use is 15, and it takes about a year before dependence sets in (Baker, Brandon, & Chassin, 2004). Among regular smokers who are 15 to 24 years old, 60 percent are addicted (Breslau et al., 2001). For many smokers, withdrawal from nicotine causes headaches, sweating, cramps, insomnia, digestive upset, irritability, and a sharp craving for cigarettes (National Institute on Drug Abuse, 2009). These symptoms may last from 2 to 6 weeks and may be worse than heroin withdrawal. Indeed, relapse patterns are nearly identical for alcoholics, heroin addicts, cocaine abusers, and smokers who try to quit (Stolerman & Jarvis, 1995). Up to 90 percent of people who

Wayne McLaren, who portrayed the rugged "Marlboro Man" in cigarette ads, died of lung cancer at age 51. A smoker for 30 years, he became an anti-smoking activist after he was diagnosed.

quit smoking relapse within a year, and 20 percent relapse even after 2 years of abstinence (Krall, Garvey, & Garcia, 2002).

Impact on Health

How serious are the health risks of smoking? If you think smoking is harmless, or that there's no connection between smoking and cancer, you're kidding yourself. A burning cigarette releases a large variety of potent *carcinogens* (car-SIN-oh-jins: cancer-causing substances). According to the U.S. Surgeon General (U.S. Department of Health and Human Services, 2004), "smoking harms nearly every organ of the body," leading to an increased risk of many cancers (such as lung cancer), cardiovascular diseases (such as stroke), respiratory diseases (such as chronic bronchitis), and reproductive disorders (such as decreased fertility). Together, these health risks combine to reduce the life expectancy of the average smoker by 10 to 15 years. Every year almost 450,000 people die from tobacco use (National Center for Chronic Disease Prevention and Health Promotion, 2010).

Anhedonia An inability to feel pleasure.
Caffeinism Excessive consumption of caffeine, leading to dependence and a variety of physical and psychological complaints.

"Not for me thanks, mate - I'm only a passive smoker."

Clive Goddard/www.CartoonStock.com

By the way, urban cowboys and Skol bandits, the same applies to chewing tobacco and snuff. A 30-minute exposure to one pinch of smokeless tobacco is equivalent to smoking three or four cigarettes. Along with all the health risks of smoking, users of smokeless tobacco also run a higher risk of developing oral cancer (American Lung Association, 2011).

Smokers don't just risk their own health; they also endanger those who live and work nearby. Secondary smoke causes about 3,000 lung cancer deaths and as many as 70,000 heart disease deaths each year in the United States alone. It is particularly irresponsible of smokers to expose young children, who are especially vulnerable, to secondhand smoke (American Lung Association, 2011).

Quitting Smoking

Is it better for a person to quit smoking abruptly or taper down gradually? Most people try to quit by themselves. Some try to quit cold turkey, whereas others try to taper down gradually. Although going cold turkey has its advocates, gradually quitting works better for more people.

Going cold turkey makes quitting an all-or-nothing proposition. Smokers who smoke even one cigarette after "quitting forever" tend to feel they've failed. Many figure they might just as well resume smoking. Those who quit gradually accept that success may take many attempts, spread over several months. If you are going to quit by going cold turkey, you will have a better chance of success if you decide to quit *now* rather than at some time in the future (West & Sohal, 2006).

The best way to taper off is *scheduled gradual reduction* (Riley et al., 2002). There are many ways in which smoking can be gradually reduced. For example, the smoker can: (1) delay having a first cigarette in the morning and then try to delay a little longer each day; (2) gradually reduce the total number of cigarettes smoked each day; or (3) quit completely, but for just 1 week, then quit again, a week at a time, for as many times as necessary to make it stick. Deliberately scheduling and then gradually stretching the length of time between cigarettes is a key part of this program. Scheduled smoking apparently helps people learn to cope with the urge to smoke. As a result, people using this method are more likely to remain permanent nonsmokers than people using other approaches (Cinciripini, Wetter, & McClure, 1997).

Whatever approach is taken, quitting smoking is not easy (Abrams et al., 2003; National Institute on Drug Abuse, 2009). Many people find that using nicotine patches or gum helps them get through the withdrawal period (Shiffman et al., 2006). Also, as we have noted, anyone trying to quit should be prepared to make several attempts before succeeding. But the good news is that tens of millions of people have quit.

BRIDGES

Behavioral self-management techniques can be very useful for breaking habits such as smoking. **See Chapter 6, pages 234–236, and Chapter 15, pages 538–540.**

Downers—Sedatives, Tranquilizers, and Alcohol

While narcotics, like *heroin* and *morphine*, may be more powerful, both as drugs of abuse and as painkillers, the most widely used downers, or depressant drugs, are alcohol, barbiturates, GHB, and benzodiazepine (ben-zoe-die-AZ-eh-peen) tranquilizers. These drugs are much alike in their effects. In fact, barbiturates and tranquilizers are sometimes referred to as "solid alcohol." Let's examine the properties of each.

Barbiturates

Barbiturates are sedative drugs that depress brain activity. Common barbiturates include amobarbital, pentobarbital, secobarbital, and tuinal. On the street they are known as "downers," "blue devils," "yellow jackets," "lows," "goof balls," "reds," "pink ladies," "rainbows," or "tooies." Medically, barbiturates are used to calm patients or to induce sleep.

Abuse

At mild dosages, barbiturates have an effect similar to alcohol intoxication. Higher dosages can cause severe mental confusion or even hallucinations. Barbiturates are often taken in excess amounts because a first dose may be followed by others, as the user becomes uninhibited or forgetful. Overdoses first cause a loss of consciousness. Then they severely depress brain centers that control heartbeat and breathing. The result is death (McKim, 2007).

GHB

Would you swallow a mixture of degreasing solvent and drain cleaner to get high? Apparently, a lot of people would. A mini-epidemic of *GHB* (gamma-hydroxybutyrate) use has taken place in recent years, especially at nightclubs and raves. GHB ("goop," "scoop," "max," "Georgia Home Boy") is a central nervous system depressant that relaxes and sedates the body. Users describe its effects as similar to those of alcohol. Mild GHB intoxication tends to produce euphoria, a desire to socialize, and a mild loss of inhibitions. GHB's intoxicating effects typically last 3 to 4 hours, depending on the dosage.

Abuse

At lower dosages, GHB can relieve anxiety and produce relaxation. However, as the dose increases, its sedative effects may result in nausea, a loss of muscle control, and either sleep or a loss of consciousness. Potentially fatal doses of GHB are only three times the amount typically taken by users. This narrow margin of safety has led to numerous overdoses, especially when GHB was combined with alcohol. An overdose causes coma, breathing failure, and death. GHB also inhibits the gag reflex, so some users choke to death on their own vomit.

In 2000, the U.S. government classified GHB as a controlled substance, making its possession a felony. Clinical evidence increasingly suggests that GHB is addictive and a serious danger to users. Two out of three frequent users have lost consciousness after taking GHB. Chronic use leads to brain damage (Pedraza, García, & Navarro, 2009). Heavy users who stop taking GHB have withdrawal symptoms that include anxiety, agitation, tremor, delirium, and hallucinations (Miotto et al., 2001).

As if the preceding weren't enough reason to be leery of GHB, here's one more to consider: GHB is often manufactured in homes with recipes and ingredients purchased on the Internet. As mentioned earlier, it can be produced by combining degreasing solvent with drain cleaner (Falkowski, 2000). If you want to degrease your brain, GHB will do the trick.

Tranquilizers

A **tranquilizer** is a drug that lowers anxiety and reduces tension. Doctors prescribe benzodiazepine tranquilizers to alleviate nervousness and stress. Valium is the best-known drug in this family; others are Xanax, Halcion, and Librium. Even at normal dosages, these drugs can cause drowsiness, shakiness, and confusion. When used at too high a dosage or for too long, benzodiazepines are addictive (McKim, 2007).

A drug sold under the trade name Rohypnol (ro-HIP-nol) has added to the problem of tranquilizer abuse. This drug, which is related to Valium, is cheap and 10 times more potent. It lowers inhibitions and produces relaxation or intoxication. Large doses induce short-term amnesia and sleep. "Roofies," as they are known on the street, are odorless and tasteless. They have been used to spike drinks, which are given to the unwary. Victims of this "date rape" drug are then sexually assaulted or raped while they are unconscious. (Be aware, however, that drinking too much alcohol is by far the most common prelude to rape.)

Abuse

Repeated use of barbiturates can cause physical dependence. Some abusers suffer severe emotional depression that may end in suicide. Similarly, when tranquilizers are used at too high a dosage or for too long, addiction can occur. Many people have learned the hard way that their legally prescribed tranquilizers are as dangerous as many illicit drugs (McKim, 2007).

Combining barbiturates or tranquilizers with alcohol is especially risky. All too often, depressants are gulped down with alcohol or added to a spiked punch bowl. This is the lethal brew that left a young woman named Karen Ann Quinlan in a coma that lasted 10 years, ending with her death. It is no exaggeration to restate that mixing depressants with alcohol can be deadly.

Alcohol

Alcohol is the common name for ethyl alcohol, the intoxicating element in fermented and distilled liquors. Contrary to popular belief, alcohol is not a stimulant. The noisy animation at drinking parties is due to alcohol's effect as a *depressant*. Small amounts of alcohol reduce inhibitions and produce feelings of relaxation and euphoria. Larger amounts cause greater impairment of the brain until the drinker loses consciousness. Alcohol is also not an aphrodisiac. Rather than enhancing sexual arousal, it usually impairs performance, especially in males. As William Shakespeare observed long ago, drink "provokes the desire, but it takes away the performance."

Some people become aggressive and want to argue or fight when they are drunk. Others become relaxed and friendly. How can the same drug have such different effects? When a person is drunk, thinking and perception become dulled or shortsighted, a condition that has been called **alcohol myopia** (my-OH-pea-ah) (Giancola et al., 2010). Only the most obvious and immediate stimuli catch a drinker's attention. Worries and "second thoughts" that would normally restrain behavior are banished from the drinker's mind. That's why many behaviors become more extreme when a person is drunk. On college campuses, drunken students tend to have accidents, get into fights, sexually assault others, or engage in risky sex. They also destroy property and disrupt the lives of students who are trying to sleep or study (Brower, 2002).

Abuse

Alcohol, the world's favorite depressant, breeds our biggest drug problem. More than 20 million people in the United States and Canada have serious drinking problems. One American dies every 20 minutes in an alcohol-related car crash. The level of alcohol abuse in America is alarming. Significant percentages of Americans of all ages abuse alcohol (● Figure 5.12).

Tranquilizer A drug that lowers anxiety and reduces tension.
Alcohol myopia Shortsighted thinking and perception that occurs during alcohol intoxication.

• Figure 5.12 Many Americans of all ages abuse alcohol. According to this 2008 survey, about 40 percent of young adults aged 18–29 admitted to heavy alcohol use or binge drinking in the month before the survey was administered (Substance Abuse and Mental Health Services Administration, 2009).

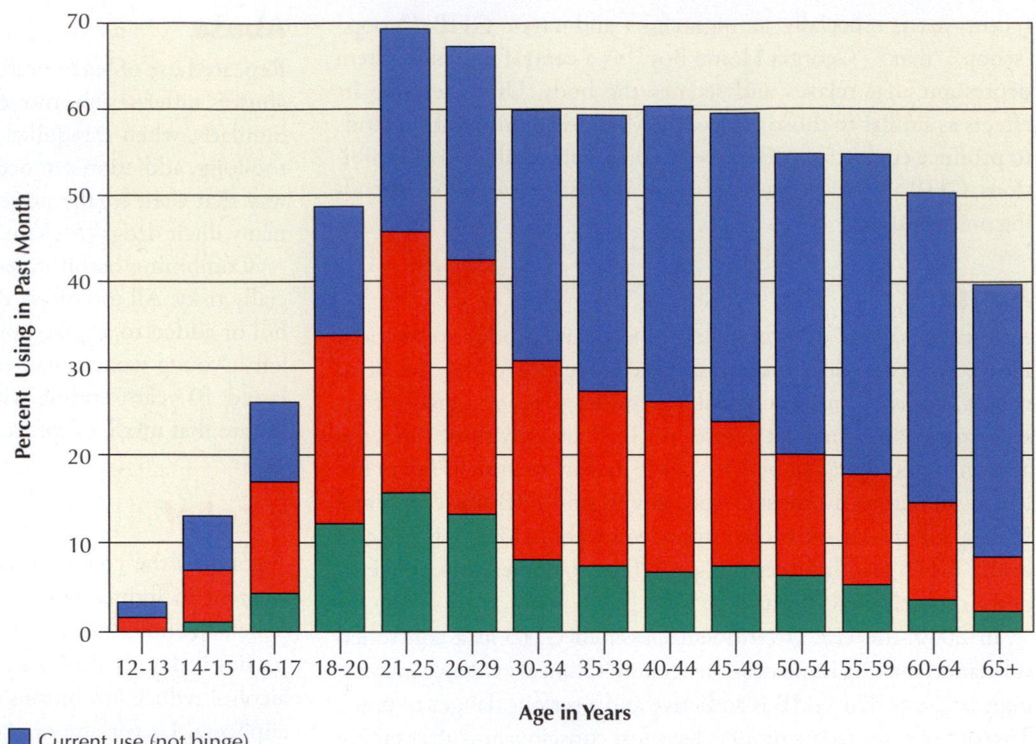

It is especially worrisome to see binge drinking among adolescents and young adults. **Binge drinking** is defined as downing five or more drinks (four drinks for women) in a short time. Apparently, many students think it's entertaining to get completely wasted and throw up on their friends. However, binge drinking is a serious sign of alcohol abuse (Beseler, Taylor, & Leeman, 2010). It is responsible for 1,800 college student deaths each year and thousands of trips to the emergency room (Mitka, 2009).

Binge drinking is of special concern because the brain continues to develop into the early twenties. Research has shown that teenagers and young adults who drink too much may lose as much as 10 percent of their brain power—especially their memory capacity (Brown et al., 2000). Such losses can have a long-term impact on a person's chances for success in life. In short, getting drunk is a slow but sure way to get stupid (Wechsler & Wuethrich, 2002).

© David Vintiner/Corbis

Binge drinking and alcohol abuse have become serious problems among college students (Tewksbury, Higgins, & Mustaine, 2008).

At Risk

Children of alcoholics and those who have other relatives who abuse alcohol are at greater risk for becoming alcohol abusers themselves. The increased risk appears to be partly genetic. It is based on the fact that some people have stronger cravings for alcohol after they drink (Hutchison et al., 2002). Women also face some special risks. For one thing, alcohol is absorbed faster and metabolized more slowly by women's bodies. As a result, women get intoxicated from less alcohol than men do. Women who drink are also more prone to liver disease, osteoporosis, and depression. Each extra drink per day adds 7 percent to a woman's risk of breast cancer (Aronson, 2003).

Positive reinforcement—drinking for pleasure—motivates most people who consume alcohol. What sets alcohol abusers apart is that they also drink to cope with negative emotions, such as anxiety and depression. That's why alcohol abuse increases with the level of stress in people's lives. People who drink to relieve bad feelings are at great risk of becoming alcoholics (Kenneth, Carpenter, & Hasin, 1998).

Recognizing Problem Drinking

What are the signs of alcohol abuse? Because alcohol abuse is such a common problem, it is important to recognize the danger signals. If you can answer yes to even one of the following questions, you may have a problem with drinking (adapted from the College Alcohol Problems Scale, revised; Maddock et al., 2001):

AS A RESULT OF DRINKING ALCOHOLIC BEVERAGES I ...

1. engaged in unplanned sexual activity.
2. drove under the influence.
3. did not use protection when engaging in sex.
4. engaged in illegal activities associated with drug use.
5. felt sad, blue, or depressed.
6. was nervous or irritable.
7. felt bad about myself.
8. had problems with appetite or sleeping.

Perhaps the simplest way to identify problem drinkers is to ask a single question: "When was the last time you had more than five drinks (four for women) in a day?" Eighty-six percent of the people who answer "less than 3 months ago" are alcohol abusers (Williams & Vinson, 2001).

Moderated Drinking

Almost everyone has been to a party spoiled by someone who drank too much too fast. Those who avoid overdrinking have a better time, and so do their friends. But how do you avoid drinking too much? After all, as one wit once observed, "The conscience dissolves in alcohol." A partial answer comes from the observation that drinking makes you feel good while blood alcohol is rising and remains below a level of about 0.05. In this range, people feel relaxed, euphoric, and sociable. At higher levels, they go from moderately intoxicated to thoroughly drunk. Later, as blood alcohol begins to fall, those who over drink become sick and miserable. ■ Table 5.4 shows the approximate amount per hour that can be consumed without exceeding the 0.05 blood alcohol level. (Beware, even at this level, driving may be impaired.) By pacing themselves, those who choose to drink can remain comfortable, pleasant, and coherent during a long social event. In short, if you drink, it might be wise to learn your "magic" number from ■ Table 5.4.

It takes skill to regulate drinking in social situations, where the temptation to drink can be strong. If you choose to drink, here are some guidelines that may be helpful (adapted from Miller & Munoz, 2005; National Institute on Alcohol Abuse and Alcoholism, 2007):

Paced Drinking

1. Think about your drinking beforehand and plan how you will manage it.
2. Drink slowly, eat while drinking or drink on a full stomach, and make every other drink (or more) a nonalcoholic beverage.
3. Limit drinking primarily to the first hour of a social event or party. Pace your drinking using the information from ■ Table 5.4.
4. Practice how you will politely but firmly refuse drinks.
5. Learn how to relax, meet people, and socialize without relying on alcohol.

And remember, research has shown that you are likely to overestimate how much your fellow students are drinking (Maddock & Glanz, 2005). So don't let yourself be lured into overdrinking just because you have the (probably false) impression that other students are drinking more than you. Limiting your own drinking may help others as well. When people are tempted to drink too much, their main reason for stopping is that "other people were quitting and deciding they'd had enough" (Johnson, 2002).

■ TABLE 5.4 Drinking in Moderation

Your Weight (pounds)	Approximate Number of Drinks per Hour to Stay below 0.05 Blood Alcohol* Male	Female
100	0.75	0.60
120	1.00	0.75
140	1.25	0.90
160	1.30	1.00
180	1.50	1.10
200	1.60	1.20
220	1.80	1.35

One drink = 12 ounces beer, 5 ounces wine, or 1.5 ounces 80 proof liquor.

*Table entries are approximate, owing to individual differences in metabolism, recency of meals, and other factors. Estimates are derived from National Institute on Alcohol Abuse and Alcoholism (2007) and Vogler & Bartz (1992).

Treatment

Treatment for alcohol dependence begins with sobering up the person and cutting off the supply. This phase is referred to as **detoxification** (literally, "to remove poison"). It frequently produces all the symptoms of drug withdrawal and can be extremely unpleasant. The next step is to try to restore the person's health. Heavy abuse of alcohol usually causes severe damage to body organs and the nervous system. After alcoholics have "dried out" and some degree of health has been restored, they may be treated with tranquilizers, antidepressants, or psychotherapy. Unfortunately, the success of these procedures has been limited.

One mutual-help approach that has been fairly successful is Alcoholics Anonymous (AA). AA takes a spiritual approach while acting on the premise that it takes a former alcoholic to understand and help a current alcoholic. Participants at AA meetings admit that they have a problem, share feelings, and resolve to stay "dry" one day at a time. Other group members provide support for those struggling to end dependency. (Other "12-step" programs, such as Cocaine Anonymous and Narcotics Anonymous, use the same approach.)

Binge drinking Consuming five or more drinks in a short time (four for women).

Detoxification In the treatment of alcoholism, the withdrawal of the patient from alcohol.

Eighty percent of those who remain in AA for more than 1 year get through the following year without a drink. However, AA's success rate may simply reflect the fact that members join voluntarily, meaning they have admitted they have a serious problem (Morgenstern et al., 1997). Sadly, it seems that alcohol abusers will often not face their problems until they have "hit rock bottom." If they are willing, though, AA presents a practical approach to the problem (Vaillant, 2005).

Other groups offer a rational, nonspiritual approach to alcohol abuse that better fits the needs of some people. Examples include Rational Recovery and Secular Organizations for Sobriety (SOS). Other alternatives to AA include medical treatment, group therapy, mindfulness meditation, and individual psychotherapy (Buddie, 2004; Jacobs-Stewart, 2010). There is a strong tendency for abusive drinkers to deny they have a problem. The sooner they seek help, the better.

Hallucinogens—Tripping the Light Fantastic

Marijuana is the most popular illicit drug in America (Substance Abuse and Mental Health Services Administration, 2010). The main active chemical in marijuana is tetrahydrocannabinol (tet-rah-hydro-cah-NAB-ih-nol), or THC for short. THC is a mild **hallucinogen** (hal-LU-sin-oh-jin: a substance that alters sensory impressions). Other hallucinogenic drugs include LSD and PCP.

LSD and PCP

The drug *LSD* (lysergic acid diethylamide or "acid") is perhaps the best-known hallucinogen. Even when taken in tiny amounts, LSD can produce hallucinations and psychotic-like disturbances in thinking and perception. Two other common hallucinogens are mescaline (peyote) and psilocybin ("magic mushrooms," or "shrooms"). Incidentally, the drug PCP (phencyclidine or "angel dust") can have hallucinogenic effects. However, PCP, which is an anesthetic, also has stimulant and depressant effects. This potent combination can cause extreme agitation, disorientation, violence—and too often, tragedy. Like other psychoactive drugs, all of the hallucinogens, including marijuana, typically affect neurotransmitter systems that carry messages between brain cells (Maisto, Galizio, & Connors, 2011).

Isaac Abrams.

Artists have tried at times to capture the effects of hallucinogens. Here, the artist depicts visual experiences he had while under the influence of LSD.

Marijuana

Marijuana and hashish are derived from the hemp plant *Cannabis sativa*. Marijuana ("pot," "grass," "Ganja," "MJ") consists of the dried leaves and flowers of the hemp plant. Hashish is a resinous material scraped from cannabis leaves. Marijuana's psychological effects include a sense of euphoria or well-being, relaxation, altered time sense, and perceptual distortions. At high dosages, however, paranoia, hallucinations, and delusions can occur (Hart, Ksir, & Ray, 2009). All considered, marijuana intoxication is relatively subtle in comparison to drugs such as LSD or alcohol. Despite this, driving a car while high on marijuana can be extremely hazardous. As a matter of fact, driving under the influence of any intoxicating drug is dangerous.

No overdose deaths from marijuana have been reported. However, marijuana cannot be considered harmless. Particularly worrisome is the fact that THC accumulates in the body's fatty tissues, especially in the brain and reproductive organs. Even if a person smokes marijuana just once a week, the body is never entirely free of THC. Scientists have located a specific receptor site on the surface of brain cells where THC binds to produce its effects (● Figure 5.13). These receptor sites are found in large numbers in the cerebral cortex, which is the seat of human consciousness (Julien, 2011). In addition, THC receptors are found in areas involved in the control of skilled movement. Naturally occurring chemicals similar to THC may help the brain cope with pain and stress. However, when THC is used as a drug, high dosages can cause paranoia, hallucinations, and dizziness.

Abuse

Does marijuana produce physical dependence? Yes, according to recent studies (Filbey et al., 2009; Lichtman & Martin, 2006). Frequent users of marijuana find it very difficult to quit, so dependence is a risk (Budney & Hughes, 2006). But marijuana's potential for abuse lies primarily in the realm of psychological dependence, not physical addiction.

For about a day after a person smokes marijuana, his or her attention, coordination, and short-term memory are impaired. Frequent marijuana users show small declines in learning, memory, attention, and thinking abilities (Solowij et al., 2002). When surveyed at age 29, nonusers are healthier, earn more, and are more satisfied with their lives than people who smoke marijuana regularly (Ellickson, Martino, & Collins, 2004). In fact, marijuana use is associated with mental health problems (Buckner, Ecker, & Cohen, 2010).

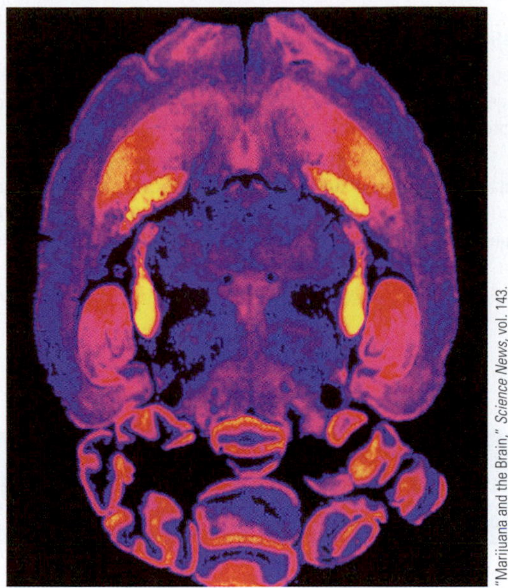

"Marijuana and the Brain," *Science News*, vol. 143.

● **Figure 5.13** This thin slice of a rat's brain has been washed with a radioactive THC-like drug. Yellowish areas show where the brain is rich in THC receptors. In addition to the cortex, or outer layer of the brain, THC receptors are found in abundance in areas involved in the control of coordinated movement. Naturally occurring chemicals similar to THC may help the brain cope with pain and stress. However, when THC is used as a drug, high doses can cause paranoia, hallucinations, and dizziness (Maisto, Galizio, & Connors, 2011).

People who smoke five or more "joints" a week score four points lower on IQ tests. This is enough to dull their learning capacity. In fact, many people who have stopped using marijuana say they quit because they were bothered by short-term memory loss and concentration problems. Fortunately, IQ scores and other cognitive measures rebound in about a month after a person quits using marijuana (Grant et al., 2001). In other words, people who smoke dope may act like dopes, but if they quit, there's a good chance they will regain their mental abilities.

Long-Term Health Risks

Marijuana's long-term effects include the following health risks:

1. Marijuana smoke contains 50 percent more cancer-causing hydrocarbons and 16 times more tar than tobacco smoke does. Thus, smoking several joints a week may be the equivalent of smoking a dozen cigarettes a day. In regular users, marijuana increases the risk of a variety of cancers, including prostate and cervical cancer (Hashibe, et al., 2005).
2. Marijuana temporarily lowers sperm production in males, and users produce more abnormal sperm. This could be a problem for a man who is marginally fertile and wants to have a family (Schuel et al., 1999).
3. In experiments with female monkeys, THC causes abnormal menstrual cycles and disrupts ovulation. Other animal studies show that THC causes a higher rate of miscarriages and that it can reach the developing fetus. As is true for so many other drugs, marijuana should be avoided during pregnancy.
4. THC can suppress the body's immune system, increasing the risk of disease.
5. In animals, marijuana causes genetic damage within cells of the body. It is not known to what extent this happens in humans, but it does suggest that marijuana can be detrimental to health.
6. Activity levels in the cerebellum are lower than normal in marijuana abusers. This may explain why chronic marijuana users tend to show some loss of coordination (Volkow et al., 1996).
7. There is some evidence that THC damages parts of the brain important for memory (Chan et al., 1998).
8. Children whose mothers smoked marijuana during pregnancy show lowered ability to succeed in challenging, goal-oriented activities (Fried & Smith, 2001; Noland et al., 2005).

Although much is still unknown, marijuana appears to pose a wide range of health risks. Only future research will tell for sure "what's in the pot."

A Look Ahead

Of the many states of consciousness we have discussed, dreaming remains one of the most familiar—and the most surprising. Are there lessons to be learned from dreams? What personal insights lie hidden in the ebb and flow of your dream images? Let's find out in the upcoming *Psychology in Action* section.

Psychoactive Drugs

RECITE

1. Addictive drugs stimulate the brain's reward circuitry by affecting
   a. neurotransmitters *b.* alpha waves *c.* tryptophan levels *d.* delta spindles
2. Which of the drugs listed below are known to cause a physical dependence?
   a. heroin *b.* morphine *c.* codeine *d.* methadone *e.* barbiturates *f.* alcohol *g.* marijuana *h.* amphetamines *i.* nicotine *j.* cocaine *k.* GHB
3. Amphetamine psychosis is similar to extreme ______________, in which the individual feels threatened and suffers from delusions.
4. Cocaine is very similar to which of the following in its effects on the central nervous system?
   a. Seconal *b.* codeine *c.* cannabis *d.* amphetamine
5. Drug interaction is a special danger when a person combines
   a. marijuana and amphetamine *b.* barbiturates and alcohol *c.* alcohol and cocaine *d.* marijuana and THC
6. College students may overdrink as they try to keep up with how much they falsely imagine that their peers drink. T or F?
7. Treatment for alcohol dependence begins with sobering up the person and cutting off the supply. This is referred to as
   a. "hitting bottom" *b.* the crucial phase *c.* detoxification *d.* clinical anhedonia

Continued

Hallucinogen A substance that alters or distorts sensory impressions.

REFLECT

Think Critically

8. The U.S. government, which helps fund antismoking campaigns and smoking-related health research, also continues to subsidize tobacco growers. Can you explain this contradiction?
9. Why do you think there is such a contrast between the laws regulating marijuana and those regulating alcohol and tobacco?

Self-Reflect

What legal drugs did you use in the last year? Did any have psychoactive properties? How do psychoactive drugs differ from other substances in their potential for abuse?

Answers: **1.** *a* **2.** All of them do **3.** paranoia **4.** *d* **5.** *b* **6.** T **7.** *c* **8.** Neither can we. **9.** Drug laws in Western societies reflect cultural values and historical patterns of use. Inconsistencies in the law often cannot be justified on the basis of pharmacology, health risks, or abuse potential.

Psychology in Action

Exploring and Using Dreams

Gateway Question 5.9: *How can dreams be used to promote personal understanding?*

No matter what theory of dreaming you favor, dreams can be thought of as a message *from* yourself *to* yourself. Thus, the way to understand dreams is to remember them, write them down, look for the messages they contain, and become deeply acquainted with *your own* symbol system. Here's how:

How to Catch a Dream

1. Before going to sleep, plan to remember your dreams. Keep a pen and paper or a voice recorder beside your bed.
2. If possible, arrange to awaken gradually without an alarm. Natural awakening almost always follows soon after a REM period.
3. If you rarely remember your dreams, you may want to set an alarm clock to go off an hour before you usually awaken. Although less desirable than awakening naturally, this may let you catch a dream.
4. Upon awakening, lie still and review the dream images with your eyes closed. Try to recall as many details as possible.
5. If you can, make your first dream record (whether by writing or by recording) with your eyes closed. Opening your eyes will disrupt dream recall.
6. Review the dream again and record as many additional details as you can remember. Dream memories disappear quickly. Be sure to describe feelings as well as the plot, characters, and actions of the dream.
7. Put your dreams into a permanent dream diary. Keep dreams in chronological order and review them periodically. This procedure will reveal recurrent themes, conflicts, and emotions. It almost always produces valuable insights.
8. Remember, a number of drugs suppress dreaming by interfering with REM sleep (see ■ Table 5.5).

Dream Work

At one time or another, almost everyone has had a dream that seemed to have deep meaning (Rock, 2004). Exploring everyday dream life can be a source of personal enrichment and personal growth (Halliday, 2010). What strategies do psychologists use to interpret dreams? Let's start with Sigmund Freud's pioneering approach.

■ TABLE 5.5 Effects of Selected Drugs on Dreaming

Drug	Effect on REM Sleep
Alcohol	Decrease
Amphetamines	Decrease
Barbiturates	Decrease
Caffeine	None
Cocaine	Decrease
Ecstasy	Decrease (by interrupting sleep)
LSD	Slight increase
Marijuana	Slight decrease or no effect
Opiates	Decrease
Valium	Decrease

To unlock dreams, Freud identified four **dream processes**, or mental filters, that disguise the meanings of dreams. The first is **condensation**, in which several people, objects, or events are combined into a single dream image. A dream character that looks like a teacher, acts like your father, talks like your mother, and is dressed like your employer might be a condensation of authority figures in your life.

Displacement is a second way of disguising dream content. Displacement may cause important emotions or actions of a dream to be redirected toward safe or seemingly unimportant images. Thus, a student angry at his parents might dream of accidentally wrecking their car instead of directly attacking them.

A third dream process is **symbolization**. As mentioned earlier, Freud believed that dreams are often expressed in images that are symbolic rather than literal. That's why it helps to ask what feelings or ideas a dream image might symbolize. Let's say, for example, that a student dreams of coming to class naked. A literal interpretation would be that the student is an exhibitionist. A more likely symbolic meaning is that the student feels vulnerable or unprepared in the class.

Secondary elaboration is the fourth method by which dream meanings are disguised. **Secondary elaboration** is the tendency to make a dream more logical and to add details when remembering it. The fresher a dream memory is, the more useful it is likely to be.

How would you try to find the meaning of a dream? A traditional approach is to look for symbolic messages, as well as literal meanings. If you find yourself wearing a mask in a dream, for instance, it could relate to important roles that you play at school, work, or home. It could also mean that you want to hide or that you are looking forward to a costume party. However, to accurately interpret a dream, it is important to learn your own "vocabulary" of dream images and meanings. Keeping a dream diary is the first step toward gaining valuable insights

Looking for condensation, displacement, symbolization, and secondary elaboration may help you unlock your dreams. But there are other techniques that may be more effective. Fritz Perls, the originator of Gestalt therapy, considered most dreams a special message about what's missing in our lives, what we avoid doing, or feelings that need to be "reowned." Perls believed that dreams are a way of filling in gaps in personal experience (Perls, 1969).

An approach that Perls found helpful is to "take the part of" or "speak for" each of the characters and objects in the dream. In other words, if you dream about a strange man standing behind a doorway, you would speak aloud to the man, then answer for him. To use Perls's method, you would even speak for the door, perhaps saying something like, "I am a barrier. I keep you safe, but I also keep you locked inside. The stranger has something to tell you. You must risk opening me to learn it."

Another theorist, Ernest Hartmann, suggests that dreams arise as our brains seek to make creative connections. Ignoring the elements of a dream which merely replay a days events and focusing instead on unusual dream elements is central to unlocking the dream's meaning (Hartmann, 2010). Hartmann adds that our emotions guide making of dream connections. Thus, the overall *emotional tone* (underlying mood) of a dream is a major clue to its meaning (Hartmann, 2008). Is the dream comical, threatening, joyous, or depressing? Were you lonely, jealous, frightened, in love, or angry?

Because each dream has several possible meanings or levels of meaning, there is no fixed way to work with it (Halliday, 2010). Telling the dream to others and discussing its meaning can be a good start. Describing it may help you relive some of the feelings in the dream. Also, family members or friends may be able to offer interpretations to which you would be blind. Watch for verbal or visual puns and other playful elements in dreams. For example, if you dream that you are in a wrestling match and your arm is pinned behind your back, it may mean that you feel someone is "twisting your arm" in real life.

The meaning of most dreams will yield to a little detective work. Try asking a series of questions about dreams you would like to understand:

Probing Dreams

1. Who was in the dream? Were there humans, animals, or mythical characters? Do you recognize any of the characters?
2. What social interactions were taking place? Were those interactions friendly? Aggressive? Sexual?
3. What activities were taking place? Were they physical activities or not?
4. Was there striving? Was the striving successful or not?
5. Was the dream about good fortune or misfortune?
6. What emotions were present in the dream? Was there anger, apprehension, confusion, happiness, or sadness?
7. What were the physical surroundings like? What was the setting? Were there any physical objects present? (Adapted from the Hall-Van de Castle system of dream content analysis; Domhoff, 2003.)

A particularly interesting dream exercise is to continue a dream as waking fantasy so that it may be concluded or carried on to a more meaningful ending. As the world of dreams and your personal dream language become more familiar, you will doubtless find many answers, paradoxes, intuitions, and insights into your own behavior.

Using Your Dreams

It is possible to learn to use dreams for our own purposes. For example, as mentioned previously, nightmare sufferers can use *imagery rehearsal* to modify their own nightmares (Germain et al., 2004; Krakow & Zadra, 2006). Similarly, it is possible to use your dreams to enhance creativity (Stickgold & Walker, 2004).

Dreams and Creativity

History is full of cases in which dreams have been a pathway to creativity and discovery. A striking example is provided by Dr. Otto Loewi, a pharmacologist and winner of a Nobel Prize. Loewi had spent years studying the chemical transmission of nerve impulses. A tremendous breakthrough in his research came when he dreamed of an experiment three nights in a row. The first two nights he woke up and scribbled the experiment on a pad. But the next morning, he couldn't tell what the notes meant. On the third night, he got up after having the dream. This time, instead of making notes he went straight to his laboratory and performed the crucial experiment. Loewi later said that if the experiment had occurred to him while awake he would have rejected it.

Dream processes Mental filters that hide the true meanings of dreams.
Condensation Combining several people, objects, or events into a single dream image.
Displacement Directing emotions or actions toward safe or unimportant dream images.
Symbolization The nonliteral expression of dream content.
Secondary elaboration Making a dream more logical and complete while remembering it.

Loewi's experience gives some insight into using dreams to produce creative solutions. Inhibitions are reduced during dreaming, which may be especially useful in solving problems that require a fresh point of view. Even unimaginative people may create amazing worlds each night in their dreams. For many of us, this rich ability to create is lost in the daily rush of sensory input.

The ability to take advantage of dreams for problem solving is improved if you "set" yourself before retiring. Before you go to bed, try to visualize or think intently about a problem you wish to solve. Steep yourself in the problem by stating it clearly and reviewing all relevant information. Then use the suggestions listed previously to catch your dreams. Although this method is not guaranteed to produce a novel solution or a new insight, it is certain to be an adventure. About half of a group of college students using the method for one week recalled a dream that helped them solve a personal problem (Barrett, 1993).

Lucid Dreaming

If you would like to press further into the territory of dreams, you may want to learn lucid dreaming, a relatively rare but fascinating experience. During a **lucid dream**, a person feels as if she or he is fully awake within the dream world and capable of normal thought and action. If you ask yourself, "Could this be a dream?" and answer "Yes," you are having a lucid dream (Holzinger, LaBerge, & Levitan, 2006; LaBerge, 2000).

Stephen LaBerge and his colleagues at the Stanford University Sleep Research Center have used a unique approach to show that lucid dreams are real and that they occur during REM sleep. In the sleep lab, lucid dreamers agree to make prearranged signals when they become aware they are dreaming. One such signal is to look up abruptly in a dream, causing a distinct upward eye movement. Another signal is to clench the right and left fists (in the dream) in a prearranged pattern. In other words, lucid dreamers can partially overcome REM sleep paralysis. Such signals show very clearly that lucid dreaming and voluntary action in dreams is possible (LaBerge, 2000).

How can a person learn to have lucid dreams? Try following this simple routine: When you awaken spontaneously from a dream, take a few minutes to try to memorize it. Next, engage in 10 to 15 minutes of reading or any other activity requiring full wakefulness. Then while lying in bed and returning to sleep, say to yourself, "Next time I'm dreaming, I want to remember I'm dreaming." Finally, visualize yourself lying in bed asleep while in the dream you just rehearsed. At the same time, picture yourself realizing that you are dreaming. Follow this routine each time you awaken (substitute a dream memory from another occasion if you don't awaken from a dream). Researchers have also found that stimulation from the vestibular system tends to increase lucidity. Thus, sleeping in a hammock, a boat, or on a waterbed might increase the number of lucid dreams you have (Leslie & Ogilvie, 1996).

Why would anyone want to have more lucid dreams? Researchers are interested in lucid dreams because they provide a tool for understanding dreaming (Paulsson & Parker, 2006). Using subjects who can signal when they are dreaming makes it possible to explore dreams with firsthand data from the dreamer's world itself.

On a more personal level, lucid dreaming can convert dreams into a nightly "workshop" for emotional growth. Consider, for example, a recently divorced woman who kept dreaming that she was being swallowed by a giant wave. The woman was asked to try swimming the next time the wave engulfed her. She did, with great determination, and the nightmare lost its terror. More important, her revised dream made her feel that she could cope with life again. For reasons such as this, people who have lucid dreams tend to feel a sense of emotional well-being (Wolpin et al., 1992). Dream expert Allan Hobson believes that learning to voluntarily enter altered states of consciousness (through lucid dreaming or self-hypnosis, for example) has allowed him to have enlightening experiences without the risks of taking mind-altering drugs (Hobson, 2001). So, day or night, don't be afraid to dream a little.

Knowledge Builder: Exploring and Using Dreams

RECITE

1. Which is NOT one of the four dream processes identified by Freud? *a.* condensation *b.* lucidity *c.* displacement *d.* symbolization
2. In secondary elaboration, one dream character stands for several others. T or F?
3. Fritz Perls's approach to dream interpretation emphasizes taking the part of characters and even objects portrayed in a dream. T or F?
4. Ernest Hartmann stresses that dreaming is a relatively mechanical process having little personal meaning. T or F?
5. Both alcohol and LSD cause a slight increase in dreaming. T or F?
6. Recent research shows that lucid dreaming occurs primarily during NREM sleep or micro-awakenings. T or F?

REFLECT

Think Critically

7. The possibility of having a lucid dream raises an interesting question: If you were dreaming right now, how could you prove it?

Self-Reflect

Some people are very interested in remembering and interpreting their dreams. Others pay little attention to dreaming. What importance do you place on dreams? Do you think dreams and dream interpretation can increase self-awareness?

Answers: 1. *b* **2.** F **3.** T **4.** F **5.** F **6.** T **7.** In waking consciousness, our actions have consequences that produce immediate sensory feedback. Dreams lack such external feedback. Thus, trying to walk through a wall or doing similar tests would reveal if you were dreaming.

Chapter in Review Gateways to Consciousness

Gateway QUESTIONS REVISITED

5.1 *What is consciousness?*

5.1.1 Consciousness is a core feature of mental life consisting of sensations and perceptions of external events as well as self-awareness of mental events including thoughts, memories, and feelings about experiences and the self.

5.1.2 States of awareness that differ from normal, alert, waking consciousness are called altered states of consciousness (ASCs). Altered states are especially associated with sleep and dreaming, hypnosis, sensory deprivation, and psychoactive drugs.

5.1.3 Cultural conditioning greatly affects what altered states a person recognizes, seeks, considers normal, and attains.

5.2 *What are the effects of sleep loss or changes in sleep patterns?*

5.2.1 Sleep is an innate biological rhythm essential for survival.

5.2.2 Moderate sleep loss mainly affects vigilance and performance on routine or boring tasks.

5.2.3 Higher animals and people deprived of sleep experience involuntary microsleeps.

5.2.4 Lowering body and brain activity and metabolism during sleep may help conserve energy and lengthen life.

5.2.5 Extended sleep loss can (somewhat rarely) produce a temporary sleep-deprivation psychosis.

5.2.6 Although sleep patterns may be modified, they cannot be disregarded.

5.2.7 Sleep patterns show some flexibility, but 7 to 8 hours remains average. The amount of daily sleep decreases steadily from birth to old age.

5.3 *What are some functions of sleep?*

5.3.1 Sleep occurs in four stages. Stage 1 is light sleep, and Stage 4 is deep sleep. The sleeper alternates between Stages 1 and 4 (passing through Stages 2 and 3) several times each night.

5.3.2 According to the dual process hypothesis, non-REM (NREM) sleep "refreshes" the body and brain and rapid eye movement (REM) sleep helps form lasting memories.

5.3.3 NREM sleep brings overall brain activation levels down, "calming" the brain.

5.3.4 REM sleep is strongly associated with dreaming. REM sleep and dreaming help us store important memories.

5.4 *What are some sleep disorders and unusual sleep events?*

5.4.1 Sleep disorders, including insomnia, sleepwalking, nightmares, night terrors, sleep apnea, and narcolepsy are serious health problems that should be corrected when they persist.

5.4.2 Insomnia may be temporary or chronic. Behavioral approaches to managing insomnia, such as sleep restriction and stimulus control, are quite effective.

5.4.3 Sleepwalking, sleeptalking, and sleepsex occur during NREM sleep.

5.4.4 Night terrors occur in NREM sleep, whereas nightmares occur in REM sleep.

5.4.5 Sleep apnea (interrupted breathing) is one source of insomnia and daytime hypersomnia (sleepiness).

5.4.6 Apnea is suspected as one cause of sudden infant death syndrome (SIDS). With only a few exceptions, healthy infants should sleep on their backs.

5.4.7 Narcolepsy (sleep attacks) and cataplexy are caused by a sudden shift to Stage 1 REM patterns during normal waking hours.

5.5 *Do dreams have meaning?*

5.5.1 REM sleep helps us form memories, and it contributes to general mental effectiveness.

5.5.2 The Freudian, or psychodynamic, view is that dreams express unconscious wishes, frequently hidden by dream symbols.

5.5.3 Many theorists have questioned Freud's view of dreams. For example, the activation-synthesis model portrays dreaming as a random physiological process.

5.5.4 The neurocognitive view of dreams holds that dreams are continuous with waking thoughts and emotions.

5.5.5 Dreams are at least as meaningful as waking thoughts. Most dream content is about familiar settings, people, and actions.

5.6 *What is hypnosis?*

5.6.1 Although not all psychologists agree, hypnosis is usually defined as an altered state characterized by narrowed attention and increased suggestibility.

5.6.2 Hypnosis appears capable of producing relaxation, controlling pain, and altering perceptions. It is also more capable of changing subjective experiences more than habits, such as smoking.

5.6.3 Stage hypnotism takes advantage of typical stage behavior and uses deception to simulate hypnosis.

Lucid dream A dream in which the dreamer feels awake and capable of normal thought and action.

5.7 *Do meditation and sensory deprivation have any benefits?*

5.7.1 Concentrative meditation can be used to focus attention, alter consciousness, and reduce stress. Mindfulness meditation widens attention to achieve similar outcomes.

5.7.2 Major benefits of meditation are its ability to interrupt anxious thoughts and to elicit the relaxation response.

5.7.3 Brief exposure to sensory deprivation can also elicit the relaxation response. Under proper conditions, sensory deprivation may help break long-standing habits.

5.7.4 Mindfulness s a positive mental state which involves an open, nonjudgmental awareness of current experience.

5.8 *What are the effects of the more commonly used psychoactive drugs?*

5.8.1 Psychoactive drugs affect the brain in ways that alter consciousness. Most psychoactive drugs can be placed on a scale ranging from stimulation to depression.

5.8.2 Psychoactive drugs are highly prone to abuse.

5.8.3 Drug abuse is related to personal maladjustment, the reinforcing qualities of drugs, peer group influences, and expectations about drug effects.

5.8.4 Drugs may cause a physical dependence (addiction), a psychological dependence, or both. The physically addicting drugs are alcohol, amphetamines, barbiturates, cocaine, codeine, GHB, heroin, marijuana, methadone, morphine, nicotine, and tranquilizers. All psychoactive drugs can lead to psychological dependence.

5.8.5 Drug use can be classified as experimental, recreational, situational, intensive, and compulsive. Drug abuse is most often associated with the last three.

5.8.6 Stimulant drugs are readily abused because of the period of depression that often follows stimulation. The greatest risks are associated with amphetamines (especially methamphetamine), cocaine, MDMA, and nicotine, but even caffeine can be a problem. Nicotine includes the added risk of lung cancer, heart disease, and other health problems.

5.8.7 Barbiturates and tranquilizers are depressant drugs whose action is similar to that of alcohol. The overdose level for barbiturates and GHB is close to the intoxication dosage, making them dangerous drugs. Mixing barbiturates, tranquilizers, or GHB and alcohol may result in a fatal drug interaction.

5.8.8 Alcohol is the most heavily abused drug in common use today. Binge drinking is a problem among college students. It is possible to pace the consumption of alcohol.

5.8.9 Marijuana is subject to an abuse pattern similar to alcohol. Studies have linked chronic marijuana use with lung cancer, various mental impairments, and other health problems.

5.9 *How can dreams be used to promote personal understanding?*

5.9.1 Collecting and interpreting your dreams can promote self-awareness.

5.9.2 Freud held that the meaning of dreams is hidden by condensation, displacement, symbolization, and secondary elaboration. Perls emphasized the technique of speaking for dream elements, and Hartmann's view of dreams as creative connections guided by emotions suggests focusing on unusual dream elements and emotions.

5.9.3 Dreams may be used for creative problem solving, especially when dream awareness is achieved through lucid dreaming.

MEDIA RESOURCES

Web Resources

Internet addresses frequently change. To find an up-to-date list of URLs for the sites listed here, visit your Psychology CourseMate.

Sleepless at Stanford What all undergraduates should know about how their sleeping lives affect their waking lives.

Sleep Patterns Are you an owl or a lark?

Sleep Paralysis Read about hypnopompic and hypnagogic experiences.

The National Sleep Foundation The NSF is dedicated to improving public health and safety by achieving understanding of sleep and sleep disorders and by supporting education, sleep-related research, and advocacy.

Sleep Apnea Find out more about sleep apnea.

Sudden Infant Death and Other Infant Death Information about SIDS, with links to related topics.

Basic Methods of Self Hypnosis Find out more about self-hypnosis.

Meditation for Stress Reduction Find out more about how to meditate.

Introduction to Floating Read more about REST (Restricted Environmental Stimulation Therapy).

Higher Education Center The Higher Education Center's purpose is to help college and community leaders develop, implement, and evaluate programs and policies to reduce student problems related to alcohol and other drug use and interpersonal violence.

National Council on Alcoholism and Drug Dependence, Inc. This site provides education, information, help, and hope to the public.

Drugs and Behavior Links Comprehensive links to topics in drugs and behavior.

Dreams and Lucid Dreams Provides links to frequently asked questions and articles regarding dreaming and lucid dreams.

Dream Dictionary One attempt to provide st andardized interpretations of common dream symbols.

How to Keep a Diary of Dreams Find out how to keep your own dream diary.

Interactive Learning

Log in to **CengageBrain** to access the resources your instructor requires. For this book, you can access:

CourseMate brings course concepts to life with interactive learning, study, and exam preparation tools that support the printed textbook. A textbook-specific website, ***Psychology CourseMate*** includes an ***integrated interactive eBook*** and other ***interactive learning tools*** including quizzes, flashcards, videos, and more.

CENGAGE**NOW**™

CengageNOW is an easy-to-use online resource that helps you study in less time to get the grade you want—NOW. Take a pre-test for this chapter and receive a personalized study plan based on your results that will identify the topics you need to review and direct you to online resources to help you master those topics. Then take a post-test to help you determine the concepts you have mastered and what you will need to work on. If your textbook does not include an access code card, go to CengageBrain.com to gain access.

WebTUTOR™

More than just an interactive study guide, **WebTutor** is an anytime, anywhere customized learning solution with an eBook, keeping you connected to your textbook, instructor, and classmates.

If your professor has assigned **Aplia** homework:

1. Sign in to your account.
2. Complete the corresponding homework exercises as required by your professor.
3. When finished, click "Grade It Now" to see which areas you have mastered and which need more work, and for detailed explanations of every answer.

Visit www.cengagebrain.com to access your account and purchase materials.

Gateway THEME

The principles of learning can be used to understand and manage behavior.

6 Conditioning and Learning

Rats!

Larry vividly remembers his mother describing how a rat had terrified her. She gestured excitedly as she relived the horror of seeing the creature scamper out of a camp stove. Although everyone else laughed, 6-year-old Larry shivered as he imagined the attacking rodent. That's the day he learned to fear rats.

Years later, while studying gorillas in Africa, he encountered his first live rat. Larry was shocked by his own reaction. Despite being a respected scientist, he ran away shrieking like a little child. After failing to control his fear a few more times (and being good-naturedly ribbed about it by others), he resolved to conquer it.

Back home, Larry read about irrational fears and realized that a form of learning called *vicarious classical conditioning* explained how he had come to dread rats. After reading several more books, he returned to the jungle, certain that he could cope with his next close encounter. However, he was shocked to discover that his newfound knowledge was no help at all.

Larry had bumped into a strange truth: All his abstract "book learning," a form of *cognitive learning*, was powerless to protect him in the presence of a rat. Chastened, he went to a therapist who used classical conditioning to help him overcome his fear. Larry eventually came to like rats and now has a pet rat named Einstein. Larry also went on to study how baby gorillas learn by observing others—much as he did when he observed his mother's story about the rat.

Different forms of learning reach into every corner of our lives. Are you ready to learn more? If so, let's begin!

Gateway QUESTIONS

6.1 *What is learning?*

6.2 *How does classical conditioning occur?*

6.3 *Does conditioning affect emotions?*

6.4 *How does operant conditioning occur?*

6.5 *Are there different kinds of operant reinforcement?*

6.6 *How are we influenced by patterns of reward?*

6.7 *What does punishment do to behavior?*

6.8 *What is cognitive learning?*

6.9 *Does learning occur by imitation?*

6.10 *How does conditioning apply to everyday problems?*

What Is Learning—Does Practice Make Perfect?

Gateway Question 6.1: *What is learning?*

Almost all human behavior is learned. Imagine if you suddenly lost all you had ever learned. What could you do? You would be unable to read, write, or speak. You couldn't feed yourself, find your way home, drive a car, play the clarinet, or "party." Needless to say, you would be totally incapacitated. (Dull, too!) **Learning** is a relatively permanent change in behavior due to experience (Domjan, 2010). Notice that this definition excludes both temporary changes and more permanent changes caused by motivation, fatigue, maturation, disease, injury, or drugs. Each of these can alter behavior, but none qualifies as learning.

Types of Learning

As Larry's rat experience illustrates, there are different types of learning (Shanks, 2010). **Associative learning** occurs whenever a person or an animal forms a simple association among various stimuli and/or responses. Humans share the capacity for associative learning with many other species. In a moment, we will explore two types of associative learning called classical conditioning and operant conditioning.

Humans also engage in **cognitive learning**, which refers to understanding, knowing, anticipating, or otherwise making use of information-rich higher mental processes. More complex forms of cognitive learning, such as learning from written language, are unique to humans. However, some animals do engage in simpler forms of cognitive learning, which we will describe later in this chapter.

Associative Learning

Isn't learning the result of practice? It depends on what you mean by practice. Merely repeating a response will not necessarily produce learning. You could close your eyes and swing a golf club hundreds of times without improving your swing. Reinforcement is the key to associative learning. **Reinforcement** refers to any event that increases the probability that a response will occur again. A response is any identifiable behavior. Responses may be observable actions, such as blinking, eating a piece of sushi, or turning a doorknob. They can also be internal, such as having a faster heartbeat.

To teach a dog a trick, we could reinforce correct responses by giving the dog some food each time it sits up. Similarly, you could teach a child to be neat by praising him for picking up his toys. Learning can also occur in other ways. For instance, if a girl gets stung by a bee, she may learn to associate pain with bees and to fear them. In this case, the girl's fear is reinforced by the discomfort she feels immediately after seeing the bee.

Unlocking the secrets of associative learning begins with noting what happens before and after a response. Events that precede a response are **antecedents**. For example, Ashleigh, who is 3 years old, has learned that when she hears a truck pull into the driveway, it means that Daddy is home. Ashleigh runs to the front door. Effects that follow a response are **consequences**. The hug she gets from her father is what reinforces Ashleigh's tendency to run to the door. As this suggests, paying careful attention to the "before and after" of associative learning is a key to understanding it.

Classical conditioning is based on what happens before we respond. It begins with a stimulus that reliably triggers a response. Imagine, for example, that a puff of air (the stimulus) is aimed at your eye. The air puff will make you blink (a response) every time. The eye blink is a **reflex** (automatic, nonlearned response). Now, assume that we sound a horn (another stimulus) just before each puff of air hits your eye. If the horn and the air puff occur together many times, what happens? Soon, the horn alone will make you blink. Clearly, you've learned something. Before, the horn didn't make you blink. Now it does.

In **classical conditioning**, an antecedent stimulus that doesn't produce a response is linked with one that does (a horn is associated with a puff of air to the eye, for example). We can say that learning has occurred when the new stimulus will also elicit (bring forth) responses (● Figure 6.1).

In **operant conditioning**, learning is based on the consequences of responding. A response may be followed by a reinforcer (such as food). Or by punishment. Or by nothing. These results determine whether a response is likely to be made again (● Figure 6.1). For example, if you wear a particular hat and get lots of compliments (reinforcement), you are likely to wear it more often. If people snicker, insult you, call the police, or scream (punishment), you will probably wear it less often.

Now that you have an idea of what happens in the two basic kinds of associative learning, let's look at classical conditioning in more detail.

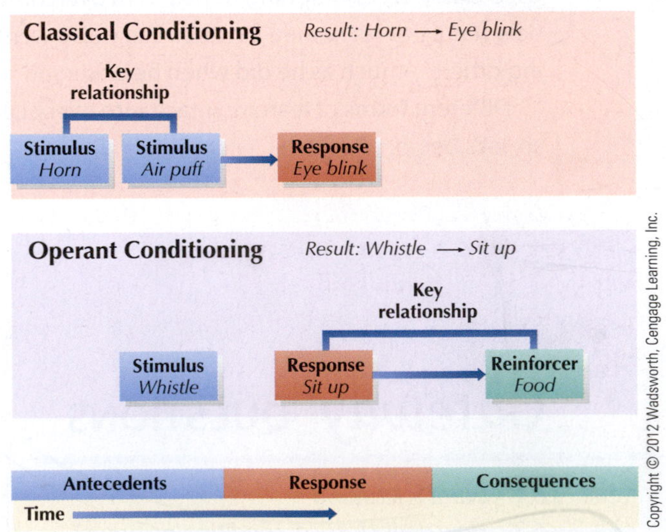

● **Figure 6.1** In classical conditioning, a stimulus that does not produce a response is paired with a stimulus that does elicit a response. After many such pairings, the stimulus that previously had no effect begins to produce a response. In the example shown, a horn precedes a puff of air to the eye. Eventually, the horn alone will produce an eye blink. In operant conditioning, a response that is followed by a reinforcing consequence becomes more likely to occur on future occasions. In the example shown, a dog learns to sit up when it hears a whistle.

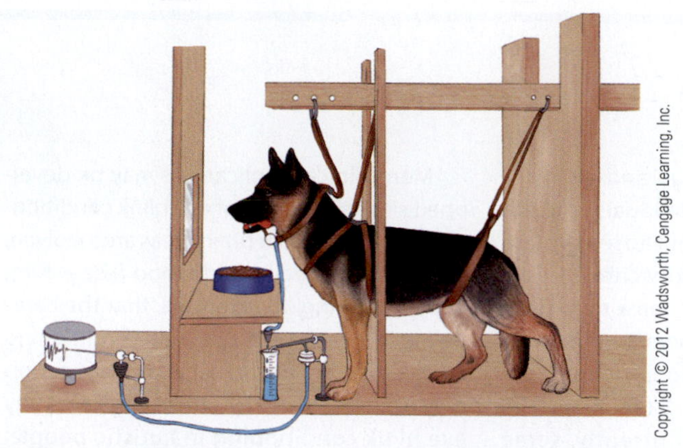

● **Figure 6.2** An apparatus for Pavlovian conditioning. A tube carries saliva from the dog's mouth to a lever that activates a recording device *(far left)*. During conditioning, various stimuli can be paired with a dish of food placed in front of the dog. The device pictured here is more elaborate than the one Pavlov used in his early experiments.

Classical Conditioning—Does the Name Pavlov Ring a Bell?

Gateway Question 6.2: *How does classical conditioning occur?*

At the beginning of the twentieth century, something happened in the lab of Russian physiologist Ivan Pavlov that brought him the Nobel Prize: Pavlov's subjects drooled at him. Actually, Pavlov was studying digestion. To observe salivation, he placed meat powder or some tidbit on a dog's tongue and measured the resulting flow of saliva. However, after repeating his procedure many times, Pavlov noticed that his dogs were salivating *before* the food reached their mouths. Later, the dogs even began to salivate when they saw Pavlov enter the room (Schultz & Schultz, 2012).

Pavlov believed that salivation is an automatic, inherited reflex. It really shouldn't change from one day to the next. His dogs were *supposed* to salivate when he put food in their mouths, but they were *not supposed* to salivate when they merely saw him. This was a change in behavior due to experience. Pavlov realized that some type of learning had occurred and soon began investigating "conditioning," as he called it (● Figure 6.2). Because of its place in history, this form of learning is now called *classical conditioning* (also known as *Pavlovian conditioning* or *respondent conditioning*) (Mackintosh, 2003).

Pavlov's Experiment

How did Pavlov study conditioning? To begin, he rang a bell. At first, the bell was a neutral stimulus (the dogs did not respond to it by salivating). Immediately after, he placed meat powder on the dogs' tongues, which caused reflex salivation. This sequence was repeated a number of times: bell, meat powder, salivation; bell, meat powder, salivation. Eventually (as conditioning took place), the dogs began to salivate when they heard the bell (● Figure 6.3). By association, the bell, which before had no effect, began to evoke the same response that food did. This was shown by sometimes ringing the bell alone. Then the dogs salivated, even though no food had been placed in their mouths.

Psychologists use several terms to describe these events. The meat powder is an **unconditioned stimulus (US)**—a stimulus innately capable of producing a response (salivation in this case). Notice that the dog did not have to learn to respond to the US. Such stimuli naturally trigger reflexes or emotional reactions. Because a reflex is innate, or "built in," it is called an **unconditioned** (nonlearned) **response (UR)**. Reflex salivation was the UR in Pavlov's experiment.

The bell starts out as a **neutral stimulus (NS)**. In time, the bell becomes a **conditioned stimulus (CS)**—a stimulus that, because of learning, will elicit a response. When Pavlov's bell also produced salivation, the dog was making a new response. Thus, salivation had also become a **conditioned** (learned) **response (CR)** (● Figure 6.3). ■ Table 6.1 summarizes the important elements of classical conditioning.

Are all these terms really necessary? Yes, because they help us recognize similarities in various instances of learning. Let's summarize the terms using an earlier example:

Before Conditioning	**Example**
US → UR	Puff of air → eye blink
NS → no effect	Horn → no effect
After Conditioning	**Example**
CS → CR	Horn → eye blink

See "In the Blink of an Eye" for an example of how classical conditioning is used to address clinical problems.

Learning Any relatively permanent change in behavior that can be attributed to experience.
Associative learning The formation of simple associations between various stimuli and responses.
Cognitive learning Higher-level learning involving thinking, knowing, understanding, and anticipation.
Reinforcement Any event that increases the probability that a particular response will occur.
Antecedents Events that precede a response.
Consequences Effects that follow a response.
Reflex An innate, automatic response to a stimulus; for example, an eye blink.
Classical conditioning A form of learning in which reflex responses are associated with new stimuli.
Operant conditioning Learning based on the consequences of responding.
Unconditioned stimulus (US) A stimulus innately capable of eliciting a response.
Unconditioned response (UR) An innate reflex response elicited by an unconditioned stimulus.
Neutral stimulus (NS) A stimulus that does not evoke a response.
Conditioned stimulus (CS) A stimulus that evokes a response because it has been repeatedly paired with an unconditioned stimulus.
Conditioned response (CR) A learned response elicited by a conditioned stimulus.

The Clinical File In the Blink of an Eye

Did you notice the eye blink example earlier in this chapter? Good. Many instructors use it because it's fairly easy for students to grasp.

OK, but is it useful for anything else? As trivial as using classical conditioning techniques to condition blinking might seem, it has great clinical potential. Remember Kate Adamson, the courageous woman with locked-in syndrome who we met in Chapter 2? Because she was totally paralyzed, doctors assumed she was brain dead. Fortunately, Kate discovered she could communicate by deliberately blinking her eyes. But what if she couldn't do even that? Worse still, what if she was only *minimally conscious* instead of brain-dead (in a *vegetative state*)?

One exciting possibility is that eye blink conditioning may be useful for distinguishing locked-in individuals from those with more severe brain damage and even severely brain-damaged individuals who are minimally conscious from those who are in a vegetative state (Bekinschtein et al., 2009). Patients who are at least minimally conscious can be conditioned and may recover some mental functions whereas patients in a vegetative state likely cannot be conditioned or recover. Currently, some minimally conscious patients are misdiagnosed and are not offered appropriate therapy.

Eye blink conditioning may also help make earlier diagnoses. For example, psychologist Diana Woodruff-Pak (2001) noticed disordered eye blink conditioning in a patient 6 years before other tests showed any signs of dementia (duh-MEN-sha). (Eventually, people with dementia suffer major declines in memory, judgment, language, and thinking abilities.)

More clinical applications may be developed since the details of eye blink conditioning, including which brain areas are involved, are now fairly well understood (Lee & Kim, 2004). Knowing, for example, that the cerebellum is involved in eye blink conditioning and suspecting that cerebellar dysfunction may be involved in, say, autism, we can study eye blink conditioning in autistic people. When psychologist Joseph Steinmetz and his colleagues did exactly that, they found that people with autism show unusual eye blink conditioning. So do people with obsessive-compulsive disorder, fetal alcohol syndrome, and schizophrenia (Bolbecker et al., 2009; Steinmetz, Tracy, & Green, 2001; Woodruff-Pak, 2001). This relationship now gives us another way to diagnose such disorders as well as to learn more about them.

Who would have thought so much could be seen "in the blink of an eye"?

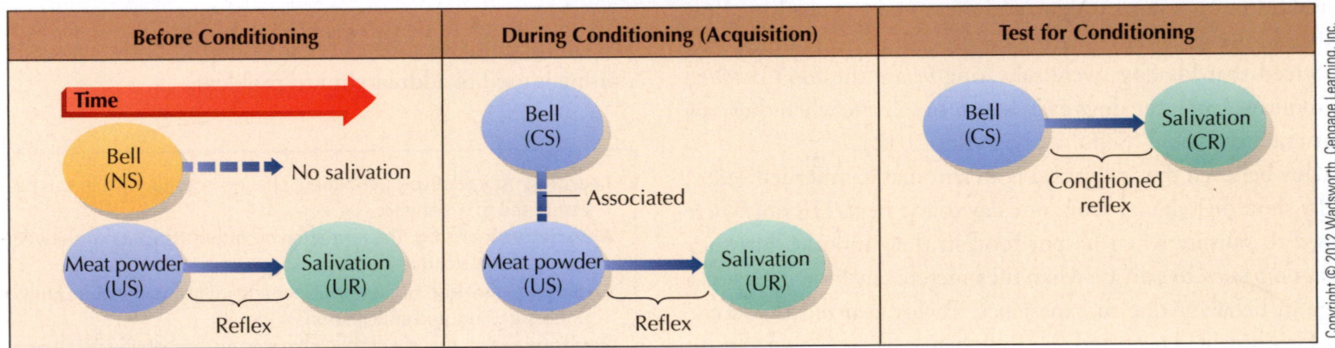

● **Figure 6.3** The classical conditioning procedure.

TABLE 6.1 Elements of Classical Conditioning

Element	Symbol	Description	Example
Unconditioned stimulus	US	A stimulus innately capable of eliciting a response	Meat powder
Unconditioned response	UR	An innate reflex response elicited by an unconditioned stimulus	Reflex salivation *to the US*
Neutral stimulus	NS	A stimulus that does not evoke the unconditioned response	Bell *before conditioning*
Conditioned stimulus	CS	A stimulus that evokes a response because it has been repeatedly paired with an unconditioned stimulus	Bell *after conditioning*
Conditioned response	CR	A learned response elicited by a conditioned stimulus	Salivation *to the CS*

Principles of Classical Conditioning—Leonard Studies Lemon Juice

Suppose a scientist named Leonard wants to study conditioning by conditioning his friend Sheldon. To observe conditioning, he could ring a bell and squirt lemon juice into Sheldon's mouth. By repeating this procedure several times, he could condition Sheldon to salivate to the bell. Sheldon might then be used to explore other aspects of classical conditioning.

Acquisition

During **acquisition**, or training, a conditioned response must be reinforced (strengthened) (● Figure 6.4). Classical conditioning is *reinforced* when the CS is followed by, or paired with, an unconditioned stimulus. This process is called **respondent reinforcement** because the US brings forth a *response*, which becomes associated with the CS. For Sheldon, the bell is the CS, salivating is the UR, and the sour lemon juice is a US. To reinforce salivating to the bell, we must link the bell with the lemon juice. Conditioning will be most rapid if the US (lemon juice) follows *immediately* after the CS (the bell). With most reflexes, the optimal delay between CS and US is from ½ second to about 5 seconds (Chance, 2009).

Higher Order Conditioning

Once a response is learned, it can bring about **higher order conditioning**. In this case, a well-learned CS is used to reinforce further learning (Lefrançois, 2006). That is, the CS has become strong enough to be used like an unconditioned stimulus. Let's illustrate again with Sheldon.

As a result of earlier learning, the bell now makes Sheldon salivate. (No lemon juice is needed.) To go a step further, Leonard could clap his hands and then ring the bell. (Again, no lemon juice would be used.) Through higher order conditioning, Sheldon would soon learn to salivate when Leonard clapped his hands (● Figure 6.5). (This little trick could be a real hit with Leonard's friends Howard and Rajesh.)

Higher order conditioning extends learning one or more steps beyond the original conditioned stimulus. Many advertisers use this effect by pairing images that evoke good feelings (such as people, including celebrities, smiling and having fun) with pictures of their products. They hope that you will learn, by association, to feel good when you see their products (Priluck & Till, 2004; Till, Stanley & Priluck, 2008).

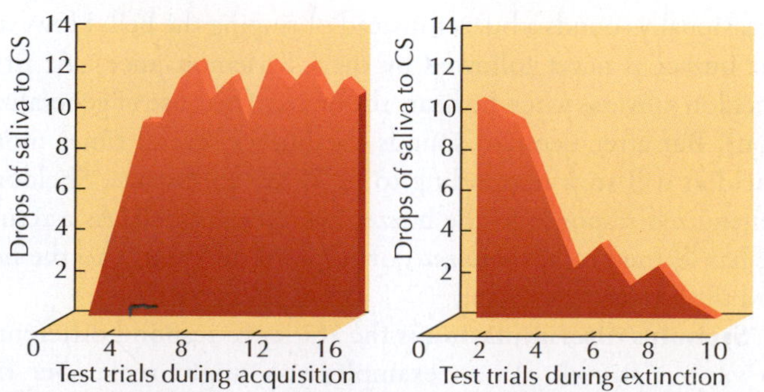

● **Figure 6.4** Acquisition and extinction of a conditioned response. (After Pavlov, 1927.)

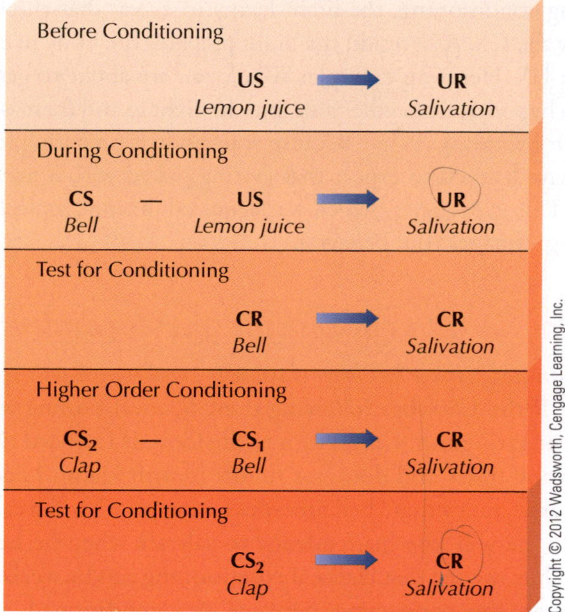

● **Figure 6.5** Higher order conditioning takes place when a well-learned conditioned stimulus is used as if it were an unconditioned stimulus. In this example, Sheldon is first conditioned to salivate to the sound of a bell. In time, the bell will elicit salivation. At that point, Leonard could clap his hands and then ring the bell. Soon, after repeating the procedure, Sheldon would learn to salivate when Leonard clapped his hands.

Expectancies

Pavlov believed that classical conditioning does not involve any higher mental processes. Today, many psychologists think that classical conditioning does have cognitive origins because it is related to information that might aid survival. According to this **informational view**, we look for associations among events. Doing so creates new mental **expectancies**, or thoughts about how events are interconnected.

How does classical conditioning alter expectancies? Notice that the conditioned stimulus reliably precedes the unconditioned stimulus. Because it does, the CS *predicts* the US (Rescorla, 1987).

Acquisition The period in conditioning during which a response is reinforced.

Respondent reinforcement Reinforcement that occurs when an unconditioned stimulus closely follows a conditioned stimulus.

Higher order conditioning Classical conditioning in which a conditioned stimulus is used to reinforce further learning; that is, a CS is used as if it were a US.

Informational view (of conditioning) Perspective that explains learning in terms of information imparted by events in the environment.

Expectancy An anticipation concerning future events or relationships.

During conditioning, the brain learns to *expect* that the US will follow the CS. As a result, the brain prepares the body to respond to the US. Here's an example: When you are about to get a shot with a hypodermic needle, your muscles tighten and there is a catch in your breathing. Why? Because your body is preparing for pain. You have learned to expect that getting poked with a needle will hurt. This expectancy, which was acquired during classical conditioning, changes your behavior.

Extinction and Spontaneous Recovery

Once an association has been classically conditioned will it ever go away? If the US stops following the CS, conditioning will fade away, or extinguish. Let's return to Sheldon. If Leonard rings the bell many times and does not follow it with lemon juice, Sheldon's expectancy that "bell precedes lemon juice" will weaken. As it does, he will lose his tendency to salivate when he hears the bell. Thus, we see that classical conditioning can be weakened by removing the connection between the conditioned and the unconditioned stimulus (see ● Figure 6.4). This process is called **extinction.**

If conditioning takes a while to build up, shouldn't it take time to reverse? Yes. In fact, it may take several extinction sessions to completely reverse conditioning. Let's say that Leonard rings the bell until Sheldon quits responding. It might seem that extinction is complete. However, Sheldon will probably respond to the bell again on the following day, at least at first (Rescorla, 2004). The return of a learned response after apparent extinction is called **spontaneous recovery**. It explains why people who have had a car accident may need many slow, calm rides before their fear of driving extinguishes.

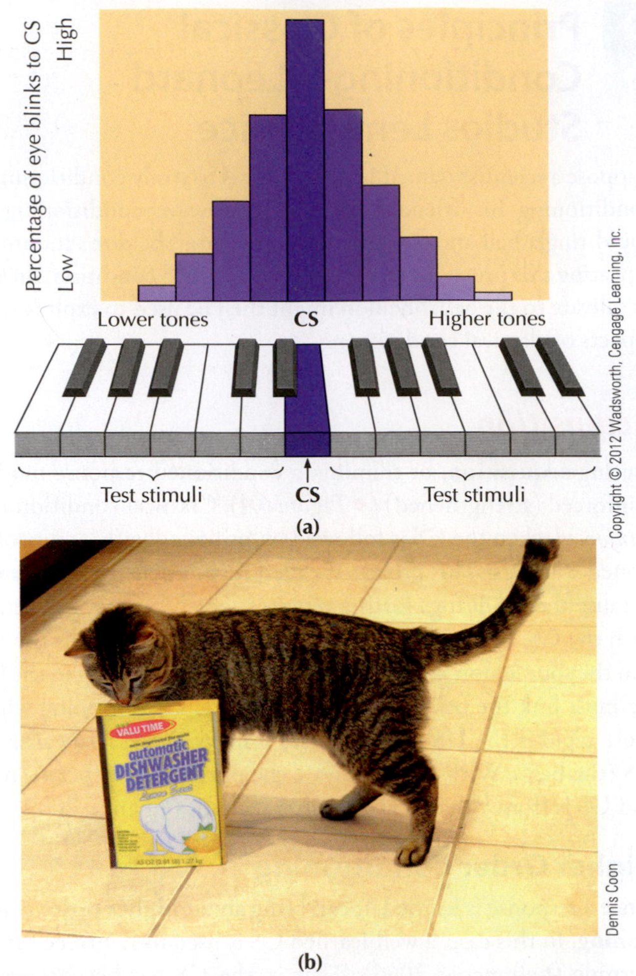

● **Figure 6.6** *(a)* Stimulus generalization. Stimuli similar to the CS also elicit a response. *(b)* This cat has learned to salivate when it sees a cat food box. Because of stimulus generalization, it also salivates when shown a similar-looking detergent box.

Generalization

After conditioning, other stimuli similar to the CS may also trigger a response. This is called **stimulus generalization**. For example, Leonard might find that Sheldon salivates to the sound of a ringing telephone or doorbell, even though they were never used as conditioning stimuli.

It is easy to see the value of stimulus generalization. Consider the child who burns her finger while playing with matches. Most likely, lighted matches will become conditioned fear stimuli for her. Because of stimulus generalization, she may also have a healthy fear of flames from lighters, fireplaces, stoves, and so forth. It's fortunate that generalization extends learning to related situations. Otherwise, we would all be far less adaptable.

As you may have guessed, stimulus generalization has limits. As stimuli become less like the original CS, responding decreases. If you condition a person to blink each time you play a particular note on a piano, blinking will decline as you play higher or lower notes. If the notes are *much* higher or lower, the person will not respond at all (● Figure 6.6). Stimulus generalization explains why many stores carry imitations of nationally known products. For many customers, positive attitudes conditioned to the original products tend to generalize to the cheaper knockoffs (Till & Priluck, 2000).

Discrimination

Let's consider one more idea with Sheldon (who by now must be ready to explode in a big bang). Suppose Leonard again conditions Sheldon, with a bell as the CS. As an experiment, he also occasionally sounds a buzzer instead of ringing the bell. However, the buzzer is never followed by the US (lemon juice). At first, Sheldon salivates when he hears the buzzer (because of generalization). But after Leonard sounds the buzzer several times more, Sheldon will stop responding to it. Why? In essence, Sheldon's generalized response to the buzzer has extinguished. As a result, he has learned to *discriminate*, or respond differently, to the bell and the buzzer.

Stimulus discrimination is the ability to respond differently to various stimuli. As an example, you might remember the feelings of anxiety or fear you had as a child when your mother's or father's voice changed to the dreaded put-away-that-Wii-controller tone. Most children quickly learn to discriminate voice tones associated with punishment from those associated with praise or affection.

Classical Conditioning in Humans—An Emotional Topic

Gateway Question 6.3: *Does conditioning affect emotions?*

Is much human learning based on classical conditioning? At its simplest, classical conditioning depends on unconditioned reflex responses. As mentioned earlier, a reflex is a dependable, inborn stimulus-and-response connection. For example, your hand reflexively draws back from pain. Bright light causes the pupil of the eye to narrow. A puff of air directed at your eye will make you blink. Various foods elicit salivation. Any of these reflexes, and others as well, can be associated with a new stimulus. At the very least, you have probably noticed how your mouth waters when you see or smell a bakery. Even pictures of food may make you salivate (a photo of a sliced lemon is great for this).

● **Figure 6.7** Hypothetical example of a CER becoming a phobia. A child approaches a dog *(a)* and is frightened by it *(b)*. This fear generalizes to other household pets *(c)* and later to virtually all furry animals *(d)*.

Conditioned Emotional Responses

More complex *emotional*, or "gut," responses may also be associated with new stimuli. For instance, if your face reddened when you were punished as a child, you may blush now when you are embarrassed or ashamed. Or think about the effects of associating pain with a dentist's office during your first visit. On later visits, did your heart pound and your palms sweat *before* the dentist began?

Many *involuntary*, autonomic nervous system, responses ("fight-or-flight" reflexes) are linked with new stimuli and situations by classical conditioning. For example, learned reactions worsen many cases of hypertension (high blood pressure). Traffic jams, arguments with a spouse, and similar situations can become conditioned stimuli that trigger a dangerous rise in blood pressure (Reiff, Katkin, & Friedman, 1999).

Of course, emotional conditioning also applies to animals. One of the most common mistakes people make with pets (especially dogs) is hitting them if they do not come when called. Calling the animal then becomes a conditioned stimulus for fear and withdrawal. No wonder the pet disobeys when called on future occasions. Parents who belittle, scream at, or physically abuse their children make the same mistake.

Learned Fears

In 1920, pioneering psychologist John Watson reported classically conditioning a young child named Little Albert to fear rats (Beck, Levinson, & Irons, 2009). Since then, it has been widely accepted that that many phobias (FOE-bee-ahs) begin as **conditioned emotional responses (CERs)**, or learned emotional reactions to a previously neutral stimulus (Field, 2006). A *phobia* is a fear that persists even when no realistic danger exists. Fears of animals, water, heights, thunder, fire, bugs, elevators, and the like, are common.

People who have phobias can often trace their fears to a time when they were frightened, injured, or upset by a particular stimulus, especially in childhood (King, Muris, & Ollendick, 2005). One bad experience in which you were frightened or disgusted by a spider may condition fears that last for years (de Jong & Muris, 2002). Stimulus generalization and higher order conditioning can spread CERs to other stimuli. As a result, what began as a limited fear may become a disabling phobia (● Figure 6.7).

During a CER, an area of the brain called the *amygdala* becomes more active, producing feelings of fear. The amygdala is part of the limbic system, which is responsible for other emotions as well (see Chapter 2). Cognitive learning has little effect on these lower brain areas (Olsson, Nearing, & Phelps, 2007). Perhaps that's why fears and phobias cannot be readily eased by merely reading about how to control fears—as our friend Larry found with his rat phobia. However, conditioned fears do respond to a therapy called **desensitization.** This is done by gradually exposing the phobic person to feared stimuli while she or he remains calm and relaxed. For example, people who fear heights can be slowly taken to ever-higher elevations until their fears extinguish. This therapy even

Extinction The weakening of a conditioned response through removal of reinforcement.

Spontaneous recovery The reappearance of a learned response after its apparent extinction.

Stimulus generalization The tendency to respond to stimuli similar to, but not identical to, a conditioned stimulus.

Stimulus discrimination The learned ability to respond differently to similar stimuli.

Conditioned emotional response (CER) An emotional response that has been linked to a previously nonemotional stimulus by classical conditioning.

Desensitization Reducing fear or anxiety by repeatedly exposing a person to emotional stimuli while the person is deeply relaxed.

works when computer graphics are used to simulate the experience of heights (Wiederhold & Wiederhold, 2005).

BRIDGES

See Chapter 15, pages 520–526, for more information about therapies based on learning principles.

Undoubtedly, we acquire many of our likes, dislikes, and fears as conditioned emotional responses. As noted before, advertisers try to achieve the same effect by pairing products with pleasant images and music. So do many students on a first date.

Vicarious, or Secondhand, Conditioning

Conditioning can also occur indirectly. Let's say, for example, that you watch another person get an electric shock. Each time, a signal light comes on before the shock is delivered. Even if you don't receive a shock yourself, you will soon develop a CER to the light. Children who learn to fear thunder by watching their parents react to it have undergone similar conditioning. Many Americans were traumatized as a consequence of watching media coverage of the September 11, 2001, terrorist attacks in New York and Washington (Blanchard et al., 2004). Similarly, people who counsel traumatized victims of sexual abuse can themselves develop vicarious trauma (Rothschild & Rand, 2006; Way et al., 2004).

Vicarious classical conditioning occurs when we learn to respond emotionally to a stimulus by observing another person's emotional reactions (Olsson, Nearing, & Phelps, 2007). Such "secondhand" learning affects feelings in many situations. Being told that "snakes are dangerous" may not explain the child's *emotional* response. More likely, the child has observed others reacting fearfully to the word *snake* or to snake images on television (King, Muris, & Ollendick, 2005). That is exactly how Larry, the researcher we met at the beginning of this chapter, developed his fear of rats. As children grow up, the emotions of parents, friends, and relatives undoubtedly add to fears of snakes, caves, spiders, heights, and other terrors. Even "horror" movies filled with screaming actors can have a similar effect.

The emotional attitudes we develop toward foods, political parties, ethnic groups, escalators—whatever—are probably conditioned not only by direct experiences but vicariously as well. No one is born prejudiced—all attitudes are learned. Parents may do well to look in a mirror if they wonder how or where a child "picked up" a particular fear or emotional attitude.

Knowledge Builder: Classical Conditioning

RECITE

1. The concept of reinforcement applies to both
   a. antecedents and consequences *b.* neutral stimuli and rewards *c.* classical and operant conditioning *d.* acquisition and spontaneous recovery
2. Classical conditioning, studied by the Russian physiologist ____________________, is also referred to as ____________________ conditioning.
3. You smell the odor of cookies being baked and your mouth waters. Apparently, the odor of cookies is a __________ and your salivation is a __________.
   a. CR, CS *b.* CS, CR *c.* consequence, neutral stimulus *d.* reflex, CS
4. The informational view says that classical conditioning is based on changes in mental ____________________ about the CS and US.
5. After you have acquired a conditioned response, it may be weakened by
   a. spontaneous recovery *b.* stimulus generalization *c.* removing reinforcement *d.* following the CS with a US
6. When a conditioned stimulus is used to reinforce the learning of a second conditioned stimulus, higher order conditioning has occurred. T or F?
7. Psychologists theorize that many phobias begin when a CER generalizes to other, similar situations. T or F?
8. Three-year-old Josh sees his 5-year-old sister get chased by a neighbor's dog. Now Josh is as afraid of the dog as his sister is. Josh's fear is a result of
   a. stimulus discrimination *b.* vicarious conditioning *c.* spontaneous recovery *d.* higher order conditioning

REFLECT

Think Critically

9. Lately you have been getting a shock of static electricity every time you touch a door handle. Now, there is a hesitation in your door-opening movements. Can you analyze this situation in terms of classical conditioning?

Self-Reflect

US, CS, UR, CR—How will you remember these terms? First, you should note that we are interested in either a stimulus (S) or a response (R). What else do we need to know? Each S or R can be either conditioned (C) or unconditioned (U).

Can a stimulus provoke a response before any learning has occurred? If it can, then it's a US. Do you have to learn to respond to the stimulus? Then it's a CS.

Does a response occur without being learned? Then it's a UR. If it has to be learned, then it's a CR.

Answers: 1. c **2.** Pavlov, Pavlovian or respondent **3.** *b* **4.** expectancies **5.** c **6.** T **7.** T **8.** *b* **9.** Door handles have become conditioned stimuli that elicit the reflex withdrawal and muscle tensing that normally follows getting a shock. This conditioned response may also have generalized to other handles.

Operant Conditioning—Can Pigeons Play Ping-Pong?

Gateway Question 6.4: *How does operant conditioning occur?*

The principles of *operant conditioning*, another form of associative learning, are among the most powerful tools in psychology. You won't regret learning how to use them. Operant conditioning applies to all living creatures and explains much day-to-day behavior. Operant conditioning can be used to alter the behavior of pets, children, other adults, and your own behavior, too.

■ **TABLE 6.2 Comparison of Classical and Operant Conditioning**

	Classical Conditioning	Operant Conditioning
Nature of response	Involuntary, reflex	Spontaneous, voluntary
Reinforcement	Occurs *before* response (CS paired with US)	Occurs *after* response (response is followed by reinforcing stimulus or event)
Role of learner	Passive (response is *elicited* by US)	Active (response is emitted)
Nature of learning	Neutral stimulus becomes a CS through association with a US	Probability of making a response is altered by consequences that follow it
Learned expectancy	US will follow CS	Response will have a specific effect

As stated earlier, in **operant conditioning** (also known as *instrumental learning*), we associate responses with their consequences. The basic principle is simple: Acts that are reinforced tend to be repeated (Chance, 2009). Pioneer learning theorist Edward L. Thorndike called this the **law of effect**: The probability of a response is altered by the effect it has (Benjafield, 2010). Learning is strengthened each time a response is followed by a satisfying state of affairs. You are much more likely to keep telling a joke if people laugh at it. If the first three people frown when they hear the joke, you may not tell it again.

In operant conditioning, the learner actively "operates on" the environment. Thus, operant conditioning refers mainly to learning *voluntary* responses. For example, pushing buttons on a TV remote control is a learned operant response. Pushing a particular button is reinforced by gaining the consequence you desire, such as changing channels or muting an obnoxious commercial. In contrast, classical conditioning is passive. It simply "happens to" the learner when a US follows a CS (see ■ Table 6.2 for a further comparison of classical and operant conditioning).

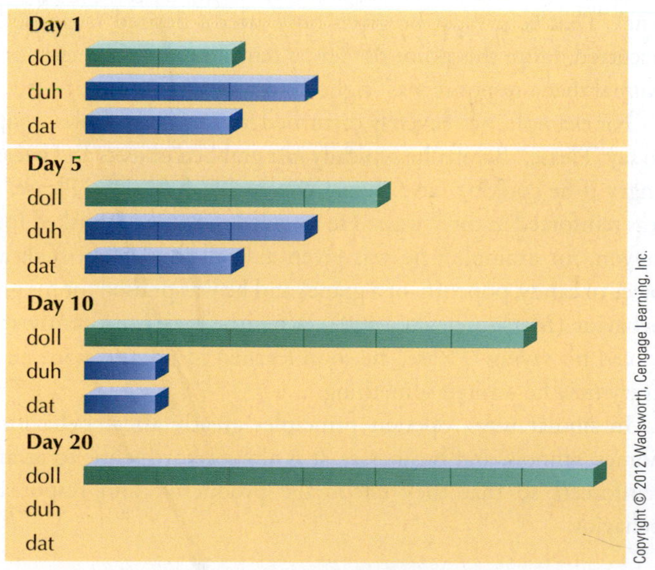

● **Figure 6.8** Assume that a child who is learning to talk points to her favorite doll and says either "doll," "duh," or "dat" when she wants it. Day 1 shows the number of times the child uses each word to ask for the doll (each block represents one request). At first, she uses all three words interchangeably. To hasten learning, her parents decide to give her the doll only when she names it correctly. Notice how the child's behavior shifts as operant reinforcement is applied. By day 20, saying "doll" has become the most probable response.

Positive Reinforcement

Isn't reinforcement another term for reward? Not exactly. To be correct, it is better to say *reinforcer*. Why? Because rewards do not always increase responding. If you give chocolate to a child as a "reward" for good behavior, it will work only if the child likes chocolate. What is reinforcing for one person may not be for another. As a practical rule of thumb, psychologists define an **operant reinforcer** as any event that follows a response and increases its probability of occurring again (● Figure 6.8).

Acquiring an Operant Response

Many studies of operant conditioning in animals make use of an **operant conditioning chamber** (Skinner, 1938). This device is also called a *Skinner box*, after B. F. Skinner, who invented it (● Figure 6.9). The walls are bare except for a metal lever and a tray into which food pellets can be dispensed. The fact that there's not much to do in a Skinner box increases the chances that a subject will make the desired response, which is pressing the bar. Also, hunger keeps the animal motivated to seek food and actively *emit*, or freely give off, a variety of responses. A look into a typical Skinner box will clarify the process of operant conditioning.

Einstein Snags a Snack

A smart and hungry rat (yes, it's Larry's rat) is placed in an operant conditioning chamber. For a while, our subject walks around, grooms, sniffs at the corners, or stands on his hind legs—all typical rat behaviors. Then it happens. He places his paw on the lever to get a better view of the top of the

Vicarious classical conditioning Classical conditioning brought about by observing another person react to a particular stimulus.

Operant conditioning Learning based on the consequences of responding.

Law of effect Responses that lead to desirable effects are repeated; those that produce undesirable results are not.

Operant reinforcer Any event that reliably increases the probability or frequency of responses it follows.

Operant conditioning chamber (Skinner box) An apparatus designed to study operant conditioning in animals; a Skinner box.

Critical Thinking: Are We Less Superstitious Than Pigeons?

Skinner once placed some pigeons in Skinner boxes and reinforced them with food every now and then no matter what they were doing (Domjan, 2010). Despite the fact that there was no real connection between their behavior and its consequences, each pigeon acted as if there was. One bird began to flap its left wing, another to hop on one leg, a third to turn around in complete circles, and so on, despite these behaviors being quite unnecessary to receive reinforcement (silly birds).

But humans wouldn't behave that way, right? Don't bet on it. When Skinner did this research, he had in mind human behavior like that of a golfer who always taps her club on the ground three times before hitting a shot. This probably started because once, by chance, the golfer tapped her club three times immediately before hitting a great shot. The tapping behavior was followed by success, and was hence reinforced, even though it had nothing to do with the great shot (which was due to her correct swing). Reinforcers affect not only the specific response they follow but also other responses that occur shortly before. After happening a few more times, this golfer ended up tapping her club three times before every shot (silly human).

Skinner even used the term **superstitious behavior** to describe a behavior that is repeated because it appears to produce reinforcement, even though it is actually unnecessary. Some examples of actual superstitious behaviors of professional baseball players include drawing four lines in the dirt before getting in the batter's box, eating chicken before each game, and always playing in the same athletic supporter—for 4 years (phew!) (Burger & Lynn, 2005; Wright, Perry, & Erdal, 2008).

Skinner's idea helps explain many human superstitions. If you walk under a ladder and then break a leg, you may avoid ladders in the future. Each time you avoid a ladder and nothing bad happens, your superstitious action is reinforced. Belief in magic can also be explained along such lines. Rituals to bring rain, ward off illness, or produce abundant crops very likely earn the faith of participants because they occasionally appear to succeed (Jahoda, 2007). So keep your fingers crossed!

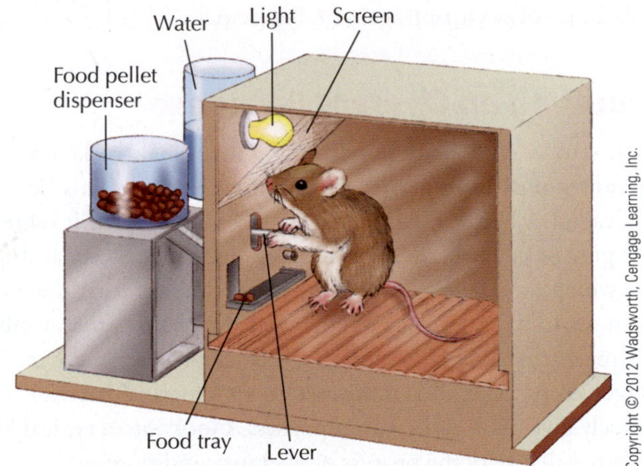

• **Figure 6.9** The Skinner box. This simple device, invented by B. F. Skinner, allows careful study of operant conditioning. When the rat presses the bar, a pellet of food or a drop of water is automatically released. (A photograph of a Skinner box appears in Chapter 1.)

cage. *Click!* The lever depresses, and a food pellet drops into the tray. The rat scurries to the tray, eats the pellet, and then grooms himself. Up and exploring the cage again, he leans on the lever. *Click!* After a trip to the food tray, he returns to the bar and sniffs it, then puts his foot on it. *Click!* Soon Einstein settles into a smooth pattern of frequent bar pressing.

Notice that the rat did not acquire a new skill in this situation. He was already able to press the bar. Reinforcement alters only how *frequently* he presses the bar. In operant conditioning, new behavior patterns are molded by changing the probability that various responses will be made.

Information and Contingency

Like classical conditioning, we can think of operant learning as based on information and expectancies (Chance, 2009). In operant conditioning, *we learn to expect that a certain response will have a certain effect at certain times.* That is, we learn that a particular response is associated with reinforcement. Further, operant reinforcement works best when it is *response contingent* (kon-TIN-jent). That is, it must be given only after a desired response has occurred. From this point of view, a reinforcer tells a person or an animal that a response was "right" and worth repeating.

For example, one severely disturbed 9-year-old child was taught to say "Please." Before, he typically just grabbed objects and became angry if he couldn't have them. When the child said "Please," he was reinforced in three ways: He received the object he asked for (a crayon, for example); he was given a small food treat, such as a piece of candy, popcorn, or a grape; and he was praised for his good behavior (Matson et al., 1990). When he was consistently reinforced for saying "Please," he soon learned to use the word nearly every time he wanted something.

In similar ways, operant principles greatly affect behavior in homes, schools, and businesses. It is always worthwhile to arrange reinforcers so that they encourage productive and responsible behavior.

The Timing of Reinforcement

Operant reinforcement is most effective when it rapidly follows a correct response (Powell, Symbaluk, & Honey, 2009). In fact, tight timing is all that is required for learning to occur (See "Are We Less

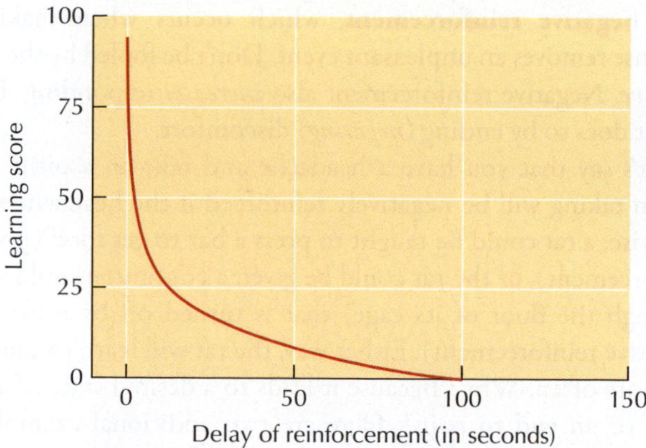

• Figure 6.10 The effect of delay of reinforcement. Notice how rapidly the learning score drops when reward is delayed. Animals learning to press a bar in a Skinner box showed no signs of learning if food reward followed a bar press by more than 100 seconds. (Adapted from Perin, 1943).

Superstitious Than Pigeons?"). For rats in a Skinner box, little or no learning occurs if the delay between bar pressing and receiving food exceeds 50 seconds. (• Figure 6.10). In general, you will be most successful if you present a reinforcer *immediately* after a response you wish to change. Thus, a child who is helpful or courteous should be immediately praised for her good behavior.

Let's say I work hard all semester in a class to get an A. Wouldn't the delay in reinforcement keep me from learning anything? No, for several reasons. First, as a mature human, you can anticipate future reward. Second, you get reinforced by quiz and test grades all through the semester. Third, a single reinforcer can often maintain a long *response chain*—a linked series of actions that lead to reinforcement.

An example of **response chaining** is provided by the sport of dog agility training. Dogs are taught to navigate a variety of obstacles. These include jumping over hurdles, walking over seesaws, climbing up and jumping off inclined walls, and running through tunnels made out of cloth (Helton, 2007, 2009). During competitions, a trainer can reinforce a dog with a snack or a hug only after the dog completes the entire response chain. The winning dog is the one who finishes the course with the fewest mistakes and the fastest time. (Good dog!)

Dogs must build up long response chains to compete in agility training competitions.

Many of the things we do every day involve similar response chains. The long series of events necessary to prepare a meal is rewarded by the final eating. A violinmaker may carry out thousands of steps for the final reward of hearing a first musical note. And as a student, you have built up long response chains for the final reward of getting good grades (right?).

Shaping

How is it possible to reinforce responses that rarely occur? Even in a barren Skinner box, it could take a long time for a rat (even one as smart as Einstein) to accidentally press the bar and get a food pellet. We might wait forever for more complicated responses to occur. For example, you would have to wait a long time for a duck to accidentally walk out of its cage, turn on a light, play a toy piano, turn off the light, and walk back to its cage. If this is what you wanted to reward, you would never get the chance.

Then how are the animals on TV and at amusement parks taught to perform complicated tricks? The answer lies in **shaping**, which is the gradual molding of responses to a desired pattern. Let's look again at our favorite rat, Einstein.

Einstein Shapes Up

Instead of waiting for Einstein's first accidental bar press, which might have taken a long time, we could have shaped his behavior. Assume that Einstein has not yet learned to press the bar. At first, we settle for just getting him to face the bar. Any time he turns toward the bar, he is reinforced with a bit of food. Soon, Einstein spends much of his time facing the bar. Next, we reinforce him every time he takes a step toward the bar. If he turns toward the bar and walks away, nothing happens. But when he faces the bar and takes a step forward, *click!* His responses are being shaped.

By changing the rules about what makes a successful response, we can gradually train the rat to approach the bar and press it. In other words, *successive approximations* (ever-closer matches) to a desired response are reinforced during shaping. B. F. Skinner once taught two pigeons to play Ping-Pong in this way (• Figure 6.11). Shaping also applies to humans (Lamb et al., 2010). Let's say you want to study more, clean the house more often, or exercise more. In each case, it would be best to set a series of gradual, daily goals. Then you can reward yourself for small steps in the right direction (Watson & Tharp, 2007).

- **Superstitious behavior** A behavior repeated because it seems to produce reinforcement, even though it is actually unnecessary.
- **Response chaining** The assembly of separate responses into a series of actions that lead to reinforcement.
- **Shaping** Gradually molding responses to a final desired pattern.

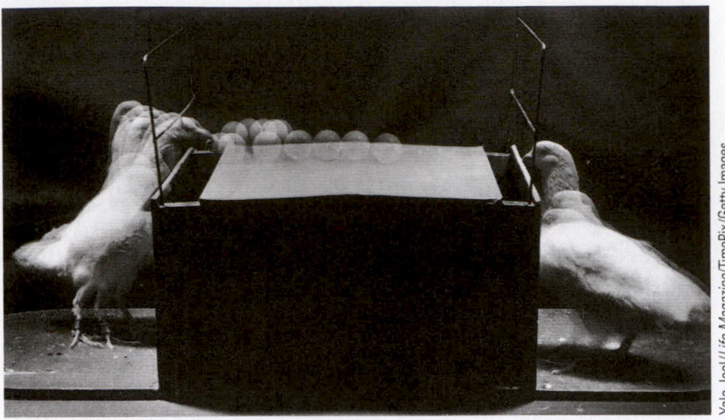
Yale Joel/Life Magazine/TimePix/Getty Images.

• **Figure 6.11** Operant conditioning principles were used to train these pigeons to play Ping-Pong.

Operant Extinction

Would a rat stop bar pressing if no more food arrived? Yes, but not immediately. Through **operant extinction**, learned responses that are not reinforced fade away gradually. Just as acquiring an operant response takes time, so does extinction. For example, if a TV program repeatedly bores you, watching the program will likely extinguish over time.

Even after extinction seems complete, the previously reinforced response may return. If a rat is removed from a Skinner box after extinction and given a short rest, the rat will press the bar again when returned to the box. Similarly, a few weeks after they give up on buying lottery tickets, many people are tempted to try again.

Does extinction take as long the second time? If reinforcement is still withheld, a rat's bar pressing will extinguish again, usually more quickly. The brief return of an operant response after extinction is another example of spontaneous recovery (mentioned earlier regarding classical conditioning). Spontaneous recovery is very adaptive. After a rest period, the rat responds again in a situation that produced food in the past: "Just checking to see if the rules have changed!"

Marked changes in behavior occur when reinforcement and extinction are combined. For example, parents often unknowingly reinforce children for *negative attention seeking* (using misbehavior to gain attention). Children are generally ignored when they are playing quietly. They get attention when they become louder and louder, yell "Hey, Mom!" at the top of their lungs, throw tantrums, show off, or break something. Granted, the attention they get is often a scolding, but attention is a powerful reinforcer nevertheless. Parents report dramatic improvements when they praise or attend to a child who is quiet or playing constructively and *ignore* their children's disruptive behavior.

Negative Reinforcement

Until now, we have stressed **positive reinforcement**, which occurs when a pleasant or desirable event follows a response. How else could operant learning be reinforced? The time has come to consider **negative reinforcement**, which occurs when making a response removes an unpleasant event. Don't be fooled by the word *negative*. Negative reinforcement also *increases* responding. However, it does so by ending (*negating*) discomfort.

Let's say that you have a headache and take an aspirin. Your aspirin taking will be negatively reinforced if the headache stops. Likewise, a rat could be taught to press a bar to get food (positive reinforcement), or the rat could be given a continuous mild shock (through the floor of its cage) that is turned off by a bar press (negative reinforcement). Either way, the rat will learn to press the bar more often. Why? Because it leads to a desired state of affairs (food or an end to pain). Here are two additional examples of negative reinforcement:

While walking outside, your hands get so cold they hurt. You take a pair of gloves out of your backpack and put them on, ending the pain. (You are *more likely* to put gloves on in the future because putting on the gloves was negatively reinforced.)

A politician who irritates you is being interviewed on the evening news. You change channels so you won't have to listen to him. (You are *more likely* to change the channel next time you see that politician because channel changing was negatively reinforced.)

Punishment

Many people mistake negative reinforcement for punishment. However, **punishment** refers to following a response with an **aversive** (unpleasant) **consequence**. Punishment *decreases* the likelihood that the response will occur again. As noted, negative reinforcement *increases* responding. The difference can be seen in a hypothetical example. Let's say you live in an apartment and your neighbor's stereo is blasting so loudly that you can't concentrate on reading this book. If you pound on the wall and the volume suddenly drops (negative reinforcement), future wall pounding will be more likely. But if you pound on the wall and the volume increases (punishment) or if the neighbor comes over and pounds on you (more punishment), wall pounding becomes less likely. Here are two more examples of punishment, in which an unpleasant result follows a response:

You are driving your car too fast. You are caught in a radar trap and given a speeding ticket. Henceforth, you will be less likely to speed. (You are *less likely* to speed next time because speeding was punished by a fine.)

Every time you give advice to a friend she suddenly turns cold and distant. Lately, you've stopped offering her advice. (You are *less likely* to offer advice to your friend in the future because giving advice was punished by rejection.)

Isn't it also punishing to have privileges, money, or other positive things taken away for making a particular response? Yes. Punishment also occurs when a reinforcer or positive state of affairs is removed, such as losing privileges. This second type of punishment is called **response cost**. Parking tickets and other fines are based on response cost. The best-known form of response cost is *time out*, in which children are removed from situations that normally allow them to gain reinforcement. When your parents put

Brainwaves Tickling Your Own Fancy

Suppose you could have an electrode implanted in your brain and connected to an iPod-style controller. Twirl the controller and electrical impulses stimulate one of your brain's "pleasure centers." The very few humans who have ever had a chance to try direct brain stimulation report feeling intense pleasure that is better than food, water, sex, drugs, or any other primary reinforcer (Heath, 1963) (● Figure 6.12).

Most of what we know about intracranial self-stimulation comes from studying rats with similar implants (Olds & Fobes, 1981). A rat "wired for pleasure" can be trained to press the bar in a Skinner box to deliver electrical stimulation to its own limbic system (refer back to ● Figure 2.26). Some rats will press the bar thousands of times per hour to obtain brain stimulation. After 15 or 20 hours of constant pressing, animals sometimes collapse from exhaustion. When they revive, they begin pressing again. If the reward circuit is not turned off, an animal will ignore food, water, and sex in favor of bar pressing.

BRIDGES

Electrical stimulation is a valuable tool for studying the functions of various brain structures. **See Chapter 2, pages 61–62.**

Many natural primary reinforcers activate the same pleasure pathways in the brain that make intracranial self-stimulation so powerful (Powell, Symbaluk, & Honey, 2009). So do psychoactive drugs, such as alcohol and cocaine (Galankin, Shekunova, & Zvartau, 2010; Rodd et al., 2005). In fact, rats will also self-administer nicotine. When they do, they are even more likely to engage in intracranial self-stimulation (Kenny & Markou, 2006). Apparently, nicotine further increases the sensitivity of pleasure pathways in the brain.

One shudders to think what might happen if brain implants were easy and practical to do. (They are not.) Every company from *Playboy* to *Microsoft* would have a device on the market, and we would have to keep a closer watch on politicians than usual!

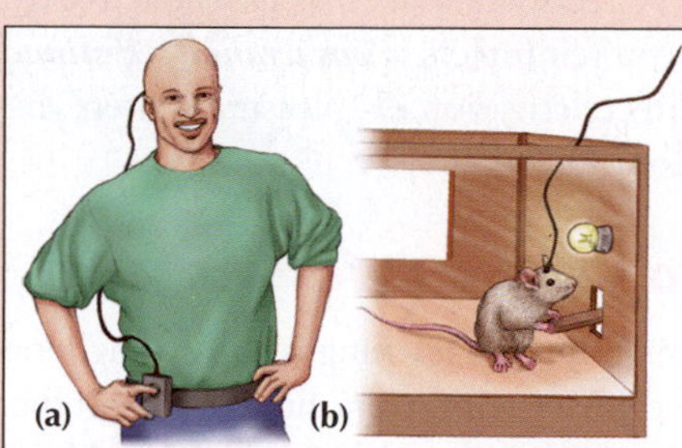

● **Figure 6.12** Humans have been "wired" for brain stimulation, as shown in *(a)*. However, in humans, this has been done only as an experimental way to restrain uncontrollable outbursts of violence. Implants have not been done merely to produce pleasure. Most research has been carried out with rats. Using the apparatus shown in *(b)*, the rat can press a bar to deliver mild electric stimulation to a "pleasure center" in the brain.

■ **TABLE 6.3 Behavioral Effects of Various Consequences**

	Consequence of Making a Response	Example	Effect on Response Probability
Positive reinforcement	Positive event begins	Food given	Increase
Negative reinforcement	Negative event ends	Pain stops	Increase
Punishment	Negative event begins	Pain begins	Decrease
Punishment (response cost)	Positive event ends	Food removed	Decrease
Nonreinforcement	Nothing	—	Decrease

you on time out by sending you to your room, they denied you the reinforcement of being with the rest of your family or hanging out with your friends. ■ Table 6.3 summarizes five basic consequences of making a response.

Operant Reinforcers—What's Your Pleasure?

Gateway Question 6.5: *Are there different kinds of operant reinforcement?*

For humans, learning may be reinforced by anything from a candy bar to a word of praise. In categorizing reinforcers, a useful distinction can be made between *primary reinforcers* and *secondary reinforcers*. It is also important to distinguish *reinforcement*, which exerts its effect through associative learning from *feedback*, a key component of cognitive learning. Let's examine reinforcement and feedback in more detail.

Operant extinction The weakening or disappearance of a nonreinforced operant response.

Positive reinforcement Occurs when a response is followed by a reward or other positive event.

Negative reinforcement Occurs when a response is followed by an end to discomfort or by the removal of an unpleasant event.

Punishment Any event that follows a response and *decreases* its likelihood of occurring again.

Aversive consequence A stimulus that is painful or uncomfortable.

Response cost Removal of a positive reinforcer after a response is made.

Primary Reinforcers

Primary reinforcers produce comfort, end discomfort, or fill an immediate physical need: They are natural, nonlearned, and rooted in biology. Food, water, and sex are obvious examples. Every time you open the refrigerator, walk to a drinking fountain, turn up the heat, or order a double latte, your actions reflect primary reinforcement.

In addition to obvious examples, there are other, less obvious, primary reinforcers, such as psychoactive drugs. One of the most powerful reinforcers is *intracranial self-stimulation*, which involves the direct activation of "pleasure centers" in the brain (see "Tickling Your Own Fancy").

Secondary Reinforcers

Although human learning is still strongly tied to food, water, and other primary reinforcers, humans also respond to a much broader range of rewards and reinforcers. Money, praise, attention, approval, success, affection, grades, and the like, all serve as learned or **secondary reinforcers.**

How does a secondary reinforcer gain its ability to promote learning? Some secondary reinforcers are simply associated with a primary reinforcer. For example, if you would like to train a dog to follow you ("heel") when you take a walk, you could reward the dog with small food treats for staying near you. If you praise the dog each time you give it a treat, praise will become a secondary reinforcer. In time, you will be able to skip giving treats and simply praise your pup for doing the right thing. The same principle applies to children. One reason that parents' praise becomes a secondary reinforcer is because it is frequently associated with food, candy, hugs, and other primary reinforcers.

Tokens

Secondary reinforcers that can be *exchanged* for primary reinforcers gain their value more directly (Powell, Symbaluk, & Honey, 2009). Printed money obviously has little or no value of its own. You can't eat it, drink it, or sleep with it. However, it can be exchanged for food, water, lodging, and other necessities.

A **token reinforcer** is a tangible secondary reinforcer, such as money, gold stars, poker chips, and the like. In a series of classic experiments, chimpanzees were taught to work for tokens. The chimps were first trained to put poker chips into a "Chimp-O-Mat" vending machine (● Figure 6.13). Each chip dispensed a few grapes or raisins. Once the animals had learned to exchange tokens for food, they would learn new tasks to earn the chips. To maintain the value of the tokens, the chimps were occasionally allowed to use the "Chimp-O-Mat" (Cowles, 1937).

A major advantage of tokens is that they don't lose reinforcing value as quickly as primary reinforcers do. For instance, if you use candy to reinforce a developmentally disabled child for correctly naming things, the child might lose interest once he is satiated (fully satisfied) or no longer hungry. It would be better to use tokens as immediate rewards for learning. Later, the child can exchange his tokens for candy, toys, or other treats.

Chimp-O-Mat, Yerkes Regional Primate Research Center, Emory University.

● **Figure 6.13** Poker chips normally have little or no value for chimpanzees, but this chimp will work hard to earn them once he learns that the "Chimp-O-Mat" will dispense food in exchange for them.

Tokens have also been used with troubled children and adults in special programs, and even in ordinary elementary school classrooms (Alberto & Troutman, 2009; Spiegler & Guevremont, 2003) (● Figure 6.14). In each case the goal is to provide an imme-

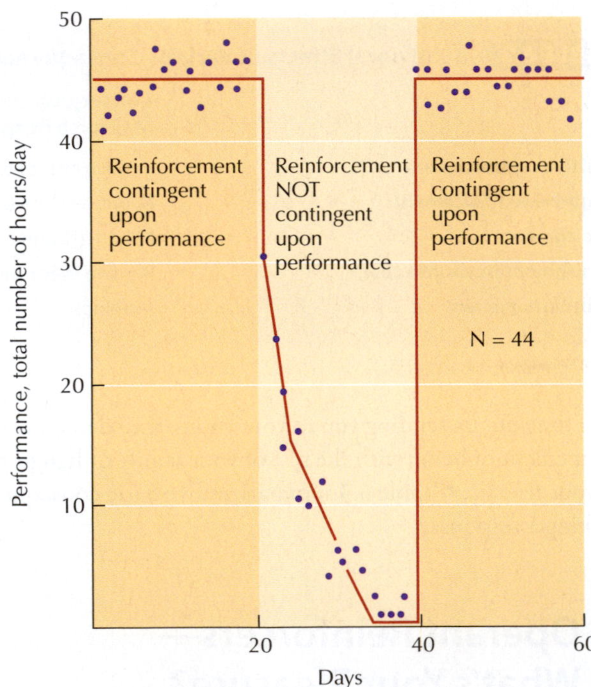

● **Figure 6.14** Reinforcement in a token economy. This graph shows the effects of using tokens to reward socially desirable behavior in a mental hospital ward. Desirable behavior was defined as cleaning, making the bed, attending therapy sessions, and so forth. Tokens earned could be exchanged for basic amenities such as meals, snacks, coffee, game-room privileges, or weekend passes. The graph shows more than 24 hours per day because it represents the total number of hours of desirable behavior performed by all patients in the ward. (Adapted from Ayllon & Azrin, 1965.)

diate reward for learning. Typically, tokens may be exchanged for food, special privileges, or trips to movies, amusement parks, and so forth. Many parents find that tokens greatly reduce discipline problems with younger children. For example, children can earn points or gold stars during the week for good behavior. If they earn enough tokens, they are allowed on Sunday to choose one item out of a "grab bag" of small prizes.

BRIDGES

A *token economy* is a system for managing and altering behavior through reinforcement of selected responses. **See Chapter 15, pages 525–526, for more information on the uses of token economies in behavior therapy.**

Social Reinforcers

As we have noted, learned desires for attention and approval, which are called **social reinforcers**, often influence human behavior. This fact can be used in a classic, if somewhat mischievous, demonstration.

Shaping a Teacher

For this activity, about one half (or more) of the students in a classroom must participate. First, select a target behavior. This should be something like "lecturing from the right side of the room." (Keep it simple, in case your teacher is a slow learner.) Begin training in this way: Each time the instructor turns toward the right or takes a step in that direction, participating students should look *really* interested. Also, smile, ask questions, lean forward, and make eye contact. If the teacher turns to the left or takes a step in that direction, participating students should lean back, yawn, check out their split ends, close their eyes, or generally look bored. Soon, without being aware of why, the instructor should be spending most of his or her time each class period lecturing from the right side of the classroom.

This trick has been a favorite of psychology graduate students for decades. For a time, one of your author's professors delivered all her lectures from the right side of the room while toying with the cords on the window shades. (We added the cords the second week!) The point to remember from this example is that attention and approval can change the behavior of children, family members, friends, roommates, and coworkers. Be aware of what you are reinforcing. And be aware that you may be unaware of some of the reinforcers that are changing your own behavior!

Feedback

His eyes, driven and blazing, dart from side to side. His body contorts while his hands furiously spin in circular motions. Does this describe some strange neurological disorder? Actually, it depicts 10-year-old Vikram as he plays his favorite Wii game, an animated snowboarding adventure!

How did Vikram learn the complex movements needed to excel at virtual snowboarding? After all, he was not rewarded with food or money. The answer lies in the fact that Vikram's favorite video game provides *feedback*, a key element that underlies learning. **Feedback**—information about the effect a response had—is particularly important in human cognitive learning (Lefrançois, 2006).

Every time a player does something, a video game responds instantly with sounds, animated actions, and a higher or lower score. The machine's responsiveness and the information flow it provides can be very motivating if you want to win. The same principle applies to many other learning situations: If you are trying to learn to use a computer, to play a musical instrument, to cook, to play a sport, or to solve math problems, feedback that you achieved a desired result can be reinforcing in its own right.

The adaptive value of feedback helps explain why much human learning occurs in the absence of obvious reinforcers, such as food or water. Humans readily learn responses that merely have a desired effect or that bring a goal closer. Let's explore this idea further.

Knowledge of Results

Imagine that you are asked to throw darts at a target. Each dart must pass over a screen that prevents you from telling if you hit the target. If you threw 1,000 darts, we would expect little improvement in your performance because no feedback is provided. Vikram's video game did not explicitly reward him for correct responses. Yet, because it provided feedback, rapid learning took place.

How can feedback be applied? Increased feedback—also called **knowledge of results (KR)**—almost always improves learning and performance (Snowman & McCown, 2011; Vojdanoska, Cranney, & Newell, 2010). If you want to learn to play a musical instrument, to sing, to speak a second language, or to deliver a speech, recorded feedback can be very helpful. In sports, video replays are used to provide feedback on everything from tennis serves to pick-off moves in baseball. Whenever you are trying to learn a complex skill, it pays to get more feedback (Eldridge, Saltzman, & Lahav, 2010; Jaehnig & Miller, 2007). See the nearby "Discovering Psychology: Learning and Conservation" box to learn more.

Learning Aids

How can feedback be applied? Since increased feedback almost always improves learning and performance, it makes sense to design learning aids to supply effective feedback (Snowman & McCown, 2011). Feedback is most effective when it is *frequent*,

Primary reinforcers Nonlearned reinforcers; usually those that satisfy physiological needs.

Secondary reinforcer A learned reinforcer; often one that gains reinforcing properties by association with a primary reinforcer.

Token reinforcer A tangible secondary reinforcer such as money, gold stars, poker chips, and the like.

Social reinforcer Reinforcement based on receiving attention, approval, or affection from another person.

Feedback Information returned to a person about the effects a response has had; also known as knowledge of results.

Knowledge of results (KR) Informational feedback.

Discovering Psychology — Learning and Conservation

Psychologists enjoy helping people solve practical problems. One area of behavior very much in need of attention is our "throw-away" society. We burn fossil fuels; destroy forests; use chemical products; and strip, clear, and farm the land. In doing so, we alter the very face of the Earth. What can be done?

One approach involves changing the *consequences* of wasteful energy use, polluting, and the like. For example, energy taxes can be used to increase the cost of using fossil fuels (response cost). On the reinforcement side of the equation, rebates can be offered for installing insulation, or buying energy-efficient appliances or cars, and tax breaks can be given to companies that take steps to preserve the environment. Recycling is also more effective when entire families participate, with some family members (usually Mom, of course) reinforcing the recycling behavior of other family members (Meneses & Beerlipalacio, 2005).

Feedback is also important. Environmental psychologists have long known that a lack of prompt feedback is a major barrier to conservation (Abrahamse et al., 2005; Carrico & Riemer, 2010). When families, work groups, factories, and dorms receive feedback, on a weekly basis, about how much they recycled, they typically recycle more. New tools, such as *ecological footprint calculators*, make it a lot easier for individuals to get feedback about their individual resource consumption (Global Footprint Network, 2010). With growing public concern over global warming, many people are now calculating their individual *carbon footprint*, the volume of greenhouse gases individual consumption adds to the atmosphere (The Nature Conservancy, 2011).

BRIDGES

See Chapter 18, pages 616–617, for more information on carbon footprints.

immediate, and *detailed*. **Programmed instruction** teaches students in a format that presents information in small amounts, gives immediate practice, and provides continuous feedback to learners. Frequent feedback keeps learners from practicing errors. It also lets students work at their own pace.

To get a sense of the programmed instruction format, finish reading the next few paragraphs and complete the *Knowledge Builder* when you encounter it (just like you do with *all* of the Knowledge Builders you come across, right?). Work through the *Recite* questions one at a time, checking your answer before moving on. (You can find the correct answers upside down at the end of the Knowledge Builder.) In this way, your correct (or incorrect) responses will be followed by immediate feedback.

Today programmed instruction is often presented via computer (Mayer, 2011; Springer & Pear, 2008). You may know it as CAI (*computer-assisted instruction*) or drill-and-practice (or, affectionately, drill-and-kill). In addition to giving learners immediate feedback, the computer can give hints about why an answer was wrong and what is needed to correct it (Timmerman & Kruepke, 2006). Increasingly, CAI programs called *serious games* are making use of game formats such as stories, competition with a partner, sound effects, and rich computer graphics to increase interest and motivation (Charsky, 2010; Westera et al., 2008; see • Figure 6.15).

Educational *simulations*, the most complex serious games, allow students to explore an imaginary situation or "microworld" to learn to solve real-world problems (• Figure 6.16). By seeing the effects of their choices, students discover basic principles of physics, biology, psychology, or other subjects (Grabe, 2006; Herold, 2010).

CAI software can save teachers and learners much time and effort, although the final level of skill or knowledge gained is not necessarily higher. In addition, people often do better with feedback from a computer because they can freely make mistakes and learn from them (Mayer, 2011; Ward & Parr, 2010).

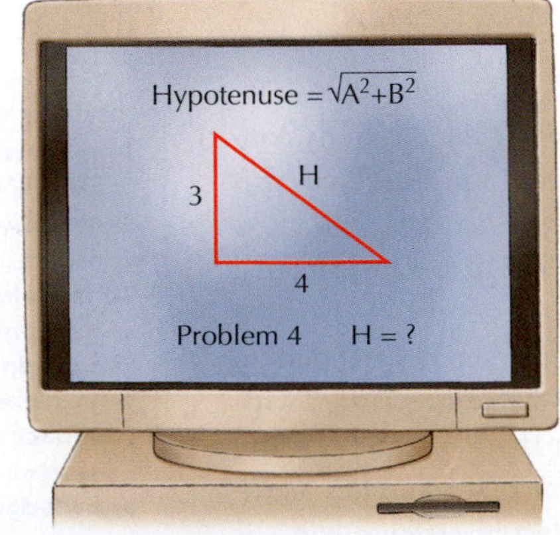

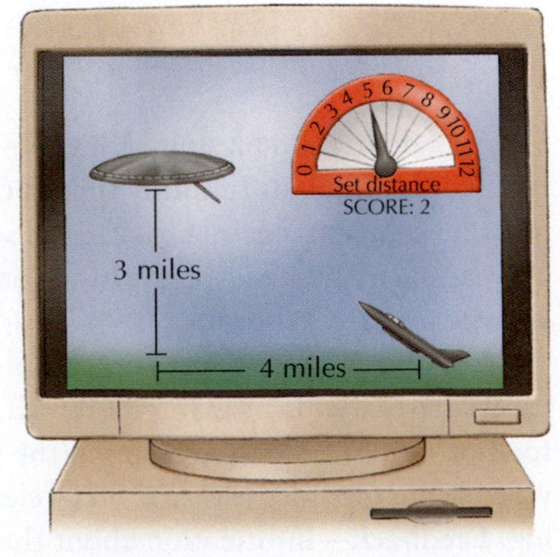

• Figure 6.15 Computer-assisted instruction. The left-hand screen shows a simplified drill-and-practice math problem, in which students must find the hypotenuse of a triangle. The right-hand screen presents the same problem as a serious game to increase interest and motivation. In the game, a child is asked to set the proper distance on a ray gun in the hovering space ship to "vaporize" an attacker.

• **Figure 6.16** Boeing 747 Airline Training Simulator. Student pilots can learn all the ins and outs of flying a jumbo jet in this flight simulator. Aren't you glad they don't have to do that with real planes (and passengers)? Your authors sure are!

Knowledge Builder — Operant Conditioning

RECITE

1. Responses in operant conditioning are ___________ or ___________, whereas those in classical conditioning are passive, ___________ or ___________ responses.
2. Changing the rules in small steps so that an animal (or person) is gradually trained to respond as desired is called ___________.
3. Extinction in operant conditioning is also subject to ___________ of a response.
   a. successive approximations *b.* shaping *c.* automation *d.* spontaneous recovery
4. Positive reinforcers increase the rate of responding and negative reinforcers decrease it. T or F?
5. Primary reinforcers are those learned through classical conditioning. T or F?
6. Which is a correct match?
   a. social reinforcer–primary reinforcement *b.* token reinforcer–secondary reinforcement *c.* intracranial stimulation–secondary reinforcement *d.* negative reinforcer–punishment
7. Superstitious responses are those that are
   a. shaped by secondary reinforcement *b.* extinguished *c.* prepotent *d.* unnecessary to obtain reinforcement
8. Knowledge of results, or KR, is also known as ___________.
9. CAI is based on the same principles as
   a. negative reinforcement *b.* programmed instruction *c.* higher order conditioning *d.* stimulus generalization

REFLECT

Think Critically

10. Can you imagine different forms of feedback?
11. Can you think of any reasons why engaging in superstitious behaviors might actually improve performance?

Self-Reflect

How have your thoughts about the effects of "rewards" changed now that you've read about operant conditioning? Can you explain the difference between positive reinforcement, negative reinforcement, and punishment? Can you give an example of each concept from your own experience?

A friend of yours punishes his dog all the time. What advice would you give him about how to use reinforcement, extinction, and shaping, instead of punishment?

Do you engage in any superstitious behaviors? Can you explain how you developed them?

Answers: 1. voluntary or emitted, involuntary or elicited **2.** shaping **3.** *d* **4.** F **5.** F **6.** *b* **7.** *d* **8.** feedback **9.** *b* **10.** Knowledge of results means you find out whether your response was right or wrong. Knowledge of correct response also tells you what the correct response should have been. Elaboration feedback adds additional information, such as an explanation of the correct answer. Adding knowledge of correct response and/or some elaboration is more effective than knowledge of results alone (Jaehnig & Miller, 2007). **11.** Even though you know tapping your club on the ground three times is not causing a better golf shot, it might nevertheless help settle you down or help you focus your attention on your swing (Damisch, Stoberock, Mussweiler, 2010).

Partial Reinforcement—Las Vegas, a Human Skinner Box?

Gateway Question 6.6: *How are we influenced by patterns of reward?*

If you would like to influence operant learning, you will need to know how patterns of reinforcement affect behavior. Imagine, for example, that a mother wants to reward her child for turning off the lights when he leaves a room. Contrary to what you might think, it is better to reinforce only some of her son's correct responses. Why should this be so? You'll find the answer in the following discussion.

Until now, we have treated operant reinforcement as if it were continuous. **Continuous reinforcement** means that a reinforcer follows every correct response. At the start, continuous reinforcement is useful for learning new responses (Domjan, 2010). To teach your dog to come to you, it is best to reinforce your dog every time it comes when called.

Curiously, once your dog has learned to come when called, it is best to shift to **partial reinforcement**, in which reinforcers do not follow every response. Responses acquired by partial reinforcement are highly resistant to extinction, a phenomenon known as the **partial reinforcement effect** (Domjan, 2010; Svartdal, 2003).

How does getting reinforced part of the time make a habit stronger? If you have ever visited a casino, you have probably seen row

Programmed instruction Any learning format that presents information in small amounts, gives immediate practice, and provides continuous feedback to learners.

Continuous reinforcement A schedule in which every correct response is followed by a reinforcer.

Partial reinforcement A pattern in which only a portion of all responses are reinforced.

Partial reinforcement effect Responses acquired with partial reinforcement are more resistant to extinction.

Noel Hendrikson/Getty Images

The one-armed bandit (slot machine) is a dispenser of partial reinforcement.

after row of people playing slot machines. To gain insight into the distinction between continuous and partial reinforcement, imagine that you put a dollar in a slot machine and pull the handle. Ten dollars spills into the tray. Let's say this continues for several minutes. Every pull is followed by a payoff. Because you are being reinforced on a continuous schedule, you quickly "get hooked" (and begin to plan your retirement).

But, alas, suddenly each pull is followed by nothing. Obviously, you would respond several times more before giving up. However, when continuous reinforcement is followed by extinction, the message quickly becomes clear: No more payoffs (or early retirement).

Contrast this with partial reinforcement. This time, imagine that you put a dollar in a slot machine five times without a payoff. You are just about to quit, but decide to play once more. Bingo! The machine returns $20. After this, payoffs continue on a partial schedule; some are large, and some are small. All are unpredictable. Sometimes you hit two in a row, and sometimes 20 or 30 pulls go unrewarded.

Now let's say the payoff mechanism is turned off again. How many times do you think you would respond this time before your handle-pulling behavior is extinguished? Because you have developed the expectation that any play may be "the one," it will be hard to resist just one more play . . . and one more . . . and one more. Also, because partial reinforcement includes long periods of nonreward, it will be harder to distinguish between periods of reinforcement and extinction. It is no exaggeration to say that the partial reinforcement effect has left many people penniless. Even psychologists visiting a casino may get "cleaned out" (not your authors, of course!).

To return to our examples, after using continuous reinforcement to teach a child to turn off the lights or a dog to come when called, it is best to shift to partial reinforcement. That way, the new behavior will become more resistant to extinction.

Schedules of Partial Reinforcement

Partial reinforcement can be given in several patterns, or partial **schedules of reinforcement** (plans for determining which responses will be reinforced) (Domjan, 2010). Let's consider the four most basic, which have some interesting effects on us. Typical responses to each pattern are shown in ● Figure 6.17. Results such as these are obtained when a *cumulative recorder* is connected to a Skinner box. The device consists of a moving strip of paper and a mechanical pen that jumps upward each time a response is made. Rapid responding causes the pen to draw a steep line; a horizontal line indicates no response. Small tick marks on the lines show when a reinforcer was given.

Fixed Ratio (FR)

What would happen if a reinforcer followed only every other response? Or what if we followed every third, fourth, fifth, or other number of responses with reinforcement? Each of these patterns is a **fixed ratio (FR) schedule**—a set number of correct responses must be made to obtain a reinforcer. Notice that in an FR schedule, the ratio of reinforcers to responses is fixed: FR-2 means that every other response is rewarded; FR-3 means that every third response is reinforced; FR-10 schedule means that 10 responses must be made to obtain a reinforcer.

Fixed ratio schedules produce *very high response rates* (see ● Figure 6.17). A hungry rat on an FR-10 schedule will quickly run off 10 responses, pause to eat, and then run off 10 more. A similar situation occurs when factory or farm workers are paid on a piecework basis. When a fixed number of items must be produced for a set amount of pay, work output is high.

Variable Ratio (VR)

In a **variable ratio (VR) schedule**, a varied number of correct responses must be made to get a reinforcer. Instead of reinforcing every fourth response (FR-4), for example, a person or animal on a VR-4 schedule gets rewarded *on the average* every fourth response. Sometimes 2 responses must be made to obtain a reinforcer; sometimes it's 5; sometimes, 4; and so on. The actual number varies, but it averages out to 4 (in this example). Variable ratio schedules also produce high response rates.

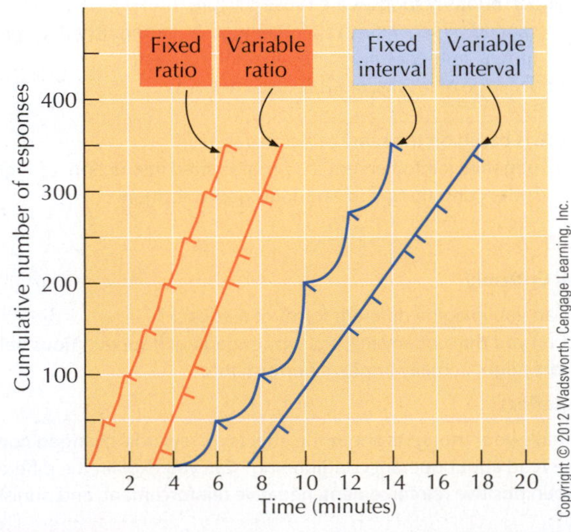

● **Figure 6.17** Typical response patterns for reinforcement schedules.

Critical Thinking: Are Animals Stuck in Time?

We humans are *cognitive time travelers*, regularly zooming back and forth through time in our minds. You can, for example, think about past events, such as what you had for breakfast this morning. We can also imagine events in the future. Brides-to-be are famous for planning their weddings down to the last detail. But what about animals? Are they cognitive time travelers, or are they less cognitive and hence "stuck in time" (Clayton, Russell, & Dickinson, 2009; Zentall, 2005)? Do dogs ever think about how hot it was yesterday or what they plan to do tomorrow? To answer such questions, psychologists have used operant conditioning as a research tool.

Conditioning studies have repeatedly shown that animals are sensitive to the passage of time (Zentall, 2005). For example, pigeons and rats reinforced on fixed interval schedules stop responding immediately after they receive a reinforcer and do not start again until just before the next scheduled reinforcement (Roberts, 2002). In one study, pigeons were put in a Skinner box with a pecking key on each wall. They quickly learned to peck only at Key 1 if it was 9:30 in the morning and at Key 3 if it was 4:00 in the afternoon (Saksida & Wilkie, 1994).

Another study focused on scrub jays. These birds are hoarders; they store excess food at different locations and then go back later to eat it. Scrub jays were allowed to hoard some nuts in one location and some worms in another. If they were released 4 hours later, they went directly to the worms. However, if they were released 5 days later, they went straight for the nuts. Worms are a scrub jay's favorite food, which explains their choice after 4 hours. But worms decay after a day or so, whereas nuts stay edible. It seems that the jays knew exactly where they stored each type of food and how much time had passed (Clayton, Yu, & Dickinson, 2001).

Although these studies are suggestive, they are part of an ongoing debate about animal cognition, including whether animals are stuck in time (Roberts & Roberts, 2002). Nevertheless, be careful if you forget to feed your beloved dog, Rover, at his usual mealtime. If he has been conditioned to think it's time to eat, he may settle for your favorite flip-flops instead of dog food!

George McCarthy/NPL/Minden Pictures

Florida scrub jays are food hoarders. Does their food hoarding behavior prove they are not "trapped in time"?

VR schedules seem less predictable than FR. Does that have any effect on extinction? Yes. Because reinforcement is less predictable, VR schedules tend to produce greater resistance to extinction than fixed ratio schedules. Playing a slot machine is an example of behavior maintained by a variable ratio schedule. Another would be our plan to only occasionally reward a child for turning off the lights, once he has learned to do so. Golf, tennis, baseball, and many other sports are also reinforced on a variable ratio basis: Even the best batters in baseball rarely get a hit more than an average of 3 out of every 10 times they are at bat.

Fixed Interval (FI)

In another pattern, reinforcement is given only when a correct response is made after a fixed amount of *time* has passed. This time interval is measured from the last reinforced response. Responses made during the time interval are not reinforced. In a **fixed interval (FI) schedule**, the first correct response made after the time period has passed is reinforced. Thus, a rat on an FI-30-second schedule has to wait 30 seconds after the last reinforced response before a bar press will pay off again. The rat can press the bar as often as it wants during the interval, but it will not be rewarded.

Fixed interval schedules produce *moderate response rates*. Animals working on an FI schedule seem to develop a keen sense of the passage of time (Eckerman, 1999). Few responses occur just after a reinforcement is delivered and a spurt of activity occurs just before the next reinforcement is due. (See "Are Animals Stuck in Time?")

Is getting paid weekly an FI schedule? Pure examples of fixed interval schedules are rare, but getting paid each week at work does come close. Notice, however, that most people do not work faster just before payday, as an FI schedule predicts. A closer parallel would be having a report due every 2 weeks for a class. Right after turning in a paper, your work would probably drop to zero for a week or more (Chance, 2009).

Schedule of reinforcement A rule or plan for determining which responses will be reinforced.

Fixed ratio (FR) schedule A set number of correct responses must be made to get a reinforcer. For example, a reinforcer is given for every four correct responses.

Variable ratio (VR) schedule A varied number of correct responses must be made to get a reinforcer. For example, a reinforcer is given after three to seven correct responses; the actual number changes randomly.

Fixed interval (FI) schedule A reinforcer is given only when a correct response is made after a set amount of time has passed since the last reinforced response. Responses made during the time interval are not reinforced.

Variable Interval (VI)

Variable interval (VI) schedules are a variation on fixed intervals. Here, reinforcement is given for the first correct response made after a varied amount of time. On a VI 30-second schedule, reinforcement is available after an interval that *averages* 30 seconds.

VI schedules produce *slow, steady response rates* and tremendous resistance to extinction (Lattal, Reilly, & Kohn, 1998). When you dial a phone number and get a busy signal, reward (getting through) is on a VI schedule. You may have to wait 30 seconds or 30 minutes. If you are like most people, you will doggedly dial over and over again until you get a connection. Success in fishing is also on a VI schedule—which may explain the bulldog tenacity of many anglers (Chance, 2009).

Stimulus Control—Red Light, Green Light

When you are driving, your behavior at intersections is controlled by the red or green light. In similar fashion, many of the stimuli we encounter each day act like stop or go signals that guide our behavior. To state the idea more formally, stimuli that consistently precede a rewarded response tend to influence when and where the response will occur. This effect is called **stimulus control**. Notice how it works with our friend Einstein.

Lights Out for Einstein

While learning the bar-pressing response, Einstein has been in a Skinner box illuminated by a bright light. During several training sessions, the light is alternately turned on and off. When the light is on, a bar press will produce food. When the light is off, bar pressing goes unrewarded. We soon observe that the rat presses vigorously when the light is on and ignores the bar when the light is off.

In this example, the light signals what consequences will follow if a response is made. Evidence for stimulus control could be shown by turning the food delivery *on* when the light is *off.* A well-trained animal might never discover that the rules had changed (Powell, Symbaluk, & Honey, 2009). A similar example of stimulus control would be a child learning to ask for candy when her mother is in a good mood, but not asking at other times. Likewise, we pick up phones that are ringing, but rarely answer phones that are silent.

Generalization

Two important aspects of stimulus control are generalization and discrimination. Let's return to dogs to illustrate these concepts. First, generalization.

Is generalization the same in operant conditioning as it is in classical conditioning? Basically, yes. **Operant stimulus generalization** is the tendency to respond to stimuli similar to those that preceded operant reinforcement. That is, a reinforced response tends to be made again when similar antecedents are present. Assume, for instance, that your dog has begun to jump up at you whenever you are eating dinner at the kitchen table (bad dog!). Mind you, that's because you have been rewarding its behavior with table scraps (bad master!). Now your dog begins to jump any time you sit at the kitchen table. The dog has learned that reinforcement tends to occur when you are at the kitchen table. The dog's behavior has come under stimulus control. Now let's say that there are some other tables in your house. Because they are similar, your dog will likely jump up if you sit at any of them because the jumping response *generalized* to other tables. Similar generalization explains why children may temporarily call all men *Daddy*—much to the embarrassment of their parents.

Discrimination

Meanwhile, back at the table. . . . As stated earlier, to discriminate means to respond differently to varied stimuli. Because one table signaled the availability of reinforcement to your dog, it began jumping up while you sat at other tables as well (generalization). If you do not feed your dog while sitting at any other table, the jumping response that originally generalized to them will extinguish because of nonreinforcement. Thus, your dog's jumping response is consistently rewarded in the presence of a specific table. The same response to different tables is extinguished. Through **operant stimulus discrimination**, your dog has learned to differentiate between antecedent stimuli that signal reward and nonreward. As a result, the dog's response pattern will shift to match these **discriminative stimuli**, stimuli that precede reinforced and nonreinforced responses.

Stimulus discrimination is aptly illustrated by the "sniffer" dogs that locate drugs and explosives at airports and border crossings. Operant discrimination is used to teach these dogs to recognize contraband. During training, they are reinforced only for approaching containers baited with drugs or explosives.

Stimulus discrimination also has a tremendous impact on human behavior. Learning to recognize different automobile

Stimulus control. Operant shaping was used to teach this whale to "bow" to an audience. Fish were used as reinforcers. Notice the trainer's hand signal, which serves as a discriminative stimulus to control the performance.

brands, birds, animals, wines, types of music, and even the answers on psychology tests all depends, in part, on operant discrimination learning.

A discriminative stimulus that most drivers are familiar with is a police car on the freeway. This stimulus is a clear signal that a specific set of reinforcement contingencies applies. As you have probably observed, the presence of a police car brings about rapid reductions in driving speed, lane changes, and tailgating.

Would using different ringtones on my cellphone be an example of using discriminative stimuli? Excellent! Suppose you use one ringtone for people you want to speak to, one for people you don't, and yet another for calls from strangers. In no time at all, you will be showing different telephone answering behavior in response to different ringtones.

Knowledge Builder

Partial Reinforcement and Stimulus Control

RECITE

1. Two aspects of stimulus control are __________ and __________.
2. Responding tends to occur in the presence of discriminative stimuli associated with reinforcement and tends not to occur in the presence of discriminative stimuli associated with nonreinforcement. T or F?
3. Stimulus generalization refers to making an operant response in the presence of stimuli similar to those that preceded reinforcement. T or F?
4. Moderate response rates that are marked by spurts of activity and periods of inactivity are characteristic of
a. FR schedules *b.* VR schedules *c.* FI schedules *d.* VI schedules
5. Partial reinforcement tends to produce slower responding and reduced resistance to extinction. T or F?
6. The schedule of reinforcement associated with playing slot machines and other types of gambling is
a. fixed ratio *b.* variable ratio *c.* fixed interval *d.* variable interval

REFLECT

Think Critically

7. A business owner who pays employees an hourly wage wants to increase productivity. How could the owner make more effective use of reinforcement?
8. How could you use conditioning principles to teach a dog or a cat to come when called?

Self-Reflect

Think of something you do that is reinforced only part of the time. Do you pursue this activity persistently? How have you been affected by partial reinforcement?

See if you can think of at least one everyday example of the five basic schedules of reinforcement (continuous reinforcement and the four types of partial reinforcement).

Doors that are meant to be pushed outward have metal plates on them. Those that are meant to be pulled inward have handles. Do these discriminative stimuli affect your behavior? (If they don't, how's your nose doing?)

Answers: 1. generalization, discrimination **2.** T **3.** T **4.** c **5.** F **6.** b **7.** Continuing to use fixed interval rewards (hourly wage or salary) would guarantee a basic level of income for employees. To reward extra effort, the owner could add some fixed ratio reinforcement (such as incentives, bonuses, commissions, or profit sharing) to employees' pay. **8.** An excellent way to train a pet to come when you call is to give a distinctive call or whistle each time you feed the animal. This makes the signal a secondary reinforcer and a discriminative stimulus for reward (food). Of course, it also helps to directly reinforce an animal with praise, petting, or food for coming when called.

Punishment—Putting the Brakes on Behavior

Gateway Question 6.7: *What does punishment do to behavior?*

Spankings, reprimands, fines, jail sentences, firings, failing grades, and the like are commonly used to control behavior. Clearly, the story of instrumental learning is unfinished without a return to the topic of punishment. Recall that **punishment** lowers the probability that a response will occur again. To be most effective, punishment must be given contingently (only after an undesired response occurs).

Punishers, like reinforcers, are defined by observing their effects on behavior. A **punisher** is any consequence that reduces the frequency of a target behavior. It is not always possible to know ahead of time what will act as a punisher for a particular person. For example, when Jason's mother reprimanded him for throwing toys, he stopped doing it. In this instance, the reprimand was a punisher. However, Chris is starved for attention of any kind from his parents, who both work full-time. For Chris, a reprimand, or even a spanking, might actually reinforce toy throwing. Remember, too, that a punisher can be either the onset of an unpleasant event or the removal of a positive state of affairs (response cost).

Variable interval (VI) schedule A reinforcer is given for the first correct response made after a varied amount of time has passed since the last reinforced response. Responses made during the time interval are not reinforced.

Stimulus control Stimuli present when an operant response is acquired tend to control when and where the response is made.

Operant stimulus generalization The tendency to respond to stimuli similar to those that preceded operant reinforcement.

Operant stimulus discrimination The tendency to make an operant response when stimuli previously associated with reward are present and to withhold the response when stimuli associated with nonreward are present.

Discriminative stimuli Stimuli that precede rewarded and nonrewarded responses in operant conditioning.

Punishment The process of suppressing a response.

Punisher Any event that decreases the probability or frequency of responses it follows.

Punishers are consequences that lower the probability that a response will be made again. Receiving a traffic citation is directly punishing because the driver is delayed and reprimanded. Paying a fine and higher insurance rates add to the punishment in the form of response cost.

Variables Affecting Punishment

How effective is punishment? The effectiveness of punishers depends greatly on their *timing, consistency,* and *intensity.* Punishment works best when it occurs as the response is being made, or *immediately* afterward (timing), and when it is given *each time* a response occurs (consistency). Thus, if simply refusing to feed your dog table scraps is not enough to stop it from jumping at you when you sit at a table, you could effectively (and humanely) punish it by spraying water on its nose each time it jumps up. About 10 to 15 such treatments are usually enough. This would not be the case if you applied punishment haphazardly or long after the jumping stopped. If you discover that your dog dug up a tree and ate it while you were gone, punishing the dog hours later will do little good. Likewise, the commonly heard childhood threat, "Wait 'til your father comes home, then you'll be sorry," just makes the father a feared brute; it doesn't effectively punish an undesirable response.

Severe punishment (following a response with an intensely aversive or unpleasant stimulus) can be extremely effective in stopping behavior. If 3-year-old Beavis sticks his finger in a light socket and gets a shock, that may be the last time he *ever* tries it. However, mild punishment only temporarily *suppresses* a response. If the response is still reinforced, punishment may be particularly ineffective.

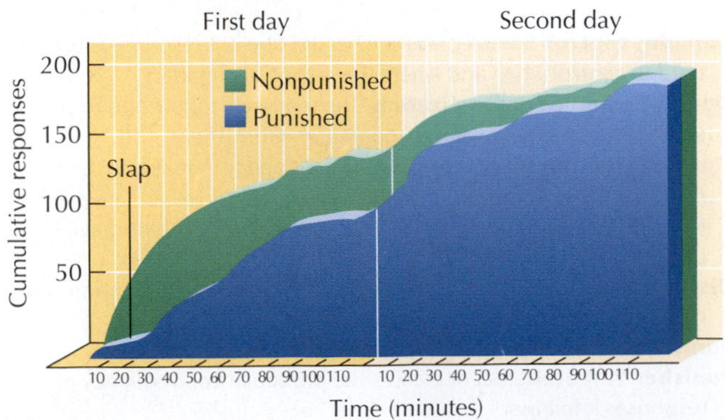

• **Figure 6.18** The effect of punishment on extinction. Immediately after punishment, the rate of bar pressing is suppressed, but by the end of the second day, the effects of punishment have disappeared. (After B. F. Skinner, 1938.)

This fact was demonstrated by slapping rats on the paw as they were bar pressing in a Skinner box. Two groups of well-trained rats were placed on extinction. One group was punished with a slap for each bar press, and the other group was not. It might seem that the slap would cause bar pressing to extinguish more quickly. Yet this was not the case, as you can see in • Figure 6.18. Punishment temporarily slowed responding, but it did not cause more rapid extinction. Slapping the paws of rats or children has little permanent effect on a reinforced response.

Similarly, if 7-year-old Alissa sneaks a snack from the refrigerator before dinner and is punished for it, she may pass up snacks for a short time. But because snack sneaking was also rewarded by the sneaked snack, she will probably try sneaky snacking again, sometime later. But seriously, to reiterate, intense punishment may permanently suppress responding, even for actions as basic as eating. Animals severely punished while eating may never eat again (Bertsch, 1976).

The Downside of Punishment

Are there drawbacks to using punishment? There are several, all of which become more of a problem as punishment increases in severity. Basically, punishment is *aversive* (painful or uncomfortable). As a result, people and situations associated with punishment tend, through classical conditioning, to become feared, resented, or disliked. The aversive nature of punishment makes it especially poor to use when teaching children to eat politely or in toilet training (Miltenberger, 2011).

Escape and Avoidance

A second major problem is that aversive stimuli encourage escape and avoidance learning (Brennan, Beck, & Servatius, 2003). In **escape learning**, we learn to make a response in order to end an aversive stimulus. Escape learning simply reflects the operation of negative reinforcement, as the following example shows.

> A dog is placed in a two-compartment cage called a shuttle box. If the dog is shocked while in one of the compartments, it will quickly learn to jump to the other compartment to *escape* the shock. If a buzzer is sounded 10 seconds before each shock begins, the dog will soon learn to associate the buzzer with shock. It will then *avoid* pain by jumping *before* the shock begins (Solomon & Wynne, 1953).

Avoidance learning—making a response in order to postpone or prevent discomfort—appears to involve *both* classical and operant conditioning (Levis, 1989). In a shuttle box a dog first learns, through classical conditioning, to fear the buzzer. (The buzzer is a CS, which is followed by shock, a US for pain and fear.) Each time the buzzer sounds, the dog becomes fearful. But by jumping to the "safe" compartment the dog can end the unpleasant fear it feels. Therefore, learning to jump *before* the onset of the shock is negatively reinforced by fear reduction. This is the operant part of avoidance learning.

Once avoidance is learned, it is very persistent. The electric shock in a shuttle box can be turned off, yet the dog will continue to leap from the compartment each time the buzzer sounds. The dog, it seems, has learned to *expect* that the buzzer will be followed by shock. If the dog leaves before the shock would normally occur, it gets no new information to change the expectancy (Chance, 2009).

Escape and avoidance learning are a regular part of daily experience (Schlund & Cataldo, 2010). For example, if you work with a loud and obnoxious person, you may at first escape from conversations with him to obtain relief. Later, you may dodge him altogether. This is an example of avoidance learning. Each time you sidestep him, your avoidance is again reinforced by a sense of relief. In many situations involving frequent punishment, similar desires to escape and avoid are activated. For example, children who run away from punishing parents (escape) may soon learn to lie about their behavior (avoidance) or to spend as much time away from home as possible (also an avoidance response).

Aggression

A third problem with punishment is that it can greatly increase *aggression*. Animals react to pain by attacking whomever or whatever else is around. A common example is the faithful dog that nips its owner during a painful procedure at the veterinarian's office. Likewise, humans who are in pain have a tendency to lash out at others.

We also know that one of the most common responses to frustration is aggression. Generally speaking, punishment is painful, frustrating, or both. Punishment, therefore, sets up a powerful environment for learning aggression. When spanked, a child may feel angry, frustrated, and hostile. What if that child then goes outside and hits a brother, a sister, or a neighbor? The danger is that aggressive acts may feel good because they release anger and frustration. If so, aggression has been rewarded and will tend to occur again in other frustrating situations.

BRIDGES

The connection between frustration and aggression is strong. But does frustration always produce aggression? **For more information, see Chapter 13, pages 451–453, and Chapter 17, pages 585–586.**

One study found that children who are physically punished are more likely to engage in aggressive, impulsive, antisocial behavior (Thomas, 2004). Similarly, a classic study of angry adolescent boys found that they were severely punished at home. This suppressed their misbehavior at home but made them more aggressive elsewhere. Parents were often surprised to learn that their "good boys" were in trouble for fighting at school (Bandura & Walters, 1959; Simons & Wurtele, 2010). Fortunately, at least for younger children, if parents change to less punitive parenting, their children's levels of aggression will decline (Thomas, 2004).

In the classroom, physical punishment, yelling, and humiliation are also generally ineffective. Positive reinforcement, in the form of praise, approval, and reward, is much more likely to quell classroom disruptions, defiance, and inattention (Alberto & Troutman, 2009).

BRIDGES

Learning principles are only one element of effective child management. **See Chapter 3, pages 117–119, for additional techniques.**

Using Punishment Wisely

In light of its limitations and drawbacks, should punishment be used to control behavior? Parents, teachers, animal trainers, and the like have three basic tools to control simple learning: (1) reinforcement strengthens responses; (2) nonreinforcement causes responses to extinguish; (3) punishment suppresses responses. (Consult ● Figure 6.19 to refresh your memory about the different types of reinforcement and punishment.) These tools work best in combination. It is usually best to begin by making liberal use of positive reinforcement, especially praise, to encourage good behavior (Martin & Pear, 2011). Also, try extinction first: See what happens if you ignore a problem behavior, or shift attention to a desirable activity and then reinforce it with praise. Remember, it is much more effective to strengthen and encourage desirable behaviors than it is to punish unwanted behaviors (Gershoff, 2002; Olson & Hergenhahn, 2009). When all else fails, it may be necessary to use punishment to help manage the behavior of an animal, child, or even another adult. For those times, here are some tips to keep in mind:

1. *Avoid harsh punishment.* Harsh or excessive punishment has serious negative drawbacks (never slap a child's face, for instance). "Sparing the rod" will not spoil a child. In fact, the reverse is true. As we just discussed, harsh punishment can lead to negative emotional reactions,

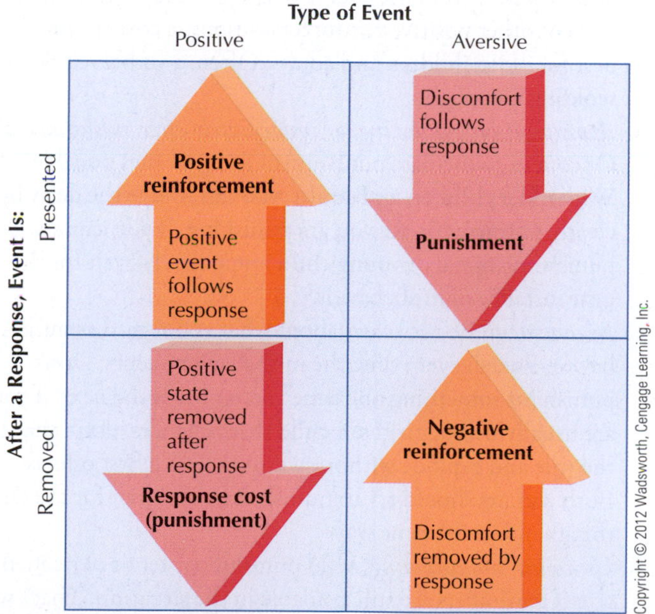

● **Figure 6.19** Types of reinforcement and punishment. The impact of an event depends on whether it is presented or removed after a response is made. Each square defines one possibility: Arrows pointing upward indicate that responding is increased; downward-pointing arrows indicate that responding is decreased.

Escape learning Learning to make a response in order to end an aversive stimulus.

Avoidance learning Learning to make a response in order to postpone or prevent discomfort.

avoidance and escape behaviors, and increased aggression (Aucoin, Frick, & Bodin, 2006; Simons & Wurtele, 2010). It can even lead to long-term mental health problems (Afifi et al., 2006).

What about spanking? Parents should minimize spanking or avoid it entirely (Gershoff, 2002). Although most children show no signs of long-term damage from spanking if it is backed up by supportive parenting, emotional damage does occur if spankings are severe, frequent, or coupled with harsh parenting (Baumrind, Larzelere, & Cowan, 2002; Stacks et al., 2009). Like all harsh punishment, frequent spanking tends to increase aggression and leads to more problem behaviors, not fewer (McLoyd & Smith, 2002; Simons & Wurtele, 2010). In fact, antispanking laws have been passed in a number of countries around the world (Gershoff & Bitensky, 2007).

2. *Use the minimum punishment necessary to suppress misbehavior.* If punishment is used at all, it should be mild. In a situation that poses immediate danger, such as when a child reaches for something hot or a dog runs into the street, mild punishment may prevent disaster. Punishment in such cases works best when it produces actions *incompatible* with the response you want to suppress. Let's say a child reaches toward a stove burner. Would a swat on the bottom serve as an effective punisher? Probably so. It would be better, however, to slap the child's outstretched hand so that it will be *withdrawn* from the source of danger. Taking away privileges or other positive reinforcers (response cost) is usually best for older children and adults. Often, a verbal rebuke or a scolding is enough.
3. *Apply punishment during, or immediately after, misbehavior.* Of course, immediate punishment is not always possible. With older children and adults, you can bridge the delay by clearly stating what act you are punishing. If you cannot punish an animal or young child immediately, wait for the next instance of misbehavior.
4. *Be consistent.* Be very clear about what you regard as misbehavior. Punish every time the misbehavior occurs. Don't punish for something one time and ignore it the next. If you are usually willing to give a child three chances, don't change the rule and explode without warning after a first offense. Both parents should try to punish their children for the same things and in the same way.
5. *Use counterconditioning.* Mild punishment tends to be ineffective if reinforcers are still available in the situation. That's why it is best to also reward an alternate, desired response. For example, Sally, who has a habit of taking toys from her sister, should not just be reprimanded for it. She should be *counter-conditioned*, or rewarded, for displaying any behavior that is counter to the unacceptable behavior, such as cooperative play or sharing her toys. As desired behaviors become more frequent, undesired behaviors become less frequent. The girl can't very well share her toys and take them from her sister at the same time.

   Remember, punishment tells a person or an animal only that a response was "wrong." Punishment does not say what the "right" response is, so it *does not teach new behaviors.* If reinforcement is missing, punishment becomes less effective (Gershoff, 2002).
6. *Expect anger from a punished person.* Briefly acknowledge this anger, but be careful not to reinforce it. Be willing to admit your mistake if you wrongfully punish someone or if you punished too severely.
7. *Punish with kindness and respect.* Avoid punishing when you are angry. It is easy to get carried away and become abusive (Gershoff & Bitensky, 2007; Gonzalez et al., 2008). Two-thirds of child abuse cases start out as attempts at physical punishment (Trocmé et al., 2001). One way to guard against doing harm is to punish with kindness and respect. Doing so also allows the punished person to retain self-respect. For instance, do not punish a person in front of others, if possible. A strong, trusting relationship tends to minimize behavior problems. Ideally, others should want to behave well to get your praise, not because they fear punishment.

To summarize, a common error is to rely too much on punishment for training or discipline. Frequent punishment makes a person or an animal unhappy, confused, anxious, aggressive, and fearful (Gershoff, 2002; Hergenhahn & Olson, 2009). The overall emotional adjustment of a child or pet disciplined mainly by reward is usually superior to one disciplined mainly by punishment.

Parents and teachers should also be aware that using punishment can be "habit forming." When children are noisy, messy, disrespectful, or otherwise misbehaving, the temptation to punish them can be strong. The danger is that punishment often works. When it does, a sudden end to the adult's irritation acts as a negative reinforcer. This encourages the adult to use punishment more often in the future (Alberto & Troutman, 2009). Immediate silence may be "golden," but its cost can be very high in terms of a child's emotional health.

Knowledge Builder: Punishment

RECITE

1. Negative reinforcement increases responding; punishment suppresses responding. T or F?
2. Three factors that greatly influence the effects of punishment are timing, consistency, and ______________.
3. Mild punishment tends to only temporarily ______________ a response that is also reinforced.
   a. enhance *b.* aggravate *c.* replace *d.* suppress
4. Three undesired side effects of punishment are (1) conditioning of fear and resentment, (2) encouragement of aggression, and (3) the learning of escape or ______________ responses.
5. Using punishment can be "habit forming" because putting a stop to someone else's irritating behavior can ______________ the person who applies the punishment.

REFLECT

Think Critically

6. Using the concept of partial reinforcement, can you explain why inconsistent punishment is especially ineffective?
7. Escape and avoidance learning have been applied to encourage automobile seat belt use. Can you explain how?

Self-Reflect

Think of how you were punished as a child. Was the punishment immediate? Was it consistent? What effect did these factors have on your behavior? Was the punishment effective? Which of the side effects of punishment have you witnessed or experienced?

Answers: **1.** T **2.** intensity **3.** *d* **4.** avoidance **5.** negatively reinforce **6.** An inconsistently punished response will continue to be reinforced on a partial schedule, which can make it even more resistant to extinction. **7.** Many automobiles have an unpleasant buzzer that sounds if the ignition key is turned before the driver's seat belt is fastened. Most drivers quickly learn to fasten the belt to stop the annoying sound. This is an example of escape conditioning. Avoidance conditioning is evident when a driver learns to buckle up before the buzzer sounds.

Cognitive Learning—Beyond Conditioning

Gateway Question 6.8: *What is cognitive learning?*

Is all learning just an association between stimuli and responses? Much learning can be explained by classical and operant conditioning. But, as we have seen, even basic conditioning has "mental" elements. As a human, you can anticipate future reward or punishment and react accordingly. (You may wonder why this doesn't seem to work when a doctor or dentist says, "This won't hurt a bit." Here's why: They lie!) There is no doubt that human learning includes a large *cognitive*, or mental, dimension (Goldstein, 2011; Lefrançois, 2006). As humans, we are greatly affected by information, expectations, perceptions, mental images, and the like.

As we mentioned at the beginning of this chapter, loosely speaking, **cognitive learning** refers to understanding, knowing, anticipating, or otherwise making use of information-rich higher mental processes. Cognitive learning extends beyond basic conditioning into the realms of memory, thinking, problem solving, and language. Because these topics are covered in later chapters, our discussion here is limited to a first look at learning beyond conditioning.

Cognitive Maps

How do you navigate around the town you live in? Have you simply learned to make a series of right and left turns to get from one point to another? More likely, you have an overall mental picture of how the town is laid out. This *cognitive map* acts as a guide even when you must detour or take a new route (Foo et al., 2005). A **cognitive map** is an internal representation of an area, such as a maze, city, or campus. Even the lowly rat—not exactly a mental giant (well, except for our Einstein)—learns *where* food is found in a maze, not just which turns to make to reach the food (Tolman, Ritchie, & Kalish, 1946). If you have ever learned your way through some of the levels found in many video games, you will have a good idea of what a cognitive map is. In a sense, cognitive maps also apply to other kinds of knowledge. For instance, it could be said that you have been developing a "map" of psychology while reading this book. That's why students sometimes find it helpful to draw pictures or diagrams of how they envision concepts fitting together.

It's easy to get lost when visiting a new place if you don't have a cognitive map of the area. Printed maps help, but they may still leave you puzzled until you begin to form a mental representation of major landmarks and directions.

'Oh no, Mr. Know-it-all isn't going to stop and ask for directions! Admit it - we're lost.'

Cognitive learning Higher-level learning involving thinking, knowing, understanding, and anticipation.

Cognitive map Internal images or other mental representations of an area (maze, city, campus, and so forth) that underlie an ability to choose alternative paths to the same goal.

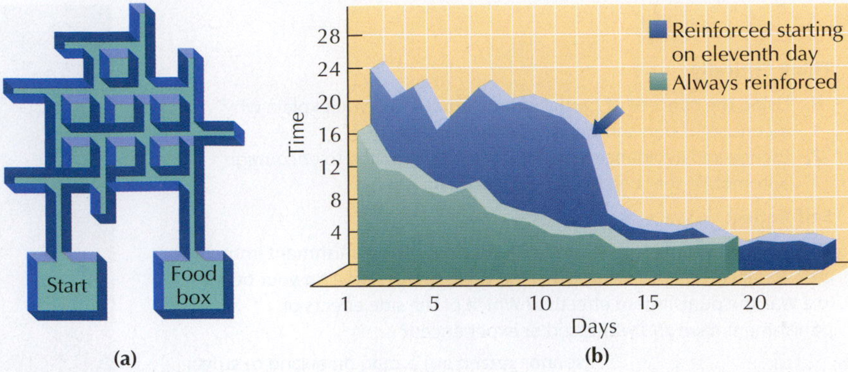

• Figure 6.20 Latent learning. *(a)* The maze used by Tolman and Honzik to demonstrate latent learning by rats. *(b)* Results of the experiment. Notice the rapid improvement in performance that occurred when food was made available to the previously unreinforced animals. This indicates that learning had occurred but that it remained hidden or unexpressed. (Adapted from Tolman & Honzik, 1930.)

Latent Learning

Cognitive learning is also revealed by latent (hidden) learning. **Latent learning** occurs without obvious reinforcement and remains hidden until reinforcement is provided (Davidson, 2000). Here's an example from a classic animal study: Two groups of rats were allowed to explore a maze. The animals in one group found food at the far end of the maze. Soon, they learned to rapidly make their way through the maze when released. Rats in the second group were unrewarded and showed no signs of learning. But later, when the "uneducated" rats were given food, they ran the maze as quickly as the rewarded group (Tolman & Honzik, 1930). Although there was no outward sign of it, the unrewarded animals had learned their way around the maze. Their learning, therefore, remained latent at first (• Figure 6.20).

How did they learn if there was no reinforcement? Just satisfying curiosity can be enough to reward learning (Harlow & Harlow, 1962). In humans, latent learning is related to higher-level abilities, such as anticipating future reward. For example, if you give an attractive classmate a ride home, you may make mental notes about how to get to his or her house, even if a date is only a remote future possibility.

Discovery Learning

Much of what is meant by cognitive learning is summarized by the word *understanding*. Each of us has, at times, learned ideas by **rote** (mechanical repetition and memorization). Although rote learning can be efficient, many psychologists believe that learning is more lasting and flexible when people *discover* facts and principles on their own. In **discovery learning**, skills are gained by *insight* and understanding instead of by rote (Snowman & McCown, 2011).

BRIDGES

Gain more insight into insight by turning to Chapter 8, pages 286–288.

As long as learning occurs, what difference does it make if it is by discovery or by rote? • Figure 6.21 illustrates the difference. Two groups of students were taught to calculate the area of a parallelogram by multiplying the height by the length of the base. Some were encouraged to see that a "piece" of a parallelogram could be "moved" to create a rectangle. Later, they were better able to solve unusual problems in which the height times base formula didn't seem to work. Students who simply memorized a rule were confused by the similar problems (Wertheimer, 1959). As this implies, discovery can lead to a better understanding of new or unusual problems. When possible, people should try new strategies and discover new solutions during learning. However, this doesn't mean that students are supposed to stumble around and redis-

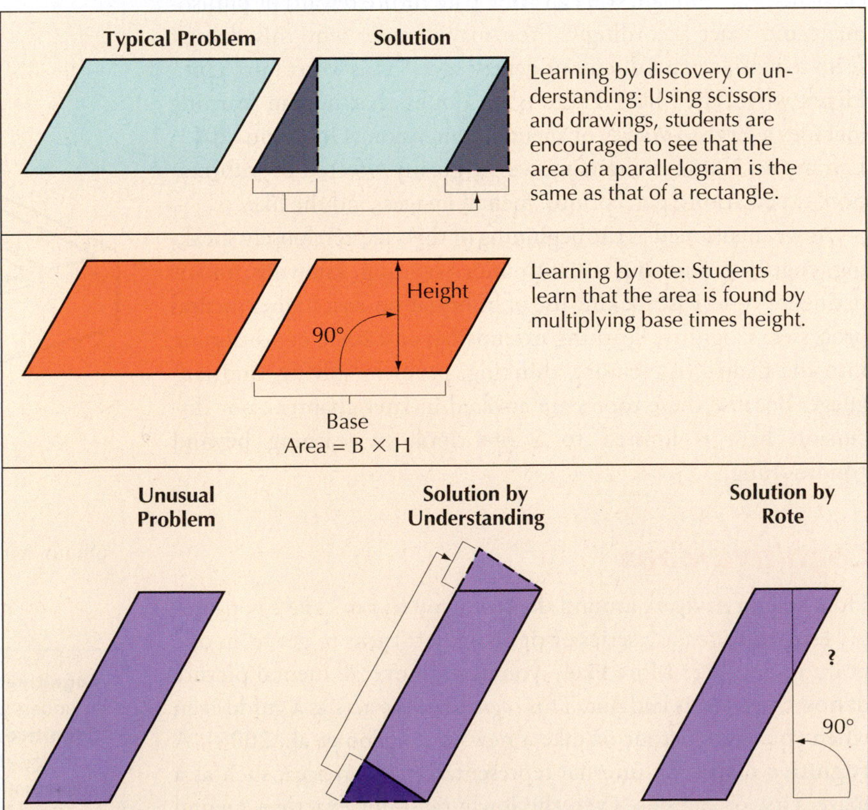

• Figure 6.21 Learning by understanding and by rote. For some types of learning, understanding may be superior, although both types of learning are useful. (After Wertheimer, 1959.)

cover the principles of math, physics, or chemistry. The best teaching strategies are based on *guided discovery*, in which students are given enough freedom to actively think about problems and enough guidance so that they gain useful knowledge (Mayer, 2004, 2011).

Modeling—Do as I Do, Not as I Say

Gateway Question 6.9: *Does learning occur by imitation?*

Many skills are learned by what Albert Bandura (1971) calls *observational learning*, or *modeling*. Watching and imitating the actions of another person or by noting the consequences of the person's actions can lead to **observational learning** (Lefrançois, 2006). We humans share the capacity for observational learning with many mammals, like Larry's gorillas (Meunier, Monfardini, & Boussaoud, 2007; Tennie et al., 2010).

BRIDGES

Learning by imitation is so important to so many mammals that the brain dedicates special neurons to this function. **For more information about mirror neurons, see Chapter 2, pages 67–68.**

The value of learning by observation is obvious: Imagine trying to *tell* someone how to tie a shoe, do a dance step, or play a guitar. Bandura believes that anything that can be learned from direct experience can be learned by observation. Often, this allows a person to skip the tedious trial-and-error stage of learning.

Stone/Getty Images.

Observational learning often imparts large amounts of information that would be difficult to obtain by reading instructions or memorizing rules.

Observational Learning

It seems obvious that we learn by observation, but how does it occur? By observing a **model** (someone who serves as an example), a person may: (1) learn new responses; (2) learn to carry out or avoid previously learned responses (depending on what happens to the model for doing the same thing); or (3) learn a general rule that can be applied to various situations (Lefrançois, 2006).

For observational learning to occur, several things must take place. First, the learner must pay *attention* to the model and *remember* what was done. (A beginning auto mechanic might be interested enough to watch an entire tune-up, but unable to remember all the steps.) Next, the learner must be able to *reproduce* the modeled behavior. (Sometimes this is a matter of practice, but it may be that the learner will never be able to perform the behavior. We may admire the feats of world-class gymnasts, but most of us could never reproduce them, no matter how much we practiced.) If a model is *successful* at a task or *rewarded* for a response, the learner is more likely to imitate the behavior. Finally, once a new response is tried, *normal reinforcement or feedback determines whether it will be repeated thereafter.* (Notice the similarity to latent learning, described earlier.)

Imitating Models

Modeling has a powerful effect on behavior. In a classic experiment, children watched an adult attack a large blow-up "Bo-Bo the Clown" doll. Some children saw an adult sit on the doll, punch it, hit it with a hammer, and kick it around the room. Others saw a movie of these actions. A third group saw a cartoon version of the aggression. Later, the children were frustrated by having some attractive toys taken away from them. Then, they were allowed to play with the Bo-Bo doll. Most imitated the adult's attack (● Figure 6.22). Some even added new aggressive acts of their own! Interestingly, the cartoon was only slightly less effective in encouraging aggression than the live adult model and the filmed model (Bandura, Ross, & Ross, 1963).

Latent learning Learning that occurs without obvious reinforcement and that remains unexpressed until reinforcement is provided.

Rote learning Learning that takes place mechanically, through repetition and memorization, or by learning rules.

Discovery learning Learning based on insight and understanding.

Observational learning Learning achieved by watching and imitating the actions of another or noting the consequences of those actions.

Model A person who serves as an example in observational learning.

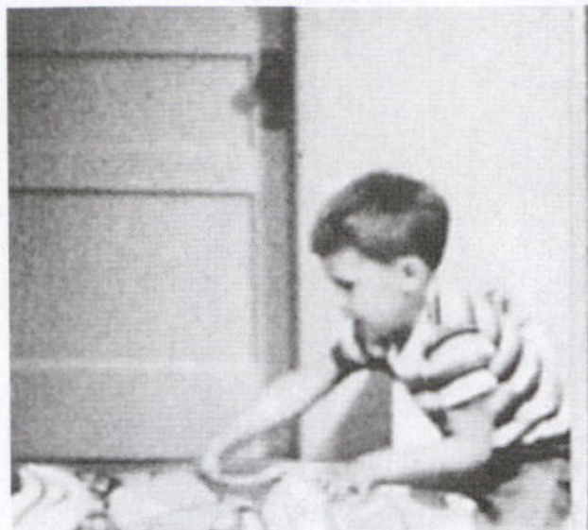

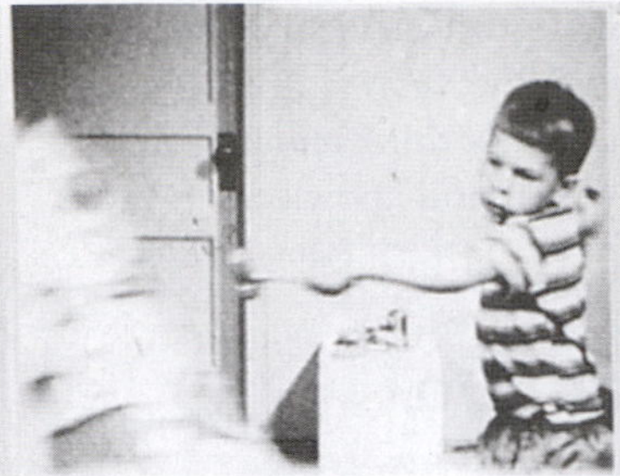
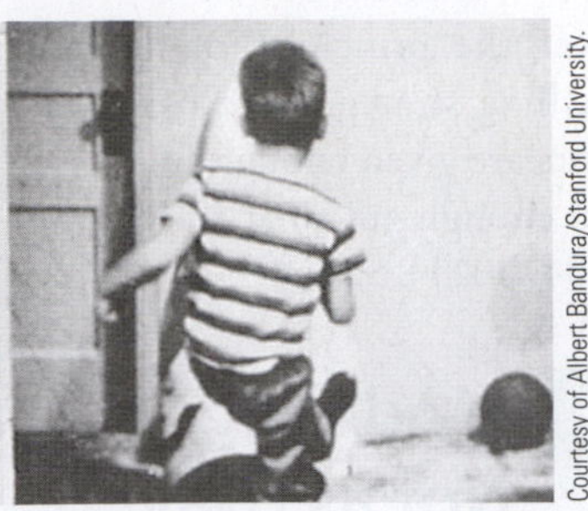

Courtesy of Albert Bandura/Stanford University.

● **Figure 6.22** A nursery school child imitates the aggressive behavior of an adult model he has just seen in a movie.

Then do children blindly imitate adults? No. Remember that observational learning only prepares a person to duplicate a response. Whether it is actually imitated depends on whether the model was rewarded or punished for what was done. Nevertheless, when parents tell a child to do one thing but model a completely different response, children tend to imitate what the parents *do,* and *not* what they *say*. Thus, through modeling, children learn not only attitudes, gestures, emotions, and personality traits, but fears, anxieties, and bad habits as well. A good example is the adolescent smoker, who is much more likely to begin smoking if her parents, siblings, and friends smoke (Wilkinson & Abraham, 2004). More tragically, children who witness domestic violence are more likely to commit it themselves (Murrell, Christoff, & Henning, 2007).

Now, consider a typical situation: Little Raymond has just been interrupted at play by his older brother, Robert. Angry and frustrated, he swats Robert. This behavior interrupts his father Frank's TV watching. Father promptly spanks little Raymond, saying, "This will teach you to hit your big brother." And it will. Because of modeling effects, it is unrealistic to expect a child to "Do as I say, not as I do." The message Frank has given the child is clear: "You have frustrated me; therefore, I will hit you." The next time little Raymond is frustrated, it won't be surprising if he imitates his father and hits his brother (so why does everybody love Raymond, anyway?).

Modeling and the Media

Does television promote observational learning? Today's 8- to 18-year-olds spend over 50 hours a week engaged with various media, including television, video games, movies, the Internet, music, and print (Rideout, Foehr, & Roberts, 2010). Although overall use is falling, television still consumes the lion's share of media attention, averaging 30 hours every week (although an ever increasing proportion of television content is being accessed through the Internet).

By the time the average person has graduated from high school, she or he will have viewed some 15,000 hours of TV, compared with only 11,000 hours spent in the classroom. In that time, viewers will have seen some 18,000 murders and countless acts of robbery, arson, bombing, torture, and beatings. Even G-rated cartoons average 10 minutes of violence per hour (Yokota & Thompson, 2000). In short, typical TV viewers are exposed to a massive dose of media violence, which tends to promote observational learning of aggression.

Televised Aggression

The last finding should come as no surprise. Studies show conclusively that if children watch a great deal of televised violence, they will be more prone to behave aggressively (Anderson et al., 2003; Anderson, Gentile, & Buckley, 2007). In other words, not all children will become more aggressive, but many will. More ominously, the effect can last into early adulthood. A group of primary school students with known television viewing habits were later contacted in early adulthood (Huesmann et al., 2003). Those who watched more violence on television as elementary schoolers were more aggressive as adults 15 years later (● Figure 6.23).

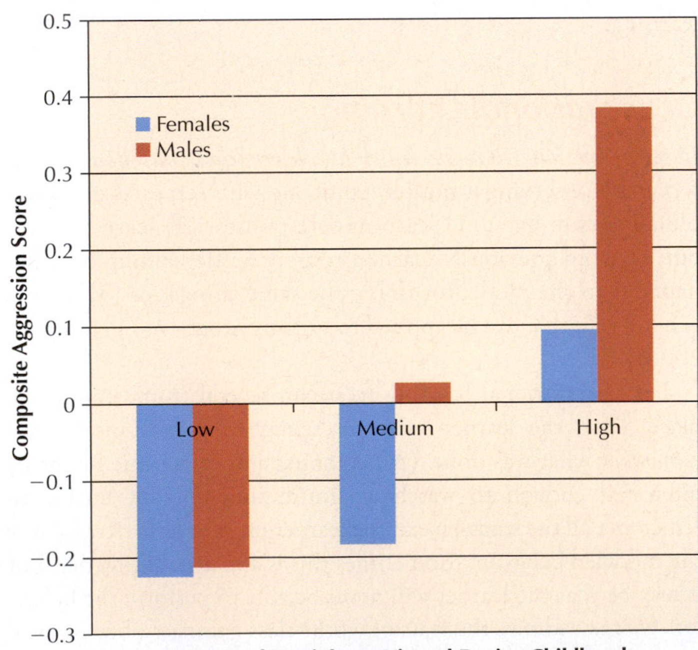

● **Figure 6.23** This graph shows that preschoolers who watched low levels of television violence were less aggressive than average as young adults when contacted 15 years later. In contrast, preschoolers who watched high levels of television violence were more aggressive than average as young adults. The composite aggression score includes measures of indirect aggression (e.g., verbal abusiveness) and direct aggression (physical aggression). (Data adapted from Huesmann et al., 2003.)

Critical Thinking — You Mean Video Games Might Be Bad for Me?

Today's kids can experience more gore in a day than most people used to experience in a lifetime, even during military combat. For example, one video game begins as zombies graphically attack a little girl, turning her into one of them. She viciously attacks her father only to be flung several stories to her death.

What effects do such experiences have on people who play violent video games? Reviews have concluded that violent video games increase aggressive behavior in children and young adults (Anderson, 2004; Krahé & Möller, 2010). As with TV, young children are especially susceptible to fantasy violence in video games (Anderson et al., 2003; Bensley & Van Eenwyk, 2001). In fact, the more personalized, intimate experience of video games may heighten their impact (Fischer, Kastenmüller, & Greitemeyer, 2010).

One classic study illustrates the impact of video game violence. First, college students played a violent *(Mortal Kombat)* or nonviolent *(PGA Tournament Golf)* video game. Next, they competed with another student (actually an actor) in a task that allowed aggression and retaliation to take place. Students who played *Mortal Kombat* were much more likely to aggress, by punishing their competitor (Bartholow & Anderson, 2002). (Don't mess with someone who just played *Mortal Kombat*!)

How does video game violence increase aggressive behavior? One possibility is that repeated exposure to violence desensitizes players, making them less likely to react negatively to violence and, hence, more prone to engage in it (Funk, 2005; Krahé et al., 2011). Another possibility is that by practicing violence against other people, players may learn to be aggressive in real life (Unsworth & Ward, 2001).

BRIDGES

Before you write off video games altogether, read "You Mean Video Games Might Be Good for Me?" in Chapter 9, pages 318–319.

Does the same conclusion apply to video games? Oh, yes. Children tend to imitate what they observe in all media. From professional wrestling (Bernthal, 2003) to rap music (Wingood et al., 2003) to video games (Carnagey & Anderson, 2004), children have plenty of opportunity to observe and imitate both the good and the bad (see "You Mean Video Games Might Be Bad for Me?" for some recent evidence).

Is it fair to say, then, that media violence causes aggression in consumers, especially children? Media violence can make aggression more *likely*, but it does not invariably "cause" it to occur for any given child (Gunter, 2008). Many other factors, such as family conflict, depression, and negative peer influences, also affect the chances that hostile thoughts will be turned into actions (Ferguson, Miguel, & Hartley, 2009). Youngsters who believe that aggression is an acceptable way to solve problems, who believe that media violence is realistic, and who identify with TV characters are most likely to copy media aggression (Huesmann et al., 2003). It is particularly troubling to find media *heroes* behaving aggressively, as well as villains. Younger children, in particular, are more likely to be influenced because they don't fully recognize that media characters and stories are fantasies.

Jon Kopaloff/Getty Images

Media heroes can act as powerful models for observational learning of aggression.

In view of such findings, it is understandable that countries like Canada, Norway, and Switzerland have restricted the amount of permissible violence on television. Should all countries do the same?

A Look Ahead

Conditioning principles are often derived from animal experiments. However, it should be apparent that the same principles apply to human behavior. Perhaps the best way to appreciate this fact is to observe how reinforcement affects your own behavior. With this in mind, the upcoming *Psychology in Action* section proposes a personal experiment in operant conditioning. Don't miss this coming attraction!

Knowledge Builder — Cognitive Learning and Imitation

RECITE

1. An internal representation of spatial relationships is referred to as a ______________ ______________.
2. Learning that suddenly appears when a reward or incentive for performance is given is called
   a. discovery learning *b.* latent learning *c.* rote learning *d.* reminiscence

Continued

3. Psychologists also use the term ____________ to describe observational learning.
4. If a model is successful or rewarded, his or her behavior is
   a. difficult to reproduce *b.* less likely to be attended to *c.* more likely to be imitated *d.* subject to positive transfer
5. Children who observed a live adult behave aggressively became more aggressive; those who observed movie and cartoon aggression did not. T or F?
6. Children are most likely to imitate media characters with whom they identify. T or F?
7. Children who watch a great deal of media violence are more prone to be aggressive, an effect that is best explained by
   a. negative reinforcement *b.* shaping and successive approximations *c.* observational learning *d.* vicarious classical conditioning

REFLECT

Think Critically

8. Draw a map of your school's campus as you picture it now. Draw a map of the campus as you pictured it after your first visit. Why do the maps differ?
9. Children who watch many aggressive programs on television tend to be more aggressive than average. Why doesn't this observation prove that televised aggression *causes* aggressive behavior?

Self-Reflect

Try to think of at least one personal example of each of these concepts: cognitive map, latent learning, discovery learning.

Describe a skill you have learned primarily through observational learning. How did modeling help you learn?

What entertainment or sports personalities did you identify with when you were a child? How did it affect your behavior?

Answers: 1. cognitive map **2.** *b* **3.** modeling **4.** c **5.** F **6.** T **7.** c **8.** Your cognitive map of the campus has undoubtedly become more accurate and intricate over time as you have added details to it. Your drawings should reflect this change. **9.** Because the observation is based on a correlation. Children who are already aggressive may choose to watch more aggressive programs, rather than being made aggressive by them. It took experimental studies to verify that televised aggression promotes aggression by viewers.

Psychology in Action

Behavioral Self-Management—A Rewarding Project

Gateway Question 6.10: *How does conditioning apply to everyday problems?*

Would you like to exercise more, attend more classes, cut down on smoking, concentrate longer, or read more books? This is an invitation to carry out a self-management project of your own. As such, this could be the start of one of the most personal applications of psychology in this book.

Self-Managed Behavior

The principles of operant conditioning can be adapted to manage your own behavior (Miltenberger, 2011; Watson & Tharp, 2007). Here's how:

1. **Choose a target behavior.** Identify the activity you want to change.
2. **Record a baseline.** Record how much time you currently spend performing the target activity or count the number of desired or undesired responses you make each day.
3. **Establish goals.** Remember the principle of shaping and set realistic goals for gradual improvement on each successive week. Also, set daily goals that add up to the weekly goal.
4. **Choose reinforcers.** If you meet your daily goal, what reward will you allow yourself? Daily rewards might be watching television, eating a candy bar, socializing with friends, listening to your iPod, or whatever you enjoy. Also establish a weekly reward. If you reach your weekly goal, what reward will you allow yourself? A movie? A dinner out? Some time playing a game like *Guitar Hero*? A weekend hike?
5. **Record your progress.** Keep accurate records of the amount of time spent each day on the desired activity or the number of times you make the desired response.
6. **Reward successes.** If you meet your daily goal, collect your reward. If you fall short, be honest with yourself and skip the reward. Do the same for your weekly goal.

"RUNNING AWAY FROM YOUR PROBLEMS DOES NOT COUNT AS EXERCISE."

7. **Adjust your plan as you learn more about your behavior.** Overall progress will reinforce your attempts at self-management.

If you have trouble thinking of rewards, remember that anything done often can serve as reinforcement. This is known as the **Premack principle**. It is named after David Premack, a psychologist who popularized its use. For example, if you like to watch television every night and want to study more, make it a rule not to turn on the set until you have studied for an hour (or whatever length of time you choose). Then lengthen the requirement each week. Here is a sample of one student's plan:

1. *Target behavior:* number of hours spent studying.
2. *Recorded baseline:* an average of 25 minutes per day for a weekly total of 3 hours.
3. *Goal for the first week:* an increase in study time to 40 minutes per day; weekly goal of 5 hours total study time. *Goal for second week:* 50 minutes per day and 6 hours per week. *Goal for third week:* 1 hour per day and 7 hours per week. *Ultimate goal:* to reach and maintain 14 hours per week study time.
4. *Daily reward for reaching goal:* 1 hour of guitar playing in the evening; no playing if the goal is not met. *Weekly reward for reaching goal:* going to a movie or buying a DVD.

Self-Recording

Even if you find it difficult to give and withhold rewards, **self-recording** (keeping records of response frequencies, a form of feedback) can make a difference all by itself. This is because we tend to react to being observed, even when we are the ones watching our own behavior. In general, when you systematically (and honestly) observe yourself, you are more likely to engage in desired behaviors and less likely to perform undesired behaviors (Fireman, Kose, & Solomon, 2003; Watson & Tharp, 2007).

Keep track of the number of times that you exercise, arrive late to class, eat vegetables, smoke a cigarette, study, watch TV, drink a cappuccino, swear, or whatever you are interested in changing. A simple tally on a piece of paper will do, or you can get a small mechanical counter like those used to keep golf scores or count calories. Record keeping helps break patterns, and the feedback can be motivating as you begin to make progress.

Good Ways to Break Bad Habits

Are there any extra tips for breaking bad habits? By using the methods, we have discussed, you can *decrease* unwanted behaviors, such as swearing, biting your nails, criticizing others, smoking, drinking coffee, watching TV too much, or engaging in any other behavior you choose to target. However, breaking bad habits may require some additional techniques. Here are four strategies to help you change bad habits.

Alternate Responses

A good strategy for change is to try to get the same reinforcement with a new response.

Example: Marta often tells jokes at the expense of others. Her friends sometimes feel hurt by her sharp-edged humor. Marta senses this and wants to change. What can she do? Usually, Marta's joke telling is reinforced by attention and approval. She could just as easily get the same reinforcement by giving other people praise or compliments. Making a change in her behavior should be easy because she will continue to receive the reinforcement she seeks.

Extinction

Try to discover what is reinforcing an unwanted response and remove, avoid, or delay the reinforcement.

Example: Fatima has developed a habit of taking longer and longer "breaks" to watch TV when she should be studying. Obviously, TV watching is reinforcing her break taking. To improve her study habits, Fatima could delay reinforcement by studying at the library or some other location a good distance from her TV.

Response Chains

Break up response chains that precede an undesired behavior; this will help break the bad habit. The key idea is to scramble the chain of events that leads to an undesired response (Watson & Tharp, 2007).

Example: Most nights Ignacio comes home from work, turns on the TV, and eats a whole bag of cookies or chips. He then takes a shower and changes clothes. By dinnertime he has lost his appetite. Ignacio realizes he is substituting junk food for dinner. Ignacio could solve the problem by breaking the response chain that precedes dinner. For instance, he could shower immediately when he gets home, or avoid turning on the television until after dinner.

Cues and Antecedents

Try to avoid, narrow down, or remove stimuli that elicit the bad habit.

Example: Brent wants to cut down on smoking. He can take many smoking cues out of his surroundings by removing ashtrays, matches, and extra cigarettes from his house, car, and office. Drug cravings are strongly related to cues conditioned to the drug, such as the odor of cigarettes. Brent can narrow antecedent stimuli even more. He could begin by smoking only in the lounge at work, never in his office or in his car. He could then limit his smoking to home. Then to only one room at home. Then to one chair at home. If he succeeds in getting this far, he may want to limit his smoking to only one unpleasant place, such as a bathroom, basement, or garage (Riley et al., 2002).

Contracting

If you try the techniques described here and have difficulty sticking with them, you may want to try behavioral contracting. In a **behavioral contract**, you state a specific problem behavior you want to control, or a goal you want to achieve. Also, state the rewards you will receive, privileges you will forfeit, or punishments you must accept. The contract should be signed by you and a person you trust.

A behavioral contract can be quite motivating, especially when mild punishment is part of the agreement. Here's a classic example reported by Nurnberger and Zimmerman (1970): A student working on his Ph.D. had completed all requirements but his dissertation, yet for 2 years had not written a single page. A contract was drawn up for him in which he agreed to meet weekly deadlines on the number of pages he would complete. To

Premack principle Any high-frequency response can be used to reinforce a low-frequency response.

Self-recording Self-management based on keeping records of response frequencies.

Behavioral contract A formal agreement stating behaviors to be changed and consequences that apply.

make sure he would meet the deadlines, he wrote postdated checks. These were to be forfeited if he failed to reach his goal for the week. The checks were made out to organizations he despised (the Ku Klux Klan and American Nazi Party). From the time he signed the contract until he finished his degree, the student's work output was greatly improved.

Getting Help

Attempting to manage or alter your own behavior may be more difficult than it sounds. If you feel you need more information, consult the books listed below. You will also find helpful advice in the Psychology in Action section of Chapter 15. If you do try a self-modification project but find it impossible to reach your goals, be aware that professional advice is available.

Where to Obtain More Information

Watson, D. L., & Tharp, R. G. (2007). *Self-directed behavior* (9th ed.). Belmont, CA: Wadsworth.

Miltenberger, R. G. (2011). *Behavior modification: Principles and procedures* (5th ed.). Belmont, CA: Cengage Learning/Wadsworth.

Knowledge Builder — Behavioral Self-Management

RECITE

1. After a target behavior has been selected for reinforcement, it's a good idea to record a baseline so that you can set realistic goals for change. T or F?
2. Self-recording, even without the use of extra rewards, can bring about desired changes in target behaviors. T or F?
3. The Premack principle states that behavioral contracting can be used to reinforce changes in behavior. T or F?
4. A self-management plan should make use of the principle of shaping by setting a graduated series of goals. T or F?
5. Eleni ends up playing solitaire on her computer each time she tries to work on a term paper. Eventually she does get to work, but only after a long delay. To break this bad habit Eleni removes the solitaire icon from her computer screen so that she won't see it when she begins work. Eleni has used which strategy for breaking bad habits? *a.* alternative responses *b.* extinction *c.* avoid cues *d.* contracting

REFLECT

Think Critically

6. How does setting daily goals in a behavioral self-management program help maximize the effects of reinforcement?

Self-Reflect

Even if you don't expect to carry out a self-management project right now, outline a plan for changing your own behavior. Be sure to describe the behavior you want to change, set goals, and identify reinforcers.

Answers: 1. T **2.** T **3.** F **4.** T **5.** c **6.** Daily performance goals and rewards reduce the delay of reinforcement, which maximizes its impact.

Chapter in Review — Gateways to Conditioning and Learning

Gateway QUESTIONS REVISITED

6.1 What is learning?

6.1.1 Learning is a relatively permanent change in behavior due to experience.

6.1.2 Associative learning is a simple type of learning that affects many aspects of daily life.

6.1.3 Cognitive learning involves making use of information-rich higher mental processes.

6.1.4 Learning resulting from conditioning depends on reinforcement. Reinforcement increases the probability that a particular response will occur.

6.1.5 Classical (or respondent) conditioning and instrumental (or operant) conditioning are two basic types of associative learning.

6.1.6 In classical conditioning, a neutral stimulus is followed by an unconditioned stimulus. With repeated pairings, the neutral stimulus begins to elicit a response.

6.1.7 In operant conditioning, responses that are followed by reinforcement occur more frequently.

6.2 How does classical conditioning occur?

6.2.1 Classical conditioning, studied by Pavlov, occurs when a neutral stimulus (NS) is associated with an unconditioned stimulus (US).

6.2.2 The US causes a reflex called the unconditioned response (UR). If the NS is consistently paired with the US, it becomes a conditioned stimulus (CS) capable of producing a conditioned (learned) response (CR).

6.2.3 When the conditioned stimulus is followed by the unconditioned stimulus, conditioning is reinforced (strengthened).

6.2.4 Higher order conditioning occurs when a well-learned conditioned stimulus is used as if it were an unconditioned stimulus, bringing about further learning.

6.2.5 From an informational view, conditioning creates expectancies, which alter response patterns. In classical conditioning, the CS creates an expectancy that the US will follow.

6.2.6 When the CS is repeatedly presented alone, conditioning is extinguished (weakened or inhibited). After extinction seems to be complete, a rest period may lead to the temporary reappearance of a conditioned response. This is called spontaneous recovery.

6.2.7 Through stimulus generalization, stimuli similar to the conditioned stimulus will also produce a response. Generalization gives way to stimulus discrimination when an organism learns to respond to one stimulus but not to similar stimuli.

6.3 *Does conditioning affect emotions?*

6.3.1 Conditioning applies to visceral or emotional responses as well as simple reflexes. As a result, conditioned emotional responses (CERs) also occur.

6.3.2 Irrational fears called phobias may begin as CERs. Conditioning of emotional responses can occur vicariously (secondhand) as well as directly.

6.4 *How does operant conditioning occur?*

6.4.1 Operant conditioning occurs when a voluntary action is followed by a reinforcer (which increases the frequency of the response) or a punisher (which decreases the frequency of the response).

6.4.2 Delaying reinforcement greatly reduces its effectiveness, but long chains of responses may be maintained by a single reinforcer.

6.4.3 Superstitious behaviors often become part of response chains because they *appear* to be associated with reinforcement.

6.4.4 By rewarding successive approximations to a particular response, behavior can be shaped into desired patterns.

6.4.5 If an operant response is not reinforced, it may extinguish (disappear). But after extinction seems complete, it may temporarily reappear (spontaneous recovery).

6.4.6 Both positive reinforcement and negative reinforcement increase the likelihood that a response will be repeated. Punishment decreases the likelihood that the response will occur again.

6.5 *Are there different kinds of operant reinforcement?*

6.5.1 Operant learning may be based on primary reinforcers, secondary reinforcers, and feedback.

6.5.2 Primary reinforcers are "natural," physiologically based rewards. Intracranial stimulation of "pleasure centers" in the brain can also serve as a primary reinforcer.

6.5.3 Secondary reinforcers are learned. They typically gain their reinforcing value by direct association with primary reinforcers or because they can be exchanged for primary reinforcers. Tokens and money gain their reinforcing value in this way.

6.5.4 Feedback, or knowledge of results, also aids learning and improves performance. It is most effective when it is immediate, detailed, and frequent.

6.5.5 Programmed instruction breaks learning into a series of small steps and provides immediate feedback. Computer-assisted instruction (CAI) does the same but has the added advantage of providing alternative exercises and information when needed.

6.6 *How are we influenced by patterns of reward?*

6.6.1 Reward or reinforcement may be given continuously (after every response) or on a schedule of partial reinforcement. Partial reinforcement produces greater resistance to extinction.

6.6.2 Five basic schedules of reinforcement are continuous, fixed ratio, variable ratio, fixed interval, and variable interval. Each produces a distinct pattern of responding.

6.6.3 Stimuli that precede a reinforced response tend to control the response on future occasions occur (stimulus control). Two aspects of stimulus control are generalization and discrimination.

6.6.4 In generalization, an operant response tends to occur when stimuli similar to those preceding reinforcement are present.

6.6.5 In discrimination, responses are given in the presence of discriminative stimuli associated with reinforcement and withheld in the presence of stimuli associated with nonreinforcement.

6.7 *What does punishment do to behavior?*

6.7.1 Punishment decreases response frequency.

6.7.2 Punishment occurs when a response is followed by the onset of an aversive event or by the removal of a positive event (response cost).

6.7.3 Punishment is most effective when it is immediate, consistent, and intense.

6.7.4 Although severe punishment can virtually eliminate a particular behavior, mild punishment usually only temporarily suppresses responding. Reinforcement must be used to make lasting changes in the behavior of a person or an animal.

6.7.5 The undesirable side effects of punishment include the conditioning of fear to punishing agents and situations associated with punishment, the learning of escape and avoidance responses, and the encouragement of aggression.

6.8 *What is cognitive learning?*

6.8.1 Cognitive learning involves higher mental processes, such as memory, thinking, problem solving, understanding, knowing, and anticipating.

6.8.2 Even in relatively simple learning situations, animals and people seem to form cognitive maps (internal representations of spatial relationships).

6.8.3 In latent learning, learning remains hidden or unseen until a reward or incentive for performance is offered.

6.8.4 Discovery learning emphasizes insight and understanding, in contrast to rote learning.

6.9 Does learning occur by imitation?

6.9.1 Learning can occur by merely observing and imitating the actions of another person or by noting the consequences of the person's actions.

6.9.2 Observational learning is influenced by the success or failure of the model's behavior. Aggression is readily learned and released by modeling.

6.9.3 Media characters can act as powerful models for observational learning. Media violence increases the likelihood of aggression by viewers.

6.10 How does conditioning apply to everyday problems?

6.10.1 By applying operant conditioning principles, it is possible to change or manage your own behavior.

6.10.2 Four strategies that can help change bad habits are reinforcing alternative responses, promoting extinction, breaking response chains, and avoiding antecedent cues.

6.10.3 When managing behavior, self-reinforcement, self-recording, feedback, and behavioral contracting are all helpful.

MEDIA RESOURCES

Web Resources

Internet addresses frequently change. To find an up-to-date list of URLs for the sites listed here, visit your Psychology CourseMate.

Ivan Pavlov Read a short biography of the man who discovered classical conditioning.

Classical Conditioning Experiment Try this demonstration of classical conditioning.

Conditioned Emotional Responses Read the classic 1920 paper on Little Albert.

B. F. Skinner: An Autobiography Read about the life and work of B. F. Skinner in his own words.

Clicker Training for Animals Read about one approach to using operant conditioning to train animals.

Hardwired for Happiness Are our brains hardwired for happiness?

Schedules of Reinforcement Read more about partial reinforcement schedules.

Stimuli Explore the different functions stimuli can serve.

Positive and Negative Discriminative Stimuli in Animal Training Read about the application of discriminative stimuli in animal training.

Ten Reasons Not to Hit Your Kids Read more about the limitations of spanking.

Guidelines for Using Time Out with Children and Preteens Read about the use of response cost as an effective form of punishment.

Reinforcement vs. Punishment in the Training of Animals Learn why punishment should be avoided in the training of animals.

Social Learning Theory and Criminality Explore the hypothesis that cognitive learning underlies much criminal behavior.

Mirror Neurons and Imitation Learning Read about a possible neural basis for imitation learning.

Media Violence How much do children learn by imitating what they see in the media?

Psychological Self-Tools An online self-help book.

Self-Management Explore some self-management techniques.

Behavior Contract An example of a behavioral contract from a school setting.

Interactive Learning

Log in to **CengageBrain** to access the resources your instructor requires. For this book, you can access:

CourseMate brings course concepts to life with interactive learning, study, and exam preparation tools that support the printed textbook. A textbook-specific website, ***Psychology CourseMate*** includes an ***integrated interactive eBook*** and other ***interactive learning tools*** including quizzes, flashcards, videos, and more.

CENGAGENOW™

CengageNOW is an easy-to-use online resource that helps you study in less time to get the grade you want—NOW. Take a pre-test for this chapter and receive a personalized study plan based on your results that will identify the topics you need to review and direct you to online resources to help you master those topics. Then take a post-test to help you determine the concepts you have mastered and what you will need to work on. If your textbook does not include an access code card, go to CengageBrain.com to gain access.

WebTUTOR™

More than just an interactive study guide, **WebTutor** is an anytime, anywhere customized learning solution with an eBook, keeping you connected to your textbook, instructor, and classmates.

If your professor has assigned **Aplia** homework:

1. Sign in to your account.
2. Complete the corresponding homework exercises as required by your professor.
3. When finished, click "Grade It Now" to see which areas you have mastered and which need more work, and for detailed explanations of every answer.

Visit www.cengagebrain.com to access your account and purchase materials.

Gateway THEME
Memory is not like a tape recorder or a video camera: Memories change as they are stored and retrieved.

7

Memory

Fuhgeddaboudit

That advice, offered New York City style, may not seem helpful at exam time. After all, the less you forget, the better, right?

Not always. Consider what Jill Price thinks about her "perfect" memory: "My memory has ruled my life.... Whenever I see a date flash on the television (or anywhere else for that matter) I automatically go back to that day and remember where I was, what I was doing, what day it fell on and on and on and on and on. It is nonstop, uncontrollable, and totally exhausting.... Most have called it a gift, but I call it a burden. I run my entire life through my head every day and it drives me crazy!!!" (Parker, Cahill, & McGaugh, 2006; Price & Davis, 2009).

Another person with an amazing memory, known as Mr. S., even made a living as a professional memorizer, or *mnemonist* (Luria, 1968). He regularly wowed audiences with his ability to memorize, with equal ease, long strings of digits, meaningless consonants, mathematical formulas, and poems in foreign languages. Don't be too quick to envy Mr. S.'s abilities either. He remembered so much that he couldn't separate important facts from trivia or facts from fantasy. His memory was so powerful that he had to devise ways to *forget*—such as writing information on a piece of paper and then burning it.

On the one hand, most people would be quite upset if they found they could no longer, for example, remember their mother. On the other hand, consider the woman pictured here. Although she lost her mother to cancer five years ago, she has been unable to "let go" and move on with her life. In a very real sense, who we are is determined by what we remember *and* what we forget. As you read this chapter on memory and forgetting, you'll almost certainly discover ways to improve your memory.

Gateway QUESTIONS

7.1 *How does memory work?*
7.2 *What are the features of short-term memory?*
7.3 *What are the features of long-term memory?*
7.4 *How is memory measured?*
7.5 *Why do we forget?*
7.6 *How does the brain form and store memories?*
7.7 *What are "photographic" memories?*
7.8 *How can I improve my memory?*
7.9 *Are there any tricks to help me with my memory?*

Stages of Memory—Do You Have a Mind Like a Steel Trap? Or a Sieve?

Gateway Question 7.1: *How does memory work?*

Do you remember what you had for breakfast this morning? Or any of what happened last month? The last friend you texted? Of course you do. But how is it possible for us to so easily travel back in time? Let's begin with a look at some basic memory concepts. An interesting series of events must occur before we can say "I remember."

Many people think of memory as "a dusty storehouse of facts." In reality, human **memory** is an active system that receives, stores, organizes, alters, and recovers information (Baddeley, Eysenck, & Anderson, 2009). To be stored for a long time (like, say, between when you study and when you need to remember for an exam), information must pass through sensory memory, short-term memory, and long-term memory. These stages are summarized by the Atkinson-Schiffrin model of memory shown in ● Figure 7.1 (Atkinson & Schiffrin, 1968; Atkinson & Schiffrin, 1968).

In some general ways, *each* of these three memory systems acts like a computer. Incoming information is first **encoded**, or changed into a usable form. This step is like entering data into a computer. Next, information is **stored**, or held, in the memory system. Finally, information must be **retrieved**, or taken out of storage, to be useful. If you're going to remember all of the 9,856 new terms on your next psychology exam, you must successfully encode them in sensory memory, move them through short-term memory, and eventually retrieve them from long-term memory. Let's trace the interesting series of memory events that must occur before you can pass that exam.

Sensory Memory

Let's say you sit down to memorize a few terms from this textbook for your exam next month. How will you remember them? Information is first encoded in **sensory memory**, which can hold an exact copy of what you see or hear, for a few seconds or less. We are normally unaware of the functioning of our sensory memories, which hold information just long enough for it to be retrieved and encoded into short-term memory (Radvansky, 2011).

For instance, look at a definition in this book and then quickly close your eyes. If you are lucky, a fleeting visual image of the letters will persist. **Iconic** (eye-KON-ick) **memories** (visual sensory images) are typically stored for about a half second (Keysers et al., 2005). Similarly, when you hear information, sensory memory stores it as an *echoic memory* for up to 2 seconds (Haenschel et al., 2005). An **echoic memory** is a brief flurry of activity in the auditory system.

If you are *selectively attending* (focusing on a selected portion of sensory input) to the terms you are trying to study, they will most likely be automatically retrieved from sensory memory and encoded in short-term memory. Background events, such as the voice on the radio saying, "Try Drizzle Diapers today," will not. However, also as shown in ● Figure 7.1, if you are just looking at the words on the page but not paying attention (maybe you are too busy listening to the radio), that does not bode well for your exam. (As your elementary teacher might have commented, reading is more than just passing your eyes over the page.)

Short-Term Memory

Even though you might normally be unaware of your sensory memory, you cannot fail to be aware of your short-term memory. Carefully read the definition contained in the next two sentences. **Short-term memory (STM)** stores small amounts of information. We are consciously aware of short-term memories for a dozen seconds or so (Jonides et al., 2008). That's right, what you're aware of right now *is* in your short-term memory. So, as you encode information in short-term memory, you become consciously aware of it.

How are short-term memories encoded? Short-term memories can be encoded as images. But more often they are encoded *phonetically* (by sound), especially when it comes to words and letters (Page et al., 2007). If you are introduced to Tim at a party and you forget his name, you are more likely to call him by a name that sounds like Tim (Jim, Kim, or Slim, for instance), rather than a name that sounds different, such as Bob or Mike. If a friend inter-

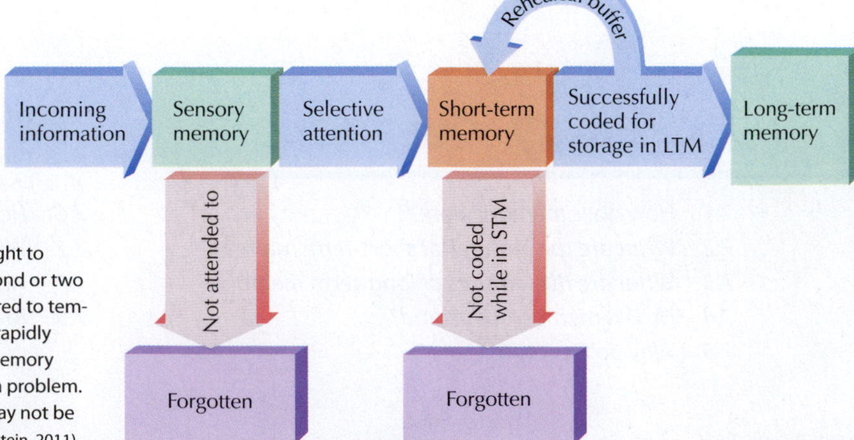

● **Figure 7.1** The Atkinson-Schiffrin model. Remembering is thought to involve at least three steps. Incoming information is first held for a second or two by sensory memory. Information selected by attention is then transferred to temporary storage in short-term memory (STM). If new information is not rapidly encoded, or rehearsed, it is forgotten. If it is transferred to long-term memory (LTM), it becomes relatively permanent, although retrieving it may be a problem. The preceding is a useful, but highly simplified, *model* of memory; it may not be literally true of what happens in the brain (Atkinson & Schiffrin, 1968; Goldstein, 2011).

rupts to ask what you are studying, you may be lucky if you don't say "axon potential" instead of "action potential," or "depression" instead of "repression"!

One nice feature of short-term memory is that it prevents our minds from more permanently storing useless names, dates, telephone numbers, and other trivia. Supposed you use STM to dial a phone number or briefly remember a shopping list. Notice that unless you *rehearse* information (silently say it over and over to yourself), it is quickly "dumped" from STM and forever lost (● Figure 7.1). Unfortunately, as you may have noticed when dialing a telephone, STM is very sensitive to *interruption*, or *interference*. You've probably had something like this happen: Someone leaves a phone number on your answering machine. You repeat the number to yourself as you start to dial. Someone asks you a question. You answer, turn to the phone, and find that you have forgotten the number. Notice again that STM can handle only small amounts of information. It is very difficult to do more than one task at a time in STM (Mercer & McKeown, 2010; Oberauer & Göthe, 2006).

Working Memory

Short-term memory is often used for more than just storing information. When STM is combined with other mental processes, it acts more like a sort of "mental scratchpad," or **working memory**, in which we do much of our thinking (Chein & Fiez, 2010). That is, working memory briefly holds the information we need when we are thinking and solving problems (Holmes & Adams, 2006). Whenever you read a book, do mental arithmetic, put together a puzzle, plan a meal, or follow directions, you are using working memory (Baddeley, 2003; Prime & Jolicoeur, 2010).

Long-Term Memory

If STM is so limited, how do we remember for longer periods? Information that is important or meaningful is retrieved from STM and encoded in **long-term memory (LTM)**, which acts as a lasting storehouse for knowledge. LTM contains everything you know about the world—from aardvark to zebra, math to *Glee*, facts to fantasy. Yet, there appears to be no danger of running out of room. LTM can store nearly limitless amounts of information. In fact, the more you know, the easier it becomes to add new information to memory. This is the reverse of what we would expect if LTM could be "filled up" (Goldstein, 2011). It is also one of many reasons for getting an education.

Are long-term memories also encoded as sounds? They can be. But typically, long-term memories are encoded on the basis of *meaning*, not sound. If you make an error in LTM, it will probably be related to meaning. For example, if you are trying to recall the phrase *test anxiety* for your psychology exam, you are more likely to mistakenly write down *test nervousness* or *test worry* than *text anxiety* or *tent anxiety*.

Back to your exam. If you can link information currently in STM to knowledge already stored in LTM, it gains meaning. This makes it easier to encode in LTM and, hence, remember. If you can relate the definition of *test anxiety* to a memory of a time when you or a friend were nervous about taking a test, you are more likely to remember the definition. As another example, try to memorize this story:

> With hocked gems financing him, our hero bravely defied all scornful laughter. "Your eyes deceive," he had said. "An egg, not a table, correctly typifies this unexplored planet." Now, three sturdy sisters sought proof. Forging along, days became weeks as many doubters spread fearful rumors about the edge. At last from nowhere welcome winged creatures appeared, signifying momentous success. (Adapted from Dooling & Lachman, 1971.)

This odd story emphasizes the impact that meaning has on memory. People given the title of the story were able to remember it far better than those not given a title. See if the title helps you as much as it did them: "Columbus Discovers America."

The Relationship Between STM and LTM

Although sensory memory is involved every time we store information, we are most likely to notice STM and LTM. To summarize their connection, picture short-term memory as a small desk at the front of a huge warehouse full of filing cabinets (LTM). As information enters the warehouse, it is first placed on the desk. Because the desk is small, it must be quickly cleared off to make room for new information. Unimportant items are simply tossed away. Meaningful or personally important information is placed in the files (LTM). (See "Horses, Memories, and Culture.") When we want to use knowledge from LTM to answer a question, the information is returned to STM. Or, in our analogy, a folder is taken out of the files (LTM) and moved to the desk (STM), where it can be used.

Now that you have a general picture of memory, it is time to explore STM and LTM in more detail. But first, here's a chance to rehearse what you've learned.

Memory The mental system for receiving, encoding, storing, organizing, altering, and retrieving information.

Encoding Converting information into a form in which it will be retained in memory.

Storage Holding information in memory for later use.

Retrieval Recovering information from storage in memory.

Sensory memory The first, normally unconscious, stage of memory, which holds an exact record of incoming information for a few seconds or less.

Iconic memory A mental image or visual representation.

Echoic memory A brief continuation of sensory activity in the auditory system after a sound is heard.

Short-term memory (STM) The memory system used to hold small amounts of information in our conscious awareness for about a dozen seconds.

Working memory Another name for short-term memory, especially as it is used for thinking and problem solving.

Long-term memory (LTM) The memory system used for relatively permanent storage of meaningful information.

Human Diversity — Horses, Memories, and Culture

If you were on a ranch and saw 20 horses walk by, do you think you could remember the age, color, gender, and condition of all of them? Unless you are a rancher, doing so would be quite a feat of memory. However, for a gaucho, a cowboy from South America, it would be easier. As noted, we are most likely to remember information that is personally important or meaningful. Horses are very important in gaucho subculture; a gaucho's self-respect is measured by his horsemanship. Thus, a gaucho is prepared to encode and store information about horses and riding that would be difficult to remember for most other people.

Culture affects our memories in other interesting ways (Ross & Wang, 2010). For example, American culture emphasizes individuals, whereas Chinese culture emphasizes membership in groups. In one study, European-American and Chinese adults were asked to recall 20 memories from any time in their lives. As expected, American memories tended to be self-centered: Most people remembered surprising events and what they did during the events. Chinese adults, in contrast, remembered important social or historical events and their own interactions with family members, friends, and others (Wang & Conway, 2004). Thus, in the United States, personal memories tend to be about "me"; in China they tend to be about "us."

Knowledge Builder — Memory Systems

RECITE

Match: **A.** Sensory memory **B.** STM **C.** LTM

1. _____ Information tends to be stored phonetically
2. _____ Holds information for a few seconds or less
3. _____ Stores an iconic memory or echoic memory
4. _____ Permanent, unlimited capacity
5. _____ Temporarily holds small amounts of information
6. _____ Selective attention determines its contents
7. STM is improved by interruption, or interference, because attention is more focused at such times. T or F?

REFLECT

Think Critically

8. Why is sensory memory important to filmmakers?

Self-Reflect

Wave a pencil back and forth in front of your eyes while focusing on something in the distance. The pencil's image looks transparent. Why? (Because sensory memory briefly holds an image of the pencil. This image persists after the pencil passes by.)

Think of a time today when you used short-term memory (such as briefly remembering a phone number, a URL, or someone's name). How long did you retain the information? How did you encode it? How much do you remember now?

How is long-term memory helping you read this sentence? If the words weren't already stored in LTM, could you read at all? How else have you used LTM today?

Answers: 1. B **2.** A **3.** A **4.** C **5.** B **6.** B **7.** F **8.** Without sensory memory, a movie would look like a series of still pictures. The split-second persistence of visual images helps blend one motion-picture frame into the next.

Short-Term Memory—Do You Know the Magic Number?

Gateway Question 7.2: *What are the features of short-term memory?*

To make good use of your memory, it is valuable to know more about the quirks and characteristics of both STM and LTM. Let's dig deeper into their inner workings.

How much information can be held in short-term memory? For an answer, read the following numbers once. Then close the book and write as many as you can in the correct order.

8 5 1 7 4 9 3

This is called a digit-span test. It is a measure of attention and short-term memory. If you were able to correctly repeat seven digits, you have an average short-term memory. Now try to memorize the following list, again reading it only once.

7 1 8 3 5 4 2 9 1 6 3 4

This series was probably beyond your short-term memory capacity. Psychologist George Miller found that short-term memory is limited to the "magic number" seven (plus or minus two) **information bits** (Miller, 1956). A bit is a single meaningful "piece" of information, such as a digit. It is as if short-term memory has seven "slots" or "bins" into which separate items can be placed. Actually, a few people can remember up to nine bits, and for some types of information five bits is the limit. Thus, an *average* of seven information bits can be stored in short-term memory (Radvansky, 2011).

When all of the "slots" in STM are filled, there is no room for new information. Picture how this works at a party: Let's say your hostess begins introducing everyone who is there, "Chun, Dasia, Sandra, Roseanna, Cholik, Shawn, Kyrene ..." "Stop," you think to yourself. But she continues, "Nelia, Jay, Frank, Patty, Amit, Ricky." The hostess leaves, satisfied that you have met everyone. And you spend the evening talking with Chun, Dasia, and Ricky, the only people whose names you remember!

Chunking

Before we continue, try your short-term memory again, this time on letters. Read the following letters once, then look away and try to write them in the proper order.

T V I B M U S N Y M C A

Notice that there are 12 letters, or "bits" of information. If you studied the letters one at a time, this should be beyond the 7-item limit of STM. However, you may have noticed that some of the letters can be grouped, or *chunked*, together. For example, you may have noticed that NY is the abbreviation for New York. If so, the two bits N and Y became one chunk. **Information chunks** are made up of bits of information grouped into larger units.

Does chunking make a difference? Yes. Chunking **recodes** (reorganizes) information into units that are already in LTM. In a classic experiment that used lists like this one, people remembered best when the letters were read as familiar meaningful chunks: TV, IBM, USN, YMCA (Bower & Springston, 1970). If you recoded the letters this way, you organized them into four *chunks* of information and probably remembered the entire list. If you didn't, go back and try it again; you'll notice a big difference.

Chunking suggests that STM holds about five to seven of whatever units we are using. A single chunk could be made up of numbers, letters, words, phrases, or familiar sentences. Picture STM as a small desk again. Through chunking, we combine several items into one "stack" of information. This allows us to place seven stacks on the desk, whereas before there was only room for seven separate items. While you are studying, try to find ways to link two, three, or more separate facts or ideas into larger chunks, and your short-term memory will improve. In fact, some psychologists believe that STM may actually hold only four items, unless some chunking has occurred (Cowan, 2005; Jonides et al., 2008). The clear message is that creating information chunks is the key to making good use of your short-term memory (Gilchrist, Cowan, & Naveh-Benjamin, 2009; Gobet, 2005). Remember, good memory results from finding or creating meaningful chunks in what you study. When meaningful organizations are elusive, even artificial ones (mnemonics—see the *Psychology in Action* section) are better than none at all.

Rehearsing Information

How long are short-term memories stored? They disappear very rapidly. However, you can prolong a memory by silently repeating it, a process called **maintenance rehearsal.** In a sense, rehearsing information allows you to "hear" it many times, not just once (Nairne, 2002). You have probably used maintenance rehearsal to keep a phone number active in your mind while looking at your cell phone and dialing it.

Isn't saying stuff to yourself over and over also a way of studying? It *is* true that the more times a short-term memory is rehearsed, the greater its chances of being stored in LTM (Goldstein, 2011). This is **rote rehearsal** or **rote learning** (learning by simple repetition). But rote learning is not a very effective way to study.

Elaborative processing, which makes information more meaningful, is a far better way to form lasting memories. When encoding information for the first time, it is best to elaborate on links between that information and memories that are already in LTM. When you are studying, you will remember more if you elaborate on the meaning of the information. As you read, try to reflect frequently. Ask yourself "why" questions, such as, "Why would that be true?" (Toyota & Kikuchi, 2005; Willoughby et al., 1997). Also, try to relate new ideas to your own experiences and knowledge (Hartlep & Forsyth, 2000).

BRIDGES

If you recognize this advice from *The Psychology of Studying—Reflective Learning* at the front of this book, good for you! If not, consider reading about reflective learning if only to elaborate on your processing of the idea of elaborative processing.

What if rehearsal is prevented, so a memory cannot be recycled or moved to LTM? Without maintenance rehearsal, STM storage is quite brief. In one experiment, subjects heard meaningless syllables like "kxw," followed by a number like 67. As soon as subjects heard the number, they began counting backward by threes (to prevent them from repeating the syllable). After a delay of between 12 and 18 seconds, their memory for the syllables fell to zero (Peterson & Peterson, 1959).

After *12 to 18 seconds* without rehearsal, the short-term memories were gone forever! Part of this rapid loss can be explained by the testing procedures used (Goldstein, 2011). In daily life, short-term memories usually last longer. Just the same, if you are introduced to someone, and the name slips out of STM, it is gone forever. To escape this awkward situation, you might try saying something like, "I'm curious, how do you spell your name?" Unfortunately, the response is often an icy reply

Information bits Meaningful units of information, such as numbers, letters, words, or phrases.

Information chunks Information bits grouped into larger units.

Recoding Reorganizing or modifying information to assist storage in memory.

Maintenance rehearsal Silently repeating or mentally reviewing information to hold it in short-term memory.

Rote rehearsal (rote learning) Learning by simple repetition.

Elaborative processing Making memories more meaningful through processing that encodes links between new information and existing memories and knowledge, either at the time of the original encoding or on subsequent retrievals.

like, "M-A-R-Y J-O-N-E-S, it's really not too difficult." To avoid embarrassment, pay careful attention to the name, repeat it to yourself several times, and try to use it in the next sentence or two—before you lose it (Radvansky, 2011).

Long-Term Memory—A Blast from the Past

Gateway Question 7.3: *What are the features of long-term memory?*

An electrode touched the patient's brain. Immediately she said, "Yes, sir, I think I heard a mother calling her little boy somewhere. It seemed to be something happening years ago. It was somebody in the neighborhood in which I live." A short time later the electrode was applied to the same spot. Again the patient said, "Yes, I hear the same familiar sounds. It seems to be a woman calling, the same lady" (Penfield, 1958). A woman made these statements while she was undergoing brain surgery. There are no pain receptors in the brain, so the patient was awake as her brain was electrically stimulated (• Figure 7.2). When activated, some brain areas seemed to produce vivid memories of long-forgotten events.

Permanence

Are all our experiences permanently recorded in memory? Results like those described led neurosurgeon Wilder Penfield to propose that the brain records the past like a "strip of movie film, complete with sound track" (Penfield, 1957). But as you already know, this is an exaggeration, since many events never get past sensory or short-term memory. Also, brain stimulation produces memory-like experiences in only about 3 percent of cases. Most reports resemble dreams more than memories, and many are clearly imaginary. Memory experts now believe that, except for a few rare individuals like Jill Price and Mr. S., who we met at the beginning of this chapter (remember?), long-term memories are only relatively permanent (Goldstein, 2011; Parker, Cahill, & McGaugh, 2006; Price & Davis, 2009).

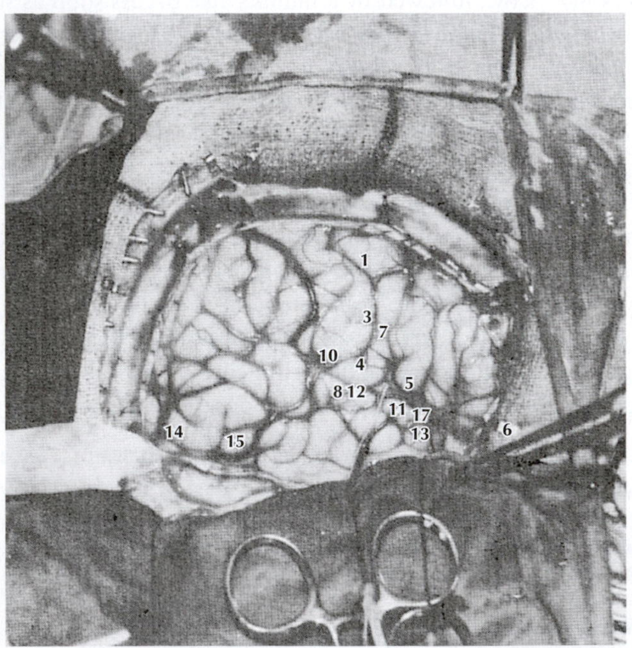

• Figure 7.2 Exposed cerebral cortex of a patient undergoing brain surgery. Numbers represent points that reportedly produced "memories" when electrically stimulated. A critical evaluation of such reports suggests that they are more like dreams than memories. This fact raises questions about claims that long-term memories are permanent. (From Penfield, 1958. Courtesy of the author and Charles C Thomas, Publisher, Springfield, Illinois.)

Try It Yourself: How's Your Memory?

To better appreciate the next topic, pause for a moment and read the words you see here. Read through the list once. Then continue reading the next section of this chapter.

bed dream blanket doze pillow nap
snore mattress alarm clock rest slumber
nod sheet bunk cot cradle groggy

Elaborating False Memories

There's another reason for doubting that all our experiences are permanently recorded. Through elaborative processing, as new long-term memories are stored, older memories are often updated, changed, lost, or *revised* (Baddeley, Eysenck, & Anderson, 2009). To illustrate this point, Elizabeth Loftus and John Palmer (1974) showed people a filmed automobile accident. Afterward, some participants were asked to estimate how fast the cars were going when they "smashed" into one another. For others the words "bumped," "contacted," or "hit" replaced "smashed." One week later, each person was asked, "Did you see any broken glass?" Those asked earlier about the cars that "smashed" into one another were more likely to say yes, even though no broken glass was shown in the film. The new information ("smashed") was included in memories and revised them, producing a **false memory.**

Try It Yourself: Old or New?

Now, without looking back to the list of words you read a few minutes ago, see if you can tell which of the following are "old" words (items from the list you read) and which are "new" words (items that weren't on the list). Mark each of the following words as old or new:

sofa sleep lamp kitchen

Gaps in memory, which are common, may be filled in by logic, guessing, or new information (Schacter, Norman, & Koutstaal, 1998). Although elaboration is helpful when you're making meaningful connections between new information and what you already know, it can also lead to false memories. Indeed, it is possible to have "memories" for things that never happened (such as remembering broken glass at an accident when there was none) (Loftus, 2003; Weinstein & Shanks, 2010). In one study, people who had visited a Disney resort were shown several fake ads for Disney that featured Bugs Bunny. Later, about 16 percent of the people who saw these fake ads claimed that they had met Bugs at Disneyland. This is impossible, of course, because Bugs Bunny is a Warner Brothers character that would never be found at Disneyland

Critical Thinking: Do You Like Jam with Your Memory?

Have you ever wondered why well-known companies that already sell huge quantities of familiar products (such as soft drinks or beer) continue to advertise as heavily as they do? If you believe that the point of the advertising is to familiarize people with a product or to inform them about it, this *is* a mystery. But if you think about the elaborative nature of memory, the mystery is solved. According to economist Jesse Shapiro (2006), the intent of much advertising is to "jam" your memory with positive impressions of a product.

How does "memory jamming" work? How many times have you had a bottle or can of your favorite beer or soft drink? And how many commercials for those beverages have you watched? Every extra commercial adds one more positive memory of the beverage to your long-term memory. Here's a typical commercial: Boy goes to cool party, sees a hot girl, flashes favorite beer, gets the girl. (Yes, beer commercials mainly target young men.) Because we cannot always easily tell which recollection is fact and which is fiction, storing enough of these commercials can eventually create "memories" that never happened. For example, you might remember that you enjoy drinking a particular beverage more than you actually do in reality.

According to Shapiro (2006), the more positive fictional commercials we see, the less likely we are to remember an actual negative experience with a product. In effect, the positive, fictional memories "jam," or block, our ability to remember actual negative memories when deciding whether to buy a product. Kathryn Braun-LaTour and Michael LaTour (2004) add that long-term advertising campaigns create a "brand" memory that can be remarkably strong. This appears to be especially true when the ads are first viewed in early childhood. So perhaps you have been having jam with your memories ever since you were a baby.

(Braun, Ellis, & Loftus, 2002). In another study, even people who were exposed to repeated warnings about a product nevertheless ended up with a more favorable impression of the product (Skurnik et al., 2005).

So elaborative processing could be used to deliberately manipulate memory? Bingo. According to one theory, advertisers do it all the time (see "Do You Like Jam with Your Memory?" for more information).

Try It Yourself: And Now, the Results

Return now and look at the labels you wrote on the "old or new" word list. Contrary to what you may think you "remembered," all of the listed words are "new." None was on the original list!

Stockbyte/Getty Images

Eyewitness memories are notoriously inaccurate. By the time witnesses are asked to testify in court, information they learned after an incident may blend into their original memories.

If you thought you "remembered" that "sleep" was on the original list, you had a false memory. The word *sleep* is associated with most of the words on the original list, which creates a strong impression that you saw it before (Roediger & McDermott, 1995).

As the preceding examples show, thoughts, inferences, and mental associations may be mistaken for true memories (Loftus, 2003). People in Elizabeth Loftus's experiments who had false memories were often quite upset to learn they had given false "testimony" (Loftus & Ketcham, 1994; Loftus & Bernstein, 2005).

False memories are a common problem in police work. For example, a witness may select a photo of a suspect from police files or see a photo in the news. Later, the witness identifies the suspect in a lineup or in court. Did the witness really remember the suspect from the scene of the crime? Or was it from the more recently seen photograph?

Does new information "overwrite" existing memories? No, the real problem is that elaborative processing makes us vulnerable to **source confusion**, which occurs when the origins of a memory are misremembered. (Simons et al., 2004; Woroch & Gonsalves, 2010). This can, for example, lead witnesses to "remember" a face that they actually saw somewhere other than the crime scene (Ruva, McEvoy, & Bryant, 2007). Many tragic cases of mistaken identity occur this way. One famous example involved memory expert Donald Thomson. After appearing live on Australian television, he was accused of rape. It turns out that the victim was watching him on television when the actual rapist broke into her apartment (Schacter, 1996). She correctly remembered his face but attributed it to the wrong *source.*

• **False memory** A memory that can seem accurate but is not.
Source confusion (in memory) Occurs when the origins of a memory are misremembered.

Critical Thinking: Telling Wrong from Right in Forensic Memory

Imagine you are a forensic psychologist, investigating a crime. Unfortunately, your witness can't remember much of what happened. As a "memory detective," what can you do to help?

Could hypnosis improve the witness's memory? It might seem so. In one case in California, 26 children were abducted from a school bus and held captive for ransom. Under hypnosis, the bus driver recalled the license plate number of the kidnappers' van. This memory helped break the case. Such successes seem to imply that hypnosis can improve memory. But does it?

Research has shown that hypnosis increases false memories more than it does true ones. Eighty percent of the new memories produced by hypnotized subjects in one classic experiment were *incorrect* (Dywan & Bowers, 1983). This is in part because a hypnotized person is more likely than normal to use imagination to fill in gaps in memory. Also, if a questioner asks misleading or suggestive questions, hypnotized persons tend to weave the information into their memories (Scoboria et al., 2002). To make matters worse, even when a memory is completely false, the hypnotized person's confidence in it can be unshakable (Burgess & Kirsch, 1999). Thus, hypnosis sometimes uncovers more information, as it did with the bus driver (Schreiber & Schreiber, 1999). However, in the absence of corroborating evidence, there is no sure way to tell which of these memories are false and which are true (Newman & Thompson, 2001).

Is there a better way to improve eyewitness memory? To help police detectives, R. Edward Geiselman and Ron Fisher created the **cognitive interview**, a technique for jogging the memory of eyewitnesses (Fisher & Geiselman, 1987). The key to this approach is recreating the crime scene. Witnesses revisit the scene in their imaginations or in person. That way, aspects of the crime scene, such as sounds, smells, and objects, provide helpful retrieval cues (stimuli associated with a memory). Back in the context of the crime, the witness is encouraged to recall events in different orders and from different viewpoints. Every new memory, no matter how trivial it may seem, can serve as a cue to trigger the retrieval of yet more memories. (Later in this chapter, we will see why such cues are so effective for jogging memories.)

When used properly, the cognitive interview produces 35 percent more correct information than standard questioning (Davis, McMahon, & Greenwood, 2005; Geiselman et al., 1986). This improvement comes without adding to the number of false memories elicited, as occurs with hypnosis (Centofanti & Reece, 2006). The result is a procedure that is more effective in actual police work and in different cultures (Memon, Meissner, & Fraser, 2010; Stein & Memon, 2006).

Is there any way to avoid such problems? Forensic psychologists have tried a variety of techniques to help improve the memory of witnesses. "Telling Wrong from Right in Forensic Memory" examines research on this important question.

To summarize, forming and using long-term memories is an active, creative, highly personal process. Our memories are colored by emotions, judgments, and quirks of personality. If you and a friend were joined at the hip and you went through life side-by-side, you would still have different memories. What we remember depends on what we pay attention to, what we regard as meaningful or important, how we elaborate our memory, and what we feel strongly about.

Organizing Memories

Long-term memory stores huge amounts of information during a lifetime. How are we able to quickly find specific memories? The answer is that each person's "memory index" is highly organized.

Does that mean that information is arranged alphabetically, as in a dictionary? Not a chance! If we ask you to name a black and white animal that lives on ice, is related to a chicken, and cannot fly, you don't have to go from aardvark to zebra to find the answer. You will probably think of only black-and-white birds living in the Antarctic. *Voilá*—the answer is a penguin.

Information in LTM may be arranged according to rules, images, categories, symbols, similarity, formal meaning, or personal meaning (Baddeley, Eysenck, & Anderson, 2009). Psychologists have begun to develop a picture of the *structure*, or organization, of memories. *Memory structure* refers to the pattern of associations among items of information. For example, assume that you are given two statements, to which you must answer yes or no: (1) *A canary is an animal.* (2) *A canary is a bird.* Which do you answer more quickly? Most people can say that *A canary is a bird* faster than they can recognize that *A canary is an animal* (Collins & Quillian, 1969).

Why should this be so? Psychologists believe that a **network model** of memory explains why. According to this view, LTM is organized as a network of linked ideas (● Figure 7.3). When ideas are "farther" apart, it takes a longer chain of associations to connect them. The more two items are separated, the longer it takes to answer. In terms of information links, *canary* is probably "close" to *bird* in your "memory files." *Animal* and *canary* are farther apart. Remember though, this has nothing to do with alphabetical order. We are talking about a system of linked meanings.

Redintegration

Networks of associated memories may also help explain a common experience: Imagine finding a picture taken on your sixth birthday or at your high school graduation. As you look at the photo, one

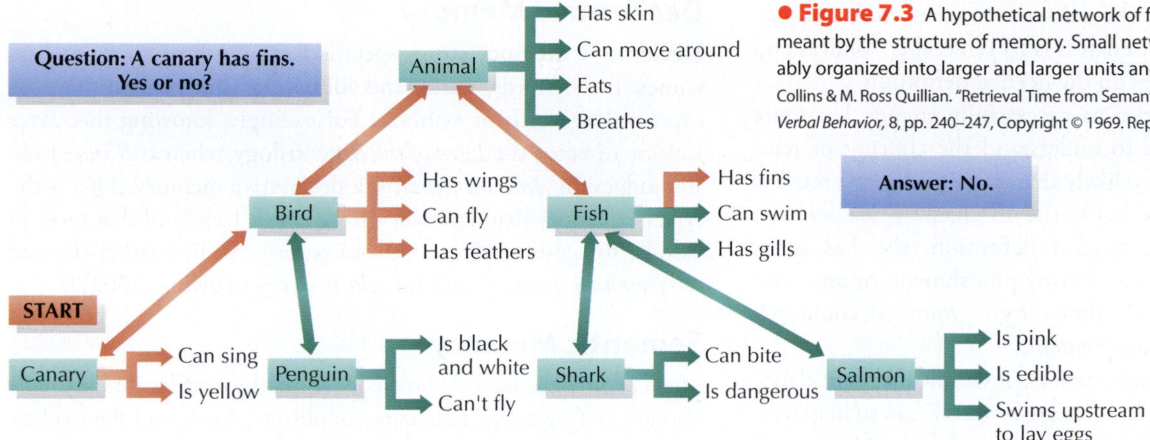

Figure 7.3 A hypothetical network of facts about animals shows what is meant by the structure of memory. Small networks of ideas such as this are probably organized into larger and larger units and higher levels of meaning. (Allan M. Collins & M. Ross Quillian. "Retrieval Time from Semantic Memory." *Journal of Verbal Learning and Verbal Behavior*, 8, pp. 240–247, Copyright © 1969. Reprinted with permission from Elsevier.)

memory leads to another, which leads to another, and another. Soon you have unleashed a flood of seemingly forgotten details. This process is called *redintegration* (reh-DIN-tuh-GRAY-shun).

Redintegration seems to spread through the "branches" of memory networks. The key idea in redintegration is that one memory serves as a cue to trigger another. As a result, an entire past experience may be reconstructed from one small recollection. Many people find that redintegration can be touched off by distinctive odors from the past—from a farm visited in childhood, Grandma's kitchen, the seashore, the perfume or aftershave of a former lover, and so on (Willander & Larsson, 2006).

From Encoding to Retrieval in Long-Term Memory

Let's get back to passing that psychology exam. On one recent exam, Jerry studied using rote learning whereas Erica made extensive use of elaborative processing. Figure 7.4 shows what their memory networks might look like for the concept of reinforcement (Chapter 6).

Because Jerry spent most of his time in rote rehearsal, his memory network for the concept of reinforcement is quite sparse. He managed to get the definition right. Also, during rote learning, it occurred to him that extra soldiers joining a battle were also reinforcements. In contrast, while studying, Erica asked herself how reinforcement and punishment differ, what kinds of reinforcement (and punishment) there are, and tried to think of personal examples. She also checked out the difference between operant and respondent senses of the term.

That must mean Erica has a better chance of doing well on the psychology exam, right? You bet. To begin, because Jerry used rote learning, his memories will be weaker since he cannot be sure he actually understood the concept of reinforcement. Also, suppose

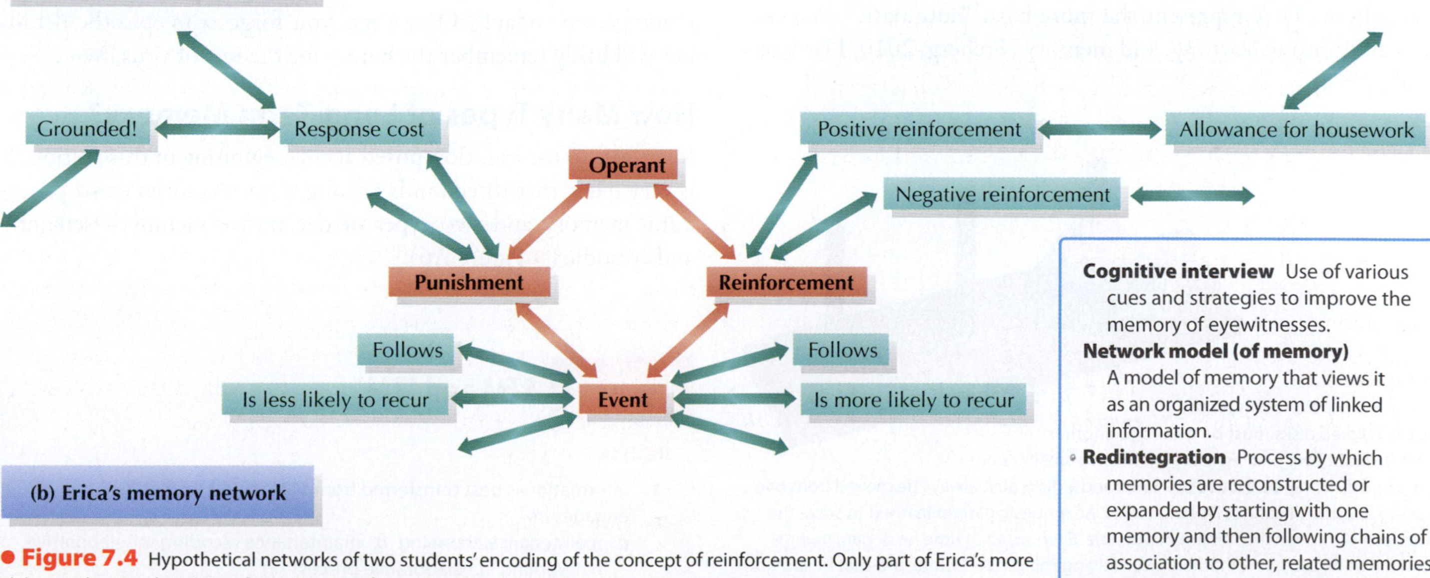

Figure 7.4 Hypothetical networks of two students' encoding of the concept of reinforcement. Only part of Erica's more elaborated network is shown here. (See text for explanation.) Copyright © 2012 Wadsworth, Cengage Learning, Inc.

Cognitive interview Use of various cues and strategies to improve the memory of eyewitnesses.

Network model (of memory) A model of memory that views it as an organized system of linked information.

Redintegration Process by which memories are reconstructed or expanded by starting with one memory and then following chains of association to other, related memories.

Jerry cannot directly retrieve the definition of reinforcement during his exam. His only other chance is to remember soldiers and hope that redintegration pops up the needed definition.

In sharp contrast, for Erica to successfully encode her more elaborated network she *had* to understand the concept of reinforcement. Hence, she is more likely than Jerry to directly retrieve that information if she needs to. On the off-chance Erica does not immediately remember the needed definition, she has many retrieval cues to help her. Remembering punishment, or an example of reinforcement, or even the time she got grounded, could well trigger redintegration of "reinforcement."

In summary, more elaborative processing results in more elaborate memory networks and, hence, more retrieval cues to help with redintegration. Time spent in elaborative processing is time well spent, at least if you want to do well on exams.

Types of Long-Term Memory

How many types of long-term memory are there? It is becoming clear that more than one type of long-term memory exists. For example, a curious thing happens to many people who develop amnesia. Amnesic patients may be unable to learn a telephone number, an address, or a person's name. Yet, the same patients can learn to solve complex puzzles in a normal amount of time (Cavaco et al., 2004) (• Figure 7.5). These and other observations have led many psychologists to conclude that long-term memories fall into at least two categories. One is called *procedural memory* (or skill memory). The other is *declarative memory* (also sometimes called fact memory).

Procedural Memory

Procedural memory includes basic conditioned responses and learned actions, such as those involved in typing, driving, or swinging a golf club. Memories such as these can be fully expressed only as actions (or "know-how"). It is likely that skill memories register in "lower" brain areas, especially the basal ganglia and the cerebellum. They represent the more basic "automatic" elements of conditioning, learning, and memory (Freberg, 2010; Hermann et al., 2004).

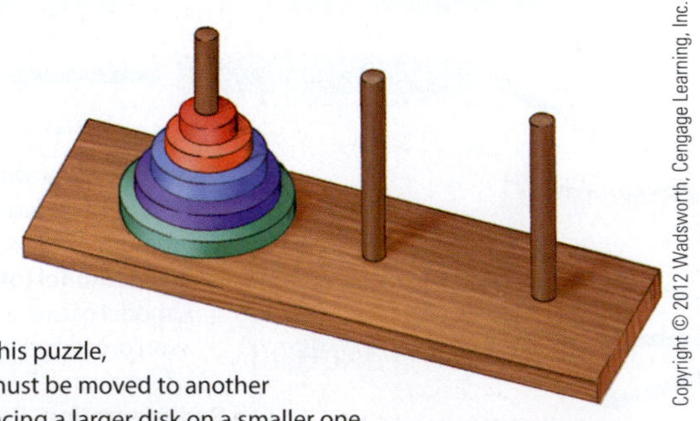

• Figure 7.5
The tower puzzle. In this puzzle, all the colored disks must be moved to another post, without ever placing a larger disk on a smaller one. Only one disk may be moved at a time, and a disk must always be moved from one post to another (it cannot be held aside). An amnesic patient learned to solve the puzzle in 31 moves, the minimum possible. Even so, each time he began, he protested that he did not remember ever solving the puzzle before and that he did not know how to begin. Evidence like this suggests that memories for skills are distinct from memories for facts.

Declarative Memory

Declarative memory stores specific factual information, such as names, faces, words, dates, and ideas. Declarative memories are expressed as words or symbols. For example, knowing that *Peter* Jackson directed the *Lord of the Rings* trilogy, whereas *Randy* Jackson judges on *American Idol*, is a declarative memory. This is the type of memory that a person with amnesia lacks and that most of us take for granted. Declarative memory can be further divided into *semantic memory* and *episodic memory* (Tulving, 2002).

Semantic Memory

Much of our basic factual knowledge about the world is almost totally immune to forgetting. The names of objects, the days of the week or months of the year, simple math skills, the seasons, words and language, and other general facts are all quite lasting. Such impersonal facts make up a part of LTM called **semantic memory**, which serves as a mental dictionary or encyclopedia of basic knowledge.

Episodic Memory

Semantic memory has no connection to times or places. It would be rare, for instance, to remember when and where you first learned the names of the seasons. In contrast, **episodic** (ep-ih-SOD-ik) **memory** is an "autobiographical" record of personal experiences. It stores life events (or "episodes") day after day, year after year. Can you remember your seventh birthday? Your first date? What you did yesterday? All are episodic memories. Note that episodic memories are about the "what," "where," and "when" of our lives. More than simply storing information, they allow us to mentally travel back in time and *re-experience* events (Kirchhoff, 2009; Tulving, 2002).

Are episodic memories as lasting as semantic memories? Either type of memory can last indefinitely. However, unless episodic memories are important, they are more easily forgotten than semantic memories. In fact, it is the forgetting of episodic information that results in the formation of semantic memories. At first, you remembered when and where you were when you learned the names of the seasons (Mommy, Mommy, guess what I learned in kindergarten today!). Over time, you forgot the episodic details but will likely remember the names for the rest of your life.

How Many Types of Long-Term Memory?

In answer to the question posed at the beginning of this section, it is very likely that three kinds of long-term memories exist: procedural memory and two types of declarative memory—semantic and episodic (• Figure 7.6).

Knowledge Builder **STM and LTM**

RECITE

1. Information is best transferred from STM to LTM when a person engages in
   a. maintenance chunking *b.* maintenance recoding *c.* elaborative networking *d.* elaborative processing

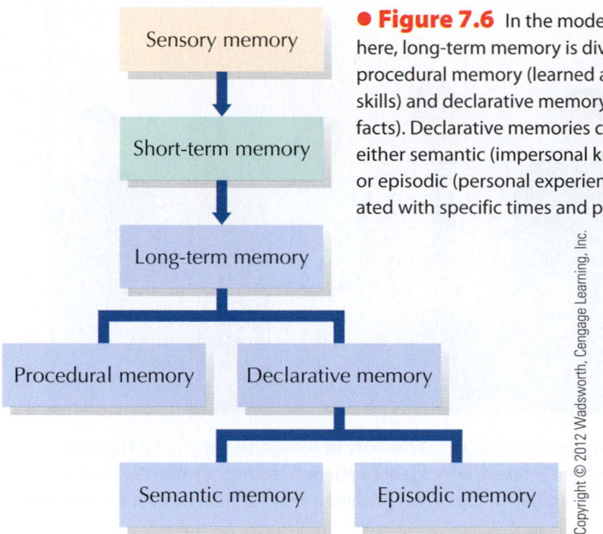

● Figure 7.6 In the model shown here, long-term memory is divided into procedural memory (learned actions and skills) and declarative memory (stored facts). Declarative memories can be either semantic (impersonal knowledge) or episodic (personal experiences associated with specific times and places).

2. Elaborative processing is often responsible for creating false memories. T or F?
3. Electrical stimulation of the brain has shown conclusively that all memories are stored permanently, but not all memories can be retrieved. T or F?
4. Memories elicited under hypnosis are more vivid, complete, and reliable than normal. T or F?
5. The existence of redintegration is best explained by ______________ models of memory.
   a. network *b.* integrative *c.* implicit *d.* chunking
6. Which of the following is a synonym for skill memory?
   a. semantic memory *b.* declarative memory *c.* episodic memory *d.* procedural memory

REFLECT

Think Critically

7. Parents sometimes warn children not to read comic books, fearing that they will learn less in school if they "fill their heads up with junk." Why is this warning unnecessary?

Self-Reflect

In the United States and Canada, telephone numbers are divided into an area code (three digits) and a seven-digit number that is divided into three digits, plus four more. Can you relate this practice to STM? How about to chunking and recoding?

Think about how you've used your memory in the last hour. See if you can identify an example of each of the following: a procedural memory, a declarative memory, a semantic memory, and an episodic memory.

Answers: 1. *d* **2.** T **3.** F **4.** F **5.** *a* **6.** *d* **7.** Because the more information you have in long-term memory, the greater the possibilities for linking new information to it. Generally, the more you know, the more you can learn—even if some of what you know is "junk."

Measuring Memory—The Answer Is on the Tip of My Tongue

Gateway Question 7.4: *How is memory measured?*

You either remember something or you don't, right? Wrong. *Partial memories* are common. For instance, have you ever tried to remember something only to find yourself stuck in a **tip-of-the-tongue (TOT) state**? This is the feeling that a memory is available but not quite retrievable (Schwartz, 2002). It is as if an answer or a memory is just out of reach—on the "tip of your tongue." In a classic TOT study, university students read the definitions of words such as *sextant, sampan,* and *ambergris.* Students who "drew a blank" and couldn't name a defined word were asked to give any other information they could. Often, they could guess the first and last letter and the number of syllables of the word they were seeking. They also gave words that sounded like or meant the same thing as the defined word (Brown & McNeill, 1966). In another study, people listened to theme music from popular TV shows. They then tried to name the program the tune came from. This produced TOT experiences for about 1 out of 5 tunes (Riefer, Keveri, & Kramer, 1995).

The items listed next may induce the TOT state. See if you can name the defined words. (*Answers are at the bottom of this page.)

What's on the Tip of Your Tongue?

1. To officially renounce a throne
2. A nylon strip surfaced with tiny hooks that fasten to another strip surfaced with uncut pile
3. Produced by humans rather than natural
4. The pictorial system of writing used in ancient Egypt
5. A small fish that attaches itself to a shark

Another example of a partial memory is the **feeling of knowing**, the fact that people can often tell beforehand if they are likely to remember something (Widner, Otani, & Winkelman, 2005). Feeling-of-knowing reactions are easy to observe on TV game shows, where they often occur just before contestants are allowed to answer. You may have experienced this yourself, perhaps during an exam. You read a question and immediately know you know the answer but the actual answer doesn't come to mind. You remember what happens next, right? As you leave the exam, the answer "pops" into your head. (Rats!)

Déjà vu, the feeling that you have already experienced a situation that you are actually experiencing for the first time, may be another example of partial memory (Brown, 2004). If a new experience triggers vague memories of a past experience, without yielding any details at all, you might be left saying to yourself, "I feel like I've seen it before." The new experience seems familiar even though the older memory is too weak to rise to the level of awareness.

---

* *1. abdicate 2. Velcro® 3. artificial 4. hieroglyphics 5. remora*

Procedural memory Long-term memories of conditioned responses and learned skills.

Declarative memory That part of long-term memory containing specific factual information.

Semantic memory A subpart of declarative memory that records impersonal knowledge about the world.

Episodic memory A subpart of declarative memory that records personal experiences that are linked with specific times and places.

Tip-of-the-tongue (TOT) state The feeling that a memory is available but not quite retrievable.

Feeling of knowing The ability to predict beforehand whether one will be able to remember something.

Déjà vu The feeling that you have already experienced a situation that you are actually experiencing for the first time.

Because memory is not an all-or-nothing event, there are several ways of measuring it. Three commonly used methods of measuring memory are *recall*, *recognition*, and *relearning*. Let's see how they differ.

Recalling Information

What is the name of the first song on your favorite playlist? Who won the World Series last year? Who wrote *Hamlet?* If you can answer these questions, you are using **recall**, a direct retrieval of facts or information. Tests of recall often require *verbatim* (word-for-word) memory. If you study a poem until you can recite it without looking at it, you are recalling it. If you complete a fill-in-the-blank question, you are using recall. When you answer an essay question by providing facts and ideas, you are also using recall, even though you didn't learn your essay verbatim.

The order in which information is memorized has an interesting effect on recall. To experience it, try to memorize the following list, reading it only once:

bread apples soda ham cookies rice lettuce beets mustard cheese oranges ice cream crackers flour eggs

If you are like most people, it will be hardest for you to recall items from the middle of the list. • Figure 7.7 shows the results of a similar test. Notice that most errors occur with middle items of an ordered list. This is the **serial position effect** (Bonk & Healy, 2010). You can remember the last items on a list because they are still in STM. The first items are also remembered well because they entered an "empty" short-term memory. This allows you to rehearse the items so they move into long-term memory (Addis & Kahana, 2004). The middle items are neither held in short-term memory nor moved to long-term memory, so they are often lost.

Recognizing Information

Try to write down everything you can remember learning from a class you took last year. If you actually did this, you might conclude that you had learned very little. However, a more sensitive test

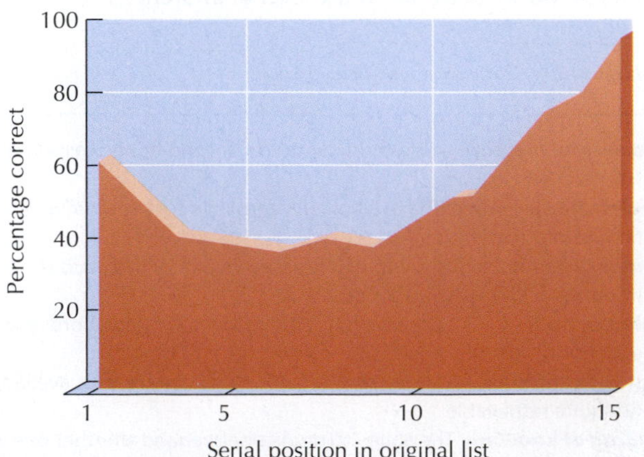

• **Figure 7.7** The serial position effect. The graph shows the percentage of subjects correctly recalling each item in a 15-item list. Recall is best for the first and last items. (Data from Craik, 1970.)

Police lineups make use of the sensitivity of recognition memory. However, unless great care is taken, false identifications are still possible (Wells, 2001). Is this a fair or an unfair lineup? What problems may be created with this lineup?

based on recognition could be used. In **recognition**, previously learned material is correctly identified. For instance, you could take a multiple-choice test on facts and ideas from the course. Because you would have to recognize only correct answers, you would probably find that you had learned a lot.

Recognition can be amazingly accurate for pictures and photographs (Whitehouse, Maybery, & Durkin, 2006). In one classic study, people viewed 2560 photographs at a rate of one every 10 seconds. Each person was then shown 280 pairs of photographs. Each pair included an "old" picture (from the first set of photos) and a similar "new" image. Subjects could tell 85 to 95 percent of the time which photograph they had seen before (Haber, 1970). This finding may explain why we rarely need to see our friends' vacation photos more than once.

Recognition is usually superior to recall. That's why people so often say, "I may forget a name, but I never forget a face." (You can't recall the name but recognize the face.) That's also why police departments use photographs or a lineup to identify criminal suspects. Witnesses who disagree when they try to recall a suspect's height, weight, age, or eye color often agree completely when they merely need to recognize the person.

Is recognition always superior? It depends greatly on the kind of *distractors* used (Flowe & Ebbese, 2007). These are false items included with an item to be recognized. If distractors are very similar to the correct item, memory may be poor. A reverse problem occurs when only one choice looks like it could be correct. This can produce a *false positive*, or false sense of recognition, like the false memory you had earlier when you thought you remembered seeing the word *sleep*.

Many hundreds of people have been put in jail on the basis of mistaken eyewitness memories (Wade, Green, & Nash, 2010; Wells, Memon, & Penrod, 2006). There have been instances in which witnesses described a criminal as black, tall, or young. Then a lineup was held in which a suspect was the only African American among whites, the only tall suspect, or the only young person. In such cases, a false identification is very likely. To avoid tragic mistakes, it's better to have *all* the distractors look like the person witnesses described. Also, to reduce false positives, witnesses should be warned that the culprit *may not be present*. It's also better to show witnesses one photo at a time (a sequential lineup). For each photo, the witness must decide whether the person is the culprit before another photo is shown (Wells, 2001; Wells & Olsen, 2003).

Relearning Information

In another classic experiment, a psychologist read a short passage in Greek to his son every day when the boy was between 15 months and 3 years of age. At age 8, the boy was asked if he remembered the Greek passage. He showed no evidence of recall. He was then shown selections from the passage he heard and selections from other Greek passages. Could he recognize the one he heard as an infant? "It's all Greek to me!" he said, indicating a lack of recognition (and drawing a frown from everyone in the room).

Had the psychologist stopped, he might have concluded that no memory of the Greek remained. However, the child was then asked to memorize the original quotation and others of equal difficulty. This time his earlier learning became evident. The boy memorized the passage he had heard in childhood 25 percent faster than the others (Burtt, 1941). As this experiment suggests, **relearning** is typically the most sensitive measure of memory.

When a person is tested by relearning, how do we know a memory still exists? As with the boy described, relearning is measured by a *savings score* (the amount of time saved when relearning information). Let's say it takes you 1 hour to memorize all the names in a telephone book. (It's a small town.) Two years later, you relearn them in 45 minutes. Because you "saved" 15 minutes, your savings score would be 25 percent (15 divided by 60 times 100). Savings of this type are a good reason for studying a wide range of subjects. It may seem that learning algebra, history, or a foreign language is wasted if you don't use the knowledge immediately. But when you do need such information, you will be able to relearn it quickly.

Implicit and Explicit Memories

Who won the half-pipe gold medal at the 2010 Winter Olympics? What did you have for breakfast today? What is the title of Taylor Swift's latest album? Explicit memory is used in answering each of these questions. **Explicit memories** are past experiences that are consciously brought to mind. Recall, recognition, and the tests you take in school rely on explicit memories.

In contrast, **implicit memories** lie outside of awareness (Roediger & Amir, 2005). That is, we are not aware that a memory exists. For example, if you know how to type, it is apparent that you know where the letters are on the keyboard. But how many typists could correctly label blank keys in a drawing of a keyboard? Many people find that they cannot directly remember such information, even though they "know" it. Nevertheless, implicit memories—such as unconsciously knowing where the letters are on a keyboard—greatly influence our behavior (Radvansky, 2011).

Can you label the letter keys on this blank keyboard? If you can, you probably used implicit memory to do it.

Priming

How is it possible to show that a memory exists if it lies outside of awareness? Psychologists first noticed implicit memory while studying memory loss caused by brain injuries. Let's say, for example, that a patient is shown a list of common words, such as *chair, tree, lamp, table,* and so on. Later, the patient fails to recall any words from the list.

Now, instead of asking the patient to explicitly recall the list, we could "prime" his memory by giving him the first two letters of each word. "Just say whatever word comes to mind that begins with these letters," we tell him. Of course, many words could be made from each pair of letters. For example, the first item (from "chair") would be the letters CH. The patient could say "child," "chalk," "chain," "check," or many other words. Instead, he says "chair," a word from the original list. The patient is not aware that he is remembering the list, but as he gives a word for each letter pair, almost all are from the list. Apparently, the letters **primed** (activated) hidden memories, which then influenced his answers.

Similar effects have been found for people with normal memories. As the preceding example implies, implicit memories are often revealed by giving a person limited cues, such as the first letter of words or partial drawings of objects. Typically, the person believes that he or she is just saying whatever comes to mind. Nevertheless, information previously seen or heard affects his or her answers (Rueckl & Galantucci, 2005).

Knowledge Builder **Measuring Memory**

RECITE

1. Four techniques for measuring or demonstrating memory are ______ ______ ______ ______

Continued

- **Recall** To supply or reproduce memorized information with a minimum of external cues.

Serial position effect The tendency to make the most errors in remembering the middle items of an ordered list.

- **Recognition** An ability to correctly identify previously learned information.
- **Relearning** Learning again something that was previously learned. Used to measure memory of prior learning.
- **Explicit memory** A memory that a person is aware of having; a memory that is consciously retrieved.
- **Implicit memory** A memory that a person does not know exists; a memory that is retrieved unconsciously.

Priming Facilitating the retrieval of an implicit memory by using cues to activate hidden memories.

2. Essay tests require ___________________ of facts or ideas.
3. As a measure of memory, a savings score is associated with
   a. recognition *b.* priming *c.* relearning *d.* reconstruction
4. The two most sensitive tests of memory are
   a. recall and redintegration *b.* recall and relearning *c.* recognition and relearning *d.* recognition and digit-span
5. Priming is used to reveal which type of memories?
   a. explicit *b.* sensory *c.* skill *d.* implicit

REFLECT

Think Critically

6. When asked to explain why they may have failed to recall some information, people often claim it must be because the information is no longer in their memory. Why does the existence of implicit memories challenge this explanation?

Self-Reflect

Have you experienced a TOT state recently? Were you able to retrieve the word you were searching for? If not, what could you remember about it?

Do you prefer tests based primarily on recall or recognition? Have you observed a savings effect while relearning information you studied in the past (such as in high school)?

Can you think of things you do that are based on implicit memories? For instance, how do you know which way to turn various handles in your house, apartment, or dorm? Do you have to explicitly think, "Turn it to the right," before you act?

What kinds of information are you good at remembering? Why do you think your memory is better for those topics?

Answers: 1. recall, recognition, relearning, priming **2.** recall **3.** *c* **4.** *c* **5.** *d* **6.** It is possible to have an implicit memory that cannot be consciously recalled. Memories like these (*available* in memory even though they are not consciously *accessible*) show that failing to recall something does not guarantee it is no longer in memory (Landau & Leynes, 2006).

Forgetting—Why We, Uh, Let's See; Why We, Uh . . . Forget!

Gateway Question 7.5: *Why do we forget?*

We don't expect sensory memories and short-term memories to remain with us for long. But when you deliberately encode and store information in long-term memory, you want it to stay there (after all, it's supposed to be *long*-term). For example, when you study for an exam, you count on your long-term memory to retain the information at least until you take your exam.

Why do we forget long-term memories? The more you know about how we "lose" memories, the better you will be able to hang on to them. Most forgetting tends to occur immediately after memorization. Herman Ebbinghaus (1885) famously tested his own memory at various intervals after learning. To be sure he would not be swayed by prior learning, he memorized *nonsense syllables.* These are meaningless three-letter words such as "cef," "wol," and "gex." The importance of using meaningless words is shown by the fact that "Vel," "Fab," and "Duz" are no longer used on memory tests. People who recognize these words as detergent names find them very easy to remember. This is another reminder that relating new information to what you already know can improve memory.

By waiting various lengths of time before testing himself, Ebbinghaus plotted a **curve of forgetting**. This graph shows the amount of information remembered after varying lengths of time (● Figure 7.8). Notice that forgetting is rapid at first and is then followed by a slow decline (Hintzman, 2005). The same applies to meaningful information, but the forgetting curve is stretched over a longer time. As you might expect, recent events are recalled more accurately than those from the remote past. Thus, you are more likely to remember that *The King's Speech* won the "Best Picture" Academy Award for 2010 than you are to remember that *Million Dollar Baby* was the 2004 winner.

As a student, you should note that a short delay between studying and taking a test minimizes forgetting. However, this is no reason for cramming. Most students make the error of *only* cramming. If you cram, you don't have to remember for very long, but you may not learn enough in the first place. If you use short, daily study sessions *and* review intensely before a test, you will get the benefit of good preparation and a minimum time lapse.

The Ebbinghaus curve shows less than 30 percent remembered after only 2 days have passed. Is forgetting really that rapid? No, not always. Meaningful information is not lost nearly as quickly as nonsense syllables. After 3 years, students who took a university psychology

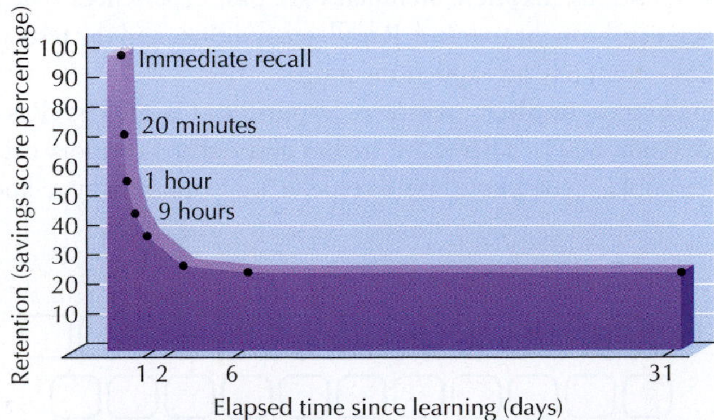

● **Figure 7.8** The curve of forgetting. This graph shows the amount remembered (measured by relearning) after varying lengths of time. Notice how rapidly forgetting occurs. The material learned was nonsense syllables. Forgetting curves for meaningful information also show early losses followed by a long gradual decline, but overall, forgetting occurs much more slowly. (After Ebbinghaus, 1885.)

Discovering Psychology — Card Magic!

● **Figure 7.9**

Pick a card from the six shown in ● Figure 7.9 above. Look at it closely and be sure you can remember which card is yours. Now, snap your fingers and look at the cards in ● Figure 7.10 below.

Poof! Only five cards remain, and the card you chose has disappeared. Obviously, you could have selected any one of the six cards in ● Figure 7.9. How did we know which one to remove?

This trick is based entirely on an illusion of memory. Recall that you were asked to concentrate on one card among the six cards in ● Figure 7.9. That prevented you from paying attention to the other cards, so they weren't stored in your memory (Mangels, Picton, & Craik, 2001; Naveh-Benjamin, Guez, & Sorek, 2007). The five cards you see below are all new (none is shown in ● Figure 7.9). Because you couldn't find it in the "remaining five," your card seemed to disappear. What looked like "card magic" is actually memory magic. Now return to "When Encoding Fails" and continue reading to learn more about forgetting.

● **Figure 7.10**

course had forgotten about 30 percent of the facts they learned. After that, little more forgetting occurred (Conway, Cohen, & Stanhope, 1992). Actually, as learning grows stronger, some knowledge may become nearly permanent (Berntsen & Thomsen, 2005).

Although the Ebbinghaus curve gives a general picture of forgetting from long-term memory, it doesn't explain it. For explanations, we must search further. (Before we do, look at "Card Magic!," in which you will find an interesting demonstration.) Earlier in this chapter, we pointed out that three processes are involved in successfully remembering: encoding, storage, and retrieval. Conversely, forgetting can be due to the failure of any one of these three processes.

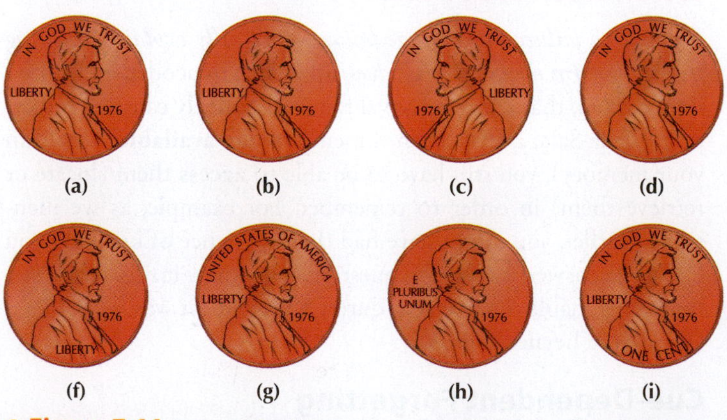

● **Figure 7.11** Some of the distractor items used in a study of recognition memory and encoding failure. Penny A is correct but was seldom recognized. Pennies G and J were popular wrong answers. (Adapted from Nickerson & Adams, 1979.)

When Encoding Fails

Whose head is on a U.S. penny? Which way is it facing? What is written at the top of a penny? Can you accurately draw and label a penny? In an interesting experiment, Ray Nickerson and Marilyn Adams (1979) asked a large group of students to draw a penny. Few could. In fact, few could even recognize a drawing of a real penny among fakes. (see ● Figure 7.11). Can you?

Curve of forgetting A graph that shows the amount of memorized information remembered after varying lengths of time.

The most obvious reason for forgetting is also the most commonly overlooked. Obviously, few of us ever encode the details of a penny. Similarly, we may not encode the details of what we are reading in a book or studying for an exam. In such cases, we "forget" because of **encoding failure**. That is, a memory was never formed in the first place (the card trick you just saw is another example). If you are bothered by frequent forgetting or absent-mindedness, it is wise to ask yourself, "Have I been encoding the information in the first place?" (Kirchhoff, 2009). By the way, if you like to study while watching television or instant messaging, beware. Dividing your attention between studying and other activities can also lead to encoding failure (Naveh-Benjamin, Guez, & Sorek, 2007).

Actively thinking about the information you are learning (elaborative processing) is a good way to prevent encoding failure (Hall et al., 2007).

BRIDGES

You'll find more memory strategies in *The Psychology of Studying—Reflective Learning* at the beginning of this book. Check it out, if you haven't already.

College Students: They're All Alike!

Encoding failures also affect our memories of people. Imagine yourself in this situation: As you are walking on campus, a young man, who looks like a college student, approaches you and asks for directions. While you are talking, two workers carrying a door pass between you and the young man. While your view is blocked by the door, another man takes the place of the first. Now you are facing a different person than the one who was there just seconds earlier. If this happened to you, do you think you would notice the change? Remarkably, only half the people tested in this way noticed the switch (Simons & Levin, 1998)!

How could anyone fail to notice that one stranger had been replaced by another? The people who didn't remember the first man were all older adults. College students weren't fooled by the switch. Apparently, older adults encoded the first man in very general terms as a "college student." As a result, that's all they remembered about him. Because his replacement also looked like a college student, they thought he was the same person (Simons & Levin, 1998).

Actually, we all tend to categorize strangers in general terms: Is the person young or old, male or female, a member of my ethnic group or another? This tendency is one reason why eyewitnesses are better at identifying members of their own ethnic group than persons from other groups (Burgess & Weaver, 2003; Michel, Caldara, & Rossion, 2006). It may seem harsh to say so, but during brief social contacts, people really do act as if members of other ethnic groups "all look alike." Of course, this bias disappears when people get acquainted and learn more about one another as individuals. (McKone et al., 2007).

When Memory Storage Fails

One view of forgetting holds that **memory traces** (changes in nerve cells or brain activity) decay (fade or weaken) over time. **Memory decay** appears to be a factor in the loss of sensory memories. Such fading also applies to short-term memory. Information stored in STM seems to initiate a brief flurry of activity in the brain that quickly dies out. Sensory memory and short-term memory, therefore, operate like "leaky buckets": New information constantly pours in, but it rapidly fades away and is replaced by still newer information.

Disuse

Does decay also occur in long-term memory? There is evidence that memories not retrieved and "used" or rehearsed become weaker over time. That is, some long-term memory traces may fade from **disuse** (infrequent retrieval) and eventually become too weak to retrieve. However, disuse alone cannot fully explain forgetting (Della Sala, 2010).

Disuse doesn't seem to account for our ability to recover seemingly forgotten memories through redintegration, relearning, and priming. It also fails to explain why some unused memories fade, whereas others are carried for life.

A third contradiction will be recognized by anyone who has spent time with the elderly. People growing senile may become so forgetful that they can't remember what happened a week ago. Unfortunately, this is often due to diseases like *Alzheimer's disease* and other *dementias*, which slowly strangle the brain's ability to process and store information (Hanyu et al., 2010).

BRIDGES

Memory can easily be disrupted by organic factors including brain injuries and disorders like Alzheimer's disease. **For more information see Chapter 14, page 485.**

Yet at the same time that your Uncle Oscar's recent memories are fading, he may have vivid memories of trivial and long-forgotten events from the past. "Why, I remember it as clearly as if it were yesterday," he will say, forgetting that the story he is about to tell is one he told earlier the same day (twice). In short, disuse offers no more than a partial explanation of long-term forgetting.

When Retrieval Fails

If encoding failure and storage failure don't fully explain forgetting from long-term memory, what does? If you have encoded and stored information, that leaves retrieval failure as a likely cause of forgetting (Della Sala, 2010). Even if memories are **available** (stored in your memory), you still have to be able to **access** them (locate or retrieve them) in order to remember. For example, as we mentioned earlier, you might have had the experience of knowing you know the answer to an exam question (you knew it was *available*), but being unable to retrieve it during the exam (it was *inaccessible*) (Landau & Leynes, 2006).

Cue-Dependent Forgetting

One reason retrieval may fail is because **retrieval cues** (stimuli associated with a memory) are missing when the time comes to retrieve information. For instance, if you were asked, "What were you doing on Monday afternoon of the third week in May, 2 years

External cues like those found in a photograph, in a scrapbook, or during a walk through an old neighborhood often aid recall of seemingly lost memories. For many veterans, finding a familiar name engraved in the Vietnam Veterans Memorial unleashes a flood of memories.

ago?" your reply might be, "Come on, how should I know?" However, if you were reminded, "That was the day the courthouse burned," or "That was the day Stacy had her automobile accident," you might remember immediately.

The presence of appropriate cues almost always enhances memory. As we saw previously, more elaborately encoded memories are more likely to be remembered because more retrieval cues are associated with any particular piece of information. Memory will even tend to be better if you study in the same room where you will be tested. Because this is often impossible, when you study, try to visualize the room where you will be tested. Doing so can enhance memory later (Jerabek & Standing, 1992). Similarly, people even remember better if the same odor (such as lemon or lavender) is present both when they study and are tested (Parker, Ngu, & Cassaday, 2001). If you wear a particular perfume or cologne while you prepare for a test, it might be wise to wear it when you take the test.

State-Dependent Learning

Have you heard the one about the drunk who misplaced his wallet and had to get drunk again to find it? Actually, this is not too far-fetched. The bodily state that exists during learning can be a strong retrieval cue for later memory, an effect known as **state-dependent learning** (Radvansky, 2011). Being very thirsty, for instance, might prompt you to remember events that took place on another occasion when you were thirsty. Because of such effects, information learned under the influence of a drug is best remembered when the drugged state occurs again (Slot & Colpaert, 1999). However, this is a laboratory finding. In school, it's far better to study with a clear mind in the first place.

A similar effect applies to emotional states (Wessel & Wright, 2004). For instance, Gordon Bower (1981) found that people who learned a list of words while in a happy mood recalled them better when they were again happy. People who learned while they felt sad remembered best when they were sad (• Figure 7.12). Similarly, if you are in a happy mood, you are more likely to remember recent happy events. If you are in a bad mood, you will tend to have unpleasant memories. Such links between emotional cues and memory could explain why couples who quarrel often end up remembering—and rehashing—old arguments.

Interference

Further insight into forgetting comes from a classic experiment in which college students learned lists of nonsense syllables. After studying, students in one group slept for 8 hours and were then tested for memory of the lists. A second group stayed awake for 8 hours and went about business as usual. When members of the second group were tested, they remembered *less* than the group that slept (• Figure 7.13). This difference is based on the fact that new learning can interfere with the ability to retrieve previous learning. **Interference** refers to the tendency for new memories to impair retrieval of older memories (and the reverse). It seems to

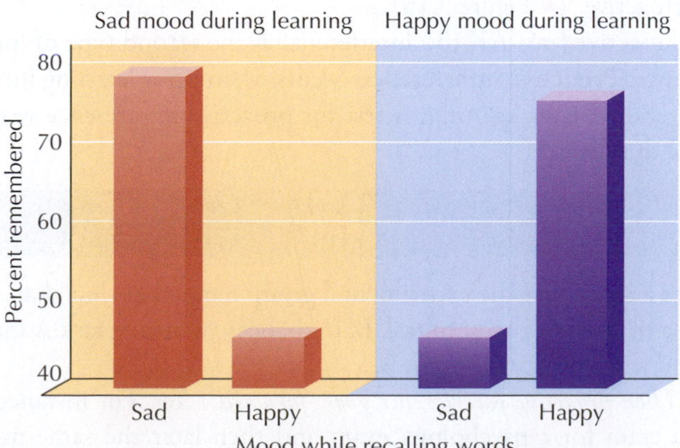

• Figure 7.12 The effect of mood on memory. Subjects best remembered a list of words when their mood during testing was the same as their mood was when they learned the list. (Adapted from Bower, 1981.)

Encoding failure Failure to store sufficient information to form a useful memory.

Memory traces Physical changes in nerve cells or brain activity that take place when memories are stored.

Memory decay The fading or weakening of memories assumed to occur when memory traces become weaker.

Disuse Theory that memory traces weaken when memories are not periodically used or retrieved.

Availability (in memory) Memories currently stored in memory are available.

Accessibility (in memory) Memories currently stored in memory which can be retrieved when necessary are both available and accessible.

Retrieval cue Stimulus associated with a memory. Retrieval cues usually enhance memory.

State-dependent learning Memory influenced by one's bodily state at the time of learning and at the time of retrieval. Improved memory occurs when the bodily states match.

Interference The tendency for new memories to impair retrieval of older memories, and the reverse.

apply to both short-term and long-term memory (Jonides et al., 2008; Nairne, 2002).

BRIDGES

Sleep can improve memory in another way: REM sleep and dreaming appear to help us form certain types of memories. **See Chapter 5, pages 172–174.**

It is not completely clear whether new memories alter existing memory traces or whether they make it harder to retrieve (or "locate") earlier memories. In any case, there is no doubt that interference is a major cause of forgetting (Radvansky, 2011). College students who memorized 20 lists of words (one list each day) were able to recall only 15 percent of the last list. Students who learned only one list remembered 80 percent (Underwood, 1957; • Figure 7.14).

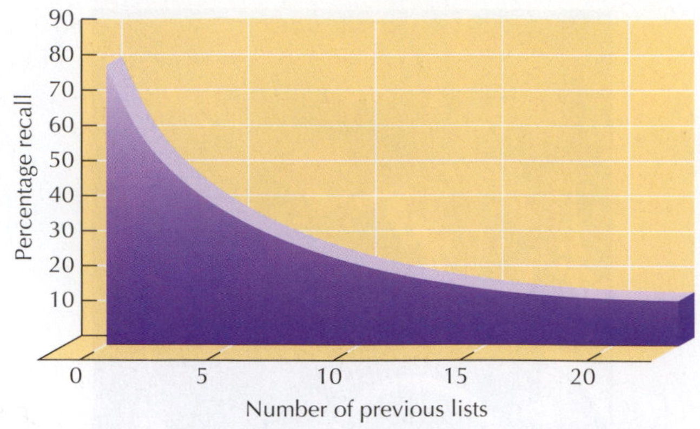

• Figure 7.14 Effects of interference on memory. A graph of the approximate relationship between percentage recalled and number of different word lists memorized. (Adapted from Underwood, 1957.)

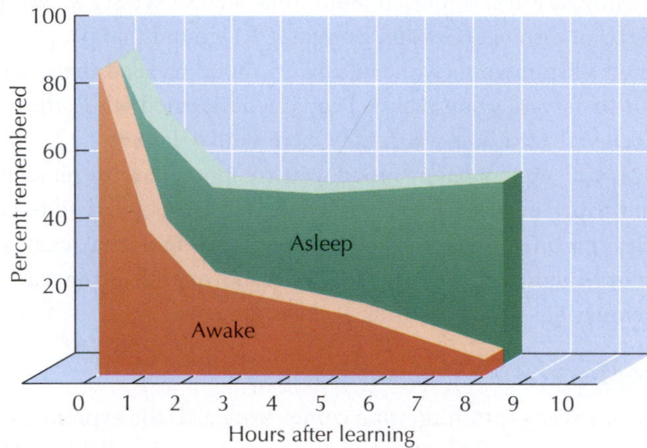

• Figure 7.13 The amount of forgetting after a period of sleep or of being awake. Notice that sleep causes less memory loss than activity that occurs while one is awake. (After Jenkins & Dallenbach, 1924.)

Duncan Mckenzie/Getty Images

How could anyone lose something as large as a car? If you park your car in a different place every day, you may have experienced forgetting caused by interference. Today's memory about your car's location is easily confused with memories from yesterday, and the day before, and the day before that.

The sleeping college students remembered more because retroactive (RET-ro-AK-tiv) interference was held to a minimum. **Retroactive interference** refers to the tendency for new learning to inhibit retrieval of old learning. Avoiding new learning prevents retroactive interference. This doesn't exactly mean you should hide in a closet after you study for an exam. However, you should, if possible, avoid studying other subjects until the exam. Sleeping after study can help you retain memories, and reading, writing, or even watching TV may cause interference.

Retroactive interference is easily demonstrated in the laboratory by this arrangement:

Experimental group:	**Learn A**	**Learn B**	**Test A**
Control group:	**Learn A**	**Rest**	**Test A**

Imagine yourself as a member of the experimental group. In task A, you learn a list of telephone numbers. In task B, you learn a list of Social Security numbers. How do you score on a test of task A (the telephone numbers)? If you do not remember as much as the control group that learns *only* task A, then retroactive interference has occurred. The second thing learned interfered with memory of the first thing learned; the interference went "backward," or was "retroactive" (• Figure 7.15).

Proactive (pro-AK-tiv) interference is the second type of interference. **Proactive interference** occurs when prior learning inhibits its recall of later learning. A test for proactive interference would take this form:

Experimental group:	**Learn A**	**Learn B**	**Test B**
Control group:	**Rest**	**Learn B**	**Test B**

Let's assume that the experimental group remembers less than the control group on a test of task B. In that case, learning task A interfered with memory for task B.

Then proactive interference goes "forward"? Yes. For instance, if you cram for a psychology exam and then later the same night cram for a history exam, your memory for the second subject studied (history) will be less accurate than if you had studied only his-

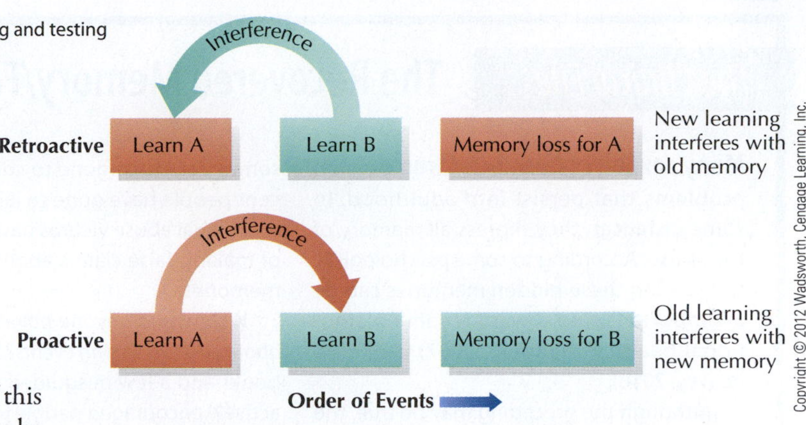

Figure 7.15 Retroactive and proactive interference. The order of learning and testing shows whether interference is retroactive (backward) or proactive (forward).

tory. (Because of retroactive interference, your memory for psychology would probably also suffer.) The greater the similarity in the two subjects studied, the more interference takes place. The moral, of course, is don't procrastinate in preparing for exams. The more you can avoid competing information, the more likely you are to recall what you want to remember (Wixted, 2004).

The interference effects we have described apply primarily to memories of verbal information, such as the contents of this chapter. When you are learning a skill, similarity can sometimes be beneficial, rather than disruptive (Osman, 2008). The next section explains how this occurs.

Transfer of Training

Two people begin mandolin lessons. One already plays the violin. The other is a trumpet player. All other things being equal, which person will initially do better in learning the mandolin? If you chose the violin player, you have an intuitive grasp of what positive transfer is. (The strings on a mandolin are tuned the same as a violin.) **Positive transfer** takes place when mastery of one task aids in mastery of a second task. Another example would be learning to balance and turn on a bicycle before learning to ride a motorcycle or motor scooter. Likewise, surfing and skateboarding skills transfer to snowboarding.

Is there such a thing as negative transfer? There is indeed. In **negative transfer**, skills developed in one situation conflict with those required to master a new task. Learning to back a car with a trailer attached to it is a good example. Normally, when you are backing a car, the steering wheel is turned in the direction you want to go, the same as when moving forward. However, when backing a trailer, you must turn the steering wheel *away* from the direction you want the trailer to go. This situation results in negative transfer, and often creates comical scenes at campgrounds and boat launching ramps.

On a more serious note, many tragic crashes caused by negative transfer finally led to greater standardization of airplane cockpits. Fortunately, negative transfer is usually brief, and it occurs less often than positive transfer. Negative transfer is most likely to occur when a new response must be made to an old stimulus (Besnard & Cacitti, 2005; Osman, 2008). If you have ever encountered a pull-type handle on a door that must be pushed open, you will appreciate this point.

Repression and Suppression of Memories

Take a moment and scan over the events of the last few years of your life. What kinds of things most easily come to mind? Many people remember happy, positive events better than disappointments and irritations (Moore & Zoellner, 2007). This tendency is called **repression**, or motivated forgetting. Through repression, painful, threatening, or embarrassing memories are held out of consciousness (Anderson et al., 2004). An example is provided by soldiers who have repressed some of the horrors they saw during combat (Anderson et al., 2004).

The forgetting of past failures, upsetting childhood events, the names of people you dislike, or appointments you don't want to keep may reveal repression (Goodman, Quas, & Ogle, 2010). People prone to repression tend to be extremely sensitive to emotional events. As a result, they use repression to protect themselves from threatening thoughts (McNally, Clancy, & Barrett, 2004). See "The Recovered Memory/False Memory Debate" for further cautions.

If I try to forget a test I failed, am I repressing it? No. Repression can be distinguished from **suppression**, an active, conscious attempt to put something out of mind. By not thinking about the test, you have merely suppressed a memory. If you choose to, you can remember the test. Clinicians consider true repression an *unconscious* event. When a memory is repressed, we may be unaware that forgetting has even occurred.

BRIDGES

Clinical psychologists regard repression as one of the major psychological defenses we use against emotional threats. **See Chapter 13, pages 456–458 for details.**

Although some psychologists have questioned whether repression exists (Court & Court, 2001), evidence suggests that we can choose to actively suppress upsetting memories (Neufeind et al., 2009). If you have experienced a painful emotional event, you will probably avoid all thoughts associated with it. This tends to keep cues out of mind that could trigger a painful memory. In time, your active suppression of the memory may become true repression (Anderson & Green, 2001).

Retroactive interference The tendency for new memories to interfere with the retrieval of old memories.

Proactive interference The tendency for old memories to interfere with the retrieval of newer memories.

Positive transfer Mastery of one task aids learning or performing another.

Negative transfer Mastery of one task conflicts with learning or performing another.

Repression Unconsciously pushing unwanted memories out of awareness.

Suppression A conscious effort to put something out of mind or to keep it from awareness.

The Clinical File: The Recovered Memory/False Memory Debate

Many sexually abused children develop problems that persist into adulthood. In some instances, they repress all memory of the abuse. According to some psychologists, uncovering these hidden memories can be an important step toward regaining emotional health (Colangelo, 2007; Haaken & Reavey, 2010).

Although the preceding may be true, the search for repressed memories of sexual abuse has itself been a problem. Families have been torn apart by accusations of sexual abuse that later turned out to be completely false. For example, when Meridith Maran thought she had recovered vivid memories of being molested by her father, she withdrew herself and her children from any further contact with him. It was not until nine years later that she realized that her "memories" were not true and finally apologized to her father (Maran, 2010). Things have gotten much worse for other people as some cases have gone to court, some innocent people have gone to jail, and some actual sexual abuse victims have been accused of making false claims about their very real memories.

Why would anyone have false memories about such disturbing events? Several popular books and a few misguided therapists have actively encouraged people to find repressed memories of abuse. Hypnosis, guided visualization, suggestion, age regression, administering the so-called "truth drug" Amytal, and similar techniques can elicit fantasies that are mistaken for real memories. As we saw earlier, it is easy to create false memories, especially by using hypnosis (Loftus & Bernstein, 2005; Weinstein & Shanks, 2010).

In an effort to illustrate how easy it is to create false memories, and to publicize *false memory syndrome*, memory expert Elizabeth Loftus once deliberately implanted a false memory in actor Alan Alda. As the host of the television series *Scientific American Frontiers*, he was scheduled to interview Loftus. Before the interview, Alda was asked to fill out a questionnaire about his tastes in food. When he arrived, Loftus told Alda that his answers revealed that he must once have gotten sick after eating hard-boiled eggs (which was false). Later that day, at a picnic, Alda would not eat hard-boiled eggs (Loftus, 2003).

Certainly, some memories of abuse that return to awareness are genuine and must be dealt with. However, there is little doubt that some "recovered" memories are pure fantasy. No matter how real a recovered memory may seem, it could be false, unless it can be verified by others or by court or medical records (Bernstein & Loftus, 2009; Otgaar & Smeets, 2010). The saddest thing about such claims is that they deaden public sensitivity to actual abuse. Childhood sexual abuse is widespread. Awareness of its existence must not be repressed.

Memory and the Brain—Some "Shocking" Findings

Gateway Question 7.6: *How does the brain form and store memories?*

One possibility overlooked in our discussion of forgetting is that memories may be lost as they are being formed (Papanicolaou, 2006). For example, a head injury may cause a "gap" in memories preceding the accident. **Retrograde amnesia**, as this is called, involves forgetting events that occurred before an injury or trauma (MacKay & Hadley, 2009). In contrast, **anterograde amnesia** involves forgetting events that follow an injury or trauma (Behrend, Beike, & Lampinen, 2004). (We will discuss an example of this type of amnesia in a moment.)

Consolidation

We can explain retrograde amnesia by assuming that it takes time to form a lasting memory, a process called **consolidation** (Vogel, Woodman, & Luck, 2006). You can think of consolidation as being somewhat like writing your name in wet concrete. Once the concrete is set, the information (your name) is fairly lasting. But while the concrete is setting, the information can be wiped out (amnesia) or scribbled over (interference).

Consider a classic experiment on consolidation, in which a rat is placed on a small platform. The rat steps down to the floor and receives a painful electric shock. After one shock, the rat can be returned to the platform repeatedly, but it will not step down. Obviously, the rat remembers the shock. Would it remember if consolidation were disturbed?

Curiously, one way to prevent consolidation is to give a different kind of shock called **electroconvulsive shock (ECS)**. ECS is a mild electric shock to the brain. It does not harm the animal, but it does destroy any memory that is being formed. If each painful shock (the one the animal remembers) is followed by ECS (which wipes out memories during consolidation), the rat will step down over and over. Each time, ECS will erase the memory of the painful shock.

BRIDGES

ECS has been used with humans as a psychiatric treatment for severe depression. Used in this way, electroshock therapy also causes memory loss. **See Chapter 15, pages 528–529.**

What would happen if ECS were given several hours after the learning? Recent memories are more easily disrupted than older memories. If enough time is allowed to pass between learning and ECS, the memory will be unaffected because consolidation is already complete. That's why people with mild head injuries lose only memories from just before the accident, whereas older memories remain intact (Baddeley, Eysenck, & Anderson, 2009). Likewise, you would forget more if you studied, stayed awake 8 hours, and then slept 8 hours than you would if you studied, slept 8 hours, and were awake for 8 hours. Either way, 16 hours would pass. However, less forgetting would occur in the second instance because more consolidation would occur before interference begins (Wixted, 2005).

Where does consolidation take place in the brain? Actually, many parts of the brain are responsible for memory, but the **hippocampus** is particularly important (Sutherland et al., 2006). The hippocampus acts as a sort of "switching station" between short-term and long-term memory (Hardt, Einarsson, & Nader, 2010). The hippocampus does this, in part, by growing new neurons (nerve cells) and by making new connections within the brain (Leuner & Gould, 2010).

If the hippocampus is damaged, patients usually develop anterograde amnesia, and show a striking inability to consolidate new memories. A man described by Brenda Milner (1965) provides a dramatic example. Two years after an operation damaged his hippocampus, the 29-year-old H. M. continued to give his age as 27 and reported that the operation had just taken place. His memory of events before the operation remained clear, but he found forming new long-term memories almost impossible. When his parents moved to a new house a few blocks away on the same street, he could not remember the new address. Month after month, he read the same magazines over and over without finding them familiar. If you were to meet this man, he would seem fairly normal because he still has short-term memory. But if you were to leave the room and return 15 minutes later, he would act as if he had never seen you before. Lacking the ability to form new lasting memories, he lived eternally in the present until his death in 2008 at the age of 82 (Bohbot & Corkin, 2007; Corkin, 2002).

Memory, Stress, and Emotion

Do you remember when you first learned about the terrorist attacks on New York City's World Trade Center in 2001? Can you recall lots of detail, including how you reacted? If so, you have a **flashbulb memory** for 9/11. A flashbulb memory is an especially vivid image that seems to be frozen in memory at times of emotionally significant personal or public events. Depending on your age, you may also have a "flashbulb" memory for the assassinations of John F. Kennedy or Martin Luther King, Jr., the *Challenger* or *Columbia* space shuttle disasters, or the death of Princess Diana (Curci & Luminet, 2006; Sharot et al., 2007).

Are flashbulb memories handled differently by the brain? Powerfully exciting or stressful experiences activate the *limbic system*, a part of the brain that processes emotions. Heightened activity in the limbic system, in turn, appears to intensify memory consolidation (LaBar, 2007; Kensinger, 2007). As a result, flashbulb memories tend to form at times of intense emotion.

Although flashbulb memories are often related to public tragedies, memories of both positive and negative events can have "flashbulb" clarity (Paradis et al., 2004). Would you consider any of the following to be a flashbulb memory? Your first kiss, a special date, or your prom night? How about a time you had to speak in front of a large audience? A car accident you were in or witnessed?

Do you have a flashbulb memory for the November 2008 election victory of President Obama? You do if someone alerted you about the news and you remember that person's call. You do if you saw the news on television and you have clear memories of how you reacted.

The term *flashbulb memories* was first used to describe recollections that seemed to be unusually vivid and permanent (Brown & Kulik, 1977). It has become clear, however, that flashbulb memories are not always accurate (Greenberg, 2004; Kensinger, 2007). More than anything else, what sets flashbulb memories apart is that we tend to place great *confidence* in them—even when they are wrong (Niedzwienska, 2004). Perhaps that's because we review emotionally charged events over and over and tell others about them. Also, public events such as wars, earthquakes, and elections reappear many times in the news, which highlights them in memory. Over time, flashbulb memories tend to crystallize into consistent, if not entirely accurate, landmarks in our lives (Schmolck, Buffalo, & Squire, 2000).

Some memories go beyond flashbulb clarity and become so intense that they may haunt a person for years. Extremely traumatic experiences, such as military combat or maltreatment as a child, can produce so much limbic system activation that the resulting

Retrograde amnesia Loss of memory for events that preceded a head injury or other amnesia-causing event.

Anterograde amnesia Loss of the ability to form or retrieve memories for events that occur after an injury or trauma.

Consolidation Process by which relatively permanent memories are formed in the brain.

Electroconvulsive shock (ECS) An electric current passed directly through the brain, producing a convulsion.

Hippocampus A brain structure associated with emotion and the transfer of information from short-term memory to long-term memory.

Flashbulb memory Memory created at times of high emotion that seems especially vivid.

Critical Thinking The Long-Term Potential of a Memory Pill

At long last, scientists may have found the chemical "signature" that records memories in everything from snails to rats to humans. If two or more interconnected brain cells become more active at the same time, the connections between them grow stronger (Xu & Yao, 2010). This process is called **long-term potentiation**. After it occurs, an affected brain cell will respond more strongly to messages from the other cells. The brain appears to use this mechanism to form lasting memories (Blundon & Zakharenko, 2008).

How has that been demonstrated? Electrically stimulating parts of the brain involved in memory, such as the hippocampus, can decrease long-term potentiation (Ivanco & Racine, 2000). As we saw earlier, using electroconvulsive shock to overstimulate memory areas in the brains of rats interferes with long-term potentiation (Trepel & Racine, 1999). It also causes memory loss—just as it does when humans are given ECS for depression.

Will researchers ever produce a "memory pill" for people with normal memory? It's a growing possibility. Drugs that *increase* long-term potentiation also tend to improve memory (Shakesby, Anwyl, & Rowan, 2002). For example, rats administered such drugs could remember the correct path through a maze better than rats not given the drug (Service, 1994). Such findings suggest that memory can be and will be artificially enhanced (McGaugh & Roozendaal, 2009). However, the possibility of something like a "physics pill" or a "math pill" still seems remote.

memories and "flashbacks" leave a person emotionally handicapped (Goodman, Quas, Ogle, 2010; Nemeroff et al., 2006).

BRIDGES

To read more about post-traumatic stress disorder, **see Chapter 14, pages 498–499.**

Long-Term Memory and the Brain

Somewhere within the 3-pound mass of the human brain lies all we know: ZIP codes, faces of loved ones, history, favorite melodies, the taste of an apple, and much, much more. Where is this information? According to neuroscientist Richard Thompson (2005), many parts of the brain become active when we form and retrieve long-term memories, but some areas are more important for different types of memory and memory process.

For example, patterns of blood flow in the cerebral cortex (the wrinkled outer layer of the brain) can be used to map brain activity. • Figure 7.16 shows the results of measuring blood flow while people were thinking about a semantic memory or an episodic memory. The resulting pattern indicates that we use the front of the cortex for episodic memory. Back areas are more associated with semantic memory (Tulving, 1989, 2002). As another example, different parts of cortex are activated when we are engaging in memory retrieval and suppression (Mecklinger, 2010).

Let's summarize (and simplify greatly). Earlier we noted that the hippocampus handles memory consolidation (Wang & Morris, 2010). Once declarative long-term memories are formed, they appear to be stored and retrieved in the cortex of the brain (episodic in the front, semantic in the back) (Mecklinger, 2010; Squire, 2004). Long-term procedural (skill) memories are stored in the basal ganglia and cerebellum, parts of the brain that are also responsible for muscular coordination (Freberg, 2010; Hermann et al., 2004).

How are memories recorded in the brain? Scientists are beginning to identify the exact ways in which nerve cells record information. For example, Eric Kandel and his colleagues have studied learning in the marine snail *aplysia* (ah-PLEEZ-yah). Learning in *aplysia* occurs when certain nerve cells in a circuit alter the amount of transmitter chemicals they release (Bailey & Kandel, 2004). Learning also alters the activity, structure, and chemistry of brain cells. Such changes determine which connections get stronger and which become weaker. This "reprograms" the brain and records information (Abraham, 2006).

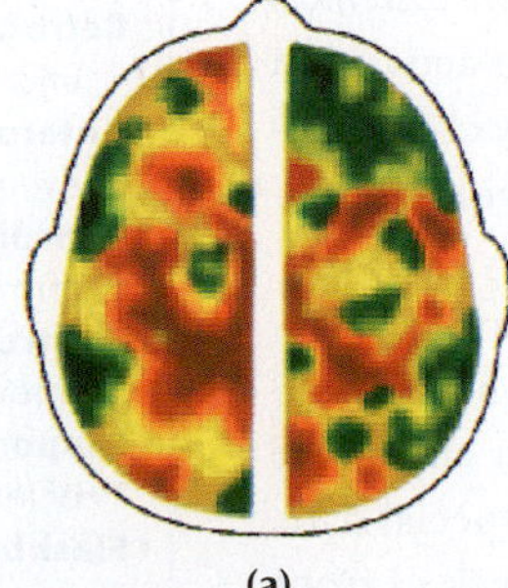
(a)

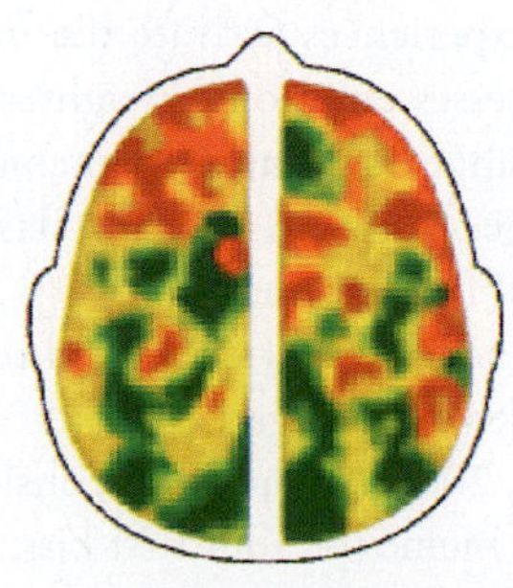
(b)

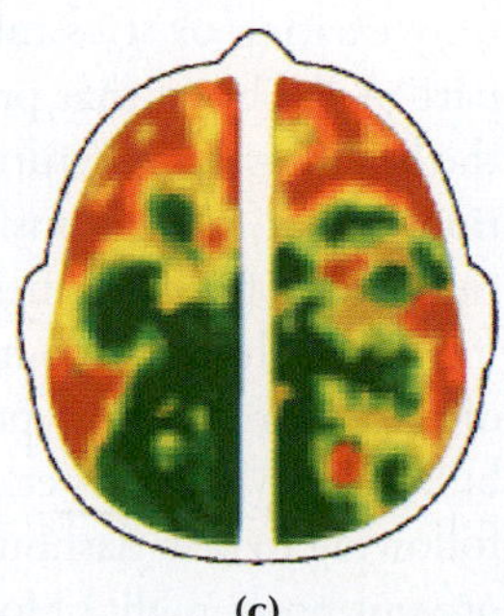
(c)

• **Figure 7.16** Patterns of blood flow in the cerebral cortex (wrinkled outer layer of the brain) change as areas become more or less active. Thus, blood flow can be used to draw "maps" of brain activity. This drawing, which views the brain from the top, shows the results of measuring cerebral blood flow while people were thinking about a semantic memory *(a)* or an episodic memory *(b)*. In the map, green indicates areas that are more active during semantic thinking. Reds show areas of greater activity during episodic thinking. The brain in view *c* shows the difference in activity between views *a* and *b*. The resulting pattern suggests that the front of the cortex is related to episodic memory. Areas toward the back and sides of the brain, especially the temporal lobes, are more associated with semantic memory (Tulving, 1989, 2002).

© Jeffrey L. Rotman/Corbis

An *aplysia.* The relatively simple nervous system of this sea animal allows scientists to study memory as it occurs in single nerve cells.

Scientists continue to study various chemicals, especially neurotransmitters, that affect memory (Xu & Yao, 2010). Their research may eventually help the millions of persons who suffer from memory impairment (Elli & Nathan, 2001; see "The Long-Term Potential of a Memory Pill").

Knowledge Builder: Forgetting

RECITE

1. According to the Ebbinghaus curve of forgetting, we forget slowly at first and then a rapid decline occurs. T or F?
2. Which explanation(s) seem(s) to account for the loss of short-term memories?
   a. decay *b.* disuse *c.* repression *d.* interference
3. When memories are available but not accessible, forgetting may be cue dependent. T or F?
4. When learning one thing makes it more difficult to recall another, forgetting may be caused by ______________________.
5. You are asked to memorize long lists of telephone numbers. You learn a new list each day for 10 days. When tested on list 3, you remember less than a person who learned only the first three lists. Your larger memory loss is probably caused by
   a. disuse *b.* retroactive interference *c.* regression *d.* proactive interference
6. If you consciously succeed at putting a painful memory out of mind, you have used
   a. redintegration *b.* suppression *c.* negative rehearsal *d.* repression
7. Retrograde amnesia results when consolidation is speeded up. T or F?

REFLECT

Think Critically

8. Based on state-dependent learning, why do you think that music often strongly evokes memories?
9. You must study French, Spanish, psychology, and biology in one evening (poor thing!). What do you think would be the best order in which to study these subjects so as to minimize interference?

Self-Reflect

Which of the following concepts best explain why you have missed some answers on psychology tests: encoding failure, decay, disuse, memory cues, interference?

Do you know someone whose name you have a hard time remembering? Do you like or dislike that person? Do you think your difficulty is an instance of repression? Suppression? Interference? Encoding failure?

Have you had a flashbulb memory? How vivid is the memory today? How accurate do you think it is?

Answers: 1. F **2.** *a* and *d* **3.** T **4.** interference **5.** *d* **6.** *b* **7.** F **8.** Music tends to affect the mood that a person is in, and moods tend to affect memory (Miranda & Kihlstrom, 2005). **9.** Any order that separates French from Spanish and psychology from biology would be better (for instance: French, psychology, Spanish, biology).

Exceptional Memory—Wizards of Recall

Gateway Question 7.7: *What are "photographic" memories?*

In this section, we will explore exceptional memories. Is superior memory a biological gift, such as having a "photographic" memory? Or do excellent memorizers merely make better-than-average use of normal memory capacities?

Can you remember how many doors there are in your house or apartment? To answer a question like this, many people form **mental images** (mental pictures) of each room and count the doorways they visualize. As this example implies, many memories are processed and stored as mental images (Shorrock & Isaac, 2010).

Stephen Kosslyn, Thomas Ball, and Brian Reiser (1978) found an interesting way to show that memories do exist as images. Participants first memorized a sort of treasure map similar to the one shown in ● Figure 7.17*a*. They were then asked to picture a black dot moving from one object, such as one of the trees, to another, such as the hut at the top of the island. Did people really form an image to do this task? It seems they did. As shown in ● Figure 7.17*b*, the time it took to "move" the dot was directly related to actual distances on the map.

Is the "treasure map" task an example of photographic memory? In some ways, internal memory images do have "photographic" qualities. However, the term *photographic memory* is more often used to describe a memory ability called *eidetic imagery*.

Eidetic Imagery

Eidetic (eye-DET-ik) **imagery** occurs when a person has visual images clear enough to be "scanned" or retained for at least 30 seconds. Internal memory images can be "viewed" mentally with the eyes closed. In contrast, eidetic images are "projected" out in front of a person. That is, they are best "seen" on a plain surface, such as a blank piece of paper. In this respect, eidetic images are somewhat

Long-term potentiation Brain mechanism used to form lasting memories by strengthening the connection between neurons that become more active at the same time.

Mental images Mental pictures or visual depictions used in memory and thinking.

Eidetic imagery The ability to retain a "projected" mental image long enough to use it as a source of information.

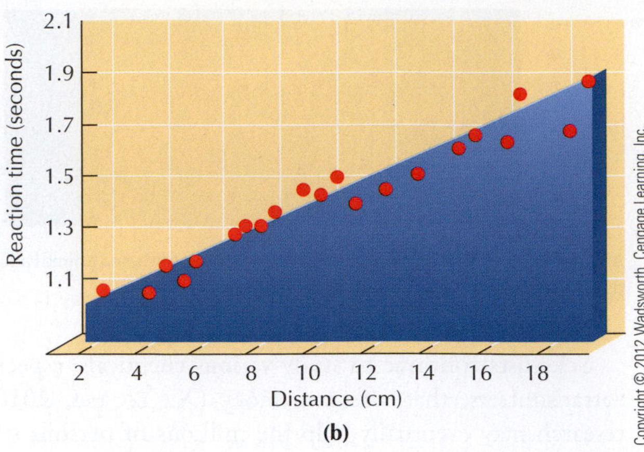

● **Figure 7.17** *(a)* "Treasure map" similar to the one used by Kosslyn, Ball, and Reiser (1978) to study images in memory. *(b)* This graph shows how long it took subjects to move a visualized spot various distances on their mental images of the map. (See text for explanation.)

like the afterimages you might have after looking at a flashbulb or a brightly lit neon sign (Haber & Haber, 2000).

In one series of tests, children were shown a picture from *Alice's Adventures in Wonderland* (● Figure 7.18). To test your eidetic imagery, look at the picture and read the instructions there.

Now, let's see how much you remember. Can you say (without looking again) which of Alice's apron strings is longer? Are the cat's front paws crossed? How many stripes are on the cat's tail? After the picture was removed from view, one 10-year-old boy correctly answered all of these questions. The boy then went on to describe the remainder of the picture in striking detail (Haber, 1969).

● **Figure 7.18** A test picture like that used to identify children with eidetic imagery. To test your eidetic imagery, look at the picture for 30 seconds. Then look at a blank surface and try to "project" the picture onto it. If you have good eidetic imagery, you will be able to see the picture in detail. Return now to the text and try to answer the questions there. (Redrawn from an illustration in Lewis Carroll's *Alice's Adventures in Wonderland*.)

Don't be disappointed if you didn't do too well when you tried your eidetic skills. Eidetic memory is more common in childhood and becomes rare by adulthood (Haber & Haber, 2000).

Photographic Memory

Let's return now to the concept of mental images. In rare instances, such images may be so vivid that it is reasonable to say that a person has "photographic memory." For example, we met Jill Price and Mr. S. at the beginning of this chapter. Besides having excellent memories, both attested to the importance of forgetting. If you didn't have selective memory, you would recall all the ingredients on your cereal box, every street number you've seen, and countless other scraps of information. Regardless, few adults in history have possessed such amazing memory abilities. Instead, most people with good memories have learned effective strategies for remembering. Let's investigate further.

Strategies for Remembering

At first, a student volunteer named Steve could remember 7 digits. Could he improve with practice? For 20 months, Steve practiced memorizing ever-longer lists of digits. Ultimately, he was able to memorize approximately 80 digits, like this sample:

92842048050842268953990190252912807999706606574717310601080585269726026357332135

How did Steve do it? Basically, he worked by chunking digits into meaningful groups containing three or four digits each. Steve's avid interest in long-distance running helped greatly. For instance, to him the first three digits above represented 9 minutes and 28 seconds, a good time for a 2-mile run. When running times wouldn't work, Steve used other associations, such as ages or dates, to chunk digits (Ericsson & Chase, 1982). It seems apparent that Steve's success was based on learned strategies. By using similar memory systems, other people have trained themselves to equal Steve's feat (Bellezza, Six, & Phillips, 1992). In fact, the ability to organize information into chunks underlies expertise in many fields (Gobet, 2005).

Psychologist Anders Ericsson believes that exceptional memory is merely a learned extension of normal memory. As evidence, he notes that Steve's short-term memory did not improve during months of practice. For example, Steve could still memorize only seven consonants. Steve's phenomenal memory for numbers grew as he figured out new ways to chunk digits at encoding and store them in LTM. Steve began with a normal memory for digits. He extended his memory by diligent practice. Clearly, exceptional memory can be learned (Ericsson et al., 2004). However, we still have to wonder, do some people have naturally superior memories?

Memory Champions

Each year, the World Memory Championship is held in England. Contestants must rapidly memorize daunting amounts of information, such as long lists of unrelated words and numbers. Psychologists John Wilding and Elizabeth Valentine saw this event as an opportunity to study exceptional memory and persuaded the contestants to take some additional memory tests. These ranged from ordinary (recall a story), to challenging (recall the telephone numbers of six different people), to diabolical (recall 48 numerals arranged in rows and columns) (Maguire et al., 2003; Wilding & Valentine, 1994).

Exceptional memorizers were found to:

- Use memory strategies and techniques;
- Have specialized interests and knowledge that make certain types of information easier to encode and recall;
- Have naturally superior memory abilities, often including vivid mental images;
- Not have superior intellectual abilities or different brains.

The first two points confirm what we learned from Steve's acquired memory ability. Many of the contestants, for example, actively used memory strategies, including special memory "tricks" called *mnemonics* (nee-MON-iks). Specialized interests and knowledge also helped for some tasks. For example, one contestant, a mathematician, was exceedingly good at memorizing numbers (Wilding & Valentine, 1994).

8 7 3 7 9 2 6 8
2 0 1 1 7 4 9 5
0 1 7 5 8 7 8 3
1 9 4 7 6 0 6 9
3 6 1 6 8 1 5 4
4 5 2 4 0 2 9 7

This number matrix is similar to the ones contestants in the World Memory Championship had to memorize. To be scored as correct, digits had to be recalled in their proper positions (Wilding & Valentine, 1994).

Several of the memory contestants were able to excel on tasks that prevented the use of learned strategies and techniques. This observation implies that superior memory ability can be a "gift" as well as a learned skill (Yi & Qian, 2009). Wilding and Valentine conclude that exceptional memory may be based on either natural ability or learned strategies. Usually it requires both.

Improving Memory—Keys to the Memory Bank

Gateway Question 7.8: *How can I improve my memory?*

Let's see how you can improve your memory. To begin, there is very little you can do to improve your brain's ability to store long-term memories. The jury is still out on the use of drugs, herbs (such as *Ginkgo biloba*), and vitamins (such as vitamin E) to improve human memory (McDaniel, Maier, & Einstein, 2002; McGaugh & Roozendaal, 2009). However, until there's a memory pill, you can immediately use meaning-based strategies to improve memory encoding and memory retrieval. Most super memorizers use these strategies to augment whatever natural talents they have. Some of their strategies are described in the remainder of this section. Later, mnemonics are explored in this chapter's *Psychology in Action* section. Please do remember to read it.

Encoding Strategies

One way to improve your memory is to be sure to fully encode information. That way you can avoid forgetting due to encoding failure. Following are some steps you can take to become a better encoder.

Elaborative Processing

The more you *rehearse* (mentally review) information as you read, the better you will remember it. But remember that rote rehearsal alone is not very effective. Elaborative processing, in which you look for connections to existing knowledge, is far better. Oddly enough, even if new information is linked to existing superstitions, the end result can be improved memory for the new information (Damisch, Stoberock, & Mussweiler, 2010; Wargo, 2008). So, for example, someone superstitious about the number 13 might show superior memory for an address like *1313 Huntington Lane*. Even repeatedly thinking about facts helps link them together in memory. To learn college-level information, you must make active use of more reflective study strategies (Santrock & Halonen, 2010).

Selection

The Dutch scholar Erasmus said that a good memory should be like a fish net: It should keep all the big fish and let the little ones escape. If you boil down the paragraphs in most textbooks to one or two important terms or ideas, your memory chores will be more manageable. Practice very selective marking in your texts and use marginal notes to further summarize ideas. Most students mark their texts too much instead of too little. If everything is underlined, you haven't been selective. And, very likely, you didn't pay much attention in the first place (Peterson, 1992).

Organization

Assume that you must memorize the following list of words: north, man, red, spring, woman, east, autumn, yellow, summer, boy, blue, west, winter, girl, green, south. This rather difficult list could be reorganized into *chunks* as follows: north-east-south-west, spring-summer-autumn-winter, red-yellow-green-blue, man-woman-boy-girl. Organizing class notes and summarizing chapters can be quite helpful (Hettich, 2005). You may even want to summarize your summaries, so that the overall network of ideas becomes clearer and simpler. Summaries improve memory by encouraging better encoding of information (Anderson, 2010).

Whole Versus Part Learning

If you have to memorize a speech, is it better to try to learn it from beginning to end? Or in smaller parts like paragraphs? Generally it is better to practice whole packages of information rather than smaller parts (*whole learning*). This is especially true for fairly short, organized information. An exception is that learning parts may be better for extremely long, complicated information. In *part learning,* subparts of a larger body of information are studied (such as sections of a textbook chapter). To decide which approach to use, remember to study the *largest meaningful amount of information* you can at one time.

For very long or complex material, try the *progressive-part method*, by breaking a learning task into a series of short sections. At first, you study part A until it is mastered. Next, you study parts A and B; then A, B, and C; and so forth. This is a good way to learn the lines of a play, a long piece of music, or a poem (Ash & Holding, 1990). After the material is learned, you should also practice by starting at points other than A (at C, D, or B, for example). This helps prevent getting "lost" or going blank in the middle of a performance.

Serial Position

Whenever you must learn something in order, be aware of the serial position effect. As you will recall, this is the tendency to make the most errors in remembering the middle of a list. If you are introduced to a long line of people, the names you are likely to forget will be those in the middle, so you should make an extra effort to attend to them. You should also give extra practice to the middle of a list, poem, or speech. Try to break long lists of information into short sublists, and make the middle sub-lists the shortest of all.

Cues

The best *memory cues* (stimuli that aid retrieval) are those that were present during encoding (Anderson, 2010). For example, students in one classic study had the daunting task of trying to recall a list of 600 words. As they read the list (which they did not know they would be tested on), the students gave three other words closely related in meaning to each listed word. In a test given later, the words each student supplied were used as cues to jog

• Figure 7.19 Actors can remember large amounts of complex information for many months, even when learning new roles in between. During testing, they remember their lines best when they are allowed to move and gesture as they would when performing. Apparently their movements supply cues that aid recall (Noice & Noice, 1999).

memory. The students recalled an astounding 90 percent of the original word list (Mantyla, 1986).

Now read the following sentence:

The fish bit the swimmer.

If you were tested a week from now, you would be more likely to recall the sentence if you were given a memory cue. And, surprisingly, the word *shark* would work better as a reminder than *fish* would. The reason for this is that most people think of a shark when they read the sentence. As a result, *shark* becomes a potent memory cue.

The preceding example shows, once again, that it often helps to *elaborate* information as you learn. When you study, try to use new names, ideas, or terms in several sentences. Also, form images that include the new information and relate it to knowledge you already have. Your goal should be to knit meaningful cues into your memory code to help you retrieve information when you need it (• Figure 7.19).

Overlearning

Numerous studies have shown that memory is greatly improved when you **overlearn** or continue to study beyond bare mastery. After you have learned material well enough to remember it once without error, you should continue studying. Overlearning is your best insurance against going blank on a test because of nervousness.

Spaced Practice

To keep boredom and fatigue to a minimum, try alternating short study sessions with brief rest periods. This pattern, called **spaced practice**, is generally superior to **massed practice**, in which little or no rest is given between learning sessions (Anderson, 2010). By improving attention and consolidation, three 20-minute study sessions can produce more learning than 1 hour of continuous study. There's an old joke that goes, "How do you get to Carnegie Hall?" The answer is, "Practice, practice, practice." A better answer would be "Practice, wait awhile, practice, wait awhile, practice" (Radvansky, 2011).

Perhaps the best way to make use of spaced practice is to *schedule* your time. To make an effective schedule, designate times during the week before, after, and between classes when you will study particular subjects. Then treat these times just as if they are classes you have to attend.

Retrieval Strategies

Once you have successfully encoded information you still have to retrieve it. Following are some strategies to help you avoid retrieval failure.

Retrieval Practice

Learning proceeds best when feedback allows you to check your progress. Feedback can help you identify ideas that need extra practice. In addition, knowing that you have remembered or answered correctly is rewarding. A prime way to provide feedback for yourself while studying is *recitation*. If you are going to remember something, eventually you will have to retrieve it. *Recitation* refers to summarizing aloud while you are learning. Recitation forces you to practice retrieving information. When you are reading a text, you should stop frequently and try to remember what you have just read by restating it in your own words. In one classic experiment, the best memory score was earned by a group of students who spent 80 percent of their time reciting and only 20 percent reading (Gates, 1917). Maybe students who talk to themselves aren't crazy after all.

Review

If you have spaced your practice and overlearned, retrieval practice in the form of review will be like icing on your study cake. Reviewing shortly before an exam cuts down the time during which you must remember details that may be important for the test. When reviewing, hold the amount of new information you try to memorize to a minimum. It may be realistic to take what you have actually learned and add a little more to it at the last minute by cramming. But remember that more than a little new learning may interfere with what you already know.

Using a Strategy to Aid Recall

Successful retrieval is usually the result of a planned *search* of memory (Herrmann et al., 2006). For example, one study found that students were most likely to recall names that eluded them if they made use of partial information (Reed & Bruce, 1982). The students were trying to answer questions such as, "He is best remembered as the boxer in the *Rocky* movies." (The answer is Sylvester Stallone.) Partial information that helped students remember included impressions about the length of the name, letter sounds within the name, similar names, and related information (such as the names of other characters in the movie). A similar helpful strategy is to go through the alphabet, trying each letter as the first sound of a name or word you are seeking.

The *cognitive interview* described earlier in this chapter (see "Telling Wrong from Right in Forensic Memory") offers some further hints for recapturing context and jogging memories:

1. Say or write down *everything* you can remember that relates to the information you are seeking. Don't worry about how trivial any of it seems; each bit of information you remember can serve as a cue to bring back others.
2. Try to recall events or information in different orders. Let your memories flow out backward or out of order, or start with whatever impressed you the most.
3. Recall from different viewpoints. Review events by mentally standing in a different place. Or try to view information as another person would remember it. When taking a test, for instance, ask yourself what other students or your professor would remember about the topic.
4. Mentally put yourself back in the situation where you learned the information. Try to mentally recreate the learning environment or relive the event. As you do, include sounds, smells, details of weather, nearby objects, other people present, what you said or thought, and how you felt as you learned the information (Fisher & Geiselman, 1987; Milne & Bull, 2002).

Extend How Long You Remember

When you are learning new information, practice retrieval repeatedly. As you do, gradually lengthen the amount of time that passes before you test yourself again. For example, if you are studying German words on flash cards, look at the first card and then move it a few cards back in the stack. Do the same with the next few cards. When you get to the first "old" card, test yourself on it and check the answer. Then, move it farther back in the stack. Do the same with other "old" cards as they come up. When "old" cards come up for the third time, put them clear to the back of the stack (Cull, Shaughnessy, & Zechmeister, 1996).

Sleep and Memory

Remember that sleeping after study reduces interference. However, unless you are a "night person," late evening may not be a very efficient time for you to study. Also, you obviously can't sleep after

Overlearn To continue to study beyond bare mastery.

Spaced practice A practice schedule that alternates study periods with brief rests.

Massed practice A practice schedule in which studying continues for long periods, without interruption.

every study session or study everything just before you sleep. That's why your study schedule should include ample breaks between subjects as described earlier (see "Spaced Practice"). The breaks and free time in your schedule are as important as your study periods.

Hunger and Memory

People who are hungry almost always score lower on memory tests. So Mother was right, it's a good idea to make sure you've had a good breakfast or lunch before you take tests at school (Smith, Clark, & Gallagher, 1999). And a cup of coffee won't hurt your test performance, either (Smith, 2005).

A Look Ahead

Psychologists still have much to learn about the nature of memory and how to improve it. For now, one thing stands out clearly: People who have good memories excel at organizing meaningful information. Sometimes, however, you are faced with the need to memorize information without much inherent meaning. For example, a shopping list is just a list of more or less unrelated items. There isn't much of a meaningful relationship between carrots, rolls of toilet paper, TV dinners, and Twinkies® except that you need more of them. With this in mind, the *Psychology in Action* discussion for this chapter tells how you can use mnemonics to better memorize when meaning-based memory strategies, like those described in this section, are not helpful.

Knowledge Builder: Improving Memory

RECITE

1. Children with eidetic imagery typically have no better than average long-term memory. T or F?
2. For most people, having an especially good memory is based on *a.* maintenance rehearsal *b.* elaborative processing *c.* phonetic imagery *d.* learned strategies
3. As new information is encoded, it is helpful to elaborate on its meaning and connect it to other information. T or F?
4. Organizing information while studying has little effect on memory because long-term memory is already highly organized. T or F?
5. The progressive-part method of study is best suited to long and complex learning tasks. T or F?
6. To improve memory, it is reasonable to spend as much or more time reciting as reading. T or F?
7. The cognitive interview helps people remember more by providing *a.* memory cues *b.* a serial position effect *c.* phonetic priming *d.* massed practice

REFLECT

Think Critically

8. Mr. S had great difficulty remembering faces. Can you guess why?
9. What advantages would there be to taking notes as you read a textbook, as opposed to underlining words in the text?

Self-Reflect

What kinds of information are you good at remembering? Why do you think your memory is better for those topics?

Return to the topic headings in the preceding pages that list techniques for improving memory. Place a check mark next to those that you have used recently. Review any you didn't mark and think of a specific example of how you could use each technique at school, at home, or at work.

Answers: 1. T **2.** *d* **3.** T **4.** F **5.** T **6.** T **7.** *a* **8.** Mr. S's memory was so specific that faces seemed different and unfamiliar if he saw them from a new angle or if a face had a different expression on it than when Mr. S last saw it. **9.** Note-taking is a form of elaborative processing and recitation; it encourages elaborative rehearsal and facilitates the organization and selection of important ideas, and your notes can be used for review.

Psychology in Action: Mnemonics—Memory Magic

Gateway Question 7.9: *Are there any tricks to help me with my memory?*

Just imagine the poor biology or psychology student who is required to learn the names of the 12 cranial nerves (in order, of course). Although the spinal nerves connect the brain to the body through the spinal cord, the cranial nerves do so directly. Just in case you wanted to know, their names are: olfactory, optic, oculomotor, trochlear, trigeminal, abducens, facial, vestibulocochlear, glossopharyngeal, vagus, spinal accessory, and hypoglossal.

As you might imagine, most of us find it difficult to successfully encode this list. In the absence of any obvious meaningful relationship among these terms, it is difficult to apply the memory strategies we discussed earlier in the chapter and tempting to resort to *rote* learning (learning by simple repetition). Fortunately, there *is* an alternative: mnemonics (nee-MON-iks) (Baddeley, Eysenck, & Anderson, 2009; Radvansky, 2011). A **mnemonic** is any kind of memory system or aid. The superiority of mnemonic learning as opposed to rote learning has been demonstrated many times (Worthen & Hunt, 2010; Saber & Johnson, 2008).

Some mnemonic systems are so common that almost everyone knows them. If you are trying to remember how many days there are in a month, you may find the answer by reciting, "Thirty days hath September . . . ." Physics teachers often help students remember the colors of the spectrum by giving them the mnemonic "Roy G. Biv": **R**ed, **O**range, **Y**ellow, **G**reen, **B**lue, **I**ndigo, **V**iolet. The budding sailor who has trouble telling port from starboard may remember that port and left

Mnemonics can be an aid in preparing for tests. However, because mnemonics help most in the initial stages of storing information, it is important to follow through with other elaborative learning strategies.

both have four letters or may remind herself, "I *left* port." And what beginning musician hasn't remembered the notes represented by the lines and spaces of the musical staff by learning "F-A-C-E" and "**E**very **G**ood **B**oy **D**oes **F**ine"?

Generations of students have learned the names of the spinal nerves by memorizing the sentence "**O**n **O**ld **O**lympus' **T**owering **T**op **A** **F**amous **V**ocal **G**erman **V**iewed **S**ome **H**ops." This mnemonic, which uses the first letter of each of the cranial nerves to generate a nonsense sentence, indeed produces better recall of the cranial nerves. Such *acrostics* are even more effective if you make up your own (Bloom & Lamkin, 2006). By practicing mnemonics, you should be able to greatly improve your memory with little effort.

Here, then, are some basic principles of mnemonics:

1. **Make things meaningful.** In general, transferring information from short-term memory to long-term memory is aided by making it meaningful. If you encounter technical terms that have little or no immediate meaning for you, *give* them meaning, even if you have to stretch the term to do so. (This point is clarified by the examples following this list.)
2. **Make information familiar.** Another way to get information into long-term memory is to connect it to information already stored there. If some facts or ideas in a chapter seem to stay in your memory easily, associate other more difficult facts with them.
3. **Use mental pictures.** Visual pictures, or images, are generally easier to remember than words. Turning information into mental pictures is, therefore, very helpful. Make these images as vivid as possible (Radvansky, 2011).
4. **Form bizarre, unusual, or exaggerated mental associations.** Forming images that make sense is better in most situations. However, when associating two ideas, terms, or especially mental images, you may find that the more outrageous and exaggerated the association, the more likely you are to remember. Bizarre images make stored information more *distinctive* and, therefore, easier to retrieve (Worthen & Marshall, 1996). Imagine, for example, that you have just been introduced to Mr. Rehkop. To remember his name, you could picture him wearing a police uniform. Then replace his nose with a ray gun. This bizarre image will provide two hints when you want to remember Mr. Rehkop's name: *ray* and *cop*. This technique works for other kinds of information, too. College students who used exaggerated mental associations to remember the names of unfamiliar animals outperformed students who just used rote memory (Carney & Levin, 2001). Bizarre images help improve mainly immediate memory, and they work best for fairly simple information (Fritz et al., 2007). Nevertheless, they can be a first step toward learning.

A sampling of typical applications of mnemonics should make these four points clearer to you.

Example 1

Let's say you have some new vocabulary words to memorize in Spanish. You can proceed by rote memorization (repeat them over and over until you begin to get them), or you can learn them with little effort by using the **keyword method**, in which a familiar word or image is used to link two other words or items (Fritz et al., 2007; Pressley, 1987). To remember that the word *pajaro* (pronounced PAH-hah-ro) means bird, you can link it to a "key" word in English: *Pajaro* sounds a bit like "parked car-o." Therefore, to remember that

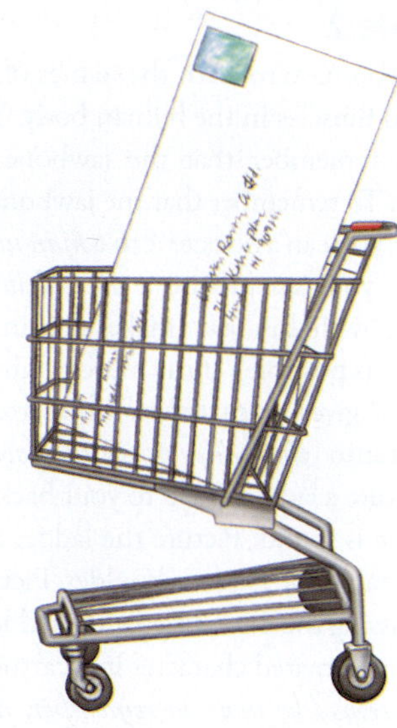

Exaggerated mental images can link two words or ideas in ways that aid memory. Here, the keyword method is used to link the English word *letter* with the Spanish word *carta*.

pajaro means bird, you might visualize a parked car jam-packed full of birds. You should try to make this image as vivid and exaggerated as possible, with birds flapping and chirping and feathers flying everywhere. Similarly, for the word *carta* (which means "letter"), you might imagine a shopping *cart* filled with postal letters.

If you link similar keywords and images for the rest of the list, you may not remember them all, but you will get most without much more practice. As a matter of fact, if you have formed the *pajaro* and *carta* images just now, it is going to be almost impossible for you to ever see these words again without remembering what they mean. The keyword method is also superior when you want to work "backward" from an English word to a foreign vocabulary word (Hogben & Lawson, 1992).

What about a year from now? How long do keyword memories last? Mnemonic memories work best in the short run. Later, they may be more fragile than conventional memories. That's why it's usually best to use mnemonics during the initial stages of learning (Carney & Levin, 2003). To create more lasting memories, you'll need to use the techniques discussed earlier in this chapter.

Mnemonic Any kind of memory system or aid.
Keyword method As an aid to memory, using a familiar word or image to link two items.

Example 2

Suppose you have to learn the names of all the bones and muscles in the human body. You are trying to remember that the jawbone is the *mandible*. To remember that the jawbone is the *mandible*, you can associate it to a *man nibbling*, or maybe you can picture a *man dribbling* a basketball with his jaw (make this image as ridiculous as possible). If the muscle name *latissimus dorsi* gives you trouble, familiarize it by turning it into "*the ladder misses the door, sigh*." Then picture a ladder glued to your back where the muscle is found. Picture the ladder leading up to a small door at your shoulder. Picture the ladder missing the door. Picture the ladder sighing like an animated character in a cartoon.

This seems like more to remember, not less; and it seems like it would cause you to misspell things. Mnemonics are an aid, not a complete substitute for normal memory. Mnemonics are not likely to be helpful unless you make extensive use of *images* (Willoughby et al., 1997; Worthen & Hunt, 2010). Your mental pictures will come back to you easily. As for misspellings, mnemonics can be thought of as a built-in hint in your memory. Often, when taking a test, you will find that the slightest hint is all you need to remember correctly. A mnemonic image is like having someone leaning over your shoulder who says, "Psst, the name of that muscle sounds like 'ladder misses the door, sigh.'" If misspelling continues to be a problem, try to create memory aids for spelling, too.

Here are two more examples to help you appreciate the flexibility of a mnemonic approach to studying.

Example 3

Your art history teacher expects you to be able to name the artist when you are shown slides as part of exams. You have seen many of the slides only once before in class. How will you remember them? As the slides are shown in class, make each artist's name into an object or image. Then picture the object *in* the paintings done by the artist. For example, you can picture Van Gogh as a *van* (automobile) *going* through the middle of each Van Gogh painting. Picture the van running over things and knocking things over. Or, if you remember that Van Gogh cut off his ear, picture a giant bloody ear in each of his paintings.

Example 4

If you have trouble remembering history, try to avoid thinking of it as something from the dim past. Picture each historical personality as a person you know right now (a friend, teacher, parent, and so on). Then picture these people doing whatever the historical figures did. Also, try visualizing battles or other events as if they were happening in your town or make parks and schools into countries. Use your imagination.

How can mnemonics be used to remember things in order? Here are three techniques that are helpful:

1. **Form a story or a chain.** To remember lists of ideas, objects, or words in order, try forming an exaggerated association (mental image) connecting the first item to the second, then the second to the third, and so on. To remember the following short list in order—elephant, doorknob, string, watch, rifle, oranges—picture a full-size *elephant* balanced on a *doorknob* playing with a *string* tied to him. Picture a *watch* tied to the string, and a *rifle* shooting *oranges* at the watch. This technique can be used quite successfully for lists of 20 or more items. In one test, people who used a linking mnemonic did much better at remembering lists of 15 and 22 errands (Higbee et al., 1990). Try it next time you go shopping and leave your list at home. Another helpful strategy is to make up a short story that links all the items on a list you want to remember (McNamara & Scott, 2001).
2. **Take a mental walk.** Ancient Greek orators had an interesting way to remember ideas in order when giving a speech. Their method was to take a mental walk along a familiar path. As they did, they associated topics with the images of statues found along the walk. You can do the same thing by "placing" objects or ideas along the way as you mentally take a familiar walk (Radvansky, 2011).
3. **Use a system.** As we have already seen, many times the first letters or syllables of words or ideas can be formed into another word that will serve as a reminder of order. "Roy G. Biv" is an example. As an alternative, learn the following: 1 is a bun, 2 is a shoe, 3 is a tree, 4 is a door, 5 is a hive, 6 is sticks, 7 is heaven, 8 is a gate, 9 is a line, 10 is a hen. To remember a list in order, form an image associating bun with the first item on your list. For example, if the first item is *frog*, picture a "frog-burger" on a bun to remember it. Then, associate shoe with the second item, and so on.

If you have never used mnemonics, you may still be skeptical, but give this approach a fair trial. Most people find they can greatly extend their memory through the use of mnemonics. But remember, like most things worthwhile, remembering takes effort.

Knowledge Builder Mnemonics

RECITE

1. Memory systems and aids are referred to as ____________.
2. Which of the following is least likely to improve memory? *a.* using exaggerated mental images *b.* forming a chain of associations *c.* turning visual information into verbal information *d.* associating new information to information that is already known or familiar
3. Bizarre images make stored information more distinctive and therefore easier to retrieve. T or F?
4. In general, mnemonics only improve memory for related words or ideas. T or F?
5. The keyword method is a commonly used *a.* cognitive interviewing technique *b.* massed practice strategy *c.* mnemonic technique *d.* first step in the progressive-part method

REFLECT

Think Critically

6. How are elaborative processing and mnemonics alike?

Self-Reflect

The best mnemonics are your own. As an exercise, see if you can create a better acrostic for the 12 cranial nerves. One student generated **O**ld **O**tto **O**ctavius **T**ried **T**rigonometry **A**fter **F**acing **V**ery **G**rim **V**irgin's **S**ad **H**usbands (Bloom & Lamkin, 2006).

Go through the glossary items in this chapter and make up mnemonics for any terms you have difficulty remembering. Here is an example to help you get started. An iconic memory is a visual image: Picture an *eye* in a *can* to remember that iconic memories store visual information.

Answers: 1. mnemonics **2.** c **3.** T **4.** F **5.** c **6.** Both attempt to relate new information to information stored in LTM that is familiar or already easy to retrieve.

Chapter in Review Gateways to Memory

Gateway QUESTIONS REVISITED

7.1 How does memory work?

7.1.1 Memory is an active, computer-like system that encodes, stores, and retrieves information.

7.1.2 The Atkinson-Schiffrin model of memory includes three stages of memory (sensory memory, short-term or working memory, and long-term memory) that hold information for increasingly longer periods.

7.1.3 Sensory memories are encoded as iconic memories or echoic memories.

7.1.4 Selective attention determines what information moves from sensory memory, which is exact but very brief, on to STM.

7.1.5 Short-term memories tend to be encoded by sound and are sensitive to interruption, or interference.

7.1.6 Long-term memories are encoded by meaning.

7.2 What are the features of short-term memory?

7.2.1 STM has a capacity of about 5 to 7 bits of information, but this limit can be extended by chunking.

7.2.2 Short-term memories are brief; however, they can be prolonged by maintenance rehearsal.

7.2.3 For transferring information to LTM, rote rehearsal is less effective than elaborative encoding.

7.3 What are the features of long-term memory?

7.3.1 Long-term memories are relatively permanent. LTM seems to have an almost unlimited storage capacity.

7.3.2 Elaborative processing can have the effect of altering memories. Remembering is an active process. Our memories are frequently lost, altered, revised, or distorted.

7.3.3 LTM is highly organized. The structure of memory networks is the subject of current research.

7.3.4 In redintegration, memories are reconstructed, as one bit of information leads to others, which then serve as cues for further recall.

7.3.5 LTM contains procedural (skill) and declarative (fact) memories. Declarative memories can be semantic or episodic.

7.4 How is memory measured?

7.4.1 The tip-of-the-tongue state shows that memory is not an all-or-nothing event. Memories may be revealed by recall, recognition, relearning, or priming.

7.4.2 In recall, memories are retrieved without explicit cues, as in an essay exam. Recall of listed information often reveals a serial position effect.

7.4.3 A common test of recognition is the multiple-choice question.

7.4.4 In relearning, material that seems to be forgotten is learned again, and memory is revealed by a savings score.

7.4.5 Recall, recognition, and relearning mainly measure explicit memories. Other techniques, such as priming, are necessary to reveal implicit memories.

7.5 Why do we forget?

7.5.1 Herman Ebbinghaus found that forgetting is most rapid immediately after learning, as shown by the curve of forgetting.

7.5.2 Forgetting can occur because of failures of encoding, of storage, or of retrieval.

7.5.3 Failure to encode information is a common cause of "forgetting."

7.5.4 Forgetting in sensory memory and STM is due to a failure of storage through a weakening (decay) of memory traces. Decay of memory traces due to disuse may also explain some LTM losses.

7.5.5 Failures of retrieval occur when information that resides in memory is nevertheless not retrieved. A lack of memory cues can produce retrieval failure. State-dependent learning is related to the effects of memory cues.

7.5.6 Much forgetting in STM and LTM is caused by interference. In retroactive interference, new learning interferes with the ability to retrieve earlier learning. Proactive interference occurs when old learning interferes with the retrieval of new learning.

7.5.7 Memories can be consciously suppressed and they may be unconsciously repressed.

7.5.8 Extreme caution is warranted when "recovered" memories are the only basis for believing that traumatic events, such as childhood sexual abuse, happened in the past.

7.6 How does the brain form and store memories?

7.6.1 It takes time to consolidate memories. In the brain, memory consolidation takes place in the hippocampus. Until they are consolidated, long-term memories are easily destroyed, resulting in retrograde amnesia.

7.6.2 Intensely emotional experiences can result in flashbulb memories.

7.6.3 After memories have been consolidated, they appear to be stored in the cortex of the brain.

7.6.4 Lasting memories are recorded by changes in the activity, structure, and chemistry of nerve cells as well as how they interconnect.

7.7 What are "photographic" memories?

7.7.1 Eidetic imagery (photographic memory) occurs when a person is able to project an image onto a blank surface. Eidetic imagery is rarely found in adults. However, many adults have internal memory images, which can be very vivid.

7.7.2 Exceptional memory may be based on natural ability or learned strategies. Usually it involves both.

7.8. How can I improve my memory?

7.8.1 Excellent memory abilities are based on using strategies and techniques that make learning efficient and that compensate for natural weaknesses in human memory.

7.8.2 Memory can be improved through better encoding strategies, such as elaborating, selecting and organizing information as well as whole learning, the progressive-part method, encoding memory cues, overlearning, and spaced practice.

7.8.3 Memory can also be improved through better retrieval strategies, such as retrieval practice, which involves feedback, recitation, and review, and active search strategies.

7.8.4 When you are studying or memorizing, you should also keep in mind the effects of serial position, sleep, and hunger.

7.9 Are there any tricks to help me with my memory?

7.9.1 Memory systems (mnemonics) greatly improve immediate memory. However, conventional learning tends to create the most lasting memories.

7.9.2 Mnemonic systems use mental images and unusual associations to link new information with familiar memories already stored in LTM.

7.9.3 Effective mnemonics tend to rely on mental images and bizarre or exaggerated mental associations.

MEDIA RESOURCES

Web Resources

Internet addresses frequently change. To find an up-to-date list of URLs for the sites listed here, visit your Psychology CourseMate.

Playing Games with Memory Try some activities to test your memory.

The Atkinson-Schiffrin Model Further explore the three-store model of memory.

Working Memory, Language and Reading Use the concept of working memory to better understand the process of reading.

The Magical Number Seven, Plus or Minus Two Read George Miller's original paper on capacity limits in short-term memory.

Questions and Answers about Memories of Childhood Abuse Read a summary of the repressed memory issue from the American Psychological Association.

False Memory Syndrome Foundation This site provides information about false memory and its devastating effects, how it works, and aid to those who are affected.

What Is Déjà Vu? Links to more information on this fascinating form of partial retrieval.

A New Theoretical Framework for Explicit and Implicit Memory An excellent article exploring a new framework for understanding and measuring explicit and implicit memory functions.

Free Recall Test Test your free recall ability.

Memory: A Contribution to Experimental Psychology Read Hermann Ebbinghaus's original article.

About Education: Fundamental Concepts of Forgetting and Learning Relate ideas about forgetting to education.

Memory Loss and the Brain Read issues of a free newsletter.

Does No One Have a Photographic Memory? A discussion of the impossibility of photographic memory.

Famous Mnemonists Read about some of history's most famous memorizers.

Memory Strategies Read a useful list of memory strategies for studying.

Memory Techniques and Mnemonics Follow links to information on mnemonics.

Memory Training Technique Test your memory using the mnemonic technique of taking a mental walk.

Online Memory Improvement Course Learn more details about several useful mnemonic techniques.

Interactive Learning

Log in to **CengageBrain** to access the resources your instructor requires. For this book, you can access:

CourseMate brings course concepts to life with interactive learning, study, and exam preparation tools that support the printed textbook. A textbook-specific website, ***Psychology CourseMate*** includes an ***integrated interactive eBook*** and other ***interactive learning tools*** including quizzes, flashcards, videos, and more.

CENGAGE**NOW**™

CengageNOW is an easy-to-use online resource that helps you study in less time to get the grade you want—NOW. Take a pre-test for this chapter and receive a personalized study plan based on your results that will identify the topics you need to review and direct you to online resources to help you master those topics. Then take a post-test to help you determine the concepts you have mastered and what you will need to work on. If your textbook does not include an access code card, go to CengageBrain.com to gain access.

WebTUTOR™

More than just an interactive study guide, **WebTutor** is an anytime, anywhere customized learning solution with an eBook, keeping you connected to your textbook, instructor, and classmates.

If your professor has assigned **Aplia** homework:

1. Sign in to your account.
2. Complete the corresponding homework exercises as required by your professor.
3. When finished, click "Grade It Now" to see which areas you have mastered and which need more work, and for detailed explanations of every answer.

Visit **www.cengagebrain.com** to access your account and purchase materials.

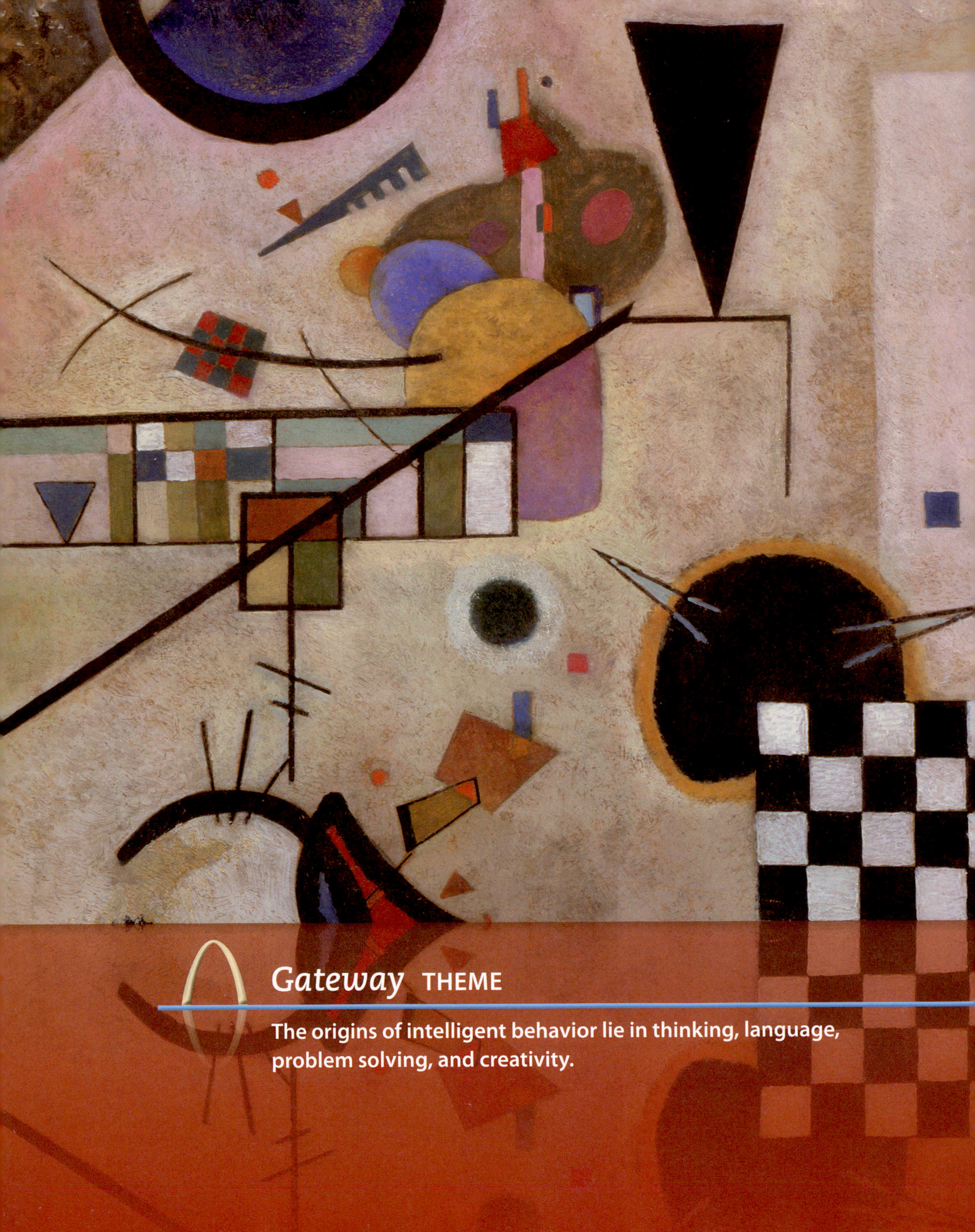
Gateway THEME
The origins of intelligent behavior lie in thinking, language, problem solving, and creativity.

8

Cognition, Language, and Creativity

Color Is the Keyboard

Russian painter Wassily Kandinsky once commented, "Color is the keyboard, the eyes are the harmonies, the soul is the piano with many strings. The artist is the hand that plays, touching one key or another, to cause vibrations in the soul." A look at one of his paintings, such as "Contrasting Sounds," shown here, suggests that he painted just like he spoke.

The creativity of individuals like Kandinsky raises many questions. Do creative people have special talents? Kandinsky himself may have had *synesthesia*—his brain allowed him to experience sounds as colors and shapes so that he was literally painting what he "saw." Or can anyone learn to be creative? Many of the painters of Kandinsky's day shared the goal of recording their subjective impressions rather than eternal objects. Surely, all of the artists who together invented *Impressionism* did not have synesthesia.

Do all people think in images, even if they are not as vivid as Kandinsky's? Is it possible to describe in language what we experience, to the point of using *metaphors*, just as Kandinsky described painting? How do we form concepts, like the concept "impressionism"?

At higher levels, these are the same abilities that define many of history's geniuses, such as Einstein, Darwin, Mozart, Newton, Michelangelo, Galileo, Madame Curie, Edison, Martha Graham, and others (Michalko, 2001; Robinson, 2010). Like all creative activities, Kandinsky's art raises questions about human cognition. How do we think? How are we able to solve problems? How do people create works of art, science, and literature? For some preliminary answers, we will investigate thinking, problem solving, and creativity in the pages that follow.

Gateway QUESTIONS

8.1 What is the nature of thought?
8.2 In what ways are images related to thinking?
8.3 What are concepts and how are they learned?
8.4 What is language and what role does it play in thinking?
8.5 What do we know about problem solving?
8.6 What is the nature of creative thinking?
8.7 How accurate is intuition?
8.8 What can be done to promote creativity?

What Is Thinking?—Brains over Brawn

Gateway Question 8.1: *What is the nature of thought?*

Humans are highly adaptable creatures. We live in deserts, jungles, mountains, frenzied cities, placid retreats, and recently, in space stations. Unlike other species, our success owes more to intelligence and thinking abilities than it does to physical strength or speed (Reed, 2010). Let's see how concepts, language, and mental images make thinking possible.

Cognition refers to mentally processing information (Sternberg, 2011). Our thoughts take many forms, including problem solving, reasoning, and even daydreaming (to name but a few). Although thinking is not limited to humans, imagine trying to teach an animal to match the feats of Shakuntala Devi, who once set a "world record" for mental calculation by multiplying two randomly chosen 13-digit numbers (7,686,369,774,870 times 2,465,099,745,779) in her head, giving the answer in 28 seconds. (That's 18,947,668,104,042,434,089,403,730 if you haven't already figured it out.)

Some Basic Units of Thought

At its most basic, thinking is an *internal representation* (mental expression) of a problem or situation. Picture a television interviewer who mentally tries out several lines of questioning before actually beginning a live interview. By *planning* her moves, she can avoid many mistakes. Imagine planning what to study for an exam, what to say at a job interview, or how to get to your spring break hotel. Better yet, in each of these cases imagine what might happen if you didn't, or couldn't, plan at all.

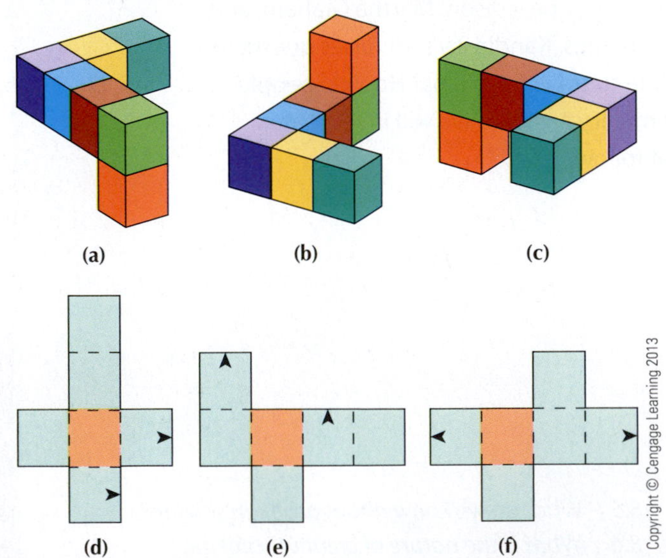

• **Figure 8.1** Imagery in thinking. *(Top)* Subjects were shown a drawing similar to *(a)* and drawings of how *(a)* would look in other positions, such as *(b)* and *(c)*. Subjects could recognize *(a)* after it had been "rotated" from its original position. However, the more *(a)* was rotated in space, the longer it took to recognize it. This result suggests that people actually formed a three-dimensional image of *(a)* and rotated the image to see if it matched (Shepard, 1975). *(Bottom)* Try your ability to manipulate mental images: Picture each of these shapes as a piece of paper that can be folded to make a cube. After they have been folded, on which cubes do the arrow tips meet (Kosslyn, 1985)?

The power of being able to mentally represent problems is dramatically illustrated by chess grand master Miguel Najdorf, who once simultaneously played 45 chess games while blindfolded. How did Najdorf do it? Like most people, he used the basic units of thought: images, concepts, and language (or symbols). **Images** are picture-like mental representations. **Concepts** are ideas that represent categories of objects or events. **Language** consists of words or symbols, and rules for combining them. Thinking often involves all three units. For example, blindfolded chess players rely on visual images, concepts ("Game 2 begins with a strategy called an English opening"), and the notational system, or "language," of chess.

In a moment we will delve further into imagery, concepts, and language. Be aware, however, that thinking involves attention, pattern recognition, memory, decision making, intuition, knowledge, and more. This chapter is only a sample of what cognitive psychology is about.

Mental Imagery—Does a Frog Have Lips?

Gateway Question 8.2: *In what ways are images related to thinking?*

Almost everyone has visual and auditory images. More than half of us have imagery for movement, touch, taste, smell, and pain. Thus, mental images are sometimes more than just "pictures." For example, your image of a bakery may also include its delicious odor. As mentioned earlier, some people, like Kandinsky, even have a rare form of imagery called **synesthesia** (sin-es-THEE-zyah). For these individuals, images cross normal sensory barriers (Cytowic & Eagleman, 2009; Kadosh & Henik, 2007). For one such person, spiced chicken tastes "pointy"; for another, pain is the color orange; and for a third, human voices unleash a flood of colors and tastes (Dixon, Smilek, & Merikle, 2004; Robertson & Sagiv, 2005). Despite such variations, most of us use images to think, remember, and solve problems. For instance, we may use mental images to:

- Make a decision or solve a problem (choosing what clothes to wear; figuring out how to arrange furniture in a room).
- Change feelings (thinking of pleasant images to get out of a bad mood; imagining yourself as thin to stay on a diet).
- Improve a skill or prepare for some action (using images to improve a tennis stroke; mentally rehearsing how you will ask for a raise).
- Aid memory (picturing Mr. Cook wearing a chef's hat so you can remember his name).

The Nature of Mental Images

Mental images are not flat, like photographs. Researcher Stephen Kosslyn showed this by asking people, "Does a frog have lips and a stubby tail?" Unless you often kiss frogs, you will probably tackle this question by using mental images. Most people picture a frog, "look" at its mouth, and then mentally "rotate" the frog in mental space to check its tail (Kosslyn, 1983). Mental rotation is partly based on imagined movements (• Figure 8.1). That is, we mentally "pick up" an object and turn it around (Wraga et al., 2005, 2010).

"Reverse Vision"

What happens in the brain when a person has visual images? Seeing something in your "mind's eye" is similar to seeing real objects. Information from the eyes normally activates the brain's primary visual area, creating an image (● Figure 8.2). Other brain areas then help us recognize the image by relating it to stored knowledge. When you form a mental image, the system works in reverse. Brain areas in which memories are stored send signals back to the visual cortex, where once again, an image is created (Ganis, Thompson, & Kosslyn, 2004; Kosslyn, 2005). For example, if you visualize a friend's face right now, the area of your brain that specializes in perceiving faces will become more active (O'Craven & Kanwisher, 2000).

Using Mental Images

How are images used to solve problems? We use *stored images* (information from memory) to apply past experiences to problem solving. Let's say you are asked, "How many ways can you use an empty egg carton?" You might begin by picturing uses you have already seen, such as sorting buttons into a carton. To give more original answers, you will probably need to use *created images*, which are assembled or invented, rather than simply remembered. Thus, an artist may completely picture a proposed sculpture before beginning work. People with good imaging abilities tend to score higher on tests of creativity (Morrison & Wallace, 2001), even if they are blind (Eardley & Pring, 2007). In fact, Albert Einstein, Thomas Edison, Lewis Carroll, and many other of history's most original intellects relied heavily on imagery (West, 1991).

Does the "size" of a mental image affect thinking? To find out, first picture a cat sitting beside a housefly. Now try to "zoom in" on the cat's ears so you see them clearly. Next, picture a rabbit sitting beside an elephant. How quickly can you "see" the rabbit's front feet? Did it take longer than picturing the cat's ears?

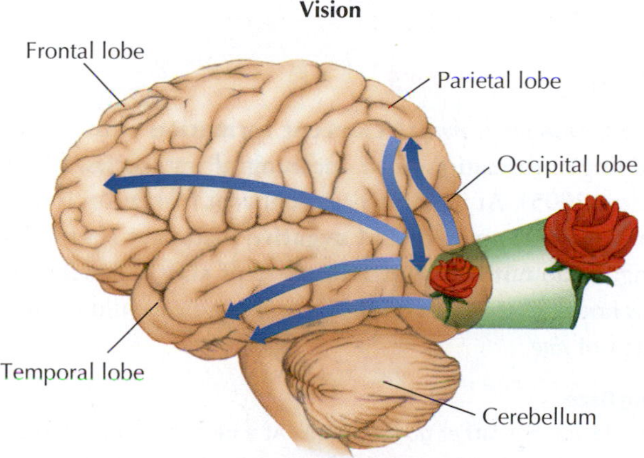

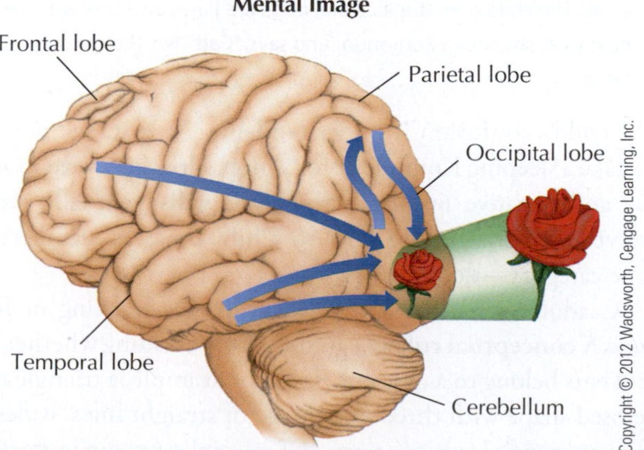

● Figure 8.2 When you see a flower, its image is represented by activity in the primary visual area of the cortex, at the back of the brain. Information about the flower is also relayed to other brain areas. If you form a mental image of a flower, information follows a reverse path. The result, once again, is activation of the primary visual area.

The Guggenheim Museum in Bilbao, Spain, was designed by architect Frank Gehry. Could a person lacking mental imagery design such a masterpiece? Three people out of 100 find it impossible to produce mental images, and 3 out of 100 have very strong imagery. Most artists, architects, designers, sculptors, and filmmakers have excellent visual imagery.

Cognition The process of thinking or mentally processing information (images, concepts, words, rules, and symbols).

Image Most often, a mental representation that has picture-like qualities; an icon.

Concept A generalized idea representing a category of related objects or events.

Language Words or symbols, and rules for combining them, that are used for thinking and communication.

Synesthesia Experiencing one sense in terms normally associated with another sense; for example, "seeing" colors when a sound is heard.

When a rabbit is pictured with an elephant, the rabbit's image must be small because the elephant is large. Using such tasks, Stephen Kosslyn (1985) found that the smaller an image is, the harder it is to "see" its details. To put this finding to use, try forming oversize images of things you want to think about. For example, to understand electricity, picture the wires as large pipes with electrons the size of golf balls moving through them; to understand the human ear, explore it (in your mind's eye) like a large cave; and so forth.

Kinesthetic Imagery

Do muscular responses relate to thinking? In a sense, we think with our bodies as well as our heads. *Kinesthetic (motor) images* are created from muscular sensations (Guillot et al., 2009). Such images help us think about movements and actions.

As you think and talk, kinesthetic sensations can guide the flow of ideas. For example, if a friend calls and asks you the combination of a lock you loaned her, you may move your hands as if twirling the dial on the lock. Or, try answering this question: Which direction do you turn the hot-water handle in your kitchen to shut off the water? Most people haven't simply memorized the words "Turn it clockwise" or "Turn it counterclockwise." Instead you will probably "turn" the faucet in your imagination before answering. You may even make a turning motion with your hand before answering.

Kinesthetic images are especially important in music, sports, dance, skateboarding, martial arts, and other movement-oriented skills. An effective way to improve such skills is to practice by rehearsing kinesthetic images of yourself performing flawlessly (Guillot & Collet, 2008).

Vixit/Shutterstock

Rock climbers use kinesthetic imagery to learn climbing routes and to plan their next few moves (Smyth & Waller, 1998).

Concepts—I'm Positive, It's a Whatchamacallit

Gateway Question 8.3: *What are concepts and how are they learned?*

As noted earlier, a **concept** is an idea that represents a category of objects or events. Concepts help us identify important features of the world. That's why experts in various areas of knowledge are good at classifying objects. Bird watchers, tropical fish fanciers, 5-year-old dinosaur enthusiasts, and other experts all learn to look for identifying details that beginners tend to miss. If you are knowledgeable about a topic, such as horses, flowers, or football, you literally see things differently than less well-informed people do (Harel et al., 2010; Ross, 2006).

Forming Concepts

How are concepts learned? **Concept formation** is the process of classifying information into meaningful categories (Ashby & Maddox, 2005). At its most basic, concept formation is based on experience with **positive** and **negative instances** (examples that belong, or do not belong, to the concept class). Concept formation is not as simple as it might seem. Imagine a child learning the concept of *dog*.

Dog Daze

A child and her father go for a walk. At a neighbor's house, they see a medium-sized dog. The father says, "See the dog." As they pass the next yard, the child sees a cat and says, "Dog!" Her father corrects her, "No, that's a *cat*." The child now thinks, "Aha, dogs are large and cats are small." In the next yard, she sees a Komondor and says, "Cat!" "No, that's a dog," replies her father.

The child's confusion is understandable. At first, she might even mistake a sleeping Komondor for a mop. However, with more positive and negative instances, the child will eventually recognize everything from Great Danes to Chihuahuas as members of the same category—dogs.

As adults, we often acquire concepts by learning or forming *rules*. A **conceptual rule** is a guideline for deciding whether objects or events belong to a concept class. For example, a triangle must be a closed shape with three sides made of straight lines. Rules are an efficient way to learn concepts, but examples remain important. It's unlikely that memorizing rules would allow a new listener to accurately categorize *rhythm and blues*, *hip-hop*, *fusion*, *salsa*, *metal*, *country*, and *rap* music.

The Komondor is the hairiest dog breed.

Types of Concepts

Are there different kinds of concepts? Yes, **conjunctive concepts**, or "and concepts," are defined by the presence of two or more features (Reed, 2010). In other words, an item must have "this feature *and* this feature *and* this feature." For example, a *motorcycle* must have two wheels *and* an engine *and* handlebars.

Relational concepts are based on how an object relates to something else, or how its features relate to one another. All of the following are relational concepts: *larger, above, left, north*, and *upside down*. Another example is *brother*, which is defined as "a male considered in his relation to another person having the same parents."

Disjunctive concepts have at *least one* of several possible features. These are "either/or" concepts. To belong to the category, an item must have "this feature *or* that feature *or* another feature." For example, in baseball, a *strike* is *either* a swing and a miss *or* a pitch over the plate *or* a foul ball. The either/or quality of disjunctive concepts makes them harder to learn.

• **Figure 8.3** When does a cup become a bowl or a vase? Deciding whether an object belongs to a conceptual class is aided by relating it to a prototype, or ideal example. Subjects in one experiment chose number 5 as the "best" cup. (After Labov, 1973.)

Prototypes

When you think of the concept *bird*, do you mentally list the features that birds have? Probably not. In addition to rules and features, we use **prototypes**, or ideal models, to identify concepts (Burnett et al., 2005; Rosch, 1977). A robin, for example, is a prototypical bird; an ostrich is not. In other words, some items are better examples of a concept than others are (Smith, Redford, & Haas, 2008). Which of the drawings in • Figure 8.3 best represents a cup? At some point, as a cup grows taller or wider, it becomes a vase or a bowl. How do we know when the line is crossed? Probably, we mentally compare objects to an "ideal" cup, like number 5. That's why it's hard to identify concepts when we can't come up with relevant prototypes. What, for example, are the objects shown in • Figure 8.4? As you can see, prototypes are especially helpful when we try to categorize complex stimuli (Minda & Smith, 2001).

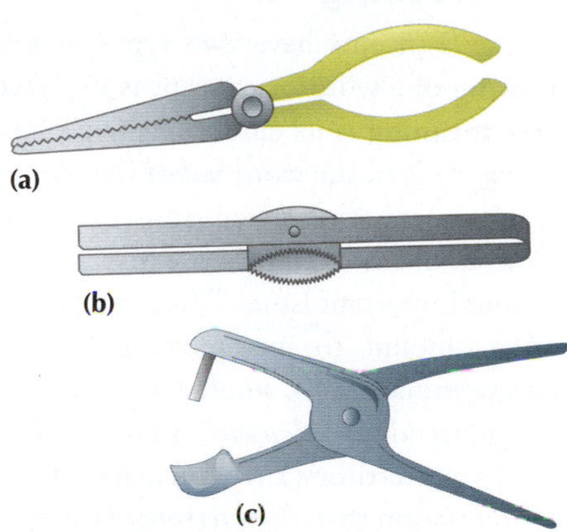

• **Figure 8.4** Use of prototypes in concept identification. Even though its shape is unusual, item *(a)* can be related to a model (an ordinary set of pliers) and thus recognized. But what are items *(b)* and *(c)*? If you don't recognize them, look ahead to • Figure 8.6. (Adapted from Bransford & McCarrell, 1977.)

Concept A generalized idea representing a class of related objects or events.

Concept formation The process of classifying information into meaningful categories.

Positive instance In concept learning, an object or event that belongs to the concept class.

Negative instance In concept learning, an object or event that does not belong to the concept class.

Conceptual rule A formal rule for deciding if an object or event is an example of a particular concept.

Conjunctive concept A class of objects that have two or more features in common. (For example, to qualify as an example of the concept an object must be both red *and* triangular.)

Relational concept A concept defined by the relationship between features of an object or between an object and its surroundings (for example, "greater than," "lopsided").

Disjunctive concept A concept defined by the presence of at least one of several possible features. (For example, to qualify an object must be either blue *or* circular.)

Prototype An ideal model used as a prime example of a particular concept.

Faulty Concepts

Using inaccurate concepts often leads to thinking errors. For example, *social stereotypes* are oversimplified concepts of groups of people (Le Pelley, et al., 2010). Stereotypes about men, African Americans, women, conservatives, liberals, police officers, or other groups often muddle thinking about members of the group. A related problem is *all-or-nothing thinking* (one-dimensional thought). In this case, we classify things as absolutely right or wrong, good or bad, fair or unfair, black or white, honest or dishonest. Thinking this way prevents us from appreciating the subtleties of most life problems (Bastian & Haslam, 2006).

BRIDGES

Stereotypes have a major impact on social behavior and frequently contribute to prejudice and discrimination. **See Chapter 17, pages 591–593, for more information.**

Connotative Meaning

Generally speaking, concepts have two types of meaning. The **denotative meaning** of a word or concept is its exact definition. The **connotative meaning** is its emotional or personal meaning. The denotative meaning of the word *naked* (having no clothes) is the same for a nudist as it is for a movie censor, but we could expect their connotations to differ. Connotative differences can influence how we think about important issues. The arts of *political spin* and *propaganda* often amount to manipulating connotations. For example, facing a terminal illness, would you rather engage in *end-of-life counseling* or attend a *death panel*? Similarly, if you are resisting an invasion of your territory, the term *defender of culture* has a more positive connotation than does *terrorist* (Payne, 2009).

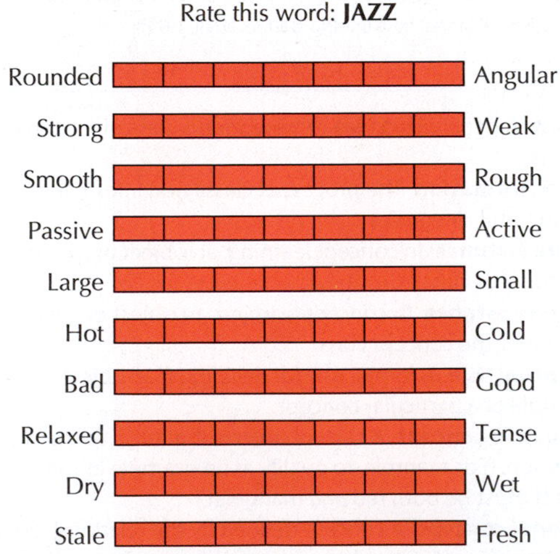

● **Figure 8.5** This is an example of Osgood's semantic differential. The connotative meaning of the word *jazz* can be established by rating it on the scales. Mark your own rating by placing dots or X's in the spaces. Connect the marks with a line; then have a friend rate the word and compare your responses. It might be interesting to do the same for *rock and roll*, *classical*, and *rap*. You also might want to try the word *psychology*. (From C. E. Osgood. Copyright © 1952 American Psychological Association. Reprinted by permission.)

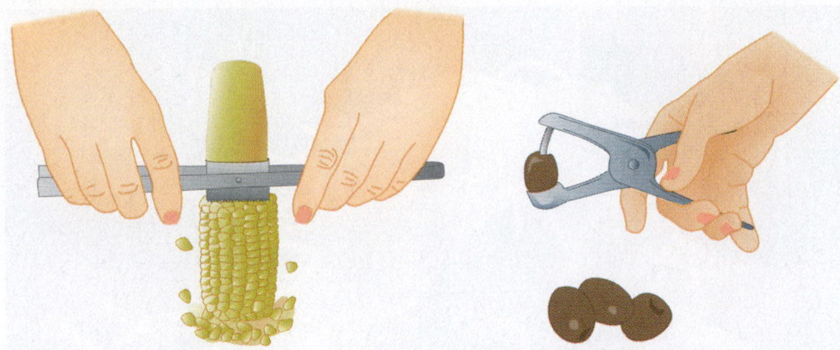

● **Figure 8.6** Context can substitute for a lack of appropriate prototypes in concept identification.

Can you clarify what a connotative meaning is? Yes, connotative meaning can be measured with a technique called the *semantic differential*, as shown in ● Figure 8.5. When we rate words or concepts, most of their connotative meaning boils down to the dimensions *good/bad*, *strong/weak*, and *active/passive*. These dimensions give words very different connotations, even when their denotative meanings are similar. For example, I am *conscientious*; you are *careful*; he is *nitpicky*! Because we are conscientious (not nitpicky, right?), let's further explore language.

Knowledge Builder: Images and Concepts

RECITE

1. List three basic units of thought: ____________, ____________, ____________
2. Synesthesia is the use of kinesthetic sensations as a vehicle for thought. T or F?
3. Humans appear capable of forming three-dimensional images that can be moved or rotated in mental space. T or F?
4. A *mup* is defined as anything that is small, blue, and hairy. *Mup* is a ____________ concept.
5. The connotative meaning of the word *naked* is "having no clothes." T or F?
6. Stereotyping is an example of oversimplification in thinking. T or F?

REFLECT

Think Critically

7. It takes longer to answer the question, "Does a frog have lips and a stubby tail?" than the question, "Does a frog have lips?" Can you think of an explanation other than mental rotation to explain this difference?
8. A Democrat and a Republican are asked to rate the word *democratic* on the semantic differential. Under what conditions would their ratings be most alike?

Self-Reflect

Name some ways in which you have used imagery in the thinking you have done today. Were the images you used created or stored? Were any synesthetic or kinesthetic?

Write a conceptual rule for the following idea: *unicycle*. Were you able to define the concept with a rule? Would positive and negative instances help make the concept clearer for others?

A true sports car has two seats, a powerful engine, good brakes, and excellent handling. What kind of a concept is the term *sports car*? What do you think of as a prototypical sports car?

Critical Thinking: What's North of My Fork?

It is clear that our thoughts influence the words we use. But might the reverse be true? Do the words we use affect our thoughts and actions? The answer may lie in a remote part of northeastern Australia. Cognitive psychologist Lera Boroditsky has reported that aboriginal children from Cape York can accurately point to any compass direction as early as age 5. In contrast, most Americans cannot do this even as adults (Boroditsky, 2011).

But why? According to Boroditsky, Kuuk Thaayorre, the language of the Cape York Australian aboriginals, relies exclusively on *absolute* directional references, unlike English. Like English, Kuuk Thaayorre has words for "north," "south," and so on. Unlike English, Kuuk Thaayorre lacks words for *relative* directional references, such as "left" and "right."

For long distances, an English speaker might say, "Chicago is north of here." But for short distances, the same speaker will shift to a relative reference and might say, "My brother is sitting to my right." In contrast, a speaker of Kuuk Thaayorre always uses absolute directional references, saying things like "My friend is sitting southeast of me" and "The dessert spoon is west of the coffee cup." If you are a young aboriginal child, you had best master your absolute directions or most conversations will be impossible to follow.

Another interesting consequence for speakers of Kuuk Thaayorre is how they arrange time. In one study, English speakers given a set of cards depicting a series of events (for example, a person getting older or a meal being cooked and eaten) and asked to put them in order usually arranged them from left to right. Hebrew speakers usually arranged the cards from right to left, presumably because this is the direction in which Hebrew is written. In contrast, speakers of Kuuk Thaayorre arrange temporal sequences from east to west. If the sorter is facing north, the cards would be arranged from right to left but if the sorter is facing south, the cards would be arranged from left to right, and so on (Boroditsky & Gaby, 2010).

Findings like these lend support to the **linguistic relativity hypothesis**, the idea that the words we use not only reflect our thoughts but can shape them as well. So the next time you think your future is "ahead" of you and your past is "behind," think again. For speakers of Aymara, a South American language, it is the past that is "ahead" (Miles et al., 2010). So watch your back.

Answers: 1. images, concepts, and language or symbols (others could be listed) **2.** F **3.** T **4.** conjunctive **5.** F **6.** T **7.** The first question could simply be more difficult. The difficulty of questions must be carefully matched in studies of mental imagery. **8.** If they both assume the word refers to a form of government, not a political party or a candidate.

Language—Say What?

Gateway Question 8.4: *What is language and what role does it play in thinking?*

As we have seen, thinking may occur without language. Everyone has searched for a word to express an idea that exists as a vague image or feeling. Nevertheless, most thinking relies heavily on language, because words *encode* (translate) the world into symbols that are easy to manipulate (● Figure 8.7). Likewise, the words we use can greatly affect our thinking (see "What's North of My Fork?").

The study of meaning in words and language is known as **semantics.** It is here that the link between language and thought becomes most evident. Has one country's army "invaded" another country or "liberated" it? Is the martini glass "half full" or "half empty"? Would you rather eat "rare prime beef" or "bloody slab of dead cow"? Suppose, on an intelligence test, you were asked to circle the word that does not belong in this series:

SKYSCRAPER CATHEDRAL TEMPLE PRAYER

Ebby May/Getty Images

● **Figure 8.7** Wine tasting illustrates the encoding function of language. To communicate their experiences to others, wine connoisseurs must put taste sensations into words. The wine you see here is "marked by deeply concentrated nuances of plum, blackberry, and currant, with a nice balance of tannins and acid, building to a spicy oak finish." (Don't try this with a Pop-tart®!)

Denotative meaning The exact, dictionary definition of a word or concept; its objective meaning.

Connotative meaning The subjective, personal, or emotional meaning of a word or concept.

Linguistic relativity hypothesis The idea that the words we use not only reflect our thoughts but can shape them as well.

Semantics The study of meanings in language.

Human Diversity

Bilingualism—*Si o No, Oui ou Non,* Yes or No?

***Are there advantages** to being able to speak more than one language?* Definitely. **Bilingualism** is the ability to speak two languages. Studies have found that students who learn to speak two languages well have better mental flexibility, general language skills, control of attention, and problem-solving abilities (Bialystok & DePape, 2009; Craik & Bialystok, 2005).

Unfortunately, millions of minority American children who do not speak English at home experience *subtractive bilingualism*. Immersed in English-only classrooms, in which they are expected to "sink or swim," they usually end up losing some of their native language skills. Such children risk becoming less than fully competent in *both* their first and second languages. In addition, they tend to fall behind educationally. As they struggle with English, their grasp of arithmetic, social studies, science, and other subjects may also suffer. In short, English-only instruction can leave them poorly prepared to succeed in the majority culture (Durán, Roseth, Hoffman, 2010; Matthews & Matthews, 2004).

For the majority of children who speak English at home, the picture can be quite different, because learning a second language is almost always beneficial. It poses no threat to the child's home language and improves a variety of cognitive skills. This has been called *additive bilingualism* because learning a second language adds to a child's overall competence (Hinkel, 2005).

An approach called **two-way bilingual education** can help children benefit from bilingualism and avoid its drawbacks (Lessow-Hurley, 2005). In such programs, majority group children and children with limited English skills are taught part of the day in English and part in a second language. Both majority and minority language speakers become fluent in two languages, and they perform as well or better than single-language students in English and general academic abilities.

Then why isn't two-way bilingual education more widely used? Bilingual education tends to be politically unpopular among majority language speakers (Garcia, 2008). Language is an important sign of group membership. Even where the majority culture is highly dominant, some of its members may feel that recent immigrants and "foreign languages" are eroding their culture. Regardless, an ability to think and communicate in a second language is a wonderful gift. Given the cognitive benefits, fostering bilingualism may also turn out to be one of the best ways to improve competitiveness in our rapidly globalizing information economy.

If you circled *prayer*, you answered as most people do. Now try another problem, again circling the odd item:

CATHEDRAL PRAYER TEMPLE SKYSCRAPER

Did you circle *skyscraper* this time? The new order subtly alters the meaning of the last word (Mayer, 1995). This occurs because words get much of their meaning from *context*. For example, the word *shot* means different things when we are thinking of marksmanship, bartending, medicine, photography, or golf (Carroll, 2008; Miller, 1999).

More subtle effects also occur. For example, most people have difficulty quickly naming the color of the ink used to print the words in the bottom two rows of • Figure 8.8. The word meanings are just too strong to ignore.

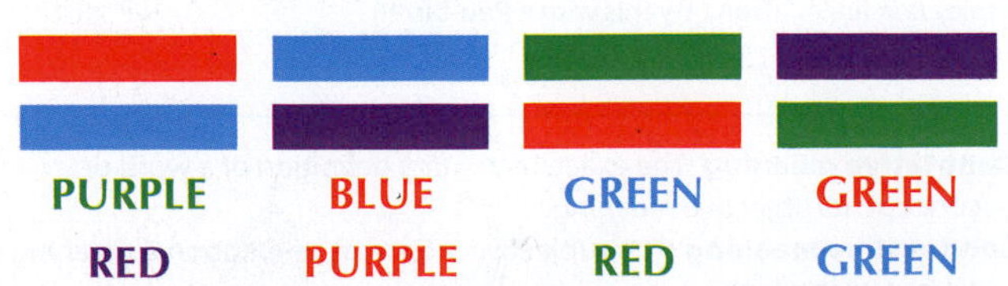

• Figure 8.8 The Stroop interference task. Test yourself by naming the colors in the top two rows as quickly as you can. Then name the colors of the *ink* used to print the words in the bottom two rows (do not read the words themselves). Was it harder to name the ink colors in the bottom rows? (Adapted from MacLeod, 2005.)

"You'll have to phrase it another way. They have no word for 'fetch.'"

Drew Dernavich/Cartoonbank

Language also plays a major role in defining ethnic communities and other social groups. Thus, language can be a bridge or a barrier between cultures. Translating languages can cause a rash of semantic problems. Perhaps the San Jose, California, public library can be excused for once displaying a large banner that was supposed to say "You are welcome" in a native Philippine language. The banner actually said "You are circumcised." Likewise, we may forgive Pepsi for translating "Come alive, you Pepsi generation," into Thai as "Pepsi brings your ancestors back from the dead." However, in more important situations, such as in international business and diplomacy, avoiding semantic confusion may be vital (see "Bilingualism—*Si o No, Oui ou Non,* Yes or No?").

The Structure of Language

What does it take to make a language? First, a language must provide symbols that can stand for objects and ideas (Jay, 2003). The symbols we call words are built out of **phonemes** (FOE-neems: basic speech sounds) and **morphemes** (MOR-feems: speech sounds collected into meaningful units, such as syllables or words). For instance, in English the sounds *m*, *b*, *w*, and *a* cannot form a syllable *mbwa*. In Swahili, they can (also, see • Figure 8.9).

Next, a language must have a **grammar**, or set of rules for making sounds into words and words into sentences (Reed, 2010). One part of grammar, known as **syntax**, concerns rules for word order. Syntax is important because rearranging words almost always changes the meaning of a sentence: "Dog bites man" versus "Man bites dog."

Traditional grammar is concerned with "surface" language—the sentences we actually speak. Linguist Noam Chomsky has focused instead on the unspoken rules we use to change core ideas into various sentences. Chomsky (1986) believes that we do not learn all the sentences we might ever say. Rather, we actively *create* them by applying **transformation rules** to universal, core patterns. We use these rules to change a simple declarative sentence to other voices or forms (past tense, passive voice, and so forth). For example, the core sentence "Dog bites man" can be transformed to these patterns (and others as well):

Past: The dog bit the man.
Passive: The man was bitten by the dog.
Negative: The dog did not bite the man.
Question: Did the dog bite the man?

Children seem to be using transformation rules when they say things such as "I runned home." That is, the child applied the normal past tense rule to the irregular verb *to run*.

A true language is also *productive*—it can generate new thoughts or ideas. In fact, words can be rearranged to produce a nearly infinite number of sentences. Some are silly: "Please don't feed me to the goldfish." Some are profound: "We hold these truths to be self-evident, that all men are created equal." In either case, the productive quality of language makes it a powerful tool for thinking.

Derek Croucher/Getty Images

Language	Sound
Albanian	mak, mak
Chinese	gua, gua
Dutch	rap, rap
English	quack, quack
French	coin, coin
Italian	qua, qua
Spanish	cuá, cuá
Swedish	kvack, kvack
Turkish	vak, vak

• **Figure 8.9** Animals around the world make pretty much the same sounds. Notice, however, how various languages use slightly different phonemes to express the sound a duck makes.

Look at

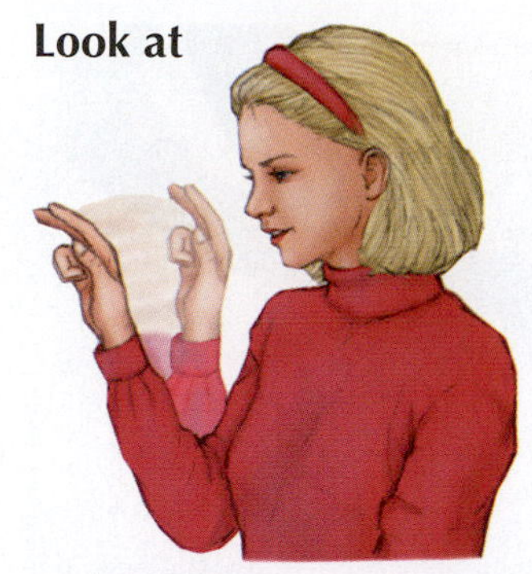

Stare

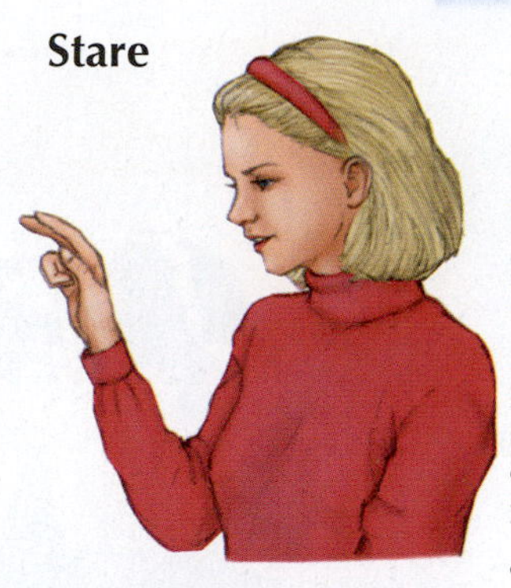

• **Figure 8.10** ASL has only 3,000 root signs, compared with roughly 600,000 words in English. However, variations in signs make ASL a highly expressive language. For example, the sign LOOK-AT can be varied in ways to make it mean look at me, look at her, look at each, stare at, gaze, watch, look for a long time, look at again and again, reminisce, sightsee, look forward to, predict, anticipate, browse, and many more variations.

Gestural Languages

Contrary to common belief, language is not limited to speech. Consider the case of Ildefonso, a young man who was born deaf. At age 24, Ildefonso had never communicated with another human, except by mime. Then at last, Ildefonso had a breakthrough: After much hard work with a sign language teacher, he understood the link between a cat and the gesture for it. At that magic moment, he grasped the idea that "cat" could be communicated to another person, just by signing the word.

American Sign Language (ASL), a gestural language, made Ildefonso's long-awaited breakthrough possible. ASL is not pantomime or a code. It is a true language, like German, Spanish, or Japanese (Liddell, 2003). In fact, those who use other gestural languages, such as French Sign, Mexican Sign, or Old Kentish Sign, may not easily understand ASL (Quinto-Pozos, 2008).

Although ASL has a *spatial* grammar, syntax, and semantics all its own (• Figure 8.10), both speech and signing follow similar universal language patterns. Signing children pass through the stages of language development at about the same age as speaking children do. Some psychologists now believe that speech evolved from gestures, far back in human history (Corballis, 2002). Gestures help us string words together as we speak (Morsella & Krauss, 2004). Some people would have difficulty speaking with their hands tied to their sides. Do you ever make hand gestures when you are speaking on the phone? If so, you may be displaying a rem-

Bilingualism An ability to speak two languages.
Two-way bilingual education A program in which English-speaking children and children with limited English proficiency are taught half the day in English and half in a second language.
Phonemes The basic speech sounds of a language.
Morphemes The smallest meaningful units in a language, such as syllables or words.
Grammar A set of rules for combining language units into meaningful speech or writing.
Syntax Rules for ordering words when forming sentences.
Transformation rules Rules by which a simple declarative sentence may be changed to other voices or forms (past tense, passive voice, and so forth).

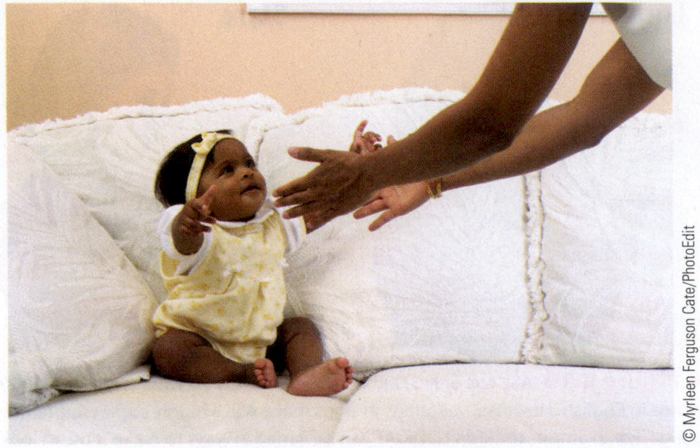

Infants can express the idea "pick me up" in gestures before they can make the same request in words. Their progression from gestures to speech may mirror the evolution of human language abilities (Genty et al., 2009).

nant of the gestural origins of language. Perhaps that's also why the same brain areas become more active when a person speaks or signs (Emmorey et al., 2003).

Sign languages naturally arise out of a need to communicate visually. But they also embody a personal identity and define a distinct community. Those who "speak" sign share not just a language, but a rich culture as well (Singleton & Newport, 2004).

Animal Language

Do animals use language? Animals do communicate. The cries, gestures, and mating calls of animals have broad meanings immediately understood by other animals of the same species (Searcy & Nowicki, 2005). For the most part, however, natural animal communication is quite limited. Even apes and monkeys make only a few dozen distinct cries, which carry messages such as "attack," "flee," or "food here." More important, animal communication lacks the productive quality of human language. For example, when a monkey gives an "eagle distress call," it means something like, "I see an eagle." The monkey has no way of saying, "I don't see an eagle," or "Thank heavens that wasn't an eagle," or "That sucker I saw yesterday was some huge eagle" (Pinker & Jackendoff, 2005). Let's consider some of psychology's experiences in trying to teach chimpanzees to use language.

Chimp Language

Early attempts to teach chimps to talk were a dismal failure. The world record was held by Viki, a chimp who could say only four words (*mama*, *papa*, *cup*, and *up*) after 6 years of intensive training (Fleming, 1974; Hayes, 1951). (Actually, all four words sounded something like a belch.) Then there was a breakthrough. In the late 1960s, Beatrix and Allen Gardner used operant conditioning and imitation to teach a female chimp named Washoe to use ASL. Washoe learned to put together primitive sentence strings like "Come-gimme sweet," "Gimme tickle," and "Open food drink." At her peak, Washoe could construct six-word sentences and use about 240 signs (Gardner & Gardner, 1989).

At around the same time, David Premack taught Sarah the chimpanzee to use 130 "words" consisting of plastic chips arranged on a magnetized board (● Figure 8.11). From the beginning of her training, Sarah was required to use proper word order. She learned to answer questions; to label things "same" or "different"; to classify objects by color, shape, and size; and to form compound sentences (Premack & Premack, 1983). Sarah even learned to use conditional sentences. A *conditional statement* contains a qualification, often in the if/then form: "If Sarah take apple, then Mary give Sarah chocolate." or "If Sarah take banana, then Mary no give Sarah chocolate."

Can it be said with certainty that the chimps understand such interchanges? Most researchers working with chimps believe that they have indeed communicated with them. Especially striking are the chimps' spontaneous responses. Washoe once "wet" on psychologist Roger Fouts' back while riding on his shoulders. When Fouts asked, with some annoyance, why she had done it, Washoe signed, "It's funny!"

Criticisms

Although such interchanges are impressive, communication and real language usage are different things. Even untrained chimps use simple gestures to communicate with humans. For example, a chimp will point at a banana that is out of reach, while glancing back and forth between the banana and a person standing nearby (Leavens & Hopkins, 1998). (The meaning of the gesture is clear. The meaning of the exasperated look on the chimp's face is less certain, but it probably means, "Give me the banana, you idiot.")

Some psychologists doubt that apes can really use language. For one thing, chimps rarely "speak" without prompting from humans. Also, the apes may be simply performing operant responses to get food or other "goodies" (Hixon, 1998). By making certain signs, the apes then manipulate their trainers to get what they want. You might say the critics believe the apes have made monkeys out of their trainers.

At this point, numerous chimps, a gorilla named Koko, and an assortment of dolphins, sea lions, and parrots have learned to communicate with word symbols of various kinds. Yet, even if some

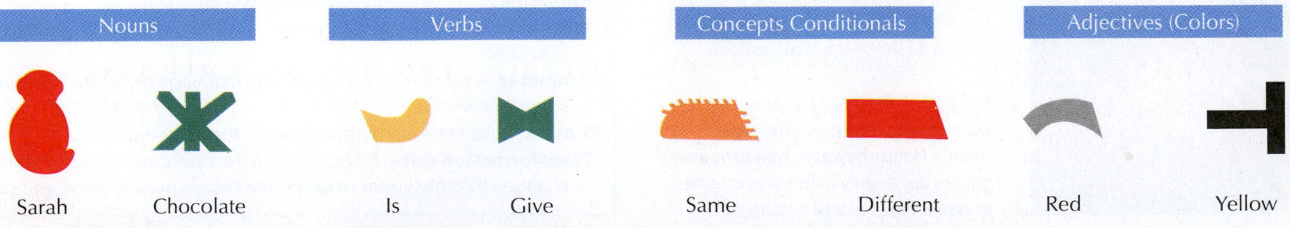

● **Figure 8.11** Here is a sample of some of the word-symbols that Sarah the chimpanzee used to communicate with humans. (After Premack & Premack, 1972).

criticisms can be answered, linguists remain unconvinced that animals can truly use language. The core issue is that problems with syntax (word order) have plagued almost all animal language studies. For example, when a chimp named Nim Chimpsky (no relation to Noam Chomsky) wanted an orange, he would typically signal a grammarless string of words: "Give orange me give eat orange me eat orange give me eat orange give me you." This might be *communication*, but it is not *language*.

Kanzi's Lexigrams

In the 1980s, Duane Rumbaugh and Sue Savage-Rumbaugh taught Kanzi, a pygmy chimpanzee, to communicate by pushing buttons on a computer keyboard. Each of the 250 buttons is marked with a **lexigram**, or geometric word-symbol (● Figure 8.12). Some of the lexigrams Kanzi knows are quite abstract, like symbols for "bad" and "good" (Lyn, Franks, & Savage-Rumbaugh, 2008). Using the lexigrams, Kanzi can create primitive sentences several words long. He can also understand about 650 spoken sentences. During testing, Kanzi hears spoken words over headphones, so his caretakers cannot visually prompt him (Savage-Rumbaugh, Shanker, & Taylor, 1998).

Kanzi's sentences consistently follow correct word order. Like a child learning language, Kanzi picked up some rules from his caregivers (Segerdahl, Fields, & Savage-Rumbaugh, 2005). However, he has developed other patterns on his own. For example, Kanzi usually places action symbols in the order he wants to carry them out, such as "chase tickle" or "chase hide." In this respect, Kanzi's grammar is on a par with that of a 2-year-old child.

Kanzi's ability to invent a simple grammar may help us better understand the roots of human language. It is certainly the strongest answer yet to critics (Benson et al., 2002). On the other hand, Chomsky insists that if chimps were biologically capable of language, they would use it on their own. Although the issue is far from resolved, such research may unravel the mysteries of language learning.

The Great Ape Trust of Iowa

● **Figure 8.12** Kanzi's language learning has been impressive. He can comprehend spoken English words. He can identify lexigram symbols when he hears corresponding words. He can use lexigrams when the objects they refer to are absent and he can, if asked, lead someone to the object. All these skills were acquired through observation, not conditioning (Segerdahl, Fields, & Savage-Rumbaugh, 2005).

Knowledge Builder **Language**

RECITE

1. True languages are ______________ because they can be used to generate new possibilities.
2. The basic speech sounds are called ______________; the smallest meaningful units of speech are called ______________.
3. Two-way bilingual education almost always has a subtractive effect on general academic abilities. T or F?
4. Noam Chomsky believes that we create an infinite variety of sentences by applying ______________ ______________ to universal language patterns.
5. ASL can be used to communicate, but it is not a true language. T or F?
6. One of the chimpanzee Sarah's most outstanding achievements was the construction of sentences involving
   a. negation *b.* conditional relationships *c.* adult grammar *d.* unprompted questions
7. Critics consider "sentences" constructed by apes to be simple ______________ responses having little meaning to the animal.
8. Kanzi's use of lexigrams has suffered from the same problems with syntax as other animal-language studies. T or F?

REFLECT

Think Critically

9. Chimpanzees and other apes are intelligent and entertaining animals. If you were doing language research with a chimp, what major problem would you have to guard against?

Self-Reflect

Here's some mnemonic help: You use a *phone* to send *phonemes*. To *morph* them into words, you have to hit them with a *grammar*. What wrong is with sentence this? (The answer is not a *sin tax*, but it still may tax you.)

Just for fun, see if you can illustrate the productive quality of language by creating a sentence that no one has ever before spoken.

You must learn to communicate with an alien life-form whose language cannot be reproduced by the human voice. Do you think it would it be better to use a gestural language or lexigrams? Why?

Answers: 1. productive **2.** phonemes, morphemes **3.** F **4.** transformation rules **5.** F **6.** *b* **7.** operant **8.** F **9.** The problem of anthropomorphizing (ascribing human characteristics to animals) is especially difficult to avoid when researchers spend many hours "conversing" with and even living with chimps.

Problem Solving—Getting an Answer in Sight

Gateway Question 8.5: *What do we know about problem solving?*

We all solve many problems every day. Problem solving can be as commonplace as figuring out how to make a nonpoisonous meal out of leftovers or as significant as developing a cure for cancer. How do we solve such problems?

Lexigram A geometric shape used as a symbol for a word.

A good way to start a discussion of problem solving is to solve a problem. Give this one a try:

A famous ocean liner (the *Queen Latifah*, of course) is steaming toward port at 20 miles per hour. The ocean liner is 50 miles from shore when a seagull takes off from its deck and flies toward port. At the same instant, a speedboat leaves port at 30 miles per hour. The bird flies back and forth between the speedboat and the *Queen Latifah* at a speed of 40 miles per hour. How far will the bird have flown when the two boats pass?

If you don't immediately see the answer to this problem, read it again. (The answer is revealed in the "Insightful Solutions" section.)

Mechanical Solutions

For routine problems, a **mechanical solution** may be adequate. Mechanical solutions are achieved by trial and error or by rote (Goldstein, 2011). If you forget the combination to your bike lock, you may be able to discover it by trial and error. In an era of high-speed computers, many trial-and-error solutions are best left to machines. A computer could generate all possible combinations of the five numbers on the lock in a split second. (Of course, it would take a long time to try them all.) When a problem is solved by *rote*, thinking is guided by an **algorithm**, or learned set of rules that always leads to an answer. A simple example of an algorithm is the steps needed to divide one number into another (by doing arithmetic, not by using a calculator). Becoming a problem-solving expert in any particular field involves, at a minimum, becoming familiar with the algorithms available in that field. Imagine wanting to be a mathematician and yet being unwilling to learn any algorithms. If you have a good background in math, you may have solved the problem of the bird and the boats by rote. (Your authors hope you didn't. There is an easier solution.)

Solutions by Understanding

Many problems cannot be solved mechanically. In that case, **understanding** (deeper comprehension of a problem) is necessary. Try this problem:

A person has an inoperable stomach tumor. A device is available that produces rays that at high intensity will destroy tissue (both healthy and diseased). How can the tumor be destroyed without damaging surrounding tissue? (Also see the sketch in ● Figure 8.13.)

What does this problem show about problem solving? German psychologist Karl Duncker gave college students this problem in a classic series of studies. Duncker asked them to think aloud as they worked. He found that successful students first had to discover the *general properties* of a correct solution. A **general solution** defines the requirements for success, but not in enough detail to guide further action. This phase was complete when students realized that the intensity of the rays had to be lowered on their way to the tumor. Then, in the second phase, they proposed a number of **functional** (workable) **solutions** and selected the best one (Duncker, 1945). (One solution is to focus weak rays on the tumor from several angles. Another is to rotate the person's body to minimize exposure of healthy tissue.)

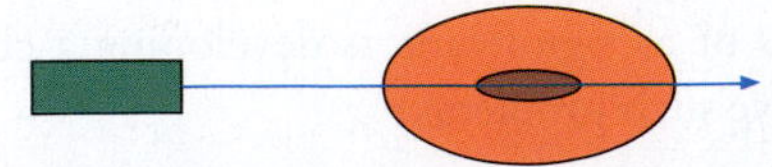

● **Figure 8.13** A schematic representation of Duncker's tumor problem. The dark spot represents a tumor surrounded by healthy tissue. How can the tumor be destroyed without injuring surrounding tissue? (After Duncker, 1945.)

It might help to summarize with a more familiar example. Almost everyone who has tried to play a poker game like Texas Hold'em begins at the mechanical, trial-and-error level. If you want to take the easy (i.e., rote) route, printed odds tables are available for every stage of play. In time, those who persist begin to understand the general properties of the game. After that, they can play fast enough to keep up with other players. With enough practice, this is exactly how novices become experts in a wide variety of fields.

Heuristics

"You can't get there from here," or so it often seems when facing a problem. Solving problems often requires a strategy. If the number of alternatives is small, a **random search strategy** may work. This is another example of trial-and-error thinking in which all possibilities are tried, more or less randomly. Imagine that you are traveling and you decide to look up an old friend, Charlie Harper, in a city you are visiting. You open the phone book and find 47 listings for C. Harper. Of course, you could dial each number until you find the right one. "Forget it," you say to yourself. "Is there any way I can narrow the search?" "Oh, yeah! I remember hearing that Charlie lives by the beach." Then you take out a map and call only the numbers with addresses near the waterfront.

The approach used in this example is a **heuristic** (hew-RIS-tik: a strategy for identifying and evaluating problem solutions). Typically, a heuristic is a "rule of thumb" that *reduces the number of alternatives* thinkers must consider (Benjafield, Smilek, & Kingstone, 2010). Although this raises the odds of success, it does not guarantee a solution. Rest assured that expert problems solvers are good at using heuristic strategies like these:

- Try to identify how the current state of affairs differs from the desired goal. Then find steps that will reduce the difference.
- Try working backward from the desired goal to the starting point or current state.
- If you can't reach the goal directly, try to identify an intermediate goal or subproblem that at least gets you closer.
- Represent the problem in other ways, with graphs, diagrams, or analogies, for instance.
- Generate a possible solution and test it. Doing so may eliminate many alternatives, or it may clarify what is needed for a solution.

Insightful Solutions

A thinker who suddenly solves a problem has experienced **insight**. Insight is so rapid and clear that we may wonder why we didn't see the solution sooner (Schilling, 2005). Insights are usually based on reorganizing a problem (Hélie & Sun, 2010). This allows us to see

Water lilies

Problem: Water lilies growing in a pond double in area every 24 hours. On the first day of spring, only one lily pad is on the surface of the pond. Sixty days later, the pond is entirely covered. On what day is the pond half-covered?

Twenty dollars

Problem: Jessica and Blair both have the same amount of money. How much must Jessica give Blair so that Blair has $20 more than Jessica?

How many pets?

Problem: How many pets do you have if all of them are birds except two, all of them are cats except two, and all of them are dogs except two?

Between 2 and 3

Problem: What one mathematical symbol can you place between 2 and 3 that results in a number greater than 2 and less than 3?

One word

Problem: Rearrange the letters NEWDOOR to make one word.

● **Figure 8.14**

problems in new ways and makes their solutions seem obvious (DeYoung, Flanders, & Peterson, 2008).

Let's return now to the problem of the boats and the bird. The best way to solve it is by insight. Because the boats will cover the 50-mile distance in exactly 1 hour, and the bird flies 40 miles per hour, the bird will have flown 40 miles when the boats meet. Very little math is necessary if you have insight into this problem. ● Figure 8.14 lists some additional insight problems you may want to try (the answers can be found in ■ Table 8.1).

The Nature of Insight

Psychologist Janet Davidson (2003) believes that insight involves three abilities. The first is *selective encoding*, which refers to selecting information that is relevant to a problem, while ignoring distractions. For example, consider the following problem:

> If you have white socks and black socks in your drawer, mixed in the ratio of 4 to 5, how many socks will you have to take out to ensure you have a pair of the same color?

A person who recognizes that "mixed in a ratio of 4 to 5" is irrelevant will be more likely to come up with the correct answer of 3 socks.

Insight also relies on *selective combination*, or bringing together seemingly unrelated bits of useful information. Try this sample problem:

> With a 7-minute hourglass and an 11-minute hourglass, what is the simplest way to time the boiling of an egg for 15 minutes?

The answer requires using both hourglasses in combination. First, the 7-minute and the 11-minute hourglasses are started. When the 7-minute hourglass runs out, it's time to begin boiling the egg. At this point, 4 minutes remain on the 11-minute hourglass. Thus, when it runs out it is simply turned over. When it runs out again, 15 minutes will have passed.

A third source of insights is *selective comparison*. This is the ability to compare new problems with old information or with problems already solved. A good example is the hat rack problem, in which subjects must build a structure that can support an overcoat in the middle of a room. Each person is given only two long sticks and a C-clamp to work with. The solution, shown in ● Figure 8.15, is to clamp

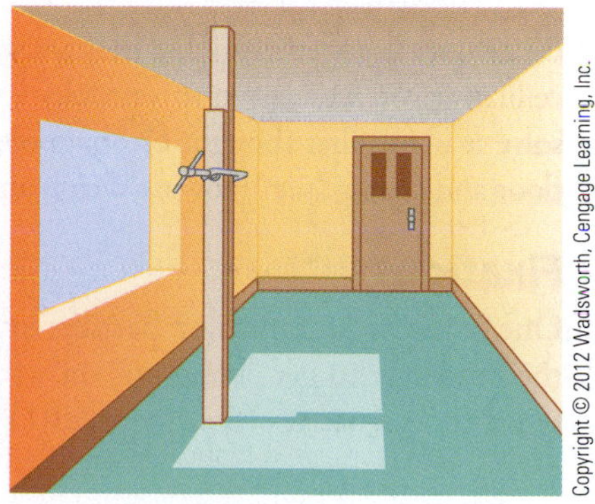

● **Figure 8.15** A solution to the hat rack problem.

Mechanical solution A problem solution achieved by trial and error or by a fixed procedure based on learned rules.

Algorithm A learned set of rules that always leads to the correct solution of a problem.

Understanding In problem solving, a deeper comprehension of the nature of the problem.

General solution A solution that correctly states the requirements for success but not in enough detail for further action.

Functional solution A detailed, practical, and workable solution.

Random search strategy Trying possible solutions to a problem in a more or less random order.

Heuristic Any strategy or technique that aids problem solving, especially by limiting the number of possible solutions to be tried.

Insight A sudden mental reorganization of a problem that makes the solution obvious.

Human Diversity: How to Weigh an Elephant

Does the culture we grow up in affect our ability to use selective comparison to solve problems? See if you can will solve this problem:

> A treasure hunter wanted to explore a cave, but he was afraid that he might get lost. Obviously, he did not have a map of the cave; all that he had with him were some common items such as a flashlight and a bag. What could he do to make sure he did not get lost trying to get back out of the cave later? (Adapted from Chen, Mo, & Honomichl, 2004.)

To solve his problem, the man could leave a trail of small objects, such as pebbles or sand, while traveling through the cave, and then follow this trail out to exit.

Seventy-five percent of American college students, but only 25 percent of Chinese students, were able to solve the cave problem. Why was there such a difference in the two groups? It seems that American students benefited from having heard the story of Hansel and Gretel when they were growing up. As you may recall, Hansel and Gretel were able to find their way out of the woods because Hansel made a trail of breadcrumbs that led back home (Chen, Mo, & Honomichl, 2004).

Now try this problem:

> In a village by a river, the chief of a tribe guards a sacred stone statue. Every year, the chief goes downriver to the next village to collect taxes. There, he places the statue in a tub at one end of a hanging balance. To pay their taxes, the villagers have to fill a tub at the other end of the scale with gold coins until the scale balances. This year, the chief forgot to bring his balance scale. How can he figure out how much gold to collect to match the statue's weight? (Adapted from Chen, Mo, & Honomichl, 2004.)

To solve this problem, the chief could put a tub in the river, and place the statue in the tub. Then he could mark the water level on the outside of the tub. To pay their taxes, the villagers would have to put gold coins in the tub until it sank to the same level as it did when the statue was in it.

Sixty-nine percent of Chinese students, but only 8 percent of American students, were able to solve this problem. Again, it seems that being exposed to a similar problem in the past was helpful. Most Chinese are familiar with a traditional tale about weighing an elephant that is too big to put on a scale. In the story, the elephant is placed in a boat and the water level is marked. After the elephant is removed, the boat is filled with small stones until the water again reaches the mark. Then, each of the stones is weighed on a small scale and the total weight of the elephant is calculated (Chen, Mo, & Honomichl, 2004).

Every culture prepares its members to solve some types of problems more easily than others (Boroditsky, 2011). As a result, learning about other cultures can make us more flexible and resourceful thinkers—and that's no fairy tale.

the two sticks together so that they are wedged between the floor and ceiling. If you were given this problem, you would be more likely to solve it if you first thought of how pole lamps are wedged between floor and ceiling (see "How to Weigh an Elephant").

Fixations

One of the most important barriers to problem solving is **fixation**, the tendency to get "hung up" on wrong solutions or to become blind to alternatives (Sternberg, 2011). Usually this occurs when we place unnecessary restrictions on our thinking (German & Barrett, 2005). How, for example, could you plant four small trees so that each is an equal distance from all the others? (The answer is shown in ● Figure 8.16.)

● **Figure 8.16** Four trees can be placed equidistant from one another by piling dirt into a mound. Three of the trees are planted equal distances apart around the base of the mound. The fourth tree is planted on the top of the mound. If you were fixated on arrangements that involve level ground, you may have been blind to this three-dimensional solution.

A prime example of restricted thinking is **functional fixedness**. This is an inability to see new uses (functions) for familiar objects or for things that were used in a particular way (German & Barrett, 2005). If you have ever used a dime as a screwdriver, you've overcome functional fixedness.

How does functional fixedness affect problem solving? Karl Duncker illustrated the effects of functional fixedness by asking students to mount a candle on a vertical board so the candle could burn normally. Duncker gave each student three candles, some matches, some cardboard boxes, some thumbtacks, and other items. Half of Duncker's subjects received these items *inside* the cardboard boxes. The others were given all the items, including the boxes, spread out on a tabletop.

Duncker found that when the items were in the boxes, solving the problem was very difficult. Why? If students saw the boxes as *containers*, they didn't realize the boxes might be part of the solution (if you haven't guessed the solution, check ● Figure 8.17). Undoubtedly, we could avoid many fixations by being more flexible in categorizing the world (Kalyuga & Hanham, 2011; Langer, 2000). For instance, creative thinking could be facilitated in the container prob-

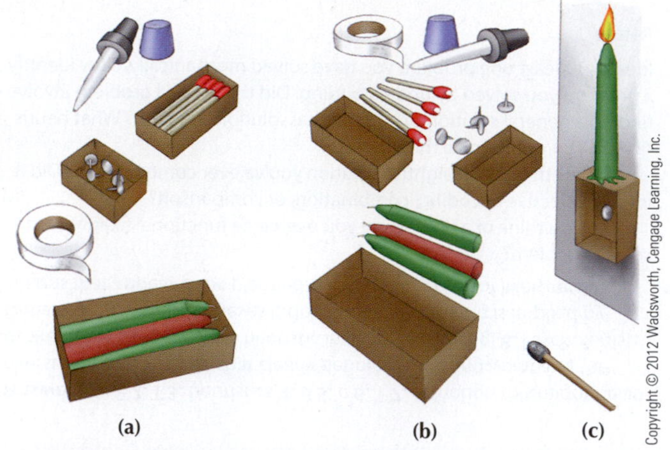

● **Figure 8.17** Materials for solving the candle problem were given to subjects in boxes *(a)* or separately *(b)*. Functional fixedness caused by condition *(a)* interfered with solving the problem. The solution to the problem is shown in *(c)*.

lem by saying "This *could be* a box," instead of "This *is* a box." When tested with the candle problem, 5-year-old children show no signs of functional fixedness. Apparently, this is because they have had less experience with the use of various objects. It is sometimes said that to be more creative, you should try to see the world without preconceptions, as if through the eyes of a child. In the case of functional fixedness that may actually be true (German & Defeyter, 2000).

Common Barriers to Problem Solving

Functional fixedness is just one of the mental blocks that prevent insight (Reed, 2010). Here's an example of another: A $5 bill is placed on a table, and a stack of objects is balanced precariously on top of the bill. How can the bill be removed without touching or moving the objects? A good answer is to split the bill on one of its edges. Gently pulling from opposite ends will tear the bill in half and remove it without toppling the objects. Many people fail to see this solution because they have learned not to destroy money (Adams, 2001). Notice again the impact of placing something in a category, in this case, "things of value" (which should not be destroyed). Other common mental blocks can hinder problem solving, too, as listed here:

1. **Emotional barriers:** inhibition and fear of making a fool of oneself, fear of making a mistake, inability to tolerate ambiguity, excessive self-criticism

   Example: An architect is afraid to try an unconventional design because she fears that other architects will think it is frivolous.

2. **Cultural barriers:** values that hold that fantasy is a waste of time; that playfulness is for children only; that reason, logic, and numbers are good; that feelings, intuitions, pleasure, and humor are bad or have no value in the serious business of problem solving

   Example: A corporate manager wants to solve a business problem but becomes stern and angry when members of his marketing team joke playfully about possible solutions.

TABLE 8.1 Solutions to Insight Problems

Water lilies: Day 59
Twenty dollars: $10
How many pets?: Three (one bird, one cat, and one dog)
Between 2 and 3: A decimal point
One word: ONE WORD (You may object that the answer is two words, but the problem called for the answer to be "one word," and it is.)

3. **Learned barriers:** conventions about uses (functional fixedness), meanings, possibilities, taboos

   Example: A cook doesn't have any clean mixing bowls and fails to see that he could use a frying pan as a bowl.

4. **Perceptual barriers:** habits leading to a failure to identify important elements of a problem

   Example: A beginning artist concentrates on drawing a vase of flowers without seeing that the "empty" spaces around the vase are part of the composition, too.

Experts and Novices

So far, we have seen that problem-solving expertise is based on *acquired strategies* (learned heuristics) and specific *organized knowledge* (systematic information). Experts are better able to see the true nature of problems and to define them more flexibly in terms of general principles (Anderson, 2010; Kalyuga, & Hanham, 2011). For example, chess experts are much more likely than novices to have heuristics available for solving problems. However, what really sets master players apart is their ability to intuitively recognize *patterns* that suggest what lines of play should be explored next. This helps eliminate a large number of possible moves. The chess master, therefore, does not waste time exploring unproductive pathways (Ross, 2006).

In other words, becoming a star performer does not come from some general strengthening of the mind. Master chess players don't necessarily have better memories than beginners (except for realistic chess positions) (Gobet & Simon, 1996; Goldstein, 2011; see ● Figure 8.18). And, typically, they don't explore more moves ahead than lesser players.

Expertise also allows more *automatic processing*, or fast, fairly effortless thinking based on experience with similar problems. Automatic processing frees "space" in short-term memory, making it easier to work on the problem (Kalyuga, Renkl, & Paas, 2010). At the highest skill levels, expert performers tend to rise above rules and plans. Their decisions, thinking, and actions become rapid, fluid, and insightful (Hélie & Sun, 2010). Thus, when a

Fixation The tendency to repeat wrong solutions or faulty responses, especially as a result of becoming blind to alternatives.

Functional fixedness A rigidity in problem solving caused by an inability to see new uses for familiar objects.

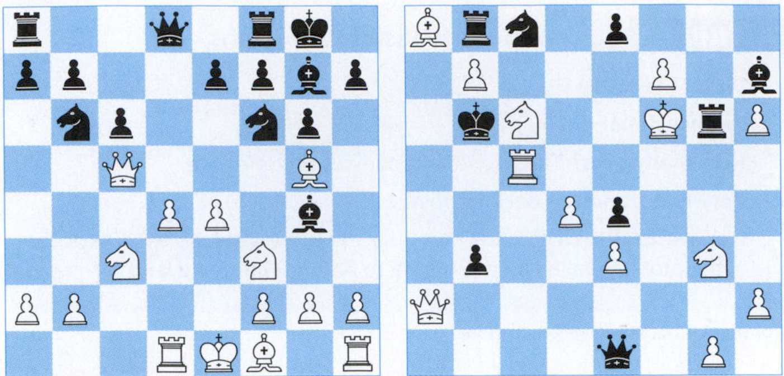

● **Figure 8.18** The left chessboard shows a realistic game. The right chessboard is a random arrangement of pieces. Expert chess players can memorize the left board at a glance, yet they are no better than beginners at memorizing the random board (Ross, 2006). Expert performance at most thinking tasks is based on acquired strategies and knowledge. If you would like to excel at a profession or a mental skill, plan on adding to your knowledge every day (Reed, 2010).

chess master recognizes a pattern on the chessboard, the most desirable tactic comes to mind almost immediately. Mind you, this capacity comes at a price. Expert chess players can automatically recognize 50,000 to 100,000 patterns, a level of skill that takes about 10 years to build up (Ross, 2006).

To develop expertise in a field, then, requires us to learn available heuristic solution strategies as well as to develop a deeper general understanding of the field. Throw into the mix that expertise also involves learning thousands of patterns and practicing solving many problems and you can see that developing expertise involves years of hard work. Think about that the next time someone says of an expert, "She makes it look easy."

Knowledge Builder: Problem Solving

RECITE

1. Insight refers to rote, or trial-and-error, problem solving. T or F?
2. The first phase in problem solving by understanding is to discover the general properties of a correct solution. T or F?
3. Problem-solving strategies that guide the search for solutions are called ______________.
4. A common element underlying insight is that information is encoded, combined, and compared
   a. mechanically *b.* by rote *c.* functionally *d.* selectively
5. Functional fixedness is a major barrier to
   a. insightful problem solving *b.* using random search strategies *c.* mechanical problem solving *d.* achieving fixations through problem solving
6. Organized knowledge, acquired heuristics, and the ability to recognize patterns are all characteristics of human expertise. T or F?

REFLECT

Think Critically

7. Do you think that it is true that "a problem clearly defined is a problem half solved"?
8. Sea otters select suitably sized rocks and use them to hammer shellfish loose for eating. They then use the rock to open the shell. Does this qualify as thinking?

Relate

Identify at least one problem you have solved mechanically. Now identify a problem you solved by understanding. Did the second problem involve finding a general solution or a functional solution? Or both? What heuristics did you use to solve the problem?

What is the most insightful solution you've ever come up with? Did it involve selective encoding, combination, or comparison?

Can you think of a time when you overcame functional fixedness to solve a problem?

Answers: 1. F **2.** T **3.** heuristics **4.** *d* **5.** *a* **6.** T **7.** Although this might be an overstatement, it is true that clearly defining a starting point and the desired goal can serve as a heuristic in problem solving. **8.** Psychologist Donald Griffin (1992) believes it does because thinking is implied by actions that appear to be planned with an awareness of likely results.

Creative Thinking—Down Roads Less Traveled

Gateway Question 8.6: *What is the nature of creative thinking?*

Original ideas have changed the course of human history. Much of what we now take for granted in art, medicine, music, technology, and science was once regarded as radical or impossible. How do creative people like Thomas Edison or Wassily Kandinsky achieve the breakthroughs that advance us into new realms? Psychologists have learned a great deal about how creativity occurs and how to promote it, as you will soon learn (Hennessey & Amabile, 2010).

We have seen that problem solving may be mechanical, insightful, or based on understanding. To this we can add that thinking may be **inductive** (going from specific facts or observations to general principles) or **deductive** (going from general principles to specific situations). Thinking may also be **logical** (proceeding from given information to new conclusions on the basis of explicit rules) or **illogical** (intuitive, associative, or personal).

What distinguishes creative thinking from more routine problem solving? Creative thinking involves all these thinking styles, plus *fluency*, *flexibility*, and *originality*. Let's say that you would like to find creative uses for the billions of plastic containers discarded each year. The creativity of your suggestions could be rated in this way: **Fluency** is defined as the total number of suggestions you are able to make. **Flexibility** is the number of times you shift from one class of possible uses to another. **Originality** refers to how novel or unusual your ideas are. By counting the number of times you showed fluency, flexibility, and originality, we could rate your creativity, or capacity for *divergent thinking* (Baer, 1993; Runco, 2004).

In routine problem solving or thinking, there is one correct answer, and the problem is to find it. This leads to **convergent thinking** (lines of thought converge on the answer). **Divergent thinking** is the reverse, in which many possibilities are developed from one starting point (Cropley, 2006; see ■ Table 8.2 for some examples). It is worth noting that divergent thinking is also a characteristic of **daydreams** (vivid waking fantasies). For most people,

© John Bryson/Sygma/Corbis

Fluency is an important part of creative thinking. Mozart produced more than 600 pieces of music. Shakespeare wrote 154 sonnets. Salvador Dali (shown here) created more than 1500 paintings as well as sculptures, drawings, illustrations, books, and even an animated cartoon. Not all of these works were masterpieces. However, a fluent outpouring of ideas fed the creative efforts of each of these geniuses.

fantasy and daydreaming are associated with greater mental flexibility or creativity (Langens & Schmalt, 2002). Regardless, no matter when or how it occurs, creative thinking produces new answers, ideas, or patterns rather than repeating learned solutions (Davidovitch & Milgram, 2006).

Problem finding is another characteristic of creative thinking. Many of the problems we solve are "presented" to us—by employers, teachers, circumstances, or life in general. **Problem finding** involves actively seeking problems to solve. When you are thinking creatively, a spirit of discovery prevails: You are more likely to find unsolved problems and *choose* to tackle them. Thus, problem finding may be a more creative act than the convergent problem solving that typically follows it (Runco, 2004).

TABLE 8.2 Convergent and Divergent Problems

Convergent Problems
What is the area of a triangle that is 3 feet wide at the base and 2 feet tall?
Erica is shorter than Zoey but taller than Carlo, and Carlo is taller than Jared. Who is the second tallest?
If you simultaneously drop a baseball and a bowling ball from a tall building, which will hit the ground first?
Divergent Problems
What objects can you think of that begin with the letters BR?
How could discarded aluminum cans be put to use?
Write a poem about fire and ice.

Tests of Creativity

Divergent thinking can be measured in several ways (Kaufman, 2009). In the *Unusual Uses Test*, you would be asked to think of as many uses as possible for some object, such as the plastic containers

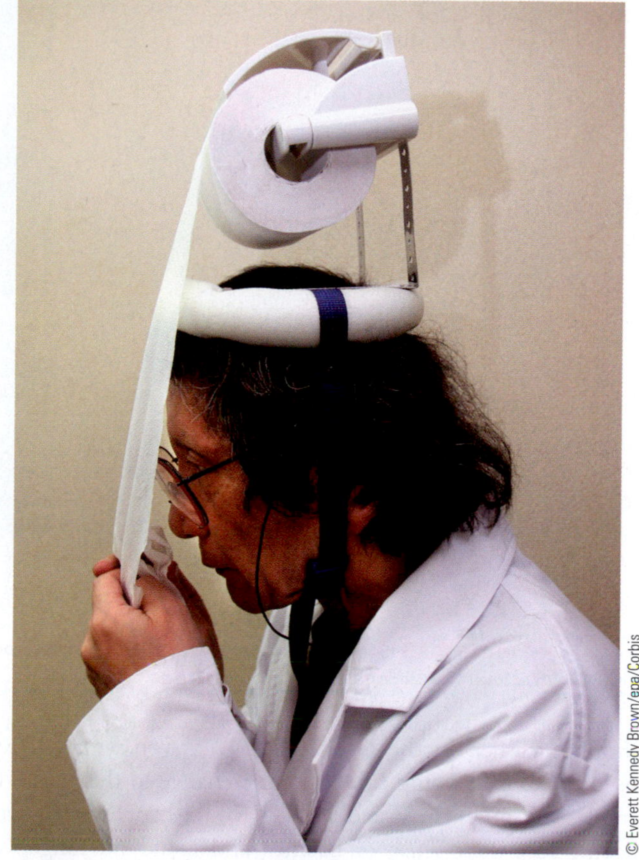
© Everett Kennedy Brown/epa/Corbis

Unorthodox Japanese inventor Kenji Kawakami created the "hay fever hat" so no one with allergies would ever have to go without tissue paper. In addition to being original or novel, a creative solution must be high quality and relevant of the problem. Is this a creative solution to the "problem" of access to tissues?

Inductive thought Thinking in which a general rule or principle is gathered from a series of specific examples; for instance, inferring the laws of gravity by observing many falling objects.

Deductive thought Thought that applies a general set of rules to specific situations; for example, using the laws of gravity to predict the behavior of a single falling object.

Logical thought Drawing conclusions on the basis of formal principles of reasoning.

Illogical thought Thought that is intuitive, haphazard, or irrational.

Fluency In tests of creativity, fluency refers to the total number of solutions produced.

Flexibility In tests of creativity, flexibility is indicated by the number of different types of solutions produced.

Originality In tests of creativity, originality refers to how novel or unusual solutions are.

Convergent thinking Thinking directed toward discovery of a single established correct answer; conventional thinking.

Divergent thinking Thinking that produces many ideas or alternatives; a major element in original or creative thought.

Daydream A vivid waking fantasy.

Problem finding The active discovery of problems to be solved.

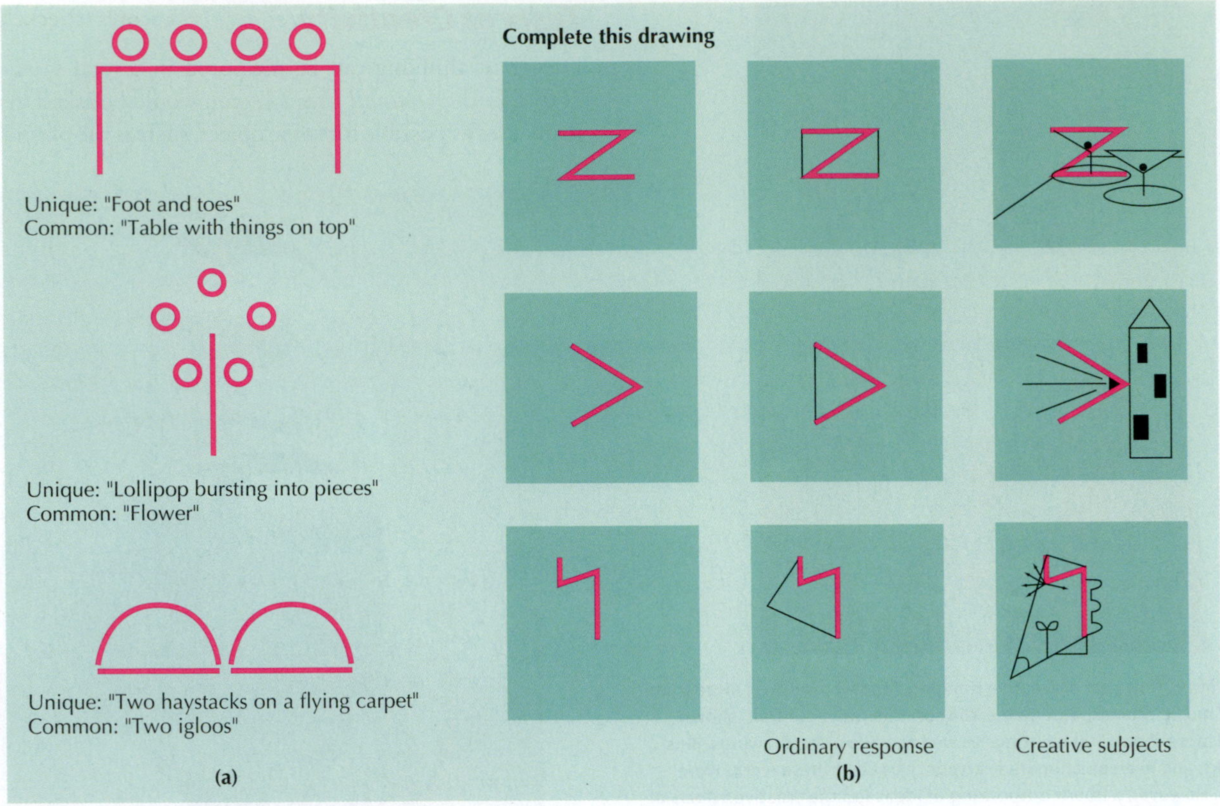

• **Figure 8.19** Some tests of divergent thinking. Creative responses are more original and more complex. (*(a)* Adapted from Wallach & Kogan, 1965; *(b)* adapted from Barron, 1958.)

mentioned earlier. In the *Consequences Test*, you would list the consequences that would follow a basic change in the world. For example, you might be asked, "What would happen if everyone suddenly lost their sense of balance and could no longer stay upright?" People try to list as many reactions as possible. If you were to take the *Anagrams Test*, you would be given a word such as *creativity* and asked to make as many new words as possible by rearranging the letters. Each of these tests can be scored for fluency, flexibility, and originality. (For an example of other tests of divergent thinking, see • Figure 8.19).

Isn't creativity more than divergent thought? What if a person comes up with a large number of useless answers to a problem? A good question. Divergent thinking is an important part of creativity, but there is more to it. To be creative, the solution to a problem must be more than novel, unusual, or original. It must also be *high quality* and *relevant* to solving the original problem (Kaufman & Sternberg, 2010). This is the dividing line between a "harebrained scheme" and a "stroke of genius." In other words, the creative person brings reasoning and critical thinking to bear on new ideas once they are produced (Runco, 2003).

Stages of Creative Thought

Is there any pattern to creative thinking? Typically, five stages occur during creative problem solving:

1. **Orientation.** As a first step, the person defines the problem and identifies its most important dimensions.
2. **Preparation.** In the second stage, creative thinkers saturate themselves with as much information about the problem as possible.
3. **Incubation.** Most major problems produce a period during which all attempted solutions will be futile. At this point, problem solving may proceed on a subconscious level: Although the problem seems to have been set aside, it is still "cooking" in the background.
4. **Illumination.** The stage of incubation is often ended by a rapid insight or series of insights. These produce the "Aha!" experience, often depicted in cartoons as a lightbulb appearing over the thinker's head.
5. **Verification.** The final step is to test and critically evaluate the solution obtained during the stage of illumination. If the solution proves faulty, the thinker reverts to the stage of incubation.

Of course, creative thought is not always so neat. Nevertheless, the stages listed are a good summary of the most typical sequence of events.

You may find it helpful to relate the stages to the following true (more or less) story. Legend has it that the king of Syracuse (a city in ancient Greece) once suspected that his goldsmith had substituted cheaper metals for some of the gold in a crown and kept the extra gold. Archimedes, a famous mathematician and thinker, was given the problem of discovering whether the king had been cheated.

Archimedes began by defining the problem (*orientation*): "How can I tell what metals have been used in the crown without damaging it?" He then checked all known methods of analyzing metals *(preparation)*. All involved cutting or melting the crown, so he was forced to temporarily set the problem aside *(incubation)*. Then one day as he stepped into his bath, Archimedes suddenly knew he had the solution *(illumination)*. He was so excited that he is said to have run naked through the streets shouting, "Eureka, eureka!" (I have found it, I have found it!).

On observing his own body floating in the bath, Archimedes realized that different metals of equal weight would displace different amounts of water. A pound of brass, for example, occupies more space than a pound of gold, which is denser. All that remained was to test the solution (*verification*). Archimedes placed an amount of gold (equal in weight to that given the goldsmith) in a tub of water. He marked the water level and removed the gold. He then placed the crown in the water. Was the crown pure gold? If it was, it would raise the water to exactly the same level. Unfortunately, the purity of the crown and the fate of the goldsmith are to this day unknown! (Too bad Archimedes didn't grow up in China. If he had heard the "weighing-the-elephant" tale, he might have quickly solved the crown problem.)

The preceding account is a good general description of creative thinking. However, rather than springing from sudden insights, much creative problem solving is **incremental**. That is, it is the end result of many small steps. This is certainly true of many inventions, which build on earlier ideas. Some authors believe that truly exceptional creativity requires a rare combination of thinking skills, personality, and a supportive social environment. This mix, they believe, accounts for creative giants such as Edison, Freud, Mozart, Picasso, and others (Robinson, 2010; Simonton, 2009).

Positive Psychology: The Creative Personality

What makes a person creative? According to the popular stereotype, highly creative people are eccentric, introverted, neurotic, socially inept, unbalanced in their interests, and on the edge of madness. After all, isn't there a "fine line between genius and insanity"? Although there is some evidence that the brain chemistry of creative people and mentally ill people is similar (de Manzano, 2010), mentally ill people are generally not creative and vice versa (Robinson, 2010).

A notable exception to the preceding conclusion concerns mood disorders. A person with a mood disorder may be manic (agitated, elated, and hyperactive), depressed, or both. One study found that parents with a history of mood swings, as well as their children, scored higher in creativity than did normal parents and their children (Simeonova et al., 2005). Further, many of history's renowned artists, writers, poets, and composers, including Vincent Van Gogh, Edgar Allan Poe, Emily Dickinson, Ernest Hemmingway, and many others, also experienced pronounced mood swings (Jamison, 1999; McDermott, 2001).

In general, however, direct studies of creative individuals paint a very different picture (Hennessey & Amabile, 2010; Robinson, 2010; Winner, 2003):

1. Although people with high IQs can be quite creative (Park, Lubinski, Benbow, 2008), there is generally little correlation between creativity tests and IQ test scores (Preckel, Holling, & Wiese, 2006).
2. Creative people usually have a greater-than-average range of knowledge and interests, and they are more fluent in combining ideas from various sources. They are also good at using mental images and metaphors in thinking (Riquelme, 2002).
3. Creative people are open to a wide variety of experiences. They accept irrational thoughts and are uninhibited about their feelings and fantasies. They tend to use broad categories, to question assumptions, to break mental sets, and they find order in chaos. They also experience more unusual states of consciousness, such as vivid dreams and mystical experiences (Ayers, Beaton, & Hunt, 1999).
4. Creative people enjoy symbolic thought, ideas, concepts, and possibilities. They tend to be interested in truth, form, and beauty, rather than in fame or success. Their creative work is an end in itself (Robinson, 2010; Sternberg & Lubart, 1995).
5. Creative people value their independence and prefer complexity. However, they are unconventional and nonconforming primarily in their work; otherwise they do not have unusual, outlandish, or bizarre personalities.

Living More Creatively

Can creativity be learned? It is beginning to look as if some creative thinking skills can be learned. In particular, you can become more creative by practicing divergent thinking and by taking risks, analyzing ideas, and seeking unusual connections between ideas (Baer, 1993; Sternberg, 2001). Don't forget to read this chapter's *Psychology in Action* module for more on creativity.

BRIDGES

Humanistic psychologist Abraham Maslow believed that we must live honestly and creatively to make full use our potentials. **See Chapter 10, pages 348–349, for a discussion of self-actualization.**

Intuition—Mental Shortcut? Or Dangerous Detour?

Gateway Question 8.7: *How accurate is intuition?*

At the same time that intuitive thought may contribute to creative problem solving, it can also lead to thinking errors. To see how this can happen, try the following problems:

Problem 1 An epidemic breaks out, and 600 people are about to die. Doctors have two choices. If they give drug A, 200 lives will be saved. If they give drug B, there is a one-third chance that 600 people will be saved, and a two-thirds chance that none will be saved. Which drug should they choose?

Problem 2 Again, 600 people are about to die, and doctors must make a choice. If they give drug A, 400 people will die. If they give drug B, there is a

Incremental problem solving Thinking marked by a series of small steps that lead to an original solution.

Critical Thinking — Have You Ever Thin Sliced Your Teacher?

Think back to your least favorite teacher (not your current one, of course!). How long did it take you to figure out that he or she wasn't going to make your list of star teachers?

In an intriguing study, psychologist Nalini Ambady asked people to watch video clips of teachers they did not know. After watching three 10-second segments, participants were asked to rate the teachers. Amazingly, their ratings correlated highly with year-end course evaluations made by actual students (Ambady & Rosenthal, 1993). Ambady obtained the same result when she presented an even thinner "slice" of teaching behavior, just three 2-second clips. A mere 6 seconds is all that participants needed to form intuitive judgments of the instructors' teaching!

In his book *Blink*, Malcolm Gladwell (2005) argues that this was not a case of hurried irrationality. Instead, it was "thin-slicing," or quickly making sense of thin slivers of experience. According to Gladwell, these immediate, intuitive reactions can sometimes form the basis of more carefully reasoned judgments. They are a testament to the power of the *cognitive unconscious*, which is a part of the brain that does automatic, unconscious processing (Wilson, 2002). Far from being irrational, intuition may be an important part of how we think.

The trick, of course, is figuring out when thin-slicing can be trusted and when it can't. After all, first impressions aren't always right. For example, have you ever had a teacher you came to appreciate only after classes were well under way or only after the course was over? In many circumstances, quick impressions are most valuable when you take the time to verify them through further observation.

one-third chance that no one will die, and a two-thirds chance that 600 will die. Which drug should they choose?

Most people choose drug A for the first problem and drug B for the second. This is fascinating because the two problems are identical. The only difference is that the first is stated in terms of lives saved, the second in terms of lives lost. Yet, even people who realize that their answers are contradictory find it difficult to change them (Kahneman & Tversky, 1972, 1973).

Intuition

As the example shows, we often make decisions intuitively, rather than logically or rationally. **Intuition** is quick, impulsive thought. It may provide fast answers, but it can also be misleading and sometimes disastrous (see "Have You Ever Thin Sliced Your Teacher?")

Two noted psychologists, Daniel Kahneman (KON-eh-man) and Amos Tversky (tuh-VER-ski) (1937–1996), studied how we make decisions in the face of uncertainty. They found that human judgment is often seriously flawed (Kahneman, 2003; Kahneman, Slovic, & Tversky, 1982). Let's explore some common intuitive thinking errors, so you will be better prepared to avoid them.

Representativeness

One very common pitfall in judgment is illustrated by the question: Which is more probable?

A. Snowboarder Shaun White will not be in the lead after the first run of a halfpipe competition but will win the competition.

B. Snowboarder Shaun White will not be in the lead after the first run of a halfpipe competition.

Tversky and Kahneman (1982) found that most people regard statements like A as more probable than B. However, this intuitive answer overlooks an important fact: The likelihood of two events occurring together is lower than the probability of either one alone. (For example, the probability of getting one head when flipping a coin is one-half, or .5. The probability of getting two heads when flipping two coins is one-fourth, or .25.) Therefore, A is less likely to be true than B.

According to Tversky and Kahneman, such faulty conclusions are based on the **representativeness heuristic**. That is, we tend to give a choice greater weight if it seems to be representative of what we already know. Thus, you probably compared the information about Shaun White with your mental model of what a snowboarding professional's behavior should be like. Answer A seems to better represent the model. Therefore, it seems more likely than answer B, even though it isn't. In courtrooms, jurors are more likely to think a defendant is guilty if the person appears to fit the profile of a person likely to commit a crime (Davis & Follette, 2002). For example, a young single male from a poor neighborhood would be more likely to be judged guilty of theft than a middle-aged married father from an affluent suburb.

Underlying Odds

Another common error in judgment involves ignoring the **base rate**, or underlying probability of an event. People in one experiment were told that they would be given descriptions of 100 people—70 lawyers and 30 engineers. Subjects were then asked to guess, without knowing anything about a person, whether she or he was an engineer or a lawyer. All correctly stated the probabilities as 70 percent for lawyer and 30 percent for engineer. Participants were then given this description:

Eric is a 30-year-old man. He is married with no children. A man of high ability and high motivation, he promises to be quite successful in his field. He is well liked by his colleagues.

Notice that the description gives no new information about Eric's occupation. He could still be either an engineer or a lawyer. Therefore, the odds should again be estimated as 70-30. However, most people changed the odds to 50-50. Intuitively, it seems that Eric has an equal chance of being either an engineer or a lawyer. But this guess completely ignores the underlying odds.

Perhaps it is fortunate that we do at times ignore underlying odds. Were this not the case, how many people would get married in the face of a 50 percent divorce rate? Or how many would start high-risk businesses? On the other hand, people who smoke, drink and then drive, or skip wearing auto seat belts ignore rather high odds of injury or illness. In many high-risk situations, ignoring base rates is the same as thinking you are an exception to the rule.

Framing

The most general conclusion about intuition is that the way a problem is stated, or **framed**, affects decisions (Tversky & Kahneman, 1981). As the first example in this discussion revealed, people often give different answers to the same problem if it is stated in slightly different ways. To gain some added insight into framing, try another thinking problem:

> A couple is divorcing. Both parents seek custody of their only child, but custody can be granted to just one parent. If you had to make a decision based on the following information, to which parent would you award custody of the child?
>
> **Parent A:** average income, average health, average working hours, reasonable rapport with the child, relatively stable social life.
>
> **Parent B:** above-average income, minor health problems, lots of work-related travel, very close relationship with the child, extremely active social life.

Most people choose to award custody to Parent B, the parent who has some drawbacks but also several advantages (such as above-average income). That's because people tend to look for *positive qualities* that can be *awarded* to the child. However, how would you choose if you were asked this question: Which parent should be denied custody? In this case, most people choose to deny custody to Parent B. Why is Parent B a good choice one moment and a poor choice the next? It's because the second question asked who should be *denied* custody. To answer this question, people tend to look for *negative qualities* that would *disqualify* a parent. As you can see, the way a question is framed can channel us down a narrow path so we attend to only part of the information provided, rather than weighing all the pros and cons (Shafir, 1993).

Usually, the *broadest* way of framing or stating a problem produces the best decisions. However, people often state problems in increasingly narrow terms until a single, seemingly "obvious" answer emerges. For example, to select a career, it would be wise to consider pay, working conditions, job satisfaction, needed skills, future employment outlook, and many other factors. Instead, such decisions are often narrowed to thoughts such as, "I like to write, so I'll be a journalist," "I want to make good money and law pays well," or "I can be creative in photography." Framing decisions so narrowly greatly increases the risk of making a poor choice. If you would like to think more critically and analytically, it is important to pay attention to how you are defining problems before you try to solve them. Remember, shortcuts to answers often short-circuit clear thinking.

"Hot" Cognition

One final factor bears mentioning: Emotions also tend to affect good judgment. When we must make a choice, our emotional reactions to various alternatives can determine what intuitively seems to be the right answer. Of course, taking action in the heat of anger, passion, or stress may not be the wisest move. It may be better to "cool down" a bit before picking that bar fight, running off and eloping, or immediately declining that daunting job offer (Johnson, Batey, & Holdsworth, 2009). Personal rituals, such as counting to ten, meditating for a moment, and even engaging in superstitious behaviors like crossing your fingers before moving ahead, can be calming (Damisch, Stoberock, & Mussweiler, 2010).

Even mild emotions, such as low-level stress, can subtly influence how we think and act (for an example, see "Extra Hot, Decaf, Double-Shot..."). Emotions such as fear, hope, anxiety, liking, or disgust can eliminate possibilities from consideration or promote them to the top of the list (Kahneman, 2003). For many people, choosing which political candidate to vote for is a good example of how emotions can cloud clear thinking. Rather than comparing candidates' records and policies, it is tempting to vote for the person we like rather than the person who is most qualified for the job.

A Look Ahead

We have discussed only some of the intuitive errors made in the face of uncertainty. In the upcoming *Psychology in Action* section, we will return to the topic of creative thinking for a look at ways to promote creativity.

Knowledge Builder — Creativity and Intuition

RECITE

1. Fluency, flexibility, and originality are characteristics of
   a. convergent thought *b.* deductive thinking *c.* creative thought *d.* trial-and-error solutions
2. List the typical stages of creative thinking in the correct order.
   ______ ______ ______ ______ ______
3. Reasoning and critical thinking tend to block creativity; these are noncreative qualities. T or F?
4. To be creative, an original idea must also be high quality and relevant. T or F?

Continued

Intuition Quick, impulsive thought that does not make use of formal logic or clear reasoning.

Representativeness heuristic A tendency to select wrong answers because they seem to match preexisting mental categories.

Base rate The basic rate at which an event occurs over time; the basic probability of an event.

Framing In thought, the terms in which a problem is stated or the way that it is structured.

Critical Thinking — Extra Hot, Decaf, Double-Shot. . .

. . . sugar-free, venti with vanilla soy, light whip, peppermint white chocolate mocha, nonfat, no foam with extra syrup, double-cupped, please. Overhearing the order while standing in line at their favorite coffee shop, the older woman remarked to her husband, "Don't you miss the days when all you could order was a coffee with cream and sugar?" Behind them, a young man whispered in his friend's ear, "Poor old people!" One stereotype of elderly people is that they have trouble coping with modern life.

But are the elderly the only ones sometimes left bewildered by tasks as simple as ordering a cup of coffee? Isn't the freedom of having a wide variety of choices a good thing (Leotti, Iyengar, & Ochsner, 2010)? Maybe not. According to behavioral economist Dilip Soman (2010), we are all struggling to make choices in an ever more complex world.

In one study, consumers were given an option to purchase jam. Half of them could choose from 6 different flavors, the other half had 24 flavors to choose from. Although consumers with more choice expressed more interest, they were actually 10 times *less* likely to purchase any jam (Iyengar & Lepper, 2000). Similarly, restaurants whose menus feature a broader variety of choices often find that patrons are more likely to order from a smaller number of familiar choices (Soman, 2010). Apparently, businesses that increase the variety of their product offerings are not guaranteed increased sales (Gourville & Soman, 2005).

It may be faintly amusing that people have trouble exercising choice in a coffee shop, grocery store, or restaurant. It's not that funny when more important issues are involved, such as choosing the best medicine or medical procedure. Imagine, for example, facing too many options when deciding whether to remove a seriously ill infant from life support (Botti, Orfali, & Iyengar, 2009).

Why are more complex choices so tough to make? Researchers like Soman have identified a number of factors, such as increased stress, cognitive overload, difficulty remembering all of the choices, and confusion about the possibilities (Soman, 2010). Although the growing complexity of modern life may increase our freedom, our choices may be expanding beyond our capacity to cope. So try ordering a coffee with cream and sugar sometime.

Diego Cervo/Shutterstock

5. Intelligence and creativity are highly correlated; the higher a person's IQ is, the more likely he or she is to be creative. T or F?
6. Kate is single, outspoken, and very bright. As a college student, she was deeply concerned with discrimination and other social issues and participated in several protests. Which statement is more likely to be true?
   a. Kate is a bank teller. *b.* Kate is a bank teller and a feminist.

REFLECT

Think Critically

7. A coin is flipped four times with one of the following results: *(a)* H T T H, *(b)* T T T T, *(c)* H H H H, *(d)* H H T H. Which sequence would most likely precede getting a head on the fifth coin flip?

Relate

Make up a question that would require convergent thinking to answer. Now do the same for divergent thinking.

Which of the tests of creativity described in the text do you think you would do best on? (Look back if you can't remember them all.)

To better remember the stages of creative thinking, make up a short story that includes these words: *orient, prepare, in Cuba, illuminate, verify.*

Explain in your own words how representativeness and base rates contribute to thinking errors.

Answers: 1. c **2.** orientation, preparation, incubation, illumination, verification **3.** F **4.** T **5.** F **6.** *a* **7.** The chance of getting heads on the fifth flip is the same in each case. Each time you flip a coin, the chance of getting a head is 50 percent, no matter what happened before. However, many people intuitively think that *b* is the answer because a head is "overdue," or that *c* is correct because the coin is "on a roll" for heads.

Psychology in Action

Enhancing Creativity—Brainstorms

Gateway Question 8.8: *What can be done to promote creativity?*

Thomas Edison explained his creativity by saying, "Genius is 1 percent inspiration and 99 percent perspiration." Many studies of creativity show that "genius" and "eminence" owe as much to persistence and dedication as they do to inspiration (Robinson, 2010; Winner, 2003). Once it is recognized that creativity can be hard work, then something can be done to enhance it. Here are some suggestions:

1. Break Mental Sets and Challenge Assumptions

A **mental set** is the tendency to perceive a problem in a way that blinds us to possible solutions. Mental sets are a major barrier to creative thinking. They usually will lead us to see a problem in preconceived terms that impede our problem solving attempts. (Fixations and functional fixedness, which were described earlier, are specific types of mental sets.)

Try the problems pictured in • Figure 8.20. If you have difficulty, try asking yourself what assumptions you are making. The problems are designed to demonstrate the limiting effects of a mental set. (The answers to these problems, along with an explanation of the sets that prevent their solution, are found in • Figure 8.21.)

Now that you have been forewarned about the danger of faulty assumptions, see if you can correctly answer the following questions. If you get caught on any of them, consider it an additional reminder of the value of actively challenging the assumptions you are making in any instance of problem solving.

1. A farmer had 19 sheep. All but 9 died. How many sheep did the farmer have left?
2. It is not unlawful for a man living in Winston-Salem, North Carolina, to be buried west of the Mississippi River. T or F?
3. Some months have 30 days, some have 31. How many months have 28 days?
4. I have two coins that together total 30 cents. One of the coins is not a nickel. What are the two coins?
5. If there are 12 one-cent candies in a dozen, how many two-cent candies are there in a dozen?

These questions are designed to cause thinking errors. Here are the answers:

1. Nineteen—9 alive and 10 dead. **2.** F. It is against the law to bury a living person anywhere. **3.** All of them. **4.** A quarter and a nickel. One of the coins is not a nickel, but the other one is! **5.** 12.

2. Define Problems Broadly

An effective way to break mental sets is to enlarge the definition of a problem. For instance, assume that your problem is to design a better doorway. This is likely to lead to ordinary solutions. Why not change the problem to design a better way to get through a wall? Now your solutions will be more original. Best of all might be to state the problem as follows: Find a better way to define separate areas for living and working. This could lead to truly creative solutions (Adams, 2001).

Let's say you are leading a group that's designing a new can opener. Wisely, you ask the group to think about *opening* in general, rather than about can openers. This was just the approach that led to the pop-top can. As the design group discussed the concept of opening, one member suggested that nature has its own openers, like the soft seam on a pea pod. Instead of a new can-opening tool, the group invented the self-opening can (Stein, 1974).

3. Restate the Problem in Different Ways

Stating problems in novel ways also tends to produce more creative solutions. See if you can cross out six letters to make a single word out of the following:

CSRIEXLEATTTERES

If you're having difficulty, it may be that you need to restate the problem. Were you trying to cross out 6 letters? The real solution is to cross out the letters in the words "six letters," which yields the word CREATE.

One way to restate a problem is to imagine how another person would view it. What would a child, engineer, professor, mechanic, artist, psychologist, judge, or minister ask about the

Mental set A predisposition to perceive or respond in a particular way.

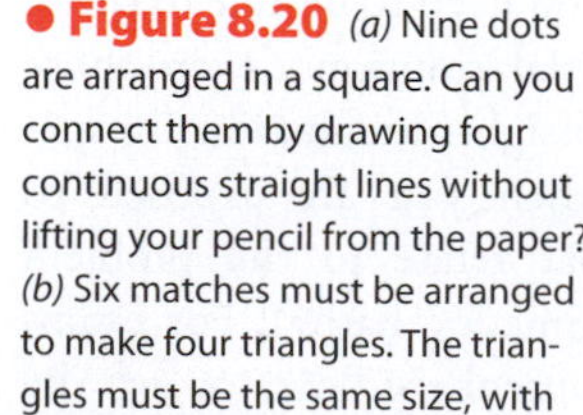

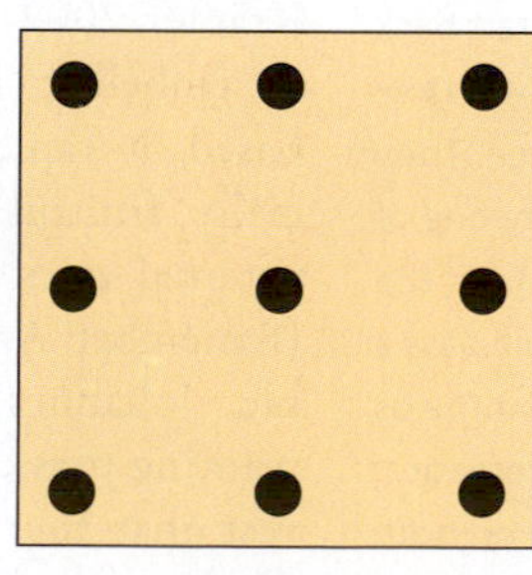

(a)

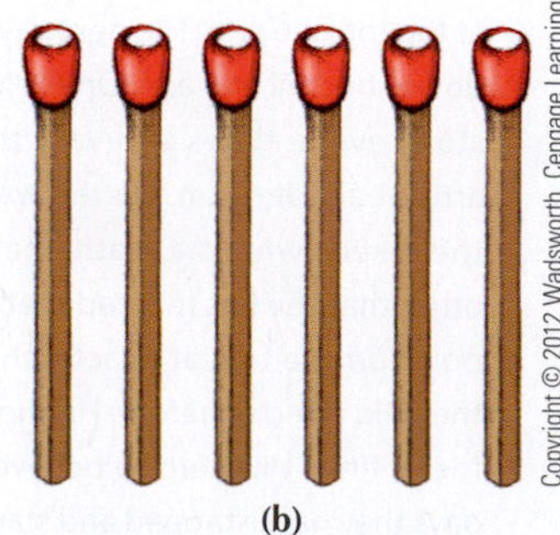

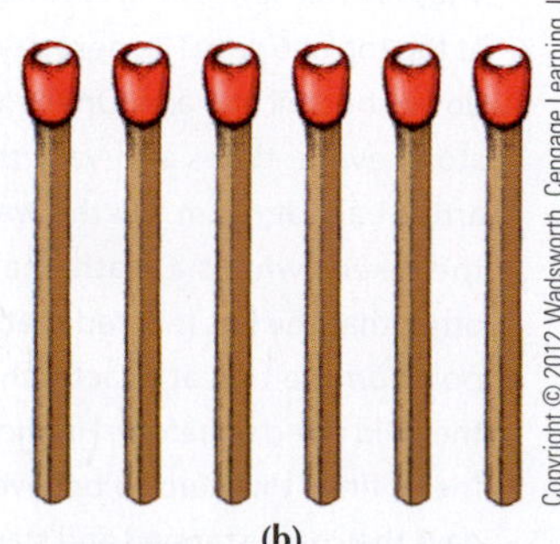

(b)

• **Figure 8.20** *(a)* Nine dots are arranged in a square. Can you connect them by drawing four continuous straight lines without lifting your pencil from the paper? *(b)* Six matches must be arranged to make four triangles. The triangles must be the same size, with each side equal to the length of one match. (The solutions to these problems appear in Fig. 8.21.)

● Figure 8.21 Problem solutions. *(a)* The dot problem can be solved by extending the lines beyond the square formed by the dots. Most people assume incorrectly that they may not do this. *(b)* The match problem can be solved by building a three-dimensional pyramid. Most people assume that the matches must be arranged on a flat surface. If you remembered the four-tree problem from earlier in the chapter, the match problem may have been easy to solve.

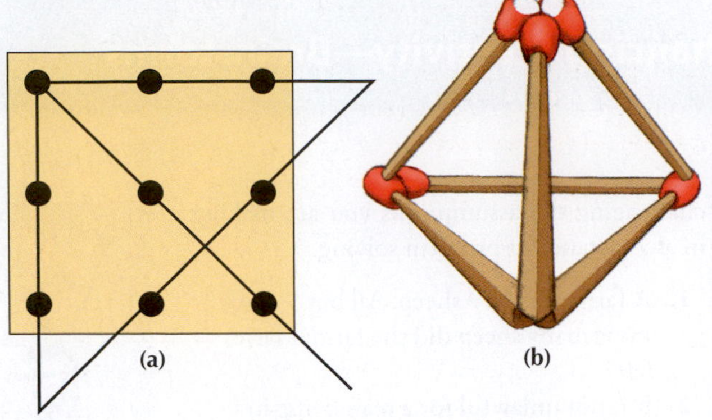

problem? Also, don't be afraid to ask "silly" or playful questions. Here are some examples:

If the problem were alive, what would it look like?

If the problem were edible, how would it taste?

How would the problem look from an airplane? How does it look from underneath?

Is any part of the problem pretty? Ugly? Stupid? Friendly?

If the problem could speak, what would it say?

At the very least, you should almost always ask the following questions:

What information do I have?

What don't I know?

What can I extract from the known information?

Have I used all of the information?

What additional information do I need?

What are the parts of the problem?

How are the parts related?

How could the parts be related?

Is this in any way like a problem I've solved before?

Remember, to think more creatively you must find ways to jog yourself out of mental sets and habitual modes of thought (Michalko, 2001; Simonton, 2009).

4. Seek Varied Input

Remember, creativity requires divergent thinking. Rather than digging deeper with logic, you are attempting to shift your mental "prospecting" to new areas. As an example of this strategy, Edward de Bono (1992) recommends that you randomly look up words in the dictionary and relate them to the problem. Often the words will trigger a fresh perspective or open a new avenue. For instance, let's say you are asked to come up with new ways to clean oil off a beach. Following de Bono's suggestion, you would read the following randomly selected words, relate each to the problem, and see what thoughts are triggered: *weed, rust, poor, magnify, foam, gold, frame, hole, diagonal, vacuum, tribe, puppet, nose, link, drift, portrait, cheese, coal.* You may get similar benefits from relating various objects to a problem. Or, take a walk, skim through a newspaper, or look through a stack of photographs to see what thoughts they trigger (Michalko, 2001). Exposing yourself to a wide variety of information is a good way to encourage divergent thinking (Clapham, 2001; Gilhooly et al., 2007).

5. Look for Analogies

Many "new" problems are really old problems in new clothing (Siegler, 1989). Representing a problem in a variety of ways is often the key to solution. Most problems become easier to solve when they are effectively represented. For example, consider this problem:

> Two backpackers start up a steep trail at 6 a.m. They hike all day, resting occasionally, and arrive at the top at 6 p.m. The next day they start back down the trail at 6 a.m. On the way down, they stop several times and vary their pace. They arrive back at 6 p.m. On the way down, one of the hikers, who is a mathematician, tells the other that she has realized that they will pass a point on the trail at exactly the same time as they did the day before. Her nonmathematical friend finds this hard to believe, since on both days they have stopped and started many times and changed their pace. The problem: Is the mathematician right?

Perhaps you will see the answer to this problem immediately. If not, think of it this way: What if there were two pairs of backpackers, one going up the trail, the second coming down, and both hiking *on the same day*? As one pair of hikers goes up the trail and the other goes down, they *must* pass one another at some point on the trail, right? Therefore, at that point they will be at the same place at the same time. Now, would your conclusion change if one of the pairs was going up the trail one day and the other was coming down the trail the next? If you mentally draw their path up the mountain and then visualize them coming back down it the next day, do you see that at some point the two paths will meet at the same point at the same time on both days? Well, what if the same pair of hikers were going up one day and coming back down the next? As you can now see, the mathematician was right.

6. Take Sensible Risks

A willingness to go against the crowd is a key element in doing creative work. Unusual and original ideas may be rejected at first by conventional thinkers. Often, creative individuals must persevere and take some risks before their ideas are widely accepted. For example, Post-It notes were invented by an engineer who accidentally created a weak adhesive. Rather than throw the mixture out, the engineer put it to a highly creative new use. However, it took him some time to convince others that a "bad" adhesive could be a useful product. Today, stick-on notepapers are one of the 3M Company's most successful products (Sternberg & Lubart, 1995).

7. Allow Time for Incubation

If you are feeling hurried by a sense of time pressure, you are almost always less likely to think creatively (Amabile, Hadley, & Kramer, 2002). You need to be able to revise or embellish initial solutions, even those based on rapid insight. Incubation is especially fruitful when you are exposed to external cues that relate to the problem (remember Archimedes' bath?). For example, Johannes Gutenberg, creator of the printing press, realized while at a wine harvest that the mechanical pressure used to crush grapes could also be used to imprint letters on paper (Dorfman, Shames, & Kihlstrom, 1996).

8. Delay Evaluation

Various studies suggest that people are most likely to be creative when they are given the freedom to play with ideas and solutions without having to worry about whether they will be evaluated. In the first stages of creative thinking, it is important to avoid criticizing your efforts. Worrying about the correctness of solutions tends to inhibit creativity (Basadur, Runco, & Vega, 2000).

Brainstorming

An alternative approach to enhancing creativity is called *brainstorming*. The essence of **brainstorming** is that producing and evaluating ideas are kept separate. This encourages divergent thinking. In group problem solving, each person is encouraged to produce as many ideas as possible without fear of criticism (Buyer, 1988). Only at the end of a brainstorming session are ideas reconsidered and evaluated. As ideas are freely generated, an interesting **cross-stimulation effect** takes place in which one participant's ideas trigger ideas from others (Brown et al., 1998).

How is brainstorming applied to individual problem solving? The essential point to remember is to *suspend judgment*. Ideas should first be produced without regard for logic, organization, accuracy, practicality, or any other evaluation. In writing an essay, for instance, you would begin by writing ideas in any order, the more the better, just as they occur to you. Later, you can go back and reorganize, rewrite, and criticize your efforts.

The basic rules for successful brainstorming are:

1. Absolutely do not criticize ideas until later in the session.
2. Modify or combine ideas freely. Don't worry about giving credit for ideas or keeping them neat. Mix them up!
3. Try to generate lots of ideas. In the early stages of brainstorming, quantity is more important than quality.
4. Let your imagination run amok! Seek unusual, remote, or wild ideas.
5. Record ideas as they occur.
6. Elaborate or improve on the most promising ideas. (Kaufman, 2009; Michalko, 2001)

Living More Creatively

Many people who think in conventional ways live intelligent, successful, and fulfilling lives. Just the same, creative thinking can add spice to life and lead to exciting personal insights (Kaufman, 2009). Psychologist Mihalyi Csikszentmihalyi (sik-sent-me-HALE-yee) (1997) makes these recommendations about how to become more creative:

- Find something that surprises you every day.
- Try to surprise at least one person every day.
- If something sparks your interest, follow it.
- Make a commitment to doing things well.
- Seek challenges.
- Take time for thinking and relaxing.
- Start doing more of what you really enjoy, less of what you dislike.
- Try to look at problems from as many viewpoints as you can.

Even if you don't become more creative by following these suggestions, they are still good advice. Life is not a standardized test with a single set of correct answers. It is much more like a blank canvas on which you can create designs that uniquely express your talents and interests. To live more creatively, you must be ready to seek new ways of doing things. Try to surprise at least one person today—yourself, if no one else.

Knowledge Builder: Enhancing Creativity

RECITE

1. Fixations and functional fixedness are specific types of mental sets. T or F?
2. The incubation period in creative problem solving usually lasts just a matter of minutes. T or F?
3. Exposure to creative models has been shown to enhance creativity. T or F?
4. In brainstorming, each idea is critically evaluated as it is generated. T or F?
5. Defining a problem broadly produces a cross-stimulation effect that can inhibit creative thinking. T or F?

REFLECT

Think Critically

6. Do you think there is any connection between your mood and your creativity?

Self-Reflect

Review the preceding pages and note which methods you could use more often to improve the quality of your thinking. Now mentally summarize the points you especially want to remember.

Answers: 1. T **2.** F **3.** T **4.** F **5.** F **6.** In general, more intense moods are associated with higher creativity (Davis, 2009).

Brainstorming Method of creative thinking that separates the production and evaluation of ideas.

Cross-stimulation effect In group problem solving, the tendency of one person's ideas to trigger ideas from others.

Chapter in Review Gateways to Cognition, Language, and Creativity

Gateway QUESTIONS REVISITED

8.1 What is the nature of thought?

8.1.1 Thinking is the manipulation of internal representations of external stimuli or situations.

8.1.2 Three basic units of thought are images, concepts, and language (or symbols).

8.2 In what ways are images related to thinking?

8.2.1 Most people have internal images of one kind or another. Sometimes they cross normal sense boundaries in a type of imagery called synesthesia.

8.2.2 Images may be three-dimensional, they may be rotated in space, and their size may change.

8.2.3 The same brain areas are involved in both vision and visual imagery.

8.2.4 Images may be stored or created.

8.2.5 Kinesthetic images are used to represent movements and actions. Kinesthetic sensations help structure the flow of thoughts for many people.

8.3 What are concepts and how are they learned?

8.3.1 A concept is a generalized idea of a class of objects or events.

8.3.2 Concept formation may be based on positive and negative instances or rule learning.

8.3.3 Concepts may be conjunctive ("and" concepts), disjunctive ("either/or" concepts), or relational.

8.3.4 In practice, concept identification frequently makes use of prototypes, or general models of the concept class.

8.3.5 Oversimplification and stereotyping contribute to thinking errors.

8.3.6 The denotative meaning of a word or concept is its dictionary definition. Connotative meaning is personal or emotional and can be measured with the semantic differential.

8.4 What is language and what role does it play in thinking?

8.4.1 Language encodes events into symbols, for easy mental manipulation. The study of meaning is called *semantics*.

8.4.2 Bilingualism is a valuable ability. Two-way bilingual education allows children to develop additive bilingualism while in school.

8.4.3 Language carries meaning by combining a set of symbols according to a set of rules (grammar), which includes rules about word order (syntax). A true language is productive and can be used to generate new ideas or possibilities.

8.4.4 Complex gestural systems, such as American Sign Language, are true languages.

8.4.5 Natural animal communication is relatively limited because it lacks symbols that can be rearranged easily.

8.4.6 Chimpanzees and other primates have been taught American Sign Language and similar systems. This suggests to some that primates are capable of very basic language use. Others question this conclusion.

8.5 What do we know about problem solving?

8.5.1 The solution to a problem may be arrived at mechanically (by trial and error or by rote application of algorithms), but mechanical solutions are often inefficient.

8.5.2 Solutions by understanding usually begin with discovery of the general properties of an answer, followed by a functional solution.

8.5.3 Problem solving is aided by heuristics, which narrow the search for solutions.

8.5.4 When understanding leads to a rapid solution, insight has occurred. Three elements of insight are selective encoding, selective combination, and selective comparison.

8.5.5 Insight and other problem solving can be blocked by fixation. Functional fixedness is a common fixation, but emotional blocks, cultural values, learned conventions, and perceptual habits are also problems.

8.5.6 Problem-solving experts also engage in automatic processing and pattern recognition.

8.6 What is the nature of creative thinking?

8.6.1 To be creative, a solution must be high quality and relevant as well as original. Creative thinking requires divergent thought, characterized by fluency, flexibility, and originality. Tests of creativity measure these qualities.

8.6.2 Five stages often seen in creative problem solving are orientation, preparation, incubation, illumination, and verification. Not all creative thinking fits this pattern.

8.6.3 Studies suggest that the creative personality has a number of characteristics, most of which contradict popular stereotypes. There is only a very small correlation between IQ and creativity.

8.6.4 Some creative thinking skills can be learned.

8.7 How accurate is intuition?

8.7.1 Intuitive thinking can be fast and accurate but also often leads to errors. Wrong conclusions may be drawn when an answer seems highly representative of what we already believe is true.

8.7.2 Another problem is ignoring the base rate (or underlying probability) of an event.

8.7.3 Clear thinking is usually aided by stating or framing a problem in broad terms.

8.7.4 Emotions also lead to intuitive thinking and poor choices.

8.8 *What can be done to promote creativity?*

8.8.1 Various strategies that promote divergent thinking tend to enhance creative problem solving.

8.8.2 In group situations, brainstorming may lead to creative solutions. The principles of brainstorming can also be applied to individual problem solving.

MEDIA RESOURCES

Web Resources

Internet addresses frequently change. To find an up-to-date list of URLs for the sites listed here, *visit your Psychology CourseMate.*

Amoeba Web Psychology Resources: Cognitive Psychology Go to the "Cognitive Psychology" link on this web page and you will find numerous other links to articles/information on many areas of cognitive psychology.

Synesthesia and the Synesthetic Experience Read first-hand accounts of the experiences of synesthetes.

Francis Galton on Mental Imagery Read a classic paper on mental imagery by one of the first psychologists.

Kinesthetic Images and the Piano Read this example of using kinesthetic imagery to improve performance.

How Does Our Language Shape the Way We Think? Read more about language and thinking.

Koko.org View the sign language (and art!) of Koko, the gorilla.

The Alex Foundation Explore the language abilities of African Gray parrots.

Classic Problems Try to solve some classic problems.

How Experts Differ from Novices Read more about the differences between experts and novices.

Functional Fixedness Read about tool use and functional fixedness.

Creativity Web Multiple links to resources on creativity.

Creative Thinking Techniques Try to apply a variety of creative thinking and lateral thinking techniques.

Thin Slicing Read what Malcolm Gladwell, the author of *Blink*, has to say about rapid cognition.

Interactive Learning

Log in to **CengageBrain** to access the resources your instructor requires. For this book, you can access:

CourseMate brings course concepts to life with interactive learning, study, and exam preparation tools that support the printed textbook. A textbook-specific website, ***Psychology CourseMate*** includes an ***integrated interactive eBook*** and other ***interactive learning tools*** including quizzes, flashcards, videos, and more.

CENGAGE**NOW**™

CengageNOW is an easy-to-use online resource that helps you study in less time to get the grade you want—NOW. Take a pre-test for this chapter and receive a personalized study plan based on your results that will identify the topics you need to review and direct you to online resources to help you master those topics. Then take a post-test to help you determine the concepts you have mastered and what you will need to work on. If your textbook does not include an access code card, go to CengageBrain.com to gain access.

WebTUTOR™

More than just an interactive study guide, **WebTutor** is an anytime, anywhere customized learning solution with an eBook, keeping you connected to your textbook, instructor, and classmates.

If your professor has assigned **Aplia** homework:

1. Sign in to your account.
2. Complete the corresponding homework exercises as required by your professor.
3. When finished, click "Grade It Now" to see which areas you have mastered and which need more work, and for detailed explanations of every answer.

Visit **www.cengagebrain.com** to access your account and purchase materials.

Gateway THEME
Measuring intelligence is worthwhile, but tests provide limited definitions of intelligent behavior.

9

Intelligence

Homo Sapiens

Unlike other species, humans owe their success more to thinking abilities and intelligence than to physical strength or speed. That's why our species is called *Homo sapiens* (from the Latin for *man* and *wise*). Our intelligence makes us highly adaptable creatures. We live in deserts, jungles, mountains, frenzied cities, placid retreats, and space stations.

Consider Stephen Hawking. He can't walk or talk. When he was 13, Lou Gehrig's disease began to slowly destroy nerve cells in his spinal cord, short-circuiting messages between his brain and muscles. Today, he is confined to a wheelchair and "speaks" by manually controlling a speech synthesizer. Yet, despite his severe disabilities, his brain is unaffected by the disease and remains fiercely active. He can still *think.* Stephen is a theoretical physicist and one of the best-known scientific minds of modern times. With courage and determination, he has used his intellect to advance our understanding of the universe.

What do we mean when we say that a person like Stephen Hawking is "smart" or "intelligent"? Can intelligence be measured? Can intelligence tests predict life success? What are the consequences of having extremely high or low intelligence? These questions and others concerning intelligence have fascinated psychologists for more than 100 years. Let's see what has been learned and what issues are still debated.

Gateway QUESTIONS

- *9.1 How do psychologists define intelligence?*
- *9.2 What are typical IQ tests like?*
- *9.3 How do IQ scores relate to sex, age, and occupation?*
- *9.4 What does IQ tell us about genius?*
- *9.5 What causes intellectual disability?*
- *9.6 How do heredity and environment affect intelligence?*
- *9.7 Are there alternate views of intelligence?*
- *9.8 Is there a downside to intelligence testing?*

Defining Intelligence—Intelligence Is . . . You Know, It's . . .

Gateway Question 9.1: *How do psychologists define intelligence?*

Like many important concepts in psychology, intelligence cannot be observed directly. Nevertheless, we feel certain it exists. Let's compare two children:

> When she was 14 months old, Anne wrote her own name. She taught herself to read at age 2. At age 5, she astounded her kindergarten teacher by bringing an iPad to class—on which she was reading an encyclopedia. At 10, she breezed through an entire high school algebra course in 12 hours.
>
> Billy, who is 10 years old, can write his name and can count, but he has trouble with simple addition and subtraction problems and finds multiplication impossible. He has been held back in school twice and is still incapable of doing the work his 8-year-old classmates find easy.

Anne is considered a genius; Billy, a slow learner. There seems little doubt that they differ in intelligence.

Wait! Anne's ability is obvious, but how do we know that Billy isn't just lazy? That's the same question that Alfred Binet faced in 1904 (Benjafield, 2010; Jarvin & Sternberg, 2003). The French minister of education wanted to find a way to distinguish slower students from the more capable (or the capable but lazy). In a flash of brilliance, Binet and an associate created a test made up of "intellectual" questions and problems. Next, they learned which questions an average child could answer at each age. By giving children the test, they could tell whether a child was performing up to his or her potential (Kaplan & Saccuzzo, 2009; Kaufman, 2000).

Binet's approach gave rise to modern intelligence tests. At the same time, it launched an ongoing debate. Part of the debate is related to the basic difficulty of defining intelligence (Sternberg, Grigorenko, & Kidd, 2005).

Defining Intelligence

Isn't there an accepted definition of intelligence? Traditionally, yes. **Intelligence** is the global capacity to act purposefully, to think rationally, and to deal effectively with the environment (Wechsler, 1939). The core of intelligence is usually thought to consist of a small set of *general mental abilities* (called the **g-factor**) in the areas of reasoning, problem solving, knowledge, memory, and successful adaptation to one's surroundings (Barber, 2010; Sternberg, 2004).

BRIDGES

Intelligence has traditionally been considered a cognitive, not an emotional, capacity. Is there such a thing as emotional intelligence?

To find out, see Chapter 10, pages 363–364.

Beyond this, however, there is much disagreement. In fact, many psychologists simply accept an **operational definition** of intelligence by spelling out the procedures they use to measure it (Neukrug & Fawcett, 2010). Thus, by selecting items for an intelligence test, a psychologist is saying in a very direct way, "This is what I mean by intelligence." A test that measures memory, reasoning, and verbal fluency offers a very different definition of intelligence than one that measures strength of grip, shoe size, length of the nose, or the person's best *Guitar Hero* score (Goldstein, 2011).

Modern intelligence tests are widely used to measure cognitive abilities. When properly administered, such tests provide an operational definition of intelligence.

Aptitudes

As a child, Hedda displayed an aptitude for art. Today, Hedda is a successful graphic artist. How does an aptitude like Hedda's differ from general intelligence? An **aptitude** is a capacity for learning certain abilities. Persons with mechanical, artistic, or musical aptitudes are likely to do well in careers involving mechanics, art, or music, respectively (● Figure 9.1).

Are there tests for aptitudes? How are they different from intelligence tests? Aptitude tests measure a narrower range of abilities than do intelligence tests (Kaplan & Saccuzzo, 2009). For example, **special aptitude tests** predict whether you will succeed in a single

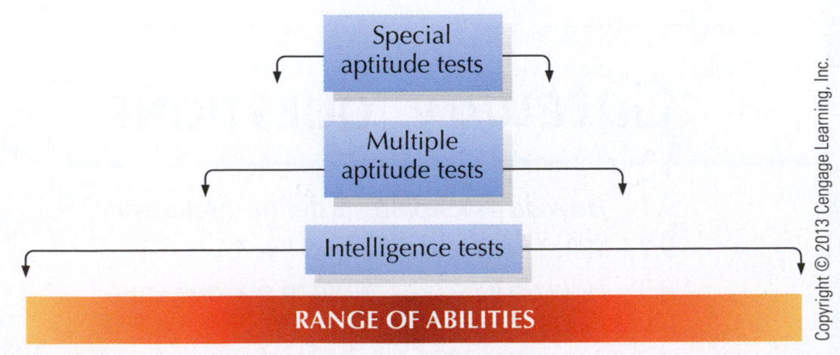

● **Figure 9.1** Special aptitude tests measure a person's potential for achievement in a limited area of ability, such as manual dexterity. Multiple aptitude tests measure potentials in broader areas, such as college work, law, or medicine. Intelligence tests measure a very wide array of aptitudes and mental abilities.

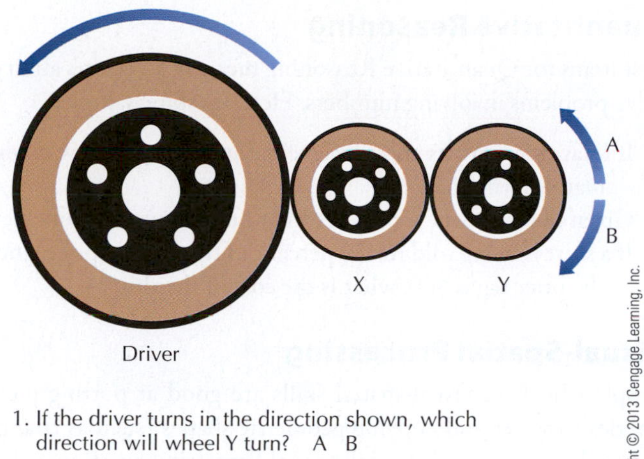

1. If the driver turns in the direction shown, which direction will wheel Y turn? A B

2. Which wheel will turn the slowest? Driver X Y

Figure 9.2 Sample questions like those found on tests of mechanical aptitude. (The answers are A and the Driver.)

area, such as clerical work or computer programming (Figure 9.2). **Multiple aptitude tests** measure two or more types of ability. These tests tend to be more like intelligence tests. The well-known *SAT Reasoning Test* (SAT), which measures aptitudes for language, math, and reasoning, is a multiple aptitude test. So are the tests required to enter graduate schools of law, medicine, business, and dentistry. The broadest aptitude measures are **general intelligence tests**, which assess a wide variety of mental abilities (Cohen & Swerdlik, 2005).

BRIDGES

Psychologists use a variety of aptitude tests to select people for employment and to advise people about choosing careers. **For more information, see Chapter 18, pages 608–611.**

Reliability and Validity

Whether it is an intelligence test or aptitude test or, for that matter, any other kind of **psychometric test**—any measurement of a person's mental functions—there will always be two questions you should ask about the test: "Is it *reliable*?" and "Is it *valid?*"

To what does reliability refer? If you weigh yourself several times in a row, a reliable bathroom scale gives the same weight each time. Likewise, a **reliable** psychometric test must give approximately the same score each time a person takes it (Kaplan & Saccuzzo, 2009). In other words, the scores should be *consistent* and highly correlated. It is easy to see why unreliable tests have little value. Imagine a medical test for pregnancy or breast cancer, for instance, which gives positive and negative responses for the same woman on the same day.

To check the reliability of a test, we could give it to a large group of people. Then, each person could be tested again a week later to establish *test-retest reliability*. We also might want to know whether scores on one half of the test items match scores on the other half (*split-half reliability*). If two versions of a test are available, we could compare scores on one version to scores on the other (*equivalent-forms reliability*).

Just because a psychometric test is reliable, however, does not mean that it should be trusted; test *validity* is also important. To see why this is the case, try creating an IQ test with ten questions *only you could possibly answer*. Your test would be very reliable. Each time you give the test, everyone scores zero, except you, who scores 100 percent (so you thereby proclaim yourself the only human with any intelligence). Even though we all have days when it seems we *are* the only smart person left on the planet, it should be obvious this is a silly example. A test must also have **validity**; it should measure what it claims to measure (Neukrug & Fawcett, 2010). By no stretch of the imagination could a test of intelligence be valid if the person who wrote it is the only one who can pass it.

How is validity established? Validity is usually demonstrated by comparing test scores to actual performance. This is called *criterion validity*. For example, scores on a test of legal aptitude might be compared with grades in law school. If high test scores correlate with high grades, or some other standard (criterion) of success, the test might be valid. Unfortunately, many "free" tests you encounter, such as those found in magazines and on the Internet, have little or no validity.

Objective Testing

Let's return to your "I'm the Smartest Person in the World IQ Test" for a final point. Is your test *objective*? Actually, it might be. If your IQ test gives the same score when corrected by different people, it is an **objective test**. However, objectivity is not enough to guarantee a fair test. Useful tests must also be *standardized* (Neukrug & Fawcett, 2010).

Test standardization refers to two things. First, it means that standard procedures are used in giving the test. The instructions, answer forms, amount of time to work, and so forth, are the same for everyone. Second, it means finding the **norm**, or average score,

Intelligence An overall capacity to think rationally, act purposefully, and deal effectively with the environment.

g-factor A general ability factor proposed to underly intelligence; the core of general intellectual ability that involves reasoning, problem-solving ability, knowledge, and memory.

Operational definition The operations (actions or procedures) used to measure a concept.

Aptitude A capacity for learning certain abilities.

Special aptitude test Test to predict a person's likelihood of succeeding in a particular area of work or skill.

Multiple aptitude test Test that measures two or more aptitudes.

General intelligence test A test that measures a wide variety of mental abilities.

Psychometric test Any scientific measurement of a person's mental functions.

Reliability The ability of a test to yield the same score, or nearly the same score, each time it is given to the same person.

Validity The ability of a test to measure what it purports to measure.

Objective test A test that gives the same score when different people correct it.

Test standardization Establishing standards for administering a test and interpreting scores.

Norm An average score for a designated group of people.

made by a large group of people like those for whom the test was designed. Without standardization, we couldn't fairly compare the scores of people taking the test at different times. And without norms, there would be no way to tell whether a score is high, low, or average.

Later in this chapter, we will address the question of whether intelligence tests are valid. For now, let's take a practical approach and learn about some popular standardized IQ tests.

Testing Intelligence—The IQ and You

Gateway Question 9.2: *What are typical IQ tests like?*

American psychologists quickly saw the value of Alfred Binet's test. In 1916, Lewis Terman and others at Stanford University revised it for use in North America. After more revisions, the *Stanford-Binet Intelligence Scales, Fifth Edition* (SB5) continue to be widely used. The original Stanford-Binet assumed that a child's intellectual abilities improve with each passing year. Today, the Stanford-Binet (or SB5) is still primarily made up of age-ranked questions. Naturally, these questions get a little harder at each age level. The SB5 is appropriate for people from age 2 to 85+ years and scores on the test are very reliable (Raid & Tippin, 2009; Roid, 2003).

Five Aspects of Intelligence

The SB5 measures five cognitive factors (types of mental abilities) that make up general intelligence. These are *fluid reasoning, knowledge, quantitative reasoning, visual-spatial processing,* and *working memory.* Each factor is measured with verbal questions (those involving words and numbers), and nonverbal questions (items that use pictures and objects). Let's see what each factor looks like.

Fluid Reasoning

Questions like the following are used to test Fluid Reasoning:

How are an apple, a plum, and a banana different from a beet?
An apprentice is to a master as a novice is to an ____________.
"I knew my bag was going to be in the last place I looked, so I looked there first." What is silly or impossible about that?

Other items ask people to fill in the missing shape in a group of shapes, and to tell a story that explains what's going on in a series of pictures.

Knowledge

The Knowledge factor assesses the person's knowledge about a wide range of topics.

Why is yeast added to bread dough?
What does cryptic mean?
What is silly or impossible about this picture? (For example, a bicycle has square wheels.)

Quantitative Reasoning

Test items for Quantitative Reasoning measure a person's ability to solve problems involving numbers. Here are some samples:

If I have six marbles and you give me another one, how many marbles will I have?
Given the numbers 3, 6, 9, 12, what number would come next?
If a shirt is being sold for 50 percent of the normal price, and the price tag is $60, what is the cost of the shirt?

Visual-Spatial Processing

People who have visual-spatial skills are good at putting picture puzzles together and copying geometric shapes (such as triangles, rectangles, and circles). Visual-Spatial Processing questions ask test takers to reproduce patterns of blocks and choose pictures that show how a piece of paper would look if it were folded or cut. Verbal questions can also require visual-spatial abilities:

Suppose that you are going east, then turn right, then turn right again, then turn left. In what direction are you facing now?

Working Memory

The Working Memory part of the SB5 measures the ability to use short-term memory. Some typical memory tasks include the following:

Correctly remember the order of colored beads on a stick.
After hearing several sentences, name the last word from each sentence.
Repeat a series of digits (forward or backward) after hearing them once.
After seeing several objects, point to them in the same order as they were presented.

If you were to take the SB5, it would yield a score for your general intelligence, verbal intelligence, nonverbal intelligence, and each of the five cognitive factors (Bain & Allin, 2005). For another perspective on the kinds of tasks used in the SB5, see "Intelligence—How Would a Fool Do It?"

The Wechsler Tests

Is the Stanford-Binet the only intelligence test? Many other IQ tests have been developed. Psychologist David Wechsler (1939) designed one widely used alternative. Whereas the original Stanford-Binet was better suited for children and adolescents, the first Wechsler test was specifically designed to test adult intelligence. The current version is the *Wechsler Adult Intelligence Scale—Fourth Edition* (WAIS-IV). With newer versions of the Stanford-Binet and a children's version of the Wechsler scales (currently the *Wechsler Intelligence Scale for Children—Fourth Edition* or WISC-IV; see Baron, 2005), both alternatives are now widely used across all ages.

■ **TABLE 9.1 Sample Items Similar to Those Used on the WAIS-IV**

Verbal Comprehension	**Sample Items or Descriptions**
Similarities	In what way are a wolf and a coyote alike?
	In what way are a screwdriver and a chisel alike?
Vocabulary	The test consists of asking, "What is a ___________?" or "What does ___________ mean?" The words range from more to less familiar and difficult.
Information	How many wings does a butterfly have?
	Who wrote *Romeo and Juliet?*
Perceptual Reasoning	
Block Design	Copy designs with blocks (as shown at right).
Matrix Reasoning	Select the item that completes the matrix.
Visual Puzzles	Choose the pieces which go together to form a figure.
Working Memory	
Digit Span	Repeat from memory a series of digits, such as 8 5 7 0 1 3 6 2, after hearing it once.
Arithmetic	Four girls divided 28 jellybeans equally among themselves. How many jellybeans did each girl receive?
	If 3 peaches take 2 minutes to find and pick, how long will it take to find and pick a dozen peaches?
Processing Speed	
Symbol Search	Match symbols appearing in separate groups.
Coding	Fill in the symbols:

Symbol Search

1	2	3	4
X	III	I	0

3	4	1	3	4	2	1	2

Adapted from Wechsler, D. (2008). *Wechsler Adult Intelligence Scale, Fourth Edition (WAIS-IV)*. San Antonio, TX: Pearson.

Like the Stanford-Binet, the Wechsler tests yield a single overall intelligence score. In addition, these tests also separate scores for **performance** (nonverbal) **intelligence** and **verbal** (language- or symbol-oriented) **intelligence**. The abilities measured by the Wechsler tests and some sample test items are listed in ■ Table 9.1.

Group Tests

The SB5 and the Wechsler tests are **individual intelligence tests**, which are given to a single person by a trained specialist. In contrast, **group intelligence tests** can be given to a large group of people with minimal supervision. Group tests usually require people to read, to follow instructions, and to solve problems of logic, reasoning, mathematics, or spatial skills. The first group intelligence test was the *Army Alpha*, developed for World War I military inductees. As you can see in ■ Table 9.2, intelligence testing has come a long way since then.

Scholastic Aptitude Tests

If you're wondering if you have ever taken an intelligence test, the answer is probably yes. As mentioned earlier, the *SAT Reasoning Test* is a multiple aptitude test. So are the *American College Test* (ACT) and the *College Qualification Test* (CQT). Each of these group tests is designed to predict your chances for success in col-

Performance intelligence Intelligence measured by solving puzzles, assembling objects, completing pictures, and other nonverbal tasks.
Verbal intelligence Intelligence measured by answering questions involving vocabulary, general information, arithmetic, and other language- or symbol-oriented tasks.
Individual intelligence test A test of intelligence designed to be given to a single individual by a trained specialist.
Group intelligence test Any intelligence test that can be administered to a group of people with minimal supervision.

Human Diversity Intelligence—How Would a Fool Do It?

You have been asked to sort some objects into categories. Wouldn't it be smart to put the clothes, containers, implements, and foods in separate piles? Not necessarily. When members of the Kpelle culture in Liberia were asked to sort objects, they grouped them together by function. For example, a potato (food) would be placed together with a knife (implement). When the Kpelle were asked why they grouped the objects this way, they often said that was how a wise man would do it. The researchers finally asked the Kpelle, "How would a fool do it?" Only then did the Kpelle sort the objects into the nice, neat categories that we Westerners prefer.

This anecdote, related by cultural psychologist Patricia Greenfield (1997), raises serious questions about general definitions of intelligence. For example, among the Cree of northern Canada, "smart" people are the ones who have the skills needed to find food on the frozen tundra (Darou, 1992). For the Puluwat people in the South Pacific, smart means having ocean-going navigation skills necessary to get from island to island (Sternberg, 2004). And so it goes, as each culture teaches its children the kinds of "intelligence" valued in that culture—how the wise man would do it, not the fool (Barber, 2010; Correa-Chávez, Rogoff, & Arauz, 2005).

Shutterstock

How important do you think the mental abilities assessed in modern intelligence tests are to this Bushman hunter in Africa's Kalahari Desert?

TABLE 9.2 Items from the Army Alpha Subtest on "Common Sense"

The *Army Alpha* was given to World War I army recruits in the United States as a way to identify potential officers. In these sample questions, note the curious mixture of folk wisdom, scientific information, and moralism (Kessen & Cahan, 1986). Other parts of the test were more like modern intelligence tests.

1. If plants are dying for lack of rain, you should
- ☐ water them
- ☐ ask a florist's advice
- ☐ put fertilizer around them

2. If the grocer should give you too much money in making change, what is the right thing to do?
- ☐ buy some candy for him with it
- ☐ give it to the first poor man you meet
- ☐ tell him of his mistake

3. If you saw a train approaching a broken track you should
- ☐ telephone for an ambulance
- ☐ signal the engineer to stop the train
- ☐ look for a piece of rail to fit in

4. Some men lose their breath on high mountains because
- ☐ the wind blows their breath away
- ☐ the air is too rare
- ☐ it is always cold there

5. We see no stars at noon because
- ☐ they have moved to the other side of the earth
- ☐ they are much fainter than the sun
- ☐ they are hidden behind the sky

© Hulton-Deusch Collection/Corbis

lege. Because the tests measure general knowledge and a variety of mental aptitudes, each can also be used to estimate intelligence.

Intelligence Quotients

What is an "IQ"? Imagine that a child named Yuan can answer intelligence test questions that an average 7-year-old can answer. We could say that 7 is her **mental age** (average intellectual performance). How smart is Yuan? Actually, we can't say yet, because we don't know how old Yuan is. If she is 10, she's not very smart. If she's 5, she is very bright. Thus, although mental age is a good measure of actual ability, it says nothing about whether overall intelligence is high or low, compared with other people of the same age.

Thus, to estimate a child's intelligence, we also need to know her **chronological age** (age in years). Then, we can relate mental age to chronological age. This yields an **IQ**, or **intelligence quotient**. A quotient results from dividing one number into another. When the Stanford-Binet was first used, IQ was defined as mental age (MA) divided by chronological age (CA) and multiplied by 100. (Multiplying by 100 changes the IQ into a whole number rather than a decimal.)

$$\frac{MA}{CA} \times 100 = IQ$$

An advantage of the original IQ was that intelligence could be compared among children with different chronological and mental ages. For instance, 10-year-old Justin has a mental age of 12. Thus, his IQ is 120:

$$\frac{(MA)\ 12}{(CA)\ 10} \times 100 = 120\ (IQ)$$

Justin's friend Suke also has a mental age of 12. However, Suke's chronological age is 12, so his IQ is 100:

$$\frac{(MA)\ 12}{(CA)\ 12} \times 100 = 100\ (IQ)$$

The IQ shows that 10-year-old Justin is brighter than his 12-year-old friend Suke, even though their intellectual skills are about the same. Notice that a person's IQ will be 100 when mental age equals chronological age. Therefore, an IQ score of 100 is defined as average intelligence.

Then does a person with an IQ score below 100 have below average intelligence? Not unless the IQ is well below 100. Average intelligence is usually defined as any score from 90 to 109. The important point is that IQ scores will be over 100 when mental age is higher than age in years. IQ scores below 100 occur when a person's age in years exceeds his or her mental age. An example of this situation would be a 15-year-old with an MA of 12:

$$\frac{12}{15} \times 100 = 80\ (IQ)$$

"The five candles represent his mental age."

Deviation IQs

Although the preceding examples may give you insight into IQ scores, it's no longer necessary to directly calculate IQs. Instead, modern tests use **deviation IQs**. Tables supplied with the test are used to convert a person's relative standing in the group to an IQ score. That is, they tell how far above or below average the person's score falls. For example, if you score at the 50th percentile, half the people your age who take the test score higher than you and half score lower. In this case, your IQ score is 100. If you score at the 84th percentile, your IQ score is 115. If you score at the 97th percentile, your IQ score is 130. (For more information, see the Statistics appendix near the end of this book.)

Mental age The average mental ability displayed by people of a given age.
Chronological age A person's age in years.
Intelligence quotient (IQ) An index of intelligence defined as mental age divided by chronological age and multiplied by 100.
Deviation IQ An IQ obtained statistically from a person's relative standing in his or her age group; that is, how far above or below average the person's score was relative to other scores.

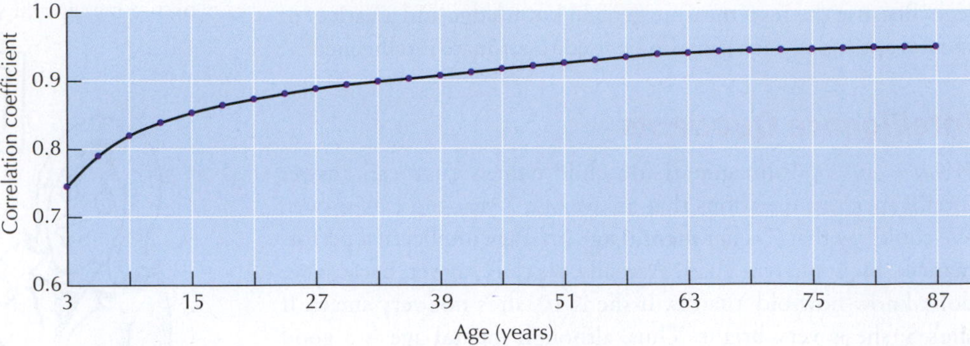

• Figure 9.3 The stability or reliability of IQ scores increases rapidly in early childhood. Scores are very consistent from early adulthood to late middle age. (Adapted from Gow et al., 2010; Larsen, Hartmann, & Nyborg, 2008; Schuerger & Witt, 1989.)

OK, so how does Stephen Hawking score? When Hawking was once asked about his IQ, he claimed he didn't know and joked, "People who boast about their IQ are losers."

The Stability of IQ

How old do children have to be before their IQ scores become stable? IQ scores are not very dependable until about age 6 (Schuerger & Witt, 1989). IQ scores measured at age 3 correlate poorly with those measured at age 27. In other words, knowing a child's IQ at age 3 tells us very little about what his or her IQ will be 24 years later. (Recall that a perfect correlation is 1.00 and a correlation of 0.00 occurs when scores are unrelated.) However, IQs do become more reliable as children grow older. Knowing a child's IQ at age 11 is a good predictor of his or her IQ later in life (Gow et al., 2010). After middle childhood, a person's IQ scores usually change very little from year to year (Canivez & Watkins, 1998; Gow et al., 2010; Larsen, Hartmann, & Nyborg, 2008). (See • Figure 9.3).

Knowledge Builder: Intelligence Tests

RECITE

1. The first successful intelligence test was developed by ____________________.
2. If we define intelligence by the obtained score on a written test, we are using
   a. a circular definition *b.* an abstract definition *c.* an operational definition *d.* a chronological definition
3. Place an "R" or a "V" after each operation to indicate whether it would be used to establish the reliability (R) or the validity (V) of a test.
   a. Compare score on one half of test items to score on the other half. ( )
   b. Compare scores on test to grades, performance ratings, or other measures. ( )
   c. Compare scores from the test after administering it on two separate occasions. ( )
   d. Compare scores on alternate forms of the test. ( )
4. Establishing norms and uniform procedures for administering a test are elements of standardization. T or F?
5. The WAIS-IV is a group intelligence test. T or F?
6. IQ was originally defined as ________________ times 100.
7. Scores on modern intelligence tests are based on one's deviation IQ (relative standing among test takers) rather than on the ratio between mental age and chronological age. T or F?

REFLECT

Think Critically

8. How well do you think a member of Kpelle culture in Liberia would score on the SB5?

Self-Reflect

If you were going to write an intelligence test, what kinds of questions would you ask? How much would your questions resemble those on standard intelligence tests? Would you want to measure any mental skills not covered by established tests?

Answers: 1. Alfred Binet **2.** c **3.** *a.* (R), *b.* (V), *c.* (R), *d.* (R) **4.** T **5.** F **6.** MA/CA **7.** T **8.** You are right if you suspect the answer is most likely "poorly." The more important question is what this means. Is the person "slow," or might there be some question about the test itself (Gardner, 2008; Henrich, Heine, & Norenzayan, 2010)? Stay tuned for more on this important issue.

Variations in Intelligence—The Numbers Game

Gateway Question 9.3: *How do IQ scores relate to sex, age, and occupation?*

IQ scores are classified as shown in ■ Table 9.3. A look at the percentages reveals a definite pattern. The distribution (or scattering) of IQ scores approximates a **normal** (bell-shaped) **curve.** That is, most

■ TABLE 9.3 Distribution of Adult IQ Scores on the WAIS-IV

IQ	Description	Percent
Above 130	Very superior	2.2
120–129	Superior	6.7
110–119	Bright normal	16.1
90–109	Average	50.0
80–89	Dull normal	16.1
70–79	Borderline	6.7
Below 70	Intellectually disabled	2.2

Derived from Wechsler, D. (2008). *Wechsler Adult Intelligence Scale, Fourth Edition (WAIS-IV)*. San Antonio, TX: Pearson.

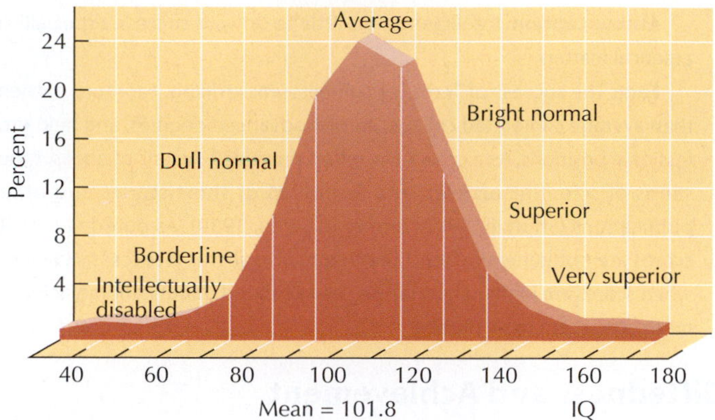

● **Figure 9.4** Distribution of Stanford-Binet Intelligence Test scores for 3184 children. (Adapted from Terman & Merrill, 1937/1960.)

scores fall close to the average and very few are found at the extremes. ● Figure 9.4 shows this characteristic of measured intelligence.

IQ and Sex

On average, do males and females differ in intelligence? IQ scores cannot answer this question because test items were selected to be equally difficult for both sexes. However, whereas males and females do not appear to differ in *overall* intelligence, general intelligence tests allow us to compare the intellectual strengths and weaknesses of men and women (Hyde, 2007). For decades, women, as a group, performed best on items that require verbal ability, vocabulary, and rote learning. Men, in contrast, were best at items that require spatial visualization and math (Clements et al., 2006; Calvin et al., 2010). Today, such male-female differences have almost disappeared among children and young adults. The small differences that remain appear to be based on a tendency for parents and educators to encourage males, more than females, to learn math and spatial skills (Ceci & Williams, 2010).

IQ and Age

How much are IQs affected by age? Don't be confused by ● Figure 9.3. The rising curve in that figure indicates that the *consistency* of IQ scores from year to year increases with age. Actual IQ test scores stay relatively stable as people age with a small, gradual increase until about age 40 and a small slow decline therafter (Larsen, Hartmann, & Nyborg, 2008; Thompson & Oehlert, 2010).

This trend, of course, is an average. Actual IQs reflect a person's education, maturity, and experience, as well as innate intelligence. Some people make fairly large gains in IQ, whereas others have sizable losses. How do the two groups differ? In general, those who gain in IQ are exposed to intellectual stimulation during early adulthood. Those who decline typically suffer from chronic illnesses, drinking problems, or unstimulating lifestyles (Honzik, 1984; Nisbett, 2009a,b).

After middle age, the picture gets a bit more complex. Intellectual skills involved in **fluid intelligence**—solving novel problems involving perceptual speed or rapid insight—decline rapidly after middle age (Brody, 1992; Lawrence, Myerson, & Hale, 1998). By way of compensation, **crystallized intelligence**—solving problems using already acquired knowledge —can actually increase or, at least, decline very little until advanced age. In other words, younger people are generally "quick learners" (fluid intelligence) but tend to be "wet behind the ears" (lack experience or crystalized intelligence). Older people might be a little "slower on the uptake" but tend to "know the ropes." Since IQ tests such as the SB5 and WAIS test for components of both fluid intelligence and crystallized intelligence, overall, age-related losses are small for most healthy, well-educated individuals (Rindermann, Flores-Mendoza, & Mansur-Alves, 2010; Weintraub 2003).

IQ and Achievement

How do IQ scores relate to success in school, jobs, and other endeavors? IQ differences of a few points tell us little about a person. But if we look at a broader ranges of scores, the differences do become meaningful. For example, a person with an IQ of 100 would probably struggle with college, whereas one with an IQ of 120 would do just fine.

The correlation between IQ and school grades is at least .50—a sizable association (Calvin et al., 2010; Mayes et al., 2009). If grades depended solely on IQ, the connection would be even stronger. However, motivation, special talents, off-campus educational opportunities, and many other factors influence grades and school success. The same is true of "real world" success beyond school (Strenze, 2007). IQ is also not a good predictor of success in art, music, writing, dramatics, science, and leadership. Tests of creativity are much more strongly related to achievement in these areas (Kaufman, 2009; Preckel, Holling, & Wiese, 2006).

As you might expect, IQ is also related to job status. Persons holding white-collar, professional positions average higher IQs than those in blue-collar settings. For example, accountants, lawyers, and engineers average about 125 in IQ. In contrast, miners and farm workers average about 90 (Brody, 1992). It is important to note, however, that a range of IQ scores can be found in all occupations. Many people of high intelligence, because of choice or circumstance, have "low-ranking" jobs.

Does the link between IQ and occupation show that professional jobs require more intelligence? Not as clearly as you might think. Higher status jobs often require an academic degree. As a result, hiring for professional jobs is biased in favor of a particular type of intelligence, namely, the kind measured by intelligence tests

Normal curve A bell-shaped curve characterized by a large number of scores in a middle area, tapering to very few extremely high and low scores.

Fluid intelligence The ability to solve novel problems involving perceptual speed or rapid insight.

Crystallized intelligence The ability to solve problems using already acquired knowledge.

(McClelland, 1994; Neisser et al., 1996). This bias probably inflates the apparent association between professional jobs and IQ. The more IQ-like tests are used to select people for jobs, the stronger the association between IQ and job status. In fact, it can be argued that high status groups use such tests to protect their "territory" (Tittle & Rotolo, 2000).

When IQs are extreme—below 70 or above 140—their link to an individual's potential for success becomes unmistakable. Only about 3 percent of the population falls in these ranges. Nevertheless, millions of people have exceptionally high or low IQs. Discussions of the intellectually gifted and intellectually disabled follow.

The Intellectually Gifted—Smart, Smarter, Smartest

Gateway Question 9.4: *What does IQ tell us about genius?*

How high is the IQ of a genius? Only 2 people out of 100 score above 130 on IQ tests. These bright individuals are usually described as "gifted." Less than one-half of one percent of the population scores above 140. These people are certainly gifted or perhaps even "geniuses." However, some psychologists reserve the term *genius* for people with even higher IQs or those who are exceptionally creative (Hallahan, Kauffman, & Pullen, 2011).

Gifted Children

Do high IQ scores in childhood predict later ability? To directly answer this question, Lewis Terman selected 1,500 children with IQs of 140 or more. Terman followed this gifted group (the "Termites," as he called them) into adulthood. By doing so, Terman corrected several popular misconceptions about high intelligence (Dai, 2010; Reis & Renzulli, 2010; Shurkin, 1992).

Misconception: The gifted tend to be peculiar, socially backward people.

Fact: On the contrary, Terman's gifted subjects, and gifted people in general, are socially skilled and above average in leadership (Feldhusen & Westby, 2003).

Misconception: Early ripe means later rot; the gifted tend to fizzle out as adults.

Fact: This is false. When they were retested as adults, Terman's subjects again scored in the upper IQ ranges.

Misconception: The very bright are physically inferior "eggheads," "nerds," or weaklings.

Fact: As a group, the gifted were above average in height, weight, and physical appearance.

Misconception: Highly intelligent persons are more susceptible to mental illness ("Genius is next to insanity").

Fact: Terman demonstrated conclusively that the gifted enjoy better than average mental health and a greater *resistance* to mental illness. In general, the highly gifted tend to be very well adjusted psychologically (Dai, 2010; Garland & Zigler, 1999).

Misconception: Intelligence has little to do with success, especially in practical matters.

Fact: The success of Terman's subjects was striking. Far more of them than average completed college, earned advanced degrees, and held professional positions. As a group, the gifted produced dozens of books, thousands of scientific articles, and hundreds of short stories and other publications (Shurkin, 1992; Terman & Oden, 1959). As noted earlier, IQ scores are not generally good predictors of real-world success. However, when scores are in the gifted range, the likelihood of outstanding achievement does seem to be higher.

Giftedness and Achievement

Were all the Termites superior as adults? No. Remember that high IQ reveals *potential.* It does not guarantee success. As adults, some of Terman's gifted subjects committed crimes, were unemployable, or were unhappy misfits. Nor does a lower IQ guarantee failure. Nobel prize-winning physicist Richard Feynman, whom many regard as a genius, had an IQ of 122 (Michalko, 2001).

How did Terman's more successful Termites differ from the less successful? Most of them had educated parents who valued learning and encouraged them to do the same. In general, successful gifted persons tend to have strong *intellectual determination*—a desire to know, to excel, and to persevere (Winner, 2003). Gifted or not, most successful persons tend to be *persistent* and *motivated* to learn (Reis & Renzulli, 2010). No one is paid to sit around being *capable* of achievement. What you do is always more important than what you should be able to do. That's why a child's talents are most likely to blossom when they are nurtured with support, encouragement, education, and effort (Callahan, 2006).

Identifying Gifted Children

How might a parent spot an unusually bright child? Early signs of giftedness are not always purely "intellectual." **Giftedness** can be either the possession of a high IQ or of special talents or aptitudes. The following signs may reveal that a child is gifted: a tendency to seek out older children and adults; an early fascination with explanations and problem solving; talking in complete sentences as early as 2 or 3 years of age; an unusually good memory; precocious talent in art, music, or number skills; an early interest in books, along with early reading (often by age 3); showing of kindness, understanding, and cooperation toward others (Dai, 2010; Distin, 2006).

Notice that this list goes beyond straight g-factor, or general "academic" intelligence. Children may be gifted in ways other than having a high IQ. In fact, if artistic talent, mechanical aptitude, musical aptitude, athletic potential, and so on are considered, many children have a special "gift" of one kind or another. Limiting giftedness to high IQ can shortchange children with special talents or potentials. This is especially true of ethnic minority children, who may be the victims of subtle biases in standardized intelligence tests. These children, as well as children with physical disabilities, are less likely to be recognized as gifted (Castellano & Frazier, 2011; Ford & Moore, 2006).

arabianEye/Photolibrary

Big Cheese Photo/SuperStock

It is wise to remember that there are many ways in which a child may be gifted. Many schools now offer Gifted and Talented Education programs for students with a variety of special abilities—not just for those who score well on IQ tests.

GATE Programs

Being exceptionally bright is not without its problems. Usually, parents and teachers must make adjustments to help gifted children make the most of their talents (Jolly et al., 2011). The gifted child may become bored in classes designed for average children. This can lead to misbehavior or clashes with teachers who think the gifted child a show-off or smart aleck. Extremely bright children may also find classmates less stimulating than older children or adults. In recognition of these problems, many schools now provide special Gifted and Talented Education (GATE) classes for gifted children. Such programs combine classroom enrichment with fast-paced instruction to satisfy the gifted child's appetite for intellectual stimulation (Dai, 2010). Since 1988, the federally funded Jacob K. Javits Gifted and Talented Children and Youth Education Act has provided ongoing funds for research into gifted and talented education programs (Reis & Renzulli, 2010).

BRIDGES

All children benefit from enriched environments. **For a discussion of enrichment and some guidelines for parents, see Chapter 3, pages 87–88.**

In the next section, we will discuss intellectual disability.

Intellectual Disability—A Difference That Makes a Difference

Gateway Question 9.5: *What causes intellectual disability?*

Before you begin, take a few moments to read "Meet the Rain Man," in which you will find information about a remarkable mixture of brilliance and intellectual disability. And please keep Kim Peek in mind as you read on. There is usually much more to intellectually disabled people than can be shown by the results of IQ testing (Treffert, 2010). It is especially important to realize that intellectually disabled persons have no handicap when feelings are concerned. They are easily hurt by rejection, teasing, or ridicule. Likewise, they respond warmly to love and acceptance. They have a right to self-respect and a place in the community (Montreal Declaration on Intellectual Disabilities, 2004). This is especially important during childhood, when support from others adds greatly to the person's chances of becoming a well-adjusted member of society.

Levels of Intellectual Disability

A person with mental abilities far below average is termed **intellectually disabled** (the former term, **mentally retarded,** is now regarded by many as offensive). According to the current definition

Kyle Nosal/AP Images

These youngsters are participants in the Special Olympics—an athletic event for the intellectually disabled. It is often said of the Special Olympics that "everyone is a winner—participants, coaches, and spectators."

Giftedness Either the possession of a high IQ or special talents or aptitudes.

Intellectual disability (formerly **mental retardation)** The presence of a developmental disability, a formal IQ score below 70, or a significant impairment of adaptive behavior.

The Clinical File: Meet the Rain Man

Meet Kim Peek, the model for Dustin Hoffman's character in the Academy Award–winning movie *Rain Man* (Peek & Hanson, 2007). Kim began memorizing books at 18 months of age. By the time of his death in 2009, he could recite from memory more than 9,000 books. He knew all the ZIP codes and area codes in the United States and could give accurate travel directions between any two major U.S. cities. He could also discuss hundreds of pieces of classical music in detail and could play most of it quite well. Amazingly, though, for someone with such skills, Kim had difficulty with abstract thinking and tests of general intelligence. He was poorly coordinated and couldn't button his own clothes (Treffert, 2010; Treffert & Christensen, 2005).

Kim Peek had **savant syndrome**, in which a person of limited intelligence shows exceptional mental ability in one or more narrow areas, such as mental arithmetic, calendar calculations, art, or music (Crane et al., 2010; Young, 2005).

Do savants have special mental powers not shared by most people? According to one theory, many savants have suffered some form of damage to their left hemispheres, freeing them from the "distractions" of language, concepts, and higher-level thought. This allows them to focus with crystal clarity on music, drawing, prime numbers, license plates, TV commercials, and other specific information (Young, 2005). Another theory holds that the performances of many savants result from intense practice (Miller, 1999). Perhaps each of us harbors embers of mental brilliance that intense practice could fan into full flame (Snyder et al., 2006; Treffert, 2010).

Although savant syndrome hasn't been fully explained, it does show that extraordinary abilities can exist apart from general intelligence.

Once, four months after reading a novel, Kim was asked about a character. He immediately named the character, gave the page number on which a description appeared, and accurately recited several paragraphs about the character (Treffert & Christensen, 2005).

listed in the American Psychiatric Association's *Diagnostic and Statistical Manual of Mental Disorders* (DSM-IV), intellectual disability begins at an IQ of approximately 70 or below and is classified as shown in ■ Table 9.4 (American Psychiatric Association, 2000). The listed IQ ranges are approximate because IQ scores normally vary a few points. The terms in the right-hand column are listed only to give you a general impression of each IQ range. Currently, a person's ability to perform *adaptive behaviors* (basic skills such as dressing, eating, communicating, shopping, and working) also figures into evaluating this disability (American Psychiatric Association, 2000; Hallahan, Kauffman, & Pullen, 2011).

A new edition of the DSM, the DSM-5, is scheduled for publication in 2012. It is quite likely that the new definitions of levels of intellectual disability will deemphasize IQ and focus more heavily on impairment of adaptive behaviors (American Psychiatric Association, 2010). After all, why label someone with fairly good adaptive skills "severely intellectually disabled" just because his or her IQ falls within a prescribed range? The end result of such labels is, too often, a placing of needless limitations on the educational goals of intellectually disabled persons (Harris, 2010; Kirk et al., 2011).

■ TABLE 9.4 Levels of Intellectual Disability

IQ Range	Degree of Intellectual Disability	Educational Classification	Required Level of Support
50–55 to 70	Mild	Educable	Intermittent
35–40 to 50–55	Moderate	Trainable	Limited
20–25 to 35–40	Severe	Dependent	Extensive
Below 20–25	Profound	Life support	Pervasive

(Adapted from American Psychiatric Association, 2000.)

Are the intellectually disabled usually placed in institutions? No. Total care is usually only necessary for the *profoundly* disabled (IQ below 25). Many of these individuals live in group homes or with their families. Those who are *severely* disabled (IQ of 25–40) and *moderately* disabled (IQ of 40–55) are capable of mastering basic language and self-help skills. Many become self-supporting by working in sheltered workshops (special simplified work environments). The *mildly* disabled (IQ of 55–70) make up about 85 percent of all those affected. This group can benefit from carefully structured education. As adults, these persons, as well as the *borderline disabled* (IQ 70–85), are capable of living alone and they may marry. However, they tend to have difficulties with many of the demands of adult life (Zetlin & Murtaugh, 1990).

Causes of Intellectual Disability

What causes intellectual disability? In 30 to 40 percent of cases, no known biological problem can be identified. In many such instances, the degree of disability is mild, in the 50–70 IQ range.

Often, other family members are also mildly disabled. **Familial intellectual disability**, as this is called, occurs mostly in very poor households, in which nutrition, intellectual stimulation, medical care, and emotional support may be inadequate. This suggests that familial intellectual disability is based largely on an impoverished environment. Thus, better nutrition, education, and early childhood enrichment programs could prevent many cases of intellectual disability (Beirne-Smith, Patton, & Shannon, 2006).

About half of all cases of intellectual disability are *organic*, or related to physical disorders (Das, 2000). These include *birth injuries* (such as lack of oxygen during delivery), and *fetal damage* (prenatal damage from disease, infection, or drugs). *Metabolic disorders*, which affect energy production and use in the body, also cause intellectual disability. Some forms of intellectual disability are linked to *genetic abnormalities*, such as missing genes, extra genes, or defective genes. Malnutrition and exposure to lead, PCBs, and other toxins early in childhood can also cause organic intellectual disability (Beirne-Smith, Patton, & Shannon, 2006). Let's briefly look at several distinctive problems.

Down Syndrome

In 1 out of 800 babies, the disorder known as **Down syndrome** causes moderate to severe intellectual disability and a shortened life expectancy of around 49 years. It is now known that Down syndrome children have an extra 21st chromosome. This condition, which is called trisomy-21, results from flaws in the parents' egg or sperm cells. Thus, although Down syndrome is *genetic*, it is not usually *hereditary* (it doesn't "run in the family").

The age of parents is a major factor in Down syndrome. As people age, their reproductive cells are more prone to errors during cell division. This raises the odds that an extra chromosome will be present. As you can see in the following figures, the older a woman is, the greater the risk (National Institute of Child Health and Human Development, 2010):

Mother's age	Incidence of Down syndrome
Under 30	1/11000
Early 40s	1/105
Late 40s	1/12

Fathers, and possibly especially older fathers, also add to the risk; in a small percentage of cases, the father is the source of the extra chromosome (National Institute of Child Health and Human Development, 2010). Older adults who plan to have children should carefully consider the odds shown here.

There is no "cure" for Down syndrome. However, these children are usually loving and responsive, and they make progress in a caring environment. At a basic level, Down syndrome children can do most of the things that other children can, only slower. The best hope for Down syndrome children, therefore, lies in specially tailored educational programs that enable them to lead fuller lives.

This young woman exhibits the classical features of Down syndrome: Distinctive features of this problem are almond-shaped eyes, a slightly protruding tongue, a stocky build, and stubby hands with deeply creased palms.

Fragile X Syndrome

The second most common form of genetic intellectual disability (after Down syndrome) is **fragile X syndrome** (Hallahan, Kauffman, & Pullen, 2011). Unlike Down syndrome, fragile X syndrome is hereditary—it *does* run in families. The problem is related to a thin, frail-looking area on the *X* (female) chromosome. Because fragile X is sex linked (like color-blindness), boys are most often affected, at a rate of about 1 out of every 3800 (National Fragile X Foundation, 2011).

Fragile X males generally have long, thin faces and big ears. Physically, they are usually larger than average during childhood, but smaller than average after adolescence. Up to three-fourths of all fragile X males suffer from hyperactivity and attention disorders. Many also have a peculiar tendency to avoid eye contact with others.

Fragile X males are only mildly intellectually disabled during early childhood, but they are often severely or profoundly intellectually disabled as adults. When learning adaptive behaviors, they tend to do better with daily living skills than with language and social skills (Hallahan, Kauffman, & Pullen, 2011).

Phenylketonuria (PKU)

The problem called **phenylketonuria** (FEN-ul-KEET-uh-NURE-ee-ah) is a genetic disease. Children who have PKU lack an important enzyme. This causes phenylpyruvic (FEN-ul-pye-ROO-vik)

Savant syndrome The possession of exceptional mental ability in one or more narrow areas, such as mental arithmetic, calendar calculations, art, or music by a person of limited general intelligence.

Familial intellectual disability Mild intellectual disability associated with homes that are intellectually, nutritionally, and emotionally impoverished.

Down Syndrome A genetic disorder caused by the presence of an extra chromosome; results in intellectual disability.

Fragile X syndrome A genetic form of intellectual disability caused by a defect in the *X* chromosome.

acid (a destructive chemical) to collect within their bodies. PKU is also linked to very low levels of dopamine, an important chemical messenger in the brain. If PKU goes untreated, severe intellectual disability typically occurs by age 3.

PKU can be detected in newborn babies by routine medical testing. Affected children are usually placed on a diet low in phenylalinine, the substance the child's body can't handle. Carefully following this diet will usually prevent intellectual disability (Grosse, 2010). (Phenylalinine is present in many foods. You might be interested to know that it is also found in Aspartame, the artificial sweetener in diet colas.)

Microcephaly

The word **microcephaly** (MY-kro-SEF-ah-lee) means small-headedness. The microcephalic person suffers a rare abnormality in which the skull is extremely small or fails to grow. This forces the brain to develop in a limited space, causing severe intellectual disability (Szabó et al., 2010). Although they are typically institutionalized, microcephalic persons are usually affectionate, well-behaved, and cooperative.

Hydrocephaly

Hydrocephaly (HI-dro-SEF-ah-lee: "water on the brain") is caused by a buildup of cerebrospinal fluid within brain cavities. Pressure from this fluid can damage the brain and enlarge the head. Hydrocephaly is not uncommon—about 10,000 hydocephalic babies are born each year in the United States and Canada. However, thanks to new medical procedures, most of these infants will lead nearly normal lives. A surgically implanted tube drains fluid from the brain into the abdomen and minimizes brain damage. Although affected children usually score below average on mental tests, severe intellectual disability usually can be prevented (Rourke et al., 2002).

Cretinism

Cretinism (KREET-un-iz-um) is another type of intellectual disability that appears in infancy. It results from an insufficient supply of thyroid hormone. In some parts of the world, cretinism is caused by a lack of iodine in the diet (the thyroid glands require iodine to function normally). Iodized salt has made this source of intellectual disability rare in developed nations. Cretinism causes stunted physical and intellectual growth that cannot be reversed. Fortunately, cretinism is easily detected in infancy. Once detected, it can be treated with thyroid hormone replacement, before permanent damage occurs.

Knowledge Builder: Variations in Intelligence

RECITE

1. The distribution of IQs approximates a normal (bell-shaped) curve.
2. Differences in the intellectual strengths of men and women have grown larger in recent years. T or F?
3. The association between IQ and high-status professional jobs proves that such jobs require more intelligence. T or F?
4. Only about 6 percent of the population scores above 140 on IQ tests. T or F?
5. An IQ score below 90 indicates intellectual disability. T or F?
6. Many cases of intellectual disability without known organic causes appear to be ________.

Match:

7. D PKU
8. B Microcephaly
9. E Hydrocephaly
10. A Cretinism
11. C Down syndrome
12. F Fragile X

A. Too little thyroid hormone
B. Very small brain
C. 47 chromosomes
D. Lack of an important enzyme
E. Excess of cerebrospinal fluid
F. Abnormal female chromosome
G. Caused by a lack of oxygen at birth

REFLECT

Think Critically

13. Lewis Terman took great interest in the lives of many of the "Termites." He even went so far as to advise them about what kinds of careers they should pursue. What error of observation did Terman make?

Self-Reflect

If you measure the heights of all the people in your psychology class, most people will be clustered around an average height. Very few will be extremely tall or extremely short. Does this ring a bell? Do you think it's normal? (It is, of course; most measured human characteristics form a normal curve, just as IQs do.)

Do you think that giftedness should be defined by high IQ or having special talents (or both)? To increase your chances of succeeding in today's society, would you prefer to be smart or talented (or both)? How about smart, talented, motivated, and lucky!?

As a psychologist you are asked to assess a child's degree of intellectual disability. Will you rely more on IQ or the child's level of adaptive behavior? Would you be more confident in your judgment if you took both factors into account?

Answers: 1. normal **2.** F **3.** F **4.** F **5.** F **6.** familial **7.** D **8.** B **9.** E **10.** A **11.** C **12.** F **13.** Terman may have unintentionally altered the behavior of the people he was studying. Although Terman's observations are generally regarded as valid, he did break a basic rule of scientific observation.

Heredity and Environment—Super Rats, Family Trees, and Video Games

Gateway Question 9.6: *How do heredity and environment affect intelligence?*

Is intelligence inherited? This seemingly simple question is loaded with controversy. Some psychologists believe that intelligence is strongly affected by heredity. Others feel that environment is dominant. Let's examine some evidence for each view.

In a classic study of genetic factors in learning, Tryon (1929) managed to breed separate strains of "maze-bright" and "maze-dull" rats (animals that were extremely "bright" or "stupid" at learning mazes). After several generations of breeding, the slowest "super rat" outperformed the best "dull" rat. This and other studies of **eugenics** (selective breeding for desirable characteristics) suggest that some traits are highly influenced by heredity.

That may be true, but is maze-learning really a measure of intelligence? No, it isn't. Tryon's study seemed to show that intelligence is inherited, but later researchers found that the "bright" rats were simply more motivated by food and less easily distracted during testing. When they weren't chasing after rat chow, the "bright" rats were no more intelligent than the supposedly dull rats. Thus, Tryon's study did demonstrate that behavioral characteristics can be influenced by heredity. However, it was inconclusive concerning intelligence. Because of such problems, animal studies cannot tell us with certainty how heredity and environment affect intelligence. Let's see what human studies reveal.

Hereditary Influences

Most people are aware of a moderate similarity in the intelligence between parents and their children, or between brothers and sisters. As ● Figure 9.5 shows, the closer two people are on a family tree, the more alike their IQs are likely to be.

Does that indicate that intelligence is hereditary? Not necessarily. Brothers, sisters, and parents share similar environments as well as similar genes (Grigorenko, 2005). To separate heredity and environment, we need to make some selected comparisons.

Twin Studies

Notice in ● Figure 9.5 that the IQ scores of fraternal twins are more alike than those of ordinary brothers and sisters. **Fraternal twins** come from two separate eggs fertilized at the same time. They are no more genetically alike than ordinary siblings. Why, then, should the twins' IQ scores be more similar? The reason is environmental: Parents treat twins more alike than ordinary siblings, resulting in a closer match in IQs.

More striking similarities are observed with **identical twins**, who develop from a single egg and have identical genes. At the top of ● Figure 9.5 you can see that identical twins who grow up in the same family have highly correlated IQs. This is what we would expect with identical heredity and very similar environments. Now, let's consider what happens when identical twins are reared apart. As you can see, the correlation drops, but only from .86 to .72. Psychologists who emphasize genetics believe figures like these show that differences in adult intelligence are roughly 50 percent hereditary (Jacobs et al., 2008; Neisser et al., 1996).

How do environmentalists interpret the figures? They point out that some separated identical twins differ by as much as 20 IQ points. In every case in which this occurs, there are large educational and environmental differences between the twins. Also, separated twins are almost always placed in homes socially and educationally similar to those of their birth parents. This would tend to inflate apparent genetic effects by making the separated

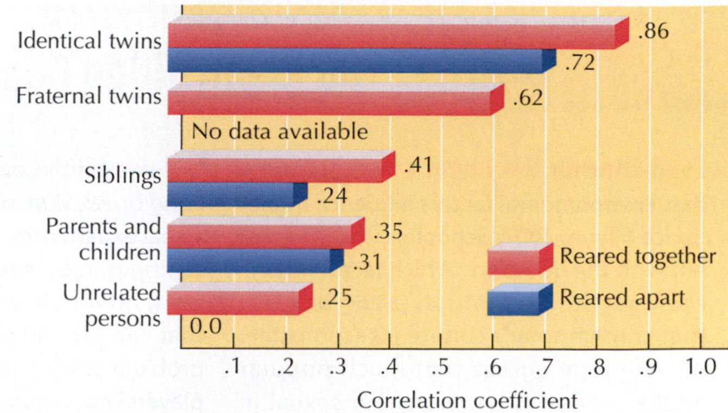

● **Figure 9.5** Approximate correlations between IQ scores for persons with varying degrees of genetic and environmental similarity. Notice that the correlations grow smaller as the degree of genetic similarity declines. Also note that a shared environment increases the correlation in all cases. (Adapted from Bouchard, 1983; Henderson, 1982.)

twins' IQs more alike. Another frequently overlooked fact is that twins grow up in the same environment *before birth* (in the womb). If this environmental similarity is taken into account, intelligence would seem to be less than 50 percent hereditary (Devlin, Daniels, & Roeder, 1997; Turkheimer et al., 2003).

BRIDGES

Identical twins also tend to have similar personality traits. This suggests that heredity contributes to personality as well as intelligence. **For more information, see Chapter 12, pages 425–427.**

Environmental Influences

Some evidence for an environmental view of intelligence comes from families having one adopted child and one biological child. As ● Figure 9.6 shows, parents contribute genes *and* environment

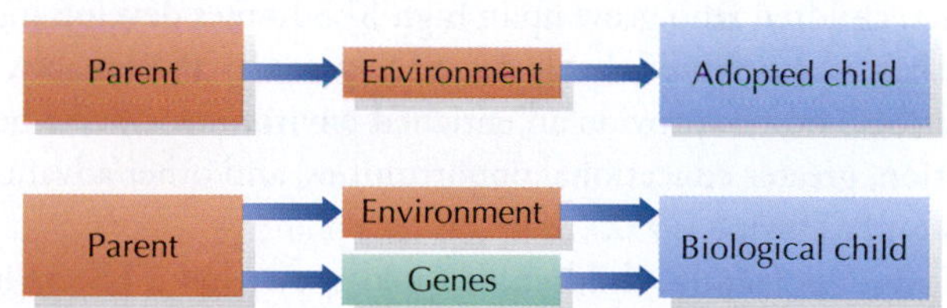

● **Figure 9.6** Comparison of an adopted child and a biological child reared in the same family. (Adapted from Kamin, 1981.)

Phenylketonuria A genetic disease that allows phenylpyruvic acid to accumulate in the body.
Microcephaly A disorder in which the head and brain are abnormally small.
Hydrocephaly A buildup of cerebrospinal fluid within brain cavities.
Cretinism Stunted growth and intellectual disability caused by an insufficient supply of thyroid hormone.
Eugenics Selective breeding for desirable characteristics.
Fraternal twins Twins conceived from two separate eggs.
Identical twins Twins who develop from a single egg and have identical genes.

Critical Thinking: You Mean Video Games Might Be Good for Me?

Even though the Flynn effect suggests that environmental factors influence intelligence (Flynn, 2007; Schooler, 1998), we are left with the question "Which factors?" Psychologist Steven Johnson (2005) believes that contemporary culture is responsible. Although he agrees that much popular media content is too violent or sexual in nature, he points out that video games, the Internet, and even television are becoming more complex. As a result, they demand ever greater cognitive effort from us. In other words, it is as important to understand *how* we experience the environment as it is to understand *what* we experience.

For example, early video games, such as *Pong* or *PacMan*, offered simple, repetitive visual experiences. In contrast, today's best-selling games, such as *Call of Duty* or *The Sims*, offer rich, complicated experiences that can take 40 or more hours of intense problem-solving to complete. Furthermore, players must usually figure out the rules by themselves. Instructions for completing popular games, which have been created by fans, are typically much longer than chapters in this textbook. Only a complex and engaging game would prompt players to use such instructions, much less write them for others to use (Johnson, 2005).

According to Johnson, other forms of popular culture have also become more complex, including the Internet and computer software. Even popular television has become more cognitively demanding. For example, compared with television dramas of the past, modern dramas weave plot lines and characters through an entire season of programs. In the end, popular culture may well be inviting us to read, reflect, and problem-solve more than ever before (Jaeggi et al., 2008). (Before you uncritically embrace video games, read "You Mean Video Games Might Be Bad for Me?" in Chapter 6.)

to their biological child. With an adopted child they contribute only environment. If intelligence is highly genetic, the IQs of biological children should be more like their parents' IQs than the IQs of adopted children are. However, studies show that children reared by the same mother resemble her in IQ to the same degree. It doesn't matter whether they share her genes (Kamin, 1981; Weinberg, 1989).

IQ and Socioeconomic Status

How much can environment alter intelligence? It depends on the quality of the environment (Turkheimer et al., 2003). One way to look at environmental effects is to compare children adopted by parents of high or low *socioeconomic status* (SES). As you might predict, children who grow up in high SES homes develop higher IQs than those reared by lower SES parents. Presumably, the higher SES homes provide an enriched environment, with better nutrition, greater educational opportunities, and other advantages (Capron & Duyme, 1992).

More importantly, children adopted *out of* low SES environments can experience great relative gains in intelligence. That is, the IQs of low SES children may be more dramatically infuenced by environmental factors than the IQs of high SES children (Henrich, Heine, & Norenzayan, 2010). In one study, striking increases in IQ occurred in 25 children who were moved from an orphanage and were eventually adopted by parents who gave them love, a family, and a stimulating home environment. Once considered intellectually disabled and unadoptable, the children gained an average of 29 IQ points. A second group of initially less intellectually disabled children, who stayed in the orphanage, *lost* an average of 26 IQ points (Skeels, 1966).

A particularly dramatic environmental effect is the fact that 14 nations have shown average IQ gains of from 5 to 25 points during the last 30 years (Dickens & Flynn, 2001; Flynn, 2007). Referred to as the *Flynn effect*, after New Zealand psychologist James Flynn, these IQ boosts, averaging 15 points, occurred in far too short a time to be explained by genetics. It is more likely that the gains reflect environmental forces, such as improved education, nutrition, and living in a technologically complex society (Barber, 2010; Johnson, 2005). If you've ever tried to play a computer game or set up a wireless network in your home, you'll understand why people may be getting better at answering IQ test questions (Neisser, 1997). The highlight "You Mean Video Games Might Be Good for Me?" explores this idea further.

If environment makes a difference, can intelligence be taught? The traditional answer is "No." Brief coaching, for instance, has little positive effect on aptitude and intelligence test scores (Brody, 1992). More encouraging results can be found in **early childhood education programs**, which provide longer-term stimulating intellectual experiences for disadvantaged children (Kirk et al., 2011). In one study, children from low-income families were given enriched environments from early infancy through preschool. By age 2, their IQ scores were already higher than those in a control group. More important, they were still 5 points higher 7 years later (Campbell & Ramey, 1994). High-quality enrichment programs such as Head Start can prevent children from falling behind in school (Barnet & Barnet, 1998; Ramey, Ramey, & Lanzi, 2001).

Later schooling can also have an impact on IQ. Stephen Ceci found that people who leave school lose up to 6 points in IQ per year. Dropping out of school in the eighth grade can reduce a person's adult IQ by up to 24 points. Conversely, IQ rises as people spend more time in school (Ceci, 1991). Israeli psychologist Reuven Feuerstein (FOY-er-shtine) and his colleagues have developed a program they call Instrumental Enrichment. Through hundreds of hours of guided problem solving, students learn to avoid the thinking flaws that lower IQ scores (Feuerstein et al., 1986). Feuerstein and others have shown that such training can improve thinking abilities and even raise IQs (Feuerstein et al., 2004; Skuy et al., 2002; Tzuriel & Shamir, 2002).

With our growing understanding of how people think and with the tireless aid of computers, it may become common in schools to "teach intelligence." Most importantly, improved education and training in thinking skills can improve the intellectual abilities of all children, regardless of what their IQ scores are (Hallahan, Kauffman, & Pullen, 2011; Hunt, 1995). Even if "teaching intelligence" doesn't raise IQ scores, it can give children the abilities they need to think better and succeed in life (Perkins & Grotzer, 1997).

Summary To sum up, few psychologists seriously believe that heredity is not a major factor in intelligence, and all acknowledge that environment affects it. Estimates of the impact of heredity and environment continue to vary. But ultimately, both camps agree that improving social conditions and education can raise intelligence.

There is probably no limit to how far *down* intelligence can go in an extremely poor environment. On the other hand, heredity does seem to impose upper limits on IQ, even under ideal conditions. It is telling, nevertheless, that gifted children tend to come from homes in which parents spend time with their children, answer their questions, and encourage intellectual exploration (Dai, 2010).

BRIDGES

Impoverished and unstimulating environments can severely restrict mental development during early childhood. **See Chapter 3, pages 87–88, for more information.**

The fact that intelligence is partly determined by heredity tells us little of any real value. Genes are fixed at birth. Improving the environments in which children learn and grow is the main way in which we can assure that they reach their full potential (Ormrod, 2011; Turkheimer, 1998).

As a final summary, it might help to think of inherited intellectual potential as a rubber band that is stretched by outside forces. A long rubber band may be stretched more easily, but a shorter one can be stretched to the same length if enough force is applied. Of course, a superior genetic gift may allow for a higher maximum IQ. In the final analysis, intelligence reflects development as well as potential, nurture as well as nature (Grigorenko, 2005; Kalat, 2009).

Beyond Psychometric Intelligence—Intelligent Alternatives to "g"

Gateway Question 9.7: *Are there alternate views of intelligence?*

Until now, we have treated intelligence *psychometrically*, as a quality that can be measured, like height or weight. Other approaches share the goal of understanding intelligence in more detail. Specifically, let's have a look at four other approaches to the study of intelligence:

- Some psychologists are investigating the neural basis for intelligence. How, they ask, does the nervous system contribute to differences in IQ?
- A second approach views intelligent behavior as an expression of thinking skills. Cognitive psychologists believe that the nervous system is like a fast computer—it's of little value unless you know how to use it.
- Speaking of computers, would it make sense to understand human intelligence by programming computers? That is one goal of the field of artificial intelligence.
- A fourth trend involves newer, broader definitions of intelligence. Many psychologists have begun to question the narrow focus on analytic thinking found in traditional IQ tests.

The Intelligent Nervous System

Do more intelligent people have superior nervous systems? It is natural to assume that intelligence, like other human abilities, can be localized in the nervous system. But where and how does Steven Hawking's nervous system allow him to be so intelligent? This is currently a vibrant research field (Banich & Compton, 2011). We can only briefly explore a few threads here.

One possibility is that intelligent people have faster nervous systems. Maybe Steven Hawking's brain is just faster than the rest of us. To investigate this possibility, researchers measure how fast people process various kinds of information (Bates, 2005). For example, psychologists have looked at people's **reaction time**, the time it takes people to respond to a stimulus (see • Figure 9.7). The flurry of brain activity that follows exposure to a stimulus can also be recorded. Such studies attempt to measure a person's

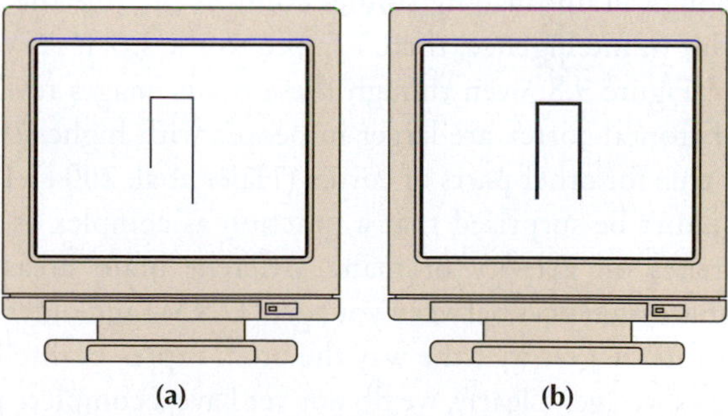

• Figure 9.7 Stimuli like those used in reaction time tasks. The participant views stimulus (a) followed almost immediately by (b), ensuring that (a) is only briefly visible. The participant's task is to press one key if the left-hand segment of (a) is shorter and another if it is longer. Participants with higher IQs are generally faster and more accurate at tasks like this (Bates, 2005; Petrill et al., 2001).

Early childhood education program Programs that provide stimulating intellectual experiences, typically for disadvantaged preschoolers.

Reaction time The amount of time a person must look at a stimulus to make a correct judgment about it.

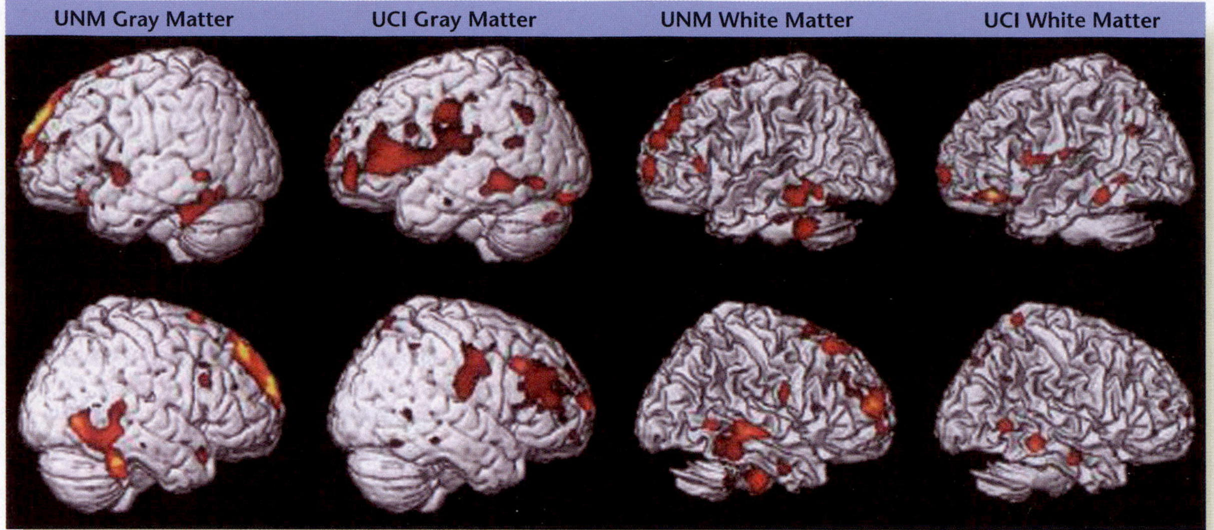

• **Figure 9.8** MRI identification of cortical areas whose size is correlated with IQ. The left hemisphere is shown in the top row; the right is on the bottom. Participants were drawn from two universities, a younger group from the University of New Mexico (UNM) and an older group from the University of California at Irvine (UCI). Brain areas pictured in red and yellow are larger in people with higher IQs. (From Haier et al., 2004).

speed of processing, which is assumed to reflect the brain's speed and efficiency (Reed, Vernon, & Johnson, 2004; Waiter et al., 2009). In general, people higher in measured IQ perform faster on reaction time tasks like that shown in • Figure 9.7 (McCrory & Cooper, 2005). In addition, brain areas that control higher mental abilities usually become more active during reaction time testing (Deary et al., 2001; Waiter et al., 2009). Such observations suggest that having a quick nervous system is part of what it means to be quick, smart, swift, or brainy.

Which brain areas control higher mental abilities? You may recall from Chapter 2 that the frontal lobes and especially prefrontal cortex are related to more complex behaviors. Maybe those parts of Steven Hawking's brain are just bigger than the rest of us.

Although brain imaging studies confirm the role the frontal lobes play in intelligence, there is more to the story. As you can see in • Figure 9.8, even though these brain images reveal that parts of frontal cortex are larger in people with higher IQs, the same is true for other parts of cortex (Haier et al, 2004). Perhaps we shouldn't be surprised that a function as complex as intelligence relies on activity of many different brain areas. Also, noticeable differences between younger (UNM) and older (UCI) participants suggest that the way the brain expresses intelligence changes as we age. Clearly, we do not yet have a complete picture of the relationship between the nervous system and intelligence.

Intelligent Information Processing

Much intelligent behavior is an expression of good thinking skills. Cognitive psychologist David Perkins believes that how smart you are depends on three factors:

- Relatively fixed **neural intelligence** (the speed and efficiency of the nervous system);
- **Experiential intelligence** (specialized knowledge and skills acquired over time);
- **Reflective intelligence** (an ability to become aware of one's own thinking habits).

Little can be done to change neural intelligence. However, by adding to personal knowledge and learning to think better, people can become more intelligent (Perkins, 1995; Ritchhart & Perkins, 2005). The effects of Feuerstein's Instrumental Enrichment program (described earlier) are a good example of how reflective intelligence can be improved.

Many psychologists now believe that to make full use of innate intelligence a person must have good **metacognitive skills.** *Meta* means "beyond," so metacognitive skills go above and beyond ordinary thinking. Such skills involve an ability to manage your own thinking and problem solving. Typically this means breaking problems into parts, establishing goals and subgoals, monitoring your progress, and making corrections. Learning metacognitive skills is the surest avenue to becoming more intelligent (Hunt, 1995; Ku & Ho, 2010).

BRIDGES

Metacognitive skills are a large part of what it means to be a reflective thinker. **See the "Psychology of Studying," pages 1–8, to remind yourself (You did read it, right?) how to sharpen your metacognitive skills to become a better student.**

Artificial Intelligence

Whereas most efforts have focused on measuring intelligence in humans, a small group of psychologists and computer scientists have taken an entirely different approach. Their basic idea is to build machines that display **artificial intelligence (AI)**. This usually refers to creating computer programs capable of doing things that require intelligence when done by people (Russell & Norvig, 2003). As computer scientist Aaron Sloman explains it, "Human brains don't work by magic, so whatever it is they do should be doable by machine" (Brooks, 2009). The resulting programs can then help us understand how people do those same things.

Consider, for example, IBM's "Watson" supercomputer, which outperforms even expert humans at playing the television game *Jeopardy* (Markoff, 2011). Similarly, Aaron Sloman's robot, the "Cubinator," does a spiffy job of solving Rubik's Cube puzzles. Sloman hopes the Cubinator's expertise will help him better understand how humans do mathematics (Sloman, 2008).

How smart are computers and robots? Don't worry, they are not very smart yet. Let's say you are exchanging instant messages with someone you don't know. You are allowed to make any comments and ask any questions you like, for as long as you like. In reality, the "person" you are communicating with is a computer. Do you think a computer could fool you into believing it was human? If it did, wouldn't that qualify it as "intelligent"? You may be surprised to learn that, to date, no machine has come close to passing this test (Moor, 2003).

The problem computers face is that we humans can mentally "shift gears" from one topic to another with incredible flexibility. In contrast, machine "intelligence" is currently "blind" outside its underlying set of rules (D'Mello, Graesser, & King, 2010). As a tiny example, u cann understnd wrds thet ar mizpeld. Computers are very literal and easily stymied by such errors.

Regardless, AI has been successful at very specific tasks (such as playing chess or solving a Rubik's Cube). Much of current AI is based on the fact that many tasks—from harmonizing music to diagnosing disease—can be reduced to a set of rules applied to a collection of information. AI is valuable in situations in which speed, vast memory, and persistence are required. In fact, AI programs are better at some tasks than humans are. An example is world chess champion Garry Kasparov's loss, in 1997, to a computer called "Deep Blue."

Bela Szandelszky/AP Images

The "Cubinator" solving a Rubik's Cube at the 2007 Rubik's Cube World Championships. The winner, in 10 seconds, was a person. The Cubinator took 26 seconds. To what extent is the way the Cubinator comes up with solutions helpful for understanding how humans do it?

Artificial Intelligence and Cognition

Although AI is a long way from duplicating general human intelligence, AI systems like the Cubinator offer a way to probe some of our specific cognitive skills, or intelligences. For instance, computer simulations and expert systems provide good examples of how AI is used as a research tool.

Computer simulations are programs that attempt to duplicate specific human behaviors, especially thinking, decision making, and problem solving. Here, the computer acts as a "laboratory" for testing models of cognition. If a computer program behaves as humans do (including making the same errors), then the program may be a good model of how we think.

Expert systems are computer programs that respond as a human expert would (Giarratano & Riley, 2005; Mahmoodabadi et al., 2010). They have demystified some human abilities by converting complex skills into clearly stated rules a computer can follow. Expert systems can predict the weather, analyze geological formations, diagnose disease, play chess, read, tell when to buy or sell stocks, and perform many other tasks.

Eventually, AI will almost certainly lead to robots that recognize voices and that speak and act "intelligently" in specific areas of ability. To achieve this, should intelligence be directly programmed into computers? Or should computers be designed to learn from experience, like the human brain does? (Sporns, 2011). Only time will tell.

Multiple Intelligences

Defining intelligence as a g-factor (general ability) has been controversial. For example, consider William, a grade-school student two years behind in reading, who shows his teacher how to solve a difficult computer-programming problem. Or what about his classmate, Malika, who is poor in math but plays intricate pieces of piano music? Both of these children show clear signs of what we earlier referred to as *aptitudes*. And, as we have seen, autistic savants like Kim Peek have even more extreme intellectual strengths and weaknesses. Such observations have convinced many psychologists that it is time to forge new, broader definitions of intelligence. Their basic goal is to better predict "real-world" success—not just the likelihood of success in school (Sternberg & Grigorenko, 2006).

Speed of processing The speed with which a person can mentally process information.

Neural intelligence The innate speed and efficiency of a person's brain and nervous system.

Experiential intelligence Specialized knowledge and skills acquired through learning and experience.

Reflective intelligence An ability to become aware of one's own thinking habits.

Metacognitive skills An ability to manage one's own thinking and problem solving efforts.

Artificial intelligence (AI) Refers to both the creation of computer programs capable of doing things that require intelligence when done by people, and to the resulting programs themselves.

Frames of Mind

One such psychologist is Howard Gardner of Harvard University. Gardner (2003, 2004, 2008) theorizes that there are actually eight distinctly different kinds of intelligence. These are different mental "languages" that people use for thinking. Each is listed below, with examples of pursuits that make use of them.

1. *Language* (linguistic abilities)—writer, lawyer, comedian.
2. *Logic and math* (numeric abilities)—scientist, accountant, programmer.
3. *Visual and spatial* (pictorial abilities)—engineer, inventor, artist.
4. *Music* (musical abilities)—composer, musician, music critic.
5. *Bodily-kinesthetic* (physical abilities)—dancer, athlete, surgeon.
6. *Intrapersonal* (self-knowledge)—poet, actor, minister.
7. *Interpersonal* (social abilities)—psychologist, teacher, politician.
8. *Naturalist* (an ability to understand the natural environment)—biologist, medicine man, organic farmer.

To simplify a great deal, people can be "word smart," "number smart," "picture smart," "music smart," "body smart," "self smart," "people smart," and/or "nature smart."

Most of us are probably strong in only a few types of intelligence. In contrast, geniuses like Albert Einstein seem to be able to use nearly all of the intelligences, as needed, to solve problems.

If Gardner's theory of **multiple intelligences** is correct, traditional IQ tests measure only a part of real-world intelligence—namely, linguistic, logical-mathematical, and spatial abilities. A further implication is that our schools may be wasting a lot of human potential (Campbell, Campbell, & Dickinson, 2003). For example, some children might find it easier to learn math or reading if these topics were tied into art, music, dance, drama, and so on. Already, many schools are using Gardner's theory to cultivate a wider range of skills and talents (Campbell, Campbell, & Dickinson, 2003; Kornhaber & Gardner, 2006).

Martin Bureau/AFP/Getty Images

According to Howard Gardner's theory, bodily-kinesthetic skills reflect one of eight distinct types of intelligence.

A Look Ahead

As promised earlier, the *Psychology in Action* section of this chapter addresses questions concerning the validity of intelligence tests and their fairness to various groups. The issues raised go to the heart of the question "What is intelligence?" In addition to being highly interesting and culturally relevant, this topics should round out your understanding of intelligence.

Knowledge Builder

Heredity, Environment, and Alternate Views of Intelligence

RECITE

1. Selective breeding for desirable characteristics is called ______________.
2. The closest similarity in IQs would be observed for
   a. parents and their children *b.* identical twins reared apart *c.* fraternal twins reared together *d.* siblings reared together
3. Most psychologists believe that intelligence is 90 percent hereditary. T or F?
4. Except for slight variations during testing, IQ cannot be changed. T or F?
5. Reaction time has been used as a measure of ______________ intelligence.
   a. experiential *b.* neural *c.* reflective *d.* analytical
6. According to Howard Gardner's theory, which of the following is not measured by traditional IQ tests?
   a. intrapersonal skills *b.* spatial skills *c.* logical skills *d.* linguistic skills

REFLECT

Think Critically

7. Dropping out of school can lower tested IQ and attending school can raise it. What do these observations reveal about intelligence *tests?*
8. Is it ever accurate to describe a machine as "intelligent"?

Self-Reflect

Why do you think studies of hereditary and environmental influences on intelligence have provoked such emotional debate? Which side of the debate would you expect each of the following people to favor: teacher, parent, school administrator, politician, medical doctor, liberal, conservative, bigot?

Would you rather have your own intelligence measured with a speed of processing test or a traditional IQ test? Why?

Here's a mnemonic: *New experiences reflect* three kinds of intelligence. Can you define *neural, experiential,* and *reflective* intelligence in your own words?

Make your own list of specialized intelligences. How many items on your list correspond to the 8 intelligences identified by Gardner?

Answers: 1. eugenics **2.** *b* **3.** F **4.** F **5.** *b* **6.** *a* **7.** Such observations remind us that intelligence tests are affected by learning and that they measure knowledge as well as innate cognitive abilities. **8.** Rule-driven expert systems may appear "intelligent" within a narrow range of problem solving. However, they are idiots at everything else. This is usually not what we have in mind when discussing human intelligence.

Psychology in Action

Intelligent Intelligence Testing—User Beware!

Gateway Question 9.8: *Is there a downside to intelligence testing?*

During their lifetimes, most people take an intelligence test, or one of the closely related scholastic aptitude tests. If you have ever taken an individually administered IQ test, you may actually know what your IQ is. If not, the following self-administered test will provide a rough estimate of your IQ. Most people are curious about how they would score on an intelligence test. Why not give the Dove test a try?

Dove Counterbalance Intelligence Test

Time limit: 5 minutes.
Circle the correct answer.

1. T-bone Walker got famous for playing what?
   a. trombone *b.* piano *c.* T-flute *d.* guitar *e.* "hambone"
2. A "gas head" is a person who has a
   a. fast-moving car. *b.* stable of "lace." *c.* "process." *d.* habit of stealing cars. *e.* long jail record for arson
3. If you throw the dice and 7 is showing on the top, what is facing down?
   a. 7 *b.* snake eyes *c.* boxcars *d.* little joes *e.* 11
4. Cheap chitlings (not the kind you purchase at a frozen-food counter) will taste rubbery unless they are cooked long enough. How soon can you quit cooking them to eat and enjoy them?
   a. 45 minutes *b.* 2 hours *c.* 24 hours *d.* 1 week (on a low flame) *e.* 1 hour
5. Bird or Yardbird was the jacket jazz lovers from coast to coast hung on
   a. Lester Young *b.* Peggy Lee *c.* Benny Goodman *d.* Charlie Parker *e.* Birdman of Alcatraz
6. A "handkerchief head" is
   a. a cool cat. *b.* a porter. *c.* an Uncle Tom. *d.* a hoddi. *e.* a preacher
7. Jet is
   a. an East Oakland motorcycle club. *b.* one of the gangs in West Side Story. *c.* a news and gossip magazine. *d.* a way of life for the very rich
8. "Bo Diddley" is a
   a. game for children. *b.* down-home cheap wine. *c.* down-home singer. *d.* new dance. *e.* Moejoe call
9. Which word is most out of place here?
   a. splib *b.* blood *c.* gray *d.* spook *e.* black
10. If a pimp is uptight with a woman who gets state aid, what does he mean when he talks about "Mother's Day"?
    a. second Sunday in May *b.* third Sunday in June *c.* first of every month *d.* none of these *e.* first and fifteenth of every month
11. Many people say that "Juneteenth" (June 10th) should be made a legal holiday because this was the day when
    a. the slaves were freed in the United States. *b.* the slaves were freed in Texas. *c.* the slaves were freed in Jamaica. *d.* the slaves were freed in California. *e.* Martin Luther King was born. *f.* Booker T. Washington died
12. If a man is called a "blood," then he is a
    a. fighter *b.* Mexican-American *c.* Black *d.* hungry hemophile *e.* red man or Indian
13. What are the Dixie Hummingbirds?
    a. a part of the KKK *b.* a swamp disease *c.* a modern gospel group *d.* a Mississippi Negro paramilitary strike force *e.* deacons
14. The opposite of square is
    a. round. *b.* up *c.* down *d.* hip *e.* lame

Answers: 1. *d* 2. *c* 3. *a* 4. *c* 5. *d* 6. *c* 7. *c* 8. *c* 9. *c* 10. *c* 11. *b* 12. *c* 13. *c* 14. *d*

If you scored 14 on this exam, your IQ is approximately 100, indicating average intelligence. If you scored 10 or less, you are intellectually disabled. With luck and the help of a special educational program, we may be able to teach you a few simple skills!

Isn't the Dove Test a little unfair? No, it is *very* unfair. It was written in 1971 by African-American sociologist Adrian Dove as "a half serious attempt to show that we're just not talking the same language." Dove tried to slant his test as much in favor of urban, African American culture as he believes the typical intelligence test is biased toward a European American, middle-class background (Jones, 2003). (Because of its age, the test is probably now also unfair even for younger African Americans.)

Dove's test is a thought-provoking reply to the fact that African American children score an average of about 15 points lower on standardized IQ tests than European American children. By reversing the bias, Dove has shown that intelligence tests are not equally valid for all groups. Psychologist Jerome Kagan once remarked, "If the Wechsler and Binet scales were translated into Spanish, Swahili, and Chinese and given to every 10-year-old in Latin America, East Africa, and China, the majority would obtain IQ scores in the mentally retarded range."

Culture-Fair Testing

Certainly we cannot believe that children of different cultures are all intellectually disabled. The fault must lie with the test (White, 2006). Cultural values, traditions, and experiences can greatly affect performance on tests designed for Western cultures (Sternberg & Grigorenko, 2005; Neisser et al., 1996). For example, our culture places a high value on logic and formal reasoning. Other cultures regard intuition as an important part of what it means to be smart (Norenzayan et al., 2002). Imagine giving the Stanford-Binet to a

Multiple intelligences Howard Gardner's theory that there are several specialized types of intellectual ability.

young Bushman hunter. If tracking prey is what he values and is good at, then what would it mean if (when?) he got a low IQ score? (Feel free to reread "Intelligence—How Would a Fool Do It?" near the beginning of this chapter.)

To avoid this problem, some psychologists have tried to develop culture-fair tests that do not disadvantage certain groups. A **culture-fair test** is designed to minimize the importance of skills and knowledge that may be more common in some cultures than in others. (For a sample of culture-fair test items, see • Figure 9.9.)

Culture-fair tests attempt to measure intelligence without, as much as possible, being influenced by a person's verbal skills, cultural background, and educational level. Their value lies not just in testing people from other cultures. They are also useful for testing children in the United States who come from poor communities, rural areas, or ethnic minority families (Stephens et al., 1999). However, no intelligence test can be entirely free of cultural influences. For instance, our culture is very "visual," because children are constantly exposed to television, movies, video games, and the like. Thus, compared with children in developing countries, a child who grows up in the United States may be better prepared to take *both* nonverbal tests and traditional IQ tests.

Since the concept of intelligence exhibits diversity across cultures, many psychologists have begun to stress the need to rethink the concept of intelligence itself (Greenfield, 1997; Sternberg & Grigorenko, 2005). If we are to find a truly culture-fair way to measure intelligence, we first need to identify those core cognitive skills that lie at the heart of human intelligence the world around (Gardner, 2008; Henrich, Heine, & Norenzayan, 2010).

IQ and Race

Historically, African American children in the United States scored an average of about 15 points lower on standardized IQ tests than European-American children. As a group, Japanese American children scored above average in IQ. Could such differences be genetic? One persistent claim is that African Americans score below average in IQ because of their "genetic heritage" and because they are genetically incapable of climbing out of poverty (Hernstein & Murray, 1994; Rushton & Jensen, 2005). Psychologists have responded to such claims with a number of counterarguments.

First, psychologists reiterate the point made by the Dove Test. The assumptions, biases, and content of standard IQ tests do not always allow meaningful comparisons between ethnic, cultural, or racial groups (White, 2006). As Leon Kamin (1981) says, "The important fact is that we cannot say which sex (or race) might be more intelligent, because we have no way of measuring 'intelligence.' We have only IQ tests."

Kamin's point is that the makers of IQ tests decided in advance to use test items that would give men and women equal IQ scores. It would be just as easy to put together an IQ test that would give African Americans and European Americans equal scores. Differences in IQ scores are not a fact of nature, but a decision by the test makers. That's why European Americans do better on IQ tests written by European Americans, and African Americans do better on IQ tests devised by African Americans. Another example of this fact is an intelligence test made up of 100 words selected from the *Dictionary of Afro-American Slang*. Williams (1975) gave the test to 100 African American and 100 European American high school students in St. Louis and found that the African American group averaged 36 points higher than the European American group.

Second, it is no secret that as a group African Americans are more likely than European Americans to live in environments that are physically, educationally, and intellectually impoverished. When unequal education is part of the equation, IQs may tell us little about how heredity affects intelligence (Sternberg, Grigorenko, & Kidd, 2005; Suzuki & Aronson, 2005). Indeed, one study found that placing poor African American children into European American adoptive families increased the children's IQs by an average of 13 points, bringing them into line with those of European American children (Nisbett, 2005). That is, providing African American children with the same environmental experiences available to European American children erased IQ differences.

A tantalizing hint that lower African American IQ scores are not genetic is provided by Ray Friedman and his colleagues at Vanderbilt University who administered a 20-item test to African American and European American students. Before the election of Barack Obama, African American students performed more poorly than European American students. During the election, African American students performed just as well as their European American counterparts. Apparently, President Obama is providing a role model, inspiring better academic performance in African American students (Tite, 2009).

Further, although IQ predicts school performance, it does not predict later career success (McClelland, 1994). In this regard, "street smarts," or what psychologist Robert Sternberg calls *practical intelligence* (Stemler & Sternberg, 2006), is often seen by minority cultures as more important than "book learning," or what Sternberg calls *analytic intelligence* (Sankofa et al., 2005).

Most psychologists have concluded that there is no scientific evidence that group differences in average IQ are based on genetics. In fact, studies that used actual blood group testing found no significant correlations between ethnic ancestry and IQ scores. This is because it does not even make genetic sense to talk about "races" at all—obvious external markers, like skin color, have little to do with underlying genetic differences (Bonham et al., 2005; Sternberg, 2007). Group differences in

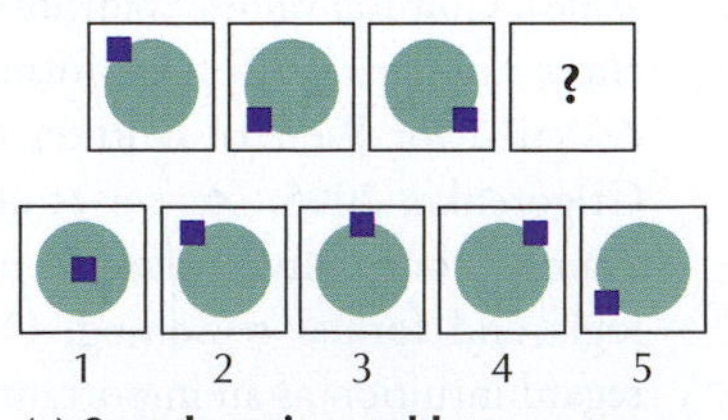

(a) Sample series problem

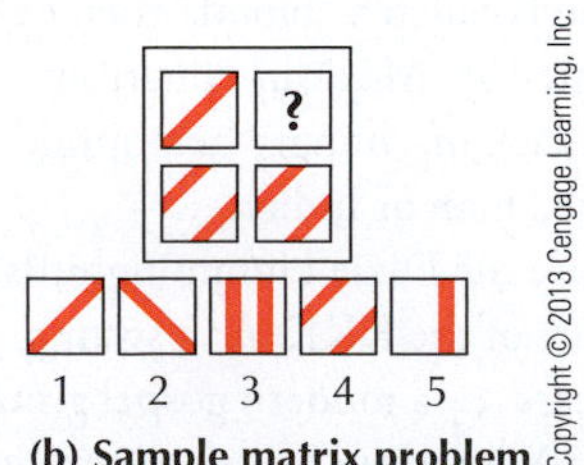

(b) Sample matrix problem

• **Figure 9.9** Sample items like those often found on culture-fair intelligence tests. (a) Sample series problem. Which pattern correctly continues the series of patterns shown at the top left? (Number 4.) (b) Sample matrix problem. Which pattern fits best completes the matrix of patterns shown at the top right? (Number 1.) The idea is that the ability to read and the mastery of culturally relevant knowledge should not be necessary to do well. Nevertheless, do you think illiterate street orphans from Sao Paulo, Brazil, or Aboriginals living in the desert of the Australian outback would find these items as easy to complete as you did? If not, can you think of any alternative truly culture-fair ways to test intelligence across different cultures?

"Yes We Can." President Obama's intelligence is inspiring millions of Americans and others around the world to aspire to greater academic success. His example is particularly important to African Americans.

AP Images

IQ scores are based on cultural and environmental diversity, as much as on heredity (Neisser et al., 1996; Nisbett, 2005). To conclude otherwise reflects political beliefs and biases, not scientific facts.

Questioning IQ—Beyond the Numbers Game

African Americans are not the only segment of the population with reason to question the validity of intelligence testing and the role of heredity in determining intelligence. The clarifications they have won extend to others as well.

Consider the 9-year-old child confronted with this question on an intelligence test: "Which of the following does not belong with the others? Roller skates, airplane, train, bicycle." If the child fails to answer "airplane," does it reveal a lack of intelligence? It can be argued that an intelligent choice could be based on any of these alternatives: Roller skates are not typically used for transportation; an airplane is the only nonland item; a train can't be steered; a bicycle is the only item with just two wheels. The parents of a child who misses this question may have reason to be angry since educational systems tend to classify children and then make the label stick.

Court decisions have led some states to outlaw the use of intelligence tests in public schools. Criticism of intelligence testing has also come from the academic community. Harvard University psychologist David McClelland believes that IQ is of little value in predicting real competence to deal effectively with the world. McClelland concedes that IQ predicts school performance, but when he compared a group of college students with straight A's to another group with poor grades, he found no differences in later career success (McClelland, 1994).

Standardized Testing

In addition to IQ tests, 400 to 500 million standardized multiple-choice tests are given in schools and workplaces around the nation each year. Many, like the *SAT Reasoning Test*, may determine whether a person is admitted to college. Other tests—for employment, licensing, and certification—directly affect the lives of thousands by qualifying or disqualifying them for jobs.

Widespread reliance on standardized intelligence tests and aptitude tests raises questions about the relative good and harm they do. On the positive side, tests can open opportunities as well as close them. A high test score may allow a disadvantaged youth to enter college, or it may identify a child who is bright but emotionally disturbed. Test scores may also be fairer and more objective than arbitrary judgments made by admissions officers or employment interviewers. Also, tests *do* accurately predict academic performance. The fact that academic performance *does not* predict later success may call for an overhaul of college course work, not an end to testing.

On the negative side, mass testing can occasionally exclude people of obvious ability. In one case, a student who was seventh in his class at Columbia University, and a member of Phi Beta Kappa, was denied entrance to law school because he had low scores on the *Law School Admissions Test*. Other complaints relate to the frequent appearance of bad or ambiguous questions on standardized tests, overuse of class time to prepare students for the tests (instead of teaching general skills), and in the case of intelligence tests, the charge that tests are often biased. Also, most standardized tests demand passive recognition of facts, assessed with a multiple-choice format. They do not, for the most part, test a person's ability to think critically or creatively or to apply knowledge to solve problems. Various "high-stakes tests," which can make or break a person's career could be improved by: (1) removing all questions that favor one group over another; (2) using digital video-based testing, when possible, to reduce the importance of verbal skills; and (3) providing a pre-test orientation for all test takers, so that people who can afford coaching won't have an unfair advantage (Sackett et al., 2001).

High Stakes Testing Intelligence tests are a double-edged sword; we have learned much from their use yet they have the potential to do great harm. In the final analysis, it is important to remember—as Howard Gardner has pointed out—that creativity, motivation, physical health, mechanical aptitude, artistic ability, and numerous other qualities not measured by intelligence tests contribute to the achievement of life goals. Also, remember that IQ is not intelligence. IQ is an *index* of intelligence (as narrowly defined by a particular test). Change the test and you change the score. An IQ is not some permanent number stamped on the forehead of a child that forever determines his or her potential. The real issue is what skills people have, not what their test scores are (Hunt, 1995).

The Whole Human: Wisdom

In the final analysis, intelligence reflects development as well as potential, nurture as well as nature (Grigorenko, 2005). Moreover, the fact that intelligence is partly determined by heredity tells us little of any real value. Genes are fixed at birth. Improving the environments in which children learn and grow is the

Culture-fair test A test designed to minimize the importance of skills and knowledge that may be more common in some cultures than in others.

main way in which we can ensure that they reach their full potential (Grigorenko & Sternberg, 2003; White, 2006).

Perhaps most importantly, people can be intelligent without being wise. For example, a person who does well in school and on IQ tests may make a total mess of her life. Likewise, people can be intelligent without being creative; and clear, rational thinking can lead to correct, but uninspired, answers (Solomon, Marshall, & Gardner, 2005). In many areas of human life, wisdom represents a mixture of convergent thinking, intelligence, and reason, spiced with creativity and originality (Meeks & Jeste, 2009). People who are wise approach life with openness and tolerance (Helson & Srivastava, 2002).

Knowledge Builder: Intelligence Testing in Perspective

RECITE

1. The WAIS-IV, Stanford-Binet 5, and Dove Test are all culture-fair intelligence scales. T or F?
2. The claim that heredity accounts for racial differences in average IQ ignores environmental differences and the cultural bias inherent in standard IQ tests. T or F?
3. IQ scores predict school performance. T or F?
4. IQ is not intelligence; it is one index of intelligence. T or F?

REFLECT

Think Critically

5. Assume that a test of memory for words is translated from English to Spanish. Would the Spanish version of the test be equal in difficulty to the English version?

Self-Reflect

Do you think it would be possible to create an intelligence test that is universally culture-fair? What would its questions look like? Can you think of any type of question that wouldn't favor the mental skills emphasized by some culture, somewhere in the world?

Funding for schools in some states varies greatly in rich and poor neighborhoods. Imagine that a politician opposes spending more money on disadvantaged students because she believes it would "just be a waste." What arguments can you offer against her assertion?

In your own opinion, what are the advantages of using standardized tests to select applicants for college, graduate school, and professional schools? What are the disadvantages?

Answers: 1. F **2.** T **3.** T **4.** T **5.** Probably not, because the Spanish words might be longer or shorter than the same words in English. The Spanish words might also sound more or less alike than words on the original test. Translating an intelligence test into another language can subtly change the meaning and difficulty of test items.

Chapter in Review: Gateways to Intelligence

Gateway QUESTIONS REVISITED

9.1 *How do psychologists define intelligence?*

9.1.1 Intelligence refers to the general capacity (or g-factor) to act purposefully, think rationally, and deal effectively with the environment.

9.1.2 In practice, intelligence is operationally defined by intelligence tests, which provide a useful but narrow estimate of real-world intelligence.

9.1.3 General intelligence is distinguished from specific aptitudes. Special aptitude tests and multiple aptitude tests are used to assess a person's capacities for learning various abilities. Aptitude tests measure a narrower range of abilities than general intelligence tests do.

9.1.4 To be of any value, a psychological test must be reliable (give consistent results). A worthwhile test must also have validity, meaning that it measures what it claims to measure. Widely used intelligence tests are also objective (they give the same result when scored by different people) and standardized (the same procedures are always used in giving the test, and norms have been established so that scores can be interpreted).

9.2 *What are typical IQ tests like?*

9.2.1 The first practical intelligence test was assembled by Alfred Binet. A modern version of Binet's test is the *Stanford-Binet Intelligence Scales—Fifth Edition* (SB5).

9.2.2 A second major intelligence test is the *Wechsler Adult Intelligence Scale-Fourth Edition (WAIS-IV)*. Wechsler's children's version is the *Wechsler Intelligence Scale for Children—Fourth Edition* (WISC-IV).

9.2.3 The SB5, WAIS-IV, and WISC-IV measure both verbal and performance intelligence.

9.2.4 In addition to individual tests, intelligence tests have also been produced for use with groups. A group test of historical interest is the *Army Alpha*. The SAT, the ACT, and the CQT are group scholastic aptitude tests. Although narrower in scope than IQ tests, they bear some similarities to them.

9.2.5 Intelligence is expressed in terms of an intelligence quotient (IQ). IQ is defined as mental age (MA) divided by chronological age (CA) and then multiplied by 100. An "average" IQ of 100 occurs when mental age equals chronological age.

9.2.6 Modern IQ tests no longer calculate IQs directly. Instead, the final score reported by the test is a deviation IQ.

9.2.7 IQ scores become fairly stable at about age 6, and they become increasingly reliable thereafter.

9.3 How do IQ scores relate to sex, age, and occupation?

9.3.1 The distribution of IQ scores approximates a normal curve.

9.3.2 There are no overall differences between males and females in tested intelligence. However, very small sex differences may result from the intellectual skills our culture encourages males and females to develop.

9.3.3 On average, IQ scores continue to gradually increase until middle age. Later intellectual declines are moderate for most people until their 70s. Aging also involves a shift from fluid intelligence to crystallized intelligence.

9.3.4 IQ is related to school grades and job status. The second association may be somewhat artificial because educational credentials are required for entry into many occupations.

9.4 What does IQ tell us about genius?

9.4.1 People with IQs in the gifted or "genius" range of above 140 tend to be superior in many respects.

9.4.2 By criteria other than IQ, a large proportion of children might be considered gifted or talented in one way or another. Intellectually gifted children often have difficulties in average classrooms and benefit from special accelerated programs.

9.5 What causes intellectual disability?

9.5.1 People with the savant syndrome combine intellectual disability with exceptional ability in a very limited skill.

9.5.2 The term intellectually disabled is applied to those whose IQ falls below 70 or who lack various adaptive behaviors.

9.5.3 Current classifications of intellectual disability are: mild (50–55 to 70), moderate (35–40 to 50–55), severe (20–25 to 35–40), and profound (below 20–25). Chances for educational success are related to the degree of intellectual disability.

9.5.4 Many cases of subnormal intelligence are thought to be the result of familial intellectual disability, a generally low level of educational and intellectual stimulation in the home, coupled with poverty and poor nutrition.

9.5.5 About 50 percent of the cases of intellectual disability are organic, caused by birth injuries, fetal damage, metabolic disorders, or genetic abnormalities. The remaining cases are of undetermined cause.

9.5.6 Six distinct forms of organic intellectual disability are Down syndrome, fragile X syndrome, phenylketonuria (PKU), microcephaly, hydrocephaly, and cretinism.

9.6 How do heredity and environment affect intelligence?

9.6.1 Studies of eugenics in animals and familial relationships in humans demonstrate that intelligence is partially determined by heredity. However, environment is also important, as revealed by changes in tested intelligence induced by schooling and stimulating environments.

9.6.2 There is evidence that some elements of intelligence can be taught. Intelligence, therefore, reflects the combined effects of both heredity and environment in the development of intellectual abilities.

9.7 Are there alternate views of intelligence?

9.7.1 Some psychologists are investigating the *neural basis* for intelligence, especially the speed of processing various kinds of information and the size of brain areas related to intelligence.

9.7.2 Cognitive psychologists believe that successful intelligence depends on thinking and problem solving skills. Metacognitive skills, in particular, contribute greatly to intelligent behavior.

9.7.3 *Artificial intelligence* refers to any artificial system that can perform tasks that require intelligence when done by people. Two principal areas of artificial intelligence research on particular human skills are computer simulations and expert systems.

9.7.4 Many psychologists have begun to forge new, broader definitions of intelligence. Howard Gardner's theory of multiple intelligences is a good example of this trend.

9.8 Is there a downside to intelligence testing?

9.8.1 Traditional IQ tests often suffer from a degree of cultural bias.

9.8.2 African Americans are unfairly stigmatized because of historically poor performance on standardized IQ tests.

9.8.3 It is wise to remember that IQ is merely an index of intelligence and that intelligence is narrowly defined by most tests.

9.8.4 The use of standard IQ tests for educational placement of students (especially into special education classes) has been prohibited by law in some states. Whether this is desirable and beneficial to students is currently being debated.

MEDIA RESOURCES

Web Resources

Internet addresses frequently change. To find an up-to-date list of URLs for the sites listed here, visit your Psychology CourseMate.

IQ Tests Provides links to a number of IQ tests.

American Mensa Mensa is an international society that has one qualification only for membership: an IQ score in the top 2 percent of the population on a standardized intelligence test.

Gifted Children Learn more about giftedness from the National Association for Gifted Children.

Helping Your Highly Gifted Child Advice for parents of gifted children.

Intellectual Disabilities Learn more about intellectual disability from the American Association on Intellectual and Developmental Disabilities (AAIDD).

Down Syndrome Find out more about Down syndrome from the National Down Syndrome Society.

Fragile X Find out more about autism and fragile X syndrome from the National Fragile X Foundation.

Mind vs. Machine Read an amusing article about the Loebner Prize, one of the holy grails of artificial intelligence.

RuBot II, The Cubinator - A Rubik's Cube Solving Robot Watch a robot solve a Rubik's cube.

Multiple Intelligences in Education Learn more about Gardner's theory of multiple intelligences and how it is being applied in education.

Be Careful of How You Define Intelligence An article about cross-cultural differences in intelligence.

The Bell Curve Flattened An article that summarizes objections to *The Bell Curve.*

The Genographic Project Trace your own ancestry.

The Knowns and Unknowns of Intelligence From the APA, what is known about intelligence and intelligence tests.

Interactive Learning

Log in to **CengageBrain** to access the resources your instructor requires. For this book, you can access:

CourseMate brings course concepts to life with interactive learning, study, and exam preparation tools that support the printed textbook. A textbook-specific website, ***Psychology CourseMate*** includes an ***integrated interactive eBook*** and other ***interactive learning tools*** including quizzes, flashcards, videos, and more.

CENGAGE**NOW**™

CengageNOW is an easy-to-use online resource that helps you study in less time to get the grade you want—NOW. Take a pre-test for this chapter and receive a personalized study plan based on your results that will identify the topics you need to review and direct you to online resources to help you master those topics. Then take a post-test to help you determine the concepts you have mastered and what you will need to work on. If your textbook does not include an access code card, go to CengageBrain.com to gain access.

WebTUTOR™

More than just an interactive study guide, **WebTutor** is an anytime, anywhere customized learning solution with an eBook, keeping you connected to your textbook, instructor, and classmates.

If your professor has assigned **Aplia** homework:

1. Sign in to your account.
2. Complete the corresponding homework exercises as required by your professor.
3. When finished, click "Grade It Now" to see which areas you have mastered and which need more work, and for detailed explanations of every answer.

Visit **www.cengagebrain.com** to access your account and purchase materials.

Gateway THEME
Our behavior is energized and directed by motives and emotions.

10

Motivation and Emotion

No Need to Tell Lady Gaga

Russian novelist Leo Tolstoy once commented, "Music is the shorthand of emotion." So true, as any American-born, Grammy Award–winning glam rocker with a wicked fashion sense could tell you. But there is more to motivation and emotion than getting you all gaga about an upcoming concert. The words *motivation* and *emotion* both derive from the Latin word *movere* (to move). Even getting out of bed in the morning can be difficult if you are unmotivated. And if you are unaware of your emotions, you will be vulnerable to health problems, such as depression or addiction.

In this chapter, you will learn how motives provide the drumbeat of human behavior and emotions color its rhythms. As we will see, both play complex roles in our daily lives. Even "simple" motivated activities, such as eating, are not solely under the control of the body. In many instances, external cues, expectations, learning, cultural values, and other factors influence our motives and emotions.

Let's begin with basic motives, such as hunger and thirst, and then explore how emotions affect us. Although emotions can be the music of life, they are sometimes the music of death as well. Read on to find out why.

Gateway QUESTIONS

10.1 *What is motivation and are there different types of motives?*

10.2 *What causes hunger, overeating, and eating disorders?*

10.3 *What kinds of biological motives are thirst, pain avoidance, and the sex drive?*

10.4 *How does arousal relate to motivation?*

10.5 *What are learned and social motives and why are they important?*

10.6 *Are some motives more basic than others?*

10.7 *What happens during emotion?*

10.8 *What physiological changes underlie emotion, and can "lie detectors" really detect lies?*

10.9 *How accurately are emotions expressed by the face and "body language"?*

10.10 *How do psychologists explain emotions?*

10.11 *What does it mean to have "emotional intelligence"?*

Motivation—Forces That Push and Pull

Gateway Question 10.1: *What is motivation and are there different types of motives?*

What are your goals? Why do you pursue them? When are you satisfied? When do you give up? These are all questions about motivation, or why we act as we do. Let's begin with a basic model of motivation and an overview of types of motives. **Motivation** refers to the dynamics of behavior—the ways in which our actions are *initiated*, *sustained*, *directed*, and *terminated* (Deckers, 2010; Franken, 2007).

Can you clarify that? Yes. Imagine that Stefani Joanne is studying biology in the library. Her stomach begins to growl and she can't concentrate. She grows restless and decides to buy a snack from a vending machine. The machine is empty, so she goes to the cafeteria. Closed. Stefani Joanne drives to a nearby fast food outlet, where she finally eats. Her hunger satisfied, she resumes studying. Notice how Stefani Joanne's food seeking was *initiated* by a bodily need. Her search was *sustained* because her need was not immediately met, and her actions were *directed* by possible sources of food. Finally, achieving her goal *terminated* her food seeking.

A Model of Motivation

Many motivated activities begin with a **need**, or internal deficiency. The need that initiated Stefani Joanne's search was a shortage of key substances in her body. Needs cause a **drive** (an energized motivational state) to develop. The drive was hunger, in Stefani Joanne's case. Drives activate a **response** (an action or series of actions) designed to push us toward a **goal** (the "target" of motivated behavior). Reaching a goal that satisfies the need will end the chain of events. Thus, a simple model of motivation can be shown in this way:

NEED → DRIVE → RESPONSE → GOAL
(NEED REDUCTION) ←

Aren't needs and drives the same thing? No, because the strength of needs and drives can differ (Deckers, 2010). For example, it is not uncommon for older people to suffer from dehydration (a bodily need for water) despite experiencing a lack of thirst (the drive to drink) (Farrell et al., 2008).

Now, let's observe Stefani Joanne again. It's a holiday weekend and she's home from school. For dinner, Stefani Joanne has soup, salad, a large steak, a baked potato, two pieces of cheesecake, and three cups of coffee. After dinner, she complains that she is "too full to move." Soon after, Stefani Joanne's aunt arrives with a strawberry pie. Stefani Joanne exclaims that strawberry pie is her favorite and eats three large pieces! Is this hunger? Certainly, Stefani Joanne's dinner already satisfied her biological needs for food.

How does that change the model of motivation? Stefani Joanne's "pie lust" illustrates that motivated behavior can be energized by the "pull" of external stimuli, as well as by the "push" of internal needs.

Incentives

The "pull" of a goal is called its **incentive value** (the goal's appeal beyond its ability to fill a need). Some goals are so desirable (strawberry pie, for example) that they can motivate behavior in the absence of an internal need. Other goals are so low in incentive value that they may be rejected even if they meet the internal need. Fresh silkworms, for instance, are highly nutritious. However, it is doubtful that you would eat one no matter how hungry you might be. Regardless, because they are also easy to grow and produce few waste products, silkworms may become the preferred food on long space voyages (Yang et al., 2009). (Attention, aspiring astronauts: Are you ready for silkworms *and* motion sickness?)

Usually, our actions are energized by a mixture of internal needs *and* external incentives. That's why a strong need may change an unpleasant incentive into a desired goal. Perhaps you've never eaten a silkworm, but we'll bet you've eaten some pretty horrible leftovers when the refrigerator was bare. The incentive value of goals also helps explain motives that don't seem to come from internal needs, such as drives for success, status, or approval (● Figure 10.1).

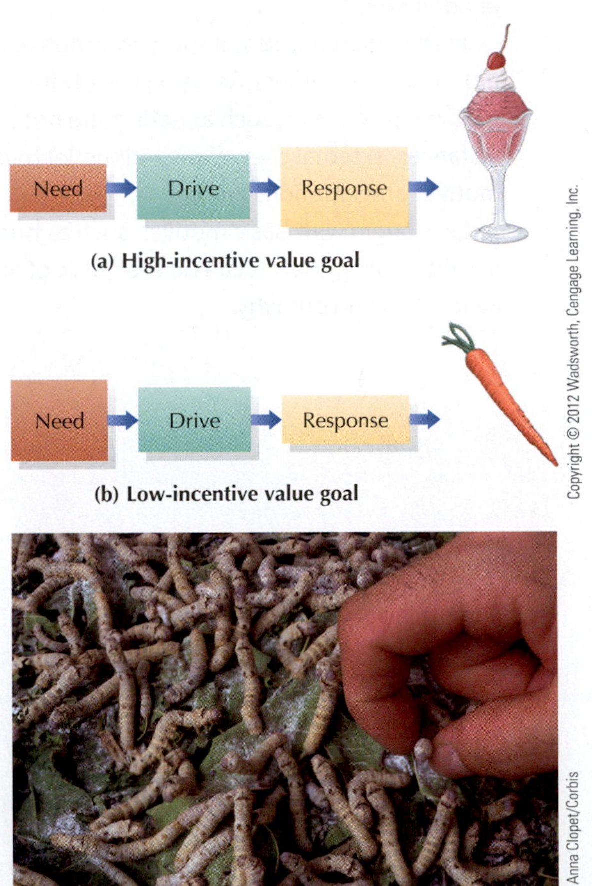

● Figure 10.1 Needs and incentives interact to determine drive strength *(above)*. *(a)* Moderate need combined with a high-incentive goal produces a strong drive. *(b)* Even when a strong need exists, drive strength may be moderate if a goal's incentive value is low. It is important to remember, however, that incentive value lies "in the eye of the beholder." No matter how hungry, few people would be able to eat the pictured silkworms.

Types of Motives

For our purposes, motives can be divided into three major categories:

1. **Biological motives** are based on biological needs that must be met for survival. The most important biological motives are hunger, thirst, pain avoidance, and needs for air, sleep, elimination of wastes, and regulation of body temperature. Biological motives are innate.
2. **Stimulus motives** express our needs for stimulation and information. Examples include activity, curiosity, exploration, manipulation, and physical contact. Although such motives also appear to be innate, they are not strictly necessary for survival.
3. **Learned motives** are based on learned needs, drives, and goals. Learned motives, which are often *social* in nature, help explain many human activities, such as standing for election or auditioning for *America's Got Talent*. Many learned motives are related to learned needs for power, affiliation (the need to be with others), approval, status, security, and achievement.

Biological Motives and Homeostasis

How important is air in your life? Water? Sleep? Food? Temperature regulation? Finding a public restroom? For most of us, satisfying biological needs is so routine that we tend to overlook how much of our behavior they direct. But exaggerate any of these needs through famine, shipwreck, poverty, near drowning, bitter cold, or drinking ten cups of coffee, and their powerful grip on behavior becomes evident.

Biological drives are essential because they maintain *homeostasis* (HOE-me-oh-STAY-sis), or bodily equilibrium (Cooper, 2008). The term **homeostasis** means "standing steady" or "steady state." Optimal levels exist for body temperature, for chemicals in the blood, for blood pressure, and so forth (Franken & Dijk, 2009; Levin, 2006). When the body deviates from these "ideal" levels, automatic reactions begin to restore equilibrium (Deckers, 2010). Thus, it might help to think of homeostasis as similar to a thermostat set at a particular temperature.

A (Very) Short Course on Thermostats

The thermostat in your house constantly compares the actual room temperature to a *set point,* or ideal temperature, which you can control. When room temperature falls below the set point, the heat is automatically turned on to warm the room. When the heat equals or slightly exceeds the set point, it is automatically turned off or the air conditioning is turned on. In this way, room temperature is kept in a state of equilibrium hovering around the set point.

The first reactions to disequilibrium in the human body are also automatic. For example, if you become too hot, more blood will flow through your skin and you will begin to perspire, thus lowering body temperature. We are often unaware of such changes, unless continued disequilibrium drives us to seek shade, warmth, food, or water.

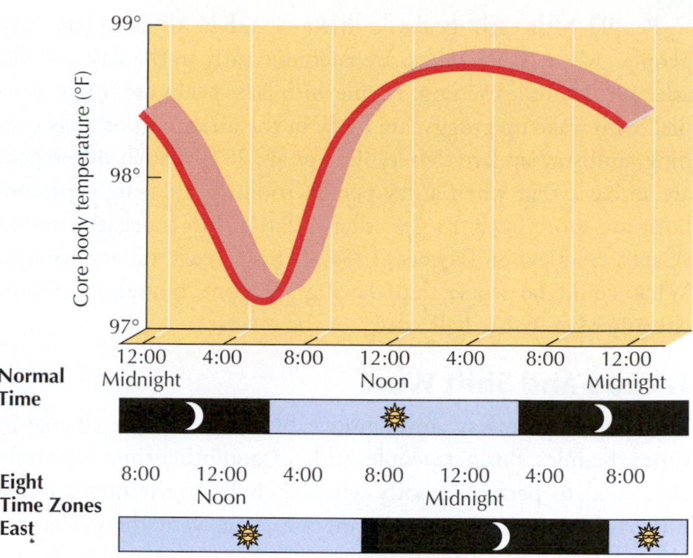

● **Figure 10.2** Core body temperature is a good indicator of a person's circadian rhythm. Rapid travel to a different time zone, shift work, depression, and illness can throw sleep and waking patterns out of synchronization with the body's core rhythm. Mismatches of this kind are very disruptive (Reinberg & Ashkenazi, 2008). Most people reach a low point 2 to 3 hours before their normal waking time. It's no wonder that both the Chernobyl and Three-Mile Island nuclear power plant accidents occurred around 4 A.M.

Circadian Rhythms

Our needs and drives can change from moment to moment. After eating, our motivation to eat more food tends to diminish, and a few minutes in the hot sun can leave us feeling thirsty. But our motivation can also vary over longer cycles. Scientists have long known that body activity is guided by internal "biological clocks." Every 24 hours, your body undergoes a cycle of changes called **circadian** (SUR-kay-dee-AN) **rhythms** (*circa:* about; *diem:* a day) (Beersma & Gordijn, 2007; Franken & Dijk, 2009). Throughout the day, activities in the liver, kidneys, and endocrine glands undergo large changes. Body temperature, blood pressure, and amino acid levels also shift from hour to hour. These activities, and many others, peak once a day (● Figure 10.2). People are usually more motivated and alert at the high point of their circadian rhythms (Bass & Takahashi, 2010; Chipman & Jin, 2009).

Motivation Internal processes that initiate, sustain, direct, and terminate activities.
Need An internal deficiency that may energize behavior.
Drive The psychological expression of internal needs or valued goals. For example, hunger, thirst, or a drive for success.
Response Any action, glandular activity, or other identifiable behavior.
Goal The target or objective of motivated behavior.
Incentive value The value of a goal above and beyond its ability to fill a need.
Biological motives Innate motives based on biological needs.
Stimulus motives Innate needs for stimulation and information.
Learned motives Motives based on learned needs, drives, and goals.
Homeostasis A steady state of body equilibrium.
Circadian rhythms Cyclical changes in body functions and arousal levels that vary on a schedule approximating a 24-hour day.

People with early peaks in their circadian rhythms are "day people," who wake up alert, are energetic early in the day, and fall asleep early in the evening. People with later peaks are "night people," who wake up groggy, are lively in the afternoon or early evening, and stay up late (Martynhak et al., 2010). Such differences are so basic that when a day person rooms with a night person, both are more likely to give their relationship a negative rating (Carey, Stanley, & Biggers, 1988). This is easy to understand: What could be worse than having someone bounding around cheerily when you're half asleep, or the reverse?

Jet Lag and Shift Work

Circadian rhythms are most noticeable after a major change in time schedules. Businesspeople, athletes, and other time zone travelers tend to perform poorly when their body rhythms are disturbed. If you travel great distances east or west, the peaks and valleys of your circadian rhythms will be out of phase with the sun and clocks. For example, you might be wide awake at midnight and feel like you're sleepwalking during the day (return to ● Figure 10.2). Shift work has the same effect, causing fatigue, irritability, upset stomach, and depression (Shen et al., 2006; Smith et al., 2011).

How fast do people adapt to rhythm changes? For major time zone shifts (5 hours or more), it can take up to 2 weeks to resynchronize. The *direction* of travel also affects adaptation (Herxheimer & Waterhouse, 2003). If you fly west, adapting is relatively easy; if you fly east, adapting takes much longer. When you fly east, the sun comes up *earlier* relative to your "home" time. Let's say that you live in San Diego and fly to Philadelphia. If you get up at 7 A.M. in Philadelphia, it's 4 A.M. back in San Diego—and your body knows it. If you fly west, the sun comes up later. In this case, it is easier for people to "advance" (stay up later and sleep in) than it is to shift backward.

Adjusting to jet lag is slowest when you stay indoors, where you can sleep and eat on "home time." Getting outdoors speeds adaptation. A few intermittent 5-minute periods of exposure to bright light early in the morning are also helpful for resetting your circadian rhythm (Dodson & Zee, 2010; Duffy & Wright, 2005). Bright light affects the timing of body rhythms by reducing the amount of melatonin produced by the pineal gland. When melatonin levels rise late in the evening, it's bedtime as far as the brain is concerned.

BRIDGES

Changes in melatonin levels are thought to partly explain winter depressions that occur when people endure several months of long dark days. **See Chapter 14, pages 494–495.**

How does this affect those of us who are not world travelers? There are few college students who have not at one time or another "burned the midnight oil," especially for final exams. At such times, it is wise to remember that departing from your regular schedule usually costs more than it's worth. You may be motivated to do as much during 1 hour in the morning as you could have done in 3 hours of work after midnight. You might just as well go to sleep 2 hours earlier. In general, if you can anticipate an upcoming body rhythm change, it is best to preadapt to your new schedule. *Preadaptation* refers to gradually matching your sleep–waking cycle to a new time schedule. Before traveling, for instance, you should go to sleep 1 hour later (or earlier) each day until your sleep cycle matches the time at your destination.

Knowledge Builder: Overview of Motivation

RECITE

1. Motives ________________, sustain, ________________, and terminate activities.
2. Needs provide the ________________ of motivation, whereas incentives provide the ________________.

Classify the following needs or motives by placing the correct letter in the blank.

A. Biological motive **B.** Stimulus motive **C.** Learned motive

3. _____ curiosity
4. _____ status
5. _____ sleep
6. _____ thirst
7. _____ achievement
8. _____ physical contact
9. The maintenance of bodily equilibrium is called thermostasis. T or F?
10. Desirable goals are motivating because they are high in
    a. secondary value *b.* stimulus value *c.* homeostatic value *d.* incentive value
11. The term *jet lag* is commonly used to refer to disruptions of
    a. the inverted U function *b.* circadian rhythms *c.* any of the episodic drives *d.* the body's set point

REFLECT

Think Critically

12. Many people mistakenly believe that they suffer from "hypoglycemia" (low blood sugar), which is often blamed for fatigue, difficulty concentrating, irritability, and other symptoms. Why is it unlikely that many people actually have hypoglycemia?

Self-Reflect

Motives help explain why we do what we do. See if you can think of something you do that illustrates the concepts of need, drive, response, and goal. Does the goal in your example vary in incentive value? What effects do high and low incentive-value goals have on your behavior?

Mentally list some biological motives you have satisfied today. Then list some stimulus motives and learned motives. How did each influence your behavior?

Answers: 1. initiate, direct **2.** push, pull **3.** B **4.** C **5.** A **6.** A **7.** C **8.** B **9.** F **10.** d **11.** b **12.** Because of homeostasis: Blood sugar is normally maintained within narrow bounds. Although blood sugar levels fluctuate enough to affect hunger, true hypoglycemia is an infrequent medical problem.

Hunger—Pardon Me, My Hypothalamus Is Growling

Gateway Question 10.2: *What causes hunger, overeating, and eating disorders?*

You get hungry, you find food, and you eat: Hunger might seem like a "simple" motive, but we have only recently begun to understand it. Hunger provides a good example of how internal and external factors direct our behavior. And, as we will see later, many

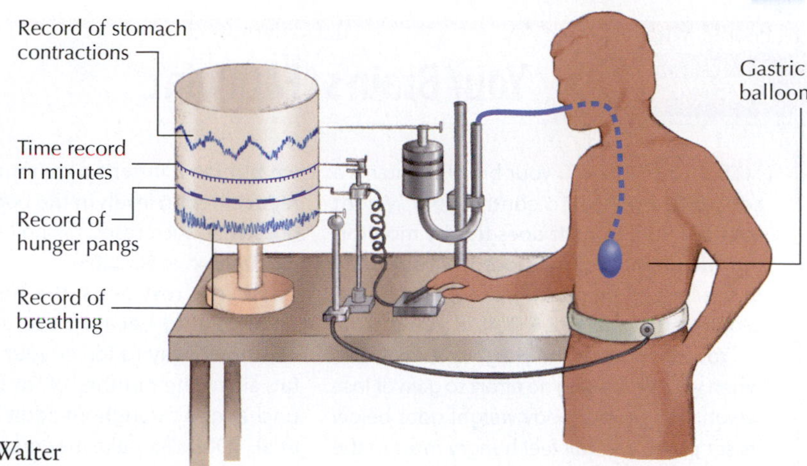

• Figure 10.3 In Walter Cannon's early study of hunger, a simple apparatus was used to simultaneously record hunger pangs and stomach contractions. (Adapted from Cannon, 1934.)

of the principles that explain hunger also apply to thirst. Like almost every other human motive, our hunger levels are affected by both internal bodily factors and external environmental and social ones. To understand how this works, let's begin with a survey of some of the internal factors controlling our hunger.

Internal Factors in Hunger

Don't feelings of hunger originate in the stomach? To find out, Walter Cannon and A. L. Washburn (1912) decided to see whether stomach contractions cause hunger. In an early study, Washburn trained himself to swallow a balloon, which could be inflated through an attached tube. (You, too, will do anything for science, right?) This allowed Cannon to record the movements of Washburn's stomach (• Figure 10.3). When Washburn's stomach contracted, he reported that he felt "hunger pangs." In view of this, the two scientists concluded that hunger is nothing more than the contractions of an empty stomach. (This, however, proved to be an inflated conclusion.)

For many people, hunger produces an overall feeling of weakness or shakiness rather than a "growling" stomach. Of course, eating *does* slow when the stomach is stretched or distended (full). (Remember last Thanksgiving?) However, we now know that the stomach is not essential for feeling hunger. Even people who have had their stomachs removed for medical reasons continue to feel hungry and eat regularly (Woods et al., 2000).

Then what does cause hunger? Many different factors combine to promote and suppress hunger (Ribeiro et al., 2009). The brain receives many signals from parts of the digestive system, ranging from the tongue and stomach to the intestines and the liver.

Brain Mechanisms

What part of the brain controls hunger? Although no single "hunger thermostat" exists, a small area called the **hypothalamus** (HI-po-THAL-ah-mus) is especially important because it regulates many motives, including hunger, thirst, and the sex drive (• Figure 10.4).

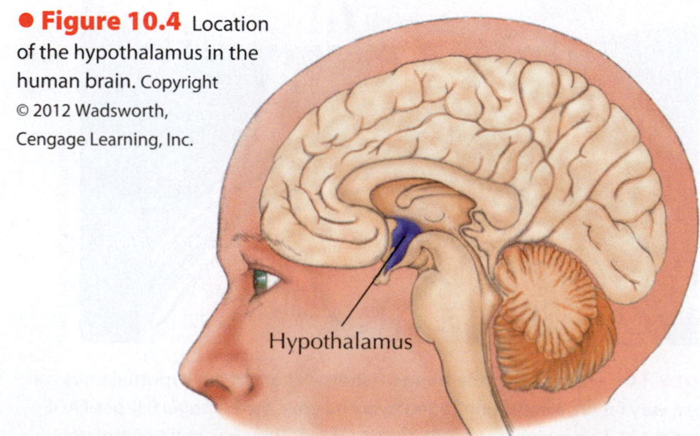

• Figure 10.4 Location of the hypothalamus in the human brain. Copyright © 2012 Wadsworth, Cengage Learning, Inc.

BRIDGES
For more information about the role of the hypothalamus in controlling behavior, see Chapter 2, pages 71–72.

The hypothalamus is sensitive to levels of sugar in the blood (and other substances described in a moment). It also receives neural messages from the liver and stomach. When combined, these signals determine whether you are hungry (Freberg, 2010; Woods et al., 2000).

One part of the hypothalamus acts as a *feeding system* that initiates eating. If the *lateral hypothalamus* is "turned on" with an electrified probe, even a well-fed animal will immediately begin eating. (The term *lateral* simply refers to the sides of the hypothalamus. See • Figure 10.5.) If the same area is destroyed, the animal may never eat again.

The lateral hypothalamus is normally activated in a variety of ways. For example, when you are hungry, your stomach lining produces ghrelin (GREL-in), a hormone that activates your lateral hypothalamus (Castañeda et al., 2010; Olszewski et al., 2003). (If your stomach is growlin', it's probably releasing ghrelin.) Ghrelin also activates parts of your brain involved in learning. This means you should consider studying before you eat, not immediately afterward (Diano et al., 2006).

How do we know when to stop eating? A second area in the hypothalamus is part of a *satiety system,* or "stop mechanism" for eating. If the *ventromedial* (VENT-ro-MEE-dee-al) *hypothalamus* is destroyed, dramatic overeating results. (*Ventromedial* refers to the bottom middle of the hypothalamus.) Rats with such damage will eat until they balloon up to weights of 1,000 grams or more (• Figure 10.6). A normal rat weighs about 180 grams. To put this weight gain in human terms, picture someone you know who weighs 180 pounds growing to a weight of 1,000 pounds.

Hypothalamus A small area at the base of the brain that regulates many aspects of motivation and emotion, especially hunger, thirst, and sexual behavior.

Brainwaves Your Brain's "Fat Point"

Like a thermostat, your brain maintains a **set point** in order to control your weight over the long term. It does this by monitoring the amount of fat stored in your body in specialized *fat cells* (Ahima & Osei, 2004; Gloria-Bottini, Magrini, & Bottini, 2009).

Your set point is the weight you maintain when you are making no effort to gain or lose weight. When your body weight goes below its set point, you will feel hungry most of the time. On the other hand, fat cells release a substance called *leptin* when your "spare tire" is well inflated. Leptin is carried in the bloodstream to the hypothalamus, where it tells us to eat less (Williams et al., 2004).

Can you change your fat set point? Good question. Your leptin levels are partly under genetic control. In rare cases, mice (and we humans) inherit a genetic defect that reduces leptin levels in the body, leading to obesity. In such cases, taking leptin can help (Williamson et al., 2005).

For the rest of us, the news is not so encouraging because there is currently no known way to lower your set point for fat, since the number of fat cells remains unchanged throughout adult life (Spalding et al., 2008). To make matters worse, radical diets do not help (but you knew that already, didn't you?). They may even raise the set point for fat, resulting in *diet-induced obesity* (Ahima & Osei, 2004). You may not be able to lose weight by resetting your hypothalamus, but psychologists have studied more effective approaches to weight loss. We will examine some later in this chapter.

AP Photo/The Rockefeller University

The mouse on the left has a genetic defect that prevents its fat cells from producing normal amounts of leptin. Without this chemical signal, the mouse's body acts as if its set point for fat storage is, shall we say, rather high.

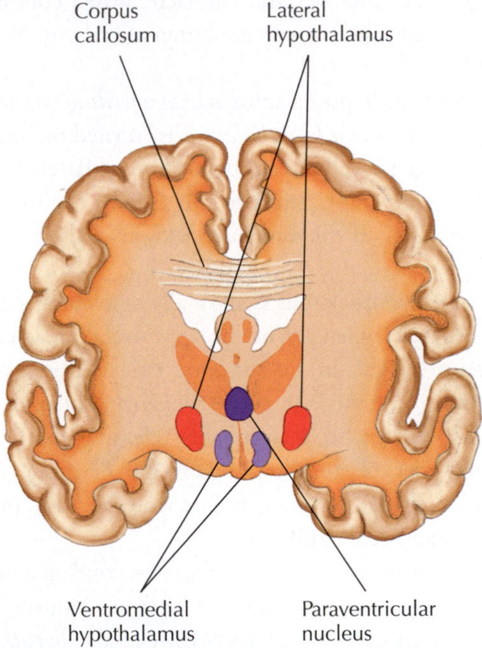

● Figure 10.5 This is a cross-section through the middle of the brain (viewed from the front of the brain). Indicated areas of the hypothalamus are associated with hunger and the regulation of body weight.

A chemical called *glucagon-like peptide 1* (GLP-1) is also involved in causing eating to cease. After you eat a meal, GLP-1 is released by the intestines. From there, it travels in the bloodstream to the brain. When enough GLP-1 arrives, your desire to eat ends (Hayes, De Jonghe, & Kanoski, 2010). As you might imagine, GLP-1 pills show promise in the treatment of obesity (Raun et al., 2007). By the way, it takes at least 10 minutes for the hypothalamus to respond after you begin eating. That's why you are less likely to overeat if you eat slowly, which gives your brain time to get the message that you've had enough (Liu et al., 2000).

The *paraventricular* (PAIR-uh-ven-TRICK-you-ler) *nucleus* of the hypothalamus also affects hunger (● Figure 10.5). This area helps keep blood sugar levels steady by both starting and stopping eating. The paraventricular nucleus is sensitive to a

John Sholtis, Rockefeller University

● Figure 10.6 Damage to the hunger satiety system in the hypothalamus can produce a very fat rat, a condition called hypothalamic *hyperphagia* (Hi-per-FAGE-yah: overeating). This rat weighs 1,080 grams. (The pointer has gone completely around the dial and beyond.) (Courtesy of Neal E. Miller, Rockefeller University.)

Discovering Psychology What's Your BMI? (We've Got Your Number.)

From the standpoint of fashion, you may already have an opinion about whether you are overweight. But how do you rate from a medical perspective? Obesity is directly linked to heart disease, high blood pressure, stroke, type 2 diabetes, and premature death. But how heavy do you have to be to endanger your health? A measure called the *body mass index (BMI)* can be used to assess where you stand on the weight scale (so to speak). You can calculate your BMI by using the following formula:

$$\text{BMI} = \frac{\text{(your weight in pounds)}}{\text{(height in inches) (height in inches)}} \times 703$$

To use the formula, take your height in inches and multiply that number by itself (square the number). Then divide the result into your weight in pounds. Multiply the resulting number by 703 to obtain your BMI. For example, a person who weighs 220 pounds and is 6 feet 3 inches tall has a BMI of 27.5.

$$\frac{\text{(220 pounds)}}{\text{(75 inches) (75 inches)}} \times 703 = 27.5$$

Now, compare your BMI to the following scale:

Underweight	less than 18.5
Normal weight	18.5 to 24.9
Overweight	25 to 29.9
Obesity	30 or greater

If your BMI is greater than 25, you should be concerned. If it is greater than 30, your weight may be a serious health risk. (There are two exceptions: The BMI may overestimate body fat if you have a muscular build, and it may underestimate body fat in older persons who have lost muscle mass.) Losing weight and keeping it off can be very challenging. However, if you're overweight, lowering your BMI is well worth the effort. In the long run, it could save your life.

substance called *neuropeptide Y (NPY)*. If NPY is present in large amounts, an animal will eat until it cannot hold another bite (Williams et al., 2004). Incidentally, the hypothalamus also responds to a chemical in marijuana, which can produce intense hunger (the "munchies") (Di Marzo et al., 2001).

In addition to knowing when to start eating, and when meals are over, your brain also controls your weight over long periods of time (see "Your Brain's 'Fat Point'").

The substances we have reviewed are only some of the chemical signals that start and stop eating (Geary, 2004; Turenius et al., 2009). Others continue to be discovered. In time, they may make it possible to artificially control hunger. If so, better treatments for extreme obesity and self-starvation could follow (Batterham et al., 2003).

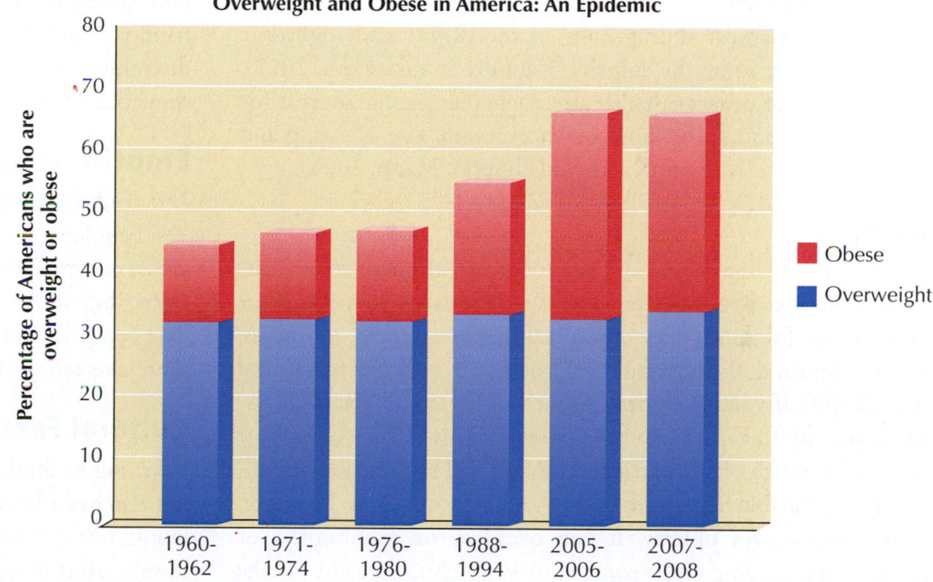

● **Figure 10.7** A near epidemic of obesity has occurred in the United States during the last 20 years, with over 65 percent of all Americans now classified as overweight or obese. (Adapted from Centers for Disease Control, 2008; Flegal et al., 2010.)

External Factors in Hunger and Obesity

As we have seen, "hunger" is affected by more than just the "push" of our biological needs for food. In fact, if internal needs alone controlled eating, many fewer people would overeat (Stroebe, Papies, & Aarts, 2008). Nevertheless, in 2006, roughly 65 percent of adults in the United States were overweight and more than one third were obese (extremely overweight) (Centers for Disease Control, 2008; Flegal et al., 2010; ● Figure 10.7). (See "What's Your BMI?") Childhood obesity has also shown a dramatic rise. As a result, obesity is overtaking smoking as a cause of needless deaths (Freedman, 2011). Let's consider some external influences on hunger and their role in obesity, a major health risk and, for many, a source of social stigma and low self-esteem.

Set point The proportion of body fat that tends to be maintained by changes in hunger and eating.

AP Photo/Haraz N. Ghanbari

Childhood obesity has reached epidemic proportions in the United States, having tripled in prevalence since 1980 (Ogden et al., 2010). In 2010, First Lady Michelle Obama launched "Let's Move," her national program to confront this problem head on.

External Eating Cues

Most of us are sensitive to the "pull" of *external eating cues,* signs and signals linked with food. For example, do you tend to eat more when food is highly visible and easy to get? In cultures like ours, in which food is plentiful, eating cues add greatly to the risk of overeating (Casey et al., 2008). Many college freshmen gain weight rapidly during their first 3 months on campus (the famous "Frosh 15"). All-you-can-eat dining halls in the dorms and nighttime snacking appear to be the culprits (Kapinos & Yakusheva, 2011). The presence of others can also affect whether people overeat (or undereat), depending on how much everyone else is eating and how important it is to impress them (Pliner & Mann, 2004).

Taste

The availability of a variety of tasty foods can also lead to overeating and obesity in societies in which such foods are plentiful. Normally, tastes for foods vary considerably. For example, if you are well fed, leptin dulls the tongue's sensitivity to sweet tastes (Kawai et al., 2000). If you have noticed that you lose your "sweet tooth" when you are full, you may have observed this effect. Actually, if you eat too much of any particular food, it will become less appealing. This probably helps us maintain variety in our diets. However, it also encourages obesity. If you overdose on hamburgers or French fries, moving on to some cookies or chocolate cheesecake certainly won't do your body much good (Pinel, Assanand, & Lehman, 2000).

It is easy to acquire a **taste aversion**, or active dislike, for a particular food. This can happen if a food causes sickness or if it is merely associated with nausea (Chance, 2009). A friend of one of your authors once became ill after eating a cheese Danish (well, actually, *several*) and has never again been able to come face to face with this delightful pastry.

If you like animals, you will be interested in an imaginative approach to an age-old problem. In many rural areas, predators are poisoned, trapped, or shot by ranchers. These practices have nearly wiped out the timber wolf, and in some areas the coyote faces a similar end. How might the coyote be saved without a costly loss of livestock?

In a classic experiment, coyotes were given lamb tainted with lithium chloride. Coyotes who took the bait became nauseated and vomited. After one or two such treatments, they developed **bait shyness**—a lasting distaste for the tainted food (Gustavson & Garcia, 1974; Nakajima & Nagaishi, 2005). If applied consistently, taste aversion conditioning might solve many predator–livestock problems.

BRIDGES

Bait shyness is similar to human aversion conditioning, which is used to help people control bad habits, such as smoking, drinking, or nail biting. **See Chapter 15, pages 521–522, to explore this connection.**

If getting sick occurs long after eating, how does it become associated with a particular food? A good question. Taste aversions are a type of classical conditioning. As stated in Chapter 6, a long delay between the conditioned stimulus (CS) and the unconditioned stimulus (US) usually prevents conditioning. However, psychologists theorize that we have a **biological preparedness** to associate an upset stomach with foods eaten earlier. Such learning usually protects us from eating unhealthy foods.

Taste aversions may also help people avoid severe nutritional imbalances. For example, if you go on a fad diet and eat only grapefruit, you will eventually begin to feel ill. In time, associating your discomfort with grapefruit may create an aversion to it and restore some balance to your diet.

Emotional Eating

Is it true that people also overeat when they are emotionally upset? Yes. People with weight problems are prone to overeat when they are anxious, angry, or sad (Macht & Simons, 2011). Furthermore, obese individuals are often unhappy in our fat-conscious culture. The result is overeating that leads to emotional distress and still more overeating (Davis & Carter, 2009).

Cultural Factors

Learning to think of some foods as desirable and others as revolting also has a large impact on what we eat. In North America, we would never consider eating the eyes out of the steamed head of a monkey, but in some parts of the world they are considered a delicacy. By the same token, vegans and vegetarians think it is barbaric to eat any kind of meat. In short, cultural values greatly affect the *incentive value* of foods.

Dieting

A diet is not just a way to lose weight. Your current diet is defined by the types and amounts of food you regularly eat. Some diets actually encourage overeating. For instance, placing animals on a "supermarket" diet leads to gross obesity. In one classic experiment, rats were given meals of chocolate chip cookies, salami, cheese, bananas, marshmallows, milk chocolate, peanut butter, and fat. These pampered rodents overate, gaining almost three times as much weight as rats that ate only laboratory chow (Sclafani & Springer, 1976). (Rat chow is a dry mixture of several bland grains. If you were a rat, you'd probably eat more cookies than rat chow, too.)

People are also sensitive to dietary content. In general, *sweetness*, high *fat content*, and *variety* tend to encourage overeating (Lucas & Sclafani, 1990). Unfortunately, North American culture provides the worst kinds of foods for people who suffer from obesity. For example, restaurant and fast food tends to be higher in fat and calories than meals made at home (Kessler, 2009). "Supersized" meals are another problem. Food portions at restaurants in the United States are 25 percent larger, or more, than they are in France. Far fewer people are obese in France, most likely because they simply eat less. The French also take longer to eat a meal, which discourages overeating (Rozin et al., 2003).

An added problem faced by people who want to control their weight concerns "yo-yo" dieting.

Pascal Le Segretain/Getty Images

Anorexia nervosa is far more dangerous than many people realize. This haunting Italian anti-anorexia poster shows 68-pound model Isabelle Caro, who suffered from anorexia for years up until her death in 2010 at age 28. Many celebrities have struggled with eating disorders, including Karen Carpenter (who died of starvation-induced heart failure), Paula Abdul, Kirstie Alley, Fiona Apple, Victoria Beckham (Posh Spice), Princess Diana, Tracey Gold, Janet Jackson, and Mary-Kate Olsen.

The Paradox of Yo-Yo Dieting

If dieting works, why are hundreds of "new" diets published each year? The answer is that although dieters do lose weight, most regain it soon after they stop dieting. In fact, many people end up weighing even more than before (Freedman, 2011). Why should this be so? Dieting (starving) slows the body's rate of metabolism (the rate at which energy is used up). In effect, a dieter's body becomes highly efficient at *conserving* calories and storing them as fat (Pinel, Assanand, & Lehman, 2000).

Apparently, evolution prepared us to save energy when food is scarce and to stock up on fat when food is plentiful. Briefly starving yourself, therefore, may have little lasting effect on weight. "Yo-yo dieting," or repeatedly losing and gaining weight, is especially dangerous. Frequent changes in weight can dramatically slow the body's *metabolic rate*. As noted earlier, this may raise the body's set point for fat and makes it harder to lose weight each time a person diets and easier to regain weight when the diet ends. Frequent weight changes also increase the risk for heart disease and premature death (Wang & Brownell, 2005). To avoid bouncing between feast and famine requires a permanent change in eating habits and exercise.

To summarize, eating and overeating are related to internal and external influences, diet, emotions, genetics, exercise, and many other factors. People become obese in different ways and for different reasons. We live in a culture that provides inexpensive, good-tasting food everywhere, and have a brain that evolved to say "Eat whenever food is available." Nevertheless, many people have learned to take control of eating by applying psychological principles (see "Behavioral Dieting").

Jason Merritt/Film Magic/Getty Images

Jon Kopalof/Film Magic/Getty Images

Singer Jennifer Hudson has been a life-long dieter who tried many different diets and experienced weight swings. As a spokeswoman for a national weight-loss program, Jennifer lost about 80 pounds. Will she maintain her weight loss over time?

Eating Disorders

Under the sheets of her hospital bed, Krystal looks like a skeleton. Victims of anorexia, who are mostly adolescent females, suffer devastating weight losses from severe, self-inflicted dieting (Cooper, 2005). If she cannot overcome her **anorexia nervosa** (AN-uh-REK-see-yah ner-VOH-sah: self-starvation), Krystal may die of malnutrition.

Taste aversion An active dislike for a particular food.

Bait shyness An unwillingness or hesitation on the part of animals to eat a particular food.

Biological preparedness (to learn) Organisms are more easily able to learn some associations (e.g., food and illness) than others (e.g., flashing light and illness). Evolution then places biological limits on what an animal or person can easily learn.

Anorexia nervosa Active self-starvation or a sustained loss of appetite that has psychological origins.

Discovering Psychology Behavioral Dieting

As we have noted, dieting is usually followed by rapid weight gain. If you really want to lose weight, you must overhaul your eating and exercise habits, an approach called **behavioral dieting** (Freedman, 2011; Roizen & Oz, 2006). Here are some helpful behavioral techniques:

1. **Get yourself committed to weight loss.** Involve other people in your efforts. Programs such as Overeaters Anonymous or Take Off Pounds Sensibly can be a good source of social support (Mitchell et al., 2010).
2. **Exercise.** No diet can succeed for long without an increase in exercise. To lose weight, you must use more calories than you take in. Burning just 200 extra calories a day can help prevent rebound weight gains. Add activity to your routine in every way you can think of. Stop saving steps and riding elevators. Buy a *step counter* to track the number of steps you take every day. Walking 10,000 steps per day will burn between 2,000 and 3,500 calories a week (depending on your weight). The more frequently and vigorously you exercise, the more weight you will lose (Jeffery & Wing, 2001).
3. **Learn your eating habits by observing yourself and keeping a "diet diary."** Begin by making a complete, 2-week record of when and where you eat, what you eat, and the feelings and events that occur just before and after eating. Is a roommate, relative, or spouse encouraging you to overeat? What are your most "dangerous" times and places for overeating?
4. **Learn to weaken your personal eating cues.** When you have learned when and where you do most of your eating, avoid these situations. Try to restrict your eating to one room, and do not read, watch TV, study, or talk on the phone while eating. Require yourself to interrupt what you are doing in order to eat.
5. **Count calories, but don't starve yourself.** To lose weight, you must eat less, and calories allow you to keep a record of your food intake. If you have trouble eating less every day, try dieting 4 days a week. People who diet intensely every other day lose as much as those who diet moderately every day (Viegener et al., 1990).
6. **Develop techniques to control the act of eating.** Whenever you can, check for nutritional information and buy groceries and meals lower in calories and fats. Begin to take smaller portions. Carry to the table only what you plan to eat. Put all other food away before leaving the kitchen. Eat slowly, sip water between bites of food, leave food on your plate, and stop eating before you are completely full. Be especially wary of the extra large servings at fast-food restaurants. Saying "supersize me" too often can, indeed, leave you supersized (Murray, 2001).
7. **Avoid snacks.** It is generally better to eat more small meals a day than fewer large ones because more calories are burned (Roizen & Oz, 2006). (No, we don't mean high-calorie snacks *in addition to* meals.) If you have an impulse to snack, set a timer for 20 minutes and see if you are still hungry then. Delay the impulse to snack several times if possible. Dull your appetite by filling up on raw carrots, bouillon, water, coffee, or tea.
8. **Chart your daily progress.** Record your weight, the number of calories eaten, and whether you met your daily goal. Set realistic goals by cutting down calories gradually. Losing about a pound per week is realistic, but remember, you are changing habits, not just dieting. Diets don't work!
9. **Set a "threshold" for weight control.** Maintaining weight loss can be even more challenging than losing weight. It is easier to maintain weight losses if you set a regain limit of 3 pounds or less. In other words, if you gain more than 2 or 3 pounds, you immediately begin to make corrections in your eating habits and amount of exercise (Kessler, 2009).

Be patient. It takes years to develop eating habits. You can expect it to take at least several months to change them. If you are unsuccessful at losing weight with these techniques, you might find it helpful to seek the aid of a psychologist familiar with behavioral weight-loss techniques.

Do anorexics lose their appetite? Although a compulsive attempt to lose weight causes them to not seek or desire food, they usually still feel physical hunger. Often, anorexia starts with "normal" dieting that slowly begins to dominate the person's life. In time, anorexics suffer debilitating health problems. From 5 to 8 percent (more than 1 in 20) die of malnutrition (Polivy & Herman, 2002). ■ Table 10.1 lists the symptoms of anorexia nervosa.

Bulimia nervosa (bue-LIHM-ee-yah) is a second major eating disorder (Bardone-Cone et al., 2008; Koda & Sugawara, 2009). Bulimic persons gorge on food, then vomit or take laxatives to avoid gaining weight (see ■ Table 10.1). As with anorexia, most victims of

TABLE 10.1 Recognizing Eating Disorders

Anorexia Nervosa
• Refusal to maintain body weight in normal range. Body weight below 85 percent of normal for one's height and age.
• Intense fear of becoming fat or gaining weight, even though underweight.
• Disturbance in one's body image or perceived weight. Self-evaluation is unduly influenced by body weight. Denial of seriousness of abnormally low body weight.
• Absence of menstrual periods (may be removed from DSM-5).
• Purging behavior (vomiting or misuse of laxatives or diuretics).
Bulimia Nervosa
• Recurring binge eating. Eating within an hour or two an amount of food that is much larger than most people would consume. Feeling a lack of control over eating.
• Purging behavior (vomiting or misuse of laxatives or diuretics). Excessive exercise to prevent weight gain. Fasting to prevent weight gain.
• Self-evaluation is unduly influenced by body weight.

Adapted from *American Psychiatric Association*, 2000, 2010.

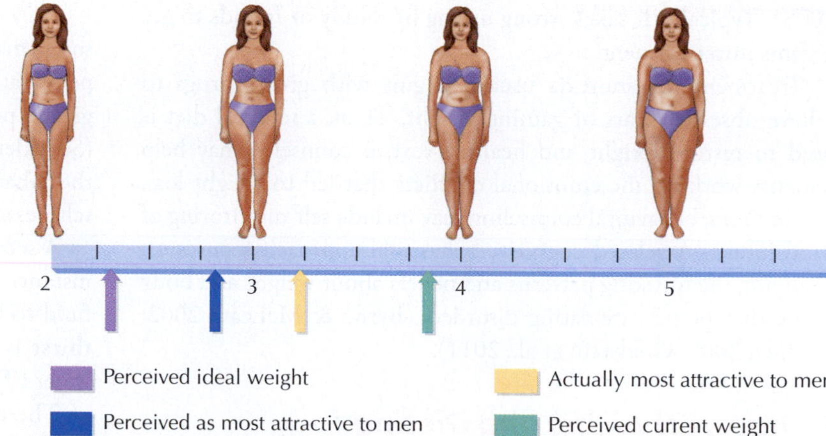

● **Figure 10.8** Women with abnormal eating habits were asked to rate their body shape on a scale similar to the one you see here. As a group, they chose ideal figures much thinner than what they thought their current weights were. (Most women say they want to be thinner than they currently are, but to a lesser degree than women with eating problems.) Notice that the women with eating problems chose an ideal weight that was even thinner than what they thought men prefer. This is not typical of most women. In this classic study, only women with eating problems wanted to be thinner than what they thought men find attractive (Zellner, Harner, & Adler, 1989).

bulimia are girls or women. Approximately 5 percent of college women are bulimic, and as many as 60 percent have milder eating problems. Bingeing and purging can seriously damage health. Typical risks include sore throat, hair loss, muscle spasms, kidney damage, dehydration, tooth erosion, swollen salivary glands, menstrual irregularities, loss of sex drive, and even heart attack.

Men and Eating Disorders

Eating disorders are on the rise among men. More and more men are experiencing *muscle dysmorphia*, excessive worry about not being muscular enough (Mosley, 2009). Currently, one third of men say they want less body fat and another third want more muscles (McCabe & Ricciardelli, 2004). As a result, many men are altering what they eat and exercising excessively. Some are going too far: About 10 percent of anorexics and 25 percent of bulimics are now males (Weltzin et al., 2005).

Causes

What causes anorexia and bulimia? People who suffer from eating disorders are extremely dissatisfied with their bodies (Crisp et al., 2006). Usually, they have distorted views of themselves, exaggerated fears of becoming fat, and low self-esteem. Many overestimate their body size by 25 percent or more. As a result, they think they are disgustingly "fat" when they are actually wasting away (● Figure 10.8) (Polivy & Herman, 2002).

Many of these problems are related to the idealized body images presented in the media (Levine & Harrison, 2004). Some websites even go so far as to celebrate anorexia and bulimia (referred to by "fans" as "Ana" and "Mia") (Borzekowski et al., 2010; Tierney, 2008). Girls who spend a lot of time reading fashion magazines or visiting these websites are more likely to have distorted body images and unrealistic ideas about how they compare with others (Martinez-Gonzalez et al., 2003).

The popularity of fitness, exercise, and sports has also contributed to eating disorders. Today, more people are changing their diets in search of a lean, muscular look. People engaged in sports that require low body fat or extreme weight loss (such as wrestling, gymnastics, pole vaulting, high jumping, and even cycling) are particularly likely to develop eating disorders (Weltzin et al., 2005).

People with eating disorders appear to be trying to gain some measure of control. Anorexic teen girls are usually described as "perfect" daughters—helpful, considerate, conforming, and obedient. They seem to be rewarded by seeking perfect control in their lives by being perfectly slim (Castro et al., 2004; Keating, 2010). People suffering from bulimia are also concerned with control (Bardone-Cone et al., 2008). Typically, they are obsessed with thoughts of weight, food, eating, and ridding themselves of food. As a result, they feel guilt, shame, self-contempt, and anxiety. Vomiting reduces their anxiety, which makes purging highly reinforcing (Powell & Thelen, 1996).

Treatment

Most people suffering from eating disorders will not seek help on their own. This is especially true for men, because eating disorders are still widely perceived to be a female problem (Weltzin et al.,

Behavioral dieting Weight reduction based on changing exercise and eating habits, rather than temporary self-starvation.

Bulimia nervosa Excessive eating (gorging) usually followed by self-induced vomiting and/or taking laxatives.

2005). Typically, it takes strong urging by family or friends to get victims into treatment.

Treatment for anorexia usually begins with giving drugs to relieve obsessive fears of gaining weight. Then, a medical diet is used to restore weight and health. Next, a counselor may help patients work on the emotional conflicts that led to weight loss. For bulimia, behavioral counseling may include self-monitoring of food intake. A related cognitive-behavioral approach focuses on changing the thinking patterns and beliefs about weight and body shape that perpetuate eating disorders (Byrne & McLean, 2002; Cooper, 2005; Goldstein et al., 2011).

Culture, Ethnicity, and Dieting

Women with eating disorders are not alone in having body image problems. In Western cultures, many women learn to see themselves as "objects" that are evaluated by others. As a result, they try to shape their bodies to the cultural ideal of slimness through dieting (Fredrickson et al., 1998).

Just looking at a fashion magazine tends to leave women less satisfied with their weight and anxious to be thinner (Simpson, 2002). However, women from some cultural backgrounds appear to be less susceptible to the glorification of slimness. For example, Asian American college students are only half as likely to diet as other college women are (Tsai, Hoerr, & Song, 1998). Within the African American and Pacific-Islander communities, there is a general preference for a fuller and shapelier figure. In these groups, a larger body size is associated with high social status, health, and beauty (Flynn & Fitzgibbon, 1998; Ofosu, Lafreniere, & Senn, 1998). Clearly, what constitutes an attractive body style is a matter of opinion.

Biological Motives Revisited—Thirst, Sex, and Pain

Gateway Question 10.3: *What kinds of biological motives are thirst, pain avoidance, and the sex drive?*

Most biological motives work in ways that are similar to hunger. For example, thirst is only partially controlled by dryness of the mouth. If you were to take a drug that made your mouth constantly wet, or dry, your water intake would remain normal. Like hunger, thirst is regulated by separate *thirst* and *thirst satiety* systems in the hypothalamus. Also like hunger, thirst is strongly affected by learning and cultural values.

Thirst

You may not have noticed, but there are actually two kinds of thirst (Thornton, 2010). **Extracellular thirst** occurs when water is lost from the fluids surrounding the cells of your body. Bleeding, vomiting, diarrhea, sweating, and drinking alcohol cause this type of thirst (Franken, 2007). When a person loses both water and minerals in any of these ways—especially by perspiration—a slightly salty liquid may be more satisfying than plain water.

Why would a thirsty person want to drink salty water? The reason is that before the body can retain water, minerals lost through perspiration (mainly salt) must be replaced. In lab tests, animals greatly prefer saltwater after salt levels in their bodies are lowered (Strickler & Verbalis, 1988). Similarly, some nomadic peoples of the Sahara Desert prize blood as a beverage, probably because of its saltiness. (Maybe they should try Gatorade?)

A second type of thirst occurs when you eat a salty meal. In this instance, your body does not lose fluid. Instead, excess salt causes fluid to be drawn out of cells. As the cells "shrink," **intracellular thirst** is triggered. Thirst of this type is best quenched by plain water (Thornton, 2010).

The drives for food, water, air, sleep, and elimination are all similar in that they are generated by a combination of activities in the body and the brain, and they are influenced by various external factors. However, the drive to avoid pain and the sex drive are more unusual.

Pain

How is the drive to avoid pain different? Hunger, thirst, and sleepiness come and go in a fairly regular cycle each day. Pain avoidance, by contrast, is an **episodic** (ep-ih-SOD-ik) **drive**. That is, it occurs in distinct episodes when bodily damage takes place or is about to occur. Most drives prompt us to actively seek a desired goal (food, drink, warmth, and so forth). Pain prompts us to *avoid* or *eliminate* sources of discomfort.

Some people feel they must be "tough" and not show any distress. Others complain loudly at the smallest ache or pain. The first attitude raises pain tolerance, and the second lowers it. As this suggests, the drive to avoid pain is partly learned. That's why members of some societies endure cutting, burning, whipping, tattooing, and piercing of the skin that would agonize most people (Chang, 2009) (but apparently not devotees of piercing and "body art"). In general, we learn how to react to pain by observing family members, friends, and other role models (McMahon & Koltzenburg, 2005).

Michael Coyne/Getty Images

Tolerance for pain and the strength of a person's motivation to avoid discomfort are greatly affected by cultural practices and beliefs, such as this penitent at a Hindu ceremony.

The Sex Drive

Sex is unlike other biological motives because sex (contrary to anything your personal experience might suggest) is not necessary for *individual* survival. It is necessary, of course, for *group* survival.

The term **sex drive** refers to the strength of one's motivation to engage in sexual behavior. In lower animals, the sex drive is directly related to hormones. Female mammals (other than humans) are interested in mating only when their fertility cycles are in the stage of **estrus**, or "heat." Estrus is caused by a release of **estrogen** (a female sex hormone) into the bloodstream. Hormones are important in males as well. In most animals, castration will abolish the sex drive. But, in contrast to females, the normal male animal is almost always ready to mate. His sex drive is aroused primarily by the behavior and scent of a receptive female. Therefore, in many species, mating is closely tied to female fertility cycles.

How much do hormones affect human sex drives? Hormones affect the human sex drive, but not as directly as in animals (Crooks & Baur, 2011). The sex drive in men is related to the amount of **androgens** (male hormones such as testosterone) provided by the testes. When the supply of androgens dramatically increases at puberty, so does the male sex drive. Likewise, the sex drive in women is related to their estrogen levels (Hyde & DeLamater, 2011). However, "male" hormones also affect the female sex drive. In addition to estrogen, a woman's body produces small amounts of androgens. When their androgen levels increase, many women experience a corresponding increase in sex drive (Van Goozen et al., 1995). Testosterone levels decline with age, and various medical problems can lower sexual desire. In some instances, taking testosterone supplements can restore the sex drive in both men and women (Crooks & Baur, 2011).

Human sexual behavior and attitudes are discussed in detail in Chapter 11. For now it is enough to note that the sex drive is largely **non-homeostatic** (relatively independent of bodily need states). In humans, the sex drive can be aroused at virtually any time by almost anything. Therefore, it shows no clear relationship to deprivation (the amount of time since the drive was last satisfied). Certainly, an increase in desire may occur as time passes. But recent sexual activity does not prevent sexual desire from occurring again. Notice, too, that people may seek to arouse the sex drive as well as to reduce it. This unusual quality makes the sex drive capable of motivating a wide range of behaviors. It also explains why sex is used to sell almost everything imaginable.

The non-homeostatic quality of the sex drive can be shown in this way: A male animal is allowed to copulate until it seems to have no further interest in sexual behavior. Then, a new sexual partner is provided. Immediately, the animal resumes sexual activity. This pattern is called the *Coolidge effect* after former U.S. President Calvin Coolidge. What, you might ask, does Calvin Coolidge have to do with the sex drive? The answer is found in the following story.

While touring an experimental farm, Coolidge's wife reportedly asked if a rooster mated just once a day. "No ma'am," she was told, "he mates dozens of times each day." "Tell that to the president," she said, with a faraway look in her eyes. When President Coolidge reached the same part of the tour, his wife's message was given to him. His reaction was to ask if the dozens of matings were with the same hen. No, he was told, different hens were involved. "Tell *that* to Mrs. Coolidge," the president is said to have replied.

Knowledge Builder: Hunger, Thirst, Pain, and Sex

RECITE

1. The hunger satiety system in the hypothalamus signals the body to start eating when it receives signals from the liver or detects changes in blood sugar. T or F?
2. Maintaining your body's set point for fat is closely linked with the amount of __________ in the bloodstream.
   a. hypothalamic factor-1 *b.* ventromedial peptide-1 *c.* NPY *d.* leptin
3. A cancer patient has little appetite for food several weeks after the nausea caused by chemotherapy has ended. Her loss of appetite is probably best explained by
   a. increased NPY in the brain *b.* a conditioned taste aversion *c.* the aftereffects of yo-yo dieting *d.* a loss of extracellular hunger
4. People who diet frequently tend to benefit from practice: They lose weight more quickly each time they diet. T or F?
5. In addition to changing eating habits, a key element of behavioral dieting is
   a. exercise *b.* well-timed snacking *c.* better eating cues *d.* commitment to "starving" every day
6. Bingeing and purging are most characteristic of people who have
   a. taste aversions *b.* anorexia *c.* bulimia *d.* strong sensitivity to external eating cues
7. Thirst may be either intracellular or ______________________.
8. Pain avoidance is a(n) ______________________ drive.
9. Sexual behavior in animals is largely controlled by estrogen levels in the female and the occurrence of estrus in the male. T or F?

REFLECT

Think Critically

10. Kim, who is overweight, is highly sensitive to external eating cues. How might her wristwatch contribute to her overeating?

Self-Reflect

Think of the last meal you ate. What caused you to feel hungry? What internal signals told your body to stop eating? How sensitive are you to external eating cues? How were you influenced by portion size? Have you developed any taste aversions?

Extracellular thirst Thirst caused by a reduction in the volume of fluids found between body cells.
Intracellular thirst Thirst triggered when fluid is drawn out of cells due to an increased concentration of salts and minerals outside the cell.
Episodic drive A drive that occurs in distinct episodes.
Sex drive The strength of one's motivation to engage in sexual behavior.
Estrus Changes in the sexual drives of animals that create a desire for mating; particularly used to refer to females in heat.
Estrogen Any of a number of female sex hormones.
Androgen Any of a number of male sex hormones, especially testosterone.
Non-homeostatic drive A drive that is relatively independent of physical deprivation cycles or bodily need states.

Courtesy of Harry F. Harlow.

● Figure 10.9 Monkeys happily open locks that are placed in their cage. Because no reward is given for this activity, it provides evidence for the existence of stimulus needs.

A friend of yours seems to be engaging in yo-yo dieting. Can you explain to her or him why such dieting is ineffective? Can you summarize how behavioral dieting is done?

If you wanted to provoke extracellular thirst in yourself, what would you do? How could you make intracellular thirst occur?

Answers: 1. F **2.** *d* **3.** *b* **4.** F **5.** *a* **6.** *c* **7.** extracellular **8.** episodic **9.** F **10.** The time of day can influence eating, especially for externally cued eaters, who tend to get hungry at mealtimes, irrespective of their internal needs for food.

Stimulus Motives—Skydiving, Horror Movies, and the Fun Zone

Gateway Question 10.4: *How does arousal relate to motivation?*

Are you full of energy right now? Or are you tired? Clearly, the level of arousal you are experiencing is closely linked with your motivation. Are there ideal levels of arousal for different people and different activities? Let's find out.

Most people enjoy a steady "diet" of new movies, novels, music, fashions, games, news, websites, and adventures. Yet *stimulus motives*, as we noted earlier, which reflect needs for information, exploration, manipulation, and sensory input, go beyond mere entertainment. Stimulus motives also help us survive. As we scan our surroundings, we constantly identify sources of food, danger, shelter, and other key details. The drive for stimulation is already present during infancy. By the time a child can walk, there are few things in the home that have not been tasted, touched, viewed, handled, or, in the case of toys, destroyed!

Stimulus motives are readily apparent in animals as well as humans. For example, monkeys will quickly learn to solve a mechanical puzzle made up of interlocking metal pins, hooks, and latches (Butler, 1954) (● Figure 10.9). No food treats or other external rewards are needed to get them to explore and manipulate their surroundings. The monkeys seem to work for the sheer fun of it.

Arousal Theory

Are stimulus motives homeostatic? Yes. According to **arousal theory**, we try to keep arousal at an optimal level (Franken, 2007; Hancock & Ganey, 2003). In other words, when your level of arousal is too low or too high, you will seek ways to raise or lower it.

What do you mean by arousal? Arousal refers to activation of the body and nervous system. Arousal is zero at death, low during sleep, moderate during normal daily activities, and high at times of excitement, emotion, or panic. Arousal theory assumes that we become uncomfortable when arousal is too low ("I'm bored") or when it is too high, as in fear, anxiety, or panic ("The dentist will see you now"). Most adults vary music, parties, sports, conversation, sleep, surfing the Web, and the like, to keep arousal at moderate levels. The right mix of activities prevents boredom *and* overstimulation (Csikszentmihalyi, Abuhamdeh, & Nakamura, 2005).

Sensation Seekers

Do people vary in their needs for stimulation? Arousal theory also suggests that people learn to seek particular levels of arousal (Lynne-Landsman et al., 2011). Where would you prefer to go on your next summer vacation? Your back yard? How about a week with your best friends at a cottage on a nearby lake? Or a shopping and museum trip to New York City? Better yet, how about cage diving with great white sharks in South Africa? If the shark adventure attracts you, you are probably high in sensation seeking and would be interested in a vacation that includes activities like bungee-jumping, scuba diving, skiing, skydiving, and white water rafting (Pizam et al., 2004).

Sensation seeking is a trait of people who prefer high levels of stimulation (Gray & Wilson, 2007). Whether you are high or low in sensation seeking is probably based on how your body responds to new, unusual, or intense stimulation (Zuckerman, 2002). People

© Jeffrey L. Rotman/Corbis

Sensation seeking is a trait of people who prefer high levels of stimulation.

● Figure 10.10
(a) The general relationship between arousal and efficiency can be described by an inverted U curve. The optimal level of arousal or motivation is higher for a simple task *(b)* than for a complex task *(c)*. Copyright © 2012 Wadsworth, Cengage Learning, Inc.

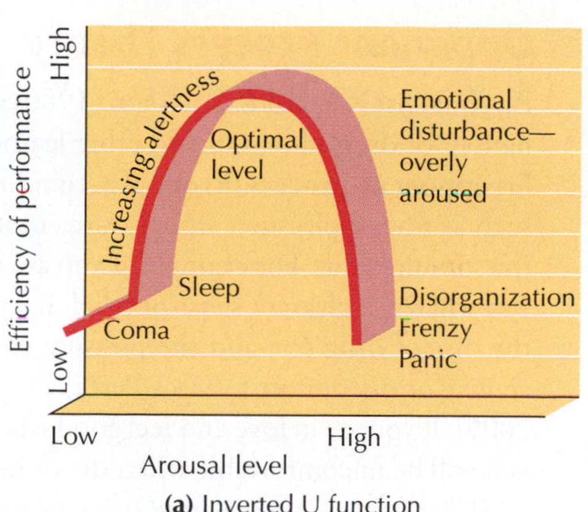

(a) Inverted U function

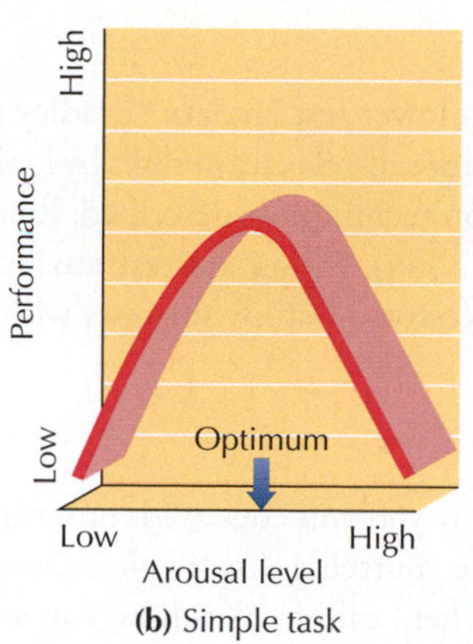

(b) Simple task

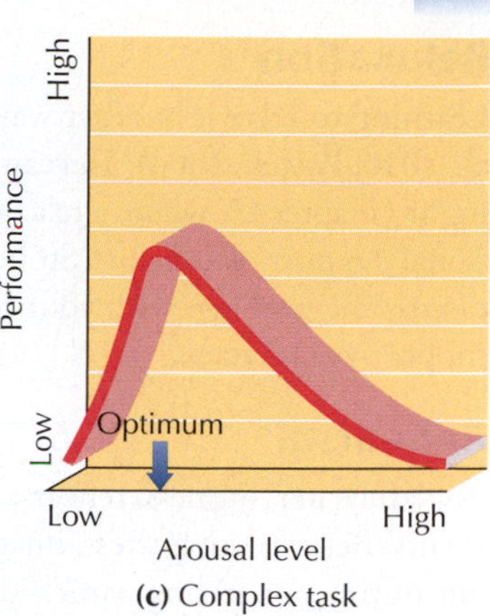

(c) Complex task

high in sensation seeking tend to be bold and independent, and value change. They also report more sexual partners, are more likely to smoke, and prefer spicy, sour, and crunchy foods over bland foods. Low sensation seekers are orderly, nurturant, and giving, and enjoy the company of others.

Exciting lives aside, there is a dark side to sensation seeking (Dunlop & Romer, 2010). High sensation seekers are more likely to engage in high-risk behaviors such as substance abuse and casual unprotected sex (Gullette & Lyons, 2005; Horvath et al., 2004).

Levels of Arousal

Is there an ideal level of arousal for peak performance? If we set aside individual differences, most people perform best when their arousal level is *moderate*. Let's say that you have to take an essay exam. If you are feeling sleepy or lazy (arousal level too low), your performance will suffer. If you are in a state of anxiety or panic about the test (arousal level too high), you will also perform below par. Thus, the relationship between arousal and performance forms an *inverted U function* (a curve in the shape of an upside-down U) (● Figure 10.10) (Hancock & Ganey, 2003).

The inverted U tells us that at very low levels of arousal, you're not sufficiently energized to perform well. Performance will improve as your arousal level increases, up to the middle of the curve. Then, it begins to drop off as you become emotional, frenzied, or disorganized. For example, imagine trying to start a car stalled on a railroad track, with a speeding train bearing down on you. That's what the high-arousal end of the curve feels like.

Is performance always best at moderate levels of arousal? No, the ideal level of arousal depends on the complexity of a task. If a task is relatively simple, it is best for arousal to be high. When a task is more complex, your best performance will occur at lower levels of arousal. This relationship is called the **Yerkes-Dodson law** (see ● Figure 10.10). It applies to a wide variety of tasks and to measures of motivation other than arousal.

For example, at a track meet, it is almost impossible for sprinters to get too aroused for a race. The task is direct and simple: Run as fast as you can for a short distance. On the other hand, a golfer making a tournament-deciding putt faces a more sensitive and complex task. Excessive arousal is almost certain to hurt his or her performance. In school, most students have had experience with "test anxiety," a familiar example of how too much arousal can lower performance.

Coping with Test Anxiety

Then is it true that by learning to calm down, a person would do better on tests? Usually, but not always. To begin with, some arousal is healthy; it focuses us on the task at hand. It is only when arousal interferes with performance that we refer to anxiety. **Test anxiety** is a mixture of *heightened physiological arousal* (nervousness, sweating, pounding heart) and *excessive worry*. This combination—arousal plus worry—tends to distract students with a rush of upsetting thoughts and feelings (Eysenck et al., 2007; Stipek, 2002).

Also, studies show that students are typically most anxious when they don't know the material (Cassady, 2004). Not studying while remaining calm simply means you will calmly fail the test. Here are some suggestions for coping with test anxiety.

Preparation

Hard work is the most direct antidote for test anxiety. Many test-anxious students simply study too little, too late. That's why improving your study skills is a good way to reduce test anxiety (Cassady, 2004).

> **BRIDGES**
> One of the best ways to avoid test anxiety is to improve your study skills. **If test anxiety is a problem for you, it would be wise to return to the Introduction in this book and review the learning and test-taking skills described there.**

The best solution is to *overprepare* by studying long before the "big day." Well-prepared students score higher, worry less, and are less likely to panic (Kaplan, 2008; Santrock & Halonen, 2010).

Arousal theory Assumes that people prefer to maintain ideal, or comfortable, levels of arousal.

Yerkes-Dodson law A summary of the relationships among arousal, task complexity, and performance.

Test anxiety High levels of arousal and worry that seriously impair test performance.

Relaxation

Learning to relax is another way to lower test anxiety (Bradley et al., 2010; Powell, 2004). You can learn self-relaxation skills by looking at Chapter 13, where a relaxation technique is described. Emotional support also helps (Stöber, 2004). If you are test anxious, discuss the problem with your professors or study for tests with a supportive classmate.

Rehearsal

To reduce nervousness, rehearse how you will cope with upsetting events. Before taking a test, imagine yourself going blank, running out of time, or feeling panicked. Then, calmly plan how you will handle each situation—by keeping your attention on the task, by focusing on one question at a time, and so forth (Watson & Tharp, 2007).

Restructuring Thoughts

Another helpful strategy involves listing the upsetting thoughts you have during exams. Then you can learn to combat these worries with calming, rational replies (Jones & Petruzzi, 1995; Olpin & Hesson, 2010). (These are called *coping statements*; see Chapter 13 for more information.) Let's say you think, "I'm going to fail this test and everybody will think I'm stupid." A good reply to this upsetting thought would be to say, "If I prepare well and control my worries, I will probably pass the test. Even if I don't, it won't be the end of the world. My friends will still like me, and I can try to improve on the next test."

Students who cope well with exams usually try to do the best they can, even under difficult circumstances. Becoming a more confident test taker can actually increase your scores because it helps you remain calm. With practice, most people can learn to be less testy at test-taking time.

Learned Motives—The Pursuit of Excellence

Gateway Questions 10.5: *What are learned and social motives and why are they important?*

Many motives are acquired directly. It is easy enough to see that praise, money, success, pleasure, and similar reinforcers affect our goals and desires. But how do people learn to enjoy activities that are at first painful or frightening? Why do people climb rocks, jump out of airplanes, run marathons, take saunas, or swim in frozen lakes? For an answer, let's examine a related situation.

When a person first tries a drug such as heroin, he or she feels a "rush" of pleasure. However, as the drug wears off, discomfort and craving occurs. The easiest way to end the discomfort is to take another dose—as most drug users quickly learn. But in time, habituation takes place; the drug stops producing pleasure, although it will end discomfort. At the same time, the after effects of the drug grow more painful. At this point, the drug user has acquired a powerful new motive. In a vicious cycle, heroin relieves discomfort, but it guarantees that withdrawal will occur again in a few hours.

Opponent-Process Theory

Psychologist Richard L. Solomon (1980) offers an intriguing explanation for drug addiction and other learned motives. According to his **opponent-process theory**, if a stimulus causes a strong emotion, such as fear or pleasure, an opposite emotion tends to occur when the stimulus ends. For example, if you are in pain and the pain ends, you will feel a pleasant sense of relief. If a person feels pleasure, as in the case of drug use, and the pleasure ends, it will be followed by craving or discomfort (Vargas-Perez, Ting-A-Kee, & van der Kooy, 2009). If you are in love and feel good when you are with your lover, you will be uncomfortable when she or he is absent.

What happens if the stimulus is repeated? Solomon assumes that when a stimulus is repeated, our response to it habituates, or gets weaker. Like almost every first-timer, our intrepid extreme skydiver Henry (who we met in Chapter 1) was terrified during his first jump. But with repeated jumps, fear decreases, until finally the skydiver feels a "thrill" instead of terror (Roth et al., 1996). In contrast, emotional after effects get stronger with repetition. After a first jump, beginners feel a brief but exhilarating sense of relief. After many such experiences, seasoned skydivers, like Henry, can get a "rush" of euphoria that lasts for hours after a jump. With repetition, the pleasurable after effect gets stronger and the initial "cost" (pain or fear) gets weaker. The opponent-process theory thus explains how skydiving, rock climbing, ski jumping, and other hazardous pursuits become reinforcing. If you are a fan of horror movies, carnival rides, or bungee jumping, your motives may be based on the same effect. (Notice, too, the strong link between motivation and emotion in such examples. We will return to this idea later.)

Social Motives

Some of your friends are more interested than others in success, achievement, competition, money, possessions, status, love, approval, grades, dominance, power, or belonging to groups—all of which are *social motives* or goals. We acquire **social motives** in complex ways, through socialization and cultural conditioning (Deckers, 2010). The behavior of outstanding artists, scientists, athletes, educators, and leaders is best understood in terms of such learned needs, particularly the need for achievement.

The Need for Achievement

To many people, being "motivated" means, like Lady Gaga, being interested in achievement (Wigfield & Eccles, 2002). In a later chapter, we will investigate aggression, helping, affiliation, seeking approval, and other social motives. For now, let's focus on the **need for achievement (nAch)**, which is a desire to meet an internal standard of excellence (McClelland, 1961). People with a high need for achievement strive to do well any time they are evaluated (Steinmayr & Spinath, 2009).

Is that like the aggressive businessperson who strives for success? Not necessarily. Needs for achievement may lead to wealth and prestige, but people who are high achievers in art, music, science, or amateur sports may excel without seeking riches. Such people typically enjoy challenges and relish a chance to test their

Discovering Psychology: True Grit

So you want to be a success. To best achieve your goals, would it be better to be naturally talented or determined? (Yes, we know you would definitely prefer to have it *both* ways. So would we.) It probably will not surprise you to learn that, in general, drive and determination, not great natural talent, lead to exceptional success (Bloom, 1985; Duckworth et al., 2007).

How can this be? When people high in need for achievement (nAch) tackle a task, they do so with perseverance, passion, and self-confidence (Duckworth et al., 2007; Munroe-Chandler, Hall, & Fishburne, 2008). They tend to complete difficult tasks, they earn better grades, and they tend to excel in their occupations. College students high in nAch attribute success to their own ability, and failure to insufficient effort. Thus, high nAch students are more likely to renew their efforts when they perform poorly. When the going gets tough, high achievers get going.

How self-confident are you? Achieving elite performance may be reserved for the dedicated few. Nevertheless, like elite athletes, you may be able to improve your motivation by increasing your self-confidence (Hanton, Mellalieu, & Hall, 2004). It is easier to perform an activity or reach a goal with perseverance and passion when you believe you can be successful.

When you tackle an important task, how many of the items on the following list can you check off? To enhance self-confidence, you would be wise to do as many as possible (Druckman & Bjork, 1994; Munroe-Chandler, Hall, & Fishburne, 2008):

- Set goals that are specific and challenging but attainable.
- Visualize the steps you need to take to reach your goal.
- Advance in small steps.
- When you first acquire a skill, your goal should be to make progress in learning. Later, you can concentrate on improving your performance compared with other people.
- Get expert instruction that helps you master the skill.
- Find a skilled model (someone good at the skill) to emulate.
- Get support and encouragement from an observer.
- If you fail, regard it as a sign that you need to try harder, not that you lack ability.

Self-confidence affects motivation by influencing the challenges you will undertake, the effort you will make, and how long you will persist when things don't go well. You can be confident that self-confidence is worth cultivating.

The Williams sisters possess high achievement motivation. They have become professional tennis champions by playing with perseverance, passion, and self-confidence.

abilities (Puca & Schmalt, 1999). (See "True Grit" for more information about the characteristics of people high in achievement motivation.)

Power

The need for achievement differs from the **need for power**, which is a desire to have impact or control over others (McClelland, 1975; Wirth, Welsh, & Schultheiss, 2006). People with strong needs for power want their importance to be visible: They buy expensive possessions, wear prestigious clothes, and exploit relationships. In some ways the pursuit of power and financial success is the dark side of the American dream. People whose main goal in life is to make lots of money tend to be poorly adjusted and unhappy (Kasser & Ryan, 1993).

The Key to Success?

Psychologist Benjamin Bloom (1985) found that the first steps toward high achievement begin when parents expose their children to music, swimming, scientific ideas, and so forth, "just for fun." At first, many of the children had very ordinary skills. One Olympic

Opponent-process theory States that strong emotions tend to be followed by an opposite emotional state; also the strength of both emotional states changes over time.

Social motives Learned motives acquired as part of growing up in a particular society or culture.

Need for achievement (nAch) The desire to excel or meet some internalized standard of excellence.

Need for power The desire to have social impact and control over others.

swimmer, for instance, remembers repeatedly losing races as a 10-year-old. At some point, however, the children began to actively cultivate their abilities. Before long, parents noticed the child's rapid progress and found an expert instructor or coach. After more successes, the youngsters began "living" for their talent and practiced many hours daily. This continued for many years before they reached truly outstanding heights of achievement.

The upshot of Bloom's work is that talent is nurtured by dedication and hard work (Beck, 2004). It is most likely to blossom when parents actively support a child's special interest and emphasize doing one's best at all times. Studies of child prodigies and eminent adults also show that intensive practice and expert coaching are common ingredients of high achievement. Elite performance in music, sports, chess, the arts, and many other pursuits requires at least 10 years of dedicated practice (Ericsson & Charness, 1994; Ross, 2006). The old belief that "talent will surface" on its own is largely a myth.

Growth Needs
- Self-actualization as expressed through meta-needs: wholeness, perfection, completion, justice, richness, simplicity, aliveness, beauty, goodness, uniqueness, playfulness, truth, autonomy, meaningfulness

Self-actualization
Esteem and self-esteem
Love and belonging
Safety and security
Physiological needs: air, food, water, sleep, sex, etc.

Basic Needs
- Esteem and self-esteem
- Love and belonging
- Safety and security
- Physiological needs

Maslow's Hierarchy of Needs

● **Figure 10.11** Maslow believed that lower needs in the hierarchy are dominant. Basic needs must be satisfied before growth motives are fully expressed. Desires for self-actualization are reflected in various meta-needs (see text).

Motives in Perspective—A View from the Pyramid

Gateway Question 10.6: *Are some motives more basic than others?*

Are all motives equally important? Abraham Maslow proposed a **hierarchy of human needs**, in which some needs are more basic or powerful than others. (As you may recall from Chapter 1, Maslow called the full use of personal potential *self-actualization*.) Think about the needs that influence your own behavior. Which seem strongest? Which do you spend the most time and energy satisfying? Now look at Maslow's hierarchy (● Figure 10.11).

Note that biological needs are at the base of the pyramid. Because these needs must be met if we are to survive, they tend to be *prepotent*, or dominant over the higher needs. That's why, when you are really hungry, you can think of little else but food. Maslow believed that higher, more fragile needs are expressed only after we satisfy our biological needs. This is also true of needs for safety and security. Until they are met, we may have little interest in higher pursuits. For instance, a person who is feeling threatened might have little interest in writing poetry or even talking with friends. For this reason, Maslow described the first four levels of the hierarchy as **basic needs**. Other basic needs are for love and belonging (family, friendship, caring) and esteem and self-esteem (recognition and self-respect).

All the basic needs are *deficiency* motives. That is, they are activated by a *lack* of food, water, security, love, esteem, or other basic needs. At the top of the hierarchy we find **growth needs**, which are expressed as a need for self-actualization. The need for self-actualization is not based on deficiencies. Rather, it is a positive, life-enhancing force for personal growth (Reiss & Havercamp, 2005). Like other humanistic psychologists, Maslow believed that people are basically good. If our basic needs are met, he said, we will tend to move on to actualizing our potentials.

How are needs for self-actualization expressed? Maslow also called the less powerful but humanly important actualization motives **meta-needs** (Maslow, 1970). Meta-needs are an expression of tendencies to fully develop your personal potentials. The meta-needs are:

1. Wholeness (unity)
2. Perfection (balance and harmony)
3. Completion (ending)

Wheelchair athletes engage in vigorous competition. Maslow considered such behavior an expression of the need for self-actualization.

4. Justice (fairness)
5. Richness (complexity)
6. Simplicity (essence)
7. Aliveness (spontaneity)
8. Beauty (rightness of form)
9. Goodness (benevolence)
10. Uniqueness (individuality)
11. Playfulness (ease)
12. Truth (reality)
13. Autonomy (self-sufficiency)
14. Meaningfulness (values)

According to Maslow, we tend to move up through the hierarchy of needs, toward the meta-needs. When the meta-needs are unfulfilled, people fall into a "syndrome of decay" marked by despair, apathy, and alienation.

BRIDGES

Maslow provided few guidelines for promoting self-actualization. However, some suggestions can be gleaned from his writings. **See Chapter 12, pages 417–418, for more about self-actualization.**

Maslow's point is that mere survival or comfort is usually not enough to make a full and satisfying life. It's interesting to note, in this regard, that college students who are concerned primarily with money, personal appearance, and social recognition score lower than average in vitality, self-actualization, and general well-being (Kasser & Ryan, 1996).

Maslow's hierarchy is not well documented by research, and parts of it are questionable. How, for instance, do we explain the actions of a person who fasts as part of a social protest? How can the meta-need for justice overcome the more basic need for food? (Perhaps the answer is that fasting is temporary and self-imposed.) Despite such objections, Maslow's views are a good way to understand and appreciate the rich interplay of human motives (Kenrick et al., 2010; Peterson & Park, 2010).

Are many people motivated by meta-needs? Maslow estimated that few people are motivated primarily by needs for self-actualization. Most of us are more concerned with esteem, love, or security. Perhaps this is because rewards in our society tend to encourage conformity, uniformity, and security in schools, jobs, and relationships. (When was the last time you met a meta-need?)

Intrinsic and Extrinsic Motivation

Some people cook for a living and consider it hard work. Others cook for pleasure and dream of opening a restaurant. For some people, mountain biking, gardening, writing, photography, or jewelry making is fun. For others the same activities are drudgery they must be paid to do. How can the same activity be "work" for one person and "play" for another?

According to *self-determination theory*, when you freely choose to do something for enjoyment or to improve your abilities, your motivation is usually *intrinsic* (Hagger & Chatzisarantis, 2010; Niemiec, Ryan, & Deci, 2009). **Intrinsic motivation** occurs when we act without any obvious external rewards (Patall, Cooper, & Robinson, 2008). We simply enjoy an activity or see it as an opportunity to explore, learn, and actualize our potentials. In contrast, **extrinsic motivation** stems from external factors, such as pay, grades, rewards, obligations, and approval. Most of the activities we think of as "work" are extrinsically rewarded (Baard, Deci, & Ryan, 2004).

Turning Play into Work

Don't extrinsic incentives strengthen motivation? Yes, they can, but not always. In fact, *excessive* rewards can decrease intrinsic motivation and spontaneous interest. For instance, in one classic study, children who were lavishly rewarded for drawing with felt-tip pens later showed little interest in playing with the pens again (Greene & Lepper, 1974). Apparently, "play" can be turned into "work" by *requiring* people to do something they would otherwise enjoy (Patall, Cooper, & Robinson, 2008). When we are coerced or "bribed" to act, we tend to feel as if we are "faking it." Employees who lack initiative and teenagers who reject school and learning are good examples of those who have such a reaction (Niemiec, Ryan, & Deci, 2009).

Creativity

People are more likely to be creative when they are intrinsically motivated. On the job, for instance, salaries and bonuses may increase the amount of work done. However, work *quality* is affected more by intrinsic factors, such as personal interest and freedom of choice (Nakamura & Csikszentmihalyi, 2003). People who are intrinsically motivated usually get personally involved in tasks, which leads to greater creativity (Ruscio, Whitney, & Amabile, 1998). Psychologist Teresa Amabile lists the following as "creativity killers" on the job:

- Working under surveillance
- Having your choices restricted by rules
- Working primarily to get a good evaluation (or avoid a bad one)
- Working mainly to get more money

Time pressure also kills creativity. Employees are less likely to solve tricky problems and come up with innovative ideas when they work "under the gun." When a person is intrinsically

Hierarchy of human needs Abraham Maslow's ordering of needs, based on their presumed strength or potency.

Basic needs The first four levels of needs in Maslow's hierarchy; lower needs tend to be more potent than higher needs.

Growth needs In Maslow's hierarchy, the higher-level needs associated with self-actualization.

Meta-needs In Maslow's hierarchy, needs associated with impulses for self-actualization.

Intrinsic motivation Motivation that comes from within, rather than from external rewards; motivation based on personal enjoyment of a task or activity.

Extrinsic motivation Motivation based on obvious external rewards, obligations, or similar factors.

People who are intrinsically motivated feel free to explore creative solutions to problems. *(right)* Dean Kaman, inventor of the Segway personal transportation device. *(below)* "The Uncatchable," an entrant in The Great Arcata to Ferndale World Championship Cross Country Kinetic Sculpture Race.

© Rick Friedman/Corbis

Matthew Filar Photography

motivated, a certain amount of challenge, surprise, and complexity makes a task rewarding. When extrinsic motivation is stressed, people are less likely to solve tricky problems and come up with innovative ideas (Amabile, Hadley, & Kramer, 2002; Hennessey & Amabile, 2010).

Should extrinsic motivation always be avoided? No, but extrinsic motivation shouldn't be overused, especially with children. In general, (1) if there's no intrinsic interest in an activity to begin with, you have nothing to lose by using extrinsic rewards; (2) if basic skills are lacking, extrinsic rewards may be necessary at first; (3) extrinsic rewards can focus attention on an activity so that real interest will develop; and (4) if extrinsic rewards are used, they should be small and phased out as soon as possible (Buckworth et al., 2007; Cameron & Pierce, 2002).

At work, it is valuable for managers to find out what each employee's interests and career goals are. People are not motivated solely by money. A chance to do challenging, interesting, and intrinsically rewarding work is often just as important. In many situations it is important to encourage intrinsic motivation, especially when children are learning new skills.

Knowledge Builder

Stimulus Motives, Learned Motives, Maslow, and Intrinsic Motivation

RECITE

1. Exploration, manipulation, and curiosity provide evidence for the existence of ____________ motives.
2. Sensation seekers tend to be extroverted, independent, and value change. T or F?
3. Complex tasks, such as taking a classroom test, tend to be disrupted by high levels of arousal, an effect predicted by
   a. sensation seeking *b.* the Yerkes-Dodson law *c.* studies of circadian arousal patterns *d.* studies of the need for achievement
4. Two key elements of test anxiety that must be controlled are ____________ and excessive ____________.
5. According to opponent-process theory, when a stimulus is repeated, our response to it gets stronger. T or F?
6. People high in nAch show high levels of perseverance, passion, and ________.
   a. control *b.* intelligence *c.* self-confidence *d.* sensation seeking
7. The highest level of Maslow's hierarchy of motives involves
   a. meta-needs *b.* needs for safety and security *c.* needs for love and belonging *d.* extrinsic needs
8. Intrinsic motivation is often undermined in situations in which obvious external rewards are applied to a naturally enjoyable activity. T or F?

REFLECT

Think Critically

9. Many U.S. college freshmen say that "being well-off financially" is an essential life goal and that "making more money" was a very important factor in their decision to attend college. Which meta-needs are fulfilled by "making more money"?

Self-Reflect

Does arousal theory seem to explain any of your own behavior? Think of at least one time when your performance was impaired by arousal that was too low or too high. Now think of some personal examples that illustrate the Yerkes-Dodson law.

Are you high or low in your need for stimulation?

Do you think you are high or low in nAch? When faced with a challenging task are you high or low in perseverance? Passion? Self-confidence?

Which levels of Maslow's hierarchy of needs occupy most of your time and energy?

Name an activity you do that is intrinsically motivated and one that is extrinsically motivated. How do they differ?

Answers: 1. stimulus **2.** T **3.** *b* **4.** arousal, worry **5.** F **6.** *c* **7.** *a* **8.** T **9.** None of them.

Inside an Emotion—How Do You Feel?

Gateway Question 10.7: *What happens during emotion?*

Picture the faces of terrified people fleeing a big disaster like the 2010 Haiti earthquake and it's easy to see that motivation and emotion are closely related. Emotions shape our relationships and color our daily activities. What are the basic parts of an emotion? How does the body respond during emotion? **Emotion** is characterized by physiological arousal, and changes in facial expressions, gestures, posture, and subjective feelings. As mentioned earlier, the word emotion derives from the Latin word meaning "to move."

What "moves" during an emotion? First of all, your body is physically aroused during emotion. Such bodily stirrings are what cause us to say we were "moved" by a play, a funeral, or an act of kindness. Second, we are often motivated, or moved to take action, by emotions such as fear, anger, or joy. Many of the goals we seek make us feel good. Many of the activities we avoid make us feel bad. We feel happy when we succeed and sad when we fail (Kalat & Shiota, 2012).

Emotions are linked to many basic **adaptive behaviors**, such as attacking, fleeing, seeking comfort, helping others, and reproducing. Such behaviors help us survive and adjust to changing conditions (Freberg, 2010). However, it is also apparent that emotions can have negative effects. Stage fright or "choking" in sports can spoil performances. Hate, anger, contempt, disgust, and fear disrupt behavior and relationships. But more often, emotions aid survival. As social animals, it would be impossible for humans to live in groups, cooperate in raising children, and defend one another without positive emotional bonds of love, caring, and friendship (Buss, 2008).

A pounding heart, sweating palms, "butterflies" in the stomach, and other bodily reactions are major elements of fear, anger, joy, and other emotions. Typical **physiological changes** take place in heart rate, blood pressure, perspiration, and other bodily stirrings. Most are caused by activity in the sympathetic nervous system and by the hormones **adrenaline** and *noradrenaline*, which the adrenal glands release into the bloodstream.

Emotional expressions, or outward signs of what a person is feeling, are another ingredient of emotion. For example, when you are intensely afraid, your hands tremble, your face contorts, your posture becomes tense and defensive, and your voice changes. In general, these expressions serve to tell others what emotions we are experiencing (Hortman, 2003).

Emotional feelings (a person's private emotional experience) are a final major element of emotion. This is the part of emotion with which we are usually most familiar.

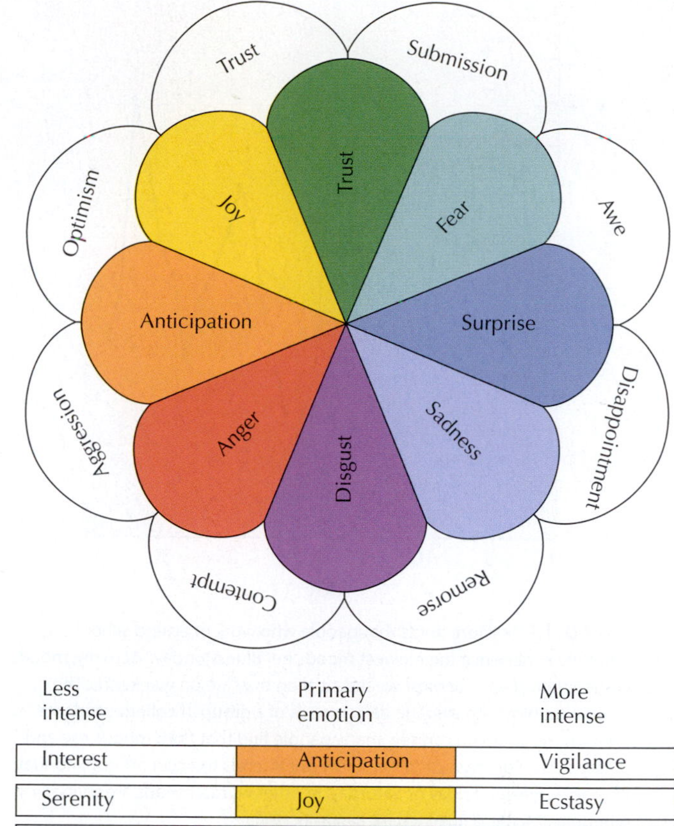

Less intense	Primary emotion	More intense
Interest	Anticipation	Vigilance
Serenity	Joy	Ecstasy
Acceptance	Trust	Admiration
Apprehension	Fear	Terror
Distraction	Surprise	Amazement
Pensiveness	Sadness	Grief
Boredom	Disgust	Loathing
Annoyance	Anger	Rage

● **Figure 10.12** Primary and mixed emotions. In Robert Plutchik's model, there are eight primary emotions, as listed in the inner areas. Adjacent emotions may combine to give the emotions listed around the perimeter. Mixtures involving more widely separated emotions are also possible. For example, fear plus anticipation produces anxiety. (Adapted from Plutchik, 2003.)

Primary Emotions

Are some emotions more basic than others? Yes. Robert Plutchik (2003) has identified eight **primary emotions**. These are fear, surprise, sadness, disgust, anger, anticipation, joy, and trust (acceptance). If the list seems too short, it's because each emotion can vary in *intensity*. When you're angry, for instance, you may feel anything from rage to simple annoyance (● Figure 10.12).

As shown in ● Figure 10.12, each pair of adjacent primary emotions can be mixed to yield a third, more complex emotion. Other mixtures are also possible. For example, 5-year-old Tupac feels both joy and fear as he eats a cookie he stole from Mom's cookie jar. The result? Guilt—as you may recall from your own childhood. Likewise, jealousy could be a mixture of love, anger, and fear.

A *mood* is the mildest form of emotion (● Figure 10.13). **Moods** are low intensity emotional states that can last for many hours, or even days. Moods often affect day-to-day behavior by preparing us to act in certain ways. For example, when your neighbor Roseanne is in an irritable mood she may react angrily to almost anything you say. When she is in a happy mood, she can easily laugh off an insult. Happy, positive moods tend to make us

Emotion A state characterized by physiological arousal, changes in facial expression, gestures, posture, and subjective feelings.

Adaptive behaviors Actions that aid attempts to survive and adapt to changing conditions.

Physiological changes (in emotion) Alterations in heart rate, blood pressure, perspiration, and other involuntary responses.

Adrenaline A hormone produced by the adrenal glands that tends to arouse the body.

Emotional expressions Outward signs that an emotion is occurring.

Emotional feelings The private, subjective experience of having an emotion.

Primary emotions According to Robert Plutchik's theory, the most basic emotions are fear, surprise, sadness, disgust, anger, anticipation, joy, and trust (acceptance).

Mood A low-intensity, long-lasting emotional state.

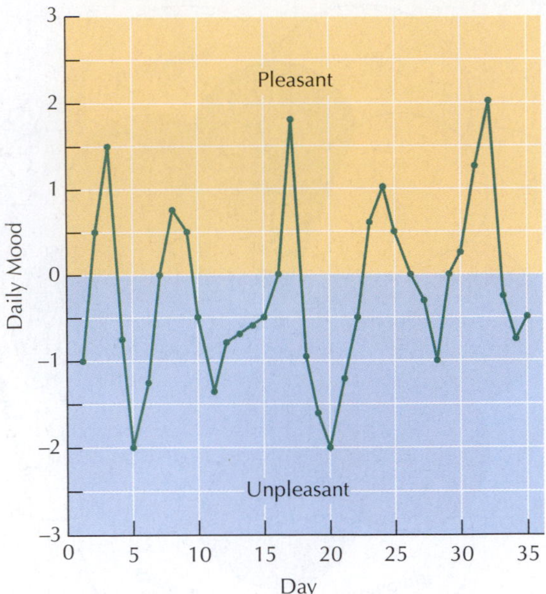

• Figure 10.13 Folklore holds that people who work or attend school on a weekly schedule experience their lowest moods on "Blue Monday." Actually, moods tend to be generally lower for *most* weekdays than they are on weekends. The graph shown here plots the average daily moods of a group of college students over a 5-week period. As you can see, many people find that their moods rise and fall on a 7-day cycle. For most students, a low point tends to occur around Monday or Tuesday and a peak on Friday or Saturday. In other words, moods are shaped by weekly schedules. (Adapted from Larsen & Kasimatis, 1990.)

more adaptable in several ways. For example, when you are in a good mood, you are likely to make better decisions, and you will be more helpful, efficient, creative, and peaceful (Compton, 2005; Fredrickson & Branigan, 2005).

Like our motives, our moods are closely tied to circadian rhythms. When your body temperature is at its daily low point, you are more likely to feel "down" emotionally. When body temperature is at its peak, your mood is likely to be positive—even if you missed a night of sleep (Boivin, Czeisler, & Waterhouse, 1997).

Emotion and the Brain

Emotions can be either positive or negative. Ordinarily, we might think that positive and negative emotions are mutually exclusive. But this is not the case. As Tupac's "cookie guilt" implies, you can have positive and negative emotions at the same time. How is that possible? In the brain, positive emotions are processed mainly in the left hemisphere. In contrast, negative emotions are processed in the right hemisphere (Hofman, 2008; Simon-Thomas, Role, & Knight, 2005). In one study, people watching their favorite soccer team play well showed activity in both hemispheres but showed activity only in the right hemisphere when they were losing (Park et al, 2009). The fact that positive and negative emotions are based in different brain areas helps explain why we can feel happy and sad at the same time. It also explains why your right foot is more ticklish than your left foot! The left hemisphere controls the right side of the body and processes positive emotions (Smith & Cahusac, 2001). Thus, most people are more ticklish on their right side. If you really want to tickle someone, be sure to "do it right."

Scientists used to think that all emotions are processed by the cerebral cortex. However, this is not always the case. Imagine this test of willpower: Go to a zoo and place your face close to the glass in front of a rattlesnake display. Suddenly, the rattlesnake strikes at your face. Do you flinch? Even though you know you are safe, Joseph LeDoux predicts that you will recoil from the snake's attack (LeDoux, 2000).

LeDoux and other researchers have found that the area of the brain called the **amygdala** (ah-MIG-duh-la) specializes in producing fear (● Figure 10.14). (See Chapter 2 for more information.) The amygdala receives sensory information very directly and quickly, bypassing the cortex (Walker & Davis, 2008). As a result, it allows us to respond to potential danger before we really know what's happening. This primitive fear response is not under the control of higher brain centers. The role of the amygdala in emotion may explain why people who suffer from phobias and disabling anxiety often feel afraid without knowing why (Fellous & Ledoux, 2005).

People who suffer damage to the amygdala become "blind" to emotion. An armed robber could hold a gun to a person's head and the person wouldn't feel fear. Such people are also unable to "read" or understand other people's emotional expressions, especially as conveyed by their eyes (Adolphs, 2008). Many lose their ability to relate normally to friends, family, and coworkers (Goleman, 1995).

Later, we will attempt to put all the elements of emotion together into a single picture. But first, we need to look more closely at bodily arousal and emotional expressions.

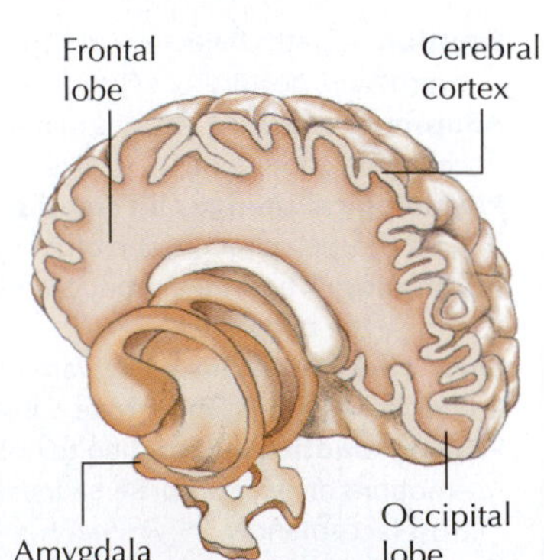

• Figure 10.14 An amygdala can be found buried within the temporal lobes on each side of the brain (see Chapter 2). The amygdala appears to provide "quick and dirty" processing of emotional stimuli that allows us to react involuntarily to danger. Copyright © 2012 Wadsworth, Cengage Learning, Inc.

Physiology and Emotion—Arousal, Sudden Death, and Lying

Gateway Questions 10.8: *What physiological changes underlie emotion, and can "lie detectors" really detect lies?*

An African Bushman frightened by a lion and a city dweller frightened by a prowler will react in much the same way. Such encounters usually produce muscle tension, a pounding heart, irritability, dryness of the throat and mouth, sweating, butterflies in the stomach, frequent urination, trembling, restlessness, sensitivity to loud noises, and numerous other body changes. These reactions are nearly universal because they are innate. Specifically, they are caused by the **autonomic nervous system (ANS)**—the neural system that connects the brain with internal organs and glands. As you may recall from Chapter 2, activity of the ANS is *automatic* rather than voluntary (Freberg, 2010).

Fight or Flight

The ANS has two divisions, the *sympathetic branch* and the *parasympathetic branch*. The two branches are active at all times. Whether you are relaxed or aroused at any moment depends on the relative activity of both branches.

What does the ANS do during emotion? In general, the **sympathetic branch** activates the body for emergency action—for "fighting or fleeing." It does this by arousing some body systems and inhibiting others (● Figure 10.15). Sugar is released into the bloodstream for quick energy, the heart beats faster to supply blood to the muscles, digestion is temporarily slowed, blood flow in the skin is restricted to reduce bleeding, and so forth. Such reactions improve the chances of surviving an emergency.

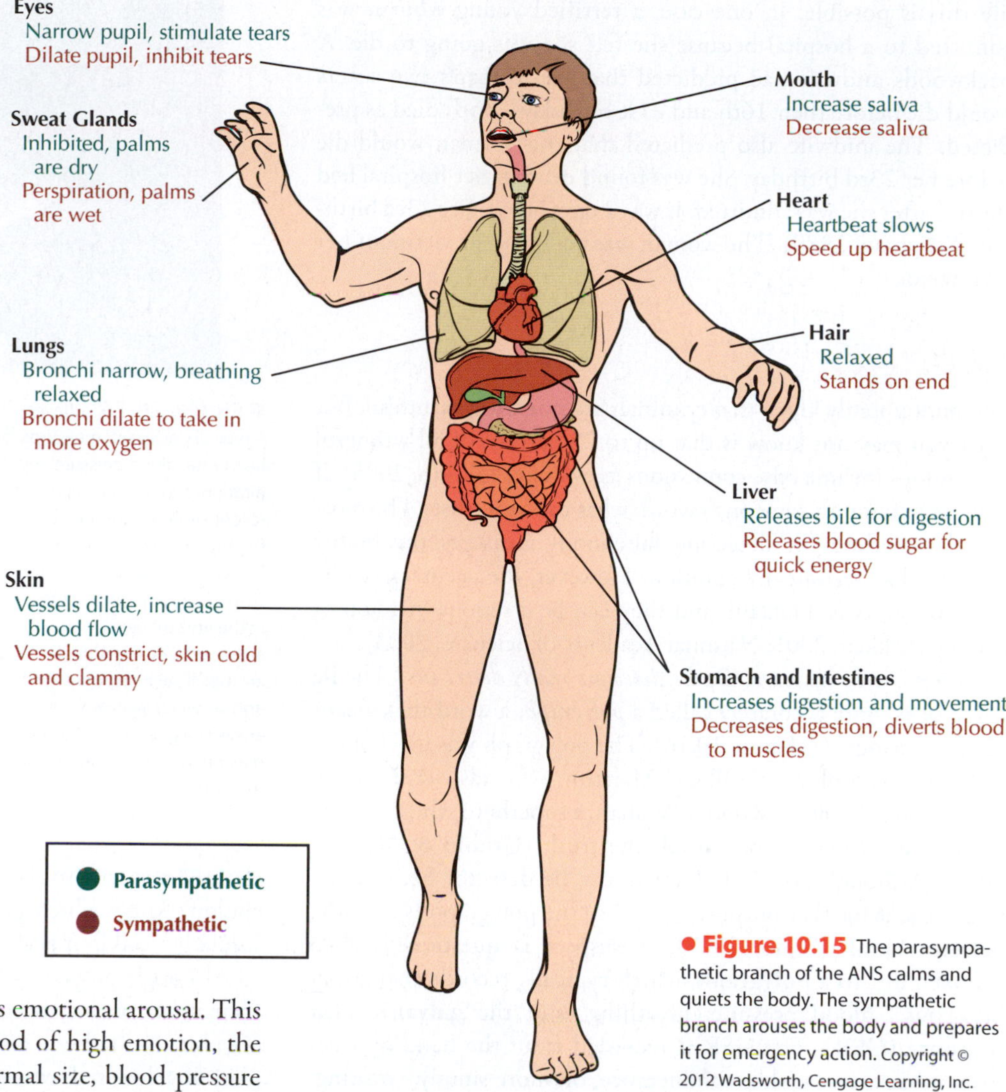

● **Figure 10.15** The parasympathetic branch of the ANS calms and quiets the body. The sympathetic branch arouses the body and prepares it for emergency action.

The **parasympathetic branch** reverses emotional arousal. This calms and relaxes the body. After a period of high emotion, the heart is slowed, the pupils return to normal size, blood pressure drops, and so forth. In addition to restoring balance, the parasympathetic system helps build up and conserve the body's energy.

The parasympathetic system responds much more slowly than the sympathetic system. That's why a pounding heart, muscle tension, and other signs of arousal don't fade for 20 or 30 minutes after you feel an intense emotion, such as fear. Moreover, after a strong emotional shock, the parasympathetic system may overreact and lower blood pressure too much. This can cause you to become dizzy or faint after seeing something shocking, such as a horrifying accident.

Sudden Death

Strong emotions can kill you in two ways. The first can occur if the sympathetic system becomes too active, resulting in excessive stress. For older persons or those with heart problems, stress-related sympathetic effects may be enough to bring about heart attack and collapse. For example, five times more people than usual died of heart attacks on the day of a major 1994 earthquake in Los Angeles (Leor, Poole, & Kloner, 1996). Similarly, in Asia, the number "4" is considered unlucky, and more heart patients die on the fourth day of the month than any other day. Because of the extra stress due to the fear that they will die on an "unlucky day," their chance of dying actually increases (Phillips et al., 2001).

Second, the **parasympathetic rebound** to sympathetic arousal can also be severe enough to cause death. In times of war, for instance, combat can be so savage that some soldiers literally die of fear (Moritz & Zamchech, 1946). Apparently, such deaths occur because the parasympathetic nervous system overreacts to the sympathetic arousal, slowing the heart to a stop. Even in civilian

Amygdala A part of the limbic system (within the brain) that produces fear responses.

Autonomic nervous system (ANS) The system of nerves that connects the brain with the internal organs and glands.

Sympathetic branch A part of the ANS that activates the body at times of stress.

Parasympathetic branch A part of the autonomic system that quiets the body and conserves energy.

Parasympathetic rebound Excess activity in the parasympathetic nervous system following a period of intense emotion.

life this is possible. In one case, a terrified young woman was admitted to a hospital because she felt she was going to die. A backwoods midwife had predicted that the woman's two sisters would die before their 16th and 21st birthdays. Both died as predicted. The midwife also predicted that this woman would die before her 23rd birthday. She was found dead in her hospital bed the day after she was admitted. It was 2 days before her 23rd birthday (Seligman, 1989). The woman was an apparent victim of her own terror.

Lie Detectors

You undoubtedly know that criminals are not always truthful. But what you may not know is that up to 25 percent of all wrongful convictions include false confessions as evidence (Kassin, 2005). If you can't count on someone's word, what can you trust? The most popular method for detecting falsehoods measures the bodily changes that accompany emotion. However, the accuracy of "lie detector" tests is doubtful, and they can be a serious invasion of privacy (Lykken, 2001; National Academy of Sciences, 2003).

What is a lie detector? Do lie detectors really detect lies? The lie detector is more accurately called a *polygraph,* a word that means "many writings" (● Figure 10.16). The polygraph was invented in 1915 by psychologist William Marston, who also created the comic book character Wonder Woman, a superhero whose "magic lasso" could force people to tell the truth (Grubin & Madsen, 2005). Although popularly known as a lie detector because the police use it for that purpose, in reality the polygraph is not a lie detector at all (Bunn, 2007). A suspect is questioned while "hooked up" to a **polygraph**, which typically records changes in heart rate, blood pressure, breathing, and the **galvanic skin response (GSR)**. The GSR is recorded from the hand by electrodes that measure skin conductance, or, more simply, sweating. Because the device records only general emotional arousal, it can't tell the difference between lying and fear, anxiety and excitement (Iacono, 2008).

So an innocent but nervous person could fail a polygraph test? Yes. A woman named Donna was arrested for violating a restraining order against Marie. Even though she claimed she was having lunch instead of harassing Marie, she failed a polygraph test (Geddes, 2008). Put yourself in her place, and it's easy to see why. Imagine the examiner asking, "Did you drive up to Marie, curse at her, and then drive away?" Because you know Marie, and you already know what you have been charged with, it's no secret that this is a critical question. What would happen to *your* heart rate, blood pressure, breathing, and perspiration under such circumstances? Psychologist David Lykken (1998, 2001) has documented many cases in which innocent people were convicted on the basis of polygraph evidence.

To minimize this problem, skilled polygraph examiners might use the **guilty knowledge test** (Hakun et al., 2009). A series of multiple-choice questions are asked; one answer is correct. For example, one question might be: "Was the gun that killed Hensley a: a) Colt; b) Smith & Wesson; c) Walther PPK; or d) Luger? A guilty person who knew which gun she had used may show an elevated response to the correct answer. Since an innocent person couldn't know which gun was involved, she could only respond similarly to all four alternatives (Iacono, 2008).

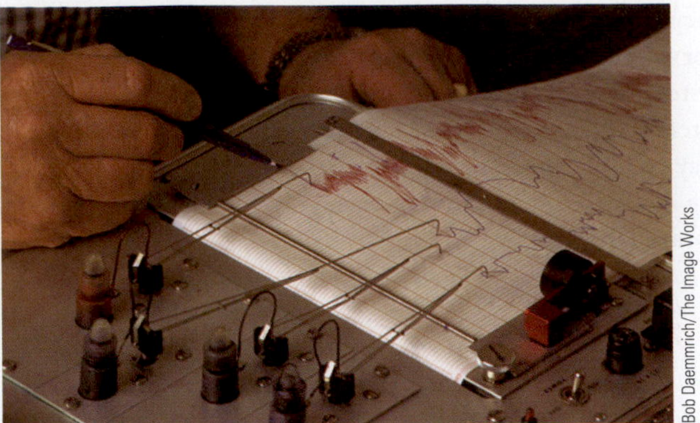

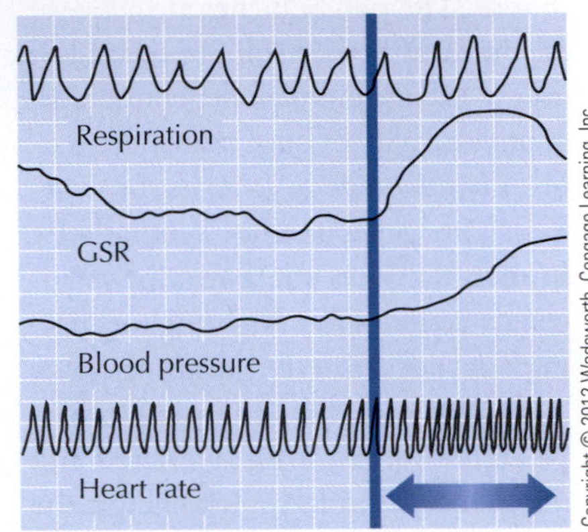

● **Figure 10.16** *(above)* A typical polygraph measures heart rate, blood pressure, respiration, and galvanic skin response. Pens mounted on the top of the machine record bodily responses on a moving strip of paper. *(right)* Changes in the area marked by the arrow indicate emotional arousal. If such responses appear when a person answers a question, he or she may be lying, but arousal may have other causes.

Although proponents of lie detection claim it is 95 percent accurate, errors may occur even when questioning is done properly (Grubin & Madsen, 2005). But in one study, accuracy was dramatically lowered when people thought about past emotional experiences as they answered irrelevant questions (Ben-Shakhar & Dolev, 1996). Similarly, the polygraph may be thrown off by self-inflicted pain, by tranquilizing drugs, or by people who can lie without anxiety (Waid & Orne, 1982). Worst of all, the test is much more likely to label an innocent person guilty rather than a guilty person innocent. In studies involving real crimes, an average of one innocent person in five was rated as guilty by the lie detector (Lykken, 2001). For such reasons, the National Academy of Sciences (2003) has concluded that polygraph tests should not be used to screen employees.

Despite the lie detector's flaws, you may be tested for employment or for other reasons. Should this occur, the best advice is to remain calm; then actively challenge the results if the machine wrongly questions your honesty.

Isn't there a better way to detect lies? Possibly. Harassment charges against Donna were dropped when a functional magnetic resonance imaging (fMRI) scan revealed she was indeed telling the truth. Brain scans like fMRI directly measure brain activity, thus bypassing the traditional approach of measuring indirect signs of emotional arousal (Hakun et al., 2009; Lefebvre et al., 2007). For example, researchers have found that different brain areas are involved in telling a lie (Abe et al., 2007). Psychiatrist Daniel Langleben (2008) theorizes that a liar must inhibit telling the truth in order to lie. Thus, extra brain areas must be activated to tell a lie, which can be seen in brain images when people are lying (see Chapter 2).

Even if new methods are used, the key problem remains: How can we avoid falsely classifying liars as truth tellers and truth tellers as liars? Until that can be done with acceptable accuracy, any new technique may have no more value than the polygraph does.

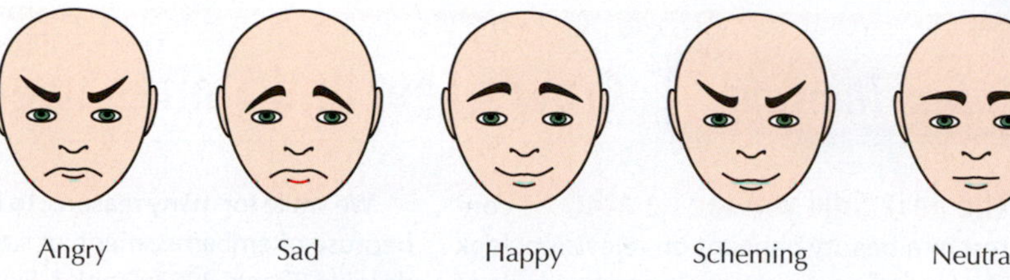

● **Figure 10.17** When shown groups of simplified faces (without labels), the angry and scheming faces "jumped out" at people faster than sad, happy, or neutral faces. An ability to rapidly detect threatening expressions probably helped our ancestors survive. (Adapted from Tipples, Atkinson, & Young, 2002.)

Knowledge Builder: Emotion and Physiological Arousal

RECITE

1. Many of the physiological changes associated with emotion are caused by secretion of the hormone
   a. atropine *b.* adrenaline *c.* attributine *d.* insulin
2. Emotional ______________ often serve to communicate a person's emotional state to others.
3. Awe, remorse, and disappointment are among the primary emotions listed by Robert Plutchik. T or F?
4. Emotional arousal is closely related to activity of the ______________ nervous system.
5. Preparing the body for "fighting or fleeing" is largely the job of the
   a. paraventricular nucleus *b.* sympathetic branch *c.* GSR *d.* left hemisphere
6. The parasympathetic system inhibits digestion and raises blood pressure and heart rate. T or F?
7. What body changes are measured by a polygraph?

REFLECT

Think Critically

8. Can you explain why people "cursed" by shamans or "witch doctors" sometimes actually die?

Self-Reflect

How did your most emotional moment of the past week affect your behavior, expressions, feelings, and bodily state? Could you detect both sympathetic and parasympathetic effects?

Make a list of the emotions you consider to be most basic. To what extent do they agree with Plutchik's list?

What did you think about lie detectors before reading this chapter? What do you think now?

Answers: 1. *b* **2.** expressions **3.** F **4.** autonomic **5.** *b* **6.** F **7.** heart rate, blood pressure, breathing rate, galvanic skin response **8.** In cultures in which there is deep belief in superstitions like magic or voodoo, a person who thinks that she or he has been cursed may become uncontrollably emotional. After several days of intense terror, the stress of sympathetic arousal may produce a heart attack. Regardless, a parasympathetic rebound is likely. If the rebound is severe enough, it can also lead to physical collapse and death.

Expressing Emotions—Making Faces and Talking Bodies

Gateway Questions 10.9: ***How accurately are emotions expressed by the face and "body language"?***

Next to our own feelings, the expressions of others are the most familiar part of emotion. Are emotional expressions a carryover from human evolution? Charles Darwin thought so. Darwin (1872) observed that angry tigers, monkeys, dogs, and humans all bare their teeth in the same way. Psychologists believe that emotional expressions evolved to communicate our feelings to others, which aids survival. Such messages give valuable hints about what other people are likely to do next (Kalat & Shiota, 2012). For instance, in one study, people were able to detect angry and scheming faces faster than happy, sad, or neutral faces (● Figure 10.17). Presumably, we are especially sensitive to threatening faces because they warn us of possible harm (Tipples, Atkinson, & Young, 2002.)

Facial Expressions

Are emotional expressions the same for all people? Basic expressions appear to be fairly universal (● Figure 10.18). Facial expressions of *fear*, *anger*, *disgust*, *sadness*, *surprise*, and *happiness* (enjoyment) are recognized around the world (Smith et al., 2005). Expressions of

● **Figure 10.18** Is anger expressed the same way in different cultures? Masks that are meant to be frightening or threatening are strikingly similar around the world. Most have an open, downward-curved mouth and diagonal or triangular eyes, eyebrows, nose, cheeks, and chin. (Keep this list in mind next Halloween.) Obviously, the pictured mask is not meant to be warm and cuddly. Your ability to "read" its emotional message suggests that basic emotional expressions have universal biological roots (Adolphs, 2008).

Polygraph A device for recording heart rate, blood pressure, respiration, and galvanic skin response; commonly called a "lie detector."

Galvanic skin response (GSR) A change in the electrical resistance (or inversely, the conductance) of the skin, due to sweating.

Guilty knowledge test Polygraph procedure involving testing people with knowledge only a guilty person could know.

Critical Thinking: Crow's-Feet and Smiles Sweet

The next time you see an athletic contest or a beauty pageant on television, look closely at the winner's smile and the smile of the runner-up. Although both people will be smiling, it is likely that the winner's smile will be authentic and the loser's smile will be forced (Thibault et al., 2009).

We smile for many reasons: to be polite or because of embarrassment, or sometimes to deceive (Frank, 2002; Frank & Ekman, 2004). These "social smiles" are often intentional or forced, and they only involve lifting the corners of the mouth. What does a genuine smile look like? A real smile involves not only the mouth, but also the small muscles around the eyes. These muscles lift the cheeks and make crow's-feet or crinkles in the outside corners of the eyes.

Dennis Coon

The face on the left shows a social smile; the one on the right is an authentic, or Duchenne, smile.

Authentic smiles are called **Duchenne smiles** (after Guilluame Duchenne, a French scientist who studied facial muscles). The muscles around the eyes are very difficult to tighten on command. Hence, to tell if a smile in authentic, or merely posed, look at the corners of a person's eyes, not the mouth (Williams et al., 2001). To put it another way, crow's-feet mean a smile is sweet.

Duchenne smiles signal genuine happiness and enjoyment (Soussignan, 2002). In one study, women who had authentic smiles in their college yearbook photos were contacted 6, 22, and 31 years later. At each interval, real smiles in college were associated with more positive emotions and a greater sense of competence. We can only speculate about why this is the case. However, it is likely that smiling signals that a person is helpful or nurturing. This leads to more supportive social relationships and, in a self-fulfilling manner, to greater happiness (Gladstone & Parker, 2002).

contempt and *interest* may also be universal, but researchers are less certain of this (Ekman, 1993). Notice that this list covers most of the primary emotions described earlier. Children who are born blind have little opportunity to learn emotional expressions from others. Even so, they also display basic expressions in the same way sighted people do (Galati, Scherer, & Ricci-Bitti, 1997). It's also nice to note that a smile is the most universal and easily recognized facial expression of emotion.

There are more than a few facial expressions, aren't there? Yes. Your face can produce some 20,000 different expressions, which makes it the most expressive part of your body. Most of these are *facial blends* (a mixture of two or more basic expressions). Imagine, for example, that you just received an "F" on an unfair test. Quite likely, your eyes, eyebrows, and forehead would reveal anger, and your mouth would be turned downward in a sad frown.

Most of us believe we can fairly accurately tell what others are feeling by observing their facial expressions. If thousands of facial blends occur, how do we make such judgments? The answer is that facial expressions can be boiled down to three basic dimensions: *pleasantness–unpleasantness, attention–rejection,* and *activation* (or arousal) (Schlosberg, 1954). By smiling when you give a friend a hard time, you add an emotional message of acceptance to the verbal insult, which changes its meaning. As they say in movie Westerns, it makes a big difference to "Smile when you say that, pardner."

Some facial expressions are shaped by learning and may be found only in specific cultures. Among the Chinese, for example, sticking out the tongue is a gesture of surprise, not of disrespect or teasing. If a person comes from another culture, it is wise to remember that you may easily misunderstand his or her expressions. At such times, knowing the social *context* in which an expression occurs helps clarify its meaning (Carroll & Russell, 1996; Kalat & Shiota, 2012). (Also, see "Crow's-Feet and Smiles Sweet.")

Cultural Differences in Emotion

How many times have you been angry this week? If it was more than once, you're not unusual. Anger is a very common emotion in Western cultures. Very likely this is because our culture emphasizes personal independence and free expression of individual rights and needs. In North America, anger is widely viewed as a "natural" reaction to feeling that you have been treated unfairly.

In contrast, many Asian cultures place a high value on group harmony. In Asia, expressing anger in public is less common and anger is regarded as less "natural." The reason for this is that anger tends to separate people. Thus, being angry is at odds with a culture that values cooperation.

Culture also influences positive emotions. In America, we tend to have positive feelings such as pride, happiness, and superiority, which emphasize our role as *individuals*. In Japan, positive feelings are more often linked with membership in groups (friendly feelings, closeness to others, and respect) (Kitayama, Markus, & Kurokawa, 2000; Markus et al., 2006). It is common to think of emotion as an individual event. However, as you can see, emotion is shaped by cultural ideas, values, and practices (Mesquita & Markus, 2004).

Gender and Emotion

Women have a reputation for being "more emotional" than men. Are they? Compared with women, men in Western cultures are more likely to have difficulty expressing their emotions. In fact, Western men are more likely than women to experience **alexithymia** (a-LEX-ih-THIGH-me-ah), from the Latin for "can't name emotions."

According to psychologist Ronald Levant and colleagues (2006, 2009), although male babies start out life more emotionally expressive than female babies, little boys soon learn to "toughen up," beginning in early childhood. As a result, men have learned to curtail the expression of most of their emotions. Whereas girls are encouraged to express sadness, fear, shame, and guilt, boys are more likely to be allowed to express only anger and hostility (Fischer et al., 2004).

But does this mean that men experience emotions less than women? Levant believes that men who fail to express emotions over time become less aware of their own emotions and, hence, less able to name them (Reker et al., 2010). For many men, a learned inability to express feelings or to even be aware of them is a major barrier to having close, satisfying relationships with others and can also lead to health problems, such as depression or addictive behaviors (Lumley, 2004; Vanheule et al., 2010). Blunted emotions may even contribute to tragedies like the mass murder at Columbine High School in Littleton, Colorado. For many young males, anger is the only emotion they can freely feel and express.

© Amy Etra/PhotoEdit, Inc.

Emotions are often unconsciously revealed by gestures and body positioning.

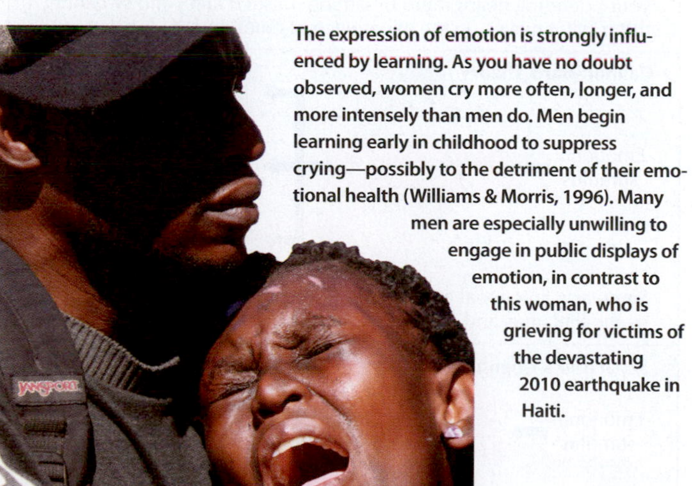

Roberto Koltun/MCT/Landov

The expression of emotion is strongly influenced by learning. As you have no doubt observed, women cry more often, longer, and more intensely than men do. Men begin learning early in childhood to suppress crying—possibly to the detriment of their emotional health (Williams & Morris, 1996). Many men are especially unwilling to engage in public displays of emotion, in contrast to this woman, who is grieving for victims of the devastating 2010 earthquake in Haiti.

Body Language

If a friend walked up to you and said, "Hey, ugly, what are you doing?" would you be offended? Probably not, because such remarks are usually delivered with a big grin. The facial and bodily gestures of emotion speak a language all their own and add to what a person says.

Kinesics (kih-NEEZ-iks) is the study of communication through body movement, posture, gestures, and facial expressions (Goman, 2008; Harrigan, 2006). Informally, we call it body language. To see a masterful use of body language, turn off the sound on a television and watch a popular entertainer or politician at work.

What kinds of messages are sent with body language? It is important to realize cultural learning also affects the meaning of gestures. What, for instance, does it mean if you touch your thumb and first finger together to form a circle? In North America, it means

Duchenne smile An authentic smile (as opposed to a posed, false smile) involving the mouth and the small muscles around the eyes.

Alexithymia A learned difficulty expressing emotions; more common in men.

Kinesics Study of the meaning of body movements, posture, hand gestures, and facial expressions; commonly called body language.

"Everything is fine" or "A-okay." In France and Belgium, it means "You're worth zero." In southern Italy, it means "You're an ass!" When the layer of culturally defined meanings is removed, it is more realistic to say that body language reveals an overall emotional tone (underlying emotional state).

The body telegraphs other feelings. The most general "messages" involve *relaxation* or *tension* and *liking* or *disliking*. Relaxation is expressed by casually positioning the arms and legs, leaning back (if sitting), and spreading the arms and legs. Liking is expressed mainly by leaning toward a person or object. Thus, body positioning can reveal feelings that would normally be concealed. Who do you "lean toward"?

Psychologist Tanya Chartrand has identified an aspect of body language they call the "chameleon effect." This refers to unconsciously imitating the postures, mannerisms, and facial expressions of other people as we interact with them (Dalton, Chartrand, & Finkel, 2010). (We change our gestures to match our surroundings, like a chameleon changes color.) Chartrand also found that if another person copies your gestures and physical postures, you are more inclined to like them (Chartrand & Bargh, 1999). This implies that to make a stronger connection with others, it helps to subtly mimic their gestures (Lakin et al., 2003).

Does body positioning or movement ever reveal lying or deception? Just as a less than genuine smile may betray a liar, so too might body language (Porter & ten Brinke, 2010). But the signs are subtle; seemingly obvious clues like shifty eyes, squirming, and nervous movements (rubbing, grooming, scratching, twisting hair, rubbing hands, biting lips, stroking the chin, and so on) are not consistently related to lying (Ekman, 2001).

On the other hand, the gestures people use to illustrate what they are saying may reveal lying. These gestures, called **illustrators**, tend to *decrease* when a person is telling a lie. In other words, persons who usually "talk with their hands" may be much less animated when they are lying (DePaulo et al., 2003).

Other movements, called *emblems*, can also reveal lying. **Emblems** are gestures that have widely understood meanings within a particular culture. Some examples are the thumbs-up sign, the A-okay sign, the middle-finger insult, a head nod for yes, and a head shake for no. Emblems tend to *increase* when a person is lying. More importantly, they often reveal true feelings contrary to what the liar is saying. For example, a person might smile and say, "Yes, I'd love to try some of your homemade candied pig's feet," while slowly shaking her head from side to side.

Theories of Emotion—Several Ways to Fear a Bear

Gateway Question 10.10: *How do psychologists explain emotions?*

Is it possible to explain what takes place during emotion? Theories of emotion offer different answers to this questions. Let's explore some prominent views. Each appears to have a part of the truth, so we will try to put them all together in the end.

The James-Lange Theory

You're hiking in the woods when a bear steps onto the trail. What will happen next? Common sense tells us that we will then feel fear, become aroused, and run (and sweat and yell). But is this the true order of events? In the 1880s, William James and Carl Lange (LON-geh) proposed that common sense had it backward (Hergenhahn, 2009). According to the **James-Lange theory**, bodily arousal (such as increased heart rate) does not *follow* a feeling such as fear. Instead, they argued, *emotional feelings follow bodily arousal.* Thus, we see a bear, run, are aroused, and *then* feel fear as we become aware of our bodily reactions (● Figure 10.19).

To support his ideas, James pointed out that we often do not experience an emotion until after reacting. For example, imagine that you are driving. Suddenly, a car pulls out in front of you. You swerve and skid to an abrupt halt. Only then do you notice your pounding heart, rapid breathing, and tense muscles—and recognize your fear.

The Cannon-Bard Theory

Walter Cannon (1932) and Phillip Bard disagreed with the James-Lange theory. According to the **Cannon-Bard theory**, emotional feelings and bodily arousal *occur at the same time.* Cannon and Bard believed that seeing a bear activates the thalamus in the brain. The thalamus, in turn, alerts the cortex and the hypothalamus for

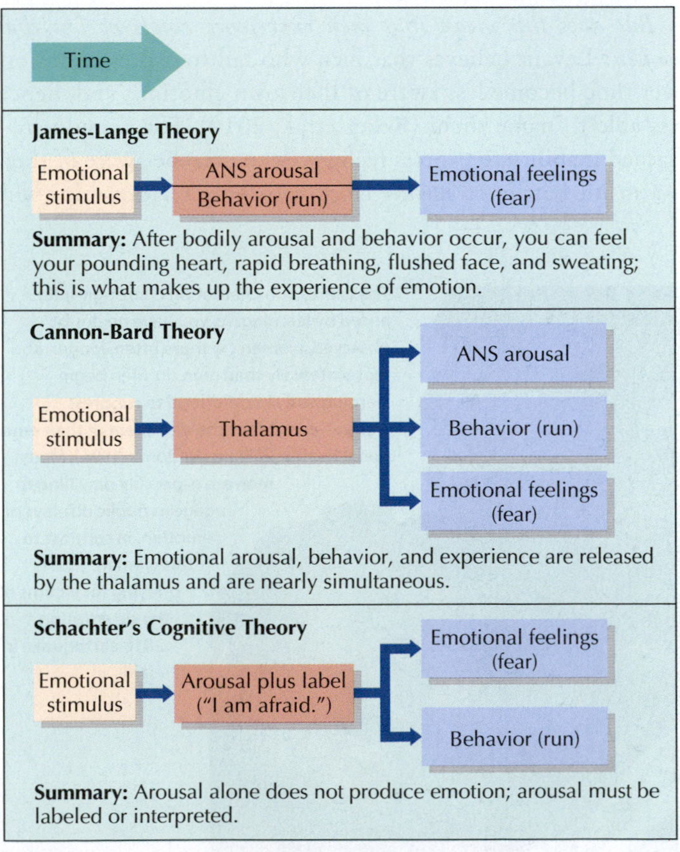

● **Figure 10.19** Theories of emotion.

action. The cortex produces our emotional feelings and emotional behavior. The hypothalamus triggers a chain of events that arouses the body. Thus, if you see a dangerous-looking bear, brain activity will simultaneously produce bodily arousal, running, and a feeling of fear (● Figure 10.19).

Schachter's Cognitive Theory of Emotion

The previous theories are concerned mostly with our physical responses. Stanley Schachter realized that cognitive (mental) factors also enter into emotion. According to **Schachter's cognitive theory**, emotion occurs when we apply a particular *label* to general physiological *arousal*. We likely choose the appropriate label through a process of **attribution**, by deciding which source is leading to the arousal (Valins, 1966).

Assume, for instance, that someone sneaks up behind you on a dark street and says, "Boo!" Your body is now aroused (pounding heart, sweating palms, and so on). If you attribute your arousal to a total stranger, you might label your arousal as fear; if you attribute your arousal to a close friend, you may experience surprise or delight. The label (such as anger, fear, or happiness) you apply to bodily arousal is influenced by your past experiences, the situation, and the reactions of others (● Figure 10.19).

Support for the cognitive theory of emotion comes from an experiment in which people watched a slapstick movie (Schachter & Wheeler, 1962). Before viewing the movie, everyone got an injection, but no one was told what he or she was injected with. One third of the people received an arousing injection of adrenaline, one third got a placebo (salt water) injection, and one third were given a tranquilizer. People who received the adrenaline rated the movie funniest and laughed the most while watching it. In contrast, those given the tranquilizer were least amused. The placebo group fell in between.

According to the cognitive theory of emotion, individuals who received adrenaline had a stirred-up body, but no explanation for what they were feeling. By attributing their arousal to the movie, they became happy and amused. This and similar experiments make it clear that emotion is much more than just an agitated body. Perception, experience, attitudes, judgment, and many other mental factors also affect the emotions we feel. Schachter's theory would predict, then, that if you met a bear, you would be aroused. If the bear seemed unfriendly, you would interpret your arousal as fear, and if the bear offered to shake your "paw," you would be happy, amazed, and relieved!

Tom Hirtreiter/Shutterstock

Which theory of emotion best describes the reactions of these people? Given the complexity of emotion, each theory appears to possess an element of truth.

Misattribution

We now move from slapstick movies and fear of bear bodies to an appreciation of bare bodies. There is no guarantee that we always make the correct attributions about our emotions. For example, Valins (1966) showed male college students a series of photographs of nude females. While watching the photographs, each student heard an amplified heartbeat that he believed was his own. In reality, students were listening to a recorded heartbeat carefully designed to beat *louder* and *stronger* when some (but not all) of the slides were shown.

After watching the slides, each student was asked to say which was most attractive. Students who heard the false heartbeat consistently rated slides paired with a "pounding heart" as the most attractive. In other words, when a student saw a slide and heard his heart beat louder, he attributed his "emotion" to the slide. His attribution seems to have been, "Now that one I like!" His next reaction, perhaps, was "But why?" Later research suggests that sub-

Illustrators Gestures people use to illustrate what they are saying.

Emblems Gestures that have widely understood meanings within a particular culture.

James-Lange theory States that emotional feelings follow bodily arousal and come from awareness of such arousal.

Cannon-Bard theory States that activity in the thalamus causes emotional feelings and bodily arousal to occur simultaneously.

Schachter's cognitive theory States that emotions occur when physical arousal is labeled or interpreted on the basis of experience and situational cues.

Attribution The mental process of assigning causes to events. In emotion, the process of attributing arousal to a particular source.

jects persuaded themselves that the slide really was more attractive in order to explain their apparent arousal (Truax, 1983).

That seems somewhat artificial. Does it really make any difference what arousal is attributed to? Yes. Attribution theory predicts that you are most likely to "love" someone who gets you stirred up emotionally (Foster et al., 1998). This is true even when fear, anger, frustration, or rejection is part of the formula. Thus, if you want to successfully propose marriage, take your intended to the middle of a narrow, windswept suspension bridge over a deep chasm and look deeply into his or her eyes. As your beloved's heart pounds wildly (from being on the bridge, not from your irresistible charms), say, "I love you." Attribution theory predicts that your companion will conclude, "Oh wow, I must love you too."

The preceding is not as farfetched as it may seem. In an ingenious classic study, a female psychologist interviewed men in a park. Some were on a swaying suspension bridge, 230 feet above a river. The rest were on a solid wooden bridge just 10 feet above the ground. After the interview, the psychologist gave each man her telephone number, so he could "find out about the results" of the study. Men interviewed on the suspension bridge were much more likely to give the "lady from the park" a call (Dutton & Aron, 1974). Apparently, these men experienced heightened arousal, which they misinterpreted as attraction to the experimenter—a clear case of love at first fright!

BRIDGES

Love is one basis for interpersonal attraction, but there are others, such as similarity and proximity. **To learn more about what brings people together, see Chapter 17, pages 576–578.**

Emotional Appraisal

According to Richard Lazarus (1991a, 1991b), the role of cognition in experiencing emotions is not restricted to making causal attributions about why arousal has occurred. The emotions you experience are also greatly influenced by your **emotional appraisal**, how you evaluate the personal meaning of a stimulus: Is it good/bad, threatening/supportive, relevant/irrelevant, and so on (León & Hernández, 1998). Some examples of emotional appraisals and the emotions they give rise to can be found in ■ Table 10.2.

BRIDGES

Emotional appraisals have a major impact on the ability to cope with threats and stress, which may ultimately affect your health. **See Chapter 13, pages 449–450.**

Our discussion suggests that emotion is greatly influenced by how you think about an event. For example, if another driver "cuts you off" on the highway, you could become very angry. But if you do, you will add 15 minutes of emotional upset to your day. By changing your attribution ("He probably didn't mean it.") and/or your emotional appraisal ("No big deal, anyway."), you could just as easily choose to brush off the other driver's behavior—and minimize your emotional wear-and-tear (Deutschendorf, 2009; Gross, 2001).

■ TABLE 10.2 Appraisals and Corresponding Emotions

Appraisal	Emotion
You have been slighted or demeaned	Anger
You feel threatened	Anxiety
You have experienced a loss	Sadness
You have broken a moral rule	Guilt
You have not lived up to your ideals	Shame
You desire something another has	Envy
You are near something repulsive	Disgust
You fear the worst but yearn for better	Hope
You are moving toward a desired goal	Happiness
You are linked with a valued object or accomplishment	Pride
You have been treated well by another	Gratitude
You desire affection from another person	Love
You are moved by someone's suffering	Compassion

Adapted from Lazarus, 1991b.

The Facial Feedback Hypothesis

Schachter and Lazarus added thinking and interpretation (cognition) to our view of emotion, but the picture still seems incomplete. What about expressions? How do they influence emotion? As Charles Darwin observed, the face is very central to emotion—perhaps it is more than just an "emotional billboard."

Psychologist Carrol Izard (1977, 1990) was among the first to suggest that the face does, indeed, affect emotion. According to Izard, emotions cause innately programmed changes in facial expression. Sensations from the face then provide cues to the brain that help us determine what emotion we are feeling. This idea is known as the **facial feedback hypothesis** (Hennenlotter et al., 2009). Stated another way, it says that having facial expressions and becoming aware of them influences our private emotional experience. Exercise, for instance, arouses the body, but we don't experience this arousal as emotion because it does not trigger emotional expressions.

Psychologist Paul Ekman takes this idea one step further. He believes that "making faces" can actually cause emotion (Ekman, 1993). In one study, participants were guided as they arranged their faces, muscle by muscle, into expressions of surprise, disgust, sadness, anger, fear, and happiness (● Figure 10.20). At the same time, each person's bodily reactions were monitored.

Contrary to what you might expect, "making faces" can affect the autonomic nervous system, as shown by changes in heart rate and skin temperature. In addition, each facial expression produces a different pattern of activity. An angry face, for instance, raises heart rate and skin temperature, whereas disgust lowers both (Ekman, Levenson, &

The Clinical File — Suppressing Emotion—Don't Turn Off the Music

According to popular media, we are supposed to be happy all the time (Hecht, 2007). However, real emotional life has its ups and downs. Often, we try to appear less emotional than we really are, especially when we are feeling negative emotions. Have you ever been angry with a friend in public? Embarrassed by someone's behavior at a party? Disgusted by someone's table manners? In such circumstances, people are quite good at suppressing outward signs of emotion.

However, restraining emotion can actually increase activity in the sympathetic nervous system. In other words, hiding emotion requires a lot of effort. Suppressing emotions can also impair thinking and memory, as you devote energy to self-control. Thus, although suppressing emotion allows us to appear calm and collected on the outside, this cool appearance comes at a high cost (Richards & Gross, 2000). People who constantly suppress their emotions cope poorly with life and are prone to depression and other problems (Haga, Kraft, Corby, 2010; Lynch et al., 2001).

Conversely, people who express their emotions generally experience better emotional and physical health (Lumley, 2004; Pennebaker, 2004). Paying attention to our negative emotions can also lead us to think more clearly about the positive *and* the negative. The end result is better decision making, which can increase our overall happiness in the long run (Deutschendorf, 2009; Norem, 2002). Usually, it's better to manage emotions than it is to suppress them. You will find some suggestions for managing emotions in the upcoming *Psychology in Action* section.

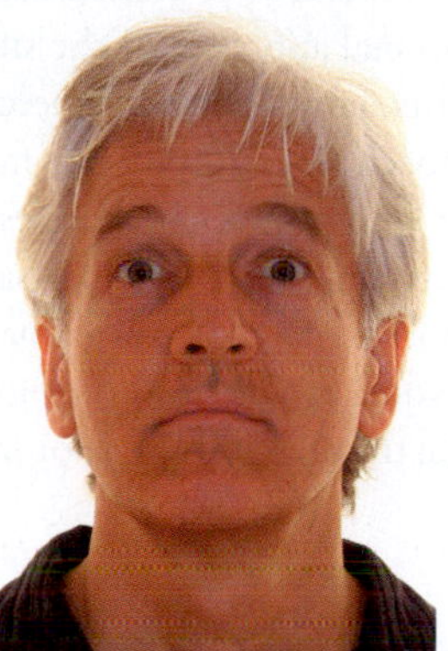
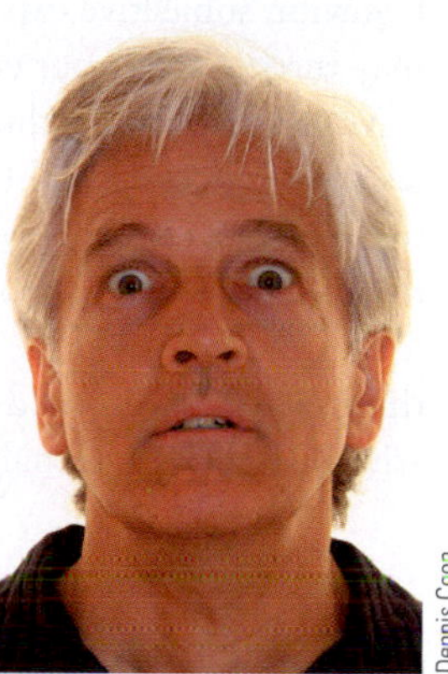

Dennis Coon

• Figure 10.20 Facial feedback and emotion. Participants in Ekman's study formed facial expressions like those normally observed during emotion. When they did this, emotion-like changes took place in their bodily activity. (Adapted from Ekman, Levenson, & Friesen, 1983.)

Friesen, 1983). Other studies have confirmed that posed expressions alter emotions and bodily activity (Duclos & Laird, 2001; Soussignan, 2002).

In a fascinating experiment on facial feedback, people rated how funny they thought cartoons were while holding a pen crosswise in their mouths. Those who held the pen in their teeth thought the cartoons were funnier than did people who held the pen in their lips. Can you guess why? The answer is that if you hold a pen with your teeth, you are forced to form a smile. Holding it with the lips makes a frown. As predicted by the facial feedback hypothesis, emotional experiences were influenced by the facial expressions that people made (Strack, Martin, & Stepper, 1988). Next time you're feeling sad, bite a pen!

Do people who have botox injected into their faces experience any less emotion? It can certainly be uncanny to watch celebrities whose faces have been injected with botox. And it is indeed possible they feel less emotion as a consequence. In one study, compared to normal participants, participants injected with Botox showed less brain activity as they imitated angry faces (Hennenlotter et al., 2009). (Ain't nothin' gonna move!) It appears, then, that not only do emotions influence expressions, but expressions influence emotions, as shown here (Duclos & Laird, 2001):

Contracted Facial Muscles	Felt Emotion
Forehead	Surprise
Brow	Anger
Mouth (down)	Sadness
Mouth (smile)	Joy

This could explain an interesting effect you have probably observed. When you are feeling "down," forcing yourself to smile will sometimes be followed by an actual improvement in your mood (Kleinke, Peterson, & Rutledge, 1998).

If smiling can improve a person's mood, is it a good idea to inhibit negative emotions? For an answer, see "Suppressing Emotion—Don't Turn Off the Music."

A Contemporary Model of Emotion

To summarize, James and Lange were right that feedback from arousal and behavior adds to our emotional experiences. Cannon and Bard were right about the timing of events. Schachter showed us that cognitive attribution is important. Richard Lazarus stressed

Emotional appraisal Evaluating the personal meaning of a stimulus or situation.

Facial feedback hypothesis States that sensations from facial expressions help define what emotion a person feels.

the importance of emotional appraisal. In fact, psychologists are increasingly aware that both the *attributions* you make and how you *appraise* a situation greatly affects your emotions (León & Hernández, 1998; Strongman, 2003). Carrol Izard focused on facial expressions. Let's put these ideas together in a single model of emotion (● Figure 10.21).

Imagine that a large snarling dog lunges at you with its teeth bared. A modern view of your emotional reactions goes something like this: An *emotional stimulus* (the dog) is *appraised* (judged) as a threat or other cause for emotion. (You think to yourself, "Uh oh, big trouble!") Your appraisal gives rise to *ANS arousal* (your heart pounds, and your body becomes stirred up) and *cognitive labeling*. At the same time, your appraisal leads to *adaptive behavior* (you run from the dog). The appraisal also releases *innate emotional expressions* (your face twists into a mask of fear, and your posture becomes tense). In addition, it causes a change in consciousness that you recognize as the subjective experience of fear. (The intensity of this *emotional feeling* is directly related to the amount of ANS arousal taking place in your body.)

Each element of emotion—ANS arousal, labeling, adaptive behavior, subjective experience, and your emotional expressions—may further alter your emotional appraisal of the situation, as well as your attributions, thoughts, judgments, and perceptions. Thus, according to the facial feedback hypothesis, your facial expression may further influence your emotion. Such changes affect each of the other reactions, which again alters your appraisal and interpretation of events. Thus, emotion may blossom, change course, or diminish as it proceeds. Note, too, that the original emotional stimulus can be external, like the attacking dog, or internal, such as a memory of being chased by a dog, rejected by a lover, or praised by a friend. That's why mere thoughts and memories can make us fearful, sad, or happy (Strongman, 2003).

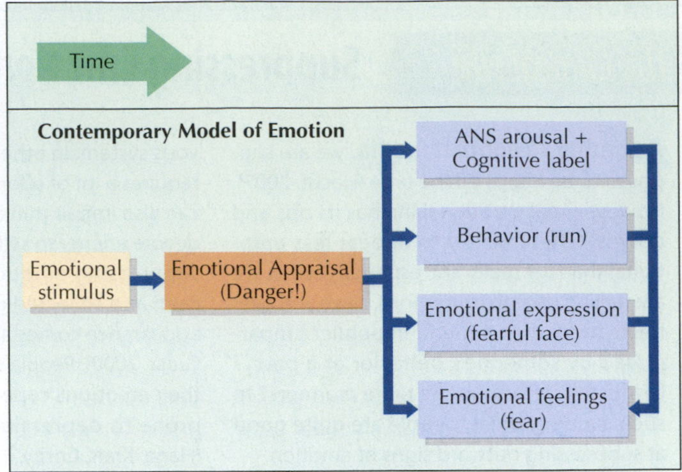

● **Figure 10.21** A contemporary model of emotion. Appraisal gives rise to arousal and cognitive labeling, behavior, facial/postural expressions, and emotional feelings. Arousal, attribution, behavior, and expressions add to emotional feelings. Emotional feelings influence appraisal, which further affects arousal, behavior, expressions, and feelings.

A Look Ahead

In the *Psychology in Action* section of this chapter, we will look further at the impact of emotional appraisals through an examination of *emotional intelligence*. Before we continue, you might want to appraise your learning with the exercises that follow.

Emotional Expression and Theories of Emotion

RECITE

1. Charles Darwin held that emotional expressions aid survival for animals. T or F?
2. Which three dimensions of emotion are communicated by facial expressions?
   a. pleasantness–unpleasantness *b.* complexity *c.* attention–rejection *d.* anger e. curiosity–disinterest f. activation
3. A formal term for "body language" is ________________.
4. According to the James-Lange theory, emotional experience precedes physical arousal and emotional behavior. (We see a bear, are frightened, and run.) T or F?
5. The Cannon-Bard theory of emotion says that bodily arousal and emotional experience occur ________________.
6. The idea that labeling arousal helps define what emotions we experience is associated with
   a. the James-Lange theory *b.* Schachter's cognitive theory *c.* the Cannon-Bard theory *d.* Darwin's theory of innate emotional expressions
7. Subjects in Valins's false heart rate study attributed increases in their heart rate to the action of a placebo. T or F?
8. As you try to wiggle your ears, you keep pulling the corners of your mouth back into a smile. Each time you do, you find yourself giggling. Which of the following provides the best explanation for this reaction?
   a. attribution *b.* the Cannon-Bard theory *c.* appraisal *d.* facial feedback

REFLECT

Think Critically

9. People with high spinal injuries may feel almost no signs of physiological arousal from their bodies. Nevertheless, they still feel emotion, which can be intense at times. What theory of emotion does this observation contradict?

Self-Reflect

Write a list of emotions that you think you can accurately detect from facial expressions. Does your list match Paul Ekman's? Would you be more confident in rating pleasantness–unpleasantness, attention–rejection, and activation? Why?

Which theory seems to best explain your own emotional experiences? Try frowning or smiling for 5 minutes. Did facial feedback have any effect on your mood? Cover the left column of ■ Table 10.2. Read each emotional label in the right column. What appraisal do you think would lead to the listed emotion?

Answers: 1. T **2.** *a, c, f* **3.** kinesics **4.** F **5.** simultaneously **6.** *b* **7.** F **8.** *d* **9.** The James-Lange theory and Schachter's cognitive theory. The facial feedback hypothesis also helps explain the observation.

Psychology in Action: Emotional Intelligence—The Fine Art of Self-Control

Gateway Question 10.11: *What does it mean to have "emotional intelligence"?*

The Greek philosopher Aristotle had a recipe for handling relationships smoothly: "Be angry with the right person, to the right degree, at the right time, for the right purpose, and in the right way." Psychologists Peter Salovey and John Mayer call such self-control **emotional intelligence**, the ability to perceive, use, understand, and manage emotions (Salovey & Mayer, 1997). In general, being emotionally intelligent means accepting that emotions are an essential part of who we are and how we survive. Being emotionally skilled can make us more flexible, adaptable, and emotionally mature (Bonanno et al., 2004; Johnson, Batey, & Holdsworth, 2009).

People who excel in life tend to be emotionally intelligent (Mehrabian, 2000). If our emotions are the music of life, then emotionally intelligent people are good musicians. They do not stifle their emotions or overindulge in them. Instead, they compose them into sustaining life rhythms that mesh well with other people. They are more *agreeable* than people with low emotional skills (Haas et al., 2007).

Indeed, the costs of poor emotional skills can be high. They range from problems in marriage and parenting to poor physical health. A lack of emotional intelligence can ruin careers and sabotage achievement (Zampetakis & Moustakis, 2011). Perhaps the greatest toll falls on children and teenagers (Alegre, 2011; Parker, 2005). For them, having poor emotional skills can contribute to depression, eating disorders, unwanted pregnancy, aggression, violent crime, and poor academic performance. Thus, in many life circumstances emotional intelligence is as important as IQ (Dulewicz & Higgs, 2000).

AP Photo/Camay Sungu

Are there specific skills that make up emotional intelligence? Many elements contribute to emotional intelligence (Deutschendorf, 2009; Larsen & Prizmic, 2004; Mayer et al., 2001). A description of some of the most important skills follows:

Perceiving emotions The foundation of emotional intelligence is the ability to perceive emotions in yourself and others. Unlike alexithymic people, emotionally intelligent people are tuned in to their own feelings (Taylor & Taylor-Allan, 2007). They are able to recognize quickly if they are angry, envious, feeling guilty, or depressed. This is valuable because many people have disruptive emotions without being able to pinpoint why they are uncomfortable. At the same time, emotionally intelligent people have *empathy*. They accurately perceive emotions in others and sense what others are feeling. They are good at "reading" facial expressions, tone of voice, and other signs of emotion.

Using Emotions People who are emotionally intelligent use their feelings to enhance thinking and decision making. For example, if you can remember how you reacted emotionally in the past, it can help you react better to new situations. You can also use emotions to promote personal growth and improve relationships with others. For instance, you may have noticed that helping someone else makes you feel better, too. Likewise, when good fortune comes their way, people who are emotionally smart share the news with others. Almost always, doing so strengthens relationships and increases emotional well-being (Gable et al., 2004).

Understanding Emotions Emotions contain useful information. For instance, anger is a cue that something is wrong; anxiety indicates uncertainty; embarrassment communicates shame; depression means we feel helpless; enthusiasm tells us we're excited. People who are emotionally intelligent know what causes various emotions, what they mean, and how they affect behavior.

Managing Emotions Emotional intelligence involves an ability to manage your own emotions and those of others. For example, you know how to calm down when you are angry and you also know how to calm others. As Aristotle noted so long ago, people who are emotionally intelligent have an ability to amplify or restrain emotions, depending on the situation (Bonanno et al., 2004).

Positive Psychology and Positive Emotions

It's obvious that joy, interest, contentment, love, and similar emotions are pleasant and rewarding. There is a natural tendency to enjoy positive emotions but to treat negative emotions as unwelcome misery. Make no mistake, though. Negative emotions can also be valuable and constructive. For example, persistent distress may motivate a person to seek help, mend a relationship, or find a new direction in life (Plutchik, 2003). Negative emotions are associated with actions that probably helped our ancestors save their skins: escaping, attacking, expelling poison, and the like. As useful as these reactions may be, they tend to narrow our focus of attention and limit our ideas about possible actions.

In contrast, positive emotions tend to broaden our focus (Fredrickson & Branigan, 2005). This opens up new possibilities and builds up our personal resources. For instance, emotions such as joy, interest, and contentment create an urge to play, to be creative, to explore, to savor life, to seek new experiences, to integrate, and to grow.

In short, positive emotions are not just a pleasant side effect of happy circumstances. They also encourage personal growth and social connection. Happiness can be cultivated by using the strengths we already possess—including kindness, originality, humor, optimism, and generosity. Such strengths are natural buffers against misfortune, and they can

Emotional intelligence The ability to perceive, use, understand, and manage emotions.

help people live more positive, genuinely happy lives (Ong, Zautra, & Reid, 2010; Seligman, 2002). A capacity for having positive emotions is a basic human strength, and cultivating good feelings is a part of emotional intelligence (Fredrickson, 2003).

Becoming Emotionally Smart

How would a person learn the skills that make up emotional intelligence? Often, the "right" choices in life can only be defined by taking personal values, needs, and emotions into account. Extremely rational approaches to making choices can produce sensible but emotionally empty decisions. Good decisions often combine emotion with reason. In short, emotional intelligence is the ability to consciously make your emotions work for you.

Psychologists are still unsure how to teach emotional intelligence. Nevertheless, it's clear that emotional skills can be learned. Accepting that emotions are valuable is an important first step. There are many valuable lessons to learn from paying close attention to your emotions and the emotions of others. It's a good bet that many of the people you admire the most are not just smart, but also emotionally smart (Lady Gaga?). They are people who know how to offer a toast at a wedding, tell a joke at a roast, comfort the bereaved at a funeral, add to the fun at a party, or calm a frightened child. These are skills worth cultivating (Deutschendorf, 2009).

Knowledge Builder: Emotional Intelligence

RECITE

1. People who rate high in emotional intelligence tend to be highly aware of their own feelings and unaware of emotions experienced by others. T or F?
2. Using the information imparted by emotional reactions can enhance thinking and decision making. T or F?
3. Positive emotions may be pleasant, but they tend to narrow our focus of attention and limit the range of possible actions we are likely to consider. T or F?
4. Which of the following is *not* an element of emotional intelligence? *a.* empathy *b.* self-control *c.* self-centeredness *d.* self-awareness

REFLECT

Think Critically

5. You are angry because a friend borrowed money from you and hasn't repaid it. What would be an emotionally intelligent response to this situation?

Self-Reflect

Think of a person you know who is smart but low in emotional intelligence. Think of another person who is smart cognitively *and* emotionally. How does the second person differ from the first? Which person do you think would make a better parent, friend, supervisor, roommate, or teacher?

Answers: 1. F **2.** T **3.** F **4.** c **5.** There's no single right answer. Rather than being angry, it might be better to reflect on whether friendship or money is more important in life. If you appreciate your friend's virtues, accept that no one is perfect, and reappraise the loan as a gift, you could save a valued relationship and reduce your anger at the same time. Alternately, if you become aware that your friend persistently manipulates other people with emotional appeals for support, it may be worth reappraising your friendship.

Chapter in Review Gateways to Motivation and Emotion

Gateway QUESTIONS REVISITED

10.1 *What is motivation and are there different types of motives?*

10.1.1 Motives initiate, sustain, and direct activities. Motivation typically involves the sequence: need, drive, goal, and goal attainment (need reduction).

10.1.2 Behavior can be activated either by needs (push) or by goals (pull).

10.1.3 The attractiveness of a goal and its ability to initiate action are related to its incentive value.

10.1.4 Three principal types of motives are biological motives, stimulus motives, and learned motives.

10.1.5 Most biological motives operate to maintain homeostasis.

10.1.6 Circadian rhythms of bodily activity are closely tied to sleep, activity, and energy cycles. Time zone travel and shift work can seriously disrupt sleep and bodily rhythms.

10.2 *What causes hunger, overeating, and eating disorders?*

10.2.1 Hunger is influenced by a complex interplay between fullness of the stomach, blood sugar levels, metabolism in the liver, and fat stores in the body.

10.2.2 The hypothalamus exerts the most direct control of eating, through areas that act like feeding and satiety systems. The hypothalamus is sensitive to both neural and chemical messages, which affect eating.

10.2.3 Other factors influencing hunger are the body's set point, external eating cues, the attractiveness and variety of diet, emotions, learned taste preferences and taste aversions, and cultural values.

10.2.4 Obesity is the result of internal and external influences, diet, emotions, genetics, and exercise.

10.2.5 The most effective way to lose weight is behavioral dieting, which is based on techniques that change eating patterns and exercise habits.

10.2.6 Anorexia nervosa and bulimia nervosa are two prominent eating disorders. Both tend to involve conflicts about self-image, self-control, and anxiety.

10.3 What kinds of biological motives are thirst, pain avoidance, and the sex drive?

10.3.1 Like hunger, thirst and other basic motives are affected by a number of bodily factors but are primarily under the central control of the hypothalamus.

10.3.2 Thirst may be either intracellular or extracellular.

10.3.3 Pain avoidance is unusual because it is episodic as opposed to cyclic. Pain avoidance and pain tolerance are partially learned.

10.3.4 The sex drive is also unusual in that it is non-homeostatic.

10.4 How does arousal relate to motivation?

10.4.1 Drives for stimulation are partially explained by arousal theory, which states that an ideal level of bodily arousal will be maintained if possible.

10.4.2 The desired level of arousal or stimulation varies from person to person.

10.4.3 Optimal performance on a task usually occurs at *moderate* levels of arousal. This relationship is described by an inverted U function. The Yerkes-Dodson law further states that for simple tasks the ideal arousal level is higher, and for complex tasks it is lower.

10.5 What are learned and social motives and why are they important?

10.5.1 Learned motives, including social motives, account for much of the diversity of human motivation.

10.5.2 Opponent-process theory explains the operation of some learned motives.

10.5.3 Social motives are learned through socialization and cultural conditioning.

10.5.4 People high in need for achievement (nAch) are successful in many situations due to their perseverance, passion, and self-confidence.

10.5.5 Self-confidence greatly affects motivation in everyday life.

10.6 Are some motives more basic than others?

10.6.1 Maslow's hierarchy of motives categorizes needs as either basic or growth oriented.

10.6.2 Lower needs in the hierarchy are assumed to be prepotent (dominant) over higher needs.

10.6.3 Self-actualization, the highest and most fragile need, is reflected in meta-needs.

10.6.4 Meta-needs are closely related to intrinsic motivation. In some situations, external rewards can undermine intrinsic motivation, enjoyment, and creativity.

10.7 What happens during emotion?

10.7.1 An emotion consists of physiological changes, adaptive behavior, emotional expressions, and emotional feelings.

10.7.2 The primary emotions of fear, surprise, sadness, disgust, anger, anticipation, joy, and trust (acceptance) can be mixed to produce more complex emotional experiences.

10.7.3 The left hemisphere of the brain primarily processes positive emotions. Negative emotions are processed in the right hemisphere.

10.7.4 The amygdala provides a "quick and dirty" pathway for the arousal of fear that bypasses the cerebral cortex.

10.8 What physiological changes underlie emotion, and can "lie detectors" really detect lies?

10.8.1 Physical changes associated with emotion are caused by activity in the autonomic nervous system (ANS).

10.8.2 The sympathetic branch of the ANS is primarily responsible for arousing the body, the parasympathetic branch for quieting it.

10.8.3 The polygraph, or "lie detector," measures emotional arousal (rather than lying) by monitoring heart rate, blood pressure, breathing rate, and the galvanic skin response (GSR). The accuracy of the lie detector can be quite low.

10.8.4 Newer brain imaging methods, such as fMRI, are showing great promise in lie detection.

10.9 How accurately are emotions expressed by the face and "body language"?

10.9.1 Basic facial expressions of fear, anger, disgust, sadness, surprise, and happiness are universally recognized. Facial expressions of contempt and interest may be universal as well.

10.9.2 Facial expressions reveal pleasantness versus unpleasantness, attention versus rejection, and a person's degree of emotional activation.

10.9.3 Social context influences the meaning of facial expressions, such as social smiles. Cultural differences in the meaning of some facial expressions also occur. Men tend to be less expressive than women.

10.9.4 The formal study of body language is known as *kinesics*. Body gestures and movements (body language) also express feelings, mainly by communicating emotional tone rather than specific universal messages.

10.9.5 Body positioning expresses relaxation or tension and liking or disliking.

10.9.6 Lying can sometimes be detected from changes in illustrators or emblems.

10.10 How do psychologists explain emotions?

10.10.1 Contrary to common sense, the James-Lange theory says that emotional experience follows bodily reactions. In contrast, the Cannon-Bard theory says that bodily reactions and emotional experiences occur at the same time.

10.10.2 Schachter's cognitive theory emphasizes that labeling bodily arousal can determine what emotion you feel. Appropriate labels are chosen by attribution (ascribing arousal to a particular source).

10.10.3 Contemporary views of emotion place greater emphasis on the effects of cognitive appraisals. Also, our feelings and actions change as each element of emotion interacts with others. One of the best ways to manage emotion is to change your emotional appraisal of a situation.

10.10.4 The facial feedback hypothesis holds that facial expressions help define the emotions we feel.

10.10.5 Contemporary views of emotion emphasize that all the elements of emotion are interrelated and interact with one another.

10.11 What does it mean to have "emotional intelligence"?

10.11.1 Emotional intelligence is the ability to consciously make your emotions work for you in a wide variety of life circumstances.

10.11.2 People who are "smart" emotionally are able to perceive, use, understand, and manage emotions. They are self-aware and empathetic; know how to use emotions to enhance thinking, decision making, and relationships; and have an ability to understand and manage emotions.

10.11.3 Positive emotions are valuable because they tend to broaden our focus and they encourage personal growth and social connection.

MEDIA RESOURCES

Web Resources

Internet addresses frequently change. To find an up-to-date list of URLs for the sites listed here, visit your Psychology CourseMate.

Theories of Motivation Because no single theory can account for all aspects of biological aspects of motivation, this site examines the major approaches to understanding motivation and includes discussions of both the strengths and weaknesses of each theory.

Sleeplessness and Circadian Rhythm Disorder Read what happens when your biological clock malfunctions and what you can do about it.

Drive Reduction Theory and Incentives in the Regulation of Food Intake Using eating behavior as an example, explore the roles of drive reduction and incentives.

Eating Disorders Website Home page of a self-help group for those afflicted with eating disorders.

Healthy Dieting Find your body mass index as you learn more about healthy dieting.

The Facts about Aphrodisiacs Find out if aphrodisiacs increase the sex drive.

Sensation Seeking Scale Find out if you are high or low in sensation seeking.

The Yerkes-Dodson Law Read more about the Yerkes-Dodson Law.

Achievement Motivation in Business Find out if people high in the need for achievement make good managers.

The Affective System Provides information about how particular parts of the brain are associated with different aspects of emotion; provides a classification of basic emotions and how emotions impact our behavior.

When a Patient Has No Story to Tell Read the case histories of several people with alexithymia.

Learn the Truth about Lie Detectors Read arguments against the use of polygraph testing.

The Expression of the Emotions in Man and Animals Read Charles Darwin's original book on this topic.

What's in a Face? Read an APA article about facial expressions.

Controlling Anger Discusses anger and some strategies for its control.

Emotional IQ Test Measure your emotional intelligence.

Emotional Intelligence This site provides information about emotional intelligence and why some people may be better at handling emotions than others and offers a useful set of guidelines for doing just this.

Emotional Intelligence Links Explore a comprehensive set of links on the topic of emotional intelligence.

Interactive Learning

Log in to **CengageBrain** to access the resources your instructor requires. For this book, you can access:

CourseMate brings course concepts to life with interactive learning, study, and exam preparation tools that support the printed textbook. A textbook-specific website, ***Psychology CourseMate*** includes an ***integrated interactive eBook*** and other ***interactive learning tools*** including quizzes, flashcards, videos, and more.

CENGAGENOW™

CengageNOW is an easy-to-use online resource that helps you study in less time to get the grade you want—NOW. Take a pre-test for this chapter and receive a personalized study plan based on your results that will identify the topics you need to review and direct you to online resources to help you master those topics. Then take a post-test to help you determine the concepts you have mastered and what you will need to work on. If your textbook does not include an access code card, go to CengageBrain.com to gain access.

WebTUTOR™

More than just an interactive study guide, **WebTutor** is an anytime, anywhere customized learning solution with an eBook, keeping you connected to your textbook, instructor, and classmates.

If your professor has assigned **Aplia** homework:

1. Sign in to your account.
2. Complete the corresponding homework exercises as required by your professor.
3. When finished, click "Grade It Now" to see which areas you have mastered and which need more work, and for detailed explanations of every answer.

Visit www.cengagebrain.com to access your account and purchase materials.

Gateway THEME

The sexes are more alike than different. Sexuality is a normal and healthy part of human behavior.

11

Sex, Gender, and Sexuality

Pink and Blue?

Girls are girls and boys are boys, right? Wrong. Even something as basic as sex is many-sided and far from black and white (pink and blue?). The complexity of sexual identity is hinted at by Elena's journey from her early life as a man to her current life as a woman. Elena is a transsexual who acted on her deeply held desire to change her sex, biologically, psychologically, and socially. About her early life, Elena remarked, "I have always known I was a girl.…In first grade I avoided boys like the plague. Boys called me 'sissy' and 'cry baby' and beat me up."

As an adult, she decided to become the woman she always felt she was. As Elena put it, "I was determined to transition. Of course, I was terrified the changes would leave me destitute and friendless, that I would wind up dead in a ditch somewhere, victim of someone else's fist.…Lucky for me, I had nothing to fear at work. When I came out to our company president, he sent an e-mail to the whole organization (with my permission) stating that I was transitioning from male to female, and that I was to be treated with the same respect and dignity [as] any other woman. My 650 coworkers fully accepted me, as did most of my family" (Kelly, 2010).

Genetically, Elena is still male, but psychologically she is female—she has female genitals, and she functions socially as a female. So is Elena female or male? You might view Elena as an unfair example because transsexuals seek to alter their "natural" sex. For most people, the indicators of maleness or femaleness are in agreement. Nevertheless, it is not unusual to find ambiguities among various aspects of a person's sex. One thing we never forget about a person is his or her sex. Considering the number of activities, relationships, conflicts, and choices influenced by sex, it is no wonder that we pay such close attention to it.

Gateway QUESTIONS

- *11.1 What are the basic dimensions of sex?*
- *11.2 What is sexual orientation?*
- *11.3 How does one's sense of maleness or femaleness develop?*
- *11.4 What is psychological androgyny (and is it contagious)?*
- *11.5 What is gender variance?*
- *11.6 What are the most typical patterns of human sexual behavior?*
- *11.7 To what extent do females and males differ in sexual response?*
- *11.8 What are the most common sexual disorders?*
- *11.9 Have recent changes in attitudes affected sexual behavior?*
- *11.10 What impacts have sexually transmitted diseases had on sexual behavior?*
- *11.11 How can couples keep their relationships sexually satisfying, and what are the most common sexual dysfunctions?*

Sexual Development—Circle One: *XX* or *XY*?

Gateway Question 11.1: *What are the basic dimensions of sex?*

The term **sex** refers to whether you are physically, biologically female or male. In contrast, **gender** refers to all the psychological and social traits associated with being male or female (Crooks & Baur, 2011). In other words, after we establish that you are male or female, gender tells us whether you are masculine or feminine (as defined by the culture in which you live). As Elena's story so clearly illustrates, biological sex does not always align with psychological and social gender. In **transsexuals**, a person's physical, biological sex conflicts with his or her preferred psychological and social gender roles (Veale, Clarke, & Lomax, 2010). For the moment, let's focus on the biology of what it means to be female or male.

Dimensions of Sex

What causes the development of sex differences? At the very least, classifying a person as female or male must take into account the following biological factors: (1) **genetic sex** (*XX* or *XY* chromosomes); (2) **hormonal sex** (predominance of androgens or estrogens); (3) **gonadal sex** (ovaries or testes); and (4) **genital sex** (clitoris and vagina in females, penis and scrotum in males). To see why sex must be defined along these four dimensions, let's trace the events involved in becoming female or male.

Genetic Sex

Becoming male or female starts simply enough. Genetic sex is determined at the instant of conception: Two ***X* chromosomes** initiate female development; an *X* chromosome plus a ***Y* chromosome** produces a male. A woman's ovum always provides an *X* chromosome, because she has two *X*'s in her own genetic makeup. In contrast, one half of the male's sperm carry *X* chromosomes and the other half carry *Y*'s.

Even at conception, variations may occur because some individuals begin life with too many or too few sex chromosomes (Crooks & Baur, 2011). For example, in *Kleinfelter's syndrome*, a boy is born XXY, with an extra X chromosome. As a result, when he matures, he may appear feminine, have undersized sexual organs, and be infertile. In *Turner's syndrome*, a girl is born with only one X chromosome and no Y chromosome. As an adolescent, she may appear boyish and she will also be infertile.

Hormonal and Gonadal Sex

Although genetic sex stays the same throughout life, it alone does not determine biological sex. In general, sexual characteristics are also related to the effects of sex hormones before birth. (Hormones are chemical substances secreted by endocrine glands.) The **gonads** (or sex glands) affect sexual development and behavior by secreting **estrogens** (female hormones) and **androgens** (male hormones). The gonads in the male are the testes; female gonads are the ovaries. The adrenal glands (located above the kidneys) also supply sex hormones.

Everyone normally produces both estrogens and androgens. Sex differences are related to the *proportion* of these hormones found in the body. In fact, prenatal development of male or female anatomy is largely due to the presence or absence of **testosterone** (tes-TOSS-teh-rone: one of the androgens, secreted mainly by the testes) (LeVay & Baldwin, 2008). For the first 6 weeks of prenatal growth, genetically female and male embryos look identical. However, if a *Y* chromosome is present, testes develop in the embryo and supply testosterone (Knickmeyer & Baron-Cohen, 2006). This stimulates growth of the penis and other male structures (● Figure 11.1). In the absence of testosterone, the embryo will

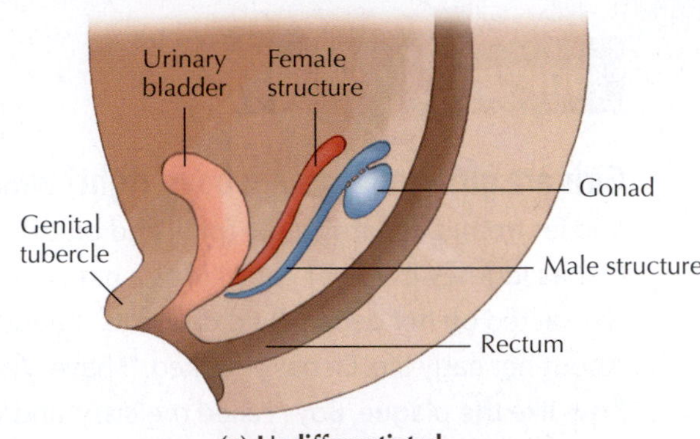

(a) Undifferentiated

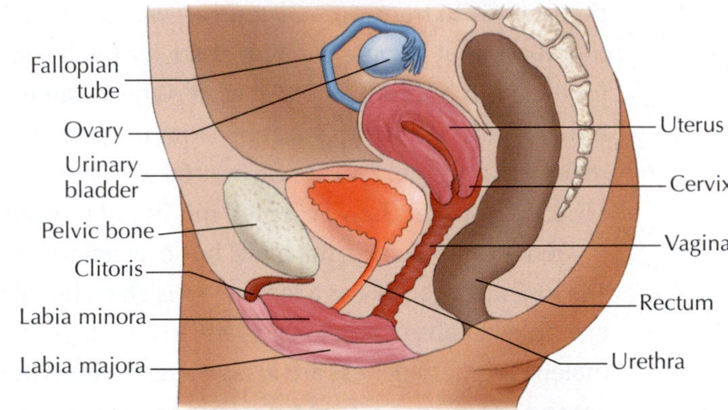

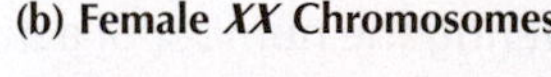

(b) Female *XX* Chromosomes

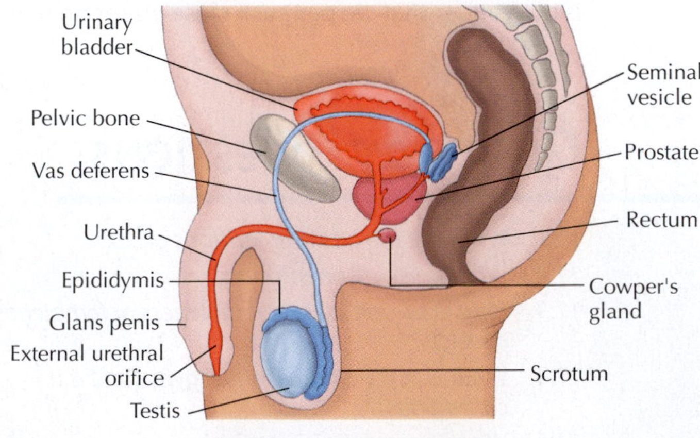

(c) Male *XY* Chromosomes

● **Figure 11.1** Prenatal development of the reproductive organs. Early development of ovaries or testes affects hormonal balance and alters sexual anatomy. *(a)* At first, the sex organs are the same in the human female and male. *(b)* When androgens are absent, female structures develop. *(c)* Male sex organs are produced when androgens are present.

TABLE 11.1 Female and Male Sexual Anatomy

Female Reproductive Structures
Cervix (SER-vix) The lower end of the uterus that projects into the vagina.
Clitoris (KLIT-er-iss) Small, sensitive organ made up of erectile tissue; located above the vaginal opening.
Fallopian tube (feh-LOPE-ee-en) One of two tubes that carry eggs from the ovaries to the uterus.
Labia majora (LAY-bee-ah mah-JOR-ah) The larger outer lips of the vulva.
Labia minora (LAY-bee-ah mih-NOR-ah) Inner lips of the vulva, surrounding the vaginal opening.
Ovary (OH-vah-ree) One of the two female reproductive glands; ovaries are the source of hormones and eggs.
Uterus (YOO-ter-us) The pear-shaped muscular organ in which the fetus develops during pregnancy; also known as the womb.
Vagina (vah-JINE-ah) Tube-like structure connecting the external female genitalia with the uterus.
Male Reproductive Structures
Cowper's glands Two small glands that secrete a clear fluid into the urethra during sexual excitement.
Epididymis (ep-ih-DID-ih-mus) A coiled structure at the top of the testes in which sperm are stored.
External urethral orifice (yoo-REE-thral OR-ih-fis) The opening at the tip of the penis through which urine and semen pass.
Glans penis (glanz PEA-nis) The tip of the penis.
Prostate (PROSS-tate) A gland located at the base of the urinary bladder that supplies most of the fluid that makes up semen.
Scrotum (SKROE-tehm) The sac-like pouch that holds the testes.
Seminal vesicles (SEM-in-uhl VES-ih-kuhlz) These two small organs (one on each side of the prostate) supply fluid that becomes part of semen.
Testis (TES-tis, singular; testes, plural) One of the two male reproductive glands; the testes are a source of hormones and sperm.
Vas deferens (vaz DEH-fur-enz) The duct that carries sperm from the testes to the urethra.

develop female reproductive organs and genitals, regardless of genetic sex (LeVay & Baldwin, 2008). It might be said, then, that nature's primary impulse is to make a female. Without testosterone, we would all be women.

Prenatal growth does not always match genetic sex. For both genetic females and males, hormonal problems before birth may produce an **intersexual person** (one who has ambiguous sexual anatomy). (The former term, **hermaphrodite**, is now regarded by many as offensive). A genetic male won't develop male genitals if too little testosterone is available. Even if testosterone is present, an inherited *androgen insensitivity syndrome* (unresponsiveness to testosterone) may exist. Again, the result is female development (Freberg, 2010).

Similarly, androgens must be at low levels or absent for an *XX* embryo to develop as a female. For instance, a developing female may be masculinized by the anti-miscarriage drug progestin, or by a problem known as *congenital adrenal hyperplasia*. In this syndrome, the child's body produces estrogen, but a genetic abnormality causes the adrenal glands to release too much androgen. In such cases, a female child may be born with genitals that are more male than female (Freberg, 2010).

Genital Sex

Mature males and females also differ in both *primary* and *secondary* sexual characteristics. **Primary sexual characteristics** refer to the sexual and reproductive organs themselves: the vagina, ovaries, and uterus in females and the penis, testes, and scrotum in males (see ■ Table 11.1). **Secondary sexual characteristics** are more superficial physical features that appear at puberty. These features develop in response to hormonal signals from the pituitary gland. In females, secondary sexual characteristics include breast development, broadening of the hips, and other changes in body shape. Males grow facial and body hair, and the voice deepens.

These changes signal that a person is biologically ready to reproduce. Reproductive maturity is especially evident in the female *menarche* (MEN-are-kee: the onset of menstruation). Soon after menarche, monthly ovulation begins. *Ovulation* refers to the release of ova (eggs) from the ovaries. From the first ovulation until *menopause* (the end of regular monthly fertility cycles, usually in the late 40s or early 50s), women can bear children.

Sexual Orientation—Who Do You Love?

Gateway Question 11.2: *What is sexual orientation?*

Another aspect of sex is **sexual orientation**, your degree of emotional and erotic attraction to members of the same sex, opposite sex, or both sexes. Just as physical sex does not fall neatly into

Sex One's physical, biological classification as female or male.

Gender Psychological and social characteristics associated with being male or female; defined especially by one's gender identity and learned gender roles.

Transsexual A person with a deep conflict between his or her physical, biological sex and preferred psychological and social gender roles.

Genetic sex Sex as indicated by the presence of *XX* (female) or *XY* (male) chromosomes.

Hormonal sex Sex as indicated by a preponderance of estrogens (female) or androgens (male) in the body.

Gonadal sex Sex as indicated by the presence of ovaries (female) or testes (male).

Genital sex Sex as indicated by the presence of male or female genitals.

***X* chromosome** The female chromosome contributed by the mother; produces a female when paired with another *X* chromosome, and a male when paired with a *Y* chromosome.

***Y* chromosome** The male chromosome contributed by the father; produces a male when paired with an *X* chromosome. Fathers may give either an *X* or a *Y* chromosome to their offspring.

Gonads The primary sex glands—the testes in males and ovaries in females.

Estrogen Any of a number of female sex hormones.

Androgen Any of a number of male sex hormones, especially testosterone.

Testosterone A male sex hormone, secreted mainly by the testes and responsible for the development of many male sexual characteristics.

Intersexual person (formerly hermaphrodite) A person who has genitals suggestive of both sexes.

Primary sexual characteristics Sex as defined by the genitals and internal reproductive organs.

Secondary sexual characteristics Sexual features other than the genitals and reproductive organs—breasts, body shape, facial hair, and so forth.

Sexual orientation One's degree of emotional and erotic attraction to members of the same sex, opposite sex, both sexes, or neither sex.

two categories—male or female—so too sexual orientation is not always exclusively heterosexual or homosexual (Carroll, 2010). **Heterosexuals** are romantically and erotically attracted to members of the opposite sex. **Homosexuals** are attracted to people whose sex matches their own. **Bisexuals** are attracted to both men and women.

It is estimated that about 3.4 percent of all adults regard themselves as homosexual or bisexual (Conron, Mimiaga, & Landers, 2010). This means about 10.5 million people in the United States alone are gay, lesbian, or bisexual. Millions of others have a family member who is homosexual. It is also worth remembering that these figures are likely on the low side since many nonheterosexuals are unwilling to identify themselves as such (Bogaert, 2006). With this in mind, here are the details:

	Men	Women
Heterosexual	95.8%	97.1%
Homosexual	3.5%	1.8%
Bisexual	.7%	1.1%

Asexuality

According to a growing number of psychologists, **asexuality**—a lack of attraction to both men and women—constitutes a fourth type of sexual orientation, accounting for about 1 percent of adults (Bogaert, 2004, 2006). Unlike *celibates*, who choose not to act on their sexual attractions, asexuals experience little or no sexual attraction in the first place. Also, unlike people who are distressed by a lack of sexual desire (see this chapter's *Psychology in Action* section), asexual individuals are comfortable with their sexual orientation (Brotto et al., 2010).

The Stability of Sexual Orientation

Sexual orientation is a deep part of personal identity and is usually quite stable. Starting with their earliest erotic feelings, most people remember being attracted to either the opposite sex or the same sex. The chances are practically nil of an exclusively heterosexual or homosexual person being "converted" from one orientation to the other (Glassgold et al., 2009). If you are heterosexual, you are probably certain that nothing could ever make you have homoerotic feelings. If so, then you know how homosexual persons feel about the prospects for changing *their* sexual orientation.

But what about people who have had both heterosexual and homosexual relationships? The fact that sexual *orientation* is usually quite stable doesn't rule out the possibility that for some people sexual *behavior* may change during the course of a lifetime. However, many such instances involve homosexual or asexual people who date or marry members of the opposite sex because of pressures to fit into heterosexual society. When these people realize they are being untrue to themselves, their identity and relationships may shift. Other apparent shifts in orientation probably involve people who are basically bisexual.

What determines a person's sexual orientation? The available evidence suggests that sexual orientation is mainly genetic and hormonal, although social, cultural, and psychological influences are also involved (LeVay, 2011; LeVay & Baldwin, 2008). See "Genes, Hormones, and Sexual Orientation," which summarizes some interesting findings about the origins of sexual orientation.

Homosexuality

As the discussion in "Genes, Hormones, and Sexual Orientation" implies, homosexuality is part of the normal range of variations in sexual orientation (Garnets, 2002; Silverstein, 2009). Historically, homosexuality has been a part of human sexuality since the dawn of time.

In contrast to heterosexuals, homosexual persons tend to confirm their sexual orientation at a fairly late date—often not until early adolescence. Very likely, this is because they are surrounded by powerful cultural images that contradict their natural feelings. However, most homosexual persons begin to sense that they are different during childhood. By early adolescence, gay men and lesbians begin to feel an attraction to members of the same sex. Gradually, this leads them to question their sexual identity and, for many, to accept their same-sex orientation (Diamond, 1998).

The problems faced by lesbians and gay men tend to be related to rejection by family and discrimination in hiring and housing. It

Jason Merritt/Wireimage/Getty Images

Contrary to the common stereotype, many homosexual couples are in long-term, committed relationships. Actress Portia de Rossi and television host Ellen Degeneres have been together since 2004 and were married in 2008.

Brainwaves: Genes, Hormones, and Sexual Orientation

Why are some people attracted to the opposite sex whereas others prefer members of the same sex? One possibility is that sexual orientation is at least partly hereditary (LeVay, 2011). One study found that if one identical twin is homosexual or bisexual, there is a 50 percent chance that the other twin is too. Similar findings lead some researchers to estimate that sexual orientation is 30 to 70 percent genetic (Mustanski, Chivers, & Bailey, 2002).

Other research suggests that sexual orientation is influenced by a gene or genes found on the X chromosome. Thus, genetic tendencies for homosexuality may be passed from mothers to their children (Rahman & Wilson, 2003). During human evolution, homosexuality may have developed to reduce competition between males for a limited number of potential female mates (Schuiling, 2004).

A different possibility is that prenatal hormone levels influence the developing fetus (LeVay, 2011). According to the *prenatal hormonal theory of homosexuality*, some male fetuses are exposed to too little testosterone. Similarly, some female fetuses are exposed to too much testosterone. These differences, in turn, can impact sexual orientation (Mustanski, Chivers, & Bailey, 2002). Regardless, homosexuality is not caused by hormone imbalances in adulthood; the hormone levels of most gay men and lesbians are within the normal range (Banks & Gartrell, 1995).

Hormonal differences during pregnancy may alter areas of the brain that orchestrate sexual behavior. Support for this idea comes from the finding that parts of the hypothalamus, which is connected with sexual activity, differ in size in heterosexuals and homosexuals (Kinnunen et al., 2004; LeVay, 2011). Furthermore, differences in neurotransmitter levels have been detected in the hypothalamus in homosexual and heterosexual persons (Kinnunen et al., 2004).

Consistent with the biological view of sexual orientation, it is unlikely that parenting makes children homosexual. There is little difference between the development of children with gay or lesbian parents and those who have heterosexual parents (Patterson, 2002; Wainwright, Russell, & Patterson, 2004). Most lesbians and gay men were raised by heterosexual parents, and most children raised by gay or lesbian parents become heterosexual (Garnets, 2002).

All these findings tend to discredit myths about parents making children homosexual or claims that homosexuality is merely a choice. Although learning contributes to one's sexual orientation, it appears that nature strongly prepares people to be either homosexual or heterosexual. In view of this, discriminating against homosexuals is much like rejecting a person for being blue eyed or left handed (Rathus, Nevid, & Fichner-Rathus, 2010).

---

is important to note that gay men, lesbians, and bisexuals encounter hostility because they are members of minority groups, not because there is anything inherently wrong with them (American Psychological Association, 2011). Such unfair treatment is based on homophobia and heterosexism in our society (Balsam & Mohr, 2007; Stefurak, Taylor & Mehta, 2010). *Homophobia* refers to prejudice, fear, and dislike directed at homosexuals. *Heterosexism* is the belief that heterosexuality is better or more natural than homosexuality.

Understandably, social rejection tends to produce higher rates of anxiety, depression, and suicidal thinking among gay and lesbian people (Cochran, 2001; Lester, 2006). However, anyone facing discrimination and stigma would react in much the same way (Jorm et al., 2002). When such stresses are factored out, homosexual persons are no more likely to have emotional problems than heterosexual people are (Goldfried, 2001).

Most homosexual people have, at one time or another, suffered verbal abuse—or worse—because of their sexual orientation (Balsam & Mohr, 2007; Cochran, 2001). Much of this rejection is based on false stereotypes about gay and lesbian people. The following points are a partial reply to such stereotypes. Gay and lesbian people:

- Do not try to convert others to homosexuality.
- Are no more likely to molest children than heterosexuals.
- Are no more likely to be mentally ill than heterosexuals.
- Do not hate persons of the opposite sex.
- Do not, as parents, make their own children gay.
- Do have long-term, caring, monogamous relationships.
- Are no less able to contribute to society than heterosexuals.

Homosexual people are found in all walks of life, at all social and economic levels, and in all cultural groups. They are as diverse in terms of race, ethnicity, age, parenthood, relationships, careers, health, education, politics, and sexual behavior as the heterosexual community (Garnets, 2002). Perhaps as more people come to see gay and lesbian people in terms of their humanity, rather than their sexuality, the prejudices they have faced will wane (Silverstein, 2009).

Heterosexual A person romantically and erotically attracted to members of the opposite sex.

Homosexual A person romantically and erotically attracted to same-sex persons.

Bisexual A person romantically and erotically attracted to both men and women.

Asexual A person not romantically or erotically attracted to either men or women.

Sexual Development and Sexual Orientation

RECITE

1. The four basic dimensions of biological sex are: ____________, ____________, ____________, ____________
2. All individuals normally produce both androgens and estrogens, although the proportions differ in females and males. T or F?
3. In females, intersexual anatomy may result from
 a. androgen insensitivity syndrome *b.* congenital adrenal hyperplasia *c.* excessive estrogen *d.* all of these
4. ____________ sexual characteristics refer to the sexual and reproductive organs; ____________ sexual characteristics refer to other bodily changes that take place at puberty.
5. Research suggests that homosexuality is closely related to hormonal imbalances found in roughly 4 percent of all adults. T or F?
6. Whether a person has erotic fantasies about women or men is a strong indicator of his or her sexual orientation. T or F?

REFLECT

Think Critically

7. Why might reaching puberty and developing secondary sexual characteristics be a mixed blessing for some adolescents?

Self-Reflect

Which of your prior beliefs about biological sex are true? Which are false? How about sexual orientation?

Answers: 1. genetic sex, gonadal sex, hormonal sex, genital sex **2.** T **3.** b **4.** Primary, secondary **5.** F **6.** T **7.** When girls reach puberty early, they may experience heightened social anxiety about their new bodies and increased sexual pressure (Deardorff et al., 2007). When boys reach it late, they may also experience social anxiety.

Gender Development—Circle One: Masculine or Feminine

Gateway Question 11.3: *How does one's sense of maleness or femaleness develop?*

Whereas the term *sex* refers to whether you are biologically female or male, your *gender* refers to whether you are masculine or feminine (as defined by the culture in which you live). A person's gender is expressed in terms of one's **gender identity** (one's subjective sense of being male or female as expressed in appearance, behavior, and attitudes). Although many men are very masculine and many women are very feminine, some are different. Some men are more feminine, some women are more masculine, and some men and women defy simple categorization because they are androgynous. Let's explore gender development and androgyny.

Is your gender identity biologically determined or is it learned? That's a good question. In animals, clear links exist between prenatal hormones and male or female behaviors. In humans, prenatal androgens and estrogens also subtly influence development of the body, nervous system, and later behavior patterns. Sex hormones may "sex-type" the brain before birth, altering the chances of developing feminine or masculine traits (Veale, Clarke, & Lomax, 2010). Evidence for this idea is provided by females exposed to androgens before birth. After birth, their hormones shift to female, and they are raised as girls. Nevertheless, the prenatal exposure to male hormones has a masculinizing effect. During childhood, such girls are typically "tomboys" who prefer the company of boys to girls.

Although it would be a mistake to ignore this **biological biasing effect**, most human sex-linked behaviors are influenced much more by learning than is the case for animals (Helgeson, 2009). For example, after adolescence, the tomboyism of masculinized girls usually gives way to more female interests and gender characteristics (Van Volkom, 2009). Cases like these make it clear that both prenatal hormones and later social factors contribute to adult sexual identity (Breedlove, Cooke, & Jordan, 1999).

At the risk of getting mired in the "battle of the sexes," let's consider the belief that the biological biasing effect imparts different thinking abilities in women and men. Women, it is said, are more often "left brained," and men, "right brained." The left brain, you may recall, is largely responsible for language and rote learning. The right brain is superior at spatial reasoning. Thus, some psychologists think that biological differences explain why men (as a group) do slightly better on spatial tasks and math and why women are slightly better at language skills (Clements et al., 2006; Hiscock, Perachio, & Inch, 2001).

BRIDGES

Differences in male and female brains may affect the chances of retaining language abilities after a person suffers a stroke or brain injury. **See "His and Her Brains?" in Chapter 2, pages 69–70.**

Others, however, reject this theory, claiming it is based on shaky evidence and sexist thinking (Fine, 2010). The most telling evidence on this point may be that female and male scores on the Scholastic Assessment Test (SAT) are rapidly becoming more alike. The same applies to tests of math ability (Ceci & Williams, 2010). The narrowing gap is probably explained by a growing similarity in male and female interests, experiences, and educational goals.

Note also that the differences that do exist between women and men are based on *averages* (● Figure 11.2). Many women are better at math than most men are. Likewise, many men are better at ver-

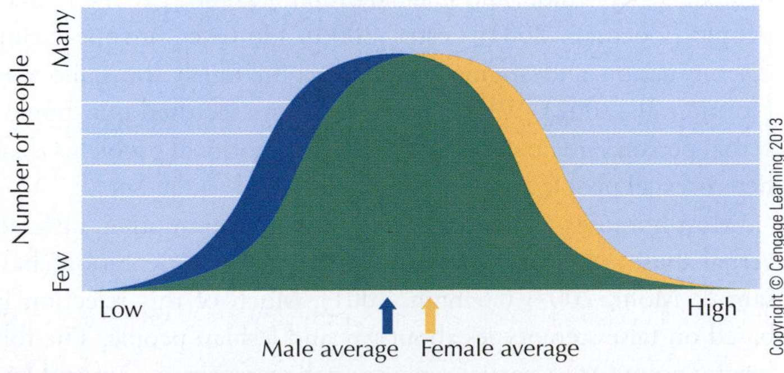

● **Figure 11.2** Recorded differences in various abilities that exist between women and men are based on *averages*. For example, if we were to record the number of men and women who have low, medium, or high scores on tests of language ability, we might obtain graphs like those shown. For other abilities, men would have a higher average. However, such average differences are typically small. As a result, the overlap in female abilities and male abilities is very large (Eliot, 2009; Fine, 2010).

Human Diversity High Test

One common gender stereotype holds that men are vulnerable to thinking with their, well,...gonads. Actually, there's a bit of truth to the stereotype and more to the story, as well. Research confirms that men may make poorer decisions about sexual behavior when they are "turned on" (Ariely & Loewenstein, 2006). Compared with unaroused men, those who are sexually excited are more willing to press women to have sex. They are also more likely to engage in risky sexual behavior. When unaroused men were asked if they thought being sexually aroused might influence their sexual choices, they predicted that arousal would have little effect. (Wrong!)

Of course, women are not immune to having their heads turned by sexual passion. However, many people see male sexual irresponsibility as part of a larger pattern that includes aggression. Some go so far as to say that men suffer from "testosterone poisoning" because men are responsible for most violence. Again, there is an element of truth to this stereotype. Men who have high testosterone levels and who are sexually aroused are more likely to make poor decisions about sexual behavior (Van den Bergh & Dewitte, 2006). They are also more likely to become aggressive (Mehta & Beer, 2010; Millet & Dewitte, 2007).

Then are high testosterone levels a problem? Not always. For example, men with low testosterone levels may have difficulty thinking and concentrating. In such cases, testosterone supplements can actually help them think *more* clearly, rather than less (Fukai et al., 2010). Furthermore, older men and women with too little testosterone tend to have memory problems and a greater risk of developing Alzheimer's disease (Janowsky, 2006).

Before we leave this topic, let's remember that we have been discussing a gender stereotype, albeit one with some truth to it. Most men, including those with high testosterone levels, manage to keep their sexual impulses and aggressiveness within acceptable limits.

Greg Gayne/© CBS/Courtesy Everett Collection

The character of Charlie Harper (played by actor Charlie Sheen), from the comedy series *Two and a Half Men*, has fun with the stereotype of a man who thinks with his gonads.

bal skills than most women are. Scores for women and men overlap so much that it is impossible to predict whether any one person will be good or bad at math or language skills simply from knowing his or her sex. There is no biological basis for the unequal treatment women have faced at work, school, and elsewhere (Eliot, 2009; Fine, 2010). Most male–female performance gaps can be traced to *social* differences in the power and opportunities given to men and women. Unequal power tends to exaggerate differences between men and women, and then makes these artificial differences appear to be real (Goodwin & Fiske, 2001).

Acquiring Gender Identity

As stated earlier, gender identity, your personal, private sense of being female or male, is at least partly learned.

How is gender identity acquired? Obviously, it begins with *labeling* ("It's a girl," "It's a boy") (Eagly, 2001). Thereafter, it is shaped by **gender role socialization** (the process of learning gender behaviors regarded as appropriate for one's sex in a given culture). Gender role socialization reflects all the subtle pressures from parents, peers, and cultural forces that urge boys to "act like boys" and girls to "act like girls." (Orenstein, 2011.) By the time they are 30 months of age, children are aware of gender role differences (Martin & Ruble, 2009). At 3 or 4 years of age, gender identity is usually well formed.

Gender Roles

Gender roles probably have as big an influence on sexual behavior as chromosomal, genital, or hormonal factors do. A **gender role** is the favored pattern of behavior expected of each sex. Traditionally, in our culture, boys are encouraged to be strong, fast, aggressive,

Gender identity One's personal, private sense of maleness or femaleness.

Biological biasing effect Hypothesized effect that prenatal exposure to sex hormones has on development of the body, nervous system, and later behavior patterns.

Gender role socialization The process of learning gender behaviors considered appropriate for one's sex in a given culture.

dominant, and achieving. Traditional females are expected to be sensitive, intuitive, passive, emotional, and "naturally" interested in child rearing. Despite much progress in the last 40 years, gender role stereotypes continue to have a major impact on women and men. **Gender role stereotypes** are oversimplified beliefs about what men and women are actually like (see "High Test").

Gender roles influence how we act. Gender role stereotypes, in contrast, turn gender roles into false beliefs about what men and women can and can't do. Are women suited to be fighter pilots, corporate presidents, military commanders, or racecar drivers? A person with strong gender role stereotypes might say, "No, because women are not sufficiently aggressive, dominant, or mechanically inclined for such roles." Yet today's women have performed successfully in virtually all realms.

Nevertheless, gender role stereotypes persist and can be a major career obstacle. For example, the United States has never had a woman president. For many jobs, your chances of being hired could be reduced by your sex, be it male or female. Unequal pay for comparable work and experience is also a major problem for women. Overall, women earn only about 77 cents for every dollar earned by men (National Committee on Pay Equity, 2010a,b). The rate for women of color is worse—64 cents for African American women and a measly 52 cents for Latinas. This wage gap can cost a woman trained in a professional school as much as $2,000,000 in lost career earnings over the course of her life. The male–female pay difference is even found in colleges, where greater awareness of gender fairness should prevail (Kite et al., 2001).

Like all stereotypes, those based on gender roles ignore the wonderful diversity of humanity. Fortunately, extreme gender stereotyping has declined somewhat in the last 20 years (Eagly & Carli, 2007; Kite et al., 2001). Just the same, in business, academia, medicine, law, sports, and politics, women continue to earn less money and achieve lower status than men. In other words, many women are still "running in place," hobbled by gender stereotyping (Brescoll, Dawson, & Uhlmann, 2010; DeArmond et al., 2006).

The Influence of Culture

A look at other cultures shows that our gender roles are by no means "natural" or universal. For example, in many cultures, women do the heavy work because men are considered too weak for it (Best, 2002). In Russia, roughly 75 percent of all medical doctors are women, and women make up a large portion of the workforce. Many more examples could be cited, but one of the most interesting is anthropologist Margaret Mead's (1935) classic observations of the Tchambuli people of New Guinea.

Gender roles for the Tchambuli are a nearly perfect reversal of North American stereotypes. Tchambuli women do the fishing and manufacturing, and they control the power and economic life of the community. Women also take the initiative in courting and sexual relations. Tchambuli men, on the other hand, are expected to be dependent, flirtatious, and concerned with their appearance. Art, games, and theatrics occupy most of the Tchambuli males' time, and men are particularly fond of adorning themselves with flowers and jewelry.

John O. Mitterer

Is this man less of a man because he sews? Behaviors that are considered typical and appropriate for each sex (gender roles) vary a great deal from culture to culture. Undoubtedly, some cultures magnify sex differences more than others (Carroll, 2010).

As the Tchambuli show, men and women are expected to act in quite different ways in various cultures. The arbitrary nature of gender roles is also apparent. A man is no less a man if he cooks, sews, or cares for children. A woman is no less a woman if she excels in sports, succeeds in business, or works as an auto mechanic. Still, adult personality and gender identity are closely tied to cultural definitions of "masculinity" and "femininity."

Gender Role Socialization

How are gender differences created? Learning gender roles begins immediately. Infant girls are held more gently and treated more tenderly than boys. Both parents play more roughly with sons than with daughters (who are presumed to be more "delicate"). Later, boys are allowed to roam over a wider area without special permission. They are also expected to run errands earlier than girls. Daughters are told that they are pretty and that "nice girls don't fight." Boys are told to be strong and that "tough guys don't cry." Sons are more often urged to control their emotions, except for anger and aggression, which parents tolerate more in boys than in girls.

Toys and sports are strongly sex typed (Hardin & Greer, 2009). Parents buy dolls for girls; trucks, tools, and sports equipment for boys. Fathers, especially, tend to encourage their children to play with "appropriate" sex-typed toys (Raag & Rackliff, 1998) (● Figure 11.3). By the time children reach kindergarten, they have learned to think that doctors, firefighters, and pilots are men and that nurses, secretaries, and hairdressers are women (Eagly, 2000). And why not? The workforce is still highly segregated by sex, and children learn from what they observe. Stereotyped gender roles are even the norm in TV commercials, children's picture books, and video games (Browne, 1998; Oppliger, 2007).

Shmeliova Natalia/Shutterstock

● Figure 11.3 One study found that the mothers interacted differently with their infant sons and daughters as they played with gender-neutral toys. Mothers of girls engaged in more interpretation and conversation, whereas mothers of boys commented more and offered more instructions (Clearfield & Nelson, 2006).

"Male" and "Female" Behavior

Overall, parents tend to encourage their sons to engage in **instrumental** (goal-directed) **behaviors**, to control their emotions, and to prepare for the world of work. Daughters, on the other hand, are encouraged in **expressive** (emotion-oriented) **behaviors** and, to a lesser degree, are socialized for motherhood (Eagly, 2009).

When parents are told they treat boys and girls differently, many explain that the sexes are just "naturally" different. But what comes first, "natural differences" or the gender-based expectations that create them? In our culture, "male" seems—for many—to be defined as "not female." That is, parents often have a vague fear of expressive and emotional behavior in male children. To them, such behavior implies that a boy is effeminate or a sissy. Many parents who would not be troubled if their daughters engaged in "masculine" play might be upset if their sons played with dolls or imitated "female" mannerisms.

Differences between boys and girls are magnified by sex-segregated play. Beginning around age 3, boys start to play mostly with boys and girls play with girls. And how do they play? Girls tend to play indoors and near adults. They like to cooperate by playing house and other games that require lots of verbal give-and-take. Boys prefer superhero games and rough-and-tumble play outdoors. They tend to be concerned with dominance or who's the boss. Thus, from an early age, males and females tend to grow up in different, gender-defined cultures (Oppliger, 2007; Shaffer & Kipp, 2010).

To summarize, gender role socialization in our society prepares children for a world in which men are expected to be instrumental, conquering, controlling, and unemotional. Women, in contrast, are expected to be expressive, emotional, passive, and dependent. Thus, gender role socialization teaches us to be highly competent in some respects and handicapped in others (Levant, 2003; Levant et al., 2009).

BRIDGES

In males, a restricted ability to express emotion is one of the costs of adopting a masculine gender role, at least as it is defined in North America. **See Chapter 10, page 357.**

Gender role The pattern of behaviors that are regarded as "male" or "female" by one's culture; sometimes also referred to as a sex role.

Gender role stereotypes Oversimplified and widely held beliefs about the basic characteristics of men and women.

Instrumental behaviors Behaviors directed toward the achievement of some goal; behaviors that are instrumental in producing some effect.

Expressive behaviors Behaviors that express or communicate emotion or personal feelings.

Of course, many people find traditional gender roles acceptable and comfortable. It seems evident, however, that many more will benefit when the more stereotyped and burdensome aspects of gender roles are set aside. The next section explains why.

Androgyny—Are You Masculine, Feminine, or Androgynous?

Gateway Question 11.4: *What is psychological androgyny (and is it contagious)?*

Are you aggressive, ambitious, analytical, assertive, athletic, competitive, decisive, dominant, forceful, independent, individualistic, self-reliant, and willing to take risks? If so, you are quite "masculine." Are you affectionate, cheerful, childlike, compassionate, flatterable, gentle, gullible, loyal, sensitive, shy, soft-spoken, sympathetic, tender, understanding, warm, and yielding? If so, then you are quite "feminine." What if you have traits from both lists? In that case, you may be *androgynous* (an-DROJ-ih-nus).

The two lists you just read are from the seminal work of psychologist Sandra Bem (1974). By combining 20 traditionally "masculine" traits (self-reliant, assertive, and so forth), 20 traditionally "feminine" traits (affectionate, gentle), and 20 neutral traits (truthful, friendly), Bem created the *Bem Sex Role Inventory* (BSRI). (Some psychologists prefer to use the term *sex role* instead of *gender role*.) Next, she and her associates gave the BSRI to thousands of people, asking them to say whether each trait applied to them. Of those surveyed, 50 percent fell into traditional feminine or masculine categories, 15 percent scored higher on traits of the opposite sex, and 35 percent were androgynous, getting high scores on both feminine and masculine items.

Psychological Androgyny

The word **androgyny** (an-DROJ-ih-nee) literally means "man-woman" and refers to having both masculine and feminine traits (Helgeson, 2009). Bem is convinced that our complex society requires flexibility with respect to gender roles. She believes that it is necessary for men to also be gentle, compassionate, sensitive, and yielding and for women to also be forceful, self-reliant, independent, and ambitious—*as the situation requires*. In short, Bem thinks that more people should feel free to be more androgynous.

Adaptability

Bem has shown that androgynous individuals are more adaptable. They seem especially to be less hindered by images of "feminine" or "masculine" behavior. For example, in one study people were given the choice of doing either a "masculine" activity (oil a hinge, nail boards together, and so forth) or a "feminine" activity (prepare a baby bottle, wind yarn into a ball, and so on). Masculine men and feminine women consistently chose to do gender-appropriate activities, even when the opposite choice paid more!

Bem has concluded that masculine males have great difficulty expressing warmth, playfulness, and concern—even when they are appropriate (Bem, 1975, 1981). Masculine men, it seems, tend to view such feelings as unacceptably "feminine." Masculine men ("manly men"?) also find it hard to accept emotional support from others, particularly from women (Levant, 2001, 2003). They tend to be interested in sports, have mostly male friends, dislike feminists, and sit with their knees wide apart (really!).

Problems faced by highly feminine women ("girlie girls"?) are the reverse of those faced by masculine men. Such women have trouble being independent and assertive, even when these qualities are desirable. In contrast, more androgynous individuals are higher in emotional intelligence (remember Chapter 10?; Guastello & Guastello, 2003).

The Whole Human

Over the years, androgyny has been variously supported, attacked, and debated. Now, as the dust begins to settle, the picture looks like this:

- Having "masculine" traits primarily means that a person is independent and assertive. Scoring high in "masculinity," therefore, is related to high self-esteem and to success in many situations (Long, 1989).
- Having "feminine" traits primarily means that a person is nurturing and interpersonally oriented. People who score high in

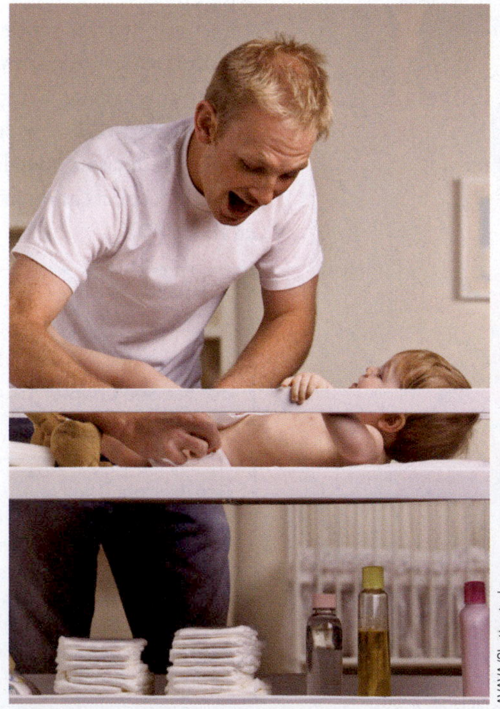

AVAVA/Shutterstock

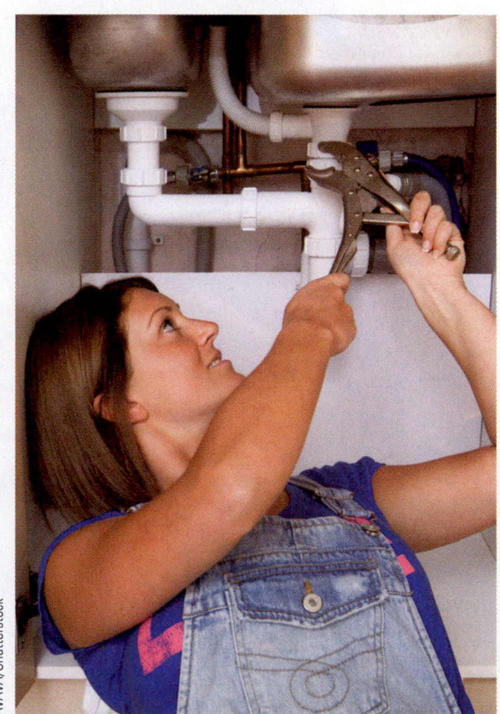

© Image Source/Corbis

Androgynous individuals adapt easily to both traditionally "feminine" and "masculine" situations.

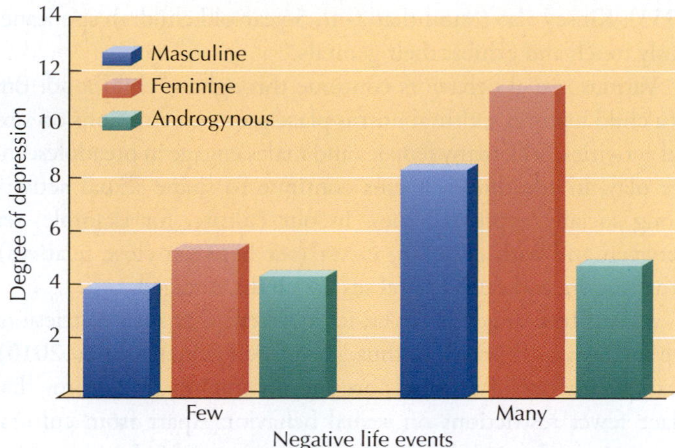

• Figure 11.4 Another indication of the possible benefits of androgyny is found in a study of reactions to stress. When confronted with an onslaught of negative events, strongly masculine or feminine persons become more depressed than androgynous individuals do. Adapted from Roos & Cohen, 1987.

"femininity," therefore, are more likely to seek and receive social support. They tend to experience greater social closeness with others and more happiness in marriage (Reevy & Maslach, 2001).

In sum, there are advantages to possessing both "feminine" and "masculine" traits (Guastello & Guastello, 2003; Lefkowitz & Zeldow, 2006). In general, androgynous persons are more flexible when it comes to coping with difficult situations (Crooks & Baur, 2011; Woodhill & Samuels, 2004; see • Figure 11.4). Androgynous persons also tend to be more satisfied with their lives. Apparently, they can use both instrumental and emotionally expressive capacities to enhance their lives and relationships (Lefkowitz & Zeldow, 2006).

Interestingly, some men appear to be moving toward more balanced definitions of manhood. For instance, older men are more accepting of androgynous traits (Strough et al., 2007). Similarly, more Mexican-American men than European-American men are androgynous (Sugihara & Warner, 1999). Along the same lines, some Asian-American men, especially those who were born in the United States, appear to be creating a more flexible masculinity free from male dominance. These men link their masculinity with a capacity for caring and they are not afraid of doing "feminine tasks," such as cooking or housework (Chua & Fujino, 1999).

It is worth saying again that many people remain comfortable with traditional views of gender. Nevertheless, "feminine" traits and "masculine" traits can exist in the same person, and androgyny can be a highly adaptive balance.

When Sex and Gender Do Not Match—The Binary Busters

Gateway Question 11.5: *What is gender variance?*

Biological sex is not binary; it comes in degrees between male and female. So, too, gender comes in shades of masculine and feminine. You will probably not be surprised, then, that the relationship between sex and gender is also a rainbow of possibility ranging from psychological androgyny and childhood tomboyism to intersexuality and transsexuality (Carroll, 2010). By adulthood, most males turn out to be more or less masculine and most females turn out to be more or less feminine. But significant numbers of people are **gender variant** in that their biological sex definitely does not match their preferred gender.

What should be done about gender variant people? This is currently a heated controversy. According to some health care professionals and gender variant people, gender variance may be unusual, but it is not pathological. Gender variant individuals deserve our understanding and support, not stigmatization (Diamond, 2009; Kaufmann, 2007). When it comes to children, many parents try to encourage what they see as gender-appropriate behavior. Others wait and see if their children will grow into more gender appropriate roles. Still others seek to accept and support their children's experiences. If there is a trend in America today, it is towards acceptance and support (Zeiler & Wickström, 2009).

To others, gender variance is a form of psychiatric illness calling out for treatment. According to the current edition of the *Diagnostic and Statistical Manual of Mental Disorders (DSM)* of the American Psychiatric Association, transsexuals like Elena, who we introduced in the beginning of the chapter, suffer from *gender identity disorder* (American Psychiatric Association, 2000; Bockting & Ehrbar, 2005). Don't expect this controversy to be resolved any time soon; the new version of the DSM, due to be published in 2013, will likely continue to include the diagnosis, although its name may be changed to *gender incongruence* (American Psychiatric Association, 2010).

In more dramatic cases, including intersexuality and transsexuality, *sex reassignment surgery* may be undertaken (Imbimbo et al., 2009). Surgery can reconfigure the external appearance of the genitals, while hormone treatments can shift the chemical balance in the body, and a deliberate effort can be made to transform the person's sense of sexual identity. Adults who deliberately seek sex reassignment are generally happy with the results (Imbimbo et al., 2009).

Sex reassignment surgery is also becoming more common with children. Supporters of early sex assignment argue that the benefits usually outweigh the long-term psychological costs (Zeiler & Wickström, 2009). Critics believe that it is better for individuals to accept who they are and to realize that some bodies do not neatly fit into the categories of male and female (Holmes, 2002). Rather than impose the choice on them as children, they argue it is better to wait until adulthood, when transsexual and intersexual individuals can choose for themselves whether to have surgery and whether to live as a man or a woman (Thyen et al., 2005).

Only time will tell which approach is more successful, and for which particular transsexual and intersex conditions. Because sex and gender are complex, the best course of treatment may prove to be different for different people (Rathus, Nevid, & Fichner-Rathus, 2010).

Androgyny The presence of both "masculine" and "feminine" traits in a single person (as masculinity and femininity are defined within one's culture).

Gender variance Condition in which a person's biological sex does not match his or her preferred gender.

Knowledge Builder: Gender Development, Androgyny, and Gender Variance

RECITE

1. For humans, the biological biasing effect of prenatal hormones tends to override all other influences. T or F?
2. One's private sense of maleness or femaleness is referred to as ______________ ______________.
3. Traditional gender role socialization encourages ______________ behavior in males.
   a. instrumental *b.* emotional *c.* expressive *d.* dependent
4. A person who is androgynous is one who scores high on ratings of traits usually possessed by the opposite sex. T or F?
5. For both women and men, having masculine traits is associated with greater happiness in marriage. T or F?
6. Sex reassignment surgery is normally undertaken to bring ______________ and ______________ into alignment.
   a. sex, intersex *b.* gender, stereotypes *c.* androgyny, sex *d.* sex, gender

REFLECT

Think Critically

7. As children are growing up, the male emphasis on instrumental behavior comes into conflict with the female emphasis on expressive behavior. At what age do you think such conflicts become prominent?
8. Could a person be androgynous in a culture in which "masculine" and "feminine" traits differ greatly from those on Bem's list?

Self-Reflect

Can you remember an example of gender role socialization you experienced as a child? Do you think you were encouraged to engage more in instrumental behaviors or expressive behaviors?

Think of three people you know, one who is androgynous, one who is traditionally feminine, and one who is traditionally masculine. What advantages and disadvantages do you see in each collection of traits? How do you think you would be classified if you took the BSRI?

In 2007, the American Medical Association changed its antidiscrimination policies to include transgender people. This means, for example, that doctors can no longer refuse medical treatment to transgender patients. Do you agree or disagree with this change?

Answers: 1. F **2.** gender identity **3.** *a* **4.** F **5.** F **6.** *d* **7.** Children segregate themselves into same-sex groups during much of childhood, which limits conflicts between male and female patterns of behavior. However, as children move into adolescence, they begin to spend more time with members of the opposite sex. This brings the dominant, competitive style of boys into conflict with the nurturing, expressive style of girls, often placing girls at a disadvantage (Maccoby, 1990). **8.** Yes. Being androgynous means having both masculine and feminine traits *as they are defined within one's culture.*

Sexual Behavior—Mapping the Erogenous Zones

Gateway Question 11.6: *What are the most typical patterns of human sexual behavior?*

Sexuality is a natural part of being human. A capacity for sexual arousal is apparent at birth or soon after. Researcher Alfred Kinsey verified instances of orgasm in boys as young as 5 months old and girls as young as 4 months (Kinsey, Pomeroy, & Martin, 1948, 1953). Kinsey also found that 2- to 5-year-old children spontaneously touch and exhibit their genitals.

Various sexual behaviors continue throughout childhood. But as a child matures, cultural norms place greater restrictions on sexual activities. Still, many females and males engage in preadolescent sex play. In adulthood, norms continue to shape sexual activity along socially approved lines. In our culture, for example, sex between and with children, incest (sex between close relatives), prostitution, and extramarital sex are all discouraged.

As was true of gender roles, it's apparent that such restrictions are somewhat arbitrary (Rathus, Nevid, & Fichner-Rathus, 2010). Sexual activities of all kinds are more common in cultures that place fewer restrictions on sexual behavior. Apart from cultural norms, it can be said that any sexual act engaged in by consenting adults is "normal" if it does not hurt anyone. (Atypical sexual behavior is discussed later in this chapter.)

Sexual Arousal

Human sexual arousal is complex. It may, of course, be produced by direct stimulation of the body's **erogenous zones** (eh-ROJ-eh-nus: productive of pleasure or erotic desire). Human erogenous zones include the genitals, mouth, breasts, ears, anus, and to a lesser degree, the entire surface of the body. It is clear, however, that more than physical contact is involved: A urological or gynecological exam rarely results in any sexual arousal. Likewise, an unwanted sexual advance may produce only revulsion. Human sexual arousal obviously includes a large mental element.

Sexual Scripts

In a restaurant, we commonly expect certain things to occur. It could even be said that each of us has a restaurant "script" that defines a plot (eating dinner outside of the home), the dialogue (ordering from the menu), and actions that should take place (paying for the dinner before leaving). We also learn a variety of **sexual scripts**, or unspoken mental plans that guide our sexual behavior. Such scripts determine when and where we are likely to express sexual feelings, and with whom (Lenton & Bryan, 2005; McCormick, 2010). They provide a "plot" for the order of events in lovemaking and they outline "approved" actions, motives, and outcomes.

When two people follow markedly different scripts, misunderstandings are almost sure to occur. Consider, for instance, what happens when a woman acting out a "romantic first date" script is paired with a man following a "friends with benefits" script: The result is often anger, hurt feelings, or worse (Schleicher & Gilbert, 2005). Even newlyweds may find that their sexual "agendas" differ. In such cases, considerable "rewriting" of scripts is often needed for sexual compatibility. For humans, the mind (or brain) is the ultimate erogenous zone. (To read more about contemporary sexual scripts, see "What's Love Got to Do with It?").

Are men more easily sexually aroused than women? Overall, women and men have equal potential for sexual arousal, and women are no less *physically* responsive than men. However, women tend to place more emphasis on emotional closeness with a lover than do men (Basson et al., 2005; Peplau, 2003).

Human Diversity: What's Love Got to Do with It?

Younger Americans are shifting toward scripts favoring casual sex (Hughes, Morrison, & Asada, 2005). One such script includes sex in a friendship, without traditional romance. According to one survey, more than half of all college students have been *friends with benefits* (friends who have sex but aren't romantically involved) (Puentes, Knox, & Zusman, 2008). Even more casual is the *hook-up* script, in which two people having sex are more or less strangers (Bradshaw, Kahn, & Saville, 2010). (Seek pleasure first, ask questions later?) In contrast, traditional sexual scripts stress courtship, romance, and marriage. Sex in such relationships might be premarital, but it is still romantic (Roese et al., 2006).

As casual sexual scripts become more common, the traditional focus on intercourse is fading in favor of oral sex, which tends to be seen as less risky, more acceptable, and "not a big deal." Casual sexual scripts are also spreading to younger children. One study found that 20 percent of American ninth graders have already had oral sex and more than 30 percent intend to try it soon (Halpern-Felsher et al., 2005).

Casual sex is often viewed as easier than facing the challenges of romantic attachment and finding a lifelong partner. However, it is not without its own risks. Casual sex is usually associated with alcohol use and unsafe sexual behaviors, such as unprotected sex (Fortunato et al., 2010; Grello, Welsh, & Harper, 2006). Although oral sex is safer than intercourse, a significant chance of getting a sexually transmitted disease remains (Boskey, 2008). Another downside of casual sex is the letdown that can occur when one person follows a romantic script and the other follows a casual script ("He [or she] is just not that into you"). For example, young women who are having casual sex are more likely to be depressed (Grello, Welsh, & Harper, 2006).

Adolescents and young adults have always engaged in experimentation and exploration. Most young people emerge unscathed from their explorations if they clearly understand that their encounters are casual and if they practice safe sex. Most eventually also "graduate" to a more traditional search for love.

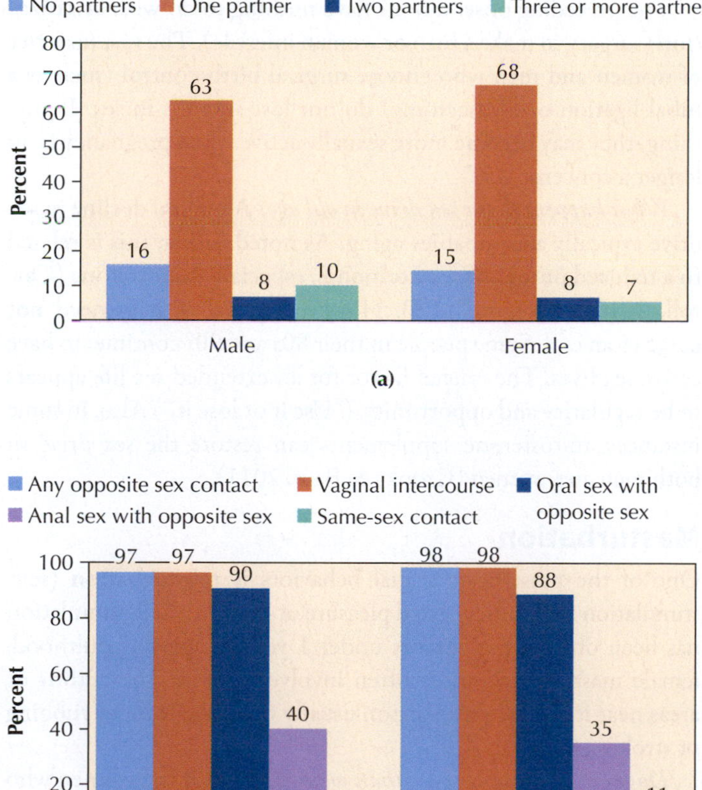

● **Figure 11.5** These graphs show the pattern of sexual behavior for American adults. *(a)* Men and women do not differ in their average number of sexual partners or *(b)* in their overall pattern of sexual activity. Adapted from Mosher, Chandra, & Jones, 2005.

In one classic study, women watched excerpts from two erotic films. One was made by a man for male viewers. The other was directed by a woman and presented from a female point of view. Although women's physical arousal was nearly identical for both films, as measured by a medical recording device, their subjective experiences differed greatly. Many women reported being repulsed, disgusted, and decidedly not aroused by the male-oriented film. When they watched the film made for women, subjects reported more subjective feelings of sexual arousal, more positive emotions, and more interest in the film (Laan et al., 1994).

Why did the women respond so differently? Basically, the male-centered film was a macho fantasy in which the woman was little more than a sexual prop—her pleasure and fulfillment were portrayed as largely unimportant. In the woman-made film, the female character took the initiative in lovemaking and obviously enjoyed it. Clearly, a woman's subjective feelings of arousal tend to be more closely tied to her emotional response to erotic cues. It would appear that many women want to be active partners in lovemaking and they want their needs and preferences to be acknowledged (Benjamin & Tlusten, 2010).

Based on the frequency of orgasm (from masturbation or intercourse), the peak of male sexual activity is at age 18. The peak rate of female sexual activity appears to occur a little later (Janus & Janus, 1993). However, male and female sexual patterns are rapidly becoming more alike. ● Figure 11.5 presents some of the data on

Erogenous zones Areas of the body that produce pleasure and/or provoke erotic desire.

Sexual script An unspoken mental plan that defines a "plot," dialogue, and actions expected to take place in a sexual encounter.

sexual behavior from a major national health survey of American men and women ages 25 to 44. As you can see, in any given year, men and women do not differ in their average number of opposite-sex partners or in their overall pattern of sexual activity (Mosher, Chandra, & Jones, 2005). Exaggerating the differences between male and female sexuality is not only inaccurate, it can also create artificial barriers to sexual satisfaction (Wiederman, 2001). For example, assuming that men should always initiate sex denies the fact that women have comparable sexual interests and needs.

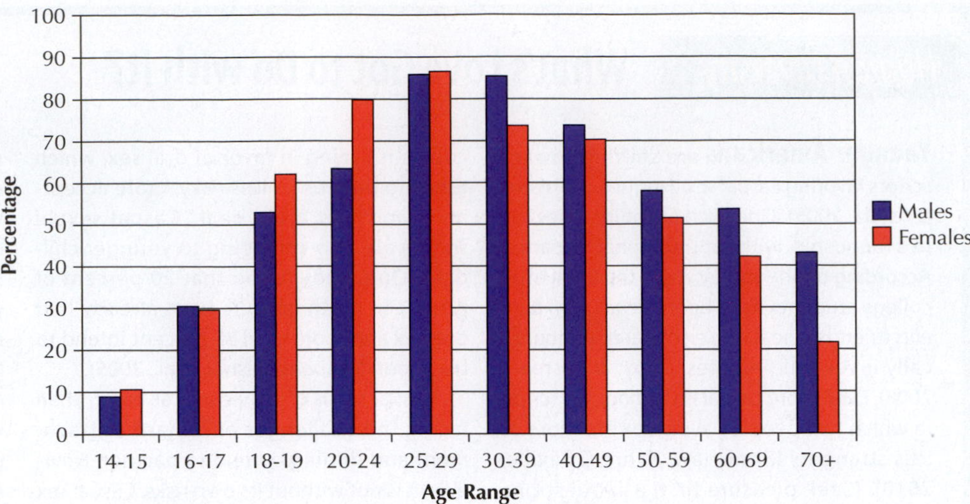

● **Figure 11.6** Percentage of men and women of various ages who experienced vaginal intercourse during the last month. Although percentages decline beginning in the 40s, significant percentages of older people remain sexually active. Data adapted from Herbenick et al., 2010.

Sex Drive

What causes differences in sex drive? The term **sex drive** refers to the strength of one's motivation to engage in sexual behavior. Attitudes toward sex, sexual experience, and recency of sexual activity are all important, but physical factors also play a role. As discussed in Chapter 10, a man's sex drive is related to the amount of androgens (especially testosterone) supplied by the testes (Crooks & Baur, 2011). The connection can be very direct: When a man chats with a woman he finds attractive, his testosterone levels actually increase (Roney, 2003). Likewise, the sex drive in women is related to estrogen levels (Graziottin, 1998). As you may recall, testosterone also plays a role in female sexuality. A woman's sex drive is closely related to the testosterone level in her bloodstream. Of course, women produce much smaller amounts of testosterone than men do. But that doesn't mean their sex drive is weaker. Women's bodies are more sensitive to testosterone, and their sex drive is comparable to males.

Does alcohol increase the sex drive? In general, no. Alcohol is a *depressant*. As such, it may, in small doses, stimulate erotic desire by lowering inhibitions. This effect no doubt accounts for alcohol's reputation as an aid to seduction. (Humorist Ogden Nash once summarized this bit of folklore by saying "Candy is dandy, but liquor is quicker.") However, in larger doses, alcohol suppresses orgasm in women and erection in men. Getting drunk *decreases* sexual desire, arousal, pleasure, and performance (McKay, 2005).

Numerous other drugs are reputed to be *aphrodisiacs* (af-ruh-DEEZ-ee-aks: substances that increase sexual desire or pleasure). However, like alcohol, many other drugs actually impair sexual response rather than enhance it (McKay, 2005). Some examples are amphetamines, amyl nitrite, barbiturates, cocaine, Ecstasy, LSD, and marijuana. (It is worth noting that, around the world, many substances are believed to be aphrodisiacs, such as oysters, chocolate, powdered rhinoceros horn, and so on. In general, these are, at best, superstitions that might produce a placebo effect.) In the end, love is the best aphrodisiac (Crooks & Baur, 2011).

Does removal of the testes or ovaries abolish the sex drive? In lower animals, **castration** (surgical removal of the testicles or ovaries) tends to abolish sexual activity in *inexperienced* animals. In humans, the effects of male and female castration vary. At first, some people experience a loss of sex drive; in others there is no change. (That's why castration of sex offenders is not likely to curb their behavior.) However, after several years, almost all subjects report a decrease in sex drive unless they take hormone supplements.

The preceding observations have nothing to do with **sterilization** (surgery to make a man or woman infertile). The vast majority of women and men who choose surgical birth control (such as a tubal ligation or a vasectomy) do not lose interest in sex. If anything, they may become more sexually active when pregnancy is no longer a concern.

What happens to the sex drive in old age? A natural decline in sex drive typically accompanies aging. As noted earlier, this is related to a reduced output of sex hormones, especially testosterone (Carroll, 2010) (● Figure 11.6). However, sexual activity need not come to an end. Some people in their 80s and 90s continue to have active sex lives. The crucial factor for an extended sex life appears to be regularity and opportunity. ("Use it or lose it.") Also, in some instances, testosterone supplements can restore the sex drive in both men and women (Crooks & Baur, 2011).

Masturbation

One of the most basic sexual behaviors is **masturbation** (self-stimulation that causes sexual pleasure or orgasm). Self-stimulation has been observed in infants under 1 year of age. In adulthood, female masturbation most often involves rubbing the clitoris or areas near it. Male masturbation usually takes the form of rubbing or stroking the penis.

Do more men masturbate than women? Yes. Of the women who took part in a national survey, 89 percent reported that they had masturbated at some time. Of the males, 95 percent reported that they had masturbated. (Some cynics add, "And the other 5 percent lied!") As ● Figure 11.7 shows, masturbation is a regular feature of the sex lives of many people (Herbenick et al., 2010).

What purpose does masturbation serve? Through masturbation, people discover what pleases them sexually. Masturbation is an important part of the psychosexual development of most adolescents. Among other things, it provides a healthy substitute for sexual involvement at a time when young people are maturing emotionally.

Is it immature for masturbation to continue after marriage? If it is, there are many "immature" people around! Approximately 70 percent of married women and men masturbate at least occasionally. Generally speaking, masturbation is valid at any age and usually has no effect on marital relationships. Contrary to popular myths, people are not always compelled to masturbate because they lack a sexual partner (Das, 2007). Masturbation is often just "one more item on the menu" for people with active sex lives.

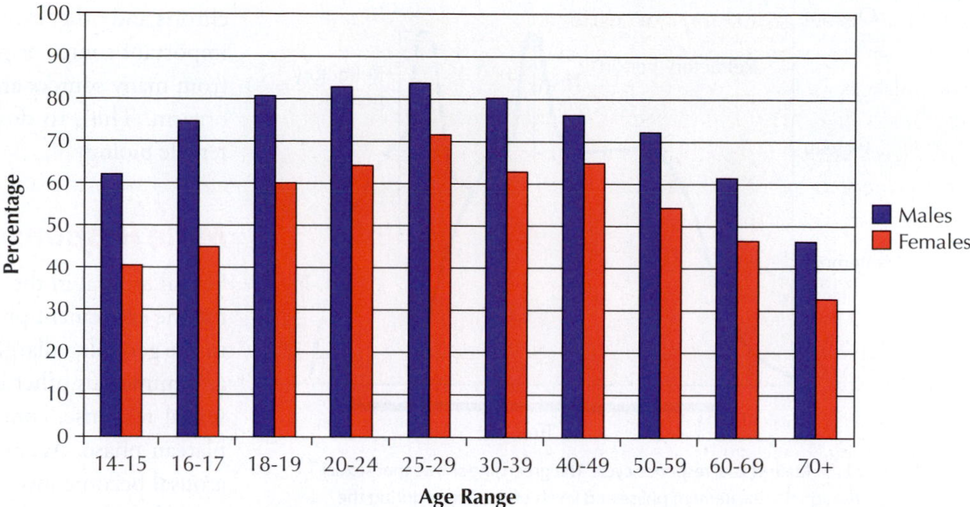

• Figure 11.7 Percentage of women and men of various ages who masturbated alone during the last year. Data adapted from Herbenick et al., 2010.

Is there any way in which masturbation can cause harm? Fifty years ago, a child might have been told that masturbation would cause insanity, acne, sterility, or other such nonsense. "Self-abuse," as it was then called, has enjoyed a long and unfortunate history of religious and medical disapproval (Carroll, 2010). The modern view is that masturbation is a normal sexual behavior (Bockting & Coleman, 2003). Enlightened parents are well aware of this fact. Still, many children are punished or made to feel guilty for touching their genitals. This is unfortunate because masturbation itself is harmless. Typically, its only negative effects are feelings of fear, guilt, or anxiety that arise from learning to think of masturbation as "bad" or "wrong." In an age when people are urged to practice "safer sex," masturbation remains the safest sex of all.

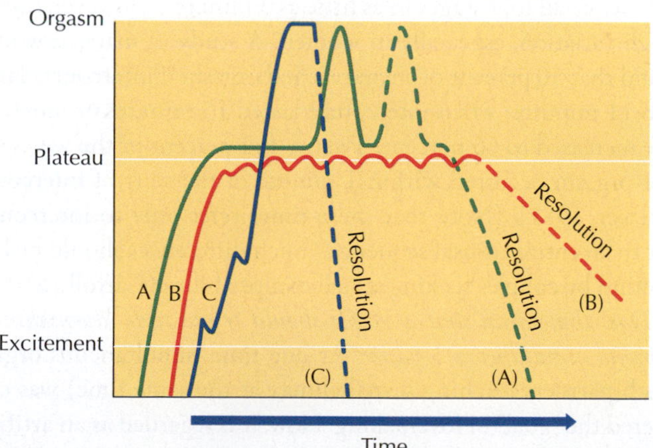

• Figure 11.8 Female sexual response cycle. The green line shows that sexual arousal rises through the excitement phase and levels off for a time during the plateau phase. Arousal peaks during orgasm and then returns to pre-excitement levels. In pattern A, arousal rises from excitement through the plateau phase and peaks in orgasm. Resolution may be immediate, or it may first include a return to the plateau phase and a second orgasm (dotted line). In pattern B, arousal is sustained at the plateau phase and slowly resolved without sexual climax. Pattern C shows a fairly rapid rise in arousal to orgasm. Little time is spent in the plateau phase, and resolution is fairly rapid. Adapted from Carroll, J. L. 2010. *Sexuality now: Embracing diversity,* 3rd ed. Cengage Learning/Wadsworth.

Human Sexual Response—Sexual Interactions

Gateway Question 11.7: *To what extent do females and males differ in sexual response?*

The pioneering work of gynecologist William Masters and psychologist Virginia Johnson greatly expanded our understanding of sexual response (Masters & Johnson, 1966, 1970). In a series of experiments, interviews, and controlled observations, Masters and Johnson directly studied sexual intercourse and masturbation in nearly 700 males and females. This objective information has given us a much clearer picture of human sexuality (Carroll, 2010).

According to Masters and Johnson, sexual response can be divided into four phases: (1) *excitement*, (2) *plateau*, (3) *orgasm*, and (4) *resolution* (• Figure 11.8 and • Figure 11.9). These four phases, which are the same for people of all sexual orientations (Garnets & Kimmel, 1991), can be described as follows:

- **Excitement phase:** The first level of sexual response, indicated by initial signs of sexual arousal.
- **Plateau phase:** The second level of sexual response, during which physical arousal intensifies.
- **Orgasm:** A climax and release of sexual excitement.
- **Resolution:** The final level of sexual response, involving a return to lower levels of sexual tension and arousal.

Sex drive The strength of one's motivation to engage in sexual behavior.
Castration Surgical removal of the testicles or ovaries.
Sterilization Medical procedures such as vasectomy or tubal ligation that make a man or a woman infertile.
Masturbation Producing sexual pleasure or orgasm by directly stimulating the genitals.
Excitement phase The first phase of sexual response, indicated by initial signs of sexual arousal.
Plateau phase The second phase of sexual response during which physical arousal is further heightened.
Orgasm A climax and release of sexual excitement.
Resolution The fourth phase of sexual response, involving a return to lower levels of sexual tension and arousal.

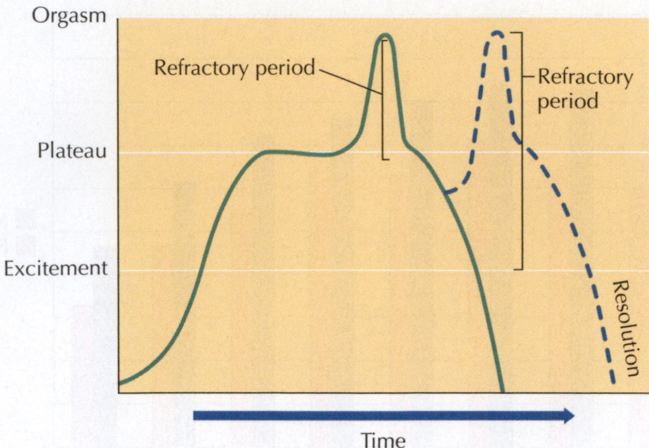

● **Figure 11.9** Male sexual response cycle. The green line shows that sexual arousal rises through the excitement phase and levels off for a time during the plateau phase. Arousal peaks during orgasm and then returns to pre-excitement levels. During the refractory period, immediately after orgasm, a second sexual climax is typically impossible. However, after the refractory period has passed, there may be a return to the plateau phase, followed by a second orgasm (dotted line). Adapted from Carroll, J. L. 2010. *Sexuality now: Embracing diversity,* 3rd ed. Cengage Learning/Wadsworth.

Female Response

In women, the excitement phase is marked by a complex pattern of changes in the body. The vagina is prepared for intercourse, the nipples become erect, pulse rate rises, and the skin may become flushed or reddened. If sexual stimulation ends, the excitement phase will gradually subside. If a woman moves into the plateau phase, physical changes and subjective feelings of arousal become more intense. Sexual arousal that ends during this phase tends to ebb more slowly, which may produce considerable frustration. Occasionally, women skip the plateau phase (see ● Figure 11.9). For some women, this is almost always the case.

During orgasm, 3 to 10 muscular contractions of the vagina, uterus, and related structures discharge sexual tension. Somewhat rarely, a small amount of fluid is released from the urethra during orgasm (Whipple, 2000). Orgasm is usually followed by resolution, a return to lower levels of sexual tension and arousal. After orgasm, about 15 percent of all women return to the plateau phase and may have one or more additional orgasms (Mah & Binik, 2001).

Before the work of Masters and Johnson, theorists debated whether "vaginal orgasms" are different from those derived from stimulation of the clitoris, a small, sensitive organ located above the vaginal opening. Sigmund Freud claimed that a "clitoral orgasm" is an "immature" form of female response. Because the clitoris is the female structure comparable to the penis, Freud believed that women who experienced clitoral orgasms had not fully accepted their femininity.

Masters and Johnson exploded the Freudian myth by showing that physical responses are the same no matter how an orgasm is produced (Carroll, 2010; Mah & Binik, 2001). As a matter of fact, the inner two thirds of the vagina is relatively insensitive to touch. Most sensations during intercourse come from stimulation of the clitoris and other external areas. For most women, the clitoris is an important source of pleasurable sensations. Apparently, sensations from many sources are fused together into the total experience of orgasm. Thus, to downgrade the "clitoral orgasm" ignores basic female biology.

Male Response

Sexual arousal in the male is signaled by erection of the penis during the excitement phase. A rise in heart rate, increased blood flow to the genitals, enlargement of the testicles, erection of the nipples, and numerous other body changes also occur. As is true of female sexual response, continued stimulation moves the male into the plateau phase. Again, physical changes and subjective feelings of arousal become more intense. Further stimulation during the plateau phase brings about a reflex release of sexual tension, resulting in orgasm.

In the mature male, orgasm is usually accompanied by **ejaculation** (release of sperm and seminal fluid). Afterward, it is followed by a short **refractory period**, during which a second orgasm is impossible. (Many men cannot even have an erection until the refractory phase has passed.) Only rarely is the male refractory period immediately followed by a second orgasm. Both orgasm and resolution in the male usually do not last as long as they do for females.

Comparing Male and Female Responses

Although male and female sexual responses are generally quite similar, the differences that do exist can affect sexual compatibility. For example, women typically go through the sexual phases more slowly than do men. During lovemaking, 10 to 20 minutes is often required for a woman to go from excitement to orgasm. Males may experience all four stages in as little as 3 minutes. However, there is much variation, especially in women. A study of married women found that 50 percent of them reached orgasm if intercourse lasted 1 to 11 minutes; when intercourse lasted 15 minutes or more, the rate increased to 66 percent. Twenty-five percent of the wives said that orgasm occurred within 1 minute of the start of intercourse (Brewer, 1981). (Note that these times refer only to intercourse, not to an entire arousal sequence.) Such differences should be kept in mind by couples seeking sexual compatibility (Carroll, 2010).

Does that mean that a couple should try to time lovemaking to promote simultaneous orgasm? At one time, simultaneous orgasm (both partners reaching sexual climax at the same time) was considered the "goal" of lovemaking. Now, it is regarded as an artificial concern that may reduce sexual enjoyment. It is more advisable for couples to seek mutual satisfaction through a combination of intercourse and erotic touching (foreplay) than it is to inhibit spontaneity, communication, and pleasure (Janus & Janus, 1993).

Does the slower female response just described mean that women are less sexual than men? Definitely not. During masturbation, 70 percent of females reach orgasm in 4 minutes or less. This casts serious doubt on the idea that women respond more slowly. Slower female response during intercourse probably occurs because stimulation to the clitoris is less direct. It might be said that men simply provide too little stimulation for more rapid female response, not that women are in any way inferior.

Does penis size affect female response? Contrary to popular belief, there is no relationship between penis size and male sexual potency. Think about it. If a woman's sexual satisfaction is related to her partner's attention to clitoral stimulation and foreplay, then why would his penis length matter? Besides, Masters and Johnson found that the vagina adjusts to the size of the penis and that subjective feelings of pleasure and intensity of orgasm are not related to penis size. They also found that although individual differences exist in flaccid penis size, there tends to be much less variation in size during erection. That's why erection has been called the "great equalizer."

Lovemaking involves the entire body. Preoccupation with the size of a woman's breasts, a man's penis, and the like, are based on myths that undermine genuine caring, sharing, and sexual satisfaction (Hyde & DeLamater, 2011).

Men almost always reach orgasm during intercourse, but many women do not. Doesn't this indicate that women are less sexually responsive? Again, the evidence argues against any lack of female sexual responsiveness. It is true that about 1 woman in 3 does not experience orgasm during the first year of marriage, and only about 30 percent regularly reach orgasm through intercourse alone. However, this does not imply lack of physical responsiveness, because 90 percent of all women reach orgasm when masturbating.

In another regard, women are clearly more responsive. Only about 5 percent of males are capable of multiple orgasm (and then only after an unavoidable refractory period). Most men are limited to a second orgasm at best. In contrast, Masters and Johnson's findings suggest that most women who regularly experience orgasm are capable of multiple orgasm. According to one survey, 48 percent of all women have had multiple orgasms (Darling, Davidson, & Passarello, 1992). Remember though, that only about 15 percent regularly have multiple orgasms. A woman should not automatically assume that something is wrong if she isn't orgasmic or multiorgasmic (Komisaruk, Beyer-Flores, & Whipple, 2006). Many women have satisfying sexual experiences even when orgasm is not involved.

Atypical Sexual Behavior—Trench Coats, Whips, Leathers, and Lace

Gateway Question 11.8: *What are the most common sexual disorders?*

By strict standards (including the law in some states), any sexual activity other than face-to-face heterosexual intercourse between married adults is atypical or "deviant." But public standards are often at odds with private behavior. Just as the hunger drive is expressed and satisfied in many ways, the sex drive also leads to an immense range of behaviors.

Then when do variations in sexual behavior become sufficiently atypical to be a disorder? Psychologically, the mark of true sexual disorders is that they are compulsive and destructive.

Paraphilias

Sexual deviance is a highly emotional subject. The sexual deviations, or **paraphilias** (PAIR-eh-FIL-ih-ahs) listed in ■ Table 11.2 cover a wide variety of behaviors (Lackamp, Osborne, & Wise, 2009). According to proposed changes to the *Diagnostic and Statistical Manual of Mental Disorders (DSM)* of the American Psychiatric Association, the paraphilias should be renamed *paraphilic disorders*, to better reflect the growing social consensus that a person engaging in unusual sexual practices does not automatically suffer from a psychiatric disorder (American Psychiatric Association, 2010). A paraphilic disorder, then, involves engaging in sexual practices *that typically cause guilt, anxiety, or discomfort for one or both participants*. For example, sadists, masochists, fetishists, and

■ **TABLE 11.2 Paraphilias**

Paraphilia (Paraphilic Disorder)	Primary Symptom
Exhibitionism (Exhibitionistic disorder)	"Flashing," or displaying the genitals to unwilling viewers
Fetishism (Fetishistic disorder)	Sexual arousal associated with inanimate objects
Frotteurism (Frotteuristic disorder)	Sexually touching or rubbing against a nonconsenting person, usually in a public place such as a subway
Pedophilia (Pedohebephilic disorder)	Sex with children, or child molesting
Sexual masochism (Sexual masochism disorder)	Desiring pain and/or humiliation as part of the sex act
Sexual sadism (Sexual sadism disorder)	Deriving sexual pleasure from inflicting pain and/or humiliation
Transvestic fetishism (Transvestic disorder)	Achieving sexual arousal by wearing clothing of the opposite sex
Voyeurism (Voyeuristic Disorder	"Peeping," or viewing the genitals of others without their permission

Paraphilia names are from the *DSM-IV-TR* (American Psychiatric Association, 2000) while the names in parentheses have been proposed for the upcoming 2013 edition, the *DSM-5* (American Psychiatric Association, 2010).

Ejaculation The release of sperm and seminal fluid by the male at the time of orgasm.

Refractory period A short period after orgasm during which males are unable to again reach orgasm.

Paraphilias (Paraphilic disorders) Compulsive or destructive deviations in sexual preferences or behavior.

transvestites voluntarily associate with people who share their sexual interests. Thus, their behavior may not harm anyone, except when it is extreme. In contrast, pedophilia, exhibitionism, voyeurism, and frotteurism do victimize unwilling participants (Crooks & Baur, 2011).

BRIDGES

See Chapter 14, page 482, for more information on the new edition of the DSM, the *DSM-5*.

Two of the most common and yet misunderstood problems are pedophilia and exhibitionism. Check your understanding against the information that follows.

Child Molestation

Child molesters, who are usually males, are often pictured as despicable perverts lurking in dark alleys. In fact, most are married, and two thirds are fathers. In most cases of pedophilia, the offender is a friend, acquaintance, or relative of the child (Abel, Wiegel, & Osborn, 2007). Molesters are also often thought of as child rapists, but most molestations rarely exceed fondling (Seto, 2008, 2009).

Many molesters are rigid, passive, puritanical, or religious. They are often consumers of child pornography (Seto, Cantor, & Blanchard, 2006). As children, child molesters themselves were often witnesses to or victims of sexual abuse (Burton, 2008).

How serious are the effects of a molestation? The impact varies widely. It is affected by how long the abuse lasts and whether genital sexual acts are involved (Freize, 1987). Many authorities believe that a single incident of fondling is unlikely to cause severe emotional harm to a child. For most children the event is frightening, but not a lasting trauma (Rind, Tromovitch, & Bauserman, 1998). That's why parents are urged not to overreact to such incidents or to become hysterical. Doing so only further frightens the child. This by no means implies, however, that parents should ignore hints from a child that a molestation may have occurred. Here are some hints of trouble that parents should watch for:

Recognizing Signs of Child Molestation

1. Unusual avoidance of, or interest in, sexual matters.
2. Secretiveness (including concerning Internet access).
3. Emotional disturbances such as depression, irritability, or withdrawal from family, friends, or school.
4. Nightmares or other sleep problems.
5. Misbehavior, such as unusual aggressiveness, suicidal behavior, or unusual risk taking such as riding a bicycle dangerously in traffic.
6. Loss of self-esteem or self-worth.

(Adapted from American Academy of Child and Adolescent Psychiatry, 2008.)

How can children protect themselves? Children should be taught to shout "No" if an adult tries to engage them in sexual activity. If children are asked to keep a secret, they should reply that they don't keep secrets. Parents and children also need to be aware that some pedophiles now try to make contact with children on the Internet. If an adult suggests to a child online that they could meet in person, the child should immediately tell his or her parents.

It also helps if children know the tactics typically used by molesters. Interviews with convicted sex offenders revealed the following (Elliott, Browne, & Kilcoyne, 1995):

Tactics of Child Molesters

1. Most molesters act alone.
2. Most assaults take place in the abuser's home.
3. Many abusers gain access to the child through caretaking.
4. Children are targeted at first through bribes, gifts, and games.
5. The abuser tries to lull the child into participation through talking about sex and persuasion. (This can take place through e-mail or chat rooms on the Internet.)
6. The abuser then uses force, anger, threats, and bribes to gain continued compliance.

Repeated molestations, those that involve force or threats, and incidents that exceed fondling can leave lasting emotional scars. As adults, many victims of incest or molestation develop sexual phobias. For them, lovemaking may evoke vivid and terrifying memories of the childhood victimization. Serious harm is especially likely to occur if the molester is someone the child deeply trusts. Molestations by parents, close relatives, teachers, priests, youth leaders, and similar persons can be quite damaging. In such cases, professional counseling is often needed (Saywitz et al., 2000).

Exhibitionism

Exhibitionism is a common disorder (Firestone et al., 2006). Between one third and two thirds of all sexual arrests are for "flashing." Exhibitionists also have high repeat rates among sexual offenders. Although it was long thought that exhibitionists are basically harmless, one recent study found that up to 40 percent of exhibitionists go on to commit more serious sexual crimes and other offenses (Firestone et al., 2006).

Exhibitionists are typically male and married, and most come from strict and repressive backgrounds. Most of them feel a deep sense of inadequacy, which produces a compulsive need to prove their "manhood" by frightening women. In general, a woman confronted by an exhibitionist can assume that his goal is to shock and alarm her. By becoming visibly upset, she actually encourages him (Hyde & DeLamater, 2011).

As the preceding discussion suggests, the picture of sexual deviance that most often emerges is one of sexual inhibition and immaturity. Typically, some relatively infantile sexual expression (like pedophilia or exhibitionism) is selected because it is less threatening than more mature sexuality.

All the paraphilias, unless they are very mild, involve compulsive behavior. As a result, they tend to emotionally handicap people. There is room in contemporary society for a large array of sexual behaviors. Nevertheless, any behavior that becomes compulsive (be it eating, gambling, drug abuse, or sex) is psychologically unhealthy.

Contemporary Attitudes and Sexual Behavior—For Better or Worse

Gateway Question 11.9: *Have recent changes in attitudes affected sexual behavior?*

If a woman and a man living in the year 1900 could be transported to the present, they would be stunned by today's North American sexual values and practices (Smith, 2006). Unmarried couples falling into bed on television; advertisements for bras, skimpy men's underwear, tampons, and cures for "jock itch"; near nudity at the beaches; sexually explicit movies, and, of course, the Internet—these and many other elements of contemporary culture would shock a person from the Victorian era.

A Sexual Revolution?

Has there been a "sexual revolution"? The word *revolution* suggests rapid change. On the one hand, a look at social changes in North America during the 1960s and early 1970s makes it clear that some fundamental alterations occurred in a relatively short time. Liberalized sexual attitudes and access to effective birth control significantly changed sexual behavior. On the other hand, many changes have occurred over longer periods. For example, traditional morality calls for female virginity before marriage. Yet even by the 1940s and 1950s, as many as 75 percent of married women had engaged in premarital sex (Smith, 2006; Regnerus & Uecker, 2011).

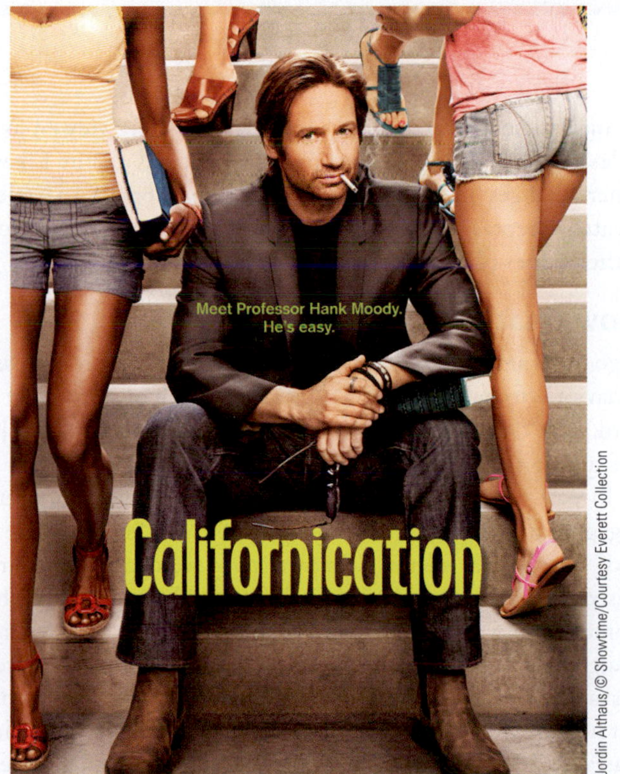

Even just 30 years ago, television soap operas were tame, gossipy melodramas. Today, they are sexy, gossipy melodramas that frequently feature steamy on-screen lovemaking.

Attitudes

Changing attitudes can be seen in national polls about premarital intercourse. In a 1959 Roper poll, 88 percent of those interviewed agreed that premarital sex is wrong. By the 1990s, more than 70 percent of young men and women approved of premarital sex (Wells & Twenge, 2005). Similar changes have occurred in attitudes toward extramarital sex, homosexuality, sex education, and related issues.

Behavior

Have changing attitudes been translated into behavior? Changes in attitudes are still larger than changes in actual sexual behavior. Mostly, there is greater *tolerance* for sexual activity, especially that *engaged in by others*. For example, a 1970s magazine poll found that 80 percent of all readers considered extramarital sex acceptable under some circumstances (Athenasiou, Shaver, & Tavris, 1970). But two other polls found that, in practice, only about 30 percent of married persons actually had extramarital sexual experience (Rubenstein, 1983; Rubenstein & Tavris, 1987). These are older studies, but the percentage has not changed greatly in the last 50 years. More importantly, faithfulness in marriage is a widely shared norm. Over a year, only about 4 percent of married people have sex partners other than their spouse. Americans actually seem to live up to the norm of marital fidelity fairly well (Mosher, Chandra, & Jones, 2005).

Teen premarital intercourse rates are a good indication of overall sexual activity. The social upheaval that began in the 1960s led to an especially sharp rise in sexual activity among teenagers. This increase continued into the 1980s but has reversed in recent years (Guttmacher Institute, 2011). In 1988, 60 percent of teenage males and 51 percent of teenage females had premarital intercourse by age 19. By 2002, the rates had dropped to 45 percent for both teenage males and females (Abma et al., 2004). The drop is especially pronounced among younger teens.

Encouragingly, the recent decline in sexual intercourse during early adolescence has been accompanied by higher rates of contraceptive use and declining rates of teen pregnancy and abortion (Guttmacher Institute, 2010; Santelli et al., 2004). Nevertheless, the United States still has one of the highest teenage pregnancy rates among all industrialized nations (Abma et al., 2004).

A partial solution to this problem may be to continue give youths a better understanding of their sexuality. Research confirms that sex education *delays* the age at which young people first engage in sexual intercourse (Kohler, Manhart, & Lafferty, 2008; Sawyer & Smith, 1996). Parents can encourage sexual responsibility in their children by providing close supervision and by stressing the value of delayed sexual involvement (Rosenthal et al., 2001).

Critical Thinking: Are We Oversexualizing Young Girls?

As the sexual double standard continues to fade, women feel freer to express their sexuality. But there is a negative side: Many experts now fear that young girls are being oversexualized by influences such as beauty pageants for very young girls, the public antics of female role models such as Paris Hilton and Britney Spears, and the availability of consumer goods such as padded bras for girls as young as six (Durham, 2009; Lerum & Dworkin, 2009). Greater sexual freedom is a positive development only for those ready for it (American Psychological Association, 2007).

© Evan Hurd/Sygma/Corbis

What messages do beauty pageants for children send to young girls?

According to an American Psychological Association Task Force, unhealthy sexualization can be distinguished from healthy sexuality when one or more of the following conditions occurs (American Psychological Association, 2007):

- A person is valued solely due to sexual appearance or behavior and not other characteristics.
- A person is led to narrowly equate sexual attractiveness with being "sexy."
- A person is objectified sexually (treated as an object for the gratification of other people).
- A person is inappropriately used sexually by another person.

From media images to popular fashions, young girls are more likely to be oversexualized than are young boys (American Psychological Association, 2007). Oversexualization leads young girls to see themselves as having value only as sexual objects. This results in low self-esteem, eating disorders, depression, and feelings of shame (Ward, 2004). Some studies have even shown that sexualized girls perform more poorly on intellectual activities (Hebl, King, & Lin, 2004). Most worrisome is an increasing tendency for young girls to engage in risky sexual behaviors, such as unprotected oral sex (Atwood, 2006; Prinstein, Meade, & Cohen, 2003).

According to the APA Task Force, parents, educators, and others should encourage young girls to develop relationships based on their personalities and interests, rather than on how they look (American Psychological Association, 2007).

Is the Revolution Over?

Talk of a sexual revolution has quieted in recent years, and a conservative counter-movement has been visible, especially among teenagers. Some of the reaction may reflect concern about sexually transmitted diseases. Regardless, it is unlikely that the United States will undergo a wholesale return to less liberal times (Janus & Janus, 1993; Smith, 2006). An interesting trend is the fact that people today spend as much of their adult lives (on average) alone as they do in marriage. As a result, many people are involved in nonmarried sexual relationships (Mahay & Laumann, 2004). This tends to increase the number of sexual partners adults encounter. Men now report having an average of seven female sexual partners in their lifetimes, whereas women report four. Further, in the past year, 17 percent of men and 10 percent of women reported having two or more sexual partners (Fryar et al., 2007).

In all, there is ample evidence that sexual behavior has generally increased in the last 40 years. Although this trend has brought problems, it does not seem to represent a wholesale move toward sexual promiscuity. Even premarital intercourse does not appear to represent a major rejection of traditional values and responsible behavior. The connection between sexuality and love or affection remains strong for most people. Both premarital sex and cohabitation are still widely viewed as preludes to marriage or as temporary substitutes for it. Likewise, other changes in attitudes and behavior appear to reflect a greater acceptance of sexuality rather than a total rejection of earlier values (Crooks & Baur, 2011).

Slow Death of the Double Standard

A good summary of one major change that has occurred in sexual behavior is found in the phrase "the slow death of the double standard." The **double standard** refers to using different rules to judge the appropriateness of male and female sexual behavior.

In past decades, for example, males were largely forgiven for engaging in premarital sex. Young males who "sowed some wild oats" were widely tolerated. In fact, many were tacitly encouraged to seek casual sex as a step toward manhood. On the other hand, women who were sexually active before marriage ran the risk of being labeled "easy," "bad," or "promiscuous." Similar differences pervade sexual mores and frequently place women in a "separate but not equal" position with regard to sexual behavior (Sprecher & Hatfield, 1996; Kreager & Staff, 2009). However, as the gap between female and male sexual patterns continues to close, it is increasingly likely that an end to the double standard is in sight (Schleicher & Gilbert, 2005).

Critical Thinking: Gender Role Stereotyping and Rape

Rape is related to traditional gender role socialization. Traditional feminine stereotypes include the idea that women should not show direct interest in sex. Traditional masculine stereotypes, on the other hand, include the ideas that a man should take the initiative and persist in attempts at sexual intimacy—even when the woman says no (Locke & Mahalik, 2005).

Psychologists James Check and Neil Malamuth (1983) believe that such attitudes create a "rape-supportive culture." In their view, rape is only an extreme expression of a system that condones coercive (forced) sexual intimacy. They point out, for instance, that the most used cries of rapists to their victims are "You know you want it," and afterward, "There now, you really enjoyed it, didn't you?"

In general, research has confirmed a link between acceptance of rape myths and sexual violence toward women (Chapleau & Oswald, 2010; Forbes, Adams-Curtis, & White, 2004). In a classic experimental confirmation of the hypothesis that stereotyped images contribute to rape, male college students were classified as either high or low in gender role stereotyping. Each student then read one of three stories: The first described voluntary intercourse; the second depicted stranger rape; and the third described date rape.

As predicted, college males high in gender role stereotyping were more aroused by the rape stories. Their arousal patterns, in fact, were similar to those found among actual rapists. Moreover, a chilling 44 percent of those tested indicated they would consider rape—especially if they could be sure of not being caught (Check & Malamuth, 1983).

In view of such findings—and the continuing widespread belief that when a woman says no she means yes—it is little wonder that rape occurs every 6 minutes in the United States. Perhaps the time has come for our culture to make it clear that no means no. Educating men about rape myths has been one of the most successful ways of preventing sexual assault (King, 2005; Reppucci, Woolard, & Fried, 1999).

Sexuality Worldwide

Our discussion has focused on sexuality in the United States and Canada. What about the rest of the world? A survey of 59 nations found that a "sexual revolution" has not occurred in most other countries (Wellings et al., 2006). People from the United States and other industrialized nations are more likely to have had two or more recent sexual partners; most people from developing countries have had only one recent sexual partner. On average, teenagers around the world have their first sexual experience at the same age as American teenagers. One finding of particular note concerns Africa, the epicenter of the AIDS epidemic. Contrary to popular opinion elsewhere, Africans are not promiscuous. They report fewer sexual partners than their counterparts in developed countries. Instead, it's likely that high rates of venereal disease in Africa result from a lack of knowledge and access to condoms.

Choices

A more comfortable acceptance of human sexuality is the positive side of changing sexual attitudes and values. The negative side is revealed by the plight of people who are not ready for, or interested in, greater sexual freedom (see "Are We Oversexualizing Young Girls?"). Apparently, some individuals feel pressured into sexual behavior because it is "expected." In fact, 6 percent of first sexual intercourse experiences are against the person's will (Bajracharya, Sarvela, & Isberner, 1995).

Pressures to engage in sex probably come as much from the individual as from others. For a greater acceptance of sexuality to be constructive, people must feel that they have the right to say no, as well as the right to choose when, where, how, and with whom they will express their sexuality. As is true elsewhere, freedom must be combined with responsibility, commitment, and caring if it is to have meaning.

The Crime of Rape

Many women believe that their chances of being raped are low, but the facts tell a different story (Centers for Disease Control, 2007, 2011; Tjaden & Thoennes, 2006):

- At least 1 woman in 6 will experience rape or attempted rape in her lifetime. Because only 1 rape in 5 is reported, the true figure is much higher.
- Pregnancy is the result of rape in 32,000 cases every year.
- Three percent of rape victims contract sexually transmitted diseases.

Although it is commonly believed that rapists are usually strangers to the women they rape, nothing could be further from the truth (Centers for Disease Control, 2009a; Martin, Taft, & Resick, 2007). Seventy-five percent of American women who have been sexually or physically assaulted reported that the perpetrator was a husband, intimate partner, or acquaintance. From 10 to 14 percent of all married women have experienced *marital rape*, which usually includes being beaten by their husbands. Similarly, 20 to 25 percent of all female college students are victims of rape or attempted

Double standard Applying different standards for judging the appropriateness of male and female sexual behavior.

rape during their time at college. Roughly one half of these rapes were **acquaintance (date) rapes** (forced intercourse that occurs in the context of a date or other voluntary encounter). In other words, they were carried out by first dates, casual dates, or romantic acquaintances (Fisher, Cullen, & Daigle, 2005; Koss, 2000).

Men who commit marital or date rape often believe they have done nothing wrong. A typical explanation is, "Her words were saying no, but her body was saying yes." (See "Gender Role Stereotyping and Rape.") But forced sex is rape, even if the rapist doesn't use a knife or become violent. The effects of rape by someone familiar are no less devastating than those of rape committed by a stranger.

Rape Myths

A study of college men found that many tend to blame *women* for date rape. According to them, women who are raped by an acquaintance actually wanted to have sex. This is just one of several widely held beliefs that qualify as **rape myths** (Forbes, Adams-Curtis, & White, 2004; Suarez & Gadalla, 2010). All these statements are myths:

- A woman who appears alone in public and dresses attractively is "asking for it."
- When a woman says no, she really means yes.
- Many women who are raped actually enjoy it.
- If a woman goes home with a man on a first date, she is interested in sex.
- If a woman is sexually active, she is probably lying if she says she was raped.

Men who believe rape myths are more likely to misread a woman's resistance to unwanted sexual advances, assuming that she really means yes when she says no (Forbes, Adams-Curtis, & White, 2004). Add some alcohol to the situation and the risk of sexual assault is even greater: Men who believe rape myths and who have been drinking are especially likely to ignore signals that a woman wants sexual advances to stop (Chapleau & Oswald, 2010; Marx, Gross, & Adams, 1999).

Forcible Rape

Date rape is coercive, but not necessarily violent. **Forcible rape**, which is distressingly common, is carried out under the threat of bodily injury. Rapists often inflict more violence on their victims than is necessary to achieve their goal.

Most psychologists no longer think of forcible rape as a primarily sexual act. Rather, it is an act of brutality or aggression based on the need to debase others. Many rapists impulsively take what they want without concern for the feelings of the victim or guilt about their deed. Others harbor deep-seated resentment or outright hatred of women.

Typical after-effects for the victim include rage, guilt, depression, loss of self-esteem, shame, sexual adjustment problems, and, in many cases, a lasting mistrust of male–female relationships. The impact is so great that most women continue to report fear, anxiety, and sexual dysfunction a year or two after being raped. Even years later, rape survivors are more likely to suffer from depression, alcohol or drug abuse, and other emotional problems.

It is also important to be aware that men can also be the victims of rape, especially homosexual rape (Centers for Disease Control, 2011; Davies & McCartney, 2003). Any man who doubts the seriousness of rape should imagine himself mistakenly placed in jail, where he is violently raped (sodomized) by other inmates. There is no pleasure in rape for victims of either sex. It is truly a despicable crime.

STDs and Safer Sex—Choice, Risk, and Responsibility

Gateway Question 11.10: ***What impacts have sexually transmitted diseases had on sexual behavior?***

In general, most adults favor greater freedom of choice for themselves, including choice about sexual behavior. Yet, as the upcoming discussion of AIDS suggests, there are new and compelling reasons for caution in sexual behavior. This is especially true for younger people who are exploring their identities, sexual or otherwise, in an era of more casual sex (Puentes, Knox, & Zusman, 2008).

A **sexually transmitted disease (STD)** is an infection passed from one person to another by intimate physical contact. Sexually active people run higher risks for chlamydia (klah-MID-ee-ah), gonorrhea, hepatitis B, herpes, syphilis, and other STDs (see ■ Table 11.3). Many people who carry STDs remain *asymptomatic* (a-SIMP-teh-mat-ik: lacking obvious symptoms). It is easy to have an infection without knowing it. Likewise, it is often impossible to tell whether a sexual partner is infectious. Thus, risky sex is a serious hazard. A study of sexually active teenage girls engaging in risky sex is a case in point. Nearly 90 percent of the girls thought that they had virtually no chance of getting an STD. In reality, over the next 18 months, 1 in 4 got chlamydia or gonorrhea (Ethier et al., 2003).

A major problem is that people who are sexually active may have indirect contact with many other people. One study of sexual relationships at a high school in a Midwestern city found long chains of sexual contact between students. Thus, a student at the end of the chain might have had sex with only one person, but in reality she or he had indirect contact with dozens or even hundreds of others (Bearman, Moody, & Stovel, 2004).

For many sexually active people, the human immunodeficiency virus (HIV) has added a new threat. HIV is a sexually transmitted disease that disables the immune system. Whereas most other STDs are treatable, HIV infections can be lethal. Check your knowledge about HIV against the following summary.

HIV/AIDS

Acquired immune deficiency syndrome (AIDS) is caused by an HIV infection. As the immune system weakens, other "opportunistic" diseases invade the body. Most AIDS victims eventually die of multiple infections (although newer multidrug therapies have greatly improved the odds of survival). The first symptoms of AIDS may show up as little as 2 months after infection, but they typically

TABLE 11.3 Common Sexually Transmitted Diseases

STD	Male Symptoms	Female Symptoms	Prevention	Treatment
Gonorrhea	Milky discharge from urethra; painful, frequent urination	Vaginal discharge and inflammation, painful urination	Condom/safer sex practices	Antibiotics
Chlamydia	Painful urination, discharge from urethra	Painful urination, discharge from vagina, abdominal pain	Condom/safer sex practices	Antibiotics
Syphilis	Painless sores on genitals, rectum, tongue, or lips; skin rash, fever, headache, aching bones and joints	Same	Condom/safer sex practices	Antibiotics
Genital herpes	Pain or itching on the penis; water blisters or open sores	Pain or itching in the genital area; water blisters or open sores	Condom/safer sex practices	Symptoms can be treated but not cured
Genital warts	Warty growths on genitals	Same	Condom/safer sex practices	Removal by surgery or laser
HIV/AIDS	Prolonged fatigue, swollen lymph nodes, fever lasting more than 10 days, night sweats, unexplained weight loss, purplish lesions on skin, persistent cough or sore throat, persistent colds, persistent diarrhea, easy bruising or unexplained bleeding	Same	Condom/safer sex practices	Can be treated with various drugs but cannot be cured
Hepatitis B	Mild cases may have no symptoms, but infection can cause chronic liver disease, cirrhosis of the liver, or liver cancer	Same	Vaccination	None available
Pelvic inflammatory disease	Does not apply	Intense pain in lower back and/or abdomen, fever	Condom/safer sex practices	Antibiotics

The AIDS Memorial Quilt was begun in 1985 to commemorate those who have died from AIDS. The photo is of the last public display of the complete quilt, in 1996. Originally the quilt memorialized only homosexual victims. It now includes heterosexual men, women, and children, signifying that AIDS respects no boundaries. Today, it is comprised of over 90,000 individual 3 ft. x 6 ft. panels (each the size of a human grave). If the quilt included panels for all 25 million of the victims of AIDs to date, it would cover a quarter of all of Washington, DC.

don't appear for 10 years. Because of this long incubation period, infected persons often pass the AIDS virus on to others without knowing it. Medical testing can detect an HIV infection. However, for at least the first 6 months after becoming infected, a person can test negative while carrying the virus. A negative test result, therefore, is no guarantee that a person is a "safe" sex partner.

HIV infections are spread by direct contact with body fluids—especially blood, semen, and vaginal secretions. The AIDS virus cannot be transmitted by casual contact. People do not get AIDS from shaking hands, touching or using objects touched by an AIDS patient, eating food prepared by an infected person, or from social kissing, sweat or tears, sharing drinking glasses, sharing towels, and so forth.

HIV can be spread by all forms of sexual intercourse, and it has affected persons of all sexual orientations. Recently, the AIDS epidemic has spread more quickly among heterosexuals, women, African Americans, Hispanics, and children (Taylor-Seehafer & Rew, 2000). Around the world, about half of all HIV cases are female (United Nations Programme on HIV/AIDS, 2009). HIV infection is the leading cause of death among women and men between the

Acquaintance (date) rape Forced intercourse that occurs in the context of a date or other voluntary encounter.

Rape myths False beliefs about rape that tend to blame the victim and increase the likelihood that some men will think that rape is justified.

Forcible rape Sexual intercourse carried out against the victim's will, under the threat of violence or bodily injury.

Sexually transmitted disease (STD) A disease that is typically passed from one person to the next by intimate physical contact; a venereal disease.

ages of 25 and 44 (Gayle, 2000). Worldwide, 2 million people die each year from HIV/AIDS, and 2.7 million new infections occur (United Nations Programme on HIV/AIDS, 2009).

Populations at Risk

In North America, those who are at greatest risk for HIV infection remain men who have had sex with other men (homosexual and bisexual men), people who have shared needles (for tattoos or for intravenous drug use), hemophiliacs (who require frequent blood transfusions), sexual partners of people in the preceding groups, and heterosexuals with a history of multiple partners. Thus, the vast majority of people are not at high risk of HIV infection. Still, 1.1 million people in the United States are now infected with HIV, of whom 26 percent are women. Each year, over 56,000 more people in the United States become infected (Centers for Disease Control, 2009b). In short, people who engage in unsafe sex are gambling with their lives—at very poor odds.

Behavioral Risk Factors for STDs

Sexually active people can do much to protect their own health. The behaviors listed here are risky when performed with an infected person:

Risky Behaviors

- Unprotected vaginal, oral, or anal sex (without a condom) with an infected partner
- Having two or more sex partners (additional partners further increase the risk)
- Sex with someone you don't know well, or with someone you know has several partners
- Sex with someone you know injects drugs (HIV/AIDS)
- Sharing drug needles and syringes (HIV/AIDS)

In the United States, between 2 and 4 of every 100 adults put themselves at high risk by engaging in the behaviors just listed (Gayle, 2000). It's important to remember that you can't tell from appearance if a person is infected. Many people would be surprised to learn that their partners have engaged in behavior that places them both at risk.

The preceding high-risk behaviors can be contrasted with the following list of safer sexual practices. Note, however, that unless a person completely abstains, sex can be made safer, but not risk-free.

Safer Sex Practices

- Not having sex
- Sex with one mutually faithful, uninfected partner
- Not injecting drugs (HIV/AIDS)
- Discussing contraception with partner
- Being selective regarding sexual partners
- Reducing the number of sexual partners
- Discussing partner's sexual health prior to engaging in sex
- Not engaging in sex while intoxicated
- Using a condom

Sexually active persons should practice safer sex until their partner's sexual history and/or health has been clearly established. And remember, a condom offers little or no protection if it is misused. Sadly, 1 of 3 sexually active teens don't know how to use a condom correctly (and virgins of both sexes are even more clueless) (Crosby & Yarber, 2001).

HIV and AIDS initially had a strong impact on sexual behavior in some groups. Among gay men, there was a sharp decrease in risky sex and an increase in monogamous relationships. Unfortunately, this trend has recently reversed. Once again, rates for many STDs are rising dramatically among gay men. In part, this may be due to the fact that new medical treatments are helping people with HIV live longer. Many victims simply do not look or act sick. This gives a false impression about the dangers of HIV infection and encourages foolish risk taking (Handsfield, 2001). The focus on HIV/AIDS prevention may also have de-emphasized the health impact of the other STDs.

Other groups are also not getting the message. The AIDS epidemic has thus far had little impact on the willingness of high school and college age students to engage in risky behavior (casual sex) or to use condoms (Bauman, Karasz, & Hamilton, 2007). A study of heterosexual adults found that the majority did not practice safer sex with their last partner. Most of these "gamblers" knew too little about their partners to be sure they were not taking a big risk. For many people, drinking alcohol greatly increases the likelihood of taking sexual risks (Corbin & Fromme, 2002).

Apparently, heterosexual people still don't feel that they are truly at risk. However, *30 percent* of new HIV infections in the United States are transmitted through heterosexual sex. Over the next 20 to 30 years, heterosexual transmission is expected to become the primary means of spreading HIV. Over the next 15 years, 65 million more people worldwide will die of AIDS unless prevention efforts are greatly expanded (Altman, 2002).

Safer Sex

The threat of HIV/AIDS has forced many people to face new issues of risk and responsibility concerning STDs in general. Those who do not ensure their own safety are playing Russian roulette with their health (Essien et al., 2010). One chilling study of HIV patients who knew they were infectious found that 41 percent of those who were sexually active did not always use condoms (Sobel et al., 1996)! Thus, responsibility for "safer sex" rests with each sexually active individual. It is unwise to count on a sexual partner for protection against STDs.

A special risk that befalls people in committed relationships is that they often interpret practicing safer sex as a sign of mistrust. Taking precautions could, instead, be defined as a way of showing that you really care about the welfare of your partner (Hammer et al., 1996). Likewise, dating couples who have high levels of emotional, social, and intellectual intimacy are more likely to use contraceptives (Davis & Bibace, 1999).

The sexual revolution was fueled, in part, by "the pill" and other birth control methods. Will the threat of AIDS reverse the tide of changes that occurred in previous decades? Will STD come to mean Sudden Total Disinterest in sex? The answers may depend on how quickly people learn to respect STDs and whether their prevention or cure can be achieved.

Knowledge Builder: Sexual Behavior, Response, Attitudes, and Consequences

RECITE

1. Areas of the body that produce erotic pleasure are called ______________ zones.
2. When exposed to erotic stimuli, men and women vary in their most common emotional reactions, but there appears to be no difference in their levels of physical arousal. T or F?
3. There is some evidence to suggest that sexual activity and sex drives peak later for males than they do for females. T or F?
4. More males than females report that they masturbate. T or F?
5. List the four phases of sexual response identified by Masters and Johnson: ______________, ______________, ______________, ______________
6. Males typically experience ______________ after ejaculation. *a.* an increased potential for orgasm *b.* a short refractory period *c.* the excitement phase *d.* muscular contractions of the uterus
7. During lovemaking, 10 to 20 minutes is often required for a woman to go from excitement to orgasm, whereas a male may experience all four stages of sexual response in as little as 3 minutes. T or F?
8. Recent research shows that more liberal views regarding sexual behavior have erased the traditional values that link sexual involvement with committed relationships. T or F?
9. The term ______________ ______________ describes the tendency for the sexual behavior of women and men to be judged differently.
10. One woman in 70 will be raped in her lifetime, and chances are greater than 50 percent that the rapist will be a friend or acquaintance. T or F?
11. Wanting to practice safe sex is an insult to your lover. T or F?

REFLECT

Think Critically

12. Why do you think that fidelity in marriage is strongly encouraged by law and custom?
13. Which do you think would be better suited to reducing STDs and unwanted pregnancies among adolescents: abstinence-only education programs or more comprehensive sex education programs?

Self-Reflect

To what extent does the discussion of sexual arousal and sex drive agree with your own experiences and beliefs? What do you want to remember that you didn't know before?

Based on your own observations of attitudes toward sex and patterns of sexual behavior, do you think there has been a sexual revolution?

To what extent do movies, music videos, and video games contribute directly to the perpetuation of rape myths? What about indirectly, by portraying gender role stereotypes?

Answers: 1. erogenous **2.** T **3.** F **4.** T **5.** excitement, plateau, orgasm, resolution **6.** *b* **7.** T **8.** F **9.** double standard **10.** F **11.** F **12.** Through marriage laws and customs, human societies tend to foster enduring bonds between sexual partners to help ensure that children are cared for and not just produced. **13.** More comprehensive programs are actually more effective at reducing STDs and unwanted pregnancies among adolescents (Kirby, 2008).

Psychology in Action: Sexual Problems—When Pleasure Fades

Gateway Question 11.11: *How can couples keep their relationship sexually satisfying, and what are the most common sexual dysfunctions?*

Keeping It Hot

Most couples find that their sexual interest and passion decline over time (Impett et al., 2008, 2010).

Is a loss of sexual interest inevitable in long-term relationships? No. But keeping passion alive does take effort, plus a willingness to resolve other types of problems in the relationship (Strong, DeVault, & Cohen, 2011). For example, conflict or anger about other issues frequently takes a toll on sexual adjustment. Conversely, couples who share positive experiences and satisfying relationships also tend to have satisfying sex lives (Algoe, Gable, & Maisel, 2010). Sex is not a performance or a skill to be mastered like playing tennis. It is a form of communication within a relationship. Couples with strong and caring relationships can probably survive most sexual problems (Impett et al., 2008, 2010). A couple with a satisfactory sex life but a poor relationship rarely lasts. Marriage expert John Gottman believes that a couple must have at least five times as many positive as negative moments in their marriage if it is to survive (Gottman, 1994).

Disagreements about Sex

When disagreements arise over issues such as frequency of lovemaking, who initiates lovemaking, or what behavior is appropriate, the rule should be, "Each partner must accept the other as the final authority on his or her own feelings." Partners are urged to give feedback about their feelings by following what therapists call the "touch and ask" rule: Touching and caressing should often be followed by questions such as, "Does that feel good?" "Do you like that?" and so forth. Satisfying erotic relationships focus on enhancing sexual pleasure for both partners, not on selfish interest in one's own gratification (Carroll, 2010; Strong, DeVault, & Cohen, 2011).

When problems do arise, partners are urged to be *responsive* to each other's needs at an *emotional* level and to recognize that all sexual problems are *mutual*. "Failures" should always be shared without placing blame. It is particularly important to avoid the "numbers game." That is, couples should avoid being influenced by statistics on the average frequency of lovemaking, by stereotypes about sexual potency, and by the superhuman sexual exploits portrayed in movies and magazines.

Bridges to Sexual Satisfaction

According to sex therapist Barry McCarthy, four elements are necessary for a continuing healthy sexual relationship:

1. **Sexual anticipation.** Looking forward to lovemaking can be inhibited by routine and poor communication between partners. It is wise for busy couples to set aside time to spend together. Unexpected, spontaneous lovemaking should also be encouraged.
2. **Valuing one's sexuality.** This is most likely to occur when you develop a respectful, trusting, and intimate relationship with your partner. Such relationships allow both partners to deal with negative sexual experiences when they occur.
3. **Feeling that you deserve sexual pleasure.** As previously noted, the essence of satisfying lovemaking is the giving and receiving of pleasure.
4. **Valuing intimacy.** A sense of closeness and intimacy with one's partner helps maintain sexual desire, especially in long-term relationships (McCarthy, 1995; McCarthy & Fucito, 2005).

Intimacy and Communication

Are there any other guidelines for maintaining a healthy relationship? A classic study that compared happily married couples with unhappily married couples found that, in almost every regard, the happily married couples showed superior *communication* skills. Three patterns that are almost always related to serious long-term problems in relationships are defensiveness (including whining), stubbornness, and refusal to talk with your partner (the "big freeze") (Gottman & Krokoff, 1989). Many couples find that communication is facilitated by observing the following guidelines.

Avoid "Gunnysacking"

Persistent feelings, whether positive or negative, need to be expressed. *Gunnysacking* refers to saving up feelings and complaints. These are then "dumped" during an argument or are used as ammunition in a fight. Gunnysacking is very destructive to a relationship.

Be Open about Feelings

Happy couples not only talk more, they convey more personal feelings and show greater sensitivity to their partners' feelings (Driver & Gottman, 2004). As one expert put it, "In a healthy relationship, each partner feels free to express his likes, dislikes, wants, wishes, feelings, impulses, and the other person feels free to react with like honesty to these. In such a relationship, there will be tears, laughter, sensuality, irritation, anger, fear, baby-like behavior, and so on" (Jourard, 1963).

Don't Attack the Other Person's Character

Whenever possible, expressions of negative feelings should be given as statements of one's own feelings, not as statements of blame. It is far more constructive to say, "It makes me angry when you leave things around the house," than it is to say, "You're a slob!" Remember too, that if you use the words "always" or "never," you are probably mounting a character attack.

Don't Try to "Win" a Fight

Constructive fights are aimed at resolving shared differences, not at establishing who is right or wrong, superior or inferior.

Recognize That Anger Is Appropriate

Constructive and destructive fights are not distinguished by whether or not anger is expressed. A fight is a fight, and anger is appropriate. As is the case with any other emotion in a relationship, anger should be expressed. However, constructive expression of anger requires that couples fight fair by sticking to the real issues and not "hitting below the belt." Resorting to threats, such as announcing, "This relationship is over," is especially damaging.

Try to See Things Through Your Partner's Eyes

Marital harmony is closely related to the ability to put yourself in another person's place (Long & Andrews, 1990). When a conflict arises, always pause and try to take your partner's perspective. Seeing things through your partner's eyes can be a good reminder that no one is ever totally right or wrong in a personal dispute (Haas et al., 2007).

Don't Be a "Mind-Reader"

The preceding suggestion should not be taken as an invitation to engage in "mind-reading." Assuming that you know what your partner is thinking or feeling can muddle or block communication. Hostile or accusatory mind-reading, as in the following examples, can be very disruptive: "You're just looking for an excuse to criticize me, aren't you?" "You don't really want my mother to visit, or you wouldn't say that." Rather than *telling* your partner what she or he thinks, *ask* her or him.

To add to these guidelines, if you really want to mess up a relationship, you can almost totally avoid intimacy and communication by doing the following (Algoe, Gable, & Maisel, 2010; Impett et al., 2010; Strong, DeVault, & Cohen, 2011).

Ten Ways to Avoid Intimacy

1. Don't talk about anything meaningful, especially about feelings.
2. Never show your feelings; remain as expressionless as possible. Never express gratitude.
3. Always be pleasant and pretend everything is okay, even if you are upset or dissatisfied.
4. Always win, never compromise.
5. Always keep busy; that way you can avoid intimacy and make your partner feel unimportant in your life.
6. Always be right; don't let on that you are human.
7. Never argue or you may have to reveal differences and make changes.

"It's a shame there isn't a pill to stimulate conversation."

8. Make your partner guess what you want. That way, you can tell your partner that she or he doesn't really understand or love you.
9. Always take care of your own needs first. Always avoid shared goals.
10. Keep the television set on. Wouldn't you rather be watching TV than talking with your partner?

Remember, to encourage intimacy, wise couples *avoid* the practices in the preceding list.

As a last point, it is worth restating that sexual adjustment and loving relationships are interdependent. When sex goes well, it's 15 percent of a relationship, and when it goes badly it's 85 percent. As a shared pleasure, a form of intimacy, a means of communication, and a haven from everyday tensions, a positive sexual relationship can do much to enhance a couple's mutual understanding and caring. Likewise, an honest, equitable, and affectionate out-of-bed relationship contributes greatly to sexual satisfaction (Rathus, Nevid, & Fichner-Rathus, 2010).

Sexual Dysfunctions

Even the best-intentioned people may nevertheless experience sexual dysfunction, which is far more common than many people realize. Most people who seek sexual counseling have one or more of the following types of problems (Crooks & Baur, 2011; American Psychiatric Association, 2000, 2010; Heiman, 2002):

1. **Desire Disorders:** The person has either little or no sexual motivation or desire or too much.
2. **Arousal Disorders:** The person desires sexual activity but does not become sexually aroused.
3. **Orgasm Disorders:** The person does not have orgasms or experiences orgasm too soon or too late.
4. **Sexual Pain Disorders:** The person experiences pain that makes lovemaking uncomfortable or impossible.

There was a time when people suffered such problems in silence. However, in recent years, effective treatments have been found for many complaints. Medical treatments or drugs (such as Viagra for men) may be helpful for sexual problems that clearly have physical causes. In other cases, counseling or psychotherapy may be the best approach. Let's briefly investigate the nature, causes, and treatments of sexual dysfunctions.

Desire Disorders

Desire disorders, like most sexual problems, must be defined in relation to a person's age, sex, partner, expectations, and sexual history. It is not at all unusual for a person to briefly lose sexual desire. Typically, erotic feelings return when anger toward a partner fades, or fatigue, illness, and similar temporary problems end. Under what circumstances, then, is loss of desire a dysfunction? First, the loss of desire must be *persistent*. Second, the person must be *troubled by it*. When these two conditions are met, **hypoactive sexual desire** is said to exist. Diminished desire can apply to both sexes. However, it is somewhat more common in women (Heiman, 2002; Segraves & Woodard, 2006).

Some people don't merely lack sexual desire; they are *repelled* by sex and seek to avoid it. A person who suffers from **sexual aversion** feels fear, anxiety, or disgust about engaging in sex. Often, the afflicted person still has some erotic feelings. For example, he or she may still masturbate or have sexual fantasies. Nevertheless, the prospect of having sex with another person causes panic or revulsion (American Psychiatric Association, 2000). According to proposed changes to the *Diagnostic and Statistical Manual of Mental Disorders (DSM)* of the American Psychiatric Association, sexual aversion disorder may be renamed as a *sexual dysfunction not otherwise specified* (American Psychiatric Association, 2010).

Sexual desire disorders are common. Possible physical causes include illness, fatigue, hormonal difficulties, and the side effects of medicines. Desire disorders are also associated with psychological factors such as depression, fearing loss of control over sexual urges, strict religious beliefs, fear of pregnancy, marital conflict, fear of closeness, and simple loss of attraction to one's partner (King, 2005). It is also not uncommon to find that people with desire disorders were sexually mistreated as children (Bakich, 1995).

Isn't it possible for someone to experience too much sexual desire? Yes it is. Another proposed change to the DSM is the addition of **hypersexual disorder**, an excess of sexual desire (American Psychiatric Association, 2010). Again, the excess must be *persistent* and the person must be *troubled by it*. Plagued by intense and recurrent and intense sexual fantasies, urges, and/or behaviors, people with hypersexual disorder are sometimes described as *sex addicts* (Kafka, 2010).

Treatment Desire disorders are complex problems. Unless they have a straightforward physical cause, they are difficult to treat. Desire disorders are often deeply rooted in a person's childhood, sexual history, personality, and relationships. In such instances, counseling or psychotherapy is recommended (King, 2005).

Arousal Disorders

A person suffering from an arousal disorder wants to make love but experiences little or no physical arousal. For men, this means an inability to maintain an erection. For women, it means vaginal dryness. Basically, in arousal disorders the body does not cooperate with the person's desire to make love.

Erectile Disorder An inability to maintain an erection for lovemaking is called **erectile disorder**. This problem, which is also known as erectile dysfunction, was once referred to as *impotence*. However, psychologists now discourage use of the term because of its many negative connotations.

Erectile disorders can be primary or secondary. Men suffering from primary erectile dysfunction have never had an erection. Those who previously performed successfully but then developed a problem suffer from secondary erectile dysfunction. Either way, persistent erectile difficulties tend to be very disturbing to the man and his sexual partner (Baldo & Eardley, 2005; Riley & Riley, 2009).

How often must a man experience failure for a problem to exist? According to the DSM, erectile disorder involves a persistent difficulty of at least six months duration, although ultimately, only the man and his partner can make this judgment (American Psychiatric Association, 2000). Repeated erectile dys-

Hypoactive sexual desire A persistent, upsetting loss of sexual desire.

Sexual aversion (One type of sexual dysfunction not otherwise specified) Persistent feelings of fear, anxiety, or disgust about engaging in sex.

Hypersexual disorder A persistent, troubling excess of sexual desire.

Erectile disorder An inability to maintain an erection for lovemaking.

function should, therefore, be distinguished from *occasional* erectile problems. Fatigue, anger, anxiety, and drinking too much alcohol can cause temporary erectile difficulties in healthy males. True erectile disorders typically persist for months or years (Rowland, 2007).

It is important to recognize that occasional erectile problems are normal. In fact, "performance demands" or overreaction to the temporary loss of an erection may generate fears and doubts that contribute to a further inhibition of arousal (Abrahamson, Barlow, & Abrahamson, 1989). At such times, it is particularly important for the man's partner to avoid expressing anger, disappointment, or embarrassment. Patient reassurance helps prevent the establishment of a vicious cycle.

What causes erectile disorders? Roughly 40 percent of all cases are *organic*, or physically caused. The origin of the remaining cases is **psychogenic** (a result of emotional factors). Even when erectile dysfunction is organic, however, it is almost always made worse by anxiety, anger, and dejection. If a man can have an erection at times other than lovemaking (during sleep, for instance), the problem probably is not physical (Baldo & Eardley, 2005).

Organic erectile problems have many causes. Typical sources of trouble include alcohol or drug abuse, diabetes, vascular disease, prostate and urological disorders, neurological problems, and reactions to medication for high blood pressure, heart disease, or stomach ulcers. Erectile problems are also a normal part of aging. As men grow older, they typically experience a decline in sexual desire and arousal and an increase in sexual dysfunction (Segraves & Segraves, 1995).

According to Masters and Johnson (1970), primary erectile disorders are often related to harsh religious training, early sexual experiences with a seductive mother, sexual molestation in childhood, or other experiences leading to guilt, fear, and sexual inhibition.

Secondary erectile disorders may be related to anxiety about sex in general, guilt because of an extramarital affair, resentment or hostility toward a sexual partner, fear of inability to perform, concerns about STDs, and similar emotions and conflicts (Shires & Miller, 1998). Often, the problem starts with repeated sexual failures caused by drinking too much alcohol or by premature ejaculation. In any event, initial doubts soon become severe fears of failure—which further inhibit sexual response.

Treatment Drugs or surgery may be used in medical treatment of organic erectile disorders. The drug Viagra is successful for about 70 to 80 percent of men with erectile disorders. However, fixing the "hydraulics" of erectile problems may not be enough to end the problem. Effective treatment should also include counseling to remove fears and psychological blocks (Heiman, 2002; Riley & Riley, 2009). It is important for the man to also regain confidence, improve his relationship with his partner, and learn better lovemaking skills. To free him of conflicts, the man and his partner may be assigned a series of exercises to perform. This technique, called **sensate focus**, directs attention to natural sensations of pleasure and builds communication skills (McCabe, 1992).

In sensate focus, the couple is told to take turns caressing various parts of each other's bodies. They are further instructed to carefully avoid any genital contact. Instead, they are to concentrate on giving pleasure and on signaling what feels good to them. This takes the pressure to perform off the man and allows him to learn to give pleasure as a means of receiving it. For many men, sensate focus is a better solution than depending on an expensive drug to perform sexually.

Over a period of days or weeks, the couple proceeds to more intense physical contact involving the breasts and genitals. As inhibitions are reduced and natural arousal begins to replace fear, the successful couple moves on to mutually satisfying lovemaking.

Female Sexual Arousal Disorder Women who suffer from **female sexual arousal disorder** respond with little or no physical arousal to sexual stimulation. The problem thus appears to correspond directly to male erectile difficulties. As in the male, female sexual arousal disorder may be primary or secondary. Also, it is again important to remember that all women occasionally experience inhibited arousal. In some instances, the problem may reflect nothing more than a lack of sufficient sexual stimulation before attempting lovemaking (King, 2005). According to proposed changes to the *Diagnostic and Statistical Manual of Mental Disorders (DSM)* of the American Psychiatric Association, female sexual arousal disorder may be renamed as a *sexual interest/arousal disorder in women* (American Psychiatric Association, 2010).

The causes of inhibited arousal in women are similar to those seen in men. Sometimes the problem is medical, related to illness or the side effects of medicines or contraceptives (Brotto, Basson, & Woo, 2009). Psychological factors include anxiety, anger or hostility toward one's partner, depression, stress, or distracting worries (Basson, & Brotto, 2009). Some women can trace their arousal difficulties to frightening childhood experiences, such as molestations (often by older relatives), incestuous relations that produced lasting guilt, a harsh religious background in which sex was considered evil, or cold, unloving childhood relationships. Also common is a need to maintain control over emotions, deep-seated conflicts over being female, and extreme distrust of others, especially males (Read, 1995).

Treatment *How does treatment proceed?* Treatment typically includes sensate focus, genital stimulation by the woman's partner, and "nondemanding" intercourse controlled by the woman (Segraves & Althof, 2002). With success in these initial stages, full intercourse is gradually introduced. As sexual training proceeds, psychological conflicts and dynamics typically appear, and as they do, they are treated in separate counseling sessions.

Orgasm Disorders

A person suffering from an orgasm disorder either fails to reach orgasm during sexual activity or reaches orgasm too soon or too late (Regev, Zeiss, & Zeiss, 2006). Notice that such disorders are very much based on expectations. For instance, if a man experiences delayed orgasm, one couple might define it as a problem but another might welcome it. It is also worth noting again that some women rarely or never have orgasm and still find sex pleasurable (King, 2005).

Female Orgasmic Disorder The most prevalent sexual complaint among women is a persistent inability to reach orgasm during lovemaking (Clayton & Hamilton, 2009). It is often clear in **female orgasmic disorder** that the woman is not completely unresponsive. Rather, she is unresponsive in the context of a relationship—she may easily reach orgasm by masturbation, but not during lovemaking with her partner.

Then couldn't the woman's partner be at fault? Sex therapists try to avoid finding fault or placing blame. However, it is true that the woman's partner must be committed to ensuring her gratification. Roughly two thirds of all women need direct stimulation of the clitoris to reach orgasm. Therefore, some apparent instances of female orgasmic disorder can be traced to inadequate stimulation or faulty technique on the part of the woman's partner. Even when this is true, sexual adjustment difficulties are best viewed as a problem the couple shares, not just as the "woman's problem," the "man's problem," or her "partner's problem."

Treatment If we focus only on the woman, the most common source of orgasmic difficulties is overcontrol of sexual response. Orgasm requires a degree of abandonment to erotic feelings. It is inhibited by ambivalence or hostility toward the relationship, by guilt, by fears of expressing sexual needs, and by tendencies to control and intellectualize erotic feelings. The woman is unable to let go and enjoy the flow of pleasurable sensations (Segraves & Althof, 2002).

Anorgasmic women (those who do not have orgasms) are first trained to focus on their sexual responsiveness through masturbation or vigorous stimulation by a partner. As the woman becomes consistently orgasmic in these circumstances, her responsiveness is gradually transferred to lovemaking with her partner. Couples also typically learn alternative positions and techniques of lovemaking designed to increase clitoral stimulation. At the same time, communication between partners is stressed, especially with reference to the woman's expectations, motivations, and preferences (Kelly, Strassberg, & Turner, 2006; Regev, Zeiss, & Zeiss, 2006).

Male Orgasmic Disorder Among males, an inability to reach orgasm was once considered a rare problem. But milder forms of **male orgasmic disorder** account for increasing numbers of clients seeking therapy (Rowland, 2007). Typical background factors are strict religious training, fear of impregnating, lack of interest in the sexual partner, symbolic inability to give of oneself, unacknowledged homosexuality, or the recent occurrence of traumatic life events. Power and commitment struggles within relationships may be important added factors.

Treatment Treatment for male orgasmic disorder (also known as retarded ejaculation) consists of sensate focus, manual stimulation by the man's partner (which is designed to orient the male to his partner as a source of pleasure), and stimulation to the point of orgasm followed by immediate intercourse and ejaculation. Work also focuses on resolving personal conflicts and marital difficulties underlying the problem (Waldinger, 2009).

Premature Ejaculation Defining premature ejaculation is tricky because of large variations in the time different women take to reach orgasm. **Premature ejaculation** exists when it occurs reflexively or the man cannot tolerate high levels of excitement at the plateau stage of arousal (Waldinger, 2009). Basically, ejaculation is premature if it consistently occurs before the man and his partner want it to occur (Rowland, 2007).

Do many men have difficulties with premature ejaculation? Approximately 50 percent of young adult men have problems with premature ejaculation. Theories advanced to explain it have ranged from the idea that it may represent hostility toward the man's sexual partner (because it deprives the partner of satisfaction) to the suggestion that most early male sexual experiences tend to encourage rapid climax (such as those taking place in the back seat of a car and masturbation). Excessive arousal and anxiety over performance are also usually present. Also, some men simply engage in techniques that maximize sensation and make rapid orgasm inevitable.

Ejaculation is a reflex. To control it, a man must learn to recognize the physical signals that it is about to occur. Some men have simply never learned to be aware of these signals. Whatever the causes, premature ejaculation can be a serious difficulty, especially in the context of long-term relationships (King, 2005).

Treatment Treatment for premature ejaculation is highly successful and relatively simple. The most common treatment is a "stop-start" procedure called the **squeeze technique** (Grenier & Byers, 1995). The man's sexual partner stimulates him manually until he signals that ejaculation is about to occur. The man's partner then firmly squeezes the tip of his penis to inhibit orgasm. When the man feels he has control, stimulation is repeated. Later, the squeeze technique is used during lovemaking. Gradually, the man acquires the ability to delay orgasm sufficiently for mutually satisfactory lovemaking. During treatment, skills that improve communication between partners are developed, along with a better understanding of the male's sexual response cues (McCarthy & Fucito, 2005).

Sexual Pain Disorders

Pain in the genitals before, during, or after sexual intercourse is called **dyspareunia** (DIS-pah-ROO-nee-ah) (Binik, 2005). Both females and males can experience dyspareunia. However, this problem is actually rare in males. In women, dyspareunia is often related to **vaginismus** (VAJ-ih-NIS-mus), a condition in which muscle spasms of the vagina prevent intercourse (American Psychiatric Association, 2000). According to proposed changes to the *Diagnostic and Statistical Manual of Mental Disorders (DSM)* of the American Psychiatric Association, dyspareunia and vaginismus may be combined and renamed *genito-pelvic pain/penetration disorder* (American Psychiatric Association, 2010).

Vaginismus is often accompanied by obvious fears of intercourse, and when fear is absent, high levels of anxiety are present (Reissing et al., 2004). Vaginismus therefore appears to be a phobic response to intercourse. Predictably, its causes include experiences of painful intercourse, rape or other brutal and frightening sexual encounters, fear of men and of penetration, misinformation about sex (belief that it is injurious), fear of pregnancy, and fear of the specific male partner (Read, 1995; Reissing et al., 2003).

Treatment Treatment of vaginismus is similar to what might be done for a nonsexual phobia. It includes extinction of conditioned muscle spasms by progressive relaxation of the

Psychogenic Having psychological origins, rather than physical causes.

Sensate focus A form of therapy that directs a couple's attention to natural sensations of sexual pleasure.

Female sexual arousal disorder (One type of sexual interest/arousal disorder in women) A lack of physical arousal to sexual stimulation.

Female orgasmic disorder A persistent inability to reach orgasm during lovemaking.

Male orgasmic disorder A persistent inability to reach orgasm during lovemaking.

Premature ejaculation Ejaculation that consistently occurs before the man and his partner want it to occur.

Squeeze technique A method for inhibiting ejaculation by compressing the tip of the penis.

Dyspareunia (One type of genito-pelvic pain/penetration disorder) Genital pain before, during, or after sexual intercourse.

Vaginismus (One type of genito-pelvic pain/penetration disorder) Muscle spasms of the vagina.

vagina, desensitization of fears of intercourse, and masturbation or manual stimulation to associate pleasure with sexual approach by the woman's partner (Bergeron & Lord, 2003). Hypnosis has also been used successfully in some cases.

Summary

Solving sexual problems can be difficult. The problems described here are rarely solved without professional help (a possible exception is premature ejaculation). If a serious sexual difficulty is not resolved in a reasonable amount of time, the aid of an appropriately trained psychologist, physician, or counselor should be sought. The longer the problem is ignored, the more difficult it is to solve. But professional help is available.

Knowledge Builder: Sexual Adjustment and Sexual Problems

RECITE

1. Sexual adjustment is best viewed as a relationship issue not just one partner's problem. T or F?
2. The term *gunnysacking* refers to the constructive practice of hiding anger until it is appropriate to express it. T or F?
3. Males suffering from primary erectile dysfunction have never been able to have or maintain an erection. T or F?
4. According to the latest figures, most erectile disorders are caused by castration fears. T or F?
5. Sensate focus is the most common treatment for premature ejaculation. T or F?
6. Premature ejaculation is considered the rarest of the male sexual adjustment problems. T or F?
7. As it is for female sexual arousal disorder, the sensate focus technique is a primary treatment mode for male sexual arousal disorder. T or F?
8. Vaginismus, which appears to be a phobic response to sexual intercourse, can also cause dyspareunia. T or F?

REFLECT

Think Critically

9. Who would you expect to have the most frequent sex and the most satisfying sex, married couples or single persons?

Self-Reflect

We all make mistakes in relationships. Using the discussion in the *Psychology in Action* as a guide, which mistakes have you avoided? Which would you like to avoid or correct?

In plain language, sexual disorders can be summarized this way: The person doesn't want to do it. The person wants to do it but can't get aroused. The person wants to do it, gets aroused, but has problems with orgasm. The person wants to do it and gets aroused, but lovemaking is uncomfortable. What are the formal terms for each of these possibilities?

Answers: 1. T **2.** F **3.** T **4.** F **5.** F **6.** F **7.** T **8.** T **9.** Contrary to mass media portrayals of sexy singles, married couples have the most sex and are most likely to have orgasms when they do. Greater opportunity, plus familiarity with a partner's needs and preferences probably account for these findings (Laumann et al., 1994).

Chapter in Review: Gateways to Sex, Gender, and Sexuality

Gateway QUESTIONS REVISITED

11.1 *What are the basic dimensions of sex?*

11.1.1 Male and female are not simple either/or categories. Sexual identity is complex, multifaceted, and influenced by biology, socialization, and learning.

11.1.2 Biological sex consists of genetic sex, gonadal sex, hormonal sex, and genital sex.

11.1.3 Sexual development begins with genetic sex (*XX* or *XY* chromosomes) and is then influenced by prenatal hormone levels.

11.1.4 Androgen insensitivity syndrome, exposure to progestin, congenital adrenal hyperplasia, and similar problems can cause a person to be born with an intersexual condition.

11.1.5 Estrogens (female sex hormones) and androgens (male sex hormones) influence the development of different primary and secondary sexual characteristics in males and females.

11.2 *What is sexual orientation?*

11.2.1 Sexual orientation refers to one's degree of emotional and erotic attraction to members of the opposite sex (heterosexuality), same sex (homosexuality, both sexes (bisexuality), or neither sex (asexuality). All four sexual orientations are part of the normal range of human variability.

11.2.2 Sexual orientation tends to be stable over time even if sexual behaviors change.

11.2.3 Similar factors (heredity, biology, and socialization) underlie all sexual orientations.

11.2.4 As a group, homosexual men and women do not differ psychologically from heterosexuals. They are, however, often the victims of homophobia and heterosexism.

11.3 *How does one's sense of maleness or femaleness develop?*

11.3.1 Male and female behavior patterns are related to learned gender identity and gender role socialization.

11.3.2 Many researchers believe that prenatal hormones exert a biological biasing effect that combines with social factors to influence psychosexual development.

11.3.3 On most psychological dimensions, women and men are more alike than they are different.

11.3.4 Gender identity usually becomes stable by age 3 or 4 years.

11.3.5 Gender role socialization seems to account for most observed female–male gender differences. Parents tend to encourage boys in instrumental behaviors and girls in expressive behaviors.

11.3.6 Gender role stereotypes often distort perceptions about the kinds activities for which men and women are suited.

11.4 *What is psychological androgyny (and is it contagious)?*

11.4.1 People who possess both masculine and feminine traits are androgynous (and is isn't contagious).

11.4.2 Roughly one third of all persons are androgynous. Approximately 50 percent are traditionally feminine or masculine.

11.4.3 Psychological androgyny is related to greater behavioral adaptability and flexibility.

11.5 *What is gender variance?*

11.5.1 Gender variant individuals experience a persistent mismatch between their biological sex and their experienced gender.

11.5.2 Sex reassignment surgery may be undertaken to help resolve the discrepancy.

11.6 *What are the most typical patterns of human sexual behavior?*

11.6.1 Although "normal" sexual behavior is defined differently by various cultures, adults typically engage in a wide variety of sexual behaviors. However, coercive and/or compulsive sexual behaviors are emotionally unhealthy.

11.6.2 Sexual arousal is related to the body's erogenous zones, but mental and emotional reactions are the ultimate source of sexual responsiveness.

11.6.3 Evidence indicates that the sex drive peaks at a later age for females than it does for males, although this difference is diminishing.

11.6.4 Castration may or may not influence sex drive in humans. Sterilization does not alter the sex drive.

11.6.5 Frequency of sexual intercourse gradually declines with increasing age. However, many elderly persons remain sexually active, and large variations exist at all ages.

11.6.6 Masturbation is a common, normal, and completely acceptable behavior.

11.7 *To what extent do females and males differ in sexual response?*

11.7.1 Sexual response can be divided into four phases: excitement, plateau, orgasm, and resolution. The similarities between female and male sexual responses far outweigh the differences.

11.7.2 There do not appear to be any differences between "vaginal orgasms" and "clitoral orgasms." Fifteen percent of women are consistently multi-orgasmic, and at least 50 percent are capable of multiple orgasm.

11.7.3 Males experience a refractory period after orgasm, and only 5 percent of men are multiorgasmic.

11.7.4 Mutual orgasm has been abandoned by most sex counselors as the ideal in lovemaking.

11.8 *What are the most common sexual disorders?*

11.8.1 Compulsive sexual behaviors (paraphilias) tend to emotionally handicap people.

11.8.2 The paraphilias include pedophilia, exhibitionism, voyeurism, frotteurism, fetishism, sexual masochism, sexual sadism, and transvestic fetishism. The most common paraphilias are pedophilia and exhibitionism.

11.8.3 The effects of child molestation vary greatly, depending on the severity of the molestation and the child's relationship to the molester.

11.8.4 Exhibitionists usually not dangerous but can escalate their sexual aggression. They and can best be characterized as sexually inhibited and immature.

11.9 *Have recent changes in attitudes affected sexual behavior?*

11.9.1 In the United States, a liberalization of attitudes toward sex has been paralleled by a gradual increase in sexual behavior over the last 50 years.

11.9.2 Adolescents and young adults engage in more frequent sexual behavior than they did 50 years ago.

11.9.3 In recent years there has been a greater acceptance of female sexuality and a narrowing of differences in female and male patterns of sexual behavior.

11.9.4 Forcible rape, acquaintance rape, and rape-supportive attitudes and beliefs are major problems in North America.

11.10 *What impacts have sexually transmitted diseases had on sexual behavior?*

11.10.1 Each person must now take responsibility for practicing safer sex and for choosing when, where, and with whom to express his or her sexuality.

11.10.2 During the last 20 years, the incidence of sexually transmitted diseases has steadily increased.

11.10.3 STDs and the spread of HIV/AIDS have had a sizable impact on patterns of sexual behavior, including some curtailment of risk taking.

11.10.4 Many sexually active people continue to take unnecessary risks with their health by failing to follow safer sex practices.

11.11 *How can couples keep their relationships more sexually satisfying, and what are the most common sexual dysfunctions?*

11.11.1 Although solutions exist for many sexual adjustment problems, good communication and a healthy relationship are the real keys to sexual satisfaction.

11.11.2 Communication skills that foster and maintain intimacy are the key to successful relationships.

11.11.3 Most sexual dysfunctions are closely linked to the general health of a couple's relationship.

11.11.4 Problems with sexual function can involve desire, arousal, orgasm, or pain. Behavioral methods and counseling techniques have been developed to alleviate many sexual problems.

MEDIA RESOURCES

Web Resources

Internet addresses frequently change. To find an up-to-date list of URLs for the sites listed here, visit your Psychology CourseMate.

Human Sexual Reproduction Read more about the biology of sex and sexual reproduction.

Simon LeVay's Home Page Read about the biology of sexual orientation.

Facts about Sexual Orientation Read about sexual prejudice in our society.

Sex and Gender Read an article about the difference between sex and gender.

Androgyny Take the *Bem Sex Role Inventory* (BSRI).

My Life as an Intersexual Read the story of one person's life as an intersexual.

Sexual Response Explore the sexual response cycle.

Sexual Scripts Read an article on sexual scripts found in *Seventeen* magazine.

Paraphilias and Sexual Disorders Read more about sexual disorders.

Sexuality and Intimacy Read a series of articles on the role of intimacy in sexuality.

Sexual Problems in Men and Women Explore this discussion of a variety of sexual problems in men and women.

Premature Ejaculation Access helpful information from causes to coping skills.

Interactive Learning

Log in to **CengageBrain** to access the resources your instructor requires. For this book, you can access:

CourseMate brings course concepts to life with interactive learning, study, and exam preparation tools that support the printed textbook. A textbook-specific website, ***Psychology CourseMate*** includes an ***integrated interactive eBook*** and other ***interactive learning tools*** including quizzes, flashcards, videos, and more.

CENGAGE**NOW**™

CengageNOW is an easy-to-use online resource that helps you study in less time to get the grade you want—NOW. Take a pre-test for this chapter and receive a personalized study plan based on your results that will identify the topics you need to review and direct you to online resources to help you master those topics. Then take a post-test to help you determine the concepts you have mastered and what you will need to work on. If your textbook does not include an access code card, go to CengageBrain.com to gain access.

WebTUTOR™

More than just an interactive study guide, **WebTutor** is an anytime, anywhere customized learning solution with an eBook, keeping you connected to your textbook, instructor, and classmates.

If your professor has assigned **Aplia** homework:

1. Sign in to your account.
2. Complete the corresponding homework exercises as required by your professor.
3. When finished, click "Grade It Now" to see which areas you have mastered and which need more work, and for detailed explanations of every answer.

Visit www.cengagebrain.com to access your account and purchase materials.

Gateway THEME

Personality refers to the consistency we see in personal behavior patterns. Measures of personality reveal individual differences and help predict future behavior.

12

Personality

At the Core

Rural Colorado. The car banged over one last, brain-jarring rut and lurched toward the dilapidated farmhouse. Annette awaited one of your authors on the porch, hooting and whooping and obviously happy to see an old friend arrive.

If anyone was suited for a move to the "wilds" of Colorado, it was Annette, a strong and resourceful woman. Still, it was hard to imagine a more radical change. After separating from her husband, she had traded a comfortable life in the city for rough times in the high country. Annette was working as a ranch hand and a lumberjack (lumberjill?), trying to make it through some hard winters. She had even recently decked a guy twice her size who was harassing her in a tavern. The changes in Annette's life were radical, and we worried that she might be entirely different. She was, on the contrary, more her "old self" than ever.

Perhaps you have had a similar experience. After several years of separation, it is always intriguing to see an old friend. At first, you may be struck by how the person has changed. ("Where did you get that haircut!?") Soon, however, you will probably be delighted to discover that the semi-stranger before you is still the person you once knew. It is exactly this core of consistency that psychologists have in mind when they use the term *personality*.

Without doubt, personality touches our daily lives. Falling in love, choosing friends, getting along with coworkers, voting for a president, or coping with your zaniest relatives all raise questions about personality.

What is personality? How does it differ from character, temperament, or attitudes? Is it possible to measure personality? Can we change our personality? We'll address these questions and more in this chapter.

Gateway QUESTIONS

12.1 How do psychologists use the term personality*?*
12.2 Are some personality traits more basic or important than others?
12.3 How do psychodynamic theories explain personality?
12.4 What are humanistic theories of personality?
12.5 What do behaviorists and social learning theorists emphasize in their approach to personality?
12.6 How do heredity and environment affect personality?
12.7 Which personality theory is right?
12.8 How do psychologists measure personality?
12.9 What causes shyness and what can be done about it?

The Psychology of Personality—Do You Have Personality?

Gateway Question 12.1: *How do psychologists use the term personality?*

"Annette has a very optimistic personality." "Ramiro's not handsome, but he has a great personality." "My father's business friends think he's a nice guy. They should see him at home where his real personality comes out." "It's hard to believe Tanya and Nikki are sisters. They have such opposite personalities."

It's obvious that we all frequently use the term *personality*. But if you think that personality means "charm," "charisma," or "style," you have misused the term. Many people also confuse personality with the term **character**, which implies that a person has been evaluated as possessing positive qualities, not just described (Bryan & Babelay, 2009). If, by saying someone has "personality," you mean the person is friendly, outgoing, and upstanding, you might be describing what we regard as good character in our culture. But in some cultures, it is deemed good for people to be fierce, warlike, and cruel.

Psychologists regard **personality** as a person's unique long-term pattern of thinking, emotions, and behavior (Burger, 2011; Ewen, 2009). In other words, personality refers to the consistency in who you are, have been, and will become. It also refers to the special blend of talents, values, hopes, loves, hates, and habits that makes each of us a unique person. So, everyone in a particular culture has personality, whereas not everyone has character—or at least not good character. (Do you know any good characters?)

Psychologists use a large number of concepts and theories to explain personality. It might be wise, therefore, to start with a few key ideas to help you keep your bearings as you read more about personality.

© Raul Vega/Corbis

Does this man have personality? Do you?

Tatiana Belova/Shutterstock

Psychologists and employers are especially interested in the personality traits of individuals who hold high-risk, high-stress positions involving public safety, such as police, firefighters, air traffic controllers, and nuclear power plant employees.

Traits

We use the idea of traits every day to talk about personality. For instance, Daryl is *sociable*, *orderly*, and *intelligent*. His sister Hollie is *shy*, *sensitive*, and *creative*. As we observed in our reunion with Annette, personality traits like these can be quite stable (Rantanen et al., 2007; Engler, 2009). Think about how little your best friends have changed in the last 5 years. It would be strange indeed to feel like you were talking with a different person every time you met a friend or an acquaintance. In general, then, **personality traits** like these are stable qualities that a person shows in most situations (Matthews, Deary, & Whiteman, 2009). As you will see when you read further into this chapter, there is considerable debate about just *why* traits are stable qualities. But more about that later.

Typically, traits are inferred from behavior. If you see Daryl talking to strangers—first at a supermarket and later at a party—you might deduce that he is "sociable." Once personality traits are identified, they can be used to predict future behavior. For example, noting that Daryl is outgoing might lead you to predict that he will be sociable at school or at work. In fact, such consistencies can span many years (Caspi, Roberts, & Shiner, 2005; Harker & Keltner, 2001). Traits even influence our health as well as our marital and occupational success (Roberts et al., 2007). For example, who do you think will be more successful in her chosen career: Jane, who is conscientious, or Sally, who is not (Brown et al., 2011; Chamorro-Premuzic & Furnham, 2003)?

Types

Have you ever asked the question, "What type of person is she (or he)?" A **personality type** refers to people who have *several traits in common* (Larsen & Buss, 2010). Informally, your own thinking might include categories such as the executive type, the athletic type, the motherly type, the hip-hop type, the techno geek, and so forth. If you tried to define these informal types, you would probably list a different collection of traits for each one.

How valid is it to speak of personality "types"? Over the years, psychologists have proposed many ways to categorize personalities into types. For example, Swiss psychiatrist Carl Jung (yoong) proposed that people are either *introverts* or *extroverts*. An **introvert** is a shy, reserved person whose attention is usually focused inward. An **extrovert** is a bold, outgoing person whose attention is usually directed outward. These terms are so widely used that you may think of yourself and your friends as being one type or the other. However, knowing if someone is extroverted or introverted tells you little about how conscientious she is, or how kind or open to new ideas he is. In short, two categories (or even several) are often inadequate to fully capture differences in personality. That's why rating people on a list of traits tends to be more informative than classifying them into two or three types (Engler, 2009).

Even though types tend to oversimplify personality, they do have value. Most often, types are a shorthand way of labeling people who have several key traits in common. For example, in the next chapter we will discuss Type A and Type B personalities. Type A's are people who have personality traits that increase their chance of suffering a heart attack; Type B's take a more laid-back approach to life (see • Figure 12.1). Similarly, you will read in Chapter 14 about unhealthy personality types such as the paranoid personality, the dependent personality, and the antisocial personality. Each problem type is defined by a specific collection of traits that are not adaptive.

Self-Concept

Self-concepts provide another way of understanding personality. The rough outlines of your self-concept could be revealed by this request: "Please tell us about yourself." In other words, your **self-concept** consists of all your ideas, perceptions, stories, and feelings about who you are. It is the mental "picture" you have of your own personality (Swann, Chang-Schneider, & Larsen McClarty, 2007).

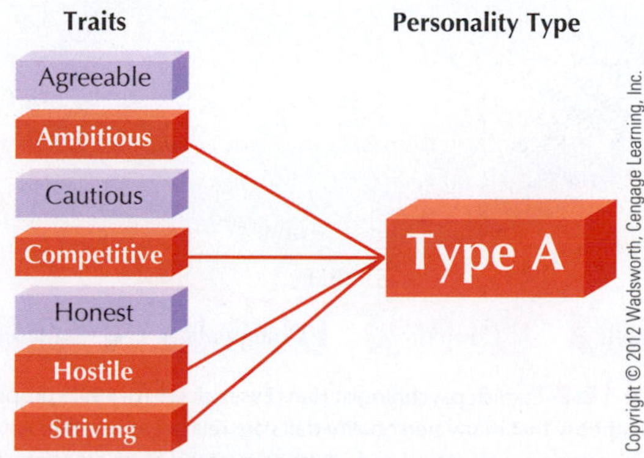

• **Figure 12.1** Personality types are defined by the presence of several specific traits. For example, several possible personality traits are shown in the left column. A person who has a Type A personality typically possesses all or most of the highlighted traits. Type A persons are especially prone to heart disease (see Chapter 13).

Self-concepts can be remarkably consistent. In an interesting study, old people were asked how they had changed over the years. Almost all thought they were essentially the same person they were when they were young (Troll & Skaff, 1997). Ninety-three-year-old Nelson Mandela, for example, has been a highly dignified and influential human rights activist for his entire adult life.

We creatively build our self-concepts out of daily experiences. Then, we slowly revise them as we have new experiences. Once a stable self-concept exists, it tends to guide what we pay attention to, remember, and think about. Because of this, self-concepts can greatly affect our behavior and personal adjustment—especially when they are inaccurate (Ryckman, 2008). For instance, Alesha is a student who thinks she is stupid, worthless, and a failure, despite getting good grades. With such an inaccurate self-concept, she tends to be depressed regardless of how well she does.

Character Personal characteristics that have been judged or evaluated; a person's desirable or undesirable qualities.
Personality A person's unique and relatively stable patterns of thinking, emotions, and behavior.
Personality trait A stable, enduring quality that a person shows in most situations.
Personality type A style of personality defined by a group of related traits.
Introvert A person whose attention is focused inward; a shy, reserved, self-centered person.
Extrovert A person whose attention is directed outward; a bold, outgoing person.
Self-concept A person's perception of his or her own personality traits.

Human Diversity: Self-Esteem and Culture—Hotshot or Team Player?

You and some friends are playing soccer. Your team wins, in part because you make some good plays. After the game, you bask in the glow of having performed well. You don't want to brag about being a hotshot, but your self-esteem gets a boost from your personal success.

In Japan, Shinobu and some of his friends are playing soccer. His team wins, in part because he makes some good plays. After the game, Shinobu is happy because his team did well. However, Shinobu also dwells on the ways in which he let his team down. He thinks about how he could improve, and he resolves to be a better team player.

These sketches illustrate a basic difference in Eastern and Western psychology. In individualistic cultures such as the United States, self-esteem is based on personal success and outstanding performance (Lay & Verkuyten, 1999). For us, the path to higher self-esteem lies in self-enhancement. We are pumped up by our successes and tend to downplay our faults and failures (Ross et al., 2005).

Japanese and other Asian cultures place a greater emphasis on collectivism, or interdependence among people. For them, self-esteem is based on a secure sense of belonging to social groups. As a result, people in Asian cultures are more apt to engage in self-criticism (Ross et al., 2005). By correcting personal faults, they add to the well-being of the group (Kitayama, Markus, & Kurokawa, 2000). And, when the *group* succeeds, individual members feel better about themselves, which raises their self-esteem.

Perhaps self-esteem is still based on success in both Eastern and Western cultures (Brown et al., 2009). However, it is fascinating that cultures define success in such different ways (Schmitt & Allik, 2005). The North American emphasis on winning is not the only way to feel good about yourself.

Self-Esteem

Note that in addition to having a faulty self-concept, Alesha has low **self-esteem** (a negative self-evaluation). A person with high self-esteem is confident, proud, and self-respecting. One who has low self-esteem is insecure, lacking in confidence, and self-critical. Like Alesha, people with low self-esteem are usually anxious and unhappy. People who have low self-esteem typically also suffer from poor self-knowledge. Their self-concepts are inconsistent, inaccurate, and confused. Problems of this type are explored later in this chapter.

Self-esteem tends to rise when we experience success or praise. It also buffers us against negative experiences (Brown, 2010). A person who is competent and effective and who is loved, admired, and respected by others will almost always have high self-esteem (Baumeister et al., 2003). The reasons for having high self-esteem, however, can vary in different cultures. See "Self-Esteem and Culture" for more information.

What if you "think you're hot," but you're not? Genuine self-esteem is based on an accurate appraisal of your strengths and weaknesses. A positive self-evaluation that is bestowed too easily may not be healthy (Kernis & Lakey, 2010; Twenge & Campbell, 2001). People who think very highly of themselves (and let others know it) may at first seem confident, but their arrogance quickly turns off other people (Paulhus, 1998).

The Whole Human: Personality Theories

As you can already see, it would be easy to get lost without a framework for understanding personality. How do our thoughts, actions, and feelings relate to one another? How does personality develop? Why do some people suffer from psychological problems? How can they be helped? To answer such questions, psychologists have created a dazzling array of theories. A **personality theory** is a system of concepts, assumptions, ideas, and principles proposed to explain personality (● Figure 12.2). In this chapter, we can explore

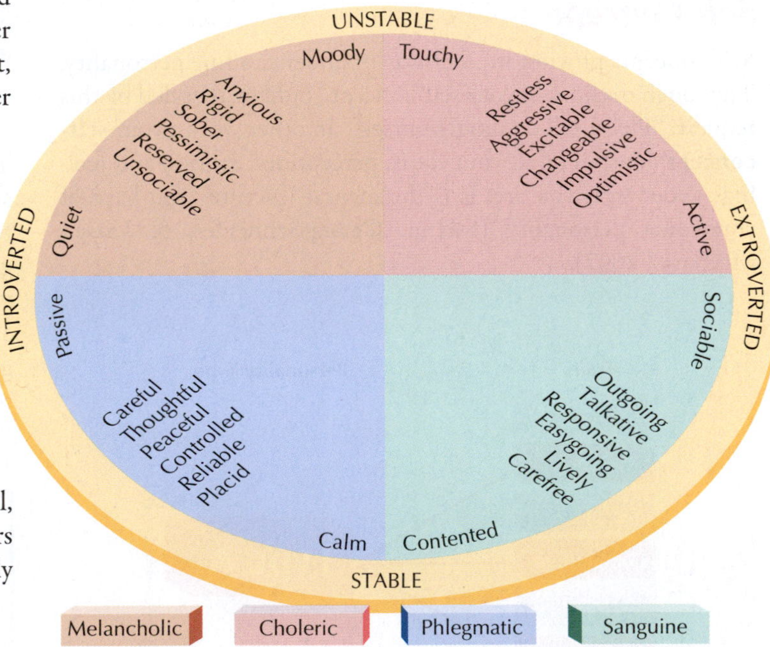

● **Figure 12.2** English psychologist Hans Eysenck (1916–1997) proposed the personality theory that many personality traits are related to whether you are mainly introverted or extroverted and whether you tend to be emotionally stable or unstable (highly emotional). These characteristics, in turn, are related to four basic types of temperament first recognized by the early Greeks. The types are *melancholic* (sad, gloomy), *choleric* (hot-tempered, irritable), *phlegmatic* (sluggish, calm), and *sanguine* (cheerful, hopeful). Adapted from Eysenck, 1981.

only a few of the many personality theories. These are the four major perspectives we will consider:

1. **Trait theories** attempt to learn what traits make up personality and how they relate to actual behavior.
2. **Psychodynamic theories** focus on the inner workings of personality, especially internal conflicts and struggles.
3. **Humanistic theories** stress private, subjective experience, and personal growth.
4. **Behaviorist and social learning theories** place importance on the external environment and on the effects of conditioning and learning. Social learning theories attribute differences in personality to socialization, expectations, and mental processes.

With these broad perspectives in mind, let's take a deeper look at personality.

The Trait Approach—Describe Yourself in 18,000 Words or Less

Gateway Question 12.2: *Are some personality traits more basic or important than others?*

The *trait approach* is currently the dominant method for studying personality. Trait theorists seek to describe personality with a small number of key traits or factors. Take a moment to check the traits in ■ Table 12.1 that describe your personality. Don't worry if some of your key traits weren't in the table. More than 18,000 English words refer to personal characteristics. Are the traits you checked of equal importance? Are some stronger or more basic than others? Do any overlap? For example, if you checked "dominant," did you also check "confident" and "bold"?

Answers to these questions would interest a trait theorist. To better understand personality, **trait theorists** attempt to analyze, classify, and interrelate traits. In addition, trait theorists often think of traits as *biological predispositions*, a hereditary readiness of humans to behave in particular ways (Ashton, 2007). (We have encountered this idea before, in Chapter 3, in which we humans were described as having a biological predisposition to learn language.) As we have noted, traits are stable dispositions that a person shows in most situations (Matthews, Deary, & Whiteman, 2009). For example, if you are usually friendly, optimistic, and cautious, these qualities are traits of your personality.

What if I am also sometimes shy, pessimistic, or uninhibited? The original three qualities are still traits as long as they are most *typical* of your behavior. Let's say our friend Annette approaches most situations with optimism, but tends to expect the worst each time she applies for a job and worries that she won't get it. If her pessimism is limited to this situation or just a few others, it is still accurate and useful to describe her as an optimistic person.

Predicting Behavior

As we have noted, separating people into broad types, such as "introvert" or "extrovert," may oversimplify personality. However, introversion/extroversion can also be thought of as a trait. Knowing how you rate on this single dimension would allow us to predict how you will behave in a variety of settings. How, for example, do you prefer to meet people—face-to-face or through the Internet? Researchers have found that students high in the trait of introversion are more likely to prefer the Internet because they find it easier to talk with people online (Koch & Pratarelli, 2004; Rice & Markey, 2009). Other interesting links exist between traits and behavior. See "What's Your Musical Personality?"

Classifying Traits

Are there different types of traits? Yes, psychologist Gordon Allport (1961) identified several kinds. **Common traits** are characteristics shared by most members of a culture. Common traits tell us how people from a particular nation or culture are similar, or which traits a culture emphasizes. In America, for example, competitiveness is a fairly common trait. Among the Hopi of northern Arizona, however, it is relatively rare.

Of course, common traits don't tell us much about individuals. Although many people are competitive in American culture, various people you know may rate high, medium, or low in this trait. Usually we are also interested in **individual traits**, which describe a person's unique qualities.

■ **TABLE 12.1 Adjective Checklist**

Check the traits you feel are characteristic of your personality. Are some more basic than others?

aggressive	organized	ambitious	clever
confident	loyal	generous	calm
warm	bold	cautious	reliable
sensitive	mature	talented	jealous
sociable	honest	funny	religious
dominant	dull	accurate	nervous
humble	uninhibited	visionary	cheerful
thoughtful	serious	helpful	emotional
orderly	anxious	conforming	good-natured
liberal	curious	optimistic	kind
meek	neighborly	passionate	compulsive

Self-esteem Regarding oneself as a worthwhile person; a positive evaluation of oneself.

Personality theory A system of concepts, assumptions, ideas, and principles used to understand and explain personality.

Trait theorist A psychologist interested in classifying, analyzing, and interrelating traits to understand personality.

Common traits Personality traits that are shared by most members of a particular culture.

Individual traits Personality traits that define a person's unique individual qualities.

Discovering Psychology What's Your Musical Personality?

Even if you like all kinds of music, you probably prefer some styles to others. Of the styles listed here, which three do you enjoy the most? (Circle your choices.)

blues jazz classical folk
rock alternative heavy metal
country soundtrack religious
pop rap/hip-hop soul/funk
electronic/dance

In one study, Peter Rentfrow and Samuel Gosling found that the types of music people prefer tend to be associated with their personality characteristics (Rentfrow & Gosling, 2003). See if your musical tastes match their findings (Rentfrow & Gosling, 2007):

- People who value aesthetic experiences, have good verbal abilities, and are liberal and tolerant of others tend to like music that is reflective and complex (blues, jazz, classical, and folk music).
- People who are curious about new experiences, enjoy taking risks, and are physically active prefer intense, rebellious music (rock, alternative, and heavy metal music).
- People who are cheerful, conventional, extroverted, reliable, helpful, and conservative tend to enjoy upbeat conventional music (country, soundtrack, religious, and pop music).
- People who are talkative, full of energy, forgiving, and physically attractive, and who reject conservative ideals tend to prefer energetic, rhythmic music (rap/hip-hop, soul/funk, and electronic/dance music).

Unmistakably, personality traits affect our everyday behavior (Rentfrow, Goldberg, & Levitin, 2011).

Here's an analogy to help you separate common traits from individual traits: If you decide to buy a pet dog, you will want to know the general characteristics of the dog's breed (its common traits). In addition, you will want to know about the "personality" of a specific dog (its individual traits) before you decide to take it home.

Allport also made distinctions between *cardinal traits, central traits,* and *secondary traits.* **Cardinal traits** are so basic that all of a person's activities can be traced to the trait. For instance, compassion was an overriding trait of Mother Teresa's personality. Likewise, Abraham Lincoln's personality was dominated by the cardinal trait of honesty. According to Allport, few people have cardinal traits.

Central Traits

How do central and secondary traits differ from cardinal traits? **Central traits** are the basic building blocks of personality. A surprisingly small number of central traits can capture the essence of a person. For instance, just six traits would provide a good description of Annette's personality: dominant, sociable, honest, cheerful, intelligent, and optimistic. When college students were asked to describe someone they knew well, they mentioned an average of seven central traits (Allport, 1961).

Secondary traits are more superficial personal qualities, such as food preferences, attitudes, political opinions, musical tastes, and so forth. In Allport's terms, a personality description might therefore include the following items:

Name: Jane Doe
Age: 22
Cardinal traits: None
Central traits: Possessive, autonomous, artistic, dramatic, self-centered, trusting
Secondary traits: Prefers colorful clothes, likes to work alone, politically liberal, always late

Source Traits

How can you tell whether a personality trait is central or secondary? Raymond B. Cattell (1906–1998) tried to answer this question by directly studying the traits of a large number of people. Cattell began by measuring visible features of personality, which he called **surface traits**. Soon, Cattell noticed that these surface traits often appeared together in groups. In fact, some traits clustered together so often that they seemed to represent a single, more basic trait. Cattell called these deeper characteristics, or dimensions, **source traits** (or **factors**) (Cattell, 1965). They are the core of each individual's personality.

How do source traits differ from Allport's central traits? Allport classified traits subjectively, and it's possible that he was wrong at times. To look for connections among traits, Cattell used **factor analysis**, a statistical technique used to correlate multiple measurements and identify general underlying factors. For example, he found that imaginative people are almost always *inventive, original, curious, creative, innovative,* and *ingenious*. If you are an imaginative person, we automatically know that you have several other traits, too. Thus, *imaginative* is a source trait. (Source traits are also called factors.)

Cattell (1973) identified 16 source traits. According to him, all 16 are needed to fully describe a personality. Source traits are measured by a test called the *Sixteen Personality Factor Questionnaire* (often referred to as the 16 PF). Like many personality tests, the 16 PF can be used to produce a **trait profile**, or graph, of a person's score on each trait. Trait profiles draw a "picture" of individual personalities, which makes it easier to compare them (● Figure 12.3).

The Big Five

Noel is outgoing and friendly, conscientious, even-tempered, and curious. His brother Joel is reserved, hostile, irresponsible, temperamental, and disinterested in ideas. You will be spending a week in a space capsule with either Noel or Joel. Who would you

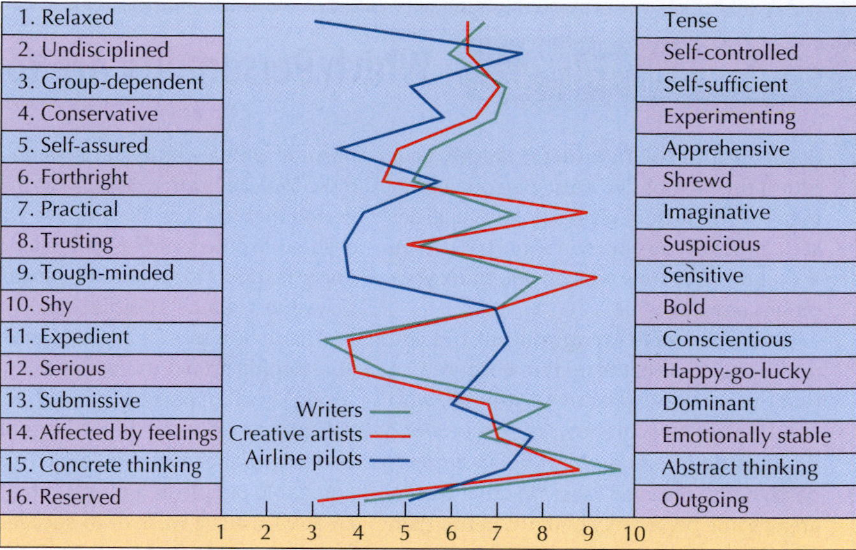

• Figure 12.3 The 16 source traits measured by Cattell's 16 PF are listed beside the graph. Scores can be plotted as a profile for an individual or a group. The profiles shown here are group averages for airline pilots, creative artists, and writers. Notice the similarity between artists and writers and the difference between these two groups and pilots. Adapted with permission from Cattell, R. B. "Personality Pinned Down," *Psychology Today*, July 1973.

choose? If the answer seems obvious, it's because Noel and Joel were described with the **five-factor model**, a system that identifies the five most basic dimensions of personality.

Five Key Dimensions

The "Big Five" factors listed in • Figure 12.4 attempt to further reduce Cattell's 16 factors to just five universal dimensions, or source traits (Costa & McCrae, 2006; Noftle & Fleeson, 2010). The Big Five may be the best answer of all to the question, What is the essence of human personality?

If you would like to compare the personalities of two people, try rating them informally on the five dimensions shown in • Figure 12.4. For Factor 1, *extroversion*, rate how introverted or extroverted each person is. Factor 2, *agreeableness*, refers to how friendly, nurturant, and caring a person is, as opposed to cold, indifferent, self-centered, or spiteful. A person who is *conscientious* (Factor 3) is self-disciplined, responsible, and achieving. People low on this factor are irresponsible, careless, and undependable. Factor 4, *neuroticism*, refers to negative, upsetting emotions. People who are high in neuroticism tend to be anxious, emotionally "sour," irritable,

Extroversion										
Loner Quiet Passive Reserved	**Low**	1	2	3	4	5	6	7	**High**	Joiner Talkative Active Affectionate

Agreeableness										
Suspicious Critical Ruthless Irritable	**Low**	1	2	3	4	5	6	7	**High**	Trusting Lenient Soft-hearted Good-natured

Conscientiousness										
Negligent Lazy Disorganized Late	**Low**	1	2	3	4	5	6	7	**High**	Conscientious Hard-working Well-organized Punctual

Neuroticism										
Calm Even-tempered Comfortable Unemotional	**Low**	1	2	3	4	5	6	7	**High**	Worried Temperamental Self-conscious Emotional

Openness to Experience										
Down-to-earth Uncreative Conventional Uncurious	**Low**	1	2	3	4	5	6	7	**High**	Imaginative Creative Original Curious

• Figure 12.4 The Big Five. According to the five-factor model, basic differences in personality can be "boiled down" to the dimensions shown here. Rate yourself on each factor. The five-factor model answers these essential questions about a person: Is she/he extroverted or introverted? Agreeable or difficult? Conscientious or irresponsible? Emotionally stable or unstable? Smart or unintelligent? These questions cover a large measure of what we might want to know about someone's personality. Trait descriptions adapted from McCrae & Costa, 2001.

Cardinal trait A personality trait so basic that all of a person's activities relate to it.

Central traits The core traits that characterize an individual personality.

Secondary traits Traits that are inconsistent or relatively superficial.

Surface traits The visible or observable traits of one's personality.

Source traits (factors) Basic underlying traits, or dimensions, of personality; each source trait is reflected in a number of surface traits.

Factor analysis A statistical technique used to correlate multiple measurements and identify general underlying factors.

Trait profile A graph of the scores obtained on several personality traits.

Five-factor model Proposes that there are five universal dimensions of personality.

Discovering Psychology: Which Personality Are You (and Which Is Best)?

According to the *five-factor model*, your rating on each of five basic personality dimensions, or factors, gives a good overall description of your personality. Try it (see ● Figure 12.4). How well do you think your ratings describe you?

When you were rating yourself, did you notice that some of the traits in ● Figure 12.4 don't seem very attractive? After all, who would want to score low in *extroversion*? What could be good about being a quiet, passive, and reserved loner? In other words, aren't some personality patterns better than others?

OK, so what is the best personality pattern? You might be surprised to learn that there is no one "best" personality pattern. For example, extroverts tend to earn more during their careers than introverts and they have more sexual partners. But they are also more likely to take risks than introverts (and to land in the hospital with an injury). Extroverts are also more likely to divorce. Because of this, extroverted men are less likely to live with their children. In other words, extroversion tends to open the doors to some life experiences and close doors to others (Nettle, 2005).

The same is true for *agreeableness*. Agreeable people attract more friends and enjoy strong social support from others. But agreeable people often put the interests of friends and family ahead of their own. This leaves agreeable people at a disadvantage. To do creative, artistic work or to succeed in the business world often involves putting your own interests first (Nettle, 2008).

How about conscientiousness? Up to a point, conscientiousness is associated with high achievement. However, having impossibly high standards, a trait called *perfectionism*, can be a problem. As you might expect, college students who are perfectionists tend to get good grades. Yet, some students cross the line into maladaptive perfectionism, which typically *lowers* performance at school and elsewhere (Accordino, Accordino, & Slaney, 2000). Authentic Navajo rugs always have a flaw in their intricate designs. Navajo weavers intentionally make a "mistake" in each rug as a reminder that humans are not perfect. There is a lesson in this: It is not always necessary, or even desirable, to be "perfect." To learn from your experiences you must feel free to make mistakes (Castro & Rice, 2003). Success, in the long run, is more often based on seeking "excellence" rather than "perfection" (Enns, Cox, & Clara, 2005).

Except for very extreme personality patterns, which are often maladaptive, most "personalities" involve a mix of costs and benefits. We all face the task of pursuing life experiences that best suit our own unique personality patterns (Nettle, 2008).

---

and unhappy. Finally, people who rate high on Factor 5, *openness to experience*, are intelligent and open to new ideas (Ashcraft, 2012).

The beauty of the Big-Five model is that almost any trait you can name will be related to one of the five factors. If you were selecting a college roommate, hiring an employee, or answering a singles ad, you would probably like to know all the personal dimensions covered by the Big Five. Now, try rating yourself as you read "Which Personality Are You (and Which Is Best)?"

The Big Five traits have been related to different brain systems and chemicals (Ashton, 2007; Nettle, 2008). They also predict how people will act in various circumstances (Sutin & Costa, 2010). For example, people who score high in conscientiousness tend to perform well at work, do well in school, and rarely have automobile accidents (Arthur & Doverspike, 2001; Brown et al., 2011; Chamorro-Premuzic & Furnham, 2003). They even live longer (Martin, Friedman, & Schwartz, 2007).

Knowing where a person stands on the "Big Five" personality factors helps predict his or her behavior. For example, people who score high on conscientiousness tend to be safe drivers who are unlikely to have automobile accidents.

Knowledge Builder: Personality and Trait Theories

RECITE

1. When someone's personality has been evaluated, we are making a judgment about his or her
   a. temperament *b.* character *c.* extroversion *d.* self-esteem
2. A personality type is usually defined by the presence of
   a. all five personality dimensions *b.* a stable self concept *c.* several specific traits *d.* a source trait
3. An individual's perception of his or her own personality constitutes that person's ______________.
4. Central traits are those shared by most members of a culture. T or F?
5. Cattell believes that clusters of ____________ traits reveal the presence of underlying ____________ traits.
6. Which of the following is *not* one of the Big Five personality factors?
   a. submissiveness *b.* agreeableness *c.* extroversion *d.* neuroticism

REFLECT

Think Critically

7. In what way would memory contribute to the formation of an accurate or inaccurate self-image?
8. Can you think of a Big Five trait besides conscientiousness that might be related to academic achievement?

Self-Reflect

See if you can define or describe the following terms in your own words: personality, character, trait, type, self-concept, self-esteem.

List six or seven traits that best describe your personality. Which system of traits seems to best match your list, Allport's, Cattell's, or the Big Five?

Answers: 1. *b* **2.** c **3.** self-concept **4.** F **5.** surface, source **6.** *a* **7.** As discussed in Chapter 7, memory is highly selective, and long-term memories are often distorted by recent information. Such properties add to the moldability of self-concept. **8.** In one study, conscientiousness was positively related to academic performance, as you might expect. Students high in neuroticism were also better academic performers, but only if they were not too stressed (Kappe & van der Flier, 2010).

Psychoanalytic Theory—Id Came to Me in a Dream

Gateway Question 12.3: *How do psychodynamic theories explain personality?*

Psychodynamic theorists are not content with studying traits. Instead, they try to probe under the surface of personality—to learn what drives, conflicts, and energies animate us. Psychodynamic theorists believe that many of our actions are based on hidden, or unconscious, thoughts, needs, and emotions. What psychodynamic theorists tend to share in common with trait theorists is the view that human personality is based on a set of biological dispositions.

As we discussed in Chapter 1, **psychoanalytic theory**, the best-known psychodynamic approach, grew out of the work of Sigmund Freud, a Viennese physician. As a doctor, Freud was fascinated by patients whose problems seemed to be more emotional than physical. From about 1890 until he died in 1939, Freud evolved a theory of personality that deeply influenced modern thought (Jacobs, 2003; Schultz & Schultz, 2009). Let's consider some of its main features.

The Structure of Personality

How did Freud view personality? Freud's model portrays personality as a dynamic system directed by three mental structures: the *id*, the *ego*, and the *superego*. According to Freud, most behavior involves activity of all three systems. (Freud's theory includes a large number of concepts. For your convenience, they are defined in ■ Table 12.2 rather than in glossary boxes.)

The Id

The **id** is made up of innate biological instincts and urges. The id operates on the **pleasure principle**. It is self-serving, irrational, impulsive, and totally unconscious. That is, it seeks to freely express pleasure-seeking urges of all kinds. If we were solely under control of the id, the world would be chaotic beyond belief.

Freud considered personality an expression of two conflicting forces, life instincts and the death instinct. Both are symbolized in this drawing by Allan Gilbert. (If you don't immediately see the death symbolism, stand farther from the drawing.)

The id acts as a power source for the entire **psyche** (sigh-KEY), or personality. This energy, called **libido** (lih-BEE-doe), flows from the **life instincts** (or **Eros**). According to Freud, libido underlies our efforts to survive, as well as our sexual desires and pleasure seeking. Freud also described a **death instinct. Thanatos**, as he called it, produces aggressive and destructive urges. Freud offered humanity's long history of wars and violence as evidence of such urges. Most id energies, then, are aimed at discharging tensions related to sex and aggression.

The Ego

The **ego** is sometimes described as the "executive," because it directs energies supplied by the id. The id is like a blind king or queen whose power is awesome but who must rely on others to carry out orders. The id can only form mental images of things it desires. The ego wins power to direct behavior by relating the desires of the id to external reality.

Are there other differences between the ego and the id? Yes. Recall that the id operates on the pleasure principle. The ego, in contrast, is guided by the **reality principle**. The ego is the system of thinking, planning, problem solving, and deciding. It is in conscious control of the personality and often delays action until it is practical or appropriate.

Psychoanalytic theory Freudian theory of personality that emphasizes unconscious forces and conflicts.

The Superego

What is the role of the superego? The **superego** acts as a judge or censor for the thoughts and actions of the ego. One part of the superego, called the **conscience**, reflects actions for which a person has been punished. When standards of the conscience are not met, you are punished internally by *guilt* feelings.

A second part of the superego is the **ego ideal**. The ego ideal reflects all behavior one's parents approved of or rewarded. The ego ideal is a source of goals and aspirations. When its standards are met, we feel *pride*.

The superego acts as an "internalized parent" to bring behavior under control. In Freudian terms, a person with a weak superego will be a delinquent, criminal, or antisocial personality. In contrast, an overly strict or harsh superego may cause inhibition, rigidity, or unbearable guilt.

TABLE 12.2 Key Freudian Concepts

Anal stage The psychosexual stage corresponding roughly to the period of toilet training (ages 1 to 3).
Anal-expulsive personality A disorderly, destructive, cruel, or messy person.
Anal-retentive personality A person who is obstinate, stingy, or compulsive, and who generally has difficulty "letting go."
Conscience The part of the superego that causes guilt when its standards are not met.
Conscious The region of the mind that includes all mental contents a person is aware of at any given moment.
Ego The executive part of personality that directs rational behavior.
Ego ideal The part of the superego representing ideal behavior; a source of pride when its standards are met.
Electra conflict A girl's sexual attraction to her father and feelings of rivalry with her mother.
Erogenous zone Any body area that produces pleasurable sensations.
Eros Freud's name for the "life instincts."
Fixation A lasting conflict developed as a result of frustration or over-indulgence.
Genital stage Period of full psychosexual development, marked by the attainment of mature adult sexuality.
Id The primitive part of personality that remains unconscious, supplies energy, and demands pleasure.
Latency According to Freud, a period in childhood when psychosexual development is more or less interrupted.
Libido In Freudian theory, the force, primarily pleasure oriented, that energizes the personality.
Moral anxiety Apprehension felt when thoughts, impulses, or actions conflict with the superego's standards.
Neurotic anxiety Apprehension felt when the ego struggles to control id impulses.
Oedipus conflict A boy's sexual attraction to his mother, and feelings of rivalry with his father.
Oral stage The period when infants are preoccupied with the mouth as a source of pleasure and means of expression.
Oral-aggressive personality A person who uses the mouth to express hostility by shouting, cursing, biting, and so forth. Also, one who actively exploits others.
Oral-dependent personality A person who wants to passively receive attention, gifts, love, and so forth.
Phallic personality A person who is vain, exhibitionistic, sensitive, and narcissistic.
Phallic stage The psychosexual stage (roughly ages 3 to 6) when a child is preoccupied with the genitals.
Pleasure principle A desire for immediate satisfaction of wishes, desires, or needs.
Preconscious An area of the mind containing information that can be voluntarily brought to awareness.
Psyche The mind, mental life, and personality as a whole.
Psychosexual stages The oral, anal, phallic, and genital stages, during which various personality traits are formed.
Reality principle Delaying action (or pleasure) until it is appropriate.
Superego A judge or censor for thoughts and actions.
Thanatos The death instinct postulated by Freud.
Unconscious The region of the mind that is beyond awareness, especially impulses and desires not directly known to a person.

The Dynamics of Personality

How do the id, ego, and superego interact? Freud didn't picture the id, ego, and superego as parts of the brain or as "little people" running the human psyche. Instead, they are conflicting mental processes. Freud theorized a delicate balance of power among the three. For example, the id's demands for immediate pleasure often clash with the superego's moral restrictions. Perhaps an example will help clarify the role of each part of the personality:

Freud in a Nutshell

Let's say you are sexually attracted to an acquaintance. The id clamors for immediate satisfaction of its sexual desires, but is opposed by the superego (which finds the very thought of sex shocking). The id says, "Go for it!" The superego icily replies, "Never even think that again!" And what does the ego say? The ego says, "I have a plan!"

This is, of course a drastic simplification, but it does capture the core of Freudian thinking. To reduce tension, the ego could begin actions leading to friendship, romance, courtship, and marriage. If the id is unusually powerful, the ego may give in and attempt a seduction. If the superego prevails, the ego may be forced to *displace* or *sublimate* sexual energies to other activities (sports, music, dancing, push-ups, cold showers). According to Freud, internal struggles and rechanneled energies typify most personality functioning.

Is the ego always caught in the middle? Basically yes, and the pressures on it can be intense. In addition to meeting the conflicting demands of the id and superego, the overworked ego must deal with external reality.

According to Freud, you feel anxiety when your ego is threatened or overwhelmed. Impulses from the id cause **neurotic anxiety** when the ego can barely keep them under control. Threats of punishment from the superego cause **moral anxiety**. Each person develops habitual ways of calming these anxieties, and many resort to using *ego-defense mechanisms* to lessen internal conflicts. Defense mechanisms are mental processes that deny, distort, or otherwise block out sources of threat and anxiety.

BRIDGES

The ego-defense mechanisms that Freud identified are used as a form of protection against stress, anxiety, and threatening events. **See Chapter 13, pages 456–458.**

Levels of Awareness

Like other psychodynamic theorists, Freud believed that our behavior often expresses unconscious (or hidden) forces. The **unconscious** holds repressed memories and emotions, plus the instinctual drives of the id. Interestingly, modern scientists have found that the brain's limbic system does, in fact, seem to trigger unconscious emotions and memories (LeDoux, 2000).

Even though they are beyond awareness, unconscious thoughts, feelings, or urges may slip into behavior in disguised or symbolic form (Reason, 2000; yes, these are *Freudian slips*). For example, if you meet someone you would like to know better, you may unconsciously leave a book or a jacket at that person's house to ensure another meeting.

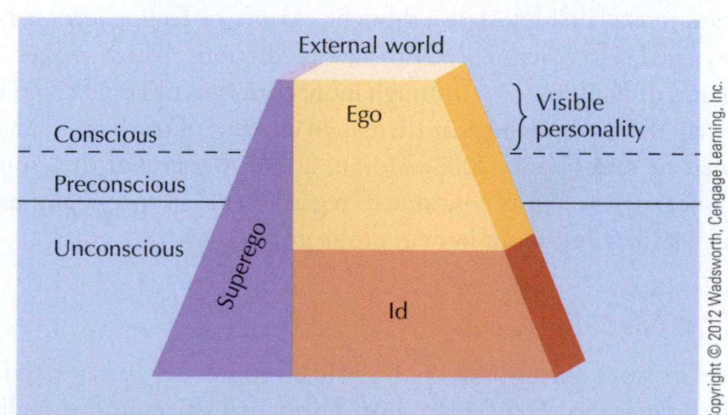

● **Figure 12.5** The approximate relationship between the id, ego, and superego, and the levels of awareness.

Are the actions of the ego and superego also unconscious, like the id? At times, yes, but they also operate on two other levels of awareness (● Figure 12.5). The **conscious** level includes everything you are aware of at a given moment, including thoughts, perceptions, feelings, and memories. The **preconscious** contains material that can be easily brought to awareness. If you stop to think about a time when you felt angry or rejected, you will be moving this memory from the preconscious to the conscious level of awareness.

The superego's activities also reveal differing levels of awareness. At times, we consciously try to live up to moral codes or standards. Yet, at other times a person may feel guilty without knowing why. Psychoanalytic theory credits such guilt to unconscious workings of the superego. Indeed, Freud believed that the unconscious origins of many feelings cannot be easily brought to awareness.

Personality Development

How does psychoanalytic theory explain personality development? Freud theorized that the core of personality is formed before age 6 in a series of **psychosexual stages**. Freud believed that erotic urges in childhood have lasting effects on development (Ashcraft, 2012). As you might expect, this is a controversial idea. However, Freud used the terms *sex* and *erotic* very broadly to refer to many physical sources of pleasure.

A Freudian Fable?

Freud identified four psychosexual stages, the **oral**, **anal**, **phallic**, and **genital**. (He also described a period of "latency" between the phallic and genital stages. Latency is explained in a moment.) At each stage, a different part of the body becomes a child's primary **erogenous zone** (an area capable of producing pleasure). Each area then serves as the main source of pleasure, frustration, and self-expression. Freud believed that many adult personality traits can be traced to **fixations** in one or more of the stages.

What is a fixation? A fixation is an unresolved conflict or emotional hang-up caused by overindulgence or by frustration. As we describe the psychosexual stages, you'll see why Freud considered fixations important.

The Oral Stage

During the first year of life, most of an infant's pleasure comes from stimulation of the mouth. If a child is overfed or frustrated, oral traits may be created. Adult expressions of oral needs include gum chewing, nail biting, smoking, kissing, overeating, and alcoholism.

Was Freud's ever-present cigar a sign of an oral fixation? Was it a phallic symbol? Was it both? Or was it neither? Once, when he was asked, Freud himself apparently replied, "Sometimes a cigar is just a cigar." An inability to say for sure is one of the shortcomings of psychoanalytic theory.

What if there is an oral fixation? Fixation early in the oral stage produces an **oral-dependent personality**. Oral-dependent persons are gullible (they swallow things easily!) and passive and need lots of attention (they want to be mothered and showered with gifts). Frustrations later in the oral stage may cause aggression, often in the form of biting. Fixations here create cynical, **oral-aggressive** adults who exploit others. They also like to argue ("Biting sarcasm" is their forte!).

The Anal Stage

Between the ages of 1 and 3, the child's attention shifts to the process of elimination. When parents attempt toilet training, the child can gain approval or express rebellion or aggression by "holding on" or by "letting go." Therefore, harsh or lenient toilet training can cause an anal fixation that may lock such responses into personality. Freud described the **anal-retentive** (holding-on) **personality** as obstinate, stingy, orderly, and compulsively clean. The **anal-expulsive** (letting-go) **personality** is disorderly, destructive, cruel, or messy.

The Phallic Stage

Adult traits of the **phallic personality** are vanity, exhibitionism, sensitive pride, and narcissism (self-love). Freud theorized that phallic fixations develop between the ages of 3 and 6. At this time, increased sexual interest causes the child to be physically attracted to the parent of the opposite sex. In males, this attraction leads to an **Oedipal conflict**. In it, the boy feels a rivalry with his father for the affection of his mother. Freud believed that the male child feels threatened by the father (specifically, the boy fears castration). To ease his anxieties, the boy must **identify** with the father. Their rivalry ends when the boy seeks to become more like his father. As he does, he begins to accept the father's values and forms a conscience.

What about the female child? Girls experience an **Electra conflict**. In this case, the girl loves her father and competes with her mother. However, according to Freud, the girl identifies with the mother more gradually.

Freud believed that females already feel castrated. Because of this, they are less driven to identify with their mothers than boys are with their fathers. This, he said, is less effective in creating a conscience. This particular part of Freudian thought has been thoroughly (and rightfully) rejected by modern experts in the psychology of women. It is better understood as a reflection of the male-dominated times in which Freud lived.

Latency

According to Freud, there is a period of **latency** from age 6 to puberty. Latency is not so much a stage as it is a quiet time during which psychosexual development is dormant. Freud's belief that psychosexual development is "on hold" at this time is hard to accept. Nevertheless, Freud saw latency as a relatively quiet time compared with the stormy first 6 years of life.

The Genital Stage

At puberty, an upswing in sexual energies activates all the unresolved conflicts of earlier years. This upsurge, according to Freud, is the reason why adolescence can be filled with emotion and turmoil. The genital stage begins at puberty. It is marked, during adolescence, by a growing capacity for responsible social–sexual relationships. The genital stage ends with a mature capacity for love and the realization of full adult sexuality.

Critical Comments

As bizarre as Freud's theory might seem, it has been influential for several reasons. First, it pioneered the idea that the first years of life help shape adult personality. Second, it identified feeding, toilet training, and early sexual experiences as critical events in personality formation. Third, Freud was among the first to propose that development proceeds through a series of stages (Shaffer, 2009).

BRIDGES

Erik Erikson's psycho*social* stages, which cover development from birth to old age, are a modern offshoot of Freudian thinking. **See Chapter 3, pages 111–113.**

Is the Freudian view of development widely accepted? Few psychologists wholeheartedly embrace Freud's theory today. In some cases, Freud was clearly wrong. His portrayal of the elementary school years (latency) as free from sexuality and unimportant for personality development is hard to believe. His idea of the role of a stern or threatening father in the development of a strong conscience in males has also been challenged. Studies show that a son is more likely to develop a strong conscience if his father is affectionate and accepting rather than stern and punishing. Freud also overemphasized sexuality in personality development. Other motives and cognitive factors are of equal importance.

Freud has been criticized for his views of patients who believed they were sexually molested as children (Marcel, 2005). Freud assumed that such events were merely childhood fantasies. This view led to a longstanding tendency to disbelieve children who have been molested and women who have been raped (Brannon, 2011).

Another important criticism is that Freud's concepts are almost impossible to verify scientifically. The theory provides numerous ways to explain almost any thought, action, or feeling *after* it has occurred. However, it leads to few predictions, which makes its claims difficult to test. Although more criticisms of Freud could be listed, the fact remains that there is an element of truth to much of what he said (Jacob, 2003; Moran, 2010). Because of this, some clinical psychologists continue to regard Freudian theory as a useful way to think about human problems.

The Neo-Freudians

Freud's ideas quickly attracted a brilliant following. Just as rapidly, the importance Freud placed on instinctual drives and sexuality caused many to disagree with him. Those who stayed close to the core of Freud's thinking are called *neo-Freudians* (*neo* means "new"). **Neo-Freudians** accepted the broad features of Freud's theory but revised parts of it. Some of the better known neo-Freudians are Karen Horney, Anna Freud (Freud's daughter), Otto Rank, and Erich Fromm. Other early followers broke away more completely from Freud and created their own opposing theories. This group includes people such as Alfred Adler, Harry Sullivan, and Carl Jung.

The full story of other psychodynamic theories must await your first course in personality. For now, let's sample three views. The first represents an early rejection of Freud's thinking (Adler). The second embraces most but not all of Freud's theory (Horney). The third involves a carryover of Freudian ideas into a related but unique theory (Jung).

Alfred Adler (1870–1937)

Adler broke away from Freud because he disagreed with Freud's emphasis on the unconscious, on instinctual drives, and on the importance of sexuality. Adler believed that we are social creatures governed by social urges, not by biological instincts (Shulman, 2004). In Adler's view, the main driving force in personality is a **striving for superiority**. This striving, he said, is a struggle to overcome imperfections, an upward drive for competence, completion, and mastery of shortcomings.

What motivates "striving for superiority"? Adler believed that everyone experiences feelings of inferiority. This occurs mainly because we begin life as small, weak, and relatively powerless children surrounded by larger and more powerful adults. Feelings of inferiority may also come from our personal limitations. The struggle for superiority arises from such feelings.

Although everyone strives for superiority, each person tries to **compensate** for different limitations, and each chooses a different pathway to superiority (Overholser, 2010). Adler believed that this situation creates a unique **style of life** (or personality pattern) for each individual. According to Adler, the core of each person's style of life is formed by age 5. (Adler also believed that valuable clues to a person's style of life are revealed by the earliest memory that can be recalled. You might find it interesting to search back to your earliest memory and contemplate what it tells you.) However, later in his life, Adler began to emphasize the existence of a **creative self**. By this, he meant that humans create their personalities through choices and experiences.

Karen Horney (1885–1952)

Karen Horney (HORN-eye) remained faithful to most of Freud's theory, but she resisted his more mechanistic, biological, and instinctive ideas. For example, as a woman, Horney rejected Freud's claim that "anatomy is destiny." This view, woven into Freudian psychology, held that males are dominant or superior to females. Horney was among the first to challenge the obvious male bias in Freud's thinking (Eckardt, 2005).

Horney also disagreed with Freud about the causes of neurosis. Freud held that neurotic (anxiety-ridden) individuals are struggling with forbidden id drives that they fear they cannot control. Horney's view was that a core of **basic anxiety** occurs when people feel isolated and helpless in a hostile world. These feelings, she believed, are rooted in childhood. Trouble occurs when an individual tries to control basic anxiety by exaggerating a single mode of interacting with others.

What do you mean by "mode of interacting"? According to Horney, each of us can move *toward* others (by depending on them for love, support, or friendship), we can move *away* from others (by withdrawing, acting like a "loner," or being "strong" and independent), or we can move *against* others (by attacking, competing with, or seeking power over them). Horney believed that emotional health reflects a balance in moving toward, away from, and against others. In her view, emotional problems tend to lock people into overuse of one of the three modes—an insight that remains valuable today (Smith, 2007).

Carl Jung (1875–1961)

Carl Jung was a student of Freud's, but the two parted ways as Jung began to develop his own ideas. Like Freud, Jung called the conscious part of the personality the *ego*. However, he further noted that a *persona,* or "mask," exists between the ego and the outside world. The **persona** is the "public self" presented to others. It is most apparent when we adopt particular roles or hide our deeper feelings. As mentioned earlier, Jung believed that actions of the ego may reflect attitudes of **introversion** (in which energy is mainly directed inward) or of **extroversion** (in which energy is mainly directed outward).

Was Jung's view of the unconscious the same as Freud's? Jung used the term *personal unconscious* to refer to what Freud simply called the unconscious (Mayer, 2002). The **personal unconscious** is a mental storehouse for a single individual's experiences, feelings, and memories. But Jung also described a deeper **collective unconscious**, or mental storehouse for unconscious ideas and images

Neo-Freudian A theorist who has revised Freud's theory, while still accepting some of its basic concepts.

Striving for superiority According to Adler, this basic drive propels us toward perfection.

Compensation Any attempt to overcome feelings of inadequacy or inferiority.

Style of life The pattern of personality and behavior that defines the pathway each person takes through life.

Creative self The "artist" in each of us that creates a unique identity and style of life.

Basic anxiety A primary form of anxiety that arises from living in a hostile world.

Persona The "mask" or public self presented to others.

Introversion Ego attitude in which energy is mainly directed inward.

Extroversion Ego attitude in which energy is mainly directed outward.

Personal unconscious A mental storehouse for a single individual's unconscious thoughts.

Collective unconscious A mental storehouse for unconscious ideas and images shared by all humans.

shared by all humans. Jung believed that, from the beginning of time, all humans have had experiences with birth, death, power, god figures, mother and father figures, animals, the earth, energy, evil, rebirth, and so on. According to Jung, such universals create **archetypes** (ARE-keh-types: original ideas, images, or patterns).

Archetypes, found in the collective unconscious, are unconscious images that cause us to respond emotionally to symbols of birth, death, energy, animals, evil, and the like (Maloney, 1999). Jung believed that he detected symbols of such archetypes in the art, religion, myths, and dreams of every culture and age. Let's say, for instance, that a man dreams of dancing with his sister. To Freud, this would probably be a sign of hidden incestuous feelings. To Jung, the image of the sister might represent an unexpressed feminine side of the man's personality and the dream might represent the cosmic dance that intertwines "maleness" and "femaleness" in all lives.

Are some archetypes more important than others? Two particularly important archetypes are the **anima** (female principle) and the **animus** (male principle). In men, the anima is an unconscious, idealized image of women. This image is based, in part, on real experiences with women (the man's mother, sister, friends). However, the experiences men have had with women throughout history form the true core of the anima. The reverse is true of women, who possess an animus, or idealized image of men. The anima in males and the animus in females enable us to relate to members of the opposite sex. The anima and animus also make it possible for people to learn to express both "masculine" and "feminine" sides of their personalities.

Jung regarded the *self archetype* as the most important of all. The **self archetype** represents the unity of the center of the self. Its existence causes a gradual movement toward balance, wholeness, and harmony within the personality. Jung felt that we become richer and more completely human when a balance is achieved between the conscious and unconscious, the anima and animus, thinking and feeling, sensing and intuiting, the persona and the ego, introversion and extroversion.

Was Jung talking about self-actualization? Essentially he was. Jung was the first to use the term *self-actualization* to describe a striving for completion and unity. He believed that the self archetype is symbolized in every culture by **mandalas** (magic circles representing the center of the self) of one kind or another.

Jung's theory may not be scientific, but clearly he was a man of genius and vision (Lawson, 2008). If you would like to know more about Jung and his ideas, a good starting place is his autobiography, *Memories, Dreams, Reflections* (Jung, 1961).

Digital Vision/Alamy

Jung regarded mandalas as symbols of the self-archetype and representations of unity, balance, and completion within the personality.

Knowledge Builder: Psychodynamic Theories

RECITE

1. List the three divisions of personality postulated by Freud. ________, ________, ________
2. Which division is totally unconscious? ________
3. Which division is responsible for moral anxiety? ________
4. Freud proposed the existence of a life instinct known as *Thanatos*. T or F?
5. Freud's view of personality development is based on the concept of ________ stages.
6. Arrange these stages in the proper order: phallic, anal, genital, oral. ________
7. Freud considered the anal-retentive personality to be obstinate and stingy. T or F?
8. Karen Horney theorized that people control basic anxiety by moving toward, away from, and ________ others.
9. Carl Jung's theory states that archetypes, which are found in the personal unconscious, exert an influence on behavior. T or F?

REFLECT

Think Critically

10. Many adults would find it embarrassing or humiliating to drink from a baby bottle. Can you explain why?

Self-Reflect

Try to think of at least one time when your thoughts, feelings, or actions seemed to reflect the workings of each of the following: the id, the ego, and the superego.

Do you know anyone who seems to have oral, anal, or phallic personality traits? Do you think Freud's concept of fixation explains their characteristics?

Do any of your personal experiences support the existence of an Oedipus conflict or an Electra conflict? If not, is it possible that you have repressed feelings related to these conflicts?

If you had to summarize your style of life in one sentence, what would it be?

Which of Horney's three modes of interacting do you think you rely on the most? Do you overuse one of the modes?

Think of the images you have seen in art, mythology, movies, and popular culture. Do any seem to represent Jungian archetypes—especially the self archetype?

Answers: 1. id, ego, superego **2.** id **3.** superego **4.** F **5.** psychosexual **6.** oral, anal, phallic, genital **7.** T **8.** against **9.** F **10.** A psychoanalytic theorist would say that it is because the bottle rekindles oral conflicts and feelings of vulnerability and dependence.

Humanistic Theory—Peak Experiences and Personal Growth

Gateway Question 12.4: *What are humanistic theories of personality?*

At the beginning of this chapter, you met Annette. A few years ago, Annette and her husband spent a year riding mules across the country as a unique way to see America and get to know themselves better. From where do such desires for personal growth come? Humanistic theories pay special attention to the fuller use of human potentials, and they help bring balance to our overall views of personality.

Humanism focuses on human experience, problems, potentials, and ideals. As we saw in Chapter 1, the core of humanism is a positive image of humans as creative beings capable of *free will*—an ability to choose that is not determined by genetics, learning, or unconscious forces. In short, humanists seek ways to encourage our potentials to blossom.

Humanism is sometimes called a "third force" in that it is opposed to both psychoanalytic and behaviorist theories of personality. Humanism is a reaction to the pessimism of psychoanalytic theory. It rejects the Freudian view of personality as a battleground for instincts and unconscious forces. Instead, humanists view **human nature**—the traits, qualities, potentials, and behavior patterns most characteristic of the human species—as inherently good. Humanists also oppose the machine-like overtones of the behaviorist view of human nature, which we will encounter shortly. We are not, they say, merely a bundle of moldable responses.

To a humanist, the person you are today is largely the product of all the choices you have made. Humanists also emphasize immediate **subjective experience** (private perceptions of reality) rather than prior learning. They believe that there are as many "real worlds" as there are people. To understand behavior, we must learn how a person subjectively views the world—what is "real" for her or him.

Who are the major humanistic theorists? Many psychologists have added to the humanistic tradition. Of these, the best known are Abraham Maslow (1908–1970) and Carl Rogers (1902–1987). Because Maslow's idea of self-actualization was introduced in Chapter 1, let's begin with a more detailed look at this facet of his thinking.

Maslow and Self-Actualization

Abraham Maslow became interested in people who were living unusually effective lives (Hoffman, 2008). How were they different? To find an answer, Maslow began by studying the lives of great men and women from history, such as Albert Einstein, William James, Jane Addams, Eleanor Roosevelt, Abraham Lincoln, John Muir, and Walt Whitman. From there, he moved on to directly study living artists, writers, poets, and other creative individuals.

Along the way, Maslow's thinking changed radically. At first, he studied only people of obvious creativity or high achievement. However, it eventually became clear that a housewife, clerk, student, or someone like our friend Annette could live a rich, creative, and satisfying life (Davidson, & Bromfield, Beck, 2007). Maslow referred to the process of fully developing personal potentials as **self-actualization** (Maslow, 1954). The heart of self-actualization is a continuous search for personal fulfillment (Ewen, 2009; Reiss & Havercamp, 2005).

Characteristics of Self-Actualizers

A self-actualizer is a person who is living creatively and fully using his or her potentials. In his studies, Maslow found that self-actualizers share many similarities. Whether famous or unknown, well-schooled or uneducated, rich or poor, self-actualizers tend to fit the following profile:

1. **Efficient perceptions of reality.** Self-actualizers are able to judge situations correctly and honestly. They are very sensitive to the fake and dishonest.
2. **Comfortable acceptance of self, others, and nature.** Self-actualizers accept their own human nature with all its flaws. The shortcomings of others and the contradictions of the human condition are accepted with humor and tolerance.
3. **Spontaneity.** Maslow's subjects extended their creativity into everyday activities. Actualizers tend to be unusually alive, engaged, and spontaneous.
4. **Task centering.** Most of Maslow's subjects had a mission to fulfill in life or some task or problem outside of themselves to pursue. Humanitarians such as Albert Schweitzer and Mother Teresa represent this quality.
5. **Autonomy.** Self-actualizers are free from reliance on external authorities or other people. They tend to be resourceful and independent.
6. **Continued freshness of appreciation.** The self-actualizer seems to constantly renew appreciation of life's basic goodness. A sunset or a flower will be experienced as intensely time after time as it was at first. There is an "innocence of vision," like that of an artist or child.

Archetype A universal idea, image, or pattern, found in the collective unconscious.

Anima An archetype representing the female principle.

Animus An archetype representing the male principle.

Self archetype An unconscious image of the center of the self, representing unity, wholeness, completion, and balance.

Mandala A circular design representing the balance, unity, and completion of the unconscious self.

Humanism An approach that focuses on human experience, problems, potentials, and ideals.

Human nature Those traits, qualities, potentials, and behavior patterns most characteristic of the human species.

Subjective experience Reality as it is perceived and interpreted, not as it exists objectively.

Self-actualization The process of fully developing personal potentials.

7. **Fellowship with humanity.** Maslow's subjects felt a deep identification with others and the human situation in general.
8. **Profound interpersonal relationships.** The interpersonal relationships of self-actualizers are marked by deep, loving bonds (Hanley & Abell, 2002).
9. **Comfort with solitude.** Despite their satisfying relationships with others, self-actualizing persons value solitude and are comfortable being alone (Sumerlin & Bundrick, 1996).
10. **Nonhostile sense of humor.** This refers to the wonderful capacity to laugh at oneself. It also describes the kind of humor a man like Abraham Lincoln had. Lincoln probably never made a joke that hurt anybody. His wry comments were a gentle prodding of human shortcomings.
11. **Peak experiences.** All of Maslow's subjects reported the frequent occurrence of **peak experiences** (temporary moments of self-actualization). These occasions were marked by feelings of ecstasy, harmony, and deep meaning. Self-actualizers reported feeling at one with the universe, stronger and calmer than ever before, filled with light, beautiful and good, and so forth.

In summary, self-actualizers feel safe, nonanxious, accepted, loved, loving, and alive.

Maslow's choice of people for study seems pretty subjective. Do they really provide a fair representation of self-actualization? Although Maslow tried to investigate self-actualization empirically, his choice of people for study was subjective. Undoubtedly, there are many ways to make full use of personal potential. Maslow's primary contribution was to draw our attention to the possibility of lifelong personal growth (Peterson & Park, 2010).

What steps can be taken to promote self-actualization? Maslow made few specific recommendations about how to proceed. There is no magic formula for leading a more creative life. Self-actualization is primarily a *process*, not a goal or an end point. As such, it requires hard work, patience, and commitment. Nevertheless, some helpful suggestions can be gleaned from his writings (Maslow, 1954, 1967, 1971). Here are some ways to begin:

1. **Be willing to change.** Begin by asking yourself, "Am I living in a way that is deeply satisfying to me and that truly expresses me?" If not, be prepared to make changes in your life. Indeed, ask yourself this question often and accept the need for continual change.
2. **Take responsibility.** You can become an architect of self by acting as if you are personally responsible for every aspect of your life. Shouldering responsibility in this way helps end the habit of blaming others for your own shortcomings.
3. **Examine your motives.** Self-discovery involves an element of risk. If your behavior is restricted by a desire for safety or security, it may be time to test some limits. Try to make each life decision a choice for growth, not a response to fear or anxiety.
4. **Experience honestly and directly.** Wishful thinking is another barrier to personal growth. Self-actualizers trust themselves enough to accept all kinds of information without distorting it to fit their fears and desires. Try to see yourself as others do. Be willing to admit, "I was wrong," or, "I failed because I was irresponsible."
5. **Make use of positive experiences.** Maslow considered peak experiences temporary moments of self-actualization. Therefore, you might actively repeat activities that have caused feelings of awe, amazement, exaltation, renewal, reverence, humility, fulfillment, or joy.
6. **Be prepared to be different.** Maslow felt that everyone has a potential for "greatness," but most fear becoming what they might. As part of personal growth, be prepared to trust your own impulses and feelings; don't automatically judge yourself by the standards of others. Accept your uniqueness.
7. **Get involved.** With few exceptions, self-actualizers tend to have a mission or "calling" in life. For these people, "work" is not done just to fill deficiency needs, but to satisfy higher yearnings for truth, beauty, community, and meaning. Get personally involved and committed. Turn your attention to problems outside yourself.
8. **Assess your progress.** There is no final point at which one becomes self-actualized. It's important to gauge your progress frequently and to renew your efforts. If you feel bored at school, at a job, or in a relationship, consider it a challenge. Have you been taking responsibility for your own personal growth? Almost any activity can be used as a chance for self-enhancement if it is approached creatively.

The Whole Person: Positive Personality Traits

It could be said that self-actualizing people are thriving, not just surviving. In recent years, proponents of positive psychology have tried to scientifically study positive personality traits that contribute to happiness and well-being (Keyes & Haidt, 2003; Seligman, 2003). Although their work does not fall within the humanistic tradition, their findings are relevant here.

Martin Seligman, Christopher Peterson, and others have identified six human strengths that contribute to well-being and life satisfaction. Each strength is expressed by the positive personality traits listed here (Peterson & Seligman, 2004):

- **Wisdom and knowledge:** Creativity, curiosity, open-mindedness, love of learning, perspective
- **Courage:** Bravery, persistence, integrity, vitality
- **Humanity:** Love, kindness, social intelligence
- **Justice:** Citizenship, fairness, leadership
- **Temperance:** Forgiveness, humility, prudence, self-control
- **Transcendence:** Appreciation of beauty and excellence, gratitude, hope, humor, spirituality

Which of the positive personality traits are most closely related to happiness? One study found that traits of hope, vitality, gratitude, love, and curiosity are strongly associated with life satisfaction (Park, Peterson, & Seligman, 2004). These characteristics, in combination with Maslow's descriptions of self-actualizers, provide a good guide to the characteristics that help people live happy, meaningful lives.

Carl Rogers' Self Theory

Carl Rogers, another well-known humanist, also emphasized the human capacity for inner peace and happiness. The **fully functioning person**, he said, lives in harmony with his or her deepest feelings and impulses. Such people are open to their experiences, and they trust their inner urges and intuitions (Rogers, 1961). Rogers believed that this attitude is most likely to occur when a person receives ample amounts of love and acceptance from others.

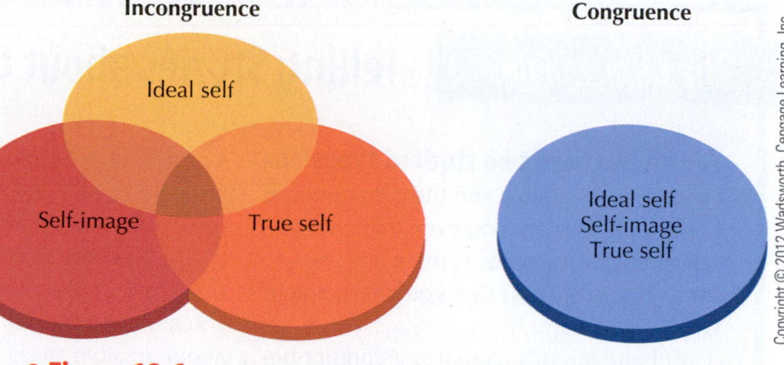

● **Figure 12.6** Incongruence occurs when there is a mismatch between any of these three entities: the ideal self (the person you would like to be), your self-image (the person you think you are), and the true self (the person you actually are). Self-esteem suffers when there is a large difference between one's ideal self and self-image. Anxiety and defensiveness are common when the self-image does not match the true self.

Personality Structure and Dynamics

Rogers' theory emphasizes the **self**, a flexible and changing perception of personal identity. Much behavior can be understood as an attempt to maintain consistency between our *self-image* and our actions. (Your **self-image** is a total subjective perception of your body and personality.) For example, people who think of themselves as kind tend to be considerate in most situations.

Let's say I know a person who thinks she is kind, but she really isn't. How does that fit Rogers' theory? According to Rogers, we allow experiences that match our self-image into awareness, where they gradually change the self. Information or feelings inconsistent with the self-image are said to be *incongruent*. Thus, a person who thinks she is kind but really isn't is in a state of **incongruence**. In other words, there is a discrepancy between her experiences and her self-image. As another example, it would be incongruent to believe that you are a person who "never gets angry" if you spend much of each day seething inside.

Experiences seriously incongruent with the self-image can be threatening and are often distorted or denied conscious recognition. Blocking, denying, or distorting experiences prevents the self from changing. This creates a gulf between the self-image and reality. As the self-image grows more unrealistic, the incongruent person becomes confused, vulnerable, dissatisfied, or seriously maladjusted (● Figure 12.6). In line with Rogers' observations, a study of college students confirmed that being *authentic* is vital for healthy functioning. That is, we need to feel that our behavior accurately expresses who we are (Sheldon et al., 1997). Please note, however, that being authentic doesn't mean you can do whatever you want. Being true to yourself is no excuse for acting irresponsibly or ignoring the feelings of others (Kernis & Goldman, 2005).

When your self-image is consistent with what you really think, feel, do, and experience, you are best able to actualize your potentials. Rogers also considered it essential to have congruence between the self-image and the *ideal self*. The **ideal self** is similar to Freud's ego ideal. It is an image of the person you would most like to be (Zentner & Renaud, 2007).

Joe McBride/Getty Images

Humanists consider self-image a central determinant of behavior and personal adjustment.

BRIDGES

Rogers and other humanistic theorists believe that some psychological disorders are caused by a faulty or incongruent self-image. **See Chapter 16, pages 552–553.**

Is it really incongruent not to live up to your ideal self? Rogers was aware that we never fully attain our ideals. Nevertheless, the greater the gap between the way you see yourself and the way you would like to be, the more tension and anxiety you will experience.

Peak experiences Temporary moments of self-actualization.

Fully functioning person A person living in harmony with her or his deepest feelings, impulses, and intuitions.

Self A continuously evolving conception of one's personal identity.

Self-image Total subjective perception of one's body and personality (another term for self-concept).

Incongruence State that exists when there is a discrepancy between one's experiences and self-image or between one's self-image and ideal self.

Ideal self An idealized image of oneself (the person one would like to be).

The Clinical File — Telling Stories about Ourselves

You know these two student types: the carefree party animal and the conscientious bookworm. Perhaps you even think of yourself as one or the other. Is there any truth to these (stereo)types? Can you change your type?

College life often creates a conflict between opportunities for fun with friends and the need to study hard. In general, our personality traits are relatively stable characteristics (McAdams & Pals, 2006). As a result, a person high in the Big Five traits of extroversion and agreeableness will tend to embrace a carefree college lifestyle. In comparison, someone high in conscientiousness will find it easier to hit the books (McGregor, McAdams, & Little, 2006).

Does that mean a partyer can't become a bookworm (or vice versa)? It depends: Do you mean over a week? Or a lifetime? Personality traits do slowly change as we age. In particular, we tend to become more agreeable, conscientious, and emotionally stable as we grow older (Roberts & Mroczek, 2008).

Oh, you need to change by the end of the semester? That's a taller order. In that case, you might want to try telling yourself stories about possible selves you could become. The *narrative approach* to personality asserts that our personalities are shaped by the stories we tell about ourselves (Lodi-Smith et al., 2009; Pals, 2006). In other words, alternate life stories are not just fantasies or daydreams. They actually influence who we are and who we become.

So, if you feel that you are being too careless and carefree at school, start imagining yourself studying more, getting to classes on time, and getting good grades. Listen to the stories of successful students and use them to revise your own story. Visit your campus counseling center to learn more about how to succeed at school. In other words, imagine yourself as a bit more of a bookworm. (Don't worry, your carefree nature won't desert you!)

If you feel you are too conscientious and working too hard, imagine yourself going out with friends more often. Listen to the stories of your extroverted classmates. Imagine the benefits of balancing work and play in your life. If you are shy or perfectionistic, visit your campus counseling center to learn how to become more sociable or relaxed. And, again, don't worry: Having more fun won't make you irresponsible.

Whatever possible self you choose to pursue, you are more likely to become what you imagine if you elaborate your story, making it more detailed and "real" as you gradually adopt new patterns. You *can* create a new narrative identity for yourself (Bauer, McAdams, & Pals, 2008).

Rogers emphasized that to maximize our potentials, we must accept information about ourselves as honestly as possible. In accord with his thinking, researchers have found that people with a close match between their self-image and ideal self tend to be socially poised, confident, and resourceful. Those with a poor match tend to be depressed, anxious, and insecure (Boldero et al., 2005).

According to psychologists Hazel Markus and Paula Nurius (1986), our ideal self is only one of a number of **possible selves** (persons we could become or are afraid of becoming). Annette, who was described earlier, is an interesting personality, to say the least. Annette is one of those people who seems to have lived many lives in the time that most of us manage only one. Like Annette, you may have pondered many possible personal identities. (See "Telling Stories about Ourselves.")

Possible selves translate our hopes, fears, fantasies, and goals into specific images of who we *could* be. Thus, a beginning law student might picture herself as a successful attorney, an enterprising college student might imagine himself as an Internet entrepreneur, and a person on a diet might imagine both slim and grossly obese possible selves. Such images tend to direct our future behavior (Oyserman et al., 2004).

Of course, almost everyone over age 30 has probably felt the anguish of realizing that some cherished possible selves will never be realized. Nevertheless, there is value in asking yourself not just "Who am I?" but also "Who would I like to become?" As you do, remember Maslow's advice that everyone has a potential for "greatness," but most fear becoming what they might.

Humanistic View of Development

Why do mirrors, photographs, video cameras, and the reactions of others hold such fascination and threat for many people? Carl Rogers' theory suggests it is because they provide information about one's self. The development of a self-image depends greatly on information from the environment. It begins with a sorting of perceptions and feelings: my body, my toes, my nose, I want, I like, I am, and so on. Soon, it expands to include self-evaluation: I am a good person, I did something bad just now, and so forth.

How does development of the self contribute to later personality functioning? Rogers believed that positive and negative evaluations by others cause children to develop internal standards of evaluation called **conditions of worth**. In other words, we learn that some actions win our parents' love and approval, whereas others are rejected. More important, parents may label some *feelings* as bad or wrong. For example, a child might be told that it is wrong to feel angry toward a brother or sister—even when anger is justified. Likewise, a little boy might be told that he must not cry or show fear, two very normal emotions.

Learning to evaluate some experiences or feelings as "good" and others as "bad" is directly related to a later capacity for self-esteem, positive self-evaluation, or **positive self-regard**, to use Rogers' term. To think of yourself as a good, lovable, worthwhile person, your behavior and experiences must match your internal conditions of worth. The problem is that this can cause incongruence by leading to the denial of many true feelings and experiences.

To put it simply, Rogers blamed many adult emotional problems on attempts to live by the standards of others (Ashcraft, 2012). He believed that congruence and self-actualization are encouraged by replacing conditions of worth with **organismic valuing** (a natural, undistorted, full-body reaction to an experience). Organismic valuing is a direct, gut-level response to life that avoids the filtering and distortion of incongruence. It involves trusting one's own feelings and perceptions. Organismic valuing is most likely to develop, Rogers felt, when children (or adults) receive **unconditional positive regard** (unshakable love and approval) from others. That is, when they are "prized" as worthwhile human beings, just for being themselves, without any conditions or strings attached. Although this may be a luxury few people enjoy, we are more likely to move toward our ideal selves if we receive affirmation and support from a close partner (Drigotas et al., 1999).

Knowledge Builder — Humanistic Theory

RECITE

1. Humanists view human nature as basically good and they emphasize the effects of subjective learning and unconscious choice. T or F?
2. Maslow used the term ______________________ to describe the tendency of certain individuals to fully use their talents and potentials.
3. According to Maslow, a preoccupation with one's own thoughts, feelings, and needs is characteristic of self-actualizing individuals. T or F?
4. Maslow thought of peak experiences as temporary moments of *a.* congruence *b.* positive self-regard *c.* self-actualization *d.* self-reinforcement
5. Which of the following is *not* one of the six human strengths identified by positive psychologists? *a.* congruence *b.* courage *c.* justice *d.* transcendence
6. According to Rogers, a close match between the self-image and the ideal self creates a condition called incongruence. T or F?
7. Markus and Nurius describe alternative self-concepts that a person may have as "possible selves." T or F?
8. Carl Rogers believed that personal growth is encouraged when conditions of worth are replaced by *a.* self-efficacy *b.* instrumental worth *c.* latency *d.* organismic valuing

REFLECT

Think Critically

9. What role would your self-image and "possible selves" have in the choice of a college major?

Self-Reflect

How do your views of human nature and free will compare with those of the humanists?

Do you know anyone who seems to be making especially good use of his or her personal potentials? Does that person fit Maslow's profile of a self-actualizer?

How much difference do you think there is between your self-image, your ideal self, and your true self? Do you think Rogers is right about the effects of applying conditions of worth to your perceptions and feelings?

Answers: 1. F **2.** self-actualization **3.** F **4.** *c* **5.** *a* **6.** F **7.** T **8.** *d* **9.** Career decisions almost always involve, in part, picturing oneself occupying various occupational roles. Such possible "future selves" play a role in many of the major decisions we make (Masters & Holley, 2006).

Learning Theories of Personality—Habit I Seen You Before?

Gateway Question 12.5: *What do behaviorists and social learning theorists emphasize in their approach to personality?*

After exploring psychodynamic theories, you might be relieved to know that behavioral theorists explain personality through straightforward concepts, such as learning, reinforcement, and imitation. Behavioral and social learning theories are based on scientific research, which makes them powerful ways of looking at personality.

How do behaviorists approach personality? According to some critics, as if people are robots. Actually, the behaviorist position is not nearly that mechanistic, and its value is well established. Behaviorists have shown repeatedly that children can *learn* things like kindness, hostility, generosity, or destructiveness. What does this have to do with personality? Everything, according to the behavioral viewpoint.

Behavioral personality theories emphasize that personality is no more (or less) than a collection of relatively stable learned behavior patterns. Personality, like other learned behavior, is acquired through classical and operant conditioning, observational learning, reinforcement, extinction, generalization, and discrimination. When Mother says, "It's not nice to make mud pies with Mommy's blender. If we want to grow up to be a big girl, we won't do it again, will we?" she serves as a model and in other ways shapes her daughter's personality.

Possible self A collection of thoughts, beliefs, feelings, and images concerning the person one could become.

Conditions of worth Internal standards used to judge the value of one's thoughts, actions, feelings, or experiences.

Positive self-regard Thinking of oneself as a good, lovable, worthwhile person.

Organismic valuing A natural, undistorted, full-body reaction to an experience.

Unconditional positive regard Unshakable love and approval given without qualification.

Behavioral personality theory Any model of personality that emphasizes learning and observable behavior.

fotostock/SuperStock

Freud believed that aggressive urges are "instinctual." In contrast, behavioral theories assume that personal characteristics such as aggressiveness are learned. Is this boy's aggression the result of observational learning, harsh punishment, or prior reinforcement?

Strict **learning theorists** reject the idea that personality is made up of traits. They would assert, for instance, that there is no such thing as a trait of "honesty" (Mischel, 2004).

Certainly some people are honest and others are not. How can honesty not be a trait? Remember, for many trait theorists, traits are biological dispositions. According to learning theorists, they are, instead, learned responses. If his parents consistently reward little Alexander for honesty, he is more likely to become an honest adult. If his parents are less scrupulous, Alexander might well grow up differently.

Lisa F. Young/Shutterstock

Seventy-five percent of American college students admit that they have been academically dishonest in one way or another. What can be done about these high rates of dishonesty? The behavioral perspective holds that honesty is determined as much by circumstances as it is by personality. In line with this, simple measures like announcing in classes that integrity codes will be enforced can significantly reduce cheating. Using multiple forms of exams and web-based plagiarism software and educating students about plagiarism also tend to deter dishonesty (Altschuler, 2001; McKeever, 2006).

Learning theorists also stress the **situational determinants** (external causes) of actions. Knowing that someone is honest does not automatically allow us to predict whether that person will be honest in a specific situation. It would not be unusual, for example, to find that a person honored for returning a lost wallet had cheated on a test, bought a term paper, or broken the speed limit. If you were to ask a learning theorist, "Are you an honest person?" the reply might be, "In what situation?"

A good example of how situations can influence behavior is a study in which people were intentionally overpaid for doing an assigned task. Under normal circumstances, 80 percent kept the extra money without mentioning it. But as few as 17 percent were dishonest if the situation was altered. For instance, if people thought the money was coming out of the pocket of the person doing the study, far fewer were dishonest (Bersoff, 1999). Thus, situations always interact with our prior learning to activate behavior.

How Situations Affect Behavior

Situations vary greatly in their impact. Some are powerful. Others are trivial and have little effect on behavior. The more powerful the situation, the easier it is to see what is meant by *situational determinants.* For example, each of the following situations would undoubtedly have a strong influence on your behavior: An armed person walks into your classroom; you accidentally sit on a lighted cigarette; you find your lover in bed with your best friend. Yet even these situations could provoke very different reactions from different personalities. That's why behavior is always a product of both prior learning and the situations in which we find ourselves (Mischel, Shoda, & Smith, 2008).

Ultimately, what is predictable about personality is that we respond in fairly consistent ways to certain *types of situations*. Consider, for example, two people who are easily angered: One person might get angry when she is delayed (for example, in traffic or a checkout line) but not when she misplaces something at home; the other person might get angry whenever she misplaces things, but not when she is delayed. Overall, the two women are equally prone to anger, but their anger tends to occur in different patterns and different types of situations (Mischel, 2004).

Personality = Behavior

How do learning theorists view the structure of personality? The behavioral view of personality can be illustrated with an early theory proposed by John Dollard and Neal Miller (1950). In their view, **habits** (learned behavior patterns) make up the structure of personality. As for the dynamics of personality, habits are governed by four elements of learning: *drive, cue, response,* and *reward.* A **drive** is any stimulus strong enough to goad a person to action (such as hunger, pain, lust, frustration, or fear). **Cues** are signals from the environment. These signals guide **responses** (actions) so that they are most likely to bring about **reward** (positive reinforcement).

How does that relate to personality? Let's say a child named Amina is frustrated by her older brother Kelvin, who takes a toy from her. Amina could respond in several ways: She could throw a temper tantrum, hit Kelvin, tell her mother, and so forth. The response she chooses is guided by available cues and the previous effects of each response. If telling her mother has paid off in the past, and her mother is present, telling again may be Amina's immediate response. If a different set of cues exists (if her mother is absent or if Kelvin looks particularly menacing), Amina may select some other response. To an outside observer, Amina's actions seem to reflect her personality. To a learning theorist, they simply express the combined effects of drive, cue, response, and reward.

BRIDGES

Behavioral theories have contributed greatly to the creation of therapies for various psychological problems and disorders. **See the discussion of behavior therapy in Chapter 15, pages 520–526.**

Doesn't this analysis leave out a lot? Yes. Learning theorists first set out to provide a simple, clear model of personality. But in recent years, they have had to face a fact that they originally tended to overlook: People think. The new breed of behavioral psychologists—whose views include perception, thinking, expectations, and other mental events—are called social learning theorists. Learning principles, modeling, thought patterns, perceptions, expectations, beliefs, goals, emotions, and social relationships are combined in **social learning theory** to explain personality (Mischel, Shoda, & Smith, 2008; Santrock, 2010).

Social Learning Theory

The "cognitive behaviorism" of social learning theory can be illustrated by three concepts proposed by Julian Rotter: the psychological situation, expectancy, and reinforcement value (Rotter & Hochreich, 1975). Let's examine each.

Someone trips you. How do you respond? Your reaction probably depends on whether you think it was planned or an accident. It is not enough to know the setting in which a person responds. We also need to know the person's **psychological situation** (how the person interprets or defines the situation). As another example, let's say you score low on an exam. Do you consider it a challenge to work harder, a sign that you should drop the class, or an excuse to get drunk? Again, your interpretation is important.

Our actions are affected by an **expectancy**, or anticipation, that making a response will lead to reinforcement. To continue the example, if working harder has paid off in the past, it is a likely reaction to a low test score. But to predict your response, we would also have to know if you *expect* your efforts to pay off in the present situation. In fact, expected reinforcement may be more important than actual past reinforcement. And what about the *value* you attach to grades, school success, or personal ability? The third concept, **reinforcement value**, states that we attach different subjective values to various activities or rewards. You will likely choose to study harder if passing your courses and obtaining a degree is highly valued. This, too, must be taken into account to understand personality.

Self-Efficacy

An ability to control your own life is the essence of what it means to be human (Corey & Corey, 2010). Because of this, Albert Bandura believes that one of the most important expectancies we develop concerns **self-efficacy** (EF-uh-keh-see: a capacity for producing a desired result). You're attracted to someone in your anthropology class. Will you ask him or her out? You're beginning to consider a career in psychology. Will you take the courses you need to get into graduate school? You'd like to exercise more on the weekends. Will you join a hiking club? In these and countless other situations, efficacy beliefs play a key role in shaping our lives (Judge et al., 2007). Believing that our actions will produce desired results influences the activities and environments we choose (Bandura, 2001; Schultz & Schultz, 2009).

Self-Reinforcement

One more idea deserves mention. At times, we all evaluate our actions and may reward ourselves with special privileges or treats for "good behavior." With this in mind, social learning theory adds the concept of self-reinforcement to the behaviorist view. **Self-reinforcement** refers to praising or rewarding yourself for having made a particular response (such as completing a school assignment). Thus, habits of self-praise and self-blame become an important part of personality (Schultz & Schultz, 2009). In fact, self-reinforcement can be thought of as the social learning theorist's counterpart to the superego.

Self-reinforcement is closely related to high self-esteem. The reverse is also true: Mildly depressed college students tend to have low rates of self-reinforcement. It is not known if low self-reinforcement leads to depression, or the reverse. In either case,

Learning theorist A psychologist interested in the ways that learning shapes behavior and explains personality.

Situational determinants External conditions that strongly influence behavior.

Habit A deeply ingrained, learned pattern of behavior.

Drive Any stimulus (especially an internal stimulus such as hunger) strong enough to goad a person to action.

Cue External stimuli that guide responses, especially by signaling the presence or absence of reinforcement.

Response Any behavior, either observable or internal.

Reward Anything that produces pleasure or satisfaction; a positive reinforcer.

Social learning theory An explanation of personality that combines learning principles, cognition, and the effects of social relationships.

Psychological situation A situation as it is perceived and interpreted by an individual, not as it exists objectively.

Expectancy Anticipation about the effect a response will have, especially regarding reinforcement.

Reinforcement value The subjective value a person attaches to a particular activity or reinforcer.

Self-efficacy Belief in your capacity to produce a desired result.

Self-reinforcement Praising or rewarding oneself for having made a particular response (such as completing a school assignment).

Diane Collins and Jordan Hollender/Getty Images

Through self-reinforcement, we reward ourselves for personal achievements and other "good" behavior.

higher rates of self-reinforcement are associated with less depression and greater life satisfaction (Seybolt & Wagner, 1997). From a behavioral viewpoint, there is value in learning to be "good to yourself."

Behaviorist View of Development

How do learning theorists account for personality development? Many of Freud's ideas can be restated in terms of learning theory. John Dollard and Neal Miller (1950) agree with Freud that the first 6 years are crucial for personality development, but for different reasons. Rather than thinking in terms of psychosexual urges and fixations, they ask, "What makes early learning experiences so lasting in their effects?" Their answer is that childhood is a time of urgent drives, powerful rewards and punishments, and crushing frustrations. Also important is **social reinforcement**, which is based on praise, attention, or approval from others. These forces combine to shape the core of personality (Shaffer, 2009).

Critical Situations

Dollard and Miller believe that during childhood, four **critical situations** are capable of leaving a lasting imprint on personality. These are (1) feeding; (2) toilet or cleanliness training; (3) sex training; and (4) learning to express anger or aggression.

Why are these of special importance? Feeding serves as an illustration. If children are fed when they cry, it encourages them to actively manipulate their parents. The child allowed to cry without being fed learns to be passive. Thus, a basic active or passive orientation toward the world may be created by early feeding experiences. Feeding can also affect later social relationships because the child learns to associate people with pleasure or with frustration and discomfort.

Toilet and cleanliness training can be a particularly strong source of emotion for both parents and children. Rashad's parents were aghast the day they found him smearing feces about with joyful abandon. They reacted with sharp punishment, which frustrated and confused Rashad. Many attitudes toward cleanliness, conformity, and bodily functions are formed at such times. Studies have also long shown that severe, punishing, or frustrating toilet training can have undesirable effects on personality development (Christophersen & Mortweet, 2003). Because of this, toilet and cleanliness training demand patience and a sense of humor.

What about sex and anger? When, where, and how a child learns to express anger and sexual feelings can leave an imprint on personality. Specifically, permissiveness for sexual and aggressive behavior in childhood is linked to adult needs for power (McClelland & Pilon, 1983). This link probably occurs because permitting such behaviors allows children to get pleasure from asserting themselves. As we saw in the last chapter, sex training also involves learning socially defined "male" and "female" gender roles—which, in turn, affects personality (Cervone & Pervin, 2010).

Personality and Gender

From birth onward, children are labeled as boys or girls and encouraged to learn sex-appropriate behavior (Denmark, Rabinowitz, & Sechzer, 2005; Oppliger, 2007).

What does it mean to have a "masculine" or "feminine" personality? According to social learning theory, identification and imitation contribute greatly to personality development and to sex training. **Identification** refers to the child's emotional attachment to admired adults, especially those who provide love and care. Identification typically encourages **imitation**, a desire to act like the admired person. Many "male" or "female" traits come from children's attempts to imitate a same-sex parent with whom they identify (Helgeson, 2009).

© Vic Lee. Reprinted with special permission of King Features Syndicate.

© Mike Powell/Corbis

Adult personality is influenced by identification with parents and imitation of their behavior.

If children are around parents of both sexes, why don't they imitate behavior typical of the opposite sex as well as of the same sex? You may recall from Chapter 6 that learning takes place vicariously as well as directly. This means that we can learn without direct reward by observing and remembering the actions of others. But the actions we choose to imitate depend on their outcomes. For example, boys and girls have equal chances to observe adults and other children acting aggressively. However, girls are less likely than boys to imitate directly aggressive behavior (shouting at or hitting another person). Instead, girls are more likely to rely on indirectly aggressive behavior (excluding others from friendship, spreading rumors). This may well be because the expression of direct aggression is thought to be inappropriate for girls.

As a consequence, girls do not as often see direct female aggression rewarded or approved (Field et al., 2009). In others words, "girlfighting" is likely a culturally reinforced pattern (Brown, 2005). Intriguingly, over the last few years, girls have become more willing to engage in direct aggression as popular culture presents more and more images of directly aggressive women (Artz, 2005).

We have considered only a few examples of the links between social learning and personality. Nevertheless, the connection is unmistakable. When parents accept their children and give them affection, the children become sociable, positive, and emotionally stable, and they have high self-esteem. When parents are rejecting, punishing, sarcastic, humiliating, or neglectful, their children become hostile, unresponsive, unstable, and dependent and have impaired self-esteem (Triandis & Suh, 2002).

Nature and Nurture—The Great Personality Debate

Gateway Question 12.6: *How do heredity and environment affect personality?*

Personality theorists have long grappled with the relative roles of nature and nurture in shaping personalities. Some theories, such as trait theory and psychoanalytic theory, stress the role of inherited biological predispositions, whereas others, including behavioral and humanist theories, stress the role of learning and life experiences. Let's look at the roles that heredity and biological predispositions (nature) and environmental situations (nurture) play in forming personality.

Do We Inherit Personality?

Even newborn babies differ in temperament, which implies that it is hereditary. **Temperament**, the "raw material" from which personalities are formed, refers to the hereditary aspects of your personality, such as biological predispositions to be sensitive, irritable, and distractible and to display a typical mood (Rothbart, 2007). Temperament has a large impact on how infants interact with their parents. Judging from Annette's adult personality, you might guess that she was an active, happy baby.

BRIDGES

Even newborn babies differ in temperament, which implies that it is hereditary. Temperament has a large impact on how infants interact with their parents. **See Chapter 3, page 89.**

At what age are personality traits firmly established? Personality starts to stabilize at around age 3 and continues to "harden" through age 50 (Caspi, Roberts, & Shiner, 2005). However, as mentioned earlier, personality slowly matures during old age as most people continue to become more conscientious, agreeable, and emotionally stable (Roberts & Mroczek, 2008). It appears that stereotypes of the "grumpy old man" and "cranky old woman" are largely unfounded.

Does the stability of personality traits mean that they are affected by heredity? Some breeds of dogs have reputations for being friendly, aggressive, intelligent, calm, or emotional. Such differences fall in the realm of **behavioral genetics**, the study of inherited behavioral traits. We know that facial features, eye color, body type, and many other physical characteristics are inherited. So are many of our behavioral dispositions (Bouchard, 2004; Kalat, 2009). Genetic studies have shown that intelligence, language, some mental disorders, temperament, and other complex qualities are influenced by heredity. In view of such findings, it wouldn't be a surprise to find that genes affect personality as well (Nettle, 2006).

Social reinforcement Praise, attention, approval, and/or affection from others.

Critical situations Situations during childhood that are capable of leaving a lasting imprint on personality.

Identification Feeling emotionally connected to a person and seeing oneself as like him or her.

Imitation An attempt to match one's own behavior to another person's behavior.

Temperament The hereditary aspects of personality, including sensitivity, activity levels, prevailing mood, irritability, and adaptability.

Behavioral genetics The study of inherited behavioral traits and tendencies.

Critical Thinking: The Amazing Twins

Many reunited twins in the Minnesota study (the Minnesota Twins?) have displayed similarities far beyond what would be expected on the basis of heredity. The "Jim twins," James Lewis and James Springer, are one famous example. Both Jims had married and divorced women named Linda. Both had undergone police training. One named his firstborn son James Allan, the other named *his* firstborn son James Alan. Both drove Chevrolets and vacationed at the same beach each summer. Both listed carpentry and mechanical drawing among their hobbies. Both had built benches around trees in their yards. And so forth (Holden, 1980).

Are all identical twins so, well, identical? No, they aren't. Consider identical twins Carolyn Spiro and Pamela Spiro Wagner who, unlike the "Jim Twins," lived together throughout their childhood. While in sixth grade, they found out that President Kennedy had been assassinated. Carolyn wasn't sure why everyone was so upset. Pamela heard voices announcing that she was responsible for his death. After years of hiding her voices from everyone, Pamela tried to commit suicide while the twins were attending Brown University. She was diagnosed with schizophrenia. Never to be cured, she has gone on to write award-winning poetry. Carolyn eventually became a Harvard psychiatrist (Spiro Wagner & Spiro, 2005). Some twins reared apart appear very similar; some reared together appear rather different.

So why are some identical twins, like the Jim Twins, so much alike even if they were reared apart? Although genetics is important, it is preposterous to suggest that there are child-naming genes and bench-building genes. How, then, do we explain the eerie similarities in some separated twins' lives? Imagine that you were separated at birth from a twin brother or sister. If you were reunited with your twin today, what would you do? Quite likely, you would spend the next several days comparing every imaginable detail of your lives. Under such circumstances, it is virtually certain that you and your twin would notice and compile a long list of similarities. ("Wow! I use the same brand of toothpaste you do!") Yet, two unrelated persons of the same age, sex, and race could probably rival your list—*if* they were as motivated to find similarities.

Identical twins Pam (left) and Carolyn (right) were raised together. Regardless, Carolyn became a psychiatrist whereas Pamela developed schizophrenia and went on to become an award-winning poet (Spiro Wagner & Spiro, 2005). Their story illustrates the complex interplay of forces that shape our adult personalities.

In fact, one study compared twins with unrelated pairs of students. The unrelated pairs, who were the same age and sex, were almost as alike as the twins. They had highly similar political beliefs, musical interests, religious preferences, job histories, hobbies, favorite foods, and so on (Wyatt et al., 1984). Why were the unrelated students so similar? Basically, it's because people of the same age and sex live in the same historical times and select from similar societal options. As just one example, in nearly every elementary school classroom, you will find several children with the same first name.

It appears then that many of the seemingly "astounding" coincidences shared by reunited twins may be yet another example of confirmation bias. Reunited twins tend to notice the similarities and ignore the differences.

BRIDGES

Confirmation bias is described in Chapter 1, pages 19–20.

BRIDGES

Behavioral genetic research has helped us better understand the hereditary origins of intelligence and psychological disorders. **See Chapter 9, pages 316–317, and Chapter 14, page 489.**

Wouldn't comparing the personalities of identical twins help answer the question? It would indeed—especially if the twins were separated at birth or soon after.

Studying Twins

For several decades, psychologists at the University of Minnesota have been studying identical twins who grew up in different homes. Medical and psychological tests reveal that reunited twins are very much alike, even when they are reared apart (Bouchard, 2004; Bouchard et al., 1990). They may even be similar in voice quality, facial gestures, hand movements, and nervous tics, such as nail biting. Separated twins also tend to have similar talents. If one twin excels at art, music, dance, drama, or athletics, the other is likely to as well—despite wide differences in childhood environment. However, as "The Amazing Twins" explains, it's wise to be cautious about some reports of extraordinary similarities in reunited twins.

Summary

Studies of twins make it clear that heredity has a sizable effect on each of us. All told, it seems reasonable to conclude that heredity is responsible for about 25 to 50 percent of the variation in many personality traits (Caspi, Roberts, & Shiner, 2005; Loehlin et al., 1998). Notice, however, that the same figures imply that personality is shaped as much, or more, by environment as it is by biological predispositions.

Each personality, then, is a unique blend of heredity and environment, nature and nurture, biology and culture. We are not—thank goodness—genetically programmed robots whose behavior and personality traits are "wired in" for life. Where you go in life is the result of the choices you make. Although these choices are influenced by inherited tendencies, they are not merely a product of your genes (Funder, 2006).

Is Personality Affected by Environment?

Remember Annette? When we heard she actually decked a man who was harassing her, we were surprised. The Annette we had known was always quite calm and peaceful. Had she changed so much? Before we try to provide an answer, take a moment to answer the questions that follow. Doing so will add to your understanding of a long-running controversy in the psychology of personality.

Rate Yourself: How Do You View Personality?

1. My friends' actions are fairly consistent from day to day and in different situations. T or F?
2. Whether a person is honest or dishonest, kind or cruel, a hero or a coward depends mainly on circumstances. T or F?
3. Most people I have known for several years have pretty much the same personalities now as they did when I first met them. T or F?
4. The reason people in some professions (such as teachers, lawyers, or doctors) seem so much alike is because their work requires that they act in particular ways. T or F?
5. One of the first things I would want to know about a potential roommate is what the person's personality is like. T or F?
6. I believe that immediate circumstances usually determine how people act at any given time. T or F?
7. To be comfortable in a particular job, a person's personality must match the nature of the work. T or F?
8. Almost anyone would be polite at a wedding reception; it doesn't matter what kind of personality the person has. T or F?

Now count the number of times you marked true for the odd-numbered items. Do the same for the even-numbered items.

If you agreed with most of the odd-numbered items, you tend to view behavior as strongly influenced by personality traits or lasting personal dispositions, whether biological or learned.

If you agreed with most of the even-numbered items, you view behavior as strongly influenced by external situations and circumstances.

What if I answered true about equally for odd and even items? Then you place equal weight on traits and situations as ways to explain behavior. This is the view now held by many personality psychologists (Funder, 2006; Mischel, Shoda, & Smith, 2008).

Traits, Consistency, and Situations

Does that mean that to predict how a person will act, it is better to focus on both personality traits and external circumstances? Yes, it's best to take both into account. Because personality *traits* are consistent, they can predict such things as job performance, dangerous driving, or a successful marriage (Burger, 2011). Yet, as we mentioned earlier in the chapter, *situations* also greatly influence our behavior. Annette's normally calm demeanor became aggressive only because the situation was unusual and extreme: The man in the bar seriously harassed her, making her uncharacteristically angry and upset.

Can all unusual behaviors be "blamed" on unusual situations? Great question. Consider Fred Cowan, a model student in school and described by those who knew him as quiet, gentle, and a man who loved children. Despite his size (6 feet tall, 250 pounds), Fred was described by a coworker as "someone you could easily push around." Two weeks after he was suspended from his job, Fred returned to work determined to get even with his supervisor. Unable to find the man, he killed four coworkers and a policeman before taking his own life (Lee, Zimbardo, & Bertholf, 1977).

Sudden murderers like Fred Cowan tend to be quiet, overcontrolled individuals. They are likely to be especially violent if they ever lose control. Although their attacks may be triggered by a minor irritation or frustration, the attack reflects years of unexpressed feelings of anger and belittlement. When sudden murderers finally release the strict controls they have maintained on their overcontrolled behavior, a furious and frenzied attack ensues (Cartwright, 2002). Usually it is totally out of proportion to the offense against them, and many have amnesia for their violent actions. So, unlike Annette, who reacted in an unexpected way to an unusual situation, Fred Cowan's overreaction was typical of people who share his personality pattern.

Trait-Situation Interactions

It would be unusual for you to dance at a movie or read a book at a football game. Likewise, few people sleep in roller coasters or tell off-color jokes at funerals. However, your personality traits may predict whether you choose to read a book, go to a movie, or attend a football game in the first place. Typically, traits *interact* with situations to determine how we will act (Mischel, 2004).

In a **trait–situation interaction**, external circumstances influence the expression of a personality trait. For instance, imagine what would happen if you moved from a church to a classroom to a party to a football game. As the setting changed, you would probably become louder and more boisterous. This change would show situational effects on behavior. At the same time, your personality traits would also be apparent: If you were quieter than average in church and class, you would probably be quieter than average in the other settings, too.

Trait-situation interaction The influence that external settings or circumstances have on the expression of personality traits.

Behavioral and Social Learning Theories

RECITE

1. Learning theorists believe that personality "traits" really are ____________ acquired through prior learning. They also emphasize ____________ determinants of behavior.
2. Dollard and Miller consider cues the basic structure of personality. T or F?
3. To explain behavior, social learning theorists include mental elements, such as ____________ (the anticipation that a response will lead to reinforcement).
4. Self-reinforcement is to behaviorist theory as superego is to psychoanalytic theory. T or F?
5. Which of the following is *not* a "critical situation" in the behaviorist theory of personality development?
   a. feeding *b.* sex training *c.* language training *d.* anger training
6. In addition to basic rewards and punishments, a child's personality is also shaped by ____________ reinforcement.
7. Social learning theories of development emphasize the impact of identification and ____________.

REFLECT

Think Critically

8. Rotter's concept of *reinforcement value* is closely related to a motivational principle discussed in Chapter 10. Can you name it?

Self-Reflect

What is your favorite style of food? Can you relate Dollard and Miller's concepts of habit, drive, cue, response, and reward to explain your preference?

One way to describe personality is in terms of a set of "If-Then" rules that relate situations to traits (Kammrath, Mendoza-Denton, & Mischel, 2005). For example, our friend Annette has a trait of independence. But she is not independent in every situation. Here are some If-Then rules for Annette: *If* Annette is working at home, *Then* she is independent. *If* Annette is in a bar being hassled by a man, *Then* she is very independent. *If* Annette has to go for a medical checkup, *Then* she is not very independent. Can you write some If-Then rules which describe your personality?

Answers: 1. habits, situational **2.** F **3.** expectancies **4.** T **5.** c **6.** social **7.** imitation **8.** Incentive value.

Personality Theories—Overview and Comparison

Gateway Question 12.7: *Which personality theory is right?*

To date, each major personality theory has added to our understanding by providing a sort of lens through which human behavior can be viewed. Nevertheless, theories often can't be fully proved or disproved. We can only ask, "Does the evidence tend to support this theory or disconfirm it?" Yet, although theories are neither true nor false, their implications or predictions may be. The best way to judge a theory, then, is in terms of its *usefulness.* Does the theory adequately explain behavior? Does it stimulate new research? Does it suggest how to treat psychological disorders? Each theory has fared differently in these areas (Cervone & Pervin, 2010).

Trait Theories

Traits are very useful for describing and comparing personalities. Many of the personality tests used by clinical psychologists are based on trait theories. However, trait theories tend to have a circular quality. For example, how do we know that a young woman named Carrie has the trait of shyness? Because we frequently observe Carrie avoiding conversations with others. And why doesn't Carrie socialize with others? Because shyness is a trait of her personality. And how do we know she has the trait of shyness? Because we observe that she avoids socializing with others. And so on.

Psychoanalytic Theory

By present standards, psychoanalytic theory seems to exaggerate the impact of sexuality and biological instincts. These distortions were corrected somewhat by the neo-Freudians, but problems remain. One of the most telling criticisms of Freudian theory is that it can explain any psychological event *after* it has occurred. But beforehand, it offers little help in predicting future behavior. For this reason, many psychoanalytic concepts are difficult or impossible to test scientifically (Schick & Vaughn, 1995).

Humanistic Theory

A great strength of the humanists is the attention they have given to positive dimensions of personality. As Maslow (1968) put it, "Human nature is not nearly as bad as it has been thought to be. It is as if Freud supplied us with the sick half of psychology, and we must now fill it out with the healthy half." Despite their contributions, humanists can be criticized for using "fuzzy" concepts that are difficult to measure and study objectively. Even so, humanistic thought has encouraged many people to seek greater self-awareness and personal growth. Also, humanistic concepts have been very useful in counseling and psychotherapy.

Behaviorist and Social Learning Theories

Learning theories have provided a good framework for personality research. Of the major perspectives, the behaviorists have made the best effort to rigorously test and verify their ideas. They have, however, been criticized for understating the impact that temperament, emotion, thinking, and subjective experience have on personality. Social learning theory answers some of these criticisms, but it may still understate the importance of private experience.

We currently need all four major perspectives to explain personality. Each provides a sort of lens through which human behavior can be viewed. In many instances, a balanced picture emerges only when each theory is considered. In the final analysis, the challenge now facing personality theorists is how to integrate the four major perspectives into a unified, systematic explanation of personality (Mayer, 2005; McAdams, & Pals, 2006). ■ Table 12.3 provides a closing overview of the principal approaches to personality.

TABLE 12.3 Comparison of Personality Theories

	Trait Theories	Psychoanalytic Theory	Humanistic Theories	Behaviorist and Social Learning Theories
Role of inheritance (genetics)	Maximized	Stressed	Minimized	Minimized
Role of environment	Recognized	Recognized	Maximized	Maximized
View of human nature	Neutral	Negative	Positive	Neutral
Is behavior free or determined?	Determined	Determined	Free will	Determined
Principal motives	Depends on one's traits	Sex and aggression	Self-actualization	Drives of all kinds
Personality structure	Traits	Id, ego, superego	Self	Habits, expectancies
Role of unconscious	Minimized	Maximized	Minimized	Practically nonexistent
Conception of conscience	Traits of honesty, etc.	Superego	Ideal self, valuing process	Self-reinforcement, punishment history
Developmental emphasis	Combined effects of heredity and environment	Psychosexual stages	Development of self-image	Critical learning situations, identification, and imitation
Barriers to personal growth	Unhealthy traits	Unconscious conflicts, fixations	Conditions of worth, incongruence	Maladaptive habits, unhealthy environment

Personality Assessment—Psychological Yardsticks

Gateway Question 12.8: *How do psychologists measure personality?*

Measuring personality can help predict how people will behave at work, at school, and in therapy. However, painting a detailed picture can be a challenge. In many instances, it requires several of the techniques described in this section. To capture a personality as unique as Annette's, it might take all of them!

How is personality "measured"? Psychologists use interviews, observation, questionnaires, and projective tests to assess personality (Burger, 2011). Each method has strengths and limitations. For this reason, they are often used in combination.

Formal personality measures are refinements of more casual ways of judging a person. At one time or another, you have probably "sized up" a potential date, friend, or roommate by engaging in conversation (interview). Perhaps you have asked a friend, "When I am delayed I get angry. Do you?" (questionnaire). Maybe you watch your professors when they are angry or embarrassed to learn what they are "really" like when they're caught off-guard (observation). Or possibly you have noticed that when you say, "I think people feel . . . ," you may be expressing your own feelings (projection). Let's see how psychologists apply each of these methods to probe personality.

Interviews

In an **interview**, direct questioning is used to learn about a person's life history, personality traits, or current mental state (Murphy & Dillon, 2011; Sommers-Flanagan & Sommers-Flanagan, 2008). In an **unstructured interview**, conversation is informal and topics are taken up freely as they arise. In a **structured interview**, information is gathered by asking a planned series of questions.

How are interviews used? Interviews are used to identify personality disturbances; to select people for jobs, college, or special programs; and to study the dynamics of personality. Interviews also provide information for counseling or therapy. For instance, a counselor might ask a depressed person, "Have you ever contemplated suicide? What were the circumstances?" The counselor might then follow by asking, "How did you feel about it?" or, "How is what you are now feeling different from what you felt then?"

In addition to providing information, interviews make it possible to observe a person's tone of voice, hand gestures, posture, and facial expressions. Such "body language" cues are important because they may radically alter the message sent, as when a person claims to be "completely calm" but trembles uncontrollably.

Computerized Interviews

If you were distressed and went to a psychologist or psychiatrist, what is the first thing she or he might do? Typically, a *diagnostic interview* is used to find out how a person is feeling and what complaints or symptoms he or she has. In many cases, such interviews are based on a specific series of questions. Because the questions are always the same, it has become commonplace to use computers to do the interviewing.

Interview (personality) A face-to-face meeting held for the purpose of gaining information about an individual's personal history, personality traits, current psychological state, and so forth.

Unstructured interview An interview in which conversation is informal and topics are taken up freely as they arise.

Structured interview An interview that follows a prearranged plan, usually a series of planned questions.

What is your impression of the person wearing the beige suit? If you think that she looks friendly, attractive, or neat, your other perceptions of her might be altered by that impression. Interviewers are often influenced by the halo effect (see text).

But do computers do as good a job as humans? Yes. For example, in one study, people were interviewed for symptoms of mania by both a computer and a human (Reilly-Harrington et al., 2010). People thought the computer conducted an acceptable interview. It was also highly accurate.

Limitations

Interviews give rapid insight into personality, but they have limitations. For one thing, interviewers can be swayed by preconceptions. A person identified as a "housewife," "college student," "high school athlete," "punk," "geek," or "ski bum" may be misjudged because of an interviewer's personal biases. Second, an interviewer's own personality, or even gender, may influence a client's behavior. When this occurs, it can accentuate or distort the person's apparent traits (Pollner, 1998). A third problem is that people sometimes try to deceive interviewers. For example, a person accused of a crime might try to avoid punishment by pretending to be mentally disabled.

A fourth problem is the **halo effect**, which is the tendency to generalize a favorable (or unfavorable) impression to an entire personality (Hartung et al., 2010). Because of the halo effect, a person who is likable or physically attractive may be rated more mature, intelligent, or mentally healthy than she or he actually is. The halo effect is something to keep in mind at job interviews. First impressions do make a difference (U.S. Department of Labor, 2009).

Even with their limitations, interviews are a respected method of assessment. In many cases, interviews are the first step in evaluating personality and an essential prelude to therapy. Nevertheless, interviews are usually not enough and must be supplemented by other measures and tests (Murphy & Dillon, 2011; Meyer et al., 2001).

Direct Observation and Rating Scales

Are you fascinated by airports, bus depots, parks, taverns, subway stations, or other public places? Many people relish a chance to observe the actions of others. When used for assessment, **direct observation** (looking at behavior) is a simple extension of this natural interest in "people watching." For instance, a psychologist might arrange to observe a disturbed child as she plays with other children. Is the child withdrawn? Does she become hostile or aggressive without warning? By careful observation, the psychologist can identify the girl's personality traits and clarify the nature of her problems.

Wouldn't observation be subject to the same problems of misperception as an interview? Yes. Misperceptions can be a difficulty, which is why rating scales are sometimes used (● Figure 12.7). A

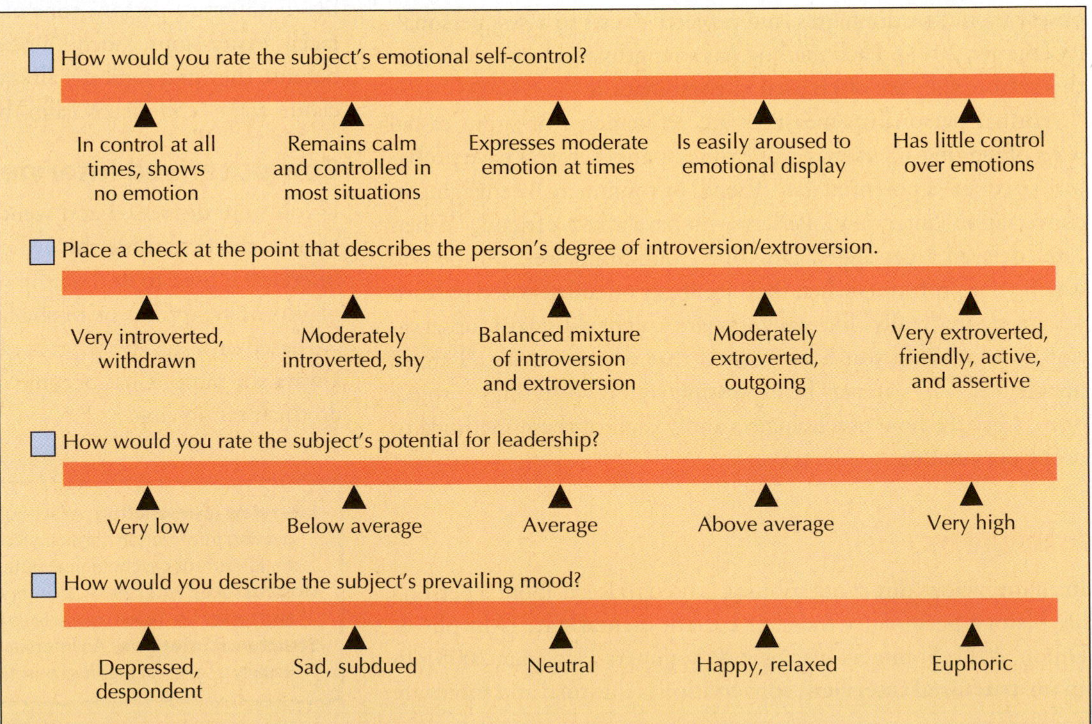

● Figure 12.7 Sample rating scale items. To understand how the scale works, imagine someone you know well. Where would you place check marks on each of the scales to rate that person's characteristics?

rating scale is a list of personality traits or aspects of behavior that can be used to evaluate a person (Siefert, 2010). Rating scales limit the chance that some traits will be overlooked while others are exaggerated (Synhorst et al., 2005). Perhaps there should be a standard procedure for choosing a roommate, spouse, or lover!

An alternative approach is to do a **behavioral assessment** by counting the frequency of specific behaviors. In this case, observers record *actions,* not what traits they think a person has (Ramsay, Reynolds, & Kamphaus, 2002). For example, a psychologist working with hospitalized mental patients might note the frequency of a patient's aggression, self-care, speech, and unusual behaviors. Behavioral assessments can also be used to probe thought processes. In one study, for example, couples were assessed while talking with each other about their sexuality. Couples with sexual difficulties were less likely to be receptive to discussing their sexuality and more likely to blame each other than were couples with no sexual difficulties (Kelly, Strassberg, & Turner, 2006).

Situational Testing

In **situational testing**, a type of direct observation, real-life conditions are simulated so that a person's spontaneous reactions can be observed. Such tests assume that the best way to learn how people react is to put them in realistic situations and watch what happens. Situational tests expose people to frustration, temptation, pressure, boredom, or other conditions capable of revealing personality characteristics (Olson-Buchanan & Drasgow, 2006; Weekley & Jones, 1997). Some popular "reality TV" programs, such as *American Idol, Survivor*, and *The Amazing Race*, bear some similarity to situational tests—which may account for their ability to attract millions of viewers.

How are situational tests done? An interesting example of situational testing is the judgmental firearms training provided by many police departments. At times, police officers must make split-second decisions about using their weapons. A mistake could be fatal. In a typical shoot/don't-shoot test, actors play the part of armed criminals. As various high-risk scenes are acted out live, or on videotape, or by computer, officers must decide to shoot or hold fire. A newspaper reporter who once took the test (and failed it) gives this account (Gersh, 1982):

> I judged wrong. I was killed by a man in a closet, a man with a hostage, a woman interrupted when kissing her lover, and a man I thought was cleaning a shotgun. . . . I shot a drunk who reached for a comb, and a teenager who pulled out a black water pistol. Looked real to me.

Larry St. Pierre/Shutterstock

A police special tactics team undergoes judgmental firearms training. Variations on this situational test are used by many police departments. All officers must score a passing grade.

Personality Questionnaires

Personality questionnaires are paper-and-pencil tests that reveal personality characteristics. Questionnaires are more objective than interviews or observation. (An **objective test** gives the same score when different people correct it.) Questions, administration, and scoring are all standardized so that scores are unaffected by any biases an examiner may have. However, this is not enough to ensure accuracy. A good test must also be reliable and valid. A test is **reliable** if it yields close to the same score each time it is given to the same person. A test has **validity** if it measures what it claims to measure. Unfortunately, many personality tests you will encounter, such as those in magazines or on the Internet, have little or no validity.

BRIDGES

Reliability and validity are important characteristics of all psychological tests, especially intelligence and aptitude tests. **See Chapter 9, pages 365–366.**

Dozens of personality tests are available, including the *Guilford-Zimmerman Temperament Survey*, the *California Psychological Inventory*, the *Allport-Vernon Study of Values*, the *16 PF*, and many more. One of the best-known and most widely used objective tests is the **Minnesota Multiphasic Personality Inventory-2 (MMPI-2)** (Butcher, 2011). The MMPI-2 is composed of 567 items to which a

Halo effect The tendency to generalize a favorable or unfavorable first impression to unrelated details of personality.
Direct observation Assessing behavior through direct surveillance.
Rating scale A list of personality traits or aspects of behavior on which a person is rated.
Behavioral assessment Recording the frequency of various behaviors.
Situational test Simulating real-life conditions so that a person's reactions may be directly observed.
Personality questionnaire A paper-and-pencil test consisting of questions that reveal aspects of personality.
Objective test A test that gives the same score when different people correct it.
Reliability The ability of a test to yield nearly the same score each time it is given to the same person.
Validity The ability of a test to measure what it purports to measure.
Minnesota Multiphasic Personality Inventory-2 (MMPI-2) One of the best-known and most widely used objective personality questionnaires.

test taker must respond "true" or "false." Items include statements such as the following:

Everything tastes the same.
I am very normal, sexually.
I like birds.
I usually daydream in the afternoon.
Mostly, I stay away from other people.
Someone has been trying to hurt me.
Sometimes I think strange thoughts.*

How can these items show anything about personality? For instance, what if a person has a cold so that "everything tastes the same"? For an answer (and a little bit of fun), read the following items. Answer "Yes," "No," or "Don't bother me, I can't cope!"

I have a collection of 1,243 old pizza cartons.
I enjoy the thought of eating liver-flavored ice cream.
I love the smell of napalm in the morning.
I hate the movie *Apocalypse Now.*
I can't add numbers correctly.
Bathing sucks.
I like rats and dry hand towels.
I absolutely adore this textbook.

These items were written by your authors to satirize personality questionnaires. (Why not try writing some of your own?) Such questions may seem ridiculous, but they are not very different from the real thing. How, then, do the items on tests such as the MMPI-2 reveal anything about personality? The answer is that a single item tells little about personality. For example, a person who agrees that "Everything tastes the same" might simply have a cold. It is only through *patterns* of response that personality dimensions are revealed.

Items on the MMPI-2 were selected for their ability to correctly identify persons with particular psychological problems (Butcher, 2011). For instance, if depressed persons consistently answer a series of items in a particular way, it is assumed that others who answer the same way are also prone to depression. As silly as the gag items in the preceding list may seem, it is possible that some could actually work in a legitimate test. But before an item could be part of a test, it would have to be shown to correlate highly with some trait or dimension of personality.

The MMPI-2 measures 10 major aspects of personality (listed in ■ Table 12.4). After the MMPI-2 is scored, results are charted graphically as an **MMPI-2 profile** (● Figure 12.8). By comparing a person's profile with scores produced by typical, normal adults, a psychologist can identify various personality disorders. Additional scales can identify substance abuse, eating disorders, Type A (heart-attack prone) behavior, repression, anger, cynicism, low self-esteem, family problems, inability to function in a job, and other problems (Butcher, 2011).

MMPI-2 statements themselves cannot be reproduced to protect the validity of the test.

■ **TABLE 12.4 MMPI-2 Basic Clinical Subscales**

1. **Hypochondriasis** (HI-po-kon-DRY-uh-sis). Exaggerated concern about one's physical health.
2. **Depression.** Feelings of worthlessness, hopelessness, and pessimism.
3. **Hysteria.** The presence of physical complaints for which no physical basis can be established.
4. **Psychopathic deviate.** Emotional shallowness in relationships and a disregard for social and moral standards.
5. **Masculinity/femininity.** One's degree of traditional "masculine" aggressiveness or "feminine" sensitivity.
6. **Paranoia.** Extreme suspiciousness and feelings of persecution.
7. **Psychasthenia** (sike-as-THEE-nee-ah). The presence of obsessive worries, irrational fears (phobias), and compulsive (ritualistic) actions.
8. **Schizophrenia.** Emotional withdrawal and unusual or bizarre thinking and actions.
9. **Mania.** Emotional excitability, manic moods or behavior, and excessive activity.
10. **Social introversion.** One's tendency to be socially withdrawn.

How accurate is the MMPI-2? Personality questionnaires are accurate only if people tell the truth about themselves. Because of this, the MMPI-2 has additional **validity scales** that reveal whether a person's scores should be discarded. The validity scales detect attempts by test takers to "fake good" (make themselves look good) or "fake bad" (make it look like they have problems). Other scales uncover defensiveness or tendencies to exaggerate shortcomings and troubles. When taking the MMPI-2, it is best to answer honestly, without trying to second-guess the test.

A clinical psychologist trying to decide whether a person has emotional problems would be wise to take more than the MMPI-2 into account. Test scores are informative, but they can incorrectly

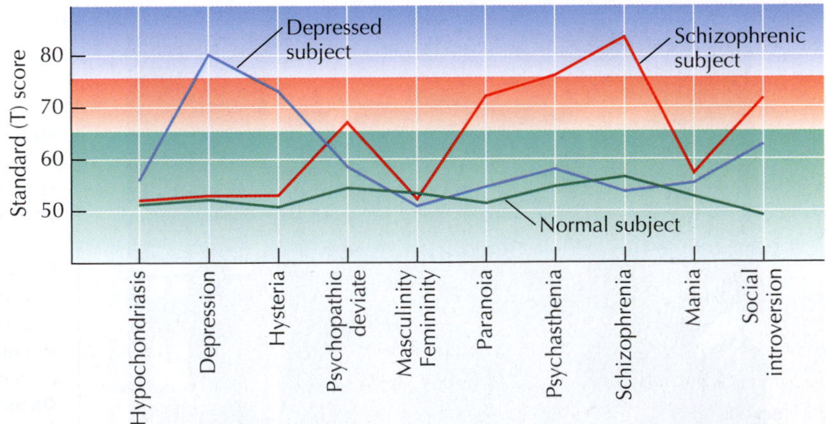

● **Figure 12.8** An MMPI-2 profile showing hypothetical scores indicating normality, depression, and psychosis. High scores begin at 66 and very high scores at 76. An unusually low score (40 and below) may also reveal personality characteristics or problems. Excerpted from the MMPI-2 (Minnesota Multiphasic Inventory 2) Manual for Administration, Scoring, and Interpretation, Revised Edition. Copyright © 2001 by the Regents of the University of Minnesota. All rights reserved. Used by permission of the University of Minnesota Press. "MMPI" and "Minnesota Multiphasic Personality Inventory" are registered trademarks owned by the Regents of the University of Minnesota.

● **Figure 12.9**
Inkblots similar to those used on the Rorschach. What do you see?

label some people (Kaplan & Saccuzzo, 2009). Fortunately, clinical judgments usually rely on information from interviews, tests, and other sources. Also, despite their limitations, it is reassuring to note that psychological assessments are at least as accurate as commonly used medical tests (Neukrug & Fawcett, 2010).

Projective Tests of Personality

Projective tests take a different approach to personality. Interviews, observation, rating scales, and inventories try to directly identify overt, observable traits (Leichtman, 2004). By contrast, projective tests seek to uncover deeply hidden or *unconscious* wishes, thoughts, and needs (Burger, 2011).

As a child you may have delighted in finding faces and objects in cloud formations. Or perhaps you have learned something about your friends' personalities from their reactions to movies or paintings. If so, you will have some insight into the rationale for projective tests. In a **projective test**, a person is asked to describe ambiguous stimuli or make up stories about them. Describing an unambiguous stimulus (a picture of an automobile, for example) tells little about your personality. But when you are faced with an unstructured stimulus, you must organize what you see in terms of your own life experiences. Everyone sees something different in a projective test, and what is perceived can reveal the inner workings of personality.

Projective tests have no right or wrong answers, which makes them difficult to fake (Leichtman, 2004). Moreover, projective tests can be a rich source of information, because responses are not restricted to simple true/false or yes/no answers.

The Rorschach Inkblot Test

Is the inkblot test a projective technique? The **Rorschach** (ROAR-shock) **Inkblot Test** is one of the oldest and most widely used projective tests. Developed by Swiss psychologist Hermann Rorschach in the 1920s, it consists of 10 standardized inkblots. These vary in color, shading, form, and complexity.

How does the test work? First, a person is shown each blot and asked to describe what she or he sees in it (● Figure 12.9). Later, the psychologist may return to a blot, asking the person to identify specific sections of it, to expand previous descriptions, or to give new impressions about what it contains. Obvious differences in content—such as "blood dripping from a dagger" versus "flowers blooming in a basket"—are important for identifying personal conflicts and fantasies. But surprisingly, content is less important than what parts of the inkblot are used to organize images. These factors allow psychologists to detect emotional disturbances by observing how a person perceives the world (Hilsenroth, 2000).

BRIDGES

Schizophrenia and other psychotic disorders are associated with severe disturbances in thinking and perception. Such disturbances are usually readily apparent during projective testing. **See Chapter 14, pages 486–488.**

The Thematic Apperception Test

Another popular projective test is the **Thematic Apperception Test (TAT)**, developed by personality theorist Henry Murray (1893–1988).

How does the TAT differ from the Rorschach? The TAT consists of 20 sketches depicting various scenes and life situations (● Figure 12.10). During testing, a person is shown each sketch and asked to make up a story about the people in it. Later, the person looks at each sketch a second or a third time and elaborates on previous stories or creates new stories.

To score the TAT, a psychologist analyzes the content of the stories. Interpretations focus on how people feel, how they interact, what events led up to the incidents depicted in the sketch, and

MMPI-2 profile A graphic representation of an individual's scores on each of the primary scales of the MMPI-2.

Validity scales Scales that tell whether test scores should be invalidated for lying, inconsistency, or "faking good."

Projective tests Psychological tests making use of ambiguous or unstructured stimuli.

Rorschach Inkblot Test A projective test comprised of 10 standardized inkblots.

Thematic Apperception Test (TAT) A projective test consisting of 20 different scenes and life situations about which respondents make up stories.

• **Figure 12.10** This is a picture like those used for the Thematic Apperception Test. If you wish to simulate the test, tell a story that explains what led up to the pictured situation, what is happening now, and how the action will end.

how the story will end. For example, TAT stories told by bereaved college students typically include themes of death, grief, and coping with loss (Balk et al., 1998).

A psychologist might also count the number of times the central figure in a TAT story is angry, overlooked, apathetic, jealous, or threatened. Here is a story written by a student to describe • Figure 12.10:

> The girl has been seeing this guy her mother doesn't like. The mother is telling her that she better not see him again. The mother says, "He's just like your father." The mother and father are divorced. The mother is smiling because she thinks she is right. But she doesn't really know what the girl wants. The girl is going to see the guy again, anyway.

As this example implies, the TAT is especially good at revealing feelings about a person's social relationships (Aronow et al, 2001; Teglasi, 2010).

Limitations of Projective Testing

Although projective tests have been popular, their validity is considered lowest among tests of personality (Wood et al., 2003). Objectivity and reliability (consistency) are also low for different users of the TAT and Rorschach. Note that after a person interprets an ambiguous stimulus, the scorer must interpret the person's (sometimes) ambiguous responses. In a sense, the interpretation of a projective test may be a projective test for the scorer!

Despite their drawbacks, projective tests still have value (Hilsenroth, 2000). This is especially true when they are used as part of a *test battery* (collection of assessment devices and interviews). In the hands of a skilled clinician, projective tests can be a good way to detect major conflicts, to get clients to talk about upsetting topics, and to set goals for therapy (O'Roark, 2001; Teglasi, 2010).

A Look Ahead

The *Psychology in Action* section that follows should add balance to your view of personality. Don't be shy. Read on!

Knowledge Builder: Personality Assessment

RECITE

1. The halo effect can be a serious problem in accurate personality assessment that is based on
   a. projective testing *b.* behavioral recording *c.* interviewing *d.* the TAT
2. Which of the following is considered the most objective measure of personality?
   a. rating scales *b.* personality questionnaires *c.* projective tests *d.* TAT
3. Situational testing allows direct _____________ of personality characteristics.
4. A psychotic person would probably score highest on which MMPI-2 scale?
   a. depression *b.* hysteria *c.* schizophrenia *d.* mania
5. The use of ambiguous stimuli is most characteristic of
   a. interviews *b.* projective tests *c.* personality inventories *d.* direct observation
6. The content of one's responses to the MMPI-2 is considered an indication of unconscious wishes, thoughts, and needs. T or F?
7. Doing a behavioral assessment requires direct observation of the person's actions or a direct report of the person's thoughts. T or F?
8. Which of the following items *does not* belong with the others?
   a. Rorschach Inkblot Test *b.* TAT *c.* MMPI-2 *d.* projective testing
9. A test is considered valid if it consistently yields the same score when the same person takes it on different occasions. T or F?

REFLECT

Think Critically

10. Can you think of one more reason why personality traits may not be accurately revealed by interviews?
11. Projective testing would be of greatest interest to which type of personality theorist?

Self-Reflect

How do *you* assess personality? Do you informally make use of any of the methods described in this chapter?

You are a candidate for a desirable job. Your personality is going to be assessed by a psychologist. What method (or methods) would you prefer that she or he use? Why?

Answers: 1. c **2.** b **3.** observation **4.** c **5.** b **6.** F **7.** T **8.** c **9.** F **10.** Because of trait-situation interactions, a person may not behave in a normal fashion while being evaluated in an interview. **11.** Psychodynamic, because projective testing is designed to uncover unconscious thoughts, feelings, and conflicts.

Psychology in Action: Barriers and Bridges—Understanding Shyness

Gateway Question 12.9: *What causes shyness and what can be done about it?*

Do you:

- Find it hard to talk to strangers?
- Lack confidence with people?
- Feel uncomfortable in social situations?
- Feel nervous with people who are not close friends?

As a personality trait, **shyness** refers to a tendency to avoid others, as well as feelings of anxiety, preoccupation, and social inhibition (uneasiness and strain when socializing) (Bruch, 2001). Shy persons fail to make eye contact, retreat when spoken to, speak too quietly, and display little interest or animation in conversations (Brunet, Mondloch, & Schmidt, 2010). Mild shyness may be no more than a nuisance. However, extreme shyness (which may be diagnosed as *social anxiety disorder*) is often associated with depression, loneliness, fearfulness, social anxiety, inhibition, and low self-esteem (Ashcraft, 2012; Stein & Stein, 2008).

Elements of Shyness

What causes shyness? To begin with, shy persons often lack **social skills** (proficiency at interacting with others). Many simply have not learned how to meet people or how to start a conversation and keep it going. **Social anxiety** (a feeling of apprehension in the presence of others) is also a factor in shyness. Almost everyone feels nervous in some social situations (such as meeting an attractive stranger). Typically, this is a reaction to **evaluation fears** (fears of being inadequate, embarrassed, ridiculed, or rejected). Although fears of rejection are common, they are much more frequent or intense for shy persons (Bradshaw, 2006; Jackson, Towson, & Narduzzi, 1997). A third problem for shy persons is a **self-defeating bias** (distortion) in their thinking. Specifically, shy persons almost always blame themselves when a social encounter doesn't go well. They are unnecessarily self-critical in social situations (Lundh et al., 2002).

Situational Causes of Shyness

Shyness is most often triggered by *novel* or *unfamiliar* social situations. A person who does fine with family or close friends may become shy and awkward when meeting a stranger. Shyness is also magnified by formality, meeting someone of higher status, being noticeably different from others, or being the focus of attention (as in giving a speech) (Larsen & Buss, 2010).

Don't most people become cautious and inhibited in such circumstances? That's why we need to see how the personalities of shy and not-shy persons differ.

Dynamics of the Shy Personality

There is a tendency to think that shy persons are wrapped up in their own feelings and thoughts. But surprisingly, researchers Jonathan Cheek and Arnold Buss (1979) found no connection between shyness and **private self-consciousness** (attention to inner feelings, thoughts, and fantasies). Instead, they discovered that shyness is linked to **public self-consciousness** (acute awareness of oneself as a social object).

Persons who rate high in public self-consciousness are intensely concerned about what others think of them (Cowden, 2005). They worry about saying the wrong thing or appearing foolish. In public, they may feel "naked" or as if others can "see through them." Such feelings trigger anxiety or outright fear during social encounters, leading to awkwardness and inhibition (Cowden, 2005). The shy person's anxiety, in turn, often causes her or him to misperceive others in social situations (Schroeder, 1995).

As mentioned, almost everyone feels anxious in at least some social situations. But there is a key difference in the way shy and not-shy persons *label* this anxiety. Shy persons tend to consider their social anxiety a *lasting personality trait.* Shyness, in other words, becomes part of their self-concept. In contrast, not-shy persons believe that *external situations* cause their occasional feelings of shyness. When not-shy persons feel anxiety or "stage fright," they assume that almost anyone would feel as they do under the same circumstances (Zimbardo, Pilkonis, & Norwood, 1978).

Labeling is important because it affects *self-esteem*. In general, not-shy persons tend to have higher self-esteem than shy persons. This is because not-shy persons give themselves credit for their social successes and recognize that failures are often due to circumstances. In

Joshua Rainey Photography/Shutterstock

Shyness A tendency to avoid others, plus uneasiness and strain when socializing.

Social skills Proficiency at interacting with others.

Social anxiety A feeling of apprehension in the presence of others.

Evaluation fears Fears of being inadequate, embarrassed, ridiculed, or rejected.

Self-defeating bias A distortion of thinking that impairs behavior.

Private self-consciousness Preoccupation with inner feelings, thoughts, and fantasies.

Public self-consciousness Intense awareness of oneself as a social object.

contrast, shy people blame themselves for social failures, never give themselves credit for successes, and expect to be rejected (Jackson et al., 2002).

Shy Beliefs

What can be done to reduce shyness? Shyness is often maintained by unrealistic or self-defeating beliefs (Antony & Swinson, 2008; Butler, 2001). Here's a sample of such beliefs:

1. *If you wait around long enough at a social gathering, something will happen.*
   Comment: This is really a cover-up for fear of starting a conversation. For two people to meet, at least one has to make an effort, and it might as well be you.
2. *Other people who are popular are just lucky when it comes to being invited to social events or asked out.*
   Comment: Except for times when a person is formally introduced to someone new, this is false. People who are more active socially typically make an effort to meet and spend time with others. They join clubs, invite others to do things, strike up conversations, and generally leave little to luck.
3. *The odds of meeting someone interested in socializing are always the same, no matter where I am.*
   Comment: This is another excuse for inaction. It pays to seek out situations that have a higher probability of leading to social contact, such as clubs, teams, and school events.
4. *If someone doesn't seem to like you right away, they really don't like you and never will.*
   Comment: This belief leads to much needless shyness. Even when a person doesn't show immediate interest, it doesn't mean the person dislikes you. Liking takes time and opportunity to develop.

Unproductive beliefs like the preceding can be replaced with statements such as the following:

1. I've got to be active in social situations.
2. I can't wait until I'm completely relaxed or comfortable before taking a social risk.
3. I don't need to pretend to be someone I'm not; it just makes me more anxious.
4. I may think other people are harshly evaluating me, but actually I'm being too hard on myself.
5. I can set reasonable goals for expanding my social experience and skills.
6. Even people who are very socially skillful are never successful 100 percent of the time. I shouldn't get so upset when an encounter goes badly. (Adapted from Antony & Swinson, 2008; Butler, 2001.)

Social Skills

Learning social skills takes practice (Carducci & Fields, 2007). There is nothing "innate" about knowing how to meet people or start a conversation. Social skills can be directly practiced in a variety of ways. It can be helpful, for instance, to get a tape recorder and listen to several of your conversations. You may be surprised by the way you pause, interrupt, miss cues, or seem disinterested. Similarly, it can be useful to look at yourself in a mirror and exaggerate facial expressions of surprise, interest, dislike, pleasure, and so forth. By such methods, most people can learn to put more animation and skill into their self-presentation.

BRIDGES

For a discussion of related skills, see the section on self-assertion in Chapter 16, pages 570–571.

Conversation

One of the simplest ways to make better conversation is by learning to ask questions. A good series of questions shifts attention to the other person and shows you are interested. Nothing fancy is needed. You can do fine with questions such as, "Where do you (work, study, live)? Do you like (dancing, travel, music)? How long have you (been at this school, worked here, lived here)?" After you've broken the ice, the best questions are often those that are *open ended* (they can't be answered yes or no):

> "What parts of the country have you seen?" (as opposed to, "Have you ever been to Florida?")
>
> "What's it like living on the West Side?" (as opposed to, "Do you like living on the West Side?")
>
> "What kinds of food do you like?" (as opposed to, "Do you like Chinese cooking?")

It's easy to see why open-ended questions are helpful. In replying to open-ended questions, people often give "free information" about themselves. This extra information can be used to ask other questions or to lead into other topics of conversation.

This brief sampling of ideas is no substitute for actual practice. Overcoming shyness requires a real effort to learn new skills and test old beliefs and attitudes. It may even require the help of a counselor or therapist. At the very least, a shy person must be willing to take social risks. Breaking down the barriers of shyness will always include some awkward or unsuccessful encounters. Nevertheless, the rewards are powerful: human companionship and personal freedom.

Knowledge Builder

Understanding Shyness

RECITE

1. Social anxiety and evaluation fears are seen almost exclusively in shy individuals; the not shy rarely have such experiences. T or F?
2. Unfamiliar people and situations most often trigger shyness. T or F?
3. Contrary to what many people think, shyness is *not* related to
   a. private self-consciousness *b.* social anxiety
   c. self-esteem *d.* blaming oneself for social failures
4. Shy persons tend to consider their social anxiety to be a
   a. situational reaction *b.* personality trait
   c. public efficacy *d.* habit
5. Changing personal beliefs and practicing social skills can be helpful in overcoming shyness. T or F?

REFLECT

Critical Thinking

6. Shyness is a trait of Vonda's personality. Like most shy people, Vonda is most likely to feel shy in unfamiliar social settings. Vonda's shy behavior demonstrates that the expression of traits is governed by what concept?

Self-Reflect

If you are shy, see if you can summarize how social skills, social anxiety, evaluation fears, self-defeating thoughts, and public self-consciousness contribute to your social inhibition. If you're not shy, imagine how you would explain these concepts to a shy friend.

Answers: 1. F **2.** T **3.** *a* **4.** *b* **5.** T **6.** trait-situation interaction (again)

Chapter in Review Gateways to Personality

Gateway QUESTIONS REVISITED

12.1 *How do psychologists use the term personality?*

12.1.1 *Personality* refers to a person's consistent and unique patterns of thinking, emotion, and behavior.

12.1.2 Character is personality evaluated, or the possession of desirable qualities.

12.1.3 Personality traits are lasting personal qualities that are inferred from behavior.

12.1.4 Personality types group people into categories on the basis of shared traits.

12.1.5 A positive self-evaluation leads to high self-esteem. Low self-esteem is associated with stress, unhappiness, and depression.

12.1.6 Each of the four major theories of personality, trait, psychodynamic, behaviorist and social learning, and humanistic, combines interrelated assumptions, ideas, and principles to explain personality.

12.2 *Are some personality traits more basic or important than others?*

12.2.1 Trait theories identify qualities that are most lasting or characteristic of a person.

12.2.2 Allport made useful distinctions between common traits and individual traits and among cardinal, central, and secondary traits.

12.2.3 Cattell's theory attributes visible surface traits to the existence of 16 underlying source traits.

12.2.4 Source traits are measured by the *Sixteen Personality Factor Questionnaire* (16 PF).

12.2.5 The five-factor model identifies five universal dimensions of personality: extroversion, agreeableness, conscientiousness, neuroticism, and openness to experience.

12.3 *How do psychodynamic theories explain personality?*

12.3.1 Like other psychodynamic approaches, Sigmund Freud's psychoanalytic theory emphasizes unconscious forces and conflicts within the personality.

12.3.2 In Freud's theory, personality is made up of the id, ego, and superego.

12.3.3 Libido, derived from the life instincts, is the primary energy running the personality. Conflicts within the personality may cause neurotic anxiety or moral anxiety and motivate us to use ego-defense mechanisms.

12.3.4 The personality operates on three levels: the conscious, preconscious, and unconscious.

12.3.5 The Freudian view of personality development is based on a series of psychosexual stages: the oral, anal, phallic, and genital stages. Fixation at any stage can leave a lasting imprint on personality.

12.3.6 Neo-Freudian theorists accepted the broad features of Freudian psychology, but developed their own views. Three representative neo-Freudians are Alfred Adler, Karen Horney, and Carl Jung.

12.4 *What are humanistic theories of personality?*

12.4.1 Humanistic theories stress subjective experience, free choice, self-actualization, and positive models of human nature.

12.4.2 Abraham Maslow's study of self-actualizers showed that they share traits that range from efficient perceptions of reality to frequent peak experiences.

12.4.3 Positive psychologists have identified six human strengths that contribute to well-being and life satisfaction: wisdom and knowledge, courage, humanity, justice, temperance, and transcendence.

12.4.4 Carl Rogers viewed the self as an entity that emerges from personal experience. We tend to become aware of experiences that match our self-image, and exclude those that are incongruent with it.

12.4.5 The incongruent person has a highly unrealistic self-image and/or a mismatch between the self-image and the ideal self. The congruent or fully functioning person is flexible and open to experiences and feelings.

12.4.6 In the development of personality, humanists are primarily interested in the emergence of a self-image and in self-evaluations.

12.4.7 As parents apply conditions of worth to children's behavior, thoughts, and feelings, children begin to do the same. Internalized conditions of worth then contribute to incongruence and disrupt the organismic valuing process.

12.5 *What do behaviorists and social learning theorists emphasize in their approach to personality?*

12.5.1 Behavioral theories of personality emphasize learning, conditioning, and immediate effects of the environment (situational determinants).

12.5.2 Learning theorists John Dollard and Neal Miller consider habits the basic core of personality. Habits express the combined effects of drive, cue, response, and reward.

12.5.3 Social learning theory adds cognitive elements, such as perception, thinking, and understanding to the behavioral view of personality.

12.5.4 Social learning theory is exemplified by Julian Rotter's concepts of the psychological situation, expectancies, and reinforcement value.

12.5.5 The behaviorist view of personality development holds that social reinforcement in four situations is critical. The critical situations are feeding, toilet or cleanliness training, sex training, and anger or aggression training.

12.5.6 Identification and imitation are of particular importance in learning to be "male" or "female."

12.6 *How do heredity and environment affect personality?*

12.6.1 Temperament refers to the hereditary and physiological aspects of one's emotional nature.

12.6.2 Behavioral genetics and studies of identical twins suggest that heredity contributes significantly to adult personality traits.

12.6.3 Biological predispositions (traits) interact with environment (situations) to explain our behavior.

12.7 *Which personality theory is right?*

12.7.1 Each of the four major theories of personality, trait, psychodynamic, behaviorist and social learning, and humanistic, is useful for understanding some aspects of personality.

12.8 *How do psychologists measure personality?*

12.8.1 Techniques typically used for personality assessment are interviews, observation, questionnaires, and projective tests.

12.8.2 Structured and unstructured interviews provide much information, but they are subject to interviewer bias and misperceptions. The halo effect may also lower the accuracy of an interview.

12.8.3 Direct observation, sometimes involving situational tests, behavioral assessment, or rating scales, allows psychologists to evaluate a person's actual behavior.

12.8.4 Personality questionnaires, such as the *Minnesota Multiphasic Personality Inventory-2* (MMPI-2), are objective and reliable, but their validity is open to question.

12.8.5 Projective tests ask a person to project thoughts or feelings to an ambiguous stimulus or unstructured situation.

12.8.6 The *Rorschach Technique,* or inkblot test, is a well-known projective technique. A second is the *Thematic Apperception Test* (TAT).

12.8.7 Projective tests are low in validity and objectivity. Nevertheless, they are considered useful by many clinicians, particularly as part of a test battery.

12.9 *What causes shyness and what can be done about it?*

12.9.1 Shyness typically involves social anxiety, evaluation fears, self-defeating thoughts, public self-consciousness, and a lack of social skills.

12.9.2 Shyness is marked by heightened public self-consciousness and a tendency to regard one's shyness as a lasting trait.

12.9.3 Shyness can be reduced by replacing self-defeating beliefs with more supportive thoughts and by learning social skills.

MEDIA RESOURCES

Web Resources

Internet addresses frequently change. To find an up-to-date list of URLs for the sites listed here, visit your Psychology CourseMate.

Personality Theories Explore an electronic textbook about personality theories.

The Personality Project Access a wide variety of information on personality.

Personality: Theory & Perspectives An undergraduate psychology course about individual differences.

Raymond Cattell Read about Raymond Cattell and his 16 Personality Factor Questionnaire.

Internet Personality Inventory Test yourself on the Big Five.

The Big Five Dimensions Provides additional information about the Big Five, with links to related sites.

Sigmund Freud and the Freud Archives This site provides an extensive collection of links to Internet resources related to Sigmund Freud and his works. Included in this collection are libraries, museums, and biographical materials as well as materials in the Brill Library archives.

Freud & Women Read about the controversy surrounding Freud's views on women.

Psychodynamic and Neo-Freudian Theories Freud's followers did not always agree with his views. Read about their views on personality.

About Humanistic Psychology Discusses the history and future of humanistic psychology.

Maslow's Hierarchy of Needs Read more about Maslow's hierarchy of needs and self-actualization.

Some Observations on the Organization of Personality Read an original article by Carl Rogers.

Information on Self-Efficacy Read about Albert Bandura and the idea of self-efficacy.

Julian Rotter Read about Julian Rotter and his Social Learning Theory.

Controlling Your Own Study Behavior Apply the concept of self-reinforcement to your own studying.

Personality and IQ Tests Multiple links to personality tests and IQ tests that are scored online.

MMPI Explore a research project about the MMPI.

Take a Rorschach Explore Hermann Rorschach's famous inkblot test.

The Shyness Home Page Try several shyness surveys.

Shake Your Shyness Get some tips for dealing with shyness.

Overcoming Shyness More on overcoming shyness.

Interactive Learning

Log in to **CengageBrain** to access the resources your instructor requires. For this book, you can access:

CourseMate brings course concepts to life with interactive learning, study, and exam preparation tools that support the printed textbook. A textbook-specific website, ***Psychology CourseMate*** includes an ***integrated interactive eBook*** and other ***interactive learning tools*** including quizzes, flashcards, videos, and more.

CENGAGE**NOW**™

CengageNOW is an easy-to-use online resource that helps you study in less time to get the grade you want—NOW. Take a pre-test for this chapter and receive a personalized study plan based on your results that will identify the topics you need to review and direct you to online resources to help you master those topics. Then take a post-test to help you determine the concepts you have mastered and what you will need to work on. If your textbook does not include an access code card, go to CengageBrain.com to gain access.

WebTUTOR™

More than just an interactive study guide, **WebTutor** is an anytime, anywhere customized learning solution with an eBook, keeping you connected to your textbook, instructor, and classmates.

If your professor has assigned **Aplia** homework:

1. Sign in to your account.
2. Complete the corresponding homework exercises as required by your professor.
3. When finished, click "Grade It Now" to see which areas you have mastered and which need more work, and for detailed explanations of every answer.

Visit **www.cengagebrain.com** to access your account and purchase materials.

Gateway THEME
Health is affected greatly by lifestyle and behavior patterns, especially those related to stress.

13

Health, Stress, and Coping

Mee Jung's Amazing Race

What a year! Mee Jung had barely managed to survive the rush of make-or-break term papers, projects, and classroom presentations. Then, it was on to the last leg of her race: final exams. Perfectly timed to inflict as much suffering as possible, her two hardest exams fell on the same day! Great.

On the last day of finals, Mee Jung got caught in a traffic jam on her way to school. Two drivers cut her off, and another gave her a one-finger salute. When Mee Jung finally got to campus, the parking lot was swarming with frantic students. Most of them, like her, were within minutes of missing a final exam. At last, Mee Jung spied an empty space. As she started toward it, a Mini Cooper darted around the corner and into "her" place. The driver of the car behind her began to honk impatiently. For a moment, Mee Jung was seized by a colossal desire to karate chop anything in sight.

Finally, after a week and a half of stress, pressure, and frustration, Mee Jung had crossed the finish line. Sleep deprivation, gallons of coffee, junk food, and equal portions of cramming and complaining had carried her through finals. She was off for a summer of karate. At last, she could kick back, relax, and have some fun. Or could she? Just 4 days after the end of school, Mee Jung got a bad cold, followed by bronchitis that lasted for nearly a month.

Mee Jung's experience illustrates what happens when stress, emotion, personal habits, and health collide. Though the timing of her cold might have been a coincidence, odds are it wasn't. Periods of stress are frequently followed by illness.

In the first part of this chapter, we will explore a variety of behavioral health risks. Then, we will look more closely at what stress is and how it affects us. After that, we will emphasize ways of coping with stress, so you can do a better job of staying healthy than Mee Jung did.

Gateway QUESTIONS

13.1 *What is health psychology and how does behavior affect health?*

13.2 *What is stress and what factors determine its severity?*

13.3 *What causes frustration and what are typical reactions to it?*

13.4 *Are there different types of conflict and how do people react to conflict?*

13.5 *What are defense mechanisms?*

13.6 *What do we know about coping with feelings of helplessness and depression?*

13.7 *How is stress related to health and disease?*

13.8 *What are the best strategies for managing stress?*

Health Psychology—Here's to Your Good Health

Gateway Question 13.1: *What is health psychology and how does behavior affect health?*

Most of us agree that our health is priceless. Yet, many diseases and half of all deaths in North America can be traced to our unhealthy behaviors (Mokdad et al., 2004). **Health psychology** aims to use behavioral principles to prevent illness and death and to promote health. Psychologists working in the allied field of **behavioral medicine** apply psychology to manage medical problems, such as diabetes or asthma. Their interests include pain control, helping people cope with chronic illness, stress-related diseases, self-screening for diseases (such as breast cancer), and similar topics (Brannon & Feist, 2010).

Behavioral Risk Factors

A century ago, people died primarily from infectious diseases and accidents. Today, people generally die from **lifestyle diseases**, which are related to health-damaging personal habits (Dombrowski et al., 2007). Examples include heart disease, stroke, HIV/AIDS, and lung cancer (● Figure 13.1). Clearly, some lifestyles promote health, whereas others lead to illness and death (Hales, 2012). As one observer put it, "If you don't take care of yourself, the undertaker will overtake that responsibility for you."

What are some unhealthy behaviors? Some causes of illness are beyond our control, but many behavioral risks can be reduced. **Behavioral risk factors** are actions that increase the chances of disease, injury, or early death. For example, approximately 443,000 people die every year from smoking-related diseases (Centers for Disease Control, 2011). Similarly, roughly 65 percent of all American adults are overweight. Of those, half are extremely overweight, or *obese* (Flegal et al., 2010). Being fat is not just a matter of fashion—in the long run, it could kill you. A person who is overweight at age 20 can expect to lose 5 to 20 years of life expectancy (Fontaine et al., 2003). Being overweight may soon overtake smoking as the main cause of preventable death (Danaei et al., 2009).

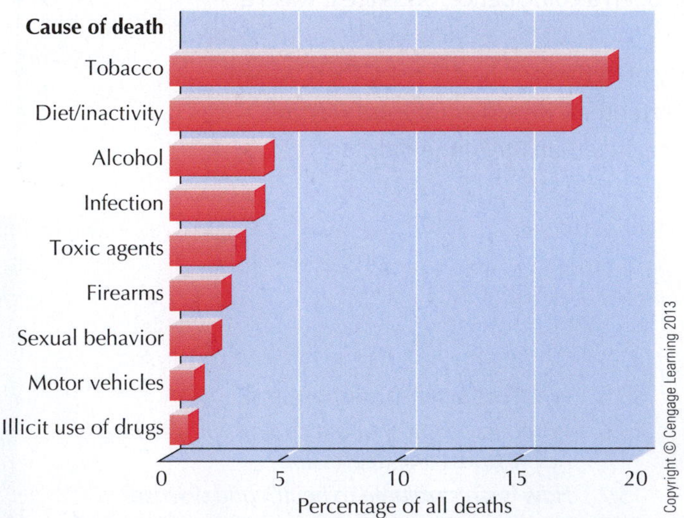

● **Figure 13.1** The nine leading causes of death in the United States are shown in this graph. As you can see, eight of the top nine causes are directly related to behavioral risk factors (infection is the exception). At least 45 percent of all deaths can be traced to unhealthful behavior. The percentage of day-to-day health problems related to unhealthful behavior is even higher (Data from Mokdad et al., 2004).

■ **TABLE 13.1 Percentage of U.S. High School Students Who Engaged in Health-Endangering Behaviors**

Risky Behavior in the Previous 30 Days	Percentage
Rode with drinking driver	28
Were in a physical fight	32
Carried a weapon	18
Drank alcohol	42
Used marijuana	20
Engaged in sexual intercourse	34
Did not use condom during last sexual intercourse	39
Smoked cigarettes	20
Did not eat enough fruits and vegetables	78
Did not get enough physical exercise	81

Source: Eaton et al., 2010.

Each of the following factors is a major behavioral risk (Brannon & Feist, 2010): high levels of stress, untreated high blood pressure, cigarette smoking, abuse of alcohol or other drugs, overeating, inadequate exercise, unsafe sexual behavior, exposure to toxic substances, violence, excess sun exposure, reckless driving, and disregarding personal safety (avoidable accidents). Seventy percent of all medical costs are related to just six of the listed factors—smoking, alcohol abuse, drug abuse, poor diet, insufficient exercise, and risky sexual practices (Brannon & Feist, 2010; Orleans, Gruman, & Hollendonner, 1999). (Unsafe sex is discussed in Chapter 11.)

The personal habits you have by the time you are 18 or 19 greatly affect your health, happiness, and life expectancy years later (Gurung, 2010; Hales, 2012). ■ Table 13.1 shows how many American high school students engage in various kinds of risky behaviors.

Specific risk factors are not the only concern. Some people have a general **disease-prone personality** that leaves them depressed, anxious, hostile, and...frequently ill. In contrast, people who are intellectually resourceful, compassionate, optimistic, and nonhostile tend to enjoy good health (Li et al., 2009; Taylor, 2009). Depression, in particular, is likely to damage health (Luppa et al., 2007). People who are depressed eat poorly, sleep poorly, rarely exercise, fail to use seat belts in cars, smoke more, and so on.

Lifestyle

In your mind's eye, fast-forward an imaginary film of your life all the way to old age. Do it twice—once with a lifestyle including a large number of behavioral risk factors, and again without them. It should be obvious that many small risks can add up, dramatically

In the long run, behavioral risk factors and lifestyles do make a difference in health and life expectancy.

© Exactostock/SuperStock

Medium Stockbyte/SuperStock

raising the chance of illness. If stress is a frequent part of your life, visualize your body seething with emotion, day after day. If you smoke, picture a lifetime's worth of cigarette smoke blown through your lungs in a week. If you drink, take a lifetime of alcohol's assaults on the brain, stomach, and liver and squeeze them into a month: Your body would be poisoned, ravaged, and soon dead. If you eat a high-fat, high-cholesterol diet, fast-forward a lifetime of heart-killing plaque clogging your arteries.

We don't mean to sermonize. We just want to remind you that risk factors make a difference. To make matters worse, unhealthy lifestyles almost always create multiple risks. That is, people who smoke are also likely to drink excessively. Those who overeat usually do not get enough exercise, and so on (Straub, 2012). Even infectious diseases are often linked to behavioral risks. For example, pneumonia and other infections occur at higher rates in people who have cancer, heart disease, lung disease, or liver disease. Thus, many deaths attributed to infections can actually be traced back to smoking, poor diet, or alcohol abuse (Mokdad et al., 2004).

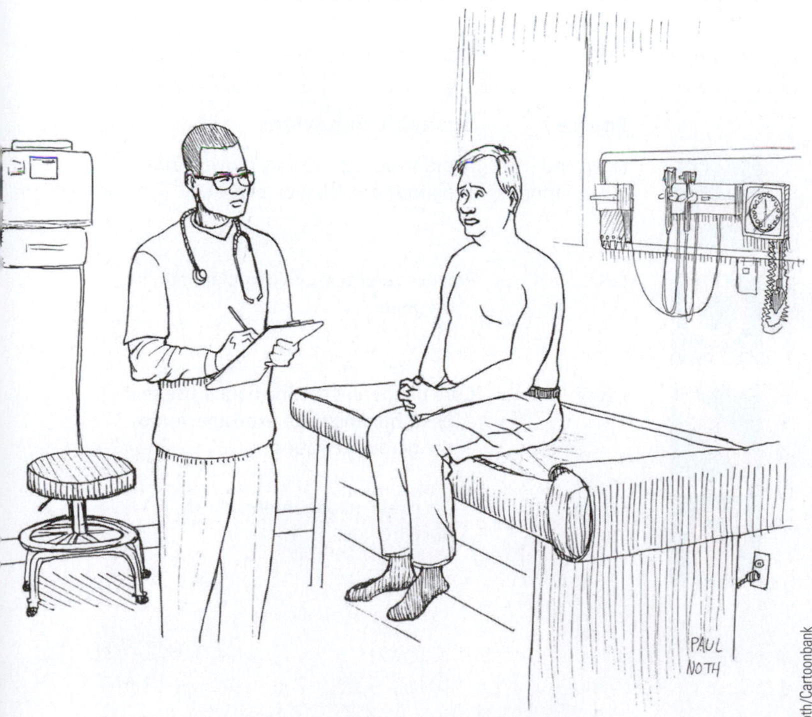

"Will I still be able to not exercise?"

Paul Noth/Cartoonbank

Health-Promoting Behaviors

To prevent disease, health psychologists first try to reduce behavioral risk factors. All the medicine in the world may not be enough to restore health without changes in behavior. We all know someone who has had a heart attack or lung disease who couldn't change the habits that led to his or her illness.

In some cases, lifestyle diseases can be treated or prevented by making specific, minor changes in behavior. For example, hypertension (high blood pressure) can be deadly. Yet, consuming less sodium (salt) can help fend off this "silent killer." (Losing weight, using alcohol sparingly, and getting more exercise will also help (Edenfield & Blumenthal, 2011; Hales, 2012.)

In addition to removing specific risk factors, psychologists are interested in getting people to increase behaviors that *promote* health. Health-promoting behaviors include such obvious practices as getting regular exercise, controlling smoking and alcohol use, maintaining a balanced diet, getting good medical care, and managing stress (Zarcadoolas, Pleasant, & Greer, 2006). In one study, the risk of dying was cut by 65 percent during a 10-year period for adults who were careful about diet, alcohol, exercise, and smoking (Knoops et al., 2004).

Health-promoting behaviors don't have to be restrictive or burdensome. For instance, maintaining a healthy diet doesn't mean surviving on tofu and wheatgrass. The healthiest people in the

Health psychology Study of the ways in which behavioral principles can be used to prevent illness and promote health.
Behavioral medicine The study of behavioral factors in medicine, physical illness, and medical treatment.
Lifestyle disease A disease related to health-damaging personal habits.
Behavioral risk factors Behaviors that increase the chances of disease, injury, or premature death.
Disease-prone personality A personality type associated with poor health; marked by persistent negative emotions, including anxiety, depression, and hostility.

Discovering Psychology: Unhealthy Birds of a Feather

Would you like to eat better, exercise more, or quit smoking? Researchers Nicholas Christakis and James Fowler believe they know why it can be difficult to alter unhealthy behaviors. Often, social factors are a barrier to change. If you are a smoker, do your friends also smoke? Are your family members fast-food junkies just like you? Are your friends all drinkers? Unhealthy behaviors such as overeating or smoking seem to spread almost like a "mental virus" (Christakis & Fowler, 2009).

One study of social contagion found that people were 57 percent more likely to become obese if they had a friend who became fat first (Christakis & Fowler, 2007). Similarly, smokers tend to "hang out" with other smokers (Christakis & Fowler, 2008). Another study found that spending time with drinkers increases alcohol consumption (Ali & Dwyer, 2010). Apparently, we tend to flock together with like-minded people and adopt many of their habits.

Does that mean I am doomed to be unhealthy if my family and friends have unhealthy habits? Not necessarily. Social networks can also spread healthy behaviors (Fowler & Christakis, 2010). If one smoker in a group of smokers quits, others are more likely to follow suit. If your spouse quits smoking, you are 67 percent more likely to quit. If a good friend quits smoking, your chances of abandoning tobacco go up by 36 percent (Christakis & Fowler, 2008). The growing social unpopularity of smoking may be the best explanation of why fewer and fewer American adults (now only 19 percent) still smoke (Schroeder, 2008).

The implication? Don't wait for your friends or family to adopt healthier habits. Take the lead and get them to join you. Failing that, start hanging out with a healthier crowd. You might catch something healthy.

study just described ate a tasty "Mediterranean diet" higher in fruit, vegetables, and fish and lower in red meat and dairy products. Likewise, you don't need to exercise like an Olympic athlete to benefit from physical activity. All you need is 30 minutes of exercise (the equivalent of a brisk walk) three or four times a week. Almost everyone can fit such "lifestyle physical activity" into their schedule (Pescatello, 2001).

What about alcohol? Moderation in drinking doesn't mean that you must be a teetotaler. Consuming one or two alcoholic drinks per day is generally safe for most people, especially if you remain alcohol free 2 or 3 days a week. A glass of red wine daily may even be healthy (Anekonda, 2006). However, having three or more drinks a day greatly increases the risk for stroke, cirrhosis of the liver, cancer, high blood pressure, heart disorders, and other diseases (Knoops et al., 2004).

To summarize, a small number of behavioral patterns accounts for many common health problems (Eaton et al., 2010; Straub, 2012). ■ Table 13.2 lists several major ways to promote good health. (To explore an interesting social factor underlying common health problems, see "Unhealthy Birds of a Feather.")

■ TABLE 13.2 Major Health-Promoting Behaviors

Source	Desirable Behaviors
Tobacco	Do not smoke; do not use smokeless tobacco.
Nutrition	Eating a balanced, low-fat diet; appropriate caloric intake; maintenance of healthy body weight.
Exercise	At least 30 minutes of aerobic exercise, 5 days per week.
Blood pressure	Lower blood pressure with diet and exercise, or medicine if necessary.
Alcohol and drugs	No more than 2 drinks per day; abstain from using drugs.
Sleep and relaxation	Avoid sleep deprivation; provide for periods of relaxation every day.
Sex	Practice safer sex; avoid unplanned pregnancy.
Injury	Curb dangerous driving habits, use seat belts; minimize sun exposure; forgo dangerous activities.
Stress	Learn stress management; lower hostility.

Early Prevention

Of the behavioral risks we have discussed, smoking is the largest preventable cause of death and the single most lethal factor (National Center for Chronic Disease Prevention and Health Promotion, 2010). As such, it illustrates the prospect for preventing illness.

What have health psychologists done to lessen the risks of smoking? Attempts to "immunize" youths against pressures to start smoking are a good example. When humorist Mark Twain said, "Giving up smoking is the easiest thing in the world. I know because I've done it thousands of times," he stated a basic truth—only 1 smoker in 10 has long-term success at quitting (Krall, Garvey, & Garcia, 2002). Thus, the best way to deal with smoking is to prevent it before it becomes a lifelong habit. For example, prevention programs in schools discourage smoking with quizzes about smoking, multiimedia presentations, antismoking art contests, poster and T-shirt giveaways, antismoking pamphlets for parents, and questions for students to ask their parents (Prokhorov et al., 2010; Zarcadoolas, Pleasant, & Greer, 2006). Such efforts are designed to persuade kids that smoking is dangerous and "uncool." Apparently, many teens are getting the message, as attitudes toward smoking are now more negative than they were 20 years ago (Chassin et al., 2003).

Some antismoking programs include **refusal skills training**. In this case, youths learn to resist pressures to begin smoking (or using other drugs). For example, junior high students can role-play ways to resist smoking pressures from peers, adults, and cigarette ads. Similar methods can be applied to other health risks, such as sexually transmitted diseases and teen pregnancy (Wandersman & Florin, 2003).

Celebrities can help persuade young people to not start smoking in the first place.

Many health programs also teach students general life skills. The idea is to give kids skills that will help them cope with day-to-day stresses. That way, they will be less tempted to escape problems through drug use or other destructive behaviors. **Life skills training** includes practice in stress reduction, self-protection, decision making, goal setting, self-control, and social skills (Corey & Corey, 2010; Tobler et al., 2000).

Community Health

In addition to early prevention, health psychologists have had some success with **community health campaigns**. These are community-wide education projects designed to lessen major risk factors (Lounsbury & Mitchell, 2009; Orleans, 2000). Health campaigns inform people of risks such as stress, alcohol abuse, high blood pressure, high cholesterol, smoking, sexually transmitted diseases, or excessive sun exposure. This is followed by efforts to motivate people to change their behavior. Campaigns sometimes provide *role models* (positive examples) who show people how to improve their own health. They also direct people to services for health screening, advice, and treatment. Health campaigns may reach people through the mass media, public schools, health fairs, workplaces, or self-help programs.

Positive Psychology: Wellness

Health is not just an absence of disease (Allen, Carlson, & Ham, 2007; Diener & Chan, 2011). People who are truly healthy enjoy a positive state of **wellness** or well-being. Maintaining wellness is a lifelong pursuit and, hopefully, a labor of love. People who attain optimal wellness are both physically and psychologically healthy. They are happy, optimistic, self-confident individuals who can bounce back emotionally from adversity (Tugade, Fredrickson, & Barrett, 2004).

People who enjoy a sense of well-being also have supportive relationships with others, do meaningful work, and live in a clean environment. Many of these aspects of wellness are addressed elsewhere in this book. In this chapter, we will pay special attention to the effect that stress has on health and sickness. Understanding stress and learning to control it can improve not only your health, but the quality of your life as well (Hales, 2012; Suinn, 2001). For these reasons, a discussion of stress and stress management follows.

Refusal skills training Program that teaches youths how to resist pressures to begin smoking. (Can also be applied to other drugs, and health risks.)

Life skills training A program that teaches stress reduction, self-protection, decision making, self-control, and social skills.

Community health campaign A community-wide education program that provides information about how to lessen risk factors and promote health.

Wellness A positive state of good health; more than the absence of disease.

Knowledge Builder Health Psychology

RECITE

1. Adjustment to chronic illness and the control of pain are topics that would more likely be of interest to a specialist in ______________ ______________ rather than a health psychologist.
2. With respect to health, which of the following is *not* a major behavioral risk factor?
   a. overexercise *b.* cigarette smoking *c.* stress *d.* high blood pressure
3. Lifestyle diseases related to just six behaviors account for 70 percent of all medical costs. The behaviors are smoking, alcohol abuse, drug abuse, poor diet, insufficient exercise, and
   a. driving too fast *b.* excessive sun exposure *c.* unsafe sex *d.* exposure to toxins
4. Health-promoting behaviors that combat hypertension include the following: lose weight, consume less sodium, use alcohol sparingly, and get more
   a. sleep *b.* exercise *c.* carbohydrates *d.* cholesterol
5. Health psychologists tend to prefer ______________ rather than modifying habits (like smoking) that become difficult to break once they are established.
6. The disease-prone personality is marked by ______________, anxiety, and hostility.

REFLECT

Think Critically

7. The general public is increasingly well informed about health risks and healthful behavior. Can you apply the concept of reinforcement to explain why so many people fail to act on this information?

Self-Reflect

If you were to work as a health psychologist, would you be more interested in preventing disease or managing it?

Make a list of the major behavioral risk factors that apply to you. Are you laying the foundation for a lifestyle disease?

Which of the health-promoting behaviors listed in Table 13.2 would you like to increase?

If you were designing a community health campaign, who would you use as role models of healthful behavior?

Answers: 1. behavioral medicine **2.** *a* **3.** *c* **4.** *b* **5.** prevention **6.** depression **7.** Many of the health payoffs are delayed by months or years, greatly lessening the immediate rewards for healthful behavior (Watson & Tharp, 2007).

Stress—Thrill or Threat?

Gateway Question 13.2: *What is stress and what factors determine its severity?*

Stress can be can be a major behavioral risk factor if it is prolonged or severe, but it isn't always bad. As Canadian stress research pioneer Hans Selye (SEL-yay) (1976) observed, "To be totally without stress is to be dead." That's because **stress** is the mental and physical condition that occurs when we adjust or adapt to the environment. Unpleasant events such as work pressures, marital problems, or financial woes naturally produce stress. But so do travel, sports, a new job, rock climbing, dating, and other positive activities. Even if you aren't a thrill seeker, a healthy lifestyle may include a fair amount of *eustress* (good stress). Activities that provoke "good stress" are usually challenging, rewarding, and energizing.

Regardless of whether it is triggered by a pleasant or an unpleasant event, a **stress reaction** begins with the same autonomic nervous system (ANS) arousal that occurs during emotion. Imagine you are standing at the top of a wind-whipped ski jump for the first time. Internally, you would experience a rapid surge in your heart rate, blood pressure, respiration, muscle tension, and other ANS responses. *Short-term* stresses of this kind can be uncomfortable, but they rarely do any damage. (Your landing might, however.) *Long-term* stresses are another matter entirely.

General Adaptation Syndrome

The impact of long-term stresses can be understood by examining the body's defenses against stress, a pattern known as the **general adaptation syndrome (GAS)**. The GAS is a series of bodily reactions to prolonged stress. Selye (1976) noticed that the first symptoms of almost any disease or trauma (poisoning, infection, injury, or stress) are almost identical. The body responds in the same way to any stress, be it infection, failure, embarrassment, a new job, trouble at school, or a stormy romance.

How does the body respond to stress? The GAS consists of three stages: an alarm reaction, a stage of resistance, and a stage of exhaustion (Figure 13.2) (Selye, 1976).

In the **alarm reaction**, your body mobilizes its resources to cope with added stress. The pituitary gland signals the adrenal glands to produce more adrenaline, noradrenaline, and cortisol. As these stress hormones are dumped into the bloodstream, some bodily processes are speeded up and others are slowed. This allows bodily resources to be applied where they are needed.

We should all be thankful that our bodies automatically respond to emergencies. But brilliant as this emergency system is, it can also cause problems. In the first phase of the alarm reaction, people have such symptoms as headache, fever, fatigue, sore muscles, shortness

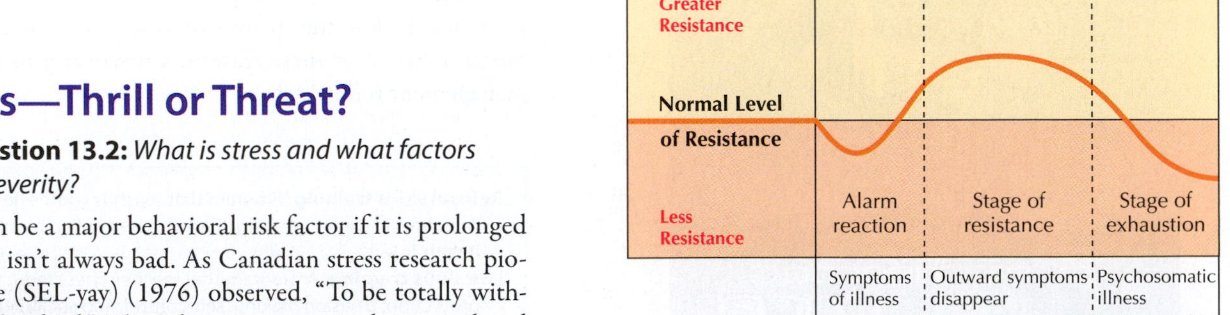

Figure 13.2 The General Adaptation Syndrome. During the initial alarm reaction to stress, resistance falls below normal. It rises again as bodily resources are mobilized, and it remains high during the stage of resistance. Eventually, resistance falls again as the stage of exhaustion is reached. From *The Stress of Life* by Hans Selye. Copyright © 1976 by Hans Selye. Used by permission of McGraw-Hill Book Company.

of breath, diarrhea, upset stomach, loss of appetite, and a lack of energy. Notice that these are also the symptoms of being sick, of stressful travel, of high-altitude sickness, of final exams week, and (possibly) of falling in love!

During the **stage of resistance**, bodily adjustments to stress stabilize. As the body's defenses come into balance, symptoms of the alarm reaction disappear. Outwardly, everything seems normal. However, this appearance of normality comes at a high cost. The body is better able to cope with the original stressor, but its resistance to other stresses is lowered. For example, animals placed in extreme cold become more resistant to the cold but more susceptible to infection. It is during the stage of resistance that the first signs of psychosomatic disorders (physical disorders triggered by psychological factors) begin to appear.

Continued stress leads to the **stage of exhaustion**, in which the body's resources are drained and stress hormones are depleted. Some of the typical signs or symptoms of impending exhaustion include the following (Friedman, 2002; Gurung, 2010):

Emotional signs: Anxiety, apathy, irritability, mental fatigue.
Behavioral signs: Avoidance of responsibilities and relationships, extreme or self-destructive behavior, self-neglect, poor judgment.
Physical signs: Excessive worry about illness, frequent illness, exhaustion, overuse of medicines, physical ailments and complaints.

The GAS may sound melodramatic if you are young and healthy or if you've never endured prolonged stress. However, you should not take stress lightly. Unless a way of relieving stress is found, the result will be a psychosomatic disease, a serious loss of health, or complete collapse. When Selye examined animals in the later stages of the GAS, he found that their adrenal glands were enlarged and discolored. There was intense shrinkage of internal organs, such as the thymus, spleen, and lymph nodes, and many animals had stomach ulcers. In addition to such direct effects, stress can disrupt the body's immune system, as described next.

Stress, Illness, and Your Immune System

How can prolonged stress result in a physical illness? An answer can be found in your body's *immune system*, which mobilizes defenses (such as white blood cells) against invading microbes and other disease agents. The immune system is regulated, in part, by the brain. Because of this link, stress and upsetting emotions can affect the immune system in ways that increase susceptibility to disease (Miller, Cohen, & Ritchey, 2002; Zachariae, 2009). By the way, the study of links among behavior, stress, disease, and the immune system is called **psychoneuroimmunology** (Daruna, 2004; Kendall-Tackett, 2010). (Try dropping that into a conversation sometime if you want to see a stress reaction!)

Studies show that the immune system is weakened in students during major exam times, as Mee Jung found out during her mad dash to the end of term. Immunity is also lowered by divorce, bereavement, a troubled marriage, job loss, poor sleep, depression, and similar stresses (Motivala & Irwin, 2007; Segerstrom & Miller, 2004). Lowered immunity explains why the "double whammy" of getting sick when you are trying to cope with prolonged or severe stress is so common (Pedersen, Bovbjerg, & Zachariae, 2011). Stress causes the body to release substances that increase inflammation. This is part of the body's self-protective response to threats, but it can prolong infections and delay healing (Wargo, 2007). It's also worth noting again the value of positive emotions. Happiness, laughter, and delight tend to strengthen immune system response. Doing things that make you happy can also protect your health (Diener & Chan, 2011; Rosenkranz et al., 2003).

Could reducing stress help prevent illness? Yes. Various psychological approaches, such as support groups, relaxation exercises, guided imagery, and stress management training, can actually boost immune system functioning (Dougall & Baum, 2003). By doing so, they help promote and restore health. For example, stress management reduced the severity of cold and flu symptoms in a group of university students (Reid, Mackinnon, & Drummond, 2001).

Stress and negative emotions lower immune system activity and increase inflammation. This, in turn, raises our vulnerability to infection, worsens illness, and delays recovery.

Stress The mental and physical condition that occurs when a person must adjust or adapt to the environment.
Stress reaction The physical response to stress, consisting mainly of bodily changes related to autonomic nervous system arousal.
General adaptation syndrome (GAS) A series of bodily reactions to prolonged stress; occurs in three stages: alarm, resistance, and exhaustion.
Alarm reaction First stage of the GAS, during which bodily resources are mobilized to cope with a stressor.
Stage of resistance Second stage of the GAS, during which bodily adjustments to stress stabilize, but at a high physical cost.
Stage of exhaustion Third stage of the GAS, at which time the body's resources are exhausted and serious health consequences occur.
Psychoneuroimmunology Study of the links among behavior, stress, disease, and the immune system.

There is even evidence that stress management can improve the chances of survival in people with life-threatening diseases, such as cancer, heart disease, and HIV/AIDS (Schneiderman et al., 2001). With some successes to encourage them, psychologists are now searching for the best combination of treatments to help people resist disease (Miller & Cohen, 2001).

When Is Stress a Strain?

It goes almost without saying that some events are more likely to cause stress than others. A **stressor** is a condition or event that challenges or threatens a person. Police officers, for instance, suffer from a high rate of stress-related diseases. The threat of injury or death—plus occasional confrontations with angry, drunk, or hostile citizens—takes a toll. A major factor is the *unpredictable* nature of police work. An officer who stops a car to issue a traffic ticket never knows if a cooperative citizen or an armed gang member is waiting inside.

A revealing study shows how unpredictability adds to stress. In a series of 1-minute trials, college students breathed air through a mask. In some trials, the air contained 20 percent more carbon dioxide (CO_2) than normal. If you were to inhale this air, you would feel anxious, stressed, and a little like you were suffocating. Students tested this way hated the "surprise" doses of CO_2. They found it much less stressful to be told in advance which trials would include a choking whiff of CO_2 (Lejuez et al., 2000).

Pressure is another element of stress, especially job stress. **Pressure** occurs when a person must meet *urgent* external demands or expectations (Szollos, 2009). For example, we feel pressured when activities must be speeded up, when deadlines must be met, when extra work is added, or when we must work near maximum capacity for long periods. Most students who have survived final exams are familiar with the effects of pressure.

© Daniel G. Lavoie/Corbis

Air traffic control is stressful work. Employees must pay intense attention for long periods, they have little control over the pace of work, and the consequences of making a mistake can be dire.

TABLE 13.3 The Top 10 Work Stresses

Work Stress	Rank
Workload	1
Feeling undervalued	2
Deadlines	3
Type of work people have to do	4
Having to take on other people's work	5
Lack of job satisfaction	6
Lack of control over the working day	7
Having to work long hours	8
Frustration with the working environment	9
Performance targets	10

Source: Data from Skillsoft, 2006.

What if I set deadlines for myself? Does it make a difference where the pressure comes from? Yes. People generally feel more stress in situations over which they have little or no control (Leiter, Gascón, & Martínez-Jarreta, 2010; Taris et al., 2005). In one study, nurses with a high sense of control (e.g., over the pacing of work and the physical arrangement of the working environment) were less likely to get sick, either physically or mentally, than nurses with a low sense of control (Ganster, Fox, & Dwyer, 2001).

To summarize, when emotional "shocks" are *intense* or *repeated, unpredictable, uncontrollable*, and linked to *pressure*, stress will be magnified, and damage is likely to result. At work, people face many of these sources of stress every day (see Table 13.3 for a list of the most common sources of stress at work). In fact, chronic job stress sometimes results in *burnout*.

Burnout

Burnout occurs when workers are physically, mentally, and emotionally drained (Leiter, Gascón, & Martínez-Jarreta, 2010). When people become burned out, they experience emotional exhaustion, cynicism or detachment, and feelings of reduced personal accomplishment (Maslach, Schaufeli, & Leiter, 2001).

Burnout may occur in any job, but it is a special problem in emotionally demanding helping professions, such as nursing, teaching, social work, childcare, counseling, or police work. Also, people who are more passionate about their work are more vulnerable to burnout (Garrosa et al., 2008; Vallerand, 2010). If we wish to keep caring people in the helping professions, it may be necessary to adjust workloads, rewards, and the amount of control people have in their jobs (Leiter & Maslach, 2005).

Can college students experience burnout? Yes, they can (Parker & Salmela-Aro, 2011). If you have a negative attitude toward your studies and feel that your college workload is too heavy, you may be vulnerable to burnout (Jacobs & Dodd, 2003). On the other hand, if you have a positive attitude toward your studies, participate in extracurricular activities, and enjoy good social support from your friends, rock on!

Appraising Stressors

It might seem that stressful events "happen to" us. Sometimes this is true, but as noted earlier, our emotions are greatly affected by how we appraise situations. That's why some people are distressed by events that others view as a thrill or a challenge (eustress). Ultimately, stress depends on how you perceive a situation. Our friend, Akihito, would find it stressful to listen to five of his son's hip-hop CDs in a row. His son, Takashi, would find it stressful to listen to *one* of his father's opera CDs. To know if you are stressed, we must know what meaning you place on events. As we will see in a moment, whenever a stressor is appraised as a *threat* (potentially harmful), a powerful stress reaction follows (Lazarus, 1991a; Smith & Kirby, 2011).

BRIDGES

See Chapter 10, pages 359–360, for a discussion of how appraisal influences emotions.

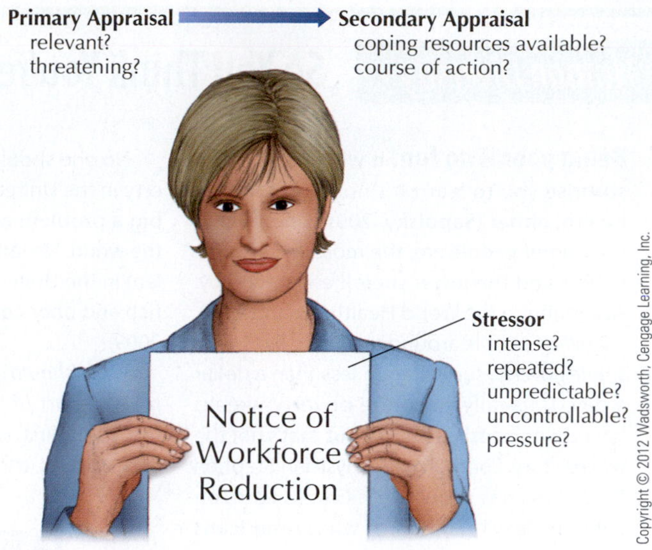

• Figure 13.3 Stress is the product of an interchange between a person and the environment.

"Am I Okay or in Trouble?"

You have been selected to give a speech to 300 people. Or a doctor tells you that you must undergo a dangerous and painful operation. Or the one true love of your life walks out the door. What would your emotional response to these events be? How do you cope with a threat?

According to Richard Lazarus (1991a), there are two important steps in managing a threat. The first is a **primary appraisal**, in which you decide whether a situation is relevant or irrelevant, positive or threatening. In essence, this step answers the question, "Am I okay or in trouble?" Then you make a **secondary appraisal**, in which you assess your resources and choose a way to meet the threat or challenge. ("What can I do about this situation?") Thus, the way a situation is "sized up" greatly affects our ability to cope with it (• Figure 13.3). Public speaking, for instance, can be appraised as an intense threat or as a chance to perform. Emphasizing the threat—by imagining failure, rejection, or embarrassment—obviously invites disaster (Strongman, 2003). (For an example of how changing your appraisal may make a big difference in your life, see "So You Think You're Poor.")

The Nature of Threat

What does it mean to feel threatened by a stressor? Certainly, in most day-to-day situations, it doesn't mean you think your life is in danger. (Unless, of course, you owe money to "The Hulk.") Threat has more to do with the idea of control. We are particularly prone to feel stressed when we can't—or think we can't—control our immediate environment. In short, a *perceived* lack of control is just as threatening as an actual lack of control. For example, college students who feel overloaded experience stress even though their workload may not actually be heavier than that of their classmates (Jacobs & Dodd, 2003).

A sense of control also comes from believing you can reach desired goals. It is threatening to feel that we lack *competence* to cope with life's demands (Bandura, 2001; Leiter, Gascón, & Martínez-Jarreta, 2010). Because of this, the intensity of your body's stress reaction often depends on what you think and tell yourself about a stressor. That's why it's valuable to learn to think in ways that ward off the body's stress response. (Some strategies for controlling upsetting thoughts are described in the *Psychology in Action* section of this chapter.)

Stressor A specific condition or event in the environment that challenges or threatens a person.

Pressure A stressful condition that occurs when a person must meet urgent external demands or expectations.

Burnout A work-related condition of mental, physical, and emotional exhaustion.

Primary appraisal Deciding if a situation is relevant to oneself and if it is a threat.

Secondary appraisal Deciding how to cope with a threat or challenge.

Human Diversity So You Think You're Poor

Being poor is no fun. It will probably not surprise you to learn it's no good for your health, either (Sapolsky, 2005). In general, the poorer people are, the more their health suffers and the lower their life expectancy. According to the World Health Organization, 1.2 *billion* people around the world live in *absolute poverty*, surviving on less than a dollar a day. Tragically, absolute poverty wreaks havoc with people's health. But that's not the whole story. For example, physician Stephen Bezruchka has shown that Greeks earn, on average, less than half of what Americans earn and yet have a longer life expectancy (Bezruchka as cited in Sapolsky, 2005).

How could this be? One possible answer is hinted at in another study that found poorer women in California are more likely to die if they live in better-off neighborhoods than if they live in poorer neighborhoods (Winkleby, Ahn, & Cubbin, 2006). Apparently, being constantly reminded that you are *relatively poor* piles on an extra measure of stress (Wilkinson & Pickett, 2006, 2007). Add to that the fact that the United States currently has the largest income inequalities in the developed world. Constantly living with an awareness of their relative poverty, then, may help explain why Americans have shorter life expectancies than Greeks.

No one should pretend that relative poverty in the United States is anywhere near as big a problem as absolute poverty around the world. Nevertheless, it is a growing problem in the United States as the gap between rich and poor continues to widen (Emerson, 2009).

What should I do if I always feel poor? That may be part of the reason you are reading this book. First, commit to changing your circumstances through education and hard work. That's called *problem-focused coping* (you'll read about it in a few paragraphs). In the meantime, remember Lazarus's (1991a,b) point about appraisal: It's only a stressor if you appraise it as one. A realistic appraisal of your situation may reveal that you are actually "richer" than you think you are. Maybe the best things in life are not all free. But why make yourself sick comparing yourself to people much better off than you (Wilkinson & Pickett, 2009)?

Zachary L. Powers/PhotoLibrary

Although being poor in the United States may mean living above an absolute poverty level, it also means constantly living with stress of dramatic income inequality (Wilkinson & Pickett, 2009).

Coping with Threat

You have appraised a situation as threatening. What will you do next? You have two major choices. Both involve thinking and acting in ways that help us handle stressors. In **emotion-focused coping**, we try to control our emotional reactions to the situation. For example, a distressed person may distract herself by listening to music, taking a walk to relax, or seeking emotional support from others. In contrast, **problem-focused coping** is aimed at managing or correcting the distressing situation itself. Some examples are making a plan of action or concentrating on your next step (Herman & Tetrick, 2009; Smith & Kirby, 2011).

Couldn't both types of coping occur together? Yes. Sometimes the two types of coping aid one another. For instance, quieting your emotions may make it easier for you to find a way to solve a problem. Say, for example, that you feel anxious as you step in front of your class to give a presentation. If you take a few deep breaths to reduce your anxiety (emotion-focused coping), you will be better able to glance over your notes to improve your delivery (problem-focused coping).

It is also possible for coping efforts to clash. For instance, if you have to make a difficult decision, you may suffer intense emotional distress. In such circumstances, there is a temptation to make a quick, ill-advised choice, just to end the suffering. Doing so may allow you to cope with your emotions, but it shortchanges problem-focused coping.

In general, problem-focused coping tends to be especially useful when you are facing a controllable stressor—that is, a situation you can actually do something about. Emotion-focused efforts are best suited to managing your reaction to stressors you cannot control (Folkman & Moskowitz, 2004; Smith & Kirby, 2011). To improve your chances of coping effectively, the stress-fighting strategies described in this chapter include a mixture of both techniques.

So far, our discussion has focused on everyday stresses. How do people react to the extreme stresses imposed by war, violence, or disaster? "Coping with Traumatic Stress" discusses this important topic.

The Clinical File Coping with Traumatic Stress

Traumatic experiences produce psychological injury or intense emotional pain. Victims of **traumatic stresses**, such as war, torture, rape, assassination, plane crashes, natural disasters, and street violence, may suffer from nightmares, flashbacks, insomnia, irritability, nervousness, grief, emotional numbing, and depression. For example, the 2011 earthquake, tsunami, and resulting nuclear crisis in Japan along with the resulting chaos has been a traumatically stressful event.

People who personally witness or survive a disaster are most affected by traumatic stress. Twenty percent of the people who lived close to the World Trade Center in New York City suffered serious stress disorders after the 9/11 terrorist attack (Galea et al., 2002). Yet, even those who experience horror at a distance may be traumatized (Galea & Resnick, 2005). Forty-four percent of U.S. adults who only saw the 9/11 attacks on television had at least some stress symptoms (Schuster et al., 2001). For example, Americans faced elevated risks of hypertension and heart problems for 3 years after 9/11 (Holman et al., 2008). Indirect exposure to such terrorist attacks, coupled with the ongoing risk of more attacks, has ensured that many people will suffer ongoing stress into the foreseeable future (Marshall et al., 2007).

Traumatic stress produces feelings of helplessness and vulnerability (Fields & Margolin, 2001). Victims realize that disaster could strike again without warning. In addition to feeling threatened, many victims sense that they are losing control of their lives (Scurfield, 2002).

What can people do about such reactions? Psychologists recommend the following:

- Identify what you are feeling and talk to others about your fears and concerns.
- Think about the skills that have helped you overcome adversity in the past and apply them to the present situation.
- Continue to do the things that you enjoy and that make life meaningful (LeDoux & Gorman, 2001).
- Get support from others. This is a major element in recovery from all traumatic events.
- Give yourself time to heal. Fortunately, most people are more resilient than they think.

When traumatic stresses are severe or repeated, some people have even more serious symptoms. They suffer from crippling anxiety or become emotionally numb. Typically, they can't stop thinking about the disturbing event, they anxiously avoid anything associated with the event, and they are constantly fearful or nervous. Such reactions can leave victims emotionally handicapped for months or years after a disaster. The consequences can last a lifetime for children who are the victims of trauma (Gillespie & Nemeroff, 2007). If you feel that you are having trouble coping with a severe emotional shock, consider seeking help from a psychologist or other professional (Bisson et al., 2007).

AP Photo/E. Pablo Kosmicki

There can be no doubt that mountain climber Aron Ralston experienced a trauma. After suffering a fall, his arm became impossibly wedged between two boulders. Left with no choice, he amputated his own arm with a dull knife. Remarkably, he survived to overcome his trauma, and the resulting disability, to climb again. Ralston (2003) told his story in his book, *Between a Rock and a Hard Place*, which inspired the 2010 film *127 Hours*.

BRIDGES

These are the symptoms of *stress disorders,* which are discussed in Chapter 14, pages 498–499.

Frustration—Blind Alleys and Lead Balloons

Gateway Question 13.3: *What causes frustration and what are typical reactions to it?*

Do you remember how frustrated Mee Jung was when she couldn't find a parking place? **Frustration** is a negative emotional state that occurs when people are prevented from reaching desired goals. In Mee Jung's case, the goal of finding a parking space was blocked by another car.

Obstacles of many kinds cause frustration. A useful distinction can be made between external and personal sources of frustration. *External frustration* is based on conditions outside a person that impede progress toward a goal. All the following are external frustrations: getting stuck with a flat tire; having a marriage proposal rejected; finding the cupboard bare when you go to get your poor dog a bone; being chased out of the house by your starving dog. In other words, external frustrations are based on *delays*, *failure*, *rejection*, *loss*, and other direct blocking of motivated behavior.

Emotion-focused coping Managing or controlling one's emotional reaction to a stressful or threatening situation.

Problem-focused coping Directly managing or remedying a stressful or threatening situation.

Traumatic stresses Extreme events that cause psychological injury or intense emotional pain.

Frustration A negative emotional state that occurs when one is prevented from reaching a goal.

Notice that external obstacles can be either *social* (slow drivers, tall people in theaters, people who cut into lines) or *nonsocial* (stuck doors, a dead battery, rain on the day of the game). If you ask your friends what has frustrated them recently, most will probably mention someone's behavior ("My sister wore one of my dresses when I wanted to wear it," "My supervisor is unfair," "My history teacher grades too hard"). As social animals, we humans are highly sensitive to social sources of frustration (Taylor, 2009). That's probably why unfair treatment associated with racial or ethnic prejudice is a major source of frustration and stress in the lives of many African Americans and other minority group members (Clark et al., 1999; Gurung, 2010).

Frustration usually increases as the *strength*, *urgency*, or *importance* of a blocked motive increases. Mee Jung was especially frustrated in the parking lot because she was late for an exam. (Likewise, an escape artist submerged in a tank of water and bound with 200 pounds of chain would become *quite* frustrated if a trick lock jammed.) Remember, too, that motivation becomes stronger as we near a goal. As a result, frustration is more intense when a person runs into an obstacle very close to a goal. If you've ever missed an A grade by five points, you were probably very frustrated. If you've missed an A by one point—well, frustration builds character, right?

A final factor affecting frustration is summarized by the old phrase "the straw that broke the camel's back." The effects of *repeated* frustrations can accumulate until a small irritation sets off an unexpectedly violent response. A case in point is the fact that people with long daily commutes are more likely to display "road rage" (angry, aggressive driving) (Sansone & Sansone, 2010).

Personal frustrations are based on personal characteristics. If you are 4 feet tall and aspire to be a professional basketball player, you very likely will be frustrated. If you want to go to medical school but can earn only D grades, you will likewise be frustrated. In both examples, frustration is actually based on personal limitations. Yet, failure may be *perceived* as externally caused. We will return to this point in a discussion of stress management. In the meantime, let's look at some typical reactions to frustration.

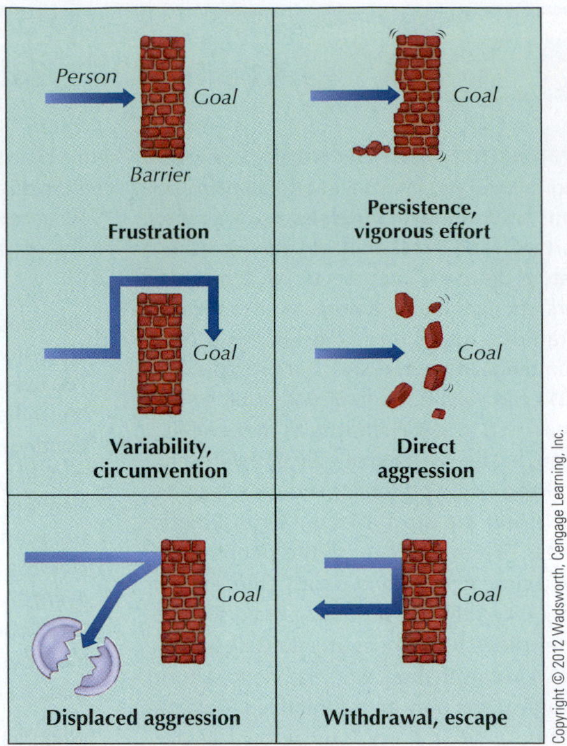

• **Figure 13.4** Frustration and common reactions to it.

Reactions to Frustration

Aggression is any response made with the intent of harming a person or an object. It is one of the most persistent and frequent responses to frustration (Anderson & Bushman, 2002; Shaver & Mikulincer, 2011).

Does frustration always cause aggression? Aren't there other reactions? Although the connection is strong, frustration does not always incite aggression. More often, frustration is met first with *persistence*, often in the form of more vigorous efforts and varied responses (• Figure 13.4). For example, if you put your last dollar in a vending machine and pressing the button has no effect, you will probably press harder and faster (vigorous effort). Then you will press all the other buttons (varied response). Persistence may help you reach your goal by getting *around* a barrier. However, if the machine *still* refuses to deliver, or return your dollar, you may become aggressive and kick the machine (or at least tell it what you think of it).

Persistence can be very adaptive. Overcoming a barrier ends the frustration and allows the need or motive to be satisfied. The same is true of aggression that removes or destroys a barrier. Picture a small band of nomadic humans, parched by thirst but separated from a water hole by a menacing animal. It is easy to see that attacking the animal may ensure their survival. In modern society, such direct aggression is seldom acceptable. If you find a long line at the drinking fountain, aggression is hardly appropriate. Because direct aggression is discouraged, it is frequently *displaced*.

How is aggression displaced? Directing aggression toward a source of frustration may be impossible, or it may be too dangerous. If you are frustrated by your boss at work or by a teacher at school, the cost of direct aggression may be too high (losing your job or failing a class). Instead, the aggression may be displaced, or redirected, toward whomever or whatever is available. Targets of **displaced aggression** tend to be safer, or less likely to retaliate, than the original source of frustration. At one time or another, you have probably lashed out at a friend or relative who was not the real cause of your annoyance. As this suggests, excessive anger over a minor irritation is a common form of displaced aggression (Miller et al., 2003).

Psychologists attribute much hostility to displaced aggression. A disturbing example is the finding that unemployment and divorce are associated with increased child abuse (Weissman, Jogerst, & Dawson, 2003). In a pattern known as **scapegoating**, a person or a group is blamed for conditions not of their making. A *scapegoat* is a person who has become a habitual target of displaced

Steve Nagy/Photolibrary

Paintball seems to bring out aggressive impulses in many players. Wild shoot-outs are part of the fun, but are some players displacing aggressive urges related to frustration in other areas of their lives?

aggression. Despite recent progress, many minority groups continue to face hostility based on scapegoating. Think, for example, about the hostility expressed toward illegal immigrants during times of economic hardship. In many communities, layoffs and job losses are closely linked to increased violence (Catalano, Novaco, & McConnell, 1997; Glick, 2008). Or think about the hostility expressed toward anyone in the United States who looked even vaguely "foreign" right after the 9/11 terrorist attacks.

I have a friend who dropped out of school to hitchhike around the country. He seemed very frustrated before he quit. What type of response to frustration is that? Another major reaction to frustration is escape, or withdrawal. It is stressful and unpleasant to be frustrated. If other reactions do not reduce frustration, a person may try to escape. **Escape** may mean actually leaving a source of frustration (dropping out of school, quitting a job, leaving an unhappy marriage), or it may mean psychologically escaping. Two common forms of psychological escape are feigned apathy (pretending not to care) and the use of drugs such as cocaine, alcohol, marijuana, or narcotics. Notice that these are examples of *ineffective* emotion-focused coping. (See ● Figure 13.4 for a summary of common reactions to frustration.)

Coping with Frustration

In a classic experiment, a psychologist studying frustration placed rats on a small platform at the top of a tall pole. Then, he forced them to jump off the platform toward two elevated doors, one locked and the other unlocked. If the rat chose the correct door, it swung open and the rat landed safely on another platform. Rats who chose the locked door bounced off it and fell into a net far below.

The problem of choosing the open door was made unsolvable and very frustrating by randomly alternating which door was locked. After a time, most rats adopted a stereotyped response. That is, they chose the same door every time. This door was then permanently locked. All the rat had to do was jump to the other door to avoid a fall, but time after time the rat bounced off the locked door (Maier, 1949).

Isn't that an example of persistence? No. Persistence that is *inflexible* can turn into "stupid," stereotyped behavior like that of a rat on a jumping platform. When dealing with frustration, you must know when to quit and establish a new direction. Here are some suggestions to help you avoid needless frustration:

1. Try to identify the source of your frustration. Is it external or personal?
2. Is the source of frustration something that can be changed? How hard would you have to work to change it? Is it under your control at all?
3. If the source of your frustration can be changed or removed, are the necessary efforts worth it?

The answers to these questions help determine whether persistence will be futile. There is value in learning to accept gracefully those things that cannot be changed.

It is also important to distinguish between *real* barriers and *imagined* barriers. All too often we create our own imaginary barriers. For example, Corazon wants a part-time job to earn extra money. At the first place she applied, she was told that she didn't have enough "experience." Now, she complains of being frustrated because she wants to work but cannot. She needs "experience" to work, but can't get experience without working. She has quit looking for a job.

Is Corazon's need for experience a real barrier? Unless she applies for *many* jobs, it is impossible to tell whether she has overestimated its importance. For her, the barrier is real enough to prevent further efforts, but with persistence she might locate an "unlocked door." If a reasonable amount of effort does show that experience is essential, it might be obtained in other ways—through temporary volunteer work, for instance.

Conflict—Yes, No, Yes, No, Yes, No, Well, Maybe

Gateway Question 13.4: *Are there different types of conflict and how do people react to conflict?*

Conflict occurs whenever a person must choose between contradictory needs, desires, motives, or demands. Choosing between college and work, marriage and single life, or study and

Aggression Any response made with the intent of causing harm.

Displaced aggression Redirecting aggression to a target other than the actual source of one's frustration.

Scapegoating Blaming a person or a group of people for conditions not of their making.

Escape Reducing discomfort by leaving frustrating situations or by psychologically withdrawing from them.

Conflict A stressful condition that occurs when a person must choose between incompatible or contradictory alternatives.

● **Figure 13.5** Three basic forms of conflict. For this woman, choosing between pie and ice cream is a minor approach-approach conflict; deciding whether to take a job that will require weekend work is an approach-avoidance conflict; and choosing between paying higher rent and moving is an avoidance-avoidance conflict.

failure are common conflicts. There are four basic forms of conflict. As we will see, each has its own properties (● Figure 13.5 and ● Figure 13.6).

Approach-Approach Conflicts

A simple **approach-approach conflict** comes from having to choose between two positive, or desirable, alternatives. Choosing between tutti-frutti-coconut-mocha-champagne ice and orange-marmalade-peanut butter-coffee swirl at the ice cream parlor may throw you into a temporary conflict. However, if you really like both choices, your decision will be quickly made. Even when more important decisions are at stake, approach-approach conflicts tend to be the easiest to resolve. The old fable about the mule that died of thirst and starvation while standing between a bucket of water and a bucket of oats is obviously unrealistic. When both options are positive, the scales of decision are easily tipped one direction or the other.

Avoidance-Avoidance Conflicts

Being forced to choose between two negative, or undesirable, alternatives creates an **avoidance-avoidance conflict**. A person in an avoidance conflict is caught between "the devil and the deep blue sea," "the frying pan and the fire," or "a rock and a hard place." In real life, double-avoidance conflicts involve dilemmas such as choosing between unwanted pregnancy and abortion, the dentist and tooth decay, a monotonous job and poverty, or dorm food and starvation.

Suppose that I consider any pregnancy sacred and not to be tampered with. Or suppose I don't object to abortion? Like many other stressful situations, these examples can be defined as conflicts only on the basis of personal needs and values. If a woman would not consider abortion under any circumstances, she experiences no conflict. If she wants to end a pregnancy and does not object to abortion, there is also no conflict.

Avoidance conflicts often have a "damned if you do, damned if you don't" quality. In other words, both choices are negative, but *not choosing* may be impossible or equally undesirable. To illustrate, imagine the plight of a person trapped in a hotel fire 20 stories from the ground. Should she jump from the window and almost surely die on the pavement? Or should she try to dash through the flames and almost surely die of smoke inhalation and burns? When faced with a choice such as this, it is easy to see why people often *freeze*, finding it impossible to decide or take action. In actual disasters of this sort, people are often found dead in their rooms, victims of an inability to take action.

Indecision, inaction, and freezing are not the only reactions to double-avoidance conflicts. Because avoidance conflicts are stressful and difficult to solve, people sometimes pull out of them entirely. This reaction, called *leaving the field*, is another form of escape. It may explain the behavior of a student who could not attend school unless he worked. However, if he worked he could not earn passing grades. His solution after much conflict and indecision? He joined the Navy.

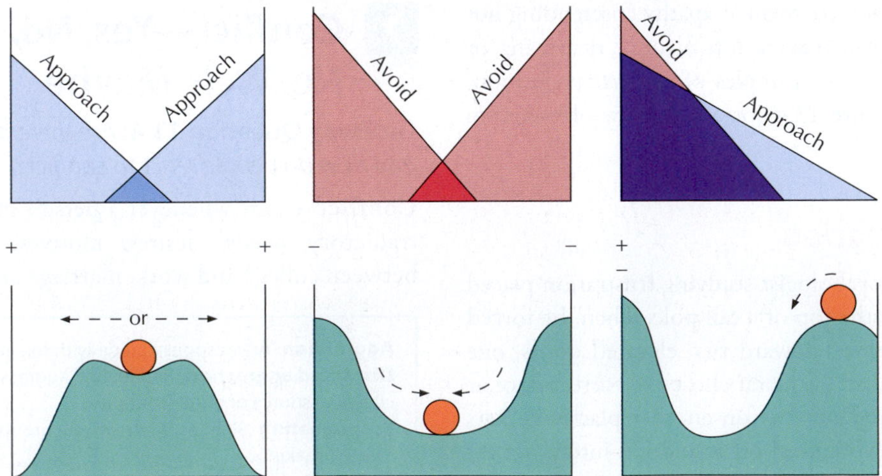

● **Figure 13.6** Conflict diagrams. As shown by the colored areas in the graphs, desires to approach and to avoid increase near a goal. The effects of these tendencies are depicted below each graph. The "behavior" of the ball in each example illustrates the nature of the conflict above it. An approach conflict *(left)* is easily decided. Moving toward one goal will increase its attraction *(graph)* and will lead to a rapid resolution. (If the ball moves in either direction, it will go all the way to one of the goals.) In an avoidance conflict *(center)*, tendencies to avoid are deadlocked, resulting in inaction. In an approach-avoidance conflict *(right)*, approach proceeds to the point at which desires to approach and avoid cancel each other. Again, these tendencies are depicted *(below)* by the action of the ball. (Graphs adapted from Miller, 1944.)

Approach-Avoidance Conflicts

Approach-avoidance conflicts are also difficult to resolve. In some ways, they are more troublesome than avoidance conflicts because people seldom escape them. A person in an **approach-avoidance conflict** is "caught" by being attracted to, and repelled by, the same goal or activity. Attraction keeps the person in the situation, but its negative aspects cause turmoil and distress. For example, a high school student arrives to pick up his date for the first time. He is met at the door by her father, who is a professional wrestler—7 feet tall, 300 pounds, and entirely covered with hair. The father gives the boy a crushing handshake and growls that he will break him in half if the girl is not home on time. The student considers the girl attractive and has a good time. But does he ask her out again? It depends on the relative strength of his attraction and his fear. Almost certainly, he will feel *ambivalent* about asking her out again, knowing that another encounter with her father awaits him.

Ambivalence (mixed positive and negative feelings) is a central characteristic of approach-avoidance conflicts. Ambivalence is usually translated into *partial approach* (Miller, 1944). Because our student is still attracted to the girl, he may spend time with her at school and elsewhere. But he may not actually date her again. Some more realistic examples of approach-avoidance conflicts are planning to marry someone your parents strongly disapprove of, wanting to be in a play but suffering stage fright, wanting to buy a car but not wanting to make monthly payments, and wanting to eat when you're already overweight. Many of life's important decisions have approach-avoidance dimensions.

Multiple Conflicts

Aren't real-life conflicts more complex than the ones described here? Yes. Conflicts are rarely as clear-cut as those described. People in conflict are usually faced with several dilemmas at once, so several types of conflict may be intermingled. The fourth type of conflict moves us closer to reality. In a **double approach-avoidance conflict** each alternative has both positive and negative qualities. For example, you are offered two jobs: One has good pay but poor hours and dull work; the second has interesting work and excellent hours, but low pay. Which do you select? This situation is more typical of the choices we must usually make. It offers neither completely positive nor completely negative options.

As with single approach-avoidance conflicts, people faced with double approach-avoidance conflicts feel ambivalent about each choice. This causes them to *vacillate*, or waver, between the alternatives. Just as you are about to choose one such alternative, its undesirable aspects tend to loom large. So, what do you do? You swing back toward the other choice.

In real life it is common to face **multiple approach-avoidance conflicts** in which several alternatives each have positive and negative features. An example would be trying to choose which automobile to buy among several brands. Another example is trying to decide between two college majors, each with advantages and disadvantages. When multiple approach-avoidance conflicts involve major life decisions, such as choosing a career, a school, a mate, or a job, they can add greatly to the amount of stress we experience.

Managing Conflicts

How can I handle conflicts more effectively? Most of the suggestions made earlier concerning frustration also apply to conflicts. However, here are some additional things to remember when you are in conflict or must make a difficult decision:

1. Don't be hasty when making important decisions. Hasty decisions are often regretted. Even if you do make a faulty decision, it will trouble you less if you know that you did everything possible to avoid a mistake.
2. Try out important decisions *partially* when possible. If you are thinking about moving to a new town, try to spend a few days there first. If you are choosing between colleges, do the same. If classes are in progress, sit in on some. If you want to learn to scuba dive, rent equipment for a reasonable length of time before buying.
3. Look for workable compromises. Again, it is important to get all available information. If you think that you have only one or two alternatives and they are undesirable or unbearable, seek the aid of a teacher, counselor, minister, or social service agency. You may be overlooking possible alternatives these people will know about.
4. When all else fails, make a decision and live with it. Indecision and conflict exact a high cost. Sometimes it is best to select a course of action and stick with it unless it is very obviously wrong after you have taken it.

Conflicts are a normal part of life. With practice, you can learn to manage many of the conflicts you will face.

Knowledge Builder: Stress, Frustration, and Conflict

RECITE

1. The first signs of psychosomatic disorders begin to appear during the stage of
   a. alarm *b.* exhaustion *c.* resistance *d.* appraisal
2. Students taking stressful final exams are more susceptible to the cold virus, a pattern best explained by the concept of
   a. the disease-prone personality *b.* psychoneuroimmunology *c.* emotion-focused coping *d.* reaction formation
3. Whereas stressful incidents suppress the immune system, stress management techniques have almost no effect on immune system functioning. T or F?

Continued

Approach-approach conflict Choosing between two positive, or desirable, alternatives.

Avoidance-avoidance conflict Choosing between two negative, or undesirable, alternatives.

Approach-avoidance conflict Being attracted to and repelled by the same goal or activity.

Ambivalence Mixed positive and negative feelings or simultaneous attraction and repulsion.

Double approach-avoidance conflict Being simultaneously attracted to and repelled by each of two alternatives.

Multiple approach-avoidance conflict Being simultaneously attracted to and repelled by each of several alternatives.

4. Emotional exhaustion, cynicism, and reduced accomplishment are characteristics of job ______________.
5. Stress tends to be greatest when a situation is appraised as a ______________ and a person does not feel ______________ to cope with the situation.
6. According to Richard Lazarus, choosing a way to meet a threat or challenge takes place during the
   a. primary stress reaction *b.* secondary stress reaction *c.* primary appraisal *d.* secondary appraisal
7. Which of the following is *not* a common reaction to frustration?
   a. ambivalence *b.* aggression *c.* displaced aggression *d.* persistence
8. Displaced aggression is closely related to the pattern of behavior known as
   a. scapegoating *b.* leaving the field *c.* stereotyped responding *d.* burnout
9. You would be most likely to experience vacillation if you found yourself in
   a. an approach-approach conflict *b.* an avoidance-avoidance conflict *c.* a double approach-avoidance conflict *d.* the condition called emotion-focused coping

REFLECT

Think Critically

10. Which do you think would produce more stress: (a) appraising a situation as mildly threatening but feeling like you are totally incompetent to cope with it, or (b) appraising a situation as very threatening but feeling that you have the resources and skills to cope with it?
11. Frustration is unpleasant. If some action, including aggression, ends frustration, why might we expect the action to be repeated on other occasions?

Self-Reflect

Can you say "psychoneuroimmunology"? Have you impressed anyone with the word yet?

What impact did pressure, control, predictability, repetition, and intensity have on your last stress reaction?

What type of coping do you tend to use when you face a stressor such as public speaking or taking an important exam?

Think of a time when you were frustrated. What was your goal? What prevented you from reaching it? Was your frustration external or personal?

Have you ever displaced aggression? Why did you choose another target for your hostility?

Review the major types of conflict and think of a conflict you have faced that illustrates each type. Did your reactions match those described in the text?

Answers: 1. *c* **2.** *b* **3.** F **4.** burnout **5.** threat, competent **6.** *d* **7.** *a* **8.** *a* **9.** *c* **10.** There is no correct answer here because individual stress reactions vary greatly. However, the secondary appraisal of a situation often determines just how stressful it is. Feeling incapable of coping is very threatening. **11.** If a response ends discomfort, the response has been negatively reinforced. This makes it more likely to occur in the future (see Chapter 6).

Psychological Defense—Mental Karate?

Gateway Question 13.5: *What are defense mechanisms?*

Threatening situations tend to produce **anxiety**. When you are anxious, you feel tense, uneasy, apprehensive, worried, and vulnerable. This unpleasant state can lead to emotion-focused coping that is *defensive* in nature (Lazarus, 1991b). Psychodynamic psychologists have identified various defense mechanisms that allow us to reduce anxiety caused by stressful situations or our own shortcomings. You might not always be aware of it, but you have probably used several of the defenses described here.

TABLE 13.4 Psychological Defense Mechanisms

Compensation Counteracting a real or imagined weakness by emphasizing desirable traits or seeking to excel in the area of weakness or in other areas.

Denial Protecting oneself from an unpleasant reality by refusing to perceive it.

Fantasy Fulfilling unmet desires in imagined achievements or activities.

Identification Taking on some of the characteristics of an admired person, usually as a way of compensating for perceived personal weaknesses or faults.

Intellectualization Separating emotion from a threatening or anxiety-provoking situation by talking or thinking about it in impersonal "intellectual" terms.

Isolation Separating contradictory thoughts or feelings into "logic-tight" mental compartments so that they do not come into conflict.

Projection Attributing one's own feelings, shortcomings, or unacceptable impulses to others.

Rationalization Justifying your behavior by giving reasonable and "rational," but false, reasons for it.

Reaction formation Preventing dangerous impulses from being expressed in behavior by exaggerating opposite behavior.

Regression Retreating to an earlier level of development or to earlier, less demanding habits or situations.

Repression Unconsciously preventing painful or dangerous thoughts from entering awareness.

Sublimation Working off unmet desires, or unacceptable impulses, in activities that are constructive.

BRIDGES

Severe anxiety can be extremely disruptive. It is the basis for some of the most common psychological disorders. **See Chapter 14, pages 496–498.**

What are psychological defense mechanisms and how do they reduce anxiety? A **defense mechanism** is any mental process used to avoid, deny, or distort sources of threat or anxiety, especially threats to one's self-image. Many of the defenses were first identified by Sigmund Freud, who assumed they operate *unconsciously*. Often, defense mechanisms create large blind spots in awareness. For instance, you might know an extremely stingy person who is completely unaware that he is a tightwad. Everyone has at one time or another used defense mechanisms. Let's consider some of the most common (a more complete listing is given in ■ Table 13.4).

Denial

One of the most basic defenses is **denial** (protecting oneself from an unpleasant reality by refusing to accept it or believe it). We are prone to deny death, illness, and similar painful and threatening events. For instance, if you were told that you had only 3 months to live, how would you react? Your first thoughts might be, "Aw, come on, someone must have mixed up the X-rays," or, "The doctor must be mistaken," or simply, "It can't be true!" Similar denial and disbelief are common reactions to the unexpected death of a friend or relative: "It's just not real. I don't believe it!"

Repression

Freud noticed that his patients had tremendous difficulty recalling shocking or traumatic events from childhood. It seemed that powerful forces were holding these painful memories from awareness. Freud called this **repression**, and said we use it to protect ourselves by blocking out threatening thoughts and impulses. Feelings of hostility toward a family member, the names of people we dislike, and past failures are common targets of repression. Research suggests that you are most likely to repress information that threatens your self-image (Axmacher et al., 2010; Mendolia, 2002).

Reaction Formation

In a **reaction formation**, impulses are not just repressed, they are also held in check by exaggerating opposite behavior. For example, a mother who unconsciously resents her children may, through reaction formation, become absurdly overprotective and overindulgent. Her real thoughts of "I hate them" and "I wish they were gone" are replaced by "I love them" and "I don't know what I would do without them." The mother's hostile impulses are traded for "smother" love, so that she won't have to admit she hates her children. Thus, the basic idea in a reaction formation is that the individual acts out an opposite behavior to block threatening impulses or feelings.

Regression

In its broadest meaning, **regression** refers to any return to earlier, less demanding situations or habits. Most parents who have a second child have to put up with at least some regression by the older child. Threatened by a new rival for affection, an older child may regress to childish speech, bed-wetting, or infantile play after the new baby arrives. If you've ever seen a child get homesick at summer camp or on a vacation, you've observed regression. The child wants to go home, where it's "safe." An adult who throws a temper tantrum or a married adult who "goes home to mother" is also regressing.

Projection

Projection is an unconscious process that protects us from the anxiety we would feel if we were to discern our faults. A person who is projecting tends to see his or her own feelings, shortcomings, or unacceptable impulses in others. **Projection** lowers anxiety by exaggerating negative traits in others. This justifies one's own actions and directs attention away from personal failings.

One of your authors once worked for a greedy shop owner who cheated many of his customers. This same man considered himself a pillar of the community and very moral and religious. How did he justify to himself his greed and dishonesty? He believed that everyone who entered his store was bent on cheating *him* any way they could. In reality, few, if any, of his customers shared his motives, but he projected his own greed and dishonesty onto them.

Rationalization

Every teacher is familiar with this strange phenomenon: On the day of an exam, an incredible wave of disasters sweeps through the city. Mothers, fathers, sisters, brothers, aunts, uncles, grandparents, friends, relatives, and pets of students become ill or die. Motors suddenly fall out of cars. Books are lost or stolen. Alarm clocks go belly-up and ring no more. All manner of computer equipment malfunctions.

The making of excuses comes from a natural tendency to explain our behavior. **Rationalization** refers to justifying personal actions by giving "rational" but false reasons for them. When the explanation you give for your behavior is reasonable and convincing—but not the real reason—you are *rationalizing*. For example, Mee Jung failed to turn in an assignment made at the beginning of the semester in one of her classes. Here's the explanation she gave her professor:

> My car broke down 2 days ago, and I couldn't get to the library until yesterday. Then I couldn't get all the books I needed because some were checked out, but I wrote what I could. Then last night, as the last straw, the ink cartridge in my printer ran out, and since all the stores were closed, I couldn't finish the paper on time.

When asked why she left the assignment until the last minute (the real reason it was late), Mee Jung offered another set of rationalizations. Like many people, Mee Jung had difficulty seeing herself without the protection of her rationalizations.

All the defense mechanisms described seem pretty undesirable. Do they have a positive side? People who overuse defense mechanisms become less adaptable, because they consume great amounts of emotional energy to control anxiety and maintain an unrealistic self-image. Defense mechanisms do have value, though. Often, they help keep us from being overwhelmed by immediate threats. This can provide time for a person to learn to cope in a more effective, problem-focused manner. If you recognize some of your own behavior in the descriptions here, it is hardly a sign that you are hopelessly defensive. As noted earlier, most people occasionally use defense mechanisms.

Two defense mechanisms that have a decidedly more positive quality are compensation and sublimation.

Compensation

Compensatory reactions are defenses against feelings of inferiority. A person who has a defect or weakness (real or imagined) may go to unusual lengths to overcome the weakness or to *compensate* for it by excelling in other areas. One of the pioneers of "pumping iron" is Jack LaLanne, who opened the first modern health club in America. LaLanne made a successful career out of bodybuilding in spite of the fact that he was thin and sickly as a young man. Or perhaps it would be more accurate to say *because* he was thin and sickly. You can find dozens of examples of **compensation** at work.

Anxiety Apprehension, dread, or uneasiness similar to fear but based on an unclear threat.

Defense mechanism A habitual and often unconscious psychological process used to reduce anxiety.

For some players—and fans—football probably allows sublimation of aggressive urges. *Call of Duty, Halo*, and similar computer games may serve the same purpose.

A childhood stutterer may excel in debate at college. As a child, Helen Keller was unable to see or hear, but she became an outstanding thinker and writer. Perhaps Ray Charles, Stevie Wonder, Andrea Bocelli, and other blind entertainers were drawn to music because of their handicap.

Sublimation

The defense called **sublimation** (sub-lih-MAY-shun) is defined as working off frustrated desires (especially sexual desires) through socially acceptable activities. Freud believed that art, music, dance, poetry, scientific investigation, and other creative activities could serve to rechannel sexual energies into productive behavior. Freud also felt that almost any strong desire could be sublimated. For example, a very aggressive person may find social acceptance as a professional soldier, boxer, or football player. Greed may be refined into a successful business career. Lying may be sublimated into storytelling, creative writing, or politics.

Sexual motives appear to be the most easily and widely sublimated (Jacobs, 2003). Freud would have had a field day with such modern pastimes as surfing, motorcycle riding, drag racing, and dancing to or playing rock music, to name but a few. People enjoy each of these activities for a multitude of reasons, but it is hard to overlook the rich sexual symbolism apparent in each.

Learned Helplessness and Depression—Is There Hope?

Gateway Question 13.6: *What do we know about coping with feelings of helplessness and depression?*

What would happen if a person's defenses failed or if the person appraised a threatening situation as hopeless? Martin Seligman studied the case of a young Marine who seemed to have adapted to the stresses of being held prisoner during the Vietnam War. The Marine's health was related to a promise made by his captors: If he cooperated, they said, he would be released on a certain date. As the date approached, his spirits soared. Then came a devastating blow. He had been deceived. His captors had no intention of ever releasing him. He immediately lapsed into a deep depression, refused to eat or drink, and died shortly thereafter.

That seems like an extreme example. Does anything similar occur outside of concentration camps? Apparently so. For example, researchers in San Antonio, Texas, asked older people if they were hopeful about the future. Those who answered "No" died at elevated rates (Stern, Dhanda, & Hazuda, 2001).

Learned Helplessness

To explain such patterns, psychologists have focused on the concept of **learned helplessness**, an acquired inability to overcome obstacles and avoid aversive stimuli (Seligman, 1989). To observe learned helplessness, let's see what happens when animals are tested in a shuttle box (• Figure 13.7). If placed in one side of a divided box, dogs will quickly learn to leap to the other side to escape an electric shock. If they are given a warning before the shock occurs (for example, a light that dims), most dogs learn to avoid the shock by leaping the barrier before the shock arrives. This is true of most dogs, but not those who have learned to feel helpless (Overmier & LoLordo, 1998).

How is a dog made to feel helpless? Before being tested in the shuttle box, a dog can be placed in a harness (from which the dog cannot escape) and then given several painful shocks. The animal is helpless to prevent these shocks. When placed in the shuttle box,

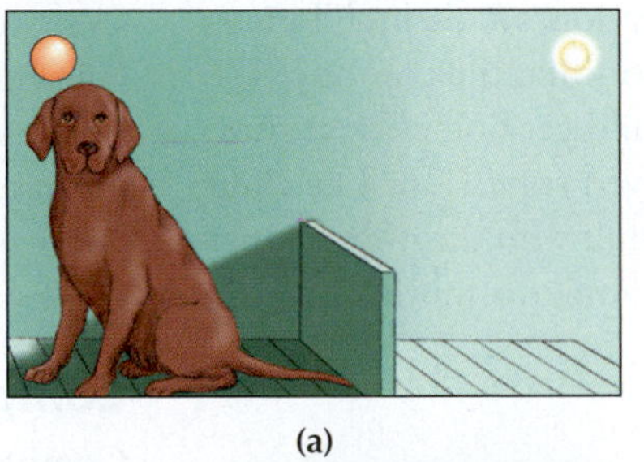
(a)

(b)

(c)

(d)

• **Figure 13.7** In the normal course of escape and avoidance learning, (a) a light dims shortly before the floor is electrified. Since the light does not yet have meaning for the dog, the dog receives a shock (noninjurious, by the way) and (b) leaps the barrier. (c) Dogs soon learn to watch for the dimming of the light and (d) to jump before receiving a shock. Dogs made to feel "helpless" rarely even learn to escape shock, much less to avoid it.

dogs prepared this way react to the first shock by crouching, howling, and whining. None of them try to escape. They helplessly resign themselves to their fate. After all, they have already learned that there is nothing they can do about shock.

As the shuttle box experiments suggest, helplessness is a psychological state that occurs when events *appear to be uncontrollable* (Seligman, 1989). Helplessness also afflicts humans (Domjan, 2010; Reivich et al., 2005). It is a common reaction to repeated failure and to unpredictable or unavoidable punishment. A prime example is college students who feel helpless about their schoolwork. Such students tend to procrastinate, give up easily, and drop out of school (Perry, 2003).

BRIDGES
Where humans are concerned, attributions have a large effect on helplessness. **See Chapter 10, pages 359–360.**

Persons who are made to feel helpless in one situation are more likely to act helpless in other situations if they attribute their failure to *lasting, general* factors. An example would be concluding, "I must be stupid," after doing poorly on a test in a biology class. In contrast, attributing a low score to specific factors in the situation ("I'm not too good at the type of test my biology professor uses" or "I'm not very interested in biology") tends to prevent learned helplessness from spreading (Peterson & Vaidya, 2001; Prochaska & Norcross, 2010).

Depression

Seligman and others have pointed out the similarities between learned helplessness and **depression**. Both are marked by feelings of despondency, powerlessness, and hopelessness. "Helpless" animals display decreased activity, lowered aggression, blunted appetite, and a loss of sex drive. Humans suffer from similar effects and also tend to see themselves as failing, even when they're not (Brown & Barlow, 2011; LoLordo, 2001).

Depression is one of the most widespread emotional problems, and it undoubtedly has many causes. However, learned helplessness seems to explain many cases of depression and hopelessness. For example, Seligman (1972) describes the fate of Archie, a 15-year-old boy. For Archie, school is an unending series of shocks and failures. Other students treat him as if he's stupid; in class, he rarely answers questions because he doesn't know some of the words. He feels knocked down everywhere he turns. These may not be electric shocks, but they are certainly emotional "shocks," and Archie has learned to feel helpless to prevent them. When he leaves school, his chances of success will be poor. He has learned to passively endure whatever shocks life has in store for him. Archie is not alone in this regard. Hopelessness is almost always a major element of depression (Ciarrochi, Dean, & Anderson, 2002; Reivich et al., 2005).

BRIDGES
Depression is a complex problem that takes many forms and has many causes. **See Chapter 14, pages 492–494.**

Mastery training can occur informally when people learn to cope with challenges. For example, 18- to 21-year-old trainees on a transatlantic sailing voyage showed marked improvements in their ability to cope with stress (Norris & Weinman, 1996).

Hope

Does Seligman's research give any clues about how to "unlearn" helplessness? With dogs, an effective technique is to forcibly drag them away from shock into the "safe" compartment. After this is done several times, the animals regain "hope" and feelings of control over the environment. Just how this can be done with humans is a question psychologists are exploring. It seems obvious, for instance, that someone like Archie would benefit from an educational program that would allow him to "succeed" repeatedly.

In **mastery training**, responses that lead to mastery of a threat or control over one's environment are reinforced. Animals who undergo such training become more resistant to learned helplessness (Volpicelli et al., 1983). For example, animals that first learn to escape shock become more persistent in trying to flee inescapable shock. In effect, they won't give up, even when the situation really is "hopeless."

Such findings suggest that we might be able to "immunize" people against helplessness and depression by allowing them to master difficult challenges (Miltenberger, 2011). The Outward Bound schools, in which people pit themselves against the rigors of mountaineering, white-water canoeing, and wilderness survival, might serve as a model for such a program.

The value of hope should not be overlooked. As fragile as this emotion seems, it is a powerful antidote to depression and helplessness (Weingarten, 2010). As an individual, you may find hope in religion, nature, human companionship, or even technology. Wherever you find it, remember its value: Hope is among the most important of all human emotions. Having positive beliefs, such as opti-

Learned helplessness A learned inability to overcome obstacles or to avoid punishment; learned passivity and inaction to aversive stimuli.
Depression A state of despondency marked by feelings of powerlessness and hopelessness.
Mastery training Reinforcement of responses that lead to mastery of a threat or control over one's environment.

mism, hope, and a sense of meaning and control, is closely related to overall well-being (Diener & Chan, 2011; Taylor et al., 2003).

Depression: Why Students Get the Blues

During the school year, many college students suffer symptoms of depression, which can exert a toll on academic performance (Lindsey, Fabiano, & Stark, 2009). In one study, students diagnosed with depression scored half a grade point below nondepressed students (Hysenbegasi, Hass, & Rowland, 2005). Why do students get "blue"? Various problems contribute to depressive feelings. Here are some of the most common:

1. Stresses from college work and pressures to choose a career can leave students feeling that they are missing out on fun or that all their hard work is meaningless.
2. Isolation and loneliness are common when students leave their support groups behind. In the past, family, a circle of high school friends, and often a boyfriend or girlfriend could be counted on for support and encouragement.
3. Problems with studying and grades frequently trigger depression. Many students start college with high aspirations and little prior experience with failure. At the same time, many lack basic skills necessary for academic success and are afraid of failure (Martin & Marsh, 2003).
4. Depression can be triggered by the breakup of an intimate relationship, either with a former boyfriend or girlfriend or with a newly formed college romance.
5. Students who find it difficult to live up to their idealized images of themselves are especially prone to depression (Enns, Cox, & Clara, 2005; Scott & O'Hara, 1993).
6. An added danger is that depressed students are more likely to abuse alcohol, which is a depressant (Weitzman, 2004).

Recognizing Depression

Most people know, obviously enough, when they are "down." You should assume that more than a minor fluctuation in mood is involved when these conditions exist (National Institute of Mental Health (2010):

1. Persistent sad, anxious or "empty" feelings.
2. Feelings of guilt, worthlessness, and/or helplessness.
3. Difficulty concentrating, remembering details, and making decisions.
4. Feelings of hopelessness and/or pessimism.
5. Loss of interest in activities or hobbies once pleasurable, including sex.

Coping with the College Blues

Bouts of the college blues are closely related to stressful events. Learning to manage college work and to challenge self-critical thinking can help alleviate mild school-related depression (Santrock & Halonen, 2010).

For example, if you don't do well on a test or a class assignment, how do you react? If you see it as a small, isolated setback, you probably won't feel too bad. However, if you feel like you have "blown it" in a big way, depression may follow. Students who strongly link everyday events to long-term goals (such as a successful career or high income) tend to overreact to day-to-day disappointments (McIntosh, Harlow, & Martin, 1995; Santrock & Halonen, 2010).

What does the preceding tell us about the college blues? The implication is that it's important to take daily tasks one step at a time and chip away at them (Watson & Tharp, 2007). That way, you are less likely to feel overwhelmed, helpless, or hopeless. When you feel "blue," you should make a *daily schedule* for yourself (Burka & Yuen, 2008). Try to schedule activities to fill up every hour during the day. It is best to start with easy activities and progress to more difficult tasks. Check off each item as it is completed. That way, you will begin to break the self-defeating cycle of feeling helpless and falling further behind. (Depressed students spend much of their time sleeping.) A series of small accomplishments, successes, or pleasures may be all that you need to get going again. However, if you are lacking skills needed for success in college, ask for help in getting them. Don't remain "helpless."

Feelings of worthlessness and hopelessness are usually supported by self-critical or negative thoughts. Consider writing down such thoughts as they occur, especially those that immediately precede feelings of sadness (Pennebaker, 2004). After you have collected these thoughts, write a rational answer to each. For example, the thought "No one loves me" should be answered with a list of those who do care. One more point to keep in mind is this: When events begin to improve, try to accept it as a sign that better times lie ahead. Positive events are most likely to end depression if you view them as stable and continuing, rather than temporary and fragile (Needles & Abramson, 1990).

Attacks of the college blues are common and should be distinguished from more serious cases of depression. Severe depression is a serious problem that can lead to suicide or a major impairment of emotional functioning. In such cases, it would be wise to seek professional help (Hollon, Stewart, & Strunk, 2006).

Knowledge Builder — Defenses, Helplessness, and Depression

RECITE

1. The psychological defense known as *denial* refers to the natural tendency to explain or justify one's actions. T or F?
2. Fulfilling frustrated desires in imaginary achievements or activities defines the defense mechanism of
   a. compensation *b.* isolation *c.* fantasy *d.* sublimation
3. In compensation, one's own undesirable characteristics or motives are attributed to others. T or F?
4. Of the defense mechanisms, two that are considered relatively constructive are
   a. compensation *b.* denial *c.* isolation *d.* projection
   e. regression *f.* rationalization *g.* sublimation

5. Depression in humans is similar to ______________ ______________ observed in animal experiments.
6. Learned helplessness tends to occur when events appear to be *a.* frustrating *b.* in conflict *c.* uncontrollable *d.* problem-focused
7. College students suffering from depression have lower grades than nondepressed students. T or F?
8. Frequent self-criticism and self-blame are a natural consequence of doing college work. T or F?

REFLECT

Think Critically

9. Learned helplessness is closely related to which of the factors that determine the severity of stress?

Self-Reflect

We tend to be blind to our own reliance on defense mechanisms. Return to the definitions in ■ Table 13.4 and see if you can think of one example of each defense that you have observed someone else using.

Have you ever felt helpless in a particular situation? What caused you to feel that way? Does any part of Seligman's description of learned helplessness match your own experience?

Imagine that a friend of yours is suffering from the college blues. What advice would you give your friend?

Answers: 1. F **2.** c **3.** F **4.** *a, g* **5.** learned helplessness **6.** *c* **7.** T **8.** F **9.** Feelings of incompetence and lack of control.

Stress and Health—Unmasking a Hidden Killer

Gateway Question 13.7: *How is stress related to health and disease?*

At the beginning of this chapter, you read about Mee Jung, our intrepid student who became ill after a stressful final exam period. Was Mee Jung's illness a coincidence? Psychologists have now firmly established that stress affects our health. Let's see how this occurs. We will also explore some factors that limit the health risks we face. Because we live in a fast-paced and often stressful society, these are topics worth stressing.

Life Events and Stress

Disaster, depression, and sorrow often precede illness (Brannon & Feist, 2010). As Mee Jung learned after finals week, stressful events reduce the body's natural defenses against disease. More surprising is the finding that *life changes*—both good and bad—can increase susceptibility to accidents or illness. Major changes in our surroundings or routines require us to be vigilant, on guard, and ready to react. Over long periods, this can be quite stressful (Sternberg, 2009).

How can I tell if I am subjecting myself to too much stress? Psychiatrist Thomas Holmes and graduate student Richard Rahe developed the first rating scale to estimate the health hazards we face when stresses add up (Holmes & Rahe, 1967). Still widely used today, a version of the ***Social Readjustment Rating Scale* (SRRS)** is reprinted in ■ Table 13.5 (Miller & Rahe, 1997; Woods, Racine, & Klump, 2010). Notice that the impact of life events is expressed in *life change units (LCUs)* (numerical values assigned to each life event).

Why is going on vacation on the list? Positive life events can be stressful as well (for example, marriage rates a 50 and Christmas a 30 even though they are usually happy events). Even a change in social activities rates 27 LCUs, whether the change is due to an improvement or a decline. A stressful adjustment may be required in either case.

To use the scale shown in ■ Table 13.5, add up the LCUs for all life events you have experienced during the last year and compare the total to the following standards:

0–149: No significant problems
150–199: Mild life crisis (33 percent chance of illness)
200–299: Moderate life crisis (50 percent chance of illness)
300 or more: Major life crisis (80 percent chance of illness)

According to Holmes, there is a high chance of illness or accident when your LCU total exceeds 300 points. A more conserva-

© Corbis

Marriage is usually a positive life event. Nevertheless, the many changes it brings can be stressful.

Social Readjustment Rating Scale (SRRS) A scale that rates the impact of various life events on the likelihood of illness.

TABLE 13.5 Social Readjustment Rating Scale

Rank	Life Event	Life Change Units	Rank	Life Event	Life Change Units
1	Death of spouse or child	119	23	Mortgage or loan greater than $10,000	44
2	Divorce	98	24	Change in responsibilities at work	43
3	Death of close family member	92	25	Change in living conditions	42
4	Marital separation	79	26	Change in residence	41
5	Fired from work	79	27	Begin or end school	38
6	Major personal injury or illness	77	28	Trouble with in-laws	38
7	Jail term	75	29	Outstanding personal achievement	37
8	Death of close friend	70	30	Change in work hours or conditions	36
9	Pregnancy	66	31	Change in schools	35
10	Major business readjustment	62	32	Christmas	30
11	Foreclosure on a mortgage or loan	61	33	Trouble with boss	29
12	Gain of new family member	57	34	Change in recreation	29
13	Marital reconciliation	57	35	Mortgage or loan less than $10,000	28
14	Change in health or behavior of family member	56	36	Change in personal habits	27
15	Change in financial state	56	37	Change in eating habits	27
16	Retirement	54	38	Change in social activities	27
17	Change to different line of work	51	39	Change in number of family get-togethers	26
18	Change in number of arguments with spouse	51	40	Change in sleeping habits	26
19	Marriage	50	41	Vacation	25
20	Spouse begins or ends work	46	42	Change in church activities	22
21	Sexual difficulties	45	43	Minor violations of the law	22
22	Child leaving home	44			

Source: Reprinted from *Journal of Psychosomatic Research*, Vol. 43, No. 3

tive rating of stress can be obtained by totaling LCU points for only the previous 6 months.

The health of college students is also affected by stressful events, such as entering college, changing majors, or breaking up in a steady relationship. (For a student-oriented stress scale, see ■ Table 13.7 in the *Psychology in Action* module.)

Evaluation

People differ greatly in their reactions to the same event. For this reason, stress scales like the SRRS at best provide a rough index of stress. Nevertheless, research has shown that if your stress level is too high, an adjustment in your activities or lifestyle may be needed. In one classic study, people were deliberately exposed to the virus that causes common colds. The results were nothing to sneeze at: If a person had a high stress score, she or he was much more likely to actually get a cold (Cohen, Tyrrell, & Smith, 1993). In view of such findings, higher levels of stress should be taken seriously (Hales, 2012). Remember, "To be forewarned is to be forearmed."

The Hazards of Hassles

There must be more to stress than major life changes. Isn't there a link between ongoing stresses and health? In addition to having a direct impact, major life events spawn countless daily frustrations and irritations (Henderson, Roberto, & Kamo, 2010). Also, many of us face ongoing stresses at work or at home that do not involve major life changes (Pett & Johnson, 2005). Such minor but frequent stresses are called **hassles**, or **microstressors**. (See ■ Table 13.6 for some examples of hassles faced by college students.)

TABLE 13.6 Examples of Common Hassles Faced by College Students

Too many things to do
Not enough money for housing
Feeling discriminated against
People making gender jokes
Communication problems with friends
Driving to school
People making fun of my religion
Fear of losing valuables
Work schedule
Getting into shape
Parents' expectations

Source: Pett & Johnson, 2005.

Human Diversity: Acculturative Stress—Stranger in a Strange Land

Around the world, an increasing number of emigrants and refugees must adapt to dramatic changes in language, dress, values, and social customs. For many, the result is a period of culture shock, or **acculturative stress** (stress caused by adapting to a foreign culture). Typical reactions to acculturative stress are anxiety, hostility, depression, alienation, physical illness, or identity confusion (Rummens, Beiser, & Noh, 2003). For many young immigrants, acculturative stress is a major source of mental health problems (Choi & Dancy, 2009; Mejía & McCarthy, 2010; Yeh, 2003).

The severity of acculturative stress is related, in part, to how a person adapts to a new culture. Four main patterns are (Berry et al., 2005; Sam & Berry, 2010):

Integration—maintain your old cultural identity but participate in the new culture.

Separation—maintain your old cultural identity and avoid contact with the new culture.

Assimilation—adopt the new culture as your own and have contact with its members.

Marginalization—reject your old culture but suffer rejection by members of the new culture.

To illustrate each pattern, let's consider a family that has immigrated to the United States from the imaginary country of Heinleinia:

The father favors integration. He is learning English and wants to get involved in American life. At the same time, he is a leader in the Heinleinian American community and spends much of his leisure time with other Heinleinian Americans. His level of acculturative stress is low.

The mother speaks only the Heinleinian language and interacts only with other Heinleinian Americans. She remains almost completely separate from American society. Her stress level is high.

The teenage daughter is annoyed by hearing Heinleinian spoken at home, by her mother's serving only Heinleinian food, and by having to spend her leisure time with her extended Heinleinian family. She would prefer to speak English and to be with her American friends. Her desire to assimilate creates moderate stress.

The son doesn't particularly value his Heinleinian heritage, yet his schoolmates reject him because he speaks with a Heinleinian accent. He feels trapped between two cultures. His position is marginal, and his stress level is high.

To summarize, those who feel marginalized tend to be highly stressed; those who seek to remain separate are also highly stressed; those who pursue integration into their new culture are minimally stressed; and those who assimilate are moderately stressed.

As you can see, integration and assimilation are the best options. However, a big benefit of assimilating is that people who embrace their new culture experience fewer social difficulties. For many, this justifies the stress of adopting new customs and cultural values (Gurung, 2010; Sam & Berry, 2010).

One of the best antidotes for acculturative stress is a society that tolerates or even celebrates ethnic diversity. Although some people find it hard to accept new immigrants, the fact is, nearly everyone's family tree includes people who were once strangers in a strange land.

In a yearlong study, 100 men and women recorded the hassles they endured. Participants also reported on their physical and mental health. Frequent and severe hassles turned out to be better predictors of day-to-day health than major life events were. However, major life events did predict changes in health 1 or 2 years after the events took place. It appears that daily hassles are closely linked to immediate health and psychological well-being (Crowther et al., 2001). Major life changes have more of a long-term impact as well as exacerbating the effects of daily hassles (Woods, Racine, & Klump, 2010).

One way to guarantee that you will experience a large number of life changes and hassles is to live in a foreign culture. "Acculturative Stress" offers a brief glimpse into some of the consequences of culture shock.

What can be done about a high LCU score or feeling excessively hassled? A good response is to use stress management skills. For serious problems, stress management should be learned directly from a therapist or a stress clinic. When ordinary stresses are involved, there is much you can do on your own. An upcoming discussion of stress management will give you a start. In the meantime, take it easy!

Psychosomatic Disorders

As we have seen, chronic or repeated stress can damage physical health as well as upset emotional well-being. Prolonged stress reactions are closely related to a large number of psychosomatic

Hassle (microstressor) Any distressing, day-to-day annoyance.
Acculturative stress Stress caused by the many changes and adaptations required when a person moves to a foreign culture.

Critical Thinking: It's All in Your Mind

Have you ever had someone dismiss a health concern by saying, "It's all in your mind," as if your problem might be imaginary? For centuries, the *medical model* has dominated Western thinking. From this perspective, health is an absence of illness and your body is a complex biological machine that can break down and become ill. Sometimes, you inflict the damage yourself through poor lifestyle choices, such as smoking or overeating. Sometimes, an external cause, such as a virus, is the culprit. In either event, the problem is physical and your mind has little to do with it. Moreover, physical problems call for physical treatments ("Take your medicine"), so your mind has little to do with your recovery. In the medical model, *any* impact of the mind on health was dismissed as a mere placebo effect.

BRIDGES
To remind yourself about placebo effects, see Chapter 1, pages 37–38.

Over the last 50 years, the medical model has slowly given way to the *biopsychosocial model*. This view states that diseases are caused by a combination of biological, psychological, and social factors. Most important, the biopsychosocial model defines health as a state of well-being that we can *actively* attain and maintain (Oakley, 2004). Instead of passively getting treatments from a doctor, this model says that you play a role in fostering your own health. Thus, it may no longer be inaccurate to say, "It's all in your mind," *if* you mean that a person's beliefs—which affect behavior—can have a dramatic impact on health (Brooks, 2008). It is becoming clear that medicine works best when doctors help people make sense of their medical condition, to maximize healing (Benedetti, 2009; Moerman, 2002). So, as you take responsibility for your own well-being, remember that in some ways health is all in your mind!

It is estimated that at least half of all patients who see a doctor have a psychosomatic disorder or an illness that is complicated by psychosomatic symptoms.

(SIKE-oh-so-MAT-ik) illnesses. In **psychosomatic disorders** (*psyche:* mind; *soma:* body), psychological factors contribute to actual bodily damage or to damaging changes in bodily functioning (Asmundson & Taylor, 2005; Bourgeois et al., 2009). Psychosomatic problems, therefore, are *not* the same as hypochondria. **Hypochondriacs** (HI-po-KON-dree-aks) imagine that they have diseases. There is nothing imaginary about asthma, a migraine headache, or high blood pressure. Severe psychosomatic disorders can be fatal. The person who says, "Oh, it's *just* psychosomatic," doesn't understand how serious stress-related diseases really are (see "It's All in Your Mind").

The most common psychosomatic problems are gastrointestinal and respiratory (stomach pain and asthma, for example), but many others exist. Typical problems include eczema (skin rash), hives, migraine headaches, rheumatoid arthritis, hypertension (high blood pressure), colitis (ulceration of the colon), and heart disease. Actually, these are only the major problems. Many lesser health complaints are also stress related. Typical examples include sore muscles, headaches, neckaches, backaches, indigestion, constipation, chronic diarrhea, fatigue, insomnia, premenstrual problems, and sexual dysfunctions (Taylor, 2009). For some of these problems, biofeedback may be helpful. The next section explains how.

Biofeedback

Psychologists have discovered that people can learn to control bodily activities once thought to be involuntary. This is done by applying informational feedback to bodily control, a process

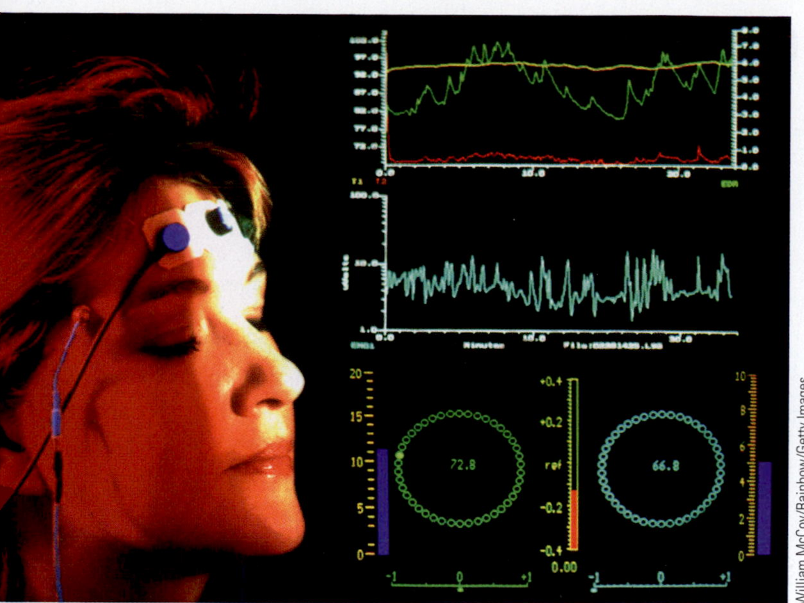

William McCoy/Rainbow/Getty Images

● **Figure 13.8** In biofeedback training, bodily processes are monitored and processed electronically. A signal is then routed back to the patient through headphones, signal lights, a computer screen, or other means. This information helps the patient alter bodily activities not normally under voluntary control. This woman is learning to control her brainwaves in order to relax.

called **biofeedback**. If I were to say to you, "Raise the temperature of your right hand," you probably couldn't, because you wouldn't know if you were succeeding. To make your task easier, we could attach a sensitive thermometer to your hand. The thermometer could be wired so that an increase in temperature would activate a signal light. Then, all you would have to do is try to keep the light on as much as possible. With practice and the help of biofeedback, you could learn to raise your hand temperature at will.

Biofeedback holds promise as a way to treat some psychosomatic problems (● Figure 13.8). For instance, people have been trained to prevent migraine headaches with biofeedback. Sensors are taped to patients' hands and foreheads. Patients then learn to redirect blood flow away from the head to their extremities. Because migraine headaches involve excessive blood flow to the head, biofeedback helps patients reduce the frequency of their headaches (Larsson et al., 2005; Stokes & Lappin, 2010).

Early successes led many to predict that biofeedback would offer a cure for psychosomatic illnesses, anxiety, phobias, drug abuse, and a long list of other problems. In reality, biofeedback has proved helpful but not an instant cure (Schwartz & Andrasik, 2003). Biofeedback can help relieve muscle-tension headaches, migraine headaches, and chronic pain (Middaugh & Pawlick, 2002; Sousa et al., 2009). It shows promise for lowering blood pressure and controlling heart rhythms (Olsson et al., 2010; Wheat & Larkin, 2010). The technique has been used with some success to control epileptic seizures and hyperactivity in children (Demos, 2005). Insomnia also responds to biofeedback therapy (Gathchel & Oordt, 2003; McLay & Spira, 2009).

How does biofeedback help? Some researchers believe that many of its benefits arise from *general relaxation*. Others stress that there is no magic in biofeedback itself. The method simply acts as a "mirror" to help a person perform tasks involving *self-regulation*. Just as a mirror does not comb your hair, biofeedback does not do anything by itself. It can, however, help people make desired changes in their behavior.

The Cardiac Personality

It would be a mistake to assume that stress is the sole cause of psychosomatic diseases. Genetic differences, organ weaknesses, and learned reactions to stress combine to do damage. Personality also enters the picture. As mentioned earlier, a general disease-prone personality type exists. To a degree, there are also "headache personalities," "asthma personalities," and so on. The best documented of such patterns is the "cardiac personality"—a person at high risk for heart disease.

Two cardiologists, Meyer Friedman and Ray Rosenman, offer a glimpse at how some people create stress for themselves. In a landmark study of heart problems, Friedman and Rosenman (1983) classified people as either **Type A personalities** (those who run a high risk for heart attack) or **Type B personalities** (those who are unlikely to have a heart attack). In an 8-year follow-up, they found more than twice the rate of heart disease in Type A's than in Type B's (Rosenman et al., 1975).

Type A

What is the Type A personality like? Type A people are hard driving, ambitious, highly competitive, achievement oriented, and striving. Type A people believe that with enough effort they can overcome any obstacle, and they "push" themselves accordingly.

Perhaps the most telltale signs of a Type A personality are *time urgency* and chronic *anger* or *hostility*. Type A's seem to chafe at the normal pace of events. They hurry from one activity to another, racing the clock in self-imposed urgency. As they do, they feel a constant sense of frustration and anger. Feelings of anger and hostility, in particular, are strongly related to increased risk for heart attack (Boyle et al., 2004; Bunde & Suls, 2006). One study found that 15 percent of a group of 25-year-old doctors and lawyers who scored high on a hostility test were dead by age 50. The most dam-

Psychosomatic disorders Illnesses in which psychological factors contribute to bodily damage or to damaging changes in bodily functioning.

Hypochondriac A person who complains about illnesses that appear to be imaginary.

Biofeedback Information given to a person about his or her ongoing bodily activities; aids voluntary regulation of bodily states.

Type A personality A personality type with an elevated risk of heart disease; characterized by time urgency, anger, and hostility.

Type B personality All personality types other than Type A; a low cardiac-risk personality.

Individuals with Type A personalities feel a continuous sense of anger, irritation, and hostility.

aging pattern may occur in hostile persons who keep their anger "bottled up." Such people seethe with anger but don't express it outwardly. This increases their pulse rate and blood pressure and puts a tremendous strain on the heart (Bongard, al'Absi, & Lovallo, 1998).

To summarize, there is growing evidence that anger or hostility may be the core lethal factor of Type A behavior (Lemogne et al., 2010; Niaura et al., 2002). To date, hundreds of studies have supported the validity of the Type A concept. In view of this, Type A's would be wise to take their increased health risks seriously.

How are Type A people identified? Characteristics of Type A people are summarized in the short self-identification test presented in ■ Table 13.7. If most of the list applies to you, you might be a Type A. However, confirmation of your type would require more powerful testing methods. Also, remember that the original definition of Type A behavior was probably too broad. The key psychological factors that increase heart disease risk appear to be anger, hostility, and mistrust (Myrtek, 2007; Smith et al., 2004). Also, although Type A behavior appears to promote heart disease, depression or distress may be what finally triggers a heart attack (Denollet & Van Heck, 2001; Dinan, 2001).

■ TABLE 13.7 Characteristics of the Type A Person

Check the items that apply to you. Do you

______	Have a habit of explosively accentuating various key words in ordinary speech even when there is no need for such accentuation (I HATE it when you do THAT!)?
______	Finish other persons' sentences for them?
______	*Always* move, walk, and eat rapidly?
______	Quickly skim reading material and prefer summaries or condensations of books?
______	Become easily angered by slow-moving lines or traffic?
______	Feel an impatience with the rate at which most events take place?
______	Tend to be unaware of the details or beauty of your surroundings?
______	Frequently strive to think of or do two or more things simultaneously?
______	Almost always feel vaguely guilty when you relax, vacation, or do absolutely nothing for several days?
______	Tend to evaluate your worth in quantitative terms (number of A's earned, amount of income, number of games won, and so forth)?
______	Have nervous gestures or muscle twitches, such as grinding your teeth, clenching your fists, or drumming your fingers?
______	Attempt to schedule more and more activities into less time and in so doing make fewer allowances for unforeseen problems?
______	Frequently think about other things while talking to someone?
______	Repeatedly take on more responsibilities than you can comfortably handle?

Source: Shortened and adapted from Friedman and Rosenman, *Type A Behavior and Your Heart*, Alfred A. Knopf, Inc., © 1983. Reprinted with permission.

Because our society places a premium on achievement, competition, and mastery, it is not surprising that many people develop Type A personalities. The best way to avoid the self-made stress this causes is to adopt behavior that is the opposite of that listed in ■ Table 13.7 (Williams, Barefoot, & Schneiderman, 2003). It is entirely possible to succeed in life without sacrificing your health or happiness in the process.

People who frequently feel angry and hostile toward others may benefit from the advice of Redford Williams (1989). According to Williams, reducing hostility involves three goals. First, you must stop mistrusting the motives of others. Second, you must find ways to reduce how often you feel anger, indignation, irritation, and rage. Third, you must learn to be kinder and more considerate. It is entirely possible to succeed in life without sacrificing your health or happiness in the process.

Hardy Personality

How do Type A people who do not develop heart disease differ from those who do? Psychologist Salvatore Maddi has studied people who have a **hardy personality**. Such people seem to be unusually resistant to stress (Maddi et al., 2009; Stix, 2011). The first study of hardiness began with two groups of managers at a large utility company. All the managers held high-stress positions. Yet some tended to get sick after stressful events, whereas others were rarely ill. How did the people who were thriving differ from their "stressed-out" colleagues? Both groups seemed to have traits typical of the Type A personality, so that wasn't the explanation. They were also quite similar in most other respects. The main difference was that the hardy group seemed to hold a worldview that consisted of three traits (Maddi, 2006; Maddi et al., 2009):

1. They had a sense of personal *commitment* to self, work, family, and other stabilizing values.
2. They felt that they had *control* over their lives and their work.
3. They had a tendency to see life as a series of *challenges*, rather than as a series of threats or problems.

How do such traits protect people from the effects of stress? Persons strong in *commitment* find ways of turning whatever they are doing into something that seems interesting and important. They tend to get involved rather than feeling alienated.

Persons strong in *control* believe that they can more often than not influence the course of events around them. This prevents them from passively seeing themselves as victims of circumstance.

Finally, people strong in *challenge* find fulfillment in continual growth. They seek to learn from their experiences, rather than accepting easy comfort, security, and routine. Indeed, many "negative" experiences can actually enhance personal growth—if you have support from others and the skills needed to cope with challenge (Garrosa et al., 2008; Stix, 2011).

Positive Psychology: Hardiness, Optimism, and Happiness

Good and bad events occur in all lives. What separates happy people from those who are unhappy is largely a matter of attitude. Happy people tend to see their lives in more positive terms, even when trouble comes their way. For example, happier people tend to find humor in disappointments. They look at setbacks as challenges. They are strengthened by losses (Lyubomirsky & Tucker, 1998). In short, happiness tends to be related to hardiness (Cohn et al., 2009; Maddi et al, 2009). Why is there a connection? As psychologist Barbara Fredrickson has pointed out, positive emotions tend to broaden our mental focus. Emotions such as joy, interest, and contentment create an urge to play, to be creative, to explore, to savor life, to seek new experiences, to integrate, and to grow. When you are stressed, experiencing positive emotions can make it more likely that you will find creative solutions to your problems. Positive emotions also tend to reduce the bodily arousal that occurs when we are stressed, possibly limiting stress-related damage (Diener & Chan, 2011; Fredrickson, 2003).

Elsewhere in this chapter, we have noted the value of optimism, which goes hand in hand with hardiness and happiness. Optimists tend to expect that things will turn out well. This motivates them to actively cope with adversity. They are less likely to be stopped by temporary setbacks, and more likely to deal with problems head-on. Pessimists are more likely to ignore or deny problems. The result of such differences is that optimists are less stressed and anxious than pessimists. They are also in better health than pessimists. In general, optimists tend to take better care of themselves because they believe that their efforts to stay healthy will succeed (Peterson & Chang, 2003).

A Look Ahead

The work we have reviewed here has drawn new attention to the fact that each of us has a personal responsibility for maintaining and promoting health. In the *Psychology in Action* section that follows, we will look at what you can do to better cope with stress and the health risks that it entails. But first, the following questions may help you maintain a healthy grade on your next psychology test.

Knowledge Builder — Stress and Health

RECITE

1. Ratings on the SRRS are based on the total number of __________ a person experienced in the preceding year.
   a. hassles *b.* LCUs *c.* STDs *d.* psychosomatic illnesses
2. The SRRS appears to predict long-range changes in health, whereas the frequency and severity of daily microstressors is closely related to immediate ratings of health. T or F?
3. Ulcers, migraine headaches, and hypochondria are all frequently psychosomatic disorders. T or F?
4. Which of the following is *not* classified as a psychosomatic disorder?
   a. hypertension *b.* colitis *c.* eczema *d.* thymus
5. Two major elements of biofeedback training appear to be relaxation and self-regulation. T or F?
6. Anger, hostility, and mistrust appear to be the core lethal factors in
   a. hypochondria *b.* learned helplessness *c.* the GAS
   d. Type A behavior
7. A sense of commitment, challenge, and control characterizes the hardy personality. T or F?

REFLECT

Think Critically

8. People with a hardy personality type appear to be especially resistant to which of the problems discussed earlier in this chapter?

Self-Reflect

Pick a year from your life that was unusually stressful. Use the SRRS to find your LCU score for that year. Do you think there was a connection between your LCU score and your health? Or have you observed more of a connection between microstressors and your health?

Continued

Hardy personality A personality style associated with superior stress resistance.

Mindy complains about her health all the time, but she actually seems to be just fine. An acquaintance of Mindy's dismisses her problems by saying, "Oh, she's not really sick. It's just psychosomatic." What's wrong with this use of the term *psychosomatic*?

Do you think you are basically a Type A or a Type B personality? To what extent do you possess traits of the hardy personality?

Answers: 1. *b* **2.** T **3.** F **4.** *d* **5.** T **6.** *d* **7.** T **8.** Learned helplessness.

Psychology in Action

Stress Management

Gateway Question 13.8: *What are the best strategies for managing stress?*

Stress management is the use of cognitive and behavioral strategies to reduce stress and improve coping skills. As promised, this section describes strategies for managing stress. Before you continue reading, you may want to assess your level of stress again, this time using a scale developed for undergraduate students (see ■ Table 13.8). Like the SRRS, high scores on the *Undergraduate Stress Questionnaire* suggest that you have been exposed to health-threatening levels of stress (Crandall, Preisler, Aussprung, 1992). But remember, stress is an internal state. If you are good at coping with stressors, a high score may not be a problem for you.

Now that you have a picture of your current level of stress, what can you do about it? The simplest way of coping with stress is to modify or remove its source—by leaving a stressful job, for example. Obviously, this is often impossible, which is why learning to manage stress is so important.

As shown in ● Figure 13.9, stress triggers *bodily effects, upsetting thoughts*, and *ineffective behavior*. Also shown is the fact that each element worsens the others in a vicious cycle. Indeed, the basic idea of the "Stress Game" is that once it begins, *you lose*—unless you take action to break the cycle. The information that follows tells how.

Managing Bodily Reactions

Much of the immediate discomfort of stress is caused by fight-or-flight emotional responses. The body is ready to act, with tight muscles and a pounding heart. If action is prevented, we merely remain "uptight." A sensible remedy is to learn a reliable, drug-free way of relaxing.

Exercise Stress-based arousal can be dissipated by using the body. Any full-body exercise can be effective. Our intrepid student, Mee Jung, enjoys karate. Swimming, dancing, jumping rope, yoga, most sports, and especially walking are valuable outlets. Regular exercise alters hormones, circulation, muscle tone, and a number of other aspects of physical functioning. Together, such changes can reduce anxiety and lower the risks for disease (Edenfield & Blumenthal, 2011; Linden, 2005).

Be sure to choose activities that are vigorous enough to relieve tension, yet enjoyable

● **Figure 13.9** The stress game. Adapted from Rosenthal and Rosenthal, 1980.

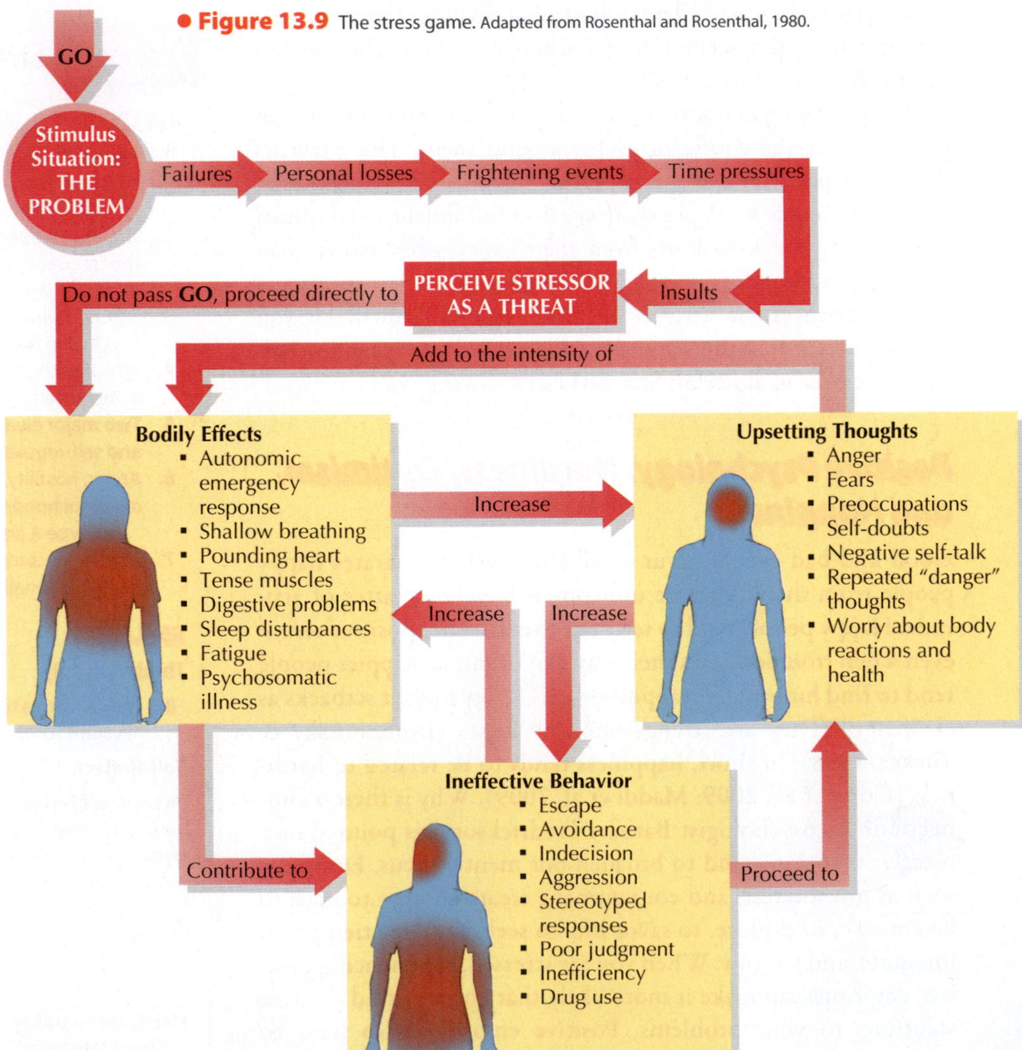

TABLE 13.8 Undergraduate Stress Questionnaire

Has this stressful event happened to you at any time during the last two weeks? If it has, please check the box next to it. If it has not, then leave it blank.

- ☐ Death (of a family member or friend)
- ☐ Death of a pet
- ☐ Working while in school
- ☐ Parents getting a divorce
- ☐ Registration for classes
- ☐ Trying to decide on a major
- ☐ Talked with a professor
- ☐ Trying to get into college
- ☐ Had a class presentation
- ☐ Had projects, research papers due
- ☐ Had a lot of tests
- ☐ It's finals week
- ☐ Applying to graduate school
- ☐ You have a hard upcoming week
- ☐ Lots of deadlines to meet
- ☐ Missed your period and waiting
- ☐ Had an interview
- ☐ Applying for a job
- ☐ Sat through a boring class
- ☐ Can't understand your professor
- ☐ Did badly on a test
- ☐ Went into a test unprepared
- ☐ Crammed for a test
- ☐ Used a fake ID
- ☐ Breaking up with boy-/girlfriend
- ☐ Holiday
- ☐ Bad haircut today
- ☐ Victim of a crime
- ☐ Can't concentrate
- ☐ Coping with addictions
- ☐ Found out boy-/girlfriend cheated on you
- ☐ Did worse than expected on a test
- ☐ Stayed up late writing a paper
- ☐ Problems with your computer
- ☐ Favorite sporting team lost
- ☐ Problems with printing things out
- ☐ Change of environment (new doctor, dentist, etc.)
- ☐ Bothered by having no social support of family
- ☐ Arguments, conflict of value with friends
- ☐ Visit from relatives and entertaining them
- ☐ Noise disturbed you while trying to study
- ☐ Maintaining a long-distance boy-/girlfriend
- ☐ Assignments in all classes due at the same time
- ☐ Dealt with incompetence at the registrar's office
- ☐ Someone borrowed something without your permission
- ☐ Exposed to upsetting TV show, book, or movie
- ☐ Problem getting home from bar when drunk
- ☐ Had confrontation with an authority figure
- ☐ Got to class late
- ☐ Parents controlling with money
- ☐ Feel isolated
- ☐ Decision to have sex on your mind
- ☐ No sex in a while
- ☐ Living with boy-/girlfriend
- ☐ Felt some peer pressure
- ☐ Felt need for transportation
- ☐ Couldn't find a parking space
- ☐ Property stolen
- ☐ Car/bike broke down, flat tire, etc.
- ☐ Got a traffic ticket
- ☐ No time to eat
- ☐ Having roommate conflicts
- ☐ Had to ask for money
- ☐ Lack of money
- ☐ Checkbook didn't balance
- ☐ You have a hangover
- ☐ Someone you expected to call did not
- ☐ Lost something (especially wallet)
- ☐ Erratic schedule
- ☐ Thoughts about future
- ☐ Dependent on other people
- ☐ No sleep
- ☐ Sick, injured
- ☐ Fought with boy-/girlfriend
- ☐ Performed poorly at a task
- ☐ Heard bad news
- ☐ Thought about unfinished work
- ☐ Feel unorganized
- ☐ Someone cut ahead of you in line
- ☐ Job requirements changed
- ☐ Someone broke a promise
- ☐ Someone did a "pet peeve" of yours
- ☐ Couldn't finish everything you needed to do

Add together the number of check marks. Students with higher scores are more likely to need health care (as measured by going to the student health center or infirmary) than students with lower scores. Adapted from Crandall, Preisler, & Aussprung, 1992.

enough to be done repeatedly. Exercising for stress management is most effective when it is done daily. As little as 30 minutes of total exercise per day, even if it occurs in short 10- to 20-minute sessions, can improve mood and energy (Hansen, Stevens, & Coast, 2001).

Meditation Many stress counselors recommend *meditation* for quieting the body and promoting relaxation. Meditation is one of the most effective ways to relax (Deckro et al., 2002; Sears & Kraus, 2009). But be aware that listening to or playing music, taking nature walks, enjoying hobbies, and the like can be meditations of sorts. Anything that reliably interrupts upsetting thoughts and promotes relaxation can be helpful. For now, it is enough to state that meditation is easy to learn—taking an expensive commercial course is unnecessary.

BRIDGES

To learn more about meditation and its effects, read Chapter 5, pages 183–184.

Progressive Relaxation It is possible to relax systematically, completely, and by choice. The basic idea of **progressive relaxation** is to tighten all the muscles in a given area of your body (the arms, for instance) and then voluntarily relax them. By first tensing and relaxing each area of the body (also called the *tension-release method*), you can learn what muscle tension feels like. Then when each area is relaxed, the change is more noticeable and more controllable. In this way it is possible, with practice, to greatly reduce tension.

BRIDGES

To learn the details of how this is done, consult Chapter 15, pages 522–523.

Guided Imagery In a technique called **guided imagery**, people visualize images that are calming, relaxing, or beneficial in other ways. Relaxation, for instance, can be promoted by visualizing peaceful scenes. Pick several places where you feel safe, calm, and at ease. Typical locations might be a beach or lake, the woods, floating on an air mattress in a warm pool, or lying in the sun at a quiet park. To relax, vividly imagine yourself in one of these locations. In the visualized scene, you should be alone and in a comfortable position. It is important to visualize the scene as realistically as possible. Try to feel, taste, smell, hear, and see what you would actually experience in the calming scene. Practice forming such images several times a day for about 5 minutes each time. When your scenes become familiar and

Stress management The application of cognitive and behavioral strategies to reduce stress and improve coping skills.

Progressive relaxation A method for producing deep relaxation of all parts of the body.

Guided imagery Intentional visualization of images that are calming, relaxing, or beneficial in other ways.

detailed they can be used to reduce anxiety and encourage relaxation (Rosenthal, 1993).

Modifying Ineffective Behavior

Stress is often made worse by our misguided responses to it. The following suggestions may help you deal with stress more effectively.

Slow Down Remember that stress can be self-generated. Try to deliberately do things at a slower pace—especially if your pace has sped up over the years. Tell yourself, "What counts most is not if I get there first, but if I get there at all," or "My goal is distance, not speed."

Organize Disorganization creates stress. Try to take a fresh look at your situation and get organized. Setting priorities can be a real stress fighter. Ask yourself what's really important and concentrate on the things that count. Learn to let go of trivial but upsetting irritations. And above all, when you are feeling stressed, remember to K.I.S: **K**eep **I**t **S**imple. (Some people prefer K.I.S.S: Keep It Simple, Stupid.)

Strike a Balance Work, school, family, friends, interests, hobbies, recreation, community, church—there are many important elements in a satisfying life. Damaging stress often comes from letting one element—especially work or school—get blown out of proportion. Your goal should be quality in life, not quantity. Try to strike a balance between challenging "good stress" and relaxation. Remember, when you are "doing nothing" you are actually doing something very important: Set aside time for "me acts" such as loafing, browsing, puttering, playing, and napping.

Recognize and Accept Your Limits Many of us set unrealistic and perfectionist goals. Given that no one can ever be perfect, this attitude leaves many people feeling inadequate, no matter how well they have performed. Set gradual, achievable goals for yourself. Also, set realistic limits on what you try to do on any given day. Learn to say no to added demands or responsibilities.

Seek Social Support **Social support** (close, positive relationships with others) facilitates good health and morale (Manne, 2003; Winfree & Jiang, 2010). People with close, supportive relationships have better immune responses and better health (Smith, Ruiz, & Uchino, 2004; Taylor & Master, 2011). Apparently, support from family, friends, and even pets serves as a buffer to cushion the impact of stressful events (Allen, Blascovich, & Mendes, 2002).

Women tend to make better use of social support than men do. Women who are stressed seek support, and they nurture others. Men are more likely to become aggressive or to withdraw emotionally (Taylor, 2009). This may be why "manly men" won't ask for help, whereas women in trouble call their friends! Where stress is concerned, many men could benefit from adopting women's tendency to tend and befriend others.

How else might social support help? Most people share positive events, such as marriages, births, graduations, and birthdays, with others. When things go well, we like to tell others. Sharing such events tends to amplify positive emotions and to further increase social support. In many ways, the sharing of good news is an important means by which positive events contribute to individual well-being (Gable et al., 2004).

Write about Your Feelings If you don't have someone you can talk to about stressful events, you might try expressing your thoughts and feelings in writing. Several studies have found that students who write about their upsetting experiences, thoughts, and feelings are better able to cope with stress. They also experience fewer illnesses, and they get better grades (Pennebaker, 2004; Smyth & Pennebaker, 2008). Writing about your feelings tends to leave your mind clearer. This makes it easier to pay attention to life's challenges and come up with effective coping strategies (Klein & Boals, 2001a,b). Thus, after you write about your feelings, it helps to make specific plans for coping with upsetting experiences (Pennebaker & Chung, 2007).

As an alternative, you might want to try writing about positive experiences. In one study, college students who wrote about intensely positive experiences had fewer illnesses over the next 3 months. Writing just 20 minutes a day for 3 days improved the students' moods and had a surprisingly long-lasting effect on their health (Burton & King, 2004).

Support from family and friends acts as a major buffer against stress.

Avoiding Upsetting Thoughts

Assume you are taking a test. Suddenly, you realize that you are running short of time. If you say to yourself, "Oh no, this is terrible, I've blown it now," your body's response will probably be sweating, tenseness, and a knot in your stomach. On the other hand, if you say, "I should have watched the time, but getting upset won't help; I'll just take one question at a time," your stress level will be much lower.

As stated earlier, stress is greatly affected by the views we take of events. Physical symptoms and a tendency to make poor decisions are increased by negative thoughts or "self-talk." In many cases, what you say to yourself can be the difference between coping and collapsing (Smith & Kirby, 2011).

Coping Statements Psychologist Donald Meichenbaum has popularized a technique called **stress inoculation**. In it, clients learn to fight fear and anxiety with an internal monologue of positive coping statements. First, clients learn to identify and monitor **negative self-statements** (self-critical thoughts that increase anxiety). Negative thoughts are a problem because they tend to directly elevate physical arousal. To counter this effect, clients learn to replace negative statements with coping statements from a supplied list. Eventually they are encouraged to make their own lists (Saunders et al., 1996).

How are coping statements applied? **Coping statements** are reassuring and self-enhancing. They are used to block out, or counteract, negative self-talk in stressful situations. Before giving a short speech, for instance, you would replace "I'm scared," "I can't do this," "My mind will go blank and I'll panic," or "I'll sound stupid and boring" with "I'll give my speech on something I like," or "I'll breathe deeply before I start my speech," or "My pounding heart just means I'm psyched up to do my best." Additional examples of coping statements follow.

Preparing for Stressful Situation

- I'll just take things one step at a time.
- If I get nervous, I'll just pause a moment.
- Tomorrow, I'll be through it.
- I've managed to do this before.
- What exactly do I have to do?

Confronting the Stressful Situation

- Relax now; this can't really hurt me.
- Stay organized; focus on the task.
- There's no hurry; take it step by step.
- Nobody's perfect; I'll just do my best.
- It will be over soon; just be calm.

Meichenbaum cautions that saying the "right" things to yourself may not be enough to improve stress tolerance. You must practice this approach in actual stress situations. Also, it is important to develop your own personal list of coping statements by finding what works for you. Ultimately, the value of learning this, and other stress management skills ties back into the idea that much stress is self-generated. Knowing that you can manage a demanding situation is in itself a major antidote for stress. In one study, college students who learned stress inoculation not only had less anxiety and depression, but better self-esteem as well (Schiraldi & Brown, 2001).

Lighten Up

Humor is worth cultivating as a way to reduce stress. A good sense of humor can lower your distress/stress reaction to difficult events (Lefcourt, 2003). In addition, an ability to laugh at life's ups and downs is associated with better immunity to disease (McClelland & Cheriff, 1997). Don't be afraid to laugh at yourself and at the many ways in which we humans make things difficult for ourselves. You've probably heard the following advice about everyday stresses: "Don't sweat the small stuff," and "It's all small stuff." Humor is one of the best antidotes for anxiety and emotional distress because it helps put things into perspective (Kuiper & McHale, 2009; Szabo, 2003). The vast majority of events are only as stressful as you allow them to be. Have some fun. It's perfectly healthy.

Knowledge Builder: Stress Management

RECITE

1. Exercise, meditation, and progressive relaxation are considered effective ways of countering negative self-statements. T or F?
2. A person using progressive relaxation for stress management is most likely trying to control which component of stress?
   a. bodily reactions *b.* upsetting thoughts *c.* ineffective behavior *d.* the primary appraisal
3. Research shows that social support from family and friends has little effect on the health consequences of stress. T or F?
4. While taking a stressful classroom test you say to yourself, "Stay organized, focus on the task." It's obvious that you are using
   a. guided imagery *b.* coping statements *c.* LCUs *d.* guided relaxation

REFLECT

Think Critically

5. Steve always feels extremely pressured when the due date arrives for his major term papers. How could he reduce stress in such instances?

Self-Reflect

If you were going to put together a "tool kit" for stress management, what items would you include?

Answers: 1. F **2.** *a* **3.** F **4.** *b* **5.** The stress associated with doing term papers can be almost completely eliminated by breaking up a long-term assignment into many small daily or weekly assignments (Anderson, 2010; Ariely & Wertenbroch, 2002). Students who habitually procrastinate are often amazed at how pleasant college work can be once they renounce "brinkmanship" (pushing things off to the limits of tolerance).

Social support Close, positive relationships with other people.

Stress inoculation Use of positive coping statements to control fear and anxiety.

Negative self-statements Self-critical thoughts that increase anxiety and lower performance.

Coping statements Reassuring, self-enhancing statements that are used to stop self-critical thinking.

Chapter in Review Gateways to Health, Stress, and Coping

Gateway QUESTIONS REVISITED

13.1 What is health psychology and how does behavior affect health?

13.1.1 Health psychologists are interested in behavior that helps maintain and promote health.

13.1.2 Studies of health and illness have identified a number of behavioral risk factors that have a major effect on general health and life expectancy.

13.1.3 At the minimum, it is important to maintain health-promoting behaviors with respect to diet, alcohol, exercise, and smoking.

13.1.4 Health psychologists have pioneered efforts to prevent the development of unhealthy habits and to improve well-being through community health campaigns.

13.1.5 Maintaining good health is a personal responsibility, not a matter of luck. Wellness is based on minimizing risk factors and engaging in health-promoting behaviors.

13.2 What is stress and what factors determine its severity?

13.2.1 Stress is a normal part of life occurring when demands are placed on an organism to adjust or adapt. However, it is also a major risk factor for illness and disease.

13.2.2 The body reacts to stress in a series of stages called the general adaptation syndrome (GAS). The stages of the GAS are alarm, resistance, and exhaustion. Bodily reactions in the GAS follow the pattern observed in the development of psychosomatic disorders.

13.2.3 Studies of psychoneuroimmunology show that stress lowers the body's resistance to disease by weakening the immune system.

13.2.4 Stress is more damaging in situations involving pressure, a lack of control, unpredictability of the stressor, and intense or repeated emotional shocks.

13.2.5 Stress is intensified when a situation is perceived as a threat and when a person does not feel competent to cope with it.

13.2.6 In work settings, prolonged stress can lead to burnout.

13.2.7 Making a primary appraisal greatly affects our emotional responses to a situation. During a secondary appraisal, we select problem-focused coping or emotion-focused coping (or both) as a way of managing stress.

13.3 What causes frustration and what are typical reactions to it?

13.3.1 Frustration is the negative emotional state that occurs when progress toward a goal is blocked.

13.3.2 External frustrations are based on delay, failure, rejection, loss, and other direct blocking of motives. Personal frustration is related to personal characteristics over which one has little control.

13.3.3 Frustrations of all types become more intense as the strength, urgency, or importance of the blocked motive increases.

13.3.4 Major behavioral reactions to frustration include persistence, more vigorous responding, circumvention, direct aggression, displaced aggression (including scapegoating), and escape or withdrawal.

13.4 Are there different types of conflict and how do people react to conflict?

13.4.1 Conflict occurs when one must choose between contradictory alternatives.

13.4.2 Four major types of conflict are approach-approach, avoidance-avoidance, approach-avoidance, and multiple conflicts (double approach-avoidance and multiple approach-avoidance).

13.4.3 Approach-approach conflicts are usually the easiest to resolve.

13.4.4 Avoidance conflicts are difficult to resolve and are characterized by inaction, indecision, freezing, and a desire to escape (called leaving the field).

13.4.5 People usually remain in approach-avoidance conflicts but fail to fully resolve them. Approach-avoidance conflicts are associated with ambivalence and partial approach.

13.4.6 Vacillation is a common reaction to double and multiple approach-avoidance conflicts.

13.5 What are defense mechanisms?

13.5.1 Defense mechanisms are mental processes used to avoid, deny, or distort sources of threat or anxiety, including threats to one's self-image.

13.5.2 Overuse of defense mechanisms makes people less adaptable.

13.5.3 A large number of defense mechanisms have been identified, including compensation, denial, fantasy, intellectualization, isolation, projection, rationalization, reaction formation, regression, repression, and sublimation.

13.6 What do we know about coping with feelings of helplessness and depression?

13.6.1 Learned helplessness can be used as a model for understanding depression. Depression is a major, and surprisingly common, emotional problem.

13.6.2 Actions and thoughts that counter feelings of helplessness tend to reduce depression. Mastery training, optimism, and hope all act as antidotes for learned helplessness.

13.6.3 The college blues are a relatively mild form of depression. Learning to manage college work and to challenge self-critical thinking can help alleviate the college blues.

13.7 How is stress related to health and disease?

13.7.1 Work with stress scales like the *Social Readjustment Rating Scale* indicates that multiple life changes tend to increase long-range susceptibility to accident or illness.

13.7.2 Immediate physical and mental health is more closely related to the intensity and severity of daily hassles (microstressors).

13.7.3 Intense or prolonged stress may cause damage in the form of psychosomatic problems.

13.7.4 During biofeedback training, bodily processes are monitored and converted to a signal that tells what the body is doing. Biofeedback allows people to alleviate some psychosomatic illnesses by altering bodily activities.

13.7.5 People with Type A personalities are competitive, striving, hostile, impatient, and prone to having heart attacks.

13.7.6 People who have traits of the hardy personality seem to be unusually resistant to stress

13.7.7 Optimism and positive emotions tend to buffer stress.

***13.8** What are the best strategies for managing stress?*

13.8.1 The damaging effects of stress can be reduced with stress management techniques.

13.8.2 A number of coping skills can be applied to manage stress. Most of these focus on one of three areas: bodily effects, ineffective behavior, and upsetting thoughts.

13.8.3 All of the following are good ways to manage bodily reactions to stress: exercise, meditation, progressive relaxation, and guided imagery.

13.8.4 To minimize ineffective behavior when you are stressed, you can slow down, get organized, balance work and relaxation, accept your limits, seek social support, and write about your feelings.

13.8.5 Learning to use coping statements is a good way to combat upsetting thoughts.

MEDIA RESOURCES

Web Resources

Internet addresses frequently change. To find an up-to-date list of URLs for the sites listed here, visit your Psychology CourseMate.

Division 38 Visit the website of the Health Psychology division of the American Psychological Association.

Careers in Health Psychology Learn more about careers in health psychology.

The Longevity Game Find out how long you might live; explore your options.

The Discovery of Stress Read more about Hans Selye's discovery of stress.

Psychoneuroimmunology Read an article on psychoneuroimmunology from the American Psychological Association.

Burnout Read about job burnout symptoms and fixes.

Defense Mechanisms Try to role play various defense mechanisms.

Learned Helplessness Read more about Seligman's discovery of learned helplessness.

Depression and Control Explore the relationship between learned helplessness and depression.

SRRS Fill out an online version of the Social Readjustment Rating Scale.

Psychosomatic Illness and Disorder More information on psychosomatic illness.

Type A Behavior Are you a Type A? Find out.

Self-Growth.Com Explore a self-improvement and personal growth website that provides many links to stress management resources, online articles, and links to related topics such as biofeedback and stress.

Preventive Health Center A general source of information on how to maintain health and prevent disease.

Stress Management Resources This site helps you deal with job-related stress.

Interactive Learning

Log in to **CengageBrain** to access the resources your instructor requires. For this book, you can access:

CourseMate brings course concepts to life with interactive learning, study, and exam preparation tools that support the printed textbook. A textbook-specific website, ***Psychology CourseMate*** includes an ***integrated interactive eBook*** and other ***interactive learning tools*** including quizzes, flashcards, videos, and more.

CENGAGE**NOW**™

CengageNOW is an easy-to-use online resource that helps you study in less time to get the grade you want—NOW. Take a pre-test for this chapter and receive a personalized study plan based on your results that will identify the topics you need to review and direct you to online resources to help you master those topics. Then take a post-test to help you determine the concepts you have mastered and what you will need to work on. If your textbook does not include an access code card, go to CengageBrain.com to gain access.

WebTUTOR™

More than just an interactive study guide, **WebTutor** is an anytime, anywhere customized learning solution with an eBook, keeping you connected to your textbook, instructor, and classmates.

If your professor has assigned **Aplia** homework:

1. Sign in to your account.
2. Complete the corresponding homework exercises as required by your professor.
3. When finished, click "Grade It Now" to see which areas you have mastered and which need more work, and for detailed explanations of every answer.

Visit **www.cengagebrain.com** to access your account and purchase materials.

Gateway THEME

Judgments of abnormality are relative, but psychological disorders clearly exist and need to be classified, explained, and treated.

14

Psychological Disorders

Beware the Helicopters

"The helicopters. Oh no, not the helicopters. Have come to tear the feathers out of my frontal lobes. Help me, nurse, help me, can't you hear them? Gotta get back into my body to save it…. The doctor is thinking I would make good glue."

These are the words of Carol North, a psychiatrist who survived schizophrenia. In addition to being plagued by hallucinated helicopters, Carol heard voices that said: "Be good," "Do bad," "Stand up," "Sit down," "Collide with the other world," "Do you want a cigar?" (North, 1987).

Carol North's painful journey into the shadows of madness left her incapacitated for nearly 20 years. Wonderfully, she has since forged a career as an eminent psychiatrist. Today, she is helping others escape the maze of mental illness that once imprisoned her (see, for example, North et al., 2008). Her case is but one hint of the magnitude of mental health problems. One quarter of American adults suffer from a diagnosable mental disorder in any given year. In 2006, about 33,300 Americans committed suicide, of whom about 90 percent had a diagnosable mental disorder (National Institute of Mental Health, 2011a).

What does it mean to be "crazy"? A hundred years ago, doctors and nonprofessionals alike used terms such as "crazy," "insane," "cracked," and "lunatic" quite freely. The "insane" were thought of as bizarre and definitely different from the rest of us. Today, our understanding of psychological disorders is more sophisticated. To draw the line between normal and abnormal, we must weigh some complex issues. We'll explore some of them in this chapter, as well as an array of psychological problems.

Gateway QUESTIONS

14.1 *How is abnormality defined?*
14.2 *What are the major psychological disorders?*
14.3 *How can psychiatric labeling be misused?*
14.4 *What are the general characteristics of psychotic disorders?*
14.5 *What is the nature of a delusional disorder?*
14.6 *What forms does schizophrenia take and what causes it?*
14.7 *What are mood disorders and what causes them?*
14.8 *What problems result when a person suffers high levels of anxiety?*
14.9 *How do psychologists explain anxiety-based disorders?*
14.10 *What is a personality disorder?*
14.11 *Why do people commit suicide and can they be stopped?*

Normality—What's Normal?

Gateway Question 14.1: *How is abnormality defined?*

"That guy is really wacko. His porch lights are dimming." "Yeah, the butter's sliding off his waffle. He's ready to go postal." Informally, it's tempting to make such snap judgments about mental health. But deciding whether a person's behavior is abnormal is harder than it might seem. To seriously classify people as psychologically unhealthy raises complex and age-old issues. The conservative, church-going housewife down the street might be flagrantly psychotic and a lethal danger to her children. The reclusive eccentric who hangs out at the park could be the sanest person in town. Let's begin our discussion with some basic factors that affect judgments of normality.

The scientific study of mental, emotional, and behavioral disorders is known as **psychopathology**. The term also refers to mental disorders themselves, such as schizophrenia or depression, and to behavior patterns that make people unhappy and impair their personal growth (Butcher, Mineka, & Hooley, 2010). Even though this definition may seem obvious, defining abnormality can be tricky (Luyten & Blatt, 2011). We might begin with the idea of statistical abnormality, which some psychologists use to define normality more objectively.

Statistical abnormality refers to scoring very high or low on some dimension, such as intelligence, anxiety, or depression. Anxiety, for example, is a feature of several psychological disorders. To measure it, we could create a test to learn how many people show low, medium, or high levels of anxiety. Usually, the results of such tests will form a *normal* (bell-shaped) *curve*. (*Normal* in this case refers only to the *shape* of the curve.) Notice that most people score near the middle of a normal curve; very few have extremely high or low scores (• Figure 14.1). A person who deviates from the average by being anxious all the time (high anxiety) might be abnormal. So, too, might a person who never feels anxiety.

Then statistical abnormality tells us nothing about the meaning of deviations from the norm? Right. It is as statistically "abnormal" (unusual) for a person to score above 145 on an IQ test as it is to score below 55. However, only the lower score is regarded as "abnormal" or undesirable. In the same sense, it is unusual for a person to speak four languages or to win an event at the Olympics, but these are desirable, if rare, accomplishments.

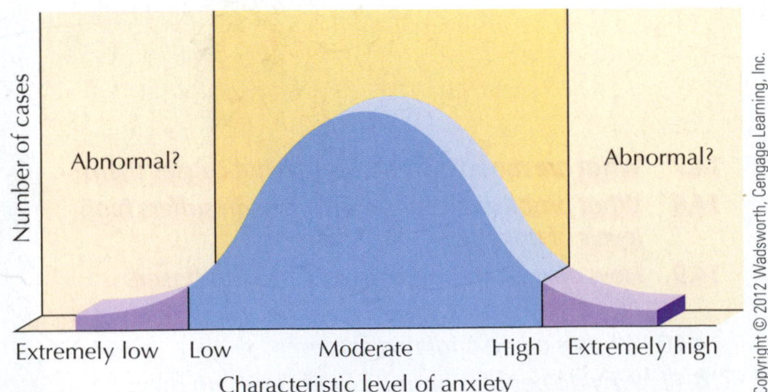

• Figure 14.1 The number of people displaying a personal characteristic may help define what is statistically abnormal.

Social nonconformity does not automatically indicate psychopathology.

Statistical definitions also can't tell us *where to draw the line* between normality and abnormality. To take a new example, we could obtain the average frequency of sexual intercourse for persons of a particular age, sex, sexual orientation, and marital status. Clearly, a person who feels driven to have sex dozens of times a day has a problem. But as we move back toward the norm, we face the problem of drawing lines. How often does a normal behavior have to occur before it becomes abnormal? As you can see, statistical boundary lines tend to be somewhat arbitrary (Comer, 2011).

Yet another approach is to focus on the atypical behavior or nonconformity that may be associated with some disorders. **Social nonconformity** refers to disobeying public standards for acceptable conduct. Extreme nonconformity can lead to destructive or self-destructive behavior. (Think, for instance, of a drug abuser or a prostitute.) However, we must be careful to separate unhealthy nonconformity from creative lifestyles. Many eccentric "characters" are charming and emotionally stable. Note, too, that strictly following social norms is no guarantee of mental health. In some cases, psychopathology involves rigid conformity (see "Crazy for a Day").

A young woman ties a thick rubber cord around her ankles, screams hysterically, and jumps headfirst off a bridge. Thirty years ago, the woman's behavior might have seemed completely crazy. Today, it is a routine form of entertainment (called "bungee jumping"). Before any behavior can be defined as abnormal, we must also consider the *situational context* (social situation, behavioral setting, or general circumstances) in which it occurs. Is it normal to stand outside and water a lawn with a hose? It depends on whether it is raining. Is it abnormal for a grown man to remove his pants and expose himself to another man or woman in a place of business? It depends on whether the other person is a bank clerk or a doctor.

Discovering Psychology Crazy for a Day

Performing a mildly abnormal behavior is a good way to get a sense of how social norms define "normality" in daily life. Here's your assignment: Do something strange in public and observe how people react to you. (Please don't do anything dangerous, harmful, or offensive—and don't get arrested!) Here are some deviant behaviors that other students have staged:

- Sit in the dining area of a fast-food restaurant and loudly carry on a conversation with an imaginary companion.
- Stand in a busy hallway on campus and adopt a kung fu stance. Remain in that position for 10 minutes.
- Walk around campus on a sunny day wearing a raincoat and carrying an open umbrella. Keep the umbrella over your head when you are inside buildings.
- Stick one finger in your nose and another in your ear. Walk through a busy shopping mall.
- Cover your head with aluminum foil for a day.

Does the idea of performing any of these actions make you uncomfortable? If so, you may not need to do anything more to appreciate how powerfully social norms constrain our actions. As we have noted, social nonconformity is just one facet of abnormal behavior. Nevertheless, actions that are regarded as "strange" within a particular culture are often the first sign to others that a person has a problem.

© John Rensten/Corbis

Almost any imaginable behavior can be considered normal in some contexts. For example, in 2003, a man sawed off his own arm. Mind you, he was a mountain climber who had fallen into a crevasse, trapping his arm between two boulders. After 5 days of trying to free his arm, and nearing unconsciousness, he did what he needed to do to survive (Ralston, 2004).

As implied by our earlier discussion of social norms, culture is one of the most influential contexts in which any behavior is judged (Fabrega, 2004). In some cultures, it is considered normal to defecate or urinate in public or to appear naked in public. In our culture, such behaviors would be considered unusual or abnormal. In some Muslim cultures, women who remain completely housebound are considered normal or even virtuous. In some Western cultures, they might be diagnosed as suffering from a disorder called agoraphobia. (Agoraphobia is described later in this chapter.)

Thus, *cultural relativity* (the idea that judgments are made relative to the values of one's culture) can affect the diagnosis of psychological disorders. Still, *all* cultures classify people as abnormal if they fail to communicate with others or are consistently unpredictable in their actions.

Yet another approach is to characterize psychopathology by *subjective discomfort* (private feelings of pain, unhappiness, or emotional distress) like Carol North endured.

But couldn't a person experience serious distress without psychopathology and couldn't someone be seriously disturbed without feeling discomfort? Yes on both counts. People who have, for example, lost a loved one or lived through a natural disaster like a hurricane will normally take quite some time to overcome their distress. Also, psychopathology doesn't always cause personal anguish. A person suffering from mania might feel elated and "on top of the world." A *lack* of discomfort may actually reveal a problem. For example, if you showed no signs of grief after the death of a close friend, we might suspect psychopathology. In practice, though, subjective discomfort explains most instances in which people voluntarily seek professional help.

Core Feature of Disordered Behavior

If abnormality is so hard to define, how are judgments of psychopathology made? Although the standards we have discussed are *relative*, psychopathological behavior does have a core feature: It is **maladaptive**. Rather than helping people cope successfully, maladaptive behavior arises from an underlying psychological or biological dysfunction that makes it more difficult for them to meet the demands of day-to-day life (American Psychiatric Association, 2000, 2010). Maladaptive behavior most often results in serious psychological discomfort, disability and/or *loss of control* of thoughts, behaviors, or feelings.

For example, gambling is not a problem if people bet for entertainment and can maintain self-control. However, compulsive gambling is a sign of psychopathology. The voices that Carol North kept hearing are a prime example of what it means to lose control of one's thoughts. In the most extreme cases, people become a danger to themselves or others, which is clearly maladaptive (Hansell & Damour, 2007).

Psychopathology The scientific study of mental, emotional, and behavioral disorders; also, abnormal or maladaptive behavior.

Statistical abnormality Abnormality defined on the basis of an extreme score on some dimension, such as IQ or anxiety.

Social nonconformity Failure to conform to societal norms or the usual minimum standards for social conduct.

Maladaptive behavior Behavior arising from an underlying psychological or biological dysfunction that makes it difficult to adapt to the environment and meet the demands of day-to-day life.

■ **TABLE 14.1 Levels of Functioning**

Scale	Level of Functioning	Examples
100	Superior functioning in a wide range of activities. No symptoms.	Life's problems never seem to get out of hand. Person is sought by others because of his or her many positive qualities.
90	Absent or minimal symptoms, functioning well in all areas, no more than everyday problems.	Has mild anxiety before exams, occasional arguments with family members.
80	If symptoms are present, they are brief and common reactions to stressors. No more than slight impairment in relationships, work, or school.	Has difficulty concentrating after family arguments, is falling behind in schoolwork.
70	Some mild symptoms, or some difficulty with relationships, work, or school.	Mood is depressed and has mild insomnia. Has been truant at school and has stolen things at home.
60	Moderate symptoms or moderate problems with relationships, work, or school.	Emotions are blunted, speech evasive, occasional panic attacks, no friends, unable to keep a job.
50	Serious symptoms or any serious impairments in relationships, work, or school.	Person has suicidal thoughts, engages in obsessional rituals, shop-lifts, has no friends, is unable to keep a job.
40	Some impairment in grasp of reality or in communication, plus major impairments in work or school relationships, judgment, thinking, or mood.	Speech is illogical, obscure, or irrelevant. Person is depressed and avoids friends, neglects family, and is unable to work.
30	Behavior is considerably affected by delusions or hallucinations; or, person is seriously impaired in communication or judgment; or, is unable to function in almost all areas.	Person is sometimes incoherent; acts grossly inappropriately; is preoccupied with suicide; stays in bed all day; has no job, home, or friends.
20	Some danger of hurting self or others; or, occasionally fails to maintain minimal personal hygiene; or, communication is grossly impaired.	Person makes tentative suicide attempts, is frequently violent and manically excited, smears own feces; is either incoherent or mute.
10	Persistent danger of severely hurting self or others; or, persistent inability to maintain minimal personal hygiene; or, serious suicidal acts.	Repeatedly violent, maintains almost no personal hygiene, has made potentially lethal suicide attempts.

Adapted from the *Global Assessment of Functioning Scale*, DSM-IV-TR (American Psychiatric Association, 2000).

Various levels of functioning—from superior to severely disturbed—are described in ■ Table 14.1. Notice that the bottom of the scale reads, "Persistent danger of severely hurting self or others." Obviously, behavior at that level is maladaptive and involves a serious loss of control.

In practice, deciding that a person needs help usually occurs when the person *does something* (assaults a person, hallucinates, stares into space, collects too many old pizza cartons, and so forth) that *annoys* or *gains the attention* of a person in a *position of power* in the person's life (an employer, teacher, parent, spouse, or the person himself or herself). That person then *does something* about it. (The person may voluntarily seek help, the person may be urged to see a psychologist, a police officer may be called, or a relative may start commitment proceedings.)

Insanity and the Insanity Defense

What are commitment proceedings? Commitment proceedings are legal proceedings that may result in the finding of **insanity**, which is a legal, not psychological, term. It refers to an inability to manage one's affairs or foresee the consequences of one's actions. People who are declared insane are not legally responsible for their actions. If necessary, they can be involuntarily committed to a mental hospital.

Legally, insanity is established by testimony from *expert witnesses* (psychologists and psychiatrists) recognized by a court of law as qualified to give opinions on a specific topic. Involuntary commitments happen most often when people are brought to emergency rooms or are arrested for committing a crime. People who are involuntarily committed are usually judged to be a danger to themselves or to others, or they are severely intellectually disabled (Luchins et al., 2004).

What is the insanity defense? Someone accused of a crime may argue that he or she is *not guilty by reason of insanity*. In practice, this means that the accused, due to a diagnosable psychological disorder, was unable to appreciate that what he or she did was wrong (Knoll & Resnick, 2008). This may be distinguished from *not guilty by reason of diminished responsibility*, which is more likely to apply in other situations, such as cases of intellectual disability, such as Down syndrome or brain damage.

You may be surprised to learn that being diagnosed with a psychological disorder does not automatically imply a successful insanity defense (Martin & Weiss, 2010). For example, someone diagnosed with, say, an anxiety disorder, who commits murder might, nevertheless, be well aware that murder is against the law. In fact, very few criminal trials end with this verdict.

Classifying Mental Disorders—Problems by the Book

Gateway Question 14.2: *What are the major psychological disorders?*

Psychological problems are classified by using the *Diagnostic and Statistical Manual of Mental Disorders* (DSM). The current edition is the DSM-IV-TR (the fourth edition, text revision) and a new edition, the DSM-5, is due to be published in 2013 (American Psychiatric Association, 2000; 2010). Regardless of the edition, the DSM influences most activities in mental health settings—from

TABLE 14.2 Some Selected Categories of Psychopathology

Problem	Primary Symptom	Typical Signs of Trouble
Schizophrenia and other psychotic disorders	Loss of contact with reality	You hear or see things that others don't; your mind has been playing tricks on you.
Mood disorders	Mania or depression	You feel sad and hopeless; or you talk too loud and too fast and have a rush of ideas and feelings that others think are unreasonable.
Anxiety disorders	High anxiety or anxiety-based distortions of behavior	You have anxiety attacks and feel like you are going to die; or you are afraid to do things that most people can do; or you spend unusual amounts of time doing things like washing your hands or counting your heartbeats.
Somatoform disorders	Bodily complaints without an organic (physical) basis	You feel physically sick, but your doctor says nothing is wrong with you; or you suffer from pain that has no physical basis; or you are preoccupied with thoughts about being sick.
Dissociative disorders	Amnesia, feelings of unreality, multiple identities	There are major gaps in your memory of events; you feel like you are a robot or a stranger to yourself; others tell you that you have done things that you don't remember doing.
Personality disorders	Unhealthy personality patterns	Your behavior patterns repeatedly cause problems at work, at school, and in your relationships with others.
Sexual and gender identity disorders	Disturbed gender identity, deviant sexual behavior, problems in sexual adjustment	You feel that you are a man trapped in a woman's body (or the reverse); or you can only gain sexual satisfaction by engaging in highly atypical sexual behavior; or you have problems with sexual desire, arousal, or performance.
Substance-related disorders	Disturbances related to drug abuse or dependence	You have been drinking too much, using illegal drugs, or taking prescription drugs more often than you should.

Source: American Psychiatric Association (2000, 2010)

diagnosis to therapy to insurance company billing (First & Pincus, 2002).

A **mental disorder** is a significant impairment in psychological functioning. If you were to glance through the DSM, you would see many disorders described. It's impossible here to discuss all these problems. However, a simplified list of some major disorders can be found in Table 14.2. Those disorders are further described in the next section.

An Overview of Psychological Disorders

People suffering from **psychotic disorders** have "retreated from reality." That is, they suffer from hallucinations and delusions and are socially withdrawn. Psychotic disorders are severely disabling and often lead to hospitalization. Typically, psychotic patients cannot control their thoughts and actions. For example, David often heard the voice of his Uncle Bill: "He told me to turn off the TV. He said, 'It's too damn loud, turn it down, turn it down.' Other times, he talks about fishing. 'Good day for fishing. Got to go fishing'" (Durand & Barlow, 2010). Psychotic symptoms occur in schizophrenia, delusional disorders, and some mood disorders. Also, psychosis may be related to medical problems, drug abuse, and other conditions.

Organic mental disorders are problems caused by brain pathology; that is, by drug damage, diseases of the brain, injuries, poisons, and so on (Figure 14.2). A person with an organic disorder may have severe emotional disturbances, impaired thinking, memory loss, personality changes, delirium, or psychotic symptoms (Nolen-Hoeksema, 2011).

In reality, almost all mental disorders are partly biological (Hansell & Damour, 2007). That's why the DSM does not list "organic mental disorders" as a separate category. Nevertheless, all the following problems are closely associated with organic damage: delirium, dementia, amnesia, and other cognitive disorders; mental disorders due to a general medical condition; and substance-related disorders (drug abuse).

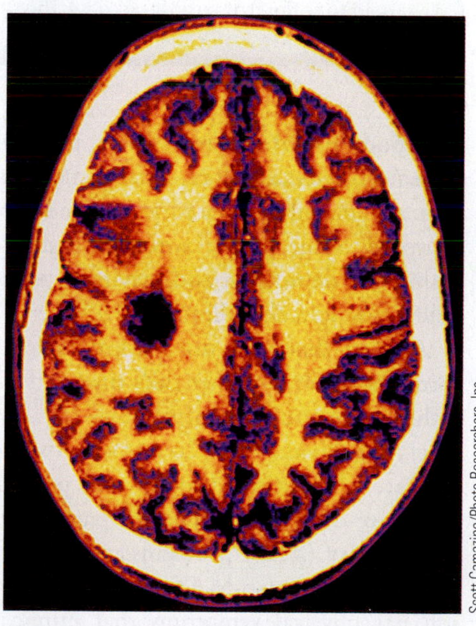

Figure 14.2 This MRI scan of a human brain (viewed from the top) reveals a tumor (dark spot). Mental disorders sometimes have organic causes of this sort. However, in many instances, no organic damage can be found.

Scott Camazine/Photo Researchers, Inc.

Insanity A legal term that refers to a mental inability to manage one's affairs or to be aware of the consequences of one's actions.

Mental disorder A significant impairment in psychological functioning.

Psychotic disorder A severe mental disorder characterized by a retreat from reality, by hallucinations and delusions, and by social withdrawal.

Organic mental disorder A mental or emotional problem caused by brain diseases or injuries.

Human Diversity Running Amok with Cultural Maladies

Every culture recognizes the existence of psychopathology, and most have at least a few folk names for afflictions you won't find in the DSM. Here are some examples of *culture-bound syndromes* from around the world (Durand & Barlow, 2010; López & Guarnaccia, 2000; Sumathipala, Siribaddana, & Bhugra, 2004; Teo & Gaw, 2010):

- **Amok** Men in Malaysia, Laos, the Philippines, and Polynesia, who believe they have been insulted are sometimes known to go amok. After a period of brooding, they erupt into an outburst of violent, aggressive, or homicidal behavior randomly directed at people and objects.
- **Susto** Among Latin Americans, the symptoms of *susto* include insomnia, irritability, phobias, and an increase in sweating and heart rate. Susto can result if someone is badly frightened by a black magic curse. In extreme cases, *voodoo death* can result, as the person is literally scared to death.
- **Ghost sickness** Among many American Indian tribes, people who become preoccupied with death and the deceased are said to suffer from ghost sickness. The symptoms of ghost sickness include bad dreams, weakness, loss of appetite, fainting, dizziness, fear, anxiety, hallucinations, loss of consciousness, confusion, feelings of futility, and a sense of suffocation.
- **Koro** In South and East Asia, a man may experience sudden and intense anxiety that his penis (or, in females, the vulva and nipples) will recede into the body. In addition to the terror this incites, victims also believe that advanced cases of *koro* can cause death. A similar fear of shrinking genitals has also been reported from West Africa (Dzokoto, & Adams, 2005).
- **Zar** In North African and Middle Eastern societies, *zar* is said to occur when spirits possess an individual. *Zar* is marked by shouting, laughing, hitting the head against a wall, singing, or weeping. Victims may become apathetic or withdrawn and may refuse to eat or carry out daily tasks.
- **Dhat** In Indian society, *dhat* is the fear of the loss of semen during nocturnal emissions. A man suffering from *dhat* will feel anxious and perhaps also guilty. He may also experience fatigue, loss of appetite, weakness, anxiety, and sexual dysfunction.
- **Hikikomori** In Japanese society, adolescents or young adults who refuse to leave their parents' homes for months at a time are experiencing an extreme form of social withdrawal called *hikikomori*.

It's clear that people everywhere have a need to label and categorize troubled behavior. On the one hand, it takes cultural sensitivity to understand these unusual experiences (Flaskerud, 2009). On the other hand, the terms listed here provide little guidance about the true nature of a person's problems or the best ways to treat them. That's why the DSM is based on empirical data and clinical observations. Otherwise, psychologists and psychiatrists would be no better than folk healers when making diagnoses (Ancis, Chen, & Schultz, 2004).

By the way, culture-bound disorders occur in all societies. For example, American psychologists Pamela Keel and Kelly Klump believe that the eating disorder bulimia is primarily a syndrome of Western cultures like the United States (Keel & Klump, 2003).

Mood disorders are defined primarily by the presence of extreme, intense, and long-lasting emotions. Afflicted persons may be *manic*, meaning agitated, elated, and hyperactive, or they may be *depressed*. Some people with mood disorders alternate between mania and depression and may have psychotic symptoms as well (Ellison-Wright & Bullmore, 2010).

Anxiety disorders are marked by fear or anxiety and by distorted behavior. Some anxiety disorders involve feelings of panic. Others take the form of phobias (irrational fears) or just overwhelming anxiety and nervousness. Two additional anxiety disorders are acute stress disorder and posttraumatic stress disorder. Obsessive-compulsive behavior patterns are also associated with high anxiety. (These problems are described later in this chapter.)

Somatoform (so-MAT-oh-form) **disorders** occur when a person has physical symptoms that mimic disease or injury (e.g., paralysis, blindness, illness, chronic pain), for which there is no identifiable physical cause. In such cases, psychological factors appear to explain the symptoms.

A person with a **dissociative disorder** may have temporary amnesia or multiple personalities. Also included in this category are frightening episodes of *depersonalization*, in which people feel like they are outside of their bodies, are behaving like robots, or are lost in a dream world.

Personality disorders are deeply ingrained, unhealthy personality patterns. Such patterns usually appear in adolescence and continue through much of adult life. They include paranoid (overly suspicious), narcissistic (self-loving), dependent, borderline, and antisocial personality types, as well as others.

Sexual and gender identity disorders include any of a wide range of difficulties with sexual identity, deviant sexual behavior, or sexual adjustment. In gender identity disorders, sexual identity does not match a person's physical sex, and the person may seek a sex-change operation. Deviations in sexual behavior known as *paraphilias* include pedophilia, exhibitionism, fetishism, voyeurism, and so on. Also found in this category are a variety of *sexual dysfunctions* (problems in sexual desire, arousal, or response).

BRIDGES

Find out more about paraphilias and sexual dysfunction in Chapter 11, pages 385–386 and 395–398.

Substance-related disorders involve abuse of, or dependence on, psychoactive drugs. Typical culprits include alcohol, barbiturates, opiates, cocaine, amphetamines, hallucinogens, marijuana, and nicotine. A person with a substance-related disorder cannot stop using the drug and may also suffer from withdrawal symp-

TABLE 14.3 Major *DSM-IV-TR* Categories

Disorders usually first diagnosed in infancy, childhood, or adolescence
- **Mental retardation (Intellectual disability)** *M
  - Example: Mild mental retardation (intellectual disability) *D
- **Learning disorders**
  - Example: Reading disorder (dyslexia)
- **Motor skills disorder**
  - Example: Developmental coordination disorder
- **Communication disorders**
  - Example: Childhood onset fluency disorder (stuttering)
- **Pervasive developmental disorders**
  - Example: Autistic disorder (Autism spectrum disorder) *M
- **Attention-deficit and disruptive behavior disorders**
  - Example: Attention-deficit/hyperactivity disorder
- **Feeding and eating disorders of infancy or early childhood** *M
  - Example: Pica (eating inedible substances) *R
- **Tic disorders**
  - Example: Tourette's disorder *R
- **Elimination disorders**
  - Example: Enuresis (bedwetting)
- **Other disorders of infancy, childhood, or adolescence**
  - Example: Separation anxiety disorder *R

Delirium, dementia, amnestic, and other cognitive disorders *M
- **Delirium**
  - Example: Delirium due to a general medical condition
- **Dementia** *D
  - Example: Dementia of the Alzheimer's type *R
- **Amnestic disorders** (memory loss) *D
  - Example: Amnestic disorder due to a general medical condition *R
- **Cognitive disorder not otherwise specified** *R

Mental disorders due to a general medical condition not elsewhere classified
- **Catatonic disorder due to a general medical condition**
- **Personality change due to a general medical condition**
- **Mental disorder not otherwise specified due to a general medical condition**

Substance-related disorders
- **Cocaine-related disorders**
  - Example: Cocaine intoxication delirium

Schizophrenia and other psychotic disorders
- **Schizophrenia**
  - Example: Schizophrenia, paranoid type *D
- **Schizophreniform disorder**
- **Schizoaffective disorder**
- **Delusional disorder**
  - Example: Delusional disorder, grandiose type
- **Brief psychotic disorder**
- **Shared psychotic disorder (folie a deux)** *R
- **Psychotic disorder due to a general medical condition**
- **Psychotic disorder not otherwise specified**

Mood disorders
- **Depressive disorders**
  - Example: Major depressive disorder
- **Bipolar disorders**
  - Example: Bipolar I disorder
- **Mood disorder due to a general medical condition**
- **Substance-induced mood disorder**
- **Depressive disorder not otherwise specified**

Anxiety disorders
- **Example: Panic disorder**

Somatoform disorders
- **Example: Conversion disorder**

Factitious disorders (faked disability or illness) *R
- **Example: Factitious disorder** *R

Dissociative disorders
- **Example: Dissociative identity disorder**

Sexual and gender identity disorders
- **Sexual dysfunctions**
  - Example: Hypoactive sexual desire disorder
- **Paraphilias** *M
  - Example: Voyeurism *M
- **Sexual disorder not otherwise specified**
- **Gender identity disorders**
  - Example: Gender identity disorder (Gender Incongruence) *M

Eating disorders
- **Example: Anorexia nervosa**

Sleep disorders
- **Primary sleep disorders**
  - Example: Primary insomnia
- **Parasomnias** *R
  - Example: Sleep terror disorder *R
- **Sleep disorders related to another mental disorder** *R
  - Example: Insomnia related to posttraumatic stress disorder *R

Impulse control disorders not elsewhere classified
- **Example: Kleptomania**

Adjustment disorders *R
- **Example: Adjustment disorder** *R

Personality disorders
- Example: **Antisocial personality disorder** *M

Source: Adapted from the DSM-IV-TR (American Psychiatric Association, 2000).

*Indictes this DSM-IV-TR category may be modified in a major way (M), reclassified (R), or deleted (D) in the forthcoming DSM-5 (American Psychiatric Association, 2010).

toms, delirium, dementia, amnesia, psychosis, emotional outbursts, sexual problems, and sleep disturbances.

BRIDGES

Problems with drug abuse and dependence are discussed in Chapter 5. **See pages 185–187.**

In upcoming sections, we will explore some disorders in more detail, beginning with psychotic disorders. (See Table 14.3 for a more detailed list of disorders, including those in Table 14.2. You don't need to memorize all of them.)

In addition to the formal mental disorders we have reviewed, many cultures have names for "unofficial" psychological "disorders." See "Running Amok with Cultural Maladies" for some examples.

Mood disorder A major disturbance in mood or emotion, such as depression or mania.

Anxiety disorder Disruptive feelings of fear, apprehension, or anxiety, or distortions in behavior that are anxiety related.

Somatoform disorder Physical symptoms that mimic disease or injury for which there is no identifiable physical cause.

Dissociative disorder Temporary amnesia, multiple personality, or depersonalization.

Personality disorder A maladaptive personality pattern.

Sexual and gender identity disorders Any of a wide range of difficulties with sexual identity, deviant sexual behavior, or sexual adjustment.

Substance-related disorder Abuse of or dependence on a mood- or behavior-altering drug.

DSM-5

Isn't neurosis a psychological disorder? You might be surprised to learn that definitions of mental disorders change over time. When the DSM was first published in 1952, **neurosis** was included. The term was dropped in later editions because it is too imprecise. "Neurotic" behavior is now part of anxiety, somatoform, or dissociative disorders. Even though *neurosis* is an outdated term, you may still hear it used to loosely refer to problems involving excessive anxiety.

As mentioned previously, a new edition, the DSM-5, is due in 2013. Like older editions, it will reflect updated research and changing social attitudes (Thomas, 2009; Ronningstam, 2009). For example, *gender identity disorder*, which was mentioned earlier, may continue to be included in the DSM-5 (American Psychiatric Association, 2010; Gever, 2009). Opponents of this term believe that many people whose physical sex does not match their sexual identity are well adjusted and should not be labeled as "disordered" (Zucker & Spitzer, 2005).

New mental disorders may also be added to the DSM-5. One possibility being considered is *post-traumatic embitterment disorder*, which occurs when a person is left so bitter after a perceived injustice that he or she cannot let it go (Linden et al., 2008). For example, Jack's wife left him 3 years ago. He is embittered, angry, and humiliated. He cannot forget or forgive her. Jack sits at home alone every night, is not seeing anyone else, is having troubles at work, and is estranged from his children.

If added, post-traumatic embitterment disorder would join an ever-growing list of recognized disorders. Other possibilities include *melancholia*, *apathy syndrome*, and *Internet addiction* (American Psychiatric Association, 2010). Such terms have led some to worry that more and more normal human behavior is being redefined as problematic (Lane, 2009). Yet each of the problems listed here can seriously disrupt a person's life and perhaps should be part of the next DSM.

General Risk Factors

What causes psychological disorders like those listed in Table 14.3? Here are some general risk factors that contribute to psychopathology:

- **Biological/physical factors:** genetic defects or inherited vulnerabilities, poor prenatal care, very low birth weight, chronic physical illness or disability, exposure to toxic chemicals or drugs, head injuries.
- **Psychological factors:** stress, low intelligence, learning disorders, lack of control or mastery.
- **Family factors:** parents who are immature, mentally disturbed, criminal, or abusive; severe marital strife; extremely poor child discipline; disordered family communication patterns.
- **Social conditions:** poverty, stressful living conditions, homelessness, social disorganization, overcrowding.

Before we go on to explore some specific problems and their causes, let's take a detour into the issues involved in psychiatric labeling.

Disorders in Perspective—Psychiatric Labeling

Gateway Question 14.3: *How can psychiatric labeling be misused?*

Before we begin our survey of psychological disorders, a caution is in order. The terms we will encounter in this chapter are meant to aid communication about human problems. But if used maliciously or carelessly, they can hurt people. (See "A Disease Called Freedom.") Everyone has felt or acted "crazy" during brief periods of stress or high emotion. People with psychological disorders have problems that are more severe or long lasting than most of us experience. Otherwise, they may not be that different from the rest of us.

A fascinating classic study carried out by psychologist David Rosenhan illustrates the impact of psychiatric labeling. Rosenhan and several colleagues had themselves committed to mental hospitals with a diagnosis of "schizophrenia" (Rosenhan, 1973). After being admitted, each of these "pseudo-patients" dropped all pretense of mental illness. Yet, even though they acted completely normal, none of the researchers was ever recognized by hospital *staff* as a phony patient. Real patients were not so easily fooled. It was not unusual for a patient to say to one of the researchers, "You're not crazy, you're checking up on the hospital!" or "You're a journalist."

To record his observations, Rosenhan took notes by carefully jotting things on a small piece of paper hidden in his hand. However, he soon learned that stealth was totally unnecessary. Rosenhan simply walked around with a clipboard, recording observations. No one questioned this behavior. Rosenhan's note taking was just regarded as a symptom of his "illness." This observation clarifies why staff members failed to detect the fake patients. Because they were in a mental ward and because they had been *labeled* schizophrenic, anything the pseudo-patients did was seen as a symptom of psychopathology.

As Rosenhan's study shows, it is far better to label *problems* than to label people. Think of the difference in impact between saying, "You are experiencing a serious psychological disorder" and, "You're a schizophrenic." Which statement would you prefer to have said about yourself?

Social Stigma

An added problem with psychiatric labeling is that it frequently leads to prejudice and discrimination. That is, the mentally ill in our culture are often *stigmatized* (rejected and disgraced). People who have been labeled mentally ill (at any time in their lives) are less likely to be hired. They also tend to be denied housing, and they are more likely to be falsely accused of crimes. Thus, people who are grappling with mental illness may be harmed as much by social stigma as they are by their immediate psychological problems (Corrigan & Penn, 1999).

Critical Thinking: A Disease Called Freedom

The year is 1840. You are a slave who has tried repeatedly to escape from a cruel and abusive master. You want to be free. An expert is consulted about your "abnormal" behavior. His conclusion? You are suffering from "drapetomania," a mental "disorder" that causes slaves to run away (Wakefield, 1992). Your "cure"? The expert will cut off your toes.

As this example suggests, psychiatric terms are easily abused. Historically, some have been applied to culturally disapproved behaviors that are not really disorders. Another of our personal favorites is the long-outdated diagnosis of "anarchia," a form of insanity that leads one to seek a more democratic society (Brown, 1990).

All of the following were also once considered disorders: childhood masturbation, lack of vaginal orgasm, self-defeating personality (applied mainly to women), homosexuality, and nymphomania (a woman with a healthy sexual appetite) (Wakefield, 1992). Even today, race, gender, and social class continue to affect the diagnosis of various disorders (Kearney & Trull, 2012; Poland & Caplan, 2004).

Gender is probably the most common source of bias in judging normality because standards tend to be based on males (Fine, 2010; Nolen-Hoeksema, 2011). According to psychologist Paula Caplan (1995) and others, women are penalized both for conforming to female stereotypes and for ignoring them. If a woman is independent, aggressive, and unemotional, she may be considered "unhealthy." Yet at the same time, a woman who is vain, emotional, irrational, and dependent on others (all "feminine" traits in our culture) may be classified as having a personality disorder (Bornstein, 1996). Indeed, a majority of persons classified as having dependent personality disorder are women. In view of this, Paula Caplan asks, why isn't there a category called "delusional dominating personality disorder" for obnoxious men (Caplan, 1995)?

Because biases can influence perceptions of disorder and normality, it is worth being cautious before you leap to conclusions about the mental health of others (American Psychiatric Association, 2000; 2010). (They might be doing an assignment for their psychology class!)

An Important Note—You're Okay, Really!

As you read the next few sections, we hope that you will not fall prey to "medical student's disease." Medical students, it seems, have a predictable tendency to notice in themselves the symptoms of each dreaded disease they study. As a psychology student, you may notice what seem to be abnormal tendencies in your own behavior. If so, don't panic. In most instances, this only shows that pathological behavior is an *exaggeration* of normal defenses and reactions, not that your behavior is abnormal.

Knowledge Builder: Normality and Psychopathology

RECITE

1. The core feature of abnormal behavior is that it is
   a. statistically unusual *b.* maladaptive *c.* socially nonconforming *d.* a source of subjective discomfort
2. Powerful contexts in which judgments of normality and abnormality are made include
   a. the family *b.* occupational settings *c.* religious systems *d.* culture
3. Which of the following is a *legal* concept?
   a. neurosis *b.* psychosis *c.* drapetomania *d.* insanity
4. People are said to have "retreated from reality" when they suffer from
   a. psychotic disorders *b.* mood disorders *c.* somatoform disorders *d.* personality disorders
5. Amnesia, multiple identities, and depersonalization are possible problems in
   a. mood disorders *b.* somatoform disorders *c.* psychosis *d.* dissociative disorders
6. Someone who engages in one of the paraphilias has what type of disorder?
   a. dissociative *b.* somatoform *c.* substance *d.* sexual
7. Koro and dhat are
   a. somatoform disorders *b.* forms of psychosis *c.* folk terminology *d.* organic mental disorders

REFLECT

Think Critically

8. Brian, a fan of grunge rock, occasionally wears a skirt in public. Does Brian's crossdressing indicate that he has a mental disorder?
9. Many states began to restrict the use of the insanity defense after John Hinkley, Jr., who tried to murder former U.S. President Ronald Reagan, was acquitted by reason of insanity. What does this trend reveal about insanity?

Self-Reflect

Think of an instance of abnormal behavior you have witnessed. By what formal standards would the behavior be regarded as abnormal? In every society? Was the behavior maladaptive in any way?

Answers: 1. *b* **2.** *d* **3.** *d* **4.** *a* **5.** *d* **6.** *d* **7.** *c* **8.** Probably not. Undoubtedly, Brian's crossdressing is socially disapproved by many people. Nevertheless, to be classified as a mental disorder, it must cause him to feel disabling shame, guilt, depression, or anxiety. The cultural relativity of behavior like Brian's is revealed by the fact that it is fashionable and acceptable for women to wear men's clothing. **9.** It emphasizes that insanity is a legal concept, not a psychiatric diagnosis. Laws reflect community standards. When those standards change, lawmakers may seek to alter definitions of legal responsibility.

Neurosis An outdated term once used to refer, as a group, to anxiety disorders, somatoform disorders, dissociative disorders, and some forms of depression.

Psychotic Disorders—The Dark Side of the Moon

Gateway Question 14.4: *What are the general characteristics of psychotic disorders?*

Psychotic disorders are among the most dramatic and serious of all mental problems. Imagine that a member of your family (Floyd?) has been hearing voices, is talking strangely, has covered his head with aluminum foil, and believes that houseflies are speaking to him in code. If you observed such symptoms, would you be concerned? Of course you would, and rightly so.

A person who is psychotic undergoes striking changes in thinking, behavior, and emotion. Basic to all these changes is the fact that **psychosis** reflects a loss of contact with shared views of reality (psycho*sis*, singular; psycho*ses*, plural). The following comments, made by a psychotic patient, illustrate what is meant by a "split" from reality (Durand & Barlow, 2010):

> When you do the 25 of the clock, it means that you leave the house 25 after 1 to mail letters so they can check on you…and they know where you're at. That's the Eagle.

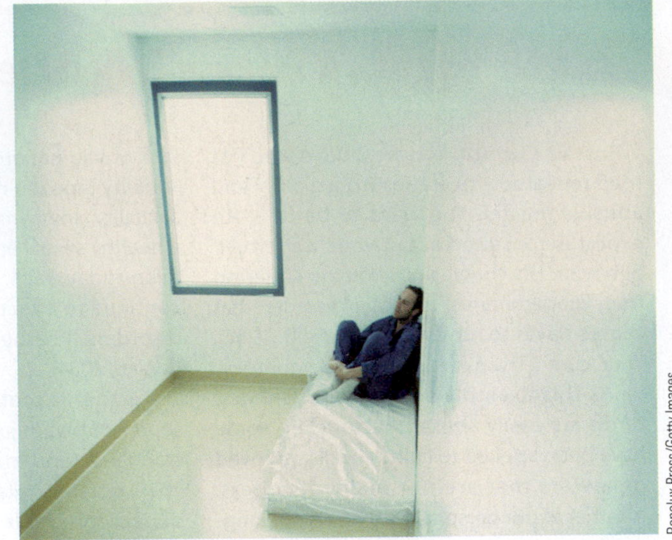

A psychotic individual in a state mental hospital.

The Nature of Psychosis

What are the major features of psychotic disorders? Delusions and hallucinations are core features, but there are others as well.

People who suffer from **delusions** hold false beliefs that they insist are true, regardless of how much the facts contradict them. An example is a 43-year-old schizophrenic man who was convinced he was pregnant (Mansouri & Adityanjee, 1995).

Are there different types of delusions? Yes, some common types of delusions are: (1) *depressive* delusions, in which people feel that they have committed horrible crimes or sinful deeds; (2) *somatic* delusions, such as believing your body is "rotting away" or that it is emitting foul odors; (3) delusions of *grandeur*, in which people think they are extremely important; (4) delusions of *influence*, in which people feel they are being controlled or influenced by others or by unseen forces; (5) delusions of *persecution*, in which people believe that others are "out to get them"; and (6) delusions of *reference*, in which people give great personal meaning to unrelated events (Kearney & Trull, 2012). For instance, delusional people sometimes think that television programs are giving them a special personal message. Regardless of their content, many delusions are very similar to superstitious, or "magical," thinking (García-Montes et al., 2008).

Hallucinations are imaginary sensations, such as seeing, hearing, or smelling things that don't exist in the real world. The most common psychotic hallucination is hearing voices, like the voice that told Carol North to "collide with the other world." Sometimes these voices command patients to hurt themselves. Unfortunately, sometimes people obey (Barrowcliff & Haddock, 2006). More rarely, psychotic people may feel "insects crawling under their skin," taste "poisons" in their food, or smell "gas" their "enemies" are using to "get" them. Sensory changes, such as anesthesia (numbness, or a loss of sensation) or extreme sensitivity to heat, cold, pain, or touch, can also occur.

During a psychotic episode, emotions are often severely disturbed. For instance, the psychotic person may be wildly elated, depressed, hyperemotional, or apathetic. Sometimes psychotic patients display *flat affect*, a condition in which the face is frozen in a blank expression. Brain images from psychotic patients with "frozen faces" reveal that their brains process emotions abnormally (Fahim et al., 2005).

Some psychotic symptoms can be thought of as a primitive type of communication. That is, many patients may be using their actions to say "I need help" or "I can't handle it anymore." This could be because disturbed verbal communication is a nearly universal symptom of psychosis. In fact, psychotic speech tends to be so garbled and chaotic that it sometimes sounds like a "word salad."

Major disturbances such as those just described—as well as added problems with thinking, memory, and attention—bring about personality disintegration and a break with reality. *Personality disintegration* occurs when a person's thoughts, actions, and emotions are no longer coordinated. When psychotic disturbances and a fragmented personality are evident for weeks or months, the person has suffered a psychosis (American Psychiatric Association, 2000, 2010; see ■ Table 14.4).

■ TABLE 14.4 Warning Signs of Psychotic Disorders and Major Mood Disorders

- You express bizarre thoughts or beliefs that defy reality.
- You have withdrawn from family members and other relationships.
- You hear unreal voices or sees things others don't.
- You are extremely sad, persistently despondent, or suicidal.
- You are excessively energetic and have little need for sleep.
- You lose your appetite, sleep excessively, and have no energy.
- You exhibit extreme mood swings.
- You believe someone is trying to get you.
- You have engaged in antisocial, destructive, or self-destructive behavior.

Sources: American Psychiatric Association, 2000, 2010; Durand & Barlow, 2010.

● **Figure 14.3** The Mad Hatter, from Lewis Carroll's *Alice's Adventures in Wonderland.* History provides numerous examples of psychosis caused by toxic chemicals. Carroll's Mad Hatter character is modeled after an occupational disease of the eighteenth and nineteenth centuries. In that era, hatmakers were heavily exposed to mercury used in the preparation of felt. Consequently, many suffered brain damage and became psychotic, or "mad" (Kety, 1979).

Organic Psychosis

In a sense, all psychoses are partly organic, involving physical changes in the brain. However, the general term *organic psychosis* is usually reserved for problems involving clear-cut brain injuries or diseases.

For example, poisoning by lead or mercury can damage the brain, causing hallucinations, delusions, and a loss of emotional control (● Figure 14.3). Children who eat leaded paint flakes or breathe leaded paint powder can become psychotic or intellectually disabled (Mielke, 1999). Children with higher levels of lead in their blood are more likely to be arrested as adults for criminal offenses (Wright et al., 2008). On a much larger scale, "poisoning" of another type, in the form of drug abuse, can also produce deviant behavior and psychotic symptoms (American Psychiatric Association, 2000; 2010).

Former U.S. President Ronald Reagan was diagnosed with Alzheimer's disease in 1995. Like many Alzheimer's victims, Reagan slipped into a slow mental decline. He died in 2004.

The most common organic problem is **dementia** (duh-MEN-sha), a serious mental impairment in old age caused by deterioration of the brain (Gatz, 2007). In dementia, we see major disturbances in memory, reasoning, judgment, impulse control, and personality. This combination usually leaves people confused, suspicious, apathetic, or withdrawn. Some common causes of dementia are circulatory problems, repeated strokes, or general shrinkage and atrophy of the brain.

The most common form of dementia is **Alzheimer's** (ALLS-hi-merz) **disease**. Alzheimer's victims slowly lose the ability to work, cook, drive, read, write, or do arithmetic. Eventually, they are mute and bedridden. Alzheimer's disease appears to be caused by unusual webs and tangles in the brain that damage areas important for memory and learning (Hanyu et al., 2010; Stix, 2010). Genetic factors can increase the risk of developing this devastating disease (Gatz, 2007).

Are there specific kinds of psychotic disorders? Two major types of psychosis are *delusional disorders* and *schizophrenia*. As you will recall, mood disorders mainly involve emotional extremes. Nevertheless, psychotic symptoms can also occur in some mood disorders. You'll find information on each of these problems in upcoming discussions.

Artist William Utermohlen painted haunting images portraying his decline into the grasp of Alzheimer's disease.

Psychosis A withdrawal from reality marked by hallucinations and delusions, disturbed thought and emotions, and personality disorganization.

Delusion A false belief held against all contrary evidence.

Hallucination An imaginary sensation, such as seeing, hearing, or smelling things that don't exist in the real world.

Dementia A serious mental impairment in old age caused by deterioration of the brain.

Delusional Disorders—An Enemy Behind Every Tree

Gateway Question 14.5: *What is the nature of a delusional disorder?*

People with delusional disorders usually do not suffer from hallucinations, emotional excesses, or personality disintegration. Even so, their break with reality is unmistakable. The main feature of **delusional disorders** is the presence of deeply held false beliefs, which may take the following forms (American Psychiatric Association, 2000; 2010):

- **Erotomanic type:** In this disorder, people have erotic delusions that they are loved by another person, especially by someone famous or of higher status. As you might imagine, some celebrity stalkers suffer from erotomania.
- **Grandiose type:** In this case, people suffer from the delusion that they have some great, unrecognized talent, knowledge, or insight. They may also believe that they have a special relationship with an important person or with God or that they are a famous person. (If the famous person is alive, the deluded person regards her or him as an imposter.)
- **Jealous type:** An example of this type of delusion would be having an all-consuming but unfounded belief that your spouse or lover is unfaithful.
- **Persecutory type:** Delusions of persecution involve belief that you are being conspired against, cheated, spied on, followed, poisoned, maligned, or harassed.
- **Somatic type:** People suffering from somatic delusions typically believe that their bodies are diseased or rotting, or infested with insects or parasites, or that parts of their bodies are defective.

Although they are false, and sometimes far-fetched, all these delusions are about experiences that could occur in real life. In other types of psychosis, delusions tend to be more bizarre (Manschreck, 1996; Brown & Barlow, 2011). For example, a person with schizophrenia might believe that space aliens have replaced all his internal organs with electronic monitoring devices. In contrast, people with ordinary delusions merely believe that someone is trying to steal their money, that they are being deceived by a lover, that the FBI is watching them, and the like.

Paranoid Psychosis

The most common delusional disorder, often called **paranoid psychosis**, centers on delusions of persecution. Many self-styled reformers, crank letter writers, conspiracy theorists, "UFO abductees," and the like suffer paranoid delusions. Paranoid individuals often believe that they are being cheated, spied on, followed, poisoned, harassed, or plotted against. Usually they are intensely suspicious, believing they must be on guard at all times.

The evidence such people find to support their beliefs usually fails to persuade others. Every detail of the paranoid person's existence is woven into a private version of "what's really going on." Buzzing during a telephone conversation may be interpreted as "someone listening"; a stranger who comes to the door asking for directions may be seen as "really trying to get information"; and so forth.

It is difficult to treat people suffering from paranoid delusions because it is almost impossible for them to accept that they need help. Anyone who suggests that they have a problem simply becomes part of the "conspiracy" to "persecute" them. Consequently, paranoid people frequently lead lonely, isolated, and humorless lives dominated by constant suspicion and hostility.

Although they are not necessarily dangerous to others, they can be. People who believe that the Mafia, "government agents," terrorists, or a street gang is slowly closing in on them may be moved to violence by their irrational fears. Imagine that a stranger comes to the door to ask a paranoid person for directions. If the stranger has his hand in his coat pocket, he could become the target of a paranoid attempt at "self-defense."

Delusional disorders are rare. By far, the most common form of psychosis is schizophrenia. Let's explore schizophrenia in more detail and see how it differs from a delusional disorder.

Schizophrenia—Shattered Reality

Gateway Question 14.6: *What forms does schizophrenia take and what causes it?*

Schizophrenia (SKIT-soh-FREN-ee-uh) is marked by delusions, hallucinations, apathy, thinking abnormalities, and a "split" between thought and emotion.

Do people with schizophrenia have two personalities? No. How many times have you heard people say something like, "David was so warm and friendly yesterday, but today he's as cold as ice. He's so schizophrenic that I don't know how to react." Such statements show how often the term *schizophrenic* is misused. As we will see later on in this chapter, a person who displays two or more personalities has a dissociative disorder and is not "schizophrenic." Neither, of course, is a person like David, whose behavior is merely inconsistent.

In schizophrenia, emotions may become blunted or very inappropriate. For example, if a person with schizophrenia is told his mother just died, he might smile, or giggle, or show no emotion at all. Schizophrenic delusions may include the idea that the person's thoughts and actions are being controlled, that thoughts are being broadcast (so others can hear them), that thoughts have been "inserted" into the person's mind, or that thoughts have been removed. In addition, schizophrenia involves withdrawal from contact with others, a loss of interest in external activities, a breakdown of personal habits, and an inability to deal with daily events (Neufeld et al., 2003; Ziv, Leiser, & Levine, 2011). One person in 100 has schizophrenia in any given year (National Institute of Mental Health, 2011a).

Many schizophrenic symptoms appear to be related to problems with *selective attention*. In other words, it is hard for people with schizophrenia to focus on one item of information at a time. Having an impaired "sensory filter" in their brains may be why they are overwhelmed by a jumble of thoughts, sensations, images, and feelings (Cellard et al., 2010; Heinrichs, 2001).

Is there more than one type of schizophrenia? Schizophrenia appears to be a group of related disturbances. It currently has four major subtypes, although these subtypes may be removed from the DSM-5 (American Psychiatric Association, 2010):

- **Disorganized type:** Schizophrenia marked by incoherence, grossly disorganized behavior, bizarre thinking, and flat or grossly inappropriate emotions.
- **Catatonic type:** Schizophrenia marked by stupor, rigidity, unresponsiveness, posturing, mutism, and, sometimes, agitated, purposeless behavior.
- **Paranoid type:** Schizophrenia marked by a preoccupation with delusions or by frequent auditory hallucinations related to a single theme, especially grandeur or persecution.
- **Undifferentiated type:** Schizophrenia in which there are prominent psychotic symptoms, but none of the specific features of catatonic, disorganized, or paranoid types.

Disorganized Schizophrenia

The disorder known as disorganized schizophrenia (sometimes called hebephrenic schizophrenia) comes close to matching the stereotyped images of "madness" seen in movies. In **disorganized schizophrenia**, personality disintegration is almost complete: Emotions, speech, and behavior are all highly disorganized. The result is silliness, laughter, and bizarre or obscene behavior, as shown by this intake interview of a patient named Edna:

> *Dr.* I am Dr. _____. I would like to know something more about you.
>
> *Patient* You have a nasty mind. Lord! Lord! Cats in a cradle.
>
> *Dr.* Tell me, how do you feel?
>
> *Patient* London's bell is a long, long dock. Hee! Hee! (Giggles uncontrollably.)
>
> *Dr.* Do you know where you are now?
>
> *Patient* D_____n! S_____t on you all who rip into my internals! The grudgerometer will take care of you all! (Shouting) I am the Queen, see my magic, I shall turn you all into smidgelings forever!
>
> *Dr.* Your husband is concerned about you. Do you know his name?
>
> *Patient* (Stands, walks to and faces the wall) Who am I, who are we, who are you, who are they, (turns) I . . . I . . . I . . . I! (Makes grotesque faces.)

Peter Granser/Laif/Aurora Photos

In disorganized schizophrenia, behavior is marked by silliness, laughter, and bizarre or obscene behavior.

Edna was placed in the women's ward where she proceeded to masturbate. Occasionally, she would scream or shout obscenities. At other times, she giggled to herself. She was known to attack other patients. She began to complain that her uterus was attached to a "pipeline to the Kremlin" and that she was being "infernally invaded" by Communism (Suinn, 1975*).

Disorganized schizophrenia typically develops in adolescence or young adulthood. Chances of improvement are limited, and social impairment is usually extreme (American Psychiatric Association, 2000).

Catatonic Schizophrenia

The catatonic person seems to be in a state of total panic (Fink, Shorter, & Taylor, 2010; Fink & Taylor, 2003). **Catatonic schizophrenia** brings about a stuporous condition in which odd positions may be held for hours or even days. These periods of rigidity may be similar to the tendency to "freeze" at times of great emergency or panic. Catatonic individuals appear to be struggling desperately to control their inner turmoil. One sign of this is the fact that stupor may occasionally give way to agitated outbursts or violent behavior. The following excerpt describes a catatonic episode:

> Manuel appeared to be physically healthy upon examination. Yet he did not regain his awareness of his surroundings. He remained motionless, speechless, and seemingly unconscious. One evening an aide turned him on his side to straighten out the sheet, was called away to tend to another patient, and forgot to return. Manuel was found the next morning, still on his side, his arm tucked under his body, as he had been left the night before. His arm was turning blue from lack of circulation, but he seemed to be experiencing no discomfort (Suinn, 1975).

All Suinn quotes in this chapter are from Fundamentals of Behavior Pathology *by R. M. Suinn. Copyright © 1975. Reprinted by permission of John Wiley & Sons, Inc.*

Alzheimer's disease An age-related disease characterized by memory loss, mental confusion, and, in its later stages, a nearly total loss of mental abilities.

Delusional disorder A psychosis marked by severe delusions of grandeur, jealousy, persecution, or similar preoccupations.

Paranoid psychosis A delusional disorder centered especially on delusions of persecution.

Schizophrenia A psychosis characterized by delusions, hallucinations, apathy, and a "split" between thought and emotion.

Disorganized schizophrenia Schizophrenia marked by incoherence, grossly disorganized behavior, bizarre thinking, and flat or grossly inappropriate emotions.

Catatonic schizophrenia Schizophrenia marked by stupor, rigidity, unresponsiveness, posturing, mutism, and, sometimes, agitated, purposeless behavior.

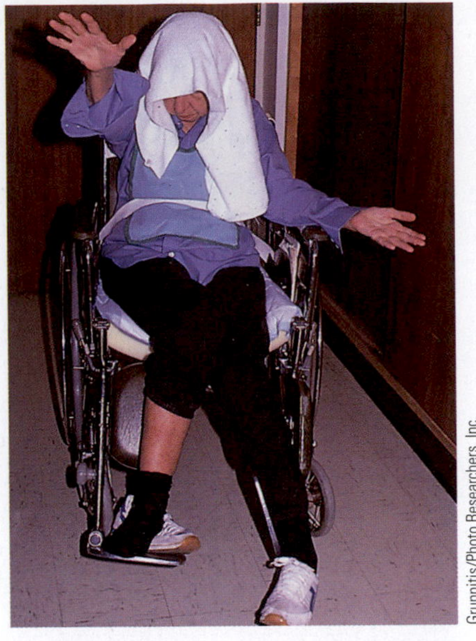

Can the catatonic's rigid postures and stupor be understood in terms of abnormal body chemistry? Environment? Heredity? As is true of other forms of schizophrenia, the answer appears to be all three factors.

Notice that Manuel did not speak. *Mutism*, along with a marked decrease in responsiveness to the environment, makes patients with catatonic schizophrenia difficult to "reach." Fortunately, this bizarre disorder has become rare in Europe and North America (American Psychiatric Association, 2000).

Paranoid Schizophrenia

Paranoid schizophrenia is the most common schizophrenic disorder (● Figure 14.4). As in paranoid delusional disorders, **paranoid schizophrenia** centers on delusions of grandeur and persecution. However, paranoid schizophrenics also hallucinate, and their delusions are more bizarre and unconvincing than those in a delusional disorder (Corcoran, 2010; Freeman & Garety, 2004).

Thinking that God, the government, or "cosmic rays from space" are controlling their minds or that someone is trying to poison them, people suffering from paranoid schizophrenia may feel forced into violence to "protect" themselves. An example is James Huberty, who brutally murdered 21 people at a McDonald's restaurant in San Ysidro, California. Huberty, who had paranoid schizophrenia, felt persecuted and cheated by life. Shortly before he announced to his wife that he was "going hunting humans," Huberty had been hearing hallucinated voices.

● Figure 14.4 Over a period of years, Theodore Kaczynski mailed bombs to unsuspecting victims, many of whom were maimed or killed. As a young adult, Kaczynski was a brilliant mathematician. At the time of his arrest, he had become the Unabomber—a reclusive "loner" who deeply mistrusted other people and modern technology. After his arrest, Kaczynski was judged to be suffering from paranoid schizophrenia.

How dangerous are the mentally ill? Horrific crimes, like the San Ysidro murders, lead many people to believe that the mentally ill are dangerous. Although sensationalized media reports tend to exaggerate the connection between mental illness and violence, the reality is just the opposite (Corrigan et al., 2005; Markowitz, 2011). According to the largest study ever conducted on this question, mentally ill individuals who are not also substance abusers are no more prone to violence than are normal individuals (Monahan et al., 2001). In general, only persons who are *actively psychotic* and *currently* experiencing psychotic symptoms are at increased risk for violence. In fact, the risk of violence from mental patients is actually many times lower than that from persons who have the following attributes: young, male, poor, and intoxicated (Corrigan & Watson, 2005).

Undifferentiated Schizophrenia

The three types of schizophrenia just described occur most often in textbooks. In reality, patients may shift from one pattern to another at different times. Many patients, therefore, are simply classified as suffering from **undifferentiated schizophrenia**, in which the specific features of catatonic, disorganized, or paranoid types are missing. Diagnosing types of schizophrenia is fairly subjective, which is why the DSM-5 may no longer make those distinctions (American Psychiatric Association, 2010). Regardless, there is no doubt that schizophrenia is real or that its treatment is a major challenge.

The Causes of Schizophrenia

What causes schizophrenia? Former British Prime Minister Winston Churchill once described a question that perplexed him as "a riddle wrapped in a mystery inside an enigma." The same words might describe the causes of schizophrenia.

Environment

An increased risk of developing schizophrenia may begin at birth or even before. Women who are exposed to the influenza (flu) virus or to rubella (German measles) during the middle of pregnancy have children who are more likely to become schizophrenic (Brown et al., 2001; Vuillermot et al., 2010). Malnutrition during pregnancy and complications at the time of birth can have a similar impact. Possibly, such events disturb brain development, leaving people more vulnerable to a psychotic break with reality (Walker et al., 2004).

Early **psychological trauma** (a psychological injury or shock) may also add to the risk. Often, the victims of schizophrenia were exposed to violence, sexual abuse, death, divorce, separation, or other stresses in childhood (Walker et al., 2004). Living in a troubled family is a related risk factor. In a disturbed family environment, stressful relationships, communication patterns, and negative emotions prevail. Deviant communication patterns cause anxiety, confusion, anger, conflict, and turmoil. Typically, disturbed families interact in ways that are laden with guilt, prying, criticism, negativity, and emotional attacks (Bressi, Albonetti, & Razzoli, 1998; Davison & Neale, 2006).

Although they are attractive, environmental explanations alone are not enough to account for schizophrenia. For example, when the children of schizophrenic parents are raised away from their chaotic home environment, they are still more likely to become psychotic (Walker et al., 2004).

Heredity

Does that mean that heredity affects the risk of developing schizophrenia? There is now little doubt that heredity is a factor in schizophrenia. It appears that some individuals inherit a *potential* for developing schizophrenia (Levy et al., 2010). They are, in other words, more *vulnerable* to the disorder (Harrison & Weinberger, 2005; Walker et al., 2004).

How has that been shown? If one identical twin becomes schizophrenic (remember, identical twins have identical genes), then the other twin has a *48 percent* chance of also becoming schizophrenic (Lenzenweger & Gottesman, 1994). The figure for twins can be compared with the risk of schizophrenia for the population in general, which is 1 percent (see ● Figure 14.5 for other relationships). In general, schizophrenia is clearly more common among close relatives and tends to run in families. There's even a case on record of *four* identical quadruplets *all* developing schizophrenia (Mirsky et al., 2000). In light of such evidence, researchers are now beginning to search for specific genes related to schizophrenia (Curtis, et al., 2011; Hyman, 2011; Roffman et al., 2011).

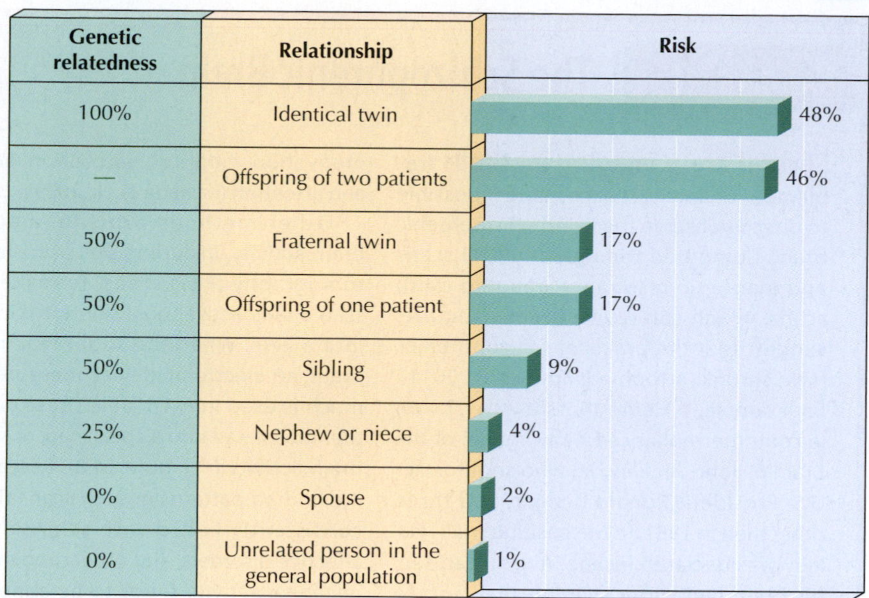

Genetic relatedness	Relationship	Risk
100%	Identical twin	48%
—	Offspring of two patients	46%
50%	Fraternal twin	17%
50%	Offspring of one patient	17%
50%	Sibling	9%
25%	Nephew or niece	4%
0%	Spouse	2%
0%	Unrelated person in the general population	1%

● **Figure 14.5** Lifetime risk of developing schizophrenia is associated with how closely a person is genetically related to a schizophrenic person. A shared environment also increases the risk. (Estimates from Lenzenweger & Gottesman, 1994.)

A problem exists with current genetic explanations of schizophrenia: Very few people with schizophrenia have children (Bundy, Stahl, & MacCabe, 2011). How could a genetic defect be passed from one generation to the next if afflicted people don't reproduce? One possible answer is suggested by the fact that the older a man is (even if he doesn't suffer from schizophrenia) when he fathers a child, the more likely it is that the child will develop schizophrenia. Apparently, genetic mutations occur in aging male reproductive cells and increase the risk of schizophrenia (as well as other medical problems) (Malaspina et al., 2005; Sipos et al., 2004).

Brain Chemistry

Amphetamine, LSD, PCP ("angel dust"), and similar drugs produce effects that partially mimic the symptoms of schizophrenia. Also, the same drugs (phenothiazines) used to treat LSD overdoses tend to alleviate psychotic symptoms. Facts such as these suggest that biochemical abnormalities (disturbances in brain chemicals or neurotransmitters) may occur in schizophrenic people. It is possible that the schizophrenic brain produces some substance similar to a *psychedelic* (mind-altering) drug. At present, one likely candidate is dopamine (DOPE-ah-meen), an important chemical messenger found in the brain.

Many researchers believe that schizophrenia is related to overactivity in brain dopamine systems (Sue, Sue, & Sue, 2010; Kapur & Lecrubier, 2003). Another possibility is that dopamine receptors become super-responsive to normal amounts of dopamine. Dopamine appears to trigger a flood of unrelated thoughts, feelings, and perceptions, which may account for the voices, hallucinations, and delusions of schizophrenia. The implication is that schizophrenic people may be on a sort of drug trip caused by their own bodies (● Figure 14.6).

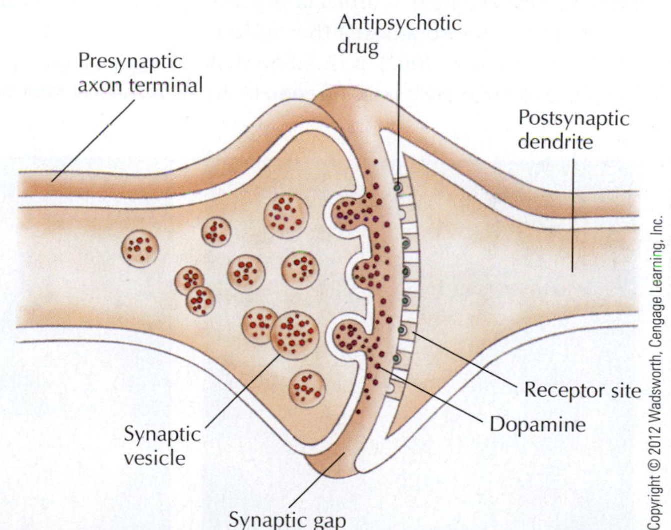

● **Figure 14.6** Dopamine normally crosses the synapse between two neurons, activating the second cell. Antipsychotic drugs bind to the same receptor sites as dopamine does, blocking its action. In people suffering from schizophrenia, a reduction in dopamine activity can quiet a person's agitation and psychotic symptoms.

Paranoid schizophrenia Schizophrenia marked by a preoccupation with delusions or by frequent auditory hallucinations related to a single theme, especially grandeur or persecution.

Undifferentiated schizophrenia Schizophrenia lacking the specific features of catatonic, disorganized, or paranoid types.

Psychological trauma A psychological injury or shock, such as that caused by violence, abuse, neglect, separation, and so forth.

Brainwaves The Schizophrenic Brain

Several brain imaging methods (remember Chapter 2?) have made it possible to directly observe the living schizophrenic brain. Computed tomography (CT) scans and magnetic resonance imaging (MRI) scans, which can reveal brain structure, suggest that the brains of schizophrenics have shrunk (atrophied; Bora et al., 2011). For example, ● Figure 14.7 shows a CT scan (a computer-enhanced X-ray image) of the brain of John Hinkley, Jr., who shot former U.S. President Ronald Reagan and three other men in 1981. In the ensuing trial, Hinkley was declared insane. As you can see, his brain had wider than normal surface fissuring.

Similarly, MRI scans indicate that schizophrenic people tend to have enlarged ventricles (fluid-filled spaces within the brain), again suggesting that surrounding brain tissue has withered (Barkataki et al., 2006). One possible explanation is that the schizophrenic brain may be unable to continually create new neurons to replace old ones that have died. In contrast, normal brains continue to produce new neurons (a process referred to as neurogenesis) throughout life (Toro & Deakin, 2007). It is telling that the affected areas are crucial for regulating motivation, emotion, perception, actions, and attention (Kawada et al., 2009).

Other methods provide images of brain activity, including positron emission tomography (PET) scans. To make a PET scan, a radioactive sugar solution is injected into a vein. When the sugar reaches the brain, an electronic device measures how much is used in each area. These data are then translated into a color map, or scan, of brain activity (● Figure 14.8). Researchers are finding patterns in such scans that are consistently linked with schizophrenia, affective disorders, and other problems. For instance, activity tends to be abnormally low in the frontal lobes of the schizophrenic brain (Durand & Barlow, 2010; Roffman et al., 2011). In the future, PET scans may be used to accurately diagnose schizophrenia. For now, such scans show that there is a clear difference in schizophrenic brain activity.

BRIDGES

Brain scans have provided valuable new insights into brain structures and activities. **See Chapter 2, pages 60–63.**

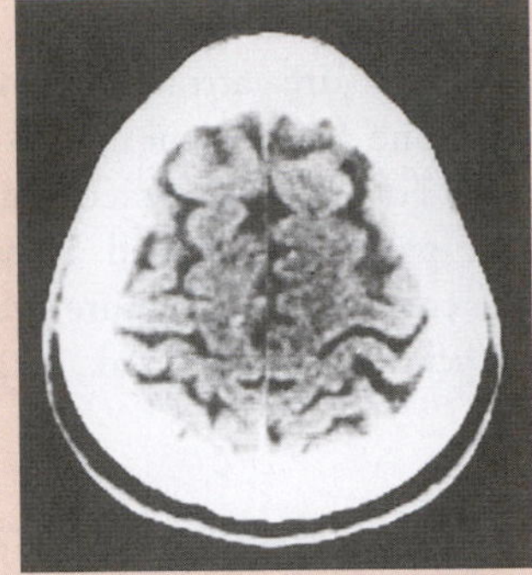

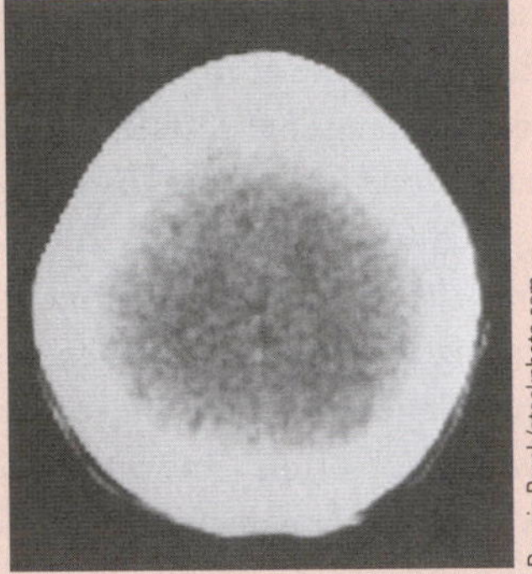

Dennis Brack/stockphoto.com

● **Figure 14.7** *(top)* CT scan of would-be presidential assassin John Hinkley, Jr., taken when he was 25. The X-ray image shows widened fissures in the wrinkled surface of Hinkley's brain. *(bottom)* CT scan of a normal 25-year-old's brain. In most young adults, the surface folds of the brain are pressed together too tightly to be seen. As a person ages, surface folds of the brain normally become more visible. Pronounced brain fissuring in young adults may be a sign of schizophrenia, chronic alcoholism, or other problems.

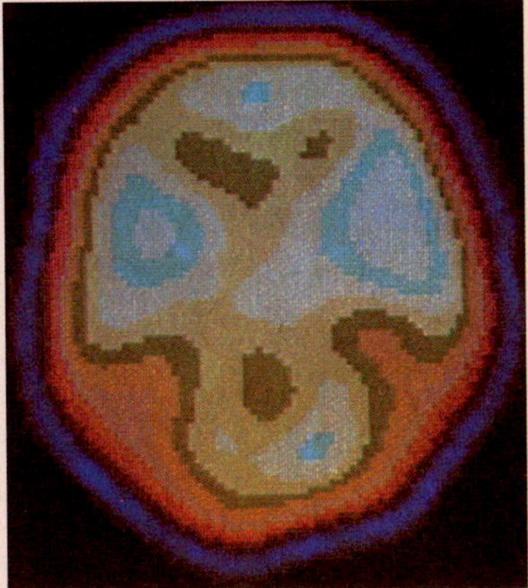

NORMAL

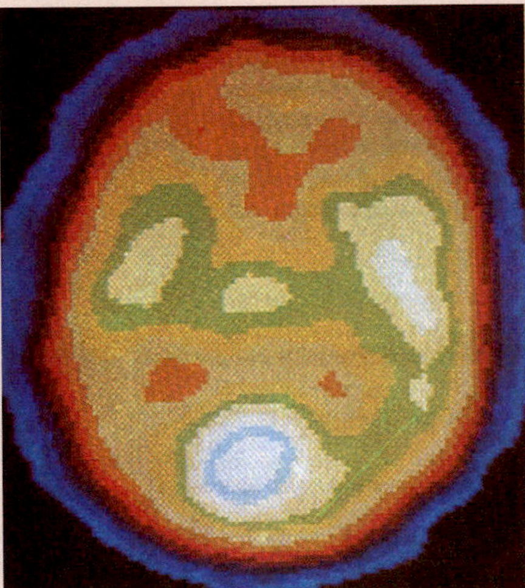

SCHIZOPHRENIC

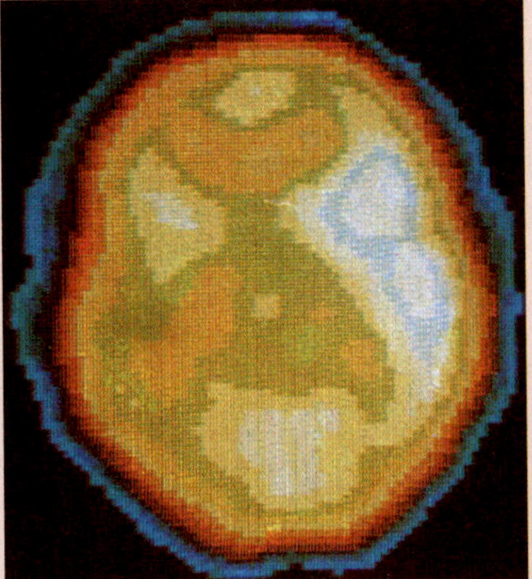

MANIC-DEPRESSIVE

The Brookhaven National Laboratory

● **Figure 14.8** Positron emission tomography produces PET scans of the human brain. In the scans shown here, red, pink, and orange indicate lower levels of brain activity; white and blue indicate higher activity levels. Notice that activity in the schizophrenic brain is quite low in the frontal lobes (top area of each scan) (Velakoulis & Pantelis, 1996). Activity in the manic-depressive brain is low in the left brain hemisphere and high in the right brain hemisphere. The reverse is more often true of the schizophrenic brain. Researchers are trying to identify consistent patterns like these to aid diagnosis of mental disorders.

Dopamine is not the only brain chemical that has caught scientists' attention. The neurotransmitter glutamate also appears to be related to schizophrenia (van Elst et al., 2005). People who take the hallucinogenic drug PCP, which affects glutamate, have symptoms that closely mimic schizophrenia (Murray, 2002). This occurs because glutamate influences brain activity in areas that control emotions and sensory information (Tsai & Coyle, 2002). Another tantalizing connection is the fact that stress alters glutamate levels, which in turn alter dopamine systems (Moghaddam, 2002). The story is far from complete, but it appears that dopamine, glutamate, and other brain chemicals partly explain the devastating symptoms of schizophrenia (Walker et al., 2004; see "The Schizophrenic Brain").

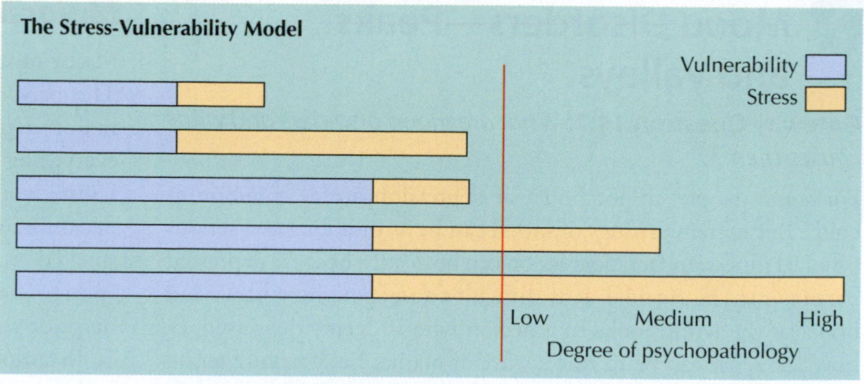

● **Figure 14.9** Various combinations of vulnerability and stress may produce psychological problems. The top bar shows low vulnerability and low stress. The result? No problem. The same is true of the next bar down, in which low vulnerability is combined with moderate stress. Even high vulnerability (third bar) may not lead to problems if stress levels remain low. However, when high vulnerability combines with moderate or high stress (bottom two bars) the person "crosses the line" and suffers from psychopathology.

Implications

In summary, the emerging picture of psychotic disorders such as schizophrenia takes this form: Anyone subjected to enough stress may be pushed to a psychotic break. (Battlefield psychosis is an example.) However, some people inherit a difference in brain chemistry or brain structure that makes them more susceptible—even to normal life stresses.

Thus, the right mix of inherited potential and environmental stress brings about mind-altering changes in brain chemicals and brain structure. This explanation is called the **stress-vulnerability model**. It attributes psychotic disorders to a blend of environmental stress and inherited susceptibility (Jones & Fernyhough, 2007; Walker et al., 2004). The model seems to apply to other forms of psychopathology as well, such as depression and anxiety (● Figure 14.9).

Despite advances in our understanding, psychosis remains "a riddle wrapped in a mystery inside an enigma." Let's hope that recent progress toward a cure for schizophrenia will continue.

Psychosis, Delusional Disorders, and Schizophrenia

RECITE

1. Angela wrongly believes that her body is "rotting away." She is suffering from
   a. depressive hallucinations *b.* a delusion *c.* flat affect *d.* Alzheimer's disease
2. Colin, who has suffered a psychotic break, is hearing voices. This symptom is referred to as
   a. flat affect *b.* hallucination *c.* a word salad *d.* organic delusions
3. A psychosis caused by lead poisoning would be regarded as an organic disorder. T or F?
4. Hallucinations and personality disintegration are the principal features of paranoid psychosis. T or F?
5. Which of the following is *not* one of the subtypes of schizophrenia?
   a. erotomanic type *b.* catatonic type *c.* paranoid type *d.* disorganized type
6. Environmental explanations of schizophrenia emphasize emotional trauma and
   a. manic parents *b.* schizoaffective interactions *c.* psychedelic interactions *d.* disturbed family relationships
7. Biochemical explanations of schizophrenia have focused on excessive amounts of _________ in the brain.
   a. radioactive sugar *b.* webs and tangles *c.* PCP *d.* dopamine and glutamate
8. The stress-vulnerability model of mental disorders explains them as a product of environmental stresses and
   a. psychological trauma *b.* deviant communication *c.* exposure to the flu virus during pregnancy *d.* heredity

REFLECT

Think Critically

9. Researchers have found nearly double the normal number of dopamine receptor sites in the brains of schizophrenics. Why might that be important?
10. Enlarged surface fissures and ventricles are frequently found in the brains of chronic schizophrenics. Why is it a mistake to conclude that such features *cause* schizophrenia?

Self-Reflect

If you were writing a "recipe" for psychosis, what would the main "ingredients" be?

If you were asked to play the role of a paranoid person for a theater production, what symptoms would you emphasize?

You have been asked to explain the causes of schizophrenia to the parents of a schizophrenic teenager. What would you tell them?

Answers: **1.** *b* **2.** *b* **3.** T **4.** F **5.** *a* **6.** *d* **7.** *d* **8.** *d* **9.** Because of the extra receptors, schizophrenics may get psychedelic effects from normal levels of dopamine in the brain. **10.** Because correlation does not confirm causation. Structural brain abnormalities are merely *correlated* with schizophrenia. They could be additional symptoms, rather than causes, of the disorder.

Stress-vulnerability model Attributes mental illness to a combination of environmental stress and inherited susceptibility.

Mood Disorders—Peaks and Valleys

Gateway Question 14.7: *What are mood disorders and what causes them?*

For some people, minor bouts of depression are as common as colds. But extreme swings of mood can be as disabling as a serious physical illness. In fact, depression can be deadly, because depressed persons may be suicidal. It is difficult to imagine how bleak and hopeless the world looks to a person who is deeply depressed, or how "crazy" it can be to ride a wave of mania. Let's explore mood disorders and their causes.

Nobody loves you when you're down and out—or so it seems. Psychologists have come to realize that **mood disorders** (major disturbances in emotion) are among the most serious of all psychological conditions. In any given year, roughly 9.5 percent of the U. S. population suffers from a mood disorder (National Institute of Mental Health, 2011a).

Two general types of mood disorder are depressive disorders and bipolar disorders. (See Table 14.5.) In **depressive disorders**, sadness and despondency are exaggerated, prolonged, or unreasonable. Signs of a depressive disorder are dejection, hopelessness, and an inability to feel pleasure or to take interest in anything. Other common symptoms are fatigue, disturbed sleep and eating patterns, feelings of worthlessness, a very negative self-image, and thoughts of suicide. In **bipolar disorders**, people go both "up" and "down" emotionally (American Psychiatric Association, 2000, 2010).

Some mood disorders are long lasting but relatively moderate. If a person is mildly depressed for at least 2 years, the problem is called a **dysthymic disorder** (dis-THY-mik). If depression alternates with periods when the person's mood is cheerful, expansive, or irritable, the problem is a **cyclothymic disorder** (SIKE-lo-THY-mik). Even at this level, mood disorders can be debilitating. However, major mood disorders are much more damaging.

Major Mood Disorders

Major mood disorders are characterized by emotional extremes. The person who only goes "down" emotionally suffers from a **major depressive disorder**. During major depressive episodes, everything looks bleak and hopeless. The person has feelings of failure, worthlessness, and total despair. Suffering is intense and the person may become extremely subdued, withdrawn, or intensely suicidal. Suicide attempted during a major depression is rarely a "plea for help." Usually, the person intends to succeed and may give no prior warning.

In a **bipolar I disorder**, people experience both extreme mania and deep depression. During manic episodes, the person is loud, elated, hyperactive, grandiose, and energetic. Manic patients may go bankrupt in a matter of days, get arrested, or go on a binge of promiscuous sex. During periods of depression, the person is deeply despondent and possibly suicidal.

In a **bipolar II disorder** the person is mostly sad and guilt ridden, but has had one or more mildly manic episodes (called *hypomania*). That is, in a bipolar II disorder, both elation and depression occur, but the person's mania is not as extreme as in a bipolar I disorder. Bipolar II patients who are hypomanic usually just manage to irritate everyone around them. They are excessively cheerful, aggressive, or irritable, and they may brag, talk too fast, interrupt conversations, or spend too much money (Nolen-Hoeksema, 2011).

In serious cases of depression, it is impossible for a person to function at work or at school. Sometimes, depressed individuals cannot even feed or dress themselves. In cases of depression and/or mania that are even more severe, the person may also lose touch with reality and display psychotic symptoms.

How do major mood disorders differ from dysthymic and cyclothymic disorders? As mentioned, the major mood disorders involve more severe emotional changes. Also, major mood disorders more often appear to be **endogenous** (en-DODGE-eh-nus: produced from within) rather than a reaction to external events.

TABLE 14.5 DSM-IV-TR Classification of Mood Disorders

Problem	Primary Symptom	Typical Signs of Trouble
Depressive Disorders		
Major depressive disorder	Extreme emotional depression for at least 2 weeks	You feel extremely sad, worthless, fatigued, and empty; you are unable to feel pleasure; you are having thoughts of suicide.
*Dysthymic disorder (chronic depressive disorder)	Moderately depressed mood on most days during the last 2 years	You feel down and depressed more days than not; your self-esteem and energy levels have been low for many months.
Bipolar Disorders		
Bipolar I disorder	Extreme mania and depression	At times you have little need for sleep, can't stop talking, your mind races, and everything you do is of immense importance; at other times you feel extremely sad, worthless, and empty.
Bipolar II disorder	Emotional depression and at least one episode of mild mania	Most of the time you feel extremely sad, worthless, fatigued, and empty; however, at times you feel unusually good, cheerful, energetic, or "high."
Cyclothymic disorder	Periods of moderate depression and moderate mania for at least 2 years	You have been experiencing upsetting emotional ups and downs for many months.

Sources: American Psychiatric Association, 2000; Durand & Barlow, 2010.

**Dysthymic disorder* may be renamed *chronic depressive disorder* in the upcoming DSM-5 (American Psychiatric Association, 2010).

© Erica Shires/Corbis

In major depressive disorders, suicidal impulses can be intense and despair total.

What Causes Mood Disorders?

Depression and other mood disorders have resisted adequate explanation and treatment. Some scientists are focusing on the biology of mood changes. They are interested in brain chemicals and transmitter substances, especially serotonin, noradrenaline, and dopamine levels. Their findings are incomplete, but progress has been made. For example, the chemical *lithium carbonate* can be effective for treating some cases of bipolar depression.

Other researchers seek psychological explanations. Psychoanalytic theory, for instance, holds that depression is caused by repressed anger. This rage is displaced and turned inward as self-blame and self-hate. As discussed in Chapter 13, behavioral theories of depression emphasize learned helplessness (LoLordo, 2001; Reivich et al., 2005). Cognitive psychologists believe that self-criticism and negative, distorted, or self-defeating thoughts underlie many cases of depression. (This view is discussed in Chapter 15.) Clearly, life stresses trigger many mood disorders (Calabrese et al., 2009). This is especially true for people who have personality traits and thinking patterns that make them vulnerable to depression (Dozois & Dobson, 2002).

Gender and Depression

Overall, women are 50 percent more likely than men to experience depression (National Institute of Mental Health, 2011a). Researchers believe that social and environmental conditions are the main reason for this difference (Cambron, Acitelli, & Pettit, 2009; Winstead & Sanchez, 2005). Factors that contribute to women's greater risk for depression include conflicts about birth control and pregnancy, work and parenting, and the strain of providing emotional support for others. Marital strife, sexual and physical abuse, and poverty are also factors. Nationwide, women and children are most likely to live in poverty. As a result, poor women frequently suffer the stresses associated with single parenthood, loss of control over their lives, poor housing, and dangerous neighborhoods (Stoppard & McMullen, 2003). One study found that women in the United States were most likely to be depressed if they lacked education, were unmarried, were Latina, had high stress levels, and experienced feelings of hopelessness (Myers et al., 2002).

Postpartum Depression

One source of women's depression is fairly easy to identify. After pregnancy and childbirth, many women face a high risk of becoming depressed (Phillips et al., 2010).

Two weeks after her child was born, Makemba realized something was wrong. She could no longer ignore that she was extremely irritable, fatigued, tearful, and depressed. "Shouldn't I be happy?" she wondered. "What's wrong with me?"

Many women are surprised to learn that they face a risk of depression after giving birth. The two most common forms of the problem are maternity blues and postpartum depression. (The term *postpartum* refers to the time following childbirth.)

An estimated 25 to 50 percent of all women experience *maternity blues*, a mild depression that usually lasts from 1 to 2 days after childbirth. These "third-day blues" are marked by crying, fitful sleep, tension, anger, and irritability. For most women, such reactions are a normal part of adjusting to childbirth. The depression is usually brief and not too severe.

For some women, maternity blues can be the beginning of a serious depression. Roughly 13 percent of all women who give birth develop **postpartum depression**, a moderately severe depression that begins within 3 months following childbirth. Typical signs of postpartum depression are mood swings, despondency, feelings of inadequacy, and an inability to cope with the new baby. Unlike other types of depression, postpartum depression also features unusually high levels of restlessness and difficulty concentrating (Bernstein et al., 2008). Depression of this kind may last any-

Mood disorder Major disturbances in mood or emotion, such as depression or mania.

Depressive disorders Emotional disorders primarily involving sadness, despondency, and depression.

Bipolar disorders Emotional disorders involving both depression and mania or hypomania.

Dysthymic disorder (Chronic depressive disorder) Moderate depression that persists for 2 years or more.

Cyclothymic disorder Moderate manic and depressive behavior that persists for 2 years or more.

Major mood disorders Disorders marked by lasting extremes of mood or emotion and sometimes accompanied by psychotic symptoms.

Major depressive disorder A mood disorder in which the person has suffered one or more intense episodes of depression.

Bipolar I disorder A mood disorder in which a person has episodes of mania (excited, hyperactive, energetic, grandiose behavior) and also periods of deep depression.

Bipolar II disorder A mood disorder in which a person is mostly depressed (sad, despondent, guilt ridden) but has also had one or more episodes of mild mania (hypomania).

Endogenous depression Depression that appears to be produced from within (perhaps by chemical imbalances in the brain), rather than as a reaction to life events.

Postpartum depression A mild to moderately severe depression that begins within 3 months following childbirth.

where from 2 months to about a year. Women are not the only ones to suffer when postpartum depression strikes. A depressed mother can seriously retard her child's rate of development (Cooper & Murray, 2001).

Stress and anxiety before birth and negative attitudes toward child rearing increase the risk of postpartum depression. (Phillips et al., 2010). A troubled marriage and lack of support from the father are also danger signs. Part of the problem may be hormonal: After a woman gives birth, her estrogen levels can drop, altering her mood (Bloch, Daly, & Rubinow, 2003).

Women who become depressed tend to see their husbands as unsupportive. Therefore, educating new parents about the importance of supporting one another may reduce the risk of depression. Groups in which new mothers can discuss their feelings are also helpful. If depression is severe or long lasting, new mothers should seek professional help.

Biology and Depression

Is heredity involved in the major mood disorders? Yes, especially in bipolar disorders (Curtis et al., 2011; Scharinger et al., 2010). As a case in point, if one identical twin is depressed, the other has a 67 percent chance of suffering depression too. For fraternal twins, the probability is 19 percent. This difference may be related to the finding that people who have a particular version of a gene are more likely to become depressed when they are stressed (Caspi et al., 2003). As we have noted, psychological causes are important in many cases of depression. But for major mood disorders, biological factors seem to play a larger role. Surprisingly, one additional source of depression is related to the seasons.

Seasonal Affective Disorder

Unless you have experienced a winter of "cabin fever" in the far north, you may be surprised to learn that the rhythms of the seasons underlie **seasonal affective disorder (SAD),** or depression that occurs only during the fall and winter months. Almost anyone can get a little depressed when days are short, dark, and cold. But when a person's symptoms are lasting and disabling, the problem may be SAD. Here are some of the major symptoms of SAD, according to Swedish psychiatrist Åsa Westrin and Canadian neuroscientist Raymond Lam (Westrin & Lam, 2007a):

- **Fatigue:** You feel too tired to maintain a normal routine.
- **Oversleeping and difficulty staying awake:** Your sleep patterns may be disturbed and waking very early in the morning is common.
- **Craving:** You hunger for carbohydrates and sweets, leading to overeating and weight gain.
- **Inability to cope:** You feel irritable and stressed.
- **Social withdrawal:** You become unsocial in the winter but are socially active during other seasons.

Starting in the fall, people with SAD sleep longer but more poorly. During the day, they feel tired and drowsy, and they tend to overeat. With each passing day, they become more sad, anxious, irritable, and socially withdrawn.

Although their depressions are usually not severe, many victims of SAD face each winter with a sense of foreboding. SAD is especially prevalent in northern latitudes (think of countries like Sweden, Greenland, and Canada), where days are very short during the winter (Michalak & Lam, 2002; Kegel et al., 2009; ● Figure 14.10). For instance, one study found that 13 percent of college students living in northern New England showed signs of suffering from SAD (Low & Feissner, 1998). The students most likely to be affected were those who had moved from the South to attend college!

Seasonal depressions are related to the release of more melatonin during the winter. This hormone, which is secreted by the pineal gland in the brain, regulates the body's response to changing light conditions (Wehr et al., 2001). That's why 80 percent of SAD patients can be helped by a remedy called phototherapy (● Figure 14.11). **Phototherapy** involves exposing SAD patients to one or more hours of very bright fluorescent light each day (Neumeister, 2004; Westrin & Lam, 2007b). This is best done early in the morning, when it simulates dawn in the summer (Avery et al., 2001). For many SAD sufferers, a hearty dose of morning "sunshine" appears to be the next best thing to vacationing in the tropics.

BRIDGES

In addition to its role in producing SAD, melatonin regulates normal circadian rhythms. **See Chapter 10, pages 333–334.**

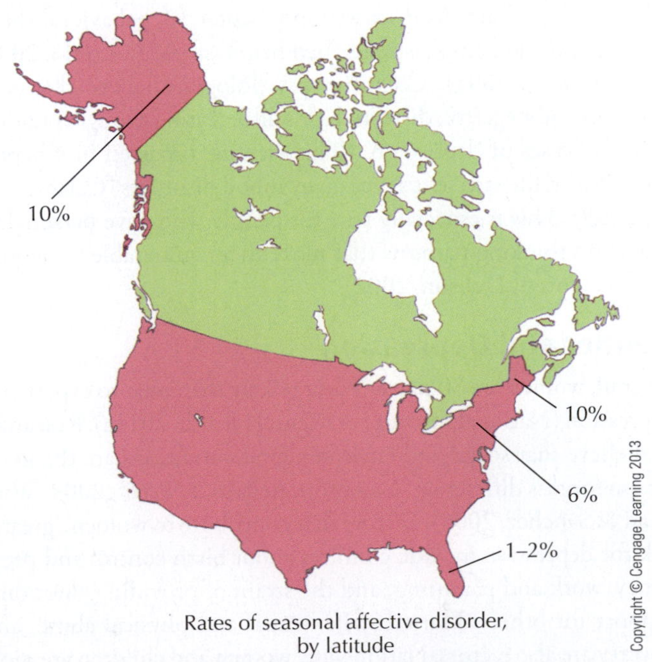

● **Figure 14.10** Seasonal affective disorder (SAD) appears to be related to reduced exposure to daylight during the winter. SAD affects 1 to 2 percent of Florida's population, about 6 percent of the people living in Maryland and New York City, and nearly 10 percent of the residents of New Hampshire and Alaska (Booker & Hellekson, 1992).

● **Figure 14.11** An hour or more of bright light a day can dramatically reduce the symptoms of seasonal affective disorder. Treatment is usually necessary from fall through spring. Light therapy typically works best when it is used early in the morning (Avery et al., 2001).

Angela Hampton/Alamy

Knowledge Builder: Mood Disorders

RECITE

1. Dysthymic disorder is to depression as cyclothymic disorder is to manic-depression. T or F?
2. Major mood disorders, especially bipolar disorders, often appear to be endogenous. T or F?
3. Learned helplessness is emphasized by ________________ theories of depression.
   a. humanistic *b.* biological *c.* behaviorist *d.* psychoanalytic
4. The main reason why women are more likely than men to become depressed is because of ________________ conditions.
   a. social and environmental *b.* existential *c.* biological *d.* postpartum
5. Roughly 13 percent of all new mothers experience the maternity blues, which are the first stage of postpartum depression. T or F?
6. Depression that occurs only in the winter is likely to be classified as
   a. SAD *b.* PTSD *c.* bipolar *d.* endogenous

REFLECT

Think Critically

7. How might relationships contribute to the higher rates of depression experienced by women?

Self-Reflect

On a piece of paper write "Bipolar Disorders" and "Depressive Disorders." How much of ■ Table 14.5 can you fill in under these headings? Keep reviewing until you can recreate the table (in your own words).

Answers: 1. T **2.** T **3.** *c* **4.** *a* **5.** F **6.** *a* **7.** Women tend to be more focused on relationships than men are. When listing the stresses in their lives, depressed women consistently report higher rates of relationship problems, such as loss of a friend, spouse, or lover, problems getting along with others, and illnesses suffered by people they care about. Depressed men tend to mention issues such as job loss, legal problems, and work problems (Cambron, Acitelli, & Pettit, 2009; Kendler, Thornton, & Prescott, 2001).

Anxiety-Based Disorders—When Anxiety Rules

Gateway Question 14.8: *What problems result when a person suffers high levels of anxiety?*

Imagine that you are waiting to take an extremely important test, waiting to give a speech to a large audience, or waiting to find out whether you or a loved one has a serious illness. You've almost certainly felt *anxiety*—feelings of apprehension, dread, or uneasiness—in similar situations.

If anxiety is a normal emotion, when does it signify a problem? It only becomes a problem when anxiety becomes so intense it prevents people from doing what they want or need to do. Also, their anxieties are out of control—they simply cannot stop worrying. An example is a college student named Jian, who became unbearably anxious when he took exams. By the time Jian went to see a counselor, he had skipped several tests and was in danger of dropping out of school. In general, people with anxiety-related problems like Jian's display the following characteristics:

- High levels of anxiety and/or restrictive, self-defeating behavior patterns.
- A tendency to use elaborate defense mechanisms or avoidance responses to get through the day.
- Pervasive feelings of stress, insecurity, inferiority, and dissatisfaction with life.

BRIDGES

Excessive use of psychological defense mechanisms is a feature of many anxiety disorders. **See Chapter 13, pages 456–458.**

People with anxiety-related problems feel threatened and often can't do anything constructive about it (Cisler & Koster, 2010). They struggle to control themselves but remain ineffective and unhappy (Cisler et al., 2010). In any given year, roughly 18 percent of the adult population suffers from an anxiety disorder (National Institute of Mental Health, 2011a).

Adjustment Disorders

Do such problems cause a "nervous breakdown"? People suffering from anxiety-based problems may be miserable, but they rarely experience a "breakdown." Actually, the term *nervous breakdown* has no formal meaning. Nevertheless, a problem known as an *adjustment disorder* does come close to being something of a "breakdown."

Adjustment disorders occur when ordinary stresses push people beyond their ability to cope with life. Examples of such stresses

Seasonal affective disorder (SAD) Depression that occurs only during fall and winter; presumably related to decreased exposure to sunlight.

Phototherapy A treatment for seasonal affective disorder that involves exposure to bright, full-spectrum light.

Adjustment disorder An emotional disturbance caused by ongoing stressors within the range of common experience.

are a job loss, intense marital strife, and chronic physical illness. People suffering from an adjustment disorder may be extremely irritable, anxious, apathetic, or depressed. They also have trouble sleeping, lose their appetite, and suffer from various physical complaints. Often, their problems can be relieved by rest, sedation, supportive counseling, and a chance to "talk through" their fears and anxieties (American Psychiatric Association, 2000; 2010).

How is an adjustment disorder different from an anxiety disorder? The outward symptoms are similar. However, adjustment disorders disappear when a person's life circumstances improve (Jones, Yates, & Zhou, 2002; Kramer et al., 2010). People suffering from anxiety disorders seem to generate their own misery, regardless of what's happening around them. They feel that they must be on guard against *future* threats that *could happen* at any time (Sue, Sue, & Sue, 2010).

Anxiety Disorders

In most anxiety disorders, distress seems greatly out of proportion to a person's circumstances. For example, consider the following description of Adrian H:

> She becomes very anxious that her children "might have been hurt or killed if they were out of the neighborhood playing and she hadn't heard from them in a couple of hours." She also worries all the time about her job performance and her relationships with men. Adrian believes that men rarely call back after a date or two because "they can sense I'm not a fun person." She never really relaxes, has difficulty focusing at work, has frequent headaches, and suffers from insomnia. (Adapted from Brown & Barlow, 2011.)

Distress like Adrian H's is a key ingredient in anxiety disorders. It also may underlie dissociative and somatoform disorders, where maladaptive behavior serves to reduce anxiety and discomfort. To deepen your understanding, let's first examine the anxiety disorders themselves (■ Table 14.6). Then we will see how anxiety contributes to other problems.

■ TABLE 14.6 DSM-IV-TR Classification of Anxiety Disorders

Type of Disorder	Typical Signs of Trouble
Generalized anxiety disorder	You have been extremely anxious or worried for 6 months.
***Panic disorder (without agoraphobia)**	You are anxious much of the time and have sudden panic attacks.
***Panic disorder (with agoraphobia)**	You have panic attacks and are afraid that they might occur in public places, so you rarely leave home.
***Agoraphobia (without a history of panic disorder)**	You fear that something extremely embarrassing will happen if you leave home (but you don't have panic attacks).
Specific phobia	You have an intense fear of specific objects, activities, or locations.
Social phobia	You fear social situations in which people can watch, criticize, embarrass, or humiliate you.
***Obsessive-compulsive disorder**	Your thoughts make you extremely nervous and compel you to rigidly repeat certain actions or routines.
Acute stress disorder	You are tormented for less than a month by the emotional after effects of horrible events you have experienced.
Post-traumatic stress disorder	You are tormented for more than a month by the emotional after effects of horrible events you have experienced.

Sources: American Psychiatric Association, 2000; Durand & Barlow, 2010.

*Several changes may be made to the DSM-5. *Panic disorder with* and *without agoraphobia* may be combined and *agoraphobia* may become a separate diagnostic category. A new category of *anxiety disorders, anxiety and obsessive-compulsive spectrum disorders* may be created, including *obsessive-compulsive disorder* (American Psychiatric Association, 2010).

Generalized Anxiety Disorder

A person with a **generalized anxiety disorder** has been extremely anxious and worried for at least 6 months. Sufferers typically complain of sweating, a racing heart, clammy hands, dizziness, upset stomach, rapid breathing, irritability, and poor concentration. Overall, more women than men have these symptoms (Brown & Barlow, 2011).

Was Adrian H's problem a generalized anxiety disorder? Yes. However, if she also experienced *anxiety attacks,* then she would likely be diagnosed with panic disorder (Batelaan et al., 2010).

Panic Disorder

In a **panic disorder (without agoraphobia)**, people are highly anxious and also feel sudden, intense, unexpected panic. During a panic attack, victims experience chest pain, a racing heart, dizziness, choking, feelings of unreality, trembling, or fears of losing control. Many believe that they are having a heart attack, are going insane, or are about to die. Needless to say, this pattern leaves victims unhappy and uncomfortable much of the time. Again, the majority of people who suffer from panic disorder are women (Foot & Koszycki, 2004).

To get an idea of how a panic attack feels, imagine that you are trapped in your stateroom on a sinking ocean liner (the Titanic?). The room fills with water. When only a small air space remains near the ceiling and you are gasping for air, you'll know what a panic attack feels like.

In a **panic disorder (with agoraphobia)**, people suffer from chronic anxiety and sudden panic. In addition, they have agoraphobia (ah-go-rah-FOBE-ee-ah), which is an intense *fear that a panic attack will occur* in a public place or unfamiliar situation. That is, agoraphobics intensely fear leaving their home and familiar surroundings. Typically, they find ways of avoiding places that frighten them—such as crowds, open roads, supermarkets, automobiles, and so on. As a result, some agoraphobics are prisoners in their own homes (American Psychiatric Association, 2000).

Agoraphobia

The problem known as **agoraphobia** can also occur without panic. In this case, people *fear that something extremely embarrassing will happen* if they leave home or enter an unfamiliar situation. For example, an agoraphobic person may refuse to go outside because he or she fears having a sudden attack of dizziness, or diarrhea, or shortness of breath. Going outside the home alone, being in a crowd, standing in line, crossing a bridge, or riding in a car can be impossible for an agoraphobic person (American Psychiatric Association, 2000). About 4.2 percent of all adults suffer from agoraphobia (with or without panic) during their lifetime (Grant et al., 2006).

Specific Phobia

As we noted earlier, phobias are intense, irrational fears that a person cannot shake off, even when there is no real danger. In a **specific phobia**, the person's fear, anxiety, and avoidance are focused on particular objects, activities, or situations. People affected by phobias recognize that their fears are unreasonable, but they cannot control them. For example, a person with a spider phobia would find it impossible to ignore a *picture* of a spider, even though a photograph can't bite anyone (Miltner et al., 2004). Specific phobias can be linked to nearly any object or situation (Stinson et al., 2007). In descending order of prevalence, the most common specific phobias among Americans are:

Fear of insects, birds, snakes, or other animals (including, of course, arachnophobia—the fear of spiders—and zoophobia—fear of animals)
Acrophobia—fear of heights
Astraphobia—fear of storms, thunder, lightning
Aquaphobia—fear of being on or in water
Aviophobia—fear of airplanes
Claustrophobia—fear of closed spaces
Agoraphobia—fear of crowds

By combining the appropriate root word with the word *phobia,* any number of fears can be named. Some are *xenophobia*, fear of strangers; *hematophobia*, fear of blood; *coulrophobia*, fear of clowns; and *arachibutyrophobia*, fear of peanut butter sticking to the roof of the mouth. One of your authors' favorites is *triskaidekaphobia*—fear of the number 13. After all, this is the 13th edition of our book (are you afraid to pick up your copy?).

Almost everyone has a few mild phobias, such as fear of heights, closed spaces, or bugs and crawly things. A phobic disorder differs from such garden-variety fears in that it produces overwhelming fear. True phobias may lead to vomiting, wild climbing and running, or fainting. For a phobic disorder to exist, the person's fear must disrupt his or her daily life. Phobic persons are so threatened that they will go to almost any length to avoid the feared object or situation, such as driving 50 miles out of the way to avoid crossing a bridge. About 8.7 percent of all adults have a specific phobic disorder in any given year (National Institute of Mental Health, 2011a).

Lucy Nicholson/Reuters/Landov

Shown here watching a basketball game, War hero Senator John McCain is no stranger to superstitions. He is, for example, no fan of the number 13. Apparently, he always carries 31 cents with him (the opposite of 13). Once, when a campaign office was located on the 13th floor of a building, the floor was quickly renamed the "Mth floor" (Wargo, 2008).

Social Phobia

In **social phobia**, people fear situations in which they can be observed, evaluated, embarrassed, or humiliated by others. This leads them to avoid certain social situations, such as eating, writing, using the rest room, or speaking in public. When such situations cannot be avoided, people endure them with intense anxiety or distress. It is common for them to have uncomfortable physical

Generalized anxiety disorder A chronic state of tension and worry about work, relationships, ability, or impending disaster.

Panic disorder (without agoraphobia) A chronic state of anxiety and also has brief moments of sudden, intense, unexpected panic.

Panic disorder (with agoraphobia) A chronic state of anxiety and brief moments of sudden panic. The person fears that these panic attacks will occur in public places or unfamiliar situations.

Agoraphobia (without panic) The fear that something extremely embarrassing will happen if one leaves the house or enters unfamiliar situations.

Specific phobia An intense, irrational fear of specific objects, activities, or situations.

Social phobia An intense, irrational fear of being observed, evaluated, embarrassed, or humiliated by others in social situations.

symptoms, such as a pounding heart, shaking hands, sweating, diarrhea, mental confusion, and blushing. Social phobias greatly impair a person's ability to work, attend school, and form personal relationships (American Psychiatric Association, 2000). About 6.8 percent of all adults are affected by social phobias in a given year (National Institute of Mental Health, 2011a).

Obsessive-Compulsive Disorder

People who suffer from **obsessive-compulsive disorder** are preoccupied with certain distressing thoughts and feel compelled to perform certain behaviors. You have probably experienced a mild obsessional thought, such as a song or stupid commercial jingle that repeats over and over in your mind. This may be irritating, but it's usually not terribly disturbing. True obsessions are images or thoughts that force their way into awareness against a person's will. They are so disturbing that they cause intense anxiety. The most common obsessions are about violence or harm (such as one's spouse being poisoned or hit by a car), about being "dirty" or "unclean," about whether one has performed some action (such as locking the door), and about committing immoral acts (Grabill et al., 2008).

Obsessions usually give rise to compulsions. These are irrational acts that a person feels driven to repeat. Often, compulsive acts help control or block out anxiety caused by an obsession. For example, a minister who finds profanities popping into her mind might start compulsively counting her heartbeat. Doing this would prevent her from thinking "dirty" words.

Some compulsive people become *hoarders*, excessively collecting various things (Hayward & Coles, 2009). Other compulsive people are *checkers* or *cleaners*. For instance, a young mother who repeatedly pictures a knife plunging into her baby might check once an hour to make sure all the knives in her house are locked away. Doing so may reduce her anxieties, but it will probably also take over her life. Likewise, a person who feels "contaminated" from touching ordinary objects because "germs are everywhere" may be driven to wash his hands hundreds of times a day.

Hulton Archive/Getty Images

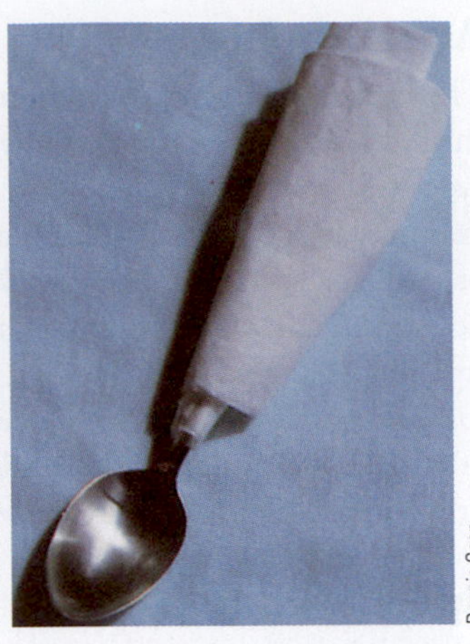

Dennis Coon

The severe obsessions and compulsions of billionaire Howard Hughes led him to live as a recluse for over 20 years. Hughes had an intense fear of contamination. To avoid infection, he constructed sterile, isolated environments in which his contact with people and objects was strictly limited by complicated rituals. Before handling a spoon, for instance, Hughes had his attendants wrap the handle in tissue paper and seal it with tape. A second piece of tissue was then wrapped around the first before he would touch it (Hodgson & Miller, 1982). A spoon prepared as Hughes required is shown at right.

Of course, not all obsessive-compulsive disorders are so dramatic. Many simply involve extreme orderliness and rigid routine. Compulsive attention to detail and rigid following of rules help keep activities totally under control and make the highly anxious person feel more secure. (If such patterns are long-standing but less intense, they are classified as personality disorders, which we will discuss later in more detail.)

Alex Garcia/MCT/Landov

Hoarders are obsessive about collecting things, which they also have great difficulty discarding (Hayward & Coles, 2009).

Stress Disorders

Stress disorders occur when people experience stresses outside the range of normal human experience, such as floods, tornadoes, earthquakes, or horrible accidents. They affect many political hostages; combat veterans; prisoners of war; victims of terrorism, torture, violent crime, child molestation, rape, or domestic violence; and people who have witnessed a death or serious injury (Brown & Barlow, 2011).

Symptoms of stress disorders include repeated reliving of the traumatic event, avoidance of reminders of the event, and blunted emotions. Also common are insomnia, nightmares, wariness, poor concentration, irritability, and explosive anger or aggression. If such reactions last *less* than a month after a traumatic event, the problem is called an **acute stress disorder**. If they last *more* than a month, the person is suffering from **post-traumatic stress disorder (PTSD)** (Nemeroff et al., 2006).

If a situation causes distress, anxiety, or fear, we tend to avoid it in the future. This is a normal survival instinct. However, victims of PTSD fail to recover from these reactions. Military combat accounts for more than a quarter of the cases of PTSD among American men (Prigerson, Maciejewski, & Rosenheck, 2002). The

Yasuyoshi Chiba/AFP/Getty Images

Natural disasters, like the catastrophic earthquake and tsunami that struck Japan in 2011, kill many people and upset the lives of many more. In the aftermath of such disasters, many survivors suffer from acute stress reactions. For some, the flare-up of anxiety and distress occurs months or years after the stressful event, an example of a post-traumatic stress reaction.

constant threat of death and the gruesome sights and sounds of war take a terrible toll. Psychologists are already seeing high rates of PTSD among soldiers involved in combat in Iraq and Afghanistan (Hoge et al., 2004; Marx, 2009). Sadly, 8 percent of military veterans still suffer from PTSD decades after they were in combat (Dirkzwager, Bramsen, & Van Der Ploeg, 2001). About 3.5 percent of adults suffer from posttraumatic stress in any given year (National Institute of Mental Health, 2011a).

Dissociative Disorders

In dissociative reactions, we see striking episodes of *amnesia*, *fugue*, or *multiple identity*. **Dissociative amnesia** is an inability to recall one's name, address, or past. **Dissociative fugue** (fewg) involves sudden, unplanned travel away from home and confusion about personal identity (This diagnosis may be classified as a subtype of dissociative amnesia in the DSM-5 [American Psychiatric Association, 2010]). Dissociations are often triggered by highly traumatic events (McLewin & Muller, 2006). In such cases, forgetting personal identity and fleeing unpleasant situations appear to be defenses against intolerable anxiety.

A person suffering from a **dissociative identity disorder** has two or more separate identities or personality states. (Don't forget that identity disorders are not the same as schizophrenia. Schizophrenia, which is a psychotic disorder, was discussed earlier in this chapter.) One famous and dramatic example of multiple identities is described in the book *Sybil* (Schreiber, 1973). Sybil reportedly had 16 different personality states. Each identity had a distinct voice, vocabulary, and posture. One personality could play the piano (not Sybil), but the others could not.

When an identity other than Sybil was in control, Sybil experienced a "time lapse," or memory blackout. Sybil's amnesia and alternate identities first appeared during childhood. As a girl she was beaten, locked in closets, perversely tortured, sexually abused, and almost killed. Sybil's first dissociations allowed her to escape by creating another person who would suffer torture in her place. Identity disorders often begin with unbearable childhood experiences, like those that Sybil endured. A history of childhood trauma, especially sexual abuse, is found in a high percentage of persons whose personalities split into multiple identities (McLewin & Muller, 2006; Simeon et al., 2002).

Flamboyant cases like Sybil's have led some experts to question the existence of multiple personalities (Casey, 2001; Piper, 2008). However, a majority of psychologists continue to believe that multiple identity is a real, if rare, problem (Cormier & Thelen, 1998; Dell, 2009).

Therapy for dissociative identity disorders may make use of hypnosis, which allows contact with the various personality states. The goal of therapy is *integration* and *fusion* of the identities into a single, balanced personality. Fortunately, multiple identity disorders are far rarer in real life than they are in TV dramas!

Somatoform Disorders

Have you ever known someone who appeared to be healthy but seemed to constantly worry about disease? These people are preoccupied with bodily functions, such as their heartbeat or breathing or digestion. Minor physical problems—even a small sore or an occasional cough—may convince them that they have cancer or some other dreaded disease. Typically, they can't give up their fears of illness, even if doctors can find no medical basis for their complaints (Korol, Craig, & Firestone, 2003).

Are you describing hypochondria? Yes. In **hypochondriasis** (HI-po-kon-DRY-uh-sis), people interpret normal bodily sensations as proof that they have a terrible disease (see "Sick of Being Sick" for a related disorder with a curious twist). In a problem called **somatization disorder** (som-ah-tuh-ZAY-shun), people

Obsessive-compulsive disorder An extreme preoccupation with certain thoughts and compulsive performance of certain behaviors.

Stress disorder A significant emotional disturbance caused by stresses outside the range of normal human experience.

Acute stress disorder A psychological disturbance lasting up to 1 month following stresses that would produce anxiety in anyone who experienced them.

Post-traumatic stress disorder (PTSD) A psychological disturbance lasting more than 1 month following stresses that would produce anxiety in anyone who experienced them.

Dissociative amnesia Loss of memory (partial or complete) for important information related to personal identity.

Dissociative fugue Sudden travel away from home, plus confusion about one's personal identity.

Dissociative identity disorder The presence of two or more distinct personalities (multiple personality).

Hypochondriasis A preoccupation with fears of having a serious disease. Ordinary physical signs are interpreted as proof that the person has a disease, but no physical disorder can be found.

Somatization disorder Afflicted persons have numerous physical complaints. Typically, they have consulted many doctors, but no organic cause for their distress can be identified.

The Clinical File Sick of Being Sick

At 14, Ben was in the hospital again for his sinus problem. He had already undergone 40 surgeries since the age of 8. In addition, he had been diagnosed at various times with bipolar disorder, oppositional defiant disorder, and attention deficit disorder. Ben was taking 19 different medications, and his mother said she desperately wanted him to be "healed." She sought numerous tests and never missed an appointment. But at long last, it became clear that there was nothing wrong with Ben. Left alone with doctors, Ben revealed that he was "sick of being sick."

In reality, it was Ben's mother who was sick. She was eventually diagnosed as suffering from **Munchausen by proxy syndrome** (Awadallah et al., 2005). This is a pattern in which a person fakes the medical problems of someone in his or her care. (In **Munchausen syndrome (factitious disorder)**, the person fakes his or her own medical problems.) As in Ben's case, most people with the syndrome are mothers who fabricate their children's illnesses (Day & Moseley, 2010). Sometimes, they even deliberately harm their children. For example, one mother injected her son with 7-Up (Reisner, 2006).

But why? People who suffer from Munchausen syndrome and Munchausen by proxy syndrome appear to have a pathological need to seek attention and sympathy from medical professionals. They may also win praise for being health conscious or a good parent (Day & Moseley, 2010).

This case illustrates another point about psychological disorders: Ben's mother was eventually diagnosed with several disorders, including Munchausen by proxy, schizoaffective disorder, and borderline personality disorder. As this suggests, many disturbed people are *comorbid*—that is, they suffer from more than one disorder at a time. Not only does comorbidity increase their misery, it makes it more difficult for health care providers to diagnose and treat them.

express their anxieties through various bodily complaints. That is, they suffer from problems such as vomiting or nausea, shortness of breath, difficulty swallowing, or painful menstrual periods. Typically, the person feels ill much of the time and visits doctors repeatedly. Most sufferers take medicines or other treatments, but no physical cause can be found for their distress. Similarly, a person with **pain disorder** is disabled by pain that has no identifiable physical basis. (This diagnosis may be renamed *complex somatic symptom disorder* in the DSM-5 [American Psychiatric Association, 2010]).

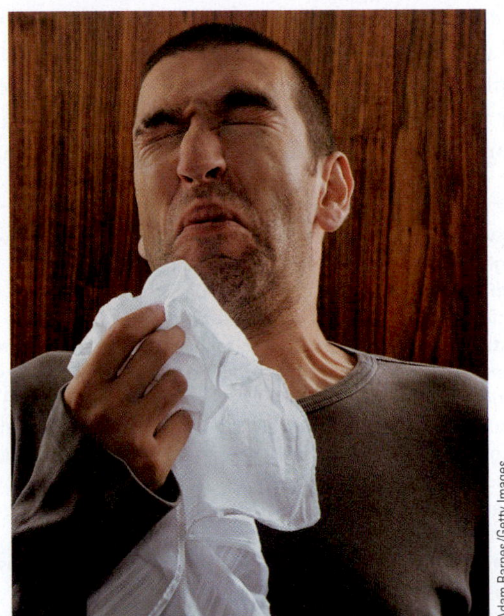

Adam Barnes/Getty Images

Uncontrollable sneezing, which may continue for days or weeks, is often a conversion disorder. In such cases, sneezing is atypical in rate and rhythm. In addition, the person's eyes do not close during a sneeze and sneezing does not occur during sleep. (A normal sneeze is shown here.) All these signs suggest that the cause of the sneezing is psychological, not physical (Fochtmann, 1995).

A rarer somatoform disorder ("body-form" disorder) is called a *conversion reaction.* In a **conversion disorder**, severe emotional conflicts are "converted" into symptoms that actually disturb physical functioning or closely resemble a physical disability. For instance, a soldier might become deaf or lame or develop "glove anesthesia" just before a battle. (This diagnosis may be renamed *functional neurological symptoms* in the DSM-5 [American Psychiatric Association, 2010]).

What is "glove anesthesia"? "Glove anesthesia" is a loss of sensitivity in the areas of the skin that would normally be covered by a glove. Glove anesthesia shows that conversion symptoms often contradict known medical facts. The system of nerves in the hands does not form a glove-like pattern and could not cause such symptoms (● Figure 14.12).

If symptoms disappear when a victim is asleep, hypnotized, or anesthetized, a conversion reaction must be suspected (Russo et al., 1998). Another sign to watch for is that victims of conversion reactions are strangely unconcerned about suddenly being disabled.

BRIDGES

Don't confuse somatoform disorders with psychosomatic illnesses, which occur when stress causes real physical damage to the body.

See Chapter 13, pages 463–464.

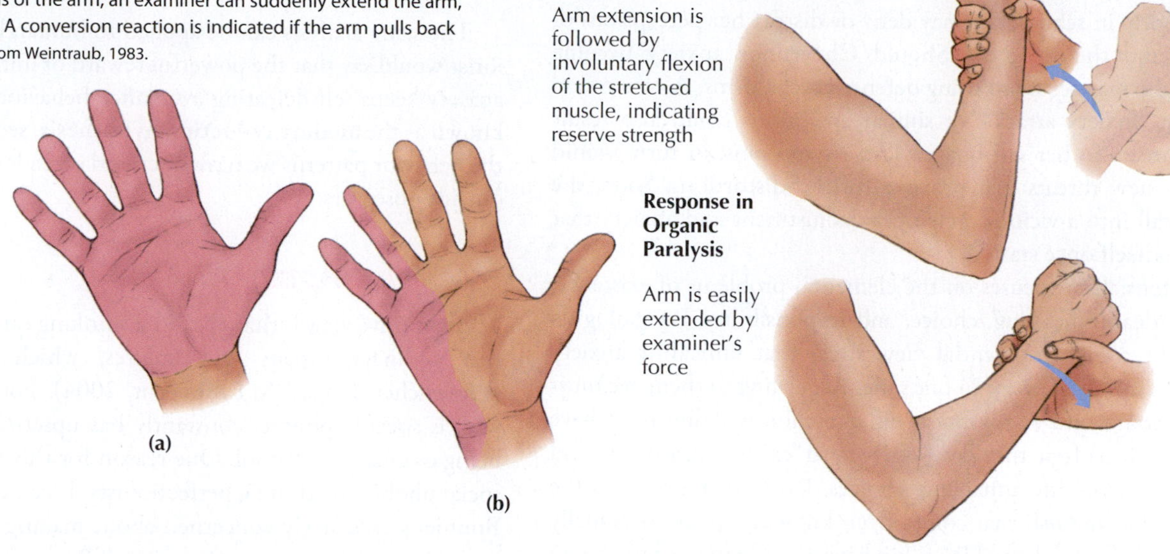

• **Figure 14.12** *(left)* "Glove" anesthesia is a conversion reaction involving loss of feeling in areas of the hand that would be covered by a glove *(a)*. If the anesthesia were physically caused, it would follow the pattern shown in *(b)*. *(right)* To test for organic paralysis of the arm, an examiner can suddenly extend the arm, stretching the muscles. A conversion reaction is indicated if the arm pulls back involuntarily. Adapted from Weintraub, 1983.

Anxiety and Disorder—Four Pathways to Trouble

Gateway Question 14.9: *How do psychologists explain anxiety-based disorders?*

What causes anxiety disorders? Anxiety disorders may also be best explained by the stress-vulnerability model. Susceptibility to anxiety-based disorders appears to be partly inherited (Rachman, 2004). Studies show that being high strung, nervous, or emotional runs in families. For example, 60 percent of children born to parents suffering from panic disorder have a fearful, inhibited temperament. Such children are irritable and wary as infants, shy and fearful as toddlers, and quiet and cautious introverts in elementary school. By the time they reach adulthood, they are at high risk for anxiety problems, such as panic attacks (Barlow, 2000; Durand & Barlow, 2010).

There are at least four major psychological perspectives on the causes of dissociative, anxiety-based, and somatoform disorders. These are (1) the *psychodynamic* approach; (2) the *humanistic-existential* approach; (3) the *behavioral* approach; and (4) the *cognitive* approach.

Psychodynamic Approach

The term *psychodynamic* refers to internal motives, conflicts, unconscious forces, and other dynamics of mental life. Freud was the first to propose a psychodynamic explanation for what he called "neurosis." According to Freud, disturbances like those we have described represent a raging conflict among subparts of the personality—the id, ego, and superego.

Freud emphasized that intense anxiety can be caused by forbidden id impulses for sex or aggression that threaten to break through into behavior. The person constantly fears doing something "crazy" or forbidden. She or he may also be tortured by guilt, which the superego uses to suppress forbidden impulses. Caught in the middle, the ego is eventually overwhelmed. This forces the person to use rigid defense mechanisms and misguided, inflexible behavior to prevent a disastrous loss of control

BRIDGES

See Chapter 13, pages 456–458, for more information on defense mechanisms.

Humanistic-Existential Approaches

Humanistic theories emphasize subjective experience, human problems, and personal potentials. Humanistic psychologist Carl Rogers regarded emotional disorders as the end product of a faulty self-image or self-concept (Rogers, 1959). Rogers believed that anxious individuals have built up unrealistic mental images of

Pain disorder Pain that has no identifiable physical cause and appears to be of psychological origin.

Munchausen by proxy syndrome An affected person fakes the medical problems of someone in his or her care in order to gain attention.

Munchausen syndrome (factitious disorder) An affected person fakes his or her own medical problems in order to gain attention.

Conversion disorder A bodily symptom that mimics a physical disability but is actually caused by anxiety or emotional distress.

themselves. This leaves them vulnerable to contradictory information. Let's say, for example, that an essential part of Cheyenne's self-image is the idea that she is highly intelligent. If Cheyenne does poorly in school, she may deny or distort her perceptions of herself and the situation. Should Cheyenne's anxiety become severe, she may resort to using defense mechanisms. A conversion reaction, anxiety attacks, or similar symptoms could also result from threats to her self-image. These symptoms, in turn, would become new threats that provoke further distortions. Soon, she would fall into a vicious cycle of maladjustment and anxiety that feeds on itself once started.

Existentialism focuses on the elemental problems of existence, such as death, meaning, choice, and responsibility. Psychologists who take a more existential view stress that unhealthy anxiety reflects a loss of *meaning* in one's life. According to them, we must show *courage* and *responsibility* in our choices if life is to have meaning. Too often, they say, we give in to "existential anxiety" and back away from life-enhancing choices. Existential anxiety is the unavoidable anguish that comes from knowing we are personally responsible for our lives. Hence, we have a crushing need to choose wisely and courageously as we face life's empty and impersonal void. Adolescents may experience considerable existential anxiety as they develop their identity (Berman, Weems, & Stickle, 2006).

From the existential view, people who are anxious are living in "bad faith;" that is, they have collapsed in the face of the awesome responsibility to choose a meaningful existence. In short, they have lost their way in life. From this point of view, making choices that don't truly reflect what you value, feel, and believe can make you sick.

Behaviorist Approach

Behaviorist approaches emphasize overt, observable behavior and the effects of learning and conditioning. Behaviorists assume that the "symptoms" we have discussed are learned, just as other behaviors are. You might recall from Chapter 6, for instance, that phobias can be acquired through classical conditioning. Similarly, anxiety attacks may reflect conditioned emotional responses that generalize to new situations and the hypochondriac's "sickness behavior" may be reinforced by the sympathy and attention he or she gets.

One point that all theorists agree on is that disordered behavior is ultimately self-defeating because it makes the person more miserable in the long run, even though it temporarily lowers anxiety.

But if the person becomes more miserable in the long run, how does the pattern get started? The behavioral explanation is that self-defeating behavior begins with avoidance learning, described in Chapter 6. Avoidance learning occurs when making a response delays or prevents the onset of a painful or unpleasant stimulus. Here's a quick review to refresh your memory:

> An animal is placed in a special cage. After a few minutes a light comes on, followed a moment later by a painful shock. Quickly, the animal escapes into a second chamber. After a few minutes, a light comes on in this chamber, and the shock is repeated. Soon the animal learns to avoid pain by moving before the shock occurs. Once an animal learns to avoid the shock, it can be turned off altogether. A well-trained animal may avoid the nonexistent shock indefinitely.

The same analysis can be applied to human behavior. A behaviorist would say that the powerful reward of immediate relief from anxiety keeps self-defeating avoidance behaviors alive. This view, known as the **anxiety reduction hypothesis**, seems to explain why the behavior patterns we have discussed often look very "stupid" to outside observers.

Cognitive Approach

The cognitive view is that distorted thinking causes people to magnify ordinary threats and failures, which leads to distress (Provencher, Dugas, & Ladouceur, 2004). For example, Bonnie, who is socially phobic, constantly has upsetting thoughts about being evaluated at school. One reason for this is that people with social phobias tend to be perfectionists. Like other social phobics, Bonnie is excessively concerned about making mistakes. She also perceives criticism when none exists. If Bonnie expects that a social situation will focus too much attention on her, she avoids it (Brown & Barlow, 2011). Even when socially phobic persons are successful, distorted thoughts lead them to believe they have failed (Barlow, 2002). In short, changing the thinking patterns of anxious individuals like Bonnie can greatly lessen their fears (Hall, 2006).

Implications

All four psychological explanations probably contain a core of truth. For this reason, understanding anxiety-based disorders may be aided by combining parts of each perspective. Each viewpoint also suggests a different approach to treatment. Because many possibilities exist, therapy is discussed later, in Chapter 15.

Personality Disorders—Blueprints for Maladjustment

Gateway Question 14.10: *What is a personality disorder?*

"Get out of here and leave me alone so I can die in peace," Judy screamed at her nurses in the seclusion room of the psychiatric hospital. On one of her arms, long dark red marks mingled with the scars of previous suicide attempts. Judy once bragged that her record was 67 stitches. Today, the nurses had to strap her into restraints to keep her from gouging her own eyes. She was given a sedative and slept for 12 hours. She woke calmly and asked for her therapist—even though her latest outburst began when he canceled a morning appointment and changed it to afternoon.

Judy has a condition called *borderline personality disorder*. Although she is capable of working, Judy has repeatedly lost jobs because of her turbulent relationships with other people. At times, she can be friendly and a real charmer. At other times, she is extremely unpredictable, moody, and even suicidal. Being a friend to Judy can be a fearsome challenge. Canceling an appointment, forgetting a special date, uttering a wrong turn of phrase—these and similar small incidents may trigger Judy's rage or a suicide attempt. Like other people with borderline personality disorder, Judy is extremely sensitive to ordinary criticism, which leaves her feeling rejected and abandoned. Typically, she reacts with anger, self-hatred, and impulsive behavior. These "emotional storms" damage her personal relationships and leave her confused about who she is (Siever & Koenigsberg, 2000).

Maladaptive Personality Patterns

As stated earlier, a person with a personality disorder has maladaptive personality traits. For example, people with a paranoid personality disorder are suspicious, hypersensitive, and wary of others. Narcissistic persons need constant admiration, and they are lost in fantasies of power, wealth, brilliance, beauty, or love. Celebrities appear to be more likely to be narcissistic than noncelebrities, perhaps because they receive so much attention (Young & Pinsky, 2006). The dependent personality suffers from extremely low self-confidence. Dependent persons allow others to run their lives and they place everyone else's needs ahead of their own. People with a histrionic personality disorder constantly seek attention by dramatizing their emotions and actions.

Typically, patterns such as the ones just described begin during adolescence or even childhood. Thus, personality disorders are deeply rooted and usually span many years.

BRIDGES
Personality patterns usually become stable by a very young age. This makes personality disorders difficult to treat. **See Chapter 12, page 425.**

The list of personality disorders is long (■ Table 14.7), so let's focus on a single frequently misunderstood problem: the antisocial personality.

■ TABLE 14.7 DSM-IV-TR Classification of Personality Disorders and Typical Degree of Impairment*

Moderate Impairment	
Dependent	You lack confidence and you are extremely submissive and dependent on others (clinging).
Histrionic	You are dramatic and flamboyant; you exaggerate your emotions to get attention from others.
Narcissistic	You think you are wonderful, brilliant, important, and worthy of constant admiration.
Antisocial	You are irresponsible, lack guilt or remorse, and engage in antisocial behavior, such as aggression, deceit, or recklessness.
High Impairment	
Obsessive-compulsive	You demand order, perfection, control, and rigid routine at all times.
Schizoid	You feel very little emotion and can't form close personal relationships with others.
Avoidant	You are timid, uncomfortable in social situations, and fear evaluation.
Severe Impairment	
Borderline	Your self-image, moods, and impulses are erratic, and you are extremely sensitive to any hint of criticism, rejection, or abandonment by others.
Paranoid	You deeply distrust others and are suspiciousness of their motives, which you perceive as insulting or threatening.
Schizotypal	You are a loner, you engage in extremely odd behavior, and your thought patterns are bizarre, but you are not actively psychotic.

Sources: American Psychiatric Association, 2000, 2010; Durand & Barlow, 2010.

*All of the personality disorders will be reformulated in the upcoming DSM-5 (American Psychiatric Association, 2010).

Antisocial Personality

What are the characteristics of an antisocial personality? A person with an **antisocial personality (antisocial/psychopathic personality)** lacks a conscience. Such people are impulsive, selfish, dishonest, emotionally shallow, and manipulative (Visser et al., 2010). Antisocial persons, who are sometimes called *sociopaths* or *psychopaths,* are poorly socialized and seem to be incapable of feeling guilt, shame, fear, loyalty, or love (American Psychiatric Association, 2000).

Are sociopaths dangerous? Sociopaths tend to have a long history of conflict with society. Many are delinquents or criminals who may be a threat to the general public (Ogloff, 2006). However, sociopaths are rarely the crazed murderers you may have seen por-

More than two thirds of all persons with antisocial personalities have been arrested, usually for crimes such as robbery, vandalism, or rape.

Anxiety reduction hypothesis Explains the self-defeating nature of avoidance responses as a result of the reinforcing effects of relief from anxiety.

Antisocial personality (antisocial/psychopathic personality) A person who lacks a conscience; is emotionally shallow, impulsive, selfish; and tends to manipulate others.

trayed on television and in movies. In fact, many sociopaths are "charming" at first. Their "friends" only gradually become aware of the sociopath's lying and self-serving manipulation. One study found that psychopaths are "blind" to signs of disgust in others. This may add to their capacity for cruelty and their ability to use others (Kosson et al., 2002). Many successful businesspersons, entertainers, politicians, and other seemingly normal people have sociopathic leanings. Basically, antisocial persons coldly use others and cheat their way through life (Ogloff, 2006).

Causes

What causes sociopathy? Typically, people with antisocial personalities showed similar problems in childhood (Burt et al., 2007). Many were emotionally deprived and physically abused as children (Pollock et al., 1990). Adult sociopaths also display subtle neurological problems (• Figure 14.13). For example, they have unusual brain-wave patterns that suggest underarousal of the brain. This may explain why sociopaths tend to be thrill seekers. Quite likely, they are searching for stimulation strong enough to overcome their chronic underarousal and feelings of "boredom" (Hare, 2006).

In a revealing study, sociopaths were shown extremely grisly and unpleasant photographs of mutilations. The photos were so upsetting that they visibly startled normal people. The sociopaths, however, showed no startle response to the photos (Levenston et al., 2000). (They didn't "bat an eyelash.") Those with antisocial personalities might, therefore, be described as *emotionally cold*. They simply do not feel normal pangs of conscience, guilt, or anxiety (Blair et al., 2006). Again, this coldness seems to account for an unusual ability to calmly lie, cheat, steal, or take advantage of others.

Can sociopathy be treated? Antisocial personality disorders are rarely treated with success (Hare, 2006). All too often, sociopaths manipulate therapy, just like any other situation. If it is to their advantage to act "cured," they will do so. However, they return to their former behavior patterns as soon as possible. On a more positive note, antisocial behavior does tend to decline somewhat after age 40, even without treatment, because people tend to become more "mellow" as they age (Laub & Sampson, 2003).

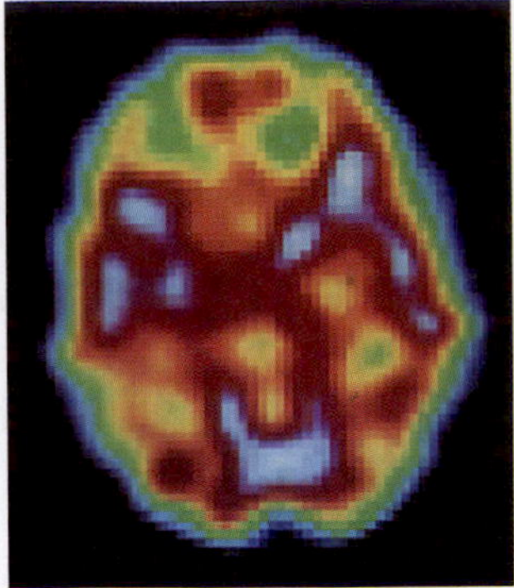

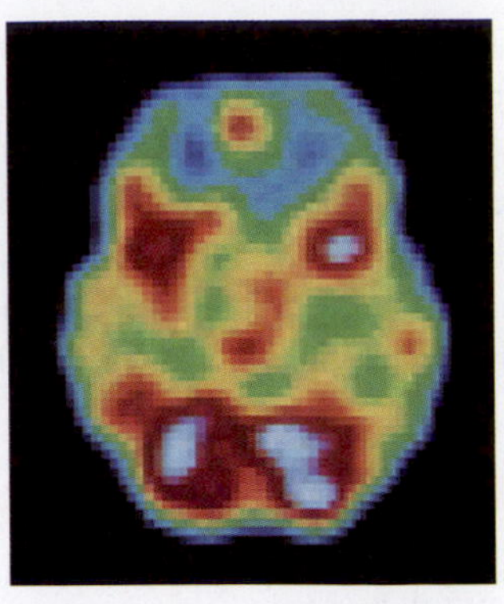

Courtesy of Robert Hare

• Figure 14.13 Using PET scans, Canadian psychologist Robert Hare found that the normally functioning brain *(left)* lights up with activity when a person sees emotion-laden words such as "maggot" or "cancer." But the brain of a psychopath *(right)* remains inactive, especially in areas associated with feelings and self-control. When Dr. Hare showed the right image to several neurologists, one asked, "Is this person from Mars?"

A Look Ahead

Treatments for psychological problems range from counseling and psychotherapy to mental hospitalization and drug therapy. Because they vary greatly, a complete discussion of therapies is found in the next chapter. For now, it's worth noting that many milder mental disorders can be treated successfully. Even major disorders may respond well to drugs and other techniques. It is wrong to fear "former mental patients" or to exclude them from work, friendships, and other social situations. A struggle with major depression or a psychotic episode does not inevitably lead to lifelong dysfunction. Too often, however, it does lead to unnecessary rejection based on groundless fears (Sarason & Sarason, 2005).

Let's conclude with a look at a widely misunderstood problem: By the time you finish reading this page, someone in the United States will have attempted suicide. What can be done about suicide? The upcoming *Psychology in Action* section provides some answers.

Knowledge Builder

Anxiety-Based Disorders and Personality Disorders

RECITE

1. When prolonged unemployment, a bad marriage, or physical illness pushes a person beyond his or her ability to cope, it is most likely that which of the following problems will occur?
   a. a dissociative disorder *b.* agoraphobia *c.* an adjustment disorder *d.* a conversion disorder
2. Panic disorder can occur with or without agoraphobia, but agoraphobia cannot occur alone, without the presence of a panic disorder. T or F?
3. Alice has a phobic fear of closed spaces. What is the formal term for her fear?
   a. nyctophobia *b.* claustrophobia *c.* pathophobia *d.* pyrophobia
4. A person who intensely fears eating, writing, or speaking in public suffers from ______________ ______________ ______________.
5. "Hoarders," "checkers," and "cleaners" suffer from which disorder?
   a. acarophobia *b.* panic disorder with agoraphobia *c.* generalized anxiety disorder *d.* obsessive-compulsive disorder
6. The symptoms of acute stress disorders last less than 1 month; posttraumatic stress disorders last more than 1 month. T or F?
7. Which of the following is *not* a dissociative disorder?
   a. fugue *b.* amnesia *c.* conversion reaction *d.* multiple identity
8. According to the ______________ view, anxiety disorders are the end result of a faulty self-image.
   a. psychodynamic *b.* humanistic *c.* behaviorist *d.* cognitive
9. Which of the following personality disorders is associated with an inflated sense of self-importance and a constant need for attention and admiration?
   a. narcissistic *b.* antisocial *c.* paranoid *d.* manipulative

10. Antisocial personality disorders are difficult to treat, but there is typically a decline in antisocial behavior a year or two after adolescence. T or F?

REFLECT

Think Critically

11. Many of the physical complaints associated with anxiety disorders are closely related to activity of what part of the nervous system?
12. How could someone get away with Munchausen by proxy syndrome? Wouldn't doctors figure out that something was fishy with Ben long before he had 40 surgeries for a faked sinus disorder? (See "Sick of Being Sick.")

Self-Reflect

Which of the anxiety disorders would you *least* want to suffer from? Why?

What minor obsessions or compulsions have you experienced?

What is the key difference between a stress disorder and an adjustment disorder? (Review both discussions if you don't immediately know the answer.)

Which of the four psychological explanations of anxiety-based disorders do you find most convincing?

Many of the qualities that define personality disorders exist to a minor degree in normal personalities. Try to think of a person you know who has some of the characteristics described for each type of personality disorder.

Answers: 1. c **2.** F **3.** b **4.** social phobia **5.** d **6.** T **7.** c **8.** b **9.** a **10.** F **11.** The autonomic nervous system (ANS), especially the sympathetic branch of the ANS. **12.** No one doctor tolerates false symptoms for long. Once a doctor refuses further treatment, the Munchausen sufferer will move on to another. Also, often more than one doctor is being seen at one time.

Psychology in Action

Suicide—Lives on the Brink

Gateway Question 14.11: *Why do people commit suicide and can they be stopped?*

Talk show host Phil Donahue once commented that "suicide is a permanent solution to a temporary problem." If this is so obvious, then why is suicide so distressingly common? In North America, for every three people who die by homicide, five will kill themselves. And there may be as many as 11 attempts for every "successful" suicide (National Institute of Mental Health, 2010). Sooner or later you are likely to be affected by the suicide attempt of someone you know.

What factors affect suicide rates? Suicide rates vary greatly, but some general patterns do emerge.

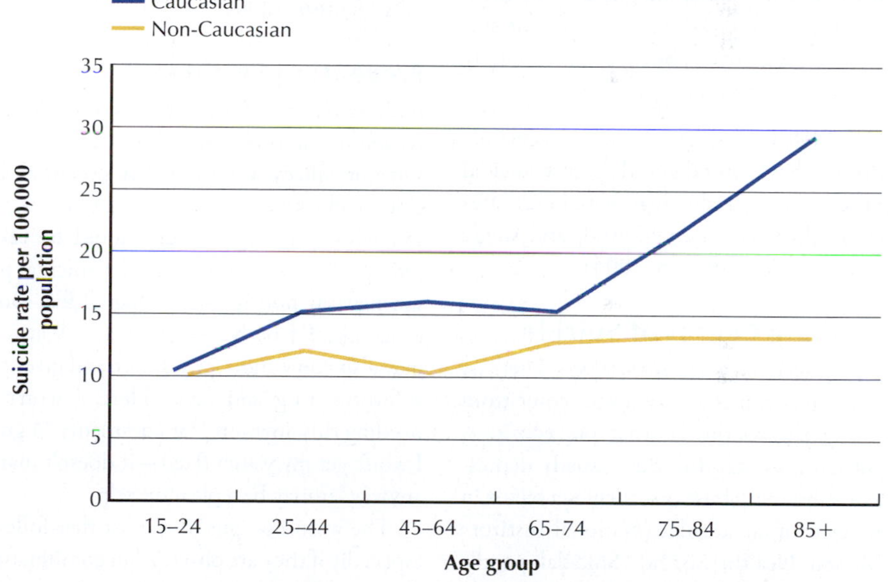

• **Figure 14.14** In the United States, in general, suicide rates for Caucasians are higher than those for non-Caucasians. Also, older people have higher suicide rates than younger people (Centers for Disease Control, 2003; National Institute of Mental Health, 2008).

Gender Men are "better" at suicide than women. Four times as many men *complete* suicide, but women make more attempts (Denney et al., 2009; National Institute of Mental Health, 2011a). Male suicide attempts are more lethal because men typically use a gun or an equally fatal method (National Institute of Mental Health, 2010). Women most often attempt a drug overdose, so there's a better chance of help arriving before death occurs. Sadly, women are beginning to use more deadly methods and may soon equal men in their likelihood of death by suicide.

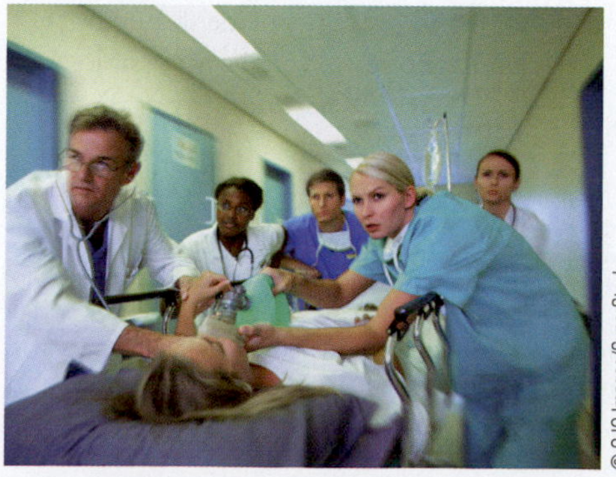

Ethnicity Suicide rates vary dramatically from country to country. The rate in the United States is almost ten times higher than the rate in Azerbaijan, and, in turn, the rate in Hungary is more than three times the U.S. rate (Lester & Yang, 2005). Within the United States, Caucasians generally have higher suicide rates than non-Caucasians (• Figure 14.14), although rates have increased among African Americans in recent years (Griffin-Fennell & Williams, 2006; National Institute of Mental

Health, 2010). Sadly, the suicide rate among Native Americans is by far the highest in the country (suicide rates are equally high among the aboriginal peoples of Australia and New Zealand) (Goldston et al., 2008; McKenzie, Serfaty, & Crawford, 2003).

Age Suicide rates increase with advancing age. More than half of all suicide victims are over 45 years old (see • Figure 14.14). White males 65 years and older are particularly at risk. Of special concern is the rate of suicide among younger people. Between 1950 and 1990, suicide rates for adolescents and young adults doubled (Durand & Barlow, 2010). In fact, suicide is the third leading cause of death among 15- to 24-year-olds (National Institute of Mental Health, 2010). School is a factor in some suicides, but only in the sense that suicidal students were not living up to their own extremely high standards. Many were good students. Other important factors in student suicide are cocaine or alcohol use (Garlow, Purselle, & Heninger, 2007), chronic health problems (real or imagined), and interpersonal difficulties (some who commit suicide are rejected lovers, but others are simply withdrawn and friendless people).

Marital Status Marriage (when successful) may be the best natural guard against suicidal impulses. Married individuals have lower rates than the divorced, the widowed, and single persons (Yip & Thorburn, 2004).

Immediate Causes of Suicide

Why do people try to kill themselves? The best explanation for suicide may simply come from a look at the conditions that precede it. A diagnosable mental disorder (usually depression or substance abuse disorder) is a factor in 90 percent of all suicides (National Institute of Mental Health, 2011a). Suicidal people usually have a history of trouble with family, a lover, or a spouse. Often they have drinking or drug abuse problems, sexual adjustment problems, or job difficulties.

The following are all major risk factors for suicide (National Institute of Mental Health, 2010; Rudd, Joiner, & Rajab, 2001): drug or alcohol abuse; a prior suicide attempt; depression or other mood disorder; feelings of hopelessness or worthlessness; antisocial, impulsive, or aggressive behavior; severe anxiety; panic attacks; a family history of suicidal behavior; shame, humiliation, failure, or rejection; and the availability of a firearm. Among ethnic adolescents, loss of face, acculturative stress, racism, and discrimination have been identified as additional risk factors (Goldston et al., 2008).

Typically, suicidal people isolate themselves from others, feel worthless, helpless, and misunderstood, and want to die. An extremely negative self-image and severe feelings of hopelessness are warnings that the risk for suicide is very high (Heisel, Flett, & Hewitt, 2003). However, a long history of such conditions is not always necessary to produce a desire for suicide. Anyone may temporarily reach a state of depression severe enough to attempt suicide. Most dangerous for the average person are times of divorce, separation, rejection, failure, and bereavement. Such situations can seem intolerable and motivate an intense desire to escape, to obtain relief, or to die (Boergers, Spirito, & Donaldson, 1998). For young people, feelings of anger and hostility add to the danger. When the impulse to harm others is turned inward, the risk for suicide increases dramatically (Jamison, 2001).

Preventing Suicide

Is it true that people who talk about or threaten suicide are rarely the ones who try it? No, this is a major fallacy. Of every ten potential suicides, eight give warning beforehand. A person who threatens suicide should be taken seriously (see • Figure 14.15). A suicidal person may say nothing more than "I feel sometimes like I'd be better off dead." Warnings may also come indirectly. If a friend gives you a favorite ring and says, "Here, I won't be needing this anymore," or comments, "I guess I won't get my watch fixed—it doesn't matter anyway," it may be a plea for help.

The warning signs in the list that follows, especially if they are observed in combination, can signal an impending suicide attempt (Leenaars, Lester, & Wenckstern, 2005; National Institute of Mental Health, 2011b):

- Direct threats to commit suicide
- Preoccupation with death
- Depression/hopelessness
- Rage/anger or seeking revenge
- Aggression and/or risk taking
- Alcohol/drug use
- Withdrawal from contact with others
- No sense of purpose in life
- Sudden swings in mood
- Personality change
- Gift giving of prized possessions
- Recent occurrence of life crisis or emotional shock

Is it true that suicide can't be prevented, that the person will find a way to do it anyway? No. Suicide attempts usually come when a person is alone, depressed, and unable to view matters objectively. You *should* intervene if someone seems to be threatening suicide.

It is estimated that about two thirds of all suicide attempts are made by people who do not really want to die. Almost a third more are *ambivalent* or undecided about dying. Only 3 to 5 percent of suicide cases involve people who really want to die. Most people, therefore, are relieved when someone comes to their aid. Remember that suicide is almost always a cry for help and that you *can* help.

How to Help

What is the best thing to do if someone hints at thinking about suicide? It helps to know some of the common characteristics of suicidal thoughts and feelings (Leenaars, Lester, & Wenckstern, 2005; Shneidman, 1987b):

1. **Escape.** At times, everyone feels like running away from an upsetting situation. Running away from home, quitting school, abandoning a marriage—these are all departures. Suicide, of course, is the ultimate escape. It helps when suicidal persons see that the natural wish for escape doesn't have to be expressed by ending it all.
2. **Unbearable psychological pain.** Emotional pain is what the suicidal person is seeking to escape. A goal of anyone hoping to prevent suicide should be to reduce the pain in any way possible. Ask the person, "Where does it hurt?"

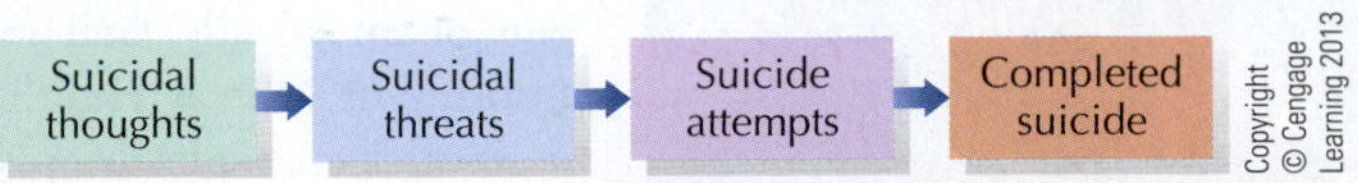

• **Figure 14.15** Suicidal behavior usually progresses from suicidal thoughts to threats to attempts. A person is unlikely to make an attempt without first making threats. Thus, suicide threats should be taken seriously (Leenaars, Lester, & Wenckstern, 2005).

Suicide occurs when pain exceeds a person's resources for coping with pain.

3. **Frustrated psychological needs.** Often, suicide can be prevented if a distressed person's frustrated needs can be identified and eased. Is the person deeply frustrated in his or her search for love, achievement, trust, security, or friendship?
4. **Constriction of options.** The suicidal person feels helpless and decides that death is the *only* solution. The person has narrowed all his or her options solely to death. The rescuer's goal, then, is to help broaden the person's perspective. Even when all the choices are unpleasant, suicidal persons can usually be made to see that their *least unpleasant option* is better than death.

Knowing these patterns will give some guidance in talking to a suicidal person. In addition, your most important task may be to establish *rapport* (a harmonious connection) with the person. You should offer support, acceptance, and legitimate caring.

Remember that a suicidal person feels misunderstood. Try to accept and understand the feelings the person is expressing. Acceptance should also extend to the idea of suicide itself. It is completely acceptable to ask, "Are you thinking of suicide?"

Establishing communication with suicidal persons may be enough to carry them through a difficult time. You may also find it helpful to get day-by-day commitments from them to meet for lunch, share a ride, and the like. Let the person know you *expect* her or him to be there. Such commitments, even though small, can be enough to tip the scales when a person is alone and thinking about suicide.

Don't end your efforts too soon. A dangerous time for suicide is when a person suddenly seems to get better after a severe depression. This often means the person has finally decided to end it all. The improvement in mood is deceptive because it comes from an anticipation that suffering is about to end.

Crisis Intervention Most cities have mental health crisis intervention teams or centers for suicide prevention trained to talk with suicidal persons over the phone. Give a person who seems to be suicidal the number of one of these services. Urge the person to call you or the other number if she or he becomes frightened or impulsive. Or better yet, help the person make an appointment to get psychological treatment (Weishaar, 2006).

The preceding applies mainly to persons who are having mild suicidal thoughts. If a person actually threatens suicide, or if a suicide attempt seems to be imminent, don't worry about overreacting. Immediately seek professional assistance by calling the police, crisis intervention, or a rescue unit. If that is infeasible, ask how the person plans to carry out the suicide. A person who has a *specific, workable plan* and the means to carry it out should be asked to accompany you to the emergency ward of a hospital.

Needless to say, you should call immediately if a person is in the act of attempting suicide or if a drug has already been taken. The majority of suicide attempts come at temporary low points in a person's life and may never be repeated. Get involved—you may save a life!

Knowledge Builder: Suicide and Suicide Prevention

RECITE

1. More women than men use guns in their suicide attempts. T or F?
2. Although the overall suicide rate has remained about the same, there has been a decrease in adolescent suicides. T or F?
3. Suicide is equally a problem in all countries. T or F?
4. The highest suicide rates are found among the divorced. T or F?
5. The majority (two thirds) of suicide attempts are made by people who do not really want to die. T or F?
6. The risk that a person may attempt suicide is greatest if the person has
   a. a concrete, workable plan *b.* had a recent life crisis *c.* withdrawn from contact with others *d.* frustrated psychological needs

REFLECT

Think Critically

7. If you follow the history of popular music, see if you can answer this question: What two major risk factors contributed to the 1994 suicide of Kurt Cobain, lead singer for the rock group Nirvana?

Self-Reflect

You're working a suicide hotline and you take a call from a very distressed young man. What risk factors will you look for as he tells you about his anguish?

What are the common characteristics of suicidal thoughts and feelings? If a friend of yours were to express any of these thoughts or feelings, how would you respond?

Answers: 1. F **2.** F **3.** F **4.** T **5.** T **6.** *a* **7.** Drug or alcohol abuse and availability of a firearm.

Chapter in Review Gateways to Psychological Disorders

Gateway QUESTIONS REVISITED

14.1 *How is abnormality defined?*

14.1.1 *Psychopathology* refers to the scientific study of mental disorders and to maladaptive behavior.

14.1.2 Factors that typically affect judgments of abnormality include statistical abnormality, nonconformity, context, culture, and subjective discomfort.

14.1.3 The key element in judgments of disorder is that a person's behavior is maladaptive. The result is usually serious psychological discomfort or disability and loss of control.

14.1.4 "Insanity" is a legal term defining whether a person may be held responsible for his or her actions. Sanity is determined in court on the basis of testimony by expert witnesses.

14.2 *What are the major psychological disorders?*

14.2.1 Psychological problems are classified by using the *Diagnostic and Statistical Manual of Mental Disorders (DSM).*

14.2.2 Major mental problems include psychotic disorders, organic disorders, mood disorders, anxiety disorders, somatoform disorders, dissociative disorders, personality disorders, sexual or gender identity disorders, and substance-related disorders.

14.2.3 Culture-bound syndromes are not found in the DSM and are unique to every culture.

14.2.4 General risk factors that contribute to psychopathology include biological/physical factors, psychological factors, family factors, and social conditions

14.3 *How can psychiatric labeling be misused?*

14.3.1 Psychiatric labels can be misused to harm and stigmatize people.

14.4 *What are the general characteristics of psychotic disorders?*

14.4.1 Psychosis is a break in contact with reality that is marked by delusions, hallucinations, sensory changes, disturbed emotions, disturbed communication, and personality disintegration.

14.4.2 An organic psychosis is based on known injuries or diseases of the brain. Some common causes of organic psychosis are poisoning, drug abuse, and dementia (especially Alzheimer's disease).

14.5 *What is the nature of a delusional disorder?*

14.5.1 Delusional disorders are almost totally based on the presence of deeply held false beliefs of grandeur, persecution, infidelity, romantic attraction, or physical disease.

14.5.2 The most common delusional disorder is paranoid psychosis. Paranoid persons may be violent if they believe they are threatened.

14.6 *What forms does schizophrenia take and what causes it?*

14.6.1 The varieties of schizophrenia all involve delusions, hallucinations, communication difficulties, and a split between thought and emotion.

14.6.2 Disorganized schizophrenia is marked by extreme personality disintegration and silly, bizarre, or obscene behavior.

14.6.3 Catatonic schizophrenia is associated with stupor, mutism, and odd postures. Sometimes violent and agitated behavior also occurs.

14.6.4 In paranoid schizophrenia (the most common type), outlandish delusions of grandeur and persecution are coupled with psychotic symptoms and personality breakdown.

14.6.5 Environmental factors that increase the risk for schizophrenia include viral infection or malnutrition during the mother's pregnancy, birth complications, early psychological trauma, and a disturbed family environment.

14.6.6 Heredity is a major factor in schizophrenia. Recent biochemical studies have focused on the neurotransmitters glutamate and dopamine and their receptor sites.

14.6.7 The dominant explanation of schizophrenia, and other problems as well, is the stress-vulnerability model which emphasizes a combination of inherited susceptibility and environmental stress.

14.7 *What are mood disorders and what causes them?*

14.7.1 Mood disorders involve primarily disturbances of mood or emotion, producing manic or depressive states. Severe mood disorders may include psychotic features.

14.7.2 In a dysthymic disorder, depression is long lasting, though moderate. In a cyclothymic disorder, people suffer from long-lasting, though moderate, swings between depression and elation.

14.7.3 Bipolar disorders combine mania and depression. In a bipolar I disorder the person swings between severe mania and severe depression. In a bipolar II disorder the person is mostly depressed but has had periods of mild mania.

14.7.4 A major depressive disorder involves extreme sadness and despondency but no signs of mania.

14.7.5 Major mood disorders are partially explained by psychological factors such as loss, anger, learned helplessness, stress, and self-defeating thinking patterns.

14.7.6 Many women experience a brief period of depression, called the maternity blues, shortly after giving birth. Some women suffer from a more serious and lasting condition called postpartum depression.

14.7.7 Major mood disorders are also partially explained by genetic vulnerability and changes in brain chemistry.

14.7.8 Seasonal affective disorder (SAD), which occurs during the winter months, is another common form of depression. SAD is typically treated with phototherapy.

14.8 *What problems result when a person suffers high levels of anxiety?*

14.8.1 Anxiety disorders, dissociative disorders, and somatoform disorders are characterized by high levels of anxiety, rigid defense mechanisms, and self-defeating behavior patterns.

14.8.2 In an adjustment disorder, ordinary stresses push people beyond their ability to cope with life.

14.8.3 Anxiety disorders include generalized anxiety disorder, panic disorder with or without agoraphobia, agoraphobia (without panic), specific phobias, social phobia, obsessive-compulsive disorders, acute stress disorder, and post-traumatic stress disorder.

14.8.4 Dissociative disorders may take the form of amnesia, fugue, or multiple identities.

14.8.5 Somatoform disorders center on physical complaints that mimic disease or disability. Four examples of somatoform disorders are hypochondriasis, somatization disorder, somatoform pain disorder, and conversion disorder.

14.9 *How do psychologists explain anxiety-based disorders?*

14.9.1 Susceptibility to anxiety-based disorders appears to be partly inherited.

14.9.2 The psychodynamic approach emphasizes unconscious conflicts as the cause of disabling anxiety.

14.9.3 The humanistic approach emphasizes the effects of a faulty self-image.

14.9.4 The behaviorists emphasize the effects of previous learning, particularly avoidance learning.

14.9.5 Cognitive theories of anxiety focus on distorted thinking and being fearful of others' attention and judgments?

14.10 *What is a personality disorder?*

14.10.1 Personality disorders are persistent, maladaptive personality patterns.

14.10.2 Sociopathy is a common personality disorder. Antisocial persons seem to lack a conscience. They are emotionally unresponsive, manipulative, shallow, and dishonest.

14.11 *Why do people commit suicide and can they be stopped?*

14.11.1 Suicide is a relatively frequent cause of death that can, in many cases, be prevented.

14.11.2 Suicide is statistically related to such factors as sex, ethnicity, age, and marital status.

14.11.3 In individual cases, the potential for suicide is best identified by a desire to escape, unbearable psychological pain, and frustrated psychological needs. People contemplating suicide narrow their options until death seems like the only way out.

14.11.4 The impulse to attempt suicide is usually temporary. Efforts to prevent suicide are worthwhile.

MEDIA RESOURCES

Web Resources

Internet addresses frequently change. To find an up-to-date list of URLs for the sites listed here, visit your Psychology CourseMate.

Against All Odds Read an article about Carol North, the psychiatrist who overcame schizophrenia.

The Insanity Defense Follow some of the history of the insanity defense.

Psychiatric Disorders Explore a complete listing of the DSM-IV diagnostic categories.

Psychotic Disorders Read more about the psychotic disorders.

William Utermohlen's Self-Portraits View more of these remarkable paintings by a man descending into Alzheimer's disease.

Schizophrenia Explore this extensive website, which includes brain images and videos about schizophrenia.

Depression Find out more about depression.

Bipolar Disorder Read more about bipolar disorder.

Seasonal Affective Disorder Explore the website of the Seasonal Affective Disorder Association.

Anxiety Disorders Explore the website of the Anxiety Disorders Association of America.

Famous People with Phobias Find out more about famous phobias and how to live with them.

Personality Disorders Read more about the ten personality disorders.

Suicide Read all about suicide.

Suicide Prevention Explore the website of the American Foundation for Suicide Prevention.

Are You Worried About a Friend or Loved One? Visit this website if you are worried about someone near you committing suicide.

Interactive Learning

Log in to **CengageBrain** to access the resources your instructor requires. For this book, you can access:

CourseMate brings course concepts to life with interactive learning, study, and exam preparation tools that support the printed textbook. A textbook-specific website, ***Psychology CourseMate*** includes an ***integrated interactive eBook*** and other ***interactive learning tools*** including quizzes, flashcards, videos, and more.

CENGAGE**NOW**™

CengageNOW is an easy-to-use online resource that helps you study in less time to get the grade you want—NOW. Take a pre-test for this chapter and receive a personalized study plan based on your results that will identify the topics you need to review and direct you to online resources to help you master those topics. Then take a post-test to help you determine the concepts you have mastered and what you will need to work on. If your textbook does not include an access code card, go to CengageBrain.com to gain access.

WebTUTOR™

More than just an interactive study guide, **WebTutor** is an anytime, anywhere customized learning solution with an eBook, keeping you connected to your textbook, instructor, and classmates.

If your professor has assigned **Aplia** homework:

1. Sign in to your account.
2. Complete the corresponding homework exercises as required by your professor.
3. When finished, click "Grade It Now" to see which areas you have mastered and which need more work, and for detailed explanations of every answer.

Visit **www.cengagebrain.com** to access your account and purchase materials.

Gateway THEME

Psychotherapies are based on a common core of therapeutic principles. Medical therapies treat the physical causes of psychological disorders. In many cases, these approaches are complementary.

15

Therapies

Paddle Like a Duck

Joe stared at some ducks through the blinds in his psychology professor's office. They were quacking as they explored the campus pond. As psychologists, we meet many students with personal problems. Still, Joe's teacher was surprised to see him at her office door. His excellent work in class and his healthy, casual appearance left her unprepared for his first words. "I feel like I'm losing my mind," he said. "Can I talk to you?"

Over the next hour, Joe described his own personal hell. In a sense, he was like the ducks outside, appearing peaceful on the surface, but madly paddling underneath. He was working hard to hide a world of crippling fear, anxiety, and depression. At work, he was deathly afraid of talking to coworkers and customers. His social phobia led to frequent absenteeism and embarrassing behavior. At school, Joe felt "different" and was sure that other students could tell he was "weird." Several disastrous romances had left him terrified of women. Lately, he had been so depressed that he thought of suicide.

Joe's request for help was a turning point. At a time when he was becoming his own worst enemy, Joe realized he needed help. In Joe's case, that person was a talented clinical psychologist to whom his teacher referred him. With psychotherapy (and some temporary help from an antidepression medication), the psychologist was able to help Joe come to grips with his emotions and regain his balance.

This chapter discusses methods used to alleviate problems like Joe's. We will begin with a look at the origins of modern therapy before describing therapies that emphasize the value of viewing personal problems with *insight* and *changing thought patterns*. Then, we will focus on *behavior therapies*, which directly change troublesome actions. After that, we will explore *medical therapies*, which are based on psychiatric drugs and other physical treatments. We conclude with a look at some contemporary issues in therapy.

Gateway QUESTIONS

- 15.1 *How did psychotherapy originate?*
- 15.2 *Is Freudian psychoanalysis still used?*
- 15.3 *How do psychotherapies differ?*
- 15.4 *What are the major humanistic therapies?*
- 15.5 *How does cognitive therapy change thoughts and emotions?*
- 15.6 *What is behavior therapy?*
- 15.7 *What role do operant principles play in behavior therapy?*
- 15.8 *How do psychiatrists treat psychological disorders?*
- 15.9 *Are various psychotherapies effective, and what do they have in common?*
- 15.10 *What will therapy be like in the future?*
- 15.11 *How are behavioral principles applied to everyday problems and how could a person find professional help?*

Origins of Therapy—Bored Out of Your Skull

Gateway Question 15.1: *How did psychotherapy originate?*

Fortunately, the odds are that you will *not* experience problems as serious as those of Joe, the student we just met. But if you did, what help is available? In most cases, it would be some form of **psychotherapy**, a psychological technique that can bring about positive changes in personality, behavior, or personal adjustment. It might, as with Joe, also include a medical therapy. Let's begin with a brief history of mental health care, including a discussion of psychoanalysis, the first fully developed psychotherapy.

Early treatments for mental problems give good reasons to appreciate modern therapies (Sharf, 2012). Archaeological findings dating to the Stone Age suggest that most primitive approaches were marked by fear and superstitious belief in demons, witchcraft, and magic. If Joe were unlucky enough to have been born several thousand years ago, his "treatment" might have left him feeling "bored." You see, one of the more dramatic "cures" practiced by primitive "therapists" was a process called *trepanning* (treh-PAN-ing), also sometimes spelled *trephining* (Terry, 2006). In modern usage, trepanning is any surgical procedure in which a hole is bored in the skull. In the hands of primitive therapists, it meant boring, chipping, or bashing holes in a patient's head. Presumably, this was done to relieve pressure or release evil spirits (• Figure 15.1).

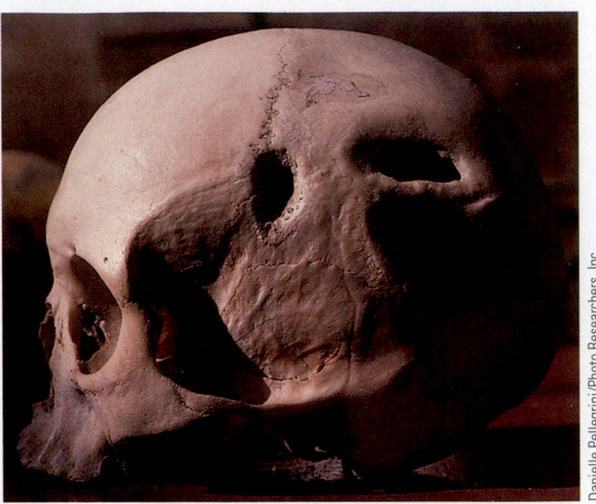

Danielle Pellegrini/Photo Researchers, Inc.

• Figure 15.1 Primitive "treatment" for mental disorders sometimes took the form of boring a hole in the skull. This example shows signs of healing, which means the "patient" actually survived the treatment. Many didn't.

Joe would not have been much better off during the Middle Ages. Then, treatments for mental illness in Europe focused on **demonology**, the study of demons and persons plagued by spirits. Medieval "therapists" commonly blamed abnormal behavior on supernatural forces, such as possession by the devil, or on curses from witches and wizards. As a cure, they used exorcism to "cast out evil spirits." For the fortunate, exorcism was a religious ritual. More often, physical torture was used to make the body an inhospitable place for the devil to reside.

One reason for the rise of demonology may lie in *ergotism* (AIR-got-ism), a psychotic-like condition caused by ergot poisoning. In the Middle Ages, rye (grain) fields were often infested with ergot fungus. Ergot, we now know, is a natural source of LSD and other mind-altering chemicals. Eating tainted bread could have caused symptoms that were easily mistaken for bewitchment or madness. Pinching sensations, muscle twitches, facial spasms, delirium, and hallucinations are all signs of ergot poisoning (Matossian, 1982). Modern analyses of "demonic possession" suggest that many victims may have been suffering from epilepsy, schizophrenia (Mirsky & Duncan, 2005), dissociative disorders (van der Hart, Lierens, & Goodwin, 1996), and depression (Thase, 2006). Thus, many people "treated" by demonologists may have been doubly victimized.

Then, in 1793, a French doctor named Philippe Pinel changed the Bicêtre Asylum in Paris from a squalid "madhouse" into a mental hospital by unchaining the inmates (Harris, 2003). Finally, the emotionally disturbed were regarded as "mentally ill" and given compassionate treatment. Although it has been more than 200 years since Pinel began more humane treatment, the process of improving care continues today.

When was psychotherapy developed? The first true psychotherapy was created by Sigmund Freud little more than 100 years ago (Jacobs, 2003). As a physician in Vienna, Freud was intrigued by cases of **hysteria**. People suffering from hysteria have physical symptoms (such as paralysis or numbness) for which no physical causes can be found.

BRIDGES

Such problems are now called somatoform disorders, as discussed in Chapter 14, pages 499–501.

Mary Evans Picture Library/Photo Researchers, Inc.

© Bettmann/Corbis

(left) **Many early asylums were no more than prisons with inmates held in chains.** ***(right)*** **One late 19th-century "treatment" was based on swinging the patient in a harness—presumably to calm the patient's nerves.**

Slowly, Freud became convinced that hysteria was related to deeply hidden unconscious conflicts and developed psychoanalysis in order to help patients gain insight into those conflicts (Knafo, 2009). Because it is the "granddaddy" of more modern therapies, let's examine psychoanalysis in some detail.

Psychoanalysis—Expedition into the Unconscious

Gateway Question 15.2: *Is Freudian psychoanalysis still used?*

Isn't psychoanalysis the therapy for which the patient lies on a couch? Freud's patients usually reclined on a couch during therapy, while Freud sat out of sight taking notes and offering interpretations. This procedure was supposed to encourage a free flow of thoughts and images from the unconscious. However, it is the least important element of psychoanalysis, and many modern analysts have abandoned it.

How did Freud treat emotional problems? Freud's theory stressed that "neurosis" and "hysteria" are caused by repressed memories, motives, and conflicts—particularly those stemming from instinctual drives for sex and aggression. Although they are hidden, these forces remain active in the personality and cause some people to develop rigid ego defenses and compulsive, self-defeating behavior. Thus, the main goal of **psychoanalysis** is to reduce internal conflicts that lead to emotional suffering (Fayek, 2010).

Freud developed four basic techniques to uncover the unconscious roots of neurosis (Freud, 1949). These are *free association, dream analysis, analysis of resistance*, and *analysis of transference*.

© Peter Aprahamian/Corbis

Pioneering psychotherapist Sigmund Freud's famous couch.

Free Association

The basis for **free association** is saying whatever comes to mind without worrying whether ideas are painful, embarrassing, or illogical. Thoughts are simply allowed to move freely from one idea to the next, without self-censorship. The purpose of free association is to lower defenses so that unconscious thoughts and feelings can emerge (Hoffer & Youngren, 2004).

Dream Analysis

Freud believed that dreams disguise consciously unacceptable feelings and forbidden desires in dream form (Rock, 2004). The psychoanalyst can use this "royal road to the unconscious" to help the patient work past the obvious, visible meaning of the dream (its *manifest content*) to uncover the hidden, symbolic meaning (its *latent content*). This is achieved by analyzing dream symbols (images that have personal or emotional meanings).

Suppose that a young man dreams of pulling a pistol from his waistband and aiming at a target as his wife watches. The pistol repeatedly fails to discharge, and the man's wife laughs at him. Freud might have seen this as an indication of repressed feelings of sexual impotence, with the gun serving as a disguised image of the penis.

BRIDGES

See Chapter 5, pages 178–179 and 198–199, for more information of Freudian dream theory.

Analysis of Resistance

When free associating or describing dreams, patients may *resist* talking about or thinking about certain topics. Such **resistances** (blockages in the flow of ideas) reveal particularly important unconscious conflicts. As analysts become aware of resistances, they bring them to the patient's awareness so the patient can deal with them realistically. Rather than being roadblocks in therapy, resistances can be clues and challenges (Engle & Arkowitz, 2006).

Psychotherapy Any psychological technique used to facilitate positive changes in a person's personality, behavior, or adjustment.

Demonology In medieval Europe, the study of demons and the treatment of persons "possessed" by demons.

Hysteria (now called somatoform disorders) An outdated term describing people with physical symptoms (such as paralysis or numbness) for which no physical causes can be found.

Psychoanalysis A Freudian therapy that emphasizes the use of free association, dream interpretation, resistances, and transference to uncover unconscious conflicts.

Free association In psychoanalysis, the technique of having a client say anything that comes to mind, regardless of how embarrassing or unimportant it may seem.

Resistance A blockage in the flow of free association; topics the client resists thinking or talking about.

Analysis of Transference

Transference is the tendency to "transfer" feelings to a therapist similar to those the patient had for important persons in his or her past. At times, the patient may act as if the analyst is a rejecting father, an unloving or overprotective mother, or a former lover, for example. As the patient re-experiences repressed emotions, the therapist can help the patient recognize and understand them. Troubled persons often provoke anger, rejection, boredom, criticism, and other negative reactions from others. Effective therapists learn to avoid reacting as others do and playing the patient's habitual resistance and transference "games." This, too, contributes to therapeutic change (Fayek, 2010).

Psychoanalysis Today

What is the status of psychoanalysis today? Traditional psychoanalysis was open-ended, calling for three to five therapy sessions a week, often for many years. Today, most patients are seen only once or twice per week, but treatment may still go on for years (Friedman et al., 1998). Because of the huge amounts of time and money this requires, psychoanalysts have become relatively rare. Nevertheless, psychoanalysis made a major contribution to modern therapies by highlighting the importance of unconscious conflicts (Friedman, 2006).

Many therapists have switched to doing time-limited **brief psychodynamic therapy**, which uses direct questioning to reveal unconscious conflicts (Binder, 2004). Modern therapists also actively provoke emotional reactions that will lower defenses and provide insights. Interestingly, brief therapy appears to accelerate recovery. Patients seem to realize that they need to get to the heart of their problems quickly (Messer & Kaplan, 2004).

Interpersonal Psychotherapy

One example of a brief dynamic therapy is **interpersonal psychotherapy (IPT)**, which was first developed to help depressed people improve their relationships with others (Teyber & McClure, 2011). Research has confirmed that IPT is effective for depressive disorders, as well as eating disorders, substance abuse, social phobias, and personality disorders (Fiore et al., 2008; Hoffart, 2005; Prochaska & Norcross, 2010; Talbot & Gamble, 2008).

Liona's therapy is a good example of IPT (Brown & Barlow, 2011). Liona was suffering from depression that a therapist helped her trace to a conflict with her parents. When her father was absent, Liona adopted the role of her mother's protector and friend. However, when her father was home, she was expected to resume her role as a daughter. She was angry with her father for frequently abandoning her mother and upset about having to switch roles so often. Liona's IPT sessions (which sometimes included her mother) focused on clarifying Liona's family roles. Her mood improved a lot after her mother urged her to "stick to being herself."

Is Traditional Psychoanalysis Effective?

The development of newer, more streamlined dynamic therapies is in part due to questions about whether traditional psychoanalysis "works." In a classic criticism, Hans Eysenck (1994) suggested that psychoanalysis simply takes so long that patients experience a **spontaneous remission** of symptoms (improvement due to the mere passage of time).

How seriously should the possibility of spontaneous remission be taken? It's true that problems ranging from hyperactivity to anxiety do improve with the passage of time. Regardless, researchers have confirmed that psychoanalysis does, in fact, produce improvement in a majority of patients (Doidge, 1997).

The real value of Eysenck's critique is that it encouraged psychologists to try new ideas and techniques. Researchers began to ask, "When psychoanalysis works, why does it work? Which parts of it are essential and which are unnecessary?" Modern therapists have given surprisingly varied answers to these questions. Let's move on to survey some of the ways modern therapies differ. Later, we will acquaint you with some of the therapies currently in use.

Dimensions of Therapy—Let Me Count the Ways

Gateway Question 15.3: *How do psychotherapies differ?*

In contrast to *medical therapies*, which are physical in nature, *psychotherapy* refers to any psychological technique that can bring about positive changes in personality, behavior, or personal adjustment. Psychotherapy is usually based on a dialogue between therapists and their clients, although some therapists also use learning principles to directly alter troublesome behaviors (Corsini & Wedding, 2011).

Therapists have many approaches to choose from: psychoanalysis, which we just discussed, as well as client-centered therapy, Gestalt therapy, cognitive therapy, and behavior therapy—to name but a few. As we will see throughout the chapter, each therapy emphasizes different concepts and methods. For this reason, the best approach for a particular person or problem may vary (Prochaska & Norcross, 2010).

Dimensions of Psychotherapy

The terms in the list that follows describe some basic aspects of various psychotherapies (Prochaska & Norcross, 2010; Sharf, 2012). Notice that more than one term may apply to a particular therapy. For example, it is possible to have a directive, action-oriented, open-ended group therapy or a nondirective, individual, insight-oriented, time-limited therapy:

- **Insight vs. action therapy:** Does the therapy aim to bring clients to a deeper understanding of their thoughts, emotions, and behavior? Or is it designed to bring about direct changes in troublesome thoughts, habits, feelings, or behavior, without seeking insight into their origins or meanings?
- **Directive vs. nondirective therapy:** Does the therapist provide strong guidance and advice? Or does the therapist merely assist clients, who are responsible for solving their own problems?

- **Individual vs. group therapy:** Does the therapy involve one therapist with one client? Or do several clients participate at the same time?
- **Open-ended vs. time-limited therapy:** Is the therapy open-ended? Or is it begun with the expectation that it will last only a limited number of sessions?

Myths

Psychotherapy has often been depicted as a complete personal transformation—a sort of "major overhaul" of the psyche. But therapy is *not* equally effective for all problems. Chances of improvement are fairly good for phobias, low self-esteem, some sexual problems, and marital conflicts. More complex problems can be difficult to solve and may, as in Joe's case, require medical treatment as well. The most extreme cases may not respond to psychotherapy at all, leaving a medical therapy as the only viable treatment option.

In short, it is often unrealistic to expect psychotherapy to undo a person's entire past. For many people, the major benefit of psychotherapy is that it provides comfort, support, and a way to make constructive changes (Bloch, 2006; Burns, 2010). Yet, even when problems are severe, therapy may help a person gain a new perspective or learn behaviors to better cope with life. Psychotherapy can be hard work for both clients and therapists, but when it succeeds, few activities are more worthwhile.

It's also a mistake to think that psychotherapy is used only to solve problems or end a crisis. Even if a person is already doing well, therapy can be a way to promote personal growth (Bloch, 2006). Therapists in the positive psychology movement are developing ways to help people make use of their personal strengths. Rather than trying to fix what is "wrong" with a person, they seek to nurture positive traits and actively solve problems (Compton, 2005). ■ Table 15.1 lists some of the elements of positive mental health that therapists seek to restore or promote. Before we dig deeper into some of the different types of psychotherapy, let's enhance your positive academic health with a short review.

■ TABLE 15.1 Elements of Positive Mental Health

- Personal autonomy and independence
- A sense of identity
- Feelings of personal worth
- Skilled interpersonal communication
- Sensitivity, nurturance, and trust
- Genuineness and honesty with self and other
- Self-control and personal responsibility
- Committed and loving personal relationships
- Capacity to forgive others and oneself
- Personal values and a purpose in life
- Self-awareness and motivation for personal growth
- Adaptive coping strategies for managing stresses and crises
- Fulfillment and satisfaction in work
- Good habits of physical health

Adapted from Bergin, 1991; Bloch, 2006.

Knowledge Builder: Treating Psychological Distress

RECITE

1. One modern scientific explanation of medieval "possessions" by "demons" is related to the effects of
   a. ergot poisoning *b.* trepanning *c.* exorcism *d.* unconscious transference
2. Pinel is famous for his use of exorcism. T or F?
3. In psychoanalysis, an emotional attachment to the therapist is called:
   a. free association *b.* manifest association *c.* resistance *d.* transference

Match:

4. _____	Directive therapies	**A.**	Change behavior
5. _____	Action therapies	**B.**	Place responsibility on the client
6. _____	Insight therapies	**C.**	The client is guided strongly
7. _____	Nondirective therapies	**D.**	Seek understanding

8. An approach that is incompatible with insight therapy is
   a. individual therapy *b.* action therapy *c.* nondirective therapy *d.* time-limited psychotherapy

REFLECT

Think Critically

9. According to Freud's concept of *transference,* patients "transfer" their feelings onto the psychoanalyst. In light of this idea, to what might the term *countertransference* refer?

Self-Reflect

The use of trepanning, demonology, and exorcism all implied that the mentally ill are "cursed." To what extent are the mentally ill rejected and stigmatized today?

Try to free associate (aloud) for 10 minutes. How difficult was it? Did anything interesting surface?

Can you explain, in your own words, the role of dream analysis, resistances, and transference in psychoanalysis?

Make a list describing what you think it means to be mentally healthy. How well does your list match the items in ■ Table 15.1?

Answers: 1. *a* **2.** F **3.** *d* **4.** C **5.** A **6.** D **7.** B **8.** *d* **9.** Psychoanalysts (and therapists in general) are also human. They may transfer their own unresolved, unconscious feelings onto their patients. This sometimes hampers the effectiveness of therapy (Kim & Gray, 2009).

Transference The tendency of patients to transfer feelings to a therapist that correspond to those the patient had for important persons in his or her past.

Brief psychodynamic therapy A modern therapy based on psychoanalytic theory but designed to produce insights more quickly.

Interpersonal psychotherapy (IPT) A brief dynamic psychotherapy designed to help people by improving their relationships with other people.

Spontaneous remission Improvement of symptoms due to the mere passage of time.

Humanistic Therapies—Restoring Human Potential

Gateway Question 15.4: *What are the major humanistic therapies?*

When most people picture psychotherapists at work, they imagine them talking with their clients. Let's sample a variety of talk-oriented approaches. *Humanistic therapies* tend to be insight therapies intended to help clients gain deeper insight into their thoughts, emotions, and behavior. In contrast, *cognitive therapies* tend to be action therapies less concerned with insight than with helping people change harmful thinking patterns. Let's start with some insight.

Better self-knowledge was the goal of traditional psychoanalysis. However, Freud claimed that his patients could expect only to change their "hysterical misery into common unhappiness"! Humanistic therapists are more optimistic, believing that humans have a natural urge to seek health and self-growth. Most assume that it is possible for people to use their potentials fully and live rich, rewarding lives. In this section, we'll discuss three of the most common humanistic therapies: client-centered therapy, existential therapy, and Gestalt therapy.

Client-Centered Therapy

What is client-centered therapy? How is it different from psychoanalysis? Whereas psychoanalysis is directive and based on insights from the *un*conscious, **client-centered therapy** (also called **person-centered therapy**) is nondirective and based on insights from *conscious* thoughts and feelings (Brodley, 2006; Wampold, 2007). The psychoanalyst tends to take a position of authority, stating what dreams, thoughts, or memories "mean." In contrast, Carl Rogers (1902–1987), who originated client-centered therapy, believed that what is right or valuable for the therapist may be wrong for the client. (Rogers preferred the term "*client*" to "*patient*" because "*patient*" implies that a person is "sick" and needs to be "cured.") Consequently, in client-centered therapy, the client determines what will be discussed during each session.

Psychotherapist Carl Rogers, who originated client-centered therapy.

Courtesy of Dr. Natalie Rogers

If the client runs things, what does the therapist do? The therapist cannot "fix" the client. Instead, the client must actively seek to solve his or her problems (Whitton, 2003). The therapist's job is to create a safe "atmosphere of growth" by providing opportunities for change.

How do therapists create such an atmosphere? Rogers believed that effective therapists maintain four basic conditions. First, the therapist offers the client **unconditional positive regard** (unshakable personal acceptance). The therapist refuses to react with shock, dismay, or disapproval to anything the client says or feels. Total acceptance by the therapist is the first step to self-acceptance by the client.

Second, the therapist attempts to achieve genuine **empathy** by trying to see the world through the client's eyes and feeling some part of what the client is feeling.

As a third essential condition, the therapist strives to be **authentic** (genuine and honest). The therapist must not hide behind a professional role. Rogers believed that phony fronts destroy the growth atmosphere sought in client-centered therapy.

Fourth, the therapist does not make interpretations, propose solutions, or offer advice. Instead, the therapist **reflects** (rephrases, summarizes, or repeats) the client's thoughts and feelings. This enables the therapist to act as a psychological "mirror" so clients can see themselves more clearly. Rogers theorized that a person armed with a realistic self-image and greater self-acceptance will gradually discover solutions to life's problems.

Existential Therapy

According to the existentialists, "being in the world" (existence) creates deep anxiety. Each of us must deal with the realities of death. We must face the fact that we create our private world by making choices. We must overcome isolation on a vast and indifferent planet. Most of all, we must confront feelings of meaninglessness (Schneider, Galvin, & Serlin, 2009).

What do these concerns have to do with psychotherapy? **Existential therapy** focuses on the problems of existence, such as meaning, choice, and responsibility. Like client-centered therapy, it promotes self-knowledge. However, there are important differences. Client-centered therapy seeks to uncover a "true self" hidden behind a screen of defenses. In contrast, existential therapy emphasizes free will, the human ability to make choices. Accordingly, existential therapists believe you can *choose to become* the person you want to be.

Existential therapists try to give clients the *courage* to make rewarding and socially constructive choices. Typically, therapy focuses on *death*, *freedom*, *isolation*, and *meaninglessness*, the "ultimate concerns" of existence (van Deurzen & Kenward, 2005). These universal human challenges include an awareness of one's mortality, the responsibility that comes with freedom to choose, being alone in your own private world, and the need to create meaning in your life.

One example of existential therapy is Victor Frankl's *logotherapy*, which emphasizes the need to find and maintain meaning in life. Frankl (1904–1997) based his approach on experiences he had as a prisoner in a Nazi concentration camp. In the camp, Frankl saw countless prisoners break down as they were stripped of all hope and human dignity (Frankl, 1955). Those who survived with their sanity did so because they managed to hang on to a sense of meaning *(logos)*. Even in less dire circumstances, a sense of purpose in life adds greatly to psychological well-being (Prochaska & Norcross, 2010).

What does the existential therapist do? The therapist helps clients discover self-imposed limitations in personal identity. To be successful, the client must fully accept the challenge of changing his or her life (Bretherton & Orner, 2004). Interestingly, Buddhists seek a similar state that they call "radical acceptance" (Brach, 2003).

A key aspect of existential therapy is *confrontation*, in which clients are challenged to be mindful of their values and choices and to take responsibility for the quality of their existence (Claessens, 2009). An important part of confrontation is the unique, intense, here-and-now *encounter* between two human beings. When existential therapy is successful, it brings about a renewed sense of purpose and a reappraisal of what's important in life. Some clients even experience an emotional rebirth, as if they had survived a close brush with death. As Marcel Proust wrote, "The real voyage of discovery consists not in seeing new landscapes but in having new eyes."

Gestalt Therapy

Gestalt therapy is based on the idea that perception, or *awareness*, is disjointed and incomplete in maladjusted persons. The German word *Gestalt* means "whole," or "complete." **Gestalt therapy** helps people rebuild thinking, feeling, and acting into connected wholes. This is achieved by expanding personal awareness; by accepting responsibility for one's thoughts, feelings, and actions; and by filling in gaps in experience (Masquelier, 2006).

What are "gaps in experience"? Gestalt therapists believe that we often shy away from expressing or "owning" upsetting feelings. This creates a gap in self-awareness that may become a barrier to personal growth. For example, a person who feels anger after the death of a parent might go for years without fully expressing it. This and similar threatening gaps may impair emotional health.

The Gestalt approach is more directive than client-centered or existential therapy, and it is less insight-oriented and instead emphasizes immediate experience. Working either one-to-one or in a group setting, the Gestalt therapist encourages clients to become more aware of their moment-to-moment thoughts, perceptions, and emotions (Staemmler, 2004). Rather than discussing *why* clients feel guilt, anger, fear, or boredom, the therapist encourages them to have these feelings in the "here and now" and become fully aware of them. The therapist promotes awareness by drawing attention to a client's posture, voice, eye movements, and hand gestures. Clients may also be asked to exaggerate vague feelings until they become clear. Gestalt therapists believe that expressing such feelings allows people to "take care of unfinished business" and break through emotional impasses (O'Leary, 2006).

Gestalt therapy is often associated with the work of Fritz Perls (1969). According to Perls, emotional health comes from knowing what you *want* to do, not dwelling on what you *should* do, *ought* to do, or *should want* to do (Brownell, 2010). In other words, emotional health comes from taking full responsibility for one's feelings and actions. For example, it means changing "I can't" to "I won't," or "I must" to "I choose to."

How does Gestalt therapy help people discover their real wants? Above all else, Gestalt therapy emphasizes *present* experience (Yontef, 2007). Clients are urged to stop intellectualizing and talking *about* feelings. Instead, they learn to live now; live here; stop imagining; experience the real; stop unnecessary thinking; taste and see; express rather than explain, justify, or judge; give in to unpleasantness and pain just as to pleasure; and surrender to being as you are. Gestalt therapists believe that, paradoxically, the best way to change is to become who you really are (Brownell, 2010).

Cognitive Therapy—Think Positive!

Gateway Question 15.5: *How does cognitive therapy change thoughts and emotions?*

Whereas humanistic therapies usually seek to foster insight, cognitive therapies usually try to directly change what people think, believe, and feel, and, as a consequence, how they act. In general, **cognitive therapy** helps clients change thinking patterns that lead to troublesome emotions or behaviors (Davey, 2008; Power, 2010).

In practice, how does cognitive therapy differ from humanistic therapy? Janice is a hoarder whose home is crammed full with things she has acquired over two decades. If she seeks help from a therapist concerned with insight, she will try to better understand why she began collecting stuff. In contrast, if she seeks help from a cognitive

Client-centered (or **person-centered) therapy** A nondirective therapy based on insights gained from conscious thoughts and feelings; emphasizes accepting one's true self.

Unconditional positive regard An unqualified, unshakable acceptance of another person.

Empathy A capacity for taking another's point of view; the ability to feel what another is feeling.

Authenticity In Carl Rogers's terms, the ability of a therapist to be genuine and honest about his or her own feelings.

Reflection In client-centered therapy, the process of rephrasing or repeating thoughts and feelings expressed by clients so they can become aware of what they are saying.

Existential therapy An insight therapy that focuses on the elemental problems of existence, such as death, meaning, choice, and responsibility; emphasizes making courageous life choices.

Gestalt therapy An approach that focuses on immediate experience and awareness to help clients rebuild thinking, feeling, and acting into connected wholes; emphasizes the integration of fragmented experiences.

Cognitive therapy A therapy directed at changing the maladaptive thoughts, beliefs, and feelings that underlie emotional and behavioral problems.

therapist, she may spend little time examining her past. Instead, she will work to actively change her thoughts and beliefs about hoarding. With either approach, the goal is to give up hoarding. Further, in practice, humanistic therapies often also result in active change and cognitive therapies often also yield deeper insight.

Cognitive therapy has been successfully used as a remedy for many problems, ranging from generalized anxiety disorder and posttraumatic stress disorder to marital distress and anger (Butler et al., 2006). For example, compulsive hand washing can be greatly reduced by changing a client's thoughts and beliefs about dirt and contamination (Jones & Menzies, 1998). Cognitive therapy has been especially successful in treating depression (Hollon, Stewart, & Strunk, 2006). Joe's clinical psychologist relied on cognitive therapy to help lift Joe (who could forget Joe?) out of his depression.

Cognitive Therapy for Depression

As you may recall from Chapter 13, cognitive psychologists believe that negative, self-defeating thoughts underlie depression. According to Aaron Beck (1991), depressed persons see themselves, the world, and the future in negative terms because of major distortions in thinking. The first is **selective perception**, which refers to perceiving only certain stimuli in a larger array. If five good things and three bad things happen during the day, depressed people focus only on the bad. A second thinking error in depression is **overgeneralization**, the tendency to think that an upsetting event applies to other, unrelated situations. An example would be Joe's considering himself a total failure, or completely worthless, if he were to lose a part-time job or fail a test. To complete the picture, depressed persons tend to magnify the importance of undesirable events by engaging in **all-or-nothing thinking**: they see events as completely good or bad, right or wrong, and themselves as either successful or failing miserably (Lam & Mok, 2008).

How do cognitive therapists alter such patterns? Cognitive therapists make a step-by-step effort to correct negative thoughts that lead to depression or similar problems. At first, clients are taught to recognize and keep track of their own thoughts. The client and therapist then look for ideas and beliefs that cause depression, anger, and avoidance. For example, here's how Joe's therapist began to challenge his all-or-nothing thinking:

Joe: I'm feeling really depressed today. No one wants to hire me, and I can't even get a date. I feel completely incompetent!

Therapist: I see. The fact that you are currently unemployed and don't have a girlfriend proves that you are completely and utterly incompetent?

Joe: Well…I can see that doesn't add up.

Next, clients are asked to gather information to test their beliefs. For instance, a depressed person might list his or her activities for a week. The list is then used to challenge all-or-nothing thoughts, such as "I had a terrible week" or "I'm a complete failure." With more coaching, clients learn to alter their thoughts in ways that improve their moods, actions, and relationships.

Cognitive therapy is at least as effective as drugs for treating many cases of depression (Butler et al., 2006; Eisendrath, Chartier, & McLane, 2011). More importantly, people who have adopted new thinking patterns are less likely to become depressed again—a benefit that drugs can't impart (Dozois & Dobson, 2004; Hollon, Stewart, & Strunk, 2006).

In an alternate approach, cognitive therapists look for an *absence* of effective coping skills and thinking patterns, not for the *presence* of self-defeating thoughts (Dobson, Backs-Dermott, & Dozois, 2000). The aim is to teach clients how to cope with anger, depression, shyness, stress, and similar problems. Stress inoculation, which was described in Chapter 13, is a good example of this approach. Joe used it to weaken his social phobia.

Cognitive therapy is a rapidly expanding specialty. Before we leave the topic, let's explore another widely used cognitive therapy.

Rational-Emotive Behavior Therapy

Rational-emotive behavior therapy (REBT) attempts to change irrational beliefs that cause emotional problems. According to Albert Ellis (1913–2007), the basic idea of REBT is as easy as A-B-C (Ellis, 1995, Ellis & Ellis, 2011). Ellis assumes that people become unhappy and develop self-defeating habits because they have unrealistic or faulty *beliefs*.

How are beliefs important? Ellis analyzes problems in this way: The letter A stands for an *activating experience*, which the person assumes to be the cause of C, an *emotional consequence*. For instance, a person who is rejected (the activating experience) feels depressed, threatened, or hurt (the consequence). Rational-emotive behavior therapy shows the client that the real problem is what comes between A and C: In between is B, the client's irrational and unrealistic *beliefs*. In this example, an unrealistic belief leading to unnecessary suffering is, "I must be loved and approved by everyone at all times." REBT holds that events do not *cause* us to have feelings. We feel as we do because of our beliefs (Dryden, 2011; Kottler & Shepard, 2011). (For some examples, see "Ten Irrational Beliefs—Which Do You Hold?")

BRIDGES

The REBT explanation of emotional distress is related to the effects of emotional appraisals. **See Chapter 10, pages 359–360.**

Ellis (1979, Ellis & Ellis, 2011) says that most irrational beliefs come from three core ideas, each of which is unrealistic:

1. I *must* perform well and be approved of by significant others. If I don't, then it is awful, I cannot stand it, and I am a rotten person.
2. You *must* treat me fairly. When you don't, it is horrible, and I cannot bear it.
3. Conditions *must* be the way I want them to be. It is terrible when they are not, and I cannot stand living in such an awful world.

Discovering Psychology — Ten Irrational Beliefs—Which Do You Hold?

Rational-emotive behavior therapists have identified numerous beliefs that commonly lead to emotional upsets and conflicts. See if you recognize any of the following irrational beliefs:

1. I must be loved and approved by almost every significant person in my life or it's awful and I'm worthless.
   Example: "One of my classmates doesn't seem to like me. I must be a big loser."
2. I should be completely competent and achieving in all ways to be a worthwhile person.
   Example: "I don't understand my physics class. I guess I really am just stupid."
3. It's terribly upsetting when things don't go my way.
   Example: "I should have gotten a B in that class. The teacher is a total creep."
4. It's not my fault I'm unhappy; I can't control my emotional reactions.
   Example: "You make me feel awful. I would be happy if it weren't for you."
5. I should never forget it if something unpleasant happens.
   Example: "I'll never forget the time my boss insulted me. I think about it every day at work."
6. It is easier to avoid difficulties and responsibilities than to face them.
   Example: "I don't know why my girlfriend is angry. Maybe it will just pass if I ignore it."
7. A lot of people I have to deal with are bad. I should severely punish them for it.
   Example: "The students renting next door are such a pain. I'm going to play my stereo even louder the next time they complain."
8. I should depend on others who are stronger than me.
   Example: "I couldn't survive if she left me."
9. Because something once strongly affected me, it will do so forever.
   Example: "My girlfriend dumped me during my junior year in college. I can never trust a woman again."
10. There is always a perfectly obvious solution to human problems, and it is immoral if this solution is not put into practice.
    Example: "I'm so depressed about politics in this country. It all seems hopeless."*

If any of the listed beliefs sound familiar, you may be creating unnecessary emotional distress for yourself by holding on to unrealistic expectations.

*Adapted from Dryden, 2011; Ellis & Ellis, 2011; Teyber & McClure, 2011).

It's easy to see that such beliefs can lead to much grief and needless suffering in a less than perfect world. Rational-emotive behavior therapists are very directive in their attempts to change a client's irrational beliefs and "self-talk." The therapist may directly attack clients' logic, challenge their thinking, confront them with evidence contrary to their beliefs, and even assign "homework." Here, for instance, are some examples of statements that dispute irrational beliefs (adapted from Dryden, 2011; Ellis & Ellis, 2011; Kottler & Shepard, 2011):

- "Where is the evidence that you are a loser just because you didn't do well this one time?"
- "Who said the world should be fair? That's your rule."
- "What are you telling yourself to make yourself feel so upset?"
- "Is it really terrible that things aren't working out as you would like? Or is it just inconvenient?"

Many of us would probably do well to give up our irrational beliefs. Improved self-acceptance and a better tolerance of daily annoyances are the benefits of doing so (see "Overcoming the Gambler's Fallacy").

The value of cognitive approaches is further illustrated by three techniques (*covert sensitization*, *thought stopping*, and *covert reinforcement*) described in this chapter's *Psychology in Action* section. A little later you can see what you think of them.

Knowledge Builder — Humanistic and Cognitive Therapies

RECITE

Match:

1. _____ Client-centered therapy
2. _____ Gestalt therapy
3. _____ Existential therapy
4. _____ REBT

A. Changing thought patterns
B. Unconditional positive regard
C. Gaps in awareness
D. Choice and becoming

5. The Gestalt therapist tries to *reflect* a client's thoughts and feelings. T or F?
6. Confrontation and encounter are concepts of existential therapy. T or F?
7. According to Beck, selective perception, overgeneralization, and ______________________ thinking are cognitive habits that underlie depression.

Continued

Selective perception Perceiving only certain stimuli among a larger array of possibilities.

Overgeneralization Blowing a single event out of proportion by extending it to a large number of unrelated situations.

All-or-nothing thinking Classifying objects or events as absolutely right or wrong, good or bad, acceptable or unacceptable, and so forth.

Rational-emotive behavior therapy (REBT) An approach that states that irrational beliefs cause many emotional problems and that such beliefs must be changed or abandoned.

The Clinical File — Overcoming the Gambler's Fallacy

Seventeen-year-old Jonathan just lost his shirt again. This time, he did it playing online Blackjack. Jonathan started out making $5 bets and then doubled his bet over and over. Surely, he thought, his luck would eventually change. However, he ran out of money after just eight straight hands, having lost more than $1000. Last week, he lost a lot of money playing Texas Hold 'Em. Now Jonathan is in tears—he has lost most of his summer earnings, and he is worried about having to drop out of school and tell his parents about his losses. Jonathan has had to admit that he is part of the growing ranks of underage gambling addicts (LaBrie & Shaffer, 2007; Wilber & Potenza, 2006).

Like many problem gamblers, Jonathan suffers from several cognitive distortions related to gambling. Here are some of his mistaken beliefs (adapted from adapted from Toneatto, 2002; Wickwire, Whelan, & Meyers, 2010):

Magnified gambling skill: Your self-confidence is exaggerated, despite the fact that you lose persistently.

Attribution errors: You ascribe your wins to skill but blame losses on bad luck.

Gambler's fallacy: You believe that a string of losses soon must be followed by wins.

Selective memory: You remember your wins but forget your losses.

Overinterpretation of cues: You put too much faith in irrelevant cues such as bodily sensations or a feeling that your next bet will be a winner.

Luck as a trait: You believe that you are a "lucky" person in general.

Probability biases: You have incorrect beliefs about randomness and chance events.

Do you have any of these mistaken beliefs? Taken together, Jonathan's cognitive distortions created an illusion of control. That is, he believed that if he worked hard enough, he could figure out how to win. Fortunately, a cognitive therapist helped Jonathan *cognitively restructure* his beliefs. He now no longer believes he can control chance events. Jonathan still gambles a bit, but he does so only recreationally, keeping his losses within his budget and enjoying himself in the process.

Gambling addiction is a growing problem among young people (LaBrie & Shaffer, 2007).

8. The B in the A-B-C of REBT stands for
   a. behavior *b.* belief *c.* being *d.* Beck

REFLECT

Think Critically

9. How might using the term *patient* affect the relationship between an individual and a therapist?
10. In Aaron Beck's terms, a belief such as "I must perform well or I am a rotten person" involves two thinking errors. What are they?

Self-Reflect

You are going to play the role of a therapist for a classroom demonstration. How would you act if you were a client-centered therapist? An existential therapist? A Gestalt therapist?

What would an existential therapist say about the choices you have made so far in your life? Should you be choosing more "courageously"?

We all occasionally engage in negative thinking. Can you remember a time recently when you engaged in selective perception? Overgeneralization? All-or-nothing thinking?

Answers: 1. B **2.** C **3.** D **4.** A **5.** F **6.** T **7.** all-or-nothing **8.** *b* **9.** The terms *doctor* and *patient* imply a large gap in status and authority between the individual and his or her therapist. Client-centered therapy attempts to narrow this gap by making the person the final authority concerning solutions to his or her problems. Also, the word *patient* implies that a person is "sick" and needs to be "cured." Many regard this as an inappropriate way to think about human problems. **10.** Overgeneralization and all-or-nothing thinking.

Therapies Based on Classical Conditioning—Healing by Learning

Gateway Question 15.6: *What is behavior therapy?*

Jay repeatedly and vividly imagined himself going into a store to steal something. He then pictured himself being caught and turned over to the police, who handcuffed him and hauled him off to jail. Once there, he imagined calling his wife to tell her he had been arrested for shoplifting. He became very distressed as he faced her anger and his son's disappointment (Kohn & Antonuccio, 2002).

Why would anyone imagine such a thing? Jay's behavior is not as strange as it may seem. His goal was self-control: Jay is a *kleptomaniac* (a compulsive thief). The method he chose (called *covert sensitization*) is a form of behavior therapy (Prochaska & Norcross, 2010).

In general, how does behavior therapy work? A breakthrough occurred when psychologists realized they could use learning principles to solve human problems. **Behavior therapy** is an action therapy that uses learning principles to make constructive changes in behavior. Behavior therapists believe that deep insight into one's problems is often unnecessary for improvement. Instead, they try to directly alter troublesome actions and thoughts. Jay

© Sidney Harris/www.CartoonStock.com

didn't need to probe into his past or his emotions and conflicts; he simply wanted to break his shoplifting habit. This and the next section describe some innovative—and very successful—behavioral therapies.

Behavior therapists assume that people have *learned* to be the way they are. If they have learned responses that cause problems, then they can change them by *relearning* more appropriate behaviors. Broadly speaking, **behavior modification** refers to any use of classical or operant conditioning to directly alter human behavior (Miltenberger, 2011; Spiegler & Guevremont, 2010). (Some therapists prefer to call this approach *applied behavior analysis*.) Behavioral approaches include aversion therapy, desensitization, token economies, and other techniques (Forsyth & Savsevitz, 2002).

How does classical conditioning work? I'm not sure I remember. Perhaps a brief review would be helpful. Classical conditioning is a form of learning in which simple responses (especially reflexes) are associated with new stimuli. In classical conditioning, a neutral stimulus is followed by an *unconditioned stimulus (US)* that consistently produces an unlearned reaction, called the *unconditioned response (UR)*. Eventually, the previously neutral stimulus begins to produce this response directly. The response is then called a *conditioned response (CR)*, and the stimulus becomes a *conditioned stimulus (CS)*. Thus, for a child the sight of a hypodermic needle (CS) is followed by an injection (US), which causes anxiety or fear (UR). Eventually, the sight of a hypodermic (the conditioned stimulus) may produce anxiety or fear (a conditioned response) *before* the child gets an injection.

BRIDGES

For a more thorough review of classical conditioning, return to Chapter 6, pages 207–212.

What does classical conditioning have to do with behavior modification? Classical conditioning can be used to associate discomfort with a bad habit, as Jay did to deal with his kleptomania. More powerful versions of this approach are called aversion therapy.

Aversion Therapy

Imagine that you are eating an apple. Suddenly, you discover that you just bit a large green worm in half. You vomit. Months later, you cannot eat an apple again without feeling ill. It's apparent that you have developed a conditioned aversion to apples. (A *conditioned aversion* is a learned dislike or negative emotional response to some stimulus.)

How are conditioned aversions used in therapy? In **aversion therapy**, an individual learns to associate a strong aversion to an undesirable habit such as smoking, drinking, or gambling. Aversion therapy has been used to cure hiccups, sneezing, stuttering, vomiting, nail-biting, bed-wetting, compulsive hair-pulling, alcoholism, and the smoking of tobacco, marijuana, or crack cocaine. Actually, aversive conditioning happens every day. For example, not many physicians who treat lung cancer patients are smokers, nor do many emergency room doctors drive without using their seat belts (Eifert & Lejuez, 2000).

Puffing Up an Aversion

The fact that nicotine is toxic makes it easy to create an aversion that helps people give up smoking. Behavior therapists have found that electric shock, nauseating drugs, and similar aversive stimuli are not required to make smokers uncomfortable. All that is needed is for the smoker to smoke—rapidly, for a long time, at a forced pace. During rapid smoking, clients are told to smoke continuously, taking a puff every 6 to 8 seconds. Rapid smoking continues until the smoker is miserable and can stand it no more. By then, most people are thinking, "I never want to see another cigarette for the rest of my life."

Rapid smoking has long been known as an effective behavior therapy for smoking (McRobbie & Hajek, 2007). Nevertheless, anyone tempted to try rapid smoking should realize that it is very unpleasant. Without the help of a therapist, most people quit too soon for the procedure to succeed. In addition, rapid smoking can be dangerous. It should be done only with professional supervision. (An alternative method that is more practical is described in the *Psychology in Action* section of this chapter.)

Aversive Therapy for Drinking

Another excellent example of aversion therapy was pioneered by Roger Vogler and his associates (1977). Vogler worked with alcoholics who were unable to stop drinking and for whom aversion therapy was a last chance. While drinking an alcoholic beverage, clients receive a painful (although not injurious) electric shock to the hand. Most of the time, these shocks occur as the client is beginning to take a drink of alcohol.

These *response-contingent shocks* (shocks that are linked to a response) obviously take the pleasure out of drinking. Shocks also

Behavior therapy Any therapy designed to actively change behavior.
Behavior modification The application of learning principles to change human behavior, especially maladaptive behavior.
Aversion therapy Suppressing an undesirable response by associating it with aversive (painful or uncomfortable) stimuli.

Discovering Psychology: Feeling a Little Tense? Relax!

The key to desensitization is relaxation. To inhibit fear, you must *learn* to relax. One way to voluntarily relax is by using the **tension-release method**. To achieve deep muscle relaxation, try the following exercise:

> Tense the muscles in your right arm until they tremble. Hold them tight as you slowly count to ten and then let go. Allow your hand and arm to go limp and to relax completely. Repeat the procedure. Releasing tension two or three times will allow you to feel whether your arm muscles have relaxed. Repeat the tension–release procedure with your left arm. Compare it with your right arm. Repeat until the left arm is equally relaxed. Apply the tension–release technique to your right leg; to your left leg; to your abdomen; to your chest and shoulders. Clench and release your chin, neck, and throat. Wrinkle and release your forehead and scalp. Tighten and release your mouth and face muscles. As a last step, curl your toes and tense your feet. Then release.

If you carried out these instructions, you should be noticeably more relaxed than you were before you began. Practice the tension-release method until you can achieve complete relaxation quickly (5 to 10 minutes). After you have practiced relaxation once a day for a week or two, you will begin to be able to tell when your body (or a group of muscles) is tense. Also, you will begin to be able to relax on command. This is a valuable skill that you can apply in any situation that makes you feel tense or anxious.

cause the alcohol abuser to develop a conditioned aversion to drinking. Normally, the misery caused by alcohol abuse comes long after the act of drinking—too late to have much effect. But if alcohol can be linked with *immediate* discomfort, then drinking will begin to make the individual very uncomfortable.

Is it really acceptable to treat clients this way? People are often disturbed (shocked?) by such methods. However, clients usually *volunteer* for aversion therapy because it helps them overcome a destructive habit. Indeed, commercial aversion programs for overeating, smoking, and alcohol abuse have attracted many willing customers. More important, aversion therapy can be justified by its long-term benefits. As behaviorist Donald Baer put it, "A small number of brief, painful experiences are a reasonable exchange for the interminable pain of a lifelong maladjustment."

Programs for treating fears of flying combine relaxation, systematic desensitization, group support, and lots of direct and indirect exposure to airliners. Many such programs conclude with a brief flight, so that participants can "test their wings."

Desensitization

How is behavior therapy used to treat phobias, fears, and anxieties? Suppose you want to help Curtis overcome fear of the high diving board. How might you proceed? Directly forcing Curtis off the high board could be a psychological disaster. A better approach would be to begin by teaching him to dive off the edge of the pool. Then he could be taught to dive off the low board, followed by a platform 6 feet above the water and then an 8-foot platform. As a last step, Curtis could try the high board.

Who's Afraid of a Hierarchy?

This rank-ordered series of steps (called a **hierarchy**) allows Curtis to undergo *adaptation*. Gradually, he adapts to the high dive and overcomes his fear. When Curtis has conquered his fear, we can say that *desensitization* (dee-SEN-sih-tih-ZAY-shun) has occurred (Spiegler & Guevremont, 2010).

Desensitization is also based on **reciprocal inhibition** (using one emotional state to block another) (Heriot & Pritchard, 2004). For instance, it is impossible to be anxious and relaxed at the same time. If we can get Curtis onto the high board in a relaxed state, his anxiety and fear will be inhibited. Repeated visits to the high board should cause fear to disappear in this situation. Again, we would say that Curtis has been desensitized. Typically, **systematic desensitization** (a guided reduction in fear, anxiety, or aversion) is attained by gradually approaching a feared stimulus while maintaining relaxation.

What is desensitization used for? Desensitization is used primarily to help people unlearn phobias (intense, unrealistic fears) or strong anxieties. For example, each of these people might be a candidate for desensitization: a teacher with stage fright; a student with test anxiety; a salesperson who fears people; or a newlywed with an aversion to sexual intimacy.

Performing Desensitization

How is desensitization done? First, the client and the therapist *construct a hierarchy*. This is a list of fear-provoking situations, arranged from least disturbing to most frightening. Second, the client is taught *exercises that produce deep relaxation* (see "Feeling a Little Tense? Relax!"). Third, once the client is relaxed, she or he tries to *perform the least disturbing item* on the list. For a fear of heights (acrophobia), this might be: "(1) Stand on a chair." The first item is repeated until no anxiety is felt. Any change from complete relaxation is a signal that clients must relax again before continuing. Slowly, clients move up the hierarchy: "(2) Climb to the top of a small stepladder"; "(3) Look down a flight of stairs"; and so on, until the last item is performed without fear: "(20) Fly in an airplane."

For many phobias, desensitization works best when people are directly exposed to the stimuli and situations they fear (Bourne, 2010; Miltenberger, 2011). For something like a simple spider phobia, this exposure can even be done in groups. Also, for some fears (such as fear of riding an elevator, or fear of spiders) desensitization may be completed in a single session (Müller et al., 2011; Sturges & Sturges, 1998).

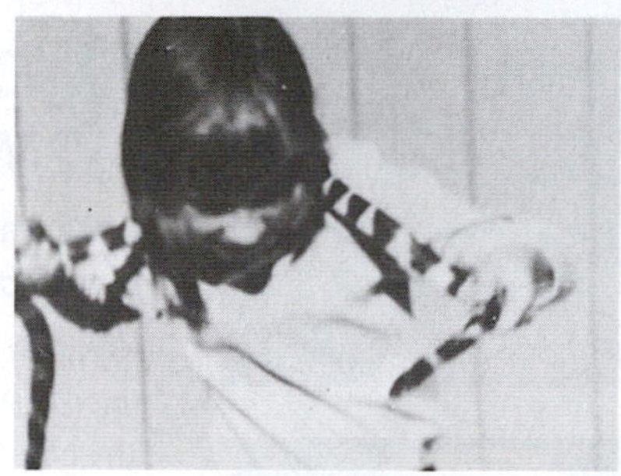

Photos courtesy of Albert Bandura.

• Figure 15.2 Treatment of a snake phobia by vicarious desensitization. These classic photographs show models interacting with snakes. To overcome their own fears, phobic subjects observed the models (Bandura, Blanchard, & Ritter, 1969).

Vicarious Desensitization

What if it's not practical to directly act out the steps of a hierarchy? For a fear of heights, the steps of the hierarchy might be acted out. However, if this is impractical, as it might be in the case of a fear of flying, the problem can be handled by having clients observe *models* who are performing the feared behavior (Eifert & Lejucz, 2000; Bourne, 2010; • Figure 15.2). A model is a person (either live or filmed) who serves as an example for observational learning. If such **vicarious desensitization** (secondhand learning) can't be used, there is yet another option. Fortunately, desensitization works almost as well when a person *vividly imagines* each step in the hierarchy (Yahnke, Sheikh, & Beckman, 2003). If the steps can be visualized without anxiety, fear in the actual situation is reduced. Because imagining feared stimuli can be done at a therapist's office, it is the most common way of doing desensitization.

Virtual Reality Exposure

Desensitization is an *exposure therapy*. Similar to other such therapies, it involves exposing people to feared stimuli until their fears extinguish. In an important recent development, psychologists are now also using virtual reality to treat phobias. Virtual reality is a computer-generated, three-dimensional "world" that viewers enter by wearing a head-mounted video display. **Virtual reality exposure** presents computerized fear stimuli to clients in a realistic, yet carefully controlled fashion (Wiederhold & Wiederhold, 2005; Riva, 2009). It has already been used to treat fears of flying, driving, and public speaking as well as acrophobia (fear of heights), claustrophobia, and spider phobias (Arbona et al., 2004; Giuseppe, 2005; Lee et al., 2002; Meyerbröker & Emmelkamp, 2010; Müller et al., 2011; see • Figure 15.3.). Virtual reality exposure has also been used to create immersive distracting environments for help patients reduce the experience of pain (Malloy & Milling, 2010).

Desensitization has been one of the most successful behavior therapies. A relatively new technique may provide yet another way to lower fears, anxieties, and psychological pain.

Eye Movement Desensitization

Traumatic events produce painful memories. Disturbing flashbacks often haunt victims of accidents, disasters, molestations, muggings, rapes, or emotional abuse. To help ease traumatic memories and post-traumatic stress, Dr. Francine Shapiro developed **eye movement desensitization and reprocessing (EMDR)**.

Hierarchy A rank-ordered series of higher and lower amounts, levels, degrees, or steps.

Reciprocal inhibition The presence of one emotional state can inhibit the occurrence of another, such as joy preventing fear or anxiety inhibiting pleasure.

Systematic desensitization A reduction in fear, anxiety, or aversion brought about by planned exposure to aversive stimuli.

Tension-release method A procedure for systematically achieving deep relaxation of the body.

Vicarious desensitization A reduction in fear or anxiety that takes place vicariously ("secondhand") when a client watches models perform the feared behavior.

Virtual reality exposure Use of computer-generated images to present fear stimuli. The virtual environment responds to a viewer's head movements and other inputs.

Eye movement desensitization and reprocessing (EMDR) A technique for reducing fear or anxiety; based on holding upsetting thoughts in mind while rapidly moving the eyes from side to side.

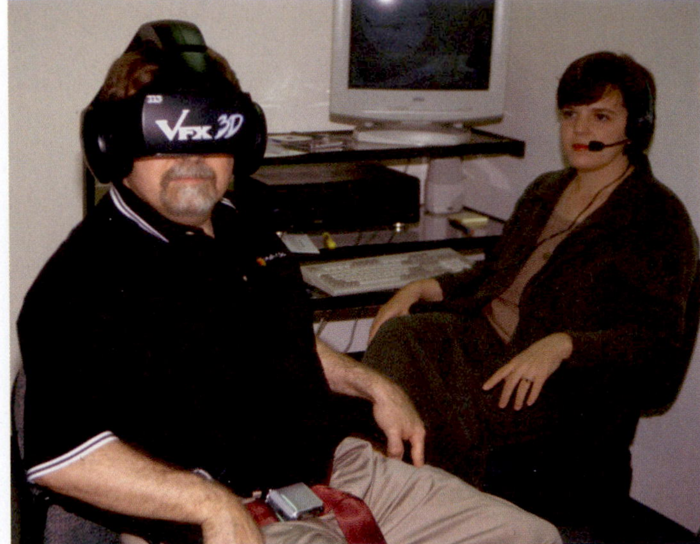

Images courtesy of Virtually Better.

• **Figure 15.3** *(top)* Dr. Larry Hodges (in the head-mounted display) and Dr. Page Anderson show how a virtual reality system is used to expose people to feared stimuli. *(bottom)* A computer image from a virtual Iraq or Afghanistan. Veterans suffering from post-traumatic stress disorder (PTSD) can re-experience their traumas. For example, someone whose Humvee was destroyed by an improvised explosive device can relive that moment complete with sights, sounds, vibrations, and even smells. Successive exposures result in a reduction of PTSD symptoms (Gerardi et al., 2008).

In a typical EMDR session, the client is asked to visualize the images that most upset her or him. At the same time, a pencil (or other object) is moved rapidly from side to side in front of the person's eyes. Watching the moving object causes the person's eyes to dart swiftly back and forth. After about 30 seconds, clients describe any memories, feelings, and thoughts that emerged and discuss them with the therapist. These steps are repeated until troubling thoughts and emotions no longer surface (Shapiro, 2001; Shapiro & Forrest, 2004).

A number of studies suggest that EMDR lowers anxieties and takes the pain out of traumatic memories (Seidler & Wagner, 2006). However, EMDR is highly controversial (Albright & Thyer, 2010). Some studies, for example, have found that eye movements add nothing to the treatment. The apparent success of EMDR may simply be based on gradual exposure to upsetting stimuli, as in other forms of desensitization (Davidson & Parker, 2001). On the other hand, some researchers continue to find that EMDR is superior to traditional therapies (Greenwald, 2006; Solomon, Solomon, & Heide, 2009).

Is EMDR a breakthrough? Given the frequency of traumas in modern society, it shouldn't be long before we find out.

Operant Therapies—All the World Is a Skinner Box?

Gateway Question 15.7: *What role do operant principles play in behavior therapy?*

Aversion therapy and desensitization are based on classical conditioning. Where does operant conditioning fit in? As you may recall, operant conditioning refers to learning based on the consequences of making a response. The operant principles most often used by behavior therapists to deal with human behavior are:

1. **Positive reinforcement.** Responses that are followed by reinforcement tend to occur more frequently. If children whine and get attention, they will whine more frequently. If you get A's in your psychology class, you may become a psychology major.
2. **Nonreinforcement and Extinction.** A response that is not followed by reinforcement will occur less frequently. If a response is not followed by reward after it has been repeated many times, it will extinguish entirely. After winning three times, you pull the handle on a slot machine 30 times more without a payoff. What do you do? You go away. So does the response of handle pulling (for that particular machine, at any rate).
3. **Punishment.** If a response is followed by discomfort or an undesirable effect, the response will be suppressed (but not necessarily extinguished).
4. **Shaping.** Shaping means reinforcing actions that are closer and closer approximations to a desired response. For example, to reward an intellectually disabled child for saying "ball," you might begin by reinforcing the child for saying anything that starts with a *b* sound.
5. **Stimulus control.** Responses tend to come under the control of the situation in which they occur. If you set your clock 10 minutes fast, it may be easier to leave the house on time in the morning. Your departure is under the stimulus control of the clock, even though you know it is fast.
6. **Time out.** A time-out procedure usually involves removing the individual from a situation in which reinforcement occurs. Time out is a variation of response cost: It prevents reward from following an undesirable response. For example, children who fight with each other can be sent to separate rooms and allowed out only when they are able to behave more calmly.

BRIDGES

For a more thorough review of operant learning, return to Chapter 6, pages 212–229.

As simple as these principles may seem, they have been used very effectively to overcome difficulties in work, home, school, and industrial settings. Let's see how.

Nonreinforcement and Extinction

An extremely overweight mental patient had a persistent and disturbing habit: She stole food from other patients. No one could persuade her to stop stealing or to diet. For the sake of her health, a behavior therapist assigned her a special table in the ward dining room. If she approached any other table, she was immediately removed from the dining room. Any attempt to steal from others caused the patient to miss her own meal (Ayllon, 1963). Because her attempts to steal food went unrewarded, they rapidly disappeared.

What operant principles did the therapist in this example use? The therapist used *nonreward* to produce *extinction*. The most frequently occurring human behaviors lead to some form of reward. An undesirable response can be eliminated by *identifying* and *removing* the rewards that maintain it. But people don't always do things for food, money, or other obvious rewards. Most of the rewards maintaining human behavior are subtler. *Attention*, *approval*, and *concern* are common yet powerful reinforcers for humans (● Figure 15.4).

Nonreward and extinction can eliminate many problem behaviors, especially in schools, hospitals, and institutions. Often, difficulties center on a limited number of particularly disturbing responses. Time out is a good way to remove such responses, usually by refusing to pay attention to a person who is misbehaving. For example, 14-year-old Terrel periodically appeared in the nude in the activity room of a training center for disturbed adolescents. This behavior always generated a great deal of attention from staff and other patients. As an experiment, the next time he appeared nude, counselors and other staff members greeted him normally and then ignored him. Attention from other patients rapidly subsided. Sheepishly, he returned to his room and dressed.

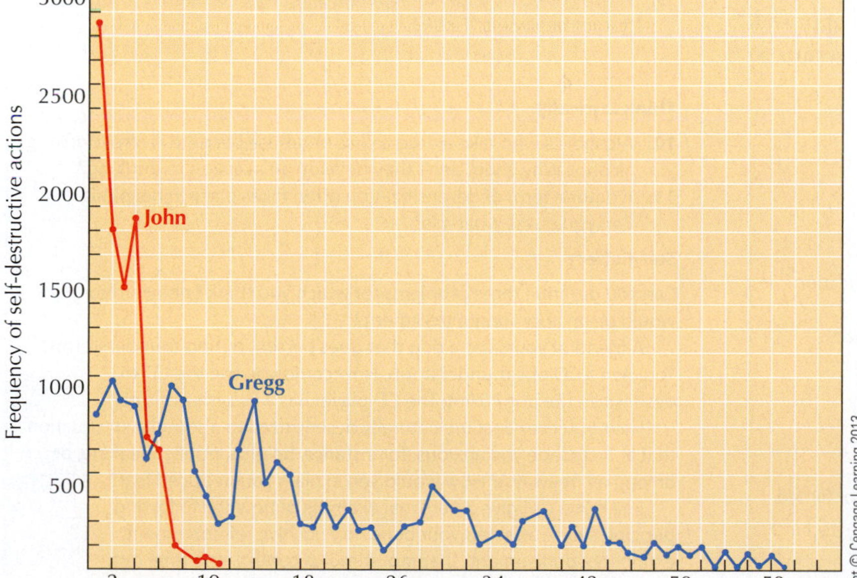

● Figure 15.4 This graph shows extinction of self-destructive behavior in two autistic boys. Before extinction began, the boys received attention and concern from adults for injuring themselves. During extinction, the adults were taught to ignore the boys' self-damaging behavior. As you can see, the number of times that the boys tried to injure themselves declined rapidly. (Adapted from Lovaas & Simmons, 1969.)

Reinforcement and Token Economies

A distressing problem therapists sometimes face is how to break through to severely disturbed patients who won't talk. Conventional psychotherapy offers little hope of improvement for such patients.

What can be done for them? One widely used approach is based on *tokens* (symbolic rewards that can be exchanged for real rewards). Tokens may be printed slips of paper, check marks, points, or gold stars. Whatever form they take, tokens serve as rewards because they may be exchanged for candy, food, cigarettes, recreation, or privileges, such as private time with a therapist, outings, or watching television. Tokens are used in mental hospitals, halfway houses, schools for the intellectually disabled, programs for delinquents, and ordinary classrooms. They usually produce improvements in behavior (Dickerson, Tenhula, & Green-Paden, 2005; Matson & Boisjoli, 2009).

BRIDGES

Tokens provide an effective way to change behavior because they are secondary reinforcers. **See Chapter 6, pages 218–220.**

By using tokens, a therapist can *immediately reward* positive responses. For maximum impact, therapists select specific *target behaviors* (actions or other behaviors the therapist seeks to modify). Target behaviors are then reinforced with tokens. For example, a mute mental patient might first be given a token each time he or she says a word. Next, tokens may be given for speaking a complete sentence. Later, the patient could gradually be required to speak more often, then to answer questions, and eventually to carry on a short conversation in order to receive tokens. In this way, deeply withdrawn patients have been returned to the world of normal communication.

The full-scale use of tokens in an institutional setting produces a *token economy*. In a **token economy**,

Token economy A therapeutic program in which desirable behaviors are reinforced with tokens that can be exchanged for goods, services, activities, and privileges.

patients are rewarded with tokens for a wide range of socially desirable or productive activities (Spiegler & Guevremont, 2010). They must *pay* tokens for privileges and when they engage in problem behaviors (● Figure 15.5). For example, tokens are given to patients who dress themselves, take required medication, arrive for meals on time, and so on. Constructive activities, such as gardening, cooking, or cleaning, may also earn tokens. Patients must *exchange* tokens for meals and private rooms, movies, passes, off-ward activities, and other privileges. They are *charged* tokens for disrobing in public, talking to themselves, fighting, crying, and similar target behaviors (Morisse et al., 1996; Spiegler & Guevremont, 2010).

Token economies can radically change a patient's overall adjustment and morale. Patients are given an incentive to change, and they are held responsible for their actions. The use of tokens may seem manipulative, but it actually empowers patients. Many "hopelessly" intellectually disabled, mentally ill, and delinquent people have been returned to productive lives by means of token economies (Field et al., 2004).

By the time they are ready to leave, patients may be earning tokens on a weekly basis for maintaining sane, responsible, and productive behavior (Miltenberger, 2011). Typically, the most effective token economies are those that gradually switch from tokens to *social rewards* such as praise, recognition, and approval. Such rewards are what patients will receive when they return to family, friends, and community.

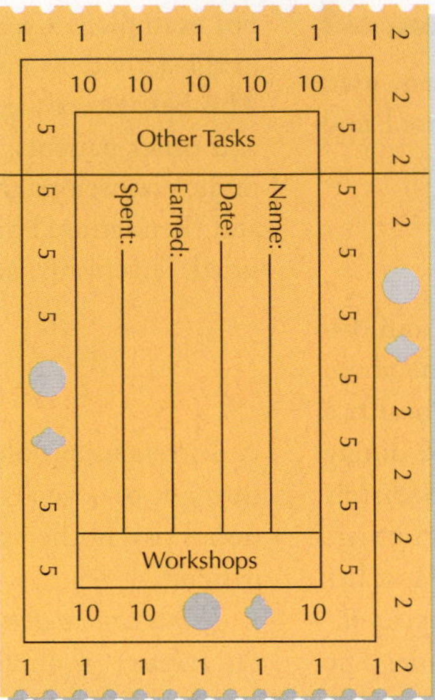

OXNARD DAY TREATMENT CENTER
CREDIT INCENTIVE SYSTEM

EARN CREDITS BY		SPEND CREDITS FOR	
MONITOR DAILY	15	COFFEE	5
MENU PLANNING CHAIRMAN	50	LUNCH	10
PARTICIPATE	5	EXCEPT THURSDAY	15
BUY FOOD AT STORE	10	BUS TRIP	5
COOK FOR/PREPARE LUNCH	5	BOWLING	8
WIPE OFF KITCHEN TABLE	3	GROUP THERAPY	5
WASH DISHES	5-10	PRIVATE STAFF TIME	5
DRY AND PUT AWAY DISHES	5	DAY OFF	5-20
MAKE COFFEE AND CLEAN URN	15	WINDOW SHOPPING	5
CLEAN REFRIGERATOR	20	REVIEW WITH DR.	10
ATTEND PLANNING CONFERENCE	1	DOING OWN THING	1
OT PREPARATION	1-5	LATE 1 PER EVERY 10 MIN	
COMPLETE OT PROJECT	5	PRESCRIPTION FROM DR.	10
RETURN OT PROJECT	2		
DUST AND POLISH TABLES	5		
PUT AWAY GROCERIES	3		
CLEAN TABLE	5		
CLEAN 6 ASH TRAYS	2		
CLEAN SINK	5		
CARRY OUT CUPS & BOTTLES	5		
CLEAN CHAIRS	5		
CLEAN KITCHEN CUPBOARDS	5		
ASSIST STAFF	5		
ARRANGE MAGAZINES NEATLY	3		
BEING ON TIME	5		
MONITOR-ANN			

● **Figure 15.5** Shown here is a token used in one token economy system. In this instance, the token is a card that records the number of credits earned by a patient. Also pictured is a list of credit values for various activities. Tokens may be exchanged for items or for privileges listed on the board. (After photographs by Robert P. Liberman.)

Knowledge Builder: Behavior Therapies

RECITE

1. What two types of conditioning are used in behavior modification? ________ and ________
2. Shock, pain, and discomfort play what role in conditioning an aversion?
   a. conditioned stimulus *b.* unconditioned response *c.* unconditioned stimulus *d.* conditioned response
3. If shock is used to control drinking, it must be ________ contingent.
4. When desensitization is carried out through the use of live or filmed models, it is called
   a. cognitive therapy *b.* flooding *c.* covert desensitization *d.* vicarious desensitization
5. The three basic steps in systematic desensitization are: constructing a hierarchy, flooding the person with anxiety, and imagining relaxation. T or F?
6. In EMDR therapy, computer-generated virtual reality images are used to expose clients to fear-provoking stimuli. T or F?
7. Behavior modification programs aimed at extinction of an undesirable behavior typically make use of what operant principles?
   a. punishment and stimulus control *b.* punishment and shaping *c.* nonreinforcement and time out *d.* stimulus control and time out
8. Attention can be a powerful ________ for humans.
9. Tokens basically allow the operant shaping of desired responses or "target behaviors." T or F?

REFLECT

Think Critically

10. Alcoholics who take a drug called Antabuse become ill after drinking alcohol. Why, then, don't they develop an aversion to drinking?
11. A natural form of desensitization often takes place in hospitals. Can you guess what it is?

Self-Reflect

Can you describe three problems for which you think behavior therapy would be an appropriate treatment?

A friend of yours has a dog that goes berserk during thunderstorms. You own a CD of a thunderstorm. How could you use the CD to desensitize the dog? (Hint: The CD player has a volume control.)

Have you ever become naturally desensitized to a stimulus or situation that at first made you anxious (for instance, heights, public speaking, or driving on freeways)? How would you explain your reduced fear?

See if you can give a personal example of how the following principles have affected your behavior: positive reinforcement, extinction, punishment, shaping, stimulus control, and time out.

Answers: 1. classical (or respondent), operant **2.** c **3.** response **4.** *d* **5.** F **6.** F **7.** C **8.** reinforcer **9.** T **10.** Committed alcoholics may actually "drink through it" and learn to tolerate the nauseating effects. **11.** Doctors and nurses learn to relax and remain calm at the sight of blood and other bodily fluids because of their frequent exposure to them.

■ **TABLE 15.2** Commonly Prescribed Psychiatric Drugs

Class	Examples (Trade Names)	Effects	Main Mode of Action
Anxiolytics (minor tranquilizers)	Ativan, Halcion, Librium, Restoril, Valium, Xanax	Reduce anxiety, tension, fear	Enhance effects of GABA
Antidepressants	Anafranil, Elavil, Nardil, Norpramin, Parnate, Paxil, Prozac, Tofranil, Zoloft	Counteract depression	Enhance effects of serotonin or dopamine
Antipsychotics (major tranquilizers)	Clozaril, Haldol, Mellaril, Navane, Risperdal, Thorazine	Reduce agitation, delusions, hallucinations, thought disorders	Reduce effects of dopamine

Source: Adapted from Freberg, 2010; Julien, 2008; Kalat, 2009.

Medical Therapies—Psychiatric Care

Gateway Question 15.8: *How do psychiatrists treat psychological disorders?*

Psychotherapy may be applied to anything from a brief crisis to a full-scale psychosis. However, most psychotherapists *do not* treat patients with major depressive disorders, schizophrenia, or other severe conditions. Major mental disorders are more often treated medically, although combinations of medication and psychotherapy are also often helpful (Beck, et al., 2009).

Three main types of **somatic** (bodily) **therapy** are *pharmacotherapy*, *electrical stimulation therapy*, and *psychosurgery*. Somatic therapy is often done in the context of psychiatric hospitalization. All the somatic approaches have a strong medical slant and are typically administered by psychiatrists, who are trained as medical doctors.

Courtesy of Rodger Casier

The work of artist Rodger Casier illustrates the value of psychiatric care. Despite having a form of schizophrenia, Casier produces artwork that has received public acclaim and has been featured in professional journals.

Drug Therapies

The atmosphere in psychiatric wards and mental hospitals changed radically in the mid-1950s with the widespread adoption of **pharmacotherapy** (FAR-meh-koe-THER-eh-pea), the use of drugs to treat psychopathology. Drugs may relieve the anxiety attacks and other discomforts of milder psychological disorders. More often, however, they are used to combat schizophrenia and major mood disorders (Julien, 2008).

What sort of drugs are used in pharmacotherapy? Three major types of drugs are used. All achieve their effects by influencing the activity of different brain neurotransmitters (Freberg, 2010). **Anxiolytics** (ANG-zee-eh LIT-iks), such as Valium, produce relaxation or reduce anxiety. **Antidepressants**, such as Prozac, are mood-elevating drugs that combat depression. **Antipsychotics** (also called **major tranquilizers**), such as Risperdal, have tranquilizing effects and reduce hallucinations and delusions. See ■ Table 15.2 for examples of each class of drugs.

Are drugs a valid approach to treatment? Yes. Drugs have shortened hospital stays, and they have greatly improved the chances that people will recover from major psychological disorders. Drug therapy has also made it possible for many people to return to the community, where they can be treated on an outpatient basis.

Limitations of Drug Therapy

Regardless of their benefits, all drugs involve risks as well. For example, 15 percent of patients taking major tranquilizers for long periods develop a neurological disorder that causes rhythmic facial

Somatic therapy Any bodily therapy, such as drug therapy, electroconvulsive therapy, or psychosurgery.

Pharmacotherapy The use of drugs to treat psychopathology.

Anxiolytics Drugs (such as Valium) that produce relaxation or reduce anxiety.

Antidepressants Mood-elevating drugs.

Antipsychotics (major tranquilizers) Drugs that, in addition to having tranquilizing effects, also tend to reduce hallucinations and delusional thinking.

and mouth movements (Chakos et al., 1996). Similarly, although the drug *clozapine* (Clozaril) can relieve the symptoms of schizophrenia, 2 out of 100 patients taking the drug suffer from a potentially fatal blood disease (Ginsberg, 2006).

Is the risk worth it? Many experts think it is, because chronic schizophrenia robs people of almost everything that makes life worth living. It's possible, of course, that newer drugs will improve the risk/benefit ratio in the treatment of severe problems like schizophrenia. For example, the drug risperidone (Risperdal) appears to be as effective as Clozaril, without the same degree of lethal risk.

But even the best new drugs are not cure-alls. They help some people and relieve some problems, but not all. It is noteworthy that for serious mental disorders a combination of medication and psychotherapy almost always works better than drugs alone (Manber et al., 2008). Nevertheless, when schizophrenia and major mood disorders are concerned, drugs will undoubtedly remain the primary mode of treatment (Vasa, Carlino, & Pine, 2006; Walker et al., 2004).

Electrical Stimulation Therapy

In contrast to drug therapies, electrical stimulation therapies achieve their effects by altering the electrical activity of the brain. Electroconvulsive therapy is the first, and most dramatic, of these therapies. Widely used since the 1940s, it remains controversial to this day (Hirshbein & Sarvananda, 2008).

Electroshock

In **electroconvulsive therapy (ECT)**, a 150-volt electrical current is passed through the brain for slightly less than a second. This rather drastic medical treatment for depression triggers a convulsion and causes the patient to lose consciousness for a short time. Muscle relaxants and sedative drugs are given before ECT to soften its impact. Treatments are given in a series of sessions spread over several weeks or months.

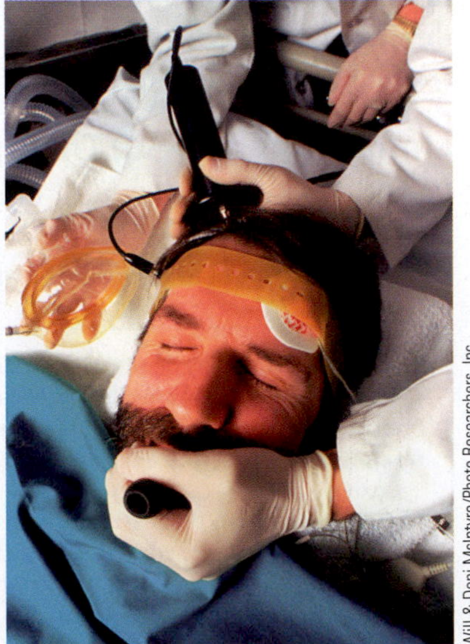

In electroconvulsive therapy, electrodes are attached to the head and a brief electrical current is passed through the brain. ECT is used in the treatment of severe depression.

Will & Deni McIntyre/Photo Researchers, Inc.

How does shock help? Actually, it is the seizure activity that is believed to be helpful. Proponents of ECT claim that shock-induced seizures alter or "reset" the biochemical and hormonal balance in the brain and body, bringing an end to severe depression and suicidal behavior (Medda et al., 2009) as well as improving long-term quality of life (McCall et al., 2006). Others have charged that ECT works only by confusing patients so they can't remember why they were depressed.

Not all professionals support the use of ECT. However, most experts seem to agree on the following: (1) At best, ECT produces only temporary improvement—it gets the patient out of a bad spot, but it must be combined with other treatments; (2) ECT can cause memory loss in some patients (Sienaert et al., 2010); (3) ECT should be used only after other treatments have failed; and (4) to lower the chance of a relapse, ECT should be followed by antidepressant drugs (Sackeim et al., 2001). All told, ECT is considered by many to be a valid treatment for selected cases of depression—especially when it rapidly ends wildly self-destructive or suicidal behavior (Medda et al., 2009; Pagnin et al., 2004). It's interesting to note that most ECT patients feel that the treatment helped them. Most, in fact, would have it done again (Bernstein et al., 1998; Smith et al., 2009).

Implanted Electrodes

Unlike ECT, implanting electrodes requires surgery but allows for electrical stimulation of precisely targeted brain regions. In some studies, depressed patients who hadn't benefited from drug therapy and ECT improved when a specific brain region was stimulated (Mayberg et al., 2005; Sartorius et al., 2010). Stimulating pleasure centers in the brains of another group of patients also relieved depression (Schlaepfer et al., 2008). Also, unlike ECT, implanted electrodes can be used to treat disorders other than depression, such as obsessive-compulsive disorder (Haq et al., 2010).

BRIDGES

Electrical stimulation of the brain is one of several methods used to investigate the brain's inner workings. **For more information, see Chapter 2, pages 60–63.**

Psychosurgery

Psychosurgery (any surgical alteration of the brain) is the most extreme medical treatment. The oldest and most radical psychosurgery is the lobotomy. In *prefrontal lobotomy*, the frontal lobes are surgically disconnected from other brain areas. This procedure was supposed to calm persons who didn't respond to any other type of treatment.

When the lobotomy was first introduced in the 1940s, there were enthusiastic claims for its success. But later studies suggested that some patients were calmed, some showed no change, and some became mental "vegetables." Lobotomies also produced a high rate of undesirable side effects, such as seizures, blunted emotions, major personality changes, and stupor. At about the same time that such problems became apparent, the first antipsychotic drugs became available. Soon after, the lobotomy was abandoned (Mashour, Walker, & Martuza, 2005).

To what extent is psychosurgery used now? Psychosurgery is still considered valid by many neurosurgeons. However, most now use *deep lesioning*, in which small target areas are destroyed in the brain's interior. The appeal of deep lesioning is that it can have value as a remedy for some very specific disorders (Mashour, Walker, & Martuza, 2005). For instance, patients suffering from a severe type of obsessive-compulsive disorder may be helped by psychosurgery (Dougherty et al., 2002).

BRIDGES

Deep lesioning is another method used to study the brain. **See Chapter 2, pages 60–63.**

It is worth remembering that psychosurgery cannot be reversed. Whereas a drug can be given or taken away and electrical stimulation can be turned off, you can't take back psychosurgery. Critics argue that psychosurgery should be banned altogether; others continue to report success with brain surgery. Nevertheless, it may have value as a remedy for some very specific disorders (Mashour, Walker, & Martuza, 2005; Sachdev & Chen, 2009).

Hospitalization

In 2008, about 3 million Americans received inpatient treatment for a mental health problem (National Institute of Mental Health, 2011a). **Mental hospitalization** involves placing a person in a protected setting where medical therapy is provided. Hospitalization, by itself, can be a form of treatment. Staying in a hospital takes patients out of situations that may be sustaining their problems. For example, people with drug addictions may find it nearly impossible to resist the temptations for drug abuse in their daily lives. Hospitalization can help them make a clean break from their self-destructive behavior patterns (André et al., 2003).

At their best, hospitals are sanctuaries that provide diagnosis, support, refuge, and therapy. This is frequently true of psychiatric units in general hospitals and private psychiatric hospitals. At worst, confinement to an institution can be a brutal experience that leaves people less prepared to face the world than when they arrived. This is more often the case in large state mental hospitals. In most instances, hospitals are best used as a last resort, after other forms of treatment within the community have been exhausted.

Another trend in treatment is **partial hospitalization**. In this approach, some patients spend their days in the hospital but go home at night. Others attend therapy sessions during the evening. A major advantage of partial hospitalization is that patients can go home and practice what they've been learning. Overall, partial hospitalization can be just as effective as full hospitalization (Drymalski & Washburn, 2011; Kiser, Heston, & Paavola, 2006).

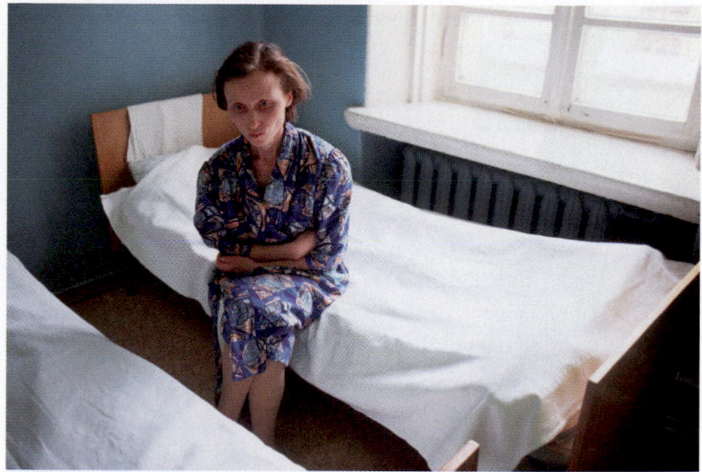

Depending on the quality of the institution, hospitalization may be a refuge or a brutalizing experience. Many state "asylums" or mental hospitals are antiquated and in need of drastic improvement.

Deinstitutionalization

In the last 50 years, the population in large mental hospitals has dropped by two thirds. This is largely a result of **deinstitutionalization**, or reduced use of full-time commitment to mental institutions. Long-term "institutionalization" can lead to dependency, isolation, and continued emotional disturbance (Novella, 2010). Deinstitutionalization was meant to remedy this problem

How successful has deinstitutionalization been? In truth, its success has been limited (Talbott, 2004). Many states reduced mental hospital populations primarily as a way to save money. The upsetting result is that many chronic patients have been discharged to hostile communities without adequate care. Many former patients have joined the ranks of the homeless. Others are repeatedly jailed for minor crimes. Sadly, patients who trade hospitalization for unemployment, homelessness, and social isolation all too often end up rehospitalized or in jail (Markowitz, 2011).

Large mental hospitals may no longer be warehouses for society's unwanted, but many former patients are no better off in bleak nursing homes, single-room hotels, board-and-care homes, shelters, or jails. For every mentally ill American in a hospital, three are trapped in the criminal justice system (National Institute of Mental Health, 2010a). These figures suggest that jails are replacing mental hospitals as our society's "solution" for mental illness (Markowitz, 2011). Yet, ironically, high-quality care is

Electroconvulsive therapy (ECT) A treatment for severe depression, consisting of an electric shock passed directly through the brain, which induces a convulsion.

Psychosurgery Any surgical alteration of the brain designed to bring about desirable behavioral or emotional changes.

Mental hospitalization Placing a person in a protected, therapeutic environment staffed by mental health professionals.

Partial hospitalization An approach in which patients receive treatment at a hospital during the day, but return home at night.

Deinstitutionalization Reduced use of full-time commitment to mental institutions to treat mental disorders.

A well-run halfway house can be a humane and cost-effective way to ease former mental patients back into the community (Soyez & Broekaert, 2003).

available in almost every community. As much as anything, a simple lack of money prevents large numbers of people from getting the help they need (Torrey, 1996).

Halfway houses may be a better way to ease a patient's return to the community (Soyez & Broekaert, 2003). **Halfway houses** are short-term group living facilities for people making the transition from an institution (mental hospital, prison, and so forth) to independent living. Typically, they offer supervision and support, without being as restricted and medically oriented as hospitals. They also keep people near their families. Most important, halfway houses can reduce a person's chances of being readmitted to a hospital (Coursey, Ward-Alexander, & Katz, 1990; Soyez & Broekaert, 2003).

Community Mental Health Programs

Community mental health centers, which offer a wide range of mental health services and psychiatric care and are a bright spot in the area of mental health care. Such centers try to help people avoid hospitalization and find answers to mental health problems (Burns, 2004; Teed et al., 2007). Typically, they do this by providing short-term treatment, counseling, outpatient care, emergency services, and suicide prevention.

Mental health centers are also concerned with *prevention*. Consultation, education, and **crisis intervention** (skilled management of a psychological emergency) are used to prevent problems before they become serious. Also, some centers attempt to raise the general level of mental health in a community by combating unemployment, delinquency, and drug abuse (Tausig, Michello, & Subedi, 2004).

Have community mental health centers succeeded in meeting their goals? In practice, they have concentrated much more on providing clinical services than they have on preventing problems. This appears to be primarily the result of wavering government support (translation: money). Overall, community mental health centers have succeeded in making psychological services more accessible than ever before. Many of their programs rely on **paraprofessionals** (individuals who work in a near-professional capacity under the supervision of more highly trained staff). Some paraprofessionals are ex-addicts, ex-alcoholics, or ex-patients who have "been there." Many more are persons (paid or volunteer) who have skills in tutoring, crafts, or counseling or who are simply warm, understanding, and skilled at communication. Often, paraprofessionals are more approachable than "doctors." This encourages people to seek mental health services that they might otherwise be reluctant to use (Everly, 2002).

Knowledge Builder — Medical Therapies

RECITE

1. Major tranquilizers are also known as
   a. anxiolytics *b.* antipsychotics *c.* antidepressants *d.* prefrontal sedatives
2. ECT is a modern form of pharmacotherapy. T or F?
3. Currently, the frontal lobotomy is the most widely used form of psychosurgery. T or F?
4. Deinstitutionalization is an advanced form of partial hospitalization. T or F?

REFLECT

Think Critically

5. Residents of Berkeley, California, once voted on a referendum to ban the use of ECT within city limits. Do you think that the use of certain psychiatric treatments should be controlled by law?

Self-Reflect

Keeping in mind that all therapies, and especially medical therapies, have side effects (see, e.g., Casselle, 2009), when is it appropriate to use a medical therapy to treat someone with a mental illness? Why not use psychotherapy instead?

Why might you choose to combine a medical therapy and psychotherapy? Can you frame your reasons in terms of the stress-vulnerability model introduced in Chapter 14?

Answers: 1. *b* **2.** F **3.** F **4.** F **5.** The question of who can prescribe drugs, perform surgery, and administer ECT *is* controlled by law. However, psychiatrists strongly object to residents, city councils, or government agencies making *medical* decisions.

Therapies—Human to the Core

Gateway Question 15.9: *Are various psychotherapies effective, and what do they have in common?*

In this section, let's ask whether the psychotherapies work and what, if anything, they have in common. We have put this section *after* the section on medical therapies to stress that human relations are at the core of healing. Whether or not a patient under medical care is receiving a somatic treatment, that treatment is administered in a human context. In that sense, it doesn't matter if the healer is a psychotherapist, psychiatrist, social worker, hospital worker, or whatever. No matter what helping specialty you might be considering as a career, information you'll encounter in this section might prove invaluable.

Critical Thinking: How Do We Know Therapy Actually Works?

Why is it risky to believe people *who say their therapy was effective?* An old joke among doctors is that a cold lasts a week without treatment and seven days with it. Perhaps the same is true of therapy. Someone who feels better after 6 months of therapy may have experienced a spontaneous remission—they just feel better because so much time has passed. Or perhaps the crisis that triggered the therapy is now nearly forgotten. Or maybe some sort of therapy placebo effect has occurred. Also, it's possible that the person has received help from other people, such as family, friends, or clergy.

To find out if therapy works, we could randomly place clients in an experimental group that receives therapy and a control group that does not. When this is done, the control group may show some improvement, even without receiving therapy (Lambert & Ogles, 2002; Schuck, Keijsers, & Rinck, 2011). Thus, we can conclude that the therapy is effective only if people in the experimental group improve more than those in the control group.

But isn't it unethical to withhold treatment from someone who really needs therapy? That's right. One way to deal with this is to use a *waiting-list control group*. In this case, people who are waiting to see a therapist are compared with those who receive therapy. Later, those on the waiting list will eventually also receive therapy.

If we combine the results of many experiments, it becomes clear that therapy *is* effective (Lipsey & Wilson, 1993). In addition, studies have revealed that some therapies work best for specific problems (Bradley et al., 2005; Eddy et al., 2004). For example, behavioral, cognitive, and drug therapies are most helpful in treating obsessive-compulsive disorder.

OK. So how effective is psychotherapy? Judging the outcome of therapy is tricky. In a national survey, 9 out of 10 people who have sought mental health care say their lives improved as a result of the treatment (Consumer Reports, 2010; Kotkin, Daviet, & Gurin, 1996). Unfortunately you can't just take people's word for it (see "How Do We Know Therapy Actually Works?").

Psychologists are making steady progress in identifying "empirically supported" (or "evidence-based") therapies (Westen & Bradley, 2005). Rather than just relying on intuition, clinicians are seeking guidance from research experiments and guidelines developed through clinical practice (Carroll & Rounsaville, 2007; Miller & Binder, 2002). The end result is a better understanding of which therapies "work" best for specific types of problems. This trend is also helping to weed out fringe "therapies" that have little or no value.

Fortunately, there is direct evidence that therapy is beneficial. Hundreds of studies show a strong pattern of positive effects for psychotherapy, counseling, and other psychological treatments (Barlow, 2004; Lambert & Cattani-Thompson, 1996; Moras, 2002). Of course, results vary in individual cases. For some people, therapy is immensely helpful; for others, it is unsuccessful. Overall, it is effective for more people than not. Speaking more subjectively, a real success, in which a person's life is changed for the better, can be worth the frustration of several cases in which little progress is made.

Although it is common to think of therapy as a long, slow process, this is not normally the case (Shapiro et al., 2003). Research shows that about 50 percent of all clients feel better after between 13 and 18 weekly 1-hour therapy sessions (Howard et al., 1986). This means that the majority of clients improve after 6 months of therapy. Such rapid improvement is impressive in view of the fact that people often suffer for several years before seeking help. Unfortunately, because of high costs and limited insurance coverage, the average client receives only 5 therapy sessions, after which only 20 percent of all patients feel better (Hansen, Lambert, & Forman, 2002).

Core Features of Psychotherapy

What do psychotherapies have in common? We have sampled only a few of the many therapies in use today. For a summary of major differences among psychotherapies, see ■ Table 15.3. To add to your understanding, let's briefly summarize what all techniques have in common.

Psychotherapies of various types share all or most of the following goals: restoring hope, courage, and optimism; gaining insight; resolving conflicts; improving one's sense of self; changing unacceptable patterns of behavior; finding purpose; mending interpersonal relations; and learning to approach problems rationally (Frank & Frank, 2004; Seligman, 1998). To accomplish these goals, psychotherapies offer the following:

1. Effective therapy provides a **therapeutic alliance**, a *caring relationship* that unites the client and therapist as they work together to solve the client's problems. The strength of this alliance has a major impact on whether therapy succeeds (Kozart, 2002; Meier et al., 2006). The basis for this relationship is emotional rapport, warmth, friendship, understanding, acceptance, and empathy.

Halfway house A community-based facility for individuals making the transition from an institution (mental hospital, prison, and so forth) to independent living.

Community mental health center A facility offering a wide range of mental health services, such as prevention, counseling, consultation, and crisis intervention.

Crisis intervention Skilled management of a psychological emergency.

Paraprofessional An individual who works in a near-professional capacity under the supervision of a more highly trained person.

Therapeutic alliance A caring relationship that unites a therapist and a client in working to solve the client's problems.

■ TABLE 15.3 Comparison of Psychotherapies

	Insight or Action?	Directive or Nondirective?	Individual or Group?	Therapy's Strength
Psychoanalysis	Insight	Directive	Individual	Searching honesty
Brief psychodynamic therapy	Insight	Directive	Individual	Productive use of conflict
Client-centered therapy	Insight	Nondirective	Both	Acceptance, empathy
Existential therapy	Insight	Both	Individual	Personal empowerment
Gestalt therapy	Insight	Directive	Both	Focus on immediate awareness
Behavior therapy	Action	Directive	Both	Observable changes in behavior
Cognitive therapy	Action	Directive	Individual	Constructive guidance
Rational-emotive behavior therapy	Action	Directive	Individual	Clarity of thinking and goals
Psychodrama	Insight	Directive	Group	Constructive re-enactments
Family therapy	Both	Directive	Group	Shared responsibility for problems

Source: Adapted from Corsini & Wedding, 2011; Prochaska & Norcross, 2010.

2. Therapy offers a *protected setting* in which emotional *catharsis* (release) can take place. Therapy is a sanctuary in which the client is free to express fears, anxieties, and personal secrets without fearing rejection or loss of confidentiality.
3. All therapies to some extent offer an *explanation* or *rationale* for the client's suffering. Additionally, they propose a line of action that will end this suffering.
4. Therapy provides clients with a *new perspective* about themselves and their situations and a chance to practice *new behaviors* (Crencavage & Norcross, 1990; Prochaska & Norcross, 2010). Insights gained during therapy can bring about lasting changes in clients' lives (Grande et al., 2003).

Master Therapists

Because therapies have much in common, a majority of psychologists have become *eclectic* in their work (Kopta et al., 1999). Eclectic therapists use whatever methods best fit a particular problem (Norcross, 2005). In addition, some seek to combine the best elements of various therapies to broaden their effectiveness.

What do the most capable therapists have in common? One study of master therapists found that they share several characteristics (Jennings & Skovholt, 1999). The most effective therapists:

- Are enthusiastic learners
- Draw on their experience with similar problems
- Value complexity and ambiguity
- Are emotionally open
- Are mentally healthy and mature
- Nurture their own emotional well-being
- Realize that their emotional health affects their work
- Have strong social skills
- Cultivate a working alliance
- Expertly use their social skills in therapy

Notice that this list also could describe the kind of person most of us would want to talk to when facing a life crisis. But what if someone else turns to you for help?

Basic Counseling Skills

If you are ever called upon to comfort a person in distress, such as a troubled friend or relative, here are some general helping skills that can be distilled from the various approaches to therapy (Kottler & Shepard, 2011; Sharf, 2012; ■ Table 15.4).

Active Listening

People frequently talk "at" each other without really listening. A person with problems needs to be heard. Make a sincere effort to listen to and understand the person. Try to accept the person's message without judging it or leaping to conclusions. Let the person know you are listening, through eye contact, posture, your tone of voice, and your replies (Kottler & Shepard, 2011).

Reflect Thoughts and Feelings

One of the best things you can do when offering support to another person is to give feedback by simply restating what is said. This is also a good way to encourage a person to talk. If your friend

■ TABLE 15.4 Helping Behaviors

To help another person gain insight into a personal problem, it is valuable to keep the following comparison in mind:

Behaviors That Help	Behaviors That Hinder
Active listening	Probing painful topics
Acceptance	Judging/moralizing
Reflecting feelings	Criticism
Open-ended questioning	Threats
Supportive statements	Rejection
Respect	Ridicule/sarcasm
Patience	Impatience
Genuineness	Placing blame
Paraphrasing	Opinionated statements

Adapted from Kottler & Shepard, 2011.

seems to be at a loss for words, *restate* or *paraphrase* his or her last sentence. Here's an example:

Friend: I'm really down about school. I can't get interested in any of my classes. I flunked my Spanish test, and somebody stole my notebook for psychology.

You: You're really upset about school, aren't you?

Friend: Yeah, and my parents are hassling me about my grades again.

You: That sucks.

Friend: Yeah.

You: That must make you angry.

As simple as this sounds, it is very helpful to someone trying to sort out feelings. Try it. If nothing else, you'll develop a reputation as a fantastic conversationalist!

Silence

Counselors tend to wait longer before responding than do people in everyday conversations. Pauses of 5 seconds or more are not unusual, and interrupting is rare. Listening patiently lets the person feel unhurried and encourages her or him to speak freely.

Questions

Because your goal is to encourage free expression, *open-ended questions* tend to be the most helpful. A *closed question* is one that can be answered yes or no. Open-ended questions call for an open-ended reply. Say, for example, that a friend tells you, "I feel like my boss has it in for me at work." A closed question would be, "Oh yeah? So, are you going to quit?" Open-ended questions such as "Do you want to talk about it?" or "How do you feel about it?" are more likely to be helpful.

BRIDGES

Open-ended questions are an effective way to begin and sustain a conversation. **See Chapter 12, page 436.**

Clarify the Problem

People who have a clear idea of what is wrong in their lives are more likely to discover solutions. Try to understand the problem from the person's point of view. As you do, check your understanding often. For example, you might ask, "Are you saying that you feel depressed just at school? Or in general?" Remember, a problem well defined is often half solved.

Focus on Feelings

Feelings are neither right nor wrong. By focusing on feelings, you can encourage the outpouring of emotion that is the basis for catharsis. Passing judgment on what is said just makes people defensive. For example, a friend confides that he has failed a test. Perhaps you know that he studies very little. If you say, "Just study more and you will do better," he will probably become defensive or hostile. Much more can be accomplished by saying, "You must feel very frustrated" or simply, "How do you feel about it?"

AFP/Getty Images

Teams of psychologists and counselors are often assembled to provide support to victims of major accidents and natural disasters. Because their work is stressful and often heart wrenching, relief workers also benefit from on-site counseling. Expressing emotions and talking about feelings are major elements of disaster counseling.

Avoid Giving Advice

Many people mistakenly think that they must solve problems for others. Remember that your goal is to provide understanding and support, not solutions. Of course, it is reasonable to give advice when you are asked for it, but beware of the trap of the "Why don't you...? Yes, but..." game. According to psychotherapist Eric Berne (1964), this "game" follows a pattern: Someone says, "I have this problem." You say, "Why don't you do thus and so?" The person replies, "Yes, but..." and then tells you why your suggestion won't work. If you make a new suggestion, the reply will once again be, "Yes, but..." Obviously, the person either knows more about his or her personal situation than you do or he or she has reasons for avoiding your advice. The student described earlier knows he needs to study. His problem is to understand why he doesn't *want* to study.

Accept the Person's Frame of Reference

Because we all live in different psychological worlds, there is no "correct" view of a life situation. A person who feels that his or her viewpoint has been understood feels freer to examine it objectively and to question it. Understanding another person's perspective is especially important when cultural differences may create a barrier between a client and therapist (Draguns, Gielen, & Fish, 2004). (See "Therapy and Culture—A Bad Case of 'Ifufunyane.'")

Maintain Confidentiality

Your efforts to help will be wasted if you fail to respect the privacy of someone who has confided in you. Put yourself in the person's place. Don't gossip.

These guidelines are not an invitation to play "junior therapist." Professional therapists are trained to approach serious problems with skills far exceeding those described here. However, the points

Human Diversity: Therapy and Culture—A Bad Case of "Ifufunyane"

At the age of 23, the patient was clearly suffering from "ifufunyane," a form of bewitchment common in the Xhosa culture of South Africa. However, he was treated at a local hospital by psychiatrists, who said he had schizophrenia and gave him antipsychotic drugs. The drugs helped, but his family shunned his fancy medical treatment and took him to a traditional healer who gave him herbs for his ifufunyane. Unfortunately, he got worse and was readmitted to the hospital. This time, the psychiatrists included the patient's family in his treatment. Together, they agreed to treat him with a combination of antipsychotic drugs *and* traditional herbs. This time, the patient got much better and his ifufunyane was alleviated, too (Niehaus et al., 2005).

As this example illustrates, **culturally skilled therapists** are trained to work with clients from various cultural backgrounds. To be culturally skilled, a counselor must be able to do all of the following (American Psychological Association, 2003, 2008; Brammer, 2012; Fowers & Davidov, 2006):

- Adapt traditional theories and techniques to meet the needs of clients from non-European ethnic or racial groups.
- Be aware of his or her own cultural values and biases.
- Establish rapport with a person from a different cultural background.
- Be open to cultural differences without resorting to stereotypes.
- Treat members of racial or ethnic communities as individuals.
- Be aware of a client's ethnic identity and degree of acculturation to the majority society.
- Use existing helping resources within a cultural group to support efforts to resolve problems.

Cultural awareness has helped broaden our ideas about mental health and optimal development (Brammer, 2012). It is also worth remembering that cultural barriers apply to communication in all areas of life, not just therapy. Although such differences can be challenging, they are also frequently enriching (Uwe et al., 2006).

made help define the qualities of a therapeutic relationship. They also emphasize that each of us can supply two of the greatest mental health resources available at any cost: friendship and honest communication.

The Future of Therapy—Magnets, Groups, and Smartphones

Gateway Question 15.10: *What will therapy be like in the future?*

Therapy has come a long way since the days of trepanning and demonology. Still, the search for ways to improve therapy remains an urgent challenge for those who devote their lives to helping others. Therapy in the future will likely include some things old and some things new (Norcross, Hedges, & Prochaska, 2002):

- More therapy provided by lower cost master's-level practitioners (counselors, social workers, and psychiatric nurses).
- Greater use of short-term therapy and solution-focused, problem-solving approaches.
- More precisely targeted medical therapies with fewer side effects.
- Greater reliance on group therapies and self-help groups run by paraprofessionals.
- Increased use of Internet services and telephone counseling to distribute mental health services.

As you might imagine, many of these predicted changes are based on pressures to reduce the cost of mental health services. Psychiatrists and clinical psychologists are expensive to train. There are too few to take on primary responsibility in all cases. Similarly, longer-term insight-oriented therapies, in particular psychoanalysis, are an expensive luxury.

New Medical Therapies

Neuroscience research continues to probe the functioning of the brain and its various parts in ever-greater detail (Freberg, 2010). As a result, more precisely targeted medical therapies with fewer side effects will continue to be discovered (Morgan & Ricke, 2008). For example, a new technique called **transcranial magnetic stimulation (TMS)** uses magnetic pulses to temporarily block activity in specific parts of the brain. Unlike surgical lesioning, TMS is noninvasive and is reversible (see • Figure 15.6).

By applying TMS to parts of the frontal lobe, Paulo Boggio and his colleagues (2010) were able to change the way people made decisions while gambling. It is not a long stretch to imagine that this technique might become a powerful adjunct therapy together with cognitive therapy to treat compulsive gambling (Ladouceur, Lachance, & Fournier, 2009). Similarly, patients with obsessive-compulsive disorder have shown marked improvement when TMS disrupted brain areas involved in compulsive behavior (Mantovani et al., 2010).

Group Therapy

Because it is cost-effective, **group therapy**, psychotherapy done with more than one person, will become more common in the future. This is a trend that began some 50 years ago when psychologists first worked with groups because there was a shortage of

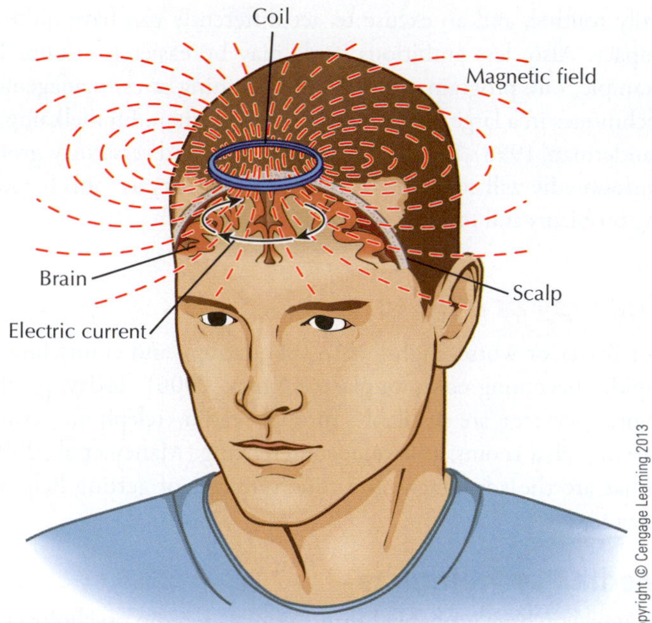

● **Figure 15.6** Transcranial magnetic stimulation (TMS) uses a small coil held near the surface of the scalp to create magnetic pulses that induce electrical activity in the underlying brain tissue. The result is a temporary blockage of normal brain activity. TMS can be used to study brain function and has already been applied as a medical therapy (Mantovani et al., 2010).

therapists. Many of the therapies we have discussed can be adapted for use in groups (Corey, 2012). Surprisingly, group therapy has turned out to be just as effective as individual therapy and has some special advantages (Burlingame, Fuhriman, & Mosier, 2003).

What are the advantages? In group therapy, a person can *act out* or directly experience problems. Doing so often produces insights that might not occur from merely talking about an issue. In addition, other group members with similar problems can offer support and useful input. Group therapy is especially good for helping people understand their personal relationships (McCluskey, 2002). For reasons such as these, a number of specialized groups have emerged. Because they range from Alcoholics Anonymous to Marriage Encounter, we will sample only a few examples.

Psychodrama

One of the first group therapies was developed by Jacob L. Moreno (1953), who called his technique psychodrama. In **psychodrama**, clients act out personal conflicts with others who play supporting roles (Blatner, 2006). Through role-playing, the client re-enacts incidents that cause problems in real life. For example, Don, a disturbed teenager, might act out a typical family fight, with the therapist playing his father and with other clients playing his mother, brothers, and sisters. Moreno believed that insights gained in this way transfer to real life situations.

Therapists using psychodrama often find that role reversals are helpful. A **role reversal** involves taking the part of another person to learn how he or she feels. For instance, Don might role-play his father or mother, to better understand their feelings. A related method is the **mirror technique**, in which clients observe another person re-enact their behavior. Thus, Don might briefly join the audience and watch as another group member plays his role. This would allow him to see himself as others do. Later, the group may summarize what happened and reflect on its meaning (Turner, 1997).

Family and Couples Therapy

Family relationships are the source of great pleasure and, all too often, of great pain. In **family therapy**, husband, wife, and children work as a group to resolve the problems of each family member. This is also called *couples therapy* when children are not involved (Scheinkman, 2008). Family and couples therapy tends to be time limited and focused on specific problems, such as frequent fights or a depressed teenager. For some types of problems, family therapy may be superior to other approaches (Capuzzi, 2003; Eisler et al., 2007).

A group therapy session. Group members offer mutual support while sharing problems and insights.

Culturally skilled therapist A therapist who has the awareness, knowledge, and skills necessary to treat clients from diverse cultural backgrounds.

Transcranial magnetic stimulation (TMS) Use of magnetic pulses to temporarily block activity in specific parts of the brain.

Group therapy Psychotherapy conducted in a group setting to make therapeutic use of group dynamics.

Psychodrama A therapy in which clients act out personal conflicts and feelings in the presence of others who play supporting roles.

Role reversal Taking the role of another person to learn how one's own behavior appears from the other person's perspective.

Mirror technique Observing another person re-enact one's own behavior, like a character in a play; designed to help persons see themselves more clearly.

Family therapy Technique in which all family members participate, both individually and as a group, to change destructive relationships and communication patterns.

Family therapists believe that a problem experienced by one family member is really the whole family's problem (Teyber & McClure, 2011). If the entire pattern of behavior in a family doesn't change, improvements in any single family member may not last. Family members, therefore, work together to improve communication, to change destructive patterns, and to see themselves and each other in new ways (Goldenberg & Goldenberg, 2004; Griffin, 2002).

Does the therapist work with the whole family at once? Family therapists treat the family as a unit, but they may not meet with the entire family at each session (Eisler et al., 2007). If a family crisis is at hand, the therapist may first try to identify the most resourceful family members, who can help solve the immediate problem. The therapist and family members may then work on resolving more basic conflicts and on improving family relationships (Griffin, 2002).

Group Awareness Training

During the 1960s and 1970s, the human potential movement led many people to seek personal growth experiences. Often, their interest was expressed by participation in sensitivity training or encounter groups.

What is the difference between sensitivity groups and encounter groups? Sensitivity groups tend to be less confrontational than encounter groups. Participants in **sensitivity groups** take part in exercises that gently enlarge self-awareness and sensitivity to others. For example, in a "trust walk," participants expand their confidence in others by allowing themselves to be led around while blindfolded.

Encounter groups are based on an honest expression of feelings, and intensely personal communication may take place. Typically, the emphasis is on tearing down defenses and false fronts. Because there is a danger of hostile confrontation, participation is safest when members are carefully screened and a trained leader guides the group. In business settings, psychologists still use the basic principles of sensitivity and encounter groups—truth, self-awareness, and self-determination—to improve employee relationships. Specially designed encounter groups for married couples are also widely held (Harway, 2004).

There has also been much public interest in various forms of large group awareness training. **Large group awareness training** refers to programs that claim to increase self-awareness and facilitate constructive personal change. The Garden Company, Lifespring, the Forum, the Hoffman Quadrinity Process, and similar commercial programs are examples. Like the smaller groups that preceded them, large-group training combines psychological exercises, confrontation, new viewpoints, and group dynamics to promote personal change.

Are sensitivity, encounter, and awareness groups really psychotherapies? These experiences tend to be positive, but they produce only moderate benefits (Faith, Wong, & Carpenter, 1995). Moreover, many of the claimed benefits may result simply from a kind of **therapy placebo effect**, in which improvement is based on a client's belief that therapy will help. Positive expectations, a break in daily routine, and an excuse to act differently can have quite an impact. Also, less ambitious goals may be easier to attain. For example, one program succeeded in teaching stress-management techniques in a large group setting (Timmerman, Emmelkamp, & Sanderman, 1998). Because of their low cost and versatility, groups undoubtedly will continue to grow in popularity as tools for solving problems and improving lives (Corey, 2012).

Therapy at a Distance

For better or worse, high-tech psychotherapy and counseling are rapidly becoming commonplace (Ormay, 2006). Today, psychological services are available through radio, telephone, e-mail, Internet chat rooms, and videoconferencing (Maheu et al., 2004). What are the advantages and disadvantages of getting help at a distance?

Media Psychologists

By now you have probably heard a phone-in radio psychologist or watched one on television. On a typical program, participants describe problems arising from child abuse, loneliness, love affairs, phobias, sexual adjustment, or depression. The media psychologist then offers reassurance, advice, or suggestions for getting help. Such talk-radio and television programs may seem harmless, but they raise some important questions. For instance, is it reasonable to give advice without knowing anything about a person's background? Could the advice do harm? What good can a psychologist do in 3 minutes or even an hour?

In their own defense, media psychologists point out that listeners and viewers may learn solutions to their problems by hearing others talk. Many also stress that their work is educational, not therapeutic. The well-known media psychologist Dr. Phil McGraw

Media psychologists have been urged to educate without actually doing therapy. Some overstep this boundary, however. Do you think popular TV psychologist Dr. Phil sometimes goes too far?

Frederick M. Brown/Getty Images

has even been awarded a President's Citation from the American Psychological Association for his work in publicizing mental health issues (Meyers, 2006).

Nevertheless, the question arises: When does advice become therapy? The American Psychological Association urges media psychologists to discuss problems only of a general nature instead of actually counseling anyone. For example, if a caller complains about insomnia, the radio psychologist should talk about insomnia in general, not probe the caller's personal life. A good guide for anyone tempted to call a radio psychologist or accept advice from a TV psychologist might be "let the consumer beware."

Telephone and Internet Therapists

The same caution applies to commercial telephone and Internet therapists. A key feature of successful face-to-face therapy is the establishment of an effective *therapeutic alliance*, a continuing relationship between two people. In this regard, distance therapies are more or less limited by a lack of interpersonal cues, such as facial expressions and body language. For example, brief e-mail messages are no way to make a diagnosis. And forget about facial expressions or body language—not even tone of voice reaches the e-mail therapist. Typing emotional icons (called *emoticons*) like little smiley faces (☺) or frowns (☹) is a poor substitute for real human interaction.

Of special concern is the fact that distance therapists may or may not be trained professionals (Bloom, 1998). And even if they are, questions exist about whether a psychologist licensed in one state can legally do therapy in another state via the telephone or the Internet.

Regardless, distance counseling and therapy services do have some advantages. For one thing, clients can more easily remain anonymous. (But beware that e-mail counseling may not be completely confidential and could be intercepted and misused.) Thus, a person who might hesitate to see a psychologist can seek help privately, on the phone or online. Likewise, people who live in rural areas can more easily work with psychologists living in large cities. And, compared with traditional office visits, distance therapies are less expensive.

Under the right circumstances, distance therapies can be successful (Day & Schneider, 2002). For example, in one study, telephone counseling helped improve success rates for smokers who wanted to quit (Rabius et al., 2004). Other studies have shown that depressed people benefit from telephone therapy (Mohr et al., 2005; Simon et al., 2004). Psychologists have also demonstrated success in providing therapy over the Internet, at least for certain types of problems (Carlbring et al., 2007; Chester & Glass, 2006; Klein, Richards, & Austin, 2006).

The Ever-Evolving Internet

The Internet continues to provide new communication tools that blend voice, text, graphics, and video. Widely available and inexpensive technologies, such as Skype, make it easy to create two-way audio-video links that allow a client and therapist to see one another on computer monitors and to talk via speakerphones. Doing therapy this way still lacks the close personal contact of face-to-face interaction. However, it does remove many of the objections to doing therapy at a distance. It's very likely that distance services will continue to evolve (Riva & Wiederhold, 2006) and become a major source of mental health care in coming years (Schopp, Demiris, & Glueckauf, 2006).

Another interesting cost-saving measure is the idea that computer software may be able to treat some relatively minor problems (Craske et al., 2009). In one study, clients worked through ten computer-guided sessions that helped them identify a problem, form a plan of action, and work through carrying out the plan. Most were satisfied with the help they received (Jacobs et al., 2001).

Implications

As you can see, psychological services that rely on electronic communication may serve some useful purposes. However, the value of therapy offered by commercial telephone "counselors" and Internet "therapists" remains open to question. The very best advice given by media psychologists, telephone "counselors," or Internet "therapists" may be, "If at all possible, you should consider discussing this problem with a psychologist or counselor in your own community."

A Look Ahead

In the *Psychology in Action* section that follows, we will return briefly to behavioral approaches. There you will find a number of useful techniques that you may be able to apply to your own behavior. You'll also find a discussion of when to seek professional help and how to find it. Here's your authors' professional advice: This is information you won't want to skip.

Knowledge Builder: Contemporary Issues in Therapy

RECITE

1. Emotional rapport, warmth, understanding, acceptance, and empathy are the core of
   a. the therapeutic alliance *b.* large-group awareness training *c.* role reversals *d.* action therapy
2. Culturally skilled therapists do all but one of the following; which does *not* apply?
   a. Are aware of the client's degree of acculturation *b.* Use helping resources within the client's cultural group *c.* Adapt standard techniques to match cultural stereotypes *d.* Are aware of their own cultural values

Continued

Sensitivity group A group experience consisting of exercises designed to increase self-awareness and sensitivity to others.

Encounter group A group experience that emphasizes intensely honest interchanges among participants regarding feelings and reactions to one another.

Large group awareness training Any of a number of programs (many of them commercialized) that claim to increase self-awareness and facilitate constructive personal change.

Therapy placebo effect Improvement caused not by the actual process of therapy but by a client's expectation that therapy will help.

3. In psychodrama, people attempt to form meaningful wholes out of disjointed thoughts, feelings, and actions. T or F?
4. Most large-group awareness trainings make use of Gestalt therapy. T or F?
5. The mirror technique is frequently used in
   a. exposure therapy *b.* psychodrama *c.* family therapy *d.* ECT
6. To date, the most acceptable type of "distance therapy" is
   a. media psychology *b.* commercial telephone counseling *c.* Internet-based cybertherapy *d.* based on videoconferencing

REFLECT

Think Critically

7. In your opinion, do psychologists have a duty to protect others who may be harmed by their clients? For example, if a patient has homicidal fantasies about his ex-wife, should she be informed?

Relate

What lies at the "heart" of psychotherapy? How would you describe it to a friend?

Which of the basic counseling skills do you already use? Which would improve your ability to help a person in distress (or even just have an engaging conversation)?

Would you rather participate in individual therapy or group therapy? What advantages and disadvantages do you think each has?

A neighbor of yours is thinking about getting counseling on the Internet. What would you tell her about the pros and cons of distance therapy?

Answers: 1. *a* **2.** *c* **3.** F **4.** F **5.** *b* **6.** *d* **7.** According to the law, there is a duty to protect others when a therapist could, with little effort, prevent serious harm. However, this duty can conflict with a client's rights to confidentiality and with client-therapist trust. Therapists often must make difficult choices in such situations.

Psychology in Action

Self-Management and Seeking Professional Help

Gateway Question 15.11: *How are behavioral principles applied to everyday problems and how could a person find professional help?*

As mentioned elsewhere in this book, you should seek professional help when a significant problem exists. For lesser difficulties you may want to try applying behavioral principles yourself (Martin & Pear, 2011; Watson & Tharp, 2007). (See also Chapter 6.)

Covert Reward and Punishment—Boosting Your "Willpower"

Behavior therapy is not a cure-all. Its use is often quite complicated and requires a great deal of expertise. Still, behavior therapy offers a straightforward solution to many problems.

Let's see how this might be done:

Therapist: "Have you ever decided to quit smoking cigarettes, watching television too much, eating too much, drinking too much, or driving too fast?"

Client: "Well, one of those applies. I have decided several times to quit smoking."

Therapist: "When have you decided?"

Client: "Usually after I am reminded of how dangerous smoking is—like when I heard that my uncle had died of lung cancer. He smoked constantly."

Therapist: "If you have decided to quit 'several times,' I assume you haven't succeeded."

Client: "No, the usual pattern is for me to become upset about smoking and then to cut down for a day or two."

Therapist: "You forget the disturbing image of your uncle's death, or whatever, and start smoking again."

Client: "Yes. I suppose if I had an uncle die every day or so, I might actually quit!"

The use of intensive behavioral principles, such as electric shock, to condition an aversion seems remote from everyday problems. Even naturally aversive actions are difficult to apply to personal behavior. As mentioned earlier, for instance, rapid smoking is difficult for most smokers to carry out on their own. And what about a problem like overeating? Indeed, it would be difficult to eat enough to create a lasting aversion to overeating (although it's sometimes tempting to try).

In view of such limitations, psychologists have developed an alternative procedure that can be used to curb smoking, overeating, and other habits (Kearney, 2006; Watson & Tharp, 2007).

Covert Sensitization In **covert sensitization,** aversive imagery is used to reduce the occurrence of an undesired response. Here's how it's done: Obtain six 3 by 5 cards and on each write a brief description of a scene related to the habit you wish to control. The scene should be so *disturbing* or *disgusting* that

© Lawrence Manning/Corbis

thinking about it would temporarily make you very uncomfortable about indulging in the habit. For smoking, the cards might read:

- "I am in a doctor's office. The doctor looks at some reports and tells me I have lung cancer. She says a lung will have to be removed and sets a date for the operation."
- "I am in bed under an oxygen tent. My chest feels caved in. There is a tube in my throat. I can barely breathe."
- "I wake up in the morning and smoke a cigarette. I begin coughing up blood."
- "My lover won't even kiss me because my breath smells bad."

Other cards would continue along the same line.

For overeating the cards might read like this:

- "I am at the beach. I get up to go for a swim and I overhear people whispering to each other, 'Isn't that fat disgusting?'"
- "I am at a store buying clothes. I try on several things that are too small. The only things that fit look like rumpled sacks. Salespeople are staring at me."
- "I can't fit into my seat at the movies."

The trick is to get yourself to imagine or picture vividly each of these disturbing scenes *several times* a day. Imagining the scenes can be accomplished by placing them under *stimulus control*. Simply choose something you do *frequently* each day (such as getting a cup of coffee or getting up from your chair). Next make a rule: Before you can get a cup of coffee or get up from your chair, or whatever you have selected as a cue, you must take out your cards and *vividly picture* yourself engaging in the action you wish to curb (eating or smoking, for example). Then *vividly picture* the scene described on the top card. Imagine the scene for 30 seconds.

After visualizing the top card, move it to the bottom so the cards are rotated. Make up new cards each week. The scenes can be made much more upsetting than the samples given here, which are toned down to keep you from being "grossed out."

Covert sensitization can also be used directly in situations that test your self-control. If you are trying to lose weight, for instance, you might be able to turn down a tempting dessert in this way: As you look at the dessert, visualize maggots crawling all over it. If you make this image as vivid and nauseating as possible, losing your appetite is almost a certainty. If you want to apply this technique to other situations, be aware that vomiting scenes are especially effective. Covert sensitization may sound as if you are "playing games with yourself," but it can be a great help if you want to cut down on a bad habit (Kearney, 2006). Try it!

Thought Stopping As discussed earlier, behavior therapists accept that thoughts, like visible responses, can also cause trouble. Think of times when you have repeatedly "put yourself down" mentally or when you have been preoccupied by needless worries, fears, or other negative and upsetting thoughts. If you would like to gain control over such thoughts, thought stopping may help you do it.

In **thought stopping**, aversive stimuli are used to interrupt or prevent upsetting thoughts (Bakker, 2009). The simplest thought-stopping technique makes use of mild punishment to suppress upsetting mental images and internal "talk." Simply place a large, flat rubber band around your wrist. As you go through the day apply this rule: Each time you catch yourself thinking the upsetting image or thought, pull the rubber band away from your wrist and snap it. You need not make this terribly painful. Its value lies in drawing your attention to how often you form negative thoughts and in interrupting the flow of thoughts.

A second thought-stopping procedure requires only that you interrupt upsetting thoughts each time they occur. Begin by setting aside time each day during which you will deliberately think the unwanted thought. As you begin to form the thought, shout "Stop!" aloud, with conviction. (Obviously, you should choose a private spot for this part of the procedure!)

Repeat the thought-stopping procedure 10 to 20 times for the first 2 or 3 days. Then switch to shouting "Stop!" covertly (to yourself) rather than aloud. Thereafter, thought stopping can be carried out throughout the day, whenever upsetting thoughts occur. After several days of practice, you should be able to stop unwanted thoughts whenever they occur.

Covert Reinforcement Earlier we discussed how punishing images can be used to decrease undesirable responses, such as smoking or overeating. Many people also find it helpful to covertly *reinforce* desired actions. **Covert reinforcement** is the use of positive imagery to reinforce desired behavior. For example, suppose your target behavior is, once again, not eating dessert. If this were the case, you could do the following (Kearney, 2006; Watson & Tharp, 2007):

> Imagine that you are standing at the dessert table with your friends. As dessert is passed, you politely refuse and feel good about staying on your diet.

These images would then be followed by imagining a pleasant, reinforcing scene:

> Imagine that you are your ideal weight. You look really slim in your favorite color and style. Someone you really like says to you, "Gee, you've lost weight. I've never seen you look so good."

For many people, of course, actual direct reinforcement is the best way to alter behavior. Nevertheless, covert or "visualized" reinforcement can have similar effects. To make use of covert reinforcement, choose one or more target behaviors and rehearse them mentally. Then follow each rehearsal with a vivid, rewarding image.

BRIDGES

Direct reinforcement is described in the *Psychology in Action* section of Chapter 6, pages 234–236.

Self-Directed Desensitization—Overcoming Common Fears

You have prepared for 2 weeks to give a speech in a large class. As your turn approaches, your hands begin to tremble. Your heart pounds and you find it difficult to breathe. You say to your body, "Relax!" What happens? Nothing! That's why the first step in desensitization is learning to relax voluntarily by using the tension-release method described earlier in this chapter. As an alternative, you might want to try imagining a very safe, pleasant, and relaxing scene. Some people find such images as relaxing as the tension-release method (Rosenthal, 1993). Another helpful technique

Covert sensitization Use of aversive imagery to reduce the occurrence of an undesired response.

Thought stopping Use of aversive stimuli to interrupt or prevent upsetting thoughts.

Covert reinforcement Using positive imagery to reinforce desired behavior.

is to do some deep breathing. Typically, a person who is breathing deeply is relaxed. Shallow breathing involves little movement of the diaphragm. If you place your hand on your abdomen, it will move up and down if you are breathing deeply.

Once you have learned to relax, the next step is to identify the fear you would like to control and construct a hierarchy.

Procedure for Constructing a Hierarchy Make a list of situations (related to the fear) that make you anxious. Try to list at least 10 situations. Some should be very frightening and others only mildly frightening. Write a short description of each situation on a separate 3-by-5 card. Place the cards in order from the least disturbing situation to the most disturbing. Here is a sample hierarchy for a student afraid of public speaking:

1. Being given an assignment to speak in class.
2. Thinking about the topic and the date the speech must be given.
3. Writing the speech; thinking about delivering the speech.
4. Watching other students speak in class the week before the speech date.
5. Rehearsing the speech alone; pretending to give it to the class.
6. Delivering the speech to my roommate; pretending my roommate is the teacher.
7. Reviewing the speech on the day it is to be presented.
8. Entering the classroom; waiting and thinking about the speech.
9. Being called; standing up; facing the audience.
10. Delivering the speech.

Using the Hierarchy When you have mastered the relaxation exercises and have the hierarchy constructed, set aside time each day to work on reducing your fear. Begin by performing the relaxation exercises. When you are completely relaxed, visualize the scene on the first card (the least frightening scene). If you can *vividly* picture and imagine yourself in the first situation twice *without a noticeable increase in muscle tension*, proceed to the next card. Also, as you progress, relax yourself between cards.

Each day, stop when you reach a card that you cannot visualize without becoming tense in three attempts. Each day, begin one or two cards before the one on which you stopped the previous day. Continue to work with the cards until you can visualize the last situation without experiencing tension (techniques are based on Wolpe, 1974).

By using this approach you should be able to reduce the fear or anxiety associated with things such as public speaking, entering darkened rooms, asking questions in large classes, heights, talking to members of the opposite sex, and taking tests (Watson & Tharp, 2007). Even if you are not always able to reduce a fear, you will have learned to place relaxation under voluntary control. This alone is valuable because controlling unnecessary tension can increase energy and efficiency.

Seeking Professional Help—When, Where, and How?

Chances are good that at some point you or someone in your family will benefit from mental health services of one kind or another. In one survey, 13.4 percent of all Americans received treatment for a mental health concern during the preceding year (National Institute of Mental Health, 2011a).

How would I know if I should seek professional help at some point in my life? Although there is no simple answer to this question, the following guidelines may be helpful:

1. If your level of psychological discomfort (unhappiness, anxiety, or depression, for example) is comparable to a level of physical discomfort that would cause you to see a doctor or dentist, you should consider seeing a psychologist or a psychiatrist.
2. Another signal to watch for is significant changes in behavior, such as the quality of your work (or schoolwork), your rate of absenteeism, your use of drugs (including alcohol), or your relationships with others.
3. Perhaps you have urged a friend or relative to seek professional help and were dismayed because he or she refused to do so. If *you* find friends or relatives making a similar suggestion, recognize that they may be seeing things more clearly than you are.
4. If you have persistent or disturbing suicidal thoughts or impulses, you should seek help immediately.

Locating a Therapist *If I wanted to talk to a therapist, how would I find one?* Here are some suggestions that could help you get started:

1. **Colleges and universities.** If you are a student, don't overlook counseling services offered by a student health center or special student counseling facilities.
2. **Workplaces.** If you have a job, check with your employer. Some employers have employee assistance programs that offer confidential free or low-cost therapy for employees.
3. **Community or county mental health centers.** Most counties and many cities offer public mental health services. (These are listed in the phone book.) Public mental health centers usually provide counseling and therapy services directly, and they can refer you to private therapists.
4. **Mental health associations.** Many cities have mental health associations organized by concerned citizens. Groups such as these usually keep listings of qualified therapists and other services and programs in the community.
5. **The Yellow Pages.** Psychologists are listed in the telephone book or on the Internet under "Psychologists," or in some cases under "Counseling Services." Psychiatrists are generally listed as a subheading under "Physicians." Counselors are usually found under the heading "Marriage and Family Counselors." These listings will usually put you in touch with individuals in private practice.
6. **Crisis hotlines.** The typical crisis hotline is a telephone service staffed by community volunteers. These people are trained to provide information concerning a wide range of mental health problems. They also have lists of organizations, services, and other resources in the community where you can go for help.

■ Table 15.5 summarizes all the sources for psychotherapy, counseling, and referrals we have discussed, as well as some additional possibilities.

Options *How would I know what kind of a therapist to see? How would I pick one?* The choice between a psychiatrist and a psycholo-

■ **TABLE 15.5 Mental Health Resources**

- Family doctors (for referrals to mental health professionals)
- Mental health specialists, such as psychiatrists, psychologists, social workers, and mental health counselors
- Religious leaders/counselors
- Health maintenance organizations (HMOs)
- Community mental health centers
- Hospital psychiatry departments and outpatient clinics
- University—or medical school—affiliated programs
- State hospital outpatient clinics
- Family service/social agencies
- Private clinics and facilities
- Employee assistance programs
- Local medical, psychiatric, or psychological societies

National Institute of Mental Health (2010b).

gist is somewhat arbitrary. Both are trained to do psychotherapy and can be equally effective as therapists (Seligman, 1995). Although a psychiatrist can administer somatic therapy and prescribe drugs, so can psychologists in New Mexico and Louisiana (Munsey, 2006). Besides, a psychologist can work in conjunction with a physician if such services are needed.

Fees for psychiatrists are usually higher, averaging about $160 to $200 an hour. Psychologists average about $100 an hour. Counselors and social workers typically charge about $80 per hour. Group therapy averages only about $40 an hour because the therapist's fee is divided among several people.

Be aware that most health insurance plans will pay for psychological services. If fees are a problem, keep in mind that many therapists charge on a sliding scale, or ability-to-pay basis, and that community mental health centers almost always charge on a sliding scale. In one way or another, help is almost always available for anyone who needs it.

Some communities and college campuses have counseling services staffed by sympathetic paraprofessionals or peer counselors. These services are free or very low cost. As mentioned earlier, paraprofessionals are people who work in a near-professional capacity under professional supervision. **Peer counselors** are nonprofessional persons who have learned basic counseling skills. There is a natural tendency, perhaps, to doubt the abilities of paraprofessionals. However, many studies have shown that paraprofessional counselors are often as effective as professionals (Christensen & Jacobson, 1994).

Also, don't overlook self-help groups, which can add valuable support to professional treatment. Members of a self-help group typically share a particular type of problem, such as eating disorders or coping with an alcoholic parent. **Self-help groups** offer members mutual support and a chance to discuss problems. In many instances, helping others also serves as therapy for those who give help (Burlingame & Davies, 2002). For some problems, self-help groups may be the best choice of all (Fobair, 1997; Galanter et al., 2005).

Qualifications You can usually find out about a therapist's qualifications simply by asking. A reputable therapist will be glad to reveal his or her background. If you have any doubts, credentials may be checked and other helpful information can be obtained from local branches of any of the following organizations. You can also browse the websites listed here:

American Association for Marriage and Family Therapy (www.aamft.org)

American Family Therapy Academy (www.afta.org)

American Psychiatric Association (www.psych.org)

American Psychological Association (www.apa.org)

Association of Humanistic Psychology (www.ahpweb.org)

Canadian Psychiatric Association (www.cpa-apc.org)

Canadian Psychological Association (www.cpa.ca)

Mental Health America (www.nmha.org)

The question of how to pick a particular therapist remains. The best way is to start with a short consultation with a respected psychiatrist, psychologist, or counselor. This will allow the person you consult to evaluate your difficulty and recommend a type of therapy or a therapist who is likely to be helpful. As an alternative you might ask the person teaching this course for a referral.

Evaluating a Therapist *How would I know whether to quit or ignore a therapist?* A balanced look at psychotherapies suggests that all *techniques* can be equally successful (Wampold et al., 1997). However, all *therapists* are not equally successful. Far more important than the approach used are the therapist's personal qualities (Okiishi et al., 2003; Prochaska & Norcross, 2010). The most consistently successful therapists are those who are willing to use whatever method seems most helpful for a client. They are also marked by personal characteristics of warmth, integrity, sincerity, and empathy. Former clients consistently rate the person doing the therapy as more important than the type of therapy used (Elliott & Williams, 2003).

It is perhaps most accurate to say that at this stage of development, psychotherapy is an art, not a science. The *relationship* between a client and therapist is the therapist's most basic tool (Hubble, Duncan, & Miller, 1999; Prochaska & Norcross, 2010). This is why you must trust and easily relate to a therapist for therapy to be effective. Here are some danger signals to watch for in psychotherapy:

- Sexual advances by therapist
- Therapist makes repeated verbal threats or is physically aggressive
- Therapist is excessively blaming, belittling, hostile, or controlling
- Therapist makes excessive small talk; talks repeatedly about his/her own problems
- Therapist encourages prolonged dependence on him/her
- Therapist demands absolute trust or tells client not to discuss therapy with anyone else

Clients who like their therapist are generally more successful in therapy (Talley, Strupp, & Morey, 1990). An especially important part of the therapeutic alliance is agreement about the goals of therapy (Meier et al., 2006). It is, therefore, a good idea to think about what you would like to accomplish by entering therapy.

Peer counselor A nonprofessional person who has learned basic counseling skills.

Self-help group A group of people who share a particular type of problem and provide mutual support to one another.

Write down your goals and discuss them with your therapist during the first session. Your first meeting with a therapist should also answer all of the following questions (Somberg, Stone, & Claiborn, 1993):

- Will the information I reveal in therapy remain completely confidential?
- What risks do I face if I begin therapy?
- How long do you expect treatment to last?
- What form of treatment do you expect to use?
- Are there alternatives to therapy that might help me as much or more?

It's always tempting to avoid facing up to personal problems. With this in mind, you should give a therapist a fair chance and not give up too easily. But don't hesitate to change therapists or to terminate therapy if you lose confidence in the therapist or if you don't relate well to the therapist as a person.

Self-Management and Seeking Professional Help

RECITE

1. Covert sensitization and thought stopping combine aversion therapy and cognitive therapy. T or F?
2. Like covert aversion conditioning, covert reinforcement of desired responses is also possible. T or F?
3. Exercises that bring about deep-muscle relaxation are an essential element in covert sensitization. T or F?
4. Items in a desensitization hierarchy should be placed in order from the least disturbing to the most disturbing. T or F?
5. The first step in desensitization is to place the visualization of disturbing images under stimulus control. T or F?
6. Persistent emotional discomfort is a clear sign that professional psychological counseling should be sought. T or F?
7. Community mental health centers rarely offer counseling or therapy themselves; they only do referrals. T or F?
8. In many instances, a therapist's personal qualities have more of an effect on the outcome of therapy than does the type of therapy used. T or F?

REFLECT

Critical Thinking

9. Would it be acceptable for a therapist to urge a client to break all ties with a troublesome family member?

Self-Reflect

How could you use covert sensitization, thought stopping, and covert reinforcement to change your behavior? Try to apply each technique to a specific example.

Just for practice, make a fear hierarchy for a situation you find frightening. Does vividly picturing items in the hierarchy make you tense or anxious? If so, can you intentionally relax using the tension-release method?

Assume that you want to seek help from a psychologist or other mental health professional. How would you proceed? Take some time to actually find out what mental health services are available to you.

Answers: 1. T **2.** T **3.** F **4.** T **5.** F **6.** T **7.** F **8.** T **9.** Such decisions must be made by clients themselves. Therapists can help clients evaluate important decisions and feelings about significant persons in their lives. However, actively urging a client to sever a relationship borders on unethical behavior.

Chapter in Review Gateways to Therapies

Gateway QUESTIONS REVISITED

15.1 *How did psychotherapy originate?*

15.1.1 Early approaches to mental illness were dominated by superstition and moral condemnation.

15.1.2 Demonology attributed mental disturbance to demonic possession and prescribed exorcism as the cure.

15.1.3 In some instances, the actual cause of bizarre behavior may have been ergot poisoning.

15.1.4 More humane treatment began in 1793 with the work of Philippe Pinel in Paris.

15.2 *Is Freudian psychoanalysis still used?*

15.2.1 As the first true psychotherapy, Freud's psychoanalysis gave rise to modern psychodynamic therapies.

15.2.2 The psychoanalyst uses free association, dream analysis, and analysis of resistance and transference to reveal health-producing insights.

15.2.3 Some critics argue that traditional psychoanalysis receives credit for spontaneous remissions of symptoms. However, psychoanalysis is successful for many patients.

15.2.4 Psychoanalysts have become relatively rare because psychoanalysis is expensive and time intensive. Brief psychodynamic therapy (which relies on psychoanalytic theory but is brief and focused) is as effective as other major therapies. One example is interpersonal psychotherapy.

15.3 How do psychotherapies differ?

15.3.1 All psychotherapy aims to facilitate positive changes in personality, behavior, or adjustment.

15.3.2 Psychotherapies may be classified as insight, action, directive, nondirective, and combinations of these.

15.3.3 Therapies may be conducted either individually or in groups, and they may be time limited.

15.4 What are the major humanistic therapies?

15.4.1 Client-centered (or person-centered) therapy is nondirective, based on insights gained from conscious thoughts and feelings, and dedicated to creating an atmosphere of growth.

15.4.2 Unconditional positive regard, empathy, authenticity, and reflection are combined to give the client a chance to solve his or her own problems.

15.4.3 Existential therapies focus on the end result of the choices one makes in life. Clients are encouraged through confrontation and encounter to exercise free will and to take responsibility for their choices.

15.4.4 Gestalt therapy emphasizes immediate awareness of thoughts and feelings. Its goal is to rebuild thinking, feeling, and acting into connected wholes and to help clients break through emotional blockages.

15.5 How does cognitive therapy change thoughts and emotions?

15.5.1 Cognitive therapy emphasizes changing thought patterns that underlie emotional or behavioral problems. Changing the thought patterns can have a positive impact on emotions and behavior.

15.5.2 Aaron Beck's cognitive therapy focuses on changing several major distortions in thinking: selective perception, overgeneralization, and all or nothing thinking.

15.5.3 In a variation of cognitive therapy called rational-emotive behavior therapy (REBT), clients learn to recognize and challenge the irrational beliefs that are at the core of their maladaptive thinking patterns.

15.6 What is behavior therapy?

15.6.1 Behavior therapists use the learning principles of classical or operant conditioning to directly change human behavior.

15.6.2 In aversion therapy, classical conditioning is used to associate maladaptive behavior (such as smoking or drinking) with pain or other aversive events in order to inhibit undesirable responses.

15.6.3 In desensitization, gradual adaptation and reciprocal inhibition break the link between fear and particular situations.

15.6.4 Typical steps in desensitization are: Construct a fear hierarchy; learn to produce total relaxation; and perform items on the hierarchy (from least to most disturbing).

15.6.5 Desensitization may be carried out with real settings or it may be done by vividly imagining the fear hierarchy or by watching models perform the feared responses.

15.6.6 In some cases, virtual reality exposure can be used to present fear stimuli in a controlled manner.

15.6.7 A newer technique called eye movement desensitization and reprocessing (EMDR) shows promise as a treatment for traumatic memories and stress disorders. At present, however, EMDR is highly controversial.

15.7 What role do operant principles play in behavior therapy?

15.7.1 Operant principles, such as positive reinforcement, nonreinforcement, extinction, punishment, shaping, stimulus control, and time out, are used to extinguish undesirable responses and to promote constructive behavior.

15.7.2 Nonreward can extinguish troublesome behaviors. Often this is done by simply identifying and eliminating reinforcers, particularly attention and social approval.

15.7.3 To apply positive reinforcement and operant shaping, tokens are often used to reinforce selected target behaviors.

15.7.4 Full-scale use of tokens in an institutional setting produces a token economy. Toward the end of a token economy program, patients are shifted to social rewards such as recognition and approval.

15.8 How do psychiatrists treat psychological disorders?

15.8.1 Medical approaches to mental disorders, such as drugs, surgery, and hospitalization, are similar to medical treatments for physical ailments. All medical treatments for psychological disorders have pros and cons. Overall, however, their effectiveness is improving.

15.8.2 Three medical, or somatic, approaches to treatment are pharmacotherapy, electrical stimulation therapy (including electroconvulsive therapy [ECT]), and psychosurgery.

15.8.3 Community mental health centers seek to avoid or minimize mental hospitalization. They also seek to prevent mental health problems through education, consultation, and crisis intervention.

15.9 Are various psychotherapies effective, and what do they have in common?

15.9.1 Effective psychotherapies are based on the therapeutic alliance, a protected setting, catharsis, insights, new perspectives, and a chance to practice new behaviors.

15.9.2 Psychotherapy is generally effective, although no single form of therapy is superior to others.

15.9.3 All of the following are helping skills that can be learned: active listening, acceptance, reflection, open-ended questioning, support, respect, patience, genuineness, and paraphrasing.

15.9.4 The culturally skilled counselor must be able to establish rapport with a person from a different cultural background and adapt traditional theories and techniques to meet the needs of clients from non-European ethnic groups.

15.10 *What will therapy be like in the future?*

15.10.1 Therapy can be done with groups of people based on a simple extension of individual methods or based on techniques developed specifically for groups.

15.10.2 In psychodrama, individuals enact roles and incidents resembling their real-life problems. In family therapy, the family group is treated as a unit.

15.10.3 Sensitivity and encounter groups encourage positive personality change. Large-group awareness training attempts to do the same, but the benefits of such programs are questionable.

15.10.4 Media psychologists, telephone counselors, and cybertherapists may, on occasion, do some good. However, each has drawbacks, and the effectiveness of telephone counseling and cybertherapy has not been established.

15.10.5 Therapy by videoconferencing shows more promise as a way to provide mental health services at a distance.

15.11 *How are behavioral principles applied to everyday problems and how could a person find professional help?*

15.11.1 Some personal problems can be successfully treated using self-management techniques, such as covert reinforcement, covert sensitization, thought stopping, and self-directed desensitization.

15.11.2 In covert sensitization, aversive images are used to discourage unwanted behavior. Thought stopping uses mild punishment to prevent upsetting thoughts. Covert reinforcement is a way to encourage desired responses by mental rehearsal.

15.11.3 Desensitization pairs relaxation with a hierarchy of upsetting images in order to lessen fears.

15.11.4 In most communities, a competent and reputable therapist can be located with public sources of information or through a referral.

15.11.5 Practical considerations such as cost and qualifications enter into choosing a therapist. However, the therapist's personal characteristics are of equal importance.

MEDIA RESOURCES

Web Resources

Internet addresses frequently change. To find an up-to-date list of URLs for the sites listed here, visit your Psychology CourseMate.

Pre-Columbian Trephination Read about the first psychosurgery as a treatment for mental illness.

Philippe Pinel Read about Pinel's contribution to the history of the treatment of mental illness.

Freud and Psychoanalysis Read about the history of psychoanalysis.

Existential Therapy Explore this extensive website about existential therapy.

The Beck Institute Read about cognitive therapy and visit the rest of the Beck Institute website.

Albert Ellis Institute Read about Albert Ellis and his Rational-Emotive Behavior Therapy.

Systematic Desensitization Explore this self-administered procedure.

Virtual Reality Therapy Learn more about VR therapy.

Token Economies Read about the use of token economies with autistic children.

Medications for Mental Illness Explore some information about different drugs used to treat mental illness.

ECT Read more about the pros and cons of ECT.

Lobotomy Read a case study of lobotomy and the history of the transorbital lobotomy procedure.

American Association for Marriage and Family Therapy Visit the website of the AAMFT.

American Self-Help Group Clearinghouse Explore this database of over 1,000 self-help groups.

Dr. Phil See for yourself how Dr. Phil publicizes mental health issues.

Therapy Effectiveness Read an article about the effectiveness of therapy.

Finding a Therapist in Your Hometown Use the Internet to locate a local therapist.

Find a Therapist Another Internet tool to help you locate a therapist.

Interactive Learning

Log in to **CengageBrain** to access the resources your instructor requires. For this book, you can access:

CourseMate brings course concepts to life with interactive learning, study, and exam preparation tools that support the printed textbook. A textbook-specific website, ***Psychology CourseMate*** includes an ***integrated interactive eBook*** and other ***interactive learning tools*** including quizzes, flashcards, videos, and more.

CENGAGE**NOW**™

CengageNOW is an easy-to-use online resource that helps you study in less time to get the grade you want—NOW. Take a pre-test for this chapter and receive a personalized study plan based on your results that will identify the topics you need to review and direct you to online resources to help you master those topics. Then take a post-test to help you determine the concepts you have mastered and what you will need to work on. If your textbook does not include an access code card, go to CengageBrain.com to gain access.

WebTUTOR™

More than just an interactive study guide, **WebTutor** is an anytime, anywhere customized learning solution with an eBook, keeping you connected to your textbook, instructor, and classmates.

If your professor has assigned **Aplia** homework:

1. Sign in to your account.
2. Complete the corresponding homework exercises as required by your professor.
3. When finished, click "Grade It Now" to see which areas you have mastered and which need more work, and for detailed explanations of every answer.

Visit www.cengagebrain.com to access your account and purchase materials.

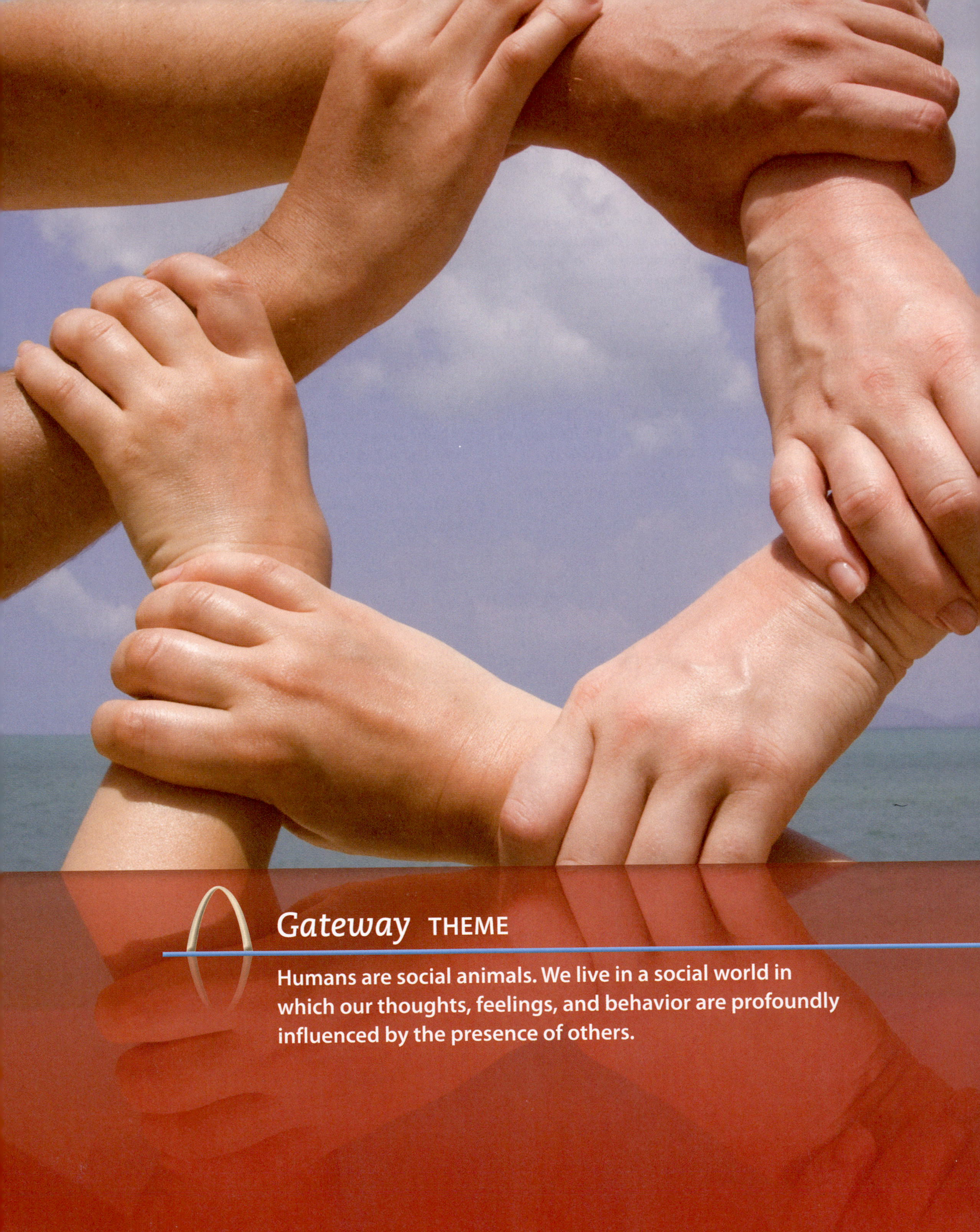

Gateway THEME

Humans are social animals. We live in a social world in which our thoughts, feelings, and behavior are profoundly influenced by the presence of others.

16 Social Thinking and Social Influence

Six Degrees of Separation

The Social Network refers to more than the name of an award-winning movie. Families, teams, crowds, tribes, companies, parties, troops, bands, sects, gangs, crews, clans, communities, and nations: we are all entwined in many, many social networks. But that's old news; nearly 400 years ago, the poet John Donne wrote, "No man is an island, entire of itself."

The "new" news is how much smaller the social world has become since the 17th century. To get some sense of this, imagine you have been given a message and the name, address, and occupation of the person who should receive it. The "target person" lives somewhere else on Earth. You can send the message with any technology you like, but only to a first-name acquaintance. That person, in turn, must forward the message to a first-name acquaintance, and so on, until it reaches the target person.

Sound impossible? Maybe in John Donne's day. More recently, social psychologist Stanley Milgram (1967) had participants use regular mail and found it took, on average, six intermediaries. Think about it: only six degrees of separation between you and pretty well everyone else on Earth. A few decades later, sociologist Duncan Watts replicated Milgram's result, this time using e-mail (Dodds, Muhamad, & Watts, 2003).

How is that possible? You almost certainly know at least dozens of people by name, who know dozens more people, who each know still more people, and so on. By following all your social links, you could reach millions of people just six "layers" out. With the recent explosion in cell phones, text messaging, and social networking sites like Facebook, our social networks will undoubtedly expand even more. At least one report has already concluded we are down to three degrees of separation (Reisinger, 2008).

Our social networks strongly influence our behavior. In this chapter, we will look at some ways we think about social situations and the various ways in which we influence others. We hope that you will find the topics interesting and thought provoking.

Gateway QUESTIONS

16.1 How does group membership affect individual behavior?

16.2 How does being social influence how we think about ourselves and others?

16.3 What are attitudes and how are they acquired?

16.4 Under what conditions is persuasion most effective and what is cognitive dissonance?

16.5 What is social influence and social power?

16.6 How does the mere presence of others affect behavior?

16.7 What have social psychologists learned about conformity?

16.8 What factors lead to increased compliance?

16.9 Can people be too obedient?

16.10 Is brainwashing actually possible and is that how people are converted to cult membership?

16.11 How does self-assertion differ from aggression?

Humans in a Social Context—People, People, Everywhere

Gateway Question 16.1: *How does group membership affect individual behavior?*

Participation in various groups is a basic fact of social life. How do groups influence our behavior? Because you are a member of a group called "psychology class," it would be wise to find out.

Social psychology is the scientific study of how individuals behave, think, and feel in social situations (that is, in the presence, actual or implied, of others) (Baron, Byrne, & Branscombe, 2009). Every day, there is a fascinating interplay between our own behavior and that of people around us. We are born into an organized society. Established values, expectations, and behavior patterns are present when we arrive. So, too, is **culture**, an ongoing pattern of life that is passed from one generation to the next. To appreciate the impact of society and culture, think about how you have been affected by language, marriage customs, concepts of ownership, and sex roles.

Roles

We all belong to many overlapping social groups, and in each, we occupy a *position* in the *structure* of the group. **Social roles** are patterns of behavior expected of persons in various social positions (Baumeister & Bushman, 2011). For instance, playing the role of mother, boss, or student involves different sets of behaviors and expectations. Some roles are *ascribed* (they are assigned to a person or are not under personal control): male or female, son, adolescent, inmate. *Achieved roles* are voluntarily attained by special effort: spouse, teacher, scientist, bandleader, criminal.

What effect does role-playing have on behavior? Roles streamline daily interactions by allowing us to anticipate what others will do. When a person is acting as a doctor, mother, clerk, or police officer, we expect certain behaviors. However, roles have a negative side, too. Many people experience **role conflicts**, in which two or more roles make conflicting demands on them (Valentine, Godkin, & Varca, 2010). Consider, for example, a teacher who must flunk a close friend's son; a mother who has a full-time job; or a soccer coach whose daughter is on the team but isn't a very good athlete. Likewise, the clashing demands of work, family, and school create role conflicts for many students (Hammer, Grigsby, & Woods, 1998; Senécal, Julien, & Guay, 2003). Role conflicts at work (such as being a good team player versus being a strong manager) lead to job burnout (Jawahar, Stone, & Kisamore, 2007) and negative health outcomes (Pomaki, Supeli, & Verhoeven, 2007).

Roles have a powerful impact on social behavior. What kinds of behavior do you expect from your teachers? What behaviors do they expect from you? What happens if either of you fails to match the other's expectations?

Survivor and other "reality" television programs offer an interesting, if voyeuristic, look at some of the best and worst aspects of human behavior. However, such programs have nothing over the most revealing experiments in social psychology. For example, a classic study done by Phil Zimbardo and his students at Stanford University showed dramatically how social settings influence our behavior.

In the study, normal healthy male college students were paid to serve as "inmates" and "guards" in a simulated prison (Zimbardo, Haney, & Banks, 1973). After just 2 days in "jail," the inmates grew restless and defiant. When they staged a disturbance, the guards unmercifully suppressed the rebellion. Over the next few days, the guards clamped down with increasing brutality. In a surprisingly short time, the fake convicts looked like real prisoners: They were dejected, traumatized, passive, and dehumanized. Four of them had to be released because they were crying, confused, or severely depressed. Each day, the guards tormented the prisoners with more commands, insults, and demeaning tasks. After 6 days, the experiment had to be halted.

What had happened? Apparently, the assigned social roles—prisoner and guard—were so powerful that in just a few days the experiment became "reality" for those involved. Afterward, it was difficult for many of the guards to believe their own behavior. As one recalls, "I was surprised at myself. I made them call one another names and clean toilets out with their bare hands. I practically considered the prisoners cattle" (Zimbardo, Haney, & Banks, 1973). We tend to think of people as inherently good or bad. But students in the Stanford prison study were randomly assigned to be prisoners or guards. Clearly, the origins of many destructive human relationships can be found in destructive roles.

Group Structure, Cohesion, and Norms

Are there other dimensions of group membership? Two important dimensions of any group are its structure and its cohesiveness (Forsyth, 2010). **Group structure** consists of the network of roles, communication pathways, and power in a group. Organized groups such as an army or an athletic team have a high degree of structure. Informal friendship groups may or may not be very structured.

Group cohesiveness refers to the degree of attraction among group members or the strength of their desire to remain in the group. Members of cohesive groups literally stick together: They

Critical Thinking: Solitude

Wrapped in ever-expanding social networks, we are never far from other people. They are always right beside us, just around the next corner, or only a phone or text message away. In our intensely social world, it is tempting to assume that a person who is alone is a loser, a loner, a social outcast or, at the very least, antisocial or shy.

But is this assumption always justified? Having read through much of this textbook (You *have* been reading this book, right?), you are likely not surprised to learn that the answer to this question is, "It depends."

On the one hand, it is true that some people are alone because they are socially fearful, self-conscious shy, or otherwise dislike social situations (Coplan & Weeks, 2010). Many of these people are lonely and/or shy (Antony & Swinson, 2008; Cacioppo & William, 2008). In more extreme cases, people who shun social interactions and are troubled by their isolation may even be diagnosed with a mental disorder such as agoraphobia.

BRIDGES

We have explored some unhealthy forms of solitude in earlier chapters. **Shyness is discussed in Chapter 12, pages 435–436, whereas agoraphobia is discussed in Chapter 14, pages 496–497.**

On the other hand, it is also true that some people are alone simply because they prefer solitude (Coplan & Weeks, 2010; Long et al., 2003). In fact, many of history's most creative and spiritual individuals have found insight in their solitude (Storr, 1988).

But can't I be around people sometimes and by myself at other times? Why not? Perhaps we could all benefit from some alone time. Quiet time for reflection does seem to be associated with creativity, spiritual growth, problem solving, and self-discovery (Long et al., 2003). In our modern, bustling world, social contact is a given. Alone time—now that's another story.

This person is alone. But is she lonely? Do you think spending time alone is healthy or unhealthy? Did you know that healthy solitude was on the minds of legislators when they passed the 1964 Wilderness Act? According to that act, national parks should serve "to preserve natural conditions, to provide opportunities for solitude, and to provide a primitive and unconfined type of recreation" (Shafer & Hammitt, 1995).

© djgis/Shutterstock

tend to stand or sit close together, they pay more attention to one another, and they show more signs of mutual affection. Also, their behavior tends to be closely coordinated (Chansler, Swamidass, & Cammann, 2003; Lin & Peng, 2010). Cohesiveness is the basis for much of the power that groups exert over us. Therapy groups, businesses, sports teams, and the like seek to increase cohesion because it helps people work together better (Casey-Campbell & Martens, 2009; Marmarosh, Holtz, & Schottenbauer, 2005). But is it ever better to work alone? See "Solitude" for some answers.

In-groups

Cohesiveness is particularly strong for **in-groups** (groups with which a person mainly identifies). Very likely, your own in-groups are defined by a combination of prominent social dimensions, such as nationality, ethnicity, age, education, religion, income, political values, gender, sexual orientation, and so forth. In-group membership helps define who we are socially. Predictably, we tend to attribute positive characteristics to our in-group and negative qualities to **out-groups** (groups with which we do not identify). We also tend to exaggerate differences between members of

Social psychology The scientific study of how individuals behave, think, and feel in social situations.
Culture An ongoing pattern of life, characterizing a society at a given point in history.
Social role Expected behavior patterns associated with particular social positions (such as daughter, worker, student).
Role conflict Trying to occupy two or more roles that make conflicting demands on behavior.
Group structure The network of roles, communication pathways, and power in a group.
Group cohesiveness The degree of attraction among group members or their commitment to remaining in the group.
In-group A group with which a person identifies.
Out-group A group with which a person does not identify.

out-groups and our own groups. This sort of "us-and-them" thinking seems to be a basic fact of social life. It also sets the stage for conflict between groups and for racial and ethnic prejudice—topics we will explore in the next chapter.

Social Status

In addition to defining roles, a person's social position within groups determines his or her **social status**, or level of social power and importance. Higher social status bestows special privileges and respect (Albrecht, & Albrecht, 2011). For example, in one experiment, a man walked into a number of bakeries and asked for a pastry while claiming he did not have enough money to pay for it. Half the time he was well dressed and half the time he was poorly dressed. If the man was polite when he asked, he was equally likely to be given a free pastry no matter how he was dressed (95 versus 90 percent). But if he was impolite when he asked, he was much less likely to get a pastry if he was poorly dressed than if he was well dressed (75 versus 20 percent) (Guéguen & Pascual, 2003).

You don't have to be in a bakery for this to work. In most situations, we are more likely to comply with a request made by a high-status (well-dressed) person (Guéguen, 2002). Perhaps the better treatment given "higher status" persons, even when they are impolite, explains some of our society's preoccupation with expensive clothes, cars, and other status symbols.

Norms

We are also greatly affected by group norms. A **norm** is a widely accepted (but often unspoken) standard for appropriate behavior. If you have the slightest doubt about the power of norms, try this test: Walk into a crowded supermarket, get in a checkout line, and begin singing loudly in your fullest voice. Are you the one person in 100 who could actually carry out these instructions?

The impact of norms is shown by an interesting study of littering. The question was, "Does the amount of trash in an area affect littering?" To find out, people were given flyers as they walked into a public parking garage. As you can see in • Figure 16.1, the more litter there was on the floor, the more likely people were to add to it by dropping their flyer. Apparently, seeing that others had already littered implied a lax norm about whether littering is acceptable. The moral? The cleaner a public area is kept, the less likely people are to "trash" it (Cialdini, Reno, & Kallgren, 1990; Göckeritz et al., 2010).

How are norms formed? One early study of group norms made use of a striking illusion called the **autokinetic effect**. In a completely darkened room, a stationary pinpoint of light will appear to drift or move about. (The light is, therefore, *autokinetic*, or "self-moving.") Muzafer Sherif (1906–1988) found that people give very different estimates of how far the light moves. However, when two or more people announce their estimates at the same time, their judgments rapidly converge. This is an example of *social influence*, in which one person's behavior is changed by the actions of others (Brehm, Kassin, & Fein, 2005). We will return to social influence later. For now, it is enough to note that a convergence of attitudes, beliefs, and behaviors tends to take place in many groups (Cialdini, 2008).

Norms are often based on our *perceptions* of what others think and do. For example, a majority of college students believe that they are more troubled about excessive drinking on campus than other students are. Apparently, many students are fooled by this false norm. Ironically, they help create this false impression by not speaking up. If disapproving students actually outnumber "party animals," then campus norms for acceptable drinking should be fairly conservative, which is usually not the case (Prentice & Miller, 1993).

The role of perception in the establishment of social norms offers a good example of **social cognition**, the process of thinking about ourselves and others in a social context (Landau, Meier, & Keefer, 2010; Strack & Förster, 2009). Despite the fact that we are immersed in social relationships with other people all of the time and can freely *observe* their behavior, as well as our own, *understanding* that behavior is another matter entirely. In the next few sections, we will consider a few examples. To begin, we'll see that we often think about ourselves in comparison with others, a form of social cognition known as *social comparison*. We'll move on to consider the process of *attribution*, one way we understand the behavior of other people. Finally, we'll have a look that *attitudes* and how we form them.

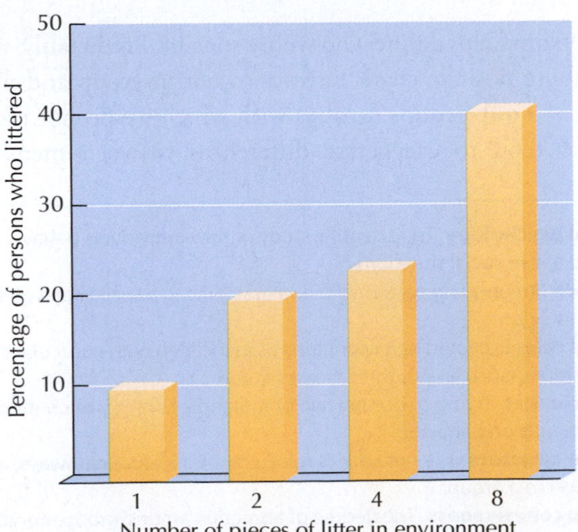

• Figure 16.1 Results of an experiment on norms concerning littering. The prior existence of litter in a public setting implies that littering is acceptable. This encourages others to "trash" the area. From Cialdini, Reno, & Kallgren, 1990.

Social Cognition—Behind Our Masks

Gateway Question 16.2: ***How does being social influence how we think about ourselves and others?***

The people around us not only affect how we behave, they also influence how we think about ourselves and others. For example, one common way that we understand ourselves is by comparing themselves to others, a process called . . . wait for it . . . *social comparison*.

Social Comparison Theory

If you want to know how heavy you are, you simply get on a scale. But how do you know if you are a good athlete, worker, parent, or friend? How do you know if your views on politics, religion, or hip-hop are unusual or widely shared? When there are no objective standards, the only available yardstick is provided by comparing yourself with others (Baumeister & Bushman, 2011; Dvash et al., 2010).

Social psychologist Leon Festinger (1919–1989) theorized that group membership fills needs for **social comparison** (comparing your own actions, feelings, opinions, or abilities to those of others). Have you ever "compared notes" with other students after taking an exam? ("How did you do?" "Wasn't that last question hard?") If you have, you were satisfying needs for social comparison (Festinger, 1957).

Typically, we don't make social comparisons randomly or on some absolute scale. Meaningful evaluations are based on comparing yourself with people of similar backgrounds, abilities, and circumstances (Stapel & Marx, 2007). To illustrate, let's ask a student named Wendy if she is a good tennis player. If Wendy compares herself with a professional, the answer will be no. But this tells us little about her *relative* ability. Within her tennis group, Wendy is regarded as an excellent player. On a fair scale of comparison, Wendy knows she is good and she takes pride in her tennis skills. In the same way, thinking of yourself as successful, talented, responsible, or fairly paid depends entirely on whom you choose for comparison. Thus, a desire for social comparison provides a motive for associating with others and influences which groups we join (Franzoi & Klaiber, 2007; Johnson & Stapel, 2010).

In addition to providing information, social comparisons may, at times, be made in ways that reflect desires for self-protection or self-enhancement (Dvash et al., 2010). If you feel threatened, you may make a **downward comparison** by contrasting yourself with a person who ranks lower on some dimension (Gibbons et al., 2002). For example, if you have a part-time job and your employer cuts your hours, you may comfort yourself by thinking about a friend who just lost a job.

Jerome Corpuz/Getty Images

High school class reunions are notorious for the rampant social comparison they often encourage. Apparently it's hard to resist comparing yourself with former classmates to see how you are doing in life.

AFP/Getty Images

Celebrities, such as Madonna and Angelina Jolie, have adopted children from third-world countries. Do you attribute their actions to selfless concern for the suffering of children? Or were they motivated by a selfish desire to hog the limelight? Such attributions greatly affect how we perceive and respond to the social behavior of others.

What about upward comparisons? Do they occur, too? As Wendy's tennis playing suggests, comparing yourself with people of much higher ability will probably just make you feel bad (Tyler & Feldman, 2006). For example, when women compare their bodies with those of beautiful women in the media, their dissatisfaction with their own bodies increases (Tiggemann & Polivy, 2010). However, **upward comparisons**, in which we compare ourselves to a person who ranks higher on some dimension, are sometimes used for self-improvement. One way that Wendy can learn to improve her tennis skills is to compare herself with players who are only a little better than she is (Huguet et al., 2001).

In general, social comparison theory holds that desires for self-evaluation self-protection, and self-enhancement provide motives for associating with others. In doing so, they influence which groups we join.

Social status An individual's position in a social structure, especially with respect to power, privilege, or importance.

Norm A widely accepted (but often unspoken) standard of conduct for appropriate behavior.

Autokinetic effect The apparent movement of a stationary pinpoint of light displayed in a darkened room.

Social cognition The process of thinking about ourselves and others in a social context.

Social comparison Making judgments about ourselves through comparison with others.

Downward comparison Comparing yourself with a person who ranks lower than you on some dimension.

Upward comparison Comparing yourself with a person who ranks higher than you on some dimension.

Let's shift gears now to examine another form of social cognition. Vonda just insulted Sutchai. But why? Why did Nick change his college major? Why does Kirti talk so fast when she's around men? In answering such questions, we *attribute* people's behavior to various causes. Whether we are right or wrong about the causes of their behavior, our conclusions affect how *we* act. To learn how we fill in the "person behind the mask," let's explore the making of attributions.

Attribution Theory

Every day we must guess how people will act, often from small shreds of evidence. We do this through a form of social cognition called **attribution**. As we observe others, we make inferences about them. For example, two people enter a restaurant and order different meals. Nell tastes her food, then salts it. Bert salts his food before he tastes it. How would you explain their behavior? In Nell's case, you might assume that the *food* needed salt. If so, you have attributed her actions to an **external cause** (one that lies outside a person). With Bert, you might be more inclined to conclude that he must really *like* salt. If so, the cause of his behavior is internal. **Internal causes**, such as needs, personality traits, and Bert's taste for salt, lie within the person.

BRIDGES

Attributing bodily arousal to various sources can also have a large impact on emotions. **See Chapter 10, pages 359–360.**

What effects do such interpretations have? It is difficult to fully understand social behavior without considering the attributions that we make. For instance, let's say that Tam, who is in one of your classes, seems to avoid you. You see Tam at a market. Do you say hello to him? It could depend on how you have explained Tam's actions to yourself. Have you assumed his avoidance is caused by shyness? Coincidence? Dislike? Many factors affect such judgments. Let's examine a few.

Making Attributions

According to Harold Kelley (1921–2003), one of the originators of attribution theory, when we make attributions, we are sensitive to how *consistent* and *distinctive* a person's behavior is (Kelley, 1967). A person's behavior is *consistent* if it changes very little when we observe it on many different occasions. The first time that Tam avoided you he might have just been in a bad mood. However, if Tam has consistently avoided you, it's not likely that he was in a bad mood every time. That rules out coincidence. Still, Tam's avoidance could mean he is shy, not that he dislikes you. That's why distinctiveness is also important. When we watch other people, *distinctiveness* refers to noting that their behavior occurs only under specific circumstances. If you notice that Tam seems to avoid other people too, you may conclude that he is shy or unfriendly. If his avoidance is consistently and distinctively linked only with you, you will probably assume he dislikes you. You could be wrong, of course, but your behavior toward him will change just the same.

To deduce causes, we typically take into account the behavior of the *actor* (the person of interest), the *object* the person's action is directed toward, and the *setting* (social or physical environment) in which the action occurs (Kelley, 1967). Imagine for example, that someone compliments you on your taste in clothes. If you are at a picnic, you may attribute this compliment to what you are wearing (the "object"), unless, of course, you're wearing your worst "grubbies." If you are, you may simply assume that the person (or "actor") is friendly or tactful. However, if you are in a clothing store and a salesperson compliments you, you will probably attribute the compliment to the setting. It's still possible that the salesperson actually likes what you are wearing. Nevertheless, when we make attributions, we are very sensitive to the *situational demands* affecting other people's behavior. **Situational demands** are pressures to behave in certain ways in particular settings and social situations. If you see Tam at a funeral and he is quiet and polite, it will tell you little about his motives and personality traits. The situation demands such behavior.

When situational demands are strong, we tend to *discount* (downgrade) internal causes as a way of explaining a person's behavior. Actually, this is true anytime strong external causes for behavior are present. For example, you have probably discounted the motives of professional athletes who praise shaving creams, hair tonics, deodorants, and the like. Obviously, the large sums of money they receive fully explain their endorsements. It's not necessary to assume they actually *like* the potions they sell. ("Self-Handicapping" discusses a related phenomenon.)

Yet another factor affecting attribution is *consensus* (or agreement). When many people act alike (there is a consensus in their behavior), it implies that their behavior is externally caused. For example, if millions of people go to see the latest Hollywood blockbuster, we tend to say *the movie* is good. If someone you know goes to see a movie six times, when others are staying away in droves, the tendency is to assume that *the person* likes "that type of movie."

Actor and Observer

Let's say that at the last five parties you've been to, you've seen a woman named Macy. Based on this, you assume that Macy likes to socialize. You see Macy at yet another gathering and mention that she seems to like parties. She says, "Actually, I hate these parties, but I get invited to play my tuba at them. My music teacher says I need to practice in front of an audience, so I keep attending these dumb events. Want to hear a Sousa march?"

We seldom know the real reasons for others' actions. That is why we tend to infer causes from *circumstances*. However, in doing so, we often make mistakes like the one with Macy. The most common error is to attribute the actions of others to internal causes (Jones & Nisbett, 1971; Riggio & Garcia, 2009). This mistake is called the **fundamental attribution error**. We tend to think the actions of others have internal causes even if they are actually caused by external forces or circumstances. One amusing example of this error is the tendency of people to attribute the actions of actors in television programs to the personality of the actor rather

The Clinical File Self-Handicapping—Smoke Screen for Failure

Have you ever known someone who got drunk before taking an exam or making a speech? Why would a person risk failure in this way? Often, the reason lies in **self-handicapping** (arranging to perform under conditions that impair performance). By providing an excuse for poor performance, self-handicapping makes people feel better in situations where they might fail (McCrea & Hirt, 2011).

What if a person succeeds while "handicapped"? Well, then, so much the better. The person's self-image then gets a boost because she or he succeeded under conditions that normally lower performance (Kimble & Hirt, 2005).

Do you believe that "you either have it or you don't" where ability is concerned? If so, you may be particularly prone to self-handicapping. By working with a handicap, people can avoid any chance of discovering that they "don't have it"! For instance, college athletes often protect their self-esteem by practicing *less* before important games or events (Kuczka & Treasure, 2005; Ntoumanis, Taylor, & Standage, 2010). That way, if they don't do well, they have an excuse for their poor performance.

Drinking alcohol is one of the most popular—and dangerous—self-handicapping strategies. A person who is drunk can attribute failure to being "loaded," but accept success if it occurs. Examples of using alcohol for self-handicapping include being drunk for school exams, job interviews, or an important first date. A person who gets drunk at such times should be aware that coping with anxiety in this way can lead to serious alcohol abuse (Zuckerman & Tsai, 2005).

Any time you set up excuses for a poor performance, you are self-handicapping. Other examples of self-handicapping include making a half-hearted effort, claiming to be ill, and procrastinating (McCrea & Hirt, 2011). Incidentally, men are more likely than women to self-handicap (Kimble & Hirt, 2005).

Most of us have used self-handicapping at times. Indeed, life would be harsh if we didn't sometimes give ourselves a break from accepting full responsibility for success or failure. Self-handicapping is mainly a problem when it becomes habitual. When it does, it typically leads to lower self-esteem poor adjustment, and poor health (Zuckerman, Kieffer, & Knee, 1998; Zuckerman & Tsai, 2005). So, watch out for self-handicapping, but try not to be too hard on yourself.

than the obvious external cause (that they are playing a character) (Tal-Or & Papirman, 2007).

When our own behavior is concerned, we are more likely to think that external causes explain our actions. In other words, there is an **actor-observer bias** in how we explain behavior. As *observers,* we attribute the behavior of others to their wants, motives, and personality traits (this is the fundamental attribution error). As *actors*, we tend to find external explanations for our own behavior (Aronson, Wilson, & Akert, 2010; Gordon & Kaplar, 2002). No doubt you chose your major in school because of what it has to offer. Other students choose *their* majors because of the kind of people they are. Other people who don't leave tips in restaurants are cheapskates. If you don't leave a tip, it's because the service was bad. And, of course, other people are always late because they are irresponsible. You are late because you were held up by events beyond your control.

As you can see, attribution theory summarizes how we think about ourselves and others, including the errors we tend to make.

Jon Cryer plays the clueless younger brother, Alan Harper, and Angus T. Jones plays his even more clueless son, Jake, in the comedy series *Two and a Half Men*. Are they clueless or are they portraying cluelessness as a part of their roles? According to Tal-Or & Papirman (2007), we are prone to attribute actors' screen actions to their personalities rather than to the personalities of the roles they are playing. Why do you think this occurs? (And then there was Charlie.)

Attribution The process of making inferences about the causes of one's own behavior, and that of others.

External cause A cause of behavior that is assumed to lie outside a person.

Internal cause A cause of behavior assumed to lie within a person—for instance, a need, preference, or personality trait.

Situational demands Unstated expectations that define desirable or appropriate behavior in various settings and social situations.

Self-handicapping Arranging to perform under conditions that usually impair performance, so as to have an excuse for a poor showing.

Fundamental attribution error The tendency to attribute the behavior of others to internal causes (personality, likes, and so forth)

Actor–observer bias The tendency to attribute the behavior of others to internal causes while attributing one's own behavior to external causes (situations and circumstances).

Knowledge Builder: Social Behavior and Cognition

RECITE

1. Research has shown that the number of first-name acquaintances needed to interconnect two widely separated strangers averages about six people. T or F?
2. Social psychology is the study of how people behave in ______________________________.
3. Male, female, and adolescent are examples of ______________ roles.
4. The Stanford prison experiment demonstrated the powerful influence of the autokinetic effect on behavior. T or F?
5. Social status refers to a set of expected behaviors associated with a social position. T or F?
6. Social comparisons are made pretty much at random. T or F?
7. When situational demands are weak, we tend to attribute a person's actions to internal causes. T or F?
8. The fundamental attribution error is to attribute the actions of others to internal causes. T or F?

REFLECT

Think Critically

9. The Stanford prison experiment also illustrates a major concept of personality theory (Chapter 12), especially social learning theory. Can you name it?
10. How could the autokinetic effect contribute to UFO sightings?

Self-Reflect

What are the most prominent roles you play? Which are achieved and which are ascribed? How do they affect your behavior? What conflicts do they create?

How has social comparison affected your behavior? Has it influenced who you associate with?

Think of a time when your attributions were affected by consistency and distinctiveness. Did situational demands also affect your judgments?

Have you ever engaged in self-handicapping? Try to relate the concept to a specific example.

How often do you commit the fundamental attribution error? Again, try to think of a specific personal example that illustrates the concept.

Answers: 1. T (so far) **2.** social situations or the presence of others **3.** ascribed **4.** F **5.** F **6.** F **7.** T **8.** T **9.** It is the idea that behavior is often strongly influenced by situations rather than by personal traits. **10.** Any point of light in the night sky may appear to move because of the autokinetic effect. This could cause a stationary light to look like it is flying or changing direction rapidly.

Attitudes—Belief + Emotion + Action

Gateway Questions 16.3: *What are attitudes and how are they acquired?*

What is your attitude toward affirmative action, euthanasia, environmental groups, the situation in the Middle East, the death penalty, legalized abortion, junk food, psychology? Your answers, which are often influenced by social situations, can have far-reaching effects on your behavior. Attitudes are intimately woven into our actions and views of the world. Our tastes, friendships, votes, preferences, goals, and behavior in many other situations are all touched by attitudes (Baumeister & Bushman, 2011). Let's see how attitudes are formed and changed.

What specifically is an attitude? An **attitude** is a mixture of belief and emotion that predisposes a person to respond to other people, objects, or groups in a positive or negative way. Attitudes summarize your *evaluation* of objects (Bohner & Dickel, 2010). As a result, they predict or direct future actions.

For example, a classic approach known as the *misdirected letter technique* shows how actions are closely linked to attitudes. During a period of violence in Northern Ireland, attitudes toward the Irish were measured in a sample of English households. Later, wrongly addressed letters were sent to the same households. Each letter had either an English name or an Irish name on it. The question was: Would the "Irish" letters be returned to the Post Office or thrown away? As predicted, letters were more often thrown away by people living in households in which anti-Irish attitudes had been measured earlier (Howitt et al., 1977).

"Your attitude is showing," is sometimes said. Actually, attitudes are expressed through beliefs, emotions, and actions. The **belief component** of an attitude is what you believe about a particular object or issue. The **emotional component** consists of your feelings toward the attitudinal object. The **action component** refers to your actions toward various people, objects, or institutions. Consider, for example, your attitude toward gun control. You will have beliefs about whether gun control would affect rates of crime or violence. You will respond emotionally to guns, finding them either attractive and desirable or threatening and destructive. And you will have a tendency to seek out or avoid gun ownership. The action component of your attitude may well include support of organizations that urge or oppose gun control. As you can see, attitudes orient us to the social world. In doing so, they prepare us to act in certain ways (Forgas, Cooper, & Crano, 2010). (For another example, see ● Figure 16.2.)

Forming Attitudes

How do people acquire attitudes? Attitudes are acquired in several basic ways. Sometimes, attitudes come from *direct contact* (personal experience) with the object of the attitude—such as opposing pollution when a nearby factory ruins your favorite river (Ajzen, 2005). Some attitudes are simply formed through chance conditioning (learning that takes place by chance or coincidence) (Albarracín, Johnson, & Zanna, 2005). Let's say, for instance, that you have had three encounters in your lifetime with psychologists. If all three were negative, you might take an unduly dim view of psychology. In the same way, people often develop strong attitudes toward cities, foods, or parts of the country on the basis of one or two unusually good or bad experiences.

Attitudes are also learned through *interaction with others*—that is, through discussion with people holding a particular attitude. For instance, if three of your good friends are volunteers at a local recycling center, and you talk with them about their beliefs, you may well come to favor recycling, too. More generally, there is little doubt that many of our attitudes are influenced by *group member-*

● Figure 16.2 Elements of positive and negative attitudes toward affirmative action.

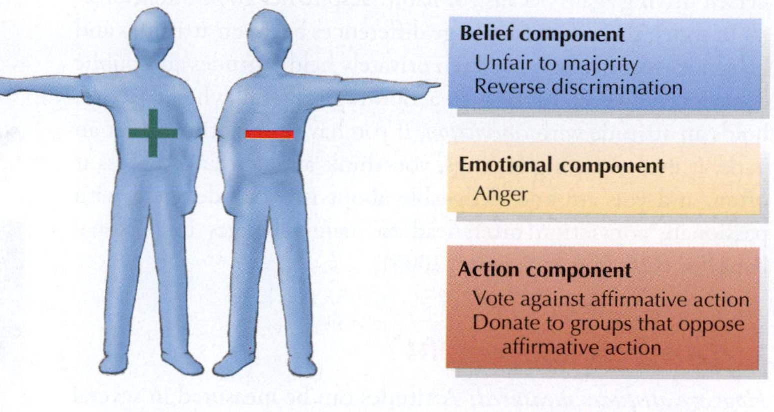

ship. In most groups, pressures to conform shape our attitudes, just as they do our behavior.

Child rearing (the effects of parental values, beliefs, and practices) also affects attitudes (Bartram, 2006). For example, if both parents belong to the same political party, chances are that their children will belong to that party as adults.

Finally, there can be no doubt that attitudes are influenced by the media, such as newspapers, television, and the Internet (Mahler, Beckerley, & Vogel, 2010). Every day we are coaxed, persuaded, and skillfully manipulated by messages in mass media. Young people today spend at least 50 hours a week immersed in media, such as television, video games, movies, the Internet, music, and print (Rideout, Foehr, & Roberts, 2010). The information thus channeled into homes has a powerful impact. For instance, frequent television viewers mistrust others and overestimate their own chances of being harmed. This suggests that a steady diet of TV violence leads some people to develop a *mean worldview*, in which they regard the world as a dangerous and threatening place (Eschholz, Chiricos, & Gertz, 2003).

Kevork Djansezian/Getty Images

Attitudes are an important dimension of social behavior. They are often greatly influenced by the attitudes of parents and the groups to which they belong.

BRIDGES

For more on media and observational learning, see Chapter 6, pages 231–233.

Attitudes and Behavior

Why are some attitudes acted on, whereas others are not? To answer this question, let's consider an example. Assume that a woman named Lorraine knows that automobiles are expensive to operate, add to air pollution, and she hates smog. Why would Lorraine continue to drive to work every day? Probably, it is because the *immediate consequences* of our actions weigh heavily on the choices we make. No matter what Lorraine's attitude may be, it is difficult for her to resist the immediate convenience of driving.

Our expectations of how *others will evaluate* our actions are also important. Lorraine may resist taking public transit to work for fear that her coworkers will be critical of her environmental stand. By taking this factor into account, researchers have been able to predict family planning choices, alcohol use by teenagers, re-enlistment in the National Guard, voting on a nuclear power plant initiative, and so forth (Cialdini, 2008). Finally, we must not overlook the effects of long-standing *habits* (Oskamp & Schultz, 2005). Let's say that after years of driving to work Lorraine finally vows to shift to public

Attitude A learned tendency to respond to people, objects, or institutions in a positive or negative way.

Belief component What a person thinks or believes about the object of an attitude.

Emotional component One's feelings toward the object of an attitude.

Action component How one tends to act toward the object of an attitude.

transit. Two months later, it would not be unusual if she found herself driving again because of habit, despite her good intentions.

In short, there are often large differences between attitudes and behavior—particularly between privately held attitudes and public behavior. However, barriers to action typically fall when a person holds an attitude with *conviction*. If you have **conviction** about an issue, it evokes strong feelings, you think about it and discuss it often, and you are knowledgeable about it. Attitudes held with passionate conviction often lead to major changes in personal behavior (Oskamp & Schultz, 2005).

Attitude Measurement

How are attitudes measured? Attitudes can be measured in several ways. In an **open-ended interview**, people are asked to freely express their attitudes toward a particular issue. For example, a person might be asked, "What do you think about freedom of speech on college campuses?" Attitudes toward social groups can be measured with a **social distance scale**. On such scales, people say how willing they are to admit members of a group to various levels of social closeness (Brown, 2011). These levels might include "would exclude from my country," "would rent a room to," or "would admit to marriage in my family." If a person has negative attitudes toward a group, she or he will prefer to remain socially distant from members of the group (Boyle, Blood, & Blood, 2009).

Attitude scales are a widely used measure. **Attitude scales** consist of statements expressing various possible views on an issue (for example, "Socialized medicine would destroy health care in this country," or "This country needs a national health care program"). People might respond to such statements on a 5-point scale, ranking it from "strongly agree" to "strongly disagree." By combining scores on all items, we can learn whether a person accepts or rejects a particular issue. When used in public polls, attitude scales provide useful information about the feelings of large segments of the population.

Attitude Change—Why the Seekers Went Public

Gateway Question 16.4: *Under what conditions is persuasion most effective and what is cognitive dissonance?*

Although attitudes are fairly stable, they do change (Forgas, Cooper, & Crano, 2010). Some attitude change can be understood in terms of **reference groups** (any group an individual uses as a standard for social comparison). It is not necessary to have face-to-face contact with other people for them to be a reference group. It depends instead on whom you identify with or whose attitudes and values you care about (Ajzen, 2005).

In the 1930s, Theodore Newcomb studied real-life attitude change among students at Bennington College (Alwin, Cohen, & Newcomb, 1991). Most students came from conservative homes, but Bennington was a very liberal school. Newcomb found that most students shifted significantly toward more liberal attitudes during their 4 years at Bennington. Those who didn't change kept their parents and hometown friends as primary reference groups. This is typified by a student who said, "I decided I'd rather stick to my father's ideas." Those who did change identified primarily with the campus community. Notice that all students could count the college and their families as *membership* groups. However, one group or the other tended to become their point of reference.

Do you exercise regularly? Like students in the Bennington study, your intentions to exercise are probably influenced by the exercise habits of your reference groups (Ajzen, 2005; Terry & Hogg, 1996).

Persuasion

What about advertising and other direct attempts to change attitudes? Are they effective? **Persuasion** is any deliberate attempt to change attitudes or beliefs through information and arguments (Brock & Green, 2005; Perloff, 2010). Businesses, politicians, and others who seek to persuade us obviously believe that attitudes can be changed. Billions of dollars are spent yearly on advertising in the United States and Canada alone. Persuasion can range from the daily blitz of media commercials to personal discussion among friends. In most cases, the success or failure of persuasion can be understood if we consider the *communicator*, the *message*, and the *audience*.

At a community meeting, let's say you have a chance to promote an issue important to you (for or against building a new mall nearby, for instance). Whom should you choose to make the presentation, and how should that person present it? Research suggests that attitude change is encouraged when the following conditions are met. You should have little trouble seeing how these principles are applied to sell everything from underarm deodorants to presidents:

1. The communicator is likable, expressive, trustworthy, an expert on the topic, and similar to the audience in some respect.
2. The communicator appears to have nothing to gain if the audience accepts the message.
3. The message appeals to emotions, particularly to fear or anxiety.

Persuasion. Would you be likely to be swayed by this group's message? Successful persuasion is related to characteristics of the communicator, the message, and the audience.

4. The message also provides a clear course of action that will, if followed, reduce fear or produce personally desirable results.
5. The message states clear-cut conclusions.
6. The message is backed up by facts and statistics.
7. The message is repeated as frequently as possible.
8. Both sides of the argument are presented in the case of a well-informed audience.
9. Only one side of the argument is presented in the case of a poorly informed audience.

(Aronson, 2008; Oskamp & Schultz, 2005; Perloff, 2010)

As we have just seen, we sometimes change our attitudes in response to external persuasion (Gass & Seiter, 2007). Sometimes, however, the internal process of *cognitive dissonance* can also lead to attitude change.

Cognitive Dissonance Theory

What happens if people act in ways that are inconsistent with their attitudes or self-images? *Cognitions* are thoughts. *Dissonance* means clashing. The influential theory of **cognitive dissonance** states that contradicting or clashing thoughts cause discomfort. That is, we have a need for *consistency* in our thoughts, perceptions, and images of ourselves (Cooper, 2007; Festinger, 1957). Inconsistency, then, can motivate people to make their thoughts or attitudes agree with their actions (Oskamp & Schultz, 2005).

For example, smokers are told on every pack that cigarettes endanger their lives. They light up and smoke anyway. How do they resolve the tension between this information and their actions? They could quit smoking, but it may be easier to convince themselves that smoking is not really so dangerous. To do this, a smoker might seek examples of heavy smokers who have lived long lives, spend time with other smokers, and avoid information about the link between smoking and cancer. According to cognitive dissonance theory, we also tend to reject new information that contradicts ideas we already hold. We're all guilty of this "don't bother me with the facts, my mind is made up" strategy at times.

A famous example of cognitive dissonance in action involves a woman named Mrs. Keech, who claimed she was in communication with beings on a planet called Clarion (Festinger, 1957). The messages foretold the destruction of North America. Mrs. Keech and her followers, the Seekers, were to be rescued by a flying saucer. The news media became involved and reported on the proceedings. When nothing happened, the Seekers suffered a bitter and embarrassing disappointment.

Did the group break up then? Amazingly, instead of breaking up, the Seekers became *more* convinced than ever before that they were right. Mrs. Keech announced that she had received a new message explaining that the Seekers had saved the world. Before, the Seekers were uninterested in persuading other people that the world was coming to an end. Now, they called newspapers and radio stations to convince others of their accomplishment.

Why did their belief in Mrs. Keech's messages *increase* after the world failed to end? Why did the group suddenly become interested in convincing others that they were right? Cognitive dissonance theory explains that after publicly committing themselves to their beliefs, they had a strong need to maintain consistency (Tavris & Aronson, 2007). In effect, convincing others was a way of adding proof that they were correct (see ■ Table 16.1).

Cognitive dissonance also underlies attempts to convince *ourselves* that we've done the right thing. Here's an example you may recognize: As romantic partners become better acquainted, they sooner or later begin to notice things they don't like about each

Conviction Beliefs that are important to a person and that evoke strong emotion.

Open-ended interview An interview in which persons are allowed to freely state their views.

Social distance scale A rating of the degree to which a person would be willing to have contact with a member of another group.

Attitude scale A collection of attitudinal statements with which respondents indicate agreement or disagreement.

Reference group Any group that an individual identifies with and uses as a standard for social comparison.

Persuasion A deliberate attempt to change attitudes or beliefs with information and arguments.

Cognitive dissonance An uncomfortable clash between self-image thoughts, beliefs, attitudes, or perceptions and one's behavior.

■ **TABLE 16.1 Strategies for Reducing Cognitive Dissonance**

LeShawn, who is a college student, has always thought of himself as an environmental activist. Recently, LeShawn "inherited" a car from his parents, who were replacing the family "barge." In the past, LeShawn biked or used public transportation to get around. His parents' old car is an antiquated gas-guzzler but he has begun to drive it every day. How might LeShawn reduce the cognitive dissonance created by the clash between his environmentalism and his use of an inefficient automobile?

Strategy	Example
Change your attitude	"Cars are not really a major environmental problem."
Add consonant thoughts	"This is an old car, so keeping it on the road makes good use of the resources consumed when it was manufactured."
Change the importance of the dissonant thoughts	"It's more important for me to support the environmental movement politically than it is to worry about how I get to school and work."
Reduce the amount of perceived choice	"My schedule has become too hectic, I really can't afford to bike or take the bus anymore."
Change your behavior	"I'm only going to use the car when it's impossible to bike or take the bus."

After Franzoi, 2002.

other. How do they reduce the cognitive dissonance and doubts caused by their partners' shortcomings? Basically, they create stories that change their partners' faults into virtues: He seems cheap, but he's really frugal; she seems egotistical, but she's really self-confident; he's not stubborn, he just has integrity; she's not undependable, she's a free spirit; and so on (Murray & Holmes, 1993).

Making choices often causes dissonance. Have you ever noticed how, once you've made a choice, it can be irksome to notice something positive about a rejected alternative (I should have bought the *blue* shirt; it had nicer buttons)? Welcome to *buyer's regret* (Godoy et al., 2010). To minimize such dissonance, we tend to emphasize positive aspects of what we choose, while downgrading other alternatives. Thus, you are more likely to think your college courses will be good *after* you have registered than you did before making a commitment.

Acting contrary to one's attitudes doesn't always bring about change. How does cognitive dissonance explain that? The amount of justification for acting contrary to your attitudes and beliefs affects how much dissonance you feel. (*Justification* is the degree to which a person's actions are explained by rewards or other circumstances.) In a classic study, college students did an extremely boring task (turning wooden pegs on a board) for a *long* time. Afterward, they were asked to help lure others into the experiment by pretending that the task was interesting and enjoyable. Students paid $20 for lying to others did not change their own negative opinion of the task: "That was *really* boring!" Those who were paid only $1 later rated the task as "pleasant" and "interesting." How can we explain these results? Apparently, students paid $20 experienced no dissonance. These students could reassure themselves that anybody would tell a little white lie for $20. Those paid $1 were faced with the conflicting thoughts: "I lied" and " I had no good reason to do it." Rather than admit to themselves that they had lied, these students changed their attitude toward what they had done (Festinger & Carlsmith, 1959; see ● Figure 16.3).

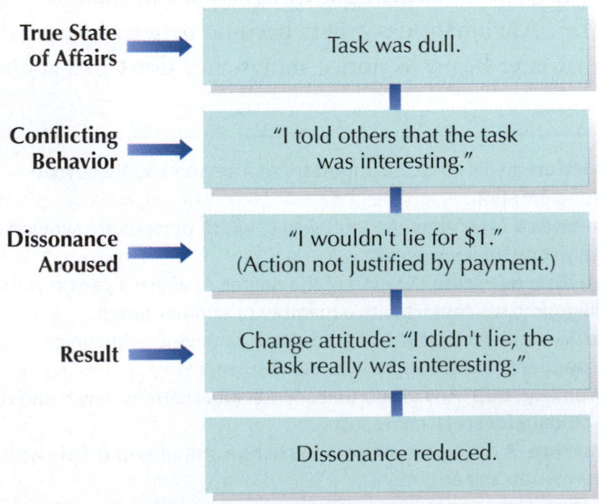

● **Figure 16.3** Summary of the Festinger and Carlsmith (1959) study from the viewpoint of a person experiencing cognitive dissonance.

Knowledge Builder

Attitudes and Attitude Change

RECITE

1. Attitudes have three parts, a ________________ component, an ________________ component, and an ________________ component.
2. Which of the following is associated with attitude formation?
   a. group membership *b.* mass media *c.* chance conditioning *d.* child rearing *e.* all of the preceding *f.* a and d only
3. Because of the immediate consequences of actions, behavior contrary to one's stated attitudes is often enacted. T or F?
4. Items such as "would exclude from my country" or "would admit to marriage in my family" are found in which attitude measure?
   a. a reference group scale *b.* a social distance scale *c.* an attitude scale *d.* an open-ended interview
5. In presenting a persuasive message, it is best to give both sides of the argument if the audience is already well informed on the topic. T or F?
6. Much attitude change is related to a desire to avoid clashing or contradictory thoughts, an idea summarized by ________________ ________________ theory.

REFLECT

Think Critically

7. Students entering a college gym are asked to sign a banner promoting water conservation. Later, the students shower at the gym. What effect would you expect signing the banner to have on how long students stay in the showers?
8. Cognitive dissonance theory predicts that false confessions obtained during brainwashing are not likely to bring about lasting changes in attitudes. Why?

Self-Reflect

Describe an attitude that is important to you. What are its three components?

Which of the various sources of attitudes best explain your own attitudes?

Who belongs to your most important reference group?

Imagine that you would like to persuade voters to support an initiative to preserve a small wilderness area by converting it to a park. Using research on persuasion as a guide, what could you do to be more effective?

How would you explain cognitive dissonance theory to a person who knows nothing about it?

Answers: 1. belief, emotional, action **2.** e **3.** T **4.** b **5.** T **6.** cognitive dissonance **7.** Cognitive dissonance theory predicts that students who sign the banner will take shorter showers to be consistent with their publicly expressed support of water conservation. This is exactly the result observed in a study done by social psychologist Elliot Aronson. **8.** Because there is strong justification for such actions, little cognitive dissonance is created when a prisoner makes statements that contradict his or her beliefs.

Social Influence—Follow the Leader

Gateway Question 16.5: *What is social influence and social power?*

No topic lies nearer the heart of social psychology than **social influence** (changes in behavior induced by the actions of others). When people interact, they almost always affect one another's behavior (Cialdini, 2008; Kassin, Fein, & Markus, 2011). For example, in a classic sidewalk experiment, various numbers of people stood on a busy New York City street. On cue, they all looked at a sixth-floor window across the street. A camera recorded how many passersby also stopped to stare. The larger the influencing group, the more people were swayed to join in staring at the window (Milgram, Bickman, & Berkowitz, 1969).

Are there different kinds of social influence? Social influence ranges from milder to stronger. The gentlest form of social influence is *mere presence* (changing behavior just because other people are nearby). We *conform* when we spontaneously change our behavior to bring it into agreement with others. Compliance is a more directed form of social influence. We *comply* when we change our behavior in response to another person who has little or no social power, or authority. Obedience is an even stronger form of social influence. We *obey* when we change our behavior in direct response to the demands of an authority. The strongest form of social influence is *coercion,* or changing behavior because you are forced to.

Social Power

The people we encounter on any given day vary in their power to influence us (Overbeck, 2010). Here's something to think about: Strength is a quality possessed by individuals; power is always social—it arises when people come together and disappears when they disperse. In trying to understand the ways in which people are able to influence one another, it is helpful to distinguish among five types of **social power** (the capacity to control, alter, or influence the behavior of another person) (Raven, 1974):

- **Reward power** lies in the ability to reward a person for complying with desired behavior. Teachers try to exert reward power over students with grades. Employers command reward power by their control of wages and bonuses.
- **Coercive power** is based on an ability to punish a person for failure to comply. Coercive power is the basis for most laws, in that fines or imprisonment are used to control behavior.
- **Legitimate power** comes from accepting a person as an agent of an established social order. For example, elected leaders and supervisors have legitimate power. So does a teacher in the classroom. Outside the classroom that power would have to come from another source.
- **Referent power** is based on respect for or identification with a person or a group. The person "refers to" the source of referent power for direction. Referent power is responsible for much of the conformity we see in groups.
- **Expert power** is based on recognition that another person has knowledge necessary for achieving a goal. We allow teachers, lawyers, and other experts to guide behavior because of their ability to produce desired results. Physicians, psychologists, programmers, and plumbers have expert power.

A person who has power in one situation may have very little in another. In those situations in which a person has power, she or he is described as an *authority*. Regardless of whether the people around you are authorities, friends, or strangers, their mere presence is likely to influence your behavior.

Social influence Changes in a person's behavior induced by the presence or actions of others.

Social power The capacity to control, alter, or influence the behavior of another person.

Reward power Social power based on the capacity to reward a person for acting as desired.

Coercive power Social power based on the ability to punish others.

Legitimate power Social power based on a person's position as an agent of an accepted social order.

Referent power Social power gained when one is used as a point of reference by others.

Expert power Social power derived from possession of knowledge or expertise.

Mere Presence—Just Because You Are There

Gateway Question 16.6: *How does the mere presence of others affect behavior?*

Suppose you just happened to be alone in a room, picking your nose (we know, none of us would do that, right?). Would you continue if a stranger entered the room? **Mere presence** refers to the tendency for people to change their behavior just because of the presence of other people. Let's explore some of the ways that mere presence can induce us to modify our behavior.

Social Facilitation and Loafing

Imagine you are out riding your mountain bike when another rider pulls up beside you. Will you pick up your pace? Slow down? Completely ignore the other rider? In 1898, psychologist Norman Triplett's investigation of just such a social situation was the first published social psychology experiment (Strubbe, 2005). According to Triplett, you are more likely to speed up. This is **social facilitation**, the tendency to perform better when in the presence of others.

Does mere presence always improve performance? No. If you are confident in your abilities, your behavior will most likely be facilitated in the presence of others. If you are not, your performance is more likely to be impaired (Uziel, 2007). Another classic study focused on college students shooting pool at a student union. Good players who were confident (sharks?) normally made 71 percent of their shots. Their accuracy improved to 80 percent when they were being watched by others. Less confident, average players (marks?) who normally made 36 percent of their shots dropped to 25 percent accuracy when someone was watching them (Michaels et al., 1982).

Social loafing is another consequence of having other people nearby. People tend to work less hard (loaf) when they are part of a group than they do when they are solely responsible for their work (Najdowski, 2010). In one study, people playing tug-of-war while blindfolded pulled harder if they thought they were competing alone. When they thought others were on their team, they made less of an effort (Ingham et al., 1974).

The use of space in public places is governed by unspoken norms, or "rules," about what is appropriate.

Personal Space

The next time you are talking with an acquaintance, move in closer and watch the reaction. Most people show signs of discomfort and step back to re-establish their original distance. Those who hold their ground may turn to the side, look away, or position an arm in front of themselves as a barrier. If you persistently edge toward your subjects, it should be easy to move them back several feet.

In this case, your mere (and close) presence amounted to an invasion of that person's **personal space**, an area surrounding the body that is regarded as private and subject to personal control (Novelli, Drury, & Reicher, 2010). Basically, personal space extends "I" or "me" boundaries past the skin to the immediate environment. Personal space is also illustrated by the fact that many train commuters prefer to stand up if it means they can avoid sitting too close to strangers (Evans & Wener, 2007). The systematic study of norms concerning the use of personal space is called **proxemics** (prok-SEE-miks) (Harrigan, 2005). Such norms may explain why people who feel offended by another person sometimes say, "Get out of my face."

Would approaching "too close" work with a good friend? Possibly not. Norms governing comfortable or acceptable distances vary according to relationships as well as activities. Hall (1966) identified four basic zones: *intimate*, *personal*, *social*, and *public* distance (● Figure 16.4).

● Figure 16.4 Typical spatial zones (in feet) for face-to-face interactions in North America. Often, we must stand within intimate distance of others in crowds, buses, subways, elevators, and other public places. At such times, privacy is maintained by avoiding eye contact, by standing shoulder-to-shoulder or back-to-back, and by positioning a purse, bag, package, or coat as a barrier to spatial intrusions.

Spatial Norms

Cultural differences also affect spatial norms. In many Middle Eastern countries, people hold their faces only inches apart while talking. In Western Europe, the English sit closer together when conversing than the French do. The Dutch, on the other hand, sit farther apart than the French (Remland, Jones, & Brinkman, 1991). In many parts of the world, merely crossing a border can dramatically change spatial behavior (Beaulieu, 2004). The distances listed below apply to face-to-face interactions in North America:

1. **Intimate distance.** For the majority of people, the most private and exclusive space extends about 18 inches out from the skin. Entry within this space (face to face) is reserved for special people or special circumstances. Lovemaking, comforting others, and cuddling children all take place within this space.
2. **Personal distance.** This is the distance maintained in comfortable interaction with friends. It extends from about 18 inches to 4 feet from the body. Personal distance basically keeps people within "arm's reach" of one another.
3. **Social distance.** Impersonal business and casual social gatherings take place in a range of about 4 to 12 feet. This distance eliminates most touching, and it formalizes conversation by requiring greater voice projection. "Important people" in many business offices use the imposing width of their desks to maintain social distance. A big smelly cigar helps, too.
4. **Public distance.** This is the distance at which formal interactions occur (about 12 feet or more from the body). When people are separated by more than 12 feet, people look "flat" and they must raise their voices to speak to one another. Formal speeches, lectures, business meetings, and the like are conducted at public distance.

Because spatial behavior is very consistent, you can learn about your relationship to others by observing the distance you comfortably hold between yourselves. But remember to be aware of cultural differences. When two people of different nationalities have different norms for personal space, both are likely to be uncomfortable when talking, as one tries to move closer and the other keeps moving back. This can lead to misunderstandings in which one person feels that the other is being too familiar at the same time as the person moving closer feels rejected (Beaulieu, 2004).

Whereas mere presence can influence our behavior in a variety of ways, conformity involves a more specific response to the presence of others.

Conformity—Don't Stand Out

Gateway Question 16.7: *What have social psychologists learned about conformity?*

We **conform** when we bring our behavior into agreement with the actions, norms, or values of others in the absence of any direct pressure. When Harry met Sally they fell in love and were not shy about expressing themselves around campus. Some students in Harry's classes advised him to be a bit more discreet. Increasingly, Sally noticed other students staring at her and Harry when they were, well, expressing their love. Although they never made a conscious decision to conform, in another week their publicly

Conformity is a subtle dimension of daily life. Notice the similarities in the clothing worn by this group of friends.

intimate moments were a thing of the past. Perhaps the most basic of all group norms is, as Harry and Sally discovered, "Thou shalt conform." Like it or not, life is filled with instances of conformity. Daily behavior is probably most influenced by group pressures for conformity (Baron, Byrne, & Branscombe, 2009).

As mentioned earlier, all groups have unspoken rules of conduct called *norms*. The broadest norms, defined by society as a whole, establish "normal" or acceptable behavior in most situations. Comparing hairstyles, habits of speech, dress, eating habits, and social customs in two or more cultures makes it clear that we all conform to social norms. In fact, a degree of uniformity is necessary if we are to interact comfortably. Imagine being totally unable to anticipate the actions of others. In stores, schools, and homes this would be frustrating and disturbing. On the highways, it would be lethal.

Mere presence The tendency for people to change their behavior just because of the presence of other people.

Social facilitation The tendency to perform better when in the presence of others.

Social loafing The tendency of people to work less hard when part of a group than when they are solely responsible for their work.

Personal space An area surrounding the body that is regarded as private and subject to personal control.

Proxemics Systematic study of the human use of space, particularly in social settings.

Intimate distance The most private space immediately surrounding the body (up to about 18 inches from the skin).

Personal distance The distance maintained when interacting with close friends (about 18 inches to 4 feet from the body).

Social distance Distance at which impersonal interaction takes place (about 4 to 12 feet from the body).

Public distance Distance at which formal interactions, such as giving a speech, occur (about 12 feet or more from the body).

Conformity Bringing one's behavior into agreement or harmony with norms or with the behavior of others in a group.

Critical Thinking Groupthink—Agreement at Any Cost

Yale psychologist Irving Janis (1918–1990) first proposed the concept of groupthink in an attempt to understand a series of disastrous decisions made by government officials (Janis, 1989, 2007). The core of **groupthink** is misguided loyalty—an urge by decision makers to maintain each other's approval, even at the cost of critical thinking (Singer, 2005). Group members are hesitant to "rock the boat," question sloppy thinking, or tolerate alternative views. This self-censorship leads people to believe they agree more than they actually do (Henningsen et al., 2006; Whyte, 2000).

Groupthink has been blamed for contributing to many crises, such as the invasion and occupation of Iraq (Houghton, 2008; Singer, 2005), the *Columbia* space shuttle disaster in 2003, and the loss of the $165 million *Mars Climate Orbiter* in 1999. An analysis of 19 international crises found that groupthink contributed to most (Schafer & Crichlow, 1996).

To prevent groupthink, group leaders should take the following steps:

- Define each group member's role as a "critical evaluator."
- Avoid revealing any personal preferences in the beginning. State the problem factually, without bias.
- Invite a group member or outside person to play devil's advocate. Make it clear that group members will be held accountable for decisions.
- Encourage open inquiry and a search for alternate solutions (Baron, 2005; Janis, 2007)

In addition, Janis suggested that there should be a "second-chance" meeting to re-evaluate important decisions; that is, each decision should be reached twice.

In fairness to our decision makers, it is worth noting that the presence of too many alternatives can lead to *deadlock*, which can delay taking necessary action (Kowert, 2002). Regardless, in an age clouded by the threat of war, global warming, and terrorism, even stronger solutions to the problem of groupthink would be welcome. Perhaps we should form a group to think about it!

The Asch Experiment

How strong are group pressures for conformity? One of the first experiments on conformity was staged by Solomon Asch (1907–1996). To fully appreciate it, imagine yourself as a subject. Assume that you are seated at a table with six other students. Your task is actually quite simple: You are shown three lines on a card and you must select the line that matches a "standard" line (● Figure 16.5).

As the testing begins, each person announces an answer for the first card. When your turn comes, you agree with the others. "This isn't hard at all," you say to yourself. For several more trials, your answers agree with those of the group. Then comes a shock: All six people announce that line 1 matches the standard, and you were about to say line 2 matches. Suddenly, you feel alone and upset. You nervously look at the lines again. The room falls silent. Everyone seems to be staring at you. The experimenter awaits your answer. Do you yield to the group?

In this study, the other "students" were all actors who gave the wrong answer on about a third of the trials to create group pressure (Asch, 1956). Real students conformed to the group on about one third of the critical trials. Of those tested, 75 percent yielded at least once. People who were tested alone erred in less than 1 percent of their judgments. Clearly, those who yielded to group pressures were denying what their eyes told them.

Are some people more susceptible to group pressures than others? People with high needs for structure or certainty are more likely to conform. So are people who are anxious, low in self-confidence or concerned with the approval of others. People who live in cultures that emphasize group cooperation (such as many Asian cultures) are also more likely to conform (Bond & Smith, 1996; Fu et al., 2007).

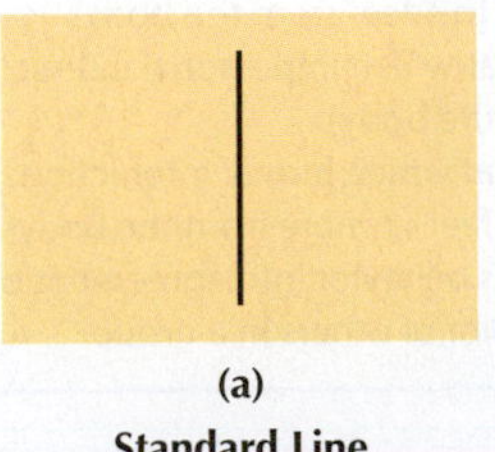

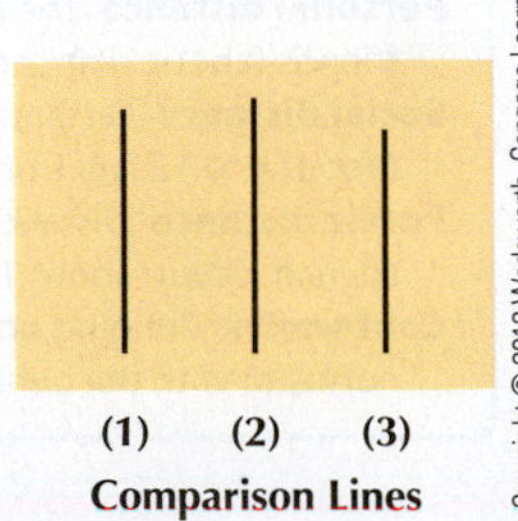

● Figure 16.5 Stimuli used in Solomon Asch's conformity experiments.

In addition to personal characteristics, certain situations tend to encourage conformity—sometimes with disastrous results. "Groupthink—Agreement at Any Cost" offers a prime example.

Group Factors in Conformity

How do groups enforce norms? In most groups, we have been rewarded with acceptance and approval for conformity and threatened with rejection or ridicule for nonconformity. These reactions are called **group sanctions**. Negative sanctions range from laughter, staring, or social disapproval to complete rejection or formal exclusion. If you've ever felt the sudden chill of disapproval by others, you will understand the power of group sanctions—just as Harry and Sally did.

Wouldn't the effectiveness of group sanctions depend on the importance of the group? Yes. The more important group membership is to a person, the more he or she will be influenced by other group members. The risk of being rejected can be a threat to our sense of personal identity (Cialdini, 2008). That's why the Asch experiments are impressive. Because these were only temporary groups, sanctions were informal and rejection had no lasting importance. Just the same, the power of the group was evident.

What other factors, besides importance of the group, affect the degree of conformity? In the sidewalk experiment described earlier, we noted that large groups had more influence. In Asch's face-to-face groups, the size of the majority also made a difference, but a surprisingly small one. In other studies, the number of people who conformed increased dramatically as the majority grew from two to three people. However, a majority of three produced about as much yielding as a majority of eight. The next time you want to talk someone into (or out of) something, take two friends along and see what a difference it makes! (Sometimes it helps if the two are large and mean looking.)

Even more important than the size of the majority is its *unanimity* (total agreement). Having at least one person in your corner can greatly reduce pressures to conform. When Asch gave participants an ally (who also opposed the majority by giving the correct answer), conformity was lessened. In terms of numbers, a unanimous majority of three is more powerful than a majority of eight with one dissenting. Perhaps this accounts for the rich diversity of human attitudes, beliefs, opinions, and lifestyles. If you can find at least one other person who sees things as you do (no matter how weird), you can be relatively secure in your opposition to other viewpoints. Incidentally, the Internet now makes it much easier to find that other like-minded person.

Knowledge Builder: Social Influence, Mere Presence, and Conformity

RECITE

1. The effect one person's behavior has on another is called ____________ ____________.
2. The mere presence of others always improves performance. T or F?
3. If two people position themselves 5 feet apart while conversing, they are separated by a gap referred to as ____________ distance.
4. Conformity is a normal aspect of social life. T or F?
5. Participants in Solomon Asch's conformity study yielded on about 75 percent of the critical trials. T or F?
6. Nonconformity is punished by negative group ____________.
7. Janis used the term ____________ to describe a compulsion among decision-making groups to maintain an illusion of unanimity.

REFLECT

Think Critically

8. Would it be possible to be completely nonconforming (that is, to not conform to any group norms)?

Self-Reflect

How do you feel about participating in group projects at college? Have you ever encountered a social loafer? (*You* were never one, right?) How did you react?

Identify a recent time when you conformed in some way. How did norms, group pressure, sanctions, and unanimity contribute to your tendency to conform?

What group sanctions have you experienced? What sanctions have you applied to others?

Have you ever been part of a group that seemed to make a bad decision because of groupthink? How could the group have avoided its mistake?

Answers: 1. social influence **2.** F **3.** social **4.** T **5.** F **6.** sanctions **7.** groupthink **8.** A person who did not follow at least some norms concerning social behavior would very likely be perceived as extremely bizarre, disturbed, or psychotic.

Compliance—A Foot in the Door

Gateway Question 16.8: *What factors lead to increased compliance?*

Pressures to "fit in" and conform are usually indirect. In contrast, the term **compliance** refers to situations in which one person bends to the requests of another person who has little or no authority (Cialdini, 2008). These more direct pressures to comply are quite common. You *passively comply* when, for example, you suffer, without protest, someone smoking near you in a nonsmoking zone or talking loudly while you are trying to study in the library. You *actively comply* when, for example, you hand over your cell phone to stranger who asks to borrow it to make a call or loan money to a coworker who requests it to buy a cappuccino.

Groupthink A compulsion by members of decision-making groups to maintain agreement, even at the cost of critical thinking.

Group sanctions Rewards and punishments (such as approval or disapproval) administered by groups to enforce conformity among members.

Compliance Bending to the requests of a person who has little or no authority or other form of social power.

What determines whether a person will comply with a request? Many factors could be listed, but three stand out as especially interesting (Cialdini & Griskevicius, 2010). We are more likely to comply with a request if it:

1. Comes from someone we know rather than a stranger.
2. Is consistent with our previous actions.
3. Allows us to reciprocate a prior gift, favor, or service.

These factors allow us to better understand several strategies that can be used to gain compliance. Since strangers must work harder to gain compliance, salespeople depend heavily on appealing to your tendency to be consistent and to reciprocate.

The Foot-in-the-Door Effect

People who sell door to door have long recognized that once they get a foot in the door, a sale is almost a sure thing. To state the **foot-in-the-door effect** more formally, a person who first agrees to a small request is later more likely, to be consistent, to comply with a larger demand (Guéguen et al., 2008). For instance, if someone asked you to put a large, ugly sign in your front yard to promote safe driving, you would probably refuse. If, however, you had first agreed to put a small sign in your window, you would later be much more likely to allow the big sign in your yard.

The Door-in-the-Face Effect

Let's say that a neighbor comes to your door and asks you to feed his dogs, water his plants, and mow his yard while he is out of town for a month. This is quite a major request—one that most people would probably turn down. Feeling only slightly guilty, you tell your neighbor that you're sorry but you can't help him. Now, what if the same neighbor returns the next day and asks if you would at least pick up his mail while he is gone. Chances are very good that you would honor this request, even if you might have originally turned it down, too.

Psychologist Robert Cialdini coined the term **door-in-the-face effect** to describe the tendency for a person who has refused a major request to agree to a smaller request. In other words, after a person has turned down a major request ("slammed the door in your face"), he or she may be more willing to comply with a lesser demand. This strategy works because a person who abandons a large request appears to have given up something. In response, many people feel that they must reciprocate by giving in to the smaller request (Cialdini, 2008; Cialdini & Goldstein, 2004). In fact, a good way to get another person to comply with a request is to first do a small favor for the person.

The Lowball Technique

Anyone who has purchased an automobile will recognize a third way of inducing compliance. Automobile dealers are notorious for convincing customers to buy cars by offering "lowball" prices that undercut the competition. The dealer first gets the customer to agree to buy at an attractively low price. Then, once the customer is committed, various techniques are used to bump the price up before the sale is concluded.

The **lowball technique** consists of getting a person committed to act and then making the terms of acting less desirable (Guéguen, Pascual, & Dagot, 2002). In this case, since you have already complied with a large request, it would be inconsistent to deny the follow-on smaller additional request. Here's another example: A fellow student asks to borrow $25 for a day. This seems reasonable and you agree. However, once you have given your classmate the money, he explains that it would be easier to repay you after payday, in 2 weeks. If you agree, you've succumbed to the lowball technique. Here's another example: Let's say you ask someone to give you a ride to school in the morning. Only after the person has agreed do you tell her that you have to be there at 6 A.M.

One of the main benefits of knowing these strategies is that you can protect yourself from being manipulated by people using them. For example, "The Car Game" explains how car salespersons use compliance techniques on customers.

In the next section we will investigate **obedience**, a special type of conformity to the demands of an authority. You've probably seen a bumper sticker that says "Question authority." Actually, that's not bad advice if it means "Think critically." However, obedience to authority is a normal part of social life. But what are the limits of obedience? When is it appropriate to resist authority? These are essential questions about how we are affected by social influence based on authority.

Obedience—Would You Electrocute a Stranger?

Gateway Question 16.9: *Can people be too obedient?*

The question is this: If ordered to do so, would you shock a man with a heart condition who is screaming and asking to be released? Certainly, few people would obey. Or would they? In Nazi Germany, obedient soldiers (once average citizens) helped slaughter more than 6 million people in concentration camps. Do such inhumane acts reflect deep character flaws? Are they the acts of heartless psychopaths or crazed killers? Or are they simply the result of obedience to authority? These are questions that puzzled social psychologist Stanley Milgram (1965) when he began a provocative series of studies on obedience.

How did Milgram study obedience? As was true of the Asch experiments, Milgram's research is best appreciated by imagining yourself as a subject. Place yourself in the following situation.

Discovering Psychology The Car Game

Your local car lot is a good place to study compliance. Automobile salespersons play the compliance game daily and get very good at it. If you understand what they are up to, and you are able to critically evaluate their tactics, you will have a far better chance of resisting their sales pressure (Cialdini, 2008; Cialdini & Goldstein, 2004).

A Foot in the Door

The salesperson offers you a test drive. If you accept, you will have made a small commitment of time to a particular car and to the salesperson. The salesperson will then ask you to go to an office and fill out some papers, "just to see what kind of a price" she or he can offer. If you go along, you will be further committed.

The Low-Ball Technique

To get things underway, the salesperson will offer you a very good price for your trade-in or will ask you to make an offer on the new car, "any offer, no matter how low." The salesperson will then ask if you will buy the car if she or he can sell it for the price you state. If you say yes, you have virtually bought the car. Most people find it very difficult to walk away once bargaining has reached this stage.

The Hook Is Set

Once buyers are "hooked" by a low-ball offer, the salesperson goes to the manager to have the sale "approved." On returning, the salesperson will tell you with great disappointment that the dealership would lose money on the deal. "Couldn't you just take a little less for the trade-in or pay a little more for the car?" the salesperson will ask. At this point many people hesitate and grumble, but most give in and accept some "compromise" price or trade-in amount.

Evening the Odds

To combat all of the preceding, you must arm yourself with accurate information. In the past, salespeople had a great advantage in negotiating because they knew exactly how much the dealership paid for each car. Now, you can obtain detailed automobile pricing information on the Internet. With such information in hand, you will find it easier to challenge a salesperson's manipulative tactics.

After you've negotiated a final "best offer," get it in writing. Then walk out. Go to another dealer and see if the salesperson will better the price, in writing. When he or she does, return to the first dealership and negotiate for an even better price. Then decide where to buy. Now that you know some of the rules of the "Car Game," you might even enjoy playing it.

Milgram's Obedience Studies

Imagine answering a newspaper ad to take part in a "learning" experiment at Yale University. When you arrive, a coin is flipped and a second subject, a pleasant-looking man in his fifties, is designated the "learner." By chance, you have become the "teacher."

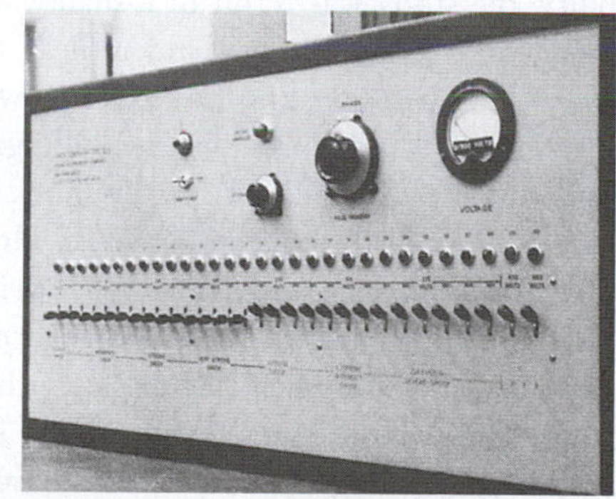

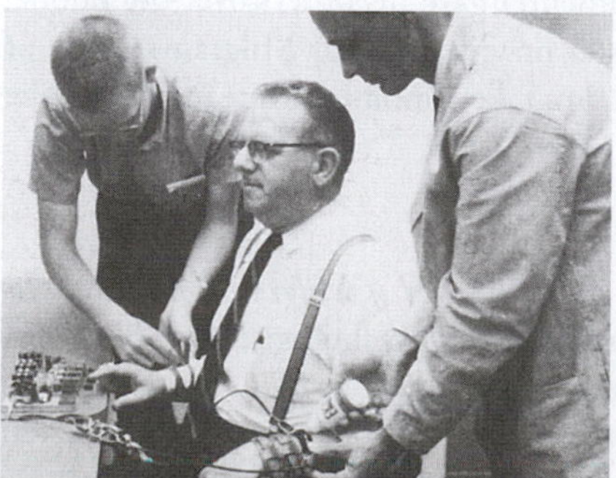

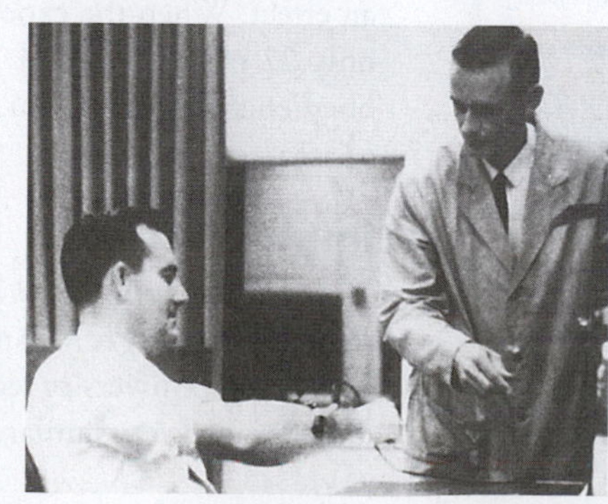

• **Figure 16.6** Scenes from Stanley Milgram's study of obedience: the "shock generator," strapping a "learner" into his chair, and a "teacher" being told to administer a severe shock to the learner. Scenes from the film "Obedience," by Stanley Milgram, The Pennsylvania State University, Audio Visual Services. Used by permission.

Your task is to read a list of word pairs. The learner's task is to memorize them. You are to punish him with an electric shock each time he makes a mistake. The learner is taken to an adjacent room and you watch as he is seated in an "electric chair" apparatus. Electrodes are attached to his wrists. You are then escorted to your position in front of a "shock generator." On this device is a row of 30 switches marked from 15 to 450 volts. Corresponding labels range from "Slight Shock" to "Extreme Intensity Shock" and finally "Danger: Severe Shock." Your instructions are to shock the learner each time he makes a mistake. You must begin with 15 volts and then move one switch (15 volts) higher for each additional mistake (• Figure 16.6).

The experiment begins, and the learner soon makes his first error. You flip a switch. More mistakes. Rapidly, you reach the 75-volt level. The learner moans after each shock. At 100 volts, he complains that he has a heart condition. At 150 volts, he says he no

Foot-in-the-door effect The tendency for a person who has first complied with a small request to be more likely later to fulfill a larger request.

Door-in-the-face effect The tendency for a person who has refused a major request to subsequently be more likely to comply with a minor request.

Low-ball technique A strategy in which commitment is gained first to reasonable or desirable terms, which are then made less reasonable or desirable.

Obedience Conformity to the demands of an authority.

Discovering Psychology: Moo Like a Cow

Imagine your response to the following events. On the first day of class, your psychology professor begins to establish the basic rules of behavior for the course. Draw a line under the first instruction you think you would refuse to carry out:

1. Seats are assigned and you are told to move to a new location.
2. You are told not to talk during class.
3. Your professor tells you that you must have permission to leave early.
4. You are told to bring your textbook to class at all times.
5. Your professor tells you to use only a pencil for taking notes.
6. You are directed to take off your watch.
7. The professor tells you to keep both hands on your desktop at all times.
8. You are instructed to keep both of your feet flat on the floor.
9. You are told to stand up and clap your hands three times.
10. Your professor says, "Stick two fingers up your nose and moo like a cow."

At what point would you stop obeying such orders? In reality, you might find yourself obeying a legitimate authority long after that person's demands had become unreasonable (Aronson, Wilson, & Akert, 2010). What would happen, though, if a few students resisted orders early in the sequence? Would that help free others to disobey? For an answer, return to the discussion of Milgram's experiment for some final remarks.

longer wants to continue and demands to be released. At 300 volts, he screams and says he can no longer give answers.

At some point, you begin to protest to the experimenter. "That man has a heart condition," you say; "I'm not going to kill that man." The experimenter says, "Please continue." Another shock and another scream from the learner and you say, "You mean I've got to keep going up the scale? No, sir. I'm not going to give him 450 volts!" The experimenter says, "The experiment requires that you continue." For a time, the learner refuses to answer any more questions and screams with each shock (Milgram, 1965). Then, he falls chillingly silent for the rest of the experiment.

It's hard to believe many people would do this. What happened? Milgram also doubted that many people would obey his orders. When he polled a group of psychiatrists before the experiment, they predicted that less than 1 percent of those tested would obey. The astounding fact is that 65 percent obeyed completely by going all the way to the 450-volt level. Virtually no one stopped short of 300 volts ("Severe Shock") (● Figure 16.7).

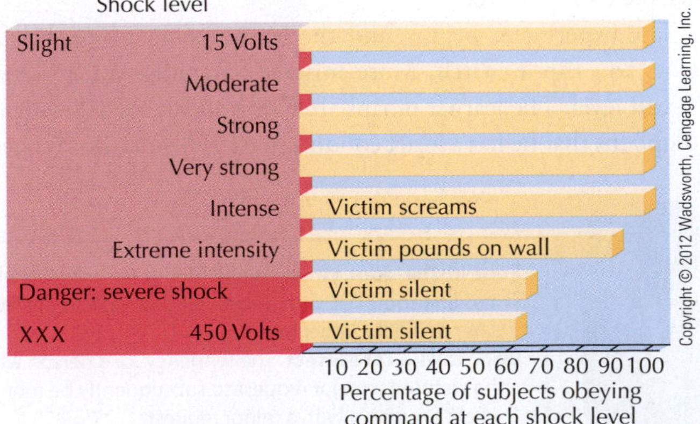

● Figure 16.7 Results of Milgram's obedience experiment. Only a minority of participants refused to provide shocks, even at the most extreme intensities. The first substantial drop in obedience occurred at the 300-volt level (Milgram, 1963).

Was the learner injured? The "learner" was actually an actor who turned a tape recorder on and off in the shock room. No shocks were ever administered, but the dilemma for the "teacher" was quite real. Participants protested, sweated, trembled, stuttered, bit their lips, and laughed nervously. Clearly, they were disturbed by what they were doing. Nevertheless, most obeyed the experimenter's orders.

Milgram's Follow-Up

Why did so many people obey? Some have suggested that the prestige of Yale University added to participants' willingness to obey. Could it be that they assumed the professor running the experiment would not really allow anyone to be hurt? To test this possibility, the study was rerun in a shabby office building in nearby Bridgeport, Connecticut. Under these conditions, fewer people obeyed (48 percent), but the reduction was minor.

Milgram was disturbed by the willingness of people to knuckle under to authority and senselessly shock someone. In later experiments, he tried to reduce obedience. He found that the distance between the teacher and the learner was important. When participants were in the *same room* as the learner, only 40 percent fully obeyed. When they were *face-to-face* with the learner and required to force his hand down on a simulated "shock plate," only 30 percent obeyed (● Figure 16.8). Distance from the authority also had an effect. When the experimenter gave his orders over the phone, only 22 percent obeyed. You may doubt that Milgram's study of obedience applies to you. If so, take a moment to read "Moo Like a Cow."

Implications

Surely people wouldn't act the same way if Milgram conducted his research today, right? Don't be so sure. Psychologist Jerry Burger of Santa Clara University recently partially replicated Milgram's study and obtained very similar results (Burger, 2009). Milgram's research

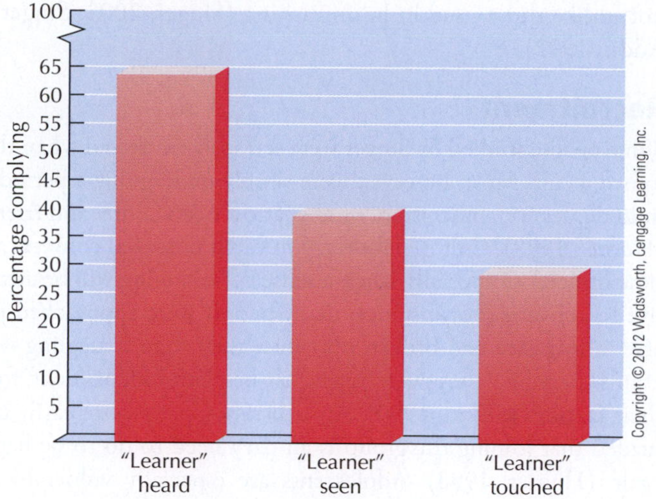

● **Figure 16.8** Physical distance from the "learner" had a significant effect on the percentage of participants obeying orders.

raises nagging questions about our willingness to commit antisocial or inhumane acts commanded by a "legitimate authority." The excuse so often given by war criminals—"I was only following orders"—takes on new meaning in this light. Milgram suggested that when directions come from an authority, people rationalize that they are not personally responsible for their actions. In locales as diverse as Cambodia, Rwanda, Bosnia, Vietnam, Darfur, Sri Lanka, and Iraq, the tragic result has been "sanctioned massacres" of chilling proportions.

Even in everyday life, crimes of obedience are common (Zimbardo, 2007). For example, in order to keep their jobs, many people obey orders to do things that they know are dishonest, unethical, or harmful.

Isn't that an overly negative view of obedience? Obedience to authority is obviously necessary and desirable in many circumstances. Just the same, it is probably true, as C. P. Snow (1961) observed, "When you think of the long and gloomy history of man, you will find more hideous crimes have been committed in the name of obedience than in the name of rebellion." With this in mind, let's end on a more positive note. In one of his experiments, Milgram found that group support can greatly reduce destructive obedience. When real participants saw two other "teachers" (both actors) resist orders and walk out of the experiment, only 10 percent continued to obey. Thus, a personal act of courage or moral fortitude by one or two members of a group may free others to disobey misguided or unjust authority.

Coercion—Brainwashing and Cults

Gateway Question 16.10: *Is brainwashing actually possible and is that how people are converted to cult membership?*

We close this section on social influence by examining some forms of *coercion*, the most extreme type of social influence. You are being **coerced** if you are forced to change your beliefs or your behavior against your will (Baumeister & Bushman, 2011; Reidy & Riker, 2008).

If you're a history enthusiast, you may associate *brainwashing* with techniques used by the Communist Chinese on prisoners during the Korean War (Jowett, 2006). Through various types of "thought reform," the Chinese were able to coerce some of these prisoners to sign false confessions. More recently, the mass murder/suicide at Jonestown, the Branch Davidian tragedy at Waco, the Heaven's Gate group suicide in San Diego, and Osama bin Laden's al-Qaeda movement have heightened public interest in coerced attitude and behavior change.

Brainwashing

How does brainwashing differ from other persuasive techniques? As we have noted, advertisers, politicians, educators, religious organizations, and others actively seek to alter attitudes and opinions. To an extent, their persuasive efforts resemble brainwashing, but there is an important difference: **Brainwashing**, or forced attitude change, requires a captive audience. If you are offended by a television commercial, you can tune it out. Prisoners in the POW camps are completely at the mercy of their captors. Complete control over the environment allows a degree of psychological manipulation that would be impossible in a normal setting.

How does captivity facilitate coercion? Brainwashing typically begins by making the target person feel completely helpless. Physical and psychological abuse, lack of sleep, humiliation, and isolation serve to *unfreeze*, or loosen, former values and beliefs. When exhaustion, pressure, and fear become unbearable, *change* occurs as the person begins to abandon former beliefs. Prisoners who reach the breaking point may sign a false confession or cooperate to gain relief. When they do, they are suddenly rewarded with praise, privileges, food, or rest. From that point on, a mixture of hope and fear, plus pressures to conform, serves to *refreeze* (solidify) new attitudes (Taylor, 2004).

How permanent are changes coerced by brainwashing? In most cases, the dramatic shift in attitudes brought about by brainwashing is temporary. Most "converted" prisoners who returned to the United States after the Korean War eventually reverted to their original beliefs. Nevertheless, brainwashing can be powerful, as shown by the success of cults in recruiting new members.

Cults

Exhorted by their leader, some 900 members of the Reverend Jim Jones's People's Temple picked up paper cups and drank purple Kool-Aid laced with the deadly poison cyanide. Some even forced their own children to join in. Psychologically, the mass suicide at

Coercion Being forced to change your beliefs or your behavior against your will.

Brainwashing Engineered or forced attitude change involving a captive audience.

© Greg Smith/Corbis

In April 1993, David Koresh and 75 members (including 21 children) of his Branch Davidian group perished in an inferno at their Waco, Texas, compound. Authorities believe the fire was set by a cult member, under the direction of Koresh. Like Jim Jones had done years before in Jonestown, Koresh took nearly total control of his followers' lives.

Jonestown in 1978 is not so incredible as it might seem (Dein & Littlewood, 2005). The inhabitants of Jonestown were isolated in the jungles of Guyana, intimidated by guards, and lulled with sedatives. They were also cut off from friends and relatives and totally accustomed to obeying rigid rules of conduct, which primed them for Jones's final "loyalty test." Of greater psychological interest is the question of how people reach such a state of commitment and dependency.

Why do people join groups such as the People's Temple? The People's Temple was a classic example of a **cult**, an authoritarian group in which the leader's personality is more important than the beliefs she or he preaches. Cult members give their allegiance to this person, who is regarded as infallible, and they follow his or her dictates without question. Almost always, cult members are victimized by their leaders in one way or another.

For example, in April 1993, David Koresh and members of his Branch Davidian group perished in a fire at their Waco, Texas, compound. As Jim Jones had done years before in Jonestown, Koresh took nearly total control of his followers' lives. He told them what to eat, dictated sexual mores, and had errant followers paddled. Followers were persuaded to surrender money, property, and even their children and wives. Like Jones, Koresh also took mistresses and had children out of wedlock. And like other cult leaders, Jones and Koresh demanded absolute loyalty and obedience to themselves and to their cult, with tragic results (Dein & Littlewood, 2005; Reiterman, 1993).

Psychologist and pioneering brainwashing expert Margaret Singer (1921–2003) studied and aided hundreds of former cult members. Her interviews reveal that in recruiting new members, cults use a powerful blend of guilt, manipulation, isolation, deception, fear, and escalating commitment. In this respect, cults employ high-pressure indoctrination techniques not unlike those used in brainwashing (Singer, 2003; Singer & Addis, 1992).

Recruitment

Some people studied by Singer were seriously distressed when they joined a cult. Most, however, were simply undergoing a period of mild depression, indecision, or alienation from family and friends (Hunter, 1998). Cult members try to catch potential converts at a time of need—especially when a sense of belonging will be attractive to converts. For instance, many people were approached just after a romance had broken up, when they were struggling with exams, or when they were trying to become independent from their families (Sirkin, 1990). At such times, people are easily persuaded that joining the group is all they need to do to be happy again (Hunter, 1998). Adolescents are especially vulnerable to recruitment into cults as they may be seeking a cause to conform to as a replacement for the parental authority they are rebelling against (Richmond, 2004).

BRIDGES

People suffering from identity confusion, which is common during adolescence, are more susceptible to recruitment by coercive groups. **See Chapter 3, pages 107–109, 112.**

Conversion

How is conversion achieved? Often it begins with intense displays of affection and understanding ("love bombing"). Next comes isolation from noncult members and drills, discipline, and rituals (all-night meditation or continuous chanting, for instance). These rituals wear down physical and emotional resistance, discourage critical thinking, and generate feelings of commitment (Langone, 2002).

Many cults make clever use of the foot-in-the-door technique (described previously). At first, recruits make small commitments (to stay after a meeting, for example). Then, larger commitments are encouraged (to stay an extra day, to call in sick at work, and so forth). Making a major commitment is usually the final step. The new devotee signs over a bank account or property to the group, moves in with the group, and so forth. Making such major public commitments creates a powerful cognitive dissonance effect. Before long, it becomes virtually impossible for converts to admit they have made a mistake.

Once in the group, members are cut off from family and friends (former reference groups), and the cult can control the flow and interpretation of information to them. Members are isolated from their former value systems and social structures. Conversion is complete when they come to think of themselves more as group members than as individuals. At this point obedience is nearly total (Wexler, 1995).

Why do people stay in cults? Most former members mention guilt and fear as the main reasons for not leaving when they wished they could. Most had been reduced to childlike dependency on the

© Bettmann/Corbis

Aftermath of the mass suicide of over 900 people at Jonestown. How do cult-like groups recruit new devotees?

group for meeting all their daily needs (Singer, 2003). After they leave, many former cult members suffer from anxiety, panic attacks, and emotional disturbances much like post-traumatic stress disorder (West, 1993).

Implications

Behind the "throne" from which Jim Jones ruled Jonestown was a sign bearing these words: "Those who do not remember the past are condemned to repeat it." Sadly, another cult-related tragedy occurred in 2001. The terrorist attacks on the United States were carried out by followers of cult leader Osama bin Laden (Olsson, 2007, 2008). At his direction, they learned hatred and contempt for everyone outside their band of true believers. If there is a lesson to be learned from such destructive cults, it is this: All true spiritual leaders have taught love and compassion. They also encourage followers to question their beliefs and to reach their own conclusions about how to live. In contrast, destructive cults show how dangerous it is to trade personal independence and critical thinking for security (Cowan & Bromley, 2008; Goldberg, 2001).

A Look Ahead

In the upcoming discussion of *Psychology in Action*, we will return to the problem of passive behavior to learn how you can better handle difficult social situations. Be assertive, and read on.

Compliance, Obedience, and Coercion

RECITE

1. An ability to punish others for failure to obey is the basis for
   a. referent power
   b. legitimate power
   c. expert power
   d. coercive power
2. The term *compliance* refers to situations in which a person complies with commands made by a person who has authority. T or F?
3. Obedience in Milgram's experiments was related to
   a. distance between learner and teacher
   b. distance between experimenter and teacher
   c. obedience of other teachers
   d. all of these
4. Obedience is conformity to the commands of an ______________________.
5. By repeating his obedience experiment in a downtown office building, Milgram demonstrated that the prestige of Yale University was the main reason for participant' willingness to obey in the original experiment. T or F?
6. Brainwashing differs from other persuasive attempts in that brainwashing requires a ______________________ ______________________.
7. Which statement about brainwashing is *false*?
   a. The target person is isolated from others.
   b. Attitude changes brought about by brainwashing are usually permanent.
   c. The first step is unfreezing former values and beliefs.
   d. Cooperation with the indoctrinating agent is rewarded.

REFLECT

Think Critically

8. Modern warfare allows killing to take place impersonally and at a distance. How does this relate to Milgram's experiments?

Self-Reflect

Return to the description of various types of social power. Can you think of a setting in which you have (to a greater or lesser degree) each type of power?

You would like to persuade people to donate to a deserving charity. How, specifically, could you use compliance techniques to get people to donate?

Are you surprised that so many people obeyed orders in Milgram's experiments? Do you think you would have obeyed? How actively do you question authority?

To what extent are governments entitled to use coercion to modify the attitudes or behavior of individuals?

Answers: 1. *d* **2.** F **3.** *d* **4.** authority **5.** F **6.** captive audience **7.** *b* **8.** There is a big difference between killing someone in hand-to-hand combat and killing someone by lining up images on a video screen. Milgram's research suggests that it is easier for a person to follow orders to kill another human when the victim is at a distance and removed from personal contact.

Cult A group that professes great devotion to some person and follows that person almost without question; cult members are typically victimized by their leaders in various ways.

Psychology in Action: Assertiveness Training—Standing Up for Your Rights

Gateway Question 16.11: *How does self-assertion differ from aggression?*

Most of us have been rewarded, first as children and later as adults, for compliant, obedient, or "good" behavior. Perhaps this is why so many people find it difficult to assert themselves. Or perhaps not asserting yourself is related to anxiety about "making a scene" or feeling disliked by others. Whatever the causes, some people suffer tremendous anguish in any situation requiring poise, self-confidence or self-assertion. Have you ever done any of the following?

- Hesitated to question an error on a restaurant bill because you were afraid of making a scene?
- Backed out of asking for a raise or a change in working conditions?
- Said yes when you wanted to say no?
- Been afraid to question a grade that seemed unfair?

If you have ever had difficulty asserting yourself in similar situations, try a technique called **assertiveness training**—instruction in how to be self-assertive (Tavakoli et al., 2009; Wolpe, 1974).

What is done in assertiveness training? Assertiveness training is a very direct procedure. By using group exercises, videotapes, mirrors, and staged conflicts, the instructor teaches assertive behavior. People learn to practice honesty, to disagree, to question authority, and to make assertive postures and gestures. As their self-confidence improves, nonassertive clients are taken on "field trips" to shops and restaurants where they practice what they have learned.

Nonassertion requiring therapy is unusual. Nevertheless, many people become tense or upset in at least some situations in which they must stand up for their rights. For this reason, many people have found the techniques and exercises of assertiveness training helpful. If you have ever eaten a carbonized steak when you ordered it rare, or stood in silent rage as a clerk ignored you, the following discussion will be of interest.

Jeff Widener/AP/Wide World Photo

Associated Press photographer Jeff Widener snapped this timeless photo of a lone protester literally standing up on his own behalf as he halted a column of tanks during the 1989 pro-democracy rallies in Tiananmen Square in Beijing, China. How many of us would find the courage to assert ourselves against such direct expressions of authority?

Self-Assertion

The first step in assertiveness training is to convince yourself of three basic rights: You have the right to refuse, to request, and to right a wrong. **Self-assertion** involves standing up for these rights by speaking out in your own behalf.

Is self-assertion just getting things your own way? Not at all. A basic distinction can be made between *self-assertion* and *aggressive* behavior. Self-assertion is a direct, honest expression of feelings and desires. It is not exclusively self-serving. People who are nonassertive are usually patient to a fault. Sometimes their pent-up anger explodes with unexpected fury, which can damage relationships. In contrast to assertive behavior, **aggression** involves hurting another person or achieving one's goals at the expense of another. Aggression does not take into account the feelings or rights of others. It is an attempt to get one's own way no matter what. Assertion techniques emphasize firmness, not attack (■ Table 16.2).

Assertiveness Training

The basic idea in assertiveness training is that each assertive action is practiced until it can be repeated even under stress. For example, let's say it really angers you when a store clerk waits on several people who arrived after you did. To improve your assertiveness in this situation, you would begin by *rehearsing* the dialogue, posture, and gestures you would use to confront the clerk or the other customer. Working in front of a mirror can be very helpful. If possible, you should *role play* the scene with a friend. Be sure to have your friend take the part of a really aggressive or irresponsible clerk, as well as a cooperative one. Rehearsal and role playing should also be used when you expect a possible confrontation with someone—for example, if you are going to ask for a raise, challenge a grade, or confront a landlord.

Is that all there is to it? No. Another important principle is **overlearning** (practice that continues after initial mastery of a skill).

■ TABLE 16.2 Comparison of Assertive, Aggressive, and Nonassertive Behavior

	Actor	Receiver of Behavior
Nonassertive behavior	Self-denying, inhibited, hurt, and anxious; lets others make choices; goals not achieved.	Feels sympathy, guilt, or contempt for actor; achieves goals at actor's expense.
Aggressive behavior	Achieves goals at others' expense; expresses feelings but hurts others; chooses for others or puts them down.	Feels hurt, defensive, humiliated, or taken advantage of; does not meet own needs.
Assertive behavior	Self-enhancing; acts in own best interests; expresses feelings; respects rights of others; goals usually achieved; self-respect maintained.	Needs respected and feelings expressed; may achieve goal; self-worth maintained.

When you rehearse or role-play assertive behavior, it is essential to continue to practice until your responses become almost automatic. This helps prevent you from getting flustered in the actual situation.

One more technique you may find useful is the **broken record**. This is a self-assertion technique involving repeating a request until it is acknowledged. (In ancient times, when people played phonograph records, the needle sometimes got "stuck in a groove." When this happened, part of a song might repeat over and over. Hence, the term *broken record* refers to repeating yourself.) Repetition is also a good way to prevent assertion from becoming aggression.

As an illustration, let's say you are returning a pair of shoes to a store. After two wearings the shoes fell apart, but you bought them 2 months ago and no longer have a receipt. The broken record could sound something like this:

Customer: I would like to have these shoes replaced.

Clerk: Do you have a receipt?

Customer: No, but I bought them here, and since they are defective, I would like to have you replace them.

Clerk: I can't do that without a receipt.

Customer: I understand that, but I want them replaced.

Clerk: Well, if you'll come back this afternoon and talk to the manager.

Customer: I've brought these shoes in because they are defective.

Clerk: Well, I'm not authorized to replace them.

Customer: Yes, well, if you'll replace these, I'll be on my way.

Notice that the customer did not attack the clerk or create an angry confrontation. Simple persistence is often all that is necessary for successful self-assertion.

How would I respond assertively to a put-down? Responding assertively to verbal aggression (a "put-down") is a real challenge. The tendency is to respond aggressively, which usually makes things worse. A good way to respond to a put-down uses the following steps: (1) If you are wrong, admit it; (2) acknowledge the person's feelings; (3) assert yourself about the other person's aggression; and (4) briskly end the interchange.

Psychologists Robert Alberti and Michael Emmons (2008) offer an example of how to use the four steps. Let's say you accidentally bump into someone. The person responds angrily, "Damn it! Why don't you watch where you're going! You fool, you could have hurt me!" A good response would be to say, "I'm sorry I bumped you. I didn't do it intentionally. It's obvious you're upset, but I don't like your calling me names, or yelling. I can get your point without that."

Now, what if someone insults you indirectly ("I love your taste in clothes, it's so 'folksy.'")? Alberti and Emmons suggest you ask for a clarification ("What are you trying to say?"). This will force the person to take responsibility for the aggression. It can also provide an opportunity to change the way the person interacts with you: "If you really don't like what I'm wearing, I'd like to know it. I'm not always sure I like the things I buy, and I value your opinion."

To summarize, self-assertion does not supply instant poise, confidence, or self-assurance. However, it is a way of combating anxieties associated with life in an impersonal and sometimes intimidating society. If you are interested in more information, you can consult a book entitled *Your Perfect Right* by Alberti and Emmons (2008).

Assertiveness training Instruction in how to be self-assertive.

Self-assertion A direct, honest expression of feelings and desires.

Aggression Hurting another person or achieving one's goals at the expense of another person.

Overlearning Learning or practice that continues after initial mastery of a skill.

Broken record A self-assertion technique involving repeating a request until it is acknowledged.

Knowledge Builder: Assertiveness Training

RECITE

1. In assertiveness training, people learn techniques for getting their way in social situations and angry interchanges. T or F?
2. Nonassertive behavior causes hurt, anxiety, and self-denial in the actor, and sympathy, guilt, or contempt in the receiver. T or F?
3. Overlearning should be avoided when rehearsing assertive behaviors. T or F?
4. The "broken record" must be avoided, because it is a basic nonassertive behavior. T or F?

REFLECT

Think Critically

5. When practicing self-assertion do you think it would be better to improvise your own responses or imitate those of a person skilled in self-assertion?

Self-Reflect

Pick a specific instance when you could have been more assertive. How would you handle the situation if it occurs again?

Think of a specific instance when you were angry and acted aggressively. How could you have handled the situation through self-assertion instead of aggression?

Answers: 1. F **2.** T **3.** F **4.** F **5.** One study found that imitating an assertive model is more effective than improvising your own responses (Kipper, 1992). If you know an assertive and self-assured person, you can learn a lot by watching how they handle difficult situations.

Chapter in Review Gateways to Social Thinking and Social Influence

Gateway QUESTIONS REVISITED

16.1 How does group membership affect individual behavior?

16.1.1 Social psychology studies humans as social animals enmeshed in complex networks of social and cultural contexts. Membership in groups and social situations in general strongly influence how people behave, think, and feel.

16.1.2 Social roles, which may be achieved or ascribed, define one's position in groups and particular behavior patterns associated with those social roles. When two or more contradictory roles are held, role conflict may occur. The Stanford prison experiment showed that destructive roles may override individual motives for behavior.

16.1.3 Group structure refers to the organization of roles, communication pathways, and power within a group. Group cohesiveness is basically the degree of attraction among group members.

16.1.4 Positions within groups typically carry higher or lower levels of social status. High social status is associated with special privileges and respect.

16.1.5 Norms are standards of conduct enforced (formally or informally) by groups. The autokinetic effect has been used to demonstrate that norms rapidly form even in temporary groups.

16.2 How does being social influence how we think about ourselves and others?

16.2.1 Social comparison theory holds that we affiliate to evaluate our actions, feelings, and abilities. Social comparisons are also made for purposes of self-protection and self-enhancement.

16.2.2 Attribution theory is concerned with how we make inferences about behavior. A variety of factors affect attribution, including consistency, distinctiveness, situational demands, and consensus.

16.2.3 Self-handicapping involves arranging excuses for poor performance as a way to protect one's self-image or self-esteem.

16.2.4 The fundamental attribution error is to ascribe the actions of others to internal causes. Because of actor–observer differences, we tend to attribute our own behavior to external causes.

16.3 What are attitudes and how are they acquired?

16.3.1 Attitudes are made up of a belief component, an emotional component, and an action component.

16.3.2 Attitudes may be formed by direct contact, chance conditioning, interaction with others, group membership, child-rearing practices, and the media.

16.3.3 Attitudes are typically measured with techniques such as open-ended interviews, social distance scales, and attitude scales. Attitudes expressed in these ways do not always correspond to actual behavior.

16.4 Under what conditions is persuasion most effective and what is cognitive dissonance?

16.4.1 Attitude change is related to reference group membership.

16.4.2 Effective persuasion occurs when characteristics of the communicator, the message, and the audience are well-matched. In general, a likable and believable communicator who repeats a credible message that arouses emotion in the audience and states clear-cut conclusions will be persuasive.

16.4.3 The maintenance and change of attitudes is closely related to needs for consistency in thoughts and actions. Cognitive dissonance theory explains the dynamics of such needs. We are motivated to reduce dissonance when it occurs, often by changing inconsistent beliefs or attitudes.

16.4.4 The amount of reward or justification for one's actions influences whether dissonance occurs.

16.5 What is social influence and social power?

16.5.1 A major fact of social life is that our behavior is influenced in numerous ways by the actions of other people.

16.5.2 Social influence ranges from mild (mere presence, conformity, and compliance) to strong (obedience and coercion). Conformity to group pressure is a familiar example of social influence.

16.5.3 A person has social power when he or she has the capacity to control, alter, or influence the behavior of another person. There are five types of social power: reward power, coercive power, legitimate power, referent power, and expert power.

16.6 How does the mere presence of others affect behavior?

16.6.1 The mere presence of others may facilitate (or inhibit) performance.

16.6.2 People may also engage in social loafing, working less hard when they are part of a group.

16.6.3 The study of personal space is called proxemics. Four basic spatial zones around each person's body are intimate distance (0–18 inches), personal distance (1½–4 feet), social distance (4–12 feet), and public distance (12 feet or more).

16.6.4 The nature of many relationships is revealed by the distance you are comfortable maintaining between yourself and another person.

16.7 What have social psychologists learned about conformity?

16.7.1 Virtually everyone conforms to a variety of broad social and cultural norms. Conformity pressures also exist within smaller groups.

16.7.2 The famous Asch experiments demonstrated that various group sanctions encourage conformity.

16.7.3 Groupthink refers to compulsive conformity in group decision making. Victims of groupthink seek to maintain one another's approval, even at the cost of critical thinking.

16.8 What factors lead to increased compliance?

16.8.1 Compliance with direct requests from a person who has little or no authority is another means by which behavior is influenced. Compliance may be active or passive.

16.8.2 Three strategies for inducing compliance are the foot-in-the-door technique, the door-in-the-face approach, and the low-ball technique.

16.9 *Can people be too obedient?*

16.9.1 Research suggests that people are excessively obedient to authority.

16.9.2 Obedience to authority has been investigated in a variety of experiments, particularly those by Milgram. Obedience in Milgram's studies decreased when the victim was in the same room, when the victim and subject were face to face, when the authority figure was absent, and when others refused to obey.

16.10 *Is brainwashing actually possible and is that how people are converted to cult membership?*

16.10.1 Coercion involves forcing people to change their beliefs or behavior against their will.

16.10.2 Brainwashing is a form of forced attitude change. Three steps in brainwashing are unfreezing, changing, and refreezing attitudes and beliefs.

16.10.3 Many cults recruit new members with high-pressure indoctrination techniques resembling brainwashing. Such groups attempt to catch people when they are vulnerable. Then they combine isolation, displays of affection, discipline and rituals, intimidation, and escalating commitment to bring about conversion.

16.11 *How does self-assertion differ from aggression?*

16.11.1 Everyone is affected by pressures to conform, comply, and obey. There are times when it is valuable to know how to recognize and resist such pressures.

16.11.2 Self-assertion as opposed to aggression, involves clearly stating one's wants and needs to others. Assertiveness is a valuable alternative to becoming aggressive or being victimized in social situations.

16.11.3 Learning to be assertive is accomplished by role-playing rehearsing assertive actions, overlearning, and use of specific techniques, such as the "broken record."

MEDIA RESOURCES

Web Resources

Internet addresses frequently change. To find an up-to-date list of URLs for the sites listed here, visit your Psychology CourseMate.

Social Psychology Network Explore this massive website devoted to social psychology.

Six Degrees of Separation Read more about the small world hypothesis.

Stanford Prison Study Explore Phil Zimbardo's classic study of the power of social roles.

Shaping Beliefs and Attitudes Attitude change strategies for teachers.

General Persuasion Techniques Explore a variety of persuasion techniques.

Cognitive Dissonance Read an original article by Festinger & Carlsmith.

Conformity and Nonconformity Read a series of interesting quotes.

Groupthink Read about and download a PowerPoint presentation about groupthink.

Milgram's Study of Obedience Listen to audio clips of this infamous experiment.

How Brainwashing Works Read more about brainwashing techniques.

Assertiveness Access a collection on virtual pamphlets on assertiveness.

Interactive Learning

Log in to **CengageBrain** to access the resources your instructor requires. For this book, you can access:

CourseMate brings course concepts to life with interactive learning, study, and exam preparation tools that support the printed textbook. A textbook-specific website, ***Psychology CourseMate*** includes an ***integrated interactive eBook*** and other ***interactive learning tools*** including quizzes, flashcards, videos, and more.

CENGAGE**NOW**™

CengageNOW is an easy-to-use online resource that helps you study in less time to get the grade you want—NOW. Take a pre-test for this chapter and receive a personalized study plan based on your results that will identify the topics you need to review and direct you to online resources to help you master those topics. Then take a post-test to help you determine the concepts you have mastered and what you will need to work on. If your textbook does not include an access code card, go to CengageBrain.com to gain access.

WebTUTOR™

More than just an interactive study guide, **WebTutor** is an anytime, anywhere customized learning solution with an eBook, keeping you connected to your textbook, instructor, and classmates.

If your professor has assigned **Aplia** homework:

1. Sign in to your account.
2. Complete the corresponding homework exercises as required by your professor.
3. When finished, click "Grade It Now" to see which areas you have mastered and which need more work, and for detailed explanations of every answer.

Visit **www.cengagebrain.com** to access your account and purchase materials.

Gateway THEME

Social life is complex, but consistent patterns can be found in our positive and negative interactions with others.

17

Prosocial and Antisocial Behavior

Love and Hate

Jasmine and Osama are tearing themselves away from home and moving to Europe. As Jasmine wryly comments, "We were naïve and thought we could win this fight, but we can't. So we have to go abroad and start a new life." The fight they lost was a struggle between love and hate. You see, Jasmine is a Jewish Israeli and Osama is a Palestinian Muslim. They met, fell in love, and were married. Since then, they have been endlessly harassed. Because of deep hatred built up during the Palestinian–Israeli conflict, both sides were hostile to the love Jasmine and Osama share. They were repeatedly insulted, threatened, shunned, and reviled. The Middle East is no place for them to live anymore (Price, 2007).

Jasmine and Osama are not alone. Prejudice and hatred between various groups around the world—from Catholics and Protestants in Northern Ireland to Hutus and Tutsis in Rwanda to African Americans and European Americans in the United States—has produced countless tragic stories like that of Jasmine and Osama. These two, at least, can be thankful they escaped with their lives.

In this chapter, we will explore the social psychology of both love and hate. Various forms of love exert a positive influence on people and generally brings them together. Hate, of course, does just the opposite. Let's start on a positive note with a look at what brings people together.

Gateway QUESTIONS

17.1 *Why do people affiliate?*

17.2 *What factors influence interpersonal attraction?*

17.3 *How do liking and loving differ?*

17.4 *Why are bystanders so often unwilling to help in an emergency?*

17.5 *How do psychologists explain human aggression?*

17.6 *What causes prejudice?*

17.7 *What can be done about prejudice and intergroup conflict?*

17.8 *How can we promote multiculturalism and social harmony?*

Prosocial Behavior—Come Together

Gateway Question 17.1: *Why do people affiliate?*

Why do we usually prefer to hang out with other people? Broadly speaking, congregating with others is a basic form of **prosocial behavior**, any behavior that has a positive impact on other people. (In contrast, **antisocial behavior** is any behavior that has a negative impact on other people.) We are social beings with a **need to affiliate** (a need to associate with other people) based on basic human desires to get and to give approval, support, friendship, and love (Baumeister & Bushman, 2011). As we saw last chapter, we also affiliate to help us think about ourselves by comparing ourselves with others. We even seek the company of others to alleviate fear or anxiety. This point is illustrated by a classic experiment in which college women were threatened with electric shock.

A Shocking Experience

Dr. Gregor Zilstein ominously explained to arriving participants, "We would like to give each of you a series of electric shocks…these shocks will hurt, they will be painful." In the room was a frightening electrical device that seemed to verify Zilstein's plans. While waiting to be shocked, each woman was given a choice of waiting alone or with other participants. Women frightened in this way more often chose to wait with others; those who expected the shock to be "a mild tickle or tingle" were more willing to wait alone. (Schachter, 1959)

Apparently, the frightened women found it comforting to be with others. Should we conclude that "misery loves company"? Actually, that's not entirely correct. In a later experiment, women who expected to be shocked were given the choice of waiting with other future shock recipients, with women waiting to see their college advisers, or alone. Most women chose to wait with other future "victims." In short, misery seems to love miserable company! In general, we prefer to be with people in circumstances similar to our own (Gump & Kulik, 1997).

Is there a reason for that? Yes. This may be an example of using social cognition to cope with personal emotions. Seeing that other people are reacting calmly can help reassure and soothe us when a situation is threatening or unfamiliar, or when we are in doubt (Kulik, Mahler, & Moore, 2003). (Of course, it is no help at all if a person trapped alongside you in an elevator begins to mutter about the end of the world as we know it.)

Don't people also affiliate out of attraction for one another? They do, of course. The next section tells why.

Interpersonal Attraction—Social Magnetism?

Gateway Question 17.2: *What factors influence interpersonal attraction?*

Interpersonal attraction (affinity to another person) is the basis for most voluntary social relationships (Berscheid, 2010; Berscheid & Regan, 2005). To form friendships, we must first identify potential friends and then get to know them. Deciding whether you would like to get to know another person can happen very quickly, sometimes within just minutes of meeting (Sunnafrank, Ramirez, & Metts, 2004). That may be because you usually don't randomly choose people to encounter.

Finding Potential Friends

What initially attracts people to each other? "Birds of a feather flock together." "Familiarity breeds contempt." "Opposites attract." Are these statements true? Actually, the folklore about friendship is, at best, a mixture of fact and fiction. As you might expect, we look for friends and lovers who will be kind and understanding and who appear to have attractive personalities (Bradbury & Karney, 2010; Park & Lennon, 2008). Let's explore the sometimes surprising variety of other factors that influence our initial attraction to people.

Familiarity

In general, we are attracted to people we are familiar with (Reis et al., 2011). (That's one reason why actors costarring in movies together often become romantically involved.) In fact, our choice of friends (and even lovers) is based more on *physical proximity* (nearness) than we might care to believe. Proximity promotes attraction by increasing the *frequency of contact* between people.

The closer people live to each other, the more likely they are to become friends. Likewise, lovers like to think they have found the "one and only" person in the universe for them. In reality, they have probably found the best match in a 5-mile radius (Reis et al., 2011). Marriages are not made in heaven—they are made in local schools, businesses, churches, bars, clubs, and neighborhoods. For example, Jasmine and Osama worked together in the same business in Jerusalem.

In short, there does seem to be a "boy-next-door" or "girl-next-door" effect in romantic attraction, and a "folks-next-door" effect in friendship. Notice, however, that the Internet is making it increasingly easier to stay in constant "virtual contact," which is leading to more and more long-distance friendships and romances (Lawson & Leck, 2006; Sautter, Tippett, & Morgan, 2010).

Similarity

Take a moment to make a list of your closest friends. What do they have in common (other than the joy of knowing you)? It is likely that their ages are similar to yours and you are of the same sex and ethnicity. There will be exceptions, of course. But similarity on these three dimensions is the general rule for friendships.

Similarity refers to how alike you are to another person in background, age, interests, attitudes, beliefs, and so forth. In everything from casual acquaintance to marriage, similar people are attracted to each other (Gonzaga, Carter, & Buckwalter, 2010; Miller, Perlman, & Brehm, 2009). And why not? It's reinforcing to see our beliefs and attitudes shared by others. It shows we are "right" and reveals that they are clever people as well!

So similarity also influences mate selection? Yes, in choosing a mate we tend to marry someone who is like us in almost every way, a pattern called **homogamy** (huh-MOG-ah-me) (Blackwell & Lichter, 2004; Kalmijn, 2010). Studies show that married couples are highly similar in age, education, ethnicity, and religion. (You go, Jasmine and Osama!) To a lesser degree, they are also similar in attitudes and opinions, mental abilities, status, height, weight, and eye color. In case you're wondering, homogamy also applies to unmarried couples who are living together (Blackwell & Lichter, 2004). Homogamy is probably a good thing. The risk of divorce is highest among couples with sizable differences in age and education (Tzeng, 1992).

Physical Attractiveness

People who are *physically attractive* are regarded as good-looking by others. Beautiful people are generally rated as more appealing than average. This is due, in part, to the *halo effect*, a tendency to generalize a favorable impression to unrelated personal characteristics. Because of it, we assume that attractive people are also likable, intelligent, warm, witty, mentally healthy, and socially skilled (Lorenzo, Biesanz, & Human, 2010). Basically, we act as if "what is beautiful is good." Even characters in Hollywood movies tend to be portrayed more favorably if they are beautiful (Smith, McIntosh, & Bazzini, 1999).

Being physically attractive can be an advantage for both males and females (Mehrabian & Blum, 2003). Good-looking people are less lonely, less socially anxious, more popular, more socially skilled, and more sexually experienced than unattractive people (Feingold, 1992). When romance is concerned, physical attractiveness has more influence on a woman's fate than on a man's (Feingold, 1990; Johnson et al., 2010). For instance, there is a strong relationship between a woman's physical beauty and her frequency of dating. For men, looks are unrelated to dating frequency. When men and women first meet, beauty affects attractiveness more for women and personality more for men (Berry & Miller, 2001).

Do these findings seem shallow and sexist? If so, it may be reassuring to know that beauty is a factor mainly in initial acquaintance (Keller & Young, 1996; Reis et al., 2011). Later, more meaningful qualities gain in importance (Berscheid, 2010; Miller, Perlman, & Brehm, 2009). As you discover that someone has a good personality, he or she will even start looking more attractive to you (Lewandowski, Aron, & Gee, 2007). It takes more than appearance to make a lasting relationship.

Chris Polk/FilmMagic/Getty Images

Physical beauty can be socially advantageous because of the widespread belief that "what is beautiful is good." However, physical beauty is generally unrelated to actual personal traits and talents.

Reciprocity

OK, so he (or she) is someone you are familiar with, appears to share a lot in common with you, and is hot to boot. What else do you need to know before taking it to the next level? Well, it would be nice to know if he or she is also the least bit interested in you (Greitemeyer, 2010). In fact, **reciprocity**, which occurs when people respond to each other in similar ways, may be the most important factor influencing the development of friendships. Most people find it easier to reciprocate to someone else's overtures than to be the initiator (Montoya & Insko, 2008). That way, at least the embarrassment of an outright rejection can be avoided.

Getting to Know One Another

Once initial contact has been made, it's time to get to know each other. This is done mainly through the process of **self-disclosure**, as you begin to share private thoughts and feelings and reveal yourself to others. To get acquainted, you must be willing to talk about more than just the weather, sports, or nuclear physics. In general, as friends talk, they gradually deepen the level of liking, trust, and self-disclosure (Levesque, Steciuk, & Ledley, 2002).We more often reveal ourselves to persons we like than to those we find unattractive. Disclosure also requires a degree of trust. Many people play it safe, or "close to the vest," with people they do not know well. Indeed, self-disclosure is governed by unspoken rules about what's acceptable (Phillips, Rothbard, & Dumas, 2009).

Moderate self-disclosure leads to increased reciprocity (a return in kind). In contrast, *overdisclosure* exceeds what is appropriate for a

Prosocial behavior Any behavior that has a positive impact on other people.

Antisocial behavior Any behavior that has a negative impact on other people.

Need to affiliate The desire to associate with other people.

Interpersonal attraction Social attraction to another person.

Homogamy Marriage of two people who are similar to one another.

Reciprocity A reciprocal exchange of feelings, thoughts, or things between people.

Self-disclosure The process of revealing private thoughts, feelings, and one's personal history to others.

Everett Collection

Excessive self-disclosure is a staple of many television talk shows. Guests frequently reveal intimate details about their personal lives, including private family matters, sex and dating, physical or sexual abuse, major embarrassments, and criminal activities. Viewers probably find such intimate disclosures entertaining, rather than threatening, because they don't have to reciprocate.

relationship or social situation, giving rise to suspicion and reducing attraction. For example, imagine standing in line at a store and having the stranger in front of you say, "Lately I've been thinking about how I really feel about myself. I think I'm pretty well adjusted, but I occasionally have some questions about my sexual adequacy."

When self-disclosure proceeds at a moderate pace, it builds trust, intimacy, reciprocity, and positive feelings. When it is too rapid or inappropriate, we are likely to "back off" and wonder about the person's motives. It's interesting to note that on the Internet (and especially on social networking websites like Facebook) people often feel freer to express their true feelings, which can lead to genuine, face-to-face friendships (Bargh, McKenna, & Fitzsimons, 2002). However, it can also lead to some very dramatic overdisclosure (George, 2006).

Is self-disclosure similar for men and women? Women and men display an interesting difference in patterns of self-disclosure as described next.

Gendered Friendships

Two male friends share lunch at a restaurant. In the next hour, they talk about sports, cars, sports cars, the *Sports Illustrated* swimsuit edition, sports, cars, and golf. (Did we mention sports and cars?) Janis, who was at a nearby table, overheard the entire conversation. Here's her summary of what the men said to each other: "Absolutely nothing!"

In North American culture, most male friendships are *activity based*. That is, men tend to do things together—a pattern that provides companionship without closeness. The friendships of women are more often based on *shared feelings and confidences*. If two female friends spent an afternoon together and did not reveal problems, private thoughts, and feelings to one another, they would assume that something was wrong. For women, friendship is a matter of talking about shared concerns and intimate matters.

Actually, the differences between male and female friendships are smaller than implied here. Men do know *something* about the private thoughts and feelings of their friends. Nevertheless, most contemporary men do not form close friendships with other men. Many could probably learn something from female friendships: Men live their friendships side by side; women live them face-to-face (Bank & Hansford, 2000).

Social Exchange Theory

Self-disclosure involves an exchange of personal information, but other exchanges also occur. In fact, many relationships can be understood as an ongoing series of **social exchanges** (transfers of attention, information, affection, favors, and the like between two people). In many social exchanges, people try to maximize their rewards while minimizing their "costs." When a friendship or love relationship ceases to be attractive, people often say, "I'm not getting anything out of it any more." Actually, they probably are, but their costs—in terms of effort, irritation, or lowered self-esteem—have exceeded their rewards.

According to **social exchange theory**, we unconsciously weigh social rewards and costs. For a relationship to last, it must be *profitable* (its rewards must exceed its costs) for both parties (Kalmijn, 2010). For instance, Troy and Helen have been dating for 2 years. Although they still have fun at times, they also frequently argue and bicker. If the friction in their relationship gets much stronger, it will exceed the rewards of staying together. When that happens, they will probably split up (Gottman, 1994).

Actually, just being profitable is not the whole story. It is more accurate to say that a relationship needs to be *profitable enough*. Generally, the balance between rewards and costs is judged in comparison with what we have come to expect from past experience. The personal standard a person uses to evaluate rewards and costs is called the **comparison level**. The comparison level is high for people with histories of satisfying and rewarding relationships. It is lower for someone whose relationships have been unsatisfying. Thus, the decision to continue a relationship is affected by your personal comparison level. A lonely person, or one whose friendships have been marginal, might stay in a relationship that you would consider unacceptable.

Loving—Dating and Mating

Gateway Question 17.3: *How do liking and loving differ?*

How does love differ from interpersonal attraction? It depends on what you mean by the word *love*. **Romantic love**, for example, is based on interpersonal attraction, but it also involves high levels of passion: emotional arousal and/or sexual desire (Berscheid & Regan, 2005; Miller, Perlman, & Brehm, 2009). You are experiencing romantic love as you are "falling in love" (Aron et al., 2008).

To get another (tri?)angle on love, psychologist Robert Sternberg (1988) created his influential *triangular theory of love*. According to Sternberg, different forms of love arise from different combinations of three basic components (see • Figure 17.1).

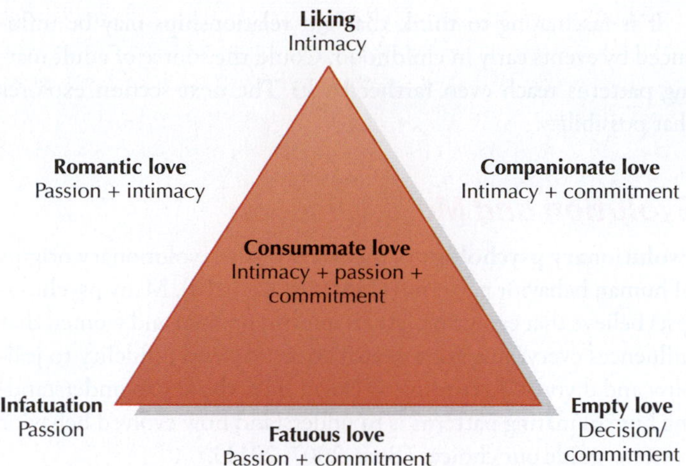

● **Figure 17.1** The Triangle of Love. Each of the three basic components of love (intimacy, passion, and commitment) appears at one corner of the triangle and is associated with a form of love. Pairs of components and their associated form of love appear on lines of the triangle. Consummate love, which involves all three components, is pictured at the center of the triangle. Adapted from Sternberg, 1988.

Intimacy refers to feelings of connectedness and affection. **Passion** refers to deep emotional and/or sexual feelings. **Commitment** involves the determination to stay in a long-term relationship with another person.

How does this triangle work? Try it for yourself. Think of a person you love. Now read ■ Table 17.1 as you ask yourself three yes/no questions: Do I feel intimate with this person? Do I feel passion for this person? Am I committed to this person? Find the kind of love that fits your answers. For example, if you answered *yes* to intimacy but *no* to passion and commitment, you **like** that person; you are friends. Alternately, if you answered *yes* to intimacy and commitment but *no* to passion, then you are feeling **companionate love**. This form of love is more common among couples who have been together for a long time. Such couples often describe themselves as "being in love" rather than "falling in love" (Riela et al., 2010).

Does that mean that the most complete form of love is consummate love? You've got it! We experience **consummate love** when we feel intimacy and passion for another person, *and* we are strongly committed to him or her. It is exactly their consummate love for each other that has allowed Jasmine and Osama to overcome all the social forces pushing them apart.

■ **TABLE 17.1 Sternberg's Triangular Theory of Love**

Combinations of intimacy, passion, and commitment

Type of love	Intimacy	Passion	Commitment
Nonlove			
Liking	Yes		
Infatuated love		Yes	
Empty love			Yes
Romantic love	Yes	Yes	
Companionate love	Yes		Yes
Fatuous love		Yes	Yes
Consummate love	Yes	Yes	Yes

Sternberg, 1988.

Romantic love differs from friendship in another interesting way. In contrast to simple liking, romantic love usually involves deep **mutual absorption**. In other words, lovers (unlike friends) attend almost exclusively to one another (Riela et al., 2010).

What do lovers see when they gaze into each other's eyes? A final interesting characteristic of romantic love is lovers' ability to see their partners in idealized ways (Barelds & Dijkstra, 2009). Nobody's perfect, of course. That's why it's no surprise that relationships are most likely to persist when lovers idealize one another. Doing so doesn't just blind them to their partner's faults, it actually helps them create the relationship they wish for (Murray, Holmes, & Griffin, 2003).

Love and Attachment

Sheela has been dating Paul for over a year. Although they have had some rough spots, Sheela is comfortable, secure, and trusting in her love for Paul. Charlene, in contrast, has had a long series of unhappy romances with men. She is basically a loner who has difficulty trusting others. Like Sheela, Eduardo has been dating the same person for a year. However, his relationship with Tanya has been stormy and troubled. Eduardo is strongly attracted to Tanya. Yet, he is also in a constant state of anxiety over whether she really loves him.

Sheela, Charlene, and Eduardo might be surprised to learn that the roots of their romantic relationships may lie in childhood. There is growing evidence that early attachments to caregivers can have a lasting impact on how we relate to others (Brumbaugh & Fraley, 2010; Nosko et al., 2011).

BRIDGES

Forming a secure attachment to a caregiver is a major event in early child development. **See Chapter 3, pages 94–95.**

Social exchange Any exchange between two people of attention, information, affection, favors, or the like.

Social exchange theory Theory stating that rewards must exceed costs for relationships to endure.

Comparison level A personal standard used to evaluate rewards and costs in a social exchange.

Romantic love Love that is associated with high levels of interpersonal attraction, heightened arousal, mutual absorption, and sexual desire.

Intimacy Feelings of connectedness and affection for another person.

Passion Deep emotional and/or sexual feelings for another person.

Commitment The determination to stay in a long-term relationship with another person.

Liking A relationship based on intimacy, but lacking passion and commitment.

Companionate love Form of love characterized by intimacy and commitment but not passion.

Consummate love Form of love characterized by intimacy, passion, and commitment.

Mutual absorption With regard to romantic love, the nearly exclusive attention lovers give to one another.

For example, studies of dating couples have identified secure, avoidant, and ambivalent attachment patterns similar to those seen in early child development (Lavy, Mikulincer, & Shaver, 2010). Nationally, about 60 percent of all adults have a secure attachment style, 25 percent are avoidant, and 10 percent have anxious attachment styles (Mickelson, Kessler, & Shaver, 1997).

Secure attachment is a stable and positive emotional bond. A secure attachment style like Sheela's is marked by caring, intimacy, supportiveness, and understanding in love relationships. Secure persons regard themselves as friendly, good natured, and likable. They think of others as generally well intentioned, reliable, and trustworthy. People with a secure attachment style find it relatively easy to get close to others. They are comfortable depending on others and having others depend on them. In general, they don't worry too much about being abandoned or about having someone become too emotionally close to them. Most people prefer to have a secure partner, whatever their own style might be (Latty-Mann, & Davis, 1996).

Charlene's **avoidant attachment** style reflects a fear of intimacy and a tendency to resist commitment to others. Avoidant persons tend to pull back when things don't go well in a relationship. The avoidant person is suspicious, aloof, and skeptical about love. She or he tends to see others as either unreliable or overly eager to commit to a relationship. As a result, avoidant persons find it hard to completely trust and depend on others. Avoidant persons get nervous when anyone gets too close emotionally. Basically, they avoid intimacy (Lavy, Mikulincer, & Shaver, 2010; Tidwell, Reis, & Shaver, 1996).

Persons like Eduardo have an **ambivalent attachment** style, marked by mixed emotions about relationships. Conflicting feelings of affection, anger, emotional turmoil, physical attraction, and doubt leave them in an unsettled, ambivalent state. Often, ambivalent persons regard themselves as misunderstood and unappreciated. They tend to see their friends and lovers as unreliable and unable or unwilling to commit themselves to lasting relationships. Ambivalent persons worry that their romantic partners don't really love them or may leave them. Although they want to be extremely close to their partners, they are also preoccupied with doubts about the partner's dependability and trustworthiness.

How could emotional attachments early in life affect adult relationships? It appears that we use early attachment experiences to build mental models about affectionate relationships. Later, we use these models as a sort of blueprint for forming, maintaining, and breaking bonds of love and affection (Sroufe, 2005). Thus, the quality of childhood bonds to parents or other caregivers may hold a key to understanding how we approach romantic relationships (Fraley & Shaver, 2000). Maybe it's no accident that persons who are romantically available are often described as "unattached."

It is fascinating to think that our relationships may be influenced by events early in childhood. Could the source of adult mating patterns reach even farther back? The next section explores that possibility.

Evolution and Mate Selection

Evolutionary psychology is the study of the evolutionary origins of human behavior patterns (Confer et al., 2010). Many psychologists believe that evolution left an imprint on men and women that influences everything from sexual attraction and infidelity to jealousy and divorce. According to David Buss, the key to understanding human mating patterns is to understand how evolved behavior patterns guide our choices (Buss, 2007, 2011).

In a study of 37 cultures on six continents, Buss found the following patterns: Compared with women, men are more interested in casual sex; they prefer younger, more physically attractive partners; and they get more jealous over real or imagined sexual infidelities than they do over a loss of emotional commitment. Compared with men, women prefer slightly older partners who appear to be industrious, higher in status, or economically successful; women are more upset by a partner who becomes emotionally involved with someone else, rather than one who is sexually unfaithful (Buss, 2000; Regan et al., 2000; • Figure 17.2).

Why do such differences exist? Buss and others believe that mating preferences evolved in response to the differing reproductive challenges faced by men and women (Buss, 2007, 2011; Confer et al., 2010). As a rule, women must invest more time and energy in reproduction and nurturing the young than men do. Consequently, women evolved an interest in whether their partners will stay with them and whether their mates have the resources to provide for their children.

In contrast, the reproductive success of men depends on their mates' fertility. Men, therefore, tend to look for health, youth, and beauty in a prospective mate as signs of suitability for reproduction. This preference, perhaps, is why some older men abandon their first wives in favor of young, beautiful "trophy wives." Evolu-

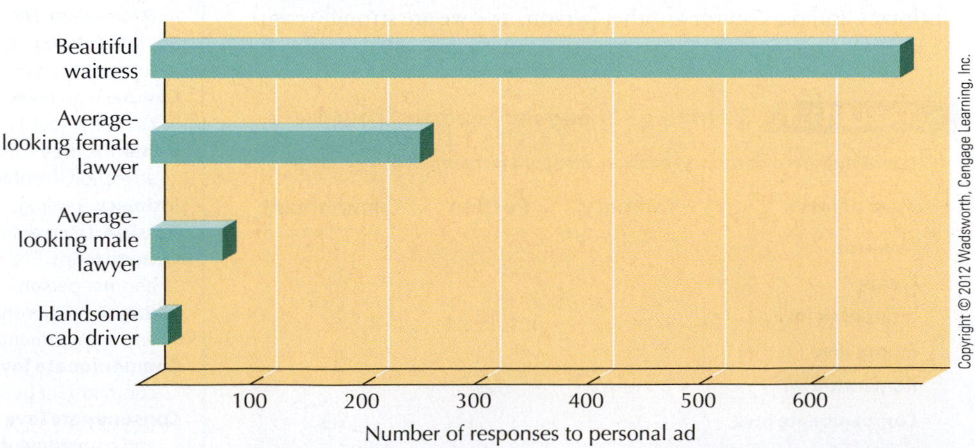

• **Figure 17.2** What do people look for when considering potential dating partners? Here are the results of a study in which personal ads were placed in newspapers. As you can see, men were more influenced by looks, and women by success (Goode, 1996).

© Monkey Business Images/Shutterstock

According to evolutionary psychologists, women tend to be concerned with whether mates will devote time and resources to a relationship. Men place more emphasis on physical attractiveness and sexual fidelity.

tionary theory further proposes that the male emphasis on mates' sexual fidelity is based on concerns about the paternity of offspring. From a biological perspective, men do not benefit from investing resources in children they did not sire (Buller, 2005).

Although some evidence supports the evolutionary view of mating, it is important to remember that evolved mating tendencies are subtle at best and easily overruled by other factors. Some mating patterns may simply reflect the fact that men still tend to control the power and resources in most societies (Feingold, 1992; Fine, 2010). Also, early research may be misleading because women tend to give "polite" answers to questions about jealousy. Privately, they may be just as furious about a mate's sexual infidelity as any man would be (Harris, 2004).

Whatever the outcome of the debate about evolution and mate selection, it is important to remember this: Potential mates are rated as most attractive if they are kind, secure, intelligent, and supportive (Klohnen & Luo, 2003; Regan et al., 2000). These qualities are love's greatest allies.

Although every society places high value on friendship and love, all would agree that the ultimate prosocial act is helping another human being, especially if he or she is a stranger in need. In the next section, we turn our attention to helping others. Before we do, here are some questions to help you help yourself.

Knowledge Builder: Affiliation, Friendship, and Love

RECITE

1. Women threatened with electric shock in an experiment generally chose to wait alone or with other women not taking part in the experiment. T or F?
2. Interpersonal attraction is increased by all but one of the following. (Which does not fit?)
   a. physical proximity *b.* competence *c.* similarity *d.* social costs
3. High levels of self-disclosure are reciprocated in most social encounters. T or F?
4. In Sternberg's triangular theory, infatuated love involves commitment but not passion or intimacy. T or F?
5. The most striking finding about marriage patterns is that most people choose mates whose personalities are quite unlike their own. T or F?
6. Both ambivalent and avoidant attachment patterns are associated with difficulties in trusting a romantic partner. T or F?
7. Compared with men, women tend to be more upset by sexual infidelity than by a loss of emotional commitment on the part of their mates. T or F?

REFLECT

Think Critically

8. How has the Internet altered the effects of proximity on interpersonal attraction?

Self-Reflect

Think of three close friends. Which of the attraction factors described earlier apply to your friendships?

To what extent does Sternberg's triangular theory of love apply to your own loving relationships with others?

Can you think of people you know whose adult relationships seem to illustrate each of the three attachments styles described in the preceding section?

Answers: 1. F **2.** d **3.** F **4.** F **5.** F **6.** T **7.** F **8.** The Internet has made actual physical proximity less crucial in interpersonal attraction because frequent contact is possible even at great distances. It has also made self-disclosure easier (be careful, it's just a click away). Internet romances are a good example of the possibilities this opens up (Lawson & Leck, 2006).

Helping Others—The Good Samaritan

Gateway Question 17.4: *Why are bystanders so often unwilling to help in an emergency?*

It's natural to act kindly towards people who you're attracted to or with whom you are friends or lovers. But what about total strangers? There is no doubt that showing kindness to strangers, especially when they are in need, is one of the most tender prosocial acts (Mikulincer & Shaver, 2010). But do we always help?

In April 2010, a homeless man helped a young woman fend off an attacker in Queens, New York. For his trouble, he was stabbed and fell to the sidewalk where he laid in a pool of his own blood. When emergency aid arrived over an hour later, Hugo Tale-Yax was already dead. Horrifyingly, surveillance video revealed that 25 people walked past him as he lay dying on the street (Livingston, Doyle, & Mangan, 2010).

Secure attachment A stable and positive emotional bond.

Avoidant attachment An emotional bond marked by a tendency to resist commitment to others.

Ambivalent attachment An emotional bond marked by conflicting feelings of affection, anger, and emotional turmoil.

Evolutionary psychology Study of the evolutionary origins of human behavior patterns.

© Robert Brenner/PhotoEdit, Inc.

Does the person lying on the ground need help? What factors determine whether a person in trouble will receive help in an emergency? Surprisingly, more potential helpers tend to lower the chances that help will be given.

This recent case, and others like it, dating back to the 1964 murder of a young woman named Kitty Genovese, which was witnessed by 38 bystanders (Manning, Levine, & Collins, 2007), make us wonder why no one helped. Perhaps it is understandable that no one wanted to get involved. After all, it might have meant risking personal injury. But what prevented these people from at least calling the police?

Isn't this an example of the alienation of city life? News reports often treat such incidents as evidence of a breakdown in social ties caused by the impersonality of the city. Although it is true that urban living can be dehumanizing, this does not fully explain such **bystander apathy** (the unwillingness of bystanders to offer help during emergencies, which is also referred to as the *bystander effect*). According to landmark work by psychologists John Darley and Bibb Latané (1968), failure to help is related to the number of people present. Over the years, many studies have shown that the *more* potential helpers present, the *less* likely people are to help (Latané, Nida, & Wilson, 1981; Miller, 2006).

Why would people be less willing to help when others are present? In Kitty Genovese's case, the answer is that everyone thought *someone else* would help. The dynamics of this effect are easily illustrated: Suppose that two motorists have stalled at the roadside, one on a sparsely traveled country road and the other on a busy freeway. Who gets help first?

On the freeway, where hundreds of cars pass every minute, each driver can assume that someone else will help. Personal responsibility for helping is spread so thin that no one takes action. On the country road, one of the first few people to arrive will probably stop, since the responsibility is clearly theirs. In general, Darley and Latané assume that bystanders are not apathetic or uncaring; they are inhibited by the presence of others.

Bystander Intervention

People must pass through four decision points before giving help. First, they must notice that something is happening. Next, they must define the event as an emergency. Then, they must take responsibility. Finally, they must select a course of action (● Figure 17.3). Laboratory experiments have shown that each step can be influenced by the presence of other people.

Noticing

What would happen if you fainted and collapsed on the sidewalk? Would someone stop to help? Would people think you were drunk? Would they even notice you? Darley and Latané suggest that if the sidewalk is crowded, few people will even see you. This has nothing to do with people blocking each other's vision. Instead, it is related to widely accepted norms against staring at others in public. People in crowds typically "keep their eyes to themselves."

Is there any way to show that this is a factor in bystander apathy? To test this idea, students were asked to fill out a questionnaire either alone or in a room full of people. As the students worked, a thick cloud of smoke was blown into the room through a vent.

Most students left alone in the room noticed the smoke immediately. Few of the people in groups noticed the smoke until it actually became difficult to see through it. Participants working in groups politely kept their eyes on their papers and avoided looking at others (or the smoke). In contrast, those who were alone scanned the room from time to time.

Defining an Emergency

The smoke-filled room also shows the influence others have on defining a situation as an emergency. When participants in groups finally noticed the smoke, they cast sidelong glances at others in the room. Apparently, they were searching for clues to help interpret what was happening. No one wanted to overreact or act like a fool if there was no emergency. However, as participants coolly surveyed the reactions of others, they were themselves being watched. In real emergencies, people sometimes "fake each other out" and underestimate the need for action because each person attempts to appear calm. In short, until someone acts, no one acts.

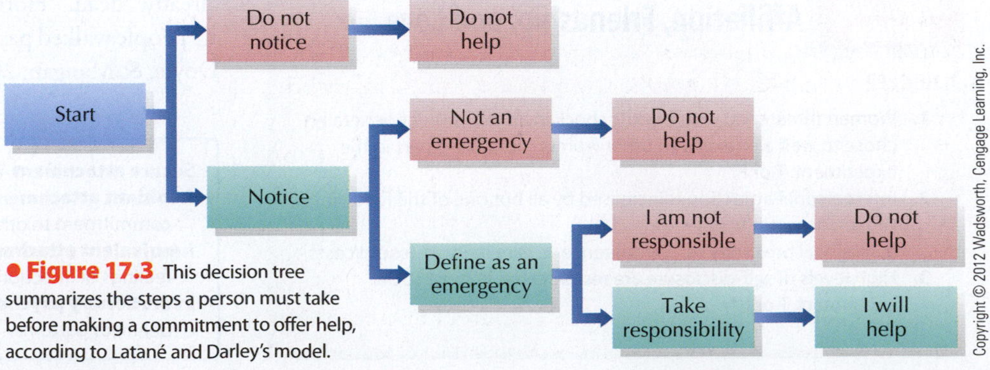

● **Figure 17.3** This decision tree summarizes the steps a person must take before making a commitment to offer help, according to Latané and Darley's model.

Taking Responsibility

Perhaps the most crucial step in helping is assuming responsibility. In this case, groups limit helping by causing a **diffusion of responsibility** (spreading responsibility among several people).

Is that like the unwillingness of drivers to offer help on a crowded freeway? Exactly. It is the feeling that no one is personally responsible for helping. This problem was demonstrated in an experiment in which students participated in a group discussion over an intercom system. Actually, there was only one real subject in each group; the others were tape-recorded actors. Each subject was placed in a separate room (supposedly to maintain confidentiality), and discussions of college life were begun. During the discussion, one of the "students" simulated an epileptic-like seizure and called out for help. In some cases, participants thought they were alone with the seizure victim. Others believed they were members of three- or six-person groups.

People who thought they were alone with the "victim" of this staged emergency reported it immediately or tried to help. Some participants in the three-person groups failed to respond, and those who did were slower. In the six-person groups, over a third of the participants took no action at all. People in this experiment were obviously faced with a conflict like that in many real emergencies: Should they be helpful and responsible, or should they mind their own business? Many were influenced toward inaction by the presence of others.

People do help in some emergencies. How are these different? It is not always clear what makes the difference. Helping behavior is complex and influenced by many variables (Baumeister & Bushman, 2011). One naturalistic experiment staged in a New York City subway gives a hint of the kinds of things that may be important. When a "victim" (actor) "passed out" in a subway car, he received more help when carrying a cane than when carrying a liquor bottle. More important, however, was the fact that most people were willing to help in either case (Piliavin, Rodin, & Piliavin, 1969).

To better answer the question we need to consider some factors not included in Latané and Darley's account of helping.

Who Will Help Whom?

Many studies suggest that when we see a person in trouble, it tends to cause *heightened arousal* (Batson, 2010; Dovidio et al., 2006). This aroused, keyed-up feeling can motivate us to give aid, but only if the rewards of helping outweigh the costs. Higher costs (such as great effort, personal risk, or possible embarrassment) almost always decrease helping. In addition to general arousal, potential helpers may also feel **empathic arousal**. This means they empathize with the person in need or feel some of the person's pain, fear, or anguish. Helping is much more likely when we are able to take the perspective of others and feel sympathy for their plight (Batson & Powell, 2003).

If people feel sad or distressed when another person is in trouble, couldn't it be that they help just to make themselves feel better? It is certainly possible that some helping is actually "selfish." But research has shown that empathy (empathic arousal) really does unleash altruistic motivation based on sympathy and compassion. Most helping, including such altruistic acts as making donations or being kind, is motivated by a true desire to relieve the distress of others (Aronson, Wilson, & Akert, 2010; Dovidio, Allen, & Schroeder, 1990).

Empathic arousal is especially likely to motivate helping when the person in need seems to be similar to ourselves (Batson, 2010; Batson & Powell, 2003). In fact, a feeling of connection to the victim may be one of the most important factors in helping. This, perhaps, is why being in a good mood also increases helping. When we are feeling successful, happy, or fortunate, we may also feel more connected to others (Dovidio & Penner, 2001). In summary, there is a strong **empathy-helping relationship**: We are most likely to help someone in need when we "feel for" that person and experience emotions such as empathy, sympathy, and compassion (Batson, 2006, 2010).

Is there anything that can be done to encourage prosocial behavior? People who see others helping are more likely to offer help themselves. Also, persons who give help in one situation tend to perceive themselves as helpful people. This change in self-image encourages them to help in other situations. One more point is that norms of fairness encourage us to help others who have helped us (Dovidio & Penner, 2001). For all these reasons, helping others not only assists them directly, it encourages others to help too.

"De-victimize" Yourself

If you should find yourself in need of help during an emergency, what can you do to avoid being a victim of bystander apathy? The work we have reviewed here suggests that you should make sure that you are noticed, that people realize there's an emergency, and that they need to take action. Being noticed can be promoted in some situations by shouting "Fire!" Bystanders who might run away from a robbery or an assault may rush to see where the fire is. At the very least, remember to not just scream. Instead, you should call out, "Help," or, "I need help right now." Whenever possible, define your situation for bystanders. Say, for instance, "I'm being attacked, call the police." Or, "Stop that man, he has my purse." You can also directly assign responsibility to a bystander by pointing to someone and saying, "You, call the police," or, "I'm injured, I need you to call an ambulance" (Cummins, 1995).

The Whole Human: Everyday Heroes

Every year awards are given to people who risk their lives while saving the lives of others. These heroes are typically honored for saving people from fires, drowning, animal attacks, electrocution, and

Bystander apathy Unwillingness of bystanders to offer help during emergencies or to become involved in others' problems.

Diffusion of responsibility Spreading the responsibility to act among several people; reduces the likelihood that help will be given to a person in need.

Empathic arousal Emotional arousal that occurs when you feel some of another person's pain, fear, or anguish.

Empathy-helping relationship Observation that we are most likely to help someone else when we feel emotions such as empathy and compassion.

suffocation. The majority of people who perform such heroic acts are men, perhaps because of the physical dangers involved. However, there are other heroic, prosocial acts that save lives and involve personal risk. Examples are kidney donors, Peace Corp volunteers, and Doctors of the World volunteers. In such endeavors, we find as many women as men, and often more. It is important to remember, perhaps, that sensational and highly visible acts of heroism are only one of many ways in which people engage in selfless, altruistic behavior (Becker & Eagly, 2004). People who serve as community volunteers, tutors, coaches, blood donors, and the like don't just help others. Often, their efforts contribute to personal growth and make themselves healthier and happier. Thus, it can be said, "We do well by doing good" (Piliavin, 2003).

Despite the many instances of prosocial behavior that occur every day, people in need are sometimes mugged or exploited rather than aided. Bluntly put, we humans are capable of hatred and cruelty as well as love (as people living in especially troubled parts of the world, such as Jasmine and Osama, know only too well). In the next few sections, we will turn our attention to the dark side of social behavior. To reiterate, **antisocial behavior** is any behavior that has a negative impact on other people. Aggression, prejudice, and intergroup conflict are all examples.

Antisocial Behavior—The World's Most Dangerous Animal

Gateway Question 17.5 : ***How do psychologists explain human aggression?***

For a time, the City Zoo of Los Angeles, California, had on display two examples of the world's most dangerous animal—the only animal capable of destroying the Earth and all other animal species. Perhaps you have already guessed which animal it was. In the cage were two college students, representing the species *Homo sapiens*!

Jon Kopaloff/Getty Images

Ritualized human aggression. Violent and aggressive behavior is so commonplace it may be viewed as entertainment. How "natural" is aggressive behavior?

Aggression refers to any action carried out with the intention of harming another person. The human capacity for aggression is staggering. About 58 million humans were killed by other humans (an average of nearly one person per minute) during the 125-year period ending with World War II. War, homicide, riots, family violence, assassination, rape, assault, forcible robbery, and other violent acts offer sad testimony to the realities of human aggression (Shaver & Mikulincer, 2011).

Bullying

Aggression is expressed in many forms. One pervasive form is **bullying**, any behavior that deliberately and repeatedly exposes a person to negative experiences (Powell & Ladd, 2010). Bullies tend to deal with everyday situations by resorting to aggression. Bullying can be *verbal* (name-calling, insults, teasing) or *physical* (hitting, pushing, confining), and it can also be *direct* ("in your face") or *indirect* (intentional exclusion, spreading rumors). Whereas male bullies are more likely to engage in direct aggression, female bullies tend to specialize in indirect aggression (Field et al., 2009). Bullying is a worldwide phenomenon. It first appears in early childhood, continues throughout adolescence into adulthood and the workplace, and can even be found online, in the form of *cyberbullying*.

Childhood bullying can have long-term consequences for the mental health of both bullies and their victims. Adolescent and adult bullying can lead to serious violence, including murder and suicide. In light of the pervasiveness of bullying, it should come as no surprise that much attention being directed at understanding the causes of bullying as well. It is especially important to understand childhood bullying in order to reduce its potential lifelong impact (Swearer, Espelage & Napolitano, 2009; Wiseman, 2009).

What causes aggression? Aggression has many potential causes (DeWall & Anderson, 2011). Brief descriptions of some of the major possibilities follow.

Instincts

Some theorists argue we are naturally aggressive creatures, having inherited a "killer instinct" from our animal ancestors. Ethologists theorize that aggression is a biologically rooted behavior observed in all animals, including humans (Blanchard & Blanchard, 2003). (An **ethologist** is a person who studies the natural behavior patterns of animals.) Noted ethologist Konrad Lorenz (1966, 1974) also believed that humans lack certain innate patterns that inhibit aggression in animals. For example, in a dispute over territory, two wolves may growl, lunge, bare their teeth, and fiercely threaten each other. In most instances, though, neither is killed or even wounded. One wolf, recognizing the dominance of the other, will typically bare its throat in a gesture of submission. The dominant wolf could kill in an instant, but it is inhibited by the other wolf's submissive gesture. In contrast, human confrontations of equal intensity almost always end in injury or death.

The idea that humans are "naturally" aggressive has an intuitive appeal, but many psychologists question it (Rhee & Waldman,

2011). Many of Lorenz's "explanations" of aggression are little more than loose comparisons between human and animal behavior. Just labeling a behavior as "instinctive" does little to explain it. More important, we are left with the question of why some individuals or human groups (the Arapesh, the Senoi, the Navajo, the Eskimo, and others) show little hostility or aggression. And, thankfully, the vast majority of humans *do not* kill or harm others.

Biology

Despite problems with the instinctive view, aggression may have biological roots (Rhee & Waldman, 2011). Physiological studies have shown that some brain areas are capable of triggering or ending aggressive behavior. Also, researchers have found a relationship between aggression and such physical factors as hypoglycemia (low blood sugar), allergy, and specific brain injuries and diseases. For both men and women, higher levels of the hormone testosterone may be associated with more aggressive behavior (McDermott et al., 2007). Perhaps because of their higher testosterone levels, men are more likely engage in physical aggression than women (Anderson & Bushman, 2002). However, none of these biological factors can be considered a direct *cause* of aggression (Moore, 2001; Popma et al., 2007). Instead, they probably lower the threshold for aggression, making hostile behavior more likely to occur (Tackett & Krueger, 2011).

The effects of alcohol and other drugs provide another indication of the role of the brain and biology in violence and aggression. A variety of studies show that alcohol is involved in large percentages of murders and violent crimes. Intoxicating drugs also seem to lower inhibitions to act aggressively—often with tragic results (Anderson & Bushman, 2002; Quigley & Leonard, 2000).

To summarize, the fact that we are biologically *capable* of aggression does not mean that aggression is inevitable or "part of human nature." In the famous Seville Statement on Violence, twenty eminent scientists who studied the question concluded that "Biology does not condemn humanity to war.... Violence is neither in our evolutionary legacy nor in our genes. The same species that invented war is capable of inventing peace" (Scott & Ginsburg, 1994; United Nations Educational, Scientific and Cultural Organization, 1990). Humans are fully capable of learning to inhibit aggression. For example, American Quakers and Amish, who live in this country's increasingly violent culture, adopt nonviolence as a way of life (Bandura, 2001).

Frustration

Step on a dog's tail and you may get nipped. Frustrate a human and you may get insulted. The **frustration-aggression hypothesis** states that frustration tends to lead to aggression.

Does frustration always produce aggression? Although the connection is strong, a moment's thought will show that frustration does not *always* lead to aggression. Frustration, for instance, may lead to stereotyped responding or perhaps to a state of "learned helplessness" (see Chapter 13, pages 458–460). Also, aggression

© Jose Luis Pelaez, Inc./Corbis

Road rage and some freeway shootings may be a reaction to the frustration of traffic congestion. The fact that automobiles provide anonymity, or a loss of personal identity, may also encourage aggressive actions that would not otherwise occur.

can occur in the absence of frustration. This possibility is illustrated by sports spectators who start fights, throw bottles, tear down goal posts, and so forth after their team has *won.*

Aversive Stimuli

Frustration probably encourages aggression because it is uncomfortable. Various *aversive stimuli,* which produce discomfort or displeasure, can heighten hostility and aggression (Anderson, Anderson, & Deuser, 1996; Morgan, 2005) (● Figure 17.4). Examples include insults, high temperatures, pain, and even disgusting scenes or odors. Such stimuli probably raise overall arousal levels so that we become more sensitive to **aggression cues** (signals that are associated with aggression) (Carlson, Marcus-Newhall & Miller, 1990). Aversive stimuli also tend to activate ideas, memories, and expressions associated with anger and aggression (Morgan, 2005).

Some cues for aggression are internal (angry thoughts, for instance). Many are external: Certain words, actions, and gestures made by others are strongly associated with aggressive responses. A raised middle finger, for instance, is an almost universal invitation to aggression in North America. Weapons serve as particularly strong cues for aggressive behavior (Morgan, 2005). The implication of this **weapons effect** seems to be that

Antisocial behavior Any behavior that has a negative impact on other people.

Aggression Any action carried out with the intention of harming another person.

Bullying The deliberate and repeated use of verbal or physical, direct or indirect, aggression as a tactic for dealing with everyday situations.

Ethologist A person who studies the natural behavior patterns of animals.

Frustration-aggression hypothesis States that frustration tends to lead to aggression.

Aggression cues Stimuli or signals that are associated with aggression and that tend to elicit it.

Weapons effect The observation that weapons serve as strong cues for aggressive behavior.

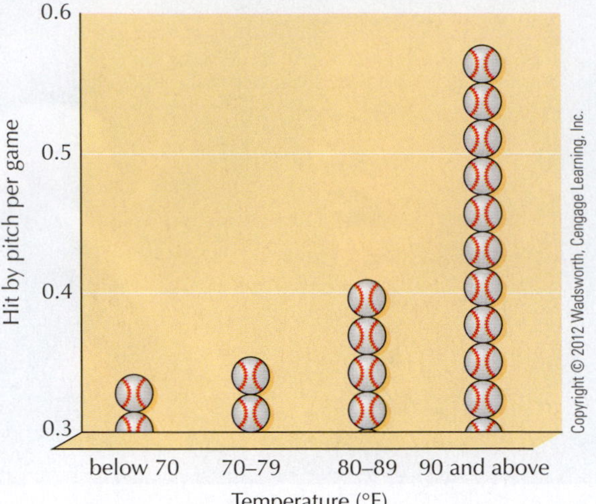

• **Figure 17.4** Personal discomfort caused by aversive (unpleasant) stimuli can make aggressive behavior more likely. For example, studies of crime rates show that the incidence of highly aggressive behavior, such as murder, rape, and assault, rises as the air temperature goes from warm to hot to sweltering (Anderson, 1989). The results you see here further confirm the heat–aggression link. The graph shows that there is a strong association between the temperatures at major league baseball games and the number of batters hit by a pitch during those games. When the temperature exceeds 90°, watch out for that fastball (Reifman, Larrick, & Fein, 1991)!

the symbols and trappings of aggression encourage aggression. A prime example is the fact that murders are more likely to occur in homes in which guns are kept (Miller, Hemenway, & Azraela, 2007).

Social Learning

One of the most widely accepted explanations of aggression is also the simplest. Social learning theory holds that we learn to be aggressive by observing aggression in others (Bandura, 2001; Lefrançois, 2006). **Social learning theory** combines learning principles with cognitive processes, socialization, and modeling to explain behavior. According to this view, there is no instinctive human programming for fistfighting, pipe bombing, knife wielding, gun loading, 95-mile-an-hour "bean balls," or other violent or aggressive behaviors. Hence, aggression must be learned (• Figure 17.5). Is it any wonder that people who were the victims of violence during childhood are likely to become violent themselves (Murrell, Christoff, & Henning, 2007)?

Social learning theorists predict that people growing up in nonaggressive cultures will themselves be nonaggressive. Those raised in a culture with aggressive models and heroes will learn aggressive responses (Bandura, 2001). Considered in such terms, it is no wonder that America has become one of the most violent of all countries. A violent crime occurred every 23 seconds in the United States during 2008 (Federal Bureau of Investigation, 2009). Approximately 38 percent of U.S. households own at least one firearm (Hepburn, 2006). Nationally, 70 percent agree that when a boy is growing up, it is "very important" for him to have a few fistfights. Children and adults are treated to an almost nonstop parade of aggressive models, in the media as well as in actual behavior. We are, without a doubt, an aggressive culture. (See "Pornography and Aggression Against Women.")

Media Violence

Today's children and adolescents spend an average of 50 hours a week exploring various media, including television, video games, movies, the Internet, music, and print media (Rideout, Foehr, & Roberts, 2010). By the time a child reaches adulthood, she or he will have viewed some 15,000 hours of television, including some 18,000 murders and countless acts of robbery, arson, bombing, torture, and beatings. Other media are no better. For example, 90 percent of popular video games contain violent content, and many popular toys are also linked to violent media (National Youth Violence Prevention Resource Center, 2008). The Internet is of special concern because it not only allows children to experience media violence, it also allows them to directly engage in *electronic aggression*, through bullying or harassment of others (David-Ferdon & Hertz, 2009).

How much does media violence affect children and adolescents? There is now little doubt that widespread exposure to media violence contributes to aggression (Anderson et al., 2003; DeGaetano, 2005; Krahé & Möller, 2010). As Albert Bandura showed in his studies of imitation, children may learn new aggressive actions by watching violent or aggressive behavior, or they may learn that violence is "okay." Either way, they are more likely to act aggressively. Heroes on television are as violent as the villains, and they usually receive praise for their violence. Boys and girls who watch a lot of violence on television are much more likely to be aggressive as adults (Huesmann et al., 2003). Violent video games are at least as problematic (Bartholow, Bushman, & Sestir, 2006), and even violent song lyrics increase aggressive tendencies (Anderson, Carnagey, & Eubanks, 2003).

BRIDGES
Modeling and observational learning explain much of television's impact on our behavior. **See Chapter 6, pages 231–233.**

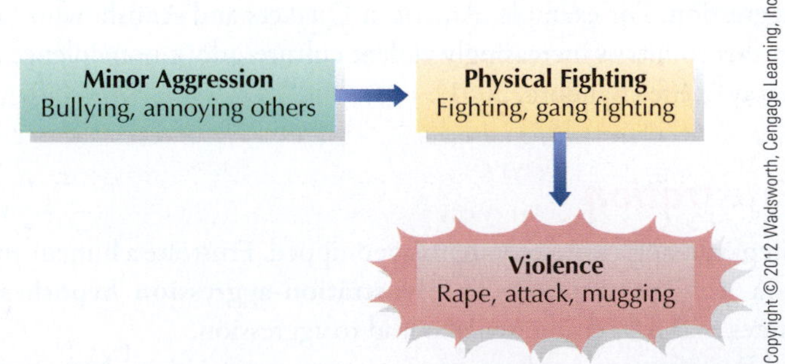

• **Figure 17.5** Violent behavior among delinquent boys doesn't appear overnight. Usually, their capacity for violence develops slowly, as they move from minor aggression to increasingly brutal acts. Overall aggression increases dramatically in early adolescence as boys gain physical strength and more access to weapons (Loeber & Hay, 1997).

Critical Thinking: Pornography and Aggression Against Women—Is There a Link?

A heated debate has raged for years about the effects of pornography. Early studies suggested that viewing pornography has no major adverse effects. This conclusion appears to remain valid for stimuli that can be described as merely erotic or sexual in content (Malamuth, Addison, & Koss, 2000). However, in recent years, there has been a dramatic increase in aggressive pornographic images in the mass media. **Aggressive pornography** refers to depictions in which violence, threats, or obvious power differences are used to force someone (usually a woman) to engage in sex (Bridges et al., 2010; Davis et al., 2006).

The main finding of studies on aggressive pornographic stimuli is that they do increase aggression against females in men who are prone to sexual violence (Hald, Malamuth, & Yuen, 2010; Malamuth, Addison, & Koss, 2000). As researchers Neil Malamuth and Ed Donnerstein (1982) concluded, "Exposure to mass media stimuli that have violent *and* sexual content increases the audience's aggressive sexual fantasies, beliefs in rape myths, and aggressive behavior." Donnerstein and Daniel Linz (1986) add that media *violence* is most damaging. As they put it, "Violent images, rather than sexual ones, are most responsible for people's attitudes about women and rape." The problem, then, extends far beyond X-rated films and books. Mainstream movies, magazines, music videos, and television programs are equally to blame for reinforcing the myth that women find force or aggression pleasurable (Donnerstein, 2001). It is telling that rapists are sexually aroused by both sexual and nonsexual violence. Clearly, violence is a major dimension of rape and sexual aggression (Forbes & Adams-Curtis 2001; Hald et al, 2010).

In addition to teaching new antisocial actions, media such as television and video games may disinhibit dangerous impulses that viewers already have. **Disinhibition** (the removal of inhibition) results in acting out behavior that normally would be restrained. For example, many television programs give the message that violence is acceptable behavior that leads to success and popularity. For some people, this message can lower inhibitions against acting out hostile feelings (Anderson et al., 2003).

Another effect of media violence is that it tends to lower sensitivity to violent acts (Funk, 2005). As anyone who has seen a street fight or a mugging can tell you, television violence is sanitized and unrealistic. The real thing is gross, ugly, and gut wrenching. Even when media violence is graphic, as it is in many video games, it is experienced in the relaxed and familiar setting of the home. For at least some viewers, this combination diminishes emotional reactions to violent scenes (Carnagey, Anderson, & Bushman, 2007). More than 30 years ago, when Victor Cline and his associates showed a bloody fight film to a group of boys, they found that heavy television viewers (averaging 42 hours a week) showed much less emotion than those who watched little or no TV (Cline, Croft, & Courrier, 1972). Media, it seems, can cause a **desensitization** (reduced emotional sensitivity) to violence (Huesmann et al., 2003; Krahé et al., 2011).

Preventing Aggression

What can be done about aggression? Social learning theory implies that "aggression begets aggression." For example, children who are physically abused at home, those who suffer severe physical punishment, and those who merely witness violence in the community are more likely to be involved in fighting, aggressive play, and antisocial behavior at school (Bartholow, Sestir, & Davis, 2005; Margolin & Gordis, 2000).

According to social learning theorists, watching a mixed martial arts fight or other violent television program may increase aggression rather than drain off aggressive urges. A case in point is provided by psychologist Leonard Eron, who spent 22 years following more than 600 children into adulthood. Eron (1987) observes, "Among the most influential models for children were those observed on television. One of the best predictors of how aggressive a young man would be at age 19 was the violence of the television programs he preferred when he was 8 years old" (● Figure 17.6). According to Eron, children learn aggressive strategies and actions from television violence. Because of this, they are more prone to aggress when they face frustrating situations or cues. Others have found that viewers who experience violent media have more aggressive thoughts. As we have noted, violent thoughts often precede violent actions (Anderson, Carnagey, & Eubanks, 2003; Ferguson, Miguel, & Hartley, 2009). Thus, the spiral of aggression might be broken if we did not so often portray it, reward it, and glorify it.

Social learning theory Combines learning principles with cognitive processes, socialization, and modeling, to explain behavior.

Aggressive pornography Media depictions of sexual violence or of forced participation in sexual activity.

Disinhibition The removal of inhibition; results in acting out behavior that normally would be restrained.

Desensitization A reduction in emotional sensitivity to a stimulus.

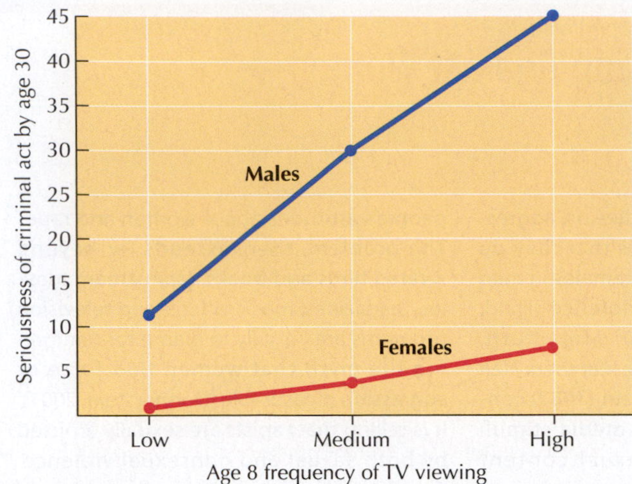

● **Figure 17.6** Although television violence does not cause aggression, it can encourage it. The likelihood of committing criminal acts by age 30 is related to the amount of television watching a person did when she or he was a child. From L. D. Eron, "The Development of Aggressive Behavior from the Perspective of a Developing Behaviorism," *American Psychologist*, May 1987, p. 435–442. Copyright © 1987 APA. Reprinted with permission of the publisher.

Parents as Media Guides

As the preceding studies show, reducing exposure to violent media is one way to lower aggression. However, other than pulling the plug, what can parents do about media's negative effects on children? Actually, quite a lot. Parents can make a big difference if they do the following (Adults and Children Together Against Violence, 2010; Frydman, 1999):

1. Start by creating a safe, warm environment at home and school and by modeling positive ways of getting along in the world. Children typically model parents' behavior, including their media viewing habits, and they are guided by parents' reactions to media.
2. Limit total media time so that television and computer games do not dominate your child's view of the world. If necessary, set schedules for when watching television or playing video games is allowed. Don't use media as a babysitter.
3. Closely monitor what your child does experience. Change channels or turn off the television if you object to a program. Be prepared to offer games and activities that stimulate your child's imagination and creativity as well as model positive behavior and social attitudes.
4. Explore media with your child so that you can counter what is shown. Help your child distinguish between reality and fantasy in media. Reply to distortions, stereotypes, and violence as they appear on screen. Encourage the child to propose more mature, realistic, and positive responses to situations.
5. Show by your own disapproval that violent television and computer game heroes are not the ones to emulate. Remember, children who identify with media characters are more likely to be influenced by media aggression.

By following these guidelines you can help children learn to enjoy television without being overly influenced by programs and advertisers. A recent study found that elementary school children become less aggressive when they decrease the amount of time they spend watching television and playing video games (Robinson et al., 2001).

Television as a Positive Model

Couldn't television's impact also be used constructively? There is no denying television's tremendous power to inform and to entertain. When these features are combined, the effect can be quite constructive. Perhaps the best examples of television as a positive social force are classic educational programs such as *Barney and Friends*, *Sesame Street*, and *Mr. Rogers' Neighborhood*. Numerous research reports have found that the impact of these programs is positive. Clearly, television can teach children while holding their interest and attention.

Prosocial behavior consists of actions toward others that are helpful, constructive, or altruistic (Penner et al., 2005). As a model for positive attitudes and responses, television could be used to promote helping, cooperation, charity, and brotherhood in the same way that it has tended to stereotype and encourage aggression. Over 200 studies have shown that prosocial behavior on television increases prosocial behavior by viewers (Hearold, 1987; Mares & Woodard, 2007).

Anger Control

On a personal level, psychologists have succeeded in teaching some people to control their anger and aggressive impulses. **Anger control** refers to personal strategies for reducing or curbing anger. The key to remaining calm is to define upsetting situations as *problems to be solved*. Therefore, to limit anger, people are taught to do the following:

1. Define the problem as precisely as possible.
2. Make a list of possible solutions.
3. Rank the likely success of each solution.
4. Choose a solution and try it.
5. Assess how successful the solution was, and make adjustments if necessary.

It also helps to learn how to avoid problematic situations or think differently about them in the first place, as well as learn how to let go of anger (Tafrate & Kassinove, 2009). Taking steps such as these has helped many people to lessen tendencies toward child abuse, family violence, and other destructive outbursts (Hall, 2009; Miltenberger, 2011).

Beyond this, the question remains: How shall we tame the world's most dangerous animal? There is no easy answer, only a challenge of pressing importance. The solution will undoubtedly involve the best efforts of thinkers and researchers from many disciplines.

Knowledge Builder

Helping Others and Aggression

RECITE

1. A ____________________ of responsibility occurs when individual bystanders in a group do not step forward to help someone in need.
2. Defining an event as an emergency is the first step toward bystander intervention. T or F?
3. Seeing that a person in need is similar to ourselves tends to increase empathic arousal and the likelihood that help will be given. T or F?
4. The position of ethologists is that there is no biological basis for aggression. T or F?
5. Higher levels of testosterone are associated with more aggressive behavior. T or F?
6. Frustration and aversive stimuli are more likely to produce aggression when cues for aggressive behavior are present. T or F?
7. Social learning theorists view aggression as primarily related to biological instincts. T or F?
8. Social learning theory holds that exposure to aggressive models helps drain off aggressive energies. T or F?
9. Heavy exposure to television results in lowered emotional sensitivity to violence. T or F?

REFLECT

Think Critically

10. If media violence contributes to aggressive behavior in our society, do you think it is possible that media could also promote prosocial behavior?

Self-Reflect

An elderly woman is at the side of the road, trying to change a flat tire. She obviously needs help. You are approaching her in your car. What must happen before you are likely to stop and help her?

Most people have been angry enough at some time to behave aggressively. Which concepts or theories do you think best explain your own aggressive actions?

Answers: 1. diffusion **2.** F **3.** T **4.** F **5.** T **6.** T **7.** F **8.** F **9.** T **10.** Yes. media could be used to promote helping, cooperation, charity, and brotherhood in the same way that it has encouraged aggression. Numerous studies show, for example, that prosocial behavior on TV increases prosocial behavior by viewers (Greitemeyer, 2009).

Prejudice—Attitudes That Injure

Gateway Question 17.6: *What causes prejudice?*

Love and friendship bring people together. Prejudice, which is marked by suspicion, fear, or hatred, has the opposite effect. **Prejudice**, an all too common part of daily life, is a negative emotional attitude held toward members of a specific social group (Whitley & Kite, 2010). What are the origins of prejudice? How can prejudice and hurtful attitudes be reduced? Psychologists have provided valuable insights into these questions (see "I'm Not Prejudiced, Right?").

Prejudices may be reflected in the policies of police departments, schools, or government institutions (Dovidio, Glick, & Rudman, 2005). In such cases, prejudice is referred to as **racism**, **sexism**, **ageism**, or **heterosexism**, depending on the group affected (Payne et al., 2010). Because sexism, ageism, and heterosexism were discussed in earlier chapters, let's focus on racism (Miller & Garran, 2008).

Both racial prejudice and racism lead to **discrimination**, or unequal treatment of people who should have the same rights as others. Discrimination prevents people from doing things they should be able to do, such as buying a house, getting a job, or attending a high-quality school (Whitley & Kite, 2010). For example, in many cities, African Americans have been the target of "racial profiling" in which they are stopped by police without reason. Sometimes, they are merely questioned, but many are cited for minor infractions, such as a cracked taillight or an illegal lane change. For many law-abiding citizens, being detained in this manner is a rude awakening (Plous, 2003). It's also one reason why many African Americans and other minority persons in America distrust police and the legal system (Dovidio et al., 2002). As distinguished African American psychologist Kenneth Clark said, "Racial prejudice...debases all human beings—those who are its victims, those who victimize, and in quite subtle ways, those who are merely accessories."

Becoming Prejudiced

How do prejudices develop? One major theory suggests that prejudice is a form of **scapegoating** (blaming a person or a group for the actions of others or for conditions not of their making). Scapegoating is a type of **displaced aggression** in which hostilities triggered by frustration are redirected at "safer" targets (Glick, 2008; Nelson, 2006). One interesting classic test of this hypothesis was conducted at a summer camp for young men. The men were given a difficult test they were sure to fail. Additionally, completing the test caused them to miss a trip to the movies, which was normally the high point of their weekly entertainment. Attitudes toward Mexicans and Japanese were measured before the test and after the men had failed the test and missed the movie. Participants in this study, all European Americans, consistently rated members of the two ethnic groups lower after being

Anger control Personal strategies for reducing or curbing anger.

Prejudice A negative emotional attitude held against members of a particular group of people.

Racism Racial prejudice that has become institutionalized (that is, it is reflected in government policy, schools, and so forth) and that is enforced by the existing social power structure.

Sexism Institutionalized prejudice against members of either sex, based solely on their gender.

Ageism An institutionalized tendency to discriminate on the basis of age; prejudice based on age.

Heterosexism The belief that heterosexuality is better or more natural than homosexuality.

Discrimination Treating members of various social groups differently in circumstances where their rights or treatment should be identical.

Scapegoating Blaming a person or a group for the actions of others or for conditions not of their making.

Displaced aggression Redirecting aggression to a target other than the actual source of one's frustration.

Discovering Psychology: I'm Not Prejudiced, Right?

Are you prejudiced against women working outside the family home? Keep in mind your answer to this question as you read on.

Below you will find a list of 12 words. Your job is to categorize the words. Suppose, for example, that one of the words is *factory*. If you feel that *factory* belongs in the category "Male or Career," then you would touch (or mark) the O to the left of the word. Otherwise, you would mark the O to the right of *factory*.

Now, take 20 seconds to classify each of the words in the list. Place them into the correct categories as quickly and accurately as you can. Got the idea? Ready, set, go!

Male or Career		Female or Family
O	Daniel	O
O	Sally	O
O	House	O
O	Kitchen	O
O	Merchant	O
O	Company	O
O	Emily	O
O	Relatives	O
O	Employment	O
O	Baby	O
O	Steven	O
O	Executive	O

Now try it again with 12 new words. The only difference is that the categories have changed. Ready, set, go!

Male or Family		Female or Career
O	Home	O
O	Manager	O
O	Domestic	O
O	Andrew	O
O	In-laws	O
O	Jane	O
O	Workplace	O
O	Sarah	O
O	Office	O
O	Corporation	O
O	Siblings	O
O	John	O

Many people notice that it takes longer to do the second list and that they make more mistakes. Even people who claim they are not prejudiced against women working outside the home will, nevertheless, be slower and less accurate in classifying words into the categories *Male or Family* as well as *Female or Career*. Why is there a difference? For many people, *Female* and *Family* seem to go together better than *Female* and *Career* do.

You just completed a pencil-and-paper version of an *implicit association test* (adapted from Nosek, Greenwald, & Banaji, 2005). If you Google the Web you will find that similar tests have been constructed for race, age, religion, ethnicity, disability, sexual orientation, weight, and many other stereotyped categories of people (Blair, 2001; Hofmann et al., 2005; Kite et al., 2005). Apparently, we can harbor implicit (hidden) prejudices even when we do not explicitly own up to them (Anderson, 2010b).

frustrated (Miller & Bugelski, 1948). This effect has been easy to observe since the September 11, 2001, terrorist attacks in the United States, as people who look "foreign" have become targets for displaced anger and hostility (Ahluwalia & Pellettiere, 2010).

At times, the development of prejudice (like other attitudes) can be traced to direct experiences with members of the rejected group. A child who is repeatedly bullied by members of a particular ethnic group might develop a lifelong dislike for all members of the group. Yet, even subtle influences, such as parents' attitudes, the depiction of people in books and on television, and exposure to children of other races can have an impact. By the time they are 3 years old, many children show signs of race bias (Katz, 2003). Sadly, once prejudices are established, they prevent us from accepting more positive experiences that could reverse the damage (Wilder, Simon, & Faith, 1996).

Distinguished psychologist Gordon Allport (1958) concluded that there are two important sources of prejudice. **Personal prejudice** occurs when members of another social group are perceived as a threat to one's own interests. For example, members of another social group may be viewed as competitors for jobs. **Group prejudice** occurs when a person conforms to group norms. Let's say, for instance, that you have no personal reason for disliking out-group members. Nevertheless, your friends, acquaintances, or coworkers expect it of you.

The Prejudiced Personality

Other research suggests that prejudice can be a general personality characteristic. Theodore Adorno and his associates (1950) described what they called the *authoritarian* (ah-thor-ih-TARE-ee-un) *personality*. These researchers started out by studying anti-Semitism. In the process, they found that people who are prejudiced against one group tend to be prejudiced against *all* out-groups (Perreault & Bourhis, 1999; Kteily, Sidanius, & Levin, 2011).

What are the characteristics of the prejudice-prone personality? The **authoritarian personality** is marked by rigidity, inhibition, prejudice, and oversimplification (black-and-white thinking). Authoritarians also tend to highly value social conformity (Feldman, 2003). More recently, this tendency been termed *right wing authoritarianism* (Duckitt & Sibley, 2010). At the same time, authoritarians also tend to be very *ethnocentric*. **Ethnocentrism** refers to placing one's own group "at the center," usually by rejecting all other groups. Put more simply, authoritarians consider their own ethnic group superior to others. In fact, authoritarians think they are superior to everyone who is different, not just other ethnic groups (Altemeyer, 2004). More recently, this has been termed *social dominance orientation* (Duckitt & Sibley, 2010).

To measure these qualities, the *F scale* was created (the *F* stands for "fascism"). This scale is made up of statements such as the ones that follow—to which authoritarians readily agree (Adorno et al., 1950):

Authoritarian Beliefs

- Obedience and respect for authority are the most important virtues children should learn.
- People can be divided into two distinct classes: the weak and the strong.
- If people would talk less and work more, everybody would be better off.
- What this country needs most, more than laws and political programs, is a few courageous, tireless, devoted leaders in whom the people can put their faith.
- Nobody ever learns anything really important except through suffering.
- Every person should have complete faith in some supernatural power whose decisions are obeyed without question.
- Certain religious sects that refuse to salute the flag should be forced to conform to such patriotic action or else be abolished.

As you can see, authoritarians are rather close-minded (Butler, 2000). As children, most were severely punished. As a result, they learned to fear authority (and to covet it) at an early age. In general, people are more likely to express authoritarian beliefs when they feel threatened. An example would be calling for more severe punishment in schools when the economy is bad and job insecurities are high. Authoritarians are not happy people.

It should be readily apparent from the list of authoritarian beliefs that the F scale is slanted toward politically conservative authoritarians. To be fair, psychologist Milton Rokeach (1918–1988) noted that rigid and authoritarian personalities can be found at both ends of the political scale. Rokeach, therefore, preferred to describe rigid and intolerant thinking as *dogmatism*. (**Dogmatism** is an unwarranted certainty in matters of belief or opinion.) Dogmatic persons find it difficult to change their beliefs, even when the evidence contradicts them (Butler, 2000).

Even if we discount the obvious bigotry of the authoritarian personality, racial prejudice runs deep in many nations. Let's probe deeper into the roots of such prejudiced behavior.

Intergroup Conflict—The Roots of Prejudice

Gateway Question 17.7: *What can be done about prejudice and intergroup conflict?*

An unfortunate byproduct of group membership is that it often limits contact with people in other groups. Additionally, groups themselves may come into conflict. Both events tend to foster hatred and prejudice toward the out-group. The bloody clash of opposing forces in the Middle East, Africa, Ireland, and Hometown, USA, are reminders that intergroup conflict is widespread. Daily, we read of jarring strife between political, religious, or ethnic groups. Suicide bombings, endless checkpoints, missiles, tanks, and a state of permanent conflict form the backdrop against which Jasmine and Osama stand out by virtue of their interethnic, interreligious relationship.

Shared beliefs concerning *superiority*, *injustice*, *vulnerability*, and *distrust* are common triggers for hostility between groups. Pick almost any group in conflict with others and you will find people

NBAE/Getty Images

● **Figure 17.7** Racial stereotypes are common in sports. For example, one study confirmed that many people actually do believe that "white men can't jump." This stereotype implies that African American basketball players are naturally superior in athletic ability. European American players, in contrast, are falsely perceived as smarter and harder working than African Americans. Such stereotypes set up expectations that distort the perceptions of fans, coaches, and sportswriters. The resulting misperceptions, in turn, help perpetuate the stereotypes (Stone, Perry, & Darley, 1997).

thinking along these lines: "We are special people who are superior to other groups, but we have been unjustly exploited, wronged, or humiliated [superiority and injustice]. Other groups are a threat to us [vulnerability]. They are dishonest and have repeatedly betrayed us [distrust]. Naturally, we are hostile toward them. They don't deserve our respect or cooperation" (Eidelson & Eidelson, 2003; Whitley & Kite, 2010).

In addition to hostile beliefs about other groups, conflicts are almost always amplified by stereotyped images of out-group members (Bar-Tal & Labin, 2001).

What exactly is a stereotype? **Social stereotypes** are oversimplified images of people in various groups There is a good chance that you have stereotyped images of some of the following: African Americans, European Americans, Hispanics, Jews, women, Christians, old people, men, Asian Americans, blue-collar workers, rednecks, politicians, business executives, teenagers, or billionaires (● Figure 17.7). In general, the top three categories on which most

Personal prejudice Prejudicial attitudes held toward persons who are perceived as a direct threat to one's own interests.
Group prejudice Prejudice held out of conformity to group views.
Authoritarian personality A personality pattern characterized by rigidity, inhibition, prejudice, and an excessive concern with power, authority, and obedience.
Ethnocentrism Placing one's own group or race at the center—that is, tending to reject all other groups but one's own.
Dogmatism An unwarranted positiveness or certainty in matters of belief or opinion.
Social stereotypes Oversimplified images of the traits of individuals who belong to a particular social group.

Human Diversity Choking on Stereotypes

Bill, a retired aircraft mechanic, has agreed to talk to a group of high school students about the early days of commercial aviation. During his talk, Bill is concerned that any slip in his memory will confirm stereotypes about older people being forgetful. Because he is anxious and preoccupied about possible memory lapses, Bill actually "chokes" as he suffers problems with his memory (Chasteen et al., 2005).

As Bill's example suggests, negative stereotypes can have a self-fulfilling quality. This is especially true in situations in which a person's abilities are evaluated. For example, African American and other minority group students must often cope with negative stereotypes about their academic abilities (Steele & Aronson, 1995; Owens & Massey, 2011). Could such stereotypes actually impair school performance?

Psychologist Claude Steele has amassed evidence that victims of stereotyping tend to feel **stereotype threat**. They can feel threatened when they think they are being judged in terms of a stereotype. The anxiety that this causes can then lower performance, seemingly confirming the stereotype. An experiment Steele did demonstrates this effect. In the study, African American and European American college students took a very difficult verbal test. Some students were told the test measured *academic ability*. Others were told that the test was a laboratory *problem-solving task* unrelated to ability. In the ability condition, African American students performed worse than European Americans. In the problem-solving condition, they performed the same as European Americans (Steele, 1997; Steele & Aronson, 1995). A similar effect occurs with women, who score lower on math and finance tests after being reminded of the stereotype that "women aren't good at math" (Cadinu et al., 2005; Carr & Steele, 2010).

In light of such findings, Steele and others are currently working on ways to remove stereotype threat, so that all students can use their potentials more fully (Alter et al., 2010; Cohen et al., 2009; Steele, 1997).

stereotypes are based are sex, age, and race (Fiske, 1993; Fiske et al., 2002).

Stereotypes tend to simplify people into "us" and "them" categories. Actually, aside from the fact that they always oversimplify, stereotypes often include a mixture of *positive* or *negative* qualities (Fiske et al., 2002). Even though stereotypes sometimes include positive traits, they are mainly used to control people. When a person is stereotyped, the easiest thing to do is to abide by others' expectations—even if they are demeaning. That's why no one likes to be stereotyped. Being forced into a small, distorted social "box" is limiting and insulting. Stereotypes rob people of their individuality (Maddox, 2004). It is especially damaging when people begin to **self-stereotype**, halfway believing the stereotypes applied to them or at least worrying about how they appear in the presence of stereotypers (Latrofa et al., 2010; Oswald & Chapleau, 2010; see "Choking on Stereotypes".) Without stereotypes, there would be far less hate, prejudice, exclusion, and conflict.

Today's racism is often disguised by **symbolic prejudice**. That is, many people realize that crude and obvious racism is socially unacceptable. However, this may not stop them from expressing prejudice in subtly veiled forms when they state their opinions about affirmative action, busing, immigration, crime, and so on (Anderson, 2010b). In effect, modern racists find ways to rationalize their prejudice so that it seems to be based on issues other than raw racism. For instance, an African American candidate and an European American candidate apply for a job. Both are only moderately qualified for the position. If the person making the hiring decision is European American, who gets the job? As you might guess, the European American candidate is much more likely to be hired. In other words, the European American candidate will be given "the benefit of the doubt" about his or her abilities, whereas the African American candidate won't. People making such decisions often believe that they aren't being prejudiced, but they unconsciously discriminate against minorities (Dovidio et al., 2002).

Stereotypes held by the prejudiced tend to be unusually irrational. When given a list of negative statements about other groups, prejudiced individuals agree with most of them. It's particularly revealing that they often agree with conflicting statements. Thus, a prejudiced person may say that Jews are both "pushy" and "standoffish" or that African Americans are both "ignorant" and "sly." In one study, prejudiced persons even expressed negative attitudes toward two nonexistent groups, the "Piraneans" and the "Danirians." (See "Terrorists, Enemies, and Infidels" for further information.) Note, too, that when a preju-

Ethnic pride is slowly replacing stereotypes and discrimination. For example, different Native American groups publicly celebrate their own festivals with pride. However, despite affirmations of ethnic heritage, the problem of prejudice is far from solved.

Critical Thinking: Terrorists, Enemies, and Infidels

During times of war, normal people are called upon to kill other humans. How do they turn off their emotions and moral standards? Actually, they don't. Instead, they convince themselves that their actions are just (Leidner et al., 2010; Osofsky, Bandura, & Zimbardo, 2005). For example, violence may be seen as necessary to eradicate evil, serve God, or to protect honor, virtue, justice, or freedom.

Whether it's Israelis and Palestinians, Sinhalese and Tamils in Sri Lanka, or al-Qaeda and the West, each side believes that attack or counterattack is morally justified. And, whether they are right or wrong, both sides use the same psychological mechanisms to justify violence (Wilmot & Hocker, 2007). In violent conflicts between groups, "the enemy" is always portrayed as evil, monstrous, or less than human (Waytz, Epley, Cacioppo, 2010). Dehumanizing others makes it seem that they *deserve* hatred and even death. Undoubtedly, this provides a degree of emotional insulation that makes it easier for soldiers to harm other humans. However, it also makes terrorism, torture, murder, and genocide possible.

A danger in demonizing "the enemy" is that it can lead to misperceptions of the motives and actions of other nations or groups. Many of the bloodiest conflicts in history have been fueled, in part, by treating "the enemy" as evil and subhuman. Those who actually do hold the moral high ground must be careful not to succumb to the same kind of blind hatred that leads to wanton violence and terrorism. It is also wise to remember that ethnic jokes, racial stereotypes, degrading names, and out-group slurs are small-scale examples of the damage that "enemy" images can do.

Issouf Sangogo/AFP/Getty Images

A long-running military conflict in the Darfur region of the Sudan, in Africa, was a genocide in which hundreds of thousands of mothers, fathers, daughters, and sons were slaughtered. Hopefully, recent political developments in the Sudan will prevent a recurrence of such a tragic scenario.

diced person meets a pleasant or likable member of a rejected group, the out-group member tends to be perceived as "an exception to the rule," not as evidence against the stereotype. Even when such "exceptional" experiences begin to stack up, a prejudiced person may not change his or her stereotyped belief (Whitley & Kite, 2010; Wilder, Simon, & Faith, 1996). Because some elements of prejudice are unconscious, they are very difficult to change (Dovidio et al., 2002).

How do stereotypes and intergroup tensions develop? Two experiments, both in unlikely settings and both using children as participants, offer some insight into these problems.

Experiments in Prejudice

What is it like to be discriminated against? In a unique experiment, elementary school teacher Jane Elliott sought to give her pupils direct experience with prejudice. On the first day of the experiment, Elliott announced that brown-eyed children were to sit in the back of the room and that they could not use the drinking fountain. Blue-eyed children were given extra recess time and got to leave first for lunch. At lunch, brown-eyed children were prevented from taking second helpings because they would "just waste it." Brown-eyed and blue-eyed children were kept from mingling, and the blue-eyed children were told they were "cleaner" and "smarter" (Peters, 1971).

Eye color might seem like a trivial basis for creating prejudices. However, people use primarily skin color to make decisions about the race of another person (Glenn, 2009). Surely this is just as superficial a way of judging people as eye color is, especially given recent biological evidence that it does not even make genetic sense to talk about "races" (Bonham, Warshauer-Baker & Collins, 2005). (See this chapter's *Psychology in Action* section for further information about the concept of race.)

John Reavenal/NTI/Landov

Are these children of different "races"? Yes, this IS a trick question. Only skin color differentiates these nonidentical twins. The odds, by the way, of mixed race parents having a pair of twins, like these two, is one in a million. How fair will it be when these two children experience differential treatment based solely on their skin color?

Self-stereotyping The tendency to apply social stereotypes to one's self.
Stereotype threat The anxiety caused by the fear of being judged in terms of a stereotype.
Symbolic prejudice Prejudice that is expressed in disguised fashion.

Human Diversity — Is America Purple?

As research shows, it is easy to create prejudice. Pick any simplistic way to divide a group of people into "us" and "them" and popularize it. That's what teacher Jane Elliott did when she divided her class into the brown-eyed kids and the blue-eyed kids. In no time at all, the groups were prejudiced against each other.

But that was just an experiment. It couldn't happen in the real world, right? According to psychologists Conor Seyle and Matthew Newman (2006), we are witnessing just such a real-world example in America today. In order to graphically convey the outcome of the presidential vote in the 2000 election, *USA Today* created a state-by-state map, color coded red and blue to denote states that had voted for the Republican candidate or the Democratic candidate.

Just a few years later, "red" and "blue" have become a national shorthand for dividing Americans into opposing camps. The "reds" are supposed to be Republican, conservative, middle-class rural, religious, and live in the American heartland. The "blues" are supposed to be Democrat, liberal, upper class, urban, nonreligious, and live on the coasts. The end result is that the complex American social world is reduced to two oversimplified stereotypes, leading to an increase in between-group prejudice (Binning et al., 2010; Mundy, 2004).

This oversimplification ignores the fact that, in many states, the presidential votes are very close. Thus, a state that is "red" by 51 percent is nevertheless 49 percent "blue." Besides, many different combinations exist. Former President Bill Clinton is originally from Arkansas (a "red" state), identifies himself as a Southern Baptist, and worships in a Methodist church. Is he "blue"? How do you categorize someone from California (a "blue" state) who is an economic conservative, attends church occasionally, lives in San Francisco, supports gay marriage, and yet votes Republican?

According to Seyle & Newman (2006), a better approach is to recognize that America is made up of a full spectrum of political, social, religious, and economic views and that most Americans are "purple." Thinking this way also highlights the fact that Americans of all political persuasions share more similarities than they do differences when compared with the citizens of other countries. This more tolerant, less polarizing view of America is reflected in the "purple America" map (● Figure 17.8) (Gastner, Shalizi, & Newman, 2005). Thinking purple just might result in a more productive national discussion about the important issues facing America today.

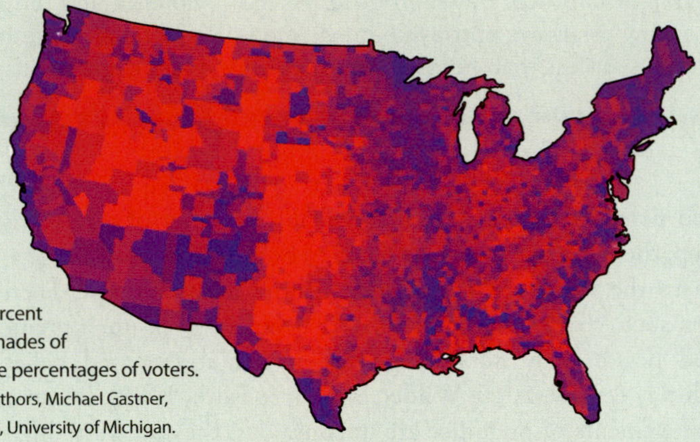

● **Figure 17.8**
Purple America map. Counties within states voting more than 70 percent Republican appear in red; areas voting more than 70 percent Democratic appear in blue. Shades of purple represent intermediate percentages of voters. Reprinted by permission of the authors, Michael Gastner, Cosma Shalizi, and Mark Newman, University of Michigan.

At first, Elliott made an effort to constantly criticize and belittle the brown-eyed children. To her surprise, the blue-eyed children rapidly joined in and were soon outdoing her in the viciousness of their attacks. The blue-eyed children began to feel superior, and the brown-eyed children felt just plain awful. Fights broke out. Test scores of the brown-eyed children fell.

How lasting were the effects of this experiment? The effects were short lived because two days later the children's roles were reversed. Before long, the same destructive effects occurred again, but this time in reverse. The implications of this experiment are unmistakable. In less than one day, it was possible to get children to hate each other because of eye color and **status inequalities** (differences in power, prestige, or privileges). Certainly, the effects of a lifetime of real life racial or ethnic prejudice are infinitely more powerful and destructive (See "Is America Purple?"). Racism is a major source of stress in the lives of many people of color. Over time, prejudice can have a negative impact on a person's physical and emotional health (Brondolo et al., 2011).

Equal-Status Contact

What can be done to combat prejudice? Progress has been made through attempts to educate the general public about the lack of justification for prejudice. Changing the belief component of an attitude is one of the most direct means of changing the entire attitude. Thus, when people are made aware that members of various racial and ethnic groups share the same goals, ambitions, feelings, and frustrations as they do, intergroup relations may be improved (Moskowitz & Li, 2011).

However, this is not the whole answer. As we noted earlier, there is often a wide difference between attitudes and actual behavior. Until nonprejudiced behavior is engineered, changes can be quite superficial. Several lines of thought (including cognitive dissonance theory) suggest that more frequent *equal-status contact* between groups in conflict should reduce prejudice and stereotyping (Olson & Zanna, 1993; Wernet et al., 2003).

Equal-status contact refers to interacting on an equal footing, without obvious differences in power or status. Much evidence

Many school districts in the United States have begun requiring students to wear uniforms. Appearance (including gang colors) is one of the major reasons why kids treat each other differently. Uniforms help minimize status inequalities and in-group/out-group distinctions. In Long Beach, California, a switch to uniforms was followed by a 91 percent drop in student assaults, thefts, vandalism, and weapons and drug violations (Ritter, 1998).

suggests that equal-status contact does, in fact, lessen prejudice. In one early study, European American women who lived in integrated and segregated housing projects were compared for changes in attitude toward their African American neighbors. Women in the integrated project showed a favorable shift in attitudes toward members of the other racial group. Those in the segregated project showed no change or actually became more prejudiced than before (Deutsch & Collins, 1951). In other studies, mixed-race groups have been formed at work, in the laboratory, and at schools. The conclusion from such research is that personal contact with a disliked group tends to induce friendly behavior, respect, and liking. However, these benefits occur only when personal contact is cooperative and on an equal footing (Grack & Richman, 1996).

To test the importance of equal-status contact directly, Gerald Clore and his associates set up a unique summer camp for children. The camp was directed by one European American male, one European American female, one African American male, and one African American female. Each campsite had three African American and three European American campers and one African American and one European American counselor. Thus, African Americans and European Americans were equally divided in number, power, privileges, and duties. Did the experience make a difference? Apparently it did: Testing showed that the children had significantly more positive attitudes toward opposite-race children after the camp than they did before (Clore, 1976; Moskowitz & Li, 2011).

Superordinate Goals

Let's now consider a revealing study done with 11-year-old boys. When the boys arrived at a summer camp, they were split into two groups and housed in separate cabins. At first, the groups were kept apart to build up separate identities and friendships. Soon each group had a flag and a name (the "Rattlers" and the "Eagles") and each had staked out its territory. At this point, the two groups were placed in competition with each other. After a number of clashes, dislike between the groups bordered on hatred: The boys baited each other, started fights, and raided each other's cabins (Sherif et al., 1961).

Were they allowed to go home hating each other? As an experiment in reducing intergroup conflict, and to prevent the boys from remaining enemies, various strategies to reduce tensions were tried. Holding meetings between group leaders did nothing. When the groups were invited to eat together, the event turned into a free-for-all. Finally, emergencies that required *cooperation* among members of both groups were staged at the camp. These emergencies created **superordinate goals** that exceeded or overrode the lesser competitive goals. For example, the water supply was damaged so that all the boys had to work together to repair it. Creating this and other superordinate goals helped restore peace between the two groups.

Cooperation and shared goals seem to help reduce conflict by encouraging people in opposing groups to see themselves as members of a single, larger group (Gaertner et al., 2000). Superordinate goals, in other words, have a "we're all in the same boat" effect on perceptions of group membership (Olson & Zanna, 1993). The power of superordinate goals can be seen in the unity that prevailed in the United States (and throughout much of the rest of the world) for months after the September 11 terrorist attacks. Superordinate goals are also an important factor in helping peacekeepers constructively engage with people from other nationalities (Boniecki & Britt, 2003; Whitley & Kite, 2010).

Can such goals exist on a global scale? One example might be a desire to deal with the current global energy and food crisis. Another that comes to mind is the need to preserve the natural environment on a global scale. Still another is the continuing threat posed by terrorism and religious extremism. Politically, such goals may be far from universal. But their superordinate quality is clearly evident.

"Jigsaw" Classrooms

Contrary to the hopes of many, integrating public schools often has little positive effect on racial prejudice. In fact, prejudice may be made worse, and the self-esteem of minority students frequently decreases (Aronson, 2008; Binder et al., 2009).

If integrated schools provide equal-status contact, shouldn't prejudice be reduced? Theoretically, yes. But in practice, minority-group

Status inequalities Differences in the power, prestige, or privileges of two or more persons or groups.

Equal-status contact Social interaction that occurs on an equal footing, without obvious differences in power or status.

Superordinate goal A goal that exceeds or overrides all others; a goal that renders other goals relatively less important.

Gage/Getty Images

In a "jigsaw" classroom, children help one another prepare for tests. As they teach one another what they know, the children learn to cooperate and to respect the unique strengths of each individual.

children often enter schools unprepared to compete on an equal footing. The competitive nature of schools almost guarantees that children will *not* learn to like and understand each other.

With the preceding in mind, social psychologist Elliot Aronson pioneered a way to apply superordinate goals to ordinary classrooms. According to Aronson, such goals are effective because they create **mutual interdependence**. That is, people must depend on one another to meet each person's goals. When individual needs are linked, cooperation is encouraged (Deutsch, 1993; Güth, Levati, & von Wangenheim, 2010).

How has that idea been applied? Aronson has successfully created "jigsaw" classrooms that emphasize cooperation rather than competition. The term *jigsaw* refers to the pieces of a jigsaw puzzle. In a **jigsaw classroom**, each child is given a "piece" of the information needed to complete a project or prepare for a test.

In a typical session, children are divided into groups of five or six and given a topic to study for a later exam. Each child is given his or her "piece" of information and asked to learn it. For example, one child might have information on Thomas Edison's invention of the light bulb; another, facts about his invention of the long-playing phonograph record; and a third, information about Edison's childhood. After the children have learned their parts, they teach them to others in the group. Even the most competitive children quickly realize that they cannot do well without the aid of everyone in the group. Each child makes a unique and essential contribution, so the children learn to listen to and respect each other.

Does the jigsaw method work? Compared with children in traditional classrooms, children in jigsaw groups are less prejudiced, they like their classmates more, they have more positive attitudes toward school, their grades improve, and their self-esteem increases (Aronson, 2008; Walker & Crogan, 1998). Such results are quite encouraging.

To summarize, prejudice will be reduced when:

- Members of different groups have equal status *within the situation* that brings them together.
- Members of all groups seek a common goal.
- Group members must cooperate to reach the goal.
- Group members spend enough time together for cross-group friendships to develop.

Sports teams are an excellent example of a situation in which all of these conditions apply. The close contact and interdependent effort required in team sports often creates lifelong friendships and breaks down the walls of prejudice.

A Look Ahead

The *Psychology in Action* section of this chapter takes a look at multiculturalism and offers some further thoughts about how to promote tolerance. Don't miss this interesting conclusion to our discussion of social psychology.

Knowledge Builder: Prejudice and Intergroup Conflict

RECITE

1. As a basis for prejudice, ____________ is frequently related to frustration and displaced ____________.
2. The authoritarian personality tends to be prejudiced against all out-groups a quality referred to as ____________.
3. Social stereotypes may be both positive and negative. T or F?
4. The stereotypes underlying racial and ethnic prejudice tend to evolve from the superordinate goals that often separate groups. T or F?
5. The term *symbolic prejudice* refers to racism or prejudice that is expressed in disguised or hidden form. T or F?
6. Jane Elliott's classroom experiment in prejudice showed that children could be made to dislike one another
   a. by setting up group competition *b.* by imposing status inequalities *c.* by role-playing *d.* by frustrating all the students
7. Research suggests that prejudice and intergroup conflict may be reduced by ____________ interaction and ____________ goals.

REFLECT

Think Critically

8. In court trials, defense lawyers sometimes try to identify and eliminate prospective jurors who have authoritarian personality traits. Can you guess why?

Self-Reflect

Mentally scan over the events of the last week. How would they have changed if prejudices of all types ceased to exist?

Think of the most rigid or dogmatic person you know. Does he or she match the profile of the authoritarian personality?

Stereotypes exist for many social categories, even ordinary ones such as "college student" or "unmarried young adult." What stereotypes do you think you face in daily life?

The director of a youth recreation center is concerned about the amount of conflict she is seeing between boys and girls from different racial and ethnic groups. What advice can you give the director?

Answers: 1. scapegoating, aggression **2.** ethnocentrism **3.** T **4.** F **5.** T **6.** *b* **7.** equal-status superordinate **8.** Because authoritarians tend to believe that punishment is effective, they are more likely to vote for conviction.

Psychology in Action

Multiculturalism—Living with Diversity

Gateway Question 17.8: *How can we promote multiculturalism and social harmony?*

Today's society is more like a "tossed salad" than a cultural "melting pot." Rather than expecting everyone to be alike, psychologists believe that we must learn to respect and appreciate our differences. **Multiculturalism**, as this is called, gives equal status to different ethnic, racial, and cultural groups. It is a recognition and acceptance of human diversity (Alleyne, 2011; Moghaddam, 2007).

Breaking the Prejudice Habit

Most people publicly support policies of equality and fairness. Yet, many still have lingering biases and negative images of African Americans, Latinos, Muslim Americans, and other ethnic minorities. How can we make sense of such conflicting attitudes? A decision to forsake prejudice does not immediately eliminate prejudiced thoughts and feelings. People who are not consciously prejudiced may continue to respond emotionally to members of other ethnic groups (Anderson, 2010b; Nosek, Greenwald, & Banaji, 2005). Quite likely, this reflects lingering stereotypes and prejudices learned in childhood (Dion, 2003).

For many people, becoming less prejudiced begins by accepting the value of *openness to the other,* the ability to genuinely appreciate those who differ from us culturally (Fowers & Davidov, 2006). It is important to remember that being open to someone else does not mean that you have to agree with that person or turn your back on your own culture. Openness, in turn, leads to the acceptance of the values of tolerance and equality. People who value tolerance resist intolerant thoughts or feelings, which motivates them to try to alter their own biased reactions (Binning et al., 2010; Dovidio & Gaertner, 1999). But doing so is not easy. Typically, it requires repeated efforts to learn to think, feel, and act differently. Nevertheless, many people have succeeded in overcoming the "prejudice habit" and becoming more open to life experiences in general (Fowers & Davidov, 2006). If you would like to be more open and tolerant, the following points may be helpful to you.

© John Wilkes/Corbis

Openness to the other is associated with values of tolerance and equality.

Beware of Stereotyping Stereotypes make the social world more manageable. But placing people in categories almost always causes them to appear more similar than they really are. As a result, we tend to see out-group members as very much alike, even when they are as varied as our friends and family. People who are not prejudiced work hard to actively inhibit stereotyped thoughts and to emphasize fairness and equality.

Seek Individuating Information A good way to tear down stereotypes is to get to know individuals from various ethnic and cultural groups (Giliovich, Keltner, & Nisbett, 2005). Typically, we are most tempted to apply stereotypes when we have only minimal information about a person. Stereotypes help us guess what a person is like and how she or he will act. Unfortunately, these inferences are usually wrong.

One of the best antidotes for stereotypes is **individuating information**, which helps us see a person as an individual, rather than as a member of a group (Cameron & Trope, 2004; Lan Yeung & Kashima, 2010). Anything that keeps us from placing a person in a particular social category tends to negate stereotyped thinking. When you meet individuals from various backgrounds, focus on the *person,* not the *label* attached to her or him.

A good example of the effects of individuating information comes from a Canadian study of English-speaking students in a French language program. Students who were "immersed" (spent most of their waking hours with French Canadians) became more positive toward them. Immersed students were more likely to say they had come to appreciate and like French Canadians; they were more willing to meet and interact with them; and they saw themselves as less different from French Canadians (Lambert, 1987). In fact, with more subtle kinds of symbolic prejudice, such contact may be the best way to reduce intergroup conflict (Dovidio & Gaertner, 1999).

Don't Fall Prey to Just-World Beliefs Do you believe that the world is basically fair? Even if you don't, you may believe that the world is sufficiently just so that people generally get what they deserve. It may not be obvious, but such beliefs can directly increase prejudiced thinking (Hafer & Bègue, 2005).

As a result of discrimination, social conditions, and circumstances (such as recent immigration), minorities may occupy lower socioeconomic positions (Whitley & Kite, 2010). **Just-world beliefs**—beliefs that people generally get what they deserve—can lead us to assume that minority group members wouldn't be in such positions if they weren't inferior in some way. This bit of faulty thinking amounts to blaming people who are *vic-*

Mutual interdependence A condition in which two or more persons must depend on one another to meet each person's needs or goals.

Jigsaw classroom A method of reducing prejudice; each student receives only part of the information needed to complete a project or prepare for a test.

Multiculturalism Giving equal status, recognition, and acceptance to different ethnic and cultural groups.

Individuating information Information that helps define a person as an individual, rather than as a member of a group or social category.

Just-world beliefs Belief that people generally get what they deserve.

tims of prejudice and discrimination for their plight. For example, assuming that a poor person is lazy may overlook the fact that discrimination in hiring has made it very difficult for him or her to find a job.

Be Aware of Self-Fulfilling Prophecies You may recall from Chapter 1 that people tend to act in accordance with the behavior expected by others. If you hold strong stereotypes about members of various groups, a vicious cycle can occur. When you meet someone who is different from yourself, you may treat her or him in a way that is consistent with your stereotypes. If the other person is influenced by your behavior, she or he may act in ways that seem to match your stereotype. For example, a person who believes that members of another ethnic group are hostile and unfriendly will probably treat people in that group in ways that provoke hostile and unfriendly response. This creates a self-fulfilling prophecy and reinforces belief in the stereotype. (A **self-fulfilling prophecy** is an expectation that prompts people to act in ways that make the expectation come true.)

Remember, Different Does Not Mean Inferior Some conflicts between groups cannot be avoided. What *can* be avoided is unnecessary **social competition** (rivalry among groups, each of which regards itself as superior to others). The concept of social competition refers to the fact that some individuals seek to enhance their self-esteem by identifying with a group. However, this works only if the group can be seen as superior to others. Because of social competition, groups tend to view themselves as better than their rivals (Baron, Byrne, & Branscombe, 2009). In one survey, every major ethnic group in the United States rated itself as better than any other group (Njeri, 1991).

A person who has high self-esteem does not need to treat others as inferior in order to feel good about himself or herself. Similarly, it is not necessary to degrade other groups in order to feel positive about one's own group identity (Fowers & Davidov, 2006). In fact, each ethnic group has strengths that members of other groups could benefit from emulating. For instance, African Americans, Asian Americans, and Latinos emphasize family networks that help buffer them from some of the stresses of daily life (Suinn, 1999).

Understand That Race Is a Social Construction From the viewpoint of modern genetics, the concept of race has absolutely no meaning (Bonham, Warshauer-Baker & Collins, 2005; Sternberg, Grigorenko, & Kidd, 2005). Members of various groups are so varied genetically and human groups have intermixed for so many centuries that it is impossible to tell, biologically, to what "race" any given individual belongs. Thus, race is an illusion based on superficial physical differences and learned ethnic identities. Certainly people *act as if* different races exist (Glenn, 2009). But this is a matter of social labeling, not biological reality. To assume that any human group is biologically superior or inferior is simply wrong. In fact, the best available evidence suggests that all people are descended from the same ancient ancestors. The origins of our species lie in Africa, about 100,000 years ago. Among early human populations, darker skin was a protective adaptation to sun exposure near the equator (Jablonski & Chaplin, 2000). Biologically, we are all brothers and sisters under the skin (Graves, 2001; Smedley & Smedley, 2005).

Look for Commonalities We live in a society that puts a premium on competition and individual effort. One problem with this is that competing with others fosters desires to demean, defeat, and vanquish them. When we cooperate with others we tend to share their joys and suffer when they are in distress (Aronson, 2008). If we don't find ways to cooperate and live in greater harmony, everyone will suffer. That, if nothing else, is one thing that we all have in common. Everyone knows what it feels like to be different. Greater tolerance comes from remembering those times.

Set an Example for Others People who act in a tolerant fashion can serve as models of tolerance for others. An example is the use of newsletters to promote understanding at an ethnically diverse high school in Houston, Texas. Students wrote stories for the newsletter about situations in which cooperation led to better understanding. For instance, a story about a Hispanic-Anglo friendship in a sports team had this headline: "Don't judge somebody until you know them. The color of the skin doesn't matter." Other stories emphasized the willingness of students to get acquainted with people from other ethnic groups and the new perceptions they had of their abilities. After just 5 months of modeling tolerance, hostility between campus ethnic groups was significantly reduced (McAlister et al., 2000).

Tolerance and Cultural Awareness

Living comfortably in a multicultural society means getting to know a little about other groups. Getting acquainted with a person whose cultural background is different from your own can be a wonderful learning experience. No one culture has all the answers or the best ways of doing things. Multicultural populations enrich a community's food, music, arts, and philosophy. Likewise, openness toward different racial, cultural, and ethnic groups can be personally rewarding (Fowers & Davidov, 2006).

The importance of cultural awareness often lies in subtleties and details. For example, in large American cities, many small stores are owned by Korean immigrants. Some of these Korean-American merchants have been criticized for being cold and hostile to their customers. Refusing to place change directly in customers' hands, for instance, helped trigger an African American boycott of Korean grocers in New York City. The core of the problem was a lack of cultural awareness on both sides.

In America, if you walk into a store, you expect the clerk to be courteous to you. One way of showing politeness is by smiling. But in the Confucian-steeped Korean culture, a smile is reserved for family members and close friends. If a Korean or Korean American has no reason to smile, he or she just doesn't smile. There's a Korean saying: "If you smile a lot, you're silly." Expressions such as "thank you" and "excuse me" are also used sparingly and strangers rarely touch each other—not even to return change.

Here's another example of how ignorance of cultural practices can lead to needless friction and misunderstanding: An African American woman who wanted to ease racial tensions took a freshly baked pie to her neighbors across the way, who were Orthodox Jews. At the front door the woman extended her hand, not knowing that Orthodox Jews don't shake women's hands, unless the woman is a close family member. Once she was inside, she picked up a kitchen knife to cut the pie, not knowing the couple kept a kosher household and used different knives for different foods. The woman's well-intentioned attempt at neighborliness ended in an argument! Knowing a little more about each other's cultures could have prevented both the conflicts just described.

We began this chapter by meeting Jasmine and Osama. What will prevail in our modern world: love, like that which binds them together, or hate, like that felt by the cultures they come from? Only time will tell.

Knowledge Builder Multiculturalism

RECITE

1. *Multiculturalism* refers to the belief that various subcultures and ethnic groups should be blended into a single emergent culture. T or F?
2. Many people who don't have prejudiced beliefs still have prejudiced thoughts and feelings in the presence of minority group individuals. T or F?
3. One of the best antidotes for stereotypes is
   a. accepting just-world beliefs *b.* individuating information
   c. accepting self-fulfilling prophecies *d.* honest social competition
4. Just-world beliefs are the primary cause of social competition. T or F?

REFLECT

Think Critically

5. Why is it valuable to learn the terms by which members of various groups prefer to be addressed (for example, Mexican American, Latino [or Latina], Hispanic, or Chicano [Chicana])?

Self-Reflect

Which strategies for breaking the prejudice habit do you already use? How could you apply the remaining strategies to become more tolerant?

Answers: 1. F **2.** T **3.** *b* **4.** F **5.** Because labels might have negative meanings that are not apparent to persons outside the group. People who are culturally aware allow others to define their own identities, rather than imposing labels on them.

Chapter in Review Gateways to Prosocial and Antisocial Behavior

Gateway QUESTIONS REVISITED

17.1 *Why do people affiliate?*

17.1.1 Affiliation is tied to needs for approval, support, friendship, and love. Also, affiliation can reduce anxiety.

17.2 *What factors influence interpersonal attraction?*

17.2.1 Initial interpersonal attractiveness is increased by familiarity, physical proximity, frequent contact, similarity, physical attractiveness, and reciprocity.

17.2.2 Relationships develop through self-disclosure which follows a reciprocity norm: Low levels of self-disclosure are met with low levels in return, whereas moderate self-disclosure elicits more personal replies. However, overdisclosure tends to inhibit self-disclosure by others.

17.2.3 In North America, male friendships tend to be activity based while female friendships tend to be based on shared feelings and confidences.

17.2.4 According to social exchange theory, we tend to maintain relationships that are profitable; that is, those for which perceived rewards exceed perceived costs.

17.3 *How do liking and loving differ?*

17.3.1 According to Sternberg's triangular theory of love, liking involves a desire for intimacy with another person while love involves desiring intimacy as well as passion and/or commitment.

17.3.2 Romantic love is based on feelings of both intimacy and passion. Companionate love involves feelings of both intimacy and commitment. Consummate love, involving intimacy, passion, and commitment, is the most complete form of love.

17.3.3 Romantic love is also associated with greater mutual absorption between people.

17.3.4 Adult love relationships tend to mirror patterns of emotional attachment observed in infancy and early childhood. Secure, avoidant, and ambivalent patterns can be defined on the basis of how a person approaches romantic and affectionate relationships with others.

17.3.5 Evolutionary psychology attributes human mating patterns to the differing reproductive challenges faced by men and women during the course of evolution.

Self-fulfilling prophecy An expectation that prompts people to act in ways that make the expectation come true.

Social competition Rivalry among groups, each of which regards itself as superior to others.

17.4 Why are bystanders so often unwilling to help in an emergency?

17.4.1 Four decision points that must be passed before a person gives help are noticing, defining an emergency, taking responsibility, and selecting a course of action. Helping is less likely at each point when other potential helpers are present.

17.4.2 Helping is encouraged by general arousal, empathic arousal, being in a good mood, low effort or risk, and perceived similarity between the victim and the helper. For several reasons, giving help tends to encourage others to help too.

17.4.3 Understanding and removing barriers to prosocial behavior can encourage acts of helping and altruism.

17.5 How do psychologists explain human aggression?

17.5.1 Aggression comes in many forms, from warfare to bullying.

17.5.2 Ethological explanations of aggression attribute it to inherited instincts. Biological explanations of aggression emphasize brain mechanisms and physical factors that lower the threshold for aggression.

17.5.3 According to the frustration-aggression hypothesis, frustration and aggression are closely linked. Frustration is only one of many aversive stimuli that can arouse a person and make aggression more likely. Aggression is especially likely to occur when aggression cues are present.

17.5.4 Social learning theory has focused attention on the role of aggressive models in the development of aggressive behavior.

17.5.5 Aggression is a fact of life, but humans are not inevitably aggressive. The same factors that help explain aggression can form the basis for preventing it.

17.6 What causes prejudice?

17.6.1 Prejudice is a negative implicit or explicit attitude held toward members of various out-groups.

17.6.2 One theory attributes prejudice to scapegoating. A second account says that prejudices may be held for personal reasons (personal prejudice) or simply through adherence to group norms (group prejudice).

17.6.3 Prejudiced individuals tend to have an authoritarian or dogmatic personality, characterized by rigidity, inhibition, intolerance, oversimplification, and ethnocentrism.

17.7 What can be done about prejudice and intergroup conflict?

17.7.1 Intergroup conflict gives rise to hostility and the formation of social stereotypes.

17.7.2 Stereotypes and self-stereotyping rob people of their individuality and can even dehumanize them.

17.7.3 Status inequalities tend to build prejudice. Prejudice is reduced by equal-status contact with other groups and by mutual interdependence, which promotes cooperation.

17.7.4 Psychologists have emphasized the concept of superordinate goals as a key to reducing intergroup conflict, be it racial, religious, ethnic, or national.

17.7.5 On a smaller scale, jigsaw classrooms (which encourage cooperation) have been shown to be an effective way of combating prejudice.

17.8 How can we promote multiculturalism and social harmony?

17.8.1 Multiculturalism is a recognition and acceptance of human diversity.

17.8.2 Multicultural harmony is attainable through conscious efforts to be more tolerant.

17.8.3 Greater tolerance can be encouraged by neutralizing stereotypes with individuating information; by looking for commonalities with others; and by avoiding the effects of just-world beliefs, self-fulfilling prophecies, and social competition.

17.8.4 Cultural awareness is a key element in promoting greater social harmony.

MEDIA RESOURCES

Web Resources

Internet addresses frequently change. To find an up-to-date list of URLs for the sites listed here, visit your Psychology CourseMate.

Real Love Read more about Sternberg's triarchic theory.

Kitty Genovese Listen to a podcast updating the famous murder case that launched research on diffusion of responsibility.

Understanding Prejudice Explore different activities that illuminate the causes and consequences of prejudice.

Authoritarian Personality Take the F Scale.

Intergroup Conflict Read an article on intergroup conflict.

Anger Management Read about anger management.

The Frustration-Aggression Hypothesis Read Neal Miller's original paper on the topic.

Media Violence Explore the debate over media violence.

Project Implicit Test yourself to see whether you are unconsciously prejudiced.

Multiculturalism Guidelines Read these guidelines from the American Psychological Association.

Diversity in College Read some relevant research about diversity in college.

Interactive Learning

Log in to **CengageBrain** to access the resources your instructor requires. For this book, you can access:

CourseMate brings course concepts to life with interactive learning, study, and exam preparation tools that support the printed textbook. A textbook-specific website, ***Psychology CourseMate*** includes an ***integrated interactive eBook*** and other ***interactive learning tools*** including quizzes, flashcards, videos, and more.

CENGAGE**NOW**™

CengageNOW is an easy-to-use online resource that helps you study in less time to get the grade you want—NOW. Take a pre-test for this chapter and receive a personalized study plan based on your results that will identify the topics you need to review and direct you to online resources to help you master those topics. Then take a post-test to help you determine the concepts you have mastered and what you will need to work on. If your textbook does not include an access code card, go to CengageBrain.com to gain access.

WebTUTOR™

More than just an interactive study guide, **WebTutor** is an anytime, anywhere customized learning solution with an eBook, keeping you connected to your textbook, instructor, and classmates.

If your professor has assigned **Aplia** homework:

1. Sign in to your account.
2. Complete the corresponding homework exercises as required by your professor.
3. When finished, click "Grade It Now" to see which areas you have mastered and which need more work, and for detailed explanations of every answer.

Visit www.cengagebrain.com to access your account and purchase materials.

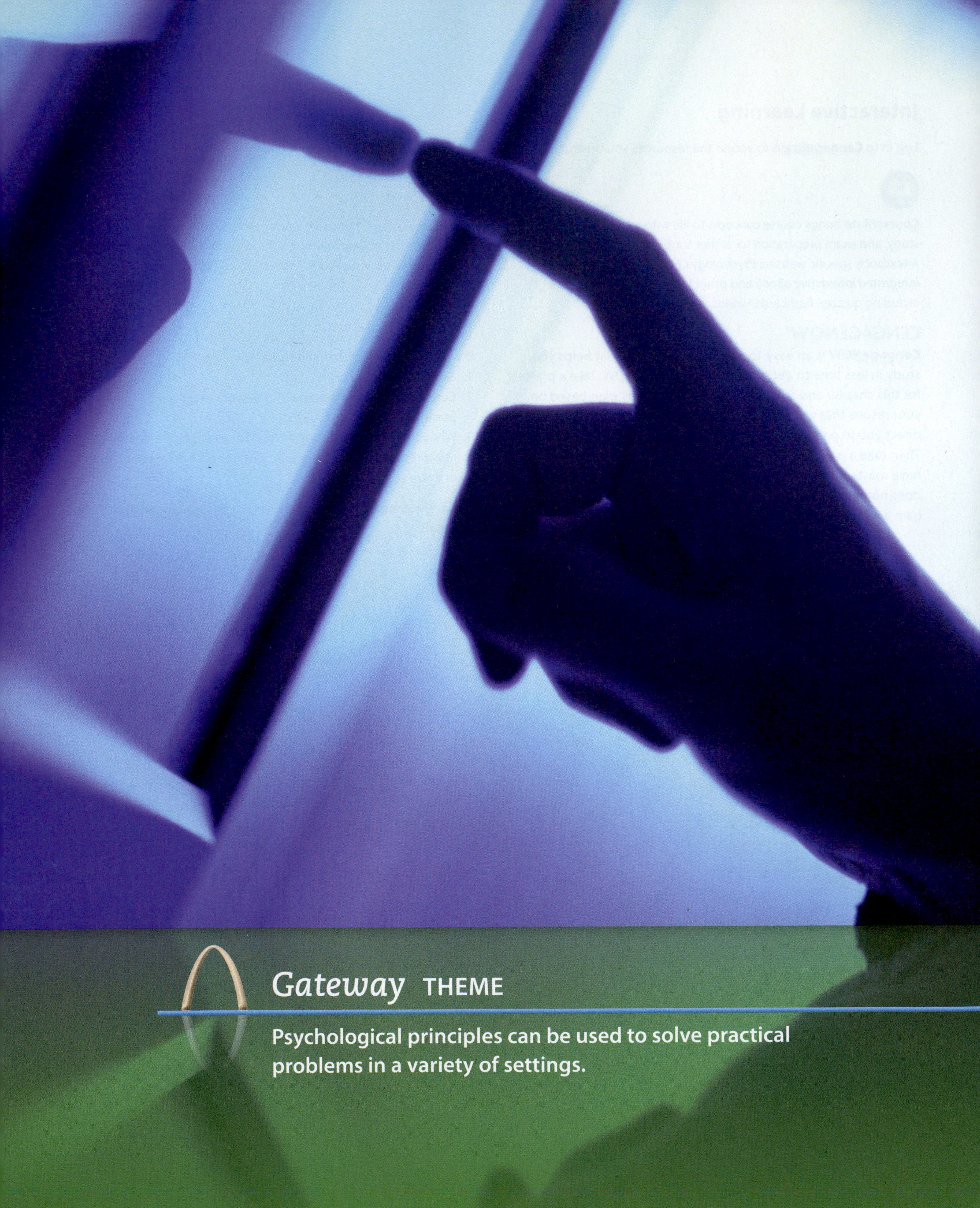

Gateway THEME

Psychological principles can be used to solve practical problems in a variety of settings.

18 Applied Psychology

In Touch with Knowledge

Laptops, smartphones, MP3 players, gaming consoles, tablet computers. By now, we're all used to the seemingly inevitable explosion of digital technologies. But it's not so easy to ignore their impact. Consumers have bought hundreds of millions of these devices. Digital gaming, social networking, the music business, the movie industry, and even book publishing will never be the same.

The success of these technologies almost always depends on engineers and psychologists coming up with ever more usable technical designs. The invention of the mouse and computer icons revolutionized personal computing. Much of the iPod's early success hinged on (rotated around?) a tiny device called a *click wheel*. This touch-sensitive ring lay at the heart of users' ability to quickly locate that one desired song among thousands. More recent touch-based devices use a *multi-touch interface* to allow easy access to the full range of available digital materials. And now, gaming systems like the Wii and Kinect can be controlled through gesture alone.

Whether it is the computer mouse, click wheel, multi-touch sensing, gestural sensing, voice-activation or computerized systems that disabled users can control with mind power alone, human factors psychologists depend on understanding human behavior to help design better computer tools.

Applied psychology refers to the use of psychological principles and research methods to solve practical problems. Designing computer interfaces is only one way to apply psychology. The largest applied areas are clinical and counseling psychology, but there are many others, such as community psychology, educational psychology, military psychology, consumer psychology, health psychology (discussed in Chapter 13), and space psychology. In this chapter we will focus on the application of psychology in six diverse areas: business, the environment, education, law, sports, and human factors.

Gateway QUESTIONS

18.1 How is psychology applied in business and industry?

18.2 What have psychologists learned about the effects of our physical and social environments?

18.3 How has psychology improved education?

18.4 What does psychology reveal about juries and court verdicts?

18.5 Can psychology enhance athletic performance?

18.6 How are tools designed to better serve human needs?

Industrial/Organizational Psychology—Psychology at Work

Gateway Question 18.1: *How is psychology applied in business and industry?*

Do you believe you should live to work or work to live? Whatever your attitude, the simple fact is that most adults work for a living. Whether you are already employed or plan to begin a career after college, it helps to know something about the psychology of work and organizations.

Industrial/organizational (I/O) psychologists study the behavior of people at work and in organizations (Aamodt, 2010; Cascio & Aguinis, 2008). Very likely, their efforts will affect how you are selected for a job and tested, trained, or evaluated for promotion. Most I/O psychologists are employed by the government, industry, and businesses. Typically, they work in two major areas: (1) studying jobs to identify underlying skills, which can then guide efforts to select people and train them for those jobs (the *industrial* part); and (2) studying organizations to understand how to create structures and company cultures that will improve worker performance (the *organizational* part). To get a better idea of what I/O psychologists do, look at ■ Table 18.1. As you can see, their interests are quite varied.

A key person in any organization is its leader (Hodson & Sullivan, 2010). Family therapist and rabbi Edwin Friedman once remarked, "Leadership can be thought of as a capacity to define oneself to others in a way that clarifies and expands a vision of the future." How do great business leaders inspire their followers?

Theories of Leadership

During many lunch hours at a major computer game developer, most of the employees, including the top executives, eat together while playing computer games (and no, the "bosses" don't always win), talking, and joking. To say the least, these are unusual working conditions. To understand the rationale behind them, let's consider two basic theories of leadership.

Theory X and Theory Y Leadership

One of the earliest attempts to improve worker efficiency was made in 1923 by Frederick Taylor, an engineer. To speed up production, Taylor standardized work routines and stressed careful planning, control, and orderliness. Today, versions of Taylor's approach are called **scientific management** (also known as **Theory X leadership**, for reasons explained shortly). Scientific management uses time-and-motion studies, task analysis, job specialization, assembly lines, pay schedules, and the like to increase productivity (Bobic & Davis, 2003; Crowley et al., 2010).

It sounds like scientific management treats people as if they were machines. Is that true? To some extent it is. In Taylor's day, many large companies were manufacturers with giant assembly lines. People had to be efficient cogs in the manufacturing machinery. Leaders who follow Theory X have a task orientation, focusing on the work to be done, rather than a person orientation, focusing on the people doing the work. As such, they tend to assume that workers must be goaded or guided into being productive. Many psychologists working in business, of course, are concerned with improving **work efficiency** (defined as maximum output at lowest cost). As a result, they alter conditions they believe will affect workers (such as time schedules, work quotas, bonuses, and so on). Some might even occasionally wish that people would act like well-oiled machines.

However, most recognize that psychological efficiency is just as important as work efficiency. **Psychological efficiency** refers to maintaining good morale, labor relations, employee satisfaction, and similar aspects of work behavior. Leadership styles that ignore or mishandle the human element can be devastatingly costly. Studies have consistently found that happy workers are productive workers (Lerner & Henke, 2008; Wright & Cropanzano, 2000).

The term *Theory X* was coined by psychologist Douglas McGregor (1960) as a way to distinguish the leadership style

■ TABLE 18.1 Topics of Special Interest to Industrial/Organizational Psychologists

Absenteeism	Minority workers
Decision making	Pay schedules
Design of organizations	Personnel selection
Employee stress	Personnel training
Employee turnover	Productivity
Interviewing	Promotion
Job enrichment	Task analysis
Job satisfaction	Task design
Labor relations	Work behavior
Leadership	Work environment
Machine design	Work motivation
Management styles	Worker evaluations

Charlie Chaplin captured the worker as machine perfectly in his 1936 film *Modern Times*. Have you ever worked at a job that made you feel like this?

Critical Thinking: From Glass Ceiling to Labyrinth

Aren't women more people-oriented than men? *And doesn't that imply that women would make better Theory Y leaders?* Good thinking. As person-oriented Theory Y leadership styles have become more popular, women are slowly gaining acceptance as leaders (Ayman & Korabik, 2010; Eagly, 2007). Nearly a quarter of all American organizations have female CEOs (Martin, 2007). Studies have even shown that companies with more women in leadership roles perform better financially (Carter, Simkins, & Simpson, 2003; Krishnan & Park, 2005).

And yet, according to psychologist Alice Eagly, women continue to face unique challenges. Increasingly, cracks are appearing in the *glass ceiling*, the invisible barrier that has prevented women from moving into leadership positions. But the glass ceiling is being replaced by a labyrinth created by a clash between leadership stereotypes and stereotypes of women (Brescoll, Dawson, & Uhlmann, 2010; Eagly & Carli, 2007). On the one hand, most people expect good leaders to be *agentic*: independent, confident, ambitious, objective, dominant, and forceful. On the other hand, they expect women to be more *communal:* dependent, caring, nurturing, tender, sensitive, and sympathetic. According to traditional gender role stereotypes (see Chapter 11), it is men who are agentic and, therefore, better leaders, despite evidence to the contrary (Eagly, 2007).

What does this mean for a woman who moves into a leadership role? If she practices communal, Theory Y leadership, she is seen as weak. She is "not tough enough" or does not "have the right stuff" to be a leader. Yet, if she acts more assertively and confidently, she is scorned for "trying to be a man" (Kark & Eagly, 2010). This conflict has been perfectly expressed by Carly Fiorina, former CEO of Hewlett-Packard, who wrote, "In the chat rooms around Silicon Valley…I was routinely referred to as either a 'bimbo' or a 'bitch'—too soft or too hard, and presumptuous, besides" (Fiorina, 2006).

As traditional gender stereotypes fade, and as Theory Y styles gain wider acceptance, perhaps women will add escaping the leadership labyrinth to their many other successes.

As the CEO of Hewlett-Packard Carly Fiorina constantly faced the incongruity between leadership stereotypes and stereotypes of women (Fiorina, 2006).

associated with scientific management from *Theory Y*, a newer approach, which emphasizes human relations at work.

How is this approach different? **Theory Y leaders** have a person orientation rather than a task orientation and tend to assume that workers enjoy autonomy and are willing to accept responsibility. They also assume that a worker's needs and goals can be meshed with the company's goals, and that people are not naturally passive or lazy. In short, Theory Y assumes that people are industrious, creative, and rewarded by challenging work.

It appears that given the proper conditions of freedom and responsibility, many people *will* work hard to gain competence and use their talents. This is especially true for **knowledge workers** (Marks & Baldry, 2009). These are people who add value to a company by creating and manipulating information and who usually think of their work as a career rather than as a job. Some examples are bankers, teachers, lawyers, computer engineers, writers, and scientists. Over the last 50 years, manufacturing has declined in North America whereas *knowledge companies* have become much more common. Today in North America, 4 of every 5 persons in the workforce are knowledge workers (Drucker, 1993).

Consider Armando, who is a software engineer. He has been working long hours trying to develop a new way to more quickly predict hurricane activity for a satellite weather system. The work efficiency of Armando's job cannot easily be measured or improved. Instead, his success depends on his own initiative, creativity, and commitment to his work. Armando quit his last job because the leaders of that company made him feel like he was "punching the clock," which is something Armando does not want to do. The woman who is the chief executive officer of his current company impresses Armando. In fact, he wonders whether women might not make better business leaders (see "From Glass Ceiling to Labyrinth").

Applied psychology The use of psychological principles and research methods to solve practical problems.

Industrial/organizational psychology A field that focuses on the psychology of work and on behavior within organizations.

Theory X leadership (scientific management) An approach to leadership that emphasizes work efficiency.

Work efficiency Maximum output (productivity) at lowest cost.

Psychological efficiency Maintenance of good morale, labor relations, employee satisfaction, and similar aspects of work behavior.

Theory Y leadership A leadership style that emphasizes human relations at work and that views people as industrious, responsible, and interested in challenging work.

Knowledge workers Workers who add value to their company by creating and manipulating information.

A Honda plant at Marysville, Ohio, illustrates many features of Theory Y. As you may already know, the automobile industry has a long history of labor-management clashes and worker discontent. In fact, outright sabotage by assembly line workers is not uncommon. To avoid such problems, Honda initiated a series of simple, seemingly successful measures. They include the following practices.

- Regardless of their position, all employees wear identical white uniforms. This allows workers and supervisors to interact on a more equal footing and builds feelings of teamwork.
- To further minimize status differences, all employees hold the title *associate*.
- Private offices, separate dining halls, and reserved parking spaces for executives were abolished.
- Employees work alongside company executives, to whom they have easy access.
- Every employee has a say in, and responsibility for, quality control and safety.
- Departmental meetings are held daily. At this time, announcements are discussed, decisions are made, and thoughts are freely shared.

Leadership Strategies

Two techniques that make Theory Y leadership methods effective are *shared leadership* and *management by objectives*. In **shared leadership (participative management)**, employees at all levels are directly involved in decision making (Pearce, Manz, & Sims, 2009). By taking part in decisions that affect them, employees like those at the Honda factory come to see work as a cooperative effort—not as something imposed on them by an egotistical leader. The benefits include greater productivity, more involvement in work, greater job satisfaction, and less job-related stress (Kim, 2002; Pearce, Conger, & Locke, 2007).

© Ghislain & Marie David de Lossy/Glow Images

Shared leadership techniques encourage employees at all levels to become involved in decision making. Quite often, this arrangement leads to greater job satisfaction.

What is "management by objectives"? In **management by objectives**, workers are given specific goals to meet so they can tell whether they are doing a good job (Antoni, 2005). Typical objectives include reaching a certain sales total, making a certain number of items, or reducing waste by a specific percentage. In any case, workers are free to choose (within limits) how they will achieve their goals. As a result, they feel more independent and take personal responsibility for their work. Workers are especially productive when they receive feedback about their progress toward goals. Clearly, people like to know what the target is and whether they are succeeding (Horn et al., 2005; Lefrançois, 2006).

Many companies also give *groups* of workers even greater freedom and responsibility. This is typically done by creating self-managed teams. A **self-managed team** is a group of employees who work together toward shared goals. Self-managed teams can typically choose their own methods of achieving results, as long as they are effective. Self-managed teams tend to make good use of the strengths and talents of individual employees. They also promote new ideas and improve motivation. Most of all, they encourage cooperation and teamwork within organizations (Woods & West, 2010). Workers in self-managed teams are much more likely to feel that they are being treated fairly at work (Chansler, Swamidass, & Cammann, 2003) and to develop a positive team atmosphere (Zárraga & Bonache, 2005).

How can workers below the management level be involved more in their work? One answer is the use of **quality circles**. These are voluntary discussion groups that seek ways to solve business problems and improve efficiency (Aamodt, 2010). In contrast to self-managed teams, quality circles usually do not have the power to put their suggestions into practice directly. But good ideas speak for themselves and many are adopted by company leaders. Quality circles have many limitations. Nevertheless, studies verify that greater personal involvement can lead to better performance and job satisfaction (Beyer et al., 2003).

Job Satisfaction

It often makes perfect sense to apply Theory X methods to work. However, doing so without taking worker needs into account can be a case of winning the battle but losing the war. That is, immediate productivity may be enhanced as job satisfaction is lowered. And when job satisfaction is low, absenteeism skyrockets, morale falls, and there is a high rate of employee turnover, leading to higher training costs and inefficiency (Wright & Bonett, 2007).

Understandably, many of the methods used by enlightened Theory Y leaders ultimately improve **job satisfaction**, or the degree to which a person is pleased with his or her work. Job satisfaction is well worth cultivating because positive moods are associated with more cooperation, better performance, a greater willingness to help others, more creative problem solving, and less absenteeism (Bowling, 2010; Brief & Weiss, 2002).

Under what conditions is job satisfaction highest? Basically, job satisfaction comes from a good fit between work and a person's interests, abilities, needs, and expectations. The major factors determining job satisfaction are listed below. Think of a job you have held. It's likely that the more these factors were present, the higher your job satisfaction was (Aamodt, 2010; Landy & Conte, 2007):

1. My job meets my expectations. Y or N?
2. My needs, values, and wants are met by my job. Y or N?
3. The tasks I have to do are enjoyable. Y or N?
4. I enjoy my supervisors and coworkers. Y or N?
5. My coworkers are outwardly happy. Y or N?
6. I am rewarded fairly for doing a good job. Y or N?
7. I have a chance to grow and be challenged. Y or N?

We should note that job satisfaction is not entirely a matter of work conditions. Anyone who has ever been employed has probably encountered at least one perpetually grumpy coworker. In other words, workers don't leave their personalities at home. Happy people are more often happy at work, and they are more likely to focus on what's good about their job rather than what's bad (Brief & Weiss, 2002). Understandably, the most productive employees are those who are happy at work (Aamodt, 2010; Elovainio et al., 2000). This connection can be seen clearly when employees are allowed to participate in various forms of *flexible work*.

Flexible Work

If you've ever worked "9 to 5" in an office, you know that traditional time schedules can be confining. They also doom many workers to a daily battle with rush-hour traffic (Lucas & Heady, 2002). To improve worker morale, I/O psychologists recommend the use of a variety of flexible work arrangements, of which the best known is **flextime**, or flexible working hours (Kossek & Michel, 2011). The basic idea of flextime is that starting and quitting times are flexible, as long as employees are present during a core work period. For example, employees might be allowed to arrive between 7:30 A.M. and 10:30 A.M. and depart between 3:30 P.M. and 6:30 P.M. In a variation called a **compressed workweek**, employees might work fewer days but put in more hours per day.

© Sullivan/Corbis

Connecting with work through the Internet makes it possible to telecommute, or work from home (Golden, Veiga, & Simsek, 2006).

A different approach to flexible work involves working at home. In knowledge companies, employees are often allowed to **telecommute**, by using a computer to remain connected to the office throughout the work day (Lautsch, Kossek, & Eaton, 2009; Golden, Veiga, & Simsek, 2006).

Is flexible work really an improvement? Generally speaking, yes (Yang & Zheng, 2011). For example, flextime typically has a positive effect on workers' productivity, job satisfaction, absenteeism, and comfort with their work schedules (Baltes et al., 1999). Similarly, telecommuting is especially effective when it allows valued employees to maintain their homes in other cities (Atkin & Lau, 2007). Psychologists theorize that flexible work lowers stress and increases feelings of independence, both of which increase productivity and job satisfaction.

Of course, not everyone wants a compressed workweek or to work from home. Ideally, flexible working arrangements should fit the needs of employees (Rothbard, Phillips, & Dumas, 2005). Regardless, most large organizations now use flexible work arrangements. Perhaps we can conclude that it is better, when possible, to bend working arrangements instead of people.

Job Enrichment

For years, the trend in business and industry was to make work more streamlined and efficient and to tie better pay to better work. There is now ample evidence that incentives such as bonuses, earned time off, and profit sharing can increase productivity. However, far too many jobs are routine, repetitive, boring, and unfulfilling. To combat the discontent this can breed, many psychologists recommend a strategy called *job enrichment*.

Job enrichment involves making a job more personally rewarding, interesting, or intrinsically motivating. Large corporations such as IBM, Maytag, Western Electric, Chrysler, and Polaroid have used job enrichment with great success. It usually leads to lower production costs, increased job satisfaction, reduced bore-

Shared leadership (participative management) A leadership approach that allows employees at all levels to participate in decision making.

Management by objectives A management technique in which employees are given specific goals to meet in their work.

Self-managed team A work group that has a high degree of freedom with respect to how it achieves its goals.

Quality circle An employee discussion group that makes suggestions for improving quality and solving business problems.

Job satisfaction The degree to which a person is comfortable with or satisfied with his or her work.

Flextime A work schedule that allows flexible starting and quitting times.

Compressed workweek A work schedule that allows an employee to work fewer days per week by putting in more hours per day.

Telecommuting An approach to flexible work that involves working from home but using a computer to stay connected to the office throughout the workday.

Job enrichment Making a job more personally rewarding, interesting, or intrinsically motivating; typically involves increasing worker knowledge.

The Clinical File: Desk Rage and Healthy Organizations

Like road rage on the highways, "desk rage," or workplace anger, is a frequent occurrence and, at times, erupts into workplace violence (Martinko, Douglas, & Harvey, 2006). It's not difficult to understand the common triggers for workplace anger: intense anger triggered by job-related stresses (such as feeling that one has been treated unfairly), perceived threats to one's self-esteem and work-related conflicts with others (Einarsen & Hoel, 2008; Glomb, 2002; Spector, 2005).

What can be done about anger and aggression at work? Most larger companies now offer mental health services to troubled employees and trauma counseling if violence erupts in the workplace. More importantly, healthy organizations actively promote the well-being of people. They do this by openly confronting problems, empowering employees, and encouraging participation, cooperation, and full use of human potential. Healthy organizations also support well-being in the following ways (Fuqua & Newman, 2002; Hodson, & Sullivan, 2010):

- Rather than always complaining and blaming, group members express sincere gratitude for the efforts of others.
- Everyone makes mistakes. The culture in caring organizations includes a capacity to forgive.
- Everyone needs encouragement at times. Encouragement can inspire workers and give them hope, confidence, and courage.
- Showing sensitivity to others can dramatically change the work environment. Sensitivity can take the form of expressing interest in others and in how they are doing. It also includes respecting the privacy of others.
- Compassion for others is a good antidote for destructive competitiveness and petty game playing.
- People have very different needs, values, and experiences. Tolerance and respect for the dignity of others goes a long way toward maintaining individual well-being.

The economic pressures that organizations face can lead to hostile and competitive work environments. However, even in economically difficult times, productivity and quality of life at work are closely intertwined. Effective organizations seek to optimize both (Fuqua & Newman, 2002). For example, companies who pay more attention to the quality of life at work generally suffer fewer productivity losses if they are forced to downsize (reduce the size of their workforce; Iverson & Zatzick, 2011).

dom, and less absenteeism (Gregory, Albritton, & Osmonbekov, 2010; Niehoff et al., 2001).

How is job enrichment done? Merely assigning a person more tasks is usually not enriching. Overloaded workers just feel stressed, and they tend to make more errors. Instead, job enrichment applies many of the principles we have discussed. Usually, it involves removing some of the controls and restrictions on employees, giving them greater freedom, choice, and authority. In some cases, employees also switch to doing a complete cycle of work. That is, they complete an entire item or project instead of doing an isolated part of a larger process. Whenever possible, workers are given direct feedback about their work or progress.

True job enrichment increases workers' feeling of *empowerment* and *knowledge*. That is, workers are encouraged to continuously learn and exercise a broad range of options, skills, and information related to their occupations (Gregory, Albritton, & Osmonbekov, 2010; Sessa & London, 2006). In short, most people seem to enjoy being good at what they do.

BRIDGES

Job enrichment can be thought of as a way of increasing intrinsic motivation. **See Chapter 10, pages 349–350.**

Organizational Culture

Businesses and other organizations, whether they are large or small, develop distinct cultures. **Organizational culture** refers to a blend of customs, beliefs, values, attitudes, and rituals. These characteristics give each organization its unique "flavor" (Chamorro-Premuzic & Furnham, 2010). Organizational culture includes such things as how people are hired and trained, disciplined, and dismissed. It encompasses how employees dress, communicate, resolve conflicts, share power, identify with organizational goals and values, negotiate contracts, and celebrate special occasions.

People who fit well into a particular organization tend to contribute to its success in ways that are not specifically part of their job description. For example, they are helpful, conscientious, and courteous. They also display good sportsmanship by avoiding pettiness, gossiping, complaining, and making small problems into big ones (see "Desk Rage and Healthy Organizations"). Like good citizens, the best workers keep themselves informed about organizational issues by attending meetings and taking part in discussions. Workers with these characteristics display what could be called **organizational citizenship**. Understandably, managers and employers highly value workers who are good organizational citizens (Woods & West, 2010).

Personnel Psychology

Companies can also enhance their chances of success by hiring the right employees in the first place. **Personnel psychology** is concerned with testing, selection, placement, and promotion of employees (Woods & West, 2010). At present, 9 out of 10 people are or will be employed in business or industry. Thus, nearly everyone who holds a job is sooner or later placed under the "psychological microscope" of personnel selection. Clearly, there is value in knowing how selection for hiring and promotion is done.

Job Analysis

How do personnel psychologists make employee selections? Personnel selection begins with **job analysis**, a detailed description of the skills, knowledge, and activities required by a particular job (Dierdorff & Wilson, 2003; Stetz, Button, & Porr, 2009). A job analysis may be done by interviewing expert workers or supervisors, giving them questionnaires, directly observing work, or identifying *critical incidents*. **Critical incidents** are situations with which competent employees must be able to cope. The ability to deal calmly with a mechanical emergency, for example, is a critical incident for airline pilots. Once job requirements are known, psychologists can state what skills, aptitudes, and interests are needed (● Figure 18.1). In addition, some psychologists are now doing a broader "work analysis." In this case, they try to identify general characteristics that a person must have to succeed in a variety of work roles, rather than in just a specific job (Sackett & Lievens, 2008).

Selection Procedures

After desirable skills and traits are identified, the next step is to learn who has them. Today, the methods most often used for evaluating job candidates include collecting *biodata*, conducting *interviews*, giving *standardized psychological tests*, and employing the *assessment center* approach. Let's see what each entails.

Biodata As simple as it may seem, one good way to predict job success is to collect **biodata** (detailed biographical information) from applicants (Schultz & Schultz, 2010). The idea behind biodata is that looking at past behavior is a good way to predict future behavior. By learning in detail about a person's life, it is often possible to say whether the person is suited for a particular type of work (Sackett & Lievens, 2008).

Tom Sheppard/Getty Images

● **Figure 18.1** Analyzing complex skills has also been valuable to the U.S. Air Force. When million-dollar aircraft and the lives of pilots are at stake, it makes good sense to do as much training and research as possible on the ground. Air Force psychologists use flight simulators like the one pictured here to analyze the complex skills needed to fly jet fighters. Skills can then be taught without risk on the ground. The flight simulator shown here uses a computer to generate full-color images that respond realistically to a pilot's use of the controls.

Some of the most useful items of biodata include past athletic interests, academic achievements, scientific interests, extracurricular activities, religious activities, social popularity, conflict with brothers and sisters, attitudes toward school, and parents' socioeconomic status (Woods & West, 2010). (It is worth pointing out that there are civil liberty and privacy concerns around the collection of sensitive biodata.) Such facts tell quite a lot about personality, interests, and abilities. In addition to past experiences, a person's recent life activities also help predict job success (Schmidt, Ones, & Hunter, 1992). For instance, you might think that college grades are unimportant, but college grade point average (GPA) predicts success in many types of work (Sackett & Lievens, 2008).

Interviews The traditional personal interview is still one of the most popular ways to select people for jobs or promotions. In a **personal interview**, job applicants are questioned about their qualifications. At the same time, interviewers gain an impression of the applicant's personality (Chamorro-Premuzic & Furnham, 2010). (Or personalities—but that's another story!)

As discussed in Chapter 12, interviews are subject to the halo effect and similar problems. (Recall that the *halo effect* is the tendency of interviewers to extend favorable or unfavorable impressions to unrelated aspects of an individual's personality, such as his or her appearance.) In addition, interviewees actively engage in *impression management*, seeking to portray a positive image to interviewers (Ellis et al., 2002; see "Surviving Your Job Interview").

It is for reasons like these that psychologists continue to look for ways to improve the accuracy of interviews. For instance, recent studies suggest that interviews can be improved by giving them more structure (Sackett & Lievens, 2008; Tsai, Chen, & Chiu, 2005). For example, each job candidate should be asked the same questions (Campion, Palmer, & Campion, 1998). However, even with their limitations, interviews can be a valid and effective way of predicting how people will perform on the job (Landy, Shankster, & Kohler, 1994).

Psychological Testing *What kinds of tests do personnel psychologists use?* General mental ability tests (intelligence tests) tell a great deal about a person's chances of succeeding in various jobs (Aamodt, 2010; Schmidt & Hunter, 1998). So do general personality tests (described in Chapter 12; Sackett & Lievens, 2008). In addition,

Organizational culture The social climate within an organization.
Organizational citizenship Making positive contributions to the success of an organization in ways that go beyond one's job description.
Personnel psychology Branch of industrial-organizational psychology concerned with testing, selection, placement, and promotion of employees.
Job analysis A detailed description of the skills, knowledge, and activities required by a particular job.
Critical incidents Situations that arise in a job, with which a competent worker must be able to cope.
Biodata Detailed biographical information about a job applicant.
Personal interview Formal or informal questioning of job applicants to learn their qualifications and to gain an impression of their personalities.

Discovering Psychology — Surviving Your Job Interview

Each year, clothing and cosmetics manufacturers spend huge sums to convince us that their products make us more attractive. Actually, such claims are somewhat justified. As we just mentioned, for instance, physically attractive people are often given more positive evaluations in interviews—even on traits that have no connection with appearance.

In general, however, indirect efforts to make a good impression, like dressing well, wearing cologne, and flattering the interviewer, are less effective in interviews than direct efforts, such as emphasizing your positive traits and past successes (Kristof-Brown, Barrick, & Franke, 2002). However, beware of blatant self-promotion. Excessively "blowing your own horn" tends to lower interviewers' perceptions of competence and suitability for a job (Howard & Ferris, 1996). According to the U. S. Department of Labor (2009), the advice that follows will help you survive your job interview.

Make sure you are prepared for your interview. Know about the company and job for which you are interviewing. Review your job qualifications and your résumé. Think about the kinds of questions you may be asked at the interview and outline broad answers. Consider practicing the interview with a family member or friend.

Be on time for your interview and bring your social security card, résumé, and references. Also, make sure you are well groomed, dressed appropriately, and well mannered. Don't smoke or chew gum. Learn your interviewer's name and shake his or her hand firmly. Relax and answer all questions politely, promptly, and concisely. Cooperate enthusiastically, use positive body language, and avoid slang.

Don't be afraid to ask questions about the potential job and the company you might be working for. Just be sure the answers aren't already easily available on the company website. And avoid questions about salary and benefits unless a job offer is coming.

personnel psychologists often use **vocational interest tests.** These tests assess people's interests and match them to interests found among successful workers in various occupations (Van Iddekinge, Putka, & Campbell, 2011). Tests such as the *Kuder Occupational Interest Survey* and the *Strong-Campbell Interest Inventory* probe interests with items like the following:

I would prefer to
a. visit a museum
b. read a good book
c. take a walk outdoors

Interest inventories typically measure six major themes identified by John Holland (■ Table 18.2). If you take an interest test and your choices match those of people in a given occupation, it is assumed that you, too, would be comfortable doing the work they do (Holland, 1997).

Aptitude tests are another mainstay of personnel psychology. Such tests rate a person's potential to learn tasks or skills used in various occupations. Tests exist for clerical, verbal, mechanical, artistic, legal, and medical aptitudes, plus many others (● Figure 18.2). For example, tests of clerical aptitude emphasize the capacity to do rapid, precise, and accurate office work. One section of a clerical aptitude test might, therefore, ask a person to mark all identical numbers and names in a long list of pairs like those shown here.

49837266	49832766
Global Widgets, Inc.	Global Wigets, Inc.
874583725	874583725
Sevanden Corp.	Sevanden Corp.
Cengage Publishing	Cengage Puhlishing

BRIDGES
Aptitude tests are related to intelligence tests. **See Chapter 9, pages 304–305, to learn how they differ.**

■ TABLE 18.2 Vocational Interest Themes

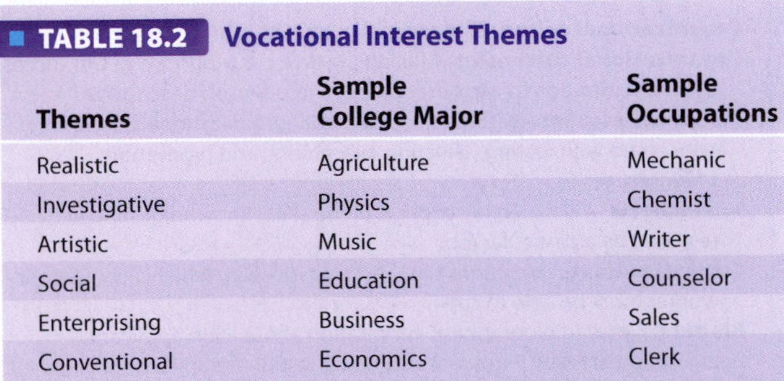

Themes	Sample College Major	Sample Occupations
Realistic	Agriculture	Mechanic
Investigative	Physics	Chemist
Artistic	Music	Writer
Social	Education	Counselor
Enterprising	Business	Sales
Conventional	Economics	Clerk

Source: Holland, 1997.

● Figure 18.2 Sample questions like those found on tests of mechanical aptitude. (The answers are A and the Driver.)

A
B
X
Y
Driver

1. If the driver turns in the direction shown, which direction will wheel Y turn? A B
2. Which wheel will turn the slowest? Driver X Y

After college, chances are good that you will encounter an *assessment center*. Many large organizations use **assessment centers** to do in-depth evaluations of job candidates. This approach has become so popular that the list of businesses using it—Ford, IBM, Kodak, Exxon, Sears, and thousands of others—reads like a corporate *Who's Who*.

How do assessment centers differ from the selection methods already described? Assessment centers are primarily used to fill management and executive positions. First, applicants are tested and interviewed. Then, they are observed and evaluated in simulated work situations. Specifically, **situational judgment tests** are used to present difficult but realistic work situations to applicants (Christian, Edwards, & Bradley, 2010; Lievens & Sackett, 2006). For example, in one exercise applicants are given an **in-basket test** that simulates the decision-making challenges executives face. The test consists of a basket full of memos, requests, and typical business problems. Each applicant is asked to quickly read all the materials and to take appropriate action. In another, more stressful test, applicants take part in a **leaderless group discussion**. This is a test of leadership that simulates group decision making and problem solving. As the group grapples with a realistic business problem, "clerks" bring in price changes, notices about delayed supplies, and so forth. By observing applicants, it is possible to evaluate leadership skills and to see how job candidates cope with stress (Chamorro-Premuzic & Furnham, 2010).

BRIDGES

Situational tests are also used to investigate personality differences. **See Chapter 12, pages 429–432.**

How well does this approach work? Assessment centers have had considerable success in predicting performance in a variety of jobs, careers, and advanced positions (Chamorro-Premuzic & Furnham, 2010; Landy, Shankster, & Kohler, 1994).

Although we have only scratched the surface of industrial/organizational psychology, it is time to move on for a look at another applied area of great personal relevance. Before we begin, here's a chance to enhance your learning.

Knowledge Builder

Industrial/Organizational Psychology

RECITE

1. Theory X leadership, or scientific management, is concerned primarily with improving ______________________.
2. Shared leadership management is often a feature of businesses with leaders who adhere to Theory Y. T or F?
3. For the majority of workers, job satisfaction is almost exclusively related to the amount of pay received. T or F?
4. Job enrichment is a direct expression of scientific management principles. T or F?
5. Identifying critical work incidents is sometimes included in a thorough ____________ ____________.
6. Detailed biographical information about a job applicant is referred to as ______________________.
7. The Strong-Campbell Inventory is a typical aptitude test. T or F?
8. A leaderless group discussion is most closely associated with which approach to employee selection?
   a. aptitude testing
   b. personal interviews
   c. job analysis
   d. assessment center

REFLECT

Think Critically

9. In what area of human behavior other than work would a careful task analysis be helpful?

Self-Reflect

If you were leading people in a business setting, which of the leadership concepts discussed in the text do you think you would be most likely to use?

Do you think women can make effective leaders? In business? In politics?

Think of a job you know well (something you have done yourself or something a person you know does). Could job enrichment be applied to the work? What would you do to increase job satisfaction for people doing similar work?

Which of the various ways of evaluating job applicants do you regard as most valid? Which would you prefer to have applied to yourself?

Answers: 1. work (or task) efficiency **2.** T **3.** F **4.** F **5.** job analysis **6.** biodata **7.** F **8.** *d* **9.** One such area is sports psychology. As described later in this chapter, sports skills can be broken into subparts, so key elements can be identified and taught. Such methods are an extension of techniques first used for job analyses. To a large extent, attempts to identify the characteristics of effective teaching also rely on task analysis.

Environmental Psychology—Life on Spaceship Earth

Gateway Question 18.2: *What have psychologists learned about the effects of our physical and social environments?*

Where do you think it is more likely that a fistfight would occur: in a church or a country-western bar? If the answer seems obvious, it is because specific environments have a significant impact on

Vocational interest test A paper-and-pencil test that assesses a person's interests and matches them to interests found among successful workers in various occupations.

Aptitude test A test that rates a person's potential to learn skills required by various occupations.

Assessment center A program set up within an organization to conduct in-depth evaluations of job candidates.

Situational judgment test Presenting realistic work situations to applicants in order to observe their skills and reactions.

In-basket test A testing procedure that simulates the individual decision-making challenges that executives face.

Leaderless group discussion A test of leadership that simulates group decision making and problem solving.

Critical Thinking Territoriality

In Chapter 16, we noted that powerful norms govern the use of the space immediately surrounding each person's body. As we move farther from the body, it becomes apparent that personal space also extends to adjacent areas that we claim as our "territory." **Territorial behavior** refers to actions that define a space as one's own or that protect it from intruders (Brown, 2009). For example, in the library, you might protect your space with a coat, handbag, book, or other personal belonging. "Saving a place" at a theater or a beach also demonstrates the tendency to identify a space as "ours." Even sports teams are territorial, usually showing a home team advantage by playing better on their own home territory than when playing in another team's territory (Neave & Wolfson, 2003; Sanchez et al., 2009).

Respect for the temporary ownership of space is also widespread. It is not unusual for a person to "take over" an entire table or study room by looking annoyed when others intrude. Your own personal territory may include your room, specific seats in many of your classes, or a particular table in the campus center or library that "belongs" to you and your friends.

Researchers have found that the more attached you are to an area, the more likely you are to adorn it with obvious **territorial markers** that signal your "ownership." Typical markers include decorations, plants, photographs, or posters. College dorms and business offices are prime places to observe this type of territorial marking. Interestingly, burglars are less likely to break into houses that have lots of obvious territorial markers, such as fences (even if small), parked cars, lawn furniture, exterior lights, and security signs (Brown & Bentley, 1993). "Gated communities" have sprung up in many cities because they mark out a "defensible space" that discourages intrusions (Low, 2001; Tijerino, 1998). (A highly territorial bulldog may help, too.)

© Imagebroker.net/PhotoLibrary

Graffiti, one of the blights of urban life, is an obvious form of territorial marking.

behavior. The reverse is also true: People have a significant impact on environments, both natural and constructed. Because of this second possibility, *environmental psychologists* are concerned with some of the most serious problems facing humanity.

© Peter M. Fisher/Corbis

Various behavioral settings place strong demands on people to act in expected ways. Consider, for example, the difference between a library and a campus center lounge. In which would a conversation be more likely to occur?

Environmental psychology is the specialty concerned with the relationship between environments and human behavior (Bell et al., 2006). Environmental psychologists are interested in both **physical environments** (natural or constructed) and **social environments** (defined by groups of people, such as a dance, business meeting, or party). They also give special attention to **behavioral settings** (smaller areas within an environment that have a well-defined use, such as an office, locker room, church, casino, or classroom). As you have no doubt noticed, various environments and behavioral settings tend to "demand" certain actions. Consider, for example, the difference between a library and a campus center lounge. In which would a conversation be more likely to occur?

Other major interests of environmental psychologists are personal space, territorial behavior (discussed in "Territoriality"), stressful environments, architectural design, environmental protection, and many related topics (■ Table 18.3).

Environmental Influences on Behavior

Much of our behavior is influenced, in part, by specific types of environments. For example, a variety of environmental factors influence the amount of vandalism that occurs in public places (Brown & Devlin, 2003). On the basis of psychological research,

TABLE 18.3 Topics of Special Interest to Environmental Psychologists

Architectural design	Noise
Behavioral settings	Personal space
Cognitive maps	Personality and environment
Constructed environments	Pollution
Crowding	Privacy
Energy conservation	Proxemics
Environmental stressors	Resource management
Heat	Territoriality
Human ecology	Urban planning
Littering	Vandalism
Natural environment	

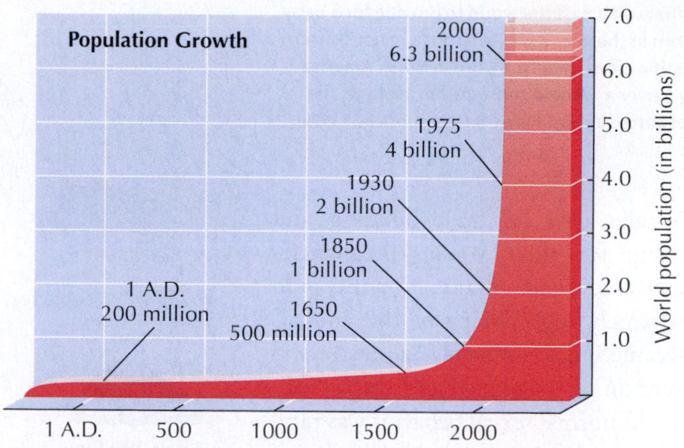

● **Figure 18.3** Population growth has exploded since 1850 and already exceeds 6 billion. Overpopulation and rapid population growth are closely connected with environmental damage, international tensions, and rapid depletion of nonrenewable resources. Some demographers predict that if population growth is not limited voluntarily before it reaches 10 billion, it will be limited by widespread food shortages, disease, infant mortality, and early death (Global Footprint Network, 2010). Population Institute, 2006

many architects now "harden" and "de-opportunize" public settings to discourage vandalism and graffiti. Some such efforts limit opportunities for vandalism (doorless toilet stalls, tiled walls). Others weaken the lure of likely targets. (Oddly enough, raised flowerbeds around signs helps protect them because people resist trampling the flowers to get to the sign.)

Similarly, many shopping malls and department stores are designed like mazes. Their twisting pathways encourage shoppers to linger and wander while looking at merchandise. Likewise, in every city more assaults and burglaries take place near the few restaurants or bars where likely offenders tend to hang out (Buchanan, 2008). Even public bathrooms influence behavior. Because the seating is limited, few people hold meetings there!

Given the personal impact that environments have, it is important to know how we are affected by stressful or unhealthy environments—a topic we will consider next.

Stressful Environments

Large cities are usually thought of as stressful places to live. Traffic congestion, pollution, crime, and impersonality are urban problems that immediately come to mind. To this list psychologists have added crowding, noise, and overstimulation as major sources of urban stress. Psychological research has begun to clarify the impact of each of these conditions on human functioning (Malan et al., 2008; Marsella, 1998).

Crowding

Overpopulation ranks as one of the most serious problems facing the world today. World population has exploded in the last 150 years (● Figure 18.3). The world's population is now more than 7 billion people and may exceed 10 billion by 2050 (UN, 2004).

How many more people can the forests, oceans, croplands, and atmosphere support? Experts estimate that the maximum sustainable population of the Earth is between 5 billion and 20 billion persons. This means the Earth has already entered the lower range of its carrying capacity. The most pessimistic experts believe we have *already* exceeded the number of people the Earth can sustain indefinitely (Global Footprint Network, 2010; Oskamp, 2000). Further population increases at the present rate could be disastrous.

Nowhere are the effects of overpopulation more evident than in the teeming cities of many underdeveloped nations. Closer to home, the jammed buses, subways, and living quarters of our own large cities are ample testimony to the stresses of crowding.

Is there any way to assess the effect crowding has on people? One approach is to study the effects of overcrowding among animals. Although the results of animal experiments cannot be considered conclusive for humans, they point to some disturbing effects.

For example? In an influential classic experiment, John Calhoun (1962) let a group of laboratory rats breed without limit in a confined space. Calhoun provided plenty of food, water, and nesting material for the rats. All that the rats lacked was space. At its peak, the colony numbered 80 rats. Yet it was housed in a cage designed to comfortably hold about 50. Overcrowding in the cage was heightened by the actions of the two most dominant males. These rascals staked out private territory at opposite ends of the cage, gathered harems of 8 to 10 females, and prospered. Their actions forced the remaining rats into a small, severely crowded middle area.

What effect did crowding have on the animals? A high rate of pathological behavior developed in both males and females.

Environmental psychology The formal study of how environments affect behavior.

Physical environments Natural settings, such as forests and beaches, as well as environments built by humans, such as buildings, ships, and cities.

Social environment An environment defined by a group of people and their activities or interrelationships (such as a parade, revival meeting, or sports event).

Behavioral setting A smaller area within an environment whose use is well defined, such as a bus depot, waiting room, or lounge.

What will it cost the world to provide for a baby born in the year 2000? Without a major conservation effort, a person born in North America will over a lifetime consume, on average, the resources shown here ("Bringing Up Baby," 1999).

© Monkey Business Images/Shutterstock

Females gave up nest building and caring for their young. Pregnancies decreased, and infant mortality ran extremely high. Many of the animals became indiscriminately aggressive and went on rampaging attacks against others. Abnormal sexual behavior was rampant, with some animals displaying hypersexuality and others total sexual passivity. Many of the animals died, apparently from stress-caused diseases. The link between these problems and overcrowding is unmistakable.

But does that apply to humans? Many of the same pathological behaviors can be observed in crowded inner-city ghettos. It is, therefore, tempting to assume that violence, social disorganization, and declining birthrates as seen in these areas are directly related to crowding. However, the connection has not been so clearly demonstrated with humans (Evans et al., 2010). People living in the inner city suffer disadvantages in nutrition, education, income, and health care. These, more than crowding, may deserve the blame. In fact, most laboratory studies using human subjects have failed to produce any serious ill effects by crowding people into small places. Most likely, this is because *crowding* is a psychological condition that is separate from **density** (the number of people in a given space).

How does crowding differ from density? **Crowding** refers to subjective feelings of being overstimulated by social inputs or a loss of privacy. Whether high density is experienced as crowding may depend on relationships among those involved. In an elevator, subway, or prison, high densities may be uncomfortable. In contrast, a musical concert, party, or reunion may be most pleasant at high density levels. Thus, physical crowding may interact with situations to intensify existing stresses or pleasures (Evans, Lercher, & Kofler, 2002). However, when crowding causes a *loss of control* over one's immediate social environment, stress is likely to result (Pandey, 1999; Steiner & Wooldredge, 2009).

Theo Wargo/Getty Images for Nivea

Times Square in New York, New Year's Eve, 2010. High densities do not automatically produce feelings of crowding. The nature of the situation and the relationships among crowd members are also important.

Stress probably explains why death rates increase among prison inmates and mental hospital patients who live in crowded conditions. Even milder instances of crowding can have a negative impact. People who live in crowded conditions often become more aggressive or guarded and withdrawn from others (Regoeczi, 2003).

Overload

One unmistakable result of high densities and crowding is a state that psychologist Stanley Milgram called **attentional overload**. This is a stressful condition that occurs when sensory stimulation, information, and social contacts make excessive demands on attention. Large cities, in particular, tend to bombard residents with continuous input. The resulting sensory and cognitive overload can be quite stressful.

Milgram (1970) believed that city dwellers learn to prevent attentional overload by engaging only in brief, superficial social contacts, by ignoring nonessential events, and by fending off others with cold and unfriendly expressions. In short, many city dwellers find that a degree of callousness is essential for survival.

USCG/Landov

AP Photo/Itsuo Inouye

In April 2010, an oil rig in the Gulf of Mexico exploded and burned, unleashing a major environmental catastrophe. In March 2011, a Japanese nuclear reactor suffered a catastrophic failure in reaction to a giant earthquake and tsunami. As the late Carl Sagan once said, "When you look closely, you find so many things going wrong with the environment, you are forced to reassess the hypothesis of intelligent life on Earth."

Kind or Callous?

Is there any evidence that such strategies are actually adopted? A fascinating study suggests they are. In several large American cities and smaller nearby towns, a young child stood on a busy street corner and asked passing strangers for help, saying, "I'm lost. Can you call my house?" About 72 percent of those approached in small towns offered to help. Only about 46 percent of those who were asked for help in the cities gave aid. In some cities (Boston and Philadelphia), only about one third were willing to help (Takooshian, Haber, & Lucido, 1977). Numerous studies confirm that country people are more likely to help than city people (Steblay, 1987; Wilson & Kennedy, 2006). The least helpful city tested was New York, where the crime rate is high and people are densely packed together (Levine, 2003). Thus, a blunting of sensitivity to the needs of others may be one of the more serious costs of urban stresses and crowding. As described next, noise also contributes to the sensory assault many people endure in urban environments.

The High Cost of Noise

How serious are the effects of daily exposure to noise? A classic study of children attending schools near Los Angeles International Airport suggests that constant noise can be quite damaging. Children from the noisy schools were compared with similar students attending schools farther from the airport (Cohen et al., 1981). The comparison students were from families of comparable social and economic makeup. Testing showed that children attending the noisy schools had higher blood pressure than those from the quieter schools. They were more likely to give up attempts to solve a difficult puzzle. And they were poorer at proofreading a printed paragraph—a task that requires close attention and concentration. Other studies of children living near other airports or in noisy neighborhoods have found similar signs of stress, poor reading skills, and other damaging effects (Evans, 2006; Sörqvist, 2010).

The tendency of the noise-battered children to give up or become distracted is a serious handicap. It may even reveal a state of "learned helplessness" caused by daily, uncontrollable blasts of sound. Even if such damage proves to be temporary, it is clear that **noise pollution** (annoying and intrusive noise) is a major source of environmental stress (Staples, 1996).

BRIDGES

Learned helplessness is described in Chapter 13, pages 458–459.

Human Influences on the Environment

Human activities drastically change the natural environment (Miller & Spoolman, 2011). We burn fossil fuels, destroy forests, use chemical products, and strip, clear, and farm the land. In doing so, we alter natural cycles, animal populations, and the very face of

Territorial behavior Any behavior that tends to define a space as one's own or that protects it from intruders.

Territorial markers Objects and other signals whose placement indicates to others the "ownership" or control of a particular area.

Density The number of people in a given space or, inversely, the amount of space available to each person.

Crowding A subjective feeling of being overstimulated by a loss of privacy or by the nearness of others (especially when social contact with them is unavoidable).

Attentional overload A stressful condition caused when sensory stimulation, information, and social contacts make excessive demands on attention.

Noise pollution Stressful and intrusive noise; usually artificially generated by machinery, but also including noises made by animals and humans.

the Earth. The long-range impact of such activities is already becoming evident through global warming, the extinction of plants and animals, a hole in the ozone layer, and polluted land, air, water, and oceans (Oskamp, 2002; Winter & Koger, 2010).

On a smaller scale there is plenty of evidence that unchecked environmental damage will be costly to our children and descendants. For example, exposure to toxic hazards, such as radiation, pesticides, and industrial chemicals, leads to an elevated risk of physical and mental disease (Evans, 2006).

Peter Ginter Material World

Peter Ginter Material World

Shown here are the Skeen family of Pearland, Texas, and the Yadev family of Ahraura, India. Each was photographed by the Material World Project, which documented typical families and their possessions around the world. Developed countries presently have much larger ecological footprints. However, population growth is fastest in developing countries, and their hunger for material possessions is rapidly expanding. Achieving sustainable levels of population and consumption are two of the greatest challenges of this century. (From Menzel et al., 1994.)

Sustainable Lifestyles

A worldwide ecological crisis is brewing, and humans must change course to avoid vast human misery and permanent damage. Of course, corporations and governments do much environmental damage. Thus, many of the solutions will require changes in politics and policies. Ultimately, it will also require changes in individual behavior. Most of the environmental problems we face can be traced back to the human tendency to overuse natural resources (Global Footprint Network, 2010; Huang & Rust, 2011).

Wasted Resources

The rapid worldwide consumption of natural resources is a devastating social problem. Resource consumption can be measured as an **ecological footprint**, the amount of land and water area required to replenish the resources that a human population consumes. According to the Global Footprint Network (2010), humans are already consuming more than the Earth can regenerate. Industrialized nations, in particular, are consuming world resources at an alarming rate. North America, for instance, has an ecological footprint about 10 times higher than that of Asia or Africa. In the face of projected shortages and squandered resources, what can be done to encourage conservation on a personal level?

Conservation

Try as you might to reduce your use of resources (electricity, for instance), you may find it difficult to do (Stall, Meadows & Hebert, 2011). Environmental psychologists have long known that a lack of *control* and *feedback* is a major barrier (Abrahamse et al., 2005). (See Chapter 6, pages 219–221, for details.)

For example, programmable home thermostats and energy saving settings on appliances and electronics make it possible for conservation-conscious consumers to more precisely control their energy consumption. Similarly, feedback about electricity use usually arrives long after the temptation to turn up the heat or to leave lights on (the monthly electricity bill). Psychologists aware of this problem have shown that lower energy bills result from simply giving families and work groups daily feedback about their use of gas or electricity (Carrico & Riemer, 2011).

Savings are magnified further with the addition of programs that give monetary rewards for energy conservation. *Smart meters*, one recent example, can provide continuous feedback about energy usage to both consumers and their energy suppliers (U.S. Department of Energy, 2010). With this information, electricity utilities can, for example, offer electricity at lower prices during periods of low demand. Savvy consumers can not only more easily conserve electricity, but they can also save even more money by, say, running their dishwasher in the evening rather than during the day.

Effective feedback about overall resource use is also finally becoming widely available as several organizations provide *ecological footprint calculators*, websites that allow individuals to calculate and, therefore, track their individual resource consumption (Global Footprint Network, 2010). With growing public concern over global warming, many people are now calculating their individual **carbon footprint**, the volume of greenhouse gases individual consumption adds to the atmosphere (The Nature Conservancy, 2011).

It is now easier than ever to conserve energy (by installing energy efficient lights, for example) and see an immediate reduction in your carbon footprint. It is also becoming more popular to offset some *carbon debt*—by planting trees, for example. Prompt and accurate information and feedback about energy use is making it possible to aspire to a *carbon-neutral lifestyle,* in which your energy consumption is reduced and the remainder offset so that your overall impact on global warming is zero. Similar factors can greatly increase recycling, as described in "Reuse and Recycle."

Discovering Psychology — Reuse and Recycle

Although reducing consumption can lighten the environmental impact of our "throw-away" society, personally reusing products and materials that would normally be thrown away is also important. In addition, we can recycle materials such as paper, steel, glass, aluminum, and plastic that can be used to make new products.

What can be done to encourage people to recycle? Psychological research has shown that all of the following strategies promote recycling (Duffy & Verges, 2009; Schmuck & Vlek, 2003; Winter & Koger, 2010):

© Philip James Corwin/Corbis.

People are much more likely to recycle if proper attention is given to psychological factors that promote recycling behavior. For example, this Washington State recycling bin is designed to be visually appealing.

- **Educate.** Learning about environmental problems and pro-environment values at school and work has been one of the most effective ways to encourage pro-environmental behavior including recycling (Carrico & Riemer, 2011; Schmuck & Vlek, 2003).
- **Provide monetary rewards.** As mentioned before, monetary rewards encourage conservation. Requiring refundable deposits on glass bottles is a good example of using incentives to increase recycling.
- **Remove barriers.** Anything that makes recycling more convenient helps. A good example is cities that offer curbside pickup of household recyclables. Another is businesses that help customers recycle old computers, printers, and the like. On campus, simply putting marked containers in classrooms is a good way to encourage recycling (Ludwig, Gray, & Rowell, 1998; Winter & Koger, 2010).
- **Use persuasion.** Many recycling programs benefit from media campaigns to persuade people to participate.
- **Obtain public commitment.** People who feel they have committed themselves to recycling are more likely to follow through and actually recycle. Sometimes, people are asked to sign "pledge cards" on which they promise to recycle. Another technique involves having people sign a list committing themselves to recycling. Such lists may or may not be published in a local newspaper. They are just as effective either way.
- **Encourage goal setting.** People who set their own goals for recycling tend to meet them. Goal setting has been used successfully with families, dorms, neighborhoods, offices, factories, and so forth.
- **Give feedback.** To reiterate, feedback proves to be very valuable. Recycling typically increases when families, work groups, dorms, and the like are simply told, on a weekly basis, how much they recycled (Keller, 2010; Schultz, 1999). Even impersonal feedback can be effective. In one study, signs were placed on recycling containers on a college campus. The signs showed how many aluminum cans had been deposited in the previous week. This simple procedure increased recycling by 65 percent (Larson, Houlihan, & Goernert, 1995).
- **Revise attitudes.** Even people who believe that recycling is worthwhile are likely to regard it as a boring task. Thus, people are most likely to continue recycling if they emphasize the sense of satisfaction they get from contributing to the environment (Nigbur, Lyons, & Uzzell, 2010; Werner & Makela, 1998).

Social Dilemmas

Why is it so difficult to get people to take better care of the environment? A pattern of behavior called a *social dilemma* contributes to many environmental problems. A **social dilemma** is any social situation that rewards actions that have undesired effects in the long run (Van Vugt, 2002, 2009). In a typical social dilemma, no one individual intentionally acts against the group interest, but if many people act alike, collective harm is done. For example, the rapid transit systems in many large cities are underused. At the same time, the roads are jammed. Why? Because too many individuals decide that it is convenient to own and drive a separate car (in order to run errands and so on). However, each person's behavior affects the welfare of others. Because everyone wants to drive for "convenience," driving becomes inconvenient: The mass of cars in most cities causes irritating traffic snarls and a lack of parking spaces. It also contributes to pollution and global warming. Each car owner has been drawn into a dilemma.

The Tragedy of the Commons

Social dilemmas are especially damaging when we are enticed into overuse of scarce resources that must be shared by many people. Again, each person acts in his or her self-interest but collectively, everyone ends up suffering. Ecologist Garrett Hardin (1968) calls such situations the **tragedy of the commons**. An example we have already discussed is the lack of individual incentives to conserve

Ecological footprint The amount of land and water area required to replenish the resources that a human population consumes.

Carbon footprint The volume of greenhouse gases individual consumption adds to the atmosphere

Social dilemma A social situation that tends to provide immediate rewards for actions that will have undesired effects in the long run.

Tragedy of the commons A social dilemma in which individuals, each acting in his or her immediate self-interest, overuse a scarce group resource.

gasoline, water, or electricity. Whenever personal comfort or convenience is involved, it is highly tempting to "let others worry about it." Yet, in the long run, everyone stands to lose (Van Vugt, 2009).

Why does such misguided behavior so often prevail? Again, we see a social dilemma at work: If one person pollutes a river or trashes the roadside, it has little noticeable effect. But as many people do the same, problems that affect everyone quickly mount. Throwing away one plastic bag may seem inconsequential, but across the world 500 billion plastic bags are used every year and it takes hundreds of years for the environment to recycle them. Plastic bags are major polluters of the world's oceans.

As another example, consider the farmer who applies pesticides to a crop to save it from insect damage. The farmer benefits immediately. However, if other farmers follow suit, the local water system may be permanently damaged. In most cases of environmental pollution, there are immediate benefits for polluting and major—but delayed—long-term costs. What can we do to avoid such dilemmas?

Escaping Dilemmas

Persuasion and education have been used with some success to get individuals and businesses to voluntarily reduce destructive activities. Effective appeals may be based on self-interest (cost savings), the collective good (protecting one's own children and future generations), or simply a personal desire to take better care of the planet (Pelletier, Baxter, & Huta, 2011; Stern, 1992; Winter & Koger, 2010). It really helps if conservation is seen as a group effort. There is evidence that in most social dilemmas, people are more likely to restrain themselves when they believe others will, too (Messick et al., 1983; Nigbur, Lyons, & Uzzell, 2010). Otherwise, they are likely to think, "Why should I be a sucker? I don't think anyone else is going to conserve" (fuel, electricity, water, paper, or whatever).

In some cases, it is possible to dismantle social dilemmas by rearranging rewards and costs. For example, many companies are tempted to pollute because it saves them money and increases profits. To reverse the situation, a pollution tax could be levied so that it would cost more, not less, for a business to pollute. Likewise, incentives can be offered for responsible behavior. An example is the rebates offered for installing insulation or buying energy-efficient appliances (Schmuck & Vlek, 2003). Another is offering lower electricity rates for shifting use to off-peak times (U.S. Department of Energy, 2010).

Some problems may be harder to solve. What, for instance, can be done about truck drivers who cause dangerous traffic jams because they will not pull over on narrow roads? How can littering be discouraged or prevented? How would you make carpooling or using public transportation the first choice for most people? Or how could people simply be encouraged to stagger their departure times to and from work? All these and more are social dilemmas that need solving. It is important that we not fall into the trap of ignoring them.

Environmental Problem Solving

How do psychologists find solutions to problems like overcrowding, pollution, and overuse of resources? Solutions can more easily be found by doing **environmental assessments** to see how environments influence the behavior and perceptions of the people using them.

For example, anyone who has ever lived in a college dorm knows that at times a dorm hall can be quite a "crazy house." In one well-known environmental assessment, Baum and Valins (1977) found that students housed in long, narrow, corridor-design dormitories often feel crowded and stressed. The crowded students tended to withdraw from others and even made more trips to the campus health center than students living in less-crowded buildings.

Through **architectural psychology**, the study of the effects buildings have on behavior, psychologists are often able to suggest design changes that solve or avoid problems (Zeisel, 2006). For example, Baum and Valins (1979) studied two basic dorm arrangements. One dorm had a long corridor with one central bathroom. As a result, residents were constantly forced into contact with one another. The other dorm had rooms clustered in threes. Each of these suites shared a small bathroom. Even though the amount of space available to each student was the same in both dorms, students in the long-corridor dorm reported feeling more crowded. They also made fewer friends in their dorm and showed greater signs of withdrawing from social contact.

What sort of solution does this suggest? A later study showed that small architectural changes can greatly reduce stress in high-density living conditions. Baum and Davis (1980) compared students living in a long-corridor dorm housing 40 students with those living in an altered long-corridor dorm. In the altered dorm, Baum and Davis divided the hallway in half with unlocked doors and made three center bedrooms into a lounge area (● Figure 18.4). At the end of the term, students living in the divided dorm reported less stress from crowding. They also formed more friendships and were more open to social contacts. In comparison, students in the long-corridor dorm felt more crowded, stressed, and unfriendly, and they kept their doors shut much more frequently—presumably because they "wanted to be alone."

Similar improvements have been made by altering the interior design of businesses, schools, apartment buildings, mental hospitals, and prisons. In general, the more spaces one must pass through to get from one part of a building to another, the less stressed and crowded people feel (Evans, Lepore, & Schroeder, 1996; Zeisel, 2006).

Conclusion

We have had room here only to hint at the creative and highly useful work being done in environmental psychology. Although many environmental problems remain, it is encouraging to see that behavioral solutions exist for at least some of them. Surely, creating and maintaining healthy environments is one of the major challenges facing coming generations (Winter & Koger, 2010; Oskamp & Schultz, 2006).

We have discussed work and the environment at some length because both have major effects on our lives. To provide a fuller account of the diversity of applied psychology, let's conclude by briefly sampling four additional topics of interest: educational psychology, legal psychology, sports psychology, and human factors psychology.

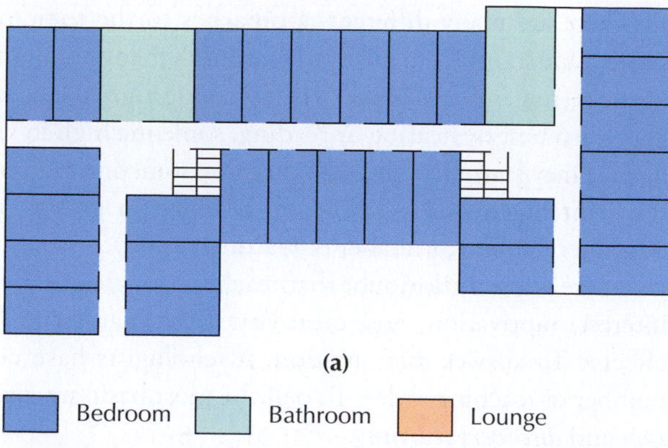

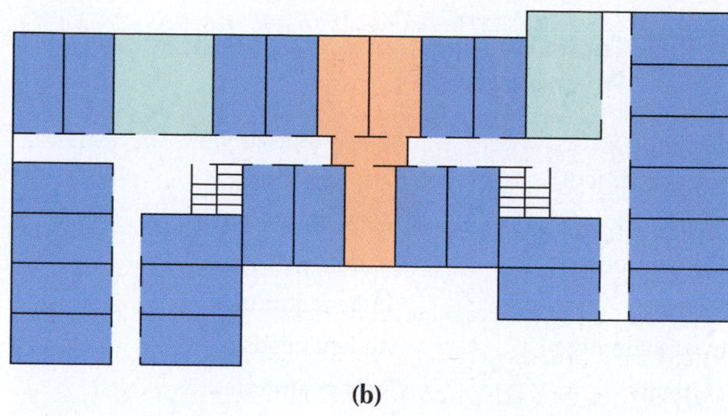

● **Figure 18.4** An architectural solution for crowding. Psychologists divided a dorm hall like that shown in the left diagram *(a)* into two shorter halls separated by unlocked doors and a lounge area *(b)*. This simple change minimized unwanted social contacts and greatly reduced feelings of crowding among dorm residents. Adapted from Baum & Davis, 1980.

Knowledge Builder — Environmental Psychology

RECITE

1. Although male rats in Calhoun's crowded animal colony became quite pathological, female rats continued to behave in a relatively normal fashion. T or F?
2. To clearly understand behavior, it is necessary to make a distinction between crowding and ____________ (the number of people in a given space).
3. Milgram believed that many city dwellers prevent attentional overload by limiting themselves to superficial social contacts. T or F?
4. Using tools like smart meters and ecological footprint calculators to provide feedback is one effective approach for bringing about energy conservation. T or F?
5. So far, the most successful approach for bringing about energy conservation is to add monetary penalties to monthly bills for excessive consumption. T or F?
6. Performing an environmental ____________ might be a good prelude to redesigning college classrooms to make them more comfortable and conducive to learning.

REFLECT

Think Critically

7. Many of the most damaging changes to the environment being caused by humans will not be felt until sometime in the future. How does this complicate the problem of preserving environmental quality?

Self-Reflect

What is the nature of the natural environment, constructed environment, social environment, and behavioral setting you are in right now?

What forms of territorial behavior are you aware of in your own actions?

Have you ever experienced a stressful level of crowding? Was density or control the key factor?

Have you ever calculated your carbon footprint? Why not try it? You might be surprised by what you find.

Answers: 1. F **2.** density **3.** T **4.** T **5.** F **6.** assessment **7.** A delay of consequences (rewards, benefits, costs, and punishers) tends to reduce their impact on immediate behavior.

Educational Psychology—An Instructive Topic

Gateway Question 18.3: *How has psychology improved education?*

You have just been asked to teach a class of fourth-graders for a day. What will you do? (Assume that bribery, showing them movies, and a field trip to an amusement park are out.) If you ever do try teaching, you might be surprised at how challenging it is. Effective teachers must understand learning, instruction, classroom dynamics, and testing.

What are the best ways to teach? Is there an optimal teaching style for different age groups, topics, or individuals? These and related questions lie at the heart of educational psychology (■ Table 18.4). Specifically, **educational psychology** seeks to understand how people learn and how teachers instruct (Snowman & McCown, 2011).

© Grantpix/PhotoLibrary

Educational psychologists are interested in enhancing learning and improving teaching.

Environmental assessment Measurement and analysis of the effects an environment has on the behavior and perceptions of people within that environment.

Architectural psychology Study of the effects buildings have on behavior and the design of buildings using behavioral principles.

Educational psychology The field that seeks to understand how people learn and how teachers instruct.

TABLE 18.4 Topics of Special Interest to Educational Psychologists

Aptitude testing	Language learning
Classroom management	Learning theory
Classroom motivation	Moral development
Classroom organization	Student adjustment
Concept learning	Student attitudes
Curriculum development	Student needs
Disabled students	Teacher attitudes
Exceptional students	Teaching strategies
Gifted students	Teaching styles
Individualized instruction	Test writing
Intellectual development	Transfer of learning
Intelligence testing	

Elements of a Teaching Strategy

Whether it's "breaking in" a new coworker, instructing a friend in a hobby, or helping a child learn to read, the fact is, we all teach at times. The next time you are asked to share your knowledge, how will you do it? One good way to become more effective is to use a specific **teaching strategy**, or planned method of instruction. The example that follows was designed for classroom use, but it applies to many other situations as well (Ormrod, 2011):

Step 1: Learner preparation. Begin by gaining the learner's attention, and focus interest on the topic at hand.

Step 2: Stimulus presentation. Present instructional stimuli (information, examples, and illustrations) deliberately and clearly.

Step 3: Learner response. Allow time for the learner to respond to the information presented (by repeating correct responses or asking questions, for example).

Step 4: Reinforcement. Give positive reinforcement (praise, encouragement) and feedback ("Yes, that's right," "No, this way," and so on) to strengthen correct responses.

Step 5: Evaluation. Test or assess the learner's progress so that both you and the learner can make adjustments when needed.

Step 6: Spaced review. Periodic review is an important step in teaching because it helps strengthen responses to key stimuli.

BRIDGES

Many effective teaching strategies apply the basic principles of operant conditioning. **See Chapter 6, pages 212–228.**

Effects of Learning and Teaching Styles

Isn't there more to teaching than following a particular teaching strategy? Effective teachers don't just use a teaching strategy to present material to their students. They also recognize that different students may have different *learning styles* and that it is possible to use different *teaching styles*.

There are many different approaches to the topic of learning styles. One stems from Howard Gardner's theory of multiple intelligences (remember Chapter 9?). Someone high in language ability may learn best by hearing or reading, someone high in visual intelligence may learn best through pictures, someone high in interpersonal intelligence may learn best working in groups, and so on (Gardner, 2008; Kornhaber & Gardner, 2006).

There is also little doubt that teachers can greatly affect student interest, motivation, and creativity. But what styles have what effects? To answer this question, psychologists have compared a number of teaching styles. Two of the most basic are *direct instruction* and *discovery learning*.

In **direct instruction**, factual information is presented by lecture, demonstration, and rote practice. In **discovery learning**, teachers create conditions that encourage students to discover or construct knowledge for themselves (Dean & Kuhn, 2007). As it turns out, both approaches have certain advantages. Students of direct instruction do slightly better on achievement tests than students in discovery classrooms (Klahr & Nigam, 2004). However, students of discovery learning do somewhat better on tests of abstract thinking, creativity, and problem solving. They also tend to be more independent, curious, and positive in their attitudes toward school (Scruggs & Mastropieri, 2007). At present, it looks as if a balance of teaching styles goes hand in hand with a balanced education.

Although we have viewed only a small sample of educational theory and research, its value for improving teaching and learning should be apparent (Snowman & McCown, 2011). Before we leave the topic of education, "Peanut Butter for the Mind: Designing Education for Everyone" offers a peek at where education is going in the future.

Psychology and Law—Judging Juries

Gateway Question 18.4: *What does psychology reveal about juries and court verdicts?*

One of the best places to see psychology in action is the local courthouse. Jury trials are often fascinating studies in human behavior. Does the defendant's appearance affect the jury's decision? Do the personality characteristics or attitudes of jurors influence how they vote? These and many more questions have been investigated by psychologists interested in law. Specifically, the **psychology of law** is the study of the behavioral dimensions of the legal system (Greene & Heilbrun, 2011; see Table 18.5).

Jury Behavior

When a case goes to trial, jurors must listen to days or weeks of testimony and then decide guilt or innocence. How do they reach their decision? Psychologists use **mock juries** (simulated juries) to probe such questions. In some mock juries, volunteers are simply given written evidence and arguments to read before making a decision. Others watch videotaped trials staged by actors. Either

Human Diversity — Peanut Butter for the Mind—Designing Education for Everyone

"Education is the key to unlock the golden door of freedom," said George Washington Carver. Born in 1860, a son of slaves, he invented that universally popular food, peanut butter. In today's ever more complicated world, Carver's words ring truer than ever. Yet, educators face an increasingly diverse mix of students: "regular" students, adult learners, students with disabilities, students who speak English as a second language, and students at risk for dropping out (Bowe, 2000). In response, educators have begun to apply an approach called *Universal Design for Instruction* (Holbrook, Moore, & Zoss, 2010; Scott, McGuire, & Shaw, 2003). The basic idea is to design lessons so richly that they will benefit most, if not all, students and their diverse needs and learning styles.

One principle of Universal Design for Instruction is to use a variety of instructional methods, such as a lecture, a podcast of the lecture, a group activity, an Internet discussion list, and perhaps student blogs. That way, for example, hearing impaired or visually impaired students can find at least one learning approach they can use. Likewise, adult learners who can't always get to class, because of work or family responsibilities, can get course information in other ways. Ultimately, everyone benefits because we all learn better if we can choose among different ways of gaining knowledge. Besides, it's not a bad idea to work through learning materials more than once in different ways.

Another principle is to make learning materials simple and intuitive by removing unnecessary complexity. For instance, students can be given clear grading standards, accurate and complete course outlines, and handbooks to guide them through difficult topics. Again, such materials are not just better for special groups of students. They make learning easier for all of us.

Are these principles being applied to learning in colleges and universities? In short, yes they are (McGuire, & Scott, 2002; Orr & Hammig, 2009). Universal instruction has broad appeal—like peanut butter—but fortunately it won't stick to the roof of your mind!

way, studying the behavior of mock juries helps us understand what determines how real jurors vote (Pezdek, Avila-Mora, & Sperry, 2010).

Some of the findings of jury research are unsettling (Levett et al., 2005). Studies show that jurors are rarely able to put aside their biases, attitudes, and values when making a decision (Buck & Warren, 2010; Devine et al., 2001). For example, appearance can be unduly influential (halo effect? Chapter 1?). Jurors are less likely to find attractive defendants guilty (on the basis of the same evidence) than unattractive defendants (Perlman & Cozby, 1983). In one mock jury study, defendants were less likely to be convicted if they wearing eyeglasses than if they were not. Presumably eye glasses imply intelligence and, hence, that the defendant wouldn't do anything as foolish as he or she was accused of (Brown, Henriquez, & Groscup, 2008).

A second major problem is that jurors are not very good at separating evidence from other information, such as their perceptions of the defendant, attorneys, witnesses, and what they think the judge wants. For example, if complex scientific evidence is presented, jurors tend to be swayed more by the expertise of the witness than by the evidence itself (Cooper, Bennett, & Sukel, 1996; Hans et al., 2011). Similarly, today's jurors place too much confidence in DNA evidence because crime-solving programs like *CSI* and *Forensic Files* make it seem simple (Myers, 2007). Further, jurors who have been exposed to pretrial publicity tend to inappropriately incorporate that information into their jury deliberations, often without being aware it has happened (Ruva, McEvoy, & Bryant, 2007).

Often the jurors' final verdict is influenced by inadmissible evidence, such as mention of a defendant's prior conviction. When jurors are told to ignore information that slips out in court, they find it very hard to do so. A related problem occurs when jurors take into account the severity of the punishment a defendant faces (Sales & Hafemeister, 1985). Jurors are not supposed to let this affect their verdict, but many do.

TABLE 18.5 Topics of Special Interest in the Psychology of Law

Arbitration	Juror attitudes
Attitudes toward law	Jury decisions
Bail setting	Jury selection
Capital punishment	Mediation
Conflict resolution	Memory
Criminal personality	Parole board decisions
Diversion programs	Police selection
Effects of parole	Police stress
Expert testimony	Police training
Eyewitness testimony	Polygraph accuracy
Forensic hypnosis	Sentencing decisions
Insanity plea	White-collar crime

Teaching strategy A plan for effective teaching.
Direct instruction Presentation of factual information by lecture, demonstration, and rote practice.
Discovery learning Instruction based on encouraging students to discover or construct knowledge for themselves.
Psychology of law Study of the psychological and behavioral dimensions of the legal system.
Mock jury A group that realistically simulates a courtroom jury.

Critical Thinking Death-Qualified Juries

People in a death-qualified jury must favor the death penalty or at least be indifferent to it. That way, jurors are capable of voting for the death penalty if they think it is justified.

In order for the death penalty to have meaning, death-qualified juries may be a necessity. However, psychologists have discovered that the makeup of such juries tends to be biased. Specifically, death-qualified juries are likely to contain a disproportionate number of people who are male, white, high income, conservative, and authoritarian. Given the same facts, jurors who favor the death penalty are more likely to read criminal intent into a defendant's actions (Goodman-Delahunty, Greene, & Hsiao, 1998; Summers, Hayward, & Miller, 2010) and are much more likely than average to convict a defendant (Allen, Mabry, & McKelton, 1998; Butler, 2007).

Could death-qualified juries be too willing to convict? It is nearly impossible to say how often the bias inherent in death-qualified juries results in bad verdicts. However, the possibility that some innocent persons have been executed may be one of the inevitable costs of using death as the ultimate punishment.

© Tim Wright/Corbis

A fourth area of difficulty arises because jurors usually cannot suspend judgment until all the evidence is in. Typically, they form an opinion early in the trial. It then becomes hard for them to fairly judge evidence that contradicts their opinion.

Problems like these are troubling in a legal system that prides itself on fairness. However, all is not lost. The more severe the crime and the more clear-cut the evidence, the less a jury's quirks affect the verdict. Although it is far from perfect, the jury system works reasonably well in most cases.

Jury Selection

In many cases, the composition of a jury has a major effect on the verdict of a trial (Lieberman & Sales, 2007). Before a trial begins, opposing attorneys are allowed to disqualify potential jurors who may be biased. For example, a person who knows anyone connected with the trial can be excluded. Beyond this, attorneys try to use jury selection to remove people who may cause trouble for them. For instance, juries composed of women are more likely to vote for conviction in child sexual assault trials (Golding et al., 2007).

Only a limited number of potential jurors can be excused. As a result, many attorneys ask psychologists for help in identifying people who will favor or harm their efforts. In **scientific jury selection**, social science principles are applied to the process of choosing a jury (Seltzer, 2006). Several techniques are typically used. As a first step, *demographic information* may be collected for each juror. Much can be guessed by knowing a juror's age, sex, race, occupation, education, political affiliation, religion, and socioeconomic status. Most of this information is available from public records.

To supplement demographic information, a *community survey* may be done to find out how local citizens feel about the case. The assumption is that jurors probably have attitudes similar to people with backgrounds like their own. Although talking with potential jurors outside the courtroom is not permitted, other information networks are available. For instance, a psychologist may interview relatives, acquaintances, neighbors, and coworkers of potential jurors.

Back in court, psychologists also often watch for *authoritarian personality* traits in potential jurors. Authoritarians tend to believe that punishment is effective, and they are more likely to vote for conviction (Devine et al., 2001). At the same time, the psychologist typically observes potential jurors' *nonverbal behavior*. The idea is to try to learn from body language which side the person favors (Sales & Hafemeister, 1985).

BRIDGES

Authoritarian personality traits are also related to ethnocentrism and racial prejudice. **See Chapter 17, pages 590–591.**

In the United States, murder trials require a special jury—one made up of people who are not opposed to the death penalty. "Death-Qualified Juries" examines the implications of this practice.

In the well-publicized case of O. J. Simpson, who was accused of brutally killing his wife and her friend, a majority of African Americans thought Simpson was innocent during the early stages of the trial. In contrast, the majority of European Americans thought he was guilty. The opinions of both groups changed little over the course of the yearlong trial. (Simpson was eventually acquitted, but he later lost a civil lawsuit brought by the victims' families.) The fact that emerging evidence and arguments had little effect on what people believed shows why jury makeup can sometimes decide the outcome of a trial (Cohn et al., 2009; Forster Lee et al., 2006).

Cases like Simpson's raise troubling ethical questions. Wealthy clients have the advantage of scientific jury selection—something most people cannot afford. Attorneys, of course, can't be blamed for trying to improve their odds of winning a case. And because both sides help select jurors, the net effect in most instances is probably a more balanced jury. At its worst, jury analysis leads to unjust verdicts. At its best, it helps to identify and remove only people who would be highly biased (Lieberman & Sales, 2007).

Jury research is perhaps the most direct link between psychology and law, but there are others. Psychologists evaluate people for sanity hearings, do counseling in prisons, profile criminals, advise lawmakers on public policy, help select and train police cadets, and more (Brewer & Williams, 2005; Wrightsman & Fulero, 2009). In the future, it is quite likely that psychology will have a growing impact on law and the courts.

Sports Psychology—The Athletic Mind

Gateway Question 18.5: *Can psychology enhance athletic performance?*

What does psychology have to do with sports? **Sports psychology** is the study of the behavioral dimensions of sports performance (Cox, 2011). As almost all serious athletes soon learn, peak performance requires more than physical training. Mental and emotional "conditioning" are also important. Recognizing this fact, many teams, both professional and amateur, now include psychologists on their staffs. On any given day, a sports psychologist might teach an athlete how to relax, how to ignore distractions, or how to cope with emotions. The sports psychologist might also provide personal counseling for performance-lowering stresses and conflicts (LeUnes, 2008). Other psychologists are interested in studying factors that affect athletic achievement, such as skill learning, the personality profiles of champion athletes, the effects of spectators, and related topics (■ Table 18.6). In short, sports psychologists seek to understand and improve sports performance and to enhance the benefits of participating in sports (Cox, 2011).

■ TABLE 18.6 Topics of Special Interest to Sports Psychologists

Achievement motivation	Hypnosis
Athletic personality	Mental practice
Athletic task analysis	Motor learning
Coaching styles	Peak performance
Competition	Positive visualization
Control of attention	Self-regulation
Coping strategies	Skill acquisition
Emotions and performance	Social facilitation
Exercise and mental health	Stress reduction
Goal setting	Team cooperation
Group (team) dynamics	Training procedures

Kenneth K. Lam/Baltimore Sun/MCT via Getty Images

Testing by psychologists has shown that umpires can call balls and strikes more accurately if they stand behind the outside corner of home plate. This position supplies better height and distance information because umpires are able to see pitches pass in front of the batter (Ford et al., 1999).

Sports often provide valuable information on human behavior in general. For example, one study of adolescents found a link between sports participation and physical self-esteem that was, in turn, linked with overall self-esteem (Bowker, 2006). In other work, psychologists have learned that such benefits are most likely to occur when competition, rejection, criticism, and the "one-winner mentality" are minimized. When working with children in sports, it is also important to emphasize fair play, intrinsic rewards, self-control of emotions, independence, and self-reliance.

Adults, of course, may also benefit from sports through reduced stress, better self-image and improved general health (Williams, 2010). Running, for instance, is associated with lower levels of tension, anxiety, fatigue, and depression than is found in the nonrunning population.

Before the advent of sports psychology, it was debatable whether athletes improved because of "homespun" coaching methods or in spite of them. For example, in early studies of volleyball and gymnastics, it became clear that people teaching these sports had very little knowledge of crucial, underlying skills (Salmela, 1974, 1975).

How has psychology helped? An ability to do detailed studies of complex skills has been one of the major contributions. In a **task analysis**, sports skills are broken into subparts, so that key elements can be identified and taught. Such methods are an extension of techniques first used for job analyses, as described earlier. For example, it doesn't take much to be off target in the Olympic sport of marksmanship. The object is to hit a bullseye the size of a dime at the end of a 165-foot-long shooting range. Nevertheless, an aver-

Scientific jury selection Using social science principles to choose members of a jury.

Death-qualified jury A jury composed of people who favor the death penalty or at least are indifferent to it.

Sports psychology Study of the psychological and behavioral dimensions of sports performance.

Task analysis Breaking complex skills into their subparts.

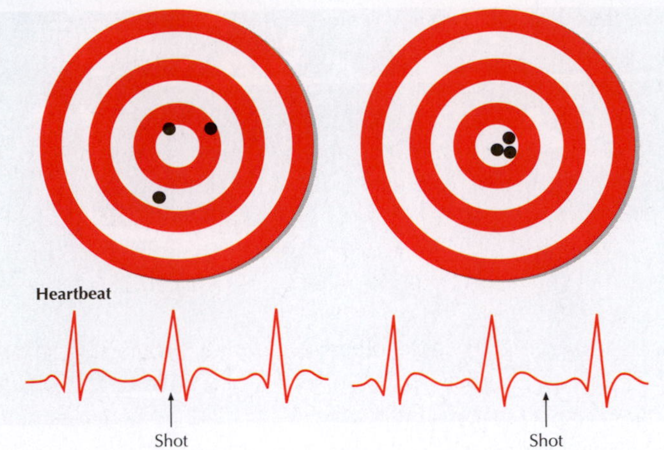

● **Figure 18.5** The target on the left shows what happens when a marksman fires during the heart's contraction. Higher scores, as shown by the three shots on the right, are more likely when shots are made between heartbeats. Adapted from Pelton, 1983.

age of 50 bullseyes out of 60 shots is not unusual in international competition (prone position).

What does it take—beyond keen eyes and steady hands—to achieve such accuracy? The answer is surprising. Sports psychologists have found that top marksmen consistently squeeze the trigger *between* heartbeats (● Figure 18.5). Apparently the tiny tremor induced by a heartbeat is enough to send the shot astray (Pelton, 1983). Without careful psychological study, it is doubtful that this element of marksmanship would have been identified. Now that its importance is known, competitors have begun to use various techniques—from relaxation training to biofeedback—to steady and control their heartbeat. In the future, the best marksmen may be those who set their sights on mastering their hearts.

Motor Skills

Sports psychologists are very interested in how we learn motor skills. A **motor skill** is a series of actions molded into a smooth and efficient performance. Typing, walking, pole-vaulting shooting baskets, playing golf, driving a car, writing, and skiing are all motor skills.

A basketball player may never make exactly the same shot twice in a game. This makes it almost impossible to practice every shot that might occur. How, then, do athletes become skillful? Typically, athletic performances involve learning *motor programs.* A **motor program** is a mental plan or model of what a skilled movement should be like. Motor programs allow an athlete—or a person simply walking across a room—to perform complex movements that fit changing conditions. If, for example, you have learned a "bike-riding" motor program, you can easily ride bicycles of different sizes and types on a large variety of surfaces.

Throughout life you will face the challenge of learning new motor skills. How can psychology make your learning more effective? Studies of sports skills suggest that you should keep the following points in mind for optimal skill learning (Karagheorgis & Terry, 2011; Williams, 2010):

1. Begin by observing and imitating a *skilled model.* Modeling provides a good mental picture of the skill. At this point, try simply to grasp a visual image of the skilled movement.
2. Learn *verbal rules* to back up motor learning. Such rules are usually most helpful in the early phases of skill learning. When first learning cross-country skiing, for example, it is helpful to say, "left arm, right foot, right arm, left foot." Later, as a skill becomes more automated, internal speech may actually get in the way.
3. Practice should be as *lifelike* as possible so that artificial cues and responses do not become a part of the skill. A competitive diver should practice on the board, not on a trampoline. If you want to learn to ski, try to practice on snow, not straw.
4. Get *feedback* from a mirror, videotape, coach, or observer. Whenever possible, get someone experienced in the skill to direct attention to *correct responses* when they occur.
5. When possible, it is better to practice *natural units* rather than breaking the task into artificial parts. When learning to type, it is better to start with real words rather than nonsense syllables.
6. Learn to *evaluate* and *analyze* your own performance. Remember, you are trying to learn a motor program, not just train your muscles. Motor skills are actually very mental.

The last point leads to one more suggestion. Research has shown that **mental practice**, or merely imagining a skilled performance, can aid learning (Short, Ross-Stewart, & Monsma, 2006). This technique seems to help by refining motor programs. Of course, mental practice is not superior to actual practice. Mental practice tends to be most valuable after you have mastered a task at a basic level (Tenenbaum, Bar-Eli, & Eyal, 1996). When you begin to get really good at a skill, give mental practice a try. You may be surprised at how effective it can be (Caliari, 2008; Morris, Spittle, & Watt, 2005).

The Whole Human: Peak Performance

One of the most interesting topics in sports psychology is the phenomenon of *peak performance.* During **peak performance**, physical, mental, and emotional states are harmonious and optimal. Many athletes report episodes during which they felt almost as if they were in a trance. The experience has also been called *flow* because the athlete becomes one with his or her performance and flows with it. At such times, athletes experience intense concentration, detachment, a lack of fatigue and pain, a subjective slowing of time, and feelings of unusual power and control (Csikszmentmihalyi, Abuhamdeh, & Nakamura, 2005; Dietrich & Stoll, 2010). It is at just such times that "personal bests" tend to occur.

A curious aspect of flow is that it cannot be forced to happen. In fact, if a person stops to think about it, the flow state goes away. Psychologists are now seeking to identify conditions that facilitate peak performance and the unusual mental state that usually accompanies it (Csikszmentmihalyi, Abuhamdeh, & Nakamura, 2005).

Even though flow may be an elusive state, there is much that athletes can do mentally to improve performance (Williams, 2010). A starting point is to make sure that their *arousal level is appropriate for the task* at hand. For a sprinter at a track meet that may mean elevating arousal to a very high level. The sprinter could, for example, try to become angry by picturing a rival cheating. For a golfer or a gymnast, lowering arousal may be crucial, in order to avoid "choking" during a big event. One way of controlling arousal is to go through a *fixed routine* before each game or event. Athletes also learn to use *imagery and relaxation techniques* to adjust their degree of arousal (LeUnes, 2008).

BRIDGES

Many of the mental strategies developed by sports psychologists are an extension of stress management techniques. **See Chapter 13, pages 468–471.**

Imaging techniques can be used to *focus attention* on the athlete's task and to *mentally rehearse* it beforehand. For example, golf great Jack Nicklaus "watches a movie" in his head before each shot. During events, athletes learn to *use cognitive-behavioral strategies to guide their efforts* in a supportive, positive way (Johnson et al., 2004). For instance, instead of berating herself for being behind in a match, a soccer player could use the time between points to savor a good shot or put an error out of mind. In general, athletes benefit from avoiding negative, self-critical thoughts that distract them and undermine their confidence (Cox, 2011). Finally, top athletes tend to use more *self-regulation strategies*, in which they evaluate their performance and make adjustments to keep it at optimum levels (Anshel, 1995; Puente & Anshel, 2010).

At present, sports psychology is a very young field and still much more an art than a science. Nevertheless, interest in the field is rapidly expanding (Gallucci, 2008).

A Look Ahead

Although we have sampled several major areas of applied psychology, they are by no means the only applied specialties. Others that immediately come to mind are community psychology, military psychology, and health psychology. The upcoming *Psychology in Action* section explores one of the most important applied fields, human factors psychology.

Psychology Applied to Education, the Law, and Sports

RECITE

1. Evaluation of learning is typically the first step in a systematic teaching strategy. T or F?
2. Compared to direct instruction, discovery learning produces better scores on achievement tests. T or F?
3. Universal Design for Instruction aims to create educational materials that are useful to ________________ students.
4. Despite their many limitations, one thing that jurors are good at is setting aside inadmissible evidence. T or F?
5. Which of the following is *not* commonly used by psychologists to aid jury selection?
   a. mock testimony *b.* information networks *c.* community surveys *d.* demographic data
6. Mental models, called ________________ ________________, appear to underlie well-learned motor skills.
7. Learning verbal rules to back up motor learning is usually most helpful in the early stages of acquiring a skill. T or F?
8. The flow experience is closely linked with instances of ________________ performance.

REFLECT

Think Critically

9. When an athlete follows a set routine before an event, what source of stress has she or he eliminated?

Self-Reflect

You are going to tutor a young child in arithmetic. How could you use a teaching strategy to improve your effectiveness?

As a student, do you prefer direct instruction or discovery learning?

What advice would you give a person who is about to serve on a jury, if she or he wants to make an impartial judgment?

How could you apply the concepts of task analysis, mental practice, and peak performance to a sport you are interested in?

Answers: 1. F **2.** F **3.** all **4.** F **5.** *a* **6.** motor programs **7.** T **8.** peak **9.** As discussed in Chapter 13, stress is reduced when a person feels in control of a situation. Following a routine helps athletes maintain a sense of order and control so that they are not overaroused when the time comes to perform.

Motor skill A series of actions molded into a smooth and efficient performance.

Motor program A mental plan or model that guides skilled movement.

Mental practice Imagining a skilled performance to aid learning.

Peak performance A performance during which physical, mental, and emotional states are harmonious and optimal.

Human Factors Psychology—Who's the Boss Here?

Gateway Question 18.6: *How are tools designed to better serve human needs?*

Should we serve machines or should they serve us? The demands that machines can make will be all too familiar if you have ever struggled with a new cell phone or failed to put together that "easy to assemble" home gym. Despite all they do for us, machines are of little value unless we humans can operate them effectively. An awkward digital camera might just as well be a paperweight. An automobile design that creates large blind spots in the driver's vision could be deadly.

"The machine's done something really weird to Mr. Hendrickson."

Designing for Human Use

The goal of **human factors psychology** (also known as **ergonomics**) is to design machines and work environments so they are *compatible* with our sensory and motor capacities (Buckle, 2011; Gamache, 2004). For example, displays must be easy to perceive, controls must be easy to use, and the tendency to make errors must be minimized (● Figure 18.6). (A *display* is any dial, screen, light, or other device used to provide information about a machine's activity to a human user. A *control* is any knob, handle, button, lever, or other device used to alter the activity of a machine.)

Psychologist Donald Norman (1994) refers to successful human factors engineering as **natural design**, because it is based on perceptual signals that people understand naturally, without needing to learn them. An example is the row of vertical buttons in elevators that mimic the layout of the floors. This is simple, natural, and clear. One way to create

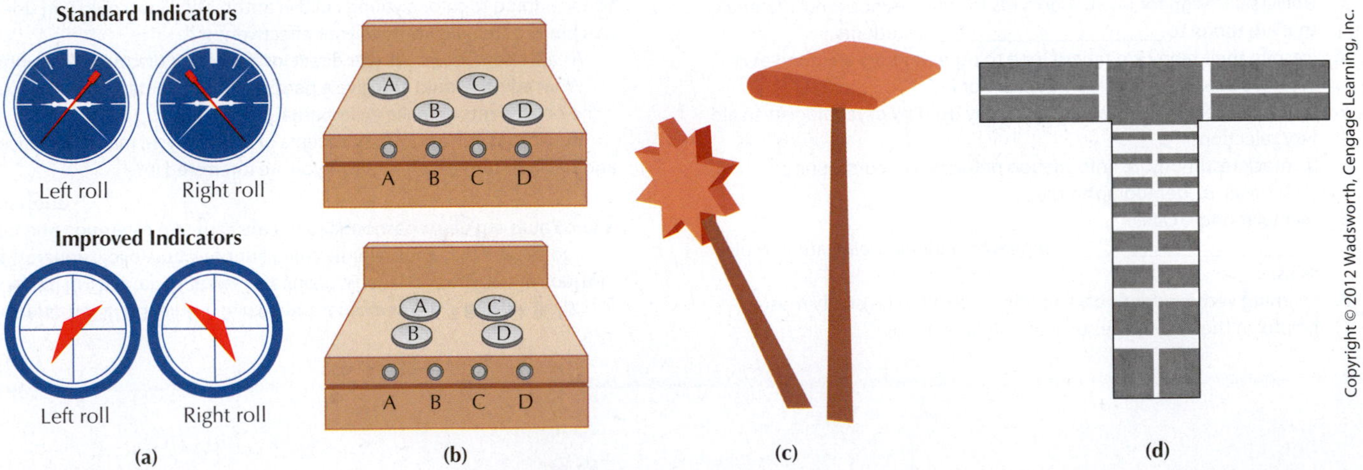

● **Figure 18.6** Human factors engineering. *(a)* Early roll indicators in airplanes were perceptually confusing and difficult to read (top). Improved displays are clear even to nonpilots. Which would you prefer if you were flying an airplane in heavy fog? *(b)* Even on a stove, the placement of controls is important. During simulated emergencies, people made no errors in reaching for the controls on the top stove. In contrast, they erred 38 percent of the time with the bottom arrangement (Chapanis & Lindenbaum, 1959). *(c)* Sometimes the shape of a control is used to indicate its function, to discourage errors. For example, the left control might be used to engage and disengage the gears of an industrial machine, whereas the right control might operate the landing flaps on an airplane. *(d)* This design depicts a street intersection viewed from above. Psychologists have found that painting white lines across the road makes drivers feel like they are traveling faster. This effect is even stronger if the lines get progressively closer together. Placing lines near dangerous intersections or sections of highway has dramatically lowered accident rates.

more natural designs is to use *metaphors* (one thing used to describe another) to create resemblances between different subjects. One famous example is the *desktop metaphor* (Kaptelinin & Czerwinski, 2007). The design of all current personal computers presents a visual "desktop" with images of "files," "folders," and even a "trashcan." That way, you can use your knowledge of real desktops to immediately begin to use the virtual "desktop" on your computer. Earlier personal computer interfaces, which required you to type in coded instructions, were much harder to use. Similarly, digital cameras are designed to look a lot like film cameras. That way people who were familiar with film cameras could use their knowledge of how such cameras work to start using a digital camera.

Effective design also provides *feedback* (information about the effect of making a response). The audible click designed into many computer keyboards is a good example. As Norman points out, the cause of many accidents is not just "human error." The real culprit is poor design. Human factors psychologists helped design many of the tools we rely on each day, such as "user-friendly" computers, home appliances, cameras, personal digital assistants (PDAs), airplane controls, and traffic signals.

Usability Testing To design useful tools, human factors psychologists do **usability testing**. That is, they directly measure the ease with which people can learn to use a machine (Bruno & Muzzupappa, 2010; Norman & Panizzi, 2006). Health and safety are also important targets of usability testing. For example, construction workers who install steel rods in the floors of large buildings spend most of their work days awkwardly bent over. To avoid injuries and to minimize fatigue, machines have been designed that allow workers to do the job while standing upright. People using these machines are faster, and they spend less time in backbreaking positions (Vi, 2006).

One interesting form of usability testing is the *thinking aloud protocol*. In this case, people are asked to say everything they are thinking as they use a machine. By comparing their actual performance with what they were thinking, it is often possible to fine-tune the details of a design (Gerjets, Kammerer, & Werner, 2011; Norman & Panizzi, 2006).

© Fred Prouser/Reuters/Corbis

Human–computer interaction designers are actively seeking new ways to interface people with computers. Microsoft's *Kinect* allows players to play games just by moving and speaking to the computer.

Human–Computer Interaction

Using human factors methods to design computers and software is referred to as **human–computer interaction (HCI)** (Fuchs & Obrist, 2010; McKay, 2008). Traditionally, machines were designed to make us stronger (such as the automobile, which moves us faster and farther than we could go on our own). In contrast, computers are meant to make us smarter (such as software that can balance a checkbook more quickly and accurately than you could on your own) (Norman, 1994). In the world of HCI, controls are also called input devices and displays are called output devices. Humans communicate with computers through the *interface,* or set of input and output devices a computer provides.

The typical laptop computer today relies on a keyboard, touch pad, and perhaps voice recognition for input. Output is handled by a display screen and audio speakers. Many experts believe that current computer interfaces are too unnatural and limited when compared with the richness of human communication (Kaptelinin & Czerwinski, 2007). Accordingly, the search is on for ways to open up new channels of communication between humans and computers. As mentioned at the beginning of this chapter, the click wheel interface and multi-touch interfaces are a key to the success of the iPod. The Nintendo Wii game console is another example. The Wii wand allows players to interface with the game through more natural hand and body movements. More recently, Microsoft's Kinect offers an even more natural interface by eliminating the hand-held controller, allowing players to play just by moving and speaking to the computer (Barras, 2010).

In addition to projecting a person's actions into a virtual world, computer interfaces can create a sense of being present in a remote location (Iastrebov, 2008). *Telepresence*, as this is called, was illustrated in 2001 when a surgeon in New York first used *telesurgery* to remove the diseased gallbladder of a patient an ocean away in France. In this instance, the surgeon controlled robotic hands to perform the surgery. Because a good surgeon relies on the sense of touch, it will be important to improve telepresence systems so they provide touch feedback to users (Jin, 2010; Kitada et al., 2010).

Using Tools Effectively

Even the best-designed tools, whether for the body or the mind, can be misused or underused. Do you feel like you are in control of the tools in your life or do you sometimes worry that they control you? Here are two tips for making sure you get the most out of the tools you use.

Understand Your Task Using a tool like a digital camera, a cell phone, or social networking software can be challenging, especially if you are not sure what it can do. Begin by finding out more about what specific tasks your new tool is designed to help you accomplish. For example, if you are buying photo editing software for your digital camera, find out what tools it offers to adjust, improve, and transform photographs. In our hectic modern world, it is often tempting to **satisfice**, or just

Human factors psychology (ergonomics) A specialty concerned with making machines and work environments compatible with human perceptual and physical capacities.

Natural design Human factors engineering that makes use of naturally understood perceptual signals.

Usability testing The empirical investigation of the ease with which users can learn to use a machine.

Human–computer interaction (HCI) The application of human factors to the design of computers and computer software.

Satisficing Engaging in behavior that achieves a minimum result, rather than maximizing the outcome of that behavior.

get by, rather than doing things really well (Güth, Levati, & Ploner, 2009). Satisficing is not just a matter of being lazy. Getting by can be a survival skill, but it does not always take full advantage of the tools available to us. For example, if you know a little about photography and jump into using your new digital camera, you may be satisfied with just being able to take a basic photo. However, if you stop there, you will have used about 10 percent of what your camera is capable of doing.

Understand Your Tools As tempting as it may be to just dive in and use your new tool, do take a peek at the instruction manual. Many modern tools, especially electronic devices, have valuable capacities hidden several layers down in menus. Without reading a manual, you might never find some of them, no matter how user friendly the device's interface may be.

© Roger Ressmeyer/Corbis

The International Space Station provides a habitat in which men and women can live and work in space for extended periods. Solving the behavioral problems of living in space will be an important step toward human exploration of the solar system.

Space Habitats

Let's conclude on a high note: Nowhere are the demands on human factors psychology greater than in space flight. Every machine, tool, and environment in a spacecraft must be carefully adapted for human use (Mulavara et al., 2010). Already, we have discovered that life on the International Space Station isn't easy, physically or mentally. For months at a time, residents are restricted to tiny living quarters with little privacy. These conditions, and other sources of stress, make it clear that the design of space habitats must take many human needs into account. For instance, researchers have learned that astronauts prefer rooms with clearly defined "up" and "down"—even in the weightlessness of space. This can be done by color-coding walls, floors, and ceilings, and by orienting furniture and controls so they all face the "ceiling" (Suedfeld & Steel, 2000).

Ideally, there should be some flexibility in the use of living and work areas inside a space station. Behavior patterns change over time, and being able to control one's environment helps lower stress. At the same time, people need stability. Psychologists have found, for instance, that eating becomes an important high point in monotonous environments. Eating at least one meal together each day can help keep crew members working as a social unit.

Sleep cycles must be carefully controlled in space to avoid disrupting body rhythms (Kanas & Manzey, 2008; Suedfeld & Steel, 2000). In past space missions, some astronauts found they couldn't sleep while other crew members continued to work and talk. Problems with sleep can be worsened by the constant noise on a space station. At first, such noise is annoying. After weeks or months, it can become a serious stressor. Researchers are experimenting with various earmuffs, eyeshades, and sleeping arrangements to alleviate such difficulties.

Sensory Restriction

Sensory monotony can be a problem in space, even with the magnificent vistas of Earth below (Kanas & Manzey, 2008). (How many times would you have to see the North American continent before you lost interest?)

Researchers are developing stimulus environments that use music, movies, and other diversions to combat monotony and boredom. Again, they are trying to provide choice and control for space crews. Studies of confined living in the Arctic and elsewhere make it clear that one person's symphony is another's grating noise. When music is concerned, individual earphones may be all that is required to avoid problems.

Most people in restricted environments find that they prefer solitary pastimes such as reading, listening to music, looking out windows, writing, and watching films or television. As much as anything, this preference may show again the need for privacy. Reading or listening to music is a good way to psychologically withdraw from the group. Experiences with confining environments on Earth (such as Biosphere 2) suggest that including live animals and plants in space habitats could reduce stress and boredom (Suedfeld & Steel, 2000).

Life on Spaceship Earth

It is curiously fitting that the dazzling technology of space travel has highlighted the inevitable importance of human behavior. Here on Earth, as in space, we cannot count on cleverly designed machines or technology alone to solve problems. The threat of nuclear war, social conflict, crime, prejudice, infectious disease, overpopulation, environmental damage, famine, homicide, economic disaster—these and most other major problems facing us are behavioral.

Will spaceship Earth endure? It's a psychological question.

Human Factors Psychology

RECITE

1. Human factors psychologists are interested in finding ways to help people adapt to working with machines. T or F?
2. According to Donald Norman, successful human factors engineering makes use of perceptual signals that people understand naturally. T or F?
3. Usability testing is used to empirically investigate machine designs. T or F?
4. To use tools effectively it is worth
   a. understanding your tool *b.* satisficing *c.* understanding your task *d.* overcoming writer's block
5. Researchers have learned that astronauts don't really care if living quarters have clearly defined "up" and "down" orientations. T or F?

REFLECT

Think Critically

6. Check out this photo of a men's urinal in Amsterdam's Schiphol Airport. Is that fly real? If not, why is it there?

Self-Reflect

Is there a machine whose design you admire? Can you express why the design works for you?

Have you thought about how you write? How does your approach differ from the one in this section? Are you using your word processor to your best advantage? What could you be improving?

Answers: 1. F **2.** T **3.** T **4.** *a* and *c* **5.** F **6.** Men tend to aim at the "fly," and hence are more accurate when they urinate. The result is much cleaner men's washrooms.

John Mitterer

This fly is not real; one is painted onto each of the men's urinals at Amsterdam's Schiphol Airport. Why?

Chapter in Review Gateways to Applied Psychology

Gateway QUESTIONS REVISITED

18.1 *How is psychology applied in business and industry?*

18.1.1 Applied psychology refers to the use of psychological principles and research to solve practical problems.

18.1.2 Industrial/organizational psychologists enhance the quality of work by studying jobs to better match people to them and by studying organizational structures and culture to improve worker performance.

18.1.3 Two basic leadership styles are Theory X (scientific management) and Theory Y (human relations approaches). Theory X is mostly concerned with work efficiency, whereas Theory Y emphasizes psychological efficiency.

18.1.4 Theory Y methods include shared leadership (participative management), management by objectives, self-managed teams, and quality circles.

18.1.5 Job satisfaction influences productivity, absenteeism, morale, employee turnover, and other factors that affect business efficiency. Job satisfaction comes from a good fit between work and a person's interests, abilities, needs, and expectations. Job enrichment tends to increase job satisfaction.

18.1.6 To match people with jobs, personnel psychologists combine job analysis with selection procedures, such as gathering biodata, interviewing, giving standardized psychological tests, and using assessment centers.

18.2 *What have psychologists learned about the effects of our physical and social environments?*

18.2.1 Humans affect the environment and environments affect humans. Many problems can be solved by understanding both relationships.

18.2.2 Environmental psychologists are interested in the effects of behavioral settings, physical or social environments, and human territoriality, among many other topics.

18.2.3 Environmental problems such as crowding, pollution, and wasted resources are based on human behavior; they can only be solved by changing behavior patterns. Overpopulation is a major world problem, often reflected at an individual level in crowding.

18.2.4 Animal experiments indicate that excessive crowding can be unhealthy. However, human research shows that psychological feelings of crowding do not always correspond to density.

18.2.5 One major consequence of crowding is attentional overload.

18.2.6 Providing feedback about resource use is an effective way to promote conservation.

18.2.7 Research has shown that various psychological strategies can promote recycling.

18.2.8 The origins of many environmental disasters lie in social dilemmas like tragedy of the commons.

18.2.9 Environmental psychologists have offered solutions to many practical problems—from noise pollution to architectural design. Their work often begins with a careful environmental assessment.

18.3 How has psychology improved education?

18.3.1 Educational psychologists improve the quality of both learning and teaching.

18.3.2 Educational psychologists seek to understand how people learn and teachers instruct. They are particularly interested in teaching strategies, learning styles, and teaching styles, such as direct instruction and discovery learning.

18.4 What does psychology reveal about juries and court verdicts?

18.4.1 The psychology of law includes studies of courtroom behavior and other topics that pertain to the legal system. Psychologists also serve various consulting and counseling roles in legal, law enforcement, and criminal justice settings.

18.4.2 Studies of mock juries show that jury decisions are often far from objective.

18.4.3 Scientific jury selection is used in attempts to choose jurors who have particular characteristics. In some instances, this may result in juries that have a particular bias or that do not represent the community as a whole.

18.4.4 A bias toward convicting defendants is characteristic of many death-qualified juries.

18.5 Can psychology enhance athletic performance?

18.5.1 Sports psychologists seek to enhance sports performance and the benefits of sports participation. A careful task analysis of sports skills is one of the major tools for improving coaching and performance.

18.5.2 A motor skill is a nonverbal response chain assembled into a smooth performance. Motor skills are guided by internal mental models called motor programs.

18.5.3 Motor skills are refined through direct practice, but mental practice can also contribute to improvement.

18.5.4 During moments of peak performance, or flow, physical, mental, and emotional states are optimal.

18.5.5 Top performers in sports often use a variety of self-regulation strategies to focus their attention and maintain optimal levels of arousal.

18.6 How are tools designed to better serve human needs?

18.6.1 Human factors psychologists (also known as ergonomists) design tools to be compatible with our sensory and motor capacities.

18.6.2 Successful human factors engineering uses natural design, which makes use of perceptual signals that people understand naturally.

18.6.3 Human factors psychologists rely on usability testing to empirically confirm that machines are easy to learn and use.

18.6.4 Human–computer interaction (HCI) is the application of human factors to the design of computers and computer software.

18.6.5 To use tools effectively it is useful to know something about the tool and the task you are using it to complete. Be aware of satisficing.

18.6.6 Space habitats must be designed with special attention to the numerous human factors issues raised by space flight.

MEDIA RESOURCES

Web Resources

Internet addresses frequently change. To find an up-to-date list of URLs for the sites listed here, visit your Psychology CourseMate.

Society for Industrial and Organizational Psychology Visit the website of APA Division 14.

Women in Management Read about how women are cracking the glass ceiling.

Job Interview Tips Further explore these tips from the U.S. Department of Labor.

Ecological Footprint Quiz Determine your ecological footprint with this quiz.

Carbon Footprint Calculator Determine your own carbon footprint.

Human Impact Read more about human influences on the biosphere.

Universal Design Education Online Read more about designing education for everyone.

The Innocence Project Read case studies of people wrongly convicted, often because of faulty eyewitness testimony.

Sports Psychology Read sports training articles.

Bad Human Factors Designs Explore these examples of poor human factors design.

Human-Computer Interaction Read about training in human-computer interaction design.

International Space Station Visit the NASA home page for the International Space Station.

Interactive Learning

Log in to **CengageBrain** to access the resources your instructor requires. For this book, you can access:

CourseMate brings course concepts to life with interactive learning, study, and exam preparation tools that support the printed textbook. A textbook-specific website, ***Psychology CourseMate*** includes an ***integrated interactive eBook*** and other ***interactive learning tools*** including quizzes, flashcards, videos, and more.

CENGAGE**NOW**™

CengageNOW is an easy-to-use online resource that helps you study in less time to get the grade you want—NOW. Take a pre-test for this chapter and receive a personalized study plan based on your results that will identify the topics you need to review and direct you to online resources to help you master those topics. Then take a post-test to help you determine the concepts you have mastered and what you will need to work on. If your textbook does not include an access code card, go to CengageBrain.com to gain access.

WebTUTOR™

More than just an interactive study guide, **WebTutor** is an anytime, anywhere customized learning solution with an eBook, keeping you connected to your textbook, instructor, and classmates.

If your professor has assigned **Aplia** homework:

1. Sign in to your account.
2. Complete the corresponding homework exercises as required by your professor.
3. When finished, click "Grade It Now" to see which areas you have mastered and which need more work, and for detailed explanations of every answer.

Visit **www.cengagebrain.com** to access your account and purchase materials.

The Whole Human: Psychology and You

At the beginning of this book we described psychology as a journey of self-discovery. It is our sincere hope that you have found enough relevance and value here to spark a lifelong interest in psychology. As your personal journey continues, one thing is certain: Many of your greatest challenges and most treasured moments will involve other people. You would be wise to continue adding to your understanding of human behavior. Psychology's future looks exciting. What role will it play in your life, real or virtual?

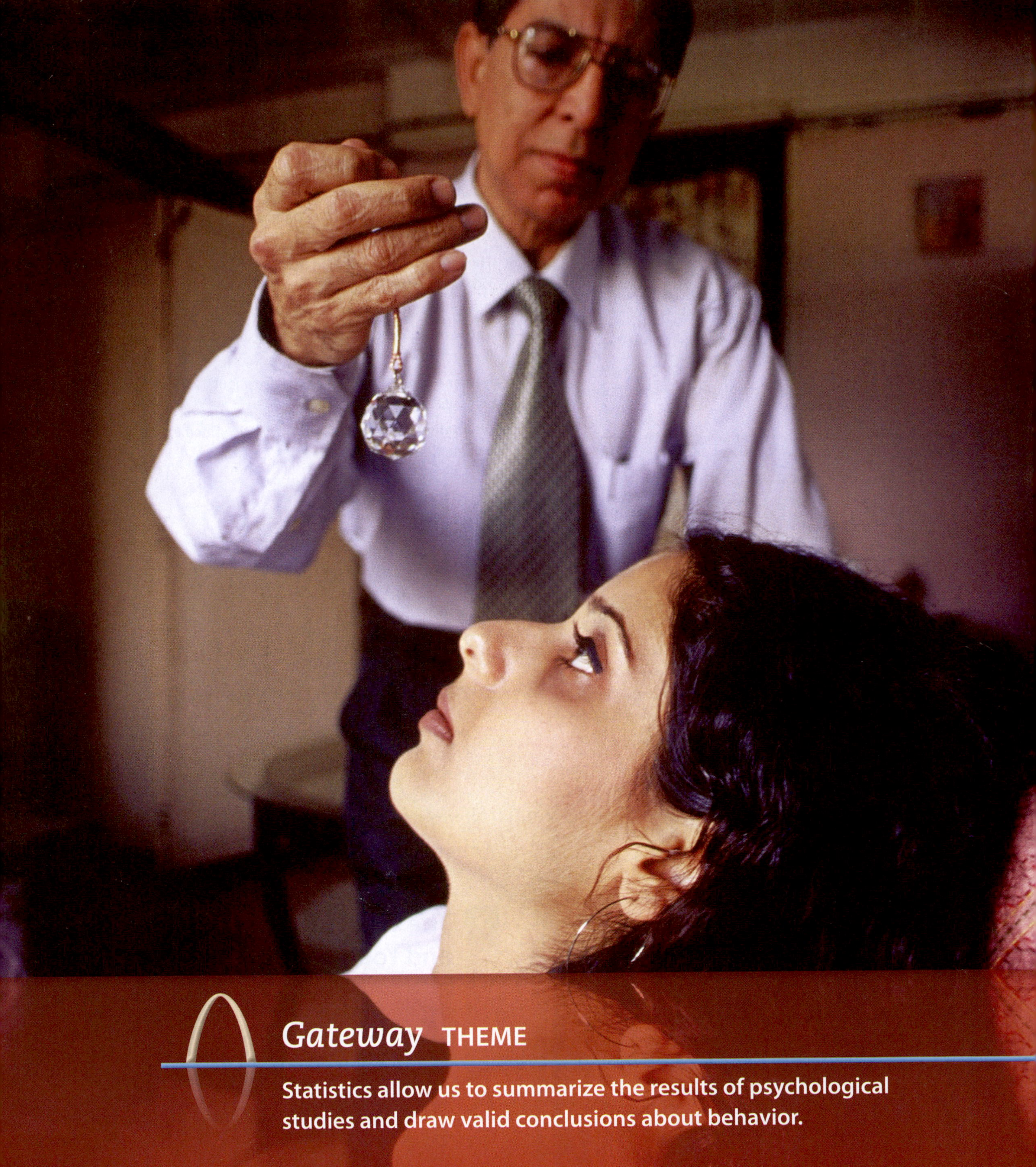

Gateway THEME

Statistics allow us to summarize the results of psychological studies and draw valid conclusions about behavior.

Appendix

Behavioral Statistics

Why Numbers?

Anita decided to major in psychology because she once went to see a hypnotist for help with problems she had falling asleep. (That's Anita starting her session in the photo on the opposite page.) She was surprised by how easily he "put her under" and even more surprised that a few hypnosis sessions actually helped improve her sleep. But her psychology studies almost came to a premature end when she found out she would need to take a statistics course to graduate. "Numbers," she muttered. "Why numbers? Doesn't psychology study people?"

Thankfully, Anita's curiosity about hypnosis in particular, and human behavior in general, was stronger than her apprehension about statistics. By the time Anita got to her third year and began to design research projects and collect data, she understood that the results of psychological studies are often expressed as numbers, which psychologists must summarize and interpret before they have any meaning.

To do so, psychologists use two major types of statistics. **Descriptive statistics** summarize or "boil down" data collected from research participants so the results become more meaningful and easier to communicate to others. In comparison, **inferential statistics** are used for decision making, for generalizing from small samples, and for drawing conclusions. Psychologists must often base decisions on limited data. Such decisions are much easier to make with the help of inferential statistics. Let's follow Anita to get an overview of how statistics are used in psychology.

Gateway QUESTIONS

A.1 What are descriptive statistics?
A.2 How are correlations used in psychology?
A.3 What are inferential statistics?

Descriptive Statistics—Psychology by the Numbers

Gateway Question A.1: *What are descriptive statistics?*

Let's say you have completed a study on human behavior. The results seem interesting, but can you really tell what your data reveal just by looking at a jumble of numbers? To get a clear picture of how people behaved, you will probably turn to descriptive statistics. By summarizing the results of your study, descriptive statistics will help you make sense of what you observed.

Statistics bring greater clarity and precision to psychological thought and research (Gravetter & Wallnau, 2010). In fact, it is difficult to make scientific arguments about human behavior without depending on statistics. To see how statistics help, let's begin by considering three basic types of descriptive statistics: *graphical statistics*, measures of *central tendency*, and measures of *variability*.

Graphical Statistics

Graphical statistics present numbers pictorially, so they are easier to visualize. At one point, Anita got a chance to study differences in hypnotizability. ■ Table A.1 shows the scores she obtained when she gave a test of hypnotic susceptibility to 100 college students. With such disorganized data, it is hard to form an overall "picture" of the differences in hypnotic susceptibility. But by using a *frequency distribution*, large amounts of information can be neatly organized and summarized. A **frequency distribution** is made by breaking down the entire range of possible scores into classes of equal size. Next, the number of scores falling into each class is recorded. In ■ Table A.2, Anita's raw data from ■ Table A.1 have been condensed into a frequency distribution. Notice how much clearer the pattern of scores for the entire group becomes.

■ **TABLE A.1 Raw Scores of Hypnotic Susceptibility**

55	86	52	17	61	57	84	51	16	64
22	56	25	38	35	24	54	26	37	38
52	42	59	26	21	55	40	59	25	57
91	27	38	53	19	93	25	39	52	56
66	14	18	63	59	68	12	19	62	45
47	98	88	72	50	49	96	89	71	66
50	44	71	57	90	53	41	72	56	93
57	38	55	49	87	59	36	56	48	70
33	69	50	50	60	35	67	51	50	52
11	73	46	16	67	13	71	47	25	77

■ **TABLE A.2 Frequency Distribution of Hypnotic Susceptibility Scores**

Class Interval	Number of Persons in Class
0–19	10
20–39	20
40–59	40
60–79	20
80–99	10

Frequency distributions are often shown *graphically* to make them more "visual." A **histogram**, or graph of a frequency distribution, is made by labeling class intervals on the *abscissa* (X axis or horizontal line) and frequencies (the number of scores in each class) on the *ordinate* (Y axis or vertical line). Next, bars are drawn for each class interval; the height of each bar is determined by the number of scores in each class (● Figure A.1). An alternate way of graphing scores is the more familiar **frequency polygon** (● Figure A.2). Here, points are placed at the center of each class interval to indicate the number of scores. Then the dots are connected by straight lines.

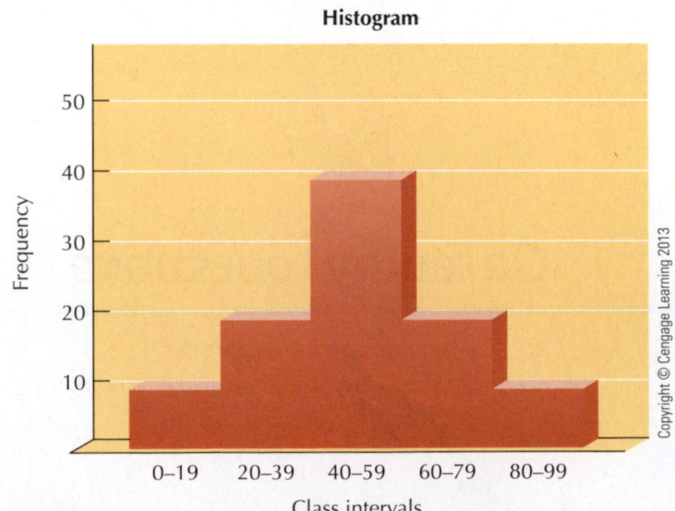

● **Figure A.1** Frequency histogram of hypnotic susceptibility scores contained in ■ Table A.2.

Measures of Central Tendency

Notice in ■ Table A.2 that more of Anita's scores fall in the 40–59 range than elsewhere. How can we show this fact? A measure of **central tendency** is simply a number describing a "typical score" around which other scores fall. A familiar measure of central tendency is the mean, or "average." But as we shall see in a moment, other types of "averages" can be used. To illustrate each we need an example: ■ Table A.3 shows the raw data for an imaginary experiment in which two groups of participants were given a test of memory. Assume that one group was given a drug that might improve memory (let's call the drug Rememberine). The second group received a placebo. Is there a difference in memory scores between the two groups? It's difficult to tell without computing an average.

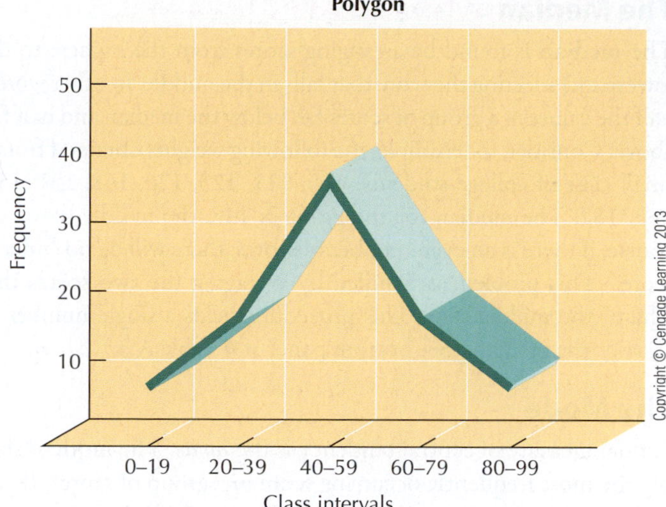

● **Figure A.2** Frequency polygon of hypnotic susceptibility scores contained in ■ Table A.2.

■ **TABLE A.3 Raw Scores on a Memory Test for Subjects Taking Rememberine or a Placebo**

Subject	Group 1 Rememberine	Group 2 Placebo
1	65	54
2	67	60
3	73	63
4	65	33
5	58	56
6	55	60
7	70	60
8	69	31
9	60	62
10	68	61
Sum	650	540
Mean	65	54
Median	66	60

$$\text{Mean} = \frac{\Sigma X}{N} \text{ or } \frac{\text{Sum of all scores, } X}{\text{number of scores}}$$

$$\text{Mean Group 1} = \frac{65+67+73+65+58+55+70+69+60+68}{10} = \frac{650}{10} = 65$$

$$\text{Mean Group 2} = \frac{54+60+63+33+56+60+60+31+62+61}{10} = \frac{540}{10} = 54$$

Median = the middle score or the mean of the two middle scores*

Median Group 1 = 55 58 60 65 [65 67] 68 69 70 73

$$= \frac{65+67}{2} = 66$$

Median Group 2 = 31 33 54 56 60 [60 60] 61 62 63

$$= \frac{60+60}{2} = 60$$

* 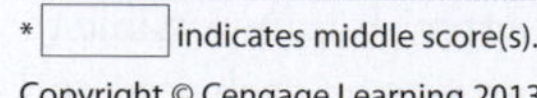 indicates middle score(s).

The Mean

As one type of "average," the **mean** is calculated by adding all the scores for each group and then dividing by the total number of scores. Notice in ■ Table A.3 that the means reveal a difference between the two groups.

The mean is sensitive to extremely high or low scores in a distribution. For this reason, it is not always the best measure of central tendency. (Imagine how distorted it would be to calculate average yearly incomes from a small sample of people that happened to include a multimillionaire, such as actor Johnny Depp.) In such cases, the middle score in a group of scores—called the *median*—is used instead.

Descriptive statistics Mathematical tools used to describe and summarize numeric data.

Inferential statistics Mathematical tools used for decision making, for generalizing from small samples, and for drawing conclusions.

Graphical statistics Techniques for presenting numbers pictorially, often by plotting them on a graph.

Frequency distribution A table that divides an entire range of scores into a series of classes and then records the number of scores that fall into each class.

Histogram A graph of a frequency distribution in which the number of scores falling in each class is represented by vertical bars.

Frequency polygon A graph of a frequency distribution in which the number of scores falling in each class is represented by points on a line.

Central tendency The tendency for a majority of scores to fall in the midrange of possible values.

Mean A measure of central tendency calculated by adding a group of scores and then dividing by the total number of scores.

The Median

The **median** is found by arranging scores from the highest to the lowest and selecting the score that falls in the middle. In other words, half the values in a group of scores fall below the median and half fall above. Consider, for example, the following weights obtained from a small class of college students: 105, 111, 123, 126, 148, 151, 154, 162, 182. The median for the group is 148, the middle score. Of course, if there is an even number of scores, there will be no "middle score." This problem is handled by averaging the two scores that "share" the middle spot. This procedure yields a single number to serve as the median. (See bottom panel of ■ Table A.3.)

The Mode

A final measure of central tendency is the *mode*. The **mode** is simply the most frequently occurring score in a group of scores. If you were to take the time to count the scores in ■ Table A.3, you would find that the mode of Group l is 65, and the mode of Group 2 is 60. Although the mode is usually easy to obtain, it can be an unreliable measure, especially in a small group of scores. The mode's advantage is that it gives the score actually obtained by the greatest number of people.

Measures of Variability

Let's say a researcher discovers two drugs that lower anxiety in agitated patients. However, let's also assume that one drug consistently lowers anxiety by moderate amounts, whereas the second sometimes lowers it by large amounts, sometimes has no effect, or may even increase anxiety in some patients. Overall, there is no difference in the *average* (mean) amount of anxiety reduction. Even so, an important difference exists between the two drugs. As this example shows, it is not enough to simply know the average score in a distribution. Usually, we would also like to know if scores are grouped closely together or scattered widely.

Measures of **variability** provide a single number that tells how "spread out" scores are. When the scores are widely spread, this number gets larger. When they are close together, it gets smaller. If you look again at the example in ■ Table A.3, you will notice that the scores within each group vary widely. How can we show this fact?

The Range

The simplest way would be to use the **range**, which is the difference between the highest and lowest scores. In Group 1 of our experiment, the highest score is 73 and the lowest is 55; thus, the range is 18 (73 − 55 = 18). In Group 2, the highest score is 63 and the lowest is 31; this makes the range 32. Scores in Group 2 are more spread out (are more variable) than those in Group 1.

The Standard Deviation

A better measure of variability is the **standard deviation** (an index of how much a typical score differs from the mean of a group of scores). To obtain the standard deviation, we find the deviation (or difference) of each score from the mean and then square it (multiply it by itself). These squared deviations are then added and averaged (the total is divided by the number of deviations). Taking the square root of this average yields the standard deviation (■ Table A.4). Notice again that the variability for Group 1 (5.4) is smaller than that for Group 2 (where the standard deviation is 11.3).

■ TABLE A.4 Computation of the Standard Deviation

Group 1 Mean = 65

Score Mean	Deviation (d)	Deviation Squared (d^2)
65 − 65 =	0	0
67 − 65 =	2	4
73 − 65 =	8	64
65 − 65 =	0	0
58 − 65 =	−7	49
55 − 65 =	−10	100
70 − 65 =	5	25
69 − 65 =	4	16
60 − 65 =	−5	25
68 − 65 =	3	9
		292

$$SD = \sqrt{\frac{\text{sum of } d^2}{n}} = \sqrt{\frac{292}{10}} = \sqrt{29.2} = 5.4$$

Group 2 Mean = 54

Score Mean	Deviation (d)	Deviation Squared (d^2)
54 − 54 =	0	0
60 − 54 =	6	36
63 − 54 =	9	81
33 − 54 =	−21	441
56 − 54 =	2	4
60 − 54 =	6	36
60 − 54 =	6	36
31 − 54 =	−23	529
62 − 54 =	8	64
61 − 54 =	7	49
		1276

$$SD = \sqrt{\frac{\text{sum of } d^2}{n}} = \sqrt{\frac{1276}{10}} = \sqrt{127.6} = 11.3$$

Standard Scores

A particular advantage of the standard deviation is that it can be used to "standardize" scores in a way that gives them greater meaning. For example, Anita and her twin sister, Amrita, both took psychology midterms, but in different classes. Anita earned a score of 118, and Amrita scored 110. Who did better? It is impossible to tell without knowing what the average score was on each test, and whether Anita and Amrita scored at the top, middle, or bottom of

■ **TABLE A.5 Computation of a z-Score**

$$z = \frac{X - \overline{X}}{SD} = or \frac{\text{score} - \text{mean}}{\text{standard deviation}}$$

$$\text{Amrita: } z = \frac{110 - 100}{10} = \frac{+10}{10} = +1.0$$

$$\text{Anita: } z = \frac{118 - 100}{18} = \frac{+18}{18} = +1.0$$

their classes. We would like to have one number that gives all this information. A number that does this is the *z-score.*

To convert an original score to a **z-score**, we subtract the mean from the score. The resulting number is then divided by the standard deviation for that group of scores. To illustrate, Amrita had a score of 110 in a class with a mean of 100 and a standard deviation of 10. Therefore, her z-score is +1.0 (■ Table A.5). Anita's score of 118 came from a class having a mean of 100 and a standard deviation of 18; thus her z-score is also +1.0. (See ■ Table A.5.) Originally it looked as if Anita did better on her midterm than Amrita did. But we now see that relatively speaking, their scores were equivalent. Compared with other students, each was an equal distance above average.

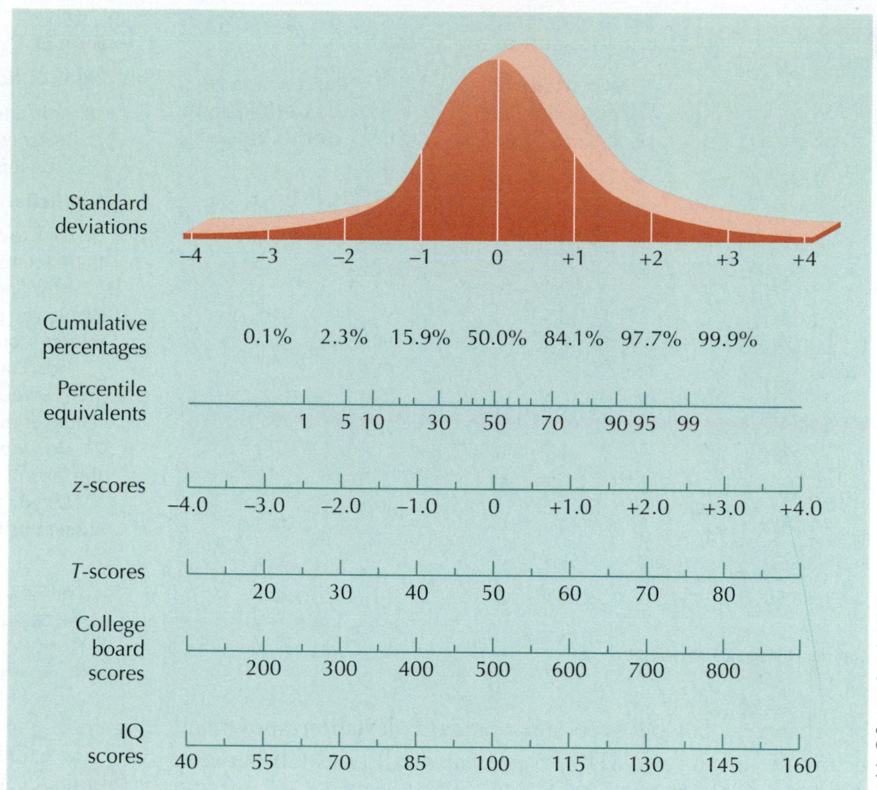

● **Figure A.3** The normal curve. The normal curve is an idealized mathematical model. However, many measurements in psychology closely approximate a normal curve. The scales you see here show the relationship of standard deviations, z-scores, and other measures to the curve.

The Normal Curve

When chance events are recorded, we find that some outcomes have a high probability and occur very often, others have a lower probability and occur infrequently; still others have little probability and occur rarely. As a result, the distribution (or tally) of chance events typically resembles a *normal curve* (● Figure A.3). A **normal curve** is bell-shaped with a large number of scores in the middle, tapering to very few extremely high and low scores. Most psychological traits or events are determined by the action of a large number of factors. Therefore, like chance events, measures of psychological variables tend to roughly match a normal curve. For example, direct measurement has shown such characteristics as height, memory span, and intelligence to be distributed approximately along a normal curve. In other words, many people have average height, memory ability, and intelligence. However, as we move above or below average, fewer and fewer people are found.

It is very fortunate that so many psychological variables tend to form a normal curve, because much is known about the curve. One valuable property concerns the relationship between the standard deviation and the normal curve. Specifically, the standard deviation measures offset proportions of the curve above and below the mean. For example, in ● Figure A.4, notice that roughly 68 percent of all cases (IQ scores, memory scores, heights,

● **Figure A.4** Relationship between the standard deviation and the normal curve.

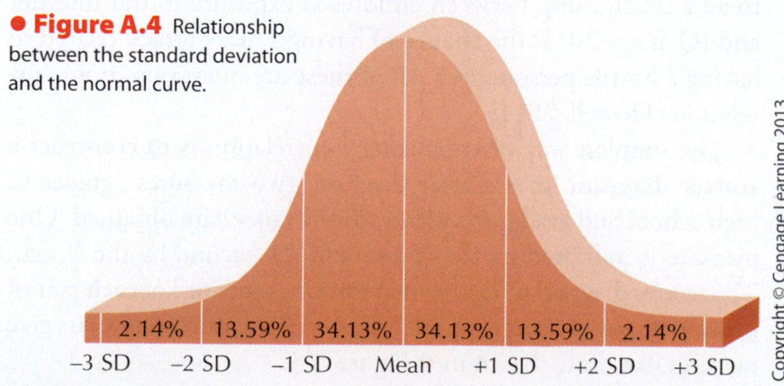

Median A measure of central tendency found by arranging scores from the highest to the lowest and selecting the score that falls in the middle. That is, half the values in a group of scores fall above the median and half fall below.

Mode A measure of central tendency found by identifying the most frequently occurring score in a group of scores.

Variability The tendency for a group of scores to differ in value. Measures of variability indicate the degree to which a group of scores differ from one another.

Range The difference between the highest and lowest scores in a group of scores.

Standard deviation An index of how much a typical score differs from the mean of a group of scores.

z-score A number that tells how many standard deviations above or below the mean a score is.

Normal curve A bell-shaped distribution, with a large number of scores in the middle, tapering to very few extremely high and low scores.

TABLE A.6 Computation of a z-Score

z-Score	Percentage of Area to the Left of this Value	Percentage of Area to the Right of this Value
−3.0 SD	00.1	99.9
−2.5 SD	00.6	99.4
−2.0 SD	02.3	97.7
−1.5 SD	06.7	93.3
−1.0 SD	15.9	84.1
−0.5 SD	30.9	69.1
0.0 SD	50.0	50.0
+0.5 SD	69.1	30.9
+1.0 SD	84.1	15.9
+1.5 SD	93.3	06.7
+2.0 SD	97.7	02.3
+2.5 SD	99.4	00.6
+3.0 SD	99.9	00.1

or whatever) fall between one standard deviation above and below the mean (± 1 SD); 95 percent of all cases fall between ± 2 SD; and 99 percent of the cases can be found between ± 3 SD from the mean.

■ Table A.6 gives a more complete account of the relationship between z-scores and the percentage of cases found in a particular area of the normal curve. Notice, for example, that 93.3 percent of all cases fall below a z-score of +1.5. A z-score of 1.5 on a test (no matter what the original, or "raw," score was) would be a good performance, because roughly 93 percent of all scores fall below this mark. Relationships between the standard deviation (or z-scores) and the normal curve do not change. This makes it possible to compare various tests or groups of scores if they come from distributions that are approximately normal.

Knowledge Builder: Descriptive Statistics

RECITE

1. ______________________ statistics summarize numbers so they become more meaningful or easier to communicate; ______________________ statistics are used for decision making, generalizing, or drawing conclusions.
2. Histograms and frequency polygons are graphs of frequency distributions. T or F?
3. Three measures of central tendency are the mean, the median, and the ______________.
4. If scores are placed in order, from the smallest to the largest, the median is defined as the middle score. T or F?
5. As a measure of variability, the standard deviation is defined as the difference between the highest and lowest scores. T or F?
6. A z-score of −1 tells us that a score fell one standard deviation below the mean in a group of scores. T or F?
7. In a normal curve, 99 percent of all scores can be found between +1 and −1 standard deviations from the mean. T or F?

REFLECT

Think Critically

8. You are asked to calculate the mean income of the following annual salaries: $2,000,000, $33,000, $27,000, $22,000, $21,000. Why might you refuse? What statistic might you propose to calculate instead?

Self-Reflect

Go back to Anita's hypnotic susceptibility data. Review how Anita showed these scores graphically.

Now find the average hypnotic susceptibility of these participants. Would you prefer to know the most frequent score (the mode), the middle score (the median), or the arithmetic average (the mean)?

How could you determine how much hypnotic susceptibility varies? That is, would you prefer to know the highest and lowest scores (the range) or the average amount of variation (the standard deviation)?

How would you feel about receiving your scores on classroom tests in the form of z-scores?

Do you think the distribution of scores in Anita's study of hypnotic susceptibility would form a normal curve? Why or why not?

Answers: 1. Descriptive, inferential **2.** T **3.** mode **4.** T **5.** F **6.** T **7.** F **8.** The single large salary in this small group will distort the mean. In cases like this, the median is a better measure of central tendency.

Correlation—Rating Relationships

Gateway Question A.2: *How are correlations used in psychology?*

As we noted in Chapter 1, many of the statements that psychologists make about behavior do not result from the use of experimental methods. Rather, they come from keen observations and measures of existing phenomena. A psychologist might note, for example, that the higher a couple's socioeconomic and educational status, the smaller the number of children they are likely to have. Or that grades in high school are related to how well a person is likely to do in college. Or even, as Anita found, that students who were more susceptible to hypnosis are also more likely to listen to music. In these instances, we are dealing with the fact that two variables are **correlating** (varying together in some orderly fashion).

Relationships

Psychologists are very interested in detecting relationships between events: Are children from single-parent families more likely to misbehave at school? Is wealth related to happiness? Is there a relationship between childhood exposure to the Internet and IQ at age 20? Is the chance of having a heart attack related to having a hostile personality? All of these are questions about correlation (Howell, 2011).

The simplest way of visualizing a correlation is to construct a **scatter diagram**. In a scatter diagram, two measures (grades in high school and grades in college, for instance) are obtained. One measure is indicated by the X axis and the second by the Y axis. The scatter diagram plots the intersection (crossing) of each pair of measurements as a single point. Many such measurement pairs give pictures like those shown in ● Figure A.5.

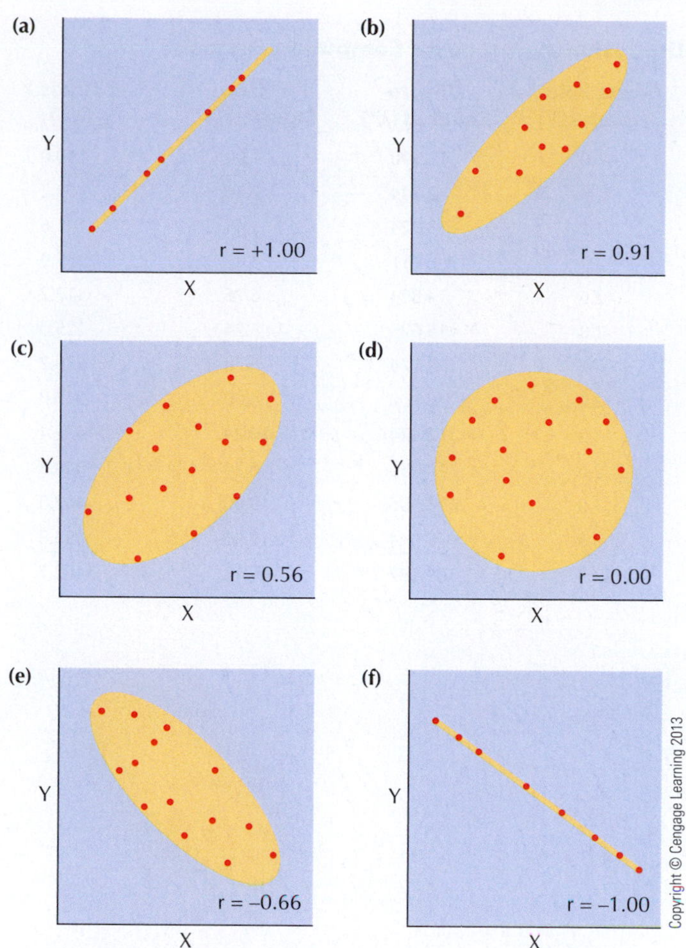

● **Figure A.5** Scatter diagrams showing various degrees of relationship for a positive, zero, and negative correlation.

Figure A.5 also shows scatter diagrams of three basic kinds of relationships between variables (or measures). Graphs *A*, *B*, and *C* show *positive relationships* of varying strength. As you can see, in a **positive relationship**, increases in the X measure (or score) are matched by increases on the Y measure (or score). An example would be finding that higher IQ scores (X) are associated with higher college grades (Y). A **zero correlation** suggests that no relationship exists between two measures (see graph *D*). This might be the result of comparing participants' hat sizes (X) to their college grades (Y). Graphs *E* and *F* both show a **negative relationship** (or correlation). Notice that as values of one measure increase, those of the second become smaller. An example might be the relationship between amount of alcohol consumed and scores on a test of coordination: Higher alcohol levels are correlated with lower coordination scores.

The Correlation Coefficient

The strength of a correlation can also be expressed as a **coefficient of correlation.** This coefficient is simply a number falling somewhere between +1.00 and −1.00. If the number is zero or close to zero, it indicates a weak or nonexistent relationship. If the correlation is +1.00, a **perfect positive relationship** exists; if the correlation is −1.00, a **perfect negative relationship** has been discovered. The most commonly used correlation coefficient is called the Pearson *r*. Calculation of the Pearson *r* is relatively simple, as shown in ■ Table A.7. (The numbers shown are hypothetical.)

As stated in Chapter 1, correlations in psychology are rarely perfect. Most fall somewhere between zero and plus or minus 1. The closer the correlation coefficient is to +1.00 or −1.00, the stronger the relationship. An interesting example of some typical correlations is provided by a study that compared the IQs of adopted children with the IQs of their biological mothers. At age 4, the children's IQs correlated .28 with their biological mothers' IQs. By age 7, the correlation was .35. And by age 13, it had grown to .38. Over time, the IQs of adopted children become more similar to the IQs of their biological mothers.

Correlations often provide highly useful information. For instance, it is valuable to know that there is a correlation between cigarette smoking and lung cancer rates. Another example is the fact that higher consumption of alcohol during pregnancy is correlated with lower birth weight and a higher rate of birth defects. There is a correlation between the number of recent life stresses experienced and the likelihood of emotional disturbance. Many more examples could be cited, but the point is, correlations help us to identify relationships that are worth knowing.

Prediction

Correlations are particularly valuable for making *predictions*. If we know that two measures are correlated, and we know a person's score on one measure, we can predict his or her score on the other. For example, most colleges have formulas that use multiple correlations to decide which applicants have the best chances for success. Usually the formula includes such predictors as high school GPA, teacher ratings, extracurricular activities, and scores on the *SAT Reasoning Test* or some similar test. Although no single predictor is perfectly correlated with success in college, together the various predictors correlate highly and provide a useful technique for screening applicants.

There is an interesting "trick" you can do with correlations that you may find useful. It works like this: If you *square* the correlation

Correlation The existence of a consistent, systematic relationship between two events, measures, or variables.

Scatter diagram A graph that plots the intersection of paired measures; that is, the points at which paired X and Y measures cross.

Positive relationship A mathematical relationship in which increases in one measure are matched by increases in the other (or decreases correspond with decreases).

Zero correlation The absence of a (linear) mathematical relationship between two measures.

Negative relationship A mathematical relationship in which increases in one measure are matched by decreases in the other.

Coefficient of correlation A statistical index ranging from −1.00 to +1.00 that indicates the direction and degree of correlation.

Perfect positive relationship A mathematical relationship in which the correlation between two measures is +1.00.

Perfect negative relationship A mathematical relationship in which the correlation between two measures is −1.00.

coefficient (multiply r by itself), you will get a number telling the **percent of variance** (amount of variation in scores) accounted for by the correlation. For example, the correlation between IQ scores and college grade point average is .5. Multiplying .5 times .5 gives .25, or 25 percent. This means that 25 percent of the variation in college grades is accounted for by knowing IQ scores. In other words, with a correlation of .5, college grades are "squeezed" into an oval like the one shown in graph C, ● Figure A.5*c*. IQ scores take away some of the possible variation in corresponding grade point averages. If there were no correlation between IQ and grades, grades would be completely free to vary, as shown in graph D, ● Figure A.5*d*.

Along the same line, a correlation of +1.00 or −1.00 means that 100 percent of the variation in the Y measure is accounted for by knowing the X measure: If you know a person's X score, you can tell exactly what the Y score is. An example that comes close to this state of affairs is the high correlation (.86) between the IQs of identical twins. In any group of identical twins, 74 percent of the variation in the "Y" twins' IQs is accounted for by knowing the IQs of their siblings (the "X's").

TABLE A.7 IQ and Grade Point Average for Computing Pearson *r*

Student No.	IQ (X)	Grade Point Average (Y)	X Score Squared (X^2)	Y Score Squared (Y^2)	X Times Y (XY)
1	110	1.0	12,100	1.00	110.0
2	112	1.6	12,544	2.56	179.2
3	118	1.2	13,924	1.44	141.6
4	119	2.1	14,161	4.41	249.9
5	122	2.6	14,884	6.76	317.2
6	125	1.8	15,625	3.24	225.0
7	127	2.6	16,124	6.76	330.2
8	130	2.0	16,900	4.00	260.0
9	132	3.2	17,424	10.24	422.4
10	134	2.6	17,956	6.76	348.4
11	136	3.0	18,496	9.00	408.0
12	138	3.6	19,044	12.96	496.8
Total	1503	27.3	189,187	69.13	3488.7

$$r = \frac{\Sigma XY - \dfrac{(\Sigma X)(\Sigma Y)}{N}}{\sqrt{\left[\Sigma X^2 - \dfrac{(\Sigma X)^2}{N}\right]\left[\Sigma Y^2 - \dfrac{(\Sigma Y)^2}{N}\right]}}$$

$$= \frac{3488.7 - \dfrac{1503(27.3)}{12}}{\sqrt{\left[189{,}187 - \dfrac{(1503)^2}{2}\right]\left[69.13\,2\dfrac{(27.3)^2}{12}\right]}}$$

$$\frac{69.375}{81.088} = 0.856 = 0.86$$

Squaring correlations to obtain the *percent variance* accounted for is a useful tool for interpreting the correlations encountered in the media and the psychological literature. For example, sweeping pronouncements about relationships are occasionally made on the basis of correlations in the .25 to .30 range even though the values mean that only 6 to 9 percent of the variance is accounted for by the observed correlation. Such correlations may document relationships worth noting, but they are rarely something to get excited about.

Correlation and Causation

It is very important to reiterate that finding a correlation between two measures does not automatically mean that one **causes** the other: Correlation does not demonstrate causation. When a correlation exists, the best we can say is that two variables are related. Of course, this does not mean that it is impossible for two correlated variables to have a cause-and-effect relationship. Rather, it means that we cannot *conclude*, solely on the basis of correlation, that a causal link exists. To gain greater confidence that a cause-and-effect relationship exists, an experiment must be performed (see Chapter 1).

Often, two correlated measures are related as a result of the influence of a third variable. For example, we might observe that the more hours students devote to studying, the better their grades. Although it is tempting to conclude that more studying produces (causes) better grades, it is possible (indeed, it is probable) that grades and the amount of study time are both related to the amount of motivation or interest a student has.

The difference between cause-and-effect data and data that reveal a relationship of unknown origin is one that should not be forgotten. Because we rarely run experiments in daily life, the information on which we act is largely correlational. This should make us more humble and more tentative in the confidence with which we make pronouncements about human behavior.

Inferential Statistics—Significant Numbers

Gateway Question A.3: *What are inferential statistics?*

You would like to know whether boys are more aggressive than girls. You observe a group of 5-year-old boys and girls on a playground. After collecting data for a week, you find that the boys committed more aggressive acts than the girls. Could this difference just be a meaningless fluctuation in aggression? Or does it show conclusively that boys are more aggressive than girls? Inferential statistics were created to answer such questions (Heiman, 2011).

Let's say that a researcher studies the effects of a new therapy on a small group of depressed individuals. Is she or he interested only in these particular individuals? Usually not, because except in rare instances, psychologists seek to discover general laws of behavior that apply widely to humans and animals (Babbie, 2011). Undoubtedly, the researcher would like to know whether the therapy holds any promise for all depressed people. As stated earlier, inferential statistics are techniques that allow us to make inferences. That is, they allow us to generalize from the behavior of small groups of participants to that of the larger groups they represent.

Samples and Populations

In any scientific study, we would like to observe the entire set, or **population**, of participants, objects, or events of interest. However, this is usually impossible or impractical. Observing all terrorists, all cancer patients, or all mothers-in-law could be both impractical (because all are large populations) and impossible (because people change political views, may be unaware of having cancer, and change their status as relatives). In such cases, **samples** (smaller cross-sections of a population) are selected, and observations of the sample are used to draw conclusions about the entire population.

For any sample to be meaningful, it must be **representative**. That is, the sample group must truly reflect the membership and characteristics of the larger population. In our earlier hypothetical study of a memory drug, it would be essential for the sample of 20 people to be representative of the general population. A very important aspect of representative samples is that their members are chosen at **random**. In other words, each member of the population must have an equal chance of being included in the sample.

Significant Differences

In our imaginary drug experiment, we found that the average memory score was higher for the group given the drug than it was for persons who didn't take the drug (the placebo group). Certainly, this result is interesting, but could it have occurred by chance? If two groups were repeatedly tested (with neither receiving any drug), their average memory scores would sometimes differ. How much must two means differ before we can consider the difference "real" (not due to chance)?

Tests of **statistical significance** provide an estimate of how often experimental results could have occurred by chance alone. The results of a significance test are stated as a probability. This probability gives the odds that the observed difference was due to chance. In psychology, any experimental result that could have occurred by chance 5 times (or less) out of 100 (in other words, a probability of .05 or less) is considered *significant*. In our memory experiment, the probability is .025 ($p = .025$) that the group means would differ as much as they do by chance alone. This allows us to conclude with reasonable certainty that the drug actually did improve memory scores.

Knowledge Builder: Correlation and Inferential Statistics

RECITE

1. A scatter diagram can be used to plot and visualize a ______________ between two groups of scores.
2. In a negative relationship, increases in X scores correspond to decreases in Y scores. T or F?
3. A perfect positive correlation exists when the correlation coefficient is 0.00. T or F?
4. It is important to remember that correlation does not demonstrate ______________.
5. In inferential statistics, observations of a ______________ are used to make inferences and draw conclusions about an entire ______________.
6. A representative sample can be obtained by selecting members of the sample at ______________.
7. If the results of an experiment could have occurred by chance alone less than 25 times out of 100, the result is considered statistically significant. T or F

REFLECT

Think Critically

8. Suppose it was found that sleeping with your clothes on is correlated with waking up with a headache. Could you conclude that sleeping with your clothes on causes headaches?

Self-Reflect

See whether you can identify at least one positive relationship and one negative relationship involving human behavior that you have observed. How strong do you think the correlation would be in each case? What correlation coefficient would you expect to see?

A woman you know drinks more coffee in the winter than she does in the summer. She also has more colds in the winter. She decides to reduce the amount of coffee she drinks to help prevent colds. What can you tell her about correlation and causation?

Informally, you have probably inferred something about a population of people based on the small sample you have observed directly. How could statistics improve the accuracy of your inferences?

If you were trying to test whether a drug causes birth defects, what level of statistical significance would you use? If you were doing a psychology experiment, what level would you be comfortable with?

Answers: 1. correlation **2.** T **3.** F **4.** causation **5.** sample, population **6.** random **7.** F **8.** No. To reiterate, correlation does not prove causality. It is more likely here that a third factor is causing *both* the sleeping with the clothes on at night *and* the headaches (too much alcohol, anyone?).

Percent of variance A portion of the total amount of variation in a group of scores.

Causation The act of causing some effect.

Population An entire group of animals, people, or objects belonging to a particular category (for example, all college students or all married women).

Sample A smaller subpart of a population.

Representative sample A small, randomly selected part of a larger population that accurately reflects characteristics of the whole population.

Random selection Choosing a sample so that each member of the population has an equal chance of being included in the sample.

Statistical significance The degree to which an event (such as the results of an experiment) is unlikely to have occurred by chance alone.

Chapter in Review Gateways to Behavioral Statistics

Gateway QUESTIONS REVISITED

A.1 ***What are descriptive statistics?***

A.1.1 Descriptive statistics organize and summarize numbers.

A.1.2 Summarizing numbers visually, by using various types of graphs such as histograms and frequency polygons, makes it easier to see trends and patterns in the results of psychological investigations.

A.1.3 Measures of central tendency define the "typical score" in a group of scores. The mean is found by adding all the scores in a group and then dividing by the total number of scores. The median is found by arranging a group of scores from the highest to the lowest and selecting the middle score. The mode is the score that occurs most frequently in a group of scores.

A.1.4 Measures of variability provide a number that shows how much scores vary. The range is the difference between the highest score and the lowest score in a group of scores. The standard deviation shows how much, on average, all the scores in a group differ from the mean.

A.1.5 To change an original score into a standard score (or z-score), you must subtract the mean from the score and then divide the result by the standard deviation. Standard scores (z-scores) tell, in standard deviation units, how far above or below the mean a score is. This allows meaningful comparisons between scores from different groups.

A.1.6 Scores that form a normal curve are easy to interpret because the properties of the normal curve are well known.

A.2 ***How are correlations used in psychology?***

A.2.1 Pairs of scores that vary together in an orderly fashion are said to be correlated.

A.2.2 The relationship between two variables or measures can be positive or negative.

A.2.3 Correlation coefficients tell how strongly two groups of scores are related.

A.2.4 Knowing a person's score on one measure allows us to predict his or her score on the second measure.

A.2.5 Correlation alone does not demonstrate cause-and-effect links between variables or measures.

A.3 ***What are inferential statistics?***

A.3.1 Inferential statistics are used to make decisions, to generalize from samples, and to draw conclusions from data.

A.3.2 Most studies in psychology are based on samples. Findings from representative samples are assumed to also apply to entire populations.

A.3.3 In psychology experiments, differences in the average performance of groups could occur purely by chance. Tests of statistical significance tell us if the observed differences between groups are common or rare. If a difference is large enough to be improbable, it suggests that the results did not occur by chance alone.

MEDIA RESOURCES

Web Resources

Internet addresses frequently change. To find an up-to-date list of URLs for the sites listed here, visit your Psychology CourseMate.

Frequency Distribution of Tossing Coins and Dice Automatically calculate frequency distributions for tossing coins or dice and plot the results as a frequency polygon.

Measures of Central Tendency Work through another example of measures of central tendency.

Descriptive Statistics Further explore descriptive statistics.

Scatter Diagram Explore correlation by better understanding scatter diagrams.

Correlations Vary the correlations and view the corresponding scatter diagram.

Concepts and Applications of Inferential Statistics Browse this full online statistics textbook.

Interactive Learning

Log in to **CengageBrain** to access the resources your instructor requires. For this book, you can access:

CourseMate brings course concepts to life with interactive learning, study, and exam preparation tools that support the printed textbook. A textbook-specific website, ***Psychology CourseMate*** includes an ***integrated interactive eBook*** and other ***interactive learning tools*** including quizzes, flashcards, videos, and more.

CENGAGE**NOW**™

CengageNOW is an easy-to-use online resource that helps you study in less time to get the grade you want—NOW. Take a pre-test for this chapter and receive a personalized study plan based on your results that will identify the topics you need to review and direct you to online resources to help you master those topics. Then take a post-test to help you determine the concepts you have mastered and what you will need to work on. If your textbook does not include an access code card, go to CengageBrain.com to gain access.

WebTUTOR™

More than just an interactive study guide, **WebTutor** is an anytime, anywhere customized learning solution with an eBook, keeping you connected to your textbook, instructor, and classmates.

If your professor has assigned **Aplia** homework:

1. Sign in to your account.
2. Complete the corresponding homework exercises as required by your professor.
3. When finished, click "Grade It Now" to see which areas you have mastered and which need more work, and for detailed explanations of every answer.

Visit **www.cengagebrain.com** to access your account and purchase materials.

References

Aamodt, M. G. (2010). *Industrial/organizational psychology: An applied approach* (6th ed.). Belmont, CA: Cengage Learning/Wadsworth.

Abe, N., Suzuki, M., Mori, E., et al. (2007). Deceiving others: Distinct neural responses of the prefrontal cortex and amygdala in simple fabrication and deception with social interactions. *Journal of Cognitive Neuroscience, 19*(2), 287–295.

Abel, G. G., Wiegel, M., & Osborn, C. A. (2007). Pedophilia and other paraphilias. In L. VandeCreek, F. L. Peterson, Jr., & J. W. Bley (Eds.), *Innovations in clinical practice: Focus on sexual health* (pp. 157–175). Sarasota, FL: Professional Resource Press.

Abma, J. C., Martinez, G. M., Mosher, W. D., et al. (2004). Teenagers in the United States: Sexual activity, contraceptive use, and childbearing, 2002. *Vital Health Statistics, 23*(24), 1–48.

Abraham, W. C. (2006). Memory maintenance: The changing nature of neural mechanisms. *Current Directions in Psychological Science, 15*(1), 5–8.

Abrahamse, W., Steg, L., Vlek, C., et al. (2005). A review of intervention studies aimed at household energy conservation. *Journal of Environmental Psychology, 25*(3), 273–291.

Abrahamson, D. J., Barlow, D. H., & Abrahamson, L. S. (1989). Differential effects of performance demand and distraction on sexually functional and dysfunctional males. *Journal of Abnormal Psychology, 98*(3), 241–247.

Abrams, D. B., Brown, R., Niaura, R. S., et al. (2003). *The tobacco dependence treatment handbook: A guide to best practices.* New York, Guilford.

Accordino, D. B., Accordino, M. P., & Slaney, R. B. (2000). An investigation of perfectionism, mental health, achievement, and achievement motivation in adolescents. *Psychology in the Schools, 37*(6), 535–545.

Adams, J. (2001). *Conceptual blockbusting* (4th ed.). New York: Basic Books.

Adamson, K. (2004). *Kate's journey: Triumph over adversity.* Redondo Beach, CA: Nosmada Press.

Adan, A., & Serra-Grabulosa, J. P. (2010). Effects of caffeine and glucose, alone and combined, on cognitive performance. *Human Psychopharmacology: Clinical & Experimental, 25*(4), 310–317.

Addis, K. M., & Kahana, M. J. (2004). Decomposing serial learning: What is missing from the learning curve? *Psychonomic Bulletin & Review, 11*(1), 118–174.

Adler, S. A., & Orprecio, J. (2006). The eyes have it: Visual pop-out in infants and adults. *Developmental Science, 9,* 189–206.

Adolphs, R. (2008). Fear, faces, and the human amygdala. *Current Opinion in Neurobiology, 18*(2), 166–172.

Adorno, T. W., Frenkel-Brunswik E., Levinson, D. J., et al. (1950). *The authoritarian personality.* New York: Harper.

Adults and Children Against Violence Together. (2010). *Violence prevention for families of young children.* Washington: Author. Retrieved March 28, 2011 from http://www.actagainstviolence.com/violprevent/index.html.

Advisory Council on the Misuse of Drugs. (2009). *MDMA ("ecstasy"): A review of its harms and classification under the Misuse of Drugs Act 1971.* London, England: Author. Retrieved January 23, 2011, from http://www.homeoffice.gov.uk/publications/drugs/acmd1/mdma-report?view=Binary.

Afifi, T. O., Brownridge, D. A., Cox, B. J., et al. (2006). Physical punishment, childhood abuse, and psychiatric disorders. *Child Abuse & Neglect, 30*(10), 1093–1103.

Ahima. R. S., & Osei, S. Y. (2004). Leptin signaling. *Physiology & Behavior, 81,* 223–241.

Ahluwalia, M. K., & Pellettiere, L. (2010). Sikh men post-9/11: Misidentification, discrimination, and coping. *Asian American Journal of Psychology, 1*(4), 303–314.

Ajzen, I. (2005). *Attitudes, personality and behaviour* (2nd ed.). New York: McGraw-Hill.

Åkerstedt, T. (2007). Altered sleep/wake patterns and mental performance. *Physiology & Behavior, 90*(2-3), 209–218.

Albarracín, D., Johnson, B. T., & Zanna, M. P. (Eds.) (2005). *The handbook of attitudes.* Mahwah, NJ: Erlbaum.

Alberti, R., & Emmons, M. (2008). *Your perfect right* (9th ed.). San Luis Obispo, CA: Impact.

Alberto, P. A., & Troutman, A. C. (2009). *Applied behavior analysis for teachers* (8th ed.). Englewood Cliffs, NJ: Prentice Hall.

Albrecht, C. M., & Albrecht, D. E. (2011). Social status, adolescent behavior, and educational attainment. *Sociological Spectrum, 31*(1), 114–137.

Albright, D. L., & Thyer, B. (2010). Does EMDR reduce post-traumatic stress disorder symptomatology in combat veterans? *Behavioral Interventions, 25*(1), 1–19.

Alcock, J. E. (2003). Give the null hypothesis a chance: Reasons to remain doubtful about the existence of psi. *Journal of Consciousness Studies, 10*(6-7), 29–50.

Alcock, J. E., Burns, J., & Freeman, A. (2003). *Psi wars: Getting to grips with the paranormal.* Exeter, UK: Imprint Academic Press.

Aldhous, P. (2010, November 11). Is this evidence that we can see the future? *New Scientist.* Retrieved December 17, 2010 from http://www.newscientist.com/article/dn19712-is-this-evidence-that-we-can-see-the-future.html.

Alegre, A. (2011). Parenting styles and children's emotional intelligence: What do we know? *The Family Journal, 19*(1), 56–62.

Algoe, S. B., Gable, S. L., & Maisel, N. (2010). It's the little things: Gratitude as a booster shot for romantic relationships. *Personal Relationships, 17*(2), 217–233.

Ali, M. M., & Dwyer, D. S. (2010). Social network effects in alcohol consumption among adolescents. *Addictive Behaviors, 35*(4), 337–342.

Allen, D., Carlson, D., & Ham, C. (2007). Well-being: New paradigms of wellness-inspiring positive health outcomes and renewing hope. *American Journal of Health Promotion, 21*(3), 1–9.

Allen, J. L., Lavallee, K. L., Herren, C., et al. (2010). DSM-IV criteria for childhood separation anxiety disorder: Informant, age, and sex differences. *Journal of Anxiety Disorders, 24*(8), 946–952.

Allen, K., Blascovich, J., & Mendes, W. B. (2002). Cardiovascular reactivity in the presence of pets, friends, and spouses: The truth about cats and dogs. *Psychosomatic Medicine, 64*(5), 727–739.

Allen, M., Mabry, E., & McKelton, D. (1998). Impact of juror attitudes about the death penalty on juror evaluations of guilt and punishment: A meta-analysis. *Law & Human Behavior, 22*(6), 715–731.

Alleyne, M. D. (Ed.). (2011). *Anti-racism and multiculturalism: Studies in international communication.* Piscataway, NJ: Transaction Publishers.

Allport, G. W. (1958). *The nature of prejudice.* Garden City, NY: Anchor Books, Doubleday.

Allport, G. W. (1961). *Pattern and growth in personality.* New York: Holt, Rinehart, & Winston.

Altemeyer, B. (2004). Highly dominating, highly authoritarian personalities. *Journal of Social Psychology, 144*(4), 421–447.

Alter, A. L., Aronson, J., Darley, J. M., et al. (2010). Rising to the threat: Reducing stereotype threat by reframing the threat as a challenge. *Journal of Experimental Social Psychology, 46,* 166–171.

Altman, L. K. (2002). AIDS threatens to claim 65M more lives by '20. *Arizona Daily Star,* July 3, A7.

Altschuler, G. C. (2001). *Battling the cheats.* The New York Times: Education, Jan. 7, 15.

Alwin, D. F., Cohen, R. L., & Newcomb, T. M. (1991). *Political attitudes over the life span: The Bennington women after fifty years.* Madison, WI: University of Wisconsin Press.

Amabile, T., Hadley, C. N., & Kramer, S. J. (2002). Creativity under the gun. *Harvard Business Review, 80*(8), 52–61.

Amato, P. R., & Fowler, F. (2002). Parenting practices, child adjustment, and family diversity. *Journal of Marriage & Family, 64*(3), 703–716.

Ambady, N., & Rosenthal, R. (1993). Half a minute: Predicting teacher evaluations from thin slices of nonverbal behavior and physical attractiveness. *Journal of Personality & Social Psychology, 64,* 431–441.

American Academy of Child and Adolescent Psychiatry. (2008). Child sexual abuse. Washington, DC: Author. Retrieved March 1, 2011 from http://www.aacap.org/cs/root/facts_for_families/child_sexual_abuse.

American Lung Association. (2011). Secondhand smoke. Retrieved January 23, 2011, from http://www.lungusa.org/stop-smoking/about-smoking/health-effects/secondhand-smoke.html.

American Psychiatric Association. (2000). *Diagnostic and statistical manual of mental disorders* (4th ed.). Washington, DC: Author.

American Psychiatric Association. (2010). *DSM-5: The future of psychiatric diagnosis.* Washington, DC: Author. Retrieved March 23, 2011 from http://www.dsm5.org/Pages/Default.aspx.

American Psychiatric Association. (2010). *Proposed draft revisions to DSM disorders and criteria.* Washington, DC: Author. Retrieved February 13, 2011 from http://www.dsm5.org/Pages/Default.aspx.

American Psychological Association. (2002). Ethical principles of psychologists and code of conduct. *American Psychologist, 57,* 1060–1073. Retrieved March 22, 2011, from http://www.apa.org/ethics/code/index.aspx.

American Psychological Association. (2003a). *Demographic shifts in psychology.* Washington, DC: Author. Retrieved March 22, 2011, from http://www.apa.org/workforce/snapshots/2003/demographic-shifts.aspx.

American Psychological Association. (2003b). Guidelines on multicultural education, training, research, practice, and organizational change for psychologists. *American Psychologist, 58*(5), 377–402.

American Psychological Association. (2007a). 2007 *APA directory survey.* Washington, DC: Author. Retrieved April 21, 2009, from http://research.apa.org/profile2007t3.pdf and http://research.apa.org/profile2007t4.pdf.

American Psychological Association. (2007b). *Report of the APA Task Force on the sexualization of girls.* Washington, DC: Author. Retrieved March 1, 2011 from http://www.apa.org/pi/women/programs/girls/report.aspx.

American Psychological Association. (2008). *Report of the Task Force on the Implementation of the Multicultural Guidelines.* Washington, DC: Author. Retrieved March 12, 2011 from http://www.apa.org/about/governance/council/policy/multicultural-report.pdf.

American Psychological Association. (2010). *Ethical principles of psychologists and code of conduct: 2010 amendments.* Washington, DC: Author. Retrieved November 28, 2010, from http://www.apa.org/ethics/code/index.aspx.

American Psychological Association. (2011). *Sexual orientation and homosexuality.* Washington, DC: Author. Retrieved February 23, 2011, from http://www.apa.org/helpcenter/sexual-orientation.aspx.

Ancis, J. R., Chen, Y., & Schultz, D. (2004). Diagnostic challenges and the so-called culture-bound syndromes. In J. R. Ancis (Ed.), *Culturally responsive interventions: Innovative approaches to working with diverse populations* (pp. 213–222). New York: Brunner-Routledge.

Andersen, M. L., Poyares, D., Alves, R. S. C., et al. (2007). Sexsomnia: Abnormal sexual behavior during sleep. *Brain Research Reviews, 56*(2), 271–282.

Anderson, C. A. (1989). Temperature and aggression. *Psychological Bulletin, 106,* 74–96.

Anderson, C. A. (2004). An update on the effects of violent video games. *Journal of Adolescence, 27,* 113–122.

Anderson, C. A., & Bushman, B. J. (2002). Human aggression. *Annual Review of Psychology, 53,* 27–51.

Anderson, C. A., Anderson, K. B., & Deuser, W. E. (1996). Examining an affective aggression framework. *Personality & Social Psychology Bulletin, 22*(4), 366–376.

Anderson, C. A., Berkowitz, L. Donnerstein, E., et al. (2003). The influence of media violence on youth. *Psychological Science in the Public Interest, 4,* 1–30.

Anderson, C. A., Carnagey, N. L., & Eubanks, J. (2003). Exposure to violent media: The effects of songs with violent lyrics on aggressive thoughts and feelings. *Journal of Personality & Social Psychology, 84*(5), 960–971.

Anderson, C. A., Gentile, D. A., & Buckley, K. E. (2007). *Violent video game effects on children and adolescents: Theory, research, and public policy.* New York: Oxford University Press.

Anderson, J. R. (2010). *Cognitive psychology and its implications* (7th ed.). New York: Worth.

Anderson, K. J. (2010). *Benign bigotry: The psychology of subtle prejudice.* New York: Cambridge University Press.

Anderson, M. C., & Green, C. (2001). Suppressing unwanted memories by executive control. *Nature, 410*(6826), 366–369.

Anderson, M. C., Ochsner, K. N., Kuhl, B., et al., (2004). Neural systems underlying the suppression of unwanted memories. *Science, 303,* 232–235.

André, C., Jaber-Filho J. A., Carvalho, M., et al. (2003). Predictors of recovery following involuntary hospitalization of violent substance abuse patients. *The American Journal on Addictions, 12*(1), 84–89.

Andresen, J. (2000). Meditation meets behavioural medicine: The story of experimental research on meditation. *Journal of Consciousness Studies, 7*(11-12), 17–73.

Anekonda, T. S. (2006). Resveratrol: A boon for treating Alzheimer's disease?. *Brain Research Reviews, 52*(2), 316–326.

Annett, M. (2002). *Handedness and brain asymmetry: The right shift theory.* Hove, UK: Psychology Press.

Annett, M., & Manning, M. (1990). Arithmetic and laterality. *Neuropsychologia, 28*(1), 61–69.

Anshel, M. H. (1995). An examination of self-regulatory cognitive-behavioural strategies of Australian elite and non-elite competitive male swimmers. *Australian Psychologist, 30*(2), 78–83.

Antoni, C. (2005). Management by objectives: An effective tool for teamwork? *International Journal of Human Resource Management, 16*(2), 174–184.

Antony, M. M., & Swinson, R. P. (2008). *The shyness and social anxiety workbook: Proven, step-by-step techniques for overcoming your fear* (2nd ed.). Oakland, CA: New Harbinger.

Arbona, C. B., Osma, J., Garcia-Palacios A., et al. (2004). Treatment of flying phobia using virtual reality: Data from a 1-year follow-up using a multiple baseline design. *Clinical Psychology & Psychotherapy, 11*(5), 311–323.

Ariely, D., & Loewenstein, G. (2006). The heat of the moment: The effect of sexual arousal on sexual decision making. *Journal of Behavioral Decision Making, 19*(2), 87–98.

Ariely, D., & Wertenbroch, K. (2002). Procrastination, deadlines, and performance: Self-control by precommitment. *Psychological Science, 13*(3), 219–224.

Arnett, J. J. (2004). *Emerging adulthood: The winding road from late teens through the twenties.* New York: Oxford University Press.

Arnett, J. J. (2010). Oh, grow up! Generational grumbling and the new life stage of emerging adulthood—Commentary on Trzesniewski & Donnellan (2010). *Perspectives on Psychological Science, 5*(1), 89–92.

Arnett, J. J., & Galambos, N. L. (Eds.). (2003). *New directions for child and adolescent development: Exploring cultural conceptions of the transition to adulthood.* San Francisco: Jossey-Bass.

Aron, A., Fisher, H. E., Strong, G., et al. (2008). Falling in love. In S. Sprecher, A. Wenzel, & J. Harvey (Eds.), *Handbook of relationship initiation* (pp. 315–336). New York: Psychology Press.

Aronow, E., Altman Weiss, K., & Reznikoff, M. (2001). *A practical guide to the Thematic Apperception Test: The TAT in clinical practice.* New York: Brunner-Routledge.

Aronson, E. (2008). *The social animal* (10th ed.). New York: Worth.

Aronson, E., Wilson, T. D., & Akert, R. M. (2010). *Social psychology* (7th ed.). Englewood Cliffs, NJ: Prentice Hall.

Aronson, K. (2003) Alcohol: A recently identified risk factor for breast cancer. *Canadian Medical Association Journal, 168*(9), 1147–1148.

Arthur, W., & Doverspike, D. (2001). Predicting motor vehicle crash involvement from a personality measure and a driving knowledge test. *Journal of Prevention & Intervention in the Community, 22*(1), 35–42.

Artz, S. (2005). To die for: Violent adolescent girls' search for male attention. In D. J. Pepler, K. C. Madsen, et al. (Eds.), *The development and treatment of girlhood aggression* (pp. 137–160). Mahwah, NJ: Erlbaum.

Ary, D. V., Duncan, T. E., Biglan, A., et al. (1999). Development of adolescent problem behavior. *Journal of Abnormal Child Psychology, 27*(2), 141–150.

Asch, S. E. (1956). Studies of independence and conformity: A minority of one against a unanimous majority. *Psychological Monographs, 70*(9, Whole No. 416).

Ash, D. W., & Holding, D. H. (1990). Backward versus forward chaining in the acquisition of a keyboard skill. *Human Factors, 32*(2), 139–146.

Ashby, F. G., & Maddox, W. T. (2005). Human category learning. *Annual Review of Psychology, 56,* 149–178.

Ashcraft, D. (2012). *Personality theories workbook* (5th ed.). Belmont, CA: Cengage Learning/Wadsworth.

Ashton, M. C. (2007). *Individual differences and personality.* San Diego: Elsevier.

Asmundson, G. J. G., & Taylor, S. (2005). *It's not all in your head.* London: Psychology Press.

Athenasiou, R., Shaver, P., & Tavris, C. (1970). Sex. *Psychology Today, 4*(2), 37–52.

Atkin, D. J., & Lau, T. Y. (2007). Information technology and organizational telework. In C. A. Lin, & D. J Atkin (Eds.), *Communication technology and social change: Theory and implications* (pp. 79–100). Mahwah, NJ: Erlbaum.

Atkinson, R.C. & Schiffrin, R.M. (1968). Human memory: A proposed system and its control processes. In K. W. Spence, & J. T. Spence (Eds.), *The psychology of learning and motivation* (Vol. 2, pp. 742–775). London: Academic Press.

Atwood, J. D. (2006). Mommy's little angel, daddy's little girl: Do you know what your preteens are doing? *American Journal of Family Therapy, 34*(5), 447–467.

Aucoin, K. J., Frick, P. J., & Bodin, S. D. (2006). Corporal punishment and child adjustment. *Journal of Applied Developmental Psychology, 27*(6), 527–541.

Avery, D. H., Eder, D. N., Bolte, M. A., et al. (2001). Dawn simulation and bright light in the treatment of SAD. *Biological Psychiatry, 50*(3), 205–216.

Awadallah, N., Vaughan, A., Franco, K., et al. (2005). Munchausen by proxy: A case, chart series, and literature review of older victims. *Child Abuse & Neglect, 29*(8), 931–941.

Axmacher, N., Do Lam, A. T. A., Kessler, H., et al. (2010). Natural memory beyond the storage model: Repression, trauma, and the construction of a personal past. *Frontiers in Human Neuroscience, 4,* 211. doi: 10.3389/fnhum.2010.00211.

Ayers, L., Beaton, S., & Hunt, H. (1999). The significance of transpersonal experiences, emotional conflict, and cognitive abilities in creativity. *Empirical Studies of the Arts, 17*(1), 73–82.

Ayllon, T. (1963). Intensive treatment of psychotic behavior by stimulus satiation and food reinforcement. *Behavior Research & Therapy, 1,* 53–61.

Ayllon, T., & Azrin, N. H. (1965). The measurement and reinforcement of behavior of psychotics. *Journal of the Experimental Analysis of Behavior, 8,* 357–383.

Ayman, R., & Korabik, K. (2010). Leadership: Why gender and culture matter. *American Psychologist, 65*(3), 157–170.

Baard, P. P., Deci, E. L., & Ryan, R. M. (2004). Intrinsic need satisfaction: A motivational basis of performance and well-being in two work settings. *Journal of Applied Social Psychology, 34*(10), 2045–2068.

Babbie, E. R. (2011). *The basics of social research* (5th ed.). Belmont, CA: Cengage Learning/Wadsworth.

Bachman, J. G., & Johnson, L. D. (1979). The freshmen. *Psychology Today, 13,* 78–87.

Baddeley, A. D. (2003). Working memory: Looking back and looking forward. *Nature Reviews Neuroscience, 4*(10), 829–839.

Baddeley, A., Eysenck, M. W., & Anderson, M. C. (2009). *Memory.* Hove, UK: Psychology Press.

Baer, J. M. (1993). *Creativity and divergent thinking.* Hillsdale, NJ: Erlbaum.

Bahr, S. J., & Hoffmann, J. P. (2010). Parenting style, religiosity, peers, and adolescent heavy drinking. *Journal of Studies on Alcohol & Drugs, 71*(4), 539–543.

Bailey, C. H., & Kandel, E. R. (2004). Synaptic growth and the persistence of long-term memory: A molecular perspective. In M. S. Gazzaniga (Ed.), *The cognitive neurosciences* (3rd ed., pp. 839–847). Cambridge, MA: MIT Press.

Bailey, L. M., & McKeever, W. F. (2004). A large-scale study of handedness and pregnancy/birth risk events: Implications for genetic theories of handedness. *Laterality: Asymmetries of Body, Brain & Cognition, 9*(2), 175–188.

Baillargeon, R. (1991). Reasoning about the height and location of a hidden object in 4.5- and 6.5-month-old infants. *Cognition, 38*(1), 13–42.

Baillargeon, R. (2004). Infants' reasoning about hidden objects: Evidence for event-general and event-specific expectations. *Developmental Science. 7*(4), 391–424.

Baillargeon, R., De Vos, J., & Graber, M. (1989). Location memory in 8-month-old infants in a nonsearch AB task. *Cognitive Development, 4*, 345–367.

Bain, S. K., & Allin, J. D. (2005). Stanford-Binet Intelligence Scales, Fifth Edition. *Journal of Psychoeducational Assessment, 23*(1), 87–95.

Bajracharya, S. M., Sarvela, P. D., & Isberner, F. R. (1995). A retrospective study of first sexual intercourse experiences among undergraduates. *Journal of American College Health, 43*(4), 169–177.

Baker, T. B., Brandon, T. H., & Chassin, L. (2004). Motivational influences on cigarette smoking. *Annual Review of Psychology, 55*, 463–491.

Bakich, I. (1995). Hypnosis in the treatment of sexual desire disorders. *Australian Journal of Clinical & Experimental Hypnosis, 23*(1), 70–77.

Bakker, G. M. (2009). In defence of thought stopping. *Clinical Psychologist, 13*(2), 59–68.

Baldo, O., & Eardley, I. (2005). Diagnosis and investigation of men with erectile dysfunction. *Journal of Men's Health & Gender, 2*(1), 79–86.

Balk, D. E., Lampe, S., Sharpe, B., et al. (1998). TAT results in a longitudinal study of bereaved college students. *Death Studies, 22*(1), 3–21.

Balsam, K. F., & Mohr, J. J. (2007). Adaptation to sexual orientation stigma: A comparison of bisexual and lesbian/gay adults. *Journal of Counseling Psychology, 54*(3), 306–319.

Baltes, B. B., Briggs, T. E., Huff, J. W., et al. (1999). Flexible and compressed workweek schedules. *Journal of Applied Psychology, 84*(4), 496–513.

Bandura, A. (1971). *Social learning theory*. New York: General Learning Press.

Bandura, A. (2001). Social cognitive theory: An agentic perspective. *Annual Review of Psychology, 52*, 1–26.

Bandura, A., & Walters, R. (1959). *Adolescent aggression*. New York: Ronald.

Bandura, A., Blanchard, E. B., & Ritter, B. (1969). Relative efficacy of desensitization and modeling approaches for inducing behavioral, affective, and attitudinal changes. *Journal of Personality & Social Psychology, 13*(3), 173–199.

Bandura, A., Ross, D., & Ross, S. A. (1963). Vicarious reinforcement and imitative learning. *Journal of Abnormal & Social Psychology, 67*, 601–607.

Banich, M. T., & Compton, R. J. (2011). *Cognitive neuroscience* (3rd ed.). Belmont, CA: Cengage Learning/ Wadsworth.

Bank, B. J., & Hansford, S. L. (2000). Gender and friendship: Why are men's best same-sex friendships less intimate and supportive? *Personal Relationships, 7*(1), 63–78.

Banks, A., & Gartrell, N. K. (1995). Hormones and sexual orientation: A questionable link. *Journal of Homosexuality, 28*(3-4), 247–268.

Barabasz, A., & Watkins, J. G. (2005). *Hypnotherapeutic techniques* (2nd ed.). Washington: Taylor & Francis.

Barber, N. (2010). Applying the concept of adaptation to societal differences in intelligence. *Cross-Cultural Research, 44*(2), 116–150.

Barber, T. X. (2000). A deeper understanding of hypnosis: Its secrets, its nature, its essence. *American Journal of Clinical Hypnosis, 42*(3–4), 208–272.

Bard, C., Fleury, M., & Goulet, C. (1994). Relationship between perceptual strategies and response adequacy in sport situations. *International Journal of Sport Psychology, 25*(3), 266–281.

Bardone-Cone, A. M., Joiner, Jr., T. E., Crosby, R. D., et al. (2008). Examining a psychosocial interactive model of binge eating and vomiting in women with bulimia nervosa and subthreshold bulimia nervosa. *Behaviour Research & Therapy, 46*(7), 887–894.

Barelds, D. P. H., & Dijkstra, P. (2009). Positive illusions about a partner's physical attractiveness and relationship quality. *Personal Relationships, 16*(2), 263–283.

Bargh, J. A., McKenna, K. Y. A., & Fitzsimons, G. M. (2002). Can you see the real me? Activation and expression of the "true self" on the Internet. *Journal of Social Issues, 58*(1), 33–48.

Barkataki, I., Kumari, V., Das, M., et al. (2006). Volumetric structural brain abnormalities in men with schizophrenia or antisocial personality disorder. *Behavioural Brain Research, 169*(2), 239–247.

Barlow, D. H. (2000). Unraveling the mysteries of anxiety and its disorders from the perspective of emotion theory. *American Psychologist, 55*, 1247–1263.

Barlow, D. H. (2002). *Anxiety and its disorders* (2nd ed.). New York: Guilford.

Barlow, D. H. (2004). Psychological treatments. *American Psychologist, 59*(9), 869–878.

Barnet, A. B., & Barnet, R. J. (1998). *The youngest minds*. New York: Touchstone.

Barnett, J., Behnke, S. H., Rosenthal, S., et al. (2007). In case of ethical dilemma, break glass: Commentary on ethical decision making in practice. *Professional Psychology: Research & Practice, 38*(1), 7–12.

Barnier, A. J., McConkey, K. M., & Wright, J. (2004). Posthypnotic amnesia for autobiographical episodes: Influencing memory accessibility and quality. *International Journal of Clinical & Experimental Hypnosis, 52*(3), 260–279.

Baron, I. S. (2005). Test review: Wechsler intelligence scale for children (4th ed.). (WISC-IV). *Child Neuropsychology, 11*(5), 471–475.

Baron, R. A., Byrne, D., & Branscombe, N. R. (2009). *Mastering social psychology* (12th ed.). Boston: Pearson/ Allyn & Bacon.

Baron, R. S. (2005). So right it's wrong: Groupthink and the ubiquitous nature of polarized group decision making. In M. P. Zanna, (Ed.), *Advances in experimental social psychology* (Vol. 37, pp. 219–253). San Diego: Elsevier.

Baron-Cohen, S. (1985). Does the autistic child have a "theory of mind"? *Cognition, 21*, 37–46.

Barras, C. (2010). Microsoft's body-sensing button-busting controller. *New Scientist, Jan 9*, 22.

Barrett, D. (1993). The "committee of sleep": A study of dream incubation for problem solving. *Dreaming, 3*(2), 115–122.

Barrett, D., Greenwood, J. G., & McCullagh, J. F. (2006). Kissing laterality and handedness. *Laterality: Asymmetries of Body, Brain & Cognition, 11*(6), 573–579.

Barron, F. (1958). The psychology of imagination. *Scientific American, 199*(3), 150–170.

Barrowcliff, A. L., & Haddock, G. (2006). The relationship between command hallucinations and factors of compliance: A critical review of the literature. *Journal of Forensic Psychiatry & Psychology, 17*(2), 266–298.

Barry, S. R., & Sacks, O. (2009). *Fixing my gaze*. New York: Basic Books.

Bar-Tal, D., & Labin, D. (2001). The effect of a major event on stereotyping: Terrorist attacks in Israel and Israeli adolescents' perceptions of Palestinians, Jordanians and Arabs. *European Journal of Social Psychology, 31*(3), 265–280.

Bartholow, B. D., & Anderson, C. A. (2002). Effects of violent video games on aggressive behavior. *Journal of Experimental Social Psychology, 38*(3), 283–290.

Bartholow, B. D., Bushman, B. J., & Sestir, M. A. (2006). Chronic violent video game exposure and desensitization to violence: Behavioral and event-related brain potential data. *Journal of Experimental Social Psychology, 42*(4), 532–539.

Bartholow, B. D., Sestir, M. A., & Davis, E. B. (2005). Correlates and consequences of exposure to video game violence: Hostile personality, empathy, and aggressive behavior. *Personality & Social Psychology Bulletin, 31*(11), 1573–1586.

Bartram, B. (2006). An examination of perceptions of parental influence on attitudes to language learning. *Educational Research, 48*(2), 211–222.

Basadur, M., Runco, M. A., & Vega, L. A. (2000). Understanding how creative thinking skills, attitudes and behaviors work together. *Journal of Creative Behavior, 34*(2), 77–100.

Basner, M., & Dinges, D. (2009). Dubious bargain: Trading sleep for Leno and Letterman. *Sleep, 32*(6), 747–752.

Bass, J., & Takahashi, J. S. (2010). Circadian integration of metabolism and energetics. *Science, 330*(6009), 1349–1354.

Basson, R., & Brotto, L. A. (2009). Disorders of sexual desire and subjective arousal in women. In R. Balon, & R. T. Segraves (Eds.), *Clinical manual of sexual disorders* (pp. 119–159). Arlington, VA: American Psychiatric Publishing.

Basson, R., Brotto, L. A., Laan, E., et al. (2005). Assessment and management of women's sexual dysfunctions: Problematic desire and arousal. *Journal of Sexual Medicine, 2*(3), 291–300.

Bastian, B., & Haslam, N. (2006). Psychological essentialism and stereotype endorsement. *Journal of Experimental Social Psychology, 42*(2), 228–235.

Batelaan, N. M., de Graaf, R., Spijker, J., et al. (2010). The course of panic attacks in individuals with panic disorder and subthreshold panic disorder: A population-based study. *Journal of Affective Disorders, 121*(1-2), 30–38.

Bates, T. C. (2005). Auditory inspection time and intelligence. *Personality & Individual Differences, 38(1)*, 115–127.

Bath, H. (1996). Everyday discipline or control with care. *Journal of Child & Youth Care, 10*(2), 23–32.

Batson, C. D. (2006). "Not all self-interest after all": Economics of empathy-induced altruism. In D. De Cremer, M. Zeelenberg, et al. (Eds.), *Social psychology and economics* (pp. 281–299). Mahwah, NJ: Erlbaum.

Batson, C. D. (2010). Empathy-induced altruistic motivation. In M. Mikulincer, & P. R. Shaver (Eds.), *Prosocial motives, emotions, and behavior: The better angels of our nature* (pp.15–34). Washington, DC: American Psychological Association.

Batson, C. D., & Powell, A. A. (2003). Altruism and prosocial behavior. In T. Millon, & M. J. Lerner (Eds.), *Handbook of psychology: Personality and social psychology* (Vol. 5, pp. 463–484). New York: Wiley.

Batterham, R. L., Cohen, M. A., Ellis, S. M., et al. (2003). Inhibition of food intake in obese subjects by peptide YY3–36. *New England Journal of Medicine, 349*(10), 941–948.

Bauer, J. J., McAdams, D. P., & Pals, J. L. (2008). Narrative identity and eudaimonic well-being. *Journal of Happiness Studies, 9*(1), 81–104.

Baum, A., & Davis, G. E. (1980). Reducing the stress of high-density living: An architectural intervention. *Journal of Personality & Social Psychology, 38*, 471–481.

Baum, A., & Valins, S. (1979). Architectural mediation of residential density and control: Crowding and the regulation of social contact. *Advances in Experimental & Social Psychology, 12*, 131–175.

Baum, A., & Valins, S. (Eds.). (1977). *Human response to crowding: Studies of the effects of residential group size.* Mahwah, NJ: Erlbaum.

Bauman, L. J., Karasz, A., & Hamilton, A. (2007). Understanding failure of condom use intention among adolescents: Completing an intensive preventive intervention. *Journal of Adolescent Research, 22*(3), 248–274.

Baumeister, R. F., & Bushman, B. (2011). *Social psychology and human nature* (2nd ed.). Belmont, CA: Cengage Learning/Wadsworth.

Baumeister, R. F., Campbell, J. D., Krueger, J. I., et al. (2003). Does high self-esteem cause better performance, interpersonal success, happiness, or healthier lifestyles? *Psychological Science in the Public Interest, 4*(1), 1–44.

Baumrind, D. (1991). The influence of parenting style on adolescent competence and substance use. *Journal of Early Adolescence, 11*(1), 56–95.

Baumrind, D. (2005). Patterns of parental authority and adolescent autonomy. In J. Smetana (Ed.), *New directions for child development: Changes in parental authority during adolescence* (pp. 61–69). San Francisco: Jossey-Bass.

Baumrind, D., Larzelere, R. E., & Cowan, P. A. (2002). Ordinary physical punishment: Is it harmful? *Psychological Bulletin, 128*(4), 580–589.

Bearman, P. S., Moody, J., & Stovel, K. (2004). Chains of affection: The structure of adolescent romantic and sexual networks. *American Journal of Sociology, 110*(1), 44–91.

Beaulieu, C. M. J. (2004). Intercultural study of personal space: A case study. *Journal of Applied Social Psychology, 34*(4), 794–805.

Beck, A. T. (1991). Cognitive therapy. *American Psychologist, 46*(4), 368–375.

Beck, A. T., Rector, N. A., Stolar, N., et al. (2009). *Schizophrenia: Cognitive theory, research, and therapy.* New York: Guilford.

Beck, B. L., Koons, S. R., & Milgrim, D. L. (2000). Correlates and consequences of behavioral procrastination. *Journal of Social Behavior & Personality, 15*(5), 3–13.

Beck, H. P., Levinson, S. & Irons, G. (2009). Finding little Albert: A journey to John B. Watson's infant laboratory. *American Psychologist, 64*(7), 605–614.

Beck, R. C. (2004). *Motivation: Theories and principles* (5th ed.). Englewood Cliffs, NJ: Prentice Hall.

Becker, S. W., & Eagly, A. H. (2004). The heroism of women and men. *American Psychologist, 59*(3), 163–178.

Beeber, L. S., Chazan-Cohen R., Squires, J., et al. (2007). The Early Promotion and Intervention Research Consortium (E-PIRC): Five approaches to improving infant/toddler mental health in Early Head Start. *Infant Mental Health Journal, 28*(2), 130–150.

Beeman, M. J., & Chiarello, C. (1998). Complementary right- and left-hemisphere language comprehension. *Current Directions in Psychological Science, 7*(1), 2–8.

Beersma, D. G. M., & Gordijn, M. C. M. (2007). Circadian control of the sleep-wake cycle. *Physiology & Behavior, 90*(2-3), 190–195.

Begley, S. (2006). *Train your mind, change your brain.* New York: Ballantine.

Behrend, D. A., Beike, D. R., & Lampinen, J. M. (2004). *The self and memory.* Hove, UK: Psychology Press.

Beirne-Smith, M., Patton, J., & Shannon, K. (2006). *Mental retardation: An introduction to intellectual disability* (7th ed.). Englewood Cliffs, NJ: Prentice Hall.

Bekinschtein, T. A., Shalom, D. E., Forcato, C., et al. (2009). Classical conditioning in the vegetative and minimally conscious state. *Nature Neuroscience 12,* 1343–1349.

Belicki, K., Chambers, E., & Ogilvie, R. (1997). Sleep quality and nightmares. *Sleep Research, 26,* 637.

Bell, P. A., Greene, T., Fisher, J., et al. (2006). *Environmental psychology* (5th ed.). Mahwah, NJ: Erlbaum.

Bellezza, F. S., Six, L. S., & Phillips, D. S. (1992). A mnemonic for remembering long strings of digits. *Bulletin of the Psychonomic Society, 30*(4), 271–274.

Belsky, J. (1996). Parent, infant, and social-contextual antecedents of father-son attachment security. *Developmental Psychology, 32*(5), 905–913.

Bem, S. L. (1974). The measurement of psychological androgyny. *Journal of Consulting & Clinical Psychology, 42*(2), 155–162.

Bem, S. L. (1975). Androgyny vs. the tight little lives of fluffy women and chesty men. *Psychology Today, 31,* 58–62.

Bem, S. L. (1981). Gender schema theory. A cognitive account of sex typing. *Psychological Review, 88,* 354–364.

Ben Abdallah, N. M.-B., Slomianka, L., Vyssotski, A. L., et al. (2010). Early age-related changes in adult hippocampal neurogenesis in C57 mice. *Neurobiology of Aging, 31*(1), 151–161.

Benbow, C. P. (1986). Physiological correlates of extreme intellectual precocity. *Neuropsychologia, 24*(5), 719–725.

Benedetti, F. (2009). *Placebo effects: Understanding the mechanisms in health and disease.* New York: Oxford University Press.

Benjafield, J. G. (2010). *A history of psychology* (4th ed.). New York: Oxford University Press.

Benjafield, J. G., Smilek, D., & Kingstone, A. (2010). *Cognition* (4th ed.). New York: Oxford University Press.

Benjamin, Jr., L. T. (2009). *A history of psychology.* London: Blackwell.

Benjamin, O., & Tlusten, D. (2010). Intimacy and/or degradation: Heterosexual images of togetherness and women's embracement of pornography. *Sexualities, 13*(5), 599–623.

Benloucif, S., Bennett, E. L., & Rosenzweig, M. R. (1995). Norepinephrine and neural plasticity: The effects of xylamine on experience-induced changes in brain weight, memory, and behavior. *Neurobiology of Learning & Memory, 63*(1), 33–42.

Bensafi, M., Zelano, C., Johnson, B., et al. (2004).Olfaction: From sniff to percept. In M. S. Gazzaniga (Ed.), *The cognitive neurosciences* (3rd ed., pp. 259–280). Cambridge, MA: MIT Press.

Ben-Shakhar, G., & Dolev, K. (1996). Psychophysiological detection through the guilty knowledge technique: Effect of mental countermeasures. *Journal of Applied Psychology, 81*(3), 273–281.

Bensley, L., & Van Eenwyk, J. (2001). Video games and real-life aggression. *Journal of Adolescent Health, 29*(4), 244–257.

Benson, H. (1977). Systematic hypertension and the relaxation response. *New England Journal of Medicine, 296,* 1152–1156.

Benson, J., Greaves, W., O'Donnell, M., et al. (2002). Evidence for symbolic language processing in a Bonobo (Pan paniscus). *Journal of Consciousness Studies, 9*(12), 33–56.

Bergeron, S., & Lord, M. J. (2003). The integration of pelvi-perineal reeducation and cognitive-behavioral therapy in the multidisciplinary treatment of the sexual pain disorders. *Sexual & Relationship Therapy, 18,* 135–141.

Bergin, A. E. (1991). Values and religious issues in psychotherapy and mental health. *American Psychologist, 46*(4), 394–403.

Berman, S. L., Weems, C. F., & Stickle, T. R. (2006). Existential anxiety in adolescents: Prevalence, structure, association with psychological symptoms and identity development. *Journal of Youth & Adolescence, 35*(3), 303–310.

Berne, E. (1964). *Games people play.* New York: Grove.

Bernstein H. J., Beale M. D., Burns C., et al. (1998). Patient attitudes about ECT after treatment. *Psychiatric Annals, 28*(9), 524–527.

Bernstein, D. M., & Loftus, E. F. (2009). How to tell if a particular memory is true or false. *Perspectives on Psychological Science, 4*(4), 370–374.

Bernstein, I. H., Rush, A. J., Yonkers, K., et al. (2008). Symptom features of postpartum depression: Are they distinct? *Depression & Anxiety, 25*(1), 20–26.

Bernthal, M. J. (2003). How viewing professional wrestling may affect children. *The Sport Journal, 6*(3). Retrieved January 19, 2011, from http://www.thesportjournal.org/article/effect-professional-wrestling-viewership-children.

Berntsen, D., & Thomsen, D. K. (2005). Personal memories for remote historical events: Accuracy and clarity of flashbulb memories related to World War II. *Journal of Experimental Psychology: General, 134*(2), 242–257.

Berry, D. S., & Miller, K. M. (2001). When boy meets girl: Attractiveness and the five-factor model in opposite-sex interactions. *Journal of Research in Personality, 35*(1), 62–77.

Berry, J. W., Phinney, J. S, Sam, D. L., et al. (2005). *Immigrant youth in cultural transition.* Mahwah, NJ: Erlbaum.

Berscheid, E. (2010). Love in the fourth dimension. *Annual Review of Psychology, 61,* 1–25.

Berscheid, E., & Regan, P. (2005). *The psychology of interpersonal relationships.* Englewood Cliffs, NJ: Prentice Hall.

Bersoff, D. M. (1999). Why good people sometimes do bad things: Motivated reasoning and unethical behavior. *Personality & Social Psychology Bulletin, 25*(1), 28–39.

Bertenthal, B. I., & Longo, M. R. (2007). Is there evidence of a mirror system from birth? *Developmental Science, 10*(5), 526–529.

Bertsch, G. J. (1976). Punishment of consummatory and instrumental behavior: A review. *Psychological Record, 26,* 13–31.

Beseler, C. L., Taylor, L. A., & Leeman, R. F. (2010). An item-response theory analysis of DSM-IV alcohol-use disorder criteria and "binge" drinking in undergraduates. *Journal of Studies on Alcohol & Drugs, 71*(3), 418–423.

Besnard, D., & Cacitti, L. (2005). Interface changes causing accidents: An empirical study of negative transfer. *International Journal of Human-Computer Studies, 62*(1), 105–125.

Best, D. (2002). Cross-cultural gender roles. In J. Worell (Ed.), *Encyclopedia of women and gender* (pp. 279–290). New York: Oxford.

Betancur, C., Velez, A., Cabanieu, G., et al. (1990). Association between left-handedness and allergy: A reappraisal. *Neuropsychologia, 28*(2), 223–227.

Beyer, M., Gerlach, F. M., Flies, U., et al. (2003). The development of quality circles/peer review groups as a tool for quality improvement in Europe: Results of a survey in 26 European countries. *Family Practice, 20,* 443–451.

Beyers, W., & Seiffge-Krenke I. (2010). Does identity precede intimacy? Testing Erikson's theory on romantic development in emerging adults of the 21st century. *Journal of Adolescent Research, 25*(3), 387–415.

Bhushan, B., & Khan, S. M. (2006). Laterality and accident proneness: A study of locomotive drivers. *Laterality: Asymmetries of Body, Brain & Cognition, 11*(5), 395–404.

Bialystok, E., & DePape, A.-M. (2009). Musical expertise, bilingualism, and executive functioning. *Journal of Experimental Psychology: Human Perception & Performance, 35*(2), 565–574.

Binder, J. L. (2004). *Key competencies in brief dynamic psychotherapy: Clinical practice beyond the manual.* New York: Guilford.

Binder, J., Zagefka, H., Brown, R., et al. (2009). Does contact reduce prejudice or does prejudice reduce contact? A longitudinal test of the contact hypothesis among majority and minority groups in three European countries. *Journal of Personality & Social Psychology, 96*(4), 843–856.

Binik, Y. M. (2005). Should dyspareunia be retained as a sexual dysfunction in

DSM-V? A painful classification decision. *Archives of Sexual Behavior, 34*(1), 11–21.

Binning, K. R., Sherman, D. K., Cohen, G. L., et al. (2010). Seeing the other side: Reducing political partisanship via self-affirmation in the 2008 presidential election. *Analyses of Social Issues & Public Policy*, (1), 276–292.

Birnbaum, M. H. (2004). Human research and data collection via the Internet. *Annual Review of Psychology, 55*, 803–832.

Biro, F. M., Galvez, M. P., Greenspan, L. C., et al. (2010). Pubertal assessment method and baseline characteristics in a mixed longitudinal study of girls. *Pediatrics, 126*(3), e583–e590.

Bisson, J. I., Ehlers, A., Matthews, R., et al. (2007). Psychological treatments for chronic post-traumatic stress disorder: Systematic review and meta-analysis. *British Journal of Psychiatry, 190*(2), 97–104.

Bjorklund, D. F. (2005). *Children's thinking* (4th ed.). Belmont, CA: Cengage Learning/Wadsworth.

Blackmore, S. (2001). What can the paranormal teach us about consciousness? *Skeptical Inquirer, 25*, 22–27.

Blackmore, S. (2004). *Consciousness: An introduction*. New York: Oxford University Press.

Blackwell, D. L., & Lichter, D. T. (2004). Homogamy among dating, cohabiting, and married couples. *Sociological Quarterly, 45*(4), 719–737.

Blair, I. V. (2001). Implicit stereotypes and prejudice. In G. B. Moscowitz (Ed.), *Cognitive social psychology* (pp. 359–374). Mahwah, NJ: Erlbaum.

Blair, K. S., Richell, R. A., Mitchell, D. G. V., et al. (2006). They know the words, but not the music: Affective and semantic priming in individuals with psychopathy. *Biological Psychology, 73*(2), 114–123.

Blakemore, C., & Cooper, G. (1970). Development of the brain depends on the visual environment. *Nature, 228*, 477–478.

Blanchard, D. C., & Blanchard, R. J. (2003). What can animal aggression research tell us about human aggression? *Hormones & Behavior, 44*(3), 171–177.

Blanchard, E. B., Kuhn, E., Rowell, D. L., et al. (2004). Studies of the vicarious traumatization of college students by the September llth attacks: Effects of proximity, exposure and connectedness. *Behaviour Research & Therapy, 42*(2), 191–205.

Blatner, A. (2006). Current trends in psychodrama. *International Journal of Psychotherapy, 10*(3), 43–53.

Bloch, M., Daly, R. C., Rubinow, D. R. (2003). Endocrine factors in the etiology of postpartum depression. *Comprehensive Psychiatry, 44*(3), 234–246.

Bloch, S. (2006). *Introduction to the psychotherapies* (4th ed.). New York: Oxford University Press.

Blood, A. J., & Zatorre, R. J. (2001). Intensely pleasurable responses to music correlate with activity in brain regions implicated in reward and emotion. *Proceedings of the National Academy of Sciences, 98*(20) 11818–11823.

Bloom, B. (1985). *Developing talent in young people*. New York: Ballantine.

Bloom, C. M., & Lamkin, D. M. (2006). The Olympian struggle to remember the cranial nerves: Mnemonics and student success. *Teaching of Psychology, 33*(2), 128–129.

Bloom, J. W. (1998). The ethical practice of WebCounseling. *British Journal of Guidance & Counselling, 26*(1), 53–59.

Blundon, J. A., & Zakharenko, S. S. (2008). Dissecting the components of long-term potentiation. *The Neuroscientist, 14*(6), 598–608.

Blunt, A., & Pychyl, T. A. (2005). Project systems of procrastinators: A personal project-analytic and action control perspective. *Personality & Individual Differences, 38*(8), 1771–1780.

Bobic, M. P. & Davis, W. E. (2003). A kind word for Theory X: or why so many newfangled management techniques quickly fail. *Journal of Public Administration Research & Theory, 13*, 239–264.

Bockting, W. O., & Coleman, E. (Eds.). (2003). *Masturbation as a means of achieving sexual health*. New York: Haworth Press.

Bockting, W. O., & Ehrbar, R. D. (2005). Commentary: Gender variance, dissonance, or identity disorder? *Journal of Psychology & Human Sexuality, 17*(3-4), 125–134.

Bodner, E. (2009). On the origins of ageism among older and younger adults. *International Psychogeriatrics, 21*(6), 1003–1014.

Boduroglu, A., Shah, P., & Nisbett, R. E. (2009). Cultural differences in allocation of attention in visual information processing. *Journal of Cross-Cultural Psychology, 40*(3), 349–360.

Boergers, J., Spirito, A., & Donaldson, D. (1998). Reasons for adolescent suicide attempts. *Journal of the American Academy of Child & Adolescent Psychiatry, 37*(12), 1287–1293.

Bogaert, A. F. (2004). Asexuality: Prevalence and associated factors in a national probability sample. *Journal of Sex Research, 41*, 279–287.

Bogaert, A. F. (2006). Toward a conceptual understanding of asexuality. *Review of General Psychology, 10*, 241–250.

Boggio, P. S., Campanhã, C., Valasek, C. A., et al. (2010). Modulation of decision-making in a gambling task in older adults with transcranial direct current stimulation. *European Journal of Neuroscience, 31*(3), 593–597.

Bohannon, J. N., & Stanowicz, L. B. (1988). The issue of negative evidence: Adult responses to children's language errors. *Developmental Psychology, 24*(5), 684–689.

Bohbot, V., & Corkin, S. (2007). Posterior parahippocampal place learning in H.M. *Hippocampus, 17*(9), 863–872.

Bohlin, G., & Hagekull, B. (2009). Socio-emotional development: From infancy to young adulthood. *Scandinavian Journal of Psychology, 50*(6), 592–601.

Bohner, G., & Dickel, N. (2010). Attitudes and attitude change. *Annual Review of Psychology, 62*, 391–417.

Boivin, D. B., Czeisler, C. A., & Waterhouse, J. W. (1997). Complex interaction of the sleep-wake cycle and circadian phase modulates mood in healthy subjects. *Archives of General Psychiatry, 54*(2), 145–152.

Boksa, P. (2009). On the neurobiology of hallucinations. *Journal of Psychiatry & Neuroscience, 34*(4), 260–262.

Bolbecker, A. R., Mehta, C. S., Edwards, C. R., et al. (2009). Eyeblink conditioning deficits indicate temporal processing abnormalities in schizophrenia. *Schizophrenia Research, 111*(1-3), 182–191.

Boldero, J. M., Moretti, M. M., Bell, R. C., et al. (2005). Self-discrepancies and negative affect: A primer on when to look for specificity and how to find it. *Australian Journal of Psychology, 57*(3), 139–147.

Bonanno, G. A., Papa, A., Lalande, K., et al. (2004). The importance of being flexible. *Psychological Science, 15*(7), 482–487.

Bond, R., & Smith, P. B. (1996). Culture and conformity: A meta-analysis of studies using Asch's (1952, 1956) line judgment task. *Psychological Bulletin, 119*(1), 111–137.

Bongard, S., al'Absi, M., & Lovallo, W. R. (1998). Interactive effects of trait hostility and anger expression on cardiovascular reactivity in young men. *International Journal of Psychophysiology, 28*(2), 181–191.

Bonham, V., Warshauer-Baker E., & Collins, F. S. (2005). Race and ethnicity in the genome era: The complexity of the constructs. *American Psychologist, 60*(1), 9–15.

Boniecki, K. A., & Britt, T. W. (2003). Prejudice and the peacekeeper. In T. W. Britt, & A. B Adler (Eds.), *The psychology of the peacekeeper: Lessons from the field* (pp. 53–70). Westport, CT: Praeger.

Bonk, W. J., & Healy, A. F. (2010). Learning and memory for sequences of pictures, words, and spatial locations: An exploration of serial position effects. *American Journal of Psychology, 123*(2), 137–168.

Bood, S., Sundequist, U., Kjellgren, A., et al. (2006). Eliciting the relaxation response with the help of flotation-REST (Restricted Environmental Stimulation Technique) in patients with stress-related ailments. *International Journal of Stress Management, 13*(2), 154–175.

Booker, J. M., & Hellekson, C. J. (1992). Prevalence of seasonal affective disorder in Alaska. *American Journal of Psychiatry, 149*(9), 1176–1182.

Bootzin, R. R., & Epstein, D. R. (2000). Stimulus control. In K. L. Lichstein, & C. M. Morin, *Treatment of late life insomnia* (pp. 167–184). Thousand Oaks, CA: Sage.

Bora, E., Fornito, A., Radua, J., et al. (2011). Neuroanatomical abnormalities in schizophrenia: A multimodal voxelwise meta-analysis and meta-regression analysis. *Schizophrenia Research, 127*(1), 46–57.

Bornstein, M. H., & Tamis-LeMonda C. S. (2001). Mother-infant interaction. In A. Fogel, & G. Bremmer (Eds.), *Blackwell handbook of infant development* (pp. 269–295). London: Blackwell.

Bornstein, R. F. (1996). Sex differences in dependent personality disorder prevalence rates. *Clinical Psychology: Science & Practice, 3*(1), 1–12.

Borod, J. C., Bloom, R. L., Brickman, A. M., et al. (2002). Emotional processing deficits in individuals with unilateral brain damage. *Applied Neuropsychology, 9*(1), 23–36.

Boroditsky, L. (2011). How language shapes thought. *Scientific American, February*, 62–65.

Boroditsky, L., & Gaby, A. (2010). Remembrances of times east: Absolute spatial representations of time in an Australian Aboriginal community. *Psychological Science, 21*(11), 1635–1639.

Borzekowski, D. L. G., Schenk, S., Wilson, J. L., et al. (2010). e-Ana and e-Mia: A content analysis of pro–eating disorder web sites. *American Journal of Public Health, 100*(8), 1526–1534.

Boskey, E. (2008). Is oral sex safe sex? Retrieved March 1, 2011, from http://std.about.com/od/riskfactorsforstds/a/oralsexsafesex.htm.

Botes, A. (2000). A comparison between the ethics of justice and the ethics of care. *Journal of Advanced Nursing, 32*(5), 1071–1075.

Botti, S., Orfali, K., & Iyengar, S. S. (2009). Tragic choices: Autonomy and emotional responses to medical decisions. *Journal of Consumer Research, 36*(3), 337–352.

Bouchard, Jr., T. J. (2004). Genetic influence on human psychological traits: A survey. *Current Directions in Psychological Science, 13*(4), 148–151.

Bouchard, Jr., T. J., Lykken, D. T., McGue, M., et al. (1990). Sources of human psychological differences: The Minnesota study of twins reared apart. *Science, 250*, 223–228.

Bouchard, Jr., T. J. (1983). Twins: Nature's twice-told tale. In *Yearbook of science and the future* (pp. 66–81). Chicago: Encyclopedia Britannica.

Bourgeois, J. A., Kahn, D., Philbrick, K. L., et al. (2009). *Casebook of psychosomatic medicine*. Washington, DC: American Psychiatric Publishing.

Bourne, E. J. (2010). *The anxiety & phobia workbook* (5th ed.). Oakland, CA: New Harbinger.

Bourne, V. J. (2008). Examining the relationship between degree of handedness and degree of cerebral lateralization for processing facial emotion. *Neuropsychology, 22*(3), 350–356.

Bowe, F. (2000). *Universal Design in education: Teaching nontraditional students*. Westport, CT: Bergin & Garvey.

Bower, G. H. (1981). Mood and memory. *American Psychologist, 36*, 129–148.

Bower, G. H., & Springston, F. (1970). Pauses as recoding points in letter series. *Journal of Experimental Psychology, 83*, 421–430.

Bowker, A. (2006). The relationship between sports participation and self-esteem during early adolescence. *Canadian Journal of Behavioural Science, 38*(3), 214–229.

Bowling, N. A. (2010). Effects of job satisfaction and conscientiousness on extra-role behaviors. *Journal of Business & Psychology, 25*(1), 119–130.

Boyle, M. P., Blood, G. W., & Blood, I. M. (2009). Effects of perceived causality on perceptions of persons who stutter. *Journal of Fluency Disorders, 34*(3), 201–218.

Boyle, S. H., Williams, R. B., Mark, D., et al. (2004). Hostility as a predictor of survival in patients with coronary artery disease. *Psychosomatic Medicine, 66*(5), 629–632.

Brach, T. (2003). *Radical acceptance*. New York: Bantam Books

Bradbury, T. N., & Karney, B. R. (2010). *Intimate relationships*. New York: Norton.

Bradley, R. T., McCraty, R., Atkinson, M., et al. (2010). Emotion self-regulation psychophysiological coherence, and test anxiety: Results from an experiment using electrophysiological measures. *Applied Psychophysiology & Biofeedback, 35*(4), 261–283.

Bradley, R., Greene, J., Russ, E., et al. (2005). A multidimensional meta-analysis of psychotherapy for PTSD. *American Journal of Psychiatry, 162*(2), 214–227.

Bradshaw, C., Kahn, A. S., & Saville, B. K. (2010). To hook up or date: Which gender benefits? *Sex Roles, 62*(9-10), 661–669.

Bradshaw, S. D. (2006). Shyness and difficult relationships: Formation is just the beginning. In D. C. Kirkpatrick, D. S. Duck, et al. (Eds.), *Relating difficulty: The processes of constructing and managing difficult interaction* (pp. 15–42). Mahwah, NJ: Erlbaum.

Brainerd, C. J. (2003). Jean Piaget, learning research, and American education. In B. J. Zimmerman, & D. H. Schunk (Eds.), *Educational psychology: A century of contributions* (pp. 251–287). Mahwah, NJ: Erlbaum.

Bramerson, A., Johansson, L., Ek, L., et al. (2004). Prevalence of olfactory dysfunction: The Skovde population-based study. *Laryngoscope, 114*(4), 733–737.

Brammer, R. (2012). *Diversity in counseling* (2nd ed.). Belmont, CA: Cengage Learning/Wadsworth.

Brand, S., Gerber, M., Beck, J., et al. (2010). High exercise levels are related to favorable sleep patterns and psychological functioning in adolescents: A comparison of athletes and controls. *Journal of Adolescent Health, 46*(2), 133–141.

Brannon, L. (2011). *Gender: Psychological perspectives*. Boston: Pearson/Allyn & Bacon.

Brannon, L., & Feist, J. (2010). *Health psychology: An introduction to behavior and health* (7th ed.). Belmont, CA: Cengage Learning/Wadsworth.

Bransford, J. D., & McCarrell, N. S. (1977). A sketch of cognitive approach to comprehension: Some thoughts about understanding what it means to comprehend. In P. N. Johnson-Laird & P. C. Wason (Eds.), *Thinking: Readings in cognitive science* (pp. 212–222). Cambridge, MA: Cambridge University Press.

Braun, K. A., Ellis, R., & Loftus, E. F. (2002). Make my memory: How advertising can change memories of the past. *Psychology & Marketing, 19*, 1–23.

Braun-LaTour, K. A., & LaTour, M. S. (2004). Assessing the long-term impact of a consistent advertising campaign on consumer memory. *Journal of Advertising, 33*(2), 49–61.

Breedlove, S. M., Cooke, B. M., & Jordan, C. L. (1999). The orthodox view of brain sexual differentiation. *Brain, Behavior & Evolution, 54*(1), 8–14.

Breedlove, S. M., Watson, N. V., & Rosenzweig, M. R. (2010). *Biological psychology: An introduction to behavioral and cognitive neuroscience* (6th ed.). Sunderland, MA: Sinauer Associates.

Brehm, S. S., Kassin, S. M., & Fein, S. (2005). *Social psychology* (6th ed.). Boston: Houghton Mifflin.

Brennan, F. X., Beck, K. D., & Servatius, R. J. (2003). Lever press escape/avoidance conditioning in rats: Safety signal length and avoidance performance. *Integrative Physiological & Behavioral Science, 38*(1), 36–44.

Brescoll, V. L., Dawson, E., & Uhlmann, E. L. (2010). Hard won and easily lost: The fragile status of leaders in gender-stereotype-incongruent occupations. *Psychological Science, 21*(11), 1640–1642.

Breslau, N., Johnson, E. O., Hiripi, E., et al. (2001). Nicotine dependence in the United States. *Archives of General Psychiatry, 58*(9), 810–816.

Bressan, P., & Pizzighello, S. (2008). The attentional cost of inattentional blindness. *Cognition, 106*(1), 370–383.

Bressi, C., Albonetti, S., & Razzoli, E. (1998). "Communication deviance" and schizophrenia. *New Trends in Experimental & Clinical Psychiatry, 14*(1), 33–39.

Bretherton, R., & Orner, R. J. (2004). Positive psychology and psychotherapy: An existential approach. In P. A. Linley, & S. Joseph (Eds.), *Positive psychology in practice* (pp. 420–430). New York: Wiley.

Brewer, J. S. (1981). Duration of intromission and female orgasm rates. *Medical Aspects of Human Sexuality, 15*(4), 70–71.

Brewer, N., & Wells, G. L. (2006). The confidence-accuracy relationship in eyewitness identification: Effects of lineup instructions, foil similarity, and target-absent base rates. *Journal of Experimental Psychology: Applied, 12*(1), 11–30.

Brewer, N., & Williams, K. D. (Eds.). (2005). *Psychology and law: An empirical perspective*. New York: Guilford.

Briand, L. A., Flagel, S. B., Seeman, P., et al. (2008). Cocaine self-administration produces a persistent increase in dopamine D2-super(High) receptors. *European Neuropsychopharmacology, 18*(8), 551–556.

Bridges, A. J., Wosnitzer, R., Scharrer, E., et al. (2010). Aggression and sexual behavior in best-selling pornography videos: A content analysis update. *Violence Against Women, 16*(10), 1065–1085.

Bridges, K. M. B. (1932). Emotional development in early infancy. *Child Development, 3*, 324–334.

Bridgett, D. J., Gartstein, M. A., Putnam, S. P., et al. (2009). Maternal and contextual influences and the effect of temperament development during infancy on parenting in toddlerhood. *Infant Behavior & Development, 32*(1), 103–116.

Brief, A. P., & Weiss, H. M. (2002). Organizational behavior. *Annual Review of Psychology, 53*, 279–307.

Bringing Up Baby. (1999). *Sierra*, Jan-Feb 17.

Brinton, R. D., & Wang, J. M. (2006). Therapeutic potential of neurogenesis for prevention and recovery from Alzheimer's disease: Allopregnanolone as a proof of concept neurogenic agent. *Current Alzheimer Research, 3*(3), 185–190.

Brock, T. C., & Green, M. C. (Eds.). (2005). *Persuasion: Psychological insights and perspectives* (2nd ed.). Thousand Oaks, CA: Sage.

Brodley, B. T. (2006). Nondirectivity in client-centered therapy. *Person-Centered & Experiential Psychotherapies, 5*(1), 36–52.

Brody, N. (1992). *Intelligence*. San Diego, CA: Academic Press.

Brondolo, E., ver Halen, N. B., L. D., et al. (2011). Racism as a psychosocial stressor. In R. J. Contrada, & A. Baum (Eds.), *The handbook of stress science: Biology, psychology, and health* (pp. 167–184). New York: Springer.

Brooks, M. (2008). The power of the placebo effect. *New Scientist*, Aug 20, 36–39.

Brooks, M. (2009). Rise of the robogeeks. *New Scientist, 2697*, 34–36.

Brooks-Gunn, J., & Warren, M. P. (1988). The psychological significance of secondary sexual characteristics in 9- to 11-year-old girls. *Child Development, 59*(4), 1061–1069.

Broom, A., & Cavenagh, J. (2010). Masculinity, moralities, and being cared for: An exploration of experiences of living and dying in a hospice. *Social Science & Medicine, 71*(5), 869–876.

Brothen, T., & Wambach, C. (2001). Effective student use of computerized quizzes. *Teaching of Psychology, 28*(4), 292–294.

Brotto, L. A., Basson, R., & Woo, J. S. T. (2009). Female sexual arousal disorders. In R. Balon, & R. T. Segraves (Eds.), *Clinical manual of sexual disorders* (pp. 185–211). Arlington, VA: American Psychiatric Publishing.

Brotto, L.A., Knudson, G., Inskip, J., et al. (2010). Asexuality: A mixed-methods approach. *Archives of Sexual Behavior, 39*(3), 599–618.

Brower, A. M. (2002). Are college students alcoholics? *Journal of American College Health, 50*(5), 253–255.

Brown, G. (2009). Claiming a corner at work: Measuring employee territoriality in their workspaces. *Journal of Environmental Psychology, 29*(1), 44–52.

Brown, G., & Devlin, A. S. (2003). Vandalism: Environmental and social factors. *Journal of College Student Development, 44*(4), 502–516.

Brown, M. J., Henriquez, E., & Groscup, J. (2008). The effects of eyeglasses and race on juror decisions involving a violent crime. *American Journal of Forensic Psychology, 26*(2), 25–43.

Brown, A. S. (2004). *The déjà vu experience*. New York: Psychology Press.

Brown, A. S., Cohen, P., Harkavy-Friedman J., et al. (2001). Prenatal rubella, premorbid abnormalities, and adult schizophrenia. *Biological Psychiatry, 49*(6), 473–486.

Brown, B. B., & Bentley, D. L. (1993). Residential burglars judge risk. *Journal of Environmental Psychology, 13*(1), 51–61.

Brown, J. D. (2010). High self-esteem buffers negative feedback: Once more with feeling. *Cognition & Emotion, 24*(8), 1389–1404.

Brown, J. D., Cai, H., Oakes, M. A., et al. (2009). Cultural similarities in self-esteem functioning: East is east and west is west, but sometimes the twain do meet. *Journal of Cross-Cultural Psychology, 40*(1), 140–157.

Brown, K. W & Ryan, R. M. (2003). The benefits of being present. *Journal of Personality & Social Psychology, 84*(4), 822–848.

Brown, L. M. (2005). *Girlfighting: Betrayal and rejection among girls*. New York: New York University Press.

Brown, P. (1990). The name game. *Journal of Mind and Behavior, 11*, 385–406.

Brown, R., & Kulik, J. (1977). Flashbulb memories. *Cognition, 5*, 73–99.

Brown, R., & McNeill, D. (1966). The "tip of the tongue" phenomenon. *Journal of Verbal Learning & Verbal Behavior, 5*, 325–337.

Brown, S. A. (2011). Standardized measures for substance use stigma. *Drug & Alcohol Dependence, 116*(1-3), 137–141.

Brown, S. A., Tapert, S. F., Granholm, E., et al. (2000). Neurocognitive functioning of adolescents: Effects of protracted alcohol use. *Alcoholism: Clinical & Experimental Research, 24*(2), 164–171.

Brown, S. D., Lent, R. W., Telander, K., et al. (2011). Social cognitive career theory, conscientiousness, and work performance: A meta-analytic path analysis. *Journal of Vocational Behavior, 79*(1), 1–302.

Brown, S. G., Roy, E., Rohr, L., et al. (2006). Using hand performance measures to predict handedness. *Laterality: Asymmetries of Body, Brain & Cognition, 11*(1), 1–14.

Brown, T. A., & Barlow, D. H. (2011). *Casebook in abnormal psychology* (4th. ed.). Belmont, CA: Cengage Learning/Wadsworth.

Brown, V., Tumeo, M., Larey, T. S., et al. (1998). Modeling cognitive interactions during group brainstorming. *Small Group Research, 29*(4), 495–526.

Browne, B. A. (1998). Gender stereotypes in advertising on children's television in the 1990s. *Journal of Advertising, 27*(1), 83–96.

Browne, N., & Keeley, S. (2010). *Asking the right questions* (9th ed.). Englewood Cliffs, NJ: Prentice Hall.

Brownell, P. (2010). *Gestalt therapy: A guide to contemporary practice.* New York: Springer.

Bruch, M. A. (2001). Shyness and social interaction. In R. Crozier, & L. Alden (Eds.), *International handbook of social anxiety* (pp. 195–215). Sussex, England: Wiley.

Brumbaugh, C. C., & Fraley, R. C. (2010). Adult attachment and dating strategies: How do insecure people attract mates? *Personal Relationships, 17*(4), 599–614.

Bruner, J. (1973). *Going beyond the information given.* New York: Norton.

Bruner, J. (1983). *Child's talk.* New York: Norton.

Brunet, P. M., Mondloch, C. J., & Schmidt, L. A. (2010). Shy children are less sensitive to some cues to facial recognition. *Child Psychiatry & Human Development, 41*(1), 1–14.

Bruno, F., & Muzzupappa, M. (2010). Product interface design: A participatory approach based on virtual reality. *International Journal of Human-Computer Studies, 68*(5), 254–269.

Bryan, C. S., & Babelay, A. M. (2009). Building character: A model for reflective practice. *Academic Medicine, 84*(9), 1283–1288.

Bryden, P. J., Bruyn, J., & Fletcher, P. (2005). Handedness and health: An examination of the association between different handedness classifications and health disorders. *Laterality: Asymmetries of Body, Brain & Cognition, 10*(5), 429–440.

Buchanan, M. (2008). Sin cities: The geometry of crime. *New Scientist, April 30*, 36–39.

Buck, J. A., & Warren, A. R. (2010). Expert testimony in recovered memory trials: Effects on mock jurors' opinions, deliberations and verdicts. *Applied Cognitive Psychology, 24*(4), 495–512.

Buckle, P. (2011). 'The perfect is the enemy of the good'—Ergonomics research and practice. *Ergonomics, 54*(1), 2011, 1–11.

Buckner, J. D., Ecker, A. H., & Cohen, A. S. (2010). Mental health problems and interest in marijuana treatment among marijuana-using college students. *Addictive Behaviors, 35*(9), 826–833.

Buckworth, J., Lee, R. E., Regan, G., et al. (2007). Decomposing intrinsic and extrinsic motivation for exercise: Application to stages of motivational readiness. *Psychology of Sport & Exercise, 8*(4), 441–461.

Buddie, A. M. (2004). Alternatives to twelvestep programs. *Journal of Forensic Psychology Practice, 4*(3), 61–70.

Budney, A. J., & Hughes, J. R. (2006). The cannabis withdrawal syndrome. *Current Opinion in Psychiatry, 19*(3), 233–238.

Buehner, M. J., & May, J. (2003). Rethinking temporal contiguity and the judgement of causality: Effects of prior knowledge, experience, and reinforcement procedure. *Quarterly Journal of Experimental Psychology A: Human Experimental Psychology, 56*(5), 865–890.

Buller, D. J. (2005). *Adapting minds: Evolutionary psychology and the persistent quest for human nature.* Cambridge, MA: MIT Press.

Bunde, J., & Suls, J. (2006). A quantitative analysis of the relationship between the cook-medley hostility scale and traditional coronary artery disease risk factors. *Health Psychology, 25*(4), 493–500.

Bundy, H., Stahl, D., & MacCabe, J. H. (2011). A systematic review and meta-analysis of the fertility of patients with schizophrenia and their unaffected relatives. *Acta Psychiatrica Scandinavica, 123*(2), 98–106.

Bunn, G. C. (2007). Spectacular science: The lie detector's ambivalent powers. *History of Psychology, 10*(2), 156–178.

Burchinal, M. R., Roberts, J. E., Riggins, R., et al. (2000). Relating quality of center-based child care to early cognitive and language development longitudinally. *Child Development, 71*(2), 339–357.

Burger, J. M. (2009). Replicating Milgram: Would people still obey today? *American Psychologist, 64*(1), 1–11.

Burger, J. M. (2011). *Personality* (8th ed.). Belmont, CA: Cengage Learning/Wadsworth.

Burger, J. M., & Lynn, A. L. (2005). Superstitious behavior among American and Japanese professional baseball players. *Basic & Applied Social Psychology, 27*(1), 71–76.

Burgess, C. A., & Kirsch, I. (1999). Expectancy information as a moderator of the effects of hypnosis on memory. *Contemporary Hypnosis, 16*(1), 22–31.

Burgess, M. C. R., & Weaver, G. E. (2003). Interest and attention in facial recognition. *Perceptual & Motor Skills, 96*(2), 467–480.

Burka, J. B., & Yuen, L. M. (2008). *Procrastination: Why you do it, what to do about it.* (2008). Cambridge, MA: Perseus.

Burke, D., Hickie, I., Breakspear, M., et al. (2007). Possibilities for the prevention and treatment of cognitive impairment and dementia. *British Journal of Psychiatry, 190*, 371–372.

Burlingame, G. M., & Davies, R. (2002). Self-help groups. In M. Hersen, & W. H. Sledge (Eds.), *Encyclopedia of psychotherapy* (pp. 601–605). San Diego: Academic Press.

Burlingame, G. M., Fuhriman, A., & Mosier, J. (2003). The differential effectiveness of group psychotherapy: A meta-analytic perspective. *Group Dynamics: Theory, Research, & Practice, 7*(1), 3–12.

Burnett, R. C., Medin, D. L., Ross, N. O., et al. (2005). Ideal is typical. *Canadian Journal of Experimental Psychology, 59*(1), 3–10.

Burns, G. W. (Ed). (2010). *Happiness, healing, enhancement: Your casebook collection for applying positive psychology in therapy.* New York: Wiley.

Burns, T. (2004). *Community mental health teams: A guide to current practices.* New York: Oxford University Press.

Burt, S. A., McGue, M., Carter, L. A., et al. (2007). The different origins of stability and change in antisocial personality disorder symptoms. *Psychological Medicine, 37*(1), 27–38.

Burton, C. M., & King, L. A. (2004). The health benefits of writing about intensely positive experiences. *Journal of Research in Personality, 38*(2), 150–163.

Burton, D. L. (2008). An exploratory evaluation of the contribution of personality and childhood sexual victimization to the development of sexually abusive behavior. *Sexual Abuse: Journal of Research & Treatment, 20*(1), 102–115.

Burtt, H. E. (1941). An experimental study of early childhood memory: Final report. *Journal of General Psychology, 58*, 435–439.

Bushnell, L. W., Sai, F., & Mullin, L. T. (1989). Neonatal recognition of the mother's face. *British Journal of Developmental Psychology, 7*(1), 3–15.

Bushnell, M. C., Villemure, C., & Duncan, G. H. (2004). Psychophysical and neurophysiological studies of pain modulation by attention. In D. D. Price & M. C. Bushnell (Eds.), *Psychological methods of pain control: Basic science and clinical perspectives* (pp. 99–116). Seattle, WA: IASP Press.

Buss, D. M. (2008). *Evolutionary psychology: The new science of the mind* (3rd ed.). Boston: Allyn & Bacon.

Buss, D. M. (2007). The evolution of human mating. *Acta Psychologica Sinica, 39*(3), 502–512.

Buss, D. M. (2008). *Evolutionary psychology: The new science of the mind* (3rd ed.). Boston: Allyn & Bacon.

Buss, D. M. (2011). *Evolutionary psychology: The new science of the mind* (4th ed.). Boston: Pearson.

Butcher, J. N. (2011). *A beginner's guide to the MMPI-2* (3rd ed.). Washington, DC: American Psychological Association.

Butcher, J. N., Mineka, S., & Hooley, J. (2010). *Abnormal psychology* (14th ed.). Boston: Allyn & Bacon.

Butler, A. C., Chapman, J. E., Forman, E. M., et al.. (2006). The empirical status of cognitive-behavioral therapy: A review of meta-analyses. *Clinical Psychology Review, 26*(1), 17–31.

Butler, B. (2007). The role of death qualification in capital trials involving juvenile defendants. *Journal of Applied Social Psychology, 37*(3), 549–560.

Butler, J. C. (2000). Personality and emotional correlates of right-wing authoritarianism. *Social Behavior & Personality, 28*(1), 1–14.

Butler, M. G. (2001). *Overcoming social anxiety and shyness: A self-help guide using cognitive behavioral techniques.* New York: New York University Press.

Butler, R. (1954). Curiosity in monkeys. *Scientific American, 190*(18), 70–75.

Buyer, L. S. (1988). Creative problem solving: A comparison of performance under different instructions. *Journal of Creative Behavior, 22*(1), 55–61.

Byrne, S. M., & McLean, N. J. (2002). The cognitive-behavioral model of bulimia nervosa: A direct evaluation. *International Journal of Eating Disorders, 31*, 17–31.

Byrnes, J. P., Miller, D. C., & Schafer, W. D. (1999). Gender differences in risk taking: A meta-analysis. *Psychological Bulletin, 125*(3), 367–383.

Cacioppo, J T., & William, P. (2008). *Loneliness: Human nature and the need for social connection.* New York: Norton.

Cadinu, M., Maass, A., Rosabianca, A., et al. (2005). Why do women underperform under stereotype threat? Evidence for the role of negative thinking. *Psychological Science, 16*(7), 572–578.

Caharel, S., Fiori, N., Bernard, C., et al. (2006). The effects of inversion and eye displacements of familiar and unknown faces on early and late-stage ERPs. *International Journal of Psychophysiology, 62*(1), 141–151.

Cahill, L. (2006). Why sex matters for neuroscience. *Nature Reviews Neuroscience, 7*(6), 477–484.

Cahn, B. R., & Polich, J. (2006). Meditation states and traits: EEG, ERP, and neuroimaging studies. *Psychological Bulletin, 132*(2), 180–211.

Calabrese, F., Molteni, R., Racagni, G., et al. (2009). Neuronal plasticity: A link between stress and mood disorders. *Psychoneuroendocrinology, 34*(Suppl 1), S208–S216.

Calabria, B., Degenhardt, L., Briegleb, C., et al. (2010). Systematic review of prospective studies investigating "remission" from amphetamine, cannabis, cocaine, or opioid dependence. *Addictive Behaviors, 35*(8), 741–749.

Calhoun, J. B. (1962). A "behavioral sink." In E. L. Bliss (Ed.), *Roots of behavior* (pp. 295–315). New York: Harper & Row.

Caliari, P. (2008). Enhancing forehand acquisition in table tennis: The role of mental practice. *Journal of Applied Sports Psychology, 20*(1), 88–96.

Callahan, C. M. (2006). Giftedness. In G. G. Bear & K. M. Minke (Eds.), *Children's needs III: Development, prevention, and intervention* (pp. 443–458). Washington, DC: National Association of School Psychologists.

Calvin, C. M., Fernandes, C., Smith, P., et al. (2010). Sex, intelligence, and educational achievement in a national cohort of over 175,000 11-year-old schoolchildren in England. *Intelligence, 38*(4), 424–432.

Calzada, E. J., Fernandez, Y., & Cortes, D. E. (2010). Incorporating the cultural value of respeto into a framework of Latino parenting. *Cultural Diversity & Ethnic Minority Psychology, 16*(1), 77–86.

Cambron, M. J., Acitelli, L. K., & Pettit, J. W. (2009). Explaining gender differences in depression: An interpersonal contingent self-esteem perspective. *Sex Roles, 61*(11-12), 751–761.

Cameron, J. A., & Trope, Y. (2004). Stereotype-biased search and processing of information about group members. *Social Cognition, 22*(6), 650–672.

Cameron, J., & Pierce, W. D. (2002). *Rewards and intrinsic motivation: Resolving the controversy*. Westport, CO: Bergin & Garvey.

Cammaroto, S., D'Aleo, G., Smorto, C., et al. (2008). Charles Bonnet syndrome. *Functional Neurology, 23*(3), 123–127.

Campbell, F. A., & Ramey, C. T. (1994). Effect of early intervention on intellectual and academic achievement. *Child Development, 65*, 684–698.

Campbell, L., Campbell, B., & Dickinson, D. (2003). *Teaching and learning through multiple intelligences* (3rd ed.). Boston: Allyn & Bacon.

Campion, M. A., & McClelland, C. L. (1993). Follow-up and extension of interdisciplinary costs and benefits of enlarged jobs. *Journal of Applied Psychology, 78*(3), 339–351.

Campion, M. A., Palmer, D. K., & Campion, J. E. (1998). Structuring employment interviews to improve reliability, validity and users' reactions. *Current Directions in Psychological Science, 7*(3), 77–82.

Canales, J. J. (2010). Comparative neuroscience of stimulant-induced memory dysfunction: Role for neurogenesis in the adult hippocampus. *Behavioural Pharmacology, 21*(5-6), 379–398.

Canivez, G. L., & Watkins, M. W. (1998). Long-term stability of the Wechsler Intelligence Scale for Children—Third Edition. *Psychological Assessment, 10*(3), 285–291.

Cannon, W. B. (1932). *The wisdom of the body*. New York: Norton.

Cannon, W. B. (1934). Hunger and thirst. In C. Murchinson (Ed.), *Handbook of general experimental psychology* (pp. 247–263). Worcester, MA: Clark University Press.

Cannon, W. B., & Washburn, A. L. (1912). An exploration of hunger. *American Journal of Physiology, 29*, 441–454.

Caplan, P. J. (1995). *They say you're crazy*. Reading, MA: Addison-Wesley.

Capron, C., & Duyme, M. (1992). Assessment of effects of socio-economic status on IQ in a full cross-fostering study. *Nature, 340*, 552–554.

Capuzzi, D. (2003). *Approaches to group counseling*. Englewood Cliffs, NJ: Prentice Hall.

Cardoso, S. H. (2000). Our ancient laughing brain. *Cerebrum, 2*(4), 15–30.

Carducci, B. J., & Fields, T. H. (2007). *The shyness workbook for teens*. Champaign, IL: Research Press.

Carey, J. C., Stanley, D. A., & Biggers, J. (1988). Peak alert time and rapport between residence hall roommates. *Journal of College Student Development, 29*(3), 239–243.

Carlbring, P., Gunnarsdóttir, M., Hedensjö, L., et al. (2007). Treatment of social phobia: Randomized trial of internet-delivered cognitive-behavioural therapy with telephone support. *British Journal of Psychiatry, 190*(2), 123–128.

Carlson, M., Marcus-Hewhall A., & Miller, N. (1990). Effects of situational aggression cues: A quantitative review. *Journal of Personality & Social Psychology, 58*(4), 622–633.

Carlson, N. R. (2010). *Physiology of behavior* (10th ed.). Boston: Allyn & Bacon.

Carnagey, N. L., & Anderson, C. A. (2004). Violent video game exposure and aggression: A literature review. *Minerva Psichiatrica, 45*(1), 1–18.

Carnagey, N. L., Anderson, C. A., & Bushman, B. J. (2007). The effect of video game violence on physiological desensitization to real-life violence. *Journal of Experimental Social Psychology, 43*(3), 489–496.

Carney, R. N., & Levin, J. R. (2001). Remembering the names of unfamiliar animals: Keywords as keys to their kingdom. *Applied Cognitive Psychology, 15*(2), 133–143.

Carney, R. N., & Levin, J. R. (2003). Promoting higher-order learning benefits by building lower-order mnemonic connections. *Applied Cognitive Psychology, 17*(5), 563–575.

Carr, P. B., & Steele, C. M. (2010). Stereotype threat affects financial decision making. *Psychological Science, 21*(10), 1411–1416.

Carrico, A. R., & Riemer, M. (2010). Motivating energy conservation in the workplace: An evaluation of the use of group-level feedback and peer education. *Journal of Environmental Psychology, 31*, 1–13.

Carroll, D. W. (2008). *Psychology of language* (5th ed.). Belmont, CA: Cengage Learning/Wadsworth.

Carroll, J. L. (2010). *Sexuality now: Embracing diversity* (3rd ed.). Belmont, CA: Cengage Learning/Wadsworth.

Carroll, J. M., & Russell, J. A. (1996). Do facial expressions signal specific emotions? Judging emotion from the face in context. *Journal of Personality & Social Psychology, 70*(2), 205–218.

Carroll, K. M., & Rounsaville, B. J. (2007). W(h)ither empirically supported therapies (ESTS)? Reply to commentaries. *Addiction, 102*(6), 867–869.

Carroll, R. T. (2010). *The skeptic's dictionary: Superstition*. Retrieved December 4, 2010 from http://www.skepdic.com/superstition.html.

Carskadon, M. A., Acebo, C., & Jenni, O. C. (2004). Regulation of adolescent sleep: Implications for behavior. *Annals of the New York Academy of Science, 1021*, 276–291.

Carter, D. A., Simkins, B. J., & Simpson, W. G. (2003). Corporate governance, board diversity, and firm value. *Financial Review, 38*, 33–53.

Cartwright, D. (2002). The narcissistic exoskeleton: The defensive organization of the rage-type murderer. *Bulletin of the Menninger Clinic, 66*(1), 1–18.

Cascio, W. F. & Aguinis, H. (2008). Industrial and organizational psychology 1963–2007: Changes, choices, and trends. *Journal of Applied Psychology, 93*, 1062–1081.

Casey, A. A., Elliott, M., Glanz, K., et al. (2008). Impact of the food environment and physical activity environment on behaviors and weight status in rural U.S. Communities. *Preventive Medicine, 47*(6), 600–604.

Casey, P. (2001). Multiple personality disorder. *Primary Care Psychiatry, 7*(1), 7–11.

Casey-Campbell, M., & Martens, M. L. (2009). Sticking it all together: A critical assessment of the group cohesion–performance literature. *International Journal of Management Reviews, 11*(2), 223–246.

Caspi, A. Sugden, K., Moffitt, T. E., et al. (2003). Influence of life stress on depression: Moderation by a polymorphism in the 5-HTT gene. *Science, 301*(5631), 386–389.

Caspi, A., Roberts, B. W., & Shiner, R. L. (2005). Personality development: Stability and change. *Annual Review of Psychology, 56*, 453–484.

Cassady, J. C. (2004). The influence of cognitive test anxiety across the learning-testing cycle. *Learning & Instruction, 14*(6), 569–592.

Casselle, G. (2009). What is it really like to have electroconvulsive therapy? *Journal of ECT, 25*(4), 289.

Castañeda, T. R., Tong, J., Datta, R., et al. (2010). Ghrelin in the regulation of body weight and metabolism. *Frontiers in Neuroendocrinology, 31*(1), 44–60.

Castellano, J. A., & Frazier, A. D. (Eds.). (2011). *Special populations in gifted education: Understanding our most able students from diverse backgrounds*. Waco, TX: Prufrock Press.

Castro, J. R., & Rice, K. G. (2003). Perfectionism and ethnicity: Implications for depressive symptoms and self-reported academic achievement. *Cultural Diversity & Ethnic Minority Psychology, 9*(1), 64–78.

Castro, J., Gila, A., Gual, P., et al. (2004). Perfectionism dimensions in children and adolescents with anorexia nervosa. *Journal of Adolescent Health, 35*(5), 392–398.

Castro-Schilo, L., & Kee, D. W. (2010). Gender differences in the relationship between emotional intelligence and right hemisphere lateralization for facial processing. *Brain & Cognition, 73*(1), 62–67.

Catalano, R., Novaco, R., & McConnell, W. (1997). A model of the net effect of job loss on violence. *Journal of Personality & Social Psychology, 72*(6), 1440–1447.

Cattell, R. B. (1965). *The scientific analysis of personality*. Baltimore: Penguin.

Cattell, R. B. (1973). Personality pinned down. *Psychology Today*, July, 40–46.

Cavaco, S., Anderson, S. W., Allen, J. S., et al. (2004). The scope of preserved procedural memory in amnesia. *Brain: A Journal of Neurology, 127*(8), 1853–1867.

Ceci, S. J. (1991). How much does schooling influence general intelligence and its cognitive components? *Developmental Psychology, 27*(5), 703–722.

Ceci, S. J., & Williams, W. M. (2010). *The mathematics of sex: How biology and society conspire to limit talented women and girls*. New York: Oxford University Press.

Cellard, C., Lefèbvre, A.-A., Maziade, M., et al. (2010). An examination of the relative contribution of saturation and selective attention to memory deficits in patients with recent-onset schizophrenia and their unaffected parents. *Journal of Abnormal Psychology, 119*(1), 60–70.

Centers for Disease Control. (2003). *Deaths, percent of total deaths, and death rates for 15 leading causes of death in 5-year age groups, by race and sex: United States, 2000*. Atlanta, GA: Author. Downloaded July 25, 2007 from http://www.cdc.gov/nchs/datawh/statab/unpubd/mortabs/lcwk1_10.htm.

Centers for Disease Control. (2007). *Sexual violence: Fact sheet*. Atlanta: Author. Retrieved March 23, 2010, from http://www.cdc.gov/ncipc/pub-res/images/SVFactsheet.pdf.

Centers for Disease Control. (2008). Prevalence of overweight, obesity and extreme obesity among adults: United States, trends 1976–1980 through 2005–2006. *NCHS Health & Stats, December*. Retrieved February 24, 2011 from http://www.cdc.gov/nchs/data/hestat/overweight/overweight_adult.pdf.

Centers for Disease Control. (2009a). *Understanding sexual violence: Fact sheet*. Atlanta: Author. Retrieved March 23, 2010, from http://www.cdc.gov/violenceprevention/pdf/SV_factsheet-a.pdf.

Centers for Disease Control. (2009b). *HIV/AIDS in the United States*. Atlanta: Author. Retrieved March 23, 2010, from http://www.cdc.gov/hiv/resources/Factsheets/PDF/us.pdf.

Centers for Disease Control. (2011a). *Adult cigarette smoking in the United States: Current estimate*. Atlanta: Author. Retrieved March 3, 2011 from http://www.cdc.gov/tobacco/data_statistics/fact_sheets/adult_data/cig_smoking/index.htm.

Centers for Disease Control. (2011b). *Understanding sexual violence: Fact sheet*. Atlanta: Author. Retrieved February 25, 2011, from http://www.cdc.gov/violenceprevention/pdf/SV_factsheet_2011-a.pdf.

Centofanti, A. T., & Reece, J. (2006). The cognitive interview and its effect on misleading postevent information. *Psychology, Crime & Law, 12*(6), 669–683.

Cervone, D., & Pervin, L. A. (2010). *Personality: Theory and research* (11th ed.). New York: Wiley.

Chabas, D., Taheri, S., Renier, C., et al. (2003). The genetics of narcolepsy. *Annual Review of Genomics & Human Genetics, 4*, 459–483.

Chaffee, J. (2010). *Thinking critically* (10th ed.). Belmont, CA: Cengage Learning/Wadsworth.

Chakos, M. H., Alvir, J. M. J., Woerner, M., et al. (1996). Incidence and correlates of tardive dyskinesia in first episode of schizophrenia. *Archives of General Psychiatry, 53*(4), 313–319.

Chalmers. D. J. (2010). *The character of consciousness*. New York: Oxford University Press.

Chambers, R. A., Taylor, J. R., & Potenza, M. N. (2003). Developmental neurocircuitry of motivation in adolescence: A critical period of addiction vulnerability. *American Journal of Psychiatry, 160*(6), 1041–1052.

Chamorro-Premuzic, T., & Furnham, A. (2003). Personality predicts academic performance. *Journal of Research in Personality, 37*(4), 319–338.

Chamorro-Premuzic, T., & Furnham, A. (2010). *The psychology of personnel selection*. New York: Cambridge University Press.

Chan, G. C.-K., Hinds, T. R., Impey, S., et al. (1998). Hippocampal neurotoxicity of Δ-9-tetrahydrocannabinol. *Journal of Neuroscience, 18*(14), 5322–5332.

Chance, P. (2009). *Learning and behavior* (6th ed.). Belmont, CA: Cengage Learning/Wadsworth.

Chandrashekar, J., Hoon, M. A., Ryba, N. J. P., et al. (2006). The receptors and cells for mammalian taste. *Nature, 444*(7117), 288–294.

Chang, J.-H. (2009). Chronic pain: Cultural sensitivity to pain. In S. Eshun, & R. A. R. Gurung (Eds.), *Culture and mental health: Sociocultural influences, theory, and practice* (pp. 71–89). New York: Wiley-Blackwell.

Chansler, P. A., Swamidass, P. M., & Cammann, C. (2003). Self-managing work teams: An empirical study of group cohesiveness in "natural work groups" at a Harley-Davidson Motor Company plant. *Small Group Research, 34*(1), 101–120.

Chao, R., & Tseng, V. (2002). Parenting of Asians. In M. H. Bornstein (Ed.), *Handbook of parenting* (Vol. 4): *Social conditions and applied parenting* (2nd ed., pp. 59–93). Mahwah, NJ: Erlbaum.

Chapanis, A., & Lindenbaum, L. E. (1959). A reaction time study of four control-display linkages. *Human Factors, 1*, 1–7.

Chapleau, K. M., & Oswald, D. L. (2010). Power, sex, and rape myth acceptance: Testing two models of rape proclivity. *Journal of Sex Research, 47*(1), 66–78.

Chapman, R. A. (Ed.). (2006). *The clinical use of hypnosis in cognitive behavior therapy: A practitioner's casebook*. New York: Springer Publishing.

Charmaraman, L., & Grossman, J. M. (2010). Importance of race and ethnicity: An exploration of Asian, Black, Latino, and multiracial adolescent identity. *Cultural Diversity & Ethnic Minority Psychology, 16*(2), 144–151.

Charsky, D. (2010). From edutainment to serious games: A change in the use of game characteristics. *Games & Culture, 5*(2), 177–198.

Chartrand, T. L., & Bargh, J. A. (1999). The chameleon effect: The perception-behavior link and social interaction. *Journal of Personality & Social Psychology, 76*(6), 893–910.

Chassin, L., Presson, C. C., Sherman, S. J., et al. (2003). Historical changes in cigarette smoking and smoking-related beliefs after two decades in a midwestern community. *Health Psychology, 22*(4), 347–353.

Chasteen, A. L., Bhattacharyya, S., Horhota, M., et al. (2005). How feelings of stereotype threat influence older adults' memory performance. *Experimental Aging Research, 31*(3), 235–260.

Chaves, J. F. (2000). Hypnosis. In A. Kazdin (Ed.), *Encyclopedia of psychology* (Vol. 4, pp. 211–216). Washington, DC: American Psychological Association.

Cheal, M. L., Cooper, S., Jacobsen, T., et al. (2009). APA membership: Past, present, and possible futures. Paper presented to the American Psychological Association annual meeting, August 6–9, Toronto, Ontario.

Check, J. V. P., & Malamuth, N. M. (1983). Sex role stereotyping and reactions to depictions of stranger versus acquaintance rape. *Journal of Personality & Social Psychology, 45*, 344–356.

Cheek, J., & Buss, A. H. (1979). *Scales of shyness, sociability and self-esteem and correlations among them*. Unpublished research, University of Texas. (Cited by Buss, 1980.)

Chein, J. M., & Fiez, J. A. (2010). Evaluating models of working memory through the effects of concurrent irrelevant information. *Journal of Experimental Psychology: General, 139*(1), 117–137.

Chen, Z., Mo, L., & Honomichl, R. (2004). Having the memory of an elephant. *Journal of Experimental Psychology: General, 133*(3), 415–433.

Cheng, H., Cao, Y., & Olson, L. (1996). Spinal cord repair in adult paraplegic rats: Partial restoration of hind limb function. *Science, 273*(5274), 510.

Chess, S., & Thomas, A. (1986). *Know your child*. New York: Basic.

Chessick, R. D. (2010). Returning to Freud. *Journal of the American Academy of Psychoanalysis & Dynamic Psychiatry, 38*(3), 413–440.

Chester, A., & Glass, C. A. (2006). Online counselling: A descriptive analysis of therapy services on the internet. *British Journal of Guidance & Counselling, 34*(2), 145–160.

Cheyne, J. A. (2005). Sleep paralysis episode frequency and number, types, and structure of associated hallucinations. *Journal of Sleep Research, 14*(3), 319–324.

Cheyne, J. A., & Girard, T. A. (2009). The body unbound: Vestibular-motor hallucinations and out-of-body experiences. *Cortex, 45*(2), 201–215.

Cheyne, J. A., Rueffer, S. D., & Newby-Clark I. R. (1999). Hypnagogic and hypnopompic hallucinations during sleep paralysis: Neurological and cultural construction of the nightmare. *Consciousness & Cognition, 8*, 319–337.

Chipman, M., & Jin, Y. L. (2009). Drowsy drivers: The effect of light and circadian rhythm on crash occurrence. *Safety Science, 47*(10), 1364–1370.

Chisolm, T. H., Willott, J. F., & Lister, J. J. (2003). The aging auditory system: Anatomic and physiologic changes and implications for rehabilitation. *International Journal of Audiology, 42*(Suppl. 2), 2S3–2S10.

Choi, H., & Dancy, B. L. (2009). Korean American adolescents' and their parents' perceptions of acculturative stress. *Journal of Child & Adolescent Psychiatric Nursing, 22*(4), 203–210.

Chomsky, N. (1975). *Reflections on language*. New York: Pantheon.

Chomsky, N. (1986). *Knowledge of language*. New York: Praeger.

Christakis, N. A., & Fowler, J. H. (2007). The spread of obesity in a large social network over 32 years. *New England Journal of Medicine, 357*(4), 370–379.

Christakis, N. A., & Fowler, J. H. (2008). The collective dynamics of smoking in a large social network. *New England Journal of Medicine, 358*(21), 2249–2258.

Christakis, N. A., & Fowler, J. H. (2009). *Connected: The surprising power of our social networks and how they shape our lives*. New York: Little, Brown.

Christensen, A., & Jacobson, N. S. (1994). Who (or what) can do psychotherapy. *Psychological Science, 5*(1), 8–14.

Christian, M. S., Edwards, B. D., & Bradley, J. C. (2010). Situational judgment tests: Constructs assessed and a meta-analysis of their criterion-related validities. *Personnel Psychology, 63*(1), 83–117.

Christian, K. M., & Thompson, R. F. (2005). Long-term storage of an associative memory trace in the cerebellum. *Behavioral Neuroscience, 119*(2), 526–537.

Christophersen, E. R., & Mortweet, S. L. (2003). *Parenting that works: Building skills that last a lifetime*. Washington: American Psychological Association.

Chua, H. F., Boland, J. E., & Nisbett, R. E. (2005). Cultural variation in eye movements during scene perception. *Proceedings of the National Academy of Sciences, 102*(35), 12629–12633.

Chua, P., & Fujino, D. C. (1999). Negotiating new Asian-American masculinities: Attitudes and gender expectations. *Journal of Men's Studies, 7*(3), 391–413.

Cialdini, R. B. (2008). *Influence: Science and practice* (5th ed.). Boston: Allyn & Bacon.

Cialdini, R. B., & Goldstein, N. J. (2004). Social influence: Compliance and conformity. *Annual Review of Psychology, 55*, 591–621.

Cialdini, R. B., & Griskevicius, V. (2010). Social influence. In R. F. Baumeister, & E. J. Finkel (Eds.), *Advanced social psychology: The state of the science* (pp. 385–417). New York: Oxford University Press.

Cialdini, R. B., Reno, R. R., & Kallgren, C. A. (1990). A focus theory of normative conduct: Recycling the concept of norms to reduce littering in public places. *Journal of Personality & Social Psychology, 58*(6), 1015–1026.

Ciarrochi, J., Dean, F. P., & Anderson, S. (2002). Emotional intelligence moderates the relationship between stress and mental health. *Personality & Individual Differences, 32*(2), 197–209.

Cinciripini, P. M., Wetter, D. W., & McClure, J. B. (1997). Scheduled reduced smoking. *Addictive Behaviors, 22*(6), 759–767.

Cisler, J. M., & Koster, E. H. W. (2010). Mechanisms of attentional biases towards threat in anxiety disorders: An integrative review. *Clinical Psychology Review, 30*(2), 203–216.

Cisler, J. M., Olatunji, B. O., Feldner, M. T., et al.. (2010). Emotion regulation and the anxiety disorders: An integrative review. *Journal of Psychopathology & Behavioral Assessment, 32*(1), 68–82.

Claessens, M. (2009). Mindfulness and existential therapy. *Existential Analysis, 20*(1), 109–119.

Clapham, M. M. (2001). The effects of affect manipulation and information exposure on divergent thinking. *Creativity Research Journal, 13*(3-4), 335–350.

Clark, D., Boutros, N., & Mendez, M. (2005). *The brain and behavior* (2nd ed.). Cambridge, MA: Cambridge University Press.

Clark, R., Anderson, N. B., Clark, V. R., et al. (1999). Racism as a stressor for African Americans. *American Psychologist, 54*(10), 805–816.

Clayton, A. H., & Hamilton, D. V. (2009). Female orgasmic disorder. In R. Balon, & R. T. Segraves (Eds.), *Clinical manual of sexual disorders* (pp. 251–271). Arlington, VA: American Psychiatric Publishing.

Clayton, N. S., Russell, J., & Dickinson, A. (2009). Are animals stuck in time or are they chronesthetic creatures? *Topics in Cognitive Science, 1*(1), 59–71.

Clayton, N. S.,Yu, K. S., & Dickinson, A. (2001). Scrub jays (Aphelocoma coerulescens) form integrated memories of the multiple features of caching episodes. *Journal of Experimental Psychology: Animal Behavior Processes*, 27, 17–29.

Clearfield, M. W., & Nelson, N. M. (2006). Sex differences in mothers' speech and play behavior with 6-, 9-, and 14-month-old infants. *Sex Roles, 54*(1-2), 127–137.

Clements, A. M., Rimrodt, S. L., Abel, J. R., et al. (2006). Sex differences in cerebral laterality of language and visuospatial processing. *Brain & Language, 98*(2), 150–158.

Cline, V. B., Croft, R. G., & Courrier, S. (1972). Desensitization of children to television violence. *Journal of Personality & Social Psychology, 27,* 360–365.

Clore, G. L. (1976). Interpersonal attraction: An overview. In *Contemporary topics in social psychology* (pp. 176–183). Morristown, NJ: General Learning Press.

Cnattingius, S., Signorello, L. B., Ammerén, G., et al. (2000). Caffeine intake and the risk of first-trimester spontaneous abortion. *New England Journal of Medicine, 343*(25), 1839–845.

Cochran, G. M., & Harpending, H. (2009). *The 10,000 year explosion.* New York: Basic Books.

Cochran, S. D. (2001). Emerging issues in research on lesbians' and gay men's mental health. *American Psychologist, 56*(11), 931–947.

Cohen, G. L., Garcia, J., Purdie-Vaughns V., et al. (2009). Recursive processes in self-affirmation: Intervening to close the minority achievement gap. *Science, 324*(5925), 400–403.

Cohen, J. E. (1995). *How many people can the earth support?* New York: Norton.

Cohen, R. J., & Swerdlik, M. E. (2005). *Psychological testing and assessment* (6th ed.). New York: McGraw-Hill.

Cohen, S., Evans, G. W., Krantz, D. S., et al. (1981). Cardiovascular and behavioral effects of community noise. *American Scientist, 69,* 528–535.

Cohen, S., Tyrrell, D. A., & Smith, A. P. (1993). Negative life events, perceived stress, negative affect, and susceptibility to the common cold. *Journal of Personality & Social Psychology, 64*(1), 131–140.

Cohn, E., Bucolo, D., Pride, M., et al. (2009). Reducing white juror bias: The role of race salience and racial attitudes. *Journal of Applied Social Psychology, 39*(8), 1953–1973.

Cohn, M. A., Fredrickson, B. L., Brown, S. L., et al. (2009). Happiness unpacked: Positive emotions increase life satisfaction by building resilience. *Emotion, 9*(3), 361–368.

Colangelo, J. J. (2007). Recovered memory debate revisited: Practice implications for mental health counselors. *Journal of Mental Health Counseling, 29*(2), 93–120.

Coles, C. D., & Black, M. M. (2006). Introduction to the special issue. *Journal of Pediatric Psychology Special Issue, 31*(1), 1–4.

Colin, A. K., & Moore, K., & West, A. N. (1996). Creativity, oversensitivity, and rate of habituation. *EDRA: Environmental Design Research Association, 20*(4), 423–427.

Collins, A. M., & Quillian, M. R. (1969). Retrieval time from semantic memory. *Journal of Verbal Learning & Verbal Behavior, 8,* 240–247.

Collins, N. L., Cooper, M. L., Albino, A., et al. (2002). Psychosocial vulnerability from adolescence to adulthood: A prospective study of attachment style differences in relationship functioning and partner choice. *Journal of Personality, 70*(6), 965–1008.

Collins, W. A., & Gunnar, M. R. (1990). Social and personality development. *Annual Review of Psychology, 41,* 387–416.

Collop, N. A. (2005). Obstructive sleep apnea: treatment overview and controversies. In P. R. Carney, J. D. Geyer, & R. B. Berry (Eds.), *Clinical sleep disorders* (pp. 278–289). Philadelphia, PA: Lippincott Williams & Wilkins.

Colvin, M. K., & Gazzaniga, M. S. (2007). *Split-brain cases.* Malden, MA: Blackwell Publishing.

Comer, R. J. (2011). *Fundamentals of abnormal psychology* (6th ed.). New York: Worth.

Compton, W. C. (2005). *An introduction to positive psychology.* Belmont, CA: Cengage Learning/Wadsworth.

Confer, J. C., Easton, J. A., Fleischman, D. S., et al. (2010). Evolutionary psychology: Controversies, questions, prospects, and limitations. *American Psychologist, 65*(2), 110–126.

Conron, K. J., Mimiaga, M. J., & Landers, S. J. (2010). A population-based study of sexual orientation identity and gender differences in adult health. *American Journal of Public Health, 100*(10), 1953–1960.

Consumer Reports. (2010). *CRH survey: Antidepressants used by 78 percent of respondents with depression or anxiety.* Yonkers, NY: Author. Retrieved March 14, 2011 from http://pressroom.consumerreports.org/pressroom/2010/06/crh-survey-antidepressants-used-by-78-percent-of-respondents-with-depression-or-anxiety-.html.

Conway, A. R. A., Cowan, N., & Bunting, M. F. (2001). The cocktail party phenomenon revisited. *Psychonomic Bulletin & Review, 8*(2), 331–335.

Conway, M. A., Cohen, G., & Stanhope, N. (1992). Very long-term memory for knowledge acquired at school and university. *Applied Cognitive Psychology, 6*(6), 467–482.

Coolican, H., Cassidy, T., Dunn, O., et al. (2007). *Applied psychology* (2nd ed.). London: Hodder Education.

Coolidge, F. L., & Wynn, T. (2009). *The rise of Homo Sapiens: The evolution of modern thinking.* New York: Wiley-Blackwell.

Cooper, H. (2010). *Research synthesis and meta-analysis.* Thousand Oaks, CA: Sage.

Cooper, J. (2007). *Cognitive dissonance: Fifty years of a classic theory.* Thousand Oaks, CA: Sage.

Cooper, J., Bennett, E. A., & Sukel, H. L. (1996). Complex scientific testimony: How do jurors make decisions? *Law & Human Behavior, 20*(4), 379–394.

Cooper, M. J. (2005). Cognitive theory in anorexia nervosa and bulimia nervosa: Progress, development and future directions. *Clinical Psychology Review, 25*(4), 511–531.

Cooper, P. J., & Murray, L. (2001). The treatment and prevention of postpartum depression and associated disturbances in child development. *Archives of Women's Mental Health, 3*(Suppl. 2), 5.

Cooper, R. P., Abraham, J., Berman, S., et al. (1997). The development of infants' preference for motherese. *Infant Behavior & Development, 20*(4), 477–488.

Cooper, S. J. (2008). From Claude Bernard to Walter Cannon: Emergence of the concept of homeostasis. *Appetite, 51*(3), 419–427.

Coplan, R. J., & Weeks, M. (2010). Unsociability and the preference for solitude in childhood. In K. H, Rubin, & R. J. Coplan (Eds.), *The development of shyness and social withdrawal* (pp. 64–83). New York: Guilford.

Corballis, M. C. (2002). *From hand to mouth: The origins of language.* Princeton, NJ: Princeton University Press.

Corbin, W. R., & Fromme, K. (2002). Alcohol use and serial monogamy as risks for sexually transmitted diseases in young adults. *Health Psychology, 21*(3), 229–236.

Corcoran, R. (2010). The allusive cognitive deficit in paranoia: The case for mental time travel or cognitive self-projection. *Psychological Medicine, 40*(8), 1233–1237.

Coren, S. (1992). *The left-hander syndrome.* New York: Free Press.

Coren, S. (1996). *Sleep thieves.* New York: Free Press.

Coren, S., Ward, L. M., & Enns, J. T. (2004). *Sensation and perception* (6th ed.). New York: Wiley.

Corey, G. & Corey, M. S. (2010). *I never knew I had a choice: Explorations in personal growth* (9th ed.). Belmont, CA: Cengage Learning/Wadsworth.

Corey, G. (2012). *Theory and practice of group counseling* (8th ed.). Belmont, CA: Cengage Learning/Wadsworth.

Corkin, S. (2002). What's new with the amnesic patient H.M.? *Nature Reviews Neuroscience, 3,* 153–160.

Cormier, J. F., & Thelen, M. H. (1998). Professional skepticism of multiple personality disorder. *Professional Psychology: Research & Practice, 29*(2), 163–167.

Correa-Chávez, M., Rogoff, B., & Arauz, R. M. (2005). Cultural patterns in attending to two events at once. *Child Development, 76*(3), 664–678.

Corrigan, P. W., & Penn, D. L. (1999). Lessons from social psychology on discrediting psychiatric stigma. *American Psychologist, 54*(9), 765–776.

Corrigan, P. W., & Watson, A. C. (2005). Findings from the National Comorbidity Survey on the frequency of violent behavior in individuals with psychiatric disorders. *Psychiatry Research, 136*(2–3), 153–162.

Corrigan, P. W., Watson, A. C., Gracia, G., et al. (2005). Newspaper stories as measures of structural stigma. *Psychiatric Services, 56*(5), 551–556.

Corsini, R. J., & Wedding, D. (2011). *Current psychotherapies* (9th ed.). Belmont, CA: Cengage Learning/Wadsworth.

Costa, Jr., P. T., & McCrae, R. R. (2006). Trait and factor theories. In J. C. Thomas, D. L. Segal, et al. (Eds.), *Comprehensive handbook of personality & psychopathology* (Vol. 1): *Personality and everyday functioning* (pp. 96–114). New York: Wiley.

Côté, J. E. (2006a). Emerging adulthood as an institutionalized moratorium: Risks and benefi ts to identity formation. In J. J. Arnett & J. L. Tanner (Eds.), *Emerging adults in America: Coming of age in the 21st century* (pp. 85–116). Washington, DC: American Psychological Association.

Côté, J. E. (2006b). Identity studies: How close are we to developing a social science of identity? An appraisal of the field. *Identity: An International Journal of Theory & Research, 6,* 3–26.

Côté, J. E., & Levine, C. (2002). *Identity formation, agency, and culture.* Mahwah, NJ: Erlbaum.

Coursey, R. D., Ward-Alexander L., & Katz, B. (1990). Cost-effectiveness of providing insurance benefits for post-hospital psychiatric halfway house stays. *American Psychologist, 45*(10), 1118–1126.

Court, J. H., & Court, P. C. (2001). Repression: R. I. P. *Australian Journal of Clinical & Experimental Hypnosis, 29*(1), 8–16.

Cowan, D. E., & Bromley, D. G. (2008). *Cults and new religions: A brief history.* Malden, MA: Blackwell.

Cowan, N. (2005). *Working memory capacity.* Hove, UK: Psychology Press.

Cowden, C. R. (2005). Worry and its relationship to shyness. *North American Journal of Psychology, 7*(1), 59–69.

Cowles, J. T. (1937). Food tokens as incentives for learning by chimpanzees. *Comparative Psychology,* Monograph, *14*(5, Whole No. 71).

Cox, J. J., Reimann, F., Nicholas, A. K., et al. (2006). An SCN9A channelopathy causes congenital inability to experience pain. *Nature, 444,* 894–898.

Cox, R. H. (2011). *Sport psychology: Concepts and applications* (6th ed.). New York: McGraw-Hill.

Craig, L. (2006). Does father care mean fathers share?: A comparison of how mothers and fathers in intact families spend time with children. *Gender & Society, 20*(2), 259–281.

Craik, F. I. M. (1970). The fate of primary items in free recall. *Journal of Verbal Learning & Verbal Behavior, 9,* 143–148.

Craik, F. I. M., & Bialystock, E. (2005). Intelligence and executive control: Evidence from aging and bilingualism. *Cortex, 41*(2), 222–224.

Crandall, C. S., Preisler, J. J., Aussprung, J. (1992). Measuring life event stress in the lives of college students: The Undergraduate Stress Questionnaire (USQ). *Journal of Behavioral Medicine, 15*(6), 627–662.

Crane, L., Pring, L., Ryder, N., et al. (2010). Executive functions in savant artists with autism. *Research in Autism Spectrum Disorders, 5*(2), 790–797.

Craske, M. G., Rose, R. D., Lang, A., et al. (2009). Computer-assisted delivery of cognitive behavioral therapy for anxiety disorders in primary-care settings. *Depression & Anxiety, 26*(3), 235–242.

Crencavage, L. M., & Norcross, J. C. (1990). Where are the commonalities among the therapeutic common factors? *Professional Psychology: Research & Practice, 21*(5), 372–378.

Crews, F. T., & Boettiger, C. A. (2009). Impulsivity, frontal lobes and risk for addiction. *Pharmacology, Biochemistry & Behavior, 93*(3), 237–247.

Crisp, A., Gowers, S., Joughin, N., et al., (2006). The enduring nature of anorexia nervosa. *European Eating Disorders Review, 14*(3), 147–152.

Crocker, J., & Park, L. E. (2004). The costly pursuit of self-esteem. *Psychological Bulletin, 130*(3), 392–414.

Crooks, R., & Baur, K. (2011). *Our sexuality* (11th ed.). Belmont, CA: Cengage Learning/Wadsworth.

Cropley, A. (2006). In praise of convergent thinking. *Creativity Research Journal, 18*, 391–404.

Crosby, R. A., & Yarber, W. L. (2001). Perceived versus actual knowledge about correct condom use among U.S. adolescents: results from a national study. *Journal of Adolescent Health, 28*(5), 415–420.

Crowley, M., Tope, D., Chamberlain, L. J., et al. (2010). Neo-Taylorism at work: Occupational change in the post-Fordist Era. *Social Problems, 57*(3), 421–447.

Crown, C. L., Feldstein, S., Jasnow, M. D., et al. (2002). The cross-modal coordination of interpersonal timing. *Journal of Psycholinguistic Research, 31*(1), 1–23.

Crowther, J. H., Sanftner, J., Bonifazi, D. Z., et al. (2001). The role of daily hassles in binge eating. *International Journal of Eating Disorders, 29*, 449–454.

Csikszentmihalyi, M. (1997). *Creativity.* New York: HarperCollins.

Csikszentmihalyi, M., Abuhamdeh, S., Nakamura, J (2005). Flow. In A. J. Elliot, & C. S. Dweck, (Eds.), *Handbook of competence and motivation* (pp. 598–608). New York: Guilford.

Cull, W. L., Shaughnessy, J. J., & Zechmeister, E. B. (1996). Expanding understanding of the expanding-pattern-of-retrieval mnemonic. *Journal of Experimental Psychology: Applied, 2*(4) 365–378.

Culver, R., & Ianna, P. (1988). *Astrology: True or false?* Buffalo, NY: Prometheus Books.

Cummings, M. R. (2011) *Human heredity: Principles and issues* (9th ed.). Belmont CA: Cengage Learning/Wadsworth.

Cummins, D. D. (1995). *The other side of psychology.* New York: St. Martins.

Curci, A., & Luminet, O. (2006). Follow-up of a crossnational comparison on flashbulb and event memory for the September 11th attacks. *Memory, 14*(3), 329–344.

Curtis, D., Vine, A. E., McQuillin, A., et al. (2011). Case–case genome-wide association analysis shows markers differentially associated with schizophrenia and bipolar disorder and implicates calcium channel genes. *Psychiatric Genetics, 21*(1), 1–4.

Cytowic, R. E., & Eagleman, D. M. (2009). *Wednesday is indigo blue: Discovering the brain of synesthesia.* Cambridge, MA: MIT Press.

Czeisler, C. A., Duffy, J. F., Shanahan, T. L., et al. (1999). Stability, precision, and near-24-hour period of the human circadian pacemaker. *Science, 284*(5423), 2177–2181.

Czeisler, C. A., Richardson, G. S., Zimmerman, J. C., et al. (1981). Entrainment of human circadian rhythms by light-dark cycles: A reassessment. *Photochemistry, Photobiology, 34*, 239–247.

Dai, D. Y. (2010). *The nature and nurture of giftedness: A new framework for understanding gifted education.* New York: Teachers College Press.

Dalton, A. N., Chartrand, T. L., & Finkel, E. J. (2010). The schema-driven chameleon: How mimicry affects executive and self-regulatory resources. *Journal of Personality & Social Psychology, 98*(4), 605–617.

Damisch, L., Stoberock, B., & Mussweiler, T. (2010). Keep your fingers crossed! How superstition improves performance. *Psychological Science, 21*(7), 1014–1020.

Danaei, G., Ding, E. L., Mozaffarian, D., et al. (2009). The preventable causes of death in the United States: Comparative risk assessment of dietary, lifestyle, and metabolic risk factors. *PLoS Med, 6*(4), e1000058. doi:10.1371/journal.pmed.1000058.

Dane, S., & Erzurumluoglu, A. (2003). Sex and handedness differences in eye-hand visual reaction times in handball players. *International Journal of Neuroscience, 113*(7), 923–929.

Dang-Vu, T. T., McKinney, S. M., Buxton, O. M., et al. (2010). Spontaneous brain rhythms predict sleep stability in the face of noise. *Current Biology, 20*(15), R626–R627, 10 August 2010 DOI: 10.1016/j.cub.2010.06.032.

Daniels, H. (2005). Vygotsky and educational psychology: Some preliminary remarks. *Educational & Child Psychology, 22*(1), 6–17.

Danziger, N., Prkachin, K. M., & Willer, J.-C. (2006). Is pain the price of empathy? The perception of others' pain in patients with congenital insensitivity to pain. *Brain: A Journal of Neurology, 129*(9), 2494–2507.

Darley, J. M. (2000). Bystander phenomenon. In A. E. Kazdin (Ed.), *Encyclopedia of psychology* (Vol. 1, pp. 493–495). Washington, DC: American Psychological Association.

Darley, J. M., & Latané, B. (1968). Bystander intervention in emergencies: Diffusion of responsibility. *Journal of Personality & Social Psychology, 8*, 377–383.

Darling, C. A., Davidson, J. K., & Passarello, L. C. (1992). The mystique of first intercourse among college youth: The role of partners, contraceptive practices, and psychological reactions. *Journal of Youth & Adolescence, 21*(1), 97–117.

Darou, W. S. (1992). Native Canadians and intelligence testing. *Canadian Journal of Counselling, 26*(2), 96–99.

Daruna, J. H. (2004). *Introduction to psychoneuroimmunology.* Amsterdam: Elsevier.

Darwin, C. (1872). *The expression of emotion in man and animals.* Chicago: University of Chicago Press.

Das, A. (2007). Masturbation in the United States. *Journal of Sex & Marital Therapy, 33*, 301–317.

Das, J. P. (2000). Mental retardation. In A. Kazdin (Ed.), *Encyclopedia of psychology* (Vol. 5, pp. 193–197). Washington, DC: American Psychological Association.

Davey, G. (2008). *Clinical psychology: Topics in applied psychology.* New York: Oxford University Press.

David-Ferdon, C., & Hertz, M. F. (2009). *Electronic media and youth violence: a CDC issue brief for researchers.* Atlanta: Centers for Disease Control. Retrieved March 28, 2011 from http://www.cdc.gov/violenceprevention/pdf/Electronic_Aggression_Researcher_Brief-a.pdf.

Davidovitch, N., & Milgram, R. M. (2006). Creative thinking as a predictor of teacher effectiveness in higher education. *Creativity Research Journal, 18*, 385–390.

Davidson, J. E. (2003). Insights about insightful problem solving. In J. E. Davidson & R. J. Sternberg (Eds.), *The psychology of problem solving* (pp. 149–175). New York: Cambridge University Press.

Davidson, P. R., & Parker, K. C. H. (2001). Eye movement desensitization and reprocessing (EMDR): A meta-analysis. *Journal of Consulting & Clinical Psychology, 69*(2), 305–316.

Davidson, R. J., Kabat-Zinn J., Schumacher, J., et al. (2003). Alternations in brain and immune function produced by mindfulness meditation. *Psychosomatic Medicine, 65*(4), 564–570.

Davidson, T. L. (2000). Latent learning. In A. E. Kazdin (Ed.), *Encyclopedia of psychology* (Vol. 4, pp. 489–492). Washington, DC: American Psychological Association.

Davidson, W. B., & Bromfield, J. M., Beck, H. P. (2007). Beneficial academic orientations and self-actualization of college students. *Psychological Reports, 100*(2), 604–612.

Davies, J. E., Pröschel, C., Zhang, N., et al. (2008). Transplanted astrocytes derived from BMP- or CNTF-treated glial-restricted precursors have opposite effects on recovery and allodynia after spinal cord injury. *Journal of Biology, 7*, 24.

Davies, M., & McCartney, S. (2003). Effects of gender and sexuality on judgements of victim blame and rape myth acceptance in a depicted male rape. *Journal of Community & Applied Social Psychology, 13*(5), 391–398.

Davis, C., & Carter, J. C. (2009). Compulsive overeating as an addiction disorder: A review of theory and evidence. *Appetite, 53*(1), 1–8.

Davis, D., & Follette, W. C. (2002). Rethinking the probative value of evidence. *Law & Human Behavior, 26*(2), 133–158.

Davis, K. C., Morris, J., George, W. H., et al. (2006). Men's likelihood of sexual aggression: The influence of alcohol, sexual arousal, and violent pornography. *Aggressive Behavior, 32*(6), 581–589.

Davis, M. A. (2009). Understanding the relationship between mood and creativity: A meta-analysis. *Organizational Behavior & Human Decision Processes, 108*(1), 25–38.

Davis, M. J., & Bibace, R. (1999). Dating couples and their relationships: Intimacy and contraceptive use. *Adolescence, 34*(133), 1–7.

Davis, M. R., McMahon, M., & Greenwood, K. M. (2005). The efficacy of mnemonic components of the cognitive interview: Towards a shortened variant for time-critical investigations. *Applied Cognitive Psychology, 19*(1), 75–93.

Davison, G. C., & Neale, J. M. (2006). *Abnormal psychology* (10th ed.). San Francisco: Jossey-Bass.

Day, D. O., & Moseley, R. L. (2010). Munchausen by proxy syndrome. *Journal of Forensic Psychology Practice, 10*(1), 13–36.

Day, S., & Schneider, P. L. (2002). Psychotherapy using distance technology. *Journal of Counseling Psychology, 49*(4), 499–503.

Dazzi, C., & Pedrabissi, L. (2009). Graphology and personality: An empirical study on validity of handwriting analysis. *Psychological Reports, 105*, 1255–1268.

de Bono, E. (1992). *Serious creativity.* New York: HarperCollins.

de C. Hamilton, A. F. (2008). Emulation and mimicry for social interaction: A theoretical approach to imitation in autism. *Quarterly Journal of Experimental Psychology, 61*(1), 101–111.

de Jong, P. J., & Muris, P. (2002). Spider phobia. *Journal of Anxiety Disorders, 16*(1), 51–65.

de Leon, C. F. M. (2005). Social engagement and successful aging. *European Journal of Ageing, 2*(1), 64–66.

de Manzano, Ö., Cervenka, S., Karabanov, A., et al. (2010). Thinking outside a less intact box: Thalamic dopamine D2 receptor densities are negatively related to psychometric creativity in healthy individuals. *PLoS ONE, 5*(5): e10670. doi:10.1371/journal.pone.0010670.

de Rios, M. D., & Grob, C. S. (2005). Editors' introduction: Ayahuasca use in crosscultural perspective. *Journal of Psychoactive Drugs, 37*(2), 119–121.

Dean, Jr., D., & Kuhn, D. (2007). Direct instruction vs. discovery: The long view. *Science Education, 91*(3), 384–397.

Deardorff, J., Hayward, C., Wilson, K. A., et al. (2007). Puberty and gender interact to predict social anxiety symptoms in early adolescence. *Journal of Adolescent Health, 41*(1), 102–104.

DeArmond, S., Tye, M., Chen, P. Y., et al. (2006). Age and gender stereotypes: New challenges in a changing workplace and workforce. *Journal of Applied Social Psychology, 36*(9), 2184–2214.

Deary, I. J., Simonotto, E., Marshall, A., et al. (2001). The functional anatomy of inspection time. *Intelligence, 29*(6), 497–510.

Deckers, L. (2010). *Motivation: Biological, psychological, and environmental* (3rd ed.). Boston: Pearson/Allyn and Bacon.

Deckro, G. R., Ballinger, K. M., Hoyt, M., et al. (2002). The evaluation of a mind/body intervention to reduce psychological distress and perceived stress in college students. *Journal of American College Health, 50*(6), 281–287.

Deeb, S. S. (2004). Molecular genetics of color-vision deficiencies. *Visual Neuroscience, 21*(3), 191–196.

DeGaetano, G. (2005). The impact of media violence on developing minds and hearts. In S. Olfman (Ed.), *Childhood lost: How American culture is failing our kids* (pp. 89–106). Westport, CT: Praeger Publishers.

Dein, S., & Littlewood, R. (2005). Apocalyptic suicide: From a pathological to an eschatological interpretation. *International Journal of Social Psychiatry, 51*(3), 198–210.

Delgado, B. M., & Ford, L. (1998). Parental perceptions of child development among low-income Mexican American families. *Journal of Child & Family Studies, 7*(4), 469–481.

Dell, P. F. (2009). The long struggle to diagnose multiple personality disorder (MPD): MPD. In P. F. Dell, & J. A. O'Neil (Eds.), *Dissociation and the dissociative disorders: DSM-V and beyond* (pp. 667–692). New York: Routledge.

Della Sala, S. (Ed.). (2010). *Forgetting*. Hove, UK: Psychology Press.

Delpero, W. T., O'Neill, H., Casson, E. et al. (2005). Aviation-relevent epidemiology of color vision deficiency. *Aviation, Space, & Environmental Medicine, 76*(2), 127–133.

Demos, J. N. (2005). *Getting started with neurofeedback*. New York: Norton.

Denmark, F. L., Rabinowitz, V. C., & Sechzer, J. A. (2005). *Engendering psychology: Women and gender revisited* (2nd ed.). Boston: Allyn & Bacon.

Denney, J. T., Rogers, R. G., Krueger, P. M., et al. (2009). Adult suicide mortality in the United States: Marital status, family size, socioeconomic status, and differences by sex. *Social Science Quarterly, 90*(5), 1167–1185.

Denollet, J., & Van Heck, G. L. (2001). Psychological risk factors in heart disease. *Journal of Psychosomatic Research, 51*(3), 465–468.

DePaulo, B. M., Undsay, J. J., Malone, B. E., et al. (2003). Cues to deception. *Psychological Bulletin, 129*, 74–118.

DeSantis, A. D., & Hane, A. C. (2010). "Adderall is definitely not a drug": Justifications for the illegal use of ADHD stimulants. *Substance Use & Misuse, 45*(1-2), 31–46.

Deutsch, M. (1993). Educating for a peaceful world. *American Psychologist, 48*(5), 510–517.

Deutsch, M., & Collins, M.E. (1951). *Interracial housing*. Minneapolis, MA: University of Minnesota.

Deutschendorf, H. (2009). *The other kind of smart: Simple ways to boost your emotional intelligence for greater personal effectiveness and success*. New York: AMACOM.

Devine, D. J., Clayton, L. D., Dunford, B. B., et al. (2001). Jury decision making: Forty-five years of empirical research on deliberating groups. *Psychology, Public Policy, & Law, 7*(3), 622–727.

Devlin, B., Daniels, M., & Roeder, K. (1997). The heritability of IQ. *Nature, 388*(6641), 468–471.

Devoto, A., Lucidi, F., Violani, C., et al. (1999). Effects of different sleep reductions on daytime sleepiness. *Sleep, 22*(3), 336–343.

DeWall, C. N., & Anderson, C. A. (2011). The general aggression model. In P. R. Shaver & M. Mikulincer (Eds.), *Human aggression and violence: Causes, manifestations, and consequences* (pp. 15–33). Washington, DC: American Psychological Association.

Dewey J. (1910). *How we think*. Lexington, MA: D.C. Health.

DeYoung, C. G., Flanders, J. L., & Peterson, J. B. (2008). Cognitive abilities involved in insight problem solving: An individual differences model. *Creativity Research Journal, 20*(3), 278–290.

Di Forti, M., Lappin, J. M., & Murray, R. M. (2007). Risk factors for schizophrenia: All roads lead to dopamine. *European Neuropsychopharmacology, 17*(Suppl. 2), S101–S107.

Di Marzo, V., Goparaju, S. K., Wang, L., et al. (2001). Leptin-regulated endocannabinoids are involved in maintaining food intake. *Nature, 410*(6830), 822–825.

Diamond, L. M. (1998). Development of sexual orientation among adolescent and young adult women. *Developmental Psychology, 34*(5), 1085–1095.

Diamond, M. (2009). Human intersexuality: Difference or disorder? *Archives of Sexual Behavior, 38*(2), 172.

Diano, S., Farr, S. A., Benoit, S. C., et al. (2006). Ghrelin controls hippocampal spine synapse density and memory performance. *Nature Neuroscience, 9*, 381–388.

Dickens, W. T., & Flynn, J. R. (2001). Heritability estimates versus large environmental effects: The IQ paradox resolved. *Psychological Review, 108*, 346–369.

Dickerson, F. B., Tenhula, W. N., & Green-Paden L. D. (2005). The token economy for schizophrenia: Review of the literature and recommendations for future research. *Schizophrenia Research, 75*(2-3), 405–416.

Dickinson, D. K., & Tabors, P. O. (Eds.). (2001). *Beginning literacy with language*. Baltimore, MD: Paul H. Brookes.

Dick-Niederhauser, A. & Silverman, W. K. (2006). Separation anxiety disorder. In J. E. Fisher, & W. T. O'Donohue (Eds.), *Practitioner's guide to evidence-based psychotherapy* (pp. 627–633). New York: Springer.

Diener, E., & Chan, M. Y. (2011). Happy people live longer: Subjective well-being contributes to health and longevity. *Applied Psychology: Health & Well-Being, 3*(1), 1–43.

Dierdorff, E. C., & Wilson, M. A. (2003). A meta-analysis of job analysis reliability. *Journal of Applied Psychology, 88*(4), 635–646.

Dieterich, S. E., Assel, M. A., Swank, P., et al. (2006). The impact of early maternal verbal scaffolding and child language abilities on later decoding and reading comprehension skills. *Journal of School Psychology, 43*(6), 481–494.

Dietrich, A., & Stoll, O. (2010). Effortless attention, hypofrontality, and perfectionism. In B. Bruya (Ed.), *Effortless attention: A new perspective in the cognitive science of attention and action* (pp. 159–178). Cambridge, MA: MIT Press.

Dinan, T. G. (2001). Stress, depression and cardiovascular disease. *Stress & Health: Journal of the International Society for the Investigation of Stress, 17*(2), 65–66.

Dingus, T. A., Klauer, S. G., Neale, V. L., et al. (2006). The 100-car naturalistic driving study: Phase II. Results of the 100-car field experiment. *National Highway Traffic Safety Administration Report No. DOT HS 810 593*. Retrieved March 22, 2011, from http://ntl.bts.gov/lib/jpodocs/repts_te/14302_files/PDFs/14302.pdf.

Dinkmeyer, D., Sr., McKay, G. D., & Dinkmeyer, Jr., D. (1997). *The parent's handbook*. Circle Pines, MN: American Guidance Service.

Dion, K. L. (2003). Prejudice, racism, and discrimination. In T. Millon, & M. J. Lerner (Eds.), *Personality and social psychology. The comprehensive handbook of psychology* (Vol. 5, pp. 507–536). New York: Wiley.

Dirkzwager, A. J. E., Bramsen, I., & Van Der Ploeg, H. M. (2001). The longitudinal course of post-traumatic stress disorder symptoms among aging military veterans. *Journal of Nervous & Mental Disease, 189*(12), 846–853.

Distin, K. (2006). *Gifted children: A guide for parents and professionals*. London: Jessica Kingsley Publishers.

Dixon, M. J., Smilek, D., & Merikle, P. M. (2004). Not all synaesthetes are created equal: Projector versus associator synaesthetes. *Cognitive, Affective, & Behavioral Neuroscience, 4*(3), 335–343.

Dixon, S. V., Graber, J. A., & Brooks-Gunn J. (2008). The roles of respect for parental authority and parenting practices in parent-child conflict among African American, Latino, and European American families. *Journal of Family Psychology, 22*(1), 1–10.

D'Mello, S. K., Graesser, A., & King, B. (2010). Toward spoken human-computer tutorial dialogues. *Human-Computer Interaction, 25*(4), 289–323.

Dobelle, W. H. (2000). Artificial vision for the blind by connecting a television camera to the visual cortex. *American Society of Artificial Internal Organs, 46*, 3–9.

Dobson, K. S., Backs-Dermott G. J., & Dozois, D. J. A. (2000). Cognitive and cognitive-behavioral therapies. In C. R. Snyder, & R. E. Ingram (Eds.), *Handbook of psychological change: Psychotherapy processes and practices for the 21st century* (pp. 409–428). New York: Wiley.

Dodds, P. S., Muhamad, R., & Watts, D. J. (2003). An experimental study of search in global social networks. *Science, 301*(5634), 827–829.

Dodson, E. R., & Zee, P. C. (2010). Therapeutics for circadian rhythm sleep disorders. *Sleep Medicine Clinics, 5*(4), 701–715.

Doherty, M. J. (2009). *Theory of mind: How children understand others' thoughts and feelings*. New York: Psychology Press.

Doidge, N. (1997). Empirical evidence for the efficacy of psychoanalytic psychotherapies and psychoanalysis. *Psychoanalytic Inquiry, (Suppl.)*, 102–150.

Dollard, J., & Miller, N. E. (1950). *Personality and psychotherapy: An analysis in terms of learning, thinking and culture*. New York: McGraw-Hill.

Dombrowski, S. U., Sniehotta, F. F., Avenell, A., et al. (2007). Current issues and future directions in psychology and health: Towards a cumulative science of behaviour change: Do current conduct and reporting of behavioural interventions fall short of best practice? *Psychology & Health, 22*(8), 869–874.

Domhoff, G. W. (2001). A new neurocognitive theory of dreams. *Dreaming, 11*, 13–33.

Domhoff, G. W. (2003). *The scientific study of dreams: neural networks, cognitive development, and content analysis*. Washington, DC: American Psychological Association.

Domhoff, G. W., & Schneider, A. (2008). Similarities and differences in dream content at the crosscultural, gender, and individual levels. *Consciousness & Cognition, 17*(4), 1257–1265.

Domingo, R. A., & Goldstein-Alpern N. (1999). "What dis?" and other toddler-initiated expressive language-learning strategies. *Infant-Toddler Intervention, 9*(1), 39–60.

Domjan, M. (2010). *The principles of learning and behavior* (6th ed.). Belmont, CA: Cengage Learning/Wadsworth.

Donate-Bartfield, E., & Passman, R. H. (2004). Relations between children's attachments to their mothers and to security blankets. *Journal of Family Psychology, 18*(3), 453–458.

Donnerstein, E. (2001). Media violence. In J. Worell (Ed.), *Encyclopedia of gender and women* (pp. 709–716). San Diego: Academic Press.

Donnerstein, E. I., & Linz, D. G. (1986). The question of pornography. *Psychology Today*, Dec., 56–59.

Dooling, D. J., & Lachman, R. (1971). Effects of comprehension on retention of prose. *Journal of Experimental Psychology, 88*, 216–222.

Doran, S. M., Van Dongen, H. P., & Dinges, D. F. (2001). Sustained attention performance during sleep deprivation. *Archives of Italian Biology, 139*, 253–267.

Dorfman, J., Shames, J., & Kihlstrom, J. F. (1996). Intuition, incubation, and insight. In G. Underwood (Ed.), *Implicit cognition* (pp. 257–296). New York: Oxford University Press.

Dorman, M. F., & Wilson, B. S. (2004). The design and function of cochlear implants. *American Scientist, 92*(Sept/Oct), 436–445.

Dougall, A. L., & Baum, A. (2003). Stress, coping, and immune function. In M. Gallagher, & R. J. Nelson (Eds.), *Handbook of psychology* (Vol. 3): *Biological psychology* (pp. 441–455). New York: John Wiley.

Dougherty, D. D., Baer, L., Cosgrove, G. R., et al. (2002). Prospective long-term follow-up of 44 patients who received cingulotomy for treatment-refractory obsessive-compulsive disorder. *American Journal of Psychiatry, 159*(2), 269–275.

Dovidio, J. F., & Gaertner, S. L. (1999). Reducing prejudice: Combating intergroup biases. *Current Directions in Psychological Science, 8*(4), 101–105.

Dovidio, J. F., & Penner, L. A. (2001). Helping and altruism. In M. Hewstone, & M. Brewer (Eds.), *Handbook of social psychology* (pp. 162–195). London: Blackwell.

Dovidio, J. F., Allen, J. L., & Schroeder, D. A. (1990). Specificity of empathy-induced helping: Evidence for altruistic motivation. *Journal of Personality & Social Psychology, 59*(2), 249–260.

Dovidio, J. F., Gaertner, S. L., Kawakami, K., et al. (2002). Why can't we just get along? *Cultural Diversity & Ethnic Minority Psychology, 8*(2), 88–102.

Dovidio, J. F., Glick, P., & Rudman, L. A. (Eds.). (2005). *On the nature of prejudice: Fifty years after Allport*. Malden, MA: Blackwell.

Dovidio, J. F., Piliavin, J. A., Schroeder, D. A., et al. (2006). *The social psychology of prosocial behavior*. Mahwah, NJ: Erlbaum.

Dowling, K. W. (2005). The effect of lunar phases on domestic violence incident rates. *Forensic Examiner, 14*(4), 13–18.

Dozois, D. J. A., & Dobson, K. S. (2002). Depression. In M. M. Antony, & D. H. Barlow (Eds.), *Handbook of assessment and treatment planning for psychological disorders* (pp. 259–299). New York: Guilford.

Dozois, D. J. A., & Dobson, K. S. (Eds.). (2004). *The prevention of anxiety and depression: Theory, research, and practice*. Washington, DC: American Psychological Association..

Draguns, J. G., Gielen, U. P., & Fish, J. M. (2004). Approaches to culture, healing, and psychotherapy. In U. P. Gielen, J. M. Fish, & J. G. Draguns (Eds.), *Handbook of culture, therapy, and healing* (pp. 1–11). Mahwah, NJ: Erlbaum.

Drews, F. A., Yazdani, H., Godfrey, C. N., et al. (2009). Text messaging during simulated driving. *Human Factors, 51*(5), 762–770.

Drigotas, S. M., Rusbult, C. E., Wieselquist, J., et al. (1999). Close partner as sculptor of the ideal self: Behavioral affirmation and the Michelangelo phenomenon. *Journal of Personality & Social Psychology, 77*(2), 293–323.

Driver, J. L., & Gottman, J. M. (2004). Daily marital interactions and positive affect during marital conflict among newlywed couples. *Family Process, 43*(3), 301–314.

Drolet, G., Dumont, E. C., Gosselin, I., et al. (2001). Role of endogenous opioid system in the regulation of the stress response. *Progress in Neuro-Psychopharmacology & Biological Psychiatry, 25*(4), 729–741.

Drucker, P. (1993). *Post-capitalist society*. New York: HarperCollins.

Druckman, D., & Bjork, R. A. (1994). *Learning, remembering, believing: Enhancing human performance*. Washington, DC: National Academy Press.

Drummond, M., Douglas, J., & Olver, J. (2007). Anosmia after traumatic brain injury: A clinical update. *Brain Impairment, 8*(1), 31–40.

Dryden, W. (2011). *Understanding psychological health: The REBT perspective*. New York: Routledge/Taylor & Francis.

Drymalski, W. M., & Washburn, J. J. (2011). Sudden gains in the treatment of depression in a partial hospitalization program. *Journal of Consulting & Clinical Psychology, 79*(3), 364–368.

Duckitt, J., & Sibley, C. G. (2010). Personality, ideology, prejudice, and politics: A dual-process motivational model. *Journal of Personality, 78*(6), 1861–1893.

Duckworth, A. L., Peterson, C., Matthews, M. D., et al. (2007). Grit: Perseverance and passion for long-term goals. *Journal of Personality & Social Psychology, 92*(6), 1087–1101.

Duclos, S. E., & Laird, J. D. (2001). The deliberate control of emotional experience through control of expressions. *Cognition & Emotion, 15*, 27–56.

Duffy, J. F., & Wright, Jr., K. P. (2005). Entrainment of the human circadian system by light. *Journal of Biological Rhythms, 20*(4), 326–338.

Duffy, S., & Verges, M. (2009). It matters a hole lot: Perceptual affordances of waste containers influence recycling compliance. *Environment & Behavior, 41*(5), 741–749.

Dulewicz, V., & Higgs, M. (2000). Emotional intelligence. *Journal of Managerial Psychology, 15*(4), 341–372.

Duncan, J. (2005). Frontal lobe function and general intelligence: Why it matters. *Cortex, 41*(2), 215–217.

Duncker, K. (1945). On problem solving. *Psychological Monographs, 58*(270).

Dunlop, S. M., & Romer, D. (2010). Adolescent and young adult crash risk: Sensation seeking, substance use propensity and substance use behaviors. *Journal of Adolescent Health, 46*(1), 90–92.

Durán, L. K., Roseth, C. J., Hoffman, P. (2010). An experimental study comparing English-only and Transitional Bilingual Education on Spanish-speaking preschoolers' early literacy development. *Early Childhood Research Quarterly, 25* (2), 207–217.

Durand, V. M., & Barlow, D. H. (2010). *Essentials of abnormal psychology* (5th ed.). Belmont, CA: Cengage Learning/Wadsworth.

Durham, M. D., & Dane, F. C. (1999). Juror knowledge of eyewitness behavior. *Journal of Social Behavior & Personality, 14*(2), 299–308.

Durham, M. G. (2009). *The Lolita effect*. New York: Overlook Press.

Durrant, J. E., & Janson, S. (2005). Legal reform, corporal punishment and child abuse: The case of Sweden. *International Review of Victimology, 12*, 139–158.

Dutta, T., & Mandal, M. K. (2005). The relationship of handedness and accidents: A meta-analytical review of findings. *Psychological Studies, 50*(4), 309–316.

Dutton, D. G., & Aron, A. P. (1974). Some evidence for heightened sexual attraction under conditions of high anxiety. *Journal of Personality & Social Psychology, 30*, 510–517.

Dvash, J., Gilam, G., Ben-Ze'ev, A., et al. (2010). The envious brain: The neural basis of social comparison. *Human Brain Mapping, 31*(11), 1741–1750.

Dwyer, W. O., Leeming, F. C., Cobern, M. K., et al. (1993). Critical review of behavioral interventions to preserve the environment. *Environment & Behavior, 25*(3), 275–321.

Dyer, K. A. (2001). Dealing with death and dying in medical education and practice. *Journey of Hearts*. Retrieved April 18, 2011 from http://www.journeyofhearts.org/kirstimd/AMSA/outline.htm.

Dyukova, G. M., Glozman, Z. M., Titova, E. Y., et al. (2010). Speech disorders in right-hemisphere stroke. *Neuroscience & Behavioral Physiology, 40*(6), 593–602.

Dywan, J., & Bowers, K. S. (1983). The use of hypnosis to enhance recall. *Science, 222*, 184–185.

Dzokoto, V. A., & Adams, G. (2005). Understanding genital-shrinking epidemics in West Africa: Koro, juju, or mass psychogenic illness? *Culture, Medicine & Psychiatry, 29*(1), 53–78.

Eagly, A. H. (2000). Gender roles. In A. Kazdin (Ed.), *Encyclopedia of psychology* (Vol. 3, pp. 448–453). Washington, DC: American Psychological Association.

Eagly, A. H. (2001). Social role theory of sex differences and similarities. In J. Worell (Ed.), *Encyclopedia of women and gender* (pp. 39–50). San Diego: Academic Press.

Eagly, A. H. (2007). Female leadership advantage and disadvantage: Resolving the contradictions. *Psychology of Women Quarterly, 31*(1), 1–12.

Eagly, A. H. (2009). The his and hers of prosocial behavior: An examination of the social psychology of gender. *American Psychologist, 64*(8), 644–658.

Eagly, A. H., & Carli, L. L. (2007). *Through the labyrinth: The truth about how women become leaders*. Watertown, MA: HBS Press Book.

Eardley, A. F., & Pring, L. (2007). Spatial processing, mental imagery, and creativity in individuals with and without sight. *European Journal of Cognitive Psychology, 19*(1), 37–58.

Eaton, D. K., Kann, L., Kinchen, S., et al. (2010). Youth risk behavior surveillance: United States, 2009. *MMWR Surveillance Summary, 59* (SS-5), 1–40. Retrieved March 4, 2011 from http://www.cdc.gov/mmwr/pdf/ss/ss5905.pdf.

Ebben, M. R., & Spielman, A. J. (2009). Non-pharmacological treatments for insomnia. *Journal of Behavioral Medicine, 32*(3), 244–254.

Ebbinghaus, H. (1885). *Memory: A contribution to experimental psychology*. (H. A. Ruger, & C. E. Bussenius, Trans.) New York: New York Teacher's College, Columbia University.

Eckardt, M. H. (2005). Karen Horney: A portrait: The 120th anniversary, Karen Horney, September 16, 1885. *American Journal of Psychoanalysis, 65*(2), 95–101.

Eckerman, D. A. (1999). Scheduling reinforcement about once a day. *Behavioural Processes, 45*(1-3), 101–114.

Eddy, K. T., Dutra, L., Bradley, R., & Westen, D. (2004). A multidimensional meta-analysis of psychotherapy and pharmacotherapy for obsessive-compulsive disorder. *Clinical Psychology Review, 24*(8), 1011–1030.

Edenfield, T. M., & Blumenthal, J. A. (2011). Exercise and stress reduction. In R. J. Contrada, & A. Baum (Eds.), *The handbook of stress science: Biology, psychology, and health* (pp. 301–319). New York: Springer.

Eidelson, R. J., & Eidelson, J. I. (2003). Dangerous ideas. *American Psychologist, 58*(3), 182–192.

Eifert, G. H., & Lejuez, C. W. (2000). Aversion therapy. In A. E. Kazdin (Ed.), *Encyclopedia of psychology* (Vol. 1, pp. 348–350). Washington, DC: American Psychological Association.

Einarsen, S. & Hoel, H. (2008). Bullying and mistreatment at work: How managers may prevent and manage such problems. In A. Kinder, R. Hughes & C. L. Cooper (Eds.), *Employee well-being support: A workplace resource* (pp. 161–173).York: Wiley.

Eisenberg, N., Valiente, C., Fabes, R. A., et al. (2003). The relations of effortful control and ego control to children's resiliency and social functioning. *Developmental Psychology, 39*(4), 761–776.

Eisendrath, S., Chartier, M., & McLane, M. (2011). Adapting mindfulness-based cognitive therapy for treatment-resistant depression. *Cognitive & Behavioral Practice, 18*(3), 362–370.

Eisler, I., Simic, M., Russell, G. F. M., et al. (2007). A randomized controlled treatment trial of two forms of family therapy in adolescent anorexia nervosa: A five-year follow-up. *Journal of Child Psychology & Psychiatry, 48*(6), 552–560.

Ekman, P. (1993). Facial expression and emotion. *American Psychologist, 48*(4), 384–392.

Ekman, P. (2001). *Telling lies: Clues to deceit in the marketplace, politics, and marriage*. New York: Norton.

Ekman, P., Levenson, R. W., & Friesen, W. V. (1983). Autonomic nervous system activity distinguishes among emotions. *Science, 221*, 1208–1210.

Elder, P. (2006). *Critical thinking: Learn the tools the best thinkers use*. Englewood Cliffs, NJ: Prentice-Hall.

Eldridge, M., Saltzman, E., & Lahav, A. (2010). Seeing what you hear: Visual feedback improves pitch recognition. *European Journal of Cognitive Psychology, 22*(7), 1078–1091.

Eliot, L. (2009). *Pink brain, blue brain*. New York: Houghton Mifflin Harcourt.

Elli, K. A., & Nathan, P. J. (2001). The pharmacology of human working memory. *International Journal of Neuropsychopharmacology, 4*(3), 299–313.

Ellickson, P. L., Martino, S. C., & Collins, R. L. (2004). Marijuana use from adolescence to young adulthood. *Health Psychology, 23*(3), 299–307.

Elliott, M., & Williams, D. (2003). The client experience of counselling and psychotherapy. *Counselling Psychology Review, 18*(1), 34–38.

Elliott, M., Browne, K., & Kilcoyne, J. (1995). Child sexual abuse prevention: What offenders tell us. *Child Abuse & Neglect, 19*(5), 579–594.

Elliott, R., Sahakian, B. J., Matthews, K., et al. (1997). Effects of methylphenidate on spatial working memory and planning in healthy young adults. *Psychopharmacology, 131*, 196–206.

Ellis, A. (1979). The practice of rational-emotive therapy. In A. Ellis, & J. Whiteley (Eds.), *Theoretical and empirical foundations of rational-emotive therapy* (pp.1–6). Monterey, CA: Brooks/Cole.

Ellis, A. (1995). Changing rational-emotive therapy (RET) to rational emotive behavior therapy (REBT). *Journal of Rational-Emotive & Cognitive Behavior Therapy, 13*(2), 85–89.

Ellis, A., & Ellis, D. J. (2011). *Rational emotive behavior therapy*. Washington, DC: American Psychological Association.

Ellis, D. (2011). *Becoming a master student: Concise* (13th ed.). Belmont, CA: Cengage Learning/Wadsworth.

Ellis, P. J., West, B. J., Ryan, A. M., et al. (2002). The use of impression management tactics in structured interviews: A function of question type. *Journal of Applied Psychology, 87*, 1200–1208.

Ellison-Wright, I., & Bullmore, E. (2010). Anatomy of bipolar disorder and schizophrenia: A meta-analysis. *Schizophrenia Research, 117*(1), 1–12.

Elovainio, M., Kivimaeki, M., Steen, N., et al. (2000). Organizational and individual factors affecting mental health and job satisfaction. *Journal of Occupational Health Psychology, 5*(2) 269–277.

Emerson, E. (2009). Relative child poverty, income inequality, wealth, and health. *Journal of the American Medical Association, 301*(4), 425–426.

Emmorey, K., Grabowski, T., McCullough, S., et al. (2003). Neural systems underlying lexical retrieval for sign language. *Neuropsychologia, 41*(1), 85–95.

Engle, D. E., & Arkowitz, H. (2006). *Ambivalence in psychotherapy: Facilitating readiness to change*. New York: Guilford.

Engler, B. (2009). *Personality theories* (5th ed.). Belmont, CA: Cengage Learning/Wadsworth.

Enns, J. T., & Coren, S. (1995). The box alignment illusion. *Perception & Psychophysics, 57*(8), 1163–1174.

Enns, M. W., Cox, B. J., & Clara, I. P. (2005). Perfectionism and neuroticism: A longitudinal study of specific vulnerability and diathesis-stress models. *Cognitive Therapy & Research, 29*(4), 463–478.

Erickson, C. D., & Al-Timimi N. R. (2001). Providing mental health services to Arab Americans. *Cultural Diversity & Ethnic Minority Psychology, 7*(4), 308–327.

Ericsson, K. A. (2000). How experts attain and maintain superior performance. *Journal of Aging & Physical Activity, 8*(4), 366–372.

Ericsson, K. A., & Charness, N. (1994). Expert performance. *American Psychologist, 49*(8), 725–747.

Ericsson, K. A., & Chase, W. G. (1982). Exceptional memory. *American Scientist, 70*, 607–615.

Ericsson, K. A., Delaney, P. F., Weaver, G., et al. (2004). Uncovering the structure of a memorist's superior "basic" memory capacity. *Cognitive Psychology, 49*(3), 191–237.

Erikson, E. H. (1963). *Childhood and society*. New York: Norton.

Erlacher, D., & Schredl, M. (2004). Dreams reflecting waking sport activities: A comparison of sport and psychology students. *International Journal of Sport Psychology, 35*(4), 301–308.

Ernst, E. (1994). Is acupuncture effective for pain control? *Journal of Pain & Symptom Management, 9*(2), 72–74.

Eron, L. D. (1987). The development of aggressive behavior from the perspective of a developing behaviorism. *American Psychologist, 42*, 435–442.

Eschholz, S., Chiricos, T., & Gertz, M. (2003). Television and fear of crime: Program types, audience traits, and the mediating effect of perceived neighborhood racial composition. *Social Problems, 50*(3), 395–415.

Essien, E. J., Monjok, E., Chen, H., et al. (2010). Correlates of HIV knowledge and sexual risk behaviors among female military personnel. *AIDS & Behavior, 14*(6), 1401–1414.

Ethier, K. A., Kershaw, T., Niccolai, L., et al. (2003). Adolescent women underestimate their susceptibility to sexually transmitted infections. *Sexually Transmitted Infections, 79*, 408–411.

Evans, G. W. (2006). Child development and the physical environment. *Annual Review of Psychology, 57*, 423–451.

Evans, G. W., Ricciuti, H. N., Hope, S., et al. (2010). Crowding and cognitive development: The mediating role of maternal responsiveness among 36-month-old children. *Environment & Behavior, 42*(1), 135–148.

Evans, G. W., & Wener, R. E. (2007). Crowding and personal space invasion on the train: Please don't make me sit in the middle. *Journal of Environmental Psychology, 27*(1), 90–94.

Evans, G. W., Lercher, P. & Kofler, W. W. (2002). Crowding and children's mental health: the role of house type. *Journal of Environmental Psychology, 22*, 221–231.

Evans, G.W., Lepore, S. J., & Schroeder, A. (1996). The role of interior design elements in human responses to crowding. *Journal of Personality & Social Psychology, 70*(1), 41–46.

Evardone, M., Alexander, G. M., & Morey, L. C. (2007). Hormones and borderline personality features. *Personality & Individual Differences, 44*(1), 278–287.

Everly, G. S. (2002). Thoughts on peer (paraprofessional) support in the provision of mental health services. *International Journal of Emergency Mental Health, 4*(2), 89–92.

Ewen, R. B. (2009). *An introduction to theories of personality* (7th ed.). Hillsdale, NJ: Lawrence Erlbaum.

Eysenck, H. J. (1994). The outcome problem in psychotherapy: What have we learned? *Behaviour Research & Therapy, 32*(5), 477–495.

Eysenck, H. J. (Ed.). (1981). *A model for personality*. New York: Springer-Verlag.

Eysenck, M. W., Derakshan, N., Santos, R., et al. (2007). Anxiety and cognitive performance: Attentional control theory. *Emotion, 7*(2), 336–353.

Fabrega, Jr., H. (2004). Culture and the origins of psychopathology. In U. P. Gielen, J. M., Fish, et al. (Eds.), *Handbook of culture, therapy, and healing* (pp. 15–35). Mahwah, NJ: Erlbaum.

Fahim, C., Stip, E., Mancini-Marïe, A., et al. (2005). Brain activity during emotionally negative pictures in schizophrenia with and without flat affect: An fMRI study. *Psychiatry Research: Neuroimaging, 140*(1), 1–15.

Fain, G. L. (2003). *Sensory transduction*. Sunderland, MA: Sinauer.

Faith, M. S., Wong, F. Y., & Carpenter, K. M. (1995). Group sensitivity training: Update, meta-analysis and recommendations. *Journal of Counseling Psychology, 42*(3), 390–399.

Falkowski, C. (2000). *Dangerous drugs*. Center City, MN: Hazelden Information Education.

Farah, M. J. (2004). *Visual agnosia* (2nd ed.). Cambridge, MA: MIT Press.

Farah, M. J. (2006). Prosopagnosia. In M. J. Farah, & T. E. Feinberg (Eds.), *Patient-based approaches to cognitive neuroscience* (2nd ed., pp. 123–125). Cambridge, MA: MIT Press.

Farah, M. J., Haimm, C., Sankoorikal, G., et al. (2009). When we enhance cognition with Adderall, do we sacrifice creativity? A preliminary study. *Psychopharmacology, 202*(1-3), 541–547.

Faraut, B., Boudjeltia, K. Z., Dyzma, M., et al. (2011). Benefits of napping and an extended duration of recovery sleep on alertness and immune cells after acute sleep restriction. *Brain, Behavior, & Immunity, 25*(1), 16–24.

Farb, N. A. S., Segal, Z. V., Mayberg, H., et al. (2007). Attending to the present: Mindfulness meditation reveals distinct neural modes of self-reference. *Social Cognitive & Affective Neuroscience, 2*(4), 313–322.

Farrell, M. J., Zamarripa, F., Shade, R., et al. (2008). Effect of aging on regional cerebral blood flow responses associated with osmotic thirst and its satiation by water drinking: A PET study. *Proceedings of the National Academy of Sciences, 105*(1), 382–387.

Farroni, T., Massaccesi, S., Pividori, D., et al. (2004). Gaze following in newborns. *Infancy, 5*(1), 39–60.

Faurie, C., Bonenfant, S., Goldberg, M., et al. (2008). Socio-economic status and handedness in two large cohorts of French adults. *British Journal of Psychology, 99*(4), 533–554.

Fayek, A. (2010). *The crisis in psychoanalysis: In search of a lost doctrine*. Austin, TX: Bridgeway Books.

Federal Bureau of Investigation. (2009). *Crime in the United States, 2008*. Washington, DC: Author. Retrieved May 1, 2010, from http://www.fbi.gov/ucr/cius2008/offenses/violent_crime/.

Feingold, A. (1990). Gender differences in effects of physical attractiveness on romantic attraction. *Journal of Personality & Social Psychology, 59*(5), 981–993.

Feingold, A. (1992). Gender differences in mate selection preferences. *Psychological Bulletin, 111*, 304–341.

Feldhusen, J. F., & Westby, E. L. (2003). Creative and affective behavior: Cognition, personality, and motivation. In J. Houtz (Ed.), *The educational psychology of creativity. Perspectives on creativity* (pp. 95–105). Cresskill, NJ: Hampton Press.

Feldman, D. H. (2004). Piaget's stages: The unfinished symphony of cognitive development. *New Ideas in Psychology, 22*(3), 175–231.

Feldman, S. (2003). Enforcing social conformity: A theory of authoritarianism. *Political Psychology, 24*(1), 41–47.

Fellous, J.-M., & Ledoux, J. E. (2005). Toward basic principles for emotional processing: What the fearful brain tells the robot. In J.-M. Fellous, & M. A.

Arbib, (Eds.), *Who needs emotions?: The brain meets the robot* (pp. 79–115). New York: Oxford University Press.

Fenn, K. M., Nusbaum, H. C., & Margoliash, D. (2003). Consolidation during sleep of perceptual learning of spoken language. *Nature, 425*(6958), 614–616.

Ferguson, C. J., Miguel, C. N., & Hartley, R. D. (2009). A multivariate analysis of youth violence and aggression: The influence of family, peers, depression, and media violence. *Journal of Pediatrics, 155*(6), 904–908.

Fernald, A. (1989). Intonation and communicative intent in mothers' speech to infants: Is the melody the message? *Child Development, 60*(6), 1497–1510.

Fernald, A., Perfors, A., & Marchman, V. A. (2006). Picking up speed in understanding: Speech processing efficiency and vocabulary growth across the 2nd year. *Developmental Psychology, 42*(1), 98–116.

Féron, F., Perry, C., Cochrane, J., et al. (2005). Autologous olfactory ensheathing cell transplantation in human spinal cord injury. *Brain: A Journal of Neurology, 128*(12), 2951–2960.

Ferrari, J. R., & Scher, S. J. (2000). Toward an understanding of academic and nonacademic tasks procrastinated by students: The use of daily logs. *Psychology in the Schools,* 37(4), 359–366.

Festinger, L. (1957). *A theory of cognitive dissonance*. Stanford, CA: Stanford University Press.

Festinger, L., & Carlsmith, J. M. (1959). Cognitive consequences of forced compliance. *Journal of Abnormal & Social Psychology, 58*, 203–210.

Feuerstein, R., Hoffman, M. B., Rand, Y., et al. (1986). Learning to learn: Mediated learning experiences and instrumental enrichment. *Special Services in the Schools,* 3(1-2), 49–82.

Feuerstein, R., Rand, Y., Hoffman, M., et al., (2004). Cognitive modifiability in retarded adolescents: Effects of Instrumental Enrichment. *Pediatric Rehabilitation,* 7(1), 20–29.

Ficca, G., & Salzarulob, P. (2004). What in sleep is for memory. *Sleep Medicine,* 5, 225–230.

Ficca, G., Axelsson, J., Mollicone, D. J., et al. (2010). Naps, cognition and performance. *Sleep Medicine Reviews, 14*(4), 249–258.

Field, A. P. (2006). Is conditioning a useful framework for understanding the development and treatment of phobias? *Clinical Psychology Review, 26*(7), 857–875.

Field, C. E., Nash, H. M., Handwerk, M. L., et al. (2004). A modification of the token economy for nonresponsive youth in family-style residential care. *Behavior Modification, 28*(3), 438–457.

Field, J. E., Kolbert, J. B., Cothers, L. M., et al. (2009). *Understanding girl bullying and what to do about it: Strategies to help heal the divide.* Thousand Oaks, CA: Corwin Press.

Fields, R. D. (2007). The shark's electric sense. *Scientific American, 297*(8), 74–81.

Fields, R. M., & Margolin, J. (2001). *Coping with trauma*. Washington, DC: American Psychological Association.

Filbey, F. M., Schacht, J. P., Myers, U. S., et al. (2009). Marijuana craving in the brain. *Proceedings of the National Academy of Sciences, 106*(31), 13016–13021.

Fine, C. (2010). *Delusions of gender*. New York: Norton.

Fink, M., & Taylor, M. A. (2003). *Catatonia: A clinician's guide to diagnosis and treatment*. London: Cambridge University Press.

Fink, M., Shorter, E., & Taylor, M. A. (2010). Catatonia is not schizophrenia: Kraepelin's error and the need to recognize catatonia as an independent syndrome in medical nomenclature. *Schizophrenia Bulletin, 36*(2), 314–320.

Fiore, D., Dimaggio, G., Nicoló, G., et al. (2008). Metacognitive interpersonal therapy in a case of obsessive-compulsive and avoidant personality disorders. *Journal of Clinical Psychology, 64*(2), 168–180.

Fiorina, C. (2006). *Tough choices: A memoir*. New York: Penguin.

Fireman, G., Kose, G., & Solomon, M. J. (2003). Self-observation and learning: The effect of watching oneself on problem solving performance. *Cognitive Development, 18*(3), 339–354.

Firestone, P., Kingston, D. A., Wexler, A., et al. (2006). Long-term follow-up of exhibitionists: Psychological, phallometric, and offense characteristics. *Journal of the American Academy of Psychiatry & the Law, 34*(3), 349–359.

First, M. B., & Pincus, H. A. (2002). The DSM-IV text revision: Rationale and potential impact on clinical practice. *Psychiatric Services, 53*, 288–292.

Fischer, A. H., Manstead, A. S. R., Rodriquez Mosquera, P. M., et al. (2004). Gender and culture differences in emotion. *Emotion, 4*(1), 87–94.

Fischer, P., Kastenmüller, A., Greitemeyer, T. (2010). Media violence and the self: The impact of personalized gaming characters in aggressive video games on aggressive behavior. *Journal of Experimental Social Psychology, 46*(1), 192–195.

Fisher, B. S., Cullen, F. T., & Daigle, L. E. (2005). The discovery of acquaintance rape: The salience of methodological innovation and rigor. *Journal of Interpersonal Violence, 20*(4), 493–500.

Fisher, R. P., & Geiselman, R. E. (1987). Enhancing eyewitness memory with the cognitive interview. In M. M. Gruneberg, P. E. Morris, et al. (Eds.), *Practical aspects of memory: Current research and issues* (pp. 34–39). Chinchester, U.K.: Wiley.

Fiske, S. T. (1993). Social cognition and social perception. *Annual Review of Psychology, 44*, 155–194.

Fiske, S. T., Cuddy, A. J. C., Glick, P., et al. (2002). A model of (often mixed) stereotype content. *Journal of Personality & Social Psychology, 82*(6), 878–902.

Flanagan, M. B., May, J. G., & Dobie, T. G. (2004). The role of vection, eye movements and postural instability in the etiology of motion sickness. *Journal of Vestibular Research: Equilibrium & Orientation, 14*(4), 335–346.

Flaskerud, J. H. (2009). What do we need to know about the culture-bound syndromes? *Issues in Mental Health Nursing, 30*(6), 406–407.

Flavell, J. H. (1992). Cognitive development: Past, present, and future. *Developmental Psychology, 28*(6), 998–1005.

Flegal, K. M., Carroll, M. D., Ogden, C. L., et al. (2010). Prevalence and trends in obesity among US adults, 1999–2008. *Journal of the American Medical Association, 303*(3), 235–241.

Fleming, J. (1974). Field report: The state of the apes. *Psychology Today, 46*, 31–38.

Florida Medical Examiners Commission. (2008). *Drugs identified in deceased persons by Florida Medical Examiners: 2008 Interim report*. Tallahassee, FL: Author. Retrieved January 23, 2011, from http://www.fdle.state.fl.us/Content/getdoc/c75b8a3c-95ea-41d1-96c5-3b00c9c6eeb4/2008InterimReport.aspx.

Flowe, H. D., & Ebbese, E. B. (2007). The effect of lineup member similarity on recognition accuracy in simultaneous and sequential lineups. *Law & Human Behavior, 31*(1), 33–52.

Flynn, J. R. (2007). *What is intelligence? Beyond the Flynn Effect*. New York: Cambridge.

Flynn, K. J., & Fitzgibbon, M. (1998). Body images and obesity risk among Black females: A review of the literature. *Annals of Behavioral Medicine, 20*(1), 13–24.

Fobair, P. (1997). Cancer support groups and group therapies. *Journal of Psychosocial Oncology, 15*(3-4), 123–147.

Fochtmann, L. J. (1995). Intractable sneezing as a conversion symptom. *Psychosomatics, 36*(2), 103–112.

Fogel, S. M., Nader, R., Cote, K. A., & et al. (2007). Sleep spindles and learning potential. *Behavioral Neuroscience, 121*(1), 1–10.

Foley, H. J., & Matlin, M. W. (2010). *Sensation and perception* (5th ed.). Boston: Pearson/Allyn and Bacon.

Folkman, S., & Moskowitz, J. T. (2004). Coping. *Annual Review of Psychology, 55*, 745–774.

Fontaine, K. R., Redden, D. T., Wang, C., et al. (2003). Years of life lost due to obesity. *Journal of the American Medical Association, 289*, 187–193.

Fontenelle, D. H. (1989). *How to live with your children*. Tucson, AZ: Fisher Books.

Foo, P., Warren, W. H., Duchon, A., et al. (2005). Do humans integrate routes into a cognitive map? Map-versus landmark-based navigation of novel shortcuts. *Journal of Experimental Psychology: Learning, Memory, & Cognition, 31*(2), 195–215.

Foot, M., & Koszycki, D. (2004). Gender differences in anxiety-related traits in patients with panic disorder. *Depression & Anxiety, 20*(3), 123–130.

Forbes, G. B., & Adams-Curtis L. E. (2001). Experiences with sexual coercion in college males and females. *Journal of Interpersonal Violence, 16*(9), 865–889.

Forbes, G. B., Adams-Curtis L. E., & White, K. B. (2004). First- and second-generation measures of sexism, rape myths and related beliefs, and hostility toward women: Their interrelationships and association with college students' experiences with dating aggression and sexual coercion. *Violence Against Women, 10(3)*, 236–261.

Ford, D. Y., & Moore, J. L. (2006). Being gifted and adolescent: Issues and needs of students of color. In F. A. Dixon & S. M. Moon (Eds.), *The handbook of secondary gifted education* (pp. 113–136). Waco, TX: Prufrock Press.

Ford, G. G., Gallagher, S. H., Lacy, B. A., et al. (1999). Repositioning the home plate umpire to provide enhanced perceptual cues and more accurate ball-strike judgments. *Journal of Sport Behavior, 22*(1), 28–44.

Forgas, J. P., Cooper, J., & Crano, W. D. (Eds.) (2010). *The psychology of attitudes and attitude change*. New York: Psychology Press.

Forney, W. S., Forney, J. C., & Crutsinger, C. (2005). Developmental stages of age and moral reasoning as predictors of juvenile delinquents' behavioral intention to steal clothing. *Family & Consumer Sciences Research Journal, 34*(2), 110–126.

ForsterLee, R., ForsterLee, L., Horowitz, I. A., et al. (2006). The effects of defendant race, victim race, and juror gender on evidence processing in a murder trial. *Behavioral Sciences & the Law, 24*(2), 179–198.

Forsyth, D. R. (2010). *Group dynamics* (5th ed.). Belmont, CA: Cengage Learning/Wadsworth.

Forsyth, J. P., & Savsevitz, J. (2002). Behavior therapy: Historical perspective and overview. In M. Hersen, & W. H. Sledge (Eds.), *Encyclopedia of psychotherapy* (Vol. 1, pp. 259–275). San Diego: Academic Press.

Fortunato, L., Young, A. M., Boyd, C. J., et al. (2010). Hook-up sexual experiences and problem behaviors among adolescents. *Journal of Child & Adolescent Substance Abuse, 19*(3), 261–278.

Foster, C. A., Witcher, B. S., Campbell, W. K., et al. (1998). Arousal and attraction. *Journal of Personality & Social Psychology, 74*(1), 86–101.

Foster, G., & Ysseldyke, J. (1976). Expectancy and halo effects as a result of artificially induced teacher bias. *Contemporary Educational Psychology, 1*, 37–45.

Fougnie, D., & Marois, R. (2007). Executive working memory load induces inattentional blindness. *Psychonomic Bulletin & Review, 14*(1), 142–147.

Fowers, B. J., & Davidov, B. J. (2006). The virtue of multiculturalism:

Personal transformation, character, and openness to the other. *American Psychologist, 61*(6), 581–594.

Fowler, J. H., & Christakis, N. A. (2010). Cooperative behavior cascades in human social networks. *Proceedings of the National Academy of Sciences, 107*(12), 5334–5338.

Foxhall, K. (2000, January). Suddenly, a big impact on criminal justice. *APA Monitor*, 36–37.

Fraley, R. C., & Shaver, P. R. (2000). Adult romantic attachment: Theoretical developments, emerging controversies, and unanswered questions. *Review of General Psychology, 4*(2), 132–154.

Frank, J. D., & Frank, J. (2004). Therapeutic components shared by all psychotherapies. In A. Freeman, M. J. Mahoney, et al. (Eds.), *Cognition and psychotherapy* (2nd ed., pp. 45–78). New York: Springer.

Frank, M. G. (2002). Smiles, lies, and emotion. In M. H. Abel (Ed.), *An empirical reflection on the smile. Mellen studies in psychology* (Vol. 4, pp. 15–43). Lewiston, NY: Edwin Mellen Press.

Frank, M. G., & Ekman, P. (2004). Appearing truthful generalizes across different deception situations. *Journal of Personality & Social Psychology, 86(3)*, 486–495.

Franken, P., & Dijk, D.-J. (2009). Circadian clock genes and sleep homeostasis. *European Journal of Neuroscience, 29*(9), 1820–1829.

Franken, R. E. (2007). *Human motivation* (6th ed.). Belmont, CA: Cengage Learning/Wadsworth.

Frankl, V. (1955). *The doctor and the soul.* New York: Knopf.

Franzoi, S. L., & Klaiber, J. R. (2007). Body use and reference group impact: With whom do we compare our bodies? *Sex Roles, 56*(3-4), 205–214.

Franzoi, S. L. (2002). *Social psychology.* New York: McGraw-Hill.

Fraser, C. (2002). Fact and fiction: A clarification of phantom limb phenomena. *British Journal of Occupational Therapy, 65*(6), 256–260.

Freberg, L.A. (2010). *Discovering biological psychology* (2nd ed.). Belmont, CA: Cengage Learning/Wadsworth.

Fredrickson, B. L. (2003). The value of positive emotions. *American Scientist, 91*, 330–335.

Fredrickson, B. L., & Branigan, C. (2005). Positive emotions broaden the scope of attention and thought-action repertoires. *Cognition & Emotion, 19*(3), 313–332.

Fredrickson, B. L., Roberts, T., Noll, S. M., et al. (1998). That swimsuit becomes you. *Journal of Personality & Social Psychology, 75*(1), 269–284.

Freedman, D. H. (2011). How to fix the obesity crisis. *Scientific American, February*, 40–47.

Freeman, D., & Garety, P. A. (2004). *Paranoia: The psychology of persecutory delusions.* New York: Routledge.

Freize, I. H. (1987). The female victim. In G. R. VandenBos, & B. K. Bryant (Eds.), *Cataclysms, crises, and catastrophes: Psychology in action* (pp. 109–145). Washington, DC: American Psychological Association.

French, C. C., Fowler, M., McCarthy, K., et al. (1991). A test of the Barnum effect. *Skeptical Inquirer, 15*(4), 66–72.

French, S. E., Kim, T. E., & Pillado, O. (2006). Ethnic identity, social group membership, and youth violence. In N. G. Guerra, & E. P. Smith (Eds.), *Preventing youth violence in a multicultural society* (pp. 47–73). Washington, DC: American Psychological Association.

Freud, S. (1900). *The interpretation of dreams.* London: Hogarth.

Freud, S. (1949). *An outline of psychoanalysis.* New York: Norton.

Freund, A. M., & Ritter, J. O. (2009). Midlife crisis: A debate. *Gerontology, 55*(5), 582–591.

Fried, P. A., & Smith, A. M. (2001) A literature review of the consequences of prenatal marihuana exposure. *Neurotoxicology & Teratology, 23*(1), 1–11.

Friedman, H. S. (2002). *Health psychology* (2nd ed.). Englewood Cliffs, NJ: Prentice-Hall.

Friedman, L. (2006). What is psychoanalysis? *Psychoanalytic Quarterly, 75*(3), 689–713.

Friedman, L. J. (2004). Erik Erikson on generativity: A biographer's perspective. In E. de St. Aubin, D. P. McAdams, et al. (Eds.), *The generative society: Caring for future generations* (pp. 257–264). Washington, DC: American Psychological Association.

Friedman, M., & Rosenman, R. H. (1983). *Type A behavior and your heart.* New York: Knopf.

Friedman, R. C., Bucci, W., Christian, C., et al. (1998). Private psychotherapy patients of psychiatrist psychoanalysts. *American Journal of Psychiatry, 155*, 1772–1774.

Fritz, C. O., Morris, P. E., Acton, M., et al. (2007). Comparing and combining retrieval practice and the keyword mnemonic for foreign vocabulary learning. *Applied Cognitive Psychology, 21*(4), 499–526.

Froufe, M., & Schwartz, C. (2001). Subliminal messages for increasing self-esteem: Placebo effect. *Spanish Journal of Psychology, 4*(1), 19–25.

Fryar, C. D., Hirsch, R., Porter, K. S., et al. (2007). Drug use and sexual behaviors reported by adults: United States, 1999-2002. *Advance data from vital and health statistics; no. 384.* Hyattsville, MD: National Center for Health Statistics. Retrieved May 17, 2008 from http://www.cdc.gov/nchs/data/ad/ad384.pdf.

Frydman, M. (1999). Television, aggressiveness and violence. *International Journal of Adolescent Medicine & Health, 11*(3-4), 335–344.

Fu, J. H., Morris, M. W., Lee, S., et al. (2007). Epistemic motives and cultural conformity: Need for closure, culture, and context as determinants of conflict judgments. *Journal of Personality & Social Psychology, 92*(2), 191–207.

Fuchs, C., & Obrist, M. (2010). HCI and society: Towards a typology of universal design principles. *International Journal of Human-Computer Interaction, 26*(6), 638–656.

Fukai, S., Akishita, M., Yamada, S., et al. (2010). Effects of testosterone in older men with mild-to-moderate cognitive impairment. *Journal of the American Geriatrics Society, 58*(7), 1419–1421.

Fukuda, K., & Ishihara, K. (2001). Age-related changes of sleeping pattern during adolescence. *Psychiatry & Clinical Neurosciences, 55*(3), 231–232.

Funder, D. C. (2006). *The personality puzzle* (4th ed.). New York: Norton.

Funk, J. B. (2005). Children's exposure to violent video games and desensitization to violence. *Child & Adolescent Psychiatric Clinics of North America, 14*(3), 387–404.

Fuqua, D. R., & Newman, J. L. (2002). Creating caring organizations. *Consulting Psychology Journal: Practice & Research, 54*(2), 131–140.

Furnham, A., Chamorro-Premuzic T., & Callahan, I. (2003). Does graphology predict personality and intelligence? *Individual Differences Research, 1(2)*, 78–94.

Gable, S. L., Reis, H. T., Impett, E. A., et al. (2004). What do you do when things go right? *Journal of Personality & Social Psychology, 87*(2), 228–245.

Gadzella, B. M. (1995). Differences in processing information among psychology course grade groups. *Psychological Reports, 77*, 1312–1314.

Gaertner, S. L., Dovidio, J. F., Banker, B. S., et al. (2000). Reducing intergroup conflict: From superordinate goals to decategorization, recategorization, and mutual differentiation. *Group Dynamics, 4*(1), 98–114.

Galambos, N. L., Barker, E. T., & Tilton-Weaver L. C. (2003). Who gets caught at maturity gap? A study of pseudomature, immature and mature adolescents. *International Journal of Behavioral Development, 27*(3), 253–263.

Galankin, T., Shekunova, E., & Zvartau, E. (2010). Estradiol lowers intracranial self-stimulation thresholds and enhances cocaine facilitation of intracranial self-stimulation in rats. *Hormones & Behavior, 58*(5), 827–834.

Galanter, M., Hayden, F., Castañeda, R, et al. (2005). Group therapy, self-help groups, and network therapy. In R. J. Frances, S. I. Miller, et al. (Eds.), *Clinical textbook of addictive disorders* (3rd ed., pp. 502–527). New York: Guilford.

Galati, D., Scherer, K. R., & Ricci-Bitti P. E. (1997). Voluntary facial expression of emotion: Comparing congenitally blind with normally sighted encoders. *Journal of Personality & Social Psychology, 73*(6), 1363–1379.

Galea, S., & Resnick, H. (2005). Posttraumatic stress disorder in the general population after mass terrorist incidents: Considerations about the nature of exposure. *CNS Spectrums, 10*(2), 107–115.

Galea, S., Ahern, J., Resnick, H., et al. (2002). Psychological sequelae of the September 11 terrorist attacks in New York City. *New England Journal of Medicine, 346*(13), 982–987.

Gallagher, S. (2004). Nailing the lie: An interview with Jonathan Cole. *Journal of Consciousness Studies, 11*(2), 3–21.

Gallucci, N. T. (2008). *Sport psychology: Performance enhancement, performance inhibition, individuals, and teams.* New York: Psychology Press.

Gamache, G. (2004). *Essentials in human factors.* San Mateo, CA: Usernomics.

Ganis, G., Thompson, W. L., & Kosslyn, S. M. (2004). Brain areas underlying visual mental imagery and visual perception: An fMRI study. *Cognitive Brain Research, 20*(2), 226–241.

Ganster, D. C., Fox, M. L., & Dwyer, D. J. (2001). Explaining employees' health care costs: A prospective examination of stressful job demands, personal control, and physiological reactivity. *Journal of Applied Psychology, 86*, 954–964.

Garcia, E. E. (2008). Bilingual education in the United States. In J. Altarriba & R. R. Heredia (Eds.), *An introduction to bilingualism: Principles and processes* (pp. 321–343). Mahwah, NJ: Erlbaum.

García-Montes, J. M., Pérez-Álvarez, M., Sass, L. A et al. (2008). The role of superstition in psychopathology. *Philosophy, Psychiatry, & Psychology, 15*(3), 227–237.

Gardner, H. (2003, April). *Multiple intelligences after twenty years.* Invited address at meeting of American Educational Research Association. Retrieved February 21, 2011, from http://www.pz.harvard.edu/PIs/HG_MI_after_20_years.pdf.

Gardner, H. (2004). *Frames of mind* (10th anniversary ed.). New York: Basic.

Gardner, H. (2008). Birth and the spreading of a "meme". In J. Q. Chen, S. Moran, & H. Gardner (Eds.), *Multiple intelligences around the world* (pp. 3–16). San Francisco: Jossey-Bass.

Gardner, R. A., & Gardner, B. T. (1989). *Teaching sign language to chimpanzees.* Albany, NY: State University of New York Press.

Garland, A. F., & Zigler, E. (1999). Emotional and behavioral problems among highly intellectually gifted youth. *Roeper Review, 22*(1), 41–44.

Garlow, S. J., Purselle, D. C., & Heninger, M. (2007). Cocaine and alcohol use preceding suicide in African American and White adolescents. *Journal of Psychiatric Research, 41*(6), 530–536.

Garnets, L. D. (2002). Sexual orientation in perspective. *Cultural Diversity & Ethnic Minority Psychology, 8*(2), 115–129.

Garnets, L. D., & Kimmel, D. (1991). Lesbian and gay male dimensions in the psychological study of human diversity. In J. D. Goodchilds (Ed.), *Psychological perspectives on human diversity in America* (pp. 137–189). Washington, DC: American Psychological Association.

Garrosa, E., Moreno-Jiménez, B., Liang, Y., et al. (2008). The relationship between socio-demographic variables, job stressors, burnout, and hardy personality in nurses: An exploratory study. *International Journal of Nursing Studies, 45*(3), 418–427.

Gass, R. H., & Seiter, J. S. (2007). Persuasion: Social influence and compliance gaining (3rd ed.). Boston: Allyn & Bacon.

Gastner, M. T., Shalizi, C. R., & Newman, M. E. J. (2005). Maps and cartograms of the 2004 US presidential election results. *Advances in Complex Systems, 8*(1), 117–123.

Gates, A. I. (1917). Recitation as a factor in memorizing. *Archives of Psychology, 40*, 104.

Gathchel, R. J., & Oordt, M. S. (2003). Insomnia. In R. J. Gatchel, & M. S. Oordt (Eds.), *Clinical health psychology and primary care: Practical advice and clinical guidance for successful collaboration* (pp. 135–148). Washington: American Psychological Association.

Gatz, M. (2007). Genetics, dementia, and the elderly. *Current Directions in Psychological Science, 16*(3), 123–127.

Gauquelin, M. (1970). *Astrology and science*. London: Peter Davies.

Gayle, H. (2000). An overview of the global HIV/AIDS epidemic, with a focus on the United States. *AIDS, 14*(Suppl. 2), S8–S17.

Gazzaniga, M. S. (1970). *The bisected brain*. New York: Plenum.

Gazzaniga, M. S. (2005). Forty-five years of split-brain research and still going strong. *Nature Reviews Neuroscience, 6*(8), 653–659.

Geary, N. (2004). Endocrine controls of eating: CCK, leptin, and ghrelin. *Physiology & Behavior, 81*(5), 719–733.

Geddes, L. (2008). Could brain scans ever be safe evidence? *New Scientist, Oct 3*, 8–9.

Gedo, J. E. (2002). The enduring scientific contributions of Sigmund Freud. *Perspectives in Biology & Medicine, 45*, 200–211.

Gegenfurtner, K. R., & Kiper, D. C. (2003). Color vision. *Annual Review of Neuroscience, 26*, 181–206.

Geiselman, R. E., Fisher, R. P., MacKinnon, D. P., et al. (1986). Eyewitness memory enhancement with the cognitive interview. *American Journal of Psychology, 99*, 385–401.

Genty, E., Breuer, T., Hobaiter, C., et al. (2009). Gestural communication of the gorilla (Gorilla gorilla): Repertoire, intentionality, and possible origins. *Animal Cognition, 12*(3), 527–546.

George, A. (2006). Living online: The end of privacy? *New Scientist*, Sept 18, 50–51.

Gerardi, M., Rothbaum, B. O., Ressler, K., et al., (2008). Virtual reality exposure therapy using a virtual Iraq: Case report. *Journal of Traumatic Stress, 21*(2), 209–213.

Gerjets, P., Kammerer, Y., & Werner, B. (2011). Measuring spontaneous and instructed evaluation processes during Web search: Integrating concurrent thinking-aloud protocols and eye-tracking data. *Learning & Instruction, 21*(2), 220–231.

Germain, A., Krakow, B., Faucher, B., et al. (2004). Increased mastery elements associated with imagery rehearsal treatment for nightmares in sexual assault survivors with PTSD. *Dreaming, 14*(4), 195–206.

German, T. P., & Barrett, H. C. (2005). Functional fixedness in a technologically sparse culture. *Psychological Science, 16*(1), 1–5.

German, T. P., & Defeyter, M. A. (2000). Immunity to functional fixedness in young children. *Psychonomic Bulletin & Review, 7*(4), 707–712.

Gersh, R. D. (1982). Learning when not to shoot. *Santa Barbara News Press*, June 20.

Gershoff, E. T. (2002). Corporal punishment by parents and associated child behaviors and experiences: A meta-analytic and theoretical review. *Psychological Bulletin, 128*(4), 539–579.

Gershoff, E. T., & Bitensky, S. H. (2007). The case against corporal punishment of children: Converging evidence from social science research and international human rights law and implications for U.S. public policy. *Psychology, Public Policy, & Law, 13*(4), 231–272.

Gerstein, E. R. (2002). Manatees, bioacoustics, and boats. *American Scientist, 90*(March–April), 154–163.

Geschwind, N. (1979). Specializations of the human brain. *Scientific American, 241*, 180–199.

Gever, J. (2009, May 19). APA: Major changes loom for bible of mental health. *MedPage Today*. Retrieved March 14, 2011, from http://www.medpagetoday.com/MeetingCoverage/APA/14270.

Giancola, P. R., Josephs, R. A., Parrott, D. J., et al. (2010). Alcohol myopia revisited: Clarifying aggression and other acts of disinhibition through a distorted lens. *Perspectives on Psychological Science, 5*(3), 265–278.

Giarratano, J. C., & Riley, G. (2005). *Expert systems, principles and programming* (4th ed.). Belmont, CA: Cengage Learning/Wadsworth.

Gibbons, F. X., Lane, D. J., Gerrard, M., et al. (2002). Comparison-level preferences after performance: Is downward comparison theory still useful? *Journal of Personality & Social Psychology, 83*(4), 865–880.

Gibson, E. J., & Walk, R. D. (1960). The "visual cliff." *Scientific American, 202*(4), 67–71.

Gilchrist, A. L., Cowan, N., & Naveh-Benjamin M. (2009). Investigating the childhood development of working memory using sentences: New evidence for the growth of chunk capacity. *Journal of Experimental Child Psychology, 104*(2), 252–265.

Gilhooly, K. J., Fioratou, E., Anthony, S. H. et al. (2007). Divergent thinking: Strategies and executive involvement in generating novel uses for familiar objects. *British Journal of Psychology*, 98, 611–625.

Giliovich, T., Keltner, D., & Nisbett, R. (2005). *Social psychology*. New York: Norton.

Gillespie, C. F., & Nemeroff, C. B. (2007). Corticotropin-releasing factor and the psychobiology of early-life stress. *Current Directions in Psychological Science, 16*(2), 85–89.

Gilligan, C. (1982). *In a different voice*. Cambridge, MA: Harvard University Press.

Gilligan, C., & Attanucci, J. (1988). Two moral orientations: Gender differences and similarities. *Merrill-Palmer Quarterly, 34*(3), 223–237.

Ginsberg, D. L. (2006). Fatal agranulocytosis four years after clozapine discontinuation. *Primary Psychiatry, 13*(2), 32–33.

Giummarra, M. J., Gibson, S. J., Georgiou-Karistianis, N., et al. (2007). Central mechanisms in phantom limb perception: The past, present and future. *Brain Research Reviews, 54*(1), 219–232.

Giuseppe, R. (2005). Virtual reality in psychotherapy: Review. *CyberPsychology & Behavior, 8*(3), 220–230.

Gladstone, G. L., & Parker, G. B. (2002). When you're smiling, does the whole world smile for you? *Australasian Psychiatry, 10*(2), 144–146.

Gladwell, M. (2005). *Blink: The power of thinking without thinking*. New York: Little, Brown.

Glass, J., & Owen, J. (2010). Latino fathers: The relationship among machismo, acculturation, ethnic identity, and paternal involvement. *Psychology of Men & Masculinity*, 11(4), 251–261.

Glassgold, J. M., Beckstead, L., Drescher, J., et al. (2009). *Report of the American Psychological Association Task Force on appropriate therapeutic responses to sexual orientation*. Washington, DC: American Psychological Association. Retrieved February 23, 2011 from http://www.apa.org/pi/lgbt/resources/therapeutic-response.pdf.

Gleason, J. B., & Ratner, N. B. (2009). *The development of language* (7th ed.). Boston: Allyn & Bacon.

Glenn, E. N. (Ed). (2009). *Shades of difference: Why skin color matters*. Palo Alto, CA: Stanford University Press.

Glick, P. (2008). When neighbors blame neighbors: Scapegoating and the breakdown of ethnic relations. In V. M. Esses, & R. A. Vernon (Eds.), *Explaining the breakdown of ethnic relations: Why neighbors kill: Social issues and interventions* (pp. 123–146). Malden, MA: Blackwell.

Global Footprint Network. (2010). *Footprint basics: Overview*. Oakland, CA: Author. Retrieved January 19, 2011, from http://www.footprintnetwork.org/en/index.php/GFN/page/footprint_basics_overview.

Glomb, T. M. (2002). Workplace anger and aggression. *Journal of Occupational Health Psychology, 7*(1), 20–36.

Gloria-Bottini, F., Magrini, A., & Bottini, E. (2009). The effect of genetic and seasonal factors on birth weight. *Early Human Development, 85*(7), 439–441.

Glover, R. J. (2001). Discriminators of moral orientation: Gender role or personality? *Journal of Adult Development, 8*(1), 1–7.

Gobet, F. (2005). Chunking models of expertise: Implications for education. *Applied Cognitive Psychology, 19*(2), 183–204.

Gobet, F., & Simon, H. A. (1996). Recall of random and distorted chess positions: Implications for the theory of expertise. *Memory & Cognition, 24*(4), 493–503.

Göckeritz, S., Schultz, P. W., Rendón, T., et al. (2010). Descriptive normative beliefs and conservation behavior: The moderating roles of personal involvement and injunctive normative beliefs. *European Journal of Social Psychology, 40*(3), 514–523.

Godnig, E. C. (2003). Tunnel vision: Its causes & treatment strategies. *Journal of Behavioral Optometry, 14*(4), 95–99.

Godoy, R., Zeinalova, E., Reyes-García V., et al. (2010). Does civilization cause discontentment among indigenous Amazonians? Test of empirical data from the Tsimane' of Bolivia. *Journal of Economic Psychology, 31*, 587–598.

Gogate, L. J., Bahrick, L. E., & Watson, J. D. (2000). A study of multimodal motherese: The role of temporal synchrony between verbal labels and gestures. *Child Development, 71*(4), 878–894.

Goldberg, C. (2001). Of prophets, true believers, and terrorists. *The Dana Forum on Brain Science, 3*(3), 21–24.

Goldberg, R. (2010). *Drugs across the spectrum* (6th ed.). Belmont, CA: Cengage Learning/Wadsworth.

Golden, J. (2005). *Message in a bottle: The making of fetal alcohol syndrome*. Cambridge, MA: Harvard University Press.

Golden, T. D., Veiga, J. F., & Simsek, Z. (2006). Telecommuting's differential impact on work-family conflict: Is there no place like home? *Journal of Applied Psychology, 91*(6), 1340–1350.

Goldenberg, H., & Goldenberg, I. (2004). *Family therapy: An overview* (6th ed.). Pacific Grove, CA: Brooks/Cole.

Goldfried, M. R. (2001). Integrating gay, lesbian, and bisexual issues into mainstream psychology. *American Psychologist, 56*(11), 977–987.

Golding, J. M., Bradshaw, G. S., Dunlap, E. E., et al. (2007). The impact of mock jury gender composition on deliberations and conviction rates in a child sexual assault trial. *Child Maltreatment, 12*(2), 182–190.

Goldstein, E. B. (2010). *Sensation and perception* (8th ed.). Belmont, CA: Cengage Learning/Wadsworth.

Goldstein, E. B. (2011). *Cognitive psychology: Connecting mind, research and everyday experience* (3rd ed.). Belmont, CA: Cengage Learning/Wadsworth.

Goldstein, M., Peters, L., Baillie, A., et al. (2011). The effectiveness of a day program for the treatment of adolescent anorexia nervosa. *International Journal of Eating Disorders, 44*(1), 29–38.

Goldston, D. B., Molock, S. D., Whitbeck, L. B., et al. (2008). Cultural considerations in adolescent suicide prevention and psychosocial treatment. *American Psychologist, 63*(1), 14–31.

Goleman, D. (1995). *Emotional intelligence*. New York: Bantam.

Goman, C. K. (2008). *The nonverbal advantage: Secrets and science of body language at work*. San Francisco: Berrett-Koehler.

Gomez, R., & McLaren, S. (2007). The inter-relations of mother and father attachment, self-esteem and aggression during late adolescence. *Aggressive Behavior, 33*(2), 160–169.

Gonzaga, G. C., Carter, S., & Buckwalter, J. G. (2010). Assortative mating, convergence, and satisfaction in married couples. *Personal Relationships, 17*(4), 634–644.

Gonzalez, M., Durrant, J. E., Chabot, M., et al. (2008).What predicts injury from physical punishment? A test of the typologies of violence hypothesis. *Child Abuse & Neglect, 32*(8), 752–765.

González-Vallejo, C., Lassiter, G. D., Bellezza, F. S., et al.. (2008). "Save angels perhaps": A critical examination of unconscious thought theory and the deliberation-without-attention effect. *Review of General Psychology, 12*(3), 282–296.

Goode, E. (1996). Gender and courtship entitlement: Responses to personal ads. *Sex Roles, 34*(3-4), 141–169.

Goodman, G. S., Quas, J. A., Ogle, C. M. (2010). Child maltreatment and memory. *Annual Review of Psychology, 61*, 325–351.

Goodman-Delahunty, J. Greene, E., & Hsiao, W. (1998). Construing motive in videotaped killings: The role of jurors' attitudes toward the death penalty. *Law & Human Behavior, 22*(3), 257–271.

Goodwin, R. D., Fergusson, D. M., & Horwood, L. J. (2005). Childhood abuse and familial violence and the risk of panic attacks and panic disorder in young adulthood. *Psychological Medicine, 35*(6), 881–890.

Goodwin, S. A., & Fiske, S. T. (2001). Power and gender. In R. K. Unger (Ed.), *Handbook of the psychology of women and gender* (pp. 358–366). New York: Wiley.

Gopnik, A. (2009). *The philosophical baby*. New York: Macmillan.

Gopnik, A., Meltzoff, A. N., & Kuhl, P. K. (2000). *The scientist in the crib: What early learning tells us about the mind*. New York: HarperCollins.

Gordon, A. K., & Kaplar, M. E. (2002). A new technique for demonstrating the actor-observer bias. *Teaching of Psychology, 29*(4), 301–303.

Gordon, I., Zagoory-Sharon O., Leckman, J. F., et al. (2010). Oxytocin and the development of parenting in humans. *Biological Psychiatry, 68*(4), 377–382.

Gordon, T. (2000). *Parent effectiveness training: The proven program for raising responsible children*. New York: Three Rivers Press.

Gottman, J. M. (1994). *Why marriages succeed or fail*. New York: Simon & Schuster.

Gottman, J. M., & Krokoff, L. J. (1989). Marital interaction and satisfaction: A longitudinal view. *Journal of Consulting & Clinical Psychology, 57*(1), 47–52.

Gourville, J. T., & Soman, D. (2005). Overchoice and assortment type: When and why variety backfires. *Marketing Science, 24*(3), 382–395.

Gow, A. J., Johnson, W., Pattie, A., et al. (2011). Stability and change in intelligence from age 11 to ages 70, 79, and 87: The Lothian birth cohorts of 1921 and 1936. *Psychology & Aging, 26*(1), 232–240.

Grabe, M. (2006). *Integrating technology for meaningful learning*. Boston: Houghton Mifflin.

Grabill, K., Merlo, L., Duke, D., et al. (2008). Assessment of obsessive-compulsive disorder: A review. *Journal of Anxiety Disorders, 22*(1), 1–17.

Grack, C., & Richman, C. L. (1996). Reducing general and specific heterosexism through cooperative contact. *Journal of Psychology & Human Sexuality, 8*(4), 59-68.

Grande, T., Rudolf, G., Oberbracht, C., et al. (2003). Progressive changes in patients' lives after psychotherapy. *Psychotherapy Research, 13*(1), 43–58.

Grandner, M. A., & Kripke, D. F. (2004). Self-reported sleep complaints with long and short sleep: A nationally representative sample. *Psychosomatic Medicine, 66*, 239–241.

Granrud, C. E. (2004). Visual metacognition and the development of size constancy. In D. T. Levin (Ed.), *Thinking and seeing: Visual metacognition in adults and children* (pp. 75–95). Cambridge, MA: MIT Press.

Granrud, C. E. (2006). Size constancy in infants: 4-month-olds' responses to physical versus retinal image size. *Journal of Experimental Psychology: Human Perception & Performance, 32*(6), 1398–1404.

Grant, B. F., Hasin, D. S., Stinson, F. S., et al. (2006). The epidemiology of DSM-IV panic disorder and agoraphobia in the United States: Results from the National Epidemiologic Survey on Alcohol and Related Conditions. *Journal of Clinical Psychiatry, 67*(3), 363–374.

Grant, I., Gonzalez, R., Carey, C., & Natarajan, L. (2001). Long-term neurocognitive consequences of marijuana. In *National Institute on Drug Abuse Workshop on Clinical Consequences of Marijuana*, August 13, 2001, Rockville, MD.

Graves, J. L. (2001). *The emperor's new clothes*. Piscataway, NJ: Rutgers University Press.

Gravetter, F. J., & Wallnau, L. B. (2010). *Statistics for the behavioral sciences* (8th ed.). Belmont, CA: Cengage Learning/Wadsworth.

Gray, J. M., & Wilson, M. A. (2007). A detailed analysis of the reliability and validity of the sensation seeking scale in a UK sample. *Personality & Individual Differences, 42*(4), 641–651.

Graziottin, A. (1998). The biological basis of female sexuality. *International Clinical Psychopharmacology, 13*(Suppl. 6), S15–S22.

Gredler, M. E. & Shields, C. C. (2008). *Vygotsky's legacy: A foundation for research and practice*. New York: Guilford.

Greenberg, D. L. (2004). President Bush's false 'flashbulb' memory of 9/11/01. *Applied Cognitive Psychology, 18*(3), 363–370.

Greene, E., & Heilbrun, K. (2011). *Wrightsman's psychology and the legal system* (7th ed.). Belmont, CA: Cengage Learning/Wadsworth.

Greene, D., & Lepper, M. R. (1974). How to turn play into work. *Psychology Today, 8*(4), 49.

Greenfield, P. M. (1997). You can't take it with you: Why abilities assessments don't cross cultures. *American Psychologist, 52*, 1115–1124.

Greenwald, R. (2006). Eye movement desensitization and reprocessing with traumatized youth. In N. B. Webb (Ed.), *Working with traumatized youth in child welfare: Social work practice with children and families* (pp. 246–264). New York: Guilford.

Greenwood, J. G., Greenwood, J. J. D., McCullagh, J. F., et al. (2006). A survey of sidedness in Northern Irish schoolchildren: The interaction of sex, age, and task. *Laterality: Asymmetries of Body, Brain & Cognition, 12*(1), 1–18.

Gregory, B. T., Albritton, M. D., & Osmonbekov, T. (2010). The mediating role of psychological empowerment on the relationships between P–O fit, job satisfaction, and in-role performance. *Journal of Business & Psychology, 25*(4), 639–647.

Gregory, R. L. (1990). *Eye and brain: The psychology of seeing*. Princeton, NJ: Princeton University Press.

Gregory, R. L. (2000). Visual illusions. In A. Kazdin (Ed.), *Encyclopedia of psychology* (Vol. 8, pp. 193–200). Washington, DC: American Psychological Association.

Gregory, R. L. (2003). Seeing after blindness. *Nature Neuroscience, 6*(9), 909–910.

Gregory, B. T., Albritton, M. D., & Osmonbekov, T. (2010). The mediating role of psychological empowerment on the relationships between P–O fit, job satisfaction, and in-role performance. *Journal of Business & Psychology, 25*(4), 639–647.

Greitemeyer, T. (2009). Effects of songs with prosocial lyrics on prosocial thoughts, affect, and behavior. *Journal of Experimental Social Psychology, 45*(1), 186–190.

Greitemeyer, T. (2010). Effects of reciprocity on attraction: The role of a partner's physical attractiveness. *Personal Relationships, 17*(2), 317–330.

Grello, C. M., Welsh, D. P., & Harper, M. S. (2006). No strings attached: The nature of casual sex in college students. *Journal of Sex Research, 43*(3), 255–267.

Grenèche, J., Krieger, J., Bertrand, F., et al. (2011). Short-term memory performances during sustained wakefulness in patients with obstructive sleep apnea–hypopnea syndrome. *Brain & Cognition, 75*(1), 39–50.

Grenier, G., & Byers, E. S. (1995). Rapid ejaculation: A review of conceptual, etiological, and treatment issues. *Archives of Sexual Behavior, 24*(4), 447–472.

Griffin, D. R. (1992). *Animal minds*. Chicago: University of Chicago Press.

Griffin, W. A. (2002). Family therapy. In M. Hersen, & W. H. Sledge (Eds.), *Encyclopedia of psychotherapy* (pp. 787–791). San Diego: Academic Press.

Griffin-Fennell, F., & Williams, M. (2006). Examining the complexities of suicidal behavior in the African American community. *Journal of Black Psychology, 32*(3), 303–319.

Grigorenko, E. L. (2005). The inherent complexities of gene-environment interactions. *Journals of Gerontology, 60B*(1), 53–64.

Grigorenko, E. L., & Sternberg, R. J. (2003). The nature-nurture issue. In A. Slater & G. Bremner (Eds.), *An introduction to developmental psychology* (pp. 64–91). Malden, MA: Blackwell.

Grobstein, P., & Chow, K. L. (1975). Perceptive field development and individual experience. *Science, 190*, 352–358.

Grodzinsky, Y., & Santi, A. (2008). The battle for Broca's region. *Trends in Cognitive Sciences, 12*(12), 474–480.

Gross, J. J. (2001). Emotion regulation in adulthood: Timing is everything. *Current Directions in Psychological Science, 10*(6), 214–219.

Grosse, S. D. (2010). Late-treated phenylketonuria and partial reversibility of intellectual impairment. *Child Development, 81*(1), 200–211.

Grubin, D., & Madsen, L. (2005). Lie detection and the polygraph: A historical review. *Journal of Forensic Psychiatry & Psychology, 16*(2), 357–369.

Guastello, D. D., & Guastello, S. J. (2003). Androgyny, gender role behavior, and emotional intelligence among college students and their parents. *Sex Roles, 49*(11-12), 663–673.

Guéguen, N. (2002). Status, apparel and touch: Their joint effects on compliance to a request. *North American Journal of Psychology, 4(2)*, 279–286.

Guéguen, N., & Pascual, A. (2003). Status and people's tolerance towards an ill-mannered person: A field study. *Journal of Mundane Behavior, 4*(1), 29–36.

Guéguen, N., Marchand, M., Pascual, A., et al. (2008). Foot-in-the-door technique using a courtship request: A field experiment. *Psychological Reports, 103*(2), 529–534.

Guéguen, N., Pascual, A., & Dagot, L. (2002). Low-ball and compliance to a request: An application in a field setting. *Psychological Reports, 91*(1), 81–84.

Guillot, A. & Collet, C. (2008). Construction of the motor imagery integrative model in sport: A review and theoretical investigation of motor imagery use. *International Review of Sport & Exercise Psychology, 1*, 31–44.

Guillot, A., Collet, C., Nguyen, V. A., et al. (2009). Brain activity during visual versus kinesthetic imagery: An fMRI study. *Human Brain Mapping, 30*(7), 2157–2172.

Gullette, D. L., & Lyons, M. A. (2005). Sexual sensation seeking, compulsivity, and HIV risk behaviors in college students. *Journal of Community Health Nursing, 22*(1), 47–60.

Gump, B. B., & Kulik, J. A. (1997). Stress, affiliation, and emotional contagion. *Journal of Personality & Social Psychology, 72*(2), 305–319.

Gündogan, N. Ü., Durmazlar, N., Gümüs, K., et al. (2005). Projected color slides as a method for mass screening test for color vision deficiency (a preliminary study). *International Journal of Neuroscience, 115*(8), 1105–1117.

Gunter, B. (2008). Media violence: Is there a case for causality? *American Behavioral Scientist, 51*(8), 1061–1122.

Gurung, R. (2010). *Health psychology: A cultural approach* (2nd ed.). Belmont, CA: Cengage Learning/Wadsworth.

Gustavson, C. R., & Garcia, J. (1974). Pulling a gag on the wily coyote. *Psychology Today*, May, 68–72.

Güth, W., Levati, M. V., & Ploner, M. (2009). An experimental analysis of satisficing in saving decisions. *Journal of Mathematical Psychology, 53*(4), 265–272.

Güth, W., Levati, M. V., & von Wangenheim, G. (2010). Mutual interdependence versus repeated interaction: An experiment studying voluntary social exchange. *Rationality & Society, 22*(2), 131–158.

Guthrie, R. V. (2004). *Even the rat was white: A historical view of psychology* (2nd ed.). Boston: Allyn & Bacon.

Guttmacher Institute. (2010). *U.S. teenage pregnancies, births and abortions: National and state trends and trends by race and ethnicity.* Washington: DC: Author. Retrieved February 25, 2011 from http://www.guttmacher.org/pubs/USTPtrends.pdf.

Guttmacher Institute. (2011). *Facts on American teens' sexual and reproductive health.* Washington: DC: Author. Retrieved February 25, 2011 from http://www.guttmacher.org/pubs/FB-ATSRH.html.

Haaken, J., & Reavey, P. (Eds.). (2010). *Memory matters: Contexts for understanding sexual abuse recollections.* New York: Routledge/Taylor & Francis.

Haas, B. W., Omura, K., Constable, R. T., et al. (2007). Is automatic emotion regulation associated with agreeableness?: A perspective using a social neuroscience approach. *Psychological Science, 18*(2), 130–132.

Haber, R. N. (1969). Eidetic images—with biographical sketches. *Scientific American, 220*(12), 36–44.

Haber, R. N. (1970). How we remember what we see. *Scientific American, 222*(5), 104–112.

Haber, R. N., & Haber, L. (2000). Eidetic imagery. In A. E. Kazdin, (Ed.), *Encyclopedia of psychology* (Vol. 3, pp. 147–149). Washington, DC: American Psychological Association.

Haenschel, C., Vernon, D. J., Dwivedi, P., et al. (2005). Event-related brain potential correlates of human auditory sensory memory-trace formation. *Journal of Neuroscience, 25*(45), 10494–10501.

Hafer, C. L., & Bègue, L. (2005). Experimental research on just-world theory: problems, developments, and future challenges. *Psychological Bulletin, 131*(1), 128–167.

Haga, S. M., Kraft, P., Corby, E.-K. (2010). Emotion regulation: Antecedents and well-being outcomes of cognitive reappraisal and expressive suppression in crosscultural samples. *Journal of Happiness Studies, 10*(3), 271–291.

Hagger, M., & Chatzisarantis, N. L.D. (2010). Causality orientations moderate the undermining effect of rewards on intrinsic motivation. *Journal of Experimental Social Psychology, 47*(2), 485–489.

Haier, R. J., Jung, R. E., Yeo, R. A., et al. (2004). Structural brain variation and general intelligence. *NeuroImage, 23*, 425–433.

Haier, R. J., Siegel, B. V., Nuechterlein, K. H., et al. (1988). Cortical glucose metabolic rate correlates of abstract reasoning and attention studied with positron emission tomography. *Intelligence, 12*, 199–217.

Haier, R. J., White, N. S., & Alkire, M. T. (2003). Individual differences in general intelligence correlate with brain function during nonreasoning tasks. *Intelligence, 31*(5), 429–441.

Hakun, J. G., Ruparel, K., Seelig, D., et al. (2009). Towards clinical trials of lie detection with fMRI. *Social Neuroscience, 4*(6), 518–527.

Hald, G. M., Malamuth, N. M., & Yuen, C. (2010). Pornography and attitudes supporting violence against women: Revisiting the relationship in nonexperimental studies. *Aggressive Behavior, 36*(1), 14–20.

Hales, D. (2012). *An invitation to health: Choosing to change* (14th ed.). Belmont, CA: Cengage Learning/Wadsworth.

Hall, E. T. (1966). *The hidden dimension.* Garden City, NY: Doubleday.

Hall, J. (2006). *What is clinical psychology?* (4th ed.). New York: Oxford University Press.

Hall, N. C., Perry, R. P., Goetz, T., et al. (2007). Attributional retraining and elaborative learning: Improving academic development through writing-based interventions. *Learning & Individual Differences, 17*(3), 280–290.

Hall, S. P. (2009). *Anger, rage, and relationships. An empathic approach to anger management.* New York: Routledge/Taylor & Francis.

Hallahan, D. P., Kauffman, J. M., & Pullen, P. C. (2011). *Exceptional learners* (12th ed.). Englewood Cliffs, NJ: Merrill/Prentice Hall.

Halliday, G. (2010). Reflections on the meanings of dreams prompted by reading Stekel. *Dreaming, 20*(4), 219–226.

Halpern, D. F. (2003). *Thought and knowledge: An introduction to critical thinking* (4th ed.). Mahwah, NJ: Erlbaum.

Halpern-Felsher, B. L., Cornell, J., Kropp, R. Y., et al. (2005). Oral versus vaginal sex among adolescents: Perceptions, attitudes, and behavior. *Pediatrics, 115*, 845–851.

Hammer, J. C., Fisher, J. D., Fitzgerald, P., et al. (1996). When two heads aren't better than one: AIDS risk behavior in college-age couples. *Journal of Applied Social Psychology, 26*(5), 375–397.

Hammer, L. B., Grigsby, T. D., & Woods, S. (1998). The conflicting demands of work, family, and school among students at an urban university. *Journal of Psychology, 132*(2), 220–226.

Hammond, D. C. (2008). Hypnosis as sole anesthesia for major surgeries: Historical & contemporary perspectives. *American Journal of Clinical Hypnosis, 51*(2), 101–121.

Hancock, P. A., & Ganey, H. C. N. (2003). From the inverted-U to the extended-U: The evolution of a law of psychology. *Journal of Human Performance in Extreme Environments, 7*(1), 5–14.

Handsfield, H. H. (2001). Resurgent sexually transmitted diseases among men who have sex with men. *Medscape Infectious Disease*, Medscape.com.

Hanley, S. J., & Abell, S. C. (2002). Maslow and relatedness: Creating an interpersonal model of self-actualization. *Journal of Humanistic Psychology, 42*(4), 37–56.

Hans, V. P., Kaye, D. H., Dann, B. M., et al. (2011). Science in the jury box: Jurors' comprehension of mitochondrial DNA evidence. *Law & Human Behavior, 35*(1), 60–71.

Hansell, J. H., & Damour, L. K, (2007). *Abnormal psychology: The enduring issues* (2nd ed.). New York: Wiley.

Hansen, C. J., Stevens, L. C., & Coast, J. R. (2001). Exercise duration and mood state. *Health Psychology, 20*(4), 267–275.

Hansen, N. B., Lambert, M. J., & Forman, E. M. (2002). The psychotherapy dose-response effect and its implications for treatment delivery services. *Clinical Psychology: Science & Practice, 9*(3), 329–334.

Hanton, S., Mellalieu, S. D., & Hall, R. (2004). Self-confidence and anxiety interpretation: A qualitative investigation. *Psychology of Sport & Exercise, 5*(4), 477–495.

Hanyu, H., Sato, T., Hirao, K., et al. (2010). The progression of cognitive deterioration and regional cerebral blood flow patterns in Alzheimer's disease: A longitudinal SPECT study. *Journal of the Neurological Sciences, 290*(1-2), 96–101.

Haq, I. U., Foote, K. D., Goodman, W. G., et al. (2010). Smile and laughter induction and intraoperative predictors of response to deep brain stimulation for obsessive-compulsive disorder. *NeuroImage, (Mar 10)*, [np].

Hardaway, C. A., & Gregory, K. B. (2005). Fatigue and sleep debt in an operational navy squadron. *International Journal of Aviation Psychology, 15*(2), 157–171.

Hardin, G. (1968). The tragedy of the commons. *Science, 162*, 1243–1248.

Hardin, M., & Greer, J. D. (2009). The influence of gender-role socialization, media use and sports participation on perceptions of gender-appropriate sports. *Journal of Sport Behavior, 32*(2), 207–226.

Harding, D. J., Fox, C., & Mehta, J. D. (2002). Studying rare events through qualitative case studies. *Sociological Methods & Research, 31*(2), 174–217.

Hardt, O., Einarsson, E. O., & Nader, K. (2010). A bridge over troubled water: Reconsolidation as a link between cognitive and neuroscientific memory research traditions. *Annual Review of Psychology, 61*, 141–167.

Hare, R. D. (2006). Psychopathy: A Clinical and forensic overview. *Psychiatric Clinics of North America, 29*(3), 709–724.

Harel, A., Gilaie-Dotan S., Malach, R., et al. (2010). Top-down engagement modulates the neural expressions of visual expertise. *Cerebral Cortex, 20*(10), 2304–2318.

Harker, L., & Keltner, D. (2001). Expressions of positive emotion in women's college yearbook pictures and their relationship to personality and life outcomes across adulthood. *Journal of Personality & Social Psychology, 80*(1), 112–124.

Harlow, H. F., & Harlow, M. K. (1962). Social deprivation in monkeys. *Scientific American, 207*, 136–146.

Harlow, J. M. (1868). Recovery from the passage of an iron bar through the head. *Publications of the Massachusetts Medical Society, 2*, 327–347.

Harm, D. L. (2002). Motion sickness neurophysiology, physiological correlates, and treatment. In K. M. Stanney (Ed.), *Handbook of virtual environments: Design, implementation, and applications* (pp. 637–661). Hillsdale, NJ: Erlbaum.

Harrigan, J. A. (2006). Proxemics, kinesics, and gaze. In J. A. Harrigan, R. Rosenthal, & R. Scherer (Eds.), *The new handbook of methods in nonverbal behavior research* (pp. 137–198). New York: Oxford University Press.

Harris, C. (2004). The evolution of jealousy. *American Scientist, 92*, 62–71.

Harris, J. C. (2003). Pinel delivering the insane. *Archives of General Psychiatry, 60*(6), 552.

Harris, J. C. (2010). *Intellectual disability: A guide for families and professionals.* New York: Oxford University Press.

Harrison, P. J., & Weinberger, D. R. (2005). Schizophrenia genes, gene expression, and neuropathology: On the matter of their convergence. *Molecular Psychiatry, 10*(1), 40–68.

Hart, B., & Risley, T. R. (1999). *The social world of children learning to talk.* Baltimore, MD: Paul H. Brookes.

Hart, C. L., Ksir, C. J., & Ray, O. S. (2009). *Drugs, society, and human* *behavior* (13th ed.). New York: McGraw-Hill.

Hart, D., & Carlo, G. (2005). Moral development in adolescence. *Journal of Research on Adolescence, 15*(3), 223–233.

Hartgens, F., & Kuipers, H. (2004). Effects of androgenic-anabolic steroids in athletes. *Sports Medicine, 34(8)*, 513–54.

Hartlep, K. L., & Forsyth, G. A. (2000). The effect of self-reference on learning and retention. *Teaching of Psychology, 27*(4), 269–271.

Hartmann, E. (2008). The central image makes "big" dreams big: The central image as the emotional heart of the dream. *Dreaming, 18*(1), 44–57.

Hartmann, E. (2010). The dream always makes new connections: The dream is a creation, not a replay. *Sleep Medicine Clinics, 5*(2), 241–248.

Hartmann, P., Reuter, M., & Nyborg, H. (2006). The relationship between date of birth and individual differences in personality and general intelligence: A large scale study. *Personality & Individual Differences, 40*(7), 1349–1362.

Hartung, C. M., Lefler, E. K., Tempel, A. B., et al. (2010). Halo effects in ratings of ADHD and ODD: Identification of susceptible symptoms. *Journal of Psychopathology & Behavioral Assessment, 32*(1), 128–137.

Harway, M. (Ed.). (2004). *Handbook of couples therapy*. San Francisco, CA: Jossey-Bass.

Hashibe, M., Straif, K., Tashkin, D. P., et al. (2005). Epidemiologic review of marijuana use and cancer risk. *Alcohol, 35*(3), 265–275.

Hashimoto, I., Suzuki, A., Kimura, T., et al. (2004). Is there training-dependent reorganization of digit representations in area 3b of string players? *Clinical Neurophysiology, 115*(2), 435–447.

Hauck, F. R., Moore, C. M., Herman, S. M., et al. (2002). The contribution of prone sleeping position to the racial disparity in sudden infant death syndrome. *Pediatrics, 110*, 772–780.

Hawks, J., Wang, E. T., Cochran, G. M., et al. (2007). Recent acceleration of human adaptive evolution. *Proceedings of the National Academy of Sciences, 104*(52), 20753–20758.

Haycraft, E., & Blissett, J. (2010). Eating disorder symptoms and parenting styles. *Appetite, 54*(1), 221–224.

Hayes, C. (1951). *The ape in our house*. New York: Harper & Row.

Hayes, M. R., De Jonghe, B. C., & Kanoski, S. (2010). Role of the glucagon-like-peptide-1 receptor in the control of energy balance. *Physiology & Behavior, 100*(5), 503–510.

Hayne, H., & Rovee-Collier C. (1995). The organization of reactivated memory in infancy. *Child Development, 66*(3), 893–906.

Hayward, L. C., & Coles, M. E. (2009). Elucidating the relation of hoarding to obsessive compulsive disorder and impulse control disorders. *Journal of Psychopathology & Behavioral Assessment, 31*(3), 220–227.

Hearold, S. L. (1987). Meta-analysis of the effects of television on social behavior. In G. Comstock (Ed.), *Public communication and behavior* (Vol. 1, pp. 65–133), NY: Academic.

Heath, R. G. (1963). Electrical self-stimulation of the brain in man. *American Journal of Psychiatry, 120*, 571–577.

Hebl, M. R., King, E. G., & Lin, J. (2004). The swimsuit becomes us all: Ethnicity, gender, and vulnerability to selfobjectification. *Personality & Social Psychology Bulletin, 30*, 1322–1331.

Hecht, J. (2007). *The happiness myth: Why what we think is right is wrong*. New York: HarperCollins.

Heiman, G. W. (2011). *Basic statistics for the behavioral sciences* (6th ed.). Belmont, CA: Cengage Learning/ Wadsworth.

Heiman, J. R. (2002). Sexual dysfunction: Overview of prevalence, etiological factors, and treatments. *Journal of Sex Research, 39(1)*, 73–78.

Heimann, M., & Meltzoff, A. N. (1996). Deferred imitation in 9- and 14-month-old infants. *British Journal of Developmental Psychology, 14*(Mar.), 55–64.

Heinrichs, R. W. (2001). *In search of madness: Schizophrenia and neuroscience*. New York: Oxford University Press.

Heisel, M. J., Flett, G. L., & Hewitt, P. L. (2003). Social hopelessness and college student suicide ideation. *Archives of Suicide Research, 7*(3), 221–235.

Helgeson, V. S. (2009). *The psychology of gender* (3rd ed.). Englewood Cliffs, NJ: Prentice Hall.

Hélie, S., & Sun, R. (2010). Incubation, insight, and creative problem solving: A unified theory and a connectionist model. *Psychological Review, 117*(3), 994–1024.

Hellige, J. B. (1993). *Hemispheric asymmetry*. Cambridge, MA: Harvard University Press.

Helson, R., & Srivastava, S. (2002). Creative and wise people. *Personality & Social Psychology Bulletin, 28*(10), 1430–1440.

Helton, W. S. (2007). Skill in expert dogs. *Journal of Experimental Psychology: Applied, 13*(3), 171–178.

Helton, W. S. (2009). Exceptional running skill in dogs requires extensive experience. *Journal of General Psychology, 136*(3), 323–332.

Henderson, N. D. (1982). Human behavior genetics. *Annual Review of Psychology, 33*, 403–440.

Henderson, T. L., Roberto, K. A., & Kamo, Y. (2010). Older adults' responses to Hurricane Katrina: Daily hassles and coping strategies. *Journal of Applied Gerontology, 29*(1), 48–69.

Hennenlotter, A., Dresel, C., Castrop, F., et al. (2009). The link between facial feedback and neural activity within central circuitries of emotion: New insights from botulinum toxin-induced denervation of frown muscles. *Cerebral Cortex, 19*(3), 537–542.

Hennessey, B. A., & Amabile, T. M. (2010). Creativity. *Annual Review of Psychology, 61*, 569–598.

Henningsen, D. D., Henningsen, M. L. M., Eden, J., et al. (2006). Examining the symptoms of groupthink and retrospective sensemaking. *Small Group Research, 37*(1), 36–64.

Henrich, J., Heine, S. J., & Norenzayan, A, (2010). The weirdest people in the world? *Behavioral & Brain Sciences, 33*, 61–135.

Henry, P. K., Murnane, K. S., Votaw, J. R., et al. (2010). Acute brain metabolic effects of cocaine in rhesus monkeys with a history of cocaine use. *Brain Imaging & Behavior, 4*(3-4), 212–219.

Hepburn, L., Miller, M, Azrael, D, et al. (2006). The US gun stock: results from the 2004 national firearms survey. *Injury Prevention, 13*, 15–19. Retrieved March 28, 2011 from http://injuryprevention.bmj.com/content/13/1/15.full.pdf.

Hepper, P. G., Wells, D. L., & Lynch, C. (2005). Prenatal thumb sucking is related to postnatal handedness. *Neuropsychologia, 43*(3), 313–315.

Herbenick, D., Reece, M., Schick, V., et al. (2010). Sexual behavior in the United States: Results from a national probability sample of men and women ages 14–94. *Journal of Sexual Medicine, 7*(suppl 5), 255–265.

Hergenhahn, B. R. (2009). *An introduction to the history of psychology* (6th ed.). Belmont, CA: Cengage Learning/ Wadsworth.

Hergenhahn, B. R., & Olson, M. (2009). *Introduction to the theories of learning* (8th ed.). Englewood Cliffs, NJ: Prentice Hall.

Heriot, S. A., & Pritchard, M. (2004). 'Reciprocal Inhibition as the Main Basis of Psychotherapeutic Effects' by Joseph Wolpe (1954). *Clinical Child Psychology & Psychiatry, 9*(2), 297–307.

Herman, J. L., & Tetrick, L. E. (2009). Problem-focused versus emotion-focused coping strategies and repatriation adjustment. *Human Resource Management, 48*(1), 69–88.

Hermann, B., Seidenberg, M., Sears, L., et al. (2004). Cerebellar atrophy in temporal lobe epilepsy affects procedural memory. *Neurology, 63*(11), 2129–2131.

Hernstein, R., & Murray, C. (1994). *The bell curve*. New York: Free Press.

Herold, D. K. (2010). Mediating media studies: Stimulating critical awareness in a virtual environment. *Computers & Education, 54*(3), 791–798.

Herrmann, D. J., Yoder, C. Y., Gruneberg, M., et al. (2006). *Applied cognitive psychology: A textbook*. Mahwah, NJ: Erlbaum.

Herxheimer, A., & Waterhouse, J. (2003). The prevention and treatment of jet lag. *British Medical Journal, 326*(7384), 296–297.

Herz, R. S. (2001). Ah sweet skunk! *Cerebrum, 3*(4), 31–47.

Hettich, P. I. (2005). *Connect college to career: Student guide to work and life transition*. Belmont, CA: Cengage Learning/Wadsworth.

Higbee, K. L., Clawson, C., DeLano, L., et al. (1990). Using the link mnemonic to remember errands. *Psychological Record, 40*(3), 429–436.

Higgins, S. T., Heil, S. H., & Lussier, J. P. (2004). Clinical implications of reinforcement as a determinant of substance use disorders. *Annual Review of Psychology, 55*, 431–461.

Higham, P. A., & Gerrard, C. (2005). Not all errors are created equal: Metacognition and changing answers on multiple-choice tests. *Canadian Journal of Experimental Psychology, 59*(1), 28–34.

Hilgard, E. R. (1968). *The experience of hypnosis*. New York: Harcourt Brace Jovanovich.

Hilgard, E. R. (1977). *Divided consciousness* (pp. 32–51). New York: Wiley.

Hilgard, E. R. (1994) Neodissociation theory. In S. J. Lynn, & J. W. Rhue (Eds.), *Dissociation: Clinical, theoretical and research perspectives* (pp. 32–51). New York: Guilford.

Hilsenroth, M. J. (2000). Rorschach test. In A. Kazdin (Ed.), *Encyclopedia of psychology* (Vol. 7, pp. 117–119). Washington, DC: American Psychological Association.

Hinkel, E. (Ed.). (2005). *Handbook of research in second language teaching and learning*. Mahwah, NJ: Erlbaum.

Hinterberger, T., Kübler, A., Kaiser, J., et al. (2003). A brain-computer interface (BCI) for the locked-in: Comparison of different EEG classifications for the thought translation device. *Clinical Neurophysiology, 114*(3), 416–425.

Hintzman, D. L. (2005). Memory strength and recency judgments. *Psychonomic Bulletin & Review, 12*(5), 858–864.

Hirshbein, L., & Sarvananda, S. (2008). History, power, and electricity: American popular magazine accounts of electroconvulsive therapy, 1940–2005. *Journal of the History of the Behavioral Sciences, 44*(1), 1–18.

Hirstein, W. (2005). *Brain fiction: Self-deception and the riddle of confabulation*. Cambridge, MA: MIT Press.

Hiscock, M., Perachio, N., & Inch, R. (2001). Is there a sex difference in human laterality? *Journal of Clinical & Experimental Neuropsychology, 23*(2), 137–148.

Hixon, M. D. (1998). Ape language research: A review and behavioral perspective. *Analysis of Verbal Behavior, 15*, 17–39.

Hobson, J. A. (2000). Dreams: Physiology. In A. Kazdin (Ed.), *Encyclopedia of psychology* (Vol. 3, pp. 78–81). Washington, DC: American Psychological Association.

Hobson, J. A. (2001). *Consciousness*. New York: Freeman.

Hobson, J. A. (2005). Sleep is of the brain, by the brain and for the brain. *Nature, 437*(7063), 1254–1256.

Hobson, J. A., Pace-Schott E. F., & Stickgold, R. (2000). Dream science 2000. *Behavioral & Brain Sciences, 23*(6), 1019–1035; 1083–1121.

Hochstenbach, J., Mulder, T., van Limbeek, J., et al. (1998). Cognitive decline following stroke: A comprehensive study of cognitive decline following stroke. *Journal of Clinical & Experimental Neuropsychology, 20*(4), 503–517.

Hodgins, H. S., & Adair, K. C. (2010). Attentional processes and meditation. *Consciousness & Cognition, 19*(4), 872–878.

Hodgson, R., & Miller, P. (1982). *Selfwatching*. New York: Facts on File.

Hodson, R., & Sullivan, T. A. (2010). *The social organization of work* (5th ed.). Belmont, CA: Cengage Learning/ Wadsworth.

Hofer, B. K., & Yu, S. L. (2003). Teaching self-regulated learning through a "Learning to Learn" course. *Teaching of Psychology, 30*(1), 30–33.

Hoff, E. (2006). How social contexts support and shape language development. *Developmental Review, 26*(1), 55–88.

Hoff, E. (2009). *Language development* (4th ed.). Belmont, CA: Cengage Learning/Wadsworth.

Hoff, E., & Tian, C. (2005). Socioeconomic status and cultural influences on language. *Journal of Communication Disorders, 38*(4), 271–278.

Hoffart, A. (2005). Interpersonal therapy for social phobia: Theoretical model and review of the evidence. In M. E. Abelian (Ed.), *Focus on psychotherapy research* (pp. 121–137). Hauppauge, NY: Nova Science Publishers.

Hoffer, A., & Youngren, V. R. (2004). Is free association still at the core of psychoanalysis? *International Journal of Psychoanalysis, 85*(6), 1489–1492.

Hoffman, E. (2008). Abraham Maslow: A biographer's reflections. *Journal of Humanistic Psychology, 48*(4), 439–443.

Hofman, D. (2008). The frontal laterality of emotion: A historical overview. *Netherlands Journal of Psychology, 64*(3), 112–118.

Hofmann, W., Gawronski, B., Gschwendner, T., et al. (2005). A meta-analysis on the correlation between the implicit association test and explicit self-report measures. *Personality & Social Psychology Bulletin, 31*(10), 1369–1385.

Hogan, E. H., Hornick, B. A., & Bouchoux, A. (2002). Focus on communications: Communicating the message: Clarifying the controversies about caffeine. *Nutrition Today, 37*, 28–35.

Hogben, D., & Lawson, M. J. (1992). Superiority of the keyword method for backward recall in vocabulary acquisition. *Psychological Reports, 71*(3, Pt 1), 880–882.

Hoge, C. W., Castro, C. A., Messer, S. C., et al. (2004). Combat duty in Iraq and Afghanistan, mental health problems, and barriers to care. *New England Journal of Medicine, 351*(1), 13–22.

Hohwy, J., & Rosenberg, R. (2005). Unusual experiences, reality testing and delusions of alien control. *Mind & Language, 20*(2), 141–162.

Holbrook, T., Moore, C., & Zoss, M. (2010). Equitable intent: Reflections on universal design in education as an ethic of care. *Reflective Practice, 11*(5), 681–692.

Holden, C. (1980). Twins reunited. *Science 80*, Nov., 55–59.

Holland, J. L. (1997). *Making vocational choices*. Odessa, FL: Psychological Assessment Resources.

Hollins, M. (2010). Somesthetic senses. *Annual Review of Psychology, 61*, 243–271.

Hollon, S. D., Stewart, M. O., & Strunk, D. (2006). Enduring effects for cognitive behavior therapy in the treatment of depression and anxiety. *Annual Review of Psychology, 57*, 285–315.

Holman, E. A., Silver, R. C., Poulin, M., et al. (2008). Terrorism, acute stress, and cardiovascular health: A 3-year national study following the September 11th attacks. *Archives of General Psychiatry, 65*(1), 73–80.

Holmes, E. K., & Huston, A. C. (2010). Understanding positive father-child interaction: Children's, father's, and mother's contributions. *Fathering, 8*(2), 203–225.

Holmes, J., & Adams, J. W. (2006). Working memory and children's mathematical skills: Implications for mathematical development and mathematics curricula. *Educational Psychology, 26*(3), 339–366.

Holmes, M. (2002). Rethinking the meaning and management of intersexuality. *Sexualities, 5*(2), 159–180,

Holmes, T. H., & Rahe, R. H. (1967). The social readjustment rating scale. *Journal of Psychosomatic Research, 11*(2), 213–218.

Holtzen, D. W. (2000). Handedness and professional tennis. *International Journal of Neuroscience, 105*(1-4), 101–111.

Holzinger, B., LaBerge, S., & Levitan, L. (2006). Psychophysiological correlates of lucid dreaming. *Dreaming, 16*(2), 88–95.

Honzik, M. P. (1984). Life-span development. *Annual Review of Psychology, 35*, 309–331.

Hooyman, N. & Kiyak, H. A. (2011). *Social gerontology: A multidisciplinary perspective* (9th ed.). Boston: Pearson/ Allyn & Bacon.

Horgan, J. (2005). The forgotten era of brain chips. *Scientific American, 293*(4), 66–73.

Horn, R. R., Williams, A. M., Scott, M. A., et al. (2005). Visual search and coordination changes in response to video and point-light demonstrations without KR. *Journal of Motor Behavior, 37*(4), 265–274.

Horne, R. S. C., Andrew, S., Mitchell, K., et al. (2001). Apnoea of prematurity and arousal from sleep. *Early Human Development, 61*(2), 119–133.

Hortman, G. (2003). What do facial expressions convey? *Emotion, 3*(2), 150–166.

Horvath, L. S., Milich, R., Lynam, D., et al. (2004) Sensation seeking and substance use: A cross-lagged panel design. *Individual Differences Research, 2*(3), 175–183.

Hosch, H. M., & Cooper, D. S. (1982). Victimization as a determinant of eyewitness accuracy. *Journal of Applied Psychology, 67*, 649–652.

Houghton, D. P. (2008). Invading and occupying Iraq: Some insights from political psychology. *Peace & Conflict: Journal of Peace Psychology, 14*(2), 169–192.

Howard, A., Pion, G. M., Gottfredson, G. D., et al. (1986). The changing face of American psychology. *American Psychologist, 41*, 1311–1327.

Howard, I. P., & Rogers, B. J. (2001a). *Seeing in depth* (Vol 1): *Basic mechanisms*. Toronto, ON: Porteous.

Howard, I. P., & Rogers, B. J. (2001b). *Seeing in depth* (Vol 2): *Depth perception*. Toronto, ON: Porteous.

Howard, J. L., & Ferris, G. R. (1996). The employment interview context. *Journal of Applied Social Psychology, 26*(2), 112–136.

Howell, D. C. (2011). *Fundamental statistics for the behavioral sciences* (7th ed.). Belmont, CA: Cengage Learning/Wadsworth.

Howitt, D., Craven, G., Iveson, C., et al. (1977). The misdirected letter. *British Journal of Social & Clinical Psychology, 16*, 285–286.

Hsia, Y., & Graham, C. H. (1997). Color blindness. In A. Byrne & D. R. Hilbert (Eds.), *Readings on color* (Vol. 2): *The science of color* (pp. 201–229). Cambridge, MA: MIT Press.

Huang, M.-H., & Rust, R. T. (2011). Sustainability and consumption. *Journal of the Academy of Marketing Science, 39*(1), 40–54.

Hubble, M.A., Duncan, B. L., & Miller, S. D. (Eds.) (1999). *The heart and soul of change: What works in therapy*. Washington, DC: American Psychological Association.

Hubel D. H., & Wiesel, W. N. (2005). *Brain & visual perception: The story of a 25-year collaboration*. New York: Oxford University Press.

Hübner, R., & Volberg, G. (2005). The integration of object levels and their content: A theory of global/local processing and related hemispheric differences. *Journal of Experimental Psychology: Human Perception & Performance, 31*(3), 520–541.

Huesmann, L. R., Moise-Titus J., Podolski, C., et al. (2003). Longitudinal relations between children's exposure to TV violence and their aggressive and violent behavior in young adulthood: 1977–1992. *Developmental Psychology, 39*(2), 201–221.

Hughes, A. (2008). The use of urban legends to improve critical thinking. In L. T. Benjamin, Jr. (Ed.). *Favorite activities for the teaching of psychology*. Washington, DC, US: American Psychological Association.

Hughes, J. R., Oliveto, A. H., Liguori, A., et al. (1998). Endorsement of DSM-IV dependence criteria among caffeine users. *Drug & Alcohol Dependence, 52*(2), 99–107.

Hughes, M., & Morrison, K., & Asada, K. J. K. (2005). What's love got to do with it? Exploring the impact of maintenance rules, love attitudes, and network support on friends with benefits relationships. *Western Journal of Communication, 69*(1), 49–66.

Huguet, P., Dumas, F., Monteil, J. M., et al. (2001). Social comparison choices in the classroom: Further evidence for students' upward comparison tendency and its beneficial impact on performance. *European Journal of Social Psychology, 31*(5), 557–578.

Huijbregts, S. C., Séguin, J. R., Zelazo, P. D., et al. (2006). Interrelations between maternal smoking during pregnancy, birth weight and sociodemographic factors in the prediction of early cognitive abilities. *Infant & Child Development, 15*(6), 593–607.

Hunt E. (1995). The role of intelligence in modern society. *American Scientist, 83*(July-August), 356–368.

Hunter, E. (1998). Adolescent attraction to cults. *Adolescence, 33*(131), 709–714.

Hunter, J. P., Katz, J., & Davis, K. D. (2003). The effect of tactile and visual sensory inputs on phantom limb awareness. *Brain, 126*(3), 579–589.

Huston, H. C., & Bentley, A. C. (2010). Human development in societal context. *Annual Review of Psychology, 61*, 411–437.

Hutchinson, S. R. (2004). Survey research. In K. deMarrais, & S. D. Lapan (Eds.), Foundations for research: *Methods of inquiry in education and the social sciences: Inquiry and pedagogy across diverse contexts* (pp. 283–301). Mahwah, NJ: Erlbaum.

Hutchinson, S., Lee, L. H. L., Gaab, N., et al. (2003). Cerebellar volume of musicians. *Cerebral Cortex, 13*(9), 943–949.

Hutchison, K. E., McGeary, J., Smolen, A., et al. (2002). The DRD4 VNTR polymorphism moderates craving after alcohol consumption. *Health Psychology, 21*(2), 139–146.

Hyde, J. S. (2007). *Half the human experience: The psychology of women* (7th ed.). Boston: Houghton Mifflin.

Hyde, J. S., & DeLamater, J. D. (2011). *Understanding human sexuality* (11th ed.). New York: McGraw-Hill.

Hyman, R. (1996a). Evaluation of the military's twenty-year program on psychic spying. *Skeptical Inquirer, 20*(2), 21–23.

Hyman, R. (1996b). The evidence for psychic functioning: Claims vs. reality. *Skeptical Inquirer, 20*(2), 24–26.

Hyman, R. (2007). Talking with the dead, communicating with the future and other myths created by cold reading. In S. Della Sala (Ed.), *Tall tales about the mind & brain: Separating fact from fiction* (pp. 218–232). New York: Oxford University Press.

Hyman, S. E. (2011). Diagnosis of mental disorders in light of modern genetics.In D. A. Regier, W. E. Narrow, E. A. Kuhl, et al. (Eds.), *The conceptual evolution of DSM-5* (pp. 3–17). Arlington, VA: American Psychiatric Publishing.

Hysenbegasi, A., Hass, S. L., & Rowland, C. R. (2005). The impact of depression on the academic productivity of university students. *Journal of Mental Health Policy & Economics, 8*(3), 145–151.

Iacono, W. G. (2008). Effective policing: Understanding how polygraph tests work and are used. *Criminal Justice & Behavior, 35*(10), 1295–1308.

Iannetti, G. D., & Mouraux, A. (2010). From the neuromatrix to the pain matrix (and back). *Experimental Brain Research, 205*(1), 1–12.

Iannone, M., Bulotta, S., Paolino, D., et al. (2006). Electrocortical effects of MDMA are potentiated by acoustic stimulation in rats. *BMC Neuroscience, February 16,* 7–13.

Iastrebov, V., Seet, G., Asokan, T., et al. (2008). Vision enhancement using stereoscopic telepresence for remotely operated underwater robotic vehicles. *Journal of Intelligent & Robotic Systems, 52*(1), 139–154.

Ida, Y., & Mandal, M. K. (2003). Cultural differences in side bias: Evidence from Japan and India. *Laterality: Asymmetries of Body, Brain & Cognition, 8*(2), 121–133.

Imbimbo, C., Verze, P., Palmieri, A., et al. (2009). A report from a single institute's 14-year experience in treatment of male-to-female transsexuals. *Journal of Sexual Medicine, 6*(10), 2736–2745.

Immordino-Yang, M. H. (2008). How we can learn from children with half a brain? *New Scientist, 2664,* 44–45.

Impett, E. A. Strachman, A., Finkel, E. J., et al. (2008). Maintaining sexual desire in intimate relationships: The importance of approach goals. *Journal of Personality & Social Psychology, 94*(5), 808–823.

Impett, E. A., Gordon, A. M., Kogan, A., et al. (2010). Moving toward more perfect unions: Daily and long-term consequences of approach and avoidance goals in romantic relationships. *Journal of Personality & Social Psychology, 99*(6), 948–963.

Ingham, A. G., Levinger, G., Graves, J., et al. (1974). The Ringelmann effect: Studies of group size and group performance. *Journal of Personality & Social Psychology, 10,* 371–384.

Iosif, A., & Ballon, B. (2005). Bad moon rising: The persistent belief in lunar connections to madness. *Canadian Medical Association Journal, 173*(12), 1498–1500.

Ivanco, T. L., & Racine, R. J. (2000). Long-term potentiation in the pathways between the hippocampus and neocortex in the chronically implanted, freely moving, rat. *Hippocampus, 10,* 143–152.

Iversen, L. (2006). *Speed, ecstasy, ritalin: The science of amphetamines.* New York: Oxford University Press.

Iverson, R. D., & Zatzick, C. D. (2011). The effects of downsizing on labor productivity: The value of showing consideration for employees' morale and welfare in high-performance work systems. *Human Resource Management, 50*(1), 29–44.

Iyengar, S. S., & Lepper, M. R. (2000). When choice is demotivating: Can one desire too much of a good thing? *Journal of Personality & Social Psychology, 79*(6), 995–1006.

Izard, C. E. (1977). *Human emotions.* New York: Plenum.

Izard, C. E. (1990). Facial expressions and the regulation of emotions. *Journal of Personality & Social Psychology, 58*(3), 487–498.

Izard, C. E., Fantauzzo, C. A., Castle, J. M., et al. (1995). The ontogeny and significance of infants' facial expressions in the first 9 months of life. *Developmental Psychology, 31*(6), 997–1013.

Jablonski, N.G., & Chaplin, G. (2000). The evolution of human skin coloration. *Journal of Human Evolution, 39*(1), 57–106.

Jackson, D., & Newberry, P. (2012). *Critical thinking: A user's manual.* Belmont, CA: Cengage Learning/Wadsworth.

Jackson, S. L. (2011). *Research methods: A modular approach* (2nd ed.). Belmont, CA: Cengage Learning/Wadsworth.

Jackson, T., Fritch, A., Nagasaka, T., et al. (2002). Towards explaining the association between shyness and loneliness. *Social Behavior & Personality, 30*(3), 263–270.

Jackson, T., Towson, S., & Narduzzi, K. (1997). Predictors of shyness. *Social Behavior & Personality, 25*(2), 149–154.

Jacob, A., Prasad, S., Boggild, M., et al. (2004). Charles Bonnet syndrome: Elderly people and visual hallucinations. *British Medical Journal, 328*(7455), 1552–1554.

Jacobs, M. (2003). *Sigmund Freud.* Thousand Oaks, CA: Sage.

Jacobs, M. K., Christensen, A., Snibbe, J. R., et al. (2001). A comparison of computer-based versus traditional individual psychotherapy. *Professional Psychology: Research & Practice, 32*(1), 92–96.

Jacobs, N., van Os, J., Derom, C., et al. (2008). Heritability of intelligence. *Twin Research & Human Genetics, 10*(Suppl), 11–14.

Jacobs, S. R., & Dodd, D. K. (2003). Student burnout as a function of personality, social support, and workload. *Journal of College Student Development, 44*(3), 291–303.

Jacobs-Stewart, T. (2010). *Mindfulness and the 12 steps: Living recovery in the present moment.* Center City, MN: Hazelden Foundation.

Jaeggi, S. M., Buschkuehl, M., Jonides, J., et al. (2008). Improving fluid intelligence with training on working memory. *Proceedings of the National Academy of Sciences, 105*(19), 6829–6833.

Jaehnig, W., & Miller, M. L. (2007). Feedback types in programmed instruction: A systematic review. *Psychological Record, 57*(2), 219–232.

Jaffe, J., Beatrice, B., Feldstein, S., et al. (2001). Rhythms of dialogue in infancy. *Monographs of the Society for Research in Child Development, 66*(2), vi–131.

Jagaroo, V. (2009). *Neuroinformatics for neuropsychology.* New York: Springer.

Jahoda, G. (2007). Superstition and belief. *The Psychologist, 20*(10), 594–595.

James, W. (1890). *The principles of psychology.* Retrieved March 22, 2011 from http://psychclassics.yorku.ca/James/Principles/.

Jamison, K. R. (1999). A magical orange grove in a nightmare: Creativity and mood disorders. In R. Conlan (Ed.), *States of mind* (pp. 53–80). New York: Wiley.

Jamison, K. R. (2001). Suicide in the young: An essay. *Cerebrum, 3*(3), 39–42.

Janis, I. L. (1989). *Crucial decisions.* New York: Free Press.

Janis, I. L. (2007). Groupthink. In R. P. Vecchio (Ed.), *Leadership: Understanding the dynamics of power and influence in organizations* (2nd ed., pp. 163–176). Notre Dame, IN: University of Notre Dame Press.

Janowsky, J. S. (2006). Thinking with your gonads: Testosterone and cognition. *Trends in Cognitive Sciences, 10*(2), 77–82.

Janssen, S. A., & Arntz, A. (2001). Real-life stress and opioid-mediated analgesia in novice parachute jumpers. *Journal of Psychophysiology, 15*(2), 106–113.

Janus, S. S., & Janus, C. L. (1993). *The Janus report.* New York: Wiley.

Jarvin, L., & Sternberg, R. J. (2003). Alfred Binet's contributions to educational psychology. In B. J. Zimmerman & D. H. Schunk (Eds.), *Educational psychology: A century of contributions* (pp. 65–79). Mahwah, NJ: Erlbaum.

Jawahar, I. M., Stone, T. H., & Kisamore, J. L. (2007). Role conflict and burnout: The direct and moderating effects of political skill and perceived organizational support on burnout dimensions. *International Journal of Stress Management, 14*(2), 142–159.

Jay, T. B. (2003). *Psychology of language.* Upper Saddle River, NJ: Prentice Hall.

Jeffery, R. W., & Wing R. R. (2001). The effects of an enhanced exercise program on long-term weight loss. *Obesity Research, 9*(3), O193.

Jellinger, K. A. (2009). Review of *Interactive atlas of the human brain. European Journal of Neurology, 16*(3), e51.

Jenkins, J. G., & Dallenbach, K. M. (1924). Oblivescence during sleep and waking. *American Journal of Psychology, 35,* 605–612.

Jennings, L., & Skovholt, T. M. (1999). The cognitive, emotional, and relational characteristics of master therapists. *Journal of Counseling Psychology, 46*(1), 3–11.

Jerabek, I., & Standing, L. (1992). Imagined test situations produce contextual memory enhancement. *Perceptual & Motor Skills, 75*(2), 400.

Jin, S.-A A. (2010). Effects of 3D virtual haptics force feedback on brand personality perception: The mediating role of physical presence in advergames. *Cyberpsychology, Behavior, & Social Networking, 13*(3), 307–311.

Jo, E. Y., Tae, W. K., Lee, M. J., et al. (2010). Reduced brain gray matter concentration in patients with obstructive sleep apnea syndrome. *Sleep: Journal of Sleep & Sleep Disorders Research, 33*(2), 235–241.

Joffe, R. T. (2006). Is the thyroid still important in major depression? *Journal of Psychiatry & Neuroscience, 31*(6), 367–368.

Johnson, J. J. M., Hrycaiko, D. W., Johnson, G. V., et al. (2004). Self-talk and female youth soccer performance. *The Sport Psychologist, 18*(1), 44–59.

Johnson, C. S., & Stapel, D. A. (2010). It depends on how you look at it: Being versus becoming mindsets determine responses to social comparisons. *British Journal of Social Psychology, 49*(4), 703–723.

Johnson, K. J., & Fredrickson, B. L. (2005). "We all look the same to me": Positive emotions eliminate the own-race bias in face recognition. *Psychological Science, 16*(11), 875–881.

Johnson, S. (2005). *Everything bad is good for you: How today's popular culture is actually making us smarter.* New York: Riverhead.

Johnson, S. J., Batey, M., & Holdsworth, L. (2009). Personality and health: The mediating role of trait emotional intelligence and work locus of control. *Personality & Individual Differences, 47*(5), 470–475.

Johnson, S. K., Podratz, K. E., Dipboye, R. L., et al. (2010). Physical attractiveness biases in ratings of employment suitability: Tracking down the "beauty is beastly" effect. *Journal of Social Psychology, 150*(3), 301–318.

Johnson, T. J. (2002). College students' self-reported reasons for why drinking games end. *Addictive Behaviors, 27*(1), 145–153.

Johnson, W., Jung, R. E., Colom, R., et al. (2008). Cognitive abilities independent of IQ correlate with regional brain structure. *Intelligence, 36*(1), 18–28.

Joinson, C., Heron, J., Von Gontard, A., et al. (2009). A prospective study of age at initiation of toilet training and subsequent daytime bladder control in school-age children. *Journal of Developmental & Behavioral Pediatrics, 30*(5), 385–393.

Jolly, J. L., Treffinger, D. J., Inman, T. F., et al. (Eds.). (2011). *Parenting gifted children: The authoritative guide from the National Association for Gifted Children.* Waco, TX: Prufrock Press.

Jones, E. E., & Nisbett, R. E. (1971). The actor and observer: Divergent perceptions of the causes of behavior. In E. E. Jones, D. E. Kanouse, et al. (Eds.), *Attribution: Perceiving the causes of behavior* (pp. 79–94). Morristown, NJ: General Learning Press.

Jones, L., & Petruzzi, D. C. (1995). Test anxiety: A review of theory and current treatment. *Journal of College Student Psychotherapy, 10*(1), 3–15.

Jones, M. K., & Menzies, R. G. (1998). Danger ideation reduction therapy (DIRT) for obsessive-compulsive washers. *Behaviour Research & Therapy, 36*(10), 959–970.

Jones, R. A. (2007). A discovery of meaning: The case of C. G. Jung's house dream. *Culture & Psychology, 13*(2), 203–230.

Jones, R. N. (2003). Racial bias in the assessment of cognitive functioning of older adults. *Aging & Mental Health, 7*(2), 83–102.

Jones, R., Yates, W. R., & Zhou, M. (2002). Readmission rates for adjustment disorders: Comparison with other mood disorders. *Journal of Affective Disorders, 71*(1–3), 199–203.

Jones, S. A. H., & Wilson, A. E. (2009). The horizon line, linear perspective, interposition, and background brightness as determinants of the magnitude of the pictorial moon illusion. *Attention, Perception, & Psychophysics, 71*(1), 131–142.

Jones, S. R., & Fernyhough, C. (2007). A new look at the neural diathesis-stress model of schizophrenia: The primacy of social-evaluative and uncontrollable situations. *Schizophrenia Bulletin, 33*(5), 1171–1177.

Jones, S. S., & Hong, H.-W. (2001). Onset of voluntary communication: Smiling looks to mother. *Infancy, 2*(3), 353–370.

Jonides, J., Lewis, R. L., Nee, D. E., et al. (2008). The mind and brain of short-term memory. *Annual Review of Psychology, 59*, 193–224.

Jorm, A. F., Korten, A. E., Rodgers, B., et al. (2002). Sexual orientation and mental health. *British Journal of Psychiatry, 180*(5), 423–427.

Jourard, S. M. (1963). *Personal adjustment*. New York: Macmillan.

Jouvet, M. (1999). *The paradox of sleep*. Boston, MA: MIT Press.

Jowett, G. S. (2006). Brainwashing: The Korean POW controversy and the origins of a myth. In G. S. Jowett, & V. O'Donnell (Eds.), *Readings in propaganda and persuasion: New and classic essays* (pp. 201–211). Thousand Oaks, CA, Sage.

Judge, T. A., Jackson, C. L., Shaw, J. C., et al. (2007). Self-efficacy and work-related performance: The integral role of individual differences. *Journal of Applied Psychology, 92*, 107–127.

Juliano, L. M., & Griffiths, R. R. (2004). A critical review of caffeine withdrawal: Empirical validation of symptoms and signs, incidence, severity, and associated features. *Psychopharmacology, 176*(1), 1–29.

Julien, R. M. (2011). *A primer of drug action*. (12th ed.). New York: Worth.

Jung, C. G. (1961). *Memories, dreams, reflections*. New York: Pantheon.

Jussim, L., & Harber, K. D. (2005). Teacher expectations and self-fulfilling prophecies: Knowns and unknowns, resolved and unresolved controversies. *Personality & Social Psychology Review, 9*(2), 131–155.

Kadosh, R. C, & Henik, A. (2007). Can synaesthesia research inform cognitive science? *Trends in Cognitive Sciences, 11*(4), 177–184.

Kafka, M. P. (2010). Hypersexual disorder: A proposed diagnosis for DSM-V. *Archives of Sexual Behavior, 39*(2), 377–400.

Kagan, J. (1971). *Change and continuity in infancy*. New York: Wiley.

Kagan, J. (2004). New insights into temperament. *Cerebrum, 6*(1), 51–66.

Kagan, J. (2005). Personality and temperament: Historical perspectives. In M. Rosenbluth, S. H. Kennedy, et al. (Eds.), *Depression and personality: Conceptual and clinical challenges* (pp. 3–18). Washington: American Psychiatric Publishing.

Kahneman, D. (2003). A perspective on judgment and choice. *American Psychologist, 58*(9), 697–720.

Kahneman, D., & Tversky, A. (1972). Subjective probability: A judgment of representativeness. *Cognitive Psychology, 3*, 430–454.

Kahneman, D., & Tversky, A. (1973). On the psychology of prediction. *Psychological Review, 80*, 237–251.

Kahneman, D., Krueger, A. B., Schkade, D., et al. (2004). A survey method for characterizing daily life experience: The day reconstruction method. *Science, 306*(5702), 1776–1780.

Kahneman, D., Slovic, P., & Tversky, A. (1982). *Judgment under uncertainty: Heuristics and biases*. Cambridge, MA: Cambridge University Press.

Kail, R. V., & Cavanaugh, J. C. (2010). *Human development: A life-span view* (5th ed.). Belmont, CA: Cengage Learning/Wadsworth.

Kalat, J. W. (2009). *Biological psychology* (10th ed.). Belmont, CA: Cengage Learning/Wadsworth.

Kalat, J. W., & Shiota, M. N. (2012). *Emotion* (2nd ed.). Belmont, CA: Wadsworth.

Kallio, S., & Revonsuo, A. (2003). Hypnotic phenomena and altered states of consciousness: A multilevel framework of description and explanation. *Contemporary Hypnosis, 20*(3), 111–164.

Kalmijn, M. (2010). Educational inequality, homogamy, and status exchange in Black-White intermarriage: A comment on Rosenfield. *American Journal of Sociology, 115*(4), 1252–1263.

Kalyuga, S., & Hanham, J. (2011). Instructing in generalized knowledge structures to develop flexible problem solving skills. *Computers in Human Behavior, 27*(1), 63–68.

Kalyuga, S., Renkl, A., & Paas, F. (2010). Facilitating flexible problem solving: A cognitive load perspective. *Educational Psychology Review, 22*(2), 175–186.

Kamimori, G. H., Johnson, D., Thorne, D., et al. (2005). Multiple caffeine doses maintain vigilance during early morning operations. *Aviation, Space, & Environmental Medicine, 76*(11), 1046–1050.

Kamin, L. J. (1981). *The intelligence controversy*. New York: Wiley.

Kammrath, L. K., Mendoza-Denton R., & Mischel, W. (2005). Incorporating If . . . Then . . . personality signatures in person perception: Beyond the person-situation dichotomy. *Journal of Personality & Social Psychology, 88*(4), 605–618.

Kampman, K. M. (2005). New medications for the treatment of cocaine dependence. *Psychiatry, 2*(12), 44–48.

Kanas, N., & Manzey, D. (2008). *Space psychology and psychiatry* (2nd ed.). New York: Springer.

Kapinos, K. A., & Yakusheva, O. (2011). Environmental influences on young adult weight gain: Evidence from a natural experiment. *Journal of Adolescent Health, 48*(1), 52–58.

Kaplan, A. (2008). Clarifying metacognition, self-regulation and self-regulated learning: What's the purpose? *Educational Psychology Review, 20*(4), 477–484.

Kaplan, P. S. (1998). *The human odyssey*. Pacific Grove, CA: Brooks/Cole.

Kaplan, R. M., & Saccuzzo, D. P. (2009). *Psychological testing: Principles, applications, and issues* (7th ed.). Belmont, CA: Cengage Learning/Wadsworth.

Kapleau, P. (1966). *The three pillars of Zen*. New York: Harper & Row.

Kappe, R., & van der Flier, H. (2010). Using multiple and specific criteria to assess the predictive validity of the big five personality factors on academic performance. *Journal of Research in Personality, 44* (1), 142–145.

Kaptelinin, V., & Czerwinski, M. (Eds.). (2007). *Beyond the desktop metaphor: Design integrated digital work environments*. Cambridge, MA: MIT Press.

Kapur, S., & Lecrubier, Y. (Eds.). (2003). *Dopamine in the pathophysiology and treatment of schizophrenia: New findings*. Washington, DC: Taylor & Francis.

Karageorgis, C. I., & Terry, P. C. (2011). *Inside sport psychology*. Champaign, IL: Human Kinetics.

Karim, A. A., Hinterberger, T., Richter, J,, et al. (2006). Neural internet: Web surfing with brain potentials for the completely paralyzed. *Neurorehabilitation & Neural Repair, 20*(4), 508–515.

Kark, R., & Eagly, A. H. (2010). Gender and leadership: Negotiating the labyrinth. In J. C. Chrisler, & D. R. McCreary (Eds.), *Handbook of gender research in psychology* (Vol 2): *Gender research in social and applied psychology* (pp. 443–470). New York: Springer.

Karpicke, J. D., & Blunt, J. R. (2011). Retrieval practice produces more learning than elaborative studying with concept mapping. *Science, January*, doi:10.1126/science.1199327.

Kasser, T., & Ryan, R. M. (1993). A dark side of the American dream: Correlates of financial success as a central life aspiration. *Journal of Personality & Social Psychology, 65*(2), 410–422.

Kasser, T., & Ryan, R. M. (1996). Further examining the American dream: Differential correlates of intrinsic and extrinsic goals. *Personality & Social Psychology Bulletin, 22*(3), 280–287.

Kassin, S. M. (2005). On the psychology of confessions: Does innocence put innocents at risk? *American Psychologist, 60*(3), 215–228.

Kassin, S. M., Fein, S., & Markus, H. R. (2011). *Social psychology* (8th ed.). Boston: Houghton Mifflin.

Kassin, S. M., Tubb, V. A., Hosch, H. M., et al. (2001). On the "general acceptance" of eyewitness testimony research. *American Psychologist, 56*(5), 405–416.

Kataria, S. (2004). A clinical guide to pediatric sleep: Diagnosis and management of sleep problems. *Journal of Developmental & Behavioral Pediatrics, 25*(2), 132–133.

Katz, P. A. (2003). Racists or tolerant multiculturalists? *American Psychologist, 58(11)*, 897–909.

Kaufman, A. S. (2000). Intelligence tests and school psychology: Predicting the future by studying the past. *Psychology in the Schools, 37*(1), 7–16.

Kaufman, A. S. (2009b). *IQ testing 101*. New York: Springer.

Kaufman, J. C. (2009a). *Creativity 101*. New York: Springer.

Kaufman, J. C., & Sternberg, R. J. (Eds.). (2010). *The Cambridge handbook of creativity*. New York: Cambridge University Press.

Kaufman, L., & Kaufman, J. H. (2000). Explaining the moon illusion. *Proceedings of the National Academy of Sciences, 97*(1), 500–505.

Kaufmann, J. (2007). Transfiguration: A narrative analysis of male-to-female transsexual. *International Journal of Qualitative Studies in Education, 20*(1), 1–13.

Kawada, R., Yoshizumi, M., Hirao, K., et al. (2009). Brain volume and dysexecutive behavior in schizophrenia. *Progress in Neuro-Psychopharmacology & Biological Psychiatry, 33*(7), 1255–1260.

Kawai, K., Sugimoto, K., Nakashima, K., et al. (2000). Leptin as a modulator of sweet taste sensitivities in mice. *Proceedings of the National Academy of Sciences, 97*(20), 11044–11049.

Kawasaki, H., Adolphs, R., Oya, H., et al. (2005). Analysis of single-unit responses to emotional scenes in human ventromedial prefrontal cortex. *Journal of Cognitive Neuroscience, 17*(10), 1509–1518.

Kearney, A. J. (2006). A primer of covert sensitization. *Cognitive & Behavioral Practice, 13*(2), 167–175.

Kearney, C. A., Sims, K. E., Pursell, C. R., et al. (2003). Separation anxiety disorder in young children: A longitudinal and family analysis. *Journal of Clinical Child & Adolescent Psychology, 32*(4), 593–598.

Kearney, C., & Trull, T. (2012). *Abnormal psychology and life: A dimensional approach*. Belmont, CA: Cengage Learning/Wadsworth.

Keating, C. (2010). Theoretical perspective on anorexia nervosa: The conflict of reward. *Neuroscience & Biobehavioral Reviews, 34*(1), 73–79.

Keefe, F. J., Abernethy, A. P., & Campbell, L. C. (2005). Psychological approaches to understanding and treating disease-related pain. *Annual Review of Psychology, 56*, 601–630.

Keegan, J., Parva, M., Finnegan, M., et al. (2010). Addiction in pregnancy.

Journal of Addictive Diseases, 29(2), 175–191.

Keel, P. K., & Klump, K. L. (2003). Are eating disorders culture-bound syndromes? Implications for conceptualizing their etiology. *Psychological Bulletin, 129*(5), 747–769.

Kegel, M., Dam, H., Ali, F., et al. (2009). The prevalence of seasonal affective disorder (SAD) in Greenland is related to latitude. *Nordic Journal of Psychiatry, 63*(4), 331–335.

Keller, E. F. (2010). Goodbye, nature vs nurture. *New Scientist, Sept 20*, 28–29.

Keller, J. J. (2010). The recycling solution: How I increased recycling on Dilworth Road. *The Behavior Analyst, 33*(2), 171–173.

Keller, M. C., & Young, R. K. (1996). Mate assortment in dating and married couples. *Personality & Individual Differences, 21*(2), 217–221.

Kelley, H. H. (1967). Attribution in social psychology. *Nebraska Symposium on Motivation, 15*, 192–238.

Kelly, E. (2010). *I always knew I was a girl.* Salon. Retrieved February 22, 2011 from http://www.salon.com/life/feature/2010/11/20/how_i_became_a_woman.

Kelly, I. W. (1999). "Debunking the debunkers": A response to an astrologer's debunking of skeptics. *Skeptical Inquirer*, Nov.–Dec., 37–43.

Kelly, M. P., Strassberg, D. S., & Turner, C. M. (2006). Behavioral assessment of couples' communication in female orgasmic disorder. *Journal of Sex & Marital Therapy, 32*(2), 81–95.

Kempermann, G. (2005). *Adult neurogenesis: Stem cells and neuronal development in the adult brain.* New York: Oxford University Press.

Kendall-Tackett, K. (Ed.). (2010). *The psychoneuroimmunology of chronic disease: Exploring the links between inflammation, stress, and illness.* Washington, DC: American Psychological Association.

Kendler, K. S., Thornton, L. M., & Prescott, C. A. (2001). Gender differences in the rates of exposure to stressful life events and sensitivity to their depressogenic effects. *American Journal of Psychiatry, 158*(4), 587–593.

Kenneth, M., Carpenter, K. M., & Hasin, D. S. (1998). Reasons for drinking alcohol. *Psychology of Addictive Behaviors, 12*(3), 168–184.

Kenny, P. J., & Markou, A. (2006). Nicotine self-administration acutely activates brain reward systems and induces a long-lasting increase in reward sensitivity. *Neuropsychopharmacology, 31*(6), 1203–1211.

Kenrick, D.T., Griskevicius, V., Neuberg, S.L., et al., (2010). Renovating the pyramid of needs: Contemporary extensions built upon ancient foundations. *Perspectives on Psychological Science, 5*, 292–314.

Kensinger, E. A. (2007). Negative emotion enhances memory accuracy: Behavioral and neuroimaging evidence. *Current Directions in Psychological Science, 16*(4), 213–218.

Kernis, M. H., & Goldman, B. M. (2005). Authenticity, social motivation, and psychological adjustment. In J. P. Forgas, K. D. Williams, & S. M. Laham (Eds.), *Social motivation: Conscious and unconscious processes* (pp. 210–227). New York: Cambridge University Press.

Kernis, M. H., & Lakey, C. E. (2010). Fragile versus secure high self-esteem: Implications for defensiveness and insecurity. In R. M. Arkin, K. C. Oleson, & P. J. Carroll (Eds.), *Handbook of the uncertain self* (pp. 360–378). New York: Psychology Press.

Kessen, W., & Cahan, E. D. (1986). A century of psychology: From subject to object to agent. *American Scientist, 74*, 640–649.

Kessler, D. A. (2009). *The end of overeating: Taking control of the insatiable American appetite.* Emmaus, PA: Rodale Press.

Kety, S. S. (1979, Sept.). Disorders of the human brain. *Scientific American, 241*, 202–214.

Keyes, C. L. M., & Haidt, J. (2003). Introduction: Human flourishing. In C. L. M. Keyes, & J. Haidt (Eds.), *Flourishing* (pp. 3–12). Washington, DC: American Psychological Association.

Keysers, C., Xiao, D.–K., Földiák, P., et al. (2005). Out of sight but not out of mind: The neurophysiology of iconic memory in the superior temporal sulcus. *Cognitive Neuropsychology, 22*(3-4), 316–332.

Khan, O., Tselis, A., & Lisak, R. (2010). Getting to grips with myelin injury in progressive multiple sclerosis. *Brain: A Journal of Neurology, 133*(10), 2845–2851.

Kida, T. E. (2006). *Don't believe everything you think.* Buffalo, NY: Prometheus.

Kim, E. H., & Gray, S. H. (2009). Challenges presenting in transference and countertransference in the psychodynamic psychotherapy of a military service member. *Journal of the American Academy of Psychoanalysis & Dynamic Psychiatry, 37*(3), 421–437.

Kim, J., Singer, R. N., & Radlo, S. J. (1996). Degree of cognitive demands in psychomotor tasks and the effects of the five-step strategy on achievement. *Human Performance, 9*(2), 155–169.

Kim, S. (2002). Participative management and job satisfaction: Lessons for management leadership. *Public Administration Review, 62*(2), 231–241.

Kimble, C. E., & Hirt, E. R. (2005). Self-focus gender, and habitual self-handicapping: Do they make a difference in behavioral self-handicapping? *Social Behavior & Personality, 33*(1), 43–56.

Kim-Cohen, J., Moffitt, T. E., Caspi, A., et al. (2004). Genetic and environmental processes in young children's resilience and vulnerability to socioeconomic deprivation. *Child Development, 75*(3), 651–668.

King, B. E. (2005). *Human sexuality today* (5th ed.). Englewood Cliffs, NJ: Prentice Hall.

King, H. E. (1961). Psychological effects of excitation in the limbic system. In D. E. Sheer (Ed.), *Electrical stimulation of the brain* (pp. 477–486). Austin: University of Texas Press.

King, N. J., Muris, P., & Ollendick, T. H. (2005). Childhood fears and phobias: Assessment and treatment. *Child & Adolescent Mental Health, 10*(2), 50–56.

King, P. M. (2009). Principles of development and developmental change underlying theories of cognitive and moral development. *Journal of College Student Development, 50*(6), 597–620.

Kingsley, C. H. & Lambert, K. G. (2006). The maternal brain. *Scientific American, 294*(1), 72–79.

Kinnunen, L. H., Moltz, H., Metz, J., et al. (2004). Differential brain activation in exclusively homosexual and heterosexual men produced by the selective serotonin reuptake inhibitor, fluoxetine. *Brain Research, 1024*(1-2), 251–254.

Kinsey, A., Pomeroy, W., & Martin, C. (1948). *Sexual behavior in the human male.* Philadelphia: Saunders.

Kinsey, A., Pomeroy, W., & Martin, C. (1953). *Sexual behavior in the human female.* Philadelphia: Saunders.

Kipper, D. A. (1992). The effect of two kinds of role playing on self-evaluation of improved assertiveness. *Journal of Clinical Psychology, 48*(2), 246–250.

Kirby, D. B. (2008). The impact of abstinence and comprehensive sex and STD/HIV education programs on adolescent sexual behavior. *Sexuality Research & Social Policy, 5*(3), 18–27.

Kirchhoff, B. A. (2009). Individual differences in episodic memory: The role of self-initiated encoding strategies. *The Neuroscientist, 15*(2), 166–179.

Kirk, S. A., Gallagher, J. J., Coleman, M. R., et al. (2011). *Educating exceptional children* (13th ed.). Belmont, CA: Cengage Learning/Wadsworth.

Kirsch, I., & Lynn, S. J. (1995). The altered state of hypnosis. *American Psychologist, 50*(10), 846–858.

Kirsch, I., & Sapirstein, G. (1998). Listening to Prozac but hearing placebo: A meta-analysis of antidepressant medication. *Prevention & Treatment, 1*, art. 0002a. Retrieved May 18, 2007, from http://journals.apa.org/prevention/volume1/pre0010002a.html.

Kirsch, I., (2005). The flexible observer and neodissociation theory. *Contemporary Hypnosis, 22*(3), 121–122.

Kirveskari, E., Salmelin, R., & Hari, R. (2006). Neuromagnetic responses to vowels vs. tones reveal hemispheric lateralization. *Clinical Neurophysiology, 117*(3), 643–648.

Kiser, L. J., Heston, J. D., & Paavola, M. (2006). Day treatment centers/ Partial hospitalization settings. In T. A. Petti, & C. Salguero (Eds.), *Community child & adolescent psychiatry: A manual of clinical practice and consultation* (pp. 189–203). Washington, DC: American Psychiatric Publishing.

Kisilevsky, B. S., Hains, S. M. J., Jacquet, A.-Y., et al. (2004). Maturation of fetal responses to music. *Developmental Science, 7(5)*, 550–559.

Kitada, R., Dijkerman, H. C., Soo, G., et al. (2010). Representing human hands haptically or visually from first-person versus third-person perspectives. *Perception, 39*(2), 236–254.

Kitayama, S., Markus, H. R., & Kurokawa, M. (2000). Culture, emotion, and well-being: Good feelings in Japan and the United States. *Cognition & Emotion, 14*, 93–124.

Kite, M. E., Russo, N. F., Brehm, S. S., et al. (2001). Women psychologists in academe. *American Psychologist, 56*(12), 1080–1098.

Kite, M. E., Stockdale, G. D., Whitley, Jr., B. E., et al. (2005). Attitudes toward younger and older adults: An updated meta-analytic review. *Journal of Social Issues, 61*(2), 241–266.

Klahr, D., & Nigam, M. (2004). The equivalence of learning paths in early science instruction: Effects of direct instruction and discovery learning. *Psychological Science, 15*, 661–667.

Klein, B., Richards, J. C., & Austin, D. W. (2006). Efficacy of internet therapy for panic disorder. *Journal of Behavior Therapy & Experimental Psychiatry, 37*(3), 213–238.

Klein, D. W., & Kihlstrom, J. F. (1986). Elaboration, organization, and the self-reference effect in memory. *Journal of Experimental Psychology: General, 115*, 26–38.

Klein, K., & Boals, A. (2001a). The relationship of life event stress and working memory capacity. *Applied Cognitive Psychology, 15*(5), 565–579.

Klein, K., & Boals, A. (2001b). Expressive writing can increase working memory capacity. *Journal of Experimental Psychology: General, 130*(3), 520–533.

Klein, L. A., & Houlihan, D. (2010). Relationship satisfaction, sexual satisfaction, and sexual problems in sexsomnia. *International Journal of Sexual Health, 22*(2), 84–90.

Kleinke, C. L., Peterson, T. R., & Rutledge, T. R. (1998). Effects of self-generated facial expressions on mood. *Journal of Personality & Social Psychology, 74*(1), 272–279.

Klohnen, E. C., & Luo, S. (2003). Interpersonal attraction and personality: What is attractive—self similarity, ideal similarity, complementarity or attachment security? *Journal of Personality & Social Psychology, 85*(4), 709–722.

Klöppel, S., Mangin, J.-F., Vongerichten, A., et al. (2010). Nurture versus nature: Long-term impact of forced right-handedness on structure of pericentral cortex and basal ganglia. *Journal of Neuroscience, 30*(9), 3271–3275.

Knafo, D. (2009). Freud's memory erased. *Psychoanalytic Psychology, 26*(2), 171–190.

Knickmeyer, R. C., & Baron-Cohen S. (2006). Fetal testosterone and sex differences. *Early Human Development, 82*(12), 755–760.

Knoll, J. L. IV., & Resnick, P. J. (2008). Insanity defense evaluations: Toward a model for evidence-based practice. *Brief Treatment & Crisis Intervention, 8*(1), 92–110.

Knoops, K. T. B., de Groot, L. C., Kromhout, D., et al. (2004). Mediterranean diet, lifestyle factors, and 10-year mortality in elderly European men and women. *Journal of the American Medical Association, 292*(12), 1433–1439.

Koch, C. (2004). *The quest for consciousness: A neurobiological approach.* Englewood, CO: Roberts and Co.

Koch, W. H., & Pratarelli, M. E. (2004). Effects of intro/extraversion and sex on social internet use. *North American Journal of Psychology, 6*(3), 371–382.

Koda, S., & Sugawara, K. (2009). The influence of diet behavior and stress on binge-eating among female college students. *Japanese Journal of Psychology, 80*(2), 83–89.

Kohlberg, L. (1969). The cognitive-developmental approach to socialization. In A. Goslin (Ed.), *Handbook of socialization theory and research* (pp. 1–134). Chicago: Rand McNally.

Kohlberg, L. (1981). *Essays on moral development* (Vol. I): *The philosophy of moral development.* San Francisco: Harper.

Kohler, P. K., Manhart, L. E., & Lafferty, W. E. (2008). Abstinence-only and comprehensive sex education and the initiation of sexual activity and teen pregnancy. *Journal of Adolescent Health, 42*(4), 344–351.

Kohn, C. S., & Antonuccio, D. O. (2002). Treatment of kleptomania using cognitive and behavioral strategies. *Clinical Case Studies, 1*(1), 25–38.

Köke, A., Schouten, J. S., Lamerichs-Geelen M. J. H., et al. (2004). Pain reducing effect of three types of transcutaneous electrical nerve stimulation in patients with chronic pain: A randomized crossover trial. *Pain, 108*(1-2), 36–42.

Kolb, B. (1990). Recovery from occipital stroke: A self-report and an inquiry into visual processes. *Canadian Journal of Psychology, 44*(2), 130–147.

Kolb, B., & Whishaw, I.Q. (2011). *Introduction to brain and behavior* (3rd ed.). New York: Freeman-Worth.

Kolb, B., Gibb, R., & Gorny, G. (2003). Experience-dependent changes in dendritic arbor and spine density in neocortex vary with age and sex. *Neurobiology of Learning & Memory, 79*(1), 1–10.

Komisaruk, B. R., Beyer-Flores C., & Whipple, B. (2006). *The science of orgasm.* Baltimore, MD: Johns Hopkins University Press.

Kopta, M. S. Lueger, R. J., Saunders, S. M., et al. (1999). Individual psychotherapy outcome and process research. *Annual Review of Psychology, 50,* 441–469.

Kornhaber, M. L., & Gardner, H. (2006). Multiple intelligences: Developments in implementation and theory. In M. A. Constas & R. J. Sternberg (Eds.), *Translating theory and research into educational practice: Developments in content domains, large-scale reform, and intellectual capacity* (pp. 255–276). Mahwah, NJ: Erlbaum.

Korol, C., Craig, K. D., & Firestone, P. (2003). Dissociative and somatoform disorders. In P. Firestone, & W. L. Marshall (Eds.), *Abnormal psychology: Perspectives* (2nd ed., pp. 183–199). Toronto: Prentice Hall.

Koss, M. P. (2000). Blame, shame, and community: Justice responses to violence against women. *American Psychologist, 55*(11), 1332–1343.

Kossek, E. E., & Michel, J. S. (2011). Flexible work schedules. In S. Zedeck (Ed.). (2011). *APA handbook of industrial and organizational psychology* (Vol 1): *Building and developing the organization* (pp. 535–572). Washington, DC: American Psychological Association.

Kosslyn, S. M. (1983). *Ghosts in the mind's machine.* New York: Norton.

Kosslyn, S. M. (1985). Stalking the mental image. *Psychology Today, 19*(5), 22–28.

Kosslyn, S. M. (2005). Mental images and the brain. *Cognitive Neuropsychology, 22*(3-4), 333–347.

Kosslyn, S. M., Ball, T. M., & Reiser, B. J. (1978). Visual images preserve metric spatial information: Evidence from studies of image scanning. *Journal of Experimental Psychology: Human Perception & Performance, 4,* 47–60.

Kosson, D. S., Suchy, Y., Mayer, A. R., et al. (2002). Facial affect recognition in criminal psychopaths. *Emotion, 2*(4), 398–411.

Kotkin, M., Daviet, C., & Gurin, J. (1996). The Consumer Reports mental health survey. *American Psychologist, 51*(10), 1080–1082.

Kottler, J. A., & Shepard, D. S. (2011). *Introduction to counseling* (7th ed.). Belmont, CA: Cengage Learning/Wadsworth.

Kowert, P. A. (2002). *Groupthink or deadlock: When do leaders learn from their advisors? SUNY series on the presidency.* Albany, NY: State University of New York Press.

Kozart, M. F. (2002). Understanding efficacy in psychotherapy. *American Journal of Orthopsychiatry, 72*(2), 217–231.

Krahé, B., & Möller, I. (2010). Longitudinal effects of media violence on aggression and empathy among german adolescents. *Journal of Applied Developmental Psychology, 31*(5), 401–409.

Krahé, B., Möller, I., Huesmann, L. R., et al. (2011). Desensitization to media violence: Links with habitual media violence exposure, aggressive cognitions, and aggressive behavior. *Journal of Personality & Social Psychology, 100*(4), 630–646.

Krakow, B., & Zadra, A. (2006). Clinical management of chronic nightmares: Imagery rehearsal therapy. *Behavioral Sleep Medicine, 4*(1), 45–70.

Krall, E. A., Garvey, A. J., & Garcia, R. I. (2002). Smoking relapse after 2 years of abstinence: Findings from the VA Normative Aging Study. *Nicotine & Tobacco Research, 4*(1), 95–100.

Kramer, U., Despland, J.-N., Michel, L., et al. (2010). Change in defense mechanisms and coping over the course of short-term dynamic psychotherapy for adjustment disorder. *Journal of Clinical Psychology, 66*(12), 1232–1241.

Kreager, D. A., & Staff, J. (2009). The sexual double standard and adolescent peer acceptance. *Social Psychology Quarterly, 72*(2), 143–164.

Krishnan, H. A., & Park, D. (2005). A few good women—on top management teams. *Journal of Business Research, 58,* 1712–1720.

Kristof-Brown, A. L., Barrick, M. R., & Franke, M. (2002). Applicant impression management: Dispositional influences and consequences for recruiter perceptions of fit and similarity. *Journal of Management, 28,* 27–46.

Kteily, N. S., Sidanius, J., & Levin, S. (2011). Social dominance orientation: Cause or 'mere effect'?: Evidence for SDO as a causal predictor of prejudice and discrimination against ethnic and racial outgroups. *Journal of Experimental Social Psychology, 47*(1), 208–214.

Ku, K. Y. L., & Ho, I. T. (2010). Metacognitive strategies that enhance critical thinking. *Metacognition & Learning, 5*(3), 251–267.

Kübler-Ross, E. (1975). *Death: The final stage of growth.* Englewood Cliffs, NJ: Prentice-Hall.

Kuczka, K. K., & Treasure, D. C. (2005). Self-handicapping in competitive sport: Influence of the motivational climate, self-efficacy and perceived importance. *Psychology of Sport & Exercise, 6*(5), 539–550.

Kuhl, P. K. (2004). Early language acquisition: Cracking the speech code. *Nature Reviews Neuroscience, 5*(11), 831–841.

Kuiper, N. A., & McHale, N. (2009). Humor styles as mediators between self-evaluative standards and psychological well-being. *Journal of Psychology: Interdisciplinary & Applied, 143*(4), 359–376.

Kulik, J., Mahler, H. I. M., & Moore, P. J. (2003). Social comparison affiliation under threat: Effects on recovery from major surgery. In P. Salovey, & A. J. Rothman (Eds.), *Social psychology of health: Key readings in social psychology* (pp. 199–226). New York: Psychology Press.

Kumaran, D., & Maguire, E. A. (2005). The human hippocampus: Cognitive maps or relational memory? *Journal of Neuroscience, 25*(31), 7254–7259.

Kunkel, M. A. (1993). A teaching demonstration involving perceived lunar size. *Teaching of Psychology, 20*(3), 178–180.

Kuther, T. L., & Morgan, R. D. (2010). *Careers in psychology: Opportunities in a changing world* (3rd ed.). Belmont, CA: Cengage Learning/Wadsworth.

Laan, E., Everaerd, W., van Bellen, G., et al. (1994). Women's sexual and emotional responses to male- and female-produced erotica. *Archives of Sexual Behavior, 23*(2), 153–169.

LaBar, K. S. (2007). Beyond fear: Emotional memory mechanisms in the human brain. *Current Directions in Psychological Science, 16*(4), 173–177.

LaBerge, S. (2000). Lucid dreaming: Evidence and methodology. In F. E. Pace-Schott M. Solms, et al. (Eds.), *Sleep and dreaming: Scientific advances and reconsiderations* (pp. 1–50). Cambridge, UK: Cambridge University Press.

Labov, W. (1973). The boundaries of words and their meanings. In C. J. N. Bailey, & R. W. Shuy (Eds.) *New ways of analyzing variation in English* (pp. 340–373). Washington, DC: Georgetown University Press.

LaBrie, R. A., & Shaffer, H. J. (2007). Gambling with adolescent health. *Journal of Adolescent Health, 40*(5), 387–389.

Lacayo, A. (1995). Neurologic and psychiatric complications of cocaine abuse. *Neuropsychiatry, Neuropsychology, & Behavioral Neurology, 8*(1), 53–60.

Lachman, M. E. (2004). Development in midlife. *Annual Review of Psychology, 55,* 305–331.

Lachman, M. E., Röcke, C., Rosnick, C., et al. (2008). Realism and illusion in Americans' temporal views of their life satisfaction: Age differences in reconstructing the past and anticipating the future. *Psychological Science, 19*(9), 889–897.

Lackamp, J. M., Osborne, C., & Wise, T. N. (2009). Paraphilic disorders. In R. Balon, & R. T. Segraves (Eds.), *Clinical manual of sexual disorders* (pp. 335–370). Arlington, VA: American Psychiatric Publishing.

Lackner, J. R., & DiZio, P. (2005). Vestibular, proprioceptive, and haptic contributions to spatial orientation. *Annual Review of Psychology, 56,* 115–147.

Ladouceur, R., Lachance, S., & Fournier, P.-M. (2009). Is control a viable goal in the treatment of pathological gambling? *Behaviour Research & Therapy, 47*(3), 189–197.

Lagos, P., Torterolo, P., Jantos, H., et al. (2009). Effects on sleep of melanin-concentrating hormone (MCH) microinjections into the dorsal raphe nucleus. *Brain Research, 1265,* 103–111.

Lakin, J. L., Jefferis, V. E., Cheng, C. M., et al. (2003). The chameleon effect as social glue: Evidence for the evolutionary significance of nonconscious mimicry. *Journal of Nonverbal Behavior, 27*(3), 145–162.

Lam, R., & Mok, H. (2008). *Depression.* New York: Oxford.

Lamb, R. J., Kirby, K. C., Morral, A. R., et al. (2010). Shaping smoking cessation in hard-to-treat smokers. *Journal of Consulting & Clinical Psychology, 78*(1), 62–71.

Lambert, M. J., & Cattani-Thompson K. (1996). Current findings regarding the effectiveness of counseling. *Journal of Counseling & Development, 74*(6), 601–608.

Lambert, M. J., & Ogles, B. M. (2002). The efficacy and effectiveness of psychotherapy. In M. J. Lambert (Ed.),

Handbook of psychotherapy and behavior change (5th ed., pp. 130–193). New York: Wiley.

Lambert, W. E. (1987). The effects of bilingual and bicultural experiences on children's attitudes and social perspectives. In P. Homel, M. Palij, & D. Aaronson (Eds.), *Childhood bilingualism* (pp. 197–221). Hillsdale, NJ: Erlbaum.

Lammers, G. J., Bassetti, C., Billiard, M., et al. (2010). Sodium oxybate is an effective and safe treatment for narcolepsy. *Sleep Medicine, 11*(1), 105–106.

Lamprecht, R., Dracheva, S., Assoun, S., et al. (2009). Fear conditioning induces distinct patterns of gene expression in lateral amygdala. *Genes, Brain & Behavior, 8*(8), 735–743.

Lan Yeung, V. W., & Kashima, Y. (2010). Communicating stereotype-relevant information: How readily can people individuate? *Asian Journal of Social Psychology, 13*(4), 209–220.

Landa, Y., Silverstein, S. M., Schwartz, F., et al. (2006). Group cognitive behavioral therapy for delusions: Helping patients improve reality testing. *Journal of Contemporary Psychotherapy, 36*(1), 9–17.

Landau, M. J., Meier, B. P., & Keefer, L. A. (2010). A metaphor-enriched social cognition. *Psychological Bulletin, 136*(6), 1045-1067.

Landau, J. D., & Bavaria A. J. (2003). Does deliberate source monitoring reduce students's misconceptions about psychology? *Teaching of Psychology, 30*, 311–314.

Landy, F. J., & Conte, J. M. (2007). *Work in the 21st century: An introduction to industrial and organizational psychology* (2nd ed.). Malden, MA: Blackwell.

Landy, F. J., Shankster, L. J., & Kohler, S. S. (1994). Personnel selection and placement. *Annual Review of Psychology, 45*, 261–296.

Lane, C. (2009). The slippery slope of bitterness disorder and other psychiatric diagnoses. *Psychology Today, June 3*, Retrieved March 14, 2011, from http://www.psychologytoday.com/blog/side-effects/200906/the-slippery-slope-bitterness-disorder-and-other-psychiatric-diagnoses.

Langens, T. A., & Schmalt, H.-D. (2002). Emotional consequences of positive daydreaming: The moderating role of fear of failure. *Personality & Social Psychology Bulletin, 28*(12), 1725–1735.

Langer, E. J. (2000). Mindful learning. *Current Directions in Psychological Science, 9*(6), 220–223.

Langleben, D. D. (2008). Detection of deception with fMRI: Are we there yet?. *Legal & Criminological Psychology, 13*(1), 1–9.

Langleben, D. D., Dattilio, F. M., & Gutheil, T. G. (2006). True lies: Delusions and lie-detection technology. *Journal of Psychiatry & Law, 34*(3), 351–370.

Langleben, D. D., Loughead, J. W., Bilker, W. B., et al. (2005). Telling truth from lie in individual subjects with fast event-related fMRI. *Human Brain Mapping, 26*(4), 262–272.

Langone, M. D. (2002). Cults, conversion, science, and harm. *Cultic Studies Review, 1*(2), 178–186.

Larsen, L., Hartmann, P., & Nyborg, H. (2008). The stability of general intelligence from early adulthood to middle-age. *Intelligence, 36*(1), 29–34.

Larsen, R. J., & Buss, D. M. (2010). *Personality psychology* (4th ed.). New York: McGraw-Hill.

Larsen, R. J., & Kasimatis, M. (1990). Individual differences in entrainment of mood to the weekly calendar. *Journal of Personality & Social Psychology, 58*(1), 164–171.

Larsen, R.J., & Prizmic, Z. (2004) Affect regulation. In R. Baumeister, & K. D. Voohs (Eds.), *Handbook of self-regulation: Research, theory, and applications* (pp. 40–61). New York: Guilford.

Larson, M. E., Houlihan, D., & Goernert, P. N. (1995). Effects of informational feedback on aluminum can recycling. *Behavioral Interventions, 10*(2), 111–117.

Larsson, B., Carlsson, J., Fichtel, Å., et al. (2005). Relaxation treatment of adolescent headache sufferers: Results from a school-based replication series. *Headache: The Journal of Head & Face Pain, 45*(6), 692–704.

Larsson, J.-O., Larsson, H., & Lichtenstein, P. (2004). Genetic and environmental contributions to stability and change of ADHD symptoms between 8 and 13 years of age: A longitudinal twin study. *Journal of the American Academy of Child & Adolescent Psychiatry, 43*(10), 1267–1275.

Latané, B., Nida, S. A., & Wilson, D. W. (1981). The effects of group size on helping behavior. In J. P. Rushton, & R. M. Sorrentino (Eds.), *Altruism and helping behavior: Social, personality and developmental perspectives* (pp. 287–313). Mahwah, NJ: Erlbaum.

LaTour, M. S., & Henthorne, T. L. (2003). Nudity and sexual appeals: Understanding the arousal process and advertising response. In T. Reichert & J. Lambioase (Eds.), *Sex in advertising: Perspectives on the erotic appeal* (pp. 91–106). Mahwah, NJ: Erlbaum.

Latrofa, M., Vaes, J., Cadinu, M., et al. (2010). The cognitive representation of self-stereotyping. *Personality & Social Psychology Bulletin, 36*(7), 911–922.

Lattal, K. A., Reilly, M. P., & Kohn, J. P. (1998). Response persistence under ratio and interval reinforcement schedules. *Journal of the Experimental Analysis of Behavior, 70*(2), 165–183.

Latty-Mann, H., & Davis, K. E. (1996). Attachment theory and partner choice. *Journal of Social & Personal Relationships, 13*(1), 5–23.

Laub, J. H., & Sampson, R. J. (2003). *Shared beginnings, divergent lives: Delinquent boys to age 70*. Cambridge, MA: Harvard University Press.

Laumann, E., Michael, R., Michaels, S., et al. (1994). *The social organization of sexuality*. Chicago: University of Chicago Press.

Laurent, G., Stopfer, M., Friedrich, R. W., et al. (2001). Odor encoding as an active, dynamical process. *Annual Review of Neuroscience, 24*, 263–297.

Laureys, S, & Boly. M. (2007). What is it like to be vegetative or minimally conscious? *Current Opinion in Neurology, 20*, 609–613.

Lautsch, B. A., Kossek, E. E., & Eaton, S. C. (2009). Supervisory approaches and paradoxes in managing telecommuting implementation. *Human Relations, 62*(6), 795–827.

Lavy, S., Mikulincer, M., & Shaver, P. R. (2010). Autonomy–proximity imbalance: An attachment theory perspective on intrusiveness in romantic relationships. *Personality & Individual Differences, 48*(5), 552–556.

Lawrence, B., Myerson, J., & Hale, S. (1998). Differential decline of verbal and visuospatial processing speed across the adult life span. *Aging, Neuropsychology, & Cognition, 5*(2), 129–146.

Lawson, H. M., & Leck, K. (2006). Dynamics of Internet dating. *Social Science Computer Review, 24*(2), 189–208.

Lawson, T. T. (2008). *Carl Jung, Darwin of the mind*. London, England: Karnac Books.

Lay, C., & Verkuyten, M. (1999). Ethnic identity and its relation to personal self-esteem. *Journal of Social Psychology, 139*(3), 288–299.

Lazar, S. W. (2005). Mindfulness research. In C. K. Germer, R. D. Siegel, et al. (Eds.), *Mindfulness and psychotherapy* (pp. 220–238). New York: Guilford.

Lazar, S. W., Bush, G., Gollub, R. L., et al. (2000). Functional brain mapping of the relaxation response and meditation. *Neuroreport, 11*(7), 1581–1585.

Lazarus, R. S. (1991a). Progress on a cognitive–motivational–relational theory of emotion. *American Psychologist, 46*(8), 819–834.

Lazarus, R. S. (1991b). Cognition and motivation in emotion. *American Psychologist, 46*(4), 352–367.

Le Pelley, M. E., Reimers, S. J., Calvini, G., et al. (2010). Stereotype formation: Biased by association. *Journal of Experimental Psychology: General, 139*(1), 138–161.

Leal, M. C., Shin, Y. J., Laborde, M.-L., et al. (2003). Music perception in adult cochlear implant recipients. *Acta Oto-Laryngologica, 123*(7), 826–835.

Leavens, D. A., & Hopkins, W. D. (1998). Intentional communication by chimpanzees. *Developmental Psychology, 34*(5), 813–822.

LeBlanc, G., & Bearison, D. J. (2004). Teaching and learning as a bi-directional activity: Investigating dyadic interactions between child teachers and child learners. *Cognitive Development, 19*(4), 499–515.

LeDoux, J. E. (2000). Emotion circuits in the brain. *Annual Review of Neuroscience, 23*, 155–184.

LeDoux, J. E., & Gorman, J. M. (2001). A call to action: Overcoming anxiety through active coping. *American Journal of Psychiatry. 158*(12), 1953–1955.

Lee, J. M., Ku, J. H., Jang, D. P., et al. (2002). Virtual reality system for treatment of the fear of public speaking using image-based rendering and moving pictures. *CyberPsychology & Behavior, 5*(3), 191–195.

Lee, M., Zimbardo, P. G., & Bertholf, M. (1977). Shy murderers. *Psychology Today, 11*, 69–70, 76, 148.

Lee, T., & Kim, J. J. (2004). Differential effects of cerebellar, amygdalar, and hippocampal lesions on classical eyeblink conditioning in rats. *Journal of Neuroscience, 24*(13), 3242–3250.

Leenaars, A. A., Lester, D., & Wenckstern, S. (2005). Coping with suicide: The art and the research. In R. I. Yufit, & D. Lester (Eds.), *Assessment, treatment, and prevention of suicidal behavior* (pp. 347–377). New York: Wiley.

Leeper, R. W. (1935). A study of a neglected portion of the field of learning: The development of sensory organization. *Pedagogical Seminary & Journal of Genetic Psychology, 46*, 41–75.

Lefcourt, H. M. (2003). Humor as a moderator of life stress in adults. In C. E. Schaefer (Ed.), *Play therapy with adults* (pp. 144–165). New York: Wiley.

Lefebvre, C. D., Marchand,Y., Smith, S. M., et al. (2007). Determining eye-witness identification accuracy using event-related brain potentials (ERPs). *Psychophysiology, 44*(6), 894–904.

Lefkowitz, E. S., & Zeldow, P. B. (2006). Masculinity and femininity predict optimal mental health: A belated test of the androgyny hypothesis. *Journal of Personality Assessment, 87*(1), 95–101.

Lefrançois, G. R. (2006). *Theories of human learning: What the old woman said* (5th ed.). Belmont, CA: Cengage Learning/Wadsworth.

Lehman, D. R., Chiu, C., & Schaller, M. (2004). Psychology and culture. *Annual Review of Psychology, 55*, 689–714.

Leichtman, M. (2004). Projective tests: The nature of the task. In M. J. Hilsenroth, & D. L. Segal (Eds.), *Comprehensive handbook of psychological assessment* (Vol. 2): *Personality assessment* (pp. 297–314). New York: Wiley.

Leidner, B., Castano, E., Zaiser, E., et al. (2010). Ingroup glorification, moral disengagement, and justice in the context of collective violence. *Personality & Social Psychology Bulletin*, 36(8), 1115–1129.

Leiter, M. P., & Maslach, C. (2005). *Banishing burnout: Six strategies for improving your relationship with work*. San Francisco, CA: Jossey-Bass.

Leiter, M. P., Gascón, S., & Martínez-Jarreta B. (2010). Making sense of work life: A structural model of burnout. *Journal of Applied Social Psychology, 40*(1), 57–75.

Lejuez, C. W., Eifert, G. H., Zvolensky, M. J., et al. (2000). Preference between onset predictable and unpredictable administrations of 20% carbon-dioxide-enriched air: Implications for better understanding the etiology and treatment of panic disorder. *Journal of Experimental Psychology: Applied, 6*(4), 349–358.

Lemogne, C., Nabi, H., Zins, M., et al. (2010). Hostility may explain the association between depressive mood and mortality: Evidence from the French GAZEL cohort study. *Psychotherapy & Psychosomatics, 79*(3), 164–171.

Lenton, A. P., & Bryan, A. (2005). An affair to remember: The role of sexual scripts in perceptions of sexual intent. *Personal Relationships, 12*(4), 483–498.

Lenzenweger, M. F., & Gottesman, I. I. (1994). Schizophrenia. In V. S. Ramachandran (Ed.), *Encyclopedia of human behavior* (Vol 4, pp. 41–59). San Diego, CA: Academic.

León, I., & Hernández, J. A. (1998). Testing the role of attribution and appraisal in predicting own and other's emotions. *Cognition & Emotion*, 12(1), 27–43.

Leor, J., Poole, W. K., & Kloner, R. A. (1996). Sudden cardiac death triggered by earthquake. *The New England Journal of Medicine, 334*(7), 413.

Leotti, L. A., Iyengar, S. S., & Ochsner, K. N. (2010). Born to choose: The origins and value of the need for control. *Trends in Cognitive Sciences, 14*(10), 457–463.

Lepage, J.-F., & Théret, H. (2007). The mirror neuron system: Grasping others' actions from birth? *Developmental Science, 10*(5), 513–523.

Lerner, D., & Henke, R. M. (2008). What does research tell us about depression, job performance, and work productivity? *Journal of Occupational & Environmental Medicine, 50*(4), 401–410.

Lerum, K., & Dworkin, S. L. (2009). "Bad girls rule": An interdisciplinary feminist commentary on the report of the APA task force on the sexualization of girls. *Journal of Sex Research, 46*(4), 250–263.

Leslie, K., & Ogilvie, R. (1996). Vestibular dreams: The effect of rocking on dream mentation. Dreaming: *Journal of the Association for the Study of Dreams, 6*(1), 1–16.

Lessow-Hurley, J. (2005). *Foundations of dual language instruction* (4th ed.). Boston: Allyn & Bacon.

Lester, D. (2006). Sexual orientation and suicidal behavior. *Psychological Reports, 99*(3), 923–924.

Lester, D., & Yang, B. (2005). Regional and time-series studies of suicide in nations of the world. *Archives of Suicide Research, 9*(2), 123–133.

Lettvin, J. Y. (1961). Two remarks on the visual system of the frog. In W. Rosenblith (Ed.), *Sensory communication* (pp. 757–776). Cambridge, MA: MIT Press.

Leuner, B., & Gould, E. (2010). Structural plasticity and hippocampal function. *Annual Review of Psychology, 61*, 111–140.

LeUnes, A. (2008). *Sport psychology* (4th ed.). New York: Psychology Press.

LeUnes, J., & Nation, J. R. (2002). *Sport psychology* (3rd ed.). Belmont, CA: Cengage Learning/Wadsworth.

Levant, R. F. (2001). Men and masculinity. In J. Worell (Ed.), *Encyclopedia of women and gender* (Vol. 2, pp. 717–727). San Diego: Academic Press.

Levant, R. F. (2003). Treating male alexithymia. In L. B. Silverstein, & T. J. Goodrich (Eds.), *Feminist family therapy: Empowerment in social context* (pp. 177–188). Washington: American Psychological Association.

Levant, R. F., Good, G. E., Cook, S. W., et al. (2006). The Normative Male Alexithymia Scale: Measurement of a gender-linked syndrome. *Psychology of Men & Masculinity, 7*(4), 212–224.

Levant, R. F., Hall, R. J., Williams, C. M., et al. (2009). Gender differences in alexithymia. *Psychology of Men & Masculinity, 10*(3), 190–203.

LeVay, S. (2011). *Gay, straight, and the reason why*. New York: Oxford University Press.

LeVay, S., & Baldwin, J. (2008). *Human sexuality* (3d ed.). Sunderland, MA: Sinauer Associates.

Levenson, M. R. (2009). Gender and wisdom: The roles of compassion and moral development. *Research in Human Development, 6*(1), 45–59.

Levenston, G. K., Patrick, C. J., Bradley, M. M., et al. (2000). The psychopathic observer. *Journal of Abnormal Psychology, 109*, 373–385.

Levesque, M. J., Steciuk, M., & Ledley, C. (2002). Self-disclosure patterns among well-acquainted individuals. *Social Behavior & Personality, 30*(6), 579–592.

Levett, L. M., Danielsen, E. M., Kovera, M. B., et al. (2005). The psychology of jury and juror decision making. In N. Brewer, & K. D. Williams, (Eds.), *Psychology and law: An empirical perspective* (pp. 365–406). New York: Guilford.

Levi, A. M. (1998). Are defendants guilty if they were chosen in a lineup? *Law & Human Behavior, 22*(4), 389–407.

Levin, B. E. (2006). Metabolic sensing neurons and the control of energy homeostasis. *Physiology & Behavior, 89*(4), 486–489.

Levin, R., & Fireman, G. (2002). Nightmare prevalence, nightmare distress, and selfreported psychological disturbance. *Sleep: Journal of Sleep & Sleep Disorders Research, 25*(2), 205–212.

Levine, M., & Harrison, K. (2004). Media's role in the perpetuation and prevention of negative body image and disordered eating. In J. K. Thompson (Ed.), *Handbook of eating disorders and obesity* (pp. 695–717). New York: Wiley.

Levine, R. V. (2003). The kindness of strangers. *American Scientist, 91*(May-June), 226–233.

Levis, D. J. (1989). The case for a return to a two-factor theory of avoidance: The failure of non-fear interpretations. In S. B Klein, & R. R. Mower (Eds.), *Contemporary learning theories* (pp. 227–277). Hillsdale, NJ: Erlbaum.

Levy, D. A. (2003). *Tools of critical thinking: Metathoughts for psychology*. Long Grove, IL: Waveland Press.

Levy, D. L., Coleman, M. J., Sung, H., et al. (2010). The genetic basis of thought disorder and language and communication disturbances in schizophrenia. *Journal of Neurolinguistics, 23*(3), 176–192.

Levy, J., & Reid, M. (1976). Cerebral organization. *Science*, 337–339.

Lewandowski, Jr., G. W., Aron, A., & Gee, J. (2007). Personality goes a long way: The malleability of opposite-sex physical attractiveness. *Personal Relationships, 14*(4), 571–585.

Lewis, I., Watson, B., & White, K. M. (2009). Internet versus paper-and-pencil survey methods in psychological experiments: Equivalence testing of participant responses to health-related messages. *Australian Journal of Psychology, 61*(2), 107–116.

Lewis, M. (1995). Self-conscious emotions. *American Scientist, 83*(Jan-Feb), 68–78.

Leyendecker, B., Harwood, R. L., Comparini, L., et al. (2005). Socioeconomic status, ethnicity, and parenting. In T. Luster, & L. Okagaki (Eds.), *Parenting: An ecological perspective* (2nd ed., pp. 319–341). Mahwah, NJ: Erlbaum.

Li, C., Ford, E. S., Zhao, G., et al. (2009). Associations of health risk factors and chronic illnesses with life dissatisfaction among U.S. adults: The Behavioral Risk Factor Surveillance System, 2006. *Preventive Medicine, 49*(2–3), 253–259.

Lichtman, A. H., & Martin, B. R. (2006). Understanding the pharmacology and physiology of cannabis dependence In R. Roffman, & R. S. Stephens (Eds.), *Cannabis dependence. Its nature, consequences and treatment* (pp. 37–57). New York: Cambridge University Press.

Lickliter, R., & Honeycutt, H. (2010). Rethinking epigenesis and evolution in light of developmental science. In M. S. Blumberg, J. H. Freeman, et al., (Eds.), *Oxford handbook of developmental behavioral neuroscience* (pp. 30–47). New York: Oxford University Press.

Liddell, S. K. (2003). *Grammar, gesture and meaning in American Sign Language*. Cambridge, MA: Cambridge University Press.

Lieberman, J. D., & Sales, B. D. (2007). *Scientific jury selection*. Washington, DC: American Psychological Association.

Lievens, F., & Sackett, P. R. (2006). Video-based versus written situational judgment tests: A comparison in terms of predictive validity. *Journal of Applied Psychology*, 91(5), 1181–1188.

Liles, E. E., & Packman, J. (2009). Play therapy for children with fetal alcohol syndrome. *International Journal of Play Therapy, 18*(4), 192–206.

Lilienfeld, S. O., Ammirati, R., & Landfield, K. (2009). Giving debiasing away: Can psychological research on correcting cognitive errors promote human welfare? *Perspectives on Psychological Science, 4*(4), 390–398.

Lilienfeld, S. O., Lynn, S. J., Ruscio, J., et al. (2010). *50 great myths of popular psychology: Shattering widespread misconceptions about human behavior*. London: Wiley-Blackwell.

Lilienfeld, S. O., Ruscio, J., & Lynn, S. J. (Eds.). (2008). *Navigating the mindfield: A user's guide to distinguishing science from pseudoscience in mental health*. Buffalo, NY: Prometheus Books.

Lin, T., & Peng, T. K. (2010). From organizational citizenship behaviour to team performance: The mediation of group cohesion and collective efficacy. *Management & Organization Review, 6*(1), 55–75.

Lindemann, B. (2001). Receptors and transduction in taste. *Nature, 413*, 219–25.

Linden, M., Baumann, K., Rotter, M., et al. (2008). Diagnostic criteria and the standardized diagnostic interview for posttraumatic embitterment disorder (PTED). *International Journal of Psychiatry in Clinical Practice, 12*(2), 93–96.

Linden, W. (2005). *Stress management: From basic science to better practice*. Thousand Oaks, CA: Sage.

Linderoth, B., & Foreman, R. D. (2006). Mechanisms of spinal cord stimulation in painful syndromes: Role of animal models. *Pain Medicine, 7*(Suppl. 1), S14–S26.

Lindsey, B. J., Fabiano, P., & Stark, C. (2009). The prevalence and correlates of depression among college students. *College Student Journal, 43*(4, PtA), 999–1014.

Lipsey, M. W., & Wilson, D. B. (1993). The efficacy of psychological, educational, and behavioral treatment: Confirmation from meta-analysis. *American Psychologist, 48*, 1181–1209.

Liu, X., Matochik, J. A., Cadet, J., et al. (1998). Smaller volume of prefrontal lobe in polysubstance abusers. *Neuropsychopharmacology, 18*(4), 243–252.

Liu, Y., Gao, J., Liu, H., et al. (2000). The temporal response of the brain after eating revealed by functional MRI. *Nature, 405*, 1058–1062.

Livingston, I, Doyle, J., & Mangan, D. (2010, April 25). Stabbed hero dies as more than 20 people stroll past him. *New York Post*. Retrieved March 28, 2011, from http://www.nypost.com/p/news/local/queens/passers_by_let_good_sam_die_5SGkf5XDP5ooudVuEd8fbI

Locke, B. D., & Mahalik, J. R. (2005). Examining masculinity norms, problem drinking, and athletic involvement as predictors of sexual aggression in college men. *Journal of Counseling Psychology, 52*(3), 279–283.

Lodi-Smith, J., Geise, A. C., Roberts, B. W., et al. (2009). Narrating personality change. *Journal of Personality & Social Psychology, 96*(3), 679–689.

Loeber, R., & Hay, D. (1997). Key issues in the development of aggression and violence from childhood to early adulthood. *Annual Review of Psychology, 48*, 371–410.

Loehlin, J. C., McCrae, R. R., Costa, P. T., et al. (1998). Heritabilities of common and measure-specific components of the Big Five personality factors.

Journal of Research in Personality, 32(4), 431–453.

Loftus, E. F. (2003). Make-believe memories. *American Psychologist, 58*(11), 867–873.

Loftus, E. F., & Bernstein, D. M. (2005). Rich false memories: The royal road to success. In A. F. Healy, (Ed.), *Experimental cognitive psychology and its applications* (pp. 101–113). Washington, DC: American Psychological Association.

Loftus, E. F., & Ketcham, K. (1994). *The myth of repressed memory: False memories and allegations of abuse* (pp. 101–113). New York: St. Martin's Press.

Loftus, E., & Palmer, J. C. (1974). Reconstruction of automobile destruction: An example of interaction between language and memory. *Journal of Verbal Learning & Verbal Behavior, 13*, 585–589.

LoLordo, V. M. (2001). Learned helplessness and depression. In M. E. Carroll, & J. B. Overmier (Eds.), *Animal research and human health: Advancing human welfare through behavioral science* (pp. 63–77). Washington: American Psychological Association.

Long, C. R., Seburn, M., Averill, J. R., et al. (2003). Solitude experiences: Varieties, settings, and individual differences. *Personality & Social Psychology Bulletin, 29*(5), 578–583.

Long, E. C., & Andrews, D. W. (1990). Perspective taking as a predictor of marital adjustment. *Journal of Personality & Social Psychology, 59*(1), 126–131.

Long, V. 0. (1989). Relation of masculinity to self-esteem and self-acceptance in male professionals, college students, and clients. *Journal of Counseling Psychology, 36*(1), 84–87.

López, S. R., & Guarnaccia, P. J. J. (2000). Cultural psychopathology. *Annual Review of Psychology, 51*, 571–598.

Lorenz, K. (1966). *On aggression*. Translated by M. Kerr-Wilson. New York: Harcourt Brace Jovanovich.

Lorenz, K. (1974). *The eight deadly sins of civilized man*. Translated by M. Kerr-Wilson. New York: Harcourt Brace Jovanovich.

Lorenzo, G. L., Biesanz, J. C., & Human, L. J. (2010). What is beautiful is good and more accurately understood: Physical attractiveness and accuracy in first impressions of personality. *Psychological Science, 21*(12), 1777–1782.

Lounsbury, D. W., & Mitchell, S. G. (2009). Introduction to special issue on social ecological approaches to community health research and action. *American Journal of Community Psychology, 44*(3–4), 213–220.

Lovaas, O., & Simmons, J. (1969). Manipulation of self-destruction in three retarded children. *Journal of Applied Behavior Analysis, 2*, 143–157.

Low, K. G., & Feissner, J. M. (1998). Seasonal affective disorder in college students: Prevalence and latitude. *Journal of American College Health, 47*(3), 135–137.

Low, S. M. (2001). The edge and the center: Gated communities and the discourse of urban fear. *American Anthropologist, 103*(1), 45–58.

Lucas, F., & Sclafani, A. (1990). Hyperphagia in rats produced by a mixture of fat and sugar. *Physiology & Behavior, 47*(1), 51–55.

Lucas, J. L., & Heady, R. B. (2002). Flextime commuters and their driver stress, feelings of time urgency, and commute satisfaction. *Journal of Business & Psychology, 16*(4), 565–572.

Luchins, D. J., Cooper, A. E., Hanrahan, P., et al. (2004). Psychiatrists' attitudes toward involuntary hospitalization. *Psychiatric Services, 55*(9), 1058–1060.

Ludwig, T. D., Gray, T. W., & Rowell, A. (1998). Increasing recycling in academic buildings. *Journal of Applied Behavior Analysis, 31*(4), 683–686.

Lum, D. (2011). *Culturally competent practice: A framework for understanding* (4th ed.). Belmont, CA: Cengage Learning/Wadsworth.

Lumley, M. A. (2004). Alexithymia, emotional disclosure, and health: A program of research. *Journal of Personality, 72*(6), 1271–1300.

Lundh, L., Berg, B., Johansson, H., et al. (2002). Social anxiety is associated with a negatively distorted perception of one's own voice. *Cognitive Behaviour Therapy, 31*(1), 25–30.

Luppa, M., Heinrich, S., Angermeyer, M. C., et al. (2007). Cost-of-illness studies of depression A systematic review. *Journal of Affective Disorders, 98*(1–2), 29–43.

Luria, A. R. (1968). *The mind of a mnemonist*. New York: Basic.

Luyten, P., & Blatt, S. J. (2011). Integrating theory-driven and empirically-derived models of personality development and psychopathology: A proposal for DSM V. *Clinical Psychology Review, 31*(1), 52–68.

Lykken, D. T. (1998). *A tremor in the blood: Uses and abuses of the lie detector*. New York, NY: Plenum.

Lykken, D. T. (2001). Lie detection. In W. E. Craighead, & C. B. Nemeroff (Eds.), *The Corsini Encyclopedia of psychology and behavioral science* (3rd ed., pp. 878–880). New York: Wiley.

Lyn, H., Franks, B., & Savage-Rumbaugh E. S. (2008). Precursors of morality in the use of the symbols "good" and "bad" in two bonobos (Pan paniscus) and a chimpanzee (Pan troglodytes). *Language & Communication, 28*(3), 213–224.

Lynch, K. B., Geller, S. R., & Schmidt, M. G. (2004). Multi-year evaluation of the effectiveness of a resilience-based prevention program for young children. *Journal of Primary Prevention, 24*(3), 335–353.

Lynch, T. R., Robins, C. J., Morse, J. Q., et al. (2001). A mediational model relating affect intensity, emotion inhibition, and psychological distress. *Behavior Therapy, 32*(3), 519–536.

Lynn, J. (2001). Serving patients who may die soon and their families. *Journal of the American Medical Association*, 285(7), 925–932.

Lynn, S. J., & Kirsch, I. (2006). Introduction: Definitions and early history. In S. J. Lynn, & I. Kirsch (Eds.), *Essentials of clinical hypnosis: An evidence-based approach* (pp. 3–15). Washington, DC: American Psychological Association.

Lynn, S. J., & O'Hagen, S. (2009). The sociocognitive and conditioning and inhibition theories of hypnosis. *Contemporary Hypnosis, 26*(2), 121–125.

Lynne-Landsman, S. D., Graber, J. A., et al. (2011). Is sensation seeking a stable trait or does it change over time? *Journal of Youth & Adolescence, 40*(1), 48–58.

Lyubomirsky, S., & Tucker, K. L. (1998). Implications of individual differences in subjective happiness for perceiving, interpreting, and thinking about life events. *Motivation & Emotion, 22*(2), 155–186.

Maas, J. (1999). *Power Sleep*. New York: HarperCollins.

Maccoby, E. E. (1990). Gender and relationships: A developmental account. *American Psychologist, 45*(4), 513–520.

MacDuffie, K., & Mashour, G. A. (2010). Dreams and the temporality of consciousness. *American Journal of Psychology, 123*(2), 189–197.

Macht, M., & Simons, G. (2011). Emotional eating. In I. NykliČek, A. Vingerhoets,, & M. Zeelenberg (Eds), *Emotion regulation and well-being* (pp. 281–295). New York: Springer.

MacKay, D. G., & Hadley, C. (2009). Supra-normal age-linked retrograde amnesia: Lessons from an older amnesic (H.M.). *Hippocampus, 19*(5), 424–445.

Mackintosh, N. J. (2003). Pavlov and associationism. *Spanish Journal of Psychology, 6*(2), 177–184.

Macklin, C. B., & McDaniel, M. A. (2005). The bizarreness effect: Dissociation between item and source memory. *Memory, 13*(7), 662–689.

MacLeod, C. M. (2005). The Stroop task in cognitive research. In A. Wenzel, & D. C. Rubin (Eds.), *Cognitive methods and their application to clinical research* (pp. 340–373). Washington, DC: American Psychological Association.

Maddi, S. R. (2006). Hardiness: The courage to grow from stresses. *Journal of Positive Psychology, 1*(3), 160–168.

Maddi, S. R., Harvey, R. H., Khoshaba, D. M., et al. (2009). The personality construct of hardiness, IV: Expressed in positive cognitions and emotions concerning oneself and developmentally relevant activities. *Journal of Humanistic Psychology, 49*(3), 292–305.

Maddock, J. E., Laforge, R. G., Rossi, J. S., et al. (2001). The College Alcohol Problems Scale. *Addictive Behaviors, 26*, 385–398.

Maddock, J., & Glanz, K. (2005). The relationship of proximal normative beliefs and global subjective norms to college students' alcohol consumption. *Addictive Behaviors, 30*(2), 315–323.

Maddox, K. B. (2004). Perspectives on racial phenotypicality bias. *Personality & Social Psychology Review, 8*(4), 383–401.

Maguire, E. A., Frackowiak, R. S. J., & Frith, C. D. (1997). Recalling routes around London: Activation of the hippocampus in taxi drivers. *Journal of Neuroscience, 17*(8), 7103.

Maguire, E. A., Valentine, E. R., Wilding, J. M., et al. (2003). Routes to remembering: The brains behind superior memory. *Nature Neuroscience, 6*(1), 90–95.

Mah, K., & Binik, Y. M. (2001). The nature of human orgasm: A critical review of major trends. *Clinical Psychology Review, 21*(6), 823–856.

Mahay, J., & Laumann, E. O. (2004). Meeting and mating over the life course. In E. O. Laumann, & R. Michael (Eds.), *The sexual organization of the city* (pp. 127–164). Chicago: University of Chicago Press.

Maheu, M. M., Pulier, M. L., Wilhelm, F. H., et al. (2004). *The mental health professional and the new technologies: A handbook for practice today*. Mahwah, NJ: Erlbaum.

Mahler, H. I. M., Beckerley, S. E., & Vogel, M. T. (2010). Effects of media images on attitudes toward tanning. *Basic & Applied Social Psychology, 32*(2), 118–127.

Mahmoodabadi, S. Z., Ahmadian, A., Abolhasani, M., et al. (2010). A fast expert system for electrocardiogram arrhythmia detection. *Expert Systems, 27*(3), 180–200.

Maier, N. R. F. (1949). *Frustration*. New York: McGraw-Hill.

Mailis–Gagnon, A., & Israelson, D. (2005). *Beyond pain: Making the mind–body connection*. Ann Arbor: University of Michigan Press.

Maisto, S. A., Galizio, M., & Connors, G. J. (2011). *Drug use and abuse* (6th ed.). Belmont, CA: Cengage Learning/Wadsworth.

Malamuth, N. M., & Donnerstein, E. (1982). The effects of aggressive-pornographic of mass media stimuli. In L. Berkowitz (Ed.), *Advances in experimental social psychology* (Vol. 15). New York: Academic Press.

Malamuth, N. M., Addison, T., & Koss, M. (2000). Pornography and sexual aggression: Are there reliable effects and can we understand them? *Annual Review of Sex Research, 11*, 26–91.

Malan, L., Malan, N. T., Wissing, M. P., et al. (2008). Coping with urbanization: A cardiometabolic risk? The THUSA study. *Biological Psychology, 79*(3), 323–328.

Malaspina, D., Reichenberg, A., Weiser, M., et al. (2005). Paternal age and intelligence: Implications for age-related genomic changes in male germ cells. *Psychiatric Genetics, 15*(2), 117–125.

Malloy, K. M., & Milling, L. S. (2010). The effectiveness of virtual reality distraction for pain reduction: A systematic review. *Clinical Psychology Review, 30*(8), 1011–1018.

Maloney, A. (1999). Preference ratings of images representing archetypal themes. *Journal of Analytical Psychology, 44*(1) 101–116.

Mamen, M. (2004). *Pampered child syndrome: How to recognize it, how to manage it and how to avoid it.* Carp, ON: Creative Bound.

Manber, R., Kraemer, H. C., Arnow, B. A., et al. (2008). Faster remission of chronic depression with combined psychotherapy and medication than with each therapy alone. *Journal of Consulting & Clinical Psychology, 76*(3), 459–467.

Mandler, J. M., & McDonough, L. (1998). On developing a knowledge base in infancy. *Developmental Psychology, 34*(6), 1274 1288.

Mangan, M. A. (2004). A phenomenology of problematic sexual behavior occurring in sleep. *Archives of Sexual Behavior, 33*(3), 287–293.

Mangels, J. A., Picton, T. W., & Craik, F. I. M. (2001). Attention and successful episodic encoding: An event-related potential study. *Brain Research, 11*, 77–95.

Manne, S. (2003). Coping and social support. In A. Nezu, C. Nezu, & P. Geller (Eds.), *Handbook of health psychology* (Vol. 9, pp. 51–74). New York: Wiley.

Manning, R., Levine, M., & Collins, A. (2007). The Kitty Genovese murder and the social psychology of helping: The parable of the 38 witnesses. *American Psychologist, 62*(6), 555–562.

Manschreck, T. C. (1996). Delusional disorder: The recognition and management of paranoia. *Journal of Clinical Psychiatry, 57*(3, Suppl), 32–38.

Manslow, C., & Vandenberghe, K. (2010). Unraveling the unknown: A therapeutic dialogue between hospice counselors and carers of people with dementia. *Illness, Crisis, & Loss, 18*(3), 185–199.

Mansouri, A., & Adityanjee. (1995). Delusion of pregnancy in males: A case report and literature review. *Psychopathology, 28*(6), 307–311.

Mantovani, A., Simpson, H. B., Fallon, B. A., et al. (2010). Randomized sham-controlled trial of repetitive transcranial magnetic stimulation in treatment-resistant obsessive-compulsive disorder. *International Journal of Neuropsychopharmacology, 13*(2), 217–227.

Mantyla, T. (1986). Optimizing cue effectiveness: Recall of 600 incidentally learned words. *Journal of Experimental Psychology: Learning, Memory, & Cognition, 12*(1), 66–71.

Maran, M. (2010). *My lie: A true story of false memory.* San Francisco: Jossey-Bass/Wiley.)

Marcel, M. (2005). *Freud's traumatic memory: Reclaiming seduction theory and revisiting Oedipus.* Pittsburgh, PA: Duquesne University Press.

Mares, M.-L., & Woodard, E. H. (2007). Positive effects of television on children's social interaction: A meta-analysis. In R. W. Preiss, W. Raymond, B. M. Gayle, et al. (Eds.), *Mass media effects research: Advances through meta-analysis* (pp. 281–300). Mahwah, NJ: Erlbaum.

Margolin, G., & Gordis, E. B. (2000). The effects of family and community violence on children. *Annual Review of Psychology, 51*, 445–479.

Markoff, J. (2011). Computer wins on 'Jeopardy!': Trivial, it's not. *New York Times, February 16*, A1. Retrieved February 21, 2011 from http://www.nytimes.com/2011/02/17/science/17jeopardy-watson.html.

Markowitz, F. E. (2011). Mental illness, crime, and violence: Risk, context, and social control. *Aggression & Violent Behavior, 16*, 36–44.

Marks, D. F. (2000). *The psychology of the psychic.* Buffalo, NY: Prometheus.

Marks, A., & Baldry, C. (2009). Stuck in the middle with who? The class identity of knowledge workers. *Work, Employment & Society, 23*(1), 49–65.

Markus H. R., Ryff, C. D., Curhan, K., et al. (2004). In their own words: Well-being at midlife among high school and college educated adults. In O. G. Brim, C. D. Ryff, & R. C. Kessler (Eds.), *How healthy are we?: A national study of well-being at midlife* (pp. 273–319). Chicago: University of Chicago Press.

Markus, H. R., Uchida, Y., Omoregie, H., et al. (2006). Going for the gold: Models of agency in Japanese and American contexts. *Psychological Science, 17*(2), 103–112.

Markus, H., & Nurius, P. (1986). Possible selves. *American Psychologist, 41*, 954–969.

Marmarosh, C., Holtz, A., & Schottenbauer, M. (2005). Group cohesiveness, group-derived collective self-esteem group-derived hope, and the well-being of group therapy members. *Group Dynamics: Theory, Research, & Practice, 9*(1), 32–44.

Marsella, A. J. (1998). Urbanization, mental health, and social deviancy. *American Psychologist, 53*(6), 624–634.

Marshall, R. D., Bryant, R. A., Amsel, L., et al. (2007). The psychology of ongoing threat: Relative risk appraisal, the September 11 attacks, and terrorism-related fears. *American Psychologist, 62*(4), 304–316.

Marsiglia, F. F., Kulis, S., Hecht, M. L., et al. (2004). Ethnicity and ethnic identity as predictors of drug norms and drug use among preadolescents in the US southwest. *Substance Use & Misuse, 39*(7), 1061–1094.

Martens, R., & Trachet, T. (1998). *Making sense of astrology.* Amherst, MA: Prometheus.

Martin, A. J., & Marsh, H. W. (2003). Fear of failure: Friend or foe? *Australian Psychologist, 38*(1), 31–38.

Martin, C. L., & Ruble, D. N. (2009). Patterns of gender development. *Annual Review of Psychology, 61*, 353–381.

Martin, E. K., Taft, C. T., & Resick, P. A. (2007). A review of marital rape. *Aggression & Violent Behavior, 12*(3), 329–347.

Martin, E., & Weiss, K. J. (2010). Knowing moral and legal wrong in an insanity defense. *Journal of the American Academy of Psychiatry & the Law, 38*(2), 286–288.

Martin, G., & Pear, J. (2011). *Behavior modification: What it is and how to do it* (9th ed.). Upper Saddle River, NJ: Prentice-Hall.

Martin, L. R., Friedman, H. S., & Schwartz, J. E. (2007). Personality and mortality risk across the life span: The importance of conscientiousness as a biopsychosocial attribute. *Health Psychology, 26*(4), 428–436.

Martin, S. (2007). The labyrinth of leadership. *Monitor on Psychology*, July/August, 90–91.

Martin, W. L. B., & Freitas, M. B. (2002). Mean mortality among Brazilian left- and right-handers: Modification or selective elimination. *Laterality, 7*(1), 31–44.

Martinez-Gonzalez, M. A., Gual, P., Lahortiga, F., et al. (2003). Parental factors, mass media influences, and the onset of eating disorders in a prospective population-based cohort. *Pediatrics, 111*, 315–320.

Martinko, M. J., Douglas, S. C., & Harvey, P. (2006). Understanding and managing workplace aggression. *Organizational Dynamics, 35*(2), 117–130

Martynhak, B. J., Louzada, F. M., Pedrazzoli, M., et al. (2010). Does the chronotype classification need to be updated? Preliminary findings. *Chronobiology International, 27*(6), 1329–1334.

Marx, B. P. (2009). Posttraumatic stress disorder and Operations Enduring Freedom and Iraqi Freedom: Progress in a time of controversy. *Clinical Psychology Review, 29*(8), 671–673.

Marx, B. P., Gross, A. M., & Adams, H. E. (1999). The effect of alcohol on the responses of sexually coercive and noncoercive men to an experimental rape analogue. *Sexual Abuse: Journal of Research & Treatment, 11*(2), 131–145.

Mashour, G. A., Walker, E. E., & Martuza, R. L. (2005). Psychosurgery: Past, present, and future. *Brain Research Reviews, 48*(3), 409–419.

Maslach, C., Schaufeli, W. B., & Leiter, M. P. (2001). Job burnout. *Annual Review of Psychology, 52*, 397–422.

Maslow, A. H. (1954). *Motivation and personality.* New York: Harper.

Maslow, A. H. (1967). Self-actualization and beyond. In J. F. T. Bugental (Ed.), *Challenges of humanistic psychology* (pp. 279–286). New York: McGraw-Hill.

Maslow, A. H. (1968). *Toward a psychology of being.* New York: Van Nostrand.

Maslow, A. H. (1969). *The psychology of science.* Chicago: Henry Regnery.

Maslow, A. H. (1970). *Motivation and personality.* New York: Harper & Row.

Maslow, A. H. (1971). *The farther reaches of human nature.* New York: Viking.

Masquelier, G. (2006). *Gestalt therapy: Living creatively today.* Hove, UK: Psychology Press.

Masse, L. C. & Tremblay, R. E. (1997). Behavior of boys in kindergarten and the onset of substance use during adolescence. *Archives of General Psychiatry, 54*(1), 62–68.

Masters, J. L., & Holley, L. M. (2006). A glimpse of life at 67: The modified future-self worksheet. *Educational Gerontology, 32*(4), 261–269.

Masters, W. H., & Johnson, V. E. (1966). *Human sexual response.* Boston: Little, Brown.

Masters, W. H., & Johnson, V. E. (1970). *The pleasure bond: A new look at sexuality and commitment.* Boston: Little, Brown.

Masuda, T., Gonzalez, R., Kwan, L., et al. (2008). Culture and aesthetic preference: Comparing the attention to context of East Asians and Americans. *Personality & Social Psychology Bulletin, 34*(9), 1260–1275.

Mather, G. (2008). *Foundations of sensation and perception.* Hove, UK: Psychology Press.

Matossian, M. K. (1982). Ergot and the Salem witchcraft affair. *American Scientist, 70*, 355–357.

Matson, J. L., & Boisjoli, J. A. (2009). The token economy for children with intellectual disability and/or autism: A review. *Research in Developmental Disabilities, 30*(2), 240–248.

Matson, J. L., Sevin, J. A., Fridley D., et al. (1990). Increasing spontaneous language in three autistic children. *Journal of Applied Behavior Analysis, 23*(2), 223–227.

Matthew, C. T., & Sternberg, R. J. (2009). Developing experience-based (tacit) knowledge through reflection. *Learning & Individual Differences, 19*, 530–540

Matthews, G., Deary, I. J., & Whiteman, M. C. (2009). *Personality traits* (3rd ed.). New York: Cambridge University Press.

Matthews, K. A., & Gallo, L. C. (2011). Psychological perspectives on pathways linking socioeconomic status and physical health. *Annual Review of Psychology, 62*, 501–530.

Matthews, P. H., & Matthews, M. S. (2004). Heritage language instruction and giftedness in language minority students: Pathways toward success. *Journal of Secondary Gifted Education, 15*(2), 50–55.

Mayberg, H., Lozano , A., Voon , V., et al. (2005). Deep brain stimulation for treatment-resistant depression. *Neuron, 45*(5), 651–660.

Mayer, E. L. (2002). Freud and Jung: the boundaried mind and the radically connected mind. *Journal of Analytical Psychology, 47*, 91–99.

Mayer, J. D. (2005). A tale of two visions: Can a new view of personality help integrate psychology? *American Psychologist, 60*(4), 294–307.

Mayer, J. D., Salovey, P., Caruso, D. R., et al. (2001). Emotional intelligence as standard intelligence. *Emotion, 1*(3), 232–242.

Mayer, R. E. (1995). *Thinking, problem solving, and cognition.* New York: Freeman.

Mayer, R. E. (2004). Should there be a three-strikes rule against pure discovery learning? *American Psychologist, 59*(1), 14–19.

Mayer, R. E. (2011). *Applying the science of learning.* Boston: Allyn & Bacon.

Mayes, S. D., Calhoun, S. L., Bixler, E. O., et al. (2009). IQ and neuropsychological predictors of academic achievement. *Learning & Individual Differences, 19*(2), 238–241.

McAdams, D. P., & Pals, J. L. (2006). A new Big Five: Fundamental principles for an integrative science of personality. *American Psychologist, 61*(3), 204–217.

McAlister, A. L., Ama, E., Barroso, C., et al. (2000). Promoting tolerance and moral engagement through peer modeling. *Cultural Diversity & Ethnic Minority Psychology, 6*(4), 363–373.

McBurney, D. H., & White, T. L. (2010). *Research methods* (8th ed.). Belmont, CA: Cengage Learning/Wadsworth.

McCabe S. E., Knight, J.R., Teter, C.J., et al. (2005). Non-medical use of prescription stimulants among US college students: prevalence and correlates from a national survey. *Addiction, 100,* 96–106.

McCabe, C., & Rolls, E. T. (2007). Umami: A delicious flavor formed by convergence of taste and olfactory pathways in the human brain. *European Journal of Neuroscience, 25*(6), 1855–1864.

McCabe, M. P. (1992). A program for the treatment of inhibited sexual desire in males. *Psychotherapy, 29*(2), 288–296.

McCabe, M. P., & Ricciardelli, L. A. (2004). Weight and shape concerns of boys and men. In Thompson, J. K. (Ed.), *Handbook of eating disorders and obesity* (pp. 606–634). New York: Wiley.

McCall, W. V., Prudic, J., Olfson, M., et al. (2006). Health-related quality of life following ECT in a large community sample. *Journal of Affective Disorders, 90*(2-3), 269–274.

McCarthy, B. W. (1995). Bridges to sexual desire. *Journal of Sex Education & Therapy, 21*(2), 132–141.

McCarthy, B. W., & Fucito, L. M. (2005). Integrating medication, realistic expectations, and therapeutic interventions in the treatment of male sexual dysfunction. *Journal of Sex & Marital Therapy, 31*(4), 319–328.

McClelland, D. C. (1961). *The achieving society*. New York: Van Nostrand.

McClelland, D. C. (1975). *Power: The inner experience*. New York: Irvington.

McClelland, D. C. (1994). The knowledge-testing-educational complex strikes back. *American Psychologist, 49*(1), 66–69.

McClelland, D. C., & Cheriff, A. D. (1997). The immunoenhancing effects of humor on secretory IgA and resistance to respiratory infections. *Psychology & Health, 12*(3), 329–344.

McClelland, D. C., & Pilon, D. A. (1983). Sources of adult motives in patterns of parent behavior in early childhood. *Journal of Personality & Social Psychology, 44,* 564–574.

McCluskey, U. (2002). The dynamics of attachment and systems-centered group psychotherapy. *Group Dynamics, 6*(2), 131–142.

McCormick, N. B. (2010). Sexual scripts: Social and therapeutic implications. *Sexual & Relationship Therapy, 25*(1), 96–120.

McCrae, R. R., & Costa, P. T. (2001). A five-factor theory of personality. In L. A. Pervin, & O. P. John (Eds.), *Handbook of personality* (pp. 139–153). New York: Guilford.

McCrea, S. M., & Hirt, E. R. (2011). Limitations on the substitutability of self-protective processes: Self-handicapping is not reduced by related-domain self-affirmations. *Social Psychology, 42*(1), 9–18.

McCrory, C., & Cooper, C. (2005). The relationship between three auditory inspection time tasks and general intelligence. *Personality & Individual Differences, 38*(8), 1835–1845.

McDaniel, M. A., Maier, S. F., & Einstein, G. O. (2002). "Brain-specific" nutrients: A memory cure? *Psychological Science in the Public Interest, 3*(1), 12–38.

McDermott, J. F. (2001). Emily Dickinson revisited: A study of periodicity in her work. *American Journal of Psychiatry, 158*(5), 686–690.

McDermott, R., Johnson, D., Cowden, J., et al. (2007). Testosterone and aggression in a simulated crisis game. *Annals of the American Academy of Political & Social Science, 614*(1), 15–33.

McGaugh, J. L., & Roozendaal, B. (2009). Drug enhancement of memory consolidation: Historical perspective and neurobiological implications. *Psychopharmacology, 202*(1-3), 3–14.

McGregor, D. (1960). *The human side of enterprise*. New York: McGraw-Hill.

McGregor, I., McAdams, D. P., & Little, B. R. (2006). Personal projects, life stories, and happiness: On being true to traits. *Journal of Research in Personality, 40*(5), 551–572.

McGuire, J., & Scott, S. (2002). Universal Design for Instruction: A promising new paradigm for higher education. *Perspectives, 28,* 27–29.

McIntosh, W. D., Harlow, T. F., & Martin, L. L. (1995). Linkers and nonlinkers: Goal beliefs as a moderator of the effects of everyday hassles on rumination, depression, and physical complaints. *Journal of Applied Social Psychology, 25*(14), 1231–1244.

McKay, A. (2005). Sexuality and substance use: The impact of tobacco, alcohol, and selected recreational drugs on sexual function. *Canadian Journal of Human Sexuality, 14*(1-2), 47–56.

McKay, E. (2008). *The human-dimensions of human-computer interaction: Balancing the HCI equation.* Amsterdam, Netherlands: IOS Press.

McKeever, L. (2006). Online plagiarism detection services: Saviour or scourge?. *Assessment & Evaluation in Higher Education, 31*(2), 155–165.

McKeever, W. F. (2000). A new family handedness sample with findings consistent with X-linked transmission. *British Journal of Psychology, 91*(1), 21–39.

McKenzie, K., Serfaty, M., & Crawford, M. (2003). Suicide in ethnic minority groups. *British Journal of Psychiatry, 183*(2), 100–101.

McKim, W. A. (2007). *Drugs and behavior* (6th ed.). Englewood Cliffs, NJ: Prentice Hall.

McKone, E., Brewer, J. L., MacPherson, S., et al. (2007). Familiar other-race faces show normal holistic processing and are robust to perceptual stress. *Perception, 36*(2), 244–248.

McLay, R. N., & Spira, J. L. (2009). Use of a portable biofeedback device to improve insomnia in a combat zone, a case report. *Applied Psychophysiology & Biofeedback, 34*(4), 319–321.

McLewin, L. A., & Muller, R. T. (2006). Childhood trauma, imaginary companions, and the development of pathological dissociation. *Aggression & Violent Behavior, 11*(5), 531–545.

McLoyd, V. C., & Smith, J. (2002). Physical discipline and behavior problems in African American, European American, and Hispanic children: Emotional support as a moderator. *Journal of Marriage & Family, 64*(1), 40–53.

McMahon, S., & Koltzenburg, M. (2005). *Wall & Melzacks textbook of pain* (5th ed.). London: Churchill Livingstone.

McNally, R. J., & Clancy, S. A. (2005). Sleep paralysis, sexual abuse, and space alien abduction. *Transcultural Psychiatry, 42(1),* 113–122.

McNally, R. J., Clancy, S. A., & Barrett, H. M. (2004). Forgetting trauma? In D. Reisberg, & P. Hertel (Eds.), *Memory & emotion* (pp. 129–154). New York: Oxford University Press.

McNamara, D. S., & Scott, J. L. (2001). Working memory capacity and strategy use. *Memory & Cognition, 29*(1), 10–17.

McRobbie, H., & Hajek, P. (2007). Effects of rapid smoking on post-cessation urges to smoke. *Addiction, 102*(3), 483–489.

Mead, M. (1935). *Sex and temperament in three primitive societies*. New York: Morrow.

Mecklinger, A. (2010). The control of long-term memory: Brain systems and cognitive processes. *Neuroscience & Biobehavioral Reviews, 34*(7), 1055–1065.

Medda, P., Perugi, G., Zanello, S., et al., (2009). Response to ECT in bipolar I, bipolar II and unipolar depression. *Journal of Affective Disorders, 118*(1-3), 55–59.

Medhus, E. (2001). *Child rearing challenges*. Retrieved May 25, 2007 from http://www.drmedhus.com/childchallenges.htm

Meeks, T. W., & Jeste, D. V. (2009). Neurobiology of wisdom: A literature overview. *Archives of General Psychiatry, 66*(4), 355–365.

Mehl, M. R., Vazire, S., Ramírez-Esparza N., et al. (2007). Are women really more talkative than men? *Science, 317*(5834), 82.

Mehrabian, A. (2000). Beyond IQ. *Genetic Social, & General Psychology Monographs, 126,* 133–239.

Mehrabian, A., & Blum, J. S. (2003). Physical appearance, attractiveness, and the mediating role of emotions. In N. J. Pallone (Ed.), *Love, romance, sexual interaction: Research perspectives from Current Psychology* (pp. 1–29). New Brunswick, NJ: Transaction Publishers.

Mehta, P. J., & Beer, J. (2010). Neural mechanisms of the testosterone-aggression relation: The role of orbitofrontal cortex. *Journal of Cognitive Neuroscience, 22*(10), 2357–2368.

Meier, P. S., Donmall, M. C., McElduff, P., et al. (2006). The role of the early therapeutic alliance in predicting drug treatment dropout. *Drug & Alcohol Dependence, 83*(1), 57–64.

Mejía, O. L., & McCarthy, C. J. (2010). Acculturative stress, depression, and anxiety in migrant farmwork college students of Mexican heritage. *International Journal of Stress Management, 17*(1), 1–20.

Meltzoff, A. N. (2005). Imitation and other minds: The "Like Me" Hypothesis. In S. Hurley, & N. Chater (Eds.), *Perspectives on imitation: From neuroscience to social science* (Vol. 2): *Imitation, human development, and culture* (pp. 55–77). Cambridge, MA: MIT Press.

Meltzoff, A. N., & Prinz, W. (2002). *The imitative mind: Development, evolution, and brain bases*. Cambridge, MA: Cambridge University Press.

Melzack, R. (1999). From the gate to the neuromatrix. *Pain, (Suppl. 6),* S121–S126.

Melzack, R., & Katz, J. (2004). The gate control theory: Reaching for the brain. In T. Hadjistavropoulos & K. D. Craig (Eds.), *Pain: Psychological perspectives* (pp. 13–34). Mahwah, NJ: Erlbaum.

Melzack, R., & Katz, J. (2006). Pain in the 21st century: The neuromatrix and beyond. In G. Young, A. W. Kane, et al. (Eds.), *Psychological knowledge in court: PTSD, pain, and TBI* (pp. 129–148). New York: Springer.

Melzack, R., & Wall, P. D. (1996). *The challenge of pain*. Harmondsworth, UK: Penguin.

Memon, A., Meissner, C. A., & Fraser, J. (2010). The Cognitive Interview: A meta-analytic review and study space analysis of the past 25 years. *Psychology, Public Policy, & Law, 16*(4), 340–372.

Mendolia, M. (2002). An index of self-regulation of emotion and the study of repression in social contexts that threaten or do not threaten self-concept. *Emotion, 2*(3), 215–232.

Meneses, G. D., & Beerlipalacio, A. (2005). Recycling behavior: A multidimensional approach. *Environment & Behavior, 37*(6), 837–860.

Menzel, P., Eisert, S., Mann, C. C., et al. (1994). *Material world: A global family portrait.* San Francisco: Sierra Club Books

Mercer, J. (2006). *Understanding attachment: Parenting, child care, and emotional development*. Westport, CT: Praeger.

Mercer, T., & McKeown, D. (2010). Interference in short-term auditory memory. *Quarterly Journal of Experimental Psychology, 63*(7), 1256–1265.

Merens, W., Booij, L., Haffmans, P. M. J., et al. (2008). The effects of experimentally lowered serotonin function on emotional information processing and memory in remitted depressed patients. *Journal of Psychopharmacology, 22*(6), 653–662.

Merhi, O., Faugloire, E., Flanagan, M., et al. (2007). Motion sickness, console video games, and head-mounted displays. *Human Factors, 49*(5), 920–934.

Merlin, D. (2008). How culture and brain mechanisms interact in decision making. In C. Engel & W. Singer (Eds.), *Better than conscious? Decision making, the human mind, and implications for institutions* (pp. 191–205). Cambridge, MA: MIT Press.

Mesquita, B., & Markus, H. R. (2004). Culture and emotion: Models of agency as sources of cultural variation in emotion. In A. S. R. Manstead, S. R. Antony, et al. (Eds.), *Feelings and emotions: The Amsterdam symposium* (pp. 341–358). New York: Cambridge University Press.

Messer, S. B., & Kaplan, A. H. (2004). Outcomes and factors related to efficacy of brief psychodynamic therapy. In D. P. Charman (Ed.), *Core processes in brief psychodynamic psychotherapy: Advancing effective practice* (pp. 103–118). Mahwah, NJ: Erlbaum.

Messick, D. M., Wilke, H., Brewer, M., et al. (1983). Individual adaptations and structural change as solutions to social dilemmas. *Journal of Personality & Social Psychology, 44*, 294–309.

Meunier, M., Monfardini, E., & Boussaoud, D. (2007). Learning by observation in rhesus monkeys. *Neurobiology of Learning and Memory, 88*(2), 243–248.

Meyer, G. J., Finn, S. E., Eyde, L. D., et al. (2001). Psychological testing and psychological assessment. *American Psychologist, 56*(2) 128–165.

Meyerbröker, K., & Emmelkamp, P. M. G. (2010). Virtual reality exposure therapy in anxiety disorders: A systematic review of process-and-outcome studies. *Depression & Anxiety, 27*(10), 933–944.

Meyers, L. (2006). Behind the scenes of the 'Dr. Phil' show. *Monitor on Psychology, 37*(9), 63.

Michaels, J. W., Blommel, J. M., Brocato, R. M., et al. (1982). Social facilitation and inhibition in a natural setting. *Replications in Social Psychology, 2*, 21–24.

Michalak, E. E., & Lam, R. W. (2002). Seasonal affective disorder: The hypothesis revisited. *Canadian Journal of Psychiatry, 47*(8), 787–788.

Michalko, M. (2001). *Cracking creativity*. Berkeley, CA: Ten Speed Press.

Michel, C., Caldara, R., & Rossion, B. (2006). Same-race faces are perceived more holistically than other-race faces. *Visual Cognition, 14*(1), 55–73.

Michel, G. F., & Tyler, A. N. (2005). Critical period: A history of the transition from questions of when, to what, to how. *Developmental Psychobiology, 46*(3), 156–162.

Mickelson, K. D., Kessler, R. C., & Shaver, P. R. (1997). Adult attachment in a nationally representative sample. *Journal of Personality & Social Psychology, 73*(5), 1092–1106.

Middaugh, S. J., & Pawlick, K. (2002). Biofeedback and behavioral treatment of persistent pain in the older adult: A review and a study. *Applied Psychophysiology & Biofeedback, 27*(3), 185–202.

Mielke, H. W. (1999). Lead in the inner cities. *American Scientist, 87*(Jan.–Feb.), 62–73.

Mignot, E. (2001). A hundred years of narcolepsy research. *Archives of Italian Biology, 139*, 207–220.

Mikolajczak, M., Pinon, N., Lane, A., et al. (2010). Oxytocin not only increases trust when money is at stake, but also when confidential information is in the balance. *Biological Psychology, 85*(1), 182–184.

Mikulincer, M. & Shaver, P. R. (Eds.). (2010). *Prosocial motives, emotions, and behavior: The better angels of our nature.* Washington, DC: American Psychological Association.

Miles, L. K., Karpinska, K., Lumsden, J., et al. (2010). The meandering mind: Vection and mental time travel. *PLoS ONE*, 5(5): e10825. doi:10.1371/journal.pone.0010825.

Milgram, S. (1963). Behavioral study of obedience. *Journal of Abnormal & Social Psychology, 67*, 371–378.

Milgram, S. (1965). Some conditions of obedience and disobedience to authority. *Human Relations, 18*, 57–76.

Milgram, S. (1967). The small-world problem. *Psychology Today*, May, 61–67.

Milgram, S. (1970). The experience of living in the cities: A psychological analysis. *Science, 167*, 1461–1468.

Milgram, S., Bickman, L., & Berkowitz, L. (1969). Note on the drawing power of crowds of different size. *Journal of Personality & Social Psychology, 13*, 79–82.

Miller, D. T. (2006). *An invitation to social psychology*. Belmont, CA: Cengage Learning/Wadsworth.

Miller, E. K., & Cohen, J. D. (2001). An integrative theory of prefrontal cortex function. *Annual Review of Neuroscience, 24*, 167–202.

Miller, G. A. (1956). The magical number seven, plus or minus two: Some limits on our capacity for processing information. *Psychological Review, 63*, 81–97.

Miller, G. A. (1999). On knowing a word. *Annual Review of Psychology, 50*, 1–19.

Miller, G. E., Cohen, S., & Ritchey, A. K. (2002). Chronic psychological stress and the regulation of pro-inflammatory cytokines. *Health Psychology, 21*(6), 531–541.

Miller, G. T., Jr., & Spoolman, S. (2011). *Environmental science* (13th ed.). Belmont, CA: Cengage Learning/Wadsworth.

Miller, J., & Garran, A. M. (2008). *Racism in the United States: Implications for the helping professions.* Belmont, CA: Cengage Learning/Wadsworth.

Miller, L. S., & Lachman, M. E. (2000). Cognitive performance and the role of control beliefs in midlife. *Aging, Neuropsychology, & Cognition, 7*(2), 69–85.

Miller, M. A., & Rahe, R. H. (1997). Life changes scaling for the 1990s. *Journal of Psychosomatic Research, 43*(3), 279–292.

Miller, M., Hemenway, D., & Azraela, D. (2007). State-level homicide victimization rates in the US in relation to survey measures of household firearm ownership, 2001–2003. *Social Science & Medicine, 64*(3), 656–664.

Miller, N. E. (1944). Experimental studies of conflict. In J. McV. Hunt (Ed.), *Personality and the behavior disorders* (Vol. 1, pp. 431–465). New York: Ronald Press.

Miller, N. E., & Bugelski. R. (1948). Minor studies of aggression: II. The influence of frustration imposed by the in-group on attitudes expressed toward out-groups. *Journal of Psychology, 25*, 437–442.

Miller, N., Pedersen, W. C., Earleywine, M., et al. (2003). A theoretical model of triggered displaced aggression. *Personality & Social Psychology Review, 7*(1), 75–97.

Miller, R., Perlman, D., & Brehm, S. S. (2009). *Intimate relationships* (5th ed.). New York: McGraw-Hill.

Miller, S. J., & Binder, J. L. (2002). The effects of manual-based training on treatment fidelity and outcome. *Psychotherapy: Theory, Research, Practice, Training, 39*(2), 184–198.

Miller, W. R., & Munoz, R. F. (2005). *Controlling your drinking: Tools to make moderation work for you*. New York: Guilford.

Miller, G. T., Jr., & Spoolman, S. (2011). *Environmental science* (13th ed.). Belmont, CA: Cengage Learning/Wadsworth.

Millet, K., & Dewitte, S. (2007). Digit ratio (2D:4D) moderates the impact of an aggressive music video on aggression. *Personality & Individual Differences, 43*(2), 289–294.

Millman, R. B., & Ross, E. J. (2003). Steroid and nutritional supplement use in professional athletes. *American Journal on Addictions, 12*(Suppl2), S48–S54.

Milne, R., & Bull, R. (2002). Back to basics: A componential analysis of the original cognitive interview mnemonics with three age groups. *Applied Cognitive Psychology, 16*(7), 743–753.

Milner, B. (1965). Memory disturbance after bilateral hippocampal lesions. In P. Milner, & S. Glickman (Eds.), *Cognitive processes and the brain* (pp. 97–111). Princeton, NJ: Van Nostrand.

Miltenberger, R. G. (2011). *Behavior modification: Principles and procedures* (5th ed.). Belmont, CA: Cengage Learning/Wadsworth.

Miltner, W. H. R., Krieschel, S., Hecht, H., et al. (2004). Eye movements and behavioral responses to threatening and nonthreatening stimuli during visual search in phobic and nonphobic subjects. *Emotion, 4*(4), 323–339.

Milton, J., & Wiseman, R. (1997). *Guidelines for extrasensory perception research*. Hertfordshire, UK: University of Hertfordshire Press.

Milton, J., & Wiseman, R. (1999). A meta-analysis of mass-media tests of extrasensory perception. *British Journal of Psychology, 90*(2), 235–240.

Minda, J. P., & Smith, J. D. (2001). Prototypes in category learning. *Journal of Experimental Psychology: Learning, Memory, & Cognition, 27*(3), 775–799.

Minton, H. L. (2000). Psychology and gender at the turn of the century. *American Psychologist, 55*(6), 613–615.

Miotto, K., Darakjian, J., Basch, J., et al. (2001). Gamma-hydroxybutyric acid: Patterns of use, effects and withdrawal. *American Journal on Addictions, 10*(3), 232–241.

Miranda, R., & Kihlstrom, J. F. (2005). Mood congruence in childhood and recent autobiographical memory. *Cognition & Emotion, 19*(7), 981–998.

Mirsky, A. F., & Duncan, C. C. (2005). Pathophysiology of mental illness: A view from the fourth ventricle. *International Journal of Psychophysiology, 58*(2-3), 162–178.

Mirsky, A. F., Bieliauskas, L. M., Van Kammen, D. P., et al. (2000). A 39-year followup of the Genain quadruplets. *Schizophrenia Bulletin, 3*, 5–18.

Mischel, W. (2004). Toward an integrative science of the person. *Annual Review of Psychology*, 55, 1–22.

Mischel, W., Shoda, Y., & Smith, R. E. (2008). *Introduction to personality: Toward an integration* (8th ed.). Hoboken, NJ: Wiley.

Mistlberger, R. E. (2005). Circadian regulation of sleep in mammals: Role of the suprachiasmatic nucleus. *Brain Research Reviews, 49*(3), 429–454.

Mitchell, D. (1987). Firewalking cults: Nothing but hot air. *Laser*, Feb., 7–8.

Mitchell, L. A., MacDonald, R. A. R., Knussen, C., et al. (2007). A survey investigation of the effects of music listening on chronic pain. *Psychology of Music, 35*(1), 37–57.

Mitchell, N. S., Dickinson, L. M., Allison Kempe, A., et al. (2010). Determining the effectiveness of Take Off Pounds Sensibly (TOPS), a nationally available nonprofit weight loss program. *Obesity, 19*, 568–573.

Mitka, M. (2009). College binge drinking still on the rise. *Journal of the American Medical Association, 302*(8), 836–837.

Moerman, D. E. (2002). The meaning response and the ethics of avoiding placebos. *Evaluation & the Health Professions, 25*(4), 399–409.

Mogg, K., Bradley, B. P., Hyare, H., et al. (1998). Selective attention to food-related stimuli in hunger. *Behaviour Research & Therapy, 36*(2), 227–237.

Moghaddam, B. (2002). Stress activation of glutamate neurotransmission in the prefrontal cortex. *Biological Psychiatry, 51*(10), 775–787.

Moghaddam, F. M. (2007). *Multiculturalism and intergroup relations: Psychological implications for democracy in global context*. Washington, DC: American Psychological Association.

Mohr, D. C., Hart, S. L., Julian, L., et al. (2005). Telephone-administered psychotherapy for depression. *Archives of General Psychiatry, 62*(9), 1007–1014.

Mokdad, A. H., Marks, J. S., Stroup, D. F., et al. (2004). Actual causes of death in the United States, 2000. *Journal of the American Medical Association, 291*, 1238–1245.

Monahan, J., Steadman, H. J., Silver, E., et al. (2001). *Rethinking risk assessment: The MacArthur Study of Mental Disorder and Violence*. New York, Oxford University Press, 2001.

Montgomery, P., & Dennis, J. (2004). A systematic review of non-pharmacological therapies for sleep problems in later life. *Sleep Medicine Reviews, 8*(1), 47–62.

Monti, M. M., Vanhaudenhuyse, A., Coleman, M. R., et al. (2010). Willful modulation of brain activity in disorders of consciousness. *New England Journal of Medicine, 362*(7), 579–589.

Montoya, R. M., & Insko, C. A. (2008). Toward a more complete understanding of the reciprocity of liking effect. *European Journal of Social Psychology, 38*, 477–498.

Montreal Declaration on Intellectual Disabilities. (2004). Retrieved February 21, 2011, from http://www.mdri.org/mdri-web-2007/pdf/montrealdeclaration.pdf.

Moor, J. (Ed.). (2003). *The Turing test: The elusive standard of artificial intelligence*. London: Kluwer Academic Publishers.

Moore, S. A., & Zoellner, L. A. (2007). Overgeneral autobiographical memory and traumatic events: An evaluative review. *Psychological Bulletin, 133*(3), 419–437.

Moore, T. O. (2001). Testosterone and male behavior: Empirical research with hamsters does not support the use of castration to deter human sexual aggression. *North American Journal of Psychology, 3*(3), 503–520.

Moran, F. (2010). *The paradoxical legacy of Sigmund Freud*. London, England: Karnac Books.

Moran, J. M., Macrae, C. N., Heatherton, T. F.. et al. (2006). Neuroanatomical evidence for distinct cognitive and affective components of self. *Journal of Cognitive Neuroscience, 18*(9), 1586–1594.

Moras, K. (2002). Research on psychotherapy. In M. Hersen, & W. H. Sledge (Eds.), *Encyclopedia of psychotherapy* (Vol 2, pp. 525–545). San Diego: Academic Press.

Moreno, J. L. (1953). *Who shall survive?* New York: Beacon.

Moreno, M. M., Linster, C., Escanilla, O., et al. (2009). Olfactory perceptual learning requires adult neurogenesis. *Proceedings of the National Academy of Sciences, 106*(42), 17980–17985.

Morgan, J. E., & Ricke, J. H. (Eds.). (2008). *Textbook of clinical neuropsychology*, Washington, DC: Taylor & Francis.

Morgan, J. P. (Ed.). (2005). *Psychology of aggression*. Hauppauge, NY: Nova Science Publishers.

Morgenstern, J., Labouvie, E., McCrady, B. S., et al. (1997). Affiliation with Alcoholics Anonymous after treatment. *Journal of Consulting & Clinical Psychology, 65*(5), 768–777.

Morin, A. (2006). Levels of consciousness and self-awareness: A comparison and integration of various neurocognitive views. *Consciousness & Cognition, 15*(2), 358–371.

Morisse, D., Batra, L., Hess, L., et al. (1996). A demonstration of a token economy for the real world. *Applied & Preventive Psychology, 5*(1), 41–46.

Moritz, A. P., & Zamchech, N. (1946). Sudden and unexpected deaths of young soldiers. *American Medical Association Archives of Pathology, 42*, 459–494.

Morris, T., Spittle, M., & Watt, T. (2005). *Imagery in sport*. Champaign, IL: Human Kinetics.

Morrison, R. G., & Wallace, B. (2001). Imagery vividness, creativity and the visual arts. *Journal of Mental Imagery, 25*(3-4), 135–152.

Morsella, E., & Krauss, R. M. (2004). The role of gestures in spatial working memory and speech. *American Journal of Psychology, 117*(3), 411–424.

Mosher, W. D., Chandra, C., & Jones, J. (2005). *Sexual behavior and selected health measures: Men and women 15–44 years of age, United States, 2002*. Atlanta, GA: Centers for Disease Control. Retrieved March 1, 2011 from http://www.cdc.gov/nchs/data/ad/ad362.pdf.

Moskowitz, G. B., & Li, P. (2011). Egalitarian goals trigger stereotype inhibition: A proactive form of stereotype control. *Journal of Experimental Social Psychology, 47*(1), 103–116.

Mosley, P. E. (2009). Bigorexia: Bodybuilding and muscle dysmorphia. *European Eating Disorders Review, 17*(3), 191–198.

Most, S. B., Scholl, B. J., Clifford, E. R., et al. (2005). What you see is what you set: Sustained inattentional blindness and the capture of awareness. *Psychological Review, 112*(1), 217–242.

Motivala, S. J., & Irwin, M. R. (2007). Sleep and immunity: Cytokine pathways linking sleep and health outcomes. *Current Directions in Psychological Science, 16*(1), 21–25.

Müller, B. H., Kull, S., Wilhelm, F. H., et al. (2011). One-session computer-based exposure treatment for spider-fearful individuals: Efficacy of a minimal self-help intervention in a randomised controlled trial. *Journal of Behavior Therapy & Experimental Psychiatry, 42*(2), 179–184.

Mulavara, A. P., Feiveson, A. H., Fiedler, J., et al. (2010). Locomotor function after long-duration space flight: Effects and motor learning during recovery. *Experimental Brain Research, 202*(3), 649–659.

Mundy, A. (2004). Divided we stand. *American Demographics, 26*(5), 26–31.

Munroe-Chandler, K., Hall, C., & Fishburne, G. (2008). Playing with confidence: The relationship between imagery use and self-confidence and self-efficacy in youth soccer players. *Journal of Sports Sciences, 26*(14), 1539–1546.

Munsey, C. (2006). RxP legislation made historic progress in Hawaii. *APA Monitor*, June, 42.

Munsey, C. (2008). Front-line psychopharmacology. *APA Monitor, February*, 56.

Murphy, B. C., & Dillon, C. (2011). *Interviewing in action in a multicultural world* (4th ed.). Belmont, CA: Cengage Learning/Wadsworth.

Murray, B. (2001). A daunting unbelievable experience. *Monitor on Psychology*, (Nov.), 18.

Murray, C. D., Pettifer, S., Howard, T., et al. (2007). The treatment of phantom limb pain using immersive virtual reality: Three case studies. *Disability & Rehabilitation, 29*(18), 1465–1469.

Murray, J. B. (2002). Phencyclidine (PCP): A dangerous drug, but useful in schizophrenia research. *Journal of Psychology, 136*(3), 319–327.

Murray, S. L., & Holmes, J. G. (1993). Seeing virtues in faults. *Journal of Personality & Social Psychology, 65*(4), 707–722.

Murray, S., Holmes, J. G., & Griffin, D. W. (2003). Reflections on the self-fulfilling effects of positive illusions. *Psychological Inquiry, 14*(3-4), 2003, 289–295.

Murrell, A. R., Christoff, K. A., & Henning, K. R. (2007). Characteristics of domestic violence offenders: Associations with childhood exposure to violence. *Journal of Family Violence, 22*(7), 523–532.

Mussen, P. H., Conger, J. J., Kagan, J., et al. (1979). *Psychological development: A life span approach*. New York: Harper & Row.

Musso, M., Weiller, C., Kiebel, S., et al. (1999). Training-induced brain plasticity in aphasia. *Brain, 122*, 1781–1790.

Mustanski, B. S., Chivers, M. L., & Bailey, J. M. (2002). A critical review of recent biological research on human sexual orientation. *Annual Review of Sex Research, 13*, 89–140.

Myers, H. F., Lesser, I., Rodriguez, N., et al. (2002). Ethnic differences in clinical presentation of depression in adult women. *Cultural Diversity & Ethnic Minority Psychology, 8*(2), 138–156.

Myers, L. (2007). The problem with DNA. *Monitor on Psychology, June*, 52–53.

Myrtek, M. (2007). Type A behavior and hostility as independent risk factors for coronary heart disease. In J. Jordan, B. Bardé, et al. (Eds.), *Contributions toward evidence-based psychocardiology: A systematic review of the literature* (pp. 159–183). Washington, DC: American Psychological Association.

Nairne, J. S. (2002). Remembering over the short-term. *Annual Review of Psychology, 53*, 53–81.

Naitoh, P., Kelly, T. L., & Englund, C. E. (1989). *Health effects of sleep deprivation*. U.S. Naval Health Research Center Report, No. 89–46.

Najdowski, C. J. (2010). Jurors and social loafing: Factors that reduce participation during jury deliberations. *American Journal of Forensic Psychology, 28*(2), 39–64.

Nakajima, S., & Nagaishi, T. (2005). Summation of latent inhibition and overshadowing in a generalized bait shyness paradigm of rats. *Behavioural Processes, 69*(3), 369–377.

Nakamura, J., & Csikszentmihalyi, M. (2003). The motivational sources of creativity as viewed from the paradigm of positive psychology. In L. G. Aspinwall, & U. M. Staudinger (Eds.), *A psychology of human strengths: Fundamental questions and future directions for a positive psychology* (pp. 257–269). Washington, DC: American Psychological Association.

National Academy of Sciences. (2003). *The polygraph and lie detection*. Washington, DC: The National Academies Press.

National Center for Chronic Disease Prevention and Health Promotion. (2010). *Tobacco use: Targeting the nation's leading killer*. Atlanta: Author. Retrieved March 7, 2011, from http://www.cdc.gov/nccdphp/publications/aag/osh.htm.

National Committee on Pay Equity. (2010a). *The wage gap over time: In real dollars, women see a continuing gap*. Washington, DC: Author. Retrieved February 23, 2011 from http://www.pay-equity.org/info-time.html.

National Committee on Pay Equity. (2010b). *Women of color in the workplace*. Washington, DC: Author. Retrieved February 23, 2011 from http://www.pay-equity.org/info-race.html.

National Fragile X Foundation. (2011). *Prevalence of Fragile X Syndrome*. Walnut Creek, CA: Author. Retrieved February 13, 2011 from http://www.nfxf.org/html/prevalence.htm.

National Institute of Child Health and Human Development. (2010a). *Link between child care and academic achievement and behavior persists into adolescence*. Washington, DC: Author. Retrieved December 31, 2010 from http://www.nichd.nih.gov/news/releases/051410-early-child-care.cfm/.

National Institute of Child Health and Human Development. (2010b). *Sudden infant death syndrome (SIDS)*. Washington, DC: Author. Retrieved January 11, 2011, from http://www.nichd.nih.gov/health/topics/sudden_infant_death_syndrome.cfm.

National Institute of Child Health and Human Development. (2010c). *Facts about Down syndrome*. Washington, DC: Author. Retrieved February 13, 2011, from http://www.nichd.nih.gov/publications/pubs/downsyndrome.cfm.

National Institute of Mental Health, (2010a). *Turning the corner, not the key, in treatment of serious mental illness*. Bethesda, MD: Author. Retrieved March 12, 2011, from http://www.nimh.nih.gov/about/director/2010/turning-the-corner-not-the-key-in-treatment-of-serious-mental-illness .shtml.

National Institute of Mental Health. (2010b). *How to find help*. Bethesda, MD: Author. Retrieved March 14, 2011, from http://www.nimh.nih.gov/health/topics/getting-help-locate-services/index.shtml.

National Institute of Mental Health. (2010c). *Depression*. Bethesda, MD: Author. Retrieved March 5, 2011, from http://www.nimh.nih.gov/health/publications/depression/complete-index.shtml#pub12.

National Institute of Mental Health. (2010d). *Suicide in the U.S.: Statistics and prevention*. Bethesda, MD: Author. Retrieved March 7, 2011, from http://www.nimh.nih.gov/health/publications/suicide-in-the-us-statistics-and-prevention/index.shtml.

National Institute of Mental Health. (2011a). *The numbers count: Mental disorders in America*. Bethesda, MD: Author. Retrieved March 7, 2011, from http://www.nimh.nih.gov/health/publications/the-numbers-count-mental-disorders-in-america/index .shtml.

National Institute of Mental Health. (2011b). *Warning signs of suicide*. Bethesda, MD: Author. Retrieved March 11, 2011, from http://www .nimh.nih.gov/health/topics/suicide-prevention/suicide-prevention-studies/warning-signs-of-suicide.shtml.

National Institute of Mental Health. (2008). *Attention deficit hyperactivity disorder*. Bethesda, MD: Author. Retrieved July 10, 2008, from http://www.nimh.nih.gov/health/publications/adhd/complete-publication.shtml.

National Institute of Neurological Disorders and Stroke. (2007). *Brain basics: Understanding sleep*. NIH Publication No.06-3440-c. Bethesda, MD: Author. Retrieved January 23, 2011 from http://www.ninds.nih.gov/disorders/brain_basics/understanding_sleep.htm.

National Institute on Alcohol Abuse and Alcoholism. (2007). *State of the science report on the effects of moderate drinking*. Bethesda, MD: Author. Retrieved January 20, 2011 from http://pubs.niaaa.nih.gov/publications/ModerateDrinking-03.htm.

National Institute on Drug Abuse. (2009). *Tobacco addiction*. Washington, DC: Author. Retrieved January 8, 2011, from http://www.drugabuse .gov/PDF/TobaccoRRS_v16.pdf.

National Institute on Drug Abuse. (2010a). *NIDA InfoFacts: MDMA (Ecstasy)*. Washington, DC: Author. Retrieved January 8, 2011, from http://www.nida.nih.gov/infofacts/ecstasy .html.

National Institute on Drug Abuse. (2010b). *Drugs, brains, and behavior: The science of addiction*. Washington, DC: Author. Retrieved January 8, 2011, from http://www.nida.nih.gov/scienceofaddiction/sciofaddiction.pdf.

National Youth Violence Prevention Resource Center (2008). *Media violence facts and statistics*. Atlanta: Author. Downloaded May 2, 2010 from http://www.safeyouth.org/scripts/faq/mediaviolstats.asp.

Nau, S. D., & Lichstein, K. L. (2005). Insomnia: Causes and treatments. In P. R. Carney, J. D. Geyer, et al. (Eds.), *Clinical sleep disorders* (pp. 157–190). Philadelphia, PA: Lippincott Williams & Wilkins.

Naveh-Benjamin, M., Guez, J., & Sorek, S. (2007). The effects of divided attention on encoding processes in memory: Mapping the locus of interference. *Canadian Journal of Experimental Psychology, 61*(1), 1–12.

Neave, N., & Wolfson, S. (2003). Testosterone, territoriality, and the 'home advantage'. *Physiology & Behavior, 78*(2), 269–275.

Needles, D. J., & Abramson, L. Y. (1990). Positive life events, attributional style, and hopefulness: Testing a model of recovery from depression. *Journal of Abnormal Psychology, 99*(2), 156–165.

Negriff, S., & Trickett, P. K. (2010). The relationship between pubertal timing and delinquent behavior in maltreated male and female adolescents. *Journal of Early Adolescence, 30*(4), 518–542.

Nehlig, A. (Ed.). (2004). *Coffee, tea, chocolate, and the brain*. Boca Raton, FL: CRC Press.

Neisser, U. (1997). Rising scores on intelligence tests. *American Scientist, 85*, 440–447.

Neisser, U., Boodoo, G., Bouchard, T. J., et al. (1996). Intelligence: Knowns & unknowns. *American Psychologist, 51*, 77–101.

Nelson, C. A. (1999). How important are the first 3 years of life? *Applied Developmental Science, 3*(4), 235–238.

Nelson, T. D. (2005). Ageism: Prejudice against our feared future self. *Journal of Social Issues, 61*(2), 207–221.

Nelson, T. D. (2006). *The psychology of prejudice* (2nd ed.). Needham Heights, MA: Allyn & Bacon.

Nemeroff, C. B., Bremner, J. D., Foa, E. B., et al. (2006). Posttraumatic stress disorder: A state-of-the-science review. *Journal of Psychiatric Research, 40*(1), 1–21.

Neter, E., & Ben-Shakhar G. (1989). The predictive validity of graphological inferences: A meta-analytic approach. *Personality & Individual Differences, 10(7)*, 737–745.

Nettle, D. (2005). An evolutionary perspective on the extraversion continuum. *Evolution & Human Behavior, 26*, 363–373.

Nettle, D. (2006). The evolution of personality variation in humans and other animals. *American Psychologist, 61*(6), 622–631.

Nettle, D. (2008). The personality factor: What makes you unique? *New Scientist, Feb 9*, 36–39.

Neubauer, A. C., & Fink, A. (2009). Intelligence and neural efficiency: Measures of brain activation versus measures of functional connectivity in the brain. *Intelligence, 37*(2), 223–229.

Neufeind, J., Dritschel, B., Astell, A. J., et al. (2009). The effects of thought suppression on autobiographical memory recall. *Behaviour Research & Therapy, 47*(4), 275–284.

Neufeld, R. W. J., Carter, J. R., Nicholson, I. R., et al. (2003). Schizophrenia. In P. Firestone, & W. L. Marshall (Eds.), *Abnormal psychology: Perspectives* (2nd ed., pp. 343–370). Toronto: Prentice Hall.

Neukrug, E. S., & Fawcett, R. C. (2010). *Essentials of testing and assessment: A practical guide for counselors, social workers, and psychologists* (2nd ed.). Belmont, CA: Cengage Learning/Wadsworth.

Neumeister, A. (2004). Neurotransmitter depletion and seasonal affective disorder: Relevance for the biologic effects of light therapy. *Primary Psychiatry, 11*(6), 44–48.

Newman, A. W., & Thompson, J. W. (2001). The rise and fall of forensic hypnosis in criminal investigation. *Journal of the American Academy of Psychiatry & the Law, 29*(1), 75–84.

Niaura, R., Todaro, J. F., Stroud, L., et al. (2002). Hostility, the metabolic syndrome, and incident coronary heart disease. *Health Psychology, 21*(6), 588–593.

Nickell, J. (2001). John Edward: Hustling the bereaved. *Skeptical Inquirer*, Nov.–Dec., 19–22.

Nickerson, R. S., & Adams, M. J. (1979). Long-term memory for a common object. *Cognitive Psychology, 11*, 287–307.

Niedzwienska, A. (2004). Metamemory knowledge and the accuracy of flashbulb memories. *Memory, 12*(5), 603–613.

Niehaus, D. J. H., Stein, D. J., Koen, L., et al. (2005). A case of "Ifufunyane": A Xhosa culture-bound syndrome. *Journal of Psychiatric Practice, 11*(6), 411–413.

Niehaus, J. L., Cruz-Bermúdez N. D., & Kauer, J. A. (2009). Plasticity of addiction: A mesolimbic dopamine short-circuit? *American Journal on Addictions, 18*(4), 259–271.

Niehoff, B. P., Moorman, R. H., Blakely, G., et al. (2001). The influence of empowerment and job enrichment on employee loyalty in a downsizing environment. *Group & Organization Management, 26*(1), 93–113.

Nielsen, M., & Dissanayake, C. (2004). Pretend play, mirror self-recognition and imitation: A longitudinal investigation through the second year. *Infant Behavior & Development, 27*(3), 342–365.

Niemiec, C. P., Ryan, R. M., & Deci, E. L. (2009). The path taken: Consequences of attaining intrinsic and extrinsic aspirations in post-college life. *Journal of Research in Personality, 43*(3), 291–306.

Nigbur, D., Lyons, E., & Uzzell, D. (2010). Attitudes, norms, identity and environmental behaviour: Using an expanded theory of planned behaviour to predict participation in a kerbside recycling programme. *British Journal of Social Psychology, 49*(2), 259–284.

Nisbett, R. E. (2005). Heredity, environment, and race differences in IQ: A commentary on Rushton and Jensen (2005). *Psychology, Public Policy, & Law, 11*(2), 302–310.

Nisbett, R. E. (2009a). *Intelligence and how to get it: Why schools and cultures count*. New York: Norton.

Nisbett, R. E. (2009b). Brighten up. *Monitor on Psychology, 40*(8), 28–30.

Nisbett, R. E., & Miyamoto, Y. (2005). The influence of culture: holistic versus analytic perception. *Trends in Cognitive Sciences, 9*(10), 467–473.

Njeri, I. (1991, January 13). Beyond the melting pot. *Los Angeles Times*, E-1 E-8.

Noftle, E. E., & Fleeson, W. (2010). Age differences in big five behavior averages and variabilities across the adult life span: Moving beyond retrospective, global summary accounts of personality. *Psychology & Aging, 25*(1), 95–107.

Noice, H., & Noice, T. (1999). Long-term retention of theatrical roles. *Memory, 7*(3), 357–382.

Noland, J. S., Singer, L. T., Short, E. J., et al. (2005). Prenatal drug exposure and selective attention in preschoolers. *Neurotoxicology & Teratology, 27*(3), 429–438.

Nolen-Hoeksema, S. (2011). *Abnormal psychology* (5th ed.). New York: McGraw-Hill.

Norcross, J. C. (2005). A primer on psychotherapy integration. In J. C. Norcross, & M. R. Goldfried (Eds.), *Handbook of psychotherapy integration* (2nd ed., pp. 3–23). London: Oxford.

Norcross, J. C., Hedges, M., & Prochaska, J. O. (2002). The face of 2010: A Delphi poll on the future of psychotherapy. *Professional Psychology: Research & Practice, 33*(3), 316–322.

Norem, J. K. (2002). *The positive power of negative thinking: Using defensive pessimism to harness anxiety and perform at your peak*. New York: Basic Books.

Norenzayan, A., & Nisbett, R. E. (2000). Culture and causal cognition. *Current Directions in Psychological Science, 9*, 132–135.

Norenzayan, A., Smith, E. E., Kim, B. J., et al. (2002). Cultural preferences for formal versus intuitive reasoning. *Cognitive Science, 26*(5), 653–684.

Norlander, T., Bergman, H., & Archer, T. (1998). Effects of flotation rest on creative problem solving and originality. *Journal of Environmental Psychology, 18*(4), 399–408.

Norlander, T., Bergman, H., & Archer, T. (1999). Primary process in competitive archery performance: Effects of flotation REST. *Journal of Applied Sport Psychology, 11*(2), 194–209.

Norman, D. A. (1994) *Things that make us smart*. Menlo Park, CA: Addison-Wesley.

Norman, K. L., & Panizzi, E. (2006). Levels of automation and user participation in usability testing. *Interacting with Computers*, 18(2), 246–264.

Norman, T. R. (2009). Melatonin: Hormone of the night. *Acta Neuropsychiatrica, 21*(5), 263–265.

Norris, R. M., & Weinman, J. A. (1996). Psychological change following a long sail training voyage. *Personality & Individual Differences, 21*(2), 189–194.

North, C. S. (1987). *Welcome silence.* NY: Simon & Schuster.

North, C. S., King, R. V., Fowler, R. L. (2008). Psychiatric disorders among transported Hurricane evacuees: Acute-phase findings in a large receiving shelter site. *Psychiatric Annals, 38*(2), 104–113.

Northcutt, R. G. (2004). Taste buds: Development and evolution. *Brain, Behavior & Evolution, 64*(3), 198–206.

Nosek, B. A., Greenwald, A. G., & Banaji, M. R. (2005). Understanding and using the implicit association test: II. Method variables and construct validity. *Personality & Social Psychology Bulletin, 31*(2), 166–180.

Nosko, A., Tieu, T.-T., Lawford, H., et al. (2011). How do I love thee? Let me count the ways: Parenting during adolescence, attachment styles, and romantic narratives in emerging adulthood. *Developmental Psychology, 47*(3), 645–657.

Novella, E. J. (2010). Mental health care in the aftermath of deinstitutionalization: A retrospective and prospective view. *Health Care Analysis, 18*(3), 222–238.

Novelli, D., Drury, J., & Reicher, S. (2010). Come together: Two studies concerning the impact of group relations on 'personal space'. *British Journal of Social Psychology, 49*(2), 223–236.

Ntoumanis, N., Taylor, I. M., & Standage, M. (2010). Testing a model of antecedents and consequences of defensive pessimism and self-handicapping in school physical education. *Journal of Sports Sciences, 28*(14), 1515–1525.

Nurnberger, J. I., & Zimmerman, J. (1970). Applied analysis of human behaviors: An alternative to conventional motivational inferences and unconscious determination in therapeutic programming. *Behavior Therapy, 1*, 59–69.

O'Conner, T. G., Marvin, R. S., Rutter, M., et al. (2003). Child-parent attachment following early institutional deprivation. *Development & Psychopathology, 15*(1), 19–38.

O'Craven, K. M., & Kanwisher, N. (2000). Mental imagery of faces and places activates corresponding stimulus-specific brain regions. *Journal of Cognitive Neuroscience, 12*(6), 1013–1023.

O'Hare, A. E., Bremner, L., Nash, M., et al. (2009). A clinical assessment tool for advanced theory of mind performance in 5 to 12 year olds. *Journal of Autism & Developmental Disorders, 39*(6), 916–928.

O'Keeffe, C., & Wiseman, R. (2005). Testing alleged mediumship: Methods and results. *British Journal of Psychology, 96*(2), 165–179.

O'Neill, B. (2003). Don't believe everything you read online. *BBC News.* Retrieved April 21, 2009, from http://newswww.bbc.net.uk/1/hi/magazine/3151595.stm.

O'Neill, P. (2005) The ethics of problem definition. *Canadian Psychology, 46*, 13–20.

O'Roark, A. M. (2001). Personality assessment, projective methods and a triptych perspective. *Journal of Projective Psychology & Mental Health, 8*(2), 116–126.

Oakley R. (2004). How the mind hurts and heals the body. *American Psychologist, 59*(1), 29–40.

Oakley, D. A., & Halligan, P. W. (2010). Psychophysiological foundations of hypnosis and suggestion. In S. J. Lynn, J. W. Rhue, & I. Kirsch (Eds.). *Handbook of clinical hypnosis* (2nd ed., pp. 79–117). Washington, DC: American Psychological Association.

Oakley, D. A., Whitman, L. G., & Halligan, P. W. (2002). Hypnotic imagery as a treatment for phantom limb pain. *Clinical Rehabilitation, 16*(4), 368–377.

Oberauer, K., & Göthe, K. (2006). Dual-task effects in working memory: Interference between two processing tasks, between two memory demands, and between storage and processing. *European Journal of Cognitive Psychology, 18*(4), 493–519.

Oberle, E. (2009). The development of Theory of Mind reasoning in Micronesian children. *Journal of Cognition & Culture, 9*(1-2), 39–56.

Ochoa, J. G., & Pulido, M. (2005). Parasomnias. In P. R. Carney, J. D. Geyer, et al. (Eds.), *Clinical sleep disorders* (pp. 224–242). Philadelphia, PA: Lippincott Williams & Wilkins.

Ofosu, H. B., Lafreniere, K. D., & Senn, C. Y. (1998). Body image perception among women of African descent: A normative context? *Feminism & Psychology, 8*(3), 303–323.

Ogden C. L., Carroll M. D., Curtin, L. R., et al. (2010). Prevalence of high body mass index in US children and adolescents, 2007–2008. *Journal of the American Medical Association, 303*(3), 242–249.

Ogloff, J. R. P. (2006). Psychopathy/antisocial personality disorder conundrum. *Australian & New Zealand Journal of Psychiatry, 40*(6), 519–528.

Okiishi, J., Lambert, M. J., Nielsen, S. L., et al. (2003). Waiting for supershrink: An empirical analysis of therapist effects. *Clinical Psychology & Psychotherapy, 10*(6), 361–373.

Olds, M. E., & Fobes, J. L. (1981). The central basis of motivation: Intracranial self-stimulation studies. *Annual Review of Psychology, 32*, 523–574.

O'Leary, E. (2006). Person-centred gestalt therapy. In E. O'Leary, & M. Murphy (Eds.), *New approaches to integration in psychotherapy* (pp. 25–37). New York: Routledge.

Olpin, M., & Hesson, M. (2010). *Stress management for life* (2nd ed.). Belmont, CA: Cengage Learning/Wadsworth.

Olson, J. M., & Zanna, M. P. (1993). Attitudes and attitude change. *Annual Review of Psychology, 44*, 117–154.

Olson, M. & Hergenhahn, B. R. (2009). *Introduction to the theories of learning* (8th ed.). Englewood Cliffs, NJ: Prentice Hall.

Olson-Buchanan, J. B., & Drasgow, F. (2006). Multimedia situational judgment tests: The medium creates the message. In J. A. Weekley, & R. E. Ployhart (Eds.), *Situational judgment tests: Theory, measurement, and application* (pp. 253–278). Mahwah, NJ: Erlbaum.

Olsson, A., Nearing, K, & Phelps, E. A. (2007). Learning fears by observing others: The neural systems of social fear transmission. *Social Cognitive & Affective Neuroscience, 2*(1), 3–11.

Olsson, E. M. G., El Alaoui, S., Carlberg, B., et al. (2010). Internet-based biofeedback-assisted relaxation training in the treatment of hypertension: A pilot study. *Applied Psychophysiology & Biofeedback, 35*(2), 163–170.

Olsson, P. A. (2007). Group death myths and terror cult groups. *Journal of Psychohistory, 34*(3), 241–254.

Olsson, P. A. (2008). *The cult of Osama: Psychoanalyzing bin Laden and his magnetism for Muslim youths.* Westport, CT: Praeger.

Olszewski, P. K., Li, D., Grace, M. K., et al. (2003). Neural basis of orexigenic effects of ghrelin acting within lateral hypothalamus. *Peptides, 24*(4), 597–602.

Ong, A. D., Zautra, A. J., & Reid, M. C. (2010). Psychological resilience predicts decreases in pain catastrophizing through positive emotions. *Psychology & Aging. 25*(3), 516–523.

Onwuegbuzie, A. J. (2000). Academic procrastinators and perfectionistic tendencies among graduate students. *Journal of Social Behavior & Personality, 15*(5), 103–109.

Ooki, S. (2005). Genetic and environmental influences on the handedness and footedness in Japanese twin children. *Twin Research & Human Genetics, 8*(6), 649–656.

Opland, D. M., Leinninger, G. M., & Myers, M. G., Jr. (2010). Modulation of the mesolimbic dopamine system by leptin. *Brain Research, 1350*, 65–70.

Oppliger, P. A. (2007). Effects of gender stereotyping on socialization. In R. W. Preiss, B. M. Gayle, et al. (Eds.), *Mass media effects research: Advances through meta-analysis* (pp. 199–214). Mahwah, NJ: Erlbaum.

Ord, T. J., Martins E. P., Thakur S., et al. (2005). Trends in animal behaviour research (1968–2002): Ethoinformatics and the mining of library databases. *Animal Behaviour, 69*(6), 1399–1413.

Orenstein, P. (2011). *Cinderella ate my daughter.* New York: HarperCollins.

Orleans, C. T. (2000). Promoting the maintenance of health behavior change. *Health Psychology, 19*(Suppl. 1), 76–83.

Orleans, C. T., Gruman, J., & Hollendonner, J. K. (1999). Rating our progress in population health promotion: Report card on six behaviors. *American Journal of Health Promotion, 14*(2), 75–82.

Ormay, T. (2006). Cybertherapy: Psychotherapy on the Internet. *International Journal of Psychotherapy, 10*(2), 51–60.

Ormrod, J. E. (2011). *Educational psychology: Developing learners* (7th ed.). Boston: Allyn & Bacon.

Orr, A. C., & Hammig, S. B. (2009). Inclusive postsecondary strategies for teaching students with learning disabilities: A review of the literature. *Learning Disability Quarterly, 32*(3), 181–196.

Osgood, C. E. (1952). The nature and measurement of meaning. *Psychological Bulletin, 49*, 197–237.

Oskamp, S. (1995). Resource conservation and recycling: Behavior and policy. *Journal of Social Issues, 51*(4), 157–177.

Oskamp, S. (2000). A sustainable future for humanity? *American Psychologist, 55*(5), 496–508.

Oskamp, S. (2002). Summarizing sustainability issues and research approaches. In P. Schmuck, & W. P. Schultz (Eds.), *Psychology of sustainable development* (pp. 301–324). Dordrecht, Netherlands: Kluwer.

Oskamp, S., & Schultz, P. W. (2005). *Attitudes and opinions* (3rd ed.). Mahwah, NJ: Erlbaum.

Oskamp, S., & Schultz, P. W. (2006). Using psychological science to achieve ecological sustainability. In S. I. Donaldson, D. E. Berger, et al. (Eds.), *Applied psychology: New frontiers and rewarding careers* (pp. 81–106). Mahwah, NJ: Erlbaum.

Osman, M. (2008). Positive transfer and negative transfer/antilearning of problem-solving skills. *Journal of Experimental Psychology: General, 137*(1), 97–115.

Osofsky, M. J., Bandura, A., & Zimbardo, P. G. (2005). The role of moral disengagement in the execution process. *Law & Human Behavior, 29*(4), 371–393.

Oster, H. (2005). The repertoire of infant facial expressions: a ontogenetic perspective. In J. Nadel, & D. Muir (Eds.), *Emotional development: Recent research advances* (pp. 261–292). New York: Oxford University Press.

Oswald, D. L., & Chapleau, K. M. (2010). Selective self-stereotyping and women's self-esteem maintenance. *Personality & Individual Differences, 49*(8), 918–922.

Otgaar, H., & Smeets, T. (2010). Adaptive memory: Survival processing increases both true and false memory in adults and children. *Journal of Experimental Psychology: Learning, Memory, & Cognition, 36*(4), 1010–1016.

Overbeck, J. R. (2010). Concepts and historical perspectives on power. In A. Guinote, & T. K. Vescio (Eds.), *The social psychology of power* (pp. 19–45). New York: Guilford.

Overholser, J. C. (2010). Psychotherapy that strives to encourage social interest: A simulated interview with Alfred Adler. *Journal of Psychotherapy Integration, 20*(4), 347–363.

Overmier, J. B., & LoLordo, V. M. (1998). Learned helplessness. In O'Donohue, W. T. (Ed.), *Learning and behavior therapy* (pp. 352–373). Boston, MA: Allyn & Bacon.

Owens, J., & Massey, D. S. (2011). Stereotype threat and college academic performance: A latent variables approach. *Social Science Research, 40*(1), 150–166.

Oyserman, D., Bybee, D., Terry, K., et al. (2004). Possible selves as roadmaps. *Journal of Research in Personality, 38*(2), 130–149.

Page, K. (1999, May 16). The graduate. *Washington Post Magazine, 152*, 18–20.

Page, M. P. A., Madge, A., Cumming, N., et al. (2007). Speech errors and the phonological similarity effect in short-term memory: Evidence suggesting a common locus. *Journal of Memory & Language, 56*(1), 49–64.

Pagnin, D., de Queiroz, V., Pini, S., et al. (2004). Efficacy of ECT in depression: A meta-analytic review. *Journal of ECT, 20*(1), 13–20.

Palmer, S. E., & Beck, D. M. (2007). The repetition discrimination task: An objective method for studying perceptual grouping. *Perception & Psychophysics, 69*(1), 68–78.

Pals, J. L. (2006). Narrative identity processing of difficult life experiences: Pathways of personality development and positive self-transformation in adulthood. *Journal of Personality, 74*(4), 1079–1110.

Pandey, S. (1999). Role of perceived control in coping with crowding. *Psychological Studies, 44*(3), 86–91.

Panksepp, J., & Pasqualini, M. S. (2005). The search for the fundamental brain/mind sources of affective experience. In J. Nadel, & D. Muir (Eds.), *Emotional development: Recent research advances* (pp. 5–30). New York: Oxford University Press.

Papadatou-Pastou, M., Martin, M., Munafò, M. R., et al. (2008). Sex differences in left-handedness: A meta-analysis of 144 studies. *Psychological Bulletin, 134*(5), 677–699.

Papanicolaou, A. C. (Ed.) (2006). *The amnesias: A clinical textbook of memory disorders*. New York: Oxford University Press.

Paquette, D. (2004). Theorizing the father-child relationship: mechanisms and developmental outcomes. *Human Development, 47*(4), 193–219.

Paquette, V., Lévesque, J., Mensour, B., et al. (2003). "Change the mind and you change the brain": Effects of cognitive-behavioral therapy on the neural correlates of spider phobia. *NeuroImage, 18*, 401–409.

Paradis, C. M., Solomon, L. Z., Florer, F., et al. (2004). Flashbulb memories of personal events of 9/11 and the day after for a sample of New York City residents. *Psychological Reports, 95*(1), 304–310.

Park, G., Lubinski, D., Benbow, C. P. (2008). Ability differences among people who have commensurate degrees matter for scientific creativity. *Psychological Science, 19*(10), 957–961.

Park, H. J., Li, R. X., Kim, J., et al. (2009). Neural correlates of winning and losing while watching soccer matches. *International Journal of Neuroscience, 119*(1), 76–87.

Park, H., & Lennon, S. J. (2008). Beyond physical attractiveness: Interpersonal attraction as a function of similarities in personal characteristics. *Clothing & Textiles Research Journal, 26*(4), 275–289.

Park, N., Peterson, C., & Seligman, M.E. P. (2004). Strengths of character and well-being. *Journal of Social & Clinical Psychology, 23*(5), 603–619.

Parke, R. D. (2004). Development in the family. *Annual Review of Psychology, 55*, 365–399.

Parker, A., Ngu, H., & Cassaday, H. J. (2001). Odour and Proustian memory. *Applied Cognitive Psychology, 15*(2), 159–171.

Parker, E. S., Cahill, L., & McGaugh, J. L. (2006). A case of unusual autobiographical remembering. *Neurocase, 12*(1), 35–49.

Parker, J. D. A. (2005). The relevance of emotional intelligence for clinical psychology. In R. Schulze, & R. D. Roberts (Eds.), *Emotional intelligence: An international handbook* (pp. 271–287). Ashland, OH: Hogrefe & Huber.

Parker, P. D., & Salmela-Aro K. (2011). Developmental processes in school burnout: A comparison of major developmental models. *Learning & Individual Differences, 21*, 244–248.

Parsons, K. M., Balcomb, K. C., III., Ford, J. K. B., et al. (2009). The social dynamics of southern resident killer whales and conservation implications for this endangered population. *Animal Behaviour, 77*(4), 963–971.

Pasupathi, M., & Staudinger, U. M. (2001). Do advanced moral reasoners also show wisdom? *International Journal of Behavioral Development, 25*(5), 401–415.

Patall, E. A., Cooper, H., & Robinson, J. C. (2008). The effects of choice on intrinsic motivation and related outcomes: A meta-analysis of research findings. *Psychological Bulletin, 134*(2), 270–300.

Paternoster, R., & Pogarsky, G. (2009). Rational choice, agency and thoughtfully reflective decision making: The short and long-term consequences of making good choices. *Journal of Quantitative Criminology, 25*(2), 103–127.

Patterson, C. J. (2002). Lesbian and gay parenthood. In M. Bornstein (Ed.), *Handbook of Parenting* (Vol. 3): *Being and becoming a parent* (2nd ed., pp. 317–338). Mahwah, NJ: Erlbaum.

Paulhus, D. L. (1998). Interpersonal and intrapsychic adaptiveness of trait self-enhancement. *Journal of Personality & Social Psychology, 74*(5), 1197–1208.

Paulsson, T., & Parker, A. (2006). The effects of a two-week reflection-intention training program on lucid dream recall. *Dreaming, 16*(1), 22–35.

Pavlov, I. P. (1927). *Conditioned reflexes*. Translated by G. V. Anrep. New York: Dover.

Payne, K. (2009). Winning the battle of ideas: Propaganda, ideology, and terror. *Studies in Conflict & Terrorism, 32*(2), 109-128.

Payne, B. K., Krosnick, J. A., Pasek, J., et al. (2010). Implicit and explicit prejudice in the 2008 American presidential election. *Journal of Experimental Social Psychology, 46*(2), 367–374.

Pearce, C. L., Conger, J. A., & Locke, E. A. (2007). Shared leadership theory. *Leadership Quarterly, 18*(3), 281–288.

Pearce, C. L., Manz, C. C., & Sims, H. P., Jr. (2009). Where do we go from here?: Is shared leadership the key to team success? *Organizational Dynamics, 38*(3), 234–238.

Pedersen, A. F., Bovbjerg, D. H., & Zachariae, R. (2011). Stress and susceptibility to infectious disease. In R. J. Contrada, & A. Baum (Eds.), *The handbook of stress science: Biology, psychology, and health* (pp. 425–445). New York: Springer.

Pedraza, C., García, F. B., & Navarro, J. F. (2009). Neurotoxic effects induced by gammahydroxybutyric acid (GHB) in male rats. *International Journal of Neuropsychopharmacology, 12*(9), 1165–1177.

Peek, F., & Hanson, L. L. (2007). *The life and message of the real Rain Man: The journey of a mega-savant*. Port Chester, NY: Dude Publishing.

Pelletier, L. G., Baxter, D., & Huta, V. (2011). Personal autonomy and environmental sustainability. In V. I. Chirkov, R. N. Ryan, & K. M. Sheldon (Eds.), *Human autonomy in cross-cultural context: Perspectives on the psychology of agency, freedom, and well-being* (pp. 257–278). New York: Springer.

Pelton, T. (1983). The shootists. *Science 83, 4*(4), 84–86.

Penfield, W. (1957). Brain's record of past a continuous movie film. *Science News Letter, April 27*, 265.

Penfield, W. (1958). *The excitable cortex in conscious man*. Springfield, IL: Charles C Thomas.

Pennebaker, J. W. (2004). *Writing to heal: A guided journal for recovering from trauma and emotional upheaval*. Oakland, CA: New Harbinger Press.

Pennebaker, J. W., & Chung, C. K. (2007). Expressive writing, emotional upheavals, and health. In H. S. Friedman, & R. C. Silver (Eds.), *Foundations of health psychology* (pp. 263–284). New York: Oxford University Press.

Penner, L. A., Dovidio, J. F., Piliavin, J. A., et al. (2005). Prosocial behavior: Multilevel perspectives. *Annual Review of Psychology, 56*, 365–392.

Peplau, L. A. (2003). Human sexuality: How do men and women differ? *Current Directions in Psychological Science, 12*(2), 37–40.

Perin, C. T. (1943). A quantitative investigation of the delay of reinforcement gradient. *Journal of Experimental Psychology, 32*, 37–51.

Perkins, D. N. (1995). *Outsmarting IQ: The emerging science of learnable intelligence*. New York: Free Press.

Perkins, D. N., & Grotzer, T. A. (1997). Teaching intelligence. *American Psychologist, 52*(10), 1125–1133.

Perlman, D., & Cozby, P. C. (1983). *Social psychology*. NY: Holt, Rinehart & Winston.

Perloff, R. M. (2010). *The dynamics of persuasion: Communication and attitudes in the 21st century*. New York: Psychology Press.

Perls, F. (1969). *Gestalt therapy verbatim*. Lafayette, CA: Real People Press.

Perreault, S., & Bourhis, R. Y. (1999). Ethnocentrism, social identification, and discrimination. *Personality & Social Psychology Bulletin, 25*(1), 92–103.

Perry, R. P. (2003). Perceived (academic) control and causal thinking in achievement settings. *Canadian Psychology, 44*(4), 312–331.

Perry, R. P., Hladkyj, S., Pekrun, R. H., et al. (2001). Academic control and action control in the achievement of college students: A longitudinal field study. *Journal of Educational Psychology, 93*(4), 776–789.

Pesant, N., & Zadra, A. (2006). Dream content and psychological well-being: A longitudinal study of the continuity hypothesis. *Journal of Clinical Psychology, 62*(1), 111–121.

Pescatello, L. S. (2001). Exercising for health. *Western Journal of Medicine, 174*(2), 114–118.

Peters, W. A. (1971). *A class divided*. Garden City, NY: Doubleday.

Peterson, C., & Chang, E. C. (2003). Optimism and flourishing. In C. L. M. Keyes, & J. Haidt (Eds.), *Flourishing* (pp. 55–79). Washington, DC: American Psychological Association.

Peterson, C., & Park, N. (2010). What happened to self-actualization? Commentary on Kenrick et al. (2010). *Perspectives on Psychological Science, 5*(3), 320–322.

Peterson, C., & Seligman, M. E. P. (2004). *Character strengths and virtues*. Washington, DC: American Psychological Association.

Peterson, C., & Vaidya, R. S. (2001). Explanatory style, expectations, and depressive symptoms. *Personality & Individual Differences, 31*(7), 1217–1223.

Peterson, D. R. (2001). Choosing the PsyD. In S. Walfish, & A. K. Hess (Eds.), *Succeeding in graduate school: The career guide for psychology students* (pp. 53–60). Mahwah, NJ: Erlbaum.

Peterson, L. R., & Peterson, M. J. (1959). Short-term retention of individual verbal items. *Journal of Experimental Psychology, 58*, 193–198.

Peterson, P. C., & Husain, A. M. (2008). Pediatric narcolepsy. *Brain & Development, 30*(10), 609–623.

Peterson, S. E. (1992). The cognitive functions of underlining as a study technique. *Reading Research & Instruction, 31*(2), 49–56.

Petrill, S. A., Luo, D., Thompson, L. A., et al. (2001). Inspection time and the relationship among elementary cognitive tasks, general intelligence and specific cognitive abilities. *Intelligence, 29*(6), 487–496.

Pett, M. A., & Johnson, M. J. M. (2005). Development and psychometric evaluation of the Revised University Student Hassles Scale. *Educational & Psychological Measurement, 65*(6), 984–1010.

Peverly, S. T., Brobst, K. E., Graham, M., et al. (2003). College adults are not good at self-regulation. *Journal of*

Educational Psychology, 95(2), 335–346.

Pezdek, K., Avila-Mora E., & Sperry, K. (2010). Does trial presentation medium matter in jury simulation research? Evaluating the effectiveness of eyewitness expert testimony. *Applied Cognitive Psychology, 24*(5), 673–690.

Phillips, D. A., & Lowenstein, A. E. (2011). Early care, education, and child development. *Annual Review of Psychology, 62*, 483–500.

Phillips, D. P., Liu, G. C., Kwok, K., et al. (2001). The Hound of the Baskervilles effect: Natural experiment on the influence of psychological stress on timing of death. *British Medical Journal, 323*(7327), 1443–1446.

Phillips, J., Sharpe, L., Matthey, S., et al. (2010). Subtypes of postnatal depression? A comparison of women with recurrent and de novo postnatal depression. *Journal of Affective Disorders, 120*(1–3), 67–75.

Phillips, K. W., Rothbard, N. P., & Dumas, T. L. (2009). To disclose or not to disclose? Status distance and self-disclosure in diverse environments. *Academy of Management Review, 34*(4), 710–732.

Piaget, J. (1951, original French, 1945). *The psychology of intelligence*. New York: Norton.

Piaget, J. (1952). *The origins of intelligence in children*. New York: International University Press.

Pickel, K. L., French, T. A., & Betts, J. M. (2003). A cross-modal weapon focus effect: The influence of a weapon's presence on memory for auditory information. *Memory, 11*(3), 277–292.

Piefke, M., Weiss, P., Markowitsch, H., et al. (2005). Gender differences in the functional neuroanatomy of emotional episodic autobiographical memory. *Human Brain Mapping, 24*, 313–324.

Piek, J. P. (2006). *Infant motor development*. Champaign, IL: Human Kinetics Publishers.

Pierrehumbert, B., Ramstein, T., Karmaniola, A., et al. (2002). Quality of child care in the preschool years. *International Journal of Behavioral Development, 26*(5), 385–396.

Piliavin, I. M., Rodin, J., & Piliavin, J. A. (1969). Good samaritanism: An underground phenomenon? *Journal of Personality & Social Psychology, 13*, 289–299.

Piliavin, J. A. (2003). Doing well by doing good: Benefits to the benefactor. In C. L. M. Keyes, & J. Haidt (Eds.), *Flourishing* (pp. 227–247). Washington, DC: American Psychological Association.

Pineda, J. A. (Ed). (2009). *Mirror neuron systems: The role of mirroring processes in social cognition*. New York: Humana Press.

Pinel, J. P. J., Assanand, S., & Lehman, D. R. (2000). Hunger, eating, and ill health. *American Psychologist, 55*(10), 1105–1116.

Pinel, P., & Dehaene, S. (2010). Beyond hemispheric dominance: Brain regions underlying the joint lateralization of language and arithmetic to the left hemisphere. *Journal of Cognitive Neuroscience, 22*(1), 48–66.

Pinker, S., & Jackendoff, R. (2005). The faculty of language: What's special about it? *Cognition, 95*(2), 201–236.

Piper, Jr., A.(2008). Multiple personality disorder: Witchcraft survives in the twentieth century. In S. O. Lilienfeld, J. Ruscio, & S. J. Lynn (Eds.), *Navigating the mindfield: A user's guide to distinguishing science from pseudoscience in mental health* (pp. 249–268). Amherst, NY: Prometheus Books.

Pizam, A., Jeong, G.-H., Reichel, A., et al. (2004). The relationship between risk-taking sensation-seeking, and the tourist behavior of young adults: A cross-cultural study. *Journal of Travel Research, 42*, 251–260.

Plassmann, H., O'Doherty, J., Shiv, B., et al. (2008). Marketing actions can modulate neural representations of experienced pleasantness. *Proceedings of the National Academy of Sciences, 105*(3), 1050–1054.

Plazzi, G., Vetrugno, R., Provini, F., et al. (2005). Sleepwalking and other ambulatory behaviours during sleep. *Neurological Sciences, 26*(Suppl3), s193–s198.

Pliner, P., & Mann, N. (2004). Influence of social norms and palatability on amount consumed and food choice. *Appetite, 42*(2), 227–237.

Plous, S. (2003). *Understanding prejudice and discrimination*. New York: McGraw-Hill.

Plutchik, R. (2003). *Emotions and life*. Washington, DC: American Psychological Association.

Poland, J., & Caplan, P. J. (2004). The deep structure of bias in psychiatric diagnosis. In P. J. Caplan, & L. Cosgrove (Eds.), *Bias in psychiatric diagnosis. A project of the association for women in psychology* (pp. 9–23). Lanham, MD: Jason Aronson.

Polemikos, N., & Papaeliou, C. (2000). Sidedness preference as an index of organization of laterality. *Perceptual & Motor Skills, 91*(3, Pt 2), 1083–1090.

Polivy, J., & Herman, C. P. (2002). Causes of eating disorders. *Annual Review of Psychology, 53*, 187–213.

Pollner, M. (1998). The effects of interviewer gender in mental health interviews. *Journal of Nervous & Mental Disease, 186*(6), 369–373.

Pollock, V. E., Briere, J., Schneider, L., et al. (1990). Childhood antecedents of antisocial behavior. *American Journal of Psychiatry, 147*(10), 1290–1293.

Pomaki, G., Šupeli, A., & Verhoeven, C. (2007). Role conflict and health behaviors: Moderating effects on psychological distress and somatic complaints. *Psychology & Health, 22*(3), 317–335.

Popma, A., Vermeiren, R., Geluk, C., et al. (2007). Cortisol moderates the relationship between testosterone and aggression in delinquent male adolescents. *Biological Psychiatry, 61*(3), 405–411.

Porter, S., & ten Brinke, L. (2010). The truth about lies: What works in detecting high-stakes deception? *Legal & Criminological Psychology, 15*(1), 57–75.

Posada, G., Jacobs, A., Richmond, M. K., et al. (2002). Maternal caregiving and infant security in two cultures. *Developmental Psychology, 38*(1), 67–78.

Powell, A. L., & Thelen, M. H. (1996). Emotions and cognitions associated with bingeing and weight control behavior in bulimia. *Journal of Psychosomatic Research, 40*(3), 317–328.

Powell, D. H. (2004). Behavioral treatment of debilitating test anxiety among medical students. *Journal of Clinical Psychology, 60*(8), 853–865.

Powell, M. D. & Ladd, L. D. (2010). Bullying: A review of the literature and implications for family therapists. *American Journal of Family Therapy, 38*(3), 189–206.

Powell, R. A., Symbaluk, D. G., & Honey, P. L. (2009). *Introduction to learning and behavior* (3rd ed.). Belmont, CA: Cengage Learning/Wadsworth.

Power, M. (2010). *Emotion-focused cognitive therapy*. New York: Wiley/Blackwell.

Preckel, F., Holling, H., & Wiese, M. (2006). Relationship of intelligence and creativity in gifted and non-gifted students: An investigation of threshold theory. *Personality & Individual Differences, 40*(1), 159–170.

Premack, A. J., & Premack, D. (1972). Teaching language to an ape. *Scientific American, 227*(4), 92–99.

Prentice, D. A., & Miller, D. T. (1993). Pluralistic ignorance of alcohol use on campus. *Journal of Personality and Social Psychology, 64*(2), 243–256.

Pressley, M. (1987). Are key-word method effects limited to slow presentation rates? An empirically based reply to Hall and Fuson (1986). *Journal of Educational Psychology, 79*(3), 333–335.

Price, J., & Davis, B. (2009). *The woman who can't forget: The extraordinary story of living with the most remarkable memory known to science—A memoir*. New York: Simon & Schuster.

Price, M. (2007). Star-crossed lovers quit West Bank. *BBC News*, Feb 28. Retrieved March 28, 2011 from http://news.bbc.co.uk/2/hi/middle_east/6405799.stm.

Prigerson, H. G., Maciejewski, P.K., & Rosenheck, R. A. (2002). Population attributable fractions of psychiatric disorders and behavioral outcomes associated with combat exposure among US men. *American Journal of Public Health, 92*, 59–63.

Priluck, R., & Till, B. D. (2004). The role of contingency awareness, involvement, and need for cognition in attitude formation. *Journal of the Academy of Marketing Science, 32*(3), 329–344.

Prime, D. J., & Jolicoeur, P. (2010). Mental rotation requires visual short-term memory: Evidence from human electric cortical activity. *Journal of Cognitive Neuroscience, 22*(11), 2437–2446.

Prinstein, M. J., Meade, C. S. & Cohen, G. L. (2003). Adolescent oral sex, peer popularity, and perceptions of best friends' sexual behavior. *Journal of Pediatric Psychology, 28*, 4, 243–249.

Prochaska, J. O., & Norcross, J. C. (2010). *Systems of psychotherapy: A transtheoretical analysis* (7th ed.). Belmont, CA: Cengage Learning/Wadsworth.

Prokhorov, A. V., Kelder, S. H., Shegog, R., et al. (2010). Project aspire: An interactive, multimedia smoking prevention and cessation curriculum for culturally diverse high school students. *Substance Use & Misuse, 45*(6), 983–1006.

Provencher, M. D., Dugas, M. J., & Ladouceur, R. (2004). Efficacy of problem-solving training and cognitive exposure in the treatment of generalized anxiety disorder: A case replication series. *Cognitive & Behavioral Practice, 11*(4), 404–414.

Puca, R. M., & Schmalt, H. (1999). Task enjoyment: A mediator between achievement motives and performance. *Motivation & Emotion, 23*(1), 15–29.

Puente, R., & Anshel, M. H. (2010). Exercisers' perceptions of their fitness instructor's interacting style, perceived competence, and autonomy as a function of self-determined regulation to exercise, enjoyment, affect, and exercise frequency. *Scandinavian Journal of Psychology, 51*(1), 38–45.

Puentes, J., Knox, D., & Zusman, M. E. (2008). Participants in "friends with benefits" relationships. *College Student Journal, 42*(1), 176–180.

Pychyl, T. A., Lee, J. M., Thibodeau, R., et al. (2000). Five days of emotion: An experience sampling study of undergraduate student procrastination. *Journal of Social Behavior & Personality, 15*(5), 239–254.

Quednow, B. B., Jessen, F., Kühn, K.-W., et al. (2006). Memory deficits in abstinent MDMA (ecstasy) users: Neuropsychological evidence of frontal dysfunction. *Journal of Psychopharmacology, 20*(3), 373–384.

Quigley, B. M., & Leonard, K. E. (2000). Alcohol, drugs, and violence. In V. B. Van Hasselt, & M. Hersen (Eds.), *Aggression and violence: An introductory text* (pp. 259–283). Boston: Allyn & Bacon.

Quinn, P. C., Bhatt, R. S., & Hayden, A. (2008). Young infants readily use proximity to organize visual pattern information. *Acta Psychologica, 127*(2), 289–298.

Quinto-Pozos, D. (2008). Sign language contact and interference: ASL and LSM. *Language in Society, 37*(2), 161–189.

Raag, T., & Rackliff, C. L. (1998). Preschoolers' awareness of social expectations of gender: Relationships to toy choices. *Sex Roles, 38*(9-10), 685–700.

Rabius, V., McAlister, A. L., Geiger, A., et al. (2004). Telephone counseling increases cessation rates among young adult smokers. *Health Psychology, 23*(5), 539–541.

Rachman, S. (2004). *Anxiety* (2nd. ed.). New York: Routledge.

Radvansky, G. A. (2011). *Human memory* (2nd ed.). Boston: Pearson/Allyn and Bacon.

Rahman, Q., & Wilson, G. D. (2003). Born gay? The psychobiology of human sexual orientation. *Personality & Individual Differences, 34*(8), 1337–1382.

Raid, G. H., & Tippin, S. M. (2009). Assessment of intellectual strengths and weaknesses with the Stanford-Binet Intelligence Scales—Fifth Edition (SB5). In J. A. Naglieri, & S. Goldstein (Eds.), *Practitioner's guide to assessing intelligence and achievement* (pp. 127–152). New York: Wiley.

Rainville, P. (2004). Pain & emotions. In D. D. Price & M. C. Bushnell (Eds.), *Psychological methods of pain control: Basic science and clinical perspectives* (pp. 117–142). Seattle, WA: IASP Press.

Ralston, A. (2004). *Between a rock and a hard place*. New York: Atria Books.

Ramachandran, V. S. & Oberman, L. (2006). Broken mirrors: A theory of autism. *Scientific American, 295*(5), 62–69.

Ramachandran, V. S. (1995). 2-D or not 2-D—that is the question. In R. Gregory, J. Harris, P. Heard, & D. Rose (Eds.), *The artful eye* (pp. 249–267). Oxford: Oxford University Press.

Ramey, C. T., Ramey, S. L., & Lanzi, R. G. (2001). Intelligence and experience. In R. J. Sternberg, & E. L. Grigorenko (Eds.), *Environmental effects on cognitive abilities* (pp. 83–115). Mahwah, NJ: Erlbaum.

Ramsay, M. C., Reynolds, C. R., & Kamphaus, R. W. (2002). *Essentials of behavioral assessment*. New York: Wiley.

Rantanen, J., Metsäpelto, R. L., Feldt, T., et al. (2007). Long-term stability in the Big Five personality traits in adulthood. *Scandinavian Journal of Psychology, 48*(6), 511–518.

Rathus, S. A. (2011). *Childhood and adolescence: Voyages in development* (4th ed.). Belmont, CA: Cengage Learning/Wadsworth.

Rau, P. R. (2005). Drowsy driver detection and warning system for commercial vehicle drivers: Field operational test design, data analyses, and progress. *National Highway Traffic Safety Administration Paper Number 05-0192.* Retrieved January 23, 2011, from http://www-nrd.nhtsa.dot.gov/pdf/nrd-01/esv/esv19/05-0192-W.pdf.

Rau, W., & Durand, A. (2000). The academic ethic and college grades: Does hard work help students to "make the grade"? *Sociology of Education, 73*(1), 19–38.

Raun, K., von Voss, P., & Knudsen, L. B. (2007). Liraglutide, a once-daily human glucagon-like peptide-1 analog, minimizes food intake in severely obese minipigs. *Obesity, 15*(7), 1710–1716.

Raven, B. H. (1974). *The analysis of power and power preference*. In J. T. Tebeschi (Ed.), *Prospectus on social power* (pp. 172–198). Chicago: Aldine.

Read, J. (1995). Female sexual dysfunction. *International Review of Psychiatry, 7*(2), 175–182.

Reason, J. (2000). The Freudian slip revisited. *The Psychologist, 13*(12), 610–611.

Reed, J. D., & Bruce, D. (1982). Longitudinal tracking of difficult memory retrievals. *Cognitive Psychology, 14*, 280–300.

Reed, S. K. (2010). *Cognition: Theory and applications* (8th ed.). Belmont, CA: Cengage Learning/Wadsworth.

Reed, T. E., Vernon, P. A., & Johnson, A. M. (2004). Confirmation of correlation between brain nerve conduction velocity and intelligence level in normal adults. *Intelligence, 32*(6), 563–572.

Reevy, G. M., & Maslach, C. (2001). Use of social support: Gender and personality differences. *Sex Roles, 44*(7-8), 437–459.

Regan, P. C., Levin, L., Sprecher, S., et al. (2000). Partner preferences: What characteristics do men and women desire in their short-term sexual and long-term romantic partners? *Journal of Psychology & Human Sexuality, 12*(3), 1–21.

Regev, L. G., Zeiss, A., & Zeiss, R. (2006). Orgasmic disorders. In J. E. Fisher, & W. T. O'Donohue (Eds.), *Practitioner's guide to evidence-based psychotherapy* (pp. 469–477). New York: Springer Science.

Regnerus, M., & Uecker, J. (2011). *Premarital sex in America: How young Americans meet, mate, and think about marrying*. New York: Oxford University Press.

Regoeczi, W. C. (2003). When context matters: A multilevel analysis of household and neighbourhood crowding on aggression and withdrawal. *Journal of Environmental Psychology, 23*(4), 457–470.

Reid, M. R., Mackinnon, L. T., & Drummond, P. D. (2001). The effects of stress management on symptoms of upper respiratory tract infection, secretory immunoglobulin A, and mood in young adults. *Journal of Psychosomatic Research, 51*(6), 721–728.

Reid, P. T. (2002). Multicultural psychology. *Cultural Diversity & Ethnic Minority Psychology, 8(2)*, 103–114.

Reidy, D. A., & Riker, W. J. (Eds.). (2008). *Coercion and the state*. New York: Springer.

Reiff, S. Katkin, E. S., & Friedman, R. (1999). Classical conditioning of the human blood pressure response. *International Journal of Psychophysiology, 34*(2), 135–145.

Reifman, A. S., Larrick, R. P., & Fein, S. (1991). Temper and temperature on the diamond: The heat-aggression relationship in major league baseball. *Personality & Social Psychology Bulletin, 17*(5), 580–585.

Reilly-Harrington, N. A., DeBonis, D., Leon, A. C., et al. (2010). The Interactive Computer Interview for mania. *Bipolar Disorders, 12*(5), 521–527.

Reinberg, A., & Ashkenazi, I. (2008). Internal desynchronization of circadian rhythms and tolerance to shift work. *Chronobiology International, 25*(4), 625–643.

Reis, H. T., Maniaci, M. R., Caprariello, P. A., et al. (2011). Familiarity does indeed promote attraction in live interaction. *Journal of Personality & Social Psychology, Mar 7*, np.

Reis, S. M., & Renzulli, J. S. (2010). Is there still a need for gifted education? An examination of current research. *Learning & Individual Differences, 20*(4), 308–317.

Reisinger, D. (2008). Six degrees of separation is now three. *TechCrunch, Sept 3.* Retrieved March 16, 2011 from http://techcrunch.com/2008/09/03/six-degrees-of-separation-is-now-three/.

Reisner, A. D. (2006). A case of Munchausen Syndrome by proxy with subsequent stalking behavior. *International Journal of Offender Therapy & Comparative Criminology, 50*(3), 245–254.

Reiss, M., Tymnik, G., Koegler, P., et al. (1999). Laterality of hand, foot, eye, and ear in twins. *Laterality, 4*(3), 287–297.

Reiss, S., & Havercamp, S. M. (2005). Motivation in developmental context: A new method for studying self-actualization. *Journal of Humanistic Psychology, 45*(1), 41–53.

Reissing, E. D., Binik, Y. M., Khalifé, S., et al. (2003). Etiological correlates of vaginismus: Sexual and physical abuse, sexual knowledge sexual self-schema and relationship adjustment. *Journal of Sex & Marital Therapy, 29*(1), 47–59.

Reissing, E. D., Binik, Y. M., Khalifé, S., et al. (2004). Vaginal spasm, pain, and behavior: An empirical investigation of the diagnosis of vaginismus. *Archives of Sexual Behavior, 33*(1), 5–17.

Reiterman, T. (1993). Parallel roads led to Jonestown, Waco. *The Los Angeles Times, April 23*, A–24.

Reivich, K., Gillham, J. E., Chaplin, T. M., et al. (2005). From helplessness to optimism: The role of resilience in treating and preventing depression in youth. In S. Goldstein, & R. B. Brooks (Eds.), *Handbook of resilience in children* (pp. 223–237). New York: Kluwer Academic Publishers.

Reker, M., Ohrmann, P., Rauch, A. V., et al. (2010). Individual differences in alexithymia and brain response to masked emotion faces. *Cortex, 46*(5), 658–667.

Remland, M. S., Jones, T. S., & Brinkman, H. (1991). Proxemic and haptic behavior in three European countries. *Journal of Nonverbal Behavior, 15*(4), 215–232.

Rentfrow, P. J. & Gosling, S. D. (2003). The do re mi's of everyday life: The structure and personality correlates of music preferences. *Journal of Personality & Social Psychology, 84*(6), 1236–1256.

Rentfrow, P. J., & Gosling, S. D. (2007). The content and validity of music-genre stereotypes among college students. *Psychology of Music, 35*(2), 306-326.

Rentfrow, P. J., Goldberg, L. R., & Levitin, D. J. (2011). The structure of musical preferences: A five-factor model. *Journal of Personality & Social Psychology, 100*(6), 1139–1157.

Reppucci, N. D., Woolard, J. L., & Fried, C. S. (1999). Social, community, and preventive interventions. *Annual Review of Psychology, 50*, 387–418.

Rescorla, R. A. (1987). A Pavlovian analysis of goal-directed behavior. *American Psychologist, 42*, 119–126.

Rescorla, R. A. (2004). Spontaneous recovery. *Learning & Memory, 11*(5), 501–509.

Restak, R. M. (2001). *The secret life of the brain*. New York: Dana Press.

Revonsuo, A., Kallio, S., & Sikka, P. (2009). What is an altered state of consciousness? *Philosophical Psychology, 22*(2), 187–204.

Rhee, S. H., & Waldman, I. D. (2011). Genetic and environmental influences on aggression. In P. R. Shaver & M. Mikulincer (Eds.), *Human aggression and violence: Causes, manifestations, and consequences* (pp. 143–163). Washington, DC: American Psychological Association.

Rhine, J. B. (1953). *New world of the mind*. New York: Sloane.

Ribeiro, A. C., LeSauter, J., Dupré, C., et al. (2009). Relationship of arousal to circadian anticipatory behavior: Ventromedial hypothalamus: One node in a hunger arousal network. *European Journal of Neuroscience, 30*(9), 1730–1738.

Rice, L., & Markey, P. M. (2009). The role of extraversion and neuroticism in influencing anxiety following computer-mediated interactions. *Personality & Individual Differences, 46*(1), 35–39.

Richards, J. M., & Gross, J. J. (2000). Emotion regulation and memory: The cognitive costs of keeping one's cool. *Journal of Personality & Social Psychology, 79*(3), 410–424.

Richmond, L. J. (2004). When spirituality goes awry: Students in cults. *Professional School Counseling, 7*(5), 367–375.

Ridenour, T. A., Maldonado-Molina M., Compton, W. M., et al. (2005). Factors associated with the transition from abuse to dependence among substance abusers: Implications for a measure of addictive liability. *Drug & Alcohol Dependence, 80*(1), 1–14.

Rideout, V., Foehr, U. G., & Roberts, D. F. (2010). *Generation M2: Media in the lives of 8–18 year-olds*. Menlo Park, CA: Kaiser Family Foundation. Retrieved January 17, 2011, from http://www.kff.org/entmedia/upload/8010.pdf.

Riefer, D. M., Keveri, M. K., & Kramer, D. L. (1995). Name that tune: Eliciting the tip-of-the-tongue experience using auditory stimuli. *Psychological Reports, 77*(3) (Pt 2), 1379–1390.

Riela, S., Rodriguez, G., Aron, A., et al. (2010). Experiences of falling in love: Investigating culture, ethnicity, gender, and speed. *Journal of Social & Personal Relationships, 27*(4), 473–493.

Rigakos, G. S., Davis, R. C., Ortiz, C., et al. (2009). Soft targets?: A national survey of the preparedness of large retail malls to prevent and respond to terrorist attack after 9/11. *Security Journal, 22*(4), 286–301.

Riggio, H. R., & Garcia, A. L. (2009). The power of situations: Jonestown and the fundamental attribution error. *Teaching of Psychology, 36*(2), 108–112.

Riley, A., & Riley, E. (2009). Male erectile disorder. In R. Balon, & R. T. Segraves (Eds.), *Clinical manual of sexual disorders* (pp. 213–249). Arlington, VA: American Psychiatric Publishing.

Riley, W., Jerome, A., Behar, A., et al. (2002). Feasibility of computerized scheduled gradual reduction for adolescent smoking cessation. *Substance Use & Misuse, 37*(2), 255–263.

Rind, B., Tromovitch, P., & Bauserman, R. (1998). A meta-analytic examination of assumed properties of child sexual abuse using college samples. *Psychological Bulletin, 124*(1), 22–53.

Rindermann, H., Flores-Mendoza C., & Mansur-Alves M. (2010). Reciprocal effects between fluid and crystallized intelligence and their dependence on parents' socioeconomic status and education. *Learning & Individual Differences, 20*(5), 544–548.

Riquelme, H. (2002). Can people creative in imagery interpret ambiguous figures faster than people less creative in imagery? *Journal of Creative Behavior, 36*(2), 105–116.

Ritchhart, R., & Perkins, D. N. (2005). Learning to think: The challenges of teaching thinking. In K. J. Holyoak, & R. G. Morrison (Eds.), *The Cambridge handbook of thinking and reasoning* (pp. 775–802). Cambridge, MA: Cambridge University Press.

Ritter, J. (1998). Uniforms changing the culture of the nation's classrooms. *USA Today*, Oct. 15, 1A, 2A.

Riva, G. (2009). Virtual reality: An experiential tool for clinical psychology. *British Journal of Guidance & Counseling, 37*(3), 337–345.

Riva, G., & Wiederhold, B. K. (2006). Emerging trends in cybertherapy: Introduction to the special issue. *Psychology Journal, 4*(2), 121–128.

Rizzolatti, G., & Craighero, L. (2004). The mirror-neuron system. *Annual Review of Neuroscience, 27*, 169–192.

Rizzolatti, G., Fogassi, L., & Gallese V. (2006). Mirrors in the mind. *Scientific American, 295*(5), 54–61.

Roberts, B. W., & Mroczek, D. (2008). Personality trait change in adulthood. *Current Directions in Psychological Science, 17*(1), 31–35.

Roberts, B. W., Kuncel, N. R., Shiner, R., et al. (2007). The power of personality: The comparative validity of personality traits, socioeconomic status, and cognitive ability for predicting important life outcomes. *Perspectives on Psychological Science, 2*(4), 313–345.

Roberts, R. E., Phinney, J. S., Masse, L. C., et al. (1999). The structure of ethnic identity of young adolescents from diverse ethnocultural groups. *Journal of Early Adolescence, 19*(3), 301–322.

Roberts, W. A. & Roberts, S. (2002). Two tests of the stuck-in-time hypothesis. *Journal of General Psychology, 129*(4), 415–429.

Roberts, W. A. (2002). Are animals stuck in time? *Psychological Bulletin, 128*(3), 473–489.

Robertson, L. C., & Sagiv, N, (2005). *Synesthesia: Perspectives from cognitive neuroscience*. New York: Oxford.

Robins, R. W., Gosling, S. D., & Craik, K. H. (1998). Psychological science at the crossroads. *American Scientist, 86*, 310–313.

Robinson, A. (2010). *Sudden genius? The gradual path to creative breakthroughs*. New York: Oxford University Press.

Robinson, D. N. (2008). *Consciousness and mental life*. New York: Columbia University Press.

Robinson, T. E., & Berridge, K. C. (2003). Addiction. *Annual Review of Psychology, 54*, 25–53.

Robinson, T. N., Wilde, M. L., Navracruz, L. C., et al. (2001). Effects of reducing children's television and video game use on aggressive behavior. *Archives of Pediatrics & Adolescent Medicine, 155*(1), 17–23.

Roca, M., Parr, A., Thompson, R., et al. (2010). Executive function and fluid intelligence after frontal lobe lesions. *Brain: A Journal of Neurology, 133*(1), 234–247.

Rock, A. (2004). *The mind at night: The new science of how and why we dream*. New York: Basic Books.

Rodd, Z. A., Bell, R. L., McQueen, V. K., et al. (2005). Chronic ethanol drinking by alcohol-preferring rats increases the sensitivity of the posterior ventral tegmental area to the reinforcing effects of ethanol. *Alcoholism: Clinical & Experimental Research, 29*(3), 358–366.

Roediger, H. L. III, & Amir, N., (2005). Implicit memory tasks: Retention without conscious recollection. In A. Wenzel, & D. C. Rubin (Eds.), *Cognitive methods and their application to clinical research* (pp. 121–127). Washington, DC: American Psychological Association.

Roediger, H. L. III, & McDermott, K. B. (1995). Creating false memories: Remembering words not presented on lists. *Journal of Experimental Psychology: Learning, Memory, and Cognition, 21*(4), 803–814.

Roese, N. J., Pennington, G. L., Coleman, J., et al. (2006). Sex differences in regret: All for love or some for lust? *Personality & Social Psychology Bulletin, 32*(6), 770–780.

Roffman, J. L., Brohawn, D. G., Friedman, J, S., et al. (2011). MTHFR 677C>T effects on anterior cingulate structure and function during response monitoring in schizophrenia: A preliminary study. *Brain Imaging & Behavior, 5*(1), 65–75.

Rogers, C. R. (1959). A theory of therapy, personality, and interpersonal relationships, as developed in the client-centered framework. In S. Koch (Ed.), *Psychology: A study of a science* (Vol.3, pp. 184–256). New York: McGraw-Hill.

Rogers, C. R. (1961). *On becoming a person: A therapist's view of psychotherapy*. Boston: Houghton Mifflin.

Rogers, P., & Soule, J. (2009). Cross-cultural differences in the acceptance of Barnum profiles supposedly derived from Western versus Chinese astrology. *Journal of Cross-Cultural Psychology, 40*(3), 381–399.

Roid, G. H. (2003). *Stanford-Binet Intelligence Scales, Fifth Edition, Examiner's Manual*. Itasca, IL: Riverside.

Roizen, M. F., & Oz, M. C. (2006). *You on a diet: The owner's manual for waist management*. New York: Free Press.

Rolls, E. T. (2008). Top-down control of visual perception: Attention in natural vision. *Perception, 37*(3), 333–354.

Roney, J. R. (2003). Effects of visual exposure to the opposite sex: Cognitive aspects of mate attraction in human males. *Personality & Social Psychology Bulletin, 29*, 393–404.

Ronningstam, E. (2009). Narcissistic personality disorder: Facing DSM-V. *Psychiatric Annals, 39*, 111–121.

Roos, P. E., & Cohen, L. H. (1987). Sex roles and social support as moderators of life stress adjustment. *Journal of Personality & Social Psychology, 52*, 576–585.

Rosch, E. (1977). Classification of real-world objects: Origins and representations in cognition. In P. N. Johnson-Laird & P. C. Wason (Eds.), *Thinking: Reading in cognitive science* (pp. 212–222). Cambridge, MA: Cambridge University Press.

Rosen, G., Hugdahl, K., Ersland, L., et al. (2001). Different brain areas activated during imagery of painful and non-painful 'finger movements' in a subject with an amputated arm. *Neurocase, 7*(3), 255–260.

Rosenberg, L. B. (1994, July). *The effect of interocular distance upon depth perception when using stereoscopic displays to perform work within virtual and telepresent environments*. USAF AMRL Technical Report (Wright-Patterson), AL/CF-TR-1994-0052.

Rosenhan, D. L. (1973). On being sane in insane places. *Science, 179*(4070), 250–258.

Rosenkranz, M.A., Jackson, D. C., Dalton, K. M., et al. (2003). Affective style and in vivo immune response: Neurobehavioral mechanisms. *Proceedings of the National Academy of Sciences, 100*, 11148–11152.

Rosenman, R. H., Brand, R. J., Jenkins, C. D., et al. (1975). Coronary heart disease in the Western Collaborative Group Study: Final follow-up experience of 8 1/2 years. *Journal of the American Medical Association, 233*, 872–877.

Rosenthal, D., & Quinn, O. W. (1977). Quadruplet hallucinations: Phenotypic variations of a schizophrenic genotype. *Archives of General Psychiatry, 34*(7), 817–827.

Rosenthal, R. (1973). The Pygmalion effect lives. *Psychology Today, Sept*, 56–63.

Rosenthal, R. (1994). Science and ethics in conducting, analyzing, and reporting psychological research. *Psychological Science, 5*, 127–134.

Rosenthal, S. L., Von Ranson, K. M., Cotton, S., et al. (2001). Sexual initiation: Predictors and developmental trends. *Sexually Transmitted Diseases, 28*(9), 527–532.

Rosenthal, T. L. (1993). To soothe the savage breast. *Behavior Research & Therapy, 31*(5), 439–462.

Rosenthal, T. L., & Rosenthal, R. (1980). *The vicious cycle of stress reaction*. Copyright, Renate & Ted Rosenthal, Stress Management Clinic, Department of Psychiatry, University of Tennessee College of Medicine, Memphis, Tennessee.

Rosnow, R. L. (2011). *Writing papers in psychology: A student guide to research papers, essays, proposals, posters, and handouts* (9th ed.). Belmont, CA: Cengage Learning/Wadsworth.

Ross, H. E., & Plug. C. (2002). *The mystery of the moon illusion*. Oxford: Oxford University Press.

Ross, M., & Wang, Q. (2010). Why we remember and what we remember: Culture and autobiographical memory. *Perspectives on Psychological Science, 5*(4), 401–409.

Ross, M., Heine, S. J., Wilson, A. E., et al. (2005). Cross-cultural discrepancies in self-appraisals. *Personality & Social Psychology Bulletin, 31*(9), 1175–1188.

Ross, P. E. (2006). The expert mind. *Scientific American, 294*(7), 64–71.

Roth, W. T., Breivik, G., Jorgensen, P. E., et al. (1996). Activation in novice and expert parachutists while jumping. *Psychophysiology, 33*(1), 63–72.

Rothbard, N. P., Phillips, K. W., & Dumas, T. L. (2005). Managing multiple roles: Work-family policies and individuals' desires for segmentation. *Organization Science, 16*(3), 243–258.

Rothbart, M. K. (2007). Temperament, development, and personality. *Current Directions in Psychological Science, 16*(4), 207–212.

Rothschild, B., & Rand, M. (2006). *Help for the helper: The psychophysiology of compassion fatigue and vicarious trauma*. New York: Norton.

Rotter, J. B. & Hochreich, D. J. (1975). *Personality*. Glenview, IL: Scott, Foresman.

Rourke, B. P., Ahmad, S. A., Collins, D. W., et al. (2002). Early hydrocephalus. *Annual Review of Psychology, 53*, 309–339.

Rowland, D. L. (2007). Sexual health and problems: Erectile dysfunction, premature ejaculation, and male orgasmic disorder. In J. E. Grant, & M. N. Potenza (Eds.), *Textbook of men's mental health* (pp. 171–203). Washington, DC: American Psychiatric Publishing.

Rozin, P., Kabnick, K., Pete, E., et al. (2003). The ecology of eating: Smaller portion sizes in France than in the United States help explain the French paradox. *Psychological Science, 14*(5), 450–454.

Rubenstein, C. (1983). The modern art of courtly love. *Psychology Today, 17*(7), 43–49.

Rubenstein, C. (2002). What turns you on? *My Generation, July-Aug*, 55–58.

Rubenstein, C., & Tavris, C. (1987). Special survey results: 2600 women reveal the secrets of intimacy. *Redbook, 159*, 147–149.

Rudd, M. D., Joiner, Jr., T. E., et al. (2001). *Treating suicidal behavior*. New York: Guilford.

Rueckl, J. G., & Galantucci, B. (2005). The locus and time course of long-term morphological priming. *Language & Cognitive Processes, 20*(1), 115–138.

Rummens, J., Beiser, M., & Noh, S. (Eds.). (2003). *Immigration, ethnicity and health*. Toronto: University of Toronto Press.

Runco, M. A. (2003). *Critical creative processes*. Cresskill, NJ: Hampton Press.

Runco, M. A. (2004). Creativity. *Annual Review of Psychology, 55*, 657–687.

Ruscio, J., Whitney, D. M., & Amabile, T. M. (1998). Looking inside the fishbowl of creativity. *Creativity Research Journal, 11*(3), 243–263.

Rushton, J. P., & Jensen, A. R. (2005). Thirty years of research on race differences in cognitive ability. *Psychology, Public Policy, & Law, 11*, 235–294.

Russell, S., & Norvig, P. (2003). *Artificial intelligence: A modern approach* (2nd ed.). Englewood Cliffs, NJ: Prentice Hall.

Russo, M. B., Brooks, F. R., Fontenot, J., et al. (1998). Conversion disorder presenting as multiple sclerosis. *Military Medicine, 163*(10), 709–710.

Rutz, C., Bluff, L.A., Reed, N., et al. (2010). The ecological significance of tool use in New Caledonian crows. *Science, 329*, 1523–1526.

Rutz, C., Bluff, L.A., Weir, A.A.S., et al. (2007). Video cameras on wild birds. *Science, 318*, 765.

Ruva, C., McEvoy, C., & Bryant, J. B. (2007). Effects of pre-trial publicity and jury deliberation on juror bias and source memory errors. *Applied Cognitive Psychology, 21*(1), 45–67.

Ryan, M. P. (2001). Conceptual models of lecture learning. *Reading Psychology, 22*(4), 289–312.

Ryckman, R. M. (2008). *Theories of personality* (9th ed.). Belmont, CA: Cengage Learning/Wadsworth.

Ryff, C. D., & Singer, B. (2009). Understanding healthy aging: Key components and their integration. In V. L. Bengston, D. Gans, D., et al. (Eds.), *Handbook of theories of aging* (2nd ed., pp. 117–144). New York: Springer.

Ryff, C. D., Singer, B. H., & Palmersheim, K. A. (2004). Social inequalities in health and well-being: The role of relational and religious protective factors. In O. G. Brim, C. D. Ryff, et al. (Eds.), *How healthy are we?: A national study of wellbeing at midlife* (pp. 90–123). Chicago, IL: University of Chicago Press.

Saber, J. L., & Johnson, R. D. (2008). Don't throw out the baby with the bathwater: Verbal repetition, mnemonics, and active learning. *Journal of Marketing Education, 30*(3), 207–216.

Sachdev, P. S., & Chen, X. (2009). Neurosurgical treatment of mood disorders: Traditional psychosurgery and the advent of deep brain stimulation. *Current Opinion in Psychiatry, 22*(1), 25–31.

Sackeim, H. A., Haskett, R. F., Mulsant, B. H., et al. (2001). Continuation pharmacotherapy in the prevention of relapse following electroconvulsive therapy. *Journal of the American Medical Association, 285*, 1299–1307.

Sackett, P. R., Schmitt, N., Ellingson, J. E., et al. (2001). High-stakes testing in employment, credentialing, and higher education. *American Psychologist, 56*(4), 302–318.

Sackett, P. R., & Lievens, F. (2008). Personnel selection. *Annual Review of Psychology, 59*, 419–450.

Sacks, O. (2010). *The mind's eye*. New York: Knopf.

Saksida, L. M., & Wilkie, D. M. (1994). Time-of-day discrimination by pigeons. *Animal Learning & Behavior, 22*, 143–154.

Salamone, J. D. (2007). Functions of mesolimbic dopamine: Changing concepts and shifting paradigms. *Psychopharmacology, 191*(3), 389.

Sales, B. D., & Hafemeister, T. L. (1985). Law and psychology. In E. M. Altmeir, & M. E. Meyer (Eds.), *Applied specialties in psychology* (pp.331–373). New York: Random House.

Sallinen, M., Holm, A., Hiltunen, J., et al. (2008). Recovery of cognitive performance from sleep debt: Do a short rest pause and a single recovery night help? *Chronobiology International, 25*(2-3), 279–296.

Salmela, J. H. (1974). An information processing approach to volleyball. *C.V.A. Technical Journal, 1*, 49–62.

Salmela, J. H. (1975). Psycho-motor task demands of artistic gymnastics. In J. H. Salmela (Ed.), *The advanced study of gymnastics: A textbook* (pp.167–182). Springfield, IL: Charles C Thomas.

Salovey, P., & Mayer, J. (1997). *Emotional development and emotional intelligence*. New York, NY: Basic.

Salthouse, T. A. (2004). What and when of cognitive aging. *Current Directions in Psychological Science, 13*(4), 140–144.

Sam, D. L., & Berry, J. W. (2010). Acculturation: When individuals and groups of different cultural backgrounds meet. *Perspectives on Psychological Science, 5*(4), 472–481.

Sánchez, P., García-Calvo T., Leo, F. M., et al. (2009). An analysis of home advantage in the top two Spanish professional football leagues. *Perceptual & Motor Skills, 108*(3), 789–797.

Sankofa, B. M., Hurley, E. A., Allen, B. A., et al. (2005). Cultural expression and black students' attitudes toward high achievers. *Journal of Psychology: Interdisciplinary & Applied, 139*(3), 247–259.

Sansone, R. A., & Sansone, L. A. (2010). Road rage: What's driving it? *Psychiatry, 7*(7), 14–18.

Santelli, J. S., Abma, J., Ventura, S., et al. (2004). Can changes in sexual behaviors among high school students explain the decline in teen pregnancy rates in the 1990s? *Journal of Adolescent Health, 35*(2), 80–90.

Santrock, J. W. (2009). *Child development* (12th ed.). New York: McGraw-Hill.

Santrock, J. W. (2010). *A topical approach to lifespan development* (5th ed.). New York, NY: McGraw-Hill.

Santrock, J. W., & Halonen, J. S. (2010). *Your guide to college success: Strategies for achieving your goals* (6th ed.). Belmont, CA: Cengage Learning/Wadsworth.

Sapolsky, R. (2005). Sick of poverty. *Scientific American, 293*(6), 92–99.

Sarason, I. G., & Sarason, B. R. (2005). *Abnormal psychology* (11th ed.). Mahwah, NJ: Prentice Hall.

Sartorius, A., Kiening, K. L., Kirsch, P., et al. (2010). Remission of major depression under deep brain stimulation of the lateral habenula in a therapy-refractory patient. *Biological Psychiatry, 67*(2), e9–e11.

Sateia, M. J., & Nowell, P. D. (2004). Insomnia. *Lancet, 364*(9449), 1959–1973.

Saunders, T., Driskell, J. E., Johnston, J. H., et al. (1996). The effect of stress inoculation training on anxiety and performance. *Journal of Occupational Health Psychology, 1*(2), 170–186.

Sautter, J. M., Tippett, R. M., & Morgan, S. (2010). The social demography of Internet dating in the United States. *Social Science Quarterly, 91*(2), 554–575.

Savage-Rumbaugh, S., Shanker, S., & Taylor, T. (1998). *Apes, language, and mind*. New York: Oxford.

Sawyer, R. G., & Smith, N. G. (1996). A survey of situational factors at first intercourse among college students. *American Journal of Health Behavior, 20*(4), 208–217.

Saxton, M., Houston-Price C., & Dawson, N. (2005). The prompt hypothesis: Clarification requests as corrective input for grammatical errors. *Applied Psycholinguistics, 26*(3), 393–414.

Saxvig, I. W., Lundervold, A. J., Gronli, J., et al. (2008). The effect of a REM sleep deprivation procedure on different aspects of memory function in humans. *Psychophysiology, 45*(2), 309–317.

Saywitz, K. J., Mannarino, A. P., Berliner, L., et al. (2000). Treatment for sexually abused children and adolescents. *American Psychologist, 55*(9), 1040–1049.

Schachter, S. (1959). *Psychology of affiliation*. Stanford, CA: Stanford University Press.

Schachter, S., & Wheeler, L. (1962). Epinephrine, chlorpromazine and amusement. *Journal of Abnormal and Social Psychology, 65*, 121–128.

Schacter, D. L. (1996). *Searching for memory: The brain, the mind, and the past*. New York: Basic Books.

Schacter, D. L., Norman, K. A., & Koutstaal, W. (1998). The cognitive neuroscience of constructive memory. *Annual Review of Psychology, 49*, 289–318.

Schafer, M., & Crichlow, S. (1996). Antecedents of groupthink: A quantitative study. *Journal of Conflict Resolution, 40*(3), 415–435.

Schaie, K. W. (1994). The course of adult intellectual development. *American Psychologist, 49*(4), 304–313.

Schaie, K. W. (2005). *Developmental influences on adult intelligence: The Seattle longitudinal study*. New York: Oxford University Press.

Scharinger, C., Rabl, U., Sitte, H. H., et al. (2010). Imaging genetics of mood disorders. *NeuroImage*, 3(3), 810–821.

Scheck, B., Neufeld, P., & Dwyer, J. (2000). *Actual innocence*. New York: Doubleday.

Scheinkman, M. (2008). The multi-level approach: A road map for couples therapy. *Family Process, 47*(2), 197–213.

Schenck, C. H., & Mahowald, M. W. (2005). Rapid eye movement and non-REM sleep parasomnias. *Primary Psychiatry, 12*(8), 67–74.

Schetter, C. D. (2011). Psychological science on pregnancy: Stress processes, biopsychosocial models, and emerging research issues. *Annual Review of Psychology, 62*, 531–558.

Schick, T., & Vaughn, L. (2011). *How to think about weird things: Critical thinking for a new age* (6th ed.). New York: McGraw-Hill.

Schilling, M. A. (2005). A "Small-World" network model of cognitive insight. *Creativity Research Journal, 17*(2-3), 131–154.

Schiraldi, G. R., & Brown, S. L. (2001). Primary prevention for mental health: Results of an exploratory cognitive-behavioral college course. *Journal of Primary Prevention, 22*(1), 55–67.

Schlaepfer, T. E., Cohen, M. X., Frick, C., et al. (2008). Deep brain stimulation to reward circuitry alleviates anhedonia in refractory major depression. *Neuropsychopharmacology, 33*(2), 368–377.

Schleicher, S. S., & Gilbert, L. A. (2005). Heterosexual dating discourses among college students: Is there still a double standard? *Journal of College Student Psychotherapy, 19*(3), 7–23.

Schlosberg, H. (1954). Three dimensions of emotion. *Psychological Review, 61*, 81–88.

Schlund, M. W. & Cataldo, M. F. (2010). Amygdala involvement in human avoidance, escape and approach behavior. *NeuroImage, 53*(2), 769–776.

Schmahmann, J. D. (2010).The role of the cerebellum in cognition and emotion: Personal reflections since 1982 on the dysmetria of thought hypothesis, and its historical evolution from theory to therapy. *Neuropsychology Review, 20*(3), 236–260.

Schmelz, M. (2010). Itch and pain. *Neuroscience & Biobehavioral Reviews, 34*(2), 171–176.

Schmidt, F. L., & Hunter, J. E. (1998). The validity and utility of selection methods in personnel psychology. *Psychological Bulletin, 124*(2), 262–274.

Schmidt, F. L., Ones, D. S., & Hunter, J. E. (1992). Personnel selection. *Annual Review of Psychology, 43*, 627–670.

Schmitt, D. P., & Allik, J. (2005). Simultaneous administration of the Rosenberg Self-Esteem Scale in 53 nations: Exploring the universal and culture-specific features of global self-esteem. *Journal of Personality & Social Psychology, 89*(4), 623–642.

Schmolck, H., Buffalo, E. A., & Squire, L. R. (2000). Memory distortions develop over time. Recollections of the O. J. Simpson trial verdict after 15 and 32 months. *Psychological Science, 11*(1), 39–45.

Schmuck, P., & Vlek, C. (2003). Psychologists can do much to support sustainable development. *European Psychologist, 8*(2), 66–76.

Schneider, K. J., Bugental, J. F. T., & Pierson, J. F. (2001). *The Handbook of Humanistic Psychology*. Thousand Oaks, CA: Sage.

Schneider, K. J., Galvin, J., & Serlin, I. (2009). Rollo May on existential psychotherapy. *Journal of Humanistic Psychology, 49*(4), 419–434.

Schneiderman, N., Antoni, M. H., Saab, P. G., et al. (2001). Health psychology: Psychological and biobehavioral aspects of chronic disease management. *Annual Review of Psychology, 52*, 555–580.

Schooler, C. (1998) Environmental complexity and the Flynn effect. In U. Neisser (Ed.), *The rising curve: Long-term gains in IQ and related measures* (pp. 67–79). Washington, DC: American Psychological Association.

Schopp, L. H., Demiris, G., & Glueckauf, R. L. (2006). Rural backwaters or front-runners? Rural telehealth in the vanguard of psychology practice. *Professional Psychology: Research & Practice, 37*(2), 165–173.

Schreiber, E. H., & Schreiber, D. E. (1999). Use of hypnosis with witnesses of vehicular homicide. *Contemporary Hypnosis, 16*(1), 40–44.

Schreiber, F. R. (1973). *Sybil*. Chicago: Regency.

Schroeder, J. E. (1995). Self-concept social anxiety, and interpersonal perception skills. *Personality & Individual Differences, 19*(6), 955–958.

Schroeder, S. (2008). Stranded in the periphery The increasing marginalization of smokers *New England Journal of Medicine, 35*(821), 2284.

Schuck, K., Keijsers, G. P. J., & Rinck, M. (2011). The effects of brief cognitive-behaviour therapy for pathological skin picking: A randomized comparison to wait-list control. *Behaviour Research & Therapy, 49*(1), 11–17.

Schuel, H., Chang, M. C., Burkman, L. J., et al. (1999). Cannabinoid receptors in sperm. In G. Nahas, K. M. Sutin, et al. (Eds.), *Marihuana and medicine* (pp. 335–345). Totowa, NJ: Humana Press.

Schuerger, J. M., & Witt, A. C. (1989). The temporal stability of individually tested intelligence. *Journal of Clinical Psychology, 45*(2), 294–302.

Schuetze, P., & Eiden, R. D. (2006). The association between maternal cocaine use during pregnancy and physiological regulation in 4- to 8-week-old infants: An examination of possible mediators and moderators. *Journal of Pediatric Psychology, 31*(1), 15–26.

Schuiling, G. A. (2004). Death in Venice: The homosexuality enigma. *Journal of Psychosomatic Obstetrics & Gynecology, 25*(1), 67–76.

Schultheiss, O. C., Wirth, M. M., & Stanton, S. J. (2004). Effects of affiliation and power motivation arousal on salivary progesterone and testosterone. *Hormones & Behavior, 46*(5), 592–599.

Schultz, D. P., & Schultz, S. E. (2010). *Psychology and work today* (10th ed.). Englewood Cliffs, NJ: Prentice Hall

Schultz, D. P., & Schultz, S. E. (2009). *Theories of personality* (9th ed.). Belmont, CA: Cengage Learning/Wadsworth.

Schultz, D. P., & Schultz, S. E. (2012). *A history of modern psychology* (10th ed.). Belmont, CA: Cengage Learning/Wadsworth.

Schultz, H. T. (2004). Good and bad movie therapy with good and bad outcomes. *The Amplifier: Official Newsletter of APA Division 46, Media Psychology, Fall/Winter*. Retrieved March 22, 2011, from http://www.apa.org/divisions/div46/Amp%20Winter%2005/for%20Website/ampwinter05.html#outcomes.

Schultz, P. W. (1999). Changing behavior with normative feedback interventions. *Basic & Applied Social Psychology, 21*(1), 25–36.

Schum T. R., Kolb, T. M., McAuliffe T. L., et al. (2002). Sequential acquisition of toilet-training skills: A descriptive study of gender and age differences in normal children. *Pediatrics, 3*, e48. Retrieved May 25, 2007, from http://pediatrics.aappublications.org/cgi/content/abstract/109/3/e48.

Schuster, M. A., Stein, B. D., Jaycox, L. H., et al. (2001). A national survey of stress reactions after the September 11, 2001, terrorist attacks. *New England Journal of Medicine, 345*(20), 1507–1512.

Schwartz, B. L. (2002). *Tip-of-the-tongue states: Phenomenology, mechanism, and lexical retrieval*. Mahwah, NJ: Erlbaum.

Schwartz, M. S., & Andrasik, F. (Eds.). (2003). *Biofeedback: A practitioner's guide* (3rd ed.). New York: Guilford.

Schwartz, S. J. (2008). Self and identity in early adolescence: Some reflections and an introduction to the special issue. *Journal of Early Adolescence, 28*(1), 5–15.

Schwitzgebel, E. (2011). *Perplexities of consciousness*. Cambridge, MA: MIT Press.

Sclafani, A., & Springer, D. (1976). Dietary obesity in adult rats: Similarities to hypothalamic and human obesity syndromes. *Psychology & Behavior, 17*, 461–471.

Scoboria, A., Mazzoni, G., Kirsch, I., et al. (2002). Immediate and persisting effects of misleading questions and hypnosis on memory reports. *Journal of Experimental Psychology: Applied, 8*(1), 26–32.

Scott, J. P., & Ginsburg, B. E. (1994). The Seville statement on violence revisited. *American Psychologist, 49*(10), 849–850.

Scott, L., & O'Hara, M. W. (1993). Self-discrepancies in clinically anxious and depressed university students. *Journal of Abnormal Psychology, 102*(2), 282–287.

Scott, S. S., McGuire, J. M., & Shaw, S. F. (2003). Universal design for instruction: A new paradigm for adult instruction in postsecondary education. *Remedial & Special Education, 24*(6), 369–379.

Scruggs, T. E. & Mastropieri, M. A. (2007). Science learning in special education: The case for constructed versus instructed learning. *Exceptionality, 15*(2), 57–74.

Scurfield, R. M. (2002). Commentary about the terrorist acts of September 11, 2001: Posttraumatic reactions and related social and policy issues. *Trauma Violence & Abuse, 3*(1), 3–14.

Searcy, W. A., & Nowicki, S. (2005). *The evolution of animal communication: Reliability and deception in signaling systems*. Princeton, NJ: Princeton University Press.

Sears, S., & Kraus, S. (2009). I think therefore I om: Cognitive distortions and coping style as mediators for the effects of mindfulness meditation on anxiety, positive and negative affect, and hope. *Journal of Clinical Psychology, 65*(6), 561–573.

Seckel, A. (2000). *The art of optical illusions*. London: Carlton Books.

Segerdahl, P., Fields, W., & Savage-Rumbaugh S. (2005). *Kanzi's primal language: The cultural initiation of primates into language*. New York: Palgrave MacMillan.

Segerstrom, S., & Miller, G. E. (2004). Psychological stress and the human immune system: A meta-analytic study of 30 years of inquiry. *Psychological Bulletin, 130*(4), 601–630.

Segraves, R. T., & Segraves, K. B. (1995). Human sexuality and aging. *Journal of Sex Education & Therapy, 21*(2), 88–102.

Segraves, R., & Woodard, T. (2006). Female hypoactive sexual desire disorder: History and current status. *Journal of Sexual Medicine, 3*(3), 408–418.

Segraves, T., & Althof, S. (2002). Psychotherapy and pharmacotherapy for sexual dysfunctions. In P. E. Nathan, & J. M. Gorman, (Eds.), *A guide to treatments that work* (2nd ed., pp. 497–524). London: Oxford.

Seidler, G. H., &Wagner, F. E. (2006). Comparing the efficacy of EMDR and trauma-focused cognitive-behavioral therapy in the treatment of PTSD: A meta-analytic study. *Psychological Medicine, 36*(11), 1515–1522.

Seidman, B. F. (2001, January-February). Medicine wars. *Skeptical Inquirer*, 28–35.

Seitz, A., & Watanabe, T. (2005). A unified model for perceptual learning. *Trends in Cognitive Sciences, 9*(7), 329–334.

Seligman, M. E. P. (1972). For helplessness: Can we immunize the weak? In *Readings in Psychology Today* (2nd ed.). Del Mar, CA: CRM.

Seligman, M. E. P. (1989). *Helplessness*. New York: Freeman.

Seligman, M. E. P. (1995). The effectiveness of psychotherapy. *American Psychologist, 50*(12), 965–974.

Seligman, M. E. P. (1998). Why therapy works. *APA Monitor, 29*(12), 2.

Seligman, M. E. P. (2002). *Authentic happiness*. New York: Free Press.

Seligman, M. E. P. (2003). Positive psychology: Fundamental assumptions. *Source Psychologist, 16*(3), 126–127.

Seligman, M. E. P., & Csikszentmihalyi, M. (2000). Positive psychology: An introduction. *American Psychologist, 55*, 5–14.

Seltzer, R. (2006). Scientific jury selection: Does it work?. *Journal of Applied Social Psychology, 36*(10), 2417–2435.

Selye, H. (1976). *The stress of life*. New York: Knopf.

Senécal, C., Julien, E., & Guay, F. (2003). Role conflict and academic procrastination: A self-determination perspective. *European Journal of Social Psychology, 33*(1), 135–145.

Service, R. F. (1994). Will a new type of drug make memory-making easier? *Science, 266*, 218–219.

Sessa, V. I., & London, M. (2006). *Continuous learning in organizations: Individual, group, and organizational perspectives*. Mahwah, NJ: Erlbaum.

Seto, M. C. (2008). *Pedophilia and sexual offending against children: Theory, assessment, and intervention*. Washington, DC: American Psychological Association.

Seto, M. C. (2009). Pedophilia. *Annual Review of Clinical Psychology, 5*, 391–407.

Seto, M. C., Cantor, J. M., & Blanchard, R. (2006). Child pornography offenses are a valid diagnostic indicator of pedophilia. *Journal of Abnormal Psychology, 115*(3), 610–615.

Seybolt, D. C., & Wagner, M. K. (1997). Self-reinforcement, gender-role and sex of participant in prediction of life satisfaction. *Psychological Reports, 81*(2) 519–522.

Seyle, D. C., & Newman, M. L. (2006). A house divided? The psychology of red and blue America. *American Psychologist, 61*(6), 571–580.

Shafer, C. S., & Hammitt, W. E. (1995). Congruency among experience dimensions, condition indicators, and coping behaviors in wilderness. *Leisure Sciences, 17*, 263–279.

Shaffer, D. R. (2009). *Social and personality development* (6th ed.). Belmont, CA: Cengage Learning/Wadsworth.

Shaffer, D. R., & Kipp, K. (2010). *Developmental psychology: Childhood and adolescence* (8th ed.). Belmont, CA: Cengage Learning/Wadsworth.

Shaffer, J. B., & Galinsky, M. D. (1989). *Models of group therapy*. Englewood Cliffs, NJ: Prentice Hall.

Shafir, E. (1993). Choosing versus rejecting: Why some options are both better and worse than others. *Memory & Cognition, 21*, 546–556.

Shafton, A. (1995). *Dream reader*. Albany, NY: SUNY Press.

Shakesby, A. C., Anwyl, R., & Rowan, M. J. (2002). Overcoming the effects of stress on synaptic plasticity in the intact hippocampus: Rapid actions of serotonergic and antidepressant agents. *Journal of Neuroscience, 22*, 3638–3644.

Shanks, D. R. (2010). Learning: From association to cognition. *Annual Review of Psychology, 61*, 273–301.

Shapiro, D. A., Barkham, M., Stiles, W. B., et al. (2003). Time is of the essence: A selective review of the fall and rise of brief therapy research. *Psychology & Psychotherapy: Theory, Research & Practice, 76*(3), 211–235.

Shapiro, F. (2001). *Eye movement desensitization and reprocessing: Basic principles, protocols and procedures* (2nd ed.). New York: Guilford.

Shapiro, F., & Forrest, M. S. (2004). *EMDR: The breakthrough therapy for overcoming anxiety, stress, and trauma.* New York: Basic Books.

Shapiro, J. M. (2006). A "memory-jamming" theory of advertising. *Social Science Research Network.* Retrieved May 12, 2011, from http://papers.ssrn.com/sol3/papers.cfm?abstract_id=903474.

Shapiro, S. L., & Walsh, R. (2006). The meeting of meditative disciplines and Western psychology: A mutually enriching dialogue. *American Psychologist, 61*(3), 227–239.

Shapiro-Mendoza, C. K., Kimball, M., et al. (2009). US infant mortality trends attributable to accidental suffocation and strangulation. *Pediatrics, 123*(2), 533–539.

Sharf, R. S. (2012). *Theories of psychotherapy & counseling: Concepts and cases* (5th ed.). Belmont, CA: Cengage Learning/Wadsworth.

Sharot, T., Martorella, E. A., Delgado, M. R., et al. (2007). How personal experience modulates the neural circuitry of memories of September 11. *Proceedings of the National Academy of Sciences, 104*(1), 389–394.

Shaver, P. R., & Mikulincer, M. (Eds.). (2011). *Human aggression and violence: Causes, manifestations, and consequences.* Washington, DC: American Psychological Association.

Shaywitz, B. A, Shaywitz, S. E., Pugh, K. R., et al. (1995). Sex differences in the functional organization of the brain for language. *Nature, 373*, 607–609.

Shaywitz, S. E., & Gore, J. C. (1995). Sex differences in functional organization of the brain for language. Nature, 373(6515), 607.

Sheldon, K. M., Ryan, R. M., Rawsthorne, L. J., et al. (1997). Trait self and true self: Cross-role variation in the Big-Five personality traits and its relations with psychological authenticity and subjective well-being. *Journal of Personality & Social Psychology, 73*(6), 1380–1393.

Shen, J., Botly, L. C. P., Chung, S. A., et al. (2006). Fatigue and shift work. *Journal of Sleep Research, 15*(1), 1–5.

Shepard, R. N. (1975). Form, formation, and transformation of internal representations. In R. L. Solso (Ed.), *Information processing and cognition: The Loyola Symposium* (pp. 87–122). Hillsdale, NJ: Erlbaum.

Shepherd, G. M. (2006). Smell images and the flavour system in the human brain. *Nature, 444*(7117), 316–321.

Sherif, M., Harvey, O. J., White, B. J., et al. (1961). *Intergroup conflict and cooperation: The Robbers Cave experiment.* University of Oklahoma, Institute of Group Relations. Retrieved March 28, 2011, from http://psychclassics.yorku.ca/Sherif/.

Shiffman, S., Scharf, D. M., Shadel, W. G., et al. (2006). Analyzing milestones in smoking cessation: Illustration in a nicotine patch trial in adult smokers. *Journal of Consulting & Clinical Psychology, 74*(2), 276 –285.

Shires, A., & Miller, D. (1998). A preliminary study comparing psychological factors associated with erectile dysfunction in heterosexual and homosexual men. *Sexual & Marital Therapy, 13*(1), 37–49.

Shneerson, J. M. (2005). *Sleep medicine: A guide to sleep and its disorders* (2nd ed.). London: Blackwell.

Shneidman, E. S. (1987b). Psychological approaches to suicide. In VandenBos, G. R., & Bryant, B. K. (Eds.), *Cataclysms, crises, and catastrophes: Psychology in action* (pp.147–184). Washington, DC: American Psychological Association.

Shorrock, S. T., & Isaac, A. (2010). Mental imagery in air traffic control. International *Journal of Aviation Psychology, 20*(4), 309–324.

Short, S. E., Ross-Stewart L., & Monsma, E. V. (2006). Onwards with the evolution of imagery research in sport psychology. *Athletic Insight: Online Journal of Sport Psychology, 8*(3), 1–15.

Shulman, B. H. (2004). Cognitive therapy and the individual psychology of Alfred Adler. In A. Freeman, M. J. Mahoney, et al. (Eds.), *Cognition and psychotherapy* (2nd ed., pp. 143–160). New York: Springer.

Shurkin, J. N. (1992). *Terman's kids.* Boston: Little, Brown.

Siefert, C. J. (2010). Screening for personality disorders in psychiatric settings: Four recently developed screening measures. In L. Baer, & M. A. Blais (Eds), *Handbook of clinical rating scales and assessment in psychiatry and mental health* (pp. 125–144). Totowa, NJ: Humana Press.

Siegel, D. J. (2007). *The mindful brain: Reflection and attunement in the cultivation of well-being.* New York: Norton.

Siegel, R. D. (2010). *The mindfulness solution: Everyday practices for everyday problems.* New York: Guilford.

Siegel, R. K. (2005). *Intoxication: The universal drive for mind-altering substances.* Rochester, VT: Park Street Press.

Siegler, R. S. (1989). Mechanisms of cognitive development. *Annual Review of Psychology, 40*, 353–379.

Siegler, R. S. (2005). *Children's thinking* (4th ed.). Mahwah, NJ: Erlbaum.

Siegler, R. S., DeLoache, J. S., & Eisenberg, N. (2011). *How children develop* (3rd ed.). New York: Worth.

Sienaert, P., Vansteelandt, K., Demyttenaere, K., et al. (2010). Randomized comparison of ultra-brief bifrontal and unilateral electroconvulsive therapy for major depression: Cognitive side-effects. *Journal of Affective Disorders, 122*(1-2), 60–67.

Siever, L. J., & Koenigsberg, H. W. (2000). The frustrating no-man's-land of borderline personality disorder. *Cerebrum, 2*(4), 85–99.

Sigelman, C. K., & Rider, E. A. (2009). *Life-span human development* (6th ed.). Belmont, CA: Cengage Learning/Wadsworth.

Silber, B. Y., & Schmitt, J. A. J. (2010). Effects of tryptophan loading on human cognition, mood, and sleep. *Neuroscience & Biobehavioral Reviews, 34*(3), 387–407.

Silverstein, C. (2009). The implications of removing homosexuality from the DSM as a mental disorder. *Archives of Sexual Behavior, 38*(2), 161–163.

Simeon, D., Guralnik, O., Knutelska, M., et al. (2002). Personality factors associated with dissociation: Temperament, defenses, and cognitive schemata. *American Journal of Psychiatry, 159*, 489–491.

Simeonova, D., Chang, K. D., Strong, C., et al. (2005). Creativity in familial bipolar disorder. *Journal of Psychiatric Research, 39*(6), 623–631.

Simister, J., & Cooper, C. (2005). Thermal stress in the U.S.A.: Effects on violence and on employee behaviour. *Stress & Health, 21*, 3–15.

Simner, M. L., & Goffin, R. D. (2003). A position statement by the international graphonomics society on the use of graphology in personnel selection testing. *International Journal of Testing, 3(4)*, 353–364.

Simon, G. E, Ludman, E. J., Tutty, S., et al. (2004). Telephone psychotherapy and telephone care management for primary care patients starting antidepressant treatment. *Journal of the American Medical Association, 292*, 935–942.

Simons, D. A., & Wurtele, S. K. (2010). Relationships between parents' use of corporal punishment and their children's endorsement of spanking and hitting other children. Child *Abuse & Neglect, 34*(9), 639–646.

Simons, D. J., & Chabris, C. F. (1999). Gorillas in our midst: Sustained inattentional blindness for dynamic events. *Perception, 28*, 1059–1074.

Simons, D. J., & Levin, D. T. (1998). Failure to detect changes to people during a real-world interaction. *Psychonomic Bulletin & Review, 5*(4), 644–649.

Simons, J. S., Dodson, C. S., Bell, D., et al. (2004). Specific- and partial-source memory: Effects of aging. *Psychology & Aging, 19*(4), 689–694.

Simon-Thomas, E. R., Role, K. O., & Knight, R. T. (2005). Behavioral and electrophysiological evidence of a right hemisphere bias for the influence of negative emotion on higher cognition. *Journal of Cognitive Neuroscience, 17*(3), 518–529.

Simonton, D. K. (2009). Varieties of (scientific) creativity: A hierarchical model of domain-specific disposition, development, and achievement. *Perspectives on Psychological Science, 4*(5), 441–452.

Simonton, D. K., & Baumeister, R. F. (2005). Positive psychology at the summit. *Review of General Psychology, 9*(2), 99–102.

Simpson, D. D., Joe, G. W., Fletcher, B. W., et al. (1999). A national evaluation of treatment outcomes for cocaine dependence. *Archives of General Psychiatry, 57*(6), 507–514.

Simpson, K. J. (2002). Anorexia nervosa and culture. *Journal of Psychiatric & Mental Health Nursing, 9*, 65–71.

Singer, J. D. (2005). Explaining foreign policy: U.S. decision-making and the Persian Gulf War. *Political Psychology, 26*(5), 831–834.

Singer, M. T. (2003). *Cults in our midst: The continuing fight against their hidden menace.* San Francisco: Jossey-Bass.

Singer, M. T., & Addis, M. E. (1992). Cults, coercion, and contumely. *Cultic Studies Journal, 9*(2), 163–189.

Singleton, J. L., & Newport, E. L. (2004). When learners surpass their models: The acquisition of American Sign Language from inconsistent input. *Cognitive Psychology, 49*(4), 370–407.

Sinha, R., Garcia, M., Paliwal, P., et al. (2006). Stress-induced cocaine craving and hypothalamic-pituitary-adrenal responses are predictive of cocaine relapse outcomes. *Archives of General Psychiatry, 63*(3), 324–331.

Sipos, A., Rasmussen, F., Harrison, G., et al. (2004). Paternal age and schizophrenia: A population based cohort study. *British Medical Journal, 329*(7474), 1070.

Sirkin, M. I. (1990). Cult involvement: A systems approach to assessment and treatment. *Psychotherapy, 27*(1), 116–123.

Sjöqvist, F., Garle, M., & Rane, A. (2008). Use of doping agents, particularly anabolic steroids, in sports and society. *Lancet, 371*(9627), 1872–1882.

Skeels, H. M. (1966). Adult status of children with contrasting early life experiences. *Monograph of the Society for Research in Child Development, 31*(3), 1–56.

Skillsoft. (2006). *IT pros more like to suffer from stress, says new survey.* Retrieved July 6, 2009 from http://www.skillsoft.com/emea/press-releases/archive/2006/19-May-06.asp.

Skinner, B. F. (1938). *The behavior of organisms.* Englewood Cliffs, NJ: Prentice-Hall.

Skurnik, I., Yoon, C., Park, D. C., et al. (2005). How warnings about false claims become recommendations. *Journal of Consumer Research, 31*(4), 713–724.

Skuy, M., Gewer, A., Osrin, Y., et al. (2002). Effects of mediated learning experience on Raven's matrices scores of African and non-African university students in South Africa. *Intelligence, 30*(3), 221–232.

Slater, A., Mattock, A., & Brown, E. (1990). Size constancy at birth:

Newborn infants' responses to retinal and real size. *Journal of Experimental Child Psychology, 49*(2), 314–322.

Sloman, A. (2008). The well-designed young mathematician. *Artifical Intelligence, 172*(18), 2015–2034.

Slot, L. A. B., & Colpaert, F. C. (1999). Recall rendered dependent on an opiate state. *Behavioral Neuroscience, 113*(2), 337–344.

Smedley, A., & Smedley, B. D. (2005). Race as biology is fiction, racism as a social problem is real. *American Psychologist, 60*(1), 16–26.

Smith, A. P. (2005). Caffeine at work. *Human Psychopharmacology: Clinical & Experimental, 20*(6), 441–445.

Smith, A. P., Clark, R., & Gallagher, J. (1999). Breakfast cereal and caffeinated coffee: Effects on working memory, attention, mood and cardiovascular function. *Physiology & Behavior, 67*(1), 9–17.

Smith, C. A., & Kirby, L. D. (2011). The role of appraisal and emotion in coping and adaptation. In R. J. Contrada, & A. Baum (Eds.), *The handbook of stress science: Biology, psychology, and health* (pp. 195–208). New York: Springer.

Smith, C. S., Folkard, S., Tucker, P., et al. (2011). Work schedules, health, and safety. In J. C. Quick, & L. E. Tetrick (Eds.), *Handbook of occupational health psychology* (2nd ed., pp. 185–204). Washington, DC: American Psychological Association.

Smith, E., & Delargy, M (2005). Locked-in syndrome. *British Medical Journal, 330*, 406–409.

Smith, J. D., Redford, J. S., & Haas, S. M. (2008). Prototype abstraction by monkeys (Macaca mulatta). *Journal of Experimental Psychology: General, 137*(2), 390–401.

Smith, J. L., & Cahusac, P. M. B. (2001). Right-sided asymmetry in sensitivity to tickle. *Laterality, 6*(3), 233–238.

Smith, M. L., Cottrell, G. W., Gosselin, F., et al. (2005). Transmitting and decoding facial expressions. *Psychological Science, 16*(3), 184–189.

Smith, M., Vogler, J., Zarrouf, F., et al. (2009). Electroconvulsive therapy: The struggles in the decision-making process and the aftermath of treatment. *Issues in Mental Health Nursing, 30*(9), 554–559.

Smith, S. M, McIntosh, W. D., & Bazzini, D. G. (1999). Are the beautiful good in Hollywood? *Basic & Applied Social Psychology, 21*(1), 69–80.

Smith, T. W. (2006). *American sexual behavior: Trends, socio-demographic differences, and risk behavior.* University of Chicago National Opinion Research Center GSS Topical Report No. 25. Retrieved February 26, 2011 from http://www.norc.org/NR/rdonlyres/2663F09F-2E74-436E-AC81-6FFBF288E183/0/AmericanSexualBehavior2006.pdf.

Smith, T. W., Glazer, K., Ruiz, J. M., et al. (2004). Hostility, anger, aggressiveness, and coronary heart disease: An interpersonal perspective on personality, emotion, and health. *Journal of Personality, 72*(6), 1217–1270.

Smith, T. W., Ruiz, J. M., & Uchino, B. N. (2004). Mental activation of supportive ties, hostility, and cardiovascular reactivity to laboratory stress in young men and women. *Health Psychology, 23*(5), 476–485.

Smith, W. B. (2007). Karen Horney and psychotherapy in the 21st century. *Clinical Social Work Journal, 35*(1), 57–66.

Smyth, J. D., Dillman, D. A., Christian, L. M., et al. (2010). Using the Internet to survey small towns and communities: Limitations and possibilities in the early 21st century. *American Behavioral Scientist, 53*(9), 1423–1448.

Smyth, J. M., & Pennebaker, J. W. (2008). Exploring the boundary conditions of expressive writing: In search of the right recipe. *British Journal of Health Psychology, 13*(1), 1–7.

Smyth, M. M., & Waller, A. (1998). Movement imagery in rock climbing. *Applied Cognitive Psychology, 12*(2), 145–157.

Snow, C. P. (1961). Either-or. *Progressive, Feb*, 24.

Snowman, J., & McCown, R. (2011). *Psychology applied to teaching* (13th ed.). Belmont, CA: Cengage Learning/Wadsworth.

Snyder, A., Bahramali, H., Hawker, T., et al. (2006). Savant-like numerosity skills revealed in normal people by magnetic pulses. *Perception, 35*(6), 837–845.

Sobel, E., Shine, D., DiPietro, D., et al. (1996). Condom use among HIV/infected patients in South Bronx, New York. *AIDS, 10*(2), 235–236.

Sobolewski, J. M., & Amato, P. R. (2005). Economic hardship in the family of origin and children's psychological well-being in adulthood. *Journal of Marriage & Family, 67*(1), 141–156.

Soderstrom, M. (2007). Beyond babytalk: Re-evaluating the nature and content of speech input to preverbal infants. *Developmental Review, 27*(4), 501–532.

Solomon, E. P., Solomon, R. M., & Heide, K. M. (2009). EMDR: An evidence-based treatment for victims of trauma. *Victims & Offenders, 4*(4), 391–397.

Solomon, J. L., Marshall, P., & Gardner, H. (2005). Crossing boundaries to generative wisdom: An analysis of professional work. In R. J. Sternberg & J. Jordan (Eds.), *A handbook of wisdom: Psychological perspectives* (pp. 272–296). New York: Cambridge University Press.

Solomon, R. C., & Wynne, L. C. (1953). Traumatic avoidance learning: Acquisition in normal dogs. *Psychological Monographs, 67*(4, Whole No. 354).

Solomon, R. L. (1980). The opponent-process theory of acquired motivation. *American Psychologist, Aug*, 691–721.

Solowij, N., Stephens, R. S., Roffman, R. A., et al. (2002). Cognitive functioning of long-term heavy cannabis users seeking treatment. *Journal of the American Medical Association, 287*, 1123–1131.

Soman, D. (2010). Option overload: How to deal with choice complexity. *Rotman Magazine, Fall*, 42–47.

Somberg, D. R., Stone, G., & Claiborn, C. D. (1993). Informed consent: Therapist's beliefs and practices. *Professional Psychology: Research & Practice, 24*(2), 153–159.

Sommers-Flanagan, J., & Sommers-Flanagan R. (2008). Clinical interviewing (4th ed.). New York: Wiley.

Sörqvist, P. (2010). Effects of aircraft noise and speech on prose memory: What role for working memory capacity? *Journal of Environmental Psychology, 30*(1), 112–118.

Sousa, K., Orfale, A. G., Meireles, S. M., et al. (2009). Assessment of a biofeedback program to treat chronic low back pain. *Journal of Musculoskeletal Pain, 17*(4), 369–377.

Soussignan, R. (2002). Duchenne smile, emotional experience, and autonomic reactivity. *Emotion, 2*(1), 52–74.

Soyez, V., & Broekaert, E. (2003). How do substance abusers and their significant others experience the re-entry phase of therapeutic community treatment: a qualitative study. *International Journal of Social Welfare, 12*(3), 211–220.

Spalding, K. L., Arner, E., Westermark, P. O., et al. (2008). Dynamics of fat cell turnover in humans. *Nature, 453*, 783–787.

Spano, R. (2005). Potential sources of observer bias in police observational data. *Social Science Research, 34*(3), 591–617.

Spector, P. E. (2005). *Industrial and organizational psychology: Research and practice* (4th ed.). New York: Wiley.

Spence, S., & David, A. (Eds.). (2004). *Voices in the brain: The cognitive neuropsychiatry of auditory verbal hallucinations.* London: Psychology Press.

Sperry, R. W. (1968). Hemisphere deconnection and unity in conscious awareness. *American Psychologist, 23*, 723–733.

Spiegler, M. D., & Guevremont, D. C. (2010). *Contemporary behavior therapy* (5th ed.). Belmont, CA: Cengage Learning/Wadsworth.

Spinella, M. (2005). Compulsive behavior in tobacco users. *Addictive Behaviors, 30*(1), 183–186.

Spiro Wagner, P., & Spiro, C. S. (2005). *Divided minds: Twin sisters and their journey through schizophrenia.* New York, St. Martin's Press.

Sporer, S. L. (2001). Recognizing faces of other ethnic groups. *Psychology, Public Policy, & Law, 7*(1), 36–97

Sporns, O. (2011). *Networks of the brain.* Cambridge, MA: MIT Press.

Sprecher, S., & Hatfield, E. (1996). Premarital sexual standards among U.S. college students. *Archives of Sexual Behavior, 25*(3), 261–288.

Springer, C. R., & Pear, J. J. (2008). Performance measures in courses using computer-aided personalized system of instruction. *Computers & Education, 51*(2), 829–835.

Springer, S. P., & Deutsch, G. (1998). *Left brain, right brain.* New York: Freeman.

Squire, L. R. (2004). Memory systems of the brain: A brief history and current perspective. *Neurobiology of Learning & Memory, 82*, 171–177.

Sroufe, L. A., Egeland, B., Carlson, E., et al. (2005). Placing early attachment experiences in developmental context: The Minnesota Longitudinal Study. In K. E. Grossmann, K. Grossmann, & E. Waters, et al. (Eds.), *Attachment from infancy to adulthood: The major longitudinal studies* (pp. 48–70). New York: Guilford.

Stacks, A. M., & Oshio, T., Gerard, J., et al. (2009). The moderating effect of parental warmth on the association between spanking and child aggression: A longitudinal approach. *Infant & Child Development, 18*(2), 178–194.

Staemmler, F.-M. (2004). Dialogue and interpretation in Gestalt therapy: Making sense together. *International Gestalt Journal, 27*(2), 33–57.

Stall-Meadows, C., & Hebert, P. R. (2011). The sustainable consumer: An in situ study of residential lighting alternatives as influenced by infield education. *International Journal of Consumer Studies, 35*(2), 164–170.

Stanovich, K. E. (2010). *How to think straight about psychology* (9th ed.). Boston: Allyn & Bacon.

Stapel, D. A., & Marx, D. M. (2007). Distinctiveness is key: How different types of self-other similarity moderate social comparison effects. *Personality & Social Psychology Bulletin, 33*(3), 439–448.

Staples, S. L. (1996). Human response to environmental noise. *American Psychologist, 51*(2), 143–150.

Steblay, N. M. (1987). Helping behavior in rural and urban environments: A meta-analysis. *Psychological Bulletin, 102*(3), 346–356.

Steele, C. M. (1997). A threat in the air. *American Psychologist, 52*(6), 613–629.

Steele, C. M., & Aronson, J. (1995). Stereotype threat and the intellectual test performance of African Americans. *Journal of Personality & Social Psychology, 69*(5), 797–811.

Stefurak, T., Taylor, C., & Mehta, S. (2010). Gender-specific models of homosexual prejudice: Religiosity, authoritarianism, and gender roles. *Psychology of Religion & Spirituality, 2*(4), 247–261.

Steiger, A. (2007). Neurochemical regulation of sleep. *Journal of Psychiatric Research, 41*, 537–552.

Stein, L. M., & Memon, A. (2006). Testing the efficacy of the cognitive interview in a developing country. *Applied Cognitive Psychology, 20*(5), 597–605.

Stein, M. B., & Stein, Dan J. (2008). Social anxiety disorder. *Lancet, 371*(9618), 1115–1125.

Stein, M. D., & Friedmann, P. D. (2005). Disturbed sleep and its relationship to alcohol use. *Substance Abuse, 26*(1), 1–13.

Stein, M. I. (1974). *Stimulating creativity* (Vol. 1). New York: Academic.

Stein, M. T., & Ferber, R. (2001). Recent onset of sleepwalking in early adolescence. *Journal of Development, Behavior, & Pediatrics, 22*, S33–S35.

Steinberg, L (2001). Adolescent development. *Annual Review of Psychology, 52*, 83–110.

Steiner, B., & Wooldredge, J. (2009). Rethinking the link between institutional crowding and inmate misconduct. *The Prison Journal, 89*(2), 205–233.

Steinmayr, R., & Spinath, B. (2009). The importance of motivation as a predictor of school achievement. *Learning & Individual Differences, 19*(1), 80–90.

Steinmetz, J. E., Tracy, J. A., & Green, J. T. (2001). Classical eyeblink conditioning: Clinical models and applications. *Integrative Physiological & Behavioral Science, 36*(3), 220–238.

Stemler, S. E., & Sternberg, R. J. (2006). Using situational judgment tests to measure practical intelligence. In J. A. Weekley & R. E. Ployhart (Eds.), *Situational judgment tests: Theory, measurement, and application* (pp. 107–131). Mahwah, NJ: Erlbaum.

Stephens, K., Kiger, L., Karnes, F. A., et al. (1999). Use of nonverbal measures of intelligence in identification of culturally diverse gifted students in rural areas. *Perceptual & Motor Skills, 88*(3, Pt 1), 793–796.

Stern, P. C. (1992). Psychological dimensions of global environmental change. *Annual Review of Psychology, 43*, 269–302.

Stern, S. L., Dhanda, R., & Hazuda, H. P. (2001). Hopelessness predicts mortality in older Mexican and European Americans. *Psychosomatic Medicine, 63*(3), 344–351.

Sternberg, E. M. (2009). *Healing spaces: The science of place and well-being.* Cambridge, MA: Harvard University Press.

Sternberg, R. J. (1988). *The triangle of love.* New York: Basic.

Sternberg, R. J. (2001). Is there a heredity-environment paradox? In R. J. Sternberg & E. L. Grigorenko (Eds.), *Environmental effects on cognitive abilities* (pp. 425–432). Mahwah, NJ: Erlbaum.

Sternberg, R. J. (2004). Culture and intelligence. *American Psychologist, 59*(5), 325–338.

Sternberg, R. J. (2007). Race and intelligence: Not a case of black and white. *New Scientist, Oct 27*, 16.

Sternberg, R. J. (2011). *Cognitive psychology* (6th ed.). Belmont, CA: Cengage Learning/Wadsworth.

Sternberg, R. J., & Grigorenko, E. L. (2005). Cultural explorations of the nature of intelligence. In A. F. Healy (Ed.), *Experimental cognitive psychology and its applications* (pp. 225–235). Washington, DC: American Psychological Association.

Sternberg, R. J., & Grigorenko, E. L. (2006). Cultural intelligence and successful intelligence. *Group & Organization Management, 31*(1), 27–39.

Sternberg, R. J., & Lubart, T. I. (1995). *Defying the crowd.* New York: The Free Press.

Sternberg, R. J., Grigorenko, E. L., & Kidd, K. K. (2005). Intelligence, race, and genetics. *American Psychologist, 60*(1), 46–59.

Sterns, H. L., & Huyck, M. H. (2001). The role of work in midlife. In M. Lachman (Ed.), *The handbook of midlife development* (pp. 447–486). New York: Wiley.

Stetz, T., Button, S. B., & Porr, W. B. (2009). New tricks for an old dog: Visualizing job analysis results. *Public Personnel Management, 38*(1), 91–100.

Stewart, A. J., & Ostrove, J. M. (1998). Women's personality in middle age. *American Psychologist, 53*(11), 1185–1194.

Stewart-Williams, S. (2004). The placebo puzzle: Putting together the pieces. *Health Psychology, 23*(2), 198–206.

Stickgold, R., & Walker, M. (2004). To sleep, perchance to gain creative insight? *Trends in Cognitive Sciences, 8*(5), 191–192.

Stinson, F. S., Dawson, D. A., Chou, S. P., et al. (2007). The epidemiology of DSM-IV specific phobia in the USA: Result from the National Epidemiologic Survey on Alcohol and Related Conditions. *Psychological Medicine, 37*(7), 1047–1059.

Stipek, D. (2002). *Motivation to learn* (4th ed.). Boston: Pearson/Allyn and Bacon.

Stix, G. (2010). Alzheimer's: Forestalling the darkness. *Scientific American, 302*, 50–57.

Stix, G. (2011).The neuroscience of true grit. *Scientific American, 304*, 28–33.

Stöber, J. (2004). Dimensions of test anxiety: Relations to ways of coping with pre-exam anxiety and uncertainty. *Anxiety, Stress & Coping, 17*(3), 213–226.

Stoffregen, T. A., Faugloire, E., Yoshida, K., et al. (2008). Motion sickness and postural sway in console video games. *Human Factors, 50*(2), 322–331.

Stokes, D. M. (2001, May-June). The shrinking filedrawer. *Skeptical Inquirer*, 22–25.

Stokes, D., & Lappin, M. (2010). Neurofeedback and biofeedback with 37 migraineurs: A clinical outcome study. *Behavioral & Brain Functions, 6*(Feb 2), ArtID 9. 10 pgs. Retrieved April 10, 2010 from http://www.ncbi.nlm.nih.gov/pmc/articles/PMC2826281/.

Stolerman, I. P., & Jarvis, M. J. (1995) The scientific case that nicotine is addictive. *Psychopharmacology, 117*(1), 2–10.

Stone, J., Perry, Z. W., & Darley, J. M. (1997). "White men can't jump." *Basic & Applied Social Psychology, 19*(3), 291–306.

Stoppard, J. M., & McMullen, L. M. (Eds.). (2003). *Situating sadness: Women and depression in social context.* New York: New York University Press.

Storr, A. (1988). *Solitude: A return to the self.* New York, Free Press.

Strack, F., & Förster, J. (Eds.). (2009). *Social cognition: The basis of human interaction.* New York: Psychology Press.

Strack. F., Martin, L. L., & Stepper, S. (1988). Inhibiting and facilitating conditions of facial expressions: A nonobtrusive test of the facial feedback hypothesis. *Journal of Personality & Social Psychology, 54*, 768–777.

Strange, J. R. (1965). *Abnormal psychology.* New York: McGraw-Hill.

Straub, R. (2012). *Health psychology* (3rd ed.). New York: Worth.

Strayer, D. L., Drews, F. A., & Crouch, D. J. (2006). A comparison of the cell phone driver and the drunk driver. *Human Factors, 48*(2), 381–391.

Strenze, T. (2007). Intelligence and socioeconomic success: A meta-analytic review of longitudinal research. *Intelligence, 35*(5), 401–426.

Strickler, E. M., & Verbalis, J. G. (1988). Hormones and behavior: The biology of thirst and sodium appetite. *American Scientist, May-June*, 261–267.

Stroebe, W., Papies, E. K., & Aarts, H. (2008). From homeostatic to hedonic theories of eating: Self-regulatory failure in food-rich environments. *Applied Psychology, 57*, 172–193.

Strong, B., DeVault, C., & Cohen, T. C. (2011). *The marriage and family experience: Intimate relationships in a changing society* (11th ed.). Belmont, CA: Cengage Learning/Wadsworth.

Strongman, K. T. (2003). *The psychology of emotion: From everyday life to theory* (5th ed.). New York: Wiley.

Strote, J., Lee, J. E., & Wechsler, H. (2002). Increasing MDMA use among college students: Results of a national survey. *Journal of Adolescent Health, 30*(1), 64–72.

Strough, J., Leszczynski, J. P., Neely, T. L., et al. (2007). From adolescence to later adulthood: Femininity, masculinity, and androgyny in six age groups. *Sex Roles, 57*(5-6), 385–396.

Strubbe, M. J. (2005). What did Triplett really find? A contemporary analysis of the first experiment in social psychology. *American Journal of Psychology, 118*, 271–286.

Sturges, J. W., & Sturges, L. V. (1998). In vivo *systematic desensitization* in a single-session treatment of an 11-year old girl's elevator phobia. *Child & Family Behavior Therapy, 20*(4), 55–62.

Stuss, D. T., & Knight, R. T. (2002). *Principles of frontal lobe function.* New York: Oxford University Press.

Stuss, D. T., & Levine, B. (2002). Adult clinical neuropsychology. *Annual Review of Psychology, 53*, 401–433.

Suarez, E., & Gadalla, T. M. (2010). Stop blaming the victim: A meta-analysis on rape myths. *Journal of Interpersonal Violence, 25*(11), 2010–2035.

Substance Abuse and Mental Health Services Administration. (2009). *Results from the 2008 National Survey on Drug Use and Health: National Findings.* Rockville, MD: Author. Retrieved January 23, 2011 from http://www.oas.samhsa.gov/nsduh/2k8nsduh/2k8Results.pdf.

Substance Abuse and Mental Health Services Administration. (2010). *Results from the 2009 National Survey on Drug Use and Health: Volume 1. Summary of National Findings.* Rockville, MD: Author. Retrieved January 8, 2011 from http://www.oas.samhsa.gov/NSDUH/2k9NSDUH/2k9ResultsP.pdf.

Sue, D., Sue, D. W., & Sue, S. (2010). *Understanding abnormal behavior* (9th ed.). Belmont, CA: Cengage Learning/Wadsworth.

Suedfeld, P. & Steel, G. D. (2000). The environmental psychology of capsule habitats. *Annual Review of Psychology, 51*, 227–253.

Suedfeld, P., & Borrie, R. A. (1999). Health and therapeutic applications of chamber and flotation restricted environmental stimulation therapy (REST). *Psychology & Health, 14*(3), 545–566.

Sugihara, Y., & Warner, J. A. (1999). Endorsements by Mexican-Americans of the Bem Sex-Role Inventory: Cross-ethnic comparison. *Psychological Reports, 85*(1), 201–211.

Sugimoto, K., & Ninomiya, Y. (2005). Introductory remarks on umami research: Candidate receptors and signal transduction mechanisms on umami. *Chemical Senses, 30*(Suppl. 1), i21–i22.

Suinn, R. M. (1975). *Fundamentals of behavior pathology* (2nd ed.). New York: Wiley.

Suinn, R. M. (1999). Scaling the summit: Valuing ethnicity. *APA Monitor, March*, 2.

Suinn, R. M. (2001). The terrible twos: Anger and anxiety. *American Psychologist, 56*(1), 27–36.

Sumathipala, A., Siribaddana, S. H., & Bhugra, D. (2004). Culture-bound syndromes: The story of dhat syndrome. *British Journal of Psychiatry, 184*(3), 200–209.

Sumerlin, J. R., & Bundrick, C. M. (1996). Brief Index of Self-Actualization: A measure of Maslow's model. *Journal of Social Behavior & Personality, 11*(2), 253–271.

Summers, A., Hayward, R. D., & Miller, M. K. (2010). Death qualification as systematic exclusion of jurors with certain religious and other characteristics. *Journal of Applied Social Psychology, 40*(12), 3218–3234.

Sunnafrank, M., Ramirez, A., & Metts, S. (2004). At first sight: Persistent relational effects of get-acquainted conversations. *Journal of Social & Personal Relationships, 21*(3), 361–379.

Sutherland, R. J., Lehmann, H., Spanswick, S. C., et al. (2006). Growth points in research on memory and hippocampus. *Canadian Journal of Experimental Psychology, 60*(2), 166–174.

Sutin, A. R., & Costa, Jr., P. T. (2010). Reciprocal influences of personality and job characteristics across middle adulthood. *Journal of Personality, 78*(1), 257–288.

Suzuki, L., & Aronson, J. (2005). The cultural malleability of intelligence and its impact on the racial/ethnic hierarchy. *Psychology, Public Policy, & Law, 11*, 320–327.

Svartdal, F. (2003). Extinction after partial reinforcement: Predicted vs. judged persistence. *Scandinavian Journal of Psychology, 44*(1), 55–64.

Swann, Jr.,W. B., Chang-Schneider C., & Larsen McClarty, K. (2007). Do people's self-views matter? Self-concept and self-esteem in everyday life. *American Psychologist, 62*(2), 84–94.

Swearer, S. M., Espelage, D. L. & Napolitano, S. A. (2009). *Bullying prevention and intervention: Realistic strategies for schools.* New York: Guilford.

Synhorst, L. L., Buckley, J. A., Reid, R., et al. (2005). Cross informant agreement of the Behavioral and Emotional Rating Scale-2nd Edition (BERS-2) parent and youth rating scales. *Child & Family Behavior Therapy, 27*(3), 1–11.

Szabo, A. (2003). The acute effects of humor and exercise on mood and anxiety. *Journal of Leisure Research, 35*(2), 152–162.

Szabó, N., Pap, C., Kóbor, J., et al. (2010). Primary microcephaly in Hungary: Epidemiology and clinical features. *Acta Paediatrica, 99*(5), 690–693.

Szollos, A. (2009). Toward a psychology of chronic time pressure: Conceptual and methodological review. *Time & Society, 18*(2–3), 332–350.

Tackett, J. L., & Krueger, R. F. (2011). Dispositional influences on human aggression. In P. R. Shaver & M. Mikulincer (Eds.), *Human aggression and violence: Causes, manifestations, and consequences* (pp. 89–104). Washington, DC: American Psychological Association.

Tafrate, R. C., & Kassinove, H. (2009). *Anger management for everyone: Seven proven ways to control anger and live a happier life.* Atascadero, CA: Impact Publishers.

Takeuchi, M. M., & Takeuchi, S. A. (2008). Authoritarian versus authoritative parenting styles: Application of the cost equalization principle. *Marriage & Family Review, 44*(4), 489–510.

Takooshian, H., Haber, S., & Lucido, D. J. (1977). Who wouldn't help a lost child? You, maybe. *Psychology Today, 88*(9), 67–89.

Talbot, N. L., & Gamble, S. A. (2008). IPT for women with trauma histories in community mental health care. *Journal of Contemporary Psychotherapy,* 38(1), 35–44.

Talbott, J. A. (2004). Deinstitutionalization: Avoiding the disasters of the past. *Psychiatric Services, 55*(10), 1112–1115.

Talley, P. F., Strupp, H. H., & Morey, L. C. (1990). Matchmaking in psychotherapy: Patient–therapist dimensions and their impact on outcome. *Journal of Consulting & Clinical Psychology, 58*(2), 182–188.

Tal-Or, N., & Papirman, Y. (2007). The fundamental attribution error in attributing fictional figures' characteristics to the actors. *Media Psychology, 9*(2), 331–345.

Tamis-LeMonda, C. S., Bornstein, M. H., & Baumwell, L. (2001). Maternal responsiveness and children's achievement of language milestones. *Child Development, 72*, 748–767.

Tamis-LeMonda, C. S., Shannon, J. D., Cabrera, N. J., et al. (2004). Fathers and mothers at play with their 2- and 3-year-olds: Contributions to language and cognitive development. *Child Development, 75*(6), 1806–1820.

Tang, C. Y., Eaves, E. L., Ng, J. C., et al. (2010). Brain networks for working memory and factors of intelligence assessed in males and females with fMRI and DTI. *Intelligence, 38*(3), 293–303.

Tanner, D. C. (2007). Redefining Wernicke's area: Receptive language and discourse semantics. *Journal of Allied Health, 36*(2), 63–66.

Tanner, J. M. (1973). Growing up. *Scientific American*, Sept., 34–43.

Taraban, R., Rynearson, K., & Kerr, M. (2000). College students' academic performance and self-reports of comprehension strategy use. *Reading Psychology, 21*(4), 283–308.

Taris, T. W., Bakker, A. B., Schaufeli, W. B., et al. (2005). Job control and burnout across occupations. *Psychological Reports, 97*(3), 955–961.

Tatum, J. L., & Foubert, J. D. (2009). Rape myth acceptance, hypermasculinity, and SAT scores as correlates of moral development: Understanding sexually aggressive attitudes in first-year college men. *Journal of College Student Development, 50*(2), 195–209.

Taub, E. (2004). Harnessing brain plasticity through behavioral techniques to produce new treatments in neurorehabilitation. *American Psychologist, 59*(8), 692–704.

Tausig, M., Michello, J., & Subedi, S. (2004). *A sociology of mental illness* (2nd ed.). Englewood Cliffs, NJ: Prentice Hall.

Tavakoli, S., Lumley, M. A., Hijazi, A. M., et al. (2009). Effects of assertiveness training and expressive writing on acculturative stress in international students: A randomized trial. *Journal of Counseling Psychology, 56*(4), 590–596.

Tavris, C., & Aronson, E. (2007). *Mistakes were made (but not by me): Why we justify foolish beliefs, bad decisions, and hurtful acts.* New York: Harcourt.

Taylor, D. J., & Roane, B. M. (2010). Treatment of insomnia in adults and children: A practice-friendly review of research. *Journal of Clinical Psychology, 66*(11), 1137–1147.

Taylor, G. J., & Taylor-Allan H. L. (2007). Applying emotional intelligence in understanding and treating physical and psychological disorders: What we have learned from alexithymia. In R. Bar-On, M. J. G. Reuven, et al. (Eds.), *Educating people to be emotionally intelligent* (pp. 211–223). Westport, CT: Praeger.

Taylor, K. (2004). *Brainwashing: The science of thought control.* New York: Oxford University Press.

Taylor, S. E. (2009). *Health psychology* (7th ed.). New York: McGraw-Hill.

Taylor, S. E., & Master, S. L. (2011). Social responses to stress: The tend-and-befriend model. In R. J. Contrada, & A. Baum (Eds.), *The handbook of stress science: Biology, psychology, and health* (pp. 101–109). New York: Springer.

Taylor, S. E., Lerner, J. S., Sherman, D. K., et al. (2003). Are self-enhancing cognitions associated with healthy or unhealthy biological profiles? *Journal of Personality & Social Psychology, 85*(4), 605–615.

Taylor-Seehafer, M., & Rew, L. (2000). Risky sexual behavior among adolescent women. *Journal of Social Pediatric Nursing, 5*(1), 15–25.

Teed, E. L., Scileppi, J. A., Boeckmann, M., et al. (2007). *The community mental health system: A navigational guide for providers.* Boston: Allyn & Bacon.

Teglasi, H. (2010). *Essentials of TAT and other storytelling assessments* (2nd ed.). Hoboken, NJ: Wiley.

Tenenbaum, G., Bar-Eli M., & Eyal, N. (1996). Imagery orientation and vividness: Their effect on a motor skill performance. *Journal of Sport Behavior, 19*(1), 32–49.

Tennesen, M. (2007). Gone today, hear tomorrow. *New Scientist, March 10*, 42–45.

Tennie, C., Greve, K., Gretscher, H., et al. (2010). Two-year-old children copy more reliably and more often than nonhuman great apes in multiple observational learning tasks. *Primates, 51*(4), 337–351.

Teo, A. R., & Gaw, A. C. (2010). Hikikomori, a Japanese culture-bound syndrome of social withdrawal? A proposal for DSM-5. *Journal of Nervous & Mental Disease, 198*(6), 444–449.

Terman, L. M., & Merrill, M. A. (1937/1960). *Stanford-Binet Intelligence Scale.* Boston: Houghton Mifflin.

Terman, L. M., & Oden, M. (1959). *The gifted group in mid-life* (Vol. 5): *Genetic studies of genius.* Stanford, CA: Stanford University Press.

Terry, C. (2006). History of treatment of people with mental illness. In J. R. Matthews, C. E. Walker, et al. (Eds.), *Your practicum in psychology: A guide for maximizing knowledge and competence* (pp. 81–103). Washington, DC: American Psychological Association.

Terry, D. J., & Hogg, M. A. (1996). Group norms and the attitude-behavior relationship. *Personality & Social Psychology Bulletin, 22*(8), 776–793.

Tewksbury, R., Higgins, G. E., & Mustaine, E. E. (2008). Binge drinking among college athletes and non-athletes. *Deviant Behavior, 29*(3), 275–293.

Teyber, E., & McClure, F. H. (2011). *Interpersonal process in therapy: An integrative model* (6th ed.). Belmont, CA: Cengage Learning/Wadsworth.

Thase, M. E. (2006). Major depressive disorder. In F. Andrasik (Ed.), *Comprehensive handbook of personality and psychopathology* (Vol. 2): *Adult psychopathology* (pp. 207–230). New York: Wiley.

The Nature Conservancy. (2011). *Carbon footprint calculator.* Arlington, VA: Author. Retrieved January 16, 2011, from http://www.nature.org/initiatives/climatechange/calculator/.

Thibault, P., Gosselin, P., Brunel, M.-L., et al. (2009). Children's and adolescents' perception of the authenticity of smiles. *Journal of Experimental Child Psychology, 102*(3), 360–367.

Thiessen, E. D., Hill, E. A., & Saffran, J. R. (2005). Infant-directed speech facilitates word segmentation. *Infancy, 7*(1), 53–71.

Thomas, E. M. (2004). *Aggressive behaviour outcomes for young children: Change in parenting environment predicts change in behaviour.* Ottawa, ON: Statistics Canada. Retrieved January 19, 2011, from http://www.statcan.ca/cgi-bin/downpub/listpub.cgi?catno=89-599-MIE2004001.

Thomas, M. (2009). Some needed changes in DSM-V: But what about children? *Clinical Psychology: Science & Practice, 16*(1), 50–53.

Thompson, A., Boekhoorn, K., Van Dam, A. M., et al. (2008). Changes in adult neurogenesis in neurodegenerative diseases: Cause or consequence? *Genes, Brain & Behavior, 7*(Suppl 1), 28–42.

Thompson, L. A., & Oehlert, J. (2010). The etiology of giftedness. *Learning & Individual Differences, 20*(4), 298–307.

Thompson, R. A., & Nelson, C. A. (2001). Developmental science and the media. *American Psychologist, 56*(1), 5–15.

Thompson, R. F. (2005). In search of memory traces. *Annual Review of Psychology, 56*, 1–23.

Thornton, S. N. (2010). Thirst and hydration: Physiology and consequences of dysfunction. *Physiology & Behavior, 100*(1), 15–21.

Thorpy, M. J. (2006). Cataplexy associated with narcolepsy: Epidemiology, pathophysiology and management. *CNS Drugs, 20*(1), 43–50.

Thorson, J. A., & Powell, F. C. (1990). Meanings of death and intrinsic religiosity. *Journal of Clinical Psychology, 46*(4), 379–391.

Thyen, U., Richter-Appelt H., Wiesemann, C., et al. (2005). Deciding on gender in children with intersex conditions: Considerations and controversies. *Treatments in Endocrinology, 4*(1), 1–8.

Tidwell, M. O., Reis, H. T., & Shaver, P. R. (1996). Attachment, attractiveness, and social interaction. *Journal of Personality & Social Psychology, 71*(4), 729–745.

Tierney, S. (2008). Creating communities in cyberspace: Pro-anorexia web sites and social capital. *Journal of Psychiatric & Mental Health Nursing, 15*(4), 340–343.

Tiggemann, M., & Polivy, J. (2010). Upward and downward: Social comparison processing of thin idealized media images. *Psychology of Women Quarterly, 34*(3), 356–364.

Tijerino, R. (1998). Civil spaces: A critical perspective of defensible space.

Journal of Architectural & Planning Research, 15(4), 321–337.

Till, B. D., & Priluck, R. L. (2000). Stimulus generalization in classical conditioning: An initial investigation and extension. *Psychology & Marketing, 17*(1), 55–72.

Till, B. D., Stanley, S. M., & Priluck, R. (2008). Classical conditioning and celebrity endorsers: An examination of belongingness and resistance to extinction. *Psychology & Marketing, 25*(2), 179–196.

Timmerman, C. K., & Kruepke, K. A. (2006). Computer-assisted instruction, media richness, and college student performance. *Communication Education, 55*(1), 73–104.

Timmerman, I. G. H., Emmelkamp, P. M. G., & Sanderman, R. (1998). The effects of a stress-management training program in individuals at risk in the community at large. *Behaviour Research & Therapy, 36*(9), 863–875.

Tipples, J., Atkinson, A. P., & Young, A. W. (2002). The eyebrow frown: A salient social signal. *Emotion, 2*(3), 288–296.

Tite, L. (2009). "The Obama Effect": Test-taking performance gap virtually eliminated during key moments of Obama's presidential run. *Research News@Vanderbilt.* Retrieved February 21, 2011, from http//news.vanderbilt.edu/2009/01/the-obama-effect-test-taking-performance-gap-story/.

Tittle, C. R., & Rotolo, T. (2000). IQ and stratification. *Social Forces, 79*(1), 1–28.

Tjaden, P., & Thoennes, N. (2006). *Extent, nature, and consequences of rape victimization: Findings from the national violence against women survey.* Washington, DC: National Institute of Justice. Retrieved February 25, 2011 from http://www.ncjrs.gov/pdffiles1/nij/210346.pdf.

Tobler, N. S., Roona, M. R., Ocshorn, P., et al. (2000). School-based adolescent drug prevention programs: 1998 meta-analysis. *Journal of Primary Prevention, 20*, 275–337.

Tolman, E. C., & Honzik, C. H. (1930). Degrees of hunger, reward and nonreward and maze performance in rats. *University of California Publications in Psychology, 4*, 21–256.

Tolman, E. C., Ritchie, B. F., & Kalish, D. (1946). Studies in spatial learning: II. Place learning versus response learning. *Journal of Experimental Psychology, 36*, 221–229.

Tomasello, M. (2003). *Constructing a language: A usage-based theory of language acquisition.* Cambridge, MA: Harvard University Press.

Toneatto, T. (2002). Cognitive therapy for problem gambling. *Cognitive & Behavioral Practice, 9*(3), 191–199.

Toneatto, T., Sobell, L. C., Sobell, M. B., & et al. (1999). Natural recovery from cocaine dependence. *Psychology of Addictive Behaviors, 13*(4), 259–268.

Tononi, G., & Cirelli, C. (2003). Sleep and synaptic homeostasis: A hypothesis. *Brain Research Bulletin, 62*(2), 143–150.

Toro, C. T., & Deakin, J. F. W. (2007). Adult neurogenesis and schizophrenia: A window on abnormal early brain development? *Schizophrenia Research, 90*(1-3), 1–14.

Torrey, E. F. (1996). *Out of the shadows.* New York: John Wiley & Sons.

Tourangeau, R. (2004). Survey research and societal change. *Annual Review of Psychology, 55*, 775–801.

Toyota, H., & Kikuchi, Y. (2005). Encoding richness of self-generated elaboration and spacing effects on incidental memory. *Perceptual & Motor Skills, 101*(2), 621–627.

Trainor, L. J., & Desjardins, R. N. (2002). Pitch characteristics of infant-directed speech affect infants' ability to discriminate vowels. *Psychonomic Bulletin & Review, 9*(2), 335–340.

Travis, F., Arenander, A., & DuBois, D. (2004). Psychological and physiological characteristics of a proposed object-referral/self-referral continuum of self-awareness. *Consciousness & Cognition, 13*, 401–420.

Treffert, D. A. (2010). *Islands of genius: The bountiful mind of the autistic, acquired, and sudden savant.* London, England: Jessica Kingsley Publishers.

Treffert, D. A., & Christensen, C. D. (2005). Inside the mind of a savant. *Scientific American, 293*(6), 108–113.

Tregear, S., Resto, J., Schoelles, K., et al. (2010). Continuous positive airway pressure reduces risk of motor vehicle crash among drivers with obstructive sleep apnea: Systematic review and meta-analysis. *Sleep: Journal of Sleep & Sleep Disorders Research, 33*(10), 1373–1380.

Trehub, S. E., Unyk, A. M., & Trainor, L. J. (1993). Adults identify infant-directed music across cultures. *Infant Behavior & Development, 16*(2), 193–211.

Trepel, C., & Racine, R. J. (1999). Blockade and disruption of neocortical long-term potentiation following electroconvulsive shock in the adult, freely moving rat. *Cerebral Cortex, 9*(3), 300–305.

Triandis, H. C., & Suh, E. M. (2002). Cultural influences on personality. *Annual Review of Psychology, 53*, 133–160.

Trocmé, N., MacLaurin, B., Fallon, B., et al. (2001). *Canadian Incidence Study of Reported Child Abuse and Neglect.* Ottawa, ON: National Clearinghouse on Family Violence. Retrieved January 19, 2011, from http://www.phac-aspc.gc.ca/publicat/cissr-ecirc/.

Troll, L. E., & Skaff, M. M. (1997). Perceived continuity of self in very old age. *Psychology & Aging, 12*(1), 162–169.

Truax, S. R. (1983). Active search, mediation, and the manipulation of cue dimensions: Emotion attribution in the false feedback paradigm. *Motivation & Emotion, 7*, 41–60.

Trujillo, L. T., Kornguth, S., & Schnyer, D. M. (2009). An ERP examination of the different effects of sleep deprivation on exogenously cued and endogenously cued attention. *Sleep, 32*(10), 1285–1297.

Tryon, R. C. (1929). The genetics of learning ability in rats. *University of California Publications in Psychology, 4*, 71–89.

Tsai, C., Hoerr, S. L., & Song, W. O. (1998). Dieting behavior of Asian college women attending a US university. *Journal of American College Health, 46*(4), 163–168.

Tsai, G., & Coyle, J. T. (2002). Glutamatergic mechanisms in schizophrenia. *Annual Review of Pharmacology & Toxicology, 42*, 165–179.

Tsai, W-C., Chen, C.-C., & Chiu, S-F. (2005). Exploring boundaries of the effects of applicant impression management tactics in job interviews. *Journal of Management, 31*(1), 108–125.

Tse, L. (1999). Finding a place to be: Ethnic identity exploration of Asian Americans. *Adolescence, 34*(133), 121–138.

Tugade, M. M., Fredrickson, B. L., & Barrett, L. F. (2004). Psychological resilience and positive emotional granularity: Examining the benefits of positive emotions on coping and health. *Journal of Personality, 72*(6), 1161–1190.

Tulving, E. (1989). Remembering and knowing the past. *American Scientist, 77*(4), 361–367.

Tulving, E. (2002). Episodic memory. *Annual Review of Psychology, 53*, 1–25.

Turenius, C. I., Htut, M. M., Prodon, D. A., et al. (2009). GABA(A) receptors in the lateral hypothalamus as mediators of satiety and body weight regulation. *Brain Research, 1262*, 16–24.

Turiel, E. (2006).Thought, emotions, and social interactional processes in moral development. In M. Killen, & J. G. Smetana, (Eds.), *Handbook of moral development* (pp. 7–35). Mahwah, NJ: Erlbaum.

Turkheimer, E. (1998). Heritability and biological explanation. *Psychological Review, 105*(4), 782–791.

Turkheimer, E., Haley, A., Waldron, M., et al. (2003). Socioeconomic status modifies heritability of IQ in young children. *Psychological Science, 14*, 623–628.

Turner, S. J. M. (1997). The use of the reflective team in a psychodrama therapy group. *International Journal of Action Methods, 50*(1) 17–26.

Tversky, A., & Kahneman, D. (1981). The framing of decisions and the psychology of choice. *Science, 211*, 453–458.

Tversky, A., & Kahneman, D. (1982). Judgments of and by representativeness. In D. Kahneman, P. Slovic, & A. Tversky (Eds.), *Judgment under uncertainty: Heuristics and biases* (pp. 84–98). Cambridge, MA: Cambridge University Press.

Twenge, J. M., & Campbell, W. K. (2001). Age and birth cohort differences in self-esteem. *Personality & Social Psychology Review, 5*(4), 321–344.

Tyler, J. M., & Feldman, R. S. (2006). Deflecting threat to one's image: Dissembling personal information as a self-presentation strategy. *Basic & Applied Social Psychology, 27*(4), 371–378.

Tzeng, M. (1992). The effects of socioeconomic heterogamy and changes on marital dissolution for first marriages. *Journal of Marriage & Family, 54*, 609–619.

Tzuriel, D., & Shamir, A. (2002). The effects of mediation in computer assisted dynamic assessment. *Journal of Computer Assisted Learning, 18*(1), 21–32.

U.S. Census Bureau. (2007). Minority population tops 100 million. *U. S. Census Bureau News, CB07-70.* Retrieved March 22, 2011, from http://www.census.gov/newsroom/releases/archives/population/cb07-70.html.

U.S. Census Bureau. (2010). *Poverty: 2008 and 2009 American Community Survey Briefs.* New York: Author. Retrieved December 18, 2010 from http://www.census.gov/prod/2010pubs/acsbr09-1.pdf.

U.S. Department of Energy Office of Science. (2008). *About the Human Genome Project.* Washington, DC: Author. Retrieved February 23, 2010, from http://www.ornl.gov/sci/techresources/Human_Genome/project/about.shtml.

U.S. Department of Energy. (2010). *Secretary Chu announces two million smart grid meters installed nationwide.* Washington, DC: Author. Retrieved March 29, 2011 from http://www.energy.gov/news/9433.htm.

U.S. Department of Health and Human Services. (2004). *The health consequences of smoking: A report of the Surgeon General, Executive summary.* Washington, DC: Author. Retrieved February 23, 2010, from http://www.cdc.gov/tobacco/data_statistics/sgr/2004/index.htm.

U.S. Department of Labor (2009). *Occupational Outlook Handbook, 2010–11 Edition: Job interview tips.* Washington, DC: Author. Retrieved May 28, 2011 from http://www.bls.gov/oco/oco20045.htm.

U.S. Department of Labor (2009). *Job interview tips.* Washington, DC: Author. Retrieved May 6, 2010 from http://www.bls.gov/oco/oco20045.htm.

Underwood, B. J. (1957). Interference and forgetting. *Psychological Review, 64*, 49–60.

United Nations. (2004). *World Population in 2300.* New York: Author. Retrieved July 12, 2008 from http://www.un.org/esa/population/publications/longrange2/2004worldpop2300reportfinalc.pdf.

United Nations Educational, Scientific and Cultural Organization. (1990). The Seville statement on violence. *American Psychologist, 45*(10), 1167–1168.

United Nations Programme on HIV/AIDS. (2009). *AIDS epidemic update.* New York: Author. Retrieved March 23, 2010 from http://www.unaids.org/en/KnowledgeCentre/HIVData/

GlobalReport/2008/2008_Global_report.asp.

Unsworth, G., & Ward, T. (2001). Video games and aggressive behaviour. *Australian Psychologist, 36*(3), 184–192.

Uwe P. Gielen, U. P., Fish, J. M., & Draguns, J. G. (Eds.) (2006). *Handbook of culture, therapy, and healing*. Mahwah, NJ: Erlbaum.

Uziel, L. (2007). Individual differences in the social facilitation effect: A review and meta-analysis. *Journal of Research in Personality, 41*(3), 579–601.

Vaillant, G. E. (2002). *Aging well*. Boston: Little, Brown.

Vaillant, G. E. (2005). Alcoholics Anonymous: Cult or cure? *Australian & New Zealand Journal of Psychiatry, 39*(6), 431–436.

Valentine, S., Godkin, L., & Varca, P. E. (2010). Role conflict, mindfulness, and organizational ethics in an education-based healthcare institution. *Journal of Business Ethics, 94*(3), 455–469.

Valins, S. (1966). Cognitive effects of false heart-rate feedback. *Journal of Personality & Social Psychology, 4*, 400–408.

Vallerand, A. H., Saunders, M. M., & Anthony, M. (2007). Perceptions of control over pain by patients with cancer and their caregivers. *Pain Management Nursing, 8*(2), 55–63.

Vallerand, R. J., Paquet, Y., Philippe, F. L., et al. (2010). On the role of passion for work in burnout: A process model. *Journal of Personality, 78*(1), 289–312.

Van Blerkom, D. L. (2011). *College study skills: Becoming a strategic learner* (7th ed.). Belmont, CA: Cengage Learning/Wadsworth.

Van den Bergh, B., & Dewitte, S. (2006). Digit ratio (2D:4D) moderates the impact of sexual cues on men's decisions in ultimatum games. *Proceedings of the Royal Society of London B, 273*, 2091–2095.

van der Hart, O., Lierens, R., & Goodwin, J. (1996). Jeanne Fery: A sixteenth-century case of dissociative identity disorder. *Journal of Psychohistory, 24*(1), 18–35.

van Deurzen, E., & Kenward, R. (2005). *Dictionary of existential psychotherapy and counselling*. Thousand Oaks, CA: Sage.

van Dierendonck, D., & Te Nijenhuis, J. (2005). Flotation restricted environmental stimulation therapy (REST) as a stress-management tool: A meta-analysis. *Psychology & Health, 20*(3), 405–412.

van Dierendonck, D., Díaz, D., Rodríguez-Carvajal R., et al. (2008). Ryff's six-factor model of psychological well-being a Spanish exploration. *Social Indicators Research, 87*(3), 473–479.

van Elst, L. T., Valerius, G., Büchert, M., et al. (2005). Increased prefrontal and hippocampal glutamate concentration in schizophrenia: Evidence from a magnetic resonance spectroscopy study. *Biological Psychiatry, 58*(9), 724–730.

Van Goozen, S. H. M., Cohen-Kettenis P. T., Gooren, L. J. G., et al. (1995). Gender differences in behaviour: Activating effects of cross-sex hormones. *Psychoneuroendocrinology, 20*(4) 343–363.

Van Iddekinge, C. H., Putka, D. J., & Campbell, J. P. (2011). Reconsidering vocational interests for personnel selection: The validity of an interest-based selection test in relation to job knowledge, job performance, and continuance intentions. *Journal of Applied Psychology, 96*(1), 13–33.

Van Lawick-Goodall J. (1971). *In the shadow of man*. New York: Houghton Mifflin.

Van Rooij, J. J. F. (1994). Introversion–extraversion: Astrology versus psychology. *Personality & Individual Differences, 16*(6), 985–988.

Van Volkom, M. (2009). The effects of childhood tomboyism and family experiences on the self-esteem of college females. *College Student Journal, 43*(3), 736–743.

Van Vugt, M. (2009). Averting the tragedy of the commons: Using social psychological science to protect the environment. *Current Directions in Psychological Science, 18*(3), 169–173.

Van Vugt, M. (2002). Central, individual, or collective control? Social dilemma strategies for natural resource management. *American Behavioral Scientist, 45*(5), 783–800.

Vandell, D. L. (2004). Early child care: The known and the unknown. *Merrill-Palmer Quarterly, 50(3)*, 387–414.

Vanheule, S., Vandenbergen, J., Verhaeghe, P., et al. (2010). Interpersonal problems in alexithymia: A study in three primary care groups. *Psychology & Psychotherapy: Theory, Research & Practice, 83*(4), 351–362.

Vargas-Perez, H., Ting-A-Kee, R., & van der Kooy, D. (2009). Different neural systems mediate morphine reward and its spontaneous withdrawal aversion. *European Journal of Neuroscience, 29*(10), 2029–2034.

Vasa, R. A., Carlino, A. R., & Pine, D. S. (2006). Pharmacotherapy of depressed children and adolescents: Current issues and potential directions. *Biological Psychiatry, 59*(11), 1021–1028.

Veale, J. F., Clarke, D. E., & Lomax, T. C. (2010). Biological and psychosocial correlates of adult gender-variant identities: A review. *Personality & Individual Differences, 48*(4), 357–366.

Velakoulis, D., & Pantelis, C. (1996). What have we learned from functional imaging studies in schizophrenia? *Australian & New Zealand Journal of Psychiatry, 30*(2), 195–209.

Venezia, M., Messinger, D. S., Thorp, D., et al. (2004). The development of anticipatory smiling. *Infancy, 6*(3), 397–406.

Vi, P. (2006). A field study investigating the effects of a rebar-tying machine on trunk flexion, tool usability and productivity. *Ergonomics, 49*(14), 1437–1455.

Videon, T. M. (2005). Parent-child relations and children's psychological well-being: Do dads matter? *Journal of Family Issues, 26*(1), 55–78.

Viegener, B. J., Perri, M. G., Nezu, A. M., et al. (1990). Effects of an intermittent, low-fat low-calorie diet in the behavioral treatment of obesity. *Behavior Therapy, 21*(4), 499–509.

Viero, C., Shibuya, I., Kitamura, N., et al. (2010). Oxytocin: Crossing the bridge between basic science and pharmacotherapy. *CNS Neuroscience & Therapeutics, 16*(5), e138–e156.

Visser, B. A., Bay, D., Cook, G. L., et al. (2010). Psychopathic and antisocial, but not emotionally intelligent. *Personality & Individual Differences, 48*(5), 644–648.

Viveros, M. P., Llorente, R., Moreno, E., et al. (2005). Behavioural and neuroendocrine effects of cannabinoids in critical developmental periods. *Behavioural Pharmacology, 16*(5–6), 353–362.

Vogel, E. K., Woodman, G. F., & Luck, S. J. (2006). The time course of consolidation in visual working memory. *Journal of Experimental Psychology: Human Perception & Performance, 32*(6), 1436–1451.

Vogler, R. E., & Bartz, W. R. (1992). *Teenagers and alcohol*. Philadelphia: Charles Press.

Vogler, R. E., Weissbach, T. A., Compton, J. V., et al. (1977). Integrated behavior change techniques for problem drinkers in the community. *Journal of Consulting & Clinical Psychology, 45*, 267–279.

Vojdanoska, M., Cranney, J., & Newell, B. R. (2010). The testing effect: The role of feedback and collaboration in a tertiary classroom setting. *Applied Cognitive Psychology, 24*(8), 1183–1195.

Volkow, N. D., Fowler, J. S., Wang, G.-J., et al. (2007). Dopamine in drug abuse and addiction: Results of imaging studies and treatment implications. *Archives of Neurology, 64*(11), 1575–1579.

Volkow, N. D., Gillespie, H., Mullani, N., et al. (1996). Brain glucose metabolism in chronic marijuana users at baseline and during marijuana intoxication. *Psychiatry Research: Neuroimaging, 67*(1), 29–38.

Volpicelli, J. R., Ulm, R. R., Altenor, A., et al. (1983). Learned mastery in the rat. *Learning & Motivation, 14*, 204–222.

Vuillermot, S., Weber, L., Feldon, J., et al. (2010). A longitudinal examination of the neurodevelopmental impact of prenatal immune activation in mice reveals primary defects in dopaminergic development relevant to schizophrenia. *Journal of Neuroscience, 30*(4), 1270–1287.

Vygotsky, L. S. (1962). *Thought and language*. Cambridge, MA: MIT Press.

Vygotsky, L. S. (1978). *Mind in society*. Cambridge, MA: Harvard University Press.

Wade, K. A., Green, S. L., & Nash, R. A. (2010). Can fabricated evidence induce false eyewitness testimony? *Applied Cognitive Psychology, 24*(7), 899–908.

Wager, T. D., Rilling, J. K., Smith, E. E., et al. (2004). Placebo-induced changes in fMRI in the anticipation and experience of pain. *Science, 303*(Feb 20), 1162–1166.

Wagstaff, G., Brunas-Wagstaff J., Cole, J., et al. (2004). New directions in forensic hypnosis: Facilitating memory with a focused meditation technique. *Contemporary Hypnosis, 21*(1), 14–27.

Waid, W. M., & Orne, M. T. (1982). The physiological detection of deception. *American Scientist, 70*(July/Aug.), 402–409.

Wainright, J. L., Russell, S. T., & Patterson, C. J. (2004). Psychosocial adjustment, school outcomes, and romantic relationships of adolescents with same-sex parents. *Child Development, 75*(6), 1886–1898.

Waiter, G. D., Deary, I. J., Staff, R. T., et al. (2009). Exploring possible neural mechanisms of intelligence differences using processing speed and working memory tasks: An fMRI study. *Intelligence, 37*(2), 199–206.

Wakefield, J. C. (1992). The concept of mental disorder. *American Psychologist, 47*(3), 373–388.

Waldinger, M. D. (2009). Delayed and premature ejaculation. In R. Balon, & R. T. Segraves (Eds.), *Clinical manual of sexual disorders* (pp. 267–292). Arlington, VA: American Psychiatric Publishing.

Walker, D. L., & Davis, M. (2008). Role of the extended amygdala in short-duration versus sustained fear: A tribute to Dr. Lennart Heimer. *Brain Structure & Function, 213*(1-2), 29–42.

Walker, E., Kestler, L. Bollini, A., et al. (2004). Schizophrenia: Etiology and course. *Annual Review of Psychology, 55*, 401–430.

Walker, I., & Crogan, M. (1998). Academic performance, prejudice, and the Jigsaw classroom. *Journal of Community & Applied Social Psychology, 8*(6), 381–393.

Walker, M. P., & Stickgold, R. (2006). Sleep, memory, and plasticity. *Annual Review of Psychology, 57*, 139–166.

Wallach, M. A., & Kogan, N. (1965). *Modes of thinking in young children*. New York: Holt.

Walton, C. E., Bower, M. L., & Bower, T. G. (1992). Recognition of familiar faces by newborns. *Infant Behavior & Development, 15*(2), 265–269.

Wampold, B. E. (2007). Psychotherapy: The humanistic (and effective) treatment. *American Psychologist, 62*(8), 857–873.

Wampold, B. E., Minami T., Tierney, S. C., et al. (2005). The placebo is powerful: Estimating placebo effects in medicine and psychotherapy from randomized clinical trials. *Journal of Clinical Psychology, 61(7)*, 835–854.

Wampold, B. E., Mondin, G. W., Moody, M., et al. (1997). A meta-analysis of outcome studies comparing bona fide psychotherapies. *Psychological Bulletin, 122*(3), 203–215.

Wan, C. Y., Demaine, K., Zipse, L., et al. (2010). From music making to speaking: Engaging the mirror neuron system in autism. *Brain Research Bulletin, 82*(3-4), 161–168.

Wandersman, A., & Florin, P. (2003). Community interventions and effective prevention. *American Psychologist, 58*(6/7), 441–448.

Wang, Q., & Conway, M. A. (2004). The stories we keep: Autobiographical memory in American and Chinese middle-aged adults. *Journal of Personality, 72*(5), 911–938.

Wang, S. S., & Brownell, K. D. (2005). Public policy and obesity: The need to marry science with advocacy. *Psychiatric Clinics of North America, 28*(1), 235–252.

Wang, S.-H., & Morris, R. G. M. (2010). Hippocampal-neocortical interactions in memory formation, consolidation, and reconsolidation. *Annual Review of Psychology, 61*, 49–79.

Ward, L. M. (2004). Wading through the stereotypes: Positive and negative associations between media use and Black adolescents' conceptions of self. *Developmental Psychology, 40*, 284–294.

Ward, L., & Parr, J. M. (2010). Revisiting and reframing use: Implications for the integration of ICT. *Computers & Education, 54*(1), 113–122.

Wargo, E. (2007). Understanding the have-knots: The role of stress in just about everything. *APS Observer, 20*(11), 18–23.

Wargo, E. (2008). The many lives of superstition. *APS Observer, 21*(9), 18–24.

Wark, G. R., & Krebs, D. L. (1996). Gender and dilemma differences in real-life moral judgment. *Developmental Psychology, 32*(2), 220–230.

Warren, D. J., & Normann, R. A. (2005). Functional reorganization of primary visual cortex induced by electrical stimulation in the cat. *Vision Research, 45*, 551–565.

Washton, A. M., & Zweben, J. E. (2009). *Cocaine and methamphetamine addiction: Treatment, recovery, and relapse prevention*. New York, Norton.

Waterfield, R. (2002). *Hidden depths: The story of hypnosis*. London: Macmillan.

Watson, D. L., & Tharp, R. G. (2007). *Self-directed behavior* (9th ed.). Belmont, CA: Cengage Learning/Wadsworth.

Watson, J. B. (1913/1994). Psychology as the behaviorist views it. *Psychological Review, 101*(2), 248–253.

Watson, J. M., & Strayer, David L. (2010). Supertaskers: Profiles in extraordinary multitasking ability. *Psychonomic Bulletin & Review, 17*(4), 479–485.

Way, I., vanDeusen, K. M., Martin, G., et al. (2004). Vicarious trauma: A comparison of clinicians who treat survivors of sexual abuse and sexual offenders. *Journal of Interpersonal Violence, 19*(1), 49–71.

Waytz, A., Epley, N., & Cacioppo, J. T. (2010). Social cognition unbound: Insights into anthropomorphism and dehumanization. *Current Directions in Psychological Science, 19*(1), 58–62.

Weaver, Y. (2009). Mid-life: A time of crisis or new possibilities? *Existential Analysis, 20*(1), 69–78.

Wechsler, D. (1939). *The measurement of adult intelligence*. Baltimore: Williams & Wilkins.

Wechsler, D. (2008). *Wechsler Adult Intelligence Scale, Fourth Edition (WAIS-IV)*. San Antonio, TX: Pearson.

Wechsler, H., & Wuethrich, B. (2002). *Dying to drink*. Emmaus, PA: Rodale Books.

Wedding, D., & Corsini, R. J. (2011). *Case studies in psychotherapy* (6th ed.). Belmont, CA: Cengage Learning/Wadsworth.

Weekley, J. A., & Jones, C. (1997). Video-based situational testing. *Personnel Psychology*, 50(1), 25–49.

Wehr, T. A., Duncan, W. C., Sher, L., et al. (2001). A circadian signal of change of season in patients with seasonal affective disorder. *Archives of General Psychiatry, 58*(12), 1108–1114.

Weidenhammer, W., Linde, K., Streng, A., et al. (2007). Acupuncture for chronic low back pain in routine care: A multicenter observational study. *Clinical Journal of Pain, 23*(2), 128–135.

Weinberg, R. A. (1989). Intelligence and IQ. *American Psychologist, 44*(2), 98–104.

Weingarten, K. (2010). Reasonable hope: Construct, clinical applications, and supports. *Family Process, 49*(1), 5–25.

Weinstein, R. S., Gregory, A., & Strambler, M. J. (2004). Intractable self-fulfilling prophesies. *American Psychologist, 59*(6), 511–520.

Weinstein, Y., & Shanks, D. R. (2010). Rapid induction of false memory for pictures. *Memory, 18*(5), 533–542.

Weintraub, M. I. (1983). *Hysterical conversion reactions*. New York: SP Medical & Scientific Books.

Weintraub, S. (2003). Cognitive aging. In G. Adelman, & B. Smith (Eds.), *Encyclopedia of Neuroscience (CD-ROM)*. New York: Elsevier Science Publishers.

Weishaar, M. E. (2006). A cognitive-behavioral approach to suicide risk reduction in crisis intervention. In A. R. Roberts, & K. R. Yeager, (Eds.), *Foundations of evidence-based social work practice* (pp. 181–193). New York: Oxford University Press.

Weisskirch, R. S. (2005). Ethnicity and perceptions relationship to ethnic identity development. *International Journal of Intercultural Relations, 29*(3), 355–366.

Weissman, A. M., Jogerst, G. J., & Dawson, J. D. (2003). Community characteristics associated with child abuse in Iowa. *Child Abuse & Neglect, 27*(10), 1145–1159.

Weitzman, E. R. (2004). Poor mental health, depression, and associations with alcohol consumption, harm, and abuse in a national sample of young adults in college. *Journal of Nervous & Mental Disease, 192*(4), 269–277.

Welch, R. D., & Houser, M. E. (2010). Extending the four-category model of adult attachment: An interpersonal model of friendship attachment. *Journal of Social & Personal Relationships, 27*(3), 351–366.

Wellings, K., Collumbien, M., Slaymaker, E., et al. (2006). Sexual behaviour in context: A global perspective. *Lancet, 368*(9548), 1706–1738.

Wells, B. E., & Twenge, J. M. (2005). Changes in young people's sexual behavior and attitudes, 1943–1999: A cross-temporal meta-analysis. *Review of General Psychology, 9*(3), 249–261.

Wells, G. L. (2001). Police lineups: Data, theory, and policy. *Psychology, Public Policy, & Law, 7*(4), 791–801.

Wells, G. L., & Olsen, E. A. (2003). Eyewitness testimony. *Annual Review of Psychology, 54*, 277–295.

Wells, G. L., Memon, A., & Penrod, S. D. (2006). Eyewitness evidence: Improving its probative value. *Psychological Science in the Public Interest, 7*(2), 45–75.

Weltzin, T. E., Weisensel, N., Franczyk, D., et al. (2005). Eating disorders in men: Update. *Journal of Men's Health & Gender, 2*(2), 186–193.

Werner, C. M., & Makela, E. (1998). Motivations and behaviors that support recycling. *Journal of Environmental Psychology, 18*(4), 373–386.

Wernet, S. P., Follman, C., Magueja, C., et al. (2003). Building bridges and improving racial harmony: An evaluation of the Bridges Across Racial Polarization Program. In J. J. Stretch, E. M. Burkemper, et al. (Eds.), *Practicing social justice* (pp. 63–79). New York: Haworth Press.

Wertheimer, M. (1959). *Productive thinking*. New York: Harper & Row.

Wesensten, N. J., Belenky, G., Kautz, M. A., et al. (2002). Maintaining alertness and performance during sleep deprivation: Modafi nil versus caffeine. *Psychopharmacology, 159*(3), 238–247.

Wessel, I., & Wright, D. B. (Eds.). (2004). *Emotional memory failures*. Hove, UK: Psychology Press.

West, L. J. (1993). A psychiatric overview of cult-related phenomena. *Journal of the American Academy of Psychoanalysis, 21*(1), 1–19.

West, R., & Sohal, T. (2006). "Catastrophic" pathways to smoking cessation: Findings from national survey. *British Medical Journal, 332*(7539), 458–460.

West, T. G. (1991). *In the mind's eye*. Buffalo, NY: Prometheus.

Westen, D., & Bradley, R. (2005). Empirically supported complexity: Rethinking evidence-based practice in psychotherapy. *Current Directions in Psychological Science, 14*(5), 266–271.

Westera, W., Nadolski, R. J., Hummel, H. G. K., et al. (2008). Serious games for higher education: A framework for reducing design complexity. *Journal of Computer Assisted Learning, 24*(5), 420–432.

Westrin, Å., & Lam, R. W. (2007a). Seasonal affective disorder: A clinical update. *Annals of Clinical Psychiatry, 19*(4), 239–246.

Westrin, Å., & Lam, R. W. (2007b). Long-term and preventative treatment for seasonal affective disorder. *CNS Drugs, 21*(11), 901–909.

Wethington, E. (2003). Turning points as opportunities for psychological growth. In C. L. M. Keyes, & J. Haidt (Eds.), *Flourishing* (pp. 37–53). Washington, DC: American Psychological Association.

Wethington, E., Kessler, R. C., & Pixley, J. E. (2004). Turning points in adulthood. In O. G. Brim, C. D. Ryff, et al. (Eds.), *How healthy are we? A national study of well-being at midlife* (pp. 425–450). Chicago, IL: University of Chicago Press.

Wexler, M. N. (1995). Expanding the groupthink explanation to the study of contemporary cults. *Cultic Studies Journal, 12*(1), 49–71.

Wheat, A. L., & Larkin, K. T. (2010). Biofeedback of heart rate variability and related physiology: A critical review. *Applied Psychophysiology & Biofeedback, 35*(3), 229–242.

Whipple, B. (2000). Beyond the G spot. *Scandinavian Journal of Sexology, 3*(2), 35–42.

White, J. (2006). *Intelligence, destiny and education: The ideological roots of intelligence testing*. New York: Brunner-Routledge.

Whitehouse, A. J. O., Maybery, M. T., & Durkin, K. (2006). The development of the picture-superiority effect. *British Journal of Developmental Psychology, 24*(4), 767–773.

Whitley, B. E., & Kite, M. E. (2010). *The psychology of prejudice and discrimination*, (2nd ed.). Belmont, CA: Cengage Learning/Wadsworth.

Whitton, E. (2003). *Humanistic approach to psychotherapy*. New York: Wiley.

Whyte, G. (2000). Groupthink. In A. E. Kazdin, (Ed.), *Encyclopedia of psychology* (Vol. 4, pp. 35–38). Washington, DC: American Psychological Association.

Wickwire, E. M., Whelan, J. P., & Meyers, A. W. (2010). Outcome expectancies and gambling behavior among urban adolescents. *Psychology of Addictive Behaviors, 24*(1), 75–88.

Widner R. L., Otani, H., & Winkelman, S. E. (2005). Tip-of-the-tongue experiences are not merely strong feeling-of-knowing experiences. *Journal of General Psychology, 132*(4), 392–407.

Wiederhold, B. K., & Wiederhold, M. D. (2005). Acrophobia. In B. K. Wiederhold & M. D. Wiederhold (Eds.), *Virtual reality therapy for anxiety disorders: Advances in evaluation and treatment* (pp. 157–164). Washington, DC: American Psychological Association.

Wiederman, M. W. (1999). Volunteer bias in sexuality research using college student participants. *Journal of Sex Research, 36*(1), 59–66.

Wiederman, M. W. (2001). Gender differences in sexuality: Perceptions, myths, and realities. *Family Journal-Counseling & Therapy for Couples & Families, 9*(4), 468–471.

Wigfield, A., & Eccles, J. (Eds.). (2002). *Development of achievement motivation*. San Diego: Academic Press.

Wilber, M. K., & Potenza, M. N. (2006). Adolescent gambling: Research and clinical implications. *Psychiatry, 3*(10), 40–46.

Wilder, D. A., Simon, A. F., & Faith, M. (1996). Enhancing the impact of counterstereotypic information. *Journal of Personality & Social Psychology, 71*(2), 276–287.

Wilding, J., & Valentine, E. (1994). Memory champions. *British Journal of Psychology, 85*(2), 231–244.

Wilkinson, D., & Abraham, C. (2004). Constructing an integrated model of the antecedents of adolescent smoking. *British Journal of Health Psychology, 9*(3), 315–333.

Wilkinson, M. (2006). The dreaming mindbrain: A Jungian perspective. *Journal of Analytical Psychology, 51*(1), 43–59.

Wilkinson, R. G., & Pickett, K. E. (2006). Income inequality and population health: A review and explanation of the evidence. *Social Science & Medicine, 62*(7), 1768–1784.

Wilkinson, R. G., & Pickett, K. E. (2007). The problems of relative deprivation: Why some societies do better than others. *Social Science & Medicine, 65*(9), 1965–1978.

Wilkinson, R. G., & Pickett, K. E. (2009). Income inequality and social dysfunction. *Annual Review of Sociology, 35*, 493–511.

Willander, J., & Larsson, M. (2006). Smell your way back to childhood: Autobiographical odor memory. *Psychonomic Bulletin & Review, 13*(2), 240–244.

Willems, R. M., Peelen, M. V., & Hagoort, P. (2010). Cerebral lateralization of face-selective and body-selective visual areas depends on handedness. *Cerebral Cortex, 20*(7), 1719–1725.

Williams, D. G., & Morris, G. (1996). Crying, weeping or tearfulness in British and Israeli adults. *British Journal of Psychology, 87*(3), 479–505.

Williams, G., Cai, X. J., Elliott, J. C., et al. (2004). Anabolic neuropeptides. *Physiology & Behavior. Special Reviews on Ingestive Science, 81*(2), 211–222.

Williams, J. M. (2010). *Applied sport psychology: Personal growth to peak performance* (6th ed.). New York: McGraw-Hill.

Williams, L. M., Senior, C. David, A. S., et al. (2001). In search of the "Duchenne Smile": Evidence from eye movements. *Journal of Psychophysiology, 15*(2), 122–127.

Williams, R. (1989). *The trusting heart: Great news about Type A behavior*. New York: Random House.

Williams, R. B., Barefoot, J. C., & Schneiderman, N. (2003). Psychosocial risk factors for cardiovascular disease: More than one culprit at work. *Journal of the American Medical Association, 290*(16), 2190–2192.

Williams, R. L. (1975). The Bitch-100: A culture-specific test. *Journal of Afro-American Issues, 3*, 103–116.

Williams, R. L., & Eggert, A. (2002). Note-taking predictors of test performance. *Teaching of Psychology, 29*(3), 234–237.

Williams, R. L., Agnew, H. W., & Webb, W. B. (1964). Sleep patterns in young adults: An EEG study. *Electroencephalography & Clinical Neurophysiology, 17*, 376–381.

Williams, R., & Vinson, D. C. (2001). Validation of a single screening question for problem drinking. *The Journal of Family Practice, 50*(4), 307–312.

Williams, J. M. (2010). *Applied sport psychology: Personal growth to peak performance* (6th ed.). New York: McGraw-Hill.

Williamson, D. A., Ravussin, E., Wong, M.-L., et al. (2005). Microanalysis of eating behavior of three leptin deficient adults treated with leptin therapy. *Appetite, 45*, 75–80.

Willoughby, T., Wood, E., Desmarais, S., et al. (1997). Mechanisms that facilitate the effectiveness of elaboration strategies. *Journal of Educational Psychology, 89*(4), 682–685.

Wilmot, W. W., & Hocker, J. L. (2007). *Interpersonal conflict* (7th ed.). Boston: McGraw-Hill.

Wilson, S. L. (2003). Post-institutionalization: The effects of early deprivation on development of Romanian adoptees. *Child & Adolescent Social Work Journal, 20*(6), 473–483.

Wilson, T. D. (2002). *Strangers to ourselves: Discovering the adaptive unconscious*. Cambridge Harvard University Press.

Wilson, T. D. (2009). Know thyself. *Perspectives on Psychological Science, 4*(4), 384–389.

Wilson, S. B., & Kennedy, J. H. (2006). Helping behavior in a rural and an urban setting: Professional and casual attire. *Psychological Reports, 98*(1), 229–233.

Wimpenny, J. H., Weir, A. A. S., Clayton, L., et al. (2009). Cognitive processes associated with sequential tool use in New Caledonian crows. *PLoS ONE, 4*(8): e6471. doi:10.1371/journal.pone.0006471. Retrieved March 22, 2011, from http://www.plosone.org/article/info%3Adoi%2F10.1371%2Fjournal.pone.0006471.

Winfree, Jr., L. T., & Jiang, S. (2010). Youthful suicide and social support: Exploring the social dynamics of suicide-related behavior and attitudes within a national sample of US adolescents. *Youth Violence & Juvenile Justice, 8*(1), 19–37.

Winger, G., Woods, J. H., Galuska, C. M., et al. (2005). Behavioral perspectives on the neuroscience of drug addiction. *Journal of the Experimental Analysis of Behavior, 84*(3), 667–681.

Wingood, G.M., DiClemente, R.J., Bernhardt, J.M., et al. (2003). A prospective study of exposure to rap music videos and African American female adolescents' health. *American Journal of Public Health, 93*, 437–439.

Winkleby, M., Ahn, D., & Cubbin, C. (2006). Effect of cross-level interaction between individual and neighborhood socioeconomic status on adult mortality rates. *American Journal of Public Health, 96*(12), 2145–2153.

Winner, E. (2003). Creativity and talent. In M. H. Bornstein, L. Davidson, C. L. M. Keyes, & K. Moore (Eds.), *Well-being: Positive development across the life course* (pp. 371–380). Mahwah, NJ: Erlbaum.

Winstead, B. A., & Sanchez, J. (2005). Gender and psychopathology. In J. E. Maddux, & B. A. Winstead (Eds.), *Psychopathology: Foundations for a contemporary understanding* (pp. 39–61). Mahwah, NJ: Erlbaum.

Winter, D. D. N., & Koger, S. M. (2010). *The psychology of environmental problems* (3rd ed.). New York: Psychology Press.

Wirth, M. M., Welsh, K. M., & Schultheiss, O. C. (2006). Salivary cortisol changes in humans after winning or losing a dominance contest depend on implicit power motivation. *Hormones & Behavior, 49*(3), 346–352.

Wise, R. A., & Safer, M. A. (2004). What U.S. judges know and believe about eyewitness testimony. *Applied Cognitive Psychology, 18*(4), 427–443.

Wise, R. A., & Safer, M. A. (2010). A comparison of what U.S. judges and students know and believe about eyewitness testimony. *Journal of Applied Social Psychology, 40*(6), 1400–1422.

Wiseman, R. (2009). *Owning up curriculum: Empowering adolescents to confront social cruelty, bullying, and injustice*. Champaign, IL: Research Press.

Wiseman, R., & Watt, C. (2006). Belief in psychic ability and the misattribution hypothesis: A qualitative review. *British Journal of Psychology, 97*(3), 323–338.

Witelson, S. F., Beresh, H., & Kigar, D. L. (2006). Intelligence and brain size in 100 postmortem brains: Sex, lateralization and age factors. *Brain: A Journal of Neurology, 129*(2), 386–398.

Witelson, S. F., Kigar, D. L., & Harvey, T. (1999). The exceptional brain of Albert Einstein. *Lancet, 353*, 2149–2153.

Witherington, D. C., Campos, J. J., Anderson, D. I., et al. (2005). Avoidance of heights on the visual cliff in newly walking infants. *Infancy, 7*(3), 285–298.

Wixted, J. T. (2004). The psychology and neuroscience of forgetting. *Annual Review of Psychology, 55*, 235–269.

Wixted, J. T. (2005). A theory about why we forget what we once knew. *Current Directions in Psychological Science, 14*(1), 6–9.

Wohl, M. J. A., Pychyl, T. A., & Bennett, S. H. (2010). I forgive myself, now I can study: How self-forgiveness for procrastinating can reduce future procrastination. *Personality & Individual Differences, 48*(7), 803–808.

Wolpe, J. (1974). *The practice of behavior therapy* (2nd ed.). New York: Pergamon.

Wolpin, M., Marston, A., Randolph, C., et al. (1992). Individual difference correlates of reported lucid dreaming frequency and control. *Journal of Mental Imagery, 16*(3-4), 231–236.

Wong, A. M., Hodges, H., & Horsburgh, K. (2005). Neural stem cell grafts reduce the extent of neuronal damage in a mouse model of global ischaemia. *Brain Research, 1063*(2), 140–150.

Wong, W. (2011). *Essential study skills* (7th ed.). Belmont, CA: Cengage Learning/Wadsworth.

Wood, E., & Willoughby, T. (1995). Cognitive strategies for test-taking. In E. Wood, V. Woloshyn, et al. (Eds.), *Cognitive strategy instruction for middle and high schools* (pp. 5–17). Cambridge, MA: Brookline Books.

Wood, J. M., Nezworski, M. T., Lilienfeld, S. O., et al. (2003). The Rorschach Inkblot test, fortune tellers, and cold reading. *Skeptical Inquirer, 27*(4), 29–33.

Woodhill, B. M., & Samuels, C. A. (2004). Desirable and undesirable androgyny: A prescription for the twenty-first century. *Journal of Gender Studies, 13*(1), 15–28.

Woodruff-Pak, D. S. (2001). Eyeblink classical conditioning differentiates normal aging from Alzheimer's disease. *Integrative Physiological & Behavioral Science, 36*(2), 87–108.

Woods, A. M., Racine, S. E., & Klump, K. L. (2010). Examining the relationship between dietary restraint and binge eating: Differential effects of major and minor stressors. *Eating Behaviors, 11*(4), 276–280.

Woods, S. C., Schwartz, M. W, Baskin, D. G., et al. (2000). Food intake and the regulation of body weight. *Annual Review of Psychology. 51*, 255–277.

Woods, S. & West, M. (2010). *The psychology of work and organizations*. Belmont, CA: Cengage Learning/Wadsworth.

Woroch, B., & Gonsalves, B. D. (2010). Event-related potential correlates of item and source memory strength. *Brain Research, 1317*, 180–191.

Worthen, J. B., & Hunt, R. R. (2010). *Mnemonology: Mnemonics for the 21st century*. Hove, UK: Psychology Press.

Worthen, J. B., & Marshall, P. H. (1996). Intralist and extralist sources of distinctiveness and the bizarreness effect. *American Journal of Psychology, 109*(2), 239–263.

Wraga, M. J., Boyle, H. K., & Flynn, C. M. (2010). Role of motor processes in extrinsically encoding mental transformations. *Brain & Cognition, 74*(3), 193–202.

Wraga, M., Shephard, J. M., Church, J. A., et al. (2005). Imagined rotations of self versus objects: An fMRI study. *Neuropsychologia, 43*(9), 1351–1361.

Wright, J. P., Dietrich, K. N., Ris, M. D., et al. (2008). Association of prenatal and childhood blood lead concentrations with criminal arrests in early adulthood. *Proceedings of the National Academy of Sciences, 5*(5), e101 doi:10.1371/journal.pmed.0050101.

Wright, Perry B., & Erdal, K. J. (2008). Sport superstition as a function of skill level and task difficulty. *Journal of Sport Behavior, 31*(2), 187–199.

Wright, T. A., & Bonett, D. G. (2007). Job satisfaction and psychological well-being as nonadditive predictors of workplace turnover. *Journal of Management, 33*(2), 141–160.

Wright, T. A., & Cropanzano, R. (2000). Psychological well-being and job satisfaction as predictors of job performance. *Journal of Occupational Health Psychology, 5*(1), 84–94.

Wrightsman, L. S., & Fulero, S. M. (2005). *Forensic psychology* (2nd ed.). Belmont, CA: Cengage Learning/Wadsworth.

Wrightsman, L. S., & Fulero, S. M. (2009). *Forensic psychology* (3rd ed.). Belmont, CA: Cengage Learning/Wadsworth.

Wu, C. W. H., & Kaas, J. H. (2002). The effects of long-standing limb loss on anatomical reorganization of the somatosensory afferents in the brainstem and spinal cord. *Somatosensory & Motor Research, 19*(2), 153–163.

Wyatt, J. W., Posey, A., Welker, W., et al. (1984). Natural levels of similarities between identical twins and between unrelated people. *The Skeptical Inquirer, 9*, 62–66.

Xu, T.-X., & Yao, W.-D. (2010). D1 and D2 dopamine receptors in separate circuits cooperate to drive associative long-term potentiation in the prefrontal cortex. Proceedings of the National Academy of Sciences, *107*(37), 16366–16371.

Yahnke, B. H., Sheikh, A. A., & Beckman, H. T. (2003). Imagery and the treatment of phobic disorders. In A. A. Sheikh (Ed.), *Healing images: The role of imagination in health* (pp. 312–342). Amityville, NY: Baywood Publishing.

Yanchar, S. C., Slife, B. D., & Warne, R. (2008). Critical thinking as disciplinary practice. *Review of General Psychology, 12*(3), 265–281.

Yang, Y., Tang, L., Tong, L., et al. (2009). Silkworms culture as a source of protein for humans in space. *Advances in Space Research, 43*(2), 1236–1242.

Yang, S., & Zheng, L. (2011). The paradox of de-coupling: A study of flexible work program and workers' productivity. *Social Science Research*, 40(1), 299–311.

Yarmey, A. D. (2003). Eyewitness identification: Guidelines and recommendations for identification procedures in the United States and in Canada. *Canadian Psychology, 44*(3), 181–189.

Yedidia, M. J., & MacGregor, B. (2001). Confronting the prospect of dying. *Journal of Pain & Symptom Management, 22*(4), 807–819.

Yeh, C. J. (2003). Age, acculturation, cultural adjustment, and mental health symptoms of Chinese, Korean, and Japanese immigrant youths. *Cultural Diversity & Ethnic Minority Psychology, 9*(1), 34–48.

Yi, H., & Qian, X. (2009). A review on neurocognitive research in superior memory. *Psychological Science (China), 32*(3), 643–645.

Yip, P. S. F., & Thorburn, J. (2004). Marital status and the risk of suicide: Experience from England and Wales, 1982–1996. *Psychological Reports, 94*(2), 401–407.

Yokota, F., & Thompson, K. M. (2000). Violence in G-rated animated films. *Journal of the American Medical Association, 283*(20), 2716.

Yonas, A., Elieff, C. A., & Arterberry, M. E. (2002). Emergence of sensitivity to pictorial depth cues: Charting development in individual infants. *Infant Behavior & Development, 25*(4), 495–514.

Yontef, G. (2007). The power of the immediate moment in gestalt therapy. *Journal of Contemporary Psychotherapy, 37*(1), 17–23.

Yost, W. A. (2007) *Fundamentals of hearing: An introduction* (5th ed.). San Diego, CA: Elsevier.

Young, R. (2005). Neurobiology of savant syndrome. In C. Stough (Ed.), *Neurobiology of exceptionality* (pp. 199–215). New York: Kluwer Academic Publishers.

Young, S. M., & Pinsky, D. (2006). Narcissism and celebrity. *Journal of Research in Personality, 40*(5), 463–471.

Yuille, J. C., & Daylen, J. (1998). The impact of traumatic events on eyewitness memory. In C. Thompson, D. Herrmann, et al. (Eds.), *Eyewitness memory: Theoretical and applied perspectives* (pp. 155–178). Mahwah, NJ: Erlbaum.

Zachariae, R. (2009). Psychoneuroimmunology: A bio-psycho-social approach to health and disease. *Scandinavian Journal of Psychology, 50*(6), 645–651.

Zampetakis, L. A., & Moustakis, V. (2011). Managers' trait emotional intelligence and group outcomes: The case of group job satisfaction. *Small Group Research, 42*(1), 77–102.

Zarcadoolas, C., Pleasant, A., & Greer, D. S. (2006). *Advancing health literacy: A framework for understanding and action*. San Francisco: Jossey-Bass.

Zarraga, C., & Bonache, J. (2005). The impact of team atmosphere on knowledge outcomes in self-managed teams. *Organization Studies, 26*(5), 661–681.

Zeidan, F., Johnson, S. K., Gordon, N. S., et al. (2010). Effects of brief and sham mindfulness meditation on mood and cardiovascular variables. *Journal of Alternative & Complementary Medicine, 16*(8), 867–873.

Zeiler, K., & Wickström, A. (2009). Why do 'we' perform surgery on newborn intersexed children? The phenomenology of the parental experience of having a child with intersex anatomies. *Feminist Theory, 10*(3), 359–377.

Zeisel, J. (2006). *Inquiry by design: Environment/behavior/neuroscience in architecture, interiors, landscape, and planning*. New York: Norton.

Zellner, D. A., Harner, D. E., & Adler, R. L. (1989). Effects of eating abnormalities and gender on perceptions of desirable body shape. *Journal of Abnormal Psychology, 98*(1), 93–96.

Zemishlany, Z., Aizenberg, D., & Weizman, A. (2001). Subjective effects of MDMA ("Ecstasy") on human sexual function. *European Psychiatry, 16*(2), 127–130.

Zentall, T. R. (2002). A cognitive behaviorist approach to the study of animal behavior. *Journal of General Psychology, 129*(4), 328–363.

Zentall, T. R. (2005). Animals may not be stuck in time. *Learning and Motivation, 36*(2), 208–225.

Zentner, M., & Renaud, O. (2007). Origins of adolescents' ideal self: An intergenerational perspective. *Journal of Personality & Social Psychology, 92*(3), 557–574.

Zetlin, A., & Murtaugh, M. (1990). Whatever happened to those with borderline IQs? *American Journal on Mental Retardation, 94*(5), 463–469.

Zhang R. L., Zhang Z. G., & Chopp, M. (2005). Neurogenesis in the adult ischemic brain: generation, migration, survival, and restorative therapy. *Neuroscientist, 11*(5), 408–416.

Zhang, B., Hao, Y. L., Jia, F. J., et al. (2010). Fatal familial insomnia: A middle-age-onset Chinese family kindred. *Sleep Medicine, 11*(5), 498–499.

Zimbardo, P. (2007). *The Lucifer Effect: Understanding how good people turn evil*. New York: Random House.

Zimbardo, P. G., Haney, C., & Banks, W. C. (1973). A Pirandellian prison. *The New York Times Magazine*, April 8.

Zimbardo, P. G., Pilkonis, P. A., & Norwood, R. M. (1978). The social disease called shyness. In *Annual editions, personality and adjustment 78/79*. Guilford, CT: Dushkin.

Ziv, I., Leiser, D., & Levine, J. (2011). Social cognition in schizophrenia: Cognitive and affective factors. *Cognitive Neuropsychiatry, 16*(1), 71–91.

Zrenner, E., Bartz-Schmidt K. U., Benav, H., et al. (2010). Subretinal electronic chips allow blind patients to read letters and combine them to words. *Proceedings of the Royal Society*, doi: 10.1098/rspb.2010.1747. Retrieved December 16, 2010 from http://rspb.royalsocietypublishing.org/content/early/2010/11/01/rspb.2010.1747.full.pdf+html.

Zucker, K. J. & Spitzer, R. L. (2005). Was the Gender Identity Disorder of Childhood Diagnosis introduced into DSM-III as a backdoor maneuver to replace Homosexuality? A historical note. *Journal of Sex & Marital Therapy, 31*(1), 31–42.

Zuckerman, M. (2002). Genetics of sensation seeking. In J. Benjamin, R. P. Ebstein, et al. (Eds.), *Molecular genetics and the human personality* (pp. 193–210). Washington, DC: American Psychiatric Publishing.

Zuckerman, M., & Tsai, F-R. (2005). Costs of self-handicapping. *Journal of Personality, 73*(2), 411–442.

Zuckerman, M., Kieffer, S. C., & Knee, C. R. (1998). Consequences of self-handicapping. *Journal of Personality & Social Psychology, 74*(6), 1619–1628.

Name Index

A
Aamodt, M. G., 604, 606–607, 609
Aarts, H., 337
Abdallah, B., 59
Abe, N., 354
Abel, J. R., 311, 374, 386
Abell, S. C., 418
Abernethy, A. P., 182
Abma, J. C., 387
Abmadian, A., 321
Abolhasani, M., 321
Abraham, C., 232
Abraham, J., 100
Abraham, W. C., 262
Abrahamse, D. J., 616
Abrahamse, L. S., 616
Abrahamse, W., 220
Abrahamson, D. J., 396
Abrahamson, L. S., 396
Abrams, D. B., 192
Abramson, L. Y., 460
Abuhamdeh, S., 344, 624
Accordino, D. B., 410
Accordino, M. P., 410
Acebo, C., 169
Acitelli, L. K., 493
Adair, K. C., 183
Adams, G., 480
Adams, H. E., 390, 499
Adams, J. W., 243, 289, 297
Adams, M., 255
Adams-Curtis, L. E., 389–390, 587
Adamson, K., 72
Adan, A., 190
Addis, K. M., 252
Addis, M. E., 568
Addison, T., 587
Adityanjee, 484
Adler, A., 26, 415
Adler, S. A., 127
Adolphs, R., 68, 352, 355
Adorno, T. W., 590–591
Adults and Children Together Against Violence, 588
Advisory Council on the Misuses of Drugs, 190
Aguinis, H., 604
Ahern, J., 451
Ahima, R. S., 336
Ahluwalia, M. K., 590
Ahmad, S. A., 316
Ahn, D., 450
Ainsworth, M., 94
Aizenberg, D., 190
Ajzen, I., 554, 556
Akerstedt, T., 171
Akert, R. M., 16, 553, 566, 583
Akishita, M., 375
al'Absi, M., 466
Al-Timimi, N. R., 98
Alaoui, S., 465
Albarracín, D., 554
Alberti, R., 571
Alberto, P. A., 218, 227–228
Albino, A., 95
Albonetti, S., 489
Albrecht, C. M., 550
Albrecht, D. E., 550
Albright, D. L., 524
Albritton, M. D., 608
Alcock, J. E., 159
Aldhous, P., 159
Alegre, A., 363
Alexander, G. M., 74
Algoe, S. B., 393–394
Ali, F., 494
Ali, M. M., 444
Alir, J. M. J., 528
Alkire, M. T., 62
Allen, B. A., 324
Allen, D., 445
Allen, J. L., 85, 94, 583
Allen, J. S., 250
Allen, K., 470
Allen, M., 622
Alleyne, M. D., 597
Allik, J., 406
Allin, J. D., 306
Allison Kempe, A., 340
Allport, G., 407–408, 590
Altemeyer, B., 590
Altenor, A., 459
Alter, A. L., 592
Althof, S., 396–397
Altman Weiss, K., 434
Altman, L. K., 392
Altschuler, G. C., 422
Alves, R. S. C., 176
Alwin, D. F., 556
Ama, E., 598
Amabile, T. M., 290, 293, 298, 349–350
Amato, P. R., 87, 118
Ambady, N., 294
American Lung Association, 192
American Psychiatric Association, 187, 314, 379, 385, 395–397, 477–479, 481–484, 486–488, 492, 496–498, 500, 503, 534
American Psychological Association, 22, 28, 30–31, 33–34, 280, 373, 388, 537
American Psychological Association Task Force, 388
Amir, N., 253
Ammerén, G., 191
Ammirati, R., 20
Amsel, L., 451
Ancis, J. R., 480
Andersen, M. L., 176
Anderson K. J., 585, 592
Anderson, C. A., 5, 232–233, 233, 246, 248, 260, 268, 289, 452, 584–857
Anderson, D. I., 149–150
Anderson, J. K, 590
Anderson, J. R., 266–267
Anderson, K. J., 597
Anderson, M. C., 242, 259
Anderson, N. B., 452
Anderson, S., 459
Anderson, S. W., 250
Andrasik, F., 465
André, C., 529
Andresen, J., 183
Andrew, D. W., 394
Andrew, S., 177, 606
Anekonda, T. S., 444
Angermeyer, M. C., 442
Annett, M., 79
Anthony, M., 141
Anthony, S. H., 298
Antoni, C., 606
Antoni, M. H., 448
Antonuccio, D. O., 520
Antony, M. M., 436, 549
Anwyl, R., 262
Arauz, R. M., 308
Arbona, C. B., 523
Archer, T., 184
Arenander, A., 183
Ariely, D., 7, 375
Aristotle, 363
Arkowitz, H., 513
Arner, E., 336
Arnett, J. J., 107, 109
Arnow, B. A., 528
Arntz, A., 56
Aron, A., 577, 579
Aron, A. P., 360
Aronow, E., 434
Aronson, E., 16, 553, 557, 566, 583, 595–596, 598
Aronson, J., 324, 592
Aronson, K., 194
Arterberry, M. E., 150
Arthur, W., 410
Artz, S., 425
Ary, D. V., 186
Asada, K.J. K., 281
Asch, S., 562
Ash, D. W., 266
Ashby, F. G., 278
Ashcraft, D., 413, 421, 435
Ashton, M. C., 55, 407
Asmundson, G. J. G., 464
Asokan, T., 627
Assanand, S., 338–339
Assel, M. A., 106
Assoun, S., 73
Astell, A. J., 259
Athenasiou, R., 387
Atkin, D. J., 607
Atkinson, A. P., 355
Atkinson, M., 346, 531
Atkinson, R. C., 242
Attanucci, J., 110
Aucoin, K. J., 118, 228
Aussprung, J., 468
Austin, D. W., 537
Avenell, A., 442
Averill, J. R., 549
Avery, D. H., 494–595
Avila-Mora, E., 621
Awadallah, N., 500
Axelsson, J., 170
Axmacher, N., 457
Ayers, L., 293
Ayllon, T/, 525
Ayman, 605
Azraela, D., 586

B
Baard, P. P., 349
Babbie, E. R., 641
Babelay, A. M., 404
Bachman, J. G., 112
Backs-Dermott, G. J., 518
Baddeley, A., 242–243, 246, 248, 260, 268
Baer, D., 522
Baer, J. M., 290, 293
Baer, L., 529
Bahr, S. J., 96
Bahramali, H., 314
Bahrick, L. E., 100
Bailey, C. H., 262
Bailey, J. M., 373
Bailey, L. M., 78
Baillargeon, R., 105
Baillie, A., 342, 506
Bain, S. K., 306
Bajracharya, S. M., 389
Baker, T. B., 191
Bakich, I., 395
Bakker, A. B., 448
Bakker, G. M., 539
Balcomb, K. C. III, 33
Baldo, O., 395–396
Baldry, C., 605
Baldwin, J., 370–372
Balk, D. E., 434
Ball, T. M., 263, 276
Ballargeon, R., 106
Ballinger, K. M., 183, 469
Ballon, B., 46
Balsam, K. F., 373
Baltes, B. B., 607
Banaji, M. R., 590, 597
Bandura, A., 227, 231, 423, 449, 523, 585–586, 593
Banich, M. T., 52, 68, 319
Bank, B. J., 578
Banker, B. S., 595
Banks, A., 373
Banks, W. C., 548
Bar-Eli, M., 624
Bar-Tal, D., 591
Barabasz, A., 180
Barber, N., 182, 304, 308, 318
Bard, C., 156
Bard, P., 358–359
Bardone-Cone, A. M., 340, 341
Barefoot, J. C., 466
Barelds, D. P. H., 579
Bargh, J. A., 578
Barkataki, L., 490
Barker, E. T., 109
Barkham, M., 531
Barlow, D. H., 396, 459, 479–480, 484, 486, 490, 496, 498, 501–502, 506, 514, 616
Barnet, A. B., 318486
Barnet, R. J., 318
Barnett, J., 34
Barnier, A. J., 182
Baron, I. S., 306
Baron, R. A., 548, 561–562, 598
Baron-Cohen, S., 105, 370
Barras, C., 627
Barrett, D., 77, 200
Barrett, H. C., 288
Barrett, H. M., 259
Barrett, L. F., 445
Barrick, M. R., 610
Barron, F., 292
Barroso, C., 598
Barrowcliff, A. L., 484
Barry, S. R., 149
Bartholow, B. D., 233, 586–587
Bartram, B., 555
Bartz-Schmidt, K. U., 128
Basadur, M., 299
Basch, J., 193
Baskin, D. G., 335
Basner, M., 170
Bass, J., 333
Bassetti, C., 177
Basson, R., 380, 396
Bastian, B., 280
Batelaan, N. M., 496

Bates, T. C., 319
Batey, M., 295, 363
Bath, H., 118
Batra, L., 526
Batson, J. A., 583
Batterham, R. L., 337
Bauer, J. J., 420
Baum, A., 447, 618–619
Bauman, K., 482
Bauman, L. J., 392
Baumeister, R. F., 30, 406, 548, 551, 554, 567, 576, 583
Baumrind, D., 96, 97, 118, 227–228
Baumwell, L., 100
Baur, K., 343, 370, 379, 382, 386, 388, 395
Bauseman, R., 386
Bavaria, A. J., 15
Baxter, D., 618
Bay, D., 503
Bazzini, D. G., 577
Bearison, D. J., 106–107
Bearman, P.S., 390
Beaton, S., 293
Beatrice, B., 100
Beck, A.T., 527
Beck, B. L., 6
Beck, D. M., 145
Beck, H. P., 211, 417
Beck, J., 175
Beck, K. D., 226
Beck, R. C., 348
Becker, S. W., 584
Beckerley, S. E., 555
Beckman, H. T., 523
Beckstead, L., 372
Beeber, L. S., 88
Beeman, M. J., 66
Beer, J., 375
Beerlipalacio, A., 220
Beersma, D. G. M., 333
Bègue, L., 597
Behar, A., 192
Behnke, S. H., 34
Behrend, D. A., 260
Beike, D. R., 260
Beirne-Smith, M., 315
Beiser, M., 463
Bekinschtein, 208
Belenky, G., 190
Belicki, K., 176
Bell, D., 247
Bell, P. A., 612
Bell, R. C., 420
Bell, R. L., 217
Bellezza, F. S., 168, 264
Belsky, J., 95
Bem, S., 378
Ben-Shakar, G., 18, 354
Ben-Ze'ev, A., 551
Benav, H., 128
Benbow, C. P., 79, 293
Benedetti, F., 38, 464
Benjafield, J. G., 24, 180, 213, 286, 304
Benjamin, L. T., Jr., 24
Benjamin, O., 281
Benloucif, S., 88
Bennett, E. A., 621
Bennett, E. L., 88
Bennett, S. H., 6
Benoit, S. C., 335
Bensafi, M., 137–138
Bensley, L., 233
Benson, H., 183
Benson, J., 285
Bentley, A. C., 87
Bentley, D. L., 612
Beresh, H., 64
Bergeron, S., 398
Bergman, H., 184
Berkowitz, L., 559
Berliner, L., 168
Berman, S., 100
Berman, S. L., 501
Bernard, C., 156
Berne, E., 533
Bernhardt, J. M., 233
Bernstein, D. M., 247, 260
Bernstein, I. H., 493, 528
Bernthal, M. J., 233
Berntsen, D., 255
Berride, K. C., 187
Berry, D. S., 577
Berry, J. W., 463
Bersceid, E., 576
Berscheid, E., 577–578
Bersoff, 422
Bertenthal, B. I., 68
Bertholf, M., 427
Bertrand, F., 176
Bertsch, G. J., 226
Beseler, C. L., 194
Besnard, D., 259
Best, D., 376
Betancur, C., 78
Betts, J. M., 161
Beyer, M., 606
Beyer-Flores, C., 385
Beyers, W., 112
Bezruchka, S., 450
Bhatt, R. S., 145
Bhattacaryya,S., 592
Bhugra, D., 480
Bhushan, B., 78
Bialystok, E., 282
Bickman, L., 559
Bieliauskas, L. M., 42, 489
Biesanz, J. C., 577
Biggers, J., 334
Biglan, A., 186
Bilbace, R., 392
Bilker, W. B., 63
Billiard, M., 177
Bilner, B., 261
Binder, J. L., 514, 531, 595
Binet, A., 304
Binik, Y. M., 384, 397
Binning, K. R., 594, 597
Birnbaum, M. H., 43
Biro, F. M., 108
Bisson, J. I., 451
Bitensky, S. H., 228
Bixler, E. O., 311
Bjork, R. A., 45
Bjorklund, D. F., 104
Black, M. M., 87
Blackmore, C., 168
Blackmore, S., 17, 183
Blackwell, D. L., 577
Blair, I. V., 590
Blair, K. S., 504
Blakely, G., 608
Blakemore, C., 127
Blanchard, D. C., 584
Blanchard, E. B., 212, 523
Blanchard, R. J., 386, 584
Blascovich, J., 470
Blatner, A., 535
Bloch, M., 494
Bloch, S., 515
Blommel, J. M., 560
Blood, A. J., 74
Blood, G. W., 556
Blood, I. M., 556
Bloom, B., 347, 537
Bloom, C. M., 269
Bloom, R. L., 66
Bluff, L. A., 39–40
Blum, J. S., 577
Blumenthal, J. A., 443, 468
Blundon, J. A., 262
Blunt, J. R., 5–6
Boals, A., 470
Bobic, M. P., 604
Bockhoorn, K., 59
Bockting, W. O., 379, 383
Bodin, S. D., 118, 228
Bodner, E., 115
Boduroglu, A, 155
Boduroglu, A., 155
Boeckmann, M., 530
Boergers, J., 506
Boettiger, C. A., 68
Bogaert, A. F., 372
Boggild, M., 144
Boggio, P., 534
Bohannon, J. N., 99
Bohlin, G., 94, 95
Bohner, G., 554
Boisjoli, 525
Boivin, D. B., 352
Boksa, P., 142
Boland, J. E., 155
Bolbecker, A. R., 208
Boldero, J. M., 420
Bollini, A., 488–489, 491, 528
Bolte, M. A., 494–495
Boly, M., 72
Bonache, J., 606
Bonanno, G. A., 363
Bond, R., 562
Bonenfant, S., 79
Bonett, D. G., 606
Bongard, S., 466
Bonham, V., 324, 593, 598
Boniecki, K. A., 595
Bonk, W. J., 252
Bood, S., 184
Boodoo, G., 312, 317, 323, 325
Booij, L., 55
Booker, J. M., 494
Bora, E., 490
Bornstein, M. H., 87, 100
Bornstein, R. F., 483
Borod, J. C., 66
Boroditsky, L., 281–282, 288
Borrie, R. A., 184
Borzekowski, D. L. G., 341
Boskey, E., 281
Botes, A., 110
Botly, L. C. P., 334
Botti, S., 296
Bottini, E., 336
Bouchard, T. L., 312, 317, 323, 325, 425
Bouchoux, A., 191
Boudjeltia, K. A., 170
Bourgeois, J. A., 464
Bourhis, R. Y., 590
Bourne, E. J., 523
Bourne, V. J., 79
Boussaud, D., 231
Boutros, N., 67
Bovbjerg, D. H., 447
Bowe, F., 621
Bower, G. H., 245, 257
Bower, M. L., 92
Bower, T. G., 92
Bowers, K. S., 248
Bowker, A., 623
Bowling, N. A., 606
Boyd, C. J., 281
Boyle, M. P., 556
Boyle, S. H., 465
Bradbury, T. N., 576
Bradely, R., 531
Bradley, J. C., 611
Bradley, M. M., 504
Bradley, R. T., 346
Bradshaw, C., 281
Bradshaw, G. S., 622
Bradshaw, S. D., 435
Braid, J., 180
Brainerd, C. J., 103
Bramerson, A., 138
Brammer, R., 534
Bramsen, L., 499
Brand, S., 175
Brandon, T. H., 191
Branigan, C., 363
Brannon, L., 414, 442, 461
Branscombe, N. R., 548, 561, 598
Bransford, J. D., 279
Braun, K. A., 247
Braun-LaTour, K. A., 247
Breakspear, M., 59
Breedlove, S. M., 52, 374
Brehm, S. S., 550, 576–578
Bremner, J. D., 262, 498
Bremner, L., 105
Brennan, F. X., 226
Bresalu, N., 191
Brescoll, V. L., 376, 605
Bressan, P., 148
Bressi, C., 489
Bretherton, R., 517
Brewer, J. L., 256
Brewer, J. S., 384
Brewer, M., 618
Brewer, N., 623
Briand, L. A., 55
Brickman, A. M., 66
Bridges, A. J., 587
Bridges, K. M. B., 92
Bridgett, D. J., 89
Brief, A. P., 606
Briere, J., 504
Brievik, G., 346
Briggs, T. E., 607
Brinkman, H., 561
Brinton, R. D., 59
Britt, T. W., 595
Brobst, K. E., 2
Brocato, R. M., 560
Brock, T. C., 556
Brodley, B. T., 516
Brody, N., 311, 318
Broekaert, E., 530
Brohawn, D. G., 489
Bromfield, J. M., 417
Bromley, D. G., 569
Brondolo, E., 594
Brooks, F. R., 500
Brooks, M., 321, 464
Brooks-Gunn, J., 97, 108
Broom, A., 116
Brothen, T., 6
Brotto, L. A., 372, 380, 396
Brower, A. M., 193
Brown, A. S., 251, 488
Brown, E., 147
Brown, G., 612
Brown, K. W., 184
Brown, M. J., 621
Brown, P., 91, 483
Brown, R., 192, 251, 261, 595
Brown, S. A., 194, 556
Brown, S. D., 404, 406, 410
Brown, S. G., 77
Brown, S. L., 467, 592, 622
Brown, T. A., 459, 486, 496, 498, 502, 514
Brown, V., 299
Browne, B. A., 377
Browne, K., 187, 386
Browne, N., 18
Brownell, K. D., 339
Brownwell, P., 517
Bruce, D., 267
Bruch, M. A., 435
Brumbaugh, C. C., 579
Brunas-Wagstaff, J., 182
Brunel, M. -L., 355
Bruner, J., 2
Brunet, P. M., 435
Bruno, F., 627

Bruyn, J., 78
Bryan, A., 380
Bryan, C. S., 404
Bryant, J. B., 247, 621
Bryant, R. A., 451
Bryden, P. J., 78
Bucci, W., 514
Büchert, M., 491
Buck, J. A., 621
Buckely, K. E., 232
Buckle, P., 626
Buckley, J. A., 431
Buckner, J. D., 196
Buckwalter, M., 576
Buckworth, J., 350
Buddie, A. M., 196
Budney, A. J., 196
Buehner, M. J., 145
Buffalo, E. A., 261
Bugelski, R., 590
Bugental, J. F. T., 27
Bull, R., 267
Buller, D. J., 581
Bullmore, E., 480
Bulotta, S., 190
Bunde, J., 465
Bundrick, C. M., 418
Bundy, H., 489
Bunn, G. C., 354
Bunting, M. F., 148
Burchinal, M. R., 95
Burger, J., 564–566
Burger, J. M., 214, 404, 427, 429, 433
Burgess, C. A., 248
Burgess, M. C. R., 256
Burka, J. B., 5, 7, 460
Burke, D., 59
Burkman, L. J., 197
Burlingame, G. M., 535, 541
Burnett, R. C., 279
Burns, G. W., 515
Burns, J., 159
Burns, T., 530
Burton, C. M., 470
Burton, D. L., 386
Burtt, H. E., 253
Buschkuehl, M., 318–319
Bush, G., 183
Bushman, B. J., 452, 548, 551, 554, 567, 576, 583, 585–586
Bushnell, M. C., 141
Buss, D. M., 351, 404, 435, 580
Butcher, J. N., 432, 476
Butler, A. C., 518
Butler, B., 622
Butler, J. C., 591
Butler, M. G., 436
Butler, R., 344
Button, S. B., 609
Buyer, L. A., 299
Bybee, D., 420
Byrne, D., 548, 561, 598
Byrne, S. M., 342
Byrnes, J. P., 37

C
Cabanieu, G., 78
Cabrera, N. J., 97
Cacioppo, J. T., 40, 549, 593
Cacitti, L., 259
Cadet, J., 68
Cadinu, M., 592
Caharel, S., 156
Cahill, L., 70, 246
Cahn, B. R., 183
Cai, H., 406
Cai, X. J., 336–337
Calabrese, F., 493
Calabria, 186
Caldara, R., 256
Calhoun, J., 613
Calhoun, S. L., 311
Caliari, P., 624
Callahan, C. M., 312
Callahan, I., 18
Calvin, C. M., 311
Calvini, G., 280
Calzada, E. J., 97
Cambron, M. J., 493
Cameron, J., 350
Cameron, J. A., 597
Cammann, C., 549, 606
Cammaroto, S., 144
Campbell, B., 322
Campbell, F. A., 318
Campbell, J. D., 406
Campbell, J. P., 610
Campbell, L. C., 182, 322
Campbell, W. K., 406
Campion, J. E., 609
Campion, M. A., 609
Campos, J. J., 149–150
Canales, J. J., 59
Canivez, G. L., 310
Cannon, W., 335, 358–359
Cantor, J. M., 386
Cao, Y., 59
Caplan, P. J., 483
Caprariello, P. A., 576
Capron, C., 318
Capuzzi, D., 535
Cardoso, S. H., 73
Carducci, B. J., 436
Carey, J. C., 334
Carlberg, B., 465
Carlbring, P., 537
Carli, L. L., 376, 605
Carlino, A. R., 528
Carlo, G., 110
Carlsmith, J. M., 558
Carlson, D., 445
Carlson, E., 95
Carlson, M., 585
Carlson, N. R., 52, 54, 70, 73–74, 139
Carlsson, J., 465
Carnagey, N. L., 232–233, 586–587
Carney, R. N., 269
Carpenter, K. M., 194, 536
Carr, P. B., 592
Carrico, A. R., 220, 616, 617
Carroll, D. W., 99, 103, 282
Carroll, J. L., 45, 372, 384
Carroll, J. M., 356
Carroll, K. M., 531
Carroll, M. D., 337, 442
Carroll, R. T., 376, 379, 382–383, 393
Carskadon, M. A., 169
Carter, D. A., 605
Carter, J. C., 338
Carter, J. E., 576
Carter, J. R., 486
Cartwright, 427
Caruso, D. R., 363
Carvalho, M., 529
Cascio, W. F., 604
Casey, A. A., 338
Casey, P., 499
Casey-Campbell, M., 549
Caspi, A., 96, 404, 425, 427, 494
Cassaday, H. J., 257
Cassady, J. C., 345
Cassidy, T., 14, 31
Casson, E., 132
Castafieda, T. R., 335
Castañfieda, R., 541
Castano, E., 593
Castellano, J. A., 312
Castle, J. M., 93
Castro, C. A., 499
Castro, J., 341
Castro, J. R., 410
Castro-Schilo, L., 66
Castrop, F., 360–361
Catalano, R., 453
Cattani-Thompson, K., 531
Cattell, R. B., 407–408
Cavaco, A., 250
Cavenaugh, J. C., 111, 116
Ceci, S. J., 311, 318, 374
Cellard, C., 486
Centers for Disease Control, 337, 389–390, 392, 442, 505
Centofanti, A. T., 248
Cervenka, S., 293
Cervone, D., 424, 428
Chabas, D., 177
Chabot, M., 228
Chabris, C. F., 148
Chaffee, J., 2
Chahusac, P. M. B., 352
Chakos, M H., 528
Challinor, M. E., 78
Chalmers, D. J., 168
Chambers, E., 176
Chambers, R. A., 186
Chamorro-Premuzic, T., 18, 404, 410, 608–609, 611
Chan, G. C.-K., 197
Chan, M. Y., 445, 447, 460, 467
Chance, P., 209, 213–214, 223–224, 227, 338
Chandra, C., 381–382, 387
Chandrashekar, J., 138
Chang, E. C., 467
Chang, J. -H., 342
Chang, M. C., 197
Chang-Schneider, C., 405
Chansler, P. A., 549, 606
Chao, R., 98
Chapanis, A., 626
Chapleau, K. M., 389–390, 592
Chaplin, G., 598
Chaplin, T. M., 459, 493
Chapman, J. E., 518
Chapman, R. A., 182
Charmaraman, L., 108
Charness, N., 348
Charsky, D., 220
Chartier, M., 518
Chartrand, T. L., 358
Chase, W. G., 264
Chassin, L., 191, 445
Chasteen, A. L., 592
Chatzisarantis, N. L. D., 349
Chaves, J. F., 181
Chazan-Cohne, R., 88
Cheal, M. L., 33
Check, J., 389
Chein, J. M., 243
Chen, C.- C., 609
Chen, H., 392
Chen, P. Y., 376
Chen, X., 529
Chen, Y., 480
Chen, Z., 288
Cheng, C. M., 358
Cheng, H., 59
Cheriff, A. D., 471
Chess, S., 89
Chessick, R. D., 26
Chester, A., 537
Cheyne, J. A., 173
Chiarello, C., 66
Chipman, M., 333
Chiricos, T., 555
Chisolm, T. H., 136
Chiu, S -F., 609
Chivers, M. L., 373
Choi, H., 463
Chomsky, N., 99, 283, 285
Chopp, M., 59
Chou, S. P., 497
Christakis, N., 444
Christensen, A., 537, 541
Christensen, C. D., 314
Christian, C., 514
Christian, K. M., 71
Christian, L. M., 43
Christian, M. S., 611
Christoff, K. A., 232, 523, 586
Christophersen, E. R., 424
Chua, H. F., 155
Chua, P., 379
Chung, C. K., 470
Chung, S. A., 334
Church, J. A., 276
Cialdini, R. B., 550, 555, 559, 563–565
Ciarrochi, J., 459
Cinciripini, P. M., 192
Cirelli, C., 172
Cisler, J. M., 495
Clancy, S. A., 173, 259
Clapham, M. M., 298
Clara, I. P., 460
Clark, D., 67
Clark, R., 268, 452
Clark, V. R., 452
Clarke, D. F., 370, 374
Classens, M., 517
Clawson, C., 270
Clayton, A. H., 396
Clayton, L. D., 40, 621–622
Clayton, N. S., 223
Clements, A. M., 311, 374
Clifford, E. R., 146, 148
Cline, V. B., 586–587
Clore, G. L., 595
Cnattingius, S., 191
Coast, J. R., 469
Cochran, G. M., 86
Cochran, S. D., 373
Cochrane, J., 59
Cohen, A. S., 196
Cohen, G. L., 255, 388, 594, 597
Cohen, L. H., 379
Cohen, M. A., 337, 592
Cohen, M. X., 528
Cohen, P., 488
Cohen, R. J., 305
Cohen, R. L., 556
Cohen, S., 447–448, 462, 615
Cohen, T. C., 393–394
Cohen-Kettenis, P. T., 343
Cohn, M. A., 467, 622
Colangelo, J. J., 260
Cole, J., 182
Coleman, J., 281
Coleman, M. J., 489
Coleman, M. R., 72, 314, 318, 383
Coles, 498
Coles, C. D., 87
Colin, A. K., 161
Collet, C., 278
Collins, A., 582
Collins, A. M., 248
Collins, D. W., 316
Collins, F. S., 324, 593, 598
Collins, M. E., 595
Collins, N. L., 95
Collins, R. L., 196
Collins, W. A., 94
Collop, N. A., 176
Collumbien, M., 389
Colom, R., 64
Colpaert, F. C., 257
Colvin, M. K., 65
Comer, R. J., 476
Comparini, L., 97–98
Compton, R. J., 52, 68, 319, 352
Compton, W. C., 30, 515
Compton, W. M., 190
Conel, J. L., 86
Confer, J. C., 580

Conger, J. J., 99
Conger, K. A., 606
Connors, G. J., 185–186, 190, 196
Conron, K. J., 372
Constable, R. T., 363, 394
Consumer Report, 531
Conte, J. M., 607
Conway, A. R. A., 148
Conway, M. A., 244, 255
Cook, G. L., 503
Cooke, B. M., 374
Coolican, H., 14, 31
Coolidge, F. L., 64
Cooper, A. E., 478
Cooper, C., 14, 320
Cooper, D. S., 161, 556
Cooper, G., 127
Cooper, H., 37, 349
Cooper, J., 554, 557, 621
Cooper, M. J., 342
Cooper, M. L., 95
Cooper, P. J., 494
Cooper, R. P., 100
Cooper, S. J., 33, 333, 339
Coplan, R. J., 549
Corballis, M. C., 283
Corbin, W. R., 392
Corby, E. -K., 361
Corcoran, R., 488
Coren, S., 78–79, 132, 157, 169
Corey, G., 423, 445, 536
Corey, M. S., 423, 445
Cormier, W. R., 499
Cornell, J., 281
Correa-Chávez, M., 308
Corrigan, P. W., 482
Corsini, R. J., 42, 514
Cortes, D. E., 97
Costa, P. T., 427
Costa, P. T., Jr., 409
Côté, J. E., 108–109, 112
Cote, K. A., 171
Cothers, L. M., 425, 584
Cotton, S., 387
Cottrell, G. W., 355
Coursey, R. D., 530
Court, J. H., 259
Court, P. C., 259
Cowan, D. E., 569
Cowan, N., 148, 245
Cowan, P. A., 118, 227–228
Cowden, C. R., 435
Cowden, J., 585
Cowles, J. T., 218
Cox, B. J., 460
Cox, J. J., 139
Cox, R. H., 623, 625
Coyle, J. T., 491
Cozby, P. C, 621
Craig, K. D., 499
Craig, L., 96–97
Craik, F. I. M., 255, 282
Craik, K. H., 30
Crandall, C. S., 468
Crane, L., 314
Cranney, J., 219
Crano, W. D., 554
Crano, W. G., 556
Craske, M. G., 537
Craven, G., 554
Crawford, M., 506
Crencavage, L. M., 532
Crews, F. T., 68
Crichlow, S., 562
Crighero, L., 68
Crisp, A., 341
Crocker, J., 118
Croft, R. G., 586–587
Crogan, M., 596
Crooks, R., 343, 370, 379, 382, 386, 388, 395
Cropanzano, R., 604
Cropley, A., 290
Crosby, R. A., 392
Crosby, R. D., 340, 341
Crouch, D. J., 36
Crowley, M., 604
Crown, C. L., 100
Crowther, 463
Crutsinger, C., 110
Cruz-Bermudez, N. D., 74, 186
Csikszentmihaly, M., 30, 299, 344, 349
Cubbin, C., 450
Cuddy, A. J. C., 592
Cull, W. L., 267
Cullen, F. T., 390
Culver, R., 19
Cumming, N., 242
Cummings, M. R., 85
Cummins, D. D., 583
Curci, A., 261
Curhan, K., 114
Curtis, D., 489, 494
Cytowic, R. E., 276
Czeisler, C. A., 170, 352
Czerwinski, M., 627

D

D'Aleo, G., 144
D'Mello, S. K., 321
Dagot, L., 564
Dai, D. Y., 312–313, 319
Daigle, L. E., 390
Dalton, A. N., 358
Dalton, K. M., 447
Daly, R. C., 494
Dam, H., 494
Damisch, L., 265, 295
Damour, L. K., 477, 479
Danaei, G., 442
Dancy, B. L., 463
Dane, S., 79
Dang-Vu, 171
Daniels, H., 106
Daniels, M., 317
Danielsen, E. M., 621
Dann, M. D., 620
Danzinger, N., 139
Darakjian, J, 193
Darley, J. M., 16, 582–583, 591, 592
Darling, C. A., 385
Darou, W. S., 308
Daruna, J. H., 447
Darwin, C., 355, 360
Das, A., 383
Das. M., 490
Datta, R., 335
Dattilio, F. M., 63
Davey, G., 517
David, A., 144
David, A. S., 356
David-Ferdon, C., 586
Davidov, B.J., 534, 597–598
Davidovitch, N., 291
Davidson, J. K., 287, 385
Davidson, P. R., 524
Davidson, R. J., 183
Davidson, W. B., 417
Davies, J. E., 59
Davies, M., 390
Davies, R., 541
Daviet, C., 531
Davis, B., 246
Davis, C., 338
Davis, D., 294
Davis, G. E., 618–619
Davis, K. C., 587
Davis, K. D., 140
Davis, K. E., 580
Davis, M., 352
Davis, M. J., 392
Davis, M. R., 248
Davis, R. C., 43
Davis, W. D., 604
Davison, G. C., 489
Dawson, D. A., 497
Dawson, E., 376, 605
Dawson, J. D., 452
Dawson, N., 99
Day, D. O., 500
Day, S., 537
Dazzi, C., 18
de Bono, E., 298
de C. Hamilton, A. F., 68
de Graaf, R., 496
de Groot, L. C., 443–444
de Jong, P. J., 211
De Jonghe, B. C., 336
de Leon, C. F. M., 114
de Manzano, Ö, 293
De Pape, A. -M., 282
de Queiroz, V., 528
de Rios, M. D., 169
De Vos, J., 106
Deakin, J. F. W., 59, 490
Dean, D., Jr., 620
Dean, F. P., 459
Deardorff, J., 108
deArmond, S., 376
Deary, I. J., 320, 404, 407
DeBonis, D., 430
Deci, E. L., 349
Deckers, L., 332–333, 346
Deckro, G. R., 183, 469
Deeb, S. S., 132
Defeyer, M. A., 289
DeGaetano, G., 586
Dehaene, S., 66
Dein, S., 568
DeLamater, J. D., 343, 385–386
Delaney, P. F., 264–265
DeLano, L., 270
Delargy, M., 72
Delgado, B. M., 97
Delgado, M. R., 261
Dell, P. F., 499
Della Sala, S., 256
DeLoache, J. S., 89
Delpero, W. T., 132
Delvin, A. S., 612
Demaine, K., 68
Dement, W., 179
Demiris, G., 537
Demos, J. N., 465
Demyttenaere, K., 528
Denmark, F. L., 28, 30, 424
Denney, J. T., 505
Dennis, J., 175
Denoller, J., 466
DePaulo, B. M., 358
Derakshan, N., 345
Derom, C., 317
DeSantis, A. D., 187
Desjardins, R. N., 100
Desmarais, S., 245, 270
Despland, J. -N., 496
Deuser, W. E., 585
Deutsch, G., 65, 66, 79
Deutsch, M., 595–596
Deutschendorf, H., 360–361, 363–364
DeVault, C., 393–394
Devine, D. J., 621
Devlin, B., 317
Devoto, A., 178
DeWall, C. N., 584
Dewitte, S., 375
DeYoung, C. G., 287
Dhanda, R., 458
Di Forti, M., 55
Di Marzo, V., 337
Diamond, L. M., 372
Diamond, M., 379
Diano, S., 335
Dick-Niederhauser, A., 94
Dickel, N., 554
Dickens, W. T., 318
Dickerson, F. B., 525
Dickinson, A., 223
Dickinson, D. K., 100, 322
Dickinson, L. M., 340
DiClemente, R. J., 233
Diener, E., 445, 447, 460, 467
Dierdorff, E. C., 609
Dietrich, A., 624
Dietrich, S. E., 106
Dijk, D. -J., 332–333
Dijkerman, H. C., 627
Dijkstra, P., 579
Dillman, D. A., 43
Dillon, C., 429–430
Dimaggio, G., 514
Dinan, T. G., 466
Ding, E. L., 442
Dinges, D., 170
Dinges, D. F., 169
Dingus, T. A., 39
Dinkmeyer, D., Jr., 117, 119
Dinkmeyer, D., Sr., 117, 119
Dion, K. L., 597
Diphboye, R. L., 577
DiPietro, D., 392
Dirkzwager, A.J. E., 499
Dissanayake, C., 105
Distin, K., 312
Dixon, M. J., 276
Dixon, S. V., 97
DiZio, P., 141
Do Lam, A. T. A., 457
Dobelle, W. H., 128
Dobie, T. G., 141
Dobon, K. S., 518
Dobson, K. S., 493
Dodd, D. K., 448–449
Dodds, P. S., 547
Dodson, C. S., 247
Dodson, E. R., 334
Doherty, M. J., 105
Doidge, N., 514
Dolev, K., 18, 354
Dollard, J., 422–423
Dombrowski, S. U., 442
Domhoff, G. W., 179, 199
Domhoff, W., 178
Domingo, R. A., 99
Domjan, M., 206, 214, 221–222, 459
Donaldson, D., 506
Donate-Bartfield, E., 94
Donmall, M. C., 531, 541
Donnerstein, E., 587
Dooling, D. J., 243
Doran, S. M., 169
Dorfman, J., 298
Dorman, M. F., 137
Dougall, A. L., 447
Dougherty, D. D., 529
Douglas, J., 138
Douglas, S. C., 608
Dourrier, S., 586–587
Dove, A., 323
Doverspike D., 410
Dovidio, J. F., 583, 588–589, 592–593, 595
Dowling, K. W., 46
Doyle, J., 581
Dozois, D. J. A., 493, 518
Dracheva, S., 73
Draguns, J. G., 533–534
Drasgow, F., 431
Drescher, J., 372
Dresel, C., 360–361
Drews, F. A., 36
Drigotas, S. M., 421
Drischel, B., 259
Driskell, J. E., 471

Driver, J. L., 394
Drolet, G., 55
Drucker, P., 605
Druckman, D., 45
Drummond, M., 138
Drummond, P. D., 447
Drury, J., 560
Drydan, W., 518–519
Drymalski, W. M., 529
DuBois, D., 183
Duchenne, G., 356
Duchon, A., 229
Duckitt, J., 590
Duckworth, A. L., 347
Duclos, S. E., 361
Duffy, J. F., 170, 334
Duffy, S., 617
Dulewicz, V., 363
Dumas, F., 551
Dumas, T. L., 577, 607
Dumont, E. C., 55
Duncan, B. L., 541
Duncan, C. C., 512
Duncan, G. H., 141
Duncan, J., 68
Duncan, T. E., 186
Duncan, W. C., 494
Duncker, K., 286, 288
Dunford, B. B., 621–622
Dunlap, E. E., 622
Dunlop, S. M., 345
Dunn, O., 14, 31
Dupré, C., 335
Durán, L. K., 282
Durand, A., 7
Durand, V. M., 479–480, 484, 490, 501, 506
Durgas, M. J., 501
Durkin, K., 252
Durmazlar, N., 132
Durnham, M. G., 388
Durrant, J. E., 228
Dutra, L., 531
Dutta, T., 78
Dutton, D. G., 360
Duyme, M., 318
Dvash, J., 551
Dwivedi, P., 242
Dworkin, S. L., 388
Dwyer, D. J., 448
Dwyer, D. S., 444
Dyer, K., 116
Dyukova, G. M., 66
Dywan, J., 248
Dzokot, V. A., 480

E
Eagleman, D. M., 276
Eagly, A. H., 375–377, 584
Eardley, I., 395–396
Earleywine, M., 452
Easton, J. A., 580
Eaton, D. K., 444
Eaton, S. E., 607
Eaves, E. L., 70
Ebben, M. R., 174–175
Ebbese, E. B., 252
Ebbinghaus, H., 254
Eccles, J., 346
Eckardt, M. H., 415
Ecker, A. H., 196
Eckerman, D. A., 223
Eddy, K. T., 531
Eden, J., 562
Edenfield, T. M., 443, 468
Eder, D. N., 494–495
Edwards, B. D., 611
Edwards, C. R., 208
Egeland, B., 95
Eggert, A., 4
Ehlers, A., 451
Ehrbar, R. D., 379
Eidelson, J. I., 591
Eidelson, R. J., 591
Eiden, R. D., 87
Eifert, G. H., 448, 521, 523
Einarsen, S., 608
Einarsson, 261
Einstein, G. O., 265
Eisenberg, N., 89, 96
Eisendrath, S., 518
Eisler, I., 535–536
Ek, L., 138
Ekman, P., 356, 358, 360–361
Elder, P., 17
Eldridge, M., 219
Elieff, C. A., 150
Eliot, L., 374–375
Elli, K. A., 263
Ellickson, P. L., 196
Ellingson, J. E., 325
Elliott, J. C., 336–337
Elliott, M., 187, 338, 386, 541
Ellis, A., 4–5, 518–519
Ellis, D. J., 519
Ellis, P. J., 609
Ellis, R., 247
Ellis, S. M., 337
Ellison-Wright, I., 480
Elovainio, M., 607
Emerson, E., 450
Emmelkamp, P. M. G., 523, 536
Emmons, M., 571
Emmorey, K., 284
Engle, D. E., 513
Engler, B., 404–405
Englund, C. E., 170
Enns, J. T., 132, 157
Enns, M. W., 460
Epley, N., 40, 593
Erasmus, 265
Erdal, K. J., 214, 485
Erickson, C. D., 98
Ericsson, K. A., 115, 264–265, 348
Erikson, E. E., 26, 111–113
Erlacher, D., 179
Ernst, E., 141
Eron, L., 587–588
Ersland, L., 140
Erzurumluoglu, A., 79
Escanilla, O., 155
Eschholz, S., 555
Espelage, D. L., 584
Essien, E. J., 392
Ethier, K. A., 390
Eubanks, J., 232–233, 586–587
Evans, G. W., 560, 614–615, 615–616
Evardone, M., 74
Everaerd, W., 381
Everly, G. S., 530
Ewen, R. B., 404
Eyal, N., 624
Eyde, L. D., 430
Eysenck, H., 406, 514
Eysnck, M. W., 242, 246, 248, 260, 268, 345

F
Fabes, R. A., 96
Fabiano, P., 460
Fabrega, H. Jr., 477
Fahim, C., 484
Fain, G. L., 126
Faith M., 590, 593
Faith, M. S., 536
Falkowski, C., 193
Fallon, B. A., 534–535
Fantauzzo, C. A., 93
Fantz, R., 91
Farah, M. J., 70, 187
Faraut, B., 170
Farb, N. A. S., 183
Farr, S. A., 335
Farrell, M. J., 332
Farroni, T., 92
Faucher, B., 199
Faugloire, E., 142
Faurie, C., 79
Fawcett, R. C., 304, 305, 333
Fayek, A., 513–514
Federal Bureau of Investigation, 586
Fein, S., 550, 559, 586
Feingold, A., 577, 581
Feissner, J. M., 494
Feist, J., 442, 461
Feiveson, A. H., 628
Feldman, D. H., 101, 104
Feldman, R. S., 551
Feldman, S., 590
Feldon, J., 488
Feldstein, S., 100
Feldt, T., 404
Fellous, J. -M., 73, 352
Fenn, K. M., 168
Ferber, R., 176
Ferguson, C. J., 233, 587
Fergusson, D. M., 87
Fernald, A., 99, 100
Fernandes, C., 311
Fernandez, Y., 97
Fernyhough, C., 491
Féron, F., 59
Ferrari, J. R., 7
Ferris, G. R., 610
Festinger, L., 551, 557–558
Feuerstein, R., 318–319
Ficca, G., 170, 172
Fichner-Rathus, L., 107, 373, 379–380, 395
Fichtel, Ä., 465
Fiedler, J., 628
Field, A. P., 211
Field, C. E., 526
Field, J. E., 425
Field, J. F., 584
Fields, R. D., 126
Fields, R. M., 451
Fields, T. H., 436
Fields, W., 285
Fiez, J. A., 243
Filbey, F. M., 196
Fine, C., 374, 483, 581
Fink, A., 62
Fink, M., 487
Finkel, E. J., 358
Finn, S. E., 430
Finnegan, M., 87
Fioratou, E., 298
Fiore, D., 514
Fiori, N., 156
Fireman, G., 176, 235
Firestone, P., 386, 499
First, 479
Firth, C. D., 74
Fischer, A. H., 357
Fischer, P., 233
Fish, J. M., 533–534
Fishburne, G., 347
Fisher, B. S., 390
Fisher, J., 612
Fisher, R., 248
Fisher, R. P., 267
Fiske, S. T., 375, 592
Fitzgibbon, M., 342
Fitzsimons, G. M., 578
Flagel, S. B., 55
Flanagan, M. B., 141–142
Flanders, J. L., 287
Flaskerud, J. H., 480
Flavell, J. H., 102
Flegal, K. M., 337, 442
Fleischman, D. S., 580
Fleming, J., 284
Fletcher, B. W., 190
Fletcher, P., 78
Flett, G. L., 506
Fleury, M., 156
Flies, U., 606
Florer, F., 261
Flores-Mendoz, C., 311
Florida Medical Examiners Commission, 187
Florina, C., 605
Flowe, H. D., 252
Floyd, 484
Flynn, J. R., 318
Flynn, K. J., 342
Foa, E. B., 262, 498
Fobair, P., 541
Fochtmann, L. J., 500
Foehr, U. G., 232, 555, 586
Fogassi, L., 68
Fogel, S. M., 171
Földiák, P., 242
Foley, H. J., 131, 137
Folkard, S., 334
Folkman, S., 450
Follette, W. C., 294
Follman, C., 594
Fontaine, K. R., 442
Fontenelle, D. H., 118–119
Fontenot, J., 500
Foo, P., 229
Foot, K. D., 528
Foot, M., 496
Forbes, G. B., 389–390, 587
Ford, D. Y., 312
Ford, E. S., 442
Ford, G. G., 623
Ford, J. K. B., 33
Ford, L., 97
Foreman, R. D., 141
Forgas, J. P., 554, 556
Forman, E. M., 518, 531
Forney, J. C., 110
Forney, W. S., 110
Fornito, A., 490
Forrest, M. S., 524
Förster, J., 550
ForsterLee, L., 622
ForsterLee, R., 622
Forsyth, D. R., 548
Forsyth, G. A., 2, 245
Forsyth, J. P., 521522
Fortunato, L., 281
Foster, G., 40
Foubert, J. D., 110
Foufe, M., 168
Fougnie, D., 148
Fourinier, P. -M., 534
Fouts, R., 284
Fowers, B. J., 534, 597–598
Fowler, F., 118
Fowler, J., 444
Fowler, J. S., 55
Fowler, M., 19
Fox, C., 41
Fox, M. L., 448
Foxhall, K., 161
Frackowiak, R. S. J., 74, 265
Fraley, R. C., 579, 580
Franco, K., 500
Franczyk, D., 341
Frank, J. D., 531
Frank, M. G., 356
Franke, M., 610
Franken, R. E., 332–333, 342, 344
Frankl, V., 516–517
Franks, B., 285
Frantz, R. L., 92
Franzoi, S. L., 551
Fraser, C., 140
Fraser, J., 248
Frazier, A. D., 312

Freberg, L. A., 55, 84, 186, 250, 262, 335, 353, 371, 527, 534
Fredrickson, B. L., 342, 363–364, 445, 467, 592, 622
Freedman, D. H., 337, 339–340
Freeman, A., 159
Freeman, D., 488
Freitas, M. B., 79
Freize, I. H., 386
French, C. C., 19
French, S. E., 108
French, T. A., 161
Frenkel-Brunswik, E., 590–591
Freud, A., 26
Freud, S., 26, 178, 198, 411, 413–415, 422, 457–458, 501, 512
Freund, A. M., 114
Frick, C., 528
Frick, P. J., 118, 228
Fridley, D., 214
Fried, C. S., 389
Fried, P. A., 197
Friedman, H. S., 410, 447
Friedman, J. S., 489
Friedman, L. J., 113
Friedman, M., 465, 466
Friedman, R., 211, 324
Friedman, R. C., 514
Friedmann, P. D., 178
Friedrich, R. W., 138
Friesen, W. V., 360–361
Frith, C. D., 265
Fritz, C. O., 269
Fromme, K., 392
Fryar, C. D., 388
Frydman, M., 588
Fu, J. H., 562
Fuchs, C., 627
Fucito, L. M., 394, 397
Fuhriman, A., 535
Fujino, D. C., 379
Fukai, S., 375
Fukuda, K., 169
Fulero, S. M., 623
Funder, D. C., 427
Funk, J. B., 233, 587
Fuqua, D. R., 608
Furnham, A., 18, 404, 410, 608–609, 611

G

Gaab, N., 71
Gable, S. L., 363, 393–394, 470
Gaby, A., 281
Gadalla, T. M., 390
Gaertner, S. L., 589, 592–593, 595, 597
Gage, P., 68
Galambos, N. L., 109
Galankin, T., 217
Galanter, M., 541
Galati, D., 356
Galea, S., 451
Galizio, M., 185–186, 190, 196
Gall, F., 18
Gallagher, J. J., 268, 314, 318
Gallagher, S. H., 139, 623
Gallese, V., 68
Gallo, L. C., 87
Gallucci, T.N., 625
Galntucci, B., 253
Galuska, C. M., 186
Galvez, M. P., 108
Galvin, J., 516
Gamble, S. A., 514
Ganey, H. C. N., 344–345
Ganis, G., 277
Ganster, D. C., 448
Garcia, A. L., 552
Garcia, E. E., 282
Garcia, F.B., 193
Garcia, J., 338
Garcia, M., 190
Garcia, R. I., 191, 445
Garcia-Calvo, T., 612
Garcia-Palacios, A., 523
Gardner, A., 284
Gardner, B., 284
Gardner, H., 322, 324–326, 620
Garety, P. A., 488
Garíca-Montes, J. M., 484
Garland, A. F., 312
Garle, M., 76
Garlow, S. J., 506
Garnets, L. D., 372, 373, 383
Garran, A. M., 589
Garrosa, M. P., 448
Gartrell, N. K., 373
Gartstein, M. A., 89
Garvey, A. J., 191, 445
Gascón, S., 448–449
Gass, R. H., 557
Gastner, M. T., 594
Gates, A. I., 267
Gathchl, R. J., 465
Gatz, M., 485
Gauquelin, M., 19, 20
Gaw, A. C., 480
Gawronski, B., 590
Gayle, H., 392
Gazzaniga, M. S., 65
Geary, N., 337
Geddes, L., 354
Gedo, J. E., 26
Gee, J., 577
Gegenfurtner, K. R., 132
Geiger, A., 537
Geise, A. C., 420
Geiselman, R. E., 248, 267
Geller, S. R., 96
Geluk, C., 585
Gentile, D. A., 232
George, A., 578
George, W. H, 587
Georgiou-Karistianis, N., 140
Gerard, J., 228
Gerardi, M., 524
Gerber, M., 175
Geriach, F. M., 606
Gerjets, P., 627
Germain, A., 199
German, T. P., 288–289
Gerrard, C., 8
Gerrard, M., 551
Gersh, R. D., 431
Gershoff, E. T., 118, 227–228
Gerstein, E. R., 126
Gertz, M., 555
Geschwind, N., 68, 79
Gever, J., 482
Gewer, A., 319
Giancola, P. R., 193
Giarratano, J. C., 321
Gibb, R., 56
Gibbons, F. X., 551
Gibson, E. J., 150
Gibson, S. J., 140
Gielen, U. P., 533, 534
Gila, A., 341
Gilaie-Dotan, S., 278
Gilam, G., 551
Gilbert, L. A., 380, 388
Gilchrist, A. L., 245
Giliovich, T., 597
Gillespie, C. F., 451
Gillham, J. E., 459, 493
Gillhooly, K. J., 298
Gilligan, C., 28, 110–111
Ginsberg, D. L., 528
Ginsburg, B. E., 585
Girard, T. A., 173
Giummarra, M. J., 140
Giuseppe, R., 523
Gladstone, G. L., 356
Gladwell, M., 294
Glanz, K., 195, 338
Glass, C. A., 537
Glass, J., 97
Glassgold, J. M., 372
Glazer, K., 466
Gleason, J. B., 99
Glenn, E. N., 593, 598
Glick, P., 453, 589, 592
Global Footprint Network, 220, 613, 615–616
Glomb, T. M., 608
Gloria-Bottini, F., 336
Glover, R. J., 110
Glozman, Z. M., 66
Glueckauf, R. L., 537
Gobet, F., 245, 265, 289
Godfrey, C. N., 36
Godkin, L., 548
Godnig, E. C., 131
Godoy, R., 558
Goernert, D. N., 617
Goetz, T., 256
Goffin, R. D., 18
Gogate, L. J., 100
Gökeritz, S., 550
Goldberg, C., 569
Goldberg, M., 79
Goldberg, R., 185
Golden, J., 87
Golden, T. D., 607
Goldenberg, H., 536
Goldenberg, I., 536
Goldfied, M. R., 373
Golding, J. M., 622
Goldman, R. M., 419
Goldstein, E. B., 29, 126, 131–132, 144, 147, 229, 243, 245–246, 286, 289, 304
Goldstein, M., 342
Goldstein, N. J., 564–565
Goldstein-Alpern, N., 99
Goldston, D. B., 506
Goleman, D., 352
Gollub, R. L., 183
Goman, C. K., 357
Gomez, R., 95
Gonsalves, B. D., 247
Gonzaga, M., 576
Gonzalez, M., 228
Gonzalez, R., 155
González-Vallejo, C., 168
Goode, E., 580
Goodman, G. S., 259, 262
Goodman, W. G., 528
Goodman-Delahunty, J., 622
Goodwin, J., 512
Goodwin, S. A., 375
Goodwin, T. D., 87
Gooren, L. J. G., 343
Goparaju, S. K., 337
Gopnik, A., 92, 99, 105
Gordijn, M. C. M., 333
Gordis, E. B., 587
Gordon, A. K., 553
Gordon, A. M., 393
Gordon, I., 75
Gordon, N. S., 183
Gordon, T., 119
Gore, J. C., 70
Gorman, J. M., 451
Gorney, G., 56
Gosgrove, G. R., 529
Gosling, S., 408
Gosling, S. D., 30
Gosselin, F., 355
Gosselin, I., 55
Gosselin, P., 355
Göthe, K., 243
Gottesman, I. I., 489
Gottfredson, G. D., 531
Gottman, J. M., 393–394, 578
Gould, 261
Goulet, C., 156
Gourville, J. T., 296
Gow, A. J., 310
Gowers, S., 341
Grabe, M., 220
Graber, J. A., 97, 344
Graber, M., 106
Grabill, 497–498
Grabowski, T., 284
Grace, M. K., 335
Grack, C., 595
Graesser, A., 321
Graham, C. H., 132
Graham, M., 2
Grande, T., 532
Grandner, M. A., 170
Granholm, E., 194
Granrud, C. E., 147
Grant, B. F., 197, 497
Graves, J., 560, 598
Gravetter, F. J., 634
Gray, J. M., 344
Gray, T. W., 617
Graziottin, A., 382
Greaves, W., 285
Gredler, M. E., 107
Green, C., 259
Green, J. T., 208
Green, M. C., 556
Green, S. I., 252
Green-Peden, L. D., 525
Greenberg, D. L., 261
Greene, D., 349
Greene, E., 620, 622
Greene, T., 612
Greenfield, 324
Greenfield, P., 308
Greenspan, L. C., 108
Greenwald, A. G., 590, 597
Greenwald, R., 524
Greenwood, J. G., 77
Greenwood, J. J. D., 77
Greenwood, K. M., 248
Greer, D. S., 443, 445
Greer, J. D., 377
Gregory, A., 38
Gregory, B. T., 608
Gregory, K. B., 169
Gregory, R. L., 142, 147, 156–157
Greitemeyer, T., 233, 577
Grello, C. M., 281
Grenèche, J., 176
Gretscher, H., 231
Greve, K., 231
Griffin, D. W., 579
Griffin-Fennell, F., 505
Griffiths, R. R., 191
Grigorenko, E. L., 304, 317, 319, 322–326
Grigsby, J. D., 548
Griskevicius, V., 349, 564
Grob, C. S., 169
Grodzinsky, Y., 68
Gronli, J., 168, 172
Groscup, J., 621
Gross, A. M., 390, 499
Gross, J. J., 360–361
Grosse, S. D., 316
Grossman, J. M., 108
Grotzer, 319
Grubin, D., 354
Gruman, J., 442
Gruneberg, M., 267
Gschwendner. T., 590
Gual, P., 341
Guarnaccia, P. J. J., 480
Guastello, D. D., 378–379
Guastello, S. J., 378–379
Guay, F., 548
Guéguen, N., 550, 564

Guevremont, D. C., 218, 521–522, 526
Guez, J., 255–256
Guillot, A., 278
Gullette, D. L., 345
Gump, B. B., 576
Gümüs, K., 132
Gündogan, N. Ü., 132
Gunnar, M. R., 94
Gunnarsdóttir, M., 537
Gunter, B., 233
Gurin, J., 531
Gurung, R., 442, 447, 452, 463
Gustavson, C. R., 338
Güth, W., 596, 628
Gutheil, T. G., 63
Guthrie, R. V., 28
Guttmacher Institute, 387

H
Haaken, J., 260
Haas, B. W., 363, 394
Haas, S. M., 279
Haber, I., 264
Haber, R. N., 252, 264
Haber, S., 615
Haddock, G., 484
Hadley, C., 260, 298
Hadley, C. N., 350
Haenschel, C., 242
Hafemeister, T. L., 621
Hafer, C. L., 597
Haffmans, P. M. J., 55
Haga, S. P., 361
Hagelkull, B., 94–95
Hagger, M., 349
Hagoort, P., 78
Haidt, J., 418
Haier, R. J., 62, 70, 320
Haimm, C., 187
Hajek, P., 521
Hakun, J. G., 354
Hald, G. M., 587
Hale, S., 311
Hales, D., 442–443, 445, 462
Haley, A., 317, 318
Hall, C., 347
Hall, J., 502
Hall, N. C., 256
Hall, R. J., 347, 377
Hall, S. P., 560, 588
Hallahan, D. P., 312, 314–315, 319
Halliday, G., 179, 198–199
Halligan, P. W., 180, 182
Halonen, J. S., 1, 5, 7, 345, 460
Halpern-Felsher, B. L., 281
Ham, C., 445
Hamilton, A., 392
Hamilton, D. V., 396
Hammer, J. C., 548
Hammig, S. B., 621
Hammitt, W. E., 549
Hammond, D. C., 182
Hancock, P. A., 344–345
Handsfield, H. H., 392
Handwerk, M. L., 526
Hane, A. C., 187
Haney, C., 548
Hanham, J., 288–289
Hanley, S. J., 418
Hanrahan, P., 478
Hans, V. D., 621
Hansell, J. H., 477, 479
Hansen, C. J., 469
Hansen, N. B., 531
Hansford, S. L., 578
Hanson, L. L., 314
Hanton, S., 347
Hanyu, H., 256, 485
Hao, Y. L., 168
Haq, I. U., 528
Harber, K. D., 38
Hardaway, C. A., 169
Hardin, G., 617
Hardin, M., 377
Harding, D. J., 41
Hardt, 261
Hare, R., 504
Harel, A., 278
Hari, R., 78
Harkavy-Friedman, J., 488
Harker, L., 404
Harlow, H., 94
Harlow, J. M., 42
Harlow, T. F., 460
Harm, D. L., 142
Harpending, H., 86
Harper, M. S., 281
Harrigan, J. A., 357, 560
Harris, C., 581
Harris, J. C., 314, 512
Harrison, G., 489
Harrison, K., 341
Harrison, P. J., 489
Hart, C. L., 186, 187, 196
Hart, D., 110
Hart, S. L., 537
Hartely, R. D., 233
Hartgens, F., 76
Hartlep, K. L., 2, 245
Hartley, R. D., 587
Hartman, E., 199
Hartman, P., 310–311
Hartmann, P., 19
Hartung, C. M., 430
Harvey, O. J., 192, 595
Harvey, P., 608
Harvey, R. H., 467
Harvey, T., 64
Harway, M., 536
Harwood, R. L., 97–98
Hashibe, M., 197
Hashimoto, I., 67
Hasin, D. S., 194, 197, 497
Haskett, R. F., 528
Haslam, N., 280
Hass, S. L., 460
Hatfield, E., 388
Hauck, F. R., 177
Havercamp, S. M., 348
Hawker, T., 314
Hawks, J., 86
Hayden, A., 145
Hayden, F., 541
Hayes, C., 284
Hayes, M. R., 336
Hayne, H., 91
Hayward, C., 108, 498
Hayward, R. D., 622
Hazuda, H. P., 458
Heady, R. B., 607
Healy, A. F., 252
Hearold, S. L., 588
Heath, R. G, 217
Heatherton, T. F., 68
Hebb, D., 84
Hebert, 616
Hebl, M. R., 388
Hecht, H., 497
Hecht, M. L., 108
Hect, J., 361
Hedensjö, L., 537
Hedges, 534
Heide, K. M., 524
Heil, S. H., 186
Heilburn, K., 620
Heiman, G. W., 640
Heiman, J. R., 395–396
Heimann, M., 91
Heine, S. J., 28, 30, 318, 324, 406
Heinrich, S., 442
Heinrichs, R. W., 486
Heisel, M. J., 506
Helgeson, V. S., 374, 378, 424
Hélie, S., 286, 289
Hellekson, C. J., 494
Hellige, J. B., 78
Helson, R., 326
Helton, W. S., 215
Hemenway, D., 586
Henderson, T. L., 462
Henik, A., 276
Heninger, M., 506
Henke, R. M., 604
Hennenlotter, A., 360–361
Hennessey, B. A., 183, 290, 293, 350
Henning, K. R., 232, 523, 586
Henningsen, D. D., 562
Henningsen, M. L. M., 562
Henrich, J., 28, 30, 318, 324
Henriquez, E, 621
Henry, P. K., 186
Hepburn, L., 586
Hepper, P. G., 78
Herbenick, D., 382–383
Hergenhahn, B. R., 24, 118, 227–228
Heriot, S. A., 522
Herman, C. P., 340–341
Herman, J. L., 450
Herman, S. M., 177
Hermann, B., 262
Hermann, R., 250
Hernández, J. A., 360, 362
Hernstein, R., 324
Herold, D. K., 220
Heron, J., 86
Herren, C., 85, 94
Herrmann, D. J., 267
Hertz, M. F., 586
Herxheimer, A., 334
Herz, R. S., 138
Hess, L., 526
Hesson, M., 346
Heston, J. D., 529
Hettich, P. I., 266
Hewitt, P. L., 506
Hickie, I., 59
Higbee, K. L., 270
Higgins, G. E., 194
Higgins, S. T., 186
Higgs, M., 363
Higham, P. A., 8
Hijazi, A. M., 570
Hilgard, E., 180
Hill, E. A., 100
Hilsenroth, M. J., 433–434
Hiltunen, J., 169
Hinds, T. R., 197
Hinkel, E., 282
Hinterberger, T., 72
Hintzman, D. L., 254
Hirao, K., 256, 485
Hiripi, E., 191
Hirsch, R., 269, 388
Hirshbein, L., 528
Hirstein, W., 63, 65
Hirt, E. R., 553
Hiscock, M., 374
Hixon, M. D., 284
Hladkyj, S., 5
Ho, I. T., 320
Hobson, A., 178, 200
Hobson, J. A., 173
Hochreich, D. J., 423
Hochstenbach, J., 70
Hocker, J. L., 593
Hodges, H., 59
Hodgins, H. S., 183
Hodson, R., 604, 608
Hoel, H., 608
Hoerr, S. L., 342
Hofer, B. K., 6
Hoff, E., 99–100
Hoffart, A., 514
Hoffer, A., 513
Hoffman, E., 417
Hoffman, M., 318
Hoffman, P., 282
Hoffmann, J. P., 96
Hofman, D., 352
Hofmann, W., 590
Hogan, E. H., 191
Hogben, D., 269
Hoge, C. W., 499
Hogg, M. A., 556
Hohwy, J., 144
Holbrook, T., 621
Holding, D. H., 266
Holdsworth, L., 295, 363
Holland, J., 610
Hollendonner, J. K., 442
Holling, H., 293, 311
Hollins, M., 139
Hollon, S. D., 460, 518
Holm, A., 169
Holmes, E. K., 97
Holmes, J., 243
Holmes, J. G., 558, 579
Holmes, M., 379
Holmes, T., 461
Holtz, A., 549
Holtzen, D. W., 79
Holzinger, B., 14, 200
Honey, P. L., 214, 217–218, 224
Hong, H.-W., 93
Honomicki, R., 288
Honzik, M. P., 311
Hooley, J., 476
Hoon, M. A., 138
Hooyman, N., 114
Hopkins, W. D., 284
Horgan, J., 54
Horn, R. S. C., 606
Horne, R. S. C., 177
Hornick, B. A., 191
Horowitz, I. A., 622
Horsburg, K., 59
Horvath, L. S., 345
Horwood, L. J., 87
Hosch, H. M., 161
Houghton, D. P., 562
Houlihan, D., 176
Houlihan, P., 617
Houser, M. E., 95
Houston-Price, C., 99
Howard, A., 531
Howard, J. L., 149–150, 610
Howard, T., 140
Howell, D. C., 638
Howitt, D., 554
Hoyt, M., 183, 469
Hsia, Y., 132
Hsiao, W., 622
Htut, M. M., 337
Huang, M. H., 616
Hubble, M. A., 541
Hubel, D. H., 127
Hübner, R., 66
Huesmann, L. R., 232–233, 586–587
Huff, J. W., 607
Hugdahl, K., 140
Hughes, A., 44
Hughes, J. R., 191, 196
Hughes, M., 281
Huguet, P., 551
Huijbregts, S. C., 87
Human, L. J., 577
Hummel, H. G. K., 220
Hunt, E., 320, 324–325
Hunt, H., 293
Hunt, R. R., 268, 270
Hunter, E., 568
Hunter, J. E., 609
Hunter, J. P., 140
Hurley, E. A., 324

Husain, A. M., 177
Huston, A. C., 97
Huston, H. C., 87
Huta, V., 618
Hutchinson, D. R., 42–43
Hutchinson, S., 71
Hutchison, K. E., 194
Huyck, M. H., 113
Hyde, J. S., 28, 311, 343, 385–386
Hyman, R., 159
Hyman, S. E., 489
Hyreaiko, D. W., 625
Hysenbegasi, A., 460

I
Iacono, W. G., 354
Ianna, P., 19
Iannetti, G. D., 140
Iannone, M., 190
Iastrebov, V., 627
Ida, Y., 78
Imbimbo, C., 379
Immordino-Yang, M. H., 56
Impett, E. A., 363, 393, 470
Impey, S., 197
Inch, R., 374
Ingham, A. G., 560
Inman, T. F., 313
Inskip, J., 372
Insko, C. A., 577
Iosif, A., 46
Irons, G., 211
Irwin, M. R., 447
Isac, A., 263
Isberner, F. R., 389
Ishihara, K., 169
Israelson, G. J., 141
Iversen, L., 187–188
Iverson, R. D., 608
Iveson, C., 554
Iyengar, S. S., 296
Izard, C., 92–93, 360, 362

J
Jaber-Filho, J. A., 529
Jablonski, N. G., 598
Jacbos, N., 317
Jackendoff, R., 284
Jackson, C. L., 423
Jackson, D., 17–18, 41
Jackson, D. C., 447
Jackson, S. L., 14, 21–22, 39–40
Jackson, T., 435–436
Jacob, A., 144
Jacob, M., 414
Jacobs, A., 95
Jacobs, M. K., 26, 411, 458, 512, 537
Jacobs, S. R., 448–449
Jacobs-Stewart, T., 196
Jacobsen, T., 33
Jacobson, N. S., 541
Jaeggi, S. M., 318
Jaehnig, W., 219
Jaffe, J., 100
Jagaroo, V., 63
Jahoda, G., 214
James, J., 24
James, W., 358
Jamison, K. R., 293, 506
Jang, D. P., 523
Janis, I., 562
Janowsky, J. S., 375
Janssen, S. A., 56
Jantos, H., 171
Janus, C. L., 381, 384, 388
Janus, S. S., 381, 384, 388
Jarvin, L., 304
Jarvis, M. J., 191
Jasnow, M. D., 100
Jawahar, I. M., 548
Jay, T. B., 283
Jaycox, L. H., 451
Jefferis, V. E., 358
Jeffery, R. W., 340
Jellinger, K. A., 63
Jenni, O. C., 169
Jennings, L., 532
Jensen, A. R., 324
Jeong, G. -H., 344
Jerabek, L., 257
Jerone, A., 192
Jessen, F., 190
Jeste, D. V, 326
Jia, F. J., 168
Jiang, S., 470
Jin, A. A., 627
Jin, Y. L., 333
Jo, E. Y., 176
Joe, G. W., 190
Joffe, R. T., 75
Jogerst, G. J., 452
Johansson, L., 138
Johnson, A. M., 320
Johnson, B., 137–138
Johnson, B.T., 554
Johnson, C. S., 551
Johnson, D., 170, 585
Johnson, E. O., 191
Johnson, G. V., 625
Johnson, J. J. M., 625
Johnson, L. D., 112
Johnson, M. J. M., 462
Johnson, R., 45
Johnson, R. D., 268
Johnson, S., 318
Johnson, S. J., 295, 363
Johnson, S. K., 183, 577
Johnson, T. J., 195
Johnson, V. E., 383–385, 396
Johnson, W., 64, 310
Johnston, J. H., 471
Joiner, T. E., Jr., 340, 341, 506
Joinson, C., 86
Jolicoeur, P., 243
Jolly, J. L., 313
Jones, C., 431
Jones, E. E., 552
Jones, J., 381–382, 387
Jones, L., 346
Jones, M. K., 518
Jones, R., 496
Jones, R. A., 178
Jones, R. N., 323
Jones, S. A. H., 153
Jones, S. R., 491
Jones, S. S., 93
Jones, T. S., 561
Jonides, J., 242, 245, 258, 318
Jordan, C. L., 374
Jorgensen, P. E., 346
Josephs, R. A., 193
Joughin, N., 341
Jourard, S. M., 394
Jouvet, M., 169
Jowett, G. S., 567
Judge, T. A., 423
Julian, L., 537
Juliano, L. M., 191
Julien, E., 548
Julien, R. M., 186, 189, 191, 196, 527
Jung, C., 26, 405, 415–416
Jung, R. E., 64, 70, 320
Jussim, L., 38

K
Kaas, J. H., 140
Kabat-Zinn, J., 183
Kabnick, K., 339
Kadosh, R. C., 276
Kafka, M. P., 395
Kagan, J., 89, 92, 99, 323
Kahana, M. J., 252
Kahn, A. S., 281
Kahn, D., 464
Kahneman, D., 43, 294–294
Kail, R. V., 111
Kalat, J. W., 55, 72, 75, 186, 319, 351, 355–356, 425
Kalish, D., 229
Kallgren, C. A., 550
Kallio, S., 168, 180–181
Kalmijn, M., 577–578
Kalyuga, S., 288–289
Kamimori, G. H., 170
Kamin, L., 324
Kamin, L. J., 317–318
Kammerer, Y., 627
Kamo, Y., 462
Kamphaus, R. W., 431
Kampman, K. M., 190
Kanas, N., 628
Kandel, E. R., 262
Kann, L., 444
Kanoski, S., 336
Kanwisher, N., 277
Kapinos, K. A., 338
Kaplan, A. H., 6, 94, 97, 99, 514
Kaplan, P. S., 345
Kaplan, R. M., 304, 305, 432
Kaplar, M. E., 553
Kapleau, P., 162
Kaptelinin, V., 627
Kapur, S., 489
Karabanov, A., 293
Karagheorgis, C. L., 624
Karasz, A., 392
Karim, A. A., 72
Kark, R., 605
Karmaniola, A., 95
Karnes, F. A., 324
Karney, B. R., 576
Karpicke, J. D., 5
Karpinska, K., 281
Kashima, Y., 597
Kasser, T., 347, 349
Kassin, S. M., 161, 354, 550, 559
Kassinove, H, 588
Kastenmüller, A., 233
Kataria, S., 176
Katkin, E. S., 211
Katz, B., 530
Katz, J., 140
Katz, P. A., 590
Kauer, J. A., 74, 186
Kauffman, J. M., 312
Kaufman, A. S., 304, 311, 314–315, 319
Kaufman, J., 379
Kaufman, J. C., 291–292, 299
Kaufman, J. H., 153
Kaufman, L., 153
Kautstaal, W., 246
Kautz, M. A., 190
Kawai, K., 338
Kawakami, K., 589, 592–593
Kawasaki, H., 68
Kearney, A. J., 538–539
Kearney, C. A., 94, 483–484
Keating, C., 341
Kee, D. W., 66
Keefe, F. J., 182
Keefer, L. A., 550
Keegan, J., 87
Keel, P. K., 480
Keeley, S., 18
Kegel, M., 494
Keijsers, G. P. J., 531
Kelder, S. H., 445
Keller, E. F., 617
Keller, M. C., 577
Kelley, H., 552
Kelly, E., 369
Kelly, I. W., 19
Kelly, M. P., 397, 431
Kelly, T. L., 170
Keltner, D., 404, 597
Kempermann, G., 59
Kendall-Tackett, K., 447
Kennedy, J. H., 615
Kenneth, M., 194
Kenny, P. J., 217
Kenrick, D. T., 349
Kensinger, E. A., 261
Kenward, R., 516
Kernis, M. H., 406, 419
Kerr, M., 3
Kershaw, T., 390
Kessler, D. A., 114, 340
Kessler, H., 457
Kessler, R. C., 580
Kestler, L., 488–489, 491, 528
Ketcham, K., 247
Kety, S. S., 485
Keveri, M. K., 251
Keyes, C. L. M., 418
Keysers, C., 242
Khalifé, S., 397
Khan, O., 54
Khan, S. M., 78
Khoshaba, D. M., 467
Kida, T. E., 17, 20, 45
Kidd, K. K., 304, 324
Kieffer, S. C., 553
Kigar, D. L., 64
Kiger, L., 324
Kihlstrom, J. F., 298
Kikuchi, Y., 245
Kilcoyne, J., 187
Kim, B. J., 323
Kim, J., 352
Kim, J. J., 208
Kim, S., 606
Kim, T. E., 108
Kim-Cohen, J., 96
Kimball, M., 177
Kimble, C. E., 553
Kimmel, D., 383
Kimura, T., 67
Kinchen, S., 444
King, B. E., 321, 389, 395–397
King, E. G., 388
King, H. E., 73
King, L. A., 470
King, N. J., 211–212
King, P. M., 110
Kingsley, C. H., 75
Kingston, D. A., 386
Kingstone, A., 286
Kinnunen, L. H., 373
Kinsey, A., 380
Kiper, D. C., 132
Kipp, K., 93, 106, 377
Kirby, K. C., 215
Kirby, K.C., 449–450
Kirby, L. D., 470
Kirchhoff, B. A., 250, 256
Kirk, S. A., 314, 318
Kirsch, I., 38, 180–181, 248
Kirveskari, E., 78
Kisamore, J. L., 548
Kiser, L. J., 529
Kitada, R., 627
Kitamura, N., 75, 406
Kite, M. E., 376, 589–591, 593, 595, 597
Kitrayama, S., 357
Kivimaeki, M., 607
Kiyak, H. A., 114
Kjellgren, A., 184
Klahr, D., 620
Klaiber, J. R., 551
Klauer, S. G., 39
Klein, B., 537
Klein, K., 470
Klein, L. A., 176

Kleinke, C. L., 361
Klohnen, E. C., 581
Kloner, R. A., 353
Klöppel, S., 78
Klump, K. L., 461, 463, 480
Knafo, D., 513
Knee, C. R., 553
Knickmeyer, R. C., 370
Knight, J. R., 187
Knight, R. T., 68, 352
Knoll, J. L., IV, 478
Knoops, K. T. B., 443–444
Knox, D., 281, 390
Knudsen, L. B., 336
Knudson, G., 372
Knussen, C., 141
Kóbor, J., 316
Koch, C., 168
Koch, W. H., 407
Koda, S., 340
Koen, L., 534
Koenigsberg, H. W., 503
Kofler, W. W., 614
Kogan, A., 393
Kogan, N., 292
Koger, S. M., 616–618
Kohlber, L., 28
Kohler, P. K., 387
Kohler, S. S., 609, 611
Kohn, C. S., 520
Kohn, J. P., 224
Köke, A., 141
Kolb, B., 51, 56, 59, 61, 64, 74
Kolb, T. M., 86
Kolbert, J. B., 425, 584
Koltzenburg, M., 139, 342
Komisaruk, B. R., 385
Koons, S. R., 6
Kopta, M. S., 532
Korabik, K., 605
Kornguth, S., 169
Kornhaber, M. L., 322, 620
Korol, C., 499
Kose, G., 235
Koss, M., 587
Koss, M. P., 390
Kossek, E. E., 607
Kosslyn, S. M., 263, 276–278
Kosson, D. S., 504
Koster, E. H. W., 495
Koszycki, D., 496
Kotkin, M., 531
Kottler, J. A., 532
Kottler, M., 518–519
Kovera, M. B., 621
Kowert, P. A., 562
Kozart, M. F., 531
Kraemer, H. C., 528
Kraft, P., 361
Krahé, B., 233, 586–587
Krakow, B., 176, 199
Krall, E. A., 191, 445
Kramer, D. L., 251, 298
Kramer, S. J., 350
Kramer, U., 496
Krantz, D. S., 615
Kraus, S., 469
Krauss, R. M., 283
Kreager, D. A., 388
Krebs, D. L., 111
Krieger, J., 176
Krieschel, S., 497
Kripke, D. F., 170
Krishnan, H. A., 605
Kristof-Brown, A. L., 610
Krokoff, L. J., 394
Kromhout, D., 443–444
Kropp, R. Y., 281
Krosnick, J. A., 589
Krueger, A. B., 43
Krueger, J. I., 406
Krueger, P. M., 505
Krueger, R. F., 585
Kruepke, K. A., 220
Ksir, C. J., 186–187, 196
Kteily, N. S., 590
Ku, J. H., 523
Ku, K. Y. L., 320
Kübler-Ross, E., 115–116
Kuczka, K. K., 553
Kuhl, B., 259
Kuhl, P. K., 92, 99
Kuhn, D., 620
Kuhn, E., 212
Kühn, K. -W., 190
Kuiper, N. A., 471
Kuipers, H., 76
Kulik, J., 261
Kulik, J. A., 576
Kulis, S., 108
Kumari, V., 490
Kuneel, N. R., 404
Kurokawa, M., 357, 406
Kwan, L., 155
Kwok, K., 353
Kysma, M., 170

L
Laan, E., 380–281
LaBar, K. S., 261
LaBerge, S., 14, 200
Labin, D., 591
Laborde, M. -L., 137
Labouvie, E., 196
Labov, W., 279
LaBrie, R. A., 520
Lacayo, A., 190
Lachance, S., 534
Lachman, M. E., 113–114
Lachman, R, 243
Lackamp, J. M., 385
Lackner, J. R., 141
Lacy, B. A., 623
Ladd, L. D., 584
Ladouceur, R., 501, 534
Laferty, W. E., 387
Laforge, R. E., 195
Lafreniere, K. D., 342
Lagos, P., 171
Lahav, A., 219
Lahortiga, F., 341
Lakey, C. E., 406
Lakin, J. L., 358
Lalande, K., 363
Lam, R. W., 494
Lamb, R. J., 215
Lambert, K. G., 75
Lambert, M. J., 531, 541
Lambert, W. E., 597
Lamerichs-Geelen, M. J. H., 141
Lamkin, D. M., 269
Lammers, G. J., 177
Lampe, S., 434
Lampinen, J. M., 260
Lamprecht, R., 73
Lan Yeung, V. W., 597
Landa, Y., 144
Landau, J. D., 15, 256, 550
Landers, S. J., 372
Landfield, K., 20
Landy, F. J., 607, 611
Landy, F.J., 609
Lane, A., 75
Lane, C., 482
Lane, D. J., 551
Lang, A., 537
Lange, C., 358
Langens, T. A., 291
Langer, E. J., 288
Langleben, D. D., 63, 354
Langone, M. D., 568
Lappin, J. M., 55
Lappin, M., 465
Larey, T. S., 299
Larid, J. D., 361
Larkin, K. T., 465
Larrick, R. P., 586
Larsen McClarty, K., 405
Larsen, L., 310–311
Larsen, R. J., 363, 404, 435
Larson, M. E, 617
Larsson, B., 465
Larsson, H., 84
Larsson, J. -O., 84
Larsson, M., 249
Larzelere, R. E., 118, 227–228
Lassiter, G. D., 168
Latané, B, 582–583
LaTour, M. S., 247
Latrofa, M., 592
Lattal, K. A., 224
Latty-Mann, H., 580
Lau, T. Y., 607
Laub, J. H., 504
Laumann, E. O., 388
Laurent, G., 138
Laureys, S., 72
Lautsch, B. A., 607
Lavalle, K. L, 85
Lavalle, K. L., 94
Lavy, S., 580
Lawandowski, G. W., Jr., 577
Lawford, H., 579
Lawrence, B., 311
Lawson, H. M., 576
Lawson, M. J., 269
Lawson, T. T., 416
Lay, C., 406
Lazar, S. W., 183
Lazarus, R., 360, 361–362, 449, 456
Lazarus, R. S., 360
Lazi, R. G., 318
Le Pelley, M. C., 280
Leal, M. C., 137
Leavens, D. A., 284
LeBlanc, G., 106–107
Lecrubier, U, 489
Ledley, C., 577
LeDoux, J. E., 73, 352, 413, 451
Lee, J. E., 190
Lee, J. M., 7, 523
Lee, L. H. L., 71
Lee, M., 427
Lee, M. J., 176
Lee, R. E., 350
Lee, S., 562
Lee, T., 208
Leek, K., 576
Leekman, J. F., 75
Leeman, R. F., 194
Leenaars, A. A., 506
Lefcourt, 471
Lefèbvre, A. -A., 486
Lefebvre, C. D., 354
Lefkowitz, E. S., 379
Lefler, E. K., 430
Lefrançois, G. R., 209, 219, 229, 231, 586, 606
Lehman, D. R., 338–339
Leichtman, M., 433
Leidner, B., 593
Leikind, B., 45
Leinninger, G. M., 55
Leiser, D., 486
Leiter, M. P., 448–449
Lejuez, C. W., 448, 521, 523
Lemogne, W. R., 466
Lennon, S. J., 576
Lent, R. W., 404, 410
Lenton, A. P., 380
Lenzenweger, M. F., 489
Leo, F. M., 612
Leon, A. C., 430
León, L., 360, 362
Leonard, K. E., 585
Leor, J., 353
Leotti, L A., 296
Lepage, J. -F., 68
Lepore, S. J., 618
Lepper, M. R., 296, 349
Lercher, P., 614
Lerner, D., 604
Lerner, J. S., 460
Lerum, K., 388
LeSauter, J., 335
Leslie, K., 200
Lesser, I., 493
Lessow-Hurley, J., 282
Lester, D., 373, 505, 506
Leszezynski, J. P., 379
Lettvin, J. Y., 127
Leuner, 261
LeUnes, A., 623, 625
Levant, R. F., 357, 377–378
Levati, M. V., 596, 628
LeVay, S., 370–373
Levenson, M. R., 110
Levenson, R. W., 360–361
Levenston, G. K., 504
Lévesque, J., 57
Levesque, M. J., 577
Levett, L. M., 621
Levin, D. T., 256
Levin, J. R., 269
Levin, L., 580–581
Levin, M., 582
Levin, R., 176
Levin, S., 590
Levine, B., 61
Levine, C., 112
Levine, J., 486
Levine, M., 341
Levine, R. V., 615
Levinger, G., 560
Levinson, D. J., 590–591
Levinson, S., 211
Levitan, L., 14, 200
Levy, D. L., 489
Levy, J., 78
Lewis, I., 43
Lewis, M., 105
Lewis, R. L., 242, 245, 258
Leyendecker, B., 97–98
Leynes, P. A., 256
Li, C., 442
Li, D., 335
Li, R. X., 352
Liberman, N. P., 526
Lichstein, K. L., 175
Lichtenstein, P., 84
Lichtman, A. H., 196
Lickter, D. T., 577
Liddell, S.K., 283
Lieberman, J. D., 622–623
Lierens, R., 512
Lievens, F., 609, 611
Liguori, A., 191
Liles, E. E., 87
Lilienfeld, S. O., 14, 20, 45–46, 158, 434
Lin, J., 388
Lin, T., 549
Linde, K., 141
Lindemann, B., 138
Linden, M., 482
Linden, W., 468
Lindenbaum, L. E., 626
Lindroth, B., 141
Lindsey, B. J., 460
Linster, C., 155
Linz, D., 587
Lipsey, M. W., 531
Lisak, R., 54
Lister, J. J., 136
Little, B. R., 420

Littlewood, R., 568
Liu, G. C., 353
Liu, X., 68
Livingston, I., 581
Llorente, R., 87
Locke, B. D., 389
Locke, E. A., 606
Lodi-Smith, J., 420
Loehlin, J. C., 427
Loewenstein, G., 375
Loewi, O., 199
Loftus, E. F., 246–247, 260
LoLordo, V. M., 458–459, 493
Lomax, T. C., 370, 374
London, M., 608
Long, C. R., 549
Long, E. C., 394
Long, V. O., 378
Longo, M. R., 68
López, S. R., 480
Lord, M. J., 398
Lorenz, 584–585
Lorenzo, G. L., 577
Loughead, J. W., 63
Lounsbury, D. W., 445
Louzada, F. M., 334
Lovaas, O., 525
Low, K. G., 494
Low, S. M., 612
Lowenstein, A. E., 88, 95
Lozano, A., 528
Lubart, T. I., 298
Lubinski, D., 293
Lucas, J. L., 607
Luchins, D. J., 478
Lucidi, F., 178
Lucido, J. D., 615
Luck, S. J., 260
Ludman, E. J., 537
Ludwig, T. D., 617
Lueger, R. J., 532
Lum, D., 28, 30
Luminer, O., 261
Lumley, M. A., 357, 361, 570
Lumsden, J., 281
Lundervold, A. J., 168, 172
Luo, S., 581
Luppa, M., 442
Luria, A. R., 241
Lussier, J. P., 186
Lykken, D., 354
Lyn, H., 285
Lynam, D., 345
Lynch, C., 78
Lynch, K. B., 96
Lynch, T. R., 361
Lynn, A. L., 214
Lynn, S. J., 14, 20, 45–46, 180–181
Lynne-Landsman, S. D., 344
Lyons, E., 617–618
Lyons, M. A., 345
Lyubomirsky, S., 467

M

Maas, J., 169
Maass, A., 592
Mabry, E., 622
MacCabe, J. H., 489
MacDonald, R. A. R., 141
MacDuffie, K., 179
MacGregor, B., 116
Macht, M., 338
Maciejewski, P. K., 498
MacKay, D. G., 260
Mackinnon, L. T., 447
Macklin, C. B., 5
MacPherson, S., 256
Macrae, C. N., 68
Maddi, S. R., 467
Maddock, J. E., 195
Maddox, K. B., 592
Maddox, W. T., 278
Madge, A., 242
Madsen, L., 354
Magrini, A., 336
Magueja, C., 594
Maguire, E. A., 74, 265
Mah, K., 384
Mahalki, J. R., 389
Mahay, J., 388
Maheu, M. M., 536
Mahler, H. I. M., 555, 576
Mahmoodabadi, S. Z., 321
Mahowald, M. W., 176
Maier, N. R. F., 453
Maier, S. F., 265
Mailis-Gagnon, M., 141
Maisel, N., 393–394
Maisto, S. A., 185–186, 190, 196
Makela, E., 617
Malach, R., 278
Malamuth, N., 389
Malamuth, N. M., 587
Malan, L., 613
Malan, N. T., 613
Malaspina, D., 489
Maldonado-Molina, M., 190
Malloy, K. M., 523
Malone, B. E., 358
Maloney, A., 416
Mamen, M., 118
Manber, R., 528
Mancini-Maríe, A., 484
Mandal, M. K., 78
Mandler, J. M., 92
Mangan, D., 581
Mangan, M. A., 176
Mangels, J. A., 255
Mangin, J. -F., 78
Manhart, L. E., 387
Maniaci, M. R., 576–577
Mann, N., 338
Mannariono, A. P., 168
Manne, S., 470
Manning, M., 79
Manning, R., 582
Manschreck, 486
Manslow, C., 116
Mansouri, A., 484
Manstead, A. S. R., 357
Mansur-Alves, M., 311
Mantovani, A., 534–535
Mantyla, T., 266
Manz, C. E., 606
Manzey, D., 628
Maoskowitz, G. B., 594–595
Maran, M., 260
Marcel, M., 414
Marchand, M., 564
Marchand, Y., 354
Marchman, V. A., 99
Marcus-Newhall, A., 585
Mares, M. -L., 588
Margoliash, D., 168
Margolin, G., 587
Margolin, J., 451
Mark, D., 465
Markey, P. M., 407
Markoff, J., 321
Markou, A., 217
Markowitsch, H., 70
Markowitz, F. E., 488, 529
Marks, A., 605
Marks, D. F., 159–160
Marks, J. S., 442–443
Markus, H. R., 114, 357, 406, 420, 559
Marmarosh, C., 549
Marois, R., 148
Marsella, A. J., 613
Marsh, H. W., 460
Marshall, A., 320
Marshall, P. H., 269, 326
Marshall, R. D., 451
Marsiglia, F. F., 108
Marston, A., 200
Martens, M. L., 549
Martens, R., 19
Martin, A. J., 460
Martin, B. R., 196
Martin, C., 380
Martin, C. L., 375
Martin, E., 478
Martin, E. K., 389
Martin, G., 212, 227, 538
Martin, L. L., 361, 460
Martin, L. R., 410
Martin, M., 78
Martin, S., 605
Martin, W. L. B., 79
Martinez, G. M., 387
Martínez-Jarreta, B., 448–449
Martinko, M. J., 608
Martino, S. C., 196
Martins, E. P., 33
Martinez-Gonzalez, M. A., 341
Martorella, E. A., 261
Martuza, R. L., 529
Martynhak, B. J., 334
Marvin, R. S., 94
Marx, B. P., 390, 499
Marx, D. M., 551
Mashour, G. A., 179, 529
Maslach, C., 379, 448
Maslow, A., 26, 161, 348–349, 417–418, 428
Masquelier, G., 517
Massaccesi, S., 92
Masse, L. C., 108, 186
Massey, D. S., 592
Master, S. L., 470
Masters, W. H., 383–385, 396
Mastropieri, M. A., 620
Masuda, T., 155
Mather, G., 128, 136, 148
Matlin, M. W., 131, 137
Matochik, J. A., 68
Matossian, M. K., 512
Matson, J. L., 214, 525
Matthews, G., 404, 407
Matthews, K. A., 87
Matthews, M. D., 347
Matthews, M. S., 282
Matthews, P. H., 282
Matthews, R., 451
Matthey, S., 493
Mattock, A., 147
May, J., 145
May, J. G., 141
Mayberg, H., 183, 528
Maybery, M. T., 252
Mayer, A. R., 504
Mayer, E. L., 415
Mayer, J. D., 363, 428
Mayer, R. E., 220, 231, 282
Mayers, A. W., 520
Mayes, S. D., 311
Maziade, M., 486
Mazzoni, G., 248
McAdams, D. P., 420, 428
McAlister, A. L., 537, 598
McAuliffe, T. L., 86
McBurney, D. H., 37
McCabe, C., 138
McCabe, M . P., 341, 396
McCabe, S. E., 187
McCall, W. V., 528
McCarley, 178
McCarrell, N. S., 279
McCarthy, B. W., 394, 397
McCarthy, C. J., 463
McCarthy, K., 19
McCartney, S., 390
McCarty, R., 531
McClelland, D. C., 312, 324–325, 346–347, 424, 471
McClure, F. H., 514, 536
McClure, J. B., 192
McCluskey, U., 535
McConkey, K. M., 182
McConnell, W., 453
McCormick, N. B., 380
McCown, R., 219, 619–620
McCrady, B. S., 196
McCrae, R. R., 409, 427
McCraty, R., 346
McCrea, S. M., 553
McCrory, C., 320
McCullagh, J. F., 77
McCullough, S., 284
McDaniel, M. A., 5, 265
McDermott, J. F., 293
McDermott, K. B., 247
McDermott, R., 585
McDonough, L., 92
McElduff, P., 531, 541
McEvoy, C., 247, 621
McGaugh, J. L., 246, 262, 265
McGeary, J., 194
McGregor, D., 604
McGregor, L., 420
McGuire, J. M., 621
McHale, N., 471
McIntosh, W. D., 460, 577
McKay, A, 382
McKay, G. D., 117, 119
McKeever, L., 78, 422
McKeever, W. F., 78
McKelton, D., 622
McKenna, K. Y. A., 578
McKenzie, K., 506
McKeown, D., 243
McKim, W. A., 192–193
McKone, E., 256
McLane, M., 518
McLaren, S., 95
McLay, R. N., 465
McLean, N. J., 342
McLewin, L. A., 499
McLoyd, V. C., 228
McMahon, M., 248
McMahon, S., 139, 342
McMullen, L. M., 493
McNally, R. J., 173, 259
McNamara, D. S., 270
McNeill, D., 251
McQueen, V. K., 217
McQuillin, A., 489, 494
McRobbie, H, 521
Mead, M., 376
Meade, C. S., 388
Meadows, 616
Mecklinger, A., 262
Medda, P., 528
Medhus, E., 98
Meeks, T. W., 326
Mehi, O., 142
Mehl, M. R., 21–22
Mehrabian, A., 363, 577
Mehta, C. S., 208
Mehta, J. D., 41
Mehta, P. J., 375
Mehta, S., 373
Meier, P. S., 531, 541, 550
Meireles, S. M., 465
Meissner, C. A., 248
Mejia, O. L., 463
Mellalieu, S. D., 347
Melnick, M., 42
Meltzoff, A. N., 91–92, 99
Melzack, R., 139–141

Memon, A., 248, 252
Mendes, W. B., 470
Mendez, M., 67
Mendolia, M., 457
Meneses, G. D., 220
Mensour, B., 57
Menzies, R. G., 518
Menziesk, R. G., 518
Mercer, J., 95
Mercer, T., 243
Merens, W., 55
Merikle, P. M., 276
Merlin, D., 74
Mesmer, F., 180
Mesquita, B., 357
Messer, S. B., 514
Messer, S. C., 499
Messinger, D. S., 93
Metsäpelto, R. L., 404
Metts, S., 576
Metz, J., 373
Meunier, M., 231
Meyer, G. J., 430
Meyerbröker, K., 523
Meyers, L., 537
Michaels, J. W., 560
Michalak, E. E., 494
Michalko, M., 298–299, 312
Michel, C., 256
Michel, G. F., 87
Michel, J. S., 607
Michel, L., 496
Michello, J., 530
Mickelson, K. D., 580
Middaugh, S. J., 465
Miechenbaum, D., 470–471
Mielke, H. W., 485
Mignot, E., 177
Miguel, C. N., 233, 587
Mikolajczak, M., 75
Mikulincer, M., 452
Mikulineer, M., 580–581, 584
Miles, L. K., 281
Milgram, R. M., 291
Milgram, S., 22, 547, 559, 564–567, 614
Milgrim, D. L., 6
Milich, R., 345
Miller, D. C., 37
Miller, D. T., 550, 582
Miller, G., 244
Miller, G. A., 282, 314
Miller, G. E., 447–448
Miller, J., 589
Miller, K. M., 577
Miller, L. S., 113
Miller, M., 586
Miller, M. A., 461
Miller, M. K., 615, 622
Miller, M. L., 219
Miller, N., 422–423, 452, 585
Miller, N. E., 336, 455, 590
Miller, R., 576–578
Miller, S. D., 541
Miller, S. J., 531
Miller, W. R., 195
Millet, K., 375
Milling, L. S., 523
Millman, R. B., 76
Milne, R., 267
Miltenberger, R. G., 226, 234, 459, 521, 523, 526, 588
Miltner, W. H. R., 497
Milton, J., 159–160
Mimiaga, M. J., 372
Minami, T., 38, 541
Minda, J. P., 279
Mineka, S., 476
Minton, H. L., 27
Miotto, K., 193
Mirsky, A. F., 42, 489, 512
Mischel, W., 422–423, 427
Missick, D. M., 618
Mistlberger, R. E., 168
Mitaka, M., 194
Mitchell, D., 45
Mitchell, D. G. V., 504
Mitchell, K., 177, 606
Mitchell, L. A., 141
Mitchell, N. S., 340
Mitchell, S. G., 445
Miyamoto, Y., 155
Mo, L., 288
Moerman, D. E., 464
Moffitt, T. E., 96, 494
Moghaddam, F. M., 491, 597
Mohr, D. C., 537
Mohr, J. J., 373
Moise-Titus, J., 232–233, 586
Moiser, J., 535
Mokdad, A. H., 442–443
Möller, I., 233, 586–587
Mollicone, D. J., 170
Molteni, R., 493
Moltz, H., 373
Monahan, J., 488
Mondloch, C. J., 435
Monfardini, E., 231
Monjok, E., 392
Monsma, E. V., 624
Monteil, J. M., 551
Montgomery, P., 175
Monti, M. M., 72
Montoya, R. M., 577
Montreal Declaration on Intellectual Disabilities, 313
Moody, J., 390
Moor, J., 321
Moore, C. M., 177, 621
Moore, J. L., 312
Moore, K., 161
Moore, P. J., 576
Moore, S. A., 259
Moore, T. O., 585
Moorman, R. H., 608
Moran, F., 26, 414
Moran, J. M., 68
Moras, K., 531
Moreno, E., 87
Moreno, J. L., 535
Moreno, M. M., 155
Moretti, M. M., 420
Morey, D. J., 541
Morey, L. C., 74
Morgan, J. E., 61, 534
Morgan, J. P., 585
Morgan, S., 576
Morgenstern, J., 196
Mori, E., 354
Morin, A., 168
Morisse, D., 526
Moritz, A. P., 353
Morral, A. R., 215
Morris, G., 357
Morris, J., 587
Morris, M. W., 562
Morris, R. G. M., 262
Morris, T., 624
Morrison, K., 281
Morrison, R. G., 277
Morse, J. Q., 361
Morsella, E., 283
Mortweet, S. L., 424
Moseley, R. L., 500
Mosher, W. D., 381–382, 387
Moskowitz, J. T., 450
Mosley, P. E., 341
Most, S. B., 146, 148
Motivala, S. J., 447
Mouraux, A., 140
Moustakis, V., 363
Mozaffarian, D., 442
Mroczek, D., 420, 425
Muhamad, R., 547
Mulavara, A. P., 628
Mulder, T., 70
Müller, A. R., 523
Muller, R. T., 499
Mulsant, B. H., 528
Munafò, M. R., 78
Munday, A., 594
Munroe-Chandler, K., 347
Munsey, C., 34, 541
Muoz, R. F., 195
Muris, P., 211–212
Murnane, K. S., 186
Murphy, B. C., 429–430
Murray, B., 340
Murray, C., 324
Murray, C. D., 140
Murray, H., 433
Murray, J. B., 491
Murray, L., 494
Murray, R. M., 55
Murray, S., 558, 579
Murrell, A. R., 232, 586
Murtaugh, M., 314
Mussen, P. H., 99
Mussweiler, T., 265, 295
Mustaine, E. E., 194
Mustanski, B. S., 373
Muzzupappa, M., 627
Myers, H. F., 493
Myers, L., 621
Myers, M. G., Jr., 55
Myers, U. S., 196
Myerson, J., 311
Myrtek, M., 466

N
Nader, R., 171, 261
Nadolski, R. J., 220
Nagaishi, T., 338
Nairne, J. S., 245, 258
Naitoh, P., 170
Najdorf, M., 276
Nakajima, S., 338
Nakamura, J., 344, 349, 624
Nakashima, K., 338
Napoliano, S. A., 584
Narduzi, K., 435–436
Nash, H. M., 526
Nash, M., 105
Nash, O., 382
Nash, R. A., 252
Nathan, P. J., 263
National Academy of Sciences, 354
National Center for Chronic Disease Prevention and Health Promotion, 191, 445
National Committee on Pay Equity, 376
National Fragile X Foundation, 315
National Institute of Child Health and Human Development, 95, 177, 315
National Institute of Mental Health, 460, 486, 492–493, 495, 497–498, 499, 505–506, 529, 540
National Institute of Neurological Disorders and Stroke, 174
National Institute on Alcohol Abuse and Alcoholism, 195
National Institute on Drug Abuse, 186, 190–192
National Youth Violence Prevention Resource Center, 586
Nature Conservancy, 220, 616
Nau, S. D., 175
Nausbaum, H. C., 168
Navaco, R., 453
Navarro, J. F., 193
Naveh-Benjamin, M., 245, 255–256
Navracruz, L. C., 588
Neal, V. L., 39
Neale, J. M., 489
Nearing, K., 211, 212
Neave, N., 612
Nee, D. E., 242, 245, 258
Needles, D. J., 460
Neely, T. L., 379
Negriff, S., 108
Nehlig, A., 190
Neisser, U., 312, 317–318, 323, 325
Nelson, C. A., 86–88
Nelson, T. D., 115, 589
Nemeroff, C. B., 262, 451, 498
Neter, E., 18
Nettle, D., 410, 425
Neuberg, S. L., 349
Neufeind, J., 259
Neufeld, R. W. J., 486
Neukrug, E. S., 304–305, 305, 333
Neurbauer, A. C., 62
Neurmeister, A., 494
Nevid, J., 107, 373, 379–300, 395
Newberry, P., 17–18, 41
Newby-Clark, I. R., 173
Newcomb, T. M., 556
Newell, B. R., 219
Newman, A. W., 248
Newman, J. L., 608
Newman, M. E. J., 594
Newport E. L., 284
Nezu, A. M., 340
Nezworski, M. T., 158, 434
Ng, J. C., 70
Ngu, H., 257
Nguyen, V. A., 278
Niaura, R. S., 192
Niccolai, L., 390
Nicholas, A. K., 139
Nicholson, I. R., 486
Nickell, J., 20, 45
Nickerson, R., 255
Nicoló, G., 514
Nida, S. A., 582
Niedzwienska, A., 261
Niehaus, D. J. H., 534
Niehaus, J. L., 74, 186
Niehoff, B. P., 608
Nielsen, M., 105
Nielsen, S. L., 541
Niemiec, C. P., 349
Nigam, M., 620
Nigbur, D., 617–618
Nisbett, R., 597
Nisbett, R. E., 155, 311, 324–325, 552
Njdowski, C. J., 560
Njeri, I., 30, 598
Noh, S., 463
Noland, J. S., 197
Nolen-Hoeksema, S., 483, 492
Noll, S. M., 342
Norcross, J. C., 459, 514, 517, 520, 532, 534, 541
Norenzayan, A., 28, 30, 155, 318, 323–324
Norlander, T., 184
Norman, D., 2, 4, 626–627
Norman, K. A., 246
Norman, T. R., 75
Normann, R. A., 128
North, C., 475, 477
Northcutt, R. G., 138
Norvig, P., 320
Norwood, R. M., 435
Nosek, B. A., 590, 597
Nosko, A., 579
Novella, E. J., 529
Novelli, D., 560
Nowell, P. D., 175
Nowicki, S., 284

Ntoumanis, N., 553
Nuechterlein, K. H., 62
Nurius, P., 420
Nurnberger, J. I., 235
Nyborg, H., 19, 310–311

O
O'Conner, T. G., 94
O'Craven, K. M., 277
O'Doherty, J., 154
O'Donnell, M., 285
O'Hagen, I., 180
O'Hare, A. E., 105
O'Keeffe, C., 159
O'Leary, E., 517
O'Neill, B., 44
O'Neill, H., 132
O'Neill, P., 15
O'Roark, A. M., 434
Oakes, M. A., 406
Oakley, D. A., 180, 182
Oakley, R., 464
Oberauer, K., 243
Oberbracht, C., 532
Oberman, L., 68
Obrist, M., 627
Ochlert, J., 311
Ochsner, K. N., 259, 296
Ocshorn, P., 445
Oden, M., 312
Ofosu, H. B., 342
Ogden, C. L., 337, 442
Ogilvie, R., 176, 200
Ogle, C. M., 259, 262
Ogles, M. B., 531
Ogloff, J. R. P., 503–504
Ohrmann, P., 357
Okiiski, J., 541
Olfson, M., 528
Oliveto, A. H., 191
Ollendick, T. H., 211–212
Olpin, M., 346
Olsen, E. A., 253
Olson, J. M.., 594–595
Olson, L., 59
Olson, M., 118, 227–228
Olson-Buchanan, J. B., 431
Olsson, A., 211, 212
Olsson, E. M. G., 465
Olsson, P. A., 569
Olszewski, P. K., 335
Olver, J., 138
Omoregie, H., 357
Omura, K., 363, 394
Ones, D. S., 609
Ong, A. D., 364
Onwuegbuzie, A. J., 6
Ooki, S., 78
Oordt, M. S., 465
Opland, D. M., 55
Oppliger, P. A., 377, 424
Ord, T. J., 33
Orenstein, P., 375
Orfale, A. G., 465
Orfall, K., 296
Orleans, C. T., 442, 445
Ormay, T., 536
Ormrod, J. E., 319, 620
Orne, M. T., 354
Orner, R. J., 517
Orprecio, J., 127
Orr, A. S., 621
Ortiz, C., 43
Osborne, C. A., 385–386
Osei, S. Y., 336
Osgood, C. E., 280
Oshio, T., 228
Osie, S. Y., 336
Oskamp, S., 555–557, 613, 616
Osma, J., 523
Osman, M., 259
Osmonbekov, T., 608
Osofsky, M. G., 593
Osrin, Y., 319
Oster, H., 92
Oswald, D. L., 389–390, 592
Otani, H., 251
Otgaar, H., 260
Overbeck, J. R., 559
Overholser, J. C., 415
Overmier, J. B., 458
Owen, J., 97
Owens, J., 592
Oya, H., 68
Oyserman, D., 420
Oz, M. C., 340

P
Paas, F., 289
Paavla, M., 529
Pace-Schott, E. F., 173
Packman, J., 87
Page, M. P. A., 109, 242
Pagnin, D., 528
Paliwal, P., 190
Palmer, D. K., 609
Palmer, S. E., 145
Palmersheim, K. A., 114
Palmieri, A., 379
Pals, J. L., 420, 428
Pandye, S., 614
Panizzi, E., 627
Panksepp, J., 92
Paolino, D., 190
Pap, C., 316
Papa, A., 363
Papaeliou, C., 79
Papanicolaou, A. C., 260
Papdatou-Pastou, M., 78
Papies, E. K., 337
Papirman, Y., 553
Paquet, Y., 448
Paquette, D., 97
Paquette, V., 57
Paradis, C. M., 261
Park, D., 605
Park, G., 293
Park, H. J., 352, 576
Park, L. E., 118
Park, N., 349, 418–419
Parke, R. D., 89, 97–98
Parker, A., 200, 257
Parker, E. S., 246
Parker, G. B., 356
Parker, K. C. H., 524
Parker, P. D., 448
Parker, R. D., 363
Parr, A., 68
Parr, J. M., 220
Parrott, D. J., 193
Parsons, K. M., 33
Parva, M., 87
Pascual, A., 550, 564
Pasek, H., 589
Pasqualini, M. S., 92
Passarello, L. C., 385
Passman, R. H., 94
Pasupathi, M. S., 111
Patall, E. A., 349
Paterson, C. J., 373
Patrick, C. J., 504
Pattie, A., 310
Patton, J., 315
Paulhus, D. L., 406
Paulsson, T., 200
Pavlov, I., 24, 207
Pawlick, K., 465
Payne, B. K., 280, 589
Pear, J. J., 220, 227, 538
Pearce, C. L., 606
Peckel, F., 293
Pedersen, A. F., 447, 452
Pedrabissi, L., 18
Pedraza, C., 193
Pedrazzoli, M., 334
Peek, K., 314
Peelen, M. V., 78
Pekrun, R. H., 5
Pelletier, L. G., 618
Pellettiere, L., 590
Pelton, T., 624
Penfield, W., 246
Peng, T. K., 549
Penn, D. L., 482
Pennebaker, J. W., 361, 460, 470
Penner, L. A., 583, 588
Pennington, G. L., 281
Penrod, S. D., 252
Peplau, L. A., 380
Perachio, N., 374
Pérez-Alvarez, M., 484
Perfors, A., 99
Perkins, D., 319–320
Perlman, D., 576–578, 621
Perloff, R. M., 556
Perls, F., 199, 517
Perreault, S., 590
Perri, M. G., 340
Perry, B., 214, 485
Perry, C., 59
Perry, R. P., 5, 256, 459
Perry, Z. W., 591
Perugi, G., 528
Pervin, L. A., 424, 428
Pesant, N., 179
Pescatello, L. S., 444
Pete, E., 339
Peters, L., 342, 506
Peters, W. A., 593
Peterson, C., 347, 349, 418–419, 459, 467
Peterson, D. R., 34
Peterson, J. B., 287
Peterson, L. R., 245
Peterson, M. J., 245
Peterson, P. C., 177
Peterson, T. R., 361
Petruzzi, D. C., 346
Pett, M. A., 462
Pettifer, S., 140
Pettit, J. W., 493
Peverly, S. T., 2
Pezdek, K., 621
Phelps, E. A., 211, 212
Philbrick, K. L., 464
Philippe, F. L., 448
Phillips, D. A., 88, 95
Phillips, D. P., 353
Phillips, D. S., 264
Phillips, J., 493–494
Phillips, K. W., 577, 607
Phinney, J. S., 108, 463
Piaget, J., 101–102, 104–106
Pickel, K. L., 161
Pickett, K. E., 450
Picton, T. W., 255
Piefke, M., 70
Piek, J. P., 91
Pierce, W. D., 350
Pierrehumbert, B., 95
Pierson, J. F., 27
Piliavin, I. M., 583, 588
Piliavin, J. A., 583–584
Pilkonis, P. A., 435
Pillado, O., 108
Pilon, D. A., 424
Pincus, 479
Pindeda, J. A., 68
Pine, D. S., 528
Pinel, J. P.J., 338–339
Pinel, P., 66, 512
Pini, S., 528
Pinker, S., 284
Pinon, N., 75
Pion, G. M., 531
Piper, A. Jr., 499
Pividori, D., 92
Pixley, J. E., 114
Pizam, A., 344
Pizzighello, S., 148
Plassmann, H., 154
Plazzi, G., 176
Pleasant, A., 443, 445
Pliner, P., 338
Ploner, M., 628
Plous, S., 589
Plug, C., 153
Plutchik, R., 351, 363
Podolski, C., 232–233, 586
Podratz, K. E., 577
Poland, J., 483
Polemikos, N., 79
Polich, J., 183
Polivy, J., 340–341, 551
Pollner, M., 430
Pollock, V. E., 504
Pomaki, G., 548
Pomeroy, W., 380
Poole, W. K., 353
Popma, A., 585
Population Institute, 613
Porr, W. B., 609
Porter, K. S., 269, 388
Porter, S., 358
Posada, G., 95
Posey, A., 426
Potenza, M. N., 176, 186, 520
Powell, A. L., 341
Powell, D. H., 346
Powell, F. C., 115
Powell, M. D., 584
Powell, R. A., 214, 217–218, 224
Power, M., 517
Poyares, D., 176
Prasad, S., 144
Pratarelli, M. E., 407
Preckel, F., 311
Preisler, J. J., 468
Premack, A. J., 284
Premack, D., 284
Prentice, D. A., 550
Presson, C. C., 445
Price, J., 246
Price, M., 575
Prigerson, H. G., 498
Priluck, R., 209
Prime, D. J., 243
Pring, L., 314
Prinstein, M. J., 388
Prinz, W., 91
Pritchard, M., 522
Prizmic, Z., 363
Prkachin, K. M., 139
Prochaska, J. O., 459, 514, 517, 520, 532, 534, 541
Prodon, D. A., 337
Prokhorov, A. V., 445
Pröschel, C., 59
Prosser, I. B., 27
Proust, M., 517
Provencher, M. D., 501
Provini, F., 176
Prudie, J., 528
Puca, R. M., 347
Puentes, J., 281, 390
Pugh, K. R., 70
Pulier, M. L., 536
Pullen, P. C., 312, 314–315, 319
Pursell, C. R., 94
Purselle, D. C., 506
Putka, D. J., 610

Putman, S. P., 89
Pychyl, T. A., 6–7

Q
Qian, X., 265
Quas, J. A., 259, 262
Quednow, B. B., 190
Quigley, B. M., 585
Quillian, M. R., 248
Quinn, O. W., 42
Quinn, P. C., 145
Quinto-Pozos, D., 283

R
Raag, T., 377
Rabinowitz, V. C., 28, 30, 424
Rabius, V., 537
Rabl, U., 494
Racagni, G., 493
Rachman, S., 501
Racine, S. E., 461, 463
Rackliff, C. L., 377
Radua, J., 490
Radvansky, G. A., 5, 242, 244, 246, 253, 257–258, 267, 269, 270
Rahe, R. H., 461
Rahman, Q., 373
Raid, G. H., 306
Rainville, P., 141
Rajab, 506
Ralston, A., 477
Ramachandran, V. S., 68
Ramey, C. T., 318
Ramey, S. L., 318
Ramirez, A., 576
Ramirez-Esparza, N., 21–22
Ramsay, M. C., 431
Ramstein, T., 95
Rand, M., 212
Rand, Y., 318–319
Randi, J., 45
Randolph, C, 200
Rane, A., 76
Rank, O., 26
Rantanen, J., 404
Rasmussen, F., 489
Rathus, R., 107–108, 373, 379–380, 395
Ratner, N. B., 99
Rau, P. R., 170
Rau, W., 7
Rauch, A. V., 357
Raun, K., 336
Raven, B. H., 559
Ravussin, E., 336
Rawsthorne, L. J., 419
Ray, O. S., 186, 187, 196
Razzoli, E., 489
Read, J., 396–397
Reavey, P., 260
Rector, N. A., 527
Redden, D. T., 442
Redford, J. S., 279
Reece, L. A., 248
Reece, M., 382
Reed, J. D., 267
Reed, N., 39–40
Reed, S. K., 276, 279, 289–290
Reed, T. E., 320
Reevy, G.M., 379
Regan, G., 350
Regan, P. C., 576, 578, 580–581
Regev, L. G., 396–397
Regnerus, M., 387
Regoeczi, W. C., 614
Reichel, A., 344
Reichenberg, A., 489
Reicher, S., 560
Reid, M., 78
Reid, M. C., 364
Reid, M. R., 447
Reid, P. T., 28
Reid, R., 431
Reidy, D. A., 567
Reiff, S., 211
Reifman, A. S., 586
Reilly, M. P., 224
Reilly-Harrington, N. A., 430
Reimann, F., 139
Reimers, S. J., 280
Reis, H. T., 95, 363, 470, 576–577, 580
Reis, S. M., 312–313
Reiser, B. J., 263, 276
Reisinger, D., 547
Reisner, A. D., 500
Reiss, S., 348
Reissing, E. D., 397
Reiterman, T., 568
Reivich, K., 459, 493
Reker, M., 357
Remer, M., 220
Remland, M. S., 561
Renaud, O., 419
Rendón, T., 550
Renier, C., 177
Renkl, A., 289
Reno, R. R., 550
Rentfrow, P., 408
Renzulli, J. S., 312–313
Reppucci, N. D., 389
Rescorla, R. A., 209–210
Resick, P. A., 389
Resnick H., 451
Resnick, P. J., 478
Ressler, K., 524
Restak, R. M., 104
Resto, J., 176
Reuffer, S. D., 173
Reuter, M., 19
Revonsuo, A., 168, 180–181
Reyes-Garcia, V., 558
Reynolds, C. R., 431
Reznikoff, M., 434
Rhee, 584–585
Rhine, J. B., 158
Ribeiro, A. C., 335
Ricci-Bitti, P. E., 356
Ricciardelli, L. A., 341
Rice, K. G., 410
Rice, L., 407
Richards, J. C., 537
Richards, J. M., 361
Richell, R. A., 504
Richman, C. L., 595
Richmond, L. J., 568
Richmond, M. K., 95
Richter, J., 72
Richter-Appelt, H., 379
Ricke, J. H., 61, 534
Ridenour, T. A., 190
Rideout, V., 232, 555, 586
Rider, E. A., 94
Riefer, D. M., 251
Riela, S., 579
Riemer, M., 616, 617
Rigakos, G. S., 43
Riggins, R., 95
Riggio, H. R., 552
Riker, W. J., 567
Riley, A., 395–396
Riley, E., 395–396
Riley, G., 321
Riley, W., 192
Rilling, J. K., 38
Rimrodt, S. L., 311, 374
Rinck, M., 531
Rind, B., 386
Rindermann, H., 311
Riquelme, H., 293
Ritche, B. F., 229
Ritchey, A. K., 447
Ritchhart, R., 320
Ritter, B., 523
Ritter, J. O., 114, 595
Riva, G., 537
Rizzolatti, G., 68
Roane, M. B., 175
Roberto, K. A., 462
Roberts, B. W., 404, 420, 425, 427
Roberts, D. F., 232, 555, 586
Roberts, J. E., 95
Roberts, R. E., 108
Roberts, S., 223
Roberts, T., 342
Roberts, W. A., 223
Robertson, L. C., 276
Robins, C. J., 361
Robins, R. W., 30
Robinson, A., 293, 297
Robinson, D. N., 168
Robinson, J. C., 349
Robinson, T. E., 187
Robinson, T. N., 588
Roca, M., 68
Rock, A., 172–173, 198, 513
Rodd, Z. A., 217
Rodin, J., 583
Rodriguez, G., 579
Rodriguez, N., 493
Rodriquez-Mosquera, P. M., 357
Roeder, K., 317
Roediger, H. L., III, 247, 253
Roese, N. J., 281
Roffman, J. L., 489–490
Roffman, R. A., 196
Rogers, C., 26, 418–421, 501, 516
Rogers, G. R., 149–150
Rogers, P., 19
Rogers, R. G., 505
Rogoff, B., 308
Rohr, L., 77
Roizen, M. F., 340
Rokeach, M., 591
Role, K. O., 352
Rolls, E. T., 138, 146
Romer, D., 345
Roney, J. R., 382
Ronningstam, E., 482
Roona, M. R., 445
Roos, P. E., 379
Roozendaal, B., 262, 265
Rorschach, H., 433
Rosabianca, A., 592
Rosch, E., 279
Rose, R. D., 537
Rosen, G., 140
Rosenberg, L. B., 151
Rosenberg, R., 144
Rosenhan, D., 482
Rosenheck, R. A., 498
Rosenkranz, M. A., 447
Rosenman, R. H., 465, 466
Rosenthal, D., 42
Rosenthal, R., 38, 294
Rosenthal, S. L., 34, 387
Rosenthal, T. L., 470, 539
Rosenzweig, M. R., 52, 88
Roseth, C. J., 282
Ross, D., 231
Ross, E. J., 76
Ross, H. E., 153
Ross, M., 244, 406
Ross, N. O., 279
Ross, P. E., 289–290, 348
Ross, S. A., 231
Ross-Stewart, L., 624
Rossi, J. S., 195
Rossion, B., 256
Roth, W. T., 346
Rothbard, N. P., 577, 607
Rothbart, M. K., 425
Rothbaum, B. O., 524
Rothschild, B., 212
Rotolo, T., 312
Rotter, J. B., 423
Rotter, M., 482
Rounsaville, B. J., 531
Rourke, B. P., 316
Rovee-Collier, C., 91
Rowan, M. J., 262
Rowell, A., 617
Rowell, D. L., 212
Rowland, C. R., 460
Rowland, D. L., 396–397
Roy, E., 77
Rozin, P., 339
Rubenstein, C., 114, 387
Rubinow, D. R., 494
Ruble, D. N., 375
Rudd, M. D., 506
Rudman, L. A., 589
Rudolf, G., 532
Rueckl, J. G., 253
Ruis, J. M., 466
Ruiz, J. M., 470
Rumbaugh, D., 285
Rummens, J., 463
Runco, M. A., 290–291, 299
Ruparel, K., 354
Rusbult, C. E., 421
Ruscio, J., 14, 20, 45–46, 349
Rush, A. J., 493–494, 528
Rushton, J. P., 324
Russell, G. F. M., 535–536
Russell, J. A., 223, 356
Russell, S. T., 320, 373
Russo, M. B., 500
Rust, R. T., 616
Rutledge, T. R., 361
Rutter, M., 94
Rutz, C., 39–40
Ruva, C., 247, 621
Ryan, A. M., 609
Ryan, M. P., 4
Ryan, R. M., 184, 347, 349, 419
Ryba, N. J. P., 138
Ryckman, R. M., 405
Ryder, N., 314
Ryff, C. D., 114
Rynearson, K., 3

S
Saab, P. G., 448
Saber, J. L., 268
Saccuzzo, D. P., 304, 305, 432
Sachdev, P. S., 529
Sackeim, H. A., 528
Sackett, P. R., 325, 609, 611
Sacks, O., 70, 149
Saffran, J. R., 100
Safton, A., 173
Sagan, C., 17, 615
Sagiv, N., 276
Saksida, L. M., 223
Salamone, J. D., 55
Sales, B. D., 621, 622–623
Sallinen, M., 169
Salmela-Aro, K., 448
Salmelin, R., 78
Salovey, P., 363
Salthouse, T. A., 114
Saltzman, E., 219
Salzarulob, P., 172
Sam, D. L., 463
Sampson, R. J., 504
Samuels, C. A., 379
Sanchez, J., 493
Sánchez, P., 612
Sanderman, R., 536
Sankofa, B. M., 324
Sankoorikal, G., 187

Sansone, L. A., 452
Sansone, R. A., 452
Santelli, J. S., 387
Santi, A., 68
Santos, R., 345
Santrock, J. W., 1, 5, 7, 96, 113–114, 345, 423, 460
Sapirstein, G., 38
Sapolsky, R., 450
Sarason, B. R., 504
Sarason, I. G., 504
Sarvananda, S., 528
Sarvela, P. D., 389
Sass, L. A., 484
Sateia, M. J., 175
Sato, T., 256, 485
Saunders, M. M., 141
Saunders, S. M., 532
Saunders, T., 471
Sautter, J. M., 576
Savage-Rumbaugh, S., 285
Saville, B. K., 281
Savsevitz, J., 521
Sawyer, R. G., 387
Saxton, M., 99
Saxvig, I. W., 168, 172
Saywitz, J., 386
Scaufeli, W. B., 448
Schacht, J. P., 196
Schachter, S., 359–360, 576
Schacter, D. L., 246, 247
Schafer, M., 562
Schafer, W. D., 37
Schaie, W., 114–115
Scharinger, C., 494
Scharrer, E., 587
Schaufeli, W. B., 448
Scheinkman, M., 535
Schenck, C. H., 176
Schenk, S., 341
Scher, S. J., 7
Scherer, K. R., 356
Schetter, C. D., 86
Schezer, J. A., 28
Schick, T., 18, 160, 428
Schick, V., 382
Schiffrin, R. M., 242
Schilling, M. E., 286
Schkade, D., 43
Schlaepfer, T. E., 528
Schleicher, S. S., 380, 388
Schlosberg, H., 356
Schlund, M. W., 73
Schmahmann, J. D., 71
Schmalt, H., 347
Schmalt, H. -D., 291
Schmeoderman, N., 448
Schmidt, F. L., 609
Schmidt, L. A., 435
Schmidt, M. G., 96
Schmitt, D. P., 406
Schmitt, J. A. J., 176
Schmitt, N., 325
Schmolck, H., 261
Schmuck, P., 617–618
Schneider, A., 179
Schneider, K. J., 27, 516
Schneider, L., 504
Schneider, P. L., 537
Schneiderman, N., 466
Schnyer, D. M., 169
Schoelles, K., 176
Scholl, B. J., 146, 148
Schooler, C., 318
Schopp, L. H., 537
Schottenbauer, M., 549
Schouten, J. S., 141
Schredl, M., 179
Schreiber, D. E., 248
Schreiber, E. H., 248
Schreiber, F. R., 499
Schroeder, A., 618
Schroeder, D. A., 583
Schroeder, J. E., 435
Schroeder, S., 444
Schuck, K., 531
Schuel, H., 197
Schuerger, J. M., 310
Schuetze, P., 87
Schulling, G. A, 373
Schultheiss, O. C., 75, 347
Schultz, D., 480
Schultz, D. P., 23, 25, 207, 411, 423, 609
Schultz, H. T., 34
Schultz, P. W., 550, 555–557, 617, 618
Schultz, S. E., 23, 25, 207, 411, 423, 609
Schum, T. R., 86
Schumacher, J., 183
Schuster, M. A., 451
Schwartz, B. L., 251
Schwartz, C., 168
Schwartz, F., 144
Schwartz, J. E., 410
Schwartz, M. S., 465
Schwartz, M. W., 335
Schwartz, S. J., 108
Schwitzgebel, E., 168
Sclafani, A., 339
Scoboria, A., 248
Scott, J. L., 270
Scott, J. P., 585
Scott, S. S., 621
Scruggs, T. E., 620
Scurfield, R. M., 451
Searcy, W. A., 284
Sears, L., 250, 262
Sears, S., 183, 469
Seburn, M., 549
Sechzer, J. A., 28, 30, 424
Seckel, A., 144
Seelig, D., 354
Seeman, P., 55
Seet, G., 627
Segal, Z. V., 183
Segerdahl, P., 285
Segerstrom, S., 447
Segraves, T., 396–397
Séguin, J. R., 87
Seidenberg, M., 250, 262
Seidler, G. H., 524
Seidman, B. F., 38
Seiffge-Krenke, I., 112
Seileppi, J. A., 530
Seiter, J. S., 557
Seitz, A., 156
Seligman, M. E. P., 30, 354, 418–419, 458–459, 531, 541
Seltzer, R., 622
Selye, H., 446–447
Senécal, S., 548
Senior, C., 356
Senn, C. Y., 342
Serfaty, M., 506
Serlin, I., 516
Serra-Grabulosa, J. P., 190
Servatius, R. J., 226
Service, R. F., 262
Sessa, V. I., 608
Sestir, M. A., 586–587
Seto, M. C., 386
Sevin, J. A., 214
Seybolt, D. C., 424
Seying, R., 621–622
Seyle, C., 594
Shade, R., 332
Shafer, C. S., 549
Shafer, H. J., 520
Shaffer, D. R., 93, 106, 377, 414, 424
Shafir, E., 295
Shafton, A., 177
Shah, P., 155
Shakesby, A. C., 262
Shalizi, C. R., 594
Shames, J., 298
Shamir, A., 319
Shanker, S., 285
Shanks, D. R., 206, 246, 260
Shankster, L. J., 609, 611
Shannon, J. D., 97
Shannon, K., 315
Shapiro, D. A., 531
Shapiro, F., 523, 524
Shapiro, J., 247
Shapiro, S., 183
Shapiro-Mendoza, C. K., 177
Sharf, R. S., 512, 514, 532
Sharot, T., 261
Sharpe, B., 434
Sharpe, L., 493
Shaughnessy, J. J., 267
Shaver, P. R., 95, 387, 452, 580–581, 584
Shaw, J. C., 423
Shaw, S. S., 621
Shaywitz, S. E., 70
Shegog, R., 445
Sheikh, A. A., 523
Shekunova, E., 217
Sheldon, K. M., 419
Shen, J., 334
Shepard, C., 518–519
Shepard, D. S., 532
Shephard, J. M., 276
Shepherd, G. M., 138
Sher, L., 494
Sherif, M., 550, 595
Sherman, D. K., 460, 594, 597
Sherman, S. J., 445, 592
Shibuya, I., 75
Shields, C. C., 107
Shiffman, S., 192
Shin, Y. J., 137
Shine, D., 392
Shiner, R. L., 404, 425, 427
Shiota, M. N., 351, 355–356
Shiv, B., 154
Shneerson, E. S., 174–175
Shneidman, E. S., 506
Shoda, Y., 422–423, 427
Shorrock, S. T., 263
Short, E. J., 197
Short, S. E., 624
Shorter, E., 487
Shulman, B. H., 415
Shurkin, J. N., 312
Sibley, C. G., 590
Sidanius, J., 590
Siefert, C. J., 431
Siegel, B. V., 62
Siegel, D. J., 2, 184
Siegel, R. K., 168–169
Siegler, R. S., 89, 298
Sienaert, P., 528
Siever, L. J., 503
Sigelman, C. K., 94
Signorello, L. B., 191
Sikka, P., 168
Silber, B. Y., 176
Silver, E., 488
Silverman, W. K., 94
Silverstein, C., 372, 373
Silverstein, S. M., 144
Simic, M., 535–536
Simister, J., 14
Simkins, B. J., 605
Simmons, J., 525
Simner, M. L., 18
Simon, A. F., 590, 593
Simon, D. J., 148
Simon, G. E., 537
Simon, H. A., 289
Simon-Thomas, E. R., 352
Simonotto, E., 320
Simons, D. A., 227–228
Simons, D. J., 256
Simons, G., 338
Simons, J. S., 247
Simonton, D. K., 30, 293, 298
Simpson, D. D., 190
Simpson, H. B., 534–535
Simpson, K. J., 342
Simpson, W. G., 605
Sims, H. P., Jr., 606
Sims, K. E., 94
Simsek, Z., 607
Singer, B. H., 114
Singer, L. T., 197
Singer, M. T., 562, 568–569
Singleton, J. L., 284
Sinha, R., 190
Siribaddana, S. H., 480
Sirkin, M. L., 568
Sitte, H. H., 494
Six, L. S., 264
Sjöqvist, F., 76
Skaff, M. M., 405
Skeels, H. M., 318
Skinner, B. F., 25, 213, 215
Skovholt, T. M., 532
Skuy, M., 319
Slaney, R. B., 410
Slater, A., 147
Slaymaker, E., 389
Slife, B. D., 17
Slot, L.A. B., 257
Slovic, P., 294
Smedley, A., 598
Smedley, B. D., 598
Smeets, T., 260
Smilek, D., 276, 286
Smith, A. M., 197
Smith, A. P., 268, 387, 462
Smith, C. A., 449–450, 470
Smith, C. S., 334
Smith, E. E., 38, 72, 323
Smith, J. D., 279
Smith, J. L., 352
Smith, M. L., 355, 528
Smith, N. G., 387
Smith, P., 311
Smith, P. B., 562
Smith, R. E., 422–423, 427
Smith, S. M., 354, 577
Smith, T. W., 466, 470
Smith. J., 228
Smolen, A., 194
Smorto, C., 144
Smyth, J. D., 43
Smyth, J. M., 470
Snibbe, J. R., 537
Sniehotta, F. F., 442
Snow, C. P., 567
Snowman, J., 219, 619–620
Snyder, A., 314
Sobel, E., 392
Sobell, L. C., 186
Sobell, M. B., 186
Sobolewski, J. M., 87
Soderstrom, M., 100
Sohal, T., 192
Solomon, E. P., 524
Solomon, J. L., 326
Solomon, L. Z., 261
Solomon, M. J., 235
Solomon, R. C., 226
Solomon, R. L., 346
Solomon, R. M., 524
Solowij, N., 196
Soman, D., 296
Sommers-Flanagan, J., 429
Sommers-Flanagan, R., 429
Song, W. O., 342
Soo, G., 627
Sorek, S., 255–256
Sörqvist, P., 615

Soule, J., 19
Sousa, K., 465
Soussignan, R., 356, 361
Soyez, V., 530
Spalding, K. L., 336
Spano, R., 40
Spector, P. E., 608
Spence, S., 144
Sperry, K., 621
Sperry, R., 66
Spiegler, M. D., 218, 521–522, 526
Spielman, A. J., 174–175
Spijker, J., 496
Spinath, B., 346
Spinella, M., 191
Spios, A., 489
Spira, J. L., 465
Spirito, A., 506
Spiro Wagner, P., 426
Spiro, C. S., 426
Spittle, M., 624
Spitzer, R. L., 482
Spoolman, S., 615
Sporer, S. L., 155
Sporns, O., 321
Spreecher, S., 388, 580–581
Springer, C. R., 220
Springer, D., 339
Springer, S. P., 65, 66, 79
Springston, f., 245
Squire, L. R., 261, 262
Squires, J., 88
Srivastava, S., 326
Sroufe, L. A., 95, 580
Stacks, A. M., 228
Staemmler, F. -M., 517
Staff, J., 388
Staff, R. T., 320
Stahl, D., 489
Stall, 616
Standage, M., 553
Standing, L., 257
Stanhope, N., 255
Stanley, D., 209–210
Stanley, D. A., 334
Stanovich, K. E., 14–15, 20, 22, 45
Stanowicz, L. B., 99
Stanton, S. J., 75
Stapel, D. A., 551
Staples, S. L., 615
Stark, C., 460
Staudiner, U. M., 111
Steadman, H. J., 488
Steblay, N. M., 615
Steciuk, M., 577
Steel, G. D., 628
Steele, C. M., 592
Steen, N., 607
Stefurak, T., 373
Steg, L., 220
Steiger, A., 171–172
Stein, B. D., 451
Stein, D. J., 435, 534
Stein, L. M., 248
Stein, M. B., 435
Stein, M. D., 178
Stein, M. I., 297
Stein, M. T., 176
Steinberg, L., 108
Steiner, B., 614
Steinmayr, R., 346
Steinmetz, J., 208
Stemler, S. E., 324
Stephens, K., 324
Stephens, R. S., 196
Stepper, S., 361
Stern, P. C., 618
Stern, S. L., 458
Sternberg, R. J., 276, 288, 292–293, 298, 304, 308, 322–324, 326, 461, 578–579
Sterns, H. L., 113
Stetz, T., 609
Stevens, L. C., 469
Stewart, M. O., 460, 518
Stewart-Williams, S., 56
Stickgold, R., 172, 173, 199
Stickle, T. R., 501
Stiles, W. B., 531
Stinson, F. S., 197, 497
Stip, E., 484
Stipek, D., 345
Stix, G., 467, 485
Stöber, J., 346
Stoberock, B., 265, 295
Stockdale, G. D., 376, 590
Stoffregen, T. A., 142
Stokes, D. M., 159, 465
Stolar, N., 527
Stoleman, I. P., 191
Stoll, O., 624
Stone, J., 591
Stone, T. H., 548
Stopfer, M., 138
Stoppard, J. M., 493
Storr, A., 549
Stovel, N., 390
Strack, F., 361, 550
Straif, K., 197
Strambler, M. J., 38
Strange, J. R., 76
Strassberg, D. S., 397, 431
Straub, R, 443–444
Strayer, D. L., 36
Streng, A., 141
Strenze, T., 311
Strickler, E. M., 342
Stroebe, W., 337
Strong, B., 393–394
Strongman, K. T., 362, 449
Strote, J., 190
Strough, J., 379
Stroup, D. F., 442–443
Strubbe, M. J., 560
Strunk, D., 460, 518
Strupp, S., 541
Sturges, J. W., 523
Sturges, L. V., 523
Stuss, D. T., 61, 68
Suarez, E., 390
Subedi, S., 530
Substance Abuse and Mental Health Services Administration, 185, 190, 196
Suchy, Y., 504
Sue, D. W., 489, 496
Sue, S., 489, 496
Suedfeld, P., 184, 628
Sugawara, K., 340
Sugden, K., 494
Sugihara, V., 379
Sugimoto, K., 338
Suh, E. M., 425
Suinn, R. M., 445, 487, 598
Sukel, H. L., 621
Sullivan, H., 415
Sullivan, P., 604
Sullivan, T.A., 608
Suls, J., 465
Sumathipala, A., 480
Sumerlin, J. R., 418
Summers, A., 622
Sumner, F. C., 27
Sun, R., 286, 289
Sundequist, U., 184
Sung, H., 489
Sunnafrank, M., 576
Supeli, A., 548
Sutherland, 261
Suzuki, A., 67
Suzuki, L., 324
Suzuki, M., 354
Svartdal, F., 221
Swamidass, P. M., 549, 606
Swank, P., 106
Swann, W. B., Jr., 405
Swearer, S. M., 584
Swerdlik, M. E., 305
Swinson, P., 549
Swinson, R. P., 436
Symbaluk, D. G., 214, 217–218, 224
Synorst, L. L., 431
Szabo, A., 471
Szabó, N., 316
Szollos, A., 448

T

Tabors, P. O., 100
Tackett, J. L., 585
Tae, W. K., 176
Tafrate, R. C., 588
Taft, C. T., 389
Taheri, S., 177
Tahlor, F., 604
Takahashi, J. S., 333
Takeuchi, M. M., 117
Takeuchi, S. A., 117
Takooshian, H., 615
Tal-Or, N., 553
Talbot, J. A., 514, 529
Talley, P. F., 541
Tamis-LeMonda, C. S., 87, 97, 100
Tang, C. Y., 70
Tang, L., 332
Tanner, D. C., 69
Tanner, J. M., 108
Tapert, S. F., 194
Taraban, R., 3
Taris, T. W., 448
Tashkin, D. P., 197
Tatum, J. L., 110
Taub, E., 59
Tausig, M., 530
Tavakoli, S., 570
Tavris, C., 387, 557
Taylor, C., 373
Taylor, D. J., 175
Taylor, G. J., 363
Taylor, I. M., 553
Taylor, J. R., 176, 186
Taylor, K., 567
Taylor, L. A., 194
Taylor, M. A., 487
Taylor, S. E., 452, 460, 464, 470
Taylor, T., 285
Taylor-Allan, H. L., 363
Te Nijenhuis, 184
Teed, E. L., 530
Telander, K., 404, 410
Telglasi, H., 434
Tempel, A. B., 430
ten Brinke, L., 358
Tenenbaum, G., 624
Tenhula, W. N., 525
Tennesen, M., 136
Tennie, C., 231
Teo, A. R., 480
Terman, L. M., 306, 312
Terry, C., 512
Terry, D. J., 556
Terry, K., 420
Terry, P. C., 624
Teter, C. J., 187
Tetrick, L. E., 450
Tewksbury, R., 194
Teyber, E., 514, 536
Thakur, S., 33
Tharp, R. G., 234–235, 346, 460, 538–540
Tharp, R. J., 215
Thelen, K., 499
Thelen, M. H., 341
Théret, H., 68
Thibault, P., 356
Thibodeau, R., 7
Thiessen, E. D., 100
Thoennes, N., 389
Thomas, A., 89
Thomas, M., 118, 227, 482
Thompson, A., 59
Thompson, K. M., 232
Thompson, L. A., 311
Thompson, R., 68, 262
Thompson, R. A., 87
Thompson, R. F., 71
Thompson, W. L., 277
Thomsen, D. K., 255
Thomson, D., 247–248
Thorne, D., 170
Thornton, S. N., 342
Thorp, D., 93
Thorphy, M. J., 177
Thorson, J. A., 115
Throburn, J., 506
Thyen, U., 379
Thyer, B., 524
Tian, C., 100
Tidwell, M. O., 95, 580
Tierney, S., 341
Tierney, S. C., 38, 541
Tieu, T. -T., 579
Tiggermann, M., 551
Tijerinoo, R., 612
Till, B., 209–210
Tilton-Weaver, L. C., 109
Timmerman, C. K., 220
Timmerman, I. G. H., 536
Ting-A-Kee, R., 346
Tippett, R. M., 576
Tippin, S. M., 306
Tipples, J., 355
Titchener, E., 24
Tite, L., 324
Titova, E. Y., 66
Tittle, R. C., 312
Tjaden, P., 389
Tlusten, D., 381
Tobler, N. S., 445
Tolman, E. C., 28, 229
Tolstoy, L., 331
Tomasello, M., 99
Toneatto, T., 186, 520
Tong, J., 335
Tong, L., 332
Tononi, G., 172
Toro, C. T., 59, 490
Torrey, E. F., 530
Torterolo, P., 171
Tourangeau, R., 42
Towson, S., 435–436
Toyota, H., 245
Trachet, T., 19
Tracy, J. A., 208
Trainor, L. J., 100
Travis, F., 183
Treasure, D. C., 553
Treffert, D. A., 313–314
Treffinger, D. J., 313
Tregear, S., 176
Trehub, S. E., 100
Tremblay, R. E., 186
Triandis, H. C., 425
Trickett, P. K., 108
Triplett, N., 560
Trocmé, 228
Troll, L. E., 405
Tromovitch, P., 386
Trope, Y., 597
Troutman, A. C., 218, 227–228
Truax, S. R., 360
Trujillo, L. T., 169
Trull, T., 483–484
Tsai, C., 342
Tsai, F. -R., 553

Tsai, W. -C., 491, 609
Tse, L., 108
Tselis, A., 54
Tseng, V., 98
Tubb, V. A., 161
Tucker, K. L., 467
Tucker, P., 334
Tugade, M. M., 445
Tulving, E., 250, 262
Tumeo, M., 299
Turenius, C. L., 337
Turiel, E., 110
Turkheimer, E., 317–318
Turner, C. M., 397, 431
Turner, S. J. M., 535
Tutty, S., 537
Tversky, A., 294–294
Twenge, J. M., 387, 406
Tye, M., 376
Tyler, A. N., 87
Tyler, J. M., 551
Tyron, 317
Tyrrell, D., 462
Tzuriel, D., 319

U

U. S. Census Bureau, 30, 88
U. S. Department of Energy, 616
U. S. Department of Health and Human Services, 191
U.S. Department of Energy Office of Science, 84
U.S. Department of Labor, 430, 610, 618
Uchida, Y., 357
Uchino, B. N., 470
Uecker, J., 387
Uhlmann, E. L., 376, 605
Ulm, R. R., 459
Underwood, B. J., 258
Undsay, J. J., 358
United Nations Educational Scientific and Cultural Organization, 585
United Nations Programme on HIV/ AIDS, 391–392
Unsworth, G., 233
Unyk, A. M., 100
Uwe, P., 534
Uziel, L., 560
Uzzell, D., 617–618

V

Vaes, J., 592
Vaidya, R. S., 459
Vaillant, G. E., 114, 196
Valentine, E. R., 265
Valentine, S., 548
Valerius, G., 491
Valiente, C., 96
Valins, S., 359, 618
Vallerand, A. H., 141
Vallerand, R. J., 448
van Bellen, G., 381
Van Blerkom, D. L., 2, 5–8
Van Dam, A. M., 59
Van Dammen, D. P., 489
Van den Bergh, B., 375
van der Hart, O., 512
van der Kooy, D., 346
Van Der Ploeg, H. M., 499
van Deurzen, E., 516
van Dierendonck, D., 114, 184
Van Dongen, H. P., 169
Van Eenwyk, J., 233
van Elst, L. T., 491
Van Goozen, S. H. M., 343
Van Heck, G. L., 466
Van Iddkinge, C. H., 610
Van Kammen, D. P., 42
Van Lawick-Goodall J., 39
Van Limbeek, J., 70
van Os, J., 317
Van Volkom, M., 374
Van Vugt, M., 617–618
Vandell, D. L., 95
Vandenbergen, J., 357
Vandenberghe, K., 116
vanDeusen, K. M., 212
Vanhaudenhuyse, A., 72
Vanheule, S., 357
Vansteelandt, K., 528
Varca, P. E., 548
Vargas-Perez, H., 346
Vasa, R. A., 528
Vaughan, A., 500
Vaughn, L., 18, 160, 428
Vazire, S., 21–22
Veale, J. F., 370, 374
Vega, L. A., 299
Veiga, J. F., 607
Velez, A., 78
Venezia, M., 93
Ventura, S., 387
ver Halen, N. B. L. D., 594
Verbalis, J. G., 342
Verges, M., 617
Verhaeghe, P., 357
Verhoeven, C., 548
Verkuyten, M., 406
Vermeiren, R., 585
Vernon, P. A., 320
Veron, D. J., 242
Verze, P., 379
Vetrugno, R., 176
Vi, P., 627
Videon, T. M., 97
Viegener, B. J., 340
Viero, C., 75
Villemure, C., 141
Vine, A. E., 489, 494
Vinson, D. C., 195
Violani, C., 178
Visser, B. A., 503
Viveros, M. P., 87
Vlek, C., 220, 617–618
Vogel, E. K., 260
Vogel, M. T., 555
Vogler, J., 528
Vogler, R., 521
Vojdanoska, M., 219
Volberg, G., 66
Volkow, N. D., 55
Volpicelli, J. R., 459
Von Gontard, A., 86
Von Ranson, K. M., 387
von Voss, P., 336
von Wangenheim, G., 596
Vongerichten, A., 78
Vonkers, K., 493–494
Voon, V., 528
Votaw, J. R., 186
Vuillermot, S., 488
Vygotsky, L., 106–107

W

Wade, K. A., 252
Wager, T. D., 38
Wagner, F. E., 524
Wagner, M. K., 424
Wagstaff, G., 182
Waid, W. M., 354
Wainwright, J. L., 373
Waiter, G. D., 320
Wakefield, J. C., 483
Waldinger, M. D., 397
Waldman, 584–585
Waldron, M., 317, 318
Walk, R. D., 150
Walker, D. L., 352
Walker, E., 488–489, 491, 528, 529
Walker, I., 596
Walker, M. P., 172, 199
Wallace, B., 277
Wallach, M. A., 292
Wallnau, L. B., 634
Walls, P., 139, 141
Walsh, R., 183
Walters, R., 227
Walton, C. E., 92
Wambach, C., 6
Wampold, B. E., 38, 516, 541
Wan, C. Y., 68
Wandersman, 445
Wang, C., 442
Wang, E. T., 86
Wang, G. -J., 55
Wang, J. M., 59
Wang, L., 337
Wang, Q., 244
Wang, S. -H., 262
Wang, S. S., 339
Ward, L. M., 132, 220, 388
Ward, T., 233
Ward-Alexander, L., 530
Wargo, E., 102, 265, 447, 497
Wark, G. R., 111
Warne, R., 17
Warner, J. A., 379
Warren, A. R., 621
Warren, D. J., 128
Warren, M. P., 108
Warren, W. H., 229
Warshauer-Baker, E., 324, 593, 598
Washburn, A. L., 335
Washburn, J. J., 529
Washburn, M., 27
Washton, A. M., 190
Watanabe, T., 156
Waterfield, R., 180
Waterhouse, J., 334
Waterhouse, J. W., 352
Watkins, J. G., 180
Watkins, M. W., 310
Watson, B., 43
Watson, D. L., 215, 234–235, 346, 460, 538–540
Watson, J., 211
Watson, J. B., 24
Watson, J. D., 100
Watson, J. M., 36
Watson, N. V., 52
Watt, C., 158
Watt, T., 624
Watts, D. J., 547
Way, L., 212
Waytz, A., 40, 593
Weaver, G., 264–265
Weaver, G. E., 256
Weaver, Y., 114
Weber, L., 488
Wechsler, D., 304, 306–307
Wechsler, H., 190, 194
Wedding, D., 42, 514
Weekley, J. A., 431
Weeks, M., 549
Weems, C. F., 501
Wehr, T. A., 494
Weidenhammer, W, 141
Weinberg, R. A., 317–318
Weinberger, D. R, 489
Weingarten, K., 459
Weinstein, R. S., 38
Weinstein, Y., 246, 260
Weintraub, M. L., 501
Weintraub, S., 311
Weir, A. A. S., 40
Weisenel, N., 341
Weiser, M., 489
Weishaar, M. E., 507
Weiss, H. M., 606
Weiss, K. J., 478
Weiss, P., 70
Weisskirch, R. S., 108
Weissman, A. M., 452
Weitzman, E. R., 460
Weizman, A., 190
Welch, R. D., 95
Welker, W., 426
Wellings, K., 389
Wells, B. E., 387
Wells, D. L., 78, 252
Wells, G. L, 253
Welsh, D. P., 281
Welsh, K. M., 347
Weltzin, T. E., 341
Wenckstern, S., 506
Wener, R. E., 560
Werner, B., 627
Werner, C. M., 617
Wernet, S. P., 594
Wertenbroch, K., 7
Wertheimer, M., 25
Wesensten, N. J., 190
Wessel, L., 257
West, A. N., 161
West, B.J., 609
West, L. J., 569
West, M., 606, 608–609
West, R., 192
West, T. G., 277
Westera, W., 220
Westermark, P. O., 336
Western, D., 531
Westrin, A., 494
Wethingon, E., 114
Wetter, D. W., 192
Wexler, A., 386
Wexler, M. N., 568
Wheat, A. L., 465
Wheeler, L., 359
Whelan, J. P., 520
Whipple, B., 384–385
Whishaw, I. Q., 74
White, B. J., 192, 595
White, J., 323–324, 326
White, K. B., 389–390
White, K. M., 43
White, N. S., 62
White, T. L., 37
Whitehouse, A. J. O., 252
Whiteman, M. C., 404, 407
Whitley, B. E., Jr., 376, 589–591, 593, 595, 597
Whitman, L. G., 182
Whitney, D. M., 349
Whitton, E., 516
Wickwire, E. M., 520
Widner, R. L., 251
Wiederhold, B. K., 523, 537
Wiederhold, M. D., 523
Wiederman, M. W., 28, 382
Wiegel, M., 386
Wiek, C., 617
Wiese, M., 293, 311
Wiesel, W. N., 127
Wieselquist, J., 421
Wiesemann, C., 379
Wigfield, A., 346
Wilber, M. K., 520
Wilde, M. L., 588
Wilder, D. A., 590, 593
Wilding, J. M., 265
Wilhelm, F. H., 536
Wilke, H, 618
Wilkie, D. M., 223
Wilkinson, D., 232
Wilkinson, M., 179
Wilkinson, R. G., 450
Willander, J., 249
Willems, R. M., 78

Willer, J. -C., 139
William, P., 549
Williams, C. M., 377
Williams, D. G., 357, 541
Williams, G., 336–337
Williams, J. M., 624–625
Williams, K. D., 623
Williams, L. M., 356
Williams, M., 505
Williams, R., 195
Williams, R. B., 465, 466
Williams, R. L., 4, 324
Williams, W. M., 311, 374
Williamson, D. A., 336
Willott, J. F., 136
Willoughby, T., 7, 245, 270
Wilmot, W. W., 593
Wilson, A. E., 153, 406
Wilson, B. S., 137
Wilson, D. B., 531
Wilson, D. W., 582
Wilson, G. D., 373
Wilson, J. L., 341
Wilson, K. A., 108
Wilson, K. B., 615
Wilson, M. A., 344, 609
Wilson, S. L., 87
Wilson, T. D., 16, 294, 553, 566, 583
Wimpenny, J. H., 40
Winfree, L. T., Jr., 470
Wing, R. R., 340
Winger, G., 186
Wingood, G. M., 233
Winkelman, S. E., 251
Winkleby, M., 450
Winner, E., 293, 297, 312
Winstead, B. A., 493
Winter, D. D. N., 616–618
Wirth, M. M., 75, 347
Wise, T. N., 385
Wiseman, R., 158–160, 584
Wissing, M. P., 613
Witelson, S. F., 64
Witherington, D. C., 149–150
Witt, A. C., 310
Wixted, J. T., 259, 261
Woerner, M., 528
Wohl, M. J. A., 6
Woldredge, J., 614
Wolfson, S., 612
Wolpe, J., 540, 570
Wolpin, M., 200
Wong, A. M., 59
Wong, F. Y., 536
Wong, M. -L., 336
Wong, W., 4
Woo, J. S. T., 396
Wood, E., 7, 245, 270
Wood, J. M., 158, 434
Woodard, E. H., 588
Woodhill, B. M., 379
Woodman, G. F., 260
Woodruff-Pak, D., 208
Woods, A. M., 461, 463
Woods, J. H., 186
Woods, P., 548
Woods, S. C., 335, 606, 608–609
Woolard, J. L., 389
Woroch, B., 247
Worthen, J. B., 268–270
Wosnitzer, R., 587
Wraga, M. J., 276
Wright, B., 214
Wright, D. B., 257
Wright, J., 182
Wright, K. P., Jr., 170, 334
Wright, P. B., 485
Wright, T. A., 604, 606
Wrightman, L. S., 623
Wu, C. W. H., 140
Wuethrich, B., 194
Wundt, W., 23–24
Wurtele, S. K., 227–228
Wyatt, J. W., 426
Wynn, T., 64
Wynne, L. C., 226

X

Xiao, D.-K., 242
Xu, T. -X., 262–263

Y

Yahnke, B. H., 523
Yakusheva, O., 338
Yamada, S., 375
Yanchar, S. C., 17
Yang, B., 505
Yang, S., 607
Yang, Y., 332
Yao, W. -D., 262–263
Yarber, W. L., 392
Yates, W. R., 496
Yazdani, H., 36
Yedidia, M. J., 116
Yeo, R. A., 70, 320
Yi, H., 265
Yip, P. S. F., 506
Yoder, C. Y., 267
Yokota, F., 232
Yonas, A., 150
Yonkers, K., 528
Yontef, G., 517
Yoshida, K., 142
Yost, W. A., 134
Young, A. M., 281
Young, A. W., 355
Young, R. K., 314, 577
Youngren, V. R., 513
Ysseldyke, J., 40
Yu, K. S., 223
Yu, S. L., 6
Yuen, C., 587
Yuen, L. M., 5, 7, 460

Z

Zachariae, R., 447
Zadra, A., 176, 179, 199
Zagefka, H., 595
Zagoory-Sharon, O., 75
Zaiser, E., 593
Zakharenko, S. S., 262
Zamarripa, F., 332
Zamchech, N., 353
Zampetakis, L. A., 363
Zanello, S., 528
Zanna, M. P., 554, 594–595
Zarcadoolas, C., 443, 445
Zárraga, C., 606
Zarrouf, F., 528
Zatorre, R. J., 74
Zatzick, C. D., 608
Zautra, A. J., 364
Zechmeister, E. B., 267
Zee, P. C., 334
Zeidan, F., 183
Zeinalova, E., 558
Zeisel, J., 618
Zeiss, A., 396–397
Zeiss, R., 396–397
Zelano, C., 137–138
Zelazo, P. D., 87
Zeldow, P. B., 379
Zemishlany, Z., 190
Zentall, T. R., 25, 223
Zentner, M., 419
Zetlin, A., 314
Zhang, B., 168
Zhang, N., 59
Zhang, R. L., 59
Zhang, Z. G., 59
Zhao, G., 442
Zheng, L., 607
Zhou, M., 496
Zigler, E., 312
Zimbardo, P. G., 427, 435, 548, 567, 593
Zimmerman, J., 235
Zinner, E., 128
Zipse, L., 68
Ziv, L., 486
Zoellner, L. A., 259
Zoss, M., 621
Zucherman, M., 553
Zucker, K. J., 482
Zuckerman, M., 344
Zusman, M. E., 281, 390
Zvartau, E., 217
Zvolensky, M. J., 448
Zweben, J. E., 190

Subject Index/Glossary

A
Ablation (ab-LAY-shun), 62. Surgical removal of tissue.
Abnormality
  core features of, 477–478
  defined, 476
  mild, 477
  statistical, 476
Absolute threshold, 126. The minimum amount of physical energy necessary to produce a sensation.
Abstracts, 22
Acceptance, 116, 417
Accessibility (in memory), 256, 257. Memories currently stored in memory which can be retrieved when necessary are both available and accessible.
Accommodation (In Piaget's theory), 101. The modification of existing mental patterns to fit new demands (that is, mental schemes are changed to accommodate new information or experiences).
Accommodation (in vision), 129. Changes in the shape of the lens of the eye.
  depth perception and, 151
Acculturative stress, 463. Stress caused by the many changes and adaptations required when a person moves to a foreign culture.
Acetylcholine (ah-SEET-ul-KOH-leen), 55. The neurotransmitter released by neurons to activate muscles.
Achievement
  giftedness and, 312
  IQ and, 311–312
  need for, 346–347
Acquaintance (date) rape, 290. Forced intercourse that occurs in the context of a date or other voluntary encounter.
Acquisition, 209. The period in conditioning during which a response is reinforced.
Acromegaly, 75
Action component, 554. How one tends to act toward the object of an attitude.
Action potential, 53–54. The nerve impulse.
Action therapy, 514
Activating experience, 518
Activation-synthesis hypothesis, 178. An attempt to explain how dream content is affected by motor commands in the brain that occur during sleep but are not carried out.
Active listener, 5. A person who knows how to maintain attention, avoid distractions, and actively gather information from lectures.
Active listening, 532
Actor-observer bias, 552–553. The tendency to attribute the behavior of others to internal causes while attributing one's own behavior to external causes (situations and circumstances).
Acupuncture, 140–141
Acute stress disorder, 498. A psychological disturbance lasting up to 1 month following stresses that would produce anxiety in anyone who experienced them.
Adamson, Kate, 72
Adaptability, 378
Adaptive behaviors, 351. Actions that aid attempts to survive and adapt to changing conditions.
Addiction. *See* Physical dependence
ADHD. *See* Attention deficit/hyperactivity disorder (ADHD)
Adjustment disorders, 495–496. An emotional disturbance caused by ongoing stressors within the range of common experience.
Adler, Alfred, 26, 415
Adolescence, 107. The culturally defined period between childhood and adulthood.
  personal identity in, 108–109, 112
  premarital intercourse rates, 387–388
  role confusion in, 112
  sexual scripts of, 381
Adrenal glands, 76. Endocrine glands that arouse the body, regulate salt balance, adjust the body to stress, and affect sexual functioning.
Adrenaline, 351. A hormone produced by the adrenal glands that tends to arouse the body.
Adulthood
  challenges of, 113
  criteria for, 107
  emerging, 109
  integrity/despair in, 113
  intimacy/isolation in, 112
  marriage and, 114
Advice giving, 523
Aerial perspective, 151
Aerophobia, 497
Affectional needs, 96. Emotional needs for love and affection.
African Americans, 97, 324
Afterimages, 132
Age
  IQ and, 311
  mental sharpness and, 114
  regression, 182
  successful, 114–115
Ageism, 115, 589. An institutionalized tendency to discriminate on the basis of age; prejudice based on age.
Aggression, 584. Any action carried out with the intention of harming another person, or achieving one's goals at the expense of another person.
  against women, 587
  assertiveness and, 570–571
  aversive stimuli and, 585–586
  biology and, 585
  causes of, 584–587
  displaced, 589
  displacement of, 452–453
  forms of, 584
  frustration and, 452, 585–586
  instincts and, 584–585
  media violence and, 586–587
  prevention of, 587–588
  punishment and, 227
  ritualized, 584
  social learning theory of, 586
  televised, 232–233
Aggression cues, 585. Stimuli or signals that are associated with aggression and that tend to elicit it.
Aggressive pornography, 587. Media depictions of sexual violence or of forced participation in sexual activity.
Agnosia, 70
Agoraphobia (without panic), 497. The fear that something extremely embarrassing will happen if one leaves the house or enters unfamiliar situations.
Agreeableness, 409
Alarm reaction, 446. First stage of the GAS, during which bodily resources are mobilized to cope with a stressor.
Alcohol
  characterization of, 193
  moderate use of, 195
  self-handicapping strategies for, 553
Alcohol abuse
  aversion therapy for, 521–522
  level of, 193–194
  recognition of, 194–195
  risk for, 194
  treatment for, 195–196
Alcohol myopia (my-OH-pea-ah), 193. Shortsighted thinking and perception that occurs during alcohol intoxication.
Alcoholics Anonymous, 195–196
Alexithymia (a-LEX-ih-THIGH-me-ah), 357. A learned difficulty expressing emotions; more common in men.
Algorithm, 286. A learned set of rules that always leads to the correct solution of a problem.
All-or-nothing thinking, 280, 518. Classifying objects or events as absolutely right or wrong, good or bad, acceptable or unacceptable, and so forth.
Alpha waves, 171. Large, slow brain waves associated with relaxation and falling asleep.
Altered states of consciousness (ACS), 168. A condition of awareness distinctly different in quality or pattern from waking consciousness.
Alternate responses, 235
Alzheimer's (ALLS-hi-merz) disease, 256, 485. An age-related disease characterized by memory loss, mental confusion, and, in its later stages, a nearly total loss of mental abilities.
Ambien, 175
Ambiguous stimuli, 146
Ambivalence, 455. Mixed positive and negative feelings or simultaneous attraction and repulsion.
Ambivalent attachment, 94–95, 580. An emotional bond marked by conflicting feelings of affection, anger, and emotional turmoil.
American College Test (ACT), 307
American Psychological Association (APA)
  divisions of, 31
  ethical guidelines of, 22
  website for, 10
American sign language, 283–284
Ames room, 143
Amnesia, 182, 260–261
Amok, 480
Amphetamine psychosis, 188
Amphetamines
  abuse of, 188–189
  characterization of, 187
  cocaine *versus,* 189
  tolerance of, 188
  types of, 187–188
Amplitude, 134
Amygdala (ah-MIG-dah-luh), 73, 211. A part of the limbic system associated with fear responses.
  emotions and, 353
Amytal, 260
Anagrams test, 292
Anal stage, 413–14. The psychosexual stage corresponding roughly to the period of toilet training (ages 1 to 3).
Anal-expulsive personality, 412. A disorderly, destructive, cruel, or messy person.
Anal-retentive personality, 412, 414. A person who is obstinate, stingy, or compulsive, and who generally has difficulty "letting go."
Analogies, 298
Analysis of resistance, 513
Analysis of transference, 514
Analyzing complex skills, 609
Androgens, 343, 370. Any of a number of male sex hormones, especially testosterone.
Androgyny (an-DROJ-ih-nee), 378–379. The presence of both "masculine" and "feminine" traits in a single person (as masculinity and femininity are defined within one's culture).
Angel dust. *See* Phencyclidine (PCP)
Anger
  impending death and, 116
  norepinephrine and, 76
  punishment and, 228
  sexual dysfunction and, 394
Anger control, 588. Personal strategies for reducing or curbing anger.
Anhedonia (an-he-DAWN-ee-ah), 190. An inability to feel pleasure.
Anima, 416. An archetype representing the female principle.
Animal language, 284–285
Animal models, 33–34. In research, an animal whose behavior is used to derive principles that may apply to human behavior. *See also* Human participants
  naturalistic observations of, 39–40
Animus, 416. An archetype representing the male principle.
Anorexia nervosa (AN-uh-REK-see-yah ner-VOH-sah), 339–340. Active self-starvation or a sustained loss of appetite that has psychological origins.

Antecedents, 206, 235. Events that precede a response.
Anterograde amnesia, 260. Loss of the ability to form or retrieve memories for events that occur after an injury or trauma.
Anthropomorphic (AN-thro-po-MORE-fik) error, 40. The error of attributing human thoughts, feelings, or motives to animals, especially as a way of explaining their behavior.
Antidepressants, 527. Mood-elevating drugs.
Antipsychotics (major tranquilizers), 489, 527. Drugs that, in addition to having tranquilizing effects, also tend to reduce hallucinations and delusional thinking.
Antisocial behavior, 576–577. Any behavior that has a negative impact on other people.
  aggression, 584–589
  anger, 588
  prejudice, 589–591
Antisocial personality (antisocial/psychopathic personality), 503–504. A person who lacks a conscience; is emotionally shallow, impulsive, selfish; and tends to manipulate others.
Anxiety Apprehension, dread, or uneasiness similar to fear but based on an unclear threat.
  basic, 415
  causes of, 456
  moral anxiety, 412
  neurotic, 412
  separation, 94
  social, 435
  test, 345–346
Anxiety disorders, 480. Disruptive feelings of fear, apprehension, or anxiety, or distortions in behavior that are anxiety related.
  effects of, 495
  humanistic-existential theory of, 501–502
  psychodynamic approach to, 501
  signs of, 496
  types of, 495–499
Anxiety reduction hypothesis, 503. Explains the self-defeating nature of avoidance responses as a result of the reinforcing effects of relief from anxiety.
Anxiolytics (ANG-zee-eh LIT-iks), 527. Drugs (such as Valium) that produce relaxation or reduce anxiety.
APA. *See* American Psychological Association (APA)
Aphasia (ah-FAZE-yah), 67. A speech disturbance resulting from brain damage.
  Broca's area and, 68
  defined, 67
  receptive, 69
Aphrodisiacs, 382
Aplysia, 262
Apparent motion, 153
Apparent-distance hypothesis, 153. An explanation of the moon illusion stating that the horizon seems more distant than the night sky.
Applied behavior analysis, 521
Applied psychology. The use of psychological principles and research methods to solve practical problems.
  areas of, 603
  educational, 619–620
  environmental, 611–619
  future of, 625
  human factors, 626–629
  industrial/organizational, 604–611
  legal, 620–623
  sports, 623–625
Appraisal, 360
Appreciation, 417
Approach-approach conflict, 454–455. Choosing between two positive, or desirable, alternatives.
Approach-avoidance conflicts, 455. Being attracted to and repelled by the same goal or activity.
Aptitude, 304. A capacity for learning certain abilities.
Aptitude tests, 610, 611. A test that rates a person's potential to learn skills required by various occupations.
  function of, 304–305
  objectivity of, 305–306
  reliability of, 305
  validity of, 305
  worksite use of, 610–611
Aquaphobia, 497
Arab-Americans, 98
Arachibutyrophobia, 497
Archetype (ARE-keh-type), 416. A universal idea, image, or pattern, found in the collective unconscious.
Archimedes, 292
Architectural psychology, 618. Study of the effects buildings have on behavior and the design of buildings using behavioral principles.
Army Alpha test, 307–308
Arousal
  ANS, 362
  disorders, 395–396
  levels of, 345–346
  sexual, 380–383
Arousal theory, 344–345. Assumes that people prefer to maintain ideal, or comfortable, levels of arousal.
Artificial hearing, 136–137
Artificial intelligence, 320–321
Asch experiment, 562–563
Asch, Solomon, 562
Asexual, 372. A person not romantically or erotically attracted to either men or women.
Asian-Americans
  emotional responses by, 356–357
  parenting by, 98
Aspartame, 316
Assertiveness training, 570–571. Instruction in how to be self-assertive.
Assessment center, 611. A program set up within an organization to conduct in-depth evaluations of job candidates.
Assimilation, 101. In Piaget's theory, the application of existing mental patterns to new situations (that is, the new situation is assimilated to existing mental schemes).
Association areas (association cortex), 67. All areas of the cerebral cortex that are not primarily sensory or motor in function.
Associative learning, 206, 212. The formation of simple associations between various stimuli and responses.
Astigmatism (ah-STIG-mah-tiz-em), 129. Defects in the cornea, lens, or eye that cause some areas of vision to be out of focus.
Astraphobia, 497
Astrology, 19–20
Atkinson-Schiffrin model, 242
Attachment
  affectional needs and, 96
  critical time for, 94
  day care and, 95
  emotional, 94–95
  love and, 579–580
  quality of, 94–95
  styles of, 94–95
  types of, 580
Attention deficit/hyperactivity disorder (ADHD), 187. A behavioral problem characterized by short attention span, restless movement, and impaired learning capacity.
Attention, selective, 148–149
Attentional bottleneck, 148
Attentional overload, 614. A stressful condition caused when sensory stimulation, information, and social contacts make excessive demands on attention.
Attentional spotlight, 148
Attitude, 554. A learned tendency to respond to people, objects, or institutions in a positive or negative way.
  behavior and, 555–556
  changing, 556–559
  characterization of, 554
  cognitive dissonance in, 557–558
  formation of, 554–555
  measurement of, 556
Attitude scale, 556. A collection of attitudinal statements with which respondents indicate agreement or disagreement.
Attraction. *See* Interpersonal attraction
Attractiveness, 577
Attribution, 552. The mental process of making inferences about the causes of one's own behavior, and that of others. In emotion, the process of attributing arousal to a particular source.
  errors in, 520
  fundamental errors of, 552–553
  making, 552
  theories of, 359–360, 552–553
Auditory ossicles, 134
Authenticity, 516. In Carl Rogers's terms, the ability of a therapist to be genuine and honest about his or her own feelings.
Authoritarian beliefs, 591
Authoritarian parents, 96. Parents who enforce rigid rules and demand strict obedience to authority.
Authoritarian personality, 591. A personality pattern characterized by rigidity, inhibition, prejudice, and an excessive concern with power, authority, and obedience.
Authoritative parents, 96, 117. Parents who supply firm and consistent guidance combined with love and affection.
Autism spectrum disorders, 68
Autokinetic effect, 550. The apparent movement of a stationary pinpoint of light displayed in a darkened room.
Autonomic nervous system (ANS), 57–58, 353. The system of nerves carrying information to and from the internal organs and glands.
Autonomy, 112, 417
Autonomy versus shame and doubt, 112. A conflict created when growing self-control (autonomy) is pitted against feelings of shame or doubt.
Availability (in memory), 257. Memories currently stored in memory are available.
Aversion therapy, 521–522. Suppressing an undesirable response by associating it with aversive (painful or uncomfortable) stimuli.
Aversive consequence, 217. A stimulus that is painful or uncomfortable.
Aversive stimuli, 585–586
Aviophobia, 497
Avoidance learning, 226–227. Learning to make a response in order to postpone or prevent discomfort.
Avoidance-avoidance conflict, 454. Choosing between two negative, undesirable, alternatives.
Avoidant attachment, 94–95, 580. An emotional bond marked by a tendency to resist commitment to others.
Awareness, levels of, 413
Axon (AK-sahn), 52. Fiber that carries information away from the cell body of a neuron.
  activity, measurement of, 53
  defined, 52
  interior of, 54
  saltatory conduction of, 54
Axon terminals, 52. Bulb-shaped structures at the ends of axons that form synapses with the dendrites and somas of other neurons.

B

Bad habits, 235–236
Bait shyness, 338. An unwillingness or hesitation on the part of animals to eat a particular food.
Barbiturates, 192
Bargaining, 116
Barnum effect, 20, 45. The tendency to consider a personal description accurate if it is stated in very general terms.
Barnum, P. T., 20
Base rate, 294. The basic rate at which an event occurs over time; the basic probability of an event.
Basic anxiety, 415. A primary form of anxiety that arises from living in a hostile world
Basic needs, 348. The first four levels of needs in Maslow's hierarchy; lower needs tend to be more potent than higher needs.
Basic suggestion effect, 181. The tendency of hypnotized persons to carry out suggested actions as if they were involuntary.
Behavior. *See also* Antisocial behavior; Prosocial behavior; Sexual behavior
  assessment of, 431
  dieting and, 340
  disordered (*See* Abnormality)
  environmental influence on, 612–613
  genetics and, 425
  healthy, 443–45
  helping, 583
  jury, 620–622
  mere presence and, 560
  personality and, 422–425
  situations effect on, 422
  social contagion and, 444
  social context of, 548–550
  target, 525
  territorial, 612
  unhealthful, 442–443
Behavior modification, 521. The application of learning principles to change human behavior, especially maladaptive behavior.
Behavior therapy, 520–521. Any therapy designed to actively change behavior.
  application of, 520–521
  aversion technique, 521–522
  characterization of, 520
  covert rewards in, 538–539
  desensitization technique, 522–524
  operant technique, 524–526
  self-directed, 539–540
Behavioral assessment, 431. Recording the frequency of various behaviors.

Behavioral contract, 235. A formal agreement stating behaviors to be changed and consequences that apply.
Behavioral dieting, 340, 341. Weight reduction based on changing exercise and eating habits, rather than temporary self-starvation.
Behavioral genetics, 425. The study of inherited behavioral traits and tendencies.
Behavioral medicine, 442. The study of behavioral factors in medicine, physical illness, and medical treatment.
Behavioral personality theory, 421. Any model of personality that emphasizes learning and observable behavior.
Behavioral risk factors, 442. Behaviors that increase the chances of disease, injury, or premature death.
Behavioral setting, 612. A smaller area within an environment whose use is well defined, such as a bus depot, waiting room, or lounge.
Behaviorism, 24–25. The school of psychology that emphasizes the study of overt, observable behavior.
Behaviorists theories
  anxiety disorders, 502
  defined, 24
  history of, 24
  personality theories of, 421–425
  strengths of, 428
  types of, 25
Behaviors
  adaptive, 351
  biological perspective of, 29
  complementary perspectives of, 28–31
  defined, 14
  helping, 532
  hormones and, 74–75
  modeling and, 231–232
  psychological perspective of, 29–30
  punishment effect on, 225
  REM disorders, 173
  self-managed, 234–236
  sociocultural perspective of, 30
  superstitious, 214
  whole human concept in, 31
Belief component, 554. What a person thinks or believes about the object of an attitude.
Beliefs
  authoritarian, 591
  irrational, 519
  just-world, 597–598
  shy, 436
  unrealistic, 518
Bem Sex Role Inventory, 378–379
Beta waves, 171. Small, fast brain waves associated with being awake and alert.
Bias
  actor-observer, 552–553
  confirmation, 19–20
  mental disorder diagnosis, 483
  observer, 40
  probability, 520
  research participant, 37
  researcher, 37
  self-defeating, 435
Biased sample, 42. A subpart of a larger population that does not accurately reflect characteristics of the whole population.
Bilingualism, 282. An ability to speak two languages.
Binge drinking, 194. Consuming five or more drinks in a short time (four for women).
Binocular depth cues, 150–151. Perceptual features that impart information about distance and three-dimensional space which require two eyes.
Biodata, 609. Detailed biographical information about a job applicant.
Biofeedback, 464–465. Information given to a person about his or her ongoing bodily activities; aids voluntary regulation of bodily states.
Biological biasing effect, 374–375. Hypothesized effect that prenatal exposure to sex hormones has on development of the body, nervous system, and later behavior patterns.
Biological motives, 333. Innate motives based on biological needs.
  sex drive, 343–344
  sexual attraction, 373
  thirst, 342
Biological perspective, 29. The attempt to explain behavior in terms of underlying biological principles.
Biological predisposition, 99. The presumed hereditary readiness of humans to learn certain skills, such as how to use language, or a readiness to behave in particular ways.
Biological preparedness (to learn), 338. Organisms are more easily able to learn some associations (e.g. food and illness) than others (e.g. flashing light and illness) Evolution then, places biological limits on what an animal or person can easily learn.
Biological rhythm, 168. Any repeating cycle of biological activity, such as sleep and waking cycles or changes in body temperature.
Biopsychology, 60
Bipolar disorders, 492–493. Emotional disorders involving both depression and mania or hypomania.
Bipolar I disorder, 492. A mood disorder in which a person has episodes of mania (excited, hyperactive, energetic, grandiose behavior) and also periods of deep depression.
Bipolar II disorder, 492. A mood disorder in which a person is mostly depressed (sad, despondent, guilt ridden) but has also had one or more episodes of mild mania (hypomania).
Birth defects. *See* Congenital problems
Bisexuals, 372. A person romantically and erotically attracted to both men and women.
Blind spots, 130
Blindness
  color, 132
  inattentional, 148
  smell, 137
Blink (Gladwell), 294
BMI. *See* Body mass index (BMI)
Bo-bo dolls, 231
Bodily reaction management, 468–469
Body language, 357–358, 429
Body mass index (BMI), 337
Borderline personality disorder, 502–503
Bottom-up processing, 144. Organizing perceptions by beginning with low-level features.
Brain dead. *See* Persistent vegetative state
Brains
  cerebral cortex of, 64–71
  efficiency of, 62
  Einstein's, 64
  emotions and, 353
  function of, 56–57, 61–62
  gender differences in, 70
  handedness and, 77–78
  hunger mechanisms, 335–337
  imaging methods, 490
  long-term memory and, 262–263
  mental abilities and, 320
  mental images and, 277
  plasticity of, 56–57
  pleasure centers in, 217
  repairing, 59
  research, 60–64
  schizophrenic, 489–491
  sensory organization by, 126
  structure, mapping of, 60–61
  subcortex of, 71–74
  white matter, 58
Brainstem, 71–72. The lowest portions of the brain, including the cerebellum, medulla, pons, and reticular formation.
Brainstorming, 297–299. Method of creative thinking that separates the production and evaluation of ideas.
Brainwashing, 567. Engineered or forced attitude change involving a captive audience.
Brief psychodynamic therapy, 514. A modern therapy based on psychoanalytic theory but designed to produce insights more quickly.
Brightness, 128
Brightness constancy, 148. The apparent (or relative) brightness of objects remains the same as long as they are illuminated by the same amount of light.
Broca's (BRO-cahs) **area**, 68. A language area related to grammar and pronunciation.
Broken record, 571. A self-assertion technique involving repeating a request until it is acknowledged.
Bulimia (bue-LIHM-ee-yah) **nervosa**, 340–341. Excessive eating (gorging) usually followed by self-induced vomiting and/or taking laxatives.
Bullying, 584
Burnout, 448. A work-related condition of mental, physical, and emotional exhaustion.
Bystander apathy, 582. Unwillingness of bystanders to offer help during emergencies or to become involved in others' problems.
Bystander intervention
  environmental factors, 615
  heroism and, 583–584
  reasons for, 581–582
  steps toward, 582–583

C
Caffeine, 190–191
Caffeinism, 191. Excessive consumption of caffeine, leading to dependence and a variety of physical and psychological complaints.
Calories, 340
Cameron, James, 150
Cannon-Bard theory, 358–359. States that activity in the thalamus causes emotional feelings and bodily arousal to occur simultaneously.
Car game, 565
Carbon debt, 616
Carbon footprint, 617, 618. The volume of greenhouse gases individual consumption adds to the atmosphere.
Carbon-neutral lifestyle, 616
Cardiac personality, 465–466
Cardinal trait, 408. A personality trait so basic that all of a person's activities relate to it.
Caring, 110
Carver, George Washington, 621
Case study, 41–42, 61. An in-depth focus on all aspects of a single person.
Castration, 382. Surgical removal of the testicles or ovaries.
Cataplexy (CAT-uh-plex-see), 177. A sudden temporary paralysis of the muscles.
Catatonic schizophrenia, 487–488. Schizophrenia marked by stupor, rigidity, unresponsiveness, posturing, mutism, and, sometimes, agitated, purposeless behavior.
Causation, 41. The act of causing some effect.
  correlation and, 640
  distinguishing, 46
Cengage's Psychology Resource Center, 9
CengageNOW, 9, 11
Central nervous system (CNS). The brain and spinal cord. *See also* Brain; Spinal cord
  commands from, 59
  components of, 56–57
Central tendency measures, 635–636
Central traits, 408. The core traits that characterize an individual personality.
Cephalocaudal pattern, 90
Cerebellum (ser-ah-BEL-uhm), 71. A brain structure that controls posture, muscle tone and coordination.
Cerebral (seh-REE-brel or ser-EH-brel) **cortex**, 64. The outer layer of the brain.
  hemispheres of, 64–67
  lobes of, 67–71
Cervix (SER-vix) The lower end of the uterus that projects into the vagina.
CERs. *See* Conditioned emotional responses (CERs)
Character, 405. Personal characteristics that have been judged or evaluated; a person's desirable or undesirable qualities.
  defined, 405
  personality and, 404
Charles Bonnet syndrome, 144
Checkers, 498
Chemical senses, 137
Child molestation, 386
Child rearing, 555
Children
  attitudes of, 555
  early education of, 318
  gifted, 312–313
  oversexualizing of, 388
  sexual abuse of, 386
  television aggression and, 232–233
Chimp language, 284
Choices, 296
Chromosomes, 84. Thread-like "colored bodies" in the nucleus of each cell that are made up of DNA.
Chronic depressive disorder. *See* Dysthymic disorders
Chronological age, 309. A person's age in years.
Chunking, 245, 266
Cigarette smoking
  abuse, 191
  health impact of, 191–192
  prevention, 445
  quitting, 192
  self-handicapping strategies for, 553
Circadian (SUR-kay-dee-AN) **rhythms**, 333–334. Cyclical changes in body functions and arousal levels that vary on a schedule approximating a 24-hour day.
Clairvoyance, 158

Classical conditioning, 206. A form of learning in which reflex responses are associated with new stimuli.
acquisition in, 209
discrimination in, 210–211
expectancies in, 209–210
extinctions in, 210
function of, 521
generalization in, 210
higher ordered, 209
in humans, 211–212
operant conditioning *versus,* 213
Pavlov's experiment, 207–208
principles of, 209–211
spontaneous recovery in, 210
therapies based on, 520–524
Claustrophobia, 497
Cleaners, 498
Click wheel, 603
Client-centered (or **person-centered**) **therapy**, 516. A nondirective therapy based on insights gained from conscious thoughts and feelings; emphasizes accepting one's true self.
Clinical case study, 61. A detailed investigation of a single person, especially one suffering from some injury or disease.
Clinical method, 41–42. Studying psychological problems and therapies in clinical settings.
Clinical psychologist, 34. A psychologist who specializes in the treatment of psychological and behavioral disturbances or who does research on such disturbances.
Clinton, Bill, 594
Clitoral orgasm, 384
Clitoris (KLIT-er-iss), 370–371. Small, sensitive organ made up of erectile tissue; located above the vaginal opening.
Closed questions, 523
Closure, 145
Cocaine
abuse of, 190
characterization of, 189
SUB, 55
Cochlea
components of, 134–135
shape of, 134
side view of, 136
Cochlear implants, 137
Cocktail party effect, 148
Coefficient of correlation, 40–41. A statistical index ranging from −1.00 to +1.00 that indicates the direction and degree of correlation.
Coercion, 567. Being forced to change your beliefs or your behavior against your will.
by brainwashing, 567
by cults, 567–569
Coercive power, 560. Social power based on the ability to punish others.
Cognition, 276, 557. The process of thinking or mentally processing information (images, concepts, words, rules, and symbols).
artificial intelligence and, 321
emotion theory of, 359
experiential, 2
social, 550–554
Cognitive behaviorism, 25, 502. An approach that combines behavioral principles with cognition (perception, thinking, anticipation) to explain behavior.
Cognitive development
concrete operational stage (7-11 years), 103
contemporary views of, 104–106
formal operational stage (11 years and up), 103–104
neonates, 91–92
overview, 101
parental guide based on, 104
preoperational stage (2-7 years), 101–103
sensorimotor stage (0-2 years), 101–102
sociocultural theory of, 106–107
Cognitive dissonance theory, 557–558. An uncomfortable clash between self-image thoughts, beliefs, attitudes, or perceptions and one's behavior.
Cognitive interview, 248, 267. Use of various cues and strategies to improve the memory of eyewitnesses.
Cognitive learning, 206, 229. Higher-level learning involving thinking, knowing, understanding, and anticipation.
discovery, 230–231
latent, 230
modeling in, 231–233
Cognitive map, 229. Internal images or other mental representations of an area (maze, city, campus, and so forth) that underlie an ability to choose alternative paths to the same goal.
Cognitive therapy, 517. A therapy directed at changing the maladaptive thoughts, beliefs, and feelings that underlie emotional and behavioral problems.
depression treatment with, 518
goals of, 517–518
REBT approach, 518–520
Cognitive time travelers, 223
Cognitive unconscious, 294. A mental storehouse for unconscious ideas and images shared by all humans.
Cold reading, 158–159
Collective unconscious, 415–416
College blues, 460–461
College Qualification Test, 307
Color blindness, 132. A total inability to perceive colors.
Color vision, 131–132
Color weakness, 132. An inability to distinguish some colors.
Columbia space shuttle, 562
Commitment, 579. The determination to stay in a long-term relationship with another person.
Common region, 145–146
Common sense beliefs, 15
Common traits, 407. Personality traits that are shared by most members of a particular culture.
Communication, 394–395
Community health campaign, 45, 445. A community-wide education program that provides information about how to lessen risk factors and promote health.
Community mental health center, 530. A facility offering a wide range of mental health services, such as prevention, counseling, consultation, and crisis intervention.
Companionate love, 579. Form of love characterized by intimacy and commitment but not passion.
Comparison level, 580. A personal standard used to evaluate rewards and costs in a social exchange.
Comparisons, 287–288, 578
Compensation, 415, 457–458. Any attempt to overcome feelings of inadequacy or inferiority.
Compliance, 563. Bending to the requests of a person who has little or no authority or other form of social power.
assertiveness training and, 570–571
car game and, 565
factors in, 563–654
Compressed workweek, 607. A work schedule that allows an employee to work fewer days per week by putting in more hours per day.
Compression, 134
Computed tomographic scans (CT scan), 60, 490. A computer-enhanced X-ray image of the brain or body.
Computer-assisted instruction, 220
Computerized interviews, 429–430
Concentrative mediation, 183. Mental exercise based on attending to a single object or thought.
Concept formation, 278. The process of classifying information into meaningful categories.
Concepts, 276. A generalized idea representing a category of related objects or events.
faulty, 280
meanings of, 280–281
protypes in, 279
types of, 279–280
Conceptual rule, 278. A formal rule for deciding if an object or event is an example of a particular concept.
Concrete operational stage (7-11 years), 103. Period of intellectual development during which children become able to use the concepts of time, space, volume, and number, but in ways that remain simplified and concrete, rather than abstract.
Condensation, 198. Combining several people, objects, or events into a single dream image.
Conditioned emotional responses (CERs), 211. An emotional response that has been linked to a previously nonemotional stimulus by classical conditioning.
Conditioned response (CR), 24. A learned response elicited by a conditioned stimulus.
behavior modification and, 521
Pavlov's experiment of, 207
Conditioned stimulus (CS), 521. A stimulus that evokes a response because it has been repeatedly paired with an unconditioned stimulus.
Conditioning. *See also* Classical conditioning; Learning; Operant conditioning
everyday problems and, 234–236
indirect, 212
time factors and, 223
types of, 206–207
Conditions of worth, 420. Internal standards used to judge the value of one's thoughts, actions, feelings, or experiences.
Conductive hearing loss, 136. Poor transfer of sounds from the eardrum to the inner ear.
Cones, 129. Visual receptors for colors and daylight visual acuity.
color vision and, 131–132
dark adaptation and, 133
firing rates of, 132
visual acuity and, 131
Confidentiality, 523
Confirmation bias, 19–20. The tendency to remember or notice information that fits one's expectations, while forgetting discrepancies.
Conflict, 453. A stressful condition that occurs when a person must choose between incompatible or contradictory alternatives.
diagrams, 454
types of, 454–455
Conformity, 561. Bringing one's behavior into agreement or harmony with norms or with the behavior of others in a group.
Asch experiment, 562–563
characterization of, 561
group factors in, 563
norms and, 561
Congenital problems, 86. Problems or defects that originate during prenatal development in the womb.
Conjunctive concepts, 279. A class of objects that have two or more features in common. (For example, to qualify as an example of the concept an object must be both red *and* triangular.)
Connotative meaning, 280. The subjective, personal, or emotional meaning of a word or concept.
Conscience, 412. The part of the superego that causes guilt when its standards are not met.
Conscientiousness, 409
Conscious, 168. The region of the mind that includes all mental contents a person is aware of at any given moment.
Conscious level, 413
Consciousness, 168. Mental awareness of sensations and perceptions of external events as well as self-awareness of internal events including thoughts, memories, and feelings about experiences and the self. *See also* Sleep
altered states of, 168
culture and, 169
drug-altered (*See* Psychoactive drugs)
sleep and, 174
Consequences, 206, 207. Effects that follow a response.
associative learning, 206
test, 292
types of, 119
Conservation, 103. In Piaget's theory, mastery of the concept that the weight, mass, and volume of matter remains unchanged (is conserved) even when the shape or appearance of objects changes.
learning and, 220
mastery of, 103
resource, 616
Consistency, 118. With respect to child discipline, the maintenance of stable rules of conduct.
Consolidation, 260. Process by which relatively permanent memories are formed in the brain.
Constancies, 147–148
Constraint-induced movement therapy, 59
Consummate love, 579. Form of love characterized by intimacy, passion, *and* commitment.
Consumption reduction, 617
Contact comfort, 94, 95. A pleasant and reassuring feeling human and animal infants get from touching or clinging to something soft and warm, usually their mother.
Contiguity, 145

Contingency, 214
Continuation, 145
Continuous positive airway pressure (CPAP), 176
Continuous reinforcement, 222. A schedule in which every correct response is followed by a reinforcer.
Contract comfort, 94
Contracting, 235
Control, 16. Altering conditions that influence behavior.
ergonomics, 626
Control group, 36, 531. In a controlled experiment, the group of subjects exposed to all experimental conditions or variables *except* the independent variable.
Conventional moral reasoning, 110. Moral thinking based on a desire to please others or to follow accepted rules and values.
Convergent thinking, 290. Thinking directed toward discovery of a single established correct answer; conventional thinking.
Conversations, 436
Conversion disorder, 500. A bodily symptom that mimics a physical disability but is actually caused by anxiety or emotional distress.
Conversions, cult, 568–569
Conviction, 556. Beliefs that are important to a person and that evoke strong emotion.
Coolidge effect, 343
Coping
frustration, 453
learned helplessness and, 458
stress, 450–451
Coping statements, 346, 470–471. Reassuring, self-enhancing statements that are used to stop self-critical thinking.
Correctional studies, 40–41, 46
Correlational method, 39. Making measurements to discover relationships between events.
Correlational study, 40, 41. A nonexperimental study designed to measure the degree of relationship (if any) between two or more events, measures, or variables.
Correlations, 640. The existence of a consistent, systematic relationship between two events, measures, or variables.
causation and, 640
coefficient, 639–640
relationships, 638–639
use of, 638
Corticalization (KORE-tih-kal-ih-ZAY-shun), 64. An increase in the relative size of the cerebral cortex.
Counseling psychologist, 34. A psychologist who specializes in the treatment of milder emotional and behavioral disturbances.
Counseling skills, 532–534
Counselors, 34. A mental health professional who specializes in helping people with problems not involving serious mental disorder; for example, marriage counselors, career counselors, or school counselors.
Counterirritation, 141
Couple-centered therapy, 536
CourseMate, 8–9, 11
Covert behaviors, 14
Covert reinforcement, 539. Using positive imagery to reinforce desired behavior.
Covert sensitization, 538–539. Use of aversive imagery to reduce the occurrence of an undesired response.
Cowper's glands, 371. Two small glands that secrete a clear fluid into the urethra during sexual excitement.
Cranial nerves, 58. Major nerves that leave the brain without passing through the spinal cord.
Creative self, 415. The "artist" in each of us that creates a unique identity and style of life.
Creativity. *See also* Problem solving
dreams and, 199–200
enhancing, 293–296
intuition in, 293–296
learning, 293
lifestyles and, 299
motivation for, 349–350
personality and, 293
problem solving *versus*, 290–291
right brain and, 67
stages of, 292–293
tests of, 291–292
Cretinism (KREET-un-iz-um), 316. Stunted growth and intellectual disability caused by an insufficient supply of thyroid hormone.
Crisis intervention, 530. Skilled management of a psychological emergency.
Crista, 141
Critical incidents, 609. Situations that arise in a job, with which a competent worker must be able to cope.
Critical situations, 424–525. Situations during childhood that are capable of leaving a lasting imprint on personality.
Critical thinking (in psychology), 296. A type of reflection involving the support of beliefs through scientific explanation and observation.
boxes, 4
characteristics of, 2
common sense beliefs, 15
function of, 17
principles of, 17–18
scientific method, 23
Cross-stimulation effect, 301. In group problem solving, the tendency of one person's ideas to trigger ideas from others.
Crowding, 613–614. A subjective feeling of being overstimulated by a loss of privacy or by the nearness of others (especially when social contact with them is unavoidable).
Cryer, Jon, 553
Crystal methamphetamine, 188
Crystallized abilities, 115
Crystallized intelligence, 311. The ability to solve problems using already acquired knowledge.
Cubinator, 321
Cue-dependent forgetting, 256–257
Cue, 422. External stimuli that guide responses, especially by signaling the presence or absence of reinforcement.
habit breaking and, 235
overinterpretation of, 520
Cults, 568. A group that professes great devotion to some person and follows that person almost without question; cult members are typically victimized by their leaders in various ways.
classical example of, 567–568
conversions to, 568–569
implications of, 569
recruitment by, 568
Cultural awareness, 598–599
Cultural factors
abnormal behavior, 477
eating disorders, 342
emotional expression, 356–357
gender roles, 376–377
identity and, 108
in parenting, 97–98
in perception, 155
self-esteem, 406
spatial norms, 560–561
stress from, 463
suicide attempts, 505–506
Cultural maladies, 480
Cultural relativity, 30, 477. The idea that behavior must be judged relative to the values of the culture in which it occurs.
Culturally skilled therapist, 534, 545. A therapist who has the awareness, knowledge, and skills necessary to treat clients from diverse cultural backgrounds.
Culture, 548, 549. An ongoing pattern of life, characterizing a society at a given point in history.
Culture factors
consciousness, 169
diet, 338
dynamics of, 548
intelligence, 308
IQ tests, 323
memory, 244
problem solving, 289
psychotherapy and, 534
selective comparison, 288
Culture-fair test, 323–324. A test designed to minimize the importance of skills and knowledge that may be more common in some cultures than in others.
Cumulative recorders, 222
Curare, 55
Curve of forgetting, 254–255. A graph that shows the amount of memorized information remembered after varying lengths of time.
Cyberbullying, 584
Cyclothymic (SIKE-lo-THY-mik) **disorders**, 492. Moderate manic and depressive behavior that persists for 2 years or more.

D

Dark adaptation, 132–133. Increased retinal sensitivity to light.
Darwin, Charles, 24
Data reduction system, 126
Date rape, 290
Date rape drug. *See* Rohypnol
Day care, 95
Daydream, 290–291. A vivid waking fantasy.
Death and dying
basic emotional reactions to, 116
impending, 115–117
sudden, 354–354
Death instinct, 411
Death-qualified jury, 622. A jury composed of people who favor the death penalty or at least are indifferent to it.
Decibels, 136
Declarative memory, 250. That part of long-term memory containing specific factual information.
Decline effect, 159
Deductive thought, 290. Thought that applies a general set of rules to specific situations; for example, using the laws of gravity to predict the behavior of a single falling object.
Deep lesioning (LEE-zhun-ing), 62. Removal of tissue within the brain by use of an electrode.
Deep sleep, 172. Stage 4 slow-wave sleep; the deepest form of normal sleep.
Defense mechanism, 456–458. A habitual and often unconscious psychological process used to reduce anxiety.
Deinstitutionalization, 529–530. Reduced use of full-time commitment to mental institutions to treat mental disorders.
Déjà view, 251
Déjà vu, 252. The feeling that you have already experienced a situation that you are actually experiencing for the first time.
Delgado, José, 54
Delta waves, 172. Large, slow brainwaves that occur in deeper sleep (stages 3 and 4).
Delusion, 484. A false belief held against all contrary evidence.
Delusional disorders, 486. A psychosis marked by severe delusions of grandeur, jealousy, persecution, or similar preoccupations.
Dementia (duh-MEN-sha), 256, 485. A serious mental impairment in old age caused by deterioration of the brain.
Demonology, 512. In medieval Europe, the study of demons and the treatment of persons "possessed" by demons.
Dendrites (DEN-drytes), 52, 86. Neuron fibers that receive incoming messages.
Denial, 116, 456–457
Denotative meaning, 280. The exact, dictionary definition of a word or concept; its objective meaning.
Density, 614, 615. The number of people in a given space or, inversely, the amount of space available to each person.
Dependence, 186–187
Dependent variable, 35–36. In an experiment, the condition (usually a behavior) that is affected by the independent variable.
Depressant (downer), 185. A substance that decreases activity in the body and nervous system.
Depression, 460. A state of despondency marked by feelings of powerlessness, worthlessness, pessimism, and hopelessness.
biology and, 494
cognitive treatment of, 518
coping with, 460–461
gender and, 493–494
impending death and, 116
learned helplessness and, 459
signs of, 460
Depressive delusions, 484
Depressive disorders, 492, 493. Emotional disorders primarily involving sadness, despondency, and depression.
Deprivation (during development), 87–88. The loss or withholding of normal stimulation, nutrition, comfort, love, and so forth; a condition of lacking.
Depth cues, 150–152. Features of the environment and messages from the body that supply information about distance and space.
Depth perception, 149. The ability to see three-dimensional space and to accurately judge distances.
apparent-distance hypothesis, 153
cures for, 150–151
development of, 149–150
moon illusion and, 152–153
tests for, 150

Description, 16. In scientific research, the process of naming and classifying.
Descriptive statistics
  central tendency measures, 635–636
  defined, 633
  graphical, 634
  types of, 634
Desensitization, 522. A reduction in emotional sensitivity to a stimulus.
  defined, 522
  exposure in, 523
  eye movement, 523–524
  hierarchy in, 522
  performing, 523
  self-directed, 539–540
  vicarious, 523
  violence, 587
Desensitization (therapy), 522. Reducing fear or anxiety by repeatedly exposing a person to emotional stimuli while the person is deeply relaxed.
Designed culture, 25
Desire disorders, 395
Desk rage, 608
Despair, 113
Determinism, 26, 27. The idea that all behavior has prior causes that would completely explain one's choices and actions if all such causes were known.
Detoxification, 195. In the treatment of alcoholism, the withdrawal of the patient from alcohol.
Development. *See* Human development
Developmental level, 89. An individual's current state of physical, emotional, and intellectual development.
Developmental psychology, 84. The study of progressive changes in behavior and abilities from conception to death.
Developmental task, 111. Any skill that must be mastered, or personal change that must take place, for optimal development.
Devi, Shakuntala, 276
Deviation IQ, 309–310. An IQ obtained statistically from a person's relative standing in his or her age group; that is, how far above or below average the person's score was relative to other scores.
Devictimization, 583
Dexterity, 67
Dhat, 480
Diagnostic and Statistical Manual of Mental Disorders (DSM-5), 482
Diagnostic interviews, 429–430
Dialogue questions, 3
Diet-induced obesity, 336
Dieting
  behavioral, 340
  cultural factors, 338
  food selection, 338–339
  healthy, 443–444
  portions and, 339
  yo-yo, 339
Difference threshold, 127. The minimum difference between two stimuli that is detectable to an observer.
Diffusion of responsibility, 583. Spreading the responsibility to act among several people; reduces the likelihood that help will be given to a person in need.
Digit-span test, 244
Digital cameras, 627–628
Digital media, 8–10
Direct instruction, 620. Presentation of factual information by lecture, demonstration, and rote practice.
Direct observation, 430. Assessing behavior through direct surveillance.
Directive therapy, 514
Discipline
  constructive, 118
  effective, 117–118
  physical, 118
  self-esteem and, 118
Discovery learning, 230–231, 620. Instruction based on encouraging students to discover or construct knowledge for themselves; learning based on insight and understanding.
Discrimination, 224–225, 589. Treating members of various social groups differently in circumstances where their rights or treatment should be identical.
Discriminative stimuli, 224. Stimuli that precede rewarded and nonrewarded responses in operant conditioning.
Disease-prone personality, 443. A personality type associated with poor health; marked by persistent negative emotions, including anxiety, depression, and hostility.
Dishabituation, 161. A reversal of habituation.
Disinhibition, 587. The removal of inhibition; results in acting out behavior that normally would be restrained.
Disjunctive concept, 279. A concept defined by the presence of at least one of several possible features. (For example, to qualify an object must be either blue *or* circular.)
Disorganized schizophrenia, 487. Schizophrenia marked by incoherence, grossly disorganized behavior, bizarre thinking, and flat or grossly inappropriate emotions.
Displaced aggression, 452, 589. Directing emotions or actions toward safe or unimportant dream images.
Displacement, 198. Directing emotions or actions toward safe or unimportant dream images.
Dissociative amnesia, 499. Loss of memory (partial or complete) for important information related to personal identity.
Dissociative disorder, 480, 499. Temporary amnesia, multiple personality, or depersonalization.
Dissociative fugue (fewg), 499. Sudden travel away from home, plus confusion about one's personal identity.
Dissociative identity disorder, 499. The presence of two or more distinct personalities (multiple personality).
Dissociative state, 180
Dissonance, 557
Disuse, 256. Theory that memory traces weaken when memories are not periodically used or retrieved.
Divergent thinking, 290. Thinking that produces many ideas or alternatives; a major element in original or creative thought.
Diversity
  acceptance of, 597–599
  broader view of, 30
  role of, 27–28
Dixon, Jeanne, 46
DNA (deoxyribonucleic acid) (dee-OX-see-RYE-bo-new-KLEE-ik), 84. A molecular structure that contains coded genetic information.
  characterization of, 84
  organization of, 84
  segments of, 84–85
Dogmatism, 591. An unwarranted positiveness or certainty in matters of belief or opinion.
Dominant gene, 84–85. A gene whose influence will be expressed each time the gene is present.
Dominant hemisphere, 77. A term usually applied to the side of a person's brain that produces language.
Door-in-the-face effect, 564–565. Being simultaneously attracted to and repelled by each of two alternatives.
Dopamine, 55, 489
Double approach-avoidance conflict, 455
Double-blind experiment, 38. An arrangement in which both participants and experimenters are unaware of whether participants are in the experimental group or the control group, including who might have been administered a drug or a placebo.
Double standard, 388. Applying different standards for judging the appropriateness of male and female sexual behavior.
Doubt, 112
Down syndrome, 315. A genetic disorder caused by the presence of an extra chromosome; results in intellectual disability.
Downward comparison, 551. Comparing yourself with a person who ranks lower than you on some dimension.
Drapetomania, 483
Dream processes, 198. Mental filters that hide the true meanings of dreams.
Dreams
  analysis of, 513
  creativity and, 199–200
  interpretation of, 198–199
  lucid, 200
  meaning of, 177
  REM sleep and, 173–174
  symbols in, 178
  theories of, 178–170
  using, 199
Dream symbols, 178. Images in dreams that serve as visible signs of hidden ideas, desires, impulses, emotions, relationships, and so forth.
Drive, 332, 422. The psychological expression of internal needs or valued goals. For example, hunger, thirst, or a drive for success.
Drug interaction, 187. A combined effect of two drugs that exceeds the addition of one drug's effects to the other.
Drug therapy. *See* Pharmacotherapy
Drug tolerance, 186. A reduction in the body's response to a drug.
Dual process hypothesis of sleep, 172–174
Duchenne smile, 356, An authentic smile (as opposed to a posed, false smile) involving the mouth and the small muscles around the eyes.
Dwarfism, 75
Dysosmia, 137–138
Dyspareunia (DIS-pah-ROO-nee-ah) **(One type of genito-pelvic pain/penetration disorder)**, 397. Genital pain before, during, or after sexual intercourse.
Dysthymic (dis-THY-mik) **disorder (Chronic depressive disorder)**, 492. Moderate depression that persists for 2 years or more.

E

Early education childhood programs, 318. Programs that provide stimulating intellectual experiences, typically for disadvantaged preschoolers.
Ears, 134–135
Eating cues, 338
Eating disorders
  causes of, 341
  cultural factors, 342
  among men, 341–342
  treatment for, 341–342
  types of, 339–341
Ebbinghaus curve, 254–255
Echoic memory, 242, 243. A brief continuation of sensory activity in the auditory system after a sound is heard.
Echolocation, 126
Ecological footprint, 616. The amount of land and water area required to replenish the resources that a human population consumes.
Ecological footprint calculators, 616
ECS. *See* Electroconvulsive shock (ECS)
Ecstasy. *See* Methylenedioxymethamphetamine (MDMA)
ECT. *See* Electroconvulsive therapy (ECT)
Education, 282, 318
Educational psychology, 619–620. The field that seeks to understand how people learn and how teachers instruct.
EEG. *See* Electroencephalograph (EEG)
Effective parents, 96
Effector cells, 59
Ego, 411. The executive part of personality that directs rational behavior.
Ego ideal, 412. The part of the superego representing ideal behavior; a source of pride when its standards are met.
Ego-defense mechanisms, 412
Egocentric thought, 102. Thought that is self-centered and fails to consider the viewpoints of others.
Eidetic (eye-DET-ik) **imagery**, 263–264. The ability to retain a "projected" mental image long enough to use it as a source of information.
Einstein, Albert, 64
Ejaculation, 384, 397. The release of sperm and seminal fluid by the male at the time of orgasm.
Elaborate processing, 245. Making memories more meaningful through processing that encodes links between new information and existing memories and knowledge, either at the time of the original encoding or on subsequent retrievals.
  effectiveness of, 265
  LTM, 246–248
  STM, 245
Elderly, 505, 592
Electra conflict, 412. A girl's sexual attraction to her father and feelings of rivalry with her mother.
Electrical stimulation of the brain (ESB), 61. Direct electrical stimulation and activation of brain tissue.
Electroconvulsive shock (ECS), 260–261. An electric current passed directly through the brain, producing a convulsion.
Electroconvulsive therapy (ECT), 528. A treatment for severe depression, consisting of an electric shock passed directly through the brain, which induces a convulsion.
Electrodes, 61. Any device (such as a wire, needle, or metal plate) used to electrically stimulate or destroy nerve tissue or to record its activity.
Electroencephalograph (EEG) (eh-LEK-tro-en-SEF-uh-lo-graf), 171. A device designed to detect, amplify, and record electrical activity in the brain.
  function of, 15–16, 62

Emblems, 358. Gestures that have widely understood meanings within a particular culture.
EMDR. *See* Eye movement desensitization and reprocessing (EMDR)
Emerging adulthood, 109. A socially tolerated period of extended adolescence now quite common in Western societies.
Emotion, 350–351. A state characterized by physiological arousal, changes in facial expression, gestures, posture, and subjective feelings. *See also* Feelings
adaptive behavior and, 351
brain and, 353
Cannon-Bard theory, 358–359
characterization of, 350–351
conditioned responses, 211–212
contemporary model of, 361–362
cultural differences in, 356–357
expression of, 355–356
facial feedback hypothesis, 360–361
gender differences, 357
infants, 92–93
James-Lange theory, 358
memory and, 261–262
misattribution of, 359–360
mixed, 351
neurotic, 409
in perceptions, 155
perceiving, 363
physiological changes, 352–353
positive, 363–364
primary, 351–352
problem solving and, 289
right brain and, 66
Schachter's cognitive theory of, 359
schizophrenia and, 486
suppressing of, 361
understanding, 363
Emotion-focused coping, 450. Managing or controlling one's emotional reaction to a stressful or threatening situation.
Emotional appraisal, 360. Evaluating the personal meaning of a stimulus or situation.
Emotional attachment, 94–95. An especially close emotional bond that infants form with their parents, caregivers, or others.
Emotional component, 554–555. One's feelings toward the object of an attitude.
Emotional consequence, 518
Emotional eating, 338
Emotional expressions, 351. Outward signs that an emotion is occurring.
Emotional feelings, 351. The private, subjective experience of having an emotion.
Emotional intelligence, 363–364. The ability to perceive, use, understand, and manage emotions.
Empathic arousal, 583. Emotional arousal that occurs when you feel some of another person's pain, fear, or anguish.
Empathy, 516. A capacity for taking another's point of view; the ability to feel what another is feeling.
Empathy-helping relationship, 583. Observation that we are most likely to help someone else when we feel emotions such as empathy and compassion.
Empirical research, 14
Employee selection, 609–611
Employees
knowledge, 605
productivity of, 606–607
selection of, 609–611
women, 605
Encoded, 242
Encoding, 243. Converting information into a form in which it will be retained in memory.
failure of, 255–256
memory cues and, 266
selective, 287
STM and, 242–243
strategies for, 265–267
Encoding failure, 255–256. Failure to store sufficient information to form a useful memory.
Encounter group, 536. A group experience that emphasizes intensely honest interchanges among participants regarding feelings and reactions to one another.
Endocrine (EN-duh-krin) **system**, 74–75. Glands whose secretions pass directly into the bloodstream or lymph system.
Endogenous (en-DODGE-eh-nus) **depression**, 492. Depression that appears to be produced from within (perhaps by chemical imbalances in the brain), rather than as a reaction to life events.
Endorphins, 55–56
Enkephalins, 55
Enrichment, 87. In development, deliberately making an environment more stimulating, nutritional, comforting, loving, and so forth.
human development and, 87–88
job, 607–608
Environmental assessment, 618. Measurement and analysis of the effects an environment has on the behavior and perceptions of people within that environment.
Environmental psychology, 612. The formal study of how environments affect behavior.
behavioral analysis by, 612–613
human influences, 615–616
impact of, 611–612
problem solving by, 618
social dilemma analysis by, 617–618
stress analysis by, 613–615
sustainability analysis by, 616–617
topics of interest to, 613
Environment ("nurture"), 87. The sum of all external conditions affecting development, including especially the effects of learning.
Environments
human development and, 86–87
human influence on, 615–616
schizophrenia and, 488–489
stressful, 613–615
types of, 86–87
Epididymis (ep-ih-DID-ih-mus), 371. A coiled structure at the top of the testes in which sperm are stored.
Epinephrine (ep-eh-NEF-rin), 76. An adrenal hormone that tends to arouse the body; epinephrine is associated with fear. (Also known as adrenaline.)
Episodic (ep-ih-SOD-ik) **drive**, 342. A drive that occurs in distinct episodes.
Episodic (ep-ih-SOD-ik) **memory**, 250. A subpart of declarative memory that records personal experiences that are linked with specific times and places.
Equal-status contact, 594–595. Social interaction that occurs on an equal footing, without obvious differences in power or status.
Equivalent-forms reliability, 305
Erasmus, 265
Erectile disorder, 395–396. An inability to maintain an erection for lovemaking.
Ergonomics. *See* Human factors psychology
Erikson's psychosocial theory, 111–112
Erikson, Erik, 26
Erogenous (eh-ROJ-eh-nus) **zones**, 380, 412. Areas of the body that produce pleasure and/or provoke erotic desire.
Eron, Leonard, 587
Eros. Freud's name for the "life instincts." *See* Life instincts
Erotomanic type disorders, 486
ESB. *See* Electrical stimulation of the brain (ESB)
Escape, 453. Reducing discomfort by leaving frustrating situations or by psychologically withdrawing from them.
Escape learning, 226. to make a response in order to end an aversive stimulus.
Escher, M. C., 152
Essay tests, 8
Estrogens, 343, 370. Any of a number of female sex hormones.
Estrus, 343. Changes in the sexual drives of animals that create a desire for mating; particularly used to refer to females in heat.
Ethics, 22–23
Ethnic pride, 592
Ethnocentrism, 590. Placing one's own group or race at the center—that is, tending to reject all other groups but one's own.
Ethologist, 584. A person who studies the natural behavior patterns of animals.
Eugenics, 317. Selective breeding for desirable characteristics.
Evaluation fears, 435. Fears of being inadequate, embarrassed, ridiculed, or rejected.
Evidence gathering, 21
Evolutionary psychology, 580–581. Study of the evolutionary origins of human behavior patterns.
Excitement phase, 383. The first phase of sexual response, indicated by initial signs of sexual arousal.
Exercise, 175, 340
Exhaustion, 447
Exhibitionism, 386
Existential therapy, 516–517. An insight therapy that focuses on the elemental problems of existence, such as death, meaning, choice, and responsibility; emphasizes making courageous life choices.
Existentialism, 501–502
Expectancies, 209–210
Expectancy, 423. An anticipation concerning future events or relationships. During learning, anticipation about the effect a response will have, especially regarding reinforcement.
Experience, 517–518
Experiences, peak, 418
Experiential cognition, 2. Style of thought arising during passive experience.
Experiential intelligence, 320. Specialized knowledge and skills acquired through learning and experience.
Experiment, 35. A formal trial undertaken to confirm or disconfirm a hypothesis about cause and effect.
cause and effect in, 36
control in, 36
double blind, 38
evaluation of, 37
single-blind, 38
subjects in, 35
variables in, 35–36
Experimental group, 36, 37. In a controlled experiment, the group of subjects exposed to the independent variable or experimental condition.
Experimental method, 39. Investigating causes of behavior through controlled experimentation.
Experimental subjects, 35. Humans (also referred to as **participants**) or animals whose behavior is investigated in an experiment.
Expert power, 559. Social power derived from possession of knowledge or expertise.
Expert systems, 321
Explicit memory, 253. A memory that a person is aware of having; a memory that is consciously retrieved.
Expressions. *See* Facial expressions
Expressive behaviors, 377. that express or communicate emotion or personal feelings.
External causes, 552. A cause of behavior that is assumed to lie outside a person.
External cues, 257
External urethral orifice (yoo-REE-thral OR-ih-fis), 371. The opening at the tip of the penis through which urine and semen pass.
Extinction, 210, 211. The weakening of a conditioned response through removal of reinforcement.
in classical conditioning, 210
example of, 525
operant, 216
responses to, 524
Extracellular thirst, 342. Thirst caused by a reduction in the volume of fluids found between body cells.
Extraneous variables, 35. Conditions or factors excluded from influencing the outcome of an experiment.
Extrasensory perception (ESP), 159. The purported ability to perceive events in ways that cannot be explained by known capacities of the sensory organs.
appraisal of, 158–160
chance in, 159
claims of, 45
defined, 159
experiments for, 159–160
forms of, 158
fraud in, 158
implications of, 159–160
Extrinsic motivation, 349–350. Motivation based on obvious external rewards, obligations, or similar factors.
Extroversion, 415. Ego attitude in which in which energy is mainly directed outward.
attitudes of, 415
characterization of, 405
dimensions of, 409
Extrovert, 405. A person whose attention is directed outward; a bold, outgoing person.
Eye blink conditioning, 208
Eye movement desensitization and reprocessing (EMDR), 523–524. A technique for reducing fear or anxiety; based on holding upsetting thoughts in mind while rapidly moving the eyes from side to side.
Eyes
depth cues and, 150
image sensors in, 129–132
shape of, 129
structure of, 129

Eyewitness memories, 252
Eyewitness testimony, 160–161
Eysenck, Hans, 514

F
Facial agnosia, 70. An inability to perceive familiar faces.
Facial blends, 356
Facial expressions
range of, 356
universality of, 355–356
Facial feedback hypothesis, 360–361. States that sensations from facial expressions help define what emotion a person feels.
Factitious disorder. *See* Munchausen syndrome
Factor analysis, 408. A statistical technique used to correlate multiple measurements and identify general underlying factors.
Fallopian (feh-LOPE-ee-en) **tube**, 371. One of two tubes that carry eggs from the ovaries to the uterus.
False memories, 246–248
False memory, 260. A memory that can seem accurate but is not.
Familial intellectual disability, 315. Mild intellectual disability associated with homes that are intellectually, nutritionally, and emotionally impoverished.
Familiarity, 576
Family-centered therapy, 535
Family therapy, 535. Technique in which all family members participate, both individually and as a group, to change destructive relationships and communication patterns.
Farsightedness. *See* Hyperopia
FAS. *See* Fetal alcohol syndrome (FAS)
Fat point, 336
Fathers' influence, 96–97
Faulty concepts, 280
Fears
amygdala and, 73
epinephrine and, 76
evaluation, 435
learned, 211–212
overcoming, 539–540
physiological reaction to, 352–353
Feedback, 360–361, 627. Information returned to a person about the effects a response has had; also known as knowledge of results.
Feeling of knowing, 251. The ability to predict beforehand whether one will be able to remember something.
Feelings. *See also* Emotions
focus on, 523
reflect, 532–533
Fellowship, 418
Female orgasmic disorder, 396–397. A persistent inability to reach orgasm during lovemaking.
Female sexual arousal disorder (One type of sexual interest/arousal disorder in women), 397. A lack of physical arousal to sexual stimulation.
Fetal alcohol syndrome (FAS), 87
Fight-or-flight, 353
Figure-ground organization, 144. Organizing a perception so that part of a stimulus appears to stand out as an object (figure) against a less prominent background (ground).
Fiorina, Carly, 605
Firewalking, 45
Five-factor model, 408–409. Proposes that there are five universal dimensions of personality.
Fixation, 288. A lasting conflict developed as a result of frustration or overindulgence; the tendency to repeat wrong solutions or faulty responses, especially as a result of becoming blind to alternatives.
myth of, 413
problem solving and, 288–289
Fixed interval (FI) schedule, 223. A reinforcer is given only when a correct response is made after a set amount of time has passed since the last reinforced response. Responses made during the time interval are not reinforced.
Fixed ratio (FR) schedule, 222. A set number of correct responses must be made to get a reinforcer. For example, a reinforcer is given for every four correct responses.
Flashbulb memory, 261. Memory created at times of high emotion that seems especially vivid.
Flat affect, 484
Flavors, 138
Flexibility, 290. In tests of creativity, flexibility is indicated by the number of different types of solutions produced.
Flextime, 607. A work schedule that allows flexible starting and quitting times.
Fluency, 290. In tests of creativity, fluency refers to the total number of solutions produced.
Fluid abilities, 115
Fluid intelligence, 311. The ability to solve novel problems involving perceptual speed or rapid insight.
Fluid reasoning, 306
Flynn effect, 318
fMRI. *See* functional magnetic resonance imaging (fMRI) scan
Food intake, 175
Foot-in-the-door effect, 564–565. The tendency for a person who has first complied with a small request to be more likely later to fulfill a larger request.
Forced teaching, 103
Forcible rape, 390. Sexual intercourse carried out against the victim's will, under the threat of violence or bodily injury.
Forebrain, 71, 73
Forensic memory, 248
Forgetting
curve of, 254
encoding failure in, 255–256
interference and, 257–259
motivation for, 259–260
reasons for, 254
state-dependent learning effect in, 257
storage failure in, 256
transfer of training and, 259
Formal operational stage, 104. Period of intellectual development characterized by thinking that includes abstract, theoretical, and hypothetical ideas.
Formal thinking, 103
Fouts, Roger, 284
Fragile X syndrome, 315. A genetic form of intellectual disability caused by a defect in the *X* chromosome.
Frames of mind, 322
Framing, 295. In thought, the terms in which a problem is stated or the way that it is structured.
Frantz, Robert, 91
Fraternal twins, 317. Twins conceived from two separate eggs.
Free association, 513. In psychoanalysis, the technique of having a client say anything that comes to mind, regardless of how embarrassing or unimportant it may seem.
Free will, 26. The idea that human beings are capable of freely making choices or decisions.
Frequency distribution, 634
Frequency theory, 135. Holds that tones up to 4,000 hertz are converted to nerve impulses that match the frequency of each tone.
Freud, Anna, 26
Freud, Sigmund, 26, 512
Freudian analysis. *See* Psychoanalysis
Freudian slips, 26, 413
Friendships, 576, 578
Frontal association areas, 67
Frontal lobes, 67–68. Areas of the cortex associated with movement, the sense of self, and higher mental functions.
Frustration, 451. A negative emotional state that occurs when one is prevented from reaching a goal.
basis of, 452
cause of, 451–452
coping with, 453
defined, 451
reactions to, 452–543
scapegoats, 452–453
Frustration-aggression hypothesis, 585–586. States that frustration tends to lead to aggression.
Fully functioning person, 419. A person living in harmony with her or his deepest feelings, impulses, and intuitions.
Functional fixedness, 288. A rigidity in problem solving caused by an inability to see new uses for familiar objects.
Functional MRI (fMRI), 61, 354. MRI technique that records brain activity.
Functional solution, 297. A detailed, practical, and workable solution.
Functionalism, 24. The school of psychology concerned with how behavior and mental abilities help people adapt to their environments.
Functioning, levels of, 478
Fundamental attribution error, 552–553. The tendency to attribute the behavior of others to internal causes (personality, likes, and so forth).

G
G-factor, 304, 319–322
GABA, 55
Gage, Phineas, 42
Gall, Franz, 18
Gallup poll, 42
Galvanic skin response (GSR), 354. A change in the electrical resistance (or inversely, the conductance) of the skin, due to sweating.
Gambler's fallacy, 520
Gamma-hydroxybutyrate (GHB), 192–193
Gaps in experience, 517
Gardner, Allen, 284
Gardner, Beatrix, 284
GAS. *See* General adaptation syndrome (GAS)
GATE. *See* Gifted and Talented Education (GATE)
Gate control theory, 139–141. Proposes that pain messages pass through neural "gates" in the spinal cord.
Gateway questions, 3–4
Gateway theme, 3
Genain sisters, 42
Gender, 370, 371. Psychological and social characteristics associated with being male or female; defined especially by one's gender identity and learned gender roles.
Gender bias in research, 28. A tendency for females and female issues to be underrepresented in research, psychological or otherwise.
Gender differences
brains, 70
depression, 493–494
eating disorders, 341–342
emotional expression, 357
expressive behaviors, 377–378
hormones and, 74–75
instrumental behaviors, 377–378
IQ, 311
leadership styles, 70
puberty, 108
reproductive anatomy, 371
scholastic, 374–375
sexual behavior, 380–383
sexual response, 383–385
suicide attempts, 505
Gender identity, 374. One's personal, private sense of maleness or femaleness.
acquiring, 374
biological bias effect, 374–375
Gender role, 375. The pattern of behaviors that are regarded as "male" or "female" by one's culture; sometimes also referred to as a sex role.
cultural influences on, 376–377
sexual behavior and, 374–375
Gender role socialization, 374, 377–378. The process of learning gender behaviors considered appropriate for one's sex in a given culture.
Gender role stereotypes, 374–375, 389. Oversimplified and widely held beliefs about the basic characteristics of men and women.
Gender variance, 379–380. Condition in which a person's biological sex does not match his or her preferred gender.
General adaptation syndrome (GAS), 446–447. A series of bodily reactions to prolonged stress; occurs in three stages: alarm, resistance, and exhaustion.
General intelligence test, 305. A test that measures a wide variety of mental abilities.
General mental abilities. *See* G-factor
General solution, 286, 287. A solution that correctly states the requirements for success but not in enough detail for further action.
Generalization, 210, 224
Generalized anxiety disorder, 496. A chronic state of tension and worry about work, relationships, ability, or impending disaster.
Generativity versus stagnation, 112–113. A conflict of middle adulthood in which self-interest is countered by an interest in guiding the next generation.
Genes, 84. Specific areas on a strand of DNA that carry hereditary information. *See also* Heredity
expression of, 84–85
Genetic disorders, 86. Problems caused by defects in the genes or by inherited characteristics.
Genetic sex, 379. Sex as indicated by the presence of *XX* (female) or *XY* (male) chromosomes.
Genital sex, 371. Sex as indicated by the presence of male or female genitals.

Genital stage, 414. Period of full psychosexual development, marked by the attainment of mature adult sexuality.
Genius. *See* Giftedness
Genovese, Kitty, 582
Gerontologist, 115. A psychologist who studies aging and the aged.
Gestalt organizing principles, 145–146
Gestalt psychology, 25–26. A school of psychology emphasizing the study of thinking, learning, and perception in whole units, not by analysis into parts.
Gestalt therapy, 517. An approach that focuses on immediate experience and awareness to help clients rebuild thinking, feeling, and acting into connected wholes; emphasizes the integration of fragmented experiences.
Gestalt, defined, 26
g-factor, 305, 306. A general ability factor proposed to underly intelligence; the core of general intellectual ability that involves reasoning, problem-solving ability, knowledge, and memory.
GHB. *See* Gamma-hydroxybutyrate (GHB)
Ghost sickness, 480
Gifted and Talented Education (GATE), 313
Giftedness, 312, 313. Either the possession of a high IQ or special talents or aptitudes.
  achievement and, 312
  identification of, 312–313
  misconceptions of, 312
  programs for, 313
Gigantism, 75
Ginkgo biloba, 265
Glans penis (glanz PEA-nis) The tip of the penis.
Glial cells, 52
Glove anesthesia, 500
Glucagon-like peptide 1 (GLP-1), 336
Glutamate, 55, 138
Goal, 332. The target or objective of motivated behavior.
  dieting, 340
  psychology, 15–16
  research, 16
  setting, 7
  success, 347
  superordinate, 595
Gonadal sex, 379. Sex as indicated by the presence of ovaries (female) or testes (male).
Gonads, 370. The primary sex glands—the testes in males and ovaries in females.
Grammar, 283. A set of rules for combining language units into meaningful speech or writing.
Grandeur, delusions of, 484
Grandiose type disorders, 486
Graphical statistics, 634
Graphology, 18
Grasping reflex, 89
Gray matter, 64
Group study, 5
Group therapy, 534–535
Group cohesiveness, 548–549. The degree of attraction among group members or their commitment to remaining in the group.
Group intelligence test, 307. Any intelligence test that can be administered to a group of people with minimal supervision.
Group prejudice, 590. Prejudice held out of conformity to group views.
Group sanctions, 563. Rewards and punishments (such as approval or disapproval) administered by groups to enforce conformity among members.
Group structure, 548. The network of roles, communication pathways, and power in a group.
Groups
  awareness training for, 536
  breakup of, 557
  conformity and, 563
  membership, 554–555
  pressure from, 562
Group therapy, 534–535. Psychotherapy conducted in a group setting to make therapeutic use of group dynamics.
Groupthink, 562. A compulsion by members of decision-making groups to maintain agreement, even at the cost of critical thinking.
Growth hormone, 75. A hormone, secreted by the pituitary gland, that promotes body growth.
Growth needs, 348. In Maslow's hierarchy, the higher-level needs associated with self-actualization.
Guided discovery, 231
Guided imagery, 469–470. Intentional visualization of images that are calming, relaxing, or beneficial in other ways.
Guilt, 112
Guilty knowledge test, 354. Polygraph procedure involving testing people with knowledge only a guilty person could know.
Gunnysacking, 394
Gustation, 137. The sense of taste.
Gutenberg, Johannes, 298

H

Habit, 422. A deeply ingrained, learned pattern of behavior.
Habituation, 156, 161–162. A decrease in perceptual response to a repeated stimulus.
Hair cells, 134. Receptor cells within the cochlea that transduce vibrations into nerve impulses.
Halcion, 193
Halfway house, 530. A community-based facility for individuals making the transition from an institution (mental hospital, prison, and so forth) to independent living.
Hallucination. 143–144. An imaginary sensation, such as seeing, hearing, or smelling things that don't exist in the real world.
  drug-induced, 489
  hypnopomic, 173
  psychotic, 484
Hallucinogen (hal-LU-sin-oh-jin), 196–197. A substance that alters or distorts sensory impressions.
Halo effect, 430. The tendency to generalize a favorable or unfavorable first impression to unrelated details of personality.
Handedness, 77. A preference for the right or left hand in most activities.
  advantages in, 78–79
  assessment of, 77
  brain dominance and, 77–78
  causes of, 78
  determination of, 77
  lateralization and, 79
Hardy personality, 467. A personality style associated with superior stress resistance.
Harris poll, 42
Hashish, 196
Hassle (microstressor), 462–463. Any distressing, day-to-day annoyance.
Hawking, Steven, 141, 303, 310, 319
Health psychology, 442, 443. Study of the ways in which behavioral principles can be used to prevent illness and promote health.
  adult challenges, 113
  approaches to, 445
  biofeedback, 464–465
  conflicts and, 454–455
  defense mechanisms, 456–458
  depression, 459–461
  frustration and, 451–453
  learned helplessness, 458–461
  personality and, 465–467
  psychosomatic disorders, 463–464
  purpose of, 442
  stress and, 446–450, 461–463
Hearing
  artificial, 136–137
  loss, 136
  mechanisms of, 134–135
  theories of, 135
Helping behaviors, 532, 583
Hematophobia, 497
Hemispheres
  connection of, 64
  damage to, 64–65
  handedness and, 77–78
  lateralization of, 79
  specialization of, 65–67
Heredity ("nature"), 84. The transmission of physical and psychological characteristics from parents to offspring through genes. *See also* Genes
  defined, 84
  depression and, 494
  intelligence and, 317
  personality and, 425–426
  schizophrenia and, 489
Hermaphrodite, 371
Heroism, 583–584
Heterosexism, 589. The belief that heterosexuality is better or more natural than homosexuality.
Heterosexual, 372. A person romantically and erotically attracted to members of the opposite sex.
Heuristic (hew-RIS-tik), 286. Any strategy or technique that aids problem solving, especially by limiting the number of possible solutions to be tried.
  defined, 286
  learned, 289
  representativeness, 294
Hidden observer, 180. A detached part of the hypnotized person's awareness that silently observes events.
Hierarchy, 522. A rank-ordered series of higher and lower amounts, levels, degrees, or steps.
  construction of, 540
  defined, 523
  desensitization, 522
  human needs, 348–349
Hierarchy of human needs, 348. Abraham Maslow's ordering of needs, based on their presumed strength or potency.
Higher order conditioning, 209
Hikikomori, 480
Hindbrain, 71
Hinkley, John, 490
Hippocampus (HIP-oh-CAMP-us), 73–74, 261. A part of the limbic system associated with emotion and the transfer of information from short-term memory to long-term memory.
Hispanics, 97
Histogram, 634
History
  defined, 513
  psychological disorders, 475–476
  structuralism, 24
HIV/AIDS
  cause of, 390
  prevention of, 392
  spread of, 391–392
  symptoms of, 390–391
Homeostasis (HOE-me-oh-STAY-sis), 333. A steady state of body equilibrium.
Homogamy (huh-MOG-ah-me), 577. Marriage of two people who are similar to one another.
Homosexual, 372. A person romantically and erotically attracted to same-sex persons.
Homosexuality, 372–373
Hope, value of, 459–460
Hormonal sex, 370. Sex as indicated by a preponderance of estrogens (female) or androgens (male) in the body
Hormone, 74. A glandular secretion that affects bodily functions or behavior.
  behavior and, 74–75
  characterization of, 74
  gender, 74–75
Horney, Karen, 26, 415
Hothousing. *See* Forced teaching
Huberty, James, 488
Hues, defined, 128
Hughes, Howard, 498
Human–computer interaction (HCI), 627. The application of human factors to the design of computers and computer software.
Human development. *See also* Cognitive development
  adolescence, 107–109
  deprivation and, 87–88
  emerging adulthood, 109
  emotions, 92–93
  enrichment and, 87–88
  environment and, 86–87
  growth sequence of, 85
  heredity and, 84–85
  language, 98–101
  lifetime milestones, 111–113
  middle age, 113–114
  moral values, 110–111
  motor skills and, 90–91
  old age, 114–115
  perceptual, 91–92
  prenatal influences on, 86–87
  psychosocial theory of, 111–112
  reaction range and, 88–89
  readiness and, 86
  sensitive periods in, 87
  social, 93–96
  theory of mind and, 105
Human diversity boxes, 28
Human factors psychology (ergonomics), 626. A specialty concerned with making machines and work environments compatible with human perceptual and physical capacities.
  computer use, 627
  goal of, 626
  sensory restriction analysis, 628
  space habitat analysis, 628
  tool use, 627–628
  usability testing by, 627
Human Genome Project, 84
Human nature, 17. Those traits, qualities, potentials, and behavior patterns most characteristic of the human species.
Human participants. *See also* Animal models
  bias of, 37–38
  diversity in, 28

Humanism, 26. An approach to psychology that focuses on human experience, problems, potentials, and ideals.
Humanistic theory
anxiety disorders, 501–502
defined, 417
history of, 26–27
perspective of, 407
self-actualization and, 417–419
strength of, 428
Humanistic therapies, 516–517
Humanity, fellowship of, 418
Humor, 418
Hunger
anorexia and, 340
external factors of, 337–344
function of, 334–335
internal factors in, 335–337
memory and, 268
Hydrocephaly (HI-dro-SEF-ah-lee), 316. A buildup of cerebrospinal fluid within brain cavities.
Hyperopia (HI-per-OPE-ee-ah), 129. Difficulty focusing nearby objects (farsightedness).
Hypersexual disorder, 396. A persistent, troubling excess of sexual desire.
Hypersexual sexual desire, 395
Hypersomnia (hi-per-SOM-nee-ah), 169. Excessive daytime sleepiness. This can result from depression, insomnia, narcolepsy, sleep apnea, sleep drunkenness, periodic limb movements, drug abuse, and other problems.
Hyperthyroidism, 75
Hypnopomic hallucinations, 173
Hypnosis, 180. An altered state of consciousness characterized by narrowed attention and increased suggestibility.
defined, 179
effects of, 181–182
history of, 180
reality of, 180–181
stage, 182
susceptibility to, 180–181
theories of, 180
Hypnotic susceptibility, 182. One's capacity for becoming hypnotized.
Hypoactive sexual desire, 395. A persistent, upsetting loss of sexual desire.
Hypochondriac (HI-po-KON-dree-ak), 464. A person who complains about illnesses that appear to be imaginary.
Hypochondriasis (HI-po-kon-DRY-uh-sis), 499. A preoccupation with fears of having a serious disease. Ordinary physical signs are interpreted as proof that the person has a disease, but no physical disorder can be found.
Hypopituitary gland, 75
Hypothalamus (HI-po-THAL-ah-mus), 73, 335. A small area at the base of the brain that regulates many aspects of motivation and emotion, especially hunger, thirst, and sexual behavior.
Hypothesis, 22. The predicted outcome of an experiment or an educated guess about the relationship between variables.
defined, 21
perceptual, 146
testing of, 21
Hypothyroidism, 75
Hysteria (now called **somatoform disorders**), 512. An outdated term describing people with physical symptoms (such as paralysis or numbness) for which no physical causes can be found.

I

I-message, 119. A message that states the effect someone else's behavior has on you.
IBM's Watson, 321
Iconic (eye-KON-ick) **memory**, 242. A mental image or visual representation.
Id, 411. The primitive part of personality that remains unconscious, supplies energy, and demands pleasure.
Ideal self, 419. An idealized image of oneself (the person one would like to be).
Identical twins, 317. Twins who develop from a single egg and have identical genes.
Identification, 424. Feeling emotionally connected to a person and seeing oneself as like him or her.
Identity. *See* Personal identity
Identity versus role confusion, 114. A conflict of adolescence, involving the need to establish a personal identity.
Ildefonso, 283
Illogical thought, 290. Thought that is intuitive, haphazard, or irrational.
Illusion, 144. A misleading or misconstructed perception.
Illusory figures, 145
Illustrators, 358. Gestures people use to illustrate what they are saying.
Imagery, 176, 263–264
Image, 276. Most often, a mental representation that has picture-like qualities; an icon. *See* Mental images
Imitation, 424. An attempt to match one's own behavior to another person's behavior.
Immune system, 447–448
Implicit association test, 590
Implicit memory, 253. A memory that a person does not know exists; a memory that is retrieved unconsciously.
Impossible figures, 147–148
In-basket test, 611. A testing procedure that simulates the individual decision-making challenges that executives face.
In-groups, 549–550. A group with which a person identifies.
Inattentional blindness, 148. A failure to notice a stimulus because attention is focused elsewhere.
Incentive value, 332. The value of a goal above and beyond its ability to fill a need.
Incongruence, 419. State that exists when there is a discrepancy between one's experiences and self-image or between one's self-image and ideal self.
Incremental problem solving, 294. Thinking marked by a series of small steps that lead to an original solution.
Incubation, 298
Incus, 134
Independent variable, 35. In an experiment, the condition being investigated as a possible cause of some change in behavior. The values that this variable takes are chosen by the experimenter.
Index of intelligence, 325
Individual intelligence test, 307. A test of intelligence designed to be given to a single individual by a trained specialist.
Individual traits, 407. Personality traits that define a person's unique individual qualities.
Individuating information, 597. Information that helps define a person as an individual, rather than as a member of a group or social category.
Inductive thought, 290. Thinking in which a general rule or principle is gathered from a series of specific examples; for instance, inferring the laws of gravity by observing many falling objects.
Industrial/organizational psychology, 606. A field that focuses on the psychology of work and on behavior within organizations.
defined, 604
job satisfaction, 606–607
leadership theories of, 604–606
organizational culture analysis by, 608
personnel analysis by, 608–611
Industry, sense of, 112
Industry versus inferiority, 114. A conflict in middle childhood centered around lack of support for industrious behavior, which can result in feelings of inferiority.
Infants. *See also* Newborns
depth perception of, 150
emotional attachment of, 94–95
emotions of, 92–93
language development in, 98–99
social development of, 93–96
sudden death of, 176–177
Inferential statistics, 633, 640–641
Inferiority, sense of, 112
Influence, delusions of, 484
Information
bits, 244
chunks, 245
opera in operant conditioning, 214
recalling, 252
recognizing, 252–253
relearning, 253
view of, 209
Information bits, 244. Meaningful units of information, such as numbers, letters, words, or phrases.
Information chunks, 246. Information bits grouped into larger units.
Informational view (of conditioning), 210. Perspective that explains learning in terms of information imparted by events in the environment.
Initiative reinforcement, 112
Initiative versus guilt, 114. A conflict between learning to take initiative and overcoming feelings of guilt about doing so.
Inkblot test, 433
Insanity, 479. A legal term that refers to a mental inability to manage one's affairs or to be aware of the consequences of one's actions.
Insanity defense, 478
Insecure-ambivalent attachment, 95. An anxious emotional bond marked by both a desire to be with a parent or caregiver and some resistance to being reunited.
Insecure-ambivalent infants, 94
Insecure-avoidant attachment, 95. An anxious emotional bond marked by a tendency to avoid reunion with a parent or caregiver.
Insecure-avoidant infants, 94
Insight, 286. A sudden mental reorganization of a problem that makes the solution obvious.
bases of, 286–287
nature of, 287–288
therapy, 514
Insomnia, 174. Difficulty in getting to sleep or staying asleep; also, not feeling rested after sleeping.
behavioral remedies for, 175–176
causes of, 175
defined, 174
types of, 175
Instrumental behaviors, 377. Behaviors directed toward the achievement of some goal; behaviors that are instrumental in producing some effect.
Instrumental learning. *See* Operant conditioning
Integrity, 113
Integrity versus despair, 113. A conflict in old age between feelings of integrity and the despair of viewing previous life events with regret.
Intellectual disability (formerly **mental retardation**), 313–314. The presence of a developmental disability, a formal IQ score below 70, or a significant impairment of adaptive behavior.
causes of, 313, 314–316
defined, 313
distinctive forms of, 315–316
familial, 315
levels of, 313–314
Intelligence, 304. An overall capacity to think rationally, act purposefully, and deal effectively with the environment.
alternative views of, 319–322
aptitude and, 304–305
artificial, 320–321
aspects of, 306
brain efficiency and, 62
culture and, 308
definitions of, 304–305
emotional, 363–364
environmental factors, 317–319
genetic factors, 316–317
gifted, 312–313
index of, 325
neonates, 91
nervous system and, 319–320
reflective, 320
standardized testing of, 325
video games and, 318
wisdom *versus*, 325–326
Intelligence quotient (IQ), 309. An index of intelligence defined as mental age divided by chronological age and multiplied by 100.
achievement and, 311–312
age and, 311
classification of, 310
defined, 309
deviation, 309–310
gender and, 311
genetic factors in, 317
race and, 324–325
ranges, 314
SES and, 318–319
stability of, 310
Intelligence tests
culture-fair, 323
reliability of, 305
types of, 306–307, 309
unfairness of, 323
Intelligent information processing, 320
Interaction with others, 554
Interference, 257. The tendency for new memories to impair retrieval of older memories, and the reverse.
defined, 257
effect of, 258
proactive, 258–259
retroactive, 258
Intergroup conflict
causes of, 591–592
experiments of, 593–596
terrorism and, 593

Internal cause, 552. A cause of behavior assumed to lie within a person—for instance, a need, preference, or personality trait.
International Space Station, 628
Internet
research information on, 44
surveys on, 43
therapists, 537
The Interpretation of Dreams (Freud), 178
Interpersonal attraction, 576. Social attraction to another person. *See also* Love
factors influencing, 576
friendships and, 576
physical aspects of, 577
reciprocity in, 577
self-disclosure in, 577–578
similarity and, 576–577
social exchange theory for, 578
Interpersonal psychotherapy (IPT), 514. A brief dynamic psychotherapy designed to help people by improving their relationships with other people.
Interpersonal relationships, 418
Intersexual person (formerly **hermaphrodite**), 371. A person who has genitals suggestive of both sexes.
Intersubjective observations, 14
Interview (personality), 429. A face-to-face meeting held for the purpose of gaining information about an individual's personal history, personality traits, current psychological state, and so forth.
cognitive, 248
employee, 609
job, 610
limitations of, 430
open-ended, 556
types of, 429–430
Intimacy, 579. Feelings of connectedness and affection for another person.
avoiding, 394–395
communication and, 394–395
defined, 579
isolation *vs.,* 112
Intimacy versus isolation, 114. The challenge of overcoming a sense of isolation by establishing intimacy with others.
Intimate distance, 561. The most private space immediately surrounding the body (up to about 18 inches from the skin).
Intracellular thirst, 342. Thirst triggered when fluid is drawn out of cells due to an increased concentration of salts and minerals outside the cell.
Intrauterine environment, 86
Intrinsic motivation, 349–350. Motivation that comes from within, rather than from external rewards; motivation based on personal enjoyment of a task or activity.
Introspection, 23. To look within; to examine one's own thoughts, feelings, or sensations.
Introversion, 405, 416. Ego attitude in which in which energy is mainly directed inward.
Introvert, 406. A person whose attention is focused inward; a shy, reserved, self-centered person.
Intuition, 294. Quick, impulsive thought that does not make use of formal logic or clear reasoning.
accuracy of, 293–294
defined, 294
framing and, 295
underlying odds of, 294–295
Intuitive thought, 104. Thinking that makes little or no use of reasoning and logic.
Iodopsin, 132
Ion channels, 54. Tiny openings through the axon membrane.
Ions, 52–53
IPT. *See* Interpersonal psychotherapy (IPT)
IQ. *See* Intelligence quotients (IQ)
Irrational beliefs, 519
Isolation, 112, 116

J
James, Henry, 24
James, Henry Sr., 24
James, William, 24
James-Lange (LON-geh) **theory**, 358. States that emotional feelings follow bodily arousal and come from awareness of such arousal.
Janis, Irving, 562
Jealous type disorders, 486
Jet leg, 334
Jigsaw classroom, 595–596. A method of reducing prejudice; each student receives only part of the information needed to complete a project or prepare for a test.
Jobs
analysis of, 609
enrichment of, 607–608
satisfaction of, 606–607
Job analysis, 609. A detailed description of the skills, knowledge, and activities required by a particular job.
Job enrichment, 607. Making a job more personally rewarding, interesting, or intrinsically motivating; typically involves increasing worker knowledge.
Job satisfaction, 606. The degree to which a person is comfortable with or satisfied with his or her work.
Johnson, Randy, 45
Jolie, Angelina, 551
Jones, Angus T., 553
Jones, Jim, 567–568
Judgment, 294–295, 611
Jung, Carl, 26, 415–416
Juries
behavior of, 620–622
death-qualified, 622
mock, 620
selection of, 622–623
Just-world beliefs, 597–598. Belief that people generally get what they deserve.
Justice, 110

K
Kaczynski, Theodore, 488
Kandinsky, Wassily, 275
Kanzi lexigrams, 285
Kawakami, Kenji, 291
Kelley, Harold, 552
Keyword method, 269. As an aid to memory, using a familiar word or image to link two items.
Kiel, Richard, 75
Kinect, 627
Kinesics (kih-NEEZ-iks), 357–358. Study of the meaning of body movements, posture, hand gestures, and facial expressions; commonly called body language.
Kinesthetic imagery, 278
Kinesthetic senses, 138. The senses of body movement and positioning.
Kleinfelter's syndrome, 370
Knowledge
builder, 3, 220
organized, 289
results, 219
workers, 605
Knowledge of results (KR), 220. Informational feedback.
Knowledge workers, 606. Workers who add value to their company by creating and manipulating information.
Kolb, Bryan, 51, 59
Koresh, David, 658
Koro, 480
Kübler-Ross, Elisabeth, 115
Kuder Occupational Interest Survey, 610–611

L
Labeling, 435–436
Labia majora (LAY-bee-ah mah-JOR-ah), 371. The larger outer lips of the vulva.
Labia minora (LAY-bee-ah mih-NOR-ah), 371. Inner lips of the vulva, surrounding the vaginal opening.
Language, 276. Words or symbols, and rules for combining them, that are used for thinking and communication.
animal, 284–285
defined, 276
gestural, 283–284
left brain and, 66
structure of, 283
study of, 281–282
thought and, 281
used in IQ test, 323–324
Language development
first words, 98
maturation and, 99
parentese and, 100
roots of, 99–100
terrible twos and, 99
Large-group awareness training, 536. Any of a number of programs (many of them commercialized) that claim to increase self-awareness and facilitate constructive personal change.
Latency, 414. According to Freud, a period in childhood when psychosexual development is more or less interrupted.
Latent content (of dreams), 178, 513. The hidden or symbolic meaning of a dream, as revealed by dream interpretation and analysis.
Latent learning, 230. Learning that occurs without obvious reinforcement and that remains unexpressed until reinforcement is provided.
Lateral hypothalamus, 335
Lateralization, 80. Differences between the two sides of the body, especially differences in the abilities of the brain hemispheres.
Law of effect, 213. Responses that lead to desirable effects are repeated; those that produce undesirable results are not.
Leaderless group discussion, 611. A test of leadership that simulates group decision making and problem solving.
Leadership
gender differences in, 605
shared, 606
theories of, 604–606
Learned fears, 211–212
Learned helplessness, 458. A learned inability to overcome obstacles or to avoid punishment; learned passivity and inaction to aversive stimuli.
causes of, 458–459
coping with, 458
defined, 458
depression and, 459
hope and, 459–460
Learned motives, 333. Motives based on learned needs, drives, and goals.
Learning, 206. Any relatively permanent change in behavior that can be attributed to experience. *See also* Conditioning
aids, 219–221
in aplysia, 262
avoidance, 226–227
cognitive, 229–231
conservation and, 220
creativity, 293
discovery, 231–232, 620
escape, 226
latent, 230
observational, 231–232
part, 266
perceptual, 155–156
rote, 230, 245
self-regulated, 6
state-dependent, 257
styles, 620
theorists, 422
types of, 206
universal design for, 621
whole, 266
Learning theorist, 422. A psychologist interested in the ways that learning shapes behavior and explains personality.
Leaving the field, 454
Legitimate power, 559. Social power based on a person's position as an agent of an accepted social order.
Lexigram, 285. A geometric shape used as a symbol for a word.
Libido (lih-BEE-doe), 411, 412. In Freudian theory, the force, primarily pleasure oriented, that energizes the personality.
Librium, 193
Lie detector tests, 354–355
Life change units (LCUs), 461
Life events, 461–463
Life instincts, 411
Life skills training, 445. A program that teaches stress reduction, self-protection decision making, self-control and social skills.
Lifestyle disease, 442. A disease related to health-damaging personal habits.
Lifestyles, 299, 442–443
Light, 128–129, 151
Light sleep, 172. Stage 1 sleep, marked by small irregular brainwaves and some alpha waves.
Liking, 579. A relationship based on intimacy, but lacking passion and commitment.
Limbic system, 73. A system in the forebrain that is closely linked with emotional response.
components of, 73
function of, 73–74
memory and, 261–262
Linear perspective, 151
Linguistic relativity hypothesis, 281. The idea that the words we use not only reflect our thoughts but can shape them as well.
Little Albert experiment, 211
Lobes
frontal, 67–68
occipital, 70
parietal, 68
temporal, 69
Lobes of the cerebral cortex, 68. Areas on the left and right cortex bordered by major fissures or defined by their functions.

Localization of function, 61. The research strategy of linking specific structures in the brain with specific psychological or behavioral functions.
Lock and key theory of olfaction, 137. Holds that odors are related to the shapes of chemical molecules.
Locked-in syndrome, 72
Logical consequences, 119. Reasonable consequences that are defined by parents.
Logical thought, 290. Drawing conclusions on the basis of formal principles of reasoning.
Logos, 517
Logotherapy, 516–517
Long sleepers, 170
Long-term memory (LTM), 243. The memory system used for relatively permanent storage of meaningful information.
brain and, 262
elaborate processing of, 246–248
extension of, 267
features of, 246
organization of, 248–250
permanence of, 246
priming of, 253
redintegration of, 248–249
retrieval of, 249–250
STM and, 243
types of, 250–251
Long-term potentiation, 262. Brain mechanism used to form lasting memories by strengthening the connection between neurons that become more active at the same time.
Long-term stress, 446
Looking chamber, 91
Loudness, 134, 136
Love
attachment and, 579–580
interpersonal attraction *vs.*, 578–579
mate selection and, 580–581
triangular theory of, 578–579
types of, 579
withdrawal of, 117–118
Lowball technique, 564–565. A strategy in which commitment is gained first to reasonable or desirable terms, which are then made less reasonable or desirable.
LSD. *See* Lysergic acid diethylamide (LSD)
LTM. *See* Long-term memory (LTM)
Lucid dream, 200, 201. A dream in which the dreamer feels awake and capable of normal thought and action.
Luck, 520
Lunesta, 175
Lying, 354–355, 358
Lysergic acid diethylamide (LSD), 196

M
Madonna, 551
Magnetic resonance imaging (MRI), 61, An imaging technique that results in a three-dimensional image of the brain or body, based on its response to a magnetic field.
Magnified gambling skills, 520
Maintenance rehearsal, 245. Silently repeating or mentally reviewing information to hold it in short-term memory.
Major depressive disorder, 492. A mood disorder in which the person has suffered one or more intense episodes of depression.
Major mood disorders, 484, 492. Disorders marked by lasting extremes of mood or emotion and sometimes accompanied by psychotic symptoms.
Major tranquilizers. *See* Antipsychotics
Maladaptive behavior, 477–478. Behavior arising from an underlying psychological or biological dysfunction that makes it difficult to adapt to the environment and meet the demands of day-to-day life.
Maladaptive personality patterns, 503
Male orgasmic disorder, 397. A persistent inability to reach orgasm during lovemaking.
Management by objectives, 606. A management technique in which employees are given specific goals to meet in their work.
Management techniques, 117–118. Combining praise, recognition, approval, rules, and reasoning to enforce child discipline.
Mandala, 416. A circular design representing the balance, unity, and completion of the unconscious self.
Mania, 432. Emotional excitability, manic moods or behavior, and excessive activity.
Manifest content (of dreams), 178, 513. The surface, "visible" content of a dream; dream images as they are remembered by the dreamer.
Mantras, 183
Marijuana
abuse of, 196–197
characterization of, 196
health risks of, 197
Marital rape, 389
Marriage
adult status and, 107
challenges of, 114
suicide and, 506
Mars Climate Orbiter, 562
Masculinity/femininity, 432. One's degree of traditional "masculine" aggressiveness or "feminine" sensitivity.
Maslow, Abraham, 26–27, 161
Massed practice, 5, 266–267. A practice schedule in which studying continues for long periods, without interruption.
Mastery learning, 459
Mastery training, 459. Reinforcement of responses that lead to mastery of a threat or control over one's environment.
Masturbation, 382–383. Producing sexual pleasure or orgasm by directly stimulating the genitals.
Mate selection, 580–581
Material World Project, 616
Maternal influences, 96. The aggregate of all psychological effects mothers have on their children.
Maternity blues. *See* Postpartum depression
Maturation, 85. The physical growth and development of the body, brain and nervous system.
McGraw, Phil, 536–537
MDMA. *See* Methylenedioxymethamphetamine (MDMA)
Mean, 635
Mean world view, 555
Measures of variability, 636
Mechanical solution, 286. A problem solution achieved by trial and error or by a fixed procedure based on learned rules.
Media
aggressive behavior and, 587
modeling behavior and, 232–233
parental guidance, 588
positive model of, 588
psychologists, 536–537
Median, 636
Medical students disease, 483
Medical therapy
community programs, 530
deinstitutionalization and, 529–530
drug classifications in, 527–528
ECT, 528
hospitalization, 529
surgery, 528–529
Meditation, 183. A mental exercise for producing relaxation or heightened awareness.
benefits of, 183
effects of, 183–184
SUB, 469
Mediterranean diet, 444
Mediumships, 158
Medulla (meh-DUL-ah), 71. The structure that connects the brain with the spinal cord and controls vital life functions.
Melatonin (mel-ah-TONE-in), 75. Hormone released by the pineal gland in response to daily cycles of light and dark.
Melnick, Michael, 42
Meltzoff, Andrew, 91
Membership groups, 556
Memories, Dreams, Reflections (Jung), 416
Memory, 242. The mental system for receiving, encoding, storing, organizing, altering, and retrieving information. *See also* Long-term memory; Recall; Short-term memory
aides, 5
cues, 257, 266
culture and, 244
defined, 242
ECS, 260–261
exceptional, 263–265
flashbulb, 261
forensic, 248
forgetting and, 254–260
gaps in, 246
hunger and, 268
hypnosis effect on, 182
illusion of, 255
improving, 265–268
long-term potentiation and, 262
measuring of, 251–254
network model of, 248
photographic, 264
recovered, 260
repression of, 259–260
selective, 520
sensory, 628
sleep and, 267–268
stages of, 242–243
structure of, 248
suppression of, 259–260
working, 306
Memory decay, 256. The fading or weakening of memories assumed to occur when memory traces become weaker.
Memory jamming, 247
Memory traces, 256. Physical changes in nerve cells or brain activity that take place when memories are stored.
Men, 341–342
Menarche, 371
Menopause, 371
Mental ability tests, 609–610
Mental age, 309. The average mental ability displayed by people of a given age.
Mental disorder, 479. A significant impairment in psychological functioning. *See also* abnormality; *specific conditions*
classification of, 478–482
general risk factors, 482
labeling of, 482–483
organic, 479
social stigma of, 482–483
treatment of, 504
Mental filters. *See* Dream process
Mental hospitalization, 529. Placing a person in a protected, therapeutic environment staffed by mental health professionals.
Mental images, 276. Mental pictures or visual depictions used in memory and thinking.
kinesthetic, 278
memory and, 263
nature of, 276
neural process of, 277
size of, 277–278
thought and, 276
use of, 277–278
Mental models. *See* Perceptual constructions
Mental practice, 624. Imagining a skilled performance to aid learning.
Mental retardation. *See* Intellectual disability
Mental set, 297. A predisposition to perceive or respond in a particular way.
Mere presence, 560. The tendency for people to change their behavior just because of the presence of other people.
Meta-analysis, 37. A statistical technique for combining the results of many studies on the same subject.
Meta-needs, 348. In Maslow's hierarchy, needs associated with impulses for self-actualization.
Metabolic rate, 339
Metacognitive skills, 320. An ability to manage one's own thinking and problem solving efforts.
Methamphetamines, 187–188
Methylenedioxymethamphetamine (MDMA), 190
Microcephaly (MY-kro-SEF-ah-lee), 316. A disorder in which the head and brain are abnormally small.
Microsleep, 169. A brief shift in brain-wave patterns to those of sleep.
Microstressors, 462–463
Mid-life crisis, 114
Milgram obedience studies
experiment, 565–566
follow-up, 566
implications of, 566–567
Milgram, Stanley, 22
Million Dollar Challenge, 45
Mind blindness. *See* Facial agnosia
Mind, frames of, 322
Mindfulness, 184, 185. A state of open, nonjudgmental awareness of current experience.
Mindfulness meditation, 183–185. Mental exercise based on widening attention to become aware of everything experienced at any given moment.
Minnesota Multiphasic Personality Inventory-2 (MMPI-2), 431. One of the best-known and most widely used objective personality questionnaires.
items in, 431–432
reliability of, 432–433
subscales of, 432
Mirror neuron, 67–68. A neuron that becomes active when a motor action is carried out *and* when another organism is observed carrying out the same action.
Mirror technique, 535. Observing another person re-enact one's own behavior, like a character in a play; designed to help persons see themselves more clearly.

Miss Cleo, 158
Mistrust, 112
Mitchell, Edgar, 159
MMPI-2 profile, 432, 433. A graphic representation of an individual's scores on each of the primary scales of the MMPI-2.
Mnemonic, 5
Mnemonics (nee-MON-ik), 265, 268–270. Any kind of memory system, aid, or strategy.
Mock jury, 620. A group that realistically simulates a courtroom jury.
Mode, 636
Model, 231. A person who serves as an example in observational learning.
Modeling, 231–233
Moderate response rates, 223
Molestation. *See* Child molestation
Monocular depth cues, 150–152. Perceptual features that impart information about distance and three-dimensional space which require just one eye.
Monosodium glutamate (MSG), 138
Mood, 351. A low-intensity long-lasting emotional state.
Mood disorders, 480, 492. A major disturbance in mood or emotion, such as depression or mania. *See also* Major mood disorders
  causes of, 493
  classification of, 492
  depression, 493–494
Moon illusion, 152–153
Moral anxiety, 412. Apprehension felt when thoughts, impulses, or actions conflict with the superego's standards.
Moral development, 110. The development of values, beliefs, and thinking abilities that act as a guide regarding what is acceptable behavior.
  characterization of, 110
  justice/caring debate in, 110–111
  levels of, 110
Moro reflex, 90
Morphemes (MOR-feems), 283. The smallest meaningful units in a language, such as syllables or words.
Motherese (or parentese), 101. A pattern of speech used when talking to infants, marked by a higher-pitched voice; short, simple sentences; repetition, slower speech; and exaggerated voice inflections.
Mothers. *See also* Parenting
  age of, Down syndrome and, 315
  attachment to, 94–95
  influence of, 96
Motion parallax. *See* Relative motion
Motion sickness, 141
Motion, apparent, 153
Motivation, 332. Internal processes that initiate, sustain, direct, and terminate activities.
  extrinsic, 349–350
  incentives, 332
  intrinsic, 349–350
  model of, 332–333
  overview of, 334
  pain avoidance, 342
  in perceptions, 155
  strengthen, 349
Motives
  biological, 333, 342–344
  examination of, 418
  learned, 346–348
  social, 346–348
  stimulus, 344–346
  types of, 333
Motor analysis, 624
Motor aphasia, 68
Motor program, 624. A mental plan or model that guides skilled movement.
Motor skill, 90–91. A series of actions molded into a smooth and efficient performance.
MSG. *See* Monosodium glutamate (MSG)
Müller-Lyer (MEOO-ler-LIE-er) **illusion**, 156–158. Two equal-length lines tipped with inward or outward pointing V's appear to be of different lengths.
Multi-touch interface, 603
Multiculturalism, 597–599. Giving equal status, recognition, and acceptance to different ethnic and cultural groups.
Multiple approach-avoidance conflict, 455. Being simultaneously attracted to and repelled by each of several alternatives.
Multiple aptitude test, 305. Test that measures two or more aptitudes.
Multiple intelligences, 321–322, 325. Howard Gardner's theory that there are several specialized types of intellectual ability.
Munchausen by proxy syndrome, 500. An affected person fakes the medical problems of someone in his or her care in order to gain attention.
Munchausen syndrome (factitious disorder), 500. An affected person fakes his or her own medical problems in order to gain attention.
Musical personality, 408
Mutual absorption, 579. With regard to romantic love, the nearly exclusive attention lovers give to one another.
Mutual interdependence, 596. A condition in which two or more persons must depend on one another to meet each person's needs or goals.
Myelin (MY-eh-lin), 54. A fatty layer coating some axons.
Myopia (my-OPE-ee-ah), 129. Difficulty focusing distant objects (nearsightedness).

N
Najdorf, Miguel, 276
Nanometers, 128
Narcissistic personality disorder, 503
Narcolepsy (NAR-koe-lep-see), 177. Sudden, irresistible, daytime sleep attacks that may last anywhere from a few minutes to a half hour. Victims may fall asleep while standing, talking, or even driving.
Nash, John, 144
Natural clinical tests, 42. An accident or other natural event that allows the gathering of data on a psychological phenomenon of interest.
Natural consequences, 119. The effects that naturally tend to follow a particular behavior.
Natural design, 626. Human factors engineering that makes use of naturally understood perceptual signals.
Natural selection, 24. Darwin's theory that evolution favors those plants and animals best suited to their living conditions.
Natural settings, 39
Naturalistic observation, 39. Observing behavior as it unfolds in natural settings.
  correctional studies, 40–41
  limitations of, 39–40
Nausea, 142
Nearness, 145
Nearsightedness. *See* Myopia
Need, 332. An internal deficiency that may energize behavior.
  basic, 348
  growth, 348
  hierarchy of, 348–349
Need for achievement (nAch), 346–347. The desire to excel or meet some internalized standard of excellence.
Need for power, 347. The desire to have social impact and control over others.
Need to affiliate, 576, 577. The desire to associate with other people.
Negative after-potential, 54. A drop in electrical charge below the resting potential.
Negative attention seeking, 216
Negative correlation, 41. A statistical relationship in which increases in one measure are matched by decreases in the other.
Negative instance, 278, 279. In concept learning, an object or event that does not belong to the concept class.
Negative reinforcement, 216. Occurs when a response is followed by an end to discomfort or by the removal of an unpleasant event.
Negative relationship, 639
Negative self-statements, 471. Self-critical thoughts that increase anxiety and lower performance.
Negative transfer, 259. Mastery of one task conflicts with learning or performing another.
Neo-Freudians, 26, 414–416. A theorist who accepts the broad features of Freud's theory but has revised the theory to fit his or her own concepts.
Neonates. *See* Newborns
Nerve, 57. A bundle of neuron axons.
Nerve cells. *See* Neurons
Nerve impulse, 52–54
Nervous system
  intelligence and, 319–320
  language development and, 99
  major parts of, 56–60
Network model (of memory), 248. A model of memory that views it as an organized system of linked information.
Neural intelligence, 320. The innate speed and efficiency of a person's brain and nervous system.
Neural networks, 56. Interlinked collections of neurons that process information in the brain.
Neural regulators, 55–56
Neurilemma (NOOR-rih-LEM-ah), 57. A layer of cells that encases many axons.
Neurocognitive dream theory, 178–179. Proposal that dreams reflect everyday waking thoughts and emotions.
Neurogenesis (noor-oh-JEN-uh-sis), 59. The production of new brain cells.
Neurological soft signs, 61. Subtle behavioral signs of brain dysfunction, including clumsiness, an awkward gait, poor hand-eye coordination, and other perceptual and motor problems.
Neuron (NOOR-on), 51. An individual nerve cell.
  action potential of, 52–54
  characterization of, 52
  communications between, 54–56
  mirror, 67–68
  parts of, 52
  sensory, 58
  vision, 66
Neuropeptide Y (NPY), 337
Neuropeptides (NOOR-oh-PEP-tides), 55. Brain chemicals, such as enkephalins (en-KEF-ah-lins) and endorphins, that regulate the activity of neurons.
Neuroplasticity, 56. The capacity of the brain to change in response to experience.
Neurosis, 482. An outdated term once used to refer, as a group, to anxiety disorders, somatoform disorders, dissociative disorders, and some forms of depression.
Neurotic anxiety, 412. Apprehension felt when the ego struggles to control id impulses.
Neuroticism, 409
Neurotransmitter (NOOR-oh-TRANS-mit-er), 54. Any chemical released by a neuron that alters activity in other neurons.
  defined, 54
  major, 55
  memory and, 262–263
  psychoactive drugs and, 186
Neutral stimulus (NS), 207. A stimulus that does not evoke a response.
Newborns
  early maturation of, 93
  face recognition by, 90
  motor skills of, 90–91
  physical capabilities of, 89–90
  temperament of, 89
  vision of, 91–92
Nicotine. *See* Cigarette smoking
Night terror, 176. A state of panic during NREM sleep
Nightmare, 176. A bad dream that occurs during REM sleep.
Nightmare disorder, 174. Vivid, recurrent nightmares that significantly disturb sleep.
Noise, 615
Noise pollution, 615. Stressful and intrusive noise; usually artificially generated by machinery, but also including noises made by animals and humans.
Noise-induced hearing loss, 136. Damage caused by exposing the hair cells to excessively loud sounds.
Non-homeostatic drive, 343. A drive that is relatively independent of physical deprivation cycles or bodily need states.
Non-REM (NREM) sleep, 172–173. Non–rapid eye movement sleep characteristic of stages 2, 3, and 4.
Nondirective therapy, 514
Nonexperimental research, 39–40
Nonreinforcement, 524–525
Norepinephrine, 55, 76. Both a brain neurotransmitter and an adrenal hormone that tends to arouse the body; norepinephrine is associated with anger. (Also known as noradrenaline.)
Normal curve, 311, 637–638
Norm, 550. A widely accepted (but often unspoken) standard of conduct for appropriate behavior.
Norm, 305. An average score for a designated group of people.
  conformity theories, 561–563
  effects of, 550
  social, 305
  spatial, 560–561
Normal curve, 311. A bell-shaped curve characterized by a large number of scores in a middle area, tapering to very few extremely high and low scores.Note taking, 4–5
NREM. *See* non-REM sleep
Nytol, 175

O
Obama, Barack, 324
Obedience, 564. Conformity to the demands of an authority.
assertiveness training and, 570–571
defined, 564
Milgram's studies of, 565–567
Obesity
diet-induced, 336
external factors of, 337–342
health risk of, 442
Obsessive-compulsive disorder, 498
Object permanence, 101. Concept, gained in infancy, that objects continue to exist even when they are hidden from view.
Objective test, 8, 431. A test that gives the same score when different people correct it.
Observational learning, 231. Learning achieved by watching and imitating the actions of another or noting the consequences of those actions.
Observational record, 40. A detailed summary of observed events or a videotape of observed behavior.
Observations, 21
Observer bias, 40. The tendency of an observer to distort observations or perceptions to match his or her expectations.
Observer effect, 39. Changes in an organism's behavior brought about by an awareness of being observed.
Obsessive-compulsive disorder,498. An extreme preoccupation with certain thoughts and compulsive performance of certain behaviors.
Occipital lobes (awk-SIP-ih-tal), 70. Portion of the cerebral cortex where vision registers in the brain.
Oedipus conflict, 412. A boy's sexual attraction to his mother, and feelings of rivalry with his father.
Olfaction, 137. The sense of smell.
Olfactory receptors, 137
Open-ended interview, 556. An interview in which persons are allowed to freely state their views.
Open-ended questions, 523
Openness to experience, 410
Operant conditioning, 206. Learning based on the consequences of responding.
classical conditioning *versus*, 213
defined, 206
positive reinforcement, 213
principles of, 212–213
response in, 213–214
stimulus control in, 224–225
therapy-based on, 524–526
Operant conditioning chamber (Skinner box), 213–215. An apparatus designed to study operant conditioning in animals; a Skinner box.
Operant extinction, 216. The weakening or disappearance of a nonreinforced operant response.
Operant reinforcer, 213. Any event that reliably increases the probability or frequency of responses it follows.
Operant reinforcement
contingency in, 214
extinction, 216
feedback, 219–221
information in, 214
negative, 216
partial, 221–224
positive, 213
primary reinforcers, 218
punishment and, 216–217
secondary reinforcers, 218
shaping in, 215–216
social reinforcers, 219
timing of, 214–215
tokens, 218–219
Operant stimulus discrimination, 224. The tendency to make an operant response when stimuli previously associated with reward are present and to withhold the response when stimuli associated with nonreward are present.
Operant stimulus generalization, 224. The tendency to respond to stimuli similar to those that preceded operant reinforcement.
Operational definition, 21, 304. Defining a scientific concept by stating the specific actions or procedures used to measure it. For example, "hunger" might be defined as "the number of hours of food deprivation."
Opponent-process theory (of emotion), 346. States that strong emotions tend to be followed by an opposite emotional state; also the strength of both emotional states changes over time.
Opponent-process theory (of vision), 131–132. Theory of color vision based on three coding systems (red or green, yellow or blue, black or white).
Optimal skills learning, 624
Optimism, 467
Oral stage, 413–414. The period when infants are preoccupied with the mouth as a source of pleasure and means of expression.
Oral-aggressive personality, 412. A person who uses the mouth to express hostility by shouting, cursing, biting, and so forth. Also, one who actively exploits others.
Oral-dependent personality, 412. A person who wants to passively receive attention, gifts, love, and so forth.
Organ of Corti (KOR-tee), 134–135. Center part of the cochlea, containing hair cells, canals, and membranes.
Organic mental disorder, 479. A mental or emotional problem caused by brain diseases or injuries.
Organic psychosis, 485
Organismic valuing, 421. A natural, undistorted, full-body reaction to an experience.
Organizational citizenship, 608. Making positive contributions to the success of an organization in ways that go beyond one's job description.
Organizational culture, 608. The social climate within an organization.
Organized knowledge, 289
Orgasm, 383. A climax and release of sexual excitement.
defined, 383
disorders, 396–397
frequency of, 381–382
types of, 384
Originality, 290. In tests of creativity, originality refers to how novel or unusual solutions are.
Otolith, 141
Out-group, 549. A group with which a person does not identify.
Oval window, 134
Ovary (OH-vah-ree), 371. One of the two female reproductive glands; ovaries are the source of hormones and eggs.
Overgeneralization, 518. Blowing a single event out of proportion by extending it to a large number of unrelated situations.
Overlap, 151
Overlearning, 6. Learning or practice that continues after initial mastery of a skill.
defined, 6
memory and, 266
skills mastery and, 570–571
Overload, 614–615
Overly permissive parents, 96. Parents who give little guidance, allow too much freedom, or do not require the child to take responsibility.
Overpopulation, 613.
Overt behaviors, 14.
Oxytocin, 75. A hormone, released by the pituitary gland, that plays a broad role in regulating pregnancy, parenthood, sexual activity, social bonding, trust, and even reducing stress reaction.

P
Pain
control of, 141
gate control theory of, 139–141
hypnosis effect on, 182
phantom, 140
types of, 139
Pain disorder, 500. Pain that has no identifiable physical cause and appears to be of psychological origin.
Palmistry, 18
Panic disorder (with agoraphobia), 496. A chronic state of anxiety and brief moments of sudden panic. The person fears that these panic attacks will occur in public places or unfamiliar situations.
Panic disorder (without agoraphobia), 496. A chronic state of anxiety and also has brief moments of sudden, intense, unexpected panic.
Paradoxical intention, 175
Paranoia, 432. Extreme suspiciousness and feelings of persecution.
Paranoid psychosis,486. A delusional disorder centered especially on delusions of persecution.
Paranoid schizophrenia, 488. Schizophrenia marked by a preoccupation with delusions or by frequent auditory hallucinations related to a single theme, especially grandeur or persecution.
Paraphilias (PAIR-eh-FIL-ih-ahs) **(Paraphilic disorders)**, 385–386. Compulsive or destructive deviations in sexual preferences or behavior.
Paraprofessional, 530. An individual who works in a near-professional capacity under the supervision of a more highly trained person.
Parasympathetic branch, 58. A part of the autonomic nervous system that quiets the body and conserves energy.
Parasympathetic rebound, 353. Excess activity in the parasympathetic nervous system following a period of intense emotion.
Paraventricular nucleus, 336
Parental influences, 96–97
Parental styles, 96. Identifiable patterns of parental caretaking and interaction with children.
Parentese, 100
Parenting
children's attitudes and, 555
communication and, 100
effective, 117–119
effective communication and, 118–119
ethnic differences in, 97–98
implications of, 98
influence, 96–97
media control by, 588
styles of, 96
Parietal (puh-RYE-ih-tal) **lobes**, 68. Areas of the cortex where bodily sensations register.
Part learning, 266
Partial hospitalization, 529. An approach in which patients receive treatment at a hospital during the day, but return home at night.
Partial reinforcement, 221. A pattern in which only a portion of all responses are reinforced.
defined, 221
effects of, 221–222
schedules of, 222–224
Partial reinforcement effect, 221–222. Responses acquired with partial reinforcement are more resistant to extinction.
Participants, 35. Humans (also referred to as **Experimental subjects**) whose behavior is investigated in an experiment.
Participative management. *See* Shared leadership
Passion, 579. Deep emotional and/or sexual feelings for another person.
Paternal influences, 96. The aggregate of all psychological effects fathers have on their children.
Passive compliance, 563
Pavlov's experiment, 207–208
Pavlov, Ivan, 24, 207
PCBs. *See* Polychlorinated biphenyls (PCBs)
PCP. *See* Phencyclidine (PCP)
Peak experiences, 418. Temporary moments of self-actualization.
Peak performance, 624–625. A performance during which physical, mental, and emotional states are harmonious and optimal.
Peek, Kim, 314, 321
Peer counselor, 541. A nonprofessional person who has learned basic counseling skills.
People's Temple, 567–569
Percent of variance, 641
Perception, 126. The mental process of organizing sensations into meaningful patterns.
accuracy in, 161–162
constancies of, 147–148
construction of, 142–143
depth, 149–154
emotion in, 155
emotional, 363
expectancies, 154–155
extrasensory, 45, 158–160
eye testimony and, 160–161
habituation and, 155–158, 161–162
misconstruction of, 143–144
motives in, 155
Müller-Lyer illusion, 156–158
organization of, 144–146
processing of, 144
reality, 417
sensory process and, 126
Perceptual construction, 143. A mental model of external events. Perceptual development, 91–92
Perceptual expectancy (or set), 154. A readiness to perceive in a particular manner, induced by strong expectations.
Perceptual features, 127. Basic elements of a stimulus, such as lines, shapes, edges, or colors.
Perceptual habits 155. Ingrained patterns of organization and attention that affect our daily experience.

Perceptual hypothesis, 146. An initial guess regarding how to organize (perceive) a stimulus pattern.
Perceptual learning, 155. Changes in perception that can be attributed to prior experience; a result of changes in how the brain processes sensory information.
Perfect negative relationships, 639
Perfect positive relationship, 639
Performance
 arousal and, 345
 desensitization, 523
 intelligence, 307
Performance intelligence, 307. Intelligence measured by solving puzzles, assembling objects, completing pictures, and other nonverbal tasks.
Periodic limb movement syndrome 174. Muscle twitches (primarily affecting the legs) that occur every 20 to 40 seconds and severely disturb sleep.
Peripheral nervous system (PNS), 57–58. All parts of the nervous system outside the brain and spinal cord.
Peripheral (side) vision, 131. Vision at the edges of the visual field.
Persecution, delusions of, 484
Persecutory type disorders, 486
Persistence, 453
Persistent vegetative state, 72
Persona, 415. The "mask" or public self presented to others.
Personal distance, 561. The distance maintained when interacting with close friends (about 18 inches to 4 feet from the body).
Personal identity
 adolescence and, 108–109
 ethnicity and, 108
 role confusion *vs.*, 112
Personal interview, 609. Formal or informal questioning of job applicants to learn their qualifications and to gain an impression of their personalities.
Personal prejudice, 590. Prejudicial attitudes held toward persons who are perceived as a direct threat to one's own interests.
Personal space, 560. An area surrounding the body that is regarded as private and subject to personal control.
Personal unconscious, 415. A mental storehouse for a single individual's unconscious thoughts.
Personality, 405, 406. A person's unique and relatively stable patterns of thinking, emotions, and behavior.
 adjective check list, 407
 assessments of, 429–434
 authoritarian, 591
 behavioral theory of, 421–425
 cardiac, 465–466
 creative, 293
 defined, 404
 disease-prone, 443
 dynamics of, 412–413, 419–420
 gender and, 424–425
 hardy, 467
 humanistic theory of, 417–421
 musical, 408
 neo-Freudian view of, 14–416
 patterns, 503
 psychoanalytic view of, 411–416
 questionnaires, 431–433
 self and, 419–421
 self-concepts, 405
 self-esteem, 406
 self-theory of, 419–421
 shy, 435–437
 social learning theory of, 423–424
 structure of, 411–412, 419–420
 theories of, 406–407
 theories, comparison of, 428–429
Personality development
 Freudian view of, 413–414
 latency in, 414
 neo-Freudian view of, 414–416
 social learning theory of, 424–425
 stages of, 413–414
Personality disorder, 480, 502. A maladaptive personality pattern.
 causes of, 504
 symptoms of, 503
 types of, 503–505
Personality questionnaire, 432. A paper-and-pencil test consisting of questions that reveal aspects of personality.
Personality theory, 406. A system of concepts, assumptions, ideas, and principles used to understand and explain personality.
Personality traits, 405, 406. A stable, enduring quality that a person shows in most situations. *See* Traits
Personality type, 404–405. A style of personality defined by a group of related traits.
Personnel psychology, 608, 609. A style of personality defined by a group of related traits.
 employee selection and, 609–611
 job analysis and, 609
Persuasion, 556–557. A deliberate attempt to change attitudes or beliefs with information and arguments.
Phallic personality, 412. A person who is vain, exhibitionistic, sensitive, and narcissistic.
Phallic stage, 413–414. The psychosexual stage (roughly ages 3 to 6) when a child is preoccupied with the genitals.
Phantom limb sensations, 140
Pharmacotherapy (FAR-meh-koe-THER-eh-pea), 527. The use of drugs to treat psychopathology.
 benefits of, 527
 limitations of, 527–528
 neurotransmitter-associated, 55
Phencyclidine (PCP), 196
Phenylketonuria (FEN-ul-KEET-uh-NURE-ee-ah), 316. A genetic disease that allows phenylpyruvic acid to accumulate in the body.
Phobias
 defined, 211
 social, 497–498
 specific, 497
Phonemes (FOE-neems), 283. The basic speech sounds of a language.
Phonetics, 242
Phosphenes, 127
Photographic memory, 264
Phototherapy, 494. A treatment for seasonal affective disorder that involves exposure to bright, full-spectrum light.
Phrenology, 18
Physical attractiveness, 577
Physical dependence (addiction), 186. Physical addiction, as indicated by the presence of drug tolerance and withdrawal symptoms.
Physical energy, 126
Physical environments, 612. Natural settings, such as forests and beaches, as well as environments built by humans, such as buildings, ships, and cities.
Physiological changes (in emotion), 351. Alterations in heart rate, blood pressure, perspiration, and other involuntary responses.
Piaget's theory
 concrete operational stage (7-11 years), 103
 contemporary views of, 104–106
 formal operational stage (11 years and up), 103–104
 overview, 101
 parental guide based on, 104
 preoperational stage (2-7 years), 101–103
 sensorimotor stage (0-2 years), 101–102
Piaget, Jean, 101
Pictorial depth cues, 151. Monocular depth cues found in paintings, drawings, and photographs that impart information about space, depth, and distance.
Picture plan, height in, 151
Pineal (pin-EE-ul) **gland**, 75. Gland in the brain that helps regulate body rhythms and sleep cycles.
Pinel, Philippe, 512
Pinna, 134
Pituitary gland, 75. The "master gland" whose hormones influence other endocrine glands.
PKU. *See* Phenylketonuria (PKU)
Place theory, 135. Theory of hearing proposing that higher and lower tones excite specific areas of the cochlea.
Placebo (plah-SEE-bo), 37, 56. An inactive substance given in the place of a drug in psychological research or by physicians who wish to treat a complaint by suggestion.
Placebo (plah-SEE-bo) **effect**, 37. Changes in behavior due to participants' expectations that a drug (or other treatment) will have some effect.
Plateau phase, 383
Pleasure principle, 411, 412. A desire for immediate satisfaction of wishes, desires, or needs.
Polychlorinated biphenyls (PCBs), 86–87
Polygenic (pol-ih-JEN-ik) **characteristics**, 86. Personal traits or physical properties that are influenced by many genes working in combination.
Polygenic traits, 85
Polygraph, 354. A device for recording heart rate, blood pressure, respiration, and galvanic skin response; commonly called a "lie detector."
Pons, 71. An area on the brainstem that acts as a bridge between the medulla and other structures.
Ponzo illusion, 153
Population, 641. An entire group of animals or people belonging to a particular category (for example, all college students or all married women).
Pornography, 587
Positive correlation, 41. A statistical relationship in which increases in one measure are matched by increases in the other (or decreases correspond with decreases).
Positive instance, 280. In concept learning, an object or event that belongs to the concept class.
Positive psychology, 30. The study of human strengths, virtues, and effective functioning.
Positive reinforcement, 213, 524. Occurs when a response is followed by a reward or other positive event.
Positive self-regard, 420–421. Thinking of oneself as a good, lovable, worthwhile person.
Positive transfer, 259. Mastery of one task aids learning or performing another.
Positron emission tomography (PET), 62–63, 490. An imaging technique that results in a computer-generated image of brain activity, based on glucose consumption in the brain.
Possible self, 420. A collection of thoughts, beliefs, feelings, and images concerning the person one could become.
Post-traumatic stress disorder, 498–499
Postconventional moral reasoning, 110. Moral thinking based on carefully examined and self-chosen moral principles.
Positive relationship, 639
Postpartum depression, 493–494. A mild to moderately severe depression that begins within 3 months following childbirth.
Posttraumatic stress disorder (PTSD), 499. A psychological disturbance lasting more than 1 month following stresses that would produce anxiety in anyone who experienced them.
Poverty, 450
Power, 117–118, 347
Power assertion 117. The use of physical punishment or coercion to enforce child discipline.
Precognition, 158
Preconscious, 413. An area of the mind containing information that can be voluntarily brought to awareness.
Preconventional moral reasoning, 110. Moral thinking based on the consequences of one's choices or actions (punishment, reward, or an exchange of favors).
Prediction, 16, 639–640. An ability to accurately forecast behavior.
Prefrontal area (prefrontal cortex), 68. The very front of the frontal lobes; involved in sense of self, reasoning, and planning.
Prejudice, 589. A negative emotional attitude held against members of a particular group of people.
 authoritarian beliefs and, 591
 development of, 589–590
 effects of, 589
 equal-status contact and, 594–595
 experiments in, 593–596
 intergroup conflict and, 591–596
 irrationality of, 592–593
 jigsaw classrooms and, 595–596
 multiculturalism and, 597–598
 superordinate goals and, 595
 symbolic, 592
 test for, 590
 types of, 589–590
Premack principle, 235. Any high-frequency response can be used to reinforce a low-frequency response.
Premack, David, 284
Premarital intercourse rates, 387–388
Premature ejaculation, 397. Ejaculation that consistently occurs before the man and his partner want it to occur.
Premature puberty, 76
Prenatal development, 86–87, 370
Prenatal hormonal theory of homosexuality, 373
Preoperational stage (2-7 years), 101–103. Period of intellectual development during which children begin to use language and think symbolically, yet remain intuitive and egocentric in their thought.

Presbyopia (prez-bee-OPE-ee-ah), 129. Farsightedness caused by aging.
Pressure, 448, 449. A stressful condition that occurs when a person must meet urgent external demands or expectations.
Prevention
aggression, 587–588
early, 445
HIV/AIDS, 392
STDs, 392
suicide, 506–507
tobacco use, 445
Primary appraisal, 449. Deciding if a situation is relevant to oneself and if it is a threat.
Primary auditory area, 69. Part of the temporal lobe where auditory information is first registered.
Primary emotions, 351–352. According to Robert Plutchik's theory, the most basic emotions are fear, surprise, sadness, disgust, anger, anticipation, joy, and acceptance.
Primary motor area (primary motor cortex), 67. A brain area associated with control of movement.
Primary reinforcers, 218. Nonlearned reinforcers; usually those that satisfy physiological needs.
Primary sexual characteristics, 371. Sex as defined by the genitals and internal reproductive organs.
Primary somatosensory area (primary somatosensory cortex) (SO-mat-oh-SEN-so-ree), 68. A receiving area for body sensations.
Primary visual area, 70, 71. The part of occipital lobe that first receives input from the eyes.
Priming, 253. Facilitating the retrieval of an implicit memory by using cues to activate hidden memories.
Private self-consciousness, 435–436. Preoccupation with inner feelings, thoughts, and fantasies.
Proactive (pro-AK-tiv) **interference**, 258–259. The tendency for old memories to interfere with the retrieval of newer memories.
Probability biases, 520
Problem clarification, 523
Problem finding, 291. The active discovery of problems to be solved.
Problem solving. *See also* Creativity
barriers to, 288–290
brainstorms and, 297–298
creative thinking *versus,* 290–291
environmental, 618
expertise in, 289–290
insights in, 286–288
process of, 290–291
strategies for, 286
Problem-focused coping, 450. Directly managing or remedying a stressful or threatening situation.
Problems
congenital, 86
defining, 21, 297
everyday, 234–236
restating, 292–293
Procedural memory, 250. Long-term memories of conditioned responses and learned skills.
Procrastination, 6–7
Programmed instruction, 220. Any learning format that presents information in small amounts, gives immediate practice, and provides continuous feedback to learners.
Progressive relaxation, 469. A method for producing deep relaxation of all parts of the body.
Projection, 457
Projective tests, 433. Psychological tests making use of ambiguous or unstructured stimuli.
Projective tests of personality
approach of, 433
limitations of, 434
types of, 433–434
Prosocial behavior, 576. Any behavior that has a positive impact on other people. *See also* Antisocial behavior
bystander interventions as, 581–584
interpersonal attraction as, 576–578
loving as, 578–580
mate selection as, 580–581
television portrayal of, 588
Prosser, Inez Beverly, 27
Prostate (PROSS-tate), 371. A gland located at the base of the urinary bladder that supplies most of the fluid that makes up semen.
Prototype, 279. An ideal model used as a prime example of a particular concept.
Proxemics (prok-SEE-miks), 560. Systematic study of the human use of space, particularly in social settings.
Proximodistal pattern, 90
Pseudopsychology (SUE-doe-psychology), 18–20. Any false and unscientific system of beliefs and practices that is offered as an explanation of behavior.
Psi (sigh) **phenomena**, 159. Events that seem to lie outside the realm of accepted scientific laws.
Psychasthenia (sike-as-THEE-nee-ah), 432. The presence of obsessive worries, irrational fears (phobias), and compulsive (ritualistic) actions.
Psyche (sigh-KEY), 411, 412. The mind, mental life, and personality as a whole.
Psychiatric social worker, 34, 35. A mental health professional trained to apply social science principles to help patients in clinics and hospitals.
Psychiatrist, 34. A medical doctor with additional training in the diagnosis and treatment of mental and emotional disorders.
Psychoactive drugs, 185. A substance capable of altering attention, memory, judgment, time sense, self-control mood, or perception.
abuse of, 187
comparison of, 188–189
dependence on, 186–187
downers, 192–196
hallucinogens, 196–200
neural effects, 186
uppers, 187–192
Psychoanalysis, 26. 27. A Freudian approach to psychotherapy that emphasizes the use of free association, dream interpretation, resistances, and transference to uncover unconscious conflicts.
basic techniques of, 513–514
criticism of, 414
effectiveness of, 514
goal of, 513
history of, 26
key concepts of, 412
modern practice of, 514
neo-Freudians, 414–416
origins of, 512
personality, 411–416
practitioners role in, 34
strength of, 428
Psychoanalyst, 34, 35. A mental health professional (usually a medical doctor) trained to practice psychoanalysis.
Psychoanalytic theory, 411. Freudian theory of personality that emphasizes unconscious forces and conflicts.
Psychodrama, 535. A therapy in which clients act out personal conflicts and feelings in the presence of others who play supporting roles.
Psychodynamic dream theory, 178
Psychodynamic theory, 407, 501. Any theory of behavior that emphasizes internal conflicts, motives, and unconscious forces.
Psychodynamic views, 30
Psychoeuroimmunology, 447
Psychogenic, 396, 397. Having psychological origins, rather than physical causes.
Psychogenic erectile disorder, 396
Psychokinesis, 158
Psycholinguists, 99
Psychological dependence, 186. Drug dependence that is based primarily on emotional or psychological needs.
Psychological disorders, 475–476
Psychological efficiency, 604. Maintenance of good morale, labor relations, employee satisfaction, and similar aspects of work behavior.
Psychological perspective, 29–30. The traditional view that behavior is shaped by psychological processes occurring at the level of the individual.
Psychological situation, 423. A situation as it is perceived and interpreted by an individual, not as it exists objectively.
Psychological trauma, 488. A psychological injury or shock, such as that caused by violence, abuse, neglect, separation, and so forth.
Psychologist, 31. A person highly trained in the methods, factual knowledge, and theories of psychology. *See also* Therapists
characterization of, 31
degrees for, 34
relative professionals, 34–35
specialties of, 32–34
Psychology, 14. The scientific study of behavior and mental processes. *See also* Applied psychology
careers in, 33
diversity in, 27–28
evolutionary, 580–581
goals of, 15–16
pioneers in, 23–27
seeking knowledge in, 14–15
Psychology of law, 620–623. Study of the psychological and behavioral dimensions of the legal system.
Psychology websites, 9–10
Psychometric tests, 305–306
Psychoneuroimmunology, 447. Study of the links among behavior, stress, disease, and the immune system.
Psychopathic deviate, 432. Emotional shallowness in relationships and a disregard for social and moral standards.
Psychopathology, 476. The scientific study of mental, emotional, and behavioral disorders; also, abnormal or maladaptive behavior.
approach to, 477
categories of, 479
Psychophysics, 126. Study of the relationship between physical stimuli and the sensations they evoke in a human observer.
Psychosexual stages, 413. The oral, anal, phallic, and genital stages, during which various personality traits are formed.
Psychosis, 188, 485. A withdrawal from reality marked by hallucinations and delusions, disturbed thought and emotions, and personality disorganization.
Psychosocial dilemmas, 111–112. A conflict between personal impulses and the social world.
Psychosocial theory, 111–113
Psychosomatic (SIKE-oh-so-MAT-ik) **disorders**, 463–464. Illnesses in which psychological factors contribute to bodily damage or to damaging changes in bodily functioning.
Psychosurgery, 528–529. Any surgical alteration of the brain designed to bring about desirable behavioral or emotional changes.
Psychotherapy, 512, 513. Any psychological technique used to facilitate positive changes in a person's personality, behavior, or adjustment.
basic skills of, 532–534
classical conditioning, 520–524
cognitive techniques, 517–520
comparison of, 530–524
core features of, 531–532
couple centered, 536
culture and, 534
development of, 512–513
dimensions of, 514–515
effectiveness of, 531–532
family centered, 535
future of, 534–538
group, 534–535
group awareness training, 536
high-tech, 536–537
humanistic techniques, 516–517
medical therapy, 527–530, 534
myths of, 515
operant techniques, 524–526
outcome comparison, 530–531
psychoanalysis, 513–514
psychodrama, 535
sources for, 540–541
Psychotic disorder. 479. A severe mental disorder characterized by a retreat from reality, by hallucinations and delusions, and by social withdrawal.
characterization of, 484
delusional, 486
nature of, 484–485
schizophrenia, 486–491
stress-vulnerability model, 491
warning signs of, 484
PsycINFO, 9–10. A searchable, online database that provides brief summaries of the scientific and scholarly literature in psychology.
PTSD. *See* Post-traumatic stress disorder
Puberty, 85. The biologically defined period during which a person matures sexually and becomes capable of reproduction.
changes during, 107
early, 108
premature, 76
Public distance, 561. Distance at which formal interactions, such as giving a speech, occur (about 12 feet or more from the body).
Public self-consciousness, 435. Intense awareness of oneself as a social object.
Punisher, 225. Any event that decreases the probability or frequency of responses it follows.

Punishment, 216. Any event that follows a response and *decreases* its likelihood of occurring again; The process of suppressing a response.
aggression and, 227
behavioral effects of, 225
downside, 226–227
limbic system and, 74
responses to, 524
types of, 216–217
variables affecting, 226
wise use of, 227–228

Q

Quality circle, 606. An employee discussion group that makes suggestions for improving quality and solving business problems.
Quantitative reasoning, 306
Questionnaires, 431–433, 469
Questions
closed, 523
dialogue, 3
gateway, 3–4
open-ended, 523
self-reflective, 3
types of, 523

R

Race. *See also specific groups*
IQ scores and, 324–325
social construction of, 598
Racism, 589. Racial prejudice that has become institutionalized (that is, it is reflected in government policy, schools, and so forth) and that is enforced by the existing social power structure.
Radical acceptance, 517
Radical behaviorism, 25
Rain Man. *See* Peek, Kim
Randi, James, 45
Random assignment, 36. The use of chance (for example, flipping a coin) to assign subjects to experimental and control groups.
Random search strategy, 286. Trying possible solutions to a problem in a more or less random order.
Random selection, 641
Range, 636
Rank, Otto, 26
Rape
crime of, 389–390
gender stereotyping and, 389
Rape myths, 390. False beliefs about rape that tend to blame the victim and increase the likelihood that some men will think that rape is justified.
Rapid eye movements (REMs), 172. Swift eye movements during sleep.
dreaming and, 173–174, 177
function of, 172–173
nightmares and, 176
Rarefaction, 134
Rating scale, 430–431. A list of personality traits or aspects of behavior on which a person is rated.
Rational-emotive behavior therapy (REBT), 518. An approach that states that irrational beliefs cause many emotional problems and that such beliefs must be changed or abandoned.
belief importance in, 518–519
goal of, 518
techniques of, 519–520
Rationalization, 457
Reaction formation, 457
Reaction range, 88–89. The limits environment places on the effects of heredity.
Reaction time, 319. The amount of time a person must look at a stimulus to make a correct judgment about it.
Readiness, 86. A condition that exists when maturation has advanced enough to allow the rapid acquisition of a particular skill.
Reagan, Ronald, 485, 490
Reality
perceptions of, 417
testing, 144
Reality principle, 411, 412. Delaying action (or pleasure) until it is appropriate.
Reality testing, 144. Obtaining additional information to check on the accuracy of perceptions.
Reasoning testing, 639–640
Reasoning types, 306
REBT. *See* Rational-emotive behavior therapy (REBT)
Recall, 252. To supply or reproduce memorized information with a minimum of external cues. *See also* Memory
defined, 252
strategies for, 264–265
Receptive aphasia, 69
Receptor sites, 55. Areas on the surface of neurons and other cells that are sensitive to neurotransmitters or hormones.
Recessive genes, 84. A gene whose influence will be expressed only when it is paired with a second recessive gene.
Reciprocal inhibition, 522. The presence of one emotional state can inhibit the occurrence of another, such as joy preventing fear or anxiety inhibiting pleasure.
Reciprocity, 577. A reciprocal exchange of feelings, thoughts, or things between people.
Recitation, 267
Recoding, 245. Reorganizing or modifying information to assist storage in memory.
Recognition, 252. An ability to correctly identify previously learned information.
Recovered memory, 260
Recycling, 617
Redintegration, 248–249. Process by which memories are reconstructed or expanded by starting with one memory and then following chains of association to other, related memories.
Reference
delusions of, 484
frame of, 523
Reference group, 556. Any group that an individual identifies with and uses as a standard for social comparison.
Referent power, 559. Social power gained when one is used as a point of reference by others.
Reflection, 516. In client-centered therapy, the process of rephrasing or repeating thoughts and feelings expressed by clients so they can become aware of what they are saying.
Reflective cognition, 2. Style of thought arising while actively thinking about an experience.
Reflective intelligence, 320. An ability to become aware of one's own thinking habits.
Reflective note taking, 4–5
Reflective SQ4R method, 2–3. An active study-reading technique based on these steps: survey, question, read, recite, reflect, and review.
Reflective test-taking 7–8
Reflective thoughts, 532–533
Reflex, 206. An innate, automatic response to a stimulus; for example, an eyeblink.
eye blink conditioning and, 208
neonates, 89–90
Reflex arc, 58. The simplest behavior, in which a stimulus provokes an automatic response.
Refractory period, 384. A short period after orgasm during which males are unable to again reach orgasm.
Refusal skills training, 445. Program that teaches youths how to resist pressures to begin smoking. (Can also be applied to other drugs, and health risks.)
Regression, 457
Rehearsal, 346
Reinforcement, 206. Any event that increases the probability that a particular response will occur. *See also* Operant reinforcement
covert, 539
token economies and, 525
Reinforcement value, 423. The subjective value a person attaches to a particular activity or reinforcer.
Relational concepts, 279. A concept defined by the relationship between features of an object or between an object and its surroundings (for example, "greater than," "lopsided").
Relationships
detecting, 638–639
empathy-helping, 583
interpersonal, 418
negative, 639
perfect negative, 639
perfect positive, 639
positive, 639
Relative motion, 151–152
Relative size, 151
Relaxation
anxiety reduction with, 346
defined, 175
tension-release method, 522
Relaxation response, 183. The pattern of internal bodily changes that occurs at times of relaxation.
Relearning, 253. Learning again something that was previously learned. Used to measure memory of prior learning.
Reliability, 305, 431. The ability of a test to yield the same score, or nearly the same score, each time it is given to the same person.
REM behavior disorder, 173. A failure of normal muscle paralysis, leading to violent actions during REM sleep.
REM rebound, 177. The occurrence of extra rapid eye movement sleep following REM sleep deprivation.
REM sleep, 172. Sleep marked by rapid eye movements and a return to stage 1 EEG patterns.
Remembering. *See* Recall
Reminding system, 139. Pain based on small nerve fibers; reminds the brain that the body has been injured.
REMs. *See* Rapid eye movements (REMs)
Repetitious stimuli, 148
Representative sample, 641. A small, randomly selected part of a larger population that accurately reflects characteristics of the whole population.
Representativeness heuristic (hew-RIS-tik), 294. A tendency to select wrong answers because they seem to match preexisting mental categories.
Repression, 457. The unconscious process by which memories, thoughts, or impulses are held out of awareness.
memory, 259–260
thoughts, 26
Reproductive organs, 370
Research
animal, 33–34
approaches to, 32
brain, 60–64
clinical method, 41–42
comparison of, 43
correlations in, 638–640
defined, 15
descriptive statistics for, 634–638
direct observations, 430
early developments in, 27
ethics of, 22–23
experimental, 35–38
gender bias in, 28
goals of, 16
history of, 23–28
inferential statistics in, 640–641
interviews, 429–430
media reports of, 44–46
nonexperimental, 39–46
rating scales, 430–431
reports of, 22
scientific method, 20–22
subjects, 28
survey method, 42–43
Research method, 15. A systematic approach to answering scientific questions.
Research participant bias, 37. Changes in the behavior of research participants caused by the unintended influence of their own expectations.
Researcher bias, 37–38. Changes in participants' behavior caused by the unintended influence of a researcher's actions.
Resistance, 447, 513. A blockage in the flow of free association; topics the client resists thinking or talking about.
Resolution, 383. The fourth phase of sexual response, involving a return to lower levels of sexual tension and arousal.
Resources, 616
Respondent reinforcement, 209. Reinforcement that occurs when an unconditioned stimulus closely follows a conditioned stimulus.
Response, 24, 332. Any action, glandular activity, or other identifiable behavior, either observable or internal.
alternate, 235
cost, 216
opera in operant conditioning, 206
Response chaining, 215, 235. The assembly of separate responses into a series of actions that lead to reinforcement.
Response cost, 216. Removal of a positive reinforcer after a response is made.
Response-contingent shocks, 521–522
Responsibility, 418, 583
REST. *See* Restricted environmental stimulation therapy (REST)
Resting potential, 53. The electrical charge of a neuron at rest.
Restless legs syndrome, 174. An irresistible urge to move the legs to relieve sensations of creeping, tingling, prickling, aching, or tension.
Restricted environmental stimulation therapy (REST), 184. A form of sensory deprivation that results in a variety of psychological benefits.
Restructuring thoughts, 346

Reticular (reh-TICK-you-ler) **activating system (RAS)**, 72–73. A part of the reticular formation that activates the cerebral cortex.
Reticular (reh-TICK-you-ler) **formation (RF)**, 72–73. A network within the medulla and brainstem; associated with attention, alertness, and some reflexes.
Retina, 129. The light-sensitive layer of cells at the back of the eye.
anatomy of, 130
blind spots in, 130
characterization of, 129
disparity in, 150
Retirement, 115
Retrieval, 243. Recovering information from storage in memory.
LTM, 249–250
memories, 242
practice, 267
Retrieval cue, 256. Stimulus associated with a memory. Retrieval cues usually enhance memory.
Retroactive (RET-ro-AK-tiv) **interference**, 258, 259. The tendency for new memories to interfere with the retrieval of old memories.
Retrograde amnesia, 260. Loss of memory for events that preceded a head injury or other amnesia-causing event.
Reverse vision, 277
Review
Reward, 422. Anything that produces pleasure or satisfaction; a positive reinforcer.
Reward power, 559. Social power based on the capacity to reward a person for acting as desired.
Rhine, J. B., 158
Ritualized aggression, 584
Rods, 129. Visual receptors for dim light that produce only black and white sensations.
function of, 129
red insensitivity of, 133
visual acuity and, 131
Rogers, Carl, 26, 419, 516
Rohypnol, 193
Role conflict, 548. Trying to occupy two or more roles that make conflicting demands on behavior.
Role reversal, 536. Taking the role of another person to learn how one's own behavior appears from the other person's perspective.
Roles. *See* Social roles
Romantic love, 578. Love that is associated with high levels of interpersonal attraction, heightened arousal, mutual absorption, and sexual desire.
Rooting reflex, 89–90
Rorschach inkblot test, 433. A projective test comprised of 10 standardized inkblots.
Rote learning, 230, 245. Learning that takes place mechanically, through repetition and memorization, or by learning rules.
Rote rehearsal (rote learning), 245, 249. Learning by simple repetition.
Run of luck, 159. A statistically unusual outcome (as in getting five heads in a row when flipping a coin) that could still occur by chance alone.

S
SAD. *See* Seasonal affective disorder (SAD)
Saltatory conduction, 54. The process by which nerve impulses conducted down the axons of neurons coated with myelin jump from gap to gap in the myelin layer.
Samples, 641
Sanctioned massacres, 567
Sarah the chimpanzee, 284
SAT. *See* Scholastic aptitude tests (SAT)
SAT Reasoning test, 307, 325
Satisficing, 627. Engaging in behavior that achieves a minimum result, rather than maximizing the outcome of that behavior.
Savant syndrome, 314. The possession of exceptional mental ability in one or more narrow areas, such as mental arithmetic, calendar calculations, art, or music by a person of limited general intelligence.
Scaffolding, 106. The process of adjusting instruction so that it is responsive to a beginner's behavior and supports the beginner's efforts to understand a problem or gain a mental skill.
Scapegoating, 452–453, 589. Blaming a person or a group for the actions of others or for conditions not of their making.
Scatter diagram, 638
Schachter's cognitive theory of emotion, 359. States that emotions occur when physical arousal is labeled or interpreted on the basis of experience and situational cues.
Schedule of reinforcement, 224. A rule or plan for determining which responses will be reinforced.
fixed interval, 223
fixed ratio, 222
variable interval, 224
variable ratio, 222–223
Schizophrenia (SKIT-soh-FREN-ee-uh), 432. A psychosis characterized by delusions, hallucinations, apathy, and a "split" between thought and emotion involving emotional withdrawal and unusual or bizarre thinking and actions.
brain chemistry and, 489, 491
brain size and, 59
emotions and, 486
environmental factors in, 488–489
heredity factors in, 489
implications of, 491
types of, 486–487
Scholastic aptitude tests (SAT), 307, 309
Science, logic of, 22
Scientific jury selection, 622. Using social science principles to choose members of a jury.
Scientific management. *See* Theory X leadership
Scientific method, 20–21. A form of critical thinking based on careful measurement and controlled observation.
critical thinking and, 23
elements of, 21
Scientific observation, 14. An empirical investigation structured to answers questions about the world in a systematic and intersubjective fashion (observations can be reliably confirmed by multiple observers).
Scrotum (SKROE-tehm), 371. The saclike pouch that holds the testes.
Seasonal affective disorder (SAD), 494–495. Depression that occurs only during fall and winter; presumably related to decreased exposure to sunlight.
Secondary appraisal, 449. Deciding how to cope with a threat or challenge.
Secondary elaboration, 198. Making a dream more logical and complete while remembering it.
Secondary reinforcers, 218. A learned reinforcer; often one that gains reinforcing properties by association with a primary reinforcer.
Secondary sexual characteristics, 371. Sexual features other than the genitals and reproductive organs—breasts, body shape, facial hair, and so forth.
Secondary traits, 408. Traits that are inconsistent or relatively superficial.
Secure attachment, 94–95, 580. A stable and positive emotional bond.
Sedatives, 192–193
Selective attention, 148–149, 486. Giving priority to a particular incoming sensory message.
Selective comparison, 287–288
Selective encoding, 287
Selective marking, 265
Selective memory, 520
Selective perception, 518. Perceiving only certain stimuli among a larger array of possibilities.
Selectively attending, 242
Self, 419. A continuously evolving conception of one's personal identity.
development of, 420–421
ideal, 419
possible, 420
theory of, 419–420
Self archetype, 416. An unconscious image representing, unity, wholeness, completion, and balance.
Self-actualization, 27. The ongoing process of fully developing one's personal potential.
characteristics of, 417–418
origins of, 417
steps to, 418
Self-assertion, 570. A direct, honest expression of feelings and desires.
Self-awareness, 105
Self-concept, 405. A person's perception of his or her own personality traits.
Self-consciousness, 435–436
Self-defeating bias, 435. A distortion of thinking that impairs behavior.
Self-directed desensitization, 539–540
Self-disclosure, 577–578. The process of revealing private thoughts, feelings, and one's personal history to others.
Self-efficacy (EF-uh-keh-see), 423. Belief in your capacity to produce a desired result.
Self-esteem, 119. Regarding oneself as a worthwhile person; a positive evaluation of oneself.
discipline and, 118
environmental factors in, 406
labeling and, 435–436
Self-fulfilling prophecy, 38, 598. A prediction or expectation that prompts people to act in ways that make the prediction or expectation come true.
Self-handicapping, 553. Arranging to perform under conditions that usually impair performance, so as to have an excuse for a poor showing.
Self-help group, 542. A group of people who share a particular type of problem and provide mutual support to one another.
Self-image, 419. Total subjective perception of one's body and personality (another term for self-concept).
Self-managed team, 606. A work group that has a high degree of freedom with respect to how it achieves its goals.
Self-recording, 235. Self-management based on keeping records of response frequencies.
Self-reference, 3. The practice of relating of new information to prior life experience.
Self-reflect questions, 3
Self-regard, 420–421
Self-regulated learning, 6–7. Deliberately reflective and active, self-guided study.
Self-reinforcement, 423. Praising or rewarding oneself for having made a particular response (such as completing a school assignment).
Self-statements, 471
Self-stereotype, 592. The tendency to apply social stereotypes to one's self.
Self-testing, 5–6. Evaluating learning by posing questions to yourself.
Semantic memory, 250. A subpart of declarative memory that records impersonal knowledge about the world.
Semantics, 281. The study of meanings in language.
differential, 280
SUB, 281–282
Semicircular canals, 141
Seminal vesicles (SEM-in-uhl VES-ih-kuhlz), 371. These two small organs (one on each side of the prostate) supply fluid that becomes part of semen.
Sensate focus, 396. A form of therapy that directs a couple's attention to natural sensations of sexual pleasure.
Sensation, 126. A sensory impression; also, the process of detecting physical energies with the sensory organs.
Sensation seekers, 344–345
Senses
chemical, 137
function of, 126
hearing, 134–137
smell, 137
somesthetic, 138–142
taste, 138
vision, 128–134
Sensible risks, 298
Sensitive periods, 87. development, a period of increased sensitivity to environmental influences. Also, a time during which certain events must take place for normal development to occur.
Sensitivity group, 536. A group experience consisting of exercises designed to increase self-awareness and sensitivity to others.
Sensitization, 538–539
Sensorimotor stage (0-2 years), 101–102. Stage of intellectual development during which sensory input and motor responses become coordinated.
Sensorineural hearing loss, 136. Loss of hearing caused by damage to the inner ear hair cells or auditory nerve.
Sensory adaptation, 126. A decrease in sensory response to an unchanging stimulus.
Sensory analysis, 127. Separation of sensory information into important elements.
Sensory changes, 182
Sensory coding, 127. Codes used by the sense organs to transmit information to the brain.
Sensory conflict theory, 141–142. Explains motion sickness as the result of a mismatch among information from vision, the vestibular system, and kinesthesis.
Sensory deprivation (SD), 183–184. Any major reduction in the amount or variety of sensory stimulation.

Sensory localization, 127
Sensory memory, 242. The first, normally unconscious, stage of memory, which holds an exact record of incoming information for a few seconds or less.
Sensory neuron, 58. A neuron that carries information from the senses toward the CNS.
Sensory overload, 168
Sensory process
adaptation, 126–127
analysis, 127
coding, 127–128
localization, 128
selection, 126
Sensory restriction, 628
Separation anxiety, 94. Distress displayed by infants when they are separated from their parents or principal caregivers.
Serial position effect, 252. The tendency to make the most errors in remembering the middle items of an ordered list.
Serotonin, 55
SES. *See* Socioeconomic status (SES)
Set point, 336. The proportion of body fat that tends to be maintained by changes in hunger and eating.
Sex, 371. One's physical, biological classification as female or male.
Sex drive, 343–344, 382. The strength of one's motivation to engage in sexual behavior.
Sexism, 589. Institutionalized prejudice against members of either sex, based solely on their gender.
Sexual and gender identity disorders, 480–481. Any of a wide range of difficulties with sexual identity, deviant sexual behavior, or sexual adjustment.
Sexual arousal, 380–383
Sexual attraction, 372–373
Sexual aversion (One type of **sexual dysfunction not otherwise specified**), 395. Persistent feelings of fear, anxiety, or disgust about engaging in sex.
Sexual behavior
atypical, 385–386
biological dimensions of, 370–371
choices in, 389
contemporary attitudes, 387–390
disagreements over, 393
double standard, 388
erogenous zones, 380
gender roles and, 374–378
global, 389
masturbation, 382–383
patterns of, 380
satisfaction in, 393–395
sex drive, 382
sexual scripts, 380–382
STDs and, 390–393
Sexual dysfunction
arousal disorders, 395–396
desire disorders, 395
orgasm disorders, 396–397
sexual pain disorders, 397–398
Sexual orientation, 371. One's degree of emotional and erotic attraction to members of the same sex, opposite sex, both sexes, or neither sex.
complexity of, 372
forms of, 372–374
stability of, 372
Sexual response, 383–385
Sexual revolution, 387–388
Sexual script, 380. An unspoken mental plan that defines a "plot," dialogue, and actions expected to take place in a sexual encounter.
adolescents, 381
defined, 380
female, 381–382
male, 380–381
Sexually transmitted diseases (STDs), 390. A disease that is typically passed from one person to the next by intimate physical contact; a venereal disease.
at risk populations, 392
behavioral risk factors, 392
characterization of, 390
common, 391
HIV/AIDS, 390–393
prevention of, 392
Shadows, 151
Shame, 112
Shape constancy, 147–148. The perceived shape of an object is unaffected by changes in its retinal image.
Shaping, 215–216, 524. Gradually molding responses to a final desired pattern.
Shared leadership (participative management), 606. A leadership approach that allows employees at all levels to participate in decision making.
Shift work, 334
Shocks, 521–522
Short sleepers, 170
Short-answer test, 8
Short-term memory (STM), 242. The memory system used to hold small amounts of information in our conscious awareness for about a dozen seconds.
encoding of, 242–243
functions of, 243
LTM and, 242
prolonging, 245–246
testing of, 244–245
Shyness, 435. A tendency to avoid others plus uneasiness and strain when socializing.
causes of, 435
dynamics of, 435–436
understanding, 436
Sidedness, 77. A combination of preference for hand, foot, eye, and ear.
SIDS. *See* Sudden infant death syndrome (SIDS)
Signal, 101. In early language development, any behavior, such as touching, vocalizing, gazing, or smiling, that allows nonverbal interaction and turn-taking between parent and child.
Silence, 532
Similarity, 145, 576–577
Singer, Margaret, 568
Single-blind experiment, 38. An arrangement in which participants remain unaware of whether they are in the experimental group or the control group.
Situational demands, 552. Unstated expectations that define desirable or appropriate behavior in various settings and social situations.
Situational determinants, 422. External conditions that strongly influence behavior.
Situational judgment test, 611. Presenting realistic work situations to applicants in order to observe their skills and reactions.
Situational test, 431. Simulating real-life conditions so that a person's reactions may be directly observed.
Sixteen Personality Factor Questionnaire, 408
Size constancy, 147. The perceived size of an object remains constant, despite changes in its retinal image.
Size-distance invariance, 156
Skin senses, 138–139. The senses of touch, pressure, pain, heat, and cold.
Skinner box. *See also* Operant conditioning
creation of, 25
cumulative recorder in, 222
design of, 213
pigeons in, 215, 223
pleasure seeking and, 217
Skinner, B. F., 25, 213–215
Sleep
consciousness and, 174
deprivation, 169
disturbances of, 174–177
dual process hypothesis of, 172–174
loss of, 168
melatonin levels and, 75
memory and, 267–268
need for, 168–170
patterns of, 170–171
repair/restorative theories of, 170
restrictions, 175
rhythms of, 170
stages of, 171–172
Sleep apnea (AP-nee-ah), 176. During sleep, breathing stops for 20 seconds or more until the person wakes a little, gulps in air, and settles back to sleep; this cycle may be repeated hundreds of times per night.
Sleep deprivation, 169. Being prevented from getting desired or needed amounts of sleep.
Sleep drunkenness, 174. A slow transition to clear consciousness after awakening; sometimes associated with irritable or aggressive behavior.
Sleep paralysis, 173
Sleep spindles, 171. Distinctive bursts of brainwave activity that indicate a person is asleep.
Sleep stages, 171. Levels of sleep identified by brain-wave patterns and behavioral changes.
Sleep terror disorder, 174. The repeated occurrence of night terrors that significantly disturb sleep.
Sleep-deprivation psychosis, 170. A major disruption of mental and emotional functioning brought about by sleep loss.
Sleep-Eze, 175
Sleep-wake schedule disorder, 174. A mismatch between the sleep-wake schedule demanded by a person's bodily rhythm and that demanded by the environment.
Sleepsex, 176
Sleeptalking, 176
Sleepwalking, 176
Sleepwalking disorder, 174. Repeated incidents of leaving bed and walking about while asleep.
Small nerve fiber pain, 139
Smell, sense of, 137–138
Smiles, types of, 356
Snacking, 340
Social anxiety, 435. A feeling of apprehension in the presence of others.
Social cognition, 550. The process of thinking about ourselves and others in a social context.
attribution theory of, 552–553
self-handicapping in, 553
social comparison theory of, 551–552
Social comparison, 551. Making judgments about ourselves through comparison with others.
Social comparison theory, 551–552
Social competition, 598. Rivalry among groups, each of which regards itself as superior to others.
Social contagion, 444
Social development, 93. The development of self-awareness attachment to parents or caregivers, and relationships with other children and adults.
attachment and, 94–96
early, 93
parental influences in, 96–98
Social dilemmas, 617. A social situation that tends to provide immediate rewards for actions that will have undesired effects in the long run.
damage from, 617–618
escaping, 618
Social distance, 561. Distance at which impersonal interaction takes place (about 4 to 12 feet from the body).
Social distance scale, 556. A rating of the degree to which a person would be willing to have contact with a member of another group.
Social environment, 612. An environment defined by a group of people and their activities or interrelationships (such as a parade, revival meeting, or sports event).
Social exchange, 578. Any exchange between two people of attention, information, affection, favors, or the like.
Social exchange theory, 578. Theory stating that rewards must exceed costs for relationships to endure.
Social facilitation, 560. The tendency to perform better when in the presence of others.
Social influence, 559. Changes in a person's behavior induced by the presence or actions of others.
Social introversion, 432. One's tendency to be socially withdrawn.
Social learning theories
personality development and, 423–424
principles of, 423–424
strengths of, 428
Social learning theory, 423–424. Combines learning principles with cognitive processes, socialization, and modeling, to explain behavior.
Social loafing, 560. The tendency of people to work less hard when part of a group than when they are solely responsible for their work.
Social motives, 346–348. Learned motives acquired as part of growing up in a particular society or culture.
Social nonconformity, 477. Failure to conform to societal norms or the usual minimum standards for social conduct.
Social norms, 30. Rules that define acceptable and expected behavior for members of a group.
Social phobia, 496. An intense, irrational fear of being observed, evaluated, embarrassed, or humiliated by others in social situations.
Social power, 559. The capacity to control, alter, or influence the behavior of another person.
Social psychology, 548, 576–584. The scientific study of how individuals behave, think, and feel in social situations.
Social Readjustment Rating Scale (SRRS), 461. A scale that rates the impact of various life events on the likelihood of illness.

Social reinforcement, 425. Praise, attention, approval, and/or affection from others.
Social reinforcer, 219, 424. Reinforcement based on receiving attention, approval, or affection from another person.
Social role, 548. Expected behavior patterns associated with particular social positions (such as daughter, worker, student).
conflicts, 548
confusion, 112
models, 445
reversal of, 535
Social skills, 435, 436. Proficiency at interacting with others.
Social smile, 93. Smiling elicited by social stimuli, such as seeing a parent's face.
Social status, 550. An individual's position in a social structure, especially with respect to power, privilege, or importance.
Social stereotypes, 280, 591–592. Oversimplified images of the traits of individuals who belong to a particular social group.
Social stigma, 482–483
Social support, 470. Close, positive relationships with other people.
Social workers, 34
Socialization, 374, 377–378
Sociocultural perspective, 30. The focus on the importance of social and cultural contexts in influencing the behavior of individuals.
Sociocultural theory
implications of, 107
principles of, 106–107
Socioeconomic status (SES), 318–319
Sociopathy, 504
Solitude, 418
Soma (SOH-mah), 52. The main body of a neuron or other cell.
Somatic delusions, 484
Somatic nervous system (SNS), 57. The system of nerves linking the spinal cord with the body and sense organs.
Somatic pain, 139
Somatic therapy, 527. Any bodily therapy, such as drug therapy, electroconvulsive therapy, or psychosurgery.
Somatic type disorders, 486
Somatization (som-ah-tuh-ZAY-shun) **disorder**, 499. Afflicted persons have numerous physical complaints. Typically, they have consulted many doctors, but no organic cause for their distress can be identified.
Somatoform (so-MAT-oh-form) **disorder**, 480, 499–500. Physical symptoms that mimic disease or injury for which there is no identifiable physical cause.
Somesthetic senses, 138. Sensations produced by the skin, muscles, joints, viscera, and organs of balance.
pain, 139–141
touch, 139
types of, 138
vestibular system, 141–142
Sominex, 175
Somnambulists (som-NAM-bue-lists), 176. People who sleepwalk; occurs during NREM sleep.
Source confusion (in memory), 247. Occurs when the origins of a memory are misremembered.
Source traits (factors), 408. Basic underlying traits, or dimensions, of personality; each source trait is reflected in a number of surface traits.
Spaced practice, 5, 266–267. A practice schedule that alternates relatively short study periods with brief rests.
Spankings, 228
Spatial neglect, 65
Spatial norms, 560–561
Special aptitude test, 305. Test to predict a person's likelihood of succeeding in a particular area of work or skill.
Specific goals, 6–7. A goal with a clearly defined and measurable outcome.
Specific phobia, 497–498. An intense, irrational fear of specific objects, activities, or situations.
Speed of processing, 320, 321. The speed with which a person can mentally process information.
Sperry, Roger, 65
Spinal cord, 58
Spinal nerves, 58. Major nerves that carry sensory and motor messages in and out of the spinal cord.
Spinocerebellar degeneration, 71
Split-brain operation, 65–66. Cutting the corpus callosum.
Split-half reliability, 305
Spontaneity, 417
Spontaneous recovery, 210. The reappearance of a learned response after its apparent extinction.
Spontaneous remission, 514. Improvement of symptoms due to the mere passage of time.
Sports psychology, 623. Study of the psychological and behavioral dimensions of sports performance.
motor analysis by, 624
peak performance analysis by, 624–625
task analysis by, 623–624
topics of interest to, 623
Squeeze technique, 397. A method for inhibiting ejaculation by compressing the tip of the penis.
Stage hypnosis, 182. Use of hypnosis to entertain; often, merely a simulation of hypnosis for that purpose.
Stage of exhaustion, 447. Third stage of the GAS., at which time the body's resources are exhausted and serious health consequences occur.
Stage of resistance, 447. Second stage of the GAS., during which bodily adjustments to stress stabilize, but at a high physical cost.
Stagnation, 112–113
Standard deviation, 636
Standard scores, 636–637
Stanford hypnotic susceptibility scale, 181
Stanford-Binet Intelligence Scales, Fifth Edition, 306
Stapes, 134
State-dependent learning, 257. Memory influenced by one's bodily state at the time of learning and at the time of retrieval. Improved memory occurs when the bodily states match.
Statistical abnormality, 476. Abnormality defined on the basis of an extreme score on some dimension, such as IQ or anxiety.
Statistical differences, 641
Statistical significance, 641. Experimental results that would rarely occur by chance alone.
Statistics, 633, 640–641
Status inequalities, 594. Differences in the power, prestige, or privileges of two or more persons or groups.
STDs. *See* Sexually transmitted diseases (STDs)
Stereocilia, 135
Stereoscopic vision, 150. Perception of space and depth due to the fact that the eyes receive different images.
Stereotyping
aging, 115
dangers of, 597
gender-based, 375
irrationality of, 592–593
oversimplification of, 594
social, 591–592
victims of, 592
Stereotype threat, 592. The anxiety caused by the fear of being judged in terms of a stereotype.
Sterilization, 382. Medical procedures such as vasectomy or tubal ligation that make a man or a woman infertile.
Stimulant (upper), 185. A substance that increases activity in the body and nervous system.
Stimulus (stimulus: singular; stimuli [STIM-you-lie]: plural), 23. Any physical energy sensed by an organism.
ambiguous, 146
discrimination, 210–211
emotional, 362
generalization, 210
unconditioned, 206–207
Stimulus control, 175. Linking a particular response with specific stimuli; stimuli present when an operant response is acquired tend to control when and where the response is made.
generalization in, 224
responses to, 524
Stimulus discrimination, 224–225. The learned ability to respond differently to similar stimuli.
Stimulus generalization, 224. The tendency to respond to stimuli similar to, but not identical to, a conditioned stimulus.
Stimulus motives, 333, 344–346. Drives based on innate needs for exploration, manipulation, curiosity, stimulation, and information.
STM. *See* Short-term memory (STM)
Storage, 243. Holding information in memory for later use.
Storage failure, 256
Stored images, 277
Stored memories, 242
Strength, 181
Stress, 446. The mental and physical condition that occurs when a person must adjust or adapt to the environment.
acculturative, 463
burnout and, 448
conflict and, 453
defined, 446
GAS and, 446–447
immune system and, 447–448
life events and, 461–463
memory and, 261–262
questionnaire, 469
signs of, 447
traumatic, 451
Stress disorder, 498–499. A significant emotional disturbance caused by stresses outside the range of normal human experience.
Stress inoculation, 470–471. Use of positive coping statements to control fear and anxiety.
Stress management, 468. The application of cognitive and behavioral strategies to reduce stress and improve coping skills.
behavior modification, 470–471, 522
bodily reactions, 468–469
guided imagery, 469–470
meditation, 469
progressive relaxation, 469
upsetting thought avoidance, 470–471
Stress reaction, 446. The physical response to stress, consisting mainly of bodily changes related to autonomic nervous system arousal.
Stress-vulnerability model, 491. Attributes mental illness to a combination of environmental stress and inherited susceptibility.
Stressor, 448. A specific condition or event in the environment that challenges or threatens a person.
appraising, 449
coping with, 450–451
hassles, 462–463
poverty as, 450
work-associated, 448
Striving for superiority, 415. According to Adler, this basic drive propels us toward perfection.
Strong-Campbell Interest Inventory, 610
Structuralism, 24. The school of thought concerned with analyzing sensations and personal experience into basic elements.
Structured interviews, 429. An interview that follows a prearranged plan, usually a series of planned questions.
Study skills, 7
Study strategies, 5–6
Style of life, 415. The pattern of personality and behavior that defines the pathway each person takes through life.
Subcortex, 71–74. All brain structures below the cerebral cortex.
Subject index/glossary, 3
Subjective experience, 417. Reality as it is perceived and interpreted, not as it exists objectively.
Sublimation, 459
Substance abuse, 442
Substance-related disorder, 481. Abuse of or dependence on a mood- or behavior-altering drug.
Success, 347–348
Successive approximations, 215
Sucking reflex, 90
Sudden infant death syndrome (SIDS), 176–177. The sudden, unexplained death of an apparently healthy infant.
Suicide
age and, 506
cause of, 505
ethnicity and, 505–506
gender and, 505
prevention, 506–507
risk factors of, 506
Sumner, Francis Cecil, 27
Superego, 412. A judge or censor for thoughts and actions.
Superiority, 415
Superordinate goals, 595. A goal that exceeds or overrides all others; a goal that renders other goals relatively less important.
Superstition, 18. Unfounded belief held without evidence or in spite of falsifying evidence.
Superstitious behavior, 214. A behavior repeated because it seems to produce reinforcement, even though it is actually unnecessary.
Suppression, 259–260. A conscious effort to put something out of mind or to keep it from awareness.
Surface traits, 408. The visible or observable traits of one's personality.

Surrogate mother, 95. A substitute mother (often an inanimate dummy in animal research).
Survey (in psychology), 42. A public polling technique used to answer psychological questions.
accuracy of, 42
Internet, 43
limitations of, 43
use of, 42
Survey method, 39. Using questionnaires and surveys to poll large groups of people.
Sustainable lifestyles, 616–617
Susto, 480
Sweat lodge ceremony, 169
Sweetness, 339
Sybil (Schreiber), 499
Symbolic prejudice, 592. Prejudice that is expressed in disguised fashion.
Symbolization, 198. The nonliteral expression of dream content.
Sympathetic branch, 58, 353. A part of the ANS that arouses the body, especially at times of stress.
Synapse (SIN-aps), 54, 86. The microscopic space between two neurons, over which messages pass.
Synesthesia (sin-es-THEE-zyah), 275–276. Experiencing one sense in terms normally associated with another sense; for example, "seeing" colors when a sound is heard.
Syntax, 283. Rules for ordering words when forming sentences.
Systematic desensitization, 522. A reduction in fear, anxiety, or aversion brought about by planned exposure to aversive stimuli.
Systematic observations, 14

T

Target behavior, 525
Task analysis, 623. Breaking complex skills into their subparts.
Task centering, 417
Taste, 338
Taste aversion, 338. An active dislike for a particular food.
Taste buds, 138. The receptor organ for taste.
Taste, sense of, 138
Teaching strategies, 620. A plan for effective teaching.
Telecommuting, 607. An approach to flexible work that involves working from home but using a computer to stay connected to the office throughout the workday.
Telepathy, 158
Telephone therapists, 536–537
Telepresence, 627
Telesurgery, 627
Television aggression, 232–233
Temperament, 89, 425. The hereditary aspects of personality, including emotional and perceptual sensitivity, activity levels, prevailing mood, irritability, adaptability, and so forth.
Temporal lobes, 69. Areas of the cortex that include the sites where hearing registers in the brain.
Tension-release method, 522. A procedure for systematically achieving deep relaxation of the body.
Teratogen (teh-RAT-uh-jen), 86. Anything capable of altering fetal development in nonheritable ways that cause birth defects.
Term schedule, 7. A written plan that lists the dates of all major assignments for each of your classes for an entire semester or quarter.
Territorial behavior, 612. Any behavior that tends to define a space as one's own or that protects it from intruders.
Territorial markers, 612. Objects and other signals whose placement indicates to others the "ownership" or control of a particular area.
Terrorism, 593
Test anxiety, 345–346. High levels of arousal and worry that seriously impair test performance.
Test standardization, 305. Establishing standards for administering a test and interpreting scores.
Testis (TES-tis, singular; testes, plural), 371. One of the two male reproductive glands; the testes are a source of hormones and sperm.
Test-retest reliability, 305
Testosterone (tes-TOSS-teh-rone), 370. A male sex hormone, secreted mainly by the testes and responsible for the development of many male sexual characteristics.
Tests
aptitude, 610–611
in-basket, 611
lie detecting, 354–355
mental ability, 609–610
natural clinical, 42
objective, 431
personality, 408, 431–434
reasoning, 639–640
scores, 374–375
situational judgment, 611
standardization of, 305–306
types of, 7–8
usability, 627
vocational interest, 610
Tetrahydrocannabinol (THC), 196–197
Texture gradients, 151
Thalamus (THAL-uh-mus), 73. A brain structure that relays sensory information to the cerebral cortex.
Thanatologist (THAN-ah-TOL-oh-jist), 115. A specialist who studies emotional and behavioral reactions to death and dying.
Thanatos, 411. The death instinct postulated by Freud.
THC. *See* Tetrahydrocannabinol (THC)
Thematic Apperception Test (TAT), 433–434. A projective test consisting of 20 different scenes and life situations about which respondents make up stories.
Theory, 21. A system of ideas designed to interrelate concepts and facts in a way that summarizes existing data and predicts future observations.
building of, 21–22
defined, 21
frequency, 135
Theory of mind, 105. The understanding that people have mental states, such as thoughts, beliefs, and intentions, and that other people's mental states can be different from one's own.
Theory X leadership (scientific management), 604–605. An approach to leadership that emphasizes work efficiency.
Theory Y leadership, 605. A leadership style that emphasizes human relations at work and that views people as industrious, responsible, and interested in challenging work.
approach of, 605–606
effectiveness of, 606
job satisfaction and, 606–607
theory X *versus,* 605
Therapeutic alliance, 531. A caring relationship that unites a therapist and a client in working to solve the client's problems.
Therapists
basic skills of, 532–534
evaluating, 541–542
finding, 540
Internet, 537
media, 536–537
qualifications, 541
telephone, 537
Therapy placebo effect, 536. Improvement caused not by the actual process of therapy but by a client's expectation that therapy will help.
Thermostats, 333
Thin-slicing, 294
Thinking critically questions, 3
Thirst, 342
Thought stopping, 539. Use of aversive stimuli to interrupt or prevent upsetting thoughts.
Thoughts
all-or-nothing, 518
basic units of, 276
concepts in, 276, 278–281
critical, 296
imagery and, 276–278
language and, 281–285
one-dimensional, 280
problem solving, 285–290
reasoning, 290
reflective, 532–533
restructuring, 346
stopping, 539
upsetting, 470–471
word use and, 281
Threshold, 53. The point at which a nerve impulse is triggered.
Thyroid gland, 74–75. Endocrine gland that helps regulate the rate of metabolism.
Time management, 6–7
Time out, 524
Time sensitivity, 223
Tip-of-the-tongue (TOT) state, 251. The feeling that a memory is available but not quite retrievable.
Titchner, Edward, 24
Tobacco. *See* Cigarette smoking
Token economy, 525. A therapeutic program in which desirable behaviors are reinforced with tokens that can be exchanged for goods, services, activities, and privileges.
Token reinforcer, 219, 220. A tangible secondary reinforcer such as money, gold stars, poker chips, and the like.
Tokens, 218–219
Tolerance, 188, 598–599
Top-down processing, 144. Applying higher-level knowledge to rapidly organize sensory information into a meaningful perception.
Touch, sense of, 139
Tragedy of the commons, 617–618. A social dilemma in which individuals, each acting in his or her immediate self-interest overuse a scarce group resource.
Trait profile, 408. A graph of the scores obtained on several personality traits.
Trait theorist, 407. A psychologist interested in classifying, analyzing, and interrelating traits to understand personality.
Trait-situation interaction, 427–428. The influence that external settings or circumstances have on the expression of personality traits.
Traits
classification of, 407–408
defined, 404
environmental factors, 427–428
five-factor model of, 409–410
heredity factors, 425–426
luck as, 520
positive, 418–419
predicting, 407
profiles, 408
self-rating of, 410
theories of, 407, 442
twin studies of, 426
Tranquilizer, 193. A drug that lowers anxiety and reduces tension.
Transcranial magnetic stimulation (TMS), 534. Uses magnetic pulses to temporarily block activity in specific parts of the brain.
Transducers, 126. Devices that convert one kind of energy into another.
Transfer of training, 259
Transference, 514. The tendency of patients to transfer feelings to a therapist that correspond to those the patient had for important persons in his or her past.
Transformation, 104. The mental ability to change the shape or form of a substance (such as clay or water) and to perceive that its volume remains the same.
Transformation rules, 283. Rules by which a simple declarative sentence may be changed to other voices or forms (past tense, passive voice, and so forth).
Transsexual, 369. A person with a deep conflict between his or her physical, biological sex and preferred psychological and social gender roles.
Traumatic stresses, 451. Extreme events that cause psychological injury or intense emotional pain.
Treasure map tasks, 263
Triangular theory of love, 578–579
Trichromatic (TRY-kro-MAT-ik) **theory**, 131. Theory of color vision based on three cone types: red, green, and blue.
Troyer, Verne, 75
Trust, 112
Trust versus mistrust, 112, 113. A conflict early in life about learning to trust others and the world.
Truth drug. *See* Amytal
Tryptophan, 176
Turner's syndrome, 370
Twelve-step programs, 195
Twin studies, 317, 426
Twixters, 109
Two-way bilingual education, 282. A program in which English-speaking children and children with limited English proficiency are taught half the day in English and half in a second language.
Tympanic membrane, 134
Type A personality, 405, 465–466. A personality type with an elevated risk of heart disease; characterized by time urgency, anger, and hostility.
Type B personality, 405, 465. All personality types other than Type A; a low cardiac-risk personality.

U

Umami, 138
Unconditional positive regard, 421, 516. Unshakable love and approval given without qualification.
Unconditioned response (UR), 207. An innate reflex response elicited by an unconditioned stimulus.

Unconditioned stimulus (US), 207, 521. A stimulus innately capable of eliciting a response.
Unconscious, 26. Contents of the mind that are beyond awareness, especially impulses and desires not directly known to a person.
awareness and, 413
collective, 415–416
defined, 26
personal, 415
personality and, 412
Unconsciousness, 294
Uncritical acceptance, 19. The tendency to believe generally positive or flattering descriptions of oneself.
Understanding (in problem solving), 286. A deeper comprehension of the nature of the problem.
Understanding (in psychology), 16. Understanding is achieved when the causes of a behavior can be stated.
Undifferentiated schizophrenia, 488. Schizophrenia lacking the specific features of catatonic, disorganized, or paranoid types.
Uniforms, 595
Universal Design for Instruction, 621
Unstructured interview, 429. An interview in which conversation is informal and topics are taken up freely as they arise.
Unusual uses test, 291–292
Upward comparison, 551. Comparing yourself with a person who ranks higher than you on some dimension.
Urban environments
attentional overload in, 614–615
bystander intervention in, 615
crowding in, 613–614
noise and, 615
Usability testing, 627. The empirical investigation of the ease with which users can learn to use a machine.
Uterus (YOO-ter-us), 371. The pear-shaped muscular organ in which the fetus develops during pregnancy; also known as the womb.

V

Vagina (vah-JINE-ah), 371. Tube-like structure connecting the external female genitalia with the uterus.
Vaginal organism, 384
Vaginismus (VAJ-ih-NIS-mus) **(One type of genito-pelvic pain/penetration disorder)**, 397. Muscle spasms of the vagina.
Validity, 305, 323–325. The ability of a test to measure what it purports to measure.
Validity scales, 432. Scales that tell whether test scores should be invalidated for lying, inconsistency, or "faking good."
Valium, 193
Values, 423, 459–460
Variability, measures of, 636
Variable, 35. Any condition that changes or can be made to change; a measure, event, or state that may vary.
Variable interval (VI) schedule, 224. A reinforcer is given for the first correct response made after a varied amount of time has passed since the last reinforced response. Responses made during the time interval are not reinforced.
Variable ratio (VR) schedule, 222–223. A varied number of correct responses must be made to get a reinforcer. For example, a reinforcer is given after three to seven correct responses; the actual number changes randomly.
Vas deferens (vaz DEH-fur-enz), 371. The duct that carries sperm from the testes to the urethra.
Ventromedial, 335
Verbal intelligence, 307. Intelligence measured by answering questions involving vocabulary, general information, arithmetic, and other language- or symbol-oriented tasks.
Vestibular senses, 138. The senses of balance, gravity and acceleration.
Vestibular system, 141–142
Vicarious classical conditioning, 212. Classical conditioning brought about by observing another person react to a particular stimulus.
Vicarious desensitization, 523. A reduction in fear or anxiety that takes place vicariously ("secondhand") when a client watches models perform the feared behavior.
Video games, 233, 318
Virtual reality exposure, 523. Use of computer-generated images to present fear stimuli. The virtual environment responds to a viewer's head movements and other inputs.
Visible spectrum, 126, 128
Vision
basic dimensions of, 128
darkness and, 132–133
deficits of, 129–130
eyes' role in, 129–132
neonates, 91–92
nerve pathways of, 66
peripheral, 131
Visual acuity, 131. The sharpness of visual perception.
Visual agnosia (ag-KNOW-zyah), 70. An inability to identify seen objects.
Visual-spatial processing, 306
Vocational interest tests, 610. A paper-and-pencil test that assesses a person's interests and matches them to interests found among successful workers in various occupations.
Vogler, Roger, 521
Vygotsky's sociocultural theory, 106–107
Vygotsky, Lev, 107

W
Waiting-list control groups, 531
Waking consciousness, 169. A state of clear, organized alertness.
Warning system, 139. Pain based on large nerve fibers; warns that bodily damage may be occurring.
Washburn, Margaret, 27
Watson, John B., 24
Weapons effect, 585–586. The observation that weapons serve as strong cues for aggressive behavior.
Wechsler Adult Intelligence Scale-Fourth Edition (WAIS-IV), 306–307, 310
Wechsler Intelligence Scale For Children-Fourth Edition (WISC-IV), 306–307
Wechsler, David, 306
Weekly time schedule, 7. A written plan that allocates time for study, work, and leisure activities during a one-week period.
Weight control threshold, 340
Weightlessness, 141
WEIRD (western, educated, industrialized, rich, and democratic), 28
Wellness, 445. A positive state of good health; more than the absence of disease.
Wernicke's (VER-nick-ees) **area**, 69. A temporal lobe brain area related to language comprehension.
Wertheimer, Max, 25
Whirling Dervishes, 168
White matter, 58
White, Betty, 115
White, Shaun, 294
Whole human concept, 31
Whole learning, 266
Wilderness Act, 549
Wisdom, 325–326
Wish fulfillment, 178. Freudian belief that many dreams express unconscious desires.
Withdrawal of love, 117–118. Withholding affection to enforce child discipline.
Withdrawal symptoms, 186. Physical illness and discomfort following the withdrawal of a drug.
Work
adult challenges, 113–114
aging and, 115
efficiency, 604
motivation for, 349–350
Work efficiency, 604. Maximum output (productivity) at lowest cost.
Working memory, 243, 306. Another name for short-term memory, especially as it is used for thinking and problem solving.
Workplace
anger, 607–608
employee selection process at, 609–611
enrichment, 607–608
satisfaction, 606–607
territorial behavior at, 612
World Memory Championship, 265
Worth, 420
Wundt, Wilhelm, 23

X
X **chromosome**, 371. The female chromosome contributed by the mother; produces a female when paired with another *X* chromosome, and a male when paired with a *Y* chromosome.
Xanax, 193
Xenophobia, 497
Xhosa, 534

Y
Y **chromosome**, 371. The male chromosome contributed by the father; produces a male when paired with an *X* chromosome. Fathers may give either an *X* or a *Y* chromosome to their offspring.
Yerkes-Dodson law, 345. A summary of the relationships among arousal, task complexity, and performance.
Yo-yo diets, 339
You-message, 119. Threatening, accusing, bossing, lecturing, or criticizing another person.

Z
Zar, 480
Zener cards, 158
Zero correlation, 639
Zone of proximal development, 106. Refers to the range of tasks a child cannot yet master alone, but that she or he can accomplish with the guidance of a more capable partner.
Zulu culture, 157